MW00633623

Achieve

for Psychology

Engaging Every Student. Supporting Every Instructor. Setting the New Standard for Teaching and Learning.

Macmillan Learning's Achieve for Psychology sets a whole new standard for integrating **assessments**, **activities**, and **analytics** into your teaching. Achieve brings together all of the high-quality features that instructors and students loved about our previous platform, LaunchPad: interactive e-book, LearningCurve adaptive quizzing and other assessments, immersive learning activities, and extensive instructor resources. This powerful platform also offers:

- A cleaner, more intuitive and **mobile-friendly** interface.
- **Powerful analytics** that track student engagement and performance.
- Self-regulated learning with **Goal-Setting and Reflection Surveys**.
- A fully integrated **iClicker** classroom response system, with questions available for each unit or the option to integrate your own.
- A **NEW Video Collection for Introductory Psychology**!

Our resources were **co-designed with instructors and students**, on a foundation of *years* of **learning research** and rigorous testing over multiple semesters. The result is superior content, organization, and functionality. Achieve's pre-built assignments engage students both *inside and outside of class*. And Macmillan Learning's Achieve is effective for students of *all levels* of motivation and preparedness, whether they are high achievers or need extra support.

Macmillan Learning offers **deep platform integration** of Achieve with all LMS providers, including Blackboard, Brightspace, Canvas, and Moodle. With integration, students can access course content and their grades through one sign-in. And you can pair Achieve with course tools from your LMS, such as discussion boards and chat and Gradebook functionality. LMS integration is also available with Inclusive Access. For more information, visit macmillanlearning.com/college/us/solutions/lms-integration or talk to your local sales representative.

Achieve was built with **accessibility** in mind. Macmillan Learning strives to create products that are usable by all learners and meet universally applied accessibility standards. In addition to addressing product compatibility with assistive technologies such as screen reader software, alternative keyboard devices, and voice recognition products, we are working to ensure that the content and platforms we provide are fully accessible. For more information, visit macmillanlearning.com/college/us/our-story/accessibility.

Macmillan Learning's Achieve for Psychology: Assessments

LearningCurve Adaptive Quizzing

Based on extensive learning and memory research, and proven effective for hundreds of thousands of students, LearningCurve focuses on the core concepts in every module, providing individualized question sets and feedback for correct and incorrect responses. The system adapts to each student's level of understanding, with follow-up quizzes targeting areas where the student needs improvement. Each question is tied to a learning objective and linked to the appropriate section of the e-book to encourage students to discover the right answer for themselves. LearningCurve has consistently been rated the #1 resource in our collection by instructors and students alike.

- LearningCurve's game-like quizzing promotes retrieval practice through its unique delivery of questions and its point system.
- Students with a firm grasp on the material get plenty of practice but proceed through the activity relatively quickly.
- Unprepared students are given more questions, requiring that they do what they should be doing anyway—practice some more.
- You can monitor results for each student and the class as a whole, to identify areas that may need more coverage in lectures and assignments.

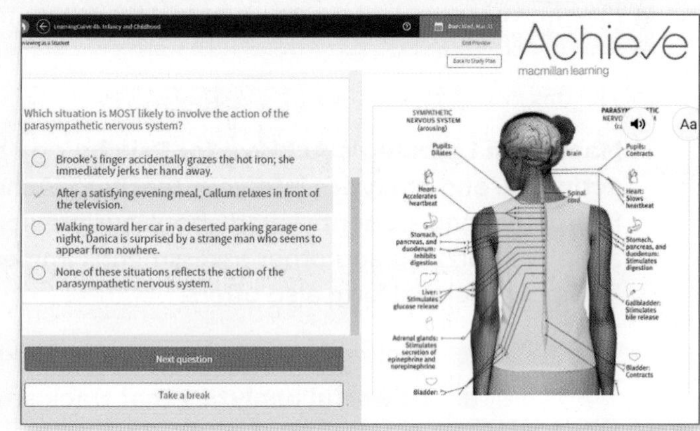
Achie/e
macmillan learning
Which situation is MOST likely to involve the action of the parasympathetic nervous system?
Brooke's finger accidentally grazes the hot iron; she immediately jerks her hand away.
After a satisfying evening meal, Callum relaxes in front of the television.
Walking toward her car in a deserted parking garage one night, Danica is surprised by a strange man who seems to appear from nowhere.
None of these situations reflects the action of the parasympathetic nervous system.
Next question
Take a break
Aa

E-book

Macmillan Learning's e-book is an interactive version of the textbook that offers highlighting, bookmarking, and note-taking. Built-in, low-stakes self-assessments allow students to test their level of understanding along the way, and learn even more in the process thanks to the testing effect. Students can download the e-book to read offline, or to have it read aloud to them. Macmillan Learning's Achieve allows you to assign modules as homework.

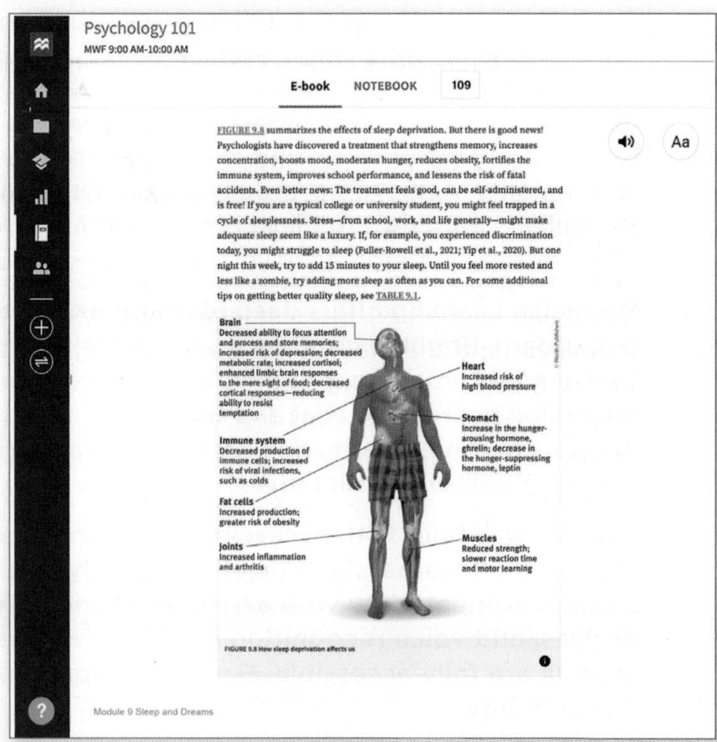
Psychology 101
MWF 9:00 AM-10:00 AM
E-book
NOTEBOOK
109
Aa
FIGURE 9.8 summarizes the effects of sleep deprivation. But there is good news! Psychologists have discovered a treatment that strengthens memory, increases concentration, boosts mood, moderates hunger, reduces obesity, fortifies the immune system, improves school performance, and lessens the risk of fatal accidents. Even better news: The treatment feels good, can be self-administered, and is free! If you are a typical college or university student, you might feel trapped in a cycle of sleeplessness. Stress—from school, work, and life generally—might make adequate sleep seem like a luxury. If, for example, you experienced discrimination today, you might struggle to sleep (Fuller-Rowell et al., 2021; Yip et al., 2020). But one night this week, try to add 15 minutes to your sleep. Until you feel more rested and less like a zombie, try adding more sleep as often as you can. For some additional tips on getting better quality sleep, see TABLE 9.1.
Brain
Decreased ability to focus attention and process and store memories; increased risk of depression; decreased metabolic rate; increased cortisol; enhanced limbic brain responses to the mere sight of food; decreased cortical responses—reducing ability to resist temptation
Heart
Increased risk of high blood pressure
Stomach
Increase in the hunger-arousing hormone, ghrelin; decrease in the hunger-suppressing hormone, leptin
Immune system
Decreased production of immune cells; increased risk of viral infections, such as colds
Fat cells
Increased production; greater risk of obesity
Joints
Increased inflammation and arthritis
Muscles
Reduced strength; slower reaction time and motor learning
FIGURE 9.8 How sleep deprivation affects us
Module 9 Sleep and Dreams

Test Bank

Psychology, Fourteenth Edition, offers the gold standard Test Bank, with its own designated editor and thousands of questions meticulously checked against the updated content of the text. You can assign out-of-the-box exams or create your own by:

- Choosing from the 8,000 multiple-choice questions (plus additional essay questions) in our database.

- Filtering questions by type, topic, difficulty, and Bloom's level.
- Customizing multiple-choice questions.
- Integrating your own questions into the exam.

Exam/Quiz results report to a Gradebook that lets you monitor student progress individually and classwide.

Practice Quizzes

Practice Quizzes mirror the experience of a test, with questions that are similar but distinct from those in the Test Bank. You can use the quizzes as is or create your own, selecting questions by question type, topic, difficulty, and Bloom's level.

Macmillan Learning's Achieve for Psychology: Activities

Achieve is designed to support and encourage active learning by connecting engaging activities and reviews out of class with effective and approachable in-class activities, curated from a variety of active learning sources.

PBS
NEWS
HOUR
PBS Newshour/BoClips

New! Video Collection for Introductory Psychology

This collection of 120 new videos (bringing our total number of videos in Macmillan Learning's Achieve to over 200!) offers classic as well as current, in-demand clips from high-quality sources, along with original content to support *Psychology*, Fourteenth Edition.

Accompanying assessments make these videos assignable, with results reporting to the Achieve Gradebook. Faculty and student advisory boards advised on topic selection and were instrumental in helping us create this diverse and engaging set of clips. The collection includes coverage of loneliness and the brain, iGen, Covid and stress, Black Lives Matter/racial trauma, online dating, and issues faced by transgender youth. All videos are closed-captioned and found only in Achieve. Instructors can review detailed video descriptions in the accompanying Faculty Guide. The video collection will be updated annually.

In addition, Garth Neufeld (Cascadia College) has created brief ***new student videos about APA's new Introductory Psychology Initiative's seven key themes***, along with an eighth video introducing the themes. These helpful resources may be found in the Welcome Unit in Macmillan Learning's Achieve, where they are accompanied by assessment so that they may be assigned and will report to the gradebook.

Immersive Learning Activities

With a focus on student engagement, these immersive learning activities invite students to apply what they are learning to their own lives, or to play the role of researcher—exploring experimental methods, analyzing data, and developing scientific literacy and critical thinking skills.

- "How Would You Know?" research activities for each group of modules allow students to play the role of researcher as they design and interpret studies. Students consider possible confounding factors and other issues that affect the interpretation of results. Students learn about how key decision points can alter the meaning and value of a psychological study, and they develop scientific literacy skills in the process. Topics include "How Would You Know If People Can Learn to Reduce Anxiety?" and "How Would You Know If Schizophrenia Is Inherited?"
- In the "Assess Your Strengths" activities, students apply what they are learning from the text to their own lives and experiences by considering key "strengths." Each activity starts with a personalized video introduction from David Myers or Nathan DeWall. Students then assess themselves on the strength (critical thinking, quality of sleep, self-control, relationship strength, belonging, hope, and more) using scales developed by researchers. Next, students get tips for nurturing that strength in their own lives, and take a quiz to help solidify their learning. This edition includes a ***new*** activity, "How Healthy Is Your Emotional Ecosystem?" by new co-author, June Gruber (University of Colorado Boulder).
- "Thinking Critically About ..." infographic activities for each group of modules teach and reinforce critical thinking skills.

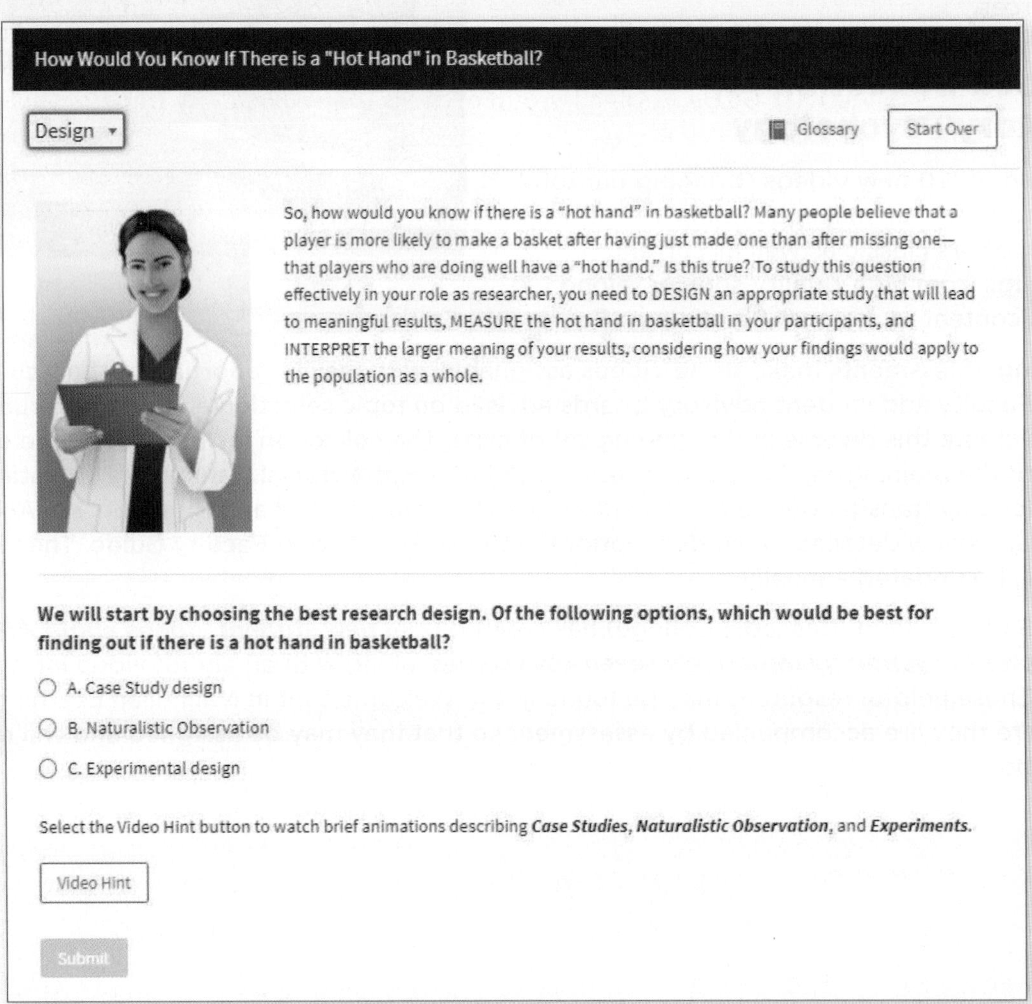
How Would You Know If There is a "Hot Hand" in Basketball?
Design
Glossary
Start Over
So, how would you know if there is a "hot hand" in basketball? Many people believe that a player is more likely to make a basket after having just made one than after missing one—that players who are doing well have a "hot hand." Is this true? To study this question effectively in your role as researcher, you need to DESIGN an appropriate study that will lead to meaningful results, MEASURE the hot hand in basketball in your participants, and INTERPRET the larger meaning of your results, considering how your findings would apply to the population as a whole.
We will start by choosing the best research design. Of the following options, which would be best for finding out if there is a hot hand in basketball?
A. Case Study design
B. Naturalistic Observation
C. Experimental design
Select the Video Hint button to watch brief animations describing Case Studies, Naturalistic Observation, and Experiments.
Video Hint
Submit

Concept Practice Tutorials

Macmillan Learning's Achieve includes dozens of these dynamic, interactive mini-tutorials that teach and reinforce the course's foundational ideas. Each of these brief activities (only 5 minutes to complete) addresses one or two key concepts in a consistent format: review, practice, quiz, and conclusion.

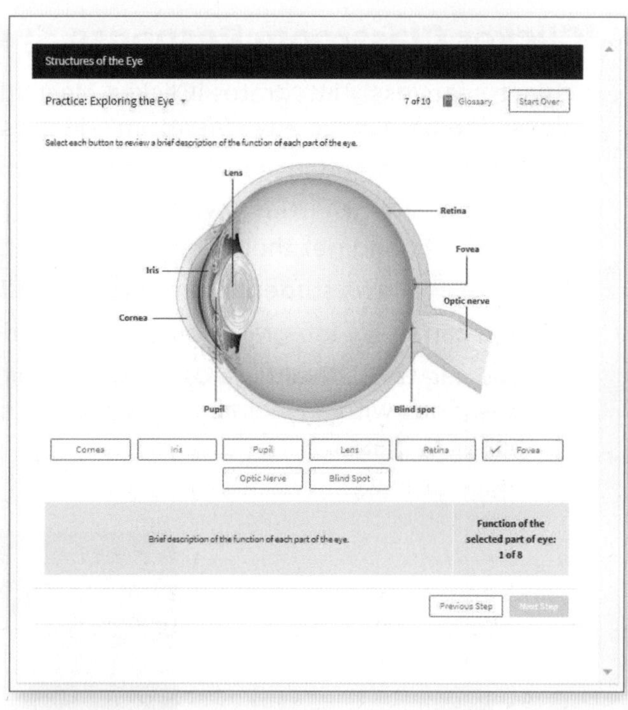
Structures of the Eye
Practice: Exploring the Eye
7 of 10
Glossary
Start Over
Select each button to review a brief description of the function of each part of the eye.
Lens
Retina
Fovea
Iris
Optic nerve
Cornea
Pupil
Blind spot
Cornea
Iris
Pupil
Lens
Retina
Fovea
Optic Nerve
Blind Spot
Brief description of the function of each part of the eye.
Function of the selected part of eye: 1 of 8
Previous Step
Next Step

PsychSim6

PsychSim for Achieve redefines what's possible with interactive psychology simulations. With a new look, new format, and updates for accessibility, the PsychSim tutorials immerse students in the world of psychological research, placing them in the role of scientist or subject in activities that highlight important concepts, processes, and experimental approaches.

Instructor Activity Guides

Instructor Activity Guides provide you with a structured plan for using Achieve's active learning opportunities in both face-to-face and remote learning courses. Each guide offers step-by-step instructions—from pre-class reflection to in-class engagement to post-class follow-up. The guides include suggestions for discussion questions, group work, presentations, and simulations, with estimated class time, implementation effort, and Bloom's taxonomy level for each activity. Myers and DeWall have created a new Instructor Activity Guide for each group of modules, showcasing some of their own favorite classroom activities.

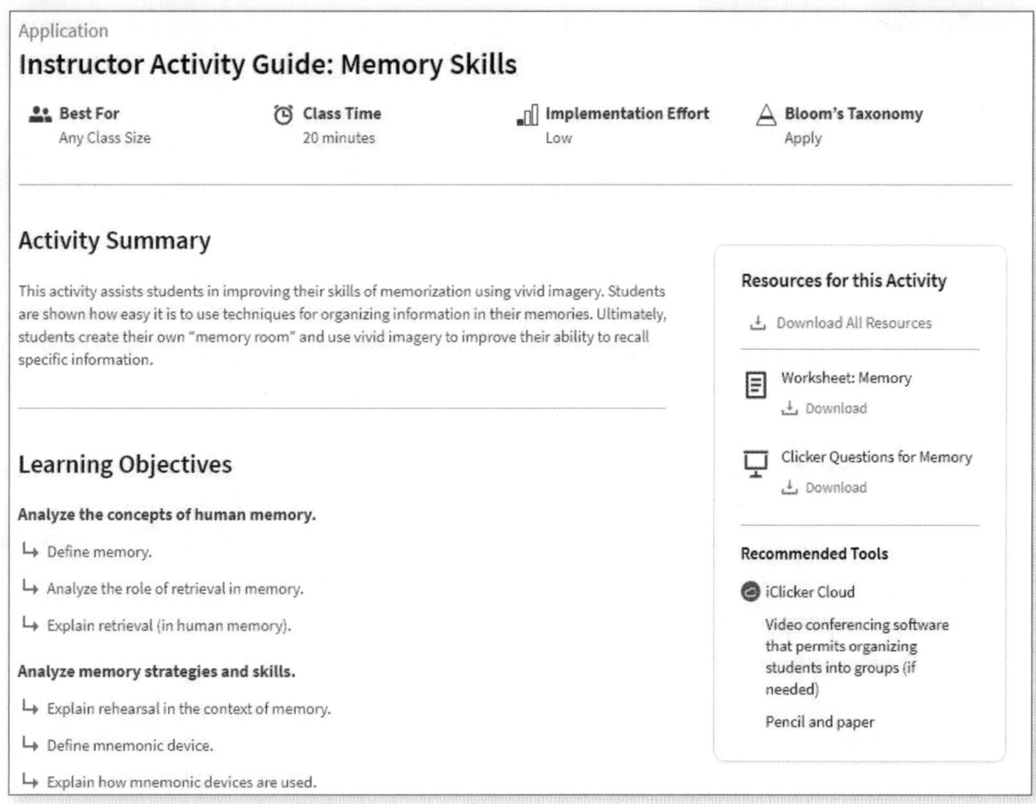

Application

Instructor Activity Guide: Memory Skills

Best For Any Class Size | **Class Time** 20 minutes | **Implementation Effort** Low | **Bloom's Taxonomy** Apply

Activity Summary

This activity assists students in improving their skills of memorization using vivid imagery. Students are shown how easy it is to use techniques for organizing information in their memories. Ultimately, students create their own "memory room" and use vivid imagery to improve their ability to recall specific information.

Learning Objectives

Analyze the concepts of human memory.

- Define memory.
- Analyze the role of retrieval in memory.
- Explain retrieval (in human memory).

Analyze memory strategies and skills.

- Explain rehearsal in the context of memory.
- Define mnemonic device.
- Explain how mnemonic devices are used.

Resources for this Activity

Download All Resources

Worksheet: Memory
Download

Clicker Questions for Memory
Download

Recommended Tools

iClicker Cloud

Video conferencing software that permits organizing students into groups (if needed)

Pencil and paper

iClicker Classroom Response System

Achieve seamlessly integrates iClicker, Macmillan Learning's highly acclaimed classroom response system. iClicker can help make any classroom—in person or virtual—more lively, engaging, and productive.

- iClicker's attendance feature helps you make sure students are actually attending in-person classes.
- You can choose from flexible polling and quizzing options to engage students, check their understanding, and get their feedback in real time.
- iClicker allows students to participate using laptops, mobile devices, or in-class remotes.
- You can easily integrate your existing slides and polling questions—there is no need to re-enter them.
- You can take advantage of the questions in our Instructor Activity Guides, and our module-specific questions within Macmillan Learning's Achieve to improve the opportunities for all students to be active in class.

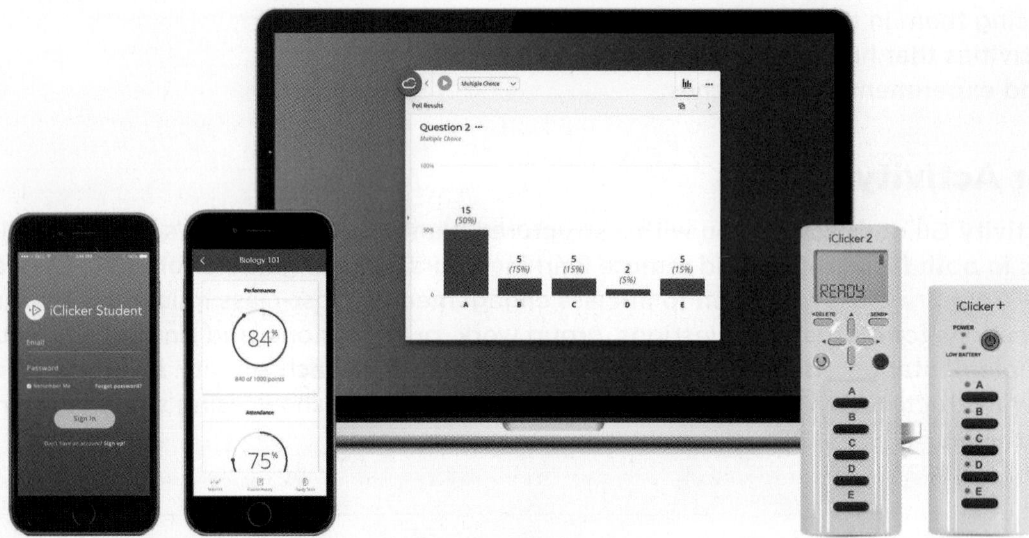
Question 2
iClicker Student
Biology 101
84%
75%
iClicker 2
READY
iClicker+

Macmillan Learning's Achieve for Psychology: Analytics

Learning Objectives, Reports, and Insights

Content in Achieve is tagged to specific Learning Objectives. Reporting within Achieve helps students see how they are performing against objectives, and it helps you determine if any student, group of students, or the class as a whole needs extra help in specific areas. This enables more efficient and effective interventions.

Macmillan Learning's Achieve provides reports on student activities, assignments, and assessments at the course level, unit level, subunit level, and individual student level, so you can identify trouble spots and adjust your efforts accordingly. Within the Reports function, the Insights section offers snapshots with high-level data on student performance and behavior, to answer such questions as:

- What are the top Learning Objectives to review in this unit?
- What are the top assignments to review?
- What is the range of performance on a particular assignment?
- How many students aren't logging in?

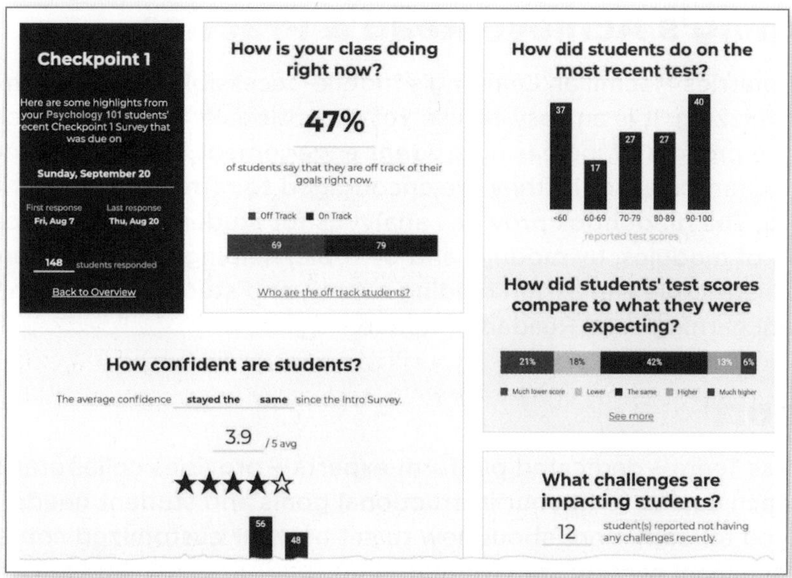
Checkpoint 1
Here are some highlights from your Psychology 101 students' recent Checkpoint 1 Survey that was due on
Sunday, September 20
First response Fri, Aug 7
Last response Thu, Aug 20
148 students responded
Back to Overview
How is your class doing right now?
47%
of students say that they are off track of their goals right now.
Off Track
On Track
69
79
Who are the off track students?
How did students do on the most recent test?
37
17
27
27
40
<60
60-69
70-79
80-89
90-100
reported test scores
How did students' test scores compare to what they were expecting?
21%
18%
42%
13%
6%
Much lower score
Lower
The same
Higher
Much higher
See more
How confident are students?
The average confidence stayed the same since the Intro Survey.
3.9 /5 avg
56
48
What challenges are impacting students?
12 student(s) reported not having any challenges recently.

Goal-Setting and Reflection surveys help students plan and direct their learning, and provide instructors with an unprecedented view into students' metacognition:

- The **Intro Survey** asks students to consider their goals for the class, providing a powerful source of intrinsic motivation. Students must then consider how they will manage their time and use learning strategies to achieve their plan.
- **Checkpoint surveys** ask students to monitor and assess their progress, and prompt them to make changes as necessary.
- **Each completed survey generates a report** for the instructor that reveals how the class is progressing—going well beyond the course grades.

These tools help students develop control over their learning and foster a growth mindset to build long-lasting academic success.

Additional Instructor Resources in Macmillan Learning's Achieve: All In One Place

Instructor's Resource Manual

We consulted with national award-winning teacher Elizabeth Hammer (Xavier University) to improve the content and organization of our Instructor's Resource Manual, available as downloadable Word files. Engage your students with this abundance of active learning opportunities, including a "Diversity in Psychology: Spotlight on Women" collection of 17 activities created by Salena Brody (University of Texas, Dallas).

Image Slides and Tables

Presentation slides feature module illustrations and tables and can be used as is or customized to fit your needs. Alt text for images is available upon request via WebAccessibility@Macmillan.com.

Lecture Slides

Accessible, downloadable presentation slides provide support for key concepts and themes from the text, and can be used as is or customized to fit your needs.

Macmillan Learning's Achieve Read & Practice

Achieve Read & Practice marries Macmillan Learning's mobile-accessible e-book with the acclaimed LearningCurve adaptive quizzing. It is an easy-to-use yet exceptionally powerful teaching and learning option that streamlines the process of increasing student engagement and understanding, and reduces cost. If students struggle with a particular topic, they are encouraged to re-read the material and answer a few short additional questions. The gradebook provides analytics for student performance individually and for the whole class, by group of modules, by module, and by topic, helping instructors prepare for class and one-on-one discussions. Instructors can assign reading simply, and students can complete assignments on any device. See MacmillanLearning.com/ReadandPractice.

Customer Support

Our Achieve Client Success Team—dedicated platform experts—provides collaboration, software expertise, and consulting to tailor each course to fit your instructional goals and student needs. Start with a demo at a time that works for you to learn more about how to set up your customized course. Talk to your sales representative or visit MacmillanLearning.com for more information.

Pricing and bundling options are available at Store.MacmillanLearning.com

FOURTEENTH EDITION

Psychology

David G. Myers
Hope College
Holland, Michigan

C. Nathan DeWall
University of Kentucky
Lexington, Kentucky

June Gruber
University of Colorado Boulder
Boulder, Colorado

worth publishers
Macmillan Learning
New York

Program Director: Suzanne Jeans
Senior Executive Program Manager: Carlise Stembridge
Executive Development Manager, Social Sciences: Christine Brune
Development Editors: Ann Kirby-Payne and Danielle Slevens
Editorial Associate: Kathryn Brownson
Assistant Editor: Talia Green
Executive Marketing Manager: Katherine Nurre
Marketing Coordinator: Claudia Cruz
Senior Media Editor, Psychology: Karissa Venne
Media Editorial Assistant: Renee Prvulov
Test Bank Editors: Betty Probert and Danielle Slevens
Senior Director, Content Management Enhancement: Tracey Kuehn
Executive Managing Editor: Michael Granger
Manager, Publishing Services: Ryan Sullivan
Senior Lead Content Project Manager: Won McIntosh
Senior Workflow Project Supervisor: Susan Wein
Senior Workflow Project Manager: Paul Rohloff
Production Supervisor: Lawrence Guerra
Director of Design, Content Management: Diana Blume
Senior Design Services Manager: Natasha A. S. Wolfe
Interior Design: Maureen McCutcheon
Senior Design Manager, Cover Design: John Callahan
Art Manager: Matthew McAdams
Interior Illustrations: Shawn Barber, Keith Kasnot, Matthew McAdams, Evelyn Pence, and Don Stewart
Senior Director of Rights and Permissions: Hilary Newman
Executive Permissions Editor: Robin Fadool
Photo Researcher and Lumina Project Manager: Cheryl DuBois
Senior Director, Digital Production: Keri deManigold
Executive Media Project Manager: Eve Conte
Composition: Lumina Datamatics, Inc.
Printing and Binding: Transcontinental

ISBN 978-1-319-42689-7 (Paperback)
ISBN 978-1-319-48983-0 (Loose-leaf)
ISBN 978-1-319-54514-7 (International)

Library of Congress Control Number: 2023940131

Printed in Canada.

1 2 3 4 5 6 28 27 26 25 24 23

David Myers' royalties from the sale of this book are assigned to the David and Carol Myers Foundation, which exists to receive and distribute funds to other charitable organizations.

Acknowledgments

Acknowledgments and copyrights appear on the same page as the text and art selections they cover; these acknowledgments and copyrights constitute an extension of the copyright page.

Worth Publishers
120 Broadway
New York, NY 10271
www.macmillanlearning.com

To Stefan von Holtzbrinck

With gratitude for his enabling educational publishing at its creative best — supporting author-editor teamwork and a prosocial sense of mission

DM

•

To Jean and Susan Rudolph

Loving in-laws and role models of patience, kindness, and integrity

ND

•

To Ansel and Silvan Gruber Saucedo

For all you bring to my life, to the end of the universe and back

JG

About the Authors

Photographer Steven Herppich, courtesy of Hope College Public Affairs and Marketing

David Myers received his B.A. in chemistry from Whitworth University, and his psychology Ph.D. from the University of Iowa. He has spent his career at Michigan's Hope College, where he has taught dozens of introductory psychology sections. Hope College students have invited him to be their commencement speaker and voted him "outstanding professor." His research and writings have been recognized by the Gordon Allport Intergroup Relations Prize, an Honored Scientist award from the Federation of Associations in Behavioral & Brain Sciences, an Award for Distinguished Service on Behalf of Social-Personality Psychology, a Presidential Citation from APA Division 2, election as an American Association for the Advancement of Science Fellow, and three honorary doctorates.

With support from National Science Foundation grants, Myers' scientific articles have appeared in three dozen scientific periodicals, including *Science, American Scientist, Psychological Science,* and *American Psychologist*. In addition to his scholarly and textbook writing, he digests psychological science for the general public. His writings have appeared in four dozen magazines, from *Today's Education* to *Scientific American*. He also has authored six general audience books, including, in 2022, *How Do We Know Ourselves? Curiosities and Marvels of the Human Mind*. And he blogs about psychology and life at TalkPsych.com.

David Myers has chaired his city's Human Relations Commission, helped found a thriving assistance center for low-income families, and spoken to hundreds of college, community, and professional groups worldwide.

Drawing on his experience of hearing loss, which now includes a cochlear implant, he also has written articles and a book (*A Quiet World*) about hearing loss, and he is advocating a transformation in U.S. assistive listening technology (see HearingLoop.org). For his leadership, he has received awards from the American Academy of Audiology, the hearing industry, and the Hearing Loss Association of America.

David and Carol Myers met and married while undergraduates, and have raised sons Peter and Andrew, and a daughter, Laura. They have one grandchild, Allie (see p. 178).

Shirley Howell

Nathan DeWall is professor of psychology at the University of Kentucky. He received his bachelor's degree from St. Olaf College, a master's degree in social science from the University of Chicago, and a master's degree and Ph.D. in social psychology from Florida State University. DeWall received the College of Arts and Sciences Outstanding Teaching Award, which recognizes excellence in undergraduate and graduate teaching. The Association for Psychological Science identified DeWall as a "Rising Star" early in his career for "making significant contributions to the field of psychological science." He has been included in the top 1 percent of all cited scientists in psychology and psychiatry on the Institute for Scientific Information list, according to the Web of Science.

DeWall conducts research on close relationships, self-control, aggression, the psychology of religion, and intellectual humility. With funding from the National Institutes of Health, the National Science Foundation, and the John Templeton Foundation, he has published 225 scientific articles and chapters. DeWall's research awards include the SAGE Young Scholars Award from the Foundation for Personality and Social Psychology, the Young Investigator Award from the International Society for Research on Aggression, and the Early Career Award from the International Society for Self and Identity. His research has been covered by numerous media and entertainment outlets, including Good Morning America, *The Wall Street Journal, Newsweek, The Atlantic Monthly, The New York Times, The Los Angeles Times, Harvard Business Review, USA Today,* National Public Radio, *The Guardian*, the BBC, and a Netflix documentary. He has lectured nationally and internationally, including in Hong Kong, China, the Netherlands, England, Greece, Hungary, Sweden, Australia, and France.

Nathan is happily married to Alice DeWall and is the proud father of Beverly "Bevy" and Ellis. He also enjoys taking care of the family dog, Artie. As an ultramarathon runner, he completed numerous races, including the Badwater 135 in 2017 (dubbed "the World's toughest foot race"). In his spare time now, he enjoys hiking, attending live concerts, setting up and maintaining aquariums, watching sports, and playing guitar and singing in local rock bands.

Molly Seeling

June Gruber is an associate professor of psychology and neuroscience at the University of Colorado Boulder. She was previously a faculty member at Yale University. She received her B.A. in psychology, and her Ph.D. in clinical psychology from the University of California Berkeley. Gruber has published over 100 articles and chapters and has edited two books—*The Oxford Handbook of Positive Emotion* and *Psychopathology and Positive Emotion: Integrating the Light Sides and Dark Sides* with Judith Moskowitz. Her research has received several honors, including the Association for Psychological Science's Rising Star Award, the Janet Taylor Spence Award for Transformative Early Career Contributions, the Society for Research in Psychopathology's Early Career Award, the NARSAD Young Investigator Award, and Yale University's Arthur Greer Memorial Prize for Outstanding Junior Faculty. Gruber has served as an Associate Editor and Interim Editor-in-Chief for *Perspectives on Psychological Science* and is currently an Associate Editor at *Emotion*.

Gruber directs the Positive Emotion and Psychopathology Laboratory, where she studies the links between positive emotions and mental health, including the "dark side" of happiness. Gruber co-led a field-wide call to action in response to the mental health crisis sparked by Covid-19 (Gruber et al., 2021).

Gruber's passion for teaching psychology and training future generations of scholars extends beyond the classroom. She has created freely available interview series and courses for the general public, including a Coursera #TalkMentalIllness course, Experts in Emotion Interview Series at Yale University, and an online course in Human Emotion. Gruber has also co-written a column for young scientists in ScienceCareers.org (from the journal *Science*) and is currently writing for *Teaching Current Directions in Psychological Science* (along with Myers and DeWall). Her teaching efforts have received several awards, including the Faculty Assembly Excellence in Teaching and Pedagogy Award, the UROP Outstanding Faculty Mentor Award, and the Cogswell Award for Inspirational Instruction at the University of Colorado, Boulder. Gruber is invested in supporting and elevating the careers of underrepresented women in the sciences. She leads workshops, publishes papers, and gives talks to raise awareness about gender disparities in the field and to chart a proactive path forward.

Gruber enjoys spending quiet days in the Colorado mountains with her two sons, Ansel and Silvan, and her husband, Raul, whom she met as an undergraduate psychology major. She enjoys taking hikes with her dogs Buddy and Eddy, making art projects with her children, traveling, and basking in the nostalgia of 80s music.

Brief Contents

Contents

Instructor Preface

Psychology is fascinating, and so relevant to our everyday lives. Psychology's insights enable students to be more successful in their courses, more tuned-in friends and partners, more effective co-workers, wiser parents, and engaged community citizens. With this new edition, we hope to help students think more like psychological scientists, and to arm them with the critical-thinking skills they need to think smart and challenge misinformation in our post-truth world. We also hope to make the *teaching* of psychology easier and more enjoyable for you, the instructor. Our integrated resources in Macmillan Learning's Achieve aim to support your class preparation, and to bring your students to class better prepared. These resources include:

- ***133 new introductory psychology videos.***
- our new "Skills for Student Success" activity.
- new student Goal-Setting and Reflection Surveys and other built-in analytics.
- my [DM] 5 new assignable *How Do We Know Ourselves?* essays (excerpted from my new general audience book), accompanied by assessment.
- the lauded LearningCurve adaptive quizzing.
- a heavily updated and improved Instructor's Resource Manual.
- our immersive learning activities ("How Would You Know?" research activities, including my [ND] new activity on social media; "Assess Your Strengths" self-assessment activities, including my [JG] new activities on healthy emotional ecosystems and on experiences of awe; and "Thinking Critically About" critical-thinking activities).

In this edition, we have decided to combine our "chapter" and "modular" formats. This offers all those using the text the opportunity to more easily assign carefully segmented portions of a chapter (modules), or to assign whole chapters if they prefer. Each module is a stand-alone teaching/learning unit that does not depend on other modules for student understanding, which facilitates flexible use. All of Macmillan Learning's Achieve resources are matched to the numbered modules, yet you still have the opportunity to use "Chapter Practice Quizzes" and to create whole chapter tests if you opt to teach all of the modules in a chapter.

From its first edition, this text has focused on teaching ***critical thinking,*** and helping students understand that psychology is a **science,** and that ***research*** underlies psychological discoveries. We've expanded that focus in this new edition. (See p. viii to learn more about the Myers/DeWall/Gruber critical-thinking story.) This new edition offers 1427 research citations dated 2019–2022, making these ***the most up-to-date introductory psychology course resources available.*** With so many exciting new findings, and every module updated with current new examples and ideas, students will see the importance and value of psychological research, and how psychology can help them make sense of the world around them. For example, we discuss new research on how the Covid-19 pandemic has affected our need to belong (What Drives Us modules), the social responsibility norm and prejudice (Social Psychology modules), and suicidal behavior (Psychological Disorders modules), and we offer several statistical examples related to the pandemic (Thinking Critically With Psychological Science modules) and cultural variations in Covid effects (Nature, Nurture, and Human Diversity modules).

APA Introductory Psychology Initiative, and Learning Goals and Outcomes for the Psychology Major

The American Psychological Association (APA) released the final results of its Introductory Psychology Initiative (IPI) in August 2021, in hopes of improving "the quality of the introductory psychology experience" (APA.org/Ed/Precollege/Undergrad/Introductory-Psychology-Initiative). The APA IPI ***Student Learning Outcomes for Introductory Psychology*** consist of three outcomes related to "Psychology Content," four outcomes related to "Scientific Thinking," and seven "Integrative Themes."

The IPI charges students to "Identify basic concepts and research findings" (Psychology Content) and to "Solve problems using psychological methods" (Scientific Thinking).

The IPI encourages instructors to incorporate and assess the ***seven Integrative Themes*** throughout the course to help students (A) adapt their thinking in response to empirical evidence; (B) recognize general principles but individual differences; (C) acknowledge biological, psychological, and social-cultural influences; (D) respect diversity, equity, and inclusion; (E) be aware of perceptual and thinking errors; (F) apply psychology's principles to improve their own lives and communities; and (G) value psychology's ethical principles. To help students understand and apply these key themes, Garth Neufeld (Cascadia College) has created a brief video about each theme, along with an introductory video about the APA IPI's Integrative Themes. These helpful resources may be found in Macmillan Learning's Achieve, where they are accompanied by assessment so that they may be assigned and will report to the gradebook.

The IPI recommends choosing course content using the ***pillar model*** (APA, 2014; Gurung et al., 2016)—and covering at least two topics from each pillar **(FIGURE 1)**.

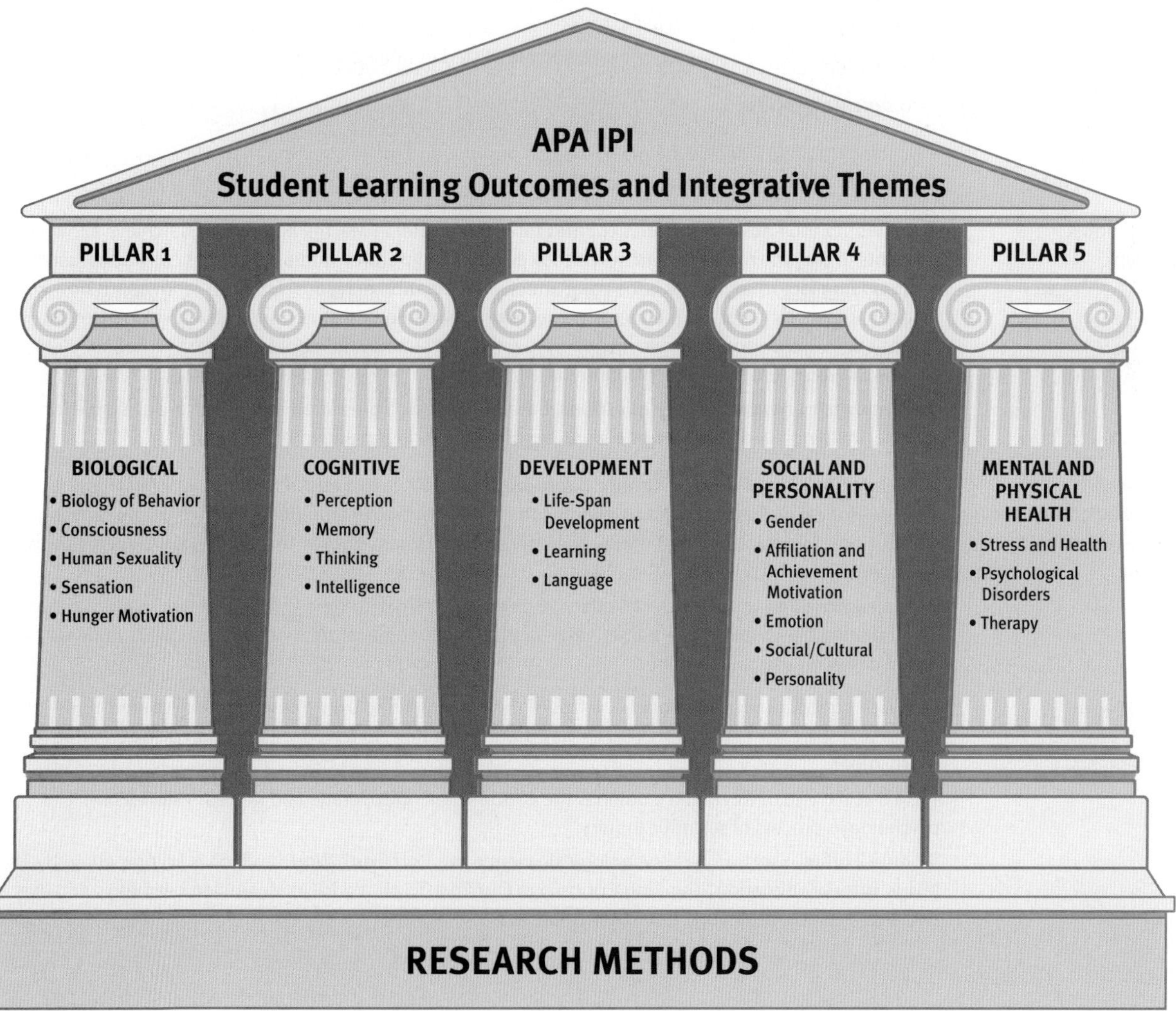
APA IPI
Student Learning Outcomes and Integrative Themes
PILLAR 1
PILLAR 2
PILLAR 3
PILLAR 4
PILLAR 5
BIOLOGICAL
• Biology of Behavior
• Consciousness
• Human Sexuality
• Sensation
• Hunger Motivation
COGNITIVE
• Perception
• Memory
• Thinking
• Intelligence
DEVELOPMENT
• Life-Span Development
• Learning
• Language
SOCIAL AND PERSONALITY
• Gender
• Affiliation and Achievement Motivation
• Emotion
• Social/Cultural
• Personality
MENTAL AND PHYSICAL HEALTH
• Stress and Health
• Psychological Disorders
• Therapy
RESEARCH METHODS

FIGURE 1
Student pillars for introductory psychology The five content pillars are built on a foundation of *research methods*, with the new *student learning outcomes* capping the structure.

Psychology, Fourteenth Edition, and its resources offer a perfect match for those interested in following these new guidelines, with full text coverage of relevant content, and abundant student and classroom activities and assessment opportunities (see **TABLES 1** and **2**).

TABLE 1 ***Psychology,*** **Fourteenth Edition, Corresponds to APA IPI Student Learning Outcomes**

APA IPI Student Learning Outcomes	*Psychology,* Fourteenth Edition, Coverage
Psychology Content: Identify basic concepts and research findings	
1.1 Define and explain basic psychological concepts.	*Psychology,* 14th Edition, offers a compelling and complete survey of the field, including all of the "Sample Concepts or Ideas" outlined in Table 2.
1.2 Interpret research findings related to psychological concepts.	• The reality that psychology is a science and that research supplies our understandings of psychology's concepts is emphasized throughout the text. See Table 6 at the end of this Preface. • In addition, David Myers regularly blogs at TalkPsych.com, where he shares the most exciting new psychological science discoveries, how the field is adapting in response, and how psychology helps explain the rapidly changing world around us.
1.3. Apply psychological principles to personal growth and other aspects of everyday life.	• Since the first edition of the text, one of the "eight guiding principles" has been "to provide applications of principles." The authors strive throughout to make psychology meaningful and memorable to students by showing how it relates to their lives. • For numerous examples, see *Psychology* coverage listed in Table 2 for Integrative Theme F.
Scientific Thinking: Solve problems using psychological methods	
2.1 Describe the advantages and limitations of research strategies.	• *Psychology* Module 2 details the main research designs, and offers a section that addresses "How would you know which research design to use?"
2.2. Evaluate, design, or conduct psychological research.	• "How Would You Know?" ***research activities*** for each chapter in Macmillan Learning's Achieve allow students to play the role of researcher as they design and interpret studies. Students consider possible confounding factors and other issues that affect interpretation of results. Students learn about how key decision points can alter the meaning and value of a psychological study, and they develop scientific literacy skills in the process. Topics include "How Would You Know If People Can Learn to Reduce Anxiety?" and "How Would You Know If Schizophrenia Is Inherited?" • ***New research-oriented iClicker questions,*** based on research presented in the text, are available for each chapter, helping build student understanding of research design and interpretation.
2.3 Draw logical and objective conclusions about behavior and mental processes from empirical evidence.	• There are ***"Thinking Critically About . . ." infographics,*** with associated activities in Macmillan Learning's Achieve, for every chapter to guide students to consider available empirical evidence before drawing conclusions. Topics include parenting styles, gender bias, sexual aggression, effects of violence-viewing, lie detection, and introversion. • Module 27 outlines the obstacles to effective decision making, judgment, and problem solving, including confirmation bias, fixation, mental set, representativeness and availability heuristics, overconfidence, belief perseverance, and framing.
2.4. Examine how psychological science can be used to counter unsubstantiated statements, opinions, or beliefs.	• "To teach critical thinking" has been the first of the "eight guiding principles" that have guided Myers' work on this text since the first edition, and in the editions that have followed with Nathan DeWall and now June Gruber. • Table 6 at the end of this Preface outlines the critical-thinking coverage and in-depth stories of psychology's process of scientific inquiry. • Module 2 offers a section on "Psychological Science in a Post-Truth World," which is accompanied by Myers' tutorial animation "Thinking Critically in Our Post-Truth World" in Macmillan Learning's Achieve, and also available at tinyurl.com/PostTruthMyers.

TABLE 2 *Psychology*, Fourteenth Edition, Corresponds to APA IPI *Integrative Themes*

APA's Seven "Integrative Themes"	APA's "Sample Concepts or Ideas"	*Psychology,* Fourteenth Edition Coverage
A. Psychological science relies on empirical evidence, and adapts as new data develop.	• Experimental methods • Statistics • Memory models • Subliminal perception • Therapy interventions	• The reality that psychology is a science and that research matters is emphasized throughout the text. See Table 6 at the end of this Preface. • In addition, David Myers regularly blogs at TalkPsych.com, where he shares the most exciting new psychological science discoveries, how the field is adapting in response, and how psychology helps explain the rapidly changing world around us.
B. Psychology explains general principles that govern behavior while recognizing individual differences.	• Intelligence • Resilience • Personality testing • Supertasters • Synesthesia	• Since the first edition of this text, one of Myers' Eight Guiding Principles has been ***"to convey respect for human unity and diversity."*** Readers will learn about human kinship in our shared biology and need for affiliation; our shared mechanisms for learning and remembering, emotional expression, and the stress response; and our shared vulnerability to perceptual and thinking errors. Yet they will learn much about our individual diversity — in development and aptitudes, temperament and characteristics, sexual orientation and gender identity, attitudes and motivations, disorders and health — and about cultural and other group variations.
C. Psychological, biological, social, and cultural factors influence behavior and mental processes.	• Psychological disorders • Aging • Health and wellness • Attachment • Personality theories	• The ***biopsychosocial approach*** is introduced in Module 1 and carried through the rest of the book, with regular narrative reflections on the biological, psychological, and social-cultural factors influencing our understanding of behavior and mental processes. The text includes flow charts outlining the biopsychosocial influences on key topics, including development, aging, disordered drug use, learning, sexual motivation, aggressive behavior, personality, and psychological disorders.
D. Psychology values diversity, promotes equity, and fosters inclusion in pursuit of a more just society.	• Racial and cultural identity • Stereotypes • Racism • Biases • Prejudice, implicit and explicit • Emotion regulation	• This text fully reflects psychology's diversity, equity, and inclusion values. The authors make no assumptions about the race/ethnicity, culture, gender identity, sexual orientation, relationship or family status, age, economic background, and cognitive or physical ability of their readers. Students of all kinds will see themselves represented in examples and illustrations throughout these resources. And the authors include important topics related to justice, including in discussions of moral development, prejudice, intelligence test bias, and legal system bias. June Gruber has added a new section on Emotion Regulation in Module 40, and a new activity in Macmillan Learning's Achieve — Assess Your Strengths: How Healthy Is Your Emotional Ecosystem?
E. Our perceptions and biases filter our experiences of the world through an imperfect personal lens.	• Perceptual illusions • Schemas • Cognitive errors • Self-serving bias • Ingroup bias	• The Module 18 discussion of "Processing Sensations and Perceptions" outlines the impressive strengths and numerous weaknesses in our ability to detect and interpret incoming stimuli. Other coverage of our "imperfect personal lens" includes: cognitive errors (Module 27), ingroup bias (Module 43), and self-serving bias (Module 47).

(Continued)		
F. Applying psychological principles can change our lives, organizations, and communities in positive ways.	• Psychotherapy • Study skills • Coping • Conflict resolution • Behavioral change	• This edition has an improved student preface — ***Student Success: How to Apply Psychology to Live Your Best Life.*** This preface offers brief discussions of "Thinking Critically and Scientifically," "Self-Control and Self-Improvement," "Time Management and Study Tips," "Social Life," and "Finding Meaning and Pursuing Goals." • ***"Ask Yourself"*** questions appear throughout each module to help students apply what they are learning to improve their own lives. This helps make the material more meaningful and memorable. • ***Self-applications*** are built into the narrative throughout the text. Examples include: "Use Psychology to Become a Stronger Person — and a Better Student" (Module 1), tips on "How to Improve Your Sleep" (Module 9), goal-setting to "Change Your Own Behavior" (Module 22), "Goal-Setting" strategies (Module 35), "Improving Memory" (Module 26), ways to "boost the creative process" (Module 27), building a "Growth Mindset" (Module 31), "Tips for Healthy Eating" (Module 33), "Connecting and Social Networking" (Module 35), "Evidence-Based Suggestions for a Happier Life" (Module 38), guidance for coping with stress (Module 40), "How to Be Persuasive" (Module 41), "Cognitive Therapy Techniques" (Module 54), "When should a person seek therapy and what should people look for when selecting a therapist?" (Module 55), "Therapeutic Lifestyle Change" (Module 56), and tips for finding "flow" (Appendix C). • In the ***"Assess Your Strengths" activities*** in Macmillan Learning's Achieve, students apply what they are learning from the text to their own lives and experiences by considering key "strengths." Students assess themselves on the strength (critical thinking, quality of sleep, self-control, relationship strength, and more), then get guidance for nurturing that strength in their own lives. • The value of ***community psychology*** and preventive mental health work is discussed in Module 1, Module 56, and Appendix B. Related discussions include: the social toxicity of extreme income inequality (Module 38), the importance of community communication (Module 44), and the relationship of income levels and community empowerment (or lack thereof) to mental disorders (Module 48).
G. Ethical principles guide psychology research and practice.	• Beneficence (do good) and nonmaleficence (do no harm) • Fidelity and responsibility • Integrity • Justice • Respect for people's rights and dignity	• Module 2 includes discussions of "Psychology's Research Ethics," "Ensuring Scientific Integrity," "Studying and Protecting Animals," "Studying and Protecting Humans," and "Values in Psychology." • Module 55 has a main section on "Ethical Principles in Psychotherapy."

In addition, **APA's 2023 Learning Goals and Outcomes** from the *APA Guidelines for the Undergraduate Psychology Major 3.0* (still in draft form at the time of this text's publication) were designed to gauge progress in students graduating with psychology majors. The new guidelines offer "Foundation Indicators" for students completing an intro course, and "Baccalaureate Indicators" for those completing a major. Many psychology departments have used these goals and outcomes in previous versions to help establish benchmarks for departmental assessment purposes. **TABLE 3** outlines the ways *Psychology*, Fourteenth Edition, can help you and your department address the Foundation Indicators for APA's Learning Goals and Outcomes 3.0. There is a detailed APA Correlation Guide in Achieve's Instructor Resources for this fourteenth edition.

TABLE 3 ***Psychology*, Fourteenth Edition, Corresponds to APA Learning Goals 3.0**[1]

Relevant Feature from *Psychology*, Fourteenth Edition	APA Learning Goals				
	Content Knowledge and Applications	**Scientific Inquiry and Critical Thinking**	**Values in Psychological Science**	**Communication, Psychological Literacy, and Technology Skills**	**Personal and Professional Development**
Text content	•	•	•	•	•
Student Success preface and Skills for Student Success activity in Macmillan Learning's Achieve	•	•	•	•	•
Myers/DeWall/Gruber's focus on research and critical thinking	•	•	•		
"Thinking Critically About . . ." infographics and their Achieve activities	•	•	•		
"Learning Objective Questions" previewing main sections	•	•			
"Retrieval Practice" self-tests throughout	•	•	•		
"Ask Yourself" questions integrated throughout	•	•	•	•	•
"Try this" style activities integrated throughout the text and Achieve resources	•	•		•	•
"Module Test" self-tests	•	•		•	
"Psychology at Work" (Appendix C)	•	•	•	•	•
"The Story of Psychology" timeline (Appendix A)	•		•		•
"Career Fields in Psychology" (Appendix B) with "Pursuing a Psychology Career" in Achieve	•		•		•
LearningCurve adaptive quizzing	•	•	•	•	•
IRM activities, including Spotlight on Women activities, and Diversity in Psychology activities	•	•	•	•	•
"Assess Your Strengths" activities in Achieve	•	•	•	•	•
"How Would You Know?" research activities in Achieve	•	•	•	•	•
New research-oriented iClicker questions	•	•	•		

[1] Information for this table is from the draft form of the APA's Learning Goals and Outcomes 3.0 that was available at the time of this text's publication.

What Should I Know About the NEW Fourteenth Edition?

In addition to our thorough, line-by-line updating of every module, and our ongoing efforts to *make no assumptions* about student readers' gender identity, sexual orientation, culture, relationship or family status, age, economic or educational background, and physical or cognitive ability, we offer much that is new or noteworthy in this fourteenth edition.

1. Over 1400 research citations dated 2019–2022. Our ongoing scrutiny of dozens of scientific periodicals and science news sources, enhanced by commissioned reviews, enables integrating our field's most important, thought-provoking, and student-relevant new discoveries. Part of the pleasure that sustains this work is learning something new every day! Ask your Macmillan Sales Representative for a module-by-module list of significant Content Changes. See also #5 in this list, "More support for teaching that psychology is a science, and that critical thinking and research matter!"

2. Macmillan Learning's Achieve for Psychology! See the section at the beginning of the text for more information about these engaging digital resources, including 133 fresh new videos, our new "Skills for Student Success" activity, a revised and thoroughly updated Instructor's Resource Manual, and new research-oriented iClicker questions (contributed by Jennifer Zwolinski, University of San Diego) that test student understanding of effective research design, the component parts of key research that's presented in the text, and the implications of research results. Achieve also retains the best from our previous teaching and learning platform: LearningCurve adaptive quizzing, "How Would You Know?" research activities, "Assess Your Strengths" self-assessment activities (including two new activities: "How Healthy Is Your Emotional Ecosystem?" and "How Much Awe Do You Experience, and How Might You Increase It?" by June Gruber), "Thinking Critically About ..." infographic activities, the popular PsychSim tutorials, and Concept Practice tutorials.

3. Continuously improving diversity, equity, and inclusion. Since this text's first edition, one of its Eight Guiding Principles has been "To convey respect for human unity and diversity." A lot has changed in the field of psychology since the last edition was written, especially in the fast-moving subfields of cultural diversity, human sexuality, and gender psychology, and in the language we use to refer to varying groups of people. We sought extra reviews from experts and instructors, and we made extensive updates to this coverage in the text and in the language used in all of our text and assessment materials. With a growth mindset, we seek ongoing conversation and constant improvement.

In Modules 13 and 34, and throughout these resources, we've worked to be appropriately inclusive and fully up-to-date in our presentation of gender, gender identity, and sexual orientation—representing the abundance of current research in these areas, but also encompassing the lived experiences of many people. Our improved photo and illustration program, and our updated examples and stories, help all students see themselves in this book and its resources. (See **TABLE 4** The Psychology of Gender, Gender Identity, and Sexuality, and **TABLE 5**, The Psychology of Culture, Ethnicity, and Race at the end of this Preface.)

4. A broad global perspective for our worldwide student audience. We continue to offer a *world-based psychology for our worldwide student readership*. Thus, we continually search the world for research findings and text and photo examples, conscious that readers may be in Melbourne, Montreal, or Memphis. Although we reside in the United States, we have traveled abroad regularly and maintain contact with colleagues in Canada (including one of our editors), Australia, Brazil, Britain, China, Hong Kong, and many other places. And we glean research from worldwide psychology and psychiatry periodicals. As a result, each new edition offers a world-based perspective, and includes research from around the world.

As global citizens, U.S. students, too, benefit from information and examples that internationalize their world-consciousness. And if psychology seeks to explain human behavior (not just American or Canadian or Australian behavior), the broader the scope of studies presented, the more accurate is our picture of this world's people. We hope to expose all students to the world beyond their own culture, and we continue to welcome input and suggestions from all readers.

The results of this effort to internationalize include dozens of Canadian examples and dozens more from other countries. Some of these examples are, by themselves, trivial. Yet by the book's end these examples accumulate, we hope, to a significant exposure to Canadian and worldwide culture and science. Mindful of the book's worldwide readership in a dozen languages, we also seek to avoid peculiarly American examples and to specify the country (rather than assume the United States) when mentioning national data.

5. More support for teaching that psychology is a science, and that critical thinking and research matter! "To teach critical thinking" has been the first of the Eight Guiding Principles that have guided our work on this text since the first edition. Chapter 1 takes a critical-thinking approach to introducing students to psychology's research methods and the idea that *psychology is a science*. Critical thinking is a key term on p. 4 and is encouraged throughout the text and its resources. For example, we offer "Thinking Critically About ..." infographics in each chapter, with accompanying activities in

Macmillan Learning's Achieve. See **TABLE 6**, Critical Thinking and Scientific Inquiry, at the end of this Preface for a deeper list of coverage. Throughout the text and its Achieve resources, students are encouraged to *think critically*, by examining sources and evidence, and to *consider other voices and ideas*, by being open to diverse perspectives.

The most important task for us as your authors is to report the current state of psychology, including each subdiscipline's latest research insights. The end-of-book ***References*** section highlights the 1427 citations from 2019–2022 in blue. With thousands of studies published each year, it takes a daily effort to keep up with all that is happening in our exciting field. In winnowing new research findings, we consider:

- *Reliability:* Does either replication or the inherent scale of the finding make it trustworthy?
- *Importance:* Is this, for psychology, a significant new finding? And is this something an educated person needs to know?
- *Clarity:* Is this something our readers could understand and remember?

The new findings met these high standards for inclusion. Each confirms key concepts or informs the way we present them. The remaining thousands of reference citations include important classic studies that have formed the structure of our discipline.

We all want students to walk away with the most accurate, current understandings of psychology to apply in their own lives and work. Having the latest research engages students so much more effectively. Here are three examples of new research areas—from just the last few years—that are important for students' understanding of psychological science and its application in their lives.

A. *People often spurn those with differing worldviews, yet the recent scientific evidence we share in this new edition demonstrates value in embracing diverse perspectives:*
    - Lower racial prejudice is linked with better personal health in that region (Michaels et al., 2022; see Module 39, Stress and Illness).
    - Children raised with competent, secure, and nurturing care can flourish regardless of parents' gender and sexual orientation (Calzo et al., 2019; see Module 15, Infancy and Childhood).
    - People who are transgender have a more positive therapeutic experience when therapists affirm them (Bettergarcia & Israel, 2018; see Module 55, Evaluating Psychotherapies).
    - Social media communication often occurs in an ideological vacuum, in which we surround ourselves with mostly like-minded individuals and become susceptible to misinformation (Hills, 2019; see Module 42, Social Influence).

B. *Social media use has soared, and the new research we present in Module 2, Research Strategies, and Module 35, Affiliation and Achievement, explores correlational, longitudinal, and experimental studies of its possible effects, such as on increasing depression and suicidal thoughts in teen girls.*

C. *Psychedelic drugs are being studied as possible safe and effective methods to treat various psychological disorders, such as depressive disorders, posttraumatic stress disorder, and substance-related and addictive disorders (see Module 56: The Biomedical Therapies and Preventing Psychological Disorders).*

Other new, student-relevant research explores

- navigating our "post-truth" world,
- understanding how gene–environment interactions affect us,
- distinguishing substance use from abuse,
- weighing parent/peer influences on our development,
- appreciating our unique sensory and perceptual windows on the world,
- figuring out how to learn and remember most effectively,
- successfully connecting socially with others to build our health and well-being,
- enjoying micro-friendships with those we encounter in our day-to-day lives,

- understanding gender identity and sexual orientation,
- learning about our hunger and sexual motivations,
- coping with stress and determining how to thrive,
- regulating our emotions effectively so that we can live our best life,
- recognizing inborn personality variations,
- dealing with the challenges of mental illness,
- appreciating neurodiversity (including those with autism spectrum disorder, and those experiencing ADHD, a specific learning disorder, or brain injury),
- finding hope in psychological and biomedical therapies, and
- seeking "flow" in our daily lives and work.

6. Improved Student Preface—Skills for Student Success: How to Apply Psychology to Live Your Best Life—With a NEW Student Success Activity in Macmillan Learning's Achieve. When we ask our teaching colleagues to share the most important lessons they wish to impart to students, they often tell us they want to teach students to think critically, and to apply psychology to their own lives so that they can live better and be more successful. This brief Student Success preface, and its interactive component in Achieve, preview relevant resources in the text and in Achieve, and help get students on the right path with sections on

- Thinking Critically and Scientifically,
- Self-Control and Self-Improvement,
- Time Management and Study Tips,
- Social Life, and
- Finding Meaning and Pursuing Goals.

In addition, students will find opportunities to *improve their everyday life* throughout the text by using evidence-based principles to boost their relationships, academic success, stress management, and so much more.

7. Improved, easier-to-use Instructor's Resource Manual. We consulted with national award-winning teacher Elizabeth Hammer (Xavier University) to radically improve the content and organization of our Instructor's Resource Manual, which offers an abundance of active learning opportunities to engage your students. The IRM includes a "Diversity in Psychology: Spotlight on Women" collection of 17 activities, as well as two new activities on diversity in psychology for use with the Timeline (Appendix A), all created by Salena Brody (University of Texas, Dallas).

8. This text offers excellent neuroscience coverage and DSM-5-TR updates, and it maps almost exactly to the MCAT Behavioral Sciences section, making it perfect for nursing and premed students. We have continued to improve our strong neuroscience, behavior genetics, and evolutionary psychology coverage in this new edition, reflecting the dynamic nature of these subfields. See **TABLE 7** and **TABLE 8** at the end of this Preface for a list of topics covered. This new edition also contains updated terminology and diagnostic criteria to match the *new* DSM-5-TR (2022).

Psychology maps well onto the new MCAT's psychology section. Since 2015, the MCAT has devoted 25 percent of its questions to the "Psychological, Social, and Biological Foundations of Behavior." The new section's topics match up almost exactly with the topics in this text. See **TABLE 9** at the end of this Preface for a sample. There is a complete pairing of the new MCAT psychology topics with this book's contents in the Instructor's Resources in Macmillan Learning's Achieve.

9. You won't find better service and support anywhere. The Macmillan Learning representatives who market and sell these resources, help set up instructors' courses, and in many other ways service instructor and student course needs, are the best in the business. Many of these folks have become personal friends. We've been grateful to be working with a family-owned publisher that has been so supportive of our teaching mission and has encouraged us to create the best teaching and learning materials.

10. This text is inclusive of all students. We have written *Psychology* with the diversity of student readers in mind:

- *Gender:* Extensive coverage of gender development, changing gender roles, and gender identity.
- *Culture:* No assumptions about readers' cultural backgrounds or experiences.
- *Economic background:* No references to backyards, summer camp, vacations.
- *Education:* No assumptions about past or current learning environments.
- *Physical and cognitive abilities:* No assumptions about full vision, hearing, movement, or other abilities.
- *Life experiences:* Our writing has a multicultural, global perspective, and our stories and examples represent diverse groups.
- *Relationship or family status:* Examples and ideas are made relevant for all students, whether they have children or are still living at home, are married or cohabiting or single; and with no assumptions about sexual orientation or gender identity.

11. This text offers abundant EVERYDAY LIFE applications. Throughout this text, we relate the findings of psychology's research to the real world. This edition includes:

- "Ask Yourself" questions throughout each module, helping students make the concepts more meaningful (and memorable), and apply psychology to improve their own lives. These questions can also be used as group discussion topics.
- "Assess Your Strengths" personal self-assessments in Macmillan Learning's Achieve, allowing students to actively apply key principles to their own experiences and develop their strengths.
- fun side notes and quotes throughout the text, applying psychology's findings to sports, literature, world religions, music, business, and more.
- an emphasis throughout the text on critical thinking in everyday life, including Module 3, "Statistical Reasoning in Everyday Life," helping students to become more informed consumers and everyday thinkers.

12. The study system follows best practices from learning and memory research. This text's learning system harnesses the *testing effect,* which documents the benefits of actively retrieving information through regular testing (**FIGURE 2**). Thus, our LearningCurve adaptive quizzing program provides a personalized study plan. In the text, each module offers **Retrieval Practice** questions interspersed throughout (**FIGURE 3**). Creating these *desirable difficulties* for students along the way optimizes the testing effect, as does *immediate feedback* via answers that are available for checking.

Make Things Memorable!
How to study and LEARN more effectively.
With David G. Myers, author

FIGURE 2
How to learn and remember For my [DM's] 5-minute animated guide to more effective studying, visit tinyurl.com/HowToRemember.

RETRIEVAL PRACTICE

RP-1 According to Kohlberg, ____________ morality focuses on self-interest, ____________ morality focuses on self-defined ethical principles, and ____________ morality focuses on upholding laws and social rules.

RP-2 How has Kohlberg's theory of moral reasoning been criticized?

ANSWERS IN APPENDIX E

FIGURE 3
Sample Retrieval Practice feature

In addition, each module begins with a numbered question that establishes a **learning objective** and directs student reading. The Module Review section repeats these questions as a further self-testing opportunity (with answers available to check). The Module Review section also offers a self-test on the **Terms and Concepts to Remember,** and **Module Test** questions in multiple formats to promote optimal retention.

Myers' Eight Guiding Principles

We have retained the goals—the guiding principles—that have animated my [DM's] text since the first edition:

Facilitating the Learning Experience

1. To teach critical thinking By presenting research as intellectual detective work, we model a scientific mindset. Students will discover how critical thinking can help them evaluate competing ideas and popular claims—from vaccine myths and memory construction to group differences in intelligence and alternative therapies. Our "Thinking Critically About" infographic features, and the accompanying activities in Macmillan Learning's Achieve, help engage students in this learning. (See Table 6 at the end of this Preface for more about critical thinking in this text.)

2. To provide applications of principles Throughout the narrative, illustrations, and other Macmillan Learning's Achieve resources we relate psychology's findings to real-world applications. We make psychology meaningful to students by showing how it relates to their lives—their lifespan development, their search for relationships and happiness, their understanding of negative forces, such as prejudice, and so much more. The "Ask Yourself" questions throughout each module, and our "Assess Your Strengths" activities in Achieve invite students to apply important concepts to their own lives, and to learn ways to develop key personal strengths. (See **TABLE 10,** Positive Psychology, for more about how we encourage understanding of happiness and human strengths, and see the Student Preface—Skills for Student Success: How to Apply Psychology to Live Your Best Life.)

TABLE 10 Positive Psychology

Coverage of *positive psychology* topics can be found in the following modules:

Topic	Module
Altruism/compassion	1, 11, 23, 38, 40, 41, 44, 46, 47, 49, 50, 56
Coping	2, 13, 14, 15, 17, 20, 21, 35, 38, 39, 40, 45, 48, 54, 55, 56
Courage	38, 42, 43, 46, 52
Creativity	2, 8, 9, 13, 24, 27, 28, 29, 30, 35, 38, 40, 42, 45, 46, 50, App. C
Emotional intelligence	29, 31
Empathy	13, 16, 20, 23, 37, 42, 43, 44, 46, 48, 54, 55
Flow	38, 47, App. C
Forgiveness	13, 38
Gratitude	36, 38, 46
Happiness/life satisfaction	1, 2, 9, 10, 11, 14, 15, 16, 17, 25, 27, 29, 34, 35, 38, 39, 40, 44, 46, 47, App. C
Humility	1, 13, 46, 47
Humor	38, 40
Integrity	16, 17, 38
Justice	14, 16, 40, 48, 55
Leadership	13, 14, 23, 30, 35, 38, 39, 40, 42, 43, 46, 47, App. C
Love	2, 13, 14, 15, 16, 17, 20, 23, 26, 32, 34, 35, 37, 40, 41, 43, 44, 46
Morality	12, 13, 14, 15, 16, 23, 27, 28, 36, 41, 48
Optimism	15, 38, 40, 46, 50, 54
Personal control	13, 35, 38, 40, 42
Resilience	11, 13, 15, 16, 17, 31, 38, 39, 49, 55
Self-awareness	7, 15, 29, 46, 47, 54
Self-control	15, 16, 21, 22, 38, 40, 47, 54
Self-discipline	14, 16, 30, 31, 35, 40
Self-efficacy	47, 55
Self-esteem	15, 16, 17, 28, 32, 35, 39, 47, 48, 54, App. C
Spirituality	10, 16, 38, 39, 40, 46, 49, 56
Toughness (also grit)	15, 29, 31, 35
Wisdom	1, 13, 15, 27, 30, 38, 46

3. To reinforce learning at every step Everyday examples and thought-provoking questions encourage students to process the material actively. Self-testing opportunities throughout the text and Macmillan Learning's Achieve resources help students learn and retain important concepts and terminology.

Demonstrating the Science of Psychology

4. To show the process of inquiry We try to show students not just the outcome of research, but how the research process works, often by putting them in the role of experimenter or participant in classic studies. We introduce research stories as mysteries that unravel as one clue after another falls into place. Our "How Would You Know?" activities in Macmillan Learning's Achieve allow students to play the role of researcher in thinking about research questions and how they may be studied effectively.

5. To be as up-to-date as possible While retaining psychology's classic studies and concepts, we also present the most important recent developments. In this edition, 1427 new references are dated 2019–2022. Likewise, new photos and new everyday examples are drawn from today's world.

6. To put facts in the service of concepts Our intention is not to overwhelm students with facts, but to reveal psychology's major concepts—to teach students how to think, and to offer psychological ideas worth thinking about. Learning Objective Questions and Retrieval Practice questions throughout each module help students focus on the most important concepts. Concept Practice activities and PsychSim tutorials in Macmillan Learning's Achieve help ensure student understanding of key points.

Promoting Big Ideas and Broadened Horizons

7. To enhance comprehension by providing continuity Many modules have a significant issue or theme that links subtopics and ties the module together. The Learning modules convey the idea that bold thinkers can serve as intellectual pioneers. The Thinking and Language modules raise the issue of human rationality and irrationality. The Psychological Disorders modules convey empathy for, and understanding of, troubled lives. Other threads, such as cognitive neuroscience, dual processing, and individual and group diversity, weave throughout the whole book, and students hear a consistent voice.

8. To convey respect for human unity and diversity Throughout the book, readers will see evidence of human kinship in our shared biology—our common mechanisms of seeing and learning, hungering and feeling, loving and hating. They will also better understand our diversity—our individual diversity in development and aptitudes, temperament and personality, and disorder and health; and our cultural diversity in attitudes and expressive styles, child raising and care for older family members, and life priorities and experiences.

In Appreciation

Aided by input from thousands of instructors and students over the years, this has become a better, more effective, more accurate book than three authors alone (these authors at least) could write. Our indebtedness continues to the innumerable researchers who have been so willing to share their time and talent to help us accurately report their research, and to the hundreds of instructors who have taken the time to offer feedback.

With this new edition, we are happy to introduce our new co-author, June Gruber (University of Colorado Boulder). We [DM and ND] admire June's dedication to rigorous research, her extensive collaborations with fellow scholars, and her passion for sharing psychological science with students and the wider world. We look forward to working together in the years ahead!

We also appreciate Salena Brody's (University of Texas, Dallas) careful work on our Psychology Timeline (Appendix A), including her added entries relating to the contributions of women and people of color, and the new Diversity in Psychology: Focus on Women activities she created for the Instructor's Resource Manual.

Our gratitude extends to the colleagues who contributed criticism, corrections, and creative ideas related to the content, pedagogy, and format of this new edition and its resources. For their expertise and encouragement, and the gift of their time to the teaching of psychology, we thank the reviewers and consultants listed here:

Jennifer Ackil
Gustavus Adolphus College

Elizabeth Arnott-Hill
College of DuPage

Christie Bartholomew
Kent State University at Kent

Stefanie S. Boswell
University of the Incarnate Word

Salena Brody
University of Texas at Dallas

Ty Brumback
Northern Kentucky University

Michelle Butler Samuels
United States Air Force Academy

Michele Camden
Stetson University

Lucy Capuano
Ventura College

Kelly L. Cate
University of North Georgia

Christie Cunningham
Pellissippi State Community College

Kilee DeBrabander
University of Texas at Dallas

Rainer Diriwächter
California Lutheran University

Hannah M. Finch
Colorado State University

Darrell W. Frost
Northern Oklahoma College

Jordan Gamache
Virginia Tech

Nathaniel R. Herr
American University

Lisa Hollis-Sawyer
Northeastern Illinois University

Bev F. Lenihan
Camosun College

Jordan Lyerly
University of North Carolina at Charlotte

Jerry Marshall
Green River Community College

Robin K. Morgan
Indiana University Southeast

Christopher Motz
Carleton University

Lauren J. Myers
Lafayette College

Jason Neill
Anderson University

Kristina Olson
Princeton University

Susana Phillips
Kwantlen Polytechnic University

Michele Poulos
ECPI University—Richmond South

Tracy Rose
Clover Park Technical College

Kenneth Thiel
Madonna University

Jason Whetten
Northern Arizona University

Rachel Wu
University of California Riverside

At Macmillan Learning, a host of people played key roles in creating this fourteenth edition.

Executive Program Manager Carlise Stembridge has been our valued and beloved team leader, thanks to her dedication, creativity, and sensitivity. Carlise oversees, encourages, and guides our author-editor team, and she serves as an important liaison with our colleagues in the field.

Karissa Venne expertly coordinated creation of the media and assessment resources. Danielle Slevens and Betty Probert thoughtfully and carefully edited the Test Bank, LearningCurve, and Practice Quiz questions. Talia Green provided invaluable support in commissioning and organizing the multitude of reviews; coordinating our development and production schedules; completing diversity, equity, and inclusion audits of our content; and providing other editorial guidance. Robin Fadool and Cheryl DuBois worked together to create the lovely photo program.

Won McIntosh, Susan Wein, and Paul Rohloff masterfully kept the book to its tight schedule, and Natasha Wolfe skillfully directed creation of the beautiful new design.

Christine Brune, chief editor for the last three decades, is a wonder worker. She offers just the right mix of encouragement, gentle admonition, attention to detail, and passion for excellence. Her authors could not ask for more. Development Editors Danielle Slevens and Ann Kirby-Payne also amazed us with their meticulous focus, impressive knowledge, and helpful editing—and with kindred spirits to our own. And Deborah Heimann did her predictably excellent copyediting.

To achieve our goal of supporting the teaching of psychology, these resources not only must be authored, reviewed, edited, and produced, but also made available to teachers of psychology, with effective guidance and professional and friendly servicing close at hand. For their exceptional success in doing all this, our author team is grateful to

Macmillan Learning's professional sales and marketing team. We are especially grateful to Executive Marketing Manager Kate Nurre, and Learning Solutions Specialists Justin Navarro and Emily White for tirelessly working to inform our teaching colleagues of our efforts to assist their teaching, and for the joy of working with them.

At Hope College, I [DM] was supported by the amazing Kathryn Brownson, who researched countless bits of information, assembled the bibliography, and edited and proofed every page. Kathryn is a knowledgeable and sensitive adviser on many matters.

Again, I [DM] gratefully acknowledge the editing assistance and mentoring of my writing coach, poet Jack Ridl, whose influence resides in the voice you will be hearing in the pages that follow. He, more than anyone, cultivated my delight in dancing with the language, and taught me to approach writing as a craft that shades into art. Likewise, I [ND] am grateful to my intellectual hero and mentor, Roy Baumeister, who taught me how to hone my writing and embrace the writing life. I'm also indebted to John Tierney, who has offered tremendous support and served as a role model of how to communicate to a general audience.

We [DM and ND] have enjoyed beginning our collaboration with June Gruber, and also our ongoing work with each other on this our twelfth co-authored book. In addition to our work together on the textbook, we contribute to the monthly "Teaching Current Directions in Psychological Science" column in the *APS Observer* (tinyurl.com/MyersDeWall). I [DM] also blog at TalkPsych.com, where I share exciting new findings, everyday applications, and observations on all things psychology.

Finally, our gratitude extends to the many students and instructors who have written to offer suggestions, or just an encouraging word. It is for them, and those about to begin their study of psychology, that we have done our best to introduce the field we love.

* * *

The day this book was released was the day we started gathering information and ideas for the next update. Your input will influence how this book continues to evolve. So, please, do share your thoughts.

David Myers
Hope College
Holland, Michigan 49422-9000 USA
DavidMyers.org
@DavidGMyers

Nathan DeWall
University of Kentucky
Lexington, Kentucky 40506-0044 USA
@cndewall

June Gruber
University of Colorado Boulder
Boulder, Colorado 80302 USA
junegruber.com
@junegruber

Tables 4, 5, 6, 7, 8, and 9

TABLE 4 The Psychology of Gender, Gender Identity, and Sexuality

Coverage of the *psychology of gender, gender identity, and sexuality* can be found in the following modules:

TABLE 5 The Psychology of Culture, Ethnicity, and Race

Coverage of *culture* can be found in the following modules:

Coverage of *ethnicity and race* can be found in the following modules:

TABLE 6 Critical Thinking and Scientific Inquiry

***Critical thinking* coverage and in-depth stories of psychology's process of *scientific inquiry* can be found in the following modules:**

TABLE 7 Neuroscience

In addition to the coverage found in Modules 4–7, *neuroscience* can be found in the following modules:

TABLE 8 Behavior Genetics and Evolutionary Psychology

Behavior genetics **is covered in the following modules:**

The *evolutionary perspective* is covered in the following modules:

TABLE 9 Sample MCAT Correlation With *Psychology,* Fourteenth Edition

From MCAT 2015 Content Category 6C: Responding to the world	*Psychology,* Fourteenth Edition, Correlations	Module
Emotion	Emotion: Arousal, Behavior, and Cognition; Embodied Emotion; Expressed and Experienced Emotion	36, 37, 38
Three components of emotion (i.e., cognitive, physiological, behavioral)	Emotion: Arousal, Behavior, and Cognition	36
Universal emotions (e.g., fear, anger, happiness, surprise, joy, disgust, and sadness)	Culture and Emotional Expression—including the universal emotions	37, 38
	Basic emotions (fear, anger, interest, surprise, joy, disgust, sadness)	38
Adaptive role of emotion	Emotion as the body's adaptive response	36, 38
	Emotions and the Autonomic Nervous System	36
Theories of emotion		
James-Lange theory	James-Lange Theory: Arousal Comes Before Emotion	36
Cannon-Bard theory	Cannon-Bard Theory: Arousal and Emotion Occur Simultaneously	36
Schachter-Singer theory	Schachter-Singer Two-Factor Theory: Arousal + Label = Emotion	36
Zajonc; LeDoux; Lazarus	Zajonc, LeDoux, and Lazarus: Does Cognition Always Precede Emotion?	36
The role of biological processes in perceiving emotion	Emotions and the Autonomic Nervous System	36
Brain regions involved in the generation and experience of emotions	Zajonc, LeDoux, and Lazarus: Does Cognition Always Precede Emotion? (Covers the brain's pathways for emotions)	36
	The Physiology of Emotions	36
The role of the limbic system in emotion	Emotions and the Autonomic Nervous System	36
	The limbic system	6, 16, 20
	The Physiology of Emotions	36
	The amygdala	6, 9, 17, 25, 36, 38, 40, 43, 49, 51, 52

Skills for Student Success: How to Apply Psychology to Live Your Best Life

As you will see in the modules to come, some things—including our temperament, body type, sexual orientation, and personality traits—are mostly beyond our power to change. In such ways it's better to accept than to fight who we are. In other ways, we can change and become the person we aspire to be. In this brief Preface, we will consider five ways we can use psychology to build ***skills for success,*** and live our best life (with more on each of these topics in the modules to come):

- thinking critically when forming judgments and making decisions,
- attending to self-control and self-improvement,
- managing our time and study,
- enjoying a satisfying social life, and
- finding meaning while pursuing goals.

Thinking Critically and Scientifically

To live your best life, you will need to learn to think critically—guidance for which you will find in every module of this book. You will need to base your hopes, your fears, and your decisions on a foundation of truth, and to understand the importance of scientific thinking and the careful research that underlies all of what we will be presenting. Alas, misinformation spreads readily. Many people fear terrorism, mass shootings, and air travel more than the vastly greater threats they face from in-home guns and car travel. In the United States, 2 in 3 people have, year after year, perceived crime as rising—even while, until 2020, it was dramatically falling (Gallup, 2021). And "how many of the world's 1-year-old children have been vaccinated against some disease"—20, 50, or 80 percent? In most countries, more than 4 in 5 people guess 20 or 50 percent, when the truth is 88 percent (Rosling et al., 2018).

Not only does it help us individually to know the truth about what threatens and benefits us, it also helps us collectively. Democracy presumes our wisdom. When we voters grasp truth—when facts prevail over false news—we can support sensible policies and elect benevolent leaders.

Misinformation comes from various sources:

- Some people or organizations aim to deceive us in order to sell a product or to undermine a political opponent.
- Sensationalized news can be misleading—vivid images of horrific shootings or plane crashes may lead us to disproportionately fear some dangers too much, and others too little.
- If we interact only with people, websites, and news sources that reflect our way of thinking, we will confirm rather than challenge our presumptions.
- We have a natural "truth bias," an inclination to believe what others say, especially when it is repeated.

Fortunately, ignorance of our ignorance can be remedied by education. And that brings you to this book and its resources, which offer psychology's contribution to critical thinking. To learn how we can protect ourselves against errors and biases that may hack our brain, and to better understand the importance of current, scientific research and the careful procedures it follows, read on. You will also want to explore the "How Would You Know?" research activities in Macmillan Learning's Achieve, which give you a hands-on opportunity to experience the value of research from the inside out. And check out my [DM's] tutorial animation, "Thinking Critically in Our Post-Truth World" in Achieve, and also at tinyurl.com/PostTruthMyers.

With a mix of open-minded curiosity and evidence-seeking questioning, we can better sift falsehood from fact. And we can live smarter and more flourishing lives.

Self-Control and Self-Improvement

We can apply our smart thinking to all aspects of living our best life, including appropriate self-care. Family, work, and school commitments can make it difficult to find time to achieve our goals, sustain our health, and have fun. But to care for others, we first need to care for ourselves.

Self-Control

Success starts with self-control—the ability to restrain impulses and delay short-term gratification for greater long-term rewards. What's your level of self-control? On a scale from 1 (not at all like me) to 5 (very much like me), indicate how much each of the following statements reflects how you typically are (Tangney et al., 2004)[1]:

1. ___ I am good at resisting temptation.
2. ___ I have a hard time breaking bad habits.
3. ___ I am lazy.
4. ___ I say inappropriate things.
5. ___ I do certain things that are bad for me, if they are fun.
6. ___ I refuse things that are bad for me.
7. ___ I wish I had more self-discipline.
8. ___ People would say that I have iron self-discipline.
9. ___ Pleasure and fun sometimes keep me from getting work done.
10. ___ I have trouble concentrating.
11. ___ I am able to work effectively toward long-term goals.
12. ___ Sometimes I can't stop myself from doing something, even if I know it is wrong.
13. ___ I often act without thinking through all the alternatives.

To tally your total score:

- Reverse your rating for items 2, 3, 4, 5, 7, 9, 10, 12, and 13 (1=5, 2=4, 3=3, 4=2, 5=1).
- Now add your ratings to establish your total score.
- Total scores range from 13 to 65, with higher scores indicating more self-control. The average score was 39 in two studies of college students (Tangney et al., 2004).

To improve your self-control, watch my [ND's] video, "Self-Control—Our Greatest Inner Strength," available in Macmillan Learning's Achieve or at tinyurl.com/DeWallSelfControl.

An important component of self-control, as we will see in Module 37, is *emotion regulation*. We do have some control over our emotions' intensity and duration (Gross et al., 2011). Healthy emotion regulation enables greater happiness, better life satisfaction, closer social relationships, and less depression and anxiety (Aldao et al., 2010; Gross, 1998). Embracing a diversity of emotions helps. We are healthier when we let ourselves feel our natural negative and positive emotions rather than pressuring ourselves to be happy all the time. (See Quoidbach et al., 2014 and emodiversity.org.)

Self-Improvement

Here are some other smart tips for improving your self-care:

- ***Set and announce your goals.*** Specific and realistic goals—such as "draft that paper by next Friday"—direct attention, promote effort, and motivate persistence. To make yourself accountable, announce your goal to friends or family.

---

[1] Reproduced with permission of June Tangney

- ***Develop an action plan.*** Specify how you will progress toward your goal. People who flesh out goals with detailed plans become more focused, and are more likely to finish on time. Fantasizing your ultimate success (a great paper turned in on time, a good course grade, a sports victory) helps. But imagining the step-by-step details helps more.
- ***Form beneficial habits.*** Is there some behavior, such as exercising, that you would like to make automatic? Make yourself do it every day for 2 months and you will have transformed a hard-to-do behavior into a must-do habit.
- ***Plan for a full night's sleep.*** Work commitments, family stresses, and other challenges can interfere with sleep. Screen time and social time can also intrude. The first step in changing your sleep routine starts with a question, "Do I want to increase my happiness, energy, focus, and health?" If so, try to find a way to give your body more of the sleep it craves. (See Module 9 for tips on how to improve sleep hygiene.)
- ***Create a supportive environment.*** It's easier to eat healthy when you don't have junk food around. At meals, control portion size by using smaller plates and bowls. To focus on a project, remove distractions. At night, stash your phone so you can sleep undisturbed. Engage with friends who bring out the best rather than the worst in you.
- ***Control substance use.*** Many psychoactive drugs, such as nicotine, are highly addictive and can readily hijack our daily lives, long-term goals, and good health. Although some drugs, such as caffeine, may be safely consumed in moderation, many others will seriously disrupt our best life unless avoided entirely. (More on this in Module 10.)
- ***Make time for exercise.*** Frequent aerobic exercise is a great time investment. Even in small amounts, aerobic exercise boosts health, increases energy, lifts mood, improves memory, and calms anxiety.
- ***Incorporate mindfulness meditation.*** Practicing mindfulness can help you manage your stress and regulate your emotions more healthfully.
- ***Build coping skills and a healthy lifestyle.*** Strengthening our resilience and managing our emotions help us cope with stress. We can also boost our mental health with lifestyle changes—daily practices that mark flourishing lives. For more information, see Module 40, and also "Thinking Critically About: Therapeutic Lifestyle Change" in Module 56.

Time Management and Study Tips

Some students fail. Some survive. And some thrive. So, what choices can you make to thrive?

You can start by making a plan for how you will manage your time and maximize your learning. As legendary basketball coach John Wooden said in 1977, "When you fail to prepare, you're preparing to fail."

It may seem as if there are not enough hours in the week to get everything done. It may be that you are not using your time as efficiently as you could. To assess your current time management and study skills, complete the survey below.[2]

Time Management Assessment Questionnaire

Rate the following items: ***Always*** (2 points), ***Sometimes*** (1 point), or ***Never*** (0 points).

1. _____I do things in order of priority.

2. _____I accomplish what needs to be done during the day.

3. _____I always get assignments done on time.

4. _____I feel I use my time effectively.

5. _____I tackle difficult or unpleasant tasks without procrastinating.

---

[2]Information from Wayne State University (2013): Advising-Time Management Questionnaire.

6. _____I force myself to make time for planning.

7. _____I prepare a daily or weekly "to do" list.

8. _____I am able to meet deadlines without rushing at the last minute.

9. _____I keep up-to-date on my reading and homework assignments.

10. _____I prevent interruptions from distracting me from high priority tasks.

11. _____I avoid spending too much time on trivial matters.

12. _____I spend enough time on academic matters.

13. _____I plan time to relax and be with family/friends in my weekly schedule.

14. _____I have a weekly schedule on which I record fixed commitments, such as classes and work hours.

15. _____I try to do the most important tasks during my most energetic periods of the day.

16. _____I make constructive use of down time (commuting, waiting in line, etc.).

17. _____I periodically re-assess my activities in relation to my goals.

18. _____I have discontinued any wasteful or unprofitable activities or routines.

19. _____I maintain control over my electronic device (phone, computer) time to avoid interruptions.

20. _____I judge myself by accomplishment of tasks rather than by amount of activity or "busy-ness."

21. _____I have a clear idea of what I want to accomplish during this course and this term.

22. _____I am satisfied with the way I use my time.

Scoring the Assessment: Give yourself 2 points for "Always," 1 point for "Sometimes," and 0 points for "Never." Then add up the total number of points to assess your current time management skills.

39–44 points: You have excellent time management skills.

24–38 points: You manage your time fairly well but should carefully consider the tips that follow to increase your skill.

0–23 points: Improving your time management skills will be a huge factor in your success in college and beyond.

We can all use a reminder of best practices. Here are a few tips.

Manage Your Time

Your time is your most precious resource. Managing your time requires intentionally planning when you will progress toward your goals. Start by carefully tracking your time use for a week—including all personal, school, and work time—and watching for patterns and opportunities. (We [DM, ND, and JG] have each done this and were surprised by how much time we were wasting!) Next, create a "time budget" that allows you to enjoy life, be energized, and complete your study, work, and family tasks. Plan time for recreation and friends; social media; sleep, eating, and personal care; class time and study; and any employment or home obligations. Determine precisely when you will do each, by creating weekly and daily schedules that make guilt-free space for each activity. To become the person you wish to be, live intentionally, day by day.

Manage Your Mental Energy

Some tasks are mentally demanding. Plan your day to make space for such tasks when you have the most energy. Allow time to rest and recover before engaging the next demanding task. By tracking your mental energy, you will know when to spend it and when to save it.

Time for success Making a realistic, day-to-day schedule will allow you time for what you need to do as well as time for what you want to do.

stock_colors/Getty Images

Play Offense

Car troubles, family problems, and work challenges happen. Sometimes we have to play "defense" against life's demands and problems, leaving us stressed and short of our goals. The solution: When possible, play "offense" against your environment. Rather than just letting the day happen to you, start each day with a plan. Control how you spend your time. Establishing routines and making decisions in advance conserves energy by reducing daily decision making. If you know you are going to study 2 hours in the morning before class, you won't waste time weighing what to do.

Study Smart

To remember what you read, use the SQ3R (Survey, Question, Read, Retrieve, Review) system: Survey the module organization. Identify Questions your reading should answer. Read actively, seeking answers. Retrieve and rehearse key ideas. Finally, Review the module's organization and concepts.

Those last two "R's" are especially important: You will retain information best through repeated self-testing and rehearsal of previously studied material. Getting immediate feedback makes this testing effect even stronger. That's the idea behind our effective online adaptive quizzing system, LearningCurve, and the frequent self-testing opportunities throughout this text.

Distributing your study time, rather than cramming, will also help. Establishing a schedule, and sticking to it, will spread the load out across the term. For more information, see "Use Psychology to Become a Stronger Person—and a Better Student" in Module 1 and "Improving Memory" in Module 26, and view my [DM's] 5-minute animation at tinyurl.com/HowToRemember.

Social Life

Living your best life requires social support. Here are some tips for forming and maintaining healthy, supportive relationships:

- ***Prioritize people.*** We humans are social animals. We need to belong. We are happier and healthier when supported by, and giving support to, our friends. So, make the effort to make friends, such as by joining a club, sports team, or fellowship group.

Get to know your instructors. And do not take your friends and loved ones for granted. Attend to them. Affirm them. Share your daily experiences and feelings with them.

- ***Embrace diversity.*** Celebrate rather than fear differences among individuals and groups. Realize that how you see the world is based on everything that makes you unique, including your age, background, culture, ethnicity, gender identity, and sexual orientation. These individual experiences may produce perspectives—conscious or unconscious—that filter how you perceive and act toward others. Surround yourself with diverse others, listen rather than lecture, and have compassion for those with whom you disagree.
- ***Enjoy social media and your phone without letting them control you.*** Use social media and your phone to stay connected with friends and family, but without hijacking your time and other priorities. And when posting on social media, remember that someday a potential employer may be Googling your name.
- ***Support a speak-up culture rather than a call-out culture.*** To disagree is to be human. You will disagree with others, and others will disagree with you. Indeed, we often learn by exploring these other perspectives. (This is why it is so important for psychological scientists to practice humility.) When you disagree, avoid calling out others (publicly shaming them). Instead, speak up: Approach the person and explain your disagreement without blaming them. We have a natural tendency to explain others' behaviors based on their personality traits ("He's a selfish jerk") rather than their situation ("He's sleep-deprived and stressed"). To resist this tendency, take the other person's perspective.
- ***It's time to be the adult in the room.*** As we grow up, we pass through different stages of development. Most adolescents seek social acceptance while still depending on family. The transition into adulthood requires becoming more independent. As adults, we need to own our goals, attitudes, values, and beliefs, and to make our own decisions and solve our own problems.

Mariusz Szczawinski/Alamy Stock Photo

Social success Nurturing relationships is an important part of a successful life. Make time and energy for important others, and you will have better physical and psychological health.

Finding Meaning and Pursuing Goals

To have meaning is to have a life filled with purpose, coherence, and significance. Most people want a meaningful life, but they report feeling unfulfilled in some area of their life. They may not be fully engaged in their work. Or they may feel stuck in a daily routine that brings money without meaning. To live your best life, take the following steps to promote meaning and pursue goals:

- ***Imagine your possible self.*** Who is the person you wish to be? Define who you hope to be and what you aim to achieve. With that vision in mind, you can then lay out specific goals and strategies that will take you where you want to go.
- ***Live your dream daily.*** Here's a good rule for success: Whatever you hope to achieve, do something toward that every day. Do you want to be kinder, more educated, more assertive? Then, every day, do a kind act, learn something new, or practice asserting yourself. Although many days you may accomplish less than you'd hoped, even small daily steps toward a goal can, over time, take you to your destination—transforming your possible self into your actual self.
- ***Adopt a "growth mindset."*** It's surprisingly powerful to believe that our abilities are changeable through energy and effort. Some things we should accept, but many things we have the power to change. If you see your math or writing or speaking ability as like a muscle—something that gets stronger with training and practice—you will, in fact, develop more skill. Your mindset matters. (More on this in Module 35.)
- ***Find your calling.*** No need to rush it. Most students change their vocational plans along the way, and you likely will, too. But notice what sorts of activities absorb you and make time fly. Is it being with people? Working with your hands? Solving problems with your mind? Watch for work and activities that will enable you to do what you love and to love what you do, and pursue those paths.

* * *

Throughout this book you will encounter additional pointers to a flourishing life: counting your blessings, expressing gratitude, finding flow, acting happy, training your willpower, becoming mindful, opting for optimism, and more. In such ways, you can not only survive, you can thrive. Don't be too hard on yourself if you experience setbacks. If you try to do a little better each day, you can, over time, accomplish goals that might seem impossible at the outset. Seek, as Reinhold Niebuhr advised, the serenity to accept things you cannot change, but also feel empowered to change the things you can.

CHAPTER
1
LumiNola/E+/Getty Images

Thinking Critically With Psychological Science (Modules 1–3)

Astronomer Owen Gingerich has described the human brain as "by far the most complex physical object known to us in the entire cosmos" (2006, p. 29). On the scale of outer space, we are less than a single grain of sand on all the oceans' beaches, and our lifetime lasts but a relative nanosecond. Yet there is nothing more awe inspiring than our own inner space. Our consciousness—our mind somehow arising from matter—remains a profound mystery. Our thinking, emotions, and actions (and their interplay with others' thinking, emotions, and actions) fascinate us. Outer space staggers us with its enormity. But inner space enthralls us. Enter psychological science.

From news and media portrayals, you might think that psychologists offer counseling, analyze personality, dispense child-raising advice, examine crime scenes, and testify in court. Do they? *Yes*—and much more. Consider some of psychology's questions that you may wonder about:

- Have you ever worried about how to act among people of a different cultural tradition, gender identity, or sexual orientation, or among people with differing abilities? *How are we alike as members of the human family? How do we differ?*

- Have you ever vowed to *never* react as one of your biological parents would—but find yourself doing so anyway—and then wondered how much of your personality you inherited? *To what extent do genes predispose our individual differences in personality? How do home and community environments shape us?*
- Have you ever awakened from a nightmare and wondered why you had such a crazy dream? *Why do we dream? Why is sleep so important?*
- Have you ever played peekaboo with a 6-month-old and wondered why the baby finds your disappearing/reappearing act so delightful? *What do babies perceive and think?*
- Have you ever wondered what fosters school and work success? *Does inborn intelligence explain why some people get richer, think more creatively, or relate more sensitively? Or does gritty effort, and a belief in the power of persistence, matter more?*
- Have you ever become depressed or anxious and wondered when, or if, it will pass? *What affects our emotional well-being? What's the line between feeling "off" and a psychological disorder?*

As we will see in Modules 1 and 2, psychology is a science that seeks to answer such questions about us all—how and why we think, feel, and act as we do.

MODULE 1 The History and Scope of Psychology

Once upon a time, on a planet in our neighborhood of the universe, there came to be people. Soon thereafter, these creatures became intensely interested in themselves and in one another: "Who are we? What produces our thoughts? Our feelings? Our actions? And how are we to understand and interact with those around us?"

Psychology Is a Science

LEARNING OBJECTIVE QUESTION LOQ 1-1 How is psychology a science?

To assist your learning, numbered *Learning Objective Questions* appear at the beginning of major sections. You can test your understanding by trying to answer the question before, and then again after, you read the section.

Underlying all science is, first, a passion for exploring and understanding without misleading or being misled. Some questions *(Is there life after death?)* are beyond science. Answering them in any way requires a leap of faith. With many other ideas *(Can some people demonstrate extrasensory perception [ESP]?)*, the proof is in the pudding. We can let the facts speak for themselves.

Magician James Randi used an **empirical approach** when testing those claiming to see glowing auras around people's bodies:

Randi: Do you see an aura around my head?

Aura seer: Yes, indeed.

Randi: Can you still see the aura if I put this magazine in front of my face?

Aura seer: Of course.

Randi: Then if I were to step behind a wall barely taller than I am, you could determine my location from the aura visible above my head, right?

Throughout the text, the most important concepts are **boldfaced**, with definitions immediately available (and in the Glossary at the end of the book).

Randi once told me [DM] that no aura seer had yet agreed to take this simple test.

No matter how sensible-seeming or how wild an idea, the smart thinker asks: *Does it work?* When put to the test, do the data support its predictions? Subjected to scrutiny, crazy-sounding ideas sometimes find support.

empirical approach an evidence-based method that draws on observation and experimentation.

More often, science becomes society's garbage disposal. It sends crazy-sounding ideas to the waste heap, atop previous claims of miracle cancer cures and out-of-body travels into centuries past. To sift reality from fantasy and fact from fiction therefore requires a *scientific attitude:* being skeptical but not cynical, open-minded but not gullible. When ideas compete, careful testing can reveal which ones best fit the facts. Do some people have a psychic power to predict an unexpected catastrophe? Is *electroconvulsive therapy* (delivering an electric shock to the brain) an effective treatment for severe depression? As we will see, putting such claims to the test has led psychological scientists to answer *No* to the first question and *Yes* to the second.

Putting a scientific attitude into practice requires not only curiosity and skepticism but also *humility*—awareness of our vulnerability to error and an openness to new perspectives. What matters is not my opinion or yours, but the truths revealed by our questioning and testing. If people or other animals don't behave as our ideas predict, then so much the worse for our ideas—and so much the better for scientific progress. One of psychology's early mottos expressed this humble attitude: "The rat is always right." (See Thinking Critically About: The Scientific Attitude.)

Humility predicts helpfulness and realistic academic confidence (Erlandsson et al., 2018). One nine-country study asked 40,000 teens which of 16 math concepts were familiar to them. The teens didn't realize that the researchers had inserted three fake terms: "proper number," "subjective scaling," and "declarative fraction." Those who arrogantly claimed to know the nonexistent concepts were often men from advantaged backgrounds (Jerrim et al., 2019). *The point to remember:* Knowing what we *don't* know enables generosity and intellectual humility, which in turn supports a healthy democracy. "Democratic citizenship," notes psychologist Fathali Moghaddam (2019), begins by "accepting that 'I could be wrong,' 'I must critically question everything' ... and 'I must revise my opinions as the evidence requires.'"

Throughout the book, information sources are cited in parentheses, with researchers' names and the date the research was published. For example, see "(Erlandsson et al., 2018)". Every citation can be found in the end-of-book References section, with complete documentation that follows American Psychological Association (APA) style.

ASK YOURSELF

Were you surprised to learn that psychology is a science? How would you explain that now if someone asked you about it?

Critical Thinking

LOQ 1-3 How does critical thinking feed a scientific attitude, and smarter thinking for everyday life?

The scientific attitude—curiosity + skepticism + humility—prepares us to think smarter. This smart thinking, called **critical thinking**, examines assumptions, appraises the source, discerns hidden biases, evaluates evidence, and assesses conclusions. When reading a research report, an online opinion, or a news story, critical thinkers ask questions: *How do they know that? What is this person's agenda? Is the conclusion based on anecdote, or evidence? Does the evidence justify a cause-effect conclusion? What alternative explanations are possible?*

From a tongue-in-cheek Twitter feed: "The problem with quotes on the internet is that you never know if they're true." — Abraham Lincoln

Critical thinkers wince when people make factual claims based on their gut: "I *feel like* climate change is [or isn't] happening." "I *feel like* self-driving cars are more [or less] dangerous." "I *feel like* I'm safe from Covid here." Such beliefs (commonly mislabeled as feelings) may or may not be true. Critical thinkers realize that they might be wrong. Sometimes, the best evidence confirms our beliefs. Other times it beckons us to a different way of thinking. Cynics sometimes seem smart, yet most demonstrate less cognitive ability and academic competence than average (Stavrova & Ehlebracht, 2019). To believe everything—or to reject everything—is to be a fool. Critical thinking, informed by science, helps check our biases. Consider: Does climate change threaten our future, and, if so, is it human-caused? Some climate-action advocates have interpreted record flooding as proof of climate change. Some climate-change skeptics have perceived a single colder-than-average winter as discounting global warming. Rather than having their understanding of climate change swayed by local weather examples, critical thinkers say, "Show me the evidence." Over time, is the Earth actually warming? Are the polar ice

critical thinking thinking that does not automatically accept arguments and conclusions. Rather, it examines assumptions, appraises the source, discerns hidden biases, evaluates evidence, and assesses conclusions.

Thinking Critically About:
The Scientific Attitude

LOQ 1-2 What are the three key elements of the scientific attitude, and how do they support scientific inquiry?

Three basic attitudes helped make modern science possible.

1 CURIOSITY:

Does it work?

When put to the test, can its predictions be confirmed?

Can some people read minds? ●
Are stress levels related to health and well-being? △
● No one has yet been able to demonstrate extrasensory mind-reading.
△ Many studies have found that higher stress relates to poorer health.

2 SKEPTICISM:

What do you mean?

How do you know?

Sifting reality from fantasy requires a healthy skepticism—an attitude that is not cynical (doubting everything), but also not gullible (believing everything).

Do our facial expressions and body postures affect how we actually feel? □
Do parental behaviors determine children's sexual orientation? ⬡

□ *Our facial expressions and body postures can affect how we feel.*

⬡ *Module 34 explains that there is not a relationship between parental behaviors and children's sexual orientation.*

3 HUMILITY:

That was unexpected! Let's explore further.

Researchers must be willing to be surprised and follow new ideas. People and other animals don't always behave as our ideas and beliefs would predict.

The rat is always right.

caps melting? Are vegetation patterns changing? Are extreme weather events becoming more frequent? And is human activity emitting atmospheric CO_2 that would lead us to expect such changes?

When contemplating such issues, critical thinkers will also consider the credibility of sources. They will look at the evidence (*Do the facts support them, or are they just makin' stuff up?*). They will recognize multiple perspectives. And they will expose themselves to news sources that challenge their preconceived ideas.

Some religious people may view critical thinking and scientific inquiry, including psychology's, as a threat. Yet many leaders of the scientific revolution, including Copernicus and Newton, were deeply religious people. U.S. astronomer Carl Sagan (1979) noted,

> My deeply held belief is that if a god anything like the traditional sort exists, our curiosity and intelligence are provided by such a god. We would be unappreciative of those gifts ... if we suppressed our passion to explore the universe and ourselves.

Critical inquiry can surprise us. Some examples from psychological science: Massive losses of brain tissue early in life may have minimal long-term effects (see Module 6). Within days, newborns can recognize their mother's odor (see Module 15). After brain damage, a person may be able to learn new skills yet be unaware of such learning (see Module 25). People of differing ages, genders, and abilities report roughly comparable levels of personal happiness (see Module 38). Depression touches many people, but most recover (see Module 50).

Other modules also illustrate how critical inquiry sometimes debunks popular presumptions, by checking intuitive fiction with empirical fact: Sleepwalkers are *not* acting out their dreams (see Module 9). Our past experiences are *not* all recorded verbatim in our brain. With brain stimulation or hypnosis, one *cannot* merely replay and relive long-buried or repressed memories (see Module 26). Opposites tend *not* to attract (see Module 44). Most people do *not* suffer from unrealistically low self-esteem, and high self-esteem is *not* all good (see Module 47). In these instances and many more, what psychological scientists have learned is not what is widely believed.

Psychology's critical inquiry can also identify effective policies. To deter crime, should we invest money in lengthening prison sentences, or should we increase the likelihood of arrest? To help people recover from a trauma, should counselors help them relive it, or not? To increase voting, should we tell people about the low turnout problem, or emphasize that their peers are voting? What matters is not what we "feel" is true, but what *is* true. When put to critical thinking's test—and contrary to common practice—the second option in each case wins (Shafir, 2013). Thinking critically can—and sometimes does—change the world.

Critical thinking can also change us, by helping us assess popular applications of psychology. Looking at a self-help blog, we can consider the author's expertise and goals. We can ask: Are the suggestions based on evidence or anecdote? And how might the author's personal values and agenda affect the advice? If you defer to guidance about how to live—how to raise children, how to achieve self-fulfillment, how to respond to sexual feelings, how to get ahead at work—you are accepting value-laden advice. A science of behavior and mental processes can help us reach our goals. But it cannot decide which goals are worth pursuing. Psychological scientists teach, but they do not preach.

Study Tip: Memory research reveals a *testing effect:* We retain information much better if we actively retrieve it by self-testing and rehearsing. (More on this at the end of this module.) To bolster your learning and memory, take advantage of the *Retrieval Practice* opportunities you'll find throughout this text—with answers for checking in Appendix E, or a click away in the e-book.

RETRIEVAL PRACTICE

RP-1 Describe what's involved in critical thinking.

ANSWERS IN APPENDIX E

Psychological Science Is Born

LOQ 1-4 What were some important milestones in psychology's early history?

To be human is to be curious about ourselves and the world around us. Before 300 B.C.E., the Greek naturalist and philosopher Aristotle theorized about learning and memory, motivation and emotion, perception and personality. Today we chuckle at some of his guesses, such as his suggestion that a meal makes us sleepy by causing gas and heat to collect around the supposed source of our personality, the heart. But credit Aristotle with asking the right questions.

Macmillan Learning

Wilhelm Wundt (1832–1920) Wundt established the first psychology laboratory at the University of Leipzig, Germany.

Macmillan Learning

Edward Bradford Titchener (1867–1927) Titchener used introspection to search for the mind's structural elements.

Psychology's First Laboratory

Philosophers' thinking about thinking continued until the birth of psychology's first laboratory. On a December day in 1879, in a small, third-floor room at Germany's University of Leipzig, two graduate students helped an austere, middle-aged professor, Wilhelm Wundt, create an experimental apparatus. Their machine measured how long it took for people to press a telegraph key after hearing a ball hit a platform (Hunt, 1993). Curiously, people responded in about one-tenth of a second when asked to press the key as soon as the sound occurred—and in about two-tenths of a second when asked to press the key as soon as they were consciously aware of perceiving the sound. (To be aware of one's awareness takes a little longer.) Wundt wanted to measure "atoms of the mind"—the fastest and simplest mental processes.

Psychology's First Schools of Thought

Before long, this new science of psychology became organized into different branches, or schools of thought, each promoted by pioneering thinkers. Two early schools were **structuralism** and **functionalism**.

STRUCTURALISM Much as chemists developed the periodic table to classify chemical elements, so psychologist Edward Bradford Titchener aimed to classify and understand elements of the mind's structure (structuralism). He engaged people in self-reflective *introspection* (looking inward), training them to report elements of their experience as they looked at a rose, listened to a metronome, smelled a scent, or tasted a substance. What were their immediate sensations, their images, their feelings? And how did these relate to one another? Alas, structuralism's technique of introspection proved somewhat unreliable. It required smart, verbal people, and its results varied from person to person and experience to experience. As introspection waned, so did structuralism. Hoping to assemble the mind's structure from simple elements was rather like trying to understand a smartphone by examining its disconnected parts.

FUNCTIONALISM Philosopher-psychologist William James sought to go beyond labeling our inner thoughts and feelings by considering their evolved *functions* (functionalism). Smelling is what the nose does; thinking is what the brain does. But *why* do the nose and brain do these things? Under the influence of evolutionary theorist Charles Darwin, James assumed that thinking, like smelling, developed because it was *adaptive*—it helped our ancestors survive and reproduce. Consciousness serves a function. It enables us to consider our past, adjust to our present, and plan our future. To explore the mind's adaptive functions, James studied emotions, memories, willpower, habits, and moment-to-moment *stream of consciousness* thinking.

James' writings moved the publisher Henry Holt to offer James a contract for a textbook on the new science of psychology. James agreed and began work in 1878, with an apology for requesting two years to finish his writing. The text proved an unexpected chore and actually took him 12 years. (Why are we authors not surprised?) More than a century later, people still read the resulting *Principles of Psychology* (1890) and marvel at the brilliance and elegance with which James introduced psychology to the educated public.

Psychology's First Women

James' legacy stems from his Harvard mentoring as well as from his writing. In 1890—thirty years before U.S. women had the right to vote—he admitted Mary Whiton Calkins into his graduate seminar over the objections of Harvard's president (Scarborough & Furumoto, 1987). When Calkins joined, the other students (all men) dropped out. So, James tutored her alone. Later, she finished all of Harvard's Ph.D. requirements, outscoring all the male students on the qualifying exams. Alas, Harvard denied her the degree she had earned, offering her instead a doctorate from Radcliffe College, its undergraduate "sister" school for women. Calkins resisted the unequal treatment and refused the degree. She nevertheless went on to become a distinguished memory researcher and, in 1905, the first female president of the American Psychological Association (APA).

The honor of being the first official female psychology Ph.D. later fell to Margaret Floy Washburn, who also wrote an influential book, *The Animal Mind*. In 1921, Washburn became the second female APA president (Fragaszy, 2021). But Washburn's gender barred

structuralism an early school of thought promoted by Wundt and Titchener; used introspection to reveal the structure of the human mind.

functionalism an early school of thought promoted by James and influenced by Darwin; explored how mental and behavioral processes function—how they enable the organism to adapt, survive, and flourish.

Macmillan Learning

Macmillan Learning

William James (1842–1910) and Mary Whiton Calkins (1863–1930) James was a legendary teacher-writer who authored an important psychology text. He mentored Calkins, a memory researcher who would become the first female president of the American Psychological Association.

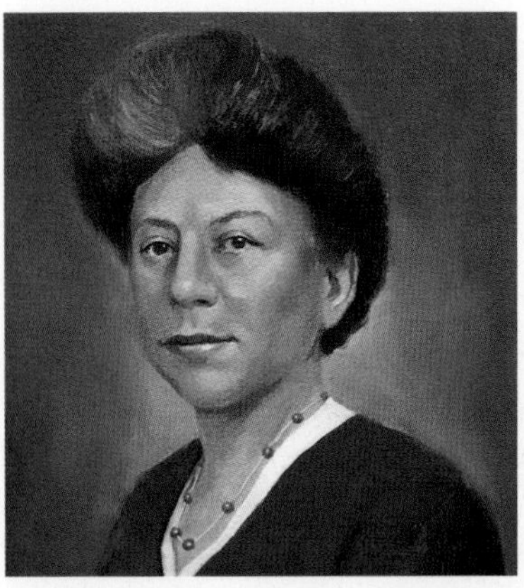

Macmillan Learning

Margaret Floy Washburn (1871–1939) The first woman to receive a psychology Ph.D., Washburn synthesized animal behavior research in *The Animal Mind* (1908).

doors for her, too. Although her thesis was the first foreign study Wundt published in his psychology journal, she could not join the all-male organization of experimental psychologists founded by Titchener, her own graduate adviser (Johnson, 1997). What a different world from the recent past: Between 1997 and 2021, more than half of the elected presidents of the science-focused Association for Psychological Science (APS) were women. In the United States, Canada, and Europe, women now earn most psychology doctorates. Nevertheless, a gender gap persists in publishing psychological research in top journals, promotion to senior professorships, and salary (Gruber et al., 2021).

1964 meeting of the Society of Experimental Psychologists in Berkeley, California. Reprinted by permission of the Society of Experimental Psychologists. http://www.sepsych.org/1964.php

(a)

Gordon B. Moskowitz, professor in Lehigh's Department of Psychology

(b)

Psychology's increasing diversity At this 1964 meeting of the Society of Experimental Psychologists (a), Eleanor Gibson was easy to spot among the many male members, all in a sea of White faces. By contrast, women are now 61 percent of APS members, including 75 percent of its psychology student affiliates, as is clear in this recent photo of APS graduate students (b). People of color have made enormous contributions to the field (see, for example, coverage of Mamie Phipps Clark and Kenneth Clark in the Chapter 1 modules), and psychology's diversity continues to grow—with one-third of recent psychology doctorates earned by people of color (APA, 2021). For more on the history of these changes, see Appendix A, the Story of Psychology: A Timeline.

behaviorism the view that psychology (1) should be an objective science that (2) studies behavior without reference to mental processes. Most psychologists today agree with (1) but not with (2).

ASK YOURSELF

How do you think psychology might change in the future as more women, and others from historically excluded groups, contribute their ideas to the field?

RETRIEVAL PRACTICE

RP-2 What event defined the start of scientific psychology?

RP-3 Why did introspection fail as a method for understanding how the mind works?

RP-4 The school of ______________ used introspection to define the mind's makeup; ______________ focused on how mental processes enable us to adapt, survive, and flourish.

ANSWERS IN APPENDIX E

Psychological Science Matures

LOQ 1-5 How did behaviorism, Freudian psychology, and humanistic psychology further the development of psychological science?

Many early psychologists shared English essayist C. S. Lewis's view that "there is one thing, and only one in the whole universe which we know more about than we could learn from external observation." That one thing, Lewis said, is ourselves. "We have, so to speak, inside information" (1960, pp. 18–19). Wundt and Titchener focused on inner sensations, images, and feelings. James also engaged in introspective examination of the stream of consciousness and of emotion, hoping to understand how they help humans survive and thrive. For these and other early pioneers, *psychology* was defined as "the science of mental life."

Behaviorism

In the 1920s, provocative U.S. psychologists began to challenge the definition of psychology as the "science of mental life." John B. Watson and, later, B. F. Skinner dismissed introspection and redefined *psychology* as "the scientific study of observable behavior." After all, they said, science is rooted in observation: What you cannot observe and measure, you cannot scientifically study. You cannot observe a sensation, a feeling, or a thought, but you *can* observe and record people's *behavior* as they are *conditioned*—as they respond to and learn in different situations. Many agreed, and **behaviorism** was increasingly influential well into the 1960s (Braat et al., 2020).

Macmillan Learning

Macmillan Learning

John B. Watson (1878–1958) and Rosalie Rayner (1898–1935) Working with Rayner, Watson championed psychology as the scientific study of behavior. In a controversial study on a baby who became famous as "Little Albert," he and Rayner showed that fear could be learned. (More about this in the Learning modules.)

Macmillan Learning

B. F. Skinner (1904–1990) This leading behaviorist rejected introspection and studied how consequences shape behavior.

Freudian (Psychoanalytic) Psychology

Another major force in psychology's development was Sigmund Freud's *psychoanalytic psychology*, which emphasized the ways our unconscious mind and childhood experiences affect our behavior. (In other modules, we'll look more closely at Freud's ideas, including his theory of personality, and his views on unconscious sexual conflicts and the mind's defenses against its own wishes and impulses.)

Macmillan Learning

Sigmund Freud (1856–1939) The controversial ideas of this famed personality theorist and therapist have influenced humanity's self-understanding.

Humanistic Psychology

As the behaviorists had rejected the early twentieth-century definition of *psychology*, other groups rejected the behaviorist definition. In the 1960s, **humanistic psychologists**, led by Carl Rogers and Abraham Maslow, found both behaviorism and Freudian psychology too limiting. Rather than focusing on conditioned responses or childhood memories, the humanistic psychologists focused on our growth potential, our needs for love and acceptance, and the environments that nurture or limit personal growth.

RETRIEVAL PRACTICE

RP-5 From the 1920s until the 1960s, the two major forces in psychology were ________ and ________ psychology.

ANSWERS IN APPENDIX E

Contemporary Psychology

LOQ 1-6 How has contemporary psychology focused on cognition, on biology and experience, on culture and gender, and on human flourishing?

Simultaneous with humanistic psychology's emergence, psychologists in the 1960s pioneered a *cognitive revolution*, which led the field back to its early interest in how our mind processes and retains information. **Cognitive psychology** today continues its scientific exploration of how we perceive, process, and remember information, and of how thinking and emotion interact in anxiety, depression, and other disorders. The marriage of cognitive psychology (mind science) and neuroscience (brain science) gave birth to **cognitive neuroscience**. This specialty, with researchers in many disciplines, studies the brain activity underlying mental activity.

Today's psychology builds on the work of many earlier scientists and schools of thought. To encompass psychology's concern with observable behavior *and* with inner thoughts and feelings, we now define **psychology** as the *science of behavior and mental processes*. Let's unpack this definition. *Behavior* is anything an organism *does*—any action we can observe and record. Yelling, smiling, blinking, sweating, talking, tweeting, and questionnaire marking are all observable behaviors. *Mental processes* are our internal, subjective experiences—our sensations, perceptions, dreams, thoughts, beliefs, and feelings.

The key word in today's definition of psychology is *science*. Psychology is less a set of findings than a way of asking and answering questions. Our aim, then, is not merely to report results but also to show you how psychologists play their game. You will see how researchers evaluate conflicting opinions and ideas. And you will learn how all of us, whether scientists or simply curious people, can think harder and smarter when experiencing and explaining the events of our lives.

Psychology—the science of behavior and mental processes—has roots in many disciplines and countries. The young science of psychology developed from the more established fields of philosophy and biology. Wundt was a German philosopher and a physiologist. James was an American philosopher. Freud was an Austrian physician. Ivan Pavlov (Learning modules), who pioneered the study of learning, was a Russian physiologist. Jean Piaget (Developing Through the Life Span modules), the last century's most influential scientific observer of children, was a Swiss biologist.

humanistic psychology a historically significant perspective that emphasized human growth potential.

cognitive psychology the study of the mental processes involved in perceiving, learning, remembering, thinking, communicating, and solving problems.

cognitive neuroscience the interdisciplinary study of the brain activity linked with cognition (perception, thinking, memory, and language).

psychology the science of behavior and mental processes.

nature–nurture issue the longstanding controversy over the relative contributions that genes and experience make to the development of psychological traits and behaviors. Today's science sees traits and behaviors arising from the interaction of nature and nurture.

natural selection the principle that the inherited traits enabling an organism to survive and reproduce in a particular environment will (in competition with other trait variations) most likely be passed on to succeeding generations.

evolutionary psychology the study of the evolution of behavior and the mind, using principles of natural selection.

behavior genetics the study of the relative power and limits of genetic and environmental influences on behavior.

Like those pioneers, today's estimated 1+ million psychologists are citizens of many lands (Zoma & Gielen, 2015). The International Union of Psychological Science has 89 member nations, from Albania to Zimbabwe. In China, the first university psychology department was established in 1978; by 2016 there were 270 (Zhang, 2016). Psychology is both *growing* and *globalizing*. The story of psychology is being written in many places, with interests ranging from the study of nerve cell activity to the study of international conflicts. Contemporary psychology, shaped by many forces, is particularly influenced by our understanding of biology and experience, culture and gender, and human flourishing.

ASK YOURSELF

How would you have defined *psychology* before taking this class?

Evolutionary Psychology and Behavior Genetics

Are our human traits inherited, or do they develop through experience? This has been psychology's biggest and most persistent issue. But the debate over the **nature–nurture issue** is ancient. The Greek philosopher Plato (428–348 B.C.E.) assumed that we inherit character and intelligence and that certain ideas are inborn. Aristotle (384–322 B.C.E.) countered that there is nothing in the mind that does not first come in from the external world through the senses.

In the 1600s, European philosophers rekindled the debate. John Locke argued that the mind is a blank slate on which experience writes. René Descartes disagreed, believing that some ideas are innate. Descartes' views gained support from a curious naturalist two centuries later. In 1831, an indifferent student but ardent collector of beetles, mollusks, and shells decided not to become a priest and instead set sail on a historic round-the-world journey. The 22-year-old voyager, Charles Darwin, pondered the incredible species variation he encountered, including tortoises on one island that differed from those on nearby islands. Darwin's *On the Origin of Species* (1859) explained this diversity by proposing the evolutionary process of **natural selection:** From among chance variations, nature selects traits that best enable an organism to survive and reproduce in a specific environment. Darwin's principle of natural selection—what philosopher Daniel Dennett (1996) has called "the single best idea anyone has ever had"—is still with us 160+ years later as biology's organizing principle. Evolution also has become an important principle for twenty-first-century psychology. This would surely have pleased Darwin, who believed his theory explained not only animal structures (such as a polar bear's white coat) but also animal behaviors (such as human mating and emotional expressions).

Macmillan Learning

Charles Darwin (1809–1882) Darwin argued that natural selection shapes behaviors as well as bodies.

The nature–nurture issue recurs throughout this text as today's psychologists explore the relative contributions of biology and experience. They ask, for example: How are we humans *alike* because of our shared biology and evolutionary history? That's the focus of **evolutionary psychology**. And how do we individually *differ* because of our differing genes and environments? That's the focus of **behavior genetics**.

We can, for example, ask: Are gender differences biologically predisposed or socially constructed? Is children's grammar mostly innate or formed by experience? How are intelligence and personality differences influenced by heredity and by environment?

rubberball/Getty Images

© Tony Freeman/PhotoEdit

A nature-made nature–nurture experiment Identical twins have the same genes. This makes them ideal participants in studies designed to shed light on hereditary and environmental influences on personality, intelligence, and other traits. Fraternal twins have different genes but often share a similar environment. Twin studies provide a wealth of findings—described in other modules—showing the importance of both nature and nurture.

Are sexual behaviors more "pushed" by inner biology or "pulled" by external incentives? Should we treat psychological disorders—depression, for example—as disorders of the brain, disorders of thought, or both?

Repeatedly we will see that in contemporary science, the nature–nurture tension dissolves: *Nurture works on what nature provides.* In other modules, you'll learn about *epigenetics*—how experience can influence genetic expression. And you will see that our species has been graced with the tremendous biological gift of *neuroplasticity*—the brain's enormous capacity to learn and adapt. Moreover, every psychological event (every thought, every emotion) is simultaneously a biological event. Thus, depression can be both a brain disorder *and* a thought disorder.

culture the enduring behaviors, ideas, attitudes, values, and traditions shared by a group of people and transmitted from one generation to the next.

ASK YOURSELF

Think of one of your own traits. (For example, are you a planner or a procrastinator—do you usually complete assignments on time, or late? Are you more an extravert or introvert—do you become energized by social interactions, or recharge by spending time alone?) How do you think that trait was influenced by nature and nurture?

RETRIEVAL PRACTICE

RP-6 How did the cognitive revolution affect the field of psychology?

RP-7 What is natural selection?

RP-8 What is contemporary psychology's position on the nature–nurture issue?

ANSWERS IN APPENDIX E

Cross-Cultural and Gender Psychology

Participants in many studies have come from the WEIRD (Western, Industrial, Rich, and Democratic) cultures—so named because they represent a mere fraction of the people on our planet (Henrich, 2020). As we will see time and again, **culture**—shared ideas and behaviors that one generation passes on to the next—matters. Our culture shapes our standards of promptness and frankness, our attitudes toward relationships, our tendency to be casual or formal, our willingness to make eye contact, our hand gestures, and much, much more. By studying people from around the world, today's researchers have observed our individual and cultural differences—in personality, in expressiveness, in attitudes and beliefs.

"All people are the same; only their habits differ." — Confucius, 551–479 B.C.E.

It is also true, however, that our shared biological heritage unites us as a universal human family. The same underlying processes guide people everywhere. Some examples:

- People diagnosed with *specific learning disorder* (formerly called dyslexia) exhibit the same brain malfunction, whether they are Italian, French, or British (Paulesu et al., 2001).
- Variation in languages may impede communication across cultures. Yet all languages share deep principles of grammar, and people from different corners of the world can communicate with a smile or a frown.
- People in different cultures vary in feelings of loneliness (Lykes & Kemmelmeier, 2014). But across cultures, loneliness is magnified by shyness and low self-esteem (Jones et al., 1985; Rokach et al., 2002).

We are each in certain respects like all others, like some others, and like no other. Studying people from all cultures helps us discern our similarities and our differences, our human kinship and our diversity.

Culture and kissing Kissing crosses cultures. Yet how we do it varies. Imagine yourself kissing someone on the lips. Do you tilt your head right or left? In Western cultures, where people read from left to right, about two-thirds of couples kiss right, as in Prince Harry and Duchess Meghan's wedding kiss and Auguste Rodin's sculpture, *The Kiss*. In one study, 77 percent of Hebrew- and Arabic-language right-to-left readers kissed tilting left (Shaki, 2013).

Jane Barlow/Getty Images

Hemis/Alamy Stock Photo

You will see throughout this book that our *gender identity*—our sense of being male, female, neither, or some combination of male and female—also matters, as does our biologically influenced *sex*. Today's researchers report gender differences in what we dream, in how we express and detect emotions, and in our risk for alcohol use disorder, depression, and eating disorders. Gender differences fascinate us, and studying them is potentially beneficial. For example, many researchers have observed that women carry on conversations more readily to build relationships, while men talk more to give information and advice (Tannen, 2001). Understanding these differences can help us prevent conflicts and misunderstandings in everyday interactions.

But again, psychologically as well as biologically, we are overwhelmingly similar. We learn to walk at about the same age. We experience the same sensations of light and sound. We remember vivid emotional events and forget mundane details. We feel the same pangs of hunger, desire, and fear. We exhibit similar overall intelligence and well-being.

The point to remember: Even when specific attitudes and behaviors vary by gender or across cultures, as they often do, the underlying processes are much the same.

Positive Psychology

Psychology's first hundred years often focused on understanding and treating troubles, such as abuse and anxiety, depression and disease, prejudice and poverty. Much of today's psychology continues the exploration of such challenges. Without slighting the need to repair damage and cure disease, Martin Seligman and others (2002, 2016) have called for more research on *human flourishing*—on understanding and developing the emotions and traits that help us to thrive. These psychologists call their approach **positive psychology**. They believe that happiness is a by-product of a pleasant, engaged, and meaningful life. Thus, positive psychology uses scientific methods to explore the building of a "good life" that engages our skills, and a "meaningful life" that points beyond ourselves.

Psychology's Three Main Levels of Analysis

LOQ 1-7 How do psychologists use the biopsychosocial approach, and how can it help us understand our diverse world?

We all share a biologically rooted human nature. Yet many psychological and social-cultural influences fine-tune our assumptions, values, and behavior. We differ individually by gender identity, physical ability, and sexual orientation. And each of us is a complex system that is part of a larger social system—family, ethnic group, culture, and *socioeconomic* status (combines education, income, and occupation). The **biopsychosocial approach** integrates these three **levels of analysis**—the biological, psychological, and social-cultural.

Consider horrific school shootings. Do they occur because the shooters have brain disorders or genetic tendencies that predispose them to violence? Because they have observed brutality in the media or played violent video games? Because they live in a gun-toting society? The biopsychosocial approach enables psychologists to move beyond labels ("school shooter") and to consider the interconnected factors that may lead to violent acts (Pryor, 2019) (**FIGURE 1.1**). Clinical psychologists use this approach to help people with mental disorders (Teachman et al., 2019).

Each level of analysis offers a perspective for looking at a behavior or mental process, yet each by itself is incomplete. Each perspective described in **TABLE 1.1** asks different questions and has its limits, but together they complement one another. Consider, for example, how they shed light on anger. Someone working from

- ***a neuroscience perspective*** might study brain circuits that cause us to be red in the face and "hot under the collar."
- ***an evolutionary perspective*** might analyze how anger facilitated the survival of our ancestors' genes.

positive psychology the scientific study of human flourishing, with the goals of discovering and promoting strengths and virtues that help individuals and communities to thrive.

biopsychosocial approach an integrated approach that incorporates biological, psychological, and social-cultural levels of analysis.

levels of analysis the differing complementary views, from biological to psychological to social-cultural, for analyzing any given phenomenon.

Biological influences:
- genetic *predispositions* (genetically influenced traits)
- genetic *mutations* (random errors in gene replication)
- natural selection of adaptive traits and behaviors passed down through generations
- genes responding to the environment

Psychological influences:
- learned fears and other learned expectations
- emotional responses
- cognitive processing and perceptual interpretations

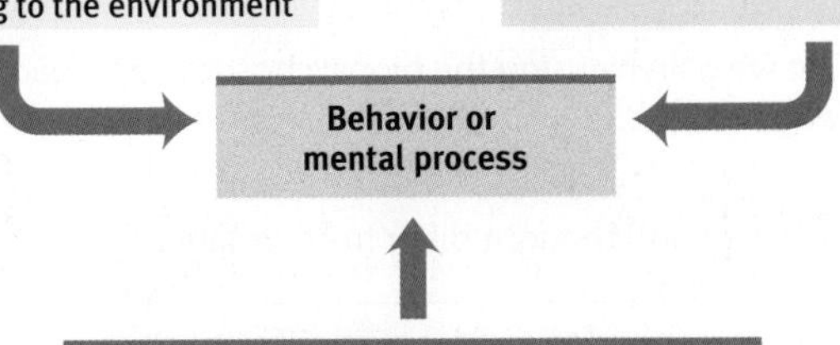
Behavior or
mental process

Social-cultural influences:
- presence of others
- cultural, societal, and family expectations
- peer and other group influences
- compelling models (such as in the media)

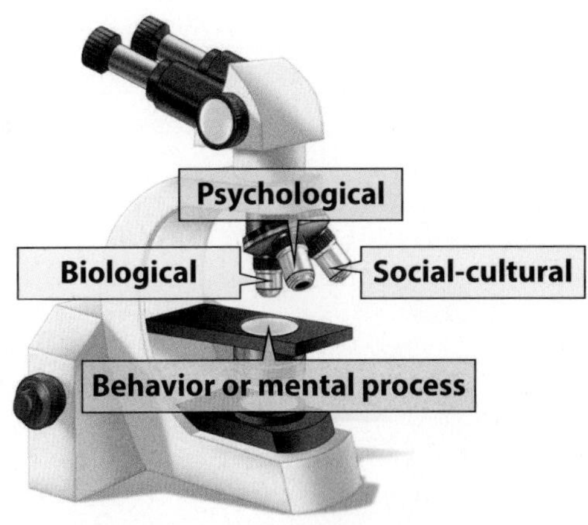
Psychological
Biological
Social-cultural
Behavior or mental process

FIGURE 1.1
Biopsychosocial approach This integrated viewpoint incorporates various levels of analysis and offers a more complete picture of any given behavior or mental process.

- ***a behavior genetics perspective*** might study how heredity and experience influence our individual differences in temperament.
- ***a psychodynamic perspective*** might view an outburst as an outlet for unconscious hostility.
- ***a behavioral perspective*** might attempt to determine what triggers aggressive acts.
- ***a cognitive perspective*** might study how our interpretation of a situation affects our anger and how our anger affects our thinking.
- ***a social-cultural perspective*** might explore how expressions of anger vary across cultural contexts.

TABLE 1.1 Psychology's Theoretical Perspectives

Perspective	Focus	Sample Questions	Examples of Subfields Using This Perspective
Neuroscience	How the body and brain enable emotions, memories, and sensory experiences	How do pain messages travel from the hand to the brain? How is blood chemistry linked with moods and motives?	Biological; cognitive; clinical
Evolutionary	How the natural selection of traits has promoted the survival of genes	How does evolution influence behavior tendencies?	Biological; developmental; social
Behavior genetics	How our genes and our environment influence our individual differences	To what extent are psychological traits, such as intelligence, personality, sexual orientation, and vulnerability to depression, products of our genes? Of our environment?	Personality; developmental; legal/forensic
Psychodynamic	How behavior springs from unconscious drives and conflicts	How can someone's personality traits and disorders be explained by unfulfilled wishes and childhood traumas?	Clinical; counseling; personality
Behavioral	How we learn observable responses	How do we learn to fear particular objects or situations? What is the most effective way to alter our behavior, say, to stop smoking?	Clinical; counseling; industrial-organizational
Cognitive	How we encode, process, store, and retrieve information	How do we use information in remembering? Reasoning? Solving problems?	Cognitive neuroscience; clinical; counseling; industrial-organizational
Social-cultural	How behavior and thinking vary across situations and cultures	How are we affected by the people around us, and by our surrounding culture?	Developmental; social; clinical; counseling

The point to remember: Like two-dimensional views of a three-dimensional object, each of psychology's perspectives is helpful. But each by itself fails to reveal the whole picture.

ASK YOURSELF

Which of psychology's theoretical perspectives do you find most interesting? Why?

RETRIEVAL PRACTICE

RP-9 What advantage do we gain by using the biopsychosocial approach in studying psychological events?

RP-10 The ________________-________________ perspective in psychology focuses on how behavior and thought differ from situation to situation and from culture to culture, while the ________________ perspective emphasizes observation of how we respond to and learn in different situations.

ANSWERS IN APPENDIX E

J.B. Handelsman/Cartoon Stock

"I'm a social scientist, Michael. That means I can't explain electricity or anything like that, but if you ever want to know about people I'm your man."

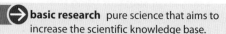

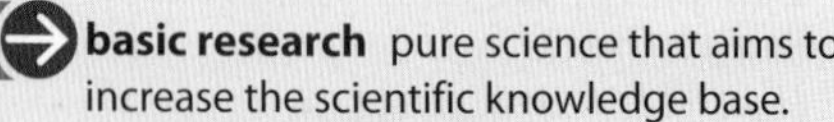

basic research pure science that aims to increase the scientific knowledge base.

applied research scientific study that aims to solve practical problems.

counseling psychology a branch of psychology that assists people with problems in living (often related to school, work, or relationships) and in achieving greater well-being.

clinical psychology a branch of psychology that studies, assesses, and treats people with psychological disorders.

psychiatry a branch of medicine dealing with psychological disorders; practiced by physicians who provide medical (for example, drug) treatments as well as psychological therapy.

community psychology a branch of psychology that studies how people interact with their social environments and how social institutions (such as schools and neighborhoods) affect individuals and groups.

Psychology's Subfields

LOQ 1-8 What are psychology's main subfields?

Picturing a chemist at work, you may envision a laboratory scientist surrounded by test tubes and high-tech equipment. Picture a psychologist at work, and you would be right to envision

- a white-coated scientist probing a rat's brain.
- an intelligence researcher measuring how quickly an infant shows boredom by looking away from a familiar picture.
- an executive evaluating a new diversity and inclusion training program for employees.
- a researcher at a computer analyzing "big data" from social media status updates, online searches, or digital traces of people's behavior.
- a therapist actively listening to an anxious client's thoughts.
- an academic studying another culture and collecting data on variations in human values and behaviors.
- a teacher or writer sharing the joy of psychology with others.

The cluster of subfields we call psychology is a meeting ground for different disciplines. Thus, it's a perfect home for those with wide-ranging interests. In its diverse activities, from biological experimentation to cultural comparisons, the tribe of psychology is united by a common quest: *describing and explaining behavior and the mind underlying it.*

Some psychologists conduct **basic research** that builds psychology's knowledge base. We will meet a wide variety of such researchers, including *biological psychologists* exploring the links between body and mind; *developmental psychologists* studying our changing abilities from womb to tomb; *cognitive psychologists* experimenting with how we perceive, think, and solve problems; *personality psychologists* investigating our persistent traits; and *social psychologists* exploring how we view and affect one another.

These and other psychologists also may conduct **applied research**, tackling practical problems. *Industrial-organizational psychologists*, for example, use psychology's concepts and methods in the workplace to help organizations and companies select and train employees, boost morale and productivity, design products, and implement systems.

Psychology is a science, but it is also a profession that helps people have healthier relationships, overcome feelings of anxiety or depression, and raise thriving children. *Counseling psychology* and *clinical psychology* grew out of different historical traditions. Early counseling psychologists offered job skills guidance, whereas clinical psychologists worked alongside psychiatrists to assess and provide psychotherapy to people in the first psychology clinics. Today's counseling psychologists and clinical psychologists have a lot in common. **Counseling psychologists** help people to cope with challenges and crises (including academic, vocational, and relationship issues) and assist those with psychological disorders to improve their personal and social functioning. **Clinical psychologists** focus on assessing and treating people with mental, emotional, and behavior disorders. Both counseling and clinical psychologists administer and interpret tests, provide therapy and advice to people with all levels of psychological difficulties, and undergo licensing exams. They sometimes also conduct basic and applied research. By contrast, **psychiatrists**, who also may provide psychotherapy, are medical doctors licensed to prescribe drugs and otherwise treat physical causes of psychological disorders.

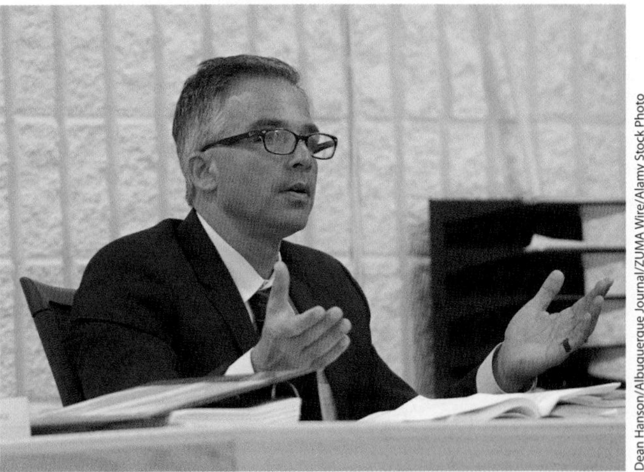

Dean Hanson/Albuquerque Journal/ZUMA Wire/Alamy Stock Photo

Psychology in court *Forensic psychologists* apply psychology's principles and methods in the criminal justice system. They may assess witness credibility or testify in court about a defendant's state of mind and future risk. This forensic psychologist testified that the defendant, who at age 15 showed no remorse after killing his parents and three younger siblings, has a *personality disorder.*

Rather than seeking to change people to fit their environment, **community psychologists** work to create social and physical environments that are healthy for all (Bradshaw et al., 2009; Trickett, 2009). To prevent bullying, for example, they might consider ways to improve the culture of a school and neighborhood, and how to increase bystander intervention (Polanin et al., 2012).

With perspectives ranging from the biological to the social, and with settings ranging from the laboratory to the clinic to the office, psychology relates to many fields. Psychologists teach in medical schools, business schools, law schools, and theological seminaries. They work in hospitals, factories, and corporate offices. And they engage in interdisciplinary studies, such as psychobiography (the study of the lives and personalities of public figures), psycholinguistics (the study of language and thinking), and psychoceramics (the study of crackpots).[1]

ASK YOURSELF

When you signed up for this course, what did you know about different psychology specialties?

Psychology also influences culture. Knowledge transforms us. Learning about the solar system and the germ theory of disease alters the way people think and act. Learning about psychology's findings also changes people: They less often judge psychological disorders as moral failings, treatable by punishment and ostracism. They less often

Psychology: A science and a profession Psychologists experiment with, observe, test, and help modify behavior. Here we see psychologists testing a child, measuring emotion-related physiology, and doing face-to-face therapy.

LAURENT/GLUCK/AGE Fotostock

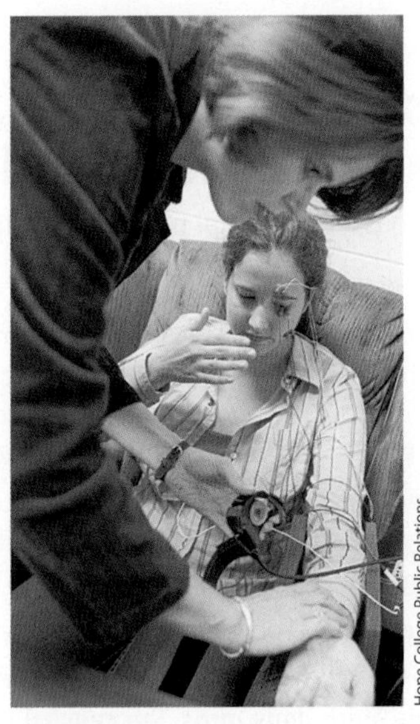

Hope College Public Relations

Scott J. Ferrell/Getty Images

[1]Confession: I [DM] wrote the last part of this sentence on April Fool's Day.

regard and treat women as men's mental inferiors. They less often view and raise children as ignorant, willful beasts in need of taming. "In each case," noted Morton Hunt (1990, p. 206), "knowledge has modified attitudes, and, through them, behavior." Once aware of psychology's well-researched ideas—about how body and mind connect, how a child's mind grows, how we construct our perceptions, how we learn and remember, how people across the world are alike (and different)—your mind may never again be the same.

"The mind, once stretched by a new idea, never returns to its original dimensions." — Ralph Waldo Emerson, 1803–1882

But bear in mind psychology's limits. Don't expect it to answer the ultimate questions, such as those posed by Russian novelist Leo Tolstoy (1904): "Why should I live? Why should I do anything? Is there in life any purpose which the inevitable death that awaits me does not undo and destroy?"

Although many of life's significant questions are beyond psychology, some very important ones are illuminated by even a first psychology course. Through painstaking research, psychologists have gained insights into brain and mind, dreams and memories, depression and joy. Even the unanswered questions can renew our sense of mystery about things we do not yet understand. Moreover, your study of psychology can help teach you how to ask and answer important questions—how to think critically as you evaluate competing ideas and claims.

"I have uttered what I did not understand, things too wonderful for me." — Job 42:3

Psychology deepens our appreciation for how we humans perceive, think, feel, and act. By so doing, it can enrich our lives and enlarge our vision. Through this book we hope to help guide you toward that end. As activist and Nobel Peace Prize winner Malala Yousafzai said, "One teacher, one book, one pen can change the world."

RETRIEVAL PRACTICE

RP-11 Match the specialty (i through iii) with the description (a through c).

i. Clinical psychology	a. works to create social and physical environments that are healthy for all
ii. Psychiatry	b. studies, assesses, and treats people with psychological disorders but usually does not provide medical therapy
iii. Community psychology	c. is a branch of medicine dealing with psychological disorders

ANSWERS IN APPENDIX E

Use Psychology to Become a Stronger Person—and a Better Student

LOQ 1-9 How can psychological principles help you learn, remember, and thrive?

Psychology is not just about understanding others; it is also about understanding ourselves. It is only through such learning that we can be—and show to the world—our best selves. Throughout this text, we will offer evidence-based suggestions that you can use to live a happy, effective, flourishing life, including the following:

- ***Manage your time to get a full night's sleep.*** Unlike sleep-deprived people, who live with fatigue and gloomy moods, well-rested people live with greater energy, happiness, and productivity.
- ***Make space for exercise.*** Aerobic activity not only increases health and energy, it also is an effective remedy for mild to moderate depression and anxiety.
- ***Set long-term goals, with daily aims.*** Successful people take time each day to work toward their goals, such as exercising or sleeping more, or eating more healthfully. Over time, they often find that their daily practice becomes a habit.

- ***Have a growth mindset.*** Rather than seeing their abilities as fixed, successful people view their mental abilities as like a muscle—something that grows stronger with effortful use.
- ***Prioritize relationships.*** We humans are social animals. We flourish when connected in close relationships. We are both happier and healthier when supported by (and when supporting) caring friends.

Psychology's research also shows how we can learn and retain information. Many students assume that the way to cement new learning is to reread. What helps more—and what this book therefore encourages—is *repeated self-testing and rehearsal* of previously studied material. Memory researchers Henry Roediger and Jeffrey Karpicke (2006) call this phenomenon the **testing effect**. (It is also sometimes called the *retrieval practice effect* or *test-enhanced learning*.) They note that "testing is a powerful means of improving learning, not just assessing it." In one study, English-speaking students who had been tested repeatedly recalled the meaning of 20 previously learned Lithuanian words better than did students who had spent the same time restudying the words (Ariel & Karpicke, 2018). Repetitive testing's rewards also make it reinforcing: Students who used repetitive testing once found that it helped, and then used it later when learning new material.

"If you read a piece of text through twenty times, you will not learn it by heart so easily as if you read it ten times while attempting to recite it from time to time and consulting the text when your memory fails." — Francis Bacon, *Novum Organum*, 1620

Many other studies, including in college classrooms, confirm that *frequent quizzing and self-testing boosts students' retention* (Yang et al., 2021).

As explained in the Memory modules, to thoroughly understand information you must *actively process it*. One digest of 225 studies showed that students engaged in active learning showed the highest examination performance in science, technology, engineering, and mathematics (the STEM fields) (Freeman et al., 2014). Active learning is particularly useful at reducing achievement gaps between underrepresented (low income, marginalized culture) and overrepresented (high income, dominant culture) STEM students (Theobald et al., 2020). So, don't treat your mind like your stomach, something to be filled passively. Instead, treat it more like a muscle that grows stronger with exercise. Countless experiments reveal that people learn and remember best when they put material in their own words, rehearse it, and then retrieve and review it again.

The **SQ3R** study method incorporates these principles (McDaniel et al., 2009; Robinson, 1970). *SQ3R* is an acronym for its five steps: Survey, Question, Read, Retrieve[2], Review.

To study a module, first *survey*, taking a bird's-eye view. Scan each module's headings, and notice the organization.

Before you read each main section, try to answer its numbered Learning Objective *Question* (for this section: "How can psychological principles help you learn, remember, and thrive?"). Researchers have found that we retain information better after generating our own questions (Ebersbach et al., 2020; Roediger & Finn, 2010). Those who test their understanding *before* reading, and discover what they don't yet know, will learn and remember better.

Then *read*, actively searching for the answer to the Learning Objective Question (LOQ). At each sitting, read only as much of the module (usually a single main section) as you can absorb without tiring. Read actively and critically. Ask questions. Take notes. Make the ideas your own: How does what you've read relate to your own life? Does it support or challenge your assumptions? How convincing is the evidence? (Our Ask Yourself questions throughout each module will help you engage personally with the material.) Write out what you know. "Writing is often a tool for learning," say researchers (Arnold et al., 2017).

Having read a section, *retrieve* its main ideas: "Active retrieval promotes meaningful learning," says Karpicke (2012). So *test yourself*. This will not only help you figure out what you know, the testing itself will help you learn and retain the information more effectively. Even better, test yourself repeatedly. To facilitate this, we offer periodic *Retrieval Practice* questions throughout each module (for example, the questions at the end of this section). After answering these questions for yourself, you can "show" the answer to check your understanding (or check the answers in Appendix E) and reread the material as needed.

testing effect enhanced memory after retrieving, rather than simply rereading, information. Also referred to as a *retrieval practice effect* or *test-enhanced learning*.

SQ3R a study method incorporating five steps: Survey, Question, Read, Retrieve, Review.

[2]Also sometimes called "Recite."

Finally, *review:* Read over any notes you have taken, again with an eye on the module's organization, and quickly review the whole module. Write or say what a concept is before rereading to check your understanding. The end-of-module *Review* is set up as an additional self-test, with the collected Learning Objective Questions, key terms, and Module Test questions.

Survey, question, read, retrieve, review. Four additional study tips may further boost your learning:

Distribute your study time. One of psychology's oldest findings is that *spaced practice* promotes better retention than *massed practice*. You'll remember material better if you space your time over several study periods—perhaps 1 hour a day, 6 days a week—rather than cram it into one week-long or all-night study blitz. For example, rather than trying to read an entire module in a single sitting, read just one main section and then turn to something else. *Interleaving* (mixing) your study of psychology with your study of other subjects boosts long-term retention and protects against overconfidence (Kornell & Bjork, 2008; Taylor & Rohrer, 2010).

Spacing your study sessions requires a disciplined approach to managing your time. For more tips on time management, see the Student Preface—Student Success: How to Apply Psychology to Live Your Best Life—at the beginning of this text.

Learn to think critically. Both inside and outside of this course, critical thinking—smart thinking—is a key to wisdom. Whether you are reading or conversing, note people's assumptions and values. What perspective or bias underlies an argument? Evaluate evidence. Is it anecdotal? Or is it based on informative experiments? Assess conclusions. Are there alternative explanations?

Process class information actively. Listen for the main ideas and sub-ideas of a lecture. *Write them down.* Ask questions during and after class. In class, as in your private study, process the information actively and you will understand and retain it better. As psychologist William James urged a century ago, "No reception without reaction, no impression without ... expression." Make the information your own. Engage with the Ask Yourself questions to relate what you read to your own life. Tell someone else about it. (As any teacher will confirm, to teach is to remember.)

Also, take notes *by hand*. Handwritten notes, in your own words, typically engage more active processing, with better retention, than does verbatim note taking on laptops (Mueller & Oppenheimer, 2014).

Macmillan Learning

More learning tips To learn more about the testing effect and the SQ3R method, watch this ***Video: Make Things Memorable*** at tinyurl.com/HowToRemember.

Overlearn. Psychology tells us that overlearning improves retention. We tend to overestimate how much we know. You may understand a module as you read it, but that feeling of familiarity can be deceptively comforting. By using all of the self-testing opportunities in the text and in Achieve, you can test your knowledge and *overlearn* in the process.

Memory experts Elizabeth Bjork and Robert Bjork (2011) offer simple, scientifically supported advice for how to improve your retention and your grades:

> Spend less time on the input side and more time on the output side, such as summarizing what you have read from memory or getting together with friends and asking each other questions. Any activities that involve testing yourself—that is, activities that require you to retrieve or generate information, rather than just representing information to yourself—will make your learning both more durable and flexible. (p. 63)

ASK YOURSELF

Of all of these helpful principles, which ones seem most relevant and important for improving your own life and studies? How will you add them to your usual routines?

RETRIEVAL PRACTICE

RP-12 The __________ __________ describes the enhanced memory that results from repeated retrieval (as in self-testing) rather than from simple rereading of new information.

RP-13 What does the acronym *SQ3R* stand for?

ANSWERS IN APPENDIX E

MODULE 1 REVIEW The History and Scope of Psychology

LEARNING OBJECTIVES

Test Yourself Answer these repeated Learning Objective Questions on your own (before "showing" the answers here, or checking the answers in Appendix D) to improve your retention of the concepts (McDaniel et al., 2009, 2015).

LOQ 1-1 How is psychology a science?

LOQ 1-2 What are the three key elements of the scientific attitude, and how do they support scientific inquiry?

LOQ 1-3 How does critical thinking feed a scientific attitude, and smarter thinking for everyday life?

LOQ 1-4 What were some important milestones in psychology's early history?

LOQ 1-5 How did behaviorism, Freudian psychology, and humanistic psychology further the development of psychological science?

LOQ 1-6 How has contemporary psychology focused on cognition, on biology and experience, on culture and gender, and on human flourishing?

LOQ 1-7 How do psychologists use the biopsychosocial approach, and how can it help us understand our diverse world?

LOQ 1-8 What are psychology's main subfields?

LOQ 1-9 How can psychological principles help you learn, remember, and thrive?

TERMS AND CONCEPTS TO REMEMBER

Test Yourself Write down the definition in your own words, then check your answer.

empirical approach, p. 2
critical thinking, p. 3
structuralism, p. 6
functionalism, p. 6
behaviorism, p. 8
humanistic psychology, p. 9
cognitive psychology, p. 9
cognitive neuroscience, p. 9
psychology, p. 9
nature–nurture issue, p. 10
natural selection, p. 10
evolutionary psychology, p. 10
behavior genetics, p. 10
culture, p. 11
positive psychology, p. 12
biopsychosocial approach, p. 12
levels of analysis, p. 12
basic research, p. 14
applied research, p. 14
counseling psychology, p. 14
clinical psychology, p. 14
psychiatry, p. 14
community psychology, p. 14
testing effect, p. 17
SQ3R, p. 17

MODULE TEST

Test Yourself Answer the following questions on your own first, then "show" the answers here, or check your answers in Appendix E.

1. How can critical thinking help you evaluate claims in the media, even if you're not a scientific expert on the issue?

2. In 1879, in psychology's first experiment, ______________ ______________ and his students measured the time lag between hearing a ball hit a platform and pressing a key.

3. William James would be considered a(n) ______________. Wilhelm Wundt and Edward Titchener would be considered ______________.
   a. functionalist; structuralists
   b. structuralist; functionalists
   c. evolutionary theorist; structuralists
   d. functionalist; evolutionary theorists

4. In the early twentieth century, ______________ redefined psychology as "the science of observable behavior."
   a. John B. Watson
   b. Abraham Maslow
   c. William James
   d. Sigmund Freud

5. Nature is to nurture as
   a. personality is to intelligence.
   b. biology is to experience.
   c. intelligence is to biology.
   d. psychological traits are to behaviors.

6. "Nurture works on what nature provides." Describe what this means, using your own words.

7. Which of the following is true regarding gender differences and similarities?
   a. Gender differences outweigh any similarities.
   b. Despite some gender differences, the underlying processes of human behavior are the same.
   c. Gender similarities and differences both depend more on biology than on environment.
   d. Gender differences are so numerous that it is difficult to make meaningful comparisons.

8. Martin Seligman and other researchers who explore various aspects of human flourishing refer to their field of study as ______________ ______________.

9. A psychologist treating emotionally troubled adolescents at a local mental health agency is most likely to be a(n)

- **a.** research psychologist.
- **b.** psychiatrist.
- **c.** industrial-organizational psychologist.
- **d.** clinical psychologist.

10. A mental health professional with a medical degree who can prescribe medication is a ____________________.

11. A psychologist conducting basic research to expand psychology's knowledge base may

- **a.** design a computer screen with limited glare and assess the effect on computer operators' eyes after a day's work.
- **b.** treat older people who experience depression.
- **c.** observe 3- and 6-year-olds solving puzzles and analyze differences in their abilities.
- **d.** interview children with behavioral problems and suggest treatments.

MODULE 2 Research Strategies: How Psychologists Ask and Answer Questions

Hoping to satisfy their curiosity about people and to relieve their own woes, millions turn to "psychology." They read advice columns aimed at helping people cope with their problems, overcome their addictions, and save their marriages. They watch "celebrity psychics" demonstrate their supposed powers. They attend stop-smoking hypnosis seminars. They play online games, hoping to strengthen their brain. They immerse themselves in self-help books, websites, and lectures that promise to teach the path to love, the road to personal happiness, and the "hacks," or shortcuts, to success.

Others, intrigued by claims of psychological truth, wonder: How—and how much—does parenting shape children's personalities and abilities? Are first-born children more driven to achieve? Do dreams have deep meaning? Do we sometimes remember events that never happened? Does psychotherapy heal?

In working with such questions, the science of psychology does more than speculate. To separate uninformed opinions from examined conclusions, psychologists use the *scientific method* to conduct research. Let's consider how psychology's researchers do their science.

The Need for Psychological Science

LOQ 2-1 How does our everyday thinking sometimes lead us to a wrong conclusion?

Some people suppose that psychology is mere common sense—documenting and dressing in jargon what people already know: "You get paid for using fancy methods to tell me what everyone knows?"

Indeed, our intuition is often right. As the baseball great Yogi Berra (1925–2015) once said, "You can observe a lot by watching." (We also have Berra to thank for other gems, such as "Nobody goes there anymore—it's too crowded," and "If the people don't want to come out to the ballpark, nobody's gonna stop 'em.") Because we're all behavior watchers, it would be surprising if many of psychology's findings had *not* been foreseen. Many people believe that love breeds happiness, for example, and they are right (we have what researchers call a deep "need to belong").

But sometimes what seems like common sense, informed by countless casual observations, is wrong. In other modules, we will see how research has overturned popular ideas—that familiarity breeds contempt, that dreams predict the future, and that most of us use only 10 percent of our brain. We will also see how research has surprised us with discoveries about how the brain's chemical messengers control our moods and memories, about other animals' abilities, and about the relationship between social media use and depression.

Other things seem like commonsense truth only because we so often hear them repeated. Mere repetition of statements—whether true or false—makes them easier to process and remember, and thus more true-seeming (Dechêne et al., 2010; Fazio et al., 2015). Easy-to-remember misconceptions ("Bundle up before you go outside, or you will catch a cold!") can therefore overwhelm hard truths. This power of familiar, hard-to-erase falsehoods is a lesson well known to political manipulators and kept in mind by critical thinkers.

Three common flaws in commonsense thinking—*hindsight bias, overconfidence,* and *perceiving order in random events*—illustrate how, as novelist Madeleine L'Engle (1973) observed, "The naked intellect is an extraordinarily inaccurate instrument."

hindsight bias the tendency to believe, after learning an outcome, that one would have foreseen it. (Also known as the *I-knew-it-all-along phenomenon.*)

Did We Know It All Along? Hindsight Bias

Consider how easy it is to draw the bull's-eye *after* the arrow strikes. After the stock market drops, people say it was "due for a correction." After an athletic match, we credit the coach if a "gutsy play" wins the game and criticize the same "stupid play" if it doesn't. After a war or an election, its outcome usually seems obvious. Although history may therefore seem like a series of inevitable events, the actual future is seldom foreseen. No one's diary recorded, "Today the Hundred Years' War began."

This **hindsight bias** is easy to demonstrate by giving half the members of a group some purported psychological finding and giving the other half an opposite result. Tell the first group, for example: "Psychologists have found that separation weakens romantic attraction. As the saying goes, 'Out of sight, out of mind.'" Ask them to imagine why this might be true. Most people can, and after hearing an explanation, nearly all will then view this true finding as unsurprising.

Tell the second group the opposite: "Psychologists have found that separation strengthens romantic attraction. As the saying goes, 'Absence makes the heart grow fonder.'" People given this untrue result can also easily imagine it, and most will also see it as unsurprising. When opposite findings both seem like common sense, there is a problem.

Such errors in people's recollections and explanations show why we need psychological research. It's not that common sense is usually wrong. Rather, common sense describes, after the fact, what *has* happened better than it predicts what *will* happen.

More than 800 scholarly papers have shown hindsight bias in people young and old from around the world (Roese & Vohs, 2012). As physicist Niels Bohr reportedly jested, "Prediction is very difficult, especially if it's about the future."

"In life as in history the unexpected lies waiting, grinning from around corners. Only with hindsight are we wise about cause and effect." — Author Penelope Lively, *Moon Tiger*

Hindsight bias As the Covid-19 pandemic began spreading in early 2020, some countries' leaders told their people not to panic over "a measly cold," assured their people that the virus was "very well under control," and encouraged people to continue to "live life as usual." In hindsight, such misjudgments cost many lives. Likewise, after the 2021 mob assault on the U.S. Capitol, it was, in hindsight, obvious that security officials should have anticipated the attack.

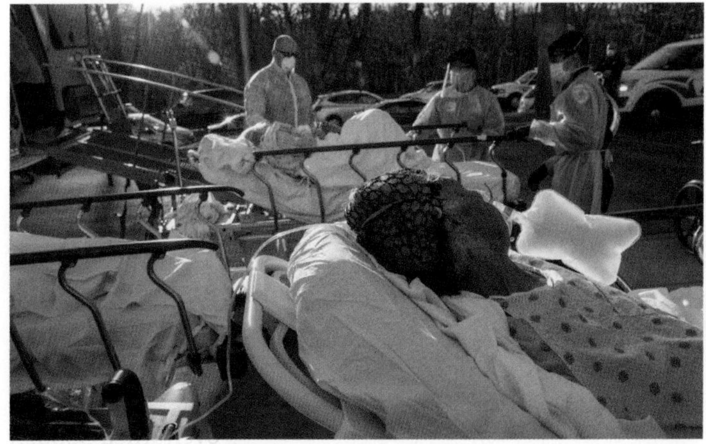
John Moore/Getty Images

Mostafa Bassim/Anadolu Agency/Getty Images

Overconfidence

We humans tend to think we know more than we do. Asked how sure we are of our answers to factual questions *(Is Boston north or south of Paris?)*, we tend to be more confident than correct.[3] And our confidence often drives us to quick—rather than correct—thinking (Rahnev et al., 2020). Consider these three anagrams, shown beside their solutions (from Goranson, 1978):

WREAT → WATER

ETRYN → ENTRY

GRABE → BARGE

Fun anagram solutions from Wordsmith (wordsmith.org):
Snooze alarms = Alas! No more z's
Dormitory = dirty room
Slot machines = cash lost in 'em

About how many seconds do you think it would have taken you to unscramble each of these? Did hindsight influence you? Knowing the answers tends to make us overconfident. (Surely, the solution would take only 10 seconds or so?) In reality, the average problem solver spends 3 minutes, as you also might, given a similar anagram without the solution: OCHSA.[4]

Are we any better at predicting social behavior? Psychologist Philip Tetlock (1998, 2005) collected more than 27,000 expert predictions of world events, such as whether Quebec would separate from Canada. His repeated finding: These predictions, which experts made with 80 percent confidence on average, were right less than 40 percent of the time.

Overconfidence in history:

"Not within a thousand years will man ever fly." —Wilbur Wright, in 1901, 2 years before he and his brother, Orville, made the first powered flight

"Computers in the future may weigh no more than 1.5 tons." —*Popular Mechanics*, 1949

"They couldn't hit an elephant at this distance." —General John Sedgwick just before being killed during a U.S. Civil War battle, 1864

"No woman in my time will be prime minister." —Margaret Thatcher, 1969 (British Prime Minister, 1979–1990)

ASK YOURSELF

Do you have a hard time believing you may be overconfident? Could overconfidence be at work in that self-assessment? How might reading this section about overconfidence help reduce your tendency to be overconfident?

RETRIEVAL PRACTICE

RP-1 Why, after friends start dating, do we often feel that we *knew* they were meant to be together?

ANSWERS IN APPENDIX E

Perceiving Order in Random Events

We're born with an eagerness to make sense of our world. People see a face on the Moon, hear Satanic messages in music, or perceive the Virgin Mary's image on a grilled cheese sandwich. Even in random data, we often find patterns, because—here's a curious fact of life—*random sequences often don't look random* (Falk et al., 2009; Nickerson, 2002, 2005). Flip a coin 50 times and you may be surprised at the streaks of heads and tails—much like supposed "hot" and "cold" streaks in basketball shooting and baseball hitting. In actual random sequences, patterns and streaks (such as repeating digits) occur more often than people expect (Oskarsson et al., 2009). That also makes it hard for people to generate random-like sequences. When embezzlers try to simulate random digits when specifying how much to steal, their nonrandom patterns can alert fraud experts (Poundstone, 2014).

Why are we so prone to pattern-seeking? For most people, a random, unpredictable world is unsettling (Tullett et al., 2015). Making sense of our world relieves stress and helps us get on with daily living (Ma et al., 2017).

Some happenings, such as winning a lottery twice, seem so extraordinary that we find it difficult to conceive an ordinary, chance-related explanation. "But with a large enough sample," say statisticians, "any outrageous thing is likely to happen" (Diaconis & Mosteller, 1989). An event that happens to but 1 in 1 billion people every day occurs about 7 times a day, more than 2500 times a year.

"The really unusual day would be one where nothing unusual happens." —Statistician Persi Diaconis (2002)

[3] Boston is south of Paris.
[4] The anagram solution: CHAOS.

The point to remember: Our commonsense thinking is flawed due to three powerful tendencies: hindsight bias, overconfidence, and our tendency to perceive patterns in random events. But scientific inquiry can help us sift reality from illusion.

Psychological Science in a Post-Truth World

LOQ 2-2 Why are we so vulnerable to believing untruths?

In 2017, the Oxford English Dictionary's word of the year was *post-truth*—describing a modern culture where people's emotions and personal beliefs often override their acceptance of objective facts.

Consider three examples of such "truth decay"(widely shared misinformation):

Belief: *The U.S. crime rate is rising.* Nearly every year since 1993, most U.S. adults have told Gallup that there is more crime "than there was a year ago" (Gallup, 2021).

Fact: For several decades, both violent and property crime rates have been *falling*. Between 1993 and 2019, the U.S. violent crime rate dropped 49 percent (Gramlich, 2020).

Belief: *Crime is common among immigrants* (McCarthy, 2017). Memorable incidents feed this narrative. Stories of an immigrant murdering, burglarizing, or lying spread through social networks and news outlets. Such fears are commonplace not only in North America, but also in Europe and Australia (Esses, 2021).

Fact: Most immigrants are *not* criminals. Compared with native-born Americans, immigrants are 44 percent *less* likely to be imprisoned (CATO, 2017; Flagg, 2018, 2019). The same has been true in Italy, the United Kingdom, and elsewhere (Di Carlo et al., 2018).

Belief: *Many people have died soon after receiving a Covid-19 vaccine.*

Fact: This statement is true, but not meaningful. With millions of people dying each year, some of those inevitably will die after receiving a vaccine, even though the vaccine itself (as of mid-2021) had caused no deaths (Rizzo, 2021).

FACTS
DON'T
MATTER!

Joe Dator/Cartoon Stock

"I'm sorry, Jeannie, your answer was correct, but Kevin shouted his incorrect answer over yours, so he gets the points."

In the United States, political party bias has distorted people's thinking. Extremely liberal and extremely conservative Americans both, with similar self-confidence, view their beliefs as superior (Harris & Van Bavel, 2021). Among single-and-looking U.S. Democrats, 71 percent said that they would not date someone who voted for Donald Trump, while 47 percent of Republicans would not date someone who voted for Hillary Clinton (Pew, 2020). When rating candidates for college scholarships, both Democrats and Republicans discriminate against those from the other party (Iyengar & Westwood, 2015). Extremely liberal people and extremely conservative people also show an equally rigid mindset and use the same amount of negative and angry language—they only differ in the issues they support (Frimer et al., 2019; Zmigrod et al., 2020). So, no American can smugly think "Yes, but bias doesn't apply to *me*." Bias goes both ways.

U.S. Democrats and Republicans share concerns about failures to separate fact from fiction. In 2021, President Joe Biden (2021) warned that favoring one's political beliefs rather than scientific research "undermines the welfare of the Nation, contributes to systemic inequities and injustices, and violates the trust that the public places in government to best serve its collective interests." Republican Senator Mitt Romney (2021) similarly expressed concern about false news, urging politicians to show people respect "by telling them the truth." Any agreement across partisan divides requires first a shared understanding of the essential facts.

So why do post-truth-era people so often, in the words of psychologist Tom Gilovich (1991), "know what isn't so?"

False news Some misinformation gets fed to us intentionally. It's "lies in the guise of news" (Kristof, 2017). In the 2016 U.S. election cycle, 6 percent of all Twitter-enabled news consumption was false news (Grinberg et al., 2019). In the United States and United Kingdom, exposure to false news related to Covid-19 vaccines was dangerous, reducing people's intention to accept a Covid vaccine (Loomba et al., 2021). And

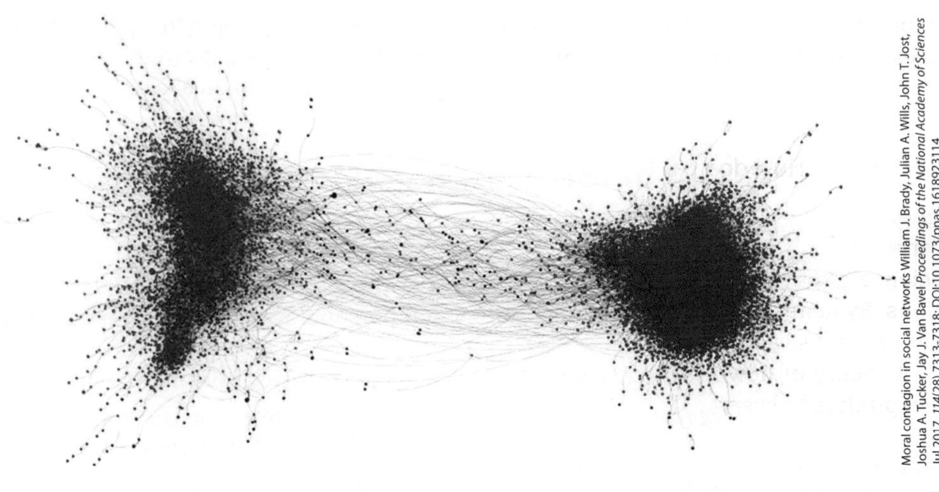

Moral contagion in social networks William J. Brady, Julian A. Wills, John T. Jost, Joshua A. Tucker, Jay J. Van Bavel *Proceedings of the National Academy of Sciences* Jul 2017, *114*(28) 7313-7318; DOI:10.1073/pnas.1618923114

FIGURE 2.1
The meeting of like minds On social media, most people discuss contentious issues with like-minded others. In this graph of politically charged Twitter activity, each node represents a user who sent a message; each line represents a user who retweeted something. As we can see, users overwhelmingly sent messages to, and retweeted messages from, those who shared their liberal (blue) or conservative (red) ideology (Brady et al., 2017).

made-up news is catchy. In one analysis of 126,000 stories tweeted by 3 million people, falsehoods—especially false political news—"diffused significantly farther, faster, deeper, and more broadly than the truth" (Vosoughi et al., 2018). Amid this sea of misinformation, we should remember Britain's scientific academy, the British Royal Society's, motto: *nullius in verba* (take nobody's word for it). The good news is that most people can tell the difference between high-quality and low-quality information sources (Pennycook & Rand, 2019). When encouraged to use slow, deliberate thinking rather than to go with their gut, people better discern fiction from fact (Bago et al., 2020).

Repetition In experiments, statements become more believable when they are repeated (De keersmaecker et al., 2020). From childhood onward, what we hear over and over—perhaps a made-up smear of a political opponent—becomes familiar, gets remembered, and comes to seem true and worth sharing (Effron & Raj, 2020; Fazio & Sherry, 2020).

Availability of powerful examples In the media, "if it bleeds it leads." Gruesome violence—a horrific murder, a mass killing, a plane crash—gets reported, with vivid images that color our judgments. No wonder Americans grossly overestimate their risk of being victimized by crime, terror, and plane crashes.

Group identity and the echo chamber of the like-minded Our social identities matter. Feeling good about our groups helps us feel good about ourselves. On social media we tend to friend and follow people who think as we do (Cinelli et al., 2021; see FIGURE 2.1). We often prefer news sources that affirm our views and demonize news sources that do not. And we often live among like-minded neighbors (Brown & Enos, 2021).

CONFIRM MY BIASES.COM

Marty Bucella/Cartoon Stock

"The best way we can transcend ideology is to teach our students, regardless of their majors, to think like scientists." —Psychologist (and Yale University President) Peter Salovey, "Knowledge Can Be Power," 2018

"We have ... become sloppier than ever: Tweet first, research later. Post first, rescind later. Guess first, confirm later." —Luvvie Ajayi, *I'm Judging You: The Do-Better Manual*, 2016

The good news is that we can build a real-truth world by embracing a scientific mindset. Mindful of our own biases, we can listen and learn. Confronted with an opposing view, we can discuss before we dismiss. And with a mix of curiosity, skepticism, and humility, we can adopt the spirit of critical thinking: *To accept everything is to be gullible; to deny everything is to be a cynic.*

The Scientific Method

The foundation of all science is a scientific attitude that combines *curiosity, skepticism,* and *humility*. Psychologists arm their scientific attitude with the *scientific method*—a self-correcting process for evaluating ideas with observation and analysis. Psychological science welcomes hunches and plausible-sounding theories. And it puts them to the test. If a theory works—if the data support its predictions—so much the better for that theory. If the predictions fail, the theory gets revised or rejected. When researchers submit their work to a scientific journal, **peer reviewers**—other scientists who are

peer reviewers scientific experts who evaluate a research article's theory, originality, and accuracy.

experts—evaluate a study's theory, originality, and accuracy. The journal editor then uses the peer reviews to decide whether the research deserves publication.

theory an explanation using an integrated set of principles that organizes observations and predicts behaviors or events.

hypothesis a testable prediction, often implied by a theory.

Constructing Theories

LOQ 2-3 How do theories advance psychological science?

In everyday conversation, we often use *theory* to mean "mere hunch." Someone might, for example, discount evolution as "only a theory"—as if it were mere speculation. In science, a **theory** explains behaviors or events by offering ideas that organize observations. By using deeper principles to organize isolated facts, a theory summarizes and simplifies. As we connect the observed dots, a coherent picture emerges.

A theory of how sleep affects memory, for example, helps us organize countless sleep-related observations into a short list of principles. Imagine that we observe over and over that people with good sleep habits tend to answer questions correctly in class and do well at test time. We might therefore theorize that sleep improves memory. So far, so good: Our principle neatly summarizes a list of observations about the effects of a good night's sleep.

Yet no matter how reasonable a theory may sound—and it does seem reasonable to suggest that sleep boosts memory—we must put it to the test. A good theory produces testable *predictions,* called **hypotheses.** Such predictions specify which results would support the theory and which results would disconfirm it. To test our theory about sleep effects on memory, we might hypothesize that when sleep deprived, people will remember less from the day before. To test that hypothesis, we might assess how well people remember course materials they studied either before a good night's sleep or before a shortened night's sleep (FIGURE 2.2). The results will either support our theory or lead us to revise or reject it.

Our theories can bias our observations. Having theorized that better memory springs from more sleep, we may see what we expect: We may perceive sleep-deprived people's answers as less accurate. The urge to see what we expect is strong, both inside and outside the laboratory, as when people's views of climate change influence their interpretation of local weather events.

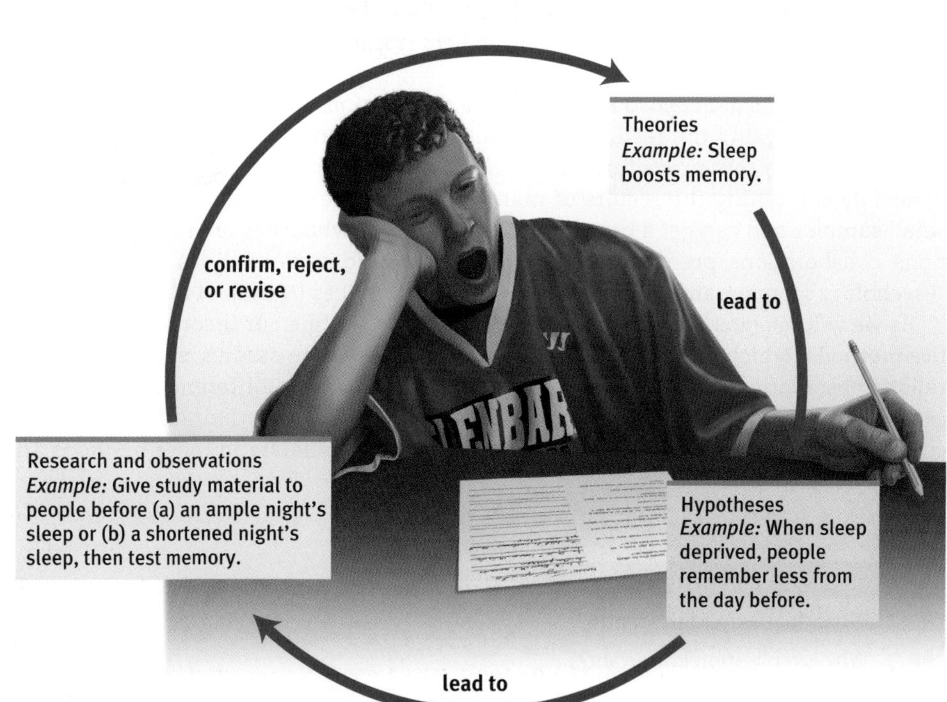
Theories
Example: Sleep boosts memory.
lead to
Hypotheses
Example: When sleep deprived, people remember less from the day before.
lead to
Research and observations
Example: Give study material to people before (a) an ample night's sleep or (b) a shortened night's sleep, then test memory.
confirm, reject, or revise

FIGURE 2.2
The scientific method This self-correcting process asks questions and observes answers.

In the end, our theory will be useful if it (1) *organizes* observations and (2) implies *predictions* that anyone can use to check the theory or to derive practical applications. (Does people's sleep predict their retention?) Eventually, our research may (3) stimulate further research that leads to a revised theory that better organizes and predicts.

As a check on their own biases, psychologists report their research with precise, measurable **operational definitions** of research procedures and concepts. *Sleep deprived,* for example, may be defined as "at least 2 hours less" than the person's natural sleep. (Likewise, a study of "aggression" may observe how many pins you stab into a doll that represents a lab partner, or a study of "helping" may record dollars donated.) By using carefully worded statements, others can **replicate** (repeat) the original observations with different participants, materials, and circumstances. If they get similar results, confidence in the finding's reliability grows. The first study of hindsight bias, for example, aroused psychologists' curiosity. Now, after many successful replications with differing people and questions, we feel sure of the phenomenon's power. Replication is confirmation.

Replication is an essential part of good science. Over the span of a decade, psychologists attempted to replicate 307 studies. They were able to reproduce similar results 64 percent of the time (Nosek et al., 2022). Replication failures often occur when samples are small, so psychologists increasingly study large samples (Blake & Gangestad, 2020; Sassenberg & Ditrich, 2019). A bigger sample = a more replicable result.

"Failure to replicate is not a bug; it is a feature. It is what leads us along the path—the wonderfully twisty path—of scientific discovery." —Lisa Feldman Barrett, "Psychology Is Not in Crisis," 2015

Today's psychological research is benefiting from more replications, more rigorous research methods, and more sharing of research data and tips on how best to analyze it (Agrawal et al., 2020; Dougherty et al., 2018; Smaldino & McElreath, 2016). Professional societies and crowdsourced projects create communities of psychological scientists who work together to improve their research methods and practices (Landy et al., 2020). More and more psychologists also use **preregistration** to publicly communicate their planned study design, hypotheses, data collection, and analyses (Nosek et al., 2018). This openness and transparency also prevents later modifications, such as changing the hypotheses to fit the data. Rather than pressuring researchers to publish only the results that support their predictions, preregistration encourages psychologists to openly report all of their results—even when that means failing to replicate earlier findings (Kristal et al., 2020). There is still a place for *exploratory research:* Investigators gather data and seek patterns that inspire theories, which can then be tested with *confirmatory research* (with preregistered hypotheses and preplanned analyses).

Psychological science also harnesses the power of *meta-analysis* (a statistical procedure for analyzing the results of multiple studies to reach an overall conclusion). Researchers use this procedure to statistically summarize a body of scientific evidence. By combining the results of many studies, researchers avoid the problem of small samples and can get a broader understanding of what they are studying. Replications, collaborations, preregistrations, explorations, and meta-analyses are all enabling "Psychology's Renaissance" of improved scientific practices (Nelson et al., 2018).

As we will see next, we can test our hypotheses and refine our theories using *descriptive* methods (which describe behaviors, often through case studies, surveys, or naturalistic observations), *correlational* methods (which associate different variables), and *experimental* methods (which manipulate variables to discover their effects). To think critically about popular psychology claims, we need to understand these methods and know what conclusions they allow.

operational definition a carefully worded statement of the exact procedures (operations) used in a research study. For example, *human intelligence* may be operationally defined as what an intelligence test measures. (Also known as *operationalization*.)

replication repeating the essence of a research study, usually with different participants in different situations, to see whether the basic finding can be reproduced.

preregistration publicly communicating planned study design, hypotheses, data collection, and analyses.

RETRIEVAL PRACTICE

RP-2 What does a good theory do?

RP-3 Why is replication important?

ANSWERS IN APPENDIX E

Description

LOQ 2-4 How do psychologists use case studies, naturalistic observations, and surveys to observe and describe behavior, and why is random sampling important?

The starting point of any science is description. In everyday life, we all observe and describe people, often drawing conclusions about why they think, feel, and act as they do. Psychologists do much the same, though more objectively and systematically, through

- ***case studies*** (in-depth analyses of individuals or groups),
- ***naturalistic observations*** (recording the natural behavior of many individuals), and
- ***surveys** and interviews* (asking people questions).

THE CASE STUDY Among the oldest research methods, the **case study** examines one individual or group in depth in the hope of revealing things true of us all. Some examples:

- ***Brain damage.*** Much of our early knowledge about the brain came from case studies of individuals who suffered particular impairments after damage to a certain brain region.
- ***Children's minds.*** Pioneering developmental psychologist Jean Piaget taught us about children's thinking after carefully observing and questioning only a few children.
- ***Animal intelligence.*** Studies of various animals, including a few chimpanzees, have revealed their capacity for understanding and language.

Intensive case studies are sometimes very revealing, and they often suggest directions for further study. But atypical individual cases may mislead us. Both in our everyday lives and in science, unrepresentative information can lead to mistaken judgments and false conclusions. Indeed, anytime a researcher mentions a finding *(Smokers die younger: 95 percent of men over 85 are nonsmokers)* someone is sure to offer a contradictory anecdote *(Well, I have an uncle who smoked two packs a day and lived to be 89!)*.

Dramatic stories and personal experiences (even psychological case examples) command our attention and are easily remembered. Journalists understand that and often begin their articles with compelling stories. Stories move us, but stories can mislead. Which of the following do you find more memorable? (1) "In one study of 1300 dream reports concerning a kidnapped child, only 5 percent correctly envisioned the child as dead" (Murray & Wheeler, 1937). (2) "I know a man who dreamed his sister was in a car accident, and two days later she died in a head-on collision!" Numbers can be numbing, but *the plural of anecdote is not evidence*. A single story of someone who supposedly changed from gay to straight is not evidence that sexual orientation is a choice. As psychologist Gordon Allport (1954, p. 9) said, "Given a thimbleful of [dramatic] facts we rush to make generalizations as large as a tub."

The point to remember: Individual cases can suggest fruitful ideas. What's true of all of us can be glimpsed in any one of us. But to find those general truths, we must employ other research methods.

Skye Hohmann/Alamy Stock Photo

Freud and Little Hans Sigmund Freud's case study of 5-year-old Hans' extreme fear of horses led Freud to his theory of childhood sexuality. He conjectured that Hans felt unconscious desire for his mother, feared castration by his rival father, and then transferred this fear into his phobia about being bitten by a horse. Today's psychological science discounts Freud's theory of childhood sexuality but does agree that much of the human mind operates outside our conscious awareness. (More on this in the Personality modules.)

RETRIEVAL PRACTICE

RP-4 We cannot assume that case studies always reveal general principles that apply to all of us. Why not?

ANSWERS IN APPENDIX E

NATURALISTIC OBSERVATION A second descriptive method involves recording responses in natural environments. These **naturalistic observations** traditionally ranged from watching chimpanzee societies in the jungle, to videotaping and analyzing parent-child interactions in different cultures, to recording racial differences in students' self-seating patterns in a school lunchroom. Until recently, such naturalistic observation was mostly "small science"—possible to do with pen and paper rather than fancy

case study a descriptive technique in which one individual or group is studied in depth in the hope of revealing universal principles. 

naturalistic observation a descriptive technique of observing and recording behavior in naturally occurring situations without changing or controlling the situation.

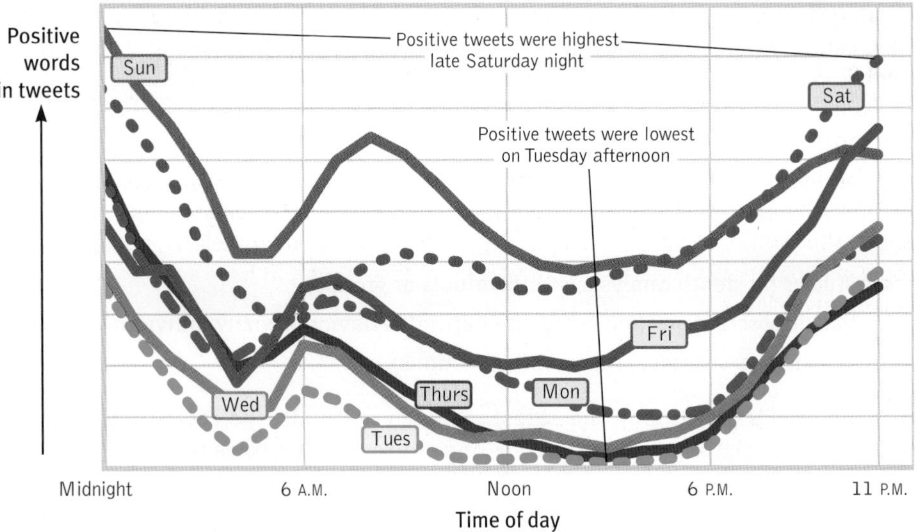
Positive words in tweets
Positive tweets were highest late Saturday night
Positive tweets were lowest on Tuesday afternoon
Sun
Sat
Fri
Wed
Thurs
Mon
Tues
Midnight
6 A.M.
Noon
6 P.M.
11 P.M.
Time of day

FIGURE 2.3
Twitter message moods, by time and by day This graph illustrates how researchers can use big data to study human behavior on a massive scale. It now is also possible to associate people's moods with, for example, their locations or with the weather, and to study the spread of ideas through social networks. (Data from Golder & Macy, 2011.)

equipment and a big budget (Provine, 2012). But today's digital technologies—thanks to "big data" harvested from phone apps, social media, online searches, and more—have transformed naturalistic observations into big science. Anonymously tapping into 15 million cell phones' GPS allowed scientists to track how often people in different geological regions obeyed stay-at-home orders and social distancing recommendations during the Covid-19 pandemic (Glanz et al., 2020). New technologies—wearable cameras and fitness sensors, and internet-connected smart-home sensors—offer increasing possibilities for people to allow accurate recording of their activity, relationships, sleep, and stress (Nelson & Allen, 2018; Yokum et al., 2019).

A natural observer "Observations, made in the natural habitat," noted chimpanzee observer Jane Goodall (1998), "helped to show that the societies and behavior of animals are far more complex than previously supposed."

The billions of people entering personal information online have also enabled big-data observations (without disclosing individual identities). One research team studied the ups and downs of human moods by counting positive and negative words in 504 million tweets from 84 countries (Golder & Macy, 2011). As **FIGURE 2.3** shows, people seemed happier on weekends, shortly after waking, and in the evenings. (Are late Saturday evenings often a happy time for you, too?) Another study found that negative emotion (especially anger-related) words in 148 million tweets from 1347 U.S. counties predicted the counties' heart disease rates *better* than smoking and obesity rates (Eichstaedt et al., 2015). Online searching enables people to learn about the world, and people's online searching enables researchers to learn about people. For example, the words people search and the questions they ask can gauge a region's level of racism and depression. But online searches also reveal our universal human likeness—as illustrated by the word *pregnant* being searched in conjunction with the same food cravings worldwide (Stephens-Davidowitz, 2017). Across the globe, we are kin beneath the skin.

Like the case study, naturalistic observation does not *explain* behavior. It *describes* it. Nevertheless, descriptions can be revealing. We once thought, for example, that only humans use tools. Then naturalistic observation revealed that chimpanzees sometimes insert a stick in a termite mound and withdraw it, eating the stick's load of termites. Such unobtrusive naturalistic observations paved the way for later studies of animal thinking, language, and emotion, which further expanded our understanding of our fellow animals. Thanks to researchers' observations, we know that chimpanzees and baboons use deception: Psychologists repeatedly saw one young baboon pretending to have been attacked by another as a tactic to get its mother to drive the other baboon away from its food (Whiten & Byrne, 1988).

Naturalistic observations also illuminate human behavior. Here are two findings you might enjoy:

- ***A funny finding.*** We humans laugh 30 times more often in social situations than in solitary situations (Provine, 2001). (Have you noticed how seldom you laugh when alone?)

- *Culture and the pace of life.* Naturalistic observation also enabled Robert Levine and Ara Norenzayan (1999) to compare the pace of life—walking speed, the accuracy of public clocks, and so forth—in 31 countries. Their conclusion: Life is fastest paced in Japan and Western Europe, and slower-paced in economically less-developed countries.

Naturalistic observation offers interesting snapshots of everyday life, but it does so without controlling for all the factors that may influence behavior. It's one thing to observe the pace of life in various places, but another to understand what makes some people walk faster than others. Nevertheless, descriptions can be revealing: The starting point of any science is description.

RETRIEVAL PRACTICE

RP-5 What are the advantages and disadvantages of naturalistic observation?

ANSWERS IN APPENDIX E

THE SURVEY A **survey** looks at many cases, asking people to report their behavior or opinions. Questions about everything from sexual practices to political opinions are put to the public. Here are some recent survey findings:

- Compared with young adults of an earlier generation (those born in the 1960s and 1970s), twice as many millennials born in the 1990s reported having no sexual partners since age 18 (Twenge, 2017). Today's less attached young adults are experiencing what one writer termed a "sex recession" (Julian, 2018).
- 1 in 2 people across 24 countries reported believing in the "existence of intelligent alien civilizations in the universe" (Lampert, 2017).
- 54 percent of all humans—some 4.1 billion people—say that religion is very important in their lives (Pew, 2019).

But asking questions is tricky. People may shade their answers in a socially desirable direction, such as by underreporting their cigarette consumption or overreporting their voting. And the answers often depend on how researchers' questions are worded and how respondents are chosen.

Wording Effects Even small changes in the order or wording of questions can make a big difference (**TABLE 2.1**). When U.S. White evangelical Christians were asked whether (1) "Humans have evolved over time" or (2) "Humans have existed in their present form since the beginning of time," only 32 percent expressed a belief in evolution (Funk, 2019). But when asked whether (1) "Humans have evolved over time due to processes such as natural selection; God or a higher power had no part in this process"; (2) "Humans have evolved over time due to processes that were guided or allowed by God or a higher power"; or (3) "Humans have existed in their present form since the beginning of time," more than twice as many—68 percent—expressed a belief in evolution. Because wording is such a delicate matter, critical thinkers will reflect on how the phrasing of a question might affect people's expressed opinions.

TABLE 2.1 Survey Wording Effects

Garners More Approval	Garners Less Approval
"aid to those in need"	"welfare"
"undocumented workers"	"illegal aliens"
"gun safety laws"	"gun control laws"
"revenue enhancers"	"taxes"
"enhanced interrogation"	"torture"

survey a descriptive technique for obtaining the self-reported attitudes or behaviors of a particular group, usually by questioning a representative, *random sample* of the group.

Random Sampling In everyday thinking, we tend to generalize from samples we observe, especially vivid cases. An administrator who reads (a) a statistical summary of an instructor's student evaluations and (b) the vivid comments of two irate students may be influenced as much by the biased sample of two unhappy students as by the many favorable evaluations in the statistical summary. The temptation to succumb to the *sampling bias*—to generalize from a few vivid but unrepresentative cases—is nearly irresistible.

So how do you obtain a *representative sample?* Say you want to learn how students at your college or university feel about online learning. It's often not possible to survey the whole group. How then could you choose a group that would represent the total student body? Typically, you would seek a **random sample**, in which every person in the entire **population** has an equal chance of being included in the sample group. You might number the names in the school's student roster and use a random-number generator to pick your survey participants. (Sending each student a questionnaire wouldn't work because the conscientious people who returned it would not be a random sample.) Large representative samples are better than small ones, but a smaller representative sample of 100 is better than a larger unrepresentative sample of 500. You cannot compensate for an unrepresentative sample by simply adding more people.

Political pollsters sample voters in national election surveys just this way. Without random sampling, large samples—such as from "opt-in" website polls—often give misleading results. But by using some 1500 randomly sampled people, drawn from all areas of a country, polls can provide a reasonably accurate snapshot of the nation's opinions. In today's world, however, with so many people not answering phones, doorknocks, and emails, getting this random sample is a challenge.

Given polling's margin of error and last-minute voter swings, political polls are good but imperfect estimates of likely outcomes. Immediately before the 2016 U.S. presidential election, popular polling analysis website FiveThirtyEight.com gave candidate Hillary Clinton an estimated 71 percent chance of winning. When Donald Trump was then elected, many regarded the prediction as a failure. But consider: When a prediction model estimates a 71 percent chance for one candidate, that candidate should *lose* nearly one third of the time. (Imagine a weather forecast that predicts a 70 percent chance of rain. If it then *always* rained, that would be a flawed forecast.) One analysis of 30,000 general election political predictions in 45 countries between 1942 and 2017 summed it up: Contrary to popular belief, polls are pretty accurate (Jennings & Wlezien, 2018).

With very large samples, estimates become quite reliable. The letter *E* is estimated to represent 12.7 percent of the letters in written English. *E*, in fact, is 12.3 percent of the 925,141 letters in Melville's *Moby-Dick*, 12.4 percent of the 586,747 letters in Dickens' *A Tale of Two Cities*, and 12.1 percent of the 3,901,021 letters in 12 of Mark Twain's works (*Chance News*, 1997).

The point to remember: Before accepting survey findings, think critically. Consider the sample. The best basis for generalizing is from a representative, random *sample*.

RETRIEVAL PRACTICE

RP-6 What is an unrepresentative sample, and how do researchers avoid it?

ANSWERS IN APPENDIX E

random sample a sample that fairly represents a population because each member has an equal chance of inclusion.

population all those in a group being studied, from which random samples may be drawn. (*Note:* Except for national studies, this does *not* refer to a country's whole population.)

correlation a measure of the extent to which two factors vary together, and thus of how well either factor *(variable)* predicts the other.

correlation coefficient a statistical index of the direction and strength of the relationship between two things (from −1.00 to +1.00).

Correlation

LOQ 2-5 What does it mean when we say two things are correlated, and what are positive and negative correlations?

Describing behavior is the first step toward predicting it. Naturalistic observation and surveys often show us that one trait or behavior tends to coincide with another. In such cases, we say the two **correlate**. A statistical measure (the **correlation coefficient**) helps us figure out the direction and strength of the relationship. Knowing how much aptitude test scores *correlate* with school success tells us how well the scores *predict* school success.

A *positive correlation* (above 0 to +1.00) indicates a *direct* relationship, meaning that two things increase together or decrease together. For example, height and weight are positively correlated.

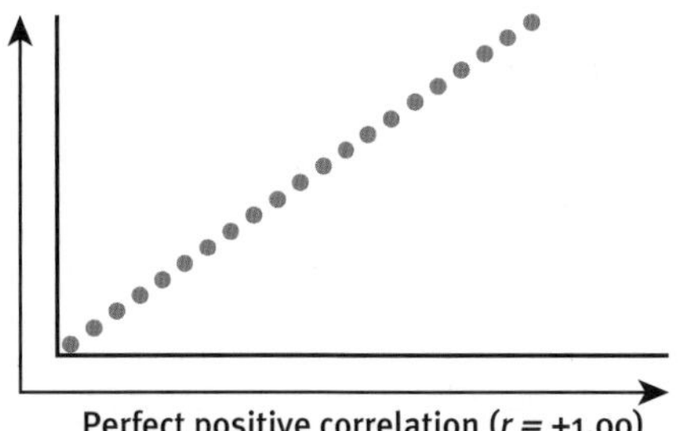
Perfect positive correlation ($r = +1.00$)

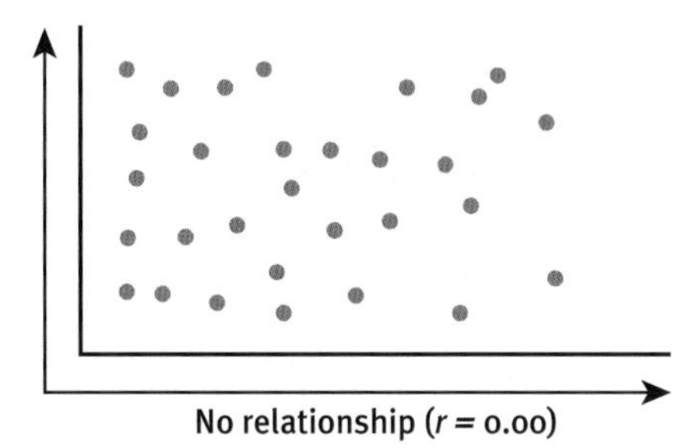
No relationship ($r = 0.00$)

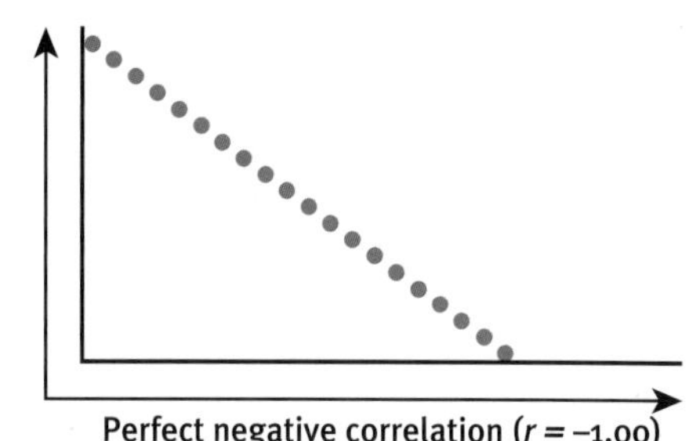
Perfect negative correlation ($r = -1.00$)

FIGURE 2.4
Scatterplots, showing patterns of correlation Correlations—abbreviated *r*—can range from +1.00 (scores for one variable increase in direct proportion to scores for another), to 0.00 (no relationship), to −1.00 (scores for one variable decrease precisely as scores for the other rise).

A *negative correlation* (below 0 to −1.00) indicates an *inverse* relationship: As one thing increases, the other decreases. Negative correlations could go as low as −1.00, which means that, like people on opposite ends of a teeter-totter, one set of scores goes down precisely as the other goes up. An example: In the fall of 2020, U.S. states' rate of mask use correlated negatively ($r = -.85$) with reported Covid-19 symptoms (CovidCast, 2020).

A coefficient near zero is a weak correlation, indicating little or no relationship.

Throughout this book, we often ask how strongly two **variables** are related: How closely related are the personality test scores for identical twins? How well do intelligence test scores predict career achievement? Do people's depression levels predict their anxiety?

In such cases, **scatterplots** can be very revealing. Each dot in a scatterplot represents the values of two variables. The three scatterplots in **FIGURE 2.4** illustrate the range of possible correlations from a perfect positive to a perfect negative. (Perfect correlations rarely occur in the real world.) A correlation is positive if two sets of scores, such as for height and weight, tend to rise or fall together.

A negative correlation isn't "bad." It simply means two sets of scores relate inversely, one set going up as the other goes down. The correlation between people's height and the distance from their head to the ceiling is strongly (perfectly, in fact) negative. Saying that a correlation is "negative" also says nothing about its strength.

Statistics can reveal what we might miss with casual observation. To demonstrate, consider the responses of 2291 Czech and Slovakian volunteers who rated, on a 1 to 7 scale, their *fear* and *disgust* related to each of 24 animals (Polák et al., 2020). With all the relevant data right in front of you (**TABLE 2.2**), can you tell whether the correlation between participants' fear and their disgust is positive, negative, or close to zero?

TABLE 2.2 People's Fear and Disgust Responses to Various Animals

Animal	Average Fear	Average Disgust
Ant	2.12	2.26
Bat	2.11	2.01
Bull	3.84	1.62
Cat	1.24	1.17
Cockroach	3.10	4.16
Dog	2.25	1.20
Fish	1.15	1.38
Frog	1.84	2.48
Snake	3.32	2.47
Horse	1.82	1.11
Lizard	1.46	1.46
Louse	3.58	4.83
Maggot	2.90	4.49
Mouse	1.62	1.78
Panda	1.57	1.17
Pigeon	1.48	2.01
Rat	2.11	2.25
Rooster	1.78	1.34
Roundworm	3.49	4.79
Snail	1.15	1.69
Spider	4.39	4.47
Tapeworm	3.60	4.83
Viper	4.34	2.83
Wasp	3.42	2.84

When comparing the columns in Table 2.2, you might not detect much of a relationship between fear and disgust. In fact, the correlation in this example is positive ($r = +.72$), as we can see if we display the data as a scatterplot (**FIGURE 2.5**).

If we don't easily recognize a strong relationship when data are presented systematically, as in Table 2.2, how much less likely are we to notice them in everyday life? To see what is right in front of us, we sometimes need statistical illumination. We can easily see evidence of gender discrimination when given statistically summarized information about job level, seniority, performance, gender, and salary. But we often see no discrimination when the same information dribbles in, case by case (Twiss et al., 1989). Single events or individuals catch our attention, especially if we want to see (or deny) bias. In contrast, statistics calculate patterns by counting every case equally.

variable anything that can vary and is practical and ethical to measure.

scatterplot a graphed cluster of dots, each of which represents the values of two variables. The slope of the points suggests the direction of the relationship between the two variables. The amount of scatter suggests the strength of the correlation (little scatter indicates high correlation).

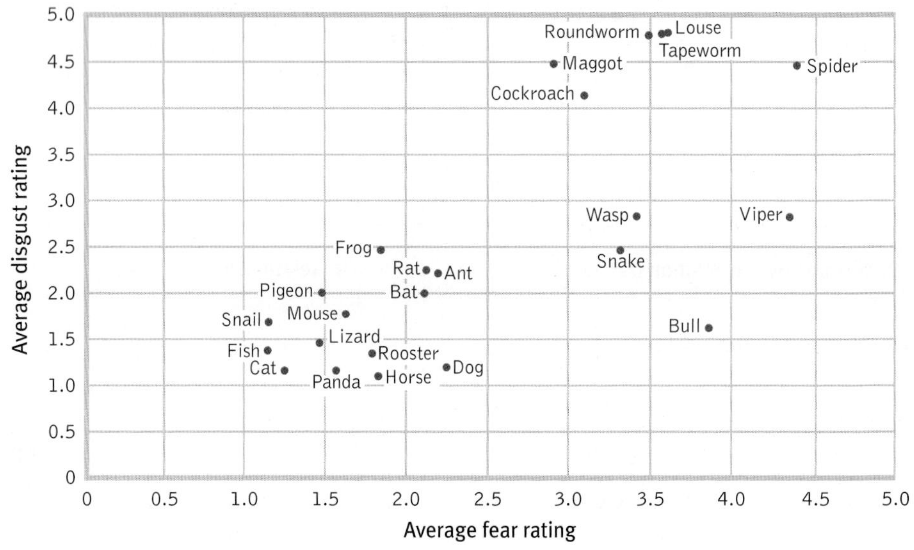

Roundworm
Louse
Tapeworm
Maggot
Spider
Cockroach
Wasp
Viper
Snake
Frog
Rat
Ant
Bat
Pigeon
Mouse
Snail
Bull
Lizard
Fish
Rooster
Cat
Dog
Panda
Horse
Average disgust rating
Average fear rating
0
0.5
1.0
1.5
2.0
2.5
3.0
3.5
4.0
4.5
5.0

FIGURE 2.5
Scatterplot for fear and disgust felt toward 24 animals This display of average self-reported fear and disgust (each represented by a data point) reveals an upward slope, indicating a positive correlation. The considerable scatter of the data indicates the correlation is much lower than +1.00.

The point to remember: Unlike experiments, correlation coefficients tell us nothing about cause and effect. But they can help us see the world more clearly by revealing the extent to which two things relate.

RETRIEVAL PRACTICE

RP-7 Indicate whether each association is a positive correlation or a negative correlation.

1. The more husbands viewed internet pornography, the worse their marital relationships (Muusses et al., 2015). ____________
2. The more time teen girls spend absorbed with online social media, the more at risk they are for depression and suicidal thoughts (Kelly et al., 2019; Twenge & Campbell, 2019). ____________
3. The longer children were breast-fed, the greater their later academic achievement (Horwood & Fergusson, 1998). ____________
4. The more leafy vegetables older adults eat, the less their mental decline over the ensuing 5 years (Morris et al., 2018). ____________

ANSWERS IN APPENDIX E

ILLUSORY CORRELATIONS AND REGRESSION TOWARD THE MEAN

LOQ 2-6 What are *illusory correlations,* and what is *regression toward the mean?*

Correlations make clear the relationships we might otherwise miss; they also keep us from falsely assuming a relationship where there is none. When we believe there is a relationship between two things, we are likely to notice and recall instances that confirm our belief. If we believe that dreams forecast actual events, we may notice and recall confirming instances more than disconfirming instances. The result is an **illusory correlation**.

Illusory correlations can feed an illusion of control—that we can personally influence chance events. Gamblers, remembering past lucky rolls, may come to believe they influenced the roll of the dice by throwing gently for low numbers and hard for high numbers. We also struggle to separate fact from fiction due to a statistical phenomenon called **regression toward the mean**. Extreme results, such as an exceptionally low exam score, are caused by unfortunate combinations—exam topic, question difficulty, sleep deprivation, the weather. The same combination likely won't occur on the next exam, raising the probability of a higher score. Simply said, extraordinary happenings tend to be followed by more ordinary ones. Unusually high or low grades will usually regress

illusory correlation perceiving a relationship where none exists, or perceiving a stronger-than-actual relationship.

regression toward the mean the tendency for extreme or unusual scores or events to fall back (regress) toward the average.

toward students' average grades. And a team's unusually poor performance in one game will usually improve in the next.

Failure to recognize regression can lead to superstitious thinking. After berating a team for poorer-than-usual performance, a coach may—when the team regresses to more typical play—think the scolding actually worked. After lavishing praise for an exceptionally fine performance, the coach may be disappointed when a team's behavior migrates back toward its average. Ironically, then, regression toward the average can mislead us into feeling rewarded after criticizing others ("That criticism really made them work harder!") and feeling punished after praising them ("All those compliments made them slack off!") (Tversky & Kahneman, 1974).

The point to remember: When a fluctuating behavior returns to average, fancy explanations for why it does so are often wrong. Regression toward the mean is probably at work.

"Once you become sensitized to it, you see regression everywhere." — Psychologist Daniel Kahneman (1985)

Moreover, although correlational research helpfully reveals relationships, it does not explain them. If teen social media use correlates with (predicts) teen risk of depression, that may—or may not—indicate that social media use affects depression risk. Other explanations are possible (see Thinking Critically About: Correlation and Causation).

RETRIEVAL PRACTICE

RP-8 You hear the school basketball coach telling her friend that she rescued her team's winning streak by yelling at the players after an unusually bad first half. What is another explanation of why the team's performance improved?

RP-9 Length of marriage positively correlates with hair loss in men. Does this mean that marriage causes men to lose their hair (or that balding men make better husbands)?

Nancy Brown/The Image Bank/Getty Images

ANSWERS IN APPENDIX E

Experimentation

LOQ 2-8 What are the characteristics of experimentation that make it possible to isolate cause and effect?

Happy are they, remarked the Roman poet Virgil, "who have been able to perceive the causes of things." How might psychologists sleuth out the causes in correlational studies, such as the small correlation between teen girls' social media use and their risk of depression and self-harm (Olgers & Jensen, 2020)?

EXPERIMENTAL MANIPULATION Our sleuthing starts with three plain facts:

1. Beginning in 2010, worldwide smart phone and social media use mushroomed.
2. Simultaneously, Canadian, American, and British teen girls' rates of depression, anxiety, self-harm, and suicide also mushroomed (Mercado et al., 2017; Morgan, 2017; Statistics Canada, 2016).
3. Moving beyond simple correlations, in seven of nine *longitudinal* (over time) studies, teens' current social media use predicted future mental health issues (Haidt & Twenge, 2021; Zhou et al., 2020).

What do such findings mean? Is there a cause-effect connection, perhaps above a certain amount of screen time? Should parents limit their children's screen time? Even big correlational data from a million teens couldn't tell us. To identify cause and effect, researchers must **experiment**. Experiments enable researchers to isolate the effects of

experiment a research method in which an investigator manipulates one or more variables (independent variables) to observe the effect on some behavior or mental process (the dependent variable). By *random assignment* of participants, the experimenter aims to control other relevant variables that may change the research outcome.

Thinking Critically About:
Correlation and Causation

LOQ 2-7 Why do correlations enable prediction but not cause-effect explanation?

Mental illness *correlates* with smoking—meaning that those who experience mental illness are also more likely to be smokers.[1] Does this tell us anything about what *causes* mental illness or smoking? **NO.**

There may be something about smoking that leads to mental illness.

Those with mental illness may be more likely to smoke.

OR

There may be some *third variable*, such as a stressful home life, for example, that triggers *both* smoking and mental illness.

So, then, how would you interpret these recent findings?

a) Sexual hook-ups correlate with college women's experiencing depression.

b) *Delaying* sexual intimacy correlates with positive outcomes such as greater relationship satisfaction and stability.[2]

Possible explanations:

1. Sexual restraint	→	Better mental health and stronger relationships
2. Depression	→	People being more likely to hook up
3. Some third factor, such as lower impulsivity	→	Sexual restraint, psychological well-being, and better relationships

Correlations do help us predict. Consider: Self-esteem correlates negatively with (and therefore predicts) depression. The lower people's self-esteem, the greater their risk for depression.

Possible interpretations:

1. Low self-esteem	→	Depression
2. Depression	→	Low self-esteem
3. Some third factor, such as distressing events or biological predisposition	→	Both low self-esteem and depression

You try it!

A survey of over 12,000 adolescents found that the more teens feel loved by their parents, the less likely they are to behave in unhealthy ways—having early sex, smoking, abusing alcohol and drugs, exhibiting violence.[3] What are three possible ways we could interpret that finding?[4]

***The point to remember:* Correlation does not prove causation.**

Correlation suggests a possible cause-effect relationship but does not prove it. Remember this principle and you will be wiser as you read and hear news of scientific studies.

1. Belluck, 2013. 2. Fielder et al., 2013; Willoughby et al., 2014. 3. Resnick et al., 1997. 4. *ANSWERS*: A. Parental love may produce healthy teens. B. Well-behaved teens may feel more parental love and approval. C. Some third factor, such as income or neighborhood, may influence both parental love AND teen behaviors.

experimental group in an experiment, the group exposed to the treatment, that is, to one version of the independent variable.

control group in an experiment, the group *not* exposed to the treatment; contrasts with the experimental group and serves as a comparison for evaluating the effect of the treatment.

random assignment assigning participants to experimental and control groups by chance, thus minimizing preexisting differences between the different groups.

one or more variables by (1) *manipulating the variables of interest* and (2) *holding constant ("controlling") other variables.* To do so, they often create an **experimental group**, in which people receive the treatment (such as reduced screen time), and a contrasting **control group** in which they do not.

To minimize any preexisting differences between the two groups, experimenters **randomly assign** people to each condition. Random assignment—whether with a random-number generator or by the flip of a coin—effectively equalizes the two groups. If one-third of the volunteers for an experiment can wiggle their ears, then about one-third of the people in each group will be ear wigglers. So, too, with age, intelligence, attitudes, and other characteristics, which will be similar in the experimental and control groups. Thus, if the groups differ at the experiment's end, we can surmise that the treatment had an effect. (Note the difference between random *sampling*—which creates a representative survey sample—and random *assignment,* which equalizes the experimental and control groups.)

So, what do *experiments* reveal about the relationship between girls' social media use and their risk of depression and self-harm? One experiment identified nearly 1700 people who agreed to deactivate their Facebook account for 4 weeks (Allcott et al., 2020). Compared with people in the control group, those randomly assigned to the deactivation group spent more time watching TV and socializing with friends and family—and they reported lower depression, and greater happiness and satisfaction with their lives (and less postexperiment Facebook use). Less Facebook time meant a happier life.

The debate over the effects of prolonged social media use is ongoing. For now, most researchers agree that unlimited teen social media use poses a modest mental health risk. With more large correlational and longitudinal studies, and more experiments, researchers will refine this tentative conclusion.

The point to remember: Correlational studies, which uncover naturally occurring relationships, are complemented by experiments, which manipulate a variable to determine its effect.

double-blind procedure an experimental procedure in which both the research participants and the research staff are uninformed (blind) about whether the research participants have received the treatment or a placebo. Commonly used in drug-evaluation studies.

placebo [pluh-SEE-bo; Latin for "I shall please"] effect experimental results caused by expectations alone; any effect on behavior caused by the administration of an inert substance or condition, which the recipient assumes is an active agent.

PROCEDURES AND THE PLACEBO EFFECT Consider, then, how we might assess therapeutic interventions. Our tendency to seek new remedies when we are ill or emotionally down can produce misleading testimonies. If three days into a cold we start taking zinc tablets and find our cold symptoms lessening, we may credit the pills rather than the cold naturally subsiding. In the 1700s, bloodletting *seemed* effective. When the patient actually survived, this "treatment" was credited for the recovery. When patients didn't survive, the practitioner inferred the disease was too advanced to be reversed. So, whether or not a remedy is truly effective, enthusiastic users will probably endorse it. To determine its effect, we must control for other variables.

And that is precisely how new drugs and new methods of psychological therapy are evaluated (more on this in the Therapy modules). Investigators randomly assign participants in these studies to research groups. One group receives a pseudotreatment—an inert *placebo* (perhaps a pill with no drug in it). The other group receives a treatment, such as an antidepressant medication. (You can think of the placebo versus the actual drug as "trick or treatment.") The participants are often *blind* (uninformed) about what treatment, if any, they are receiving. If the study is using a **double-blind procedure**, neither the participants nor those who administer the drug and collect the data will know which group is receiving the treatment.

In double-blind studies, researchers check a treatment's actual effects apart from the participants' and the staff's belief in its healing powers. Just *thinking* you are getting a treatment can boost your spirits, relax your body, and relieve your symptoms. This **placebo effect** is well documented in reducing pain, depression, anxiety, and auditory hallucinations in schizophrenia (Dollfus et al., 2016; Kirsch, 2010). Athletes have run faster when given a supposed performance-enhancing drug (McClung & Collins, 2007). Decaf-coffee drinkers have reported increased vigor and alertness when they thought their brew had caffeine in it (Dawkins et al., 2011). People have felt better after receiving a phony mood-enhancing drug (Michael et al., 2012). And the more expensive the placebo, the more "real" it seems to us—a fake pill that costs $2.50 worked better than one costing 10 cents (Waber et al., 2008). To know how effective a therapy really is, researchers must control for a possible placebo effect.

HOW DO I KNOW MY CLIENT DIDN'T DO IT? BECAUSE HE'S A PLACEBO! HE'S NEVER DONE ANYTHING!

RETRIEVAL PRACTICE

RP-10 What measures do researchers use to prevent the *placebo effect* from confusing their results?

ANSWERS IN APPENDIX E

independent variable in an experiment, the variable that is manipulated; the variable whose effect is being studied.

confounding variable in an experiment, a variable other than the variable being studied that might influence a study's results.

dependent variable in an experiment, the variable that is measured; the variable that may change when the independent variable is manipulated.

INDEPENDENT AND DEPENDENT VARIABLES Here is an even more potent example: The drug Viagra was approved for use after 21 clinical trials. One trial was an experiment in which researchers randomly assigned 329 men with erectile disorder to either an experimental group (Viagra takers) or a control group (placebo takers given an identical-looking pill). The procedure was double-blind—neither the men taking the pills nor the person giving them knew what participants were receiving. The result: At peak doses, 69 percent of Viagra-assisted attempts at intercourse were successful, compared with 22 percent for men receiving the placebo (Goldstein et al., 1998). Follow-up experiments replicated Viagra's helpful effect (Fink et al., 2002). Viagra performed.

These simple experiments manipulated just one variable: the drug (Viagra versus no Viagra). We call this experimental variable the **independent variable** because we can vary it *independently* of other variables, such as the men's age, weight, and personality. Other variables that can potentially influence a study's results are called **confounding variables**. Random assignment controls for possible confounding variables.

A similar experiment on a drug approved to increase women's sexual arousal produced a result described as, um, anticlimactic—an additional "half of one satisfying sexual encounter a month" (Ness, 2016; Tavernise, 2016).

Experiments examine the effect of one or more independent variables on some measurable behavior, called the **dependent variable** because it can vary *depending* on what occurs during the experiment. Both variables are given precise *operational definitions*, which specify the procedures that manipulate the independent variable (the exact drug dosage and timing in this study) or measure the dependent variable (the men's responses to questions about their sexual performance). These definitions offer a level of precision that enables others to replicate the study. (See **FIGURE 2.6** for the Facebook experiment design.)

Let's pause to check your understanding using a simple psychology experiment: To test the effect of perceived ethnicity on the availability of rental housing, Adrian Carpusor and William Loges (2006) sent identically worded email inquiries to 1115 Los Angeles-area landlords. The researchers varied the sender's name and tracked the percentage of positive replies (invitations to view the apartment in person). "Patrick McDougall," "Said Al-Rahman," and "Tyrell Jackson" received, respectively, 89 percent, 66 percent, and 56 percent invitations. In this experiment, what was the independent variable? The dependent variable?[5]

"[We must guard] against not just racial slurs, but ... against the subtle impulse to call Johnny back for a job interview, but not Jamal." — U.S. President Barack Obama, eulogy for state senator and church-shooting victim Clementa Pinckney, June 26, 2015

Experiments can also help us evaluate social programs. Do early childhood education programs boost impoverished children's chances for success? What are the effects of different antismoking campaigns? Do school sex-education programs reduce teen pregnancies? To answer such questions, we can experiment: If an intervention is welcomed but resources are scarce, we could use a lottery to randomly assign some people (or regions) to experience the new program and others to a control condition. If later the two groups differ, the intervention's effect will be supported (Passell, 1993).

Let's recap. A *variable* is anything that can vary (social media exposure, erectile function, landlord responses—anything within the bounds of what is feasible and ethical to measure). Experiments aim to *manipulate* an *independent* variable, *measure* a *dependent* variable, and *control confounding* variables. An experiment has at least two different conditions: an *experimental condition* and a *comparison* or *control condition*. *Random assignment*

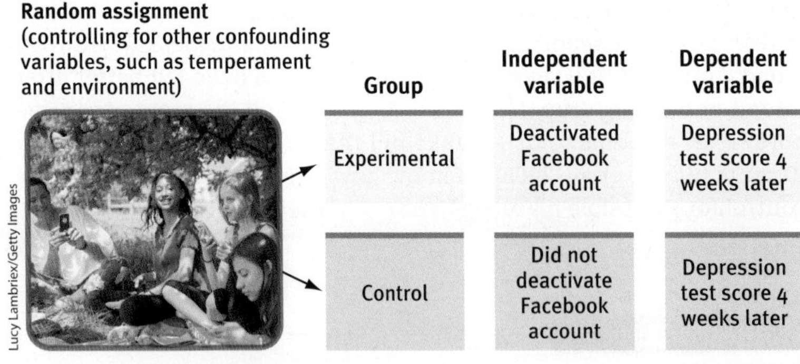
Random assignment (controlling for other confounding variables, such as temperament and environment)
Group
Independent variable
Dependent variable
Experimental
Deactivated Facebook account
Depression test score 4 weeks later
Control
Did not deactivate Facebook account
Depression test score 4 weeks later
Lucy Lambriex/Getty Images

FIGURE 2.6
Experimentation To establish causation, psychologists control for confounding variables by randomly assigning some participants to an experimental group, others to a control group. Measuring the dependent variable (depression score) will determine the effect of the independent variable (social media exposure).

[5]The independent variable, which the researchers manipulated, was the implied ethnicity of the applicants' names. The dependent variable, which researchers measured, was the rate of positive responses from the landlords.

works to minimize preexisting differences between the groups before any treatment effects occur. In this way, an experiment tests the effect of at least one independent variable (what we manipulate) on at least one dependent variable (the outcome we measure).

RETRIEVAL PRACTICE

RP-11 By using *random assignment,* researchers are able to control for ____________ ____________, which are other variables besides the independent variable(s) that may influence research results.

RP-12 Match the term on the left (i through iii) with the description on the right (a through c).

i. Double-blind procedure	a. helps researchers generalize from a small set of survey responses to a larger population
ii. Random sampling	b. helps minimize preexisting differences between experimental and control groups
iii. Random assignment	c. controls for the placebo effect; neither researchers nor participants know who receives the real treatment

RP-13 Why, when testing a new drug to control blood pressure, would we learn more about its effectiveness from giving it to half the participants in a group of 1000 than to all 1000 participants?

ANSWERS IN APPENDIX E

Research Design

LOQ 2-9 How would you know which research design to use?

Throughout this book, you will read about amazing psychological science discoveries. But how do psychological scientists choose research methods and design their studies in ways that provide meaningful results? Understanding how research is done—how testable questions are developed and studied—is key to appreciating all of psychology. **TABLE 2.3** compares the features of psychology's main research methods. In other modules, you will read about other research designs, including *twin studies* and *cross-sectional* and *longitudinal research.*

In psychological research, no questions are off limits, except untestable (or unethical) ones: Does free will exist? Are people born evil? Is there an afterlife? Psychologists can't

TABLE 2.3 Comparing Research Methods

Research Method	Basic Purpose	How Conducted	What Is Manipulated	Weaknesses
Descriptive	To observe and record behavior	Do case studies, naturalistic observations, or surveys	Nothing	No control of variables; single cases may be misleading
Correlational	To detect naturally occurring relationships; to assess how well one variable predicts another	Collect data on two or more variables; no manipulation	Nothing	Cannot specify cause and effect
Experimental	To explore cause and effect	Manipulate one or more variables; use random assignment	The independent variable(s)	Sometimes not feasible; results may not generalize to other contexts; not ethical to manipulate certain variables

test those questions. But they *can* test whether free-will beliefs, aggressive personalities, and a belief in life after death influence how people think, feel, and act (Dechesne et al., 2003; Shariff et al., 2014; Webster et al., 2014).

Having chosen their question, psychologists then select the most appropriate research design—*experimental, correlational, case study, naturalistic observation, twin study, longitudinal,* or *cross-sectional*—and determine how to set it up most effectively. They consider how much money and time are available, ethical issues, and other limitations. For example, it wouldn't be ethical for a researcher studying child development to use the experimental method and randomly assign children to loving versus abusive homes.

Next, psychological scientists decide how to measure the behavior or mental process being studied. For example, researchers studying aggressive behavior could measure participants' willingness to blast a stranger with supposed intense noise.

Researchers want to have confidence in their findings, so they carefully consider confounding variables—variables other than those being studied that may affect their interpretation of results.

Psychological research is a creative adventure. Researchers *design* each study, *measure* target behaviors, *interpret* results, and learn more about the fascinating world of behavior and mental processes along the way.

ASK YOURSELF

If you could conduct a study on any psychological question, which question would you choose? How would you design the study?

Predicting Everyday Behavior

LOQ 2-10 How can simplified laboratory experiments help us understand general principles of behavior?

When you see or hear about psychological research, do you ever wonder whether people's behavior in the lab will predict their behavior in everyday life? Does detecting the blink of a faint red light in a dark room say anything useful about flying an airplane at night? After viewing a violent, sexually explicit film, does a man's increased willingness to push buttons that he thinks will deliver a noise blast to a woman really say anything about whether viewing violent pornography makes a man more likely to abuse a woman?

Before you answer, consider: The experimenter *intends* the laboratory environment to be a simplified reality—one that simulates and controls important features of everyday life. Just as a wind tunnel lets airplane designers re-create airflow forces under controlled conditions, a laboratory experiment lets psychologists re-create psychological forces under controlled conditions. An experiment's purpose is not to re-create the exact behaviors of everyday life, but to test *theoretical principles* (Mook, 1983). In aggression studies, deciding whether to push a button that delivers a noise blast may not be the same as slapping someone in the face, but the principle is the same. *It is the resulting principles—not the specific findings—that help explain everyday behaviors.*

When psychologists apply laboratory research on aggression to actual violence, they are applying theoretical principles of aggressive behavior, principles they have refined through many experiments. Similarly, it is the principles of the visual system, developed from experiments in artificial settings (such as looking at red lights in the dark), that researchers apply to more complex behaviors such as night flying. And many investigations show that principles derived in the laboratory do typically generalize to the everyday world (Mitchell, 2012).

The point to remember: Psychological science focuses less on specific behaviors than on revealing general principles that help explain many behaviors.

Psychology's Research Ethics

LOQ 2-11 Why do psychologists study animals, and what ethical research guidelines safeguard human and animal welfare? How do psychologists' values influence what they study and how they apply their results?

We have reflected on how a scientific approach can restrain biases. We have seen how case studies, naturalistic observations, and surveys help us describe behavior. We have also noted that correlational studies assess the association between two variables, showing how well one predicts another. We have examined the logic that underlies experiments, which use control conditions and random assignment of participants to isolate the causal effects of an independent variable on a dependent variable.

Yet even knowing this much, you may still be approaching psychology with a mixture of curiosity and apprehension. So, before we plunge in, let's entertain some common questions about psychology's ethics and values.

Studying and Protecting Animals

Many psychologists study nonhuman animals because they find them fascinating. They want to understand how different species learn, think, and behave. Psychologists also study animals to learn about people. We humans are not *like* animals; we *are* animals, sharing a common biology. Animal experiments have therefore led to treatments for human diseases—insulin for diabetes, vaccines to prevent polio and rabies, transplants to replace defective organs.

"Rats are very similar to humans except that they are not stupid enough to purchase lottery tickets." — Dave Barry, 2002

Humans are complex. But some of the same processes by which we learn are present in other animals, even sea slugs and honeybees. The simplicity of the sea slug's nervous system is precisely what makes it so revealing of the neural mechanisms of learning. Ditto for the honeybee, which resembles us humans in how it learns to cope with stress (Dinges et al., 2017).

Sharing such similarities, should we not respect our animal relatives? The animal protection movement protests the use of animals in psychological, biological, and medical research. "We cannot defend our scientific work with animals on the basis of the similarities between them and ourselves and then defend it morally on the basis of differences," noted Roger Ulrich (1991). In U.S. national surveys, half of adults oppose and half favor "the use of animals in scientific research"—with support greater among those most informed about science (Strauss, 2018).

Out of this heated debate, two issues emerge. The basic one is whether it is right to place the well-being of humans above that of other animals. In experiments on stress and cancer, is it right that mice get tumors in the hope that people might not? Was it right that researchers exposed monkeys to a coronavirus in the search for a Covid-19 vaccine (Shandrashekar et al., 2020)? Humans slaughter for meat 80 billion animals a year (Ritchie & Roser, 2019). Is our use and consumption of other animals as natural as the behavior of carnivorous hawks, cats, and whales?

"Please do not forget those of us who suffer from incurable diseases or disabilities who hope for a cure through research that requires the use of animals." — Psychologist Dennis Feeney (1987)

For those who give human life top priority, a second issue emerges: What safeguards should protect the well-being of animals in research? One survey of animal researchers gave an answer. Some 98 percent supported government regulations protecting primates, dogs, and cats, and 74 percent also supported regulations providing for the humane care of rats and mice (Plous & Herzog, 2000). Many professional associations and funding agencies already have such guidelines. British Psychological Society (BPS) guidelines call for housing animals under reasonably natural living conditions, with companions for social animals (Lea, 2000). American Psychological Association (APA) guidelines state that researchers must provide "humane care and healthful conditions" and that testing should "minimize discomfort" (APA, 2012). The European Parliament also mandates standards for animal care and housing (Vogel, 2010). Most universities screen research proposals, often through an animal care ethics committee, and laboratories are regulated and inspected.

"The greatness of a nation can be judged by the way its animals are treated." — Mahatma Gandhi, 1869–1948

MARY ALTAFFER/AP Photo

Animal research benefiting animals Psychologists have helped zoos enrich animal environments—for example, by giving animals more choices to reduce the *learned helplessness* of captivity (Kurtycz, 2015; Weir, 2013). Thanks partly to research on the benefits of novelty, control, and stimulation, these gorillas are enjoying an improved quality of life in New York's Bronx Zoo.

Animals have themselves benefited from animal research. One Ohio team of research psychologists measured stress hormone levels in samples of millions of dogs brought each year to animal shelters. They devised handling and stroking methods to reduce stress and ease the dogs' transition to adoptive homes (Tuber et al., 1999). Other studies have helped improve care and management in animals' natural habitats. By revealing our behavioral kinship with animals and the remarkable intelligence of chimpanzees, gorillas, and other animals, experiments have also led to increased empathy and protection for them. At its best, a psychology concerned for humans and sensitive to animals serves the welfare of both.

Studying and Protecting Humans

What about human participants? Does the image of white-coated scientists seeming to deliver electric shocks trouble you? Actually, most psychological studies are free of such stress. Blinking lights, flashing words, and pleasant social interactions are more common.

Occasionally, researchers do temporarily stress or deceive people, but only when they believe it is essential to a justifiable end, such as understanding and controlling violent behavior or studying mood swings. Many experiments won't work if participants know everything beforehand. (Wanting to be helpful, the participants might try to confirm the researcher's predictions.)

Some of psychology's famous experiments used stressful and deceptive methods that are considered unacceptable today. These early psychologists deprived baby monkeys of their mothers, conditioned human babies to burst into tears, and semistarved conscientious objectors. More to come on each of these in other modules.

Today's ethics codes, from the APA and Britain's BPS, urge researchers to (1) obtain potential participants' **informed consent** to take part, (2) protect participants from greater-than-usual harm and discomfort, (3) keep information about individual participants confidential, and (4) fully **debrief** people (explain the research afterward, including any temporary deception). To enforce these ethical standards, universities and research organizations have *Institutional Review Boards* that screen research proposals and safeguard "the rights, welfare and well-being of human research participants" (NIEHS, 2019).

RETRIEVAL PRACTICE

RP-14 How are animal and human research participants protected?

ANSWERS IN APPENDIX E

Ensuring Scientific Integrity

In science, as in everyday life, mistakes happen. When data get accidentally miscomputed or misreported, that's forgivable and correctable. What's not acceptable—and will get a scientist banished from the profession—is fraud. Leading scientists cite honesty as the most important scientific value, followed by curiosity and perseverance (*Nature*, 2016). The worldwide general public rates doctors and scientists as the most trusted professionals, followed by judges and members of the armed forces (Ipsos, 2019). To seek career advancement by plagiarizing another's words or ideas, or to make up data, is to risk finding one's career ended. This was the case when a Dutch psychologist fabricated data that made it into 58 research articles—fakery that was sniffed out by alert colleagues (Retraction Watch, 2015).

Fake science also has the potential to cause great harm. This happened in 1998 when a now-disbarred British physician published an article in the prestigious *Lancet*, reporting a dozen cases in which British children given the measles, mumps, and rubella (MMR) vaccine supposedly developed autism afterward. Other studies failed to reproduce the finding (replication matters!) (Hviid et al., 2019). An investigation revealed a fraud—with falsified data—and the journal retracted the report (Godlee, 2011). Alas, by then the widely publicized finding—"the most damaging medical hoax of the last 100 years" (Flaherty, 2011)—had produced an "anti-vax" movement and declining vaccination

informed consent giving potential participants enough information about a study to enable them to choose whether they wish to participate.

debriefing the postexperimental explanation of a study, including its purpose and any deceptions, to its participants.

rates. Instead of following the typical path toward disease elimination, U.S. measles rates in 2019 rose to their highest levels in 25 years (CDC, 2019; Graham et al., 2019). Unvaccinated children may suffer long-term harm or even death, as well as placing at risk those children too young to be fully vaccinated. Though the science was self-correcting, the damage lingers on. Today, the discredited Wakefield continues to urge people to avoid other vaccines, including those for Covid-19 (Jamison, 2020). (In September 2020, only one-third of Americans said they would get a Covid-19 vaccine as soon as they could [Elbeshbihi & King, 2020].) Nevertheless, the good news is that scientific scrutiny, complete with replication, can inform and protect us.

(a)

(b)

Mike Kemp/Rubberball/Getty Images

FIGURE 2.7
What do you see? Our expectations influence what we perceive in (a). Did you see a duck or a rabbit? Show some friends this image with the rabbit photo (b) covered up and see if they are more likely to perceive a duck. (Inspired by Shepard, 1990.)

Values in Psychology

Values affect what we study, how we study it, and how we interpret results. Researchers' values influence choice of research topics. Should we study worker productivity or worker morale? Cultural differences or social injustice? Conformity or independence? Values can also color "the facts"—our observations and interpretations. Sometimes we see what we want or expect to see (**FIGURE 2.7**).

Even the words we use to describe traits and tendencies can reflect our values. In psychology and in everyday speech, labels describe and labels evaluate: One person's *rigidity* is another's *consistency*. One person's *faith* is another's *fanaticism*. One person's *adultery* is another's *open marriage*. Our labeling someone as *firm* or *stubborn*, *careful* or *picky*, *discreet* or *secretive* reveals our own attitudes.

So, values inform psychological science—and psychological science has the power to persuade. This may lead some to feel distrustful: Is psychology dangerously powerful? Might it be used to manipulate people? Knowledge, like all power, can be used for good or evil. Nuclear power has been used to light up cities—and to demolish them. Persuasive power has been used to educate people—and to deceive them. Although psychology does have the power to deceive, its purpose is to enlighten. Every day, psychologists explore ways to enhance learning, creativity, and compassion. Psychology speaks to many of our world's great problems—extremist terrorism, political corruption, economic inequality, climate change, prejudice, refugee crises—all of which involve attitudes and behaviors. Psychology also speaks to our deepest longings—for love, for happiness, for meaning. Psychology cannot address all of life's great questions, but it speaks to some mighty important ones.

ASK YOURSELF

What other questions or concerns do you have about psychology?

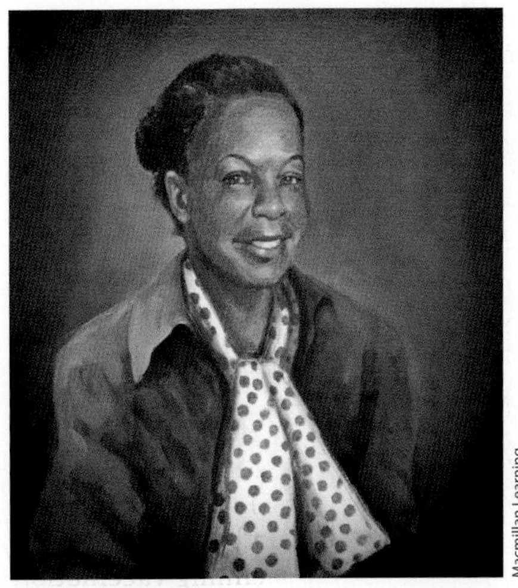

Macmillan Learning

Macmillan Learning

Courtesy of and copyright The Gordon Parks Foundation

Psychology speaks In making its historic 1954 school desegregation decision, the U.S. Supreme Court cited the expert testimony and research of psychologists Mamie Phipps Clark and Kenneth Clark (1947). The Clarks reported that, when given a choice between Black and White dolls, most African American children chose the White doll, which indicated that they had likely absorbed and internalized anti-Black prejudice.

MODULE

2 REVIEW Research Strategies: How Psychologists Ask and Answer Questions

LEARNING OBJECTIVES

Test Yourself Answer these repeated Learning Objective Questions on your own (before "showing" the answers here, or checking the answers in Appendix D) to improve your retention of the concepts (McDaniel et al., 2009, 2015).

LOQ 2-1 How does our everyday thinking sometimes lead us to a wrong conclusion?

LOQ 2-2 Why are we so vulnerable to believing untruths?

LOQ 2-3 How do theories advance psychological science?

LOQ 2-4 How do psychologists use case studies, naturalistic observations, and surveys to observe and describe behavior, and why is random sampling important?

LOQ 2-5 What does it mean when we say two things are correlated, and what are positive and negative correlations?

LOQ 2-6 What are *illusory correlations,* and what is *regression toward the mean?*

LOQ 2-7 Why do correlations enable prediction but not cause-effect explanation?

LOQ 2-8 What are the characteristics of experimentation that make it possible to isolate cause and effect?

LOQ 2-9 How would you know which research design to use?

LOQ 2-10 How can simplified laboratory experiments help us understand general principles of behavior?

LOQ 2-11 Why do psychologists study animals, and what ethical research guidelines safeguard human and animal welfare? How do psychologists' values influence what they study and how they apply their results?

TERMS AND CONCEPTS TO REMEMBER

Test Yourself Write down the definition in your own words, then check your answer.

MODULE TEST

Test Yourself Answer the following questions on your own first, then "show" the answers here, or check your answers in Appendix E.

1. ______________ ______________ refers to our tendency to perceive events as obvious or inevitable after the fact.

2. As scientists, psychologists

a. keep their methods private so others will not repeat their research.

b. assume the truth of articles published in leading scientific journals.

c. reject evidence that competes with traditional findings.

d. are willing to ask questions and to reject claims that cannot be verified by research.

3. A theory-based prediction is called a(n) ______________.

4. Which of the following is NOT one of the *descriptive* methods psychologists use to observe and describe behavior?

a. A case study
b. Naturalistic observation
c. Correlational research
d. A phone survey

5. For your survey, you need to establish a group of people who represent your country's entire adult population. To do this, you will need to question a ______________ sample of the population.

6. A study finds that the more childbirth training classes women attend, the less pain medication they require during childbirth. This finding can be stated as a ______________ (positive/negative) correlation.

7. A ______________ provides a visual representation of the direction and the strength of a relationship between two variables.

8. In a ______________ correlation, the scores rise and fall together; in a(n) ______________ correlation, one score falls as the other rises.

a. positive; negative
b. positive; illusory
c. negative; weak
d. strong; weak

9. In a study, people who were afraid of cockroaches tended also to be disgusted by them. This suggests that the correlation between fear of and disgust for cockroaches is ______________ (positive/negative).

10. How can regression toward the mean influence our interpretation of events?

11. Knowing that two events are correlated provides

a. a basis for prediction.

b. an explanation of why the events are related.

c. proof that as one increases, the other also increases.

d. an indication that an underlying third variable is at work.

12. Here are some recently reported correlations, with interpretations drawn by journalists. Knowing just these correlations, can you come up with other possible explanations for each of these?

a. Alcohol use is associated with violence. (One interpretation: Drinking triggers or unleashes aggressive behavior.)

b. Educated people live longer, on average, than less-educated people. (One interpretation: Education lengthens life and enhances health.)

c. Teens engaged in team sports are less likely to use drugs, smoke, have sex, carry weapons, and eat junk food than are teens who do not engage in team sports. (One interpretation: Team sports encourage healthy living.)

d. Adolescents who frequently see smoking in movies are more likely to smoke. (One interpretation: Movie stars' behavior influences impressionable teens.)

13. To explain behaviors and clarify cause and effect, psychologists use ____________________.

14. To test the effect of a new drug on depression, we randomly assign people to control and experimental groups. Those in the control group take a pill that contains no medication. This pill is a ____________________.

15. In a double-blind procedure,

a. only the participants know whether they are in the control group or the experimental group.

b. experimental and control group members will be carefully matched for age, sex, income, and education level.

c. neither the participants nor the researchers know who is in the experimental group or control group.

d. someone separate from the researcher will ask people to volunteer for the experimental group or the control group.

16. A researcher wants to determine whether noise level affects workers' blood pressure. In one group, the researcher varies the level of noise in the environment and records participants' blood pressure. In this experiment, the level of noise is the ____________________ ____________________.

17. The laboratory environment is designed to

a. exactly recreate the events of everyday life.

b. recreate psychological forces under controlled conditions.

c. recreate psychological forces under random conditions.

d. minimize the use of animals and humans in psychological research.

18. In defending their experimental research with animals, psychologists have noted that

a. animals' physiology and behavior can tell us much about our own.

b. animal experimentation sometimes helps animals as well as humans.

c. animals are fascinating creatures and worthy of study.

d. all of these statements are correct.

MODULE

3 Statistical Reasoning in Everyday Life

For psychological scientists, **statistics** are important tools. Yet a basic ability to understand statistics can benefit *anyone*. To be an educated critical thinker is to apply simple statistical principles to everyday reasoning. And there's good news: To think smarter about data, we needn't memorize complicated formulas. We need merely to be statistically literate.

Statistical Literacy

LOQ **3-1** Why does statistical literacy matter?

"There are guys that've been vaccinated that have contracted Covid," exclaimed vaccine-shunning, Covid-infected Green Bay Packers quarterback Aaron Rodgers (2021a). "This idea that it's the pandemic of the unvaccinated, it's just a total lie" (2021b).

statistics using mathematical methods to understand numerical information *(data).* 

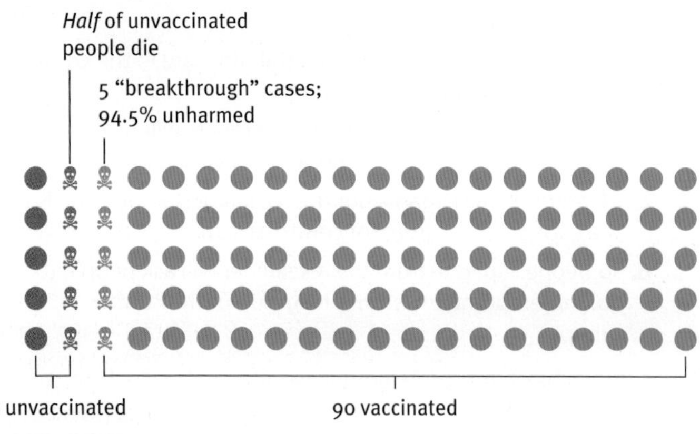
Half of unvaccinated people die
5 "breakthrough" cases; 94.5% unharmed
10 unvaccinated
90 vaccinated

FIGURE 3.1

Statistical literacy for vaccines Imagine that you live in a town with a population of 100 people. Your local media announce that, among people dying of a pandemic virus, half were vaccinated. So, the vaccine was useless, concludes your neighbor, Bea Ware. But Bea fails to consider the *vaccination* base rate of 90 percent. The death rate among the vaccinated is 5 of 90 (5.5 percent). The death rate among the *unvaccinated* is 5 of 10 (50 percent). That's 9 times as great![6] Statistically literate people consider not just simple numbers, but also *rates*.

Rogers could have benefited from *statistical literacy*—understanding statistics and what they mean. Like many who refused to take the vaccine, Rodgers not only doubted the vaccine's effectiveness, he also felt confident in his power to avoid the disease. But even among those who got the vaccine, many doubted its efficacy. Consider the irony, noted U.S. Surgeon General Vivek Murthy (2021): "Vaccinated people may overestimate their peril, just as unvaccinated people may underestimate it."

National surveys consistently revealed that those unvaccinated were, like Aaron Rodgers, *much* less likely to fear the virus (CBS, 2021; KFF, 2021; YouGov, 2021). You read that right: A slight majority of those who were protected by vaccination still feared the virus, while most of those unvaccinated did not fear it. Moreover, those who were unvaccinated—and thus at vastly greater risk of contracting, transmitting, and being seriously sickened by the virus—were also much *less* likely to protect themselves and others by wearing masks (Tyson et al., 2021).

The confusion over Covid's risks and the vaccines' protectiveness stemmed partly from a lack of statistical literacy. Many people simply did not comprehend this key finding: Of 74,000 participants in the clinical trials of five Covid vaccines, the number who were hospitalized or died of Covid was ... zero (Leonhardt, 2021).

Translating statistical data into clear language is a challenge, and those who try sometimes mess up. For example, National Public Radio (2020) explained that, with a 50 percent effective vaccine, "If you vaccinate 100 people, 50 people will not get the disease." This implied that with a 95 percent effective vaccine, we have a 5 percent chance of getting the disease. Actually, the news was much, much better: During the Pfizer/BioNTech clinical trial, for example, only 8 of 170 Covid cases (5 percent) were among vaccinated people, making the vaccine "95 percent effective." But that's 8 out of nearly 22,000—less than 1/10th of one percent—of the vaccinated clinical trial participants (none of whom got sick enough to be hospitalized). To assess vaccine effectiveness, it isn't enough to know simply what percent of sick or hospitalized people were vaccinated. We must also know what percent of the whole population is vaccinated (**FIGURE 3.1**). Moreover, for Covid-19, given that older people are at more risk—but also more likely to have been vaccinated—we would need to compare illness or death rates among vaccinated and unvaccinated people *of the same age*.

We need to look beyond simple numbers, such as the mere number of "breakthrough" Covid cases (those that occur in the vaccinated). Failing to reason statistically can lead us to fear some health dangers too little, which contributed to more than 800,000 Americans dying of Covid by the end of 2021—more than died in all twentieth century U.S. wars combined.

A lack of statistical literacy can also lead us to fear other supposed health dangers *too much* (Gigerenzer, 2010). In the 1990s, the British press reported a study showing that women taking a particular contraceptive pill had a 100 percent increased risk of blood clots that could produce strokes. The story went viral, causing thousands of women to stop taking the pill. What happened as a result? A wave of unwanted pregnancies and an estimated 13,000 additional abortions (which, like other medical procedures, also are associated with increased blood-clot risk). Distracted by big, round numbers, few people focused on the study's actual findings: A 100 percent increased risk, indeed—but only from 1 in 7000 to 2 in 7000. Such false alarms underscore the need to think critically, to teach statistical reasoning, and to present statistical information more transparently.

Statistical misinformation also gets fed by off-the-top-of-the-head estimates. Someone throws out a big, round number. Others echo it, and before long the big, round number becomes public misinformation. Three examples:

- ***Ten percent of people are gay.*** Or is it 2 to 4 percent, as suggested by various national surveys?

[6]The example is inspired by ourworldindata.org/covid-deaths-by-vaccination, which also documented that the U.S. Covid-19 death rate, as of October 2, 2021, was 13 times greater among the unvaccinated than the vaccinated.

- ***We ordinarily use only 10 percent of our brain.*** Or is it closer to 100 percent?
- ***To be healthy, walk 10,000 steps a day.*** Or will 8500 or 13,000 steps do the trick? How about swimming or jogging (Mull, 2019)?

If you find an attention-grabbing headline presented *without evidence*—that nationally there are 1 million teen pregnancies, 2 million homeless seniors, or 3 million alcohol-related motor vehicle accidents—you can be pretty sure that someone is estimating. If they want to emphasize the problem, they will be motivated to estimate high. If they want to minimize the problem, they will estimate low. *The point to remember:* Think critically when you encounter big, round, undocumented numbers.

descriptive statistics using statistical methods to provide a simple summary of data.

When setting goals, we love big, round numbers. We're far more likely to want to lose 20 pounds than 19 or 21 pounds (or an even 10 kilograms rather than 9.07 kilograms). And U.S. high school students are more likely to retake the Scholastic Aptitude Test (SAT) if they score just below a round number, such as 1100, rather than just above (Pope & Simonsohn, 2011).

Descriptive Statistics

Once researchers have gathered their data, they may organize that data using **descriptive statistics**. One way to do this is to convert the data into a simple *bar graph*, as in FIGURE 3.2, which displays a distribution of different brands of trucks still on the road after a decade. When reading statistical graphs such as this one, take care. It's easy to design a graph to make a difference look big (Figure 3.2a) or small (Figure 3.2b). The secret lies in how you label the vertical scale (the *y-axis*).

The point to remember: Think smart. When interpreting graphs, consider the scale labels and note their *range.*

ASK YOURSELF

Think of a time when you used statistics to make a point—maybe in class, in a paper, or in a discussion with a friend or family member. Looking back, were the data you cited credible and accurate? How do you know?

RETRIEVAL PRACTICE

RP-1 A truck manufacturer offered Figure 3.2's graph (a)—with actual brand names included—to suggest the much greater durability of its trucks. What does graph (b) make clear about the varying durability, and how is this accomplished?

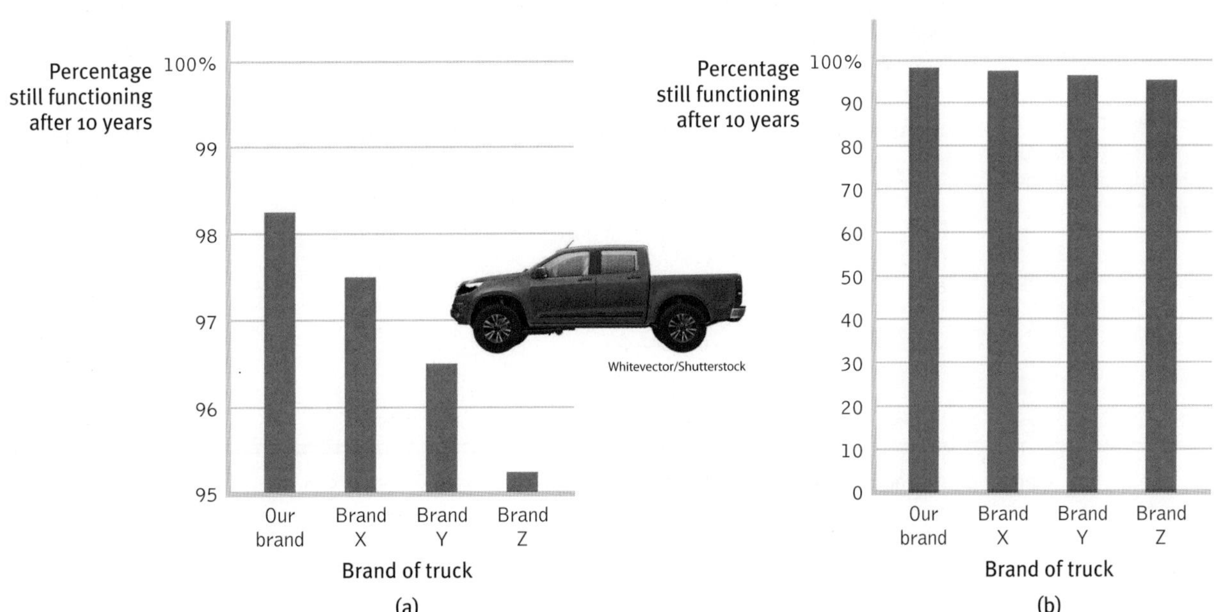
Percentage still functioning after 10 years
100%
99
98
97
96
95
Our brand
Brand X
Brand Y
Brand Z
Brand of truck
(a)
Whitevector/Shutterstock
Percentage still functioning after 10 years
100%
90
80
70
60
50
40
30
20
10
0
Our brand
Brand X
Brand Y
Brand Z
Brand of truck
(b)

FIGURE 3.2
Read the scale labels

ANSWERS IN APPENDIX E

mode the most frequently occurring score(s) in a distribution.

mean the arithmetic average of a distribution, obtained by adding the scores and then dividing by the number of scores.

median the middle score in a distribution; half the scores are above it and half are below it.

range the difference between the highest and lowest scores in a distribution.

Measures of Central Tendency

LOQ 3-2 How do we describe data using three measures of central tendency?

The next step is to summarize the data using a *measure of central tendency*—a single score that represents a whole *distribution* of scores. The simplest measure is the **mode**, the most frequently occurring score or scores. (A *bimodal distribution* occurs when there are two most frequently occurring scores.) What is your favorite number? One global survey found that the most frequently occurring response—the mode—was *seven* (Bellos, 2014). (Was that yours?) The most familiar measure is the **mean**, or arithmetic average—the total sum of all the scores divided by the number of scores. The midpoint—the 50th percentile—is the **median**. On a divided highway, the median is the middle. So, too, with data: If you arrange all the scores in order from the highest to the lowest, half will be above the median and half will be below it.

The average person has one ovary and one testicle.

WHAT IS THE NORMAL TEMPERATURE FOR THIS TIME OF THE YEAR?
USUALLY ANYTHING ABOVE NORMAL OR BELOW NORMAL.
BUS STOP

Dave Carpenter/Cartoon Stock

Measures of central tendency neatly summarize data. But consider what happens to the mean when a distribution is lopsided—when it's *skewed* by a few way-out scores. With income data, for example, the mode, median, and mean often tell very different stories (**FIGURE 3.3**). This happens because a few extreme incomes bias the mean. When Elon Musk (in 2022, the worlds' richest person) sits down in a small café, its average (mean) customer instantly becomes a billionaire. But median customer wealth remains unchanged. Understanding this, you can see why, according to the 2020 U.S. Census, over 60 percent of U.S. households have "below average" income. The bottom half of earners receive much less than half of the total national income. So, most Americans make less than average (the mean). Mean and median tell different true stories. Think of it this way: Calling someone average is a mean thing.

The point to remember: Always note which measure of central tendency is reported. If it is a mean, consider whether a few atypical scores could be distorting it.

Measures of Variation

LOQ 3-3 What is the relative usefulness of the two measures of variation?

Knowing the value of an appropriate measure of central tendency can tell us a great deal. But the single number omits other information. It helps to know something about the amount of *variation* in the data—how similar or diverse the scores are. Averages derived from scores with low variability are more reliable than averages based on scores with high variability. Consider a basketball player who scored between 13 and 17 points in each of the season's first 10 games. Knowing this, we would be more confident that she would score near 15 points in her next game than if her scores had varied from 5 to 25 points.

The **range** of scores—the difference between the lowest and highest—provides only a crude estimate of variation. A couple of extreme scores in an otherwise similar group,

FIGURE 3.3
A skewed distribution This graphic representation of the distribution of a village's incomes illustrates the three measures of central tendency: mode, median, and mean. Note how just a few high incomes make the mean—the fulcrum point that balances the incomes above and below—deceptively high.

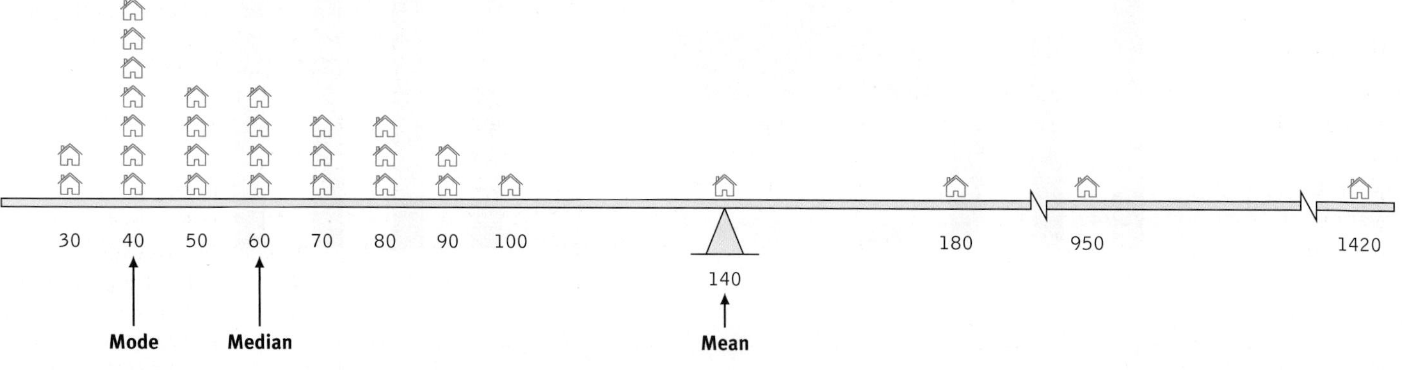
30
40
50
60
70
80
90
100
140
180
950
1420
Mode
Median
Mean
One family's income
Income per family in thousands of dollars

such as the $950,000 and $1,420,000 incomes in Figure 3.3, will create a deceptively large range.

It's good to know the range of scores, but we often want to know how much scores vary in relation to a population's average. The **standard deviation** measures how much scores deviate (differ) from the mean. It better gauges whether scores are packed together or dispersed, because it uses information from each score. The standard deviation is derived from a mathematical formula[7] that assembles information about how much individual scores differ from the mean, which can be very telling. Let's say test scores from Class A and Class B both have the same mean (75 percent correct), but very different standard deviations (5.0 for Class A and 15.0 for Class B). Have you ever had test experiences like that—where two-thirds of your classmates in one course score in the 70 to 80 percent range, with scores in another course more spread out (two-thirds between 60 and 90 percent)? The standard deviation, as well as the mean score, tell us about how each class is faring.

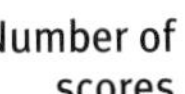
Number of scores

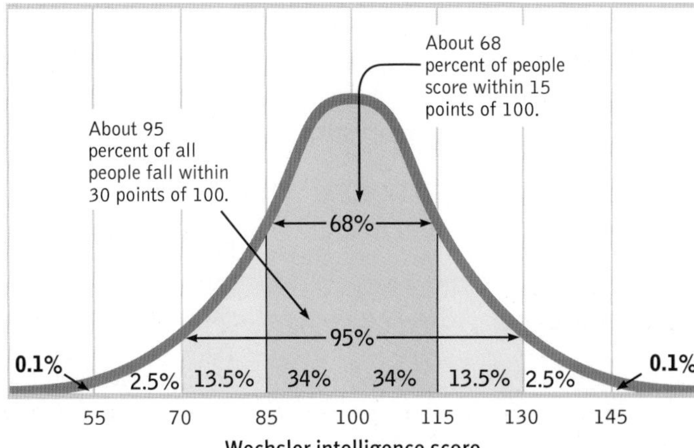
About 68 percent of people score within 15 points of 100.
About 95 percent of all people fall within 30 points of 100.
68%
95%
0.1%
2.5%
13.5%
34%
34%
13.5%
2.5%
0.1%
55
70
85
100
115
130
145
Wechsler intelligence score

FIGURE 3.4
The normal curve Scores on aptitude tests tend to form a normal, or bell-shaped, curve. The most commonly used intelligence test, the Wechsler Adult Intelligence Scale, calls the average score 100.

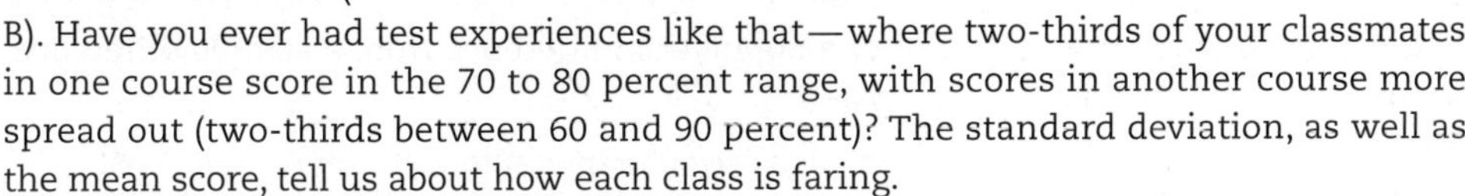

You can grasp the meaning of the standard deviation if you consider how scores naturally tend to be distributed. Large numbers of data—heights, intelligence scores, life expectancy (though not incomes)—often form a symmetrical, *bell-shaped* distribution. Most cases fall near the mean, and fewer cases fall near either extreme. This bell-shaped distribution is so typical that we call the curve it forms the **normal curve**.

As **FIGURE 3.4** shows, a useful property of the normal curve is that roughly 68 percent of the cases fall within one standard deviation on either side of the mean. About 95 percent of cases fall within two standard deviations. Thus, as Module 30 notes, about 68 percent of people taking an intelligence test will score within 15 points—either above or below—of 100. About 95 percent will score within ±30 points.

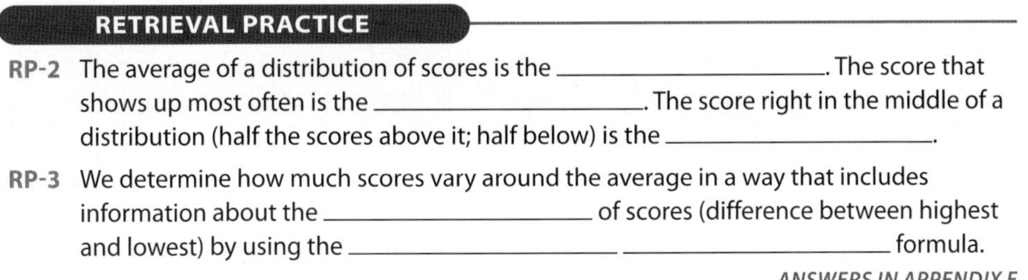

RETRIEVAL PRACTICE

RP-2 The average of a distribution of scores is the ______________. The score that shows up most often is the ______________. The score right in the middle of a distribution (half the scores above it; half below) is the ______________.

RP-3 We determine how much scores vary around the average in a way that includes information about the ______________ of scores (difference between highest and lowest) by using the ______________ ______________ formula.

ANSWERS IN APPENDIX E

Inferential Statistics

LOQ 3-4 How do we know whether an observed difference can be generalized to other populations?

From moment to moment, people's behaviors may vary. Thus, one group's average score could conceivably differ from another group's average score not because of any real difference, but merely because of chance fluctuations in the people sampled. **Inferential statistics** use the results from a sample to inform us about a larger population (everybody in some group). When we infer that our sample's difference reflects a true population difference, we are saying the difference is **statistically significant**. When we

standard deviation a computed measure of how much scores vary around the mean score.

normal curve a symmetrical, bell-shaped curve that describes the distribution of many types of data; most scores fall near the mean (about 68 percent fall within one standard deviation of it) and fewer and fewer near the extremes. (Also called a *normal distribution.*)

inferential statistics using statistical methods to interpret data meaningfully.

statistical significance a statistical statement of how likely it is that an obtained result (such as a difference between samples) occurred by chance, assuming there is no difference between the populations being studied.

[7]The actual standard deviation formula is: $\sqrt{\frac{\text{Sum of (deviations from mean)}^2}{\text{Number of scores} - 1}}$

meta-analysis a statistical procedure for analyzing the results of multiple studies to reach an overall conclusion.

conclude that our sample's difference is likely just a fluke, we're saying it's not statistically significant. (We will focus only on this part of inferential statistics.)

Significant Differences

Imagine a prospective student who visits two similar universities. At the first school, the student randomly samples two classes and finds that both instructors are witty and engaging. At the second school, the two sampled instructors seem dull and uninspiring. Should the student conclude that the first school's teachers are "great" and the second school's teachers are "bores"? You might respond that the student should sample more classes—and you'd be right. It's possible that the populations of teachers at the two universities are equal. Just by chance, the student could have sampled two great (and two boring) teachers.

How confidently can we infer that some observed difference in a sample (such as a couple of teachers) reflects the larger population it comes from (all the teachers at the school)?

In deciding when it is safe to infer a population difference from a sample difference, we should keep three principles in mind:

1. ***Representative samples are better than biased (unrepresentative) samples.*** The best basis for generalizing is not from the exceptional and memorable cases one finds at the extremes but from a representative sample of cases. Research never randomly samples the whole human population. Thus, it pays to keep in mind what population a study has sampled.
2. ***Bigger samples are better than smaller ones.*** We know it but we ignore it: *Averages based on many cases are more reliable* than averages based on only a few. If you select a certain instructor's class based on conversations with three people, you can't conclude much. A set of 50 class evaluations will give you a better estimate of an instructor's performance. More (randomly sampled) cases make the sample's estimate more reliable. Larger samples also make for a more *replicable* study—one that will find a similar estimate the next time.
3. ***More estimates are better than fewer estimates.*** A study gives one brief peek at what's going on in the population. But the best thing to do is conduct multiple studies and combine all the estimates, using **meta-analysis**. Better to consider an entire forest of findings rather than focusing on a single study.

The point to remember: Smart thinkers are not overly impressed by a few anecdotes. Estimates based on a few unrepresentative cases are unreliable.

Let's consider another significant differences example. Say you sampled men's and women's scores on a laboratory test of aggression and found a gender difference. But samples can vary. So how likely is it that your observed gender difference was just a fluke?

Researchers use statistical testing to estimate the probability of the result occurring by chance. They begin with the assumption that no difference exists between groups,

PEANUTS

BONK
6-17

LUCY, YOU'RE THE WORST PLAYER IN THE HISTORY OF THE GAME!

YOU CAN'T PROVE THAT! YOU SHOULD NEVER SAY THINGS THAT YOU CAN'T PROVE!

IN ALL PROBABILITY, YOU ARE THE WORST PLAYER IN THE HISTORY OF THE GAME!

I CAN ACCEPT THAT..
SCHULZ

an assumption called the *null hypothesis*. Then, using statistics, they evaluate whether the observed gender difference is so big that it's unlikely to fit the null hypothesis. If so, they reject the null hypothesis of no differences, and they say that the result is statistically significant. Such a large difference would support an *alternative hypothesis*—that the populations of men and women really do differ in aggression.

What factors determine statistical significance? When averages from two samples are each reliable measures of their respective populations (as when each is based on many observations that have low variability), then any difference between the two samples is more likely to be statistically significant. (For our example: The less the variability in women's and in men's aggression scores, and the more scores we observe, the more confidence we would have that our observed gender difference is real.) When the difference we estimate is *large*, it's also more likely to reflect a real difference in the population.

In short, when estimates are reliable and when the difference between them is relatively large, we're more likely to find that the difference is statistically significant. This means that the observed difference in the sample is probably more than just chance variation, so we reject the original null hypothesis of no existing differences.

In judging statistical significance, psychologists are conservative. They are like juries that must presume innocence until guilt is proven. Many psychological tests provide *p*-values, which indicate the probability of the result, given the null hypothesis. For most psychologists, strong evidence that we can reject the null (no-difference) hypothesis occurs when the probability (*p*-value) of that result is very low. "Very low" is usually set at less than 5 percent ($p < .05$). When a sample's result would occur less than 5 percent of the time assuming the null hypothesis, we say it is significant.

When learning about research, you should remember that a "statistically significant" result may have little *practical significance*. Especially when a sample is very large, a result might be statistically significant but have a tiny *effect* size. One large study tested the intelligence of first-born and later-born individuals. Researchers revealed a statistically significant tendency for first-born individuals to have higher average scores than their later-born siblings (Rohrer et al., 2015; Zajonc & Markus, 1975). But the difference was only about 1.5 IQ points. There were 20,000 people in the study, so this difference was "significant," but it had little practical importance.

The point to remember: Statistical significance indicates the likelihood that the result would have happened by chance if the null hypothesis (of no difference) were true. But statistically significant is not the same as *important* or *strong*.

ASK YOURSELF

Can you think of a situation where you were fooled by a writer or speaker's attempts to persuade you with statistics? What have you learned in this module that will be most helpful in the future to avoid being misled?

RETRIEVAL PRACTICE

RP-4 Can you solve this puzzle?

The registrar's office at the University of Michigan has found that usually about 100 students in Arts and Sciences have perfect marks at the end of their first term. However, only about 10 to 15 students graduate with perfect marks. What do you think is the most likely explanation for the fact that there are more perfect marks after one term than at graduation (Jepson et al., 1983)?

RP-5 ________________ statistics summarize data, while ________________ statistics determine if data can be generalized to other populations.

ANSWERS IN APPENDIX E

MODULE

3 REVIEW Statistical Reasoning in Everyday Life

LEARNING OBJECTIVES

Test Yourself Answer these repeated Learning Objective Questions on your own (before "showing" the answers here, or checking the answers in Appendix D) to improve your retention of the concepts (McDaniel et al., 2009, 2015).

LOQ 3-1 Why does statistical literacy matter?

LOQ 3-2 How do we describe data using three measures of central tendency?

LOQ 3-3 What is the relative usefulness of the two measures of variation?

LOQ 3-4 How do we know whether an observed difference can be generalized to other populations?

TERMS AND CONCEPTS TO REMEMBER

Test Yourself Write down the definition in your own words, then check your answer.

statistics, p. 43
descriptive statistics, p. 45
mode, p. 46
mean, p. 46
median, p. 46
range, p. 46
standard deviation, p. 47
normal curve, p. 47
inferential statistics, p. 47
statistical significance, p. 47
meta-analysis, p. 48

MODULE TEST

Test Yourself Answer the following questions on your own first, then "show" the answers here, or check your answers in Appendix E.

1. Which of the three measures of central tendency is most easily distorted by a few very high or very low scores?
   a. The mode
   b. The mean
   c. The median
   d. They are all equally vulnerable to distortion from atypical scores.

2. The standard deviation is the most useful measure of variation in a set of data because it tells us
   a. the difference between the highest and lowest scores in the set.
   b. the extent to which the sample being used deviates from the bigger population it represents.
   c. how much individual scores differ from the mode.
   d. how much individual scores differ from the mean.

3. Another name for a bell-shaped distribution, in which most scores fall near the middle and fewer scores fall at each extreme, is a ________________.

4. When sample averages are ________________ and the difference between them is ________________, we can say the difference is more likely to be statistically significant.
   a. reliable; large
   b. reliable; small
   c. due to chance; large
   d. due to chance; small

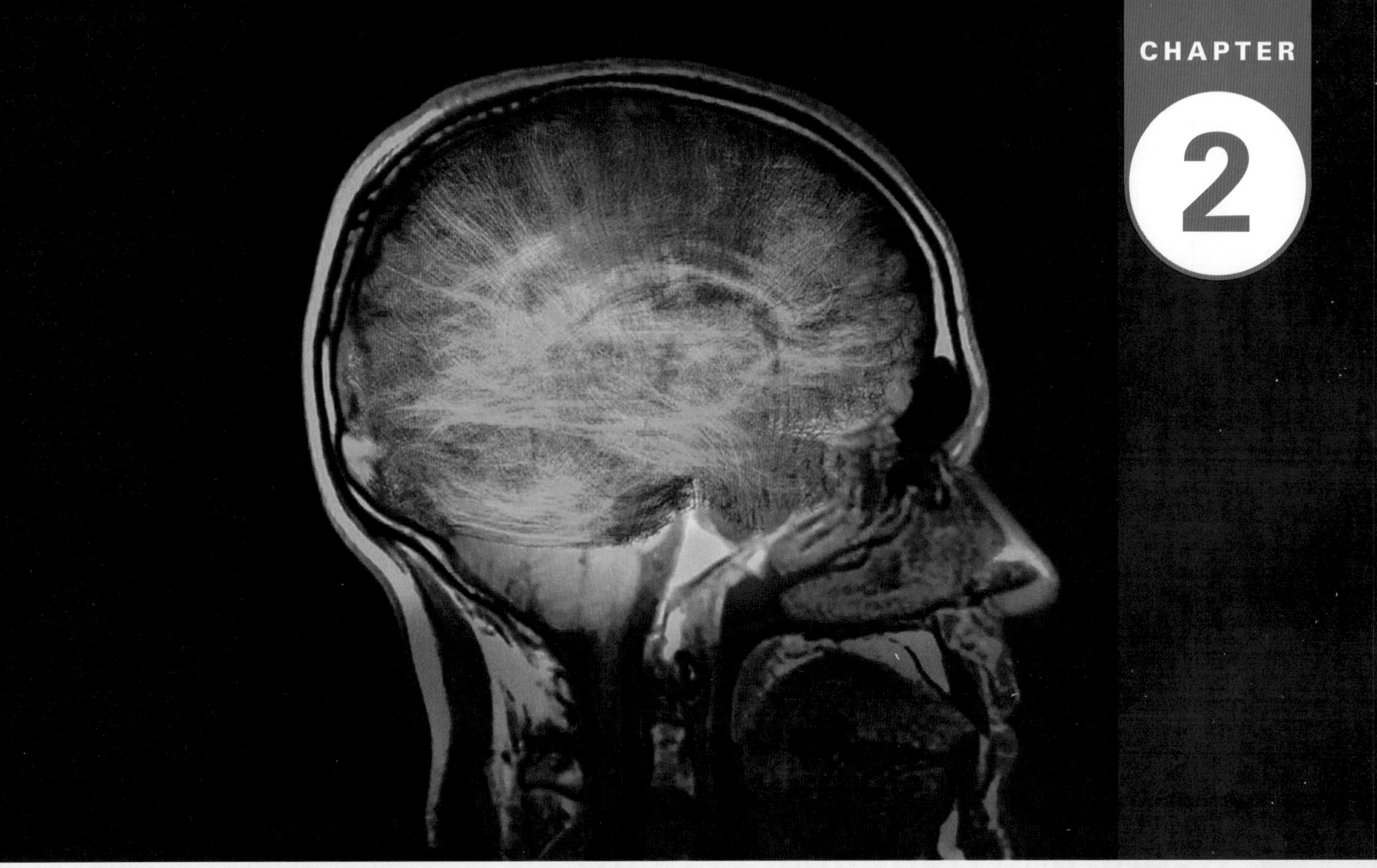
CHAPTER
2
ALFRED PASIEKA/Science Source

The Biology of Mind (Modules 4–7)

Wang Huanming, a man paralyzed from the neck down in a 2010 wrestling accident, made news when he volunteered to participate in an audacious medical venture: a head transplant. A transplant surgeon has offered to surgically transfer Wang's fully functioning head to a brain-dead person's still-functioning body (Tatlow, 2016).

Ignore for the moment the ethical issues of such an experiment, which some have called "reckless and ghastly" and part of the scientists' "ghoulish fantasies" (Illes & McDonald, 2017; Wolpe, 2018). Ignore the procedure's cost, estimated at up to $100 million (Hjelmgaard, 2019). And ignore the seeming impossibility of precisely connecting the head-to-spinal-cord nerves. Imagine, just imagine, that the procedure could work. With the same brain and a new body, would Wang still be Wang? To whose home should he return? If the old Wang was a skilled guitarist, would the new Wang conceivably retain that skill—or would he have to train his new body to play? If he later fathered a child, whom should the birth certificate list as the parent?

Most of us twenty-first-century people (you, too?) presume that, even with a new body, Wang would still be Wang. We presume that our brain, designed by our genes and sculpted by our experiences, provides our identity and enables our mind. No brain, no mind.

We are, indeed, living brains, but more. We are bodies alive. No principle is more central to today's psychology, or to this book, than this: *Everything psychological is simultaneously biological.* Your every idea, every mood, every urge is also a biological happening. You love, laugh, and cry with your body. Thinking, feeling, or acting without a body would be like running without legs. Without your body—your genes, your nervous system, your hormones, your appearance—you truly would be nobody. Moreover, your body and your brain influence and are influenced by your experiences. Throughout this book, you will find many examples of the interplay between biology and psychology.

As you will also see throughout this book, we humans share the same basic biological design. Yet thanks to our individual genes, experiences, and cultural traditions and teachings, we differ from one another. Our traits and behaviors arise from the interaction of nature and nurture. Our thoughts, feelings, and actions influence our blood pressure, hormones, and brain. As we wend our way from the cradle to the grave, our biology changes in response to our behaviors and environments.

In these Biology of Mind modules, we ask a profound question: How does matter make mind? To answer this question, we explore the mind's biology. We start small and build from the bottom up—from nerve cells up to the brain. But we'll also discuss how our behavior and environment can influence our biology from the top down. Life changes us. You've heard it before and will hear it again: *Nurture works on what nature provides.*

MODULE 4 Neural and Hormonal Systems

Let's begin by exploring why psychologists study biology and how their scientific discoveries have improved our understanding of how matter makes mind.

Biology, Behavior, and Mind

LEARNING OBJECTIVE QUESTION LOQ 4-1 Why are psychologists concerned with human biology?

Our understanding of the relationship between brain and mind has come a long way. The ancient Greek physician, Hippocrates, correctly located the mind in the brain. His contemporary, the philosopher Aristotle, believed the mind was in the heart, which pumps warmth and vitality to the body. The heart remains our symbol for love, but psychological science has long since taught us an important lesson: It's your brain, not your heart, that falls in love.

In the early 1800s, German physician Franz Gall proposed that *phrenology*, studying bumps on the skull, could reveal a person's mental abilities and character traits (**FIGURE 4.1**). At one point, Britain had 29 phrenological societies. Phrenologists also traveled North America to give skull readings (Dean, 2012; Hunt, 1993). Using a false name, writer Mark Twain put one famous phrenologist to the test. "He found a cavity [and] startled me by saying that that cavity represented the total absence of the sense of humor!" Three months later, Twain sat for a second reading, this time identifying himself. Now "the cavity was gone, and in its place was . . . the loftiest bump of humor he had ever encountered in his life-long experience!" (Lopez, 2002). The "science" of phrenology remains known today as a reminder of our need for critical thinking and scientific analysis. Phrenology did at least succeed in focusing attention on the *localization of function*—the idea that various brain regions have particular functions.

biological psychology the scientific study of the links between biological (genetic, neural, hormonal) and psychological processes. Some biological psychologists call themselves *neuroscientists, neuropsychologists, behavior geneticists, physiological psychologists,* or *biopsychologists.*

Today's psychologists live in a world that Gall could only dream about. **Biological psychologists** use advanced technologies to study the links between biological (genetic,

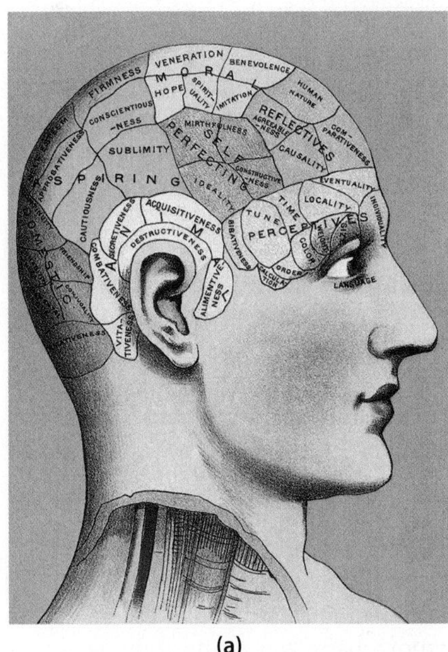
VENERATION
BENEVOLENCE
HOPE
SUBLIMITY
CONSCIENTIOUS -NESS
FIRMNESS
LANGUAGE

(a)

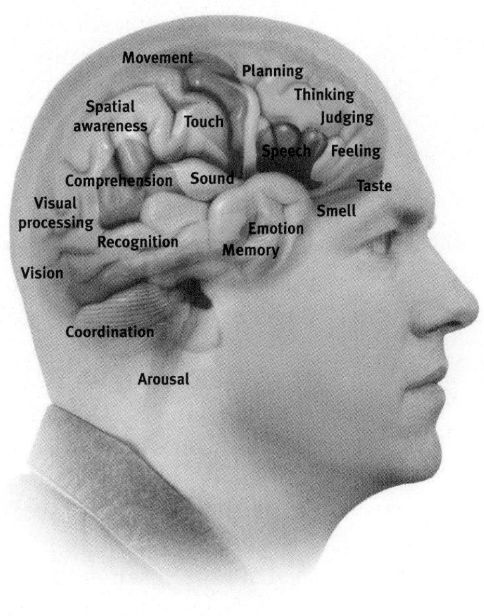
Movement
Planning
Thinking
Judging
Spatial awareness
Touch
Speech
Feeling
Comprehension
Sound
Taste
Smell
Visual processing
Emotion
Recognition
Memory
Vision
Coordination
Arousal

(b)

FIGURE 4.1
A wrongheaded theory (a) Despite initial acceptance of Franz Gall's speculations, bumps on the skull tell us nothing about the brain's underlying functions. Nevertheless, some of his assumptions have held true. Though they are not the functions Gall proposed, different parts of the brain do contribute to different aspects of behavior, as suggested in (b) (from *The Human Brain Book*), and as you will see throughout these Biology of Mind modules.

neural, hormonal) processes and psychological processes. They and other researchers working from a biological perspective are announcing discoveries about the interplay of our biology and our behavior and mind at an exhilarating pace. Within little more than the past century, researchers seeking to understand the biology of the mind have discovered that

- our experiences wire our adaptive brain.
- among the body's cells are nerve cells that conduct electricity and "talk" to one another by sending chemical messages across a tiny gap that separates them.
- specific brain systems serve specific functions (though not the functions Gall supposed).
- we integrate information processed in these different brain systems to construct our experience of sights and sounds, meanings and memories, pain and passion.
- our emotions, like our thoughts and memories, are supported by brain networks.

We have also realized that we are each a system composed of subsystems that are, in turn, composed of even smaller subsystems. Tiny cells organize to form body organs. These organs form larger systems for digestion, circulation, and information processing. And those systems are part of an even larger system—the person, who in turn is a part of a family, community, and culture. Thus, we are *biopsychosocial* systems (Engel, 1981). To understand our behavior, we need to study how these biological, psychological, and social-cultural systems work and interact, and how they form us over time. We are formed by ancient evolution, by our enduring cultures, by our daily experiences, by our fluctuating hormones, and by our immediate neural activity (Sapolsky, 2017).

RETRIEVAL PRACTICE

RP-1 What do phrenology and biological psychology have in common?

ANSWERS IN APPENDIX E

The Power of Neuroplasticity

LOQ 4-2 How do biology and experience together enable neuroplasticity?

Your brain is sculpted not only by your genes but also by your life. Under the surface of your awareness, your brain constantly changes, building new pathways as it adjusts to new experiences. This neural change is called **neuroplasticity**. Neuroplasticity is greatest early in life but continues over the life span (Lindenberger & Lövdén, 2019; Walasek et al., 2022).

neuroplasticity the brain's ability to change, especially during childhood, by reorganizing after damage or by building new pathways based on experience.

Skyler Williams/Touch The Top, Inc.

The mind's eye Erik Weihenmayer, who is completely blind, has rappelled into active volcanos and summited the tallest mountain peaks on every continent (Chesnutt, 2013; Valluzzo, 2021). To stay safe, he uses a guide and echolocation, the navigation method used by bats (Sulser et al., 2022). Blind echolocation engages the brain's visual centers—the same centers that sighted people use when looking at stimuli (Norman & Thaler, 2019). Weihenmayer's flexible brain transforms sound to help him "see."

To see neuroplasticity at work, consider London's taxi driver trainees. They spend years learning and remembering the city's 26,000 street locations and connections. For the half who pass the difficult final test, big rewards are in store: a better income and an enlarged hippocampus, one of the brain's memory centers that processes spatial memories. London's bus drivers, who navigate a smaller set of roads, gain no similar neural rewards (Griesbauer et al., 2022; Maguire et al., 2000).

We also see neuroplasticity in well-practiced pianists, who have a larger-than-usual auditory cortex area, a sound-processing region (Bavelier et al., 2000; Pantev et al., 1998). Practice likewise sculpts the brains of ballerinas, jugglers, and unicyclists (Draganski et al., 2004; Hänggi et al., 2010; Weber et al., 2019).

Your brain is a work in progress. The brain you were born with is not the brain you will die with. Even limited practice times may produce neural benefits. If you spend 45 minutes learning how to play the piano, as did participants in one study, you may grow your motor learning-related brain areas (Tavor et al., 2020). Mere minutes of word learning produce subtle brain changes (Vukovic et al., 2021). Remember that the next time you attend class!

Neuroplasticity underlies interventions aimed at reducing child poverty. In one experiment, families experiencing poverty with a newborn baby were randomly assigned to receive either large ($333) or small ($20) unconditional monthly cash transfers (Troller-Renfree et al., 2022). A year later, researchers examined how the children's brain activity adapted to these financial changes in their family environment. Compared with children whose families received small cash transfers, those whose families received large cash transfers showed more brain activity in regions associated with language, thinking, and social understanding.

Neuroplasticity is part of what makes humans exceptional (Gómez-Robles et al., 2015). Think of how much the world has changed over the past 50 years, and how much more it will change in the next 50. We can barely imagine a past without smartphones, or a future where most people use self-driving cars. Our neuroplasticity enables us, more than other species, to adapt to our rapidly changing world (Roberts & Stewart, 2018).

Cultural neuroscientists argue that experiencing different cultural traditions, beliefs, and rituals can create distinct behaviors and brain activation patterns (Gao et al., 2022; Pugh et al., 2022). For example, people in the United States and Mexico tend to value expressing positive emotions, while people in China view emotional expression more negatively (Ma et al., 2018; Rychlowska et al., 2015; Senft et al., 2021). Adapting to these different cultural norms helps explain why those in the United States and Mexico, compared with those in China, show more brain activation in emotion expression areas when viewing emotion-arousing photos (Hampton et al., 2021).

Luna Productions

Marian Diamond (1926–2017) Marian Diamond worked during an era when female scientists experienced tremendous discrimination. She overcame these biases and was among the first scientists to explore how experience changes the brain (Diamond et al., 1964). Her research, for example, showed how exposing rats to different environments produced changes in their brain structure (Diamond et al., 1966). Diamond also analyzed Albert Einstein's brain after his death, which helped unlock the neural mechanics of his mind. Diamond noted, "The brain is a three-pound mass you can hold in your hand that can conceive of a universe a hundred billion light years across."

ASK YOURSELF

What skills did you practice the most as a child—sports, music, cooking, video gaming? How do you think this affected your brain development? How will you continue to develop your brain with new learning and new skills?

RETRIEVAL PRACTICE

RP-2 How does learning a new skill affect the structure of our brain?

ANSWERS IN APPENDIX E

Neural Communication

For scientists, it is a happy fact of nature that the information systems of humans and other animals operate similarly—so much so that you could not distinguish between small samples of brain tissue from a human and a monkey. This similarity allows researchers to study much simpler animals, such as squids and sea slugs, to discover how our neural systems operate. It allows them to study other mammals' brains to

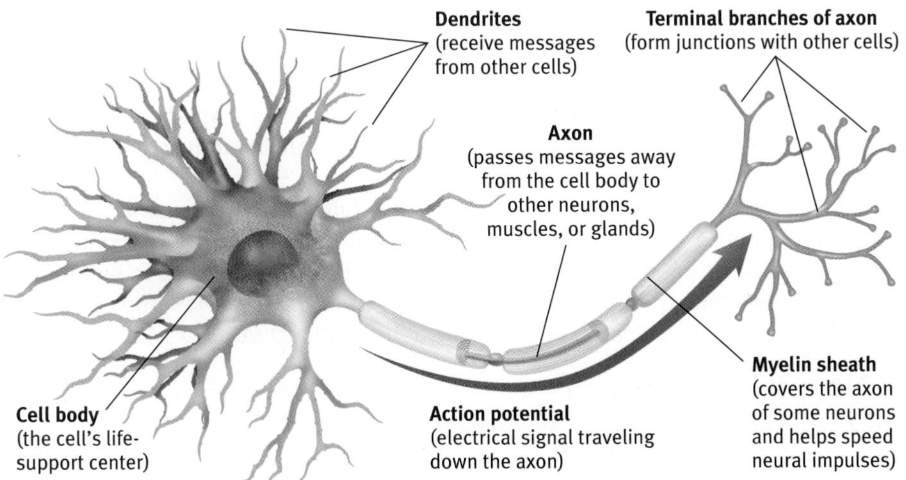
Dendrites
(receive messages
from other cells)
Terminal branches of axon
(form junctions with other cells)
Axon
(passes messages away
from the cell body to
other neurons,
muscles, or glands)
Myelin sheath
(covers the axon
of some neurons
and helps speed
neural impulses)
Cell body
(the cell's life-
support center)
Action potential
(electrical signal traveling
down the axon)

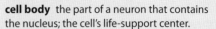

FIGURE 4.2
A motor neuron

neuron a nerve cell; the basic building block of the nervous system.

cell body the part of a neuron that contains the nucleus; the cell's life-support center.

dendrites a neuron's often bushy, branching extensions that receive and integrate messages from axons, conducting impulses toward the cell body.

axon the segmented neuron extension that passes messages through its branches to other neurons, muscles, or glands.

myelin [MY-uh-lin] **sheath** a fatty tissue layer segmentally encasing the axons of some neurons; enables vastly greater transmission speed as neural impulses hop from one node to the next.

understand the organization of our own. Cars differ, but all have accelerators, steering wheels, and brakes. A space alien could study any one of them and grasp the operating principles. Likewise, animals differ, yet their nervous systems operate similarly.

Neurons

LOQ 4-3 What are *neurons*, and how do they transmit information?

Our body's neural information system is complexity built from simplicity. Its building blocks are **neurons** or nerve cells. Throughout life, new neurons are born and unused neurons wither away (O'Leary et al., 2014; Shors, 2014). To fathom our thoughts and actions, our memories and moods, we must first understand how neurons work and communicate.

Neurons differ, but all are variations on the same theme (**FIGURE 4.2**). Each consists of a **cell body** and its branching fibers. The often bushy **dendrite** fibers receive and integrate information, conducting it toward the cell body (Poirazi & Papoutsi, 2020). From there, the cell's single lengthy **axon** fiber passes the message through its terminal branches to other neurons, muscles, or glands (**FIGURE 4.3**). Dendrites listen. Axons speak.

Unlike the short dendrites, axons may be very long, projecting several feet through the body. A human neuron carrying orders from the brain to a leg muscle, for example, has a cell body and axon roughly on the scale of a basketball attached to a rope that's 4 miles (6.4 kilometers) long. Much as home electrical wire is insulated, some axons are encased in a **myelin sheath**, a layer of fatty tissue that insulates them and speeds their impulses. As myelin is laid down up to about age 25, neural efficiency, judgment, and self-control grow (Nakamura et al., 2018; Van Munster et al., 2015). If the myelin sheath degenerates, *multiple sclerosis* results. Communication to muscles and brain regions slows. The result: diminished muscle control and sometimes impaired cognition.

John Shearer/Getty Images

Managing multiple sclerosis Actor Selma Blair's multiple sclerosis results from a loss of the myelin sheath that insulates her motor axons and speeds their neural impulses. She has discussed her challenges openly, including difficulty speaking and walking with a cane. Researchers are exploring myelin repair therapies for people with multiple sclerosis (Hoojimans et al., 2019).

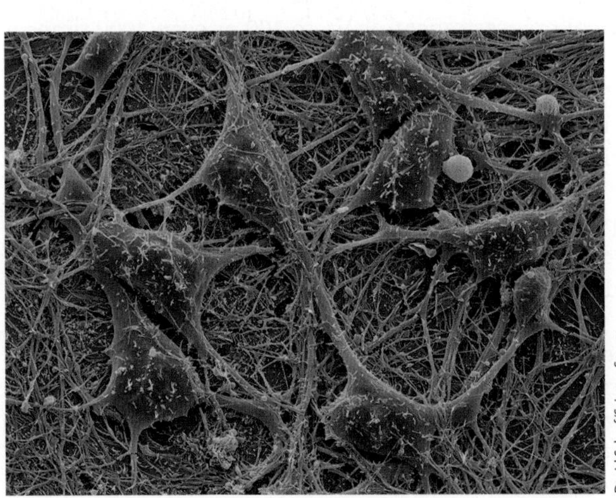

David Scharf/Science Source

FIGURE 4.3
Neurons communicating Our billions of neurons exist in a vast and densely interconnected web. As part of a fascinating electrochemical communication process, one neuron's *terminal branches* send messages to neighboring dendrites.

glial cells (glia) cells in the nervous system that support, nourish, and protect neurons; they also play a role in learning, thinking, and memory.

action potential a neural impulse; a brief electrical charge that travels down an axon.

threshold the level of stimulation required to trigger a neural impulse.

refractory period in neural processing, a brief resting pause that occurs after a neuron has fired; subsequent action potentials cannot occur until the axon returns to its resting state.

all-or-none response a neuron's reaction of either firing (with a full-strength response) or not firing.

Supporting these billions of nerve cells are spidery **glial cells** ("glue cells"). Neurons are like queen bees; on their own they cannot feed or sheathe themselves. Glial cells are worker bees. They provide nutrients and insulating myelin, guide neural connections, and mop up *ions* and *neurotransmitters*. Glia also play a role in learning, thinking, and memory. By "chatting" with neurons, they participate in information transmission and memory (Fields, 2013; Martín et al., 2015).

In more complex animal brains, the proportion of glia to neurons increases. Marian Diamond and other researchers' postmortem analyses of Albert Einstein's brain did not find more or larger-than-usual neurons. They did, however, reveal a much greater concentration of glial cells than found in an average person's head (Diamond et al., 1985; Fields, 2004). Einstein's glial cells kept his brain abuzz with activity.

The Neural Impulse

Neurons transmit messages when stimulated by our senses or by neighboring neurons. A neuron sends a message by firing an impulse, called the **action potential**—a brief electrical charge that travels down its axon.

Depending on the type of fiber, a neural impulse travels at speeds ranging from a sluggish 2 miles (3 kilometers) per hour to more than 200 miles (320 kilometers) per hour. But even its top speed is 3 million times slower than that of electricity through a wire. We measure brain activity in milliseconds (thousandths of a second) and computer activity in nanoseconds (billionths of a second). Unlike a computer's nearly instantaneous reaction, your response to a sudden event, such as a child darting in front of your car, may take a quarter-second or more. Your brain is vastly more complex than a computer, but slower at executing simple responses. And if you were an elephant—whose round-trip message travel time from a yank on the tail to the brain and back to the tail is 100 times longer than that of a tiny shrew—your reflexes would be slower yet (More et al., 2010).

Like batteries, neurons generate electricity from chemical events. The neuron's chemistry-to-electricity process exchanges ions (electrically charged atoms). The fluid outside an axon's membrane has mostly positively charged sodium ions. A resting axon's fluid interior (which includes both large, negatively charged protein ions and smaller, positively charged potassium ions) has a mostly negative charge. Like a tightly guarded facility, the axon's surface is selective about what it allows through its gates. We say the axon's surface is *selectively permeable*. This positive-outside/negative-inside state is called the *resting potential*.

When a neuron fires, however, the security parameters change: The first section of the axon opens its gates, like a storm sewer cover flipping open, and positively charged sodium ions (attracted to the negative interior) flood in through the now-open channels (**FIGURE 4.4**). The loss of the inside/outside charge difference, called *depolarization*, causes the next section of axon channels to open, and then the next, like falling dominos. This temporary inflow of positive ions is the neural impulse—the action potential. Each neuron is itself a miniature decision-making device performing complex calculations as it receives signals from hundreds, even thousands, of other neurons. The mind boggles when imagining this electrochemical process repeating up to 100 or even 1000 times a second.

"I sing the body electric." —Walt Whitman, "Children of Adam," 1855

Most neural signals are *excitatory*, somewhat like pushing a neuron's accelerator. Some are *inhibitory*, more like pushing its brake. If excitatory signals exceed the inhibitory signals by a minimum intensity, or **threshold** (see Figure 4.4), the combined signals trigger an action potential. (Think of it this way: If the excitatory party animals outvote the inhibitory party poopers, the party's on.) The action potential then travels down the axon, which branches into junctions with hundreds or thousands of other neurons or with the body's muscles and glands.

"What one neuron tells another neuron is simply how much it is excited." —Francis Crick, *The Astonishing Hypothesis*, 1994

Neurons need short breaks (a tiny fraction of an eyeblink). During a resting pause called the **refractory period**, subsequent action potentials cannot occur until the axon returns to its resting state. Then the neuron can fire again.

Increasing the stimulation above the threshold will not increase the neural impulse's intensity. The neuron's reaction is an **all-or-none response**: Like guns, neurons either fire or they don't. How, then, do we detect the intensity of a stimulus? How do we distinguish

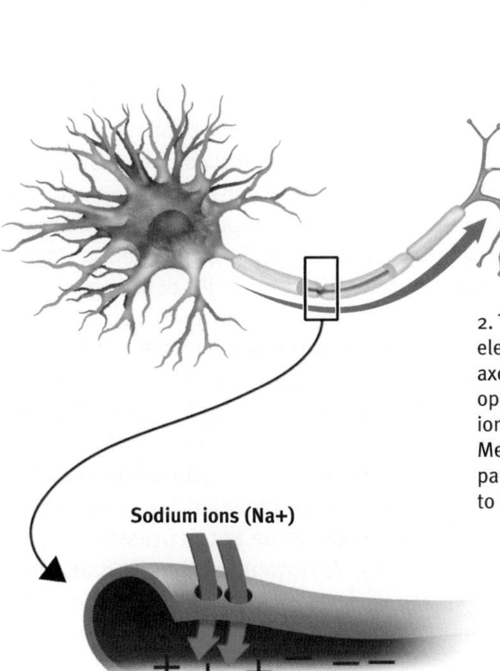

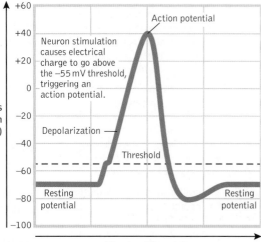

Axon membrane's electrical charge in millivolts (mV)

+60
+40
+20
0
−20
−40
−60
−80
−100

Action potential

Neuron stimulation causes electrical charge to go above the −55 mV threshold, triggering an action potential.

Depolarization

Threshold

Resting potential

Resting potential

Time in milliseconds

2. This initial depolarization influences the electrical charge of the next portion of the axon. Gates in this neighboring area now open, allowing positively charged sodium ions to flow in and depolarize that area. Meanwhile, other gates open in the first part of the axon, allowing potassium ions to flow out, repolarizing this section.

Sodium ions (Na+)

Potassium (K+)

Na+

1. Neuron stimulation causes a brief change in electrical charge. If strong enough, this opens gates to allow positively charged sodium ions to flood in, producing a momentary depolarization called the action potential.

3. As the action potential moves speedily down the axon, sodium/potassium pumps in the cell membrane finish restoring the first section of the axon to its resting potential.

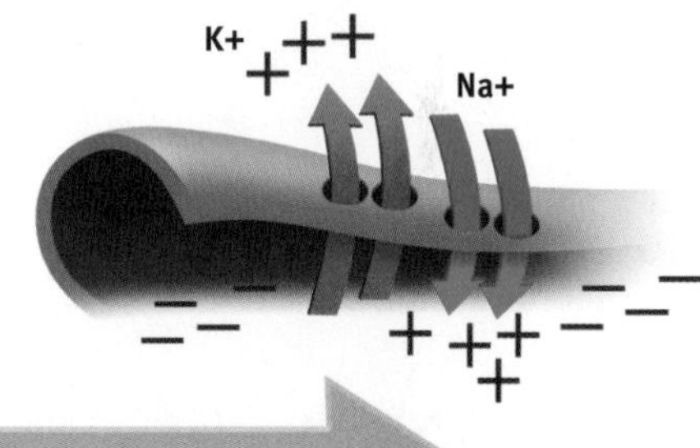
K+
Na+

Direction of action potential: toward axon terminals

FIGURE 4.4
Action potential Bodily sensations and actions—detecting an ant crawling on your foot or kicking a soccer ball—happen when our neurons are stimulated enough that their membrane's electrical charge reaches a threshold (–55 mV in this example—see graph). This prompts each of those neurons to "fire" an impulse—an action potential—which travels down its axon (see numbered drawings) and transmits a message to other neurons, muscles, or glands.

a gentle touch from a big hug? A strong stimulus can trigger *more* neurons to fire, and to fire more often. But it does not affect the action potential's strength or speed. Squeezing a trigger harder won't make a bullet go faster.

ASK YOURSELF

Does it surprise you to learn that your reaction time is slower than a computer's? Does this suggest which tasks might be more readily performed by computers?

RETRIEVAL PRACTICE

RP-3 When a neuron fires an action potential, the information travels through the axon, the dendrites, and the cell body, but not in that order. Place these three structures in the correct order.

RP-4 How does our nervous system allow us to experience the difference between a slap and a tap on the back?

ANSWERS IN APPENDIX E

How Neurons Communicate

LOQ 4-4 How do nerve cells communicate with other nerve cells?

Neurons interweave so intricately that even with a microscope, you would struggle to see where one neuron ends and another begins. Scientists once believed that the axon of one cell fused with the dendrites of another in an uninterrupted fabric. Then British physiologist Sir Charles Sherrington (1857–1952) noticed that neural impulses

synapse [SIN-aps] the junction between the axon tip of the sending neuron and the dendrite or cell body of the receiving neuron. The tiny gap at this junction is called the *synaptic gap* (or *synaptic cleft*).

neurotransmitters chemical messengers that cross the synaptic gap between neurons. When released by the sending neuron, neurotransmitters travel across the synapse and bind to receptor sites on the receiving neuron, thereby influencing whether that neuron will generate a neural impulse.

reuptake a neurotransmitter's reabsorption by the sending neuron.

"All information processing in the brain involves neurons 'talking to' each other at synapses." —Neuroscientist Solomon H. Snyder (1984)

were taking an unexpectedly long time to travel a neural pathway. Inferring that there must be a brief interruption in the transmission, Sherrington drew on the Greek word *synaptein* (meaning "fasten together") when he defined the meeting point between neurons as a **synapse**.

We now know that the axon terminal of one neuron is in fact separated from the receiving neuron by a tiny—less than a millionth of an inch wide—*synaptic gap* (or *synaptic cleft*). Spanish anatomist Santiago Ramón y Cajal (1852–1934) marveled at these near-unions of neurons, calling them "protoplasmic kisses." "Like elegant ladies air-kissing so as not to muss their makeup, dendrites and axons don't quite touch," noted poet Diane Ackerman (2004, p. 37). How do the neurons execute this protoplasmic kiss, sending information across the synaptic gap? The answer is one of the important scientific discoveries of our age.

When an action potential reaches the button-like terminals at an axon's end, it triggers the release of chemical messengers, called **neurotransmitters** (**FIGURE 4.5**). Within 1/10,000th of a second, the neurotransmitter molecules cross the synaptic gap and bind to receptor sites on the receiving neuron—as precisely as a key fits a lock. For an instant, the neurotransmitter unlocks tiny channels at the receiving site, and electrically charged atoms flow in, exciting or inhibiting the receiving neuron's readiness to fire. The excess neurotransmitters finally drift away, are broken down by enzymes, or are reabsorbed by the sending neuron—a process called **reuptake**. Some antidepressant medications partially block the reuptake of mood-enhancing neurotransmitters (**FIGURE 4.6**).

RETRIEVAL PRACTICE

RP-5 What happens in the *synaptic gap*?

RP-6 What is *reuptake*? What two other things can happen to excess neurotransmitters after a neuron reacts?

ANSWERS IN APPENDIX E

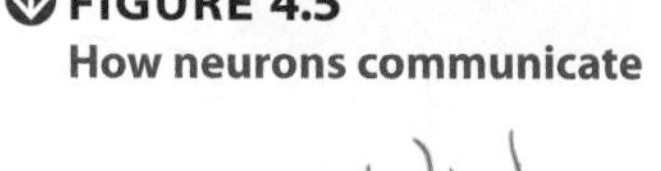
1. Electrical impulses (action potentials) travel down a neuron's axon until reaching a tiny junction known as a *synapse*.
Sending neuron
Action potential
Receiving neuron
Synapse
Sending neuron
Action potential
Reuptake
Synaptic gap
Axon terminal
Receptor sites on receiving neuron
Neurotransmitter
2. When an action potential reaches an axon's end (terminal), it stimulates the release of neurotransmitter molecules. These molecules cross the synaptic gap and bind to receptor sites on the receiving neuron. This allows electrically charged atoms to enter the receiving neuron and excite or inhibit a new action potential.
3. Excess neurotransmitters are reabsorbed (a process called *reuptake*), drift away, or are broken down by enzymes.

FIGURE 4.5
How neurons communicate

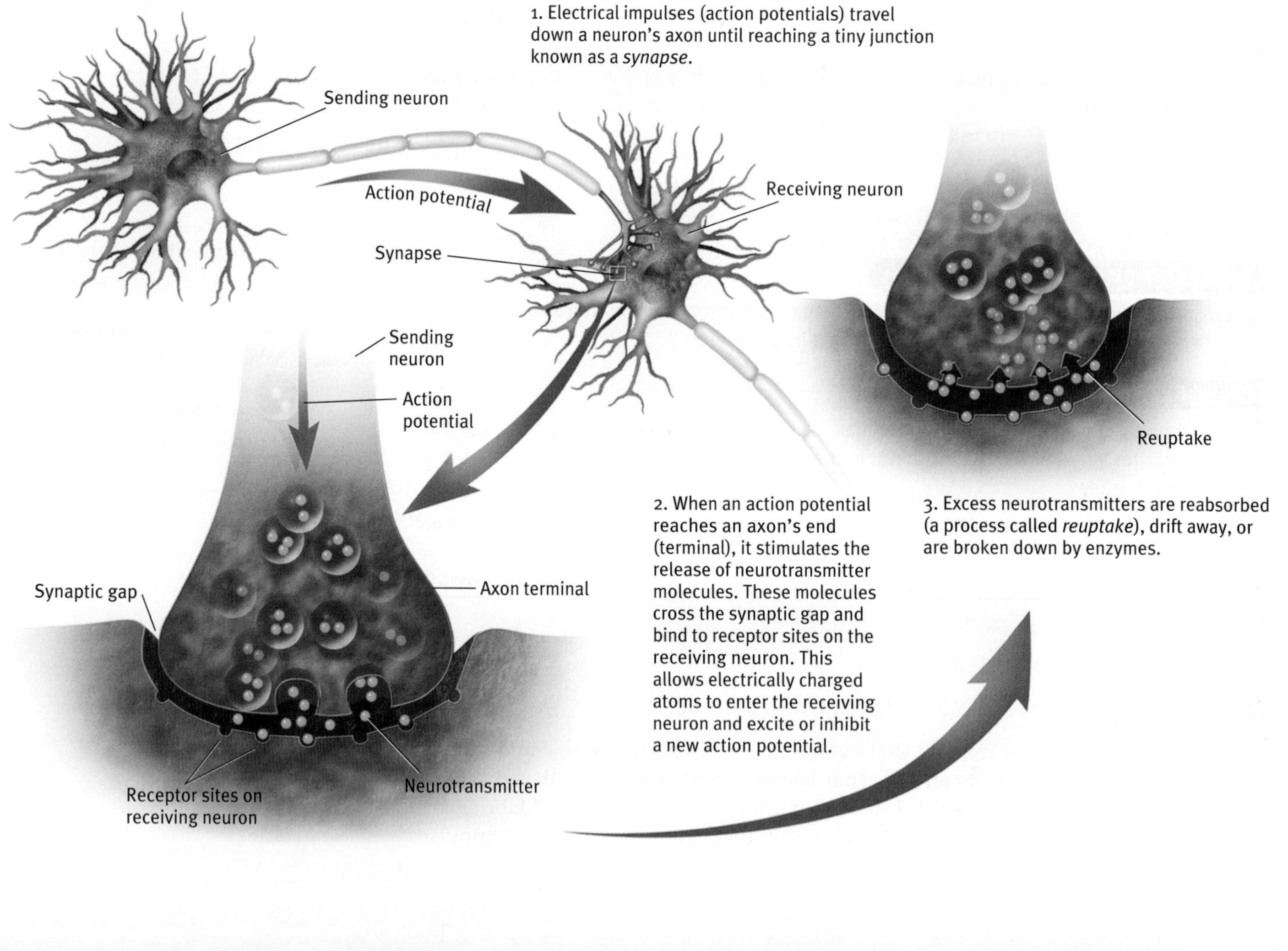

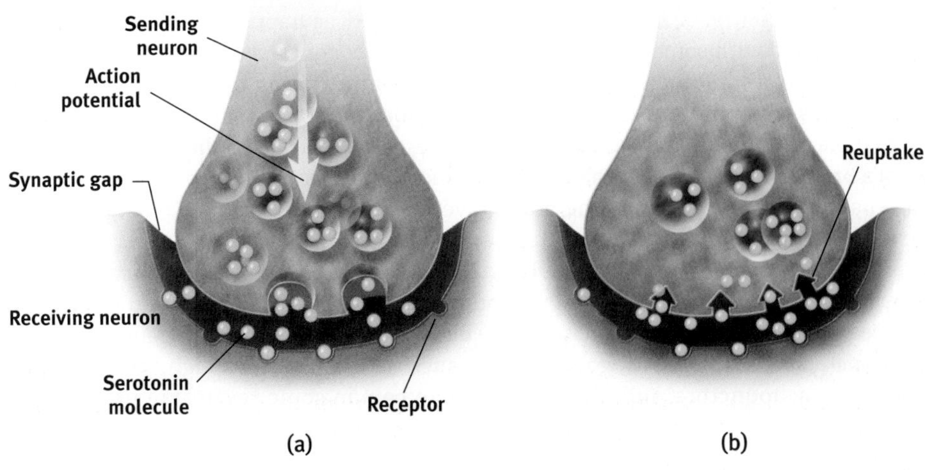
Message is sent across synaptic gap.
Message is received; excess serotonin molecules are reabsorbed by sending neuron.
Sending neuron
Action potential
Synaptic gap
Receiving neuron
Serotonin molecule
Receptor
Reuptake
(a)
(b)

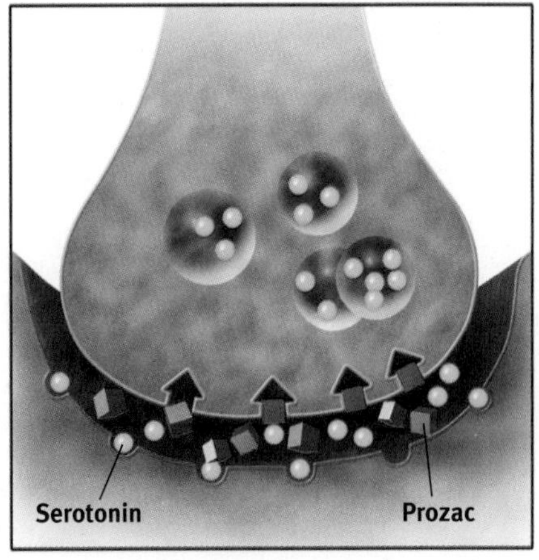
Prozac partially blocks normal reuptake of the neurotransmitter serotonin; excess serotonin in synapse enhances its mood-lifting effect.
Serotonin
Prozac
(c)

FIGURE 4.6
Biology of antidepressants Selective serotonin reuptake inhibitors (SSRIs) are popularly prescribed antidepressants. They are designed to relieve depression by partially blocking the reuptake of the neurotransmitter serotonin. Shown here is the action of the SSRI Prozac.

How Neurotransmitters Influence Us

LOQ 4-5 How do neurotransmitters influence behavior, and how do drugs and other chemicals affect neurotransmission?

In their quest to understand neural communication, researchers have discovered several dozen neurotransmitters and as many new questions: Are certain neurotransmitters found only in specific places? How do neurotransmitters affect our moods, memories, and mental abilities? Can we boost or diminish these effects through drugs or diet?

Other modules explore how neurotransmitters influence our hunger and thinking, depression and euphoria, addictions and therapy. In this module, we'll see how neurotransmitters affect our motions and emotions. A particular brain pathway may use only one or two neurotransmitters, such as serotonin and dopamine, and certain neurotransmitters affect specific behaviors and emotions (**TABLE 4.1**). But neurotransmitter systems don't operate in isolation; they interact, and their effects vary with the receptors they stimulate.

"When it comes to the brain, if you want to see the action, follow the neurotransmitters." —Neuroscientist Floyd Bloom (1993)

TABLE 4.1 Commonly Studied Neurotransmitters and Their Functions

Neurotransmitter	Function	Examples of Malfunctions
Acetylcholine (ACh)	Enables muscle action, learning, and memory	With Alzheimer's disease, ACh-producing neurons deteriorate.
Dopamine (DOH-puh-meen)	Influences movement, learning, attention, and emotion	Oversupply linked to schizophrenia. Undersupply linked to tremors and decreased mobility in Parkinson's disease.
Serotonin (ser-uh-TOH-nin)	Affects mood, hunger, sleep, and arousal	Undersupply linked to depression. Some drugs that raise serotonin levels are used to treat depression.
Norepinephrine	Helps control alertness and arousal	Undersupply can depress mood.
GABA (gamma-aminobutyric acid)	A major inhibitory neurotransmitter	Undersupply linked to seizures, tremors, and insomnia.
Glutamate (GLUE-tuh-mate)	A major excitatory neurotransmitter; involved in learning and memory	Oversupply can overstimulate the brain, producing migraines or seizures.
Endorphins	Neurotransmitters that influence the perception of pain or pleasure	Oversupply with opioid drugs can suppress the body's natural endorphin supply.

Dependent upon dopamine The neurotransmitter dopamine helps us move, think, and feel. Too little dopamine may produce the tremors and loss of motor control of Parkinson's disease (Wang et al., 2022). More than 8.5 million people worldwide have Parkinson's disease, including musical artist and reality show actor Ozzy Osbourne, shown here with the rest of *The Osbournes* (Ou et al., 2021).

One of the best-understood neurotransmitters, *acetylcholine (ACh),* plays a role in learning and memory. ACh also enables muscle action, by acting as the messenger at every junction between motor neurons (which carry information from the brain and spinal cord to the body's tissues) and skeletal muscles. When ACh is released to our muscle cell receptors, the muscle contracts. If ACh transmission is blocked, as happens during some kinds of anesthesia and with some poisons, the muscles cannot contract and we are paralyzed.

Candace Pert and Solomon Snyder (1973) made an exciting discovery about neurotransmitters when they attached a harmless radioactive tracer to morphine, an opioid drug that elevates mood and eases pain. As the researchers tracked the morphine in an animal's brain, they noticed it was binding to receptors in areas linked with mood and pain sensations. But why would the brain have these "opioid receptors"? Why would it have a chemical lock, unless it also had a key to open it?

Researchers soon confirmed that the brain does indeed produce its own naturally occurring opioids. Our body releases several neurotransmitter molecules similar to morphine in response to pain and vigorous exercise. These **endorphins** (short for *endo*genous [produced within] m*orphine*) help explain good feelings such as the "runner's high," the painkilling effects of acupuncture, and the indifference to pain in some severely injured people (Boecker et al., 2008; Fuss et al., 2015). But once again, new knowledge led to new questions.

ASK YOURSELF

Can you recall a time, perhaps after a workout, when you felt the effects of endorphins? How would you describe those feelings?

RETRIEVAL PRACTICE

RP-7 Serotonin, dopamine, and endorphins are all chemical messengers called ____________.

ANSWERS IN APPENDIX E

HOW DRUGS AND OTHER CHEMICALS ALTER NEUROTRANSMISSION If natural endorphins lessen pain and boost mood, why not increase this effect by flooding the brain with artificial opioids, thereby intensifying the brain's own "feel-good" chemistry? Because it would disrupt the brain's chemical balancing act. When flooded with opioid drugs such as heroin, morphine, and fentanyl (a powerful synthetic opioid), the brain—to maintain its chemical balance—may stop producing its own natural opioids. When the drug is withdrawn, the brain may then be deprived of *any* form of opioid, causing intense discomfort. For suppressing the body's own neurotransmitter production, nature charges a price.

Drugs and other chemicals affect brain chemistry. **Agonist** molecules *increase* a neurotransmitter's action. Some agonists may increase the production or release of neurotransmitters, or block reuptake in the synapse. Other agonists may be similar enough to a neurotransmitter to bind to its receptor and mimic its excitatory or inhibitory effects. Some opioid drugs, then, are agonists and produce a temporary "high" by amplifying normal sensations of arousal or pleasure.

Antagonists *decrease* a neurotransmitter's action by blocking production or release. An antagonist is enough like the natural neurotransmitter to occupy its receptor site and block its effect, but it is not similar enough to stimulate the receptor (rather like foreign coins that fit into, but won't operate, a vending machine). Botulin, a poison that can form in improperly canned food, causes paralysis by blocking ACh release. (Small injections of botulin—Botox—smooth wrinkles by paralyzing the underlying facial muscles.) Curare, a poison some South American Indigenous people have applied to hunting-dart tips, also occupies and blocks ACh receptor sites on muscles, producing paralysis in their prey.

RETRIEVAL PRACTICE

RP-8 Curare poisoning paralyzes animals by blocking ACh receptors involved in muscle movement. Morphine mimics endorphin actions. Which is an agonist, and which is an antagonist?

ANSWERS IN APPENDIX E

endorphins [en-DOR-fins] "morphine within"—natural, opioid-like neurotransmitters linked to pain control and to pleasure.

agonist a molecule that increases a neurotransmitter's action.

antagonist a molecule that inhibits or blocks a neurotransmitter's action.

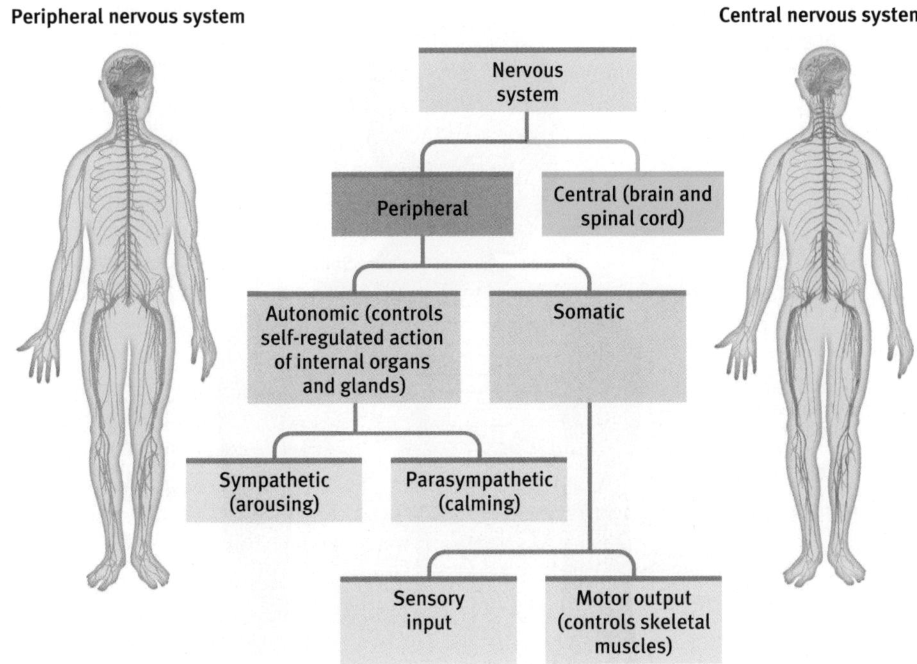
Peripheral nervous system
Central nervous system
Nervous system
Peripheral
Central (brain and spinal cord)
Autonomic (controls self-regulated action of internal organs and glands)
Somatic
Sympathetic (arousing)
Parasympathetic (calming)
Sensory input
Motor output (controls skeletal muscles)

FIGURE 4.7
The functional divisions of the human nervous system

The Nervous System

LOQ 4-6 What are the functions of the nervous system's main divisions, and what are the three main types of neurons?

Neurons communicating via neurotransmitters make up our body's **nervous system**, a communication network that takes in information from the world and the body's tissues, makes decisions, and sends back information and orders to the body's tissues (FIGURE 4.7).

A quick overview: The brain and spinal cord form the **central nervous system (CNS)**, the body's decision maker. The **peripheral nervous system (PNS)** is responsible for gathering information and transmitting CNS decisions to our body parts. **Nerves**, electrical cables formed from bundles of axons, link the CNS with the body's sensory receptors, muscles, and glands. The optic nerve, for example, bundles a million axons into a single cable carrying the messages from the eye to the brain (Mason & Kandel, 1991).

Information travels in the nervous system through three types of neurons. **Sensory neurons** carry messages from the body's tissues and sensory receptors inward (what biologists term *afferent*) to the brain and spinal cord for processing. **Motor neurons** (which are *efferent*) carry instructions from the central nervous system outward to the body's muscles and glands. Between the sensory input and motor output, information is processed via **interneurons**. Our complexity resides mostly in these interneurons. Our nervous system has a few million sensory neurons, a few million motor neurons, and billions and billions of interneurons.

The Peripheral Nervous System

Our peripheral nervous system has two components—somatic and autonomic. Our **somatic nervous system** enables voluntary control of our skeletal muscles. When your friend taps your shoulder, your somatic nervous system reports to your brain the current state of your skeletal muscles and carries instructions back, triggering your head to turn.

Our **autonomic nervous system (ANS)** controls our glands and our internal organ muscles. The ANS influences functions such as glandular activity, heartbeat, and digestion. (*Autonomic* means "self-regulating.") As with a self-driving car, we may consciously override the system, but it usually operates on its own (autonomously).

The autonomic nervous system's subdivisions serve two important functions (FIGURE 4.8). The **sympathetic nervous system** arouses and expends energy. Imagine an

nervous system the body's speedy, electrochemical communication network, consisting of all the nerve cells of the peripheral and central nervous systems.

central nervous system (CNS) the brain and spinal cord.

peripheral nervous system (PNS) the sensory and motor neurons that connect the central nervous system (CNS) to the rest of the body.

nerves bundled axons that form neural cables connecting the central nervous system with muscles, glands, and sensory organs.

sensory (afferent) neurons neurons that carry incoming information from the body's tissues and sensory receptors to the brain and spinal cord.

motor (efferent) neurons neurons that carry outgoing information from the brain and spinal cord to the muscles and glands.

interneurons neurons within the brain and spinal cord; they communicate internally and process information between the sensory inputs and motor outputs.

somatic nervous system the division of the peripheral nervous system that controls the body's skeletal muscles. Also called the *skeletal nervous system*.

autonomic [aw-tuh-NAHM-ik] **nervous system (ANS)** the part of the peripheral nervous system that controls the glands and the muscles of the internal organs (such as the heart). Its *sympathetic* division arouses; its *parasympathetic* division calms.

sympathetic nervous system the division of the autonomic nervous system that arouses the body, mobilizing its energy.

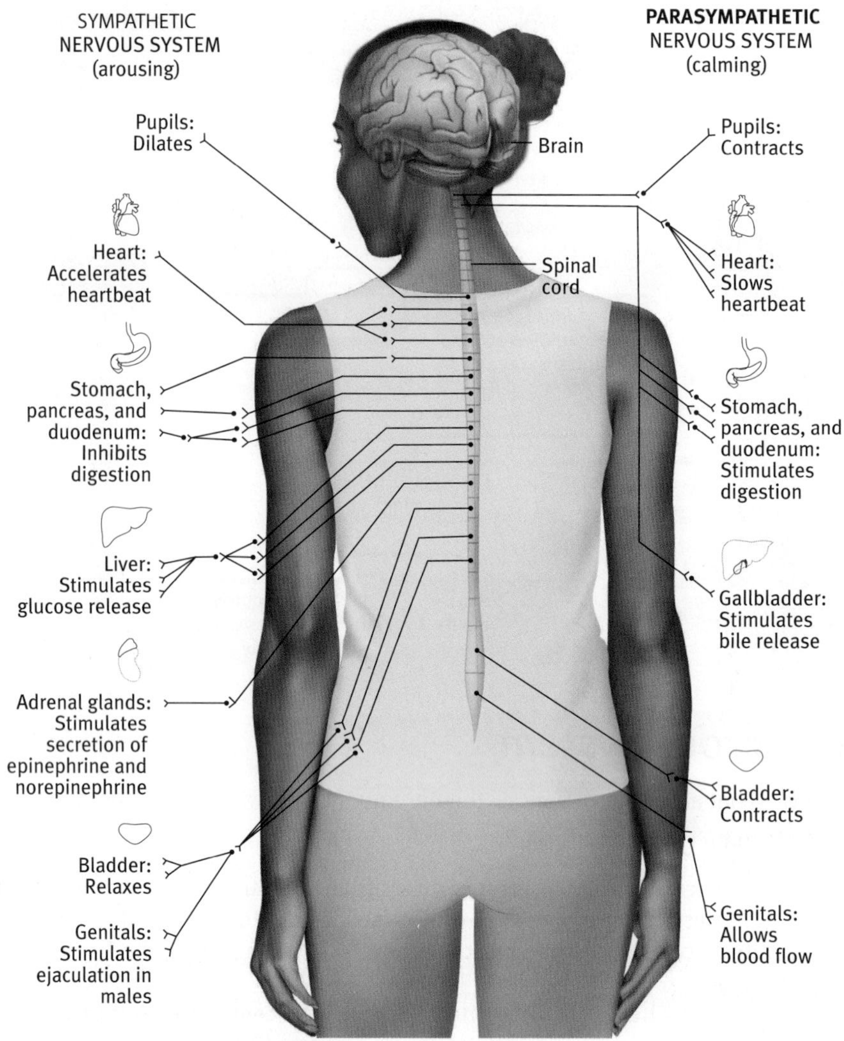

SYMPATHETIC NERVOUS SYSTEM (arousing)
PARASYMPATHETIC NERVOUS SYSTEM (calming)
Pupils: Dilates
Brain
Pupils: Contracts
Heart: Accelerates heartbeat
Spinal cord
Heart: Slows heartbeat
Stomach, pancreas, and duodenum: Inhibits digestion
Stomach, pancreas, and duodenum: Stimulates digestion
Liver: Stimulates glucose release
Gallbladder: Stimulates bile release
Adrenal glands: Stimulates secretion of epinephrine and norepinephrine
Bladder: Contracts
Bladder: Relaxes
Genitals: Allows blood flow
Genitals: Stimulates ejaculation in males

FIGURE 4.8
The dual functions of the autonomic nervous system The autonomic nervous system controls the more autonomous (or self-regulating) internal functions. Its sympathetic division arouses the body and expends energy. Its parasympathetic division calms the body and conserves energy, allowing routine maintenance activity. For example, sympathetic stimulation accelerates heartbeat, whereas parasympathetic stimulation slows it.

activity that alarms or challenges you, such as a longed-for job interview. Your sympathetic nervous system accelerates your heartbeat, raises your blood pressure, slows your digestion, raises your blood sugar, and cools you with sweat, making you alert and ready for action. When the stress subsides after the interview, your **parasympathetic nervous system** will produce the opposite effects, conserving your energy as it decreases your heartbeat, lowers your blood sugar, and enables you to rest and digest. The sympathetic and parasympathetic nervous systems work together, as accelerator and brake, to keep us in a steady internal state called *homeostasis* (more on this in the "What Drives Us" modules).

Several years ago, I [DM] experienced my ANS in action. Before sending me into an MRI machine for a shoulder scan, the technician asked if I had issues with claustrophobia. "No, I'm fine," I assured her. Moments later, as I found myself on my back, stuck deep inside a coffin-sized box and unable to move, my sympathetic nervous system had a different idea. Claustrophobia overtook me. My heart began pounding, and I felt a desperate urge to escape. Just as I was about to cry out for release, I felt my calming parasympathetic nervous system kick in. My heart rate slowed and my body relaxed, though my arousal surged again before the 20-minute confinement ended. "You did well!" the technician said, unaware of my ANS roller-coaster ride.

ASK YOURSELF

Think back to a stressful moment when you felt your sympathetic nervous system kick in. What was your body preparing you for? Were you able to sense your parasympathetic nervous system's response when the challenge had passed?

parasympathetic nervous system the division of the autonomic nervous system that calms the body, conserving its energy.

RETRIEVAL PRACTICE

RP-9 Match the type of neuron (i–iii) to its description (a–c).

Type	Description
i. Motor neurons	a. Carry incoming messages from sensory receptors to the CNS.
ii. Sensory neurons	b. Communicate within the CNS and process information between incoming and outgoing messages.
iii. Interneurons	c. Carry outgoing messages from the CNS to muscles and glands.

RP-10 How was the ANS involved in Hawaiians' terrified responses, and in calming their bodies once they realized it was a false alarm?

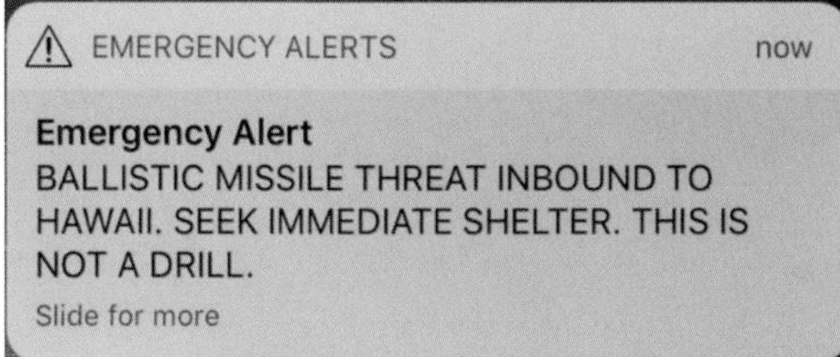
EMERGENCY ALERTS
now
Emergency Alert
BALLISTIC MISSILE THREAT INBOUND TO HAWAII. SEEK IMMEDIATE SHELTER. THIS IS NOT A DRILL.
Slide for more

Ballistic stress In 2018, Hawaiians received this terrifying alert, amid concerns about North Korean nuclear warheads. "We fully felt we were about to die," reported one panicked mother (Nagourney et al., 2018). Thirty-eight minutes later, the alert was declared a false alarm.

ANSWERS IN APPENDIX E

The Central Nervous System

From neurons "talking" to other neurons arises the complexity of the central nervous system's brain and spinal cord.

The brain enables our humanity—our thinking, feeling, and acting. Tens of billions of neurons, each communicating with thousands of other neurons, yield an ever-changing wiring web. By one estimate—projecting from neuron counts in small brain samples—our brain has some 128 billion neurons (Feldman Barrett, 2020). (Although that's a lot, the world's 10 richest people, as we write, each have more dollars than brain cells.)

Just as individual pixels combine to form a picture, the brain's individual neurons cluster into work groups called *neural networks*. To understand why, Stephen Kosslyn and Olivier Koenig (1992, p. 12) have invited us to "think about why cities exist; why don't people distribute themselves more evenly across the countryside?" Like people networking with people, neurons network with nearby neurons with which they can have short, fast connections; each layer's cells connect with various cells in the neural network's next layer. Learning—to play the violin, speak a foreign language, or solve a math problem—occurs as experience strengthens connections. To paraphrase one neuropsychologist, neurons that fire together wire together (Hebb, 1949).

BIOLOGY

"The body is made up of millions and millions of crumbs."

The other part of the CNS, the *spinal cord*, connects the peripheral nervous system and the brain. Ascending neural fibers send up sensory information, and descending fibers send back motor-control information. The neural pathways governing our **reflexes**, our automatic responses to stimuli, illustrate the spinal cord's work. A simple spinal reflex pathway is composed of a single sensory neuron and a single motor neuron. These often communicate through an interneuron. The knee-jerk reflex, for example, involves one such simple pathway. A headless warm body could do it.

Another neural circuit enables the pain reflex (**FIGURE 4.9**). When your finger touches a flame, neural activity (excited by the heat) travels via sensory neurons to interneurons in your spinal cord. These interneurons respond by activating motor neurons leading to the muscles in your arm. Because the simple pain-reflex pathway runs through the spinal cord and right back out, your hand jerks away from the candle's flame *before* your brain receives and responds to the information that causes you to feel pain. That's why it feels as if your hand jerks away not by your choice, but on its own.

reflex a simple, automatic response to a sensory stimulus, such as the knee-jerk reflex.

FIGURE 4.9
A simple reflex

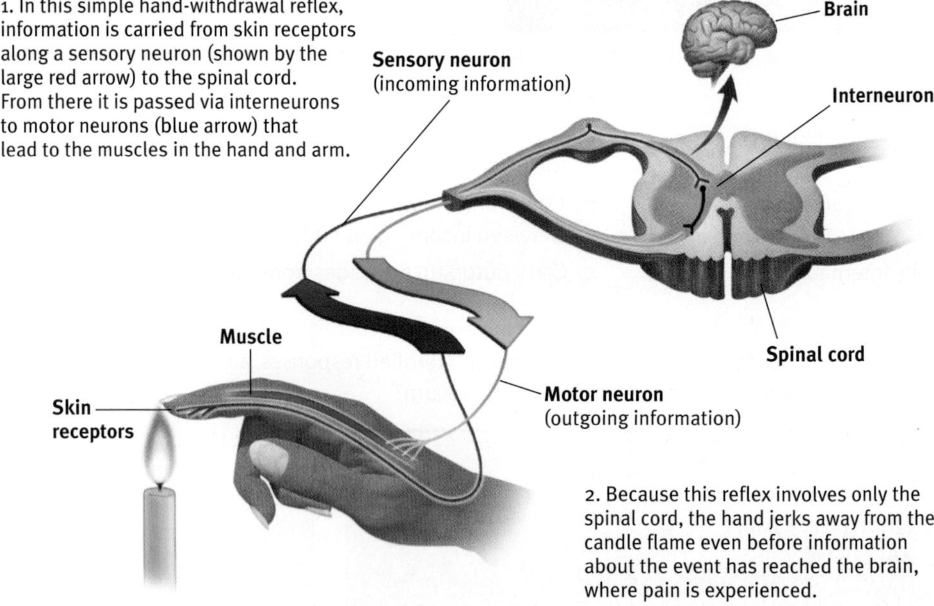
1. In this simple hand-withdrawal reflex, information is carried from skin receptors along a sensory neuron (shown by the large red arrow) to the spinal cord. From there it is passed via interneurons to motor neurons (blue arrow) that lead to the muscles in the hand and arm.
Brain
Sensory neuron (incoming information)
Interneuron
Muscle
Spinal cord
Skin receptors
Motor neuron (outgoing information)
2. Because this reflex involves only the spinal cord, the hand jerks away from the candle flame even before information about the event has reached the brain, where pain is experienced.

Information travels to and from the brain by way of the spinal cord. Were the top of your spinal cord severed, you would not feel pain from your paralyzed body below. Nor would you feel pleasure. With your brain literally out of touch with your body, you would lose all sensation and voluntary movement in body regions with sensory and motor connections to the spinal cord below its point of injury. You would exhibit the knee-jerk reflex without feeling the tap. Men paralyzed below the waist may be capable of an erection (a simple reflex) if their genitals are stimulated (Gomes et al., 2017; Hess & Hough, 2012). Women who are similarly paralyzed may respond with vaginal lubrication. But, depending on where and how completely their spinal cord is severed, they may be genitally unresponsive to erotic images and have no genital feelings (Kennedy & Over, 1990; Sipski et al., 1999). To produce bodily pain or pleasure, the sensory information must reach the brain.

"If the nervous system be cut off between the brain and other parts, the experiences of those other parts are nonexistent for the mind. The eye is blind, the ear deaf, the hand insensible and motionless." —William James, *Principles of Psychology,* 1890

The Endocrine System

LOQ 4-7 How does the endocrine system transmit information and interact with the nervous system?

So far, we have focused on the body's speedy electrochemical information system. Interconnected with your nervous system is a second communication system, the **endocrine system** (FIGURE 4.10). The endocrine system contains glands and fat tissue that secrete another form of chemical messenger, **hormones**. Hormones travel through the bloodstream and affect other tissues, including the brain. When hormones act on the brain, they influence our interest in sex, food, and aggression.

Some hormones are chemically identical to neurotransmitters (the chemical messengers that diffuse across a synapse and excite or inhibit an adjacent neuron). The endocrine system and nervous system are therefore close relatives: Both produce molecules that act on receptors elsewhere. Like many relatives, they also differ. The speedier nervous system zips messages from eyes to brain to hand in a fraction of a second. Endocrine messages trudge along in the bloodstream, taking several seconds or more to travel from the gland to the target tissue. If the nervous system transmits information with text-message speed, the endocrine system delivers an old-fashioned letter.

But slow and steady sometimes wins the race. Endocrine messages tend to outlast the effects of neural messages. Have you ever felt angry long after the cause of your angry feelings was resolved (say, your friend apologized for their rudeness)? You may have experienced an "endocrine hangover" from lingering emotion-related hormones. The persistence of emotions—even without conscious awareness of what

endocrine [EN-duh-krin] **system** the body's "slow" chemical communication system; glands and fat tissue that secrete hormones into the bloodstream.

hormones chemical messengers that are manufactured by the endocrine glands, travel through the bloodstream, and affect other tissues.

adrenal [ah-DREEN-el] **glands** a pair of endocrine glands that sits just above the kidneys and secretes hormones (epinephrine and norepinephrine) that help arouse the body in times of stress.

pituitary gland the endocrine system's most influential gland. Under the influence of the hypothalamus, the pituitary regulates growth and controls other endocrine glands.

caused them—was dramatically evident in one ingenious experiment. Brain-damaged patients unable to form new conscious memories watched a sad film and later a happy film. After each viewing, they did not consciously recall the films, but the sad or happy emotion persisted (Feinstein et al., 2010).

In a moment of danger, the ANS orders the **adrenal glands** on top of the kidneys to release *epinephrine* and *norepinephrine* (also called *adrenaline* and *noradrenaline*). These hormones increase heart rate, blood pressure, and blood sugar, providing a surge of energy to power our *fight-or-flight* response. When the emergency passes, the hormones—and the feelings—linger for a few moments before the parasympathetic system calms you.

The most influential endocrine gland is the **pituitary gland**, a pea-sized structure located in the core of the brain, where it is controlled by an adjacent brain area, the *hypothalamus* (more on that shortly). Among the hormones released by the pituitary is a growth hormone that stimulates physical development. Another is *oxytocin*, which enables orgasm, and, in women, labor contractions and (while nursing) milk flow. Oxytocin also aids social connection. For example, while bonding with their offspring through grooming, male baboons' oxytocin levels surge (Rincon et al., 2020). Children with autism spectrum disorder, who experience atypical social connections, have lower oxytocin levels than do their non-autistic peers (John & Jaeggi, 2021).

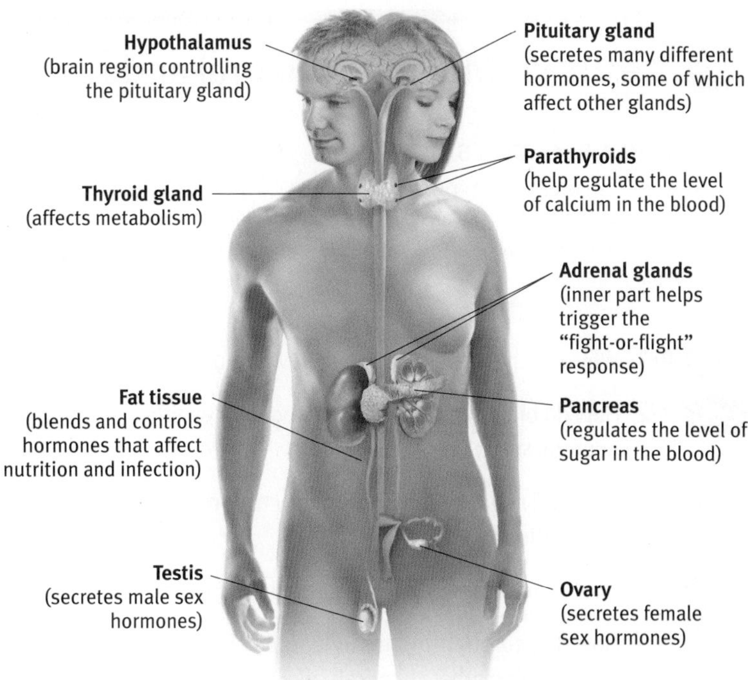
Hypothalamus
(brain region controlling the pituitary gland)
Pituitary gland
(secretes many different hormones, some of which affect other glands)
Parathyroids
(help regulate the level of calcium in the blood)
Thyroid gland
(affects metabolism)
Adrenal glands
(inner part helps trigger the "fight-or-flight" response)
Fat tissue
(blends and controls hormones that affect nutrition and infection)
Pancreas
(regulates the level of sugar in the blood)
Testis
(secretes male sex hormones)
Ovary
(secretes female sex hormones)

FIGURE 4.10
The endocrine system

Pituitary secretions also direct other endocrine glands to release their hormones. The pituitary, then, is a *master gland* (whose own master is the hypothalamus). For example, under the brain's influence, the pituitary triggers your sex glands to release sex hormones. These in turn influence your brain and behavior (Goetz et al., 2014). So, too, with stress. A stressful event triggers your hypothalamus to instruct your pituitary to release a hormone that causes your adrenal glands to flood your body with *cortisol*, a stress hormone that increases blood sugar. Sustained stress also increases adolescents' and adults' risk for later depression (Kennis et al., 2020; Zajkowska et al., 2022). Stressed body → depressed mind.

This feedback system (brain → pituitary → other glands → hormones → body and brain) reveals the intimate connection of the nervous and endocrine systems. The nervous system directs endocrine secretions, which then affect the nervous system. Conducting and coordinating this whole electrochemical orchestra is that flexible maestro we call the brain.

ASK YOURSELF

Do you remember feeling the lingering emotional effects related to a hormonal response, such as anger or anxiety after a particularly upsetting event? How did it feel? How long did it last?

RETRIEVAL PRACTICE

RP-11 Why is the pituitary gland called the *master gland?*

RP-12 How are the nervous and endocrine systems alike, and how do they differ?

ANSWERS IN APPENDIX E

Brittainy Newman/The New York Times/Redux Pictures

Prejudice causes stress Experiencing prejudice triggers the release of the stress hormone cortisol (Palmer-Bacon et al., 2020; Seaton & Zeiders, 2021). In 2020, Christian Cooper experienced prejudice and stress while bird-watching in New York's Central Park. After politely asking a White woman to leash her dog, the woman yelled at him and threatened to call the police and tell them that "an African American man is threatening my life" (Nir, 2020). A video of the stressful interaction went viral, attracting more than 40 million views in 2 days. The woman was later arrested on charges of filing a false police report.

REVIEW Module 4: Neural and Hormonal Systems

LEARNING OBJECTIVES

Test Yourself Answer these repeated Learning Objective Questions on your own (before "showing" the answers here, or checking the answers in Appendix D) to improve your retention of the concepts (McDaniel et al., 2009, 2015).

LOQ 4-1 Why are psychologists concerned with human biology?

LOQ 4-2 How do biology and experience together enable neuroplasticity?

LOQ 4-3 What are *neurons*, and how do they transmit information?

LOQ 4-4 How do nerve cells communicate with other nerve cells?

LOQ 4-5 How do neurotransmitters influence behavior, and how do drugs and other chemicals affect neurotransmission?

LOQ 4-6 What are the functions of the nervous system's main divisions, and what are the three main types of neurons?

LOQ 4-7 How does the endocrine system transmit information and interact with the nervous system?

TERMS AND CONCEPTS TO REMEMBER

Test Yourself Write down the definition in your own words, then check your answer.

biological psychology, p. 52
neuroplasticity, p. 53
neuron, p. 55
cell body, p. 55
dendrites, p. 55
axon, p. 55
myelin [MY-uh-lin] sheath, p. 55
glial cells (glia), p. 56
action potential, p. 56
threshold, p. 56
refractory period, p. 56
all-or-none response, p. 56
synapse [SIN-aps], p. 58
neurotransmitters, p. 58
reuptake, p. 58
endorphins [en-DOR-fins], p. 60
agonist, p. 60
antagonist, p. 60
nervous system, p. 61
central nervous system (CNS), p. 61
peripheral nervous system (PNS), p. 61
nerves, p. 61
sensory (afferent) neurons, p. 61
motor (efferent) neurons, p. 61
interneurons, p. 61
somatic nervous system, p. 61
autonomic [aw-tuh-NAHM-ik] nervous system (ANS), p. 61
sympathetic nervous system, p. 61
parasympathetic nervous system, p. 62
reflex, p. 63
endocrine [EN-duh-krin] system, p. 64
hormones, p. 64
adrenal [ah-DREEN-el] glands, p. 64
pituitary gland, p. 64

MODULE TEST

Test Yourself Answer the following questions on your own first, then "show" the answers here, or check your answers in Appendix E.

1. What do psychologists mean when they say the brain is "plastic"?

2. The neuron fiber that passes messages through its branches to other neurons or to muscles and glands is the ____________.

3. The tiny space between the axon of one neuron and the dendrite or cell body of another is called the
   a. axon terminal.
   b. branching fiber.
   c. synaptic gap.
   d. threshold.

4. Regarding a neuron's response to stimulation, the intensity of the stimulus determines
   a. whether or not an impulse is generated.
   b. how fast an impulse is transmitted.
   c. how intense an impulse will be.
   d. whether reuptake will occur.

5. In a sending neuron, when an action potential reaches an axon terminal, the impulse triggers the release of chemical messengers called ____________.

6. Endorphins are released in the brain in response to
   a. morphine or heroin.
   b. pain or vigorous exercise.
   c. the all-or-none response.
   d. all of the above.

7. The autonomic nervous system controls internal functions, such as heart rate and glandular activity. The word *autonomic* means
   a. calming.
   b. voluntary.
   c. self-regulating.
   d. arousing.

8. The sympathetic nervous system arouses us for action and the parasympathetic nervous system calms us down. Together, the two systems make up the ____________ nervous system.

9. The neurons of the spinal cord are part of the ____________ nervous system.

10. The most influential endocrine gland, known as the *master gland*, is the
    a. pituitary.
    b. hypothalamus.
    c. thyroid.
    d. pancreas.

11. The ____________ ____________ secrete(s) epinephrine and norepinephrine, helping to arouse the body during times of stress.

MODULE

5 Tools of Discovery: Having Our Head Examined

LOQ 5-1 How do neuroscientists study the brain's connections to behavior and mind?

When you think *about* your brain, you're thinking *with* your brain—by releasing billions of neurotransmitter molecules across trillions of synapses. The effect of hormones on experiences such as love reminds us that we would not be of the same mind if we were a bodiless brain. Nevertheless, brain, behavior, and cognition are an integrated whole. But precisely where and how are the mind's functions tied to the brain? Let's consider how scientists explore such questions.

"I am a brain, Watson. The rest of me is a mere appendix." —Sherlock Holmes, in Arthur Conan Doyle's "The Adventure of the Mazarin Stone," 1921

For most of human history, scientists had no tools high-powered yet gentle enough to reveal a living brain's activity. Early case studies helped localize some brain functions. Damage to one side of the brain often caused numbness or paralysis on the body's opposite side, suggesting that the body's right side is wired to the brain's left side, and vice versa. Damage to the back of the brain disrupted vision, and to the left-front part of the brain produced speech difficulties. Gradually, these early explorers were mapping the brain.

Now the human brain has invented new ways to study itself. A new generation of neural mapmakers is charting the known universe's most amazing organ. Scientists can selectively **lesion** (destroy) tiny clusters of normal or defective brain cells, observing any effect on brain function. In the laboratory, such studies have revealed, for example, that damage to one area of the hypothalamus in a rat's brain reduces eating, to the point of starvation, whereas damage in another area produces overeating.

Today's neuroscientists can *stimulate* various brain parts—electrically, chemically, or magnetically—and note the effect. Depending on the stimulated brain part, people may—to name a few examples—giggle, hear voices, turn their head, feel themselves falling, or have an out-of-body experience (Selimbeyoglu & Parvizi, 2010).

Scientists can even snoop on the messages of individual neurons. With tips small enough to detect the electrical pulse in a single neuron, modern microelectrodes can, for example, now detect exactly where the information goes in a rat's brain when someone tickles its belly (Ishiyama & Brecht, 2017). Promising new tools include *optogenetics*, a technique that allows neuroscientists to control the activity of individual neurons (Boyden, 2014). By programming neurons to become receptive to light, researchers can examine the biological basis of sensations, fear, depression, and substance use disorders (Dygalo & Shishkina, 2019; Firsov, 2019; Juarez et al., 2019; Nikitin et al., 2019).

Researchers can also eavesdrop on the chatter of billions of neurons. Right now, your mental activity is emitting telltale electrical, metabolic, and magnetic signals that would enable neuroscientists to observe your brain at work. Electrical activity in your brain's billions of neurons sweeps in regular waves across its surface. An **EEG (electroencephalogram)** is an amplified readout of such waves. Researchers record the brain waves through a shower-cap-like hat that is filled with electrodes covered with a conductive gel. Studying an EEG of the brain's activity is like studying a blender's motor by listening to its hum. With no direct access to the brain, researchers present a stimulus repeatedly and have a computer filter out brain activity unrelated to the stimulus. What remains is the electrical wave evoked by the stimulus.

A related technique is **MEG (magnetoencephalography)**. To isolate the brain's magnetic fields, researchers create special rooms that cancel out other magnetic signals, such as the Earth's magnetic field. Participants sit underneath a head coil that resembles a hair salon hairdryer. While participants complete activities, tens of thousands of neurons create electrical pulses, which in turn create magnetic fields. The speed and strength of the magnetic fields enable researchers to understand how certain tasks influence brain activity (Samuelsson et al., 2020). Other researchers have stimulated people's brains and noted what they experience, such as fear, a funny smell, sexual excitement, or a sense of calm (Koch, 2021).

Neuroimaging techniques give us a superhero-like ability to see inside the living brain. One such tool, **PET (positron emission tomography)** (FIGURE 5.1), depicts brain

lesion [LEE-zhuhn] tissue destruction. Brain lesions occur naturally (disease or trauma), in surgery, or experimentally (using electrodes to destroy brain cells).

EEG (electroencephalogram) an amplified recording of the waves of electrical activity sweeping across the brain's surface. These waves are measured by electrodes placed on the scalp.

MEG (magnetoencephalography) a brain-imaging technique that measures magnetic fields from the brain's natural electrical activity.

PET (positron emission tomography) a technique for detecting brain activity that displays where a radioactive form of glucose goes while the brain performs a given task.

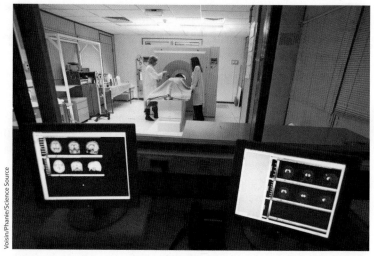

FIGURE 5.1
The PET scan

Voisin/Phanie/Science Source

activity by showing each brain area's consumption of its chemical fuel, the sugar glucose. Active neurons gobble glucose. Our brain, though only about 2 percent of our body weight, consumes 20 percent of our calorie intake. After a person receives temporarily radioactive glucose, the PET scan can track the gamma rays released by this "food for thought" as a task is performed. Rather like weather radar showing rain activity, PET-scan "hot spots" show the most active brain areas as the person does mathematical calculations, looks at images of faces, or daydreams.

Understanding the non-WEIRD brain Most neuroscience research studies people from Western, Educated, Industrialized, Rich, and Democratic (WEIRD) populations (Falk et al., 2013). Using functional near-infrared spectroscopy (fNIRS), the researchers shown here were able to identify brain areas involved in persuasion among a Jordanian sample (Burns et al., 2019).

Mark Straccia/UCLA Social Cognitive Neuroscience Laboratory

In **MRI (magnetic resonance imaging)** brain scans, the person's head is put in a strong magnetic field, which aligns the spinning atoms of brain molecules. Then, a radio-wave pulse momentarily disorients the atoms. When the atoms return to their typical spin, they emit signals that provide a detailed picture of soft tissues, including the brain. MRI scans have revealed a larger-than-average neural area in the left hemisphere of musicians who display perfect pitch (Yuskaitis et al., 2015). They have also revealed enlarged *ventricles*—fluid-filled brain areas (marked by the red arrows in **FIGURE 5.2**)—in some patients who have *schizophrenia*.

A special application of MRI—**fMRI (functional MRI)**—can reveal the brain's functioning as well as its structure. Where the brain is especially active, blood goes. By comparing successive MRI scans, researchers can watch as specific brain areas activate, showing increased oxygen-laden blood flow. As a person looks at a scene, for example, the fMRI machine detects blood rushing to the back of the brain, which processes visual information. Another tool, *functional near-infrared spectroscopy (fNIRS)*, uses infrared light that shines onto blood molecules to identify brain activity. The fNIRS equipment can fit in a large backpack, enabling researchers to study the biology of mind in difficult-to-reach populations (Burns et al., 2019; Perdue et al., 2019).

See **TABLE 5.1** for a comparison of some of these imaging techniques.

MRI (magnetic resonance imaging) a technique that uses magnetic fields and radio waves to produce computer-generated images of soft tissue. MRI scans show brain anatomy.

fMRI (functional MRI) a technique for revealing blood flow and, therefore, brain activity by comparing successive MRI scans. fMRI scans show brain function as well as structure.

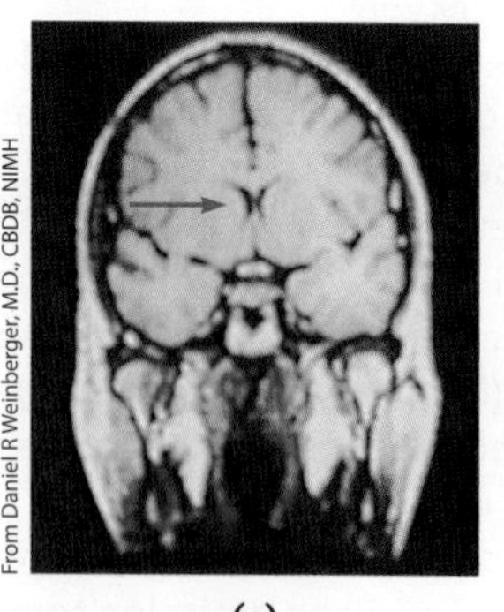

(a)

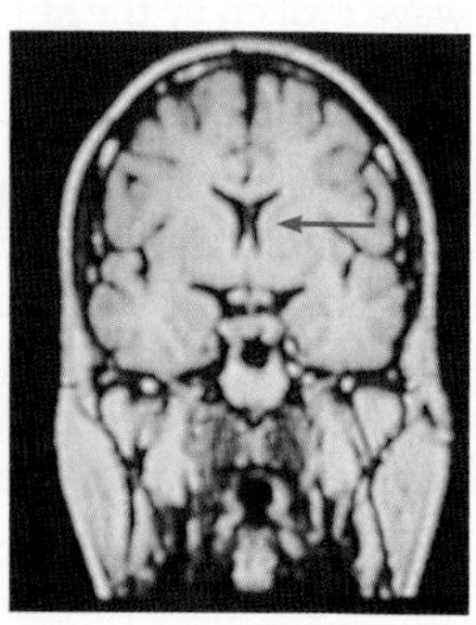

(b)

From Daniel R Weinberger, M.D., CBDB, NIMH

FIGURE 5.2
MRI scans of individuals without schizophrenia (a) and with schizophrenia (b) Note the enlarged ventricle—the fluid-filled brain region at the tip of the arrow in the image—in the brain of the person with schizophrenia (b).

TABLE 5.1 Common Types of Neural Measures

Name	How Does It Work?	Sample Finding
EEG (electroencephalogram)	Electrodes placed on the scalp measure electrical activity in neurons.	Symptoms of depression and anxiety correlate with increased activity in the right frontal lobe, a brain area associated with behavioral withdrawal and negative emotion (Thibodeau et al., 2006).
MEG (magnetoencephalography)	A head coil records magnetic fields from the brain's natural electrical currents.	Soldiers with posttraumatic stress disorder (PTSD), compared with soldiers who do not have PTSD, show stronger magnetic fields in the visual cortex when they view trauma-related images (Todd et al., 2015).
PET (positron emission tomography)	Tracks where in the brain a temporarily radioactive form of glucose goes while the person given it performs a task.	Monkeys with an anxious temperament have brains that use more glucose in regions related to fear, memory, and expectations of reward and punishment (Fox et al., 2015).
MRI (magnetic resonance imaging)	People sit or lie down in a chamber that uses magnetic fields and radio waves to provide a map of brain structure.	People with a history of violence tend to have smaller frontal lobes, especially in regions that aid moral judgment and self-control (Glenn & Raine, 2014).
fMRI (functional magnetic resonance imaging)	Measures blood flow to brain regions by comparing continuous MRI scans.	Years after surviving a near plane crash, passengers who viewed material related to their trauma showed greater activation in the brain's fear, memory, and visual centers than when they watched footage related to the 9/11 terrorist attacks (Palombo et al., 2015).

Such snapshots of the brain's changing activity provide new insights into how the brain divides its labor and reacts to changing needs. A mountain of recent fMRI studies tells us which brain areas are most active when people feel pain or rejection, listen to angry voices, think about scary things, feel happy, or become sexually aroused. fMRI can even reveal what happens if we deliberately suppress our own personality, as actors do (Brown et al., 2019).

Can brain imaging enable mind reading? fMRI technology has enabled a very basic sort of eavesdropping on the mind. One neuroscience team scanned 129 people's brains as they did eight different mental tasks (such as reading, gambling, or rhyming). Later, they were able, with 80 percent accuracy, to identify which of these mental activities their participants had been doing (Poldrack, 2018).

You've seen the pictures—of colorful "lit up" brain regions with accompanying headlines, such as "your brain on music." Although brain areas don't actually light up, vivid brain-scan images seem impressive. People rated scientific explanations as more believable and interesting when they contained neuroscience (Fernandez-Duque et al., 2015; Im et al., 2017). But "neuroskeptics" caution against overblown claims about any ability to predict customer preferences, to detect lies, and to foretell crime (Schwartz et al., 2016). Neuromarketing, neuroleadership, neurolaw, and neuropolitics are often neurohype. Imaging techniques illuminate brain structure and activity, and sometimes help us test different theories of behavior (Mather et al., 2013). But given that all human experience is brain-based, it's no surprise that different brain areas become active when one listens to a lecture or lusts for a lover.

* * *

Today's techniques for peering into the thinking, feeling brain are doing for psychology what the microscope did for biology and the telescope did for astronomy. From them we have learned more about the brain in the last 100 years than in the previous 10,000. And the next decade will reveal much more, as each year massive funding goes into brain research. To advance brain science, researchers from across Europe have undertaken a $1 billion Human Brain Project (Salles et al., 2019). Another project explores brain aging from ages 3 to 96 (Pomponio et al., 2020). These massive undertakings harness the collective power of hundreds of scientists from dozens of countries (Thompson et al., 2020) (**FIGURE 5.3**). "Individually, we contribute little or nothing to the truth," said Aristotle. "By the union of all a considerable amount is amassed."

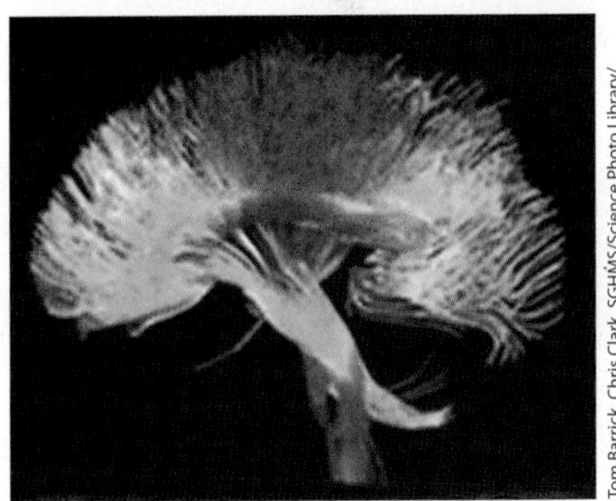

Tom Barrick, Chris Clark, SGHMS/Science Photo Library/Science Source

FIGURE 5.3
Beautiful brain connections The Human Connectome Project is using cutting-edge *diffusion tensor imaging* MRI methods to map the brain's interconnected network of neurons (Glasser et al., 2016; Wang & Olson, 2018). Such efforts have led to the creation of a new brain map with 100 neural centers not previously described (Glasser et al., 2016). Scientists used the technique to create this multicolored "symphony" of neural fibers transporting water through different brain regions.

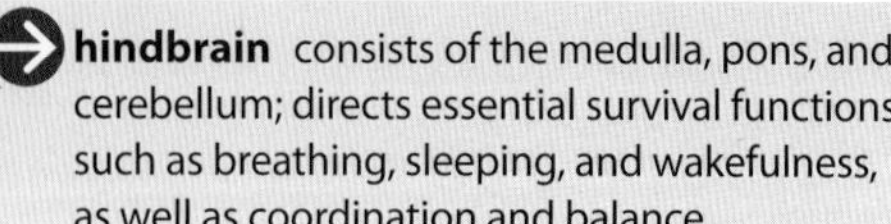

hindbrain consists of the medulla, pons, and cerebellum; directs essential survival functions, such as breathing, sleeping, and wakefulness, as well as coordination and balance.

midbrain found atop the brainstem; connects the *hindbrain* with the *forebrain,* controls some motor movement, and transmits auditory and visual information.

ASK YOURSELF

Were you surprised to learn that there are so many technologies to study the brain's structures and functions? Which techniques do you find most interesting? Why?

RETRIEVAL PRACTICE

RP-1 Match the scanning technique (i–iii) with the correct description (a–c).

Technique	Description
i. fMRI scan	a. Tracks radioactive glucose to reveal brain *activity.*
ii. PET scan	b. Tracks successive images of brain tissue to show brain *function.*
iii. MRI scan	c. Uses magnetic fields and radio waves to show brain *anatomy.*

ANSWERS IN APPENDIX E

MODULE 5 REVIEW Tools of Discovery: Having Our Head Examined

LEARNING OBJECTIVES

Test Yourself Answer this repeated Learning Objective Question on your own (before "showing" the answer here, or checking the answer in Appendix D) to improve your retention of the concepts (McDaniel et al., 2009, 2015).

LOQ 5-1 How do neuroscientists study the brain's connections to behavior and mind?

TERMS AND CONCEPTS TO REMEMBER

Test Yourself Write down the definition in your own words, then check your answer.

lesion [LEE-zhuhn], p. 67
EEG (electroencephalogram), p. 67
MEG (magnetoencephalography), p. 67
PET (positron emission tomography), p. 67
MRI (magnetic resonance imaging), p. 68
fMRI (functional MRI), p. 68

MODULE TEST

Test Yourself Answer the following questions on your own first, then "show" the answers here, or check your answers in Appendix E.

1. Selectively destroying brain cells, which enables scientists to note the resulting effect on brain function, is called ____________.

2. The neuroimaging technique that measures magnetic fields from the brain's natural electrical activity is called

a. MEG.
b. PET.
c. MRI.
d. fMRI.

3. If a researcher wanted to see which brain areas become active when a person writes a poem, the best technique to use would be

a. PET.
b. MRI.
c. fMRI.
d. lesioning.

4. The neuroimaging technique that uses magnetic fields and radio waves to produce computer-generated images of soft tissue is called

a. MEG.
b. PET.
c. MRI.
d. fMRI.

MODULE 6 Brain Regions and Structures

LOQ 6-1 What are the *hindbrain, midbrain,* and *forebrain?*

Vertebrate brains have three main divisions. The **hindbrain** contains brainstem structures that direct essential survival functions, such as our breathing, sleeping, arousal, coordination, and balance. The **midbrain**, atop the brainstem, connects the hindbrain with the forebrain; it also controls some movement and transmits information that

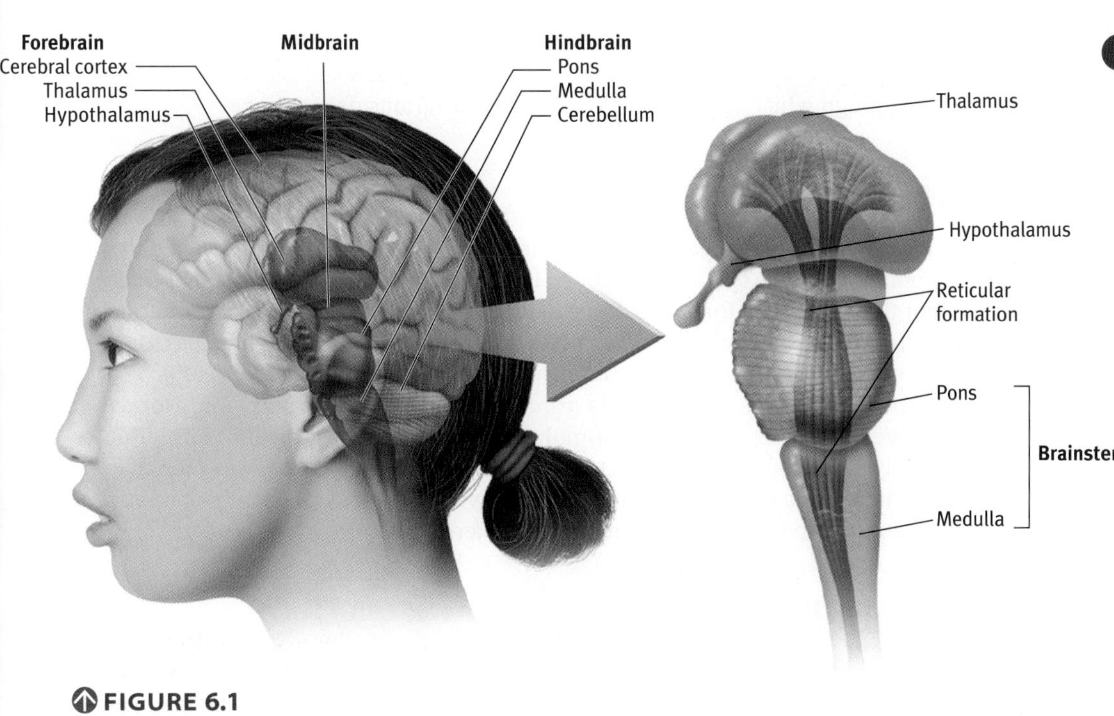
Forebrain
Cerebral cortex
Thalamus
Hypothalamus
Midbrain
Hindbrain
Pons
Medulla
Cerebellum
Thalamus
Hypothalamus
Reticular formation
Pons
Brainstem
Medulla

FIGURE 6.1
Brain divisions: forebrain, midbrain, hindbrain In the hindbrain, the brainstem (including the pons and medulla) is an extension of the spinal cord. The thalamus is attached to the top of the brainstem. The reticular formation passes through both structures.

enables our seeing and hearing. The **forebrain** manages complex cognitive activities, sensory and associative functions, and voluntary motor activities (FIGURE 6.1). Individual organisms' brains have evolved to best suit their environment (Cesario et al., 2020). We humans, for example, have extremely well-developed forebrains, allowing us an unparalleled ability to make complex decisions and judgments. Predatory sharks have complex hindbrains, supporting their impressive ability to chase down prey (Yopak et al., 2010).

RETRIEVAL PRACTICE

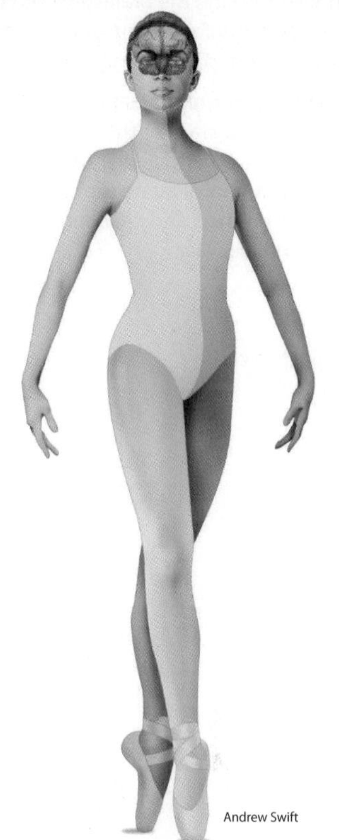
Andrew Swift

FIGURE 6.2
The body's wiring

RP-1 The ________________ is a crossover point where nerves from the left side of the brain are mostly linked to the right side of the body, and vice versa.

ANSWERS IN APPENDIX E

The Brainstem

LOQ 6-2 What structures make up the brainstem, and what are the functions of the brainstem, thalamus, reticular formation, and cerebellum?

The **brainstem** is the brain's innermost region. Its base is the **medulla**, the slight swelling in the spinal cord just after it enters the skull (see Figure 6.1). Here lie the controls for your heartbeat and breathing. As some patients with severe brain damage illustrate, we do not need a conscious mind to orchestrate our heart's pumping and lungs' breathing. The brainstem handles those tasks. Just above the medulla sits the *pons*, which helps coordinate movements and control sleep.

If a cat's brainstem were cut off from the rest of its brain, the cat would still breathe and live—and even run, climb, and groom (Klemm, 1990). But cut off from its midbrain and forebrain, the cat would not *purposefully* run or climb to get food.

The brainstem is also a crossover point, where most nerves to and from each side of the brain connect with the body's opposite side (FIGURE 6.2). This peculiar cross-wiring is but one of the brain's many surprises.

The Thalamus

Sitting atop the brainstem is the forebrain's **thalamus**, a pair of egg-shaped structures that acts as the brain's sensory control center (see Figure 6.1). The thalamus receives information from all the senses except smell, and routes that information to the brain regions that deal with seeing, hearing, tasting, and touching. The thalamus also receives

forebrain consists of the cerebral cortex, thalamus, and hypothalamus; manages complex cognitive activities, sensory and associative functions, and voluntary motor activities.

brainstem the central core of the brain, beginning where the spinal cord swells as it enters the skull; the brainstem is responsible for automatic survival functions.

medulla [muh-DUL-uh] the hindbrain structure that is the brainstem's base; controls heartbeat and breathing.

thalamus [THAL-uh-muss] the forebrain's sensory control center, located on top of the brainstem; it directs messages to the sensory receiving areas in the cortex and transmits replies to the cerebellum and medulla.

reticular formation a nerve network that travels through the brainstem into the thalamus; filters information and plays an important role in controlling arousal.

cerebellum [sehr-uh-BELL-um] the hindbrain's "little brain" at the rear of the brainstem; functions include processing sensory input, coordinating movement output and balance, and enabling nonverbal learning and memory.

some of the replies, which it then directs to the medulla and to the hindbrain's *cerebellum*. For sensory information, your thalamus is something like what Seoul is to South Korea's trains: a hub through which traffic passes on its way to various destinations.

The Reticular Formation

Inside the brainstem, between your ears, lies the **reticular** ("netlike") **formation**, a nerve network extending from the spinal cord right up through the thalamus. As the spinal cord's sensory input flows up to the thalamus, some of it travels through the reticular formation, which filters incoming stimuli and relays important information to other brain areas. Have you multitasked today? You can thank your reticular formation (Wimmer et al., 2015).

The reticular formation also controls arousal, as Giuseppe Moruzzi and Horace Magoun discovered in 1949. Electrically stimulating a sleeping cat's reticular formation almost instantly produced an awake, alert animal. When Magoun *severed* a cat's reticular formation without damaging nearby sensory pathways, the effect was equally dramatic: The cat lapsed into a coma from which it never awakened.

The Cerebellum

Extending from the rear of the brainstem is the hindbrain's baseball-sized **cerebellum**, meaning "little brain," which is what its two wrinkled halves resemble (**FIGURE 6.3**). The cerebellum (along with the *basal ganglia*—deep brain structures involved in motor movement) enables nonverbal learning and skill memory. With assistance from the pons, it also coordinates voluntary movement. When a soccer player skillfully controls the ball, give their cerebellum some credit. Under alcohol's influence, coordination suffers. And if you injured your cerebellum, you would have difficulty walking, keeping your balance, or texting your friend. Your movements would be jerky and exaggerated. Gone would be any dreams of being a dancer or guitarist.

The cerebellum, which has more than half your brain's neurons, operates just outside your awareness. Quickly answer these questions: How long have you been reading this text? Do your clothes feel loose or tight? How's your mood? You probably answered easily, thanks to your cerebellum.

* * *

Note: The brain functions we've discussed so far all occur without any conscious effort. This illustrates another of our recurring themes: *Our brain processes most information outside of our awareness.* We are aware of the *results* of our brain's labor—say, our current visual experience—but not *how* we construct the visual image. Likewise, whether we

FIGURE 6.3
The brain's organ of agility Hanging at the back of the brain, the cerebellum coordinates our voluntary movements, as when tennis player Naomi Osaka returns the ball.

mirates
LY BETTER

WILLIAM WEST/AFP/Getty Images

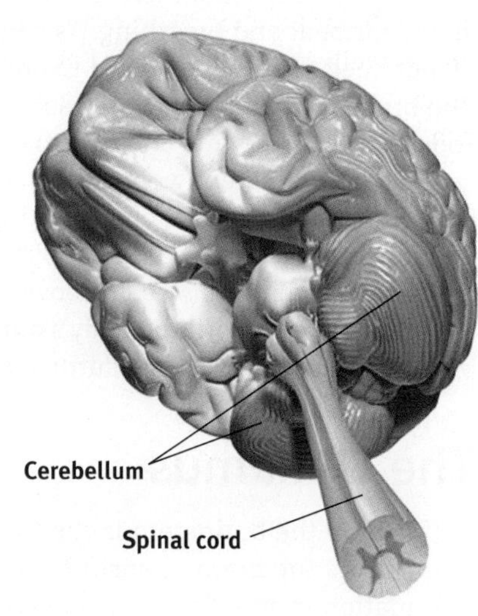
Cerebellum
Spinal cord

are asleep or awake, our brainstem manages its life-sustaining functions, freeing our conscious brain regions to think, talk, dream, or savor a memory.

RETRIEVAL PRACTICE

RP-2 In what brain region would damage be most likely to (a) disrupt your ability to jump rope? (b) disrupt your ability to hear? (c) leave you in a coma? (d) cut off the very breath and heartbeat of life?

ANSWERS IN APPENDIX E

Hypothalamus
Pituitary gland
Amygdala
Hippocampus

FIGURE 6.4
The limbic system This neural system is located mostly in the forebrain. The limbic system's hypothalamus controls the nearby pituitary gland.

The Limbic System

LOQ 6-3 What are the limbic system's structures and functions?

A skeleton walks into a café. "What would you like?" asks the barista. The skeleton replies, "I'll take a latte and a mop."

We can thank our **limbic system** for that wonderful emotion when we enjoy a joke. This system, which is associated with emotions and drives, contains the *amygdala,* the *hypothalamus,* and the *hippocampus* (**FIGURE 6.4**).

The Amygdala

The **amygdala**—two almond-shaped neural clusters—enables aggression and fear. In 1939, psychologist Heinrich Klüver and neurosurgeon Paul Bucy surgically removed a rhesus monkey's amygdala, turning the normally ill-tempered animal into the most mellow of creatures. In studies with other wild animals, including the lynx, wolverine, and wild rat, researchers noted the same effect. So, too, with humans. After a rare genetic disease destroyed one woman's amygdala, she no longer experienced fear. Facing a snake, speaking in public, even being threatened with a gun—she is not afraid (Feinstein et al., 2013). Even healthy people who have a smaller-than-average amygdala display reduced arousal to threatening stimuli (Foell et al., 2019). Little amygdala, little fear.

What then might happen if we electrically stimulated the amygdala of a normally placid domestic animal, such as a cat? Do so in one spot and the cat prepares to attack, hissing with its back arched, its pupils dilated, its hair on end. Move the electrode only slightly within the amygdala, cage the cat with a small mouse, and now it cowers in terror.

These and other experiments have confirmed the amygdala's role in fear and rage. Monkeys and humans with amygdala damage become less fearful of strangers (Harrison et al., 2015). Other studies link criminal behavior with amygdala dysfunction (Dotterer et al., 2017; Ermer et al., 2012). When people view angry and happy faces, only the angry ones increase activity in the amygdala (Mende-Siedlecki et al., 2013). And when negative events energize the amygdala, they become more memorable (Admon et al., 2018).

But we must be careful. The brain is not neatly organized into structures that correspond to our behavior categories. The amygdala is engaged with other mental phenomena as well. And when we feel afraid or act aggressively, there is neural activity in many areas of our brain—not just the amygdala. If you destroy a car's battery, the car won't run. But the battery is merely one link in an integrated system.

RETRIEVAL PRACTICE

GK Hart/Vikki Hart/Getty Images

RP-3 Electrical stimulation of a cat's amygdala provokes angry reactions. Which *autonomic nervous system* division is activated by such stimulation?

ANSWERS IN APPENDIX E

limbic system neural system located mostly in the forebrain—below the cerebral hemispheres—that includes the *amygdala, hypothalamus,* and *hippocampus;* associated with emotions and drives.

amygdala [uh-MIG-duh-la] two almond-shaped neural clusters in the limbic system; linked to emotion.

hypothalamus [hi-po-THAL-uh-muss] a limbic system neural structure lying below *(hypo)* the thalamus; it directs several maintenance activities (eating, drinking, body temperature), helps govern the endocrine system via the pituitary gland, and is linked to emotion and reward.

hippocampus a neural center located in the limbic system that helps process explicit (conscious) memories—of facts and events—for storage.

The Hypothalamus

Just below the thalamus is the **hypothalamus**, an important link in the command chain governing bodily maintenance. Some neural clusters in the hypothalamus influence hunger; others regulate thirst, body temperature, and sexual behavior. Together, they help maintain a steady *(homeostatic)* internal state.

To monitor your body state, the hypothalamus tunes in to your blood chemistry and any incoming orders from other brain parts. For example, picking up signals from your brain's cerebral cortex that you are thinking about sex, your hypothalamus will secrete hormones. These hormones will, in turn, trigger the adjacent *master gland* of the endocrine system, your pituitary (see Figure 6.4), to influence your sex glands to release *their* hormones. These hormones will intensify the thoughts of sex in your cerebral cortex. (Note the interplay between the nervous and endocrine systems: The brain influences the endocrine system, which in turn influences the brain.)

A remarkable discovery about the hypothalamus illustrates how progress in science often occurs—when curious, open-minded investigators make an unexpected observation. Two young McGill University neuropsychologists, James Olds and Peter Milner (1954), were trying to implant an electrode in a rat's reticular formation when they made a magnificent mistake: They placed the electrode incorrectly (Olds, 1975). Curiously, as if seeking more stimulation, the rat kept returning to the location in the cage where it had been stimulated. On discovering that they had actually placed the device in a region of the hypothalamus, Olds and Milner realized they had stumbled upon a brain center that provides pleasurable rewards.

Later experiments located other "pleasure centers" (Olds, 1958). (What the rats actually experience only they know, and they aren't telling. Rather than attribute human feelings to rats, today's scientists refer to *reward centers*.) Just how rewarding are these reward centers? Enough to cause rats to self-stimulate these brain regions more than 1000 times per hour.

In other species, including dolphins and monkeys, researchers later discovered other limbic system reward centers, such as the *nucleus accumbens* in front of the hypothalamus (Hamid et al., 2016). Animal research has also revealed both a general dopamine-related reward system and specific centers associated with the pleasures of eating, drinking, and sex. Animals, including us, seem to come equipped with built-in systems that reward activities essential to survival.

"If you were designing a robot vehicle to walk into the future and survive, ... you'd wire it up so that behavior that ensured the survival of the self or the species—like sex and eating—would be naturally reinforcing." —Neuroscientist Candace Pert (1986)

Researchers have experimented with ways of using brain stimulation to control nonhuman animals' actions in search-and-rescue operations. By rewarding rats for turning left or right, one research team trained previously caged rats to navigate natural environments (Talwar et al., 2002). By pressing buttons on a laptop, the researchers were then able to direct the rat—which carried a receiver, power source, and video camera all in a tiny backpack—to turn on cue, climb trees, scurry along branches, and return.

When we meet likable people or read affirming messages from friends, our brain buzzes with reward center activity (Inagaki et al., 2019; Zerubavel et al., 2018). But as one neurosurgeon found by implanting electrodes in violent patients' reward center areas, the patients reported only mild pleasure. Unlike Olds and Milner's rats, the patients were not driven to a frenzy (Deutsch, 1972; Hooper & Teresi, 1986). Stimulating the brain's "hedonic hot spots" (its reward circuits) produces more *desire* than pure enjoyment (Kringelbach & Berridge, 2012).

Experiments have also revealed the effects of a dopamine-related reward system in people. For example, experimentally boosting dopamine levels increases the pleasurable "chills" response to a favorite piece of music, whereas reducing dopamine levels decreases musical pleasure (Ferreri et al., 2019). Some researchers believe that many disordered behaviors may stem from malfunctions in natural brain systems for pleasure and well-being. People genetically predisposed to this *reward deficiency syndrome* may crave whatever provides that missing pleasure or relieves negative feelings, such as aggression, fattening food, or drugs and alcohol (Blum et al., 1996, 2014; Chester et al., 2016).

The Hippocampus

The **hippocampus** is a curved brain structure that processes conscious, explicit memories. Humans who lose their hippocampus to surgery or injury lose their ability to form

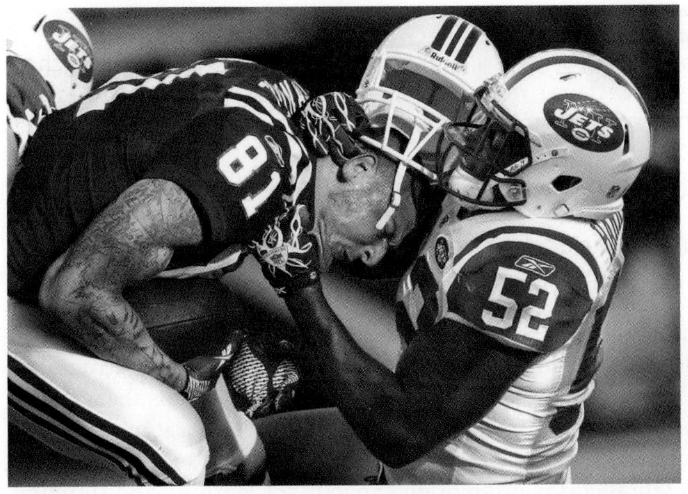
81
52
JETS

Elise Amendola/AP Photo

Are football players' brains protected? When researchers analyzed the brains of 111 deceased National Football League players, 99 percent showed signs of degeneration related to frequent head trauma (Mez et al., 2017). In 2017, NFL player Aaron Hernandez (#81) died by suicide while imprisoned for murder. An autopsy revealed that his brain, at age 27, was already showing advanced degeneration (Kilgore, 2017). In hopes of protecting players, some teams use more protective gear and portable brain-imaging tools to quickly identify potential injuries (Canadian Press, 2018).

new memories of facts and events (Clark & Maguire, 2016). Those who survive a hippocampal brain tumor in childhood struggle to remember new information in adulthood (Jayakar et al., 2015). Athletes who experience repeated brain trauma may later have a shrunken hippocampus and poor memory (Futterman, 2021; Tharmaratnam et al., 2018). Hippocampus size and function decrease as we grow older, which furthers cognitive decline (O'Callaghan et al., 2019). The Memory modules explain how our two-track mind uses the hippocampus to process our memories.

* * *

FIGURE 6.5 locates the brain areas we've discussed, as well as the *cerebral cortex*—the body's ultimate control and information-processing center.

FIGURE 6.5
Brain structures and their functions

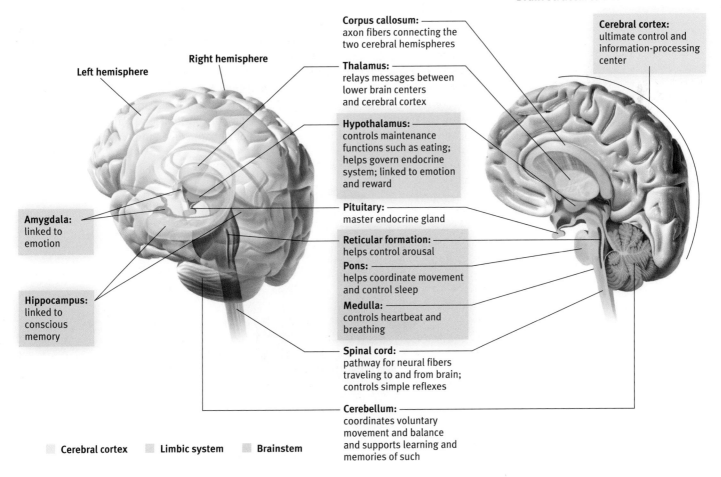

Left hemisphere

Right hemisphere

Amygdala: linked to emotion

Hippocampus: linked to conscious memory

Corpus callosum: axon fibers connecting the two cerebral hemispheres

Thalamus: relays messages between lower brain centers and cerebral cortex

Hypothalamus: controls maintenance functions such as eating; helps govern endocrine system; linked to emotion and reward

Pituitary: master endocrine gland

Reticular formation: helps control arousal

Pons: helps coordinate movement and control sleep

Medulla: controls heartbeat and breathing

Spinal cord: pathway for neural fibers traveling to and from brain; controls simple reflexes

Cerebellum: coordinates voluntary movement and balance and supports learning and memories of such

Cerebral cortex: ultimate control and information-processing center

Cerebral cortex Limbic system Brainstem

cerebral [seh-REE-bruhl] **cortex** the intricate fabric of interconnected neural cells covering the forebrain's cerebral hemispheres; the body's ultimate control and information-processing center.

frontal lobes the portion of the cerebral cortex lying just behind the forehead; involved in speaking and muscle movements and in making plans and judgments.

parietal [puh-RYE-uh-tuhl] **lobes** the portion of the cerebral cortex lying at the top of the head and toward the rear; receives sensory input for touch and body position.

occipital [ahk-SIP-uh-tuhl] **lobes** the portion of the cerebral cortex lying at the back of the head; includes areas that receive information from the visual fields.

The people who first dissected and labeled the brain used the language of scholars—Latin and Greek. Their words are actually attempts at graphic description: For example, *cortex* means "bark," *cerebellum* is "little brain," and *thalamus* is "inner chamber."

RETRIEVAL PRACTICE

RP-4 What are the three key structures of the limbic system, and what functions do they serve?

ANSWERS IN APPENDIX E

The Cerebral Cortex

LOQ 6-4 What four lobes make up the cerebral cortex, and what are the functions of the motor cortex, somatosensory cortex, and association areas?

The *cerebrum*—the two cerebral hemispheres that contribute 85 percent of the brain's weight—enables our perceiving, thinking, and speaking. Like other brain structures, including the thalamus, hippocampus, and amygdala, the cerebral hemispheres come as a pair. Covering those hemispheres, like bark on a tree, is the **cerebral cortex**, a thin surface layer of interconnected neural cells.

Mammals' complex cerebral cortex offers high capacity for learning and thinking, enabling them to adapt to ever-changing environments. What makes humans distinct is the size and interconnectivity of our cerebral cortex (Donahue et al., 2018). Let's take a look at its structure and function.

RETRIEVAL PRACTICE

RP-5 Which part of the human brain distinguishes us most from other animals?

ANSWERS IN APPENDIX E

Structure of the Cortex

If you opened a human skull, exposing the brain, you would see a wrinkled organ, shaped like the meat of an oversized walnut. Without these wrinkles, a flattened cerebral cortex would require triple the area—roughly that of a large pizza. The brain's left and right hemispheres are filled mainly with axons connecting the cortex to the brain's other regions. The cerebral cortex—that thin surface layer—contains some 20 to 23 billion of the brain's nerve cells and 300 trillion synaptic connections (de Courten-Myers, 2005). Being human takes a lot of nerve.

Each hemisphere's cortex is subdivided into four *lobes*, separated by prominent *fissures*, or folds (**FIGURE 6.6**). Starting at the front of your brain and moving over the top, there are the **frontal lobes** (behind your forehead), the **parietal lobes** (at the top and to the rear), and the **occipital lobes** (at the back of your head). Reversing direction and moving

FIGURE 6.6
The cortex and its basic subdivisions

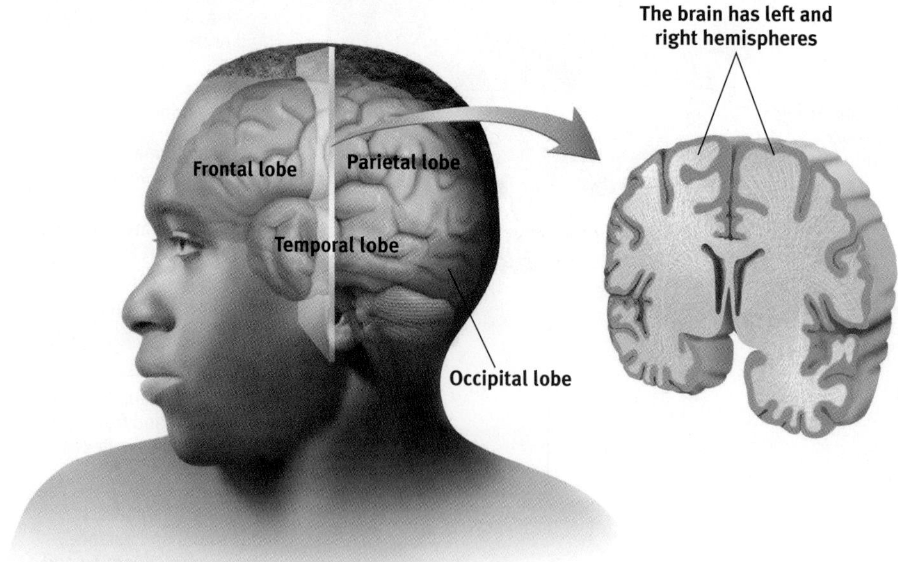
The brain has left and right hemispheres
Frontal lobe
Parietal lobe
Temporal lobe
Occipital lobe

forward, just above your ears, you find the **temporal lobes**. Each of the four lobes carries out many functions, and many functions require the interplay of several lobes.

temporal lobes the portion of the cerebral cortex lying roughly above the ears; includes the auditory areas, each receiving information primarily from the opposite ear.

motor cortex a cerebral cortex area at the rear of the frontal lobes that controls voluntary movements.

Functions of the Cortex

More than a century ago, surgeons found damaged cortical areas during autopsies of people who had been partially paralyzed or speechless. This rather crude evidence did not prove that specific parts of the cortex control complex functions like movement or speech. A laptop with a broken power cord might go dead, but we would be fooling ourselves if we thought we had "localized" the internet in the cord.

MOTOR FUNCTIONS Scientists had better luck in localizing simpler brain functions. For example, in 1870, German physicians Gustav Fritsch and Eduard Hitzig made an important discovery: Mild electrical stimulation to parts of an animal's cortex made parts of its body move. The effects were selective: Stimulation caused movement only when applied to an arch-shaped region at the back of the frontal lobe, running roughly ear to ear across the top of the brain. Moreover, stimulating parts of this region in the left or right hemisphere caused movements of specific body parts on the *opposite* side of the body. Fritsch and Hitzig had discovered what is now called the **motor cortex**.

MAPPING THE MOTOR CORTEX Lucky for brain surgeons and their patients, the brain has no sensory receptors. Knowing this, in the 1930s, Otfrid Foerster and Wilder Penfield were able to map the motor cortex in hundreds of wide-awake patients by stimulating different cortical areas and observing responses. They discovered that body areas requiring precise control, such as the fingers and mouth, occupy the greatest amount of cortical space (**FIGURE 6.7**). In one of his many demonstrations of motor behavior mechanics, Spanish neuroscientist José Delgado stimulated a spot on a patient's left motor cortex, triggering the right hand to make a fist. Asked to keep the fingers open during the next stimulation, the patient, whose fingers closed despite his best efforts, remarked, "I guess, Doctor, that your electricity is stronger than my will" (Delgado, 1969, p. 114).

Scientists can predict a monkey's arm motion *just before* it moves—by repeatedly measuring motor cortex activity preceding specific arm movements (Livi et al., 2019). Scientists have also observed monkeys' motor cortex neurons responding differently when executing a social act (putting an object in an experimenter's hand) rather than a nonsocial act (putting something in a container or in their own mouth) (Coudé et al., 2019). Such findings have opened the door to research on brain-controlled computer technology.

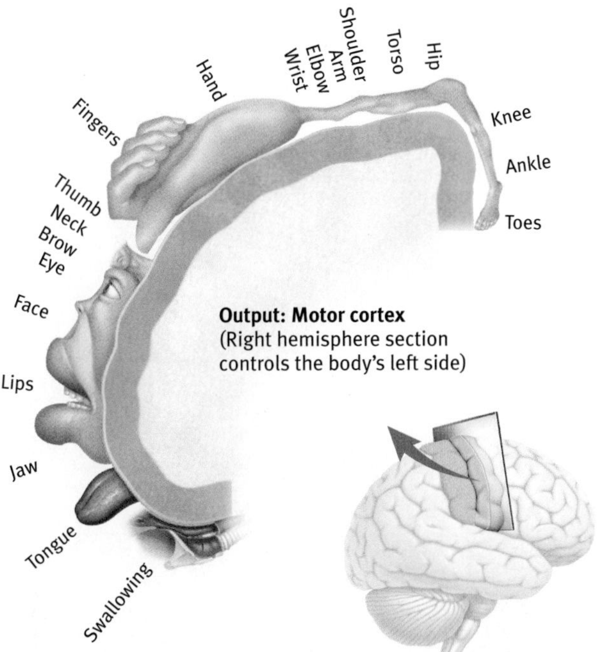
Hand
Shoulder
Arm
Elbow
Wrist
Torso
Hip
Knee
Ankle
Toes
Fingers
Thumb
Neck
Brow
Eye
Face
Lips
Jaw
Tongue
Swallowing
Output: Motor cortex
(Right hemisphere section controls the body's left side)

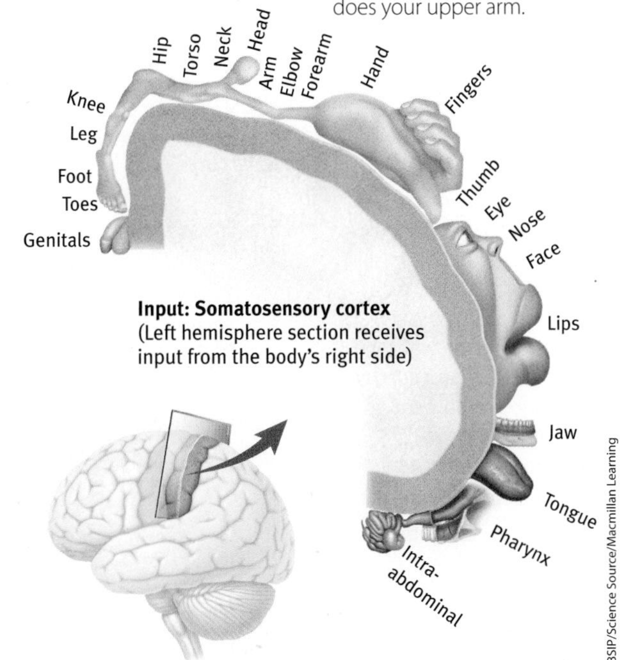
Hip
Torso
Neck
Head
Arm
Elbow
Forearm
Hand
Fingers
Knee
Leg
Foot
Toes
Genitals
Thumb
Eye
Nose
Face
Lips
Jaw
Tongue
Pharynx
Intra-abdominal
Input: Somatosensory cortex
(Left hemisphere section receives input from the body's right side)
BSIP/Science Source/Macmillan Learning

FIGURE 6.7
Motor cortex and somatosensory cortex tissue devoted to each body part As you can see from this classic though inexact representation, the amount of cortex devoted to a body part in the motor cortex (in the frontal lobes) or in the somatosensory cortex (in the parietal lobes) is not proportional to that body part's size. Rather, the brain devotes more tissue to sensitive areas and to areas requiring precise control. So, your fingers have a greater representation in the cortex than does your upper arm.

RETRIEVAL PRACTICE

RP-6 If you are able, try moving your right hand in a circular motion, as if cleaning a table. Then start your right foot doing the same motion, synchronized with your hand. Now reverse the right foot's motion, but not the hand's. Finally, try moving the *left* foot opposite to the right hand.

a. Why is reversing the right foot's motion so hard?

b. Why is it easier to move the left foot opposite to the right hand?

ANSWERS IN APPENDIX E

BRAIN-MACHINE INTERFACES What might happen if researchers implant a device to detect motor cortex activity in humans? Could such devices help people with paralysis learn to command a cursor or write email or work online? Clinical trials of such *cognitive neural prosthetics* have been under way with people who have severe paralysis or have lost a limb (Andersen et al., 2010; Rajangam et al., 2016). The first patient, a 25-year-old man with paralysis, was able to mentally control a TV, draw shapes on a computer screen, and play video games—all thanks to an aspirin-sized chip with 100 microelectrodes recording activity in his motor cortex (Hochberg et al., 2006). Others with paralysis who have received implants have learned to direct robotic arms with their thoughts (Clausen et al., 2017).

And then there is Ian Burkhart, who lost the use of his arms and legs at age 19. Ohio State University brain researchers implanted recording electrodes in his motor cortex (Schwemmer et al., 2018). Using computer *machine learning,* they instructed Burkhart to stare at a screen that showed a moving hand. Next, Burkhart imagined moving his own hand. Brain signals from his motor cortex began feeding into the computer, which got the message that he wanted to move his arm and thus stimulated those muscles. The result? Burkhart, with his very own paralyzed arm, grasped a bottle, dumped out its contents, and picked up a stick. He can even play the video game *Guitar Hero.* By learning Burkhart's unique brain response patterns, the computer can predict his brain activity to help him make these movements. "It's really restored a lot the hope I have for the future to know that a device like this will be possible to use in everyday life," Burkhart says, "for me and for many other people" (Wood, 2018). (See tinyurl.com/ControlMotorCortex.)

If everything psychological is also biological—if, for example, every thought is also a neural event—microelectrodes could someday detect complex thoughts well enough to enable many people to control their environment with ever-greater precision (see **FIGURE 6.8**). Scientists have even created a prosthetic voice, which creates (mostly) understandable speech by detecting activity in the brain area that normally controls vocalizing, and converting that activity to computer speech (Anumanchipalli et al., 2019).

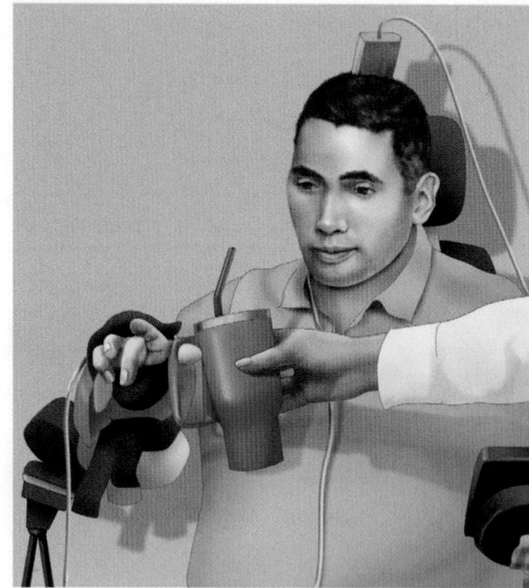

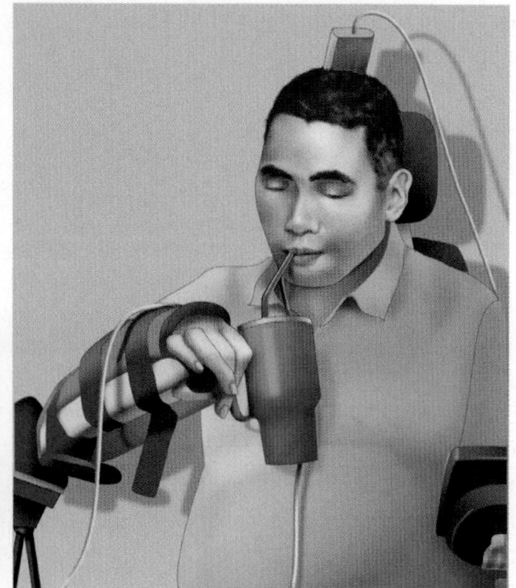

FIGURE 6.8
Brain-machine interaction Electrodes planted in the hand area of the motor cortex, and in the hand, elbow, and shoulder muscles helped a man with paralysis in all four limbs use his paralyzed arm to take a drink of coffee (Ajiboye et al., 2017). Such research advances are paving the way for restored movement in daily life, outside the controlled laboratory environment (Andersen, 2019; Andersen et al., 2010). People's ability to control a robotic arm improves when it also provides touch sensations (Flesher et al., 2021).

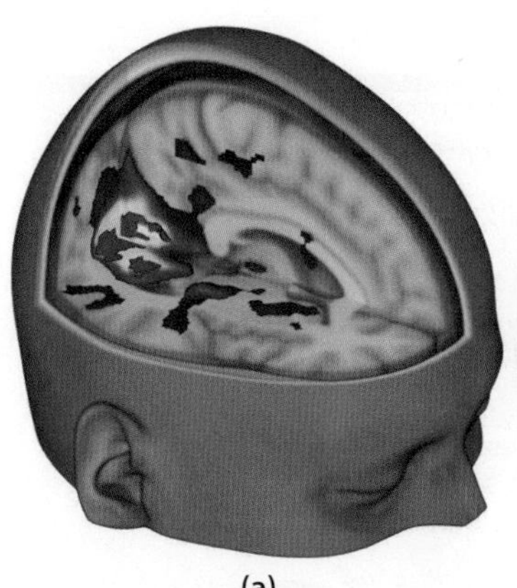
(a)

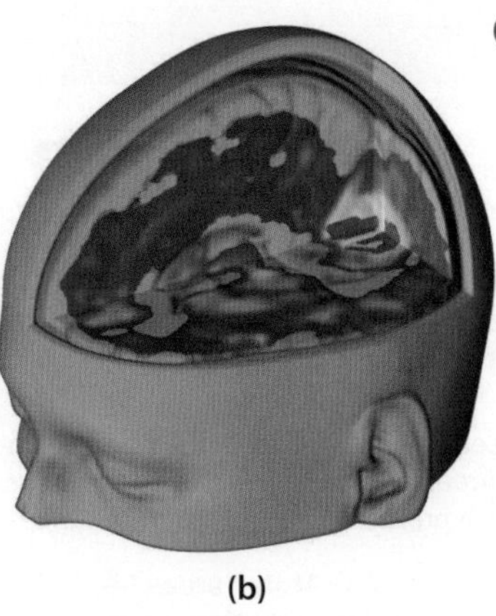
(b)

Imperial College London

FIGURE 6.9
Seeing without eyes The psychoactive drug LSD often produces vivid *hallucinations*. Why? Because it dramatically increases communication between the visual cortex (in the occipital lobe) and other brain regions. These fMRI (functional MRI) scans show (a) a research participant with closed eyes who has been given a placebo and (b) the same person under the influence of LSD. Color represents increased blood flow (Carhart-Harris et al., 2016). Other researchers have confirmed that LSD increases communication between brain regions (Preller et al., 2019; Timmermann et al., 2018).

SENSORY FUNCTIONS If the motor cortex sends messages out to the body, where does the cortex receive incoming messages? Wilder Penfield identified a cortical area—at the front of the parietal lobes, parallel to and just behind the motor cortex—that specializes in receiving information from the skin senses, such as touch and temperature, and from the movement of body parts. We now call this area the **somatosensory cortex**. Stimulate a point on the top of this band of tissue and a person may report being touched on the shoulder; stimulate some point on the side and the person may feel something on the face.

The more sensitive the body region, the larger the somatosensory cortex area devoted to it (see Figure 6.7). Your supersensitive lips project to a larger brain area than do your toes, which is one reason we kiss rather than touch toes. Rats have a large area of the brain devoted to their whisker sensations, and owls to their hearing sensations.

Scientists have identified additional areas where the cortex receives input from senses other than touch. Any visual information you are receiving now is going to the visual cortex in your occipital lobes, at the back of your brain (**FIGURES 6.9** and **6.10**). If you have normal vision, you might see flashes of light or dashes of color if stimulated in your occipital lobes. (In a sense, we *do* have eyes in the back of our head!) Having lost much of his right occipital lobe to a tumor removal, a friend of mine [DM's] was blind to the left half of his field of vision. Visual information travels from the occipital lobes to other areas that specialize in tasks such as identifying words, detecting emotions, and recognizing faces.

Any sound you now hear is processed by your auditory cortex in your temporal lobes (just above your ears; see Figure 6.10). Most of this auditory information travels a circuitous route from one ear to the auditory receiving area above your opposite ear. If stimulated in your auditory cortex, you might hear a sound. fMRI scans of people with schizophrenia reveal active auditory areas in the temporal lobes (Lennox et al., 1999). Even the phantom ringing sound experienced by people with hearing loss (tinnitus) is—if heard in one ear—associated with activity in the temporal lobe on the brain's opposite side (Muhlnickel, 1998).

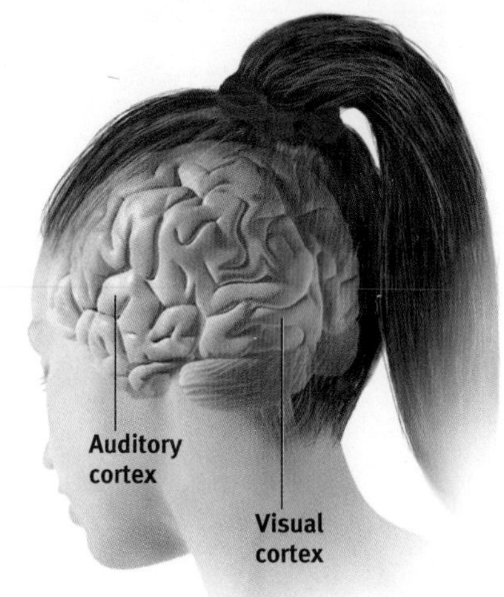
Auditory cortex
Visual cortex

FIGURE 6.10
The visual cortex and auditory cortex
The visual cortex in the occipital lobes at the rear of your brain receives input from your eyes. The auditory cortex in your temporal lobes—above your ears—receives information from your ears.

RETRIEVAL PRACTICE

RP-7 Our brain's ____________ cortex registers and processes body touch and movement sensations. The ____________ cortex controls our voluntary movements.

ANSWERS IN APPENDIX E

ASSOCIATION AREAS So far, we have pointed out small cortical areas that either receive sensory input or direct muscular output. Together, these occupy about one-fourth of the human brain's thin, wrinkled cover. What, then, goes on in the remaining vast regions of the cortex? In these **association areas**, neurons are busy with higher mental functions—many of the tasks that make us human. Electrically probing an association area won't trigger any observable response. So, unlike the somatosensory and motor areas, association area functions cannot be neatly mapped. Does this mean we don't use

somatosensory cortex a cerebral cortex area at the front of the parietal lobes that registers and processes body touch and movement sensations.

association areas areas of the cerebral cortex that are not involved in primary motor or sensory functions; rather, they are involved in higher mental functions such as learning, remembering, thinking, and speaking.

Thinking Critically About: Do We Use Only 10 Percent of Our Brain?

LOQ 6-5 Is it true that 90 percent of our brain isn't really used?

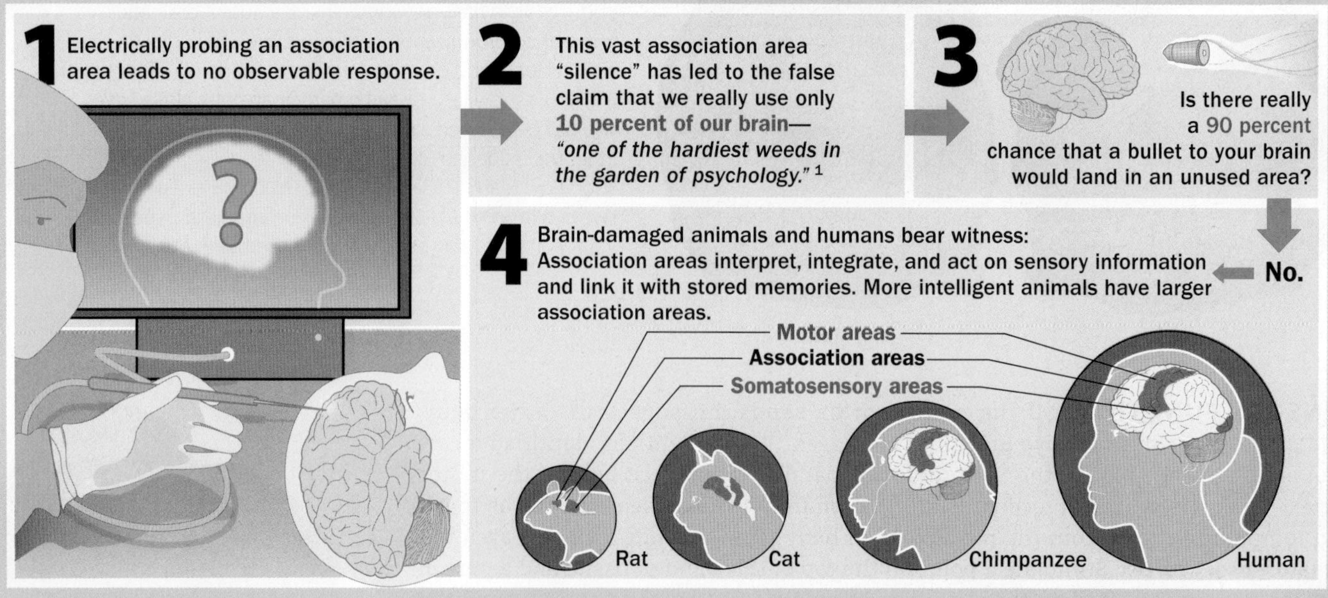

1 Electrically probing an association area leads to no observable response.
2 This vast association area "silence" has led to the false claim that we really use only 10 percent of our brain—"one of the hardiest weeds in the garden of psychology."[1]
3 Is there really a 90 percent chance that a bullet to your brain would land in an unused area?
No.
4 Brain-damaged animals and humans bear witness: Association areas interpret, integrate, and act on sensory information and link it with stored memories. More intelligent animals have larger association areas.
Motor areas
Association areas
Somatosensory areas
Rat
Cat
Chimpanzee
Human

1. McBurney, 1996, p. 44

them—or that, as some 4 in 10 people agreed in two surveys, "We use only 10 percent of our brains" (Furnham, 2018; Macdonald et al., 2017)? (See Thinking Critically About: Do We Use Only 10 Percent of Our Brain?)

Association areas are found in all four lobes. The *prefrontal cortex* in the forward part of the frontal lobes enables our forward thinking—our planning, judgment, social interactions, and processing of new memories (Panichello & Buschman, 2021). People with damage to this area may have high intelligence test scores and great cake-baking skills. Yet they would not be able to plan ahead to *begin* baking a birthday cake or remember a new recipe (MacPherson et al., 2016). And if they fail to deliver a promised birthday cake, they may feel no regret (Bault et al., 2019).

Frontal lobe damage also can alter personality and remove a person's inhibitions. Consider the classic case of railroad worker Phineas Gage. One afternoon in 1848, Gage, then 25 years old, was using a tamping iron to pack gunpowder into a rock. A spark ignited the gunpowder, shooting the rod up through his left cheek and out the top of his skull, leaving his frontal lobes damaged (**FIGURE 6.11**). To everyone's amazement, Gage was immediately able to sit up and speak, and after the wound healed, he returned to work. But the blast had damaged connections between his frontal lobes and brain regions that control emotion and decision making (Thiebaut de Schotten et al., 2015; Van Horn et al., 2012). How did this damage affect Gage's personality? The usually friendly, soft-spoken man was now irritable, profane, and dishonest. Gage, said his friends, was "no longer Gage." Most of his mental abilities and memories were intact, but for the next few years his personality was not. (Gage later lost his railroad job, but over time he adapted to his disability and found work as a stagecoach driver [Macmillan & Lena, 2010].)

FIGURE 6.11
A blast from the past (a) Phineas Gage's skull was kept as a medical record. Using measurements and modern neuroimaging techniques, researchers have reconstructed the probable path of the rod through Gage's brain (Van Horn et al., 2012). (b) This photo shows Gage after his accident. (The image has been reversed to show Gage's features correctly. Early photos, including this one, were actually mirror images.)

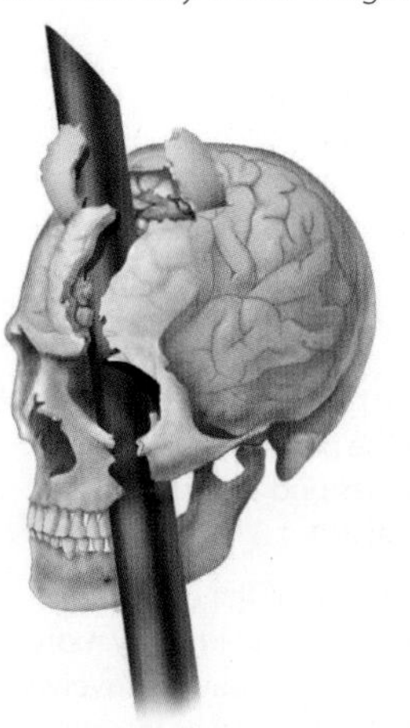

(a) (b)

Warren Anatomical Museum in the Francis A. Countway Library of Medicine. Gift of Jack and Beverly Wilgus.

Studies of others with damaged frontal lobes have revealed similar impairments. Not only do they become less inhibited (without the frontal lobe brakes on their impulses), but their moral judgments also seem unrestrained. Cecil Clayton lost 20 percent of his left frontal lobe in a 1972 sawmill accident. Thereafter, his intelligence test score dropped to an elementary school level and he displayed increased impulsivity. In 1996, he fatally shot a deputy sheriff. In 2015, when he was 74, the State of Missouri executed him (Williams, 2015).

The frontal lobes help steer us toward kindness and away from violence (Achterberg et al., 2020; Lieberman et al., 2019). With their frontal lobes ruptured, people's moral compass seems separated from their actions. They know right from wrong but often don't care.

Association areas also perform other mental functions. The parietal lobes, parts of which were large and unusually shaped in Einstein's normal-weight brain, enable mathematical and spatial reasoning (Amalric & Dehaene, 2019; Wilkey et al., 2018). Stimulation of one parietal lobe area in brain-surgery patients produced a feeling of wanting to move an upper limb, the lips, or the tongue without any actual movement. With increased stimulation, patients falsely believed they *had* moved. Curiously, when surgeons stimulated a different association area near the motor cortex in the frontal lobes, the patients did move but had no awareness of doing so (Desmurget et al., 2009). These head-scratching findings suggest that our perception of moving flows not from the movement itself, but rather from our intention and the results we expected.

"We held Einstein's brain in our hands and realized that this is the organ that was responsible for changing our perceptions of the universe . . . we were in awe."
—Neuroscientist Sandra Witelson (2011)

On the underside of the right temporal lobe, another association area enables us to instantly recognize faces (Retter et al., 2020). If a stroke or head injury destroyed this area of your brain, you would still be able to describe facial features and to recognize someone's feminine or masculine features and approximate age, yet be strangely unable to identify the person as, say, Ariana Grande, or even your grandmother.

Nevertheless, to reemphasize, we should be wary of using pictures of brain "hot spots" to create a new phrenology that locates complex functions in precise brain areas (Beck, 2010; Shimamura, 2010; Uttal, 2001). During a complex task, a brain scan shows many islands of brain activity working together—some running automatically in the background, and others under conscious control (Chein & Schneider, 2012). Your memory, language, attention, and social skills result from *functional connectivity*—communication among distinct brain areas and neural networks (Bassett et al., 2018; Silston et al., 2018). What happens when brain areas struggle to communicate with each other? People are at increased risk for mental disorders (J. Baker et al., 2019; Zhang et al., 2019).

The point to remember: Our mental experiences—and our psychological health—rely on coordinated brain activity.

RETRIEVAL PRACTICE

RP-8 Why are association areas important?

ANSWERS IN APPENDIX E

MODULE 6 REVIEW Module 6: Brain Regions and Structures

LEARNING OBJECTIVES

Test Yourself Answer these repeated Learning Objective Questions on your own (before "showing" the answers here, or checking the answers in Appendix D) to improve your retention of the concepts (McDaniel et al., 2009, 2015).

LOQ 6-1 What are the *hindbrain, midbrain,* and *forebrain*?

LOQ 6-2 What structures make up the brainstem, and what are the functions of the brainstem, thalamus, reticular formation, and cerebellum?

LOQ 6-3 What are the limbic system's structures and functions?

LOQ 6-4 What four lobes make up the cerebral cortex, and what are the functions of the motor cortex, somatosensory cortex, and association areas?

LOQ 6-5 Is it true that 90 percent of our brain isn't really used?

TERMS AND CONCEPTS TO REMEMBER

Test Yourself Write down the definition in your own words, then check your answer.

MODULE TEST

Test Yourself Answer the following questions on your own first, then "show" the answers here, or check your answers in Appendix E.

1. The part of the brainstem that controls heartbeat and breathing is the
   - a. cerebellum.
   - b. medulla.
   - c. cortex.
   - d. thalamus.
2. The thalamus functions as a
   - a. memory bank.
   - b. balance center.
   - c. breathing regulator.
   - d. sensory control center.
3. The lower brain structure that governs arousal is the
   - a. spinal cord.
   - b. cerebellum.
   - c. reticular formation.
   - d. medulla.
4. The part of the brain that coordinates voluntary movement and enables nonverbal learning and memory is the ________________.
5. Two parts of the limbic system are the amygdala and the
   - a. cerebral hemispheres.
   - b. hippocampus.
   - c. thalamus.
   - d. cerebellum.
6. A cat's ferocious response to electrical brain stimulation would lead you to suppose the electrode had touched the ________________.
7. The neural structure that most directly regulates eating, drinking, and body temperature is the
   - a. endocrine system.
   - b. hypothalamus.
   - c. hippocampus.
   - d. amygdala.
8. The initial reward center discovered by Olds and Milner was located in the ________________.
9. If a neurosurgeon stimulated your right motor cortex, you would most likely
   - a. see light.
   - b. hear a sound.
   - c. feel a touch on the right arm.
   - d. move your left leg.
10. How do different neural networks communicate with one another to let you respond when a friend greets you at a party?
11. Which of the following body regions has the greatest representation in the somatosensory cortex?
    - a. Upper arm
    - b. Toes
    - c. Lips
    - d. All regions are equally represented.
12. Judging and planning are enabled by the ________________ lobes.
13. The "uncommitted" areas that make up about three-fourths of the cerebral cortex are called ________________ ________________.

MODULE 7 Damage Responses and Brain Hemispheres

Earlier, we learned about *neuroplasticity*—how our brain adapts to new situations. What happens when we experience mishaps, big and little? Let's explore the brain's ability to modify itself after damage.

Responses to Damage

LOQ 7-1 To what extent can a damaged brain reorganize itself, and what is *neurogenesis*?

Most brain-damage effects can be traced to two hard facts: (1) Severed brain and spinal cord neurons, unlike cut skin, usually do not regenerate. (If your spinal cord were severed, you would probably be permanently paralyzed.) And (2) some brain functions seem preassigned to specific areas. One newborn who experienced damage to temporal lobe facial recognition areas was never able to recognize faces (Farah et al., 2000). But there is good news: Some neural tissue can *reorganize* in response to damage.

Neuroplasticity may also occur after serious damage, especially in young children whose undamaged hemisphere develops extra connections (Lindenberger & Lövdén,

2019; see also **FIGURE 7.1**). *Constraint-induced therapy* aims to rewire brains and improve the dexterity of a brain-damaged child or even an adult stroke victim (Taub, 2004). By restraining a fully functioning limb, therapists force patients to use the "bad" hand or leg, gradually reprogramming the brain. One stroke victim, a surgeon in his fifties, was put to work cleaning tables, with his good arm and hand restrained. Slowly, the bad arm recovered its skills. As damaged-brain functions migrated to other brain regions, he gradually learned to write again and even to play tennis (Doidge, 2007).

The brain's plasticity is good news for those who are blind or deaf. Blindness or deafness makes unused brain areas available for other uses, such as sound and smell (Amedi et al., 2005; Bauer et al., 2017). If a blind person uses one finger to read Braille, the brain area dedicated to that finger expands as the sense of touch invades the visual cortex that typically helps people see (Barinaga, 1992; Sadato et al., 1996). In sighted people, Braille-reading training produces similar brain changes (Debowska et al., 2016). Neuroplasticity also helps explain why blind people display superior ability to locate sounds, and why deaf people who learned sign language before another language may have enhanced peripheral and motion-detection vision (Battal et al., 2020; Brooks et al., 2020). In deaf people whose native language is sign, the temporal lobe area typically dedicated to hearing waits in vain for stimulation. Finally, it looks for other signals to process, such as those from the visual system used to see and interpret signs.

Joe McNally/Hulton Archive/Getty Images

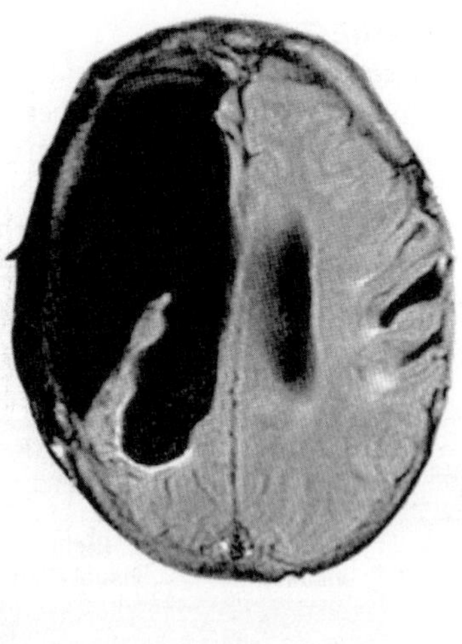

Living Art Enterprises, LLC/Science Source

FIGURE 7.1
Half a brain At age 3, Jodie Miller started having life-threatening seizures. To save her life, doctors removed most of her right hemisphere (see MRI of hemispherectomy). Jodie's remaining hemisphere compensated by putting other areas to work, enabling this dance recital at age 6. Today, even without a left hemisphere, Jodie is, so to speak, all-right: She lives a meaningful life, is happily married, and speaks publicly about the power of neuroplasticity. "I have half a brain," she says. "When people meet me, they have no idea" (BBC, 2017).

Similar reassignment may occur when disease or damage frees up other brain areas typically dedicated to specific functions. If a slow-growing left hemisphere tumor disrupts language (which resides mostly in the left hemisphere), the right hemisphere may compensate (Thiel et al., 2006). When people who are born without hands use their feet to perform everyday tasks, their somatosensory cortex for the hand area becomes active—even though they have never had hands (Striem-Amit et al., 2018). So what do you suppose was the sexual intercourse experience of one patient whose lower leg had been amputated? "I actually experience my orgasm in my [phantom] foot. And there it's much bigger than it used to be because it's no longer just confined to my genitals" (Ramachandran & Blakeslee, 1998, p. 36). Note that in Figure 6.8 the toes region is adjacent to the genitals.

Although the brain often attempts self-repair by reorganizing existing tissue, researchers are debating whether it can also mend itself through **neurogenesis**—producing new neurons that may mature more and grow larger than the neurons we are born with (Cole et al., 2020). Neurogenesis happens in part thanks to *stem cells*—special cells that can develop into different types of cells, including brain cells. Researchers have found baby neurons deep in the brain of adult mice, birds, monkeys, and humans (He & Jin, 2016; Jessberger et al., 2008). These neurons may then form connections with neighboring neurons (Gould, 2007; Luna et al., 2019). Neurogenesis varies among individuals, offering another example of how we experience a common process in our own unique way (Kempermann, 2018).

Courtesy of Dr. Danielle Bassett

Physics of the mind Physicist and neuroscientist Danielle Bassett, whose work crosses disciplines, was the youngest person to receive a MacArthur "Genius Grant" in 2014. She applies concepts from physics and mathematics to explain the brain's neural network connections.

The Divided Brain

LOQ 7-2 What do split brains reveal about the functions of our two brain hemispheres?

Our brain's look-alike left and right hemispheres serve differing functions. This *lateralization* is apparent after brain damage. Research spanning more than a century has

neurogenesis the formation of new neurons.

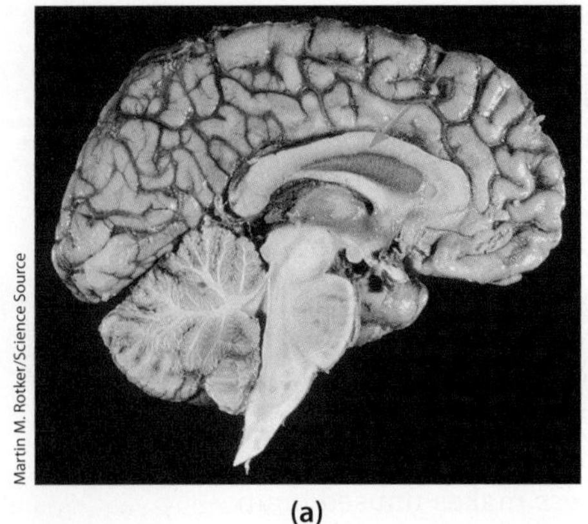
Martin M. Rotker/Science Source

(a)

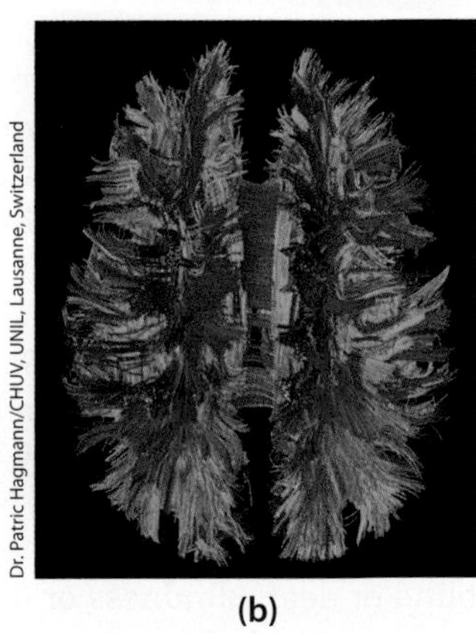
Dr. Patric Hagmann/CHUV, UNIL, Lausanne, Switzerland

(b)

FIGURE 7.2
The corpus callosum This large band of neural fibers connects the two brain hemispheres. (a) To photograph this half brain, a surgeon separated the hemispheres by cutting through the corpus callosum (see blue arrow) and lower brain regions. (b) This high-resolution diffusion spectrum image, showing a top-facing brain from above, reveals brain neural networks within the two hemispheres, and the corpus callosum neural bridge between them.

shown that left hemisphere accidents, strokes, and tumors can impair reading, writing, speaking, arithmetic reasoning, and understanding. Similar right hemisphere damage has less visibly dramatic effects. Does this mean that the right hemisphere is just along for the ride? Many believed this was the case until the 1960s, when a fascinating chapter in psychology's history began to unfold: Researchers found that the "minor" right hemisphere was not so limited after all.

Splitting the Brain

In the early 1960s, two neurosurgeons speculated that major epileptic seizures were caused by an amplification of abnormal brain activity bouncing back and forth between the two cerebral hemispheres, which work together as a whole system (Bogen & Vogel, 1962). They wondered if they could end this biological tennis match by severing the **corpus callosum**, the wide band of axon fibers connecting the two hemispheres and carrying messages between them (see **FIGURE 7.2**). The neurosurgeons knew that psychologists Roger Sperry, Ronald Myers, and Michael Gazzaniga had divided cats' and monkeys' brains in this manner, with no serious ill effects.

So the surgeons operated. The result? The seizures all but disappeared. The patients with these **split brains** were surprisingly healthy, their personality and intellect hardly affected. Waking from surgery, one even joked that he had a "splitting headache" (Gazzaniga, 1967). By sharing their experiences, these patients have greatly expanded our understanding of interactions between the intact brain's two hemispheres.

To appreciate these findings, we need to focus for a minute on the peculiar nature of our visual wiring, illustrated in **FIGURE 7.3**. Note that each eye receives sensory information from the entire visual field. But in each eye, information from the left half of your field of vision goes to your right hemisphere, and information from the right half of your visual field goes to your left hemisphere, which usually controls speech. Information received by either hemisphere is quickly transmitted to the other across the corpus callosum. In a person with a severed corpus callosum, this information-sharing does not take place.

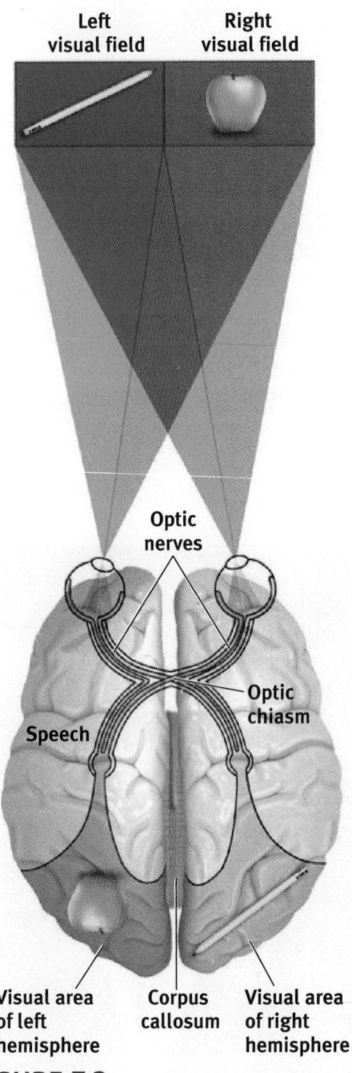
Left visual field
Right visual field
Optic nerves
Optic chiasm
Speech
Visual area of left hemisphere
Corpus callosum
Visual area of right hemisphere

FIGURE 7.3
The information highway from eye to brain

Knowing these facts, Sperry and Gazzaniga could send information to a patient's left or right hemisphere. As the person stared at a spot, they flashed a stimulus to its right or left. They could do this with you, too, but in your intact brain, the hemisphere receiving the information would instantly pass the news to the other side. Because the split-brain surgery had cut the communication lines between the hemispheres, the researchers could, with these patients, quiz each hemisphere separately.

In an early experiment, Gazzaniga (1967) asked split-brain patients to stare at a dot as he flashed HE•ART on a screen (**FIGURE 7.4**). Thus, HE appeared in their left visual field (which transmits to the right hemisphere) and ART in the right field (which transmits to the left hemisphere). When he then asked them to *say* what they had seen, the patients reported that they had seen ART. But when asked to *point* with their left hand to what they had seen, they were startled when their hand (controlled by the right hemisphere) pointed to HE. Given an opportunity to express itself, each hemisphere indicated what it had seen. The right hemisphere (controlling the left hand) intuitively knew what it could not verbally report.

corpus callosum [KOR-pus kah-LOW-sum] the large band of neural fibers connecting the two brain hemispheres and carrying messages between them.

split brain a condition resulting from surgery that separates the brain's two hemispheres by cutting the fibers (mainly those of the corpus callosum) connecting them.

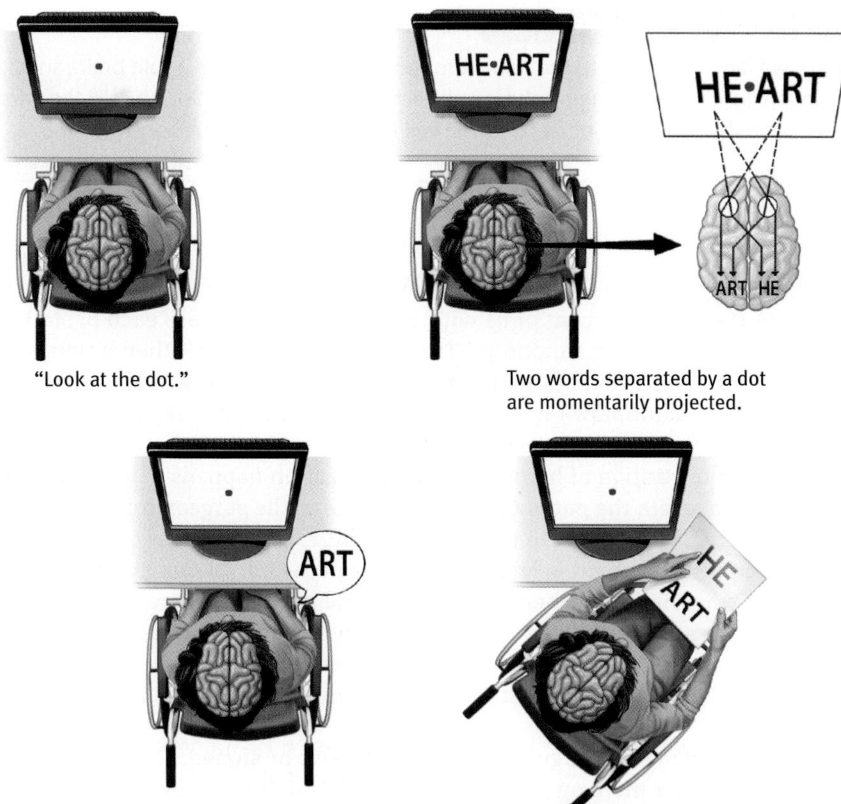
HE•ART
HE•ART
ART HE
"Look at the dot."
Two words separated by a dot are momentarily projected.
ART
HE
ART
"What word did you see?"
or
"Point with your left hand to the word you saw."

FIGURE 7.4
One skull, two minds When an experimenter flashes HE•ART across the visual field, a woman with a split brain verbally reports seeing the word transmitted to her left hemisphere. However, if asked to indicate with her left hand what she saw, she points to the word transmitted to her right hemisphere (Gazzaniga, 1983).

When a picture of a spoon was flashed to their right hemisphere, the patients could not *say* what they had viewed. But when asked to *identify* what they had viewed by feeling an assortment of hidden objects with their left hand, they readily selected the spoon. If the experimenter said, "Correct!" the patient might reply, "What? Correct? How could I possibly pick out the correct object when I don't know what I saw?" It is, of course, the left hemisphere doing the talking here, bewildered by what the nonverbal right hemisphere knows.

A few people who have had split-brain surgery have been for a time bothered by the unruly independence of their left hand. It seemed the left hand truly didn't know what the right hand was doing. The left hand might unbutton a shirt while the right hand buttoned it, or put grocery store items back on the shelf after the right hand put them in the cart. It was as if each hemisphere was thinking, "I've half a mind to wear my green (blue) shirt today." Indeed, said Sperry (1964), split-brain surgery leaves people "with two separate minds." With a split brain, both hemispheres can comprehend and follow an instruction to copy—*simultaneously*—different figures with the left and right hands (Franz et al., 2000; see also **FIGURE 7.5**). Today's researchers believe that a split-brain patient's mind resembles a river that has branched into separate streams, each unaware of the other (Pinto et al., 2017). (Reading these reports, can you imagine a patient enjoying a solitary game of "rock, paper, scissors"—left versus right hand?)

FIGURE 7.5
Try this! People who have had split-brain surgery can simultaneously draw two different shapes.

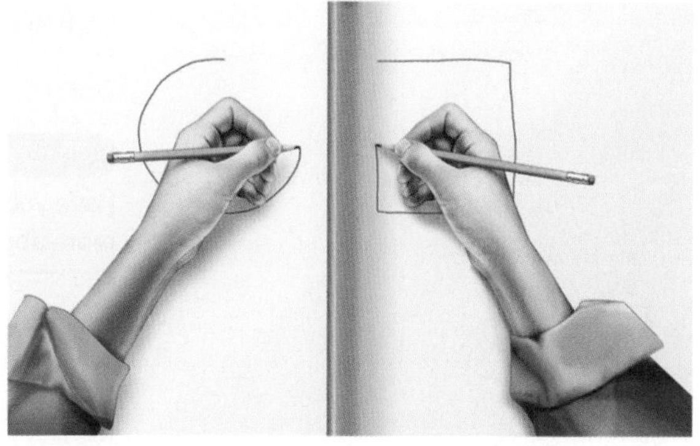

When the "two minds" are at odds, the left hemisphere does mental gymnastics to rationalize reactions it does not understand. If a patient follows an order ("Walk") sent to the right hemisphere, a strange thing happens. The left hemisphere, unaware of the order, doesn't know why the patient begins walking. But if asked, the patient doesn't reply, "I don't know." Instead, the left hemisphere improvises—"I'm going into the house to get a Coke." Gazzaniga (2006), who described these patients as "the most fascinating people on earth," realized that the conscious left hemisphere resembles an interpreter that instantly constructs explanations. The brain, he concluded, often runs on autopilot; it acts first and then explains itself.

RETRIEVAL PRACTICE

RP-1 (a) If we flash a red light to the right hemisphere of a person with a split brain, and flash a green light to the left hemisphere, will each observe its own color? (b) Will the person be aware that the colors differ? (c) What will the person verbally report seeing?

ANSWERS IN APPENDIX E

Right-Left Differences in the Intact Brain

So, what about the 99.99+ percent of us with undivided brains? Does each of *our* hemispheres also perform distinct functions? The short answer is *Yes*. When a person performs a *perceptual* task, a brain scan often reveals increased activity (brain waves, blood flow, and glucose consumption) in the *right* hemisphere. When the person speaks or does a math calculation, activity usually increases in the *left* hemisphere.

A dramatic demonstration of hemispheric specialization happens before some types of brain surgery. To locate the patient's language centers, the surgeon injects a sedative into the neck artery feeding blood to the left hemisphere, which usually controls speech. Before the injection, the patient is lying down, arms in the air, chatting with the doctor. Can you predict what happens when the drug puts the left hemisphere to sleep? Within seconds, the person's right arm falls limp. If the left hemisphere is controlling language, the patient will be speechless until the drug wears off. If the drug is injected into the artery to the right hemisphere, the left arm will fall limp, but the person will still be able to speak.

To the brain, language is language, whether spoken or signed. (The Thinking and Language modules offer more on how and where the brain processes language.) Just as hearing people usually use the left hemisphere to process spoken language, deaf people use the left hemisphere to process sign language (Corina et al., 1992; Hickok et al., 2001). Thus, a left hemisphere stroke disrupts a deaf person's signing, much as it would disrupt a hearing person's speaking (Corina, 1998).

Although the left hemisphere is skilled at making quick, literal interpretations of language, the right hemisphere

- *excels in making inferences* (Beeman & Chiarello, 1998; Bowden & Beeman, 1998; Mason & Just, 2004). When given an insight-like problem—"What word goes with *boot, summer,* and *ground?*"—the right hemisphere more quickly comes to a reasoned conclusion and recognizes the solution: *camp*. As one patient explained after a right hemisphere stroke, "I understand words, but I'm missing the subtleties."
- *helps us modulate our speech* to make meaning clear—as when we say, "Let's eat, Grandpa!" instead of "Let's eat Grandpa!" (Heller, 1990).
- *helps orchestrate our self-awareness*. People who have partial paralysis will sometimes stubbornly deny their impairment—constantly claiming they can move a paralyzed limb—if the damage is to the right hemisphere (Berti et al., 2005).

Simply looking at the two hemispheres, so alike to the naked eye, who would suppose they each contribute uniquely to the harmony of the whole? Yet a variety of observations—of people with split brains, of people with intact brains, and even of other species' brains—converge beautifully, leaving little doubt that we have unified brains with specialized parts (Hopkins & Cantalupo, 2008; MacNeilage et al., 2009).

ASK YOURSELF

Have you ever been asked if you are "left-brained" or "right-brained"? Now that you understand more about hemispheric functioning, how might you respond to this popular misconception?

7 REVIEW Module 7: Damage Responses and Brain Hemispheres

LEARNING OBJECTIVES

Test Yourself Answer these repeated Learning Objective Questions on your own (before "showing" the answers, or checking the answers in Appendix D) to improve your retention of the concepts (McDaniel et al., 2009, 2015).

LOQ 7-1 To what extent can a damaged brain reorganize itself, and what is *neurogenesis*?

LOQ 7-2 What do split brains reveal about the functions of our two brain hemispheres?

TERMS AND CONCEPTS TO REMEMBER

Test Yourself Write down the definition in your own words, then check your answer.

neurogenesis, p. 83

corpus callosum [KOR-pus kah-LOW-sum], p. 84

split brain, p. 84

MODULE TEST

Test Yourself Answer the following questions on your own first, then "show" the answers, or check your answers in Appendix E.

1. The flexible brain's ability to respond to damage is especially evident in the brains of
   a. split-brain patients.
   b. young adults.
   c. young children.
   d. right-handed people.

2. An experimenter flashes the word HER•ON across the visual field of a man whose corpus callosum has been severed. HER is transmitted to his right hemisphere and ON to his left hemisphere. When asked to indicate what he saw, the man says he saw ____________, but his left hand points to ____________.

3. Studies of people with split brains and brain scans of those with undivided brains indicate that the left hemisphere excels in
   a. processing language.
   b. visual perceptions.
   c. making inferences.
   d. neurogenesis.

4. Damage to the brain's right hemisphere is most likely to reduce a person's ability to
   a. recite the alphabet rapidly.
   b. make inferences.
   c. understand verbal instructions.
   d. solve arithmetic problems.

CHAPTER

3

wavebreakmedia/Shutterstock

Consciousness and the Two-Track Mind (Modules 8–10)

Consciousness is a funny thing. It offers us weird experiences, as when entering sleep or leaving a dream. And sometimes it leaves us wondering who is really in control. After zoning me [DM] out with nitrous oxide, my dentist tells me to turn my head to the left. My conscious mind resists: "No way," I silently say. "You can't boss me around!" Whereupon my robotic head, ignoring my conscious mind, turns obligingly under the dentist's control.

Playing basketball, I have sometimes been mildly irritated as my body passes the ball while my conscious mind says, "No, stop! Sarah is going to intercept!" Alas, my body completes the pass. Other times, as psychologist Daniel Wegner (2002) noted in *The Illusion of Conscious Will*, people believe their conscious mind is controlling their actions when it isn't. In one experiment, two people jointly controlled a computer mouse. Even when their partner (who was actually the experimenter's accomplice) caused the mouse to stop on a predetermined square, the participants perceived that *they* had caused it to stop there.

Then there are those times when consciousness seems to split. Sometimes, my [ND's] mind wanders while singing portions of the *Trolls World Tour* soundtrack daily with my young children. So, if a friend interrupts you mid-text to ask what you're doing for lunch, it's not a problem. Your thumbs complete their keyboard dance as you suggest getting tacos.

What do such experiences tell us? Does the mind's wandering while singing or texting reveal a split in consciousness (Module 8)? How do our states of consciousness play out in our sleep and dreams (Module 9)? And was that drug-induced dental episode akin to people's experiences with other mood- and perception-altering *psychoactive drugs* (Module 10)? Before considering these questions and more, let's start with a fundamental question: What is *consciousness?*

MODULE 8 Basic Consciousness Concepts

Every science has concepts so fundamental they are nearly impossible to define. Biologists agree on what is alive but not on precisely what *life* is. In physics, *matter* and *energy* elude simple definition. To psychologists, *consciousness* is similarly a fundamental yet slippery concept.

THE MIND-BODY PROBLEM
Get up.
No.
Roz Chast/Cartoon Stock

Defining Consciousness

LEARNING OBJECTIVE QUESTION LOQ 8-1 What is the place of *consciousness* in psychology's history?

At its beginning, *psychology* was "the description and explanation of states of consciousness" (Ladd, 1887). But during the first half of the twentieth century, the difficulty of scientifically studying consciousness led many psychologists—including those in the emerging school of *behaviorism* (Learning modules)—to turn to direct observations of behavior. By 1960, psychology had nearly lost consciousness, defining itself as "the science of behavior." Like a car's speedometer, consciousness "just reflects what's happening" (Seligman, 1991, p. 24).

But in the 1960s, mental concepts reemerged. Neuroscience advances linked brain activity to sleeping, dreaming, and other mental states. Researchers began studying consciousness altered by drugs, hypnosis, and meditation. (More on meditation in the Emotions, Stress, and Health modules.) Psychologists of all persuasions were affirming the importance of *cognition*, or mental processes. Psychology was regaining consciousness.

Today, consciousness is a thriving area of study (Michel et al., 2019). By **consciousness**, most psychologists mean our subjective awareness of ourselves and our environment (Feinberg & Mallatt, 2016).

- Conscious awareness helps us make sense of our life, including our sensations, emotions, and choices (Weisman et al., 2017). It allows us to set and achieve goals as we reflect on our past, adapt to our present, and plan for our future. Most conscious thoughts focus on the present and the future (Baumeister et al., 2020).
- When learning a behavior, conscious awareness focuses our attention (Logan et al., 2018). Over time, our mind tends to run on autopilot (Logan, 2018; Rand et al., 2017). When learning to drive, we focus on the car and the traffic. With practice, driving becomes semiautomatic. We may find our mind wandering on a long stretch of highway—only to have our attention jolted back to the car and the traffic when someone cuts in front of us and we need to react.
- Over time, we flit between different *states of consciousness,* including typical waking awareness and various altered states (**FIGURE 8.1**).

Hypnosis

Through **hypnosis**, we may experience an altered state of consciousness involving changes in perceptions, feelings, thoughts, or behaviors. Researchers and health care

consciousness our subjective awareness of ourselves and our environment.

hypnosis a social interaction in which one person (the hypnotist) suggests to another (the subject) that certain perceptions, feelings, thoughts, or behaviors will spontaneously occur.

FIGURE 8.1
Altered states of consciousness In addition to normal, waking awareness, consciousness comes to us in altered states, including daydreaming, sleeping, drug-induced hallucinating, and meditating.

Some states occur spontaneously	Daydreaming and drowsiness	Flow	Dreaming
Some are physiologically induced	Hallucinations	Orgasm	Food or oxygen starvation
Some are psychologically induced	Sensory deprivation	Hypnosis	Meditation

INSADCO Photography/Alamy Stock Photo

providers have for many years used hypnosis to lessen pain related to medical procedures, headaches, burn injuries, heart disease, and dental issues (Milling et al., 2002; Montgomery et al., 2000; Patterson & Jensen, 2003). Hypnosis can also reduce emotional distress, unpleasant thinking, and the pain of social rejection (Rainville et al., 1997; Raz et al., 2005; Schnur et al., 2008). For people who are obese, hypnosis can aid weight loss, especially when used with *psychotherapy* (Milling et al., 2018). (More on hypnosis in the Sensation and Perception modules.)

Cognitive Neuroscience

How does the brain make the mind? Researchers call this the "hard problem": How do brain cells jabbering to one another create our awareness of the taste of toast, the idea of infinity, the feeling of fright? The question of how consciousness arises from the material brain is one of life's deepest mysteries. Even with all the world's technology, we still don't have a clue *how* to make a conscious robot. Such questions are at the heart of **cognitive neuroscience**—the interdisciplinary study of the brain activity linked with our mental processes.

If you just *think* about kicking a soccer ball, an fMRI scan could detect increased blood flow to the brain region that plans such action. In one study, researchers asked skilled soccer players to imagine they were making either creative moves (complex bicycle kicks) or ordinary moves (simply kicking the ball from foot to foot). Scans showed that thinking of creative moves produced the most coordinated brain activity across different brain regions (Fink et al., 2019).

If brain activity can reveal conscious thinking, could brain scans allow us to discern mental activity in unresponsive patients? *Yes.* A stunning demonstration of consciousness appeared in brain scans of a noncommunicative patient—a 23-year-old woman who had been in a car accident and showed no outward signs of conscious awareness (Owen, 2017a; Owen et al., 2006). When researchers asked her to *imagine* playing tennis, fMRI scans revealed activity in a brain area that controls arm and leg movements (**FIGURE 8.2**). Even in a motionless, noncommunicative body, researchers concluded, the brain—and the mind—may still be active. Follow-up studies of brain activity in dozens of unresponsive patients suggest that 15 to 30 percent may be experiencing meaningful conscious awareness (Claassen et al., 2019; Owen, 2017b).

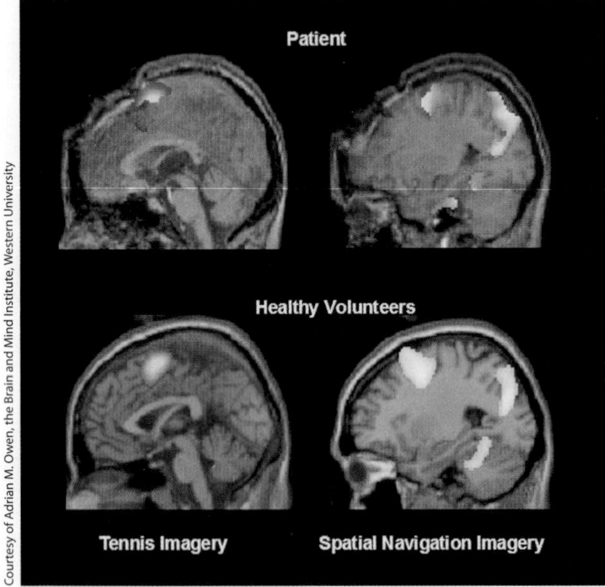
Patient
Healthy Volunteers
Tennis Imagery
Spatial Navigation Imagery

Courtesy of Adrian M. Owen, the Brain and Mind Institute, Western University

FIGURE 8.2
Evidence of awareness When a noncommunicative patient was asked to imagine playing tennis or walking, her brain (top) exhibited activity similar to a healthy person's brain (bottom). Such fMRI scans enable a "conversation" with some unresponsive patients, by instructing them, for example, to answer *yes* to a question by imagining playing tennis (top and bottom left), and *no* by imagining walking (top and bottom right).

cognitive neuroscience the interdisciplinary study of the brain activity linked with cognition (thinking, knowing, remembering, and communicating).

Many cognitive neuroscientists are exploring and mapping the conscious functions of the cortex. Based on your cortical activation patterns, they can now, in limited ways, read your mind (Bor, 2010). They could, for example, tell which of 10 similar objects (hammer, drill, and so forth) you were viewing (Shinkareva et al., 2008).

Conscious experience arises from synchronized activity across the brain (Mashour, 2018; Vaz et al., 2019). If a stimulus activates enough cortex-wide coordinated neural activity—as strong signals in one brain area trigger activity elsewhere—it crosses a threshold for consciousness. A weaker stimulus—perhaps a word flashed too briefly to be consciously perceived—may trigger only visual cortex activity that quickly fades.

A stronger visual stimulus will engage other brain areas, such as those involved with language, attention, and memory. Such reverberating activity detected by brain scans is a telltale sign of conscious awareness (Boly et al., 2011; Silverstein et al., 2015). Coordinated activity across brain areas can therefore provide another indication of awareness in unresponsive patients (Demertzi et al., 2019). How the synchronized activity produces awareness remains a mystery. One theory proposes that consciousness occurs when incoming information activates the cerebral "workspace," a super network that distributes information to and from other brain networks (Baars, 2002; Dehaene & Changeux, 2011). Still, one wonders: How does matter make mind?

RETRIEVAL PRACTICE

RP-1 Those working in the interdisciplinary field called ____________ ____________ study the brain activity associated with the mental processes of thinking, knowing, remembering, and communicating.

ANSWERS IN APPENDIX E

Selective Attention

LOQ 8-2 How does *selective attention* direct our perceptions?

Through **selective attention**, our awareness focuses, like a flashlight beam, on a minute aspect of all that we experience. We may think we can fully attend to a conversation or a class lecture while checking and returning text messages. Actually, our consciousness focuses on but one thing at a time.

By one estimate, our five senses take in 11,000,000 bits of information per second, of which we consciously process about 40 (Wilson, 2002). Yet our mind's unconscious track intuitively makes great use of the other 10,999,960 bits.

What captures our limited attention? Things we deem important. A classic example of selective attention is the *cocktail party effect*—your ability to attend to only one voice within a sea of many as you chat with a party guest. But what happens when another voice speaks your name? Your cognitive radar, operating on your mind's other track, instantly brings that unattended voice into consciousness. Even cats selectively respond to their own names (Saito et al., 2019). This effect might have prevented an embarrassing and dangerous situation in 2009, when two Northwest Airlines pilots "lost track of time." Focused on their laptops and in conversation, they ignored alarmed air traffic controllers' attempts to reach them and overflew their Minneapolis destination by 150 miles. If only the controllers had known and spoken the pilots' names.

Selective Attention and Accidents

Have you, like 60 percent of U.S. drivers, read or sent a text message or used your phone's GPS while driving in the last month (Gliklich et al., 2016)? If so, you may have thought—wrongly—that you could simultaneously attend to the road. Such digital distraction can have tragic consequences, as our selective attention shifts more than we realize (Stavrinos et al., 2017). One study left people in a room for 28 minutes with both internet and television access. On average, they guessed their attention switched 15 times. But they were not even close. Eye-tracking revealed eight times that many attentional switches—120 on average (Brasel & Gips, 2011).

Natalie Dupille/Cartoon Stock

"Are you O.K.? You're barely paying attention to your book, phone, show, laptop, and the crossword you started ten minutes ago."

Rapid toggling between activities is today's great enemy of sustained, focused attention. The more we mindlessly check our phone, the more we're distracted from our everyday tasks (Marty-Dugas et al., 2018). When we switch attentional gears, and especially when we shift to and from complex tasks such as noticing and avoiding cars around us, we pay a toll—a slight and sometimes fatal delay in coping (Rubenstein et al., 2001). When a driver attends to a conversation, activity in brain areas vital to driving decreases an average of 37 percent (Just et al., 2008).

Just how dangerous is distracted driving? Each day, distracted driving kills about 9 Americans (CDC, 2018). One video cam study of teen drivers found that driver distraction from passengers or phones occurred right before 58 percent of their crashes (AAA, 2015).

selective attention focusing conscious awareness on a particular stimulus.

THIS LANE FOR
CALLING AND TEXTING
WHILE DRIVING
ONLY

Talking with passengers makes the risk of an accident 1.6 times higher than normal. Using a phone (even hands-free) makes the risk 4 times higher than normal—equal to the risk of drunk driving (McEvoy et al., 2005, 2007). And while talking is distracting, texting wins the danger game. One 18-month video cam study tracked the driving habits of long-haul truckers. When they were texting, their risk of a collision increased 23 times (Olson et al., 2009)!

Inattentional Blindness

At the level of conscious awareness, we are "blind" to all but a tiny sliver of visual stimuli. Ulric Neisser (1979) and Robert Becklen and Daniel Cervone (1983) demonstrated this **inattentional blindness** dramatically by showing people a 1-minute video of basketball players, three in black shirts and three in white shirts, tossing a ball. Researchers told viewers to press a key every time they saw a black-shirted player pass the ball. Most were so intent on their task that they failed to notice a young woman carrying an umbrella saunter across the screen midway through the video (**FIGURE 8.3**). Watching a replay, viewers were astonished to see her (Mack & Rock, 2000). This inattentional blindness is a by-product of what we are really good at: focusing attention on some part of our environment.

In a repeat of the experiment, smart-aleck researchers sent a gorilla-suited assistant through the swirl of players (Simons & Chabris, 1999). During its 5- to 9-second cameo appearance, the gorilla paused and thumped its chest. But the gorilla did not steal the show: Half the conscientious pass-counting viewers failed to see it. Inattentional blindness struck again in a study of 50 radiologists who were asked to search for cancer in lung scans. Two out of three radiologists missed a large breast mass, indicating cancer (Williams et al., 2021). They did, however, spot the much tinier groups of lung cancer cells, which were the focus of their attention.

FIGURE 8.3
Inattentional blindness Viewers who attended to basketball tosses among the black-shirted players usually failed to spot the umbrella-toting woman sauntering across the screen (Neisser, 1979).

This phenomenon extends to *inattentional numbness.* Pickpockets have long understood that bumping into people makes them unlikely to notice a hand slipping into their pocket. British researchers experimented with this tactile inattention: Sure enough, when distracted, participants failed to perceive an otherwise easily noticed vibration to their hand (Murphy & Dalton, 2016, 2018). Inattentional numbness can lead us to ignore information right beneath our noses. When people focused on a distracting task, they failed to notice a coffee scent in the room (Forster & Spence, 2018). Our attention is a wonderful gift, given to one thing at a time.

Knowing that most people miss someone in a gorilla suit while their attention is riveted elsewhere, imagine the fun that magicians can have by manipulating our selective attention. "Every time you perform a magic trick, you're engaging in experimental psychology," says magician Teller (2009), a master of mind-messing methods. Clever thieves know this, too. One Swedish psychologist was surprised in Stockholm by a woman suddenly exposing herself; only later did he realize that he had been pickpocketed, outwitted by thieves who understood the limits of our selective attention (Gallace, 2012).

In other experiments, people exhibited a form of inattentional blindness called **change blindness**. Viewers failed to notice that, after a brief visual interruption, a big Coke bottle had disappeared, a railing had risen, clothing had changed color, and someone they'd been talking to had been replaced by a different person (**FIGURE 8.4**) (Chabris & Simons, 2010; Resnick et al., 1997). Out of sight, out of mind.

inattentional blindness failing to see visible objects when our attention is directed elsewhere.

change blindness failing to notice changes in the environment; a form of *inattentional blindness.*

ASK YOURSELF

Can you recall a recent time when, as your attention focused on one thing, you were oblivious to something else—perhaps to pain, to someone's approach, or to music lyrics? (If you're reading this while listening to exciting music, you may have struggled to understand the question 😊 [Vasilev et al., 2018]).

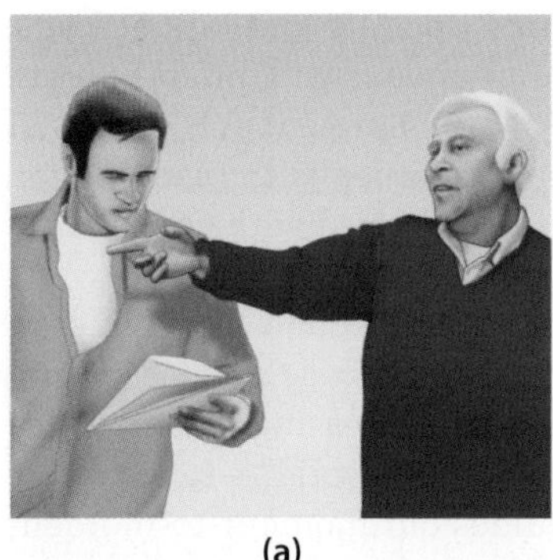
(a)

(b)

(c)

FIGURE 8.4
Change blindness While a man (in red) provides directions to another (a), two experimenters rudely pass between them carrying a door (b). During this interruption, the original direction seeker switches places with another person wearing different-colored clothing (c). Most people, focused on their direction giving, do not notice the switch (Simons & Levin, 1998).

RETRIEVAL PRACTICE

RP-2 Explain two attentional principles that magicians may use to fool us.

ANSWERS IN APPENDIX E

Dual Processing: The Two-Track Mind

LOQ 8-3 What is the *dual processing* being revealed by today's cognitive neuroscience?

Discovering which brain regions become active with a particular conscious experience strikes many people as interesting, but not mind-blowing. If everything psychological is simultaneously biological, then our ideas, emotions, and spirituality must all, somehow, be embodied. What is mind-blowing to many of us is evidence that we have, so to speak, two minds, each supported by its own neural equipment.

At any moment, we are aware of little more than what's on the screen of our consciousness. But beneath the surface, unconscious information processing occurs simultaneously on many parallel tracks. When we look at a bird flying, we are consciously aware of the result of our cognitive processing *(It's a hummingbird!)* but not of our subprocessing of the bird's color, form, movement, and distance. One of the grand ideas of today's cognitive neuroscience is that much of our brain work occurs off stage, out of sight. Thinking, knowing, remembering, and communicating all operate on two independent levels—a conscious, deliberate "high road," and an unconscious, automatic "low road." The high road is reflective, the low road intuitive—together making what researchers call **dual processing** (Kahneman, 2011; Pennycook et al., 2018). We know more than we know we know.

If you are a driver, consider how you move into the right lane. Drivers know this unconsciously but cannot accurately explain it (Eagleman, 2011). Most say they would bank to the right, then straighten out—a procedure that would actually steer them off the road. In reality, an experienced driver, after moving right, automatically reverses the steering wheel just as far to the left of center, only then returning to center. The lesson: The human brain is a device for converting conscious into unconscious knowledge.

Or consider this story, which illustrates how science can be stranger than science fiction. During my sojourns at Scotland's University of St Andrews, I [DM] came to know cognitive neuroscientists David Milner and Melvyn Goodale (2008). They studied a local woman, D. F., who experienced brain damage when overcome by carbon monoxide, leaving her unable to recognize and discriminate objects visually. Consciously, D. F. could see nothing. Yet she exhibited **blindsight**—she acted as though she *could* see. Asked to slip a postcard into a vertical or horizontal mail slot, she could do so without error. Asked the width of a block in front of her, she was at a loss, but she could grasp it with just the proper finger–thumb distance. Likewise, if our right and left eyes view different scenes, we will only be consciously aware of one at a time. Yet we will display some blindsight awareness of the other (Baker & Cass, 2013).

dual processing the principle that information is often simultaneously processed on separate conscious and unconscious tracks.

blindsight a condition in which a person can respond to a visual stimulus without consciously experiencing it.

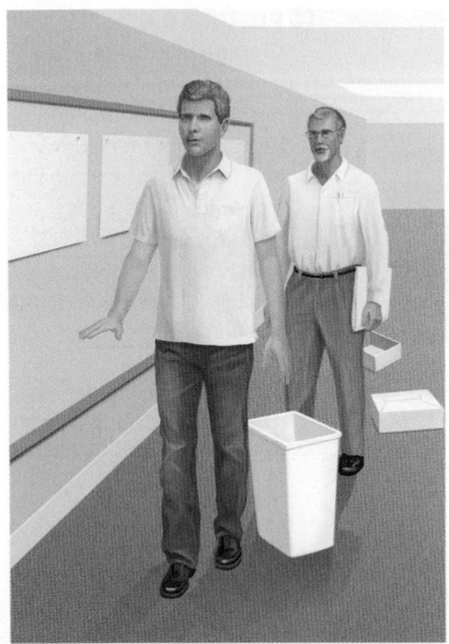

FIGURE 8.5
When the blind can "see" In this compelling demonstration of blindsight and the two-track mind, researcher Lawrence Weiskrantz trailed a blindsight patient down a cluttered hallway. Although told the hallway was empty, the patient meandered around all the obstacles without any awareness of them.

How could this be? Don't we have one visual system? Goodale and Milner knew from animal research that the eye sends information simultaneously to different brain areas, which support different tasks (Weiskrantz, 2009, 2010). Sure enough, a scan of D. F.'s brain activity revealed normal activity in the area concerned with reaching for, grasping, and navigating objects, but damage in the area concerned with consciously recognizing objects.[1] (See another example in FIGURE 8.5.)

How strangely intricate is this thing we call vision, conclude Goodale and Milner in their aptly titled book, *Sight Unseen* (2004). We may think of our vision as a single system that controls our visually guided actions. Actually, it is a dual-processing system (Foley et al., 2015). A *visual perception track* enables us "to think about the world"—to recognize things and to plan future actions. A *visual action track* guides our moment-to-moment movements.

The dual-track mind also appeared in a patient who lost all of his left visual cortex, leaving him blind to objects and faces presented on the right side of his field of vision. He nevertheless could sense the emotion expressed in faces that he did not consciously perceive (de Gelder, 2010). The same is true of normally sighted people whose visual cortex has been disabled with magnetic stimulation. Such findings suggest that brain areas below the cortex process emotion-related information.

Much of our everyday thinking, feeling, and acting operates outside our conscious awareness (Bargh & Chartrand, 1999). Some "80 to 90 percent of what we do is unconscious," says Nobel laureate and memory expert Eric Kandel (2008). Sometimes our unconscious biases *(I prefer to hire a female nanny)* do not match our conscious beliefs *(I am not biased)* (Greenwald & Lai, 2020). Other times, we're motivated to avoid thinking, especially when careful thought *(How many calories are in that dessert?)* conflicts with temptations *(I want that piece of cake!)* (Woolley & Risen, 2018). Yet most people, most of the time, mistakenly believe that their intentions and deliberate choices rule their lives. They don't.

Although consciousness enables us to exert voluntary control and to communicate our mental states to others, it is but the tip of the information-processing iceberg. Just ask the volunteers who chose a card after watching a magician shuffle through the deck (Olson et al., 2015). In nearly every case, the magician swayed participants' decisions by subtly allowing one card to show for longer—but 91 percent of the participants believed they had made the choice on their own. Being intensely focused on an activity (such as reading about consciousness, we hope) increases your total brain activity no more than 5 percent above its baseline rate. Even when you rest, activity whirls inside your head (Raichle, 2010).

This unconscious parallel processing is faster than conscious sequential processing, but both are essential. **Parallel processing** enables your mind to take care of routine business (more on this in the Sensation and Perception modules). **Sequential processing** is best for solving new problems, which requires our focused attention on one thing at a time. Try this if you are able: If you are right-handed, move your right foot in a smooth counterclockwise circle and write the number 3 repeatedly with your right hand—at the same time. Or try something equally difficult: Tap a steady beat three times with your left hand while tapping four times with your right hand. Both tasks require conscious attention, which can be in only one place at a time. If time is nature's way of keeping everything from happening at once, then consciousness is nature's way of keeping us from thinking and doing everything at once.

parallel processing processing multiple aspects of a stimulus or problem simultaneously.

sequential processing processing one aspect of a stimulus or problem at a time; generally used to process new information or to solve difficult problems.

RETRIEVAL PRACTICE

RP-3 What are the mind's two tracks, and what is *dual processing*?

ANSWERS IN APPENDIX E

[1] So, would the reverse damage lead to the opposite symptoms? Indeed, there are a few such patients—who can see and recognize objects but have difficulty pointing toward or grasping them.

REVIEW Module 8: Basic Consciousness Concepts

LEARNING OBJECTIVES

Test Yourself Answer these repeated Learning Objective Questions on your own (before "showing" the answers here, or checking the answers in Appendix D) to improve your retention of the concepts (McDaniel et al., 2009, 2015).

LOQ 8-1 What is the place of *consciousness* in psychology's history?

LOQ 8-2 How does *selective attention* direct our perceptions?

LOQ 8-3 What is the *dual processing* being revealed by today's cognitive neuroscience?

TERMS AND CONCEPTS TO REMEMBER

Test Yourself Write down the definition in your own words, then check your answer.

consciousness, p. 89	change blindness, p. 92
hypnosis, p. 89	dual processing, p. 93
cognitive neuroscience, p. 90	blindsight, p. 93
selective attention, p. 91	parallel processing, p. 94
inattentional blindness, p. 92	sequential processing, p. 94

MODULE TEST

Test Yourself Answer the following questions on your own first, then "show" the answers here, or check your answers in Appendix E.

1. Failure to see visible objects because our attention is occupied elsewhere is called ________________.
2. We register and react to stimuli outside of our awareness by means of ________ processing. When we devote deliberate attention to stimuli, we use ________ processing.
3. Inattentional blindness is a product of our ________ attention.

MODULE 9 Sleep and Dreams

LOQ 9-1 What is *sleep*?

We humans have about a 16-hour battery life before we lie down on our comfy wireless charging pad and slip into sleep. **Sleep**—the irresistible tempter that commands a third of our lives—matters more than you think. Sleep strengthens our mind and body. It can make or break our ability to remember things, manage our feelings, and even stay alive. "The best bridge between despair and hope," says sleep researcher Matthew Walker (2007), "is a good night's sleep."

Sleep's mysteries puzzled scientists for centuries. Now, in laboratories worldwide, some of these mysteries are being solved as people sleep, while devices measure their bodily and brain activity. By recording brain waves and muscle movements, and by watching and sometimes waking sleepers, researchers are glimpsing things that a thousand years of common sense never told us.

Why is it that the roar of my [ND's] neighbor's motorcycle leaves me undisturbed, but my child's cry will shatter my sleep? While sleeping, we may feel "dead to the world," but we are not. Even when you are deeply asleep, your perceptual window remains open a crack, and some part of you still attends to your environment. You move around on the bed but manage not to fall out. You maintain a sense of time, perhaps even awakening when you wish without an alarm. EEG recordings confirm that the brain's auditory cortex responds to sound stimuli even during sleep (Kutas, 1990). And when you sleep, as when awake, you process most information outside your conscious awareness.

"I love to sleep. . . . It really is the best of both worlds. You get to be alive and unconscious."—Comedian Rita Rudner, 1993

sleep a periodic, natural loss of consciousness—as distinct from unconsciousness resulting from a coma, general anesthesia, or hibernation. (Information from Dement, 1999.)

circadian [ser-KAY-dee-an] **rhythm** our biological clock; regular bodily rhythms (for example, of temperature and wakefulness) that occur on a 24-hour cycle.

REM sleep rapid eye movement sleep; a recurring sleep stage during which vivid dreams commonly occur. Also known as *paradoxical sleep,* because the muscles are relaxed (except for minor twitches) but other body and brain systems are active. (Sometimes called *R sleep.*)

alpha waves the relatively slow brain waves of a relaxed, awake state.

By recording the brain waves and muscle movements of sleeping participants, and by observing and occasionally waking them, researchers are solving some of sleep's deepest mysteries. Perhaps you can anticipate some of their discoveries. Are the following statements true or false?

1. When people dream of performing some activity, their limbs often move in concert with the dream.
2. Older adults sleep more than young adults.
3. Sleepwalkers are acting out their dreams.
4. Sleep experts recommend treating insomnia with an occasional sleeping pill.
5. Some people dream every night; others seldom dream.

All these statements (adapted from Palladino & Carducci, 1983) are *false*. To see why, read on.

Biological Rhythms and Sleep

Like the ocean, life has its rhythmic tides. Over varying time periods, our bodies fluctuate, and with them, our minds. Let's look more closely at two of those biological rhythms—our 24-hour *circadian rhythm* and our 90-minute sleep cycle.

Circadian Rhythm

LOQ 9-2 How do our biological rhythms influence our daily functioning?

The rhythm of the day parallels the rhythm of life—from our waking at a new day's birth to our nightly return to what Shakespeare called "death's counterfeit." Our bodies roughly synchronize with the 24-hour cycle of day and night thanks to our internal biological clock called the **circadian rhythm** (from the Latin *circa,* "about," and *diem,* "day"). Our body temperature is lowest at night and begins to rise steadily after we get out of bed, as our grogginess transforms into alertness throughout the morning. Our temperature then plateaus for a time in the afternoon and drops back down in the evening as we wind down for bedtime (Refinetti & Menaker, 1992). Thinking and memory improve as we approach our daily peak in circadian arousal. Have you ever pulled an all-nighter? You might remember feeling groggiest in the middle of the night, but gaining a sense of new alertness with the arrival of your regular wake-up time. Even our happy moods peak in the afternoon and decline into the evening hours (Murray et al., 2002).

Age and experience can alter our circadian rhythm. Most 20-year-olds are evening-energized "owls," with performance improving across the day (May & Hasher, 1998). Older adults tend to become morning-loving "larks." For our ancestors (and for today's hunter-gatherers), a grandparent who awakened easily and early helped protect the family from predators (Samson et al., 2017). By mid-evening, when the night has hardly begun for many young adults, retirement homes are typically quiet. After about age 20 (slightly earlier for women), we gradually shift from being owls to being larks (Wallace et al., 2022). Night owls tend to be smart and creative (Giampietro & Cavallera, 2007). Morning types tend to do better in school, take more initiative, be more punctual, and be less vulnerable to depression (Preckel et al., 2013; Randler, 2008, 2009; Werner et al., 2015).

Take the test: Morning lark or night owl? Would you consider yourself a night owl or a morning lark? When do you usually feel most energetic? What time of day works best for you to study? This simple quiz from the Sleep Health Foundation will tell you if you are more like a night owl or a morning lark: https://tinyurl.com/4btct7nw.

Peter Chadwick/Science Source

Morning lark

Eric Isselee/Shutterstock

Night owl

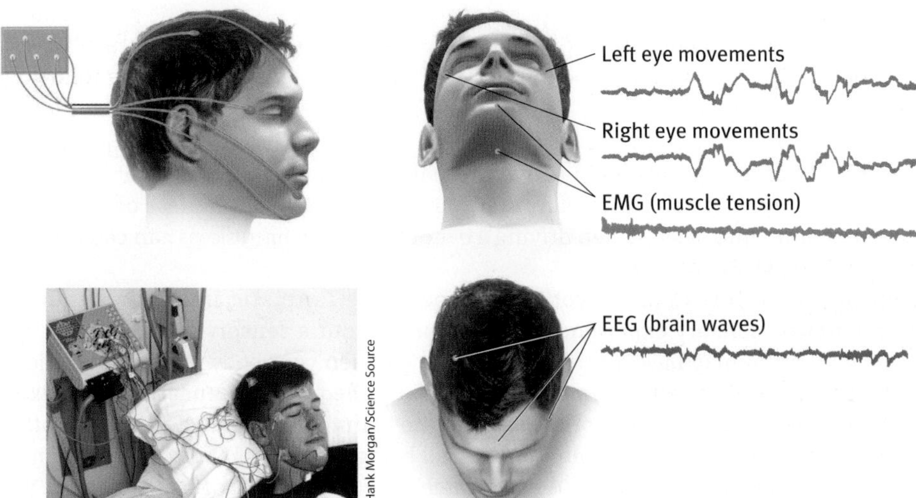
Left eye movements
Right eye movements
EMG (muscle tension)
EEG (brain waves)
Hank Morgan/Science Source

FIGURE 9.1
Measuring sleep activity Sleep researchers measure brain-wave activity, eye movements, and muscle tension with electrodes that pick up weak electrical signals from the brain, eyes, and facial muscles (Dement, 1978).

Sleep Stages

LOQ 9-3 What is the biological rhythm of our sleeping and dreaming stages?

Seeking sleep, we crawl into bed, shut our eyes, and wait. Eventually, sleep overtakes us, and consciousness fades as different parts of our brain's cortex stop communicating (Massimini et al., 2005). Sleep may feel like time-traveling a few hours into the future. Yet the sleeping brain remains active and has its own biological rhythm.

About every 90 minutes, we cycle through distinct sleep stages. This fact came to light when 8-year-old Armond Aserinsky went to bed one night in 1952. His father, Eugene, a University of Chicago graduate student, needed to test an electroencephalograph he had repaired that day (Aserinsky, 1988; Seligman & Yellen, 1987). Placing electrodes near Armond's eyes to record the rolling eye movements then believed to occur during sleep, Aserinsky watched the machine go wild, tracing deep zigzags on the graph paper. Could the machine still be broken? As the night proceeded and the activity recurred, Aserinsky realized that the periods of fast, jerky eye movements were accompanied by energetic brain activity. Awakened during one such episode, Armond reported having a dream, Aserinsky recalled 65 years later, of "a chicken walking through a barnyard" (Nichols, 2018). He had discovered what we now know as **REM sleep** (rapid eye movement sleep; sometimes called *R sleep*).

Similar procedures used with thousands of volunteers showed the cycles were a regular part of sleep (Kleitman, 1960). To appreciate these studies, imagine yourself as a paid participant in this dream job. As the hour grows late, you feel sleepy and yawn in response to reduced brain metabolism. (Yawning stretches your neck muscles and increases your heart rate, which helps keep you awake and alert [Moorcroft, 2003].) When you are ready for bed, a researcher comes in and tapes electrodes to your scalp (to detect your brain waves), on your chin (to detect muscle tension), and just outside the corners of your eyes (to detect eye movement; **FIGURE 9.1**). Other devices may record your heart rate, respiration rate, blood oxygen, and genital arousal while you sleep. A tracker worn around your wrist records when you are awake or asleep based on your movements.

When you are in bed with your eyes closed, the researcher in the next room sees on the EEG the relatively slow **alpha waves** of your awake but relaxed state (**FIGURE 9.2**). As time wears on, you adapt to all this equipment, grow tired, and, in an unremembered moment, slip into sleep (**FIGURE 9.3**). This transition is marked by the slowed breathing and irregular brain waves of what the American Academy of Sleep Medicine classifies as N1 sleep—the first stage of non-REM (NREM) sleep (Silber et al., 2007).

In one of his 15,000 research participants, William Dement (1999) observed the moment the brain's perceptual window to the outside world slammed shut. Dement asked a sleep-deprived young man with eyelids taped open to press a button every time a strobe light flashed in his eyes (about every 6 seconds). After a few minutes, the young man missed one. Asked why, he said, "Because there was no flash." But there was a flash.

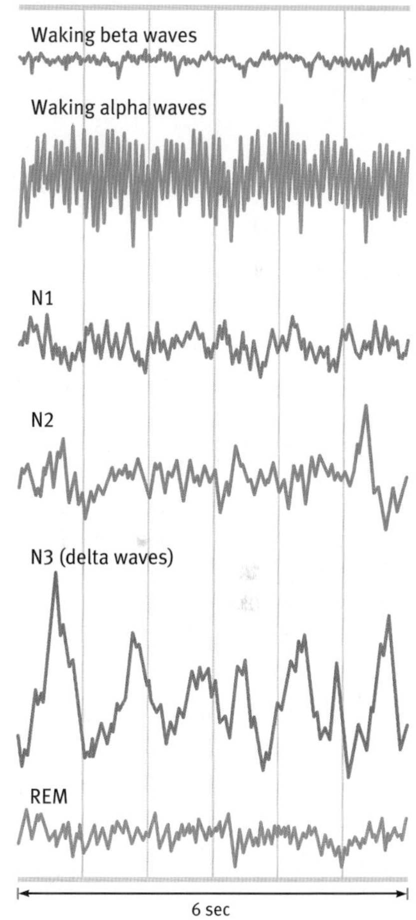
Waking beta waves
Waking alpha waves
N1
N2
N3 (delta waves)
REM
6 sec

FIGURE 9.2
Brain waves and sleep stages The beta waves of an alert, waking state and the regular alpha waves of an awake, relaxed state differ from the slower, larger delta waves of deep Stage 3 (or N3) sleep. Although the rapid REM sleep waves resemble the near-waking Stage 1 (N1) sleep waves, the body is more internally aroused during REM sleep than during NREM sleep (the N1, N2, and N3 stages).

Dolphins, porpoises, and whales sleep with one side of their brain at a time (Mascetti, 2019).

FIGURE 9.3
The moment of sleep We seem unaware of the moment we fall into sleep, but someone watching our brain waves could tell (Dement, 1999).

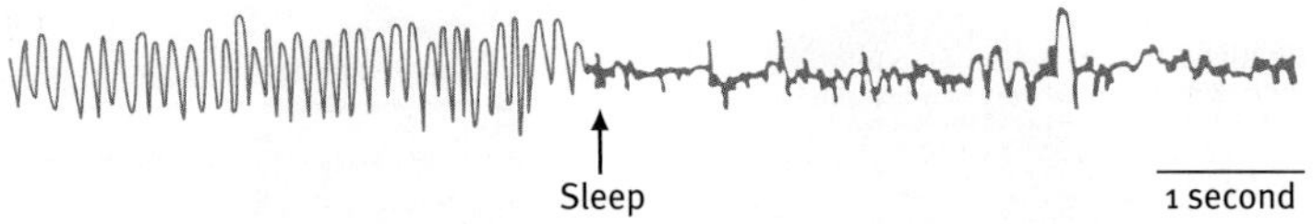

Sleep
1 second

He missed it because (as his brain activity revealed) he had fallen asleep for 2 seconds, missing not only the flash 6 inches from his nose but also the awareness of the abrupt moment of entry into sleep. When driving a car or train such *microsleeps* can cause disaster (Koch, 2016; McGeehan, 2018).

During this brief N1 sleep you may experience fantastic images resembling **hallucinations**—sensory experiences that occur without a sensory stimulus from the outside world. You may have a sensation of falling (when your body may suddenly jerk) or of floating weightlessly. These *hypnagogic* (also called *hypnic*) sensations may later be incorporated into your memories. People who claim aliens abducted them—often shortly after getting into bed—commonly recall being floated off of or pinned down on their beds (Clancy, 2005; McNally, 2012). (To catch your own hypnagogic experiences, you might use your alarm's snooze function.)

You then relax more deeply and begin about 20 minutes of N2 sleep, with its periodic *sleep spindles*—bursts of rapid, rhythmic brain-wave activity that aid memory processing (Studte et al., 2017). Although you could still be awakened without too much difficulty, you are now clearly asleep.

Then you transition to the deep sleep of N3. During this slow-wave sleep, which lasts for about 30 minutes, your brain emits large, slow **delta waves** and you are hard to awaken. Have you ever said, "That thunder was so loud last night!" only to have a friend respond, "What thunder?" Those who missed the storm may have been in delta sleep. (It is at the end of this stage that children may wet the bed.)

REM Sleep

About an hour after you first fall asleep, a strange thing happens. Rather than continuing in deep slumber, you ascend from your initial sleep dive. Returning through N2 (where you'll ultimately spend about half your night), you enter the most fascinating sleep phase—REM sleep. For about 10 minutes, your brain waves become rapid and saw-toothed, more like those of the nearly awake N1 sleep. But unlike N1, during REM sleep your heart rate rises, your breathing becomes rapid and irregular, and every half-minute or so your closed eyes dart around in momentary bursts of activity. These eye movements announce the beginning of a dream—often emotional, usually storylike, and richly hallucinatory. Dreams aren't real, but REM sleep tricks your brain into responding as if they were (Andrillon et al., 2015). Anyone watching a sleeper's eyes can notice these REM bursts, but it wasn't until Aserinsky attached his probes to little Armond's eyelids in 1952 that scientists made the connection between these movements and dreaming.

Your genitals may become aroused during REM sleep. You may have an erection or increased vaginal lubrication and clitoral engorgement, regardless of whether the dream's content is sexual (Karacan et al., 1966). During REM sleep, your brain's motor cortex is active, but your brainstem blocks its messages. This leaves your muscles relaxed, so much so that, except for an occasional finger, toe, or facial twitch, you are essentially paralyzed. Moreover, you cannot easily be awakened. (This immobility may occasionally linger as you awaken from REM sleep, producing a disturbing experience of *sleep paralysis* [Santomauro & French, 2009].) REM sleep is thus sometimes called *paradoxical sleep:* The body is internally aroused, with waking-like brain activity, yet asleep and externally immobile. We spend about 600 hours a year experiencing some 1500 dreams, or more than 100,000 dreams over a typical lifetime—dreams swallowed by the night but not acted out, thanks to REM's protective paralysis.

People rarely snore during dreams. When REM starts, snoring stops.

The sleep cycle repeats itself about every 90 minutes (with shorter, more frequent cycles for very young children and older adults). As the night goes on, deep N3 sleep grows shorter and disappears, and REM and N2 sleep periods get longer (**FIGURE 9.4**). By morning, we have spent 20 to 25 percent of an average night's sleep—some 100 minutes—in REM sleep. In sleep lab studies, 37 percent of participants have reported rarely or never having dreams that they "can remember the next morning" (Moore, 2004). Yet even they, more than 80 percent of the time, could recall a dream after being awakened during REM

hallucinations sensory experiences without sensory stimulation, such as seeing something in the absence of an external visual stimulus.

delta waves the large, slow brain waves associated with deep sleep.

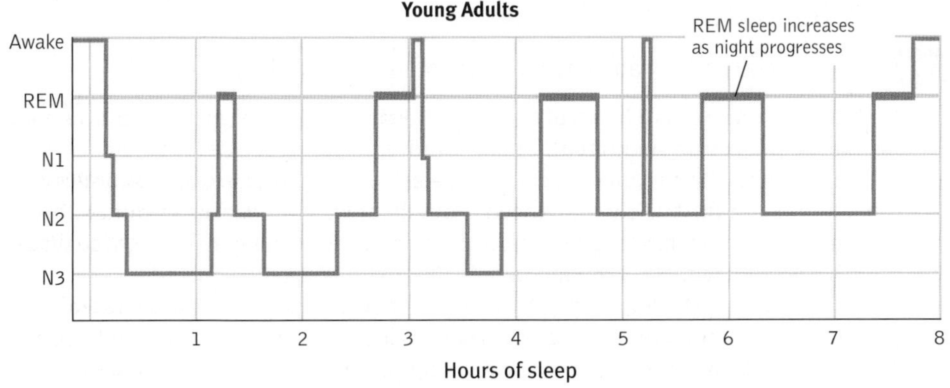
Young Adults
REM sleep increases as night progresses
Awake
REM
N1
N2
N3
1
2
3
4
5
6
7
8
Hours of sleep

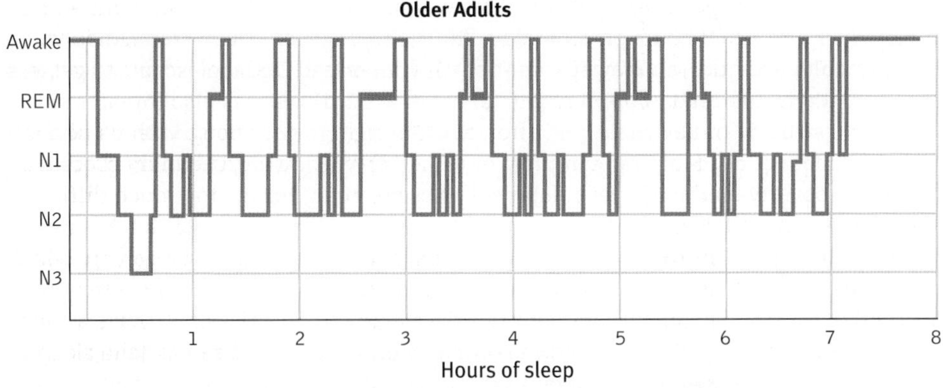
Older Adults
Awake
REM
N1
N2
N3
1
2
3
4
5
6
7
8
Hours of sleep

FIGURE 9.4
The stages in a typical night's sleep
People pass through a multistage sleep cycle several times each night. As the night goes on, periods of deep sleep diminish and, for younger adults, REM sleep increases. As people age, sleep becomes more fragile, with awakenings more common among older adults (Kamel & Gammack, 2006; Li et al., 2022).

sleep. Neuroscientists have also identified brain regions that are active during dreaming, which enables them to detect when dreaming occurs (Siclari et al., 2017).

REM sleep is not only the place where dreams are made, it's also where healing happens. Feelings of tension between you and your roommate may not be as tense after a good night's sleep. Some research suggests that REM sleep offers overnight therapy by calming the days' emotions (Walker, 2010). People who were disrupted during REM sleep were later more emotionally reactive and less attuned to other's emotions (Talbot et al., 2010; van der Helm et al., 2011). Likewise, having our emotions charged up just before bedtime can disrupt both the quality and quantity of our sleep. As psychologist Roxanne Prichard wisely observed: "Nothing gets worse with sleep, and a lot of things get better" (quoted in Brody, 2018). Our sleep and feelings intertwine (Palmer & Alfano, 2017).

RETRIEVAL PRACTICE

Tatan Syuflana/AP Photo

RP-1 Why would communal sleeping provide added protection for those whose safety depends on vigilance, such as these Rohingya refugees at a temporary shelter in Indonesia?

RP-2 What are the sleep stages, and in what order do we typically travel through those stages?

RP-3 Match the sleep stage (i–iii) with the cognitive experience (a–c).

Sleep stage:	**Cognitive experience:**
i. N1	**a.** story-like dream
ii. N3	**b.** fleeting images
iii. REM	**c.** minimal awareness

ANSWERS IN APPENDIX E

suprachiasmatic nucleus (SCN) a pair of cell clusters in the hypothalamus that controls circadian rhythm. In response to light, the SCN causes the pineal gland to adjust melatonin production, thus modifying our feelings of sleepiness.

What Affects Our Sleep Patterns?

LOQ 9-4 How do biology and environment interact in our sleep patterns?

Is it true that everyone needs 8 hours of sleep? *No.* Newborns often sleep two-thirds of their day, but most adults sleep no more than one-third. And some people wake up between nightly sleep periods—sometimes called "first sleep" and "second sleep" (Randall, 2012).

Sleep patterns are genetically influenced (Hayashi et al., 2015; Mackenzie et al., 2015). Identical twins are more similar than fraternal twins in their sleep habits (O'Callaghan et al., 2021). One analysis of 1.3 million people identified 956 genes related to sleep patterns such as *insomnia* (Jansen et al., 2019). Another identified genes associated with being a morning person (Jones et al., 2019). Genes also influence how much people sleep (Ashbrook et al., 2019).

Sleep patterns are also culturally, socially, and economically influenced. In Britain, Canada, Germany, Japan, and the United States, adults average 7 hours of sleep a night on workdays and 7 to 8 hours on other days (NSF, 2013). Earlier school start times, more extracurricular activities, and fewer parent-set bedtimes lead U.S. adolescents to get less sleep than their Australian counterparts (Short et al., 2013). Stress also impacts sleep. Those who struggle to pay their bills often also struggle to get enough sleep (Johnson et al., 2018; Mai et al., 2019; Vancampfort et al., 2018). Worldwide, urban dwellers who experience poverty tend to be sleep deprived (Bessone et al., 2021).

With sleep, as with waking behavior, biology and environment interact. Thanks to modern lighting, shift work, and media diversions, many who might have gone to bed at 9:00 P.M. in days past are now up until 11:00 P.M. or later.

Whether for work or play, bright light tweaks the circadian clock by activating light-sensitive retinal proteins. These proteins control the circadian clock by triggering signals to the brain's **suprachiasmatic nucleus (SCN)**—a pair of grain-of-rice-sized, 10,000-cell clusters in the hypothalamus (FIGURE 9.5). The SCN does its job partly by causing the brain's pineal gland to decrease its production of the sleep-promoting hormone *melatonin* in the morning and to increase it in the evening (Chang et al., 2015; Gandhi et al., 2015). (A 2017 Nobel Prize was awarded for research on the molecular biology that runs our biological clock.)

Being bathed in (or deprived of) light disrupts our 24-hour biological clock (Czeisler et al., 1999; Dement, 1999). Night-shift workers may experience a chronic state of *desynchronization*. As a result, they become more likely to develop fatigue, stomach problems, heart disease, and cancer (Garcia-Saenz et al., 2018; Knutsson & Bøggild, 2010; Lin et al., 2015; Maria et al., 2020; Puttonen et al., 2009).

Our ancestors' body clocks were attuned to the rising and setting Sun of the 24-hour day, leading them to get more sleep during the dark winter months and less during the sunny summer months (van Egmond et al., 2019). Today's young adults adopt something closer to a 25-hour day, by staying up too late to get 8 hours of sleep. Approximately 90 percent of Americans report using a light-emitting electronic device 1 hour before

FIGURE 9.5
The biological clock (a) Light striking the retina signals the suprachiasmatic nucleus (SCN) to suppress the pineal gland's production of the sleep hormone melatonin. (b) At night, the SCN quiets down, allowing the pineal gland to release melatonin into the bloodstream.

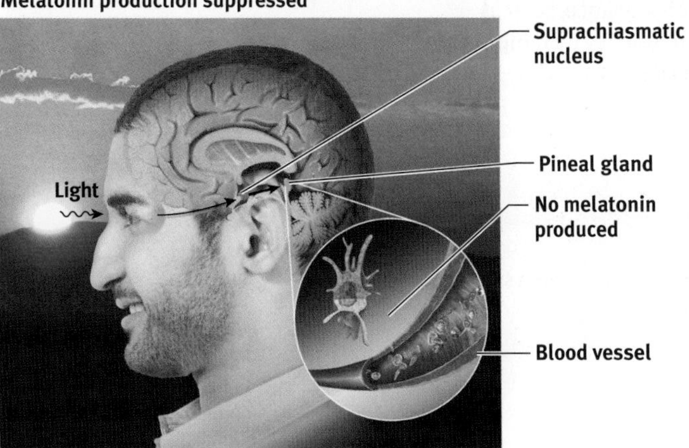
Melatonin production suppressed
Suprachiasmatic nucleus
Pineal gland
No melatonin produced
Light
Blood vessel
(a)

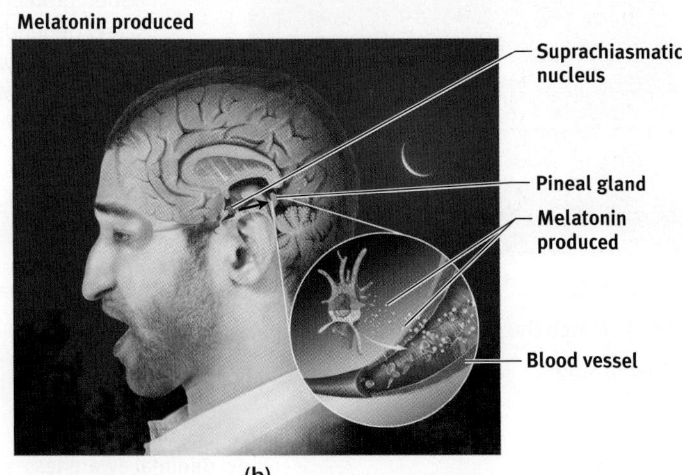
Melatonin produced
Suprachiasmatic nucleus
Pineal gland
Melatonin produced
Blood vessel
(b)

going to sleep (Chang et al., 2015). Such artificial light delays sleep and affects sleep quality. For college students in one study, staying up late engaged with digital entertainment interfered with the onset, quality, and duration of their sleep (Exelmans & Van den Bulck, 2018). Streaming disrupts dreaming.

Sleep often eludes those who stay up late and sleep in on weekends, then go to bed earlier on Sunday evening in preparation for the week ahead (Oren & Terman, 1998). Like New Yorkers readjusting after a trip to California, they experience a kind of jet lag. For North Americans who fly to Europe and need to be up when their circadian rhythm cries "*SLEEP*," bright light (spending the next day outdoors) helps reset the biological clock (Czeisler et al., 1986, 1989; Eastman et al., 1995).

"I'M LOOKING UP SLEEPING TIPS."

© JIMMYTRIED/Jimmy Craig

Circadian disadvantage: Major League Baseball, National Basketball Association, and National Hockey League teams crossing three time zones have a nearly 60 percent chance of losing their next game (Roy & Forest, 2018; Winter et al., 2009).

ASK YOURSELF

How does your need for sleep compare with that of others you know? Do you see age-related differences among your friends and family?

RETRIEVAL PRACTICE

RP-4 The ______________ nucleus helps monitor the brain's release of melatonin, which affects our ______________ rhythm.

ANSWERS IN APPENDIX E

Why Do We Sleep?

LOQ 9-5 What are sleep's functions?

So, our sleep patterns differ from person to person and from culture to culture. But why do we have this need for sleep? Psychologists offer five possible reasons:

1. ***Sleep protects.*** When darkness shut down the day's hunting, gathering, and travel, our distant ancestors were better off asleep in a cave, out of harm's way. Those who didn't wander around dark cliffs were more likely to leave descendants. This fits a broader principle: A species' sleep pattern tends to suit its ecological niche (Siegel, 2009). Animals with the greatest need to graze and the least ability to hide tend to sleep less. Animals also sleep less, with no ill effects, during times of mating and migration (Siegel, 2012). (For a sampling of animal sleep times, see **FIGURE 9.6**.)
2. ***Sleep helps us recuperate.*** Sleep gives our body and brain the chance to repair, rewire, and reorganize. It helps the body heal from infection and restores the immune system (Dimitrov et al., 2019; Walker, 2007). Sleep gives resting neurons time to repair themselves, while pruning or weakening unused connections (Ascády & Harris, 2017; Ding et al., 2016; Li et al., 2017). Bats and other animals with high waking metabolism burn a lot of calories, producing *free radicals,* molecules that are toxic to neurons. Sleep sweeps away this toxic waste along with protein fragments that for humans can cause Alzheimer's disease (Beil, 2018; Lewis, 2021). Imagine that when consciousness leaves your house, a cleanup crew comes in and says, "Good night. Sleep tidy."
3. ***Sleep helps restore and rebuild our fading memories of the day's experiences.*** Our memories are *consolidated* during slow-wave deep sleep by replaying recent learning and strengthening neural connections (Paller & Oudiette, 2018; Todorova & Zugaro, 2019; Walker, 2010). Sleep reactivates recent experiences stored in the hippocampus and shifts them for permanent storage elsewhere in the cortex (Girardeau &

FIGURE 9.6
Animal sleep time Would you rather be a brown bat that sleeps 20 hours a day or a giraffe that sleeps 2 hours a day? (Data from NIH, 2010.)

20 hours
Kruglov_Orda/Shutterstock

16 hours
Andrew D. Myers

12 hours
Utekhina Anna/Shutterstock

10 hours
Steffen Foerster/Shutterstock

8 hours
RubberBall Productions/Getty Images

4 hours
Eric Isselee/Shutterstock

2 hours
pandapaw/Shutterstock

How to sleep like an MVP Sleep scientist Cheri Mah and NBA star Andre Iguodala have spoken to many groups about his sleep success story, including remotely for this Time for Health Talk.

Lopes-dos-Santos, 2021; Ikegaya & Matsumoto, 2019). Adults and children trained to perform tasks therefore recall them better after a night's sleep, or even after a short nap, than after several hours awake (He et al., 2020; Seehagen et al., 2015; Werchan et al., 2021). When sleep deprived, people learn and remember less (Newbury et al., 2021). Older adults' more frequently disrupted sleep also disrupts their memory consolidation (Boyce et al., 2016; Pace-Schott & Spencer, 2011).

"Remember to sleep because you have to sleep to remember." —James B. Maas and Rebecca S. Robbins, *Sleep for Success*, 2010

4. ***Sleep feeds creative thinking.*** Dreams can inspire noteworthy artistic and scientific achievements, such as the dreams that inspired novelist Stephanie Meyer to write the first book in the *Twilight* series (CNN, 2009) and inspired medical researcher Carl Alving (2011) to invent the vaccine patch. More commonplace is the boost that a complete night's sleep gives to our thinking and learning. After working on a task, then sleeping on it, people solve difficult problems more insightfully than do those who stay awake (Barrett, 2011; Sio et al., 2013). They also are better at spotting connections among novel pieces of information (Ellenbogen et al., 2007; Whitehurst et al., 2016). To think smart and see connections, it often pays to ponder a problem just before bed and then sleep on it.
5. ***Sleep supports growth.*** During slow-wave sleep, which occurs mostly in the first half of a night's sleep, the pituitary gland releases a human growth hormone that is necessary for muscle development.

A regular full night's sleep can "*dramatically* improve your athletic ability," report James Maas and Rebecca Robbins (2010). REM sleep and N2 sleep—which occur mostly in the final hours of a long night's sleep—help strengthen the neural connections that build enduring memories, including the "muscle memories" learned while practicing tennis or shooting baskets. Sleep scientist Cheri Mah and her colleagues (2011) advise athletes on how to build sleep into their training. She helped professional basketball player Andre Iguodala to transform himself from an afternoon-napping, late-night videogamer into someone with healthy sleep habits (Gonzalez, 2018). The result? Iguodala played more minutes, shot more effectively, and received the 2015 National Basketball Association Finals Most Valuable Player award. Given all the benefits of sleep, it's no wonder that sleep loss hits us so hard.

RETRIEVAL PRACTICE

RP-5 What are five proposed reasons for our need for sleep?

ANSWERS IN APPENDIX E

Sleep Deprivation and Sleep Disorders

LOQ 9-6 How does sleep loss affect us, and what are the major sleep disorders?

When our body yearns for sleep but does not get it, we begin to feel terrible. Trying to stay awake, we will eventually lose. The longer we're awake, the more the inescapable drive to sleep beckons us. Even when sleep seems elusive, it ultimately finds us. In the tiredness battle, sleep always wins.

Effects of Sleep Loss

Modern sleep patterns—the "Great Sleep Recession"—leave us not only sleepy but drained of energy and our sense of well-being (Keyes et al., 2015; Thorarinsdottir et al., 2019). After several 5-hour short sleeping nights, we accumulate a sleep debt that cannot be satisfied by one long sleep. "The brain keeps an accurate count of sleep debt for at least two weeks," reported sleep researcher William Dement (1999, p. 64).

Obviously, then, we need sleep. Allowed to sleep unhindered, most adults paying off a sleep debt will sleep at least 9 hours a night (Coren, 1996). One experiment demonstrated the benefits of unrestricted sleep by having volunteers spend 14 hours daily in bed for at least a week. For the first few days, the volunteers averaged 12 hours of sleep or more per day, apparently paying off a sleep debt that averaged 25 to 30 hours. That accomplished, they settled back to 7.5 to 9 hours nightly and felt energized and happier (Dement, 1999).

College and university students are especially sleep deprived; 69 percent in one U.S. survey reported "feeling tired" or "having little energy" on at least several days during the previous 2 weeks (AP, 2009). One in four Chinese university students has serious sleep problems (L. Li et al., 2018). And 75 percent of U.S. high school students report getting fewer than 8 hours nightly, with 28 percent admitting they fall asleep in class at least once a week (CDC, 2019; NSF, 2006). The going needn't get boring before students start snoring.

Sleep loss affects our mood. Tiredness triggers testiness—less sleep predicts more anger (Keller et al., 2019; Krizan & Hisler, 2019). On the days after U.S. President Donald Trump was tweeting during the night, his interviews and speeches were three times more likely to display anger (Almond & Du, 2020).

Depression disrupts sleep, but sleep disturbance also contributes to depression (Plante, 2021). Sleep deprivation makes us more vulnerable to mood disruption and intrusive negative memories (Fang et al., 2021; Harrington et al., 2021). Studies show that sleep loss not only increases teens' fatigue but also depresses their mood and aggravates their sense of worthlessness—and (good news) that sleep improvements "alleviate depression symptoms" (Gradisar et al., 2022). Among a half million people from China, those who slept 5 or fewer hours a night had a more than doubled rate of depression (Sun et al., 2018). Modern psychological treatments now focus on treating sleep difficulties to help lessen depression (Kaplan, 2020).

When youth are followed through time, sleep loss predicts depression (Gregory et al., 2009). For people at risk for suicide, a night of poor sleep increases their next-day suicidal thinking (Littlewood et al., 2019).

But there is hope: In particular, REM sleep's processing of emotional experiences helps protect against depression (Walker & van der Helm, 2009). Later secondary school start times consistently produce more sleep, better and more on-time attendance, and less negative mood (Morgenthaler et al., 2016; Yip et al., 2022). When Minneapolis/St. Paul high schools shifted to an hour-later start time, students stayed up no later—and thus got more sleep (Berry et al., 2021). And when the Seattle School District moved secondary school start times about an hour later, the results were clear: more sleep and better grades (Dunster et al., 2018). The same applies to later-starting Italian high school students (Alfonsi et al., 2020). The American Academy of Pediatrics recommends that middle and high schools start at 8:30 A.M. or later—which, alas, only 7 percent of U.S. high schools do (CDC, 2020). Other sleep experts advocate year-round standard time: better to align students' body clocks with the sun than to awaken to the dark mornings of early spring daylight savings time (Turgeon & Wright, 2022). As sleep experts Michael Grandner and Fabian-Xosé Fernandez (2021) concluded, sleep is a "major contributor" to our health and exerts a "tremendous influence on our well-being."

Lack of sleep can also make you gain weight. Sleep deprivation messes with our hormones, our metabolism, and our brain's responses to food by

- increasing *ghrelin,* a hunger-arousing hormone, and decreasing its hunger-suppressing partner, *leptin* (Shilsky et al., 2012).
- increasing *cortisol,* a stress hormone that stimulates the body to make fat, and decreasing metabolic rate (Potter et al., 2017; Schmid et al., 2015).

- disrupting gene expression, which increases risk for heart disease and other negative health outcomes (Möller-Levet et al., 2013; Mure et al., 2018).
- enhancing limbic brain responses to the mere sight of food and decreasing cortical responses that help us resist temptation (Benedict et al., 2012; Greer et al., 2013; St-Onge et al., 2012).

Thus, children and adults who sleep less are heavier than average, and in recent decades people have been sleeping less and weighing more (Hall et al., 2018; M. Miller et al., 2018). Moreover, experimental sleep deprivation increases appetite and junk food eating; our tired brain finds fatty foods more enticing (Fang et al., 2015; Rihm et al., 2019). So, sleep loss may help explain the weight gain common among sleep-deprived college students (Hull et al., 2007).

Short sleep short-circuits our body's immune system. When we get sick, we typically sleep more, boosting our immune cells. Sleep deprivation can suppress immune cells that battle viral infections and cancer (Opp & Krueger, 2015). One experiment exposed volunteers to a cold virus. Those who averaged less than 5 hours sleep a night were 4.5 times more likely to develop a cold than were those who slept more than 7 hours a night (Prather et al., 2015). Sleep-deprived people's vulnerability to illness helps explain a recent Gallup survey finding: Self-described poor sleepers reported 2.3 unplanned missed workdays in the past month—more than double that of other workers (Witters & Agrawal, 2022).

Short sleep can also shorten our lives. Sleep's protective effect may help explain why people who sleep 7 to 8 hours a night tend to outlive those who are chronically sleep deprived (Dew et al., 2003; Parthasarathy et al., 2015; Scullin & Bliwise, 2015). When sustained, sleep deprivation produces brain cell death in mice and increased risk of human brain disorders such as neurocognitive disorder (Sabia et al., 2021; Zamore & Veasey, 2022).

Although short-term sleep deprivation does not injure the brain, it does slow reactions and increase errors on visual attention tasks similar to those involved in screening airport baggage, performing surgery, and reading X-rays (Caldwell, 2012; Lim & Dinges, 2010).

For many North Americans, a semi-annual sleep-manipulation experiment is the "spring forward" to daylight saving time and "fall back" to standard time. A review of millions of Canadian and U.S. records revealed that accidents increased immediately after the spring-forward time change, which shortens sleep (Fritz et al., 2020; Kolla et al., 2020; **FIGURE 9.7**). While it seems like a minor annoyance, the 1-hour time change shift associated with daylight savings has been linked with a 24 percent increase in heart attacks the following day (Sandhu et al., 2014).

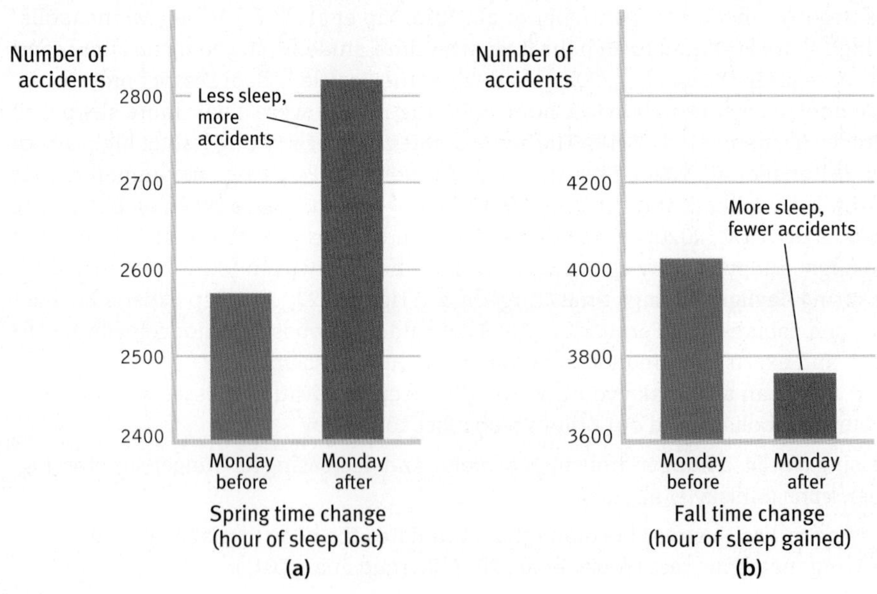

Number of accidents
2800
2700
2600
2500
2400
Less sleep, more accidents
Monday before
Monday after
Spring time change (hour of sleep lost)
(a)
Number of accidents
4200
4000
3800
3600
More sleep, fewer accidents
Monday before
Monday after
Fall time change (hour of sleep gained)
(b)

FIGURE 9.7
Less sleep = more accidents (a) On the Monday after the spring time change, when people lose 1 hour of sleep, accidents increased, as compared with the Monday before. (b) In the fall, traffic accidents typically increase because of more snow, ice, and darkness, but they diminished after the time change. (Data from Coren, 1996.)

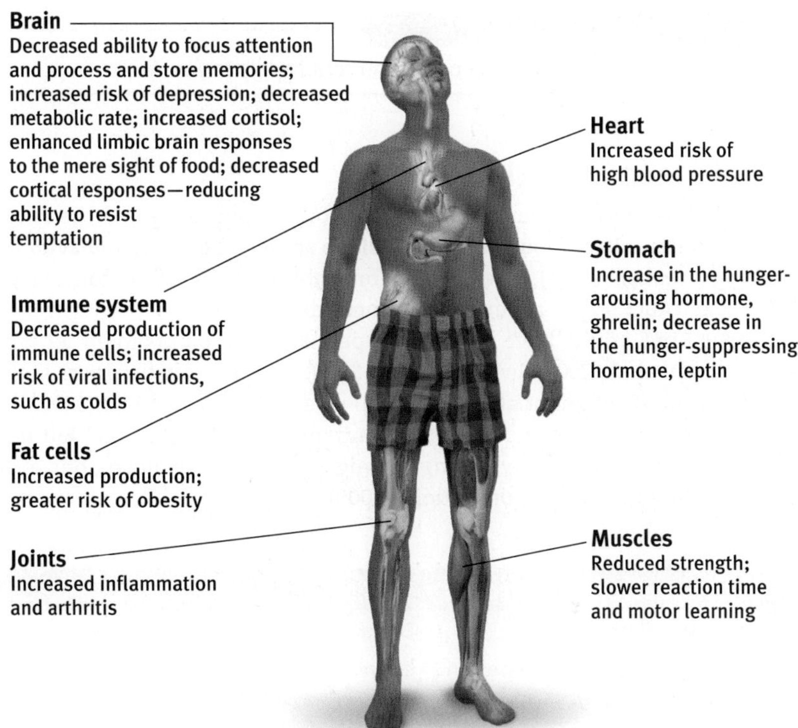

Brain
Decreased ability to focus attention and process and store memories; increased risk of depression; decreased metabolic rate; increased cortisol; enhanced limbic brain responses to the mere sight of food; decreased cortical responses—reducing ability to resist temptation
Immune system
Decreased production of immune cells; increased risk of viral infections, such as colds
Fat cells
Increased production; greater risk of obesity
Joints
Increased inflammation and arthritis
Heart
Increased risk of high blood pressure
Stomach
Increase in the hunger-arousing hormone, ghrelin; decrease in the hunger-suppressing hormone, leptin
Muscles
Reduced strength; slower reaction time and motor learning

FIGURE 9.8
How sleep deprivation affects us

FIGURE 9.8 summarizes the effects of sleep deprivation. But there is good news! Psychologists have discovered a treatment that strengthens memory, increases concentration, boosts mood, moderates hunger, reduces obesity, fortifies the immune system, improves school performance, and lessens the risk of fatal accidents. Even better news: The treatment feels good, can be self-administered, and is free! If you are a typical college or university student, you might feel trapped in a cycle of sleeplessness. Stress—from school, work, and life generally—might make adequate sleep seem like a luxury. If, for example, you experienced discrimination today, you might struggle to sleep (Fuller-Rowell et al., 2021; Yip et al., 2020). But one night this week, try to add 15 minutes to your sleep. Until you feel more rested and less like a zombie, try adding more sleep as often as you can. For some additional tips on getting better quality sleep, see **TABLE 9.1**.

BLOPER

Brendan Loper/Cartoon Stock

"Wow it's only 11:30, that still leaves time for me to ruin tomorrow by staying up doing nothing on the Internet."

TABLE 9.1 How to Improve Your Sleep

Better sleep requires a good sleep routine. Here are some tips for improving yours.

- ***Avoid arousing activities, foods, and beverages before bedtime.*** Exercise regularly but not in the late evening—late afternoon is best (Lowe et al., 2019). Avoid caffeine after the early afternoon, and avoid food and drink near bedtime.
- ***Go to the dark side of the room (when sleeping).*** Darkness increases production of the sleep-promoting hormone melatonin. Turn off the lights when you sleep, and avoid bright lights or screens an hour before bedtime. Wear a sleep mask to cover your eyes if there is light you can't control. Consider ear plugs if you can't control noise.
- ***Rise, rest, repeat.*** Wake up and go to bed at the same time, even on weekends and holidays. Use reminders on your phone to stay on schedule both for waking and for getting ready for bed. Patterns yield payoffs. Just say no to naps (Jansson-Fröjmark et al., 2019).
- ***Keep it cool.*** Your body and brain sleep better when it is cooler. Aim for a temperature around 65 degrees F (18 degrees C). Use lighter blankets and bedtime clothing when it's a hot night.
- ***Don't worry.*** Reassure yourself that temporary sleep loss happens, and it's normal to struggle to sleep sometimes. Try not to overthink your sleep, because doing so might keep you awake (Baron et al., 2017).
- ***Embrace a wind down routine.*** Try to relax at least a half-hour before your bedtime. Winding down helps your mind and body calm down before falling asleep. Focus your mind on nonarousing thoughts, such as a relaxing hobby (Gellis et al., 2013).
- ***Don't stay in bed awake.*** Your bed is meant for sleep. If you really can't sleep, get out of bed and go to another room. Come back when you are ready to fall asleep.
- ***Manage stress.*** Realize that for any stressed organism, being vigilant is natural and adaptive. Less stress = better sleep.

insomnia recurring problems in falling or staying asleep.

narcolepsy a sleep disorder characterized by uncontrollable sleep attacks. The sufferer may lapse directly into REM sleep, often at inopportune times.

sleep apnea a sleep disorder characterized by temporary cessations of breathing during sleep and repeated momentary awakenings.

REM sleep behavior disorder a sleep disorder characterized by acting out dreams while sleeping, through physical movements (such as kicking or striking out) and vocal behaviors (such as talking or yelling).

night terrors a sleep disorder characterized by high arousal and an appearance of being terrified; unlike nightmares, night terrors occur during N3 sleep, within 2 or 3 hours of falling asleep, and are seldom remembered.

ASK YOURSELF

What have you learned about sleep that you could apply to yourself?

Major Sleep Disorders

An occasional loss of sleep is nothing to worry about. But for those who have a major sleep disorder—**insomnia**, **narcolepsy**, **sleep apnea**, **REM sleep behavior disorder**, sleepwalking *(somnambulism)*, sleeptalking, or **night terrors**—trying to sleep can be a nightmare. (See **TABLE 9.2** for a summary of these disorders.)

About 1 in 5 adults have insomnia—persistent problems in either falling or staying asleep (Irwin et al., 2006; Sivertsen et al., 2020). The result is tiredness and increased risk of depression (Baglioni et al., 2016). Sleep researcher Wilse Webb (1992) likened sleep to love or happiness: "If you pursue it too ardently it will elude you." But from middle age on, awakening occasionally during the night becomes the norm, not something to fret over or treat with medication (Vitiello, 2009).

TABLE 9.2 Sleep Disorders

Disorder	Rate	Description	Effects
Insomnia	1 in 5 adults (based on past year's symptoms)	Ongoing difficulty falling or staying asleep.	Chronic tiredness, increased risk of depression, obesity, hypertension, and arthritic and fibromyalgia pain (Olfson et al., 2018).
Narcolepsy	1 in 2000 adults	Sudden attacks of overwhelming sleepiness.	Risk of falling asleep at a dangerous moment. Narcolepsy attacks usually last less than 5 minutes, but they can happen at the worst and most emotional times. Everyday activities, such as driving, require extra caution.
Sleep apnea	1 in 20 adults	Stopping breathing repeatedly while sleeping.	Fatigue and depression as a result of slow-wave sleep deprivation. Associated with obesity, especially among men.
REM sleep behavior disorder	1 in 100 adults; 2 in 100 older adults (APA, 2022)	Dream-enacting behaviors—loud, sometimes profane vocalizations and dramatic motor behaviors during REM sleep	May cause serious injury to self or bed partner, and associated distress and embarrassment.
Sleepwalking and sleeptalking	1–15 in 100 in the general population for sleepwalking (NSF, 2020); about half of young children for sleeptalking (Reimão & Lefévre, 1980)	Doing regular waking activities (sitting up, walking, speaking) while asleep. Sleeptalking can occur during any sleep stage. Sleepwalking happens in N3 sleep.	Few serious concerns. Sleepwalkers return to their beds on their own or with the help of a family member, rarely remembering their trip the next morning.
Night terrors	1 in 100 adults; 1 in 30 children	Appearing terrified, talking nonsense, sitting up, or walking around during N3 sleep; different from nightmares.	Doubling of a child's heart and breathing rates during the attack. Luckily, children remember little or nothing of the fearful event the next day. As people age, night terrors become increasingly rare.

Ironically, insomnia becomes worse when we fret about it. In laboratory studies, people with insomnia do sleep less than others. But even they typically overestimate how long it takes them to fall asleep and underestimate how long they actually have slept (te Lindert et al., 2020). Even if we have been awake only an hour or two, we may *think* we have had very little sleep because it's the waking part we remember.

The most common quick fixes for true insomnia, sleeping pills and alcohol, typically aggravate the problem by reducing REM sleep, causing concentration and memory problems, and leaving the person with next-day blahs. Such aids can also lead to *tolerance*—a state in which increasing doses are needed to produce an effect. Better to visit a sleep specialist to obtain a healthy long-term treatment plan.

RETRIEVAL PRACTICE

RP-6 A well-rested person would be more likely to have __________ (trouble concentrating/quick reaction times) and a sleep-deprived person would be more likely to __________ (gain weight/fight off a cold).

ANSWERS IN APPENDIX E

Dreams

LOQ 9-7 What do we dream, and what functions have theorists proposed for dreams?

Now playing at an inner theater near you: the premiere of a sleeping person's vivid dream. This never-before-seen mental movie features captivating characters wrapped in a plot so original and unlikely, yet so intricate and so seemingly real, that the viewer later marvels at its creation.

REM **dreams** are vivid, emotional, and often bizarre (Loftus & Ketcham, 1994). Waking from one, we may wonder how our brain can so creatively, colorfully, and completely construct this alternative world. In the shadowland between our dreaming and waking consciousness, we may even wonder for a moment which is real. Awakening from a nightmare, a 4-year-old may be sure there is a bear in the house.

Discovering the link between REM sleep and dreaming began a new era in dream research. Instead of relying on someone's hazy recall hours later, researchers could catch dreams as they happened, awakening people during or shortly after a REM sleep period to hear a vivid account.

What We Dream

Most of the dreams we can remember are anything but sweet. For women and men, 8 in 10 reported dreams are marked by at least one negative event or emotion (Domhoff, 2007). Common themes include repeatedly failing in an attempt to do something; being attacked, pursued, or rejected; or experiencing misfortune (Hall et al., 1982). Most people experience erotic dreams, but less often than you might think (Van den Bulck et al., 2016). In one study, only 1 in 10 reported dreams among young men and 1 in 30 among young women had sexual content (Domhoff, 1996).

More commonly, a dream's story line incorporates traces of previous days' nonsexual experiences and preoccupations (Nikles et al., 2017):

- ***Trauma and dreams*** After suffering a trauma, people commonly report nightmares, which help extinguish daytime fears (Petrov & Robinson, 2020). Auschwitz concentration camp inmates, Palestinian children living amid conflict, and people living in the United States after the 9/11 terrorist attacks all have experienced frequent trauma-related dreams (Owczarski, 2018; Propper et al., 2007; Punamäki & Joustie, 1998).
- ***Music and dreams*** Compared with nonmusicians, musicians report twice as many dreams of music (Uga et al., 2006). For many, listening to music before bed can produce an "earworm"—a tune that sticks and replays in the mind when trying to sleep (Scullin et al., 2021).

dream a sequence of images, emotions, and thoughts passing through a sleeping person's mind. 

FINAL
EXAM
Meredith Southard/Cartoon Stock

"I'd like to extend a special welcome for those of you who are joining us for the first time, as part of a nightmare you're having."

- ***Vision loss and dreams*** Studies in four countries have found people who are blind mostly dreaming of using their nonvisual senses (Buquet, 1988; Taha, 1972; Vekassy, 1977). But even people born blind sometimes "see" in their dreams (Bértolo, 2005). Likewise, people born paralyzed below the waist sometimes dream of walking, standing, running, or cycling (Saurat et al., 2011; Voss et al., 2011).
- ***Media experiences and dreams*** In a study of 1287 Turkish people, participants who reported viewing violent media during daytime hours tended to have violent dreams, and those who reported viewing sexual media tended to have sexual dreams (Van den Bulck et al., 2016).

Our two-track mind continues to monitor our environment while we sleep. Sensory stimuli—a particular odor or a phone's chime—may be instantly and ingeniously woven into the dream story itself. In a classic experiment, researchers lightly sprayed cold water on dreamers' faces (Dement & Wolpert, 1958). Compared with sleepers who did not get the cold-water treatment, these people were more likely to dream about a waterfall, a leaky roof, or even about being sprayed by someone.

So, could we learn a foreign language by hearing it played while we sleep? If only! While sleeping, we can learn to associate a sound with a mild electric shock (and to react to the sound accordingly). We can also learn to associate a particular sound with a pleasant or unpleasant odor (Arzi et al., 2012). But we do not remember recorded information played while we are soundly asleep (Eich, 1990; Wyatt & Bootzin, 1994). In fact, anything that happens during the moments before we fall asleep is typically lost from memory (Roth et al., 1988). This explains why sleep apnea patients, who repeatedly awaken with a gasp and then immediately fall back to sleep, do not recall the episodes. Ditto someone who awakens momentarily, sends a text message, and the next day can't remember doing so. It also explains why dreams that momentarily awaken us are mostly forgotten by morning. To remember a dream, get up and stay awake for a few minutes.

Sleeping superstition: If you dream you are falling and hit the ground, or if you dream of dying, you die. Unfortunately, those who could confirm these ideas are not around to do so. Many people, however, have had such dreams and are alive to report them.

Why We Dream

Dream theorists have proposed several explanations of why we dream, including these:

FREUD'S WISH FULFILLMENT THEORY Sigmund Freud considered dreams the key to understanding our inner conflicts. He proposed that dreams provide a psychic safety valve that discharges otherwise unacceptable feelings. He viewed a dream's **manifest content** (the apparent and remembered story line) as a censored, symbolic version of its **latent content**, the unconscious drives and wishes (often erotic) that would be threatening if expressed directly. However, modern psychologists largely disregard Freud's dream theory. "There is no reason to believe any of Freud's specific claims about dreams and their purposes," observed dream researcher William Domhoff (2003).

INFORMATION-PROCESSING THEORY The *information-processing* perspective proposes that dreams help sift, sort, and fix the day's experiences in our memory. In contrast to Freud's theories, there is research that supports this view. When tested the day after learning a task, those deprived of both slow-wave and REM sleep did not do as well as those who had slept undisturbed (Zadra & Stickgold, 2021). Other studies have shown similar memory lapses for new material among people awakened every time they began REM sleep (Empson & Clarke, 1970; Karni & Sagi, 1994).

Brain scans confirm the link between REM sleep and memory. The brain regions that were active as rats learned to navigate a maze, or as people learned to perform a visual-discrimination task, became active again later during REM sleep (Louie & Wilson, 2001; Maquet, 2001). So precise were these activity patterns that scientists could tell where in the maze the rat would be if awake. To sleep, perchance to remember.

This is important news for students, many of whom are sleep deprived on weekdays and binge sleep on the weekend (Stickgold, 2000). High school students with high grades sleep more than their lower-achieving classmates (Wolfson & Carskadon, 1998; see **FIGURE 9.9**). Sacrificing sleep time to study actually *worsens* academic performance, by making it harder the next day to understand class material or do well on a test (Gillen-O'Neel et al., 2013). When one psychology professor challenged students to sleep at least 8 hours each night during final exams week, those who completed the challenge

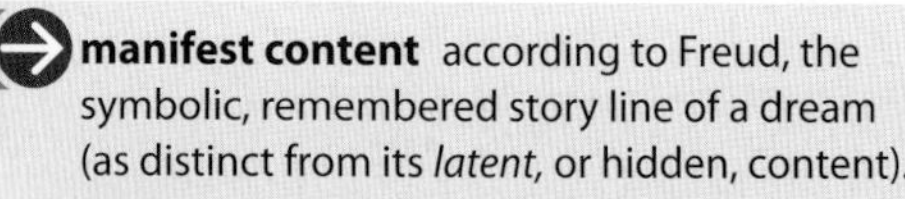
manifest content according to Freud, the symbolic, remembered story line of a dream (as distinct from its *latent*, or hidden, content).

latent content according to Freud, the underlying meaning of a dream (as distinct from its *manifest content*).

(a) Learning.

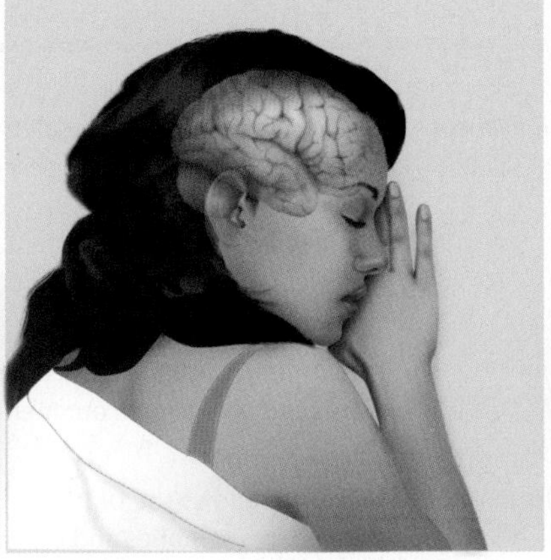
(b) Sleep consolidates our learning into long-term memory.

(c) Learning is retained.

FIGURE 9.9
A sleeping brain is a working brain

earned higher final exam grades than those who did not (Scullin, 2019). *The bottom line:* Sleep better to perform better.

NEUROCOGNITIVE FUNCTION THEORY Perhaps dreams, or the brain activity associated with REM sleep, serve a *neurocognitive* function, providing the sleeping brain with an opportunity to consolidate memories and process emotional information (Walker & van der Helm, 2009). Researchers have found that infants, whose neural networks are fast developing and rapidly processing new emotional events, spend much of their abundant sleep time in REM sleep (**FIGURE 9.10**).

Rapid eye movements also stir the liquid behind the cornea; this delivers fresh oxygen to corneal cells, preventing their suffocation.

ACTIVATION-SYNTHESIS THEORY Other researchers propose that dreams erupt from *neural activation* spreading upward from the brainstem (Antrobus, 1991; Hobson, 2009). According to the *activation-synthesis theory,* dreams are the brain's attempt to synthesize random neural activity. Much as a neurosurgeon can produce hallucinations by stimulating different parts of a patient's cortex, so can stimulation originating within the brain. PET scans of sleeping people also reveal increased activity in the emotion-related limbic system (in the amygdala) during emotional dreams (Schwartz, 2012). In contrast, frontal lobe regions responsible for inhibition and logical thinking seem to idle, which may explain why we are less inhibited when dreaming than when awake (Maquet et al., 1996). Add the limbic system's emotional tone to the brain's visual bursts and—voila!—we dream. Damage either the limbic system or the visual centers active during dreaming, and dreaming itself may be impaired (Domhoff, 2003).

COGNITIVE DEVELOPMENT THEORY Some dream researchers focus on dreams as part of brain maturation and cognitive development (Domhoff, 2010, 2011; Foulkes, 1999).

FIGURE 9.10
Sleep across the life span As we age, our sleep patterns change. During infancy and our first 2 years, we spend progressively less time in REM sleep. During our first 20 years, we spend progressively less time asleep. (Data from Snyder & Scott, 1972.)

swissmacky/Shutterstock

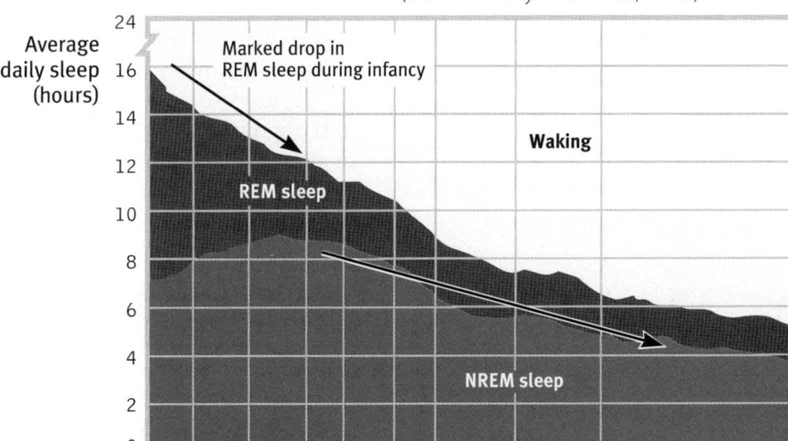
Average daily sleep (hours)
24
16
14
12
10
8
6
4
2
0
Marked drop in REM sleep during infancy
Waking
REM sleep
NREM sleep
1–15 days
3–5 mos.
6–23 mos.
2 yrs.
3–4 yrs.
5–13 yrs.
14–18 yrs.
19–30 yrs.
31–45 yrs.
90 yrs.
Age

TABLE 9.3 Dream Theories

Theory	Explanation	Critical Considerations
Freud's wish fulfillment	Dreams provide a "psychic safety valve"—expressing otherwise unacceptable feelings; dreams contain manifest (remembered) content and a deeper layer of latent content (a hidden meaning).	Lacks any scientific support; dreams may be interpreted in many different ways.
Information processing	Dreams help us sort out the day's events and consolidate our memories.	But why do we sometimes dream about things we have not experienced and about past events?
Neurocognitive function	REM sleep allows the brain to consolidate memories and process emotional information.	This does not explain why we experience *meaningful* dreams.
Activation synthesis	REM sleep triggers neural activity that evokes random visual memories, which our sleeping brain weaves into stories.	The individual's brain is weaving the stories, which still tells us something about the dreamer.
Cognitive development	Dream content reflects dreamers' level of cognitive development—their knowledge and understanding. Dreams simulate our lives, including worst-case scenarios.	Does not propose an adaptive function of dreams.

For example, prior to age 9, children's dreams seem more like a slide show and less like an active story in which the dreamer is an actor. Dreams overlap with waking cognition and they feature coherent speech. They *simulate reality* by drawing on our concepts and knowledge. They engage brain networks that also are active during daydreaming—and so may be viewed as intensified mind-wandering, enhanced by visual imagery (Fox et al., 2013). Unlike the idea that dreams arise from bottom-up brain activation, the cognitive perspective emphasizes our mind's top-down control of our dream content (Nir & Tononi, 2010). "[Dreams] dramatize our wishes, fears, concerns, and interests in striking scenarios that we experience as real events" (Domhoff, 2014).

Question: Does eating spicy foods cause us to dream more?

Answer: No, but a spicy food that causes you to awaken more increases your chance of *recalling* a dream (Moorcroft, 2003).

TABLE 9.3 compares these major dream theories. Although today's sleep researchers debate dreams' function—and some are skeptical that dreams serve any function—there is one thing they agree on: We need REM sleep. Deprived of it by repeated awakenings, people return more and more quickly to the REM stage after falling back to sleep. When finally allowed to sleep undisturbed, they literally sleep like babies—with increased REM sleep, a phenomenon called **REM rebound**. Most other mammals also experience REM rebound, suggesting that the causes and functions of REM sleep are deeply biological. (That REM sleep occurs in mammals—and not in animals such as fish, whose behavior is less influenced by learning—fits the information-processing theory of dreams.)

So, does this mean that because dreams serve physiological functions and support our cognition, they are psychologically meaningless? Not necessarily. Every psychologically meaningful experience involves an active brain. We are once again reminded of a basic principle: *Biological and psychological explanations of behavior work together to help us understand our experiences.*

ASK YOURSELF

Which explanation for why we dream makes the most sense to you? How well does it explain your own dreams?

RETRIEVAL PRACTICE

RP-7 What are five theoretical explanations for why we dream?

ANSWERS IN APPENDIX E

REM rebound the tendency for REM sleep to increase following REM sleep deprivation.

MODULE 9 REVIEW Sleep and Dreams

LEARNING OBJECTIVES

Test Yourself Answer these repeated Learning Objective Questions on your own (before "showing" the answers here, or checking the answers in Appendix D) to improve your retention of the concepts (McDaniel et al., 2009, 2015).

LOQ 9-1 What is *sleep*?

LOQ 9-2 How do our biological rhythms influence our daily functioning?

LOQ 9-3 What is the biological rhythm of our sleeping and dreaming stages?

LOQ 9-4 How do biology and environment interact in our sleep patterns?

LOQ 9-5 What are sleep's functions?

LOQ 9-6 How does sleep loss affect us, and what are the major sleep disorders?

LOQ 9-7 What do we dream, and what functions have theorists proposed for dreams?

TERMS AND CONCEPTS TO REMEMBER

Test Yourself Write down the definition in your own words, then check your answer.

sleep, p. 95
circadian [ser-KAY-dee-an] rhythm, p. 96
REM sleep, p. 97
alpha waves, p. 97
hallucinations, p. 98
delta waves, p. 98
suprachiasmatic nucleus (SCN), p. 100
insomnia, p. 106
narcolepsy, p. 106
sleep apnea, p. 106
REM sleep behavior disorder, p. 106
night terrors, p. 106
dream, p. 107
manifest content, p. 108
latent content, p. 108
REM rebound, p. 110

MODULE TEST

Test Yourself Answer the following questions on your own first, then "show" the answers here, or check your answers in Appendix E.

1. Our body temperature tends to rise and fall in sync with a biological clock, which is referred to as the ______________.

2. During the N1 sleep stage, a person is most likely to experience
a. sleep spindles.
b. hallucinations.
c. night terrors or nightmares.
d. rapid eye movements.

3. The brain emits large, slow delta waves during ______________ sleep.

4. As the night progresses, what happens to the REM stage of sleep?

5. Which of the following is NOT one of the reasons that have been proposed to explain why we need sleep?
a. Sleep has survival value.
b. Sleep helps us recuperate.
c. Sleep rests the eyes.
d. Sleep plays a role in the growth process.

6. What is the difference between narcolepsy and sleep apnea?

7. In interpreting dreams, Freud was most interested in their
a. information-processing function.
b. neurocognitive function.
c. manifest content, or story line.
d. latent content, or hidden meaning.

8. How has the activation-synthesis theory been used to explain why we dream?

9. "For what one has dwelt on by day, these things are seen in visions of the night" (Menander of Athens [342–292 B.C.E.], *Fragments*). How might we use the information-processing perspective on dreaming to interpret this ancient Greek quote?

10. The tendency for REM sleep to increase following REM sleep deprivation is referred to as ______________.

MODULE 10 Drugs and Consciousness

Mood- and perception-altering psychoactive drugs affect our state of consciousness and may even lead to substance use disorders.

psychoactive drug a chemical substance that alters the brain, causing changes in perceptions and moods.

substance use disorder a disorder characterized by continued substance use despite significant life disruption.

tolerance the diminishing effect with regular use of the same dose of a drug, requiring the user to take larger and larger doses before experiencing the drug's effect.

addiction an everyday term for compulsive substance use (and sometimes for dysfunctional behavior patterns, such as out-of-control gambling) that continues despite harmful consequences. (See also *substance use disorder.*)

withdrawal the discomfort and distress that follow discontinuing an addictive drug or behavior.

Tolerance and Addiction in Substance Use Disorders

LOQ **10-1** What are *substance use disorders*?

Let's imagine a day in the life of a make-believe drug-using student. It begins with a few cups of coffee to feel alert, then Adderall to help focus on a morning lecture. At midday, an energy drink offsets post-lunch drowsiness, and a little vaping calms frazzled nerves before a class presentation. An after-dinner study session means another Adderall, followed by marijuana with friends before heading to the bar. It used to take only a drink or two to feel relaxed, but now it's three or four. Back home, two Advil PMs help induce sleep. The alarm clock beeps just a few hours later, and the daily cycle of drug use resumes. Over time, our imagined student—and many actual students—may struggle to keep up with school, work, and family responsibilities; experience strained relationships; and have difficulty limiting their substance use. How do we know when substance use becomes a problem?

The substances our imaginary student uses are **psychoactive drugs**, chemicals that alter the brain, producing changes in perceptions and moods. Most of us manage to use some psychoactive drugs in moderation and without disrupting our lives. But sometimes, drug use crosses the line between recreational or moderate use and **substance use disorder** (TABLE 10.1).

Today's psychiatric diagnostic system identifies separate categories for *substance/medication-induced disorders* (APA, 2022). A substance/medication-induced disorder occurs when people misuse drugs and alcohol, causing changes that resemble various psychological disorders. These include sexual dysfunctions, obsessive-compulsive disorder (OCD), depression, psychosis, and sleep and neurocognitive disorders.

TABLE 10.1 When Is Drug Use a Disorder?

According to the American Psychiatric Association (2013), a person may be diagnosed with *substance use disorder* when drug use continues despite significant life disruption. Resulting brain changes may persist after quitting use of the substance (thus leading to strong cravings when exposed to people and situations that trigger memories of drug use). The severity of substance use disorder varies from *mild* (two to three of the indicators listed below) to *moderate* (four to five indicators) to *severe* (six or more indicators). If you are concerned about your substance use or that of a loved one, contact your school counseling center, health clinic, or physician.

Indicators
Diminished Control
1. Uses more substance or for longer than intended.
2. Tries unsuccessfully to regulate use of substance.
3. Spends much time acquiring, using, or recovering from effects of substance.
4. Craves the substance.
Diminished Social Functioning
5. Use disrupts commitments at work, school, or home.
6. Continues use despite social problems.
7. Causes reduced social, recreational, and work activities.
Hazardous Use
8. Continues use despite hazards.
9. Continues use despite worsening physical or psychological problems.
Drug Action
10. Experiences tolerance (needing more substance for the desired effect).
11. Experiences withdrawal (unpleasant mental or physical reactions) when attempting to end use.

Thinking Critically About: Tolerance and Addiction

LOQ 10-2 What roles do tolerance and addiction play in substance use disorders, and how has the concept of *addiction* changed?

Tolerance

With continued use of alcohol and some other drugs, users develop **tolerance** as their brain chemistry adapts to offset the drug effect (*neuroadaptation*). To experience the same effect, users require larger and larger doses, which increase the risk of becoming **addicted** and developing a *substance use disorder*.

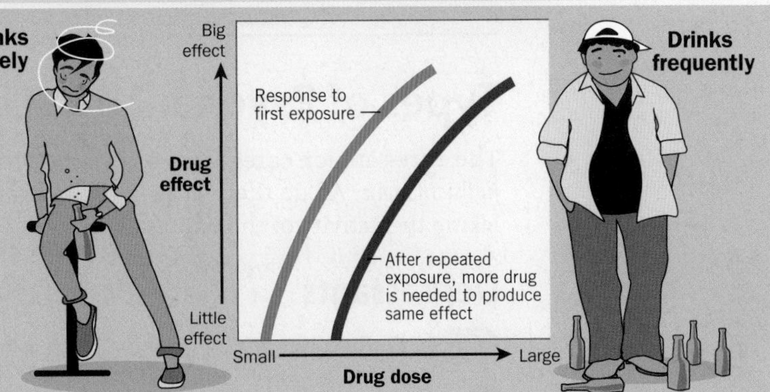

Drinks rarely
Big effect
Drug effect
Little effect
Response to first exposure
After repeated exposure, more drug is needed to produce same effect
Small
Large
Drug dose
Drinks frequently

Addiction

Caused by ever-increasing doses of most psychoactive drugs (including prescription painkillers). Prompts user to crave the drug, to continue use despite adverse consequences, and to struggle when attempting to **withdraw** from it. These behaviors suggest a substance use disorder. Once in the grip of addiction, people *want* the drug more than they *like* the drug.[1]

4% of the world's people have an alcohol use disorder.[2]

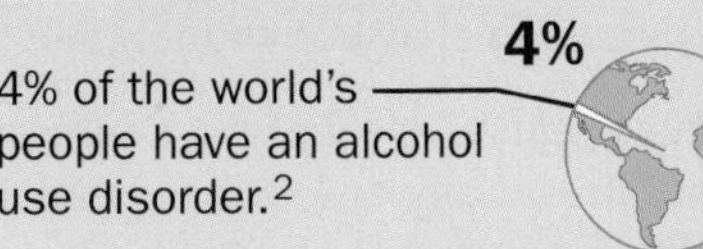

4%

The lifetime odds of getting hooked after using various drugs:

Marijuana	9%
Cocaine	21%
Alcohol	23%
Tobacco	68%

Source: National Epidemiologic Survey on Alcohol and Related Conditions[3]

Therapy or group support, such as from Alcoholics Anonymous, may help. It also helps to believe that addictions are controllable and that people can change. Many people do voluntarily stop using addictive drugs without any treatment. "Most people who successfully quit smoking kicked the habit on their own."[4]

Behavior Addictions

Psychologists try to avoid using "addiction" to label driven, excessive behaviors such as eating, work, sex, and accumulating wealth.

I'm ADDICTED to cheeseburgers!

Yet some behaviors can become compulsive and dysfunctional—similar to problematic alcohol and drug use.[5] Behavior addictions include *gambling disorder. Internet gaming disorder* is also now a diagnosable condition.[6] Such gamers display a consistent inability to resist logging on and staying on, even when this excessive use impairs their work and relationships. One international study of 19,000 gamers found that 1 in 3 had at least one symptom of the disorder. But fewer than 1 percent met criteria for a diagnosis.[7]

Psychological and drug therapies may be "highly effective" for problematic internet use.[8]

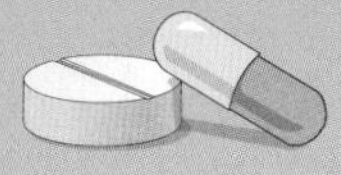

1. Berridge et al., 2009; Robinson & Berridge, 2003. 2. WHO, 2014. 3. Lopez-Quintero et al., 2011. 4. Newport, 2013. 5. Gentile, 2009; Griffiths, 2001; Hoeft et al., 2008. 6. WHO, 2018. 7. Przybylski et al., 2017. 8. Winkler et al., 2013.

A drug's overall effect depends not only on its biological effects but also on the user's expectations, which vary with social and cultural contexts (Gu et al., 2015; Ward, 1994). If one culture assumes that a particular drug produces euphoria (or aggression or sexual arousal) and another does not, each culture may find its expectations fulfilled. We'll take a closer look at these interacting forces in the use and potential abuse of particular psychoactive drugs. But first, to consider what contributes to the disordered use of various substances, see Thinking Critically About: Tolerance and Addiction.

RETRIEVAL PRACTICE

RP-1 What is the process that generally leads to drug tolerance?

RP-2 Can someone become "addicted" to shopping?

ANSWERS IN APPENDIX E

Types of Psychoactive Drugs

The three major categories of psychoactive drugs are *depressants, stimulants,* and *hallucinogens*. All do their work at the brain's synapses, stimulating, inhibiting, or mimicking the activity of the brain's own chemical messengers, the neurotransmitters.

Depressants

LOQ 10-3 What are *depressants,* and what are their effects?

Depressants are drugs such as alcohol, barbiturates (tranquilizers), and opioids that calm neural activity and slow body functions.

ALCOHOL True or false? Alcohol is a depressant in large amounts but is a stimulant in small amounts. *False.* In any amount, alcohol is a depressant. Low doses of alcohol may enliven a drinker, but they do so by acting as a *disinhibitor*—they slow brain activity that controls judgment and inhibitions, causing 3 million yearly deaths worldwide (WHO, 2018).

Alcohol is an equal-opportunity drug: It increases (disinhibits) helpful tendencies—as when tipsy restaurant patrons leave extravagant tips and members of a group bond over drinks (Fairbairn & Sayette, 2014; Lynn, 1988). And it increases harmful tendencies, as when sexually aroused men become more disposed to sexual aggression. Drinking increases men's and women's desire for casual sex and perception of attractiveness in others (Bowdring & Sayette, 2018; Johnson & Chen, 2015). *The bottom line:* The urges you would feel if sober are the ones you will more likely act upon when intoxicated.

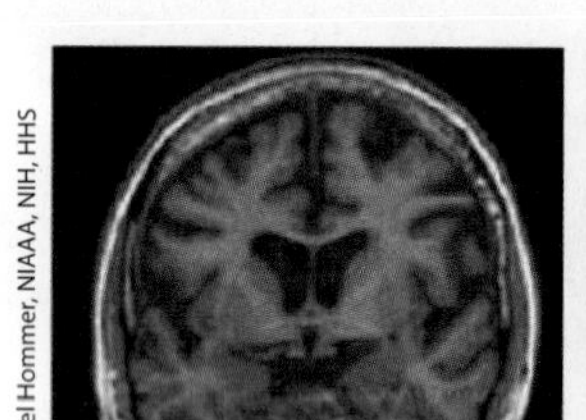

Daniel Hommer, NIAAA, NIH, HHS

Scan of woman with alcohol use disorder (a) | Scan of woman without alcohol use disorder (b)

FIGURE 10.1
Disordered drinking shrinks the brain MRI scans show brain shrinkage in a woman with alcohol use disorder (a) compared with a woman in a control group (b).

The prolonged and excessive drinking that characterizes **alcohol use disorder** (commonly referred to as *alcoholism*) contributes to more than 200 diseases, and can even shrink the brain and contribute to premature death (Kendler et al., 2016; Mackey et al., 2019; WHO, 2018). Girls and young women (who have less of a stomach enzyme that digests alcohol) can become addicted to alcohol more quickly than boys and young men do, and they are at risk for lung, brain, and liver damage at lower consumption levels (CASA, 2003). Heavy drinking has increased among women of all ages, with life-or-death consequences: Canadian women's risk for alcohol-related death between 2001 and 2017 increased at five times the rate of men's (Tam, 2018) (**FIGURE 10.1**). Canadian and Australian researchers are now using computer-based *machine learning* to identify other risk factors and to predict problem alcohol use (Afzali et al., 2019).

Slowed Neural Processing Alcohol slows sympathetic nervous system activity. Larger doses cause reactions to slow, speech to slur, and skilled performance to deteriorate. Alcohol is a potent sedative, especially when paired with sleep deprivation. Add these physical effects to lowered inhibitions, and the result can be deadly. As blood-alcohol levels rise and judgment falters, people's qualms about drinking and driving lessen. When drunk, people aren't aware of how drunk they are (Moore et al., 2016). Virtually all drinkers insist when sober that they would not drive under the influence later. Yet, in experiments, the majority of intoxicated participants decided to drink and drive (MacDonald et al., 1995; Ouimet et al., 2020). Alcohol can also be life-threatening when heavy drinking depresses the vomiting response. People may poison themselves with an overdose that their bodies would normally throw up.

depressants drugs (such as alcohol, barbiturates, and opioids) that reduce neural activity and slow body functions.

alcohol use disorder (commonly known as *alcoholism*) alcohol use marked by a combination of symptoms that may include tolerance, withdrawal, and a drive to continue problematic use.

Memory Disruption Alcohol can disrupt memory formation, and heavy drinking can also have long-term effects on the brain and cognition. In rats, at a developmental period corresponding to human adolescence, binge drinking contributes to nerve cell

ITALIA'S
PIZZERIA
MARYSVILLE FD

Lon Clark Diehl

Drinking disaster demo Firefighters reenacted the trauma of an alcohol-related car accident, providing a memorable demonstration for these high school students. Alcohol consumption leads to feelings of invincibility, which become especially dangerous behind the wheel of a car.

death and reduces the birth of new nerve cells. It also impairs the growth of synaptic connections (Crews et al., 2006, 2007). In humans, heavy drinking may lead to blackouts, in which drinkers continue to interact but are unable to later recall people they met or what they said or did while intoxicated.

Reduced Self-Awareness In one experiment, those who consumed alcohol (rather than a placebo beverage) were doubly likely to be caught mind-wandering during a reading task, yet were *less* likely to notice that they zoned out (Sayette et al., 2009). Sometimes we mind-wander to give our brains a break, but unintentional zoning out—while driving, for example—can cause later regret (Seli et al., 2016). Alcohol also focuses attention on an immediate arousing situation (say, provocation) and distracts it from normal inhibitions and future consequences (Giancola et al., 2010; Steele & Josephs, 1990).

Reduced self-awareness may help explain why people who want to suppress their awareness of failures or shortcomings often drink more than do those who feel good about themselves. Losing a business deal, a game, or a romantic partner sometimes elicits binge drinking.

Expectancy Effects Expectations influence behavior. Adolescents—presuming that alcohol will lift their spirits—sometimes drink when they're upset and alone (Bresin et al., 2018). But solitary drinking just boosts their chance of developing a substance use disorder (Creswell et al., 2014; Fairbairn & Sayette, 2014).

Simply *believing* we're consuming alcohol can cause us to act out alcohol's presumed influence (Christiansen et al., 2016; Moss & Albery, 2009). In a classic experiment, researchers gave male students at Rutgers University either an alcoholic or a nonalcoholic drink (Abrams & Wilson, 1983). (Both had a strong flavor that masked the taste and smell of alcohol.) After watching an erotic movie clip, the men who *thought* they had consumed alcohol were more likely to report having strong sexual fantasies and feeling guilt free. *The point to remember:* Alcohol's effect lies partly in that powerful sex organ, the mind.

BARBITURATES Like alcohol, the **barbiturate** drugs, which are *tranquilizers,* depress nervous system activity. Barbiturates such as Nembutal, Seconal, and Amytal are sometimes prescribed to induce sleep or reduce anxiety. In larger doses, they can impair memory and judgment. If combined with alcohol—say, a sleeping pill after an evening of heavy drinking—the total depressive effect on body functions can be lethal.

OPIOIDS The **opioids**—opium and its derivatives—also depress neural functioning. Opioids include *heroin* and its medically prescribed synthetic substitute, *methadone.*

barbiturates drugs that depress central nervous system activity, reducing anxiety but impairing memory and judgment.

opioids opium and its derivatives, such as morphine and heroin; depress neural activity, temporarily lessening pain and anxiety.

Theo Wargo/WireImage/Getty Images

Jerod Harris/Getty Images

Lives lost to opioids Prince and Tom Petty are among those who have died of opioid overdoses. Both musicians had been prescribed narcotic painkillers for chronic pain conditions.

They also include pain-relief *narcotics* such as codeine, OxyContin, Vicodin, and morphine (and morphine's dangerously powerful synthetic counterpart, fentanyl). As blissful pleasure replaces pain and anxiety, the user's pupils constrict and breathing slows, and lethargy sets in. Those who become addicted to this short-term pleasure may pay a long-term price: a gnawing craving for another fix, a need for progressively larger doses (as tolerance develops), and the extreme discomfort of withdrawal. When repeatedly flooded with a synthetic opioid, the brain eventually stops producing *endorphins*, its own natural opioids. If the artificial opioid is then withdrawn, the brain will lack the normal level of these painkilling neurotransmitters.

An alarming number of Americans have been unable or unwilling to tolerate this state, and have paid an ultimate price—death by overdose. Between 2013 and 2016, the U.S. rate of opioid overdose deaths increased almost *ten times* to 43,036 (NIDA, 2018; NSC, 2019). "For the first time in U.S. history, a person is more likely to die from an accidental opioid overdose than from a motor vehicle crash," reported the National Safety Council in 2019. The Covid pandemic increased stress, uncertainty, and social isolation that may have contributed to even more U.S. and Canadian opioid-related deaths in 2020 (Katz et al., 2020; Schmunk, 2020).

What started the opioid crisis? Drug companies played a large part by aggressively promoting opioid drugs while downplaying the dangers, and by sending millions of pills to pharmacies known to sell the drugs illegally (Rashbaum, 2019). As a result, pharmaceutical companies have been fined billions of dollars, including one company in 2019 for "false, misleading, and dangerous marketing" of opioids (Hoffman, 2019). Some doctors have overprescribed pills, making their patients more likely to become addicted (Tompkins et al., 2017). Social influence also matters. People with parents and friends who use opioids are more likely to use opioids (Griesler et al., 2019; Keyes et al., 2014).

RETRIEVAL PRACTICE

RP-3 Alcohol, barbiturates, and opioids are all in a class of drugs called ___________.

ANSWERS IN APPENDIX E

Stimulants

LOQ 10-4 What are *stimulants,* and what are their effects?

A **stimulant** excites neural activity and speeds up body functions. Pupils dilate, heart and breathing rates increase, and blood sugar levels rise, reducing appetite. Energy and self-confidence also rise.

Stimulants include caffeine, nicotine, and the more powerful cocaine, **amphetamines**, methamphetamine (also known as "speed"), and Ecstasy. People use stimulants to feel alert, lose weight, or boost mood or athletic performance. Some students resort to stronger stimulant drugs in hopes of boosting their grades, even though the drugs offer little or no benefit (Ilieva et al., 2015; Teter et al., 2018). Stimulants can be addictive, as many know from the fatigue, headaches, irritability, and depression that result from missing their usual caffeine dose (Silverman et al., 1992). A mild dose typically lasts three or four hours, which—if taken in the evening—may impair sleep.

stimulants drugs (such as caffeine, nicotine, and the more powerful cocaine, amphetamines, methamphetamine, and Ecstasy) that excite neural activity and speed up body functions.

amphetamines drugs (such as *methamphetamine*) that stimulate neural activity, causing accelerated body functions and associated energy and mood changes.

ASK YOURSELF

Have you ever relied on caffeinated drinks to stay awake for a late-night study session, and then struggled to fall asleep? How might you plan your caffeine intake and study sessions better?

NICOTINE Tobacco products deliver highly addictive **nicotine**. Imagine that cigarettes were harmless—except, once in every 25,000 packs, an occasional innocent-looking one was filled with dynamite instead of tobacco. Not such a bad risk of having your head blown off. But with 250 million packs a day consumed worldwide, we could expect more than 10,000 gruesome daily deaths—surely enough to have cigarettes banned everywhere.[1]

The lost lives from these dynamite-loaded cigarettes approximate those from today's actual cigarettes. A teen-to-the-grave smoker has a 50 percent chance of dying from the habit, and each year, tobacco kills nearly 7 million people worldwide, with another 1.2 million people killed due to exposure to second-hand smoke (WHO, 2020). By 2030, annual tobacco deaths are expected to increase to 8 million. That means that 1 *billion* twenty-first-century people may be killed by tobacco (WHO, 2012). Most tobacco deaths will occur in low- and middle-income countries, where 80 percent of the world's smokers live (Akanbi et al., 2019).

Tobacco products include cigarettes, cigars, chewing tobacco, pipe tobacco, snuff, and—most recently—e-cigarettes. Inhaling e-cigarette vapor (vaping) gives users a jolt of nicotine without cancer-causing tar. Thanks to vaping's rapid increase—the fastest drug use increase on record—U.S. high school students in 2019 used e-cigarettes at five times the rate of traditional cigarettes (Miech et al., 2019).

In one survey of regular e-cigarette users from the United States, England, Canada, and Australia, 85 percent reported they vaped because they believed it would help them cut down on smoking traditional cigarettes (Yong et al., 2019). Experts continue to debate whether e-cigarettes can help smokers quit smoking (Hajek et al., 2019; HHS, 2020). But they agree that e-cigarettes are addictive nicotine dispensers that introduce nonsmokers to smoking (Prochaska, 2019). In a British study, nonsmoking teens who started vaping became four times more likely to move on to cigarette smoking (Miech et al., 2017).

"No adult who has never used nicotine should ever use our product." —Ashley Gould, Chief Administrative Officer of e-cigarette company Juul Labs, 2018

Teen use has prompted legal restrictions as well as investigations, including one by the U.S. Food and Drug Administration on whether e-cigarette companies target teenage users (Richtel & Kaplan, 2018). Fruity flavors, for example, increases teen use (Buckell & Sindelar, 2019; O'Connor et al., 2019). These troubling trends prompted U.S. Surgeon General Jerome Adams to "officially declar[e] e-cigarette use among youth an epidemic" (Stein, 2018).

Smoke a cigarette and nature will charge you 12 minutes—about double the length of time you spend smoking it (*Discover,* 1996). (Researchers don't yet know how e-cigarette use affects life expectancy.) Compared with nonsmokers, smokers' life expectancy is "at least 10 years shorter" (CDC, 2013). Eliminating smoking would increase life expectancy more than any other preventive measure. Why, then, do so many people smoke?

Tobacco products are as powerfully and quickly addictive as heroin and cocaine. Attempts to quit tobacco use, even within the first weeks, often fail (DiFranza, 2008). And, as with other addictions, users develop *tolerance.* Those who attempt to quit will experience nicotine withdrawal symptoms—craving, insomnia, anxiety, irritability, and distractibility. When trying to focus on a task, their mind wanders at three times the normal rate (Sayette et al., 2010). When not craving a cigarette, they tend to underestimate the power of such cravings (Sayette et al., 2008).

All it takes to relieve the aversive state of craving is a single inhale. With that inhale, a rush of nicotine will signal the central nervous system to release a flood of neurotransmitters (**FIGURE 10.2**): Epinephrine and norepinephrine diminish appetite and boost alertness and mental efficiency. Dopamine and opioids temporarily calm anxiety and reduce sensitivity to pain (Ditre et al., 2011; Gavin, 2004). No wonder some ex-users, under stress, resume their habit—as did some 1 million Americans after the 9/11 terrorist attacks (Pesko, 2014). Ditto for people experiencing major depressive disorder, who are more likely than others to see their efforts to quit go up in smoke (Zvolensky et al., 2015).

Cigarette smoking is the leading cause of preventable death in the United States, killing 480,000 people each year (CDC, 2020). Although 3 in 4 smokers wish they could stop, each year fewer than 1 in 7 will be successful (Newport, 2013). Even those who know that smoking is slow-motion suicide may be unable to stop (Saad, 2002).

[1]This analogy, adapted here with world-based numbers, was suggested by mathematician Sam Saunders, as reported by K. C. Cole (1998).

nicotine a stimulating and highly addictive psychoactive drug in tobacco products.

FIGURE 10.2
Physiological effects of nicotine
Nicotine reaches the brain within 7 seconds, twice as fast as intravenous heroin. Within minutes, the amount in the blood soars.

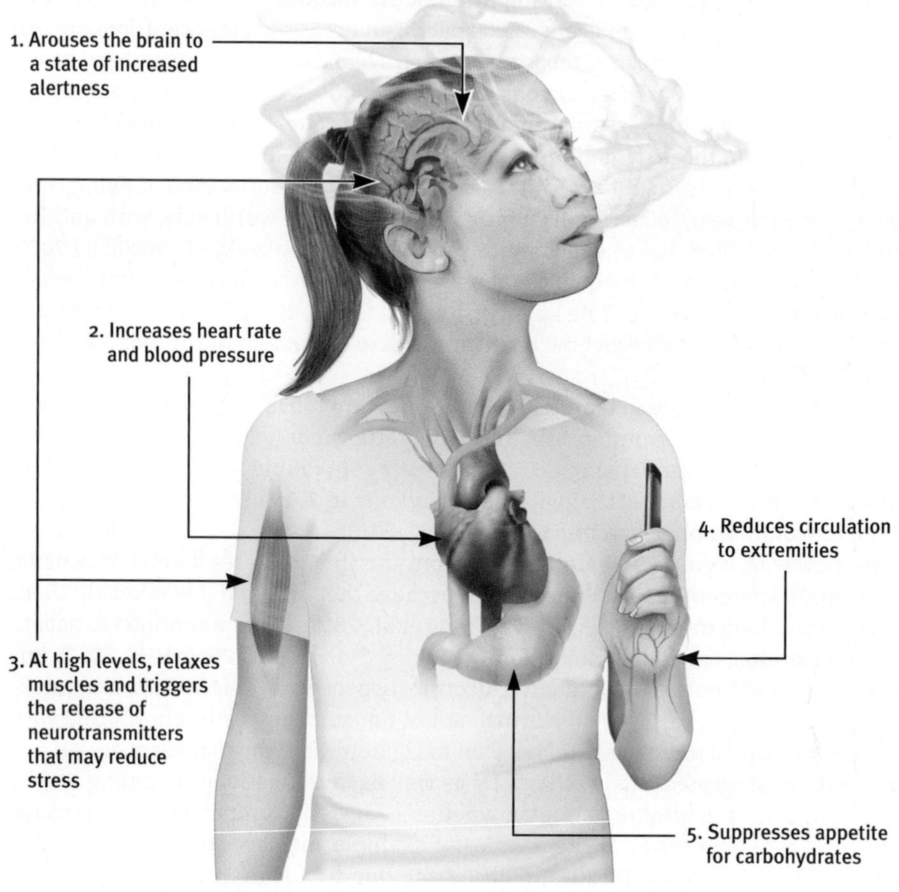
1. Arouses the brain to a state of increased alertness
2. Increases heart rate and blood pressure
3. At high levels, relaxes muscles and triggers the release of neurotransmitters that may reduce stress
4. Reduces circulation to extremities
5. Suppresses appetite for carbohydrates

Nevertheless, repeated attempts seem to pay off. The worldwide smoking rate—25 percent among men and 5 percent among women—is down about 30 percent since 1990 (GBD, 2017). The U.S. smoking rate plummeted from 45 percent in 1955 to 15 percent in 2019 (Saad, 2019). Half of all Americans who have ever smoked have quit, sometimes aided by a nicotine replacement drug and with encouragement from a counselor or support group. Some researchers argue that it is best to quit abruptly—to go "cold turkey" (Lindson-Hawley et al., 2016). Others suggest that success is equally likely whether smokers quit abruptly or gradually (Fiore et al., 2008; Lichtenstein et al., 2010). *The point to remember:* If you want to quit using tobacco, there is hope regardless of how you choose to quit.

For those who endure, the acute craving and withdrawal symptoms slowly dissipate over the ensuing 6 months (Ward et al., 1997). After a year's abstinence, only 10 percent will relapse in the next year (Hughes, 2010). These nonsmokers may live not only healthier but also happier lives. Smoking correlates with higher rates of depression, chronic disabilities, and divorce (Doherty & Doherty, 1998; Edwards & Kendler, 2012; Vita et al., 1998). Healthy living seems to add both years to life and life to years. Awareness of nonsmokers' better health and happiness has contributed to U.S. twelfth graders' 88 percent disapproval of smoking a pack or more a day, and also to a plunge in their daily smoking rate, from 25 percent in 1997 to 2 percent in 2019 (Johnston et al., 2020).

Humorist Dave Barry (1995) recalling why he smoked his first cigarette the summer he turned 15: "Arguments against smoking: 'It's a repulsive addiction that slowly but surely turns you into a gasping, gray-skinned, tumor-ridden invalid, hacking up brownish gobs of toxic waste from your one remaining lung.' Arguments for smoking: 'Other teenagers are doing it.' Case closed! Let's light up!"

ASK YOURSELF

Think of a friend or family member who is addicted to nicotine. What do you think would be most effective to say to that person to convince them to try to quit?

RETRIEVAL PRACTICE

RP-4 What withdrawal symptoms should your friend expect when quitting smoking?

ANSWERS IN APPENDIX E

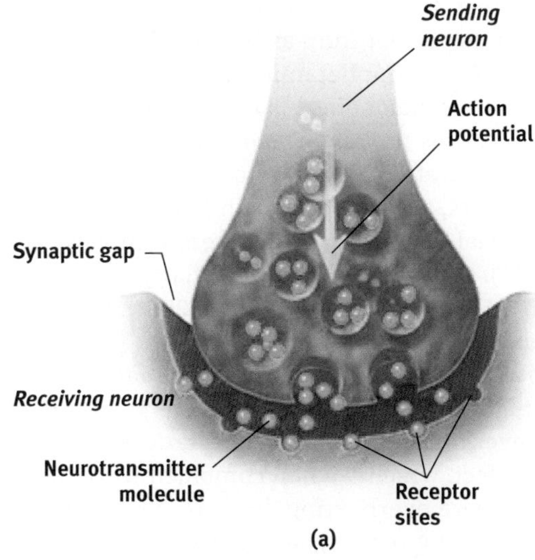
Sending neuron
Action potential
Synaptic gap
Receiving neuron
Neurotransmitter molecule
Receptor sites

(a)

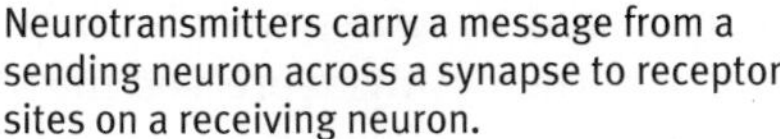

Neurotransmitters carry a message from a sending neuron across a synapse to receptor sites on a receiving neuron.

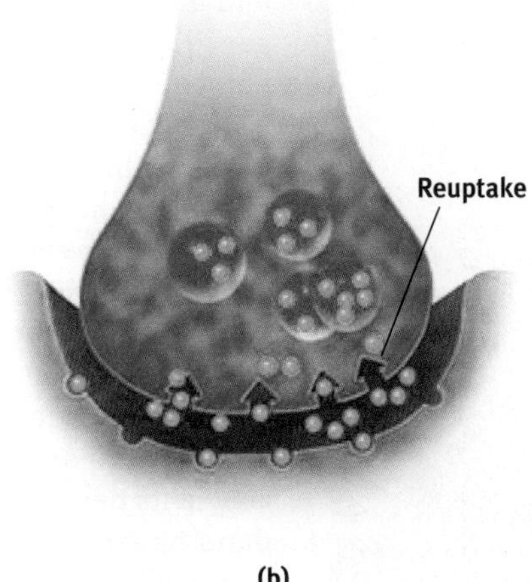
Reuptake

(b)

The sending neuron normally reabsorbs excess neurotransmitter molecules, a process called *reuptake.*

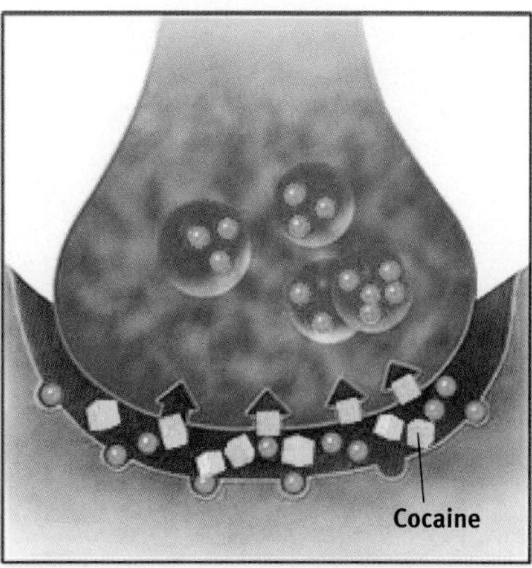
Cocaine

(c)

By binding to the sites that normally reabsorb neurotransmitter molecules, cocaine blocks reuptake of dopamine, norepinephrine, and serotonin (Ray & Ksir, 1990). The extra neurotransmitter molecules therefore remain in the synapse, intensifying their normal mood-altering effects and producing a euphoric rush. When the cocaine level drops, the absence of these neurotransmitters produces a crash.

FIGURE 10.3
Cocaine euphoria and crash

COCAINE **Cocaine** is a powerfully addictive stimulant derived from the coca plant. The recipe for Coca-Cola originally included coca extract, creating a mild cocaine tonic intended for tired older people. Between 1896 and 1905, Coke was indeed "the real thing." Today, cocaine is snorted, injected, or smoked (sometimes as *crack cocaine,* a faster-working crystallized form that produces a briefer but more intense high, followed by a more intense crash). Cocaine enters the bloodstream quickly, producing a rush of euphoria that depletes the brain's supply of the neurotransmitters dopamine, serotonin, and norepinephrine (FIGURE 10.3). Within the hour, a crash of agitated depression follows as the drug's effect wears off. After several hours, the craving for more wanes, only to return several days later (Gawin, 1991).

cocaine a powerful and addictive stimulant derived from the coca plant; produces temporarily increased alertness and euphoria.

methamphetamine a powerfully addictive drug that stimulates the central nervous system, with accelerated body functions and associated energy and mood changes; over time, reduces baseline dopamine levels.

In situations that trigger aggression, ingesting cocaine may heighten reactions. Caged rats fight when given foot shocks, and they fight even more when given cocaine *and* foot shocks. Likewise, humans who voluntarily ingest high doses of cocaine in laboratory experiments impose higher shock levels on a presumed opponent than do those receiving a placebo (Licata et al., 1993). Cocaine use may also lead to emotional disturbances, suspiciousness, convulsions, cardiac arrest, or respiratory failure.

Cocaine powerfully stimulates brain reward pathways (Keramati et al., 2017; Walker et al., 2018). Alcohol or nicotine use, which often precedes cocaine use, amplifies the brain's response to cocaine (Griffin et al., 2017). Cocaine's psychological effects vary with the dosage and form consumed, but the situation and the user's expectations and personality also play a role. Given a placebo, cocaine users who *thought* they were taking cocaine often had a cocaine-like experience (Van Dyke & Byck, 1982).

In national surveys, 2 percent of American twelfth graders and 6 percent of British 18- to 24-year-olds reported having tried cocaine during the past year (ACMD, 2009; Johnston et al., 2020).

Dramatic drug-induced decline In the 18 months between these two mug shots, this woman's methamphetamine addiction led to obvious physical changes.

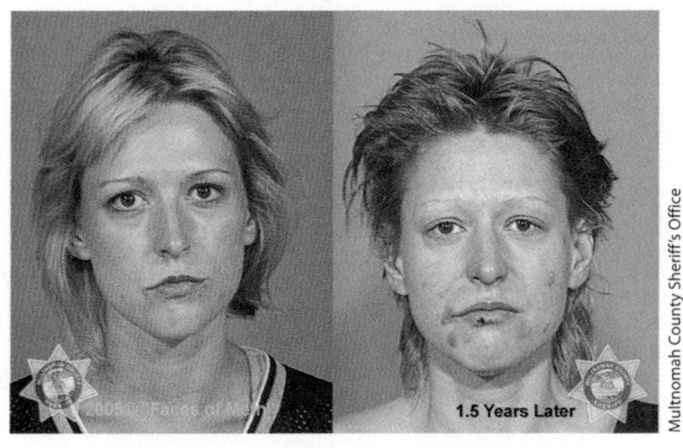
1.5 Years Later

Multnomah County Sheriff's Office

METHAMPHETAMINE Amphetamines stimulate neural activity. As body functions speed up, the user's energy rises and mood soars. Amphetamines are the parent drug for the highly addictive **methamphetamine**, which is chemically similar but has greater effects (NIDA, 2002, 2005). Methamphetamine triggers the release of the neurotransmitter dopamine, which stimulates brain cells that enhance energy and mood, leading to 8 hours or so of heightened energy and euphoria. Its aftereffects may include irritability, insomnia, hypertension, seizures, social isolation, depression, and occasional violent outbursts (Homer et al., 2008). Over time, methamphetamine reduces baseline dopamine levels, leaving the user with continuing depressed functioning.

Malthe Ivarsson/Gonzales Photo/Alamy Stock Photo

The hug drug MDMA, known as Ecstasy and often taken at clubs, produces a euphoric high and feelings of intimacy. But repeated use can destroy serotonin-producing neurons, impair memory, and permanently deflate mood.

ECSTASY **Ecstasy**, a street name for **MDMA** (*methylenedioxymethamphetamine*, also known in its powder form as *Molly*), is both a stimulant and a mild hallucinogen. As an amphetamine derivative, Ecstasy triggers dopamine release, but its major effect is releasing stored serotonin and blocking its reuptake, thus prolonging serotonin's feel-good flood (Braun, 2001). Users feel the effect about a half-hour after taking an Ecstasy pill. For 3 or 4 hours, they experience high energy, emotional elevation, and (given a social context) connectedness with those around them ("I love everyone!"). Octopuses became similarly sociable when researchers gave them MDMA (Edsinger & Dölen, 2018). Eight arms + MDMA = a lot of reaching out.

Ecstasy's popularity first soared globally in the late 1990s as a "club drug" taken at nightclubs and all-night dance parties (Landry, 2002). There are, however, reasons not to be ecstatic about Ecstasy. One is its dehydrating effect, which—when combined with prolonged dancing—can lead to severe overheating, increased blood pressure, and death. Another is that long-term, repeated leaching of brain serotonin can damage serotonin-producing neurons, leading to decreased output and increased risk of permanently depressed mood (Croft et al., 2001; McCann et al., 2001; Roiser et al., 2005). Ecstasy also suppresses the immune system, impairs memory, slows thought, and disrupts sleep by interfering with serotonin's control of the circadian clock (Laws & Kokkalis, 2007; Schilt et al., 2007; Wagner et al., 2012). Ecstasy delights for the night but dispirits the morrow.

Hallucinogens

LOQ 10-5 What are *hallucinogens*, and what are their effects?

Hallucinogens distort perceptions and evoke sensory images in the absence of sensory input (which is why these drugs are also called *psychedelics*, meaning "mind-manifesting"). Some, such as LSD and MDMA (Ecstasy), are synthetic. Others, including psilocybin, ayahuasca, and the mild hallucinogen marijuana, are natural substances. Researchers are exploring psilocybin and ayahuasca as possible treatments for persistent depression.

Whether provoked to hallucinate by drugs, loss of oxygen, or extreme sensory deprivation, the brain hallucinates in basically the same way (Martial et al., 2019; Siegel, 1982). The experience typically begins with simple geometric forms, such as a spiral. Then come more meaningful images, which may be superimposed on a tunnel; others may be replays of past emotional experiences. Brain scans of people on LSD reveal that their visual cortex becomes hypersensitive and strongly connected to their brain's emotion centers (Carhart-Harris et al., 2016). As the hallucination peaks, people frequently feel separated from their body and experience dreamlike scenes. Their sense of self dissolves, as does the border between themselves and the external world (Lebedev et al., 2015).

These sensations are strikingly similar to the **near-death experience**, an altered state of consciousness reported by 10 to 23 percent of those revived from cardiac arrest (Martial et al., 2020). Many describe visions of tunnels (**FIGURE 10.4**), bright lights, a replay of old memories, and out-of-body sensations (Siegel, 1980). These experiences can later enhance spirituality and promote feelings of personal growth (Khanna & Greyson, 2014, 2015). Given that oxygen deprivation and other insults to the brain are known to produce hallucinations, we may wonder: Does a brain under stress manufacture the near-death experience? During epileptic seizures and migraines, people may experience similar hallucinations of geometric patterns (Billock & Tsou, 2012). So have solitary sailors and polar explorers while enduring monotony, isolation, and cold (Suedfeld & Mocellin, 1987). The philosopher-neuroscientist Patricia Churchland has called such experiences "neural funny business" (Churchland, 2013, p. 70).

LSD Chemist Albert Hofmann created—and on one Friday afternoon in April 1943 accidentally ingested—**LSD (lysergic acid diethylamide)**. The result—"an uninterrupted

Ecstasy (MDMA) a synthetic stimulant and mild hallucinogen. Produces euphoria and social intimacy, but with short-term health risks and longer-term harm to serotonin-producing neurons and to mood and cognition.

hallucinogens psychedelic ("mind-manifesting") drugs, such as LSD, that distort perceptions and evoke sensory images in the absence of sensory input.

near-death experience an altered state of consciousness reported after a close brush with death (such as cardiac arrest); often similar to drug-induced hallucinations.

LSD (lysergic acid diethylamide) a powerful hallucinogenic drug; also known as *acid*.

stream of fantastic pictures, extraordinary shapes with intense, kaleidoscopic play of colors"—reminded him of a childhood mystical experience that had left him longing for another glimpse of "a miraculous, powerful, unfathomable reality" (Siegel, 1984; Smith, 2006).

The emotions of an LSD (or *acid*) trip vary from euphoria to detachment to panic. Users' mood and expectations (their "high hopes") color the emotional experience, but the perceptual distortions and hallucinations have some commonalities.

NUMAX3D/Shutterstock

FIGURE 10.4
Near-death vision or hallucination? Psychologist Ronald Siegel (1977) reported that people under the influence of hallucinogenic drugs often see "a bright light in the center of the field of vision. . . . The location of this point of light create[s] a tunnel-like perspective." This is very similar to others' near-death experiences.

MARIJUANA The straight dope on marijuana: Marijuana leaves and flowers contain **THC (delta-9-tetrahydrocannabinol)**. Whether inhaled (getting to the brain quickly) or consumed (traveling through the body slowly), THC produces a mix of effects. An analysis of 15 studies showed that the THC of a single joint may induce psychiatric symptoms such as hallucinations, delusions, and anxiety (Hindley et al., 2020).

Marijuana amplifies sensitivity to colors, sounds, tastes, and smells. But like the depressant alcohol, it relaxes, disinhibits, and may produce a euphoric high. As with alcohol, people sometimes consume marijuana to help them sleep or improve their mood, even though marijuana use often predicts worse sleep and mood (Buckner et al., 2019; Wong et al., 2019). Both alcohol and marijuana impair the motor coordination, perceptual skills, and reaction time necessary for safely operating a vehicle or other machine. "THC causes animals to misjudge events," reported Ronald Siegel (1990, p. 163). "Pigeons wait too long to respond to buzzers or lights that tell them food is available for brief periods; and rats turn the wrong way in mazes."

Marijuana and alcohol also differ. The body eliminates alcohol within hours, while THC and its by-products linger in the body for more than a week. Although marijuana users develop tolerance—a lesser high for a single dose—repeated short-term use increases the drug's presence in the body (Volkow et al., 2014).

Synthetic cannabinoids (also known as *synthetic marijuana, Spice,* or *K2*) mimic THC. Their harmful side effects can include agitation and hallucinations (Fattore, 2016; Sherif et al., 2016).

After considering more than 10,000 scientific reports, the U.S. National Academies of Sciences, Engineering, and Medicine (2017) concluded that marijuana use

- alleviates chronic pain, chemotherapy-related nausea, and muscle soreness among people with multiple sclerosis;
- may offer short-term sleep improvements;
- does not increase risk for tobacco-related diseases such as lung cancer;
- predicts increased risk of traffic accidents;
- predicts increased risk of chronic bronchitis, psychosis, social anxiety disorder, and suicidal thoughts; and
- likely contributes to impaired attention, learning, and memory, and possibly to academic underachievement.

The more often the person uses marijuana, especially during adolescence, the greater the risk of anxiety, depression, psychosis, and suicidal behavior (Gage, 2019; Gobbi et al., 2019; Huckins, 2017). One study of nearly 4000 Canadian seventh graders concluded that marijuana use at that early age was "neurotoxic": It predicted long-term cognitive impairment (Harvey, 2019). Marijuana can also function as a "gateway drug" for future alcohol and opioid use (Gunn et al., 2018; Olfson et al., 2018). "Nearly 1 in 5 people who begin marijuana use during adolescence become addicted," warned U.S. Surgeon General Jerome Adams (Aubrey, 2019).

Americans' attitudes toward marijuana use have changed remarkably—from 12 percent support for legalizing marijuana in 1969 to 66 percent in 2019 (De Pinto, 2019; McCarthy, 2018). Some countries and U.S. states have legalized marijuana possession. Greater legal acceptance may explain why rates of Americans who have tried marijuana rose dramatically between 1969 and 2019, from 4 to 45 percent, with 12 percent saying they now smoke marijuana (Gallup, 2019).

* * *

Despite their differences, the psychoactive drugs summarized in **TABLE 10.2** share a common feature: They trigger changes to the brain and body that grow stronger with repetition. This helps explain both tolerance and withdrawal.

THC (delta-9-tetrahydrocannabinol) the major mind-altering ingredient in marijuana. 

TABLE 10.2 A Guide to Selected Psychoactive Drugs

Drug	Type	Pleasurable Effects	Possible Negative Effects
Alcohol	Depressant	Initial high followed by relaxation and disinhibition	Depression, memory loss, organ damage, impaired reactions
Heroin	Depressant	Rush of euphoria, relief from pain	Depressed physiology, loss of natural endorphin function
Caffeine	Stimulant	Increased alertness and wakefulness	Anxiety, restlessness, and insomnia in high doses
Nicotine	Stimulant	Arousal and relaxation, sense of well-being	Heart disease, cancer
Cocaine	Stimulant	Rush of euphoria, confidence, energy	Cardiovascular stress, suspiciousness, depressive crash
Methamphetamine	Stimulant	Euphoria, alertness, energy	Irritability, insomnia, hypertension, seizures
Ecstasy (MDMA)	Stimulant; mild hallucinogen	Emotional elevation, disinhibition	Dehydration, overheating, depressed mood, impaired cognitive and immune functioning
LSD	Hallucinogen	Visual "trip"	Risk of panic
Marijuana (THC)	Mild hallucinogen	Enhanced sensation, relief of pain, distortion of time, relaxation	Impaired learning and memory, increased risk of psychological disorders

RETRIEVAL PRACTICE

"How curiously [pleasure] is related to what is thought to be its opposite, pain! . . . Wherever the one is found, the other follows up behind." (Plato, *Phaedo*, fourth century B.C.E.)

RP-5 How does this pleasure-pain description apply to the repeated use of psychoactive drugs?

ANSWERS IN APPENDIX E

Influences on Drug Use

LOQ 10-6 Why do some people become regular users of consciousness-altering drugs?

Drug use by North American youth increased during the 1970s. Then, with increased drug education and a more realistic and deglamorized media depiction of taking drugs, drug use declined sharply (except for a small rise in the mid-1980s). After the early 1990s, the cultural antidrug voice softened, and some drugs for a time were again glamorized in music and films. Consider these historical trends in the use of marijuana:

- In the University of Michigan's annual survey of 15,000 U.S. twelfth graders, the proportion who said there is "great risk" in regular marijuana use rose from 35 percent in 1978 to 79 percent in 1991, then retreated to 30 percent in 2019 (Johnston et al., 2020).
- After peaking in 1978, marijuana use by U.S. twelfth graders declined through 1992, then rose and held steady until beginning to trend back up in 2015. Canadian use among 15- to 24-year-olds has been similarly trending upward since 2012 (CCSA, 2017), and by late 2019 was 16 percent among Canadians age 15 and older (CBC, 2019). European teen drug use is lower, but with trends mirroring those in North America: rising marijuana and declining cigarette use (Wadley & Lee, 2016).

Adolescents sometimes experiment with mind-altering drugs, unaware or unconvinced that doing so increases their risk of developing a substance use disorder. So why do some teens, but not others, become regular drug users? In search of answers, researchers have engaged biological, psychological, and social-cultural levels of analysis.

Biological Influences

Some people are biologically vulnerable to particular drugs:

- ***Genetics***. Heredity influences some aspects of substance use problems, especially those appearing by early adulthood (Crabbe, 2002). Researchers have identified genes associated with alcohol use disorder, and they are discovering genes that contribute to nicotine and cannabis use disorders (Erzurumluoglu et al., 2019; Sanchez-Roige et al., 2019).

- ***Brain differences.*** These culprit genes seemingly produce deficiencies in the brain's natural dopamine reward system: While triggering temporary dopamine-produced pleasure, the addictive drugs disrupt normal dopamine balance. Studies of how drugs reprogram the brain's reward systems raise hopes for anti-addiction drugs that might block or blunt the effects of alcohol and other drugs (Volkow & Boyle, 2018). Neuroscientists have also discovered a brain circuit that may predict compulsive drinking. In mice, the circuit's activity in response to drinking alcohol predicts which mice will become excessive alcohol drinkers (Siciliano, 2019).
- ***Twin studies.*** If an identical rather than fraternal twin is diagnosed with alcohol use disorder, the other twin is at increased risk for alcohol problems (Verhulst et al., 2015). In marijuana use, too, identical twins more closely resemble each other than do fraternal twins.
- ***Adoption studies.*** One study tracked 18,115 Swedish adoptees. Those with drug-abusing biological parents were at doubled risk of drug abuse, indicating a genetic influence—a finding confirmed in another Swedish study of 14,000+ twins and 1.3 million other siblings. But then those with drug-abusing adoptive siblings also had a doubled risk of drug abuse, indicating an environmental influence (Kendler et al., 2012; Maes et al., 2016). So, what might those environmental influences be?

Warning signs of alcohol use disorder:

- Drinking binges (five drinks for men and four for women over 2 hours)
- Craving alcohol
- Use results in unfulfilled work, school, or home tasks
- Failing to honor a resolve to drink less
- Continued use despite health risk
- Avoiding family or friends when drinking

Psychological and Social-Cultural Influences

Throughout this text, you will see that biological, psychological, and social-cultural factors interact to produce behavior. An example is problematic drug use (**FIGURE 10.5**). Those without close, secure attachments with family and friends are more likely to turn to substance use (Fairbairn et al., 2018). So, too, are those who find their lives meaningless and directionless (Kim et al., 2020).

Sometimes the psychological influence is obvious. Many heavy users of alcohol, marijuana, and cocaine have experienced trauma or failure and are depressed. Girls with a history of depression, eating disorders, or sexual or physical abuse are at increased risk for substance misuse. So are youth undergoing school or neighborhood transitions (CASA, 2003; Logan et al., 2002). Undergraduates who have not yet achieved a clear identity are also at greater risk (Bishop et al., 2005). By temporarily dulling the pain of self-awareness, psychoactive drugs may offer a way to avoid coping with depression, anger, anxiety, or insomnia. (As the learning modules explain, behavior is often controlled more by its immediate consequences than by its later ones.)

Smoking and vaping usually begin during early adolescence. (If you are in college or university, and tobacco product companies haven't yet made you their devoted

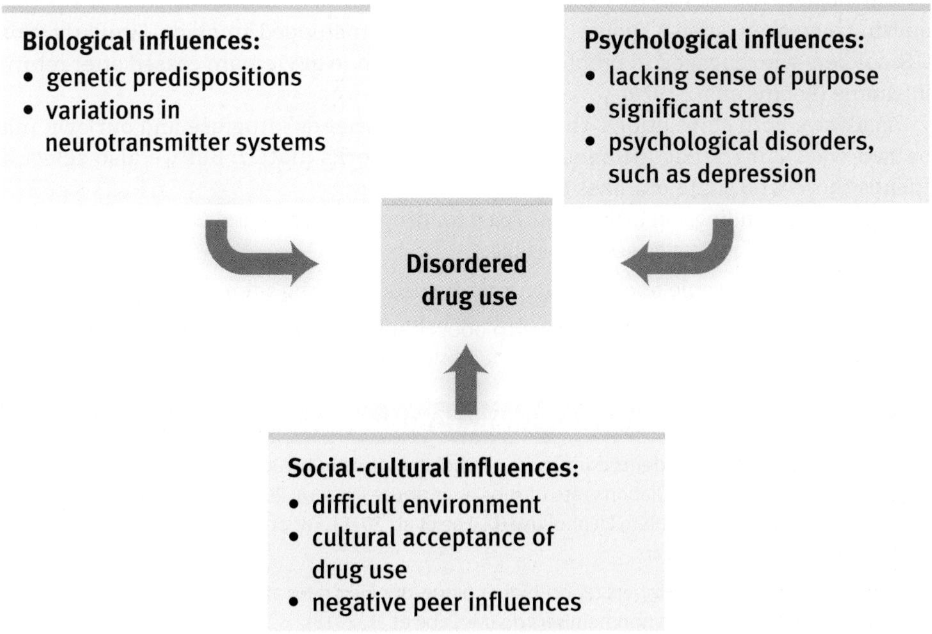

Biological influences:
- genetic predispositions
- variations in neurotransmitter systems

Psychological influences:
- lacking sense of purpose
- significant stress
- psychological disorders, such as depression

Disordered drug use

Social-cultural influences:
- difficult environment
- cultural acceptance of drug use
- negative peer influences

FIGURE 10.5
Levels of analysis for disordered drug use The *biopsychosocial approach* enables researchers to investigate disordered drug use from complementary perspectives.

FIGURE 10.6
Peer influence Kids don't smoke if their friends don't (Philip Morris, 2003).

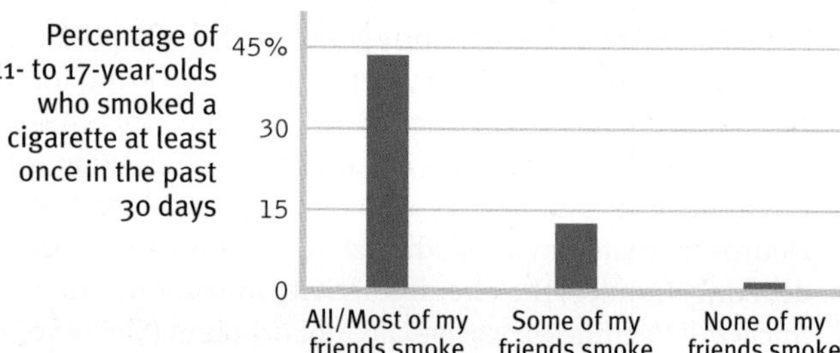
Percentage of 11- to 17-year-olds who smoked a cigarette at least once in the past 30 days
45%
30
15
0
All/Most of my friends smoke
Some of my friends smoke
None of my friends smoke

VYPE/MEGA/Newscom

Nic-A-Teen Seeing celebrities like singer Lily Allen vaping or smoking may tempt young people in the vulnerable teen and early-adult years to imitate. In 2017, more than a third of youth-rated (G, PG, PG-13) American movies showed smoking (CDC, 2020).

customer, they almost surely never will.) Adolescents, self-conscious and often thinking the world is watching their every move, are especially vulnerable. They may first light up to imitate glamorous celebrities, to project a particular image, to handle stress, or to get the social reward of acceptance by other users (Cin et al., 2007; DeWall & Pond, 2011; Tickle et al., 2006). Mindful of these tendencies, tobacco companies have effectively modeled their products with themes that appeal to youth: attractiveness, independence, adventurousness, social approval (Surgeon General, 2012).

Rates of drug use vary across cultural and ethnic groups. One survey of European teens found that lifetime marijuana use ranged from 5 percent in Norway to more than eight times that in the Czech Republic (Romelsjö et al., 2014). Alcohol and other drug addiction rates have been low among actively religious people, with extremely low rates among Orthodox Jews, Mormons, Mennonites, and the Amish (DeWall et al., 2014; Salas-Wright et al., 2012). Among Americans aged 12 and older, illicit drug use is higher for people who are White or Indigenous compared with those who are Black or Hispanic (NSDUH, 2020).

Among teens whose parents and best friends are nonsmokers, the smoking rate is close to zero (Moss et al., 1992; also see **FIGURE 10.6**). If teens' friends misuse drugs, the odds are double that they will, too (Liu et al., 2017). Peers throw the parties and provide (or don't provide) the drugs. Teens who come from happy families, who do not begin drinking before age 15, and who do well in school tend not to use drugs, largely because they rarely associate with those who do (Bachman et al., 2007; Hingson et al., 2006; Odgers et al., 2008).

Adolescents' expectations—what they *believe* friends do and like—also influence their behavior (Vitória et al., 2009). University students are not immune to such misperceptions: Drinking can dominate social occasions partly because students overestimate their peers' enthusiasm for alcohol and underestimate their views of its risks (Prentice & Miller, 1993; Self, 1994) (**TABLE 10.3**). When students' overestimates of peer drinking are corrected, alcohol use often subsides (Moreira et al., 2009).

People whose beginning use of drugs was influenced by their peers are more likely to stop using when friends stop or their social network changes (Chassin & MacKinnon, 2015). One study that followed 12,000 adults over 32 years found that smokers tend to quit in clusters (Christakis & Fowler, 2008). Within a social network, the odds of a person quitting increased when a spouse, friend, or co-worker stopped smoking. Similarly, most U.S. soldiers who engaged in problematic drug use while in Vietnam ceased after returning home (Robins et al., 1974).

As always with correlations, the traffic between friends' drug use and our own may be two-way: Our friends influence us. Social networks matter. But we also select as friends those who share our likes and dislikes.

What do the findings on drug use suggest for drug prevention and treatment programs? Three channels of influence seem possible:

- Educate young people about the long-term costs of a drug's temporary pleasures.
- Help young people find other ways to boost their self-esteem and discover their purpose in life.

TABLE 10.3 Facts About U.S. "Higher" Education

• College and university students drink more alcohol than their nonstudent peers and exhibit 2.5 times the general population's rate of substance abuse (NCASA, 2007). After college, many adults "mature out" of problem alcohol use (M. Lee et al., 2018). For others, problems with alcohol haunt their postcollege years.
• Fraternity and sorority members report higher binge-drinking rates and more alcohol abuse symptoms later in life than nonmembers do (McCabe et al., 2018).

- Attempt to modify peer associations or to "inoculate" youth against peer pressures by training them in refusal skills.

People rarely abuse drugs if they understand the physical and psychological costs, feel good about themselves and the direction their lives are taking, and are in a peer group that disapproves of using drugs.

"Substance use disorders don't discriminate; they affect the rich and the poor; they affect all ethnic groups. This is a public health crisis, but we do have solutions." —U.S. Surgeon General Vivek Murthy, 2016

RETRIEVAL PRACTICE

RP-6 Why do tobacco product companies try so hard to get customers hooked as teens?

RP-7 Studies have found that people who begin drinking in their early teens are much more likely to develop alcohol use disorder than are those who begin at age 21 or after. What possible explanations might there be for this correlation?

ANSWERS IN APPENDIX E

MODULE

10 REVIEW Drugs and Consciousness

LEARNING OBJECTIVES

Test Yourself Answer these repeated Learning Objective Questions on your own (before "showing" the answers here, or checking the answers in Appendix D) to improve your retention of the concepts (McDaniel et al., 2009, 2015).

LOQ 10-1 What are *substance use disorders*?

LOQ 10-2 What roles do tolerance and addiction play in substance use disorders, and how has the concept of *addiction* changed?

LOQ 10-3 What are *depressants*, and what are their effects?

LOQ 10-4 What are *stimulants*, and what are their effects?

LOQ 10-5 What are *hallucinogens*, and what are their effects?

LOQ 10-6 Why do some people become regular users of consciousness-altering drugs?

TERMS AND CONCEPTS TO REMEMBER

Test Yourself Write down the definition in your own words, then check your answer.

psychoactive drug, p. 112
substance use disorder, p. 112
tolerance, p. 113
addiction, p. 113
withdrawal, p. 113
depressants, p. 114
alcohol use disorder, p. 114
barbiturates, p. 115
opioids, p. 115
stimulants, p. 116
amphetamines, p. 116
nicotine, p. 117
cocaine, p. 119
methamphetamine, p. 119
Ecstasy (MDMA), p. 120
hallucinogens, p. 120
near-death experience, p. 120
LSD (lysergic acid diethylamide), p. 120
THC (delta-9-tetrahydrocannabinol), p. 121

MODULE TEST

Test Yourself Answer the following questions on your own first, then "show" the answers here, or check your answers in Appendix E.

1. After continued use of a psychoactive drug, the drug user needs to take larger doses to get the desired effect. This is referred to as ____________.
2. The depressants include alcohol, barbiturates,
   a. and opioids.
   b. cocaine, and morphine.
   c. caffeine, nicotine, and marijuana.
   d. and amphetamines.
3. Why might alcohol make a person more helpful *or* more aggressive?
4. Long-term use of Ecstasy can
   a. depress sympathetic nervous system activity.
   b. deplete the brain's supply of epinephrine.
   c. deplete the brain's supply of dopamine.
   d. damage serotonin-producing neurons.
5. Near-death experiences are strikingly similar to the experiences evoked by ____________ drugs.
6. Use of marijuana
   a. impairs motor coordination, perception, reaction time, and memory.
   b. inhibits people's emotions.
   c. leads to dehydration and overheating.
   d. stimulates brain cell development.
7. An important psychological contributor to drug use is
   a. inflated self-esteem.
   b. the feeling that life is meaningless and directionless.
   c. a genetic predisposition.
   d. overprotective parents.

CHAPTER

4

jacoblund/iStock/Getty Images

Nature, Nurture, and Human Diversity (Modules 11–13)

What makes you *you*? In important ways, we are each unique. We are each a one-of-a-kind package of looks, personality, feelings, interests, abilities, cultural background, and language. For example, consider how you greet people. Your affiliative motivation is common, but how you express it is unique. North Americans often ask, "How are you?" Members of an Aboriginal community in remote Australia, in contrast, typically ask, "Which way are you going?" (Boroditsky, 2017). Our cultural values — such as prioritizing our feelings or our sense of direction — interact with our hard-wired traits to make each of us distinct.

Yet we are also the leaves of one tree. Our human family shares not only a common biological heritage — cut us and we bleed — but also common behavioral tendencies. Our shared brain architecture disposes us to sense the world, develop language, and feel hunger through identical mechanisms. Whether we live by the Arctic Ocean or the Atacama Desert, we prefer sweet tastes to sour. We divide the color spectrum into similar colors. And we affiliate, conform, return favors, punish offenses, organize hierarchies of status, and anguish over a child's death. A visitor from outer space could drop in anywhere and find humans dancing and feasting, singing and worshiping, playing sports and games, laughing and crying, living in families and forming groups. Taken together, such universal behaviors define our human nature.

What causes our striking diversity, and also our shared human nature? How much are our individual differences shaped by our differing genes? And how much by our environment—by every external influence, from maternal nutrition while in the womb to social support while near the tomb? Modules 11, 12, and 13 tell the scientific story of how our genes (nature) and environments (nurture) together knit us.

MODULE

11 Behavior Genetics: Predicting Individual Differences

LEARNING OBJECTIVE QUESTION LOQ 11-1 What are *chromosomes, DNA, genes,* and the human *genome*? How do behavior geneticists explain our individual differences?

If Beyoncé and JAY-Z's eldest daughter, Blue Ivy, becomes a popular recording artist, should we attribute her musical talent to her "superstar genes"? To her growing up in a musically rich environment? To high expectations? To her parents' financial resources? Such questions intrigue **behavior geneticists**, who study our differences and weigh the effects and the interplay of **heredity** and **environment**.

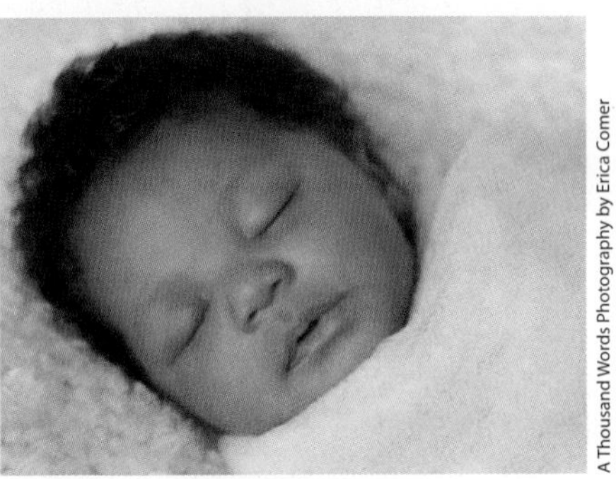

A Thousand Words Photography by Erica Comer

The nurture of nature Parents everywhere wonder: Will my baby grow up to be agreeable or aggressive? Successful or struggling? What comes built in, and what is nurtured—and how? Research reveals that both nature and nurture shape our development—every step of the way.

Genes: Our Codes for Life

Behind the story of our body and its brain—surely the most awesome thing on our little planet—is the heredity that interacts with our experience to create both our universal nature and our individual and social diversity. On the eve of the twentieth century, few would have guessed that every cell nucleus in your body contains your genetic master code. It's as if every room in Dubai's Burj Khalifa (the world's tallest structure) contained a book detailing the architect's plans for the entire structure. The plans for your own book of life run to 46 chapters—23 donated by your mother's egg and 23 by your father's sperm. Each of these 46 chapters, called a **chromosome**, is composed of a coiled chain of the molecule **DNA (deoxyribonucleic acid). Genes**, small segments of the giant DNA molecules, form the words of those chapters (**FIGURE 11.1**). Altogether, you have some 20,000 genes, which are either active *(expressed)* or inactive. Environmental events "turn on" genes. When turned on, genes provide the code for creating *protein molecules*, our body's building blocks.

Genetically speaking, every other human is nearly your identical twin. Human **genome** researchers have discovered a common sequence within human DNA. We share most of our genes with most people, creating a common genetic profile that makes us humans, rather than tulips, bananas, or chimpanzees.

Yet we aren't all that different from our chimpanzee cousins. At a genetic level, humans and chimpanzees are 96 percent identical (Mikkelsen et al., 2005). At "functionally important" DNA sites (those that play a key role in our evolution), this number reaches 99.4 percent (Wildman et al., 2003)! Yet that wee 0.6 percent difference matters a lot. It took a human, Shakespeare, to do what our chimpanzee cousins cannot—intricately weave 17,677 words into literary masterpieces.

Slight differences matter among other species, too. Chimpanzees and bonobos resemble each other in many ways. They should—their genomes differ by much less than 1 percent. But they display markedly different behaviors. Chimpanzees are often aggressive and male-dominated. Bonobos are peaceable and female-led.

Consider how improbable you are. "Each pair of parents," notes behavior geneticist Kathryn Paige Harden (2021), "could produce over 70 *trillion* unique offspring."

"Your DNA and mine are 99.9 percent the same. ... At the DNA level, we are clearly all part of one big worldwide family." —Francis Collins, Human Genome Project director, 2007

behavior genetics the study of the relative power and limits of genetic and environmental influences on behavior.

heredity the genetic transfer of characteristics from parents to offspring.

environment every nongenetic influence, from prenatal nutrition to the people and things around us.

chromosomes threadlike structures made of DNA molecules that contain the genes.

DNA (deoxyribonucleic acid) a complex molecule containing the genetic information that makes up the chromosomes.

genes the biochemical units of heredity that make up the chromosomes; small segments of DNA capable of synthesizing proteins.

genome the complete instructions for making an organism, consisting of all the genetic material in that organism's chromosomes.

FIGURE 11.1
The life code The nucleus of every human cell contains chromosomes, each comprising two strands of DNA connected in a double helix. Genes are DNA segments that, when expressed (turned on), direct the development of proteins that influence a person's individual development.

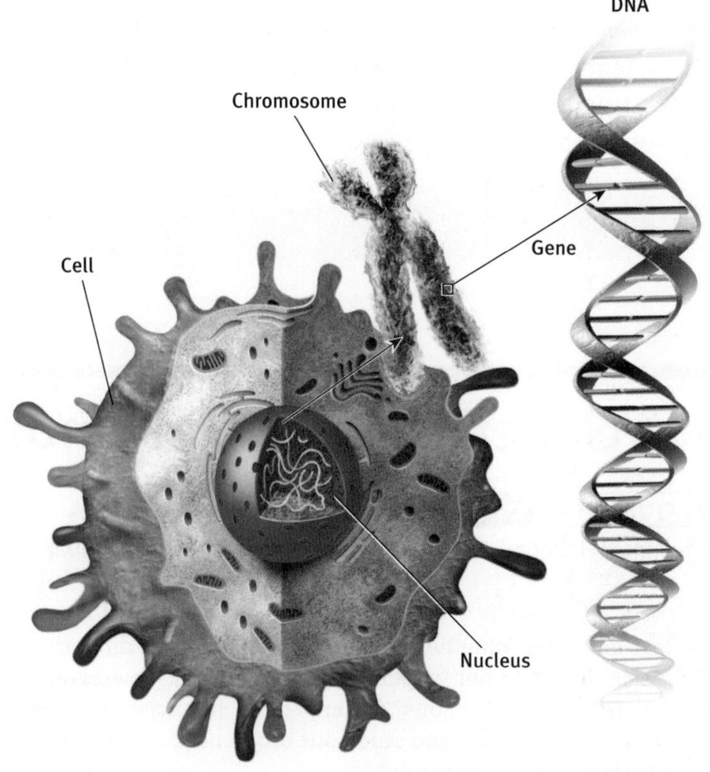
DNA
Chromosome
Gene
Cell
Nucleus

"We share half our genes with the banana." —Evolutionary biologist Robert May, president of Britain's Royal Society, 2001

When your biological parents shuffled their gene decks and dealt your hand, the highly unlikely result was you—with your special combination of traits and abilities. Slight person-to-person variations from the common pattern give clues to our uniqueness—why one person is more susceptible than others to certain psychological disorders, or why one person's face is long and another's is wide (Grotzinger et al., 2022; Zhang et al., 2022).

Most of our traits have complex genetic roots. Your height, for example, reflects the size of your face, vertebrae, leg bones, and so forth—each of which may be influenced by different genes interacting with your specific environment. Your leadership ability, intelligence, aggressiveness, and even happiness are each similarly affected by a whole orchestra of genes (Holden, 2008; Song et al., 2022). Indeed, one of the big take-home findings of today's behavior genetics is that no single gene predicts your smarts, sexual orientation, or personality. Gene analyses of more than 300,000 people have, for example, identified 120 genes associated with schizophrenia (Trubetskoy et al., 2022). Another study of 1.1 million people identified 1271 gene variations that together predicted about 12 percent of the differences in people's years of schooling (J. J. Lee et al., 2018). *The bottom line:* Our differing traits are *polygenic*—influenced by many genes that each have a small effect (Plomin, 2018; von Stumm & d'Apice, 2022).

So, our many genes help explain both our shared human nature and our human diversity. But—another take-home finding—knowing our heredity tells only part of our story. To form us, environmental influences interact with our genetic predispositions.

Nature or nurture or both? When talent runs in families—as with musician Lenny Kravitz, actor Lisa Bonet, and their daughter, actor Zoë Kravitz—how do heredity and environment together do their work?

Jon Kopaloff/FilmMagic/Getty Images

RETRIEVAL PRACTICE

RP-1 Put the following cell structures in order from smallest to largest: nucleus, gene, chromosome.

ANSWERS IN APPENDIX E

Twin and Adoption Studies

LOQ 11-2 How do twin and adoption studies help us understand the effects and interactions of nature and nurture?

To scientifically tease apart the influences of heredity and environment, behavior geneticists could wish for two types of experiments. The first would control heredity while varying the home environment. The second would control the home environment while varying heredity. Such experiments with human infants would be unethical, but nature has done this work for us.

Identical Versus Fraternal Twins

Identical (monozygotic) twins develop from a single fertilized egg that splits. Thus, they are *genetically* identical—nature's own human clones (**FIGURE 11.2**). Indeed, they are clones who share not only the same genes but the same conception and uterus, and usually the same birth date. Two slight qualifications:

- Although identical twins have the same genes, they don't always have the same *number of copies* of those genes repeated within their genome, and they sometimes differ in their brain's tiny wiring structures. These variations help explain why one twin may have a greater risk for certain illnesses and disorders, including schizophrenia (Lee et al., 2019; Maiti et al., 2011).
- During prenatal development, most identical twins share a *placenta* (which transfers nutrients and oxygen from mother to embryo), but one of every three sets has separate placentas. One twin's placenta may provide slightly better nourishment, contributing to a few identical twin differences (Marceau et al., 2016; van Beijsterveldt et al., 2016).

Fraternal (dizygotic) twins develop from two separate fertilized eggs. Although they share a prenatal environment, they are genetically no more similar than ordinary siblings.

Shared genes can translate into shared experiences. A person whose identical twin has *autism spectrum disorder,* for example, has about a 3 in 4 risk of being similarly diagnosed. If the affected twin is fraternal, the co-twin has about a 1 in 3 risk (Tick et al., 2016). To study the effects of genes and environments, several thousand medical and psychological researchers have studied nearly 15 million identical and fraternal twin pairs (Polderman et al., 2015).

Are genetically identical twins also behaviorally and emotionally more similar than fraternal twins? Compared with fraternal twins, identical twins are much more alike in their personality, their emotions, their politics, and even their marijuana use (Choi et al., 2022; Hufer et al., 2020; Schaefer et al., 2021).

Identical twins, more than fraternal twins, look alike—so much so that most have difficulty distinguishing a flashed photo of their face from their co-twin's face (Martini et al., 2015). So, do people's responses to their looks account for their similarities? *No.* In a clever approach, researcher (and fraternal twin) Nancy Segal (2013) compared personality similarity between identical twins and unrelated look-alike pairs. Only the identical twins reported similar personalities. Other studies have shown that identical twins whose parents treated them alike (for example, dressing them identically) were *not* psychologically more alike than other identical twins (Kendler et al., 1994; Loehlin & Nichols, 1976). In explaining individual differences, identical genes matter more than identical jeans.

Separated Twins

Imagine the following science fiction experiment: A mad scientist, given two pairs of identical twins, swaps one in each pair. The resulting pairs are then raised in separate environments as if they were fraternal twins. Better yet, consider a *true* story (Dominus, 2015; Segal & Montoya, 2018):

In 2015, William Velasco was working as a butcher in Bogotá, Colombia. One day, customer Laura Vega Garzón mistook him for her colleague, Jorge, who looked the same—same high cheekbones, same smile, same walking style. Was it Jorge, pretending to be someone else? Confused, she returned to the butcher shop to show William a picture of his look-alike, Jorge. William laughed and didn't take it seriously, but Laura later showed her colleague Jorge a photograph of William, the butcher. "That's me!" Jorge exclaimed.

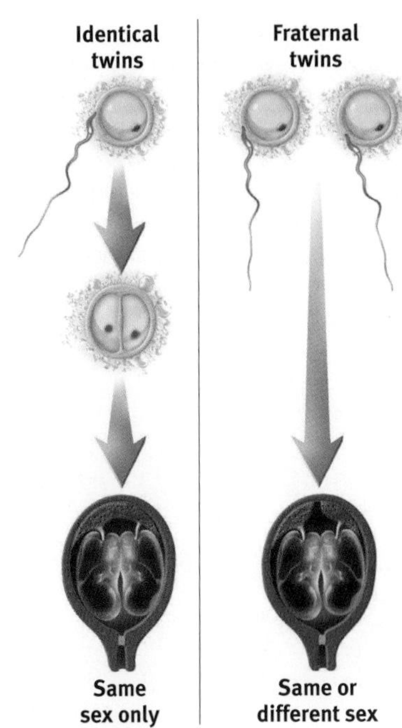
Identical twins
Fraternal twins
Same sex only
Same or different sex

FIGURE 11.2
Same fertilized egg, same genes; different eggs, different genes Identical twins develop from a single fertilized egg, fraternal twins from two.

The Salyers Family

Double twins When identical twins Brittany and Briana married identical twins Josh and Jeremy, their baby boys became legal cousins, but genetic brothers.

identical (monozygotic) twins individuals who developed from a single fertilized egg that split in two, creating two genetically identical organisms. 

fraternal (dizygotic) twins individuals who developed from separate fertilized eggs. They are genetically no closer than ordinary siblings, but shared a prenatal environment.

Charlie Riedel/AP Photo

Ole Miss
39

Bobby McDuffie/Icon Sportswire/Getty Images

Do look-alikes act alike? Genetically unrelated look-alikes, called doppelgangers, tend not to have notably similar personalities (Segal, 2013). Amazingly, these two bearded, red-haired, 6′4″ minor league baseball pitchers also share the same unusual name—Brady Feigl—but grew up unaware of each other. Genetic testing confirmed that the two Brady Feigls are unrelated (Gaydos, 2019).

Scrolling through William's social media photos, Jorge found another surprise: his look-alike, William, was sitting next to a mirror image of Jorge's fraternal twin brother.

Until then, William and Jorge had lived utterly separate lives. William grew up in a rural village, whereas Jorge was city-raised. William and Jorge both—thanks to a colossal hospital mistake—believed they had fraternal twin brothers, Wilber and Carlos, respectively. In reality, Wilber and Carlos, like William and Jorge, were identical twins. The hospital had sent William home with Wilber, and Carlos home with Jorge.

Although they were raised apart, William and Jorge both were jokesters, physically strong, and supportive. Wilber and Carlos were moody and serious, always organized, and prone to crying, and they had the same speech impediment. Each of the four had wondered why he felt so different from his supposed fraternal twin. Meeting their identical twins revealed the power of genetics.

Genes matter, but so does environment. Urban dwellers Jorge and Carlos had better nutrition, and were taller than rural-raised William and Wilber. Wilber didn't have access to the speech therapy that Carlos did, which meant that only Wilber struggled with speaking as an adult.

The remarkable story of the "Bogotá brothers" (see tinyurl.com/BogotaBrothers for photos and more) resembles that of many separated twin pairs. When tested by psychologists Thomas Bouchard and Nancy Segal, separated identical twins exhibited similarities not only of tastes and physical attributes but also of personality, abilities, attitudes, interests, and fears.

Fly Emirates

Nancy L. Segal, PhD.

Bogotá brothers When two pairs of accidentally switched Colombian identical twins were reunited, the power of nature was evident. But the twins also witnessed the impact of their different childhood environments and family circumstances. Nature and nurture matter.

Stories of startling twin similarities have not impressed critics, who remind us that "the plural of *anecdote* is not *data*." They note that if researchers created a control group of biologically unrelated pairs of the same age, sex, and ethnicity, who had not grown up together but who were as similar to one another in economic and cultural background as are many of the separated twin pairs, these pairs would also exhibit striking, yet coincidental, similarities (Joseph, 2001). Twin researchers reply that separated fraternal twins do not, however, exhibit similarities comparable to those of separated identical twins.

Even the impressive data from personality assessments are clouded by the reunion of many of the separated twins some years before they were tested. Moreover, when adoption agencies are involved, separated twins tend to be placed in similar homes. Despite these criticisms, the striking twin-study results helped shift scientific thinking toward a greater appreciation of genetic influences.

Separated Jims
In 1979, Jim Lewis awoke next to his second wife, for whom he often left love notes around the house. As he lay in bed, he thought about his son, James Alan, and his dog, Toy. Jim enjoyed building furniture in his basement woodworking shop, including a white bench encircling a tree in his front yard. He also liked driving his Chevy, watching stock-car racing, and drinking Miller Lite beer.

Shockingly, there existed another Jim for whom all these things were also true![1] Thirty-seven days after their birth, identical twins Jim Lewis and Jim Springer were adopted separately and raised with no knowledge of each other until the day Jim Lewis received a call from his genetic clone (who, having been told he had a twin, set out to find him). The 39-year-old brothers became the first of 74 separated twin pairs tested by psychologist Thomas Bouchard and his colleagues (2009; P. Miller, 2012).

Biological Versus Adoptive Relatives

For behavior geneticists, nature's second real-life experiment—adoption—creates two groups: *genetic relatives* (biological parents and siblings) and *environmental relatives* (adoptive parents and siblings). For personality or any other given trait, we can ask whether adopted children are more like their biological parents, who contributed their genes, or their adoptive parents, who contribute a home environment. And while sharing that home environment, do adopted siblings come to share traits?

The stunning finding from studies of hundreds of adoptive families is that, apart from identical twins, people who grow up together—whether biologically related or not—do not much resemble one another in personality (McGue & Bouchard, 1998; Plomin, 2011; Rowe, 1990). In personality traits such as extraversion and agreeableness, for example, people who have been adopted are more similar to their *biological* parents than to their caregiving adoptive parents.

The finding is important enough to bear repeating: Unless an environment is extreme (such as conditions of war or famine), *shared family environment has little discernible impact on children's personality.* Two adopted children raised in the same home are no more likely to share personality traits with each other than with the child down the block.

Heredity shapes other primates' personalities, too. Macaque monkeys raised by foster mothers exhibit social behaviors that resemble their biological, rather than foster, mothers (Maestripieri, 2003).

The genetic leash may limit the family environment's influence on personality, but it does not mean that adoptive parenting is a fruitless venture. One study followed more than 3000 Swedish children with at least one biological parent who had depression. Compared with their not-adopted siblings, those raised by an adoptive family were about 20 percent less likely to develop depression (Kendler et al., 2020). As an adoptive parent, I [ND] find it heartening to know that parents do influence their children's attitudes, values, manners, politics, education, and faith (Gould et al., 2019; Willoughby et al., 2021). This was dramatically illustrated during World War II by separated identical twins Jack Yufe, who was Jewish, and Oskar Stöhr, a member of Germany's Hitler Youth. After later reuniting, Oskar mused to Jack: "If we had been switched, I would have been the Jew, and you would have been the Nazi" (Segal, 2005, p. 70). Parenting—and the cultural environments in which parents place children—matters!

Siblings so different: Hermann Goering was outgoing, loved crowds, and became Hitler's right-hand man and founder of the Nazi Gestapo. His younger brother Albert Goering was quiet and reclusive, and worked to save the Jewish people that brother Hermann's regime was killing (Brennan, 2010).

Moreover, child neglect and abuse and even parental divorce are rare in adoptive homes. (Adoptive parents are carefully screened; biological parents are not.) One study looked at biological mothers with multiple children who were raised apart—some of whom they parented, and some of whom an adoptive mother parented (Natsuaki et al., 2019). Compared with the biological mothers, the adoptive mothers used gentler parenting and gave more guidance. So it is not surprising that most adopted children thrive, especially when adopted as infants (Loehlin et al., 2007; van IJzendoorn & Juffer, 2006; Wierzbicki, 1993). Seven in eight adopted children have reported feeling strongly attached to one or both adoptive parents. As children of self-giving parents, they have

[1]Actually, this description of the two Jims errs in one respect: Jim Lewis named his son James Alan. Jim Springer named his James Allan.

Guillaume Collet/Sipa/Shutterstock

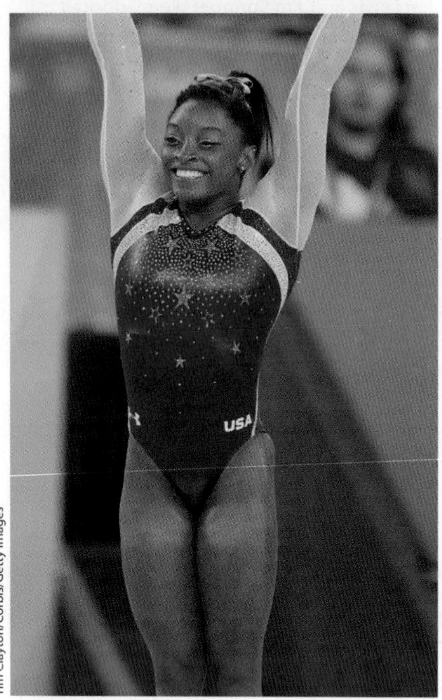
USA

Tim Clayton/Corbis/Getty Images

Adoption matters Oscar-winning actor Frances McDormand and Olympic gold medal gymnast Simone Biles both benefited from one of the biggest gifts of love: adoption.

grown up to be more self-giving and altruistic than average (Sharma et al., 1998). Many scored higher than their biological parents and raised-apart biological siblings on intelligence tests, and most grew into happier and more stable adults (Kendler et al., 2015; van Ijzendoorn et al., 2005). In one Swedish study, children adopted as infants grew up with fewer problems than were experienced by children whose biological mothers initially registered them for adoption but then decided to raise the children themselves (Bohman & Sigvardsson, 1990). *The bottom line:* Most adopted children benefit from adoption.

ASK YOURSELF

Do you know biological siblings who, despite having been raised together, have very different personalities? (Are *you* one of these siblings, perhaps?) Knowing what you do of their lives and upbringing, what do you think contributed to these differences?

RETRIEVAL PRACTICE

RP-2 How do researchers use twin and adoption studies to learn about psychological principles?

ANSWERS IN APPENDIX E

Temperament and Heredity

LOQ 11-3 What have psychologists learned about temperament?

As most parents with multiple children report, babies differ right out of the womb (Willoughby et al., 2019). One aspect of personality—**temperament** (emotional reactivity and intensity)—is quickly apparent, and it is genetically influenced (Kandler et al., 2012; Raby et al., 2012). Identical twins, more than fraternal twins, often have similar temperaments (Fraley & Tancredy, 2012; Kandler et al., 2013). Temperament differences typically persist. Emotionally reactive infant monkeys tend to become reactive adults (Fox et al., 2021). Ditto for emotionally intense preschoolers, who tend to become relatively intense young adults (Larsen & Diener, 1987). One study of 1037 New Zealanders found that a 45-minute assessment of 3-year-olds' frustration tolerance, impulsivity, and intelligence could predict "with considerable accuracy" which of them would, by age 38, consume the most welfare benefits, parent and then abandon the most children, and commit the most crime (Caspi et al., 2016).

The genetic effect appears in physiological differences. Anxious, inhibited infants have high and variable heart rates and a reactive nervous system. When facing new or strange situations, they become more physiologically aroused (Kagan & Snidman, 2004; Roque et al., 2012).

Heritability

LOQ 11-4 What is *heritability*, and how does it relate to individuals and groups?

So, our biology helps form our personality. Yet asking whether our personality is more a product of our genes or our environment is like asking whether a basketball court's size is more the result of its length or its width. However, we could ask whether different court sizes are more the result of *differences* in their length or width. Similarly, we can ask whether person-to-person personality differences are influenced more by nature or by nurture.

Using twin and adoption studies, behavior geneticists can mathematically estimate the **heritability** of a trait—the extent to which variation among individuals in a group can be attributed to their differing genes. For many personality traits, heritability is about 40 percent (Weinschenk et al., 2022). For major depressive disorder, heritability is about 30 percent (Pettersson et al., 2019). For adult intelligence, heritability is about 60 percent (Plomin et al., 2016). This does *not* mean that *your* intelligence is 40–60 percent genetic. Rather, it means that genetic influence explains 60 percent of

temperament a person's characteristic emotional reactivity and intensity.

heritability the proportion of variation among individuals in a group that we can attribute to genes. The heritability of a trait may vary, depending on the range of populations and environments studied.

the observed *variation* among adults. We can never say what percentage of an *individual's* personality or intelligence is inherited. It makes no sense to say that your personality is due x percent to your heredity and y percent to your environment. This point is so often misunderstood that we repeat: Heritability refers to how much *differences among people* are due to genes.

The heritability of traits such as intelligence varies from study to study. Consider humorist Mark Twain's (1835–1910) fictional idea of raising boys in barrels until age 12, feeding them through a hole. If we followed his suggestion, the boys would all emerge with lower-than-average intelligence scores at age 12. Yet, given their equal environments, their test score differences could be explained only by their heredity. With the same environment, heritability—differences due to genes—would be nearly 100 percent.

As environments become more similar, heredity becomes the primary source of differences. If all schools were of uniform quality, all families equally loving, and all neighborhoods equally healthy, then heritability would *increase* (because differences due to environment would *decrease*). But consider the other extreme: If all people had similar heredities but were raised in drastically different environments (some in barrels, some in luxury homes), heritability would be much lower. So, heritability is not a single fixed score; it varies with changing environments.

If genetic influences help explain variations in traits among individuals in a group, can the same be said of trait differences *between* groups? Not necessarily. Height is 90 percent heritable, yet nutrition (an environmental factor) rather than genes explains why, as a group, today's adults are taller (Floud et al., 2011). In 1896, the global average height for men was 5 feet 3 inches (162 centimeters) and for women was 4 feet 10 inches (151 centimeters) (Our World in Data, 2019). In the 1990s, their male and female counterparts stood 3.5 inches (9 centimeters) taller. The two groups differ, but not because human genes have changed in this eyeblink of time. With their better diets, South Korean men and women now average 6 inches (15 centimeters) taller than genetically similar North Koreans (Johnson et al., 2009). Genes matter, but so does environment.

As with height, so with personality and intelligence scores: Heritable individual differences need not imply heritable group differences. And, if some *individuals* are genetically disposed to be more aggressive than others, that needn't explain why some *groups* are more aggressive than others. Putting people in a new social context can change their aggressiveness. Today's peaceful Scandinavians carry many genes inherited from their Viking warrior ancestors.

AMY HWANG
Amy Hwang/Cartoon Stock

"You can be whatever you want to be, but you'll probably turn out like me."

RETRIEVAL PRACTICE

RP-3 Those studying the *heritability* of a trait try to determine how much of the person-to-person variation in that trait among members of a specific group is due to their differing ______________.

ANSWERS IN APPENDIX E

Gene–Environment Interaction

Among our similarities, the most important—the behavioral hallmark of our species—is our enormous adaptive capacity. Some human traits develop the same way in virtually every environment. But other traits are expressed only in particular environments. Go barefoot for a summer and you will develop toughened, callused feet—a biological adaptation to friction. Meanwhile, your shod neighbor will remain a tenderfoot. The difference between the two of you is an effect of the environment. But it is the product of a biological mechanism—*adaptation*. Our shared biology enables our developed diversity (Buss, 1991). Thus, to say that genes and experience are *both* important is true. But more precisely, they **interact**.

Just *how* our genes and our experiences interact to form us is one of psychology's hottest topics. Gene–environment interaction studies reveal that family genetics help predict child abuse and neglect, which in turn predicts poor mental health (Warrier et al., 2021). These studies also demonstrate who is most at risk of permanent harm from

interaction the interplay that occurs when the effect of one factor (such as environment) depends on another factor (such as heredity).

WEST ORANGE

Derek Storm/Splash News/Newscom

An out-of-this-world study of genes and environments In 2015, Scott Kelly (left) spent 340 days orbiting the planet in the International Space Station. His identical twin, Mark Kelly (right), remained on Earth. Both twins underwent the same physical and psychological testing (Garrett-Bakelman et al., 2019). Only Scott Kelly's immune system temporarily went into overdrive, possibly due to the stresses of living in space and exposure to greater-than-average levels of radiation.

stress or abuse and who is most likely to benefit from interventions (Byrd et al., 2019; Manuck & McCaffery, 2014). The National Institutes of Health *All of Us* research program is now studying 1 million people from all backgrounds to pinpoint precisely how their genes and environment interact to predict physical and mental health (NIH, 2022).

Molecular Behavior Genetics

LOQ 11-5 How is molecular genetics research changing our understanding of the effects of nature and nurture?

Behavior geneticists have progressed well beyond asking "Do genes influence behavior?" The newest frontier of behavior-genetic research draws on "bottom-up" **molecular genetics**, which studies the molecular structure and function of genes.

SEARCHING FOR SPECIFIC GENES INFLUENCING BEHAVIOR As we've seen, genes typically are not solo players. For example, twin and adoption studies have revealed no single "obesity gene." Some genes influence how quickly the stomach tells the brain, "I'm full" (Adetunji, 2014). Others might dictate how much fuel the muscles need, how many calories are burned off by fidgeting, and how efficiently the body converts extra calories into fat. So, one goal of **molecular behavior genetics** is to find some of the many genes that together orchestrate complex traits such as body weight, sexual orientation, and impulsivity.

GENOME-WIDE STUDIES Most genes have tiny effects, which means it makes little sense to look for a single "smart gene" or "optimism gene." The human traits we care about, observes Kathryn Paige Harden (2021), "are influenced by many (very, very, very many) genetic variants, each of which contributes only a drop of water to the swimming pool of genes that make a difference." Nevertheless, these tiny effects can add up to big effects—shaping our personality, mental health, and longevity.

Genome-wide association studies (GWAS) study the entire genome of a large group of people to find genetic variations associated with an observed trait or behavior (a *phenotype*). Copious correlations from thousands of these variants combine to predict meaningful differences among people. In one large study, only 11 percent of high school students with the lowest genome-wide scores predicting school success later graduated from college—as did 55 percent of those with the highest combined genome score (Lee et al., 2018). Controlling for individual genetic differences, using a GWAS measure, can even promote social equity by identifying who is most likely to benefit from environmental interventions such as school programs or income support (Harden, 2021). In this way, scientists can use genetics to improve lives rather than to classify people as genetically superior or deficient.

EPIGENETICS: TRIGGERS THAT SWITCH GENES ON AND OFF Genes can be either active (expressed, as hot water activates a tea bag) or inactive. **Epigenetics** (meaning "in addition to" or "above and beyond" genetics) studies the molecular mechanisms by which environments can trigger or block genetic expression. Genes are *self-regulating*. Rather than acting as blueprints that lead to the same result no matter the context, genes react. An African butterfly that is green in summer turns brown in fall, thanks to a temperature-controlled genetic switch. The same genes that produce green in one situation produce brown in another.

The molecules that trigger or block genetic expression are called *epigenetic marks*. These marks tell the associated genes "what to do, where to do it, and when to do it" (NIH, 2021). For example, when one of these molecules attaches to part of a DNA segment, it may "turn off" the gene at that site (**FIGURE 11.3**). As one geneticist explained, "Things written in pen you can't change. That's DNA. Things written in pencil you can. That's epigenetics" (Reed, 2012).

Environmental factors such as diet, drugs, and stress can affect the epigenetic molecules that regulate gene expression. Mother rats normally lick their infants. In experiments, infant rats deprived of this licking had more epigenetic molecules blocking access to their brain's "on" switch for developing stress hormone receptors. When stressed, animals with above-average levels of free-floating stress hormones displayed more stress (Champagne et al., 2003; Champagne & Mashoodh, 2009).

molecular genetics the subfield of biology that studies the molecular structure and function of genes.

molecular behavior genetics the study of how the structure and function of genes interact with our environment to influence behavior.

epigenetics "above" or "in addition to" *(epi)* genetics; the study of the molecular mechanisms by which environments can influence gene expression (without a DNA change).

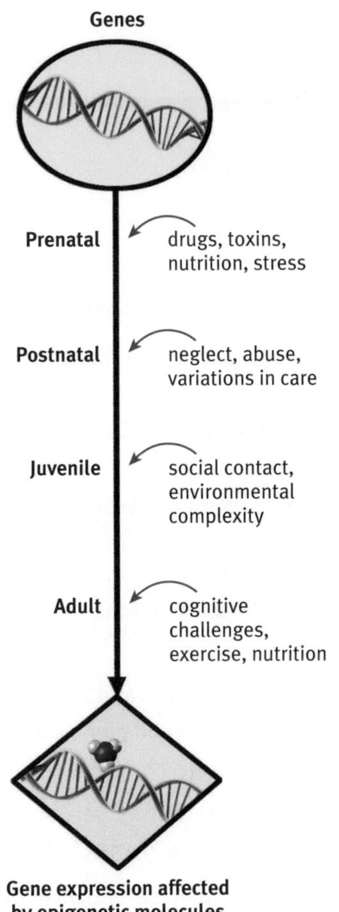
Genes
Prenatal
drugs, toxins, nutrition, stress
Postnatal
neglect, abuse, variations in care
Juvenile
social contact, environmental complexity
Adult
cognitive challenges, exercise, nutrition
Gene expression affected by epigenetic molecules

FIGURE 11.3
Epigenetic expression Beginning in the womb, life experiences lay down *epigenetic marks*—often organic methyl molecules—that can influence the expression of any gene in the DNA segment they affect. (Research from Champagne, 2010.)

TRUTH & RECONCILIATION COMMISSION OF CANADA

Adrian Wyld/The Canadian Press/AP Photo

Lasting effects Former Canadian Senator Murray Sinclair led an in-depth investigation on Canada's residential school program, which, for more than a century, removed Indigenous children from their families. Disease and abuse were common, with an estimated 10,000 students dying or missing (Austen, 2022). In 2022, Pope Francis visited Canada to apologize for the Roman Catholic Church's extensive involvement in the program (Picheta et al., 2022). Although the program shut down in 1996, its devastating effects on Indigenous Canadians continue to fuel income inequality, prejudice, and discrimination (Greenwood, 2021).

Thanks to epigenetics, the effects of our experiences can last a lifetime—and beyond. Traumatic experiences, such as childhood trauma, poverty, or malnutrition, for example, may leave their fingerprints in a person's genome (Nugent et al., 2016; Peter et al., 2016; Swartz et al., 2016). While some people experience prolonged distress and related epigenetic changes, for others, traumatic experiences increase the expression of genes related to psychological resilience (Smeeth et al., 2021). Epigenetic changes like these may get passed down to future generations, leading some evolutionary biologists to theorize that inheritance occurs not only through gene transmission, but also through experience (Uller & Laland, 2019). Evolution, they argue, predisposes human culture and experiences, which then influence evolution. Other scientists dispute the idea that children can inherit their parents' epigenetic changes (Horsthemke, 2018; Ryan & Kuzawa, 2020). Stay tuned: This scientific story is still being written.

Epigenetics research may solve some scientific mysteries, such as why only one member of an identical twin pair may develop a genetically influenced mental disorder (Spector, 2012). Epigenetics can also help explain why identical twins may look slightly different. Researchers studying mice have found that in utero exposure to certain chemicals can cause genetically identical twins to have different-colored fur (Dolinoy et al., 2007).

RETRIEVAL PRACTICE

RP-4 Match the following terms (i–iii) to the correct definition (a–c).

Term:	**Definition:**
i. Epigenetics	a. Study of the relative effects of our genes and our environment on our behavior.
ii. Molecular behavior genetics	b. Study of how the structure and function of specific genes interact with our environment to influence behavior.
iii. Behavior genetics	c. Study of environmental factors that affect how our genes are *expressed*.

ANSWERS IN APPENDIX E

MODULE

11 REVIEW Behavior Genetics: Predicting Individual Differences

LEARNING OBJECTIVES

Test Yourself Answer these repeated Learning Objective Questions on your own (before "showing" the answers here, or checking the answers in Appendix D) to improve your retention of the concepts (McDaniel et al., 2009, 2015).

LOQ 11-1 What are *chromosomes, DNA, genes*, and the human *genome*? How do behavior geneticists explain our individual differences?

LOQ 11-2 How do twin and adoption studies help us understand the effects and interactions of nature and nurture?

LOQ 11-3 What have psychologists learned about temperament?

LOQ 11-4 What is *heritability*, and how does it relate to individuals and groups?

LOQ 11-5 How is molecular genetics research changing our understanding of the effects of nature and nurture?

TERMS AND CONCEPTS TO REMEMBER

Test Yourself Write down the definition in your own words, then check your answer.

behavior genetics, p. 127
heredity, p. 127
environment, p. 127
chromosomes, p. 127
DNA (deoxyribonucleic acid), p. 127
genes, p. 127
genome, p. 127
identical (monozygotic) twins, p. 129
fraternal (dizygotic) twins, p. 129
temperament, p. 132
heritability, p. 132
interaction, p. 133
molecular genetics, p. 134
molecular behavior genetics, p. 134
epigenetics, p. 134

MODULE TEST

Test Yourself Answer the following questions on your own first, then "show" the answers here, or check your answers in Appendix E.

1. The threadlike structures made largely of DNA molecules are called ________________.
2. A small segment of DNA that codes for particular proteins is referred to as a ________________.
3. When the mother's egg and the father's sperm unite, each contributes
   a. one chromosome pair.
   b. 23 chromosomes.
   c. 23 chromosome pairs.
   d. 25,000 chromosomes.
4. Fraternal twins result when
   a. a single egg is fertilized by a single sperm and then splits.
   b. a single egg is fertilized by two sperm and then splits.
   c. two eggs are fertilized by two sperm.
   d. two eggs are fertilized by a single sperm.
5. ________________ twins share the same DNA.
6. Adoption studies seek to understand genetic influences on personality. They do this mainly by
   a. comparing adopted children with nonadopted children.
   b. evaluating whether adopted children's personalities more closely resemble those of their adoptive parents or those of their biological parents.
   c. studying the effect of prior neglect on adopted children.
   d. studying the effect of children's age at adoption.
7. From the very first weeks of life, infants differ in their characteristic emotional reactions, with some infants being intense and anxious, while others are easygoing and relaxed. These differences are usually explained as differences in ________________.
8. ________________ is the proportion of variation among individuals in groups that we can attribute to genes.
9. Epigenetics is the study of the molecular mechanisms by which ________________ trigger or block genetic expression.

MODULE

12 Evolutionary Psychology: Explaining Human Nature and Nurture

evolutionary psychology the study of the evolution of behavior and the mind, using principles of natural selection.

natural selection the principle that inherited traits that better enable an organism to survive and reproduce in a particular environment will (in competition with other trait variations) most likely be passed on to succeeding generations.

LOQ 12-1 How do evolutionary psychologists use natural selection to explain behavior tendencies?

Behavior geneticists explore the genetic and environmental roots of human differences. **Evolutionary psychologists** instead focus mostly on what makes us so much alike as humans. They use Charles Darwin's principle of **natural selection**—"arguably the most momentous idea ever to occur to a human mind," said Richard Dawkins (2007)—to understand the roots of behavior and mental processes. The idea, simplified, is this:

- Organisms' varied offspring compete for survival.
- Certain biological and behavioral variations increase organisms' reproductive and survival chances in their particular environment.
- Offspring that survive are more likely to pass their genes to ensuing generations.
- Thus, over time, population characteristics may change.

To see these principles at work, let's consider a straightforward example in foxes.

Natural Selection and Adaptation

A fox is a wild and wary animal. If you capture a fox and try to befriend it, be careful: If the timid fox cannot flee, it may snack on your fingers. In the early 1950s, Russian scientist Dmitry Belyaev wondered how our human ancestors had domesticated dogs from their equally wild wolf forebears. Might he, within a comparatively short stretch of time, accomplish a similar feat by transforming the fearful fox into a friendly fox?

To find out, Belyaev set to work with 100 female and 30 male foxes selected from fox farms (where some domestication would have already occurred [Gorman, 2019]). From their offspring he selected and mated the tamest 20 percent of females and 5 percent of males. (He measured tameness by the foxes' responses to attempts to feed, handle, and stroke them.) Over 57 generations of foxes, Belyaev and his successor, Lyudmila Trut, have repeated that simple procedure (Dugatkin & Trut, 2017). After 40 years and 45,000 foxes, they had a new breed of foxes that, in Trut's (1999) words, were "docile, eager to please, and unmistakably domesticated.... Before our eyes, 'the Beast' has turned into 'beauty,' as the aggressive behavior of our herd's wild [ancestors] entirely disappeared." So friendly and eager for human contact were these animals, so inclined to whimper to attract attention and to lick people like affectionate dogs, that the cash-strapped institute seized on a way to raise funds—marketing its friendly foxes as house pets.

Courtesy Institute of Cytology and Genetics, SB RAS

How to tame a fox Over six decades, geneticist Lyudmila Trut has bred silver foxes into friendly human companions.

Does the same process work with naturally occurring selection? Does natural selection explain our human tendencies? Nature has indeed selected advantageous variations from the new gene combinations produced at each human conception, plus occasional **mutations** (random errors in gene replication that become nature's preliminary tests of alternative possibilities). But the tight genetic leash that predisposes a dog's retrieving, a cat's pouncing, or a bird's nesting is looser on humans. The genes selected during our ancestral history provide more than a long leash; they give us a great capacity to learn and therefore to *adapt* to life in varied environments, from the tundra to the jungle. Genes and experience together wire the brain. Our adaptive flexibility in responding to different environments contributes to our *fitness*—our ability to survive and reproduce.

RETRIEVAL PRACTICE

RP-1 How are Belyaev and Trut's breeding practices similar to, and how do they differ from, the way natural selection normally occurs?

ANSWERS IN APPENDIX E

Evolutionary Success Helps Explain Similarities

Human differences grab our attention. Guinness World Records entertain us with the tallest, oldest, longest-haired, and most-tattooed humans. But our deep similarities also demand explanation. At the Amsterdam Airport's international arrivals area, one sees the same delighted joy on the faces of Indonesian grandmothers, Chinese children, and homecoming Dutch. "Even at a time when everything seems to be changing," notes physician-sociologist Nicholas Christakis (2019), "fundamental ways that humans live together remain constant."

mutation a random error in gene replication that leads to a change.

Our Genetic Legacy

Our similarities arise from our shared human *genome,* our common genetic profile. No more than 5 percent of the genetic differences among humans arise from population group differences. Some 95 percent of genetic variation exists *within* populations (Rosenberg et al., 2002). The typical genetic difference between two South Africans or between two Singaporeans is much greater than the *average* difference between the two groups. Thus, if after a worldwide catastrophe only South Africans or Singaporeans survived, the human species would suffer only "a trivial reduction" in its genetic diversity (Lewontin, 1982).

And how did we develop this shared human genome? At the dawn of human history, our ancestors faced certain questions: Who is my ally, who is my foe? With whom should I mate? What food should I eat? Some individuals answered those questions more successfully than others. For example, women who experienced nausea in the critical first three months of pregnancy were genetically predisposed to avoid certain bitter, strongly flavored, and novel foods. Avoiding such foods had survival value, since they are the very foods most often toxic to prenatal development (Profet, 1992; Schmitt & Pilcher, 2004). Early humans disposed to eat nourishing rather than poisonous foods survived to contribute their genes to later generations. Those who deemed leopards "nice to pet" often did not.

Similarly successful were those whose mating helped them produce and nurture offspring. Over generations, the genes of individuals not disposed to mate or nurture tended to be lost from the human gene pool. As success-enhancing genes continued to be selected, behavioral tendencies and learning capacities emerged that prepared our Stone Age ancestors to survive, reproduce, and send their genes into the future—and into you.

Consider yourself fortunate: Despite high infant mortality and rampant disease in past millennia, not one of your countless ancestors died childless.

Across our cultural differences, we even share a "universal moral grammar" (Mikhail, 2007). Men and women, young and old, liberal and conservative, living in Sydney or Seoul, all respond negatively when asked, "If a lethal gas is leaking into a vent and is headed toward a room with seven people, is it okay to push someone into the vent—saving the seven but killing the one?" And they all respond more approvingly when asked if it's okay to *allow* someone to fall into the vent, again sacrificing one life but saving seven. Our shared moral instincts survive from a distant past where we lived in small groups in which direct harm-doing was punished. For all such universal human tendencies, from our intense need to give parental care to our shared fears and lusts, evolutionary theory proposes a one-stop-shopping explanation (Schloss, 2009).

As heirs to this prehistoric legacy, we were not born as unprogrammed "blank slates." Instead, we are genetically predisposed to think and act in ways that promoted our biological ancestors' surviving and reproducing. But in some ways, we are biologically prepared for a world that no longer exists. We love the taste of sweets and fats, nutrients that prepared our physically active ancestors to survive food shortages. Few of us now gather and hunt for our food; instead, we too readily find sweets and fats in fast-food outlets and vending machines. Our deeply rooted natural dispositions are mismatched with today's junk food and often inactive lifestyle.

Evolutionary Psychology Today

Darwin's theory of evolution has become one of biology's fundamental organizing principles and lives on in the *second Darwinian revolution:* the application of evolutionary principles to psychology. In concluding *On the Origin of Species,* Darwin (1859, p. 346) anticipated this, foreseeing "open fields for far more important researches. Psychology will be based on a new foundation."

Those who are troubled by an apparent conflict between scientific and religious accounts of human origins may find it helpful to consider that different perspectives on life can be complementary. For example, the scientific account attempts to tell us *when* and *how;* religious creation stories usually aim to tell about an ultimate *who* and *why*. As Galileo explained to the Grand Duchess Christina, "The Bible teaches how to go to heaven, not how the heavens go."

Elsewhere in this text, we address questions that intrigue evolutionary psychologists: Why do infants start to fear strangers about the time they become mobile? Why do more people develop a *specific phobia* in response to spiders, snakes, and heights than to modern threats such as guns? And why do we fear commercial air travel more than much riskier driving?

To see how evolutionary psychologists think and reason, let's pause to explore their answers to two questions: How are men and women alike? How and why does their sexuality differ?

An Evolutionary Explanation of Human Sexuality

LOQ 12-2 How might an evolutionary psychologist explain male-female differences in sexuality and mating preferences?

Having faced many similar challenges throughout history, all genders have adapted in similar ways: We eat the same foods, avoid the same dangers, and perceive, learn, and remember similarly. When looking for a mate, we all prize many of the same traits—kindness, honesty, and intelligence—and we avoid our close genetic relatives (Dandine-Roulland et al., 2019). It is only in those domains where we have faced differing adaptive challenges—most obviously in behaviors related to reproduction—that we differ, say evolutionary psychologists.

Male-Female Differences in Sexuality

And differ we do. Consider sex drives. Men and women are sexually motivated, some women more so than many men. Yet on average, who thinks more about sex? Hooks up more often? Masturbates more often? Views more pornography? The answers worldwide: *men, men, men,* and *men* (Baumeister et al., 2001; Hall et al., 2017; Lippa, 2009; Petersen & Hyde, 2010). Even among 65- to 80-year-old Americans, 12 percent of women and 50 percent of men reported being "very" or "extremely" interested in sex (Malani et al., 2018).

Unattached straight men are alert for women's interest, and often misperceive a woman's friendliness as a sexual come-on (Abbey, 1987). This *sexual overperception bias* was evident in speed-dating men, who believed their dating partners expressed more sexual interest than the partners reported actually expressing (Perilloux et al., 2012). (This may be partially explained by unattached straight women underreporting their own sexual interests [Engeler & Raghubir, 2018]). Long-term couples do better at gauging their partners' sexual interest (Dobson et al., 2018).

Many gender similarities and differences transcend sexual orientation. Compared with gay women, gay men (like straight men) report more responsiveness to visual sexual stimuli, and more concern with their partner's physical attractiveness (Bailey et al., 1994; Doyle, 2005; Schmitt, 2007; Sprecher et al., 2013). Gay male couples also report having sex more often than do gay female couples (Peplau & Fingerhut, 2007). And men, regardless of sexual orientation, report more interest in uncommitted sex than do women (Schmitt, 2003).

Natural Selection and Mating Preferences

Natural selection is nature selecting traits and appetites that contribute to survival and reproduction. Evolutionary psychologists use the principle of *sex selection* to explain how females and males tend to differ in dating and mating patterns, whether they're chimpanzees or elephants, farmworkers or corporate presidents (Buss & Schmitt, 2019; Hughes et al., 2021). Our natural yearnings, they say, are our genes' way of reproducing themselves.

Why do women tend to be choosier than men when selecting sexual partners? Women have more at stake. To send her genes into the future, a woman conceives and protects a fetus growing inside her body for up to 9 months, and may nurse for months following birth. No surprise then, that straight women prefer partners who will offer their joint offspring support and protection—stick-around dads over likely cads (Meeussen et al., 2019). Straight women are attracted to tall men with slim waists and broad shoulders—all signs of reproductive success (Sidari et al., 2021). And straight women worldwide prefer men who seem affluent (Walter et al., 2020). One study of hundreds of Welsh pedestrians asked people to rate a driver pictured at the wheel of a humble Ford Fiesta or a swanky Bentley. Men said a female driver was equally attractive in both cars. Women, however, found a male driver more attractive if he was in the luxury car

Carolita Johnson/Cartoon Stock

"Is that all you can think about?"

(Dunn & Searle, 2010). Similarly, when people viewed pictures of others in luxury or standard apartments, women found men more attractive when they appeared in the luxury apartment, but men's perceptions were not affected by the backdrop (Dunn & Hill, 2014).

The data are in, say evolutionists: Men pair widely; women pair wisely. And what traits do straight men find desirable? Some traits, such as smooth skin and a youthful shape, are culturally universal, and they convey health and fertility (Buss & Von Hippel, 2018). Mating with such women might increase a man's chances of sending his genes into the future. And sure enough, men feel most attracted to women whose waist is roughly a third narrower than their hips—a fertility indicator (Lassek & Gaulin, 2018, 2019; Lewis et al., 2015). Even blind men show this preference for women with a low waist-to-hip ratio (Karremans et al., 2010). Men are most attracted to women whose ages in the ancestral past (when ovulation began later than today) would be associated with peak fertility (Kenrick et al., 2009). Thanks to males' sensitivity to fertility cues, teen boys are most attracted to women several years older than themselves; mid-twenties men to women around their own age; and older men to younger women. This pattern consistently appears across European singles ads, Indian marital ads, and marriage records from North and South America, Africa, and the Philippines (Singh, 1993; Singh & Randall, 2007).

MGP/Photodisc/Getty Images

Nature selects behaviors that increase genetic success. As mobile gene machines, say evolutionary psychologists, we are designed to prefer whatever worked for our ancestors in their environments. Had they not been genetically predisposed to act in ways that would produce children, we wouldn't be here. As carriers of their genetic legacy, we are similarly predisposed.

Critiquing the Evolutionary Perspective

LOQ 12-3 What are the key criticisms of evolutionary explanations of human sexuality, and how do evolutionary psychologists respond?

Most psychologists agree that natural selection prepares us for survival and reproduction. But critics say there is a weakness in evolutionary psychology's explanation of our mating preferences. Let's consider how an evolutionary psychologist might explain the findings in a startling, classic study of straight women and men (Clark & Hatfield, 1989), and how a critic might object.

In this experiment, a woman or man posing as an interested stranger approached men or women and remarked, "I have been noticing you around campus. I find you to be very attractive." The "stranger" then asked a question, which was sometimes "Would you go to bed with me tonight?" What percentage of women and men do you think agreed? An evolutionary explanation of sexuality would predict that women would be choosier than men in selecting their sexual partners. Indeed, not a single woman agreed—but 70 percent of the men did. A French replication of this study produced a similar result (Guéguen, 2011).

Did the research support evolutionary psychology? Critics note that evolutionary psychologists start with an effect—in this case, the survey result showing that men were more likely to accept casual sex offers—and work backward to explain what happened. What if research showed the opposite effect? If men refused an offer for casual sex, might we not reason that men who partner with one woman for life make better fathers, whose children more often survive?

Other critics ask why we should try to explain today's behavior based on our ancestors' decisions thousands of years ago. Don't cultural expectations also bend the genders? Alice Eagly and Wendy Wood (1999, 2013) point to the smaller behavioral differences between women and men in cultures with greater gender equality. Such critics believe that *social learning theory* offers a better, more immediate explanation. We all learn **social scripts**—our culture's guide to how people should act in certain situations. By watching and imitating others in their culture, women may learn that sexual encounters with strange men can be dangerous, that casual sex may not offer much sexual pleasure, and that women (more than men) who engage in casual sexual activity have low self-esteem (Conley, 2011; Krems et al., 2021). This alternative explanation suggests that women are reacting to sexual encounters in socially scripted ways. And men's

social script a culturally modeled guide for how to act in various situations.

reactions may reflect *their* learned social scripts: "Real men" take advantage of every opportunity to have sex.

A third criticism focuses on evolutionary psychology's possible social effects. Are straight men truly hardwired to have sex with any woman who approaches them? If so, does it mean that men have no moral responsibility to remain faithful to their partners? Does this explanation excuse inappropriate sexual behavior as men's evolutionary legacy? Might evolutionary psychology weaken social movements aimed at reducing *sexual aggression*, such as #MeToo?

Evolutionary psychologists agree that much of who we are is *not* hardwired. Our destiny is not written in our genes. Instead, our environment shaped how our ancestors cooperated and competed (Geary, 2021). And evolutionary psychology research confirms that men and women, having faced similar adaptive problems, are far more alike than different. Natural selection has prepared us to be flexible. Thanks to our neuroplasticity, we humans have a great capacity for learning and social progress. We adjust and respond to varied environments. We adapt and survive, whether we live in the arctic or the desert.

Evolutionary psychologists also agree with their critics that some traits and behaviors, such as suicide, are hard to explain in terms of natural selection (Barash, 2012; Confer et al., 2010). But they ask us to remember evolutionary psychology's scientific goal: to explain behaviors and mental traits by offering testable predictions using principles of natural selection (Lewis et al., 2017). We may, for example, predict that people are more likely to perform favors for those who share their genes or can later return those favors. Is this true? (The answer is *Yes*.) And evolutionary psychologists remind us that studying how we *came to be* need not dictate how we *ought to be*. Understanding our questionable tendencies can help us overcome them.

ASK YOURSELF

Based on what you've learned so far, how would you say that genes and environment work together to influence sexual behavior?

RETRIEVAL PRACTICE

RP-2 How do evolutionary psychologists explain male-female differences in sexuality?

RP-3 What are the three main criticisms of the evolutionary explanation of human sexuality?

ANSWERS IN APPENDIX E

MODULE 12 REVIEW Evolutionary Psychology: Explaining Human Nature and Nurture

LEARNING OBJECTIVES

Test Yourself Answer these repeated Learning Objective Questions on your own (before "showing" the answers here, or checking the answers in Appendix D) to improve your retention of the concepts (McDaniel et al., 2009, 2015).

LOQ 12-1 How do evolutionary psychologists use natural selection to explain behavior tendencies?

LOQ 12-2 How might an evolutionary psychologist explain male-female differences in sexuality and mating preferences?

LOQ 12-3 What are the key criticisms of evolutionary explanations of human sexuality, and how do evolutionary psychologists respond?

TERMS AND CONCEPTS TO REMEMBER

Test Yourself Write down the definition in your own words, then check your answer.

evolutionary psychology, p. 136
natural selection, p. 136
mutation, p. 137
social script, p. 140

MODULE TEST

Test Yourself Answer the following questions on your own first, then "show" the answers here, or check your answers in Appendix E.

1. Behavior geneticists are most interested in exploring ____________ (commonalities/differences) in our behaviors. Evolutionary psychologists are most interested in exploring ____________ (commonalities/differences).

2. Evolutionary psychologists are most likely to focus on

a. how individuals differ from one another.

b. the social consequences of learned behaviors.

c. the natural selection of traits that helped our ancestors survive and reproduce.

d. social scripts.

3. How do evolutionary psychologists use the principle of *natural selection* to explain differences in mating preferences in women and men?

MODULE

13 Cultural and Gender Diversity: Understanding Nature and Nurture

From conception onward, we are the product of accumulating *interactions* between our genes and our environment (McGue, 2010). Our genes affect how people react to and influence us. And they affect our family environment (Barlow, 2019; Kong et al., 2018). Forget nature *versus* nurture; think nature *via* nurture.

Imagine two babies, one genetically predisposed to be attractive, friendly, and easy-going, the other less so. Assume further that the first baby attracts more affection and care from others, and so develops into a warmer and more outgoing person. As the two children grow older, the more naturally outgoing child may seek activities and friends that encourage even more social confidence.

What has caused their resulting personality differences? Neither heredity nor experience acts alone. Environments trigger gene activity. And our genetically influenced traits *evoke* significant responses in others. Thus, a child's impulsivity and aggression may evoke an angry reaction from a parent or teacher, who reacts warmly to well-behaved children in the family or classroom. In such cases, the child's nature and the parents' nurture interact. Gene and scene dance together.

Identical twins not only share the same genetic predispositions; they also seek and create similar experiences that express their shared genes (Kandler et al., 2012). Identical twins raised in different families have recalled their parents' warmth as remarkably similar—almost as similar as if they had been raised by the same parents (Plomin et al., 1988, 1991, 1994). Fraternal twins have more differing recollections of their early family life—even if raised in the same family. "Children experience us as different parents, depending on their own qualities," noted Sandra Scarr (1990).

How Does Experience Influence Development?

Our genes, when expressed in specific environments, influence our developmental differences. We are like coloring books, with certain lines predisposed and experience filling in the full picture. The formative nurture that conspires with nature begins at conception, with the prenatal environment in the womb, where embryos receive differing nutrition and varying levels of exposure to toxic agents. Nurture continues outside the womb, where our early experiences foster brain development.

Experience and Brain Development

LOQ 13-1 How do early experiences modify the brain?

How do early experiences leave their fingerprints in the brain? Mark Rosenzweig, David Krech, and their colleagues (1962) opened a window on that process when they raised some young rats in solitary confinement and others in a communal rat playground. The rats living in the enriched social environment often developed a heavier and thicker brain cortex (**FIGURE 13.1**).

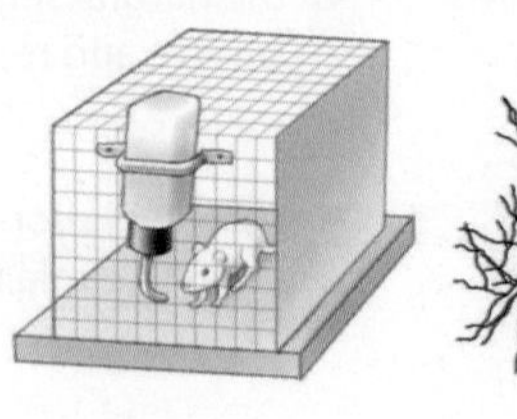
Impoverished environment
Impoverished rat brain cell

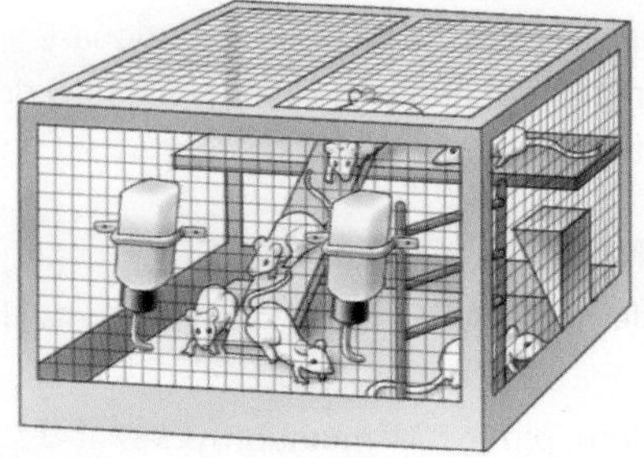
Enriched environment

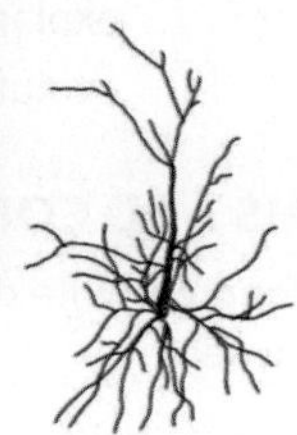
Enriched rat brain cell

FIGURE 13.1
Experience affects brain development Researchers raised rats either alone in an environment without playthings, or with other rats in an environment enriched with playthings that changed daily (Rosenzweig et al., 1962). In 14 of 16 replications of this basic experiment, rats in the enriched environment developed significantly more cerebral cortex than did those in the impoverished environment.

Rosenzweig was so surprised that he repeated the experiment several times before publishing his findings (Renner & Rosenzweig, 1987; Rosenzweig, 1984). So great were the effects that, shown brief video clips of the rats, you could tell from their activity and curiosity whether their environment had been impoverished or enriched (Renner & Renner, 1993). After 60 days in the enriched environment, the rats' brain weights increased 7 to 10 percent and the number of brain *synapse* connections ballooned by about 20 percent (Kolb & Whishaw, 1998). The enriched environment literally increased brain power. In humans, lack of stimulation can also slow brain and cognitive development (Farah, 2017).

Such results have motivated improvements in environments for laboratory, farm, and zoo animals—and for children in institutions. Infant rats and premature babies also benefit from touch and massage (Charpak et al., 2021; Sarro et al., 2014). "Handled" infants of both species develop faster neurologically and gain weight more rapidly. Preemies who have had skin-to-skin contact with their parents show better cognitive development, lower aggressiveness, and lower hyperactivity 20 years later (Charpak et al., 2017).

Nature and nurture interact to sculpt our synapses. Brain maturation provides us with an abundance of neural connections. Experiences—sights and smells, touches and tastes, music and movement—activate and strengthen some neural pathways while others weaken from disuse. Similar to paths through a forest, less-traveled neural pathways gradually disappear and popular ones are strengthened (Dahl et al., 2018; Gopnik et al., 2015). By puberty, this *pruning process* results in a massive loss of underused connections.

At the juncture of nurture and nature is the biological reality of early childhood learning. During early childhood—while excess connections are still on call—youngsters can most easily master such skills as the grammar and accent of another language. Lacking any exposure to language before adolescence, a person will never become proficient in any language. Likewise, lacking visual experience during the early years, a person whose vision is later restored by cataract removal will never achieve typical perceptions (Gregory, 1978; Wiesel, 1982). Without that early visual stimulation, the brain cells usually assigned to vision will die or be diverted to other uses. The maturing brain's rule: Use it or lose it.

Although normal stimulation during the early years is critical, brain development does not end with childhood. Thanks to the brain's remarkable neuroplasticity, our neural tissue is ever changing and reorganizing in response to new experiences. New neurons are also born. If a monkey pushes a lever with the same finger many times a day, brain tissue controlling that finger will change to reflect the experience (Karni et al., 1998). Human brains work similarly. Whether learning to play a musical instrument or to navigate London's streets, we perform with increasing skill as our brain incorporates the learning (Bianco et al., 2022; Maguire et al., 2000).

Courtesy of C. Brune

Stringing the circuits young String musicians who started playing before age 12 have larger and more complex neural circuits controlling the note-making left-hand fingers than do string musicians whose training started later (Elbert et al., 1995).

"Genes and experiences are just two ways of doing the same thing—wiring synapses." —Joseph LeDoux, *The Synaptic Self*, 2002

ASK YOURSELF

What skills did you practice the most as a child—sports, music, art, cooking, video gaming? How do you think this affected your brain development? How will you continue to develop your brain with new learning and new skills?

How Much Credit or Blame Do Parents Deserve?

LOQ 13-2 In what ways do parents and peers shape children's development?

Biological parents shuffle their gene decks and deal a life-forming hand to their child-to-be, who is then subjected to countless influences beyond their control. But all parents—whether biological or adoptive—feel enormous satisfaction in their children's successes, and guilt over their failures. They beam over the child who wins trophies and titles. They wonder where they went wrong with the child who is repeatedly in trouble.

Do parents really produce wounded future adults by being (take your pick from the toxic-parenting lists) overbearing—or uninvolved? Pushy—or indecisive? Overprotective—or

Barbara Smaller/Cartoon Stock

"Nature, nurture—either way, it's still all your fault."

culture the enduring behaviors, ideas, attitudes, values, and traditions shared by a group of people and transmitted from one generation to the next.

SUITS

Julia Suits/Cartoon Stock

"To be frank, officer, my parents never set boundaries."

distant? Should we then blame our parents for our failings, and ourselves for our children's failings? Or does talk of wounding fragile children through normal parental mistakes trivialize the brutality of real abuse? To paraphrase developmental psychologist Alison Gopnik (2016), parents may be less like potters who mold clay, and more like gardeners who provide the soil for their children's natural growth.

Parents matter. But parenting wields its largest effects at the extremes: the abused children who become abusive, the deeply loved but firmly handled children who become self-confident and socially competent. The power of the family environment also appears in the remarkable academic and vocational successes of many children of people who leave their home countries, such as those of refugees who fled war-torn Vietnam and Cambodia—successes attributed to close-knit, supportive, even demanding families (Caplan et al., 1992). Parents' power also appears in their children's tendency to share their politics, religion, and values (O'Reilly, 2021).

Yet in personality measures, shared environmental influences from the womb onward typically account for less than 10 percent of children's differences. Referring to our traits rather than our values, behavior geneticist Robert Plomin (2018) noted, "We would essentially be the same person if we had been adopted at birth and raised in a different family." (Rub your eyes and read that last sentence again.)

Peer Influence

As children mature, what other experiences do the work of nurturing? At all ages, but especially during childhood and adolescence, we seek to fit in with our groups (Blakemore, 2018; Harris, 1998, 2000):

- Preschoolers who dislike a certain food often will eat that food if put at a table with a group of children who like it.
- Children who hear English spoken with one accent at home and another in the neighborhood and at school will invariably adopt the accent of their peers, not their parents. Accents (and slang) reflect culture, "and children get their culture from their peers," as Judith Rich Harris (2007) has noted.
- Teens who start smoking or vaping typically have friends who model smoking, suggest its pleasures, and offer cigarettes or pods (Liu et al., 2017). Part of this peer similarity may result from a *selection effect,* as adolescents seek out peers with similar attitudes, interests, and traits (Domingue et al., 2018). Those who smoke (or don't) may select as friends those who also smoke (or don't).

RETRIEVAL PRACTICE

RP-1 What is the *selection effect,* and how might it affect a teen's decision to join a school sports team?

ANSWERS IN APPENDIX E

Humans are cultural animals More than any other species, humans imitate and invent. They absorb the wisdom of previous generations, build upon it, and pass it along through teaching.

Staffan Widstrand/The Image Bank Unreleased/Getty Images

Cultural Influences

LOQ 13-3 How does culture affect our behavior?

Compared with the narrow path taken by flies, fish, and foxes, the road along which environment drives humans is wider. Our species' success is born of our ability to imitate and invent. We absorb the collective wisdom of those who came before us, and we sometimes improve upon it. We come equipped with a powerful cerebral mobile device, ready to download cultural apps.

How do you cook rice? Dry your wet clothes? What type of treatment do you seek when you're sick? Rather than use trial and error, we imitate people close to us. **Culture** consists of the behaviors, ideas, and values shared by a group of people and passed down from generation to generation (Brislin, 1988; Cohen, 2009). Wolves are social animals; they live and hunt in packs. Ants are incessantly social, never alone. Humans are social animals, but more.

Humans' social nature helps us exploit accumulated cultural know-how. While wolves function pretty much as they did 10,000 years ago, humans enjoy microwave ovens, clothes dryers, and antibiotics—things unknown to most of our ancestors. Culture also enables an efficient *division of labor*. Although three lucky people get their names on this book (which transmits accumulated cultural wisdom), it actually results from the coordination and commitment of a team of gifted people, no one of whom could produce it alone.

Across cultures, we differ in our language, money, sports, religion, and customs. But beneath these differences lies our great similarity—our capacity for culture. Culture works. It transmits the customs and beliefs that enable us to communicate, to exchange money for things, to play, to eat, and to drive with agreed-upon rules and without crashing into one another.

"We will lead not merely by the example of our power but by the power of our example." —U.S. President Joe Biden, Inaugural Address, 2021

Variation Across Cultures

We see our adaptability in cultural variations among our beliefs and our values, in how we nurture our children and bury our dead, and in what we wear (or whether we wear anything at all). We are always mindful that this book's worldwide readers are culturally diverse. You and your ancestors reach from Australia to Algeria and from Singapore to Samoa. Cultures influence how we sleep, eat, dress, learn, love, and worship.

Gender equity: Among the Aka people of Central Africa, men and women interchangeably perform roles such as hunting and child care. As a result, fathers form an especially close bond with their infants, even suckling the babies with their own nipples when hunger makes the child impatient for Mother's return. Fathers in this culture are holding or within reach of their babies 47 percent of the time (Hewlett, 1991).

Riding along with your culture is like biking with the wind. As it carries us along, we hardly notice it. When we try traveling against the wind, we feel its force. Face-to-face with a different culture, we become aware of the cultural winds. Visiting Europe, someone from the United States may notice the small cars and tiny coffee cups. Visiting North America, someone from Japan may wonder why people wear their shoes in the house and can't seem to line up properly.

But humans in varied cultures nevertheless share some basic moral ideas. Even before they can walk, babies prefer helpful people over naughty ones (Hamlin et al., 2011). Worldwide, people prize honesty, fairness, and kindness (McGrath, 2015). Yet each cultural group also evolves its own **norms**. The British have a norm for orderly waiting in line. Many in South Asia, Africa, and the Middle East use only the right hand for eating. Sometimes social expectations seem oppressive: "Why should it matter how I dress?" Yet, norms—how to greet, how to eat—grease the social machinery. Norms also served our ancestors by encouraging food sharing and fostering communal defense, notes Joseph Henrich (2020): "Norms create communities in which the health and survival of each individual depend on almost everyone else." If someone were to invent a drug that made people unresponsive to social norms, cultures would collapse. We are cultural animals.

Cultures also differ in how strictly people follow norms. In **tight cultures**, people more often obey social norms: A pedestrian might wait for the light to say "WALK," even on a deserted corner at midnight. In such cultures, people arrive on time, rarely drop a piece of trash, and might not kiss their sweetheart in public. **Loose cultures** have norms, too (as drivers appreciate), but people expect variability (Gelfand, 2018). In loose cultures, people tolerate some jaywalking, late arrivals, littering, and public affection. Each cultural pattern has benefits: Tight cultures coordinate their actions well, ensuring reliable public transportation and clean streets—and fewer Covid-19 cases and deaths (Gelfand et al., 2021). In contrast, looseness allows for creativity, innovation, and self-expression.

When we don't understand what's expected or accepted, we may experience *culture shock*. People from Mediterranean cultures have perceived northern Europeans as efficient but cold, and preoccupied with punctuality (Triandis, 1981). People from time-conscious Japan—where pedestrians walk briskly and postal clerks fill requests speedily—have found themselves growing impatient when visiting Indonesia, where the pace of life is more leisurely (Levine & Norenzayan, 1999). Someone from the European community, which requires 20 paid vacation days each year, may also experience culture shock when working in the United States, which does not guarantee workers any paid vacation (Ray et al., 2013).

norms understood rules for accepted and expected behavior. Norms prescribe "proper" behavior.

tight culture places with clearly defined and reliably imposed norms.

loose culture places with flexible and informal norms.

Variation Over Time

Like biological creatures, cultural groups vary, compete for resources, and, over time, evolve (Mesoudi, 2009). Cultures change when many people copy the innovations of a few. Not long ago, humans roamed Earth in groups of 150; today, we mostly live in stable, cooperative societies of millions (Dunbar, 1993; Johnson & Earle, 2000). What changed? The cultural inventions of agriculture and animal domestication provided dependable sources of calories (Diamond, 1997). And when religion encouraged people to control their selfish impulses and cooperate, settlements typically grew and became more successful (Henrich, 2020; Norenzayan et al., 2016).

Cultures can change rapidly. At the beginning of the last century, people lived in a world without cars, radio broadcasting, or electric lighting. If you could sit down to chat with your great-great-grandparents, you might even have trouble understanding one another's accents, words, and expressions. And in the thin slice of history since 1960, most Western cultures have changed with astonishing speed. People enjoy expanded human rights. Middle-class people earn twice as much as they did then. They also enjoy the convenience of air-conditioned housing, online shopping, and anywhere-anytime electronic communication.

But some changes seem not so wonderfully positive. Had you fallen asleep in the United States in 1960 and awakened today, you would open your eyes to a culture where more people experience depression and economic inequality. You would also find U.S. people—like their counterparts in Britain, Australia, and New Zealand—spending more hours working, fewer hours with friends and family, and fewer hours asleep (BLS, 2011; Twenge, 2017).

Whether we love or loathe these changes, we cannot fail to be impressed by their breathtaking speed. And we cannot explain them by changes in the human gene pool, which evolves too slowly to account for high-speed cultural transformations. Cultures vary. Cultures change. Cultures shape our lives.

Culture and the Self

LOQ 13-4 How do individualist and collectivist cultures shape values and goals?

A little quiz: In each statement pair, choose the statement that best describes you.

- "I value self-sufficiency and being unique" or "I value loyalty and getting along with others."
- "I experience pride more often than shame" or "I experience shame more often than pride."
- "I aim to stand out and to win" or "I aim to fit in and cooperate."

If you grew up in a city in Canada, the United States, the United Kingdom, Australia, or New Zealand, you likely expressed **individualism** by preferring the first options. If you grew up in rural Japan, China, India, Guatemala, or Indonesia, you more likely expressed **collectivism**, as reflected in your preferring the second options.

Another question to ponder: Imagine that someone ripped away your social connections, making you a solitary refugee in a foreign land. How much of your identity would remain intact?

If you are an individualist, a great deal. You would have an independent sense of "me," and an awareness of your unique personal convictions and values. Individualists prioritize personal goals. They seek personal control and individual achievement. They define their identity mostly in terms of personal traits. (Ask some friends to complete this sentence with three answers: "I am ____________." If they're from an individualist culture, they likely will respond with personal descriptors such as "passionate," "outgoing," or "tall" rather than defining themselves in terms of their relationships or group memberships, such as "a daughter" or "a brother.")

The human need to belong is universal. So, even in individualist cultures, people seek out and join groups. But individualists focus less on group harmony or social duty (Brewer & Chen, 2007). As children, they value a sense of free will (Chernyak et al., 2019). Being more self-contained, individualists move in and out of social groups more easily. They feel relatively free to switch places of worship, change jobs, or even leave their extended families and migrate to a new place. Marriage is often for as long as they both shall love.

When individualists feel coerced, they often rebel—sometimes with devastating consequences. Individualist cultures suffered the worst Covid-19 death rates, with many

individualism a cultural pattern that emphasizes people's own goals over group goals and defines identity mainly in terms of unique personal attributes.

collectivism a cultural pattern that prioritizes the goals of important groups (often one's extended family or work group).

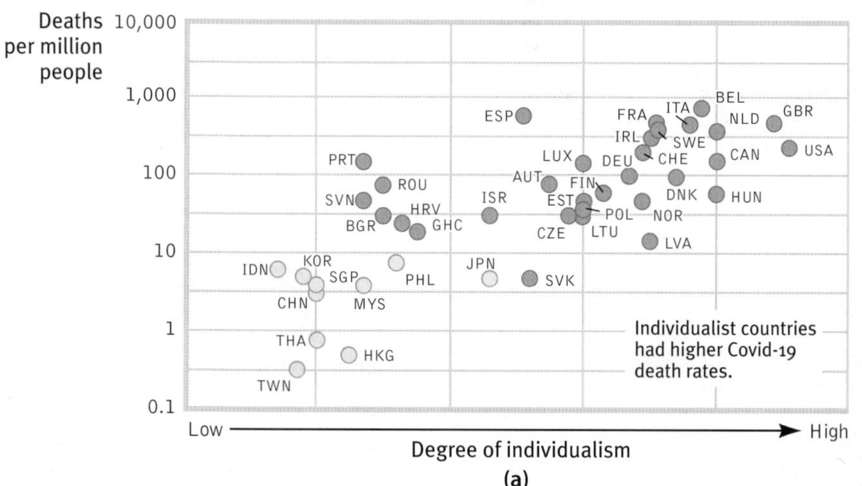
Deaths per million people
10,000
1,000
100
10
1
0.1
ESP
FRA
ITA
BEL
NLD
GBR
IRL
SWE
USA
LUX
DEU
CHE
CAN
PRT
AUT
FIN
ROU
ISR
EST
DNK
HUN
SVN
HRV
POL
NOR
BGR
GHC
CZE
LTU
LVA
IDN
KOR
JPN
SGP
PHL
SVK
CHN
MYS
THA
HKG
TWN
Individualist countries had higher Covid-19 death rates.
Low
High
Degree of individualism
(a)

Takashi Aoyama/Getty Images
(b)

FIGURE 13.2
Deadly individualism Worldwide, countries' levels of individualism correlated positively with Covid-19 death rates ($r = .75$). (Data from Garland et al., 2020.)

citizens rejecting distancing, vaccines, and masking (Fischer & Karl, 2022; Huang et al., 2022) (**FIGURE 13.2**). Japan, by contrast, experienced one-twelfth of the U.S. Covid-19 death rate, thanks to people's support for the common good—as shown by a 90 percent masking rate on public transit (Rich & Dooley, 2022). Within the United States, people living in the most individualist regions (such as Florida and Louisiana) were most likely to contract and die from the virus (Bazzi et al., 2020; CovidCast, 2020). Promoting collectivism, suggested one group of psychological researchers, "may be a way to increase engagement with efforts to reduce the spread of Covid-19" (Biddlestone et al., 2020, p. 663).

If set adrift in a foreign land as a collectivist, you might experience a greater loss of identity. Cut off from family, groups, and loyal friends, you would lose the connections that have defined who you are. *Group identifications* provide a sense of belonging, a set of values, and an assurance of security. Collectivists have deep attachments to their groups—their family, clan, company, or country. Elders receive respect. Adults in collectivist countries often feel duty-bound to support their aging parents, such as by paying for some of their living expenses (Sethi, 2021; Yang, 2015).

Sportscasters in collectivist contexts credit coaches and teammates as much as individual athletes for success (Markus et al., 2006). Collectivists find satisfaction in advancing their groups' interests while keeping their personal needs in the background. They may preserve group spirit by avoiding direct confrontation, blunt honesty, and uncomfortable topics. Norms favor humility, not self-importance (Bond et al., 2012). Collectivists view forgiveness as a way to strengthen group harmony (Joo et al., 2019). Given the priority on "we," not "me," that satisfying, super-customized latte in Seattle might seem selfishly demanding in Seoul (Kim & Markus, 1999).

Culture teaches us which behaviors are "good" and "bad." What do you think of people who willingly change their behavior to suit different people and situations? Or of people who say one thing ("We should all do our part to address the climate crisis") and do another (drive a gas-guzzling SUV)? People in largely individualist countries, such as the United States, tend to see traits as fixed and believe that people cannot have seemingly opposite traits, such as being both extraverted and introverted (Choi & Choi, 2002). People from these countries are also more likely to judge others harshly when they are not true to their word—when they don't "practice what they preach" (Dong et al., 2022; Levine, 2016). Traditionally collectivist cultures (China and Japan, for example) emphasize adopting more flexible perceptions (Peng & Nisbett, 1999). Thus, people in collectivist countries view personality traits as more fluid, and more often perceive disagreement between one's words and one's deeds as indicative of being "mature," "honest," "trustworthy," and "sincere." A country's cultural values are powerful, but not absolutely so. Even though Christmas permeates U.S. spaces every December, many Americans do not celebrate it. Similarly, even when a country's dominant messages are collectivist (or individualist), its people vary. All countries host distinct subcultures related to religion, economic status, and region (Cohen, 2009).

Collectivism varies across cultures, but also *within* cultures. Southern Chinese farmers typically grow rice, a crop that requires intense labor and rewards farmers'

ME

WE

Changing ME to WE To transform individualism to collectivism, rotate the letter M 180 degrees.

"One needs to cultivate the spirit of sacrificing the *little me* to achieve the benefits of the *big me*." —Chinese saying

"I'D LIKE A DECAFFACINNO FRAPPA CHAPPA DAPPA DINGO ICE BLENDED LAST OF THE MOCCA-HICANS VANILLA ICE ICE BETTER LATTE' THAN NEVER SMOOTHIE WITH A SHOT OF SELF-EXPRESSO."
hickerson
Cartoon by Buddy Hickerson
The tolerance of a Starbucks barista is severely tested.

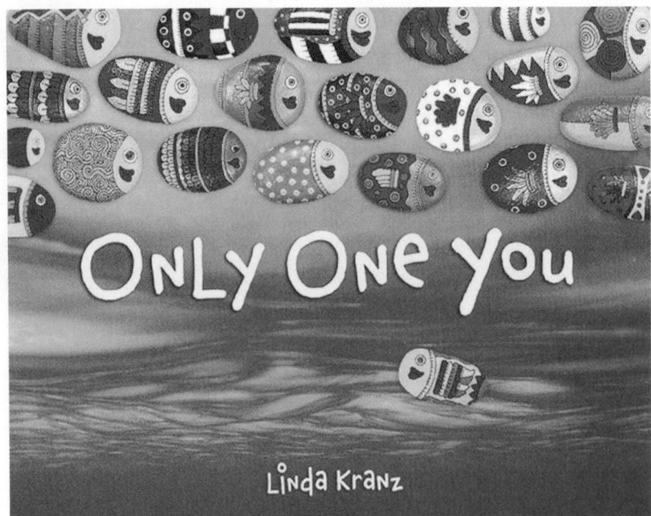
Only One You
Linda Kranz

Me or we? U.S. school systems are likely to favor books, such as *Only One You*, that encourage individuality and taking pride in one's personal identity. In contrast, Japanese stories, such as *A Big Turnip*, often describe how groups are stronger together (Imada, 2012).

coordinating with one another. Northern Chinese farmers often grow wheat, a crop that can be farmed independently (Dong et al., 2019; Obschonka et al., 2018; Talhelm et al., 2014). In one clever study, researchers used chairs to block aisles in Starbucks coffeehouses across China. They observed who acted like a typical individualist, controlling the environment by moving chairs out of the way, and who acted like a typical collectivist, adapting to the environment by squeezing through the chairs (Talhelm et al., 2018). Compared with the more collectivist Southern Chinese, the Northern Chinese were more likely to simply move the chair.

In collectivist Japan, a spirit of individualism marks the "northern frontier" island of Hokkaido (Kitayama et al., 2006). And even in the most individualist countries, people hold some collectivist values. *E pluribus unum,* says the U.S. motto: "Out of many, one." But in general (especially for men), competitive, individualist cultures encourage more personal freedom and independence from family, enable more privacy, and induce folks to take pride in personal achievements (**TABLE 13.1**).

People even value unusual names in individualist contexts, as psychologist Jean Twenge noticed while seeking a name for her first child. When she and her colleagues analyzed the first names of 358 million U.S. babies born between 1880 and 2015, they discovered that the most common baby names had become less common (Twenge et al., 2010, 2016). As **FIGURE 13.3** illustrates, the percentage of boys and girls given one of the 10 most common names for their birth year has plunged. Collectivist Japan provides

TABLE 13.1 Value Contrasts Between Individualism and Collectivism

Concept	Individualism	Collectivism
Self	Independent (identity from internal, individual traits)	Interdependent (identity from group roles)
Life task	Discover and express one's uniqueness	Maintain connections, fit in, perform role
What matters	Me — personal achievement and fulfillment; rights and liberties; self-esteem	Us — group goals and solidarity; responsibilities and relationships; family duty
Coping method	Change reality	Accommodate to reality
Morality	Defined by the individual (choice-based)	Defined by social networks (duty-based)
Relationships	Easier to enter and leave relationships	Fewer but closer and more stable relationships
Attributing behavior	Behavior reflects the individual's personality and attitudes	Behavior also reflects social norms and roles

Information from Thomas Schoeneman (1994) and Harry Triandis (1994).

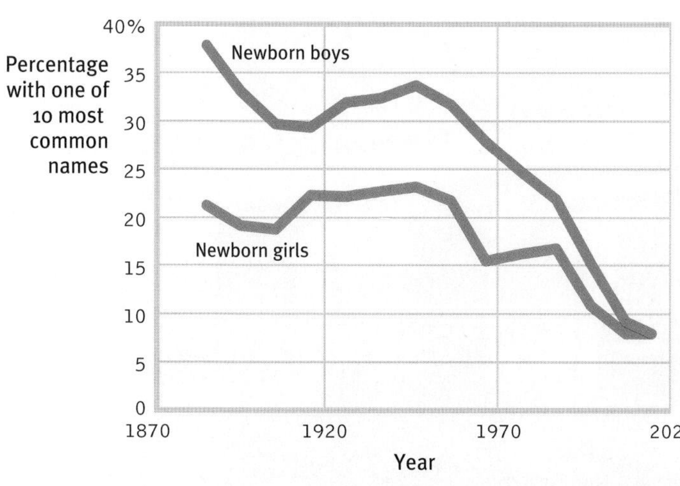
Percentage with one of 10 most common names
40%
35
30
25
20
15
10
5
0
Newborn boys
Newborn girls
1870
1920
1970
2020
Year

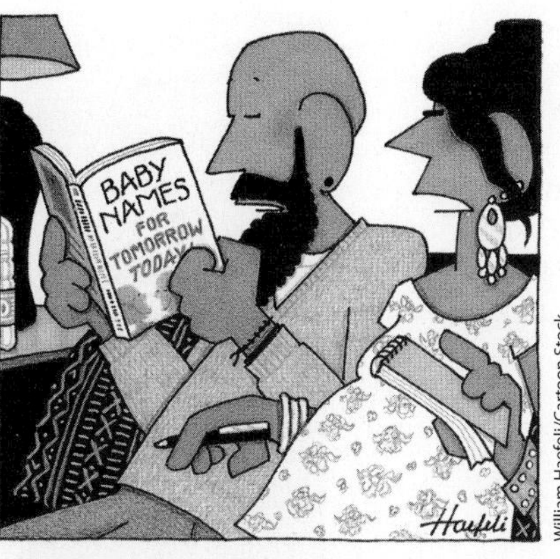
BABY NAMES FOR TOMORROW TODAY
William Haefeli/Cartoon Stock

"Remember—we want her to stand out and fit in."

FIGURE 13.3 **A child like no other** In recent years, the percentage of U.S. babies receiving one of that year's 10 most common names has plunged, reflecting the nation's individualist tendencies. (Data from Twenge et al., 2010, 2016.)

a contrast: Half of Japanese baby names are among the country's 10 most common names, though unique names are also increasing in that culture (Ogihara et al., 2015).

The individualist-collectivist divide appears in reactions to Olympic medals received. U.S. gold medal winners and the U.S. media covering them have attributed the achievements mostly to the athletes themselves (Markus et al., 2006). "I think I just stayed focused," explained swimming gold medalist Misty Hyman. "It was time to show the world what I could do." Japan's gold medalist in the women's marathon, Naoko Takahashi, had a different explanation: "Here is the best coach in the world, the best manager in the world, and all of the people who support me—all of these things ... became a gold medal."

Individualists frequently demand romance and personal fulfillment in marriage (Dion & Dion, 1993). In contrast, collectivist love songs have often expressed enduring commitment and friendship, as in this one from China: "We will be together from now on. ... I will never change from now to forever" (Rothbaum & Tsang, 1998).

What predicts cultural change over time, or differences between cultures? Social history matters. Individualism and independence have been fostered by mobility and emigration, a capitalist economy, and a sparsely populated, challenging environment (Buttrick & Oishi, 2021; Kitayama et al., 2009, 2010). Worldwide, individualism has increased, following increasing affluence (Grossmann & Varnum, 2015; Hamamura, 2012; Santos et al., 2017).

ASK YOURSELF

Is the culture you live in more collectivist or individualist? How have your culture's values influenced your behavior, emotions, and thoughts?

Culture and Child Raising

Child-raising values reflect cultural similarity and diversity. Across cultures, most mothers want to establish rules, ensure child safety, encourage socializing, and teach right

Sam Harrel/ZUMA Press/Newscom

Collectivist culture Although the United States emphasizes individualism, many cultural subgroups remain collectivist. This is true for Alaska Natives, who demonstrate respect for tribal elders, and whose identity springs largely from their group affiliations.

Licensed Grocer 50 Self Service Store

Stephen H. Reehl

Cultures vary Parents everywhere care about their children, but raise and protect them differently depending on the surrounding culture. In big cities, parents keep children close. In smaller, close-knit communities, such as Scotland's Orkney Islands' town of Stromness, social trust has enabled parents to park their toddlers outside shops.

from wrong (Cho et al., 2021). Yet cultural traditions also differ in parental preferences. Do your parents prefer children who are independent, or children who comply with what others think? Compared with families in Asian cultures, families in Western cultures more often prefer independence: "You are responsible for yourself. Follow your conscience. Be true to yourself. Discover your gifts." Some Western parents go even further, telling their children, "You are more special than other children" (Brummelman et al., 2015).

But that was not always so. Western cultures formerly prioritized obedience, respect, and sensitivity to others (Alwin, 1990; Remley, 1988). In the 1950s, Western parents were more likely to teach their children, "Be true to your traditions. Be loyal to your heritage and country. Show respect toward your parents and other superiors." Cultures vary. And cultures change.

Children across place and time have thrived under various child-raising systems. Upper-class British parents traditionally handed off routine caregiving to nannies, then sent their 10-year-olds away to boarding school.

Those from Asian and African cultures more often value physical closeness and shared emotions. Children often sleep with their parents and spend their days close to a family member (Shweder et al., 1995; Xiong et al., 2020). Many of these cultures encourage a strong sense of *family self—meaning* that what shames children shames their parents, and what brings honor to children brings honor to their parents (Chen & Zhou, 2021).

In western Kenya's traditional Gusii society, babies nurse freely but spend most of the day on their mother's or a sibling's back—with lots of body contact but little face-to-face and language interaction. To these Gusii parents, what would seem weird is Westerners' lesser body contact as they push babies in strollers, plant them in car seats, and leave them in playpens (Small, 1997). Diversity in child raising cautions us against presuming that any one culture's way is the only way to raise children successfully.

Developmental Similarities Across Groups

Mindful of how others differ from us, we often fail to notice the similarities predisposed by our shared biology. Regardless of our culture, we humans are more alike than different. We share the same life cycle. We speak to our infants in similar ways and respond similarly to their coos and cries (Bornstein et al., 1992a,b).

Even differences *within* a culture, such as those sometimes attributed to race, are often easily explained by an interaction between our biology and our culture. Consider this illustration (Rowe et al., 1994, 1995): Black men tend to have higher blood pressure than White men. Suppose that (1) in both groups, salt consumption correlates with blood pressure, and (2) salt consumption is higher among Black men than among White men. The blood pressure "race difference" might then actually, at least partly, reflect nothing about race—and more about a difference in diet.

And that parallels psychological findings. Ethnic groups sometimes differ, such as in average school achievement. But such differences are, as the researchers noted, "no more than skin deep." To the extent that family structure, peer influences, and parental education predict behavior in one of these ethnic groups, they do so for the others.

So as members of different ethnic and cultural groups, we may differ in surface ways. But as members of one species, we are subject to the same psychological forces. Our outward reactions vary, yet our basic emotions are universal. Our tastes vary, yet they reflect common principles of hunger. Our social behaviors vary, yet they reflect pervasive principles of human influence. Cross-cultural research helps us appreciate both our cultural diversity *and* our human similarity.

sex in psychology, the biologically influenced characteristics by which people define *male, female,* and *intersex.*

gender in psychology, the behavioral characteristics that people associate with *boy, girl, man,* and *woman.* (See also *gender identity.*)

intersex possessing male and female biological sexual characteristics at birth.

RETRIEVAL PRACTICE

RP-2 How do individualist and collectivist cultures encourage people to see themselves?

ANSWERS IN APPENDIX E

Gender Development

LOQ 13-5 How does the meaning of *gender* differ from the meaning of *sex*?

We humans share an irresistible urge to organize our worlds into simple categories. Among the ways we classify people—as tall or short, dull or smart, cheerful or churlish—one stands out. It's what everyone first wanted to know about you: "Boy or girl?" Your parents may have offered clues about your assigned **sex** through your clothing and name. For most people, biological traits help define their assigned **gender**, their culture's expectations about what it means to be a man or a woman. In recent years, cultural and scientific understandings of gender development have grown.

Simply said, your body defines your sex; your mind defines your gender. But your mind's understanding of gender arises from the interplay between your biology and your experiences (Eagly & Wood, 2013). Before we consider that interplay, let's look at some ways that males and females are alike, and some ways that they differ.

Boy or Girl?

Michael Allen/Shutterstock

Is it a boy or a girl? Some people question an early emphasis on gender; others enjoy celebrations such as U.S. "gender reveal" parties.

Similarities and Differences

LOQ 13-6 What are some of the ways males and females tend to be alike and to differ?

Whether male, female, or **intersex**, most of us receive 23 chromosomes from each parent. Of those 46 chromosomes, 45 are *unisex*—*the* same for everyone. Our similar biology helped our evolutionary ancestors face similar adaptive challenges. For example, survival for men and women involved traveling long distances (migration, outrunning threats), which today is reflected biologically in men's and women's similar finishing times for ultralong-distance races. Everyone needed to survive, reproduce, and avoid predators, and so we are in most ways alike. How you identify yourself—as male, female, neither, or some combination of the two—gives no clue to your vocabulary, happiness, or ability to see, learn, and remember, report gender researcher Janet Shibley Hyde and her colleagues (2019). Whatever our gender, we are, on average, comparably creative and intelligent and feel similar emotions and longings (Hyde, 2014; Lauer et al., 2019; Reilly et al., 2019).

But in some areas, female and male traits do differ, and differences command attention. Some oft-noted differences (like women being more helpful than men) are actually quite modest (Olsson et al., 2021). Others are more striking. The average female enters puberty about two years earlier than the average male, and her

Cultural norms vary and change. "The generally accepted rule is pink for the boy and blue for the girl," declared the *Earnshaw's Infants' Department* in 1918 (Frassanito & Pettorini, 2008). "Pink being a more decided and stronger color is more suitable for the boy, while blue, which is more delicate and dainty, is prettier for the girls."

life expectancy is 4 years longer. She expresses most emotions more freely, smiling and crying more, and, in social media updates, more often expresses "love" and being "sooo excited!!!" (Fischer & LaFrance, 2015; Schwartz et al., 2013). She is better at spelling and reading (Reilly et al., 2019). Ms. Average can detect fainter odors and become sexually re-aroused sooner after orgasm, but she also has twice the risk of developing depression and anxiety, and 10 times the risk of developing an eating disorder. Yet the average male is 4 times more likely to die by suicide, to abuse tobacco products, and to develop an alcohol use disorder. Mr. Average also has greater size and strength, but is more likely to be diagnosed with autism spectrum disorder, color-deficient vision, and antisocial personality disorder. And Mr. Average more often becomes Mr. Extreme, with males displaying greater variability than do females in their risk-taking and patience (Thöni & Volk, 2022). Whatever our gender, we come predisposed to certain rewards and risks.

AGGRESSION To a psychologist, **aggression** is any physical or verbal behavior intended to hurt someone physically or emotionally (Bushman & Huesmann, 2010). Try this: Pause to picture in your mind an aggressive person.

Is the person a man? Likely yes. Men generally admit to more aggression, especially extreme physical violence (Yount et al., 2017). Nearly half of 14- to 19-year-old U.S. boys feel pressure to be "willing to punch someone if provoked" (PLAN USA, 2018). In romantic relationships between women and men, minor acts of physical aggression, such as slaps, are roughly equal, but the most violent acts are mostly committed by men (Archer, 2000; Buss, 2021). Domestic abuse is usually hidden. As a result of home confinement, unemployment, and food insecurity during the Covid pandemic, violence against women and children increased in more than two dozen countries (Bourgault et al., 2021).

Men worldwide commit more violent crimes and represent 90 percent of those convicted of murder (UNODC, 2019). Men also take the lead in hunting, fighting, warring, and supporting war (Liddle et al., 2012; Wood & Eagly, 2002, 2007). Such gender differences are not limited to physical aggression. In laboratory experiments, men have been more willing to blast people with what they believed was intense and prolonged noise (Bushman et al., 2007).

Here's another situation to consider: Picture in your mind a person who harms others by passing along hurtful gossip, socially rejecting others, or bullying people online.

Was the person a woman? Perhaps. Those behaviors are acts of **relational aggression**, and women have been slightly more likely than men to commit some forms of them (Archer, 2004, 2007, 2009).

SOCIAL POWER Imagine you've walked into a job interview and are taking your first look at the two interviewers. The unsmiling person on the left oozes self-confidence and independence, maintaining steady eye contact. The person on the right gives you a warm, welcoming smile, but makes less eye contact and seems to expect the other interviewer to take the lead.

Which interviewer is male?

If you said the person on the left, you're not alone. Around the world, from Nigeria to New Zealand, people have perceived gender differences in power (Williams & Best, 1990). Even in 2020, a United Nations global survey found that almost half of humanity believed men to be superior political leaders, and more than 40 percent believed them to be better business executives (UNDP, 2020). These biased perceptions can start from an early age, with 6- to 10-year-olds in one study associating power with being male (Reyes-Jaquez & Koenig, 2022). (For more on this topic, see Thinking Critically About: Gender Bias in the Workplace.)

Now picture a heterosexual couple negotiating a car purchase price. "If you won't lower your price, we're leaving," says one of them to the salesperson.

Which member of the couple—male or female—made the demand?

If you said the male, you're again in good company. People tend to associate negotiation with males, and men often have an advantage in negotiation outcomes (Mazei et al., 2015).

"I hate to say there are female and male ways of dealing with power, because I think each of us has a male and a female part. But based on my own experience, women will tend to be inclusive, to reach out more, to care a little more." —Christine Lagarde, president of the European Central Bank, 2011

aggression any physical or verbal behavior intended to harm someone physically or emotionally.

relational aggression an act of aggression (physical or verbal) intended to harm a person's relationship or social standing.

Thinking Critically About:
Gender Bias in the Workplace

LOQ 13-7 What factors contribute to gender bias in the workplace?

Differences in PERCEPTION

She's so aggressive!
He's so take-charge!

Among politicians who seem power-hungry, women are less successful than men.[1]

Most political leaders are men:

men
Political leaders
women

Men held 74% of seats in the world's governing parliaments in 2022.[2]

People around the world tend to see men as more powerful.[3]

When groups form, whether as juries or companies, leadership tends to go to males.[4] In a study of 2000+ U.S. companies, male CEOs outnumbered female CEOs 17 to 1.[5]

Differences in COMPENSATION

Women in traditionally male occupations have received less than their male colleagues.[6]

Medicine Over their careers, how much more male doctors will earn than female doctors:[7] **$2,000,000**

Academia Female research grant applicants have received lower quality of researcher ratings and have been less likely to be funded.[8] (But as we will see, gender attitudes and roles are changing.)

Differences in FAMILY-CARE RESPONSIBILITY

U.S. mothers still do nearly **twice** as much child care as **fathers**.[9] In the workplace, women are less often driven by money and status, compromise more, and more often opt for reduced work hours.[10]

What else contributes to WORKPLACE GENDER BIAS?

Social norms

In most societies, men place more importance on power and achievement, and are socially dominant.[11]

Leadership styles

Men are more *directive*, telling people what to do and how to do it.

Women are more *democratic*, welcoming others' input in decision making.[12]

Interaction styles

Women are more likely to express support.[13]

Men are more likely to offer opinions.[13]

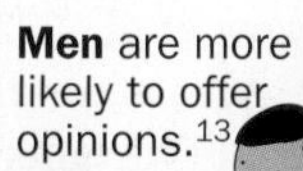

Everyday behavior

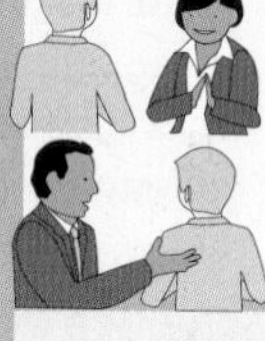

Women smile and apologize more than men.[14]

Men are more likely to talk assertively, interrupt, initiate touches, and stare.[14]

Yet GENDER ROLES VARY WIDELY across place and time.

Women are increasingly represented in leadership (now 50% of Canada's cabinet ministers) and in the workforce. In 1963, the Harvard Business School admitted its first women students. Among its Class of 2020, 41% were women.[15] In 1960, women were 6% of U.S. medical students. Today they are slightly more than half.[16]

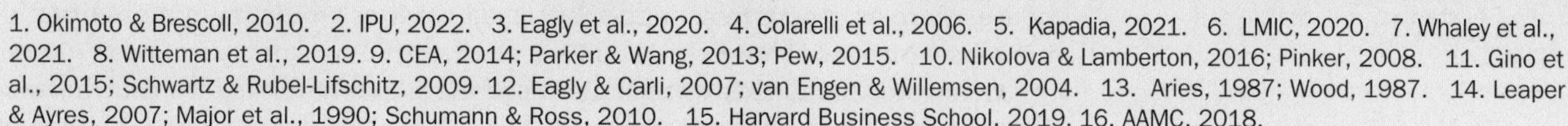

1. Okimoto & Brescoll, 2010. 2. IPU, 2022. 3. Eagly et al., 2020. 4. Colarelli et al., 2006. 5. Kapadia, 2021. 6. LMIC, 2020. 7. Whaley et al., 2021. 8. Witteman et al., 2019. 9. CEA, 2014; Parker & Wang, 2013; Pew, 2015. 10. Nikolova & Lamberton, 2016; Pinker, 2008. 11. Gino et al., 2015; Schwartz & Rubel-Lifschitz, 2009. 12. Eagly & Carli, 2007; van Engen & Willemsen, 2004. 13. Aries, 1987; Wood, 1987. 14. Leaper & Ayres, 2007; Major et al., 1990; Schumann & Ross, 2010. 15. Harvard Business School, 2019. 16. AAMC, 2018.

When asked a difficult question to which they don't know the answer—"Do you have any idea why the sky is blue?"—men are more likely than women to hazard answers than to admit they don't know, a phenomenon researchers have called the *male answer syndrome*. This tendency is related to "mansplaining" (men's explaining something to women in a condescending and sometimes inaccurate manner) (Giuliano et al., 1998; Tramontana, 2020).

Emily Bernstein/The New Yorker Collection/The Cartoon Bank

"Oh, you've read it? I'll just describe it to you as if you hadn't."

Cadet Hallie H. Pound/U.S. Army

Making history In 2019, West Point's 34 Black female cadets, many shown here, were part of its most diverse graduating class in history. These newly commissioned officers will add to a growing body of female military leaders.

SOCIAL CONNECTEDNESS Whatever our gender, we all have a need to belong, though we may satisfy this need in different ways (Baumeister, 2010). Males tend to be *independent*. Even as children, males typically form large play groups that brim with activity and competition, with little intimate discussion (Rose & Rudolph, 2006). As adults, men usually enjoy side-by-side activities, and their conversations often focus on problem solving (Baumeister, 2010; Tannen, 1990).

A neuroscientist could not tell whether a brain is male or female just by looking. Brain scans show few structural male-female differences, apart from male brains being a tad larger and female brains having thicker cortexes (Ritchie et al., 2018; van Eijk et al., 2021; Wierenga et al., 2019). "Human brains cannot be categorized into two distinct classes—male brain/female brain," reported neuroscientist Daphna Joel and her colleagues (2015).

Brain scans do, however, show some male-female differences. For example, a female's brain, more than a male's, is usually wired in a way that enables social relationships (Kiesow et al., 2020). This finding helps explain why females tend to be more *interdependent*. Across nearly a thousand studies, women have been characterized as "more communal than men" (Hsu et al., 2021). In childhood, girls usually play in small groups, often with one friend. They compete less and imitate social relationships more (Maccoby, 1990; Roberts, 1991). Teen girls spend more time with friends and less time alone (Wong & Csikszentmihalyi, 1991). In late adolescence, they spend more time on social media and enjoy it more (Rideout et al., 2022). Girls' and women's friendships are more intimate, with more conversation that explores relationships (Maccoby, 2002). In one analysis of 10 million posts to Facebook (which more women use), women's status updates were as assertive as men's, but used warmer words; men more often swore or expressed anger (Gramlich, 2018; Park et al., 2016). An analysis of over 700 million Facebook words found that women also used more family-related words, whereas men used more work-related words (Schwartz et al., 2013). In an analysis of 1.9 billion phone conversations, women's calls were longer (Dunbar, 2021).

When searching for understanding from someone who will share their worries and hurts, people usually turn to women. Women and men have reported that their friendships with women are more intimate, enjoyable, and nurturing (Kuttler et al., 1999; Rubin, 1985; Sapadin, 1988). Bonds and feelings of support are stronger among women than among men (Rossi & Rossi, 1993). Women's ties—as mothers, daughters, sisters, aunts, and grandmothers—can bind families together. As friends, women talk more often and more openly (Berndt, 1992; Dindia & Allen, 1992). "Perhaps because of [women's] greater desire for intimacy," reported Joyce Benenson and colleagues (2009), first-year

Anthony Asael/Danita Delimont Stock Photography

© 2/Rob Van Petten/Ocean/Corbis

Free-for-all, or tend and befriend? Gender differences in the way we interact with others begin to appear at a very young age.

college and university women are twice as likely as men to change roommates. When stressed, women are also more likely than men to turn to others for support. They *tend and befriend* (Tamres et al., 2002; Taylor, 2002).

Gender differences in both social connectedness and power are greatest in adolescence and early adulthood—the prime years for dating and mating (Hoff et al., 2018). By their teen years, girls appear less assertive and more insecure, and boys seem more dominant and less expressive (Chaplin, 2015). In adulthood, attitude and behavior differences often peak with parenthood. Mothers especially may express more traditionally female attitudes and behaviors (Ferriman et al., 2009; Katz-Wise et al., 2010). By age 50, most gender differences subside. Men become less domineering and more empathic, and women—especially those with paid employment—become more assertive and self-confident (Kasen et al., 2006; Maccoby, 1998). Worldwide, fewer women than men work for pay. But, like men, women tend to be more satisfied with their lives when gainfully employed (Ryan, 2016).

"In the long years liker must they grow;
The man be more of woman, she of man."
—Alfred Lord Tennyson, *The Princess*, 1847

So, although women and men are more alike than different, there are some behavior differences between the average woman and man—and likewise, between male and female nonhuman primates (de Waal, 2022). Psychologists Alice Eagly and William Revelle (2022) remind us that gender equality does not require gender similarity. Differences are not deficits. Indeed, they note, "groups composed of diverse individuals are more effective in solving problems."

Are gender differences dictated by our biology? Shaped by our cultures and other experiences? Read on.

RETRIEVAL PRACTICE

RP-3 ______________ (Men/Women) are more likely to commit relational aggression, and ______________ (men/women) are more likely to commit physical aggression.

ANSWERS IN APPENDIX E

The Nature of Gender

LOQ 13-8 How do sex hormones influence prenatal and adolescent sexual development?

In most physical ways—regulating heat with sweat, preferring energy-rich foods, growing calluses where the skin meets friction—we are all alike. Although biology does not *dictate* gender, it can influence our gender psychology in two ways:

- *Genetically*—We have differing sex chromosomes.
- *Physiologically*—We have differing concentrations of sex hormones, which trigger other anatomical differences.

These two influences began to form you long before you were born.

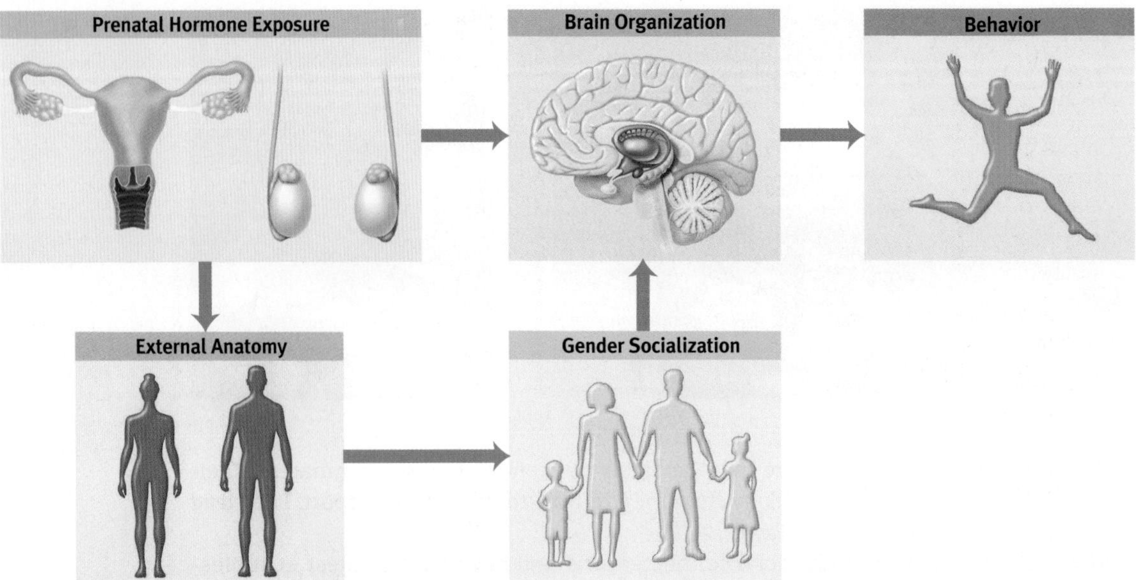
Prenatal Hormone Exposure
Brain Organization
Behavior
External Anatomy
Gender Socialization

FIGURE 13.4 From hormones to behavior Researchers are exploring how nature (prenatal exposure to male hormones, plus external anatomy, and brain organization) and nurture (gender socialization) contribute to male- or female-typical behaviors.

Pubertal boys may not at first like their sparse beard. (But then it grows on them.)

X chromosome the sex chromosome found in females and males. Females typically have two X chromosomes; males typically have one. An X chromosome from each parent produces a female child.

Y chromosome the sex chromosome typically found only in males. When paired with an X chromosome from the mother, it produces a male child.

testosterone the most important male sex hormone. Males and females have it, but the additional testosterone in males stimulates the growth of the male sex organs during the fetal period, and the development of the male sex characteristics during puberty.

estrogens sex hormones, such as estradiol, that contribute to female sex characteristics and are secreted in greater amounts by females than by males.

puberty the period of sexual maturation, when a person usually becomes capable of reproducing.

primary sex characteristics the body structures (ovaries, testes, and external genitalia) that make sexual reproduction possible.

secondary sex characteristics non-reproductive sexual traits, such as female breasts and hips, male voice quality, and body hair.

spermarche [sper-MAR-key] the first ejaculation.

menarche [meh-NAR-key] the first menstrual period.

PRENATAL SEXUAL DEVELOPMENT Six weeks after you were conceived, you looked much the same as any other tiny embryo. Then, as your genes kicked in, your biological sexual characteristics—determined by your twenty-third pair of chromosomes (the two sex chromosomes)—became more apparent. If you are male or female, your mother's contribution to that chromosome pair was an **X chromosome**. From your father, you received the 1 chromosome out of the usual 46 that is not unisex—either another X chromosome, making you female, or a **Y chromosome**, making you male.

About seven weeks after conception, a single gene on the Y chromosome throws a master switch, which triggers the testes to develop and to produce **testosterone**, the main *androgen* (male hormone) that promotes male sex organ development. Females also have testosterone, but less of it; the main female sex hormones are the **estrogens**, such as *estradiol*.

Later, during the fourth and fifth prenatal months, sex hormones bathe the fetal brain and influence its wiring. Gender-typical male and female traits develop under the influence of the male's greater testosterone and the female's estrogens (see **FIGURE 13.4**) (Hines, 2004; Udry, 2000). Females who are prenatally exposed to unusually high male hormone levels tend to grow up with more male-typical interests (Berenbaum & Beltz, 2021; Endendijk et al., 2016). Likewise, males prenatally exposed to *low* male hormone levels tend to grow up with more female-typical interests (Shirazi et al., 2022).

ADOLESCENT SEXUAL DEVELOPMENT A flood of hormones triggers another period of dramatic physical change when we enter **puberty**. In this 2-year period of rapid sexual maturation, pronounced female-male differences emerge. A variety of changes begin at about age 10 in girls and at about age 12 in boys (Biro et al., 2012; Herman-Giddens et al., 2012). A year or two before visible physical changes, we often feel the first stirrings of sexual attraction (McClintock & Herdt, 1996).

Girls' earlier entry into puberty can at first propel them to greater height than boys of the same age. But boys catch up when they begin puberty, and by age 14 they are usually taller than girls. During these growth spurts, the **primary sex characteristics**—the reproductive organs and external genitalia—develop dramatically. So do the nonreproductive **secondary sex characteristics**. Pubic and underarm hair emerges. Girls develop breasts and larger hips. Boys' facial hair begins growing and their voices deepen (**FIGURE 13.5**).

For boys, puberty's landmark is the first ejaculation, which often occurs first during sleep (as a "wet dream"). This event, called **spermarche**, usually happens by about age 14.

In girls, the landmark is the first menstrual period, **menarche**, usually within a year of age 12-1/2 (Anderson et al., 2003). Scientists have identified nearly 250 genes that predict age at menarche (Day et al., 2017). But environment matters, too. Early menarche is more likely following stresses related to poverty, father absence, sexual abuse, insecure attachments, or a history of a mother's smoking during pregnancy (Richardson et al., 2018; Shrestha et al., 2011; Sun et al., 2017). Girls in various countries are reaching

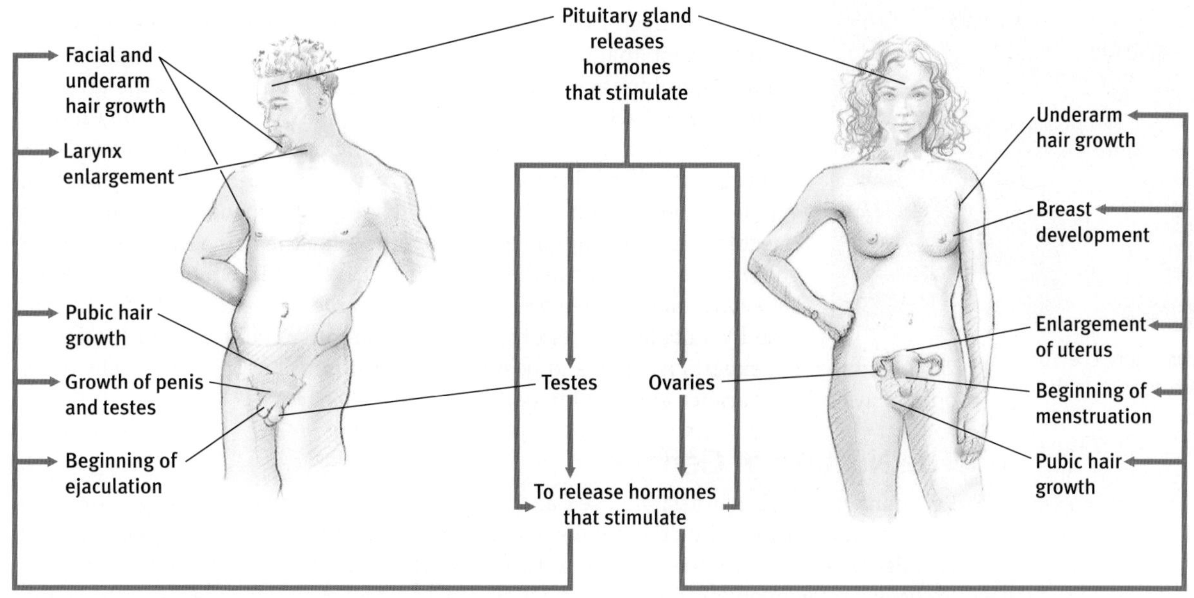
Pituitary gland releases hormones that stimulate
Facial and underarm hair growth
Larynx enlargement
Pubic hair growth
Growth of penis and testes
Beginning of ejaculation
Testes
Ovaries
To release hormones that stimulate
Underarm hair growth
Breast development
Enlargement of uterus
Beginning of menstruation
Pubic hair growth

FIGURE 13.5
Body changes at puberty

puberty earlier today than in the past. Suspected triggers include increased body fat, increased hormone-mimicking chemicals in the diet, and increased stress related to family disruption (Biro et al., 2010, 2012; Ellis et al., 2012; Herman-Giddens, 2013). But there is good news for children with a secure child-mother attachment: This bond can provide a buffer against childhood stresses, including those related to early puberty (Sung et al., 2016). Remember: *Nature and nurture interact.*

RETRIEVAL PRACTICE

RP-4 Prenatal sexual development begins about ________________ weeks after conception. Adolescence is marked by the onset of ________________.

ANSWERS IN APPENDIX E

SEXUAL DEVELOPMENT VARIATIONS Nature may blur the biological line between males and females. People who are intersex may be born with combinations of male and female chromosomes, hormones, and anatomy. For example, a genetic male may be born with two or more X chromosomes as well as a Y chromosome *(Klinefelter syndrome)*, often resulting in sterility and small testes. Genetic females born with only one normal X chromosome *(Turner syndrome)* may not have menstrual periods, develop breasts, or be able to have children without reproductive assistance. Such individuals may struggle with their *gender identity.*

In the 1970s, physician Julianne Imperato-McGinley discovered one of the rarest sexual development variations. She traveled to a remote village in the Dominican Republic, where she had learned that some seemingly female children became male children at the beginning of puberty. These children—called *güevedoces,* meaning "penis at 12"—were born with an apparent vagina, and neither a visible penis nor testes. The children were raised as girls until puberty, when they grew a penis and testes and developed male-typical secondary sex characteristics. Through genetic and biological analysis, Imperato-McGinley showed that these children had XY sex chromosomes—typical of genetic males—but lacked an enzyme that converts testosterone to form visible male genitalia (Imperato-McGinley et al., 1974). So puberty's testosterone surge prompted not only the usual development of secondary sex characteristics (such as deepening voice), but also the belated development of male genitalia. This rare genetic condition was widespread in the village, affecting 1 in 90 children.

Despite being raised as girls, güevedoces children often display male-typical childhood interests, and most eventually self-identify as males. Carlos, named Carla at birth, was more interested in playing soccer than in playing with dolls (Ennis, 2015). At the beginning of puberty, he told his dad he no longer wanted to have long hair or "to be a girl anymore" (Univision, 2015). Johnny, who grew up as Felicita, noted that "I never

Jon Sayers/BBC

The amazing *güevedoces* Catherine and Carla, pictured here, are cousins with güevedoces syndrome. Born without visible male reproductive organs at birth, they were raised as girls. At the onset of puberty, they grew a penis and testes and asked people to call them Cástulo and Carlos, respectively.

liked to dress as a girl and when they bought me toys for girls I never bothered playing with them—when I saw a group of boys I would stop to play ball with them." Like many güevedoces children, when his characteristics changed to become typically male, Johnny was bullied by peers.

In the past, medical professionals often recommended surgery to create an unambiguous sex identity for children with conditions affecting their external anatomy. In one famous case, when a baby boy named Bruce Reimer lost his penis in a botched circumcision, his parents followed a psychologist's advice to seek surgery and raise him as a girl, "Brenda." When Reimer learned as a teenager what had happened, he immediately rejected the assigned female identity, choosing the name David and undergoing surgery to remove the breasts he'd developed from hormone therapy. He eventually married a woman and became a stepfather. Sadly, he later died by suicide—as had his depressed identical twin brother (Colapinto, 2000). Today, most experts recommend postponing surgery until people's naturally developing physical appearance and gender identity become clear.

The Nurture of Gender

For many people, birth-assigned sex and gender coexist in harmony. Biology draws the outline, and culture paints the details. The physical traits that define a newborn as male, female, or intersex are the same worldwide. But the gender traits that define how men (or boys) and women (or girls) should act, interact, or feel about themselves differ across time and place (Zentner & Eagly, 2015).

role a set of expectations (norms) about a social position, defining how those in the position ought to behave.

gender role a set of expected behaviors, attitudes, and traits for men and for women.

GENDER ROLES

LOQ 13-9 What are some cultural influences on gender roles?

Cultures shape our behaviors by defining how we ought to behave in a particular social position, or **role**. We can see this shaping power in **gender roles**—the social expectations that guide people's behavior as men or as women.

In just a thin slice of history, gender roles worldwide have undergone an extreme makeover. At the beginning of the twentieth century, only one country in the world—New Zealand—granted women the right to vote (Briscoe, 1997). By 2015, that right existed in all countries. A century ago, U.S. women could not vote in national elections, serve in the military, or divorce a husband without cause. If a woman worked for pay, she would more likely have been a maid than a manager. Between 2007 and 2018, 1.4 million tests of attitudes toward gender roles showed decreasing endorsement of traditional stereotypes, such as associating men with "career" and "science" and women with "family" and "arts" (Charlesworth & Banaji, 2022).

MARWAN NAAMANI/AFP/Getty Images

Driving change Thanks to the advocacy of Manal al-Sharif and others, driving a car became a universal right for women in 2018, when Saudi Arabia lifted its ban. She said, "The fight for women's rights anywhere contributes to the fight for women's rights everywhere" (2019).

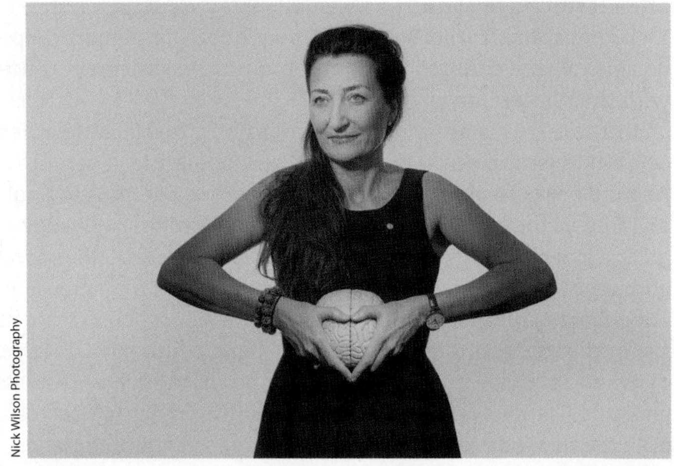
Nick Wilson Photography

Benefits of belonging Women are gaining ground in STEM fields, as illustrated by the 2014 Nobel Prize in medicine going to neuroscientist May-Britt Moser (who was a psychology major). Moser credits her passion for studying the brain to having capable and encouraging mentors: "I was not always the best student, but my teachers saw something in me and tried to encourage me" (Moser, 2014).

Gender roles also vary from one place to another. Nomadic societies of food-gathering people have had little division of labor by sex. Boys and girls receive much the same upbringing. In agricultural societies, where women typically work in the nearby fields and men roam while herding livestock, cultures have shaped children to assume more distinct gender roles (Segall et al., 1990; Van Leeuwen, 1978).

Take a minute to check your own gender expectations. Would you agree that "When jobs are scarce, men should have more right to a job"? In Sweden and Spain, barely more than 10 percent of adults agreed. In Egypt and Jordan, about 90 percent agreed (UNFPA, 2016). We're all human, but my, how our views differ.

Cultural expectations about gender roles also factor into **sexual aggression**. In the United States, 1 in 5 women and 1 in 16 men are sexually assaulted while in college (Lisak et al., 2010). In the aftermath of credible accusations of sexual aggression by famous and powerful men, many countries are making efforts to reduce sexual harassment and assault. Still, the problem persists, with a survey of nearly 10,000 in the Hollywood entertainment industry revealing the power of harassers: "You can fire somebody, you can influence their ability to get another job, or you can just destroy their reputation" (Noveck, 2020). (See Thinking Critically About: Sexual Aggression.)

Suvra Kanti Das/Abaca Press/Alamy Stock Photo

The gendered pandemic As the Covid pandemic devastated people's careers, many more women than men were forced to reduce their work hours or leave the workplace. Women more often work in low-paying jobs that offer few benefits and little flexibility, such as remote work or paid leave to care for sick relatives. In 2020, women worldwide lost 64 million jobs and $800 billion in income (Oxfam International, 2021). These unemployed domestic workers in Dhaka, Bangladesh, wait to receive food aid.

RETRIEVAL PRACTICE

RP-5 What are gender roles, and what do their variations tell us about our human capacity for learning and adaptation?

ANSWERS IN APPENDIX E

GENDER IDENTITY

LOQ 13-11 How do we form our gender identity?

A *gender role* describes how others expect us to think, feel, and act. Our **gender identity**, when *binary* (involving only two options), is our personal sense of being male or female. Those with a *nonbinary* gender identity may not feel male or female, or they may identify as some combination of male *and* female. How do we develop our gender identity?

Social learning theory assumes that we acquire our identity in childhood, by observing and imitating others' gender-linked behaviors and by being rewarded or punished for acting in specific ways. ("Tatiana, you're such a good mommy to your dolls"; "You're such a tough kid, Armand.") But there's more to gender identity than imitation and reward. **Gender typing**—taking on a traditional female or male role—varies from child to child (Tobin et al., 2010).

Parents help transmit their culture's views on gender. In one analysis of 43 studies, parents with traditional gender views were more likely to have gender-typed children who shared their expectations about how males and females should act (Tenenbaum & Leaper, 2002). When fathers share equally in housework, their daughters develop higher aspirations for work outside the home (Croft et al., 2014).

But no matter how much parents encourage or discourage traditional gender behavior, children may drift toward what feels right to them. Some organize themselves into "boy worlds" and "girl worlds," each guided by their understanding of the rules. Others conform to these rules more flexibly. Still others prefer **androgyny**: A blend of male and female roles feels right to them. Androgyny has benefits. As adults, androgynous people are more adaptable. They are more flexible in their actions and in their career choices (Bem, 1993). From childhood onward, they tend to be more resilient and self-accepting, and they experience less depression (Lam & McBride-Chang, 2007; Mosher & Danoff-Burg, 2008; Pauletti et al., 2017).

Feelings matter, but so does how we think. Early in life, we all form *schemas*, or concepts that help us make sense of our world. Our *gender schemas* organize our experiences of male-female characteristics and help us think about our gender identity, about who we are as unique individuals (Bem, 1987, 1993; Martin et al., 2002).

As young children, we were "gender detectives" (Martin & Ruble, 2004). Before our first birthday, we knew the difference between a typically male and female voice or face

"You cannot put women and men on an equal footing. It is against nature." —Turkish President Recep Tayyip Erdoğan, 2014

"We need to keep changing the attitude that raises our girls to be demure and our boys to be assertive, that criticizes our daughters for speaking out and our sons for shedding a tear." —Former U.S. President Barack Obama, 2016

sexual aggression any physical or verbal behavior of a sexual nature that is unwanted or intended to harm someone physically or emotionally. Can be expressed as either *sexual harassment* or *sexual assault.*

gender identity our personal sense of being male, female, neither, or some combination of male and female.

social learning theory the theory that we learn social behavior by observing and imitating and by being rewarded or punished.

gender typing the acquisition of a traditional masculine or feminine role.

androgyny blending traditionally masculine and traditionally feminine psychological characteristics.

Thinking Critically About:
Sexual Aggression

LOQ 13-10 What are the effects of sexual aggression? How have cultural views changed, and how can we reduce sexual aggression?

Definition of Sexual Aggression

Sexual harassment involves making unwanted sexual advances, obscene remarks, or requests for sexual favors.[1]

Sexual assault is "any type of sexual contact or behavior that occurs without the explicit consent of the recipient," such as unwanted touching, molestation, and attempted or completed rape.[2]

Cultural Effects on Our Views

By Place: Some cultures view victims of sexual aggression as guilty of disgracing their families. In India and Pakistan, male family members kill an unknown number of women—one source estimates 1000 annually in each country[10]—for dishonoring their families.

Over Time: Changes in global norms have made it less acceptable to blame victims of sexual aggression.

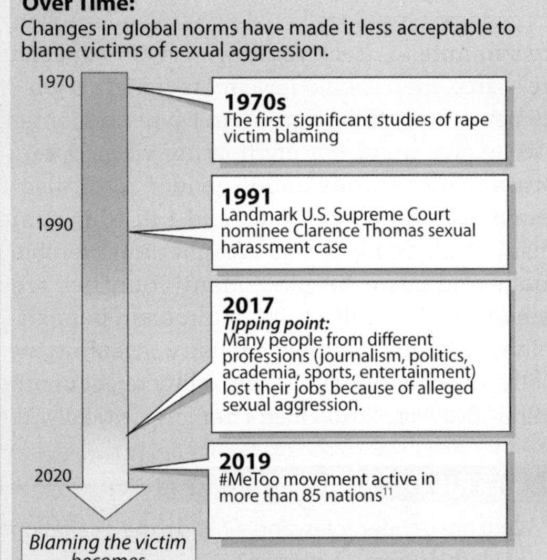

1970
1990
2020
1970s
The first significant studies of rape victim blaming
1991
Landmark U.S. Supreme Court nominee Clarence Thomas sexual harassment case
2017
Tipping point:
Many people from different professions (journalism, politics, academia, sports, entertainment) lost their jobs because of alleged sexual aggression.
2019
#MeToo movement active in more than 85 nations[11]
Blaming the victim becomes less acceptable.

Victims

In the U.S., **81%** of women and **43%** of men report having experienced sexual aggression in their lifetime.[3]

Sexual aggression affects people of *all ethnic groups*.[4]

Nearly **70%** of rape victims are between the ages of 11 and 24.[4]

In a National School Climate survey, **8** out of **10** gay or lesbian adolescents reported experiencing sex-related harassment in the prior year.[5]

Effects on Well-Being

Thanks to human resilience, victims of sexual aggression often recover and lead healthy and meaningful lives. Yet many also suffer serious setbacks, including:

- Greater anxiety, depression, and risk for posttraumatic stress disorder6
- Disrupted sleep[7]
- Poor physical health[8]
- Difficulty trusting new relationship partners[9]

How to Reduce Sexual Aggression

Therapy to treat sexual aggressors has not been very effective.[12] However, other, broader-based strategies do work:

Encourage victims to report their experiences to authority figures (parents, supervisors, law enforcement officials) and to share their experiences publicly.[13]

Empower victims to take control of their situation and refuse to let their perpetrators dominate or manipulate them. Adjust social norms so that victims feel safe reporting their experiences.

Educate people about preventive bystander intervention strategies, such as "Green Dot," which has reduced sexual aggression in communities by as much as 20%.[14]

Person of the Year
TIME
The Silence Breakers
2017

THE INDIANAPOLIS STAR
Disgraced Dr. Nassar...sexual abuse
... 332 victims[15]

1. McDonald, 2012; U.S.E.E.O.C., 2018. 2. U.S.D.O.J., 2018. 3. Stop Street Harassment, 2018. 4. Black et al., 2011. 5. GLSEN, 2012. 6. Choudhary et al., 2012; Krahé & Berger, 2017; Snipes et al., 2017; Zanarini et al., 1997. 7. Krakow et al., 2001, 2002. 8. Schuyler et al., 2017; Zinzow et al., 2011. 9. Muldoon et al., 2016; Starzynski et al., 2017. 10. HBVA, 2018. 11. Stone & Vogelstein, 2019. 12. Grønnerød et al., 2015; Klapilová et al., 2019. 13. Holland et al., 2020. 14. Coker et al., 2017. 15. Jesse, 2019.

(Martin et al., 2002). After we turned 2, language forced us to label the world in terms of gender. The English language has classified people as *he* and *she*, though *they* is increasingly used as a gender-neutral pronoun. Other languages classify objects as masculine ("*le* train") or feminine ("*la* table").

For young children, gender looms large. Children tend to learn that two sorts of people exist and they begin to search for clues about gender. In every culture, people communicate their gender in many ways. Their *gender expression* drops hints not only in their language but also in their clothing, interests, and possessions. Having picked up such clues, 3-year-olds may divide the human world in half. "Girls," they may decide, are the ones who love *Frozen* and have longer hair. "Boys" think *Captain Underpants* is hilarious and don't wear dresses. Armed with their newly collected "proof," they then adjust their behaviors to fit their concept of gender. These stereotypes are most rigid at about age 5 or 6. If the new neighbor is a girl, a 6-year-old boy may assume he cannot share her interests.

transgender an umbrella term describing people whose gender identity differs from that associated with their sex assigned at birth. 

What children learn has, however, slowly been broadening from the "two sorts of people" found in the animated classics and separate toy aisles for dolls and action heroes. In 2022, the popular Pixar film *Lightyear* portrayed two female characters in a same-sex relationship, including a scene where they kiss. "We're reflecting the world around us," said producer Gayle Susman (Cavna, 2022).

For people who are *cisgender*, gender identity corresponds with their sex assigned at birth. For those who are **transgender**, gender identity differs from what's typical for that person's assigned sex (APA, 2010; Bockting, 2014). For example, a person assigned female at birth may identify as a male from childhood onward. Others first identify as transgender in adolescence or adulthood. One study of 300 transgender girls and boys found them to be as strongly gender-typed and gender-identified as cisgender children (Gülgöz et al., 2019).

In most countries, it's not easy being transgender. Cisgender people often perceive transgender people as mentally ill or confused (Howansky et al., 2021). In North America, Europe, and Asia, transgender people frequently experience verbal harassment, prejudice, and discrimination (James et al., 2016; Spielmann et al., 2022). Transgender people may experience distress due to this mistreatment, increasing their risk of depression and suicidal thinking (de Graaf et al., 2022; Pellicane & Ciesla, 2022). Perhaps due to experiencing or anticipating prejudice, U.S. transgender veterans have twice the risk of dying by suicide as cisgender military veterans (Tucker, 2019). Some transgender people may develop *gender dysphoria*, which involves clinical levels of distress associated with dissimilarity between a person's experienced or expressed gender and their sex assigned at birth. This distress may impact their ability to work, interact with loved ones, or experience satisfying sexual relationships (APA, 2022; Lindley et al., 2022). But when accepted by their families, transgender youth are not at higher risk for depression, and experience only slightly higher levels of anxiety than their cisgender peers (Durwood et al., 2017; Gibson et al., 2021).

Transgender people may undergo a social transition, changing their hairstyles, clothing, first names, or pronouns to align with their gender identity. After the start of puberty, transgender people may use medical interventions to align their outward appearance and everyday lives with their gender identity. Gender-affirming medical procedures (including hormone use and surgery) reduce transgender people's depression, anxiety, and posttraumatic stress (Almazan & Keuroghlian, 2021; Baker et al., 2021; Tomita et al., 2019). Only 1 percent of transgender people report regretting their gender-affirming medical procedure (Bustos et al., 2021). Younger people have begun to seek these medical procedures, sparking debates within psychology and medical communities about what age to begin use of "puberty blocker" medication, administer gender-affirming hormones, or undergo genital surgery (Tavris, 2022; Temming, 2021).

Gender identity is distinct from *sexual orientation* (the direction of one's sexual attraction). Transgender people may be sexually attracted to people of any gender or to no one at all, just as cisgender people may be. Your sexual orientation is who you fantasize going to bed *with;* your gender identity is who you go to bed *as*.

Worldwide, an estimated 25 million people are transgender (WHO, 2016). That's 0.4 percent of humans, which is a number similar to that reported in an Alberta census (Frew, 2022). About 1.6 million people in the United States (0.6 percent) are transgender (Herman et al., 2022). Roughly 30 percent of those not identifying with their assigned

Erich Bartlebaugh/BuzzFeed News/Redux Pictures

Nonbinary on the big screen Asia Kate Dillon is a nonbinary actor whose films include *John Wick 3.* Dillon describes educating others about gender identity as "a dialogue . . . about what pronouns are, what gender identity is, the fact that we're all assigned a sex, but that everyone actually has the autonomy to [determine] how they identify" (Soloski, 2019).

"It is no lie nor fable, that females may turn to be males." —Pliny the Elder, *Natural History*, 77 C.E. (quoted in Wilkinson, 2021).

sex have a nonbinary gender identity (Barr et al., 2016; James et al., 2016; Mikalson et al., 2012).

In North America and Europe, the number of transgender people is rising, most notably among adolescents who were assigned female at birth (Thompson et al., 2022). Referrals to UK clinics for adolescents seeking gender-affirming medical care increased from 250 in 2011 to 5000 in 2021, with two-thirds of patients having been assigned female at birth (Ghorayshi, 2022). In a 2022 U.S. survey, 3.1 percent of 18- to 24-year-olds identified as transgender—six times the proportion of those aged 25 to 29 and 16 times the proportion of those aged 50 and older (Brown, 2022). Thus, half of U.S. young adults, but only one in five of those over 65, personally know someone who is transgender (McCarthy, 2021).

The large differences among age groups have sparked debate: Is the increase in youth and young adults who identify as transgender a healthy trend, with greater awareness and acceptance of transgender people, more of whom feel comfortable sharing their identities? Or is the multiplying number a social phenomenon? Or both (Tavris, 2022)? Regardless, early childhood gender identity tends to be stable: Transgender youth who socially transitioned at an early age rarely retransition to a cisgender identity (Olson et al., 2022).

ASK YOURSELF

How gender-typed are you? What has influenced your feelings of being male, female, neither, or some combination of male and female?

Reflections on Nature, Nurture, and Their Interaction

LOQ 13-12 How do nature, nurture, and our own choices influence gender roles and sexuality?

"There are trivial truths and great truths," reflected the physicist Niels Bohr on the paradoxes of science. "The opposite of a trivial truth is plainly false. The opposite of a great truth is also true." Our ancestral history helped form us as a species. Where there is variation, natural selection, and heredity, there will be evolution. Our genes form us. This is a great truth about human nature.

But our experiences also shape us. Our families and peer relationships teach us how to think and act. Differences initiated by our nature may be amplified by our nurture. If their genes and hormones predispose males to be more physically aggressive than females, culture can amplify this gender difference through norms that reward macho men and gentle women. If men are encouraged toward roles that demand physical power, and women toward more nurturing roles, each may act accordingly. Roles remake their players. Lawyers in time become more lawyerly, professors more professorial. Gender roles similarly shape us.

In many modern cultures, gender roles are merging. Brute strength has become less important for power and status (think of how climate activist Greta Thunberg has galvanized millions of people worldwide to environmental protest and action). From 1965 to 2021, women soared from 9 percent to 56 percent of U.S. medical students (AAMC, 2014, 2021). In the quarter century since 1996, U.S. partnered heterosexual men have been doing more and more of the laundry, cleaning, and cooking—though still less than women contribute (Brenan, 2020). A 30-country survey shows that women complete two more hours of unpaid daily work than do men, but the gender gap is shrinking (OECD, 2022). Such swift changes signal that biology does not define gender roles.

San Diego Museum of Man, photograph by Rose Tyson

Culture matters As this exhibit at a San Diego museum illustrates, children learn their culture. A baby's foot can step into any culture.

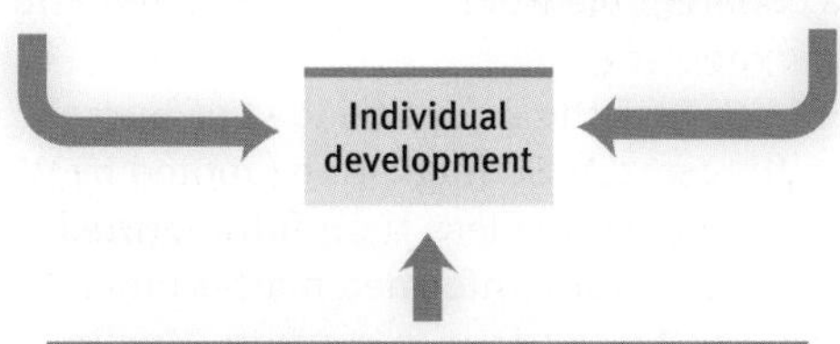
Biological influences:
• Shared human genome
• Individual genetic variations
• Prenatal environment
• Sex-related genes, hormones, and physiology
Psychological influences:
• Gene–environment interaction
• Neurological effect of early experiences
• Responses evoked by our own temperament, gender, etc.
• Beliefs, feelings, and expectations
Individual development
Social-cultural influences:
• Parental influences
• Peer influences
• Cultural individualism or collectivism
• Cultural gender norms

FIGURE 13.6
The biopsychosocial approach to development

If nature and nurture jointly form us, are we "nothing but" the product of nature and nurture? Are we rigidly determined?

We *are* the product of nature and nurture, but we are also an open system (**FIGURE 13.6**). Genes are all-pervasive but not all-powerful. People may reject their evolutionary role as transmitters of genes and choose not to reproduce. Culture, too, is all-pervasive but not all-powerful. People may defy peer pressures and resist social expectations.

Moreover, we cannot excuse our failings by blaming them solely on bad genes or bad influences. In reality, we are both creatures and creators of our worlds. So many things about us—including our gender roles—are the products of our genes and environments. Yet the stream that runs into the future flows through our present choices. Our decisions today design our environments tomorrow. We are the architects. Our hopes, goals, and expectations influence our destiny. And that is what enables cultures to vary and to change. Mind matters.

NED HELPED OUT

Ellis Rosen/Cartoon Stock

RETRIEVAL PRACTICE

RP-6 How does the biopsychosocial approach explain our individual development?

ANSWERS IN APPENDIX E

* * *

We know from our correspondence and from surveys that some readers are troubled by the naturalism and evolutionism of contemporary science. (A note to readers from other nations: In the United States there can be a gulf between scientific and lay thinking about evolution.) "The idea that human minds are the product of evolution is ... unassailable fact," declared a 2007 editorial in *Nature,* a leading science journal. In *The Language of God,* Human Genome Project director Francis Collins (2006, pp. 141, 146), a self-described Christian, compiled the "utterly compelling" evidence that led him to conclude that Darwin's big idea is "unquestionably correct." Yet Gallup pollsters report that 40 percent of U.S. adults believe that humans were created "pretty much in their present form" within the last 10,000 years (Brenan, 2019). Many people who dispute the scientific story worry that a science of behavior (and evolutionary science in particular) will destroy our sense of human beauty, mystery, and spiritual significance. For those concerned, we offer some reassuring thoughts.

When Isaac Newton explained the rainbow in terms of light of differing wavelengths, the British poet John Keats feared that Newton had destroyed the rainbow's mysterious beauty. Yet, as evolutionary biologist Richard Dawkins (1998) noted in *Unweaving the Rainbow,* Newton's analysis led to an even more profound mystery—Einstein's theory of special relativity. Nothing about Newton's optics need diminish our appreciation for the dramatic elegance of a rainbow arching across a brightening sky.

"Let's hope that it's not true; but if it is true, let's hope that it doesn't become widely known." —Lady Ashley, commenting on Darwin's theory

"Is it not stirring to understand how the world actually works—that white light is made of colors, that color measures light waves, that transparent air reflects light ... ? It does no harm to the romance of the sunset to know a little about it." —Carl Sagan, *Skies of Other Worlds,* 1988

When Galileo assembled evidence that the Earth revolved around the Sun, not vice versa, he did not offer irrefutable proof for his theory. Instead, he provided a coherent explanation for a variety of observations, such as the changing shadows cast by the Moon's mountains. His explanation eventually won the day because it described and explained things in a way that made sense, that hung together. Darwin's theory of evolution likewise is a coherent view of natural history. It offers an organizing principle that unifies various observations.

Many people of faith find the scientific idea of human origins congenial with their spirituality. In the fifth century, St. Augustine (quoted by Wilford, 1999) wrote, "The universe was brought into being in a less than fully formed state, but was gifted with the capacity to transform itself from unformed matter into a truly marvelous array of structures and life forms." In the fourteenth century, Muslim historian Ibn Khaldun (1377) wrote, "One should then look at the world of creation. It started out from the minerals and progressed, in an ingenious, gradual manner to plants and animals." Some 800 years later, Pope Francis in 2015 welcomed a science–religion dialogue, saying, "Evolution in nature is not inconsistent with the notion of creation, because evolution requires the creation of beings that evolve."

heromen30/Shutterstock

Meanwhile, many people of science are awestruck at the emerging understanding of the universe and the human creature. It boggles the mind—the entire universe popping out of a point some 14 billion years ago, and instantly inflating to cosmological size. Had the energy of this Big Bang been the tiniest bit less, the universe would have collapsed back on itself. Had it been the tiniest bit more, the result would have been a soup too thin to support life. Astronomer Sir Martin Rees has described *Just Six Numbers* (1999), any one of which, if changed ever so slightly, would produce a cosmos in which life could not exist. Had gravity been a tad stronger or weaker, or had the weight of a carbon proton been a wee bit different, our universe just wouldn't have worked.

What caused this almost too-good-to-be-true, finely tuned universe? Why is there something rather than nothing? How did it come to be, in the words of Harvard-Smithsonian astrophysicist Owen Gingerich (1994), "so extraordinarily right, that it seemed the universe had been expressly designed to produce intelligent, sentient beings"? On such matters, a humble, awed, scientific silence is appropriate, suggested philosopher Ludwig Wittgenstein: "Whereof one cannot speak, thereof one must be silent" (1922, p. 189).

Rather than fearing science, we can welcome its enlarging our understanding and awakening our sense of awe. In *The Fragile Species,* Lewis Thomas (1992) described his utter amazement that the Earth in time gave rise to bacteria and eventually to Bach's Mass in B Minor. In a short 4 billion years, life on Earth has come from nothing to structures as complex as a 6-billion-unit strand of DNA and the incomprehensible intricacy of the human brain. Atoms no different from those in a rock somehow formed dynamic entities that produced extraordinary, self-replicating, information-processing systems—us (Davies, 2007). Although we appear to have been created from dust, over eons of time, the end result is a priceless creature, rich with potential beyond our imagination.

"The possession of knowledge does not kill the sense of wonder and mystery. There is always more mystery." —Anaïs Nin, *The Diary of Anaïs Nin*, 1934

MODULE

13 REVIEW Cultural and Gender Diversity: Understanding Nature and Nurture

LEARNING OBJECTIVES

Test Yourself Answer these repeated Learning Objective Questions on your own (before "showing" the answers here, or checking the answers in Appendix D) to improve your retention of the concepts (McDaniel et al., 2009, 2015).

LOQ **13-1** How do early experiences modify the brain?

LOQ **13-2** In what ways do parents and peers shape children's development?

LOQ **13-3** How does culture affect our behavior?

LOQ **13-4** How do individualist and collectivist cultures shape values and goals?

LOQ **13-5** How does the meaning of *gender* differ from the meaning of *sex*?

LOQ **13-6** What are some of the ways males and females tend to be alike and to differ?

LOQ **13-7** What factors contribute to gender bias in the workplace?

LOQ **13-8** How do sex hormones influence prenatal and adolescent sexual development?

LOQ **13-9** What are some cultural influences on gender roles?

LOQ **13-10** What are the effects of sexual aggression? How have cultural views changed, and how can we reduce sexual aggression?

LOQ **13-11** How do we form our gender identity?

LOQ **13-12** How do nature, nurture, and our own choices influence gender roles and sexuality?

TERMS AND CONCEPTS TO REMEMBER

Test Yourself Write down the definition in your own words, then check your answer.

culture, p. 144
norms, p. 145
tight culture, p. 145
loose culture, p. 145
individualism, p. 146
collectivism, p. 146
sex, p. 151
gender, p. 151
intersex, p. 151
aggression, p. 152
relational aggression, p. 152
X chromosome, p. 156
Y chromosome, p. 156
testosterone, p. 156
estrogens, p. 156
puberty, p. 156
primary sex characteristics, p. 156
secondary sex characteristics, p. 156
spermarche [sper-MAR-key], p. 156
menarche [meh-NAR-key], p. 156
role, p. 158
gender role, p. 158
sexual aggression, p. 159
gender identity, p. 159
social learning theory, p. 159
gender typing, p. 159
androgyny, p. 159
transgender, p. 161

MODULE TEST

Test Yourself Answer the following questions on your own first, then "show" the answers here, or check your answers in Appendix E.

1. Individualist cultures tend to value ________; collectivist cultures tend to value ________.
   - **a.** interdependence; independence
   - **b.** independence; interdependence
   - **c.** solidarity; uniqueness
   - **d.** duty; fulfillment

2. In psychology, ________ is the biologically influenced characteristics by which people define *male, female*, and *intersex*. The behavioral characteristics that people associate with *boy, girl, man*, and *woman* is ________.

3. Females and males are very similar, but one way they differ is that
   - **a.** females interrupt more often than males.
   - **b.** males are more democratic than females in their leadership roles.
   - **c.** as children, females tend to play in small groups, while males tend to play in large groups.
   - **d.** females are more likely to die by suicide.

4. A fertilized egg will develop into a male if it receives a/n ________ chromosome from its father.

5. Primary sex characteristics relate to ________; secondary sex characteristics refer to ________.
   - **a.** spermarche; menarche
   - **b.** breasts and facial hair; ovaries and testes
   - **c.** emotional maturity; hormone surges
   - **d.** reproductive organs; nonreproductive traits

6. On average, girls begin puberty at about the age of ________, boys at about the age of ________.

7. A person born with a combination of male and female biological sexual characteristics is ________.

8. *Gender role* refers to our
   - **a.** sense of being male, female, neither, or some combination of male and female.
   - **b.** culture's expectations about the "right" way for men and women to behave.
   - **c.** assigned sex at birth—our chromosomes and anatomy.
   - **d.** gender identity.

9. Our personal sense of being male, female, neither, or some combination of male and female is known as our ________ ________.

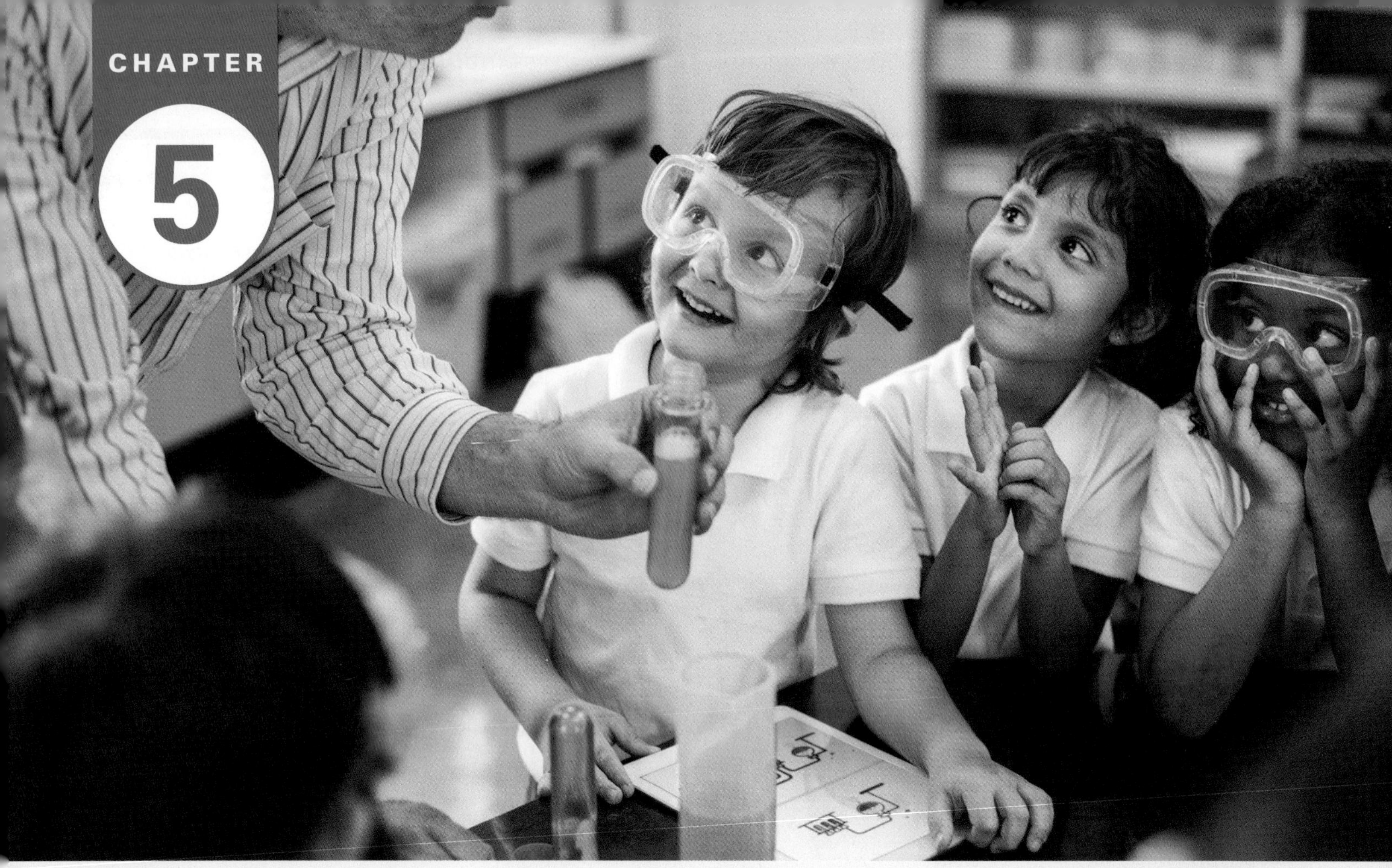
CHAPTER
5

Rawpixel.com/Shutterstock

Developing Through the Life Span (Modules 14–17)

Life is a journey, from womb to tomb. So it is for me [DM], and so it will be for you. My story, and yours, began when a man and a woman together contributed 20,000+ genes to an egg that became a unique person. Those genes coded the protein building blocks that, with astonishing precision, form our body and predispose our traits. My grandmother bequeathed to my mother a rare hearing-loss pattern, which she, in turn, gave to me (the least of her gifts). My father was an amiable extravert, and sometimes I forget to stop talking (although as a child, my talking was impeded by stuttering, for which Seattle Public Schools provided speech therapy).

Along with my parents' nature, I also received their nurture. Like you, I was born into a particular family and culture, with its own way of viewing the world. My values have been shaped by a family culture filled with talking and laughter, by a religious culture that speaks of love and justice, and by an academic culture that encourages critical thinking (asking, *What do you mean? How do you know?*).

We are formed by our genes and by our contexts, so our stories all differ. But in many ways we are each like nearly everyone else on Earth. Being human, you and I have a need to belong. My mental video library, which began after age 4, is filled with scenes of social attachment. Over time, my attachments to parents loosened as peer friendships grew. After lacking the confidence to date in high school, I fell in love with a college classmate and married at age 20. Natural selection predisposes us to survive and perpetuate our genes. Sure enough, two years later a child entered our lives, and I experienced a new form of love that surprised me with its intensity.

But life is marked by change. That child and his brother now live 2000 miles away, and their sister has found her calling in South Africa. The tight rubber bands linking parent and child have loosened, as yours likely have as well.

Change also marks most vocational lives, which for me transitioned from a teen working in the family insurance agency, to a premed chemistry major and hospital aide, to (after discarding my half-completed medical school applications) a psychology professor and author. I predict that in 10 years, you will also be doing things you do not currently anticipate.

Stability also marks our development: Our life situations change, but we experience a continuous self. When I look in the mirror, I do not see the person I once was, but I feel like the person I have always been. I am the same person who, as a late teen, played basketball and discovered love. Sixty years later, I still enjoy basketball and still love (with less passion but more security) the life partner with whom I have shared life's griefs and joys.

Continuity morphs through stages—for me, growing up, raising children, enjoying a career, and, eventually, life's final stage, which will demand my presence. As I wend my way through this cycle of life and death, I am mindful that life is a journey, a continuing process of development, seeded by nature and shaped by nurture, animated by love and focused by work, begun with wide-eyed curiosity and completed, for those blessed to live to a good old age, with peace and never-ending hope.

Across the life span, we grow from newborn to toddler, from toddler to teenager, and from teenager to mature adult. At each stage of life there are physical, cognitive, and social milestones. We begin with prenatal development and the newborn (Module 14). Then we'll turn our attention to infancy and childhood (Module 15), adolescence (Module 16), and adulthood (Module 17).

MODULE 14 Developmental Issues, Prenatal Development, and the Newborn

Researchers find human development interesting for the same reasons most of us do—they want to understand more about how we've become our current selves, and how we may change in the years ahead.

Developmental Psychology's Major Issues

LEARNING OBJECTIVE QUESTION LOQ 14-1 What three issues have engaged developmental psychologists?

Developmental psychologists often do **cross-sectional studies** (comparing people of different ages) and **longitudinal studies** (following people across time) to explore three major issues:

1. *Nature and nurture:* How does our genetic inheritance (our nature) interact with our experiences (our nurture) to influence our development? (This is our focus in the Nature, Nurture, and Human Diversity modules.)

developmental psychology a branch of psychology that studies physical, cognitive, and social development throughout the life span.

cross-sectional study research that compares people of different ages at the same point in time.

longitudinal study research that follows and retests the same people over time.

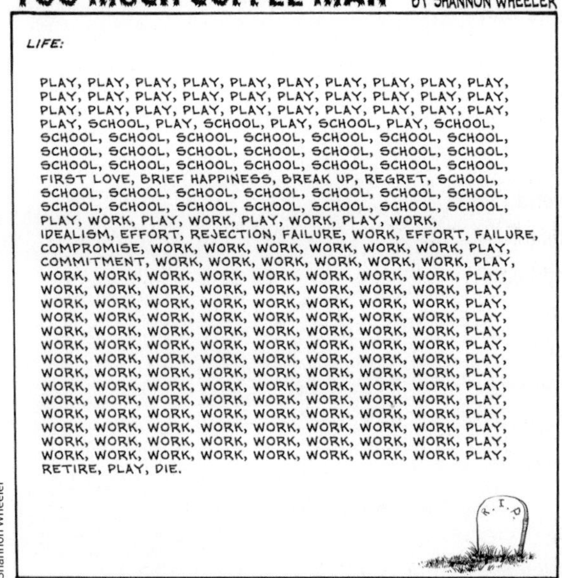
TOO MUCH COFFEE MAN BY SHANNON WHEELER
LIFE:
PLAY, PLAY, PLAY, PLAY, PLAY, PLAY, PLAY, PLAY, PLAY, PLAY,
PLAY, PLAY, PLAY, PLAY, PLAY, PLAY, PLAY, PLAY, PLAY, PLAY,
PLAY, PLAY, PLAY, PLAY, PLAY, PLAY, PLAY, PLAY, PLAY, PLAY,
PLAY, SCHOOL, PLAY, SCHOOL, PLAY, SCHOOL, PLAY, SCHOOL,
SCHOOL, SCHOOL, SCHOOL, SCHOOL, SCHOOL, SCHOOL, SCHOOL,
SCHOOL, SCHOOL, SCHOOL, SCHOOL, SCHOOL, SCHOOL, SCHOOL,
SCHOOL, SCHOOL, SCHOOL, SCHOOL, SCHOOL, SCHOOL, SCHOOL,
FIRST LOVE, BRIEF HAPPINESS, BREAK UP, REGRET, SCHOOL,
SCHOOL, SCHOOL, SCHOOL, SCHOOL, SCHOOL, SCHOOL, SCHOOL,
SCHOOL, SCHOOL, SCHOOL, SCHOOL, SCHOOL, SCHOOL, SCHOOL,
PLAY, WORK, PLAY, WORK, PLAY, WORK, PLAY, WORK,
IDEALISM, EFFORT, REJECTION, FAILURE, WORK, EFFORT, FAILURE,
COMPROMISE, WORK, WORK, WORK, WORK, WORK, WORK, PLAY,
COMMITMENT, WORK, WORK, WORK, WORK, WORK, WORK, PLAY,
WORK, WORK, WORK, WORK, WORK, WORK, WORK, WORK, PLAY,
WORK, WORK, WORK, WORK, WORK, WORK, WORK, WORK, PLAY,
WORK, WORK, WORK, WORK, WORK, WORK, WORK, WORK, PLAY,
WORK, WORK, WORK, WORK, WORK, WORK, WORK, WORK, PLAY,
WORK, WORK, WORK, WORK, WORK, WORK, WORK, WORK, PLAY,
WORK, WORK, WORK, WORK, WORK, WORK, WORK, WORK, PLAY,
WORK, WORK, WORK, WORK, WORK, WORK, WORK, WORK, PLAY,
WORK, WORK, WORK, WORK, WORK, WORK, WORK, WORK, PLAY,
WORK, WORK, WORK, WORK, WORK, WORK, WORK, WORK, PLAY,
WORK, WORK, WORK, WORK, WORK, WORK, WORK, WORK, PLAY,
WORK, WORK, WORK, WORK, WORK, WORK, WORK, WORK, PLAY,
WORK, WORK, WORK, WORK, WORK, WORK, WORK, WORK, PLAY,
WORK, WORK, WORK, WORK, WORK, WORK, WORK, WORK, PLAY,
WORK, WORK, WORK, WORK, WORK, WORK, WORK, WORK, PLAY,
RETIRE, PLAY, DIE.
R.I.P.

Shannon Wheeler

Stages of the life cycle

2. ***Continuity and stages:*** What parts of development are gradual and continuous, like riding an escalator? What parts change abruptly in separate stages, like climbing rungs on a ladder?
3. ***Stability and change:*** Which of our traits persist through life? How do we change as we age?

Continuity and Stages

Do adults differ from infants as a giant redwood differs from its seedling—a difference created mainly by gradual, cumulative growth? Or do they differ as a butterfly differs from a caterpillar—a difference of distinct stages?

Researchers who emphasize experience and learning typically see development as a slow, continuous shaping process. Those who emphasize biological maturation tend to see development as a sequence of genetically predisposed stages or steps: Although progress through the various stages may be quick or slow, everyone passes through the stages in the same order.

Are there clear-cut stages of psychological development, as there are physical stages such as walking before running? The *stage theories* we will consider—of Jean Piaget on cognitive development, Lawrence Kohlberg on moral development, and Erik Erikson on psychosocial development—propose developmental stages (summarized in **FIGURE 14.1**). But as we will also see, some research casts doubt on the idea that life proceeds through neatly defined age-linked stages.

Although many modern developmental psychologists do not identify as stage theorists, the stage concept remains useful. The human brain does experience growth spurts during childhood and puberty that correspond roughly to Piaget's stages (Thatcher et al., 1987). And stage theories contribute a developmental perspective on the whole life span, by suggesting how people of one age might come to think and act differently when they arrive at a later age.

Stability and Change

As we follow lives through time, do we find more evidence for stability or change? If reunited with a long-lost childhood friend, do we instantly realize that "it's the same old Jordan"? Or do long-ago friends now seem like strangers? (At least one acquaintance of mine [DM's] would choose the second option. At his 40-year college reunion, he failed to recognize a former classmate. The understandably appalled classmate was his first wife!)

We experience both stability and change. Some of our characteristics, such as *temperament,* are very stable. Following thousands of people in New Zealand and the United States over several decades, researchers have been struck by the consistency of temperament and emotionality across time (Kassing et al., 2019; Moffitt et al., 2013; Slutske et al., 2012). Inhibited 14-month-olds mostly grow up to be reserved, introverted

FIGURE 14.1
Comparing the stage theories (With thanks to Dr. Sandra Gibbs, Muskegon Community College, for inspiring this illustration.)

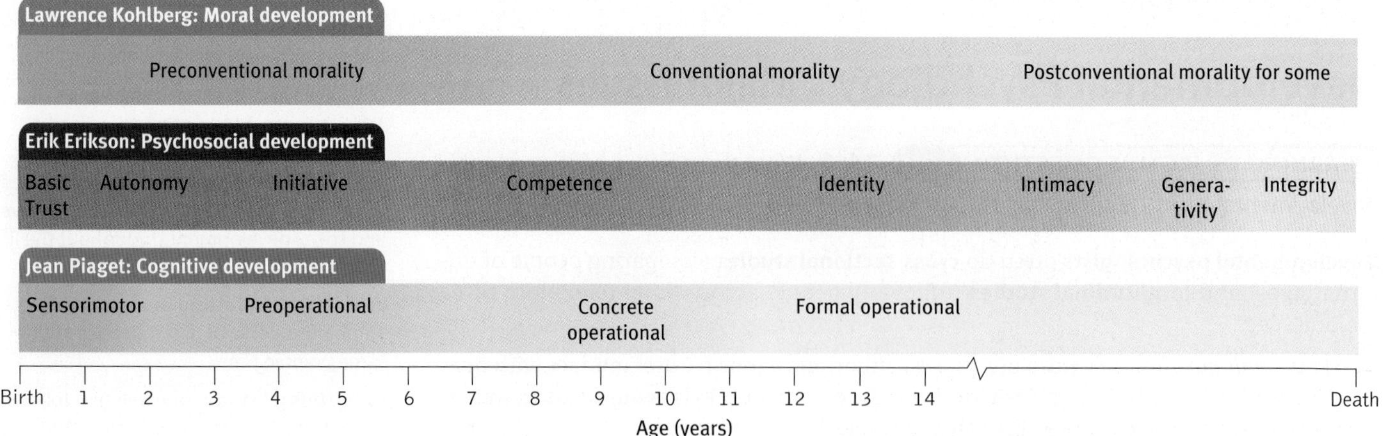
Lawrence Kohlberg: Moral development
Preconventional morality
Conventional morality
Postconventional morality for some
Erik Erikson: Psychosocial development
Basic Trust
Autonomy
Initiative
Competence
Identity
Intimacy
Genera-tivity
Integrity
Jean Piaget: Cognitive development
Sensorimotor
Preoperational
Concrete operational
Formal operational
Birth 1 2 3 4 5 6 7 8 9 10 11 12 13 14 Death
Age (years)

adults (Tang et al., 2020). Out-of-control preschoolers are later the most likely to engage in teen smoking, adult criminal behavior, or out-of-control gambling. From age 10 to 22, most people become nicer, though the meaner kids tend also to become the meaner adults (Vaillancourt & Farrell, 2021). Inattentive Canadian kindergarteners are less likely to earn high salaries in their adult careers (Vergunst et al., 2019). Moreover, children observed being repeatedly cruel to animals often became violent adults (Hensley et al., 2018). But on a happier note, the widest smilers in childhood and college photos are the ones most likely to enjoy enduring marriages (Hertenstein et al., 2009).

We cannot, however, predict all aspects of our future selves based on our early life. Our social attitudes, for example, are much less stable than our temperament, especially during the impressionable late adolescent years (Krosnick & Alwin, 1989; Rekker et al., 2015). Older children and adolescents learn new ways of coping. Although delinquent children have elevated rates of later problems, many confused and troubled children blossom into mature, successful adults (Moffitt et al., 2002; Roberts et al., 2013; Thomas & Chess, 1986). Life is a process of becoming. Our present struggles may lay the foundation for a happier tomorrow.

In some ways, we *all* change with age. Most shy, fearful toddlers begin opening up by age 4, and after adolescence people gradually become more conscientious and self-disciplined (Richmond-Rakerd et al., 2021). Risk-prone adolescents tend, as adults, to become more cautious (Mata et al., 2016). Indeed, many irresponsible 18-year-olds have matured into 40-year-old business or cultural leaders. (If you are the former, you aren't done yet.) But when asked how they have changed in the last decade and will change in the next decade, people—both young and old—exhibit an *end of history illusion*. They recognize that they have changed but expect they will change little in the future (Quoidbach et al., 2013).

Life requires *both* stability and change. Stability provides our identity. Change gives us our hope for a brighter future, allowing us to adapt and grow from experience.

Tom Prokop/Shutterstock

(a)

Photodisc/Getty Images

(b)

Perks of temperament stability In one study of 306 U.S. college graduates, 1 in 4 with yearbook expressions like the one in photo (a) later had divorced, as had only 1 in 20 with smiles like the one in photo (b) (Hertenstein et al., 2009).

"As at 7, so at 70."—Jewish proverb

BEFORE
AFTER
MUELLER
Peter Mueller/Cartoon Stock

As adults grow older, there is continuity of self.

ASK YOURSELF

Are you the same person you were as a preschooler? As an 8-year-old? As a 12-year-old? How are you different? How are you the same?

RETRIEVAL PRACTICE

RP-1 Developmental researchers who emphasize learning and experience are supporting ____________; those who emphasize biological maturation are supporting ____________.

RP-2 What findings in psychology support (1) the stage theory of development and (2) the idea of stability in personality across the life span?

ANSWERS IN APPENDIX E

Prenatal Development and the Newborn

LOQ 14-2 What is the course of prenatal development, and how do teratogens affect that development?

Conception

Nothing is more natural than a species reproducing itself. And nothing is more wondrous. For you, the process started inside your *grandmother*—as an egg formed inside a developing female fetus inside of her. (Your mother was born with all the immature eggs she would ever have.) Your father, in contrast, began producing sperm cells nonstop at puberty—in the beginning at a rate of more than 1000 sperm during the second it takes to read this phrase.

Some time after puberty, your mother's ovary released a mature egg—a cell roughly the size of the period that ends this sentence. Like space voyagers approaching a huge

FIGURE 14.2
Life is sexually transmitted (a) Sperm cells surround an egg. (b) One sperm penetrates the egg's jellylike outer coating, triggering a series of chemical events that will cause sperm and egg to fuse into a single cell. If all goes well, that cell will subdivide again and again to emerge 9 months later as a 37-trillion-cell human being (Bianconi et al., 2013).

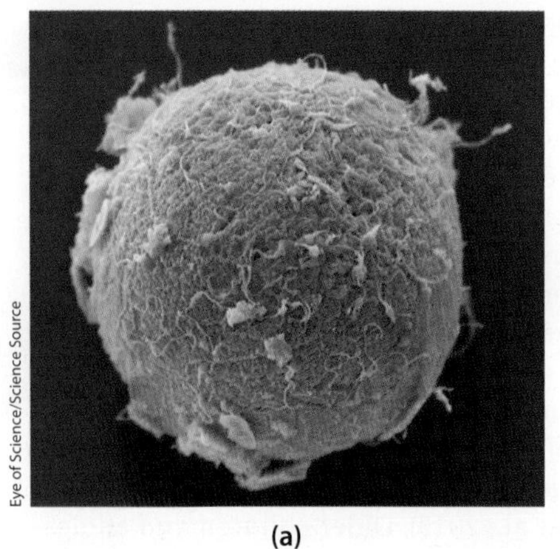

Eye of Science/Science Source

(a)

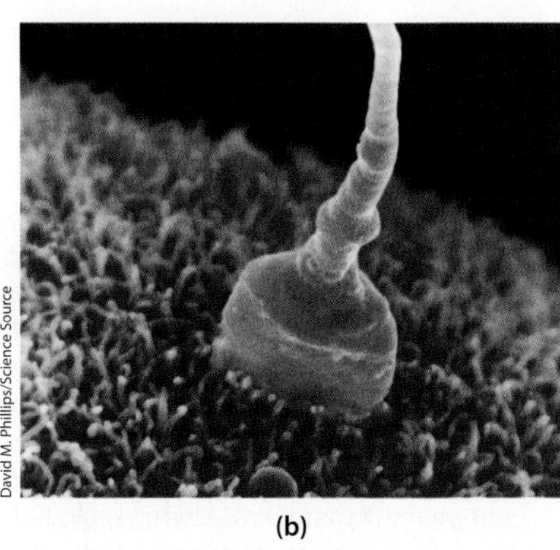

David M. Phillips/Science Source

(b)

zygote the fertilized egg; it enters a 2-week period of rapid cell division and develops into an embryo.

embryo the developing human organism from about 2 weeks after fertilization through the second month.

planet, some 250 million deposited sperm began their frantic race upstream, approaching a cell 85,000 times their own size. The small number reaching the egg released digestive enzymes that ate away the egg's protective coating (**FIGURE 14.2a**). As soon as the one winning sperm penetrated that coating and was welcomed in (Figure 14.2b), the egg's surface blocked out the others. Before half a day elapsed, the egg nucleus and the sperm nucleus fused: The two became one.

Consider it your most fortunate of moments. Among some 250 million sperm, the one needed to make you, in combination with that one particular egg, won the race. (As individual humans, we do not reproduce, we recombine.) And so it was for innumerable generations before us. If any one of our ancestors had been conceived with a different sperm or egg, or died before conceiving, or not chanced to meet their partner, or . . . . The mind boggles at the improbable, unbroken chain of events that produced us.

Prenatal Development

How many fertilized eggs, called **zygotes**, survive beyond the first 2 weeks? Fewer than half (Grobstein, 1979; Hall, 2004). But for us, good fortune prevailed. One cell became 2, then 4—each just like the first—until this cell division had produced some 100 identical cells within the first week. Then the cells began to differentiate—to specialize in structure and function ("I'll become a brain, you become intestines!").

About 10 days after conception, the zygote attaches to the mother's uterine wall, beginning approximately 37 weeks of the closest human relationship. Near the beginning of this maternal bodybuilding feat, the tiny clump of cells forms two parts. The inner cells become the **embryo** (**FIGURE 14.3a**). Many outer cells become the *placenta*, the life-link that transfers nutrients and oxygen from mother to embryo. Over the next 6 weeks, the embryo's organs begin to form and function. The heart begins to beat.

FIGURE 14.3
Prenatal development (a) The embryo grows and develops rapidly. At 40 days, the spine is visible and the arms and legs are beginning to grow. (b) By the start of the ninth week, when the fetal period begins, facial features, hands, and feet have formed. (c) As the fetus enters the sixteenth week, its 3 ounces could fit in the palm of your hand.

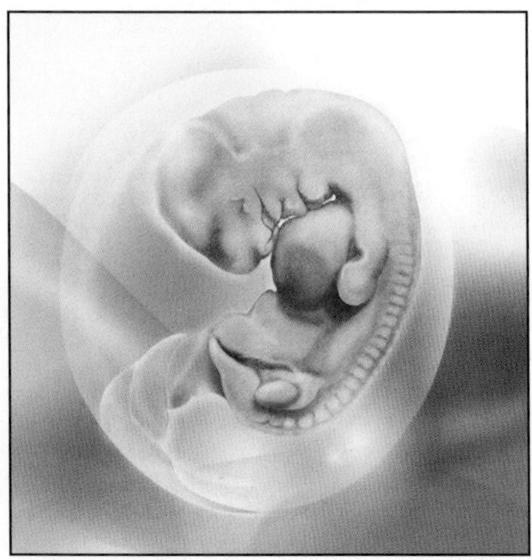

(a)

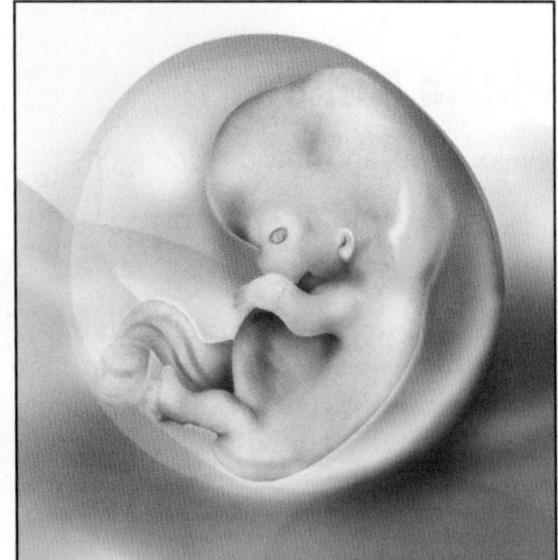

(b)

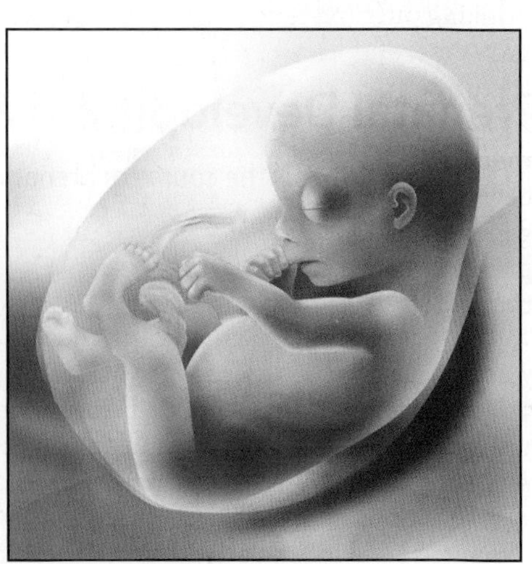

(c)

By 9 weeks after conception, an embryo looks unmistakably human (Figure 14.3b). It is now a **fetus** (Latin for "offspring" or "young one"). During the sixth month, organs such as the stomach develop enough to give the fetus a good chance of surviving and thriving if born prematurely.

At each prenatal stage, genetic and environmental factors affect our development. By the sixth month, the fetus is responsive to sound. Microphone readings taken inside the uterus reveal that the fetus is exposed to the sound of its mother's muffled voice (Ecklund-Flores, 1992; Hepper, 2005). Immediately after emerging from their underwater world, newborns prefer their mother's voice to another woman's, or to their father's (DeCasper et al., 1986, 1994; Lee & Kisilevsky, 2014).

Review prenatal development:

Zygote:	Conception to 2 weeks
Embryo:	2 weeks through 8 weeks
Fetus:	9 weeks to birth

They also prefer hearing their mother's language. In one study, day-old American and Swedish newborns paused more in their pacifier sucking when listening to familiar vowels from their mother's language (Moon et al., 2013). After repeatedly hearing a fake word *(tatata)* in the womb, Finnish newborns' brain waves displayed recognition when hearing the word after birth (Partanen et al., 2013). If their mother spoke two languages during pregnancy, newborns displayed interest in both (Byers-Heinlein et al., 2010). And just after birth, the melodic ups and downs of newborns' cries bear the tuneful signature of their mother's native tongue (Mampe et al., 2009). Babies born to French-speaking mothers tended to produce cries with the rising intonation of French; babies born to German-speaking mothers produced cries with the falling tones of German (Mampe et al., 2009). Would you have guessed? The learning of language begins in the womb.

In the 2 months before birth, fetuses demonstrate learning in other ways, as when they adapt to a vibrating, honking device placed on their mother's abdomen (Dirix et al., 2009). Like people who adapt to the sound of trains in their neighborhood, fetuses get used to the honking. Moreover, 4 weeks later, they recall the sound (as evidenced by their blasé response, compared with the reactions of those fetuses not previously exposed).

Sounds are not the only environmental factors that impact fetal development. In addition to transferring nutrients and oxygen from mother to fetus, the placenta screens out many harmful substances. But some slip by. **Teratogens**, agents such as viruses and drugs, can damage an embryo or fetus. This is one reason pregnant people are advised not to drink alcoholic beverages or use nicotine or marijuana (Kuehn, 2019; Saint Louis, 2017). A pregnant person never smokes, vapes, or drinks alone: When alcohol, nicotine, or other drugs enter their bloodstream, and that of the fetus, activity is affected in the parent *and* the baby's central nervous systems. Those exposed to alcohol in the womb may be primed to like alcohol, which may put them at risk for heavy drinking and alcohol use disorder during their teen years. In experiments, when pregnant rats drank alcohol, their young offspring later displayed a liking for alcohol's taste and odor (Youngentob & Glendinning, 2009; Youngentob et al., 2007).

Worldwide, 1 in 10 women report consuming alcohol while pregnant (S. Popova et al., 2019). Even light drinking, occasional binge drinking, or marijuana smoking can affect the fetal brain (CDC, 2018; Ghazi Sherbaf et al., 2019; Lees et al., 2020). Persistent heavy drinking puts the fetus at risk for *congenital* (present at birth) disorders, future behavior problems, and lower intelligence. For 1 in about 130 children worldwide and 1 in 30 in the United States, the effects are visible as *fetal alcohol spectrum disorder* (Lange et al., 2017; May et al., 2018). Its most serious form is **fetal alcohol syndrome (FAS)**, which is marked by lifelong physical and mental function deficits. The fetal damage may occur because alcohol has an *epigenetic effect:* It leaves chemical marks on DNA that switch genes abnormally on or off (Liu et al., 2009). Smoking cigarettes or marijuana during pregnancy also leaves epigenetic scars that may increase vulnerability to stress or addiction (Stroud et al., 2014; Szutorisz & Hurd, 2016).

fetus the developing human organism from 9 weeks after conception to birth.

teratogens agents, such as chemicals and viruses, that can reach the embryo or fetus during prenatal development and cause harm.

fetal alcohol syndrome (FAS) physical and cognitive function deficits in children caused by their mother's heavy drinking during pregnancy. In severe cases, symptoms include a small, out-of-proportion head and distinct facial features.

RETRIEVAL PRACTICE

RP-3 The first 2 weeks of prenatal development is the period of the ________. The period of the ________ lasts from 9 weeks after conception until birth. The time between those two prenatal periods is considered the period of the ________.

ANSWERS IN APPENDIX E

habituation decreasing responsiveness with repeated stimulation. As infants gain familiarity with repeated exposure to a stimulus, their interest wanes and they look away sooner.

The Competent Newborn

LOQ 14-3 What are some newborn abilities, and how do researchers explore infants' mental abilities?

Babies come with apps preloaded. Having survived prenatal hazards, we as newborns came equipped with automatic reflex responses ideally suited for our survival. We withdrew our limbs to escape pain. If a cloth over our face interfered with our breathing, we turned our head from side to side and swiped at it.

New parents are often in awe of the coordinated sequence of reflexes by which their baby gets food. When something touches their cheek, babies turn toward that touch, open their mouth, and vigorously *root* for a nipple. Finding one, they automatically close on it and begin *sucking*. (Failing to find satisfaction, the hungry baby may cry—a behavior parents find highly unpleasant, and very rewarding to relieve.) Other adaptive reflexes include the *startle* reflex (when arms and legs spring out, quickly followed by fist clenching and loud crying) and the surprisingly strong *grasping* reflex, both of which may have helped infants stay close to their caregivers.

The pioneering American psychologist William James presumed that the newborn experiences a "blooming, buzzing confusion," an assumption few people challenged until the 1960s. But then scientists discovered that babies can tell you a lot—if you know how to ask. To ask, you must capitalize on what babies can do—gaze, suck, and turn their heads. So, equipped with eye-tracking machines and pacifiers wired to electronic gear, researchers set out to answer parents' age-old questions: What can my baby see, hear, smell, and think?

FIGURE 14.4
Newborns' preference for faces When shown these two images with the same three elements, Italian newborns spent nearly twice as many seconds looking at the face-like image (Valenza et al., 1996). Newborns—average age 53 minutes in one Canadian study—have an apparently inborn preference for looking toward faces (Mondloch et al., 1999).

Consider how researchers exploit **habituation**—a decrease in responding with repeated stimulation. We saw this earlier when fetuses adapted to a vibrating, honking device placed on their mother's abdomen. The novel stimulus gets attention when first presented. With repetition, the response weakens. This seeming boredom with familiar stimuli gives us a way to ask infants what they see and remember.

As newborns, we prefer sights and sounds that facilitate social responsiveness. We turn our head in the direction of human voices. And we prefer face-like images over abstract images (**FIGURE 14.4**). Even late-stage fetuses look more at face-like patterns in red lights shined into the womb (Reid et al., 2017). As young infants, we also prefer to look at objects 8 to 12 inches away, which—wonder of wonders—just happens to be about the distance between a nursing infant's eyes and its mother's (Maurer & Maurer, 1988). Our brain's default settings help us connect socially.

Within days after birth, our brain's neural networks were stamped with the smell of our mother's body. Week-old nursing babies, placed between a gauze pad from their mother's bra and one from another nursing mother, have usually turned toward the smell of their own mother's pad (MacFarlane, 1978). What's more, that smell preference lasts. One experiment capitalized on the fact that some nursing mothers in a French maternity ward used a chamomile-scented balm to prevent nipple soreness (Delaunay-El Allam et al., 2010). Twenty-one months later, their toddlers preferred playing with chamomile-scented toys! Their peers who had not sniffed the scent while breast-feeding showed no such preference. (This makes us wonder: Will these children grow up to become devoted chamomile tea drinkers?) Such studies reveal the remarkable abilities with which we enter our world.

JamesBrey/E+/Getty Images

Alice DeWall

Prepared to feed and eat Like birds and other animals, we are predisposed to respond to our offspring's cries for food—even if we are in the middle of a 314-mile ultramarathon, as I [ND] was when my 18-month-old, Bevy, decided that only Daddy could feed her.

RETRIEVAL PRACTICE

RP-4 Infants' ____________________ to repeated stimulation helps developmental psychologists study what infants can learn and remember.

ANSWERS IN APPENDIX E

MODULE 14 REVIEW Developmental Issues, Prenatal Development, and the Newborn

LEARNING OBJECTIVES

Test Yourself Answer these repeated Learning Objective Questions on your own (before "showing" the answers here, or checking the answers in Appendix D) to improve your retention of the concepts (McDaniel et al., 2009, 2015).

LOQ 14-1 What three issues have engaged developmental psychologists?

LOQ 14-2 What is the course of prenatal development, and how do teratogens affect that development?

LOQ 14-3 What are some newborn abilities, and how do researchers explore infants' mental abilities?

TERMS AND CONCEPTS TO REMEMBER

Test Yourself Write down the definition in your own words, then check your answer.

developmental psychology, p. 167
cross-sectional study, p. 167
longitudinal study, p. 167
zygote, p. 170
embryo, p. 170
fetus, p. 171
teratogens, p. 171
fetal alcohol syndrome (FAS), p. 171
habituation, p. 172

MODULE TEST

Test Yourself Answer the following questions on your own first, then "show" the answers here, or check your answers in Appendix E.

1. How do cross-sectional and longitudinal studies differ?

2. The three major issues that interest developmental psychologists are nature/nurture, stability/change, and ________________/________________.

3. Although development is lifelong, there is stability of personality over time. For example,
   a. most personality traits emerge in infancy and persist throughout life.
   b. temperament tends to remain stable throughout life.
   c. few people change significantly after adolescence.
   d. people tend to undergo greater personality changes as they age.

4. Body organs first begin to form and function during the period of the ________________; within 6 months, during the period of the ________________, the organs are sufficiently functional to provide a good chance of surviving and thriving.
   a. zygote; embryo
   b. zygote; fetus
   c. embryo; fetus
   d. placenta; fetus

5. Chemicals that the placenta isn't able to screen out that can harm an embryo or fetus are called ________________.

6. Stroke a newborn's cheek and the infant will root for a nipple. This illustrates
   a. a reflex.
   b. nurture.
   c. a preference.
   d. continuity.

MODULE 15 Infancy and Childhood

As a flower unfolds in accord with its genetic instructions, so do we. **Maturation**—the orderly sequence of biological growth—decrees many of our commonalities. Babies stand, then walk. Toddlers use nouns, then verbs. Severe deprivation or abuse can slow development, but genetic growth patterns come "factory-installed"—they are inborn. Maturation (nature) sets the basic course of development; experience (nurture) adjusts it. Genes and scenes interact.

maturation biological growth processes that enable orderly changes in behavior, relatively uninfluenced by experience.

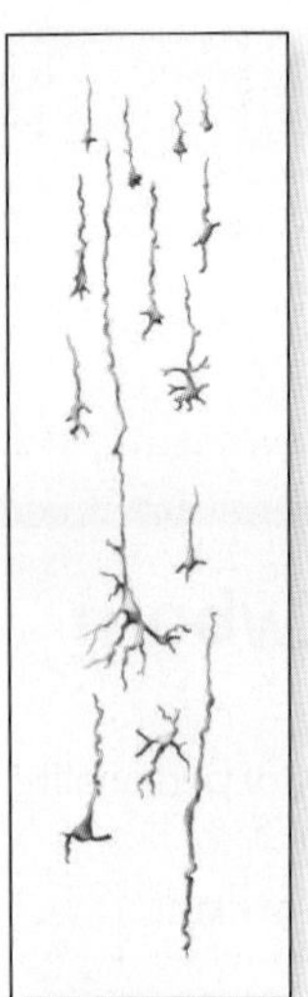
Newborn

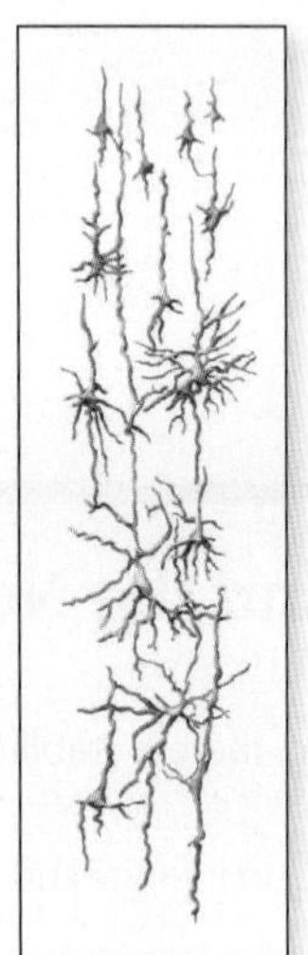
3 months

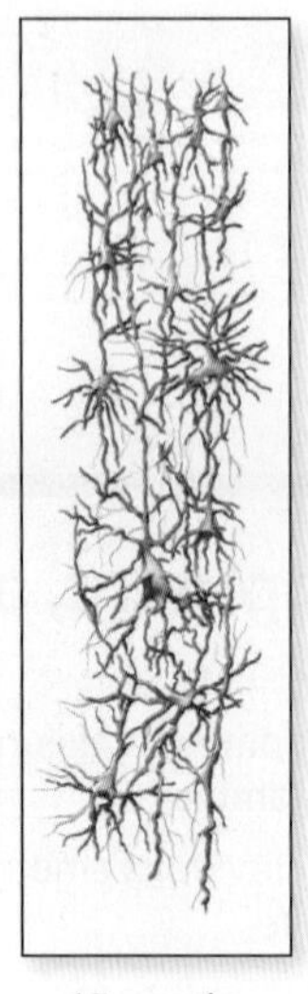
15 months

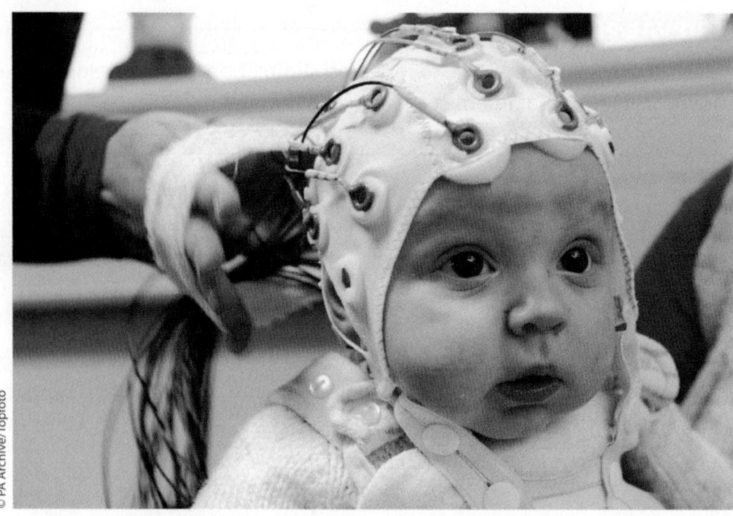
© PA Archive/Topfoto

FIGURE 15.1
Mapping infant brain development By fitting infants with an electrode cap, researchers are able to detect changes in their brain activity triggered by different stimuli. The brain is immature at birth, but as the child matures, the neural networks grow increasingly complex.

Physical Development

LOQ 15-1 During infancy and childhood, how do the brain and motor skills develop?

Brain Development

In your mother's womb, your developing brain formed nerve cells at the explosive rate of nearly one-quarter million per minute. On the day you were born, you had most of the brain cells you would ever have. However, your nervous system was immature: After birth, the branching neural networks that eventually enabled all your abilities had a wild growth spurt (**FIGURE 15.1**). This rapid development helps explain why infant brain size increases rapidly in the early days after birth (Holland et al., 2014). From ages 3 to 6, the most rapid growth was in your frontal lobes, which enable rational planning. During those years, your brain required vast amounts of energy (Kuzawa et al., 2014). This energy-intensive process caused rapid progress in your ability to control your attention and behavior (Garon et al., 2008; Thompson-Schill et al., 2009).

The brain's association areas—those linked with thinking, memory, and language—were the last cortical areas to develop. As they did, your mental abilities surged (Chugani & Phelps, 1986; Thatcher et al., 1987). Fiber pathways supporting agility, language, and self-control proliferated into puberty. Under the influence of adrenal hormones, tens of billions of synapses formed and organized, while a use-it-or-lose-it *synaptic pruning* process shut down unused links (Paus et al., 1999; Thompson et al., 2000).

Motor Development

The developing brain enables physical coordination. Skills emerge as infants exercise their maturing muscles and nervous system. With occasional exceptions, the motor development sequence is universal. Babies roll over before they sit unsupported, and they usually crawl before they walk. These behaviors reflect not imitation but a maturing nervous system; blind children, too, crawl before they walk.

Genes guide motor development. In the United States, 25 percent of all babies walk by age 11 months, 50 percent within a week after their first birthday, and 90 percent by age 15 months (Frankenburg et al., 1992). Identical twins typically begin walking on nearly the same day (Wilson, 1979). Maturation—including the rapid development of the cerebellum at the back of the brain—creates our readiness to learn walking at about age 1. The same is true for other physical skills, including bowel and bladder control. Before necessary muscular and neural maturation, neither pleading nor punishment will produce successful toilet training. You can't rush a child's first flush.

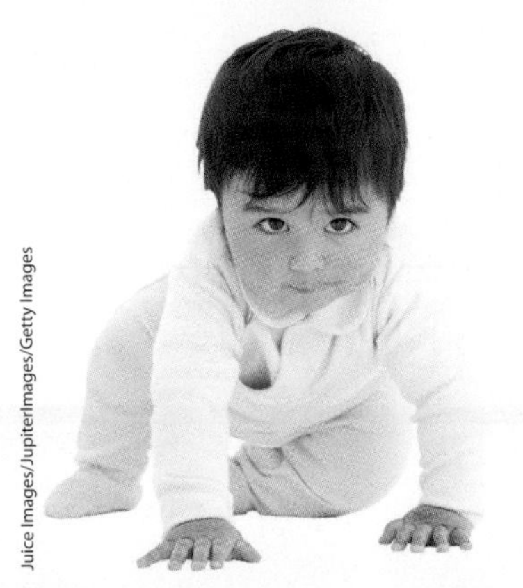
Juice Images/JupiterImages/Getty Images

Physical development Sit, crawl, walk, run—the sequence of these motor development milestones is the same around the world, though babies reach them at varying ages.

Still, nurture may amend what nature intends. In some regions of Africa, the Caribbean, and India, caregivers often massage and exercise babies, which can accelerate the process of learning to walk (Karasik et al., 2010). The recommended infant *back to sleep position* (putting babies to sleep on their backs to reduce crib-death risk) has been associated with somewhat later crawling but not with later walking (Davis et al., 1998; Lipsitt, 2003).

DON'T LISTEN TO THEM - YOU'RE ALREADY WALKING JUST FINE.

Dave Coverly/Speed Bump

In the 8 years following the 1994 launch of a U.S. Back to Sleep educational campaign, the number of infants sleeping on their stomach dropped from 70 to 11 percent—and sudden infant deaths fell significantly (Braiker, 2005).

RETRIEVAL PRACTICE

RP-1 The biological growth process called ______________ explains why most children begin walking by about 12 to 15 months.

ANSWERS IN APPENDIX E

Brain Maturation and Infant Memory

Can you recall your third birthday? Most of us *consciously* remember little from before age 4. Mice and monkeys also forget their early life, as rapid neuron growth disrupts the circuits that stored old memories (Akers et al., 2014). But as children mature, this *infantile amnesia* wanes, and they become increasingly capable of remembering experiences, even for a year or more (Bauer & Larkina, 2014; Morris et al., 2010). The brain areas underlying memory, such as the hippocampus and frontal lobes, continue to mature during and after adolescence (Luby et al., 2016; Murty et al., 2016).

Despite consciously recalling little from our early years, our brain was processing and storing information. While finishing her doctoral work in psychology, Carolyn Rovee-Collier observed nonverbal infant memory in action. Her 2-month-old, Benjamin, could be calmed by a moving crib mobile. Hoping to keep the baby entertained while she worked, she strung a cloth ribbon connecting the mobile to Benjamin's foot. Soon, he was kicking his foot to move the mobile. Thinking about her unintended home experiment, Rovee-Collier realized that, contrary to popular opinion in the 1960s, babies can learn and remember. To know for sure that her son wasn't just a whiz kid, she repeated the experiment with other infants (Rovee-Collier, 1989, 1999). Sure enough, they, too, soon kicked more when hitched to a mobile, both on the day of the experiment and the day after. If, however, she hitched them to a different mobile the next day, the infants showed no learning, indicating that they remembered the original mobile and recognized the difference. Moreover, when tethered to the familiar mobile a month later, they remembered the association and again began kicking.

Traces of forgotten childhood languages may also persist. One study tested English-speaking British adults who had no conscious memory of the Hindi or Zulu they had spoken as children. Yet up to age 40, they could relearn subtle sound contrasts in these languages that other English speakers could *not* learn (Bowers et al., 2009). Chinese adoptees living in Canada since age 1 process Chinese sounds as do fluent Chinese speakers, even if they have no conscious recollection of Chinese words (Pierce et al., 2014). We see our two-track mind at work here: What the conscious mind does not know and cannot express in words, the nervous system and unconscious mind somehow remember.

ASK YOURSELF

What do you regard as your earliest memory? Now that you know about infantile amnesia, has your opinion changed about the accuracy of that memory?

Cognitive Development

LOQ 15-2 How did Piaget broaden our understanding of the way a child's mind develops, and how have today's researchers built on his work?

Somewhere on your precarious journey "from egghood to personhood" (Broks, 2007), you became conscious. When was that? And once conscious, how did your mind grow? Developmental psychologist Jean Piaget [pee-ah-ZHAY] spent his life searching for the answers. He studied children's developing **cognition**—all the mental activities associated with thinking, knowing, remembering, and communicating. His interest in

cognition all the mental activities associated with thinking, knowing, remembering, and communicating.

FIGURE 15.2
A changing marriage schema Most people once had a *marriage* schema as a union between a man and a woman. By 2021, 29 countries had legalized same-sex marriage. Marriage equality laws are both informed by and inform a culture's changing marriage schema.

Image Ideas/Getty Images

Christian L Birmele

children's cognitive development began in 1920, when he was in Paris developing questions for children's intelligence tests. While administering the tests, Piaget became intrigued by children's wrong answers, which were often strikingly similar among same-age children. Where others saw childish mistakes, Piaget saw developing intelligence at work. Such accidental discoveries are among the fruits of psychological science.

A half-century spent with children convinced Piaget that a child's mind is not a miniature model of an adult's. Thanks partly to his careful observations, we now understand that children reason differently than adults, in "wildly illogical ways" (Brainerd, 1996).

Bill Anderson/Science Source

Jean Piaget (1896–1980) "If we examine the intellectual development of the individual or of the whole of humanity, we shall find that the human spirit goes through a certain number of stages, each different from the other" (1930).

Piaget's studies led him to believe that a child's mind develops through a series of stages, in an upward march from the newborn's simple reflexes to the adult's abstract reasoning power. Thus, an 8-year-old can comprehend things a toddler cannot, such as the analogy that "getting an idea is like having a light turn on in your head."

Piaget's core idea was that our intellectual progression reflects an unceasing struggle to make sense of our experiences. To this end, the maturing brain builds **schemas**—concepts or mental molds into which we pour our experiences (**FIGURE 15.2**).

To explain how we use and adjust our schemas, Piaget proposed two more concepts. First, we **assimilate** new experiences—we interpret them according to our current schemas (understandings). Having a simple schema for *dog*, for example, a toddler may call all four-legged animals *dogs*. But as we interact with the world, we also adjust, or **accommodate**, our schemas to incorporate information provided by new experiences. Thus, the child soon learns that the original *dog* schema is too broad and accommodates by refining the category.

ASK YOURSELF

Can you recall a time when you misheard some song lyrics because you assimilated them into your own schema? (For hundreds of examples of this, visit KissThisGuy.com.)

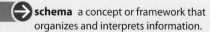

schema a concept or framework that organizes and interprets information.

assimilation interpreting our new experiences in terms of our existing schemas.

accommodation adapting our current schemas (understandings) to incorporate new information.

sensorimotor stage in Piaget's theory, the stage (from birth to nearly 2 years of age) at which infants know the world mostly in terms of their sensory impressions and motor activities.

object permanence the awareness that things continue to exist even when not perceived.

Piaget's Theory and Current Thinking

Piaget believed that children construct their understanding of the world while interacting with it. Their mind experiences spurts of change, followed by greater stability as they move from one cognitive plateau to the next, each with distinctive characteristics that permit specific kinds of thinking. In Piaget's view, cognitive development consisted of four major stages—*sensorimotor, preoperational, concrete operational,* and *formal operational.*

SENSORIMOTOR STAGE In the **sensorimotor stage**, from birth to nearly age 2, babies take in the world through their senses and actions—through looking, hearing, touching, mouthing, and grasping. As their hands and limbs begin to move, they learn to make things happen.

Very young babies seem to live in the present: Out of sight is out of mind. In one test, Piaget showed an infant an appealing toy and then flopped his beret over it. Before the age of 6 months, the infant acted as if the toy ceased to exist. Young infants

© Doug Goodman/Science Source

FIGURE 15.3
Object permanence Infants younger than 6 months seldom understand that things continue to exist when they are out of sight. But for this older infant, out of sight is definitely not out of mind.

lack **object permanence**—the awareness that objects continue to exist even when not perceived. By 8 months, infants begin exhibiting memory for things no longer seen. If you hide a toy, the infant will momentarily look for it (**FIGURE 15.3**). Within another month or two, the infant will look for it even after being restrained for several seconds.

So, does object permanence in fact blossom suddenly at 8 months, much as tulips blossom in spring? Today's researchers believe object permanence unfolds gradually, and they see development as more continuous than Piaget did. Even young infants will momentarily look for a toy where they saw it hidden a second before (Wang et al., 2004). And infants with impaired vision rely on their hearing and touch to understand object permanence, resulting in a slight developmental delay (Bruce & Vargas, 2012; Ihsen et al., 2010).

Today's researchers also believe Piaget and his followers underestimated young children's competence. Young children think like little scientists. They test ideas, make causal inferences, and learn from statistical patterns (Gopnik et al., 2015). Consider these simple experiments:

- ***Baby physics:*** Like adults staring in disbelief at a magic trick (the "*Whoa!*" look), infants look longer at and explore impossible scenes—a car seeming to pass through a solid object, a ball stopping in midair, or an object violating object permanence by magically disappearing (Shuwairi & Johnson, 2013; Stahl & Feigenson, 2015). Why do infants show this visual bias? Because impossible events violate infants' expectations (Baillargeon et al., 2016).
- ***Baby math:*** Karen Wynn (1992, 2000, 2008) showed 5-month-olds one or two objects (**FIGURE 15.4a**). Then she hid the objects behind a screen, and visibly removed or added one (Figure 15.4d). When she lifted the screen, the infants sometimes did a double take, staring longer when shown a wrong number of objects (Figure 15.4f). But were they just responding to a greater or smaller *mass* of objects, rather than a change in *number* (Feigenson et al., 2002)? Later experiments showed that babies' number sense extends to larger numbers, to ratios, and to such things as drumbeats

FIGURE 15.4
Baby math Shown a numerically impossible outcome, 5-month-old infants stare longer (Wynn, 1992). Clearly, infants are smarter than Piaget appreciated. Even as babies, we had a lot on our minds.

(a) Objects placed in case

(b) Screen comes up

(c) Empty hand enters

(d) One object removed

Then either: possible outcome

(e) Screen drops revealing 1 object

or: impossible outcome

(f) Screen drops revealing 2 objects

"It is a rare privilege to watch the birth, growth, and first feeble struggles of a living human mind." —Annie Sullivan, in Helen Keller's *The Story of My Life*, 1903

and motions (Libertus & Brannon, 2009; McCrink & Wynn, 2004; Spelke et al., 2013). If accustomed to a Daffy Duck puppet jumping three times on stage, they showed surprise if it jumped only twice.

PREOPERATIONAL STAGE Piaget believed that until about age 6 or 7, children are in a **preoperational stage**—able to represent things with words and images but too young to perform *mental operations* (such as imagining an action and mentally reversing it).

Pretend Play Symbolic thinking and *pretend play* occur at this stage, at an earlier age than Piaget supposed. Judy DeLoache (1987) discovered this when she showed children a model of a room and hid a miniature stuffed dog behind its miniature couch. The 2½-year-olds easily remembered where to find the miniature toy, but they could not use the model to locate an actual stuffed dog behind a couch in a real room. Three-year-olds—only 6 months older—usually went right to the actual stuffed animal in the real room, showing they *could* think of the model as a symbol for the room. Another study with 3-year-olds involved pretending to play firefighter (Kalkusch et al., 2020). The researchers found that the kids were actively making up stories—they knew they weren't actually firefighters, but that didn't stop them from pretending to fight fires and rescue princes and princesses from burning towers. Although Piaget did not view the stage transitions as abrupt, he probably would have been surprised to see symbolic thinking at such an early age.

Dave Myers

Egocentrism in action "Look, Granddaddy, a match!" So said my [DM's] granddaughter, Allie, at age 4, when showing me two memory game cards with matching pictures—that faced her.

Egocentrism Piaget taught us that preschool children are **egocentric**: They have difficulty perceiving things from another's perspective. They are like the person who, when asked by someone across a river, "How do I get to the other side?" answered, "You're *on* the other side." Asked to "show Mommy your picture," 2-year-old Gabriella holds the picture up facing her own eyes. Asked what he would do if he saw a bear, 3-year-old Grant replies, "We cover our eyes so the bear can't see us."

Children's conversations also reveal their egocentrism, as one young boy demonstrated (Phillips, 1969, p. 61):

"Do you have a brother?"

"Yes."

"What's his name?"

"Jim."

"Does Jim have a brother?"

"No."

Like Gabriella, TV-watching preschoolers who block your view of the TV assume that you see what they see. They simply have not yet developed the ability to take another's viewpoint. Even adolescents egocentrically overestimate how much others are noticing them (Lin, 2016). And adults may overestimate the extent to which others share their opinions, knowledge, and perspectives. We assume that something will be clear to others if it is clear to us, or that email recipients will "hear" our "just kidding" intent (Epley et al., 2004; Kruger et al., 2005). Perhaps you can recall asking someone to guess a simple tune such as "Happy Birthday" as you clapped or tapped it out. With the tune in your head, it seemed so obvious! But you suffered from the egocentric *curse of knowledge*, assuming that what was in your head was also in someone else's.

CONCRETE OPERATIONAL STAGE By about age 7, said Piaget, children enter the **concrete operational stage**. Given concrete (physical) materials, they begin to grasp complex operations, such as spatial and mathematical relationships.

Consider a 5-year-old, who tells you there is too much milk in a tall, narrow glass. "Too much" may become just right if you pour that milk into a short, wide glass. Focusing only on the height dimension, the child cannot perform the operation of mentally pouring the milk back into the tall glass. Before about age 6, said Piaget, young children lack the concept of **conservation**—the idea that the amount remains the same even if it changes shape (**FIGURE 15.5**).

preoperational stage in Piaget's theory, the stage (from about 2 to 6 or 7 years of age) at which a child learns to use language but does not yet comprehend the mental operations of concrete logic.

egocentrism in Piaget's theory, the preoperational child's difficulty taking another's point of view.

concrete operational stage in Piaget's theory, the stage of cognitive development (from about 7 to 11 years of age) at which children gain the mental operations that enable them to think logically about concrete events.

conservation the principle (which Piaget believed to be a part of concrete operational reasoning) that properties such as mass, volume, and number remain the same despite changes in the forms of objects.

Bianca Moscatelli/Macmillan Learning

FIGURE 15.5

Piaget's test of conservation This visually focused preoperational child does not yet understand the principle of conservation. When the milk is poured into a tall, narrow glass, it suddenly seems like "more" than when it was in the shorter, wider glass. In another year or so, she will understand that the amount stays the same.

Understanding that change in form does not mean change in quantity, they can mentally pour milk back and forth between glasses of different shapes. They also enjoy jokes that use this new understanding:

> Mr. Jones went into a restaurant and ordered a whole pizza for his dinner. When the waiter asked if he wanted it cut into 6 or 8 pieces, Mr. Jones said, "Oh, you'd better make it 6, I could never eat 8 pieces!" (McGhee, 1976)

Piaget believed that during the concrete operational stage, children become able to comprehend mathematical transformations and conservation. When my [DM's] daughter, Laura, was 6, I was surprised at her inability to reverse simple arithmetic. Asked, "What is 8 plus 4?" she required 5 seconds to compute "12," and another 5 seconds to then compute 12 minus 4. By age 8, she could answer a reversed question instantly.

FORMAL OPERATIONAL STAGE By age 12, our reasoning expands from the purely concrete (involving actual experience) to encompass abstract thinking (involving imagined realities and symbols). As children approach adolescence, said Piaget, they can ponder hypothetical propositions and deduce consequences: *If* this, *then* that. Systematic reasoning, what Piaget called **formal operational** thinking, is now within their grasp.

Although full-blown logic and reasoning await adolescence, the rudiments of formal operational thinking begin earlier than Piaget realized. Consider this simple problem:

> If John is in school, then Mary is in school. John is in school. What can you say about Mary?

Formal operational thinkers have no trouble answering correctly. But neither do most 7-year-olds (Suppes, 1982). **TABLE 15.1** summarizes the four stages in Piaget's theory.

formal operational stage in Piaget's theory, the stage of cognitive development (usually beginning about age 12) at which people begin to think logically about abstract concepts.

TABLE 15.1 Piaget's Stages of Cognitive Development

Typical Age Range	Stage and Description	Key Milestones
Birth to nearly 2 years	*Sensorimotor* Experiencing the world through senses and actions (looking, hearing, touching, mouthing, and grasping)	• Object permanence • Stranger anxiety
About 2 to 6 or 7 years	*Preoperational* Representing things with words and images; using intuitive rather than logical reasoning	• Pretend play • Egocentrism
About 7 to 11 years	*Concrete operational* Thinking logically about concrete events; grasping concrete analogies and performing arithmetical operations	• Conservation • Mathematical transformations
About 12 through adulthood	*Formal operational* Reasoning abstractly	• Abstract logic • Potential for mature moral reasoning

Liz Banfield/Getty Images

Pretend play

RETRIEVAL PRACTICE

RP-2 Object permanence, pretend play, conservation, and abstract logic are developmental milestones for which of Piaget's stages, respectively?

RP-3 Label each of the following developmental phenomena (i–vi) with the correct cognitive developmental stage: (a) sensorimotor, (b) preoperational, (c) concrete operational, or (d) formal operational.

i. Thinking about abstract concepts, such as "freedom."
ii. Enjoying imaginary play (such as dress-up).
iii. Understanding that physical properties stay the same even when objects change form.
iv. Having the ability to reverse math operations.
v. Understanding that something is not gone for good when it disappears from sight.
vi. Having difficulty taking another's point of view (as when blocking someone's view of the TV).

ANSWERS IN APPENDIX E

Reflecting on Piaget's Theory

What remains of Piaget's ideas about the child's mind? Plenty—enough to merit his being singled out by *Time* magazine as one of the twentieth century's 20 most influential scientists and thinkers, and his being rated in a survey of British psychologists as the last century's greatest psychologist (*Psychologist*, 2003). Piaget identified significant cognitive milestones and stimulated worldwide interest in how the mind develops. His emphasis was less on the ages at which children typically reach specific milestones than on their sequence. Worldwide studies, from Australia to Algeria to North America, have confirmed that human cognition unfolds basically in the sequence Piaget described (Lourenco & Machado, 1996; Segall et al., 1990).

"Assessing the impact of Piaget on developmental psychology is like assessing the impact of Shakespeare on English literature." —Developmental psychologist Harry Beilin (1992)

However, today's researchers see development as more continuous than did Piaget. By detecting the beginnings of each type of thinking at earlier ages, they have revealed conceptual abilities Piaget missed. Moreover, they see formal logic as a smaller part of cognition than he did. Today, as part of our own cognitive development, we are adapting Piaget's ideas to accommodate new findings.

"Childhood has its own way of seeing, thinking, and feeling, and there is nothing more foolish than the attempt to put ours in its place." —Philosopher Jean-Jacques Rousseau, 1798

IMPLICATIONS FOR PARENTS AND TEACHERS Future parents and teachers, remember: Young children are incapable of adult logic. Preschoolers who block one's view of the TV simply have not learned to take another's viewpoint. What seems simple and obvious to us—getting off a seesaw will cause a friend on the other end to crash—may be incomprehensible to a 3-year-old. And all of us need to remember that children are not passive receptacles waiting to be filled with knowledge. Better to build on what they already know, engaging them in concrete demonstrations and stimulating them to think for themselves. Finally, accept children's cognitive immaturity as adaptive. It is nature's strategy for keeping children close to protective adults and providing time for learning and socialization (Bjorklund & Green, 1992).

An Alternative Viewpoint: Lev Vygotsky and the Social Child

LOQ 15-3 How did Vygotsky view children's cognitive development?

As Piaget was forming his theory of cognitive development, Russian psychologist Lev Vygotsky was also studying how children think and learn. Where Piaget emphasized how the child's mind grows through interaction with the physical environment, Vygotsky emphasized how the child's mind grows through interaction with the *social* environment. If Piaget's child was a young scientist, Vygotsky's was a young apprentice. By giving children new words and mentoring them, parents, teachers, and other children provide what we now call a temporary **scaffold** from which children can step to higher levels of thinking (Renninger & Granott, 2005; Wood et al., 1976). Children learn

scaffold in Vygotsky's theory, a framework that offers children temporary support as they develop higher levels of thinking.

best when their social environment presents them with something in the sweet spot between too easy and too difficult.

Language, an important ingredient of social mentoring, provides the building blocks for thinking, noted Vygotsky (who was born the same year as Piaget, but died prematurely of tuberculosis). By age 7, children increasingly think in words and use words to solve problems. They do this, Vygotsky said, by internalizing their culture's language and relying on inner speech (Fernyhough, 2008). Parents who say, "No, no, Bevy!" when pulling their child's hand away from a cup of hot coffee are giving their child a self-control tool. When Bevy later needs to resist temptation, she may likewise think, *"No, no, Bevy!"* Second graders who muttered to themselves while doing math problems grasped third-grade math better the following year (Berk, 1994). Whether out loud or inaudibly, talking to themselves helps children control their behavior and emotions and master new skills. (It helps adults, too. Adults who motivate themselves using self-talk—"You can do it!"—experience better performance [Kross et al., 2014].)

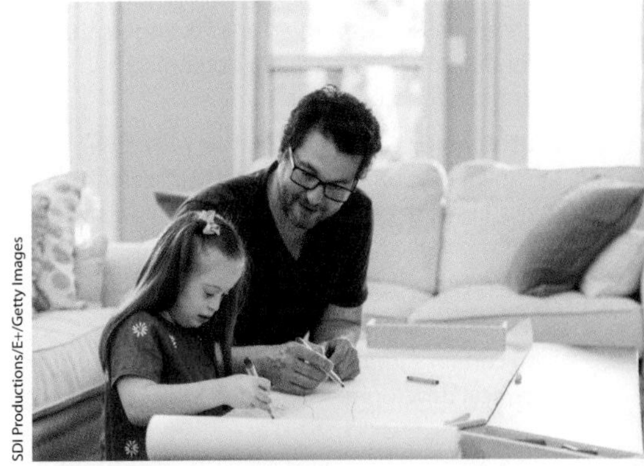
SDI Productions/E+/Getty Images

Scaffolding in action

Theory of Mind

LOQ 15-4 What does it mean to develop a *theory of mind*, and how is this impaired in those with autism spectrum disorder?

When Little Red Riding Hood realized her "grandmother" was really a wolf, she swiftly revised her ideas about the creature's intentions and raced away. Preschoolers, although still egocentric, develop this ability to infer others' mental states when they begin forming a **theory of mind** (Premack & Woodruff, 1978).

Infants as young as 7 months show some knowledge of others' beliefs (Kovács et al., 2010). With time, the ability to take another's perspective develops. They come to understand what made a playmate angry, when a sibling will share, and what might make a parent buy a toy. They begin to tease, empathize, and persuade. And when making decisions, they use their understanding of how their actions will make others feel (Repacholi et al., 2016). Preschoolers and young children who have an advanced ability to understand others' minds tend to be well-liked (McElwain et al., 2019; Slaughter et al., 2015).

Between about ages 3 and 4½, children come to realize that others may hold false beliefs (Callaghan et al., 2005; Rubio-Fernández & Geurts, 2013; Sabbagh et al., 2006). Jennifer Jenkins and Janet Astington (1996) showed Canadian children a Band-Aid box and asked them what was inside. Expecting Band-Aids, the children were surprised to discover that the box actually contained pencils. Asked what a child who had never seen the box would think was inside, 3-year-olds typically answered "pencils." By age 4 to 5, the children's theory of mind had leapt forward, and they anticipated their friends' false belief that the box would hold Band-Aids.

In a follow-up experiment, children viewed a doll named Sally leaving her ball in a red cupboard (**FIGURE 15.6**). Another doll, Anne, then moved the ball to a blue cupboard. Researchers then posed a question: When Sally returns, where will she look for the ball? Children with *autism spectrum disorder* (discussed in the Psychological Disorders modules) had difficulty understanding that Sally's state of mind differed from their own—that Sally, not knowing the ball had been moved, would return to the red cupboard. They also have difficulty reflecting on their own mental states. They are, for example, less likely to use the personal pronouns *I* and *me*. Deaf children with hearing parents and minimal communication opportunities have had similar difficulty inferring others' states of mind (Peterson & Siegal, 1999).

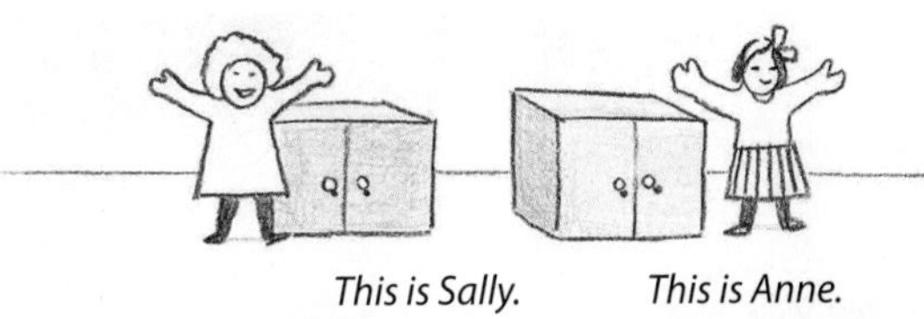
This is Sally. *This is Anne.*

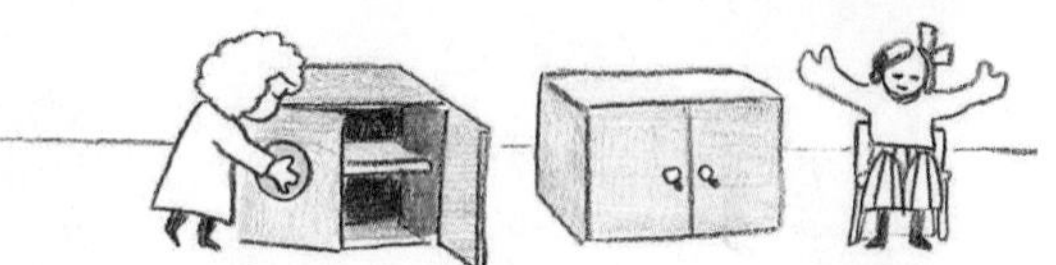
Sally puts her ball in the red cupboard.

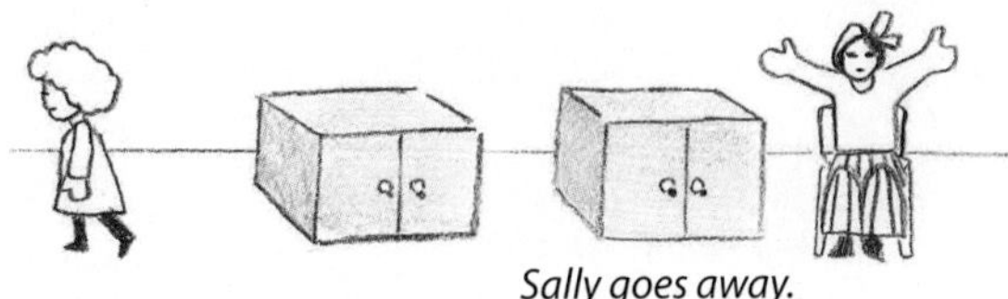
Sally goes away.

Anne moves the ball to the blue cupboard.

Where will Sally look for her ball?

FIGURE 15.6
Testing children's theory of mind This simple problem illustrates how researchers explore children's presumptions about others' mental states. (Inspired by Baron-Cohen et al., 1985.)

RETRIEVAL PRACTICE

RP-4 What does *theory of mind* have to do with autism spectrum disorder?

ANSWERS IN APPENDIX E

theory of mind people's ideas about their own and others' mental states—about their feelings, perceptions, and thoughts, and the behaviors these might predict.

stranger anxiety the fear of strangers that infants commonly display, beginning by about 8 months of age.

attachment an emotional tie with others; shown in young children by their seeking closeness to caregivers and showing distress on separation.

critical period an optimal period early in the life of an organism when exposure to certain stimuli or experiences produces typical development.

Social Development

LOQ **15-5** How do caregiver-infant attachment bonds form?

From birth, most babies are social creatures, developing an intense attachment to their caregivers. (Infancy is the time of life when we get the most kisses.) Infants come to prefer familiar faces and voices, then to coo and gurgle when given a caregiver's attention. By 4.5 months, infants can tell apart familiar and unfamiliar languages (Fecher & Johnson, 2019). After about 8 months, soon after object permanence emerges and children become mobile, a curious thing happens: They develop **stranger anxiety**. They may greet strangers by crying and reaching for familiar caregivers, as if to say "No! Don't leave me!" Children this age have schemas for familiar faces, and may resist being handed to someone unfamiliar (Quinn et al., 2019). Once again, we see an important principle: *The brain, mind, and social-emotional behavior develop together.*

Origins of Attachment

One-year-olds typically cling tightly to a caregiver when they are frightened or expect separation. Reunited after being apart, they often shower the caregiver with smiles and hugs. This striking caregiver-infant **attachment** bond is a powerful survival impulse that keeps infants close to their caregivers. Infants usually become attached to those—typically their parents—who are comfortable and familiar. For many years, psychologists reasoned that infants became attached to those who satisfied their need for nourishment. But an accidental finding overturned this explanation.

BODY CONTACT During the 1950s, psychologists Harry Harlow and Margaret Harlow bred monkeys for their learning studies. To equalize experiences and to isolate any disease, they separated the infant monkeys from their mothers shortly after birth and raised them in individual cages, each including a cheesecloth baby blanket (Harlow et al., 1971). Then came a surprise: When their soft blankets were taken to be washed, the monkeys became distressed.

The Harlows recognized that this intense attachment to the blanket contradicted the idea that attachment derives from an association with nourishment. But how could they show this more convincingly? To pit the drawing power of a food source against the comfort of the blanket, they created two artificial mothers. One was a bare wire cylinder with a wooden head and an attached feeding bottle; the other a cylinder with no bottle, but covered with foam rubber and wrapped with terry cloth.

When raised with both, the monkeys overwhelmingly preferred the comfy cloth mother (FIGURE 15.7). Like other infants clinging to their live mothers, anxious monkey babies would cling to their cloth mothers, soothed by this *contact comfort*. When exploring their environment, they used her as a *secure base*, as if attached to her by an invisible elastic band that stretched only so far before pulling them back. Researchers soon learned that other qualities—rocking, warmth, and feeding—made the cloth mother even more appealing.

Photo Researchers/Science History Images/Alamy Stock Photo

FIGURE 15.7
The Harlows' monkey mothers The Harlows' discovery surprised many psychologists: The infants much preferred contact with the comfortable cloth mother, even while feeding from the nourishing wire mother.

Human infants, too, become attached to parents who are soft and warm and who rock, feed, and pat. Much parent-infant emotional communication occurs via touch, which can be either soothing (snuggles) or arousing (tickles) (Hertenstein et al., 2006). People across the globe agreed that the ideal mother "shows affection by touching" (Mesman et al., 2015). Such parental affection not only feels good, it boosts brain development and later cognitive ability (Davis et al., 2017).

Human attachment also consists of one person providing another with a secure base from which to explore and a safe haven when distressed. As we mature, our secure base shifts—from parents to peers and partners (Mikulincer & Shaver, 2020; A. Schmidt et al., 2019). But at all ages we are social creatures. We gain strength when someone offers, by words and actions, a safe haven: "I will be here. I am interested in you. Come what may, I will support you" (Crowell & Waters, 1994).

FAMILIARITY Contact is one key to attachment. Another is familiarity. In many animals, attachments based on familiarity form during a **critical period**—an optimal period when certain events must take place to facilitate proper development (Bornstein, 1989).

For goslings, ducklings, or chicks, that period falls in the hours shortly after hatching, when the first moving object they see is typically their mother. From then on, the young fowl follow her, and her alone.

Konrad Lorenz (1937) explored this rigid attachment process, called **imprinting**. He wondered: What would ducklings do if he was the first moving creature they observed? What they did was follow him around: Everywhere that Konrad went, the ducks were sure to go. Although baby birds imprint best to their own species, they also will imprint to a variety of moving objects—an animal of another species, a box on wheels, or a bouncing ball (Colombo, 1982; Johnson, 1992). Once formed, this attachment is difficult to reverse.

Nina Leen/The LIFE Picture Collection/Getty Images

Daddy duck? Konrad Lorenz demonstrated that ducks will imprint on the first moving thing they see, which in this case was him!

Children—unlike ducklings—do not imprint. However, they do become attached to what they've known. *Mere exposure* to people and things fosters fondness. Children like to reread the same books, rewatch the same movies, reenact family traditions. They prefer to eat familiar foods, live in the same familiar neighborhood, attend school with the same old friends. Familiarity is a safety signal. Familiarity breeds content.

For some people, a perceived relationship with God functions as do other attachments, by providing a secure base for exploration and a safe haven when threatened (Granqvist et al., 2010; Kirkpatrick, 1999).

RETRIEVAL PRACTICE

RP-5 What distinguishes imprinting from attachment?

ANSWERS IN APPENDIX E

Attachment Differences

LOQ 15-6 How have psychologists studied attachment differences, and what have they learned?

What accounts for children's attachment differences? To answer this question, Mary Ainsworth (1979) designed the *strange situation* experiment. She observed mother-infant pairs at home during their first 6 months. Later she observed the 1-year-old infants in a strange situation (usually a laboratory playroom) with and without their mothers. Such research has shown that about 60 percent of infants and young children display *secure attachment* (Moulin et al., 2014). In their mother's presence they play comfortably, happily exploring their new environment. When she leaves, they become distressed; when she returns, they seek contact with her.

Other infants show *insecure attachment,* marked by either anxiety or avoidance of trusting relationships. These infants are less likely to explore their surroundings. Anxious infants may cling to their mother. When she leaves, they might cry loudly and remain upset. Avoidant infants seem not to notice or care about her departure and return (Ainsworth, 1973, 1989; Kagan, 1995; van Ijzendoorn & Kroonenberg, 1988). Ainsworth and others found that sensitive, responsive mothers—those who noticed what their babies were doing and responded appropriately—had infants who exhibited secure attachment (De Wolff & van IJzendoorn, 1997). Insensitive, unresponsive mothers—mothers who attended to their babies when they felt like doing so but ignored them at other times—often had infants who were insecurely attached. The Harlows' monkey studies, with unresponsive artificial mothers, produced even more striking effects. When put in strange situations without their artificial mothers, the deprived infants were terrified (**FIGURE 15.8**).

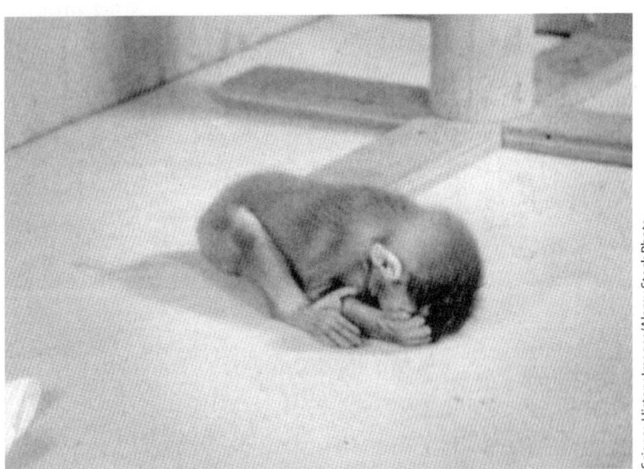

Science History Images/Alamy Stock Photo

FIGURE 15.8
Social deprivation and fear In the Harlows' experiments, monkeys raised with artificial mothers were overwhelmed when placed in strange situations without those mothers.

Many remember Harry Harlow as the researcher who tortured helpless monkeys, and today's climate of greater respect for animal welfare would likely prevent such primate studies. But Harlow defended his methods: "Remember, for every mistreated monkey there exist a million mistreated children," he said, expressing the hope that his research would sensitize people to child abuse and neglect. "No one who knows Harry's work could ever argue that babies do fine without companionship, that a caring mother

imprinting the process by which certain animals form strong attachments during early life.

doesn't matter," noted Harlow biographer Deborah Blum (2011, pp. 292, 307). "And since we . . . didn't fully believe that before Harry Harlow came along, then perhaps we needed—just once—to be smacked really hard with that truth so that we could never again doubt."

So, caring parents (and other caregivers) matter. But is attachment style the result of parenting? Or is attachment style the result of genetically influenced *temperament?* Studies reveal that heredity affects temperament, and that temperament affects attachment style (Picardi et al., 2011; Raby et al., 2012). Shortly after birth, some babies are noticeably *difficult*—irritable, intense, and unpredictable. Others are *easy*—cheerful, relaxed, and on predictable feeding and sleeping schedules (Chess & Thomas, 1987). By neglecting such inborn differences, the parenting studies, noted Judith Harris (1998), are like "comparing foxhounds reared in kennels with poodles reared in apartments." So, to separate nature and nurture, we would need to vary parenting while controlling temperament. Pause and think: If you were the researcher, how might you do this?

Dutch researcher Dymphna van den Boom's (1994) solution was to randomly assign 100 temperamentally difficult 6- to 9-month-olds to either an experimental group, in which mothers received personal training in sensitive responding, or to a control group, in which they did not. At 12 months of age, 68 percent of the infants in the experimental group were securely attached, as were only 28 percent of the control-group infants. Other studies confirm that intervention programs can increase parental sensitivity and, to a lesser extent, infant attachment security (Bakermans-Kranenburg et al., 2003; Van Zeijl et al., 2006). Such "positive parenting" interventions seem to be especially beneficial for children with difficult temperaments (Slagt et al., 2016).

As these examples indicate, researchers have more often studied mother care than father care. Infants who lack a caring mother are said to suffer "maternal deprivation"; those lacking a father's care merely experience "father absence." This reflects a wider attitude in which "fathering a child" has meant impregnating, and "mothering" has meant nurturing. But fathers are more than just mobile sperm banks. Across nearly 100 studies worldwide, a father's love and acceptance have been comparable with a mother's love in predicting their offspring's health and well-being (Rohner & Veneziano, 2001; see also **TABLE 15.2**). Fathers matter.

A large British study following 7259 children from birth to adulthood showed that those whose fathers were most involved in parenting (through outings, reading to them, and taking an interest in their education) tended to achieve more in school, even after controlling for other factors such as parental education and family wealth (Flouri & Buchanan, 2004). Fathers can also help children cope with stress. Among children who grew up in Belfast, Northern Ireland, during the violent conflict, those with engaged fathers experienced fewer mental health problems (Luningham et al., 2021). Girls with supportive fathers expect that other men will treat them with care and respect, and they are less prone to risky sexual behavior (DelPriore et al., 2017, 2019). Increasing

TABLE 15.2 Dual Parenting Positives

- *Active dads are caregiving more.* Today's co-parenting fathers are more engaged, with a doubling in the weekly hours spent with their children, compared with fathers in 1965 (Livingston & Parker, 2011).
- *Couples that share housework and child care are happier in their relationships and less divorce-prone* (Wilcox & Marquardt, 2011).
- *Dual parenting supports children.* After controlling for other factors, children average better life outcomes "if raised by both parents" (Taylor, 2014).
- *Parents' gender and sexual orientation do not affect children's well-being.* The American Academy of Pediatrics (2013) reports that what matters is competent, secure, nurturing parents. The American Sociological Association (2013) concurs: Parental stability and resources matter, but "whether a child is raised by same-sex or opposite-sex parents has no bearing on a child's well-being." One analysis of 21,000 American children aged 4 to 17 found that, compared to those with straight parents, children with gay or lesbian parents experienced similar levels of well-being (Calzo et al., 2019).

Lorie Hailey

nonmarital births and the greater instability of cohabiting versus married partnerships has, however, meant more father-absent families (Hymowitz et al., 2013). In Europe and the United States, for example, children born to married parents (compared to cohabiting parents) are about half as likely to experience their parents' separation, which often entails diminished father care (Brown et al., 2016; Wilcox & DeRose, 2017). Even after controlling for parents' income, education, and race, children whose parents are married experience a lower rate of school problems (Zill, 2020).

Children's anxiety over separation from parents peaks at around 13 months, then gradually declines (**FIGURE 15.9**). This happens whether they live with one parent or two, are cared for at home or in day care, live in North America, Guatemala, or the Kalahari Desert. Does this mean our need for and love of others also fades away? Hardly. Our capacity for love grows, and our pleasure in touching and holding those we love never ceases.

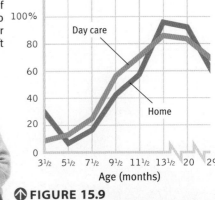

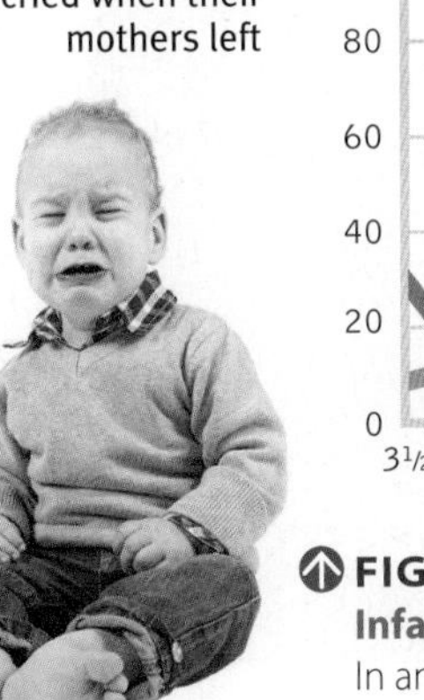
Jouke van Keulen/Shutterstock

Percentage of infants who cried when their mothers left

100%, 80, 60, 40, 20, 0

Day care

Home

3½ 5½ 7½ 9½ 11½ 13½ 20 29

Age (months)

FIGURE 15.9
Infants' distress over separation
In an experiment, infants were left by their mothers in an unfamiliar room. Regardless of whether the infant had experienced day care, the percentage who cried when the mother left peaked at about 13 months of age (Kagan, 1976).

ATTACHMENT STYLES AND LATER RELATIONSHIPS Developmental psychologist Erik Erikson (1902–1994), working with his wife, Joan Erikson (1902–1997), believed that securely attached children approach life with a sense of **basic trust**—a sense that the world is predictable and reliable. He attributed basic trust not to environment or inborn temperament, but to early parenting. He theorized that infants blessed with sensitive, loving caregivers form a lifelong attitude of trust rather than fear.

Many researchers now believe that our early attachments form part of the foundation for our adult relationships and our comfort with affection and intimacy (Fraley et al., 2021). People who report secure relationships with their parents tend to enjoy secure friendships (Gorrese & Ruggieri, 2012). Students leaving home to attend college or university—another kind of "strange situation"—tend to adjust well if they have been closely attached to parents (Mattanah et al., 2011). Children with sensitive, responsive mothers tend to flourish socially and academically (Raby et al., 2014).

Feeling insecurely attached to others may take either of two main forms (Fraley, 2019). One is *anxious attachment,* in which people constantly crave acceptance but remain vigilant to signs of possible rejection. (Being sensitive to threat, anxiously attached people also tend to be skilled lie detectors and poker players [Ein-Dor & Perry, 2012, 2013].) The other is *avoidant attachment,* in which people experience discomfort getting close to others and use avoidant strategies to maintain distance from others. In romantic relationships, an anxious attachment style creates constant concern over rejection, leading people to cling to their partners. An avoidant style decreases commitment and increases conflict (DeWall et al., 2011; Girme et al., 2021).

Adult attachment styles can also affect relationships with one's own children. But say this for those (nearly half of all people) who exhibit wary, insecure attachments: Anxious or avoidant tendencies have helped our groups detect or escape dangers (Ein-Dor et al., 2010).

ASK YOURSELF

How has your upbringing affected your attachment style?

Facing Adversity

LOQ 15-7 How does experiencing adversity affect children's social development?

DEPRIVATION OF ATTACHMENT

If secure attachment nurtures social competence, what happens when circumstances prevent a child's forming any attachments? In all of psychology, there is no sadder research literature. Babies locked away at home under conditions of abuse or extreme neglect are often withdrawn, frightened, even silent. The same is true of those raised in institutions without the stimulation and attention of a regular caregiver, as was tragically illustrated during the 1970s and 1980s in Romania. Having decided that

basic trust according to Erik Erikson, a sense that the world is predictable and trustworthy; said to be formed during infancy by appropriate experiences with responsive caregivers.

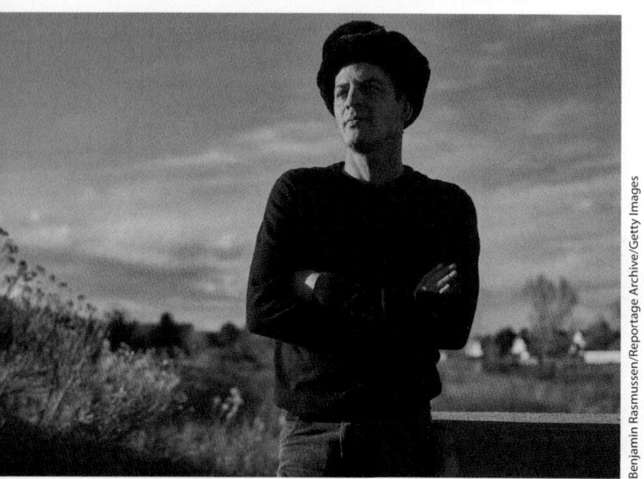
Benjamin Rasmussen/Reportage Archive/Getty Images

Starved of love Izidor Ruckel spent most of his early years in a Romanian orphanage, deprived of close attachment until his adoption at age 10 by a loving U.S. family. But Ruckel's early neglect left lasting psychological scars, leaving him to assume "there would be no human being who would ever want to get close to me. . . . If someone tries to get close, I get away" (Greene, 2020).

economic growth for his impoverished country required more human capital, Nicolae Ceauşescu, Romania's Communist dictator, outlawed contraception, forbade abortion, and taxed families with fewer than five children. The birthrate skyrocketed. But unable to afford the children they had been coerced into having, many families had to leave them at government-run orphanages with untrained and overworked staff. Child-to-caregiver ratios often were 15 to 1, so the children were deprived of healthy attachments with at least one adult.

When tested after Ceauşescu's 1989 execution, and compared with children assigned to quality foster care, the socially deprived children had lower intelligence scores, abnormal stress responses, and quadruple the rate of attention-deficit/hyperactivity disorder (ADHD) (van IJzendoorn et al., 2020). Hundreds of studies have shown that orphaned children generally fare better on later physical health and intelligence tests when raised in family homes from an early age (van IJzendoorn et al., 2020).

TRAUMA, ABUSE, AND POVERTY Most children growing up under adversity (including child survivors of the Holocaust) are *resilient*—they withstand the trauma and become well-adjusted adults (Helmreich, 1992; Masten, 2001). So do most survivors of childhood sexual abuse (Clancy, 2010). Hardship short of trauma often boosts mental toughness (Seery, 2011). Children who have coped with some adversity become hardier when facing future stresses, much like children's immunity to disease builds from exposure to germs (Ellis et al., 2017).

But many who experience enduring abuse don't bounce back so readily. The Harlows' monkeys raised in total isolation, without even an artificial mother, bore lifelong scars. As adults, when placed with other monkeys their age, they either cowered in fright or lashed out in aggression. When they reached sexual maturity, most were incapable of mating. If artificially impregnated, the female monkeys often were neglectful, abusive, even murderous toward their first-born. Another primate experiment confirmed the abuse-breeds-abuse phenomenon: 9 of 16 female monkeys who had been abused by their mothers became abusive parents, as did *none* of the females raised by a nonabusive mother (Maestripieri, 2005).

In humans, too, the abused may become the abusers. Most abusive parents—and many condemned murderers—have reported being neglected or battered as children (Kempe & Kempe, 1978; Lewis et al., 1988). Some 30 percent of people who have been abused later abuse their children—four times the U.S. national rate of child abuse (Dumont et al., 2007; Widom, 1989). And abusive parents tend to abuse their own children in the ways they were abused as children, such as through neglect, emotional abuse, physical abuse, or sexual abuse (Madigan et al., 2019).

Although most abused children do *not* later become violent criminals or abusive parents, extreme early trauma may nevertheless leave footprints on the brain (McLaughlin et al., 2019). Like battle-stressed soldiers, abused children's brains respond to angry faces with heightened activity in threat-detecting areas (McCrory et al., 2011). In conflict-plagued homes, even sleeping infants' brains show heightened reactivity to hearing angry speech (Graham et al., 2013). As adults, abused children are more uncomfortable when touched (Maier et al., 2020). Abused children tend to struggle in adulthood to regulate their negative emotions. They exhibit stronger startle responses, and are twice as likely to attempt suicide (Angelakis et al., 2019; Jovanovic et al., 2009; Lavi et al., 2019).

If repeatedly threatened and attacked while young, normally placid golden hamsters grow up to be cowards when caged with same-sized hamsters, or bullies when caged with weaker ones (Ferris, 1996). Such animals show changes in the brain chemical serotonin, which calms aggressive impulses. A similarly sluggish serotonin response has been found in abused children who become aggressive teens and adults. By sensitizing the stress response system, early stress can permanently heighten reactions to later stress and increase stress-related disease (Fagundes & Way, 2014; van Zuiden et al., 2012; Wei et al., 2012). Child abuse can also leave epigenetic marks—chemical tags—that can alter normal gene expression (Lutz et al., 2017; McKinney, 2017).

Such findings help explain why young children who have survived severe or prolonged physical abuse, sexual abuse, bullying, or wartime atrocities are at increased risk for health problems, psychological disorders, substance abuse, criminality, and, for women, earlier death (E. Chen et al., 2016; Jakubowski et al., 2018; J. Schaefer et al., 2018). Among 135,000 adolescents in 48 countries, those who were bullied had triple the normal rate of attempted suicide (Koyanagi et al., 2019). In one national study of 43,093 U.S. adults, 8 percent reported experiencing physical abuse at least fairly often before age 18 (Sugaya et al., 2012). Among these, 84 percent had experienced at least one psychiatric disorder. Moreover, the greater the abuse, the greater the odds of anxiety, depression, substance use disorder, and attempted suicide. Childhood abuse survivors also experience more troubled adult romantic relationships (Labella et al., 2018).

Childhood abuse survivors have a tripled risk of adult depression (Nelson et al., 2017). Abuse survivors are at especially heightened risk for depression if they carry a gene variation that spurs stress-hormone production (Bradley et al., 2008). As we will see again and again, behavior and emotion arise from a particular environment interacting with particular genes.

Children raised in poverty face unique hardships. They complete less schooling, and as adolescents and adults commit more crimes and have more problems with anxiety, depression, substance abuse, and getting a job (Akee et al., 2010; National Academy of Sciences, 2019). The Covid-19 pandemic increased unemployment and closed schools, which led to more child poverty and child hunger (Sinha et al., 2020).

We adults also suffer when our attachment bonds are severed. Whether through death or separation, a break produces a predictable sequence. Agitated preoccupation with the lost partner is followed by deep sadness and, eventually, the beginnings of emotional detachment and a return to normal living (Hazan & Shaver, 1994). Newly separated couples who have long ago ceased feeling affection are sometimes surprised at their desire to be near the former partner. Detaching is a process, not an event.

Developing a Self-Concept

LOQ 15-8 How do children's self-concepts develop?

Infancy's major social achievement is attachment. *Childhood's* major social achievement is a positive sense of self. By the end of childhood, at about age 12, most children have developed a **self-concept**—an understanding and assessment of who they are. Parents often wonder when and how this sense of self develops. "Is my baby aware of herself—does she know she is a person distinct from everyone else?"

Of course we cannot ask the baby directly, but we can again capitalize on what she can do—letting her *behavior* provide clues to the beginnings of her self-awareness. In 1877, biologist Charles Darwin offered one idea: Self-awareness begins when we recognize ourselves in a mirror. To see whether a child recognizes that the girl in the mirror is indeed herself, researchers sneakily dabbed color on her nose. At about 6 months, children reach out to touch their mirror image as if it were another child (Courage & Howe, 2002; Damon & Hart, 1982, 1988, 1992). By 15 to 18 months, they begin to touch their own noses when they see the colored spot in the mirror (Butterworth, 1992; Gallup & Suarez, 1986). Apparently, 18-month-olds have a schema of how their face should look, and they wonder, "What is that spot doing on *my* face?"

By school age, children's self-concept has blossomed. It now includes their gender identity, group memberships, psychological traits, and similarities and differences compared with other children (Newman & Ruble, 1988; Stipek, 1992). They come to see themselves as good and skillful in some ways but not others. They form a concept of which traits, ideally, they would like to have. By age 8 or 10, their self-image is quite stable.

Kate Nurre

Self-awareness Mirror images fascinate infants from the age of about 6 months. Only at about 18 months, however, does the child recognize that the image in the mirror is "me."

self-concept all our thoughts and feelings about ourselves, in answer to the question, "Who am I?"

Children's views of themselves affect their actions. Children who form a positive self-concept are more confident, independent, optimistic, assertive, and sociable (Maccoby, 1980). So how can parents encourage a positive yet realistic self-concept?

Parenting Styles

LOQ 15-9 What are the four main parenting styles?

Some parents spank; others reason. Some are strict; others are lax. Some show little affection; others liberally hug and kiss. How do parenting-style differences affect children?

The most heavily researched aspect of parenting has been how, and to what extent, parents seek to control their children. Parenting styles can be described as a combination of two traits: how *responsive* and how *demanding* parents are (Kakinami et al., 2015). Investigators have identified four parenting styles (Baumrind, 1966, 1989, 1991; Maccoby & Martin, 1983; Steinberg et al., 1994):

12345678910
William Haefeli/Cartoon Stock

"We've created a safe, nonjudgmental environment that will leave you child ill-prepared for real life."

1. ***Authoritarian*** parents are *coercive*. They impose rules and expect obedience: "Don't interrupt." "Keep your room clean." "Don't stay out late or you'll be grounded." "Why? Because I said so."
2. ***Permissive*** parents are *unrestraining*. They make few demands, set few limits, and use little punishment.
3. ***Neglectful*** parents are *uninvolved*. They are neither demanding nor responsive. They are careless, inattentive, and do not seek a close relationship with their children.
4. ***Authoritative*** parents are *confrontive*. They are both demanding and responsive. They exert control by setting rules, but, especially with older children, they encourage open discussion and allow exceptions.

For more on parenting styles and their associated outcomes, see Thinking Critically About: Parenting Styles.

Parents who struggle with conflicting advice should remember that *all advice reflects the advice-giver's values*. For parents who prize unquestioning obedience, or whose children live in dangerous environments, an authoritarian style may have the desired effect. For those who value children's sociability and self-reliance, there is wisdom in authoritative firm-but-open parenting.

"Before I got married I had six theories about bringing up children; now I have six children and no theories." —attributed to John Wilmot, 2nd Earl of Rochester (1647–1680)

The investment in raising a child buys many years of joy and love, but also of worry and irritation. Yet for most people who become parents, a child is one's legacy—one's personal investment in the human future. To paraphrase psychiatrist Carl Jung, we reach backward into our parents and forward into our children, and through their children into a future we will never see, but about which we must therefore care.

"You are the bows from which your children as living arrows are sent forth." —Kahlil Gibran, *The Prophet*, 1923

ASK YOURSELF

What mistakes do you think parents of the past most often made? What mistakes do you think today's parents might be making, and that as a parent you would want to (or already try to) avoid?

RETRIEVAL PRACTICE

RP-6 For those who value children's self-reliance, the four parenting styles may be described as "too hard, too soft, too uncaring, and just right." Which parenting style goes with each of these descriptions, and how do children benefit from the "just right" style?

ANSWERS IN APPENDIX E

LOQ 15-10 What outcomes are associated with each parenting style?

Thinking Critically About:

Parenting Styles—Too Hard, Too Soft, Too Uncaring, and Just Right?

Researchers have identified four parenting styles,[1] which have been associated with varying outcomes.

1 Authoritarian parents

↕ *Children with less social skill and self-esteem, and a brain that overreacts when they make mistakes[2]*

2 Permissive parents

↕ *Children who are more aggressive and immature[3]*

HOWEVER, Correlation ≠ Causation!

What other factors might explain this parenting-competence link?

- Children's traits may influence parenting. Parental warmth and control vary somewhat from child to child, even in the same family.[6] Maybe socially mature, agreeable, easygoing children get greater trust and warmth from their parents? Twin studies have supported this possibility.[7]
- Some underlying third factor may be at work. Perhaps, for example, competent parents and their competent children share genes that make social competence more likely. Twin studies have also supported this possibility.[8]

CHORES
dishes
SCHEDULE
soccer practice

3 Neglectful parents

↕ *Children with poor academic and social outcomes[4]*

4 Authoritative parents

↕ *Children with the highest self-esteem, self-reliance, self-regulation, and helpfulness[5]*

1. Kakinami et al., 2015. 2. Meyer et al., 2019. 3. Luyckx et al., 2011. 4. Pinquart, 2016; Steinberg et al., 1994. 5. Baumrind, 1996, 2013; Buri et al., 1988; Coopersmith, 1967; Wong et al., 2021. 6. Holden & Miller, 1999; Klahr & Burt, 2014. 7. Kendler, 1996. 8. South et al., 2008.

MODULE 15

REVIEW Infancy and Childhood

LEARNING OBJECTIVES

Test Yourself Answer these repeated Learning Objective Questions on your own (before "showing" the answers here, or checking the answers in Appendix D) to improve your retention of the concepts (McDaniel et al., 2009, 2015).

LOQ **15-1** During infancy and childhood, how do the brain and motor skills develop?

LOQ **15-2** How did Piaget broaden our understanding of the way a child's mind develops, and how have today's researchers built on his work?

LOQ **15-3** How did Vygotsky view children's cognitive development?

LOQ **15-4** What does it mean to develop a *theory of mind*, and how is this impaired in those with autism spectrum disorder?

LOQ **15-5** How do caregiver-infant attachment bonds form?

LOQ **15-6** How have psychologists studied attachment differences, and what have they learned?

LOQ **15-7** How does experiencing adversity affect children's social development?

LOQ **15-8** How do children's self-concepts develop?

LOQ **15-9** What are the four main parenting styles?

LOQ **15-10** What outcomes are associated with each parenting style?

TERMS AND CONCEPTS TO REMEMBER

Test Yourself Write down the definition in your own words, then check your answer.

maturation, p. 173
cognition, p. 175
schema, p. 176
assimilation, p. 176
accommodation, p. 176
sensorimotor stage, p. 176
object permanence, p. 176
preoperational stage, p. 178
egocentrism, p. 178
concrete operational stage, p. 178
conservation, p. 178
formal operational stage, p. 179
scaffold, p. 180
theory of mind, p. 181
stranger anxiety, p. 182
attachment, p. 182
critical period, p. 182
imprinting, p. 183
basic trust, p. 185
self-concept, p. 187

MODULE TEST

Test Yourself Answer the following questions on your own first, then "show" the answers here, or check your answers in Appendix E.

1. Between ages 3 and 6, the human brain experiences the greatest growth in the ____________ lobes, which enable reasoning and planning.
2. Which of the following is true of motor-skill development?
   a. It is determined solely by genetic factors.
   b. The sequence, but not the timing, is universal.
   c. The timing, but not the sequence, is universal.
   d. It is determined solely by environmental factors.
3. Why can't we consciously recall learning to walk?
4. Use Piaget's first three stages of cognitive development to explain why young children are not just miniature adults in the way they think.
5. Although Piaget's stage theory continues to inform our understanding of children's thinking, many researchers believe that
   a. Piaget's stages begin earlier and development is more continuous than he realized.
   b. children do not progress as rapidly as Piaget predicted.
   c. few children progress to the concrete operational stage.
   d. there is no way of testing much of Piaget's theoretical work.
6. An 8-month-old infant who reacts to a new babysitter by crying and clinging to his father's shoulder is showing ____________ ____________.
7. In a series of experiments, the Harlows found that monkeys raised with artificial mothers tended, when afraid, to cling to their cloth mother rather than to a wire mother holding the feeding bottle. Why was this finding important?

MODULE 16

Adolescence and Emerging Adulthood

LOQ **16-1** How is *adolescence* defined, and how do physical changes affect developing teens?

Many psychologists once believed that childhood sets our traits. Today's developmental psychologists see development as lifelong. As this *developmental life-span perspective* emerged, psychologists began to look at how maturation and experience shape us not only in infancy and childhood, but also—after we are no longer handed the children's menu—in adolescence and beyond. **Adolescence**—the years spent morphing from child to adult—starts with the physical beginnings of sexual maturity and ends with social independence. Thus, adolescence hardly exists in cultures where post-pubertal teens are self-supporting (Schlegel & Barry, 1991). And in Western cultures, where sexual maturation occurs earlier and independence later, adolescence is lengthening and can happen anywhere between the ages of 10 and 19 (Sawyer et al., 2018; Worthman & Trang, 2018).

"Somewhere between the ages of 10 and 13 (depending on how hormone-enhanced their beef was), children entered adolescence, a.k.a. 'the de-cutening.'" —Jon Stewart et al., *Earth (The Book)*, 2010

In industrialized countries, what are the teen years like? In Leo Tolstoy's *Anna Karenina*, the teen years were "that blissful time when childhood is just coming to an end, and out of that vast circle, happy and gay, a path takes shape." But another teenager, Anne Frank, writing in her diary while hiding from the Nazis, described tumultuous teen emotions:

> My treatment varies so much. One day Anne is so sensible and is allowed to know everything; and the next day I hear that Anne is just a silly little goat who doesn't know anything at all and imagines that she's learned a wonderful lot from books. . . . Oh, so many things bubble up inside me as I lie in bed, having to put up with people I'm fed up with, who always misinterpret my intentions.

G. Stanley Hall (1904), one of the first psychologists to describe adolescence, believed that this tension between biological maturity and social dependence creates a period of "storm and stress."

It's a time of diminishing parental control (Lionetti et al., 2019). It's also a time when teens crave social acceptance, but often feel socially disconnected. Three in four U.S. friendships started in seventh grade dissolve by the end of eighth grade (Hartl et al., 2015). Such social disconnection hits adolescents hard—increasing their risk for substance abuse and depressive and anxiety symptoms (Hussong et al., 2020; McLaughlin & King, 2015). No wonder that, after age 30, many who grow up in independence-fostering Western cultures look back on their teenage years as a time they would not want to relive—a time when their peers' social approval was imperative, their sense of direction in life was in flux, and their feeling of alienation from their parents was deepest (Arnett, 1999; Macfarlane, 1964). For those who grow up in non-Western Latinx cultures fostering more interdependence, adolescence may be a time of increased family responsibilities (Fuligni & Pederson, 2002). Adolescents in Japan, who are now raised at the intersection of traditional Japanese collectivism and growing Western-world influences, may focus on making decisions on their own while also considering the perspective of a parent or teacher (Sugimura, 2020).

But for others, adolescence is a time of vitality without the cares of adulthood—a time of rewarding friendships, heightened idealism and defining one's identity, and a growing sense of life's exciting possibilities. Adolescence is complicated.

ASK YOURSELF

How do you look back on your early teen years? What would you change, and what would you keep the same?

Physical Development

"Let me just say for the record that I think middle school is the dumbest idea ever invented. You got kids like me who haven't hit their growth spurt yet mixed in with these gorillas who need to shave twice a day." —Jeff Kinney, *Diary of a Wimpy Kid* (2010)

Adolescence begins with **puberty**, the time when we mature sexually. Puberty follows a surge of hormones, which may intensify moods and trigger the bodily changes discussed in the Cultural and Gender Diversity module. I [JG] remember being confronted with a changing female body that felt confusing and even foreign at first. Suddenly my female peers were buying bras and talking about their body size and shape. Ideas about what becoming a woman meant came to life in school hallway conversations. The transition for me and many of my friends was complex, confusing, and full of questions.

adolescence the transition period from childhood to young adulthood, extending from puberty to independence.

puberty the period of sexual maturation, during which a person usually becomes capable of reproducing.

The Timing of Puberty

Just as in the earlier life stages, the *sequence* of physical changes in puberty (for example, breast buds and visible pubic hair before *menarche*—the first menstrual period) is far more predictable than their *timing* (when they first begin). Over recent decades, puberty worldwide has been starting earlier, with obesity, stress, and chemical exposure offered as possible explanations (Eckert-Lind et al., 2000; Ghorayshi, 2022). Some girls start their puberty at age 8 or 9, some boys as late as age 16.

Early maturation can be a challenge. Early maturing adolescents are at increased risk for mental health problems (Hamlat et al., 2022; Pfeifer & Allen, 2021; Ullsperger & Nikolas, 2017). This vulnerability is greatest for adolescents who experience childhood trauma (such as abuse) or who have emotionally reactive temperaments. For girls in particular, physical development that outpaces emotional maturity can have lasting effects. In that case, girls may suffer teasing or sexual harassment, engage in harmful thinking, and bully or physically harm others (Nolen-Hoeksema et al., 2007; Skoog & Kapetanovic, 2022).

The Teenage Brain

The adolescent brain is a mind-boggling mix of great strength and vulnerability. It's also a remarkable work in progress: Teen brains have ever increasing reasoning ability but their self-control lags.

Until puberty, brain cells increase their connections, like trees growing more roots and branches. Then during adolescence comes a *selective pruning* of unused neurons and connections (Blakemore, 2008). What we don't use, we lose. As teens mature, their frontal lobes also continue to develop. The continuing growth of *myelin* (the fatty tissue that forms around axons and speeds neurotransmission) and *glial cells* (providing an immune defense of the central nervous system) enables better communication with other brain regions and aids cognitive development (Schalbetter et al., 2022; Whitaker et al., 2016). These developments bring improved judgment, impulse control, emotion regulation, and long-term planning. A landmark study following 11,000 youth from late childhood to early adulthood is examining influences on teens' brain development, such as drugs, screen time, and sleep (NIMH, 2019; Wadman, 2018).

Frontal lobe maturation nevertheless lags behind the emotion-controlling limbic system's development. Puberty's hormonal surge and this developing brain imbalance help explain teens' occasional impulsiveness, risky behaviors, and emotional extremes—slamming doors, and turning up the music (Casey, 2015; Smith, 2018; Steinberg & Icenogle, 2019). This developmental imbalance increases during the teenage years and then tapers off after that (**FIGURE 16.1**).

Teens don't underestimate the risks of vaping, drinking, fast driving, or unprotected sex. But their brains are attuned toward immediate rewards, which helps explain why teens worldwide struggle with self-control (Hansen et al., 2019; Steinberg et al., 2018). The teenage brain is like a car with a forceful accelerator and unreliable brakes (Dahl, 2004).

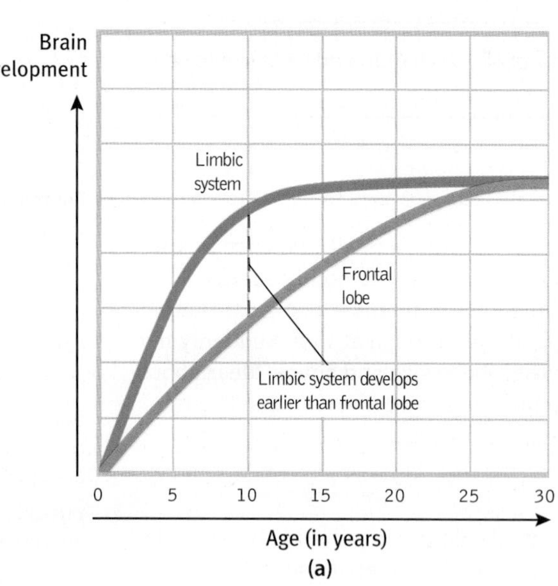

Brain development
Limbic system
Frontal lobe
Limbic system develops earlier than frontal lobe
0
5
10
15
20
25
30
Age (in years)
(a)

ViewStock/Getty Images
(b)

FIGURE 16.1
Riding on the edge
Our brain's emotion-controlling limbic system develops earlier than the future-thinking frontal lobes. No wonder young teens (whose frontal lobes are still developing) are more likely to succumb to the lure of risky behaviors. Information from: Casey (2015).

So, when a teen drives recklessly and academically self-destructs, should their parents reassure themselves that "they can't help it; their frontal cortex isn't yet fully grown"? Parents can at least take hope: Brain changes underlie teens' new self-consciousness about what others are thinking as well as their valuing of risky rewards (Barkley-Levenson & Galván, 2014; Somerville et al., 2013). Parental warmth and support help teenagers become more emotionally resilient (Butterfield et al., 2021). And the brain with which youths begin their teens differs from the brain with which they will end their teens. Unless they slow their brain development with heavy alcohol use—making them more prone to impulsivity and addiction—their frontal lobes will continue maturing until about age 25 (Crews et al., 2007; Giedd, 2015). They will also become better connected with the limbic system, enabling better emotion regulation (Cohen et al., 2016; Steinberg, 2012).

Barbara Smaller/Cartoon Stock

"Young man, go to your room and stay there until your cerebral cortex matures."

In 2004, the American Psychological Association (APA) joined seven other medical and mental health associations in filing U.S. Supreme Court briefs arguing against the death penalty for 16- and 17-year-olds. The briefs documented the teen brain's immaturity "in areas that bear upon adolescent decision making." Brain scans of young teens reveal that frontal lobe immaturity is most evident among juvenile offenders and drug users (Shannon et al., 2011; Whelan et al., 2012). Thus, teens are "less guilty by reason of adolescence," suggested psychologist Laurence Steinberg and law professor Elizabeth Scott (2003; Steinberg et al., 2009). Some researchers have argued that teenagers, whose brains are still developing, should not incur the same penalties that adults do when they are convicted of a crime (Casey, 2015). In 2005, by a 5-to-4 margin, the Court concurred, declaring juvenile death penalties unconstitutional. In 2012, the APA offered similar arguments against sentencing juveniles to life without parole (Banville, 2012; Steinberg, 2013). Once again, the Court, by a narrow 5-to-4 vote, concurred.

BJ Casey

Betty Jo (BJ) Casey This influential developmental neuroscientist uses neuroimaging to explore the mysteries of the teen brain. Courts have used Casey's research when sentencing adolescents convicted of a crime.

Cognitive Development

LOQ 16-2 How did Piaget, Kohlberg, and later researchers describe adolescent cognitive and moral development?

During the early teen years, *egocentrism* endures, and reasoning is often self-focused. Capable of thinking about their own and others' thinking, teens also begin imagining what others think about *them* and develop an intense awareness of this *imaginary audience*. (They might worry less if they understood their peers' similar self-focus: Few people will remember our awkward moments because they're too busy remembering their own.) Teens also tend to develop a *personal fable*—believing that they are unique and special and what happens to "most people" would never happen to them. "I vape for fun; I would never become addicted to nicotine."

"When the pilot told us to brace and grab our ankles, the first thing that went through my mind was that we must all look pretty stupid." —Jeremiah Rawlings, age 12, after surviving a plane crash in Sioux City, Iowa

Developing Reasoning Power

When adolescents achieve the intellectual summit that Jean Piaget called *formal operations*, they apply their new abstract reasoning tools to the world around them. They may think about what is possible and compare that with the imperfect reality of their society, their parents, friends, and themselves. They may debate human nature, good and evil, truth and justice. Their sense of what's fair changes from simple equality to equity—to what's proportional to merit (Almås et al., 2010). Having left behind the concrete images of early childhood, they may search for spirituality and the deeper meaning of life (Boyatzis, 2012; Elkind, 1970). They assess their social worth and place in society, figuring out who their friends are and what they want to do with their life (Choudhury et al., 2006). Reasoning hypothetically and deducing consequences also enables adolescents to detect inconsistencies and spot hypocrisy in others' reasoning. This can lead to heated family debates and silent vows to never lose sight of their own ideals (Peterson et al., 1986).

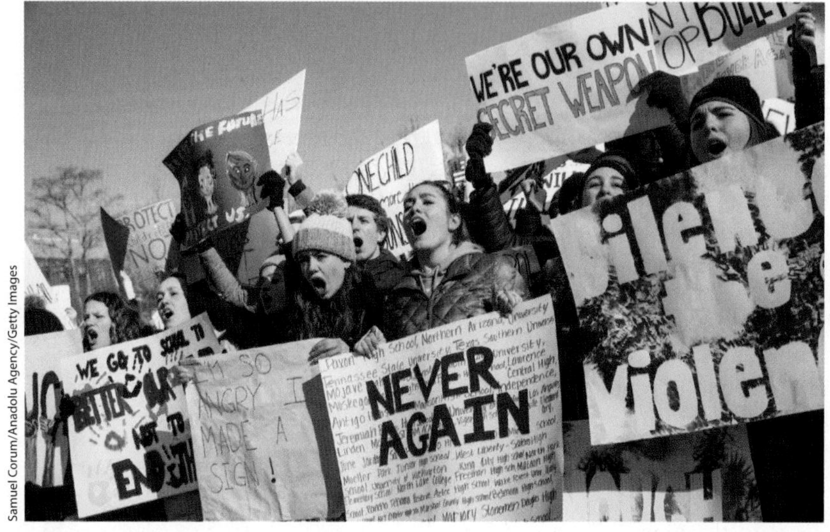
WE'RE OUR OWN
NEVER
AGAIN

Samuel Corum/Anadolu Agency/Getty Images

A generation fed up with firearms Hundreds of thousands of teens have participated in school walkouts and marches to protest gun violence, demonstrating their ability to think logically about abstract topics and to voice their ideals. According to Piaget, these teens are in the final cognitive stage, formal operations.

"I helped a so-called friend commit armed robbery and murder. . . . I was just 17 years old. . . . Been in prison for over 20 years . . . longer than I was ever free. . . . I am among the 300 plus "Juvenile Lifers" in Michigan prisons. I learned and matured a lot since my time incarcerated. I experience great remorse and regret over the tragedy that I ashamedly participated in. But I salvage this experience by learning and growing from it." —M. H., Michigan prison inmate, personal correspondence, 2015

Developing Morality

Two crucial tasks of childhood and adolescence are discerning right from wrong and developing character—the psychological muscles for controlling impulses. Children learn to empathize with others, an ability that continues to develop in adolescence. To be a moral person is to *think* morally and *act* accordingly. Jean Piaget and Lawrence Kohlberg proposed that moral reasoning guides moral actions. A newer view builds on psychology's game-changing recognition that much of our functioning occurs not on the "high road" of deliberate, conscious thinking but on the "low road," unconscious and automatic.

MORAL REASONING Piaget (1932) believed that children's moral judgments build on their cognitive development. Agreeing with Piaget, Lawrence Kohlberg (1981, 1984) described the development of *moral reasoning*, the thinking that occurs as we consider right and wrong. Kohlberg posed moral dilemmas (for example, whether a person should steal medicine to save a loved one's life) and asked children, adolescents, and adults whether the action was right or wrong. His analysis of their answers led him to propose three basic levels of moral thinking: *preconventional*, *conventional*, and *postconventional* (**TABLE 16.1**). Kohlberg claimed these levels form a moral ladder. As with all stage theories, the sequence is unvarying. We begin on the bottom rung and rise to varying heights. Infants recognize right and wrong, preferring moral over immoral action (Cowell & Decety, 2015). Preschoolers, typically identifying with their cultural group, conform to and enforce its moral norms (Tomasello, 2019; Yudkin et al., 2019). When those norms reward kind actions, preschoolers help others (Carragan & Dweck, 2014). From a young age, we seem hard-wired to dislike unfairness and to value morally good or kind characters (Elenbaas, 2019; Hamlin et al., 2007).

TABLE 16.1 Kohlberg's Levels of Moral Thinking

Kohlberg posed moral dilemmas, such as: "Is it okay to steal medicine to save a loved one?"

Level (approximate age)	Focus	Example of Moral Reasoning
Preconventional morality (before age 9)	Self-interest; obey rules to avoid punishment or gain concrete rewards.	"If you steal the medicine, you'll go to jail."
Conventional morality (early adolescence)	Uphold laws and rules to gain social approval or maintain social order.	"If you steal the medicine, everyone will think you're a criminal."
Postconventional morality (adolescence and beyond)	Actions reflect belief in basic rights and self-defined ethical principles.	"People's right to live matters more than property or profits."

Kohlberg's critics have noted that the postconventional stage is culturally limited. It appears mostly among people from large *individualist* societies that prioritize personal goals, rather than from *collectivist* societies that place more value on social or group goals (Barrett et al., 2016; Eckensberger, 1994). In more collectivist India, morality is less a matter of personal choice and more a role-related duty (Miller et al., 2017). Some also view Kohlberg's theory as male-focused, given women's tendency to emphasize care for others in need over what is "fair" (Gilligan, 1982, 2015).

Ramon Espinosa/AP Photo

Moral reasoning Bahamians faced a moral dilemma in 2019 when Hurricane Dorian devastated their northern islands. As many took in family and friends who now had no home, their reasoning likely reflected different levels of moral thinking, even if they behaved similarly.

MORAL INTUITION Psychologist Jonathan Haidt [pronounced HITE] (2001) believes that much of our morality is rooted in *moral intuitions*—"quick gut feelings." According to this intuitionist view, the mind makes moral judgments quickly and automatically, relying largely on feelings. Feelings of disgust or of elation trigger moral reasoning (Inbar & Pizarro, 2022).

One woman recalled traveling through her snowy neighborhood with three young men as they passed "an elderly woman with a shovel in her driveway. . . . [O]ne of the guys . . . asked the driver to let him off there. . . . [M]y mouth dropped in shock as I realized that he was offering to shovel her walk for her." Witnessing this unexpected goodness triggered elevation: "I felt like jumping out of the car and hugging this guy. I felt like singing and running, or skipping and laughing. I felt like saying nice things about people" (Haidt, 2000).

"Could human morality really be run by the moral emotions," Haidt wonders, "while moral reasoning struts about pretending to be in control?" Consider the desire to punish. Laboratory games reveal that the desire to punish wrongdoing is mostly driven not by reason (such as an objective calculation that punishment deters crime) but rather by emotional reactions, such as moral outrage and the pleasure of revenge (Chester & DeWall, 2016; Crockett, 2017). After the emotional fact, moral reasoning—our mind's press secretary—aims to convince us and others of the logic of what we have intuitively felt.

This intuitionist perspective on morality finds support in a study of moral paradoxes. Imagine seeing a runaway trolley headed for five people. All will certainly be killed unless you throw a switch that diverts the trolley onto another track, where it will kill one person. Should you throw the switch? Most say *Yes*. Kill one, save five.

THE LITTLE ENGINE THAT FACED A TOUGH MORAL DILEMMA
SPAULDING

Trevor Spaulding/Cartoon Stock

Now imagine the same dilemma, with one change. You must save the five this time by pushing a large male stranger onto the tracks, where he will die as his body stops the trolley. In both versions of this famous "trolley problem," the logic is the same—kill one, save five. But worldwide, half say *No* in this second dilemma (Awad et al., 2020). One brain-imaging study showed that only the body-pushing type of moral dilemma activated emotion-relevant brain responses (Greene et al., 2001). Thus, our moral judgments provide another example of the two-track mind—of dual processing (Feinberg et al., 2012). We may liken our moral cognition to our phone's camera settings. Usually, we rely on the default settings. Yet sometimes, we use reason to override those settings manually or to adjust the resulting image (Greene, 2010; May, 2019).

MORAL ACTION Our moral thinking and feeling surely affect our moral talk. But sometimes talk is cheap and emotions are fleeting. Morality involves *doing* the right thing; what we do also depends on social influences. As political theorist Hannah Arendt (1963) observed, many Nazi concentration camp guards during World War II were ordinary "moral" people corrupted by a powerfully evil situation.

Today's character education programs focus on the whole moral package—thinking, feeling, and *doing* the right thing. In service-learning programs, teens have tutored, cleaned up their neighborhoods, and assisted older adults. The result? The teens' sense of competence and desire to serve has increased, school absenteeism and dropout rates have fallen, and violent behavior has diminished (Andersen, 1998; Heller, 2014; Piliavin, 2003). *Moral action* feeds moral attitudes.

These programs also teach the self-discipline needed to restrain one's own impulses. Those who have learned to *delay gratification*—to live with one eye on the future—have become more socially responsible, academically successful, and productive (Daly et al., 2015;

Sawyer et al., 2015). A preference for large-later rather than small-now rewards also minimizes one's risk of problem gambling and delinquency (Callan et al., 2011; Lee et al., 2017).

In one of psychology's best-known experiments, Walter Mischel (2014) gave 4-year-olds a choice between one marshmallow now, or two marshmallows when he returned a few minutes later. The children who delayed gratification went on to have higher college completion rates and incomes, and less often suffered addiction problems. A replication of this famous study found a more modest effect (Watts et al., 2018; Watts & Duncan, 2020). But the big idea remains: Maturity and life success grow from the ability to spurn small pleasures now in favor of greater pleasures later (Baird et al., 2021; Robson et al., 2020; Yanaoka et al., 2022). Think of it this way: Immediate gratification makes today easy but tomorrow difficult; self-discipline—delayed gratification—makes today difficult and tomorrow easy. Marshmallows—and so much more—come to those who wait.

"The best time to plant a tree was 20 years ago. The second best time is now." —Chinese proverb

ASK YOURSELF

Think about a difficult decision you had to make in early adolescence and later regretted. What did you do? How would you do things differently now?

RETRIEVAL PRACTICE

RP-1 According to Kohlberg, ____________ morality focuses on self-interest, ____________ morality focuses on self-defined ethical principles, and ____________ morality focuses on upholding laws and social rules.

RP-2 How has Kohlberg's theory of moral reasoning been criticized?

ANSWERS IN APPENDIX E

Social Development

LOQ 16-3 What are the social tasks and challenges of adolescence?

Psychologist Erik Erikson (1963) contended that each stage of life has its own *psychosocial* task, a crisis that needs resolution. Young children wrestle with issues of *trust*, then *autonomy* (independence), then *initiative*. School-age children strive for *competence*, feeling able and productive. The adolescent's task is to synthesize past, present, and future possibilities into a clearer sense of self (**TABLE 16.2**). Adolescents wonder, "Who am I as

TABLE 16.2 Erikson's Stages of Psychosocial Development

Stage (approximate age)	Issue	Description of Task
Infancy (to 1 year)	Trust vs. mistrust	If needs are dependably met, infants develop a sense of basic trust.
Toddlerhood (1 to 3 years)	Autonomy vs. shame and doubt	Toddlers learn to exercise their will and do things for themselves, or they doubt their abilities.
Preschool (3 to 6 years)	Initiative vs. guilt	Preschoolers learn to initiate tasks and carry out plans, or they feel guilty about their efforts to be independent.
Elementary school (6 years to puberty)	Competence vs. inferiority	Children learn the pleasure of applying themselves to tasks, or they feel inferior.
Adolescence (teen years into 20s)	Identity vs. role confusion	Teenagers work at refining a sense of self by testing roles and then integrating them to form a single identity, or they become confused about who they are.
Young adulthood (20s to early 40s)	Intimacy vs. isolation	Young adults learn to form close relationships and gain the capacity for intimate love, or they feel socially isolated.
Middle adulthood (40s to 60s)	Generativity vs. stagnation	Middle-aged people discover a sense of contributing to the world, usually through family and work, or they may feel a lack of purpose.
Late adulthood (late 60s and up)	Integrity vs. despair	Reflecting on their lives, older adults may feel a sense of satisfaction or failure.

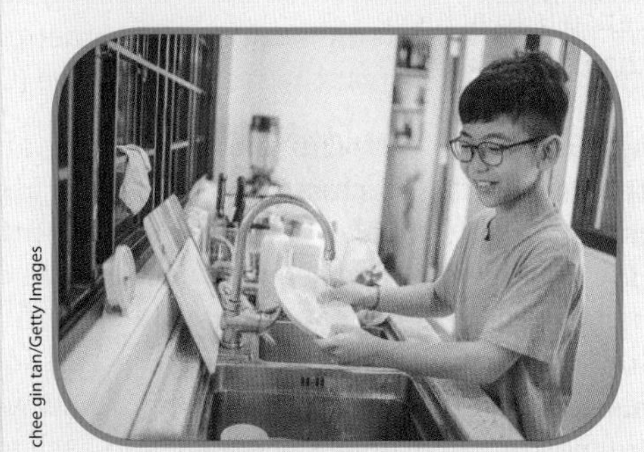
chee gin tan/Getty Images

Competence vs. inferiority

an individual? What do I want to do with my life? What values should I live by? What do I believe in?" Erikson called this quest the adolescent's *search for identity.*

As sometimes happens in psychology, Erikson's interests were bred by his own life experience. As the son of a Jewish mother and a Danish Gentile father, Erikson was "doubly an outsider," reported Morton Hunt (1993, p. 391). He was "scorned as a Jew in school but mocked as a Gentile in the synagogue because of his blond hair and blue eyes." Such episodes fueled his interest in the adolescent struggle for identity.

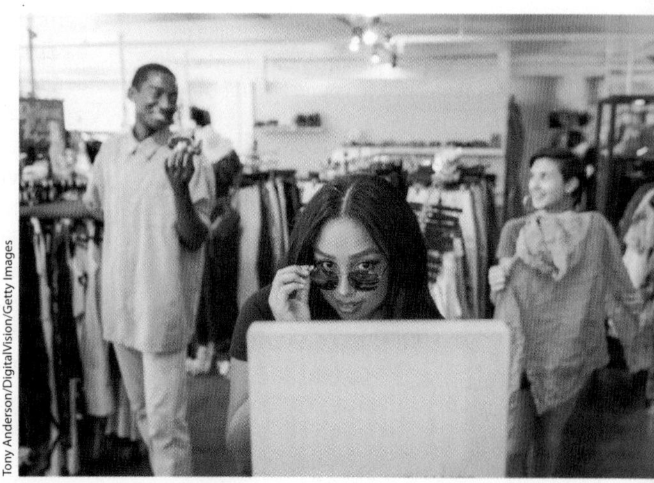
Tony Anderson/DigitalVision/Getty Images

Who shall I be today? By varying the way they look, adolescents try out different "selves." Although we eventually form a consistent and stable sense of identity, the self we present may change with the situation.

Forming an Identity

Erikson noticed that some adolescents forge their identity by adopting their parents' values and expectations. Other adolescents may adopt the identity of a particular peer group—as an athlete or an artist, a tech geek or a science fiction buff. Traditional, collectivist cultures teach adolescents to adopt a certain identity, rather than encouraging them to decide on their own.

Adolescents in individualist cultures usually try out different "selves" to refine their sense of identity. They may act out one self at home, another with friends, another online, and still another at school. If two situations overlap—as when a teenager brings new friends home—the discomfort can be considerable (Klimstra et al., 2015). The teen often wonders, "Which self should I be? Which is the real me?" The eventual resolution is a self-definition that unifies the various selves into a consistent and comfortable sense of who one is—an **identity**. In collectivist cultures such as Japan, where less emphasis is placed on individual identity, teens spend more time in adolescence and are less certain about who they are (Hatano et al., 2020; Sugimura, 2020). In such cultures, adolescents who are immigrants (or the children of immigrants) form complex identities as they adopt new languages and integrate group memberships (Aumann et al., 2022; Marks et al., 2011).

"I don't think any of us like to be reduced to just one label." —Actor Riz Ahmed, 2016

For adolescents and adults, group identities are often formed by how we differ from those around us—in gender identity and sexual orientation, age and relative wealth, abilities and beliefs. When living in Britain, I [DM] became conscious of my Americanness. When spending time in Hong Kong, I [ND] became conscious of my White race. When I [JG] joined this all-male author team, I became conscious of being a woman. For international students, for those of a minority ethnic or religious group, for members of the LGBTQ community, or for people with a disability, a **social identity** often forms around their distinctiveness. (Stay tuned for more on social identity and prejudice in the Social Psychology modules.)

Most young people develop a sense of contentment with their lives. Which statement best describes you: "I would choose my life the way it is right now" or "I wish I were somebody else"? When American teens answered, 81 percent picked the first, and 19 percent the second (Lyons, 2004). Reflecting on their existence, 76 percent of U.S. college and university students say they "discuss religion/spirituality" with friends (Stolzenberg et al., 2019). This would not surprise researchers who have contended that a key task of adolescence is to achieve a purpose—a desire to accomplish something personally meaningful that contributes to the world beyond oneself (Fuligni, 2019; Sumner et al., 2018).

Interventions that aim to boost adolescents' health and well-being work best when appealing to their desires for self-esteem, status, and respect (Yeager et al., 2018). Rather than saying "Eating well is important for your health," a more effective message would be "Buying junk food gives money to rich adults who disrespect you by thinking you don't know better."

During the early teen years, self-esteem typically falls and, for girls, depression often increases (Kwong et al., 2019; Salk et al., 2017). Teen depression and suicide rates have also increased since the spread of social media and the peer comparisons they enable (more on this in the Affiliation and Achievement module). To sustain mental health, hanging out with friends beats scrolling through Instagram (Twenge, 2022). But there's good news: Self-image rebounds during the late teens and twenties, and self-esteem gender differences shrink (Orth et al., 2021; Zuckerman et al., 2016). Agreeableness and emotional stability scores also increase in late adolescence (Klimstra et al., 2009).

These are the years when many people in industrialized countries begin exploring new opportunities by attending college or working full time. Many college and university

identity our sense of self; according to Erikson, the adolescent's task is to solidify a sense of self by testing and integrating various roles.

social identity the "we" aspect of our self-concept; the part of our answer to "Who am I?" that comes from our group memberships.

intimacy in Erikson's theory, the ability to form close, loving relationships; a primary developmental task in young adulthood.

seniors have achieved a clearer identity and a more positive self-concept than they had as first-year students (Jones & Abes, 2013; Waterman, 1988). Those who have a clear sense of identity are less prone to alcohol misuse (Bishop et al., 2005).

Erikson contended that adolescent identity formation (which continues into adulthood) is followed in young adulthood by a developing capacity for **intimacy**, the ability to form emotionally close relationships. When Mihaly Csikszentmihalyi [chick-SENT-me-hi] and Jeremy Hunter (2003) used a beeper to sample the daily experiences of U.S. teens, they found them unhappiest when alone and happiest when with friends. Romantic relationships, which tend to be emotionally intense, are reported by two in three North American 17-year-olds, but by fewer in collectivist countries such as China (Collins et al., 2009; Li et al., 2010). Those who enjoy high-quality (intimate, supportive) relationships with family and friends also tend to enjoy similarly high-quality romantic relationships in adolescence, which set the stage for healthy adult relationships and fewer behavior problems (Aikins et al., 2010). Such relationships are, for most of us, a source of great pleasure. As Aristotle long ago recognized, we humans are "the social animal." We have a deep need to belong. Relationships matter.

Parent and Peer Relationships

LOQ 16-4 How do parents and peers influence adolescents?

Adolescence is typically a time of diminishing parental influence and growing peer influence (Blakemore, 2018). The preschooler who can't be close enough to her mother, who loves to touch and cling to her, becomes the 14-year-old who wouldn't be caught dead holding hands with Mom in front of their friends. The transition occurs gradually (**FIGURE 16.2**). As children, we recognize adult faces more readily than other children's faces; by adolescence, we display superior recognition for our peers' faces (Picci & Scherf, 2016; Somerville et al., 2011). Puberty alters attachments and primes perceptions.

FIGURE 16.2
The changing parent-child relationship In a large national study of Canadian families, the typically close, warm relationships between children and their parents loosened as they became teens (Pepler & Craig, 2012).

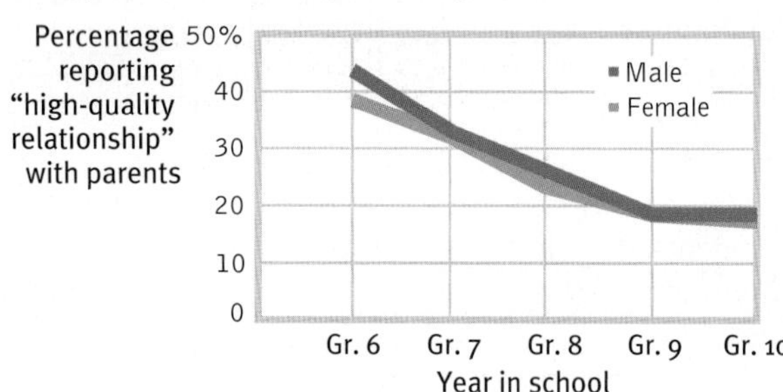
Percentage reporting "high-quality relationship" with parents
50%
40
30
20
10
0
Male
Female
Gr. 6
Gr. 7
Gr. 8
Gr. 9
Gr. 10
Year in school

By adolescence, parent-child arguments occur more often, usually over mundane things—household chores, bedtime, homework (Steinberg & Morris, 2001; Tesser et al., 1989). Conflict during the transition to adolescence tends to be greater with first-born than with second-born children, and greater with mothers than with fathers (Burk et al., 2009; Shanahan et al., 2007).

For a minority of parents and their adolescent children, differences lead to real splits and great stress (Steinberg & Morris, 2001). But many disagreements are at the level of harmless bickering about relationships. With sons, the issues are often about behavior problems, such as acting out or hygiene; for daughters, the issues commonly involve relationships, such as dating and friendships (Schlomer et al., 2011). In a survey of nearly 6000 adolescents in 10 countries—from Australia to Bangladesh to Turkey—most said they like their parents (Offer et al., 1988). "We usually get along but . . . ," adolescents often reported (Galambos, 1992; Steinberg, 1987).

Positive parent-teen relations and positive peer relations often go hand in hand. High school girls who have the most affectionate relationships with their mothers also tend to enjoy the most intimate friendships with girlfriends (Gold & Yanof, 1985). And teens (including transgender teens) who feel close to their parents have tended to be healthy and happy and to do well in school (Olson et al., 2016; Resnick et al., 1997). Of course, we can state this correlation the other way: Misbehaving teens are more likely to have tense relationships with parents and other adults.

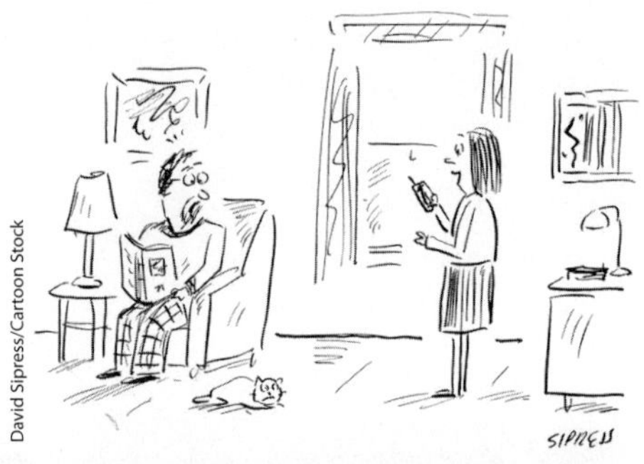
SIPRESS
David Sipress/Cartoon Stock

"She says she's someone from your past who gave birth to you, and raised you, and sacrificed everything so you could have whatever you wanted."

Heredity does much of the heavy lifting in forming individual temperament and personality differences, and peer influences do much of the rest. When with peers, teens discount the future and focus more on immediate rewards (O'Brien et al., 2011). Most teens are herd animals. They talk, dress, and act more like their peers than their parents. They often become what their friends are, and what "everybody's doing," they usually do. Teens' social media use illustrates the power of peer influence. Compared to photos with few likes, teens prefer photos with many likes. Moreover, when viewing many-liked photos, teens' brains become more active in areas associated with reward processing and imitation (Sherman et al., 2016). Liking and doing what everybody else likes and does feels good.

The pain is acute for those who feel excluded and bullied by their peers, both online and face-to-face. Most excluded "students suffer in silence. . . . A small number act out in violent ways against their classmates" (Aronson, 2001). The pain of exclusion also persists. In large longitudinal studies, those who were bullied as children showed poorer physical health, greater psychological distress, and an increased risk of dying by suicide several decades later (Geoffrey et al., 2022; Takizawa et al., 2014).

ASK YOURSELF

What are the most positive and the most negative things you remember about your own adolescence? Who do you credit or blame more—your parents or your peers?

Emerging Adulthood

LOQ 16-5 What is *emerging adulthood*?

In the Western world, adolescence now roughly corresponds to the teen years. At earlier times, and in other parts of the world today, this slice of life has been much smaller (Baumeister & Tice, 1986). Shortly after sexual maturity, young people would assume adult responsibilities and status. The event might be celebrated with an elaborate initiation—a public rite of passage. The new adult would then work, partner, and have children.

When schooling became compulsory in many Western countries, independence was put on hold until after graduation. Adolescents are now taking more time to establish themselves as adults. Today's adolescents are less likely to work for pay, drive, or have romantic attachments (Twenge & Park, 2019). In the United States, the average age at first marriage has increased more than 5 years since 1960, to 29 for men, and 27 for women. In 1960, three in four women and two in three men had, by age 30, finished school, left home, become financially independent, married, and had a child. In the early twenty-first century, this was true for fewer than half of 30-year-old women and one-third of 30-year-old men (Henig, 2010). In 2016, 15 percent of 25- to 35-year-old Americans—double the 1981 proportion—were living in their parents' home (Fry, 2017).

CAMPUS EVENTS

Barbara Smaller/Cartoon Stock

"I just don't know what to do with myself in that long stretch after college but before social security."

We noted that later independence and earlier sexual maturity have widened the once-brief interlude between biological maturity and social independence. In prosperous communities, the time from age 18 to the mid-twenties is an increasingly not-yet-settled phase of life, now often called **emerging adulthood** (Arnett, 2006, 2007; Reitzle, 2006). No longer adolescents, these emerging adults—having not yet assumed full adult responsibilities and independence—feel "in between." Those furthering their education or working may manage their own time and priorities. Yet they may be doing so from their parents' home, unable to afford their own place and perhaps still emotionally dependent (Fry, 2017). Recognizing today's more gradually emerging adulthood, the U.S. government now allows dependent children up to age 26 to remain on their parents' health insurance (HHS, 2020). Research suggests that emerging adulthood may be shorter or nonexistent in non-Western cultures that may emphasize a swifter transition to adulthood (Arnett, 2015; Nelson & Chen, 2007).

"Emerging adulthood is a time of life when many different directions remain possible, when little about the future has been decided for certain, when the scope of independent exploration of life's possibilities is greater for most people than it will be at any other period of the life course." —Psychologist Jeffrey Jensen Arnett, 2000

ASK YOURSELF

What do you think makes a person an adult? Do you feel like an adult? Why or why not?

RETRIEVAL PRACTICE

RP-3 Match the psychosocial development stage below (i–viii) with the issue that Erikson believed we wrestle with at that stage (a–h).

i. Infancy	a. Generativity vs. stagnation
ii. Toddlerhood	b. Integrity vs. despair
iii. Preschool	c. Initiative vs. guilt
iv. Elementary school	d. Intimacy vs. isolation
v. Adolescence	e. Identity vs. role confusion
vi. Young adulthood	f. Competence vs. inferiority
vii. Middle adulthood	g. Trust vs. mistrust
viii. Late adulthood	h. Autonomy vs. shame and doubt

ANSWERS IN APPENDIX E

emerging adulthood a period from about age 18 to the mid-twenties, when many in Western cultures are no longer adolescents but have not yet achieved full independence as adults.

MODULE 16 REVIEW Adolescence and Emerging Adulthood

LEARNING OBJECTIVES

Test Yourself Answer these repeated Learning Objective Questions on your own (before "showing" the answers here, or checking the answers in Appendix D) to improve your retention of the concepts (McDaniel et al., 2009, 2015).

LOQ 16-1 How is *adolescence* defined, and how do physical changes affect developing teens?

LOQ 16-2 How did Piaget, Kohlberg, and later researchers describe adolescent cognitive and moral development?

LOQ 16-3 What are the social tasks and challenges of adolescence?

LOQ 16-4 How do parents and peers influence adolescents?

LOQ 16-5 What is *emerging adulthood*?

TERMS AND CONCEPTS TO REMEMBER

Test Yourself Write down the definition in your own words, then check your answer.

adolescence, p. 191
puberty, p. 191
identity, p. 197
social identity, p. 197
intimacy, p. 198
emerging adulthood, p. 199

MODULE TEST

Test Yourself Answer the following questions on your own first, then "show" the answers here, or check your answers in Appendix E.

1. Adolescence is marked by the onset of
   a. an identity crisis.
   b. puberty.
   c. moral reasoning.
   d. parent-child conflict.
2. According to Piaget, a person who can think logically about abstractions is in the ________________ stage.
3. In Erikson's stages, the primary task during adolescence is
   a. attaining formal operations.
   b. forging an identity.
   c. developing a sense of intimacy with another person.
   d. living independent of parents.
4. Some developmental psychologists refer to the period that occurs in some Western cultures from age 18 to the mid-twenties as ________________.

MODULE 17 Adulthood

Billy Bennight/The Photo Access/Alamy Stock Photo and Impress/United Archives GmbH/Alamy Stock Photo

To live is to age Actor Tom Hanks hanging out with his younger self.

The unfolding of our lives continues across the life span. It is, however, more difficult to generalize about adulthood stages than about life's early years. If you know that James is a 1-year-old and Jamal is a 10-year-old, you could say a great deal about each child. Not so with adults who differ by a similar number of years. The boss may be 30 or 60; the marathon runner may be 20 or 50; the 19-year-old may be a parent who supports a child or a child who receives an allowance. Yet our life courses are in some ways similar. Physically, cognitively, and especially socially, we differ at age 50 from our 25-year-old selves. In the discussion that follows, we recognize these differences and use three terms: *early adulthood* (roughly twenties and thirties), *middle adulthood* (to age 65), and *late adulthood* (the years after 65). Within each of these stages, people vary widely in physical, psychological, and social development.

ASK YOURSELF

Imagining the future, how do you think you might change? How might you stay the same? In what ways do you most want to grow as a person?

Physical Development

LOQ 17-1 What physical changes occur during middle and late adulthood?

Like the declining daylight after the summer solstice, our physical abilities—muscular strength, reaction time, sensory keenness, and cardiac output—all begin an almost imperceptible decline in our mid-twenties. Athletes are often the first to notice. Baseball players peak at about age 27—with 60 percent of Major League Baseball's Most Valuable Player awardees since 1985 coming within 2 years of that age (Silver, 2012). But most of us—especially those of us whose daily lives do not require top physical performance—hardly perceive the early signs of decline.

Adult abilities vary widely George Blair was, at age 92, the world's oldest barefoot water skier. He is shown here in 2002 when he first set the record, at age 87. (He died at age 98.)

Rick Doyle/Getty Images

Physical Changes in Middle Adulthood

Athletes over 40 know all too well that physical decline gradually accelerates. As a lifelong basketball player, I [DM] am playing less often and no longer racing for that loose ball. But even diminished vigor is sufficient for typical activities. During early and middle adulthood, physical vigor has less to do with age than with a person's health and exercise habits. Many physically fit 50-year-olds run 4 miles with ease, while sedentary 25-year-olds find themselves huffing and puffing up two flights of stairs.

Aging also brings a gradual decline in fertility, especially for women. For a 35- to 39-year-old woman, the chance of getting pregnant after a single act of intercourse is half that of a woman aged 19 to 26 (Dunson et al., 2002). **Menopause** (when menstrual cycles end) usually occurs within a few years of age 50. Worldwide, early menopause increases women's risk for depression (Georgakis et al., 2016; Zeng et al., 2019). Men experience a gradual decline in sperm count, testosterone level, and speed of erection and ejaculation. With declining virility and changing appearance, some people may experience distress. Seeing their first gray hairs, they may just want to dye.

Sexual activity remains satisfying, though less frequent, after middle age. This was true of 70 percent of Canadians surveyed (ages 40 to 64) and 75 percent of Finns (ages 65 to 74) (Kontula & Haavio-Mannila, 2009; Wright, 2006). In an American Association of Retired Persons sexuality survey, it was not until age 75 or older that most women and nearly half of men reported little sexual desire (DeLamater, 2012; DeLamater & Sill, 2005). As Alex Comfort (2002, p. 226) jested, "The things that stop you having sex with age are exactly the same as those that stop you riding a bicycle (bad health, thinking it looks silly, no bicycle)."

"Happy fortieth. I'll take the muscle tone in your upper arms, the girlish timbre of your voice, your amazing tolerance for caffeine, and your ability to digest french fries. The rest of you can stay."

Physical Changes in Late Adulthood

Is old age "more to be feared than death" (Juvenal, *The Satires*)? Or is life "most delightful when it is on the downward slope" (Seneca, *Epistulae ad Lucilium*)? What is it like to grow old?

LIFE EXPECTANCY From 1950 to 2015, worldwide life expectancy at birth increased from 50 to 73 years (Dicker et al., 2018). (See **FIGURE 17.1**.) What a gift—two decades more of life! In China, the United States, the United Kingdom, Canada, and Australia (to name some countries where students read this book), life expectancy had by 2019 (World Bank, 2019) risen to 76, 79, 81, 82, and 82, respectively (though the opioid epidemic and Covid-19 pandemic have reduced some of those gains). This increasing life expectancy (humanity's greatest achievement, say some) combines with decreasing birthrates: Older adults are a growing population segment, creating an increasing demand for hearing aids, retirement villages, and nursing homes. Today, 13 percent of people worldwide are 60 or older. The United Nations (2017) projects that proportion will more than double by 2100.

Throughout the life span, males are more prone to dying. Although 126 male embryos begin life for every 100 females, the sex ratio is down to 105 males for every 100 females at birth (Strickland, 1992). During the first year, male infants' death rates exceed females'

menopause the time of natural cessation of menstruation; also refers to the biological changes a woman experiences as her ability to reproduce declines. 

FIGURE 17.1
Life expectancy since 1770, by world regions With improved sanitation, modern medicine, and the introduction of antibiotics, infant mortality declined during the twentieth century and life expectancy increased (Roser, 2019).

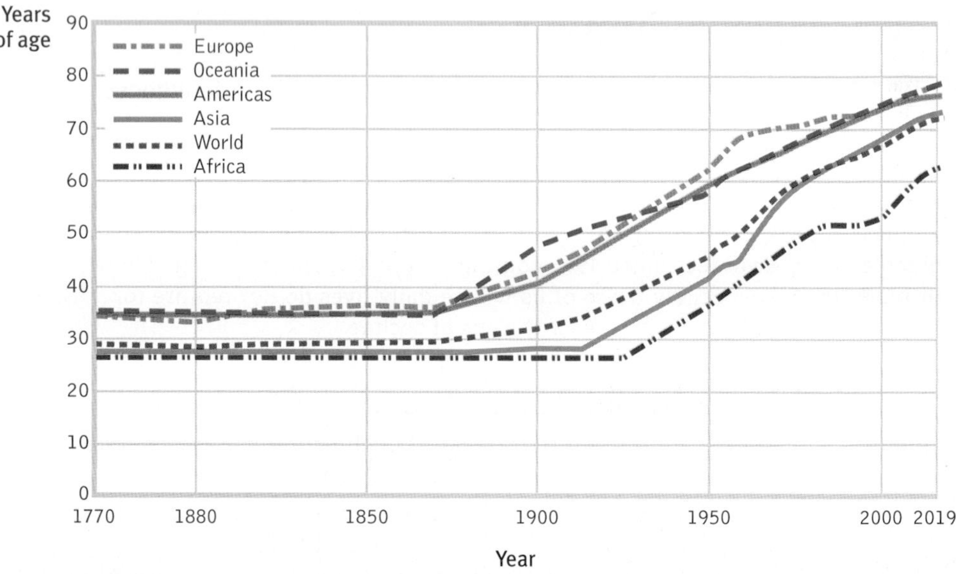
Years of age
90
80
70
60
50
40
30
20
10
0
Europe
Oceania
Americas
Asia
World
Africa
1770
1880
1850
1900
1950
2000
2019
Year

Pascal Parrot/Getty Images

Pascal Parrot/Getty Images

World record for longevity? French woman Jeanne Calment, the oldest human in history with authenticated age, died in 1998 at age 122 (Robine & Allard, 1999). At age 100, she was still riding a bike.

by one-fourth. Worldwide, women outlive men by 4.4 years (WHO, 2019). By age 100, women outnumber men 5 to 1.

But few of us live to 100. Disease strikes. The body ages. Its cells stop reproducing. It becomes frail and vulnerable to tiny insults—hot weather, a fall, a mild infection—that at age 20 would have been trivial. Tips of chromosomes, called *telomeres,* wear down, much as the tip of a shoelace frays. This wear is accelerated by smoking, obesity, or stress. Breast-fed children have longer telomeres, while those who suffer frequent abuse or bullying exhibit the biological scars of shortened telomeres (Shalev et al., 2013). As telomeres shorten, aging cells may die without being replaced with perfect genetic replicas (Epel, 2009).

Chronic anger and depression increase our risk of premature death. But low stress and good health habits enable longevity, as does a positive spirit. Researchers have even observed an intriguing *death-deferral* phenomenon (Shimizu & Pelham, 2008). Across one 15-year period, 2000 to 3000 more Americans died on the 2 days after Christmas than on Christmas and the 2 days before. The death rate also increases when people reach their birthdays, and when they survive until after other milestones, like the first day of the new millennium.

SENSORY ABILITIES, STRENGTH, AND STAMINA Although physical decline begins in early adulthood, we are not usually acutely aware of it until later in life, when the stairs get steeper, the print gets smaller, and other people seem to mumble more. Visual sharpness diminishes, as does distance perception and adaptation to light-level changes. Muscle strength, reaction time, and stamina also diminish, as do smell, hearing, and touch. In Wales, teens' loitering around a convenience store has been discouraged by a device that emits an aversive high-pitched sound that almost no one over 30 can hear (Lyall, 2005).

With age, the eye's pupil shrinks and its lens becomes less transparent, reducing the amount of light reaching the retina. A 65-year-old retina receives only about one-third as much light as its 20-year-old counterpart (Kline & Schieber, 1985). Thus, to see as well as a 20-year-old when reading or driving, a 65-year-old needs three times as much light—a reason for buying cars with untinted windshields. This also explains why older people sometimes ask younger people, "Don't you need better light for reading?"

"For some reason, possibly to save ink, the restaurants had started printing their menus in letters the height of bacteria."—Dave Barry, *Dave Barry Turns Fifty*, 1998

HEALTH As people age, they care less about what their bodies look like and more about how their bodies function. For those growing older, there is both bad and good news about health. The bad news: The body's disease-fighting immune system weakens, making older adults more susceptible to life-threatening ailments such as cancer

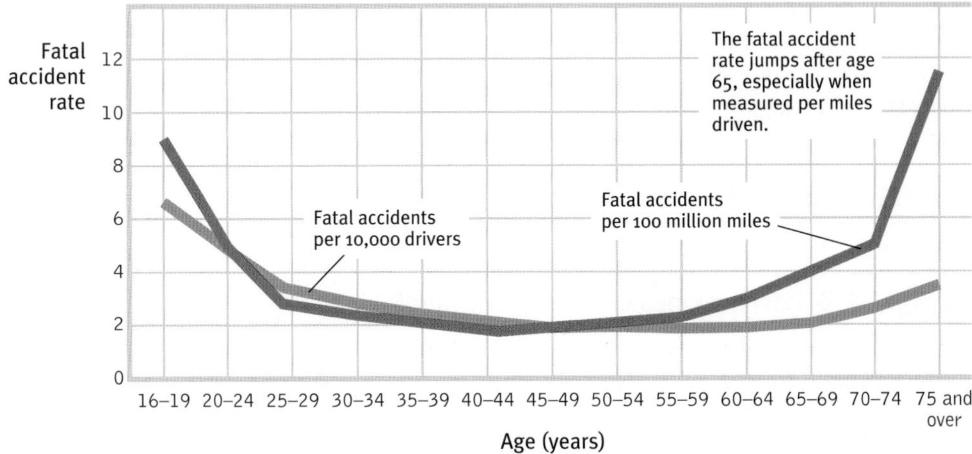

Fatal accident rate
12
10
8
6
4
2
0
The fatal accident rate jumps after age 65, especially when measured per miles driven.
Fatal accidents per 10,000 drivers
Fatal accidents per 100 million miles
16–19 20–24 25–29 30–34 35–39 40–44 45–49 50–54 55–59 60–64 65–69 70–74 75 and over
Age (years)

FIGURE 17.2
Age and driver fatalities Slowing reactions contribute to increased accident risk among those 75 and older, and older adults' greater fragility increases their risk of death when accidents happen (NHTSA, 2000). Would you favor driver exams based on performance, not age, to screen out those whose slow reactions or sensory impairments indicate accident risk?

and Covid-19. The good news: Thanks partly to a lifetime's accumulation of antibodies, people over 65 suffer fewer short-term ailments, such as common flu and cold viruses. One study found they were half as likely as 20-year-olds and one-fifth as likely as preschoolers to suffer upper respiratory infections each year (National Center for Health Statistics, 1990).

THE AGING BRAIN Up to the teen years, we process information with greater and greater speed (Fry & Hale, 1996; Kail, 1991). But compared with teens and young adults, older people take a bit more time to react, to solve perceptual puzzles, even to remember names (Bashore et al., 1997; Verhaeghen & Salthouse, 1997). At video games, most 70-year-olds are no match for a 20-year-old. This processing lag can also have deadly consequences (Aichele et al., 2016). As **FIGURE 17.2** indicates, fatal accident rates per mile driven increase sharply after age 75. By age 85, they exceed the 16-year-old level. Older drivers appear to focus well on the road ahead, but attend less to other vehicles approaching from the side (Pollatsek et al., 2012).

Brain regions important to memory begin to atrophy during aging (Fraser et al., 2015; Ritchie et al., 2015). The blood-brain barrier also breaks down, beginning in the hippocampus, which furthers cognitive decline (Montagne et al., 2015). No wonder older adults feel even older after taking a memory test: It's like "aging 5 years in 5 minutes," joked one research team (Hughes et al., 2013). In early adulthood, a small, gradual net loss of brain cells begins, contributing by age 80 to a brain-weight reduction of 5 percent or so. We know that our frontal lobes help us override undesirable urges—their slow development (not fully mature until about age 25) helps account for teen impulsivity. Late in life, some of that impulsiveness often returns as those same frontal lobes begin to atrophy, seemingly explaining older people's occasional blunt questions ("Have you put on weight?") or inappropriate comments (von Hippel, 2007, 2015). But good news: There is still some *neuroplasticity* in the aging brain, which partly compensates for what it loses by recruiting and reorganizing neural networks (Park & McDonough, 2013). During memory tasks, for example, the left frontal lobes are especially active in young adult brains, while older adult brains use both left and right frontal lobes.

EXERCISE AND AGING And more good news: Exercise slows aging, as shown in studies of identical twin pairs in which only one twin exercised (Iso-Markku et al., 2016; Rottensteiner et al., 2015). Older adults who exercise more tend to be mentally quick (Sinha et al., 2021). Physical exercise not only increases blood flow to the brain and enhances physical health, it maintains the *telomeres* that protect the chromosome ends and can slow the progression of Alzheimer's disease (Kivipelto & Håkansson, 2017; Loprinzi et al., 2015; Smith et al., 2014).

Exercise also appears to stimulate *neurogenesis*—the development of new brain cells—and neural connections, thanks perhaps to increased oxygen and nutrient flow (Ansere & Freeman, 2020; Wang, 2020). Sedentary older adults randomly assigned to aerobic exercise programs exhibited enhanced memory, sharpened judgment, and reduced risk of severe cognitive decline (Northey et al., 2018; Raji et al., 2016; G. Smith,

Hafeez

"I've been working out for six months, but all my gains have been in cognitive function."

2016). In the aging brain, exercise reduces brain shrinkage (Domingos et al., 2021). And it increases the cellular mitochondria that help power both muscles and brain cells (Steiner et al., 2011). We are more likely to rust from disuse than to wear out from overuse. Fit bodies support fit minds.

Cognitive Development

Aging and Memory

LOQ 17-2 How does memory change with age?

Among the most intriguing developmental psychology questions is whether adult cognitive abilities, such as memory, intelligence, and creativity, parallel the gradually accelerating decline of physical abilities.

"I am still learning." —Michelangelo, 1560, at age 85

As we age, we remember some things well. Looking back in later life, adults asked to recall the one or two most important events over the last half-century tend to name events from their teens or twenties (Conway et al., 2005; Rubin et al., 1998). They also display this "reminiscence bump" when asked to name their all-time favorite music, movies, and athletes (Janssen et al., 2012). Whatever people experience around this time—the Vietnam War, the space shuttle *Challenger* explosion, the Covid-19 pandemic—becomes pivotal (Pillemer, 1998; Schuman & Scott, 1989). Our teens and twenties hold so many memorable "firsts"—first kiss, first job, first day at college or university, first apartment.

If you are within 5 years of 20, what experiences from the past year will you likely never forget? (This is the time of your life you may best remember when you are 50.)

Early adulthood is indeed a peak time for some types of learning and remembering. In one test of recall, people watched video clips as 14 strangers said their names, using a common format: "Hi, I'm Larry" (Crook & West, 1990). As **FIGURE 17.3** shows, even after a second and third replay of the introductions with more personal information, younger adults consistently remembered more names than older adults did. How well older people remember depends, in part, on the task. In another experiment, when asked to *recognize* 24 words they had earlier tried to memorize, older adults showed no memory decline. When asked to *recall* that information without clues, however, the decline was greater (**FIGURE 17.4**).

Teens and young adults surpass both young children and 70-year-olds at *prospective memory* ("Remember to . . .") (Zimmermann & Meier, 2006). But older people's prospective memory remains strong when events help trigger a memory (as when walking

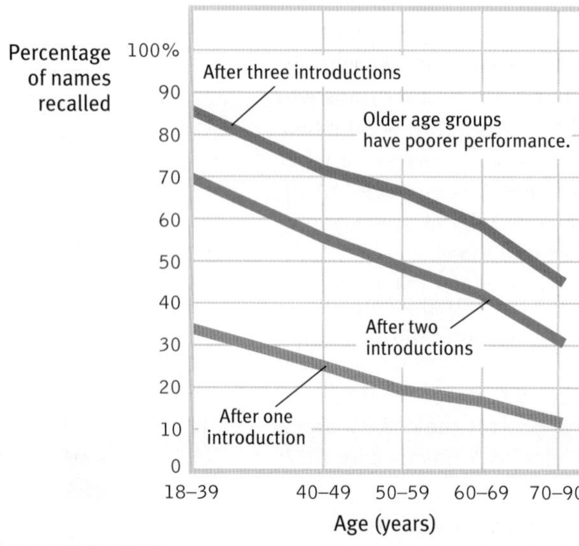
Percentage of names recalled
100%
90
80
70
60
50
40
30
20
10
0
After three introductions
Older age groups have poorer performance.
After two introductions
After one introduction
18–39
40–49
50–59
60–69
70–90
Age (years)

FIGURE 17.3
Tests of recall Recalling new names introduced once, twice, or three times is easier for younger adults than for older ones. (Data from Crook & West, 1990.)

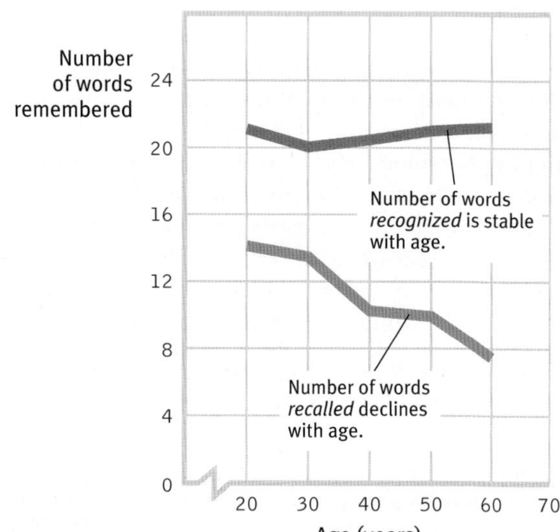
Number of words remembered
24
20
16
12
8
4
0
Number of words *recognized* is stable with age.
Number of words *recalled* declines with age.
20
30
40
50
60
70
Age (years)

FIGURE 17.4
Recall and recognition in adulthood In this experiment, the ability to *recall* new information declined during early and middle adulthood, but the ability to *recognize* new information did not. (Data from Schonfield & Robertson, 1966.)

by a convenience store triggers "Pick up milk!"). Time-based tasks ("Client meeting at 3:00 P.M.") and especially habitual tasks ("Take medications at 9:00 A.M., 2:00 P.M., and 6:00 P.M.") can be challenging (Einstein & McDaniel, 1990; Einstein et al., 1995, 1998). To minimize such problems, older adults rely more on time management and reminder cues, such as notes to themselves, and Alexa and other reminder apps (Henry et al., 2004). This might have helped John Basinger, who, at age 76, memorized all 12 volumes of John Milton's epic poem *Paradise Lost* and became the subject of a psychology journal article (Seamon et al., 2010; Weir, 2010). A local paper scheduled an interview with Basinger, which he forgot to attend. Calling the reporter to apologize, he noted the irony of forgetting his interview about memory!

In our capacity to learn and remember, as in other areas of development, we show individual differences. Younger adults vary in their abilities to learn and remember, but 70-year-olds vary much more. "Differences between the most and least able 70-year-olds become much greater than between the most and least able 50-year-olds," reported Oxford researcher Patrick Rabbitt (2006). Some 70-year-olds perform below nearly all 20-year-olds; other 70-year-olds match or outdo the average 20-year-old.

No matter how quick or slow we are, remembering seems also to depend on the type of information we are trying to retrieve. If the information is meaningless—nonsense syllables or unimportant events or experiences—then the older we are, the more errors we are likely to make (Ward et al., 2020). If the information is *meaningful,* as was *Paradise Lost* for John Basinger, older people's rich web of existing knowledge will help them to hold it. But they may take longer than younger adults to *produce* the words and things they know. Older adults also more often experience *tip-of-the-tongue* forgetting (Ossher et al., 2012). Quick-thinking game show winners have usually been young or middle-aged adults (Burke & Shafto, 2004).

Maintaining Mental Abilities

More education earlier in life predicts better cognitive ability late in life (Lövdén et al., 2020). Psychologists who study the aging mind therefore debate whether computer-based "brain fitness" training programs can simulate education, by building mental muscles that stave off cognitive decline. Our brain remains plastic throughout life (Gutchess, 2014). So, can exercising our brains on a "cognitive treadmill"—with memory, visual tracking, and problem-solving exercises—help us avoid losing our minds? One analysis of cognitive training programs showed that they consistently improved scores on tests related to their training (Simons et al., 2016). Video game playing may also enhance people's attention (Bediou et al., 2018).

Based on such findings, some computer game makers have been marketing daily brain-exercise programs for older adults. But researchers, after reviewing all the available studies, advise skepticism (Horne et al., 2021; Sala et al., 2021). Across more than 200 studies, brain-exercise programs improved performance on closely related tasks but not on unrelated tasks (Basak et al., 2020). As researcher Zach Hambrick (2014) explains, "Play a video game and you'll get better at that video game, and maybe at very similar video games"—but not at driving a car or filling out your tax return.

The Intelligence modules explore another dimension of cognitive development. As we will see, *cross-sectional studies* and *longitudinal studies* have identified mental abilities that do and do not change as people age. Age is less a predictor of memory and intelligence than is proximity to a natural death, which does give a clue to someone's mental ability. In the last three or four years of life, and especially as death approaches, cognitive decline typically accelerates (Vogel et al., 2013; Wilson et al., 2007). Researchers call this near-death drop *terminal decline* (Backman & MacDonald, 2006). Our goals also shift: We're driven less to learn and more to connect socially (Carstensen, 2011).

Markian Lozowchuk/Redux Pictures

Smart centenarian "I am very curious. . . . I wouldn't still be working if I didn't find it exciting," said pioneering neuropsychologist Brenda Milner (2017). Her landmark contributions to cognitive psychology continued at age 103 in her McGill University lab.

"The sudden knowledge of the fragility of his life narrowed his focus and altered his desires. . . . It made him visit with his grandchildren more often, put in an extra trip to see his family in India, and tamp down new ventures." —Atul Gawande, *Being Mortal: Medicine and What Matters in the End*, 2014, describing his father's terminal condition

Neurocognitive Disorders and Alzheimer's Disease

LOQ 17-3 How do neurocognitive disorders and Alzheimer's disease affect cognitive ability?

Most people who live into their nineties do so with clear minds. Some, unfortunately, suffer substantial psychological decline that is *not* typical aging. Among older adults,

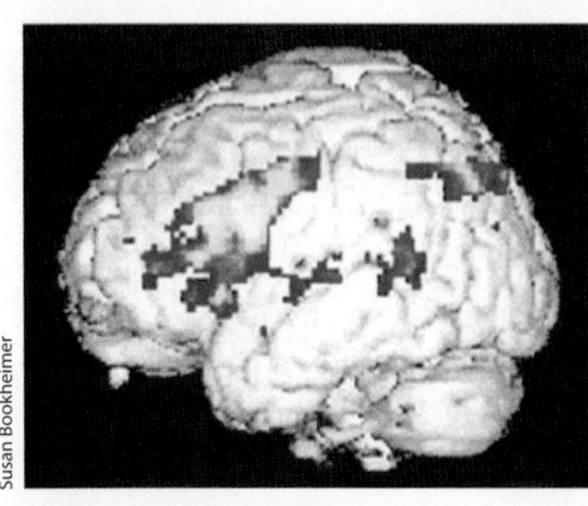
(a)

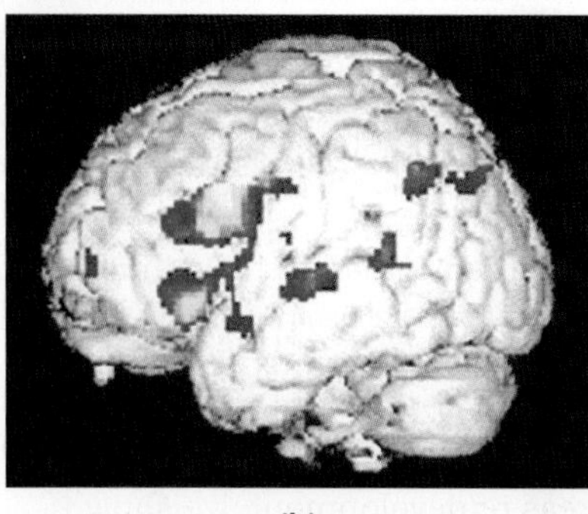
(b)

Susan Bookheimer

FIGURE 17.5
Predicting Alzheimer's disease During a memory test, MRI scans of the brains of people at risk for Alzheimer's (a) revealed more intense activity (yellow, followed by orange and red) when compared with healthy brains (b). As brain scans and genetic tests make it possible to identify those likely to suffer Alzheimer's, would you want to be tested? At what age?

hearing loss, and its associated social isolation, predicts risk of depression and accelerated mental decline (Lin et al., 2011a,b, 2013; Loughrey et al., 2018). Compared with people with good hearing, those with hearing loss show declines in memory, attention, and learning about three years earlier—but less if they get hearing aids (Maharani et al., 2018). A series of small strokes, a brain tumor, or alcohol use disorder can progressively damage the brain, causing that mental erosion we call a **neurocognitive disorder (NCD**, also called *dementia*). Heavy midlife smoking more than doubles later risk of the disorder (Rusanen et al., 2011). A common cause of NCDs is the feared brain ailment **Alzheimer's disease**, which strikes 3 percent of the world's population by age 75. Up to age 95, the incidence of mental disintegration doubles roughly every 5 years.

Alzheimer's destroys even the brightest of minds. First memory deteriorates, then reasoning. (Occasionally forgetting where you laid the car keys—the sort of "episodic memory" that subsides with typical aging—is no cause for alarm. Forgetting how to get home may suggest Alzheimer's.) Robert Sayre (1979) recalled his father shouting at his afflicted mother to "think harder," while his mother, confused, embarrassed, on the verge of tears, randomly searched the house for lost objects. As the disease runs its course, after 5 to 20 years, the person becomes emotionally flat, then disoriented and disinhibited, then incontinent, and finally mentally vacant—a sort of living death, a mere body stripped of its humanity.

Underlying the symptoms of Alzheimer's are a loss of brain cells and a deterioration of neurons that produce the neurotransmitter acetylcholine, which is vital to memory and thinking. An autopsy reveals two telltale abnormalities in these acetylcholine-producing neurons: shriveled protein filaments in the cell body, and clumps of a free-floating protein fragment that accumulate as plaque at neuron tips where synaptic communication typically occurs. Long before symptoms appear, new technologies can now test for the Alzheimer's susceptibility gene or check spinal fluid for the culprit protein fragments (De Meyer et al., 2010; Luciano et al., 2009). Such discoveries have stimulated a race to invent and test drugs that may forestall the disease, such as by reducing the activity of a memory-inhibiting neurotransmitter called GABA (Chen et al., 2014). The discovery of 21 associated genes may help (Lambert et al., 2013).

A diminishing sense of smell and slowed or wobbly walking may foretell Alzheimer's (Belluck, 2012; Wilson et al., 2007). In people at risk for Alzheimer's, brain scans (FIGURE 17.5) have also revealed—before symptoms appear—the degeneration of critical brain cells and diminished activity in Alzheimer's-related brain areas (Apostolova et al., 2006; Johnson et al., 2006; Wu & Small, 2006). When people memorized words, scans also showed diffuse brain activity in those with Alzheimer's, as if more exertion was required to achieve the same performance (Bookheimer et al., 2000).

Alzheimer's is somewhat less common among those who sleep well and who keep their minds and bodies active, through activities like reading, attending educational lectures, and running or lifting weights (Agrigoroaei & Lachman, 2011; Noble & Spires-Jones, 2019; Reynolds, 2019). In one four-decade-long study that followed nearly 1500 middle-aged Swedish women, a high fitness level delayed the onset of dementia by 9.5 years (Hörder et al., 2018). As with muscles, so with the brain: Those who use it less often lose it.

neurocognitive disorders (NCDs) acquired (not lifelong) disorders marked by cognitive deficits; often related to Alzheimer's disease, brain injury or disease, or substance abuse. Also called *dementia* in older adults.

Alzheimer's disease a neurocognitive disorder marked by neural plaques, often with onset after age 80, and entailing a progressive decline in memory and other cognitive abilities.

Social Development

LOQ 17-4 What themes and influences mark our social journey from early adulthood to death?

Try completing this statement five times: "I am ________."

In response, teens mostly describe their individual traits. Young adults more often define themselves in terms of their social roles, such as their occupation or being a parent (Hards et al., 2019). Many differences between teens, younger adults, and older adults are created by significant life events. A new job means new relationships, new expectations, and new demands. Marriage brings the joy of intimacy and the stress of merging two lives. The 3 years surrounding the birth of a child bring increased life satisfaction for most couples (Dyrdal & Lucas, 2011). The death of a loved one creates an irreplaceable loss. How do these life events shape the course of our adulthood?

social clock the culturally preferred timing of social events such as marriage, parenthood, and retirement.

Adulthood's Ages and Stages

As people enter their forties, they undergo a transition to middle adulthood, a time when they realize that life will soon be mostly behind instead of ahead of them. Some psychologists have argued that for many the *midlife transition* is a crisis, a time of great struggle, regret, or even feeling struck down by life. The popular image of the midlife crisis—an early-forties man who forsakes his family for a younger romantic partner and a hot sports car—is more a myth than reality. In surveys in many countries, unhappiness does *not* surge during the early forties (Galambos et al., 2020). One study of emotional instability in nearly 10,000 men and women found "not the slightest evidence" that distress peaks anywhere in the midlife age range (McCrae & Costa, 1990).

For the 1 in 4 middle-aged adults who report experiencing a life crisis, the trigger is not age, but a major event, such as illness, divorce, or job loss (Lachman, 2004). Some middle-aged adults describe themselves as a "sandwich generation," simultaneously supporting their aging parents and their emerging adult children or grandchildren (Riley & Bowen, 2005). With others depending on their support, middle-aged adults become especially sensitive to their social status rising or falling (Weiss & Kunzmann, 2020). Later in life, status changes matter less for people's happiness.

Life events trigger transitions to new life stages at varying ages. The **social clock**—the definition of "the right time" to leave home, get a job, marry, have children, and retire—varies from era to era and culture to culture. The once-rigid sequence has loosened; the social clock still ticks, but people feel freer to keep their own time.

Rick Cruz/Pacific Daily News/AP Photo

Social-clock adjustment We don't always follow the social clock, as Genevie Chiguina and her daughter Genaray Chiguina made clear when they graduated from Guam Community College, together!

Even *chance events* can have lasting significance, by deflecting us down one road rather than another. Albert Bandura (1982, 2005) recalled the ironic true story of a book editor who came to one of Bandura's lectures on the "Psychology of Chance Encounters and Life Paths"—and ended up marrying the woman who happened to sit next to him. The sequence that led to my [DM's] authoring this book (which was not my idea) began with my being seated near, and getting to know, a distinguished colleague at an international conference. The road to my [ND's] co-authoring this book began in a similarly unplanned manner: After stumbling on an article about my professional life, DM invited me to visit his college. There, we began a conversation that resulted in our collaboration. Chance events can change our lives.

"The important events of a person's life are the products of chains of highly improbable occurrences." —Joseph Traub, "Traub's Law," 2003

Adulthood's Commitments

Two basic aspects of our lives dominate adulthood. Erik Erikson called them *intimacy* (forming close relationships) and *generativity* (being productive and supporting future generations). Sigmund Freud (1935/1960) put this more simply: The healthy adult, he said, is one who can *love* and *work*.

LOVE More and more people live single lives, supported by close and loving friendships. Most eventually also pair up romantically. People typically flirt, fall in love, and commit—one person at a time. "Pair-bonding is a trademark of the human animal," observed anthropologist Helen Fisher (1993). From an evolutionary perspective, relatively monogamous pairing makes sense: Parents who cooperated to nurture their children to maturity were more likely to have their genes passed along to posterity than were parents who didn't.

Adult bonds of love are most satisfying and enduring when marked by a similarity of interests and values, a sharing of emotional and material support, and intimate self-disclosure. And for better or for worse, our standards have risen over the years: We now hope not only for an enduring bond, but also for a mate who is a wage earner, caregiver, intimate friend, and warm and responsive lover (Finkel, 2017). There also appears to be "vow power." Straight and gay relationships sealed with commitment more often endure

Andersen Ross/Blend Images/Alamy Stock Photo

Love Intimacy, attachment, commitment—love by whatever name—is central to healthy and happy adulthood.

"Still married after all these years?
No mystery.
We are each other's habit,
And each other's history."
—Judith Viorst, "The Secret of Staying Married," 2007

(Rosenfeld, 2014; Wilcox et al., 2019). Such bonds are especially likely to last when couples marry after age 20 and are well educated. Compared with their counterparts of 70 years ago, people in Western countries *are* better educated and marrying much later—7–8 years later for first marriages in the United States (U.S. Census Bureau, 2021). These trends may help explain why the U.S. divorce rate, which surged from 1960 to 1980, has since declined.

Might test-driving life together minimize divorce risk? In Europe, Canada, and the United States, those who live together before marriage (and especially before engagement) have had *higher* rates of divorce and marital dysfunction than those who did not (Rosenfeld & Roesler, 2019, 2021). Across developed countries, cohabiting partners were more likely than married spouses to agree that they have had recent serious doubts their relationship will last (Wang & Wilcox, 2019). Three factors contribute. First, those who live together tend to be initially less committed to the idea of enduring marriage. Second, they may become even less marriage-supporting while living together. Third, it's more awkward to break up with a cohabiting partner than with a dating partner, leading some cohabiters to marry someone "they otherwise would have left behind" (Stanley & Rhoades, 2016a,b).

Although there is more variety in relationships today, the institution of marriage endures. In Western countries, what counts as a "very important" reason to marry? Among Americans, 31 percent say financial stability, and 93 percent say love (Cohn, 2013). And marriage is a predictor of happiness, sexual satisfaction, income, and physical and mental health (Scott et al., 2010; Wilcox & Wolfinger, 2017). Between 1972 and 2018, surveys of more than 60,000 Americans revealed that 40 percent of married adults were "very happy," compared with 23 percent of those never married (NORC, 2019). Gay and lesbian adults similarly report greater happiness if married. Moreover, neighborhoods with high marriage rates typically have low rates of social pathologies such as crime, delinquency, and emotional disorders among children (Myers & Scanzoni, 2005; Wilcox et al., 2018).

What do you think? Does marriage correlate with happiness because marital support and intimacy breed happiness, because happy people more often marry and stay married, or both?

Relationships that last are not always devoid of conflict. Some couples fight but also shower each other with affection. Other couples never raise their voices yet also seldom praise each other or nuzzle. Both styles can last. After observing the interactions of 2000 couples, John Gottman and Julie Gottman (2018) reported one indicator of marital success: at least *a five-to-one ratio of positive to negative interactions*. Stable marriages provide five times more instances of smiling, touching, complimenting, and laughing than of sarcasm, criticism, and insults. So, if you want to predict which couples will stay together, don't pay attention to how passionately they are in love. The pairs who make it are more often those who refrain from putting down their partners. To prevent a cancerous negativity, successful couples learn to fight fair (to state feelings without insulting) and to steer conflict away from chaos with comments like "I know it's not your fault" or "I'll just be quiet for a moment and listen."

"To understand your parents' love, bear your own children." —Chinese proverb

Often, love bears children. For most people, this most enduring of life changes is a happy event—one that adds occasional stress but also meaning, joy (Nelson-Coffey et al., 2019; Witters, 2014). "I feel an overwhelming love for my children unlike anything I feel for anyone else," said 93 percent of U.S. mothers in a national survey (Erickson & Aird, 2005). Many fathers feel the same. A few weeks after the birth of my first child I [DM] was suddenly struck by a realization: "So *this* is how my parents felt about me!"

"Our love for children is so unlike any other human emotion. I fell in love with my babies so quickly and profoundly, almost completely independently of their particular qualities. And yet 20 years later I was (more or less) happy to see them go—I had to be happy to see them go. We are totally devoted to them when they are little and yet the most we can expect in return when they grow up is that they regard us with bemused and tolerant affection." —Developmental psychologist Alison Gopnik, "The Supreme Infant," 2010

When children begin to absorb time, money, and emotional energy, parents' satisfaction with their own relationship may decline (Doss et al., 2009). This is especially likely among employed women who, more than they expected, may also carry the burden of doing more chores at home. Putting effort into creating an equitable relationship can thus pay double dividends: greater satisfaction, which breeds better parent-child relations (Erel & Burman, 1995).

Eventually, children leave home. This departure is a significant and sometimes difficult event. But for most people, an empty nest is a happy place (Adelmann et al., 1989; Gorchoff et al., 2008). Many parents experience a "postlaunch honeymoon," especially if they maintain close relationships with their children (White & Edwards, 1990). As Daniel Gilbert (2006) said, "The only known symptom of 'empty nest syndrome' is increased smiling."

© Jose Luis Pelaez Inc/Blend Images/Corbis

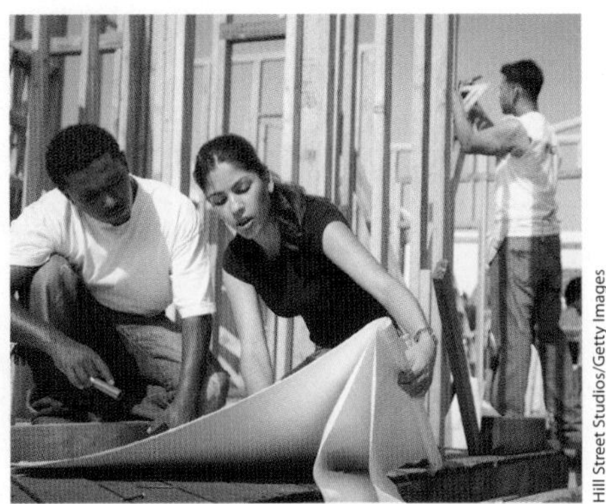
Hill Street Studios/Getty Images

Job satisfaction and life satisfaction Work can provide us with a sense of identity and competence, and opportunities for accomplishment. Perhaps this is why challenging and interesting occupations enhance people's happiness. For more on work, including discovering your own strengths, see Appendix C, Psychology at Work.

WORK For many adults, the answer to "Who are you?" depends a great deal on the answer to "What do you do?" Choosing a career path is difficult, especially during uncertain economic times. Even in the best of times, few students in their first 2 years of college or university can predict their later careers.

In the end, happiness is about having work that fits your interests and provides you with a sense of competence and accomplishment. It is giving generously of your time and resources (Mogilner & Norton, 2016; Whillans et al., 2016). It is having a close, supportive companion, or family and friends, who notice and cheer your accomplishments (Campos et al., 2015). And for some, it includes having children who love you and whom you love and feel proud of.

RETRIEVAL PRACTICE

RP-1 Freud defined the healthy adult as one who is able to ________________ and to ________________.

ANSWERS IN APPENDIX E

Well-Being Across the Life Span

LOQ 17-5 How does our well-being change across the life span?

To live is to grow older. This moment marks the oldest you have ever been and the youngest you will henceforth be. That means we all can look back with satisfaction or regret, and forward with hope or dread. When asked what they would have done differently if they could relive their lives, people's most common answer has been "taken my education more seriously and worked harder at it" (Kinnier & Metha, 1989; Roese & Summerville, 2005). Other regrets—"I should have told my father I loved him," "I regret that I never went to Europe"—have also focused less on mistakes made than on the things one *failed* to do (Gilovich & Medvec, 1995).

Cultures differ in their expectations for old age. Older adults from a Western cultural tradition tend to live independently and to seek experiences, such as ticking off items on their "bucket list" (Kitayama et al., 2020; Tsai et al., 2018). My [ND] own grandmother fit this mold, by living independently until age 97. In East Asian cultures, older adults more often live with family and help care for grandkids.

Until the very end, the over-65 years are not notably unhappy. Self-esteem and psychological well-being remain stable (Jebb et al., 2020). Gallup asked 952,739 people in 150 countries to rate their lives on a ladder from 0 ("the worst possible life") to 10 ("the best possible life"). Age—from 15 to over 90 years—gave no clue to life satisfaction (Joshanloo & Jovanović, 2021). Positive feelings, supported by enhanced emotional control, tend to grow after midlife, and negative feelings subside (Stone et al., 2010; Urry & Gross, 2010). Compared with younger Chinese and U.S. adults, for example, older adults are *more* attentive to positive news (Isaacowitz, 2012; J. Wang et al., 2015). And while young adults' depression levels rose during the Covid-19 pandemic, older adults were more emotionally resilient (Daly et al., 2021; Klaiber et al., 2021; Pierce et al., 2020).

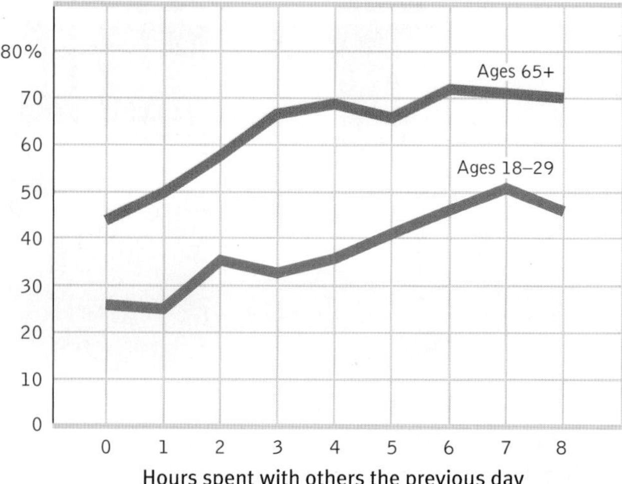
In the U.S., percentage reporting a lot of stress-free enjoyment and happiness the previous day
80%
70
60
50
40
30
20
10
0
Ages 65+
Ages 18–29
0 1 2 3 4 5 6 7 8
Hours spent with others the previous day

FIGURE 17.6
We are social creatures Both younger and older adults report greater happiness when spending time with others. (Note: This correlation could also reflect happier people being more social.) (Gallup survey data reported by Crabtree, 2011).

Like people of all ages, older adults are happiest when not alone (**FIGURE 17.6**). Compared with teens and young adults, older adults do tend to have a smaller social network, with fewer friendships and greater loneliness (Luhmann & Hawkley, 2016; Wagner et al., 2016). Older adults become less extraverted with a shrinking social network (Dunbar, 2021; Oltmanns et al., 2020), but they experience fewer problems in their relationships—less attachment anxiety, stress, and anger (Chopik et al., 2013; Fingerman & Charles, 2010). With age, we become more trusting, more helpful, and more generous (Bailey & Leon, 2019; Mayr & Freund, 2020; Sparrow et al., 2021).

The aging brain may help nurture positive feelings. Brain scans of older adults show that the amygdala, a neural processing center for emotions, responds less actively to negative events, but still responds to positive events (Mather et al., 2004). Brain-wave reactions to negative images also diminish with age (Kisley et al., 2007). As we reach the later chapters of our lives, our brain enables a contented culmination (Mather, 2016).

Moreover, unlike younger people, older adults remember the good more than the bad events of their lives (Addis et al., 2010). This happy phenomenon leaves most older people with the comforting feeling that life, on balance, has been mostly good. Biological, psychological, and social-cultural influences help explain why more and more people flourish into later life (**FIGURE 17.7**).

"At 70, I would say the advantage is that you take life more calmly. You know that 'this, too, shall pass'!" —Eleanor Roosevelt, 1954

The resilience of well-being across the life span obscures some interesting age-related emotional differences. As the years go by, feelings mellow (Brose et al., 2015). Highs become less high, lows less low. Compliments provoke less elation and criticisms less despair, as both become merely additional feedback atop a mountain of accumulated praise and blame. As we age, life therefore becomes less of an emotional roller coaster.

"The best thing about being 100 is *no peer pressure*." —Lewis W. Kuester, 2005, on turning 100

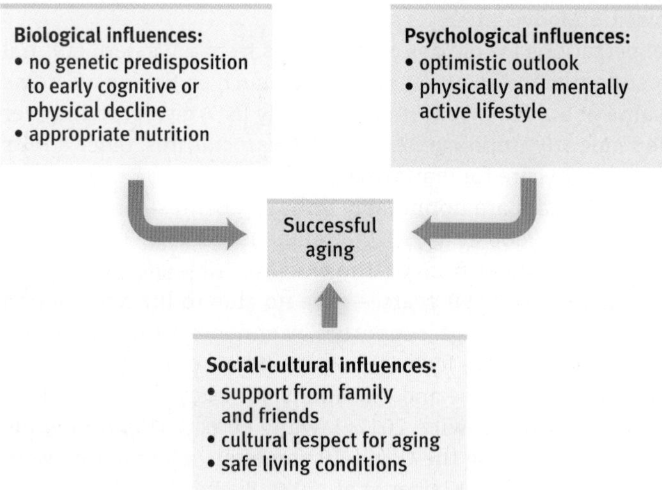
Biological influences:
• no genetic predisposition to early cognitive or physical decline
• appropriate nutrition
Psychological influences:
• optimistic outlook
• physically and mentally active lifestyle
Successful aging
Social-cultural influences:
• support from family and friends
• cultural respect for aging
• safe living conditions

FIGURE 17.7
Biopsychosocial influences on successful aging

RETRIEVAL PRACTICE

RP-2 What are some of the most significant challenges and rewards of growing old?

ANSWERS IN APPENDIX E

Death and Dying

LOQ 17-6 What range of reactions does a loved one's death trigger?

"Time is a great teacher," noted the nineteenth-century composer Hector Berlioz, "but unfortunately it kills all its pupils" (Citron, 1989).

Most of us will also cope with the deaths of relatives and friends. Typically, the most difficult separation a person experiences is the death of a partner—a loss suffered by four times more women than men. That's because it's common for women to marry men who are older than them, and also because, as noted earlier, women worldwide outlive men by more than 4 years (Ritchie, 2019; WHO, 2019).

Maintaining everyday engagements and relationships increases resilience in the face of such a loss (Infurna & Luthar, 2016). But grief is the price of love. And for some, grief is severe, especially when a loved one's death comes suddenly and before its expected time on the social clock. I [ND] experienced this when a tragic accident claimed the life of my mother at age 60. Such tragedies may trigger a year or more of memory-laden mourning, especially for those with few close, supportive relationships (Lehman et al., 1987; Smith et al., 2020).

Some losses can be unbearable. For example, one Danish long-term study of more than 1 million people found that about 17,000 of them had suffered the death of a child under 18. In the 5 years following that death, 3 percent of them had a first psychiatric hospitalization—a 67 percent higher rate than among other parents (Li et al., 2005).

Reactions to a loved one's death range more widely than most suppose. Some cultures encourage public weeping and wailing; others hide grief. Within any culture, individuals differ. Given similar losses, some people grieve hard and long, others less so (Ott et al., 2007). Some popular misconceptions persist, however:

- ***Are there stages of grieving?*** Terminally ill and bereaved people do not go through identical predictable stages, such as denial before anger (Friedman & James, 2008; Nolen-Hoeksema & Larson, 1999).
- ***Should we purge our grief?*** Those who express the strongest grief immediately do not purge their grief more quickly (Bonanno & Kaltman, 1999; Wortman & Silver, 1989). But grieving parents who try to protect their partner by "staying strong" and not discussing their child's death may actually prolong the grieving (Stroebe et al., 2013).
- ***Is therapy needed?*** Bereavement therapy and self-help groups offer support, but there is similar healing power in the passing of time, the support of friends, and the act of giving support and help to others (Baddeley & Singer, 2009; Brown et al., 2008; Neimeyer & Currier, 2009). Grieving spouses who talk often with others or receive grief counseling adjust about as well as those who grieve more privately (Bonanno, 2004; Stroebe et al., 2005).
- ***Is impending death terrifying?*** Compared to what people *imagine* they would feel when facing death, those actually facing imminent death due to terminal illness are more positive and less sad and despairing. After studying terminally ill patients' blog posts and death row inmates' last words, Amelia Goranson and her colleagues (2017) concluded that "Meeting the grim reaper may not be as grim as it seems."

Facing death with dignity and openness helps people complete the life cycle with a sense of life's meaningfulness and unity—the sense that their existence has been good and that life and death are parts of an ongoing cycle. Although death may be unwelcome, life itself can be affirmed even at death. This is especially so for people who review their lives not with despair but with what Erik Erikson called a sense of *integrity*—a feeling that one's life has been meaningful and worthwhile.

"When you were born, you cried and the world rejoiced. Live your life in a manner so that when you die the world cries and you rejoice." —Cherokee proverb

"When you're young and strong and healthy, and life stretches ahead of you, living isn't really important at all. . . . But old people know how valuable life is and how interesting." —Agatha Christie's Miss Marple, in *A Caribbean Mystery*, 1964

MODULE

17 REVIEW Adulthood

LEARNING OBJECTIVES

Test Yourself Answer these repeated Learning Objective Questions on your own (before "showing" the answers here, or checking the answers in Appendix D) to improve your retention of the concepts (McDaniel et al., 2009, 2015).

LOQ **17-1** What physical changes occur during middle and late adulthood?

LOQ **17-2** How does memory change with age?

LOQ **17-3** How do neurocognitive disorders and Alzheimer's disease affect cognitive ability?

LOQ **17-4** What themes and influences mark our social journey from early adulthood to death?

LOQ **17-5** How does our well-being change across the life span?

LOQ **17-6** What range of reactions does a loved one's death trigger?

TERMS AND CONCEPTS TO REMEMBER

Test Yourself Write down the definition in your own words, then check your answer.

menopause, p. 201

neurocognitive disorders (NCDs), p. 206

Alzheimer's disease, p. 206

social clock, p. 207

MODULE TEST

Test Yourself Answer the following questions on your own first, then "show" the answers here, or check your answers in Appendix E.

1. By age 65, a person would be most likely to experience a cognitive decline in the ability to
  a. recall and list all the important terms and concepts in a text module.
  b. select the correct definition in a multiple-choice question.
  c. recall their own birth date.
  d. practice a well-learned skill, such as knitting.

2. Freud defined the healthy adult as one who is able to love and work. Erikson agreed, observing that the adult struggles to attain intimacy and ______________.

3. Contrary to what many people assume,
  a. older people are significantly less happy than adolescents are.
  b. people become less happy as they move from their teen years into midlife.
  c. positive feelings tend to grow after midlife.
  d. those whose children have recently left home—the empty nesters—have the lowest level of happiness of all groups.

CHAPTER 6

E+/Getty Images

Sensation and Perception (Modules 18–20)

Indiana Adams awoke on New Year's Day in 2020, wanting to buy her husband exercise equipment. As she scrolled through the social media marketplace, a used psychology textbook cover caught her attention. Adams' vision is perfect, but her perception is not. A former model and actor, Adams noted that the woman on the textbook cover wore clothes that evoked memories of one of her photoshoots. But Adams has *prosopagnosia*—face blindness—which means she can't even recognize her own face.

She went into her bedroom and showed her husband the picture. "That's you!" he said. And we [DM and ND] were that textbook's authors.

People with face blindness sometimes struggle socially. On one occasion, Adams was shopping and complimented another woman on her cute clothes. When the woman didn't respond, Adams quickly realized she was actually looking at herself in the mirror—and talking to her own reflection! Others with face blindness report experiencing distress when they confuse coworkers and strangers with loved ones. Face blind people sometimes pretend to recognize people, just in case they turn out to be someone they know. One woman found a way to use her face blindness to build friendships (Dingfelder, 2019). "When I was walking to class, if someone seemed to look my way, I smiled. If they smiled, I stopped to chat," she said. "Before long, the whole campus was brimming with close, personal friends of mine."

David G. Myers C. Nathan DeWall PSYCHOLOGY 12th edition

Could that be me?

Unlike people with face blindness, most of us have a functioning area on the underside of our brain's right hemisphere that helps us recognize a familiar human face, including our own, as soon as we detect it—in only one-seventh of a second (Jacques & Rossion, 2006).

Our remarkable ability illustrates a broader principle: *Nature's sensory gifts enable each animal to obtain essential information.* Other examples:

- Human ears are most sensitive to sound frequencies that include human voices, especially a baby's cry.
- Frogs, which feed on flying insects, have cells in their eyes that fire only in response to small, dark, moving objects. A frog could starve to death knee-deep in motionless flies. But let one zoom by and the frog's "bug detector" cells snap awake. (As Kermit the Frog said, "Time's fun when you're having flies.")
- Male silkworm moths' odor receptors can detect one-billionth of an ounce of chemical sex attractant per second, released by a female silkworm one mile away (Sagan, 1977). That is why there continue to be silkworms.

In these modules, we'll look at what psychologists have learned about how we sense and perceive our world. Module 18 begins by considering some basic principles. In Module 19, we take a close look at sensory and perceptual processes in vision. Finally, Module 20 reviews our hearing, skin, chemical, and body senses.

MODULE 18 Basic Concepts of Sensation and Perception

How do we create meaning from the blizzard of sensory stimuli that bombards our bodies 24 hours a day? In its silent, cushioned, inner world, our brain floats in utter darkness. By itself, it sees nothing. It hears nothing. It feels nothing. *So, how does the world out there get in?* To phrase the question scientifically: How do we construct our representations of the external world? How do a campfire's flicker, crackle, heat, and smoky scent activate neural connections? And how, from this living neurochemistry, do we create our conscious experience of the fire's motion and temperature, its aroma and beauty?

Processing Sensations and Perceptions

LEARNING OBJECTIVE QUESTION LOQ **18-1** What are *sensation* and *perception?* What do we mean by *bottom-up processing* and *top-down processing?*

Indiana Adams' curious mix of "perfect vision" and face blindness illustrates the distinction between *sensation* and *perception*. When she looks at a friend, her **sensation** is normal. Her **sensory receptors** detect the same information any sighted person's would, and her nervous system transmits that information to her brain. Her **perception**—the processes by which her brain organizes and interprets sensory input—is *almost* normal. Thus, she may recognize people from their hair, gait, voice, or particular physique, just not from their face. Her experience is much like the struggle any human would have trying to recognize a specific penguin.

Under normal circumstances, sensation and perception blend into one continuous process. As your brain absorbs the information in FIGURE 18.1, **bottom-up processing** enables your sensory systems to detect the lines, angles, and colors that form the images. Using **top-down processing**, you interpret what your senses detect. Our perceived world is our brain's explanation of incoming sensations.

sensation the process by which our sensory receptors and nervous system receive and represent stimulus energies from our environment.

sensory receptors sensory nerve endings that respond to stimuli.

perception the process by which our brain organizes and interprets sensory information, enabling us to recognize objects and events as meaningful.

bottom-up processing information processing that begins with the sensory receptors and works up to the brain's integration of sensory information.

top-down processing information processing guided by higher-level mental processes, as when we construct perceptions drawing on our experience and expectations.

Transduction

LOQ 18-2 What three steps are basic to all of our sensory systems?

Your sensory systems perform an amazing feat: They convert outside energy into a form our brain can use. Vision processes light energy. Hearing processes sound waves. All our senses

- ***receive*** sensory stimulation, often using specialized receptor cells,
- ***transform*** that stimulation into neural impulses, and
- ***deliver*** the neural information to our brain.

The process of converting one form of energy into another that our brain can use is called **transduction**. Transduction is rather like translation—of a physical energy such as light waves into the brain's electrochemical language. **Psychophysics** studies the relationships between the physical energy we can detect and its effects on our psychological experiences.

How do we see? Hear? Feel pain? Taste? Smell? Keep our balance? In each case, one of our sensory systems receives, transforms, and delivers the information to our brain. And our senses work together.

Let's first explore some strengths and weaknesses in our ability to detect and interpret stimuli in the sea of energy around us.

FIGURE 18.1
What's going on here? Our sensory and perceptual processes work together to help us sort out complex images, including the hidden donkey rider in Sandro Del-Prete's drawing, *Homage to Leonardo da Vinci.*

RETRIEVAL PRACTICE

RP-1 What is the rough distinction between sensation and perception?

ANSWERS IN APPENDIX E

Thresholds

LOQ 18-3 How do *absolute thresholds* and *difference thresholds* differ?

At this moment, we are being struck by X-rays and radio waves, ultraviolet and infrared light, and sound waves of very high and very low frequencies. To all of these we are blind and deaf. Other animals with differing needs detect a world that lies beyond our experience. Migrating birds stay on course aided by an internal magnetic compass. Bats and dolphins locate prey using sonar, bouncing echoing sound off objects. Bees navigate on cloudy days by detecting invisible (to us) polarized light.

Our senses open the shades just a crack, allowing us a restricted awareness of this vast sea of energy. But for our needs, this is enough.

transduction conversion of one form of energy into another. In sensation, the transforming of physical energy, such as sights, sounds, and smells, into neural impulses our brain can interpret.

psychophysics the study of relationships between the physical characteristics of stimuli, such as their intensity, and our psychological experience of them.

absolute threshold the minimum stimulus energy needed to detect a particular stimulus 50 percent of the time.

Absolute Thresholds

To some stimuli we are exquisitely sensitive. Standing atop a mountain on an utterly dark, clear night, most of us could see a candle flame atop another mountain 30 miles (nearly 50 kilometers) away. We could feel the wing of a bee falling on our cheek. We could smell a single drop of perfume in a three-room apartment (Galanter, 1962).

German scientist and philosopher Gustav Fechner (1801–1887) studied the edge of our awareness of these faint stimuli, which he called an **absolute threshold**. To test your absolute threshold for sounds, a hearing specialist would send tones, at varying levels, into each of your ears and record whether you could hear each tone (**FIGURE 18.2**). The test results would show the point where, for any sound frequency, half the time you could detect the sound and half the time you could not. That 50-50 point would define your absolute threshold.

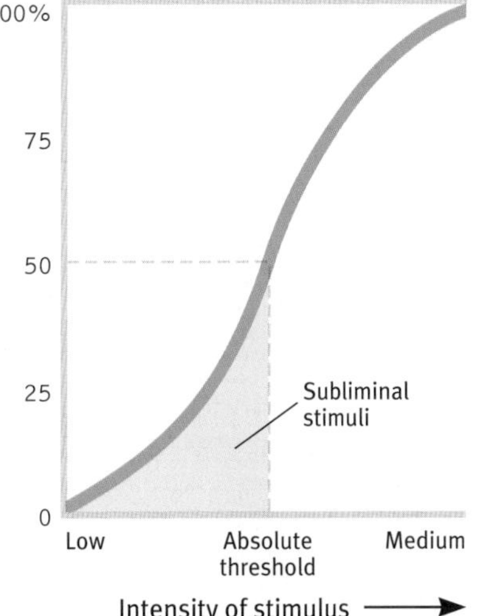
Percentage of correct detections
100%
75
50
25
0
Subliminal stimuli
Low
Absolute threshold
Medium
Intensity of stimulus

FIGURE 18.2
Threshold detected Hearing tests locate our thresholds for various sound frequencies.

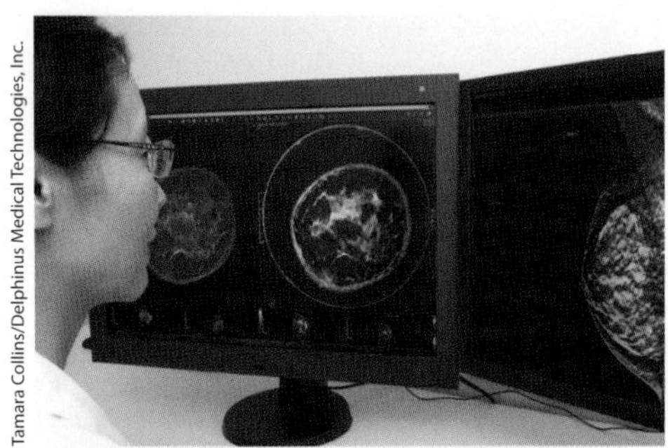

Tamara Collins/Delphinus Medical Technologies, Inc.

Signal success When reading mammograms, health professionals seek to detect the presence of a faint cancer stimulus *(signal)* amid background stimulation *(noise)*, and without raising false alarms. New 3-D ultrasound breast-imaging technologies aim to clarify the signal and reduce the rate of false positive results.

signal detection theory a theory predicting how and when we detect the presence of a faint stimulus *(signal)* amid background stimulation *(noise)*. Assumes there is no single absolute threshold and that detection depends partly on a person's experience, expectations, motivation, and alertness.

subliminal stimulation presenting something below one's absolute threshold for conscious awareness.

priming the activation, often unconsciously, of certain associations, thus predisposing one's perception, memory, or response.

difference threshold the minimum difference between two stimuli required for detection 50 percent of the time. We experience the difference threshold as a *just noticeable difference* (or *jnd*).

Weber's law the principle that, to be perceived as different, two stimuli must differ by a constant minimum percentage (rather than a constant amount).

Detecting a weak stimulus, or signal (such as a hearing-test tone), depends not only on its strength but also on our psychological state—our experience, expectations, motivation, and alertness. **Signal detection theory** predicts when we will detect weak signals (measured as our ratio of "hits" to "false alarms"). Signal detection theorists seek to understand why people respond differently to the same stimuli, and why the same person's reactions vary as circumstances change.

Stimuli you cannot consciously detect 50 percent of the time are **subliminal**—below your absolute threshold (Figure 18.2). One experiment using subliminal stimuli illustrated the deep reality of sexual orientation. As people gazed at the center of a screen, a nude person's photo was flashed on one side and a scrambled version of the photo on the other side (Jiang et al., 2006). Because a colored checkerboard immediately masked the nude images, viewers consciously perceived nothing but flashes of color and so were unable to state on which side the nude had appeared. To test whether this unseen image had unconsciously attracted their attention, the experimenters then flashed a geometric figure on one side or the other. This, too, was quickly followed by a masking stimulus. When asked to give the figure's angle, straight men guessed more accurately when it appeared where a nude *woman* had been a moment earlier. Gay men and straight women guessed more accurately when the geometric figure replaced a nude *man*. Though not consciously perceived, the more appealing sexual image had drawn their attention.

This experiment indicates that sexual orientation is something deeper than a conscious choice. And it illustrates how the unconscious mind is like the wind: We don't see it, but we see its effects. When your own face appears on a screen faster than you can perceive it consciously, researchers can nevertheless detect your brain's response (Wójcik et al., 2019). The brain knows what the conscious mind doesn't. So, can we be *controlled* by subliminal messages? (See Thinking Critically About: Subliminal Stimulation and Subliminal Persuasion.)

Difference Thresholds

To function effectively, we need absolute thresholds low enough to allow us to detect important sights, sounds, textures, tastes, and smells. We also need to detect small differences among stimuli. A musician must detect minute discrepancies when tuning an instrument. Parents must detect the sound of their own child's voice amid other children's voices. Even after 2 years of living in Scotland, all lamb *baas* sounded alike to my [DM's] ears. But not to lamb mothers. After shearing, I observed, each ewe would streak directly to the *baa* of *her* lamb amid the chorus of other distressed lambs.

Eric Isselee/Shutterstock

The **difference threshold** (or the *just noticeable difference [jnd]*) is the minimum stimulus difference a person can detect half the time. That detectable difference increases with the size of the stimulus. If we listen to our music at 40 decibels, we might barely detect an added 5 decibels (the jnd). But if we increase the volume to 110 decibels, we probably won't detect an additional 5-decibel change.

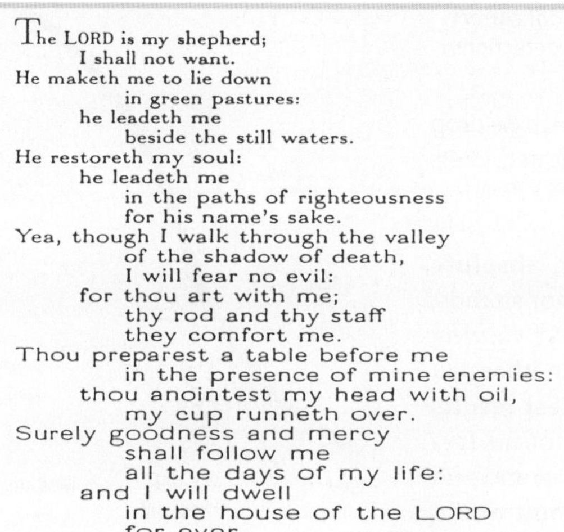

The LORD is my shepherd;
I shall not want.
He maketh me to lie down
in green pastures:
he leadeth me
beside the still waters.
He restoreth my soul:
he leadeth me
in the paths of righteousness
for his name's sake.
Yea, though I walk through the valley
of the shadow of death,
I will fear no evil:
for thou art with me;
thy rod and thy staff
they comfort me.
Thou preparest a table before me
in the presence of mine enemies:
thou anointest my head with oil,
my cup runneth over.
Surely goodness and mercy
shall follow me
all the days of my life:
and I will dwell
in the house of the LORD
for ever.

The difference threshold In this copy of the Twenty-third Psalm, each line of the typeface increases in size slightly. How many lines are required for you to experience a just noticeable difference?

In the late 1800s, German physician Ernst Weber described a principle so simple and so widely applicable that we still refer to it as **Weber's law**: For an average person to perceive a difference, two stimuli must differ by a constant minimum *percentage* (not a constant *amount*). The exact percentage varies, depending on the stimulus.

LOQ 18-4 How are we affected by subliminal stimulation?

Thinking Critically About:
Subliminal Stimulation and Subliminal Persuasion

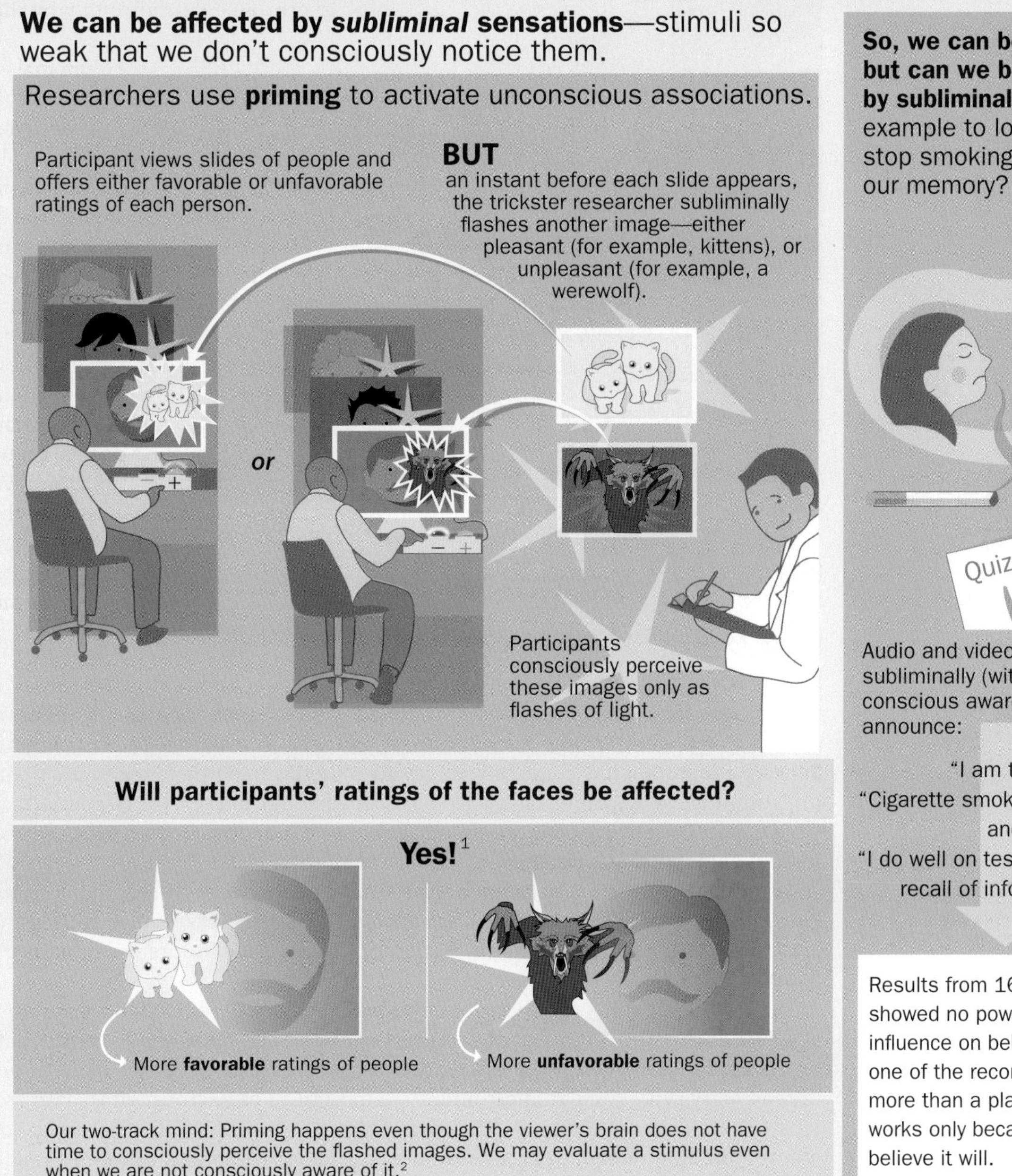

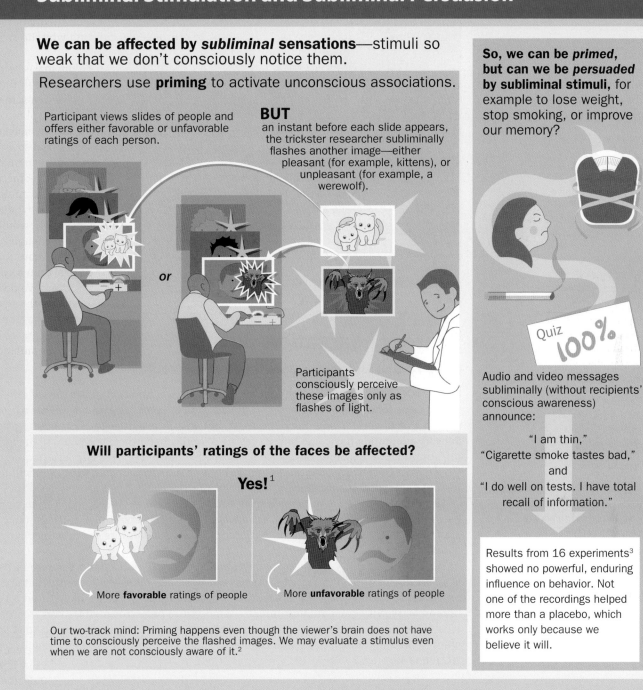

We can be affected by *subliminal* sensations—stimuli so weak that we don't consciously notice them.
Researchers use **priming** to activate unconscious associations.
Participant views slides of people and offers either favorable or unfavorable ratings of each person.
BUT
an instant before each slide appears, the trickster researcher subliminally flashes another image—either pleasant (for example, kittens), or unpleasant (for example, a werewolf).
or
Participants consciously perceive these images only as flashes of light.
Will participants' ratings of the faces be affected?
Yes![1]
More **favorable** ratings of people
More **unfavorable** ratings of people
Our two-track mind: Priming happens even though the viewer's brain does not have time to consciously perceive the flashed images. We may evaluate a stimulus even when we are not consciously aware of it.[2]
So, we can be *primed*, but can we be *persuaded* by subliminal stimuli, for example to lose weight, stop smoking, or improve our memory?
Quiz
100%
Audio and video messages subliminally (without recipients' conscious awareness) announce:
"I am thin,"
"Cigarette smoke tastes bad,"
and
"I do well on tests. I have total recall of information."
Results from 16 experiments[3] showed no powerful, enduring influence on behavior. Not one of the recordings helped more than a placebo, which works only because we believe it will.

1. Krosnick et al., 1992. 2. Ferguson & Zayas, 2009. 3. Greenwald et al., 1991, 1992.

Two lights, for example, must differ in intensity by 8 percent. Two objects must differ in weight by 2 percent. And two tones must differ in frequency by only 0.3 percent (Teghtsoonian, 1971).

RETRIEVAL PRACTICE

RP-2 Using sound as your example, explain how these concepts differ: *absolute threshold, subliminal stimulation*, and *difference threshold*.

ANSWERS IN APPENDIX E

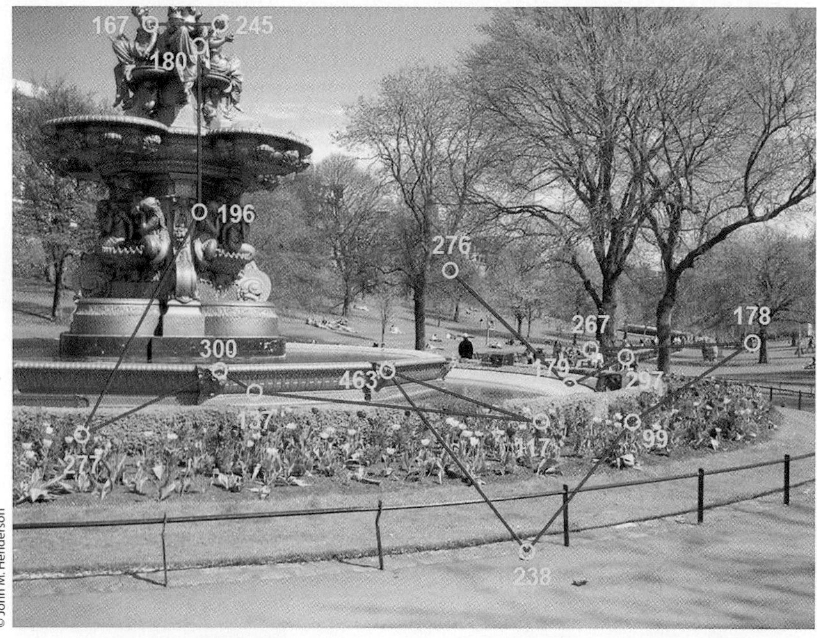
167
245
180
196
276
267
178
300
463
99
238
© John M. Henderson

FIGURE 18.3
The jumpy eye Our gaze jumps from one spot to another every third of a second or so. Eye-tracking equipment recorded a person's eye movements while they looked at this photograph of Edinburgh's Princes Street Gardens (Henderson, 2007). The circles represent visual fixations, and the numbers indicate the time of fixation in milliseconds (300 milliseconds = 3/10ths of a second).

Sensory Adaptation

LOQ 18-5 What is the function of sensory adaptation?

It's one of life's little curiosities: You may not notice a fan's noise until it's turned off. The same is true for odors. Sitting down on the bus, you are struck by your seatmate's heavy perfume. You wonder how they endure it, but within minutes you no longer notice. **Sensory adaptation** has come to your rescue. When constantly exposed to an unchanging stimulus, we become less aware of it because our nerve cells fire less frequently. (To experience sensory adaptation, put a rubber band around your wrist. You will feel it—but only for a few moments.)

"We need above all to know about changes; no one wants or needs to be reminded 16 hours a day that [their] shoes are on." —Neuroscientist David Hubel (1979)

Why, then, if we stare at an object without flinching, does it *not* vanish from sight? Because, unnoticed by us, our eyes are always moving. This continual flitting from one spot to another ensures that stimulation on the eyes' receptors continually changes (FIGURE 18.3).

What if we actually could stop our eyes from moving? Would sights seem to vanish, as odors do? To find out, psychologists have devised ingenious instruments that maintain a constant image on the eye's inner surface. Imagine that we have fitted a volunteer, Mary, with such an instrument—a miniature projector mounted on a contact lens. When Mary's eye moves, the image from the projector moves as well. So everywhere that Mary looks, the scene is sure to go. Can you guess the weird result? (See FIGURE 18.4.)

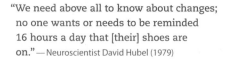

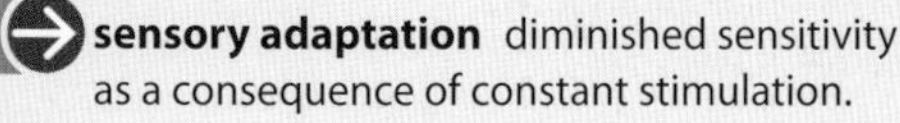
sensory adaptation diminished sensitivity as a consequence of constant stimulation.

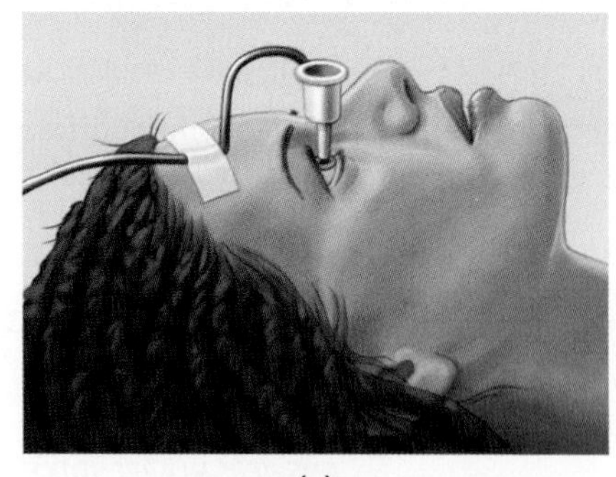
(a)

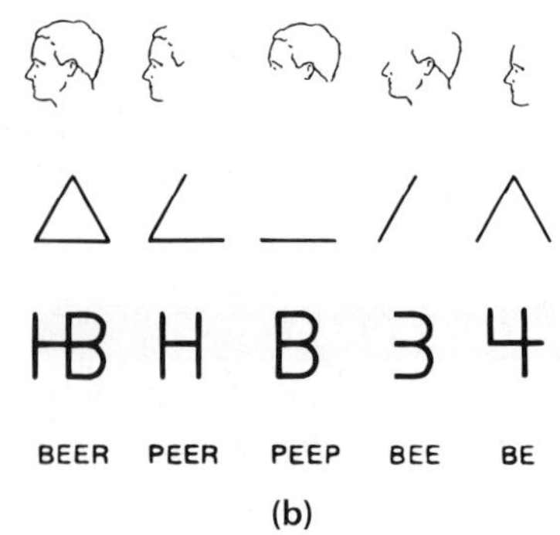
HB H B 3 4
BEER PEER PEEP BEE BE
(b)

FIGURE 18.4
Sensory adaptation: Now you see it, now you don't! (a) A projector mounted on a contact lens makes the projected image move with the eye. (b) Initially, the person sees the stabilized image. But thanks to sensory adaptation, her eye soon becomes accustomed to the unchanging stimulus. Rather than the full image, she begins to see fragments fading and reappearing.

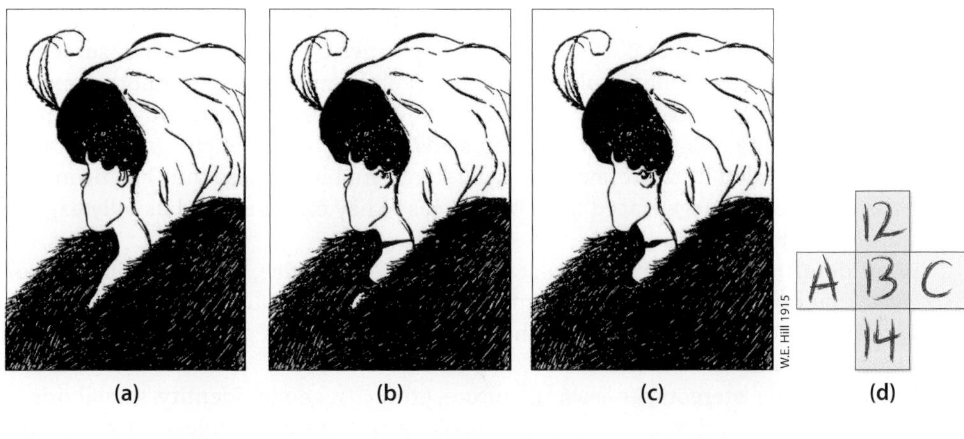
W.E. Hill 1915
12
A
C
14
(a)
(b)
(c)
(d)

FIGURE 18.5
Two examples of perceptual set Show a friend *either* image (a) or image (c). Then show image (b) and ask, "What do you see?" Whether your friend reports seeing an old woman's face or young woman's profile may depend on which of the other two drawings they viewed first. In images (a) and (c), the meaning is clear, and it will establish perceptual expectations (Boring, 1930). In image (d), do you perceive a number or letter in the middle? If you read from left to right, you likely perceive a letter. But if you read from top to bottom, you may perceive the same center image as a number.

Although sensory adaptation reduces our sensitivity, it offers an important benefit: freedom to focus on our environment's informative changes. Technology companies understand the attention-grabbing power of changing stimulation: Our phone's notifications are hard to ignore. If we're performing other tasks, these intrusions can harm our performance (Stothart et al., 2015).

The point to remember: Our sensory system is alert to novelty; bore it with repetition and it frees our attention for more important things. *We perceive the world not exactly as it is, but as it is useful for us to perceive it.*

ASK YOURSELF

In the last day, what types of sensory adaptation have you experienced?

RETRIEVAL PRACTICE

RP-3 Why is it that after wearing shoes for a while, you cease to notice them (until questions like this draw your attention back to them)?

ANSWERS IN APPENDIX E

Perceptual Set

LOQ 18-6 How do our expectations, contexts, motivation, and emotions influence our perceptions?

perceptual set a mental predisposition to perceive one thing and not another.

To see is to believe. As we less fully appreciate, to believe is to see. Through experience, we come to expect certain results. Those expectations may give us a **perceptual set**, a set of mental tendencies and assumptions that affects, top-down, what we hear, taste, feel, and see. Consider **FIGURE 18.5**.

Everyday examples abound of perceptual set—of "mind over mind." In 1972, a British newspaper published unretouched photographs of a "monster" in Scotland's Loch Ness, proclaiming them "the most amazing pictures ever taken." If this information creates in you the same expectations it did in most of the paper's readers, you, too, will see the monster in a similar photo in **FIGURE 18.6**. But when a skeptical researcher approached the original photos with different expectations, he saw a curved tree limb—as had others the day that photo was shot (Campbell, 1986). What a difference a new perceptual set makes.

Perceptual set also affects what we hear—"stuffy nose" or "stuff he knows"? Consider the kindly airline pilot who, on a takeoff run, looked over at his sad co-pilot and said, "Cheer up." Expecting to hear the usual "Gear up," the co-pilot promptly raised the wheels—before they left the ground (Reason & Mycielska, 1982). Or ask the little boy who loved the prelude to Major League Baseball games when people rose to sing to him: "José, can you see?" Or tell people about a couple who suffered from their experience with some "bad sects" and (depending on what's on their mind) they may hear something quite different ("bad sex").

FIGURE 18.6
Believing is seeing What do you perceive? Is this Nessie, the Loch Ness monster, or a log?

Keystone/ Hulton Archive/Getty Images

Will Santino/CartoonStock

"Can I see your I.D? Wait, never mind. Wait—yeah, I need to see your I.D? Wait—"

Our expectations can influence our taste perceptions, too. In one experiment, by a 6-to-1 margin, preschool children thought french fries tasted better when served in a McDonald's bag rather than a plain white bag (Robinson et al., 2007). Another experiment invited campus bar patrons at Massachusetts Institute of Technology to sample free beer (Lee et al., 2006). When researchers added a few drops of vinegar to a brand-name beer and called it "MIT brew," the tasters preferred it—unless they had been told they were drinking vinegar-laced beer. In that case, they expected, and usually experienced, a worse taste.

What determines our perceptual set? Through experience, we form concepts, or *schemas,* that organize and interpret unfamiliar information. Our preexisting schemas for monsters and tree limbs influence how we apply top-down processing to interpret ambiguous sensations.

In everyday life, stereotypes—about culture, ethnicity, gender identity, sexual orientation, income, age, abilities, and more—can color perception. People (especially children) have, for example, perceived new baby "David" as bigger and stronger than when the same infant was called "Diana" (Stern & Karraker, 1989). Some differences, it seems, exist merely in the eyes of their beholders.

FIGURE 18.7
Culture and context effects What is above the woman's head? In one classic study, most rural East Africans questioned said the woman was balancing a metal box or can on her head (a typical way to carry water at that time). They also perceived the family as sitting under a tree. Westerners, used to tap water and box-like homes with corners, were more likely to perceive the family as being indoors, with the woman sitting under a window (Gregory & Gombrich, 1973).

Context, Motivation, and Emotion

Perceptual set influences how we interpret stimuli. But our immediate context, and the motivation and emotion we bring to a situation, also affect our interpretations.

Context

Social psychologist Lee Ross invites us to recall our own perceptions in different contexts: "Ever notice that when you're driving you hate . . . the way [pedestrians] saunter through the crosswalk, almost daring you to hit them, but when you're walking you hate drivers?" (Jaffe, 2004). Our expectations influence our perceptions constantly: Why is that person standing so close while speaking to me *(is this a threat, or just a cultural difference)*? Or so far away *(is it disinterest, or just their usual behavior)*?

Some other examples of the power of context:

- Imagine that you are exposed to only part of a conversation and hear the words "eel is on the wagon." Likely, you would actually perceive the first word as *wheel.* If, however, you'd heard the words "eel is on the orange," you would more likely perceive the first word as *peel.* In each case, the context creates an expectation that, top-down, influences our perception (Grossberg, 1995).
- Cultural context helps inform our perceptions, so it's not surprising that people's varying cultures may cause them to view things differently, as in **FIGURE 18.7**.

Inti St. Clair/Getty Images

Hearing hype Why do people pay millions of dollars for old Italian violins? Many people believe the sound quality is unmatched. But a recent study showed that, under blind conditions, expert violin soloists generally preferred the sound of less expensive, modern violins over expensive, old Italian violins (C. Fritz et al., 2017).

- How is the woman in **FIGURE 18.8** feeling? The context provided in **FIGURE 18.9** will leave no doubt.

Craig Klomparens/Hope College

FIGURE 18.8
What emotion is this? (See Figure 18.9)

ASK YOURSELF

Can you think of a time when your expectations caused you to misperceive the intentions of a person or a group? How might you use awareness of *context effects* to modify your expectations next time?

RETRIEVAL PRACTICE

RP-4 Does *perceptual set* involve bottom-up or top-down processing? Why?

ANSWERS IN APPENDIX E

Motivation

Motives give us energy as we work toward a goal. Like context, they can bias our interpretations of neutral stimuli:

- Desirable objects, such as a water bottle viewed by a thirsty person, seem closer than they really are (Balcetis & Dunning, 2010). And closeness can increase desire itself. Straight men, for example, find women who are physically closer more desirable than those who are further away (Shin et al., 2019).
- A to-be-climbed hill can seem steeper when we are carrying a heavy backpack, and a walking destination further away when we are feeling tired (Burrow et al., 2016; Philbeck & Witt, 2015; Proffitt, 2006a,b). When heavy people lose weight, hills and stairs no longer seem so steep (Taylor-Covill & Eves, 2016).
- A softball appears bigger when you're hitting well, as researchers observed after asking players to choose a circle the size of the ball they had just hit well or poorly. There's also a reciprocal phenomenon: Seeing a target as bigger—as happens when athletes focus directly on a target—improves performance (Witt et al., 2012).

"When you're hitting the ball, it comes at you looking like a grapefruit. When you're not, it looks like a black-eyed pea." —Former Major League Baseball player George Scott

Emotion

Other studies have demonstrated that emotions can shove our perceptions in one direction or another:

- Hearing sad music can predispose people to perceive a sad meaning in spoken homophonic words—*mourning* rather than *morning*, *die* rather than *dye*, *pain* rather than *pane* (Halberstadt et al., 1995). And hearing major-key (bright, cheery-sounding) music, such as Beyoncé's "Single Ladies," speeds up identification of happy emotion words (Tay & Ng, 2019).
- When angry, people more often perceive neutral objects as guns (Baumann & DeSteno, 2010). When hungry, people tend to find larger bodies more attractive (Saxton et al., 2020).
- Worry about a panic attack (as with panic disorder) leads people to misperceive common physical sensations (heart pounding, breathlessness) as a panic attack (Maisto et al., 2021).
- When made to feel mildly upset by subliminal exposure to a scowling face, people perceive a neutral face as less attractive and less likable (Anderson et al., 2012).

The point to remember: Much of what we perceive comes not just from what's "out there," but also from what's behind our eyes and between our ears. Our experiences, assumptions, expectations—and even our context, motivation, and emotions—can shape and color our views of reality through top-down processing.

FIGURE 18.9
Context makes clearer The Hope College volleyball team celebrates its national championship-winning moment.

Craig Klomparens/Hope College

MODULE 18 REVIEW Basic Concepts of Sensation and Perception

LEARNING OBJECTIVES

Test Yourself Answer these repeated Learning Objective Questions on your own (before "showing" the answers here, or checking the answers in Appendix D) to improve your retention of the concepts (McDaniel et al., 2009, 2015).

LOQ 18-1 What are *sensation* and *perception*? What do we mean by *bottom-up processing* and *top-down processing*?

LOQ 18-2 What three steps are basic to all our sensory systems?

LOQ 18-3 How do *absolute thresholds* and *difference thresholds* differ?

LOQ 18-4 How are we affected by subliminal stimulation?

LOQ 18-5 What is the function of sensory adaptation?

LOQ 18-6 How do our expectations, contexts, motivation, and emotions influence our perceptions?

TERMS AND CONCEPTS TO REMEMBER

Test Yourself Write down the definition in your own words, then check your answer.

sensation, p. 214
sensory receptors, p. 214
perception, p. 214
bottom-up processing, p. 214
top-down processing, p. 214
transduction, p. 215
psychophysics, p. 215
absolute threshold, p. 215
signal detection theory, p. 216
subliminal stimulation, p. 216
priming, p. 216
difference threshold, p. 216
Weber's law, p. 216
sensory adaptation, p. 218
perceptual set, p. 219

MODULE TEST

Test Yourself Answer the following questions on your own first, then "show" the answers here, or check your answers in Appendix E.

1. Sensation is to ____________ as perception is to ____________.
   a. absolute threshold; difference threshold
   b. bottom-up processing; top-down processing
   c. interpretation; detection
   d. grouping; priming
2. The process by which we organize and interpret sensory information is called ____________.
3. Subliminal stimuli are
   a. too weak to be processed by the brain.
   b. consciously perceived more than 50 percent of the time.
   c. strong enough to affect our behavior at least 75 percent of the time.
   d. below our absolute threshold for conscious awareness.
4. Another term for *difference threshold* is the ____________ ____________ ____________.
5. Weber's law states that for a difference to be perceived, two stimuli must differ by
   a. a fixed or constant energy amount.
   b. a constant minimum percentage.
   c. a constantly changing amount.
   d. more than 7 percent.
6. Sensory adaptation helps us focus on
   a. visual stimuli.
   b. auditory stimuli.
   c. constant features of the environment.
   d. important changes in the environment.
7. Our perceptual set influences what we perceive. This mental tendency reflects our
   a. experiences, assumptions, and expectations.
   b. sensory adaptation.
   c. priming ability.
   d. difference thresholds.

19 Vision: Sensory and Perceptual Processing

For those of us with vision, our eyes receive light energy and *transduce* (transform) it into neural messages. Our brain—in one of life's greatest wonders—then creates what we consciously see. How does such a taken-for-granted yet extraordinary thing happen?

wavelength the distance from the peak of one light or sound wave to the peak of the next. Electromagnetic wavelengths vary from the short blips of gamma rays to the long pulses of radio transmission.

hue the dimension of color that is determined by the wavelength of light; what we know as the color names *blue, green,* and so forth.

intensity the amount of energy in a light wave or sound wave, which influences what those with typical vision or hearing perceive as brightness or loudness. Intensity is determined by the wave's amplitude (height).

Light Energy and Eye Structures

LOQ 19-1 What are the characteristics of the energy that we see as visible light? What structures in the eye help focus that energy?

The Stimulus Input: Light Energy

When those with vision look at a bright red tulip, the stimuli striking the eyes are not particles of the color red, but pulses of electromagnetic energy that the visual system *perceives* as red. What we see as visible light is but a thin slice of the wide spectrum of electromagnetic energy, ranging from imperceptibly short gamma waves to the very long waves of radio transmission (**FIGURE 19.1**). Other portions are visible to other animals. Bees, for instance, cannot see what we perceive as red, but they can see ultraviolet light.

Light travels in waves, and the shape of those waves influences what we see. Light's **wavelength** is the distance from one wave peak to the next (**FIGURE 19.2A**). Wavelength determines **hue**, the color we experience, such as the tulip's red petals or green leaves. A light wave's *amplitude,* or height, determines its **intensity**—the amount of energy the wave contains. Intensity influences *brightness* (**FIGURE 19.2B**).

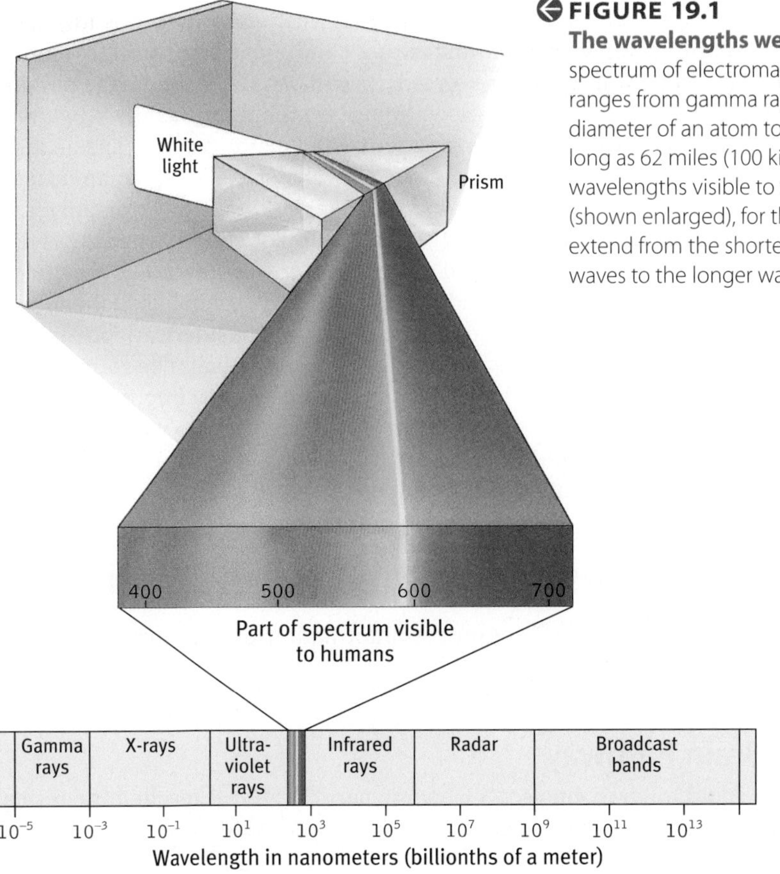
White light
Prism
400
500
600
700
Part of spectrum visible to humans
Gamma rays
X-rays
Ultra-violet rays
Infrared rays
Radar
Broadcast bands
10^{-5}
10^{-3}
10^{-1}
10^{1}
10^{3}
10^{5}
10^{7}
10^{9}
10^{11}
10^{13}
Wavelength in nanometers (billionths of a meter)

FIGURE 19.1
The wavelengths we see The wide spectrum of electromagnetic energy ranges from gamma rays as short as the diameter of an atom to radio waves as long as 62 miles (100 kilometers). The wavelengths visible to the human eye (shown enlarged), for those with vision, extend from the shorter blue-violet light waves to the longer waves of red light.

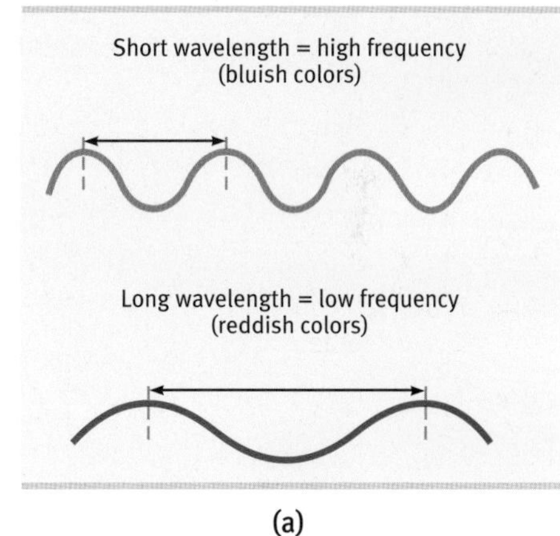
Short wavelength = high frequency (bluish colors)
Long wavelength = low frequency (reddish colors)

(a)

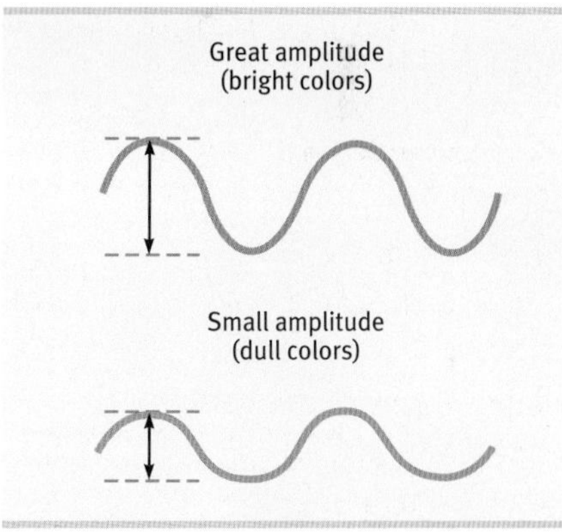
Great amplitude (bright colors)
Small amplitude (dull colors)

(b)

FIGURE 19.2
The physical properties of waves
(a) Waves vary in *wavelength* (the distance between successive peaks). *Frequency,* the number of complete wavelengths that can pass a point in a given time, depends on the wavelength. The shorter the wavelength, the higher the frequency. Wavelength determines the perceived *color* of light.
(b) Waves also vary in *amplitude* (the height from peak to trough). Wave amplitude influences the perceived *brightness* of colors.

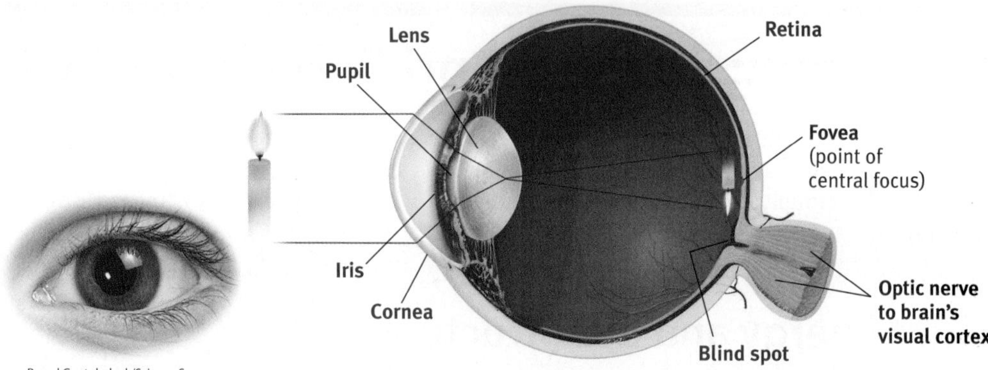
Lens
Retina
Pupil
Fovea
(point of
central focus)
Iris
Cornea
Optic nerve
to brain's
visual cortex
Blind spot
Pascal Goetgheluck/Science Source

FIGURE 19.3
The eye Light rays reflected from a candle pass through the cornea, pupil, and lens. The curvature and thickness of the lens change to bring nearby or distant objects into focus on the retina. Rays from the top of the candle strike the bottom of the retina, and those from the left side of the candle strike the right side of the retina. The candle's image on the retina thus appears upside down and reversed.

The Eye

Light enters the eye through the *cornea,* which bends light to help provide focus. The light then passes through the *pupil,* a small adjustable opening. Surrounding the pupil and controlling its size is the *iris,* a colored muscle that dilates or constricts in response to light intensity. Each iris is so distinctive that iris-scanning technology can often confirm your identity.

The iris responds to our cognitive and emotional states. If you have vision, imagine a sunny sky and your iris will constrict, making your pupil smaller; imagine a dark room and it will dilate, enlarging your pupil (Laeng & Sulutvedt, 2014). The iris also constricts when we are about to answer *No* to a question, or when we feel disgust (de Gee et al., 2014; Goldinger & Papesh, 2012). And when we're feeling amorous or trusting, our telltale dilated pupils subtly signal our feelings (Attard-Johnson et al., 2016, 2017; Kret & De Dreu, 2019; Prochanzkova et al., 2018).

After passing through our pupil, light hits the transparent *lens* in our eye. The lens then focuses the light rays into an image on our **retina**, the multilayered tissue lining the back inner surface of the eyeball. To focus the rays, the lens changes its curvature and thickness in a process called **accommodation**. If the lens focuses the image on a point in front of the retina, we see near objects clearly but not distant objects. This nearsightedness—*myopia*—can be remedied with glasses, contact lenses, or surgery.

For centuries, scientists knew that an image of a candle passing through a small opening will cast an inverted mirror image on a dark wall behind. If the image passing through the pupil casts this sort of upside-down image on the retina, as in **FIGURE 19.3**, how can we see the world right side up? The ever-curious Leonardo da Vinci had an idea: Perhaps the eye's watery fluids bend the light rays, reinverting the image to an upright position as it reaches the retina. Unfortunately for da Vinci, that idea was disproved in 1604, when the astronomer and optics expert Johannes Kepler showed that the retina *does* receive upside-down images of the world (Crombie, 1964). So how could we understand such a world? "I leave it," said the befuddled Kepler, "to natural philosophers."

Today's answer: The retina doesn't "see" a whole image. Consider the four-tenths of a second a baseball batter takes to respond to a pitcher's fastball. The retina's millions of receptor cells convert the particles of light energy into neural impulses and forward those to the brain, which reassembles them, right side up, into what the batter perceives—incoming fastball! Visual information processing percolates through progressively more abstract levels, all at astonishing speed.

Information Processing in the Eye and Brain

LOQ 19-2 How do the rods and cones process information, and what is the path information travels from the eye to the brain?

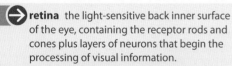

retina the light-sensitive back inner surface of the eye, containing the receptor rods and cones plus layers of neurons that begin the processing of visual information.

accommodation the process by which the eye's lens changes shape to focus near or far objects on the retina.

The Eye-to-Brain Pathway

Imagine that you could follow a single light-energy particle after it reached the retina. First, you would thread your way through the retina's sparse outer layer of cells. Then,

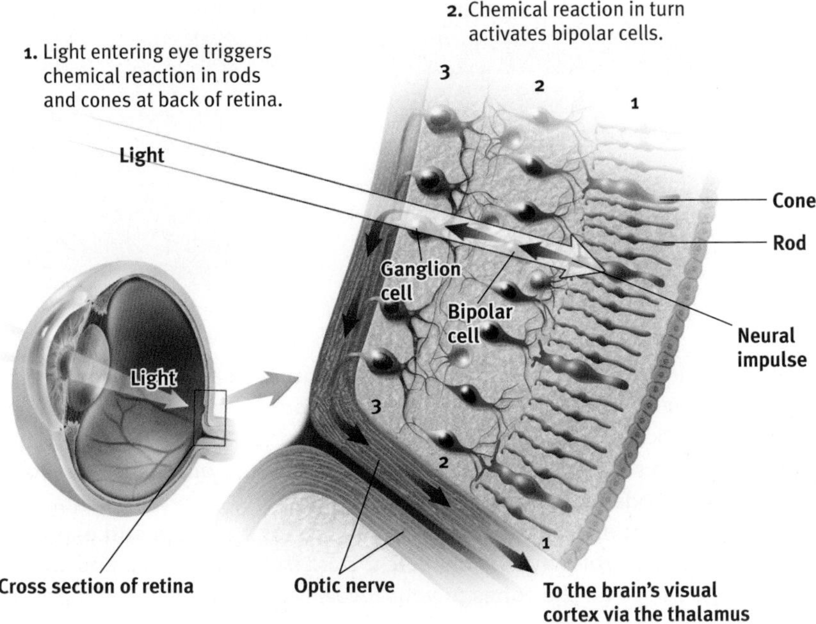
1. Light entering eye triggers chemical reaction in rods and cones at back of retina.
2. Chemical reaction in turn activates bipolar cells.
Light
Cone
Rod
Ganglion cell
Bipolar cell
Neural impulse
Light
Cross section of retina
Optic nerve
To the brain's visual cortex via the thalamus
3. Bipolar cells then activate the ganglion cells, whose combined axons form the optic nerve. This nerve transmits information (via the thalamus) to the brain's visual cortex.

FIGURE 19.4
The retina's reaction to light

reaching the very back of the eye, you would encounter the retina's nearly 130 million buried photoreceptor cells, the **rods** and **cones** (FIGURE 19.4). There, you would see the light energy trigger chemical changes. That chemical reaction would spark neural signals in nearby *bipolar cells*. You could then watch the bipolar cells activate neighboring *ganglion cells,* whose axons twine together like the strands of a rope to form the **optic nerve**. After a momentary stopover at the thalamus, the information would fly on to the final destination, the visual cortex, in the occipital lobe at the back of the brain.

The optic nerve is an information highway from the eye to the brain. This nerve can send nearly 1 million messages at once through its nearly 1 million ganglion fibers. (The auditory nerve, which enables hearing, carries much less information through its mere 30,000 fibers.) We pay a price for this high-speed connection. Our eye has a **blind spot**, with no receptor cells, where the optic nerve leaves the eye (FIGURE 19.5). If you have vision, close one eye. Do you see a black hole? No—because without seeking your approval, your brain fills in the hole.

rods retinal receptors that detect black, white, and gray, and are sensitive to movement. Rods are necessary for peripheral and twilight vision, when cones don't respond.

cones retinal receptors that are concentrated near the center of the retina and that function in daylight or in well-lit conditions. Cones detect fine detail and give rise to color sensations.

optic nerve the nerve that carries neural impulses from the eye to the brain.

blind spot the point at which the optic nerve leaves the eye, creating a "blind" spot because no receptor cells are located there.

fovea the central focal point in the retina, around which the eye's cones cluster.

RETRIEVAL PRACTICE

FIGURE 19.5
The blind spot

RP-1 There are no receptor cells where the optic nerve leaves the eye. This creates a blind spot if you have vision. To demonstrate, close your left eye, stare at the black dot, and slowly move the image closer to and then further from your face until one of the cars briefly disappears. (Which one do you predict it will be?) Repeat with your right eye closed—and note that now the other car disappears. Can you explain why?

ANSWERS IN APPENDIX E

Rods and cones differ in where they're found and in what they do (TABLE 19.1). *Cones* cluster in and around the **fovea**, the retina's area of central focus (Figure 19.3). Many cones have their own hotline to the brain: One cone transmits its message to a single bipolar cell, which relays the message to the visual cortex (where a large area receives input from the fovea). These direct connections preserve the cones' precise information, making them better able to detect fine detail. Cones can detect white and enable us to perceive color—but not at night (Sabesan et al., 2016).

TABLE 19.1 Receptors in the Human Eye: Rod-Shaped Rods and Cone-Shaped Cones

	Cones	Rods
Number	6 million	120 million
Location in retina	Center	Periphery
Sensitivity in dim light	Low	High
Color sensitivity	High	Low
Detail sensitivity	High	Low

Omikron/Science Source

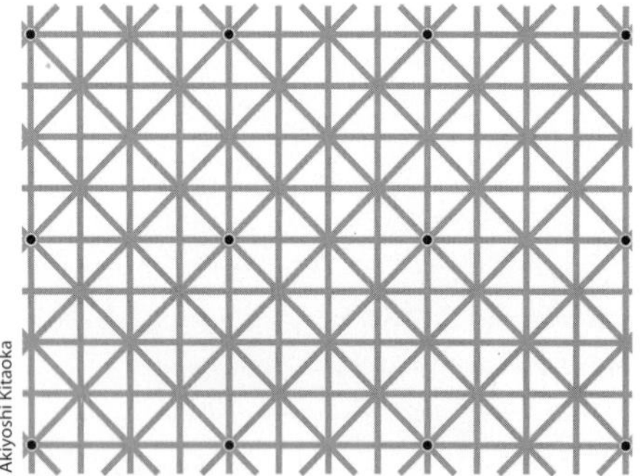
Akiyoshi Kitaoka

FIGURE 19.6
Disappearing dots If you have vision, look at or near any of the 12 black dots and you can see them, but not in your peripheral vision (Kitaoka, 2016, adapting Ninio & Stevens, 2000).

Rods, which (unlike cones) reside in the retina's periphery, remain sensitive in dim light, and they enable black-and-white vision. Rods have no hotline to the brain. If cones are soloists, rods perform as a chorus. Several rods pool their faint energy output and funnel it onto a single bipolar cell, which sends the combined message to our brain.

Cones and rods each provide a special sensitivity—cones to detail and color, and rods to faint light and peripheral motion. Stop for a minute and experience this rod–cone difference. If you have vision, pick a word in this sentence and stare directly at it, focusing its image on the cones in your fovea. Notice that words distant from it appear blurred? They lack detail because their image is striking your retina's outer regions, where rods predominate. Thus, when you drive or bike, rods help you detect a car in your peripheral vision well before you perceive its details. How many of the black dots can you see at once in **FIGURE 19.6**?

When we enter a darkened theater or turn off the light at night, our pupils dilate to allow more light to reach our retina. Our eyes adapt, but fully adapting typically takes 20 minutes or more. This period of dark adaptation matches the average natural twilight transition between the Sun's setting and darkness. How wonderfully made we are.

At the entry level, the retina's neural layers don't just pass along electrical impulses; they also help to encode and analyze sensory information. (The third neural layer in a frog's eye, for example, contains those "bug detector" cells that fire only in response to moving fly-like stimuli.) In human eyes, any given retinal area relays its information to a corresponding location in the visual cortex, in the occipital lobe. The brain's peculiar wiring means that half of each eye's sensory information arrives in the opposite side of the brain, by crossing the X-shaped *optic chiasm* (**FIGURE 19.7**).

FIGURE 19.7
Pathway from the eyes to the visual cortex The retina's ganglion axons form the optic nerve. It runs to the thalamus, where the axons synapse with neurons that run to the visual cortex.

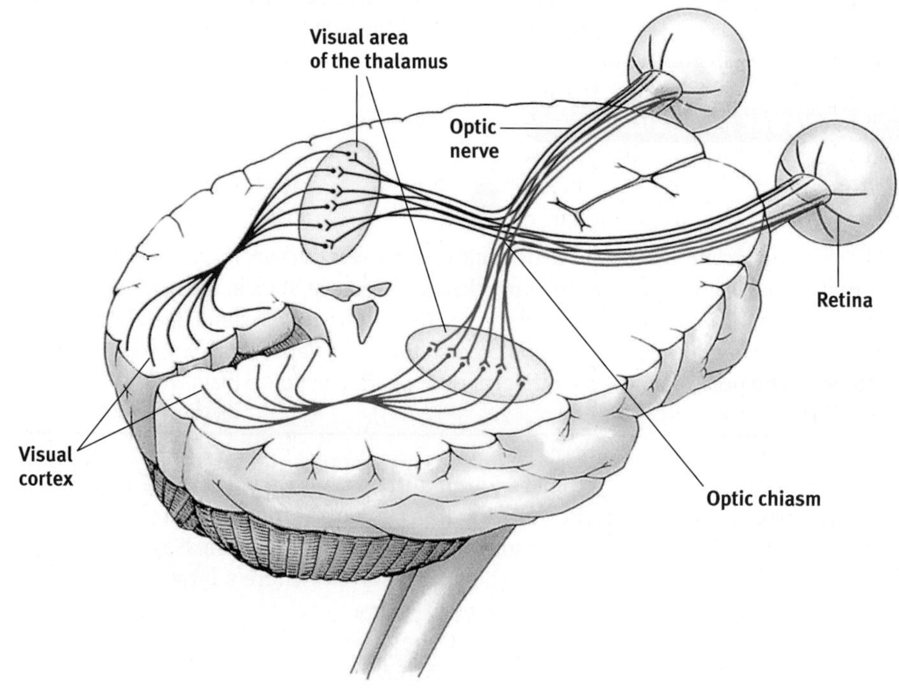
Visual area of the thalamus
Optic nerve
Retina
Visual cortex
Optic chiasm

The same sensitivity that enables retinal cells to fire messages can lead them to misfire, as you can demonstrate. If you have typical vision, turn your eyes to the left, close them, and then gently rub the right side of your right eyelid with your fingertip. Note the patch of light to the left, moving as your finger moves. Why do you see light? Why at the left? This happens because the retinal cells are so responsive that even pressure triggers them. And the brain interprets their firing as light. Moreover, it interprets the light as coming from the left—the normal direction of light that activates the right side of the retina.

ASK YOURSELF

Consider your activities in the last day. If you have vision, which of them relied on your rods? Which relied on your cones? How would these activities be different—or impossible—without these cells' different abilities?

RETRIEVAL PRACTICE

RP-2 Some nocturnal animals, such as toads, mice, rats, and bats, have impressive night vision thanks to having many more ____________ (rods/cones) than ____________ (rods/cones) in their retinas. These creatures probably have very poor ____________ (color/black-and-white) vision.

RP-3 Cats are able to open their ____________ much wider than we can, which allows more light into their eyes so they can see better at night.

ANSWERS IN APPENDIX E

Kruglov_Orda/Shutterstock

Color Processing

LOQ 19-3 How do we perceive color in the world around us?

Those of us with typical color vision talk as though objects possess color: "A tomato is red." Recall the old question, "If a tree falls in the forest and no one hears it, does it make a sound?" We can ask the same of color: If no one sees the tomato, is it red?

The answer is *No*. First, the tomato is everything *but* red, because it *rejects* (reflects) the long wavelengths of red. Second, the tomato's color is our mental construction. As Sir Isaac Newton (1704) noted, "The [light] rays are not colored." Like all aspects of vision, perception of color resides not in the object itself but in the theater of the brain; even while dreaming, those of us with color vision usually perceive things in color. Likewise, air molecules striking the eardrum are silent and scent molecules have no smell. Our brain creates experiences of sight, sound, and smell.

"It is in the brain that the poppy is red, that the apple is odorous, that the skylark sings."—Oscar Wilde, love letter to Alfred Douglas, 1896

One of vision's most basic and intriguing mysteries is how we see the world in color. How, from the light energy striking the retina, does our brain construct our experience of such a multitude of colors?

Modern detective work on the mystery of color vision began in the nineteenth century, when German scientist Hermann von Helmholtz built on the insights of an English physicist, Thomas Young. They knew that any color can be created by combining the light waves of three primary colors—red, green, and blue. So Young and von Helmholtz's research led to a hypothesis: The eye must have three corresponding types of color receptors.

Researchers later confirmed the **Young-Helmholtz trichromatic (three-color) theory** by measuring the response of various cones to different color stimuli. The retina does indeed have three types of color receptors, each especially sensitive to the wavelengths of red, green, or blue. When light stimulates combinations of these cones, we see other colors. For example, the retina has no separate receptors especially sensitive to yellow. But when red and green wavelengths stimulate both red-sensitive and green-sensitive cones, we see yellow. Said differently, when our eyes see red and green without blue, our brain says *yellow*.

In Singapore, yellow taxis—which are strikingly visible—have had 9 percent fewer accidents than blue taxis (Ho et al., 2017).

Young-Helmholtz trichromatic (three-color) theory the theory that the retina contains three different types of color receptors—one most sensitive to red, one to green, one to blue—which, when stimulated in combination, can produce the perception of any color. 

Worldwide, about 1 in 12 men and 1 in 200 women have the genetically sex-linked condition of *color-deficient vision*. Most are not entirely "color blind": They simply lack functioning red- or green-sensitive cones, or sometimes both. Their vision—perhaps unknown to them, because their lifelong vision is normal to them—is monochromatic (one-color) or

BEN SOLOMON/The New York Times/Redux Pictures

(a) (b)

FIGURE 19.8
Color-deficient vision The photo in image (a) shows how people with red-green deficiency perceived a 2015 Buffalo Bills versus New York Jets football game. "For the 8 percent of Americans like me that are red-green colorblind, this game is a nightmare to watch," tweeted one fan. "Everyone looks like they're on the same team," said another. The photo in image (b) shows how the game looked for those with typical color vision.

dichromatic (two-color) instead of trichromatic, making it impossible to distinguish the red and green in **FIGURE 19.8** (Boynton, 1979). Dogs, too, lack receptors for the wavelengths of red, giving them only limited, dichromatic color vision (Neitz et al., 1989).

But why do people blind to red and green often still see yellow? And why does yellow appear to be a pure color and not a mixture of red and green, the way purple is a blend of red and blue? As physiologist Ewald Hering—a contemporary of von Helmholtz—noted, trichromatic theory leaves some parts of the color vision mystery unsolved.

Hering found a clue in *afterimages*. If a person with color vision stares at a green shape for a while and then looks at a white sheet of paper, they will see red, green's *opponent color*. If they stare at a yellow shape, its opponent color, blue, will appear on the white paper (**FIGURE 19.9**). Hering formed another hypothesis: Color vision must involve two *additional* color processes, one responsible for red-versus-green perception, and one for blue-versus-yellow perception.

•

FIGURE 19.9
Afterimage effect If you have full color vision, stare at the center of the flag for a minute and then shift your eyes to the dot in the white space below it. What do you see? (After tiring your neural response to black, green, and yellow, you should see their opponent colors.) Stare at a white wall and note how the size of the flag grows with the projection distance.

Indeed, a century later, researchers also confirmed Hering's hypothesis, now called the **opponent-process theory**. This concept is tricky, but here is the gist: Color vision depends on three sets of opposing retinal processes—*red-green, blue-yellow,* and *white-black*. As impulses travel to the visual cortex, some neurons in both the retina and the thalamus are turned "on" by red but turned "off" by green. Others are turned on by green but off by red (DeValois & DeValois, 1975). Like red and green marbles sent down a narrow tube, "red" and "green" messages cannot both travel simultaneously. Those with color vision see either red or green, not a reddish-green mixture. But red and blue travel in separate channels, so we *can* see a reddish-blue magenta.

So how does opponent-process theory help us understand negative afterimages, as in the flag demonstration? Here's the answer (for the green changing to red): First, we stared at green bars, which tired our green response. Then we stared at a white area. White contains all colors, including red. Because we had tired our green response, only the red part of the green-red pairing fired normally.

The present solution to the mystery of color vision is roughly this: *Color processing occurs in two stages.*

1. The retina's red-, green-, and blue-sensitive cones respond in varying degrees to different color stimuli, as the Young-Helmholtz trichromatic theory suggested.
2. The cones' responses are then processed by opponent-process cells, as Hering's opponent-process theory proposed.

ASK YOURSELF

Does it surprise you to learn that, for those of us with color vision, colors don't "live" in the objects we perceive—that in fact, these objects are everything but the color we experience? If someone had asked you, "Is grass green?" before you read this section, how would you have responded?

RETRIEVAL PRACTICE

RP-4 What are two key theories of color vision? Are they contradictory or complementary? Explain.

ANSWERS IN APPENDIX E

opponent-process theory the theory that opposing retinal processes (red-green, blue-yellow, white-black) enable color vision. For example, some cells are stimulated by green and inhibited by red; others are stimulated by red and inhibited by green.

Giant

Patrick McDermott/Getty Images

Supercells score In this National Hockey League game, Alex Ovechkin (in red) instantly processed visual information about the positions and movements of three opponents. By using his pattern-detecting supercells, Ovechkin somehow managed to get the puck into the net.

Feature Detection

LOQ 19-4 Where are feature detectors located, and what do they do?

Scientists once likened the brain to a movie screen on which the eye projected images. Then along came David Hubel and Torsten Wiesel (1979), who showed that our visual processing deconstructs visual images and then reassembles them. Hubel and Wiesel received a Nobel Prize for their work on **feature detectors**, nerve cells in the occipital lobe's visual cortex that respond to a scene's specific visual features—to particular edges, lines, angles, and movements.

Using microelectrodes, they had discovered that some neurons fired actively when cats were shown lines at one angle, while other neurons responded to lines at a different angle. They surmised that these specialized neurons, now known as feature detectors, receive information from individual ganglion cells in the retina. Feature detectors pass this specific information to other cortical areas, where teams of cells *(supercell clusters)* respond to more complex patterns.

For biologically important objects and events, monkey brains (and surely ours as well) have a "vast visual encyclopedia" distributed as specialized cells (Perrett et al., 1990, 1992, 1994). These cells respond to one type of stimulus, such as a specific gaze, head angle, posture, or body movement. Other supercell clusters integrate this information and fire only when the cues collectively indicate the direction of someone's attention and approach. This instant analysis, which aided our ancestors' survival, also helps a hockey player anticipate where to shoot the puck, and a driver to anticipate a pedestrian's next movement.

One temporal lobe area by our right ear (**FIGURE 19.10**) typically enables us to perceive faces and, thanks to a specialized neural network, to recognize them from varied viewpoints (Connor, 2010). This *fusiform face area* helps us recognize friends (Wiese et al., 2019). If you have vision and your fusiform face area were stimulated, you might spontaneously see faces. One participant reported to an experimenter, "You just turned into someone else. Your face metamorphosed" (Koch, 2015).

When researchers temporarily disrupt the brain's face-processing areas with magnetic pulses, people cannot recognize faces. But they can still recognize other objects, such as houses, because the brain's face perception occurs separately from its object perception (McKone et al., 2007; Pitcher et al., 2007). Thus, functional MRI (fMRI) scans have shown different brain areas activating when people viewed varied objects (Downing et al., 2001). Brain activity is so specific that, with the help of brain scans, researchers can tell whether people are "looking at a shoe, a chair, or a face, based on the pattern of their brain activity" (Haxby, 2001).

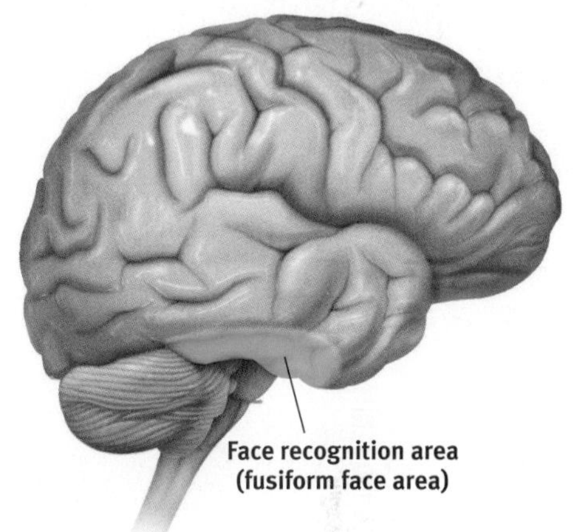
Face recognition area
(fusiform face area)

FIGURE 19.10
How our brain processes faces In social animals such as humans, a large right temporal lobe area (shown here in a right-facing brain) is dedicated to the crucial task of face recognition. Viewing famous people's faces, compared with famous buildings, increases activation in this fusiform face area (Gorno-Tempini & Price, 2001).

Parallel Processing

LOQ 19-5 How does the brain use parallel processing to construct visual perceptions?

Our brain achieves these and other remarkable feats by **parallel processing**: doing many things at once. To analyze a visual scene, the brain processes its subdimensions—motion, form, depth, color—simultaneously.

feature detectors nerve cells in the brain's visual cortex that respond to specific features of the stimulus, such as shape, angle, or movement.

parallel processing processing multiple aspects of a stimulus or problem simultaneously.

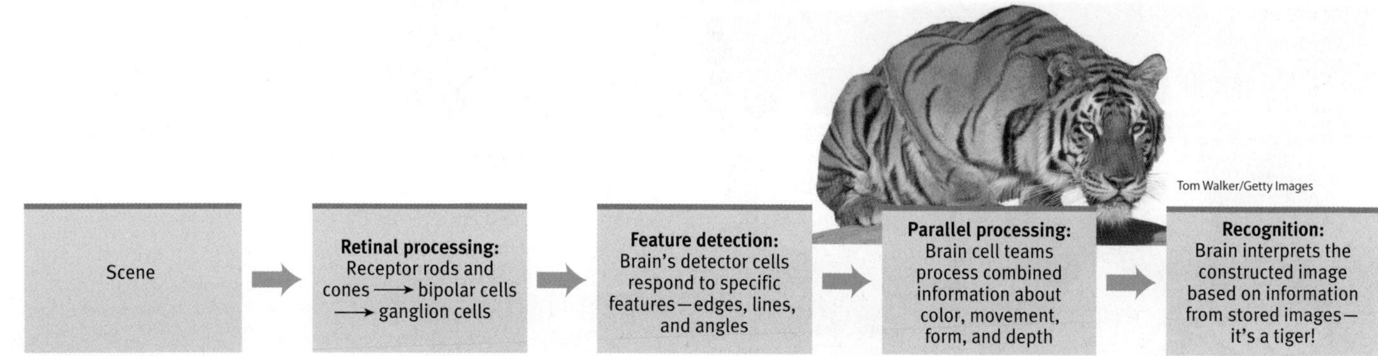
Tom Walker/Getty Images
Scene
Retinal processing: Receptor rods and cones ⟶ bipolar cells ⟶ ganglion cells
Feature detection: Brain's detector cells respond to specific features—edges, lines, and angles
Parallel processing: Brain cell teams process combined information about color, movement, form, and depth
Recognition: Brain interprets the constructed image based on information from stored images—it's a tiger!

FIGURE 19.11
A simplified summary of visual information processing

To recognize a face, our brain integrates information projected by our retinas to several visual cortex areas and compares it with stored information, thus enabling our fusiform face area to recognize the face: *Grandma!* Scientists have debated whether this stored information is contained in a single cell or, as now seems more likely, distributed over a network of cells that build a facial image bit by bit (Tsao, 2019). But some supercells—actually nicknamed *"grandmother cells"*—do appear to respond very selectively to 1 or 2 faces in 100 (Bowers, 2009; Quiroga et al., 2013). The whole face-recognition process involves connections between visual, memory, social, and auditory networks (Ramot et al., 2019). Supercells require super-sized brain power.

Destroy or disable the neural workstation for a visual subtask, and something peculiar results, as happened to "Mrs. M." (Hoffman, 1998). After a stroke damaged areas near the rear of both sides of her brain, she could not perceive motion. People in a room seemed "suddenly here or there but I [had] not seen them moving." Pouring tea into a cup was a challenge because the fluid appeared frozen—she could not perceive it rising in the cup.

After stroke or surgery has damaged the brain's visual cortex, others have experienced *blindsight* (see The Biology of Mind modules). Shown a series of sticks, they report seeing nothing. Yet when asked to guess whether the sticks are vertical or horizontal, their visual intuition typically offers the correct response. When told, "You got them all right," they are astounded. There is, it seems, a second "mind"—a parallel processing system—operating unseen. These separate visual systems for perceiving and for acting illustrate once again the astonishing dual processing of our two-track mind.

* * *

Think about the wonders of visual processing. If you have vision, as you read these words, the letters reflect light rays onto your retina, which triggers a process that sends formless nerve impulses to several areas of your brain, integrating the information and decoding its meaning. The amazing result: We have transferred information across time and space, from our minds to yours (**FIGURE 19.11**). That all of this happens instantly, effortlessly, and continuously is indeed awesome. As Roger Sperry (1985) observed, the "insights of science give added, not lessened, reasons for awe, respect, and reverence."

"I am . . . wonderfully made." —King David, Psalm 139:14

RETRIEVAL PRACTICE

RP-5 What is the rapid sequence of events that occurs when those with vision see and recognize a friend?

ANSWERS IN APPENDIX E

gestalt an organized whole. Gestalt psychologists emphasized our tendency to integrate pieces of information into meaningful wholes.

figure-ground the organization of the visual field into objects (the *figures*) that stand out from their surroundings (the *ground*).

grouping the perceptual tendency to organize stimuli into coherent groups.

Perceptual Organization

LOQ 19-6 How did the Gestalt psychologists understand perceptual organization, and how do figure-ground and grouping principles contribute to our perceptions?

How do those of us with vision organize and interpret sights so that they become *meaningful* perceptions—a rose in bloom, a familiar face, a sunset? Early in the twentieth century some German psychologists noticed that people tend to organize visual sensations into a **gestalt**, a German word meaning a "form" or a "whole." As we look straight ahead, we cannot separate the perceived scene into our left and right fields of view. Our conscious perception is, at every moment, a seamless scene—an integrated whole.

Consider **FIGURE 19.12:** The individual elements of this figure are really nothing but eight hexagons, each containing three converging white lines. What happens when we view these elements together? The resulting *Necker cube* nicely illustrates a favorite saying of Gestalt psychologists: *In perception, the whole may exceed the sum of its parts.*

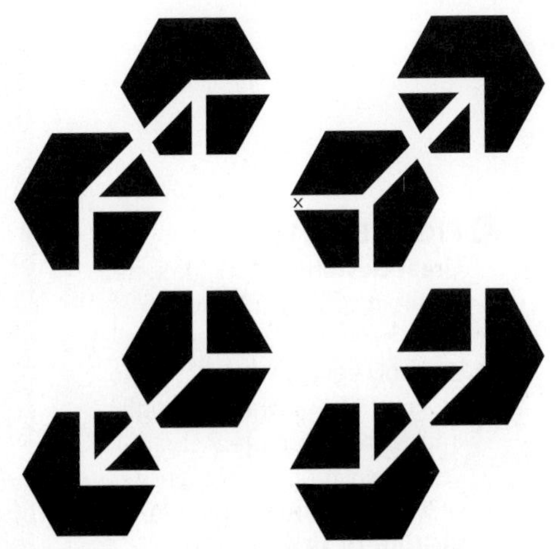

FIGURE 19.12
A Necker cube If you have vision, what do you see: hexagons with white lines, or a cube? If you stare at the cube, you may notice that it reverses location, moving the tiny X from the front edge to the back. At times, the cube may seem to float forward, with hexagons behind it. At other times, the hexagons may become holes through which the cube appears, as though it were floating behind them. There is far more to perception than meets the eye. (From Bradley et al., 1976.)

Over the years, the Gestalt psychologists demonstrated many principles we use to organize our sensations into perceptions (Wagemans et al., 2012a,b). Underlying all of them is a fundamental truth: *Our brain does more than register information about the world.* Perception is not a picture printing itself on the brain. We filter incoming information and *construct* perceptions. Mind matters.

Form Perception

You may be familiar with facial-recognition technology that can unlock your phone, or automatically tag your favorite people in photos. Newer phones' camera-software system, like our eye-brain system, recognizes faces at a glance. What abilities go into the design of these phone systems?

FIGURE AND GROUND To start with, the camera-software system needs to perceive **figure-ground**—to separate faces from their backgrounds. In our eye-brain system, this is our first perceptual task—perceiving any object (the *figure*) as distinct from its surroundings (the *ground*). For sighted readers, the words are the figure; the white space is the ground. This perception applies for those listening to the text, too. If you listen in a noisy coffee shop, the text reading you are attending to becomes the figure; all other sounds are part of the ground. Sometimes the same stimulus can trigger more than one perception. In **FIGURE 19.13**, the figure-ground relationship continually reverses. First, we may see the vase (or the faces), then the faces (or the vase), but sighted viewers always organize the stimulus into a figure seen against a ground.

FIGURE 19.13
Reversible figure and ground

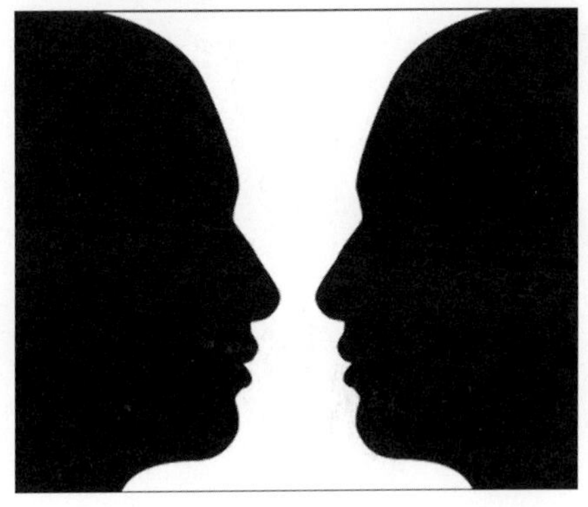

GROUPING Having discriminated figure from ground, we (and our camera-software system) must also organize the figure into a *meaningful* form. Some basic features of a scene—such as color, movement, and light-dark contrast—we typically process instantly and automatically (Parrish & Beran, 2021). Our mind brings order and form to other stimuli by following certain rules for **grouping**, also identified by the Gestalt psychologists. These rules, which we apply even as infants and even in our touch perceptions, illustrate how the perceived whole differs from the sum of its parts, rather as water differs from its hydrogen and oxygen parts (Gallace & Spence, 2011; Quinn et al., 2002; Rock & Palmer, 1990). See **FIGURE 19.14** for three examples.

Such principles usually help us construct reality. Sometimes, however, they lead us astray, as when we look at the doghouse in **FIGURE 19.15.**

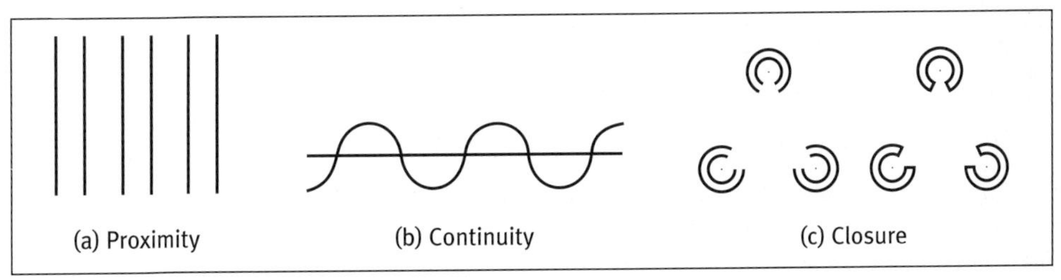
(a) Proximity
(b) Continuity
(c) Closure

FIGURE 19.14
Three principles of grouping (a) Thanks to *proximity,* we group nearby figures together. We see not six separate lines, but three sets of two lines. (b) Through *continuity,* we perceive smooth, continuous patterns rather than discontinuous ones. This pattern could be a series of alternating semicircles, but we perceive it as two continuous lines—one wavy, one straight. (c) Using *closure,* we fill in gaps to create a complete, whole object. Thus, we assume that the circles on the left are complete but partially blocked by the (illusory) triangle. Add nothing more than little line segments to close off the circles and your brain may stop constructing a triangle.

depth perception the ability to see objects in three dimensions, although the images that strike the retina are two-dimensional; allows us to judge distance.

visual cliff a laboratory device for testing depth perception in infants and young animals.

FIGURE 19.15
Great Gestalt! What's the secret to this impossible doghouse? If you have typical vision, you probably perceive this doghouse as a gestalt — a whole (though impossible) structure. Actually, your brain imposes this sense of wholeness on the picture. As **FIGURE 19.19** shows, Gestalt grouping principles such as closure and continuity are at work here.

Photo by Walter Wick. Reprinted by permission from GAMES Magazine © 1983 PCS Games Limited Partnership

RETRIEVAL PRACTICE

RP-6 In terms of perception, a band's lead singer would be considered ________ (figure/ground), and the other musicians would be considered ________ (figure/ground).

RP-7 What do we mean when we say that, in perception, "the whole may exceed the sum of its parts"?

ANSWERS IN APPENDIX E

Depth Perception

LOQ 19-7 How do binocular and monocular cues enable three-dimensional vision, and how does motion perception occur?

For those of us with typical vision, the eye-brain system performs many remarkable feats, among which is **depth perception**. From the two-dimensional images falling on our retinas, we somehow organize three-dimensional perceptions that, for example, let us estimate the distance of an oncoming car. How do we acquire this ability? Are we born with it? Did we learn it?

As psychologist Eleanor Gibson picnicked on the rim of the Grand Canyon, her scientific curiosity kicked in. She wondered: *Would a toddler peering over the rim perceive the dangerous drop-off and draw back?* To answer that question and others, Gibson and Richard Walk (1960) designed a series of experiments in their Cornell University laboratory using a **visual cliff**—a model of a cliff with a "drop-off" area that was actually covered by sturdy glass. They placed 6- to 14-month-old infants on the edge of the "cliff" and had a parent coax the infants to lean over the glass or crawl out onto it (**FIGURE 19.16**). Most infants refused to do so, indicating that they could perceive depth.

Creating three-dimensional perceptions from two dimensions Several of the world's cities slow traffic with illusory 3-D crosswalk paintings, thanks to artists Saumya Pandya Thakkar and Shakuntala Pandyaand, who created the first of these in India.

Monika Skolimowska/picture-alliance/dpa/AP Photo

Had they *learned* to perceive depth? Learning appears also to be part of the human story. Years after Gibson and Walk's classic visual cliff studies, psychologist Karen Adolph continued to study infant motor development (Adolph & Hoch, 2019). Adolph and others showed that crawling, no matter when it begins, seems to increase an infant's wariness of heights (Adolph et al., 2014; Campos et al., 1992). Crawling infants tend to gaze downward, making it more likely for them to stare at possible hazards they are approaching (Kretch et al., 2014). They likely evolved this tendency because learning to avoid cliffs helped them survive. Mobile newborn animals—even those with no visual experience (including young kittens, a day-old goat, and newly hatched chicks)—also refuse to venture across the visual cliff. Thus, biology prepares us to be wary of heights, and experience amplifies that fear.

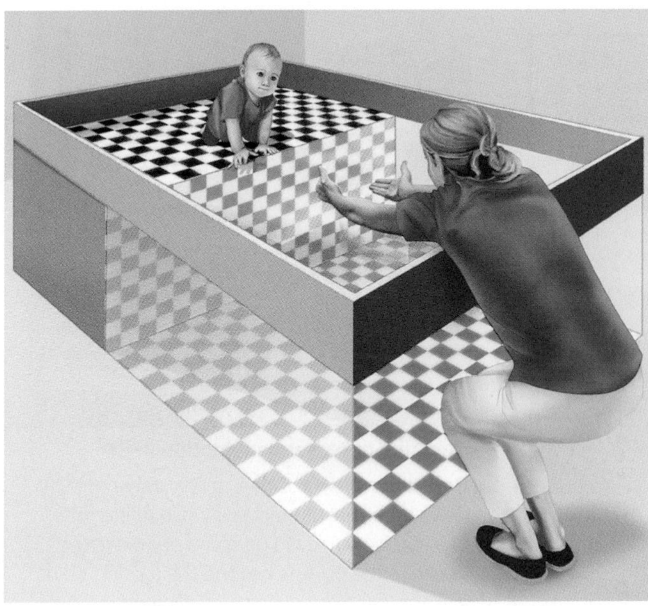

FIGURE 19.16 Gibson and Walk's visual cliff

If we were to build the ability to perceive depth into our camera-software system, what rules might enable it to convert two-dimensional images into a single three-dimensional perception? A good place to start would be the depth cues our brain receives from information supplied by one or both eyes.

BINOCULAR CUES People who see with two eyes perceive depth thanks partly to **binocular cues**. Here's a demonstration you might try: With both eyes open, hold two pens or pencils in front of you and touch their tips together. Now do so with one eye closed. A more difficult task, yes?

We use binocular cues to judge the distance of nearby objects. One such cue is *convergence,* the inward angle of the eyes focusing on a near object. Another is **retinal disparity**. Because there is space between our eyes, each retina receives a slightly different image of the world. By comparing these two images, our brain can judge how close an object is to us. The greater the disparity (difference) between the two retinal images, the closer the object. Try it. Hold your two index fingers about 5 inches (12 centimeters) in front of your eyes, with their tips half an inch (1 centimeter) apart. Your retinas will receive quite different views. If you close one eye and then the other, you can see the difference. Now look beyond your fingers and note the weird result. Move your fingers out farther and the retinal disparity—and the finger sausage—will shrink (FIGURE 19.17).

We could easily include retinal disparity in our camera-software system. Movie directors sometimes film a scene through two lenses placed a small distance apart. Viewers

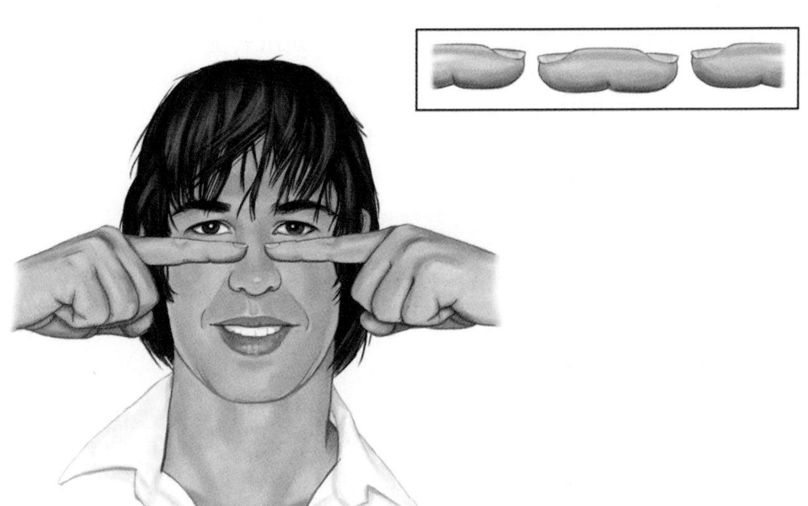

FIGURE 19.17 The floating finger sausage

binocular cue a depth cue, such as retinal disparity, that depends on the use of two eyes.

retinal disparity a binocular cue for perceiving depth. By comparing retinal images from the two eyes, the brain computes distance—the greater the disparity (difference) between the two images, the closer the object.

Relative height We perceive objects higher in our field of vision as farther away. Because we assume the lower part of a figure-ground illustration is closer, we perceive it as figure (Vecera et al., 2002). Invert this illustration and the black will become ground, like a night sky.

I have no depth perception. Is there a cop standing on the corner, or do you have a tiny person in your hair?

Relative size If we assume two objects are similar in size, *most* people perceive the one that casts the smaller retinal image as farther away.

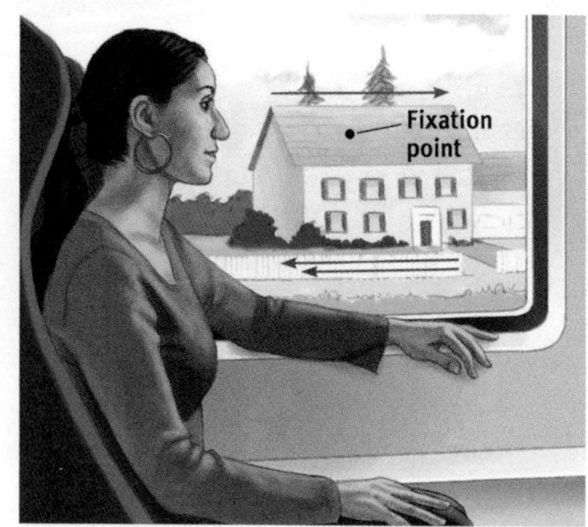
Fixation point

Direction of passenger's motion →

Relative motion As we move, stable objects may also appear to move. If while riding on a bus you fix your gaze on some point—say, a house—the objects beyond the fixation point will appear to move with you. Objects in front of the point will appear to move backward. The farther an object is from the fixation point, the faster it will seem to move.

ROAD NARROWS
ROAD NARROWS

Linear perspective Parallel lines appear to meet in the distance. The sharper the angle of convergence, the greater the perceived distance.

Interposition If one object partially blocks our view of another, we perceive it as closer.

FIGURE 19.18
Monocular depth cues

then watch the film through glasses that allow the left eye to see only the image from the left camera, and the right eye to see only the image from the right camera. As 3-D movie fans know, the resulting effect mimics or exaggerates normal retinal disparity, giving the perception of depth. (And as someone who is *not* a fan of 3-D movies, I [ND] can confirm another, less pleasant effect: motion sickness.)

Unlike carnivores, whose eyes enable forward focus on prey and offer binocular vision-enhanced depth perception, grazing herbivores typically have eyes on either side of their skull. Although lacking superior depth perception, herbivores have sweeping peripheral vision, all the better to detect predators.

MONOCULAR CUES How do those of us with typical vision judge whether a person is 10 or 100 meters away? Retinal disparity won't help us here, because there won't be much difference between the images cast on our right and left retinas. At such distances, we depend on **monocular cues** (depth cues available to each eye separately). See **FIGURE 19.18** for some examples.

RETRIEVAL PRACTICE

RP-8 How do people typically perceive depth?

ANSWERS IN APPENDIX E

Motion Perception

Imagine that, like Mrs. M. described earlier, you could perceive the world as having color, form, and depth but that you could not see motion. Not only would you be unable to bike or drive, you would have trouble writing, eating, and walking.

monocular cue a depth cue, such as interposition or linear perspective, available to either eye alone.

The brain typically computes motion based partly on its assumption that shrinking objects are retreating (not getting smaller) and enlarging objects are approaching. In young children, this ability to correctly perceive approaching (and enlarging) vehicles is not yet fully developed, which puts them at risk for pedestrian accidents (Wann et al., 2011). But it's not just children who have occasional difficulties with motion perception. Our adult brain is sometimes tricked into believing what it is not seeing. When large and small objects move at the same speed, the large objects appear to move more slowly. Thus, trains seem to move slower than cars, and jumbo jets seem to land more slowly than little jets.

If you have vision, have you noticed how often you interrupt that vision with a 0.1 second blink—about 15 times per minute, or 15,000 unnoticed missing time slices per day (Grossman et al., 2019)? Probably not. Our brain perceives a rapid series of slightly varying images as continuous movement (a phenomenon called *stroboscopic movement*). As film animators know well, a superfast slide show of 24 still pictures a second will create an illusion of movement. We construct that motion in our head, just as we construct movement in blinking marquees and holiday lights. We perceive two adjacent stationary lights blinking on and off in quick succession as one single light jumping back and forth. Lighted signs exploit this **phi phenomenon** with a succession of lights that creates the impression of, say, a moving arrow.

Photo by Walter Wick. Reprinted from GAMES Magazine ©1983 PCS Games Limited Partnership

FIGURE 19.19
The solution Another view of the impossible doghouse in Figure 19.15 reveals the secrets of this illusion. From the photo angle, the grouping principles of closure and continuity lead us to perceive the boards as continuous.

Perceptual Constancy

LOQ 19-8 How do perceptual constancies help us construct meaningful perceptions?

So far, we have noted that our camera-software system must perceive objects as we typically do—as having a distinct form, location, and motion. Its next task is to recognize objects without being deceived by changes in their color, brightness, shape, or size—a *top-down* process called **perceptual constancy**. Regardless of the viewing angle, distance, and illumination, those of us with typical vision can identify people and things in less time than it takes to draw a breath. This feat is a huge challenge for a camera-software system.

COLOR AND BRIGHTNESS CONSTANCIES James Gibson (1979) argued for an *ecological approach* to perception, in which our perceptions depend on an object's context. If you have full color vision, consider how you experience the color of a tomato—and how it would change if you viewed it through a paper tube over the course of a day. As the light—and thus the tomato's reflected wavelengths—changed, the tomato's color would also seem to change. But if you discarded the paper tube and viewed the tomato as one item in a salad bowl, its perceived color would remain constant, a consistent perception we call *color constancy*.

"From there to here, from here to there, funny things are everywhere."—Dr. Seuss, *One Fish, Two Fish, Red Fish, Blue Fish*, 1960

Though we may take color constancy for granted, this ability is truly remarkable. Under indoor lighting, a blue poker chip reflects wavelengths that match those reflected by a sunlit gold chip (Jameson, 1985). Yet bring a goldfinch indoors and it won't look like a bluebird. The color is not in the bird's feathers. We see color thanks to our brain's computations of the light reflected by an object *relative to the objects surrounding it*. For those with color vision, **FIGURE 19.20** dramatically illustrates the ability of a blue object

R. Beau Lotto/LottoLab

(a) (b)

FIGURE 19.20
Color depends on context (a) Believe it or not, these three blue disks are identical in color. (b) Remove the surrounding context and see what results.

phi phenomenon an illusion of movement created when two or more adjacent lights blink on and off in quick succession.

perceptual constancy perceiving objects as unchanging (having consistent color, brightness, shape, and size) even as illumination and retinal images change.

Seeing color? Surprise! This is actually a black and white photo. If you have full color vision, did the colorful, overlaid grid lines trick your eyes, too?

Photo by Manuel Schmalsteig/Color Illusory color remix by Øyvind Kolås

FIGURE 19.21
Relative luminance
Because of its surrounding context, those with vision perceive Square A as lighter than Square B. But believe it or not, they are identical. To channel comedian Richard Pryor, "Who you gonna believe: me, or your lying eyes?" If you believe your lying eyes—actually, your lying brain—you can photocopy (or screen-capture and print) the illustration, then cut out the squares and compare them. (Information from Edward Adelson.) Such human mistakes are so reliable that computer systems use them to identify human website users—knowing that computer spam robots answer *correctly*.

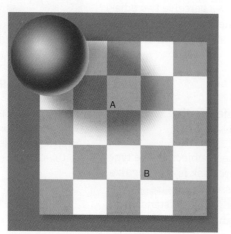

to appear very different in three different contexts. Knowing the truth—that these disks are identically colored—does not diminish our perception that they are quite different. Because we construct our perceptions, we can simultaneously accept alternative objective and subjective realities.

Brightness constancy (also called *lightness constancy*) similarly depends on context. If we have typical vision, we perceive an object as having a constant brightness even as its illumination varies. This perception of constancy depends on *relative luminance*—the amount of light an object reflects *relative to its surroundings* (**FIGURE 19.21**). White paper reflects 90 percent of the light falling on it; black paper, only 10 percent. Although black paper viewed in sunlight may reflect 100 times more light than does white paper viewed indoors, it will still look black (McBurney & Collings, 1984). But try viewing sunlit black paper through a narrow tube moved just slightly away from the paper, but close enough so nothing else is visible. Now it may look gray, because in bright sunshine it reflects a fair amount of light. View it without the tube and it is again black, because it reflects much less light than the objects around it.

This principle—that we perceive objects not in isolation but in their environmental context—matters to artists, interior decorators, and clothing designers. Our perception of the color and brightness of a wall or of a streak of paint on a canvas is determined not just by the paint itself but by the surrounding colors. The take-home lesson: *Context governs our perceptions.*

SHAPE AND SIZE CONSTANCIES Thanks to *shape constancy,* those with typical vision perceive the form of familiar objects, such as the door in **FIGURE 19.22**, as constant even while the retinas receive changing images of them. The brain manages this feat because visual cortex neurons rapidly learn to associate different views of an object (Li & DiCarlo, 2008).

Thanks to *size constancy,* those with typical vision perceive an object as having an unchanging size, even while distance from it varies. We assume a bus is large enough to carry people, even when we see its tiny image from two blocks away. This assumption also illustrates the close connection between perceived *distance* and perceived *size.* Perceiving an object's distance gives us cues to its size. Likewise, knowing its general size—that the object is a bus—provides us with cues to its distance. To our distant ancestors, the similar-sized Sun and Moon likely seemed equally distant.

"Sometimes I wonder: Why is that Frisbee getting bigger? And then it hits me." —Anonymous

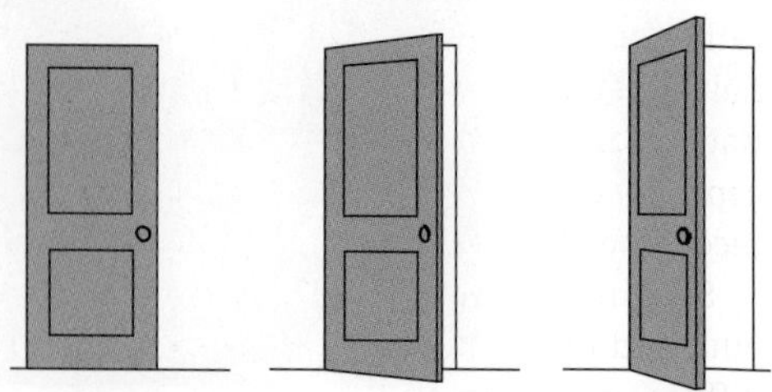

FIGURE 19.22
Shape constancy A door casts an increasingly trapezoidal image on our retinas as it opens. Yet we still perceive it as rectangular.

Even in size-distance judgments, however, we consider an object's context. This interplay between perceived size and perceived distance helps explain several well-known illusions, including the *Moon illusion:* The Moon looks up to 50 percent larger when near the horizon than when high in the sky. Can you imagine why?

For at least 22 centuries, scholars have wondered (Hershenson, 1989). One reason is that monocular cues to an object's distance make the horizon Moon seem farther away. If it's farther away, our brain assumes, it must be larger than the Moon high in the night sky (Kaufman & Kaufman, 2000). But again, if we use a paper tube to take away the distance cue, the horizon Moon will immediately seem smaller.

Perceptual illusions reinforce a fundamental lesson: Perception is not merely a projection of the world onto our brain. Rather, our sensations are disassembled into information bits that our brain then reassembles into its own functional model of the external world. During this reassembly process, our assumptions—such as the usual relationship between distance and size—can lead us astray. *Our brain constructs our perceptions.*

* * *

Form perception, depth perception, motion perception, and perceptual constancies illuminate how we typically organize our visual experiences. Perceptual organization applies to our other senses, too. Listening to an unfamiliar language, those of us with hearing have trouble detecting where one word stops and the next one begins. Listening to our own language, we automatically hear distinct words. This, too, reflects perceptual organization. But it is more, for we even organize a string of letters—THEDOGATEMEAT—into words that make an intelligible phrase; it's more likely "The dog ate meat" than "The do gate me at" (McBurney & Collings, 1984). This process involves not only the organization we've been discussing, but also interpretation—discerning meaning in what we perceive.

Perceptual Interpretation

Philosophers have debated whether our perceptual abilities should be credited to our nature or our nurture. To what extent do we *learn* to perceive? German philosopher Immanuel Kant (1724–1804) maintained that knowledge comes from our *inborn* ways of organizing sensory experiences. Indeed, we typically come equipped to process sensory information. But British philosopher John Locke (1632–1704) argued that through our experiences we also *learn* to perceive the world. Indeed, we learn to link an object's distance with its size. So, just how important is experience? How radically does it shape our perceptual interpretations?

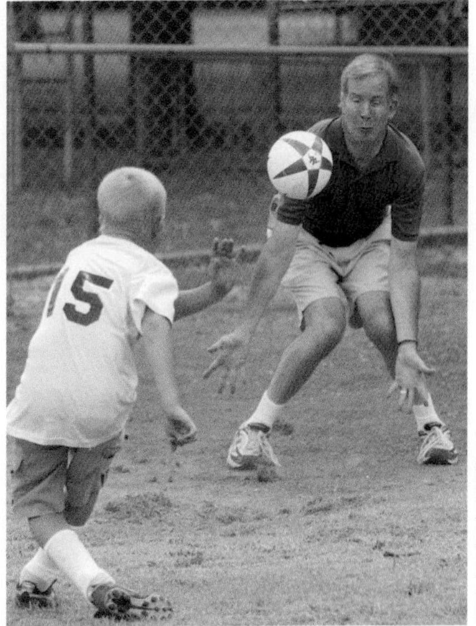
Marcio Jose Sanchez/AP Photo

Learning to see At age 3, Mike May lost his vision in an explosion. Decades later, after a new cornea restored vision to his right eye, he got his first look at his wife and children. Alas, although signals were now reaching his visual cortex, it lacked the experience to interpret them. May could not recognize expressions or faces, apart from features such as hair. Yet he can see an object in motion and has learned to navigate his world and to marvel at such things as dust floating in sunlight (Abrams, 2002; Gorlick, 2010; Huber et al., 2015).

Experience and Visual Perception

LOQ 19-9 What does research on restored vision, sensory restriction, and perceptual adaptation reveal about the effects of experience on perception?

RESTORED VISION AND SENSORY RESTRICTION Writing to John Locke, William Molyneux wondered whether a person "*born* blind, and now adult, taught by . . . *touch* to distinguish between a cube and a sphere" could, if made to see, visually distinguish the two. Locke's answer was *No,* because the person would never have *learned* to see the difference.

Molyneux's hypothetical case has since been tested with people who, though blind from birth, later gained sight (Gandhi et al., 2017; Gregory, 1978; von Senden, 1932). Most were born with cataracts—clouded lenses that allowed them to see only diffused light, rather as a sighted person might see a foggy image through a table-tennis ball sliced in half. After cataract surgery, the patients could distinguish figure from ground, differentiate colors, and distinguish faces from nonfaces—suggesting that these aspects of perception are innate. But much as Locke supposed, they often remained unable to visually recognize objects that were familiar by touch.

Seeking to gain more control than is provided by clinical cases, researchers have outfitted infant kittens and monkeys with goggles through which they could see only diffuse, unpatterned light (Hubel & Wiesel, 1963). After infancy, when their vision was

perceptual adaptation the ability to adjust to changed sensory input, including an artificially displaced or even inverted visual field.

"Let us then suppose the mind to be, as we say, white paper void of all characters, without any ideas: How comes it to be furnished? . . . To this I answer, in one word, from EXPERIENCE." —John Locke, *An Essay Concerning Human Understanding*, 1690

restored, the kittens behaved much like the humans born with cataracts. They could distinguish color and brightness, but not a circle from a square. Their eyes had not degenerated; their retinas still relayed signals to their visual cortex. But lacking early stimulation, their brain's cortical cells had failed to develop the necessary connections. Thus, the animals remained functionally blind to shape.

Surgery on children in India reveals that those who are blind from birth can benefit from removal of cataracts, and the younger they are, the more they benefit. But their visual acuity (sharpness) may never match the acuity of those born with full vision (Chatterjee, 2015; Gandhi et al., 2014). For sensory and perceptual development, there is a *critical period*—an optimal period when exposure to certain stimuli or experiences is required.

Once this critical period has passed, sensory restrictions later in life do no permanent harm. When researchers cover an adult animal's eye for several months, its vision will be unaffected after the eye patch is removed. When surgeons remove cataracts that developed during late adulthood, most people are thrilled at the return to full vision.

Courtesy of Hubert Dolezal

Perceptual adaptation "Oops, missed," thought researcher Hubert Dolezal as he attempted a handshake while viewing the world through inverting goggles. Yet, believe it or not, kittens, monkeys, and humans can adapt to an inverted world.

PERCEPTUAL ADAPTATION Given a new pair of prescription eyeglasses, we may feel slightly disoriented, even dizzy. Within a day or two, we adjust. Our **perceptual adaptation** to changed visual input makes the world seem normal again. But if you are sighted, imagine wearing a far more dramatic new pair of glasses—one that shifts the apparent location of objects 40 degrees to the left. When you first toss a ball to a friend, it sails off to the left. Walking forward to shake hands with someone, you veer to the left.

Could you adapt to this distorted world? Not if you were a baby chicken. When fitted with such lenses, baby chicks continue to peck where food grains *seem* to be (Hess, 1956; Rossi, 1968). But we humans adapt to distorting lenses quickly. Within a few minutes your throws would again be accurate, your stride on target. Remove the lenses and you would experience an aftereffect: At first your throws would err in the *opposite* direction, sailing off to the right; but again, within minutes you would readapt.

Indeed, given an even more radical pair of glasses—one that literally turns the world upside down—you could still adapt. Psychologist George Stratton (1896) experienced this. He invented, and for 8 days wore, optical headgear that flipped left to right *and* up to down, making him the first person to experience a right-side-up retinal image while standing upright. The ground was up, the sky was down.

At first, when Stratton wanted to walk, he found himself searching for his feet, which were now "up." Eating was nearly impossible. He became nauseated and depressed. But he persisted, and by the eighth day he could comfortably reach for an object and, if his hands were in view, could walk without bumping into things. When Stratton finally removed the headgear, he readapted quickly. So did research participants who later wore such gear—while riding a motorcycle, skiing the Alps, or flying an airplane (Dolezal, 1982; Kohler, 1962). By actively moving about in their topsy-turvy world, they adapted to their new context and learned to coordinate their movements.

So, do we learn to perceive the world? In part we do, as we constantly adjust to changing sensory input. Research on critical periods teaches us that early nurture sculpts what nature has provided. In less dramatic ways, nurture continues to do so throughout our lives. Radiologists, who spend their careers inspecting complex visual patterns, outperform novices in detecting unfamiliar visual information (Hussain, 2020). Likewise, portrait artists, who devote their careers to drawing faces, outperform nonartists on facial recognition tests (Hsia et al., 2021). Experience guides, sustains, and maintains the brain pathways that enable our perceptions.

ASK YOURSELF

Consider someone you know (could be yourself) who has a visual disability of some kind. What sort of disruption in the visual process might be causing that disability?

19 REVIEW Vision: Sensory and Perceptual Processing

LEARNING OBJECTIVES

Test Yourself Answer these repeated Learning Objective Questions on your own (before "showing" the answers here, or checking the answers in Appendix D) to improve your retention of the concepts (McDaniel et al., 2009, 2015).

LOQ 19-1 What are the characteristics of the energy that we see as visible light? What structures in the eye help focus that energy?

LOQ 19-2 How do the rods and cones process information, and what is the path information travels from the eye to the brain?

LOQ 19-3 How do we perceive color in the world around us?

LOQ 19-4 Where are feature detectors located, and what do they do?

LOQ 19-5 How does the brain use parallel processing to construct visual perceptions?

LOQ 19-6 How did the Gestalt psychologists understand perceptual organization, and how do figure-ground and grouping principles contribute to our perceptions?

LOQ 19-7 How do binocular and monocular cues enable three-dimensional vision, and how does motion perception occur?

LOQ 19-8 How do perceptual constancies help us construct meaningful perceptions?

LOQ 19-9 What does research on restored vision, sensory restriction, and perceptual adaptation reveal about the effects of experience on perception?

TERMS AND CONCEPTS TO REMEMBER

Test Yourself Write down the definition in your own words, then check your answer.

wavelength, p. 223
hue, p. 223
intensity, p. 223
retina, p. 224
accommodation, p. 224
rods, p. 225
cones, p. 225
optic nerve, p. 225
blind spot, p. 225
fovea, p. 225
Young-Helmholtz trichromatic (three-color) theory, p. 227
opponent-process theory, p. 228
feature detectors, p. 229
parallel processing, p. 229
gestalt, p. 230
figure-ground, p. 230
grouping, p. 230
depth perception, p. 232
visual cliff, p. 232
binocular cue, p. 233
retinal disparity, p. 233
monocular cue, p. 234
phi phenomenon, p. 235
perceptual constancy, p. 235
perceptual adaptation, p. 238

MODULE TEST

Test Yourself Answer the following questions on your own first, then "show" the answers here, or check your answers in Appendix E.

1. The characteristic of light that determines the color we experience, such as blue or green, is its ________________.

2. The amplitude of a light wave determines our perception of
   a. brightness.
   b. color.
   c. meaning.
   d. distance.

3. The blind spot in our retina is located where
   a. there are rods but no cones.
   b. there are cones but no rods.
   c. the optic nerve leaves the eye.
   d. the bipolar cells meet the ganglion cells.

4. Cones are the eye's receptor cells that are especially sensitive to ________________ light and are responsible for our ________________ vision.
   a. bright; black-and-white
   b. dim; color
   c. bright; color
   d. dim; black-and-white

5. Two theories together account for color vision. The Young-Helmholtz trichromatic theory shows that the eye contains ________________, and Hering's theory accounts for the nervous system's having ________________.
   a. opposing retinal processes; three pairs of color receptors
   b. opponent-process cells; three types of color receptors
   c. three pairs of color receptors; opposing retinal processes
   d. three types of color receptors; opponent-process cells

6. What mental processes allow sighted viewers to perceive a lemon as yellow?

7. The cells in the visual cortex that respond to certain lines, edges, and angles are called ________________.

8. The brain's ability to process many aspects of an object or a problem simultaneously is called ________________.

9. In listening to a concert, we attend to the solo instrument and perceive the orchestra as accompaniment. This illustrates the organizing principle of
   a. figure-ground.
   b. shape constancy.
   c. grouping.
   d. depth perception.

10. Our tendencies to fill in the gaps and to perceive a pattern as continuous are two different examples of the organizing principle called
   a. interposition.
   b. depth perception.
   c. shape constancy.
   d. grouping.

11. The visual cliff experiments suggest that
   a. infants have not yet developed depth perception.
   b. crawling human infants and very young animals perceive depth.
   c. we have no way of knowing whether infants can perceive depth.
   d. unlike other species, humans are able to perceive depth in infancy.

12. Depth perception underlies our ability to
   a. group similar items in a gestalt.
   b. perceive objects as having a constant shape or form.
   c. judge distances.
   d. fill in the gaps in a figure.

13. Two examples of ________________ depth cues are interposition and linear perspective.

14. Perceiving a tomato as consistently red, despite lighting shifts, is an example of
   a. shape constancy.
   b. perceptual constancy.
   c. a binocular cue.
   d. continuity.

15. After surgery to restore vision, adults who had been blind from birth had difficulty
   a. recognizing objects by touch.
   b. recognizing objects by sight.
   c. distinguishing figure from ground.
   d. distinguishing between bright and dim light.

16. In experiments, people have worn glasses that turned their visual fields upside down. After a period of adjustment, they learned to function quite well. This ability is called ________________.

MODULE 20 Hearing, Skin, Chemical, and Body Senses

Hearing

Like our other senses, our hearing—**audition**—helps us adapt and survive. Hearing provides information and enables relationships. Hearing humanizes: People seem more thoughtful, competent, and likable when we hear, not just read, their words (Schroeder & Epley, 2015, 2016). And hearing is pretty spectacular. It lets us communicate invisibly—by shooting unseen air waves across space and receiving the same from others. Hearing loss is the great invisible disability. To not catch someone's name, to not grasp what someone is asking, and to miss the hilarious joke is to be deprived of what others know, and sometimes to feel excluded. As a person with inherited hearing loss, I [DM] know the feeling and understand why adults with significant hearing loss experience increased risk of depression and anxiety (Blazer & Tucci, 2019; Scinicariello et al., 2019).

Most of us, however, can hear a wide range of sounds, and the ones we hear best are those in the range of the human voice. With normal hearing, we are remarkably sensitive to faint sounds, such as a child's whimper. (If our ears were only slightly more sensitive, we would hear a constant hiss from the movement of air molecules.) Our distant ancestors' survival depended on this keen hearing when hunting or being hunted.

We are also remarkably attuned to sound variations. Among thousands of possible voices, we easily recognize an unseen friend's. Moreover, hearing is fast. "It might take you a full second to notice something out of the corner of your eye, turn your head toward it, recognize it, and respond to it," notes auditory neuroscientist Seth Horowitz (2012). "The same reaction to a new or sudden sound happens at least 10 times as fast." A fraction of a second after such events stimulate your ear's receptors, millions of neurons have simultaneously coordinated in extracting the essential features, comparing them with past experience, and identifying the stimulus (Freeman, 1991). For hearing, as for our other senses, we wonder: How do we do it?

audition the sense or act of hearing.

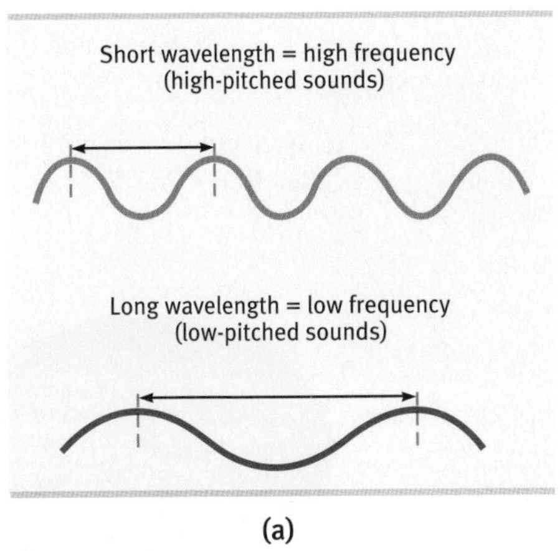
Short wavelength = high frequency
(high-pitched sounds)
Long wavelength = low frequency
(low-pitched sounds)
(a)

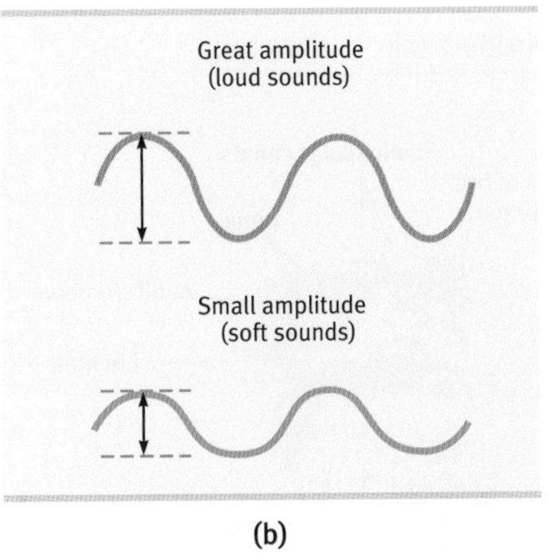
Great amplitude
(loud sounds)
Small amplitude
(soft sounds)
(b)

FIGURE 20.1
The physical properties of waves
(a) Waves vary in *wavelength* (the distance between successive peaks). *Frequency,* the number of complete wavelengths that can pass a point in a given time, depends on the wavelength. The shorter the wavelength, the higher the frequency. Wavelength determines the *pitch* of sound. (b) Waves also vary in *amplitude* (the height from peak to trough). Wave amplitude influences sound *intensity.*

The Stimulus Input: Sound Waves

LOQ 20-1 What are the characteristics of the air pressure waves that we hear as sound?

Draw a bow across a violin, and you will unleash the energy of sound waves. Air molecules, each bumping into the next, create waves of compressed and expanded air, like the ripples on a pond circling out from a tossed stone. As we swim in our ocean of moving air molecules, our ears detect these brief air pressure changes.

Like light waves, sound waves vary in shape (**FIGURE 20.1**). The height, or *amplitude,* of sound waves determines their perceived *loudness.* Their **frequency** (measured in *hertz*) determines the **pitch** (the high or low tone) we experience. Long waves have low frequency—and low pitch. Short waves have high frequency—and high pitch. Sound waves produced by a soprano are much shorter and faster than those produced by a baritone singer.

Vereshchagin Dmitry/Shutterstock

Courtesy of Eric Richmond/The Chineke! Foundation

The sounds of music A violin's short, fast waves create a high pitch. The longer, slower waves of Chi-chi Nwanoku OBE's double bass create a lower pitch. Differences in the waves' height, or amplitude, also create differing degrees of loudness.

We measure sound intensity in *decibels,* with zero decibels representing the absolute threshold for hearing. Every 10 decibels corresponds to a tenfold increase in sound intensity. Thus, normal conversation (60 decibels) is 10,000 times more intense than a 20-decibel whisper. And a temporarily tolerable 100-decibel passing subway train is 10 billion times more intense than the faintest detectable sound. If prolonged, exposure to sounds above 85 decibels can produce hearing loss. Tell that to basketball fans at the University of Kentucky who, in 2017, broke the Guinness World Record for the noisiest indoor stadium at 126 decibels (WKYT, 2017). Hear today, gone tomorrow.

The Ear

LOQ 20-2 How does the ear transform sound energy into neural messages?

How does vibrating air trigger nerve impulses that your brain can decode as sounds? The process begins when sound waves strike your *eardrum,* causing this tight membrane to vibrate (**FIGURE 20.2**).

In your **middle ear**, a piston made of three tiny bones—the *hammer* (malleus), *anvil* (incus), and *stirrup* (stapes)—picks up the vibrations and transmits them to the **cochlea**, a snail-shaped tube in your **inner ear**.

The incoming vibrations then cause the cochlea's membrane-covered opening (the *oval window*) to vibrate, jostling the fluid inside the cochlea. This motion causes ripples in the *basilar membrane,* bending the *hair cells* lining its surface, rather like grass blades bending in the wind.

frequency the number of complete wavelengths that pass a point in a given time (for example, per second).

pitch a tone's experienced highness or lowness; depends on frequency.

middle ear the chamber between the eardrum and cochlea containing three tiny bones—hammer (malleus), anvil (incus), and stirrup (stapes)—that concentrate the vibrations of the eardrum on the cochlea's oval window.

cochlea [KOHK-lee-uh] a coiled, bony, fluid-filled tube in the inner ear; sound waves traveling through the cochlear fluid trigger nerve impulses.

inner ear the innermost part of the ear, containing the cochlea, semicircular canals, and vestibular sacs.

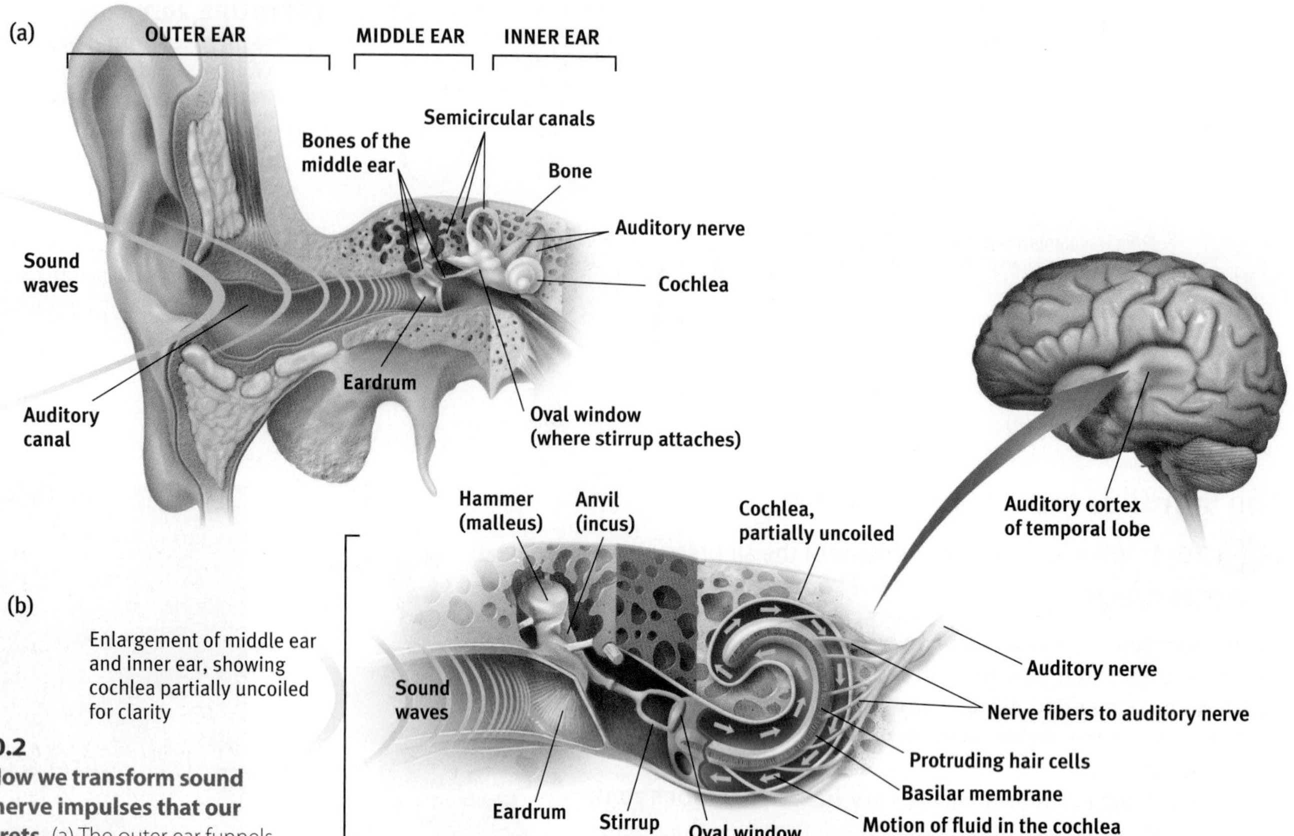
(a)
OUTER EAR
MIDDLE EAR
INNER EAR
Semicircular canals
Bones of the middle ear
Bone
Auditory nerve
Sound waves
Cochlea
Eardrum
Auditory canal
Oval window (where stirrup attaches)
Hammer (malleus)
Anvil (incus)
Cochlea, partially uncoiled
Auditory cortex of temporal lobe
(b)
Enlargement of middle ear and inner ear, showing cochlea partially uncoiled for clarity
Sound waves
Auditory nerve
Nerve fibers to auditory nerve
Protruding hair cells
Basilar membrane
Eardrum
Stirrup (stapes)
Oval window
Motion of fluid in the cochlea

FIGURE 20.2
Hear here: How we transform sound waves into nerve impulses that our brain interprets (a) The outer ear funnels sound waves to the eardrum. The bones of the middle ear (malleus, incus, and stapes) amplify and relay the eardrum's vibrations through the oval window into the fluid-filled cochlea. (b) As shown in this detail of the middle ear and inner ear, the cochlear fluid's resulting pressure changes cause the basilar membrane to ripple, bending the hair cells on its surface. Hair cell movements trigger impulses at the nerve cells' base, whose fibers converge to form the auditory nerve. That nerve sends neural messages to the thalamus and on to the auditory cortex.

The hair cell movements in turn trigger impulses in adjacent nerve cells, whose axons converge to form the *auditory nerve*. The auditory nerve carries the neural messages to your thalamus and then on to the *auditory cortex* in your brain's temporal lobe. From vibrating air, to tiny moving bones, to fluid waves, to electrical impulses to the brain: Voila! You hear!

Perhaps the most intriguing part of the hearing process is the hair cells—"quivering bundles that let us hear" thanks to their "extreme sensitivity and extreme speed" (Goldberg, 2007). A cochlea has 16,000 of them, which sounds like a lot until we compare that with an eye's 130 million or so photoreceptors. But consider a hair cell's responsiveness. Deflect the tiny bundles of *cilia* on its tip by only the width of an atom, and the alert hair cell, thanks to a special protein, will trigger a neural response (Corey et al., 2004).

Worldwide, 1.57 billion people are challenged by hearing loss and about half a billion have a disabling hearing loss (Global Burden of Disease, 2021; Wilson et al., 2017). Damage to the cochlea's hair cell receptors or the auditory nerve can cause **sensorineural hearing loss** (or nerve deafness). With auditory nerve damage, people may hear sound but have trouble discerning what someone is saying (Liberman, 2015). Sensorineural hearing loss is more common than **conduction hearing loss**, which is caused by damage to the mechanical system—the eardrum and middle ear bones—that conducts sound waves to the cochlea. Occasionally, disease damages hair cell receptors, but more often the culprit is biological changes linked with heredity and aging. I [DM] understand—as one who lives with severe hearing loss passed down from my grandmother and mother, thanks to a single gene mutation.

Toxic noise, such as prolonged exposure to ear-splitting music, is another culprit. The cochlea's hair cells have been likened to carpet fibers. Walk around on them and they will spring back. But leave a heavy piece of furniture on them and they may never rebound. As a general rule, any noise we cannot talk over (loud machinery, fans screaming at a concert or sports event, our daily music mix blasting at maximum volume) may be harmful, especially if prolonged and repeated (Roesser, 1998) (**FIGURE 20.3**). And if our ears ring after such experiences, we have been bad to our unhappy hair cells. As pain alerts us to

sensorineural hearing loss the most common form of hearing loss, caused by damage to the cochlea's receptor cells or to the auditory nerve; also called *nerve deafness*.

conduction hearing loss a less common form of hearing loss, caused by damage to the mechanical system that conducts sound waves to the cochlea.

possible bodily harm, ringing of the ears alerts us to possible hearing damage. It is hearing's equivalent of bleeding.

Since the early 1990s, teen hearing loss has risen by a third, now affecting 1 in 6 teens (Shargorodsky et al., 2010; Weichbold et al., 2012). After three hours of a rock concert averaging 99 decibels, 54 percent of teens reported temporarily not hearing as well, and 1 in 4 had ringing in their ears (Derebery et al., 2012). Teen boys more than teen girls or adults blast themselves with loud volumes for long periods (Widén et al., 2017; Zogby, 2006). Greater noise exposure may help explain why men's hearing tends to be less acute than women's. People who spend many hours working in a noisy environment should wear earplugs, or risk needing a hearing aid later (Zhou et al., 2021). "Condoms," say sex educators. "Earplugs or walk away," say hearing educators.

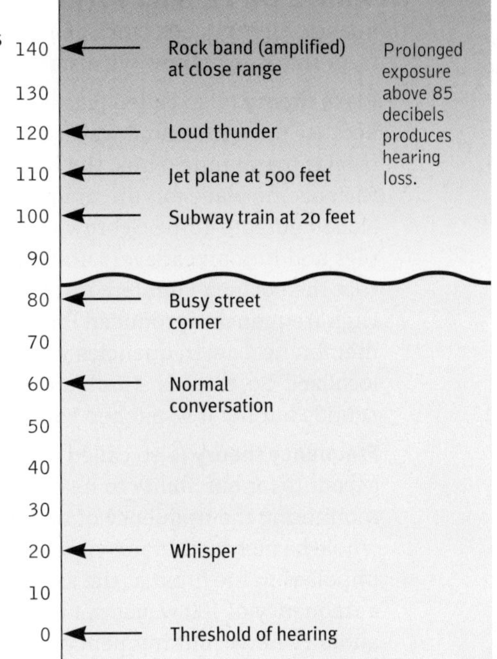
Decibels
140 Rock band (amplified) at close range
130
120 Loud thunder
110 Jet plane at 500 feet
100 Subway train at 20 feet
90
80 Busy street corner
70
60 Normal conversation
50
40
30
20 Whisper
10
0 Threshold of hearing
Prolonged exposure above 85 decibels produces hearing loss.

FIGURE 20.3
The intensity of some common sounds One study found 3 million professional musicians with almost four times the normal rate of noise-induced hearing loss (Schink et al., 2014). Noise-blocking earpieces and headphones reduce the need to blast the music at dangerous volumes.

Nerve deafness cannot, as yet, be reversed. One way to restore hearing is a sort of bionic ear—a **cochlear implant**. The implants translate sounds into electrical signals that, wired into the cochlea's nerves, convey information about sound to the brain (**FIGURE 20.4**). When given to deaf kittens and human infants, cochlear implants have seemed to trigger an "awakening" of the pertinent brain area (Klinke et al., 1999; Sireteanu, 1999). These devices can help children become proficient in oral communication (especially if they receive them as preschoolers or ideally before age 1) (Dettman et al., 2007; Schorr et al., 2005). Hearing, like vision, has a *critical period.* As I [DM] can attest, cochlear implants can help restore hearing for most adults, but only if their brain learned to process sound during childhood. The restored hearing can also reduce social isolation and the risk of depression (Mosnier et al., 2015).

cochlear implant a device for converting sounds into electrical signals and stimulating the auditory nerve through electrodes threaded into the cochlea.

RETRIEVAL PRACTICE

RP-1 The amplitude of a sound wave determines our perception of ________ (loudness/pitch).

RP-2 The longer the sound waves, the ________ (lower/higher) their frequency and the ________ (higher/lower) their pitch.

ANSWERS IN APPENDIX E

FIGURE 20.4
Hardware for hearing Cochlear implants work by translating sounds into electrical signals that are transmitted to the cochlea and, via the auditory nerve, relayed to the brain.

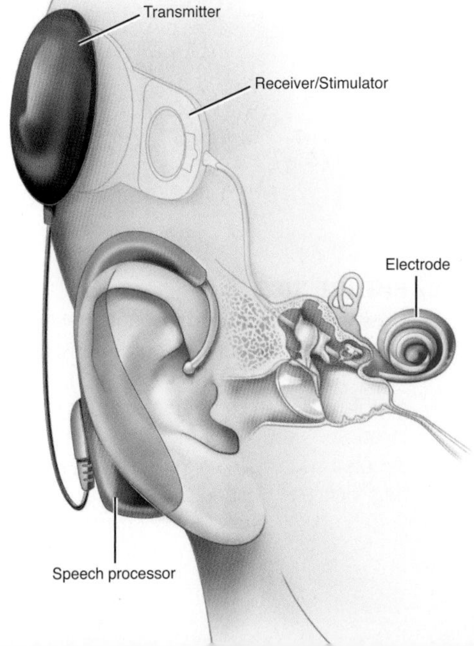
Transmitter
Receiver/Stimulator
Electrode
Speech processor

Perceiving Loudness, Pitch, and Location

LOQ 20-3 How do we detect loudness, discriminate pitch, and locate sounds?

RESPONDING TO LOUD AND SOFT SOUNDS How do we detect loudness? If you guessed that it's related to the *intensity* of a hair cell's response, you'd be wrong. Rather, a soft, pure tone activates only the few hair cells attuned to its frequency. Given louder sounds, neighboring hair cells also respond. Thus, your brain interprets loudness from the *number* of activated hair cells.

If a hair cell loses sensitivity to soft sounds, it may still respond to loud sounds. This helps explain another surprise: Really loud sounds may seem loud to people with or without normal hearing. Given my hearing loss, I [DM] have wondered what really loud music must sound like to people with normal hearing. Now I realize it sounds much the same; where we differ is in our perception of soft sounds (and our ability to isolate one sound amid noise). This is why we hard-of-hearing people do not want *all* sounds (loud and soft) amplified. We like sound *compressed,* which means harder-to-hear sounds are amplified more than loud sounds (a feature of today's digital hearing aids).

place theory in hearing, the theory that links the pitch we hear with the place where the cochlea's membrane is stimulated. (Also called *place coding.*)

frequency theory in hearing, the theory that the rate of nerve impulses traveling up the auditory nerve matches the frequency of a tone, thus enabling us to sense its pitch. (Also called *temporal coding.*)

HEARING DIFFERENT PITCHES How do we know whether a sound is the high-frequency, high-pitched chirp of a bird or the low-frequency, low-pitched roar of a truck? Current thinking on how we discriminate pitch combines two theories.

- **Place theory** (also called *place coding*) presumes that we hear different pitches because different sound waves trigger activity at different places along the cochlea's basilar membrane. Thus, the brain determines a sound's pitch by recognizing the specific place (on the membrane) that is generating the neural signal. When Nobel laureate-to-be Georg von Békésy (1957) cut holes in the cochleas of guinea pigs and human cadavers and looked inside with a microscope, he discovered that the cochlea vibrated, rather like a shaken bedsheet, in response to sound. High frequencies produced large vibrations near the beginning of the cochlea's membrane. Low frequencies vibrated more of the membrane and were not so easily localized. So, there is a problem: Place theory can explain how we hear high-pitched sounds but not low-pitched sounds.
- **Frequency theory** (also called *temporal coding*) suggests another explanation that accounts for our ability to hear low-pitched sounds: The brain reads pitch by monitoring the frequency of neural impulses traveling up the auditory nerve. The whole basilar membrane vibrates with the incoming sound wave, triggering neural impulses to the brain at the same rate as the sound wave. If the sound wave has a frequency of 100 waves per second, then 100 pulses per second travel up the auditory nerve. But frequency theory also has a problem: An individual neuron cannot fire faster than 1000 times per second. How, then, can we sense sounds with frequencies above 1000 waves per second (roughly the upper third of a piano keyboard)? Enter the *volley principle:* Like soldiers who alternate firing so that some can shoot while others reload, neural cells can alternate firing. By firing in rapid succession, they can achieve a *combined frequency* above 1000 waves per second.

So, place theory and frequency theory work together to enable our perception of pitch. Place theory best explains how we sense *high pitches*. Frequency theory, extended by the volley principle, explains how we sense *low pitches*. Finally, some combination of place and frequency theories likely explains how we sense *pitches in the intermediate range*.

RETRIEVAL PRACTICE

RP-3 Which theory of pitch perception would best explain a symphony audience's enjoyment of a high-pitched piccolo? How about a low-pitched cello?

ANSWERS IN APPENDIX E

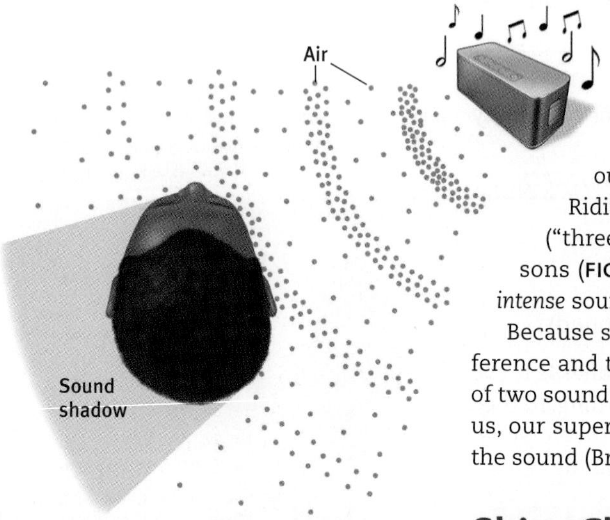

LOCATING SOUNDS Why don't we have one big ear—perhaps above our one nose? "All the better to hear you with," as the wolf said to Little Red Riding Hood. Thanks to the placement of our two ears, we enjoy stereophonic ("three-dimensional") hearing. Two ears are better than one for at least two reasons (**FIGURE 20.5**). If a car to your right honks, your right ear will receive a more *intense* sound, and it will receive the sound slightly *sooner* than your left ear.

Because sound travels fast and human ears are not very far apart, the intensity difference and the time lag are extremely small. A *just noticeable difference* in the direction of two sound sources corresponds to a time difference of just 0.000027 second! Lucky for us, our supersensitive auditory system can detect such minute differences and locate the sound (Brown & Deffenbacher, 1979; Middlebrooks & Green, 1991).

Air
Sound shadow

FIGURE 20.5
How we locate sounds Sound waves strike one ear sooner and more intensely than the other. From this information, our nimble brain can compute the sound's location. As you might therefore expect, people who lose all hearing in one ear often have difficulty locating sounds.

Skin, Chemical, and Body Senses

Sharks and dogs rely on their outstanding sense of smell, aided by large smell-related brain areas. Our human brain allocates more real estate to seeing and hearing. But extraordinary happenings also occur within our skin (touch and pain), chemical (taste and smell), and body (position and movement) senses. Without these other senses, we humans would be seriously hampered, and our capacity for enjoying the world would be greatly diminished.

Touch

LOQ 20-4 What are the four basic touch sensations, and how do we sense touch?

Touch, our tactile sense, is vital. From infancy to adulthood, affectionate touches promote our well-being (Jakubiak & Feeney, 2017). Right from the start, touch aids our development. Infant rats deprived of their mother's grooming produce less growth hormone and have a lower metabolic rate—a good way to keep alive until the mother returns, but a reaction that stunts growth if prolonged. Infant monkeys that are allowed to see, hear, and smell—but not touch—their mother become desperately unhappy (Suomi et al., 1976). Premature human babies gain weight faster and go home sooner if they are stimulated by hand massage (Field et al., 2006). Coping with disaster or grieving a death, we may find comfort in a hug. As adults, we still yearn to touch—to kiss, to stroke, to snuggle.

Humorist Dave Barry (1985, p. 2) was perhaps right to jest that your skin "keeps people from seeing the inside of your body, which is repulsive, and it prevents your organs from falling onto the ground." But skin does much more. Touching various spots on the skin with a soft hair, a warm or cool wire, and the point of a pin reveals that some spots are especially sensitive to *pressure*, others to *warmth*, others to *cold*, still others to *pain*. Our "sense of touch" is actually a mix of these four basic and distinct skin senses, and our other skin sensations are variations of pressure, warmth, cold, and pain. For example, stroking adjacent pressure spots creates a tickle. Repeated gentle stroking of a pain spot creates an itching sensation. Touching adjacent cold and pressure spots triggers a sense of wetness (which you can experience by touching dry, cold metal).

© Jose Luis Pelaez/Blend Images/Corbis

The precious sense of touch As William James wrote in his *Principles of Psychology* (1890), "Touch is both the alpha and omega of affection."

Touch sensations involve more than tactile stimulation, however. A self-administered tickle produces less somatosensory cortex activation than does the same tickle from something or someone else (Blakemore et al., 1998). Likewise, a sensual leg caress evokes a different somatosensory cortex response when a heterosexual man believes it comes from an attractive woman rather than a man (Gazzola et al., 2012). Such responses reveal how quickly cognition influences our brain's sensory response.

Pain

LOQ 20-5 What biological, psychological, and social-cultural influences affect our experience of pain? How do placebos, distraction, and hypnosis help control pain?

Be thankful for occasional pain. Pain is your body's way of telling you something has gone wrong. Drawing your attention to a burn, a break, or a sprain, pain orders you to change your behavior—"Stay off that ankle!"

The rare people born without the ability to feel pain may experience pain-free childbirth, but also are at risk of severe injury or even early death (Habib et al., 2019). Without the discomfort that makes us shift position, their joints can fail from excess strain. Without the warnings of pain, infections can run wild and injuries can accumulate (Neese, 1991).

More numerous are those who live with chronic pain, which is like an alarm that won't shut off. Persistent backaches, arthritis, headaches, and cancer-related pain prompt two questions: What is pain? How might we control it?

Photo by Jeff Riedel/Contour by Getty Images

"Pain is a gift." So said a doctor studying Ashlyn Blocker, who has a rare genetic mutation that prevents her from feeling pain. At birth, she didn't cry. As a child, she ran around for 2 days on a broken ankle. She has put her hands on a hot machine and burned the flesh off. And she has reached into boiling water to retrieve a dropped spoon. "Everyone in my class asks me about it, and I say, 'I can feel pressure, but I can't feel pain.' *Pain!* I cannot feel it!" (Heckert, 2012).

UNDERSTANDING PAIN Our experience of pain reflects both *bottom-up* sensations and *top-down* cognition. Pain is a biopsychosocial phenomenon (Hadjistavropoulos et al., 2011). As such, pain experiences vary widely, from group to group and from person to person. Viewing pain from the biological, psychological, and social-cultural perspectives can help us better understand it, and also help us cope with it and treat it (**FIGURE 20.6**).

FIGURE 20.6
Biopsychosocial approach to pain Our experience of pain is much more than the neural messages sent to our brain.

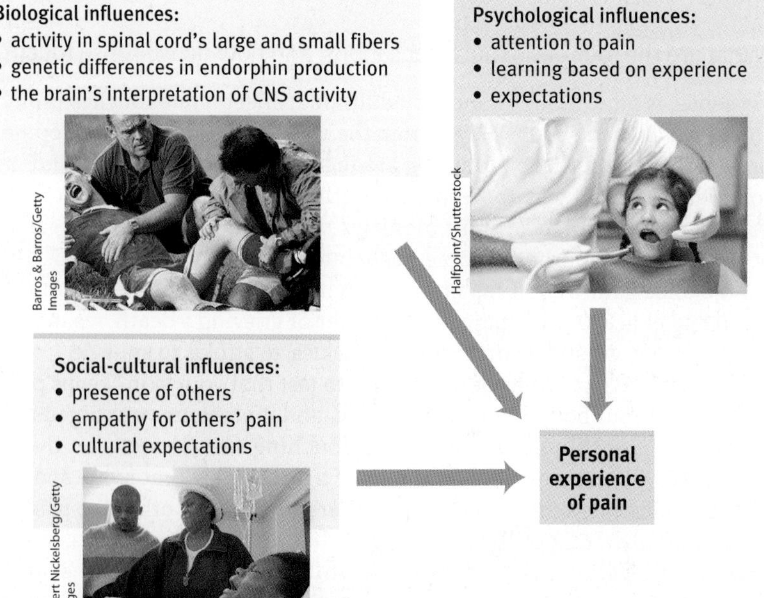
Biological influences:
• activity in spinal cord's large and small fibers
• genetic differences in endorphin production
• the brain's interpretation of CNS activity
Barros & Barros/Getty Images
Psychological influences:
• attention to pain
• learning based on experience
• expectations
Halfpoint/Shutterstock
Social-cultural influences:
• presence of others
• empathy for others' pain
• cultural expectations
Robert Nickelsberg/Getty Images
Personal experience of pain

gate-control theory the theory that the spinal cord contains a neurological "gate" that blocks pain signals or allows them to pass on to the brain. The "gate" is opened by the activity of pain signals traveling up small nerve fibers and is closed by activity in larger fibers or by information coming from the brain.

Biological Influences Pain is a physical event produced by your senses. But pain differs from some of your other sensations. No one type of stimulus triggers pain the way light triggers vision. And no specialized receptors process pain signals the way your retina receptors react to light rays. Instead, sensory receptors called *nociceptors*—mostly in your skin, but also in your muscles and organs—detect hurtful temperatures, pressure, or chemicals (**FIGURE 20.7**). Your brain's neural networks process these sensations and produce perceptions of pain (Tan & Kuner, 2021).

FIGURE 20.7
The pain circuit Sensory receptors *(nociceptors)* respond to potentially damaging stimuli by sending an impulse to the spinal cord, which passes the message to the brain, which interprets the signal as pain.

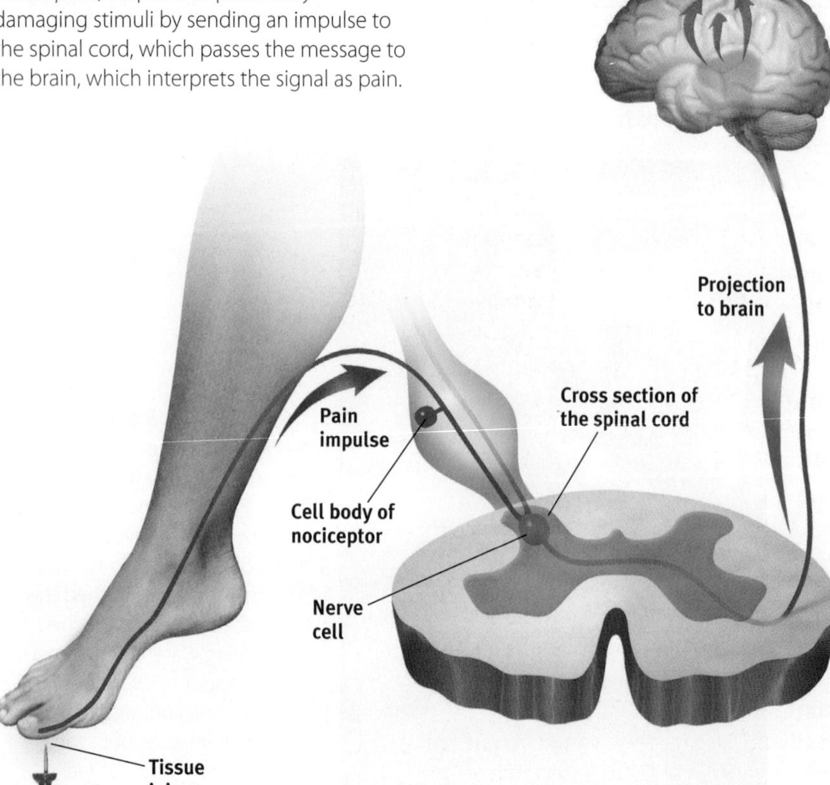
Projection to brain
Pain impulse
Cross section of the spinal cord
Cell body of nociceptor
Nerve cell
Tissue injury

People's pain experiences differ. Those who *fear* pain the most tend to *feel* pain the most (Markfelder & Pauli, 2020). Your experience of pain depends in part on the genes you inherited and on your physical characteristics (Gatchel et al., 2007; Reimann et al., 2010). Women are more sensitive to pain than men are (their senses of hearing and smell also tend to be more sensitive) (Ruau et al., 2012; Wickelgren, 2009).

No pain theory can explain all available findings. One useful model, **gate-control theory**, suggests that the spinal cord contains a neurological "gate" that controls the transmission of pain messages to the brain (Melzack & Katz, 2013; Melzack & Wall, 1965, 1983).

Small spinal cord nerve fibers conduct most pain signals. An injury activates the small fibers and opens the gate. The pain signals can then travel to your brain, and you feel pain. But large-fiber activity (stimulated by massage, electrical stimulation, or acupuncture) can close the pain gate by blocking pain signals. Brain-to-spinal-cord messages can also close the gate. Thus, chronic pain can be treated both by gate-closing stimulation, such as massage, and by mental activity, such as distraction (Wall, 2000).

We also benefit from our own natural painkillers, *endorphins,* which are released in response to severe pain or vigorous exercise. People who carry a gene that boosts the availability of endorphins are less bothered by pain, and their brain is less responsive to pain (Zubieta et al., 2003). Others, who carry a mutated gene that disrupts pain circuit neurotransmission, may not experience pain (Cox et al., 2006). Such discoveries point the way toward future pain medications that mimic these genetic effects.

Pain is not merely a physical phenomenon of injured nerves sending impulses to a definable brain or spinal cord area—like pulling on a rope to ring a bell. The brain can also create pain, as it does in *phantom limb sensations*. Without normal sensory input from a missing limb, the brain may misinterpret and amplify spontaneous but irrelevant central nervous system activity. As the dreamer sees with eyes closed, so 7 in 10 people who have undergone limb amputation feel pain or movement in nonexistent limbs (Melzack, 1992, 2005). Some may even try to lift a cup with a phantom hand, or step off a bed onto a phantom leg. Even those born without a limb sometimes perceive sensations from the absent arm or leg; the brain comes prepared to anticipate "that it will be getting information from a body that has limbs" (Melzack, 1998).

Phantoms may haunt other senses, too. People with hearing loss often experience the sound of silence. *Tinnitus*, the phantom sound of ringing in the ears, is not produced by vibrating air molecules but is accompanied by auditory brain activity (Sedley et al., 2015). Those who lose vision to glaucoma, cataracts, diabetes, or macular degeneration may experience phantom sights—nonthreatening hallucinations (Painter et al., 2018). Others with nerve damage in the tasting and smelling systems have experienced phantom tastes or smells, such as ice water that seems sickeningly sweet or fresh air that reeks of rotten food (Goode, 1999). *The point to remember*: We feel, see, hear, taste, and smell with our brain.

Reinhold Matay/AP Photo

Distracted from the pain After a tackle in the first half of a competitive game, Mohammed Ali Khan (here playing for BK Häcken in white) said he "had a bit of pain" but thought it was "just a bruise." With his attention focused on the game, he played on. In the second half he was surprised to learn from an attending doctor that his leg was broken.

Psychological Influences One powerful influence on our perception of pain is the attention we focus on it. Athletes, focused on winning, may perceive pain differently and play through it. Injured soldiers, caught up in battle, may feel little or no pain until they reach safety.

We also seem to edit our *memories* of pain, which often differ from the pain we actually experienced. In experiments, and after painful medical procedures or childbirth, people overlook a pain's duration. Instead, their memory snapshots record two factors: their pain's *peak* moment (which can lead them to recall variable pain, with peaks, as worse [Chajut et al., 2014; Stone et al., 2005]), and how much pain they felt at the *end*. In one experiment, people immersed one hand in painfully cold water for 60 seconds followed by a slightly less painful 30 seconds more (Kahneman et al., 1993). Which experience would you expect they recalled as most painful?

"Pain is increased by attending to it." —Charles Darwin, *The Expression of the Emotions in Man and Animals*, 1872

Curiously, when asked which trial they would prefer to repeat, most preferred the 90-second trial, with more net pain—but less pain at the end. Physicians have used this principle with patients undergoing sedation-free colon exams—lengthening the discomfort by a minute but lessening its intensity at the end (Kahneman, 1999). Imagine undergoing a painful procedure and having the doctor ask if you'd rather go home now or bear a few more minutes of milder discomfort. There's a case to be made for prolonging a tapered hurt.

The end of an experience can color our memory of pleasures, too. In one simple experiment, some people, on receiving a fifth and last piece of chocolate, were told it was their "next" one. Others, told it was their "last" piece, liked it better and rated the whole experiment as being more enjoyable (O'Brien & Ellsworth, 2012). Endings matter.

Social-Cultural Influences Pain is a product of our attention, our expectations, and also our culture (Gatchel et al., 2007; Reimann et al., 2010). Not surprisingly, then, our perception of pain varies with our social situation and our cultural traditions. We tend to perceive more pain when others also seem to be experiencing pain (Symbaluk et al., 1997). This may help explain the apparent social aspects of pain, as when groups of Australian keyboard operators during the mid-1980s suffered outbreaks of severe pain while typing or performing other repetitive work—without any discernible physical abnormalities (Gawande, 1998). Sometimes the pain in a sprain is mainly in the brain—literally. When people feel empathy for another's pain, their own brain activity partly mirrors the activity of the actual brain in pain (Singer et al., 2004).

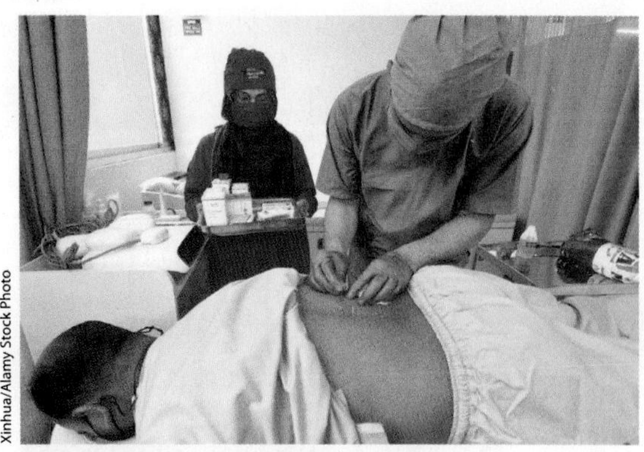

Xinhua/Alamy Stock Photo

Acupuncture: A jab well done Kawsar Ali Sardar began experiencing severe headaches in 2021 after having Covid. Acupuncture treatments, received near his home in Dhaka, Bangladesh, brought some relief.

Ellis Rosen/Cartoon Stock

"It's like I'm actually walking."

CONTROLLING PAIN If pain is where body meets mind—if it is both a physical and a psychological phenomenon—then it should be treatable both physically and psychologically. Depending on the symptoms, pain control therapies may include drugs, surgery, acupuncture, electrical stimulation, massage, exercise, hypnosis, relaxation training, meditation, and thought distraction.

Placebos Even *placebos* can help, by dampening the central nervous system's attention and responses to painful experiences—mimicking painkilling drugs (Eippert et al., 2009; Wager & Atlas, 2013). After being injected in the jaw with a stinging saltwater solution, men in one experiment received a placebo they had been told would relieve the pain. It did—they immediately felt better. "Nothing" worked. The men's belief in the fake painkiller triggered their brain to respond by dispensing endorphins, as revealed by activity in an area that releases natural painkilling opiates (Scott et al., 2007; Zubieta et al., 2005).

Distraction Have you ever had a health care professional suggest that you focus on a pleasant image ("Think of a warm, comfortable environment") during a procedure, or perform some distracting task ("Count backward by 3s") while receiving an unpleasant treatment? Drawing attention away from the painful stimulation is an effective way to activate brain pathways that inhibit pain and increase pain tolerance (Edwards et al., 2009). For burn victims receiving excruciating wound care, an even more effective distraction is escaping into virtual reality. Functional MRI (fMRI) scans have revealed that playing in a computer-generated 3-D world reduces the brain's pain-related activity (Hoffman, 2004). Because pain is in the brain, diverting the brain's attention may bring relief. Being "fully immersed in a virtual environment [is] like a 'brain hack,'" said one doctor who uses virtual reality to treat pain. "You can't be engaged in anything else" (Brody, 2019).

Hypnosis Better yet, research suggests, try maximizing pain relief by combining a placebo with distraction (Buhle et al., 2012) and amplifying their effects with **hypnosis**. Imagine you are about to be hypnotized. The hypnotist invites you to sit back, fix your gaze on a spot high on the wall, and relax. You hear a quiet, low voice suggest, "Your eyes are growing tired. . . . Your eyelids are becoming heavy . . . now heavier and heavier. . . . They are beginning to close. . . . You are becoming more deeply relaxed. . . . Your breathing is now deep and regular. . . . Your muscles are becoming more and more relaxed. . . . Your whole body is beginning to feel like lead." After a few minutes of this *hypnotic induction*, you may experience hypnosis. Words can temporarily change your brain activity.

Hypnotists have no magical mind-control power; they merely focus people's attention on certain images or behaviors. To some extent, we are all open to suggestion. But highly hypnotizable people—such as the 20 percent who can carry out a suggestion not to react to an open bottle of smelly ammonia—are especially suggestible and imaginative (Barnier & McConkey, 2004; Silva & Kirsch, 1992). Their brain also displays altered activity when under hypnosis (Jiang et al., 2016).

Can hypnosis relieve pain? *Yes*. When unhypnotized people put their arm in an ice bath, they felt intense pain within 25 seconds (Elkins et al., 2012; Jensen, 2008). When hypnotized people did the same after being given suggestions to feel no pain, they indeed reported feeling little pain. Hypnosis can also reduce some forms of chronic and disability-related pain (Adachi et al., 2014; Bowker & Dorstyn, 2016).

In surgical experiments, hypnotized patients have required less medication, recovered sooner, and left the hospital earlier than unhypnotized control patients (Askay & Patterson, 2007; Hammond, 2008; Spiegel, 2007). Nearly 10 percent of us can become so deeply hypnotized that even major surgery can be performed without anesthesia. Half of us can gain at least some pain relief from hypnosis. The surgical use of hypnosis has flourished in Europe, where one Belgian medical team has performed more than 5000 surgeries with a combination of hypnosis, local anesthesia, and a mild sedative (Facco, 2016; Song, 2006).

Psychologists have proposed two explanations for how hypnosis works:

- *Social influence theory* contends that hypnosis is a by-product of normal social and mental processes (Lynn et al., 1990, 2015; Spanos & Coe, 1992). In this view,

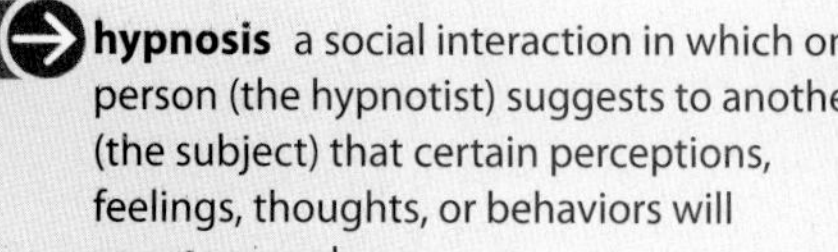

hypnosis a social interaction in which one person (the hypnotist) suggests to another (the subject) that certain perceptions, feelings, thoughts, or behaviors will spontaneously occur.

hypnotized people, like actors caught up in a role, begin to feel and behave in ways appropriate for "good hypnotic subjects." They may allow the hypnotist to direct their attention away from pain.

- *Dissociation theory* proposes that hypnosis is a special dual-processing state of **dissociation**—a split between different levels of consciousness. Dissociation theory seeks to explain why, when no one is watching, previously hypnotized people may later carry out **posthypnotic suggestions** (Perugini et al., 1998). It also explains why people hypnotized for pain relief may show brain activity in areas that receive sensory information, but not in areas that normally process pain-related information (Rainville et al., 1997).

Selective attention (see the Consciousness and the Two-Track Mind modules) may also play a role in hypnotic pain relief. Brain scans show that hypnosis increases activity in frontal lobe attention systems (Oakley & Halligan, 2013). So, while hypnosis does not block sensory input itself, it may redirect our attention to other stimuli.

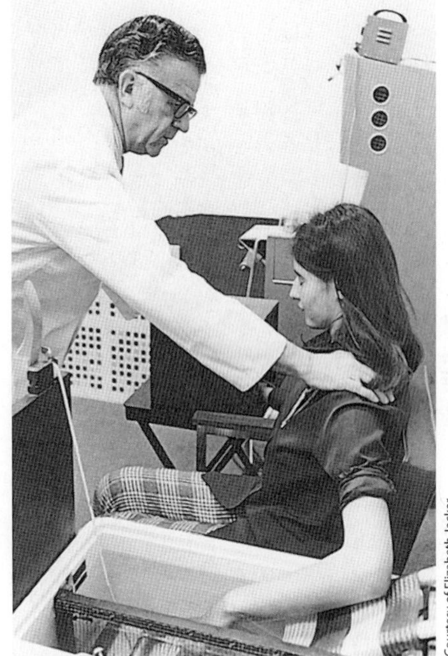
Courtesy of Elizabeth Jecker

Dissociation or social influence? This hypnotized woman being tested by researcher Ernest Hilgard showed no pain when her arm was placed in an ice bath. She said the water felt cold, but not painful. But asked to press a key if some part of her felt the pain, she did so. Although Hilgard (1986, 1992) argued that this was evidence of "dissociation," the social influence perspective assumes that the woman was simply caught up in playing the role of "good subject."

ASK YOURSELF

What methods of pain control do you usually turn to when you need it? Has learning about these ways to control pain given you some new ideas about other strategies to try?

RETRIEVAL PRACTICE

RP-4 Which of the following options has NOT been proven to reduce pain?

a. Distraction b. Hypnosis c. Phantom limb sensations d. Endorphins

ANSWERS IN APPENDIX E

Chemical Senses: Taste and Smell

LOQ 20-6 In what ways are our senses of taste and smell similar, and how do they differ?

TASTE Like touch, **gustation**—our sense of taste—involves several basic sensations. Taste's sensations were once thought to be *sweet, sour, salty,* and *bitter,* with all others stemming from mixtures of these four (McBurney & Gent, 1979). Then, as investigators searched for specialized nerve fibers for the four taste sensations, they encountered a receptor for what we now know is a fifth—the savory, meaty taste of *umami,* best experienced as the flavor enhancer monosodium glutamate (MSG).

Tastes exist for more than our pleasure (see **TABLE 20.1**). Pleasureful tastes attracted our ancestors to energy- or protein-rich foods that enabled their survival. Aversive tastes deterred them from new foods that might be toxic. We see the inheritance of this biological wisdom in today's 2- to 6-year-olds, who are typically fussy eaters, especially when offered new meats or bitter-tasting vegetables, such as spinach and brussels sprouts (Cooke et al., 2003). Meat and plant toxins were both potentially dangerous sources of food poisoning for our ancestors, especially children. Given repeated small tastes of disliked but safe new foods, however, most children begin to accept them (Wardle et al., 2003). We come to like what we eat. Compared with breast-fed babies, German babies bottle-fed vanilla-flavored milk grew up to be adults with a striking preference for vanilla flavoring (Haller et al., 1999). The taste-exposure phenomenon even extends to

TABLE 20.1 The Survival Functions of Basic Tastes

Taste	Indicates
Sweet	Energy source
Salty	Sodium essential to physiological processes
Sour	Potentially toxic acid
Bitter	Potential poisons
Umami	Proteins to grow and repair tissue

dissociation a split in consciousness, which allows some thoughts and behaviors to occur simultaneously with others. 

posthypnotic suggestion a suggestion, made during a hypnosis session, to be carried out after the subject is no longer hypnotized; used by some clinicians to help control undesired symptoms and behaviors.

gustation our sense of taste.

Macmillan Learning

Linda Bartoshuk As a student in the late 1950s era of gender discrimination, Bartoshuk (2010) abandoned her interest in astronomy when she learned that "women weren't allowed to use the big telescopes." This led her to *psychophysics*—the study of how physical stimuli, such as substances on the tongue, create our subjective experience. While studying taste experiences, she discovered *supertasters*.

the womb. In one experiment, babies whose mothers drank carrot juice during the end of pregnancy and the early weeks of nursing developed a liking for carrot-flavored cereal (Mennella et al., 2001).

Taste is a chemical sense. Inside each little bump on the top and sides of your tongue are 200 or more taste buds, each containing a pore that catches food chemicals and releases neurotransmitters (Roper & Chaudhari, 2017). In each taste bud pore, 50 to 100 taste receptor cells project antenna-like hairs that sense food molecules. Some receptors respond mostly to sweet-tasting molecules, others to salty-, sour-, umami-, or bitter-tasting ones. Each receptor transmits its message to a matching partner cell in your brain's temporal lobe (Barretto et al., 2015). Some people have more taste buds than others, enabling them to experience more intense tastes. Psychologist Linda Bartoshuk (2000) has researched these *supertasters* and how they can taste some things that the rest of us cannot.

For most people, it doesn't take much to trigger a taste response. If a stream of water is pumped across your tongue, the addition of a concentrated salty or sweet taste for but one-tenth of a second will get your attention (Kelling & Halpern, 1983). When a friend asks for "just a taste" of your smoothie, a few drops from your straw is all they'll need.

Taste receptors reproduce themselves every week or two, so if you burn your tongue it hardly matters. However, as you grow older, the number of taste buds decreases, as does taste sensitivity (Cowart, 1981). (No wonder adults enjoy strong-tasting foods that children resist.) Smoking and alcohol use accelerate these declines. Those who have lost their sense of taste have reported that food tastes like "straw" and is hard to swallow (Cowart, 2005).

There's more to taste than meets the tongue. Wear a blindfold when eating a meal and you will attend more to (and savor) its taste (O'Brien & Smith, 2019). Expectations also influence taste. When told a sausage roll was "vegetarian," nonvegetarian people judged it decidedly inferior to its identical partner labeled "meat" (Allen et al., 2008). In another experiment, hearing that a wine cost $90 rather than its real $10 price made it taste better and triggered more activity in a brain area that responds to pleasant experiences (Plassmann et al., 2008). Contrary to Shakespeare's presumption (in *Romeo and Juliet*) that "A rose by any other name would smell as sweet," labels matter. And speaking of smell . . .

SMELL Inhale, exhale. Between birth's first inhale and death's last exhale, an average 500 million breaths of life-sustaining air bathe human nostrils in a stream of scent-laden molecules. The resulting experience of smell—**olfaction**—is strikingly intimate. With every breath, you inhale something of whatever or whoever it is you smell.

Smell, like taste, is a chemical sense. We smell something when molecules of a substance carried in the air reach a tiny cluster of receptor cells at the top of each nasal cavity (**FIGURE 20.8**). By sniffing, you swirl air up to those receptors, enhancing the aroma. These 20 million olfactory receptors, waving like sea anemones on a reef, respond selectively—to the aroma of a cake baking, to a wisp of smoke, to a friend's fragrance. Instantly, they alert the brain through their axon fibers.

Impress your friends with your new word for the day: People unable to see are said to experience blindness. People unable to hear experience deafness. People unable to smell experience *anosmia*. The 1 in 7500 people born with anosmia not only have trouble cooking and eating, but also are somewhat more prone to depression, accidents, and relationship insecurity (Croy et al., 2012, 2013). The loss of smell and taste have been commonly reported symptoms of Covid-19.

Being part of an old, primitive sense, olfactory neurons bypass the brain's sensory control center, the thalamus. Eons before our cerebral cortex had fully evolved, our mammalian ancestors sniffed for food—and for predators. They also smelled molecules called *pheromones*, especially those secreted by other members of their species. Some pheromones now serve as sexual attractants. When straight men smelled ovulating women's T-shirts, the men became more sexually interested and experienced increased testosterone (Miller & Maner, 2010, 2011).

Odor molecules come in many shapes and sizes—so many, in fact, that it takes many different receptors to detect them. A large family of genes designs the 350 or so receptor proteins that recognize particular odor molecules (Miller, 2004). Linda Buck and Richard Axel (1991) discovered (in work for which they received a 2004 Nobel Prize) that these receptor proteins are embedded on the surface of nasal cavity neurons. As a key slips into a lock, so odor molecules slip into these receptors. Yet we don't seem to have a distinct receptor for each detectable odor. Odors trigger combinations of receptors, in patterns that are interpreted by the olfactory cortex. As the English alphabet's 26 letters can

olfaction our sense of smell.

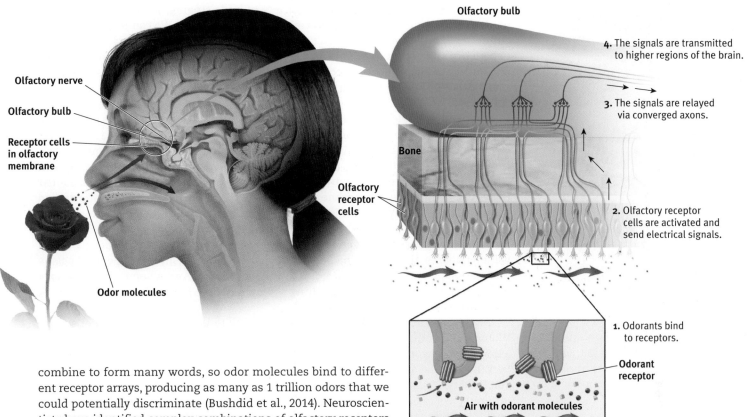

Olfactory nerve
Olfactory bulb
Receptor cells in olfactory membrane
Odor molecules
Olfactory bulb
Bone
Olfactory receptor cells
4. The signals are transmitted to higher regions of the brain.
3. The signals are relayed via converged axons.
2. Olfactory receptor cells are activated and send electrical signals.
1. Odorants bind to receptors.
Odorant receptor
Air with odorant molecules

FIGURE 20.8
The sense of smell Olfactory receptor cells receive airborne molecules and then send messages to the brain's olfactory bulb, which then sends them to the temporal lobe's primary smell cortex and to the parts of the limbic system involved in memory and emotion.

combine to form many words, so odor molecules bind to different receptor arrays, producing as many as 1 trillion odors that we could potentially discriminate (Bushdid et al., 2014). Neuroscientists have identified complex combinations of olfactory receptors that trigger different neural networks, allowing us to distinguish between delightful and disagreeable odors (Zou et al., 2016).

Animals that have many times more olfactory receptors than we do also use their sense of smell to survive, to communicate, and to navigate. Elephants can smell the difference between small and large amounts of food—letting them know whether they have enough to feed themselves or their herd (Plotnik et al., 2019). And long before a shark can see its prey, or a moth its mate, olfactory cues direct their way, as they also do for migrating salmon returning to their home stream. After being exposed in a hatchery to one of two odorant chemicals, returning salmon will later seek whichever stream was spiked with the familiar smell (Barinaga, 1999).

Aided by smell, a mother fur seal returning to a beach crowded with pups will find her own. Human mothers and nursing infants also quickly learn to recognize each other's scents (McCarthy, 1986). When people in loving relationships catch a whiff of their romantic partner's scent, their stress hormone levels drop (Granqvist et al., 2019; Hofer et al., 2018). As any dog or cat with a good nose could tell us, we each have our own identifiable chemical signature. (One noteworthy exception: A dog will follow the tracks of one identical twin as though they had been made by the other person [Thomas, 1974].)

The brain knows what the nose knows (Cook et al., 2017; Zou et al., 2016). When mice sniff a predator's scent, their brain instinctively sends signals to stress-related neurons (Kondoh et al., 2016). But smell expert Rachel Herz (2001) has noted that a smell's appeal—or lack of it—also depends on cultural experiences. In North America, people associate the smell of wintergreen with candy and gum, and they tend to like it. In Britain, wintergreen often is associated with medicine, and people find it less appealing. Odors also evoked unpleasant emotions when researchers frustrated Brown University students with a rigged computer game in a scented room (Herz et al., 2004). Later, if exposed to the same odor while working on a verbal task, the students' frustration was rekindled and they gave up sooner than others exposed to a different odor or no odor.

Although important, our sense of smell is less acute than our senses of seeing and hearing. Looking out across a garden, we see its forms and

The nose knows Humans have some 20 million olfactory receptors. A bloodhound has 220 million (Herz, 2007).

Layne Bailey/The Charlotte Observer/AP Photo

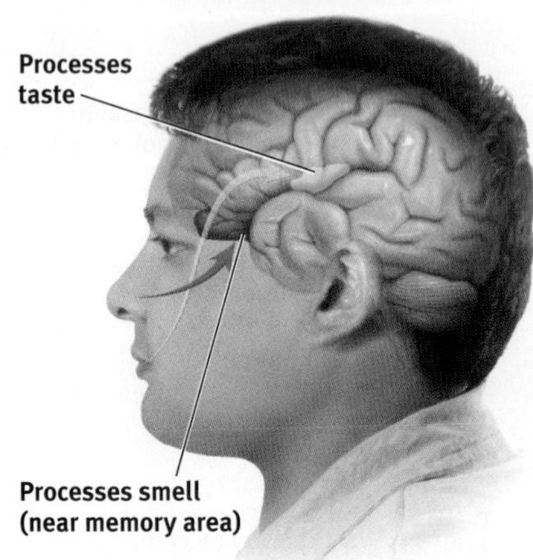
Processes taste
Processes smell (near memory area)

FIGURE 20.9
Taste, smell, and memory Information from the taste buds travels to an area between the brain's frontal and temporal lobes (yellow arrow). It registers in an area not far from where the brain receives information from our sense of smell (red area), which interacts with taste. The brain's circuitry for smell also connects with areas involved in memory storage, which helps explain why a smell can trigger a memory.

colors in exquisite detail and hear a variety of birds singing, yet we miss some of a garden's scents unless we stick our nose into the blossoms. We can learn to identify subtle smell differences, but it isn't easy (Al Aïn et al., 2019). Compared with how we experience and remember sights and sounds, smells are harder to describe and recall (Richardson & Zucco, 1989; Zucco, 2003). Test it yourself: Which is easier, describing the *sound* of coffee brewing, or the *aroma* of coffee? For most people in Western cultures, it's the sound.

We might struggle to recall odors by name, but we have a remarkable capacity to recognize long-forgotten odors and their associated memories (Engen, 1987; Schab, 1991). Our brain's circuitry helps explain why the smell of the sea, the scent of a perfume, or an aroma of a favorite relative's kitchen can bring to mind a happy time. Other odors remind us of traumatic events, activating brain regions related to fear (Kadohisa, 2013). Indeed, a hotline runs between the brain area receiving information from the nose and the brain's limbic centers associated with memory and emotion (FIGURE 20.9). Thus, when put in a foul-smelling room, people have expressed harsher judgments of other people and of immoral acts (such as lying or keeping a found wallet) (Inbar et al., 2012; Schnall et al., 2008). Exposed to a fishy smell, people became more suspicious (Lee et al., 2015; Lee & Schwarz, 2020). And when riding in a train car with the citrus scent of a cleaning product, people have left behind less trash (de Lange et al., 2012).

Gender, age, and expertise influence our ability to identify and remember scents. Women and young adults tend to have the best sense of smell (Wysocki & Gilbert, 1989). Physical condition also matters. Smokers and people with Alzheimer's disease, Parkinson's disease, or alcohol use disorder typically have a diminished sense of smell (Doty, 2001). Moreover, the smells we detect and the ways we experience them differ, thanks to our individual genes (Trimmer et al., 2019). The scent of a flower may be different for you than for a friend. For all of us, however, the sense of smell tends to peak in early adulthood and gradually declines thereafter (Doty, 2001; Wickelgren, 2009).

"[I] use my memory of how things smell and taste to recreate the experience, because otherwise I would not want to eat." —Meema Spadola, describing her loss of smell and taste after contracting Covid-19 (Zhang, 2021).

RETRIEVAL PRACTICE

RP-5 How does our system for sensing smell differ from our systems for touch and taste?

ANSWERS IN APPENDIX E

Body Position and Movement

LOQ 20-7 How do we sense our body's position and movement?

Without sensing your body's position and movement, you could not put food in your mouth, stand up, or reach out and touch someone. Nor could you perform the "simple" act of taking one step forward. That act requires feedback from, and instructions to, some 200 muscles, and it engages brain power that exceeds the mental activity involved in reasoning. Millions of position and motion sensors in muscles, tendons, and joints all over your body, called *proprioceptors,* provide constant feedback to your brain. This enables your sense of **kinesthesia**, which keeps you aware of your body parts' position and movement. Twist your wrist one degree and your brain receives an immediate update.

If you are able to experience sight and sound, you can momentarily imagine being blind and deaf by closing your eyes and plugging your ears to experience the dark silence. But what would it be like to live without touch or kinesthesia—without being able to sense the positions of your limbs when you wake during the night? Ian Waterman of Hampshire, England, knows. At age 19, Waterman contracted a rare viral infection that destroyed the nerves enabling his sense of light touch *and* of body position and movement. People with this condition report feeling disembodied, as though their body is dead, not real, not theirs (Sacks, 1985). With prolonged practice, Waterman learned to walk and eat—by visually focusing on his limbs and directing them accordingly. But if the lights went out, he would crumple to the floor (Azar, 1998).

kinesthesia [kin-ehs-THEE-zhuh] our movement sense—our system for sensing the position and movement of individual body parts.

Vision interacts with kinesthesia for you, too. If you are able, stand with your right heel in front of your left toes. Easy. Now close your eyes and try again. Did you wobble?

A companion **vestibular sense** monitors your head's (and thus your body's) position and movement. The biological gyroscopes for this sense of equilibrium are two structures in your inner ear. The first, your fluid-filled *semicircular canals,* look like a three-dimensional pretzel (see Figure 20.2a). The second structure is the pair of calcium-crystal–filled *vestibular sacs.* When your head rotates or tilts, the movement of these organs stimulates hair-like receptors, which send nerve signals to your cerebellum at the back of your brain, enabling you to sense your body position and maintain your balance.

CHINE NOUVELLE/SIPA/Shutterstock

Twisting in space By using information from the inner ears, U.S. gymnast Simone Biles' brain expertly monitors her body position. In the 2020 Tokyo Olympics, Biles withdrew from the vault competition after experiencing the "twisties," in which she felt unable to accurately sense and perceive her body position. "I had no idea where I was in the air," Biles said (Giamalvo, 2021).

If you twirl around and then come to an abrupt halt, neither the fluid in your semicircular canals nor your kinesthetic receptors will immediately return to their neutral state. The dizzy aftereffect fools your brain with the sensation that you're still spinning. This illustrates a principle that underlies perceptual illusions: *Mechanisms that normally give us an accurate experience of the world can, under special conditions, fool us.* Understanding how we get fooled provides clues to how our perceptual system works.

Your vestibular sense is super speedy. If you slip, your vestibular sensors automatically and instantly order your skeletal response, well before you have consciously decided how to right yourself. You might try this: Hold one of your thumbs in front of your face, then move it rapidly right to left and back. Notice how your thumb blurs (your vision isn't fast enough to track it). Now hold your thumb still and swivel your *head* from left to right—just as fast. Voila! Your thumb stays clear—because your vestibular system, which is monitoring your head position, speedily moves the eyes. Head moves right, eyes move left. Vision is fast, but the vestibular sense is faster.

* * *

For a summary of our sensory systems, see **TABLE 20.2.**

RETRIEVAL PRACTICE

RP-6 Where are the kinesthetic receptors and the vestibular sense receptors located?

ANSWERS IN APPENDIX E

vestibular sense our balance sense—our sense of body movement and position that enables our sense of balance.

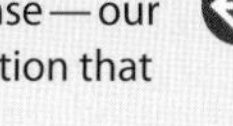

TABLE 20.2 Summarizing the Senses

Sensory System	Source	Receptors	Key Brain Areas
Vision	Light waves striking the eye	Rods and cones in the retina	Occipital lobes
Hearing	Sound waves striking the outer ear	Cochlear hair cells *(cilia)* in the inner ear	Temporal lobes
Touch	Pressure, warmth, cold, harmful chemicals	Receptors (including pain-sensitive *nociceptors*), mostly in the skin, which detect pressure, warmth, cold, and pain	Somatosensory cortex
Taste	Chemical molecules in the mouth	Basic taste receptors for sweet, sour, salty, bitter, and umami	Frontal/temporal lobe border
Smell	Chemical molecules breathed in through the nose	Millions of receptors at top of nasal cavities	Olfactory bulb
Kinesthesia—position and movement	Any change in position of a body part, interacting with vision	Kinesthetic sensors in joints, tendons, and muscles *(proprioceptors)*	Cerebellum
Vestibular sense—balance and movement	Movement of fluids in the inner ear caused by head/body movement	Hair-like receptors *(cilia)* in the ears' semicircular canals and vestibular sacs	Cerebellum

sensory interaction the principle that one sense can influence another, as when the smell of food influences its taste.

embodied cognition the influence of bodily sensations, gestures, and other states on cognitive preferences and judgments.

Sensory Interaction

LOQ 20-8 How does *sensory interaction* influence our perceptions, and what is *embodied cognition?*

We have seen that vision and kinesthesia interact. Actually, none of our senses act alone. All our senses—seeing, hearing, tasting, smelling, touching—eavesdrop on one another, and our brain blends their inputs to interpret the world (Rosenblum, 2013). This is **sensory interaction** at work. One sense can influence another.

Consider how smell sticks its nose into the business of taste. Hold your nose, close your eyes, and have someone feed you various foods. A slice of apple may be indistinguishable from a chunk of raw potato. A cracker may taste like cardboard. Without their smells, a cup of cold coffee may be hard to distinguish from a glass of red wine.

Contrary to Aristotle's presumption that taste sensors were only on the tongue, our taste experience is also affected by inhaling a substance's aroma through our nose—a scientific fact not understood until 1812 (Bartoshuk et al., 2019). Like smoke rising in a chimney, food molecules released by chewing rise into our nasal cavity. This is why food tastes bland when you have a bad cold. Smell can also change our perception of taste: A drink's strawberry odor enhances our perception of its sweetness. Even touch can influence our taste. Depending on its texture, a potato chip "tastes" fresh or stale (Smith, 2011). Smell + texture + taste = flavor. Yet perhaps you have noticed: Flavor *feels* located in the mouth (Stevenson, 2014).

Vision and hearing may similarly interact. Baseball umpires' vision informs their hearing of when the ball hits a player's glove, influencing their judgments of whether baserunners are safe or out (Krynen & McBeath, 2019). Likewise, a weak flicker of light becomes more visible when accompanied by a short burst of sound (Kayser, 2007). The reverse is also true: Soft sounds are more easily heard when paired with a visual cue. If I [DM], as a person with hearing loss, watch a video with on-screen captions, I have no trouble hearing the words I am seeing. But if I then decide I don't need the captions and turn them off, I quickly realize I do need them. The eyes guide the ears (**FIGURE 20.10**).

So, our senses do not function in isolation; they interact. But what happens if they disagree? What if our eyes *see* a speaker form one sound but our ears *hear* another sound? Surprise: Our brain may perceive a third sound that blends both inputs. Seeing mouth movements for *ga* while hearing *ba*, we may perceive *da*. This phenomenon is known as the *McGurk effect,* after Scottish psychologist Harry McGurk, who, with his assistant John MacDonald, discovered the effect (1976). For most of us, lip reading is part of hearing, which is why mask wearing during the Covid-19 pandemic has made communication more challenging (Spitzer, 2020).

FIGURE 20.10
Sensory interaction Seeing the speaker forming the words in video chats—better yet reading captions of the conversation—helps people with hearing loss understand.

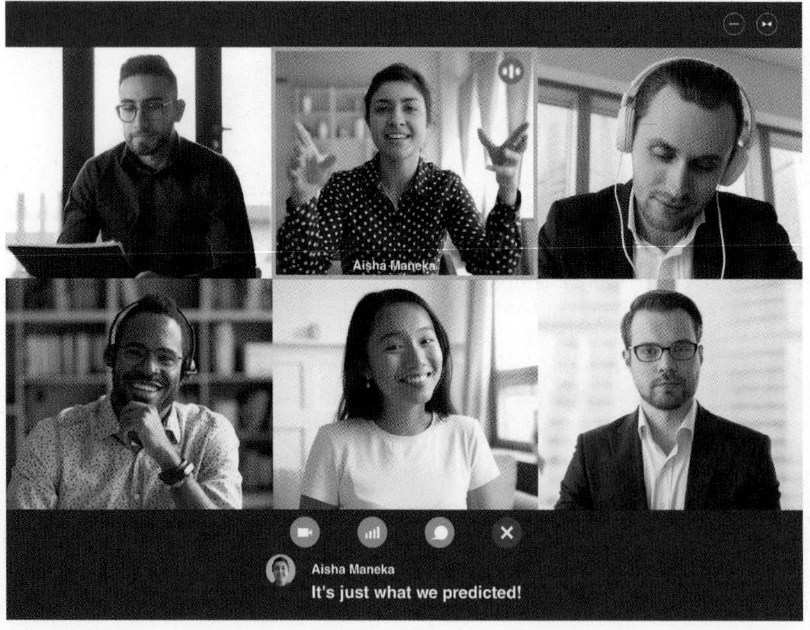
Aisha Maneka
Aisha Maneka
It's just what we predicted!

fizkes/Shutterstock

We have seen that our perceptions have two main ingredients: Our bottom-up sensations and our top-down cognitions (such as expectations, attitudes, thoughts, and memories). In everyday life, sensation and perception are two points on a continuum. It's not surprising, then, that the brain circuits processing our physical sensations sometimes interact with brain circuits responsible for cognition. The result is **embodied cognition**. We think from within a body. A few examples:

- ***Judgments may mimic body sensations.*** Sitting at a wobbly desk and chair may make relationships seem less stable (Forest et al., 2015; Kille et al., 2013).
- ***Hard chair, hard on crime.*** People who sat in a hard chair, compared with a soft chair, gave harsher punishments to people convicted of a crime (M. Schaefer et al., 2018).

- ***Upright is honorable.*** Chinese and American participants associated honor-related phrases ("maintains honor" and "respects me") with arrows pointing up (↑) and right (→) (Lin & Oyserman, 2021).

As we attempt to decipher our world, our brain blends inputs from multiple channels. For example, more than 100 studies reveal captioned videos don't just boost speech comprehension among those with hearing loss, they benefit everyone (Gernsbacher, 2015). Captions help hearing children learn to read (by connecting sound to text). They enhance comprehension for those who are not native speakers of that language. And they boost attention and memory—of both TV commercials and course lectures.

But in a few select individuals, the brain circuits for two or more senses become joined in a phenomenon called *synesthesia,* where the stimulation of one sense triggers an experience of another (**FIGURE 20.11**). Early in life, "exuberant neural connectivity" produces some arbitrary associations among the senses, which later are normally—but not always—pruned (Wagner & Dobkins, 2011). In a brain that blends sensations, hearing music may activate color-sensitive cortex regions and trigger a sensation of color (Brang et al., 2008; Hubbard et al., 2005). Seeing a number may evoke a taste or color sensation (Newell & Mitchell, 2016; Ranzini & Girelli, 2019). People with synesthesia experience such sensory blends.

Think of even numbers

2 4 6

Person without synesthesia

Person with synesthesia

FIGURE 20.11
Synesthesia's symphony A person with synesthesia experiences blended sensations. For example, hearing numbers may evoke an experience of specific colors or smells or musical notes.

ASK YOURSELF

When have you experienced a feeling that you think could be explained by embodied cognition?

Perception Without Sensation?

LOQ 20-9 What are the claims of ESP, and what have most research psychologists concluded after putting these claims to the test?

The river of perception is fed by sensation, cognition, and emotion. If perception is the product of these three sources, what can we say about **extrasensory perception (ESP)**, which claims that perception can occur without sensory input? Are there indeed people—any people—who can read minds, see through walls, or foretell the future? Nearly half of Americans surveyed believe we are capable of ESP, and 41 percent believe in psychics (Gecewicz, 2018; Kim et al., 2015).

If ESP is real, we would need to overturn the scientific understanding that we are creatures whose minds are tied to our physical brains and whose perceptual experiences of the world are built of sensations. The most testable and, for this discussion, most relevant ESP claims are

- *telepathy:* mind-to-mind communication.
- *clairvoyance:* perceiving remote events, such as a house on fire across the country.
- *precognition:* perceiving future events, such as an unexpected death in the next month.

Closely linked to these ESP claims is *psychokinesis,* or "mind moving matter," such as levitating a table or controlling the roll of a die. (The claim, also called *telekinesis,* is illustrated by the wry request, "Will all those who believe in psychokinesis please raise my hand?") In Britain, psychologists created a "mind machine" to see if festival visitors could influence or predict a coin toss (Wiseman & Greening, 2002). Participants were given four attempts to call heads or tails, playing against a computer. By the time the experiment ended, nearly 28,000 people had predicted 110,959 tosses—with 49.8 percent correct, almost exactly as chance would predict.

8
7
8
PSYCHIC DIVING COMPETITION.
carter

Jon Carter/Cartoon Stock

extrasensory perception (ESP) the controversial claim that perception can occur apart from sensory input; includes telepathy, clairvoyance, and precognition.

parapsychology the study of paranormal phenomena, including ESP and psychokinesis (also called *telekinesis*).

Most psychological scientists are skeptical that paranormal phenomena exist. But in several reputable universities, **parapsychology** researchers search for possible ESP phenomena by performing scientific experiments (Cardeña, 2018; Storm et al., 2010a,b; Turpin, 2005). Before seeing how they conduct their research, let's consider some popular beliefs.

Premonitions or Pretensions?

Can psychics see into the future? No greedy—or charitable—psychic has been able to make billions on the stock market. Where were the psychics the day before the 9/11 terrorist attacks? Why could no psychics help locate Osama bin Laden afterward? Why did none of them prepare us for the Covid-19 pandemic?

Psychic visions offered to police departments have been no more accurate than guesses made by others (Nickell, 2005; Palmer, 2013; Radford, 2010). But their sheer volume increases the odds of an occasional correct guess, which psychics can then report to the media. Such visions can sound amazingly correct when later retrofitted to match events. Nostradamus, a sixteenth-century French psychic, explained in an unguarded moment that his ambiguous prophecies "could not possibly be understood till they were interpreted after the event and by it." Shoot, and then call whatever you hit the target.

A headline you've never seen: "Psychic wins lottery."

Are everyday people's "visions" any more accurate than psychic predictions? Do our dreams foretell the future, as people from both Eastern and Western cultures tend to believe (Morewedge & Norton, 2009)? Or do they only seem to do so when we recall or reconstruct them in light of what has already happened? Are our remembered visions merely revisions? After famed aviator Charles Lindbergh's baby son was kidnapped and murdered in 1932, but before the body was discovered, two Harvard psychologists invited people to report their dreams about the child (Murray & Wheeler, 1937). How many visionaries replied? 1300. How many accurately envisioned the child dead? Five percent. How many also correctly anticipated the body's location—buried among trees? Only 4. Although this number was surely no better than chance, to those 4 dreamers, the accuracy of their apparent precognitions must have seemed uncanny.

"A person who talks a lot is sometimes right." —Spanish proverb

Given countless daily events, and given enough days, some stunning coincidences are bound to occur. By one careful estimate, chance alone would predict that more than a thousand times per day, someone on Earth will think of another person and then, within the next 5 minutes, learn of that person's death (Charpak & Broch, 2004). Thus, when explaining an astonishing event, we should "give chance a chance" (Lilienfeld, 2009). With enough time and people, the improbable becomes inevitable.

"It's not *impossible*, my dear. It's just a very remarkable coincidence—and remarkable coincidences do happen." —Agatha Christie's Miss Marple in *Sleeping Murder*, 1976

Putting ESP to Experimental Test

When faced with claims of mind reading or out-of-body travel or communication with the dead, how can we separate fiction from strange-but-true fact? Psychological science offers a simple answer: *Test claims to see if they work*. If they do, so much the better for the ideas. If they don't, so much the better for our skepticism.

Both believers and skeptics agree that what parapsychology needs is a reproducible phenomenon and a theory to explain it. Parapsychologist Rhea White (1998) spoke for many in saying that "the image of parapsychology that comes to my mind, based on nearly 44 years in the field, is that of a small airplane [that] has been perpetually taxiing down the runway of the Empirical Science Airport since 1882 . . . its movement punctuated occasionally by lifting a few feet off the ground only to bump back down on the tarmac once again. It has never taken off for any sustained flight."

How might we test ESP claims in a controlled, reproducible experiment? An experiment differs from a staged demonstration. In the laboratory, the experimenter controls what the "psychic" sees and hears. On stage, the psychic controls what the audience sees and hears.

Daryl Bem, a respected social psychologist, once quipped that "a psychic is an actor playing the role of a psychic" (1984). Yet this one-time skeptic reignited hopes for replicable evidence of ESP with nine experiments that seemed to show people anticipating future events (Bem, 2011). In one, when an erotic scene was about to appear on a screen in one of two randomly selected positions, Cornell University participants guessed the right placement 53.1 percent of the time (beating chance by a small but statistically significant margin).

Despite Bem's research surviving critical reviews by a top-tier journal, critics found Bem's methods and statistical analyses "badly flawed" and "biased" (Alcock, 2011; Wagenmakers et al., 2011). And so, conclude parapsychology's critics, after "nearly 150 years of efforts" to document ESP, "there has been, literally, no progress" (Reber & Alcock, 2020). Anticipating such skepticism, Bem made his research materials available to anyone who wished to replicate his studies. Multiple attempts have met with minimal success and continuing controversy (Bem et al., 2015; Ritchie et al., 2012; Wagenmakers, 2014). Regardless, science is doing its work:

- It has been open to a finding that challenges its own assumptions.
- Through follow-up research, it has assessed the reliability and validity of that finding.

And that is how science sifts crazy-sounding ideas, leaving most on the historical waste heap while occasionally surprising us.

For 19 years, the late skeptic and magician James Randi offered $1 million "to anyone who proves a genuine psychic power under proper observing conditions" (Randi, 1999; Thompson, 2010). French, Australian, and Indian groups have made similar offers of up to 200,000 euros (CFI, 2003). Large as these sums are, the scientific seal of approval would be worth far more. To refute those who say there is no ESP, one need only produce a single person who can demonstrate a single, reproducible ESP event. (To refute those who say pigs can't talk would take but one talking pig.) So far, after more than a thousand aspirants, no such person (or pig) has emerged (Fox, 2020).

"At the heart of science is an essential tension between two seemingly contradictory attitudes—an openness to new ideas, no matter how bizarre or counterintuitive they may be, and the most ruthless skeptical scrutiny of all ideas, old and new." —Carl Sagan (1987)

RETRIEVAL PRACTICE

RP-7 If an ESP event did occur under controlled conditions, what would be the next step to confirm that ESP really exists?

ANSWERS IN APPENDIX E

* * *

To feel awe, mystery, and a deep reverence for life, we need look no further than our own perceptual system and its capacity for organizing formless nerve impulses into colorful sights, vivid sounds, and evocative smells. As Shakespeare's Hamlet recognized, "There are more things in Heaven and Earth, Horatio, than are dreamt of in your philosophy." Within our ordinary sensory and perceptual experiences lies much that is truly extraordinary—surely much more than has so far been dreamt of in our psychology.

MODULE

20 REVIEW Hearing, Skin, Chemical, and Body Senses

LEARNING OBJECTIVES

Test Yourself Answer these repeated Learning Objective Questions on your own (before "showing" the answers here, or checking the answers in Appendix D) to improve your retention of the concepts (McDaniel et al., 2009, 2015).

LOQ 20-1 What are the characteristics of the air pressure waves that we hear as sound?

LOQ 20-2 How does the ear transform sound energy into neural messages?

LOQ 20-3 How do we detect loudness, discriminate pitch, and locate sounds?

LOQ 20-4 What are the four basic touch sensations, and how do we sense touch?

LOQ 20-5 What biological, psychological, and social-cultural influences affect our experience of pain? How do placebos, distraction, and hypnosis help control pain?

LOQ 20-6 In what ways are our senses of taste and smell similar, and how do they differ?

LOQ 20-7 How do we sense our body's position and movement?

LOQ 20-8 How does *sensory interaction* influence our perceptions, and what is *embodied cognition*?

LOQ 20-9 What are the claims of ESP, and what have most research psychologists concluded after putting these claims to the test?

TERMS AND CONCEPTS TO REMEMBER

Test Yourself Write down the definition in your own words, then check your answer.

audition, p. 240
frequency, p. 241
pitch, p. 241
middle ear, p. 241
cochlea [KOHK-lee-uh], p. 241
inner ear, p. 241
sensorineural hearing loss, p. 242
conduction hearing loss, p. 242
cochlear implant, p. 243
place theory, p. 244
frequency theory, p. 244
gate-control theory, p. 246
hypnosis, p. 248
dissociation, p. 249
posthypnotic suggestion, p. 249
gustation, p. 249
olfaction, p. 250
kinesthesia [kin-ehs-THEE-zhuh], p. 252
vestibular sense, p. 253
sensory interaction, p. 254
embodied cognition, p. 254
extrasensory perception (ESP), p. 255
parapsychology, p. 256

MODULE TEST

Test Yourself Answer the following questions on your own first, then "show" the answers here, or check your answers in Appendix E.

1. The snail-shaped tube in the inner ear, where sound waves are converted into neural activity, is called the ________________.
2. What are the basic steps in transforming sound waves into perceived sound?
3. ________________ theory explains how we hear high-pitched sounds, and ________________ theory, extended by the ________________ principle, explains how we hear low-pitched sounds.
4. The sensory receptors that are found mostly in the skin and that detect painful temperatures, pressure, or chemicals are called ________________.
5. The gate-control theory of pain proposes that
   - **a.** special pain receptors send signals directly to the brain.
   - **b.** the pain gate is controlled by the thalamus.
   - **c.** small spinal cord nerve fibers conduct most pain signals, but large-fiber activity can close access to those pain signals.
   - **d.** pain can often be controlled and managed effectively through the use of relaxation techniques.
6. How does the biopsychosocial approach explain our experience of pain? Provide examples.
7. We have specialized nerve receptors for detecting which five tastes? How did this ability aid our ancestors?
8. ________________ is your sense of body position and movement. Your ________________ ________________ specifically monitors your head's movement, with sensors in the inner ear.
9. Why do you feel a little dizzy immediately after a roller-coaster ride?
10. A food's aroma can greatly enhance its taste. This is an example of
    - **a.** olfaction.
    - **b.** synesthesia.
    - **c.** kinesthesia.
    - **d.** sensory interaction.
11. Which of the following ESP phenomena is supported by solid, replicable scientific evidence?
    - **a.** Telepathy
    - **b.** Clairvoyance
    - **c.** Precognition
    - **d.** None of these answers

CHAPTER
7
Ippei Naoi/Moment/Getty Images

Learning (Modules 21–23)

In the early 1940s, University of Minnesota graduate students Marian Breland and Keller Breland witnessed the power of an exciting new learning technique. Their mentor, B. F. Skinner, would become famous for *shaping* rat and pigeon behaviors by delivering well-timed rewards as the animals inched closer and closer to a desired behavior. Impressed by Skinner's results, the Brelands began shaping the behavior of cats, chickens, parakeets, turkeys, pigs, ducks, and hamsters (Bailey & Gillaspy, 2005). The company they formed spent the next half-century training more than 15,000 animals from 140 species. Their efforts helped pave the way for training animals to assist police officers and people with vision loss.

Like other animals, humans learn from experience. Indeed, nature's most important gift may be our *adaptability*—our capacity to learn new behaviors that help us cope with our changing world. We can learn how to build grass huts or snow shelters, submarines, or space stations, thereby adapting to almost any environment.

Oprah Winfrey is a living example of adaptability. Growing up in poverty with her grandmother, Winfrey wore dresses made of potato sacks. She experienced constant racism and was molested by a cousin, an uncle, and a family friend, beginning at age 9. Winfrey ran away from home at age 13 and became pregnant at age 14, but her son died shortly after birth.

To overcome such tremendous adversity, Winfrey learned how to adapt to new situations. She joined her high school speech team and used this talent to win a college scholarship. After graduating, she moved to Chicago and took over as the host of a struggling television show, transforming it into the most popular daytime talk show in America. Winfrey continues to influence the world as a media executive, philanthropist, and political activist. "Education," said Winfrey, "is the key to unlocking the world, a passport to freedom."

Learning breeds hope. What is learnable we may be able to teach — a fact that encourages animal trainers, and also parents, educators, and coaches. What has been learned we may be able to change by new learning — an assumption underlying stress management and counseling programs. No matter how unhappy or unsuccessful or unloving we are, that need not be the end of our story. Our species' success lies in our ability to learn, and to pass our learning on to others.

Here in Modules 21–23, we examine the heart of learning: classical conditioning, operant conditioning, the effects of biology and cognition on learning, and learning by observation.

MODULE 21 Basic Learning Concepts and Classical Conditioning

No topic is closer to the heart of psychology than learning. Psychologists study infants' learning, and the learning of visual perceptions, of a drug's expected effect, and of gender roles. They also consider how learning shapes our thoughts and language, our motivations and emotions, our personalities, and attitudes.

How Do We Learn?

LEARNING OBJECTIVE QUESTION LOQ **21-1** How do we define *learning*, and what are some basic forms of learning?

By **learning**, we humans adapt to our environments. We learn to expect and prepare for significant events such as the arrival of food or pain *(classical conditioning)*. We learn to repeat acts that bring rewards and avoid acts that bring unwanted results *(operant conditioning)*. We learn new behaviors by observing events and people, and through language, we learn things we have neither experienced nor observed *(cognitive learning)*. But *how* do we learn?

One way we learn is by *association*. Our mind naturally connects events that occur in sequence. Learned associations feed our habitual behaviors (Urcelay & Jonkman, 2019; Wood, 2017). Habits can form when we repeat behaviors in a given context—sleeping in a certain position in bed, biting our nails when taking an exam, or switching off the lights when leaving a room. As behavior becomes linked with the context, our next experience of that context will evoke our habitual response. That's true of both good habits (eating fruit) and bad (overindulging in alcohol) (Graybiel & Smith, 2014). To increase your self-control, and to achieve your academic goals, the key is to form helpful habits (Fiorella, 2020).

How long does it take to form a beneficial habit? To find out, one British research team asked 96 university students to choose a healthy behavior (such as running before dinner or eating fruit with lunch), to do it daily for 84 days, and to record whether the behavior felt automatic (something they did without thinking and would find it hard not to do). On average, behaviors became habitual after about 66 days (Lally et al., 2010). Is there something you'd like to make a routine or essential part of your life? Just do it every day for two months, or a bit longer for exercise, and you likely will find yourself with a new habit. This happened for two of your authors—with a midday workout [DM] and a late afternoon guitar practice session [ND] having long ago become an automatic daily routine.

learning the process of acquiring through experience new and relatively enduring information or behaviors.

Two related events:

Stimulus 1:
Lightning
Stimulus 2:
Thunder
BOOM!
Response:
Startled reaction; wincing

Result after repetition:

Stimulus:
Lightning

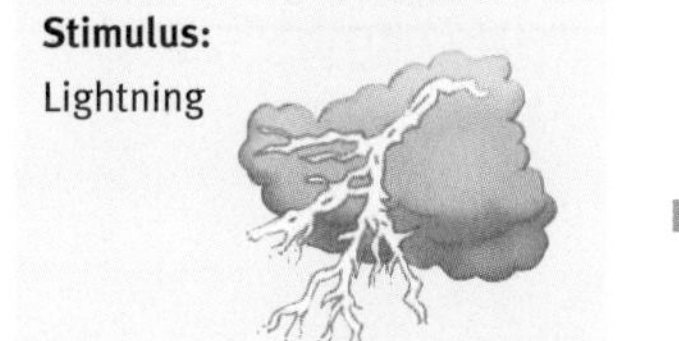

Response:
Anticipation of booming thunder; wincing

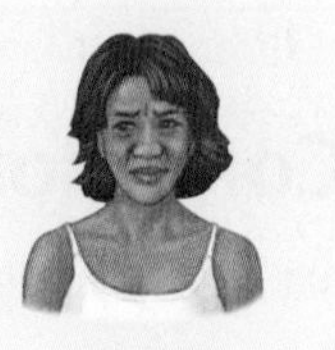

FIGURE 21.1
Classical conditioning

Other animals also learn by association. Disturbed by a squirt of water, the sea slug *Aplysia* protectively withdraws its gill. If the squirts continue, as happens naturally in choppy water, the withdrawal response diminishes. But if the sea slug repeatedly receives an electric shock just after being squirted, its protective response to the squirt instead grows stronger. The animal has associated the squirt with the impending shock.

Complex animals can learn to associate their own behavior with its outcomes. An aquarium seal will repeat behaviors, such as slapping and barking, that prompt people to toss it a herring. After five speech-imitating African gray parrots were adopted and housed together at England's Lincolnshire Wildlife Park, they started using obscenities, which put the park staff into hysterics. The birds' "fowl" language prompted moving them from public display. "The more they swear, the more you usually laugh, which then triggers them to swear again," explained the park manager (Franklin & Merrifield, 2020).

By linking two events that occur close together, sea slugs, seals, and parrots are exhibiting **associative learning**. The sea slug associates the squirt with an impending shock; the seal associates slapping and barking with a herring treat; and the parrot associates uttering an obscenity with a positive reaction from humans. Each animal has learned something important to its survival: anticipating the immediate future.

This process of learning associations is *conditioning*. It takes two main forms:

- In *classical conditioning* (FIGURE 21.1), we learn to associate two stimuli and thus to anticipate events. (A **stimulus** is any event or situation that evokes a response.) We learn that a flash of lightning signals an impending crack of thunder; when lightning flashes nearby, we start to brace ourselves. We associate stimuli that we do not control, and we respond automatically (exhibiting **respondent behavior**).
- In *operant conditioning*, we learn to associate a response (our behavior) and its consequence. Thus, we (and other animals) learn to repeat acts followed by good results (FIGURE 21.2) and avoid acts followed by bad results. These associations produce **operant behaviors** (which operate on the environment to produce consequences).

To simplify, we will explore these two types of associative learning separately. Often, though, they occur together, as on one Japanese cattle ranch, where the clever rancher outfitted his herd with electronic pagers, which he called from his cell phone. After a week of training, the animals learned to associate two stimuli—the beep of their pager and the arrival of food (classical conditioning). But they also learned to associate their hustling to the food trough with the pleasure of eating (operant conditioning), which simplified the rancher's work. Classical conditioning + operant conditioning did the trick.

associative learning learning that certain events occur together. The events may be two stimuli (as in classical conditioning) or a response and its consequence (as in operant conditioning).

stimulus any event or situation that evokes a response.

respondent behavior behavior that occurs as an automatic response to some stimulus.

operant behavior behavior that operates on the environment, producing a consequence.

Most of us could not list in order the songs on our favorite album or playlist. Yet hearing the end of one piece cues (by association) an anticipation of the next. Likewise, when singing your national anthem, you associate the end of each line with the beginning of the next. (Pick a line out of the middle and notice how much harder it is to recall the *previous* line.)

FIGURE 21.2
Operant conditioning

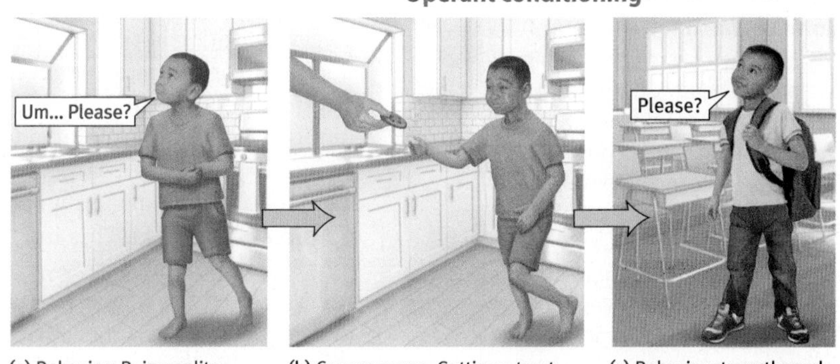
Um... Please?
Please?

(a) Behavior: Being polite (b) Consequence: Getting a treat (c) Behavior strengthened

cognitive learning the acquisition of mental information, whether by observing events, by watching others, or through language.

classical conditioning a type of learning in which we link two or more stimuli; as a result, to illustrate with Pavlov's classic experiment, the first stimulus (a tone) comes to elicit behavior (drooling) in anticipation of the second stimulus (food).

behaviorism the view that psychology (1) should be an objective science that (2) studies behavior without reference to mental processes. Most research psychologists today agree with (1) but not with (2).

Conditioning is not the only form of learning. Through **cognitive learning**, we acquire mental information that guides our behavior. *Observational learning,* one form of cognitive learning, lets us learn from others' experiences. Chimpanzees, for example, sometimes learn behaviors merely by watching other chimpanzees perform them. If one animal sees another solve a puzzle and gain a food reward, the observer may perform the trick more quickly. So, too, in humans: We look and we learn.

RETRIEVAL PRACTICE

RP-1 Why are habits, such as having something sweet with that cup of coffee, so hard to break?

ANSWERS IN APPENDIX E

Classical Conditioning

LOQ 21-2 What is behaviorism's view of learning?

For many people, the name Ivan Pavlov (1849–1936) rings a bell. The Russian physiologist's early twentieth-century experiments—now psychology's most famous research—are classics, and the phenomenon he explored we justly call **classical conditioning**.

Pavlov's work laid the foundation for many of psychologist John B. Watson's ideas. In searching for laws underlying learning, Watson (1913) urged his colleagues to discard reference to inner thoughts, feelings, and motives. The science of psychology should instead study how organisms respond to stimuli in their environments, said Watson: "Its theoretical goal is the prediction and control of behavior. Introspection forms no essential part of its methods." Simply said, psychology should be an objective science—based on observable behavior.

This view, which Watson called **behaviorism**, influenced North American psychology, especially during the first half of the twentieth century. Pavlov and Watson came to share both a disdain for "mentalistic" concepts (such as consciousness) and a belief that the basic laws of learning were the same for all animals—whether sea slugs or dogs or humans. Few researchers today agree that psychology should ignore mental processes, but most do agree that classical conditioning is a basic form of learning by which all organisms adapt to their environments.

Macmillan Learning

Ivan Pavlov "Experimental investigation . . . should lay a solid foundation for a future true science of psychology" (1927).

Pavlov's Experiments

LOQ 21-3 Who was Pavlov, and what are the basic components of classical conditioning?

Pavlov was driven by a lifelong passion for research. After setting aside his initial plan to follow his father into the Russian Orthodox priesthood, Pavlov earned a medical degree at age 33 and spent the next two decades studying dogs' digestive system. This work earned him, in 1904, Russia's first Nobel Prize. But Pavlov's novel experiments on learning, which consumed the last three decades of his life, earned this feisty, intense scientist his place in history (Todes, 2014).

Pavlov's new direction came when his creative mind seized on an incidental observation. Without fail, putting food in a dog's mouth caused the animal to salivate. Moreover, the dog began salivating not only to the taste of the food, but also to the mere sight of the food, or the food dish, or the person delivering the food, or even the sound of that person's approaching footsteps. At first, Pavlov considered these "psychic secretions" an annoyance—until he realized they pointed to a simple but fundamental form of learning.

Pavlov and his team of researchers—over half of whom were women (Hill, 2019)—tried to imagine what the dog was thinking and feeling as it drooled in anticipation of the food. This only led them into fruitless debates. So, to explore the phenomenon more objectively, they experimented. To eliminate other possible influences, they isolated the dog in a small room, secured it in a harness, and attached a device to divert its saliva to a measuring instrument (**FIGURE 21.3**). From the next room, they presented food—first by sliding in a food bowl, later by blowing meat powder into the dog's

Macmillan Learning

John B. Watson Watson (1924) admitted to "going beyond my facts" when offering his famous boast: "Give me a dozen healthy infants, well-formed, and my own specified world to bring them up in and I'll guarantee to take any one at random and train him to become any type of specialist I might select—doctor, lawyer, artist, merchant-chief, and, yes, even beggar-man and thief, regardless of his talents, penchants, tendencies, abilities, vocations, and race of his ancestors."

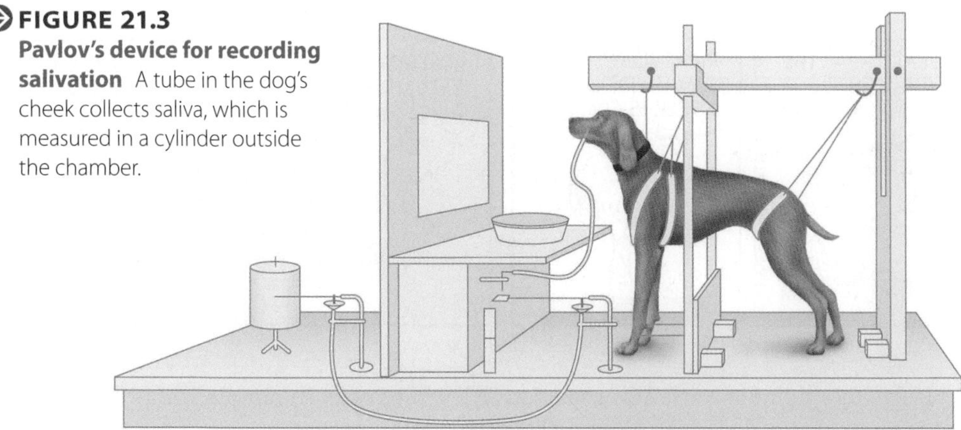

FIGURE 21.3
Pavlov's device for recording salivation A tube in the dog's cheek collects saliva, which is measured in a cylinder outside the chamber.

neutral stimulus (NS) in classical conditioning, a stimulus that elicits no response before conditioning.

unconditioned response (UR) in classical conditioning, an unlearned, naturally occurring response (such as salivation) to an unconditioned stimulus (US) (such as food in the mouth).

unconditioned stimulus (US) in classical conditioning, a stimulus that unconditionally—naturally and automatically—triggers an unconditioned response (UR).

conditioned response (CR) in classical conditioning, a learned response to a previously neutral (but now conditioned) stimulus (CS).

conditioned stimulus (CS) in classical conditioning, an originally neutral stimulus that, after association with an unconditioned stimulus (US), comes to trigger a conditioned response (CR).

mouth at a precise moment. They then paired various **neutral stimuli (NS)**—events the dog could see or hear but didn't associate with food—with food in the dog's mouth. If a sight or sound regularly signaled the arrival of food, would the dog learn the link? If so, would it begin salivating in anticipation of the food?

The answers proved to be *Yes* and *Yes*. Just before placing food in the dog's mouth to produce salivation, Pavlov sounded a tone. After several pairings of tone and food, the dog, now anticipating the meat powder, began salivating to the tone alone. In later experiments, a buzzer,[1] a light, a touch on the leg, even the sight of a circle set off the drooling. (This procedure works with people, too. When hungry young Londoners viewed abstract figures before smelling peanut butter or vanilla, their brain soon responded in anticipation to the abstract images alone [Gottfried et al., 2006].)

A dog does not learn to salivate in response to food in its mouth. Rather, food in the mouth automatically, *unconditionally*, triggers a dog's salivary reflex (FIGURE 21.4). Thus, Pavlov called this drooling an **unconditioned response (UR)**. And he called the food an **unconditioned stimulus (US)**.

Salivation in response to a tone, however, is learned. It is *conditional* upon the dog's associating the tone with the food. Thus, we call this response the **conditioned response (CR)**. The stimulus that used to be neutral (in this case, a previously meaningless tone that now triggers salivation) is the **conditioned stimulus (CS)**. Distinguishing these two kinds of stimuli and responses is easy: conditioned = learned; *un*conditioned = *un*learned.

FIGURE 21.4
Pavlov's classic experiment Pavlov presented a neutral stimulus (a tone) just before an unconditioned stimulus (food in mouth). The neutral stimulus then became a conditioned stimulus, producing a conditioned response.

BEFORE CONDITIONING

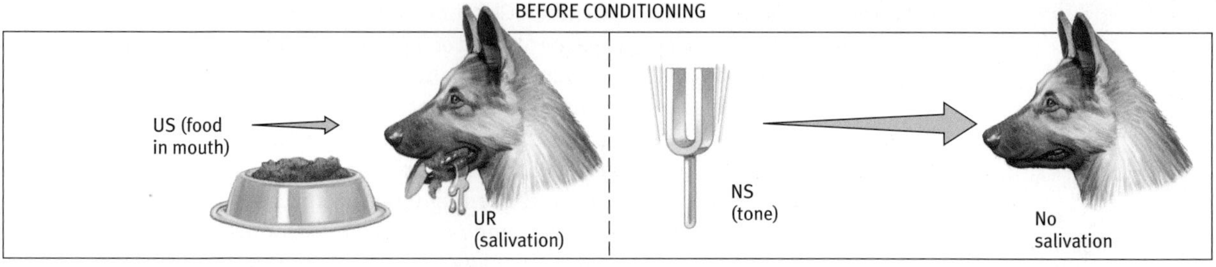
US (food
in mouth)
UR
(salivation)
NS
(tone)
No
salivation

An unconditioned stimulus (US) produces an unconditioned response (UR).

A neutral stimulus (NS) produces no salivation response.

DURING CONDITIONING

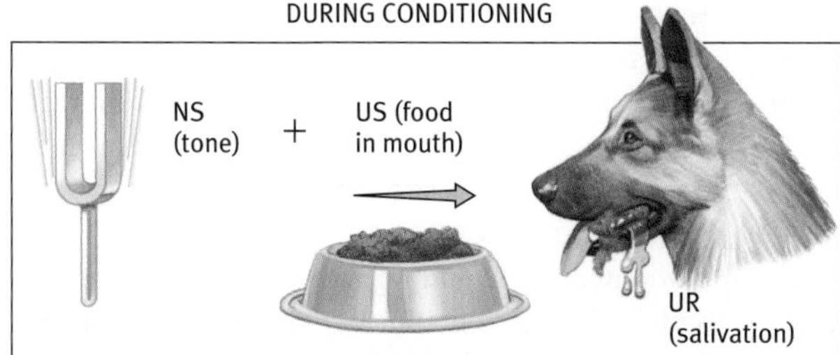
NS
(tone)
+
US (food
in mouth)
UR
(salivation)

The US is repeatedly presented just after the NS. The US continues to produce a UR.

AFTER CONDITIONING

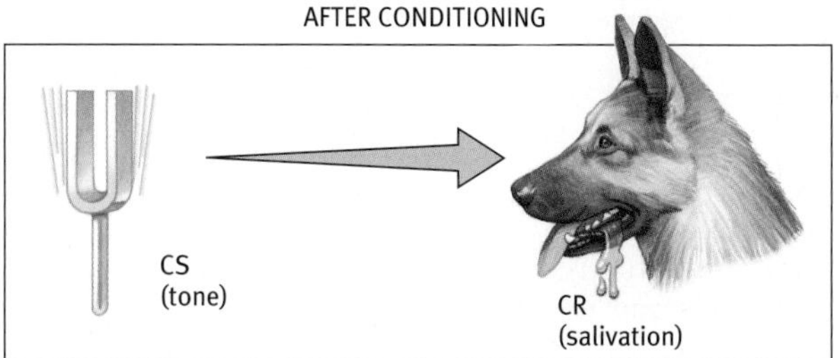
CS
(tone)
CR
(salivation)

The previously neutral stimulus alone now produces a conditioned response (CR), thereby becoming a conditioned stimulus (CS).

[1] The "buzzer" (English translation) was perhaps the bell people commonly associate with Pavlov (Tully, 2003). Pavlov used various stimuli, but some have questioned whether he used a bell.

THE EARS HEAR THE CAN OPENER..
© 1969 United Feature Syndicate, Inc

RIGHT AWAY THE STOMACH KNOWS THAT SUPPER IS COMING..

HOW DO THE EARS TELL THE STOMACH?

I'VE NEVER BEEN ABLE TO FIGURE THAT OUT..
5-17

If Pavlov's demonstration of associative learning was so simple, what did he do for the next three decades? What discoveries did his research factory publish in his 532 papers on salivary conditioning (Windholz, 1997)? He and his associates explored five major conditioning processes: *acquisition, extinction, spontaneous recovery, generalization,* and *discrimination.*

RETRIEVAL PRACTICE

RP-2 An experimenter sounds a tone just before delivering an air puff that causes your eye to blink. After several repetitions, you blink to the tone alone. What is the NS? The US? The UR? The CS? The CR?

ANSWERS IN APPENDIX E

ACQUISITION

LOQ 21-4 In classical conditioning, what are the processes of *acquisition, extinction, spontaneous recovery, generalization,* and *discrimination?*

To understand the **acquisition**, or initial learning, of the stimulus-response relationship, Pavlov and his associates wondered: How much time should elapse between presenting the NS (the tone, the light, and the touch) and the US (the food)? In most cases, not much—half a second usually works well.

What do you suppose would happen if the food (US) appeared before the tone (NS) rather than after? Would conditioning occur? Not likely. Conditioning usually won't occur when the NS follows the US. Remember: *Classical conditioning is biologically adaptive because it helps humans and other animals prepare for good or bad events.* To Pavlov's dogs, the originally neutral tone became a CS after signaling an important biological event—the arrival of food (US). To deer in the forest, a snapping twig (CS) may signal a predator's approach (US).

Research on male Japanese quail shows how a CS can signal another important biological event (Domjan, 1992, 1994, 2005). Just before presenting a sexually approachable female quail, the researchers turned on a red light. Over time, as the red light continued to herald the female's arrival, the light alone caused the male quail to become excited. They developed a preference for their cage's red-light district, and when a female appeared, they mated with her more quickly and released more semen and sperm (Matthews et al., 2007). This capacity for classical conditioning supports reproduction.

In humans, too, objects, smells, sounds, and sights associated with sexual pleasure—even a geometric figure, in one experiment—can become conditioned stimuli for sexual arousal (Byrne, 1982; Hoffman, 2012, 2017). Onion breath, for example, is an NS—it does not typically produce sexual arousal. But when repeatedly paired with a passionate kiss, it can become a CS and do just that (**FIGURE 21.5**).

The larger lesson: *Conditioning helps an animal survive and reproduce—by responding to cues that help it gain food, avoid dangers, locate mates, and produce offspring* (Hollis, 1997). Learning makes for yearning.

Through **higher-order conditioning**, a new NS can become a new CS without the presence of a US. All that's required is for it to become associated with a previously conditioned stimulus. If a tone regularly signals food and produces salivation, then a light that becomes associated with the tone (light → tone → food) may also begin to trigger

acquisition in classical conditioning, the initial stage—when one links a neutral stimulus and an unconditioned stimulus so that the neutral stimulus begins triggering the conditioned response. (In operant conditioning, the strengthening of a reinforced response.)

higher-order conditioning a procedure in which the conditioned stimulus in one conditioning experience is paired with a new neutral stimulus, creating a second (often weaker) conditioned stimulus. For example, an animal that has learned that a tone predicts food might then learn that a light predicts the tone and begin responding to the light alone. (Also called *second-order conditioning*.)

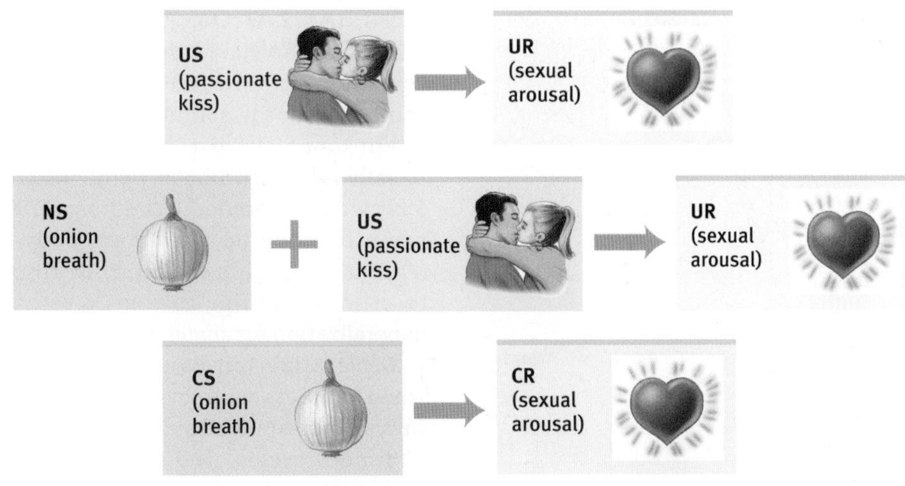
US
(passionate
kiss)
UR
(sexual
arousal)
NS
(onion
breath)
+
US
(passionate
kiss)
UR
(sexual
arousal)
CS
(onion
breath)
CR
(sexual
arousal)

FIGURE 21.5
An unexpected CS Psychologist Michael Tirrell (1990) recalled: "My first girlfriend loved onions, so I came to associate onion breath with kissing. Before long, onion breath sent tingles up and down my spine. Oh what a feeling!"

salivation. Although this higher-order conditioning (also called *second-order conditioning*) tends to be weaker than first-order conditioning, it influences our everyday lives. If a dog bites you, just the sound of a barking dog may later make you feel afraid.

Remember:
NS = Neutral Stimulus
US = Unconditioned Stimulus
UR = Unconditioned Response
CS = Conditioned Stimulus
CR = Conditioned Response

ASK YOURSELF

A psychologist recalled coming to associate his girlfriend's onion breath with arousal. Can you remember ever experiencing something that would normally be neutral (or even unpleasant) but came to mean something special to you?

EXTINCTION AND SPONTANEOUS RECOVERY What would happen, Pavlov wondered, if, after conditioning, the CS occurred repeatedly without the US? If the tone sounded again and again, but no food appeared, would the tone still trigger salivation? The answer was mixed. The dogs salivated less and less, a reaction known as **extinction**. Extinction is diminished responding that occurs when the CS (tone) no longer signals an impending US (food). But if Pavlov sounded the tone again after several hours' delay, the dogs drooled in response (FIGURE 21.6). This **spontaneous recovery**—the reappearance of a (weakened) CR after a pause—suggested to Pavlov that extinction was suppressing the CR rather than eliminating it.

extinction in classical conditioning, the diminishing of a conditioned response—when an unconditioned stimulus does not follow a conditioned stimulus. (In operant conditioning, when a response is no longer reinforced.)

spontaneous recovery the reappearance, after a pause, of a weakened conditioned response.

RETRIEVAL PRACTICE

RP-3 A baker loves the taste and aroma of apple pie. Every time the baker sees a photo of apple pie, he salivates. In this situation, what is the US? The CS? The CR?

RP-4 The first step of classical conditioning, when an NS becomes a CS, is called ____________. When a US no longer follows the CS, and the CR becomes weakened, this is called ____________.

ANSWERS IN APPENDIX E

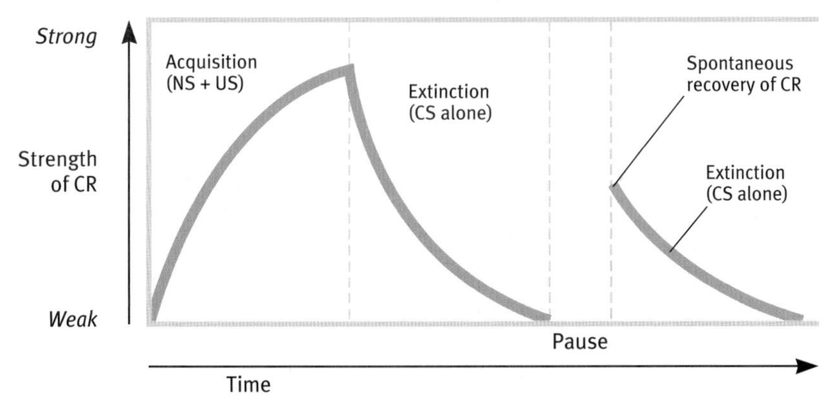
Strong
Strength
of CR
Weak
Acquisition
(NS + US)
Extinction
(CS alone)
Spontaneous
recovery of CR
Extinction
(CS alone)
Pause
Time

FIGURE 21.6
Idealized curve of acquisition, extinction, and spontaneous recovery The rising curve shows the CR rapidly growing stronger as the NS becomes a CS due to repeated pairing with the US *(acquisition)*. The CR then weakens rapidly as the CS is presented alone *(extinction)*. After a pause, the (weakened) CR reappears *(spontaneous recovery)*.

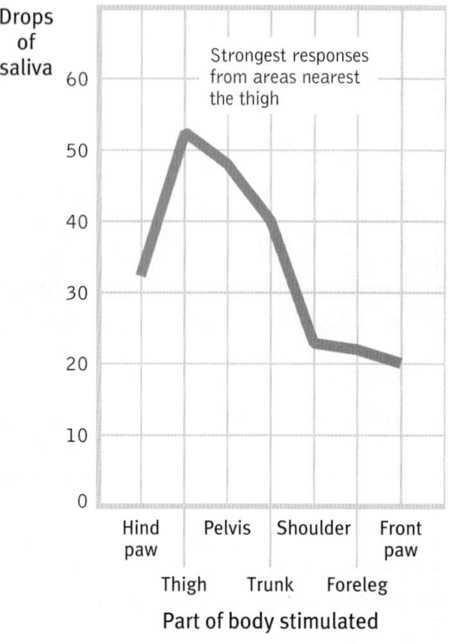
Drops of saliva
60
50
40
30
20
10
0
Strongest responses from areas nearest the thigh
Hind paw
Pelvis
Shoulder
Front paw
Thigh
Trunk
Foreleg
Part of body stimulated

FIGURE 21.7
Generalization Pavlov demonstrated generalization by attaching miniature vibrating devices to various parts of a dog's body. After conditioning salivation to stimulation of the thigh, he stimulated other areas. The closer a stimulated spot was to the dog's thigh, the stronger the conditioned response. (Data from Pavlov, 1927.)

GENERALIZATION Pavlov and his students noticed that a dog conditioned to the sound of one tone also responded somewhat to the sound of a new and different tone. Likewise, a dog conditioned to salivate when rubbed would also drool a bit when scratched (Windholz, 1989) or when touched on a different body part (**FIGURE 21.7**). This tendency to respond to stimuli similar to the CS is called **generalization** (or *stimulus generalization*).

Generalization can be adaptive, as when toddlers who learn to fear moving cars also become afraid of moving trucks and motorcycles. And generalized fears can linger, sticking in our memory (Simon-Kutscher et al., 2019; Stout et al., 2018). For two months after being in a car collision, sensitized young drivers are less vulnerable to repeat collisions (O'Brien et al., 2017). Years after being tortured in an Argentinean prison, one journalist reported still flinching with fear at the sight of black shoes—his first glimpse of his torturers as they approached his cell (Timerman, 1980). Generalized anxiety reactions have been demonstrated in laboratory studies comparing children who have been abused with children who have not (**FIGURE 21.8**).

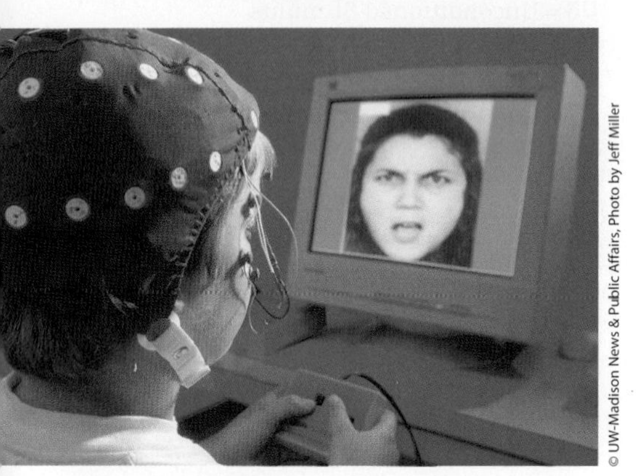

© UW-Madison News & Public Affairs, Photo by Jeff Miller

FIGURE 21.8
Child abuse leaves tracks in the brain Abused children's sensitized brains react more strongly to angry faces (Pollak et al., 1998). This generalized anxiety response may help explain their greater risk of psychological disorder.

Stimuli related to naturally disgusting or morally objectionable objects will, by association, also evoke some physical or moral disgust. Would most people eat otherwise desirable fudge shaped to resemble dog feces? Or hold an English dictionary apparently owned and used by Adolf Hitler? Or wrap themselves in a blanket thought to be previously owned by members of the al-Qaeda terrorist group? *No, No,* and *No.* These situations cause people to feel repulsed (Fedotova & Rozin, 2018; Rozin et al., 1986, 2015). These examples show how people's emotional reactions to one stimulus can generalize to other, related stimuli.

DISCRIMINATION Pavlov's dogs also learned to respond to the sound of a particular tone and *not* to other tones. One stimulus (tone) predicted the US, and the others did not. This learned ability to *distinguish* between a conditioned stimulus (which predicts the US) and other, irrelevant stimuli is called **discrimination**. Being able to recognize differences is adaptive: Slightly different stimuli can cause vastly different consequences. After eating a butterfly that makes them sick, birds will generalize—they will avoid preying on similar butterflies. But they will also discriminate such butterflies from other butterfly species that are edible (Sims, 2018). Kenyan elephants flee the scent of Maasai hunters, whom they have learned to fear, but not the scent of the nonthreatening Kamba people (Rhodes, 2017). Facing a guard dog, your heart may race; facing a guide dog, it probably will not.

generalization (also called *stimulus generalization*) in classical conditioning, the tendency, once a response has been conditioned, for stimuli similar to the conditioned stimulus to elicit similar responses. (In operant conditioning, when responses learned in one situation occur in other, similar situations.)

discrimination in classical conditioning, the learned ability to distinguish between a conditioned stimulus and similar stimuli that do not signal an unconditioned stimulus. (In operant conditioning, the ability to distinguish responses that are reinforced from similar responses that are not reinforced.)

RETRIEVAL PRACTICE

RP-5 What conditioning principle is influencing the snail's affections?

Sam Gross/Cartoon Stock

"I don't care if she's a tape dispenser. I love her."

ANSWERS IN APPENDIX E

Pavlov's Legacy

LOQ 21-5 Why does Pavlov's work remain so important?

What remains today of Pavlov's ideas? A great deal. Most psychologists now agree that classical conditioning is a basic form of learning. Modern neuroscience has also supported Pavlov's ideas—by identifying neural circuits that link a conditioned stimulus (warning signal) with an impending unconditioned stimulus (threat) (Harnett et al., 2016; Yau & McNally, 2018). Other researchers have applied Pavlov's ideas to shopping. Conditioning neutral brand logos with positive or negative images can cause people to like or loathe those brands (Alves et al., 2020). Judged with today's knowledge of the interplay of our biology, psychology, and social-cultural environment, some of Pavlov's ideas were incomplete. But if we see further than Pavlov did, it is because we stand on his shoulders.

Why does Pavlov's work remain so important? If he had merely taught us that old dogs can learn new tricks, his experiments would long ago have been forgotten. Why should we care that dogs can be conditioned to salivate to the sound of a tone? The importance lies first in the finding that *many other responses to many other stimuli can be classically conditioned in many other organisms*—in fact, in every species tested, from microscopic creatures to earthworms to fish to dogs to monkeys to people (Schwartz, 1984; S. Zhou et al., 2019). Thus, classical conditioning is one way that virtually all organisms learn to adapt to their environment.

Second, *Pavlov showed us how a process such as learning can be studied objectively.* He was proud that his methods involved virtually no subjective judgments or guesses about what went on in a dog's mind. The salivary response is a behavior measurable in cubic centimeters of saliva. Pavlov's success suggested a scientific model for how the young discipline of psychology might proceed—by isolating the basic building blocks of complex behaviors and studying them with objective laboratory procedures.

RETRIEVAL PRACTICE

RP-6 Companies often pay to make their products visible in popular movies and television shows—such as when beloved characters drive particular car brands. (Have you noticed that the Avengers all drive Audis?) Based on classical conditioning principles, what might be an effect of this pairing?

ANSWERS IN APPENDIX E

APPLICATIONS OF CLASSICAL CONDITIONING

LOQ 21-6 What have been some applications of Pavlov's work to human health and well-being? How did Watson apply Pavlov's principles to learned fears?

In many areas of psychology, including consciousness, motivation, emotion, health, psychological disorders, and therapy, Pavlov's principles are used to influence human health and well-being. Three examples:

- ***Drug cravings:*** Classical conditioning may inform treatments for *substance use disorder*. People who formerly misused drugs often feel a craving when they are again in the drug-using context, because their brain has become conditioned to associate that context with a drug's reward (X. Wang et al., 2018; Wilar et al., 2019). Breaking this association can reduce cravings (Ananth et al., 2019; Martínez-Rivera et al., 2019). Many drug counselors advise clients to steer clear of the people and settings associated with previous highs (NIDA, 2017; Siegel, 2005). (The Therapy modules illustrate how behavior therapists apply classical conditioning to treat other psychological disorders.)
- ***Food cravings:*** Classical conditioning makes avoiding sweets difficult. Sugary substances evoke sweet sensations. Researchers have conditioned healthy volunteers to experience cravings after only one instance of eating a sweet food (Blechert et al., 2016). So, the next time you think "I can definitely eat just one cookie," you might be wise to think twice.

- ***Immune responses:*** Classical conditioning even works on the body's disease-fighting immune system. When a particular taste accompanies a drug that influences immune responses, the taste by itself may come to produce an immune response (Ader & Cohen, 1985).

Pavlov's work also provided a basis for Watson's (1913) idea that human emotions and behaviors, though biologically influenced, are mainly a bundle of conditioned responses. Working with an 11-month-old, Watson and his graduate student Rosalie Rayner (1920; Harris, 1979) showed how specific fears might be conditioned. Like most infants, "Little Albert" feared loud noises but not white rats. Watson and Rayner presented a white rat and, as Little Albert reached to touch it, struck a hammer against a steel bar just behind his head. After seven repeats of seeing the rat and hearing the frightening noise, Albert burst into tears at the mere sight of the rat. Five days later, he reportedly generalized this startled fear reaction to the sight of a rabbit, a dog, and even a furry coat. A modern reanalysis questioned Watson's evidence for Albert's conditioning, but the case remains legendary (Powell & Schmaltz, 2021).

People later wondered what became of Watson. After losing his Johns Hopkins professorship over an affair with Rayner (whom he later married), he joined an advertising agency as the company's resident psychologist. There, he used his knowledge of associative learning to conceive many successful advertising campaigns, including one for Maxwell House that helped make the "coffee break" an American custom (Hunt, 1993).

Macmillan Learning

Mary Cover Jones (1897–1987) At a time when men dominated the field of psychology, Jones' pioneering behavior therapy research made her a rare female contributor. In her most famous study, she used conditioning to help a 3-year-old named Peter to overcome his fear of white rabbits.

Critics have questioned the strength and reliability of Watson and Rayner's findings (Ginsburg et al., 2020; Powell & Schmaltz, 2021). (These experiments would also be unethical by today's standards, making replication studies difficult.) Nevertheless, the case remains legendary. Little Albert's learned fears led many psychologists to wonder whether each of us might be a walking warehouse of conditioned emotions. If so, might extinction procedures or new conditioning help us change our unwanted responses to emotion-arousing stimuli? Psychologist Mary Cover Jones (1924) was the first to extend Watson and Rayner's results by showing how conditioning can also reduce children's fear.

Therapists began using conditioning to reduce their clients' fears. One person used his therapist's conditioning strategy to treat a longtime fear of entering an elevator. For 10 days, the client entered 20 elevators a day. By the end of the treatment, the client's fear of elevators had nearly vanished (Ellis & Becker, 1982). Comedian-writer Mark Malkoff extinguished his fear of flying by taking 135 flights in 30 days, spending 14 hours a day in the air (NPR, 2009). After a week and a half, his fears had faded, and he began playing games with fellow passengers. His favorite was the "toilet paper experiment": Put one end of a roll in the toilet, unroll the rest down the aisle, and flush, sucking down the whole roll in three seconds! In the Therapy modules, we see more examples of how psychologists use behavioral techniques such as *counterconditioning* to treat psychological disorders and promote personal growth.

RETRIEVAL PRACTICE

RP-7 In Watson and Rayner's experiments, "Little Albert" learned to fear a white rat after repeatedly experiencing a loud noise as the rat was presented. In these experiments, what was the US? The UR? The NS? The CS? The CR?

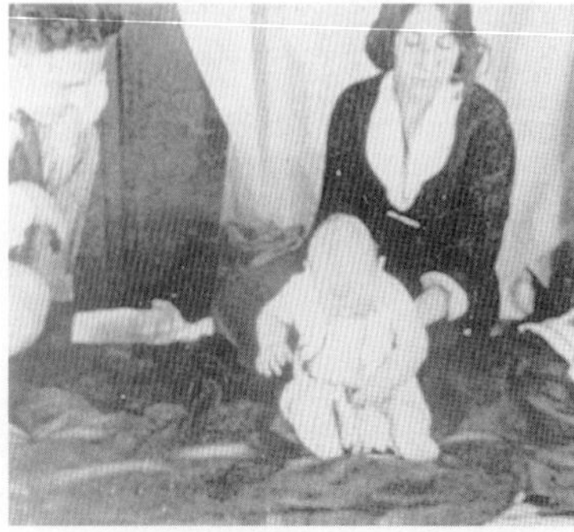

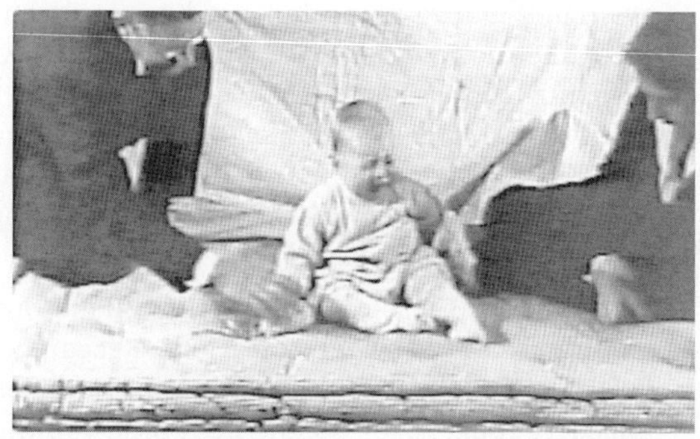
Archives of the History of American Psychology, The Center for the History of Psychology, The University of Akron

ANSWERS IN APPENDIX E

MODULE 21 REVIEW Basic Learning Concepts and Classical Conditioning

LEARNING OBJECTIVES

Test Yourself Answer these repeated Learning Objective Questions on your own (before "showing" the answers here, or checking the answers in Appendix D) to improve your retention of the concepts (McDaniel et al., 2009, 2015).

LOQ 21-1 How do we define *learning*, and what are some basic forms of learning?

LOQ 21-2 What is behaviorism's view of learning?

LOQ 21-3 Who was Pavlov, and what are the basic components of classical conditioning?

LOQ 21-4 In classical conditioning, what are the processes of *acquisition, extinction, spontaneous recovery, generalization*, and *discrimination*?

LOQ 21-5 Why does Pavlov's work remain so important?

LOQ 21-6 What have been some applications of Pavlov's work to human health and well-being? How did Watson apply Pavlov's principles to learned fears?

TERMS AND CONCEPTS TO REMEMBER

Test Yourself Write down the definition in your own words, then check your answer.

learning, p. 260
associative learning, p. 261
stimulus, p. 261
respondent behavior, p. 261
operant behavior, p. 261
cognitive learning, p. 262
classical conditioning, p. 262
behaviorism, p. 262
neutral stimulus (NS), p. 263
unconditioned response (UR), p. 263
unconditioned stimulus (US), p. 263
conditioned response (CR), p. 263
conditioned stimulus (CS), p. 263
acquisition, p. 264
higher-order conditioning, p. 264
extinction, p. 265
spontaneous recovery, p. 265
generalization, p. 266
discrimination, p. 266

MODULE TEST

Test Yourself Answer the following questions on your own first, then "show" the answers here, or check your answers in Appendix E.

1. Learning is defined as "the process of acquiring through experience new and relatively enduring ____________ or ____________."

2. Two forms of associative learning are classical conditioning, in which the organism associates ____________, and operant conditioning, in which the organism associates ____________.
   a. two or more responses; a response and its consequence
   b. two or more stimuli; two or more responses
   c. two or more stimuli; a response and its consequence
   d. two or more responses; two or more stimuli

3. In Pavlov's experiments, the tone started as a neutral stimulus, and then became a(n) ____________ stimulus.

4. Dogs have been taught to salivate to a circle but not to a square. This process is an example of ____________.

5. After Watson and Rayner classically conditioned Little Albert to fear a white rat, the child later showed fear in response to a rabbit, a dog, and a furry coat. This illustrates
   a. extinction.
   b. generalization.
   c. spontaneous recovery.
   d. discrimination between two stimuli.

6. "Sex sells!" is a common assumption in advertising. Using classical conditioning terms, explain how sexual images in advertisements can condition your response to a product.

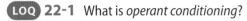

MODULE 22 Operant Conditioning

LOQ 22-1 What is *operant conditioning*?

It's one thing to classically condition a dog to salivate to the sound of a tone, or a child to fear moving cars. But to teach an elephant to **learn** to walk on its hind legs or a child to say *please*, we turn to operant conditioning.

Classical conditioning and operant conditioning are both forms of **associative learning**, yet their differences are straightforward:

- *Classical conditioning* forms associations between **stimuli** (a CS and the US it signals). It also involves **respondent behavior**—automatic responses to a stimulus (such as salivating in response to meat powder and later in response to a tone).

learning the process of acquiring through experience new and relatively enduring information or behaviors.

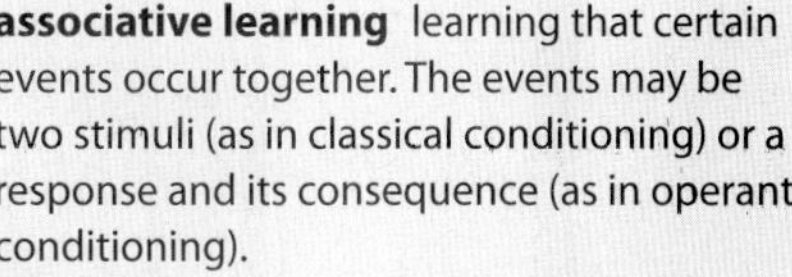

associative learning learning that certain events occur together. The events may be two stimuli (as in classical conditioning) or a response and its consequence (as in operant conditioning).

stimulus any event or situation that evokes a response.

respondent behavior behavior that occurs as an automatic response to some stimulus.

operant conditioning a type of learning in which a behavior becomes more likely to recur if followed by a reinforcer or less likely to recur if followed by a punisher.

operant behavior behavior that operates on the environment, producing a consequence.

law of effect Thorndike's principle that behaviors followed by favorable consequences become more likely, and that behaviors followed by unfavorable consequences become less likely.

operant chamber in operant conditioning research, a chamber (also known as a *Skinner box*) containing a bar or key that an animal can manipulate to obtain a food or water reinforcer; attached devices record the animal's rate of bar pressing or key pecking.

reinforcement in operant conditioning, any event that *strengthens* the behavior it follows.

shaping an operant conditioning procedure in which reinforcers guide behavior toward closer and closer approximations of the desired behavior.

positive reinforcement increasing behaviors by presenting a pleasurable stimulus. A positive reinforcer is any stimulus that, when *presented* after a response, strengthens the response.

- In **operant conditioning**, organisms associate their own actions with consequences. Actions followed by reinforcers increase; those followed by punishments often decrease. Behavior that *operates* on the environment to produce rewarding or punishing stimuli is called **operant behavior**.

RETRIEVAL PRACTICE

RP-1 With classical conditioning, we learn associations between events we ____________ (do/do not) control. With operant conditioning, we learn associations between our behavior and ____________ (resulting/random) events.

ANSWERS IN APPENDIX E

Skinner's Experiments

LOQ 22-2 Who was Skinner, and how is operant behavior reinforced and shaped?

B. F. Skinner (1904–1990), initially a college English major and aspiring writer, went on to become modern behaviorism's most influential and controversial figure. Skinner's work elaborated on what psychologist Edward L. Thorndike (1874–1949) called the **law of effect**: Rewarded behavior tends to recur (**FIGURE 22.1**). Using Thorndike's law of effect as a starting point, Skinner developed a behavioral technology that revealed principles of *behavior control*. Working from a rooftop office in a Minneapolis flour mill in 1943, Skinner and his students Keller Breland and Norman Guttman looked at the flocks of pigeons sitting on the windowsills and jokingly wondered, "Could we teach a pigeon how to bowl?" (Goddard, 2018; Skinner, 1960). By shaping pigeons' natural walking and pecking behaviors, they did just that (Peterson, 2004). Skinner later used his new learning principles to teach pigeons other unpigeon-like behaviors, including how to walk in a figure 8, play table tennis, and keep a missile on course by pecking at a screen target.

For his pioneering studies, Skinner designed an **operant chamber**, popularly known as a *Skinner box* (**FIGURE 22.2**). The box has a bar (a lever) that an animal presses—or a key (a disc) the animal pecks—to release a reward of food or water. It also has a device that records these responses. This creates a stage on which rats and other animals act out Skinner's concept of **reinforcement**: any event that strengthens (increases the frequency of) a preceding response. What is reinforcing depends on the animal and the conditions. For some people, it may be praise, attention, or a paycheck. For others, it may be drugs that reduce distress or produce euphoria (Bechara et al., 2019). For hungry and thirsty rats, food and water work well. Skinner's experiments have done far more than teach us how to pull habits out of a rat. They have explored the precise conditions that foster efficient and enduring learning.

Shaping Behavior

Imagine that you wanted to condition a hungry rat to press a bar. Like Skinner, you could tease out this action with **shaping**, gradually guiding the rat's actions toward the desired behavior. First, you would observe the animal's natural behavior in order to build on its

FIGURE 22.1
Cat in a puzzle box Thorndike used a fish reward to entice cats to find their way out of a puzzle box through a series of maneuvers. The cats' performance tended to improve with successive trials, illustrating Thorndike's *law of effect*. (Data from Thorndike, 1898.)

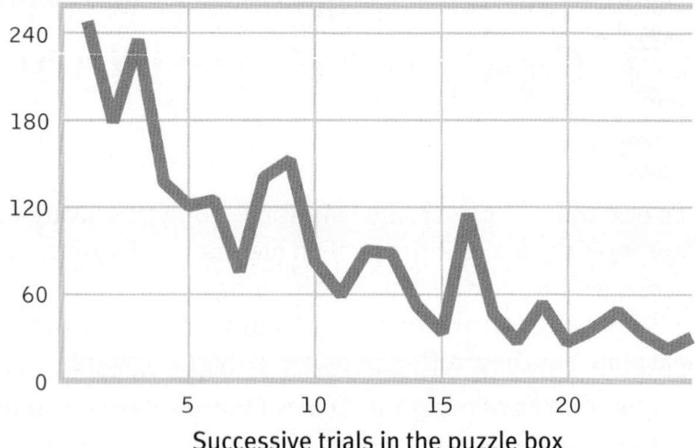
Time required to escape (seconds)
240
180
120
60
0
5
10
15
20
Successive trials in the puzzle box

existing behaviors. You might give the rat a bit of food each time it approaches the bar. Once the rat is approaching regularly, you would give the food only when it moves close to the bar, then closer still. Finally, you would require it to touch the bar to get food. By rewarding *successive approximations,* you reinforce responses that are ever-closer to the final desired behavior, and you ignore all other responses. By making rewards contingent on desired behaviors, researchers and animal trainers gradually shape complex behaviors.

We can also shape our own behavior. Let's say you want to train for your first 5K race. You set up a daily plan with a mixture of walking and running. At each stage, you give yourself a nice reward—perhaps first for a 15-minute walk, then for walking and jogging that distance, then for running it, then for running a bit more each week—rewarding successive approximations of your target behavior.

Speaker
Light
Bar
Water
Food dispenser

FIGURE 22.2
A Skinner box Inside the box, the rat presses a bar for a food reward. Outside, measuring devices (not shown here) record the animal's accumulated responses.

Shaping can also help us understand what nonverbal organisms can perceive. Can a dog distinguish red and green? Can a baby hear the difference between lower- and higher-pitched tones? If we can shape them to respond to one stimulus and not to another, then we know they can perceive the difference. Such experiments have even shown that some nonhuman animals can form concepts. When experimenters reinforced pigeons for pecking after seeing a human face, but not after seeing other images, the pigeons' behavior showed that they could recognize human faces (Herrnstein & Loveland, 1964). In this experiment, the human face was a *discriminative stimulus.* Like a green traffic light, discriminative stimuli signal that a response will be reinforced. After being trained to discriminate among classes of events or objects—flowers, people, cars, and chairs—pigeons can usually identify the category in which a new pictured object belongs (Bhatt et al., 1988; Wasserman, 1993). They have even been trained to discriminate between the music of Bach and Stravinsky (Porter & Neuringer, 1984).

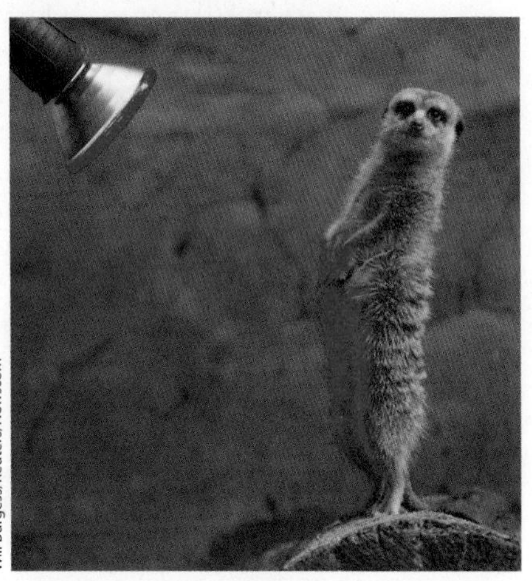
Will Burgess/Reuters/Newscom

Reinforcers vary with circumstances What is reinforcing (a heat lamp) to one animal (a cold meerkat) may not be to another (an overheated bear). What is reinforcing in one situation (a cold snap at the Taronga Zoo in Sydney) may not be in another (a sweltering summer day). Reinforcers also vary among humans. A chocolate treat that is reinforcing to Clarice might not be to Clarence, who prefers vanilla.

Skinner noted that we continually reinforce and shape others' everyday behaviors, though we may not mean to do so. Erlinda's nagging annoys her mom, for example, but consider how Mom typically responds:

ERLINDA: *Could you take me to the store?*
MOM: *(Continues checking her phone.)*
ERLINDA: *Mom, I need to go to the store.*
MOM: *Uh, yeah, in a few minutes.*
ERLINDA: *MOM! The store!*
MOM: *Show some manners! Okay, where are my keys . . .*

Erlinda's nagging is reinforced, because she gets something desirable—a drive to the store. Mom's response is reinforced, because it gets rid of something aversive—Erlinda's nagging.

Or consider a teacher who sticks gold stars on a wall chart beside the names of children scoring 100 percent on spelling tests. As everyone can then see, some children consistently do perfect work. The others, who may have worked harder than the academic all-stars, get no rewards. The teacher would be better advised to apply the principles of operant conditioning—to reinforce all spellers for gradual improvements (successive approximations toward perfect spelling of words they find challenging).

Bird brains spot tumors After being rewarded with food when correctly spotting breast tumors in scans, pigeons became as skilled as humans at discriminating cancerous from healthy tissue (Levenson et al., 2015). Other animals have been shaped to sniff out explosives and drugs or to locate people amid rubble (La Londe et al., 2015).

Levenson RM, Krupinski EA, Navarro VM, Wasserman EA (2015) Pigeons (Columba livia) as Trainable Observers of Pathology and Radiology Breast Cancer Images. PLoS ONE 10(11): e0141357.

ASK YOURSELF

Can you recall a time when a teacher, coach, family member, or employer helped you learn something by shaping your behavior in little steps until you achieved your goal?

Types of Reinforcers

LOQ 22-3 How do positive and negative reinforcement differ, and what are the basic types of reinforcers?

Until now, we've mainly been discussing **positive reinforcement**, which strengthens responding by *presenting* a typically *pleasurable* stimulus immediately after a response. But, as the rude Erlinda story illustrates, there are two basic kinds of reinforcement

TABLE 22.1 Ways to Increase Behavior

Operant Conditioning Term	Description	Examples
Positive reinforcement	Add a desirable stimulus	Pet a dog that comes when you call it; pay someone for work done.
Negative reinforcement	Remove an aversive stimulus	Take painkillers to end pain; fasten seat belt to end loud beeping.

(TABLE 22.1). **Negative reinforcement** strengthens a response by *reducing or removing* something *negative*. Erlinda's nagging was *positively* reinforced, because Erlinda got something desirable—a ride to the store. Her mom's response (doing what Erlinda wanted) was *negatively* reinforced, because it ended an aversive event—Erlinda's nagging. Similarly, taking aspirin may relieve your headache, giving your dog a treat may silence its barking, and fastening your car seat belt will silence the annoying sound. These welcome results provide negative reinforcement and increase the odds that you will repeat these behaviors. For those with an opioid addiction, the negative reinforcement of ending withdrawal pangs can be a compelling reason to resume using (Pantazis et al., 2021). It is very important to understand and remember that *negative reinforcement is not punishment*. Rather, negative reinforcement—psychology's most misunderstood concept—*removes* a punishing (aversive) event. Think of negative reinforcement as something that provides relief—from that bad headache, yapping dog, or annoying seat belt alert.

Sometimes negative and positive reinforcement coincide. Imagine a worried student who, after goofing off and getting a bad exam grade, studies harder for the next exam. This increased effort may be *negatively* reinforced by reduced anxiety, and *positively* reinforced by a better grade. We reap the rewards of escaping the aversive stimulus, which increases the chances that we will repeat our behavior. *The point to remember:* Whether it works by reducing something aversive, or by providing something desirable, *reinforcement is any consequence that strengthens behavior.*

RETRIEVAL PRACTICE

RP-2 How is operant conditioning at work in this cartoon?

THIS IS GREAT!
CHANCE BROWNE
©1992 by King Features Syndicate, Inc. World rights reserved.

I'LL HAVE TO WAKE UP CRYING IN THE MIDDLE OF THE NIGHT MORE OFTEN
3-9

ANSWERS IN APPENDIX E

negative reinforcement increasing behaviors by stopping or reducing an aversive stimulus. A negative reinforcer is any stimulus that, when *removed* after a response, strengthens the response. (*Note:* Negative reinforcement is not punishment.)

primary reinforcer an innately reinforcing stimulus, such as one that satisfies a biological need.

conditioned reinforcer a stimulus that gains its reinforcing power through its association with a primary reinforcer. (Also known as a *secondary reinforcer*.)

PRIMARY AND CONDITIONED REINFORCERS Getting food when hungry or having a painful headache go away is innately satisfying. These **primary reinforcers** are unlearned. **Conditioned reinforcers**, also called *secondary reinforcers*, get their power through learned association with primary reinforcers. If a rat in a Skinner box learns that a light reliably signals a food delivery, the rat will work to turn on the light (see Figure 22.2). The light has become a conditioned reinforcer. Our lives are filled with conditioned reinforcers—money, good grades, approving words, and social media "likes" (Lindström et al., 2021).

IMMEDIATE AND DELAYED REINFORCERS Let's return to the imaginary shaping experiment in which you were conditioning a rat to press a bar. In addition to performing this "wanted" behavior, the hungry rat will engage in other "unwanted" behaviors—scratching, sniffing, and moving around. If you present food immediately after any one of these behaviors, the rat will likely repeat that rewarded behavior. But what if the rat presses the bar while you are distracted, and you delay giving the reinforcer? If the delay lasts longer than about 30 seconds, the rat will not learn to press the bar (Austen & Sanderson, 2019; Cunningham & Shahan, 2019). Delays also decrease human learning. Students learn class material better when they complete frequent quizzes that provide them with immediate feedback (Healy et al., 2017). Immediate feedback produces immediate learning.

But unlike rats, humans *can* respond to delayed reinforcers: the paycheck at the end of the week, the good grade at the end of the term, and the trophy at the end of the sports season. Indeed, to function effectively we must accomplish the difficult task of delaying gratification. In one of psychology's most famous studies, some 4-year-olds showed this ability. In choosing a piece of candy or a marshmallow, these impulse-controlled children preferred having a big one tomorrow to munching on a small one right away. The children who delayed gratification tended to become socially competent and high-achieving adults (Mischel, 2014). Later studies showed a similar (though weaker) relationship between delay of gratification and achievement later (Watts et al., 2018). Learning to control our impulses in order to earn more valued future rewards reduces later likelihood of committing impulsive crimes (Åkerlund et al., 2016; Logue, 1998a,b). *The bottom line:* It pays to delay.

To our detriment, small but immediate pleasures (late-night binge-watching) are sometimes more alluring than big but delayed rewards (feeling rested for a big exam tomorrow). For many teens, the immediate gratification of risky, unprotected sex in passionate moments prevails over the delayed gratifications of safe or saved sex. And for many people, the immediate rewards of today's gas-guzzling vehicles and air conditioning prevail over the bigger future consequences of the global climate crisis, with rising seas and extreme weather.

reinforcement schedule a pattern that defines how often a desired response will be reinforced.

continuous reinforcement schedule reinforcing the desired response every time it occurs.

partial (intermittent) reinforcement schedule reinforcing a response only part of the time; results in slower acquisition of a response but much greater resistance to extinction than does continuous reinforcement.

fixed-ratio schedule in operant conditioning, a reinforcement schedule that reinforces a response only after a specified number of responses.

Reinforcement Schedules

LOQ 22-4 How do different reinforcement schedules affect behavior?

In most of our examples, the desired response has been reinforced every time it occurs. But **reinforcement schedules** vary. With **continuous reinforcement**, learning occurs rapidly, which makes it the best choice for acquiring a behavior. But extinction also occurs rapidly. When reinforcement stops—when we stop delivering food after the rat presses the bar—the behavior soon stops (is *extinguished*). If a normally dependable vending machine fails to deliver a chocolate bar twice in a row, we stop putting money into it (although a week later we may exhibit *spontaneous recovery* by trying again).

Real life rarely provides continuous reinforcement. Salespeople do not make a sale with every pitch. But they persist because their efforts are occasionally rewarded. This persistence is typical with **partial (intermittent) reinforcement schedules**, in which responses are sometimes reinforced, sometimes not. Learning is slower to appear, but *resistance to extinction* is greater than with continuous reinforcement. Imagine a pigeon that has learned to peck a key to obtain food. If you gradually phase out the food delivery until it occurs only rarely, in no predictable pattern, the pigeon may peck 150,000 times without a reward (Skinner, 1953). Slot machines reward gamblers in much the same way—occasionally and unpredictably. And like pigeons, slot players keep trying, time and time again. With intermittent reinforcement, hope springs eternal.

Lesson for parents: Whether intended or not, partial reinforcement also works with children. *Occasionally* giving in to children's tantrums for the sake of peace and quiet intermittently reinforces the tantrums. This is the very best procedure for making a behavior persist!

Skinner (1961) and his collaborators compared four schedules of partial reinforcement and their effects on behavior:

Fixed-ratio schedules reinforce behavior after a set number of responses. Coffee shops may reward us with a free coffee after every 10 purchased. Once conditioned, rats may be reinforced on a fixed ratio of, say, one food pellet for every 30 responses. Once conditioned, animals will pause only briefly after a reinforcer before returning to a high rate of responding.

CHENEY

"Oh, not bad. The light comes on, I press the bar, they write me a check. How about you?"

variable-ratio schedule in operant conditioning, a reinforcement schedule that reinforces a response after an unpredictable number of responses.

fixed-interval schedule in operant conditioning, a reinforcement schedule that reinforces a response only after a specified time has elapsed.

variable-interval schedule in operant conditioning, a reinforcement schedule that reinforces a response at unpredictable time intervals.

TABLE 22.2 Schedules of Partial Reinforcement

	Fixed	Variable
Ratio	*Every so many:* reinforcement after every *nth* behavior, such as "buy 10 coffees, get 1 free" offer, or paying workers per product unit produced	*After an unpredictable number:* reinforcement after a random number of behaviors, as when playing slot machines or fishing
Interval	*Every so often:* reinforcement for behavior after a fixed time, such as Tuesday discount prices	*Unpredictably often:* reinforcement for behavior after a random amount of time, as when checking for a social media update

Variable-ratio schedules provide reinforcers after a seemingly unpredictable number of responses. This unpredictable reinforcement is what slot-machine players and anglers experience, and it's what makes gambling and fishing so hard to extinguish even when they don't produce the desired results. Because reinforcers increase as the number of responses increases, variable-ratio schedules produce high rates of responding.

Fixed-interval schedules reinforce a response after a fixed time period. Animals on this type of schedule tend to respond more frequently as the anticipated time for reward draws near. People check more frequently for the mail as the delivery time approaches. Pigeons peck keys more rapidly as the time for reinforcement draws closer. This produces a choppy stop-start pattern rather than a steady rate of response (**FIGURE 22.3**).

Variable-interval schedules reinforce the first response after *varying* time intervals. At unpredictable times, a food pellet rewarded Skinner's pigeons for persistence in pecking a key. Like the longed-for message that finally rewards persistence in checking our phone, variable-interval schedules tend to produce slow, steady responding. This makes sense, because there is no knowing when the waiting will be over (**TABLE 22.2**). Pigeons keep pecking—and we keep checking—hoping that *this time* we'll get the reward.

In general, response rates are higher when reinforcement is linked to the number of responses (a ratio schedule) rather than to time (an interval schedule). But responding is more consistent when reinforcement is unpredictable (a variable schedule) than when it is predictable (a fixed schedule). (See Figure 22.3.) Animal behaviors differ, yet Skinner (1956) contended that the reinforcement principles of operant conditioning are universal. It matters little, he said, what response, what reinforcer, or what species. The effect of a given reinforcement schedule is pretty much the same: "Pigeon, rat, monkey, which is which? It doesn't matter. . . . Behavior shows astonishingly similar properties."

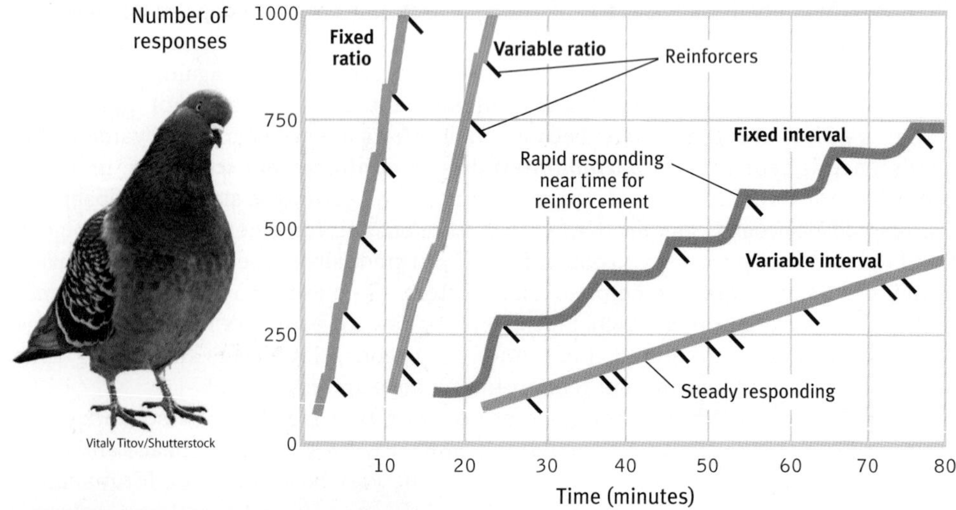
Number of responses
1000
750
500
250
0
Fixed ratio
Variable ratio
Reinforcers
Fixed interval
Rapid responding near time for reinforcement
Variable interval
Steady responding
10
20
30
40
50
60
70
80
Time (minutes)
Vitaly Titov/Shutterstock

FIGURE 22.3
Intermittent reinforcement schedules
Skinner's laboratory pigeons produced these response patterns to each of four reinforcement schedules. (Reinforcers are indicated by diagonal marks.) For people, as for pigeons, reinforcement linked to number of responses (a *ratio* schedule) produces a higher response rate than reinforcement linked to amount of time elapsed (an *interval* schedule). But the predictability of the reward also matters. An unpredictable *(variable)* schedule produces more consistent responding than does a predictable *(fixed)* schedule. (Data from Skinner, 1961.)

RETRIEVAL PRACTICE

RP-3 People who send spam email are reinforced by which schedule? Home bakers checking the oven to see if the cookies are done are reinforced on which schedule? Sandwich shops that offer a free sandwich after every 10 purchased are using which reinforcement schedule?

ANSWERS IN APPENDIX E

Punishment

LOQ 22-5 How does punishment differ from negative reinforcement, and how does punishment affect behavior?

positive punishment an event that decreases a behavior by administering a negative stimulus.

negative punishment an event that decreases behavior by removing a rewarding stimulus.

Reinforcement increases a behavior; punishment does the opposite. A *punisher* is any consequence that *decreases* the frequency of the behavior it follows (**TABLE 22.3**). **Positive punishment** is punishing by adding (administering) an unpleasant stimulus. **Negative punishment** is punishing by subtracting (taking away) a rewarding stimulus. Swift and sure punishers can powerfully restrain unwanted behavior. The rat that is shocked after touching a forbidden object and the child who is burned by touching a hot stove will learn not to repeat those behaviors.

Criminal behavior, much of it impulsive, is also influenced more by swift and sure punishers than by the threat of severe sentences (Darley & Alter, 2013). Thus, when Arizona introduced an exceptionally harsh sentence for first-time drunk drivers, the drunk-driving rate changed very little. But when Kansas City police started patrolling a high crime area to increase the swiftness and sureness of punishment, that city's crime rate dropped dramatically.

What do punishment studies imply for parenting? One analysis of over 160,000 children found that physical punishment rarely corrects unwanted behavior (Gershoff & Grogan-Kaylor, 2016). A second analysis of 131,000 children from 49 countries found that, even after accounting for other family differences such as economic status, children who were hit and spanked fared more poorly (Cuartas, 2021). With support from an American Psychological Association resolution on the ineffectiveness and potential harm of physical punishment, psychologists have noted five major drawbacks (APA, 2019; Finkenauer et al., 2015; Gershoff et al., 2018, 2019; Marshall, 2002):

1. ***Punished behavior is suppressed, not forgotten. This temporary state may (negatively) reinforce parents' punishing behavior.*** The child swears, the parent swats, the child stops swearing when the parent is nearby, so the parent believes the punishment successfully stopped the behavior. No wonder spanking is a hit with so many parents—with more than two in three children in less developed countries spanked or otherwise physically punished (UNICEF, 2020).
2. ***Physical punishment does not replace the unwanted behavior.*** Physical punishment may reduce or even eliminate unwanted behavior, but it does not provide direction for appropriate behavior. A child who is slapped for screaming in the car may stop yelling but continue to throw her food or steal her brother's toys.
3. ***Punishment teaches discrimination among situations.*** In operant conditioning, *discrimination* occurs when an organism learns that certain responses, but not others, will be reinforced. Did the punishment effectively end the child's swearing? Or did the child simply learn that it's not okay to swear in front of parents?
4. ***Punishment can teach fear.*** In operant conditioning, *generalization* occurs when an organism's response learned in one situation occurs in other, similar situations. A punished child may associate fear not only with the undesirable behavior but also with the person who delivered the punishment or where it occurred. Thus, children may learn to fear a punishing teacher and try to avoid school, or may become anxious (Gershoff et al., 2010). For such reasons, most European countries and 31 U.S. states now ban hitting children in public schools (EndCorporalPunishment.org). As of 2021, 62 countries had outlawed all corporal punishment of children, including in the home. A large survey in Finland, the second country to pass such a law, revealed that children born after the law passed were, indeed, less often slapped and beaten (Österman et al., 2014).
5. ***Physical punishment may increase aggression by modeling violence as a way to cope with problems.*** Studies find that spanked children are at increased risk

TABLE 22.3 Ways to Decrease Behavior

Type of Punisher	Description	Examples
Positive punishment	Administer an aversive stimulus.	Spray water on a barking dog; give a traffic ticket for speeding.
Negative punishment	Withdraw a rewarding stimulus.	Take away a misbehaving teen's driving privileges; block a rude commenter on social media.

for aggression (MacKenzie et al., 2013). We know, for example, that many aggressive adults come from abusive families (Fitton et al., 2020).

Some researchers question this logic. Physically punished children may be more aggressive, they say, for the same reason that people who have undergone psychotherapy are more likely to experience depression—because they had preexisting problems that triggered the treatments (Ferguson, 2013; Larzelere, 2000; Larzelere et al., 2019). So, does spanking cause misbehavior, or does misbehavior trigger spanking? Or do physically aggressive parents give their children aggression-disposing genes? Correlations don't hand us an answer.

How *should* parents and caregivers discipline children? Many psychologists encourage *time-out from positive reinforcement:* removing a misbehaving child from access to desired stimuli such as siblings' and parents' attention (Dadds & Tully, 2019). Effective time-outs come with clear expectations for replacing problem behavior (hitting siblings) with alternative positive behaviors (telling siblings they have hurt your feelings) (O'Leary et al., 1967; Patterson et al., 1968). Children learn that time-out helps the family enjoy positive and caring interactions.

Some parents may not know how to discourage bad behavior without screaming, hitting, or threatening their children with punishment (Patterson et al., 1982). Training programs can help transform dire threats ("You clean up your room this minute or no dinner!") into positive incentives ("You're welcome at the dinner table after you get your room cleaned up"). Stop and think about it. Aren't many threats of punishment just as forceful, and perhaps more effective, when rephrased positively? Thus, "If you don't get your homework done, there'll be no car" could be phrased more positively as . . .

In classrooms, too, teachers can give feedback by saying, "No, but try this . . ." and "Yes, that's it!" Such responses reduce unwanted behavior while reinforcing more desirable alternatives. Other studies show that people learn and grow more from feedback that tells them where they've succeeded rather than where they have failed (Eskreis-Winkler & Fishbach, 2019). Remember: *Punishment tells you what not to do; reinforcement tells you what to do.* Thus, punishment trains a particular sort of morality—one focused on prohibition (what *not* to do) rather than positive obligations (Sheikh & Janoff-Bulman, 2013).

"A pat on the back, though only a few vertebrae removed from a kick in the pants, is miles ahead in results." —Attributed to publisher Bennett Cerf (1898–1971)

What punishment often teaches, said Skinner, is how to avoid it. *The bottom line:* Most psychologists now favor an emphasis on reinforcement: Focus on what people do right and praise them for it.

RETRIEVAL PRACTICE

RP-4 Fill in the blanks with one of the following terms: positive reinforcement (PR), negative reinforcement (NR), positive punishment (PP), or negative punishment (NP). We have provided the first answer (PR) for you.

Type of Stimulus	Give It	Take It Away
Desired (for example, a teen's use of the car)	1. PR	2.
Undesired/aversive (for example, an insult)	3.	4.

ANSWERS IN APPENDIX E

Skinner's Legacy

LOQ 22-6 Why did Skinner's ideas provoke controversy, and how might his operant conditioning principles be applied?

B. F. Skinner stirred a hornet's nest with his outspoken beliefs. He repeatedly insisted that external influences, not internal thoughts and feelings, shape behavior. He argued that brain science isn't needed for psychological science, saying that "a science of behavior is independent of neurology" (Skinner, 1938/1966, pp. 423–424). And he urged people to use operant conditioning principles to influence others' behavior at school, work, and home. Knowing that behavior is shaped by its results, he argued that we should use rewards to evoke more desirable behavior.

Skinner's critics objected, saying that he dehumanized people by neglecting their personal freedom and by seeking to control their actions. Skinner's reply: External consequences already haphazardly control people's behavior. Why not administer those consequences toward human betterment? Wouldn't reinforcers be more humane than the punishments used in homes, schools, and prisons? And if it is humbling to think that our history has shaped us, doesn't this very idea give us hope that we can apply operant conditioning to shape our future?

Macmillan Learning

B. F. Skinner "I am sometimes asked, 'Do you think of yourself as you think of the organisms you study?' The answer is yes. So far as I know, my behavior at any given moment has been nothing more than the product of my genetic endowment, my personal history, and the current setting" (1983).

Applications of Operant Conditioning

Psychologists apply operant conditioning principles to help people improve their health or gain social skills. Reinforcement techniques are also at work in schools, sports, computer programs, workplaces, and homes, and these principles can support our self-improvement as well (Flora, 2004).

AT SCHOOL More than 50 years ago, Skinner and others envisioned a day when "machines and textbooks" would shape learning in small steps, by immediately reinforcing correct responses. Such machines and textbooks, they said, would revolutionize education and free teachers to focus on each student's special needs. "Good instruction demands two things," said Skinner (1989). "Students must be told immediately whether what they do is right or wrong and, when right, they must be directed to the step to be taken next."

Skinner might be pleased to know that many of his ideals for education are now possible. Teachers used to find it difficult to pace material to each student's learning rate and provide prompt feedback. Online adaptive quizzing, such as the LearningCurve system in Achieve available with this text, do both. Students move through quizzes at their own pace, according to their own level of understanding. And they get immediate feedback on their efforts, including personalized study plans.

IN SPORTS The key to shaping behavior in athletic performance, as elsewhere, is first reinforcing small successes and then gradually increasing the challenge. Golf students can learn putting by starting with very short putts, and then, as they build competence, stepping back farther and farther. Novice batters can begin with half swings at an oversized ball pitched from 10 feet away, giving them the immediate pleasure of smacking the ball. As the hitters' confidence builds with their success and they achieve competence at each level, the pitcher gradually moves back and eventually introduces a standard baseball. Compared with children taught by conventional methods, those trained by this behavioral method have shown faster skill improvement (Simek & O'Brien, 1981, 1988).

Immediate reinforcement Muffet McGraw, the coach of Notre Dame's 2018 national championship women's basketball team, spent her career focusing on catching her players doing something right and applauding them for it on the spot.

Chuck Burton/AP Photo

IN VIDEO GAMES Game developers use reinforcement principles to create computer programs that mimic human learning. Such *artificial intelligence (AI)* programs perform actions—playing chess, poker, or a multiplayer videogame—enabling the programs to quickly learn to repeat reinforced actions (what leads to winning) and avoid punished responses (what leads to losing) (Botvinick et al., 2019; Jaderberg et al., 2019).

AT WORK How might managers successfully motivate their employees? People do respond to delayed positive and negative reinforcement, but it's better to make the reinforcement *immediate.* It's also better to reward specific, achievable behaviors rather than vaguely defined "merit." General Motors CEO Mary Barra understood this. In 2015, she observed workers' high performance and awarded record bonuses (Vlasic, 2015). But rewards don't have to be monetary. An effective manager may simply chime in on group chats, sincerely praising people for good work.

IN PARENTING As we have seen, parents can learn from operant conditioning practices. Parent-training researchers remind us that by saying, "Get ready for bed" and then caving in to protests or defiance, parents reinforce such whining and arguing (Wierson & Forehand, 1994). Exasperated, they may then yell or gesture menacingly. When the child, now frightened, obeys, that reinforces the parent's angry behavior. Over time, a destructive parent-child relationship develops.

To disrupt this cycle, parents should remember the basic rule of shaping: *Notice people doing something right and affirm them for it.* Give children attention and other reinforcers when they are behaving *well.* If you want your teen to drive safely, reward them for safe driving (Hinnant et al., 2019). Target a specific behavior, reward it, and watch it increase. Ask your child to make their bed, say "thank you" and smile when they make it, and they may make the bed more often on their own. When children misbehave, don't yell at them or hit them. Use punishment gently to reduce future unwanted behavior. Simply explain the misbehavior and take away their screen time, remove a misused toy, or give a brief time-out.

TO CHANGE YOUR OWN BEHAVIOR Finally, we can use operant conditioning in our own lives. To reinforce your own desired behaviors (perhaps to improve your study habits) and extinguish the undesired ones (to stop vaping, for example), psychologists suggest taking these steps:

1. ***State a realistic goal in measurable terms and announce it.*** You might, for example, aim to boost your study time by an hour a day. To increase your commitment and odds of success, share that goal with friends.
2. ***Decide how, when, and where you will work toward your goal.*** Plan when and where you will complete assigned reading and other homework. From North American undergraduates to Swedish entrepreneurs, those who specify how they will implement goals become more focused on those goals and more likely to fulfill them (Gollwitzer & Oettingen, 2012; van Gelderen et al., 2018).
3. ***Monitor how often you engage in your desired behavior.*** You might log your current study time, noting under what conditions you do and don't study. See how many days in a row you can meet your study goal. (When we began writing textbooks, we each logged our time and were amazed to discover how much time we were wasting.)
4. ***Reinforce the desired behavior.*** People's persistence toward long-term goals is powered mostly by immediate rewards (Woolley & Fishbach, 2017). So, to increase your study time, reward yourself (a snack, a nap, or 15 minutes goofing off online) only after you finish your extra hour of study. Use apps that reward your progress toward desired goals, whether to meditate regularly, get more sleep, or drink more water. Agree to join your friends for weekend activities only if you have met your realistic weekly studying goal.
5. ***Reduce the rewards gradually.*** As your new behaviors become more habitual, separate the behaviors from the rewards. Give yourself a mental pat on the back instead of a cookie.

ASK YOURSELF

Think of a personal bad habit you'd like to break. How could you use operant conditioning to break it?

RETRIEVAL PRACTICE

RP-5 Joslyn constantly misbehaves at preschool even though her teacher scolds her repeatedly. Why does Joslyn's misbehavior continue, and what can her teacher do to stop it?

ANSWERS IN APPENDIX E

Contrasting Classical and Operant Conditioning

LOQ **22-7** How does operant conditioning differ from classical conditioning?

Both classical and operant conditioning are forms of *associative learning*. Both involve *acquisition, extinction, spontaneous recovery, generalization,* and *discrimination*. But these two forms of learning also differ. Through classical (Pavlovian) conditioning, we associate different stimuli we do not control, and we respond automatically *(respondent behaviors)* (**TABLE 22.4**). Through operant conditioning, we associate our own behaviors—which act on our environment to produce rewarding or punishing stimuli *(operant behaviors)*—with their consequences.

TABLE 22.4 Comparison of Classical and Operant Conditioning

	Classical Conditioning	Operant Conditioning
Basic idea	Learning associations between events we do not control.	Learning associations between our behavior and its consequences.
Response	Involuntary, automatic.	Voluntary, operates on environment.
Acquisition	Associating events; NS is paired with US and becomes CS.	Associating a response with a consequence (reinforcer or punisher).
Extinction	CR decreases when CS is repeatedly presented alone.	Responding decreases when reinforcement stops.
Spontaneous recovery	The reappearance, after a rest period, of a weakened CR.	The reappearance, after a rest period, of a weakened response.
Generalization	The tendency to respond to stimuli similar to the CS.	Responses learned in one situation occurring in other, similar situations.
Discrimination	Learning to distinguish between a CS and other stimuli that do not signal a US.	Learning that some responses, but not others, will be reinforced.

As we shall see next, our biology and cognitive processes influence both classical and operant conditioning.

"O! This learning, what a thing it is."
—William Shakespeare, *The Taming of the Shrew*, 1597

RETRIEVAL PRACTICE

RP-6 Salivating in response to a tone paired with food is a(n) ________ behavior; pressing a bar to obtain food is a(n) ________ behavior.

ANSWERS IN APPENDIX E

MODULE 22 REVIEW Operant Conditioning

LEARNING OBJECTIVES

Test Yourself Answer these repeated Learning Objective Questions on your own (before "showing" the answers here, or checking the answers in Appendix D) to improve your retention of the concepts (McDaniel et al., 2009, 2015).

LOQ **22-1** What is *operant conditioning*?

LOQ **22-2** Who was Skinner, and how is operant behavior reinforced and shaped?

LOQ **22-3** How do positive and negative reinforcement differ, and what are the basic types of reinforcers?

LOQ **22-4** How do different reinforcement schedules affect behavior?

LOQ **22-5** How does punishment differ from negative reinforcement, and how does punishment affect behavior?

LOQ **22-6** Why did Skinner's ideas provoke controversy, and how might his operant conditioning principles be applied?

LOQ **22-7** How does operant conditioning differ from classical conditioning?

TERMS AND CONCEPTS TO REMEMBER

Test Yourself Write down the definition in your own words, then check your answer.

learning, p. 269
associative learning, p. 269
stimulus, p. 269
respondent behavior, p. 269
operant conditioning, p. 270
operant behavior, p. 270
law of effect, p. 270
operant chamber, p. 270
reinforcement, p. 270
shaping, p. 270
positive reinforcement, p. 270
negative reinforcement, p. 272
primary reinforcer, p. 272
conditioned reinforcer, p. 272
reinforcement schedule, p. 273
continuous reinforcement schedule, p. 273
partial (intermittent) reinforcement schedule, p. 273
fixed-ratio schedule, p. 273
variable-ratio schedule, p. 274
fixed-interval schedule, p. 274
variable-interval schedule, p. 274
positive punishment, p. 275
negative punishment, p. 275

MODULE TEST

Test Yourself Answer the following questions on your own first, then "show" the answers here, or check your answers in Appendix E.

1. Thorndike's law of effect was the basis for ________'s work on operant conditioning and behavior control.

2. One way to change behavior is to reward natural behaviors in small steps, as the organism gets closer and closer to a desired behavior. This process is called ______________.

3. Your dog is barking so loudly that it's making your ears ring. You clap your hands, the dog stops barking, your ears stop ringing, and you think to yourself, "I'll have to do that when she barks again." The clapping was for your dog a
   - **a.** positive reinforcer.
   - **b.** negative reinforcer.
   - **c.** positive punishment.
   - **d.** negative punishment.

4. How do hungry babies negatively reinforce their caregivers to feed them?

5. Reinforcing a desired response only some of the times it occurs is called ______________ reinforcement.

6. A restaurant delivery service is running a special deal. After you buy four meals at full price, you will get a free appetizer. This is an example of a ______________-______________ schedule of reinforcement.
   - **a.** fixed-ratio
   - **b.** variable-ratio
   - **c.** fixed-interval
   - **d.** variable-interval

7. The partial reinforcement schedule that reinforces a response after unpredictable time periods is a ______________-______________ schedule.

8. A medieval proverb notes that "a burnt child dreads the fire." In operant conditioning, getting burned would be an example of a
   - **a.** primary reinforcer.
   - **b.** negative reinforcer.
   - **c.** punisher.
   - **d.** positive reinforcer.

MODULE 23

Biology, Cognition, and Learning

From drooling dogs, running rats, and pecking pigeons we have learned much about the basic processes of **learning**. But conditioning principles don't tell us the whole story. Today's learning theorists recognize that learning is the product of the interaction of biological, psychological, and social-cultural influences (**FIGURE 23.1**).

Biological Constraints on Conditioning

LOQ 23-1 How do biological constraints affect classical and operant conditioning?

Ever since Charles Darwin, scientists have assumed that all animals share a common evolutionary history and thus share commonalities in their makeup and functioning. Pavlov, Watson, and Skinner believed the basic laws of learning were essentially similar in all animals. So, it should make little difference whether one studied pigeons or people. Moreover, it seemed that any natural response could be conditioned to any neutral stimulus.

Biological influences:
- genetic predispositions
- unconditioned responses
- adaptive responses
- neural mirroring

Psychological influences:
- previous experiences
- predictability of associations
- generalization
- discrimination
- expectations

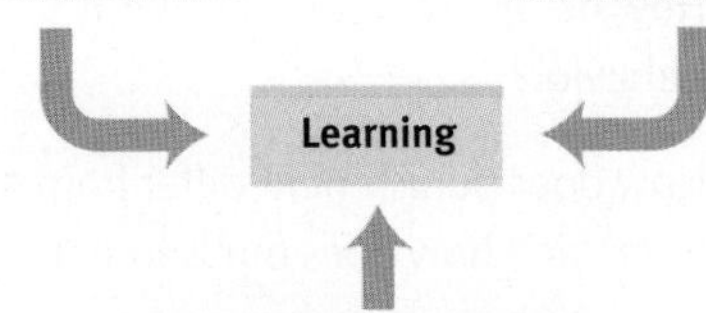
Learning

Social-cultural influences:
- culturally learned preferences
- motivation, affected by presence of others
- modeling

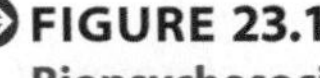
FIGURE 23.1
Biopsychosocial influences on learning Our learning results not only from environmental experiences, but also from cognitive and biological influences.

learning the process of acquiring through experience new and relatively enduring information or behaviors.

Biological Limits on Classical Conditioning

Macmillan Learning

John Garcia As the laboring son of California farmworkers, Garcia attended school only in the off-season during his early childhood years. After entering junior college in his late twenties, and earning his Ph.D. in his late forties, he received the American Psychological Association's Distinguished Scientific Contribution Award "for his highly original, pioneering research in conditioning and learning." He was also elected to the National Academy of Sciences.

In 1956, learning researcher Gregory Kimble proclaimed, "Just about any activity of which the organism is capable can be conditioned and . . . these responses can be conditioned to any stimulus that the organism can perceive" (p. 195). Twenty-five years later, he humbly acknowledged that "half a thousand" scientific reports had proven him wrong (Kimble, 1981). More than the early behaviorists realized, an animal's capacity for conditioning is limited by biological constraints. For example, each species' predispositions *prepare* it to learn the associations that enhance its survival—a phenomenon called **preparedness**. Environments are not the whole story. Biology matters.

John Garcia (1917–2012) was among those who challenged the prevailing idea that all associations can be learned equally well. While researching the effects of radiation on laboratory animals, Garcia and Robert Koelling (1966) noticed that rats began to avoid drinking water from the plastic bottles in radiation chambers. Could classical conditioning be the culprit? Might the rats have linked the plastic-tasting water (a CS) to the sickness (UR) triggered by the radiation (US)?

Classical Conditioning Review:
NS = Neutral Stimulus
US = Unconditioned Stimulus
UR = Unconditioned Response
CS = Conditioned Stimulus
CR = Conditioned Response

To test their hunch, Garcia and Koelling exposed the rats to a particular taste, sight, or sound (CS) and later also to radiation or drugs (US) that led to nausea (UR). Two startling findings emerged: First, even if sickened as late as several hours after tasting a particular novel flavor, the rats thereafter avoided that flavor. This appeared to violate the notion that for conditioning to occur, the US must immediately follow the CS.

Second, the sickened rats developed aversions to tastes but not to sights or sounds. This contradicted the behaviorists' idea that any perceivable stimulus could serve as a CS. But it made adaptive sense. For rats, the easiest way to identify tainted food is to taste it; if sickened after sampling a new food, they thereafter avoid it. This response, called *taste aversion,* makes it difficult to eradicate a population of "bait-shy" rats by poisoning.

Humans, too, seem biologically prepared to learn some associations rather than others. If you become violently ill four hours after eating contaminated oysters, you will probably develop an aversion to the *taste* of oysters more readily than to the sight of the associated restaurant, the people you ate with, or the music you listened to while eating. (In contrast, birds, which hunt by sight, appear biologically primed to develop aversions to the *sight* of tainted food [Nicolaus et al., 1983].)

Jose Oto/BSIP SA/Alamy Stock Photo

Taste aversion Our biology prepares us to learn taste aversions to toxic foods.

"Once bitten, twice shy." —G. F. Northall, *Folk-Phrases,* 1894

Garcia's early findings on taste aversion were met with an onslaught of criticism. As the German philosopher Arthur Schopenhauer (1788–1860) once said, important ideas are first ridiculed, then attacked, and finally taken for granted. Leading journals refused to publish Garcia's work: The findings are impossible, said some critics. But, as sometimes happens in science, Garcia and Koelling's taste-aversion research replicated often, from the simple snail to the complex human (Aonuma et al., 2018). Conditioned taste aversion is now basic textbook material.

It is also a good example of experiments that begin with the discomfort of some laboratory animals and end by enhancing many others' welfare. In one conditioned taste-aversion study, coyotes and wolves were tempted into eating sheep carcasses

preparedness a biological predisposition to learn associations, such as between taste and nausea, that have survival value.

FIGURE 23.2
Nausea conditioning in cancer patients

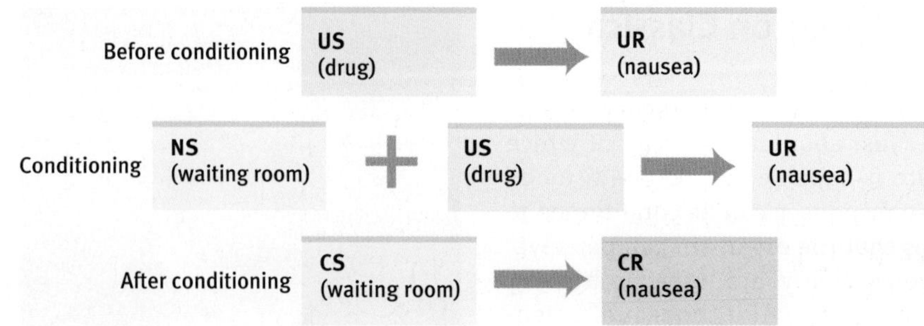

Before conditioning
US (drug)
UR (nausea)
Conditioning
NS (waiting room)
US (drug)
UR (nausea)
After conditioning
CS (waiting room)
CR (nausea)

laced with a sickening poison. Thereafter, they developed an aversion to sheep meat; two wolves later penned with a live sheep seemed actually to fear it (Gustavson et al., 1974, 1976). These studies not only saved the sheep from their predators, but also saved the sheep-shunning coyotes and wolves from angry ranchers and farmers who had wanted to destroy them. Similar applications have prevented baboons from raiding African gardens, raccoons from attacking chickens, and ravens and crows from feeding on crane eggs. In all these cases, research helped preserve both the prey and their predators, all of which occupy an important ecological niche (Dingfelder, 2010; Garcia & Gustavson, 1997).

Such research supports Darwin's principle that natural selection favors traits that aid survival. Our ancestors learned to avoid foods and situations that made them sick, which helped them survive and leave descendants (Bernal-Gamboa et al., 2018). Nausea, like anxiety, pain, and other bad feelings, serves a good purpose. Like a "malware detected" message that pops up on your computer, each alerts the body to a threat (Davidson & Riley, 2015; Neese, 1991).

Our preparedness to associate a CS with a US that follows predictably and immediately is adaptive. Causes often do immediately precede effects. But as we saw in the taste-aversion findings, our predisposition to associate an effect with a preceding event can trick us. When chemotherapy triggers nausea and vomiting more than an hour following treatment, cancer patients may, over time, develop classically conditioned nausea (and sometimes anxiety) to the sights, sounds, and smells associated with the clinic (Hall, 1997) (**FIGURE 23.2**). Merely returning to the clinic's waiting room or seeing the nurses can provoke these conditioned feelings (Burish & Carey, 1986; Davey, 1992). Under normal circumstances, such revulsion to sickening stimuli would be adaptive.

RETRIEVAL PRACTICE

RP-1 How did Garcia and Koelling's taste-aversion studies help disprove Gregory Kimble's early claim that "just about any activity of which the organism is capable can be conditioned . . . to any stimulus that the organism can perceive"?

ANSWERS IN APPENDIX E

Biological Limits on Operant Conditioning

Nature also constrains each species' capacity for operant conditioning. Science fiction writer Robert Heinlein (1973) said it well: "Never try to teach a pig to sing; it wastes your time and annoys the pig."

We most easily learn and retain behaviors that reflect our biological and psychological predispositions (Iliescu et al., 2018). Thus, using food as a reinforcer, you could easily condition a hamster to dig or to rear up, because these are among the animal's natural food-searching behaviors. But you won't be so successful if you use food as a reinforcer to shape face washing and other hamster behaviors that aren't typically associated with food or hunger (Shettleworth, 1973). Similarly, you could easily teach pigeons to flap their wings to avoid being shocked, and to peck to obtain food: Fleeing with their wings and eating with their beaks are natural pigeon behaviors. However, pigeons would have a hard time learning to peck to avoid a shock, or to flap their wings to obtain food (Foree & LoLordo, 1973). *The bottom line:* Biological constraints predispose organisms to learn associations that are naturally adaptive.

In the early years of their work, animal trainers Marian Breland and Keller Breland presumed that operant principles would work on almost any response an animal could make. But along the way, they too learned about biological constraints. In one act, pigs trained to pick up large wooden "dollars" and deposit them in a piggy bank began to drift back to their natural ways. They dropped the coin, pushed it with their snouts as pigs are prone to do, picked it up again, and then repeated the sequence—delaying their food reinforcer. This **instinctive drift** occurred as the animals reverted to their biologically predisposed patterns.

Jeffery Jones/The Gallup Independent/AP Photo

Natural athletes Animals can most easily learn and retain behaviors that draw on their biological predispositions, such as this horse's inborn ability to move around obstacles with speed and agility.

Cognition's Influence on Conditioning

LOQ **23-2** How do cognitive processes affect classical and operant conditioning?

Cognition and Classical Conditioning

In their dismissal of "mentalistic" concepts such as consciousness, Pavlov and Watson underestimated the importance of not only biological constraints such as preparedness and instinctive drift, but also the effects of cognitive processes (thoughts, perceptions, expectations). The early behaviorists believed that rats' and dogs' learned behaviors could be reduced to mindless mechanisms, so there was no need to consider cognition. But Robert Rescorla and Allan Wagner (1972) argued that an animal can learn an event's *predictability.* If a shock always is preceded by a tone, and then may also be preceded by a light that accompanies the tone, a rat will react with fear to the tone but not to the light. Although the light is always followed by the shock, it adds no new information; the tone is a better predictor. The more predictable the association, the stronger the conditioned response. It's as if the animal learns an *expectancy*, an awareness of how likely it is that the US will occur.

"All brains are, in essence, anticipation machines." —Daniel C. Dennett, *Consciousness Explained,* 1991

Classical conditioning treatments that ignore cognition often have limited success. For example, people receiving therapy for alcohol use disorder may be given alcohol spiked with a nauseating drug. Will they then associate alcohol with sickness? If classical conditioning were merely a matter of "stamping in" stimulus associations, we might hope so, and to some extent this does occur. However, one's awareness that the drug, not the alcohol, induces nausea often weakens the association between drinking alcohol and feeling sick, reducing the treatment's effectiveness. So, even in classical conditioning, it is—especially with humans—not simply the CS-US association, but also the thought that counts.

Cognition and Operant Conditioning

B. F. Skinner acknowledged the biological underpinnings of behavior and the existence of private thought processes. Nevertheless, many psychologists criticized him for discounting cognition's importance.

A mere 8 days before dying of leukemia at age 86, Skinner stood before the American Psychological Association convention. In this final address, he still resisted the growing belief that cognition has a necessary place in the science of psychology and even in our

instinctive drift the tendency of learned behavior to gradually revert to biologically predisposed patterns.

understanding of conditioning. He viewed "cognitive science" as a throwback to early twentieth-century introspectionism. For Skinner, thoughts and emotions were behaviors that follow the same laws as other behaviors.

Nevertheless, the evidence of cognitive processes cannot be ignored. For example, rats exploring a maze, given no obvious rewards, seem to develop a **cognitive map**, a mental representation of the maze. When an experimenter then places food in the maze's goal box, these rats run the maze as quickly as other rats that were previously reinforced with food for this result. Like people sightseeing in a new town, the exploring rats seemingly experienced **latent learning** during their earlier tours (Tolman & Honzik, 1930). That learning became apparent only when there was some incentive to demonstrate it. Children, too, may learn from watching a parent but demonstrate the learning only much later, as needed.

P. BYRNES.

Pat Byrnes/Cartoon Stock

"Bathroom? Sure, it's just down the hall to the left, jog right, left, another left, straight past two more lefts, then right, and it's at the end of the third corridor on your right."

The point to remember: There is more to learning than associating a response with a consequence; there is also cognition. In the Thinking and Language modules, we encounter more striking evidence of animals' cognitive abilities in solving problems and in using aspects of language. And in the Affiliation and Achievement module, we see how, due to cognition, excessive rewards can make us *less* motivated to perform a desired behavior.

TABLE 23.1 compares the biological and cognitive influences on classical and operant conditioning.

TABLE 23.1 Biological and Cognitive Influences on Conditioning

	Classical Conditioning	Operant Conditioning
Biological influences	Natural predispositions constrain what stimuli and responses can easily be associated.	Organisms most easily learn behaviors similar to their natural behaviors; unnatural behaviors instinctively drift back toward natural ones.
Cognitive influences	Organisms develop an expectation that a CS signals the arrival of a US.	Organisms develop an expectation that a response will be reinforced or punished; they also exhibit latent learning, without reinforcement.

ASK YOURSELF

Can you remember examples from your childhood of learning through *classical conditioning* (salivating at the sound or smell of some delicious food cooking in the kitchen?), *operant conditioning* (deciding not to repeat a behavior because you disliked its consequence?), and *cognitive learning* (repeating or avoiding what you watched someone else do)?

RETRIEVAL PRACTICE

RP-2 Instinctive drift and latent learning are examples of what important idea?

ANSWERS IN APPENDIX E

cognitive map a mental representation of the layout of one's environment. For example, after exploring a maze, rats act as if they have learned a cognitive map of it.

latent learning learning that occurs but is not apparent until there is an incentive to demonstrate it.

observational learning learning by observing others. (Also called *social learning*.)

modeling the process of observing and imitating a specific behavior.

Learning by Observation

LOQ 23-3 What is *observational learning?*

Cognition supports **observational learning** (also called *social learning*). A child who sees their sister burn her fingers on a hot stove learns not to touch it. Likewise, nonhuman animals learn by observing others responding to threats, such as predators (Olsson et al., 2020). Observational learning does have its limits: Merely observing someone who is proficient at, say, dart-throwing, can lead people to overestimate their talent at doing the same (Kardas & O'Brien, 2018). Imitative *practice* matters, too. We learn our native languages and various other specific behaviors by observing and by imitating others, a process called **modeling**.

Polaris/Newscom

Albert Bandura An analysis of citations, awards, and textbook coverage identified Bandura — shown here receiving a 2016 U.S. National Medal of Science from President Barack Obama — as the world's most eminent psychologist (Diener et al., 2014).

Picture this scene from an experiment by Albert Bandura (1925–2021), the pioneering researcher of observational learning (Bandura et al., 1961): A preschool child works on a drawing. An adult in another part of the room builds with Tinkertoys. As the child watches, the adult gets up and for nearly 10 minutes pounds, kicks, and throws around the room a large inflated toy clown called a Bobo doll, yelling, "Sock him in the nose. . . . Hit him down. . . . Kick him."

The child is then taken to another room filled with appealing toys. Soon the experimenter returns and tells the child she has decided to save these good toys "for the other children." She takes the now-frustrated child to a third room containing a few toys, including a Bobo doll. Left alone, what does the child do?

Unlike children not exposed to the adult model (none of whom acted aggressively), those who viewed the model's actions often lashed out at the doll (Bandura, 2017). Observing the aggressive outburst apparently lowered their inhibitions. But *something more* was also at work, for the children imitated the very acts they had observed and used the very words they had heard (**FIGURE 23.3**). Additionally, reported Bandura (2017), the children displayed other "non-modeled" aggressive behaviors, such as "assaults with dart guns and fights among toy animals."

That "something more," Bandura suggests, was this: By watching models, we experience *vicarious reinforcement* or *vicarious punishment,* and we learn to anticipate a behavior's consequences in situations like those we are observing. We are especially likely to learn from people we perceive as powerful, successful, or similar to ourselves. Thus, children may acquire fears vicariously, by observing their parents' fearful reactions (Marin et al., 2020). fMRI scans show that when people observe someone winning a reward (and especially when it's someone likable and similar to themselves), their own brain reward systems activate, much as if they themselves had won the reward (Mobbs et al., 2009). When we identify with someone, we experience their outcomes vicariously. Even our learned fears may extinguish as we observe someone else safely navigating the feared

"The Bobo doll follows me wherever I go. The photographs are published in every introductory psychology text and virtually every undergraduate takes introductory psychology. I recently checked into a Washington hotel. The clerk at the desk asked, 'Aren't you the psychologist who did the Bobo doll experiment?' I answered, 'I am afraid that will be my legacy.' He replied, 'That deserves an upgrade. I will put you in a suite in the quiet part of the hotel.'" — Albert Bandura (2005)

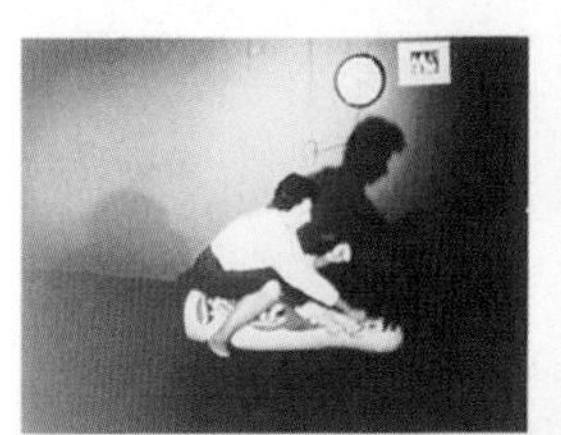

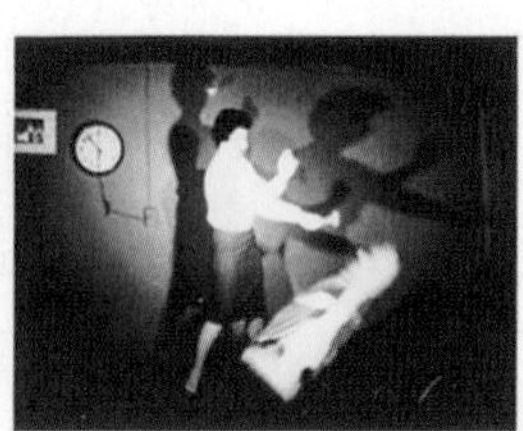
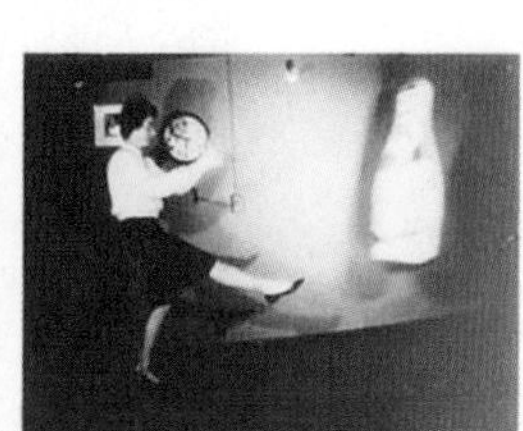
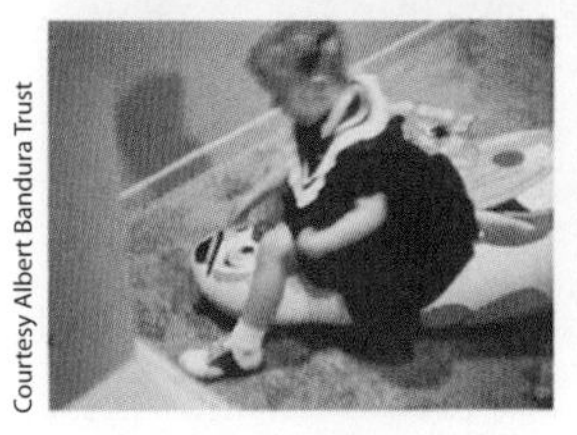

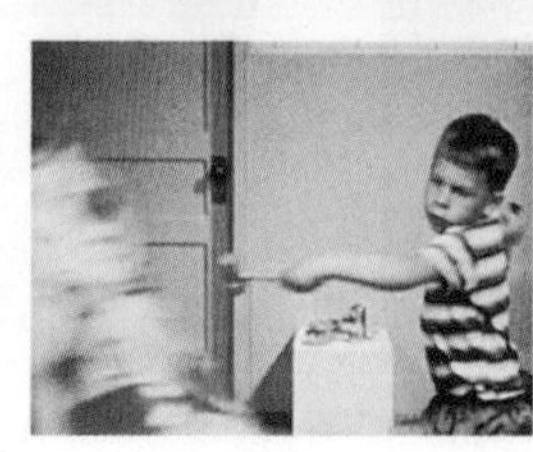
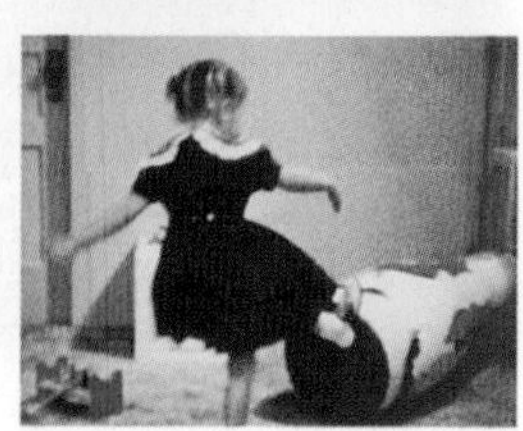

Courtesy Albert Bandura Trust

FIGURE 23.3 The famous Bobo doll experiment Notice how the children's actions directly imitate the adult's.

situation (Golkar et al., 2013). Lord Chesterfield (1694–1773) had the idea: "We are, in truth, more than half what we are by imitation."

Bandura's work provides an example of how basic research "pursued for its own sake" can have a broader purpose. Insights derived from his research have been used not only to restrain televised violence, but also to offer social models in African, Asian, and Latin American television and radio series that have helped reduce unplanned childbearing, protect against AIDS, and promote environmental conservation.

mirror neurons frontal lobe neurons that some scientists believe fire when we perform certain actions or observe another doing so. The brain's mirroring of another's action may enable imitation and empathy.

Mirrors and Imitation in the Brain

LOQ 23-4 How may observational learning be enabled by neural mirroring?

In 1991, on a hot summer day in Parma, Italy, a lab monkey awaited its researchers' return from lunch. The researchers had implanted electrodes next to its motor cortex, in a frontal lobe brain region that enabled the monkey to plan and enact movements. The monitoring device would alert the researchers to activity in that region of the monkey's brain. When the monkey moved a peanut into its mouth, for example, the device would buzz. That day, as one of the researchers reentered the lab, ice cream cone in hand, the monkey stared at him. As the researcher raised the cone to lick it, the monkey's monitor buzzed—as if the motionless monkey had itself moved (Blakeslee, 2006; Iacoboni, 2008, 2009).

The same buzzing had been heard earlier, when the monkey watched humans or other monkeys move peanuts to their mouths. The flabbergasted researchers, led by Giacomo Rizzolatti (2002, 2006), had, they believed, stumbled onto a previously unknown type of neuron. These presumed **mirror neurons**, they argued, provide a neural basis for everyday imitation and observational learning. When one monkey sees, its neurons mirror what another monkey does. (Other researchers continue to debate the existence and importance of mirror neurons and related networks [Bekkali et al., 2021; Fox et al., 2016].)

Imitation is widespread in other species. Primates observe and imitate all sorts of behaviors, such as how to crack nuts using stone hammers (Fragaszy et al., 2017). These types of behaviors are then transmitted from generation to generation within their local culture (Hopper et al., 2008; Whiten et al., 2007). In one 27-year analysis of 73,790 humpback whale observations, a single whale in 1980 whacked the water to drive prey fish into a clump. In the years since, this "lobtail" technique spread among other whales (Allen et al., 2013).

So, too, with monkeys. Erica van de Waal and her co-researchers (2013) trained groups of vervet monkeys to prefer either blue or pink corn by soaking one color in a disgusting-tasting solution. Four to six months later, after a new generation of monkeys was born, the adults stuck with whatever color they had learned to prefer—and, on observing them, so did all but 1 of 27 infant monkeys. Moreover, when blue- (or pink-) preferring male monkeys migrated to the other group, they switched preferences and began eating as the other group did. Monkey see, monkey do.

David Sipress/Cartoon Stock

"Your back is killing me!"
Mirror neurons at work?

Animal social learning Whacking the water to boost feeding has spread among humpback whales through social learning (Allen et al., 2013). Likewise, monkeys learn to prefer whatever color corn they observe other monkeys eating.

Masa Ushioda/AGE Fotostock

(a)

Erica van de Waal

(b)

Meltzoff, A. N., Kuhl, P. K., Movellan, J. & Sejnowski, T. J. (2009). Foundations for a new science of learning. Science, 325, 284–288.

FIGURE 23.4
Imitation This 12-month-old infant sees an adult look left, and immediately follows her gaze (Meltzoff et al., 2009).

In humans, imitation is pervasive. Our catchphrases, fashions, ceremonies, foods, traditions, morals, and fads all spread by one person copying another. Children, and even infants, are natural imitators (Marshall & Meltzoff, 2014). From 8 to 16 months, infants come to imitate various novel gestures (Jones, 2007, 2017). By 12 months (**FIGURE 23.4**), they look where an adult is looking (Meltzoff et al., 2009). And by 14 months, children imitate acts modeled on TV (Meltzoff, 1988; Meltzoff & Moore, 1989, 1997). Even as 2½-year-olds, when many of their mental abilities are near those of adult chimpanzees, young humans surpass chimps at social tasks such as imitating another's solution to a problem (Herrmann et al., 2007). Children see, children do.

So strong is the human predisposition to learn from watching adults that 2- to 5-year-old children *overimitate*. Whether living in urban Australia or a rural region of Africa, they copy even irrelevant adult actions. Before reaching for a toy in a plastic jar, they will first stroke the jar with a feather if that's what they have observed (Lyons et al., 2007). Or, imitating an adult, they will wave a stick over a box and then use the stick to push on a knob that opens the box—when all they needed to do to open the box was to push on the knob (Nielsen & Tomaselli, 2010).

Humans, like monkeys, have brains that support empathy and imitation. Researchers cannot insert experimental electrodes in human brains, but they can use fMRI scans to see brain activity associated with performing and with observing actions. So, is the human capacity to simulate another's action and to share in another's experience due to specialized mirror neurons? Or is it due to distributed brain networks? That issue is under debate (Bekkali et al., 2021; Jeon & Lee, 2018). Regardless, children's brains do enable their empathy and their ability to infer another's mental state, an ability known as *theory of mind*.

Our brain's response to observing others makes emotions contagious. Our brain simulates and vicariously experiences what we observe. So real are these mental instant replays that we may misremember an action we have observed as one we have performed (Lindner et al., 2010). When research participants watched someone experience electric shocks, they became more fearful in their own choices—as if they had experienced the shocks (Lindström et al., 2019). Through these reenactments, we grasp others' states of mind. As we observe others' postures, faces, voices, and writing styles, we unconsciously mimic them. When others yawn, primates, dogs, and we humans often yawn, too (Palagi et al., 2020). Such mimicry helps us grasp others' states of mind and we feel what they feel (Bernieri et al., 1994; Ireland & Pennebaker, 2010). Imitation helps us gain friends, leading us to mimic those we like, who then like us more in return (Chartrand & Lakin, 2013; Salazar Kämpf, 2018).

Seeing a loved one's pain, our faces mirror their emotion. But as **FIGURE 23.5** shows, so do our brains. Ditto for mice brains when observing other mice experiencing pain (Smith et al., 2021). Observing others' pain also releases our body's natural painkillers, thus calming our distress and enabling our helping (Haaker et al., 2017). Even fiction reading may trigger such activity, as we mentally simulate (and vicariously experience) the experiences described (Mar & Oatley, 2008; Speer et al., 2009). In a series of experiments, reading about kid wizard Harry Potter and his acceptance of people such as the "Mudbloods" reduced readers' prejudice against immigrants, refugees, and gay people (Vezzali et al., 2015).

"Children need models more than they need critics."—Joseph Joubert, *Pensées*, 1842

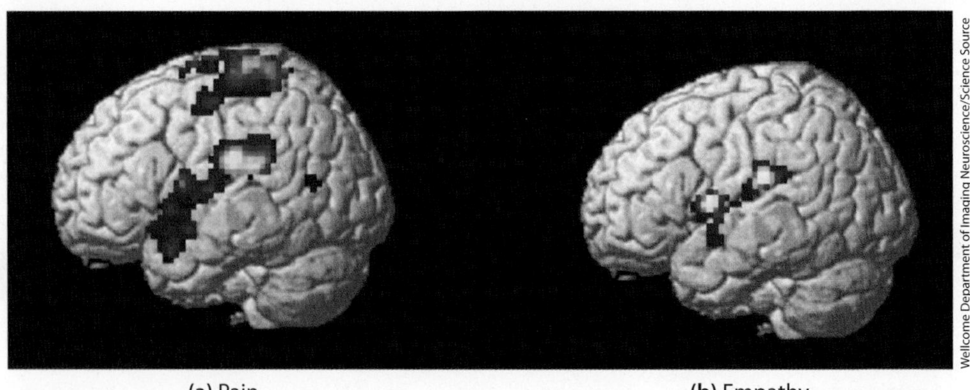

Wellcome Department of Imaging Neuroscience/Science Source

(a) Pain (b) Empathy

FIGURE 23.5
Experienced and imagined pain in the brain In these fMRI scans, brain activity related to actual pain (a) is mirrored in the brain of an observing loved one (b) (Singer et al., 2004). Empathy in the brain shows up in areas that process emotions, but not in the somatosensory cortex, which receives the physical pain input.

Applications of Observational Learning

LOQ 23-5 What is the impact of prosocial modeling and of antisocial modeling?

The big news from Bandura's studies and mirror-neuron research is that we look, we mentally imitate, and we learn. Models—in our family, our neighborhood, or the media we consume—have effects, good and bad.

PROSOCIAL EFFECTS The good news is that people's modeling of **prosocial** (positive, helpful) **behaviors** can have prosocial effects. Many business organizations effectively use *behavior modeling* to help new employees learn communications, sales, and customer service skills (Taylor et al., 2005). Trainees gain these skills faster when they can observe the skills being modeled effectively by experienced workers (or actors simulating them).

People who exemplify nonviolent, helpful behavior can also prompt similar behavior in others (Jung et al., 2020). After observing someone helping (assisting a woman with dropped books), people became more helpful, such as by assisting someone who dropped a dollar (Burger et al., 2015). India's Mahatma Gandhi and America's Martin Luther King, Jr., both drew on the power of modeling, making nonviolent action a powerful, enduring force for social change in both countries (Matsumoto et al., 2015). The media offer models. Across many countries and dozens of studies, exposure to prosocial TV, movies, and video games boosted later helping behavior (Coyne et al., 2018; Prot et al., 2014).

Parents are also powerful models. European Christians who risked their lives to rescue Jews from the Nazis usually had a close relationship with at least one parent who modeled a strong moral or humanitarian concern; this was also true for U.S. civil rights activists in the 1960s (London, 1970; Oliner & Oliner, 1988). The observational learning of morality begins early. Socially responsive toddlers, who readily imitate their parents, tend to become preschoolers with a strong internalized conscience (Forman et al., 2004). To encourage children's honesty, let them overhear adults praising honesty (Sai et al., 2020).

Models are most effective when their actions and words are consistent. To encourage children to read, read to them and surround them with books and people who read. To increase the odds that your children will practice your religion, worship and attend religious activities with them (Lowicki & Zajenkowski, 2020). To teach your children persistence, let them see *you* practice persistence (Butler, 2017).

Zumapress/Newscom

A model caregiver This girl is learning orphan-nursing skills, as well as compassion, by observing her mentor in this Humane Society program. As a sixteenth-century proverb states, "Example is better than precept."

Sometimes, however, models say one thing and do another. Many parents seem to operate according to the principle "Do as I *say*, not as I *do*." Experiments suggest that children learn to do both (Rice & Grusec,

1975; Rushton, 1975). Exposed to a hypocrite, they tend to imitate the hypocrisy—by doing what the model did and saying what the model said. Actions often speak louder than words.

prosocial behavior positive, constructive, helpful behavior. The opposite of antisocial behavior.

antisocial behavior negative, destructive, harmful behavior. The opposite of prosocial behavior.

RETRIEVAL PRACTICE

RP-3 Hannah's parents and older friends all drive over the speed limit, but they advise her not to. Breonna's parents and friends drive within the speed limit, but they say nothing to deter her from speeding. Will Hannah or Breonna be more likely to speed?

ANSWERS IN APPENDIX E

ANTISOCIAL EFFECTS The bad news is that observational learning can increase **antisocial behavior**. This helps us understand why abusive parents might have aggressive children, why children who are lied to become more likely to cheat and lie, and why many men who abuse their wives are themselves the children of wife-abusing fathers (Hays & Carver, 2014; Jung et al., 2019; Stith et al., 2000). Aggressiveness could have a genetic link. But with monkeys, we know it can be environmental. In study after study, young monkeys separated from their mothers and subjected to high levels of aggression grew up to be aggressive themselves (Chamove, 1980). The lessons we learn as children are not easily replaced as adults, and they are sometimes visited on future generations.

Observational learning influences adults, too. Those repeatedly exposed to hate speech become desensitized to hateful words. And they become more prejudiced toward its targets (Soral et al., 2018). As social psychologists Chris Crandall and Mark White (2016) remind us, political leaders have the power to influence *norms*, and norms matter: "People express the prejudices that are socially acceptable and they hide the ones that are not."

"This instinct to humiliate, when it's modeled by someone in the public platform, by someone powerful, it filters down into everybody's life, because it . . . gives permission for other people to do the same thing." —Meryl Streep, U.S. Golden Globe Award speech, 2017

TV shows, movies, and videos are sources of observational learning. While watching, children may learn that bullying is an effective way to control others, that free-and-easy sex brings pleasure without consequence, or that men should be tough and women gentle. Do films that glorify high-speed and risky driving teach viewers that such driving is acceptable? An analysis of nearly 200,000 speeding tickets showed increased average speed among drivers who received them on the weekends following the release of the *Fast and the Furious* films (Jena et al., 2018). And most U.S. children have ample time to learn such lessons.

Viewers are learning about life from a peculiar storyteller, one that reflects the culture's mythology rather than its reality. Between 1998 and 2006, prime-time violence on TV reportedly increased 75 percent (PTC, 2007). An analysis of more than 3000 network and cable programs aired during one closely studied year revealed that nearly 6 in 10 featured violence, that 74 percent of the violence went unpunished, that 58 percent did not show the victims' pain, that nearly half the incidents involved "justified" violence, and that nearly half involved an attractive perpetrator. These conditions define the recipe for the *violence-viewing effect* described in many studies around the world and recognized by most media researchers (Anderson et al., 2017; Bushman, 2018; Martins & Weaver, 2019; Teng et al., 2019). (See Thinking Critically About: The Effects of Viewing Media Violence.)

* * *

Bandura's work—like that of Ivan Pavlov, John Watson, B. F. Skinner, and thousands of others who advanced our knowledge of learning principles—illustrates the impact that can result from single-minded devotion to a few well-defined problems and ideas. These researchers defined the issues and impressed on us the importance of learning. As their legacy demonstrates, intellectual history is often made by people who risk going to extremes in pushing ideas to their limits (Simonton, 2000).

READ
PAUL NOTH

Paul Noth/Cartoon Stock

"Screen time . . . screen time . . ."

The Effects of Viewing Media Violence

LOQ 23-6 What is the violence-viewing effect?

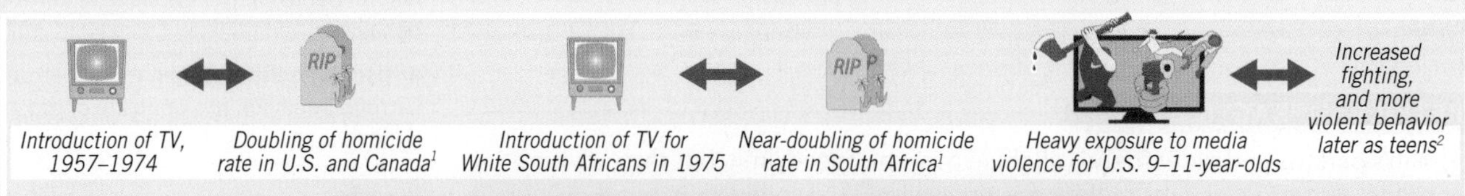
RIP
RIP
Introduction of TV, 1957–1974
Doubling of homicide rate in U.S. and Canada[1]
Introduction of TV for White South Africans in 1975
Near-doubling of homicide rate in South Africa[1]
Heavy exposure to media violence for U.S. 9–11-year-olds
Increased fighting, and more violent behavior later as teens[2]

BUT, CORRELATION ≠ CAUSATION!

***Experimental* studies have also found that media violence viewing can cause aggression:**
Viewing violence (compared to entertaining nonviolence) → participants react more cruelly when provoked. (Effect is strongest if the violent person is attractive, the violence seems justified and realistic, the act goes unpunished, and the viewer does not see pain or harm caused.)

What prompts the *violence-viewing effect*?

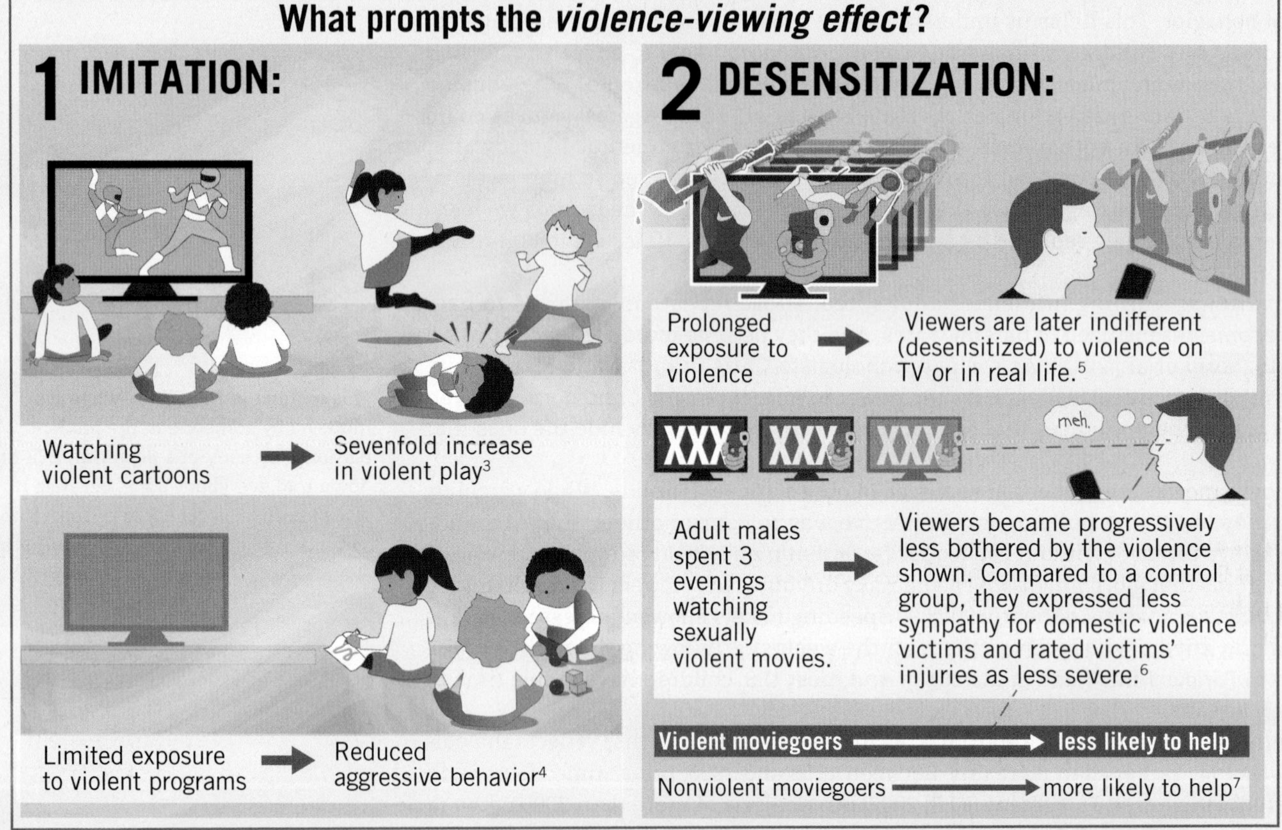
1 IMITATION:
Watching violent cartoons → Sevenfold increase in violent play[3]
Limited exposure to violent programs → Reduced aggressive behavior[4]
2 DESENSITIZATION:
Prolonged exposure to violence → Viewers are later indifferent (desensitized) to violence on TV or in real life.[5]
XXX
XXX
XXX
meh.
Adult males spent 3 evenings watching sexually violent movies. → Viewers became progressively less bothered by the violence shown. Compared to a control group, they expressed less sympathy for domestic violence victims and rated victims' injuries as less severe.[6]
Violent moviegoers → less likely to help
Nonviolent moviegoers → more likely to help[7]

- **APA Task Force on Violent Media (2015)** found that the "research demonstrates a consistent relation between violent video game use and increases in aggressive behavior, aggressive cognitions, and aggressive affect, and decreases in prosocial behavior, empathy, and sensitivity to aggression."
- **American Academy of Pediatrics (2009)** has advised pediatricians that "media violence can contribute to aggressive behavior, desensitization to violence, nightmares, and fear of being harmed."

Critics suggest that these statements may ignore some weakness in media violence research, such as reliability and the size of the effect. They also note that some places, such as Japan, have similarly violent media but much less violent behavior.[8]

1. Centerwall, 1989. 2. Boxer et al., 2009; Gentile et al., 2011; Gentile & Bushman, 2012. 3. Boyatzis et al., 1995. 4. Christakis et al., 2013.
5. Fanti et al., 2009; Jin et al., 2018; Rule & Ferguson, 1986. 6. Mullin & Linz, 1995. 7. Bushman & Anderson, 2009. 8. Elson et al., 2019; Ferguson et al., 2020

ASK YOURSELF

Most of us spend plenty of time on screens. What prosocial and antisocial role models do you see on your screens? Which ones have you chosen to imitate? For whom are you a role model? How might you become a better role model for others?

RETRIEVAL PRACTICE

RP-4 Match the examples (i–v) to the appropriate underlying learning principle (a–e):

i. Knowing the way from your bed to the bathroom in the dark
ii. Your little brother getting in a fight after watching a violent action movie
iii. Salivating when you smell brownies in the oven
iv. Disliking the taste of chili after becoming violently sick a few hours after eating chili
v. Your dog racing to greet you on your arrival home

a. Classical conditioning
b. Operant conditioning
c. Latent learning
d. Observational learning
e. Biological predispositions

ANSWERS IN APPENDIX E

MODULE

23 REVIEW Biology, Cognition, and Learning

LEARNING OBJECTIVES

Test Yourself Answer these repeated Learning Objective Questions on your own (before "showing" the answers here, or checking the answers in Appendix D) to improve your retention of the concepts (McDaniel et al., 2009, 2015).

LOQ 23-1 How do biological constraints affect classical and operant conditioning?

LOQ 23-2 How do cognitive processes affect classical and operant conditioning?

LOQ 23-3 What is *observational learning*?

LOQ 23-4 How may observational learning be enabled by neural mirroring?

LOQ 23-5 What is the impact of prosocial modeling and of antisocial modeling?

LOQ 23-6 What is the violence-viewing effect?

TERMS AND CONCEPTS TO REMEMBER

Test Yourself Write down the definition in your own words, then check your answer.

learning, p. 280
preparedness, p. 281
instinctive drift, p. 283
cognitive map, p. 284
latent learning, p. 284
observational learning, p. 284
modeling, p. 284
mirror neurons, p. 286
prosocial behavior, p. 289
antisocial behavior, p. 289

MODULE TEST

Test Yourself Answer the following questions on your own first, then "show" the answers here, or check your answers in Appendix E.

1. Garcia and Koelling's ____________-____________ studies showed that conditioning can occur even when the unconditioned stimulus (US) does not immediately follow the neutral stimulus (NS).

2. Taste-aversion research has shown that some animals develop aversions to certain tastes but not to sights or sounds. Which of Darwin's principles does this support?

3. Evidence that cognitive processes play an important role in learning comes in part from studies in which rats running a maze develop a ____________ ____________ of the maze.

4. Rats that explored a maze without any reward were later able to run the maze as well as other rats that had received food rewards for doing so. The rats that had learned without reinforcement demonstrated ____________ ____________.

5. Children learn many social behaviors by imitating parents and other models. This type of learning is called ____________ ____________.

6. According to Bandura, we learn by watching models because we experience ____________ reinforcement or ____________ punishment.

7. Parents are most effective in getting their children to imitate them if

a. their words and actions are consistent.

b. they have outgoing personalities.

c. they do *not* have outgoing personalities.

d. they carefully explain why a behavior is acceptable in adults but not in children.

8. Some scientists believe that the brain has ____________ neurons that enable empathy and imitation.

9. Most experts agree that repeated viewing of media violence

a. makes all viewers significantly more aggressive.

b. has little effect on viewers.

c. is a risk factor for viewers' increased aggression.

d. makes viewers angry and frustrated.

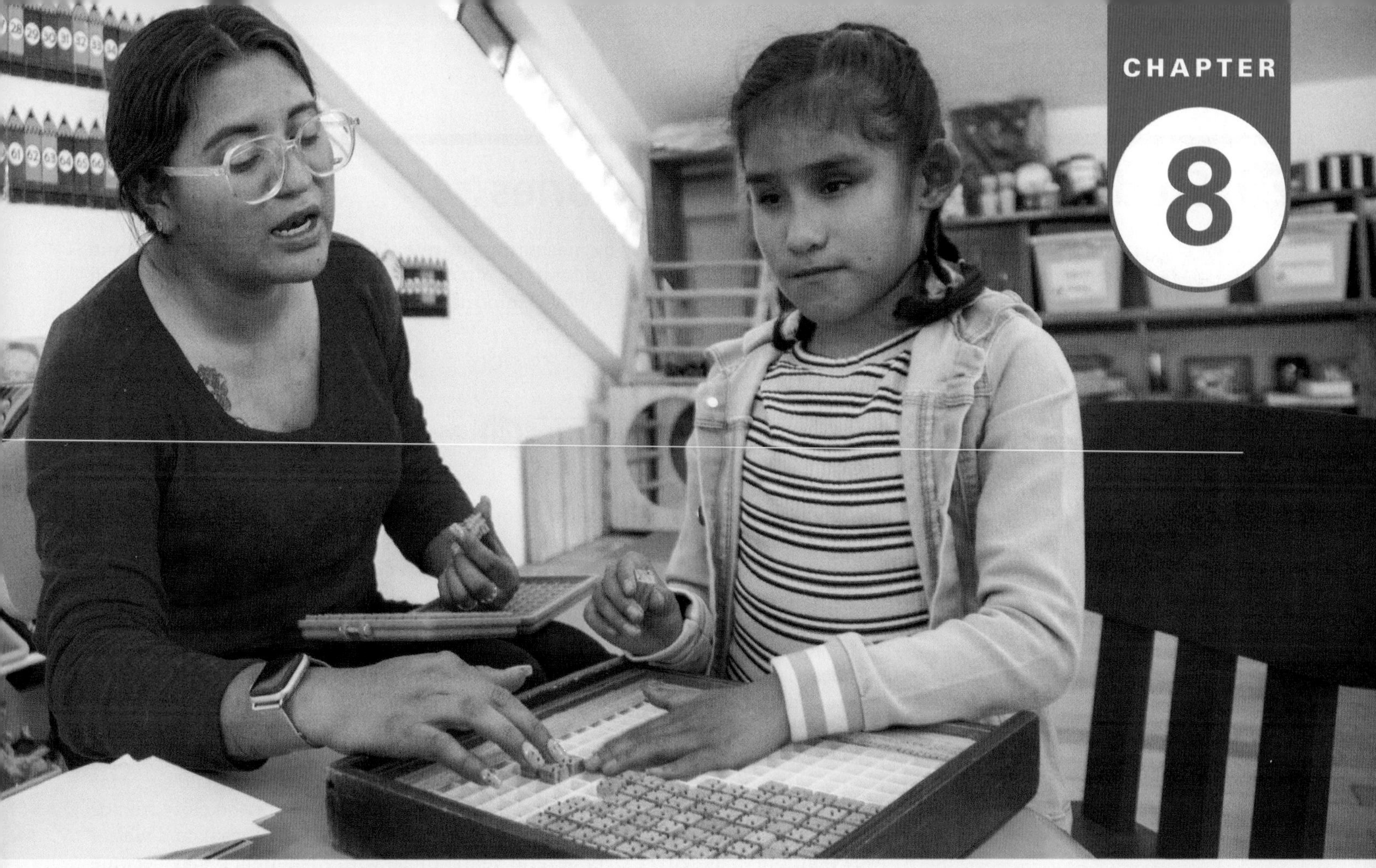

CHAPTER 8

DarioGaona/E+/Getty Images

Memory (Modules 24–26)

Be thankful for your memory. We often take memory for granted, except when it malfunctions. But it is our memory that accounts for time and defines our life. It is our memory that enables us to recognize family members, speak our language, and find our way home. It is our memory that enables us to enjoy an experience and then mentally replay it to enjoy again. It is our memory that enables us to build histories with those we love. And it is our shared memories that bind us together as Irish or Iranian, Somalian or Samoan — and occasionally pit us against others whose offenses we cannot forget.

In large part, we are what we remember. Without memory — our archive of accumulated learning — there would be no savoring of past joys, no guilt or anger over painful recollections. We would instead live in an enduring present, each moment unfamiliar. Each person would be a stranger, every language foreign, every task — dressing, cooking, and biking — a new challenge. You would even be a stranger to yourself, lacking that continuous sense of self that extends from your distant past to your momentary present.

Researchers study memory from many perspectives. Module 24 introduces the measuring, modeling, and encoding of memories. Module 25 examines how memories are stored and retrieved. Module 26 explores what happens when our memories fail us, and looks at ways to improve memory.

MODULE

24 Studying and Encoding Memories

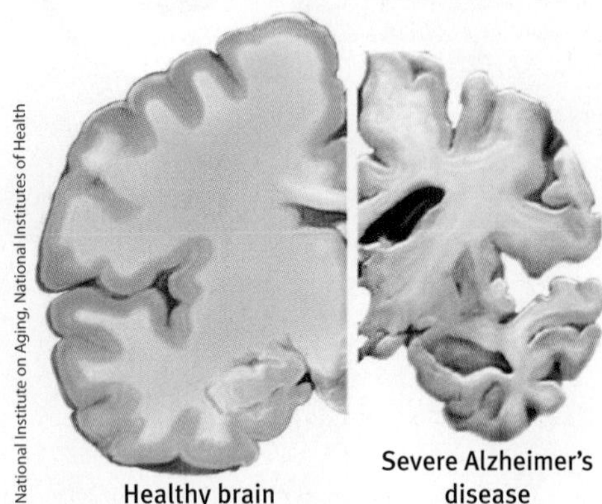
Healthy brain
Severe Alzheimer's disease

National Institute on Aging, National Institutes of Health

FIGURE 24.1
Extreme forgetting Alzheimer's disease severely damages the brain, and in the process strips away memory.

Psychologists study memory by measuring our retention of learned information and creating models that help us understand our brain's memory-making process. Such models begin with encoding, when new information enters our memory system.

Studying Memory

LEARNING OBJECTIVE QUESTION LOQ **24-1** What is *memory*, and how is it measured?

Memory is learning that persists over time; it is information that has been acquired and stored and can be retrieved. Research on memory's extremes has helped us understand how memory works. At age 92, my [DM's] father experienced a small stroke-like brain event that had but one peculiar effect. His genial personality was intact. He knew us and enjoyed poring over family photo albums and reminiscing about his past. But he had lost most of his ability to form new memories of conversations and everyday episodes. He could not tell me what day of the week it was, or what he'd had for lunch. Told repeatedly of his brother-in-law's recent death, he was surprised and saddened each time he heard the news.

Some disorders slowly strip away memory (**FIGURE 24.1**). *Alzheimer's disease* begins as difficulty remembering new information, progressing to an inability to do everyday tasks. Complex speech becomes simple sentences; family members and close friends become strangers; the brain's memory centers, once strong, become weak and wither away (Rathore et al., 2017). Over several years, those with Alzheimer's may become unknowing and unknowable. Their sense of self fades, leaving them wondering, "Who am I?" (Ben Malek et al., 2019). Lost memory strikes at the core of their humanity, robbing them of their joy, meaning, and companionship.

Want to test your memory? Try to memorize the first 10 digits of pi (π): 3.141592653. In 2015, Rajveer Meena of India broke the world record by reciting 70,000 digits of pi (*Guinness World Records*, 2019).

At the other extreme are people who win memory competitions. When two-time World Memory Champion Feng Wang was a 21-year-old college student, he didn't need help from his phone to remember his friends' numbers. The average person could parrot back a string of about 7—maybe even 9—digits. If numbers were read to him about 1 per second, Feng could reliably repeat up to 200 (Ericsson et al., 2017).

Amazing? Yes, but consider your own impressive memory. You remember countless faces, places, and happenings; tastes, smells, and textures; and voices, sounds, and songs. One study asked students to listen to snippets—a mere four-tenths of a second—from popular songs. How often did they recognize the artist and song? More than 25 percent of the time (Krumhansl, 2010). We often recognize songs as quickly as we recognize a familiar voice.

So, too, with faces and places. Imagine viewing more than 2500 slides of faces and places for 10 seconds each. Later, you see 280 of these slides, paired with others you've never seen. Actual participants recognized 90 percent of the slides they had viewed in the first round (Haber, 1970). In a follow-up experiment, people who viewed 2800 images for only 3 seconds each later spotted the repeats with 82 percent accuracy (Konkle et al., 2010). Look for a target face in a sea of faces and you later will recognize other faces from the scene as well (Kaunitz et al., 2016).

FIGURE 24.2
Other animals also display face smarts After food rewards are repeatedly associated with some sheep and human faces, but not with others, sheep remember food-associated faces for 2 years (Kendrick & Feng, 2011; Knolle et al., 2017).

A. Jennifer Morton/University of Cambridge

The average person permanently stores and recognizes about 5000 faces (Jenkins et al., 2018). But some *super-recognizers* display an extraordinary face-recognition ability. By watching street footage, super-recognizers have helped British, Asian, and German police to solve difficult cases (Keefe, 2016; NPR, 2018). Eighteen months after viewing a video of an armed robbery, one super-recognizer police officer spotted and arrested the robber walking on a busy street (Davis et al., 2013). And it's not just humans who have shown remarkable memory for faces. Sheep remember faces, too (**FIGURE 24.2**). And so has at least one fish species—as demonstrated by their spitting at familiar faces to trigger a food reward (Newport et al., 2016).

How do we humans accomplish such memory feats? How does our brain pluck information out of the world around us and tuck it away for later use? How can we remember things we have not thought about for years, yet forget the name of someone we just met? How are memories stored in our brain? Why will you be likely, later in this module, to misrecall this sentence: *"The angry rioter threw the rock at the window"*?

ASK YOURSELF

Imagine having an injury that significantly impairs your ability to form new memories. Now imagine having a record-setting ability to remember, like Feng Wang. How would each condition affect your daily routine?

memory the persistence of learning over time through the encoding, storage, and retrieval of information.

recall a measure of memory in which the person must retrieve information learned earlier, as on a fill-in-the-blank test.

recognition a measure of memory in which the person identifies items previously learned, as on a multiple-choice test.

relearning a measure of memory that assesses the amount of time saved when learning material again.

Measuring Retention

To a psychologist, evidence that learning persists includes these three *retention measures:*

- **recall**—*retrieving* information that is not currently in your conscious awareness but that was learned at an earlier time. A fill-in-the-blank question tests your recall.
- **recognition**—*identifying* items previously learned. A multiple-choice question tests your recognition.
- **relearning**—*learning something more quickly* when you learn it a second or later time. When you review the first weeks of course work to prepare for your final exam, or engage a language used in early childhood, it will be easier to relearn the information than it was to learn it initially.

"If any one faculty of our nature may be called *more* wonderful than the rest, I do think it is memory." —Jane Austen, *Mansfield Park*, 1814

Long after you cannot recall most of the people in your high school graduating class, you may still be able to recognize their yearbook pictures and spot their names in a list of names. In one experiment, people who had graduated 25 years earlier could not recall many of their old classmates. But they could *recognize* 90 percent of their pictures and names (Bahrick et al., 1975). If you are like most students, you, too, could probably recognize more names of Snow White's seven dwarfs than you could recall (Miserandino, 1991).

National News/Zuma Press//Newscom

Globe Photos/Zuma Press

Remembering faces Even if Taylor Swift and Denzel Washington had not become famous, their high school classmates would most likely still recognize them in these photos.

Our recognition memory is impressively quick and vast. "Is your friend wearing a new or old outfit?" *Old.* "Have you read this textbook material before?" *No.* "Have you ever seen this person before?" *No.* Before the mouth can form our answer to any of millions of such questions, the mind knows, and knows that it knows.

Our response speed when recalling or recognizing information indicates memory strength, as does our speed at *relearning.* Pioneering memory researcher Hermann Ebbinghaus (1850–1909) showed this in the nineteenth century using nonsense syllables. He randomly selected a sample of syllables, practiced them, and tested himself. To get a feel for his experiments, rapidly read aloud, eight times over, the following list of syllables (from Baddeley, 1982), then look away and try to recall the items:

JIH, BAZ, FUB, YOX, SUJ, XIR, DAX, LEQ, VUM, PID, KEL, WAV, TUV, ZOF, GEK, HIW.

The day after learning such a list, Ebbinghaus could recall few of the syllables. But they weren't entirely forgotten. As **FIGURE 24.3** portrays, the more frequently he repeated the list aloud on Day 1, the less time he required to relearn the list on Day 2. Additional rehearsal *(overlearning)* of verbal information increases retention, especially when practice is distributed over time. For students, this means that it helps to rehearse course material over time, even after you know it. Better to rehearse and overlearn than relax and remember too little.

The point to remember: Tests of recognition and of time spent relearning demonstrate that we remember more than we can recall.

FIGURE 24.3
Ebbinghaus' retention curve (Data from Baddeley, 1982.)

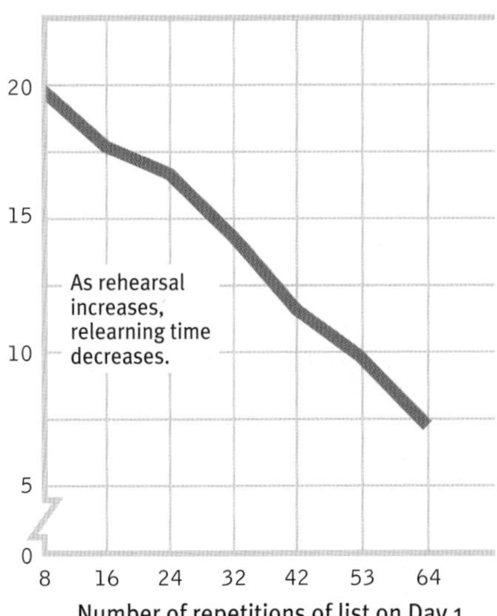
Time in minutes taken to relearn list on Day 2
20
15
10
5
0
As rehearsal increases, relearning time decreases.
8
16
24
32
42
53
64
Number of repetitions of list on Day 1

encoding the process of getting information into the memory system—for example, by extracting meaning.

storage the process of retaining encoded information over time.

retrieval the process of getting information out of memory storage.

parallel processing processing multiple aspects of a stimulus or problem simultaneously.

sensory memory the immediate, very brief recording of sensory information in the memory system.

short-term memory briefly activated memory of a few items (such as digits of a phone number while calling) that is later stored or forgotten.

long-term memory the relatively permanent and limitless archive of the memory system. Includes knowledge, skills, and experiences.

RETRIEVAL PRACTICE

RP-1 Multiple-choice questions test our ________. Fill-in-the-blank questions test our ________.

RP-2 If you want to be sure to remember what you're learning for an upcoming test, would it be better to use *recall* or *recognition* to check your memory? Why?

ANSWERS IN APPENDIX E

Memory Models

LOQ 24-2 How do memory models help us study memory, and how has later research updated the three-stage information-processing model?

Architects create virtual models to help clients imagine their future homes. Similarly, psychologists create memory models. Such models aren't perfect, but they help us think about how our brain forms and retrieves memories. History has offered varied memory models: a wax tablet (Aristotle); a "mystic writing pad" (Freud); a house, a library, a telephone switchboard, a videotape (Roediger, 1980). Today's *information-processing model* likens human memory to computer operations. Thus, to remember, we must

- **encode**—get information into our brain.
- **store**—retain that information.
- **retrieve**—later get the information back out.

Like all analogies, computer models have their limits. Our memories are less literal and more fragile than a computer's. Most computers also process information *sequentially*, even while alternating between tasks. Our agile brain processes many things *simultaneously* (some of them unconsciously) using **parallel processing**. To focus on this multitrack processing, one information-processing model, *connectionism*, views memories as products of interconnected neural networks. Specific memories arise from particular activation patterns within these networks. Every time you learn something new, your brain's neural connections change—an example of *neuroplasticity*—forming and strengthening pathways that allow you to interact with and learn from your constantly changing environment.

To explain our memory-forming process, Richard Atkinson and Richard Shiffrin (1968, 2016) proposed a three-stage information-processing model:

1. We first record to-be-remembered information as a fleeting **sensory memory**.
2. From there, we process information into **short-term memory**, where we encode it through *rehearsal*.
3. Finally, information moves into **long-term memory** for later retrieval.

This model has been updated (**FIGURE 24.4**) with important newer concepts, including *working memory* and *automatic processing*.

ASK YOURSELF

What has your memory system encoded, stored, and retrieved today?

FIGURE 24.4
A modified three-stage information-processing model of memory Atkinson and Shiffrin's classic three-stage model helps us to think about how memories are processed, but researchers now recognize other ways that long-term memories form. For example, some information slips into long-term memory via a "back door," without our consciously attending to it *(automatic processing)*. And so much active processing occurs in the short-term memory stage that we now call it *working memory*.

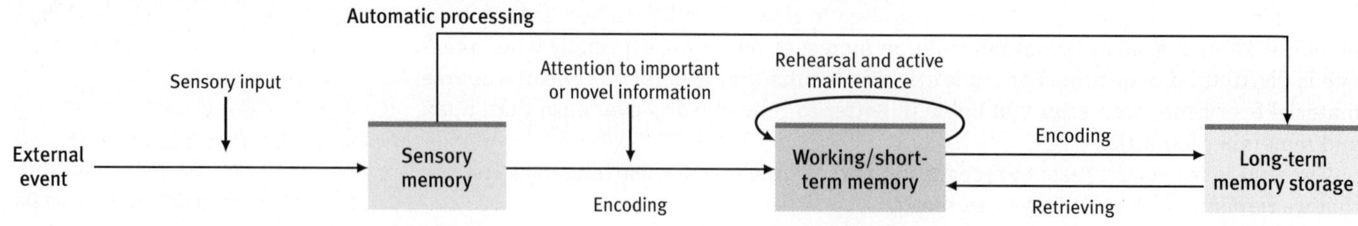
Automatic processing
Sensory input
External event
Sensory memory
Attention to important or novel information
Encoding
Rehearsal and active maintenance
Working/short-term memory
Encoding
Retrieving
Long-term memory storage

WORKING MEMORY Atkinson and Shiffrin saw short-term memory merely as a space for briefly storing recent thoughts and experiences. Alan Baddeley and others (Baddeley, 2002; Barrouillet et al., 2011; Engle, 2002) extended our understanding. They began calling this stage **working memory**, a stage where short-term memories combine with long-term memories. Baddeley likened working memory to an active "scratch pad" where our brain makes sense of new experiences and links them with our long-term memories. This "system for holding information in mind and working on it" (Oberauer et al., 2018) also functions in the opposite direction, by retrieving and processing previously stored information.

As you integrate new information with your existing long-term memory, your attention is focused. In Baddeley's (2002) model, a *central executive* coordinates this focused processing. Without focused attention, information typically fades. If you think you can look something up later, you attend to it less and forget it more quickly. In one experiment, people read and typed new bits of trivia they would later need, such as "an ostrich's eye is bigger than its brain." If they knew the information would be available online, they invested less energy and remembered it less well (Wegner & Ward, 2013). Online, out of mind.

Right now, your working memory is actively linking what you're reading with what you already know (Cowan, 2010, 2016; deBettencourt et al., 2019). If you hear "eye-screem," you may encode it as *ice cream* or *I scream,* depending on both your experiences and the context (snack shop or horror film).

Cultural traditions influence how we encode and retrieve information (Wang, 2021). For many of you, what you are reading enters working memory through vision. You might also repeat the information using auditory rehearsal. Some groups, such as Inuit in northern Canada, use repeated oral histories to help younger group members remember important information. In one dramatic case, repeated information passed down through many generations was crucial to the archeological discovery of the doomed ships of the 1845 Franklin Expedition, which sank near where local Inuit lived (Neatby & Mercer, 2018). Whether we soak up information with our eyes or our ears, working memory helps us integrate our previous experiences to make smart decisions.

RETRIEVAL PRACTICE

RP-3 How does the *working memory* concept update the classic Atkinson-Shiffrin three-stage information-processing model?

RP-4 What are two basic functions of working memory?

ANSWERS IN APPENDIX E

Encoding Memories

How do we *encode* information, and how does this process differ for *explicit* versus *implicit* memories?

Dual-Track Memory: Effortful Versus Automatic Processing

LOQ 24-3 How do explicit and implicit memories differ?

Explicit *(declarative)* **memories** are the facts and experiences that we can consciously know and "declare." We encode many explicit memories through conscious **effortful processing**. But our mind has a second, unconscious track. Behind the scenes, other information skips the conscious encoding track and barges directly into storage. This **automatic processing**, which happens without our awareness, produces some things we can know without actively thinking about them (the shape of the cafeteria tray in our hands), and also produces our **implicit** *(nondeclarative)* **memories**.

Our two-track mind, then, helps us encode, store, and retrieve information through both effortful and automatic tracks. Let's see how automatic processing assists the formation of implicit memories.

working memory a newer understanding of short-term memory; conscious, active processing of both (1) incoming sensory information and (2) information retrieved from long-term memory. 

explicit memory retention of facts and experiences that we can consciously know and "declare." (Also called *declarative memory.*)

effortful processing encoding that requires attention and conscious effort.

automatic processing unconscious encoding of incidental information, such as space, time, and frequency, and of familiar or well-learned information, such as sounds, smells, and word meanings.

implicit memory retention of learned skills or classically conditioned associations independent of conscious recollection. (Also called *nondeclarative memory.*)

Automatic Processing and Implicit Memories

LOQ 24-4 What information do we process automatically?

Our implicit memories include *procedural* memory for automatic skills (such as how to ride a bike) and classically conditioned *associations* among stimuli. If once attacked by a dog, years later you may, without recalling the conditioned association, automatically tense up as a dog approaches. Such memories are implicit because we react automatically and without conscious effort.

You also automatically process information about

- ***space.*** While studying, if you are reading visually, you often encode the place on the page or screen where certain material appears; later, you may visualize its location when you want to retrieve the information.
- ***time.*** While going about your day, you unintentionally note the sequence of its events. Later, realizing you've left your phone somewhere, the event sequence your brain automatically encoded will enable you to retrace your steps.
- ***frequency.*** You effortlessly keep track of how many times things happen, as when you realize, "This is the third time I've run into her today!"

Our two-track mind engages in impressively efficient information processing. As one track automatically tucks away routine details, the other track is free to focus on conscious, effortful processing. Mental feats, such as vision, thinking, and memory, may seem to be single abilities, but they are not. Rather, we split information into different components for separate and simultaneous processing.

Effortful Processing and Explicit Memories

Automatic processing happens effortlessly. When you see familiar words on the side of a delivery truck, you can't help but read them and register their meaning. *Learning* to read wasn't automatic. You may recall working hard to pick out letters and connect them to certain sounds. But with experience and practice, your reading became automatic. Imagine now learning to read sentences in reverse:

.citamotua emoceb nac gnissecorp luftroffE

At first, this requires effort, but after enough practice, you would also perform this task much more automatically. We develop many skills in this way: driving, texting, and speaking a new language.

ASK YOURSELF

Does it surprise you to learn how much of your memory processing is automatic? What might life be like if *all* memory processing were effortful?

SENSORY MEMORY

LOQ 24-5 How does sensory memory work?

Sensory memory (recall Figure 24.4) feeds our active working memory, recording momentary images, sounds, and strong scents. But sensory memory, like a lightning flash, is fleeting. How fleeting? In one experiment, people viewed three rows of three letters each, for only one-twentieth of a second (**FIGURE 24.5**). After the nine letters disappeared, they could recall only about half of them.

Was it because they had insufficient time to glimpse them? *No.* People actually *could* see and recall all the letters but only momentarily. We know this because rather than ask them to recall all nine letters at once, researcher George Sperling sounded a high, medium, or low tone immediately *after* flashing the nine letters. The pitch of the tone directed participants to report *only* the top, middle, or bottom row letters, respectively. Now, they rarely missed a letter, showing that all nine letters were momentarily available for recall.

FIGURE 24.5
Total recall—briefly

K	Z	R
Q	B	T
S	G	N

Sperling's experiment demonstrated **iconic memory**, a fleeting sensory memory of visual stimuli. For a few tenths of a second, our eyes register a picture-image memory of a scene, and we can recall any part of it in amazing detail. But delaying the tone signal by more than half a second caused the image to fade and memory to suffer. We also have an impeccable, though fleeting, memory for auditory stimuli, called **echoic memory** (Cowan, 1988; Lu et al., 1992). Picture yourself in class being distracted by a text message. If your mildly irked instructor tests you by asking, "What did I just say?" you can recover the last few words from your mind's echo chamber. Auditory echoes tend to linger for 3 or 4 seconds.

iconic memory a momentary sensory memory of visual stimuli; a photographic or picture-image memory lasting no more than a few tenths of a second.

echoic memory a momentary sensory memory of auditory stimuli; if attention is elsewhere, sounds and words can still be recalled within 3 or 4 seconds.

SHORT-TERM MEMORY CAPACITY

LOQ 24-6 What is our short-term memory capacity?

Recall that short-term memory—and working memory, its processing manager—refers to what we can briefly retain for just a few seconds. What are the limits of what we can hold in this middle, short-term stage?

George Miller (1956) proposed that we can store about seven pieces of information (give or take two) in short-term memory. Miller's magical number seven is psychology's contribution to the list of magical sevens—the seven wonders of the world, the seven seas, the seven deadly sins, the seven colors of the rainbow, the seven-note musical scale, and the seven days of the week—seven magical sevens.

After Miller's 2012 death, his daughter recalled his best moment of golf: "He made the one and only hole-in-one of his life at the age of 77, on the seventh green . . . with a seven iron. He loved that" (quoted by Vitello, 2012).

Other research confirms that we can, if nothing distracts us, recall about seven bits of information. But the number varies by task; we tend to remember about six letters and only about five words (Baddeley et al., 1975; Cowan, 2015). And how quickly do our short-term memories disappear? To find out, Lloyd Peterson and Margaret Peterson (1959) asked people to remember three-consonant groups, such as *CHJ*. To prevent rehearsal, the researchers distracted participants (asking them, for example, to start at 100 and begin counting aloud backward by threes). After 3 seconds, people recalled the letters only about half the time; after 12 seconds, they seldom recalled them at all (**FIGURE 24.6**). Without the active processing that we now understand to be a part of our working memory, short-term memories have a limited life.

Working memory capacity varies, depending on age and other factors. Young adults tend to have greater working memory capacity—the ability to juggle multiple items while processing information—than do children and older adults (Bopp & Verhaeghen, 2020; Jaroslawska & Rhodes, 2019). This helps young adults to better retain information and to solve problems creatively (De Dreu et al., 2012; Fenn & Hambrick, 2012; Wiley & Jarosz, 2012). But because task-switching reduces working memory, everyone does better and more efficient work when focused, without distractions, on one task at a time (Steyvers et al., 2019). *The bottom line:* It's probably a bad idea to simultaneously watch a live stream, text your friends, and study psychology, with your attention switching among them (Willingham, 2010)!

Working memory capacity appears to reflect intelligence level (Cowan, 2008; Shelton et al., 2010). Imagine seeing a letter of the alphabet, then a simple question, then another letter, followed by another question, and so on. In such experiments, those who could juggle the most mental balls—who could remember the most letters despite the interruptions—tended in everyday life to exhibit high intelligence and an ability to maintain their focus (Kane et al., 2007; Unsworth & Engle, 2007). When beeped to report in at various times, they were less likely than others to report that their mind was wandering.

FIGURE 24.6
Short-term memory decay (Data from Peterson & Peterson, 1959; see also Brown, 1958.)

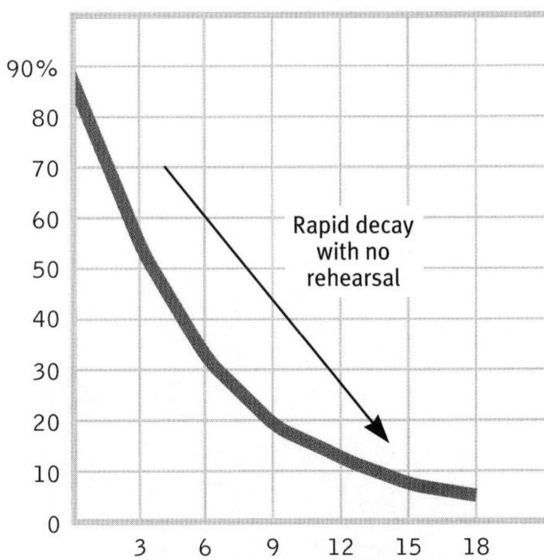
Percentage who recalled consonants
90%
80
70
60
50
40
30
20
10
0
Rapid decay with no rehearsal
3
6
9
12
15
18
Time in seconds between presentation of consonants and recall request (no rehearsal allowed)

RETRIEVAL PRACTICE

RP-5 What is the difference between *automatic* and *effortful* processing, and what are some examples of each?

RP-6 At which of Atkinson-Shiffrin's three memory stages would *iconic* and *echoic* memory occur?

ANSWERS IN APPENDIX E

chunking organizing items into familiar, manageable units; often occurs automatically.

mnemonics [nih-MON-iks] memory aids, especially those techniques that use vivid imagery and organizational devices.

EFFORTFUL PROCESSING STRATEGIES

LOQ 24-7 What are some effortful processing strategies that can help us remember new information?

Several effortful processing strategies boost our ability to form new memories. Later, when we try to retrieve a memory, these strategies can make the difference between success and failure.

1. W G V S R M T
2. W G V S R M T

3. VRESLI UEGBN GSORNW CDOUL LWLE NTOD WTO
4. SILVER BEGUN WRONGS CLOUD WELL DONT TWO

5. SILVER BEGUN WRONGS CLOUD DONT TWO
HALF MAKE WELL HAS A
EVERY IS RIGHT A DONE LINING

6. WELL BEGUN IS HALF DONE
EVERY CLOUD HAS A SILVER LINING
TWO WRONGS DONT MAKE A RIGHT

FIGURE 24.7
Chunking effects Organizing information into meaningful units, such as letters, words, and phrases, helps us recall it more easily (Hintzman, 1978).

Chunking Glance for a few seconds at the first set of letters (row 1) in **FIGURE 24.7**, then look away and try to reproduce what you saw. Impossible, yes? But you can easily reproduce set 2, which is no less complex. Similarly, you will probably remember sets 4 and 6 more easily than the same elements in sets 3 and 5. As this demonstrates, **chunking** information into familiar segments enables us to recall it more easily (Thalmann et al., 2019). Try remembering 43 individual numbers and letters. It would be impossible, unless chunked into, say, seven meaningful chunks, such as "Try remembering 43 individual numbers and letters." ☺

Chunking usually occurs so naturally that we take it for granted. Native English speakers can reproduce perfectly the 150 or so line segments that make up the words in the three phrases of set 6 in Figure 24.7. Similarly amazing is a Chinese reader's ability to glance at **FIGURE 24.8** and then reproduce all the strokes, or a varsity basketball player's recall of all the players' positions after a 4-second peek at a picture of a basketball play (Allard & Burnett, 1985). We all remember information best when we can organize it into personally meaningful arrangements.

FIGURE 24.8
An example of chunking—for those who read Chinese After looking at these characters, can you reproduce them exactly? If so, you likely are fluent in Chinese.

Mnemonics To help encode lengthy passages and speeches, ancient Greek scholars and orators developed **mnemonics**. Many of these memory aids use vivid imagery, because we are particularly good at remembering mental pictures. We more easily remember concrete, visualizable words than we do abstract words (Akpinar & Berger, 2015). (When we quiz you later, which three of these words—*bicycle, void, cigarette, inherent, fire, process*—will you most likely recall?) If you still recall the rock-throwing rioter sentence, it is probably not only because of the meaning you encoded but also because the sentence painted a mental image.

Memory whizzes understand the power of such systems. Star performers in the World Memory Championships do not usually have exceptional intelligence but rather are superior at using mnemonic strategies (Maguire et al., 2003). Frustrated by his ordinary memory, science writer Joshua Foer wanted to see how much he could improve it. After a year of intense practice, he won the U.S. Memory Championship, memorizing a pack of 52 playing cards in under 2 minutes. How did Foer do it? He added vivid new details to memories of a familiar place—his childhood home. Each card, presented in any order, could then match up with the clear picture in his head. As the test subject of his own wild memory experiment, he learned the power of painting pretty pictures in his mind (Foer, 2011).

When combined, chunking and mnemonic techniques can be great memory aids for unfamiliar material. Want to remember the planets in order of distance from the Sun? Think of the mnemonic My Very Educated Mother Just Served Us Noodles (Mercury, Venus, Earth, Mars, Jupiter, Saturn, Uranus, and Neptune). Need to recall the names of North America's five Great Lakes? Just remember HOMES (Huron, Ontario, Michigan, Erie, and Superior). In many cases, we chunk information into a more familiar form by creating a word or phrase from the first letters of the to-be-remembered items.

IT'S EASY TO GET CONFUSED, SO I USE A SIMPLE MNEMONIC: THE FRIDGE ON THE LEFT IS FOR LUNCH, AND THE FRIDGE ON THE RIGHT IS FOR REALLY, REALLY POISONOUS SUBSTANCES.
Tom Gauld/Heart Agency

Hierarchies When people develop expertise in an area, they often process information in *hierarchies* composed of a few broad concepts divided and subdivided into narrower concepts and facts. Organizing knowledge in hierarchies helps us retrieve information efficiently, as Gordon Bower and his colleagues (1969) demonstrated by presenting words either randomly or grouped into categories. When the words were grouped, recall was two to three times better. Such results show the benefits of organizing what you study—of giving special attention to module headings, and, in this text, to numbered Learning Objective Questions. Taking lecture and text notes in outline format—a type of hierarchical organization—may also prove helpful.

ASK YOURSELF

How have you used hierarchies to organize material that you are trying to remember? How would you do so for one of this text's modules?

spacing effect the tendency for distributed study or practice to yield better long-term retention than is achieved through massed study or practice.

testing effect enhanced memory after retrieving, rather than simply rereading, information. Also sometimes referred to as a *retrieval practice effect* or *test-enhanced learning*.

shallow processing encoding on a basic level, based on the structure or appearance of words.

deep processing encoding semantically, based on the meaning of the words; tends to yield the best retention.

DISTRIBUTED PRACTICE

LOQ 24-8 How do distributed practice, deep processing, and making new material personally meaningful aid memory?

We retain information better when our encoding is distributed over time. Experiments have consistently revealed the benefits of this **spacing effect** (Cepeda et al., 2006; Soderstrom et al., 2016). *Massed practice* (cramming) can produce speedy short-term learning and an inflated feeling of confidence. But to paraphrase early memory researcher Hermann Ebbinghaus (1885), those who learn quickly also forget quickly. *Distributed practice* produces better long-term recall. After you've studied long enough for competence with the material, further study at that time becomes inefficient. Better to spend that extra reviewing time later—a day later if you need to remember something 10 days hence, or a month later if you need to remember something 6 months hence (Cepeda et al., 2008). The spacing effect is one of psychology's most reliable findings, and it extends to motor skills and online game performance, too (Stafford & Dewar, 2014). Memory researcher Henry Roediger (2013) sums it up: "Hundreds of studies have shown that distributed practice leads to more durable learning."

"The mind is slow in unlearning what it has been long in learning." —Roman philosopher Seneca (4 B.C.E.–65 C.E.)

One effective way to distribute practice is *repeated* self-testing, a phenomenon that researchers have called the **testing effect** (Roediger & Karpicke, 2006; Yang et al., 2021). Testing does more than assess learning and memory: It improves them (Su et al., 2021). In this book, the Retrieval Practice questions and Review sections, including the Module Test questions, offer opportunities to improve learning and memory. "Practicing retrieval facilitates learning," notes memory expert Kathleen McDermott (2021). Better to practice retrieval (as any exam will demand) than to merely reread material (which may lull you into a false sense of competence). Roediger (2013) explains, "Two techniques that students frequently report using for studying—highlighting (or underlining) text and rereading text—[have been found] ineffective." As another memory expert explained, "What we recall becomes more recallable" (Bjork, 2011). No wonder daily quizzing improves introductory psychology students' course performance (Batsell et al., 2017; Pennebaker et al., 2013). So, too, can teaching the material to someone else, self-testing with flash cards, and responding to teacher questions with a clicker (Fazio & Marsh, 2019).

The point to remember: Spaced study and self-assessment beat cramming and rereading. Practice may not make perfect, but smart practice—occasional rehearsal with self-testing—makes for lasting memories.

Make Things Memorable My [DM's] animated tutorial (tinyurl.com/HowToRemember) offers suggestions on how to apply the *testing effect* to your own learning.

LEVELS OF PROCESSING Memory researchers have discovered that we process verbal information at different levels and that depth of processing affects our long-term retention. **Shallow processing** encodes on an elementary level, such as a word's letters or, at a more intermediate level, a word's sound. Thus, we may type *there* when we mean *their*, *write* when we mean *right*, and *two* when we mean *too*. **Deep processing** encodes *semantically*, based on the meaning of the words. The deeper (more meaningful) the processing, the better our retention.

In one classic experiment, researchers Fergus Craik and Endel Tulving (1975) flashed words at viewers. Then they asked them questions that would elicit different levels of processing. To experience the task yourself, rapidly answer the questions in **TABLE 24.1**.

TABLE 24.1

Sample Questions to Elicit Different Levels of Processing	Word Flashed	Yes	No
Shallowest: Is the word in capital letters?	CHAIR	________	________
Shallow: Does the word rhyme with train?	brain	________	________
Deep: Would the word fit in this sentence? The girl put the ________ on the table.	puzzle	________	________

Which type of processing would best prepare you to recognize the words at a later time? In this experiment, the deeper, semantic processing triggered by the third question yielded a much better memory than did the shallower processing elicited by the second question or the very shallow processing elicited by the first question (which was especially ineffective).

MAKING MATERIAL PERSONALLY MEANINGFUL If new information is neither meaningful nor related to our experience, we have trouble processing it. Imagine being asked to remember the following recorded passage:

> The procedure is actually quite simple. First, you arrange things into different groups. Of course, one pile may be sufficient depending on how much there is to do . . . . After the procedure is completed, one arranges the materials into different groups again. Then they can be put into their appropriate places. Eventually, they will be used once more and the whole cycle will then have to be repeated. However, that is part of life.

When some students heard the paragraph you have just read, without a meaningful context, they remembered little of it (Bransford & Johnson, 1972). When others were told the paragraph described washing clothes (something meaningful), they remembered much more of it—as you probably could now after rereading it.

Can you repeat the sentence about the angry rioter that we gave you at this module's beginning?

Perhaps, like those in an experiment by William Brewer (1977), you recalled the sentence by the meaning you encoded when you read it (for example, "The angry rioter threw the rock *through* the window") and not as it was written ("The angry rioter threw the rock *at* the window"). Referring to such mental mismatches, some researchers have likened our minds to theater directors who, given a raw script, imagine the finished stage production (Bower & Morrow, 1990). Asked later what we heard or read, we recall not the literal text but what we encoded. Thus, studying for an exam, you may remember your lecture notes rather than the lecture itself.

We can avoid significant mismatches by rephrasing what we see and hear into meaningful terms. From his experiments on himself, Ebbinghaus estimated that, compared with learning nonsense syllables, learning meaningful material required one-tenth the effort. As memory researcher Wayne Wickelgren (1977, p. 346) noted, "The time you spend thinking about material you are reading and relating it to previously stored material is about the most useful thing you can do in learning any new subject matter."

Psychologist-actor team Helga Noice and Tony Noice (2006) have described how actors inject meaning into the daunting task of learning "all those lines." They do it by first coming to understand the flow of meaning: "One actor divided a half-page of dialogue into three [intentions]: 'to flatter,' 'to draw him out,' and 'to allay his fears.'" With this meaningful sequence in mind, the actor more easily remembered the lines.

Most people excel at remembering personally relevant information. Asked how well certain adjectives describe a stranger, we often forget them; asked how well the adjectives describe us, we often remember them. To remember their passwords, people (you, too?) often use self-relevant information (Taylor & Garry, 2019). The tendency to remember self-relevant information, called the *self-reference effect,* is especially strong in individualist Western cultures (Jiang et al., 2019; Zhang & Tullis, 2021).

The point to remember: You can profit from taking time to find personal meaning in what you are studying.

In the discussion of mnemonics, we gave you six words and told you we would quiz you about them later. How many of these words can you now recall? Of these, how many are high-imagery words? How many are low-imagery?[1]

[1]The words were bicycle, void, cigarette, inherent, fire, and process.

RETRIEVAL PRACTICE

RP-7 Which strategies are better for long-term retention: cramming and rereading material or spreading out learning over time and repeatedly testing yourself?

RP-8 If you try to make the material you are learning personally meaningful, are you processing at a shallow or a deep level? Which level leads to greater retention?

ANSWERS IN APPENDIX E

MODULE

24 REVIEW Studying and Encoding Memories

LEARNING OBJECTIVES

Test Yourself Answer these repeated Learning Objective Questions on your own (before "showing" the answers here, or checking the answers in Appendix D) to improve your retention of the concepts (McDaniel et al., 2009, 2015).

LOQ 24-1 What is *memory*, and how is it measured?

LOQ 24-2 How do memory models help us study memory, and how has later research updated the three-stage information-processing model?

LOQ 24-3 How do explicit and implicit memories differ?

LOQ 24-4 What information do we process automatically?

LOQ 24-5 How does sensory memory work?

LOQ 24-6 What is our short-term memory capacity?

LOQ 24-7 What are some effortful processing strategies that can help us remember new information?

LOQ 24-8 How do distributed practice, deep processing, and making new material personally meaningful aid memory?

TERMS AND CONCEPTS TO REMEMBER

Test Yourself Write down the definition in your own words, then check your answer.

memory, p. 294
recall, p. 295
recognition, p. 295
relearning, p. 295
encoding, p. 296
storage, p. 296
retrieval, p. 296
parallel processing, p. 296
sensory memory, p. 296
short-term memory, p. 296
long-term memory, p. 296
working memory, p. 297
explicit memory, p. 297
effortful processing, p. 297
automatic processing, p. 297
implicit memory, p. 297
iconic memory, p. 299
echoic memory, p. 299
chunking, p. 300
mnemonics [nih-MON-iks], p. 300
spacing effect, p. 301
testing effect, p. 301
shallow processing, p. 301
deep processing, p. 301

MODULE TEST

Test Yourself Answer the following questions on your own first, then "show" the answers here, or check your answers in Appendix E.

1. A psychologist who asks you to write down as many objects as you can remember having seen a few minutes earlier is testing your ____________.
2. The psychological terms for taking in information, retaining it, and later getting it back out are ____________, ____________, and ____________.
3. The concept of working memory
   a. clarifies the idea of short-term memory by focusing on the active processing that occurs in this stage.
   b. splits short-term memory into two substages—sensory memory and iconic memory.
   c. splits short-term memory into two types: implicit and explicit memory.
   d. clarifies the idea of short-term memory by focusing on space, time, and frequency.
4. Sensory memory may be visual (____________ memory) or auditory (____________ memory).
5. Our short-term memory for new information is limited to about ____________ bits of information.
6. Memory aids that use visual imagery or other organizational devices are called ____________.

MODULE 25 Storing and Retrieving Memories

Once information is encoded, how does our brain process and store it? What can affect our memory processing? And once a memory is stored, how do we get it back out? What influences memory retrieval?

Memory Storage

LOQ 25-1 What is the capacity of long-term memory? Are our long-term memories processed and stored in specific locations?

In Arthur Conan Doyle's *A Study in Scarlet,* Sherlock Holmes offers a popular theory of memory capacity:

> [A] brain originally is like a little empty attic, and you have to stock it with such furniture as you choose . . . . It is a mistake to think that that little room has elastic walls and can distend to any extent. Depend upon it, there comes a time when for every addition of knowledge you forget something that you knew before.

Contrary to Holmes' "memory model," our brain is *not* like an attic, which once filled can store more items only if we discard old ones. Our capacity for storing long-term memories is essentially limitless. After studying the brain's neural connections, researchers estimated its storage capacity as "in the same ballpark as the World Wide Web" (Sejnowski, 2016).

Retaining Information in the Brain

I [DM] marveled at my aging mother-in-law, a retired pianist and organist. At age 88, her blind eyes could no longer read music. But let her sit at a keyboard and she would flawlessly play any of hundreds of hymns, including ones she had not thought of for 20 years. Where did her brain store those thousands of sequenced notes?

For a time, some surgeons and memory researchers marveled at patients' apparently vivid memories triggered by brain stimulation during surgery. Did this prove that our whole past, not just well-practiced music, is "in there," in complete detail, just waiting to be relived? On closer analysis, the seeming flashbacks appeared to have been invented, not a vivid reliving of long-forgotten experiences (Loftus & Loftus, 1980). In a further demonstration that memories do not reside in single, specific spots, psychologist Karl Lashley (1950) trained rats to find their way out of a maze, then surgically removed pieces of their brain's cortex and retested their memory. No matter which small brain section he removed, the rats retained at least a partial memory of how to navigate the maze. Memories *are* brain based, but the brain distributes the components of a memory across a network of locations. These specific locations include some of the neural circuitry involved in the original experience: Some brain cells that fire when we experience something fire again when we recall it (G. Miller, 2012; Miller et al., 2013).

The point to remember: Despite the brain's vast storage capacity, we do not store information as libraries store their books, in single, precise locations. Instead, brain networks encode, store, and retrieve the information that forms our complex memories.

EXPLICIT MEMORY SYSTEM: THE FRONTAL LOBES AND HIPPOCAMPUS

LOQ 25-2 What roles do the frontal lobes and hippocampus play in memory processing?

Explicit, conscious memories are either **semantic** (facts and general knowledge) or **episodic** (experienced events). The network that processes and stores new explicit memories for facts and episodes includes your frontal lobes and hippocampus. When you summon up a mental encore of a past experience, many brain regions send input to your *prefrontal cortex* (the front part of your frontal lobes) for working memory processing

semantic memory explicit memory of facts and general knowledge; one of our two conscious memory systems (the other is *episodic memory*).

episodic memory explicit memory of personally experienced events; one of our two conscious memory systems (the other is *semantic memory*).

(de Chastelaine et al., 2016; Michalka et al., 2015). The left and right frontal lobes process different types of memories. Recalling a password and holding it in working memory, for example, would activate the left frontal lobe. Calling up a visual party scene would more likely activate the right frontal lobe. And women, whose episodic memory surpasses men's, are most likely to accurately remember what happened at the party (Asperholm et al., 2019).

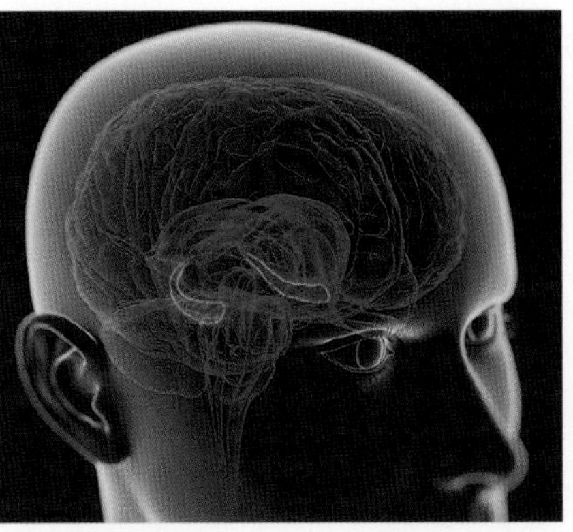

Roger Harris/Science Source

FIGURE 25.1
The hippocampus Explicit memories for facts and episodes are processed in the hippocampus (purple structures) and fed to other brain regions for storage.

Cognitive neuroscientists have found that the **hippocampus**, a temporal lobe neural structure located in the limbic system, can be likened to a "save" button for explicit memories (**FIGURE 25.1**). As children mature, their hippocampus grows, enabling them to construct detailed memories (Keresztes et al., 2017). Brain scans reveal activity in the hippocampus and nearby brain networks as people form explicit memories of names, images, and events (Norman et al., 2019).

Damage to this structure therefore disrupts the formation and recall of explicit memories. If their hippocampus is severed, chickadees and other birds will continue to cache food in hundreds of places, but later cannot find the places (Kamil & Cheng, 2001; Sherry & Vaccarino, 1989). With left-hippocampus damage, people have trouble remembering verbal information, but they have no trouble recalling visual designs and locations. With right-hippocampus damage, the problem is reversed (Schacter, 1996).

So the hippocampus is complex, with subregions that serve different functions. One part is active as people and mice learn social information (Okuyama et al., 2016; Zeineh et al., 2003). Another part is active as memory champions engage in spatial mnemonics (Maguire et al., 2003). The rear area processes spatial memory, and it grows bigger as London cabbies memorize the names and layout of 26,000 streets and thousands of popular city locations (Woollett & Maguire, 2011).

Memories are not permanently stored in the hippocampus. Instead, the hippocampus acts as a loading dock where the brain registers and temporarily holds the elements of a to-be-remembered episode—its smell, feel, sound, and location. Then, like older files shifted to be archived, memories migrate to the cortex for storage. This storage process is called **memory consolidation**.

Tim Zurowski/All Canada Photos

Hippocampus hero One contender for champion memorist is a mere birdbrain—the Clark's Nutcracker—which can locate up to 6000 caches of pine seed it had previously buried (Gould et al., 2013; Shettleworth, 1993).

Sleep supports memory consolidation. In one experiment, students who learned material in a study/sleep/restudy condition remembered material better, both a week and 6 months later, than did students who studied in both the morning and evening without intervening sleep (Mazza et al., 2016). During deep sleep, the hippocampus processes memories for later retrieval. After a training experience, the greater one's hippocampus activity during sleep, the better the next day's memory will be (Peigneux et al., 2004; Whitehurst et al., 2016). Researchers have watched the hippocampus and brain cortex displaying simultaneous activity rhythms during sleep, as if they were having a dialogue (Euston et al., 2007; Khodagholy et al., 2017). The brain seems to replay the day's experiences as it transfers them to the cortex for long-term storage (Squire & Zola-Morgan, 1991). When our learning is distributed over days rather than crammed into a single day, we experience more sleep-induced memory consolidation. And that helps explain the spacing effect.

IMPLICIT MEMORY SYSTEM: THE CEREBELLUM AND BASAL GANGLIA

LOQ 25-3 What roles do the cerebellum and basal ganglia play in memory processing?

Your hippocampus and frontal lobes are processing sites for your *explicit* memories. But you could lose those newer areas of the brain and still, thanks to automatic processing, lay down *implicit* memories for skills and newly conditioned associations. Joseph LeDoux (1996) recounted the story of a patient with brain damage whose amnesia left her unable to recognize her physician as, each day, he shook her hand and introduced himself. One day, she yanked her hand back, for the physician had pricked her with a tack in his palm. The next time he returned to introduce himself, she refused to shake his hand but couldn't explain why. Having been classically conditioned, she just wouldn't do it. Implicitly, she felt what she could not explain.

hippocampus a neural center located in the limbic system; helps process explicit (conscious) memories—of facts and events—for storage.

memory consolidation the neural storage of a long-term memory.

flashbulb memory a clear memory of an emotionally significant moment or event.

long-term potentiation (LTP) an increase in a nerve cell's firing potential after brief, rapid stimulation; a neural basis for learning and memory.

The *cerebellum* plays a key role in forming and storing the implicit memories created by classical conditioning. With a damaged cerebellum, people cannot develop certain conditioned reflexes, such as associating a tone with an impending puff of air—and thus, do not blink in anticipation of the puff (Daum & Schugens, 1996; Green & Woodruff-Pak, 2000). Implicit memory formation needs the cerebellum.

The *basal ganglia,* deep brain structures involved in motor movement, facilitate formation of our procedural memories for skills (Mishkin, 1982; Mishkin et al., 1997). The basal ganglia receive input from the cortex but do not return the favor by sending information back to the cortex for conscious awareness of procedural learning. If you have learned how to ride a bike, thank your basal ganglia.

Our implicit memory system, enabled by these brain areas, helps explain why the reactions and skills we learned during infancy reach far into our future. Yet as adults, our *conscious* memory of our first 4 years is largely blank due to *infantile amnesia.* As an adult, my [ND's] son, Ellis, will not consciously remember his happy visit to Disney World at age 2. Two influences contribute to infantile amnesia: First, we index much of our explicit memory with a command of language that young children do not possess. Second, the hippocampus is one of the last brain structures to mature, and as it does, more gets retained (Akers et al., 2014).

RETRIEVAL PRACTICE

RP-1 Which parts of the brain are important for *implicit* memory processing, and which parts play a key role in *explicit* memory processing?

RP-2 Leslie, who has experienced brain damage in an accident, can remember how to tie shoes but has a hard time remembering anything you say during a conversation. How can implicit versus explicit information processing explain what's going on here?

ANSWERS IN APPENDIX E

Which do you feel is more important—your experiences or your memories of them?

THE AMYGDALA, EMOTIONS, AND MEMORY

LOQ 25-4 How do emotions affect our memory processing?

Our emotions trigger stress hormones that influence memory formation. When we are excited or stressed, these hormones make more glucose energy available to fuel brain activity, signaling the brain that something important is happening. Moreover, stress hormones focus memory. Stress provokes the *amygdala* (two limbic system, emotion-processing clusters) to initiate a *memory trace*—a lasting physical change as the memory forms—that boosts activity in the brain's memory-forming areas (Buchanan, 2007; Kensinger, 2007) (**FIGURE 25.2**). It's as if the amygdala says, "Brain, encode this moment for future reference!" The result? Emotional arousal can sear certain events into the brain, while disrupting memory for irrelevant events (Brewin et al., 2007; McGaugh, 2015).

FIGURE 25.2
Review key memory structures in the brain
Frontal lobes and *hippocampus:* explicit memory formation
Cerebellum and *basal ganglia:* implicit memory formation
Amygdala: emotion-related memory formation

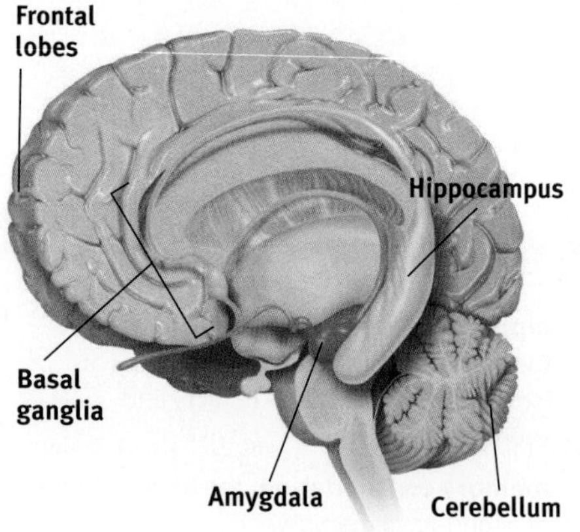
Frontal lobes
Hippocampus
Basal ganglia
Amygdala
Cerebellum

Significantly stressful events can form unforgettable memories. After a traumatic experience—a school shooting, a house fire, a sexual assault—vivid recollections of the horrific event may intrude again and again. "Stronger emotional experiences make for stronger, more reliable memories," noted James McGaugh (1994, 2003). Such experiences even strengthen recall for relevant, immediately preceding events (Dunsmoor et al., 2015; Jobson & Cheraghi, 2016). This makes adaptive sense: By waving warning flags, memory protects us from future dangers (Leding, 2019).

But emotional events produce tunnel vision memory. They focus our attention and recall on high-priority information and reduce our recall of irrelevant details (Mather & Sutherland, 2012). Whatever captures our attention gets well recalled, at the expense of the surrounding context.

Flashbulb memories form when we create mental snapshots of exciting or shocking events, such as our first kiss or our whereabouts when learning of a loved one's death (Brown & Kulik, 1977; Muzzulini et al., 2020). In a 2006 Pew survey, 95 percent of U.S. adults said they could recall exactly where they were or what they were doing when they first heard the news of the 9/11 terrorist attacks.

Our flashbulb memories are noteworthy for their vividness and our confidence in them. But as we relive, rehearse, and discuss them, even our flashbulb memories may become inconsistent, especially among older people (Kopp et al., 2020). With time, some errors crept into people's 9/11 recollections (compared with their earlier reports taken right afterward). Mostly, however, people's memories of 9/11 remained consistent over the next 10 years (Hirst et al., 2015).

Dramatic experiences remain clear in our memory in part because we rehearse them (Hirst & Phelps, 2016). We think about them and describe them to others. Memories of personally important experiences also endure (Storm & Jobe, 2012; Talarico & Moore, 2012). When their team won, fans enjoyed recalling and recounting the victory, leading to longer-lasting memories.

Renata Rodrigues Pereira/Shutterstock

Not-so-sluggish synapses The California sea slug, which neuroscientist Eric Kandel studied for 45 years, has increased our understanding of the neural basis of learning and memory.

Synaptic Changes

LOQ 25-5 How do changes at the synapse level affect our memory processing?

As you now think and learn about memory processes, your flexible brain is changing. Given increased activity in particular pathways, neural interconnections are forming and strengthening.

The quest to understand the physical basis of memory—how information becomes embedded in brain matter—has sparked study of the synaptic meeting places where neurons communicate with one another via their neurotransmitter messengers. Eric Kandel and James Schwartz (1982) recruited a seemingly unlikely candidate for this research: the California sea slug, a simple animal with a mere 20,000 or so unusually large and accessible nerve cells. It can be classically conditioned (with mild electric shock) to reflexively withdraw its gills when squirted with water, much as a soldier traumatized by combat might jump at the sound of a firecracker. When learning occurs, the researchers discovered, the slug releases more of the neurotransmitter *serotonin* into certain neurons. These cells' synapses then become more efficient at transmitting signals. Experience and learning can increase—even double—the number of synapses, even in slugs (Kandel, 2012).

In experiments with people, rapidly stimulating certain memory-circuit connections has increased their sensitivity for hours or even weeks to come. The sending neuron now needs less prompting to release its neurotransmitter, and more connections exist between neurons. This increased efficiency of potential neural firing, called **long-term potentiation (LTP)**, provides a neural basis for learning and remembering associations (Lynch, 2002; Whitlock et al., 2006) (**FIGURE 25.3**). Several lines of evidence confirm that LTP is a physical basis for memory. For example, drugs that block LTP interfere with learning (Lynch & Staubli, 1991). Drugs that mimic what happens during learning increase LTP (Harward et al., 2016). And rats given a drug that enhanced synaptic efficiency (LTP) learned a maze with half the usual number of mistakes (Service, 1994).

After LTP has occurred, passing an electric current through the brain won't disrupt old memories. But the current will wipe out very recent memories. Such is the experience both of laboratory animals and of severely depressed people given *electroconvulsive therapy (ECT)*. A blow to the head can do the same. Football players and boxers momentarily knocked unconscious typically have no memory of events just before the knockout (Yarnell & Lynch, 1970). Their working memory had no time to consolidate the information into long-term memory before the lights went out.

Recently, I [DM] did a little test of memory consolidation. While on an operating table for a basketball-related tendon repair, I was given a face mask and soon could smell the anesthesia gas. "So how much longer will I be with you?" I asked the anesthesiologist (knowing that our last seconds before falling asleep go unremembered). My last moment of memory was her answer: "About 10 seconds." My brain spent

FIGURE 25.3
Doubled receptor sites An electron microscope image (a) shows just one receptor site (gray) reaching toward a sending neuron before long-term potentiation. Image (b) shows that, after LTP, the receptor sites have doubled. This means the receiving neuron has increased sensitivity for detecting the presence of the neurotransmitter molecules that may be released by the sending neuron (Toni et al., 1999).

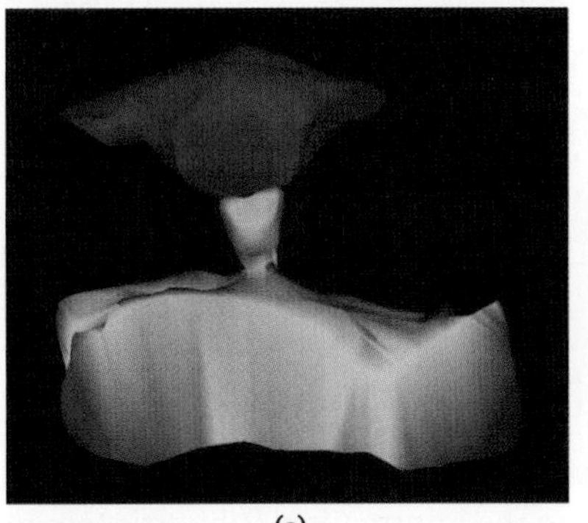

(a)

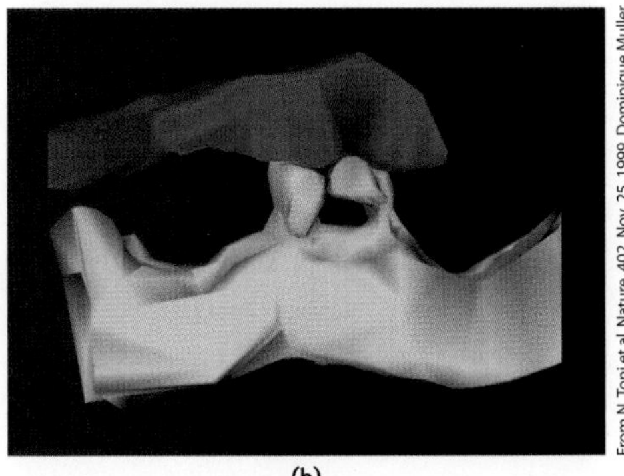

(b)

From N. Toni et al, Nature, 402, Nov. 25, 1999. Dominique Muller

FIGURE 25.4
Our two memory systems

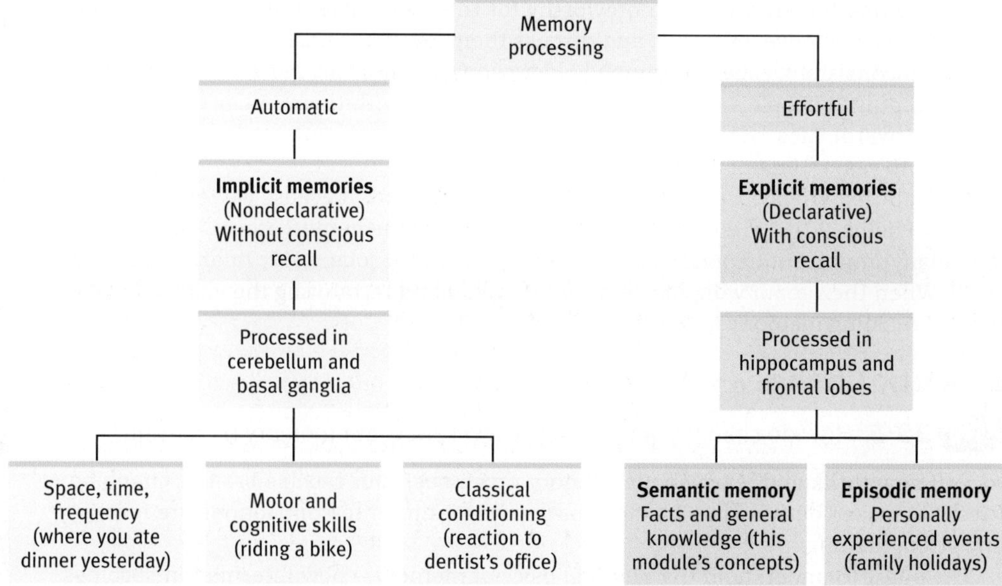
Memory processing
Automatic
Effortful
Implicit memories (Nondeclarative) Without conscious recall
Explicit memories (Declarative) With conscious recall
Processed in cerebellum and basal ganglia
Processed in hippocampus and frontal lobes
Space, time, frequency (where you ate dinner yesterday)
Motor and cognitive skills (riding a bike)
Classical conditioning (reaction to dentist's office)
Semantic memory Facts and general knowledge (this module's concepts)
Episodic memory Personally experienced events (family holidays)

that 10 seconds consolidating a memory for her 2-second answer, but could not tuck any further memory away before I was out cold.

Some memory-biology explorers have helped found companies that are competing to develop memory-altering drugs. The target market for memory-boosting drugs is massive: people with Alzheimer's disease or the *mild cognitive impairment* that often becomes Alzheimer's, people with more typical age-related memory decline, and anyone who simply wants a better memory. Meanwhile, students already have free access to one safe, proven memory enhancer: effective study techniques followed by adequate *sleep!*

One approach to improving memory focuses on drugs that boost the LTP-enhancing neurotransmitter *glutamate* (Lynch et al., 2011). Another approach involves developing drugs that boost production of CREB, a protein that also enhances the LTP process (Fields, 2005). Boosting CREB production might trigger increased production of other proteins that help reshape synapses and transfer short-term memories into long-term memories.

Some of us may wish for memory-*blocking* drugs that could blunt intrusive memories when taken after a traumatic experience (Adler, 2012; Kearns et al., 2012). In experiments, survivors of events such as car accidents and sexual assault received, afterward, several doses of one such drug (propranolol) or a placebo. Later testing revealed more stress reduction in the drug-treated group (Brunet et al., 2018; Pitman et al., 2002).

FIGURE 25.4 summarizes the brain's two-track memory processing and storage system for implicit (automatic) and explicit (effortful) memories. *The bottom line:* Learn something and you can change your brain a little.

RETRIEVAL PRACTICE

RP-3 Which brain area responds to stress hormones by helping to create stronger memories?

RP-4 Increased efficiency at the synapses is evidence of the neural basis of learning and memory. This is called ________________-________________ ________________.

ANSWERS IN APPENDIX E

Memory Retrieval

After the magic of brain encoding and storage, we still have the daunting task of retrieving the information. What triggers retrieval?

Retrieval Cues

LOQ 25-6 How do external cues, internal emotions, and order of appearance influence memory retrieval?

Imagine a spider suspended in the middle of her web, held up by the many strands extending outward from her in all directions to different points. If you were to trace a pathway to the spider, you would first need to locate an anchor point and then follow the strand into the web.

The process of retrieving a memory follows a similar principle, because memories are held in storage by a web of associations, each piece of information interconnected with others. When you encode into memory a target piece of information, such as the name of the person sitting next to you in class, you associate with it other bits of information about your surroundings, mood, seating position, and so on. These bits can serve as *retrieval cues*—like passwords that open memories. The more retrieval cues you have, the better your chances of finding a route to the suspended memory. The best retrieval cues come from associations we form when we encode a memory—smells, tastes, and sights that can evoke our memory of the associated person or event (Tamminen & Mebude, 2019).

"Memory is not like a container that gradually fills up; it is more like a tree growing hooks onto which memories are hung." —Peter Russell, *The Brain Book*, 1979

To call up visual cues when trying to recall something, we may mentally place ourselves in the original context. After losing his sight, British scholar John Hull (1990, p. 174) described his difficulty recalling such details:

> I knew I had been somewhere, and had done particular things with certain people, but where? I could not put the conversations . . . into a context. There was no background, no features against which to identify the place. Normally, the memories of people you have spoken to during the day are stored in frames which include the background.

To help people recall older memories, *reminiscence therapy* uses the power of retrieval cues (İnel Manav & Simsek, 2019; Park et al., 2019). One study had older people with Alzheimer's disease spend time in a room styled as a 1950s museum, filled with sights, sounds, and smells that triggered their youthful memories (Kirk et al., 2019). Compared with people who received standard assistive care, those who experienced the immersive reminiscence therapy performed better on memory tests. Retrieval cues helped them regain memories.

We need to retrieve memories for both our past (called *retrospective memory*) and our intended future actions *(prospective memory)*. To remember to do something (say, to get the mail), one effective strategy is to mentally associate the act with a cue (perhaps putting your mailbox key by the door) (Rogers & Milkman, 2016). It pays to plan ahead, which helps explain why most people spend more time thinking about their future than their past (Anderson & McDaniel, 2019).

Robert Leighton/Cartoon Stock

"Oh, is that today?"

Does the unprepared astronaut illustrate a failure of retrospective or prospective memory?[2]

PRIMING Often our associations are activated without our awareness. Philosopher-psychologist William James referred to this process, which we call **priming**, as the "wakening of associations." After seeing or hearing the word *rabbit*, we are later more likely to spell the spoken word *hair/hare* as *h-a-r-e*, even if we don't recall seeing or hearing *rabbit* (Bower, 1986) (**FIGURE 25.5**).

Seeing or hearing the word *rabbit*

Activates concept

Primes spelling the spoken word *hair/hare* as *h-a-r-e*

FIGURE 25.5 Priming associations unconsciously activates related associations

priming the activation, often unconsciously, of particular associations in memory.

[2]It was this astronaut's prospective memory that failed.

Priming is often "memoryless memory"—an implicit, invisible memory, without your conscious awareness. If you see a poster of a missing child, you may then unconsciously be primed to interpret an ambiguous adult-child interaction as a possible kidnapping (James, 1986). Although you no longer have the poster in mind, it predisposes your interpretation. Priming can also influence behaviors (Weingarten et al., 2016). Adults and children primed with money-related words and materials change their behavior in various ways, such as by becoming less helpful (Gasiorowska et al., 2016; Lodder et al., 2019). Money may prime our materialism and self-interest. And priming people with threatening (versus pleasant) images causes them to evaluate other people negatively (Lai & Wilson, 2021). Similarly, our learned stereotypes—of which we may not be consciously aware—can prime our perceptions and actions that feed prejudice and discrimination (see the Social Psychology modules).

Ask a friend three rapid-fire questions:

1. **What color is snow?**
2. **What color are clouds?**
3. **What do cows drink?**

If your friend answers "milk" to the third question, you have demonstrated priming.

CONTEXT-DEPENDENT MEMORY Have you noticed? Putting yourself back in the context where you earlier experienced something can prime your memory retrieval. Remembering, in many ways, depends on our environment (Palmer, 1989). When you visit your childhood home or neighborhood, old memories surface. When scuba divers listened to a word list in one of two different settings (either 10 feet underwater or sitting on the beach), they recalled more words when later tested in the same place where they first heard the list (Godden & Baddeley, 1975).

By contrast, experiencing something outside the usual setting can be confusing. Have you ever run into a former teacher in an unusual place, such as at a store or park? Perhaps you felt a glimmer of recognition but struggled to realize who it was and how you were acquainted. The **encoding specificity principle** helps us understand how *specific* cues will most effectively trigger that memory. In new settings, you may be missing the memory cues needed for speedy face recognition. Our memories are *context-dependent* and are affected by the cues we have associated with that context.

In several experiments, Carolyn Rovee-Collier (1993) found that a familiar context activated memories even in 3-month-olds. After infants learned that kicking would make a crib mobile move (via a connecting ribbon from their ankle), the infants kicked more when tested again in the same crib than when in a different context.

David Sipress/Cartoon Stock

"I can't remember what we're arguing about, either. Let's keep yelling, and maybe it will come back to us."

STATE-DEPENDENT MEMORY Closely related to context-dependent memory is *state-dependent memory.* What we learn in one state may be more easily recalled when we are again in that state. What people learn when drunk they don't recall well in *any* state (alcohol disrupts memory storage). But they recall it slightly better when again drunk. Someone who hides money when drunk may forget the location until drunk again.

Moods also provide an example of memory's state dependence. Emotions that accompany good or bad events become retrieval cues (Gaddy & Ingram, 2014). Thus, our memories are somewhat **mood congruent**. If you've had a bad day—you argued with a friend, made a big mistake at work, and got a poor grade on your midterm—your gloomy mood may facilitate recalling other bad times. Depression sours memories by priming negative associations, which we then use to explain our current mood (Mihailova & Jobson, 2020). In many experiments, people put in a buoyant mood—whether under hypnosis or just by the day's events (a World Cup soccer victory for German participants in one study)—recall the world through rose-colored glasses (DeSteno et al., 2000; Forgas et al., 1984; Schwarz et al., 1987). They recall their behaviors as competent and effective, other people as benevolent, happy events as more frequent.

Have you ever noticed that how you feel influences how you perceive others? In one study, adolescents' ratings of parental warmth in 1 week gave little clue to how they would rate their parents 6 weeks later (Bornstein et al., 1991). When teens were down, their parents seemed cruel; as their mood brightened, their parents morphed from devils into angels. And at age 26, people's recall of their parents' caregiving during their childhood were linked less with the actual caregiving (which had been assessed years earlier) than with their *current* moods and parental relationship (Nivison et al., 2021). We may nod our heads knowingly. Yet, in a good or bad mood, we persist in attributing to reality our own changing judgments, memories, and interpretations. In a bad mood, we may read someone's look as a glare and feel even worse. In a good mood, we may encode the same look as interest and feel even better.

encoding specificity principle the idea that cues and contexts specific to a particular memory will be most effective in helping us recall it.

mood-congruent memory the tendency to recall experiences that are consistent with one's current good or bad mood.

Mood effects on retrieval help explain why our moods persist. When happy, we recall pleasant events and, therefore, see the world as a wonderful place, which helps prolong our good mood. When depressed, we recall sad events, which darkens our interpretations of current events. For those of us predisposed to depression, this process can help maintain a vicious, dark cycle. Moods magnify.

"When a feeling was there, they felt as if it would never go; when it was gone, they felt as if it had never been; when it returned, they felt as if it had never gone." —George MacDonald, *What's Mine's Mine*, 1886

ASK YOURSELF

What sort of mood have you been in lately? How has your mood colored your memories, perceptions, and expectations?

SERIAL POSITION EFFECT Another memory-retrieval quirk, the **serial position effect**, explains why we may have large holes in our memory of a list of recent events. Imagine it's your first day in a new job, and your manager is introducing you to your co-workers. As you meet each person, you silently repeat everyone's name, starting from the beginning. As the last person smiles and turns away, you feel confident you'll be able to greet your new co-workers by name the next day.

Don't count on it. Because you have spent more time rehearsing the earlier names than the later ones, those are the names you'll probably recall more easily the next day. In experiments, when people viewed a list of items (words, names, dates) or experienced a series of odors or tastes, and then immediately tried to recall them in any order, they fell prey to the serial position effect (Daniel & Katz, 2018; Dimsdale-Zucker et al., 2019). They briefly recalled the last items especially quickly and well (a *recency effect*), perhaps because those last items were still in working memory. But after a delay, when their attention was elsewhere, their recall was best for the first items (a *primacy effect*; see **FIGURE 25.6**).

RETRIEVAL PRACTICE

RP-5 What is *priming*?

RP-6 When tested immediately after viewing a list of words, we tend to recall the first and last items best, which is known as the ____________ ____________ effect.

ANSWERS IN APPENDIX E

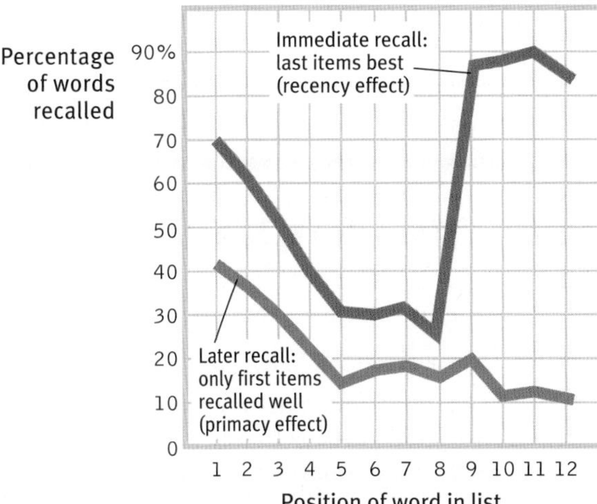
Percentage of words recalled
90%
80
70
60
50
40
30
20
10
0
Immediate recall: last items best (recency effect)
Later recall: only first items recalled well (primacy effect)
1 2 3 4 5 6 7 8 9 10 11 12
Position of word in list

Kevork Djansezian/Getty Images

FIGURE 25.6
The serial position effect Immediately after Mahershala Ali made his way down the red carpet at the 2019 Academy Awards, he would probably have best recalled the names of the last few people he greeted *(recency effect)*. But later, he may only have been able to recall the first few people best *(primacy effect)*. Memory "sags in the middle," leading us to remember best the first and last people we meet.

serial position effect our tendency to recall best the last *(recency effect)* and first *(primacy effect)* items in a list.

MODULE 25 REVIEW Storing and Retrieving Memories

LEARNING OBJECTIVES

Test Yourself Answer these repeated Learning Objective Questions on your own (before "showing" the answers here, or checking the answers in Appendix D) to improve your retention of the concepts (McDaniel et al., 2009, 2015).

LOQ 25-1 What is the capacity of long-term memory? Are our long-term memories processed and stored in specific locations?

LOQ 25-2 What roles do the frontal lobes and hippocampus play in memory processing?

LOQ 25-3 What roles do the cerebellum and basal ganglia play in memory processing?

LOQ 25-4 How do emotions affect our memory processing?

LOQ 25-5 How do changes at the synapse level affect our memory processing?

LOQ 25-6 How do external cues, internal emotions, and order of appearance influence memory retrieval?

TERMS AND CONCEPTS TO REMEMBER

Test Yourself Write down the definition in your own words, then check your answer.

semantic memory, p. 304
episodic memory, p. 304
hippocampus, p. 305
memory consolidation, p. 305
flashbulb memory, p. 306
long-term potentiation (LTP), p. 306
priming, p. 309
encoding specificity principle, p. 310
mood-congruent memory, p. 310
serial position effect, p. 311

MODULE TEST

Test Yourself Answer the following questions on your own first, then "show" the answers here, or check your answers in Appendix E.

1. The hippocampus seems to function as a
a. temporary processing site for explicit memories.
b. temporary processing site for implicit memories.
c. permanent storage area for emotion-based memories.
d. permanent storage area for unconscious memories.

2. Hippocampus damage typically leaves people unable to learn new facts or recall recent events. However, they may be able to learn new skills, such as riding a bicycle, which is an ________________ (explicit/implicit) memory.

3. Long-term potentiation (LTP) refers to
a. emotion-triggered hormonal changes.
b. the role of the hippocampus in processing explicit memories.
c. an increase in a cell's firing potential.
d. the potential for learning in late adulthood.

4. Specific odors, visual images, emotions, or other associations that help us access a memory are examples of ________________________.

5. When you feel sad, why might it help to look at pictures that reawaken some of your best memories?

6. When tested immediately after viewing a list of words, people tend to recall the first and last items more readily than those in the middle. When retested after a delay, they are most likely to recall
a. the first items on the list.
b. the first and last items on the list.
c. a few items at random.
d. the last items on the list.

MODULE 26 Forgetting, Memory Construction, and Improving Memory

Our memories are amazing, but they are not perfect. We may forget, fail to encode, or find ourselves unable to retrieve information. We might misremember what we've seen or heard, or "remember" things that are false. What influences these errors in memory? And how can we use research findings to improve our memories?

Forgetting

LOQ 26-1 Why do we forget?

Amid all the applause for memory—all the efforts to understand it, all the books on how to improve it—have any voices been heard in praise of forgetting? William James

(1890, p. 680) was such a voice: "If we remembered everything, we should on most occasions be as ill off as if we remembered nothing." Psychologists Robert Bjork and Elizabeth Bjork (2019) agree, calling forgetting "the friend of learning." Indeed, the ability to forget out-of-date information—where we parked yesterday, an old phone number, meals prepared and eaten—is a blessing (Nørby, 2015). Forgetting unimportant information helps us remember what matters most (Murphy & Castel, 2021). So the next time you fret about forgetting, remember that letting go of bad memories is good for our mental well-being (Stramaccia et al., 2021).

"Amnesia seeps into the crevices of our brains, and amnesia heals."—Joyce Carol Oates, "Words Fail, Memory Blurs, Life Wins," 2001

Yet some people seem unable to forget. In the 1920s, Russian journalist and memory whiz Solomon Shereshevsky had merely to listen while other reporters scribbled notes. Performing in front of a crowd, he could memorize streams of nonsensical or random information, such as long sections from Dante's *Inferno* in Italian—despite not knowing Italian (Johnson, 2017). But his junk heap of memories dominated his conscious mind (Luria, 1968). He had difficulty thinking abstractly—generalizing, organizing, evaluating. After reading a story, he could recite it but would struggle to summarize its gist.

Jill Price's incredibly accurate memory of her life's events since age 14 has been closely studied by a University of California at Irvine research team. She reports that her super-memory, called *highly superior autobiographical memory*, interferes with her life, with one memory cuing another (McGaugh & LePort, 2014; Parker et al., 2006): "It's like a running movie that never stops . . . . It is nonstop, uncontrollable, and totally exhausting." Although their memories are not perfect, people like Price are prone to having their mind fill up with information that most people ignore—shoes worn on a first date, the day of the week that you first ate at a favorite childhood restaurant—and that, once in memory storage, never leaves (Frithsen et al., 2019; Patihis, 2016). In such rare individuals—60 of whom have been identified worldwide—researchers have found enlarged brain areas and increased brain activity in memory centers (Dutton, 2018; Santangelo et al., 2020). A good memory is helpful but so is the ability to forget. If a memory-enhancing pill ever becomes available, it had better not be *too* effective.

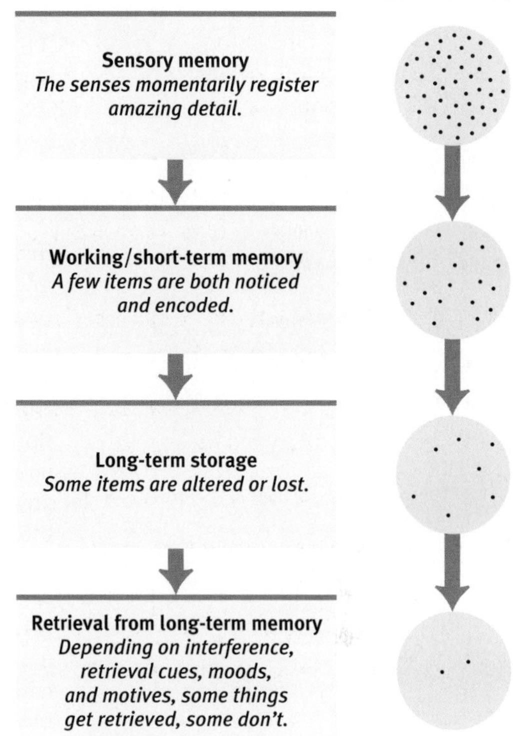
Information bits
Sensory memory
The senses momentarily register amazing detail.
Working/short-term memory
A few items are both noticed and encoded.
Long-term storage
Some items are altered or lost.
Retrieval from long-term memory
Depending on interference, retrieval cues, moods, and motives, some things get retrieved, some don't.

FIGURE 26.1
When do we forget? Forgetting can occur at any memory stage.

More often, however, our unpredictable memory dismays and frustrates us. Memories are quirky. My [DM's] own memory can easily call up such episodes as that wonderful first kiss with the woman I love, or trivial facts like the mileage from Los Angeles to New York. Then it abandons me when I fail to encode, store, or retrieve a student's name or where I left my keys. See how you do with remembering this sentence when we ask you about it later: *The fish attacked the swimmer.*

As we process information, we filter, alter, or lose most of it (**FIGURE 26.1**).

Forgetting and the Two-Track Mind

For some, memory loss is severe and permanent. Consider Henry Molaison (or H. M., as he was known until his 2008 death). Surgeons removed much of his hippocampus to stop persistent seizures. This resulted "in severe disconnection of the remaining hippocampus" from the rest of the brain (Annese et al., 2014). For his remaining 55 years, he was unable to form new conscious memories. Molaison suffered from **anterograde amnesia**—he could remember his past, but he could not form new memories. (Those who *cannot* remember their past—the old information stored in long-term memory—suffer from **retrograde amnesia**.) Molaison was, as before his surgery, intelligent and did daily crossword puzzles. Yet, reported neuroscientist Suzanne Corkin (2005, 2013), "I've known H. M. since 1962, and he still doesn't know who I am." For about half a minute he could keep something in mind, enough to carry on a conversation. When distracted, he would lose what was just said or what had just occurred. Without the neural tissue for turning new information into long-term memories, he never could name the current U.S. president (Ogden, 2012).

Neurologist Oliver Sacks (1985, pp. 26–27) described another patient, Jimmie, who had anterograde amnesia resulting from brain damage. Jimmie had no memories—thus, no sense of elapsed time—beyond his injury in 1945.

When Jimmie gave his age as 19, Sacks set a mirror before him: "Look in the mirror and tell me what you see. Is that a 19-year-old looking out from the mirror?"

anterograde amnesia an inability to form new memories. 

retrograde amnesia an inability to remember information from one's past.

Jimmie turned ashen, gripped the chair, cursed, then became frantic: "What's going on? What's happened to me? Is this a nightmare? Am I crazy? Is this a joke?" When his attention was diverted to some children playing baseball, his panic ended, the dreadful mirror forgotten.

Sacks showed Jimmie a photo from *National Geographic*. "What is this?" he asked.

"It's the Moon," Jimmie replied.

"No, it's not," Sacks answered. "It's a picture of the Earth taken from the Moon."

"Doc, you're kidding! Someone would've had to get a camera up there!"

"Naturally."

"Hell! You're joking—how the hell would you do that?" Jimmie's wonder was that of a bright young man from the 1940s, amazed by his travel back to the future.

Careful testing of these unique people reveals something even stranger: Although incapable of recalling new facts or anything they have done recently, Molaison, Jimmie, and others with similar conditions can learn nonverbal tasks. Shown hard-to-find figures in pictures (in the *Where's Waldo?* series, for example), they can quickly spot them again later. They can find their way to the bathroom, though without being able to tell you where it is. They can learn to read mirror-image writing or do a jigsaw puzzle, and they have even learned complicated *procedural* job skills (Schacter, 1992, 1996; Xu & Corkin, 2001). They can be classically conditioned. However, *they do all these things with no awareness of having learned them.* "Well, this is strange," Molaison said, after demonstrating his nondeclarative memory of skillful mirror tracing. "I thought that would be difficult. But it seems as though I've done it quite well" (Shapin, 2013).

Molaison and Jimmie lost their ability to form new explicit memories, but their automatic processing ability remained intact. Like Alzheimer's patients, whose *explicit* memories for new people and events are lost, they could form new *implicit* memories (Lustig & Buckner, 2004). These patients can learn *how* to do something, but they will not consciously recall learning their new skill. Such sad case studies confirm that we have two distinct memory systems, controlled by different parts of the brain.

For most of us, forgetting is a less drastic process. Let's consider some of the reasons we forget.

MEMORIES START TO FADE

Lightspring/Shutterstock

Encoding Failure

Much of what we sense we never notice, and what we fail to encode, we will never remember (**FIGURE 26.2**). English novelist and critic C. S. Lewis (1967, p. 107) described the enormity of what we never encode:

> [We are] bombarded every second by sensations, emotions, thoughts . . . nine-tenths of which [we] must simply ignore. The past [is] a roaring cataract of billions upon billions of such moments: Any one of them too complex to grasp in its entirety, and the aggregate beyond all imagination . . . . At every tick of the clock, in every inhabited part of the world, an unimaginable richness and variety of "history" falls off the world into total oblivion.

Age can affect encoding efficiency. The brain areas that jump into action when young adults encode new information are less responsive in older adults. This slower encoding helps explain age-related memory decline (Ward et al., 2020). (For more on aging's effect on memory, see the Developing Through the Life Span modules.)

But no matter how young we are, we selectively attend to few of the myriad sights and sounds continually bombarding us. Consider: You have surely seen the Apple logo thousands of times. Can you draw it? In one study, only 1 of 85 UCLA students (including 52 Apple users) could do so accurately (Blake et al., 2015). Without encoding effort, many potential memories never form.

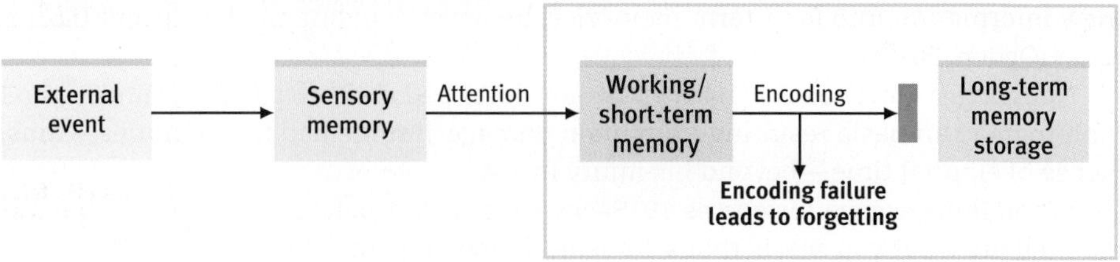
External event
Sensory memory
Attention
Working/ short-term memory
Encoding
Long-term memory storage
Encoding failure leads to forgetting

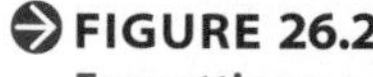
FIGURE 26.2
Forgetting as encoding failure We cannot remember what we have not encoded.

diego_cervo/iStock/Getty Images

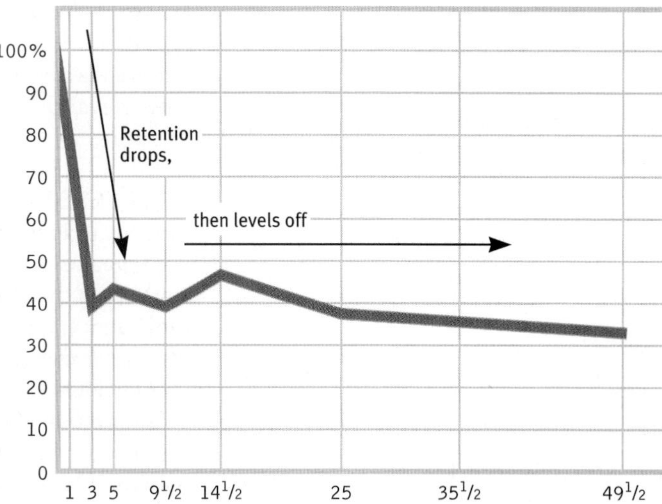
Percentage of original vocabulary retained
100%
90
80
70
60
50
40
30
20
10
0
Retention drops,
then levels off
1 3 5 9½ 14½ 25 35½ 49½
Time in years after completion of Spanish course

FIGURE 26.3
The forgetting curve for Spanish learned in school

Storage Decay

"You are already beginning to forget the material you just read." So said famed memory researcher Gordon Bower (1973). Indeed, even after encoding something well, we sometimes later forget it. To study the durability of stored memories, Hermann Ebbinghaus (1885) learned lists of nonsense syllables, such as *YOX* and *JIH*, and measured how much he retained when relearning each list, from 20 minutes to 30 days later. The result was his famous forgetting curve: *The course of forgetting is initially rapid, then levels off with time* (Wixted & Ebbesen, 1991). Another study found a similar forgetting curve for Spanish vocabulary learned in school (Bahrick, 1984). Compared with those just completing a high school or college Spanish course, people 3 years out of school had forgotten much of what they had learned (**FIGURE 26.3**). However, what people remembered then, they still mostly remembered 25+ years later. Their forgetting had leveled off.

One explanation for these forgetting curves is a gradual fading of the physical *memory trace*. Cognitive neuroscientists are getting closer to solving the mystery of memory's physical storage and are increasing our understanding of how memory storage could decay. Like books you can't find in your campus library, memories may be inaccessible for many reasons. Some were never acquired (not encoded). Others were discarded (stored memories decay). And others are out of reach because we can't retrieve them.

Retrieval Failure

Often, forgetting is not memories faded but memories unretrieved. We store in long-term memory what's important to us or what we've rehearsed. But sometimes important events defy our attempts to access them (**FIGURE 26.4**). How frustrating when a name lies poised on the tip of our tongue, just beyond reach. Given retrieval cues *(It begins with an M)*, we may easily retrieve the elusive memory. Retrieval problems contribute to the occasional memory failures of older adults, who more frequently are frustrated by tip-of-the-tongue forgetting (Abrams, 2008; Salthouse & Mandell, 2013).

Do you recall the gist of the sentence about the attacked swimmer that we asked you to remember? If not, does the word *shark* serve as a retrieval cue? Experiments show

People who are deaf and fluent in sign language experience a parallel "tip of the fingers" phenomenon (Thompson et al., 2005).

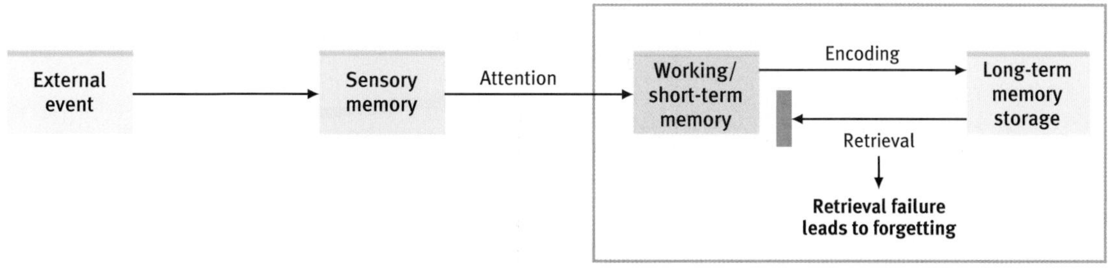
External event
Sensory memory
Attention
Working/ short-term memory
Encoding
Long-term memory storage
Retrieval
Retrieval failure leads to forgetting

FIGURE 26.4
Retrieval failure
Sometimes even stored information cannot be accessed, which leads to forgetting.

proactive interference the forward-acting disruptive effect of older learning on the recall of *new* information.

retroactive interference the backward-acting disruptive effect of newer learning on the recall of *old* information.

that *shark* (likely what you visualized) more readily retrieves the image you stored than does the sentence's actual word, *fish* (Anderson et al., 1976). (The sentence was, *The fish attacked the swimmer.*)

Retrieval problems occasionally stem from interference and even from motivated forgetting.

INTERFERENCE As you collect more and more information, your mental attic never fills, but it does get cluttered. Your brain tries to keep things tidy: Using a new password weakens your memory of competing old passwords (Wimber et al., 2015). But sometimes the clutter wins, and new and old learning collide. **Proactive** *(forward-acting)* **interference** occurs when prior learning disrupts your recall of new information. If you buy a new combination lock, your well-rehearsed old combination may interfere with your retrieval of the new one.

Retroactive *(backward-acting)* **interference** occurs when new learning disrupts your recall of old information. If someone sings new lyrics to an old song's tune, you may have trouble remembering the original words. Imagine a second stone tossed in a pond, disrupting the waves rippling out from the first.

Information presented in the hour before sleep suffers less retroactive interference because the opportunity for interfering events is minimized (Mercer, 2015). In a classic experiment, two people each learned some nonsense syllables (Jenkins & Dallenbach, 1924). Then they tried to recall them after a night's sleep or after remaining awake. As FIGURE 26.5 shows forgetting occurred more rapidly after being awake and involved with other activities. The investigators surmised that "forgetting is not so much a matter of the decay of old impressions and associations as it is a matter of interference, inhibition, or obliteration of the old by the new" (1924, p. 612).

The hour before sleep is a good time to commit information to memory (Scullin & McDaniel, 2010), though information presented in the *seconds* just before sleep is seldom remembered (Wyatt & Bootzin, 1994). If you're considering learning *while* sleeping, forget it. We have little memory for information played aloud in the room during sleep, although the ears do register it (Wood et al., 1992).

Old and new learning do not always compete. Previously learned information (Latin) often facilitates our learning of new information (French). This phenomenon is called *positive transfer.*

MOTIVATED FORGETTING To remember our past is often to revise it. Years ago, the huge cookie jar in my [DM's] kitchen was jammed with freshly baked chocolate chip cookies. Still, more were cooling across racks on the counter. Twenty-four hours later, not a crumb was left. Who had taken them? During that time, my wife, three children, and I were the only people in the house. So while memories were still fresh, I conducted a little memory test. Andy admitted wolfing down as many as 20. Peter thought he had

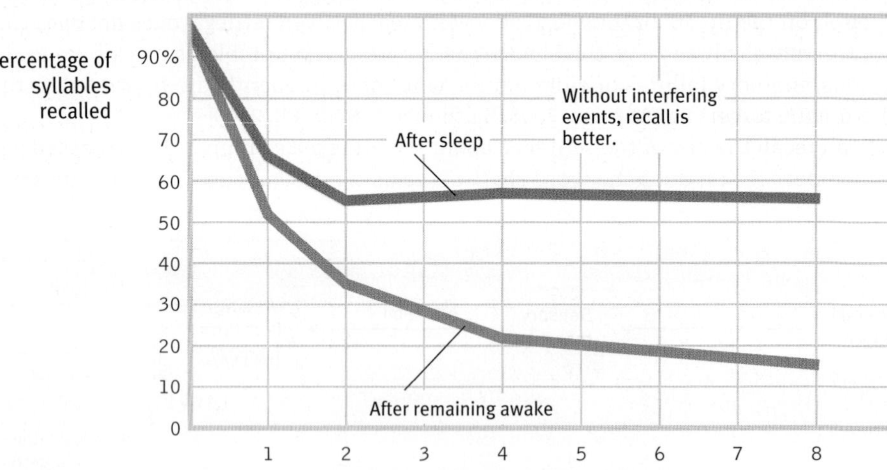
Percentage of syllables recalled
90%
80
70
60
50
40
30
20
10
0
Without interfering events, recall is better.
After sleep
After remaining awake
1
2
3
4
5
6
7
8
Hours elapsed after learning syllables

FIGURE 26.5
Retroactive interference More forgetting occurred when a person stayed awake and experienced other new material. (Data from Jenkins & Dallenbach, 1924.)

European Pressphoto Agency/Lages/PORTUGAL/Newscom

Do people vividly remember — or repress — traumatic experiences? Imagine yourself several hours into Flight AT236 from Toronto to Lisbon. A fractured fuel line begins leaking. Soon the engines go silent and primary electrical power is lost. In the eerie silence, the pilots instruct you and other terrified passengers to don life jackets and prepare for ocean impact. Before long, the pilot declares, above the passengers' screams and prayers, "About to go into the water." Death awaits.

But no! "We have a runway! Brace! Brace! Brace!" The plane makes a hard landing at an Azores airbase, averting death for all 305 on board.

Among the passengers thinking "I'm going to die" was psychologist Margaret McKinnon. Seizing the opportunity, four years later she tracked down 15 of her fellow passengers to test their trauma memories. Did they repress the experience? *No.* All exhibited vivid, detailed memories. With trauma comes not repression, but, far more often, "robust" memory (McKinnon et al., 2015).

eaten 15. Laura guessed she had stuffed her then-6-year-old body with 15 cookies. My wife, Carol, recalled eating 6, and I remembered consuming 15 and taking 18 more to the office. We sheepishly accepted responsibility for 89 cookies. Still, we had not come close; there had been 160.

Peter Johansky/Photolibrary/Getty Images

Why do our memories fail us? This happens in part because memory is an "unreliable, self-serving historian" (Tavris & Aronson, 2007, p. 6). Consider one study, in which researchers told some participants about the benefits of frequent toothbrushing. Those individuals then recalled (more than others did) having frequently brushed their teeth in the preceding 2 weeks (Ross et al., 1981).

So why were my family and I so far off in our cookie-consumption estimates? Was it an *encoding* problem? (Did we just not notice what we had eaten?) Was it a storage problem? (Might our memories of cookies, like Ebbinghaus' memory of nonsense syllables, have melted away almost as fast as the cookies themselves?) Or was the information still intact but not *retrievable.*[2]

Sigmund Freud might have argued that our memory systems self-censored this information. He proposed that we **repress** painful or unacceptable memories to protect our self-concept and to minimize anxiety. But the repressed memory lingers, he believed, and can be retrieved by some later cue or during therapy. Repression was central to Freud's psychoanalytic theory and remains a popular idea. Indeed, many people, including many clinicians, continue to believe that people repress their traumatic memories (Otgaar et al., 2021; Wake et al., 2020). However, memory experts think repression rarely, if ever, occurs (Patihis et al., 2021). Consider the words people later remember. People who have experienced sexual assault, for example, succeed in forgetting neutral words *(salt, plant)*, but they struggle to forget trauma-related words *(intercourse, assault)* (Blix & Brennen, 2011). Trauma releases stress hormones, which cause trauma survivors to attend to and remember the threat (Quaedflieg & Schwabe, 2017). Thus, people often have intrusive, persistent memories of the very same traumatic experiences they would most like to forget (Marks et al., 2018).

RETRIEVAL PRACTICE

RP-1 What are three ways we forget, and how does each of these happen?

RP-2 Freud believed (though many researchers doubt) that we ______ unacceptable memories to minimize anxiety.

ANSWERS IN APPENDIX E

repression in psychoanalytic theory, the basic defense mechanism that banishes from consciousness anxiety-arousing thoughts, feelings, and memories.

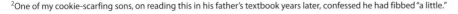

[2]One of my cookie-scarfing sons, on reading this in his father's textbook years later, confessed he had fibbed "a little."

Memory Construction Errors

LOQ 26-2 How do misinformation, imagination, and source amnesia influence our memory construction? How do we decide whether a memory is real or false?

Nearly two-thirds of Americans agree: "Human memory works like a video camera, accurately recording the events we see and hear so that we can review and inspect them later" (Simons & Chabris, 2011). Actually, memory is not so precise. Like scientists who infer a dinosaur's appearance from its remains, we infer our past from stored information, plus what we later imagined, expected, saw, and heard. Memories are constructed: We don't just retrieve memories, we reweave them.

Our memories are like Wikipedia pages, capable of constant revision. When we "replay" a memory, we often replace the original with a slightly modified version, rather like what happens in the telephone game, as a whispered message gets progressively altered when passed from person to person (Hardt et al., 2010). Memory researchers call this **reconsolidation** (Elsey et al., 2018). So, in a sense, said Joseph LeDoux (2009), "your memory is only as good as your last memory. The fewer times you use it, the more pristine it is." This means that, to some degree, "all memory is false" (Bernstein & Loftus, 2009).

"Our memories are flexible and superimposable, a panoramic blackboard with an endless supply of chalk and erasers." — Elizabeth Loftus and Katherine Ketcham, *The Myth of Repressed Memory*, 1994

Despite knowing all this, I [DM] rewrote my own past at an international conference, where memory researcher Elizabeth Loftus (2012) spoke. Loftus showed attendees a handful of individual faces that we were later to identify, as if in a police lineup. She then showed us some pairs of faces—one face we had seen earlier and one we had not—and asked us to identify the one we had seen. But one pair she had slipped in included *two* new faces, one of which was rather *like* a face we had seen earlier. Most of us understandably but wrongly identified this face as one we had previously seen. To climax the demonstration, she showed us the originally seen face and the previously chosen wrong face and asked us to choose the original face we had seen. Again, most of us picked the wrong face! As a result of our memory reconsolidation, we—an audience of psychologists who should have known better—had replaced the original memory with a false memory.

Neuroscientists are identifying relevant brain regions and neurochemicals that help or hinder memory consolidation (Bang et al., 2018). And clinical researchers have been experimenting. They ask people to recall a traumatic or negative experience and then disrupt the reconsolidation of that memory with a drug (such as propranolol), a brief, painless electroconvulsive shock, or novel distracting images (Phelps & Hofmann, 2019; Scully et al., 2017; Treanor et al., 2017). Someday it might become possible to use memory reconsolidation to erase specific traumatic memories. Would you wish to do this if you could? If brutally assaulted, would you welcome having your memory of the attack and its associated fears deleted?

Misinformation and Imagination Effects

In more than 200 experiments involving more than 20,000 people, Loftus has shown how eyewitnesses reconstruct their memories after a crime or accident. In one classic study, two groups of people watched a traffic accident film clip and then answered questions about what they had seen (Loftus & Palmer, 1974). Those asked, "About how fast were the cars going when they *smashed* into each other?" gave higher speed estimates than those asked, "About how fast were the cars going when they *hit* each other?" A week later, when asked whether they recalled seeing any broken glass, people who had heard *smashed* were more than twice as likely to report seeing glass fragments (**FIGURE 26.6**). In fact, the film showed no broken glass.

In many follow-up experiments worldwide, others have witnessed an event, received or not received misleading information about it, and then taken a memory test. The repeated result is a **misinformation effect**: After exposure to subtly misleading information, we may confidently misremember what we've seen or heard (Anglada-Tort et al., 2019; Loftus et al., 1992). Across studies, about half of people show some vulnerability to the misinformation effect (Brewin & Andrews, 2017; Scoboria et al., 2017). A yield sign becomes a stop sign, hammers become screwdrivers, Coke cans become peanut

reconsolidation a process in which previously stored memories, when retrieved, are potentially altered before being stored again.

misinformation effect occurs when a memory has been corrupted by misleading information.

Leading question:
"About how fast were the cars going when they smashed into each other?"
Image of actual accident
Memory construction

FIGURE 26.6
Memory construction

cans, breakfast cereal becomes eggs, and a clean-shaven man morphs into a man with a mustache. These false memories wither away once the trickster researchers *debrief* research participants, revealing that the study's purpose was to demonstrate the human mind's built-in photo-editing software (Murphy et al., 2020).

So powerful is the misinformation effect that it can influence later attitudes and behaviors (Bernstein & Loftus, 2009). One experiment falsely suggested to some Dutch university students that, as children, they became ill after eating spoiled egg salad (Geraerts et al., 2008). After absorbing that suggestion, they were less likely to eat egg salad sandwiches, both immediately and 4 months later.

Even repeatedly *imagining* nonexistent actions and events can create false memories. In real life, some people, after suggestive interviews, have even vividly recalled murders or other crimes they didn't commit (Aviv, 2017; Shaw, 2018; Wade et al., 2018).

"Memory is insubstantial. Things keep replacing it. Your batch of snapshots will both fix and ruin your memory . . . . You can't remember anything from your trip except the wretched collection of snapshots." —Annie Dillard, "To Fashion a Text," 1988

Misinformation and imagination effects occur partly because visualizing something and actually perceiving it activate similar brain areas (Gonsalves et al., 2004). Imagined events also later seem more familiar, and familiar things seem more real. The more vividly we can imagine things, the more likely they are to become memories (Loftus, 2001; Porter et al., 2000). Telling lies can likewise alter people's memories of the truth (Otgaar & Baker, 2018). Fibbing feeds falsehoods.

In experiments, researchers have altered photos from a family album to show some family members taking a hot-air balloon ride. After viewing these photos (rather than photos showing just the balloon), children reported more false memories of the balloon ride and indicated high confidence in those memories. *Imagination inflation* was evident several days later, when they reported even richer details of their false memories (Strange et al., 2008; Wade et al., 2002). In British and Canadian university surveys, nearly one-fourth of students have reported personal memories that they later realized were not accurate (Foley, 2015; Mazzoni et al., 2010). *The bottom line:* Don't believe everything you remember.

Evan Agostini/Invision/AP Photo

FEDERAL
MF 56401232 A
F6
THIS NOTE IS LEGAL TENDER FOR ALL DEBTS, PUBLIC AND PRIVATE
10
TEN
HAMILTON
YamabikaY/Shutterstock

Was Alexander Hamilton a U.S. president? Sometimes our mind tricks us into misremembering dates, places, and names. This often happens because we misuse familiar information. In one study, many Americans mistakenly recalled Alexander Hamilton—whose face appears on the U.S. $10 bill, and who is the subject of Lin-Manuel Miranda's popular Broadway musical—as a U.S. president (Roediger & DeSoto, 2016).

source amnesia faulty memory for how, when, or where information was learned or imagined. (Also called *source misattribution.*) Source amnesia, along with the misinformation effect, is at the heart of many false memories.

déjà vu that eerie sense that "I've experienced this before." Cues from the current situation may unconsciously trigger retrieval of an earlier experience.

Source Amnesia

What is the frailest part of a memory? Its source. An example: On a recent anniversary of the 9/11 terrorist attack, I [DM] mentioned to my wife my vivid memory of our Manhattan daughter's call as she witnessed—while we talked—the horror of the second tower's collapse. But no, replied my wife, whose memory is usually far more reliable than mine: "She made that call to *me*."

Clearly, one of us had reported the call to the other, who was now misattributing the source. ("I was definitely speaking to Dad," our daughter later informed us, triggering a smug smile from her error-prone father.) We may cite a statistic when arguing a point but be unable to recall where we read or heard it. We may dream an event and later be unsure whether it really happened. We may tell a friend some gossip, only to learn we got the news from that friend. Famed child psychologist Jean Piaget was startled as an adult to learn that a vivid, detailed memory from his childhood—a nursemaid's thwarting his kidnapping—was utterly false. He apparently constructed the memory from repeatedly hearing the story (which his nursemaid, after undergoing a religious conversion, later confessed had never happened). In attributing his "memory" to his own experiences, rather than to his nursemaid's stories, Piaget exhibited **source amnesia** (also called *source misattribution*). Misattribution is at the heart of many false memories. Authors, songwriters, and comedians sometimes suffer from it. They think an idea came from their own creative imagination, when in fact they are unintentionally plagiarizing something they earlier read or heard.

Source amnesia also helps explain **déjà vu** (French for "already seen"). Two-thirds of us have experienced this fleeting, eerie sense that "I've been in this exact situation before." The key to déjà vu seems to be familiarity with a stimulus coupled with uncertainty about where we encountered it before (Cleary & Claxton, 2018; Urquhart et al., 2018). Normally, we experience a feeling of *familiarity* (thanks to temporal lobe processing) before we consciously remember details (thanks to hippocampus and frontal lobe processing). When these functions (and brain regions) are out of sync, we may experience a feeling of familiarity without conscious recall. Our amazing brains try to make sense of such an improbable situation, and we get an eerie feeling that we're reliving some earlier part of our life. Our source amnesia forces us to do our best to make sense of an odd moment.

"Do you ever get that strange feeling of vujà dé? Not déjà vu; vujà dé. It's the distinct sense that, somehow, something just happened that has never happened before. Nothing seems familiar. And then suddenly the feeling is gone. Vujà dé." —Comedian George Carlin, *Funny Times*, December 2001

Discerning True and False Memories

Since memory is reconstruction as well as reproduction, we can't be sure whether a memory is real by how real it feels. Much as perceptual illusions may seem like real perceptions, unreal memories *feel* like real memories. Because the misinformation effect and source amnesia happen outside our awareness, it is hard to separate false memories from real ones (Schooler et al., 1986). You can likely recall describing a childhood experience to a friend and filling in memory gaps with reasonable guesses and assumptions. We all do it. After more retellings, those guessed details—now absorbed into your memory—may feel as real as if you had actually experienced them (Roediger et al., 1993). False memories, like fake diamonds, seem so real.

False memories can be persistent, especially when they align with our beliefs. Such was the case when, in one large experiment, Irish people retained inaccurate memories of false news related to Ireland's 2018 abortion referendum—especially when the false news supported their own views (Murphy et al., 2019).

False memories often retain a false association. Imagine that we were to read aloud a list of words, such as *candy, sugar, honey,* and *taste.* Later, we ask you to recognize the presented words from a larger list. If you are at all like the people tested by Henry Roediger and Kathleen McDermott (1995), you would err three out of four times—by falsely remembering a nonpresented similar word, such as *sweet.* We more easily remember the gist than the words themselves.

False memories are socially contagious. When we hear others falsely remember events, we tend to make the same memory mistakes (Roediger et al., 2001). We get confused about where we originally learned about the false event—*Did I already know that or am I learning it from others?*—and adopt others' false memories (Hirst & Echterhoff, 2012). It's easy to see how false memories can spread as online misinformation.

Memory construction errors also help explain why some people have been sent to prison for crimes they never committed. Of 375 people (60 percent of whom were African American) who were later proven not guilty by DNA testing, 69 percent had been convicted because of faulty eyewitness identification (Innocence Project, 2021; Wells, 2020). It explains why "hypnotically refreshed" memories of crimes so easily incorporate errors, some of which may originate with the hypnotist's leading questions *(Did you hear loud noises?)*. Memory construction errors also seem to be at work in many "recovered" memories of childhood abuse. (See Thinking Critically About: Can Memories of Childhood Sexual Abuse Be Repressed and Then Recovered?)

Eyewitness accuracy is also influenced by our tendency to recall faces of our own race more accurately than faces of other races (see the Social Psychology modules' discussion of the *other-race effect*). Among criminal suspects exonerated with DNA evidence after eyewitness misidentification, more than 40 percent were falsely accused after a cross-racial misidentification (Innocence Project, 2021).

Memory construction errors explain why dating partners now in love *over*estimate their first impressions of one another *(It was love at first sight)*, while those who have broken up *under*estimate their earlier liking *(We never really clicked)* (McFarland & Ross, 1987). When we love someone, our memory extinguishes the negative and shines a light on the positive (Cortes et al., 2018). And it explains why people asked how they felt 10 years ago about marijuana or gender issues recalled attitudes closer to their current views than to the views they had actually reported a decade earlier (Markus, 1986). In one experiment, students who chose to write an essay supporting a higher tuition policy constructed a false memory of previously supporting the policy, despite initially opposing it (Rodriguez & Strange, 2015). People tend to recall having always felt as they feel today (Mazzoni & Vannucci, 2007). As George Vaillant (1977, p. 197) noted after following adult lives through time, "It is all too common for caterpillars to become butterflies and then to maintain that in their youth they had been little butterflies. Maturation makes liars of us all."

ASK YOURSELF

Think of a memory you frequently recall. How might you have changed it without conscious awareness?

Children's Eyewitness Recall

LOQ 26-4 How reliable are young children's eyewitness descriptions?

If memories can be sincere, yet sincerely wrong, how can jurors decide cases in which children's memories of sexual abuse are the only evidence? "It would be truly awful to ever lose sight of the enormity of child abuse," observed Stephen Ceci (1993). Yet Ceci and Maggie Bruck's (1993, 1995) studies of children's memories made them aware of how easily children's memories can err. For example, they asked 3-year-olds to show on anatomically correct dolls where a pediatrician had touched them. Of the children who had not received genital examinations, 55 percent pointed to either genital or anal areas.

The researchers also studied the effect of suggestive interviewing techniques (Bruck & Ceci, 1999, 2004). In one experiment, children chose a card from a deck containing events that, according to their parents, had and had not happened. An adult then asked them a question about the event on the card—for example, "Think real hard, and tell me if this ever happened to you. Can you remember going to the hospital with a mousetrap on your finger?" In subsequent interviews, the same adult repeatedly asked the children to think about the same events, both real and fictitious. After 10 weeks of this, a new adult asked the original question: "Can you remember going to the hospital with a mousetrap on your finger?" The stunning result: 58 percent of preschoolers produced false (often vivid) stories regarding one or more events they had never experienced (Ceci et al., 1994). Here's one:

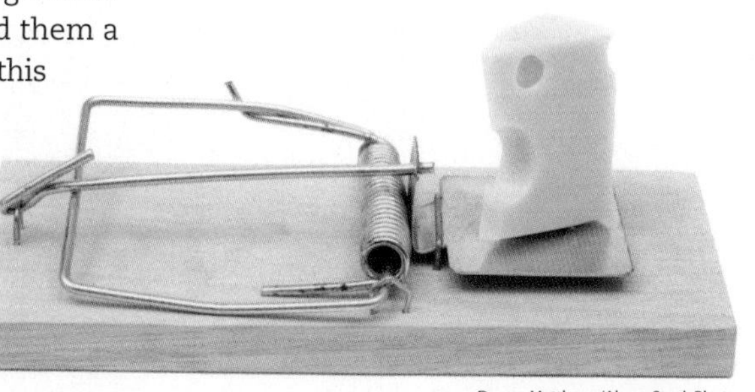

Darren Matthews/Alamy Stock Photo

> My brother Colin was trying to get Blowtorch [an action figure] from me, and I wouldn't let him take it from me, so he pushed me into the wood pile where the mousetrap was. And then my finger got caught in it. And then we went to the hospital, and my mommy, daddy, and Colin drove me there, to the hospital in our van, because it was far away. And the doctor put a bandage on this finger.

Given such detailed stories, professional psychologists who specialize in interviewing children could not reliably separate the real memories from the false ones. Nor could

LOQ 26-3 Why have reports of repressed and recovered memories been so hotly debated?

Thinking Critically About:

Can Memories of Childhood Sexual Abuse Be Repressed and Then Recovered?

Two Possible Tragedies:

1. People doubt childhood sexual abuse survivors who tell their secret.

2. Innocent people are falsely accused, as therapists prompt "recovered" memories of childhood sexual abuse:

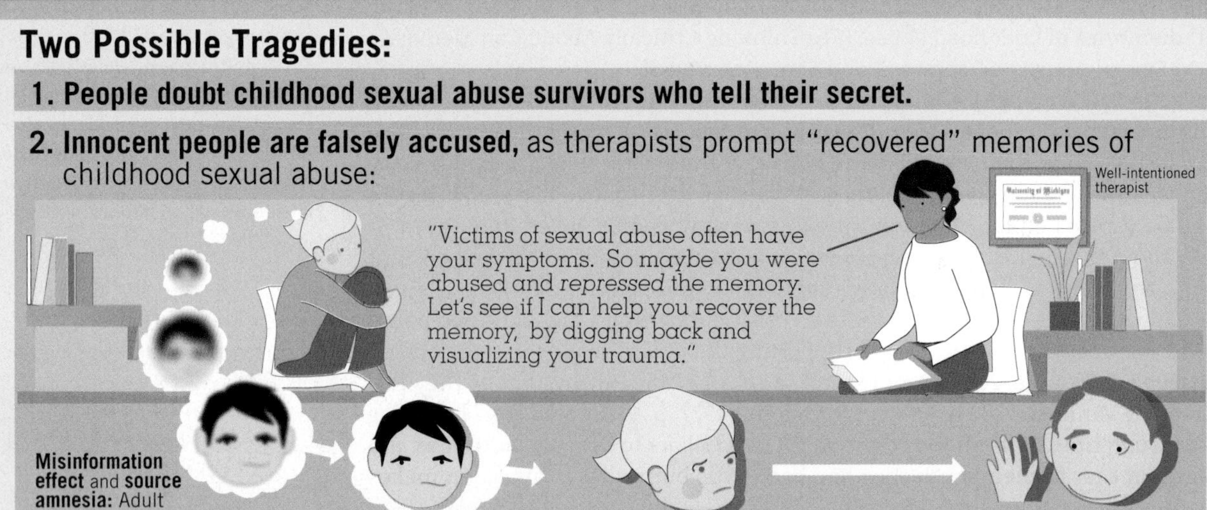

Well-intentioned therapist
"Victims of sexual abuse often have your symptoms. So maybe you were abused and *repressed* the memory. Let's see if I can help you recover the memory, by digging back and visualizing your trauma."

Misinformation effect and **source amnesia:** Adult client may form image of threatening person.

With *rehearsal* (repeated therapy sessions), the image grows more vivid.

Client is stunned, angry, and ready to confront or sue the remembered abuser.

Accused person is equally stunned and vigorously denies the accusation of long-ago abuse.

Professional organizations (including the American Medical, American Psychological, and American Psychiatric Associations) are working to find sensible common ground to resolve psychology's "memory war":[1]

- **Childhood sexual abuse happens** and can leave its victims at risk for problems ranging from sexual dysfunction to depression.[2] But there is no "survivor syndrome"—no group of symptoms that lets us spot victims of sexual abuse.[3]
- **Injustice happens.** Innocent people have been falsely convicted. And guilty people have avoided punishment by casting doubt on their truth-telling accusers.
- **Forgetting happens.** Children abused when very young may not have understood the meaning of their experience or remember it. Forgetting long-ago good and bad events is an ordinary part of everyday life.
- **Recovered memories are common.** Cued by a remark or an experience, we may recover pleasant or unpleasant memories of long-forgotten events. But does the unconscious mind forcibly repress painful experiences, and can these experiences be recovered by therapist-aided techniques?[4] Memories that surface naturally are more likely to be true.[5]
- **Memories of events before age 4 are unreliable.** Infantile amnesia results from not yet developed brain pathways. Most psychologists therefore doubt "recovered" memories of abuse during infancy.[6] The older a child was when suffering sexual abuse, and the more severe the abuse, the more likely it is to be remembered.[7]
- **Memories "recovered" under hypnosis are especially unreliable.**
- **Memories, whether real or false, can be emotionally upsetting.** What was born of mere suggestion can become, like an actual event, a stinging memory that drives bodily stress.[8]

Psychologists question whether *repression* ever occurs.
(See thePsychologicalDisorders modules for more on this concept, which is central to Freud's theory.)

Traumatic experiences (witnessing a loved one's murder, being terrorized by a hijacker or rapist, losing everything in a natural disaster) → **TYPICALLY LEAD TO** → **vivid, persistent, haunting memories[9]**

The Royal College of Psychiatrists Working Group on Reported Recovered Memories of Child Sexual Abuse advised that "when memories are 'recovered' after long periods of amnesia, particularly when extraordinary means were used to secure the recovery of memory, there is a high probability that the memories are false." [10]

1. Patihis et al., 2014. 2. Freyd et al., 2007. 3. Kendall-Tackett et al., 1993. 4. McNally & Geraerts, 2009. 5. Geraerts et al., 2007. 6. Gore-Felton et al., 2000; Knapp & VandeCreek, 2000. 7. Goodman et al., 2003. 8. McNally, 2003, 2007. 9. Porter & Peace, 2007; Goldfarb et al., 2019. 10. Brandon et al., 1998.

the children themselves. The above child, reminded that his parents had told him several times that the mousetrap incident never happened—that he had imagined it—protested, "But it really did happen. I remember it!" This misinformation effect is common. In one analysis of eyewitness data from over 20,000 participants, children regularly identified innocent suspects as guilty (Fitzgerald & Price, 2015). "[The] research," said Ceci (1993), "leads me to worry about the possibility of false allegations. It is not a tribute to one's scientific integrity to walk down the middle of the road if the data are more to one side."

With carefully trained interviewers, however, both adults and children can be accurate eyewitnesses (Wixted et al., 2018). When questioned about their experiences in neutral words they understand, children often accurately recall what happened and who did it (Brewin & Andrews, 2017; Goodman, 2006). When interviewers have used less suggestive, more effective techniques, even 4- to 5-year-old children have produced more accurate recall (Holliday & Albon, 2004; Pipe et al., 2004). Children are especially accurate when they haven't talked with involved adults prior to the interview, and when their disclosure was made in a first interview with a neutral person who asked nonleading questions.

"Older adults—especially those whose frontal lobe functioning has declined—are more susceptible than young adults to false memories. This makes older adults more vulnerable to scams, as when a caller falsely claims, "Remember that lottery you entered? You won $4.5 million! To process and deliver your winnings, this lottery requires you to send a $4,500 deposit" (Jacoby & Rhodes, 2006; Roediger & McDaniel, 2007).

RETRIEVAL PRACTICE

RP-3 What might life be like if we remembered all our waking experiences and all our dreams?

RP-4 Imagine being a jury member in a trial for a parent accused of sexual abuse based on a recovered memory. What insights from memory research should you share with the rest of the jury?

ANSWERS IN APPENDIX E

Improving Memory

LOQ 26-5 How can you use memory research findings to do better in this and other courses?

Biology's findings benefit medicine. Botany's findings benefit agriculture. So, too, can memory researchers' findings benefit education. And they can boost your performance in class and on tests. Here, for easy reference, is a summary of some research-based suggestions that can help you remember information when you need it. The SQ3R—Survey, Question, Read, Retrieve, Review—study technique used in this book incorporates several of these strategies.

Rehearse repeatedly. To thoroughly comprehend material, remember the *spacing effect*—use *distributed (spaced) practice*. To learn a concept, give yourself many separate study sessions. Take advantage of life's little intervals—riding a bus, walking across campus, waiting for class to start. New memories are weak; if you exercise them, they will strengthen. Experts recommend retrieving a to-be-remembered item three times before you stop studying it (Miyatsu et al., 2018). Reading complex material with minimal rehearsal yields little retention. Rehearsal and critical reflection help more. As the *testing effect* has shown, it pays to study actively. Mentally saying, writing, or typing information beats silently reading it (MacLeod & Bodner, 2017).

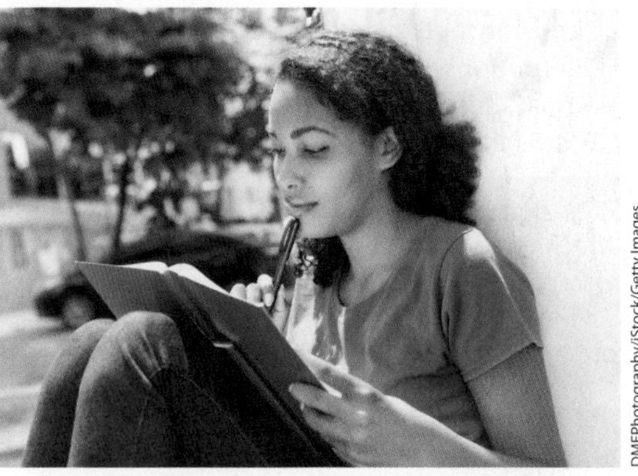

DMEPhotography/iStock/Getty Images

Thinking and memory Think actively as you read, by rehearsing and relating ideas, and by making the material personally meaningful. This will yield the best retention.

This *production effect* explains why we so often learn something best when teaching it, explaining it to ourselves, or rehearsing it out loud (Bisra et al., 2018; Forrin & Macleod, 2018; Koh et al., 2018).

The learning power of actively explaining or rehearsing information often goes unnoticed. One experiment randomly assigned students to experience either passive lectures or active learning. The students learned more in the active classroom—but *believed* they learned less (Deslauriers et al., 2019). So you might form a study group where you can verbalize your class material and reap the rewards of social support.

Laptop distraction? In one study of introductory psychology students in a large university course, the average student spent one-third of the class hour browsing online. More time spent online predicted poorer exam performance, even after controlling for aptitude and expressed interest (Ravizza et al., 2017).

Make the material meaningful. Space it. Rehearse it. And also personalize it. You can build a network of retrieval cues by forming as many associations as possible. Apply the concepts to your own life. Understand and organize information. Relate the material to what you already know or have experienced. As William James (1890) suggested, "Knit each new thing on to some acquisition already there." You can even try *drawing* the concept (Fernandes et al., 2018). Mindlessly repeating someone else's words without taking the time to really understand what they mean won't supply many retrieval cues. On an exam, you may find yourself stuck when a question uses phrasing different from the words you memorized.

Activate retrieval cues. Remember the importance of *context-dependent* and *state-dependent memory.* Mentally re-create the situation and the mood in which your original learning occurred. Jog your memory by allowing one thought to cue the next.

Use mnemonic devices. Make up a story that incorporates *vivid images* of the concepts. *Chunk* information. Create a memorable mnemonic. (Did you learn Never Eat Soggy Waffles for the four directions clockwise—*north, east, south,* and *west?*)

Minimize proactive and retroactive interference. Study before sleep. Do not schedule back-to-back study times for topics that are likely to interfere with each other, such as Spanish and French.

Sleep more. During sleep, the brain reorganizes and *consolidates* information for long-term memory. Sleeping more will help you remember what you've learned, and also what you're planning to do tomorrow (Cousins et al., 2021; Leong et al., 2020). Sleep deprivation disrupts this process (Frenda et al., 2014; Lo et al., 2016).

Test your own knowledge, both to rehearse it and to find out what you don't yet know. The testing effect is real, and it is powerful. Don't be lulled into overconfidence by your ability to *recognize* information. Test your *recall* using the periodic Retrieval Practice items, and the numbered Learning Objective and Module Test questions in the Review sections. Outline modules using a blank page. Define the terms and concepts listed at each module's end by yourself before turning back to their definitions. Take practice tests; the online resources that accompany many texts, including this text, are a good source.

ASK YOURSELF

Which three of these study and memory strategies will be most important for you to start using to improve your own learning and retention?

RETRIEVAL PRACTICE

RP-5 Which memory strategies can help you study smarter and retain more information?

ANSWERS IN APPENDIX E

26 REVIEW Forgetting, Memory Construction, and Improving Memory

LEARNING OBJECTIVES

Test Yourself Answer these repeated Learning Objective Questions on your own (before "showing" the answers here, or checking the answers in Appendix D) to improve your retention of the concepts (McDaniel et al., 2009, 2015).

LOQ 26-1 Why do we forget?

LOQ 26-2 How do misinformation, imagination, and source amnesia influence our memory construction? How do we decide whether a memory is real or false?

LOQ 26-3 Why have reports of repressed and recovered memories been so hotly debated?

LOQ 26-4 How reliable are young children's eyewitness descriptions?

LOQ 26-5 How can you use memory research findings to do better in this and other courses?

TERMS AND CONCEPTS TO REMEMBER

Test Yourself Write down the definition in your own words, then check your answer.

anterograde amnesia, p. 313
retrograde amnesia, p. 313
proactive interference, p. 316
retroactive interference, p. 316
repression, p. 317
reconsolidation, p. 318
misinformation effect, p. 318
source amnesia, p. 320
déjà vu, p. 320

MODULE TEST

Test Yourself Answer the following questions on your own first, then "show" the answers here, or check your answers in Appendix E.

1. When forgetting is due to encoding failure, information has not been transferred from
   a. the environment into sensory memory.
   b. sensory memory into long-term memory.
   c. long-term memory into short-term memory.
   d. short-term memory into long-term memory.
2. Ebbinghaus' forgetting curve shows that after an initial decline, memory for novel information tends to
   a. increase slightly.
   b. decrease noticeably.
   c. decrease greatly.
   d. level off.
3. You will experience less ________ (proactive/retroactive) interference if you learn new material in the hour before sleep than you will if you learn it before turning to another subject.
4. Freud proposed that painful or unacceptable memories are blocked from consciousness through a mechanism called ________.
5. One reason false memories form is our tendency to fill in memory gaps with our reasonable guesses and assumptions, sometimes based on misleading information. This tendency is an example of
   a. proactive interference.
   b. the misinformation effect.
   c. retroactive interference.
   d. the forgetting curve.
6. Eliza's family loves to tell the story of how she "stole the show" as a 2-year-old, dancing at her aunt's wedding reception. Even though she was so young, Eliza says she can recall the event clearly. How might Eliza have formed this memory?
7. We may recognize a face at a social gathering but be unable to remember how we know that person. This is an example of ________ ________.
8. When a situation triggers the feeling that "I've been here before," you are experiencing ________ ________.
9. Children can be accurate eyewitnesses if
   a. interviewers give the children hints about what really happened.
   b. a neutral person asks nonleading questions soon after the event.
   c. the children have a chance to talk with involved adults before the interview.
   d. interviewers use precise technical and medical terms.
10. Memory researchers involved in the study of memories of abuse tend to *disagree* with some therapists about which of the following statements?
    a. Memories of events that happened before age 4 are not reliable.
    b. We tend to repress extremely upsetting memories.
    c. Memories can be emotionally upsetting.
    d. Sexual abuse happens.

CHAPTER
9
E+/Getty Images

Thinking and Language (Modules 27–28)

Throughout history, we humans have both celebrated our wisdom and bemoaned our foolishness. Shakespeare's Hamlet extolled the human species as "noble in reason! . . . infinite in faculties! . . . in apprehension how like a god!" But the poet T. S. Eliot was struck by "the hollow men . . . Headpiece filled with straw." Throughout this text, we likewise marvel at both our abilities and our errors.

We study the human brain — three pounds of tissue the size of a head of lettuce, yet containing staggeringly complex circuitry. We appreciate the amazing abilities of newborns. We marvel at our visual system, which converts physical stimuli into nerve impulses, distributes them for parallel processing, and reassembles them into colorful perceptions. We ponder our memory's enormous capacity, and the ease with which our two-track mind processes information, with and without our awareness. Little wonder that our species has had the collective genius to invent the camera, the car, and the computer; to unlock the atom and modify our genetic code; to travel out to space and into our brain's depths.

Yet we also see that in some other ways, we are less than noble in reason. Our species is kin to the other animals, influenced by the same principles that produce learning in rats and pigeons. We note that we not-always-wise humans are easily deceived by perceptual illusions, misinformation, and false memories.

In Modules 27 and 28, we encounter further instances of these two aspects of the human condition—the rational and the irrational. We will first consider *thinking*: how we use—and sometimes ignore or misuse—information about the world around us (Module 27). And we will look at our gift for *language* and consider how and why it develops (Module 28). Finally, we will reflect on how deserving we are of our species name, *Homo sapiens*—"wise human."

MODULE 27 Thinking

How do we use—and sometimes ignore or misuse—information about the world around us as we solve problems, make judgments, and find creative solutions? Do other species share our cognitive skills?

cognition all the mental activities associated with thinking, knowing, remembering, and communicating.

metacognition cognition about our cognition; keeping track of and evaluating our mental processes.

concept a mental grouping of similar objects, events, ideas, or people.

prototype a mental image or best example of a category. Matching new items to a prototype provides a quick and easy method for sorting items into categories (as when comparing feathered creatures to a prototypical bird, such as a crow).

Concepts

LEARNING OBJECTIVE QUESTION LOQ **27-1** What are *cognition* and *metacognition*, and what are the functions of concepts?

Psychologists who study **cognition** focus on the mental activities associated with thinking, knowing, remembering, and communicating information. One of these activities is **metacognition**. Metacognition is cognition about cognition, or thinking about our thinking. Students who use metacognition—who monitor and evaluate their learning—perform better academically (de Boer et al., 2018). (To improve your grades, it helps to figure out what you *don't* know. The LearningCurve adaptive quizzing available with this text can help.)

At a basic level, we form **concepts**—mental groupings of similar objects, events, ideas, or people. The concept *chair* includes many items—a baby's high chair, a reclining chair, and a dentist's chair—all for sitting. Concepts simplify our thinking. Imagine life without them. We could not ask a child to "throw the ball" because there would be no concept of *throw* or *ball*. We could not say "I want to earn money" because people aren't born with a concept of *earn* or *money*. Concepts, such as *ball* and *money*, give us much information with little cognitive effort.

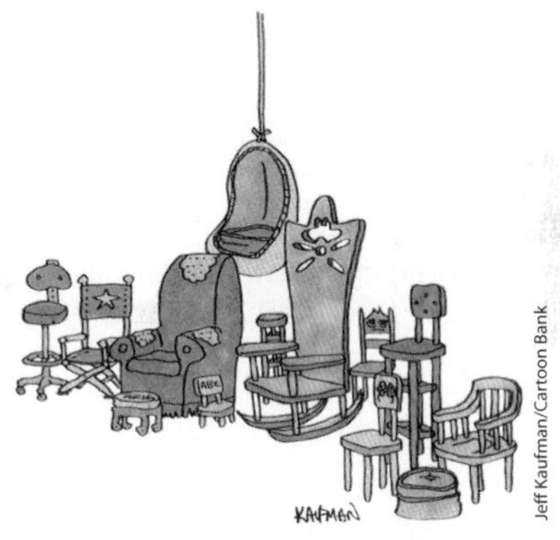
KAUFMAN
Jeff Kaufman/Cartoon Bank

"Attention, everyone! I'd like to introduce the newest member of our family."

We often form our concepts by developing a **prototype**—a mental image or best example of a category (Rosch, 1978). People more quickly agree that "a crow is a bird" than that "a penguin is a bird." For most of us, the crow is the birdier bird; it more closely resembles our *bird* prototype. When something closely matches our prototype of a concept, we more readily recognize it as an example of the concept.

When we categorize people, we mentally shift them toward our category prototypes. Such was the experience of Belgian students who viewed ethnically blended faces. When viewing a blended face in which 70 percent of the features were prototypically White and 30 percent were Asian, the students categorized the face as White (**FIGURE 27.1**). Later, as their memory shifted toward the White prototype, they were more

FIGURE 27.1
Categorizing faces influences recollection Shown a face that was 70 percent White, people tended to classify the person as White and to recollect the face as more White than it was. (Re-creation of experiment courtesy of Olivier Corneille.)

90% WH

80% WH

70% WH

60% WH

50%/50%

60% AS

70% AS

80% AS
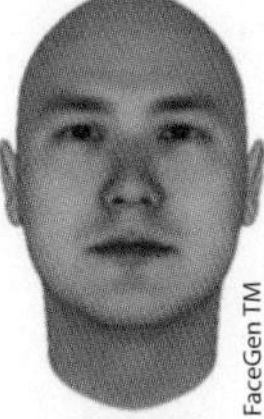
90% AS

FaceGen TM

algorithm a methodical, logical rule, or procedure that guarantees solving a particular problem. Contrasts with the usually speedier—but also more error-prone—use of *heuristics*.

heuristic a simple thinking strategy—a mental shortcut—that often allows us to make judgments and solve problems efficiently; usually speedier but also more error-prone than an *algorithm*.

insight a sudden realization of a problem's solution; contrasts with strategy-based solutions.

likely to remember an 80 percent White face than the 70 percent White face they had actually seen (Corneille et al., 2004). Likewise, if shown a 70 percent Asian face, they later remembered a more prototypically Asian face. So, too, with gender: People who viewed 70 percent male faces later misremembered them as even more prototypically male (Huart et al., 2005).

Move away from our prototypes, and category boundaries may blur. Is a tomato a fruit? Is a 17-year-old a girl or a woman? Is a whale a fish or a mammal? Because a whale fails to match our *mammal* prototype, we are slower to recognize it as a mammal. Similarly, when symptoms don't fit one of our disease prototypes, we are slow to perceive an illness (Bishop, 1991). People whose heart attack symptoms (shortness of breath, exhaustion, a dull weight in the chest) don't match their *heart attack* prototype (sharp chest pain) may not seek help. And when behaviors don't fit our *discrimination* prototypes, of White against Black, men against women, young against old, we often fail to notice prejudice. People more easily detect men's prejudice against women than women's prejudice against men or women's prejudice against other women (Cunningham et al., 2009; Inman & Baron, 1996). Although concepts speed and guide our thinking, they don't always make us wise.

Problem Solving: Strategies and Obstacles

LOQ 27-2 What cognitive strategies assist our problem solving, and what obstacles hinder it?

One tribute to our rationality is our problem-solving skill. What's the best route around this traffic jam? How should we handle a friend's criticism? How, without our keys, can we get into the house?

Some problems we solve through *trial and error*. Thomas Edison tried thousands of light bulb filaments before stumbling upon one that worked. For other problems, we use **algorithms**, step-by-step procedures that guarantee a solution. But step-by-step algorithms can be laborious and exasperating. To find a word using the 10 letters in *SPLOYOCHYG*, for example, you could try each letter in each of the 10 positions—907,200 permutations in all. Rather than give you a computing brain the size of a beach ball, nature resorts to **heuristics**, simpler thinking strategies. Thus, you might reduce the number of options in the *SPLOYOCHYG* example by grouping letters that often appear together (*CH* and *GY*) and excluding rare letter combinations (such as *YY*). By using heuristics and then applying trial and error, you may hit on the answer. Have you guessed it?[1]

Sometimes, we puzzle over a problem and the pieces suddenly fall together in a flash of **insight**—an abrupt, true-seeming, and often satisfying solution (Topolinski & Reber, 2010; Webb et al., 2019). Ten-year-old Johnny Appleton had one of these Aha! moments and solved a problem that had stumped construction workers: how to rescue a young robin from a narrow 30-inch-deep hole in a cement-block wall. The child's solution: Slowly pour in sand, giving the bird enough time to keep its feet on top of the constantly rising pile (Ruchlis, 1990). Insights aren't always perfect, but they often lead to correct solutions (Danek & Salvi, 2020).

What happens in the brain when people experience an Aha! moment? Brain scans show bursts of activity associated with sudden flashes of insight (Kounios & Beeman, 2014). In one study, researchers asked people to think of a word that forms a compound word or phrase with each of three other words in a set (such as *pine, crab,* and *sauce*) and to press a button to sound a bell when they knew the answer. (Need a hint? The word is a fruit.[2]) A sudden Aha! insight led to about half the solutions. Before the Aha! moment, the problem solvers' frontal lobes (involved in focusing attention) were active. At the instant of discovery, there was a burst of activity in the right temporal lobe, just above the ear (**FIGURE 27.2**).

FIGURE 27.2
The Aha! moment A burst of right temporal lobe activity accompanied insight solutions to word problems (Jung-Beeman et al., 2004). The red dots designate EEG electrodes. The light gray lines show the distribution of high-frequency activity accompanying insight. The insight-related activity is centered in the right temporal lobe (yellow area).

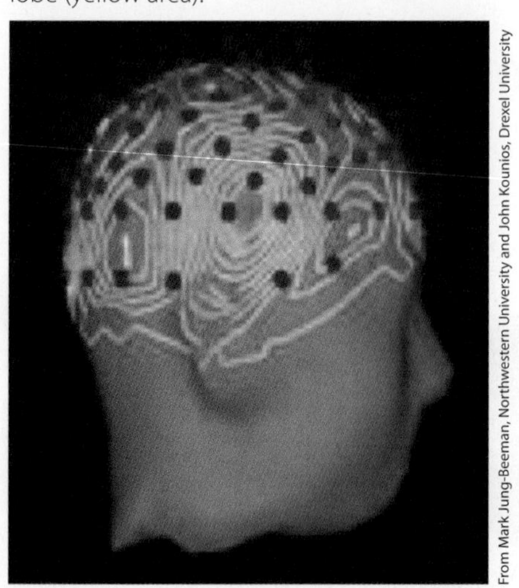

From Mark Jung-Beeman, Northwestern University and John Kounios, Drexel University

[1] Answer to SPLOYOCHYG anagram: PSYCHOLOGY.
[2] The word is *apple*: pineapple, crabapple, applesauce.

Insight often strikes suddenly, creating a happy sense of satisfaction (Knoblich & Oellinger, 2006; Metcalfe, 1986). When the answer pops into mind *(apple!)*, we feel a happy sense of satisfaction. The joy of a joke may similarly lie in our sudden comprehension of an unexpected ending or a double meaning (as "aha" becomes "ha ha"): "When a clock is hungry, it goes back 4 seconds" or "The only thing flat-earthers fear is sphere itself." The grim reaper also strikes with a surprise ending: "You don't need a parachute to skydive. You only need a parachute to skydive twice."

UNPLEASANT TRUTHS
COMFORTING LIES
S.H. Chambers

Insightful as we are, other cognitive tendencies may lead us astray. We seek news that not only informs us but also affirms us. **Confirmation bias**, for example, leads us to seek evidence *for* our ideas more eagerly than we seek evidence *against* them (Klayman & Ha, 1987; Skov & Sherman, 1986). In a classic study, Peter Wason (1960) gave British university students a set of three numbers (2-4-6) and told them the series was based on a rule. Their task was to guess the rule. (It was simple: any three ascending numbers.) Before submitting answers, students generated their own three-number sets, and Wason told them whether their sets conformed to his rule. Once *certain* they had the rule, they could announce it. The result? Most students formed a wrong idea *("Maybe it's counting by twos")* and then searched *only* for confirming evidence (by testing 6-8-10, 100-102-104, and so forth). Seldom right but never in doubt.

"The human understanding, when any proposition has been once laid down . . . forces everything else to add fresh support and confirmation." —Francis Bacon, *Novum Organum*, 1620

In real life, having formed a belief—that people can (or cannot) change their sexual orientation, that gun control fails (or does not fail) to save lives—we prefer information that supports our belief. And once we get hung up on an incorrect view of a problem, it's hard to approach it from a different angle. This obstacle to problem solving is called **fixation**, an inability to come to a fresh perspective. See if fixation prevents you from solving the matchstick problem in FIGURE 27.3. (For the solution, see FIGURE 27.4.)

A prime example of fixation is **mental set**, our tendency to approach a problem with the mindset of what has worked for us previously. Indeed, solutions that worked in the past often do work on new problems. Consider:

Given the sequence O-T-T-F-?-?-?, what are the final three letters?

Most people have difficulty recognizing that the three final letters are F(ive), S(ix), and S(even). But solving this problem may make the next one easier:

Given the sequence *J-F-M-A-?-?-?*, what are the final three letters? (If you don't get this one, ask yourself what month it is.)

As a *perceptual set* predisposes what we perceive, a mental set predisposes how we think. Sometimes this can be an obstacle to problem solving, as when our mental set from our past experiences with matchsticks predisposes us to arrange them in two dimensions.

Macmillan Learning

FIGURE 27.3
The matchstick problem How would you arrange six matches to form four equilateral triangles?

Forming Good (and Bad) Decisions and Judgments

LOQ 27-3 What is *intuition*, and how can the representativeness and availability heuristics influence our decisions and judgments?

When making each day's hundreds of judgments and decisions *(Should I take a jacket? Can I trust this person? Is that a friendly dog?)*, we seldom take the time and effort to reason systematically. We follow our **intuition**, our fast, automatic, unreasoned feelings and thoughts. After interviewing policy makers in government, business, and education, social psychologist Irving Janis (1986) concluded that they "often do not use a reflective problem-solving approach. How do they usually arrive at their decisions? If you ask, they are likely to tell you . . . they do it mostly by the *seat of their pants*."

Two Quick But Risky Shortcuts

When we need to make snap judgments, *heuristics* enable quick thinking that often serves us well (Gigerenzer, 2015). But as cognitive psychologists Amos Tversky and Daniel Kahneman (1974) showed, some intuitive mental shortcuts—the *representativeness* and *availability heuristics*—can lead even the smartest people into dumb decisions.

confirmation bias a tendency to search for information that supports our preconceptions and to ignore or distort contradictory evidence. 

fixation in cognition, the inability to see a problem from a new perspective; an obstacle to problem solving.

mental set a tendency to approach a problem in one particular way, often a way that has been successful in the past.

intuition an effortless, immediate, automatic feeling or thought, as contrasted with explicit, conscious reasoning.

representativeness heuristic judging the likelihood of events in terms of how well they seem to represent, or match, particular prototypes; may lead us to ignore other relevant information.

availability heuristic judging the likelihood of events based on their availability in memory; if instances come readily to mind (perhaps because of their vividness), we presume such events are common.

overconfidence the tendency to be more confident than correct—to overestimate the accuracy of our beliefs and judgments.

Macmillan Learning

"In creating these problems, we didn't set out to fool people. All our problems fooled us, too."—Amos Tversky (1985)

Carsten Rehder/KIEL/European Pressphoto Agency/Newscom

"Intuitive thinking [is] fine most of the time. . . . But sometimes that habit of mind gets us in trouble."—Daniel Kahneman (2005)

Few would have predicted Tversky and Kahneman's becoming friends and collaborators (Lewis, 2016; Sunstein & Thaler, 2016). When they met, Tversky was a war hero with a confident swagger who studied decision making; Kahneman was a chronic worrier who studied vision. Setting aside their differences, Tversky and Kahneman would sequester themselves in a small seminar room, where they argued, laughed, and ultimately changed the way that people view thinking and decision making (Dean & Ortoleva, 2019). Their joint efforts earned the ultimate award: a 2002 Nobel Prize. (Sadly, only Kahneman was alive to receive the honor.) As Kahneman wrote in a vignette for my [DM's] *Social Psychology* text, "Amos and I shared the wonder of together owning a goose that could lay golden eggs—a joint mind that was better than our separate minds."

"Kahneman and his colleagues and students have changed the way we think about the way people think." —American Psychological Association President Sharon Brehm, 2007

THE REPRESENTATIVENESS HEURISTIC To judge the likelihood of something by intuitively comparing it to particular prototypes is to use the **representativeness heuristic**. Imagine someone who is short, slim, and likes to read poetry. Is this person more likely to be an Ivy League university English professor or a truck driver (Nisbett & Ross, 1980)?

Many people guess English professor—because the person better fits their prototype of professor than of truck driver. In doing so, they fail to consider the *base rate* number of Ivy League English professors (fewer than 400) and truck drivers (3.5 million in the United States alone). Instead, they recall situations that confirm their professor prototype (Bordalo et al., 2021). Thus, even if the description is 50 times more typical of English professors than of truck drivers, the fact that there are about 7000 times more truck drivers means that the poetry reader is many times more likely to be a truck driver.

Some prototypes have social consequences. One mother of two Black and three White teens asked other parents: "Do store personnel follow your children when they are picking out their Gatorade flavors? They didn't follow my White kids. . . . When your kids trick-or-treat dressed as a ninja and a clown, do they get asked who they are with and where they live, door after door? My White kids didn't get asked" (Roper, 2016). If people have a prototype—a *stereotype*—of delinquent Black teens—they may unconsciously use the representativeness heuristic when judging individuals. The result is racial bias.

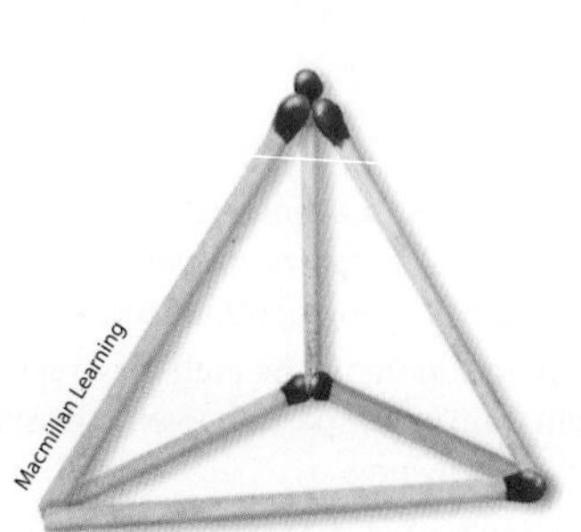

Macmillan Learning

FIGURE 27.4
Solution to the matchstick problem To solve this problem, you must view it from a new perspective, breaking the fixation of limiting solutions to two dimensions.

THE AVAILABILITY HEURISTIC The **availability heuristic** operates when we evaluate the commonality of an event *based on its mental availability*. Anything that makes information pop into mind—its vividness, recency, or distinctiveness—can make it seem commonplace. Exceptional happenings may, therefore, seem typical. Watching a horrific terrorist beheading online implants a fear of global terrorism that lingers for 2 or more years (Redmond et al., 2019). Sometimes photos—say, of terrified children separated from their parents at the U.S. border, or of the mother of seven children being appointed to the U.S. Supreme Court—can change thinking for years. As climate change has become more vividly associated with extreme weather—fires, floods, and hurricanes—public concern has risen. For worse or for better, the incidents that we see often overwhelm the larger realities we don't see.

The availability heuristic distorts our judgments of risks. Nonstop news coverage of the dangerous Covid-19 pandemic distorted young people's judgments of how Covid-19 might affect them. Asked whether they were worried about their health during the Covid-19 pandemic, younger (ages 18 to 29) respondents reported equal levels of worry as older respondents (ages 65 and older) (Rothwell, 2020). Yet Americans aged 18 to 29 were 180 times *less* likely to die from Covid-19 than were Americans aged 65 and older (CDC, 2021). (Younger adults were nonetheless well advised to protect themselves from contracting and spreading the virus to others.)

The bottom line: We often fear the wrong things (see Thinking Critically About: The Fear Factor).

"Don't believe everything you think."
—Bumper sticker

The lack of available images of a *future* climate change disaster—a climate crisis described by scientists as "Armageddon in slow motion"—has left some people unconcerned. Moreover, climate beliefs can shift with the day's hot or cold weather, which, though more cognitively available, tells us zilch about long-term planetary trends (Egan & Mullin, 2012; Kaufmann et al., 2017; Zaval et al., 2014). As Stephen Colbert (2014) tweeted, "Global warming isn't real because it was cold today! Also great news: World hunger is over because I just ate."

Over 40 nations have sought to harness the positive power of vivid, memorable images by putting eye-catching warnings and graphic photos on cigarette packages (Riordan, 2013). This campaign has worked because we reason emotionally (Huang et al., 2013). In 2015, a viral photo of a Syrian child lying dead on a beach had massive impact. Red Cross donations to Syrian refugees were 55 times greater in response to that photo than in response to "psychically numbing" statistics describing the hundreds of thousands of other refugee deaths (Slovic et al., 2017). Dramatic incidents make us gasp ("four deaths!"); probabilities we barely grasp ("per million"). It's so easy to scare people with a horrific happening and then harder to unscare them with representative data.

Emily Flake/Cartoon Stock

"Don't let this beautiful weather fool you into thinking everything's fine."

ASK YOURSELF

How has your family managed risk related to Covid-19? Have some of your fears been excessive, or have you not feared enough? How have heuristics influenced your thinking?

RETRIEVAL PRACTICE

RP-1 Why can news be described as "something that hardly ever happens"? How does knowing this help us assess our fears?

ANSWERS IN APPENDIX E

To offer a vivid depiction of climate crisis, Cal Tech scientists created and continue to update an interactive map of global temperatures since 1884 (see tinyurl.com/TempChange).

Overconfidence

LOQ 27-5 How are our decisions and judgments affected by overconfidence, belief perseverance, and framing?

Sometimes we are more confident than correct. When answering factual questions, such as "Is absinthe a liqueur or a precious stone?" only 60 percent of people in one study answered correctly. (It's a licorice-flavored liqueur.) Yet those answering felt, on average, 75 percent confident (Fischhoff et al., 1977). This tendency to overestimate the accuracy of our knowledge and judgments is **overconfidence**.

It is overconfidence that drives stockbrokers and investment managers to market their ability to outperform stock market averages—which, as a group, they cannot do (Malkiel, 2016). And it is overconfidence that so often leads us to succumb to a *planning fallacy* (Zauberman & Lynch, 2005). Students and others often expect to finish assignments ahead of schedule (Buehler et al., 1994, 2002). In fact, such projects generally take about twice the predicted time. Anticipating how much more time we will have next month, we happily accept invitations. And believing we'll surely have more money next year, we take out loans or buy on credit.

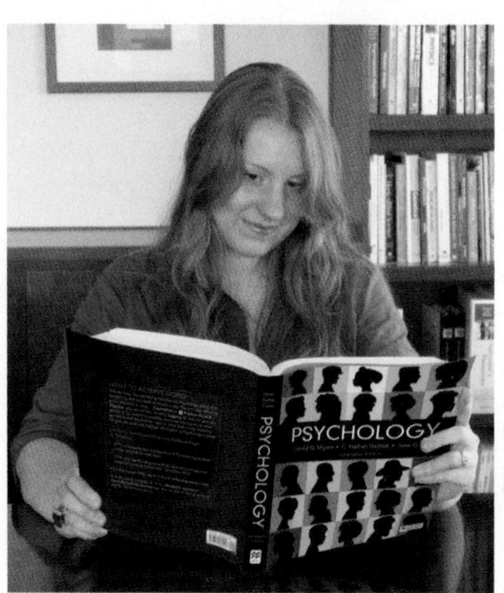
PSYCHOLOGY
PSYCHOLOGY
Bianca Moscatelli/Macmillan Learning

Predict your own behavior When will you finish reading this module?

Overconfidence—the bias that Kahneman (2015), if given a magic wand, would most like to eliminate—affects life-or-death decisions. History is full of leaders who, when faced with potential war, were more confident than correct. On December 4, 1941,

Thinking Critically About:
The Fear Factor

LOQ 27-4 What factors exaggerate our fear of unlikely events?

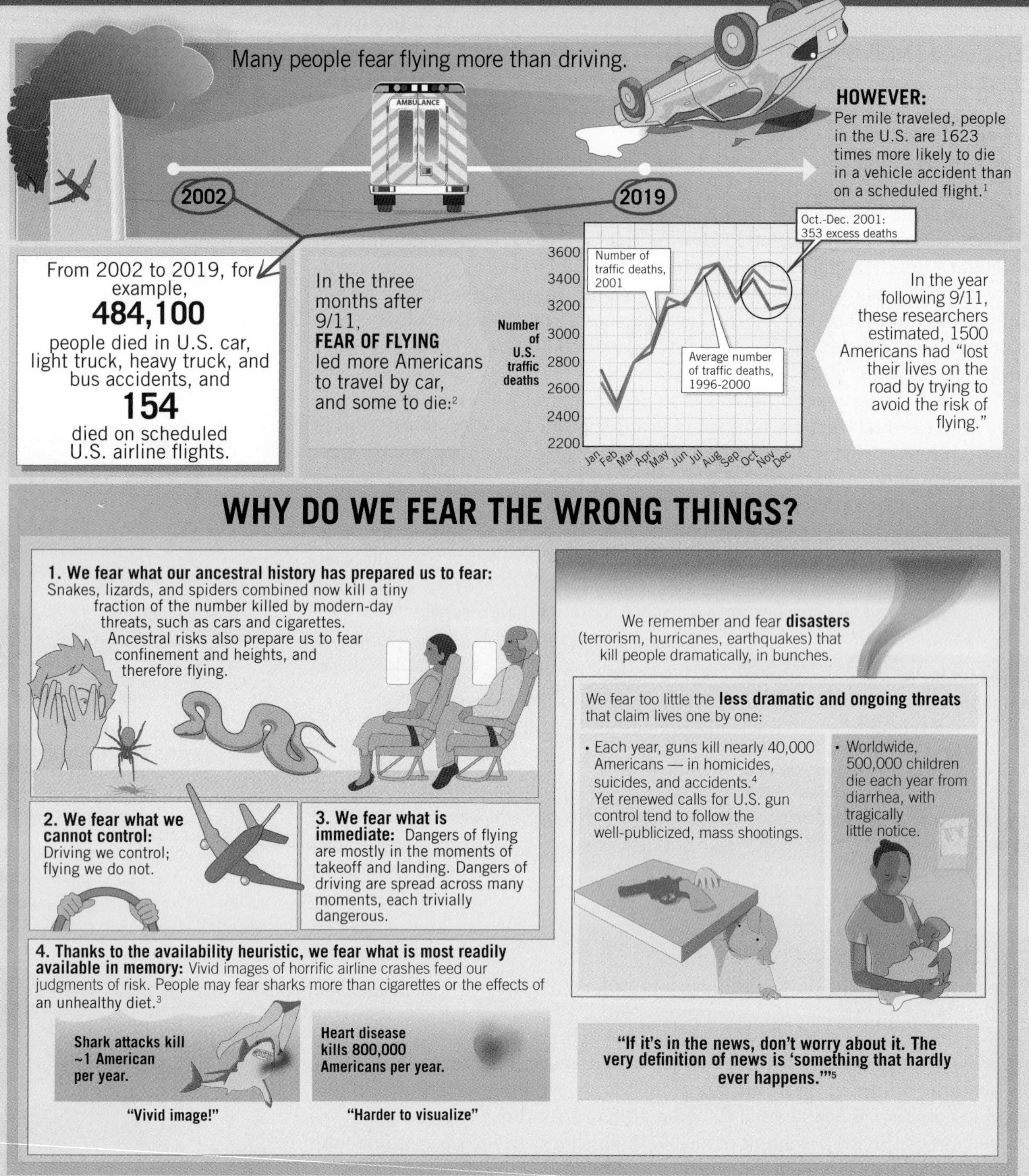

Many people fear flying more than driving.
AMBULANCE
HOWEVER:
Per mile traveled, people in the U.S. are 1623 times more likely to die in a vehicle accident than on a scheduled flight.[1]
2002
2019
From 2002 to 2019, for example,
484,100
people died in U.S. car, light truck, heavy truck, and bus accidents, and
154
died on scheduled U.S. airline flights.
In the three months after 9/11, FEAR OF FLYING led more Americans to travel by car, and some to die:[2]
Number of U.S. traffic deaths
3600
3400
3200
3000
2800
2600
2400
2200
Jan Feb Mar Apr May Jun Jul Aug Sep Oct Nov Dec
Number of traffic deaths, 2001
Average number of traffic deaths, 1996-2000
Oct.-Dec. 2001: 353 excess deaths
In the year following 9/11, these researchers estimated, 1500 Americans had "lost their lives on the road by trying to avoid the risk of flying."
WHY DO WE FEAR THE WRONG THINGS?
1. We fear what our ancestral history has prepared us to fear: Snakes, lizards, and spiders combined now kill a tiny fraction of the number killed by modern-day threats, such as cars and cigarettes. Ancestral risks also prepare us to fear confinement and heights, and therefore flying.
2. We fear what we cannot control: Driving we control; flying we do not.
3. We fear what is immediate: Dangers of flying are mostly in the moments of takeoff and landing. Dangers of driving are spread across many moments, each trivially dangerous.
4. Thanks to the availability heuristic, we fear what is most readily available in memory: Vivid images of horrific airline crashes feed our judgments of risk. People may fear sharks more than cigarettes or the effects of an unhealthy diet.[3]
Shark attacks kill ~1 American per year.
"Vivid image!"
Heart disease kills 800,000 Americans per year.
"Harder to visualize"
We remember and fear disasters (terrorism, hurricanes, earthquakes) that kill people dramatically, in bunches.
We fear too little the less dramatic and ongoing threats that claim lives one by one:
• Each year, guns kill nearly 40,000 Americans — in homicides, suicides, and accidents.[4] Yet renewed calls for U.S. gun control tend to follow the well-publicized, mass shootings.
• Worldwide, 500,000 children die each year from diarrhea, with tragically little notice.
"If it's in the news, don't worry about it. The very definition of news is 'something that hardly ever happens.'"[5]

1. National Safety Council, 2023; National Highway Traffic Safety Administration, 2021. 2. Gaissmaier & Gigerenzer, 2012; Gigerenzer, 2004, 2006. 3. Daley, 2011. 4. USA Facts, 2021. 5. Schneider, 2007.

"Hofstadter's Law: It always takes longer than you expect, even when you take into account Hofstadter's Law." — Douglas Hofstadter, *Gödel, Escher, Bach: The Eternal Golden Braid*, 1979

U.S. Secretary of the Navy Frank Knox said, "Whatever happens, the U.S. Navy is not going to be caught napping" (Warren, 2019). Three days later, the Japanese attacked Pearl Harbor, killing more than 2300 U.S. service members. In politics, overconfidence feeds extreme political views. In medicine, overconfidence can lead to incorrect diagnoses (Saposnik et al., 2016). One research team tested 743 U.S. federal intelligence analysts' ability to predict future events—predictions that typically are overconfident. Those whose predictions most often failed tended to be inflexible and closed-minded (Mellers et al., 2015).

Nevertheless, overconfidence sometimes has adaptive value. Believing that their decisions are right and they have time to spare, self-confident people tend to live more happily. They make tough decisions more easily, and they seem competent (Anderson et al., 2012). Given prompt and clear feedback, we can also learn to be more realistic about the accuracy of our judgments (Fischhoff, 1982). The wisdom to know when we know a thing and when we do not is born of experience.

J.A.K.

Jason Adam Katzenstein/Cartoon Stock

"Let me interrupt your expertise with my confidence."

Belief Perseverance

Our overconfidence is startling. Equally so is our **belief perseverance**—our tendency to stick to our beliefs, even when faced with evidence that disproves them. A classic study of belief perseverance engaged people with opposing views of capital punishment (Lord et al., 1979). After studying two supposedly new research findings, one supporting and the other refuting the claim that the death penalty deters crime, each side was more impressed by the study supporting its own beliefs. And each readily disputed the other study. Thus, showing the pro- and anti-capital-punishment groups the *same* mixed evidence actually *increased* their disagreement. Rather than using evidence to draw conclusions, they used their conclusions to assess evidence—a phenomenon also known as *motivated reasoning.*

"When you know a thing, to hold that you know it; and when you do not know a thing, to allow that you do not know it; this is knowledge." —Confucius (551–479 B.C.E.), *Analects*

In other studies and in everyday life, people have similarly welcomed belief-supportive logic and evidence—about climate change, same-sex marriage, or politics—while discounting challenging evidence (Friesen et al., 2015; Gampe et al., 2019; Sunstein et al., 2016). Often, prejudice persists. Beliefs persevere. It's hard to teach old dogma new tricks.

To rein in belief perseverance, a simple remedy exists: *Consider the opposite.* When the same researchers repeated the capital-punishment study, they asked some participants to be "as *objective* and *unbiased* as possible" (Lord et al., 1984). The plea did nothing to reduce biased evaluations of evidence. They also asked another group to consider "whether you would have made the same high or low evaluations had exactly the same study produced results on the *other* side of the issue." Having imagined and pondered *opposite* findings, these people became much less biased. Newer studies confirm the point: Considering opposing arguments reduces bias (Catapano et al., 2019; Van Boven et al., 2019).

Ellis Rosen/Cartoon Stock

"And in this corner, still undefeated, Frank's long-held beliefs."

Once beliefs take root, it takes more compelling evidence to change them than it did to create them. We often label evidence that contradicts our beliefs as "weak" (Anglin, 2019). Climate change skeptics, for example, tend to view evidence of the climate crisis as inaccurate or untrustworthy (Druckman & McGrath, 2019). As an old Chinese proverb says, "Two-thirds of what we see is behind our eyes."

The Effects of Framing

Framing—the way we present an issue—can be a powerful tool of persuasion for good or ill, as psychologists and economists have together learned. Long before the Covid-19 pandemic, Tversky and Kahneman (1981) asked people to consider a scenario: How should the United States prepare for the outbreak of an unusual disease that could kill 600 people? Participants strongly preferred solutions framed as *gains* ("200 people will be saved") rather than *losses* ("400 people will die.").

As a young scholar, behavioral economist Richard Thaler worked closely with cognitive psychologists Tversky and Kahneman. Thaler and others have shown how the framing of options can **nudge** people toward beneficial decisions (Benartzi et al., 2017; Daniels & Zlatev, 2019; Thaler & Sunstein, 2008).

- ***Healthier eating.*** Knowing that many people prefer tasty to healthy foods, researchers have nudged healthy choices with tasty-sounding food labels. The university dining hall turnips got chosen more when labeled "Herb n' Honey Balsamic Glazed Turnips" (Turnwald et al., 2019).
- ***Making moral decisions.*** Imagine an experimenter gives you $5.00 and asks how much (if any) you want to donate to charity, then asks, "What do you personally think is

belief perseverance the persistence of one's initial conceptions after the basis on which they were formed has been discredited.

framing the way an issue is posed; how an issue is framed can significantly affect decisions and judgments.

nudge framing choices in a way that encourages people to make beneficial decisions.

the morally right thing to do in this situation?" Researchers did just that and found that nudging people to take a moral mindset made them more generous, increasing donations by 44 percent (Capraro et al., 2019).

- ***Becoming an organ donor.*** In many countries, people renewing their driver's license can decide whether to be organ donors. Sometimes, the default option is *Yes,* but people can opt out. Nearly 100 percent of the people in opt-out countries have agreed to be donors. In countries where the default option is *No,* most do *not* agree to be donors (Hajhosseini et al., 2013; Johnson & Goldstein, 2003). One way or the other, the default option nudges people's organ donation choices.

The point to remember: Framing can nudge our attitudes and decisions.

The Perils and Powers of Intuition

LOQ 27-6 How do smart thinkers use intuition?

It's clear that very smart people can make not-so-smart judgments. So, are our heads indeed "filled with straw," as T. S. Eliot suggested? Good news: Cognitive scientists are also revealing intuition's powers.

- ***Intuition is recognition born of experience.*** It is implicit (unconscious) knowledge—what we've recorded in our brains but can't fully explain (Chassy & Gobet, 2011; Gore & Sadler-Smith, 2011). We see it in the smart and quick judgments of experienced nurses, firefighters, art critics, car mechanics, and athletes who react *without thinking.* Indeed, conscious thinking may disrupt well-practiced movements, leading skilled athletes to choke under pressure, as when shooting free throws (Beilock, 2010). And we would see this instant intuition in you, too, for anything in which you have developed knowledge based on experience.
- ***Intuition is usually adaptive.*** Our fast and frugal heuristics let us intuitively rely on learned associations that surface as gut feelings, right or wrong: Seeing a stranger who resembles someone who has harmed or threatened us previously, we may automatically react with distrust. Our intuition aids our survival, and it can also steer us toward more satisfying relationships: Newlyweds' implicit, gut-level attitudes toward their new spouse predict their future marital happiness (McNulty et al., 2017). Smart thinking often means having smart intuitions (Raoelison et al., 2020).
- ***Intuition is huge.*** Unconscious, automatic influences constantly affect our judgments (Custers & Aarts, 2010; Kihlstrom, 2019). Consider: Most people guess that the more complex the choice, the smarter it is to make decisions rationally rather than intuitively (Inbar et al., 2010). Actually, in making complex decisions, we sometimes benefit by letting our brain work on a problem without consciously thinking about it (Strick et al., 2010, 2011). In one series of experiments, three groups of people read complex information (for example, about apartments or European football matches). Those in the first group stated their preference immediately after reading information about four possible options. The second group, given several minutes to analyze the information, made slightly smarter decisions. But wisest of all, in several studies, were those in the third group, whose attention was distracted for a time, enabling their minds to engage in automatic, unconscious processing of the complex information. The practical lesson: Letting a problem incubate while we attend to other things can pay dividends (Dijksterhuis & Strick, 2016). Facing a difficult decision involving a lot of facts, we're wise to gather all the information we can and then say, "Give me some time to *not* think about this." Even sleeping on it can help. Thanks to our ever-active brain, nonconscious thinking (reasoning, problem solving, decision making, planning) can be surprisingly astute (Creswell et al., 2013; Hassin, 2013; Lin & Murray, 2015).

"The heart has its reasons which reason does not know." —Blaise Pascal, *Pensées,* 1670

Critics note that some studies have not found the supposed power of unconscious thought, and they remind us that deliberate, conscious thought also furthers smart thinking (Newell, 2015; Nieuwenstein et al., 2015; Phillips et al., 2016). In challenging situations—making the best chess move, distinguishing between false and real news headlines—deliberate thinking beats instant intuition (Bago et al., 2020; Moxley et al., 2012).

Consider:

1. A bat and a ball together cost 110 cents. The bat costs 100 cents more than the ball. How much does the ball cost?
2. Emily's father has three daughters. The first two are named April and May. What is the third daughter's name?

Most people's intuitive responses—10 cents and June—are wrong, and a few moments of deliberate thinking reveals why.[3]

The bottom line: Our two-track mind makes sweet harmony as smart, critical thinking listens to the creative whispers of our vast unseen mind and then evaluates evidence, tests conclusions, and plans for the future.

ASK YOURSELF

Can you recall a time when contradictory information challenged one of your views? Was it hard for you to consider the opposite view? What caused you to change your thinking or keep your opinion?

Thinking Creatively

LOQ 27-7 What is *creativity*, and what fosters it?

Creativity is the ability to produce novel and valuable ideas (Hennessey & Amabile, 2010). Consider Princeton mathematician Andrew Wiles' incredible, creative moment. *Fermat's last theorem* (dreamed up by seventeenth-century mischievous genius Pierre de Fermat) had baffled the greatest mathematical minds for centuries—even after a $2 million prize (in today's dollars) for the first proof was offered in 1908.

Wiles had pondered Fermat's theorem for more than 30 years. One morning, out of the blue, the final "incredible revelation" struck him. "It was so indescribably beautiful; it was so simple and so elegant. I couldn't understand how I'd missed it.... It was the most important moment of my working life" (Singh, 1997, p. 25). Likewise, creative writers and physicists experience many significant ideas, unbidden, during mind wandering (Gable et al., 2019). (Perhaps, you can recall such an experience?)

Creativity is supported by a certain level of *aptitude* (ability to learn). Those who score exceptionally high in quantitative aptitude as 13-year-olds, for example, are later more likely to create published or patented work (Bernstein et al., 2019; Lubinski et al., 2014). Yet there is more to creativity than aptitude, or what intelligence tests reveal. Indeed, brain activity associated with intelligence differs from that associated with creativity (Jung & Haier, 2013; Shen et al., 2017).

Aptitude tests (such as the SAT) typically require **convergent thinking**—an ability to provide a single correct answer. Creativity tests *(How many uses can you think of for a brick?)* require **divergent thinking**—the ability to consider many different options and to think in novel ways. Injury to certain areas of the frontal lobes can leave reading, writing, and arithmetic skills intact but destroy imagination (Kolb & Whishaw, 2006).

Robert Sternberg and his colleagues believe creativity has five components (Sternberg, 1988, 2003; Sternberg & Lubart, 1991, 1992):

1. *Expertise*—well-developed knowledge—furnishes the ideas, images, and phrases, we use as mental building blocks. "Chance favors only the prepared mind" observed Louis Pasteur. The longer we work on a problem, the more creative are our solutions (Lucas & Nordgren, 2020).
2. *Imaginative thinking skills* provide the ability to see things in novel ways, to recognize patterns, and to make connections. Having fully understood a problem's basic elements, we can redefine or explore it in a new way.
3. *A venturesome personality* seeks new experiences, tolerates ambiguity and risk, and perseveres in overcoming obstacles.

[3] The first answer is 5 cents. The bat would then cost $1.05, for a $1.10 total. If the ball cost the *intuitive* answer of 10 cents, the bat would then have to cost $1.10 (for a bat-and-ball total of $1.20, not $1.10). The second answer is Emily. If you answered incorrectly, don't fret—so do many others (Frederick, 2005; Thomson & Oppenheimer, 2016).

PETER MUHLY/Getty Images

Creative women Researcher Sally Reis (2001) found that notably creative women were typically "intelligent, hardworking, imaginative, and strong willed" as girls. In her 2013 Nobel Prize for Literature acceptance speech, author Alice Munro, shown here, described the creative process as hard work: "The part that's hardest is when you go over the story and realize how bad it is. You know, the first part, excitement, the second, pretty good, but then you pick it up one morning and you think, 'what nonsense,' and that is when you really have to get to work."

creativity the ability to produce new and valuable ideas.

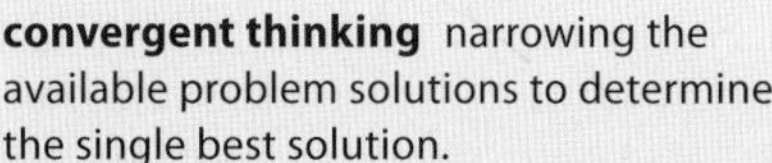

convergent thinking narrowing the available problem solutions to determine the single best solution.

divergent thinking expanding the number of possible problem solutions; creative thinking that diverges in different directions.

Christopher Weyant/Cartoon Stock

"For the love of God, is there a doctor in the house?"

WELL, I TOLD YOU TO ADD YEAST TO YOUR SHAMPOO.
© Dave Coverly/speedbump.com

Imaginative thinking Cartoonists often display creativity as they see things in new ways or make unusual connections.

4. ***Intrinsic motivation*** is the quality of being driven more by interest, satisfaction, and challenge than by external pressures (Amabile & Hennessey, 1992). Creative people focus less on extrinsic motivators—meeting deadlines, impressing people, or making money—than on the pleasure and stimulation of the work itself.
5. ***A creative environment*** sparks, supports, and refines creative ideas. Wiles stood on the shoulders of others and collaborated with a former student. A study of the careers of 2026 prominent scientists and inventors revealed that the most eminent were mentored, challenged, and supported by their colleagues (Simonton, 1992). Creativity-fostering environments support innovation, team building, and communication (Hülsheger et al., 2009). They also minimize anxiety and foster contemplation (Byron & Khazanchi, 2011).

For those seeking to boost the creative process, research offers some ideas:

- ***Develop your expertise.*** Ask yourself what you care about and most enjoy. Follow your passion by broadening your knowledge base and becoming an expert at something.
- ***Allow time for incubation.*** Think hard on a problem, but then set it aside and come back to it later. Periods of inattention to a problem ("sleeping on it") allow for automatic processing to form associations (Zhong et al., 2008).
- ***Set aside time for the mind to roam freely.*** Creativity springs from "defocused attention" (Simonton, 2012a,b). So, detach from attention-grabbing TV shows, social media, and video gaming. Jog, go for a long walk, or meditate. Serenity seeds spontaneity. "Time alone is . . . the font of creativity," says playwright and musician Lin-Manuel Miranda (Hainey, 2016).
- ***Experience other cultures and ways of thinking.*** Viewing life from a different perspective sometimes sets the creative juices flowing. Students who spend time in other cultures learn how to blend new norms with those from their home culture, which increases creativity (Godart et al., 2015; Lu et al., 2018). Even getting out of your neighborhood or embracing intercultural friendships fosters flexible thinking (Kim et al., 2013; Ritter et al., 2012).

For a summary of some key ideas from this section, see **TABLE 27.1**.

RETRIEVAL PRACTICE

RP-2 Match the process or strategy listed below (i–xi) with its description (a–k).

i. Algorithm	a. Inability to view problems from a new angle; focuses thinking but hinders creative problem solving
ii. Intuition	b. Methodological rule or procedure that guarantees a solution but requires time and effort
iii. Insight	c. Your fast, automatic, effortless feelings, and thoughts based on your experience; huge and adaptive but can lead you to overfeel and underthink
iv. Heuristic	d. Simple thinking shortcut that lets you act quickly and efficiently but puts you at risk for errors
v. Fixation	e. Sudden Aha! reaction that instantly reveals the solution
vi. Confirmation bias	f. Tendency to search for support for your own views and to ignore contradictory evidence
vii. Overconfidence	g. Holding on to your beliefs even after they are proven wrong; closing your mind to new ideas
viii. Creativity	h. Overestimating the accuracy of your beliefs and judgments; allows you to be happier and to make decisions more easily but puts you at risk for errors
ix. Framing	i. Wording a question or statement so that it evokes a desired response; can mislead people and influence their decisions
x. Belief perseverance	j. The ability to produce novel and valuable ideas
xi. Nudge	k. Framing choices to encourage certain decisions

ANSWERS IN APPENDIX E

TABLE 27.1 Comparing Cognitive Processes and Strategies

Process or Strategy	Description	Powers	Perils
Algorithm	Methodical rule or procedure	Guarantees solution	Requires time and effort
Heuristic	Simple thinking shortcut, such as the availability heuristic (which estimates likelihood based on how easily events come to mind)	Lets us act quickly and efficiently	Puts us at risk for errors
Insight	Sudden Aha! reaction	Provides instant realization of solution	May not happen
Confirmation bias	Tendency to search for support for our own views and ignore contradictory evidence	Lets us quickly recognize supporting evidence	Hinders recognition of contradictory evidence
Fixation	Inability to view problems from a new angle	Focuses thinking	Hinders creative problem solving
Intuition	Fast, automatic feelings and thoughts	Is based on our experience; huge and adaptive	Can lead us to overfeel and underthink
Overconfidence	Overestimating the accuracy of our beliefs and judgments	Allows us to live more happily and to make decisions easily	Puts us at risk for errors
Belief perseverance	Ignoring evidence that contradicts our beliefs	Supports our enduring beliefs	Closes our mind to new ideas
Framing	Wording a question or statement so that it evokes a desired response	Can influence others' decisions	Can produce a misleading result
Creativity	Ability to innovate valuable ideas	Produces new insights and products	May distract from structured, routine work

Do Other Species Share Our Cognitive Skills?

LOQ 27-8 What do we know about thinking in other species?

Other animals are surprisingly smart (de Waal, 2016). In her 1908 book, *The Animal Mind*, pioneering psychologist Margaret Floy Washburn argued that animal consciousness and intelligence can be inferred from their behavior. In 2012, neuroscientists convening at the University of Cambridge added that animal consciousness can also be inferred from their brains: "Nonhuman animals, including all mammals and birds," possess the neural networks "that generate consciousness" (Herculano-Houzel, 2020). Consider, then, what animal brains can do.

Using Concepts and Numbers

By touching screens in quest of a food reward, black bears have learned to sort pictures into animal and nonanimal categories, or concepts (Vonk et al., 2012). The great apes—a group that includes chimpanzees and gorillas—also form concepts, such as *cat* and *dog*. After monkeys have learned these concepts, certain frontal lobe neurons in their brain fire in response to new "cat-like" images, others to new "dog-like" images (Freedman et al., 2001). Even pigeons—mere birdbrains—can sort objects (pictures of cars, cats, chairs, flowers) into categories. Shown a picture of a never-before-seen chair, pigeons will reliably peck a key that represents *chairs* (Wasserman, 1995).

Animal cognition in action Alex, an African Grey parrot, could categorize and name objects (Pepperberg, 2009, 2012, 2013). Among his jaw-dropping numerical skills was the ability to comprehend numbers up to 8. He could speak the number of objects. He could add two small clusters of objects and announce the sum. He could indicate which of two numbers was greater. And he gave correct answers when shown various groups of objects. Asked, for example, "What color four?" (meaning "What's the color of the objects of which there are four?"), he could speak the answer.

Mike Lovett

Tomas Persson/PLoS ONE
(a)

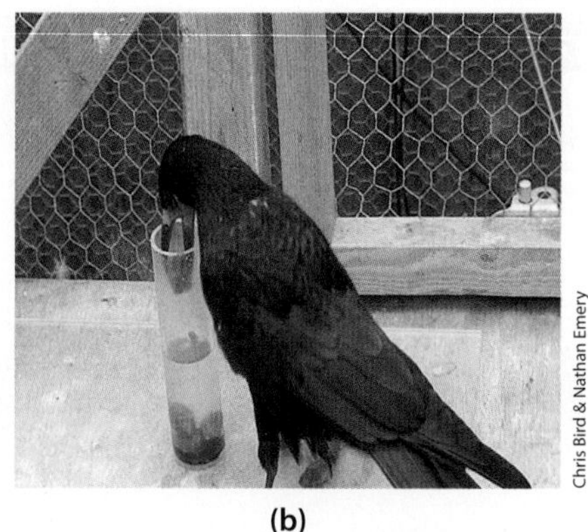
Chris Bird & Nathan Emery
(b)

FIGURE 27.5
Animal talents (a) One male chimpanzee in Sweden's Furuvik Zoo was observed every morning collecting stones, which later in the day he used as ammunition to pelt visitors (Osvath & Karvonen, 2012). (b) Crows quickly learned to raise the water level in a tube and nab a floating worm by dropping in stones (Bird & Emery, 2009).

Displaying Insight

Psychologist Wolfgang Köhler (1925) showed that humans are not the only creatures to display insight. He placed a piece of fruit and a long stick outside the cage of a chimpanzee named Sultan, beyond his reach. Inside the cage, Köhler placed a short stick, which Sultan grabbed, using it to try to reach the fruit. After several failed attempts, the chimpanzee dropped the stick and seemed to survey the situation. Then suddenly (as if thinking *Aha!*), Sultan jumped up and seized the short stick again. This time, he used it to pull in the longer stick—which he then used to reach the fruit. Apes have even exhibited foresight by storing a tool they could use to retrieve food the next day (Mulcahy & Call, 2006). (For one example of a chimpanzee's use of foresight, see **FIGURE 27.5a**.)

Birds, too, have displayed insight. One experiment, by (yes) Christopher Bird and Nathan Emery (2009), brought to life an Aesop fable in which a thirsty crow is unable to reach the water in a partly filled pitcher. See the crow's solution (exactly as in the fable) in **FIGURE 27.5b**. Other crows have fashioned wire or sticks for extracting food, such as insects in rotting logs (Jelbert et al., 2018; Rutz et al., 2016). In one study, an African gray parrot equaled or bettered the performance of Harvard students at a complex shell game testing visual memory (Pailian et al., 2020).

Transmitting Culture

Like humans, other species invent behaviors and transmit cultural patterns to their observing peers and offspring (Boesch-Achermann & Boesch, 1993). Orca whales may look similar, but each subpopulation has its own language, social behaviors, and food preferences—all of which are transmitted across generations (Mapes, 2021). The Pacific Northwest southern resident orcas find Chinook salmon tasty, while their transient orca cousins dine on seals and other sea mammals. And similar to human accents, naked mole-rats' vocal "chirps" mirror those of other nearby mole-rats (Barker et al., 2021).

Forest-dwelling chimpanzees select different tools for different purposes—a heavy stick for making holes, a light, flexible stick for fishing for termites, or a pointed stick for roasting marshmallows. (Just kidding: They don't roast marshmallows, but they have surprised us with their sophisticated tool use [Sanz et al., 2004]). Researchers have found at least 39 local customs related to chimpanzee tool use, grooming, and courtship (Claidière & Whiten, 2012; Whiten, 2021a,b). One group may slurp termites directly from a stick, while another group may pluck them off individually. One group may break nuts with a stone, while their neighbors use a piece of wood. One chimpanzee discovered that tree moss could absorb water for drinking from a waterhole, and within 6 days, seven other observant chimpanzees began using moss in the same way (Hobaiter et al., 2014). Along with differing communication and hunting styles, these transmitted behaviors are the chimpanzee version of cultural diversity, a diversity that is threatened by habitat loss.

Other Cognitive Skills

Great apes, dolphins, magpies, and elephants recognize themselves in a mirror, demonstrating self-awareness (Boyle, 2021). Elephants also display abilities to learn, remember, discriminate smells, empathize, cooperate, teach, and spontaneously use tools (Byrne et al., 2009). Chimpanzees show altruism, cooperation, and group aggression. Like humans, they may purposefully kill their neighbor, and they grieve over dead relatives (D. Biro et al., 2010; Mitani et al., 2010).

* * *

Thinking about other species' abilities brings us back to our initial question: How deserving are we of the label *Homo sapiens*—wise human? On decision making and risk assessment, our smart but error-prone species might rate a B–. On problem solving, where humans are inventive yet vulnerable to confirmation bias and fixation, we would probably receive a better mark, perhaps a B+. And on cognitive efficiency and creativity, our quick (though sometimes faulty) heuristics and divergent thinking would surely earn us an A.

What time is it now? When we asked you (in the section on overconfidence) to estimate how quickly you would finish this module, did you underestimate or overestimate?

MODULE

27 REVIEW Thinking

LEARNING OBJECTIVES

Test Yourself Answer these repeated Learning Objective Questions on your own (before "showing" the answers here, or checking the answers in Appendix D) to improve your retention of the concepts (McDaniel et al., 2009, 2015).

LOQ 27-1 What are *cognition* and *metacognition*, and what are the functions of concepts?

LOQ 27-2 What cognitive strategies assist our problem solving, and what obstacles hinder it?

LOQ 27-3 What is *intuition*, and how can the representativeness and availability heuristics influence our decisions and judgments?

LOQ 27-4 What factors exaggerate our fear of unlikely events?

LOQ 27-5 How are our decisions and judgments affected by overconfidence, belief perseverance, and framing?

LOQ 27-6 How do smart thinkers use intuition?

LOQ 27-7 What is *creativity*, and what fosters it?

LOQ 27-8 What do we know about thinking in other species?

TERMS AND CONCEPTS TO REMEMBER

Test Yourself Write down the definition in your own words, then check your answer.

cognition, p. 327
metacognition, p. 327
concept, p. 327
prototype, p. 327
algorithm, p. 328
heuristic, p. 328
insight, p. 328
confirmation bias, p. 329
fixation, p. 329
mental set, p. 329
intuition, p. 329
representativeness heuristic, p. 330
availability heuristic, p. 330
overconfidence, p. 330
belief perseverance, p. 333
framing, p. 333
nudge, p. 333
creativity, p. 335
convergent thinking, p. 335
divergent thinking, p. 335

MODULE TEST

Test Yourself Answer the following questions on your own first, then "show" the answers here, or check your answers in Appendix E.

1. A mental grouping of similar things is called a ____________________.

2. The most systematic procedure for solving a problem is a(n) ____________________.

3. Omar describes his political beliefs as "strongly liberal," but he is interested in exploring opposing viewpoints. How might he be affected by confirmation bias and belief perseverance?

4. A major obstacle to problem solving is fixation, which is a(n)
   a. tendency to base our judgments on vivid memories.
   b. tendency to wait for insight to occur.
   c. inability to view a problem from a new perspective.
   d. rule of thumb for judging the likelihood of an event in terms of our mental image of it.

5. Foreign terrorist attacks made Americans more fearful of being victimized by foreign terrorism than of other, greater threats. Such exaggerated fear after dramatic events illustrates the ____________________ heuristic.

6. When consumers respond more positively to ground beef described as "75 percent lean" than to the same product labeled "25 percent fat," they have been influenced by ____________________.

7. Which of the following is NOT a characteristic of a creative person?
   a. Expertise
   b. Extrinsic motivation
   c. A venturesome personality
   d. Imaginative thinking skills

8. In the early twentieth century, some psychologists noted that animal consciousness can be inferred from their behavior. In the early twenty-first century, other scientists argued that animal consciousness can be inferred from their brain's ______ ______.

MODULE

28 Language and Thought

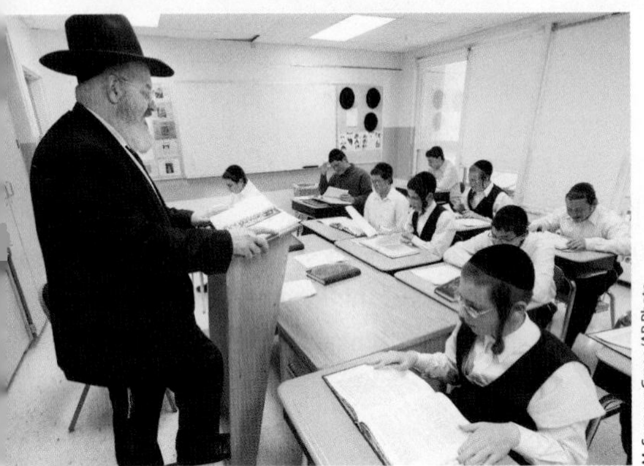

M. Spencer Green/AP Photo

Language transmits knowledge Whether spoken, written, or signed, language — the original wireless communication — enables mind-to-mind information transfer and with it the transmission of civilization's accumulated knowledge across generations.

Imagine an alien species that could pass thoughts from one head to another merely by pulsating air molecules in the space between them. Perhaps, these weird creatures could inhabit a future science fiction movie? Actually, we are those creatures! When we speak, our brain and voice apparatus transmit air pressure waves that we send banging against another's eardrum—enabling us to transfer thoughts from our brain into theirs. As cognitive psychologist Steven Pinker (1998) noted, we sometimes sit for hours "listening to other people make noise as they exhale, because those hisses and squeaks contain *information*." Depending on how you vibrate the air, you may get a scowl or a kiss.

Language is more than vibrating air—it is our spoken, written, or signed words, and the ways we combine them to communicate meaning. When I [DM] created this paragraph, my fingers on the keyboard generated electronic binary numbers that morphed into the squiggles before you. These squiggles trigger formless nerve impulses that travel to several areas of your brain, which integrate the information, compare it to stored information, and decode meaning. Thanks to language, information is moving from our minds to yours. Many animals know little more than what they sense. Thanks to language, we comprehend much that we've never seen and that our distant ancestors never knew. And thanks to technology, we can use language to communicate across vast distances—through spoken, written, and even pictorial words (including the 2015 *Oxford English Dictionary* "Word" of the Year, the emoji: 😂).

Let's begin our study of language by examining some of its components.

Language Structure

LOQ 28-1 What are the structural components of a language?

Consider how we might go about inventing a language. For a spoken language, we would need three building blocks:

- **Phonemes** are the smallest distinctive sound units in a language. The word *that* has three phonemes—*th, a,* and *t*. Each *e* in *Mercedes* is a different phoneme because each is pronounced differently. Linguists surveying nearly 500 languages have identified 869 different phonemes in human speech, but no language uses all of them (Holt, 2002; Maddieson, 1984). Those 800+ sounds "can form all the words in every language of the world," notes child language researcher Patricia Kuhl (2015). English uses about 40 phonemes; other languages use anywhere from half to more than twice as many. Consonant phonemes generally carry more information than do vowel phonemes. *The treth ef thes stetement shed be evedent frem thes bref demenstretien.*
- **Morphemes** are the smallest language units that carry meaning. In English, a few morphemes are also phonemes—the article *a*, for instance. But most morphemes combine two or more phonemes. The word *readers*, for example, contains three morphemes: *read, er* (that is, "one who reads"), and *s* (not one but multiple readers). Every word in a language contains one or more morphemes.
- **Grammar** is a language's set of rules that enable people to communicate. Grammatical rules guide us in deriving meaning from sounds *(semantics)* and in ordering words into sentences *(syntax)*.

language our spoken, written, or signed words and the ways we combine them to communicate meaning.

phoneme in a language, the smallest distinctive sound unit.

morpheme in a language, the smallest unit that carries meaning; may be a word or a part of a word (such as a prefix).

grammar in a language, a system of rules that enables us to communicate with and understand others. *Semantics* is the language's set of rules for deriving meaning from sounds, and *syntax* is its set of rules for combining words into grammatically sensible sentences.

Like life constructed from the genetic code's simple alphabet, language is complexity built of simplicity. In English, for example, 40 or so phonemes can be combined to form more than 100,000 morphemes, which alone or in combination produce the 600,000 variations of past and present words in the *Oxford English Dictionary*. Using those words, we can then create an infinite number of sentences, most of which (like this one) are original. We know that you can know why we worry that you think this sentence is starting to get too complex; but that complexity—and our capacity to communicate and comprehend it—is what distinguishes our human language capacity (Hauser et al., 2002; Premack, 2007).

syntax the correct way to string words together to form sentences for a given language.

RETRIEVAL PRACTICE

RP-1 How many morphemes are in the word *cats*? How many phonemes?

ANSWERS IN APPENDIX E

Language Acquisition and Development

We humans have an astonishing knack for language. With little effort, we draw from tens of thousands of words in our memory, assemble them on the fly with near-perfect **syntax**, and spew them out, three words a second (Vigliocco & Hartsuiker, 2002). Given how many ways we can mess up, our language capacity is truly amazing.

"Language is a uniquely human gift, central to our experience of being human."
—Cognitive scientist Lera Boroditsky (2009)

Language Acquisition: How Do We Learn Language?

LOQ 28-2 How do we acquire language, and what did Chomsky mean by *universal grammar*?

Linguist Noam Chomsky has argued that language is an unlearned human trait, separate from other parts of human cognition. He theorized that a built-in predisposition to learn grammar rules, which he called *universal grammar,* helps explain why preschoolers pick up language so readily and use grammar so well. It happens so naturally—as naturally as birds learn to fly—that training hardly helps. Whether in Indiana or Indonesia, we intuitively follow similar syntax rules (Aryawibawa & Ambridge, 2018). All human languages—and there are more than 6000 of them—have nouns, verbs, and adjectives as grammatical building blocks, and they use words in some common ways (Blasi et al., 2016; Futrell et al., 2015).

Other researchers note that children learn grammar as they discern patterns in the language they hear (Ibbotson & Tomasello, 2016). And Chomsky agrees that we are not born with a built-in *specific* language or *specific* set of grammatical rules. The world's languages are structurally very diverse—more so than the universal grammar idea implies (Bergen, 2014). Whatever language we experience as children, whether spoken or signed, we will readily learn its specific grammar and vocabulary (Bavelier et al., 2003). And we always start speaking mostly in nouns (*kitty, da-da*) rather than in verbs and adjectives (Bornstein et al., 2004). Biology and experience work together.

Creating a language Brought together as if on a desert island (actually a school), Nicaragua's young deaf children over time drew upon sign gestures from home to create their own Nicaraguan Sign Language, complete with words and intricate grammar. Activated by a social context, nature and nurture work creatively together (Osborne, 1999; Sandler et al., 2005; Senghas & Coppola, 2001).

RETRIEVAL PRACTICE

RP-2 What was Noam Chomsky's view of language learning?

ANSWERS IN APPENDIX E

Language Development: When Do We Learn Language?

LOQ 28-3 What are the milestones in language development, and when is the critical period for acquiring language?

Make a quick guess: How many words of your native language did you learn between your first birthday and your high school graduation? Although you use only 150 words for about half of what you say, you probably learned about 60,000 words (Bloom, 2000;

babbling stage the stage in speech development, beginning around 4 months, during which an infant spontaneously utters various sounds that are not all related to the household language.

one-word stage the stage in speech development, from about age 1 to 2, during which a child speaks mostly in single words.

two-word stage the stage in speech development, beginning about age 2, during which a child speaks mostly in two-word sentences.

telegraphic speech the early speech stage in which a child speaks like a telegram—"go car"—using mostly nouns and verbs.

McMurray, 2007). That averages (after age 2) to nearly 3500 words each year, or about 10 each day! How you did it—how those 3500 words could so far outnumber the roughly 200 words your schoolteachers consciously taught you each year—is one of the great human wonders.

Could you even now state the rules of syntax (the correct way to string words together to form sentences) for the language(s) you speak fluently? Most of us cannot. Yet before you could add 2 + 2, you were creating your own original sentences and applying these rules. As a preschooler, you comprehended and spoke with a facility that far outpaced even the brightest adult's ability to learn a new language.

RECEPTIVE LANGUAGE Children's language development moves from simplicity to complexity. Babies are born prepared to learn any language, with a slight bent toward the language they heard in the womb. By 4 months of age, babies can recognize differences in speech sounds (Stager & Werker, 1997). They can also read lips. We know this because in experiments by Patricia Kuhl and Andrew Meltzoff (1982), babies have preferred looking at a face that matches a sound—an *"ah"* coming from wide open lips and an *"ee"* from a mouth with corners pulled back. Recognizing such differences marks the beginning of the development of babies' *receptive language,* their ability to understand what is said to and about them. At 7 months and beyond, they grow in their power to do what adults find difficult when listening to an unfamiliar language: to segment spoken sounds into individual words.

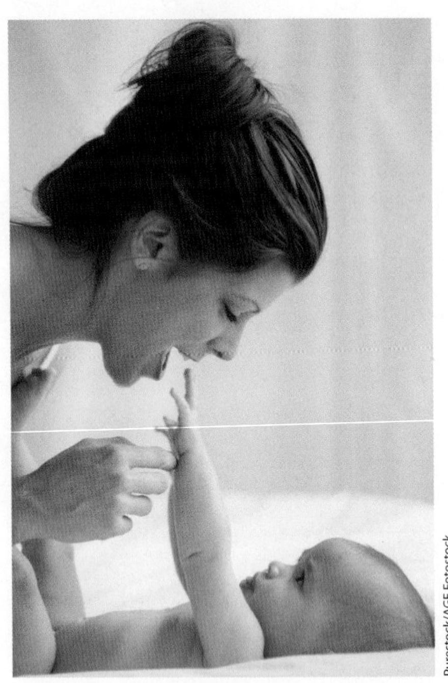
Purestock/AGE Fotostock

A natural talent Human infants come with a remarkable capacity to soak up language. But the particular language they learn will reflect their unique interactions with others.

When adults listen to an unfamiliar language, the syllables all run together. A young Sudanese couple new to North America and unfamiliar with English might, for example, hear *United Nations* as "Uneye Tednay Shuns." Their 7-month-old daughter would not have this problem. Human infants display a remarkable ability to learn statistical aspects of human speech (Batterink, 2017; Werker et al., 2012). Their brains not only discern word breaks, they statistically analyze which syllables—as in *hap-py-ba-by*—most often go together. After just 2 minutes of exposure to a computer voice speaking an unbroken, monotone string of nonsense syllables *(bidakupadotigolabubidaku . . .)*, 8-month-olds were able to recognize (as indicated by their attention) three-syllable sequences that appeared repeatedly (Saffran, 2009; Saffran et al., 1996).

PRODUCTIVE LANGUAGE Long after the beginnings of receptive language, babies' *productive language*—their ability to produce words—matures. Before nurture molds babies' speech, nature enables a wide range of possible sounds in the **babbling stage**, beginning around 4 months. In this stage, babies seem to sample all the sounds they can make, such as *ah-goo*. Babbling does not imitate the adult speech babies hear—it includes sounds from various languages. From this early babbling, a listener could not identify an infant as being, say, French, Korean, or Ethiopian.

By about 10 months, infants' babbling has changed so that a trained ear can identify the household language (de Boysson-Bardies et al., 1989). Deaf infants who observe their deaf parents using sign language begin to babble more with their hands (Petitto & Marentette, 1991). Without exposure to other languages, babies lose their ability to do what we cannot—to discriminate and produce sounds and tones found outside their native language (Kuhl et al., 2014; Meltzoff et al., 2009). Thus, by adulthood, those who speak only English cannot discriminate certain sounds in Japanese speech. Nor can Japanese adults with no training in English hear the difference between the English *r* and *l*. For a Japanese-speaking adult, *"la-la-ra-ra"* may sound like the same syllable repeated.

Around their first birthday, most children enter the **one-word stage**. They know that sounds carry meanings, and they begin to use sounds—usually only one barely recognizable syllable, such as *ma* or *da*—to communicate meaning. But gradually the infant's language conforms more to the family's language. Across the world, baby's first words are often nouns that label objects or people (Tardif et al., 2008). At this one-word stage, *"Doggy!"* may mean *"Look at the dog out there!"*

Care to guess babies' most common first words? In English, Croatian, French, Italian, and Kiswahili, they are *mommy* and *daddy* (Frank et al., 2019).

At about 18 months, children's word learning explodes from about a word per week to a word per day. By their second birthday, most have entered the **two-word stage** (TABLE 28.1). They start uttering two-word sentences in **telegraphic speech**. Like

TABLE 28.1 Summary of Language Development

Month (approximate)	Stage
4	Babbles many speech sounds ("ah-goo")
10	Babbling resembles household language ("ma-ma")
12	One-word speech ("Kitty!")
24	Two-word speech ("Get ball.")
24+	Rapid development into complete sentences

yesterday's telegrams that charged by the word ("TERMS ACCEPTED. SEND MONEY"), a 2-year-old's speech contains mostly nouns and verbs (*"Want juice"*). Also like telegrams, their speech follows rules of syntax, arranging words in a sensible order. English-speaking children typically place adjectives before nouns—*white house* rather than *house white*. Spanish reverses this order, as in *casa blanca*.

Sidney Harris/Cartoon Stock

"Got idea. Talk better. Combine words. Make sentences."

Moving out of the two-word stage, children quickly begin uttering longer phrases (Fromkin & Rodman, 1983). By early elementary school, they understand complex sentences and begin to enjoy the humor conveyed by double meanings: "You never starve in the desert because of all the sand-which-is there."

RETRIEVAL PRACTICE

RP-3 What is the difference between *receptive* language and *productive* language, and when do children typically hit these milestones in language development?

ANSWERS IN APPENDIX E

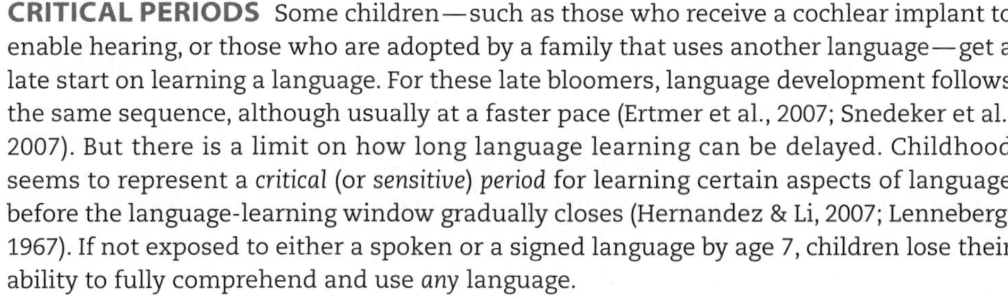

CRITICAL PERIODS Some children—such as those who receive a cochlear implant to enable hearing, or those who are adopted by a family that uses another language—get a late start on learning a language. For these late bloomers, language development follows the same sequence, although usually at a faster pace (Ertmer et al., 2007; Snedeker et al., 2007). But there is a limit on how long language learning can be delayed. Childhood seems to represent a *critical* (or *sensitive*) *period* for learning certain aspects of language before the language-learning window gradually closes (Hernandez & Li, 2007; Lenneberg, 1967). If not exposed to either a spoken or a signed language by age 7, children lose their ability to fully comprehend and use *any* language.

Cultural and other environmental variations affect children's language exposure. Children exposed to less complex language—such as U.S. 4-year-olds in classrooms with 3-year-olds, or some children from impoverished homes—often display less language skill (Ansari et al., 2015; Hirsh-Pasek et al., 2015). Reading to children increases language exposure. Jessica Logan and her colleagues (2019) found that frequent exposure to children's books boosts children's school readiness. "Kids who hear more vocabulary words are going to be better prepared to see those words in print when they enter school."

Language-learning ability is universal, but it is easiest when we're children. If we learn a new language as adults, we will usually speak it with the accent of our native language and with imperfect grammar (Hartshorne et al., 2018). In one experiment, U.S. immigrants from South Korea and China considered 276 English sentences (*"Yesterday the hunter shoots a deer"*) and decided whether each was grammatically correct or incorrect (Johnson & Newport, 1991). All had been in the United States for approximately 10 years; some had arrived in early childhood, others as adults. As **FIGURE 28.1** reveals, those who learned their second language early learned it best.

RETRIEVAL PRACTICE

RP-4 Why is it so difficult to learn a new language in adulthood?

ANSWERS IN APPENDIX E

FIGURE 28.1
Our ability to learn a new language diminishes with age Ten years after coming to the United States, Asian immigrants took an English grammar test. Those who arrived before age 8 understood American English grammar as well as native speakers. Those who arrived later did not. (Data from Johnson & Newport, 1991.)

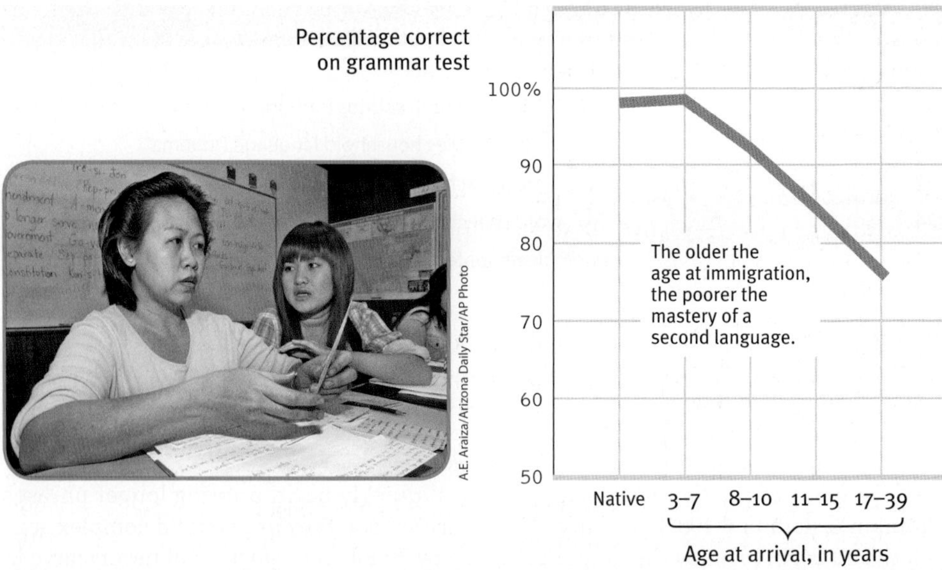
Percentage correct on grammar test
100%
90
80
70
60
50
The older the age at immigration, the poorer the mastery of a second language.
Native
3–7
8–10
11–15
17–39
Age at arrival, in years
A.E. Araiza/Arizona Daily Star/AP Photo

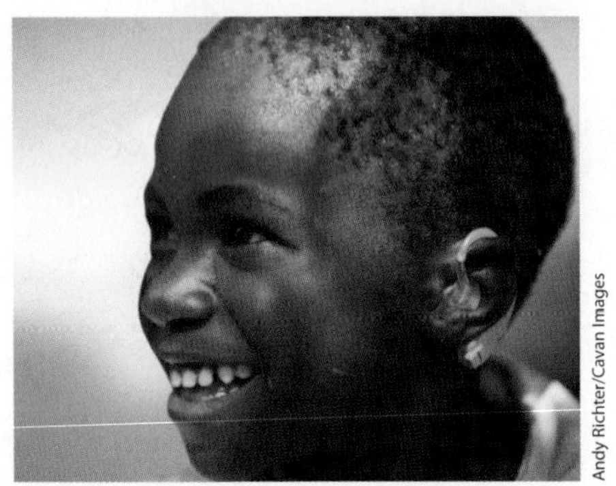
Andy Richter/Cavan Images
Hearing improved A boy in Malawi experiences new hearing aids.

Deafness and Language Development

The impact of early experiences is evident in language learning in deaf children of hearing-nonsigning parents. These children typically do not experience language during their early years. For example, natively deaf children who learn sign language after age 9 never learn it as well as those who learned it early in life. Those who learn to sign as teens or adults never become as fluent as native signers in producing and comprehending subtle grammatical differences (Newport, 1990). As a flower's growth requires nourishment, so, too, children's language acquisition requires early-life language exposure.

More than 90 percent of all deaf children are born to hearing parents. Most of these parents want their children to experience their world of sound and talk. Cochlear implants enable this by converting sounds into electrical signals and stimulating the auditory nerve by means of electrodes threaded into the child's cochlea. But if an implant is to help children become proficient in oral communication, parents cannot delay the surgery until their child reaches the age of consent. Giving cochlear implants to children is hotly debated. Deaf culture advocates object to giving implants to children who were deaf prelingually. The National Association of the Deaf, for example, argues that deafness is *not* a disability because native signers are not linguistically disabled. More than five decades ago, Gallaudet University linguist William Stokoe (1960) showed that sign is a complete language with its own grammar, syntax, and meanings. Deaf culture advocates sometimes further contend that deafness could as well be considered "vision enhancement" as "hearing impairment." Close your eyes and immediately you, too, will notice your attention being drawn to your other senses. In one experiment, people who had spent 90 minutes sitting quietly blindfolded became more accurate in their location of sounds (Lewald, 2007). When kissing, lovers minimize distraction and increase sensitivity by closing their eyes.

People who lose one channel of sensation compensate with a slight enhancement of their other sensory abilities (Backman & Dixon, 1992; Levy & Langer, 1992). Those who have been deaf from birth exhibit enhanced visual processing (Almeida et al., 2015). Their auditory cortex, starved for sensory input, remains largely intact but becomes responsive to touch and to visual input (Karns et al., 2012). Once repurposed, the auditory cortex becomes less available for hearing—which helps explain why cochlear implants are most effective when given before age 2 (Geers & Nicholas, 2013; Niparko et al., 2010).

LIVING IN A SILENT WORLD Worldwide, 466 million people live with hearing loss (WHO, 2019). Some are profoundly deaf; most (more men than women) have hearing loss (Agrawal et al., 2008). Some were deaf from birth; others have known the hearing world. Some sign and identify with the language-based Deaf culture. Others, especially those who lost their hearing after speaking a language, are "oral" and converse with the hearing world by reading lips or written notes. Still others move between the two cultures.

The challenges of life without hearing may be greatest for children. Unable to communicate in customary ways, signing playmates may struggle to coordinate their play with speaking playmates. School achievement may also suffer; academic subjects are rooted in *spoken* languages. Adolescents may feel socially excluded, with a resulting low self-confidence. Deaf children who grow up around other deaf people more often identify with Deaf culture and feel positive self-esteem. If raised in a signing household, whether by deaf or hearing parents, they also express higher self-esteem and feel more accepted (Bat-Chava, 1993, 1994).

Adults who lose hearing late in life also face challenges. Expending effort to hear words drains their capacity to perceive, comprehend, and remember them (Wingfield et al., 2005). In several studies, people with hearing loss, especially those not wearing hearing aids, have reported more sadness, less social engagement, and worrying that they irritate others (Kashubeck-West & Meyer, 2008; National Council on Aging, 2000). They also may experience a sort of shyness: "It's almost universal among the deaf to want to cause hearing people as little fuss as possible," observed Henry Kisor (1990, p. 244), a Chicago newspaper editor and columnist who lost his hearing at age 3. "We can be self-effacing and diffident to the point of invisibility. Sometimes this tendency can be crippling. I must fight it all the time." Helen Keller, both blind and deaf, noted that "blindness cuts people off from things. Deafness cuts people off from people."

I [DM] understand. My mother, with whom we communicated by writing notes on an erasable "magic pad," spent her last dozen years in an utterly silent world, largely withdrawn from the stress and strain of trying to interact with people outside a small circle of family and old friends. My own hearing is declining on a trajectory toward hers (with my hearing aid and cochlear implant receiver out at night, I cannot understand my wife speaking from her adjacent pillow). Even with hearing aids, I sit front and center at plays and meetings and seek quiet corners in restaurants. I do benefit from cool technology (see HearingLoop.org) that, at the press of a button, can transform my hearing aid into an in-the-ear loudspeaker for the broadcast of phone, TV, and public address system sound. Yet I still experience frustration when I can't hear the joke everyone else is guffawing over; when, after repeated tries, I just can't catch that exasperated person's question and can't fake my way around it; when family members give up and say, "Oh, never mind" after trying three times to tell me something unimportant.

As she aged, my mother came to feel that seeking social interaction was simply not worth the effort. I share newspaper columnist Kisor's belief that communication is worth the effort (p. 246): "So, . . . I will grit my teeth and plunge ahead." To reach out, to connect, to communicate with others, even across a chasm of silence, is to affirm our humanity as social creatures.

Jim Cummins/Getty Images

Talking hands Human language appears to have evolved from gestured communications (Corballis, 2002, 2003; Pollick & de Waal, 2007). Even today, gestures are naturally associated with spontaneous speech, and similarly so for blind and sighted speakers of a given language (Özçaliskan et al., 2016). Both gesture and speech communicate, and when they convey the same rather than different information (as they do in baseball's sign language), we humans understand faster and more accurately (Dargue et al., 2019; Hostetter, 2011; Kelly et al., 2010). Outfielder William Hoy, the first deaf player to join the major leagues (1892), reportedly helped invent hand signals for "Strike!" "Safe!" (shown here) and "Yerr out!" (Pollard, 1992). Referees in all sports now use invented signs, and fans are fluent in sports sign language.

The Brain and Language

LOQ 28-4 What brain areas are involved in language processing and speech?

We think of speaking and reading, or writing and reading, or singing and speaking as merely different examples of the same general ability—language. But consider this curious finding: Damage to any of several cortical areas can produce **aphasia**, impairment of language. Even more curious, some people with aphasia can speak fluently but cannot read (despite good vision). Others can comprehend what they read but cannot speak. Still others can write but not read, read but not write, read numbers but not letters, or sing but not speak. These cases suggest that language is complex and that different brain areas must serve different language functions.

Indeed, in 1865, French physician Paul Broca confirmed a fellow physician's observation that after damage to an area of the left frontal lobe (later called **Broca's area**) a person would struggle to *speak* words, yet could sing familiar songs and comprehend speech. A decade later, German investigator Carl Wernicke discovered that after damage to a specific area of the left temporal lobe (**Wernicke's area**), people could not *understand* others' sentences and could speak only meaningless sentences.

aphasia impairment of language, usually caused by left hemisphere damage either to Broca's area (impairing speaking) or to Wernicke's area (impairing understanding).

Broca's area a frontal lobe brain area, usually in the left hemisphere, that helps control language expression by directing the muscle movements involved in speech.

Wernicke's area a brain area, usually in the left temporal lobe, involved in language comprehension and expression.

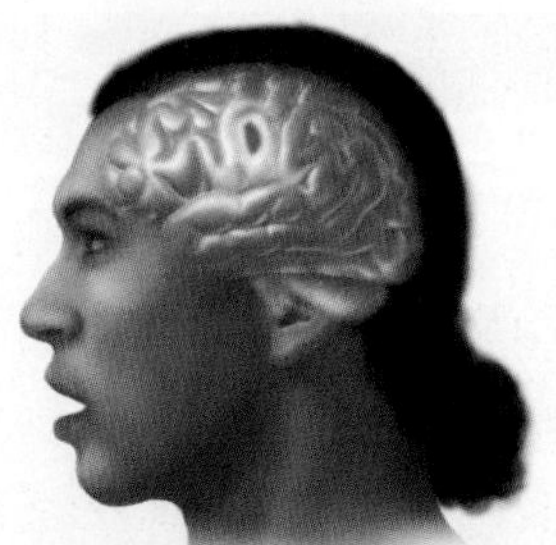

(a)
Speaking words
(Broca's area and the motor cortex)

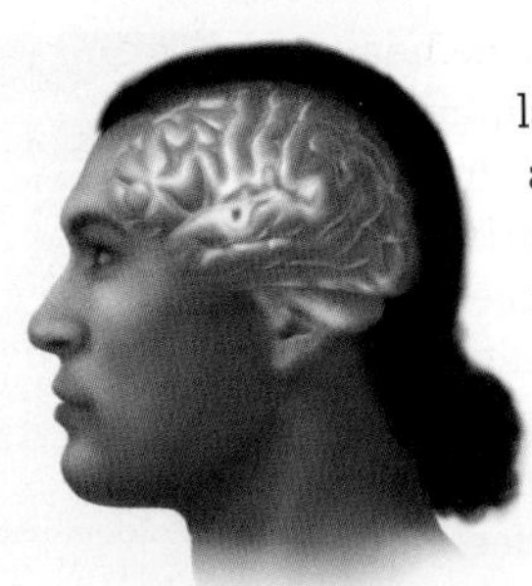

(b)
Hearing words
(Wernicke's area and the auditory cortex)

FIGURE 28.2
Brain activity when speaking and hearing words

Brain scans have confirmed activity in Broca's and Wernicke's areas during language processing (**FIGURE 28.2**). (For those with a larger-than-average Broca's area, grammar learning is a breeze [Novén et al., 2019].) For people with aphasia, electrical stimulation of Broca's area can help restore their speaking abilities (Marangolo et al., 2016). One man, whose stroke eliminated his ability to speak, allowed researchers to implant an electrode array over his speech motor cortex (Moses et al., 2021). By decoding the man's brain activity, researchers could understand what he was trying to say about half of the time—even though he could not utter a single word. "Not to be able to communicate with anyone, to have a normal conversation and express yourself in any way," the man noted, using a head-controlled mouse to type key-by-key, "it's devastating, very hard to live with" (Belluck, 2021).

The brain's processing of language is complex. Broca's area coordinates with the brain's processing of language in other areas as well (Flinker et al., 2015; Tremblay & Dick, 2016). Although you experience language as a single, unified stream, fMRI scans would show that your brain is busily multitasking and networking. Different neural networks are activated by nouns and verbs (or objects and actions); by different vowels; by stories of visual versus motor experiences; by who spoke and what was said; and by many other stimuli (Perrachione et al., 2011; Shapiro et al., 2006; Speer et al., 2009). And these same networks become activated whether you're reading or listening to the words (Deniz et al., 2019).

Moreover, if you're lucky enough to be natively fluent in two languages, your brain processes them in similar areas (Kim et al., 2017). But your brain doesn't use the same areas if you learned a second language *after* the first or if you sign rather than speak your second language (Berken et al., 2015; Kovelman et al., 2014).

The point to remember: In processing language, as in other forms of information processing, the brain operates by dividing its mental functions—speaking, perceiving, thinking, and remembering—into subfunctions. Your conscious experience of learning about the brain and language *seems* indivisible, but thanks to your parallel processing, many different neural networks are pooling their work to give meaning to the words, sentences, and paragraphs (Fedorenko et al., 2016; Snell & Grainger, 2019). *E pluribus unum*: Out of many, one.

RETRIEVAL PRACTICE

RP-5 __________ __________ is one part of the brain that, if damaged, might impair your ability to speak words. Damage to __________ __________ might impair your ability to understand language.

ANSWERS IN APPENDIX E

Thinking and Language

LOQ 28-5 What is the relationship between thinking and language, and what is the value of thinking in images?

Thinking and language—which comes first? This is one of psychology's great chicken-and-egg questions. Do our ideas come first and then the words to name them? Or are our thoughts conceived in words and unthinkable without them?

The theory of **linguistic determinism** was developed by linguist Benjamin Lee Whorf (1956), who believed that those using languages with no past tense, such as the Hopi, could not readily *think* about the past. But Whorf's theory was too extreme. We all think about things for which we have no words. (Can you think of a shade of blue you cannot name? Can you imagine wondering if someone might fall?)

A less extreme idea, **linguistic relativism**, recognizes that our words *influence* our thinking (Gentner, 2016). To those who speak two dissimilar languages, such as English and Japanese, this point seems obvious (Brown, 1986). Unlike English, which has a rich vocabulary for self-focused emotions such as anger, Japanese has more words for interpersonal emotions such as sympathy (Markus & Kitayama, 1991). Many bilingual individuals report

linguistic determinism Whorf's hypothesis that language determines the way we think.

linguistic relativism the idea that language influences the way we think.

that they have different senses of self—that they feel like different people—depending on which language they are using (Matsumoto, 1994; Pavlenko, 2014).

Bilingual individuals may even reveal different personality profiles when taking the same test in two languages, with their differing cultural associations (Chen & Bond, 2010; Dinges & Hull, 1992). When China-born, bilingual University of Waterloo students described themselves in English, their responses fit typical Canadian profiles, expressing mostly positive self-statements and moods. When responding in Chinese, the same students gave typically Chinese self-descriptions, reporting more agreement with Chinese values and roughly equal positive and negative self-statements and moods (Ross et al., 2002). Similar attitude and personality changes have been shown when switching between Spanish and English or Arabic and English (Ogunnaike et al., 2010; Ramírez-Esparza et al., 2006). "Learn a new language and get a new soul," says a Czech proverb.

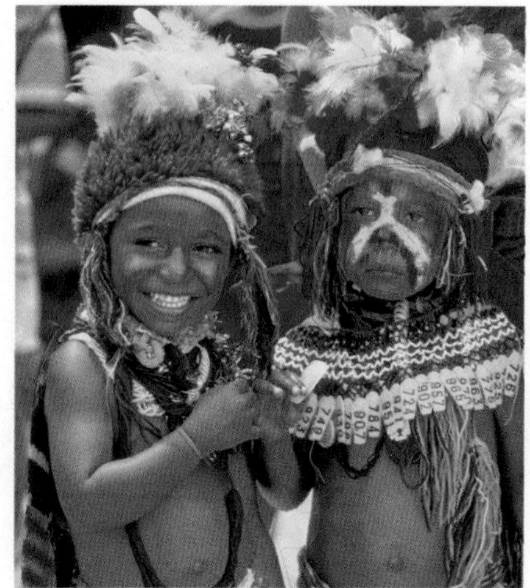

Prisma by Dukas Presseagentur GmbH/Alamy Stock Photo

Culture and color In Papua New Guinea, Berinmo children have words for different shades of yellow, which might enable them to spot and recall yellow variations more quickly. Here and everywhere, "the languages we speak profoundly shape the way we think, the way we see the world, the way we live our lives," noted psychologist Lera Boroditsky (2009).

So, our words do influence our thinking (Boroditsky, 2011). Words define our mental categories. Whether we live in New Mexico, New South Wales, or New Guinea, we *see* the same colors, but we use our native language to *classify* and *remember* them (Davidoff, 2004; Roberson et al., 2004, 2005). Imagine viewing three colors and calling two of them "yellow" and one of them "blue." Later you would likely see and recall the yellows as being more similar. But if you speak the language of Papua New Guinea's Berinmo people, which has words for two different shades of yellow, you would more speedily perceive and better recall the variations between the two yellows. And if your native language is Russian or Greek, which have distinct names for various shades of blue, you would perceive and recall the yellows as more similar and remember the blues better (Maier & Abdel Rahman, 2018). Words matter.

On the color spectrum, blue blends into green—until we draw a dividing line between the portions we call "blue" and "green." Although equally different on the color spectrum, two different items that share the same color name (as the two "blues" do in **FIGURE 28.3**, contrast B) are harder to distinguish than two items with different names ("blue" and "green," as in Figure 28.3, contrast A) (Özgen, 2004). Likewise, $4.99 perceptually differs more from $5.01 than from $4.97. And to doctors, a patient who is 80 seems, relative to a 79-year-old, older than does a 79-year-old compared to one who is 78 (Olenski et al., 2020).

Given their subtle influence on thinking, we do well to choose our words carefully. When hearing the generic *he* (as in "the artist and his work"), people are more likely to picture a man (Henley, 1989; Ng, 1990). If *he* and *his* were truly gender free, we shouldn't skip a beat when hearing that "man, like other mammals, nurses his young." Pronoun usage can also influence how we feel about ourselves. Transgender and gender nonconforming youth report feeling respected and included when their preferred pronouns are used—*he/she, him/her, they/their* (Olson & Gülgöz, 2018; Rae et al., 2019). And consider: Gender prejudice also occurs more in gendered languages, such as French, in which, for example, *la table* is feminine and *le téléphone* is masculine (DeFranza et al., 2020; Lewis & Lupyan, 2020).

To expand language is to expand the ability to think. Young children's thinking develops hand in hand with their language (Gopnik & Meltzoff, 1986). Indeed, it is very difficult to think about or conceptualize certain abstract ideas (*commitment, freedom,* or *rhyming*) without language. And what is true for preschoolers is true for everyone: *It pays to increase your word power.* That's why most textbooks, including this one, introduce new words—to teach new ideas and new ways of thinking.

"All words are pegs to hang ideas on."
—Henry Ward Beecher, *Proverbs from Plymouth Pulpit*, 1887

Increased word power helps explain some benefits of bilingualism. McGill University researcher Wallace Lambert (1992; Lambert et al., 1993) reported that bilingual people are

A

B

FIGURE 28.3
Language and perception When people view blocks of equally different colors, they perceive those with different names as more different. Thus, the "green" and "blue" in contrast A may appear to differ more than the two equally different blues in contrast B (Özgen, 2004).

skilled at inhibiting one language while using another—for example, inhibiting "crayón amarillo" while saying "yellow crayon" to English speakers, then doing the reverse for Spanish speakers (Tsui et al., 2019). Bilingual children also exhibit enhanced social skill by being better able to understand another's perspective (Fan et al., 2015; Gampe et al., 2019). Bilingual preschool children have also displayed less racial bias (Singh et al., 2020).

Working with bilingual education advocates Olga Melikoff, Valerie Neale, and Murielle Parkes, Lambert helped implement a Canadian program that has given millions of English-speaking children a natural French fluency via French-immersion schooling (Statistics Canada, 2019). Compared with similarly capable children in control groups, these children exhibit no loss of English fluency. They also display increased creativity and appreciation for French-Canadian culture (Genesee & Gándara, 1999; Lazaruk, 2007).

One lingering dispute concerns whether there exists, as some have claimed, a "bilingual advantage" in cognitive tasks such as planning, focusing attention, and then, when needed, switching attention (Antoniou, 2019; Bialystok, 2017). After reviewing all the available research, critics argue that any bilingual advantage on overall cognitive performance is unreliable and small (Gunnerud et al., 2020; Nichols et al., 2020). Stay tuned: This research story is still being written.

ASK YOURSELF

Have you tried to learn a new language after learning your first language? If so, how did learning this other language differ from learning your first language? Does speaking it feel different?

RETRIEVAL PRACTICE

RP-6 Benjamin Lee Whorf's controversial hypothesis, called ________________ ________________, suggested that we cannot think about things unless we have words for those concepts or ideas.

ANSWERS IN APPENDIX E

Thinking in Images

To turn on the cold water in your bathroom, in which direction do you turn the handle? To answer, you probably thought not in words but with *implicit* (nondeclarative, procedural) memory—a mental picture of how you do it.

Indeed, we often think in images; mental practice relies on it. Pianist Liu Chi Kung harnessed this power. One year after placing second in the 1958 Tchaikovsky piano competition, Liu was imprisoned during China's cultural revolution. Soon after his release, after 7 years without touching a piano, he was back on tour. Critics judged Liu's musicianship as better than ever. How did he continue to develop without practice? "I did practice," said Liu, "every day. I rehearsed every piece I had ever played, note by note, in my mind" (Garfield, 1986).

Blend Images/Getty Images

For someone who has learned a skill, such as ballet dancing, even *watching* the activity will activate the brain's internal simulation of it (Calvo-Merino et al., 2004). So, too, will *imagining* a physical experience, which activates some of the same neural networks that are active during the actual experience (Grèzes & Decety, 2001). Small wonder, then, that mental practice has become a standard part of training for Olympic athletes (Blumenstein & Orbach, 2012; Ungerleider, 2005).

One experiment on mental practice and basketball free-throw shooting tracked the University of Tennessee women's team over 35 games (Savoy & Beitel, 1996). During that time, the team's free-throw accuracy increased from approximately 52 percent in games following standard physical practice, to some 65 percent after mental practice. Players had repeatedly imagined making free throws under various conditions, including being "trash-talked" by their opposition. In a dramatic conclusion, Tennessee won the national championship game in overtime, thanks in part to their free-throw shooting.

Researchers demonstrated academic benefits of mental rehearsal with two groups of introductory psychology students facing a midterm exam 1 week later (Taylor et al., 1998). (Students not engaged in any mental rehearsal formed a third control group.)

The first group spent 5 minutes daily visualizing themselves scanning the posted grade list, seeing their A, beaming with joy, and feeling proud. This daily *outcome simulation* added only 2 points to their exam-score average. The second group spent 5 minutes daily visualizing themselves reading their text, going over notes, eliminating distractions, declining an invitation out. This daily *process simulation* paid off: The group began studying sooner, spent more time at it, and beat the others' average score by 8 points. *The point to remember:* It's better to imagine *how* to reach your goal than merely to fantasize your desired destination.

* * *

Psychological research on thinking and language mirrors the mixed impressions of our species by those in fields such as literature and religion. Our misjudgments are commonplace and our intellectual failures striking. Yet our problem-solving ingenuity and our extraordinary power of language mark humankind as (in Shakespeare's words) almost "infinite in faculties."

ASK YOURSELF

How could you use mental practice to improve your performance in some area of your life—for example, in your schoolwork, personal relationships, or hobbies?

RETRIEVAL PRACTICE

RP-7 What is mental practice, and how can it help you to prepare for an upcoming event?

ANSWERS IN APPENDIX E

Do Other Species Have Language?

LOQ 28-6 What do we know about other species' capacity for language?

Humans, more than other animals, can take others' perspectives and regulate themselves with a moral sense (Li & Tomasello, 2021). Humans also have long proclaimed that language sets us above other animals. "When we study human language," asserted linguist Noam Chomsky (1972), "we are approaching what some might call the 'human essence,' the qualities of mind that are, so far as we know, unique [to humans]." Is it true that humans, alone, have language?

Some animals display basic language processing. Pigeons can learn the difference between words and nonwords, but they could never read this book (Scarf et al., 2016). Various monkey species sound different alarm cries for different predators. Hearing the leopard alarm, vervets climb the nearest tree. Hearing the eagle alarm, they rush into the bushes. Hearing the snake alarm, they stand up and scan the ground (Byrne, 1991; Clarke et al., 2015; Coye et al., 2015). To indicate multiple threats (some combination of eagle, leopard, falling tree, and neighboring group), monkeys will combine 6 different calls into a 25-call sequence (Balter, 2010). But are such communications language?

In the late 1960s, psychologists Allen Gardner and Beatrix Gardner (1969) aroused enormous scientific and public interest with their work with Washoe, a young chimpanzee. Building on chimpanzees' natural tendencies for gestured communication, they taught Washoe sign language. After 4 years, Washoe could use 132 signs; by her life's end in 2007, she was using 250 signs (Metzler, 2011; Sanz et al., 1998).

During the 1970s, some chimpanzees reportedly began stringing signs together to form sentences. Washoe, for example, signed "You me go out, please." Some word combinations seemed creative—saying *water bird* for "swan" or *apple-which-is-orange* for "orange" (Patterson, 1978; Rumbaugh, 1977).

But by the late 1970s, other psychologists were growing skeptical. Were the chimps language champs or were the researchers chumps? Consider, said the skeptics:

- Ape vocabularies and sentences are simple—rather like those of a 2-year-old child. And unlike children, apes gain their limited vocabularies only with great difficulty (Wynne, 2004, 2008). Apes' signing might also be nothing more than aping their trainers' signs and learning that certain arm movements produce rewards (Terrace, 1979).

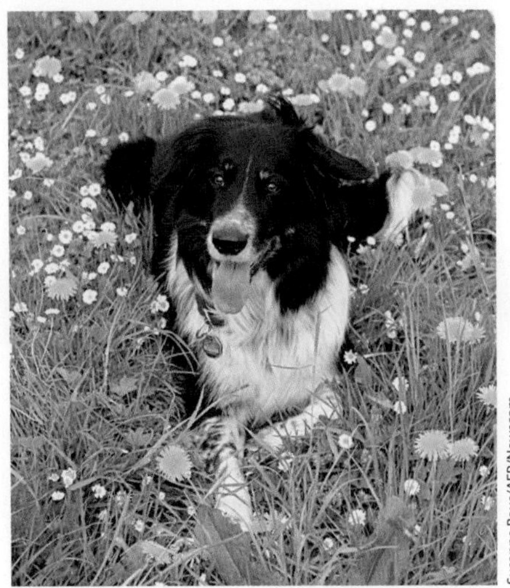

Susanne Baus/AFP/Newscom

Comprehending canine Border collie Rico had a vocabulary of 200 human words. If asked to retrieve a toy with a name he had never heard, Rico would pick out a new toy from a group of familiar items (Kaminski et al., 2004). Hearing that name for the second time 4 weeks later, Rico more often than not would retrieve the same toy. Another border collie, Chaser, set an animal record by learning 1000 object names (Pilley, 2013). Like a 3-year-old child, she could also categorize them by function and shape and could "fetch a ball" or "fetch a doll."

- When information is unclear, we are prone to *perceptual set*—a tendency to see what we want or expect to see. Interpreting chimpanzee signs as language may have been little more than the trainers' wishful thinking (Terrace, 1979). When Washoe seemingly signed *water bird,* she may actually have been separately naming *water* and *bird*.
- "Give orange me give eat orange me eat orange . . ." is a far cry from the exquisite syntax of a 3-year-old (Anderson, 2004; Pinker, 1995). Rules of syntax in human language govern the order of words in sentences. So to a child, "You tickle" and "Tickle you" communicate different ideas. Not so to a chimpanzee.

Controversy can stimulate progress, and in this case, it triggered more evidence of other species' abilities to think and communicate. One surprising finding was that Washoe trained her adopted son Loulis to use the signs she had learned. Without human assistance, Loulis eventually picked up 68 signs, simply by observing Washoe and three other language-trained chimps signing together. Even more stunning was a later report: Kanzi, a bonobo with a reported 384-word vocabulary, could understand syntax in spoken English (Savage-Rumbaugh et al., 1993, 2009). Kanzi, who appears to have the receptive language ability of a human 2-year-old, has responded appropriately when asked, "Can you show me the light?" and "Can you bring me the [flash]light?" and "Can you turn the light on?" Given stuffed animals and asked—for the first time—to "make the dog bite the snake," he put the snake to the dog's mouth.

So, are humans the only language-using species? If by *language* we mean an ability to communicate through a meaningful sequence of symbols, then apes are indeed capable of language. But if we mean a verbal or signed expression of complex grammar that enables us to exchange thoughts, most psychologists would now agree that humans alone possess language (Suddendorf, 2018).

One thing is certain: Studies of animal language and thinking have moved psychologists toward a greater appreciation of other species' remarkable abilities (de Waal, 2019; Wilson et al., 2015). In the past, many psychologists doubted that other species could plan, form concepts, count, use tools, or show compassion (Thorpe, 1974). Today, thanks to animal researchers, we know better. When communicating, chimps seem to consider what others know—*Does my friend know a snake is nearby?* (Crockford et al., 2017). Nonhuman animals exhibit insight, show family loyalty, care for one another, and transmit cultural patterns across generations. Working out what this means for the moral rights of other animals is an unfinished task.

ASK YOURSELF

Can you think of a time when you believed an animal was communicating with you? How might you put that to a test?

RETRIEVAL PRACTICE

RP-8 If your dog barks at a stranger at the door, does this qualify as language? What if the dog yips in a telltale way to let you know she needs to go out?

ANSWERS IN APPENDIX E

28 REVIEW Language and Thought

LEARNING OBJECTIVES

Test Yourself Answer these repeated Learning Objective Questions on your own (before "showing" the answers here, or checking the answers in Appendix D) to improve your retention of the concepts (McDaniel et al., 2009, 2015).

LOQ 28-1 What are the structural components of a language?

LOQ 28-2 How do we acquire language, and what did Chomsky mean by *universal grammar*?

LOQ 28-3 What are the milestones in language development, and when is the critical period for acquiring language?

LOQ 28-4 What brain areas are involved in language processing and speech?

LOQ 28-5 What is the relationship between thinking and language, and what is the value of thinking in images?

LOQ 28-6 What do we know about other species' capacity for language?

TERMS AND CONCEPTS TO REMEMBER

Test Yourself Write down the definition in your own words, then check your answer.

language, p. 340	two-word stage, p. 342
phoneme, p. 340	telegraphic speech, p. 342
morpheme, p. 340	aphasia, p. 345
grammar, p. 340	Broca's area, p. 345
syntax, p. 341	Wernicke's area, p. 345
babbling stage, p. 342	linguistic determinism, p. 346
one-word stage, p. 342	linguistic relativism, p. 346

MODULE TEST

Test Yourself Answer the following questions on your own first, then "show" the answers here, or check your answers in Appendix E.

1. Children reach the one-word stage of speech development at about
   a. 4 months.
   b. 6 months.
   c. 1 year.
   d. 2 years.

2. The three basic building blocks of language are ____________, ____________, and ____________.

3. When young children speak in short phrases using mostly verbs and nouns, this is referred to as ____________ ____________.

4. According to Chomsky, humans have a built-in predisposition to learn grammar rules. He called this trait ____________ ____________.

5. Most researchers agree that apes can
   a. communicate through symbols.
   b. gain vocabulary with little difficulty.
   c. comprehend language in adulthood.
   d. surpass a human 3-year-old in language skills.

CHAPTER
10

RealPeopleGroup/E+/Getty Images

Intelligence (Modules 29–31)

Little Natey's parents never thought he'd excel in the classroom. They were just being realistic: Their son often seemed bored at school. He was never the "smart" kid. Natey overwhelmingly preferred sports to studying. Eventually, he became a skilled musician, learning how to sing and to play multiple instruments. College wasn't in Natey's plans. He definitely wanted a music career. Then Natey's father suggested, "Maybe try a year of college. It can't hurt." So, Natey agreed.

To fill his course schedule, Natey registered for Introduction to Psychology. The assigned text — an earlier edition of the very book you're reading now — left him abuzz with excitement: "I had no idea you could use science to understand people!" Although he did not earn an A, Natey learned something that forever changed his life: Hard work and persistence could grow his knowledge.

With his new mindset, Natey immersed himself in psychology. He read dozens of psychology books and began to excel in his classes. He gained research experience and attended academic conferences. Natey went on to earn two master's degrees and a Ph.D. in psychology and became a professor — and one of your authors. Yes, that's correct: Natey (a family nickname) is me [ND].

Few topics have sparked more debate than intelligence: Does each of us have an inborn general mental capacity (intelligence)? Can we quantify this capacity as a meaningful number? How much does intelligence vary within and between groups, and why? Do beliefs about intelligence—whether it is unchangeable or can grow through experience—influence academic achievement?

Modules 29–31 offer answers, by identifying a variety of mental gifts and concluding that the recipe for high achievement blends talent, grit, and life circumstances.

MODULE 29 What Is Intelligence?

LEARNING OBJECTIVE QUESTION LOQ 29-1 How do psychologists define *intelligence*?

In many studies, *intelligence* has been defined as whatever *intelligence tests* measure, which has tended to be school smarts. But intelligence is not a quality like height or weight, which has the same meaning to everyone worldwide. Intelligence describes the qualities that enable people to achieve success in their own time and place (Sternberg & Kaufman, 1998). In Cameroon's equatorial forest, *intelligence* may reflect understanding the medicinal qualities of local plants. In a North American high school, it may reflect mastering difficult concepts in calculus or chemistry. In both places, **intelligence** is the ability to learn from experience, solve problems, and use knowledge to adapt to new situations.

You probably know some people with talents in science, others who excel in the humanities, and still others gifted in athletics, art, music, or dance. You may also know a talented artist who is stumped by the simplest math problem, or a brilliant math student who struggles when discussing literature. Are all these people intelligent? Could you rate their intelligence on a single scale? Or would you need several different scales?

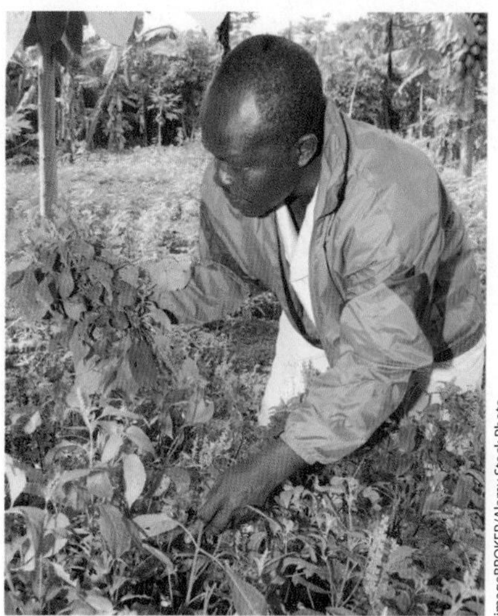

imageBROKER/Alamy Stock Photo

Hands-on healing The socially constructed concept of intelligence varies from culture to culture. This natural healer in Cameroon displays intelligence in his knowledge about medicinal plants and his understanding of the needs of the people he is helping.

Is Intelligence One General Ability?

LOQ 29-2 What are the arguments for *g*?

Charles Spearman (1863–1945) believed we have one **general intelligence** (often shortened to *g*) that is at the heart of all our intelligent behavior, from sailing the sea to sailing through school. He granted that people often have special, outstanding abilities. But he noted that those who score high in one area, such as verbal intelligence, typically score higher than average in other areas, such as spatial or reasoning ability.

Spearman's (1904) belief stemmed in part from his work with *factor analysis,* a statistical procedure that identifies clusters of related variables. His idea of a general mental capacity expressed by a single intelligence score was controversial in Spearman's day, and so it remains. One of Spearman's early critics was L. L. Thurstone (1887–1955). Thurstone gave 56 different tests to people and mathematically identified seven clusters of *primary mental abilities* (word fluency, verbal comprehension, spatial ability, perceptual speed, numerical ability, inductive reasoning, and memory). Thurstone did not rank people on a single scale of general aptitude. But when other investigators studied these profiles, they detected a persistent tendency: Those who excelled in one of the seven clusters generally scored well on the others. So, the investigators concluded, there was still some evidence of a *g* factor.

"*g* is one of the most reliable and valid measures in the behavioral domain . . . and it predicts important social outcomes such as educational and occupational levels far better than any other trait." —Behavior geneticist Robert Plomin (1999)

We might, then, liken mental abilities to physical abilities: Athleticism is not one thing, but many. The ability to run fast is distinct from the eye-hand coordination required to throw a ball on target. Yet there remains some tendency for good things to come packaged together—for running speed and throwing accuracy to correlate. So, too, with intelligence. Several distinct abilities tend to cluster together and to correlate enough to define a general intelligence factor. Distinct brain networks enable distinct abilities, with *g* explained by their coordinated activity (Cole et al., 2015; Kocevar et al., 2019).

intelligence the ability to learn from experience, solve problems, and use knowledge to adapt to new situations.

general intelligence *(g)* according to Spearman and others, underlies all mental abilities and is, therefore, measured by every task on an intelligence test.

fluid intelligence *(Gf)* our ability to reason speedily and abstractly; tends to decrease with age, especially during late adulthood.

crystallized intelligence *(Gc)* our accumulated knowledge and verbal skills; tends to increase with age.

Cattell-Horn-Carroll (CHC) theory the theory that our intelligence is based on general intelligence *(g)* as well as specific abilities, bridged by fluid intelligence *(Gf)* and crystallized intelligence *(Gc)*.

The Cattell-Horn-Carroll Intelligence Theory

LOQ 29-3 How have the concepts of *fluid intelligence* and *crystallized intelligence,* and the *CHC theory,* affected our understanding of intelligence?

Raymond Cattell (1905–1998) and his student, John Horn (1928–2006) simplified Thurstone's primary mental abilities into two factors: **fluid intelligence *(Gf)***—our ability to reason speedily and abstractly, as when solving logic problems—and **crystallized intelligence *(Gc)***—our accumulated knowledge as reflected in vocabulary and applied skills (Cattell, 1963). A mathematician may use her *Gf* to develop new theories of mathematics. Her *Gc* may be evident in the way she expertly discusses her research when teaching college math classes. Our *Gf* and *Gc* often work together, as when we solve problems by drawing on our accumulated knowledge.

The idea of a single intelligence factor *(g)* received support from hundreds of intelligence studies. But studies also confirm the distinction between fluid and crystallized intelligence, and more specific abilities (Carroll, 1993). The **Cattell-Horn-Carroll (CHC) theory** brings all of these abilities together in one cumulative framework, affirming a general intellectual ability factor and the existence of *Gf* and *Gc*. And it identifies more specific abilities, such as reading and writing ability, memory capacity, and processing speed (Schneider & McGrew, 2012). The CHC theory remains influential because it recognizes that intelligence comprises many abilities but that these specific abilities exist under a broader umbrella of general intelligence. This expanded view of intelligence has inspired other psychologists, particularly since the mid-1980s, to extend the definition of *intelligence* beyond the idea of academic smarts (Caemmerer et al., 2020).

Theories of Multiple Intelligences

LOQ 29-4 How do Gardner's and Sternberg's theories of multiple intelligences differ, and what criticisms have they faced?

Gardner's Multiple Intelligences

Howard Gardner has identified eight *relatively independent intelligences,* including the verbal and mathematical aptitudes assessed by standardized tests (**FIGURE 29.1**). Thus, the app developer, the poet, the street-smart adolescent, and the basketball team's playmaking point guard exhibit different kinds of intelligence (Gardner, 1998). Gardner (1999) has also proposed a ninth possible intelligence—*existential intelligence*—the ability "to ponder large questions about life, death, and existence." Gardner's notion of multiple

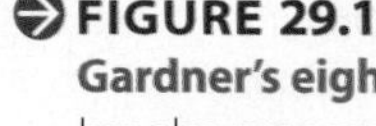

FIGURE 29.1
Gardner's eight intelligences Gardner has also proposed *existential intelligence* (the ability to ponder deep questions about life) as a ninth possible intelligence.

NATURALIST
LINGUISTIC
INTERPERSONAL
LOGICAL-MATHEMATICAL
INTRAPERSONAL
MUSICAL
BODILY-KINESTHETIC
SPATIAL

intelligences continues to influence many educators' belief that children have different "learning styles," such as visual and auditory (Newton & Miah, 2017). In one study, 93 percent of British teachers agreed that "individuals learn better when they receive information in their preferred Learning Style" (Dekker et al., 2012). Increasingly, however, research casts doubt on the idea of boosting comprehension in this way (Nancekivell et al., 2019; Papadatou-Pastou et al., 2018).

Gardner (1983, 2006, 2011; Davis et al., 2011) views intelligence domains as multiple abilities that come in different packages. Brain damage, for example, may destroy one ability but leave others intact. One man, Dr. P., had damage to a visual brain area. He spoke fluently and could walk a straight line. But his facial recognition ability suffered, causing him to mistake his wife for, of all things, a hat (Sacks, 1985). And consider people with **savant syndrome**, who have an island of brilliance but often score low on intelligence tests and may have limited or no language ability (Treffert, 2010). Some can compute complicated calculations almost instantly, or identify the day of the week of any given historical date, or render incredible works of art or music (Miller, 1999).

Then Chih Wey/Xinhua News Agency/Newscom

Islands of genius: savant syndrome After a brief helicopter ride over Singapore followed by 5 days of drawing, British savant artist Stephen Wiltshire accurately reproduced an aerial view of the city from memory.

The late memory whiz Kim Peek inspired the 1988 movie *Rain Man*. In 8 to 10 seconds, he could read and remember a page. During his lifetime, he memorized 9000 books, including Shakespeare's works and the Bible. He could provide GPS-like travel directions within any major U.S. city. Yet he could not button his clothes, and he had little capacity for abstract concepts. Asked by his father at a restaurant to lower his voice, he slid down in his chair to lower his voice box. Asked for Lincoln's Gettysburg Address, he responded, "227 North West Front Street. But he only stayed there one night—he gave the speech the next day" (Treffert & Christensen, 2005).

Sternberg's Three Intelligences

Robert Sternberg (1985, 2015, 2017) agrees with Gardner that there is more to success than academic intelligence and that we have multiple intelligences. But Sternberg's *triarchic theory* proposes three, not eight or nine, reliably measured intelligences:

- ***Analytical (academic problem-solving) intelligence*** is assessed by intelligence tests, which present well-defined problems having a single right answer. Such tests predict school grades reasonably well and vocational success more modestly.
- ***Creative intelligence*** is demonstrated in innovative smarts: the ability to adapt to new situations and generate novel ideas.
- ***Practical intelligence*** is required for everyday tasks that may be poorly defined and may have multiple solutions.

Gardner and Sternberg agree on two important points: Multiple abilities can contribute to life success, and differing varieties of giftedness bring both spice to life and challenges for education. Trained to appreciate such variety, many teachers have applied multiple intelligence theories in their classrooms.

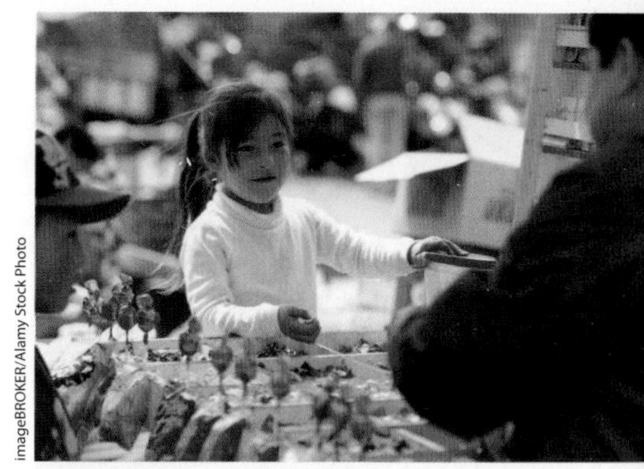

imageBROKER/Alamy Stock Photo

Street smarts This child selling candy on the streets of Bogota, Colombia, is developing practical intelligence at a very young age.

ASK YOURSELF

The concept of multiple intelligences assumes that the analytical school smarts measured by traditional intelligence tests are important, but that other abilities are also important. Different people have different gifts. What are yours?

General Intelligence, Grit, and Deliberate Practice

Wouldn't it be nice if the world were so fair that a weakness in one area would be compensated by genius in another? Alas, say scientists, the world is not fair (Brown et al., 2021; Ferguson, 2009). There is a general intelligence factor: g matters (Johnson et al., 2008). It predicts performance on various complex tasks and in various jobs (Gottfredson, 2002a,b, 2003a,b). Studies of nearly 70,000 people from 19 countries find that g predicts

savant syndrome a condition in which a person otherwise limited in mental ability has an exceptional specific skill, such as in computation or drawing. 

FIGURE 29.2
Smart and rich? Jay Zagorsky (2007) tracked 7403 participants in the U.S. National Longitudinal Survey of Youth across 25 years. As shown in this illustrative scatterplot, their intelligence scores correlated +.30 (a moderate positive correlation) with their later income.

Annual income: $275,000; 250,000; 225,000; 200,000; 175,000; 150,000; 125,000; 100,000; 75,000; 50,000; 25,000; 0

Score on intelligence test: 75 80 85 90 95 100 105 110 115 120 125 130

Higher childhood intelligence test scores predict higher adult income.

"I happen to have a talent for allocating capital. But my ability to use that talent is completely dependent on the society I was born into. If I'd been born into a tribe of hunters . . . I'd probably end up as some wild animal's dinner."—Warren Buffett, multibillionaire stock investor (2006)

higher incomes (Ganzach & Patel, 2018; see also **FIGURE 29.2**). And extremely high cognitive ability scores predict exceptional achievements, such as doctoral degrees and publications (Kuncel & Hezlett, 2010).

Even so, "success" is not a one-ingredient recipe. Although high academic intelligence will help you get into a profession (via schools and training programs), it alone won't make you successful once there. Success is a combination of talent and *grit:* Highly successful people tend also to be conscientious and doggedly energetic.

Skills that breed success seldom sprout spontaneously. It takes time to cultivate a seedling of talent. K. Anders Ericsson and others proposed a *10-year rule:* A common ingredient of expert performance in chess, dance, sports, computer programming, music, and medicine is "about 10 years of intense, daily practice" (Ericsson & Pool, 2016). Becoming a professional musician, chess player, or elite athlete requires, first, native ability (Macnamara et al., 2014, 2016; Vaci et al., 2019). But it also requires years of *deliberate practice*—about 11,000 hours on average (Campitelli & Gobet, 2011). The recipe for success is a gift of nature plus a whole lot of nurture.

For more on how self-disciplined grit feeds achievement, see the What Drives Us modules.

Christopher Lee/The New York Times/Redux Pictures

Talent + opportunity + practice After winning the New York State chess championship for kindergarten through third grade, Tanitoluwa ("Tani") Adewumi lugged his trophy to his home at the time—a homeless shelter. In the prior year, after his family fled terrorists in northern Nigeria, Tani learned chess at his elementary school, then began hours of daily practice. "He does 10 times more chess puzzles than the average kid," said his chess teacher, after Tani bested privately tutored children from elite schools (Kristof, 2019).

RETRIEVAL PRACTICE

RP-1 How does the existence of savant syndrome support Gardner's theory of multiple intelligences?

ANSWERS IN APPENDIX E

Emotional Intelligence

LOQ 29-5 What are the four components of emotional intelligence?

Social intelligence is the know-how involved in understanding social situations and managing yourself successfully (Cantor & Kihlstrom, 1987). Psychologist Edward Thorndike first proposed the concept in 1920, noting that "the best mechanic in a factory may fail as a [supervisor] for lack of social intelligence" (Goleman, 2006, p. 83).

A critical part of social intelligence, **emotional intelligence**, consists of four abilities (Mayer et al., 2002, 2012, 2016):

- ***Perceiving emotions*** (recognizing them in faces, music, and stories, and identifying our own emotions),
- ***Understanding emotions*** (predicting them and how they may change and blend),
- ***Managing emotions*** (knowing how to express them in varied situations, and how to handle others' emotions), and
- ***Using emotions*** to facilitate adaptive or creative thinking.

Emotionally intelligent people are both socially aware and self-aware. They avoid being hijacked by overwhelming depression, anxiety, or anger. They can read others' emotional cues and know what to say to soothe a grieving friend, encourage a workmate, and manage a conflict. They can delay gratification in pursuit of long-range rewards. Thus, emotionally intelligent people tend to succeed in relationship, career, and parenting situations where academically smarter but less emotionally intelligent people may fail (Cherniss, 2010a,b; Czarna et al., 2016; Miao et al., 2016). They also tend to be happy and healthy (Sánchez-Álvarez et al., 2016; Sarrionandia & Mikolajczak, 2020). And they do somewhat better academically (MacCann et al., 2020). Aware of these benefits, school-based programs have sought to increase teachers' and students' emotional intelligence (Mahoney et al., 2021).

* * *

For a summary of these theories of intelligence, see **TABLE 29.1**.

Donald Reilly/Cartoon Stock

"You're wise, but you lack tree smarts."

TABLE 29.1 Comparing Theories of Intelligence

Theory	Summary	Strengths	Other Considerations
Spearman's general intelligence (g)	A basic intelligence predicts our abilities in varied academic areas.	Different abilities, such as verbal and spatial, do have some tendency to correlate.	Human abilities are too diverse to be encapsulated by a single general intelligence factor.
Thurstone's primary mental abilities	Our intelligence may be broken down into seven distinct factors.	A single *g* score is not as informative as scores for seven primary mental abilities.	Even Thurstone's seven mental abilities show a tendency to cluster, suggesting an underlying *g* factor.
Cattell-Horn-Carroll (CHC) theory	Our intelligence is based on a general ability factor as well as other specific abilities, bridged by crystallized and fluid intelligence.	Intelligence is composed of broad and narrow abilities, such as reading ability, memory capacity, and processing speed.	The specific abilities outlined by the CHC theory may be too narrowly cognitive.
Gardner's multiple intelligences	Our abilities are best classified into eight or nine independent intelligences, which include a broad range of skills beyond traditional school smarts.	Intelligence is more than just verbal and mathematical skills. Other abilities are equally important to our human adaptability.	Should all our abilities be considered *intelligences?* Shouldn't some be called less vital *talents?*
Sternberg's triarchic theory	Our intelligence is best classified into three areas that predict real-world success: analytical, creative, and practical.	These three domains can be reliably measured.	These three domains may be less independent than the theory suggests, and may actually share an underlying *g* factor.
Emotional intelligence	Social intelligence is an important indicator of life success. Emotional intelligence is a key aspect of it, consisting of perceiving, understanding, managing, and using emotions.	These four components predict social success and emotional well-being.	Does this stretch the concept of intelligence too far?

RETRIEVAL PRACTICE

RP-2 How does the Cattell-Horn-Carroll theory of intelligence integrate the idea of having general intelligence as well as specific abilities?

ANSWERS IN APPENDIX E

emotional intelligence the ability to perceive, understand, manage, and use emotions.

MODULE

29 REVIEW What Is Intelligence?

LEARNING OBJECTIVES

Test Yourself Answer these repeated Learning Objective Questions on your own (before "showing" the answers here, or checking the answers in Appendix D) to improve your retention of the concepts (McDaniel et al., 2009, 2015).

LOQ **29-1** How do psychologists define *intelligence*?

LOQ **29-2** What are the arguments for *g*?

LOQ **29-3** How have the concepts of *fluid intelligence* and *crystallized intelligence*, and the *CHC theory*, affected our understanding of intelligence?

LOQ **29-4** How do Gardner's and Sternberg's theories of multiple intelligences differ, and what criticisms have they faced?

LOQ **29-5** What are the four components of emotional intelligence?

TERMS AND CONCEPTS TO REMEMBER

Test Yourself Write down the definition in your own words, then check your answer.

intelligence, p. 353
general intelligence *(g)*, p. 353
fluid intelligence *(Gf)*, p. 354
crystallized intelligence *(Gc)*, p. 354
Cattell-Horn-Carroll (CHC) theory, p. 354
savant syndrome, p. 355
emotional intelligence, p. 357

MODULE TEST

Test Yourself Answer the following questions on your own first, then "show" the answers here, or check your answers in Appendix E.

1. Charles Spearman suggested we have one ______________________ underlying success across a variety of intellectual abilities.
2. The existence of savant syndrome seems to support
   a. Sternberg's distinction among three types of intelligence.
   b. criticism of multiple intelligence theories.
   c. theories of multiple intelligences.
   d. Thorndike's view of social intelligence.
3. Sternberg's three types of intelligence are ______________, ______________, and ______________.
4. Emotionally intelligent people tend to
   a. seek immediate gratification.
   b. understand their own emotions but not those of others.
   c. understand others' emotions but not their own.
   d. succeed in their careers.

MODULE

30 Intelligence Assessment and Dynamics

LOQ **30-1** What is an *intelligence test,* and how do *achievement tests* and *aptitude tests* differ?

An **intelligence test** assesses people's mental aptitudes and compares them with those of others, using numerical scores. How do psychologists design such tests, and what makes them credible?

In your lifetime, you've taken dozens of mental ability tests: school tests of basic reading and math skills, course exams, intelligence tests, driver's license exams. These tests fall under two general categories:

- **Achievement tests**, which are intended to *reflect* what you have learned. Your final exam will measure what you learned in this class.
- **Aptitude tests**, which are intended to *predict* what you will be able to learn. If you took an entrance exam, it was designed to predict your ability to do college or university work.

An aptitude test is a "thinly disguised intelligence test," says Howard Gardner (1999). Indeed, report Meredith Frey and Douglas Detterman (2004), total scores on the U.S. SAT have correlated +0.82 with general intelligence test scores in a national sample of 14- to 21-year-olds (FIGURE 30.1). Aptitude also supports achievement: People who learn quickly are also better at retaining information (Zerr et al., 2018).

intelligence test a method for assessing an individual's mental aptitudes and comparing them with those of others, using numerical scores.

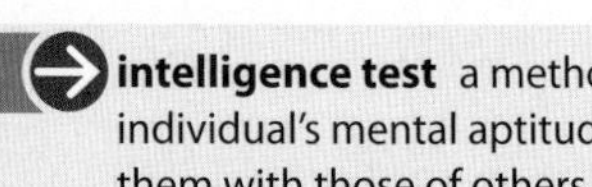

achievement test a test designed to assess what a person has learned.

aptitude test a test designed to predict a person's future performance; *aptitude* is the capacity to learn.

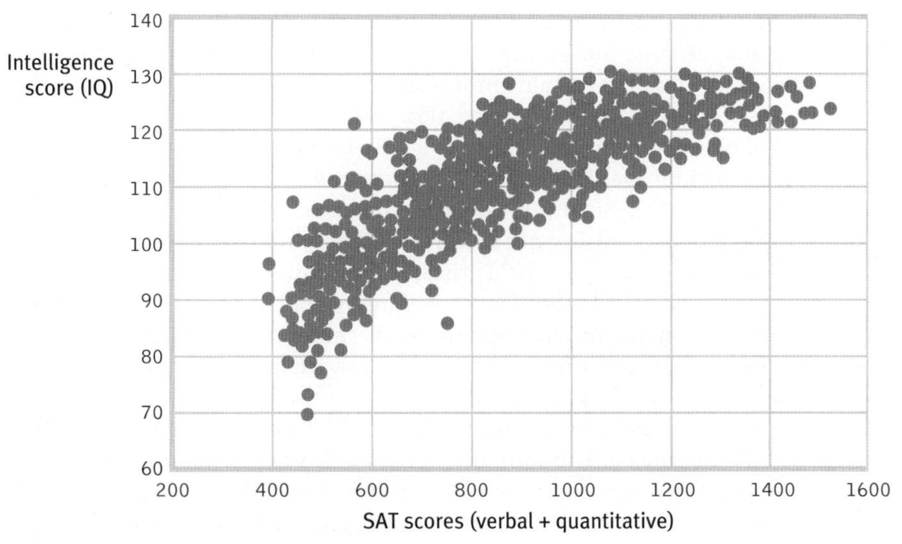
Intelligence score (IQ)
140
130
120
110
100
90
80
70
60
200
400
600
800
1000
1200
1400
1600
SAT scores (verbal + quantitative)

FIGURE 30.1
Close cousins: Aptitude and intelligence test scores A scatterplot shows the close correlation that has existed between intelligence test scores and verbal and quantitative SAT scores. (Data from Frey & Detterman, 2004.)

ASK YOURSELF

What achievement or aptitude tests have you taken? In your opinion, how well did these tests assess what you'd learned or predict what you were capable of learning?

Early and Modern Tests of Mental Abilities

LOQ 30-2 When and why were intelligence tests created, and how do today's tests differ from early intelligence tests?

Francis Galton: Presuming Hereditary Genius

Western attempts to assess such differences began in earnest with English scientist Francis Galton (1822–1911), who was fascinated with measuring human traits. When his cousin Charles Darwin proposed that nature selects successful traits through the survival of the fittest, Galton wondered if it might be possible to measure "natural ability" and to encourage those of high ability to mate with one another. At the 1884 London Health Exhibition, more than 10,000 visitors received his assessment of their "intellectual strengths" based on such things as reaction time, sensory acuity, muscular power, and body proportions. But alas, on these measures, well-regarded adults and students did not outscore others. Nor did the measures correlate with each other.

Although Galton's quest for a simple intelligence measure failed, he gave us some statistical techniques that we still use (as well as the phrase *nature and nurture*). And his persistent belief in the inheritance of genius—reflected in his book, *Hereditary Genius* (1869)—illustrates an important lesson from both the history of intelligence research and the history of science: Although science itself strives for objectivity, individual scientists are affected by their own assumptions and attitudes.

Alfred Binet (1857–1911) "Some recent philosophers have given their moral approval to the deplorable verdict that an individual's intelligence is a fixed quantity, one which cannot be augmented. We must protest and act against this brutal pessimism" (Binet, 1909, p. 141).

Macmillan Learning

Alfred Binet: Predicting School Achievement

Modern intelligence testing traces its birth to early twentieth-century France, where a new law required all children to attend school. French officials knew that some children, including many newcomers to Paris, would need special classes. But how could the schools make fair judgments about children's learning potential? Teachers might assess children who had little prior education as slow learners. Or they might sort children into classes by their social backgrounds. To minimize such bias, France's minister of public education gave psychologist Alfred Binet the task of designing fair tests.

Binet and his student, Théodore Simon, began by assuming that all children follow the same course of intellectual development but that some develop more rapidly (Nicolas & Levine, 2012). A child with an intellectual developmental disorder should score much

mental age a measure of intelligence test performance devised by Binet; the level of performance typically associated with children of a certain chronological age. Thus, a child who does as well as an average 8-year-old is said to have a mental age of 8.

Stanford-Binet the widely used U.S. revision (by Terman at Stanford University) of Binet's original intelligence test.

intelligence quotient (IQ) defined originally as the ratio of mental age *(ma)* to chronological age *(ca)* multiplied by 100 (thus, IQ = *ma*/*ca* × 100). On contemporary intelligence tests, the average performance for a given age is assigned a score of 100.

like a typical younger child, and an intellectually gifted child like a typical older child. Thus, their goal became measuring each child's **mental age**, the level of performance typically associated with a certain chronological age. The average 8-year-old, then, has a mental age of 8. An 8-year-old with a below-average mental age (perhaps performing at the level of typical 6-year-old) would struggle with age-appropriate schoolwork.

To measure mental age, Binet and Simon theorized that mental aptitude, like athletic aptitude, is a general capacity that shows up in various ways. They tested a variety of reasoning and problem-solving questions on Binet's two daughters, and then on what they called "backward" and "bright" Parisian schoolchildren. Items answered correctly could then predict how well other French children would handle their schoolwork.

Binet and Simon made no assumptions concerning *why* a particular child was slow, average, or precocious. Binet personally leaned toward an environmental explanation. To raise the capacities of low-scoring children, he recommended "mental orthopedics" that would help develop their attention span and self-discipline. He believed his intelligence test did not measure inborn intelligence as a scale measures weight. Rather, it had a single practical purpose: to identify French schoolchildren needing special attention. Binet hoped his test would be used to improve children's education, but he also feared it would be used to label children and limit their opportunities (Gould, 1981).

RETRIEVAL PRACTICE

RP-1 What did Binet hope to achieve by establishing a child's mental age?

ANSWERS IN APPENDIX E

Lewis Terman: Measuring Innate Intelligence

After Binet's death in 1911, others adapted his tests for use as a numerical measure of intelligence. Lewis Terman (1877–1956) was an ambitious Stanford University professor who sought to bring intelligence testing to the United States. At a young age, Terman presumed he wasn't destined for an intellectual life (Terman, 1930). He grew up the twelfth of fourteen children, the son of farmers who had little education. Terman overcame being burned in a fire, breaking a hip, and tuberculosis (Boring, 1959). His persistence and unquenchable reading appetite led him out of his one-room schoolhouse to a local college and later to Stanford University to study children who, like him, were born with high general intelligence *(g)*.

To achieve his goal, Terman tried the Paris-developed questions and age norms with California kids. Adapting some of Binet's original items, adding others, and establishing new age norms, Terman extended the upper end of the test's range from age 12 to "superior adults." He also gave his revision the name today's version retains—the **Stanford-Binet**.

So, how were these intelligence tests scored? The **intelligence quotient (IQ)** was a formula developed by German psychologist William Stern. The IQ was simply a person's mental age divided by chronological age, multiplied by 100. Thus, the average 8-year-old child, whose mental age and chronological age match, has an IQ of 100. But an 8-year-old who answers questions as would a typical 10-year-old has an IQ of 125:

$$\text{IQ} = \frac{\text{mental age of 10}}{\text{chronological age of 8}} \times 100 = 125$$

This original IQ formula worked fairly well for children but not for adults. (Should a 40-year-old who does as well on the test as an average 20-year-old be assigned an IQ of only 50?) Most current intelligence tests, including the Stanford-Binet, no longer compute an IQ in this manner (though the term *IQ* still lingers as a shorthand expression for "intelligence test score"). Instead, they assign a score that represents a test-taker's performance *relative to the average performance* (arbitrarily set at 100) of others the same age. Most people—about 68 percent of those taking an intelligence test—fall between 85 and 115.

Terman assumed that intelligence tests revealed a mental capacity present from birth. He also assumed that some ethnic groups were naturally more intelligent than

THAT'S MY BOY, MARK... HE'S 39, BUT HE'S ALREADY READING AT A 42-YEAR-OLD LEVEL...
© Dave Coverly/speedbump.com

Mrs. Randolph takes mother's pride too far.

others. And he supported *eugenics,* the discriminatory nineteenth- and twentieth-century movement that proposed measuring human traits and encouraging only those deemed "fit" to reproduce—as well as preventing those deemed "inferior" from doing so.

With Terman's help, the U.S. government developed new tests to evaluate both newly arriving immigrants and World War I army recruits—the world's first mass administration of an intelligence test. To some psychologists, the results indicated the inferiority of people not sharing their Anglo-Saxon heritage. Abuses of the early intelligence tests serve to remind us that science can be value laden. Behind a screen of scientific objectivity, ideology may lurk.

RETRIEVAL PRACTICE

RP-2 What is the IQ score of a 4-year-old with a mental age of 5?

ANSWERS IN APPENDIX E

David Wechsler: Testing Separate Strengths

Psychologist David Wechsler created what is now the most widely used individual intelligence test, the **Wechsler Adult Intelligence Scale (WAIS)**, together with a version for school-age children (the *Wechsler Intelligence Scale for Children [WISC]*), and another for preschool children (Evers et al., 2012). The 2008 edition of the WAIS consists of 15 subtests, including these:

- ***Similarities***—reasoning the commonality of two objects or concepts ("In what way are wool and cotton alike?")
- ***Vocabulary***—naming pictured objects, or defining words ("What is a guitar?")
- ***Block design***—visual abstract processing ("Using the four blocks, make one just like this.")

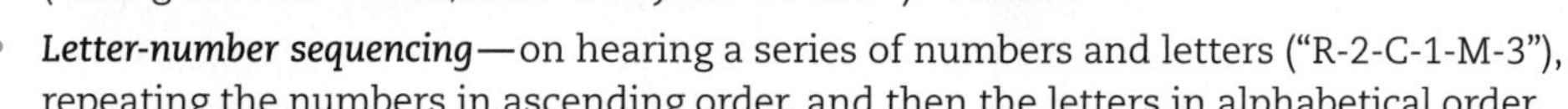

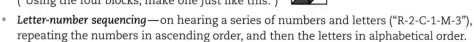

- ***Letter-number sequencing***—on hearing a series of numbers and letters ("R-2-C-1-M-3"), repeating the numbers in ascending order, and then the letters in alphabetical order.

The WAIS yields not only an overall intelligence score, as does the Stanford-Binet, but also separate scores for verbal comprehension, perceptual reasoning, *working memory,* and processing speed. In such ways, this test helps realize Binet's aim: to identify those who could benefit from special educational opportunities for improvement.

Richard T. Nowitz/The Image Bank/Getty Images

Matching patterns Block-design puzzles test visual abstract processing ability. Wechsler's individually administered intelligence test comes in forms suited for adults and children.

RETRIEVAL PRACTICE

RP-3 An employer with a pool of applicants for a single available position is interested in testing each applicant's potential. To determine that, she should use an ____________ (achievement/aptitude) test. That same employer, wishing to test the effectiveness of a new, on-the-job training program, would be wise to use an ____________ (achievement/aptitude) test.

ANSWERS IN APPENDIX E

Principles of Test Construction

LOQ 30-3 What is a *normal curve,* and what does it mean to say that a test has been *standardized* and is *reliable* and *valid*?

To be widely accepted, a psychological test must meet three criteria: It must be *standardized, reliable,* and *valid.* The Stanford-Binet and Wechsler tests meet these requirements.

Standardization

To know how well you performed on an intelligence test, you would need some basis for comparison. That's why test-makers give new tests to a representative sample of people. The scores from this pretested group become the basis for future

Wechsler Adult Intelligence Scale (WAIS)  the WAIS and its companion versions for children are the most widely used intelligence tests; they contain verbal and performance (nonverbal) subtests.

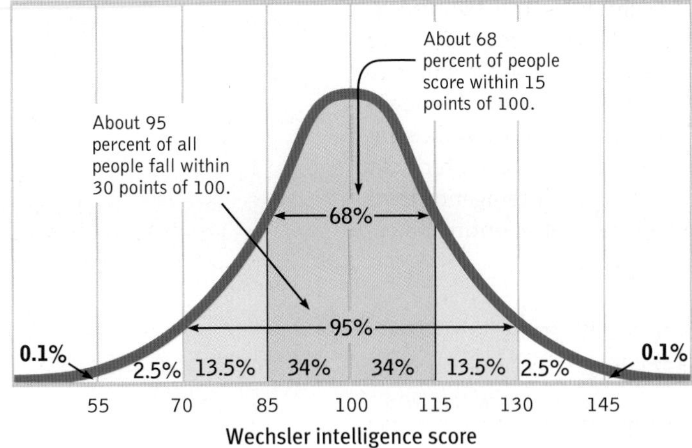
Number of scores
About 68 percent of people score within 15 points of 100.
About 95 percent of all people fall within 30 points of 100.
68%
95%
0.1%
2.5%
13.5%
34%
34%
13.5%
2.5%
0.1%
55
70
85
100
115
130
145
Wechsler intelligence score

FIGURE 30.2
The normal curve Scores on aptitude tests tend to form a normal, or bell-shaped, curve around an average score. For the Wechsler scale, for example, the average score is 100. Note: Numbers do not add up to 100 percent due to rounding.

comparisons. If you then take the test following the same procedures, your score, when compared with others, will be meaningful. This process is called **standardization**.

For many human attributes—height, weight, and mental aptitude—people's scores typically form a bell-shaped pattern called the *bell curve,* or **normal curve**. The curve's highest point is the average score. On an intelligence test, we give this average score a value of 100 (**FIGURE 30.2**). Moving out from the average toward either extreme, we find fewer and fewer people. For both the Stanford-Binet and Wechsler tests, a person's score indicates whether that person's performance fell above or below the average. A score of 130 would indicate that only 2.5 percent of test-takers performed better. About 95 percent of all people score within 30 points of 100.

To keep the average score near 100, the Stanford-Binet and Wechsler scales are periodically restandardized. If you recently took the WAIS, Fourth Edition, your performance was compared with a standardization sample who took the test during 2007, not to David Wechsler's initial 1930s sample. If you compared the performance of the most recent standardization sample with that of the 1930s sample, do you suppose you would find rising or declining test performance? Amazingly—given that college entrance aptitude scores have sometimes dropped, such as during the 1960s and 1970s—intelligence test performance has improved. This worldwide phenomenon is called the *Flynn effect,* in honor of New Zealand researcher James Flynn (1987, 2012, 2018), who first calculated its magnitude. Flynn observed that the average person's intelligence test score rose three points per decade. Thus, an average person in 1920 would—by today's standard—score only a 76! Such rising performance has been observed in 49 countries, from Sweden to Sudan (Dutton et al., 2018; Wongupparaj et al., 2015). Countries that have shown the greatest growth in IQ score over time have also experienced more economic growth (Rindermann & Becker, 2018). Although there have been some regional reversals, the historic increase is now widely accepted as an important phenomenon (Lynn, 2009; Teasdale & Owen, 2008).

The Flynn effect's cause has been a psychological mystery. Did it result from greater test sophistication? *No.* Gains appeared before testing was widespread. Perhaps better nutrition? Thanks to improved nutrition, people have gotten taller as well as smarter. But in postwar Britain, noted Flynn (2009), children in families with lower income gained the most from improved nutrition, yet the intelligence performance gains were greater among children in families with higher income. Might the explanation be greater educational opportunities, smaller families, and rising living standards (Pietschnig & Voracek, 2015; Rindermann et al., 2016)? For example, children around the world now have access to educational programs such as *Sesame Street* that increase their intellectual performance and reduce their prejudice toward children from different ethnic backgrounds (Kwauk et al., 2016). Flynn (2012) attributes the IQ score increases to our need to develop new mental skills to cope with modern environments. Regardless of what combination of factors explains the rise in intelligence test scores, the phenomenon counters one concern of some hereditarians—that the higher twentieth-century birthrates among those with lower scores would shove human intelligence scores downward (Lynn & Harvey, 2008).

standardization defining uniform testing procedures and meaningful scores by comparison with the performance of a pretested group.

normal curve the bell-shaped curve that describes the distribution of many physical and psychological attributes. Most scores fall near the average, and fewer and fewer scores lie near the extremes.

reliability the extent to which a test yields consistent results, as assessed by the consistency of scores on two halves of the test, on alternative forms of the test, or on retesting.

Reliability

Knowing where you stand in comparison to a standardization group still won't say much about your intelligence unless the test has **reliability**. A reliable test, when retaken, gives consistent scores. To check a test's reliability, researchers test people many times. They may split the test in half (*split-half:* agreement of odd-question scores and even-question scores), test with alternative forms of the test, or retest with the same test *(test-retest)*. The higher the *correlation* between the two scores, the higher the test's reliability. The tests we have considered—the Stanford-Binet, the WAIS, and the WISC—are very reliable after early childhood (with *correlation coefficients* of about +.9). In retests, sometimes decades later, people's scores are generally similar to their first score (Deary et al., 2009; Lyons et al., 2017).

validity the extent to which a test measures or predicts what it is supposed to. (See also *predictive validity*.)

predictive validity the success with which a test predicts the behavior it is designed to predict; it is assessed by computing the correlation between test scores and the criterion behavior. (Also called *criterion-related validity*.)

Validity

High reliability does not ensure a test's **validity**—the extent to which the test actually measures or predicts what it promises. Imagine using a tape measure with faulty markings. If you use it to measure people's heights, your results will be very reliable. No matter how many times you measure a person's height, you will get a consistent result. But those results will not be valid.

We expect intelligence tests to have **predictive validity**: They should predict the criterion of future performance, and to some extent they do. In one analysis of 223,000 students from 171 colleges and universities, SAT aptitude scores correlated +.5 with first-year college grade-point average (Westrick et al., 2019). Higher SAT aptitude scores also predict a greater likelihood of returning for a second year of college. Thus, the SAT has predictive validity of first-year college success and retention. And SAT aptitude scores correlate about +.8 with those for the Graduate Record Examination (the GRE; an aptitude test similar to the SAT but for those applying to graduate school) (Wai et al., 2018).

Are general aptitude tests as predictive as they are reliable? *No.* Aptitude test scores do predict school grades (Roth et al., 2015). But as critics are fond of noting, the predictive power of aptitude tests peaks in the early school years and weakens later. Academic aptitude test scores are reasonably good predictors of school achievement for children ages 6 to 12, where the correlation between intelligence score and school performance is about +.6 (Jensen, 1980). Intelligence scores correlate even more closely with scores on later achievement tests: +.81 in one comparison of 70,000 English children's intelligence scores at age 11 with their academic achievement in national exams at age 16 (Deary et al., 2007, 2009). The SAT, used in the United States as a college entrance exam, has been less successful in predicting first-year college grades. (The correlation, less than +.5, has been, however, a bit higher when adjusting for high scorers electing tougher courses [Berry & Sackett, 2009; Willingham et al., 1990].) By the time we get to the GRE, the correlation with graduate school performance is an even more modest but still significant +.4 (Kuncel & Hezlett, 2007).

Why does the predictive power of aptitude scores diminish as students move up the educational ladder? Consider a parallel situation: Among all U.S. and Canadian football linemen, body weight correlates with success. A 300-pound player tends to overwhelm a 200-pound opponent. But within the narrow 280- to 320-pound range typically found at the professional level, the correlation between weight and success becomes negligible (FIGURE 30.3). The narrower the *range* of weights, the lower the predictive power of body weight becomes. If an elite university takes only those students who have very high aptitude scores, and then gives them a restricted range of high grades, those scores cannot possibly predict much. This will be true even if the test has excellent predictive validity with a more diverse sample of students. Likewise, modern grade inflation has produced less diverse high school grades. With their diminished range, high school grades now predict college grades no better than have SAT scores (Sackett et al., 2012). So, when we validate a measure using a wide range of scores but then use it with a restricted range of scores, it loses much of its predictive validity.

Michael Ciaglo/Colorado Springs Gazette/MCT/Getty Images

FIGURE 30.3

Diminishing predictive power Let's imagine a correlation between football linemen's body weight and their success on the field. Note how insignificant the relationship becomes when we narrow the range of weight to 280 to 320 pounds. As the range of data under consideration narrows, its predictive power diminishes.

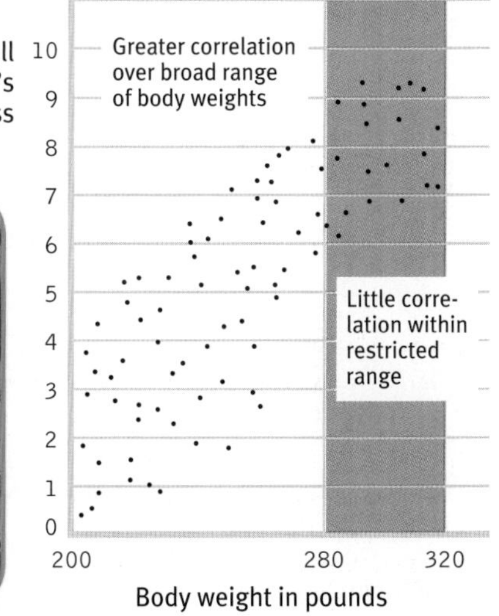
Football linemen's success
10
9
8
7
6
5
4
3
2
1
0
Greater correlation over broad range of body weights
Little correlation within restricted range
200
280
320
Body weight in pounds

RETRIEVAL PRACTICE

RP-4 What are the three criteria that a psychological test must meet in order to be widely accepted? Explain.

RP-5 Correlation coefficients were used in this section. Here's a quick review: Correlations do not indicate cause-effect, but they do tell us whether two things are associated in some way. A correlation of −1.00 represents perfect ________________ (agreement/disagreement) between two sets of scores: As one score goes up, the other score goes ________________ (up/down). A correlation of ________________ represents no association. The highest correlation, +1.00, represents perfect ________________ (agreement/disagreement): As the first score goes up, the other score goes ________________ (up/down).

ANSWERS IN APPENDIX E

Extremes of Intelligence

LOQ 30-4 What are the traits of those at the low and high intelligence extremes?

One way to glimpse the validity and significance of any test is to compare people who score at the two extremes of the normal curve. The two groups should differ noticeably, and on intelligence tests, they do.

The Low Extreme

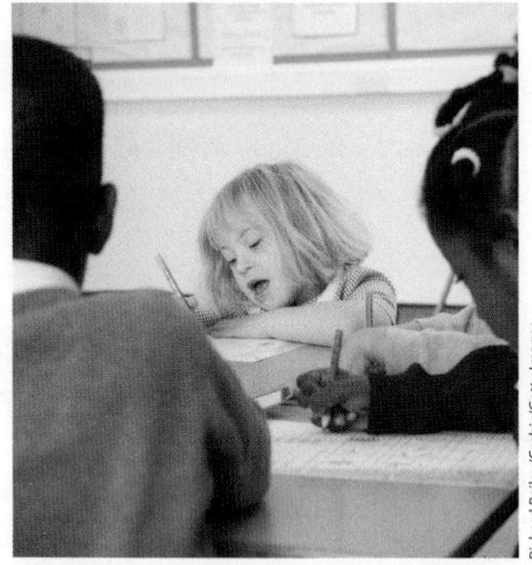
Richard Bailey/Corbis/Getty Images

Integrated intelligence Many U.S. classrooms combine children with differing intellectual abilities, providing additional support services as needed.

Intellectual developmental disorder is a neurodevelopmental disorder that is apparent before age 18, sometimes with a known physical cause. To be diagnosed with an intellectual developmental disorder, a person must—among other criteria (see the Psychological Disorders modules)—have a test score of 70 or below. For some, intelligence test scores can mean life or death. In the United States (one of the only industrialized countries with the death penalty), the Flynn effect means fewer people are now eligible for execution. Why? Because in 2002, the U.S. Supreme Court ruled that the execution of people with an intellectual developmental disorder is "cruel and unusual punishment." For Teresa Lewis, that test score cutoff was 70. Lewis, a "dependent personality" with limited intellect (a reported intelligence test score of 72), allegedly agreed to a plot in which two men killed her husband and stepson in exchange for a split of a life insurance payout (Eckholm, 2010). The State of Virginia executed Lewis in 2010. If only she had scored 69.

In 2014, the U.S. Supreme Court recognized the imprecision and arbitrariness of a fixed cutoff score of 70, and required states with death row inmates who have scored just above 70 to consider other evidence. Thus, Ted Herring, who had scored 72 and 74 on intelligence tests—but didn't know that summer follows spring or how to transfer between buses—was taken off Florida's death row (Alvarez & Schwartz, 2014).

The High Extreme

Barbara Smaller/Cartoon Stock

"Zach is in the gifted-and-talented-and-you're-not class."

Children whose intelligence test scores indicate extraordinary academic gifts mostly thrive. In one famous project begun in 1921, Lewis Terman studied more than 1500 California schoolchildren with IQ scores over 135. These high-scoring children (later called the "Termites") were—like those in later studies—healthy, well-adjusted, and unusually successful academically (Friedman & Martin, 2012; Lubinski, 2016). Their success continued over the next seven decades. Most had attained high levels of education, and many were doctors, lawyers, professors, scientists, and writers (Austin et al., 2002; Holahan & Sears, 1995).

Other studies have followed the lives of precocious youths who had aced the math SAT at age 13—by scoring in the top 1 percent of their age group. By their fifties, these math whizzes had secured 681 patents and many had achieved eminence, often in STEM (science, technology, engineering, and math) fields (Bernstein et al., 2019; Lubinski et al., 2014). About 1 percent of Americans earn doctorates. But for the 12- and 13-year-olds who scored in the top 1 in 10,000 among those of their age taking the SAT, about 40 percent had done so (Kell et al., 2013; Makel et al., 2016). Among U.S. high-scoring whiz kids were Google co-founder Sergey Brin and musician Stefani Germanotta (Lady Gaga) (Clynes, 2016).

Schooling and Intelligence

"Gifted child" programs tend to segregate high-scoring children in special classes, often giving them academic enrichment not available to their peers. "Remedial" programs generally mainstream children, but give them access to resources that help them overcome challenges. Critics note that grouping ("tracking") students by aptitude sometimes creates a self-fulfilling prophecy: Implicitly labeling some children as "ungifted" and denying them enrichment opportunities can widen the achievement gap between ability groups (Batruch et al., 2019). Because minority and low-income youth are more often placed in lower academic groups, tracking can also promote segregation and prejudice—hardly, note critics, a healthy preparation for working and living in a modern world.

Critics and proponents of gifted education do, however, agree on this: Children have differing gifts, whether at math, verbal reasoning, art, or social leadership. Educating children as if all were alike is as naive as assuming that giftedness is something, like curly hair, that you either have or do not have. One need not stick labels on children to affirm their special talents or their challenges, and to reach them all at the frontiers of their own ability and understanding. By providing *appropriate placement* suited to each child's talents (as when allowing a math whiz to study math at a higher level, or providing extra resources to children struggling to read), we can promote both equity and excellence for all (Subotnik et al., 2011).

Intelligence Across the Life Span

What happens to our intellectual muscles as we age? Do they gradually decline, as does our body strength? Or do they remain constant? To see how psychologists have studied intelligence across the life span—and for an illustration of psychology's self-correcting process—see Thinking Critically About: Cross-Sectional and Longitudinal Studies.

Stability or Change?

LOQ 30-6 How stable are intelligence test scores over the life span?

What can we predict from a child's early-life intelligence scores? Will a precocious 2-year-old mature into a talented college student and a brilliant senior citizen? Maybe—or maybe not. For most children, intelligence assessments before age 3 only modestly predict future aptitudes (Humphreys & Davey, 1988; Tasbihsazan et al., 2003; Yu et al., 2018). Some precocious preschoolers become brilliant adults, but even Albert Einstein was once thought "slow"—as he was in learning to talk (Quasha, 1980).

By age 4, however, children's performance on intelligence tests begins to predict their adolescent and adult scores. The consistency of scores over time increases with the age of the child (Tucker-Drob & Briley, 2014). By age 11, the stability becomes impressive, as Ian Deary and his colleagues (2004, 2009, 2013) discovered when they retested the same **cohort**—the same group of people—over many years. Their amazing longitudinal studies have been enabled by their country, Scotland, doing something no nation has done before or since. On June 1, 1932, essentially every child in the country born in 1921—87,498 children around age 11—took an intelligence test. The aim was to identify working-class children who would benefit from further education. Sixty-five years later to the day, Deary's colleague Lawrence Whalley and Whalley's wife Patricia scoured the dusty storeroom shelves at the Scottish Council for Research in Education, not far from Deary's Edinburgh University office. At the last possible moment, Patricia uncovered the test results tucked away in a brown paper sack (Carpenter, 2001). "This will change our lives," Deary replied when Whalley told him the news.

21 Day $1,608,627

The stability of intelligence At age 4, James Holzhauer was featured in a *Chicago Tribune* article about his math ability. By age 7, he was in the fifth grade (Jacobs, 2019). At age 34, he won 32 consecutive appearances on the quiz show *Jeopardy!*

cohort a group of people sharing a common characteristic, such as being from a given time period. 

Thinking Critically About:
Cross-Sectional and Longitudinal Studies

LOQ 30-5 What are *cross-sectional studies* and *longitudinal studies*, and why is it important to know which method was used?

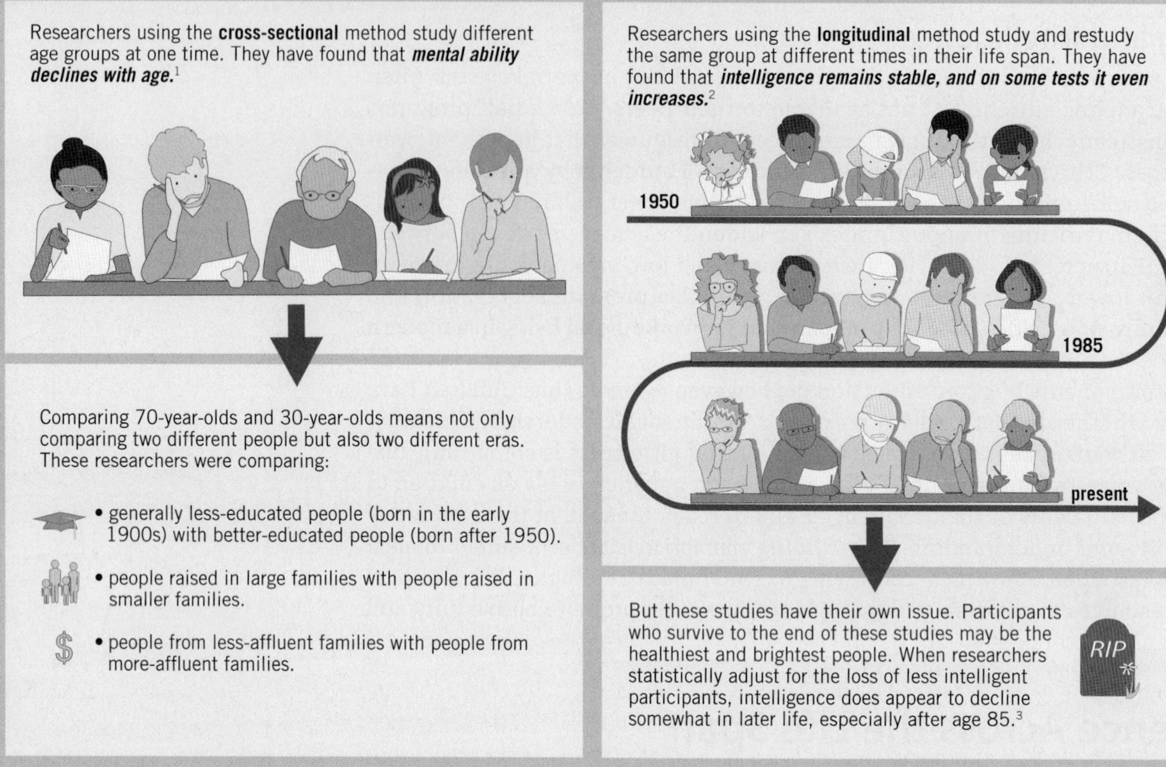

Researchers using the **cross-sectional** method study different age groups at one time. They have found that ***mental ability declines with age.***[1]
Comparing 70-year-olds and 30-year-olds means not only comparing two different people but also two different eras. These researchers were comparing:
• generally less-educated people (born in the early 1900s) with better-educated people (born after 1950).
• people raised in large families with people raised in smaller families.
• people from less-affluent families with people from more-affluent families.
Researchers using the **longitudinal** method study and restudy the same group at different times in their life span. They have found that ***intelligence remains stable, and on some tests it even increases.***[2]
1950
1985
present
But these studies have their own issue. Participants who survive to the end of these studies may be the healthiest and brightest people. When researchers statistically adjust for the loss of less intelligent participants, intelligence does appear to decline somewhat in later life, especially after age 85.[3]
RIP

1. Wechsler, 1972. 2. Salthouse, 2010, 2014; Schaie & Geiwitz, 1982. 3. Brayne et al., 1999.

cross-sectional study research that compares people of different ages at the same point in time.

longitudinal study research that follows and retests the same people over time.

And so it has, with dozens of studies of the stability and the predictive capacity of these early test results. One of Deary's studies, for example, retested 542 survivors from the 1932 test group now at age 80. The correlation between the two sets of scores—after nearly 70 years of varied life experiences—was striking (**FIGURE 30.4**). Ditto when 106 survivors were retested at age 90 (Deary et al., 2013). Another study that followed Scots born in 1936 from ages 11 to 70 confirmed the remarkable stability of intelligence, independent of life circumstance (Johnson et al., 2010).

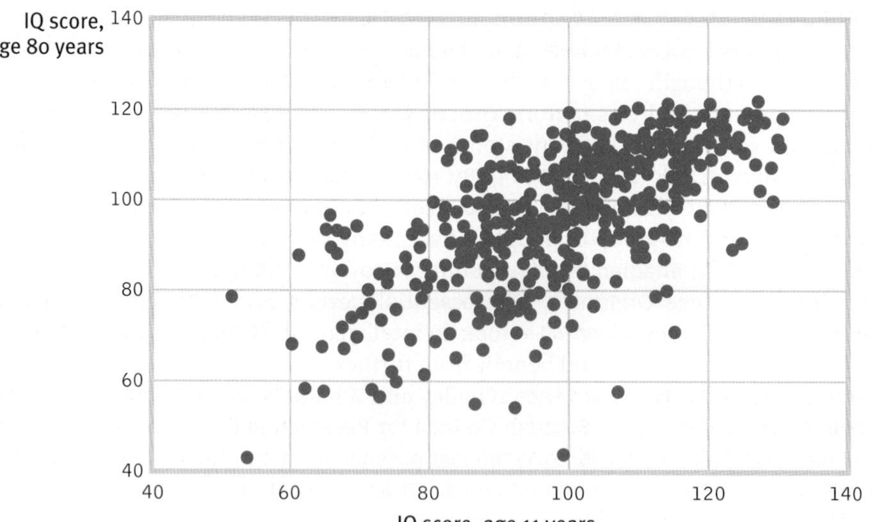

IQ score, age 80 years
140
120
100
80
60
40
40
60
80
100
120
140
IQ score, age 11 years

FIGURE 30.4
Intelligence endures When Ian Deary and his colleagues retested 80-year-old Scots, using an intelligence test they had taken as 11-year-olds, their scores across seven decades correlated +.66, as shown here. (Data from Deary et al., 2004.) When 106 survivors were again retested at age 90, the correlation with their age 11 scores was +.54 (Deary et al., 2013).

Children and adults who are more intelligent tend to live healthier and longer lives (Cadar et al., 2020; Geary, 2019). High-scoring adolescents, 50 years later, even *feel* younger than their age (Stephan et al., 2018). Why might this intelligence-health link exist? Deary (2008) has proposed four possible explanations:

1. Intelligence facilitates more education, better jobs, and a healthier environment.
2. Intelligence encourages healthy living: less smoking, better diet, and more exercise.
3. Prenatal events or early childhood illnesses can influence both intelligence and health.
4. A "well-wired body," as evidenced by fast reaction speeds, perhaps fosters both intelligence and longevity.

"Whether you live to collect your old-age pension depends in part on your IQ at age 11." —Ian Deary, "Intelligence, Health, and Death," 2005

GLASBERGEN
© Randy Glasbergen

"We're looking for someone with the wisdom of a 50-year-old, the experience of a 40-year-old, the drive of a 30-year-old, and the payscale of a 20-year-old."

Aging and Intelligence

LOQ 30-7 How does aging affect crystallized intelligence *(Gc)* and fluid intelligence *(Gf)*?

It matters what questions psychological scientists ask, but as we've seen, sometimes it matters even more *how* they ask them—the research methods they use. Cross-sectional studies had shown that older adults gave fewer correct answers on intelligence tests than did younger adults. These findings caused WAIS-creator David Wechsler (1972) to conclude that "the decline of mental ability with age is part of the general [aging] process of the organism as a whole." For a long time, this rather dismal view went unchallenged. Many corporations established mandatory retirement policies, assuming the companies would benefit by replacing aging workers with younger, more capable employees. This thinking persists today, with some countries requiring professors to retire by age 60 (Hong Kong) or 65 (the Netherlands). As "everyone knows," you can't teach an old dog new tricks. But after colleges in the 1920s began giving intelligence tests to entering students, psychologists using longitudinal studies (retesting the same cohorts over a period of years) discovered that intelligence remained stable. On some tests, scores even increased, due partly to experience with the tests (Salthouse, 2014) (**FIGURE 30.5**). Methods matter.

"Knowledge is knowing a tomato is a fruit; wisdom is not putting it in a fruit salad." —Anonymous

The more optimistic results from longitudinal studies challenged the presumption that intelligence sharply declines with age. Famed painter Anna Mary Robertson Moses ("Grandma Moses") took up painting in her seventies, and at age 88 a popular magazine named her "Young Woman of the Year." At age 89, architect Frank Lloyd Wright designed New York City's Guggenheim Museum. At age 101, neuropsychologist Brenda Milner was still conducting research and supervising students. As everyone knows, given good health, you're never too old to learn.

For most people, aging leads to losses and gains. We simultaneously lose recall memory and processing speed but gain vocabulary and knowledge (Ackerman, 2014; Tucker-Drob et al., 2019; **FIGURE 30.6**). *Crystallized intelligence (Gc)*—our accumulated knowledge as reflected in vocabulary and analogies tests—increases up to old age. *Fluid intelligence (Gf)*—our ability to reason speedily and abstractly, as when solving novel logic problems—may decline, but older adults' social reasoning skills increase, as shown by an ability to take multiple perspectives, to appreciate knowledge limits, and to offer helpful wisdom in times of social conflict (Grossmann et al., 2010). Decisions also become less distorted by negative emotions, such as anxiety, depression, and anger (Blanchard-Fields, 2007; Carstensen & Mikels, 2005).

FIGURE 30.5
Cross-sectional versus longitudinal testing of intelligence at various ages In this test of one type of verbal intelligence (inductive reasoning), the cross-sectional method showed declining scores with age. The longitudinal method (in which the same people were retested over a period of years) showed a slight rise in scores well into adulthood. (Data from Schaie, 1994.)

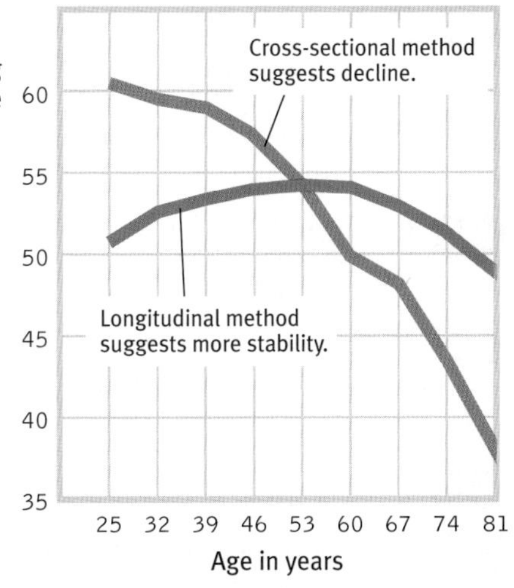
Reasoning ability score
60
55
50
45
40
35
Cross-sectional method suggests decline.
Longitudinal method suggests more stability.
25 32 39 46 53 60 67 74 81
Age in years
Cross-sectional method
Longitudinal method

These life-span differences in mental abilities help explain why older adults are less likely to embrace new technologies and have more difficulty detecting lies (Brashier & Schacter, 2020; Charness & Boot, 2009; Pew, 2017). These cognitive differences also help explain why mathematicians and scientists produce much of their most creative work, and chess players' performance peaks, during their late twenties or early thirties, when *Gf* is at its highest point (Jones et al., 2014; Strittmatter et al., 2020). In contrast, authors, historians, and philosophers tend to produce their best work in their forties, fifties, and beyond—after building their *Gc*, or accumulated knowledge (Simonton, 1988, 1990).

FIGURE 30.6
With age, we lose and we win When Joe Biden assumed the U.S. presidency at age 78, many wondered: Would he have the mental agility to be entrusted with the cognitive demands of national and world leadership? With age comes diminishing physical capabilities and a lessening ability to think speedily (fluid intelligence). But later life also offers an accumulation of applicable knowledge (crystallized intelligence) along with an enhanced wisdom that enables older adults to navigate conflicts, to respond with emotional composure, and to appreciate the limits of their knowledge. "In youth we learn, in age we understand," observed the nineteenth-century novelist Marie Von Ebner-Eschenbach.

Joe Raedle/Getty Images

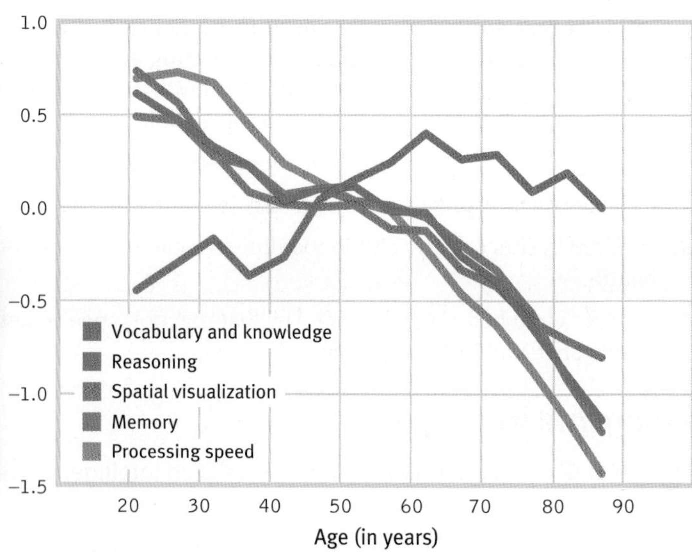
Relative performance above or below average (with average test-taker's score as zero)
1.0
0.5
0.0
−0.5
−1.0
−1.5
Vocabulary and knowledge
Reasoning
Spatial visualization
Memory
Processing speed
20
30
40
50
60
70
80
90
Age (in years)

RETRIEVAL PRACTICE

RP-6 Researcher A wants to study how intelligence changes over the life span. Researcher B wants to study the intelligence of people who are now at various life stages. Which researcher should use the cross-sectional method, and which the longitudinal method?

ANSWERS IN APPENDIX E

MODULE 30 REVIEW Intelligence Assessment and Dynamics

LEARNING OBJECTIVES

Test Yourself Answer these repeated Learning Objective Questions on your own (before "showing" the answers here, or checking the answers in Appendix D) to improve your retention of the concepts (McDaniel et al., 2009, 2015).

LOQ 30-1 What is an *intelligence test*, and how do *achievement tests* and *aptitude tests* differ?

LOQ 30-2 When and why were intelligence tests created, and how do today's tests differ from early intelligence tests?

LOQ 30-3 What is a *normal curve*, and what does it mean to say that a test has been *standardized* and is *reliable* and *valid*?

LOQ 30-4 What are the traits of those at the low and high intelligence extremes?

LOQ 30-5 What are *cross-sectional studies* and *longitudinal studies*, and why is it important to know which method was used?

LOQ 30-6 How stable are intelligence test scores over the life span?

LOQ 30-7 How does aging affect crystallized intelligence *(Gc)* and fluid intelligence *(Gf)*?

TERMS AND CONCEPTS TO REMEMBER

Test Yourself Write down the definition in your own words, then check your answer.

intelligence test, p. 358
achievement test, p. 358
aptitude test, p. 358
mental age, p. 360
Stanford-Binet, p. 360
intelligence quotient (IQ), p. 360
Wechsler Adult Intelligence Scale (WAIS), p. 361
standardization, p. 362
normal curve, p. 362
reliability, p. 362
validity, p. 363
predictive validity, p. 363
cohort, p. 365
cross-sectional study, p. 366
longitudinal study, p. 366

MODULE TEST

Test Yourself Answer the following questions on your own first, then "show" the answers here, or check your answers in Appendix E.

1. The IQ score of 6-year-old Shanice, who has a measured mental age of 9, would be
   a. 67.
   b. 133.
   c. 86.
   d. 150.

2. The Wechsler Adult Intelligence Scale (WAIS) is best able to tell us
   a. about innate intelligence among groups.
   b. whether the test-taker will succeed in a job.
   c. how the test-taker compares with other adults in vocabulary and arithmetic reasoning.
   d. whether the test-taker has specific skills for music and the performing arts.
3. The Stanford-Binet, the Wechsler Adult Intelligence Scale, and the Wechsler Intelligence Scale for Children yield consistent results, for example on retesting. In other words, these tests have high ________________.
4. Which of the following is NOT a possible explanation for the fact that people with higher intelligence scores tend to live longer, healthier lives?
   a. Intelligence facilitates more education, better jobs, and a healthier environment.
   b. Intelligence encourages a more health-promoting lifestyle.
   c. Intelligent people have slower reaction times, so are less likely to put themselves at risk.
   d. Prenatal events or early childhood illnesses could influence both intelligence and health.
5. Use the concepts of *Gc* and *Gf* to explain why writers tend to produce their most creative work later in life, while scientists often hit their peak much earlier.

MODULE

31 Genetic and Environmental Influences on Intelligence

Intelligence runs in families. But why? Are our intellectual abilities mostly inherited? Or are they molded by our environment?

Heredity and Intelligence

LOQ 31-1 What is *heritability*, and what do twin and adoption studies tell us about the nature and nurture of intelligence?

Heritability is the portion of variation among individuals in a group that we can attribute to genes. Estimates of the heritability of intelligence—the extent to which intelligence test score variation within a group can be attributed to genetic variation—range from 50 percent to 80 percent (Madison et al., 2016; Plomin et al., 2016; Plomin & von Stumm, 2018). Does this mean that we can assume that 50 percent to 80 percent of *your* intelligence is due to your genes, and the rest to your environment? *No.* Heritability never applies to an individual, only to *why people in a group differ from one another.*

Identical twins share the same genes; do they also share mental abilities? As you can see from **FIGURE 31.1**, which summarizes many studies, the answer is clearly *Yes.* Even when adopted by two different families, their intelligence test scores are very similar. When raised together, their scores are nearly as similar as those of the same person taking the same test twice (Haworth et al., 2009; Lykken, 2006; Plomin et al., 2016). Identical twins also exhibit substantial similarity (and heritability) in specific talents, such as music, math, and sports.

Are there known genes for genius? When 100 researchers pooled their data on 269,867 people, all of the gene variations analyzed accounted for only about 5 percent of the differences in educational achievement (Savage et al., 2018). Another analysis of genes from 1.1 million people accounted for about 12 percent of their educational attainment differences (J. J. Lee et al., 2018). Like height, which is predicted by nearly 10,000 known DNA sequences, intelligence is *polygenic,* involving many genes (Kaiser, 2020). What matters for intelligence (as for height, personality, sexual orientation, or just about any human trait), as well as for disorders such as schizophrenia, is the combination of many genes.

heritability the proportion of variation among individuals in a group that we can attribute to genes. The heritability of a trait may vary, depending on the range of populations and environments studied.

© Christopher Fitzgerald/Topfoto

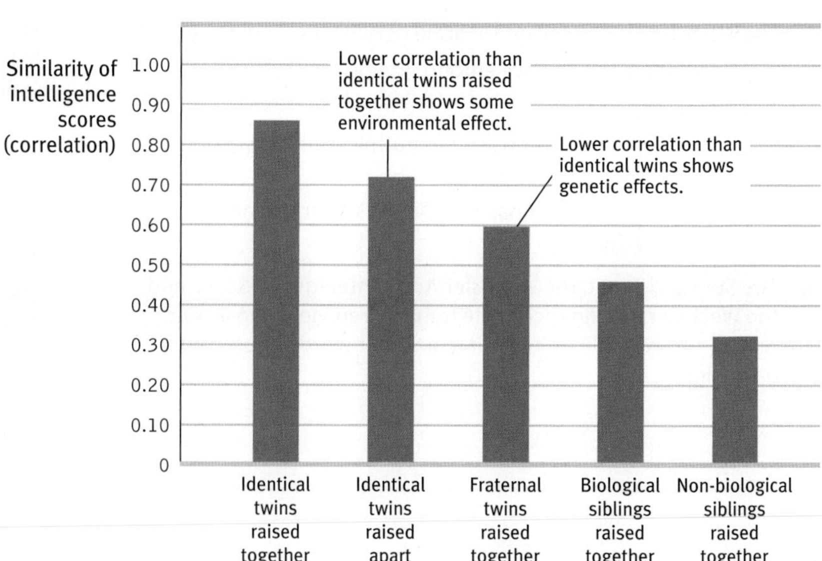
Similarity of intelligence scores (correlation)
1.00
0.90
0.80
0.70
0.60
0.50
0.40
0.30
0.20
0.10
0
Lower correlation than identical twins raised together shows some environmental effect.
Lower correlation than identical twins shows genetic effects.
Identical twins raised together
Identical twins raised apart
Fraternal twins raised together
Biological siblings raised together
Non-biological siblings raised together

FIGURE 31.1
Intelligence: nature and nurture The most genetically similar people have the most similar intelligence scores. Remember: 1.00 indicates a perfect positive correlation; zero indicates no correlation at all. (Data from McGue et al., 1993.)

Environment and Intelligence

Fraternal twins are genetically no more alike than other biological siblings, but they usually share an environment and are often treated similarly. Their intelligence test scores are also more alike than are the scores of nontwin siblings (see Figure 31.1). So, environment does have some effect. Adoption studies help us assess the influence of environment. Seeking to untangle genes and environment, researchers have also compared the intelligence test scores of adopted children with those of (a) their *biological parents,* who provided their genes, (b) *adoptive parents,* who provided their home environment, and (c) *adoptive siblings,* who shared that home environment.

Several studies suggest that a shared environment exerts a modest influence on intelligence test scores:

- Adoption from poverty into financially secure homes enhances children's intelligence test scores (Nisbett et al., 2012). One large Swedish study looked at this effect among children adopted into wealthier families with more educated parents. The adopted children's IQ scores were higher, by an average of 4.4 points, than those of their non-adopted biological siblings (Kendler et al., 2015).
- Adoption of mistreated or neglected children enhances their intelligence scores (Almas et al., 2017).
- The intelligence scores of "virtual twins"—same-age, unrelated children adopted as infants and raised together as siblings—correlate positively: +.28 (Segal et al., 2012).

During childhood, adoptive siblings' test scores correlate modestly. Over time, adopted children accumulate experience in their differing adoptive families. So, would you expect the shared-environment effect to grow with age and the genetic-legacy effect to shrink?

If you would, behavior geneticists have a stunning surprise for you. Adopted children's intelligence scores resemble those of their biological parents much more than those of their adoptive parents (Loehlin, 2016). And over time, adopted children's verbal ability scores become *more* like those of their biological parents (**FIGURE 31.2**). Mental ability similarities between adopted children and their adoptive families wane with age (McGue et al., 1993). Who would have guessed?

Genetic influences become more apparent as we accumulate life experience. Identical twins' similarities, for example, continue or increase into their eighties. In one massive study of 11,000 twin pairs in four countries, the heritability of general intelligence *(g)* increased from 41 percent in middle childhood to 55 percent in adolescence to 66 percent in young adulthood (Haworth et al., 2010). Thus, report Ian Deary and his colleagues (2009, 2012), the heritability of general intelligence increases from "about 30 percent" in early childhood to "well over 50 percent in adulthood."

Leo Cullum/Cartoon Stock

"Selective breeding has given me an aptitude for the law, but I still love fetching a dead duck out of freezing water."

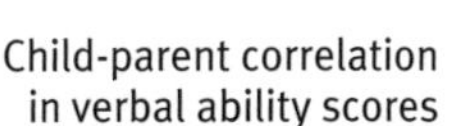
Child-parent correlation
in verbal ability scores

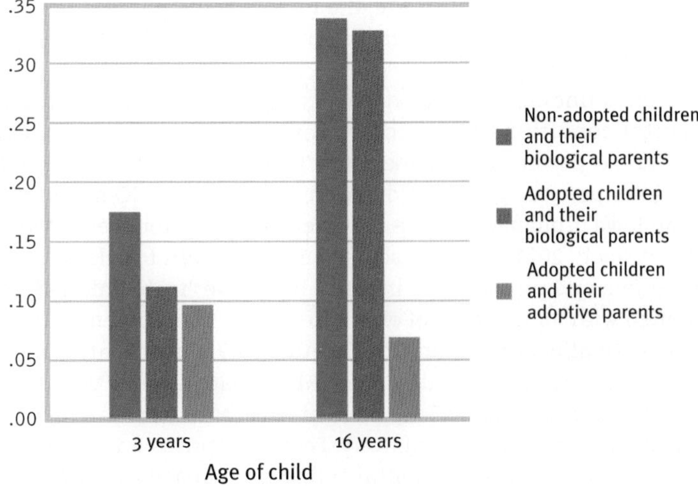
.35
.30
.25
.20
.15
.10
.05
.00
3 years
16 years
Age of child
Non-adopted children and their biological parents
Adopted children and their biological parents
Adopted children and their adoptive parents

FIGURE 31.2
In verbal ability, whom do adopted children resemble? As the years went by in their adoptive families, children's verbal ability scores became more like their *biological* parents' scores. (Data from Plomin & DeFries, 1998; Plomin et al., 2016.)

RETRIEVAL PRACTICE

RP-1 A check on your understanding of heritability: If environments become more equal, the heritability of intelligence will

a. increase. **b.** decrease. **c.** be unchanged.

ANSWERS IN APPENDIX E

Gene–Environment Interactions

LOQ 31-2 How can environmental influences affect cognitive development?

Genes and experience together weave the fabric of intelligence. *Epigenetics* studies part of the dynamic biology of this nature–nurture meeting place. With all our abilities—whether mental or physical—*our genes shape the experiences that shape us.* If you have a natural aptitude for dance, you will probably perform more often than others (getting more practice, instruction, and experience). Or, if you have a natural aptitude for academics, you will more likely stay in school, read books, and ask questions—all of which will increase your brain power. The same would be true for your identical twin—who might, not just for genetic reasons, also become a star performer. In these gene–environment interactions, small genetic advantages can trigger social experiences that multiply our original skills (Cheesman et al., 2020; Sauce & Matzel, 2018).

Sometimes, however, environmental conditions work in reverse, depressing physical or cognitive development. Severe deprivation leaves footprints on the human brain. Nowhere is the intertwining of biology and experience more apparent than in the most hopeless human environments, such as J. McVicker Hunt (1982) observed in a destitute Iranian orphanage. The typical child Hunt observed there could not sit up unassisted at age 2 or walk at age 4. The minimal care infants received was not in response to their crying, cooing, or other behaviors, so the children developed little sense of personal control over their environment. Extreme deprivation had crushed their native intelligence—a finding confirmed by other studies of children raised in poorly run orphanages in Romania and elsewhere (Nelson et al., 2009, 2013; van IJzendoorn et al., 2008).

Aware of both the dramatic effects of early experiences and the impact of early intervention, Hunt began a training program for the Iranian caregivers, teaching them to play language-fostering games with 11 infants. They imitated the babies' babbling, engaged them in vocal follow-the-leader, and, finally, they taught the infants sounds from the Persian language. The results were

Devastating neglect Some Romanian orphans, such as these children in the Leaganul Pentru Copii orphanage in 1990, had minimal interaction with caregivers and suffered delayed development.

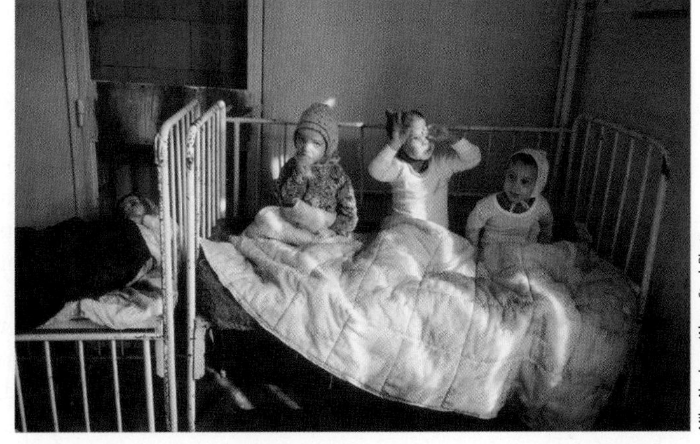

Mike Abrahams/Alamy Stock Photo

dramatic. By 22 months of age, the infants could name more than 50 objects and body parts, and so charmed visitors that most were adopted—an unprecedented success for the orphanage.

Hunt's findings are an extreme case of a more general finding: The poor environmental conditions that accompany poverty can depress cognitive development (Heberle & Carter, 2015; Tuerk, 2005). The environment's influence was strikingly apparent after psychologist Harold Skeels in 1934 did an IQ assessment of two toddler girls at an Iowa orphanage, where they were "scarcely touched, never held, rarely spoken to" (Brookwood, 2021). With IQ scores below 50, both toddlers were deemed ineligible for adoption, and placed in an institution for the "feebleminded" to be cared for by adult women with mental ages of only 5 to 9 years. The women lavished their new foster children with affection. When Skeels returned 9 months later, he was amazed to find the girls "alert, attractive, [and] playful. After nearly 2 years with their new caregivers, their IQs had risen to 95 and 93. By their late 20s, both were married and with children in loving households." Nurture matters. People's worries and distractions can also consume cognitive bandwidth and diminish thinking capacity. On tests of cognitive functioning, sugar cane farmers in India scored better after being paid for their harvest—when their money worries dropped (Mani et al., 2013).

If extreme conditions—sensory deprivation, social isolation, poverty—can slow brain development, could the reverse also be true? Could an "enriched" environment amplify development and give very young children a superior intellect? Most experts doubt it (DeLoache et al., 2010; Reichert et al., 2010; Vance, 2018). There is no environmental recipe for fast-forwarding a normal infant into a genius. All babies should have normal exposure to sights, sounds, and speech. Beyond that, Sandra Scarr's (1984) verdict still is widely shared: "Parents who are very concerned about providing special educational lessons for their babies are wasting their time."

More encouraging results have come from intensive, post-babyhood enrichment programs (Dodge et al., 2017; Sasser et al., 2017; Tucker-Drob, 2012). This is particularly true of preschool programs for children living in poverty (Gormley et al., 2013; Heckman & Karapakula, 2019; Magnuson et al., 2007). Intelligence scores also rise with nutritional supplements for pregnant people and newborns (3.5 points), with quality preschool experiences (4 points), and with interactive reading programs (6 points) (Protzko et al., 2013).

It pays to view intelligence as expandable Psychologist Carol Dweck has shown several benefits of adopting a growth mindset—believing that intelligence grows through motivated effort. Companies with mission statements that endorse a growth mindset, for example, have more trusting and committed employees (Canning et al., 2020).

Courtesy Dr. Carol Dweck

Growth Mindset

Schooling and intelligence interact, and both enhance later income (Ceci & Williams, 1997, 2009). But what we accomplish with our intelligence depends also on our own beliefs and motivation. One analysis of 72,431 undergraduates found that study motivation and study skills rivaled aptitude and previous grades as predictors of academic achievement (Credé & Kuncel, 2008). Even intelligence test performance can be affected by motivation. Four dozen studies show that, when promised money for doing well, adolescents score higher on such tests (Duckworth et al., 2011).

These observations would not surprise psychologist Carol Dweck (2018; Dweck & Yeager, 2019). She reports that believing intelligence is changeable fosters a **growth mindset**, a focus on learning and growing. Conversely, believing that intelligence is innately fixed fosters less optimism about people's capacity for change and growth (Tao et al., 2021). Teachers who adopt a growth mindset tend to view their schools as more likely to improve (Rechsteiner et al., 2021).

Researcher Gregory Walton (2020) teaches a growth mindset to his young children when they tire while biking home: "It's when you're tired and you keep going that your muscles get stronger." Dweck likewise teaches young teens that the brain is like a muscle, growing stronger with use as neuron connections grow: "Learning how to do a new kind of problem grows your math brain!" Receiving praise for *effort* and for tackling challenges, rather than for being smart or accomplished, helps teens understand the link between hard work and success (Gunderson et al., 2013).

growth mindset a focus on learning and growing rather than viewing abilities as fixed.

A growth mindset doesn't alter inborn intelligence, so its benefits should not be overstated or lead children to blame themselves for their struggles. But it can make children and youth more resilient when confronted with difficult learning material or frustrating people (Peng & Tullis, 2020; Walton & Wilson, 2018). One national experiment with 6320 lower-achieving U.S. high school students showed that viewing two 25-minute videos fostering a growth mindset modestly improved grades (Yeager et al., 2019). Mindset is only part of the story, but it does matter.

More than 300 studies confirm that ability + opportunity + motivation = success in fields from sports to science to music (Ericsson et al., 2007). Extremely high intelligence-test-scoring 12-year-olds are much more likely than the average person to earn doctorates and hold patents—if their ability is "coupled with commitment" (Makel et al., 2016). High school students' math proficiency and college students' grades reflect their aptitude but also their self-discipline, their belief in the power of effort, and a curious, "hungry mind" (Murayama et al., 2013; Richardson et al., 2012; von Stumm et al., 2011). Consider Zaila Avant-garde, who in 2021 became the first African American winner of the U.S. national spelling bee contest. For 2 years, she studied tens of thousands of words with her father and participated in 18 spelling competitions. Not only is she America's best speller; Avant-garde also holds three world records for basketball dribbling (Cramer & Yuhas, 2021). Zaila Avant-garde shows us how to realize our potential: *Believe* in your ability to learn, and *apply* yourself with sustained effort.

Scott McIntyre/The New York Times/Redux Pictures

U.S. national spelling bee champion Zaila Avant-garde

These repeated findings—that a growth mindset and disciplined effort enhance achievement—have generated attention. Applying growth mindset findings in large-scale interventions with at-risk students can have a downside: the social cost of blaming struggling individuals for their circumstances (Ikizer & Blanton, 2016). And researchers and educators sometimes overstate the modest growth-mindset benefit (Burgoyne et al., 2020). Overemphasizing growth-mindset power can, as with the motivational concept of grit, leave some students feeling that their disappointments reflect a moral flaw. Sometimes people need more than the power of positive thinking to overcome their harsh conditions.

"When you [fail], embrace it; learn from it. Don't think . . . that's going to hinder you from becoming whoever you want to become . . . . I wake up every day telling the world: Come on baby, let's ride. What you got for me?" —Recording artist Pitbull, 2019

ASK YOURSELF

Are you working to the potential reflected in your standardized aptitude test scores? What, other than your aptitude, is affecting your school performance?

Group Differences in Intelligence Test Scores

If there were no group differences in intelligence test scores, psychologists would have less debate over hereditary and environmental influences. But there are group differences. What are they? And what shall we make of them?

Gender Similarities and Differences

LOQ 31-3 How and why do the genders differ in mental ability scores?

In science, as in everyday life, it is differences—not similarities—that excite interest. Men's self-estimated intelligence is often higher than women's self-estimated intelligence, which may fuel a false perception that men are smarter than women (Furnham, 2016). In truth, men's and women's intelligence differences are minor. For example, in that 1932 testing of all Scottish 11-year-olds, boys' intelligence scores averaged 100.5 and girls' 100.6 (Deary et al., 2003). As far as *g* is concerned, the genders are the same.

Testosterone therapy for those transitioning from female to male results in brain language-processing areas that become more male-like, as well as some gray matter loss (Hahn et al., 2016).

Yet most people find differences more newsworthy. In cultures where both girls and boys are educated, girls tend to outpace boys in spelling, verbal fluency, and reading—skills that may affect their career choices, some researchers suspect (Breda & Napp, 2019; Reilly et al., 2019). They are better emotion detectors and are more sensitive to touch, taste, and color (Halpern et al., 2007).

Which one of the options below matches the Original?

Original

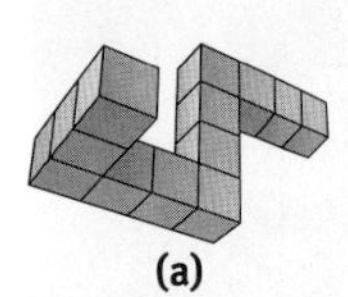
(a)

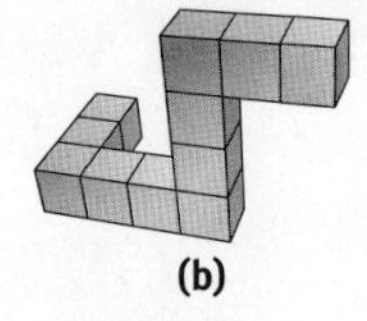
(b)

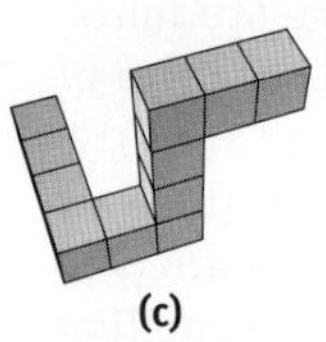
(c)

FIGURE 31.3
A mental rotation test These kinds of items are often found on spatial abilities tests. See answer in footnote.[1]

In math computation and overall math performance, girls and boys hardly differ (Else-Quest et al., 2010; Hyde & Mertz, 2009; Lindberg et al., 2010). On complex math problems, men outperform women. But the most reliable male edge appears in spatial ability tests like the one shown in **FIGURE 31.3** (Lauer et al., 2019). The solution requires speedy mental rotation of three-dimensional objects. Male mental ability scores (and brains) also vary more (Wierenga et al., 2022). Worldwide, boys and men outnumber girls and women at both the low and high extremes (Ball et al., 2017; Baye & Monseur, 2016). Boys, for example, are more likely than girls to need remedial math classes. But they are also more likely to earn the highest math scores.

Psychologist Steven Pinker (2005) has argued for the evolutionary perspective—that biology affects gender differences in life priorities (women's somewhat greater interest in people versus men's in money and things), in risk-taking (with men more reckless), and in math reasoning and spatial abilities. Such differences are, he noted, observed across cultures, stable over time, influenced by prenatal hormones, and observed in boys raised as girls.

But social expectations and opportunities also construct gender by shaping interests and abilities (Jiang et al., 2020). Stephen Ceci and Wendy Williams (2010, 2011) reported that culturally influenced preferences help explain why U.S. women, more than men, avoid math-intensive vocations. In Asia and Russia, teen girls have outperformed boys in an international science exam; in North America and Britain, boys have scored higher (Fairfield, 2012).

More gender-equal cultures, such as Sweden and Iceland, exhibit little of the gender math gap found in gender-unequal cultures, such as Turkey and Korea (Guiso et al., 2008; Kane & Mertz, 2012). Since the 1970s, as gender equity has increased in the United States, the boy-to-girl ratio among 12- to 14-year-olds with very high SAT math scores (above 700) has declined from 13 to 1 to 3 to 1 (Makel et al., 2016; Nisbett et al., 2012). And in psychology, there's been a dramatic change in the ratio of women to men earning doctorates—from 17 percent women in 1958 to 71 percent in 2018 (Burelli, 2008; NSF, 2019). As we have seen in so many areas of life, cultural expectations and opportunities matter.

Punch Cartoon Library/TopFoto

"That's an excellent suggestion, Miss Triggs. Perhaps one of the men would like to suggest it."

Stanford News Service/Zuma Press/Newscom

(a)

Henrik Montgomery/AP Photo

(b)

Henrik Montgomery/AP Photo

(c)

Shrinking the STEM gap In 2014, Iranian math professor Maryam Mirzakhani (1977–2017) became the first woman to win math's most admired award, the Fields Medal (a). In 2018, physicist Donna Strickland (b) and chemist Frances C. Arnold (c) were each awarded a Nobel Prize in scientific fields where women have rarely won. In her acceptance speech, Strickland said, "Not everyone thinks physics is fun, but I do."

Racial and Ethnic Similarities and Differences

LOQ 31-4 How and why do racial and ethnic groups differ in mental ability scores?

Fueling the group-differences debate are two other disturbing but scientifically agreed-upon facts:

- Racial and ethnic groups differ in their average intelligence test scores.
- High-scoring people (and groups) are more likely to attain high levels of education and income.

[1] The correct answer is c.

There are many group differences in average intelligence test scores. New Zealanders of European descent outscore native Maori New Zealanders. Israeli Jews outscore Israeli Arabs. Most Japanese outscore most Burakumin, a stigmatized Japanese minority. And White Americans have outscored Black Americans, although this difference has diminished, especially among children (Dickens & Flynn, 2006; Nisbett et al., 2012). Such *group* differences provide little basis for judging individuals. Worldwide, women outlive men by 5 years, but knowing only an individual's gender won't tell us how long that person will live.

We have seen that heredity contributes to *individual* differences in intelligence. But group differences in a heritable trait may be entirely environmental. Consider one of nature's experiments: Allow some children to grow up hearing their culture's dominant language, while others, born deaf, do not. Then give both groups an intelligence test rooted in the dominant language. The result? No surprise: Those with expertise in the dominant language will score higher than those who were born deaf (Braden, 1994; Steele, 1990; Zeidner, 1990).

Might the racial and ethnic gap be similarly environmental? Consider:

Genetics research reveals that under the skin, we humans are remarkably alike. Despite some racial variation, such as in health risks, the average genetic difference between two Icelandic villagers or between two Kenyans greatly exceeds the average group difference between Icelanders and Kenyans (Cavalli-Sforza et al., 1994; Rosenberg et al., 2002). Moreover, looks can deceive. Light-skinned Europeans and dark-skinned Africans are genetically closer than are dark-skinned Africans and dark-skinned Aboriginal Australians.

Race is not a neatly defined biological category. Race is primarily a social construction without well-defined physical boundaries; each race blends seamlessly into the race of its geographical neighbors (Helms et al., 2005; Smedley & Smedley, 2005). In one genetic analysis of more than 160,000 people living in the United States, most with less than 28 percent African ancestry said they were White; those with more than 28 percent mostly said they were African American (Byrc et al., 2015). Moreover, with increasingly mixed ancestries, more and more people defy neat racial categorization and self-identify as multiracial (Pauker et al., 2009).

Within the same populations, there are generation-to-generation differences in test scores. Test scores of today's better-fed, better-educated, and more test-prepared populations exceed those of 1930s populations—by a greater margin than the score difference between today's average-scoring Black Americans and average-scoring White Americans (Flynn, 2012; Pietschnig & Voracek, 2015; Trahan et al., 2014). The average intelligence test performance of today's sub-Saharan Africans is the same as that of British adults in 1948 (Wicherts et al., 2010). No one credits genetics for such generation-to-generation differences.

Schools and culture matter. Countries whose economies create a large wealth gap between rich and poor tend also to have a large rich-versus-poor intelligence test score gap (Nisbett, 2009). In the United States, rising income inequality has meant less equal access to a college education (Jackson & Holzman, 2020). And fewer educational opportunities can result in lower intelligence test scores. One analysis of 600,000 students showed that each additional year of school predicted 1 to 5 additional IQ points (Ritchie & Tucker-Drob, 2018). Starting and staying in school secures superior smarts.

Larry Williams/The Image Bank/Getty Images

HOSHANG HASHIMI/AFP/Getty Images

Intelligence allowed to flourish The famed all-women Afghan robotics team stood as a symbol of progress for women in Afghanistan. With the Taliban's return to power in 2021 and the team's welfare and educational opportunities endangered, humanitarian groups helped the team escape the country.

"Do not obtain your slaves from Britain, because they are so stupid and so utterly incapable of being taught." —Cicero, 106–43 B.C.E.

Math achievement, aptitude test differences, and especially grades may reflect conscientiousness more than competence (Poropat, 2014). Women in college and university outperform equally able men, thanks partly to their greater conscientiousness (Keiser et al., 2016). Students in Asia, who have largely outperformed North American students on such tests, have also spent more time in school and much more time studying in and out of school (CMEC, 2018; Larson & Verma, 1999; NCEE, 2018). These differences persist within the United States, where Asian American students devote the most time to studying and earn the highest grades (Hsin & Xie, 2014).

In different eras, different ethnic groups have experienced golden ages—periods of remarkable achievement. Twenty-five hundred years ago, it was the Greeks and the Egyptians, then the Romans. In the eighth and ninth centuries, genius seemed to reside in the Arab world, leading one Muslim scholar of the era to say of the English and the Dutch, "They lack keenness of understanding and clarity of intelligence and are overcome by ignorance and apathy, lack of discernment, and stupidity" (Henrich, 2020). Five hundred years ago, the Aztec Indians and the peoples of Northern Europe were the superachievers. While the gene pool remained relatively stable, cultures rose and fell.

RETRIEVAL PRACTICE

RP-2 The heritability of intelligence scores will be greater in a society of equal opportunity than in a society of extreme inequality between the working poor and billionaires. Why?

ANSWERS IN APPENDIX E

The Question of Bias

LOQ 31-5 Are intelligence tests biased or unfair? What is *stereotype threat*, and how does it affect test-takers' performance?

Knowing there are group differences in intelligence test scores leads to the question of whether those differences are built into the tests. Are intelligence tests biased? The answer depends on how we define bias.

The *scientific* meaning of *bias* hinges solely on whether a test predicts future behavior for all groups of test-takers, not just for some. For example, if the SAT accurately predicted the college achievement of women but not that of men, then the test would be biased. In this scientific meaning of the term, the near-consensus among psychologists (as summarized by the U.S. National Research Council's Committee on Ability Testing and the American Psychological Association's Task Force on Intelligence) has been that the major U.S. aptitude tests are *not* biased (Berry & Zhao, 2015; Neisser et al., 1996; Wigdor & Garner, 1982). The tests' predictive validity is roughly the same, regardless of gender, race, ethnicity, or socioeconomic level. If an intelligence test score of 95 predicts slightly below-average grades, that rough prediction usually applies equally to all.

But in everyday language, we sometimes use the word "bias" to describe things that are *unfair.* For example, if scores will be influenced by the test-takers' cultural or life experiences, then intelligence tests may be considered unfair, even if scientifically unbiased. Why? Because they measure the test-takers' developed abilities, which reflect, in part, their education and experiences. Being able to answer "Who wrote *Hamlet?*" relies more on educational exposure than on innate intellectual ability (Zoref & Williams, 1980). Some researchers, therefore, recommend culture-neutral questions—such as those that assess people's ability to learn novel words, sayings, and analogies—to enable *culture-fair* aptitude tests (Fagan & Holland, 2007, 2009). Today's standardized tests are rigorously reviewed to attempt to eliminate cultural bias.

Testing proponents caution us against blaming tests for exposing unequal experiences and opportunities. If, because of malnutrition, people were to suffer stunted growth, should we blame the measuring stick that reveals it? If unequal past experiences predict unequal future achievements, a valid aptitude test will detect such inequalities.

RETRIEVAL PRACTICE

RP-3 What is the difference between a test that is culturally biased and a test that is scientifically biased?

ANSWERS IN APPENDIX E

TEST-TAKERS' EXPECTATIONS Throughout this text, you have seen that expectations and attitudes can influence our perceptions and behaviors. For test-makers, expectations can introduce bias. For test-takers, they can become self-fulfilling prophecies. In one study, equally capable men and women took a difficult math test. The women did not do as well as the men—except when they were led to expect that women usually do as well as men on the test (Spencer et al., 1999). Otherwise, something affected their performance, leading the women to confirm societal expectations that they would not perform as well as the men. There was a "threat in the air" (Spencer et al., 2016). This self-fulfilling **stereotype threat** appeared again when Black students who were reminded of their race just before taking verbal aptitude tests performed worse than those who hadn't been reminded (Steele et al., 2002).

Such studies suggest that negative stereotypes may undermine people's academic and professional potential (Grand, 2016; Nguyen & Ryan, 2008; Walton & Spencer, 2009). If you worry that your group or "type" often doesn't do well on a certain kind of test or task, your self-doubts and self-monitoring may hijack your working memory and impair attention, performance, and learning (Hutchison et al., 2013; Inzlicht & Kang, 2010; Rydell et al., 2010). Critics argue that stereotype threat effects are weaker than originally thought (Flore & Wicherts, 2015; Flore et al., 2019).

Stereotype threat, like growth mindset and grit, is a modest phenomenon that often gets overstated (Flore et al., 2019). Yet it helps explain why Black Americans have scored higher when test administrators were Black than when test administrators were White (Danso & Esses, 2001). It gives us insight into why women have scored higher on math tests when there are no test-takers who are men present (Doyle & Voyer, 2016). Avoiding the presence of others who are expected to perform better can give you the confidence to do your best.

"Math class is tough!" —"Teen Talk" talking Barbie doll (introduced July 1992, recalled 3 months later)

From such studies, some researchers have concluded that making students believe they probably won't succeed—an unintended effect of some remedial programs—can function as a stereotype and weaken performance (Steele, 1995, 2010).

Other research teams have demonstrated the benefits of self-affirmation exercises that engage students in writing about their most important values (Borman et al., 2019; Ferrer & Cohen, 2018; Logel et al., 2019). When challenged to believe in their potential, think positively about their diverse life experiences, or increase their sense of belonging, disadvantaged university students have earned higher grades and have had lower drop-out rates (Binning et al., 2020; Broda et al., 2018; Townsend et al., 2019).

* * *

Perhaps, then, our goals for tests of mental abilities should be threefold. First, we should realize the benefits that intelligence-testing pioneer Alfred Binet foresaw—to enable schools to recognize who might profit most from early intervention. Second, we must remain alert to Binet's wish that intelligence test scores not be misinterpreted as literal measures of a person's worth and potential. Third, we must remember that the competence that general intelligence tests sample is important; it helps enable success in some life paths. But these tests reflect only one important aspect of personal competence (Stanovich et al., 2016). Our rationality, practical intelligence, and emotional intelligence matter, too, as do other forms of creativity, talent, and character.

"Almost all the joyful things of life are outside the measure of IQ tests." —Madeleine L'Engle, *A Circle of Quiet*, 1972

The point to remember: There are many ways of being successful; our differences are variations of human adaptability. Life's great achievements result not only from "can do" abilities and fair opportunity but also from "will do" motivation. Competence + Opportunity + Diligence = Accomplishment.

"[Einstein] showed that genius equals brains plus tenacity squared." —Walter Isaacson, "Einstein's Final Quest," 2009

RETRIEVAL PRACTICE

RP-4 What psychological principle may help explain why women tend to score higher on math tests when none of their fellow test-takers are men?

ANSWERS IN APPENDIX E

stereotype threat a self-confirming concern that one will be evaluated based on a negative stereotype. 

MODULE

31 REVIEW Genetic and Environmental Influences on Intelligence

LEARNING OBJECTIVES

Test Yourself Answer these repeated Learning Objective Questions on your own (before "showing" the answers here, or checking the answers in Appendix D) to improve your retention of the concepts (McDaniel et al., 2009, 2015).

LOQ 31-1 What is *heritability*, and what do twin and adoption studies tell us about the nature and nurture of intelligence?

LOQ 31-2 How can environmental influences affect cognitive development?

LOQ 31-3 How and why do the genders differ in mental ability scores?

LOQ 31-4 How and why do racial and ethnic groups differ in mental ability scores?

LOQ 31-5 Are intelligence tests biased or unfair? What is *stereotype threat*, and how does it affect test-takers' performance?

TERMS AND CONCEPTS TO REMEMBER

Test Yourself Write down the definition in your own words, then check your answer.

heritability, p. 369
growth mindset, p. 372
stereotype threat, p. 377

MODULE TEST

Test Yourself Answer the following questions on your own first, then "show" the answers here, or check your answers in Appendix E.

1. To say that the heritability of intelligence is about 50 percent means that 50 percent of
   a. an individual's intelligence is due to genetic factors.
   b. the similarities between two groups of people are attributable to genes.
   c. the variation in intelligence within a group of people is attributable to genetic factors.
   d. an individual's intelligence is due to each parent's genes.

2. The strongest support for heredity's influence on intelligence is the finding that
   a. identical twins, but not other siblings, have nearly identical intelligence test scores.
   b. the correlation between intelligence test scores of fraternal twins is not higher than that for other siblings.
   c. similarity of mental abilities between adopted siblings increases with age.
   d. children in impoverished families have similar intelligence scores.

3. The environmental influence that has the clearest, most profound effect on intellectual development is
   a. exposing infants to enrichment programs before age 1.
   b. growing up in an economically disadvantaged home.
   c. being raised in conditions of extreme deprivation.
   d. being an identical twin.

4. ______________________ can lead to poor performance on tests by undermining test-takers' belief that they can do well on the test.

CHAPTER
11
E+/Getty Images

What Drives Us: Hunger, Sex, Belongingness, and Achievement (Modules 32–35)

How well I [DM] remember asking my first discussion question in a new introductory psychology class. Several hands rose, along with one left foot. The foot belonged to Chris Klein, who was the unlikeliest person to have made it to that class. At birth, Chris suffered oxygen deprivation that required 40 minutes of CPR. "One doctor wanted to let him go," recalled his mother.

The result was severe cerebral palsy. With damage to the brain area that controls muscle movement, Chris can't contain his constantly moving hands. He cannot feed, dress, or care for himself. And he cannot speak. But Chris can control his keen mind and his left foot. With that blessed foot, he operates the joystick on his motorized wheelchair. Using his left big toe, he can type sentences, which his communication system can store, send, or speak. And Chris is motivated—very motivated.

When Chris was a high school student in suburban Chicago, three teachers doubted he could leave home for college. Yet he persisted, and, with much support, attended my college

Katie Green © 2023 MLive Media Group. All rights reserved. Used with permission.

A motivated man: Chris Klein To see and hear Chris presenting his story, visit https://www.youtube.com/watch?v=3H3e2MXV6iY.

called Hope. Five years later, as his left foot drove him across the stage to receive his diploma, Chris's admiring classmates honored his achievement with a spontaneous standing ovation.

Today, Chris is an inspirational speaker for schools, churches, universities, and community events, giving "a voice to those that have none, and a helping hand to those with disabilities." He maintains a website, LessonsFromTheBigToe.com. And he has found love and married.

Few of us face Chris Klein's challenges. But we all seek to direct our energy in ways that will produce satisfaction and success. We are pushed by biological motives, such as hunger and sex (Modules 33–34), and social ones, such as the needs to belong and to achieve (Module 35). Chris Klein's fierce will to live, learn, and love highlights the essence of our own *motivations*, which energize and direct our lives.

Let's begin by looking at how psychologists have approached the study of motivation (Module 32).

MODULE 32 Basic Motivational Concepts

LEARNING OBJECTIVE QUESTION LOQ **32-1** How do psychologists define *motivation*? What are four key motivation theories?

Our **motivations** arise from the interplay between nature (the bodily "push") and nurture (the "pulls" from our personal experiences, thoughts, and culture). Our motives drive our behavior. That is usually, but not always, for the better. If our motivations get hijacked, our lives go awry. Those with *substance use disorder*, for example, may find their cravings for an addictive substance override their longings for sustenance, safety, and social support.

In their attempts to understand motivated behavior, psychologists have viewed it from four perspectives:

- *Instinct theory* (now replaced by the *evolutionary perspective*) focuses on genetically predisposed behaviors.
- *Drive-reduction theory* focuses on how we respond to inner pushes and external pulls.
- *Arousal theory* focuses on finding the right level of stimulation.
- Abraham Maslow's *hierarchy of needs* focuses on the priority of some needs over others.

Instincts and Evolutionary Theory

To qualify as an **instinct**, a complex behavior must have a fixed pattern throughout a species and be unlearned (Tinbergen, 1951). Such unlearned behaviors include *imprinting* in birds and the return of salmon to their birthplace. A few human behaviors, such as infants' innate reflexes to root for a nipple and suck, also exhibit unlearned fixed patterns. *Instinct theory*, popular in the early twentieth century, viewed our instincts as the source of our motivations. But many more behaviors are directed by both physiological needs and psychological wants.

motivation a need or desire that energizes and directs (or *pushes*) behavior.

instinct a complex behavior that is rigidly patterned throughout a species and is unlearned.

Annika Erickson/Getty Images

James Warwick/Science Source

Same motive, different wiring The more complex the nervous system, the more adaptable the organism. Both humans and weaverbirds satisfy their need for shelter in ways that reflect their inherited capacities. Human behavior is flexible; we can learn whatever skills we need to build a house. The bird's behavior pattern is fixed; it can build only this kind of nest.

Although instincts cannot explain most human motives, the underlying assumption endures in *evolutionary psychology*: Genes do predispose some species-typical behavior. Psychologists might apply this perspective, for example, to explain our human similarities, animals' biological predispositions, and the influence of evolution on our fears, helping behaviors, and romantic attractions.

Drives and Incentives

In addition to our predispositions, we have *drives*. **Physiological needs** (such as for food or water) create an aroused, motivated state—a drive (such as hunger or thirst)—that pushes us to reduce the need. **Drive-reduction theory** explains that, with few exceptions, when a physiological need increases, so does our psychological drive to reduce it.

Drive reduction is one way our bodies strive for **homeostasis** (literally "staying the same")—the maintenance of a steady internal state. For example, our body regulates its temperature in a way similar to a room's thermostat. Both systems operate through feedback loops: Sensors feed room temperature to a control device. If the room's temperature cools, the control device switches on the furnace. Likewise, if our body's temperature cools, our blood vessels constrict to conserve warmth, and we feel driven to put on more clothes or seek a warmer environment (**FIGURE 32.1**).

Need (food, water)
Drive (hunger, thirst)
Drive-reducing behaviors (eating, drinking)

FIGURE 32.1
Drive-reduction theory Drive-reduction motivation arises from *homeostasis*—our body's natural tendency to maintain a steady internal state. Thus, if we are water-deprived, our thirst drives us to drink to restore the body's normal state.

Not only are we *pushed* by our need to reduce drives, we are also motivated (or *pulled*) by **incentives**—positive or negative environmental stimuli that lure or repel us. Such stimuli (when positive) increase our dopamine levels, causing our underlying drives (such as for food or sex) to become active impulses (Hamid et al., 2016). And the more these impulses are satisfied and reinforced, the stronger the drive—the next time it arises—may become: As Roy Baumeister (2015) noted, "Getting begets wanting." If you are hungry, the aroma of good food will motivate you. Whether that aroma comes from roasted peanuts or toasted tarantula will depend on your culture and experience. Incentives can also be negative: If teasing others on social media causes others to unfollow or unfriend us, we may feel motivated to treat others better.

When there is both a need and an incentive, we feel strongly driven. The food-deprived person who smells pizza baking may feel an intense hunger drive, and the baking pizza may become a compelling incentive. For each motive, we can ask, "How is it pushed by our inborn physiological needs and pulled by learned incentives in the environment?"

"Nature often equips life's essentials—sex, eating, nursing—with built-in gratification."
—Frans de Waal, "Morals Without God?," 2010

Arousal Theory

We are much more than calm homeostatic systems, however. Some motivated behaviors actually *increase* rather than decrease arousal. Well-fed animals will leave their shelter to explore and gain information, seemingly in the absence of any need-based drive. Curiosity drives monkeys to monkey around trying to figure out how to unlock a latch that opens nothing or how to open a window that allows them to see outside their room (Butler, 1954). It drives newly mobile human infants to investigate every accessible corner of the house. It drives the scientists whose work this text discusses. And it drives explorers and adventurers such as mountaineer George Mallory. Asked why he wanted to climb Mount Everest, Mallory famously answered, "Because it's there." Sometimes uncertainty brings excitement, which amplifies motivation (Shen et al., 2015). Those who, like Mallory, enjoy high arousal are most likely to seek out intense music, novel foods, and risky behaviors and careers (Roberti et al., 2004; Zuckerman, 1979, 2009). Although they have been called *sensation-seekers*, risk takers may also be motivated to gain control over their emotions and actions (Barlow et al., 2013).

So, human motivation aims not to eliminate arousal but to seek optimum levels of arousal. Having all our biological needs satisfied, we feel driven to experience stimulation. Lacking stimulation, we feel bored and look for a way to increase arousal. Most people, worldwide, prefer to *do* something—even (when given no other option while

physiological need a basic bodily requirement.

drive-reduction theory the idea that a physiological need creates an aroused state (a drive) that motivates an organism to satisfy the need.

homeostasis a tendency to maintain a balanced or constant internal state; the regulation of any aspect of body chemistry, such as blood glucose, around a particular level.

incentive a positive or negative environmental stimulus that motivates (or *pulls*) behavior.

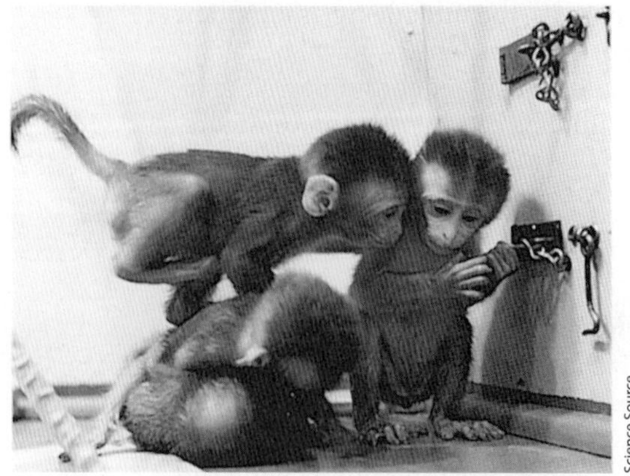
Science Source

Glenn Swier

Driven by curiosity Young monkeys and children are fascinated by the unfamiliar. Their drive to explore maintains an optimum level of arousal. It is one of several motives that do not fill any immediate physiological need.

waiting in a lab) to self-administer mild electric shocks (Buttrick et al., 2019; Wilson et al., 2014). Why might people seek to increase their arousal? Moderate arousal and even anxiety can be motivating—leading to higher levels of math achievement, for example (Z. Wang et al., 2015). Yet *too much* stimulation or stress motivates us to decrease arousal. In experiments, people have felt less stress when they limited email-checking and phone notifications to three times a day rather than being continually accessible (Fitz et al., 2019; Kushlev & Dunn, 2015).

Two early-twentieth-century psychologists studied the relationship of arousal to performance and identified the **Yerkes-Dodson law**: *moderate arousal leads to optimal performance* (Yerkes & Dodson, 1908). When taking an exam, it pays to be moderately aroused—alert but not trembling with nervousness. (If you're already nervous, it's better to avoid becoming further aroused with caffeine.) Between bored low arousal and anxious hyperarousal lies a flourishing life. Even people visiting a haunted house attraction enjoy it most when aroused, with an elevated heart rate, but not terrified (Andersen et al., 2020). As with Goldilocks' porridge, what's best is not too cold and not too hot. Optimal arousal levels depend on the task, with more difficult tasks requiring lower arousal for best performance (Hembree, 1988).

ASK YOURSELF

Does boredom ever motivate you to do things just to figure out something new? When was the last time that happened, and what did you find?

RETRIEVAL PRACTICE

RP-1 Performance peaks at lower levels of arousal for difficult tasks, and at higher levels for easy or well-learned tasks. (a) How might this affect marathon runners? (b) How might this affect anxious test-takers facing a difficult exam?

ANSWERS IN APPENDIX E

A Hierarchy of Needs

"Hunger is the most urgent form of poverty."
—Alliance to End Hunger, 2002

Some needs take priority. At this moment, with your needs for air and water hopefully satisfied, other motives—such as your desire to learn and achieve—are energizing and directing your behavior. Let your need for water go unsatisfied, however, and your thirst will preoccupy you. Deprived of air, your thirst will disappear.

Abraham Maslow (1970) described these priorities as a **hierarchy of needs**, which others later portrayed as a pyramid (Bridgman et al., 2019; **FIGURE 32.2**). Our physiological needs, such as for food and water, form the pyramid's base. As these needs become met, our focus shifts to our need for safety, and then to satisfying our needs to give and receive love and to enjoy self-esteem. Beyond this, said Maslow (1971), lies the need to actualize one's full potential.

Near the end of his life, Maslow proposed that some people also reach a level of *self-transcendence*. At the self-actualization level, people seek to realize their own potential. At the self-transcendence level, people strive for meaning, purpose, and communion in

Yerkes-Dodson law the principle that performance increases with arousal only up to a point, beyond which performance decreases.

hierarchy of needs Maslow's five levels of human needs, beginning with physiological needs. Often visualized as a pyramid, with basic needs providing the foundation supporting higher-level needs.

Self-transcendence needs
Need to find meaning and identity beyond the self

Self-actualization needs
Need to live up to our fullest and unique potential

Esteem needs
Need for self-esteem, achievement, competence, and independence; need for recognition and respect from others

Belongingness and love needs
Need to love and be loved, to belong and be accepted; need to avoid loneliness and separation

Safety needs
Need to feel that the world is organized and predictable; need to feel safe, secure, and stable

Physiological needs
Need to satisfy hunger and thirst

Jalal Morchidi/Anadolu Agency/Getty Images

FIGURE 32.2
Maslow's hierarchy of needs During the month of Ramadan, many Muslims refrain from eating and drinking from dawn to sunset. They end their daily fast by satisfying their lower-level needs for food and drink and engaging their middle-level needs for belongingness and love, often having a large communal meal (called *iftar*, meaning "break fast").

a way that is transpersonal—beyond the self (Kaufman, 2020). Maslow's contemporary, psychiatrist Viktor Frankl (1962), a Nazi concentration camp survivor, concurred that the search for meaning is an important human motive: "Life is never made unbearable by circumstances, but only by lack of meaning and purpose."

"Do you feel your life has an important purpose or meaning?" When Gallup asked this of people in 132 countries, 91 percent answered *Yes* (Oishi & Diener, 2014). People sense meaning when they experience their life as having *purpose* (goals), *significance* (value), and *coherence* (sense)—sentiments that may be nourished by strong social connections, a religious faith, an orderly world, and social status (King et al., 2016; Martela & Steger, 2016). People's sense of life's meaning predicts their psychological and physical well-being, and their capacity to delay gratification (Heine et al., 2006; Van Tongeren et al., 2018). Meaning matters.

The order of Maslow's hierarchy is not universally fixed: U.S. suffragist Alice Paul starved herself to make a political statement (enduring force-feeding by her jailers). Culture also influences our priorities: Self-esteem matters most in modern individualist nations, where people prioritize personal achievements more than family and community identity (Oishi et al., 1999). And, while agreeing with Maslow's basic levels of need, today's psychologists note that gaining and retaining mates, parenting offspring, and desiring social status are also basic human motives (Anderson et al., 2015; Kenrick et al., 2010).

Nevertheless, the simple idea that some motives are more compelling than others provides a framework for thinking about motivation. Worldwide life-satisfaction surveys support this basic idea (Oishi et al., 1999; Tay & Diener, 2011). In lower-income nations that lack easy access to money and the food and shelter it buys, financial satisfaction more strongly predicts feelings of well-being. In wealthy countries, where most can meet their basic needs, social connections better predict well-being.

With these classic motivation theories in mind (**TABLE 32.1**), the remaining What Drives Us modules consider four representative motives, beginning at the physiological level with hunger and working up through sexual motivation to the higher-level needs to belong and to achieve. At each level, we can see how experience interacts with biology.

TABLE 32.1 Classic Motivation Theories

Theory	Its Big Idea
Instincts and evolutionary theory	There is a genetic basis for unlearned, species-typical behavior (such as birds building nests or infants rooting for a nipple).
Drive-reduction theory	Physiological needs (such as hunger and thirst) create an aroused state that drives us to reduce the need (for example, by eating or drinking).
Arousal theory	Our need to maintain an optimal level of arousal motivates behaviors that meet no physiological need (such as our yearning for stimulation and our hunger for information).
Maslow's hierarchy of needs	We prioritize survival-based needs and then social needs more than the needs for esteem and meaning.

ASK YOURSELF

Consider your own experiences in terms of Maslow's hierarchy of needs. Do you remember experiencing hunger or thirst that displaced your concern for other, higher-level needs? Do you usually feel safe? Loved? Confident? How often can you address what Maslow called "self-actualization" needs? What about "self-transcendence" needs?

RETRIEVAL PRACTICE

RP-2 After hours of driving alone in an unfamiliar city, you finally see a diner. Although it looks deserted and a little creepy, you stop because you are *really* hungry and thirsty. How would Maslow's hierarchy of needs explain your behavior?

ANSWERS IN APPENDIX E

MODULE 32 REVIEW Basic Motivational Concepts

LEARNING OBJECTIVES

Test Yourself Answer these repeated Learning Objective Questions on your own (before "showing" the answers here, or checking the answers in Appendix D) to improve your retention of the concepts (McDaniel et al., 2009, 2015).

LOQ 32-1 How do psychologists define *motivation*? What are four key motivation theories?

TERMS AND CONCEPTS TO REMEMBER

Test Yourself Write down the definition in your own words, then check your answer.

motivation, p. 380	homeostasis, p. 381
instinct, p. 380	incentive, p. 381
physiological need, p. 381	Yerkes-Dodson law, p. 382
drive-reduction theory, p. 381	hierarchy of needs, p. 382

MODULE TEST

Test Yourself Answer the following questions on your own first, then "show" the answers here, or check your answers in Appendix E.

1. Today's evolutionary psychology shares an idea that was an underlying assumption of instinct theory. This idea is that
   - **a.** physiological needs arouse psychological states.
   - **b.** genes predispose species-typical behavior.
   - **c.** physiological needs increase arousal.
   - **d.** external needs energize and direct behavior.

2. An example of a physiological need is __________. An example of a psychological drive is __________.
   - **a.** hunger; a "push" to find food
   - **b.** a "push" to find food; hunger
   - **c.** curiosity; a "push" to reduce arousal
   - **d.** a "push" to reduce arousal; curiosity

3. Danielle walks into a friend's kitchen, smells cookies baking, and begins to feel very hungry. The smell of baking cookies is a(n) __________ (incentive/drive).

4. __________ theory attempts to explain behaviors that do NOT reduce physiological needs.

5. With a challenging task, such as taking a difficult exam, performance is likely to peak when arousal is
   - **a.** very high.
   - **b.** moderate.
   - **c.** very low.
   - **d.** absent.

6. According to Maslow's hierarchy of needs, our most basic needs are physiological, including the need for food and water; just above these are __________ needs.
   - **a.** safety
   - **b.** self-esteem
   - **c.** belongingness
   - **d.** self-transcendence

MODULE 33 Hunger

glucose the form of sugar that circulates in the blood and provides the major source of energy for body tissues. When its level is low, we feel hunger.

Physiological needs are powerful. In a vivid demonstration, Ancel Keys and his research team (1950) studied semistarvation among wartime volunteers, who participated as an alternative to military service. After feeding 200 men normally for 3 months, researchers halved the food intake for 36 of them. These semistarved men became listless and apathetic as their bodies conserved energy. Eventually, their body weights stabilized about 25 percent below their starting weights.

More dramatic were the psychological effects. Consistent with Abraham Maslow's idea of a needs hierarchy, the men became food-obsessed. They talked food. They daydreamed food. They collected recipes, read cookbooks, and feasted their eyes on delectable forbidden foods. Preoccupied with their unfulfilled basic need, they lost interest in sex and social activities. As one participant reported, "If we see a show, the most interesting part of it is contained in scenes where people are eating. I couldn't laugh at the funniest picture in the world, and love scenes are completely dull." The men's preoccupations illustrate how powerful motives can hijack our consciousness.

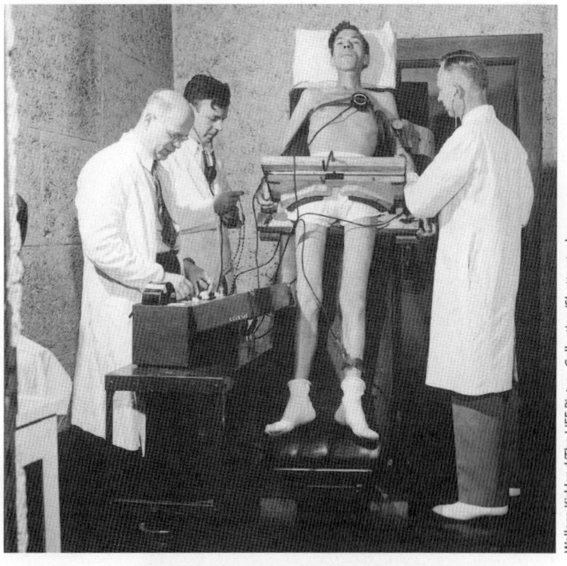
Wallace Kirkland/The LIFE Picture Collection/Shutterstock

Studying starvation in conscientious objectors Researchers carefully recorded and analyzed the physiological and psychological effects of 6 months of starvation, and various methods for rehabilitation. They hoped to support the recovery of World War II famine survivors.

The Physiology of Hunger

LOQ 33-1 What physiological factors produce hunger?

Keys' semistarved volunteers felt their hunger because of a homeostatic system that maintains one's normal body weight and an adequate nutrient supply. But what precisely triggers hunger? Is it the pangs of an empty stomach? So it seemed to A. L. Washburn. Working with Walter Cannon, Washburn agreed to swallow a balloon attached to a recording device (Cannon & Washburn, 1912) (**FIGURE 33.1**). When inflated to fill his stomach, the balloon transmitted his stomach contractions. Washburn supplied information about his *feelings* of hunger by pressing a key each time he felt a hunger pang. The discovery: Whenever Washburn felt hungry, he was indeed having stomach contractions.

Can hunger exist without stomach pangs? To answer that question, researchers removed some rats' stomachs, creating a direct path to their small intestines (Tsang, 1938). Did the rats continue to eat? Indeed they did. Some hunger similarly persists in humans whose stomachs have been removed due to ulcers or cancer.

If the pangs of an empty stomach are not the only source of hunger, what else matters?

"Hunger, real hunger, provokes desperation and leads to choices that might otherwise be unfathomable." —Mikki Kendall, "Hood Feminism," 2020

"The full person does not understand the needs of the hungry." —Irish proverb

Body Chemistry and the Brain

People and other animals automatically regulate their caloric intake to prevent energy deficits and maintain a stable body weight. This suggests that your body is keeping tabs on its available resources. The blood sugar **glucose** is one such resource. Increases in the hormone *insulin* (secreted by the pancreas) diminish blood glucose, partly by converting it to stored fat. If your blood glucose level drops, you won't consciously feel the lower blood sugar. But your brain, which is automatically monitoring your blood chemistry and your body's internal state, will trigger hunger. Signals from your stomach, intestines, and liver (indicating whether glucose is being deposited or withdrawn) all signal your brain to motivate eating or not.

"Never hunt when you're hungry."
Mike Twohy//Cartoon Stock

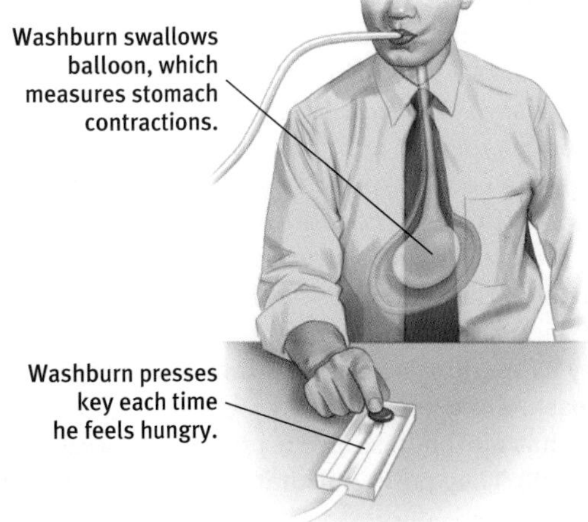
Washburn swallows balloon, which measures stomach contractions.
Washburn presses key each time he feels hungry.

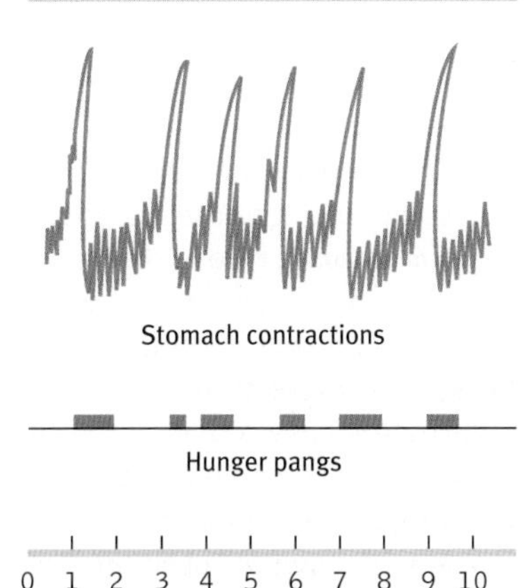
Stomach contractions
Hunger pangs
0 1 2 3 4 5 6 7 8 9 10
Time in minutes

FIGURE 33.1
Monitoring stomach contractions
(Information from Cannon, 1929.)

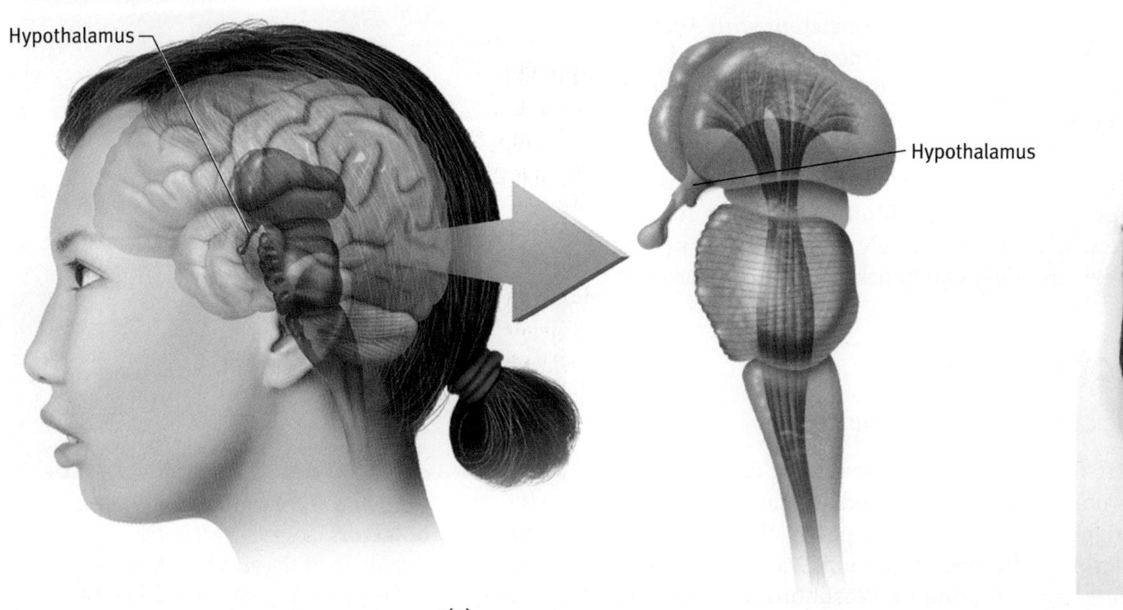
Hypothalamus
Hypothalamus
(a)
(b)

FIGURE 33.2
The hypothalamus (a) The hypothalamus performs various body maintenance functions, including control of hunger. Blood vessels supply the hypothalamus, enabling it to respond to our current blood chemistry as well as to incoming neural information about the body's state. (b) The overweight mouse on the left has nonfunctioning receptors in the appetite-suppressing part of the hypothalamus.

How does the brain integrate these messages and sound the alarm? Several neural areas—some housed deep in the hippocampus and within the hypothalamus, a neural traffic intersection—do the work (Stevenson & Francis, 2017; **FIGURE 33.2**). For example, one neural network in the hypothalamus (called the *arcuate nucleus*) has a center that secretes appetite-stimulating hormones. When stimulated electrically, well-fed animals begin to eat. If the area is destroyed, even starving animals have no interest in food. Another neural center secretes appetite-suppressing hormones. When electrically stimulated, animals will stop eating. Destroy this area and animals can't stop eating and will become obese (see Figure 33.2b) (Duggan & Booth, 1986; Hoebel & Teitelbaum, 1966).

Blood vessels connect the hypothalamus to the rest of the body, so it can respond to our current blood chemistry and other incoming information. One of its tasks is monitoring levels of appetite hormones, such as *ghrelin*, a hunger-arousing hormone secreted by an empty stomach. During bypass surgery for severe *obesity*, surgeons seal off or remove part of the stomach. The remaining stomach then produces much less ghrelin, reducing the person's appetite and making food less enticing (Ammori, 2013; Lemonick, 2002; Scholtz et al., 2013). The result, for most, is "profound improvements in psychosocial functioning" (Sarwer & Henberg, 2020). Other appetite hormones include *orexin, leptin,* and *PYY*; **FIGURE 33.3** describes how these hormones influence our feelings of hunger.

THANKS FOR COMING, EVERYONE.
I CALLED YOU HERE TO DECIDE WHETHER
OR NOT WE'RE ACTUALLY HUNGRY.

If you lose some extra weight and later find it creeping back, you can also blame your brain for your weight regain (Cornier, 2011). The complex interaction of appetite hormones and brain activity helps explain the body's predisposition to maintain a particular weight. When semistarved rats fall below their normal weight, their "weight thermostat" signals the body to restore the lost weight. It's as though fat cells cry out "Feed me!" and grab glucose from the bloodstream (Ludwig & Friedman, 2014). Hunger increases and energy expenditure decreases. This stable weight toward which semistarved rats return is their **set point** (Keesey & Corbett, 1984; Yeo & O'Rahilly, 2021). In rats and humans, heredity influences body type and approximate set point.

Our bodies regulate weight through the control of food intake, energy output, and **basal metabolic rate**—the resting rate of energy expenditure for maintaining basic body functions. By the end of their 6 months of semistarvation, the men who participated in Keys' experiment had stabilized at three-quarters of their normal weight, even though they took in only *half* their previous calories. How did they achieve this dieter's nightmare? They reduced their energy expenditure, partly through inactivity but partly because of a 29 percent drop in their basal metabolic rate.

Some researchers, however, doubt that our bodies have a preset tendency to maintain a given weight (Assanand et al., 1998). They point out that slow, sustained changes

set point the point at which the "weight thermostat" may be set. When the body falls below this weight, increased hunger and a lowered metabolic rate may combine to restore lost weight.

basal metabolic rate the body's resting rate of energy output.

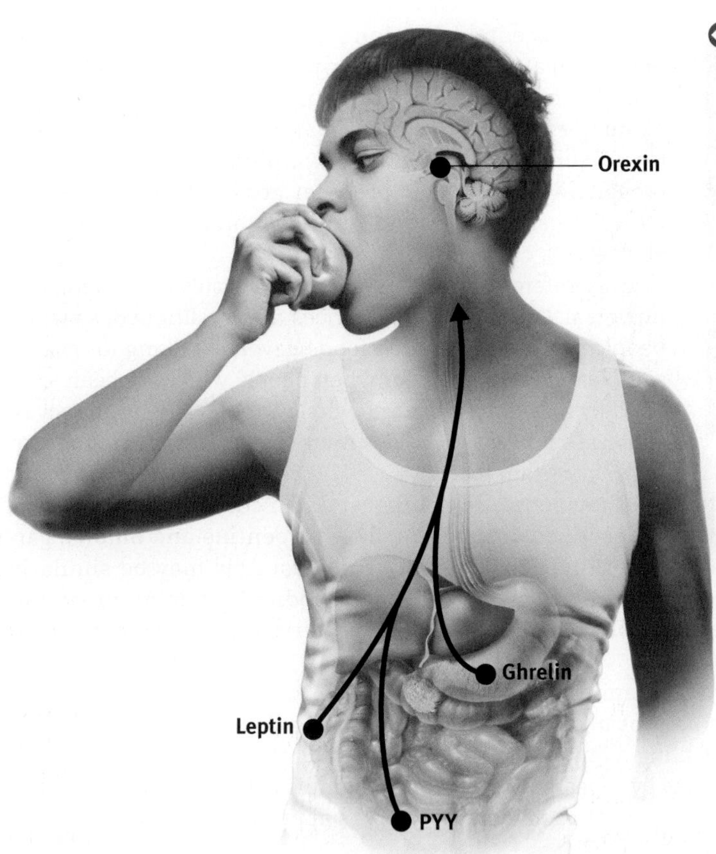
Orexin
Ghrelin
Leptin
PYY

FIGURE 33.3
The appetite hormones

Increases appetite
- *Ghrelin:* Hormone secreted by empty stomach; sends "I'm hungry" signals to the brain.
- *Orexin:* Hunger-triggering hormone secreted by hypothalamus.

Decreases appetite
- *Leptin:* Protein hormone secreted by fat cells; when abundant, causes brain to increase metabolism and decrease hunger.
- *PYY:* Digestive tract hormone; sends "I'm *not* hungry" signals to the brain.

in body weight can alter one's set point, and that psychological factors also sometimes drive our feelings of hunger. Given unlimited access to a wide variety of tasty foods, people and other animals tend to overeat and gain weight (Raynor & Epstein, 2001). Thus, many researchers prefer the term *settling point* to indicate the level at which a person's weight settles in response to caloric intake and expenditure (which are influenced by environment as well as biology).

RETRIEVAL PRACTICE

RP-1 Hunger occurs in response to ____________ (low/high) blood glucose and ____________ (low/high) levels of ghrelin.

ANSWERS IN APPENDIX E

The Psychology of Hunger

LOQ 33-2 What cultural and situational factors influence hunger?

Our internal hunger is pushed by our physiology—our body chemistry and hypothalamic activity. Yet there is more to hunger than meets the stomach. This was strikingly apparent when Paul Rozin and his colleagues (1998) tested two patients with amnesia who had no memory for events occurring more than a minute ago. If, 20 minutes after eating a normal lunch, the patients were offered another, both readily consumed it . . . and usually a third meal offered 20 minutes after the second was finished. This suggests that part of knowing when to eat is our memory of our last meal. As time passes since we last ate, we anticipate eating again and start feeling hungry.

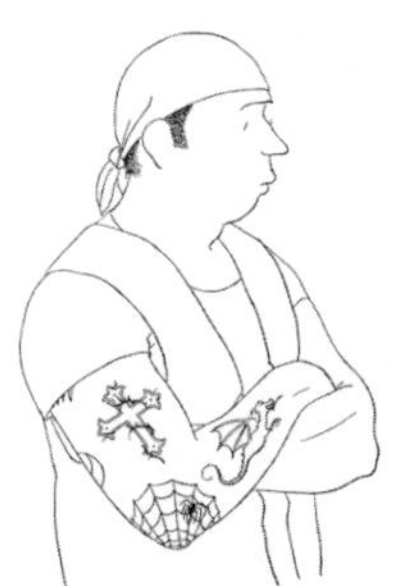

I LOVE PEACH COBBLER

Alex Gregory/Cartoon Stock

"Never get a tattoo when you're drunk and hungry."

Taste Preferences: Biology and Culture

Body cues and environmental factors together influence not only the *when* of hunger, but also the *what—our* taste preferences. When feeling tense or depressed, do you tend

Bryan and Cherry Alexander/Science Source

(a)

Mark Bowler/Alamy Stock Photo

(b)

An acquired taste People everywhere learn to enjoy the fatty, bitter, or spicy foods common in their culture. (a) For these Alaska Natives, but not for most other North Americans, whale blubber is a tasty treat. (b) For Peruvians, roasted guinea pig is similarly delicious.

to take solace in high-calorie foods, as ardent football fans have done after a big loss (Cornil & Chandon, 2013)? Carbohydrates boost the neurotransmitter serotonin, which has calming effects. When dieting and stressed, both rats and many humans find it extra rewarding to gobble up Oreos (Boggiano et al., 2005; Sproesser et al., 2014). And people living stressed lives tend to put on more weight (Mehlig et al., 2020).

Our preferences for sweet and salty tastes are genetic and universal. Other taste preferences are conditioned, as when people given highly salted foods develop a liking for excess salt (Beauchamp, 1987), or when people who have been sickened by a food develop an aversion to it. (The frequency of children's illnesses provides many chances for them to learn to avoid certain foods.)

Culture affects taste, too. Many people in Southeast Asian countries enjoy *durian*, a fruit that a detractor has described as smelling like "turpentine and onions, garnished with a gym sock" (Sterling, 2003). People from East Asia may be similarly repulsed by what many Westerners love—"the rotted bodily fluid of an ungulate" (a.k.a. cheese, some varieties of which have the same bacteria and odor as stinky feet) (Herz, 2012).

Spices per recipe

The hotter the climate, the more spices used.

Mean annual temperature (degrees Celsius)

FIGURE 33.4
Hot climates and hot spices Countries with hot climates, in which food historically spoiled more quickly, feature recipes with more bacteria-inhibiting spices (Sherman & Flaxman, 2001). India averages nearly 10 spices per meat recipe; Finland, 2 spices.

Rats tend to avoid unfamiliar foods (Sclafani, 1995). So do we, especially animal-based foods. Such *neophobia* (dislike of unfamiliar things) surely was adaptive for our ancestors, protecting them from potentially toxic substances. We can overcome harmless food dislikes by repeatedly trying small samples of an unfamiliar food or drink. In experiments, this tends to increase people's appreciation for the new taste (Pliner, 1982; Pliner et al., 1993).

Other taste preferences also are adaptive. For example, the spices most commonly used in hot-climate recipes—where food, especially meat, is at risk of spoiling more quickly—inhibit bacteria growth (**FIGURE 33.4**). Pregnancy-related nausea and food aversions peak about the tenth week, when the developing embryo is most vulnerable to toxins. Thus, many pregnant women naturally avoid potentially harmful foods and other substances, such as alcoholic and caffeinated beverages (Forbes et al., 2018; Gaskins et al., 2018).

Situational Influences on Eating

To a surprising extent, situations also control our eating—a phenomenon psychologists have called the *ecology of eating*. Here are four situational influences you may have noticed but underestimated:

- ***Friends and food*** Do you eat more when eating with friends? Most of us do (Cummings & Tomiyama, 2019). But when we're trying to impress an attractive date, we often eat less (M. Baker et al., 2019).
- ***Serving size*** Researchers studied the effects of portion size by offering people varieties of free snacks (Geier et al., 2006). For example, in an apartment building's lobby, they laid out full or half pretzels, big or little Tootsie Rolls, or a small or large serving scoop by a bowl of M&M'S. Their consistent result: Offered a supersized portion, people put away more calories. Larger portions induce bigger bites, which may increase intake by decreasing oral exposure time (Herman et al., 2015). Children also eat more when using adult-sized (rather than child-sized) dishware (DiSantis et al., 2013). Portion size matters.
- ***Stimulating selections*** Food variety also stimulates eating. Offered a dessert buffet, people eat more than they do when choosing a portion from one favorite dessert. For our early ancestors, variety was healthy. When foods were abundant and varied, eating more provided a wide range of vitamins and minerals and produced protective fat for winter cold or famine. When a bounty of varied foods was unavailable, eating less extended the food supply until winter or famine ended (Polivy et al., 2008; Remick et al., 2009).

- ***Nudging nutrition*** When carrots appeared early (rather than late) in a lunch line, schoolchildren took four times more carrots (Redden et al., 2015). In other ways, too—nutrition labeling, healthy food defaults, taxing what's unhealthy—we can structure an environment that promotes healthier eating (Roberto, 2020). Such "nudges" show how psychological science can improve our everyday life.

ASK YOURSELF

Do you usually eat only when your body sends hunger signals? How much does the sight or smell of delicious food tempt you even when you're full?

RETRIEVAL PRACTICE

RP-2 After an 8-hour hike without food, your long-awaited favorite dish is placed in front of you, and your mouth waters in anticipation. Why?

ANSWERS IN APPENDIX E

* * *

To consider how hunger and other factors affect our risk for **obesity**, see Thinking Critically About: The Challenges of Obesity and Weight Control. And for tips on healthy eating and weight management, see **TABLE 33.1**.

TABLE 33.1 Tips for Healthy Eating

For those seeking healthier eating habits that can boost energy and longevity, here are some evidence-based guidelines (Moss et al., 2022; Sole-Smith, 2020):

- ***Healthy eating requires a healthy attitude.*** Absent a lifestyle change, there's a slim chance of permanent weight loss (Rothblum, 2018). Yet those most likely to successfully monitor and manage a healthier weight are those who believe their weight is changeable (Ehrlinger et al., 2017).
- ***Exercise and get enough sleep.*** Especially when supported by 7 to 8 hours of sleep a night, exercise empties fat cells, builds muscle, speeds up metabolism, helps lower your settling point, and reduces stress and stress-induced craving for carbohydrate-rich comfort foods (Bennett, 1995; Ruotsalainen et al., 2015; Thompson et al., 1982). Among TV's *Biggest Loser* competitors, exercise predicted less weight regain (Kerns et al., 2017). During the more sedentary months of the Covid pandemic, most people gained some weight (Woolford et al., 2021).
- ***Minimize exposure to unhealthy food cues.*** Food-shop on a full stomach. Stock healthy foods, such as fruits and vegetables. Keep unhealthy foods out of your home, and tuck away special-occasion foods. You can't eat it if you can't reach it.
- ***Limit variety and eat healthy foods.*** Given more variety, people consume more. So, eat simple meals with protein, vegetables, fruits, and whole grains. Healthy fats, such as those found in olive oil and fish, help regulate appetite (Taubes, 2001, 2002). Water- and vitamin-rich veggies can fill the stomach with few calories. Better crispy greens than Krispy Kremes.
- ***Reduce portion sizes and relabel your portions.*** Offered less, people consume less. People also eat less when they think of a portion as a number of items (10 chips) rather than as a general quantity (1 serving of chips) (Lewis & Earl, 2018).
- ***Time your intake.*** We tend to have a healthier weight (and better sleep) when we eat our last meal in the early evening and then hold off eating or drinking more until the next morning's breakfast (Wilkinson et al., 2020). Eating our heavier meals earlier in the day boosts metabolism, and eating a balanced breakfast helps us to feel more alert and less fatigued by late morning (Spring et al., 1992).
- ***Monitor your moods.*** Drinking alcohol or feeling anxious or depressed can unleash the urge to eat unhealthfully (Herman & Polivy, 1980; Mehlig et al., 2020).
- ***Eat unhurriedly.*** Eating slowly often means eating less (Hurst & Fukuda, 2018; Martin et al., 2007). Instead of wolfing down your meal, take time to savor each bite.
- ***Before eating with others, decide what and how much you want to eat.*** Eating with friends can distract us from monitoring our own eating (Ward & Mann, 2000).
- ***Allow for an occasional treat.*** In a healthy lifestyle, a lapse need not become a collapse.
- ***Chart and share your progress.*** Those who record and publicly disclose their progress toward a goal more often achieve it (Harkin et al., 2016).
- ***Connect to a support group.*** Join with others, either face-to-face or online, to share goals and progress updates (Freedman, 2011).

obesity defined as a body mass index (BMI) measurement of 30 or higher, which is calculated from our weight-to-height ratio. (Individuals who are *overweight* have a BMI of 25 or higher.)

Thinking Critically About:

The Challenges of Obesity and Weight Control

LOQ 33-3 How does obesity affect physical and psychological health? What factors are involved in weight management?

Obesity and Its Health Effects

Obesity is associated with:

- **physical health risks**, including diabetes, high blood pressure, heart disease, gallstones, arthritis, and certain types of cancer.[1]
- **increased depression,** especially among women.[2]
- **bullying,** outranking race and sexual orientation as the biggest reason for youth bullying in Western cultures.[3]

Percentage Overweight in 195 Countries Studied[4]

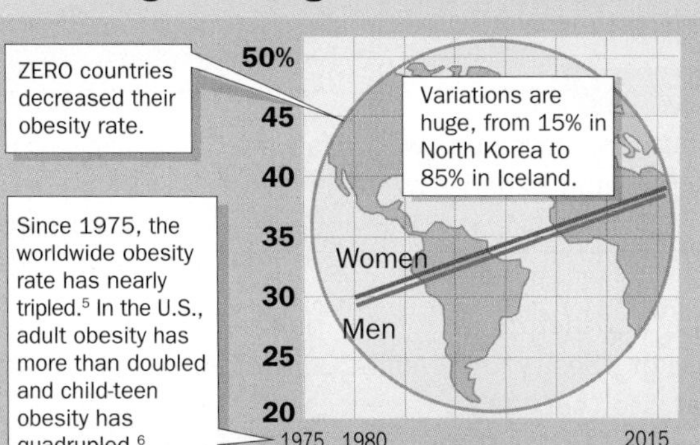

ZERO countries decreased their obesity rate.
Variations are huge, from 15% in North Korea to 85% in Iceland.
Since 1975, the worldwide obesity rate has nearly tripled.5 In the U.S., adult obesity has more than doubled and child-teen obesity has quadrupled.6
50%
45
40
35
30
25
20
Women
Men
1975
1980
2015
Year

Body Mass Index (BMI)

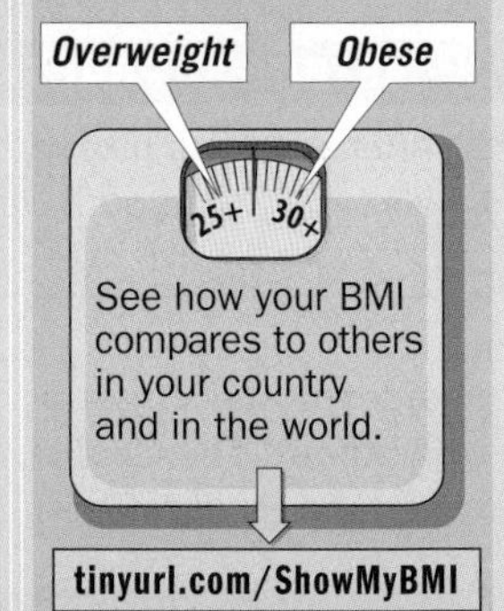

Overweight
Obese
25+
30+
See how your BMI compares to others in your country and in the world.
tinyurl.com/ShowMyBMI

How Did We Get Here?

Does obesity reflect a simple lack of willpower, as some people presume?[7] ***No.*** Many factors contribute to obesity.

PHYSIOLOGY FACTORS

Storing fat was adaptive.

- This ideal form of stored energy carried our ancestors through periods of famine. People in some impoverished places still find heavier bodies attractive, as plumpness signals affluence and status.[8]
- In food-rich countries, the drive for fat has become dysfunctional.[9]

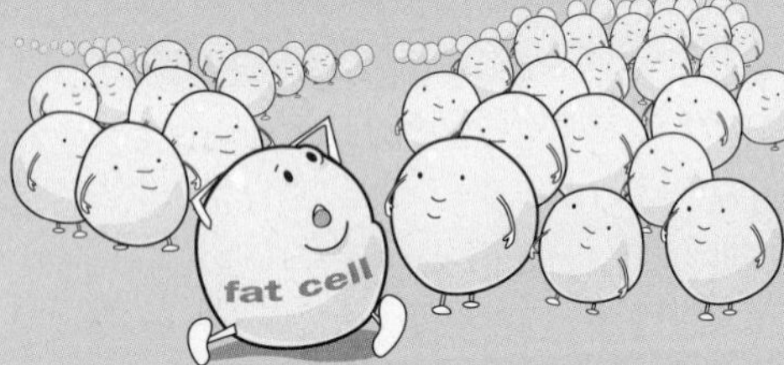

fat cell

Set point and metabolism matter.

- Fat (lower metabolic rate than muscle) requires less food intake to maintain than it did to gain.
- If weight drops below *set point/settling point*, the brain triggers more hunger and a slowed metabolism.
  - Body perceives STARVATION; adapts by burning fewer calories. Most dieters in the long run regain what they lose on weight-loss programs.[10]
  - After 30 weeks of competition on TV's *The Biggest Loser*, 6 years later only 1 of 14 contestants had kept the weight off. On average, they regained 70% of what they lost, and their metabolism remained slow.[11]

Genes influence us.

- Lean people seem naturally disposed to move about, burning more calories than energy-conserving overweight people, who tend to sit still longer.[12]
- Adoptive siblings' body weights are uncorrelated with one another or with their adoptive parents, instead resembling their biological parents' weight.[13]
- Identical twins have closely similar weights, even if raised apart.[14] Much lower *fraternal* twin weight correlation suggests genes explain 2/3 of our varying body mass.[15]
- More than 100 genes have been identified as each affecting weight in some small way.[16]

ENVIRONMENTAL FACTORS

- **Sleep loss** makes us more vulnerable to obesity.[17]

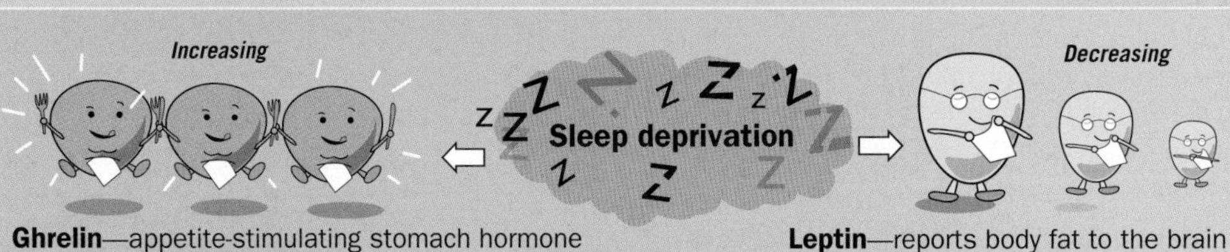

Increasing
Sleep deprivation
Decreasing
Ghrelin—appetite-stimulating stomach hormone
Leptin—reports body fat to the brain

- **Social influences:** Our own odds of becoming obese triple if a close friend becomes obese.[18]
- **Food and activity levels:** Worldwide, we eat more energy-dense foods and we move less, with 31% of adults (including 43% of Americans and 25% of Europeans) now sedentary—averaging <20 minutes per day of moderate activity such as walking.[19]

NOTE: With weight, as with intelligence and other characteristics, there can be high levels of *heritability* (genetic influence on *individual* differences) without heredity explaining *group* differences. Genes mostly determine why one person is heavier than another. Environment mostly determines why people today are heavier than people were 50 years ago.

1. Kitahara et al., 2014. 2. Haynes et al., 2019; Jung et al., 2017; Rivera et al., 2017. 3. Puhl et al., 2015. 4. GBD, 2017. 5. NCD, 2016. 6. Flegal et al., 2010, 2012, 2016. 7. NORC, 2016. 8. Furnham & Baguma, 1994; Nettle et al., 2017; Swami, 2015. 9. Hall, 2016. 10. Mann et al., 2015. 11. Fothergill et al., 2016. 12. Levine et al., 2005. 13. Grilo & Pogue-Geile, 1991. 14. Hjelmborg et al., 2008; Plomin et al., 1997. 15. Maes et al., 1997. 16. Akiyama et al., 2017. 17. Keith et al., 2006; Nedeltcheva et al., 2010; Taheri, 2004; Taheri et al., 2004. 18. Christakis & Fowler, 2007. 19. Hallal et al., 2012.

ASK YOURSELF

How would you rate your eating habits? What would you like to improve, and which healthy-eating strategies would help you the most?

RETRIEVAL PRACTICE

RP-3 Why can two people of the same height, age, and activity level maintain the same weight, even if one of them eats much less than the other does?

ANSWERS IN APPENDIX E

MODULE 33 REVIEW Hunger

LEARNING OBJECTIVES

Test Yourself Answer these repeated Learning Objective Questions on your own (before "showing" the answers here, or checking the answers in Appendix D) to improve your retention of the concepts (McDaniel et al., 2009, 2015).

LOQ 33-1 What physiological factors produce hunger?

LOQ 33-2 What cultural and situational factors influence hunger?

LOQ 33-3 How does obesity affect physical and psychological health? What factors are involved in weight management?

TERMS AND CONCEPTS TO REMEMBER

Test Yourself Write down the definition in your own words, then check your answer.

glucose, p. 384
set point, p. 386
basal metabolic rate, p. 386
obesity, p. 389

MODULE TEST

Test Yourself Answer the following questions on your own first, then "show" the answers here, or check your answers in Appendix E.

1. Journalist Dorothy Dix once remarked, "Nobody wants to kiss when they are hungry." Which motivation theory best supports her statement?
2. According to the concept of ______________ point, our body maintains itself at a particular weight level.
3. Which of the following is a genetically predisposed response to food?
   a. An aversion to eating cats and dogs
   b. An interest in novel foods
   c. A preference for sweet and salty foods
   d. An aversion to carbohydrates
4. Blood sugar provides the body with energy. When it is ______________ (low/high), we feel hungry.
5. The rate at which your body expends energy while at rest is referred to as the ______________ ______________ rate.
6. People who are significantly overweight often struggle to lose weight permanently. This is due to several factors, including the fact that
   a. trying to lose weight triggers neophobia.
   b. the set point of people with a higher body weight is lower than average.
   c. with food restriction, metabolism increases.
   d. there is a genetic influence on body weight.
7. Sanjay eats a diet high in processed foods, fat, and sugar. He knows he may gain weight, but he figures it's no big deal because he can simply lose it in the future. How would you evaluate Sanjay's plan?

MODULE 34 Sexual Motivation

Sex is a part of life. For all but the 1 percent of us who are **asexual** (Bogaert, 2004, 2015), dating and mating often become a high priority from puberty on. Pioneering sex researcher Alfred Kinsey (1894–1956) stumbled into studying sex. Raised in a religious home where money was tight, he was fascinated by nature (PBS, 2019). He spent the first 20 years of his career as a biologist collecting and categorizing insects, but he became concerned that people knew more about insects than about the then-taboo topic of sex. Kinsey's experience teaching a marriage and family course motivated him to spend the rest of his career collecting and categorizing people's sex histories. Kinsey and his colleagues' findings ignited debate and controversy, but they also paved the way for future research on the sexual behavior of men and women. Our **sexuality** consists of feelings and behaviors that reflect both physiological and psychological influences.

asexual having no sexual attraction toward others.

sexuality our thoughts, feelings, and actions related to our physical attraction to another.

The Physiology of Sex

Unlike hunger or sleep, sex is not an actual *need*. (Without sex, we may feel like dying, but we will not.) Yet sex motivates behavior. Had this not been so for your biological ancestors, you would not be alive and reading these words. Sexual motivation is nature's clever way of making people procreate, thus enabling our species' survival. Life is sexually transmitted.

Hormones and Sexual Behavior

LOQ 34-1 How do hormones influence human sexual motivation?

Among the forces driving sexual behavior are the *sex hormones*. The main male sex hormone is *testosterone*, and the main female sex hormones are the *estrogens*, such as estradiol. Sex hormones influence us at several points in the life span:

- During the prenatal period, they direct our sexual development.
- During puberty, a sex hormone surge ushers us into adolescence. In adolescent males, higher testosterone levels predict more male-typical traits and disorders (Vosberg et al., 2021).

After puberty and well into the late adult years, sex hormones facilitate sexual behavior.

In most mammals, nature neatly synchronizes sex with fertility. Females become sexually receptive when their estrogens peak at ovulation, and researchers can cause female animals to become receptive by injecting them with estrogens. Male hormone levels are more constant, and hormone injection does not so easily affect the sexual behavior of male animals. Nevertheless, male hamsters that have had their testosterone-making testes surgically removed will gradually lose interest in receptive females. They slowly regain it if injected with testosterone (Piekarski et al., 2009).

Hormones do influence human sexual behavior, but more loosely. Researchers have explored whether women's mating preferences change across the menstrual cycle, especially at ovulation, when both estrogens and testosterone rise (Arslan et al., 2021; Boudesseul et al., 2019). Worldwide, women's sexual behavior decreases during menstruation, when estrogen and testosterone levels are low (Pierson et al., 2021).

Women have much less testosterone than men do. But more than other mammalian females, women are responsive to their own testosterone level (Davison & Davis, 2011; Edelstein, 2022). If a woman's natural testosterone drops, as happens with the removal of the ovaries or adrenal glands, her sexual interest may wane. And as experiments with surgically or naturally menopausal women have demonstrated, testosterone-replacement therapy sometimes helps restore diminished arousal, desire, and sexual activity (Braunstein et al., 2005; Buster et al., 2005; Petersen & Hyde, 2011).

In human males with abnormally low testosterone levels, testosterone-replacement therapy often increases sexual desire and also energy and vitality (Khera et al., 2011). But typical fluctuations in testosterone levels, from man to man and hour to hour, have little effect on men's sex drive (Byrne, 1982). Indeed, male hormones sometimes vary in *response* to sexual stimulation (Escasa et al., 2011). In one study, Australian skateboarders' testosterone surged in the presence of an attractive female, contributing to riskier moves and more crash landings (Ronay & von Hippel, 2010). Thus, sexual arousal can be a *cause* and a consequence of increased testosterone levels.

Large hormonal surges or declines affect sexual desire at two predictable points in the life span, and sometimes at an unpredictable third point:

1. ***The pubertal surge in sex hormones triggers the development of sex characteristics and sexual interest.*** If puberty's hormonal surge is precluded—as it was during the 1600s and 1700s for prepubertal boys who were castrated to preserve their soprano voices for Italian opera—sex characteristics and sexual desire do not develop normally (Peschel & Peschel, 1987).
2. ***In later life, sex hormone levels fall.*** Women experience menopause as their estrogen levels decrease; men experience a more gradual change. Sex remains a part of life, but as hormone levels decline, sexual fantasies and intercourse also decline (Frankenbach et al., 2022).

3. ***For some, surgery or drugs may cause hormonal shifts.*** When adult men were castrated, their sex drive typically fell as testosterone levels declined sharply (Hucker & Bain, 1990). Likewise, when male sex offenders took a drug that reduced their testosterone level to that of a prepubertal boy, they also lost much of their sexual desire (Bilefsky, 2009; Money et al., 1983). Similar effects occur in women. For example, if a woman's testosterone level drops, as happens with the removal of the ovaries or adrenal glands, her sexual interest may wane (Davison & Davis, 2011; Lindau et al., 2007).

To summarize: We might compare human sex hormones, especially testosterone, to the fuel in a car. Without fuel, a vehicle will not run. But if the fuel level is minimally adequate, adding more won't change how the vehicle runs. The analogy is imperfect because hormones and sexual motivation interact. However, it correctly suggests that biology is a necessary but incomplete explanation of human sexual behavior. The hormonal fuel is essential, but so are the psychological stimuli that turn on the engine, keep it running, and shift it into high gear.

RETRIEVAL PRACTICE

RP-1 The primary female sex hormones are the ____________________. The primary male sex hormone is ____________________.

ANSWERS IN APPENDIX E

The Sexual Response Cycle

LOQ 34-2 What is the human *sexual response cycle,* and how do sexual dysfunctions and paraphilias differ?

The scientific process often begins with careful observations of complex behaviors. When William Masters and Virginia Johnson (1966) applied this process to human sexual intercourse in the 1960s, they made headlines. They recorded the physiological responses of volunteers who came to their lab to masturbate or have intercourse. (The volunteers—382 women and 312 men—were a somewhat atypical sample, consisting only of people able and willing to display arousal and orgasm while scientists observed.) Masters and Johnson reported observing more than 10,000 sexual "cycles." Their description of the **sexual response cycle** identified four stages:

1. *Excitement:* The genital areas become engorged with blood, causing a woman's clitoris and a man's penis to swell. A woman's vagina expands and secretes lubricant; her breasts and nipples may enlarge.
2. *Plateau:* Excitement peaks as breathing, pulse, and blood pressure rates continue to increase. A man's penis becomes fully engorged—to an average length of 5.6 inches, in a study of 1661 men (Herbenick et al., 2014). Some fluid—frequently containing enough live sperm to enable conception—may appear at its tip. A woman's vaginal secretion continues to increase, and her clitoris retracts. Orgasm feels imminent.
3. *Orgasm:* Muscle contractions appear all over the body and are accompanied by increased breathing, pulse, and blood pressure rates. The pleasurable feeling of sexual release is much the same for men and women. One panel of experts could not reliably distinguish between descriptions of orgasm written by men and those written by women (Vance & Wagner, 1976). In both female and male animals, sexual climax is directed by spinal cord neurons linked with the brain's thalamus region (McKenna, 2022).
4. *Resolution:* The body gradually returns to its unaroused state as the genital blood vessels release their accumulated blood. For men, this happens relatively quickly if an orgasm has occurred, relatively slowly otherwise. (It's like the nasal tickle that goes away rapidly if you have sneezed, slowly otherwise.) Men then enter a **refractory period** that lasts from a few minutes to a day or more, during which they are incapable of another orgasm. A woman's much shorter refractory period may enable her, if restimulated during or soon after the resolution, to have more orgasms (Prause, 2011).

sexual response cycle the four stages of sexual responding described by Masters and Johnson—excitement, plateau, orgasm, and resolution. 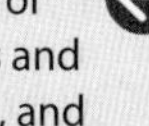

refractory period in human sexuality, a resting period that occurs after orgasm, during which a person cannot achieve another orgasm.

People vary in how often they repeat this sexual response cycle. In a U.S. sample of 1029 adults, participants reported an average of 10 orgasms each month, through both masturbation and partnered activity (Peters et al., 2022). One in 6 men and 1 in 10 women experienced seven or more orgasms each week (Kingston & Bradford, 2013).

Sexual Dysfunctions and Paraphilias

Masters and Johnson sought not only to describe the human sexual response cycle but also to understand and treat the inability to complete it. **Sexual dysfunctions** are problems that consistently impair sexual arousal or functioning at any point in this cycle. Some involve sexual motivation, especially lack of sexual energy and arousability. About 1 in 5 men have **erectile disorder** (inability to have or maintain an erection) (Selvin et al., 2007). Another problem is *premature ejaculation*—reaching a sexual climax before the man or his partner wishes. For women, the problem may be pain or **female orgasmic disorder** (distress over weak orgasmic feelings or infrequently or never experiencing orgasm). In separate surveys of some 3000 Boston women and 32,000 other U.S. women, about 4 in 10 reported a sexual problem, such as orgasmic disorder or low desire. Among more than 20,000 Australians surveyed, 52 percent of women—and 28 percent of men—reported a lack of interest in having sex (Richters et al., 2022). Most women who experience sexual distress relate it to their emotional relationship with their partner during sex (Bancroft et al., 2003).

Psychological and medical therapies can help men and women with sexual dysfunctions (Frühauf et al., 2013). In behaviorally oriented therapy, for example, men learn ways to control their urge to ejaculate, and women are trained to bring themselves to orgasm. Starting with the introduction of Viagra in 1998, erectile disorder has been routinely treated by taking a pill. Researchers have struggled to develop reliable drug treatments for *female sexual interest/arousal disorder* (Chivers & Brotto, 2017).

Sexual dysfunction involves problems with arousal or sexual functioning. People with **paraphilias** (primarily men) experience sexual desire, but they direct it in unusual ways that may cause harm (Baur et al., 2016). The American Psychiatric Association (2013) only classifies such behavior as disordered if

- a person experiences distress from an unusual sexual interest *or*
- it entails harm or risk of harm to one's self or to others.

The serial killer Jeffrey Dahmer had *necrophilia*, a sexual attraction to corpses. Those with *exhibitionism* derive pleasure from exposing themselves sexually to others without consent. People with the paraphilic disorder *pedophilia* experience sexual arousal toward children who haven't entered puberty.

RETRIEVAL PRACTICE

RP-2 Someone who is distressed by impaired sexual arousal may be diagnosed with a ______________ ______________. Exhibitionism would be considered a ______________.

ANSWERS IN APPENDIX E

sexual dysfunction a problem that consistently impairs sexual arousal or functioning at any point in the sexual response cycle.

erectile disorder inability to develop or maintain an erection due to insufficient blood flow to the penis.

female orgasmic disorder distress due to weak orgasmic feelings or infrequently or never experiencing orgasm.

paraphilias sexual arousal from fantasies, behaviors, or urges involving nonhuman objects, the suffering of self or others, and/or nonconsenting persons.

Sexually Transmitted Infections

LOQ 34-3 How can sexually transmitted infections be prevented?

Every day, more than 1 million people worldwide acquire a *sexually transmitted infection* (*STI;* also called *STD,* for *sexually transmitted disease*). Common STIs include chlamydia, gonorrhea, herpes simplex virus (HSV), and human papillomavirus (HPV) infection. In 2019, the Centers for Disease Control and Prevention reported that compared with older adults, sexually active adolescents (aged 15 to 19 years) and early adults (aged 20 to 24 years) are at higher risk. Teenage girls, for example, are at heightened risk given their not yet fully mature anatomy and lower levels of protective antibodies (Dehne & Riedner, 2005; Guttmacher Institute, 1994).

Condoms offer only limited protection against certain skin-to-skin STIs, such as herpes; but when used correctly, they do reduce other risks (NIH, 2001). The effects were clear when Thailand promoted condom use by sex workers. Over four years, as condom use soared from 14 to 94 percent, the annual number of bacterial STIs plummeted by 93 percent (WHO, 2000). When used by people with an infected partner, condoms have also been 80 percent effective in preventing the transmission of *HIV (human immunodeficiency virus)*—the virus that causes **AIDS** (Weller & Davis-Beaty, 2002; WHO, 2003). Although HIV can be transmitted by other means, such as needle sharing during drug use, its sexual transmission is most common. Half of all those with HIV (and 1 in 5 Americans recently diagnosed with HIV) are women (CDC, 2020). Because the virus is spread more easily from men to women than from women to men, women's proportion of the worldwide AIDS population is growing.

Having sex with one person means also partnering with that person's past partners—any one of whom might have unknowingly transmitted an STI. So, the first step in preventing STIs is knowing one's status, and telling one's sexual partner.

AIDS (acquired immune deficiency syndrome) a life-threatening condition caused by the *human immunodeficiency virus (HIV)*, a sexually transmitted infection. AIDS depletes the immune system, leaving the person vulnerable to infections.

The Psychology of Sex

LOQ 34-4 How do external and imagined stimuli contribute to sexual arousal?

Biological factors powerfully influence our sexual motivation and behavior. Yet the wide variations over time, across place, and among individuals also document the great influence of psychological factors (**FIGURE 34.1**). What motivates people to have sex? The 281 reasons offered by people in one study ranged widely—from "it feels good" to "to get closer to God" to "I was drunk" (Buss, 2008; Meston & Buss, 2007).

External Stimuli

Men and women become aroused when they see, hear, or read erotic material (Heiman, 1975; Stockton & Murnen, 1992). In men more than in women, feelings of sexual arousal closely mirror their (more obvious) physical genital responses (Chivers et al., 2010).

People may find sexual arousal either pleasing or disturbing. (Those who wish to control their arousal often limit their exposure to arousing materials, just as those wishing to avoid overeating limit their exposure to tempting food cues.) With repeated exposure to any stimulus, including an erotic stimulus, the emotional response lessens, or *habituates*. During the 1920s, when Western women's hemlines rose to the knee, an exposed leg made hearts flutter. Today, many would barely notice.

Can exposure to sexually explicit material have other effects? Research indicates that it can, in four ways.

- ***Accelerating sexual activity*** When followed over time, teens with high exposure to pornography later engaged in sexual activity earlier and more often (Pirrone et al., 2022).
- ***Believing rape is acceptable*** Although some modern pornography portrays women in powerful roles, mostly it presents women as subservient sexual objects (Fritz & Paul, 2018; Jones, 2018). Four in 10 pornographic scenes from two major online sites involve physical aggression, such as choking, slapping, and gagging (Fritz et al.,

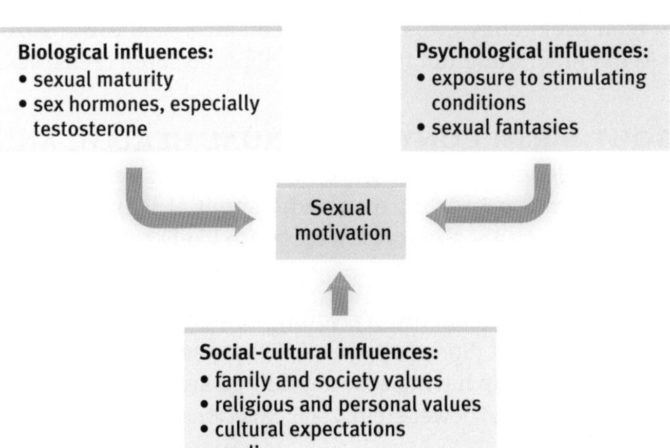
Biological influences:
• sexual maturity
• sex hormones, especially testosterone
Psychological influences:
• exposure to stimulating conditions
• sexual fantasies
Sexual motivation
Social-cultural influences:
• family and society values
• religious and personal values
• cultural expectations
• media

Digital Vision./Getty Images

FIGURE 34.1 Biopsychosocial influences on sexual motivation Compared with our motivation for eating, our sexual motivation is less influenced by biological factors. Psychological and social-cultural factors play a bigger role.

2020). Across 166 studies with 125,000 participants, exposure to violent sexual media increased participants' aggressive thoughts, feelings, and actions (Burnay et al., 2022). Depictions of violence toward women feed the false belief that women want to be sexually overpowered, increasing their risk of sexual victimization.

- ***Reducing satisfaction with a partner's appearance or with a relationship*** After viewing erotic films of sexually attractive women and men, people have judged their own relationship as less satisfying (Perry, 2020). Perhaps reading or watching erotica's unlikely scenarios creates expectations that few people can fulfill.
- ***Desensitization*** Extensive online pornography viewing can warp expectations and desensitize people to normal sexuality. Repeated exposure to this distorted sexual world may contribute to greater risk of psychological distress, lowered sexual desire and satisfaction, diminished brain activation in response to sexual images, and, for men, erectile problems (Mennig et al., 2022; Wright et al., 2018). "Porn is messing with your manhood," argued Philip Zimbardo and colleagues (2016).

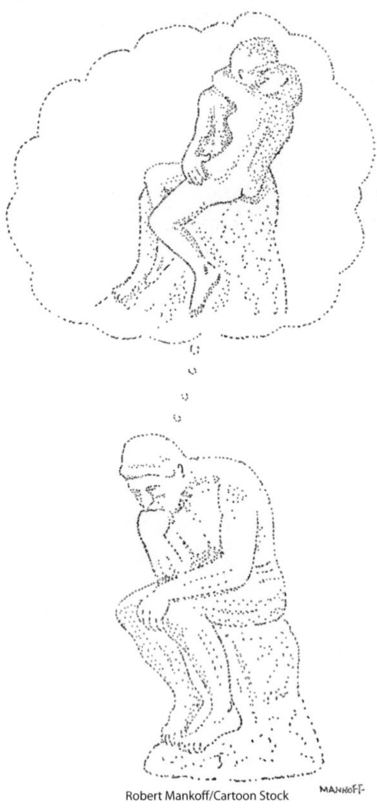
Robert Mankoff/Cartoon Stock

Imagined Stimuli

The brain, it has been said, is our most significant sex organ. The stimuli inside our head—our imagination—can influence sexual arousal and desire. Lacking genital sensation because of a spinal-cord injury, people can still feel sexual desire (Willmuth, 1987).

All genders report having sexual fantasies and watching pornography, and have similar brain responses to sexual imagery (Mitricheva et al., 2019; Solano et al., 2018; Wright & Vangeel, 2019). While men and most women need genital stimulation to produce orgasm, sexual fantasies alone can cause some women to experience orgasms (Komisaruk & Whipple, 2011). Men, regardless of sexual orientation, tend to have more frequent, more physical, and more aggressive sexual fantasies (Apostolou & Khalil, 2019; Canivet et al., 2022). They also prefer less personal and faster-paced sexual content in books and videos (Leitenberg & Henning, 1995). Fantasizing about sex does *not* indicate a sexual problem or dissatisfaction. If anything, sexually active people have more sexual fantasies.

RETRIEVAL PRACTICE

RP-3 What factors influence our sexual motivation and behavior?

ANSWERS IN APPENDIX E

Teen Sexual Risk Taking

LOQ 34-5 What factors influence teenagers' sexual behaviors and use of contraceptives?

Sexual attitudes and behaviors vary dramatically across cultures and eras. "Sex between unmarried adults" is "morally unacceptable," agreed 97 percent of Indonesians and 6 percent of Germans (Pew, 2014). Thanks mostly to decreased sexual activity—from 54 percent of high school students in 1991 reporting ever having had intercourse to 38 percent in 2019—U.S. teen pregnancy rates have halved since 2008 (CDC, 2020; Livingston & Thomas, 2019). What environmental factors contribute to some teens' sexual risk taking?

COMMUNICATION ABOUT BIRTH CONTROL, SEXUAL HEALTH, AND DISEASE PREVENTION Many teenagers are uncomfortable discussing sex and contraception with parents, partners, and peers. But teens who spent at least 10 hours talking freely and openly with their parents about sex were more likely to use contraceptives (Widman et al., 2019).

IMPULSIVITY When reflecting on their sexual history, young women, more often than men, regret the timing of their sexual debut (Sprecher et al., 2022). If passion overwhelms intentions to use contraceptives or to delay having sex, unplanned sexual activity may result in unsafe sex and pregnancy (Ariely & Loewenstein, 2006; MacDonald & Hynie, 2008).

"Condoms should be used on every conceivable occasion."—Anonymous

ALCOHOL USE Among older teens and young adults, most sexual hook-ups (casual encounters outside of a relationship) occur after alcohol use, often without *affirmative consent* (Fielder et al., 2013; Garcia et al., 2013; Johnson & Chen, 2015). Those who use alcohol prior to sexual activity are less likely to use condoms (Kotchick et al., 2001). By depressing the brain centers that control judgment, inhibition, and self-awareness, alcohol disarms normal restraints—a phenomenon well known to sexually coercive people.

MASS MEDIA Popular media influence teens by providing *social scripts* for sexual behavior. Media also affect peer perceptions: The more sexual content adolescents and young adults view or read (even when controlling for other predictors of early sexual activity), the more likely they are to perceive their peers as sexually active, to develop sexually permissive attitudes, to experience early intercourse, and to use condoms inconsistently (Escobar-Chaves et al., 2005; O'Hara et al., 2012; Parkes et al., 2013; Ward et al. 2018). Perceived peer norms influence teens' sexual behavior (Lyons, 2015; van de Bongardt et al., 2015).

Frank Schuermann/dpa/picturealliance/Newscom

Distorted social scripts An analysis of the 60 top-selling video games found 489 characters, 86 percent of whom were male (like most of the game players). The female characters were much more likely than the male characters to be hypersexualized—partially nude or revealingly clothed, with large breasts and tiny waists (Downs & Smith, 2010). Such depictions can lead to unrealistic expectations about sexuality and body ideals, and contribute to the early sexualization of girls (Karsay et al., 2018).

SEXUAL RESTRAINT What are the characteristics of teens who delay having sex?

- ***High intelligence*** Teens with high rather than average intelligence test scores more often delay sex, partly because they consider possible negative consequences and delay gratification (Harden & Mendle, 2011).
- ***Religious engagement*** Actively religious teens more often reserve sexual activity for adulthood or long-term relationships (Hull et al., 2011; Schmitt & Fuller, 2015; Štulhofer et al., 2011).
- ***Father presence*** In studies that followed hundreds of New Zealand and U.S. girls from age 5 to 18, having Dad in the household reduced the risk of teen pregnancy and of sexual activity before age 16 (Ellis et al., 2003). These associations held even after adjusting for other influences, such as poverty. Close family attachments—as in families that spend time together and where parents know their teens' activities and friends—also predict later sexual initiation (Coley et al., 2008).
- ***Comprehensive sex education*** Irish teens who received comprehensive sex education at school (including discussion of feelings, relationships, safe sex, and sexual orientation), compared with those who did not, were more likely to delay having sex until they were older (Bourke et al., 2014).
- ***Service-learning participation*** U.S. teens who volunteered as tutors or teachers' aides, or participated in community projects, had lower pregnancy rates than did comparable teens randomly assigned to control conditions (Kirby, 2002; O'Donnell et al., 2002). Researchers are unsure why. Does service learning promote a sense of personal competence, control, and responsibility? Does it encourage more future-oriented thinking? Or does it simply reduce opportunities for unprotected sex? (After-school activities and later school start times also reduced unplanned pregnancies [Bryan et al., 2016; Steinberg, 2015].)

Shutterstock

Father presence

ASK YOURSELF

What strategies could your community use to reduce teen pregnancy?

RETRIEVAL PRACTICE

RP-4 Which *three* of the following five factors contribute to sexual risk taking among some teens?

a. Alcohol use
b. Higher intelligence level
c. Father absence
d. Mass media models
e. Participating in service-learning programs

ANSWERS IN APPENDIX E

Sexual Orientation

LOQ 34-6 What do we know about sexual orientation?

To motivate is to energize and direct behavior. So far, we have considered the energizing of sexual motivation but not its *direction*, which is our **sexual orientation**—sexual attraction that may be female-male (*heterosexual* orientation), to our own sex (*same-sex* orientation), to males and females (*bisexual* orientation), or to no one at all (*asexual* orientation). We experience such attractions in our interests and fantasies. (Who appears in your imagination?)

Note that sexual orientation is distinct from *gender identity* (including *transgender* identity).

In one British survey of 18,876 people (and in other surveys since), about 1 percent identified themselves as asexual, having "never felt sexually attracted to anyone at all" (Bogaert, 2004, 2015). People with an asexual orientation are, however, nearly as likely as others to report masturbating, noting that it feels good, reduces anxiety, or "cleans out the plumbing." Those who are asexual may enjoy nonsexual aspects of relationships (emotional closeness, companionship); 1 in 3 reports being in a romantic relationship (Carvalho & Rodrigues, 2022).

Cultures vary in their attitudes toward same-sex attractions. Should society accept such attractions? *Yes*, say 94 percent of Swedes and 7 percent of Nigerians. Acceptance, however, is increasing worldwide, with women and younger, educated adults being more accepting (Poushter & Kent, 2020). Yet whether a culture condemns or accepts same-sex unions, heterosexuality is most common and same-sex attraction and other variations exist. In the African countries in which same-sex relationships are illegal, the ratio of gay and bisexual people "is no different from other countries in the rest of the world," reports the Academy of Science of South Africa (2015). And in cultures in which same-sex behavior is expected of boys before marriage, most men nevertheless grow up to be heterosexual—or *straight*—adults (Hammack, 2005; Money, 1987). So, same-sex activity spans human history, and sexual behaviors need not indicate *orientation*.

How many people have exclusively same-sex attractions? According to more than a dozen national surveys in Europe and the United States, about 3 or 4 percent of men and 2 percent of women (Chandra et al., 2011; Copen et al., 2016; Savin-Williams et al., 2012). But the percentages vary somewhat over time, with the percentage who feel comfortable self-reporting as gay or bisexual gradually increasing with increased social acceptance. In 2021, 5.2 percent of Americans reported being gay or bisexual (Jones, 2021). Percentages are also slightly higher when reporting is anonymous (Copen et al., 2016). A larger number of Americans—17 percent of women and 6 percent of men—say they have had some same-sex sexual contact during their lives (Copen et al., 2016). Psychologists have only recently begun to research the experiences of those who are bisexual (Borgogna et al., 2018; Greaves et al., 2019; House et al., 2022; Torres, 2019).

In less tolerant places, people are more likely to hide their sexual orientation. About 3 percent of California men express same-sex attraction on Facebook, for example, as do only about 1 percent in Mississippi. Yet about 5 percent of Google pornography searches in both states are for gay porn. And online ads for men seeking "casual encounters" with other men tend to be at least as common in less tolerant states, where there are also more Google searches for "gay sex" and "Is my husband gay?" (MacInnis & Hodson, 2015; Stephens-Davidowitz, 2013).

What would it be like to be straight in a majority gay culture? If you are straight, imagine that you have found "the one"—your perfect other-sex partner. How would you feel if you weren't sure who you could trust with knowing you had these feelings? How would you react if you overheard people telling crude jokes about straight people, or if most movies, TV shows, and advertisements showed only same-sex relationships? How would you like hearing that many people wouldn't vote for a political candidate who favors other-sex marriage? And how would you feel if children's organizations and adoption agencies thought you might not be safe or trustworthy because you are attracted to people of another sex?

Facing such reactions, some people with same-sex attractions may at first try to ignore or deny their desires, hoping they will go away. But they don't. And these people may—particularly if they live in a region or a country that condemns same-sex attractions—conceal their orientation, which can harm their mental health (Pachankis et al., 2020). Especially during adolescence or when feeling rejected by their parents or peers, people may struggle against same-sex attractions. Some may wish to change their orientation, but the feelings are typically as enduring as those of straight people—who are similarly unable to change who they are (Haldeman, 1994, 2002; Myers & Scanzoni, 2005).

sexual orientation the direction of our sexual attractions, as reflected in our longings and fantasies.

In surveys of U.S. high schoolers, gay youth have been twice as likely as straight youth to report being bullied, feeling unsafe, and experiencing violence. They have also been 3.6 times more likely to report persistent feelings of sadness or hopelessness in the past 12 months, and 4.5 times more likely to have "seriously considered attempting suicide" (CDC, 2020). When including a wider range of sexual orientations (gay, lesbian, bisexual, queer, questioning, asexual), the risk for attempted suicide is even greater, with 20 percent of these teens having attempted suicide over the past year (Trevor Project, 2022).

Today's psychologists view sexual orientation as neither willfully chosen nor willfully changed. In 1973, the American Psychiatric Association dropped "homosexuality" from its list of mental illnesses. In 2009, the American Psychological Association declared that "Efforts to change sexual orientation are unlikely to be successful and involve some risk of harm." A consensus of British mental health organizations agreed that such attempts are "unethical and potentially harmful" (Gale et al., 2017). Recognizing this, some countries and U.S. states and cities have banned "conversion therapy"—which aims to change people's sexual orientation—with minors.

"There is no sound scientific evidence that sexual orientation can be changed."
—UK Royal College of Psychiatrists, 2014

Sexual orientation in some ways is like handedness: Most people are one way, some the other. A smaller group experiences some form of ambidexterity. Regardless, the way we are endures, especially in men (Dickson et al., 2013; Norris et al., 2015). Women's sexual orientation tends to be less strongly felt than men's and, for some women, is more *fluid* and changing. For example, 1 in 10 straight U.S. women report having had at least one same-sex sexual partner, which is five times greater than the rate among straight men (Silva, 2022). Straight women may experience genital arousal to either male or female sexual stimuli (Chivers, 2017). Transgender men (assigned a female sex at birth but identifying as male) similarly seem to experience genital arousal to both male and female sexual stimuli (Raines et al., 2021). But transgender men tend to show much stronger sexual arousal toward whatever gender they are attracted to, as is the case for cisgender men.

In general, men are sexually simpler. Across time, cultures, situations, differing levels of education, religious observance, and peer influence, men's sexual drive and interests have been less flexible and varying than have women's. Women, for example, more often prefer to alternate periods of high sexual activity with periods of almost none (Mosher et al., 2005). Roy Baumeister (2000) calls this flexibility *erotic plasticity*.

Origins of Sexual Orientation

So, if we do not choose our sexual orientation and (especially for men) cannot change it, where do these feelings come from? In an early search for possible environmental influences on sexual orientation, Kinsey Institute investigators in the 1980s interviewed nearly 1000 lesbian/gay and 500 heterosexual people. They assessed nearly every imaginable psychological "cause" of same-sex attraction—parental relationships, childhood sexual experiences, peer relationships, and dating experiences (Bell et al., 1981; Hammersmith, 1982). Their findings: Gay people were no more likely than straight people to have been smothered by maternal love or neglected by their father. And consider this: If "distant fathers" were more likely to produce gay sons, then shouldn't boys growing up in father-absent homes more often be gay? (They are not.) And shouldn't the rising number of such homes have led to a noticeable increase in the gay population? (It did not.) Most children raised by gay or lesbian parents display gender-typical behavior and are heterosexual (Farr et al., 2018; Gartrell & Bos, 2010). And they grow up with health and emotional well-being similar to children with straight parents (Bos et al., 2016; Farr, 2017).

So, what else might influence sexual orientation? One theory has proposed that people develop same-sex erotic attachments if segregated by sex at the time their sex drive matures (Storms, 1981). Indeed, gay men tend to recall going through puberty somewhat earlier, when peers are more likely to be all male (Bogaert et al., 2002). Moreover, though peers' attitudes predict teens' sexual attitudes and behavior, they do not predict same-sex attraction. "Peer influence has little or no effect" on sexual orientation (Brakefield et al., 2014).

Environment likely contributes to sexual orientation—nature and nurture work together—but the inability to pin down specific environmental influences has led researchers to explore several lines of biological evidence. These include same-sex attraction in other species, brain differences, and genetic and prenatal influences.

SAME-SEX ATTRACTION IN OTHER SPECIES In Boston's Public Gardens, caretakers solved the mystery of why a much-loved swan couple's eggs never hatched. Both swans

SEA LIFE Sydney Aquarium

Dad and dad At Sydney's SEA LIFE Aquarium, Sphen and Magic, a bonded same-sex penguin pair, successfully raised a foster chick (appropriately named "Sphengic").

were female. In New York City's Central Park Zoo, penguins Silo and Roy spent several years as devoted same-sex partners. Same-sex sexual behaviors have been observed in several hundred other species, including grizzlies, gorillas, giraffes, monkeys, flamingos, and owls (Bagemihl, 1999). Among rams, for example, some 7 to 10 percent display same-sex attraction by shunning ewes and seeking to mount other males (Perkins & Fitzgerald, 1997). Same-sex sexual behavior seems a natural part of the animal world.

BRAIN DIFFERENCES Might the structure and function of gay and straight brains differ? Neuroscientist Simon LeVay (1991) studied sections of the hypothalamus taken from deceased gay and straight people. His discovery: a cell cluster that was indeed reliably larger in straight men than in straight women and gay men.

It should not surprise us that brains differ with sexual orientation. Remember: *Everything psychological is simultaneously biological.* But when did the brain difference begin? At conception? During childhood or adolescence? Did experience produce the difference? Or was it genes or prenatal hormones (or genes activating prenatal hormones)?

LeVay does not view the hypothalamus cell network as a sexual orientation center. Rather, he sees it as an important part of the neural pathway linked to sexual behavior. He acknowledges that sexual behavior patterns may influence the brain's anatomy. In fish, birds, rats, and humans, brain structures vary with experience—including sexual experience (Breedlove, 1997). But LeVay believes it is more likely that brain anatomy influences sexual orientation. His hunch seems confirmed by the discovery of a similar hypothalamic difference between male sheep that do and don't display same-sex attraction (Larkin et al., 2002; Roselli et al., 2002, 2004). Moreover, such differences seem to develop soon after birth, and perhaps even before birth (Rahman & Wilson, 2003).

Since LeVay's brain *structure* discovery, other researchers have reported differences in how gay and straight brains *function*. One is in an area of the hypothalamus that governs sexual arousal (Savic et al., 2005). This brain area became active when straight women were given a whiff of a scent derived from men's sweat. Gay men's brains responded similarly to the men's scent. But straight men's brains showed the arousal response only to a female hormone derivative. In a similar study, gay women's responses differed from those of straight women (Kranz & Ishai, 2006; Martins et al., 2005). Researcher Qazi Rahman (2015) sums it up: Compared with straight men and women, "gay men appear, on average, more 'female typical' in brain pattern responses and [gay] women are somewhat more 'male typical.'"

On several traits, the average gay man and gay woman fall midway between the average straight man and straight woman. Consider the gay-straight difference in spatial abilities. On mental rotation tasks such as the one in **FIGURE 34.2**, straight men tend to outscore straight women, and gay men fall in between (Xu et al., 2020). But straight women and gay men have both outperformed straight men at remembering objects' spatial locations in memory game tasks (Hassan & Rahman, 2007).

FIGURE 34.2
Spatial abilities and sexual orientation Which of the three figures can be rotated to match the Original figure?[1] Straight men tend to find this type of mental rotation task easier than do straight women, with gay men and gay women falling in between (see graph) (Rahman et al., 2004).

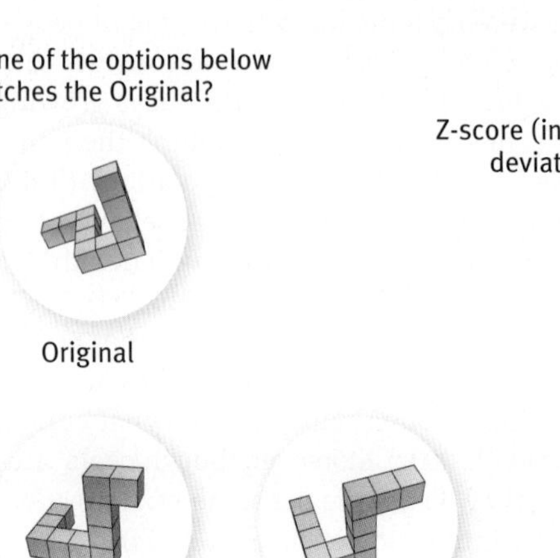
Which one of the options below matches the Original?
Original
(a)
(b)
(c)

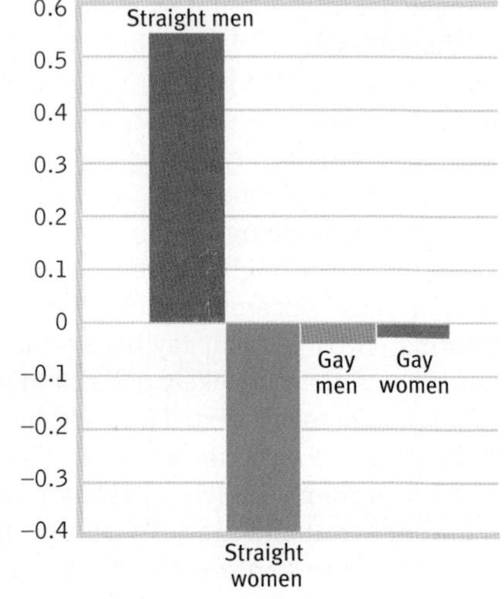
Z-score (in standard deviation units)
0.6
0.5
0.4
0.3
0.2
0.1
0
–0.1
–0.2
–0.3
–0.4
Straight men
Straight women
Gay men
Gay women

[1] Answer: Figure (c).

GENETIC INFLUENCES Studies indicate that "about a third of variation in sexual orientation is attributable to genetic influences" (Bailey et al., 2016). A same-sex orientation does tend to run in families. And identical twins are somewhat more likely than fraternal twins to share a same-sex orientation (Alanko et al., 2010; Långström et al., 2010). But because sexual orientations differ in many identical twin pairs, especially female twins, we know that other factors besides genes are also at work—including, it appears, *epigenetic marks* that help distinguish gay and straight twins (Balter, 2015; Gavrilets et al., 2018).

By altering a single gene in fruit flies, experimenters have changed the flies' sexual orientation and behavior (Dickson, 2005). In search of genes that influence human sexual orientation, researchers have analyzed the genomes of 409 pairs of gay brothers, and of 1231 straight men and 1077 gay men. They found links between sexual orientation and two genes on chromosomes 13 and 14. The first of those chromosome regions influences a brain area that varies in size with sexual orientation. The second influences thyroid function, which has also been associated with sexual orientation (Sanders et al., 2015, 2017). But we should also recall a familiar lesson: Human traits are *polygenic*—influenced by *many genes having small effects*. Indeed, a giant study of nearly 500,000 peoples' genes confirmed that "Same-sex behavior is influenced by not one or a few genes but many" (Ganna et al., 2019).

Researchers have speculated about possible reasons why same-sex attraction persists, given that it involves a "reproductive cost" (because same-sex couples cannot naturally reproduce) (Apostolou, 2022). One possible answer is *kin selection*. Evolutionary psychologists remind us that many of our genes also reside in our biological relatives. Perhaps, then, gay people's genes live on by supporting their relatives' survival and reproduction. Another possible answer comes from a study that analyzed the entire genome of 360,000 participants, who also reported their same-sex and other-sex sexual behavior (Zietsch et al., 2021). The results were striking: The same genetic patterns that predispose some people to be gay are also found in some straight people who tend to have more sexual partners, thus leading to more offspring.

A *fertile females theory* suggests that maternal genetics may also be at work (Bocklandt et al., 2006). Around the world, gay men tend to have more gay relatives on their mother's side than on their father's (Camperio-Ciani et al., 2004, 2009, 2012; VanderLaan et al., 2012; VanderLaan & Vasey, 2011). And the relatives on the mother's side also produce more offspring than do the maternal relatives of straight men. Perhaps the genes that dispose some women to conceive more children with men also dispose some men to be attracted to men (LeVay, 2011). Thus, the decreased reproduction by gay men appears to be offset by the increased reproduction by their maternal extended family.

"Modern scientific research indicates that sexual orientation is . . . partly determined by genetics, but more specifically by hormonal activity in the womb." —Glenn Wilson and Qazi Rahman, *Born Gay: The Psychobiology of Sex Orientation*, 2005

PRENATAL INFLUENCES Recall that in the womb, sex hormones direct our male and female development. In animals and some humans, prenatal hormone conditions have altered a fetus' sexual orientation, most clearly so for females (Breedlove, 2017). When pregnant sheep were injected with testosterone during a critical period of fetal development, their female offspring later showed same-sex sexual behavior (Money, 1987). A critical period in the human brain's neural-hormonal control system may exist during the second trimester (Ellis & Ames, 1987; Garcia-Falgueras & Swaab, 2010; Meyer-Bahlburg, 1995). Exposure to the hormone levels typically experienced by female fetuses during this period may predispose females later to become attracted to males (Tasos, 2022). And female fetuses most exposed to testosterone appear most likely later to exhibit gender-atypical traits and to experience same-sex desires. "Prenatal sex hormones control the sexual differentiation of brain centers involved in sexual behaviors," noted Simon LeVay (2011, p. 216).

The mother's immune system may also play a role in determining the sexual orientation of the fetus. In a curious but amazingly reliable finding from 35 of 36 samples studied, men with older brothers have been somewhat more likely to be gay, reports Ray Blanchard (2004, 2018, 2019)—about one-third more likely for each additional older brother (see also Bogaert, 2003). A similar, though weaker, effect is found among men with older sisters (Blanchard & Skorska, 2022). The odds of same-sex attraction are roughly 2 percent among first sons, and they rise to about 2.6 percent among second sons, 3.5 percent for third sons, and so on for each additional older brother (Bailey et al., 2016). This is called the *older-brother effect* (also called the *fraternal birth order effect;* see **FIGURE 34.3**).

FIGURE 34.3
The older-brother effect These approximate curves depict a man's likelihood of same-sex attraction as a function of the number of biological (not adopted) older brothers he has (Blanchard, 2008; Bogaert, 2006). This correlation has been found in several studies, but only among right-handed men (as about 9 in 10 men are). A similar, though weaker, effect occurs among men with older sisters.

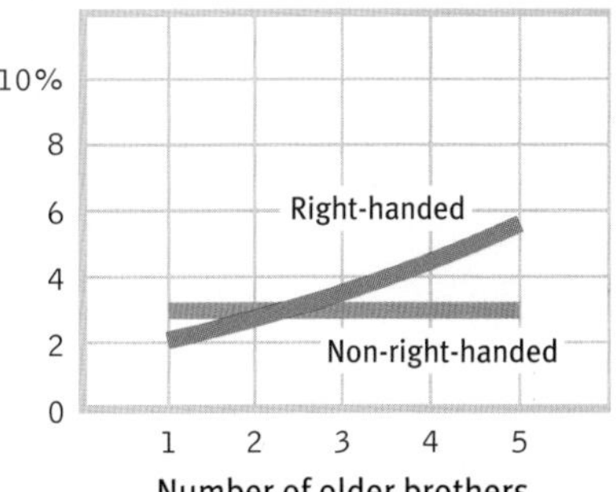

Probability of same-sex attraction
10%
8
6
4
2
0
Right-handed
Non-right-handed
1
2
3
4
5
Number of older brothers

William Haefeli/Cartoon Stock

"Thanks, but I'm in the midst of a lesbian phase that started the day I was born."

A recent study of more than 9 million Dutch people born between 1940 and 1990—60,000+ of whom had same-sex marriages—strongly confirmed the older-brother effect (Ablaza et al., 2022). The more older brothers, the more likely a same-sex marriage. Although the older-brother effect is but one of several biological contributions to sexual orientation, it is no longer a mere hypothesis; it is an established fact. (Curiously, in this study, women with older brothers were also more likely to enter a same-sex marriage.) The researchers believe their Dutch data add evidence "that sexual orientation is an innate trait and a reflection of individuals' true selves, rather than the product of lifestyle choices."

The reason for this older-brother effect is unclear. Blanchard and his colleagues (2021) offer a *maternal immune hypothesis:* Male fetuses may stimulate the maternal immune system to produce antibodies. With each pregnancy with a male fetus, the maternal antibodies accumulate and divert brain development from the male-typical pattern (Bogaert et al., 2018). Consistent with this biological explanation, in men, the effect occurs only with older brothers born to the same mother (whether raised together or not). Sexual orientation is unaffected by adoptive brothers (Bogaert, 2006).

The point to remember: Taken together, the brain, genetic, and prenatal findings offer strong support for a biological explanation of sexual orientation, especially for men (LeVay, 2011; Rahman & Koerting, 2008). Women's greater sexual fluidity suggests there are psychosocial influences as well (Diamond et al., 2017).

Note that the scientific question is not "What causes same-sex orientation?" (or "What causes heterosexual orientation?") but "What causes differing sexual orientations?" In pursuit of answers, psychological science compares the backgrounds and physiology of people whose sexual orientations *differ*.

* * *

Still, some people wonder: Should the cause of sexual orientation matter? Perhaps it shouldn't, but people's assumptions matter. Those who believe sexual orientation is a lifestyle choice often oppose equal rights for gay people. For example, in signing a 2014 bill that made some same-sex sexual acts punishable by life in prison, Uganda's president denied that same-sex attraction is inborn, declaring it a matter of "choice" (Balter, 2014; Landau et al., 2014). Those who instead understand sexual orientation as inborn—as shaped by biological and prenatal influences—more often favor equal rights for gay, lesbian, and bisexual people (Bailey et al., 2016).

ASK YOURSELF

How has learning more about what contributes to sexual orientation influenced your views? How might your learning from this module influence your interactions with people whose sexual orientation differs from yours?

RETRIEVAL PRACTICE

RP-5 Which *three* of the following five factors have researchers found to have an effect on sexual orientation?

a. An over-involved mother
b. The size of a certain cell cluster in the hypothalamus
c. Prenatal hormone exposure
d. A distant or ineffectual father
e. Having multiple older biological brothers

ANSWERS IN APPENDIX E

Sex and Human Relationships

LOQ 34-7 What role do social factors play in our sexuality?

Scientific research on sexual motivation does not aim to define the personal meaning of sex in our own lives. You could know every available fact about sex—that the initial spasms of male and female orgasm come at 0.8-second intervals, that female nipples can expand 10 millimeters at the peak of sexual arousal, that systolic blood pressure can rise some 60 points and respiration rate can reach 40 breaths per minute—but fail to understand the human significance of sexual intimacy.

Sexual desire motivates people to form intimate, committed relationships, which in turn enable satisfying sex (Birnbaum, 2018). Relationship satisfaction and sexual satisfaction often go hand in hand. A loving relationship enhances sex. And good sex, with a lingering "afterglow," enhances a loving relationship (Maxwell & McNulty, 2019). Surely one meaning of such intimacy is its expression of our profoundly social nature.

In one study that followed U.S. participants to age 30, later first sex predicted greater satisfaction with one's marriage or partnership (Harden, 2012). Another study asked 2035 married people when they started having sex (while controlling for education, religious engagement, and relationship length). Those whose relationship first developed to a deep commitment reported greater relationship satisfaction and stability, and also better sex (Busby et al., 2010; Galinsky & Sonenstein, 2013). For men and women, but especially for women, sex is more satisfying (with more orgasms and less regret) when in a committed relationship, rather than a brief sexual hook-up (Armstrong et al., 2012; Benidixen et al., 2017; Dubé et al., 2017). Partners who share regular meals are more likely than one-time dinner companions to understand what seasoning touches suit each other's food tastes; so, too, with the touches of loyal partners who share a bed.

Sex is more than an itch that begs to be scratched. It is a socially significant act. Men and women can achieve orgasm alone, yet most people find greater satisfaction—and experience a much greater surge in *prolactin*, the hormone associated with sexual satisfaction and satiety—after intercourse and orgasm with their loved one (Brody & Tillmann, 2006). Among newlyweds in one study, the sexual afterglow lasted 48 hours and increased marital satisfaction (Meltzer et al., 2017). Thanks to their overlapping brain reward areas, sexual desire and love feed each other (Cacioppo et al., 2012). Sex at its human best is life uniting and love renewing.

We realize that sexuality research may create discomfort and invite disagreement. Some may find it awkward to speak frankly about sex and sexuality. Others may feel that acceptance of diverse sexual orientations challenges their personal beliefs (Wilkins et al., 2022). Yet we believe that learning about our sexual motivation can predict positive outcomes, such as greater appreciation of our bodies and brains and greater respect for ourselves and others. We hope you have found the material enriching.

skynesher/iStock/Getty Images

Life-uniting and love-renewing Being in a committed relationship before having sex leads to better relationships, and better sex.

Increased sex ≠ more happiness
Among married couples, more frequent sex correlates with happiness (Muise et al., 2016). So, would systematically increasing sexual frequency *cause* people to be happier? Alas, heterosexual married couples randomly assigned to double their intercourse frequency over 3 months became slightly *less* happy (Loewenstein et al., 2015).

MODULE 34 REVIEW Sexual Motivation

LEARNING OBJECTIVES

Test Yourself Answer these repeated Learning Objective Questions on your own (before "showing" the answers here, or checking the answers in Appendix D) to improve your retention of the concepts (McDaniel et al., 2009, 2015).

LOQ 34-1 How do hormones influence human sexual motivation?

LOQ 34-2 What is the human *sexual response cycle*, and how do sexual dysfunctions and paraphilias differ?

LOQ 34-3 How can sexually transmitted infections be prevented?

LOQ 34-4 How do external and imagined stimuli contribute to sexual arousal?

LOQ 34-5 What factors influence teenagers' sexual behaviors and use of contraceptives?

LOQ 34-6 What do we know about sexual orientation?

LOQ 34-7 What role do social factors play in our sexuality?

TERMS AND CONCEPTS TO REMEMBER

Test Yourself Write down the definition in your own words, then check your answer.

asexual, p. 391
sexuality, p. 391
sexual response cycle, p. 393
refractory period, p. 393
sexual dysfunction, p. 394
erectile disorder, p. 394
female orgasmic disorder, p. 394
paraphilias, p. 394
AIDS (acquired immune deficiency syndrome), p. 395
sexual orientation, p. 398

MODULE TEST

Test Yourself Answer the following questions on your own first, then "show" the answers here, or check your answers in Appendix E.

1. A striking effect of hormonal changes on human sexual behavior is the
a. end of sexual desire in men over 60.
b. sharp rise in sexual interest at puberty.
c. decrease in women's sexual desire at the time of ovulation.
d. increase in testosterone levels in castrated men.

2. In describing the sexual response cycle, Masters and Johnson noted that
a. a plateau phase follows orgasm.
b. people experience a refractory period during which they cannot experience orgasm.
c. the feeling that accompanies orgasm is stronger in men than in women.
d. testosterone is released equally in women and men.

3. What is the difference between sexual dysfunctions and paraphilias?

4. Using condoms during sex ________ (does/doesn't) reduce the risk of getting HIV and ________ (does/doesn't) fully protect against skin-to-skin STIs.

5. An example of an external stimulus that might influence sexual behavior is

a. the level of testosterone in the bloodstream.
b. the onset of puberty.
c. a sexually explicit film.
d. an erotic fantasy or dream.

6. Which factors have researchers so far found to be *unrelated* to the development of our sexual orientation?

MODULE 

Affiliation and Achievement

Affiliation and achievement are among the strongest human motivations. Let's investigate how people fulfill these motivations—and what happens when people's affiliation and achievement needs are not met.

The Need to Belong

LOQ 35-1 What evidence points to our human affiliation need—our need to belong?

Separated from friends or family—at a new school, alone in prison or a foreign land, or isolating to prevent the spread of Covid-19—most people keenly feel their loss of social connection. We are what the ancient Greek philosopher Aristotle called the *social animal*. "Without friends," he wrote in *Nicomachean Ethics*, "no one would choose to live, though he had all other goods." This deep *need to belong*—our **affiliation need**—is a key human motivation (Baumeister & Leary, 1995). Even a chat with a stranger—though we may fear it will be awkward—often gives us an emotional boost (Kardas et al., 2022). It is common and healthy to seek privacy and solitude (Nguyen et al., 2019). But most of us also seek to affiliate—to become strongly attached to certain others in enduring, close relationships. Across 27 countries, people were most strongly motivated to maintain their romantic relationships and to care for family members (Ko et al., 2020).

The Benefits of Belonging

Social bonds boosted our early ancestors' survival chances. Adults who formed attachments were more likely to survive, reproduce, and co-nurture their offspring to maturity. Attachment bonds motivated caregivers to keep children close, calming and protecting them from threats (Esposito et al., 2013). Indeed, to be "wretched" literally means, in its Middle English origin *(wrecched)*, to be without kin nearby.

Cooperating with friends and acquaintances also enhanced survival. As hunters, our ancestors learned that six hands were better than two. As food gatherers, they gained protection from two-footed and four-footed enemies by traveling in groups. Those who cooperated survived and reproduced most successfully, and their cooperative genes now predominate (Rand & Nowak, 2013). Our innate need to belong drives us to befriend people who cooperate and to avoid those who exploit (Feinberg et al., 2014; Kashima et al., 2019). People in every society on Earth belong to groups and prefer and favor "us" over "them." Having a *social identity*—feeling part of a group—boosts people's health and well-being (Allen et al., 2015; Haslam et al., 2019).

Do you have close friends—people to whom you freely disclose your ups and downs? Having someone who listens and rejoices with us over good news helps us feel better about both the news and the friendship (Itzchakov et al., 2022). Such companionship creates connection and cooperation (Canavello & Crocker, 2017). Warmth and social connection go hand in hand: Feeling physically warm makes us feel socially connected to

affiliation need the need to build and maintain relationships and to feel connected to a group.

self-determination theory the theory that we feel motivated to satisfy our needs for competence, autonomy, and relatedness.

close others, and close others make us feel physically warm (Inagaki et al., 2019; Inagaki & Ross, 2021). The need to belong runs deeper, it seems, than any need to be rich. Very happy university students are marked not by the amount of money they have but by their "strong social relationships" (Diener et al., 2018).

The need to belong colors our thoughts and emotions. We spend a great deal of time thinking about actual and hoped-for relationships. When new relationships form, we often feel joy. Falling in mutual love, people's cheeks may ache from their irrepressible grins. Asked, "What is necessary for your happiness?" or "What is it that makes your life meaningful?" most people mention—before anything else—close, satisfying relationships with family, friends, or romantic partners (Berscheid, 1985). Happiness hits close to home.

Consider: What was your most satisfying moment this past week? Researchers asked that question of U.S. and South Korean university students, then asked them to rate how much that moment had satisfied various needs (Sheldon et al., 2001). In both countries, the peak moment had satisfied self-esteem, relatedness, and belonging needs. Our drive to connect with others runs deep.

Keith Birmingham/MediaNews Group/Pasadena Star-News/Getty Images

Creative graduation "ceremonies" As social animals with a need to belong, we thrive on our connections with others. During the Covid pandemic, social distancing slowed the spread of the virus, but it disrupted our everyday relationships and challenged us to come up with new ways to celebrate important events together.

According to **self-determination theory**, we strive to satisfy three needs: *competence*, *autonomy* (a sense of personal control), and *relatedness* (Deci & Ryan, 2012; Ryan & Deci, 2000). Fulfilling these motives reduces stress and boosts health and self-esteem (Guertin et al., 2017; Uysal et al., 2020). One analysis of 200,000 people from nearly 500 studies concluded that "self-determination is key to explaining human motivation" (Howard et al., 2017, p. 1346).

Self-determination theory can help leaders motivate people. Employees who feel empowered perform better. They also feel more autonomous, competent, and socially included (Slemp et al., 2018; Van den Broeck et al., 2016). This also holds true for teachers motivating their students and military leaders motivating their soldiers (Bakadorova & Raufelder, 2018; Chambel et al., 2015; Hagger & Chatzisarantis, 2016). An empowered mindset fuels motivation by giving people the perception that they have unlimited energy (Sieber et al., 2019).

Small wonder, then, that our social behavior often aims to increase our feelings of belonging, and spending more time with friends and family increases happiness (Li & Kanazawa, 2016; Rohrer et al., 2018). To gain acceptance, we generally conform to group standards. We wait in lines and obey laws. We monitor our behavior, hoping to make a good impression. We spend billions on clothes, cosmetics, and diet and fitness aids—all motivated, in part, by our search for love and acceptance.

Thrown together in groups at school or at work, we form bonds. Parting, we feel distressed. We promise to stay in touch and return for reunions. By drawing a sharp circle around "us," the need to belong feeds both deep attachments to those inside the circle (loving families, faithful friendships, team loyalty) and hostilities toward those outside (as happens with rival gangs, ethnic conflicts, and fanatic nationalism; see the Social Psychology modules). Feeling close with our relationship partner, we expand our self-concept to overlap with theirs (Aron et al., 1991; [**FIGURE 35.1**]). Feelings of love activate brain reward and safety systems. In one experiment, deeply in love university students exposed to heat felt less pain when looking at their beloved's picture (Younger et al.,

"When my brothers try to draw a circle to exclude me, I shall draw a larger circle to include them." —Lawyer and civil rights activist Pauli Murray, "An American Credo," 1945

Self Other

Self Other

Self Other

Self Other

Self Other

Self Other

FIGURE 35.1
Inclusion of Other in Self (IOS) Scale Psychologist Arthur Aron developed the IOS scale to measure people's feelings of closeness with others. The more a person's self-concept overlaps with a romantic partner, friend, or acquaintance, the closer they feel and the more they like that other person. Think of a relationship partner and choose the pair of overlapping circles that best describes your relationship. (Information from Aron et al., 1992 and Gächter et al., 2015.)

2010). Pictures of our loved ones activate a brain region—the prefrontal cortex—that dampens feelings of physical pain (Eisenberger et al., 2011). Love is a natural painkiller.

When relationships end, people may suffer. In one 16-nation survey, and in repeated U.S. surveys, separated and divorced people have been half as likely as married people to say they are "very happy" (Inglehart, 1990; NORC, 2022). Is that simply because happy people more often marry and stay married? A national study following British lives through time revealed that, even after controlling for premarital life satisfaction, "the married are still more satisfied, suggesting a causal effect" of marriage (Grover & Helliwell, 2014). Divorce also predicts earlier mortality. Data from more than 600 million(!) people in 24 countries reveal that, compared with married people, separated and divorced people are at greater risk for early death (Shor et al., 2012). This massive study's finding was no fluke: An independent study of 7.8 million people replicated the association between being separated or divorced and the risk of early death (Wang et al., 2020). A happy marriage is, as one data scientist noted, "perhaps as important as not smoking, which is to say: huge" (Ungar, 2014).

Children who endure a series of foster homes or repeated family relocations experience frequent disruptions of budding relationships. They may then have difficulty forming deep connections with others (Oishi & Schimmack, 2010). The evidence is clearest at the extremes. Children who grow up in institutions without a sense of belonging to anyone, or who are locked away at home and severely neglected tend to become withdrawn, frightened, even speechless.

No matter how secure our early years were, we all—when something threatens or dissolves our social ties—experience anxiety, loneliness, jealousy, or guilt. Much as life's best moments occur when close relationships begin—making a new friend, falling in love, having a baby—life's worst moments happen when close relationships end (Beam et al., 2016). Bereaved, we may feel life is empty or pointless, and we may overeat to fill that emptiness (Yang et al., 2016). Even the first months of living on campus can be distressing, when new social ties have not yet formed (English et al., 2017).

Gregory Walton and Timothy Wilson (2018) note that a lonely new college student may wonder, "Can people like me belong here?" Entering Black American students who experienced a 1-hour session explaining the commonness of that worry, with reassuring stories from older peers, achieved higher grades over the next 3 years—and greater life and career satisfaction after college. Boosting a sense of belonging had big benefits.

Social isolation can put our mental and physical health at risk (Cacioppo et al., 2015; Cheek et al., 2019). Lonely older adults, for example, make more doctor visits and are at greater risk for dementia (Gerst-Emerson & Jayawardhana, 2015; Holwerda et al., 2014). In separate U.S. surveys during the early months of the Covid pandemic,

- 48 percent of 18- to 29-year-olds reported repeatedly feeling lonely or isolated (Cox & Bowman, 2020);
- 70 percent of all adults reported experiencing "moderate or severe distress"—triple the 22 percent in a prior survey (Twenge & Joiner, 2020); and
- 36 percent of all adults showed signs of clinical depression or anxiety—again, triple the level of a year earlier (NCHS, 2020).

UK, Asian, European, and New Zealand researchers also reported that mental distress surged during the Covid pandemic restrictions (Prati & Mancini, 2021). The benefits of belonging make it worth the effort to nurture our relationships with family and friends.

The Pleasure of Micro-Friendships

We are made for relationships—not just with our nearest and dearest, but also in our fleeting connections. That's the consistent lesson of experiments on *micro-friendships*.

Connecting while commuting Nicholas Epley and Juliana Schroeder (2014) offered Chicago commuters a $5 gift card to complete a randomly assigned task: to (a) do as they would usually do on their train or bus, (b) sit in solitude, or (c) strike up a conversation with a stranger. Although most expected the attempted conversation would be awkward, it typically was not. Moreover, upon finishing the ride, the talkers were in a happier mood.

Bantering with a barista Gillian Sandstrom and Elizabeth Dunn (2014) similarly offered Starbucks patrons a $5 gift card to participate in an experiment. They asked half of the patrons, when interacting with the barista, to act respectful but *efficient* ("have your money ready, and avoid unnecessary conversation"). They assigned the others to act *social* ("smile, make eye contact to establish a connection, and have a brief conversation"). When later exiting the store, those tasked with being social reported feeling happier and more satisfied.

Complimenting a stranger In five experiments, Erica Boothby and Vanessa Bohns (2021) observed the unexpected power of compliments. For example, they instructed compliment-givers to approach strangers, observe "something about them that you like" (often their hair or clothing), and compliment them. Inevitably, the little act of kindness was warmly received, leaving the compliment-giver feeling better afterward.

The bottom line: Micro-friendships can brighten others' days, and our own.

Easy enough for extraverts, you say? Perhaps, but intentional micro-friendly acts have been found to create an equally happy experience for both extraverts and introverts.

A suggestion: *Try it.* Greet a service worker with a smile. Chat up the ride-share driver. Ask the checkout clerk how their day is going. Can you replicate the happy science of micro-friendships in your daily encounters?

CBS/Photofest

Social acceptance and rejection Successful participants on the reality TV show *Survivor* form alliances and gain acceptance among their peers. The rest receive the ultimate social punishment by being "voted off the island."

The Pain of Being Shut Out

Recall a time when you felt excluded, ignored, or shunned. Perhaps your texts went unanswered, or you were unfriended or ghosted online. Perhaps others gave you the silent treatment, avoided you, looked away, mocked you, or excluded you in some other way. Or perhaps you have felt excluded among people speaking an unfamiliar language (Dotan-Eliaz et al., 2009). We feel the sting even from small-scale exclusions like being *phubbed*—an Australian-coined term meaning *phone-snubbed*—when our conversation partner seems more interested in gazing at their phone than interacting with us (Roberts & David, 2016). Frequent phubbing distracts attention and predicts a less satisfying relationship, as well as lower self-esteem and greater suicidal thinking among those feeling ignored (Sbarra et al., 2019; Wang & Qiao, 2022).

"If we truly want to be healthy, happy and fulfilled as a society, we have to restructure our lives around people . . . . We have this powerful force for enhancing health and well-being, in their relationships." —U.S. Surgeon General Vivek Murthy (Leland, 2022).

These situations are forms of **ostracism**, or social exclusion (Williams, 2007, 2009). Worldwide, humans use many forms of ostracism—shunning, exile, imprisonment, solitary confinement—to punish, and therefore control, social behavior. For children, even a brief time-out in isolation can be punishing. In experiments with adults, simply being excluded from ball tosses during a video game increased suicidal thinking (Chen et al., 2021). Loneliness is less a matter of being alone than of feeling ignored, dismissed, or not cared about.

Being ostracized threatens one's basic need to belong (Vanhalst et al., 2015). "It's the meanest thing you can do to someone, especially if you know they can't fight back. I never should have been born," said Lea, a lifelong victim of the silent treatment by her mother and grandmother (Wirth et al., 2010). Like Lea, people often respond to ostracism with initial efforts to restore social acceptance, followed by depressed mood and, finally, withdrawal into solitude (Ren et al., 2021). To many, social exclusion is an inhumane sentence. After more than a quarter century in solitary confinement, Dennis Hope petitioned the U.S. Supreme Court to consider whether such isolation is cruel and unusual punishment. Having "watched men commit suicide, mutilate themselves, try to overdose on pills and slowly lose their minds," he stated, "I said to myself that I was going to try to make a positive change in the way we are housed and treated if it was the last thing I did" (Liptak, 2022).

The Granger Collection

Enduring the pain of ostracism White cadets at the U.S. Military Academy at West Point ostracized Henry Flipper for years, hoping he would drop out. Somehow, he withstood their cruelty, and in 1877, he became the first African American West Point graduate.

To experience ostracism is to experience real pain, as social psychologist Kipling Williams and his colleagues were surprised to discover in their studies of exclusion on social media (Gonsalkorale & Williams, 2006). Such ostracism elicits increased activity in brain areas, such as the *anterior cingulate cortex*, that also respond to physical pain (Lieberman & Eisenberger, 2015; Rotge et al., 2015).

When people view pictures of romantic partners who broke their heart, their brain and body begin to ache (Kross et al., 2011). This result helps explain some other surprising findings: The pain reliever acetaminophen (as in Tylenol) lessens *social* and physical pain (DeWall et al., 2010). Ditto for marijuana (Deckman et al., 2014). Across cultures,

ostracism deliberate social exclusion of individuals or groups.

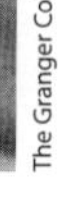

people use the same words (for example, *hurt* or *crushed*) for social pain and physical pain (MacDonald & Leary, 2005). Psychologically, we seem to experience social pain with the same unpleasantness that marks physical pain. Compared with collectivist cultures, rejection tends to hurt more in individualist cultures—where people have weaker social support networks (Heu et al., 2019; Uskul & Over, 2017).

Ostracism can make people disagreeable, uncooperative, and hostile, leading to further ostracism (Rudert et al., 2019; Walasek et al., 2019). In one series of experiments, researchers told some students that people they had met earlier didn't want them in a group that was forming (Gaertner et al., 2008; Twenge et al., 2001).[1] Others heard good news: "Everyone chose you as someone they'd like to work with." Those who were excluded became much more likely to engage in self-defeating behaviors, and to disparage or act aggressively toward those who had excluded them (blasting them with noise, for example).

"If no one turned around when we entered, answered when we spoke, or minded what we did, but if every person we met 'cut us dead,' and acted as if we were non-existing things, a kind of rage and impotent despair would ere long well up in us." —William James, *Principles of Psychology*, 1890/1950, pp. 293–294

ASK YOURSELF

Have there been times when you felt lonely or ostracized? What are some strategies that might help you to cope the next time you feel this way? On the other hand, can you think of a time when you ostracized or ignored someone? How do you think this made them feel?

RETRIEVAL PRACTICE

RP-1 How have students reacted in studies when they were made to feel rejected and unwanted? What helps explain these results?

ANSWERS IN APPENDIX E

Connecting and Social Networking

LOQ 35-2 How does social networking influence us?

As social creatures, we live for connection. Researcher George Vaillant (2013) was asked what he had learned from studying 238 Harvard University men from the 1930s to the end of their lives. His reply: "Happiness is love." A South African Zulu saying captures the idea: *Umuntu ngumuntu ngabantu*—"a person is a person through other persons."

MOBILE NETWORKS AND SOCIAL MEDIA Look around and see humans connecting: talking, tweeting, texting, posting, gaming, emailing. Today, have you observed more students engaging with each other face-to-face or silently checking their phones—as one research team's phone app counted students doing 56 times per day (Elias et al., 2016)? The changes in how we connect have been fast and vast:

- ***Mobile phones*** By 2021's end, 95 percent of the world's 7.96 billion people lived in an area covered by a mobile-cellular network, and most humans—6.61 billion—had broadband mobile subscriptions (ITU, 2021).
- ***Texting and instant messaging*** In 2020, people in the United States alone sent 2.2 trillion texts and instant messages, up from 1.5 trillion in 2017 (Statista, 2022).
- ***Social networking*** More than half of entering U.S. college students report using social media at least 6 hours per week (Stolzenberg et al., 2020). With our friends online, it's hard to avoid social networks: Check in or miss out.

Increased online time displaces other activities. Compared to teens before 2010, today's teens spend fewer hours dating, driving, talking face-to-face, reading books, and working (Livingston et al., 2019; Twenge, 2019). Technology has radically changed the teen experience.

MUELLER
P.S. Mueller/Cartoon Stock

"A bunch of friends are coming over to stare at their phones."

THE NET RESULT: SOCIAL EFFECTS OF SOCIAL NETWORKING By connecting like-minded people, the internet serves as a social amplifier. In times of social crisis or personal stress, it provides information and supportive connections. The internet can also help you find a romantic partner (as I [ND] can attest: I met my wife online). Keep in

[1] The researchers later *debriefed* and reassured the participants.

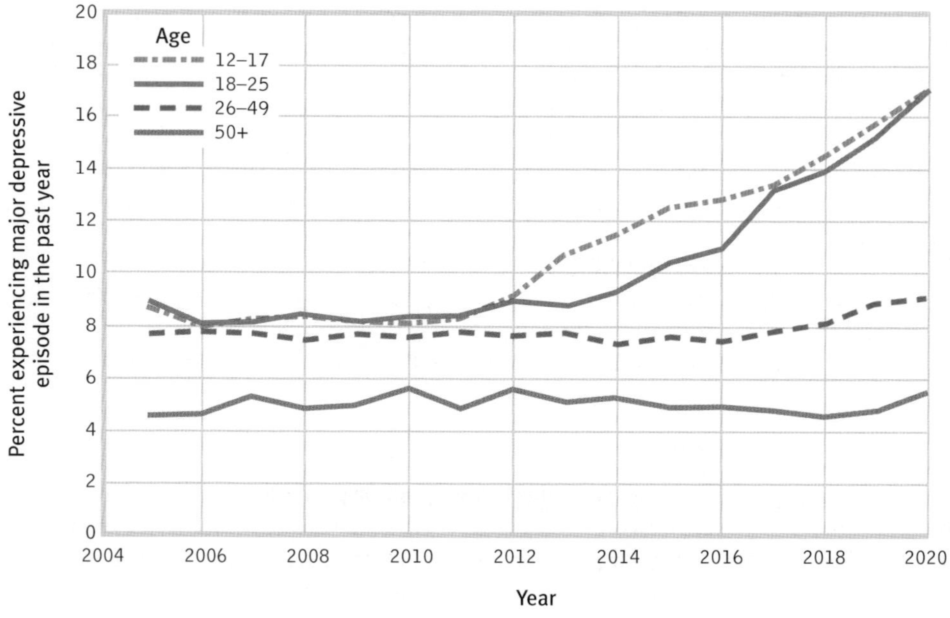
Age
12–17
18–25
26–49
50+
Percent experiencing major depressive episode in the past year
Year

FIGURE 35.2
Depression has risen sharply among teens and young adults, coinciding with the rise of smartphones (SAMHSA, 2021)

mind: Although dating websites aren't adept at matchmaking, they do expand the pool of potential romantic matches (Joel et al., 2017).

But social media also leads people to compare their lives with others. When others—sharing their best and most perfect-looking moments—seem happier, more popular, or more successful, this can trigger envy and depressed feelings (Verduyn et al., 2022; Whillans et al., 2017). In study after study, most people perceive that others' social lives are more active than their own (Deri et al., 2017). Perhaps you have noticed? Do others seem to party more, dine out more, and have more friends and fun? Take comfort: Most of your friends are thinking the same.

Maddie Dai/Cartoon Stock

"Well, if it's any consolation, your social media makes it look like you're absolutely thriving."

Smartphones have become pervasive—their number tripled between 2011 and 2018 in the United States and rose similarly elsewhere. Worldwide, one meta-analysis suggested that 1 in 4 people now have "smartphone addiction" (Meng et al., 2022). Simultaneously—and merely coincidentally?—teen depression, anxiety, self-harm, and suicide rates have mushroomed (**FIGURE 35.2**). From the first decade of the twenty-first century to the second, the number of adolescents worldwide with depression symptoms increased from 24 percent to 37 percent (Shorey et al., 2022). From 2012 to 2018, loneliness at school also increased globally among 15- and 16-year-old students (Twenge et al., 2022). Rates of depression, anxiety, self-injury, and suicidal thinking have similarly increased for college students (Duffy et al., 2019).

So, is there a causal connection between these concurrent increases in screen time and mental health problems? Under the leadership of Jonathan Haidt and Jean Twenge (2021), researchers are accumulating and debating findings. They have tentative conclusions from three types of explorations:

- **Correlational studies ask:** *Is social media use associated with teen mental health problems?* To an extent, *Yes*. Studies vary, but overall, a small positive correlation exists between adolescents' social media time and their risk of depression, anxiety, and self-harm. The screen time–disorder association is stronger for social media use than for other kinds of screen time, including TV and gaming time (Twenge et al., 2022). The link is greater for teen girls, especially during early puberty (Orben et al., 2022). And it increases only with daily screen time of 3 hours or more—leading some mental health experts to ask social media companies to enforce time limits for teen use (Twenge, 2021). "Any platform that encourages children to upload photos of themselves, to be rated and commented on by strangers, is likely to harm many kids," surmises Haidt (2021a). (See **FIGURE 35.3**.)
- **Longitudinal studies ask:** *Does teen social media use predict teens' future mental health?* The answer is *Maybe*. Of 34 studies, 20 confirmed that excessive teen social media use (defined as more than 3 hours per day) predicted worse future mental health.

MODERN GIRL
Erika Sjule/Cartoon Stock

"... and, what felt for the millionth time, she opened her phone for the diminishing dopamine hit that never satisfied."

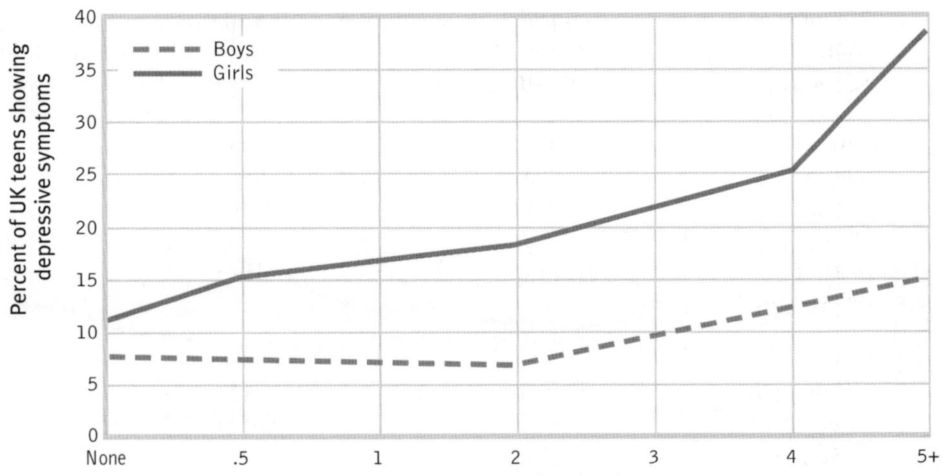
Boys
Girls
Percent of UK teens showing depressive symptoms
40
35
30
25
20
15
10
5
0
None
.5
1
2
3
4
5+
Hours spent on social media per weekday

FIGURE 35.3
Depression and teen screens In 2022, psychologist Jonathan Haidt testified before the U.S. Congress: "The United States is experiencing a catastrophic wave of mood disorders (anxiety and depression) and related behaviors (self-harm and suicide).... The crisis emerged in the exact years when American teens were getting smartphones and becoming daily users of social media platforms such as Instagram. Correlational, experimental, and eye-witness testimony points to social media as a major cause of the crisis. I do not believe that social media is the only cause of the crisis, but there is no alternative hypothesis that can explain the suddenness, enormity, and international similarity" (Haidt, 2022).

Leigh Vogel/WireImage/Getty Images

- **Experiments ask:** *Do volunteers randomly assigned to restricted social media use fare better than those not assigned on outcomes such as loneliness and depression?* On balance, *Probably*. Of 15 experiments, 11 have indicated a causal effect of social media use on diminished mental health. One experiment, which randomly assigned nearly 3000 paid volunteers to either deactivate their Facebook account or not, found that "four weeks without Facebook improves subjective well-being" (Allcott et al., 2020).

Is solitary screen time the primary culprit because of its "opportunity cost"—the other healthy activities it displaces, including face-to-face connection, sleep, exercise, reading, and spending time outdoors? Or is social media emotionally toxic, triggering envy when comparing one's own humdrum life with the lives of cooler-seeming others? If increased screen time—especially social media time—isn't responsible for the surging teen mental health crisis, what is? What other social forces—common to Canada, the UK, Australia, New Zealand, and the United States—would you suppose might be at work (Haidt, 2021b)? And what can be done to protect and improve youth and young adult well-being? Stay tuned: This important story is still being written.

Online networking is double-edged. Nature has designed us for face-to-face relationships, and people who spend hours online and texting daily are *less* likely to know and draw help from their real-world neighbors. They are also more likely to experience online bullying, which can increase anxiety, depression, and suicidal thinking (Giumetti et al., 2022; Nesi et al., 2021). But social media and mobile phones do help us connect with friends, stay in touch with family, and find support when facing challenges (Clark et al., 2018; Jensen et al., 2021). *When used in moderation*, social networking supports our face-to-face relationships and therefore predicts longer life—especially among middle-aged and older adults (Hobbs et al., 2016; Waytz & Gray, 2018; Wang et al., 2022).

Walsh

Liam Francis Walsh/Cartoon Stock

"The women on these dating sites don't seem to believe I'm a prince."

Does Electronic Communication Stimulate Healthy Self-Disclosure? *Self-disclosure* is sharing ourselves—our joys, worries, and weaknesses—with others. Confiding can be a healthy way of coping with day-to-day challenges. When communicating electronically rather than face-to-face, we often focus less on others' reactions. We are less self-conscious, and thus less inhibited. Sometimes, disinhibitions become toxic: Political extremists post inflammatory messages, online bullies hound their targets, hate groups promote bigotry, and people send selfies they later regret (Frimer et al., 2019). But more often, the increased self-disclosure strengthens friendships (Valkenburg & Peter, 2009).

Does Social Networking Promote Narcissism? **Narcissism** is self-esteem gone wild. Narcissistic people are self-important, self-focused, and self-promoting. To measure your narcissistic tendencies, you might rate your agreement with personality test items such as "I like to be the center of attention." People who agree with such statements tend to have high narcissism scores—and they are especially active on social

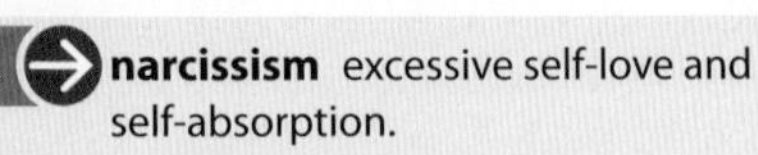
narcissism excessive self-love and self-absorption.

networking sites (Casale & Banchi, 2020). They collect more superficial "friends." They offer more staged, glamorous photos. They retaliate more against negative comments. And, not surprisingly, they *seem* more narcissistic to strangers (Buffardi & Campbell, 2008; Weiser, 2015).

For narcissists, social networking sites are more than a gathering place; they are a feeding trough. In one study, college students were randomly assigned either to edit and explain their online profiles for 15 minutes, or to use that time to study and explain a Google Maps routing (Freeman & Twenge, 2010). After completing their tasks, all were tested. Who then scored higher on a narcissism measure? Those who had spent the time focused on themselves.

BROOK PIFER/Getty Images

Self-esteem or narcissism? Social networking can help people share self-relevant information and stay connected with family and friends. But it can also feed narcissistic tendencies and enable self-glamorization.

MAINTAINING BALANCE AND FOCUS It will come as no surprise that excessive online socializing and gaming have correlated with lower grades and with increased anxiety and depression (Brooks, 2015; Lepp et al., 2014; Walsh et al., 2013). In one U.S. survey, 47 percent of the heaviest internet and other media users received mostly C grades or lower, as did just 23 percent of the lightest users (Kaiser Family Foundation, 2010). In another national survey, young adults who used seven or more social media platforms were three times more likely to be depressed or anxious than those who used two or fewer (Primack et al., 2016).

In today's world, it can be challenging to maintain a healthy balance between our real-world and online time. Experts offer some practical suggestions:

- ***Monitor your time.*** Use a time-tracking app to measure your time online. Then ask yourself, "Does my time use reflect my priorities? Am I spending more time online than I intended? Does it interfere with my school or work performance or my relationships?"
- ***Monitor your feelings.*** Ask yourself, "Am I emotionally distracted by my online interests? Do my online activities cause negative emotions (jealousy or loneliness when comparing myself to others; anger when engaging with combative people)? When I disconnect and move to another activity, how do I feel?"
- ***Break the phone-checking habit.*** Selective attention—the flashlight of your mind—can be in only one place at a time. When we try to do two things at once, we don't do either very well (Willingham, 2010). If you want to study or work productively—or just give a friend your full attention—resist the temptation always to be available. Disable sound alerts, vibrations, and pop-ups. Change your online status to unavailable when you don't want to be contacted. (To reduce distraction, I [ND] am working on this module while using an app that blocks distracting websites.)
- ***Refocus by taking a nature walk.*** People learn better after connecting with nature, which—unlike a walk on a busy street—refreshes our capacity for focused attention (Berman et al., 2008). Connecting with nature boosts our spirits and sharpens our mind (Pritchard et al., 2019; Zelenski & Nisbet, 2014).

As psychologist Steven Pinker (2010) said, "The solution is not to bemoan technology but to develop strategies of self-control, as we do with every other temptation in life."

ASK YOURSELF

Do your connections on social media increase your sense of belonging? Sometimes, do they make you feel lonely? Which of the strategies discussed will you find most useful to maintain balance and focus?

RETRIEVAL PRACTICE

RP-2 Social networking tends to ____________ (strengthen/weaken) your relationships with people you already know, and ____________ (increase/decrease) your self-disclosure.

ANSWERS IN APPENDIX E

Achievement Motivation

LOQ 35-3 What is *achievement motivation,* and what are some ways to encourage achievement?

Some motives seem to have little obvious survival value. Billionaires may be motivated to make more money, internet celebrities to attract more social media followers, politicians to achieve more power. And motives vary across cultures. In individualist cultures, employees may work to receive an "employee of the month" award; in collectivist cultures, they may strive to join a company's hardest-working team. The more we achieve, the more we may need to achieve. Psychologist Henry Murray (1938) called this **achievement motivation**.

Achievement motivation matters. One famous study followed the lives of 1528 California children whose intelligence test scores were in the top 1 percent. Forty years later, researchers compared those who were most and least successful professionally. What did the researchers discover? A motivational difference. The most successful were more ambitious, energetic, and persistent. As children, they had more active hobbies. As adults, they participated in more groups and sports (Goleman, 1980). Gifted children are able learners. Accomplished adults are tenacious doers. Most of us are energetic doers when starting and when finishing a project. It's easiest—have you noticed?—to get stuck in the middle. That's when high achievers keep going (Bonezzi et al., 2011). Once they get in a groove, their motivation keeps them engaged in goal striving (Foulk et al., 2019; Miller et al., 2021). No wonder people with high achievement motivation tend to have greater financial success, healthy social relationships, and good physical and mental health (Steptoe & Wardle, 2017).

In studies of both secondary school and university students, self-discipline has surpassed intelligence test scores in predicting school performance, attendance, and graduation honors. For school performance, "discipline outdoes talent," concluded researchers Angela Duckworth and Martin Seligman (2005, 2017).

"Genius is 1% inspiration and 99% perspiration." —Thomas Edison (1847–1931)

Discipline focuses and refines talent. By their early twenties, top violinists have fiddled away thousands of lifetime practice hours—in fact, double the practice time of other violin students aiming to be teachers (Ericsson, 2001, 2006, 2007). A study of outstanding scholars, athletes, and artists found that all were highly motivated and self-disciplined, willing to dedicate hours every day to the pursuit of their goals (Bloom, 1985). But as young Mozart composing at age 8 illustrates, native talent matters, too (Hambrick & Meinz, 2011; Ruthsatz & Urbach, 2012). In sports, music, and chess, people's practice-time differences, while significant, account for a third or less of their performance differences (Hambrick et al., 2014a,b; Macnamara et al., 2014, 2016; Ullén et al., 2016). High achievers benefit from their passion and perseverance, but the superstars among them are also distinguished by their extraordinary natural talent.

Cultures differ in their achievement motivation. Western, individualist cultures emphasize the need for people to "follow their passion." To achieve success, individualists believe they need to experience enjoyment, interest, and confidence. Eastern, collectivist cultures focus less on personal passion and more on fulfilling one's duty and obligations to family and friends. Analyzing 1.2 million students' responses from 59 societies, passion was a greater predictor of high achievement scores in individualist cultures than in collectivist cultures (Li et al., 2021). In collectivist cultures, parental emotional support was more important than passion in predicting students' success.

"It's just perseverance, isn't it, that leads to things." —Agatha Christie's Miss Marple, in *Nemesis*

Duckworth (2016) has a name for dedication to an ambitious, long-term goal: **grit**. Other researchers see grit as similar to conscientiousness and less important than intelligence (Ponnock et al., 2021; Zisman & Ganzach, 2021). Researchers have begun to sleuth the neural and genetic markers of grit (Takahashi et al., 2021; Wang et al., 2018). Passion and perseverance fuel gritty goal-striving, which can produce great achievements (Jachimowicz et al., 2018; Muenks et al., 2018). Consider Elinor Ostrom: After working her way through college, she was rejected from an economics Ph.D. program. She obtained a Ph.D. in political science instead, and in 2009—four decades later—became the first woman to receive the Nobel Prize in economics.

achievement motivation the desire for significant accomplishment, for mastery of skills or ideas, for control, and for attaining a high standard.

grit in psychology, passion and perseverance in the pursuit of long-term goals.

Calum's Road: What grit can accomplish Having spent his life on the Scottish island of Raasay, farming a small patch of land, tending its lighthouse, and fishing, Malcolm ("Calum") MacLeod (1911–1988) felt anguished. His local government repeatedly refused to build a road enabling vehicles to reach his island's north end. With the once-flourishing population there having dwindled to two — MacLeod and his wife — he responded with heroic determination. One spring morning in 1964, MacLeod, then in his fifties, gathered a pick-axe, a shovel, and a wheelbarrow. By hand, he began to transform the existing footpath into a 1.75-mile road (Miers, 2009).

"With a road," a former neighbor explained, "he hoped new generations of people would return to the north end of Raasay," restoring its culture (Hutchinson, 2006). Day after day he worked through rough hillsides, along hazardous cliff faces, and over peat bogs. Finally, 10 years later, he completed his supreme achievement. The road, which the government has since surfaced, remains a visible example of what vision plus determined grit can accomplish. It bids us each to ponder: What "roads" — what achievements — might we, with sustained effort, build in the years to come?

Gritty students are most likely to avoid burnout and persist in school (Saunders-Scott et al., 2018; Tang et al., 2021). As basketball star Damian Lillard (2015) said, "If you want to look good in front of thousands, you have to outwork thousands in front of nobody."

"You may have to fight a battle more than once to win it." — Former British Prime Minister Margaret Thatcher

Although intelligence is distributed like a bell curve (see the Intelligence modules), achievements are not. This tells us that achievement involves much more than raw ability. Sometimes, our motivation stems from a natural curiosity and drive to accomplish a goal. At other times, we're driven to please others, receive awards, or make money.

Promising people a reward for an enjoyable task can backfire. Excessive rewards can destroy **intrinsic motivation**. In experiments, children have been promised a payoff for playing with an interesting puzzle or toy. Later, they played with the toy *less* than did unpaid children (Deci et al., 1999; Tang & Hall, 1995). Likewise, rewarding children with toys or candy (or money or screen time) for reading diminishes the time they spend reading (Marinak & Gambrell, 2008). It is as if they think, "If I have to be bribed into doing this, it must not be worth doing!"

To sense the difference between intrinsic motivation and **extrinsic motivation**, think about your experience in this course. Like most students, you probably want to earn a high grade. But what motivates your actions to achieve your goal? Do you feel pressured to finish this reading before a deadline? Are you worried about your grade? Eager for the credits that will count toward graduation? Hoping to do well to please your family? If *Yes*, then you are extrinsically motivated (as, to some extent, all students must be). Do you also find the material interesting? Does learning it make you feel more competent? If there were no grade at stake, might you be curious enough to want to learn the material for its own sake? If *Yes*, intrinsic motivation also fuels your efforts.

People who focus on their work's meaning and significance do better work *and* ultimately earn more extrinsic rewards (Wrzesniewski et al., 2014). Elementary school students with greater-than-average academic intrinsic motivation — who love learning for its own sake — go on to perform better in school, take more challenging classes, and earn more advanced degrees (Fan & Williams, 2018; Gottfried et al., 2006). *Wanting* to do something, rather than having to do something, seems to pay off (Converse et al., 2019).

Extrinsic rewards work well when people perform tasks that don't naturally inspire complex, creative thinking (Hewett & Conway, 2015). They're also effective when used to signal a job well done (rather than to bribe or control someone) (Boggiano et al., 1985). When administered wisely, rewards can improve performance and spark creativity (Eisenberger & Aselage, 2009; Henderlong & Lepper, 2002). "Most improved player" awards, for example, can boost feelings of competence and increase enjoyment of

intrinsic motivation the desire to perform a behavior effectively for its own sake. 

extrinsic motivation the desire to perform a behavior to receive promised rewards or avoid threatened punishment.

a sport. And the rewards that often follow academic achievement, such as scholarships and job opportunities, can have long-lasting benefits.

Organizational psychologists seek ways to engage and motivate ordinary people doing ordinary jobs (see Appendix C: Psychology at Work).

Goal Setting

Do you have a specific goal you'd like to achieve? Each of us can adopt some research-based strategies for achieving our goals:

1. ***Make that resolution.*** Challenging goals motivate achievement (Harkin et al., 2016). SMART goals are specific, measurable, achievable, realistic, and timely. Such goals—"finish my psychology assignment by Tuesday"—direct attention and motivate persistence.
2. ***Announce the goal to friends or family.*** We're more likely to follow through after making a public commitment.
3. ***Develop an implementation plan.*** Be specific about when, where, and how you'll progress toward your goal. Identify potential challenges and how you'll revisit and adjust your plan. People who flesh out goals with detailed plans become more focused and more likely to succeed (Duckworth et al., 2018; Gollwitzer & Oettingen, 2012). Better to concentrate on small steps—spending 5 to 10 minutes learning words from a foreign language each week—than to fantasize about speaking that language fluently.
4. ***Create short-term rewards that support long-term goals.*** Although delayed rewards motivate us to set goals, immediate rewards best predict our persistence toward those goals (Woolley & Fishbach, 2018).
5. ***Monitor and record progress.*** For example, if you are striving for more exercise, use a fitness tracker or enter your activity in a free fitness app. It's even more motivating when progress is shared rather than hidden (Harkin et al., 2016).
6. ***Create a supportive environment.*** When trying to eat healthily, keep junk food out of the cupboards. When focusing on a project, hole up in the library. When sleeping, shut off your phone. Have your gym bag ready the night before. Such "situational self-control strategies" prevent tempting impulses (Duckworth et al., 2016; Schiffer & Roberts, 2018).
7. ***Transform the hard-to-do behavior into a must-do habit.*** Habits form when we repeat behaviors in a given context. Do something every day for about two months and see it become an ingrained habit.

To achieve important life goals, we often know what to do. We *know* that a full night's sleep boosts our alertness, energy, and mood. We *know* that exercise lessens depression and anxiety, builds muscle, and strengthens our heart and mind. We *know* that what we put into our body—junk food or balanced nutrition, addictive substances or clean air—affects our health and longevity. Alas, as T. S. Eliot foresaw, "Between the idea/And the reality . . . / Falls the Shadow." Nevertheless, we can create a bridge between the idea and reality by taking these seven steps: resolving, announcing, planning, rewarding, monitoring, controlling, and persistently acting.

ASK YOURSELF

What goal would you like to achieve? How might you use the seven strategies offered in this section to meet that goal?

RETRIEVAL PRACTICE

RP-3 What have researchers found to be an even better predictor of school performance than intelligence test scores?

ANSWERS IN APPENDIX E

35 REVIEW Affiliation and Achievement

LEARNING OBJECTIVES

Test Yourself Answer these repeated Learning Objective Questions on your own (before "showing" the answers here, or checking the answers in Appendix D) to improve your retention of the concepts (McDaniel et al., 2009, 2015).

LOQ **35-1** What evidence points to our human affiliation need—our need to belong?

LOQ **35-2** How does social networking influence us?

LOQ **35-3** What is *achievement motivation*, and what are some ways to encourage achievement?

TERMS AND CONCEPTS TO REMEMBER

Test Yourself Write down the definition in your own words, then check your answer.

affiliation need, p. 404
self-determination theory, p. 404
ostracism, p. 407
narcissism, p. 410
achievement motivation, p. 412
grit, p. 412
intrinsic motivation, p. 413
extrinsic motivation, p. 413

MODULE TEST

Test Yourself Answer the following questions on your own first, then "show" the answers here, or check your answers in Appendix E.

1. Which of the following is NOT evidence supporting the view that humans are strongly motivated by a need to belong?
   a. Students who rated themselves as "very happy" also tended to have satisfying close relationships.
   b. Social exclusion—such as exile or solitary confinement—is considered a severe form of punishment.
   c. As adults, adopted children tend to resemble their biological parents.
   d. Children who are extremely neglected become withdrawn, frightened, and sometimes even speechless.

2. What are some ways to manage our social networking time successfully?

3. If we want to increase our chance of success in achieving a new goal, such as stopping smoking, we ____________ (should/should not) announce the goal publicly, and we ____________ (should/should not) share with others our progress toward achieving that goal.

CHAPTER 12

FG Trade/E+/Getty Images

Emotions, Stress, and Health (Modules 36–40)

No one needs to tell you that feelings add color to your life, or that in times of stress they can disrupt your life, or save it. Fear, anger, sadness, joy, and love are psychological states that also entail physical reactions. Nervous about an important encounter, we feel stomach butterflies. Anxious over public speaking, we frequent the bathroom. Smoldering over a family conflict, we get a splitting headache.

You can surely recall a time when emotion overwhelmed you. I [DM] retain a flashbulb memory of the day I went to a huge store and brought along Peter, my toddler first-born child. As I set Peter down on his feet for a moment to do some paperwork, a passerby warned, "You'd better be careful or you'll lose that boy!" Not more than a few breaths later, I turned and found no Peter beside me.

With mild anxiety, I looked around one end of the customer service counter. No Peter in sight. With slightly more anxiety, I peered around the other side. No Peter there, either. Now, with my heart accelerating, I circled the neighboring counters. Still no Peter anywhere. As anxiety turned to panic, I began racing up and down the store aisles. He was nowhere to be found. The alerted store manager used the intercom to ask customers to assist in looking for a missing child. Soon after, I passed the customer who had warned me. "I told you that you were going to lose him!" he now scolded. With visions of kidnapping (strangers routinely adored that beautiful child), I braced for the unthinkable possibility that my negligence had caused me to lose what I loved above all else, and that I might have to return home and face my wife without our only child.

But then, as I passed the customer service counter yet again, there he was, having been found and returned by some obliging customer. In an instant, the arousal of terror spilled into ecstasy. Clutching my son, with tears suddenly flowing, I found myself unable to speak my thanks and stumbled out of the store awash in grateful joy.

Emotions are subjective. But they are real. As researcher Lisa Feldman Barrett (2012, 2013) noted, "My experience of anger is not an illusion. When I'm angry, I feel angry. That's real." Where do our emotions come from? Why do we have them? What are they made of?

Emotions are an adaptive response—"our body's way of ensuring we do what is best for us," noted primate researcher Frans de Waal (2019). Anger can elicit a concession. Gratitude strengthens relationships. Pride motivates hard work (Weidman & Kross, 2021). When we face challenges, emotions focus our attention and energize our actions (Cyders & Smith, 2008). Our heart races. Our pace quickens. All our senses go on high alert. By integrating data from our environment, our body, and our experiences, we feel emotional stress (Francis, 2018).

Emotions can also be positive. Receiving unexpected good news, we may find our eyes tearing up. We raise our hands triumphantly. We feel exuberance and a newfound confidence. Yet negative and prolonged emotions can harm our health.

In Modules 36, 37, and 38, we explore how psychologists think about and study our emotional expression and experiences. In Modules 39 and 40, we take a close look at the challenges of stress and some ways of coping that help us meet those challenges.

Courtesy of David Myers

MODULE 36 Introduction to Emotion

Like most psychological phenomena—vision, sleep, memory, sex—emotion can be approached in three ways: physiologically, behaviorally, and cognitively. Researchers explore these manifestations of emotion and their interactions.

Emotion: Arousal, Behavior, and Cognition

LEARNING OBJECTIVE QUESTION LOQ 36-1 How do arousal, expressive behavior, and cognition interact in emotion?

As my [DM's] panicked search for Peter illustrates, **emotions** are a mix of

- *bodily arousal* (heart pounding),
- *expressive behaviors* (quickened pace), and
- *conscious experience* (Is this a kidnapping?) *and feelings* (panic, fear, joy).

The puzzle for psychologists is fitting these three pieces together. To do that, the first researchers of emotion considered two big questions:

1. A chicken-and-egg debate: Does your bodily arousal come *before* or *after* your emotional feelings? (Did I first notice my racing heart and faster step, and then feel terror about losing Peter? Or did my sense of fear come first, stirring my heart and legs to respond?)
2. How do *thinking* (cognition) and *feeling* interact? Does cognition always come before emotion? (Did I think about a kidnapping threat before I reacted emotionally?)

The psychological study of emotion began with the first question: How do bodily responses relate to emotions? Two of the earliest emotion theories offered different answers.

emotion a response of the whole organism, involving (1) physiological arousal, (2) expressive behaviors, and, most importantly, (3) conscious experience resulting from one's interpretations. 

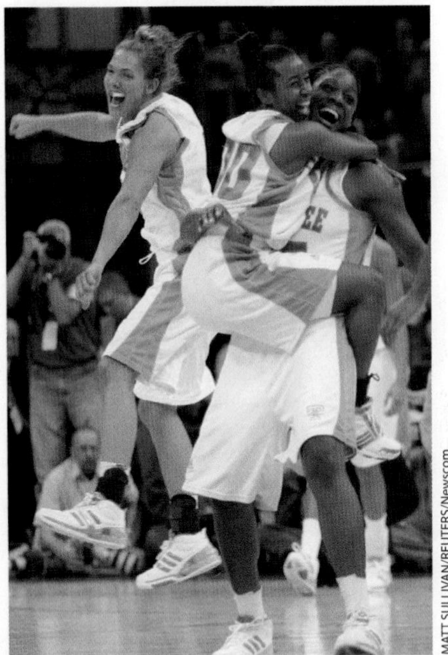
MATT SULLIVAN/REUTERS/Newscom

Joy expressed According to the James-Lange theory, we don't just smile because we share our teammates' joy. We also share the joy because we are smiling with them.

James-Lange Theory: Arousal Comes Before Emotion

Common sense tells most of us that we cry because we are sad, lash out because we are angry, tremble because we are afraid. But to pioneering psychologist William James, this commonsense view of emotion had things backward. Rather, "We feel sorry because we cry, angry because we strike, afraid because we tremble" (1890, p. 1066). To James, emotions result from attention to our bodily activity. James' idea was also proposed by Danish physiologist Carl Lange, and so is called the **James-Lange theory**. James and Lange would have guessed that I noticed my racing heart and then, shaking with fright, felt the whoosh of emotion—that my feeling of fear *followed* my body's response.

Cannon-Bard Theory: Arousal and Emotion Occur Simultaneously

Physiologist Walter Cannon (1871–1945) disagreed with the James-Lange theory. Does a racing heart signal fear or anger or love? The body's responses—heart rate, perspiration, and body temperature—are too similar, and they change too slowly, to *cause* the different emotions, said Cannon. He, and later another physiologist, Philip Bard, concluded that our bodily responses and experienced emotions occur separately but simultaneously. So, according to the **Cannon-Bard theory**, my heart began pounding *as* I experienced fear. The emotion-triggering stimulus traveled to my sympathetic nervous system, causing my body's arousal. *At the same time*, it traveled to my brain's cortex, causing my awareness of my emotion. My pounding heart did not cause my feeling of fear, nor did my feeling of fear cause my pounding heart.

But are they really independent of each other? Countering the Cannon-Bard theory are studies of people with severed spinal cords, including a survey of 25 World War II soldiers (Hohmann, 1966). Those with *lower-spine injuries*, who had lost sensation only in their legs, reported little change in their emotions' intensity. Those with *high spinal cord injury*, who could feel nothing below the neck, did report changes: Some of their reactions were much less intense than before the injuries. Anger, one man with this injury type revealed, "just doesn't have the heat to it that it used to. It's a mental kind of anger." Other emotions, those expressed mostly in body areas above the neck, were felt *more* intensely. These men reported increases in weeping, lumps in the throat, and getting choked up when saying good-bye, worshiping, or watching a touching movie. Such evidence has led some researchers to view feelings as "mostly shadows" of our bodily responses and behaviors (Damasio, 2003).

But our emotions also involve cognition (Averill, 1993; Feldman Barrett, 2006, 2017). Here we arrive at psychology's second big emotion question: How do thinking and feeling interact? Whether we fear the person behind us on a dark street depends entirely on whether or not we interpret them as threatening.

RETRIEVAL PRACTICE

RP-1 According to the Cannon-Bard theory, (a) our *physiological response* to a stimulus (for example, a pounding heart), and (b) the *emotion we experience* (for example, fear) occur ________________ (simultaneously/sequentially). According to the James-Lange theory, (a) and (b) occur ________________ (simultaneously/sequentially).

ANSWERS IN APPENDIX E

James-Lange theory the theory that our experience of emotion occurs when we become aware of our physiological responses to an emotion-arousing stimulus.

Cannon-Bard theory the theory that an emotion-arousing stimulus simultaneously triggers (1) physiological responses and (2) the subjective experience of emotion.

two-factor theory the Schachter-Singer theory that to experience emotion one must (1) be physically aroused and (2) cognitively label the arousal.

Schachter-Singer Two-Factor Theory: Arousal + Label = Emotion

LOQ 36-2 To experience emotions, must we consciously interpret and label them?

Stanley Schachter and Jerome Singer (1962) demonstrated that how we *appraise* (interpret) our experiences also matters. Our physical reactions *and our thoughts* (perceptions, memories, and interpretations) together create emotion. In their **two-factor theory**, emotions have two ingredients: physical arousal and cognitive appraisal. An emotional experience, they argued, requires a conscious interpretation of arousal.

Consider how arousal spills over from one event to the next. Imagine completing an intense session at the gym and then receiving a message that you got your dream job. With arousal lingering from the workout, would you feel more elated than if you heard this news after staying awake all night studying?

To explore this *spillover effect*, Schachter and Singer injected college men with the hormone epinephrine, which triggers feelings of arousal. One group of men was told to expect feelings of arousal from the injection. Others were told by the trickster researchers that it would help test their eyesight. Picture yourself as a participant: After receiving the injection, you go to a waiting room, where you find yourself with another person (actually an accomplice of the experimenters) who is acting either euphoric or irritated. As you observe this person, you begin to feel your heart race, your skin flush, and your breathing become more rapid. What would you feel if you had been in the group told to expect these effects from the injection?

In the experiment, these volunteers felt little emotion—because they correctly attributed their arousal to the drug. But if you had been told the injection would help assess your eyesight, what would you feel? Perhaps you would react as this group of participants did. They "caught" the apparent emotion of the other person in the waiting room. They became happy if the accomplice was acting euphoric, and testy if the accomplice was acting irritated.

This discovery—that a stirred-up state can be experienced as one emotion or another, depending on how we interpret and label it—has been replicated in dozens of experiments and continues to influence modern emotion research (MacCormack & Lindquist, 2016; Reisenzein, 1983; Sinclair et al., 1994). *The point to remember:* Arousal fuels emotion; cognition channels it.

The spillover effect Arousal from a soccer match can fuel anger, which can descend into rioting or other violent confrontations.

RETRIEVAL PRACTICE

RP-2 According to Schachter and Singer, two factors lead to our experience of an emotion: (a) physiological arousal and (b) ________________ appraisal.

ANSWERS IN APPENDIX E

Zajonc, LeDoux, and Lazarus: Does Cognition Always Precede Emotion?

But is the heart always subject to the mind? Must we *always* interpret our arousal before we can experience an emotion? Robert Zajonc [ZI-yence] (1923–2008) didn't think so. He contended that we actually have many emotional reactions apart from, or even before, our conscious interpretation of a situation (1980, 1984). Perhaps you can recall liking (or disliking) something or someone immediately, without knowing why.

Thanks to the *mere exposure effect* (see the Social Psychology modules), we come to like what is familiar. Even when people repeatedly view stimuli flashed too briefly for them to interpret, they come to prefer those stimuli (Kunst-Wilson & Zajonc, 1980). Unaware of having previously seen them, they nevertheless like them. We also have an acutely sensitive automatic radar for emotionally significant information; even a subliminally flashed stimulus can prime us to feel better or worse about a follow-up stimulus (Murphy et al., 1995; Zeelenberg et al., 2006).

Neuroscientists are charting the neural pathways of emotions (Ochsner et al., 2009). Our emotional responses can follow two different brain pathways. Some emotions (especially more complex feelings like hatred and love) travel a "high road." A stimulus following this path would travel (by way of the thalamus) to the brain's cortex (**FIGURE 36.1**). There, it would be analyzed and labeled before the response command is sent out, via the amygdala (an emotion-control center).

But sometimes our emotions (especially simple likes, dislikes, and fears) take what Joseph LeDoux (2002, 2015) has called the more direct "low road," a neural shortcut that bypasses the cortex. Following the low road, a fear-provoking stimulus would travel from the eye or ear (again via the thalamus) directly to the amygdala (Figure 36.1b). This shortcut enables our lightning-quick emotional response before our intellect intervenes. Like speedy reflexes (that also operate separately from the brain's thinking cortex),

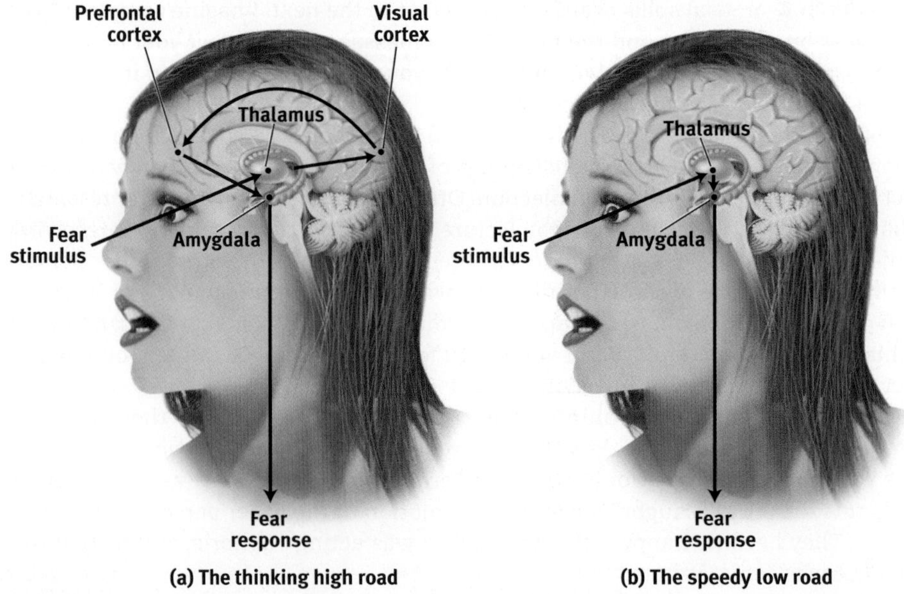
Prefrontal cortex
Visual cortex
Thalamus
Fear stimulus
Amygdala
Fear response
(a) The thinking high road
Thalamus
Fear stimulus
Amygdala
Fear response
(b) The speedy low road

FIGURE 36.1
The brain's pathways for emotions In the two-track brain, sensory input may be routed (a) to the cortex (via the thalamus) for analysis and then transmission to the amygdala; or (b) directly to the amygdala (via the thalamus) for an instant emotional reaction.

the amygdala's reactions are so fast that we may be unaware of what's transpired (Dimberg et al., 2000). A conscious fear experience then occurs as we become aware that our brain has detected danger (LeDoux & Brown, 2017).

The amygdala sends more neural projections up to the cortex than it receives back, which makes it easier for our feelings to hijack our thinking than for our thinking to rule our feelings (LeDoux & Armony, 1999). Thus, in the forest, we can jump at the sound of rustling bushes nearby, leaving it to our cortex to decide later whether the sound was made by a snake or by the wind. Such experiences support Zajonc's and LeDoux's belief that *some* of our emotional reactions involve no deliberate thinking.

Emotion researcher Richard Lazarus (1991, 1998) agreed that our brain processes vast amounts of information without our conscious awareness, and that some emotional responses do not require *conscious* thinking. Much of our emotional life operates via the automatic, speedy low road. But he further wondered: How would we *know* what we are reacting to if we did not in some way appraise the situation? The appraisal may be effortless and unconscious, but it is still a mental function. To know whether a stimulus is good or bad, the brain must have some idea of what it is (Storbeck et al., 2006). Thus, said Lazarus, emotions arise when we *appraise* an event as harmless or dangerous. We appraise the sound of the rustling bushes as the presence of a threat. Then we realize that it was "just the wind."

So, let's sum up (see also **TABLE 36.1**). As Zajonc and LeDoux have demonstrated, some simple emotional responses involve no conscious thinking. When I [ND] see a big spider trapped behind glass, I experience fear, even though I *know* the spider can't

TABLE 36.1 Summary of Emotion Theories

Theory	Explanation of Emotions	Example
James-Lange	Emotions arise from our awareness of our specific bodily responses to emotion-arousing stimuli.	We observe our heart racing after a threat and then feel afraid.
Cannon-Bard	Emotion-arousing stimuli trigger our bodily responses and simultaneous subjective experience.	Our heart races at the same time that we feel afraid.
Schachter-Singer	Our experience of emotion depends on two factors: general arousal and a conscious cognitive label.	We may interpret our arousal as fear or excitement, depending on the context.
Zajonc; LeDoux	Some embodied responses happen instantly, without conscious appraisal.	We automatically feel startled by a sound in the forest before labeling it as a threat.
Lazarus	Cognitive appraisal ("Is it dangerous or not?") — sometimes without our awareness — defines emotion.	We feel frightened when we believe the rustling in the bushes signals a wild animal; we feel relieved when we realize it's just the wind.

hurt me. Such responses are difficult to alter by changing our thinking. Within a fraction of a second, we may perceive one person as more likable or trustworthy than another (Willis & Todorov, 2006). This instant appeal can even influence our political decisions if we vote (as many people do) for the candidate we *like* over the candidate who expresses positions closer to our own (Westen, 2007).

But other emotions—including depressive moods and complex feelings—are greatly affected by our conscious and unconscious information processing: our memories, expectations, and interpretations. For these emotions, we have more conscious control. When we feel emotionally overwhelmed, we can change our interpretations (Gross, 2013). Such *reappraisal* often reduces distress and the corresponding amygdala response (Ford & Troy, 2019; Liu et al., 2019). Reappraisal not only reduces stress, it also helps students achieve better school performance (Borman et al., 2019). So don't stress about your stress. Embrace it, and approach your next exam with this mindset, "Stress evolved to help maintain my focus and solve problems." Although the emotional low road functions automatically, the thinking high road allows us to retake some control over our emotional life. *The bottom line:* Together, automatic emotion and conscious thinking weave the fabric of our emotional lives.

RETRIEVAL PRACTICE

RP-3 Emotion researchers have disagreed about whether emotional responses occur in the absence of cognitive processing. How would you characterize the approach of each of the following researchers: Zajonc, LeDoux, Lazarus, Schachter, and Singer?

ANSWERS IN APPENDIX E

Embodied Emotion

Whether you are falling in love or grieving a death, you need little convincing that emotions involve the body. Feeling without a body is like breathing without lungs. Some physical responses are easy to notice. Other emotional responses we experience without awareness.

Emotions and the Autonomic Nervous System

LOQ 36-3 What is the link between emotional arousal and the autonomic nervous system?

In a crisis, the *sympathetic division* of your *autonomic nervous system (ANS)* mobilizes your body for action (**FIGURE 36.2**). It directs your adrenal glands to release the stress hormones epinephrine (adrenaline) and norepinephrine (noradrenaline). To provide energy, your liver pours extra sugar (glucose) into your bloodstream. To help burn the sugar, your respiration increases to supply needed oxygen. Your heart rate and blood pressure increase. Your digestion slows, diverting blood from your internal organs to your muscles. With blood sugar driven into the large muscles, action becomes easier. Your pupils dilate, letting in more light. To cool your stirred-up body, you perspire. If wounded, your blood would clot more quickly.

"Fear lends wings to his feet." —Virgil, *Aeneid*, 19 B.C.E.

When the crisis passes, the *parasympathetic division* of your ANS gradually calms your body, as stress hormones slowly leave your bloodstream. After your next crisis, think of this: Without any conscious effort, your body's response to danger is wonderfully coordinated and adaptive—preparing you to *fight* or *flee*. So, do the different emotions have distinct arousal fingerprints?

ASK YOURSELF

Can you think of a time when you noticed your body's reactions to an emotionally charged situation, such as a tense social setting, or perhaps before an important test or performance? How would you describe your sympathetic nervous system's responses?

Autonomic Nervous System Controls Physiological Arousal

Sympathetic division (arousing)		Parasympathetic division (calming)
Pupils dilate	EYES	Pupils contract
Decreases	SALIVATION	Increases
Perspires	SKIN	Dries
Increases	RESPIRATION	Decreases
Accelerates	HEART	Slows
Inhibits	DIGESTION	Activates
Secrete stress hormones	ADRENAL GLANDS	Decrease secretion of stress hormones
Reduced	IMMUNE SYSTEM FUNCTIONING	Enhanced

FIGURE 36.2
Emotional arousal Like a crisis management center, the autonomic nervous system arouses the body in a crisis and calms it when danger passes.

The Physiology of Emotions

LOQ 36-4 How do emotions activate different physiological and brain-pattern responses?

Imagine conducting an experiment measuring the physiological responses of different emotions. In each room, participants watch one of four movies: a horror film, an anger-provoking film, a sexually arousing film, or an utterly boring film. From the control center, you monitor participants' perspiration, pupil size, breathing, and heart rate. Could you tell who is frightened? Who is angry? Who is sexually aroused? Who is bored?

With training, you could probably pick out the bored viewer. But discerning physiological differences among fear, anger, and sexual arousal is much more difficult (Siegel et al., 2018). Different emotions can share common biological signatures.

"No one ever told me that grief felt so much like fear. I am not afraid, but the sensation is like being afraid. The same fluttering in the stomach, the same restlessness, the yawning. I keep on swallowing." —C. S. Lewis, *A Grief Observed*, 1961

A single brain region can also serve as the seat of seemingly different emotions. Consider the broad emotional portfolio of the *insula*, a neural center deep inside the brain. The insula is activated when we experience various negative social emotions, such as lusting after another's partner, pridefulness, and disgust. In brain scans, it becomes active when people bite into some disgusting food, smell disgusting food, think about biting into a disgusting cockroach, or feel moral disgust over a sleazy businessperson exploiting a saintly widow (Sapolsky, 2010). Similar multitasking regions are found in other brain areas.

Yet our varying emotions *feel* different to us, and they often *look* different to others. We may appear "paralyzed with fear" or "ready to explode." Fear and joy prompt a similar increased heart rate, but they stimulate different facial muscles. When fearful, your brow muscles tense. When joyful, muscles in your cheeks and under your eyes pull into a smile (Witvliet & Vrana, 1995). When guppies get ready to attack, their eye color changes from silver to black (Heathcote et al., 2018).

Scary thrills Elated excitement and panicky fear involve similar physiological arousal. This allows us to flip rapidly between the two emotions.

Jacob Lund/Shutterstock

Some of our emotions also have distinct brain circuits (Dixon et al., 2017; Panksepp, 2007). Observers watching fearful faces show more amygdala activity than do other observers who view angry faces (Whalen et al., 2001). Emotions also activate different areas of the brain's cortex. When you experience a negative emotion such as disgust, your right prefrontal cortex tends to be more active than the left. Depression-prone people, and those with generally negative perspectives, have also shown more right frontal lobe activity (Harmon-Jones et al., 2002).

Positive moods tend to trigger more left frontal lobe activity. People with positive personalities—from exuberant infants to alert, energized, and persistently goal-directed adults—have also shown more activity in the left frontal lobe than in the right (Davidson et al., 2000; Urry et al.,

Thinking Critically About: Lie Detection

LOQ 36-5 How effective are polygraphs in using body states to detect lies?

Polygraphs are not actually lie detectors, but rather arousal detectors. They measure emotion-linked changes in breathing, heart rate, and perspiration. Can we use these results to detect lies?

In the last 20 years, have you ever taken something that didn't belong to you?
No!
EEG
Did you ever steal anything from your previous employer?
Uh, no.
EEG

Many people tell a little white lie in response to this *control question*, prompting elevated arousal readings that give the examiner a baseline for comparing responses to other questions.

This person shows greater arousal in response to the *critical question* than she did to the control question, so the examiner may infer she is lying.

But is it true that *only a thief becomes nervous when denying a theft?*

1. We have similar bodily arousal in response to anxiety, irritation, and guilt. So, is she really guilty, or just anxious?
2. Many innocent people do get tense and nervous when accused of a bad act. (Many of those sexually assaulted, for example, have "failed" these tests because they had strong emotional reactions while telling the truth about the event.[1])

About one-third of the time, polygraph test results are ***just wrong***.[2]

Innocent people

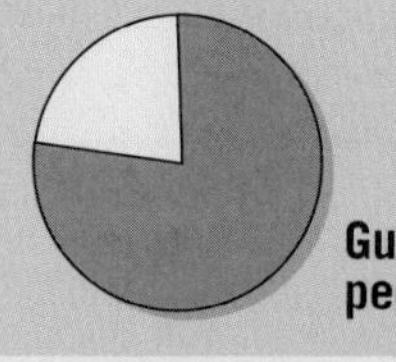

Guilty people

○ Judged innocent by polygraph ● Judged guilty by polygraph

If these polygraph experts had been the judges, more than one-third of the innocent would have been declared guilty, and nearly one-fourth of the guilty would have gone free.

The CIA and other U.S. agencies have spent millions of dollars testing tens of thousands of employees. Yet the U.S. National Academy of Sciences (2002) has reported that "no spy has ever been caught [by] using the polygraph."

***The Concealed Information Test* is more effective.** Innocent people are seldom wrongly judged to be lying.

Questions focus on specific crime-scene details known only to the police and the guilty person.[3] (If a camera and computer had been stolen, for example, only a guilty person should react strongly to the brand names of the stolen items. A slow response time may also indicate a lie. It typically takes less time to tell the truth than to make up a lie.[4])

1. Lykken, 1991. 2. Kleinmuntz & Szucko, 1984. 3. Ben-Shakhar & Elaad, 2003; Verschuere & Meijer, 2014; Vrij & Fisher, 2016. 4. Suchotzki et al., 2017.

2004). Indeed, the more a person's baseline frontal lobe activity tilts left—or is made to tilt left by perceptual activity—the more upbeat the person typically is (Drake & Myers, 2006).

To sum up, we can't easily see differences in emotions from tracking heart rate, breathing, and perspiration. But facial expressions and brain activity can vary with the emotion. So, do we, like Pinocchio, give off telltale signs when we lie? (For more on that question, see Thinking Critically About: Lie Detection.)

polygraph a machine used in attempts to detect lies; measures emotion-linked changes in perspiration, heart rate, and breathing.

RETRIEVAL PRACTICE

RP-4 What roles do the two divisions of the autonomic nervous system play in our emotional responses?

ANSWERS IN APPENDIX E

MODULE 36 REVIEW Introduction to Emotion

LEARNING OBJECTIVES

Test Yourself Answer these repeated Learning Objective Questions on your own (before "showing" the answers here, or checking the answers in Appendix D) to improve your retention of the concepts (McDaniel et al., 2009, 2015).

LOQ 36-1 How do arousal, expressive behavior, and cognition interact in emotion?

LOQ 36-2 To experience emotions, must we consciously interpret and label them?

LOQ 36-3 What is the link between emotional arousal and the autonomic nervous system?

LOQ 36-4 How do emotions activate different physiological and brain-pattern responses?

LOQ 36-5 How effective are polygraphs in using body states to detect lies?

TERMS AND CONCEPTS TO REMEMBER

Test Yourself Write down the definition in your own words, then check your answer.

emotion, p. 417
James-Lange theory, p. 418
Cannon-Bard theory, p. 418
two-factor theory, p. 418
polygraph, p. 423

MODULE TEST

Test Yourself Answer the following questions on your own first, then "show" the answers here, or check your answers in Appendix E.

1. The ____________-____________ theory of emotion maintains that our emotional experience occurs after our awareness of a physiological response.

2. Imagine that after returning from an hour-long run, you receive a letter saying that your scholarship application has been approved. The two-factor theory of emotion would predict that your physical arousal will
   - **a.** weaken your happiness.
   - **b.** intensify your happiness.
   - **c.** transform your happiness into relief.
   - **d.** have no particular effect on your happiness.

3. Zajonc and LeDoux have maintained that some emotional reactions occur before we have had the chance to consciously label or interpret them. Lazarus noted the importance of how we appraise events. These psychologists differ in the emphasis they place on ____________ in emotional responses.
   - **a.** physical arousal
   - **b.** the hormone epinephrine
   - **c.** cognitive processing
   - **d.** learning

4. What does a polygraph measure, and why are its results questionable?

MODULE 

Expressing Emotion

Expressions imply emotions. Sloths, with serene smiles seemingly plastered on their faces, appear happy. Basset hounds, with their long faces and droopy eyes, seem sad. Are our own faces a window into our feelings? To decipher people's emotions, we study their faces. We listen to their vocal tones. We read their bodies. Does nonverbal language vary with culture—or is it universal? Are women more emotional and empathic than men—or are all people roughly equal? And do our outward emotional expressions influence our internally experienced emotions—or are our bodies and minds separate?

Detecting Emotion in Others

LOQ 37-1 How do we communicate emotions nonverbally?

To people from Western cultures, a firm handshake conveys an outgoing, expressive personality (Chaplin et al., 2000). A gaze can communicate intimacy, while darting eyes may signal anxiety (Kleinke, 1986; Perkins et al., 2012). When two people are in love, they often gaze into each other's eyes, smile, and nod (Bolmont et al., 2014; Cowen & Keltner, 2020; Gonzaga et al., 2001). Would such gazes stir loving feelings between strangers? To find out, researchers have placed unacquainted straight people in pairs and asked them to gaze intently for 2 minutes either at each other's hands, or into each other's eyes. After separating, the eye gazers reported feeling a tingle of attraction and affection (Kellerman et al., 1989).

GeorgePeters/Getty Images

Petrut Romeo Paul/Shutterstock

Our brain is an amazing detector of subtle expressions. We are adept at detecting a hint of a smile (Maher et al., 2014). Shown 10 seconds of video from the end of a speed-dating interaction, people can often tell

Paul Ekman, Ph.D./Paul Ekman Group, LLC.

FIGURE 37.1
Experience influences how we perceive emotions Viewing the morphed middle face, evenly mixing anger with fear, children who had been physically abused were more likely than other children to perceive the face as angry.

whether one person is attracted to another (Place et al., 2009). Observing *thin slices* of behavior (brief samples) revealed that the intensity of women's high school yearbook smiles predicted their well-being and marital satisfaction up to 30 years later (Harker & Keltner, 2001). More cheerful smiles in kindergarteners' class photos reflected warmer family relationships (Oveis et al., 2009). Even brief smiles convey more than meets the eye.

Signs of status are also easy to spot. When shown someone with arms raised, chest expanded, and a downward head tilt, people from diverse cultures—including Fijian villagers, Canadian undergraduates, and Indigenous peoples of Nicaragua—perceive that person as experiencing pride and having dominant status (Tracy et al., 2013; Witkower et al., 2022). Even a fleeting tenth-of-a-second glimpse of a face has enabled viewers to judge people's trustworthiness, or to rate politicians' competence and predict their voter support (Willis & Todorov, 2006). "First impressions . . . occur with astonishing speed," noted Christopher Olivola and Alexander Todorov (2010).

We also excel at quickly detecting nonverbal threats. An angry face can "pop out" of a crowd (Öhman et al., 2001; Stjepanovic & LaBar, 2018). Even children as young as 2 years old attend to angry faces, suggesting that we instinctively detect threats (Burris et al., 2019).

Zohaib Hussain/Getty Images

A silent language of emotion Hindu classic dance uses the face and body to effectively convey 10 different emotions (Hejmadi et al., 2000).

Experience sensitizes us to particular emotions, as shown by experiments using a series of faces (like those in **FIGURE 37.1**) that morph from anger to fear (or sadness). Shown a face that is 50 percent fear and 50 percent anger, children who have been physically abused are more likely than other children to perceive anger (Pollak & Kistler, 2002; Pollak & Tolley-Schell, 2003). Their perceptions become attuned to swiftly spotting glimmers of danger.

Hard-to-control facial muscles can reveal signs of emotions you may be trying to conceal. Lifting just the inner part of your eyebrows, which few people do consciously, reveals distress or worry. Eyebrows raised and pulled together signal fear. Raised cheeks and activated muscles under the eyes suggest a natural smile, called a *Duchenne* smile (in honor of the French physician who described it). These authentic smiles reveal our honest positive emotions (Sheldon et al., 2021). While a fake smile—such as one we make for a photographer—is often frozen in place for several seconds, then suddenly switched off, genuine happy smiles tend to be briefer but to fade less abruptly (Ekman et al., 1990) (**FIGURE 37.2**). True smiles cause others to perceive us as trustworthy, authentic, and attractive (Gunnery & Ruben, 2016). When smiling, we can fake it, but our facial muscles won't make it.

Despite our brain's emotion-detecting skill, we find it difficult to discern deceit. Computer algorithms outperform humans when detecting deception, because liars' and truth-tellers' behavioral differences are often too minute for the human eye (Hartwig & Bond, 2011; Monaro et al., 2022). One digest of 206 studies found that people were just 54 percent accurate in discerning truth from lies—barely better than a coin toss (Bond & DePaulo, 2006). Virtually no one—except perhaps police professionals in high-stakes situations—beats chance by much, not even when detecting children's lies (Gongola et al., 2017; O'Sullivan et al., 2009; ten Brinke et al., 2016).

Gestures, facial expressions, and vocal tones, which are absent in written communication, convey important information.

FIGURE 37.2
Which smile is natural, which is feigned? Smile (a) engages the facial muscles of a natural smile.

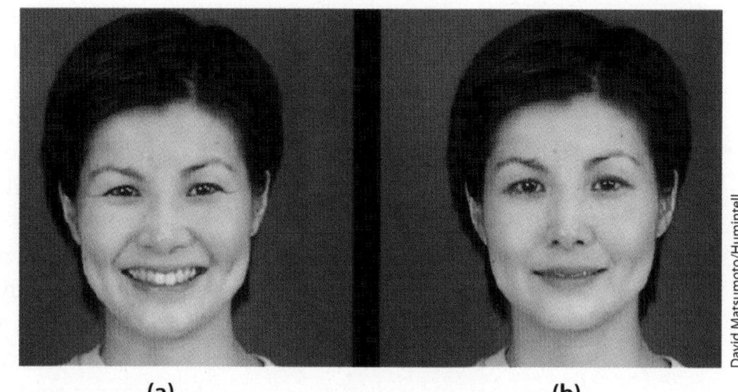

David Matsumoto/Humintell

(a) (b)

The difference was clear when study participants in one group heard 30-second recordings of people describing their marital separations. Participants in the other group read a transcript of the recording. Compared with those who had read it, participants who *heard* the description were better able to predict the people's current and future adjustment (Mason et al., 2010). Just hearing a stranger say "hello" is enough to give listeners some clue to the speaker's personality.

Our texts, emails, and other online communications lack vocal and facial emotional nuances. Without the usual expressive cues, we run the risk of what developmental psychologist Jean Piaget called *egocentrism*—difficulty taking another's point of view. We may, for example, fail to perceive how others interpret our "just kidding" message (Kruger et al., 2005). So, to help people understand our personality and whether our online comment is serious, kidding, or sarcastic, we may insert emojis (Kaye et al., 2017). ☺

Gender, Emotion, and Nonverbal Behavior

LOQ 37-2 How do men and women differ in nonverbal communication?

Do women have greater sensitivity than men to nonverbal cues? An analysis led by Judith Hall (2016) of 176 thin slice studies indicated that women outperformed men at emotion detection. This advantage emerges early in infancy (McClure, 2000). Women's nonverbal sensitivity might explain their greater emotional literacy.

When invited to describe how they would feel in certain situations, men tend to describe simpler emotional reactions (Barrett et al., 2000). You might like to try this yourself: Ask some people how they might feel when saying good-bye to friends after graduation. Research suggests men are more likely to say, simply, "I'll feel bad," and women to express more complex emotions: "It will be bittersweet; I'll feel both happy and sad."

Women's skill at decoding others' emotions may also contribute to their greater emotional responsiveness and expressiveness, especially for positive emotions (Fischer & LaFrance, 2015; McDuff et al., 2017). In studies of 23,000 people from 26 cultures, women more than men reported themselves open to feelings (Costa et al., 2001). Girls tend to express stronger emotions than boys do, hence the extremely strong perception that emotionality is "more true of women"—a perception expressed by nearly 100 percent of U.S. 18- to 29-year-olds (Chaplin & Aldao, 2013; Newport, 2001). In conversation, young girls and their parents—more than young boys and their parents—tend to discuss emotions and use more emotion-related words (Fivush et al., 2000).

One exception: Quickly—imagine an angry face. What gender is the person? If you're like 3 in 4 Arizona State University students, you imagined a man (Becker et al., 2007). The same researchers also manipulated a computer-generated, gender-neutral face to display different emotions. People were more likely to perceive the face as male when it wore an angry expression and as female when it wore a smile (Becker et al., 2007). Anger strikes most people as a more masculine emotion. Women who express "male-typed" anger pay a penalty in the workplace, such as being labeled "out of control" (Brescoll & Uhlmann, 2008).

The perception of women's emotionality also feeds—and is fed by—people's attributing women's emotionality to their disposition and men's to their circumstances: "She's emotional" versus "He's having a bad day" (Feldman Barrett & Bliss-Moreau, 2009). Nevertheless, there are some gender differences in descriptions of emotional experiences. When surveyed, women are far more likely than men to describe themselves as empathic (Benenson et al., 2021). If you have *empathy*, you identify with others and imagine being in their skin. You appraise a situation as they do, rejoicing with those who rejoice and weeping with those who weep (Wondra & Ellsworth, 2015). Fiction readers, who immerse themselves in others' lives, report higher empathy levels (Mar et al., 2009).

"Empathy's most important role . . . is to inspire kindness: our tendency to help each other, even at a cost to ourselves."
—Jamil Zaki, *The War for Kindness*, 2019

Women are also more likely to *express* empathy—to display more emotion when observing others' emotions (Depow et al., 2021). This gender difference was clear when college students watched film clips that were sad (children with a dying parent), happy (slapstick comedy), or frightening (a man nearly falling off the ledge of a tall building) (Kring & Gordon, 1998; Vigil, 2009).

You may wonder: Are gender differences in empathy the result of nature or nurture? As we have seen repeatedly, nature and nurture often interact. Evolutionary biologists and neuroscientists note that similar female-male empathy differences occur in nonhuman animals (Christov-Moore et al., 2014). To these researchers, biology powerfully predicts empathy. But cultural learning also matters. People with high power and privilege are less motivated to empathize (Dietze & Knowles, 2021; Kraus et al., 2012). Those lower in power, as women historically have been, may feel a strong motivation to understand others' emotions (Dietze & Knowles, 2016).

RETRIEVAL PRACTICE

RP-1 ____________ (Women/Men) report experiencing emotions more deeply, and they tend to be more adept at reading nonverbal behavior.

ANSWERS IN APPENDIX E

Culture and Emotional Expression

LOQ 37-3 How are gestures and facial expressions understood within and across cultures?

Where you live, do people often smile when passing a stranger on an otherwise empty sidewalk? Where your authors live—in the U.S. Midwest [DM], the Rocky Mountains [JG], and the U.S. South [ND]—that's the norm. Elsewhere, making eye contact and smiling at a stranger might seem strange, or even suspicious (Niedenthal, et al., 2019). Culture matters.

The meaning of *gestures* also varies from culture to culture. In 1968, North Korea publicized photos of supposedly happy officers from a captured U.S. Navy spy ship. In the photo, three men had raised their middle finger, telling their captors it was a "Hawaiian good luck sign" (Fleming & Scott, 1991). I [ND] have taught my young children the thumbs-up gesture so they can let me know that something is good. But I will also teach them not to make that gesture if we travel to certain West African and Middle Eastern countries, where it can mean "up yours!" (Koerner, 2003).

Do *facial expressions* also have different meanings in different cultures? To find out, researchers have traveled the world, showing people photos of different posed faces and asking them to guess the emotion (Ekman & Friesen, 1975; Izard, 1994; Mesquita, 2022). You can try one such task yourself by labeling the emotions in **FIGURE 37.3**.

Rotman Institute of Philosophy

Emotion construction Pioneering emotion researcher Lisa Feldman Barrett is exploring how people construct emotions based on their body, brain, and culture.

(a) (b) (c)

(d) (e) (f)

David Matsumoto/Humintell, LLC

FIGURE 37.3
Culture-specific or culturally universal expressions? Which face expresses disgust? Anger? Fear? Happiness? Sadness? Surprise?[1]

[1](a) happiness, (b) surprise, (c) fear, (d) sadness, (e) anger, (f) disgust.

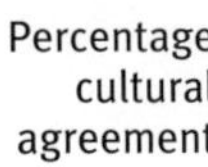
Percentage
cultural
agreement

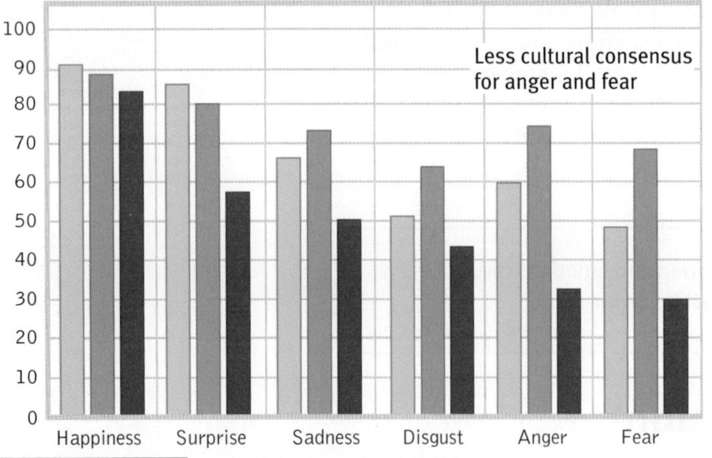
100
90
80
70
60
50
40
30
20
10
0
Less cultural consensus
for anger and fear
Happiness
Surprise
Sadness
Disgust
Anger
Fear
Facial expression label chosen
Literate, non-Western cultures
Literate, Western cultures
Illiterate, isolated cultures

Roman Samborskyi/Alamy Stock Photo

FIGURE 37.4
Cultural consensus in question In global studies, most people agree that a smiling face represents happiness. Other expressions, such as in the face shown here, have offered less cross-cultural consensus (Nelson et al., 2013). What emotion do you see in this face?

You probably labeled the smiling face as "happiness"—and so would most people worldwide. One analysis of 6 million videos from 144 countries found reliable associations between facial expressions and social contexts (Cowen et al., 2021). Across humanity, expressions conveying amusement occurred in videos with practical jokes, pained expressions with weight training, and triumphant expressions with sports.

But people also differ in some expressions, especially anger and fear, even when matching exaggerated poses to a limited set of emotion words (Crivelli et al., 2016a; **FIGURE 37.4**). We're also better at judging faces from our own culture; it's as if we learn a local emotional dialect (Crivelli et al., 2016b; Elfenbein & Ambady, 2002; Laukka & Elfenbein, 2021).

"For news of the heart, ask the face."
—Guinean proverb

Some emotion categories are clear universals: A smile's a smile the world around. The same with laughter: People everywhere can discriminate real from fake laughs (Bryant et al., 2018). Even people blind from birth spontaneously exhibit the common facial expressions associated with such emotions as joy, sadness, fear, anger, and pride (Galati et al., 1997; Tracy & Matsumoto, 2008).

Such results would not have surprised evolutionary theorist Charles Darwin (1809–1882), who argued that before our prehistoric ancestors communicated in words, they communicated threats, greetings, and submission with facial expressions. These shared expressions helped them survive (Hess & Thibault, 2009). In confrontations, for example, a human sneer retains elements of an animal baring its teeth in a snarl (**FIGURE 37.5**). Emotional expressions may enhance our survival in other ways, too. Surprise raises the eyebrows and widens the eyes, enabling us to take in more information. Disgust wrinkles the nose and sticks out the tongue, reducing intake of foul odors or foods.

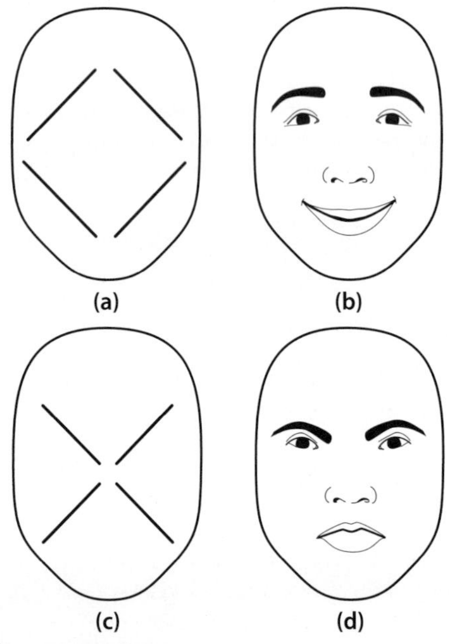
(a)
(b)
(c)
(d)

FIGURE 37.5
Anger expressed Cover up faces (c) and (d) and ask a friend if they would select image (a) or image (b) as the angry one. Even without the obvious facial cues, most people choose (b) (Franklin et al., 2019).

Yet facial expressions are not crystal balls to our emotions. We routinely control our faces to fit in with, influence, or deceive others. Euphoric Olympic gold-medal winners typically don't smile when they are waiting alone for their award ceremony. But they wear broad grins when interacting with officials and when facing the crowd and cameras (Fernández-Dols & Ruiz-Belda, 1995). Depending on the situation, the same expression may also convey different messages (Feldman Barrett et al., 2019). When worn by a villain, a smile may be terrifying. A fearful face set in a painful situation looks pained (Carroll & Russell, 1996). Film directors harness this phenomenon by creating scenes and soundtracks that amplify our perceptions of particular emotions.

Facial expressions are also cultural occurrences, with *display rules* guiding *when* to express an emotion, *which* emotion is appropriate, and *how much* of an emotion to express. Compared with job applicants in Hong Kong, where calmness is emphasized, European American applicants use excited smiles and words more frequently. Likewise, European American leaders showed broad smiles six times more frequently in their official photos (Bencharit et al., 2019; **FIGURE 37.6**).

Peter Probst/Alamy Stock Photo

AP Photo

FIGURE 37.6
Culture and smiling U.S. President Joe Biden's broad smile and Chinese President Xi Jinping's more reserved one illustrate a cultural difference in facial expressiveness. (Stimuli from Tsai et al., 2016.)

In cultures that encourage individuality and personal influence, as in Western Europe, Australia, New Zealand, and North America, people prefer high-intensity positive emotions (Tsai, 2007). Cultures that encourage collectivism with a focus on others, as in Japan, China, and Korea, often value less intense emotional displays (Cordaro et al., 2018; Matsumoto et al., 2009). Moreover, in Japan, the mouth—often so expressive in North Americans—conveys less emotion than do the telltale eyes (Masuda et al., 2008; Yuki et al., 2007). If we're happy and we know it, our culture will teach us how to show it.

Cultural differences also exist *within* nations. Irish people and their Irish American descendants have tended to be more expressive than Scandinavian people and their Scandinavian American descendants, even though both groups share a common nationality (Tsai & Chentsova-Dutton, 2003). And that reminds us of a familiar lesson: Like most psychological events, facial expressions are best understood not only as biological and cognitive phenomena, but also as social-cultural phenomena.

RETRIEVAL PRACTICE

RP-2 How are facial expressions rooted in biology and culture?

ANSWERS IN APPENDIX E

The Effects of Facial Expressions

LOQ 37-4 How do our external facial expressions influence our internal feelings?

As William James (1890) struggled with feelings of depression and grief, he came to believe that we can control emotions by going "through the outward movements" of any emotion we want to experience. "To feel cheerful," he advised, "sit up cheerfully, look

Masashi Hara/Getty Images

(a)

Elsa/Getty Images

(b)

Display rules differ Soccer players from more collectivist cultures, such as Japanese Yū Kobayashi, tend to celebrate a goal with fellow players in a way that deflects attention from themselves (a). Those from more individualist cultures, such as American Megan Rapinoe—shown here after scoring at the 2019 Women's World Cup—are more comfortable making themselves distinct (b).

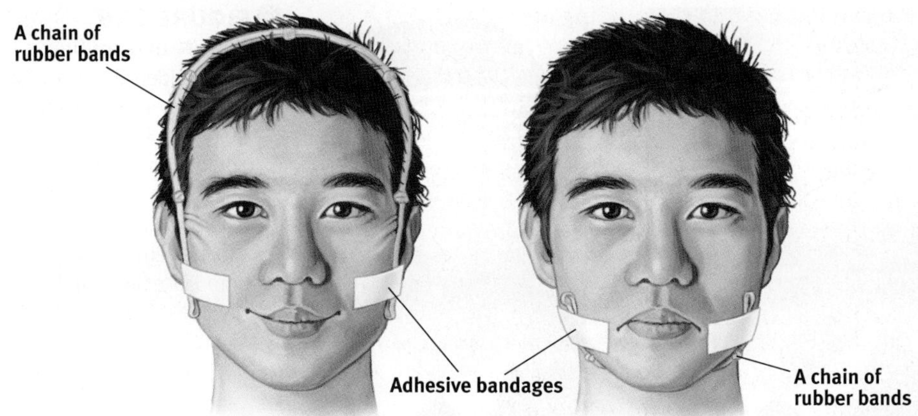
A chain of rubber bands
Adhesive bandages
A chain of rubber bands

FIGURE 37.7
How to make people smile without telling them to smile Do as Kazuo Mori and Hideko Mori (2009) did with students in Japan: Attach rubber bands to the sides of the face with adhesive bandages, and then run them either over the head or under the chin.

around cheerfully, and act as if cheerfulness were already there." In *The Expression of the Emotions in Man and Animals*, Charles Darwin (1872) contended that "the free expression by outward signs of an emotion intensifies it. . . . He who gives way to violent gestures will increase his rage."

Were they right? You can test their hypothesis: Fake a big grin. Now scowl. Can you feel the "smile therapy" difference? Participants in dozens of experiments have felt a difference. Researchers subtly induced students to make a frowning expression by asking them to contract certain muscles and pull their brows together (supposedly to help the researchers attach facial electrodes) (Laird, 1974, 1984; Laird & Lacasse, 2014). The results? The students reported feeling a little angry, as do people naturally frowning (by squinting) when facing the Sun (Marzoli et al., 2013). So, too, for other basic emotions. For example, people reported feeling more fear than anger, disgust, or sadness when made to construct a fearful expression: "Raise your eyebrows. And open your eyes wide. Move your whole head back, so that your chin is tucked in a little bit, and let your mouth relax and hang open a little" (Duclos et al., 1989).

James and Darwin had it right: Expressions not only communicate emotion, they also amplify and regulate it. This **facial feedback effect** has been found many times, in many places, for many basic emotions (Coles et al., 2019; see **FIGURE 37.7**). We're just a little happier when smiling, angrier when scowling, and sadder when frowning. Merely activating one of the smiling muscles by holding a pen in the teeth (rather than gently between the lips, which produces a neutral expression) makes stressful situations less upsetting (Kraft & Pressman, 2012). A hearty smile—made not just with the mouth but with raised cheeks that crinkle the eyes—enhances positive feelings even more when you are reacting to something pleasant or funny (Soussignan, 2001). When happy we smile, and when smiling we become happier, unless we're distracted by being videotaped (Marsh et al., 2019; Noah et al., 2018; Strack, 2016). In a saying often attributed to Vietnamese Buddhist monk Thích Nhất Hạnh, "Sometimes your joy is the source of your smile, but sometimes your smile can be the source of your joy."

So, your face is more than a billboard that displays your feelings; it also fuels your feelings. Scowl and the whole world scowls back. No wonder some people with depression or borderline personality disorder have reported feeling better after Botox injections paralyzed their facial frowning muscles (Kruger et al., 2022; Schultze et al., 2021). However, Botox paralysis of the frowning muscles also slows activity in emotion-related brain circuits and weakens emotional experiences (Davis et al., 2010; Hennenlotter et al., 2008). The opposite happens when Botox paralyzes laughter muscles: People feel worse (Lewis, 2018).

A request from your authors: Smile often as you read this book.

Researchers have also observed a broader **behavior feedback effect** (Carney et al., 2015; Flack, 2006). You can duplicate the participants' experience: Walk for a few minutes with short, shuffling steps, keeping your eyes downcast. Now walk around taking long strides, with your arms swinging and your eyes looking straight ahead. Can you feel your mood shift? Or when angry, lean back in a reclined sitting position and feel the anger lessen (Krahé et al., 2018). Going through the motions awakens the emotions. The next time you're angry or stressed, lean back and take a few deep breaths.

facial feedback effect the tendency of facial muscle activation, alone, to trigger corresponding feelings such as fear, anger, or happiness.

behavior feedback effect the tendency of behavior to influence our own and others' thoughts, feelings, and actions.

You can use your understanding of feedback effects to become more empathic: Let your own face mimic another person's expression. Acting as another acts helps us feel what another feels (Hess & Fischer, 2016; Iacoboni, 2009). Losing this ability to mimic others can leave us struggling to make emotional connections, as social worker Kathleen Bogart, who has Moebius syndrome (a rare facial paralysis disorder), discovered while working with Hurricane Katrina refugees: When people made a sad expression, "I wasn't able to return it. I tried to do so with words and tone of voice, but it was no use. Stripped of the facial expression, the emotion just dies there, unshared" (Carey, 2010).

ASK YOURSELF

Imagine a situation in which you would like to change the way you feel. How could you do so by altering your facial expressions or the way you carry yourself? In what other settings could you apply your knowledge of these feedback effects?

RETRIEVAL PRACTICE

RP-3 (a) Based on the *facial feedback effect*, how might students report feeling when the rubber bands raise their cheeks as though in a smile? (b) How might students report feeling when the rubber bands pull their cheeks downward?

ANSWERS IN APPENDIX E

MODULE 37 REVIEW Expressing Emotion

LEARNING OBJECTIVES

Test Yourself Answer these repeated Learning Objective Questions on your own (before "showing" the answers here, or checking the answers in Appendix D) to improve your retention of the concepts (McDaniel et al., 2009, 2015).

LOQ 37-1 How do we communicate emotions nonverbally?

LOQ 37-2 How do men and women differ in nonverbal communication?

LOQ 37-3 How are gestures and facial expressions understood within and across cultures?

LOQ 37-4 How do our external facial expressions influence our internal feelings?

TERMS AND CONCEPTS TO REMEMBER

Test Yourself Write down the definition in your own words, then check your answer.

facial feedback effect , p. 430

behavior feedback effect , p. 430

MODULE TEST

Test Yourself Answer the following questions on your own first, then "show" the answers here, or check your answers in Appendix E.

1. When people are induced to assume a fearful expression, they often report feeling some fear. This result is known as the ________ ________ effect.
2. Aiden has a bad cold and finds himself shuffling to class with his head down. How might his posture, as well as his cold, affect his emotional well-being?

MODULE 38 Experiencing Emotion

LOQ 38-1 What are some of the basic emotions?

How many distinct emotions are there? When surveyed, most emotion scientists agreed on five basic emotions: anger, fear, disgust, sadness, and happiness (Ekman, 2016). Carroll Izard (1977) isolated 10: joy, interest-excitement, surprise, sadness, anger, disgust, contempt, fear, shame, and guilt, most present in infancy (**FIGURE 38.1**). Others recognize as many as 28, including different flavors of happiness like awe, love, and pride (Cowen & Keltner, 2020).

FIGURE 38.1
Some naturally occurring infant emotions To identify the emotions generally present in infancy, Carroll Izard analyzed the facial expressions of infants.

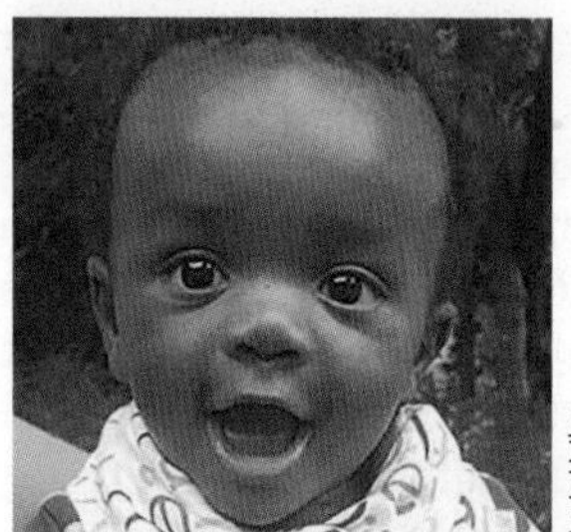
Lorie Hailey
Joy (mouth forming smile, cheeks lifted, twinkle in eye)

Patrick Donehue/Science Source
Anger (brows drawn together and downward, eyes fixed, mouth squarish)

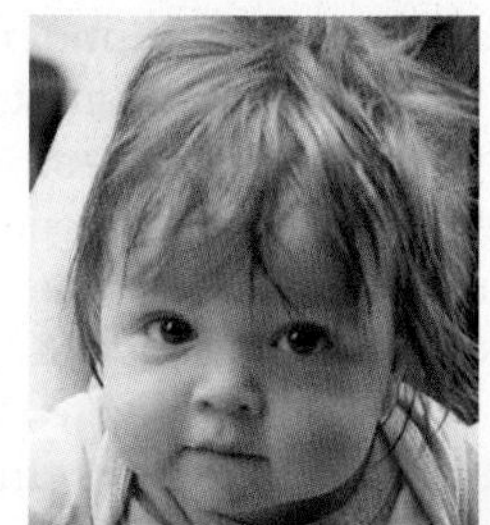
Raul Saucedo
Interest (brows raised or knitted, mouth softly rounded, lips may be pursed)

lina aidukaite/Getty Images
Disgust (nose wrinkled, upper lip raised, tongue pushed outward)

Samuel Borges Photography/Shutterstock
Surprise (brows raised, eyes widened, mouth rounded in oval shape)

bendao/Getty Images
Sadness (brows' inner corners raised, mouth corners drawn down)

Vladimir Godnik/Getty Images
Fear (brows level, drawn in and up, eyelids lifted, mouth corners retracted)

Emotions are categorized along two dimensions: *valence* (positive versus negative) and *arousal* (low versus high) (Feldman Barrett & Russell, 1998; Tsai et al., 2006; **FIGURE 38.2**). But are emotions biologically distinct? Does our body, for example, know the difference between fear and anger? Can our brain distinguish happiness from interest?

Let's take a closer look at anger and happiness. What functions do they serve? What influences our experience of each?

FIGURE 38.2
A tale of two emotional dimensions You can feel good with little arousal (the calmness that often accompanies meditation) or lots of arousal (excitement at seeing friends). Likewise, negative feelings can involve low arousal (boredom during a long-winded lecture) or high arousal (nervousness before a job interview).

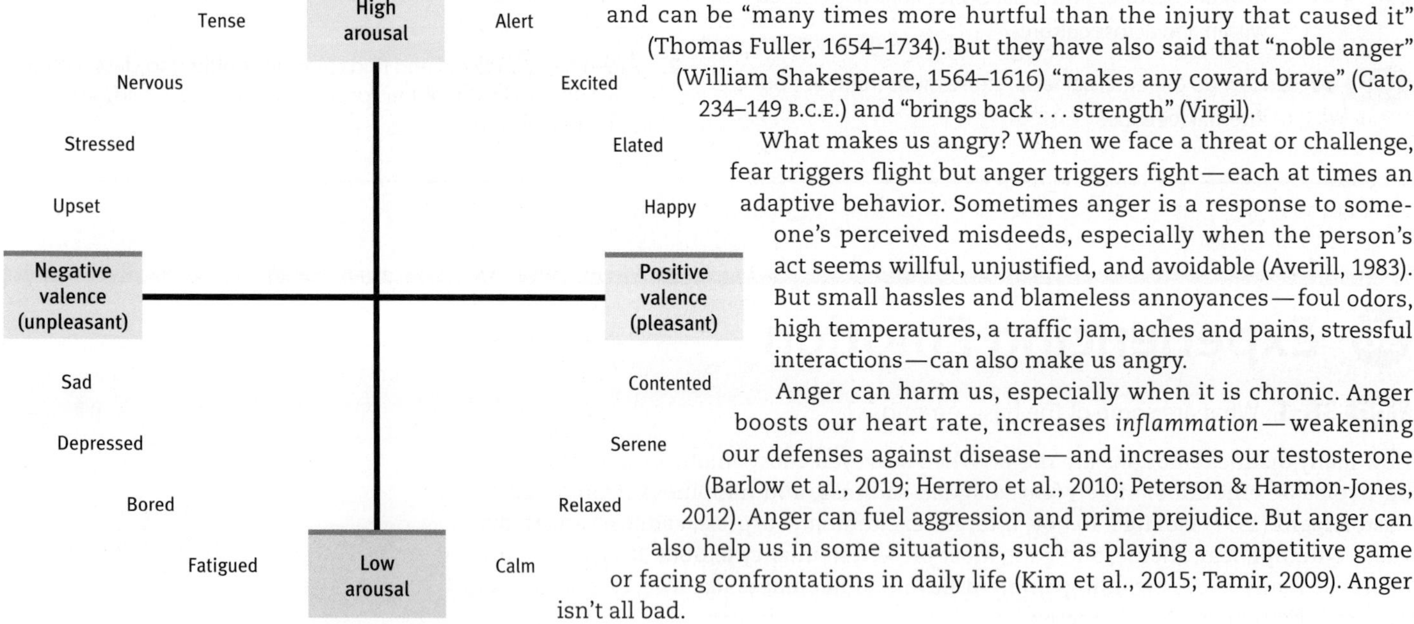
High arousal
Tense
Alert
Nervous
Excited
Stressed
Elated
Upset
Happy
Negative valence (unpleasant)
Positive valence (pleasant)
Sad
Contented
Depressed
Serene
Bored
Relaxed
Fatigued
Calm
Low arousal

Anger

LOQ 38-2 What are the causes and consequences of anger?

Anger, the sages have said, "carries the mind away" (Virgil, 70–19 B.C.E.) and can be "many times more hurtful than the injury that caused it" (Thomas Fuller, 1654–1734). But they have also said that "noble anger" (William Shakespeare, 1564–1616) "makes any coward brave" (Cato, 234–149 B.C.E.) and "brings back . . . strength" (Virgil).

What makes us angry? When we face a threat or challenge, fear triggers flight but anger triggers fight—each at times an adaptive behavior. Sometimes anger is a response to someone's perceived misdeeds, especially when the person's act seems willful, unjustified, and avoidable (Averill, 1983). But small hassles and blameless annoyances—foul odors, high temperatures, a traffic jam, aches and pains, stressful interactions—can also make us angry.

Anger can harm us, especially when it is chronic. Anger boosts our heart rate, increases *inflammation*—weakening our defenses against disease—and increases our testosterone (Barlow et al., 2019; Herrero et al., 2010; Peterson & Harmon-Jones, 2012). Anger can fuel aggression and prime prejudice. But anger can also help us in some situations, such as playing a competitive game or facing confrontations in daily life (Kim et al., 2015; Tamir, 2009). Anger isn't all bad.

How do we manage our anger? Individualist cultures encourage people to vent their rage. The Western vent-your-anger advice presumes that aggression enables emotional release, or *catharsis*. Joining others in venting shared angry feelings can increase our feelings of closeness, intimacy, and attachment (Fischer & Roseman, 2007). But does this venting calm us (Bushman, 2002)? Researchers report that *sometimes* when people retaliate against a provoker, they may calm down if they direct their counterattack toward the provoker, their retaliation seems justifiable, and their target is not intimidating. Expressing anger can be temporarily calming if it does not leave us feeling guilty or anxious (Geen & Quanty, 1977; Hokanson & Edelman, 1966; Verona & Sullivan, 2008). However, *acting* angry more often makes us *feel* angrier (Flack, 2006; Snodgrass et al., 1986). Anger's backfire potential appeared in a study of people asked to wallop a punching bag while ruminating about a person who had recently angered them (Bushman, 2002). Had the opportunity to "drain off" their anger reduced it? Quite the contrary. Later, when given a chance for revenge, those who had vented their anger became even more aggressive.

MIKE HUTCHINGS/REUTERS/Newscom

When anger is all the rage Fans seem to experience a *temporary* release while cheering at World Cup soccer matches, such as this one in South Africa. My [DM's] daughter, a resident, noted, "Every time I got angry at Uruguay, blowing that vuvuzela and joining the chorus of dissent released something in me."

Advice to release anger is seldom heard in cultures where people's identity is centered more on "we" than "me." People who keenly sense their *inter*dependence see anger as a threat to group harmony (Markus & Kitayama, 1991). In Tahiti, for instance, people learn to be considerate and gentle. In Japan, from infancy on, angry expressions are less common than in Western cultures.

What are some healthy ways to manage your anger? Experts offer these suggestions:

- ***Wait.*** Doing so will reduce your physiological arousal. "What goes up must come down," noted Carol Tavris (1982). "Any emotional arousal will simmer down if you just wait long enough."
- ***Think about the situation differently.*** Reappraisal—thinking about things in a different way—can reduce anger and help us tolerate frustration (Szasz et al., 2011). The next time you're angry about something, consider: In the long run, will this matter? Is there another side to the story?
- ***Find a healthy distraction or support instead of ruminating.*** Calm yourself by exercising, reading, or talking things through with a friend. Brain scans show that ruminating inwardly about why you are angry increases blood flow to the brain's anger-processing amygdala (Fabiansson et al., 2012).
- ***Distance yourself.*** Try to move away from the situation mentally, as if you are watching it unfold from a distance or the future. Self-distancing reduces rumination, anger, and aggression (Kross & Ayduk, 2011; Mischkowski et al., 2012; White et al., 2015).

"Anger will never disappear so long as thoughts of resentment are cherished in the mind." —The Buddha, 500 B.C.E.

Used wisely, anger communicates strength and competence (Tiedens, 2001). Anger also motivates people to act courageously and achieve goals (Aarts & Custers, 2012; Halmburger et al., 2015). Controlled expressions of anger are more adaptive than either hostile outbursts or pent-up angry feelings. Civility means not only keeping silent about trivial irritations but also communicating important ones clearly and assertively. A nonjudgmental statement of feeling—perhaps letting a roommate know that "I feel upset when I have to clean up your dirty dishes"—can help resolve conflicts. Anger that expresses a grievance in ways that promote reconciliation and cooperation rather than retaliation can benefit a relationship (Van Kleef & Côté, 2007).

What if someone's behavior really hurts you, and you cannot resolve the conflict? Research commends the age-old response of forgiveness (Worthington & Wade, 2019). Without letting the offender off the hook or inviting further harm (sometimes we need to distance ourselves from an abusive person), forgiveness may release anger and calm the body. Forgiveness doesn't just apply to other people: We also benefit from forgiving ourselves (Webb et al., 2017). One summary of 17 studies reported that self-forgiveness predicted less suicidal ideation and self-harm (Cleare et al., 2019).

RETRIEVAL PRACTICE

RP-1 Which one of the following is an effective strategy for reducing angry feelings?

a. Retaliate verbally or physically.
b. Wait or "simmer down."
c. Express anger in our behavior.
d. Review the grievance silently.

ANSWERS IN APPENDIX E

happiness an enduring prevalence of positive emotions.

feel-good, do-good phenomenon our tendency to be helpful when in a good mood.

positive psychology the scientific study of human flourishing, with the goals of discovering and promoting strengths and virtues that help individuals and communities to thrive.

subjective well-being self-perceived satisfaction with life. Used along with measures of objective well-being (for example, physical and economic indicators) to judge our quality of life.

Happiness and Well-Being

LOQ 38-3 What is happiness? Why does happiness matter?

The Greek philosopher Aristotle (350 B.C.E.) believed that "happiness is the meaning and the purpose of life, the whole aim and end of human existence." The psychologist William James (1902) called happiness "the secret for all [we] do." The Dalai Lama (2009) agreed: "The very purpose of our life is to seek happiness."

Happiness (our having more positive than negative feelings) matters in our daily lives. Our happiness or unhappiness colors our thoughts and our actions. Happy people perceive the world as safer (Cunningham & Kirkland, 2014). They also smile more, and act more playfully (Gardiner et al., 2022). Their eyes are drawn toward emotionally positive images (Raila et al., 2015). Positive feelings enhance our memory of positive facts and pleasant times (Bower, 1981; Isen et al., 1978). Happy feelings also "broaden and build" our thinking, allowing us to relax, become more creative, and connect more easily with others (Fredrickson, 2013; Shiota et al., 2017).

Happiness also promotes a flourishing life. Happy babies tend to become successful adults, and happier adults experience more career success (Coffey, 2020; Walsh et al., 2018). Happier adults also live healthier and more satisfied lives (Boehm et al., 2015; Kushlev et al., 2020; Willroth et al., 2020). When researchers surveyed thousands of U.S. college students in 1976 and restudied them 2 decades later, happy students had gone on to earn significantly more money than their less-happy-than-average peers (Diener et al., 2002). When we are happy, our relationships, self-image, and hopes for the future also seem more promising.

Happiness benefits society, too. Happy people not only feel good, they also do good. This **feel-good, do-good phenomenon** is one of psychology's most consistent findings (Salovey, 1990). Happier people are more helpful and kind to others (Kushlev et al., 2022). A mood-boosting experience (finding money, succeeding on a challenging task, recalling a happy event) has made people more likely to give money, pick up someone's dropped papers, and volunteer time (Isen & Levin, 1972).

The reverse is also true: Doing good also promotes good feeling. Spending money on others, rather than on ourselves, increases happiness (Aknin et al., 2020). Young children also show more positive emotion when they give, rather than receive, gifts (Aknin et al., 2015). In a Spanish corporate workplace, employees who helped their co-workers experienced greater well-being, and those they helped also became happier and more helpful (Chancellor et al., 2018). Even donating a kidney, despite the pain, leaves donors feeling good (Brethel-Haurwitz & Marsh, 2014). The benefits of helping are not limited to exceptional altruists. People with a history of criminal behavior also feel good when they do good (Hanniball et al., 2019). *The bottom line:* Helping others helps us all feel happy.

Why does doing good feel so good? One reason is that it strengthens our social relationships (Aknin & Human, 2015; Yamaguchi et al., 2015). Some happiness coaches assign people to perform a daily "random act of kindness" and to record the results.

Martin E. P. Seligman "The main purpose of a positive psychology is to measure, understand, and then build the human strengths and the civic virtues."

Courtesy of Martin Seligman

Positive Psychology

Psychologist William James was writing about the importance of happiness ("the secret motive for all [we] do") as early as 1902. By the 1960s, the *humanistic psychologists* were interested in advancing human fulfillment. In the twenty-first century, under the leadership of American Psychological Association past-president Martin Seligman, **positive psychology** is using scientific methods to study human flourishing. This rapidly growing subfield includes studies of **subjective well-being**. One ongoing longitudinal study is following 240,000 people in 24 countries to understand the key elements in human experience that help us thrive and feel a greater sense of purpose and meaning (VanderWeele, 2021).

Taken together, satisfaction with the past, happiness with the present, and optimism about the future define the positive psychology movement's first pillar: *positive well-being.*

Positive psychology is about building not just a pleasant life, says Seligman, but also a good life that engages one's skills, and a meaningful life that points beyond oneself.

Thus, the second pillar, *positive traits*, focuses on exploring and enhancing creativity, courage, compassion, integrity, self-control, leadership, wisdom, and spirituality. Happiness is a by-product of a pleasant, engaged, and meaningful life.

The third pillar, *positive groups, communities, and cultures*, seeks to foster a positive social world. This includes healthy families, supportive neighborhoods, effective schools, socially responsible media, and civil dialogue.

"Positive psychology," Seligman and colleagues have said (2005), "is an umbrella term for the study of positive emotions, positive character traits, and enabling institutions." Its focus differs from psychology's traditional interests in understanding and alleviating negative states—abuse and anxiety, depression and disease, prejudice and poverty. (Psychology articles published since 1887 mentioning "depression" still outnumber those mentioning "happiness" by about 16 to 1.) The positive psychology movement has gained strength, with supporters in more than 100 countries (IPPA, 2022). Worldwide, centers such as the Greater Good Science Center in Berkeley, California, support the science of thriving and happiness.

adaptation-level phenomenon our tendency to form judgments (of sounds, of lights, of income) relative to a neutral level defined by our prior experience.

When Are We Happiest?

LOQ 38-4 How do time, wealth, adaptation, and comparison affect our happiness levels?

So, happiness matters. But what factors influence when people are happiest? For example, are some days of the week happier than others? One social psychologist (Kramer, 2010) did a *naturalistic observation* of emotion words in billions (!) of Facebook posts. He tracked the frequency of people's positive and negative emotion words by day of the week. The days with the most positive moods? Friday and Saturday (**FIGURE 38.3**). Similar analyses of questionnaire responses and 59 million Twitter messages found Friday, Saturday, and Sunday to be the week's happiest days (Golder & Macy, 2011; Helliwell & Wang, 2015; Young & Lim, 2014). For you, too?

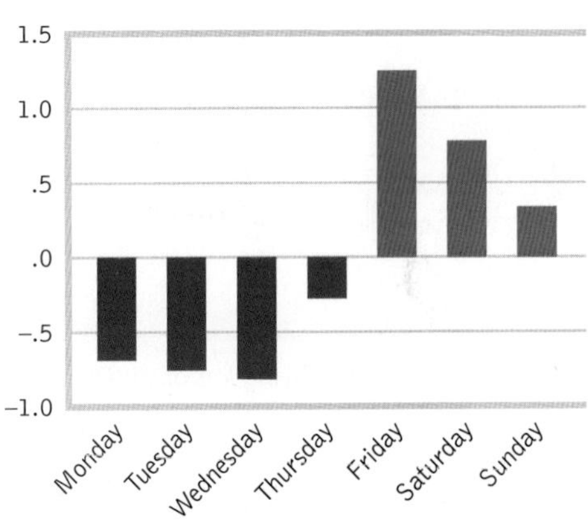
Happiness factor
1.5
1.0
.5
.0
–.5
–1.0
Monday
Tuesday
Wednesday
Thursday
Friday
Saturday
Sunday

FIGURE 38.3
Emotion notification A pattern emerged in tracked positive and negative emotion words in many "billions" (the exact number is proprietary information) of status updates of U.S. Facebook users over a 3-year period (Kramer, 2010).

Positive emotions also tend to rise in the early to middle part of most days, and they tend to decline later in the day (Kahneman et al., 2004; Watson, 2000). So, too, with day-to-day moods. A stressor—an argument, a bad test grade, a car problem—triggers a bad mood. No surprise there. But by the next day, the gloom nearly always lifts (Affleck et al., 1994; Bolger et al., 1989; Stone & Neale, 1984). Our overall judgments of our lives often show lingering effects of good or bad events, but our daily moods typically rebound (Luhmann et al., 2012). If anything, people tend to bounce back from a bad day to a *better-than-usual* good mood the following day. Sadness helps us appreciate happiness. The surprising reality: *We overestimate the duration of our emotions and underestimate our resiliency and capacity to adapt.* (As one who inherited hearing loss with a trajectory toward that of my mother, who spent the last 13 years of her life completely deaf, I [DM] take heart from these findings.)

Our current happiness is also shaped by our recent experience. Psychologist Harry Helson (1898–1977) identified this **adaptation-level phenomenon**: We judge new events by comparing them with our past experiences. Our past experiences define neutral levels—sounds that seem neither loud nor soft, temperatures that seem neither hot nor cold, events that seem neither pleasant nor unpleasant. We then notice and react to variations up or down from these levels. Have you noticed how a chilly fall day, after summer, feels colder than the same temperature in late winter?

People who have experienced a recent windfall—from the lottery, an inheritance, or a surging economy—typically feel joy and satisfaction (Diener & Oishi, 2000; Gardner & Oswald, 2007; Lindqvist et al., 2020). You would, too, if you woke up tomorrow with all your wishes granted—perhaps a world with no bills, no ills, and perfect grades? But eventually, you would adapt to this new normal. Before long, you would again sometimes feel joy and satisfaction (when events exceed your expectations), sometimes feel let down (when they fall below), and sometimes feel neither up nor down. *The point to remember*: Feelings of satisfaction and dissatisfaction, success and failure are based partly on expectations formed by our recent experience (Rutledge et al., 2014).

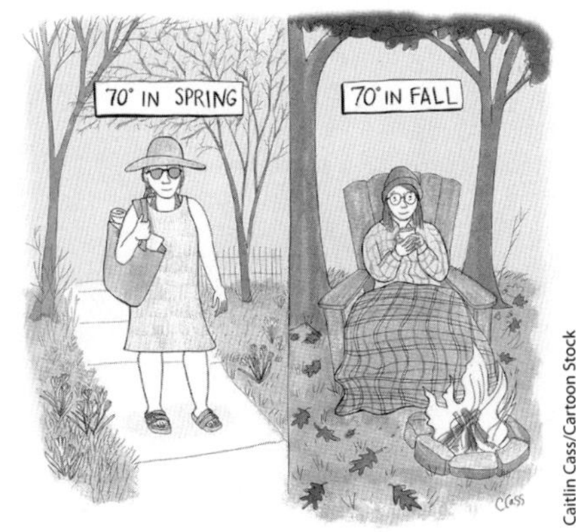
70° IN SPRING
70° IN FALL

Caitlin Cass/Cartoon Stock

What Predicts Happiness?

LOQ 38-5 What predicts happiness, and how can we be happier?

Happy people share many characteristics (**TABLE 38.1**). But what makes one person filled with joy, day after day, while others seem dark or aloof? Here, as in so many other areas, the answer is found in the interplay between nature and nurture.

Genes matter. In one analysis of over 55,000 identical and fraternal twins, 36 percent of the differences among people's happiness ratings was heritable—attributable to genes (Bartels, 2015). Even identical twins raised apart have similar happiness levels. The challenging quest for specific genes that influence happiness confirms a familiar lesson: Human traits are influenced by many genes having small effects (Røysamb & Nes, 2019).

Matthew Diffee/Cartoon Stock

"Have you ever tried buying lots of stuff?"

But our personal history and our culture matter, too. Values vary; one group's recipe for happiness might differ from another group's. Self-esteem matters more in Western cultures, which value individualism. Social acceptance and harmony matter more in communal cultures, such as Japan, that stress family and community (Diener et al., 2003; Fulmer et al., 2010; Uchida & Kitayama, 2009). In East Asia, most people prefer a "calm" to an "exciting" life (Crabtree & Lai, 2021).

Depending on our genes, outlook, and recent experiences, our happiness seems to fluctuate around a "happiness set point," which disposes some people to be more upbeat and others, more negative. Even so, our satisfaction with life can change (Sheldon & Lyubomirsky, 2021). Happiness rises and falls, and we can control some of what makes us more or less happy on a given day or in a given situation.

Your happiness, like your cholesterol level, is partially shaped by genetics. Yet as cholesterol is also influenced by diet and exercise, some of your happiness is under your personal control (Nes, 2010; Sin & Lyubomirsky, 2009). See **TABLE 38.2** for some research-based suggestions to build your personal strengths and increase your happiness and well-being.

If we can enhance our happiness on an *individual* level, could we use happiness research to refocus our *collective* priorities? Psychologists believe we could. Thanks to information resources such as the Gallup World Poll, researchers can track human happiness and misery over time (2021 was the unhappiest year of the past two decades). Many political leaders are also making use of such research: 43 nations have begun measuring their citizens' well-being, and many have undertaken interventions to boost national well-being (Diener et al., 2015, 2019). Britain's Annual Population Survey, for example, asks its citizens how satisfied they are with their lives, how worthwhile they judge their lives, and how happy and how anxious they felt yesterday (ONS, 2018).

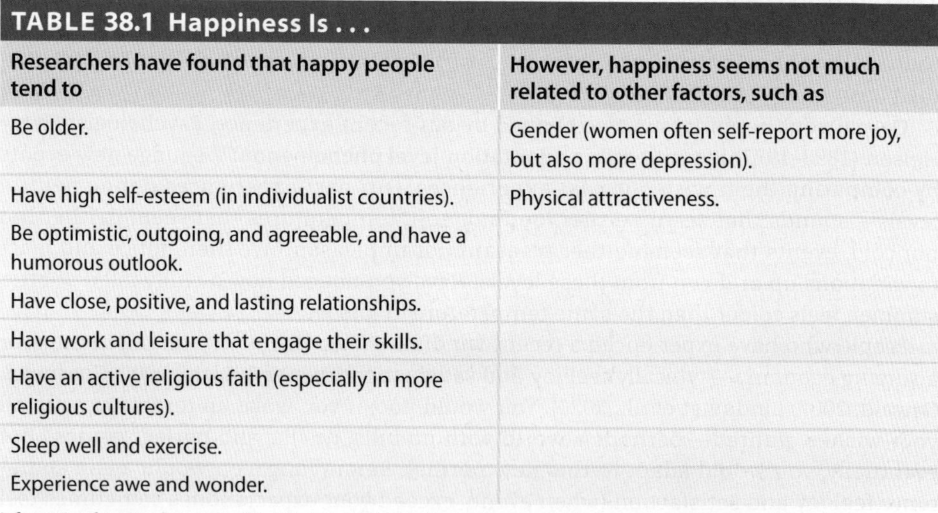

TABLE 38.1 Happiness Is . . .

Researchers have found that happy people tend to	However, happiness seems not much related to other factors, such as
Be older.	Gender (women often self-report more joy, but also more depression).
Have high self-esteem (in individualist countries).	Physical attractiveness.
Be optimistic, outgoing, and agreeable, and have a humorous outlook.	
Have close, positive, and lasting relationships.	
Have work and leisure that engage their skills.	
Have an active religious faith (especially in more religious cultures).	
Sleep well and exercise.	
Experience awe and wonder.	

Information from Anglim et al., 2020; Bai et al., 2021; Batz-Barbarich et al., 2018; Carstensen et al., 2011; De Neve & Cooper, 1998; Diener et al., 2003, 2011; Headey et al., 2010; Lucas et al., 2004; Lyubomirsky, 2013; Myers, 1993, 2000; Myers & Diener, 1995, 1996; Newport, 2022; Steel et al., 2008. Veenhoven, 2014, 2015 offers a database of 13,000+ correlates of happiness at WorldDatabaseofHappiness.eur.nl

TABLE 38.2 Evidence-Based Suggestions for a Happier Life

- ***Take control of your time.*** Happy people feel in control of their lives and less time-stressed (Whillans, 2019). Too little time is stressful; too much is boring. So, set goals and divide them into manageable daily aims. We all tend to overestimate how much we will accomplish in any given day, but the good news is that we generally *underestimate* how much we can accomplish in a year, given just a little daily progress.
- ***Label your feelings.*** Research shows that people who chose a word that fit their feelings actually felt more positive and less negative (Vlasenko et al., 2021). So, label your feelings. We can often find our way into a happier state of mind by understanding what we are feeling.
- ***Seek work and leisure that engage your skills.*** Happy people often are in a zone called *flow*—absorbed in tasks that challenge but don't overwhelm them. Passive forms of leisure (streaming movies and television shows) often provide less flow experience than exercising, socializing, or expressing artistic interests.
- ***Seek experiences rather than things.*** For those who are not struggling financially, money buys more happiness when spent on experiences—especially socially shared experiences—that you look forward to, enjoy, remember, and talk about (Caprariello & Reis, 2013; Kumar & Gilovich, 2013, 2015; J. C. Lee et al., 2018). As pundit Art Buchwald said, "The best things in life aren't things."
- ***Join the "movement" movement.*** Aerobic exercise not only promotes health and energy, it also helps relieve mild depression (McIntyre et al., 2020; Willis et al., 2018). Researchers have found that certain kinds of body movement while exercising, such as reaching our arms up or bouncing to a beat, may be especially good at elevating feelings of joy (McGonigal, 2019; Shafir et al., 2013). Sound minds often reside in sound bodies.
- ***Give your body the sleep it wants.*** Happy people live active lives yet reserve time for renewing, refreshing sleep. Sleep debt results in fatigue, diminished alertness, poor physical health, and gloomy moods. If you sleep now, you'll smile later.
- ***Give priority to close relationships.*** Compared with unhappy people, happy people engage in more meaningful conversations (Milek et al., 2018). Resolve to nurture your closest relationships by *not* taking your loved ones for granted: Give them the sort of kindness and affirmation you give others. Relationships matter.
- ***Focus and find meaning beyond self.*** Reach out to those in need. Perform acts of kindness. Happiness increases helpfulness, but doing good for others also fills us with happiness, meaning, and purpose (Kumar & Epley, 2022). And meaning matters mightily: A meaningful life is often a long, active, and healthy life (Alimujiang et al., 2019; Hooker & Masters, 2018).
- ***Challenge your negative thinking.*** Remind yourself that a disappointment today may not seem like that big a deal in a month, or a year.
- ***Count your blessings and record your gratitude.*** Keeping a gratitude journal heightens well-being (Davis et al., 2016). Take time to savor positive experiences and achievements, and to appreciate why they occurred (Sheldon & Lyubomirsky, 2012). Share your gratitude with others and prepare for smiles all around (Dickens, 2017; Kumar & Epley, 2018).
- ***Nurture your spiritual self.*** Relaxation and meditation help us stay emotionally steady. And for many people, faith provides a support community, a reason to focus beyond self, and a sense of purpose and hope. That helps explain why, worldwide, people active in faith communities report greater-than-average happiness and often cope well with crises (Pew, 2019).
- ***Take an "awe walk."*** Experiencing a sense of awe or wonder can reduce stress and increase well-being (Bai et al., 2021; Sturm et al., 2020). Taking a 15-minute outdoor awe walk can help you appreciate the presence of something bigger than yourself.

Happy societies are not only prosperous, but also places where people trust one another, feel free, and enjoy close relationships (Helliwell et al., 2013; Oishi & Schimmack, 2010). This knowledge may guide nations toward policies that decrease stress, foster human flourishing, and promote "the pursuit of happiness." Debates about economic inequality, tax rates, divorce laws, parental leave, health care, and city planning can all consider people's psychological well-being.

nortonrsx/iStock/Getty Images

Experiencing awe in nature improves well-being.

Questioning Some Myths About Happiness

People believe many myths about happiness. Let's review the most common and see what the science has to say.

DOES MONEY BUY US HAPPINESS? Would you be happier if you made more money? How important is "Being very well off financially"? "Very important" or "essential," say 84 percent of entering U.S. college students (Stolzenberg et al., 2019). But *can* money buy happiness?

Personal income predicts happiness—but the more you have, the more it takes to raise your happiness. Having enough money to eat, to feel control over your life, and to occasionally treat yourself to something special predicts greater happiness (Fischer & Boer, 2011; Ruberton et al., 2016). This is especially true for people during their midlife working years (Cheung & Lucas, 2015). But money's power to buy happiness also depends on your current income. Although nearly everyone welcomes more money, a $3000 wage increase does much more for someone making $30,000 per year than for someone making $300,000 (Killingsworth, 2021).

Those living in countries where most people have a secure livelihood tend to be happier than those living in very low-income countries (Diener & Tay, 2015). Money may not buy happiness, but extreme poverty often means misery, which can be lessened by more fairly distributed economic growth (Roser, 2021). Once we have enough money for comfort and security, however, we reach an "income satiation" point beyond which piling up more and more matters less and less (Donnelly et al., 2018; Jebb et al., 2018).

Economic growth in higher-income countries has provided no apparent boost to people's morale or social well-being. Since the late 1950s, the average U.S. citizen's buying power has almost tripled, and with it came new home entertainment systems, safer cars, fresh fruit in winter, and easy information access. Did it also buy more happiness? As **FIGURE 38.4** shows, Americans have become no happier. In 1957, some 35 percent said they were "very happy," as did slightly fewer—31 percent—in 2018 (and 19 percent during the Covid pandemic in 2021). The same thing happened in China and India, where living standards have risen but happiness and life satisfaction have not (Easterlin & O'Connor, 2020). The good life is not the goods life.

Extreme inequality is socially toxic. Why has economic growth not made us happier? Economic growth has been accompanied by rising *inequality*, which, across time and place, predicts unhappiness (Cheung & Lucas, 2016; Graafland & Lous, 2019). In countries such as the United States, China, and India, the last half-century's rising economic tide has lifted the yachts faster than the rowboats (Hasell, 2018). In countries and states with greater inequality, people with lower incomes tend to experience more physical, emotional, and social problems than they do in places with less inequality (Payne, 2017; Sommet et al., 2018; Vyas et al., 2022). One study following over 40,000 Canadian children found that those experiencing poverty had greater odds of having asthma and a psychological disorder, and were less ready for school (Roos et al., 2019).

Thus, the more unequal a country's income, the more money predicts happiness (Macchia, 2020; Quispe-Torreblanca et al., 2021). Across the world, we seem to understand that extreme inequality is socially toxic. Regardless of their political party, most

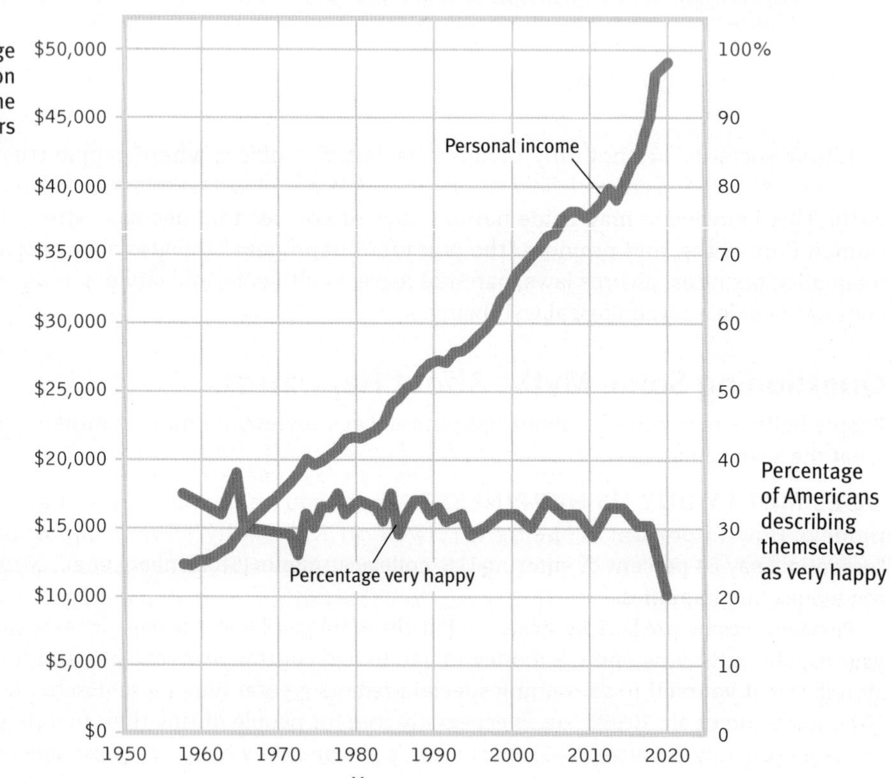

Average per-person after-tax income in 2012 dollars
$50,000
$45,000
$40,000
$35,000
$30,000
$25,000
$20,000
$15,000
$10,000
$5,000
$0
100%
90
80
70
60
50
40
30
20
10
0
Personal income
Percentage very happy
Percentage of Americans describing themselves as very happy
1950
1960
1970
1980
1990
2000
2010
2020
Year

FIGURE 38.4
Money didn't buy happiness
(Happiness data from National Opinion Research Center surveys; income data from *Historical Statistics of the United States and Economic Indicators.*)

people say they would prefer smaller pay gaps between people with high incomes and people with low incomes (Arsenio, 2018; Kiatpongsan & Norton, 2014).

Ironically, in every culture, those who strive hardest for wealth have tended to live with lower well-being, especially when they seek money to prove themselves, gain power, or show off rather than support their families (Donnelly et al., 2016; Niemiec et al., 2009; Srivastava et al., 2001). Those who instead strive for intimacy, personal growth, and community contribution experience a higher quality of life (Kasser, 2018; Ward et al., 2020).

The bottom line: Money by itself does not *buy* happiness, but if you spend it on others in ways that promote kindness, it can *predict* happiness.

relative deprivation the perception that we are worse off relative to those with whom we compare ourselves.

IS OUR HAPPINESS INDEPENDENT OF OTHERS? Are you happy? Many people, especially those from individualist cultures, believe our happiness is independent of others. "If you want to live a happy life, tie it to a goal, not to people," advised Albert Einstein.

Yet the reality is that we are social animals. We often compare ourselves to others—our looks, our achievements, and our happiness. Whether we feel good or bad depends on our perception of just how successful those others are (Lyubomirsky, 2001). Most new university students perceive their peers as more socially connected, which diminishes their well-being and makes it harder to form friendships (Whillans et al., 2017; Zell et al., 2018). Across many studies, people ranging from mall shoppers to online respondents have perceived others' social lives as more active than their own (Deri et al., 2017). Do such social comparisons—which social media may encourage—leave you, too, feeling like your life is a bit dull and unromantic compared to that of your friends? If so, you likely are experiencing **relative deprivation**.

Students tend to have a higher academic self-concept if they attend a school where most other students are not exceptionally able (Marsh et al., 2020, 2021). If you were near the top of your graduating class, you might feel inferior or discouraged upon entering a college or university where all students were near the top of their class. As Theodore Roosevelt reportedly observed, "Comparison is the thief of joy."

When expectations soar above attainments, we feel disappointed. Worldwide, life satisfaction suffers when people with low incomes compare themselves to those with higher incomes (Macchia et al., 2020). One analysis of 2.4 million participants in 357 studies found that happiness depended less on actual financial success than on how participants *compared* themselves financially to their peers (Tan et al., 2020). As British philosopher Bertrand Russell (1930/1985) noted, "Napoleon envied Caesar, Caesar envied Alexander, and Alexander, I daresay, envied Hercules, who never existed. You cannot, therefore, get away from envy by means of success alone, for there will always be in history or legend some person even more successful than you are" (pp. 68–69).

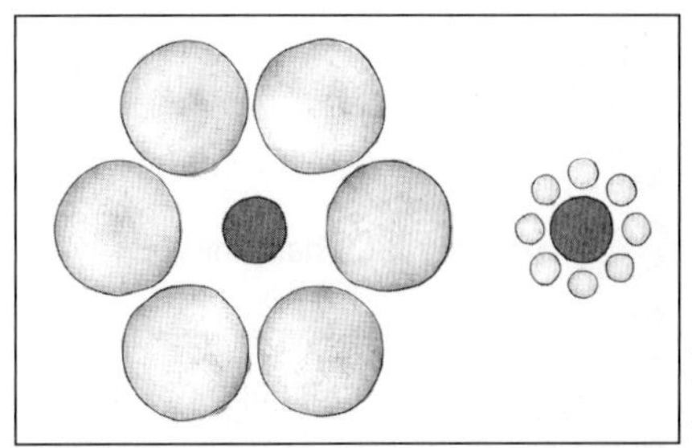

Adam Sacks

"Two dark circles that are the same size.
or
Would I be happier if i had less successful friends?"

Relative deprivation Comparing ourselves with more successful others, we feel diminished; comparing ourselves with those who are worse off, we feel contented. How does the cartoon illustrate this *relative deprivation* principle?

Just as comparing ourselves with those who are better off creates envy, so counting our blessings as we compare ourselves with those worse off boosts our contentment. In one study, when mildly depressed people read about someone who was even more depressed, they felt somewhat better (Gibbons, 1986). "I cried because I had no shoes," states a Persian saying, "until I met a man who had no feet."

MUST BAD EVENTS CAUSE LONG-TERM UNHAPPINESS? Extremely stressful events—the loss of a spouse or a job—can drag us down for a long time (Infurna & Luthar, 2016). But eventually, most bad moods end. We may feel that our heart has broken during a romantic breakup, but in time the wound heals. In one study, faculty members up for tenure expected a negative decision would deflate their lives. Actually, 5 to 10 years later, their happiness level was about the same as for those who received tenure (Gilbert et al., 1998).

Grief over the loss of a loved one or anxiety after a severe trauma can linger. But tragedy and trauma are usually not permanently depressing. People who become blind or paralyzed may not completely recover their previous well-being, but many—especially those with an agreeable personality—eventually approach their prior levels of day-to-day happiness (Bonanno, 2004; Boyce & Wood, 2011; Hall et al., 1999). Although the 9/11 terrorist attacks and Covid-19 pandemic caused widespread immediate distress, a year later many people had returned to their baseline levels of happiness (Aknin et al., 2021). "Distress is a normal reaction to mass tragedy," said psychologist George Bonanno (2021), "but so is a relatively prompt climb back to good mental health." In the poetry of an ancient Psalm, "Weeping may linger for the night, but joy comes with the morning."

Think back to some significant event that either elated or depressed you. How long did your extreme emotions last before returning to more typical levels?

Bonanno (2021) told the story of Jed, who lost his leg when he was run over by a garbage truck. Despite this traumatic accident and the challenges he faced adapting to life with

resilience the personal strength that helps people cope with stress and recover from adversity and even trauma.

one less limb, Jed demonstrated **resilience**. After recovery, he returned to being a happy person whose endless optimism could light up a room. Overcoming serious setbacks, as Jed did, can even foster a deeper sense of life's purpose and meaning (Seery, 2011).

ASK YOURSELF

Were you surprised by any of the findings related to happiness? How might you increase your happiness?

RETRIEVAL PRACTICE

RP-2 Which of the following factors does *not* predict self-reported happiness?

a. Age
b. Personality traits
c. Sleep and exercise
d. Active religious faith

ANSWERS IN APPENDIX E

MODULE 38 REVIEW Experiencing Emotion

LEARNING OBJECTIVES

Test Yourself Answer these repeated Learning Objective Questions on your own (before "showing" the answers here, or checking the answers in Appendix D) to improve your retention of the concepts (McDaniel et al., 2009, 2015).

LOQ 38-1 What are some of the basic emotions?

LOQ 38-2 What are the causes and consequences of anger?

LOQ 38-3 What is happiness? Why does happiness matter?

LOQ 38-4 How do time, wealth, adaptation, and comparison affect our happiness levels?

LOQ 38-5 What predicts happiness, and how can we be happier?

TERMS AND CONCEPTS TO REMEMBER

Test Yourself Write down the definition in your own words, then check your answer.

happiness, p. 434
feel-good, do-good phenomenon, p. 434
positive psychology, p. 434
subjective well-being, p. 434
adaptation-level phenomenon, p. 435
relative deprivation, p. 439
resilience, p. 440

MODULE TEST

Test Yourself Answer the following questions on your own first, then "show" the answers here, or check your answers in Appendix E.

1. One of the most consistent findings of psychological research is that happy people are also
a. more likely to express anger.
b. generally luckier than others.
c. concentrated in the wealthier nations.
d. more likely to help others.

2. ________________ psychology is a scientific field of study focused on how humans thrive and flourish.

3. After moving to a new apartment, you find the street noise irritatingly loud, but after a while it no longer bothers you. This reaction illustrates the
a. relative deprivation principle.
b. adaptation-level phenomenon.
c. feel-good, do-good phenomenon.
d. catharsis principle.

4. There will always be someone more successful, more accomplished, or more popular with whom to compare ourselves. In psychology, this phenomenon is referred to as the ________________ ________________ principle.

MODULE 39 Stress and Illness

"It's killing me inside. I'm kind of broken. I'm broken. And my colleagues are broken. And people say, 'It's not that big a deal.' And I want to take them by the collar and say you don't know what you're talking about. Come see my world." So explained Montana nurse Joey Traywick (2020), choking back tears while his hospital's intensive care unit was overwhelmed with Covid patients.

When restricted from visiting, patients' loved ones also experienced deep distress. Such was witnessed by Nebraska nurse Antonia Brune (2021) as she accompanied a patient to life's finish line: "I could feel how my patient's three daughters were tormented by not being able to be there physically with their mom." Brune used an iPad to enable the daughters to spend "the whole night talking to their mother—sharing stories, laughter, tears, memories, and music." When their mother's breathing ceased, Brune recalled, "[the daughters] asked me, 'Could you touch her face?' I softly stroked her forehead. 'Could you touch her cheek?' I caressed her cheek. 'Could you hold her hand?' I took her hand. Her daughters gained peace from the sense that they were touching their mom, through me. We were all united in a beautiful, ephemeral moment—patient, family, and caregiver—as they said their final goodbyes."[1]

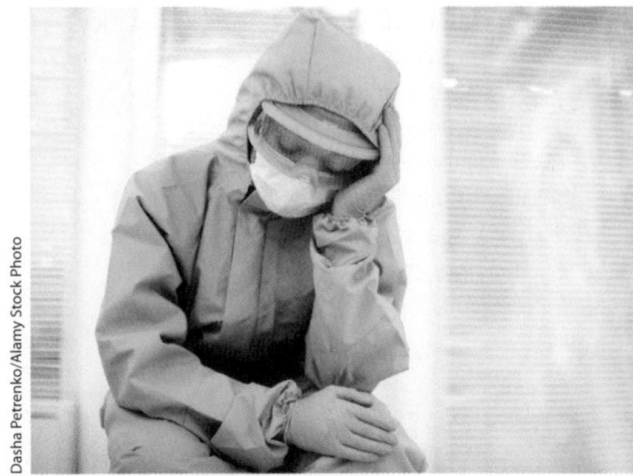
Dasha Petrenko/Alamy Stock Photo

Covid nursing stress

The Covid pandemic caused major stress: loss of loved ones, illness, fear of becoming ill, social isolation, job loss, and the upheaval of normal routines. How did you cope? The impact of Covid illustrates what this module explores: what causes stress, and how stress affects us.

To live is to experience stress. Worldwide, 41 percent of people reported experiencing "a lot of stress" the day before (Gallup, 2022). People from Afghanistan and Lebanon (74 percent) were the most stressed. Those from Uzbekistan and Kazakhstan were the least stressed (12 percent). People from the United States (52 percent) and Canada (49 percent) were about in the middle. A third of U.S. college students recently considered withdrawing from school, reported a Gallup survey—and 7 in 10 blamed emotional stress (Marken, 2022).

Some stresses we anticipate. An important exam is not an unexpected event, but it will still make you tense. Although well-intended, *trigger warnings* that alert people to possibly disturbing content do little to prevent distress, and may even increase anxiety (Bellet et al., 2020; Sanson et al., 2019). Even when trigger-warned about a literary passage describing an assault (and given the option of reading a neutral passage), 96 percent of students in one study chose to read the triggering passage. Two weeks later, the students (even those with preexisting posttraumatic stress disorder) showed no increased distress (Kimble et al., 2021).

Other stress strikes without warning. Imagine being 21-year-old Ben Carpenter, who experienced the world's wildest and fastest wheelchair ride. As he was crossing a highway intersection, the light changed, and a big truck moved into the intersection. When they bumped, Carpenter's wheelchair handles got stuck in the truck's grille. The driver, who hadn't seen Carpenter and couldn't hear his cries for help, took off down the highway, pushing the wheelchair at 50 miles per hour until, after two miles, passing police flagged down the truck. Meanwhile, Carpenter reacted to the loss of control: His heart raced, his hands sweated, and his breathing sped up. "It was very scary," he recalled.

Stress may be extreme but brief, as Carpenter experienced. It may be deep and prolonged, as Covid nurses Traywick and Brune endured. Ordinary life transitions and everyday hassles also cause stress and produce similar, though weaker, physical and psychological responses. And as we will see, stress—from the catastrophic to the everyday—can harm our health.

Stress: Some Basic Concepts

LOQ 39-1 How does our appraisal of an event affect our stress reaction, and what are the three main types of stressors?

Stress is a slippery concept. We sometimes use the word informally to describe threats or challenges ("Nurse Brune was under a lot of stress"), and at other times to describe our responses ("She felt very stressed"). Psychologists use more precise terms. The challenge or event (Brune's distressing time treating Covid patients) is a *stressor*. Her physical and emotional responses are a *stress reaction*. And the process by which she interpreted the threat was *stress*.

stress the process by which we perceive and respond to certain events, called *stressors*, that we appraise as threatening or challenging.

[1]Credit: Nebraska Nurses Association

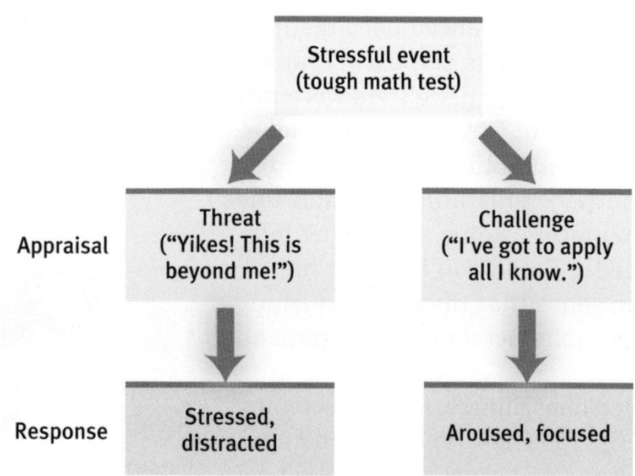
Stressful event
(tough math test)
Appraisal
Threat
("Yikes! This is beyond me!")
Challenge
("I've got to apply all I know.")
Response
Stressed, distracted
Aroused, focused

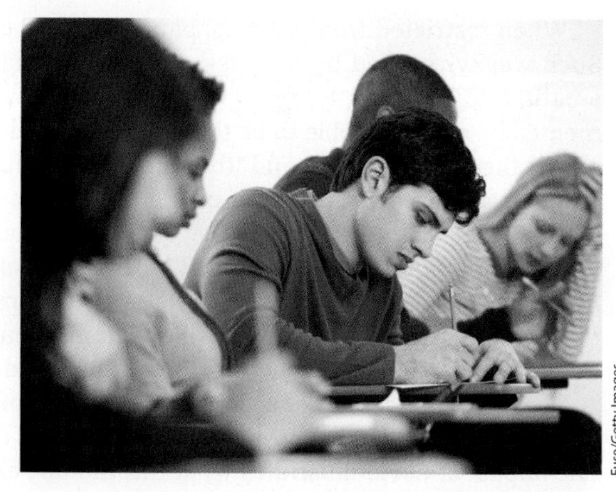
Fuse/Getty Images

FIGURE 39.1
Stress appraisal The events of our lives flow through a psychological filter. How we appraise an event influences how much stress we experience and how effectively we respond.

Stress often arises less from events themselves than from how we think about or *appraise* them (Lazarus, 1998). One person, alone in a house, ignores its creaking sounds and experiences no stress; another suspects an intruder and becomes alarmed. One person regards a difficult new class as a welcome challenge; another appraises it as risking failure (**FIGURE 39.1**). Once we've appraised an event as a stressor (the *primary appraisal*), we assess our ability to respond to it (the *secondary appraisal*).

When short-lived, or when perceived as challenges, stressors can have positive effects. Momentary stress can mobilize the immune system to fend off infections and heal wounds (Segerstrom, 2007). Stress also arouses and motivates us to conquer problems. In a Gallup World Poll, those who were stressed, but not depressed, reported being energized and satisfied with their lives. This is the opposite of the lethargy reported by those who were depressed, but not stressed (Ng & Feldman, 2009).

Championship athletes, successful entertainers, motivated students, and great teachers and leaders often thrive and excel when aroused by a challenge (Blascovich & Mendes, 2010; Z. Wang et al., 2015). When we think about our stress as being helpful to us, we show less cardiovascular stress and even attend less to negativity (Jamieson et al., 2012). In games and athletic contests, the stress of not knowing who will win makes the competition enjoyable (Abuhamdeh et al., 2015). Having conquered cancer or rebounded from a lost job, some people emerge with stronger self-esteem and a deepened spirituality and sense of purpose. Indeed, experiencing some stress builds *resilience—our* ability to adapt to, cope with, and rebound from life's challenges (Bonanno, 2021; Wu et al., 2019). When we experience hardship, we sometimes discover the hidden power of our talents and relationships (Nuñez et al., 2022; Schwartz et al., 2022). By teaching us how to cope with life's twists and turns, occasional stressors can even build a healthier immune system (Epel et al., 1998). Adversity can produce growth.

"Too many parents make life hard for their children by trying, too zealously, to make it easy for them." —German author Johann Wolfgang von Goethe (1749–1832)

But stress can also harm us. Stress can trigger risky decisions and unhealthy behaviors (Cohen et al., 2016; Starcke & Brand, 2016). And stress can affect health directly, by increasing infectious-disease-related illnesses and even deaths (Epel et al., 2004; Hamer et al., 2019). Those who endure extreme stress during pregnancy tend to have shorter pregnancies, which pose health risks for infants (Ding et al., 2021). What is your perceived stress level (**FIGURE 39.2**)?

So, there is an interplay between our head and our health. That isn't surprising: *Mind and body interact; everything psychological is simultaneously physiological.* Before exploring that interplay, let's look more closely at stressors and stress reactions.

Stressors—Things That Push Our Buttons

Stressors fall into three main types: catastrophes, significant life changes, and daily hassles (including social stress).

CATASTROPHES Catastrophes are large-scale disasters: think earthquakes, hurricanes, wildfires, wars. Their damage to emotional and physical health can be significant. In the four months after Hurricane Katrina in 2005, New Orleans' suicide rate tripled (Saulny, 2006). And in surveys taken in the three weeks after the 9/11 terrorist attacks,

Perceived Stress Scale

The questions in this scale ask about your feelings and thoughts *during the last month.* In each case, indicate how often you felt or thought a certain way.

0	1	2	3	4
Never	**Almost never**	**Sometimes**	**Fairly often**	**Very often**

In the last month...

1. ___ ...how often have you been upset because of something that happened unexpectedly?
2. ___ ...how often have you felt that you were unable to control the important things in your life?
3. ___ ...how often have you felt nervous and "stressed"?
4. ___ ...how often have you felt confident about your ability to handle your personal problems?
5. ___ ...how often have you felt that things were going your way?
6. ___ ...how often have you found that you could not cope with all the things you had to do?
7. ___ ...how often have you been able to control irritations in your life?
8. ___ ...how often have you felt that you were on top of things?
9. ___ ...how often have you been angered because of things that were outside of your control?
10. ___ ...how often have you felt difficulties were piling up so high that you could not overcome them?

SCORING:

- First, reverse your scores for questions 4, 5, 7, and 8.
  On these four questions, change the scores like this: 0 = 4, 1 = 3, 2 = 2, 3 = 1, 4 = 0.
- Next, add up your scores to get a **total score**.
- Scores range from 0 to 40, with higher scores indicating higher perceived stress.
- Scores ranging from 0-13 would be considered *low perceived stress.*
- Scores ranging from 14-26 would be considered *moderate perceived stress.*
- Scores ranging from 27-40 would be considered *high perceived stress.*

Scale data from Cohen, S., Kamarck, T., & Mermelstein, R. (1983). A global measure of perceived stress. *Journal of Health and Social Behavior, 24,* 385-396.

FIGURE 39.2
Perceived Stress Scale

58 percent of Americans said they were experiencing greater-than-average arousal and anxiety (Silver et al., 2002). People were especially likely to report such symptoms in the New York City area, and sleeping pill prescriptions rose by 28 percent (HMHL, 2002; NSF, 2001). Worldwide, a similar uptick in anxiety and depression occurred during the initial months of the Covid pandemic (Aknin et al., 2022).

For those who respond to catastrophes, the stress may be twofold. The trauma of uprooting and family separation may combine with the challenges of adjusting to a new culture's language, ethnicity, and social norms (Pipher, 2002). Newcomers often feel marginalized and experience culture shock, leading to stress-related inflammation (Gonzales et al., 2018; Scholaske et al., 2018). This *acculturative stress* can decline over time, especially when people engage in meaningful activities and connect socially (Bostean & Gillespie, 2017; Kim et al., 2012).

SIGNIFICANT LIFE CHANGES Life transitions—leaving home, having a loved one die, taking on student debt, losing a job, getting divorced—are often keenly felt. Even happy transitions, such as graduating or getting married, can be stressful. Many stresses peak during adolescence and young adulthood: A massive Canadian survey investigating people's responses to difficult problems revealed that adolescents struggled the most (Statistics Canada, 2019). In another survey, nearly two-thirds of U.S. 15- to 29-year-olds—but less than half of those over 50—reported experiencing stress during "a lot of the day yesterday" (Ray, 2019).

Some psychologists study the health effects of life changes by following people over time. Others compare the life challenges previously endured by those who have (or have not) experienced a health problem, such as a heart attack. In such studies, recently widowed, fired, or divorced people have been more vulnerable to disease (Dohrenwend et al., 1982; Sbarra et al., 2015; Strully, 2009). One Finnish study of 96,000 widowed people found that the survivor's

A hurricane of stress and destruction
Hurricane Ian raged across Florida in 2022, killing more than 100 people and destroying the homes and possessions of thousands more. Alice Pujols (shown here) survived the storm but her home was destroyed. "I'm trying to make it to the next day," she said. "That's all I can do. It's really depressing" (Calvan & Melley, 2022).

Marta Lavandier/AP Photo

approach and avoidance motives the drive to move toward (approach) or away from (avoid) a stimulus.

risk of death doubled in the week following a partner's death (Kaprio et al., 1987). A cluster of crises—losing a job, home, and partner—puts one at even greater risk.

DAILY HASSLES AND SOCIAL STRESS Events don't have to remake our lives to cause stress. Stress also comes from *daily hassles*—aggravating housemates, incessant social media notifications, bumper-to-bumper traffic, and overflowing to-do lists (Lazarus, 1990; Pascoe & Richman, 2009; Ruffin, 1993). We might have to give a speech or do difficult math problems (Dickerson & Kemeny, 2004; Meier et al., 2022; **FIGURE 39.3**).

Some people shrug off such hassles; others cannot. Daily pressures can become especially toxic when they are serious and ongoing. Chronic workplace stress can cause worker "burnout"—feeling ineffective, emotionally depleted, and disconnected (Guthier et al., 2020). Others may wake up each day facing housing problems, unreliable child care, budgets that won't stretch to the next payday, physical or emotional challenges, or poor health. Such daily hassles can harm physical health years later—and even shorten life (Chiang et al., 2018; Leger et al., 2022).

Daily pressures may be compounded by social stressors, such as prejudice. Like other stressors, prejudice can have significant psychological and physical consequences (Michaels et al., 2022; Pascoe et al., 2022). Thinking that some of the people you encounter each day will dislike, distrust, or doubt you is a toxic stressor. Many transgender and gender-nonconforming people experience the stress of stigma and discrimination (Valentine & Shipherd, 2018). People with a same-sex sexual orientation who face frequent prejudice in their communities have died, on average, 12 years earlier than have those who live in more accepting communities (Hatzenbueler, 2014). For many Black Americans, the stress of racial discrimination can lead to unhealthy blood pressure and insulin levels and inflammation (Ajilore & Thames; 2020; Brody et al., 2018; Lawrence et al., 2022). Black Americans who have experienced police brutality are also at greater risk of depression, anxiety, and heart disease (Alang et al., 2022; Freedman et al., 2022).

Stress also arises from the daily conflicts we face between our different **approach and avoidance motives** (Hovland & Sears, 1938; Lewin, 1935). Least stressful are the

FIGURE 39.3
Studying stress Most people experience stress when giving a public speech. To study stress, researchers re-create this type of situation. At the end, they *debrief* and reassure each participant.

1. Participants chew gum so that collecting saliva is easy. The researcher takes a saliva sample from each participant at the beginning of the experiment to measure levels of the stress hormone *cortisol*.

What is 1223 minus 37?

2. Participant gives simulated job interview speech to a critical panel. Next, the participant is asked to complete difficult math problems out loud.

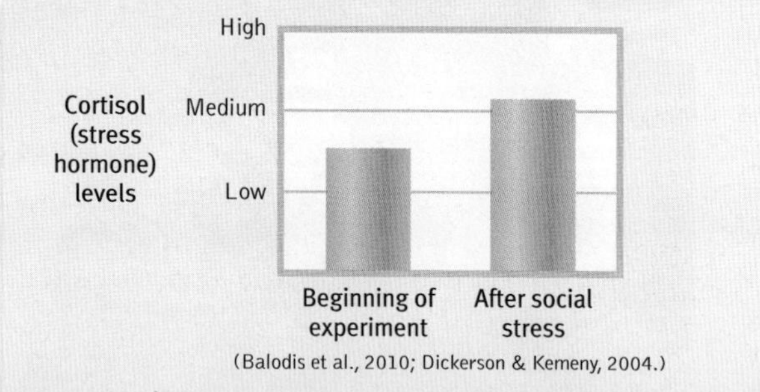
High
Medium
Low
Cortisol (stress hormone) levels
Beginning of experiment
After social stress
(Balodis et al., 2010; Dickerson & Kemeny, 2004.)

3. Measuring cortisol in participants' saliva before and after tells us that although they enter the lab experiencing some stress, that level goes up 40 percent after they experience social stress.

THANK YOU!

4. Research team thanks and *debriefs* the participant—explaining the purpose of the experiment and the role she played.

approach-approach conflicts, in which two attractive but incompatible options pull us—to choose tacos or pizza, a dance or music class, the green or the gray hoodie. Other times, we face an *avoidance-avoidance* conflict between two undesirable alternatives. Do you avoid studying a disliked subject, or avoid failure by doing your reading? Do you suffer someone's wrath for admitting the truth, or feelings of guilt for having lied?

In times of *approach-avoidance* conflict, we feel simultaneously attracted and repelled. You may enjoy your job but dislike its lack of remote work flexibility. From a distance, the goal—making a good living—looks appealing. But as you approach that goal, your avoidance tendency may begin to overtake your approach tendency and you feel an urge to escape. Stepping back, the negative aspects fade, and you again feel attracted. Stress multiplies when we face several approach-avoidance conflicts simultaneously—where to work, which courses to take, whom to date.

The Stress Response System

LOQ 39-2 How do we respond and adapt to stress?

Medical interest in stress began with Hippocrates (460–377 B.C.E.). Centuries later, Walter Cannon (1929) confirmed that the stress response is part of a unified mind-body system. He observed that extreme cold, lack of oxygen, and emotion-arousing events all trigger an outpouring of the adrenal stress hormones epinephrine and norepinephrine. When alerted by any of a number of brain pathways, the sympathetic nervous system arouses us, preparing the body for the wonderfully adaptive response Cannon called the **fight-or-flight response**. It increases heart rate and breathing, diverts blood from digestion to the skeletal muscles for greater mobility, dulls feelings of pain, and releases sugar and fat from the body's energy stores. The sympathetic nervous system helps more with immediate or *acute* threats (a poisonous snake nearby) than with distant or looming threats (a climate apocalypse). By fighting or fleeing, we increase our chances of survival.

Since Cannon's time, physiologists have identified an additional stress response system. On orders from the cerebral cortex (via the hypothalamus and pituitary gland), the outer part of the adrenal glands secretes *glucocorticoid* stress hormones such as *cortisol*. The two systems work at different speeds, explained biologist Robert Sapolsky (2003): "In a fight-or-flight scenario, epinephrine is the one handing out guns; glucocorticoids are the ones drawing up blueprints for new aircraft carriers needed for the war effort." The epinephrine guns were firing at high speed during an experiment inadvertently conducted on a British Airways San Francisco to London flight. Three hours after takeoff, a mistakenly played message told passengers the plane was about to crash into the sea. Although the flight crew immediately recognized the error and tried to calm the terrified passengers, several required medical assistance (Associated Press, 1999).

Canadian scientist Hans Selye's (1936, 1976) 40 years of research on stress extended Cannon's findings. Selye's studies of animals' reactions to various stressors, such as electric shock and surgery, helped make stress a major concept in both psychology and medicine. Selye proposed that the body's adaptive response to stress is so general that, like a burglar alarm, it sounds, no matter what intrudes. He named this response the **general adaptation syndrome (GAS)**, which he saw as a three-phase process.

HOW IS YOUR TERROR TODAY?
1
2
3
4
5
Shhh. I am sleeping.
I am awake.
What?
WHAT?!?
WHAT?!?!

Roz Chast/Cartoon Stock

Let's say you're experiencing physical or emotional trauma:

- In *Phase 1*, you have an ***alarm reaction***, as your sympathetic nervous system is suddenly activated. Your heart rate zooms. Blood is diverted to your skeletal muscles. With your resources mobilized, you are now ready to fight back.
- During *Phase 2, **resistance***, your temperature, blood pressure, and respiration remain high. Your adrenal glands pump epinephrine and norepinephrine into your bloodstream. You are fully engaged, summoning all your resources to meet the challenge. As time passes, with no relief from stress, your body's reserves begin to dwindle.
- You have reached *Phase 3, **exhaustion***. With exhaustion, you become more vulnerable to illness or, in extreme cases, collapse and even death.

Selye's basic point: Although the human body copes well with temporary stress, prolonged stress can damage it. Syria's civil war, for example, has taken a toll on Syrians'

fight-or-flight response an emergency response, including activation of the sympathetic nervous system, that mobilizes energy and activity for attacking or escaping a threat.

general adaptation syndrome (GAS) Selye's concept of the body's adaptive response to stress in three phases—alarm, resistance, exhaustion.

Sultan Kitaz/Reuters/Newscom

Sebastiano Tomada/Getty Images

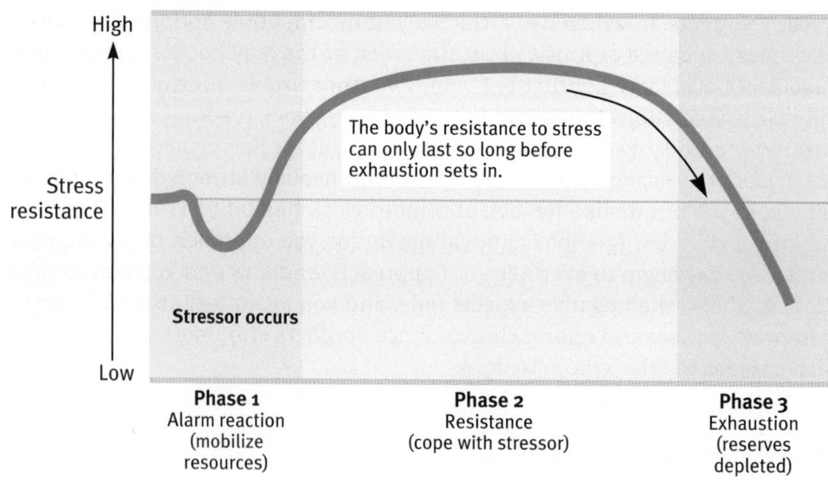
High
Stress resistance
Low
The body's resistance to stress can only last so long before exhaustion sets in.
Stressor occurs
Phase 1
Alarm reaction (mobilize resources)
Phase 2
Resistance (cope with stressor)
Phase 3
Exhaustion (reserves depleted)

FIGURE 39.4
Selye's general adaptation syndrome
Due to ongoing conflict, Syria's White Helmets (volunteer rescuers) were perpetually in "alarm reaction" mode, rushing to pull victims from the rubble after each fresh attack. As their resistance depleted, they risked exhaustion.

physical health and increased their risk for PTSD (Al Ibraheem et al., 2017; **FIGURE 39.4**). Severe childhood stress gets under the skin, leading to greater adult stress, sleeplessness, and heart disease (Jakubowski et al., 2018; Puterman et al., 2016; Talvitie et al., 2019). Some examples:

- In one 2-decade study, severely stressed Welsh children were three times more likely to develop heart disease as adults (Ashton et al., 2016).
- Black Americans who experience frequent racial discrimination develop shorter *telomeres*—DNA pieces protecting the chromosome ends (Chae et al., 2020). That helps explain why, compared with White Americans, Black Americans have a shorter life expectancy (CDC, 2020; Puterman et al., 2020).
- In studies of abused youth and stressed caregivers, those who were most stressed had cells that looked older than their chronological age (Nelles-McGee et al., 2022).

Severe stress ages people.

We respond to stress in other ways, too. One response is common after severe stress: Withdraw. Isolate. Conserve energy. Or act like a mouse, whose stressed-out brain induces them to recharge by taking a nap (Yu et al., 2022). (Do you also get sleepy when you're stressed?) Faced with an extreme disaster, such as a ship sinking, some people become paralyzed by fear. Another response, found among women more often than men, is to give and receive support—what's called the **tend-and-befriend response** (Lim & DeSteno, 2016; Taylor, 2006; von Dawans et al., 2019).

"We sleep afraid, we wake up afraid, and leave our homes afraid."—15-year-old girl's Facebook post, describing her family's daily life in war-torn Yemen (al-Asaadi, 2016).

Bring to mind a personal experience related to the Covid pandemic. What stressors affected you? What stress responses did you experience? How did you cope?

RETRIEVAL PRACTICE

RP-1 When alerted to a negative, uncontrollable event, our __________ nervous system arouses us. Heart rate and respiration __________ (increase/decrease). Blood is diverted from digestion to the skeletal __________. The body releases sugar and fat. All this prepares the body for the __________-__________-__________ response.

ANSWERS IN APPENDIX E

Stress and Vulnerability to Disease

LOQ 39-3 How does stress make us more vulnerable to disease?

It often pays to spend our resources in fighting or fleeing an external threat. But we do so at a cost. When stress is momentary, the cost is small. When stress persists, the cost may be greater, in the form of lowered resistance to infections and other threats to mental and physical well-being.

To study how stress—and healthy and unhealthy behaviors—influence health and illness, psychologists and physicians created the interdisciplinary field of *behavioral*

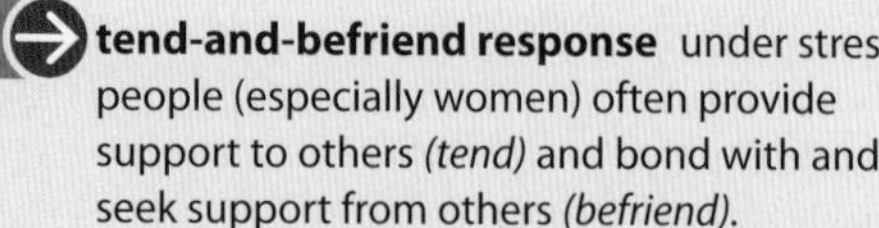

tend-and-befriend response under stress, people (especially women) often provide support to others *(tend)* and bond with and seek support from others *(befriend)*.

medicine, integrating behavioral and medical knowledge. **Health psychology** provides psychology's contribution to behavioral medicine. A branch of health psychology called **psychoneuroimmunology** focuses on mind-body interactions (Kiecolt-Glaser, 2009; Kipnis, 2018). This awkward name makes sense: Your thoughts and feelings *(psycho)* influence your brain *(neuro)*, which influences the endocrine hormones that affect your disease-fighting *immune* system. And this subfield is the study *(ology)* of those interactions.

If you've ever had a stress headache, or felt your blood pressure rise with anger, you know that our psychological states have physiological effects. Stress can even leave you less able to fight off disease because your nervous and endocrine systems influence your immune system (Sternberg, 2009). You can think of the immune system as a complex surveillance system. When it functions properly, it keeps you healthy by isolating and destroying bacteria, viruses, and other invaders. Four types of cells are active in these search-and-destroy missions (**FIGURE 39.5**).

Your age, nutrition, genetics, and stress level all influence your immune system's activity. When your immune system doesn't function properly, it can err in two directions:

1. ***Overreacting.*** The immune system may attack the body's own tissues, causing an allergic reaction or a self-attacking disease, such as lupus, multiple sclerosis, or some forms of arthritis. Women, who are immunologically stronger than men, are more susceptible to such *autoimmune diseases* (Nussinovitch & Schoenfeld, 2012; Schwartzman-Morris & Putterman, 2012).
2. ***Underreacting.*** The immune system may allow a bacterial infection to flare, a dormant virus to erupt, or cancer cells to multiply. To protect transplanted organs, which the recipient's body treats as foreign invaders, a patient's immune system may be deliberately suppressed.

Immune system suppression has been observed in animals stressed by physical restraints, unavoidable electric shocks, noise, crowding, cold water, social defeat, or separation from their mothers (Maier et al., 1994). One study monitored immune responses in 43 monkeys over 6 months (Cohen et al., 1992). Half were left in stable groups. The rest

London 2012
GOUCHER
London 2012
FLANAGAN
Streeter Lecka/Getty Images

Friendly foes Tending and befriending helped U.S. marathon rivals and good friends Kara Goucher and Shalane Flanagan cope with stress and excel. During the 2012 London Olympic Marathon, they battled intense rain and physical pain, finishing 1 second apart.

"I've stopped turning the telly on. I've had to because the news was making me ill." —U.K. nurse explaining how she coped with stress during the Covid pandemic (Kinsella et al., 2022).

Intruders!
Is it a bacterial infection?
Is it a cancer cell, virus, or other "foreign substance"?
Is it some other harmful intruder, or perhaps a worn-out cell needing to be cleaned up?
Are there diseased cells (such as those infected by viruses or cancer) that need to be cleared out?
Possible Responses:
Send in: *B lymphocytes,* which fight bacterial infections. (This one is shown in front of a macrophage.)
Send in: *T lymphocytes,* which attack cancer cells, viruses, and foreign substances.
Send in: *macrophage cells* ("big eaters"), which attack harmful invaders and worn-out cells. (This one is engulfing tuberculosis bacteria.)
Send in: *natural killer cells* (NK cells), which attack diseased cells. (These two are attacking a cancer cell.)
Romariolen/Shutterstock

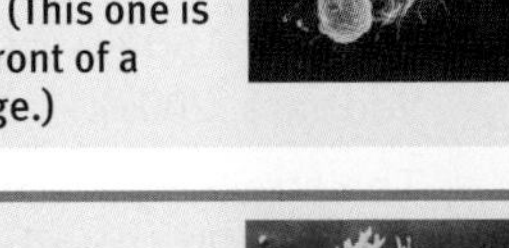
CNRI/Science Source

NIBSC/Science Source

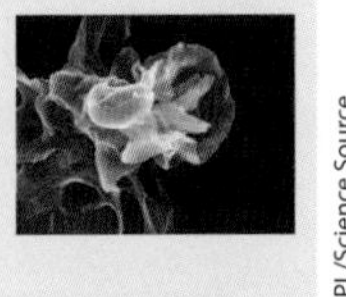
SPL/Science Source

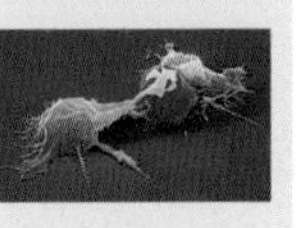
Eye of Science/Science Source

FIGURE 39.5
A simplified view of immune responses

health psychology a subfield of psychology that contributes to behavioral medicine.

psychoneuroimmunology the study of how psychological, neural, and endocrine processes together affect our immune system and resulting health.

FIGURE 39.6
Stress and colds People with the highest life stress scores were also most vulnerable when exposed to an experimentally delivered cold virus (Cohen et al., 1991).

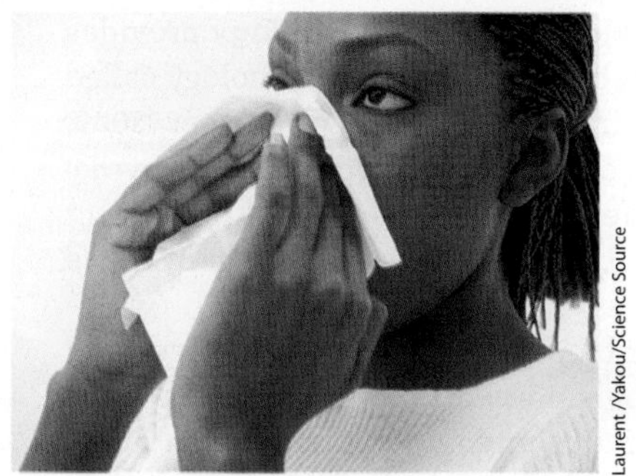
Laurent/Yakou/Science Source

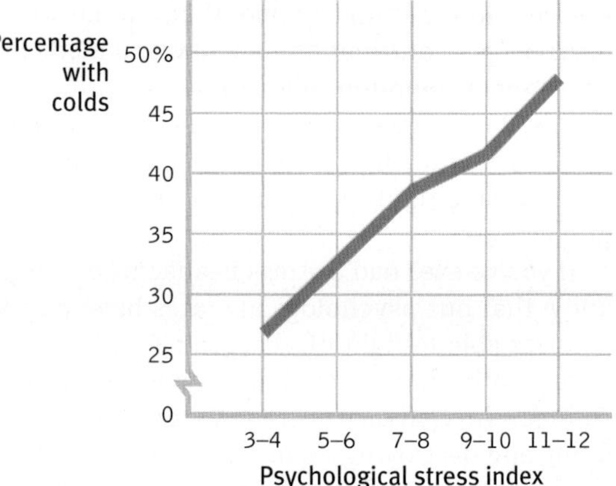
Percentage with colds
50%
45
40
35
30
25
0
3–4
5–6
7–8
9–10
11–12
Psychological stress index

were stressed by being housed with new roommates—three or four new monkeys each month. By the end of the experiment, the socially disrupted monkeys had weaker immune systems.

Human immune systems react similarly. Three examples:

- ***Surgical wounds heal more slowly in stressed people.*** In one experiment, dental students received punch wounds (precise small holes punched in the skin). Compared with wounds placed during summer vacation, those placed three days before a major exam healed 40 percent more slowly (Kiecolt-Glaser et al., 1998). In other studies, marriage conflict has also slowed punch-wound healing (Kiecolt-Glaser et al., 2005).
- ***Stressed people are more vulnerable to illness.*** Major life stress increases the risk of a respiratory infection (Pedersen et al., 2010). When psychologist Sheldon Cohen and his colleagues dropped a cold virus into people's noses, 47 percent of those living stress-filled lives developed colds (**FIGURE 39.6**). Among those living relatively free of stress, only 27 percent did. In a U.K. study, high stress levels at the outset of the Covid pandemic predicted a greater likelihood of Covid infection eight months later (Ayling et al., 2022).
- ***Stress can hasten the course of disease.*** As its name tells us, *AIDS (acquired immune deficiency syndrome)* is an immune disorder, caused by the *human immunodeficiency virus (HIV)*. Stress cannot give people AIDS. But a global analysis of 33,252 found that stress and negative emotions sped the transition from HIV infection to AIDS. And stress predicted a faster decline in those with AIDS (Chida & Vedhara, 2009).

The stress effect on immunity makes physiological sense. It takes energy to track down invaders, produce swelling, and maintain fevers. Thus, when diseased, your body reduces its muscular energy output by decreasing activity (and increasing sleep). Stress creates a competing energy need. During an aroused fight-or-flight reaction, your stress responses divert energy from your disease-fighting immune system and send it to your muscles and brain. This renders you more vulnerable to illness. Even within twin pairs, the less happy twin tends to die first (Saunders et al., 2018). *The point to remember:* Stress gets under the skin. It does not make us sick, but it does alter our immune functioning, which leaves us less able to fight infection and more likely to get sick.

RETRIEVAL PRACTICE

RP-2 The field of ____________________ studies mind-body interactions, including the effects of psychological, neural, and endocrine functioning on the immune system and overall health.

RP-3 What general effect does stress have on our health?

ANSWERS IN APPENDIX E

Stress and Heart Disease

LOQ 39-4 Why are some of us more prone than others to coronary heart disease?

Imagine a world where you wake up each day, make your breakfast, and check the news. Among the headlines, you see that 64 jumbo jets crashed again yesterday, killing another 25,000 passengers. You finish your breakfast and go on with your morning. It's just an average day.

Replace airline crashes with **coronary heart disease**, the United States' leading cause of death, and you have reentered reality. More than 9 million people die annually from heart disease (Roth et al., 2020). High blood pressure and a family history of the disease increase the risk. So do smoking, obesity, an unhealthy diet, physical inactivity, and a high cholesterol level. Such factors—along with more opioid deaths, the Covid pandemic, and economic inequality—help explain why, despite spending much more on health care, U.S. life expectancy is lower than in other high-income countries, and has been declining since 2014 (Rabin, 2022; Roser, 2021). Worldwide, coronary heart disease kills more men than women (Zhang et al., 2021).

Stress and personality also play a big role in heart disease. The more ongoing stress people experience, the more their bodies generate inflammation, which is associated with heart and other health problems, including depression (Madison et al., 2022). Plucking a hair and measuring its level of the stress hormone cortisol can help indicate whether women were exposed to violence or children have experienced prolonged stress (Bürgin et al., 2022; Lynch et al., 2022). Cortisol in a fingernail clipping can also indicate people's prior stress exposure and current heart problems and depression (Izawa et al., 2017; Phillips et al., 2021).

THE EFFECTS OF PERSONALITY, PESSIMISM, AND DEPRESSION In a classic study, Meyer Friedman, Ray Rosenman, and their colleagues tested the idea that stress increases vulnerability to heart disease. At different times of the year, they measured the blood cholesterol level and clotting speed of 40 U.S. male tax accountants (Friedman & Ulmer, 1984). The test results were initially typical, but as the accountants scrambled to finish their clients' tax returns before the April 15 filing deadline, their cholesterol and clotting measures rose to dangerous levels. After the deadline, the measures returned to typical levels. For these men, stress predicted heart attack risk.

The researchers then launched a *longitudinal study* of more than 3000 healthy middle-aged men. They interviewed each man for 15 minutes, noting his work and eating habits, manner of talking, and other behavior patterns, and then identified him as either **Type A** or **Type B** (with a roughly equal number of each type).

Nine years later, 257 men had experienced heart attacks—69 percent of them Type A. Moreover, not one of the "pure" Type Bs—the most mellow and laid-back of their group—had experienced a heart attack.

As often happens in science, this exciting discovery provoked both enormous public interest and researchers' curiosity. Was the finding reliable? If so, what was the toxic component of the Type A profile? Time-consciousness? Competitiveness? Anger?

Hundreds of other studies have since explored possible psychological predictors of cardiovascular disease (Chida & Hamer, 2008; Chida & Steptoe, 2009). These reveal that Type A's toxic core is negative emotions—especially the anger associated with an aggressively reactive temperament. Their often-active sympathetic nervous system redistributes blood flow to their muscles, pulling it away from their internal organs. The liver, which usually removes cholesterol and fat from the blood, can't do its job. Thus, excess cholesterol and fat may continue to circulate in the blood and later get deposited around the heart. Hostility also correlates with other risk factors, such as smoking, drinking, and obesity (Bunde & Suls, 2006). Our mind and heart interact.

In Western cultures, suppressing negative emotions increases gloomy moods, relationship problems, and health risks (Cameron & Overall, 2018; Kitayama et al., 2015). Many studies have also found that people who react with anger over little things are the most coronary-prone. Rage "seems to lash back and strike us in the heart muscle" (Spielberger & London, 1982). To have a healthy body and mind, learn how to reframe unpleasant events ("I have overcome obstacles like this before" or "There are other

In India and the United States, Type A bus drivers are literally hard-driving: They brake, pass, and honk their horns more often than their more easygoing Type B colleagues (Evans et al., 1987).

coronary heart disease the clogging of the vessels that nourish the heart muscle; a leading cause of death in many developed countries.

Type A Friedman and Rosenman's term for competitive, hard-driving, impatient, verbally aggressive, and anger-prone people.

Type B Friedman and Rosenman's term for easygoing, relaxed people.

"A cheerful heart is a good medicine, but a downcast spirit dries up the bones."
—Proverbs 17:22

positive aspects of my life") and pause when agitated rather than letting your anger erupt. (For some tips on managing anger, see Module 38.)

ASK YOURSELF

Do you think you are Type A, Type B, or somewhere in between? In what ways has this tendency been helpful to you, and in what ways has it been a challenge?

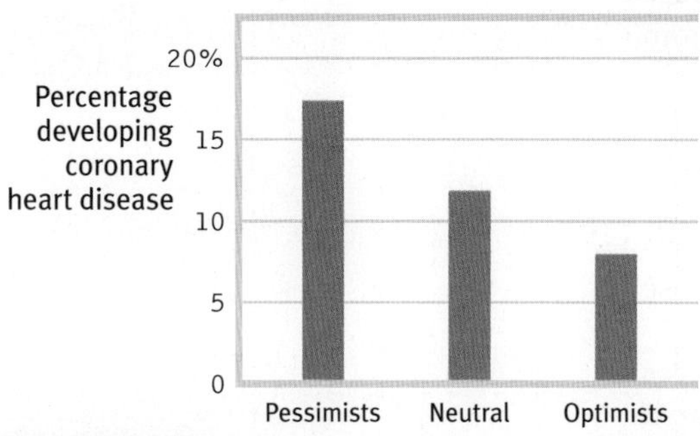
20%
Percentage developing coronary heart disease
15
10
5
0
Pessimists
Neutral
Optimists

FIGURE 39.7
Pessimism and heart disease (Data from Krittanawong et al., 2022.)

Chronic pessimism may be similarly toxic. In 10 longitudinal studies, researchers compared health records among 215,000 people who scored as optimists, pessimists, or neither (Krittanawong et al., 2022). When the researchers followed up with participants years later, they found that pessimists were 43 percent more likely than optimists to develop heart disease and 13 percent more likely to be dead (**FIGURE 39.7**). Pessimism's pestilence even emerged among people in their eighties and nineties, with pessimistic participants at greater risk of dying over the next 5 years (Jacobs et al., 2021).

Happiness also matters. Happy and consistently satisfied people tend to be healthy and to outlive their unhappy peers (Diener et al., 2017; Gana et al., 2016; Martín-María et al., 2017). People with big smiles tend to have extensive social networks, which predict longer life (Hertenstein et al., 2009). Boosting people's happiness (with a 10-week educational and skills-building experimental intervention) reduced their subsequent sick days (Kushlev et al., 2020). Having a happy spouse also predicts better health (Chopik & O'Brien, 2017). Happy you, healthy me.

As we noted earlier, depressed people tend to age faster and die sooner (Han et al., 2018). This is in part because depressed people often smoke more and exercise less (Whooley et al., 2008). In one study, nearly 4000 English adults (ages 52 to 79) provided mood reports from a single day. Compared with those in a good mood, those in a depressed mood were twice as likely to be dead 5 years later (Steptoe & Wardle, 2011). In a U.S. survey of 164,102 adults, those who had experienced a heart attack were twice as likely to report also having been depressed at some point in their lives (Witters & Wood, 2015). And in the years following a heart attack, people with high scores for depression were four times more likely than their low-scoring counterparts to develop further heart problems (Frasure-Smith & Lesperance, 2005). Depression is disheartening.

RETRIEVAL PRACTICE

RP-4 Which component of the Type A personality has been linked most closely to coronary heart disease?

ANSWERS IN APPENDIX E

A broken heart? Two days after Irma Garcia was tragically killed in the Uvalde, Texas, elementary school massacre, her husband Joe Garcia died of a heart attack at age 50. Might grief-related depression and stress hormones have contributed to his death? In a British study, older adults were at increased risk for a stroke or heart attack in the month following a partner's death (Carey et al., 2014).

Robin Jerstad/ZUMAPRESS/Newscom

Stress and Inflammation

Stress is also disheartening: Work stress, involuntary job loss, and trauma-related stress symptoms increase heart disease risk (Allesøe et al., 2010; Gallo et al., 2006; Kubzansky et al., 2009; Slopen et al., 2010).

Both heart disease and depression may result when chronic stress triggers blood vessel inflammation, disrupting the body's disease-fighting immune system (Miller & Blackwell, 2006; Mommersteeg et al., 2016). People who experience social threats, including harshly raised children, are more prone to inflammation responses (Chiang et al., 2022; Dickerson et al., 2009). So are bereaved spouses experiencing severe grief (Brown et al., 2022). Inflammation fights infections. But persistent inflammation can produce problems such as asthma or clogged arteries, and worsen depression (Enache et al., 2019; Sforzini et al., 2019).

So, stress can affect our health in many ways. (See Thinking Critically About: Stress and Health.) The stress-illness connection is a price we pay for the benefits of stress. Stress invigorates our lives by arousing and motivating us (see the What Drives Us modules for a discussion of motivation). An unstressed life would hardly be challenging, productive, or even safe.

Thinking Critically About: Stress and Health

LOQ **39-5** So, does stress *cause* illness?

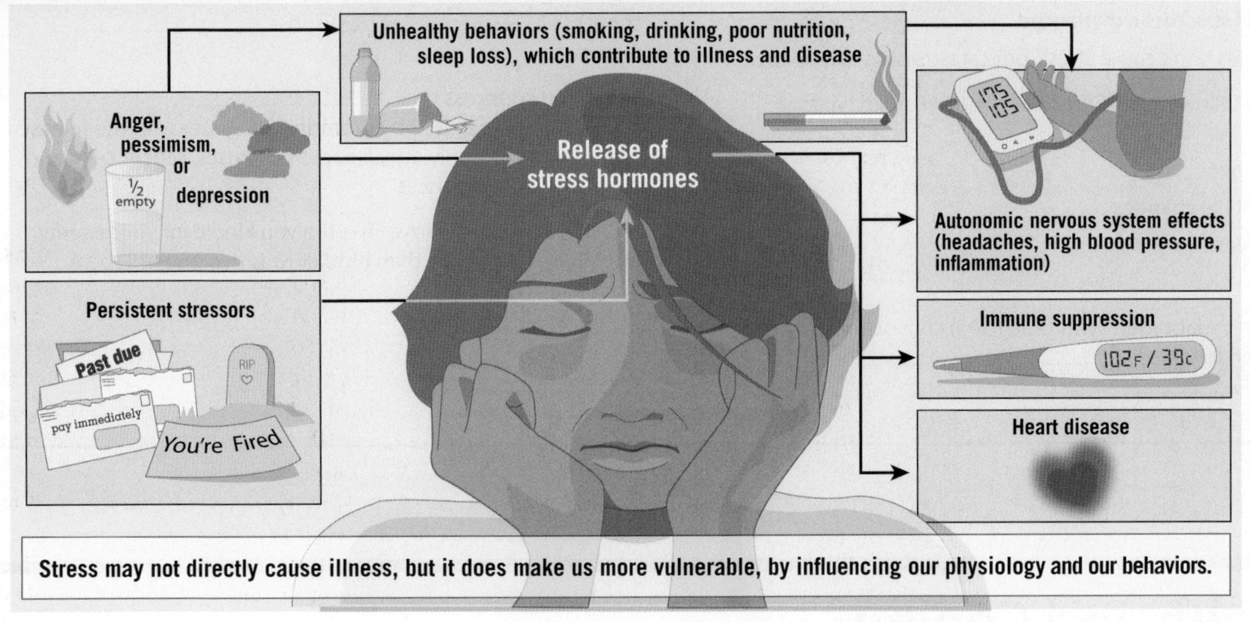

Unhealthy behaviors (smoking, drinking, poor nutrition, sleep loss), which contribute to illness and disease
Anger, pessimism, or depression
1/2 empty
Release of stress hormones
Persistent stressors
Past due
pay immediately
RIP
You're Fired
Autonomic nervous system effects (headaches, high blood pressure, inflammation)
175
105
Immune suppression
102F / 39c
Heart disease
Stress may not directly cause illness, but it does make us more vulnerable, by influencing our physiology and our behaviors.

* * *

Research on stress and health reminds us that psychological states are physiological events that influence other parts of our physiological system. Just pausing to *think* about biting into an orange wedge—imagine the sweet, tangy juice from the pulpy fruit flooding across your tongue—can trigger salivation. As the ancient Indian text the Mahābhārata recognized, "Mental disorders arise from physical causes, and likewise physical disorders arise from mental causes." We are biopsychosocial systems.

MODULE

39 REVIEW Stress and Illness

LEARNING OBJECTIVES

Test Yourself Answer these repeated Learning Objective Questions on your own (before "showing" the answers here, or checking the answers in Appendix D) to improve your retention of the concepts (McDaniel et al., 2009, 2015).

LOQ **39-1** How does our appraisal of an event affect our stress reaction, and what are the three main types of stressors?

LOQ **39-2** How do we respond and adapt to stress?

LOQ **39-3** How does stress make us more vulnerable to disease?

LOQ **39-4** Why are some of us more prone than others to coronary heart disease?

LOQ **39-5** So, does stress *cause* illness?

TERMS AND CONCEPTS TO REMEMBER

Test Yourself Write down the definition in your own words, then check your answer.

stress, p. 441
approach and avoidance motives, p. 444
fight-or-flight response, p. 445
general adaptation syndrome (GAS), p. 445
tend-and-befriend response, p. 446
health psychology, p. 447
psychoneuroimmunology, p. 447
coronary heart disease, p. 449
Type A, p. 449
Type B, p. 449

MODULE TEST

Test Yourself Answer the following questions on your own first, then "show" the answers here, or check your answers in Appendix E.

1. The number of short-term illnesses and stress-related psychological disorders was higher than usual in the months following an earthquake. Such findings suggest that

a. daily hassles have adverse health consequences.

b. experiencing a very stressful event increases a person's vulnerability to illness.

c. the amount of stress a person feels is directly related to the number of stressors experienced.
d. daily hassles don't cause stress, but catastrophes can be toxic.

2. Which of the following is NOT one of the three main types of stressors?
   a. Catastrophes
   b. Significant life changes
   c. Daily hassles
   d. Pessimism

3. Selye's general adaptation syndrome (GAS) consists of an alarm reaction followed by ______________, then ______________.

4. When faced with stress, women are more likely than men to show a ______________-and-______________ response.

5. Stress can suppress the ______________ ______________ by prompting a decrease in the release of cells that ordinarily attack bacteria, viruses, cancer cells, and other foreign substances.

6. A Chinese proverb warns, "The fire you kindle for your enemy often burns you more than him." How is this true of Type A people?

MODULE

40 Health and Coping

Promoting health begins with implementing strategies that prevent illness and enhance wellness. Traditionally, people have thought about their health only when something goes wrong and they visit a physician. That, say health psychologists, is like ignoring a car's maintenance and going to a mechanic only when the car breaks down. Health maintenance includes alleviating stress, preventing illness, and promoting well-being.

Coping With Stress

LOQ 40-1 In what two ways do people try to alleviate stress?

Stressors are unavoidable. This fact, coupled with the fact that persistent stress correlates with heart disease, depression, and lowered immunity, gives us a clear message. We need to learn to **cope** with the stress in our lives.

Coping Strategies

We address some stressors directly, with **problem-focused coping**. If our impatience leads to a family fight, we may go directly to that family member to work things out. We tend to use problem-focused strategies when we feel a sense of control over a situation and think we can change the circumstances, or at least change ourselves to deal with the circumstances more capably. We turn to **emotion-focused coping** when we believe we cannot change a situation. If, despite our best efforts, we cannot get along with that family member, we may relieve stress by reaching out to friends for support and comfort. Some emotion-focused strategies can harm our health, such as when we respond by eating unhealthy comfort foods. When challenged, some of us tend to respond with problem-focused coping, others with emotion-focused coping (Connor-Smith & Flachsbart, 2007). Our feelings of personal control, our explanatory style, our sense of humor, and our supportive connections all influence our ability to cope successfully.

coping alleviating stress using emotional, cognitive, or behavioral methods.

problem-focused coping attempting to alleviate stress directly—by changing the stressor or the way we interact with that stressor.

emotion-focused coping attempting to alleviate stress by avoiding or ignoring a stressor and attending to emotional needs related to our stress reaction.

RETRIEVAL PRACTICE

RP-1 To cope with stress when we feel in control of our world, we tend to use ______________ (emotion/problem)-focused strategies. To cope with stress when we believe we cannot change a situation, we tend to use ______________ (emotion/problem)-focused strategies.

ANSWERS IN APPENDIX E

Perceived Lack of Control

LOQ 40-2 How does a perceived lack of control affect health?

personal control our sense of being in charge of our environment rather than feeling helpless.

learned helplessness the hopelessness and passive resignation humans and other animals learn when unable to avoid repeated aversive events.

Picture the scene: Two rats receive simultaneous shocks. Only one of them can turn a wheel to stop the shocks. The helpless rat, but not the wheel turner, becomes more susceptible to ulcers and lowered immunity to disease (Laudenslager & Reite, 1984). In humans, too, uncontrollable threats trigger the strongest stress responses (Dickerson & Kemeny, 2004).

Any of us may feel helpless, hopeless, and depressed after experiencing a series of bad events beyond our **personal control**. One Syrian refugee in Canada reflected on life during the Covid-19 pandemic: "We have all been made refugees by this virus, trapped and terrified. We are all in this together, facing the same pandemic" (Al-Kontar, 2020). Martin Seligman and his colleagues have shown that for some animals and people, a series of uncontrollable events creates a state of **learned helplessness**. In experiments (which likely would not be repeated today), dogs were strapped in a harness and given repeated shocks, with no opportunity to avoid them (Seligman & Maier, 1967). Later, when placed in another situation where they *could* escape the punishment by simply leaping a hurdle, the dogs displayed learned helplessness; they cowered as if without hope. Other dogs that had been able to escape the first shocks reacted differently. They had learned they were in control and easily escaped the shocks in the new situation (Seligman & Maier, 1967). People have shown similar patterns of learned helplessness (Abramson et al., 1978, 1989; Seligman, 1975).

Perceiving a loss of control, we become more vulnerable to ill health. This is an especially serious problem for older people, who are highly susceptible to health problems and also perceive the greatest loss of control (Drewelies et al., 2017). In a famous study of elderly nursing home residents, those who perceived the least amount of control over their activities declined faster and died sooner than those given more control (Rodin, 1986). Workers able to adjust office furnishings and control interruptions and distractions in their work environment have also experienced less stress (O'Neill, 1993). Such findings help explain why British executives have tended to outlive those in clerical or laboring positions, and why Finnish workers with low job stress have been less than half as likely to die of stroke or heart disease as those with a demanding job and little control. The more control workers have, the longer they live (Bosma et al., 1997, 1998; Kivimaki et al., 2002; Marmot et al., 1997).

Poverty entails less control of one's life, which helps explain a link between economic status and longevity (Jokela et al., 2009). In one study of 843 grave markers in an old cemetery in Glasgow, Scotland, those with the costliest, highest pillars (indicating the most affluence) tended to have lived the longest (Carroll et al., 1994). Likewise, U.S. presidents, who are generally high-income and well-educated, have had above-average life spans (Olshansky, 2011). Across cultures, high economic status predicts a lower risk of heart and respiratory diseases (Sapolsky, 2005). High-income parents also tend to have healthy, advantaged children (Savelieva et al., 2016). With higher economic status comes reduced risk of low birth weight, infant mortality, smoking, and violence. Even among other primates, those at the bottom of the social pecking order have been more likely than their higher-status counterparts to become sick when exposed to a cold virus (Cohen et al., 1997).

Separation stress In 2018, new U.S. immigration policies led to thousands of immigrating children being separated from their parents at the southern border. Children isolated from parents and held in detention camps lose a sense of control, making them vulnerable to physical and psychological problems.

Adrees Latif/Reuters/Newscom

When rats cannot control shock or when humans or other primates feel unable to control their environment, stress hormone levels rise, blood pressure increases, and immune responses drop (Rodin, 1986; Sapolsky, 2005). The greater nurses' workload, the higher their cortisol level and blood pressure—but only among nurses who reported little control over their environment (Fox et al., 1993). The crowding in high-density neighborhoods, prisons, and college and university dorms is another source of diminished feelings of control—and of elevated levels of stress hormones and blood pressure (Fleming et al., 1987; Ostfeld et al., 1987).

BENEFITS OF BOOSTING CONTROL Increasing control—allowing prisoners to move chairs and to control room lights and the TV, having workers participate in decision making, allowing people to personalize their workspace—has often improved health and morale (Humphrey et al., 2007; Ng et al., 2012; Ruback et al., 1986). In the case of nursing home residents, 93 percent of those who were given more control over how they arranged their room and spent their time became more alert, active, and happy (Langer & Rodin, 1976). As researcher Ellen Langer concluded, "Perceived control is basic to human functioning" (1983, p. 291). "For the young and old alike," she suggested, environments should enhance people's sense of control over their world. No wonder mobile devices and online streaming, which enhance our control of the content and timing of our entertainment, are so popular.

People thrive when they live in conditions of personal freedom and empowerment. At the national level, citizens of stable democracies report higher levels of happiness (Inglehart et al., 2008). Freedom and personal control foster human flourishing. But does ever-increasing choice breed ever-happier lives? Today's Western cultures may offer an "excess of freedom"—too many choices. The result can be decreased life satisfaction, increased depression, or even behavior paralysis (Schwartz, 2000, 2004). In one study, people offered a choice of one of 30 brands of jam or chocolate were less satisfied with their decision than were others who had chosen from only 6 options (Iyengar & Lepper, 2000). This *tyranny of choice* brings information overload and a greater likelihood that we will feel regret over some of the things we left behind (Chernev et al., 2015). Do you, too, ever waste time agonizing over too many choices?

INTERNAL VERSUS EXTERNAL LOCUS OF CONTROL Consider your own perceptions of control, and how they have been influenced by your upbringing and culture. Do you believe that your life is beyond your control? That getting a good job depends mainly on being in the right place at the right time? Or do you more strongly believe that you control your own fate? That being a success is a matter of hard work?

Hundreds of studies have compared people who differ in their perceptions of control. On one side are those who have what psychologist Julian Rotter called an **external locus of control**. In one study of more than 1200 Israeli people exposed to missile attacks, those with an external locus of control experienced the most *posttraumatic stress* symptoms (Hoffman et al., 2016). On the other side are those who perceive an **internal locus of control**. In study after study, the "internals" have achieved more in school and work, acted more independently, enjoyed better health, and felt less depressed than did the "externals" (Lefcourt, 1982; Ng et al., 2006). In longitudinal research on more than 7500 people, those who had expressed a more internal locus of control at age 10 exhibited less obesity, lower blood pressure, and less distress at age 30 (Gale et al., 2008). Compared with nonleaders, military and business leaders have lower-than-average levels of stress hormones and report less anxiety, thanks to their greater sense of control (Sherman et al., 2012).

Compared with their parents' generation, today's U.S. youth more often express an external locus of control (Twenge et al., 2004). This shift may help explain an associated increase in rates of depression and other psychological disorders in young people (Twenge et al., 2010).

We tend to believe we are in control of our own life when we say we have *free will*. Studies show that people who believe they have free will behave more helpfully, learn better, and persist and perform better at work (Job et al., 2010; J. Li et al., 2018; Stillman et al., 2010). Across varied cultures, those who believe in free will also experience greater job satisfaction (Feldman et al., 2018). Belief in free will feeds *self-control*—to which we turn next.

ASK YOURSELF

How much control do you have over your life? How much do others (family members, friends, work supervisors) control your life? What changes could you make to increase your sense of control?

external locus of control the perception that outside forces beyond our personal control determine our fate.

internal locus of control the perception that we control our own fate.

BUILDING SELF-CONTROL

LOQ 40-3 Why is self-control important, and can our self-control be depleted?

When we have a sense of personal control over our lives, we are more likely to develop **self-control**—the ability to control impulses and delay short-term gratification for longer-term rewards. Self-control predicts good health, higher income, and better school performance (Bub et al., 2016; Keller et al., 2016; Moffitt et al., 2011). In studies of American, Asian, and New Zealander children, self-control outdid intelligence test scores in predicting future academic and life success (Duckworth & Seligman, 2005, 2017; Poulton et al., 2015; Wu et al., 2016).

Strengthening self-control is key to coping effectively with stress. Doing so requires attention and energy—similar to strengthening a muscle. It's easy to form bad habits, but it takes hard work to break them. With frequent practice in overcoming unwanted urges, people have improved their self-management of anger, dishonesty, smoking, and impulsive spending (Beames et al., 2017; Wang et al., 2017).

Although self-control grows stronger with exercise, it may also weaken after use and need rest to recover (Baumeister & Vohs, 2016). While some researchers debate the reliability of this effect (Hagger et al., 2016), others have shown that exercising willpower can temporarily consume the mental energy we need for self-control on other tasks (Dang et al., 2021; Vohs et al., 2021). In one famous experiment, hungry people expended willpower to resist eating tasty cookies. They then abandoned a frustrating task sooner than those who hadn't had to deal with the cookies (Baumeister et al., 1998).

The bottom line: Research on self-control teaches us that developing self-discipline can lead to a healthier, happier, and more successful life (Baumeister et al., 2018; Tuk et al., 2015). Delaying a little fun now can lead to bigger future rewards. And persevering through today's struggles builds an inner strength that enables us to tackle tomorrow's challenges.

Brian Fairbrother/LatitudeStock/Alamy Stock Photo

Extreme self-control Our ability to exert self-control increases with practice, and some of us have a lot of practice! This performer has made her living as a very convincing human statue on The Royal Mile in Edinburgh, Scotland.

Explanatory Style: Optimism Versus Pessimism

LOQ 40-4 How does an optimistic outlook affect health and longevity?

Our outlook—what we expect from the world—influences how we cope with stress. Pessimists expect things to go badly (Aspinwall & Tedeschi, 2010). They attribute their poor performance to a basic lack of ability ("I can't do this") or to situations enduringly beyond their control ("There is nothing I can do about it"). Optimists do the opposite by expecting more control, coping ability, and better health (Aspinwall & Tedeschi, 2010; Boehm & Kubzansky, 2012; Hernandez et al., 2015). During a semester's final month, optimistic students reported the least fatigue and fewer coughs, aches, and pains. And during the stressful first few weeks of law school, optimists enjoyed better moods and stronger immune systems (Segerstrom et al., 1998). Optimists tend to have optimal health.

Optimists have tended to get better grades because they respond to setbacks with a hopeful attitude that they can improve (Noel et al., 1987; Peterson & Barrett, 1987). Optimists and their romantic partners generally manage conflict constructively, resulting in feeling more supported and satisfied with the resolution and with their relationship (Srivastava et al., 2006). Optimism relates to well-being and success in many places, from Europe and North America to China and Japan (Qin & Piao, 2011).

"I do the very best I can to look upon life with optimism and hope and looking forward to a better day." —Civil rights activist Rosa Parks, "Standing Up for Freedom," 2005

Consider the consistency and startling magnitude of the optimism and positive emotions factor in several longitudinal studies:

- *Long lives.* One research team followed 70,021 nurses over time; those scoring in the top quarter on optimism were nearly 30 percent less likely to have died than those scoring in the bottom quarter (Kim et al., 2017). Even greater optimism-longevity differences have been found in studies of Finnish men and U.S. Vietnam War veterans (Everson et al., 1996; Phillips et al., 2009). In long-term studies of nurses and veterans, the most optimistic were 50 to 70 percent more likely than pessimists to live beyond age 85 (Lee et al., 2019). In fact, just being not-pessimistic predicts good health (Scheier et al., 2021).

self-control the ability to control impulses and delay short-term gratification for greater long-term rewards.

emotion regulation how we manage our emotions, including which emotions we allow ourselves to feel, when we feel them, and how we express those emotions.

- *The famous "Nuns Study."* A classic study followed up on 180 Catholic nuns who had written brief autobiographies at about 22 years of age and had thereafter lived similar lifestyles. Those who had expressed happiness, love, and other positive feelings in their autobiographies lived an average 7 years longer than their more dour counterparts (Danner et al., 2001). By age 80, some 54 percent of those expressing few positive emotions had died, as had only 24 percent of the most positive-spirited.
- *Optimism and the end of life.* Optimists not only live longer lives, they approach the end of life positively. One study followed more than 68,000 U.S. women, ages 50 to 79 years, for nearly 2 decades (Zaslavsky et al., 2015). As death grew nearer, the optimists tended to feel more life satisfaction than did the pessimists.

Optimism runs in families, so some people are born with a sunny, hopeful outlook. If one identical twin is optimistic, the other typically will be, too (Bates, 2015; Mosing et al., 2009).

The good news is that all of us, even the most pessimistic, can learn to become more optimistic. Compared with a control group of pessimists who simply kept diaries of their daily activities, pessimists in a skill-building group—who learned ways of seeing the bright side of difficult situations and of viewing their goals as achievable—reported lower levels of depression (Sergeant & Mongrain, 2014). In other experiments, people instructed to imagine their best possible future—one where they have worked hard and succeeded in all their life goals—became more optimistic (Malouff & Schutte, 2017). Positive expectations often motivate eventual success: Optimism is the light bulb that can brighten anyone's life.

Emotion Regulation

"Getting angry . . . is easy and everyone can do it; but doing it . . . in the right amount, at the right time, and for the right end, and in the right way is no longer easy, nor can everyone do it." —Aristotle, *Nicomachean Ethics* (II.9, 1109a27)

LOQ 40-5 How does controlling our feelings affect our well-being and health?

Life is full of emotions. A frustrating conversation with a friend can throw us off for the rest of the day. An upcoming class presentation can strike us with fear and get our heart pounding. People vary in how often and how well we manage our feelings. And how we navigate our emotional ups and downs matters for our health.

Our emotions can be our best friends or our worst enemies—it all depends how well we manage them (Gross, 2013). Think back to a time when you felt really upset. Were you able to control your feelings? Healthy **emotion regulation** enables more happiness, better life satisfaction, closer social relationships, and even less depression and anxiety (Aldao et al., 2010; Gross, 1998).

In what ways do we change our feelings? We can increase or decrease emotional intensity and how long our feelings last, and we can control which kinds of emotions

Control contrasts Some actors seem to have complete control over their feelings (Leonard Nimoy, who was nearly as calm in real life as his *Star Trek* character, Spock). Others seem to have much less emotional control (Tom Cruise famously expressing his feelings for a new girlfriend on the Oprah Winfrey Show).

LLAP
David Livingston/Getty Images

Photofest

we feel (Gross et al., 2011). People most often report trying to decrease their negative feelings (sadness, anger, worry) and increase their positive feelings (joy, love, contentment) (Gross et al., 2006; Quoidbach et al., 2010). But sometimes people aim for the reverse: They may embrace their anger at social justice protests. And any parent knows the importance of helping young children calm excited feelings before bedtime (**FIGURE 40.1**).

The idea that changing our thoughts upstream can shape our moods and feelings downstream is at the heart of modern-day cognitive therapy for depression and anxiety (see the Therapy modules). Psychologist James Gross (1998, 2015) describes three strategies people often use—with the first two usually being more helpful than the third.

- ***Situation selection*** Change your situation to alter your feelings, such as by getting new roommates.
- ***Cognitive reappraisal*** Think about a situation in a more neutral way to dampen its negativity, such as reminding yourself that a mediocre grade on an exam could have been worse.
- ***Suppression*** Contain those feelings, as when forcing a smile after an argument. (As we will see, this strategy can backfire.)

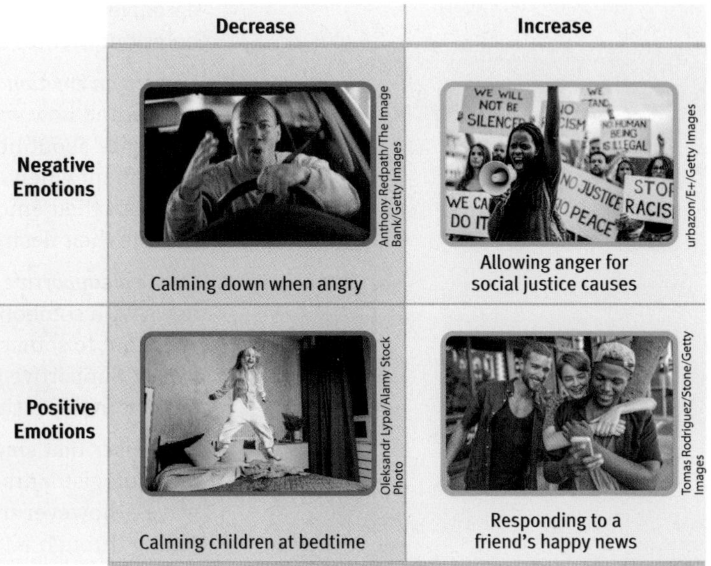
Decrease
Increase
Negative Emotions
Positive Emotions
Calming down when angry
Allowing anger for social justice causes
Calming children at bedtime
Responding to a friend's happy news
WE WILL NOT BE SILENCED
NO JUSTICE NO PEACE
STOP RACISM
WE CAN DO IT
Anthony Redpath/The Image Bank/Getty Images
urbazon/E+/Getty Images
Oleksandr Lypa/Alamy Stock Photo
Tomas Rodriguez/Stone/Getty Images

FIGURE 40.1
How do we change our feelings? We can decrease or increase all of our feelings, both negative and positive.

Some strategies seem to benefit us more than others. In one study, participants watched a disturbing video of a gory medical procedure. Researchers had asked some viewers to step back and "adopt a detached and unemotional attitude" *(reappraisal)*, and others to "behave so that someone watching you would not know that you are feeling anything at all" *(suppression)*. Compared with those in the emotion suppression group, participants who used the reappraisal strategy had a lower bodily stress response and experienced fewer negative emotions (Gross, 1998). Using reappraisal regularly also promotes health and well-being. Using *situation selection* is associated with greater emotional well-being and happiness, and less depression (Webb et al., 2017; **TABLE 40.1**).

FOUR TIPS FOR MANAGING EMOTIONS Psychology's toolkit offers four tips for managing your emotions.

1. ***Accept rather than criticize your feelings, and embrace a diversity of emotions.*** We navigate many emotional ups and downs throughout our day. That is perfectly okay—our emotions are pieces of information about our world that help us get through tough times and appreciate good ones. A sad mood may remind us of what matters to us, and a dose of fear can keep us alert and safe. We are healthier when we let ourselves feel our natural negative and positive emotions rather than pressuring ourselves to be happy all the time (Quoidbach et al., 2014; see also

Farley Katz/Cartoon Stock

"This is the barn where we keep our feelings. If a feeling comes to you, bring it out here and lock it up."
Unhealthy emotion regulation

TABLE 40.1 Consequences of Three Emotion Regulation Strategies

Emotion Regulation Strategy	Definition	Consequences
Situation selection	Changing your situation to influence your feelings	• Greater well-being and happiness • More positive emotions; fewer negative emotions • Less depression
Reappraisal	Changing how you *think* about a situation to influence your feelings	• Better social relationships • Better coping with stress • More positive emotions
Suppression	Hiding or dampening your emotional expression	• Feeling less authentic in social life • Poorer coping with stress • Fewer positive emotions; more negative emotions

emodiversity.org). Adopting an accepting, matter-of-fact attitude toward emotions helps our mental and physical health.

2. ***Develop an emotion road map.*** Rather than wandering among emotions, decide when, where, and how you can enable your desired emotions. For example, you might strategize about how to reduce angry outbursts or how to replace jealousy with excitement when congratulating a friend on their accomplishments. People who flesh out their emotional goals with detailed plans more often stay on track and achieve their desired emotional endpoint (Mauss & Tamir, 2014).
3. ***Create a supportive environment.*** When something good happens, share the joyful news with someone to feel even better (Peters et al., 2018). When feeling upset, reach out to someone close for perspective and social support. Choose your friends wisely. Supportive friends can help you sustain the good feelings longer and bounce back from down times more quickly.
4. ***Remember that emotions are temporary.*** Emotions are usually short-lived. As psychologist Marsha Linehan (2016) explains: Emotions are like an ocean wave—however intense and high they peak they will eventually come down. Riding through an emotional wave may mean sitting with that emotion until it passes.

ASK YOURSELF

Which of these tips will you employ to improve your own emotion regulation?

RETRIEVAL PRACTICE

RP-2 Which of the following emotion regulation strategies tends to lead to *fewer* positive emotions and *more* negative emotions?

a. Reappraisal

b. Suppression

c. Situation selection

ANSWERS IN APPENDIX E

Social Support

LOQ 40-6 How does social support promote good health?

Social support—feeling liked, encouraged, and helped-when-needed by friends and family—promotes both happiness and health. When randomly prompted by a researcher's phone app, people report more happiness when with others (Quoidbach et al., 2019). In international studies following thousands of people over several years, close relationships have predicted happiness and health in both individualist and collectivist cultures (Brannan et al., 2013; Chu et al., 2010; Rueger et al., 2016). People supported by close relationships tend to enjoy better health and longer lives (Holt-Lunstad, 2021; Vila, 2021). When researchers combined data from 70 studies of 3.4 million people worldwide, they confirmed a striking social support benefit: Compared with those who had ample social connections, socially isolated or lonely people had a 30 percent greater death rate during the 7-year study period (Holt-Lunstad et al., 2010, 2015, 2017). "Loneliness [predicts] a reduction of life span," former U.S. Surgeon General Vivek H. Murthy (2017) noted, that is "similar to that caused by smoking 15 cigarettes a day."

To combat social isolation, we need to do more than collect acquaintances. We need people who genuinely care about us (Cacioppo et al., 2014; Hawkley et al., 2008). Some fill this need by connecting with friends, family, co-workers, members of a faith community, or support groups. Others connect in positive, supportive marriages. Happy marriages bathe us in social support, leading to less weight gain and a longer life (Chen et al., 2018; VanderWeele, 2017). One 7-decade-long study found that at age 50, healthy aging was better predicted by a good marriage than by a low cholesterol level (Vaillant, 2002). On the flip side, divorce predicts poor health. In one analysis of 600 million people in 24 countries, separated and divorced people were more likely to die early (Shor et al., 2012). But it's less marital status than marital *quality* that predicts health—to about

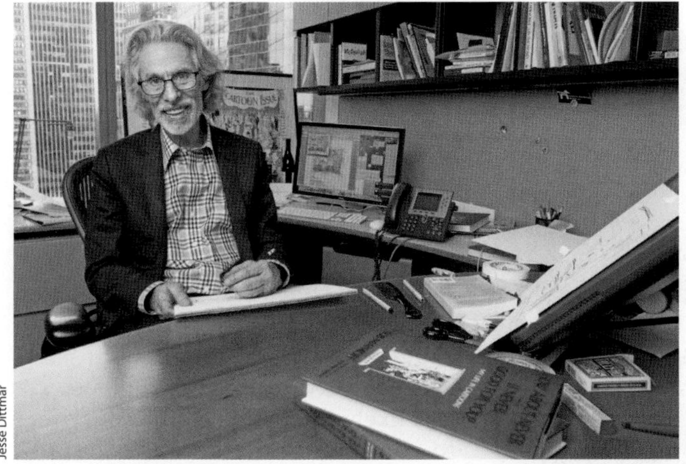
Jesse Dittmar

Funny business Part of our pleasure in authoring this text—and, we hope, yours in reading it—is finding cartoons that offer comic relief while illustrating and reinforcing psychological concepts. Many have come from the *New Yorker*, whose longtime cartoonist and cartoon editor was Bob Mankoff—a former psychology major who lectures on the psychology of humor and is president of CartoonCollections.com. Mankoff explains: "Humor, like other forms of play, has three main benefits. First, it's physically and psychologically healthy, especially in the way it blocks stress. Second, humor makes us mentally flexible—able to manage change, take risks, and think creatively. And third, humor serves as a social lubricant, making us more effective in dealing with colleagues and clients."

the same extent as a healthy diet and physical activity do (Bookwala & Gaugler, 2020; Smith & Baucom, 2017).

Research suggests that social support has many health benefits:

Social support calms us, improves our sleep, and reduces blood pressure (Baron et al., 2016; Kent de Grey et al., 2018; Uchino & Way, 2017). To see if social support might calm people's response to threats, one research team asked happily married women to lie in an fMRI machine, and subjected them to the threat of electric shock to an ankle (Coan et al., 2006). During the experiment, some women held their husband's hand. Others held a stranger's hand or no one's hand. While awaiting the occasional shocks, women holding their husband's hand showed less activity in threat-responsive brain areas. This soothing benefit was greatest for those reporting the highest-quality marriages. Simply holding your romantic partner's hand while resolving a conflict may help you handle stress and improve communication (Jakubiak & Feeney, 2019).

Social support fosters stronger immune functioning. Stress hampers immune functioning, but social connections strengthen it (Leschak & Eisenberger, 2019). Recognizing this, some physicians have begun providing "social prescriptions" for patients that advise connecting with others. These have helped people with conditions ranging from dementia to diabetes to Parkinson's disease (Hanc, 2021). Volunteers exposed to cold viruses showed the health-promoting effect of social support while being quarantined for 5 days (Cohen, 2004; Cohen et al., 1997). (In these experiments, the more than 600 participants were well-paid volunteers.) Age, race, sex, and health habits being equal, those with close social ties were least likely to catch a cold. People whose daily life included frequent hugs likewise experienced fewer cold symptoms (Cohen et al., 2015). The cold fact: The effect of social ties is nothing to sneeze at!

Close relationships give us an opportunity for "open heart therapy"—a chance to confide painful feelings (Frattaroli, 2006). Talking about a stressful event can temporarily arouse us, but in time it calms us (Lieberman et al., 2007; Mendolia & Kleck, 1993; Niles et al., 2015). In one study, 33 Holocaust survivors spent 2 hours recalling their experiences, many in intimate detail never before disclosed (Pennebaker et al., 1989). Those who disclosed the most had the most improved health 14 months later. In another study of surviving spouses of people who had died by suicide or in car accidents, those who bore their grief alone had more health problems than those who shared it with others

Tim Robberts/Getty Images

Laughter among friends is good medicine Laughter arouses us, massages muscles, and leaves us feeling relaxed (Robinson, 1983). Humor (though not hostile sarcasm) may ease pain, and strengthen immune activity (Ayan, 2009; Berk et al., 2001; Dunbar et al., 2011). Humor buffers stress (H. Fritz et al., 2017). People who laugh a lot have also tended to have lower rates of heart disease (Clark et al., 2001).

Scientists: Holding Hands With Loved Ones* Lowers Blood Pressure
Weekly Woman
Horoscope Capricorn
Horoscope Aquarius
Horoscope Pisces

* May not include small children
DUH.
www.babyblues.com
Kirkman & Scott

Baby Blues: © 2010 Baby Blues Partnership Distributed by King Features Syndicate, Inc

FluxFactory/E+/Getty Images

Pets are friends, too Having a pet may increase the odds of survival after a heart attack, relieve depression among people with AIDS, and lower blood pressure and other coronary risk factors (Allen, 2003; McConnell et al., 2011; Wells, 2009). Pets are no substitute for effective drugs and exercise. But for people who enjoy animals, and especially for those who live alone, pets are a healthy pleasure (Reis et al., 2017; Siegel, 1990). The Covid-19 pandemic made many of us new pet owners, as we sought to cope with stress and social isolation.

(Pennebaker & O'Heeron, 1984). Confiding is good for the body and the soul (see the Therapy modules).

Suppressing emotions can be detrimental to physical health. When psychologist James Pennebaker (1985) surveyed more than 700 undergraduate women, those who had experienced a traumatic sexual experience in childhood reported more headaches and stomach ailments than those who had experienced other traumas—possibly because survivors of sexual abuse are less likely than other trauma survivors to confide in others. Another study, of 437 Australian ambulance drivers, confirmed the ill effects of suppressing one's emotions after witnessing traumas (Wastell, 2002).

Even writing about personal traumas in a diary can help (Burton & King, 2008; Kállay, 2015; Lyubomirsky et al., 2006). For trauma survivors, writing therapy reduces posttraumatic stress (Pavlacic et al., 2019). In one experiment, volunteers who kept trauma diaries had fewer health problems during the ensuing 4 to 6 months (Pennebaker, 1990). As one participant explained, "Although I have not talked with anyone about what I wrote, I was finally able to deal with it, work through the pain instead of trying to block it out. Now it doesn't hurt to think about it."

"Woe to one who is alone and falls and does not have another to help." —Ecclesiastes 4:10

If we are aiming to exercise more, drink less, quit smoking, or be a healthy weight, our social ties can tug us away from, or toward, our goal. If you are trying to achieve some goal, think about whether your social network is helping or hindering you.

ASK YOURSELF

Can you remember a time when you felt better after discussing a problem with a friend or family member? How did doing so help you to cope—either emotionally (emotion-focused), or by resolving the problem (problem-focused)?

Reducing Stress

Having a sense of control, developing more optimistic thinking, and building social support can help us experience less stress and thus improve our health. People who have been upbeat about themselves and their future also have tended to enjoy health-promoting social ties (Stinson et al., 2008). But sometimes we cannot alleviate stress and simply need to *manage* our stress. Aerobic exercise, relaxation, meditation, and spiritual communities have helped people gather inner strength and lessen stress effects.

"These mountains that you are carrying, you were only supposed to climb." —Poet Najwa Zebian, *The Nectar of Pain*, 2016

Aerobic Exercise

LOQ 40-7 How effective is aerobic exercise as a way to manage stress and improve well-being?

It's hard to find a medicine that works for most people most of the time. But **aerobic exercise**—sustained, oxygen-consuming exertion—is one of those rare near-perfect "medicines." Estimates vary, but some studies suggest that exercise adds to your quantity of life—about *7 hours longer life for every exercise hour* (Lee et al., 2017; Mandsager et al., 2018; Zahrt & Crum, 2017). Think about it: Nature generously gives a 7-to-1 return for time spent exercising. It also boosts your quality of life, with more energy, better mood, and stronger relationships (Buecker et al., 2020; Wiese et al., 2018). As author Bill Bryson (2019) noted, "If someone invented a pill that could do for us all that a moderate amount of exercise achieves, it would instantly become the most successful drug in history."

**aerobic exercise** sustained exercise that increases heart and lung fitness; also helps alleviate depression and anxiety.

In the late 1940s, British government doctor Jeremy Morris and his colleagues (1953) sought a low-cost way to test their belief that exercise reduced people's risk of heart attacks. While riding the bus to work one day, Morris realized that every double-decker bus offered a perfect laboratory: Each had a driver who sat while working, and a conductor who moved constantly and climbed 600 steps in a typical shift. After following 31,000 drivers and conductors for 2 years and adjusting for other factors, he had the first causal evidence of exercise affecting health: Compared with drivers, the conductors experienced fewer than half as many heart attacks.

Exercise helps fight heart disease by strengthening the heart, increasing blood flow, keeping blood vessels open, lowering blood pressure, and reducing the hormone and blood pressure reaction to stress (Ford, 2002; Manson, 2002). Compared with inactive adults, people who exercise experience about half as many heart attacks (Evenson et al., 2016; Visich & Fletcher, 2009). Among older women, those who take 4400 steps per day have a lower risk of death than those who take 2700 or fewer steps (Lee et al., 2019). Until 7500 or so steps, the risk continues to drop; more steps = less death.

It's a fact: Fitness predicts longevity (Moholdt et al., 2018). Dietary fat contributes to clogged arteries, but exercise makes our muscles hungry for those fats and cleans them out of our arteries (Barinaga, 1997). A study of 1.44 million Americans and Europeans found that exercise predicted "lower risks of many cancer types" (Moore et al., 2016). Scottish mail carriers, who spend their days walking, have lower heart disease risk than Scottish mail office workers (Tigbe et al., 2017). Regular exercise in later life also predicts better cognitive functioning and reduced risk of neurocognitive disorder and Alzheimer's disease (Kramer & Erickson, 2007).

The genes passed down to us from our distant ancestors enabled the physical activity essential to hunting, foraging, and farming (Raichlen & Polk, 2013; Shave et al., 2019). In muscle cells, those genes, when activated by exercise, respond by producing proteins. We are made for exercise. In the modern inactive person, these genes produce lower quantities of proteins and leave us susceptible to more than 20 chronic diseases, such as type 2 diabetes, coronary heart disease, stroke, and cancer (Booth & Neufer, 2005). Inactivity is thus potentially toxic. Physical activity can weaken the influence of some genetic risk factors. In one analysis of 45 studies, the risk of obesity fell by 27 percent (Kilpeläinen et al., 2012).

Does exercise also boost the spirit? In a 21-country survey of university students, physical exercise was a strong and consistent predictor of life satisfaction (Grant et al., 2009). People from the United States, Canada, and the United Kingdom who do aerobic exercise at least three times a week manage stress better, exhibit more self-confidence, have more vigor, and feel less depressed and fatigued than their inactive peers (Rebar et al., 2015; Smits et al., 2011). One analysis of 1.2 million Americans compared exercisers with nonexercisers. After controlling for other physical and social differences among them, the exercisers experienced 43 percent "fewer days of poor mental health in the last month" (Chekroud et al., 2018). "Exercise has a large and significant antidepressant effect," concluded one digest of 49 controlled studies (Schuch et al., 2018).

But remember, correlation does not imply causation. We could state this observation another way: Stressed and depressed people exercise less. To sort out cause and effect, researchers experiment. They *randomly assign* stressed, depressed, or anxious people either to an aerobic exercise group or to a control group. Next, they measure whether aerobic exercise (compared with a control activity not involving exercise) produces a change in stress, depression, anxiety, or some other health-related outcome. One classic experiment randomly assigned mildly depressed female college students to three groups. One-third participated in a program of aerobic exercise. Another third took part in a program of relaxation exercises. The remaining third (the control group) formed a no-treatment group (McCann & Holmes, 1984). As **FIGURE 40.2** shows, 10 weeks later, the women in the aerobic exercise program reported the greatest decrease in depression. Many had, quite literally, run away from their troubles.

Dozens of other experiments and longitudinal studies confirm that exercise reduces or prevents depression and anxiety (Catalan-Matamoros et al., 2016; Harvey et al., 2018; Stubbs et al., 2017). When experimenters randomly assigned depressed people to an exercise group, an antidepressant group, or a placebo pill group, exercise diminished depression as effectively as antidepressants—and with longer-lasting effects (Hoffman et al., 2011).

Paik Photography/Alamy Stock Photo

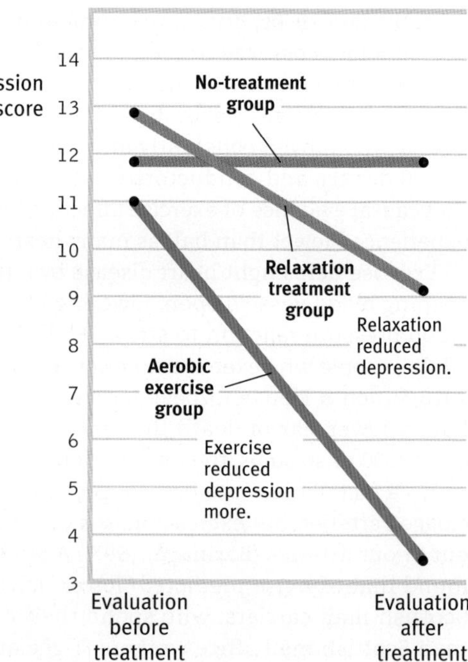
Depression score
14
13
12
11
10
9
8
7
6
5
4
3
No-treatment group
Relaxation treatment group
Relaxation reduced depression.
Aerobic exercise group
Exercise reduced depression more.
Evaluation before treatment
Evaluation after treatment

FIGURE 40.2
Aerobic exercise reduces mild depression (Data from McCann & Holmes, 1984.)

Vigorous exercise provides a substantial and immediate mood boost (Watson, 2000). Even a 10-minute walk stimulates 2 hours of increased well-being by raising energy levels and lowering tension (Thayer, 1987, 1993). Exercise works its magic in several ways. It increases arousal, thus counteracting depression's low arousal state. It enables muscle relaxation and sounder sleep. It produces toned muscles, which filter out a depression-causing toxin (Agudelo et al., 2014). Like an antidepressant drug, it orders up mood-boosting chemicals from our body's internal pharmacy—neurotransmitters such as norepinephrine, serotonin, and the endorphins (Jacobs, 1994; Salmon, 2001). Exercise also fosters *neurogenesis*. In mice, exercise causes the brain to produce a molecule that stimulates the production of new, stress-resistant neurons (Hunsberger et al., 2007; Reynolds, 2009; van Praag, 2009).

On a simpler level, the sense of accomplishment and improved physique and body image that often accompany a successful exercise routine may enhance one's self-image, leading to a better emotional state. Frequent exercise is like a drug that prevents and treats disease, increases energy, calms anxiety, and boosts mood—a drug we would all take, if available. Yet few people (only 1 in 4 in the United States) take advantage of it (Mendes, 2010).

Relaxation and Meditation

LOQ 40-8 In what ways might relaxation and meditation influence stress and health?

Knowing the damaging effects of stress, could we learn to counteract our stress responses by altering our thinking and lifestyle? In the late 1960s, psychologists began experimenting with *biofeedback*, a system of recording, amplifying, and feeding back information about subtle physiological responses in an effort to help people control them. After a decade of study, however, the initial claims for biofeedback seemed overblown and oversold (Miller, 1985).

Simple relaxation methods, which require no expensive equipment, produce many of the results biofeedback once promised. Massage relaxes both premature infants and those experiencing pain, and it also helps reduce depression (Hou et al., 2010). Figure 40.2 pointed out that aerobic exercise reduces depression. But did you notice in that figure that depression also decreased among women in the relaxation treatment group? More than 60 studies have found that relaxation procedures can also relieve headaches, hypertension, anxiety, and insomnia (Nestoriuc et al., 2008; Stetter & Kupper, 2002).

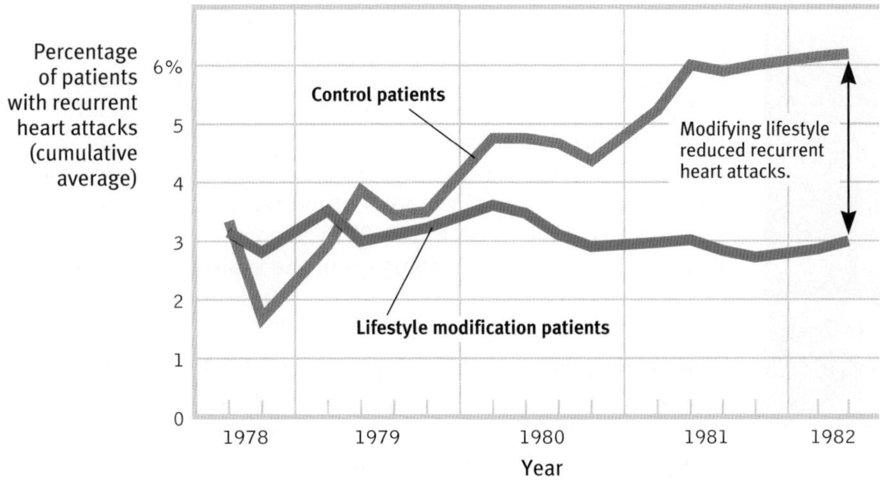
Percentage of patients with recurrent heart attacks (cumulative average)
6%
5
4
3
2
1
0
Control patients
Modifying lifestyle reduced recurrent heart attacks.
Lifestyle modification patients
1978
1979
1980
1981
1982
Year

FIGURE 40.3
Recurrent heart attacks and lifestyle modification (Data from Friedman & Ulmer, 1984.)

Such findings would not surprise Meyer Friedman, Ray Rosenman, and their colleagues. They tested relaxation in a program designed to help hard-driving *Type A* heart attack survivors (who are more prone to heart attacks than their relaxed *Type B* peers) reduce their risk of future attacks. Among hundreds of randomly assigned middle-aged men, half received standard advice from cardiologists about medications, diet, and exercise habits. The other half received similar advice, but they also learned to slow down and relax by walking, talking, and eating more slowly; to smile at others and laugh at themselves; to admit their mistakes; to take time to enjoy life; and to renew their religious faith. The training paid off (**FIGURE 40.3**). During the next 3 years, those who learned to modify their lifestyle had half as many repeat heart attacks as did the group that received standard advice. This, wrote the exuberant Friedman, was an unprecedented, spectacular reduction in heart attack recurrence. A smaller-scale British study spanning 13 years similarly showed a halved death rate among high-risk people trained to alter their thinking and lifestyle (Eysenck & Grossarth-Maticek, 1991). After experiencing a heart attack at age 55, Friedman started taking his own behavioral medicine—and lived to age 90 (Wargo, 2007). Learning to chill → less risk of getting ill.

shapecharge/Getty Images

Is music a natural antistress medicine? One analysis of more than 100 studies showed that listening to music (especially slower tempo music) reduced heart rate, blood pressure, and psychological distress (de Witte et al., 2019). The next time you find yourself stressed, remember that music may help you mellow out. When exercising, however, up-tempo music is energizing — it reduces perceived exertion (Terry et al., 2020).

Time may heal all wounds, but relaxation can help speed that process. In one study, surgery patients were randomly assigned to two groups. Both groups received standard treatment, but the second group also experienced a 45-minute relaxation session and received relaxation recordings to use before and after surgery. A week after surgery, patients in the relaxation group reported lower stress and showed better wound healing (Broadbent et al., 2012).

Meditation is a practice with a long history. In many world religions, meditation has been used to reduce suffering and improve awareness, insight, and compassion. Today, meditation apps offer free, guided techniques that can improve health (Adams et al., 2018). Numerous studies have confirmed meditation's benefits (Goyal et al., 2014; Rosenberg et al., 2015; Sedlmeier et al., 2012). One type, **mindfulness meditation**, has found a new home in stress management programs. If you learned this practice, you would relax and silently attend to your inner state, without judging it (Goldberg et al., 2018, 2019; Kabat-Zinn, 2001). You would sit down, close your eyes, and mentally scan your body from head to toe. Zooming in on certain body parts and responses, you would remain aware and accepting. You would also pay attention to your breathing, attending to each breath as if it were a material object.

Meditation is an ancient practice with deep roots in many world religions. Gregory of Sinai (d. 1346) offered this guidance: "Sit down alone and in silence. Lower your head, shut your eyes, breathe out gently, and imagine yourself looking into your own heart. . . . As you breathe out, say 'Lord Jesus Christ, have mercy on me.' . . . Try to put all other thoughts aside. Be calm, be patient, and repeat the process very frequently."

For many people, practicing mindfulness boosts happiness and lessens anxiety and depression (Goldberg et al., 2021; van Agteren et al., 2021). In one experiment, Korean participants were asked to think about their own mortality. Compared with nonmeditators, those who meditated were less anxious when reminded of their inevitable death (Park & Pyszczynski, 2019). Mindfulness practices have also been linked with improved sleep, helpfulness, and immune system functioning (Donald et al., 2018; Rusch et al., 2019; Villalba et al., 2019). They also increase the length of the *telomeres* protecting our chromosome tips, which reduces the risk of cancer and heart disease (Conklin et al., 2018). Just a few minutes of daily mindfulness

mindfulness meditation a reflective practice in which people attend to current experiences in a nonjudgmental and accepting manner.

AP Photo

Furry friends relieve stress Some schools bring cuddly critters on campus to help students relax and lower disruptive stress levels. In one study, exam-stressed college students who interacted with therapy dogs felt less stressed 10 hours later (Ward-Griffin et al., 2018).

meditation is enough to improve concentration and decision making (Hafenbrack et al., 2014; Rahl et al., 2017).

Nevertheless, some researchers caution that mindfulness is overhyped (Britton, 2019; Van Dam et al., 2018). For some people, mindfulness meditation produces self-absorption or even adverse effects (Britton, 2019; Van Dam et al., 2018; Vonk & Visser, 2021). Moreover, say critics, meditation's stress relief is mirrored by mere solitude, which can similarly relax us and reduce stress (Nguyen et al., 2018). Even so, meditation's positive results make us wonder: What's going on in the brain as we practice mindfulness? Correlational and experimental studies offer three explanations. Mindfulness

- ***strengthens connections among brain regions.*** The affected regions are those associated with focusing our attention, processing what we see and hear, and being reflective and aware (Berkovich-Ohana et al., 2014; Ives-Deliperi et al., 2011; Kilpatrick et al., 2011).
- ***activates brain regions associated with emotion regulation*** (Davidson et al., 2003; Way et al., 2010). When labeling emotions, mindful people show less activation in the amygdala, a brain region associated with fear, and more activation in the prefrontal cortex, which aids emotion regulation (Creswell et al., 2007; Gotink et al., 2016).
- ***calms brain activation in emotional situations.*** This lower activation was clear in one study in which participants watched two movies—one sad, one neutral. Those in the control group, who were not trained in mindfulness, showed strong brain activation differences when watching the two movies. Those who had received mindfulness training showed little change in brain response to the two movies (Farb et al., 2010). Emotionally unpleasant images also trigger weaker electrical brain responses in mindful people than in their less mindful counterparts (Brown et al., 2013).

A mindful brain is strong, reflective, and calm.

And then there are the mystics who seek to use the mind's power to enable Novocain-free cavity repair. Their aim: transcend dental medication.

Faith Communities and Health

LOQ 40-9 What is the *faith factor,* and what are some possible explanations for the link between faith and health?

A wealth of studies—more than 2000 in the twenty-first century's first two decades alone—has revealed a curious correlation called the *faith factor* (Oman & Syme, 2018; VanderWeele, 2018). Religiously active people (especially in more religious cultures) tend to live longer than those not religiously active (Ebert et al., 2020). One such study compared the death rates for 3900 people living in two Israeli communities. The first contained 11 religiously orthodox collective settlements; the second contained 11 matched, nonreligious collective settlements (Kark et al., 1996). Over a 16-year period, "belonging to a religious collective was associated with a strong protective effect" not explained by age or economic differences. In every age group, religious community members were about half as likely to have died as were their nonreligious counterparts. This difference is roughly comparable to the gender difference in mortality. Another study followed 74,534 U.S. nurses over 20 years. When controlling for various health risk factors, those who attended religious services more than weekly were a third less likely to have died than were nonattenders, and were much less likely to have died by suicide (Li et al., 2016; VanderWeele et al., 2016). In U.S. obituaries, mention of a religious affiliation predicted 7.5 years of additional life compared with no religious affiliation (Wallace et al., 2018).

Barbara Smaller/Cartoon Stock

"We don't have a time-out chair in our Classroom Community. That's our mindfulness chair."

How should we interpret such findings, recalling that researchers cannot randomly assign people to be religiously engaged or not? Correlations are not cause-effect statements, and they leave many factors uncontrolled (Sloan, 2005; Sloan & Bagiella, 2002; Sloan et al., 1999, 2000). Here is another possible interpretation:

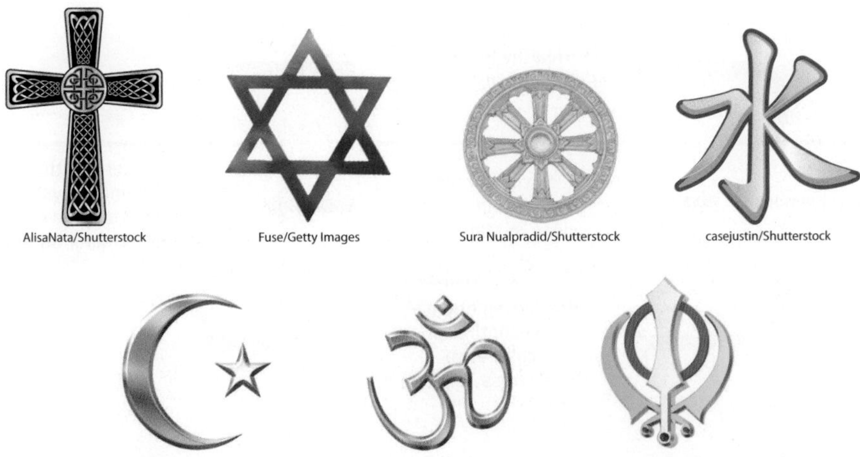
AlisaNata/Shutterstock Fuse/Getty Images Sura Nualpradid/Shutterstock casejustin/Shutterstock
Georgios Kollidas/Alamy Stock Photo Georgios Kollidas/Shutterstock ppart/Shutterstock

Women are more religiously active than men, and women outlive men. Might religious involvement merely reflect this gender-longevity link?

Apparently not. One 8-year National Institutes of Health study followed 92,395 women, ages 50 to 79. After controlling for many factors, researchers found that women attending religious services at least weekly experienced an approximately 20 percent reduced risk of death during the study period (Schnall et al., 2010). Moreover, the association between religious involvement and life expectancy is also found among men (Benjamins et al., 2010; McCullough et al., 2000; McCullough & Laurenceau, 2005). A 28-year study that followed 5286 Californians found that, after controlling for age, gender, ethnicity, and education, frequent religious attenders were 36 percent less likely to have died in any year (**FIGURE 40.4**). In another 8-year controlled study of more than 20,000 people (Hummer et al., 1999), this effect translated into a life expectancy of 83 years for those frequently attending religious services and 75 years for nonattenders.

Research points to three possible explanations for the religiosity-longevity correlation (**FIGURE 40.5**):

- ***Healthy behaviors*** Religion promotes self-control (DeWall et al., 2014; McCullough & Willoughby, 2009). This helps explain why religiously active people tend to smoke and drink much less and to have healthier lifestyles (Islam & Johnson, 2003; Koenig & Vaillant, 2009; Masters & Hooker, 2013; Park, 2007). In one large U.S. Gallup survey, 15 percent of the very religious were smokers, as were 28 percent of the nonreligious (Newport et al., 2010). But such lifestyle differences are not great enough to explain the dramatically reduced mortality in the Israeli religious settlements. In U.S. studies, too, about 75 percent of the longevity difference remained when researchers controlled for unhealthy behaviors, such as inactivity and smoking (Musick et al., 1999).
- ***Social support*** To belong to a faith community is to participate in a support network. Religiously active people are often there for one another when misfortune strikes.

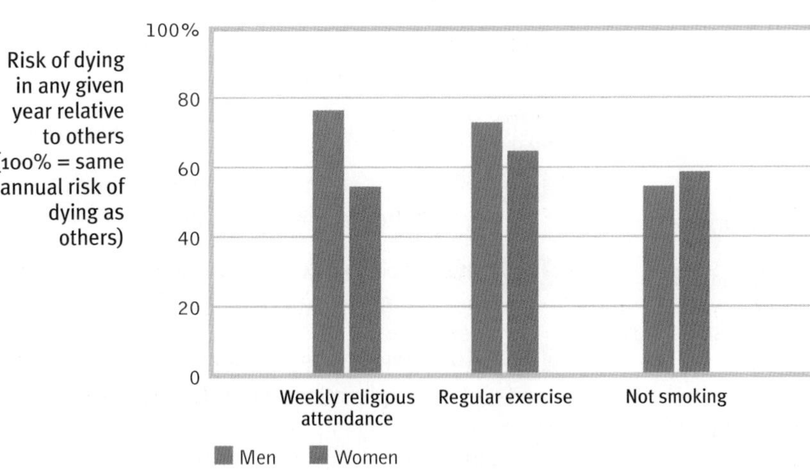
Risk of dying in any given year relative to others (100% = same annual risk of dying as others)
100%
80
60
40
20
0
Weekly religious attendance
Regular exercise
Not smoking
Men
Women

FIGURE 40.4
Predictors of longer life Researchers found that among adult participants, religious attendance, regular exercise, and not smoking all predicted a lowered risk of death in any given year (Oman et al., 2002; Strawbridge, 1999; Strawbridge et al., 1997). Women attending weekly religious services, for example, were only 54 percent as likely to die in a typical study year as were nonattenders.

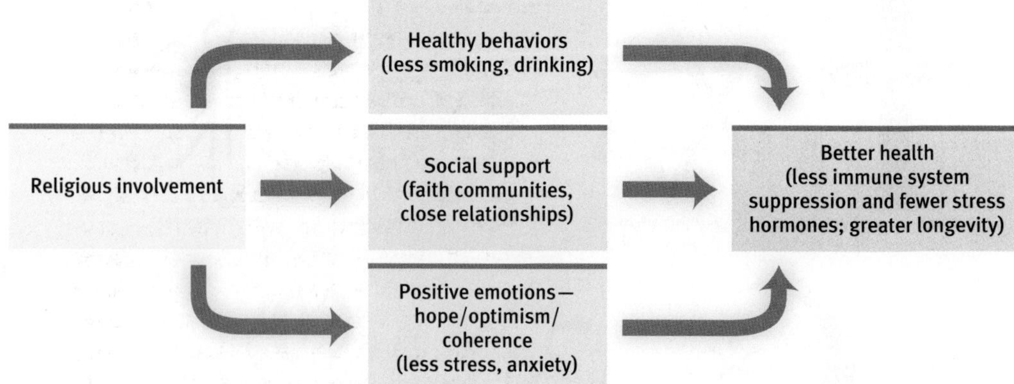
Healthy behaviors
(less smoking, drinking)
Religious involvement
Social support
(faith communities,
close relationships)
Better health
(less immune system
suppression and fewer stress
hormones; greater longevity)
Positive emotions—
hope/optimism/
coherence
(less stress, anxiety)

FIGURE 40.5
Possible explanations for the correlation between religious involvement and health/longevity

In the 20-year nurses study, for example, religious people's social support was the best predictor of their good health. Moreover, religion encourages marriage, another predictor (when happy) of health and longevity (Bookwala & Gaugler, 2020).

- ***Positive emotions*** Even after controlling for social support, unhealthy behaviors, gender, and preexisting health problems, studies have found that religiously engaged people tend to live longer (Chida et al., 2009). Researchers speculate that religiously active people may benefit from a stable, coherent worldview, a sense of hope for the long-term future, feelings of ultimate acceptance, and the relaxed meditation of prayer or other religious observances. The religiously active have had healthier immune functioning, fewer hospital admissions, and, for people with AIDS, fewer stress hormones and longer survival (Ironson et al., 2002; Koenig & Larson, 1998; Lutgendorf et al., 2004).

ASK YOURSELF

What strategies have you used to cope with stress in your life? How well have they worked? What other strategies could you try?

RETRIEVAL PRACTICE

RP-3 What are some of the tactics we can use to successfully manage the stress we cannot avoid?

ANSWERS IN APPENDIX E

MODULE 40 REVIEW Health and Coping

LEARNING OBJECTIVES

Test Yourself Answer these repeated Learning Objective Questions on your own (before "showing" the answers here, or checking the answers in Appendix D) to improve your retention of the concepts (McDaniel et al., 2009, 2015).

LOQ 40-1 In what two ways do people try to alleviate stress?

LOQ 40-2 How does a perceived lack of control affect health?

LOQ 40-3 Why is self-control important, and can our self-control be depleted?

LOQ 40-4 How does an optimistic outlook affect health and longevity?

LOQ 40-5 How does controlling our feelings affect our well-being and health?

LOQ 40-6 How does social support promote good health?

LOQ 40-7 How effective is aerobic exercise as a way to manage stress and improve well-being?

LOQ 40-8 In what ways might relaxation and meditation influence stress and health?

LOQ 40-9 What is the *faith factor,* and what are some possible explanations for the link between faith and health?

TERMS AND CONCEPTS TO REMEMBER

Test Yourself Write down the definition in your own words, then check your answer.

coping, p. 452
problem-focused coping, p. 452
emotion-focused coping, p. 452
personal control, p. 453
learned helplessness, p. 453
external locus of control, p. 454
internal locus of control, p. 454
self-control, p. 455
emotion regulation, p. 456
aerobic exercise, p. 460
mindfulness meditation, p. 463

MODULE TEST

Test Yourself Answer the following questions on your own first, then "show" the answers here, or check your answers in Appendix E.

1. When faced with a situation over which you feel you have little control, you are more likely to turn to ________ (emotion/problem)-focused coping.

2. Seligman's classic research showed that a dog will respond with learned helplessness if it has received repeated shocks and has had

a. the opportunity to escape.
b. no control over the shocks.
c. pain or discomfort.
d. no food or water prior to the shocks.

3. When nursing home residents take an active part in managing their own care and surroundings, their morale and health tend to improve. Such findings indicate that people do better when they experience an ________ (internal/external) locus of control.

4. How does accepting our feelings help us regulate our emotions more healthfully?

5. People who have close relationships are less likely to die prematurely than are those who do not, supporting the idea that

a. social ties can be a source of stress.
b. gender influences longevity.
c. Type A behavior is responsible for many premature deaths.
d. social support has a beneficial effect on health.

6. Because it triggers the release of mood-boosting neurotransmitters, such as norepinephrine, serotonin, and the endorphins, ________ exercise raises energy levels and helps alleviate depression and anxiety.

7. Research on the faith factor has found that

a. pessimists tend to be healthier than optimists.
b. our expectations influence our feelings of stress.
c. religiously active people tend to outlive those who are not religiously active.
d. religious engagement promotes social isolation and repression.

CHAPTER
13

Maskot/Getty Images

Social Psychology (Modules 41–44)

Dirk Willems faced a moment of decision in 1569. Threatened with torture and death as a member of a persecuted religious group, he escaped from his Asperen, Holland, prison and fled across an ice-covered pond. His stronger and heavier jailer pursued him but fell through the ice. Unable to climb out, the jailer pleaded for help.

With his freedom in front of him, Willems acted with ultimate selflessness. He turned back and rescued his pursuer, who, under orders, took him back to captivity. A few weeks later Willems was condemned to be "executed with fire, until death ensues." For his martyrdom, present-day Asperen has a street named in honor of its folk hero (Toews, 2004).

What drives groups, such as Willems' community, to act so heartlessly toward those who differ from them? What motivates people, such as Willems' jailer, to carry out unjust orders? And what inspired the selflessness of Willems' response, and the selflessness of so many who have died trying to save others? Indeed, what motivates any of us who volunteer kindness and generosity?

We are social animals. We cannot live for ourselves alone. Many of us felt this keenly during the Covid-19 pandemic, when social distancing meant going without the face-to-face social interactions we'd once taken for granted. *Social psychologists* explore our connections by scientifically studying how we *think about* and *influence* others (Modules 41 and 42), and also how we *relate* to one another (Modules 43 and 44).

MODULE

41 Social Thinking

LEARNING OBJECTIVE QUESTION LOQ **41-1** What do social psychologists study? How do we tend to explain others' behavior and our own?

Personality psychologists focus on the person. They study the personal traits and dynamics that explain why, in a given situation, *different people* act differently. (Would you have helped your jailer out of the icy water?) **Social psychologists** focus on the situation. They study the social influences that explain why *the same person* acts differently in *different situations*. (Might Willems' jailer have released him under other circumstances?)

Unlike sociology, which studies societies and social groupings, social psychologists focus more on how *individuals* view and affect one another.

The Fundamental Attribution Error

Dirk Willemſz. 1569.

Mennonite Library and Archives/Bethel College

An etching of Dirk Willems by Dutch artist Jan Luyken (From *The Martyrs Mirror*, 1685.)

Our social behavior arises from our social cognition. We all want to understand and explain why people act as they do. After studying how people explain others' behavior, Fritz Heider (1958) proposed an **attribution theory**: We can attribute the behavior to the person's stable, enduring traits (a *dispositional attribution*), or we can attribute it to the situation (a *situational attribution*).

For example, in class, we notice that Jill seldom talks. Over coffee, Jack talks nonstop. That must be the sort of people they are, we decide. Jill must be shy and Jack outgoing. Such attributions—to their dispositions—can be valid. People do have enduring personality traits. But sometimes we fall prey to the **fundamental attribution error** (Ross, 1977, 2018). In class, Jack may be as quiet as Jill. Catch Jill at a party and you may hardly recognize your quiet classmate.

Researchers demonstrated this tendency in an experiment with college students (Napolitan & Goethals, 1979). Students talked, one at a time, with a woman who acted either cold and critical or warm and friendly. Before the conversations, the researchers told half the students that the woman's behavior would be spontaneous. They told the other half the truth—that they had instructed her to *act* friendly or unfriendly.

Did hearing the truth affect students' impressions of the woman? Not at all! If the woman acted friendly, both groups decided she was a warm person. If she acted unfriendly, both decided she was a cold person. They attributed her behavior to her personal disposition *even when told that her behavior was situational*—that she was merely acting that way for the experiment.

We all commit the fundamental attribution error. Consider: Is your psychology instructor shy or outgoing? If you answer "outgoing," remember that you know your instructor from one situation—the classroom, where teaching demands talking. Your instructor might disagree: "Me, outgoing? It all depends on the situation. In class or with good friends, yes, I'm outgoing. But at professional meetings I'm really rather shy." Outside their assigned roles, professors seem less professorial, presidents less presidential, managers less managerial.

What Factors Affect Our Attributions?

One factor is culture. Westerners more often attribute behavior to people's personal traits. People in China and Japan are more sensitive to the power of the situation (Feinberg et al., 2019; Miyamoto & Kitayama, 2018). In experiments in which people viewed scenes, such as a big fish swimming among smaller fish and plants, Americans focused more on the attributes of the big fish. Japanese viewers focused more on the setting and context—the situation (Chua et al., 2005; Nisbett, 2003).

Whose behavior also matters. When we explain *our own* behavior, we are sensitive to how behavior changes with the situation (Idson & Mischel, 2001). We also are sensitive to the power of the situation when we explain the behavior of people we have seen

social psychology the scientific study of how we think about, influence, and relate to one another.

attribution theory the theory that we explain someone's behavior by crediting either the situation or the person's disposition.

fundamental attribution error the tendency, when analyzing others' behavior, to underestimate the impact of the situation and to overestimate the impact of personal disposition.

Keith Srakocic/AP Photo

Personal versus situational attributions Should the 2018 slaughter of 11 Jewish worshippers at Pittsburgh's Tree of Life synagogue be attributed to the shooter's hateful disposition? To social media, where the shooter and like-minded others promoted anti-Semitism and white nationalism? To the U.S. gun culture? (The shooter used four guns.) Or to all of these? And to what should we attribute the compassion of the emergency room nurse (a Jewish person and the son of a rabbi) who treated the hate-spewing shooter (Flynn, 2018)?

Some 7 in 10 college women report having experienced a man misattributing her friendliness as a sexual come-on (Jacques-Tiura et al., 2007).

in many different contexts. We more often commit the fundamental attribution error when a stranger behaves badly. Having only seen that enraged fan screaming at the referee in the heat of competition, we may assume a negative, disagreeable temperament. But outside the stadium, this person may be a good neighbor and a loving parent.

Would taking an observer's viewpoint make us more aware of our own behavior? Researchers tested this idea by using separate cameras to film two people interacting. When they showed each person a replay of the interaction—filmed from the other person's perspective—participants credited their own behavior more to their *disposition* (personal character), much as an observer typically would (Lassiter & Irvine, 1986; Storms, 1973). Similarly, when people assess a police officer's actions from the officer's body cam perspective (rather than a dashcam that also shows the officer), they become more attuned to the situation—and more sympathetic to the officer (Turner et al., 2019).

Two important exceptions to our usual view of our own actions: Our deliberate and *admirable* actions we often attribute to our own good reasons, not to the situation (Malle, 2006; Malle et al., 2007). And as we age, we tend to attribute our younger selves' behavior mostly to our traits (Pronin & Ross, 2006). In 5 or 10 years, your current self may seem like another person.

How Do Our Attributions Matter?

The way we explain others' actions, attributing them to the person or the situation, can have important real-life effects (Fincham & Bradbury, 1993; Fletcher et al., 1990). Does a warm greeting reflect romantic interest or social courtesy? Does a manager's tart-tongued remark reflect a job threat or just a bad day? Was a shooting malicious or an act of self-defense? In one study, 181 U.S. state judges gave lighter sentences to a violent offender who a scientist testified had a gene that altered brain areas related to aggressiveness (Aspinwall et al., 2012). Attributions matter.

Do you attribute poverty and unemployment to social circumstances, or to personal traits and bad choices? In Britain, India, Australia, and the United States, political conservatives have tended to attribute responsibility to the personal dispositions of people who are unemployed or living in poverty (Dunn, 2018; Furnham, 1982; Pandey et al., 1982; Wagstaff, 1982; Zucker & Weiner, 1993). They assume that people make their choices and that anybody who works hard can still get ahead. In experiments, those who reflect on the power of choice—either by recalling their own choices or by taking note of another's choices—become more likely to think that people get what they deserve (Savani & Rattan, 2012). Political liberals, and those not primed to consider the power of choice, are more likely to blame past and present situations. They assume that anyone who lacks access to quality education and other opportunities, and faces discrimination, would struggle to get ahead, no matter how hard they work.

The point to remember: Our attributions—to a person's disposition or to the situation—have real consequences.

Attitudes and Actions

LOQ 41-2 How do attitudes and actions interact?

Attitudes predispose our reactions to objects, people, and events. If we *believe* someone is threatening us, we may *feel* fear and anger toward the person and *act* defensively. The traffic between our attitudes and our actions is two-way. Our attitudes affect our actions. Hateful attitudes feed violent behavior. And our actions affect our attitudes (much as our emotional expressions affect our emotions).

attitude feelings, often influenced by our beliefs, that predispose us to respond in a particular way to objects, people, and events.

Attitudes Affect Actions

Attitudes affect our behavior. U.S. regions where people most often express hostile attitudes toward women (as evident in 1.8 billion tweets) are also regions that have high rates of domestic violence against women (Blake et al., 2021). But situational factors, such as intense social pressures, can override the attitude-behavior connection (Wallace et al., 2005). Politicians may vote as their supporters demand, despite privately disagreeing (Nagourney, 2002). Or they may publicly espouse behaviors they don't privately practice (as when one adulterous member of the U.S. Congress was said to be "pro-life in the streets, pro-choice in the sheets" [Weiner, 2017]).

Attitudes are especially likely to affect behavior when external influences are minimal, and when the attitude is stable, specific to the behavior, and easily recalled (Glasman & Albarracín, 2006). One experiment used vivid, easily remembered information to convince White sun-tanning college students that repeated tanning put them at risk for future skin cancer. One month later, 72 percent of the participants, and only 16 percent of those in a control group, had lighter skin (McClendon & Prentice-Dunn, 2001). Changed attitudes (about skin cancer risk) changed behavior (less tanning).

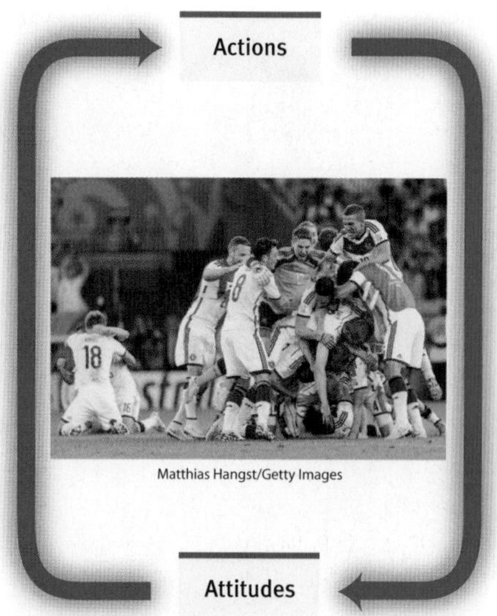
Actions
Attitudes

Matthias Hangst/Getty Images

FIGURE 41.1
Attitudes follow behavior Cooperative actions, such as those performed by people on sports teams (including Germany's, shown here celebrating a World Cup victory), feed mutual liking. Such attitudes, in turn, promote positive behavior.

Actions Affect Attitudes

Now consider a more surprising principle: Not only will we stand up for what we believe, but we also will more strongly believe in what we have stood up for. Many streams of evidence confirm the *attitudes follow behavior* principle (**FIGURE 41.1**).

THE FOOT-IN-THE-DOOR PHENOMENON How would you react if someone induced you to act against your beliefs? In many cases, people adjust their attitudes. During the Korean war, many U.S. prisoners were held in Chinese communist war camps. The captors secured prisoners' collaboration in various activities, ranging from simple tasks (running errands to gain privileges) to more serious actions (false confessions, informing on other prisoners, and divulging U.S. military information). After doing so, the prisoners sometimes adjusted their beliefs to be more consistent with their public acts (Lifton, 1961). When the war ended, 21 prisoners chose to stay with the communists. Some others returned home convinced that communism was good for Asia (though not actually "brainwashed," as has often been said).

The Chinese captors succeeded in part thanks to the **foot-in-the-door phenomenon**: They knew that people who agreed to a small request would find it easier to comply later with a larger one. The captors began with harmless requests, such as copying a trivial statement, but gradually escalated their demands (Schein, 1956). The next statement to be copied might list flaws of capitalism. Then, to gain privileges, the prisoners would move up to participating in group discussions, writing self-criticisms, and, finally, uttering public confessions. The point is simple: To get people to agree to something big, start small and build (Cialdini, 1993). A small lie paves the way to a bigger lie. Fibbers may become fraudsters. Succumb to a temptation and the next temptation becomes harder to resist.

Experiments also reveal a *door-in-the-face* effect (Cialdini et al., 1975; Genschow et al., 2021): Approach someone with an unreasonable request ("Could you volunteer daily for the next two weeks?"). After you get turned down (the door in the face), a follow-up moderate request becomes more acceptable ("Could you volunteer for the next 30 minutes?").

In dozens of experiments, researchers have coaxed people into acting against their attitudes or violating their moral standards, with the same result: Doing becomes believing. After giving in to an order to harm an innocent victim—by making nasty comments or delivering presumed electric shocks—people begin to disparage their victim. After speaking or writing on behalf of a position they have qualms about, they begin to believe their own words.

Fortunately, the attitudes-follow-behavior principle works with good deeds as well. In one classic experiment, researchers sought permission to place a large "Drive Carefully" sign in people's front yards (Freedman & Fraser, 1966). The 17 percent rate of agreement soared to 76 percent among those who first did a small favor—placing a 3-inch-high "Be a Safe Driver" sign in their window.

IS IT OKAY WITH YOU IF WE GO UP ON THE ROOF AND SHOOT OFF THESE HIGHLY ILLEGAL FIREWORKS?
WHAT? NO!!

THEN CAN I STAY OUT PAST MY CURFEW TO WATCH THE PUBLIC DISPLAY AT THE PARK?
OKAY

OPEN WITH THE OUTRAGEOUS, SETTLE FOR YOUR GOAL.
I TAUGHT YOU THAT!

King Features Syndicate

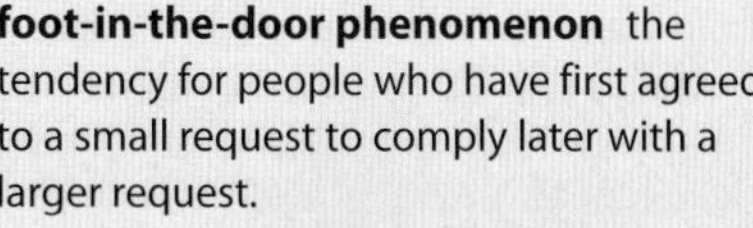

foot-in-the-door phenomenon the tendency for people who have first agreed to a small request to comply later with a larger request.

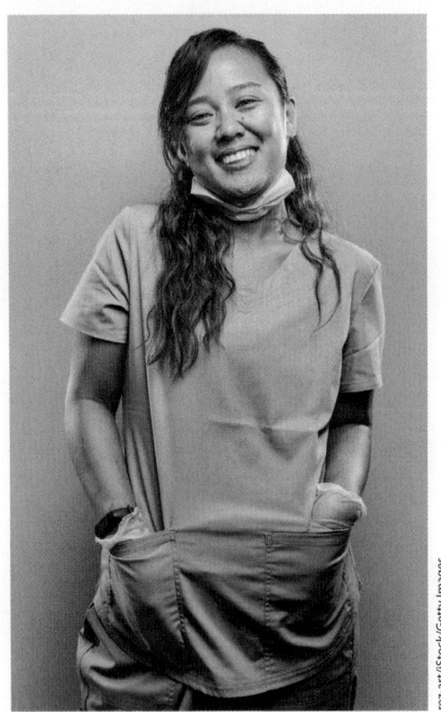
rez-art/iStock/Getty Images

New nurse Pulling on scrubs for the first time can feel like playing dress-up. But over time, that role defines the players, as they jump into the day-to-day work and follow the social cues in their new environment.

"Fake it until you make it." — Alcoholics Anonymous saying

The foot-in-the-door tactic has helped boost charitable contributions and blood donations. When mandates required seat belt use or Covid vaccination, many people at first protested—but then, after behaving in accord with the mandate—came to accept it. Behaving became believing.

Likewise, after U.S. schools were desegregated and Congress passed the 1964 Civil Rights Act, White Americans expressed diminishing racial prejudice. And as Americans in different regions came to *act* more alike—thanks to more uniform national standards against discrimination—they began to *think* more alike. Experiments confirm the point: *Moral actions strengthen moral convictions.*

ASK YOURSELF

Do you have an attitude or tendency you would like to change? Using the attitudes-follow-behavior principle, how might you go about changing that attitude?

ROLE-PLAYING AFFECTS ATTITUDES When you adopt a new **role**—when you become a college student, become a parent, or begin a new job—you strive to follow the social prescriptions. At first, your behaviors may feel phony, because you are acting a role. Soldiers may at first feel they are playing war games. Before long, however, what began as play-acting in the theater of life becomes *you*. To choose a vocation is also to choose who you will become (Woods et al., 2020).

Step-by-step role-playing has even been used to train torturers (Staub, 1989). In the early 1970s, the Greek military government eased men into their roles. First, a trainee played the role of guard outside an interrogation cell. After this foot-in-the-door step, he stood guard inside. Only then was he ready to become actively involved in the questioning-and-torture role. In one study of German men, military training toughened their personalities, leaving them less agreeable even 5 years later, after leaving the military (Jackson et al., 2012). What we do, we gradually become: Every time we act like the people around us, we slightly change ourselves to be more like them and less like who we used to be.

Yet people differ. In real-life atrocity-producing situations, some people have succumbed to the situation and others have not (Haslam & Reicher, 2007, 2012; Mastroianni & Reed, 2006; Zimbardo, 2007). Person and situation interact.

COGNITIVE DISSONANCE: RELIEF FROM TENSION We have seen that actions can affect attitudes, sometimes turning prisoners into collaborators and role-players into believers. But why? One explanation is that when we become aware that our attitudes and actions don't coincide, we experience tension, or *cognitive dissonance*. To relieve this mental tension, according to Leon Festinger's (1957) **cognitive dissonance theory**, we often bring our attitudes into line with our past actions.

Dozens of experiments have tested cognitive dissonance theory (Levy et al., 2018). Many have made people feel responsible for behavior that clashed with their attitudes and had foreseeable consequences. As a participant in one of these experiments, you might agree, for a small sum of money, to write an essay supporting something you don't believe in (perhaps a tuition increase). Feeling responsible for your written statements (which are inconsistent with your attitudes), you would probably feel dissonance, especially if you thought your essay might influence an administrator. To reduce the uncomfortable tension, you might start believing your phony words. It's as if we rationalize, "If I chose to do it (or say it), I must believe in it." The less coerced and more responsible we feel for a troubling act, the more dissonance we feel. The more dissonance we feel, the more motivated we are to find and project consistency, such as changing our attitudes to justify the act.

The attitudes-follow-behavior principle has a heartening implication: We cannot directly control all our feelings, but we can influence them by altering our behavior. If we are depressed, we can change our attributions and explain events in more positive terms, with more self-acceptance and fewer self-put-downs (Rubenstein et al., 2016). If we are unloving, we can become more loving by behaving *as if* we were—by doing thoughtful things, expressing affection, giving affirmation. We can stay home or wear

role a set of expectations *(norms)* about a social position, defining how those in the position ought to behave.

cognitive dissonance theory the theory that we act to reduce the discomfort (dissonance) we feel when two of our thoughts (cognitions) are inconsistent. For example, when we become aware that our attitudes and our actions clash, we can reduce the resulting dissonance by changing our attitudes.

a mask when feeling sick. "Each time you ask yourself, 'How should I act?,'" observes Robert Levine (2016), "you are also asking, 'Who is the person I want to become?'" That helps explain why teens doing volunteer work promotes a compassionate identity. Act as if you like someone, and you soon may. Pretense can become reality. Conduct sculpts character. What we do we become.

The point to remember: Not only can we think ourselves into action, but we can also act ourselves into a way of thinking.

"Sit all day in a moping posture, sigh, and reply to everything with a dismal voice, and your melancholy lingers. . . . If we wish to conquer undesirable emotional tendencies in ourselves, we must . . . go through the outward movements of those contrary dispositions which we prefer to cultivate." —William James, *Principles of Psychology* (1890)

RETRIEVAL PRACTICE

RP-1 Driving to school one snowy day, Marco narrowly misses a car that slides through a red light. "Slow down! What a terrible driver," he thinks. Moments later, Marco himself slips through an intersection and yelps, "Wow! These roads are awful. The city plows need to get out here." What social psychology principle has Marco just demonstrated? Explain.

RP-2 How do our attitudes and our actions affect each other?

RP-3 When people act in a way that is not in keeping with their attitudes, and then change their attitudes to match those actions, ____________________ ____________________ theory attempts to explain why.

ANSWERS IN APPENDIX E

Persuasion

LOQ 41-3 How do *peripheral route persuasion* and *central route persuasion* differ?

Often, people may try to influence our actions by *persuading* us to change our attitudes. Public health officials aimed to persuade people of the Covid pandemic's threat, and of the protective power of vaccination and mask-wearing. Persuasion efforts generally take two forms:

- **Peripheral route persuasion** uses attention-getting cues to trigger speedy, emotion-based judgments. One experiment gave some people information that debunked the vaccines-cause-autism myth; others viewed photos of unvaccinated children suffering mumps, measles, or rubella, along with a parent's description of their child's suffering with measles. Only those given the vivid photos and description became more supportive of vaccines (Horne et al., 2015). Endorsements by beautiful or famous people can also influence people, whether they're choosing a political candidate or a perfume. When environmental activist and actor Cate Blanchett urges action to counter climate change disaster, or when Pope Francis (2015) states that "Climate change is a global problem with grave implications," they hope to harness their appeal for peripheral route persuasion. The same is true of advertisements that use heart-tugging imagery to sell products.
- **Central route persuasion** offers evidence and arguments that trigger careful thinking. To persuade consumers to purchase a new gadget, an ad might itemize all the latest features. To marshal support for climate change intervention, convincing arguments have focused on the accumulating greenhouse gases, melting arctic ice, rising world temperatures and seas, and increasing extreme weather (van der Linden et al., 2015). Central route persuasion works well for people who are naturally analytical or involved in an issue. And because it is more thoughtful and less superficial, it is more durable. When people actively process a message—when they mentally elaborate on it—they more often retain it (a phenomenon described by the *elaboration likelihood model*).

With time and persuasion, attitudes can change dramatically. What yesterday's people accepted without question—slavery, climate destruction, anti-gay policies, orca captures—today's people mostly mourn. So how can we be more successful at getting others to see our point of view? And how can we more effectively counter misinformation, such as from anti-vaccine activists or conspiracy theorists? For more on effective persuasion strategies, see Thinking Critically About: How to Be Persuasive.

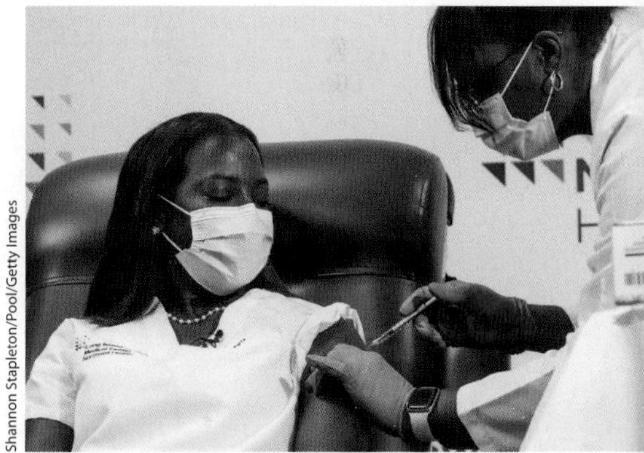

Shannon Stapleton/Pool/Getty Images

Peripheral route persuasion New York nurse Sandra Lindsay made history when she became the first American vaccinated for the coronavirus. Mindful of historically unequal and racist medical treatment of people of color, Lindsay said she wanted to "inspire people who look like me, who are skeptical in general about taking vaccines" (Otterman, 2020).

"Have you ever noticed how one example—good or bad—can prompt others to follow? How one illegally parked car can give permission for others to do likewise? How one racial joke can fuel another?" —Marian Wright Edelman, *The Measure of Our Success*, 1994

peripheral route persuasion occurs when people are influenced by attention-getting cues, such as a speaker's attractiveness. 

central route persuasion occurs when interested people's thinking is influenced by considering evidence and arguments.

Thinking Critically About: How to Be Persuasive

LOQ 41-4 How can we share our views more effectively?

Do not:

Loudly argue your position before listening. But do use respectful questions that help people assess the evidence, such as "What evidence might change your mind?"[1]

Humiliate people, or imply that they are ignorant. Insults breed defensiveness.

^%*&#!!
idiot
#&#!!
Stupid

Bore people with complex and forgettable information. But do "pre-suade" people by "prebunking" misinformation before they encounter it.[2]

Therefore, with that said, direct your attention to this very dull and wonky and boring statistic that you will never remember. Now, however, on the other hand, here are yet more data points that are even more dry and overly complicated than the last... Let us continue...

Do:

Identify your shared values or goals, such as, "Do we both value people's right to health and life, and their freedom to be free of disease?"

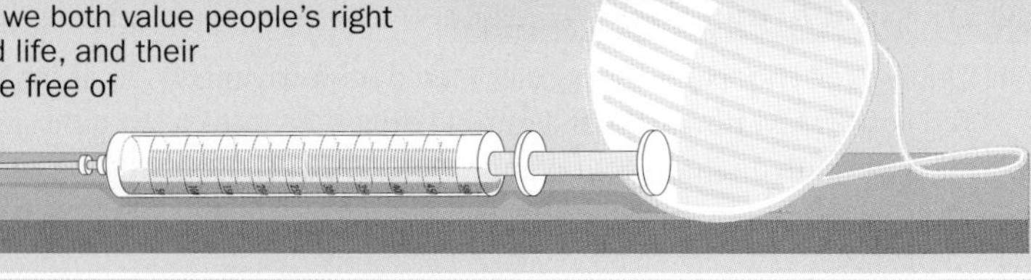

Appeal to others' admirable motives. Relate your aims to their yearnings.[3] For example:

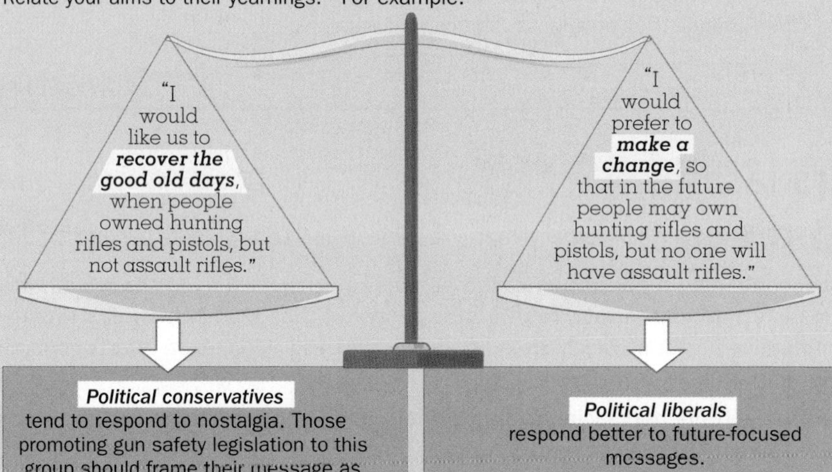

"I would like us to ***recover the good old days***, when people owned hunting rifles and pistols, but not assault rifles."
"I would prefer to ***make a change***, so that in the future people may own hunting rifles and pistols, but no one will have assault rifles."

Political conservatives tend to respond to nostalgia. Those promoting gun safety legislation to this group should frame their message as an affirmation of yesteryear.

Political liberals respond better to future-focused messages.

Make your message vivid. People remember dramatic visual examples. Pictures of unvaccinated children suffering from preventable diseases, or hungry children starving speak to the heart as well as the head.

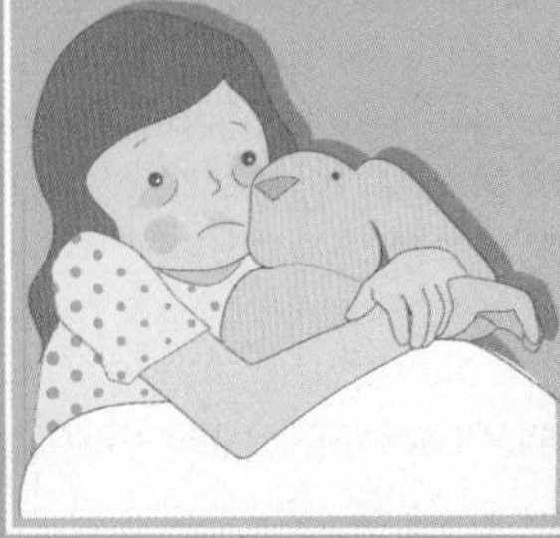

Repeat your message. People often come to believe repeated falsehoods, but they also tend to believe oft-repeated truths.

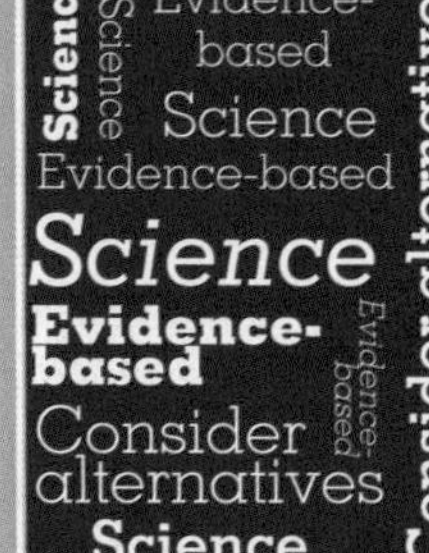

Science
Science
Evidence-based
Science
Evidence-based
Science
Evidence-based
Evidence-based
Consider alternatives
Science
Consider alternatives

Engage your audience in restating your message or, better yet, acting on it. Engage them in actively owning it—not just passively listening.

1. McIntyre, 2021. 2. Jolley & Douglas, 2017. 3. Lammers & Baldwin, 2018.

ASK YOURSELF

Have you found yourself using any of the ineffective persuasive strategies identified in the infographic? How might you improve your approach the next time you are having an important discussion?

RETRIEVAL PRACTICE

RP-4 What are some evidence-based ways to effectively persuade others?

ANSWERS IN APPENDIX E

MODULE 41 REVIEW Social Thinking

LEARNING OBJECTIVES

Test Yourself Answer these repeated Learning Objective Questions on your own (before "showing" the answers here, or checking the answers in Appendix D) to improve your retention of the concepts (McDaniel et al., 2009, 2015).

LOQ 41-1 What do social psychologists study? How do we tend to explain others' behavior and our own?

LOQ 41-2 How do attitudes and actions interact?

LOQ 41-3 How do *peripheral route persuasion* and *central route persuasion* differ?

LOQ 41-4 How can we share our views more effectively?

TERMS AND CONCEPTS TO REMEMBER

Test Yourself Write down the definition in your own words, then check your answer.

social psychology, p. 469
attribution theory, p. 469
fundamental attribution error, p. 469
attitude, p. 470
foot-in-the-door phenomenon, p. 471
role, p. 472
cognitive dissonance theory, p. 472
peripheral route persuasion, p. 473
central route persuasion, p. 473

MODULE TEST

Test Yourself Answer the following questions on your own first, then "show" the answers here, or check your answers in Appendix E.

1. A study indicated that most teen boys and girls believe the women they see in online porn are experiencing real sexual pleasure (Jones, 2018). But the situation—being in front of the camera—suggests the women are acting their role. Social psychologists might explain the teens' misperception as the ________ ________ error.
2. We tend to agree to a larger request more readily if we have already agreed to a small request. This tendency is called the ________-________-________-________ phenomenon.
3. Jamala's therapist has suggested that Jamala should "act as if" she is confident, even though she feels insecure and shy. Which social psychological theory would best support this suggestion, and what might the therapist be hoping to achieve?
4. Celebrity endorsements in advertising often lead consumers to purchase products through ________ (central/peripheral) route persuasion.

MODULE 42 Social Influence

Social psychology's great lesson is the enormous power of social influence. This influence stems in part from social **norms**. On campus, workout clothes are the norm; on New York's Wall Street or London's Bond Street, business attire is expected. When we know how to act, how to groom, how to talk, life functions smoothly.

But sometimes social pressure moves people in dreadful directions. Isolated with others who share their grievances, dissenters may gradually become rebels, and rebels may become terrorists. Shootings, suicides, and bomb threats all have a curious tendency to come in clusters. After a mass killing (of four or more people), the probability of another such attack increases for the ensuing 13 days (Towers et al., 2015). Let's examine the pull of these social strings. How strong are they? How do they operate? When do we break them?

norms understood rules for accepted and expected behavior. Norms prescribe "proper" behavior.

I CAN'T STOP YAWNING, EITHER...
CLAMS
© Dave Coverly/speedbump.com

Conformity: Complying With Social Pressures

LOQ 42-1 How is social contagion a form of conformity, and how do conformity experiments reveal the power of social influence?

Social Contagion

Fish swim in schools. Birds fly in flocks. And humans, too, tend to go with their group, to do what it does and think what it thinks. Behavior is influenced by *social contagion*. A lion that sees another member of its pride yawn becomes 100+ times more likely to yawn in the next 3 minutes (Casetta et al., 2021). If one of us humans yawns, laughs, coughs, scratches, stares at the sky, or checks our phone, others in our group will often do the same (Holle et al., 2012). Even just reading about yawning increases people's yawning (Provine, 2012), as perhaps you've just noticed?

Tanya Chartrand and John Bargh (1999) call this social contagion the *chameleon effect*, likening it to chameleon lizards' ability to mimic the color of their surroundings. They captured the effect by having students work in a room alongside another person (actually an *accomplice* working for the experimenters). Sometimes the accomplices rubbed their own face. Sometimes they shook their foot. Sure enough, students tended to rub their face along with the face-rubbing person and shake their foot along with the foot-shaking person.

Social contagion also affects emotions. We human chameleons take on the emotional tones of those around us—their expressions, postures, inflections—and even their grammar (Ireland & Pennebaker, 2010). Just hearing someone reading a neutral text in either a happy- or sad-sounding voice creates *mood contagion* in listeners (Neumann & Strack, 2000).

This natural mimicry enables us to *empathize*. We smile and frown when others do, and then feel what others feel. This helps explain why we feel happier around happy people than around depressed people. It also helps explain why studies of groups of British workers have revealed *mood linkage,* the sharing of moods (Totterdell et al., 1998). Empathic mimicking—as when a conversation partner nods their head as you do—fosters fondness (Chartrand & van Baaren, 2009; Lakin et al., 2008). We tend to mimic those we like, and to like those who mimic us (Kämpf et al., 2018). Just going for a walk with someone—perhaps someone with whom you disagreed—not only synchronizes your movements but increases rapport and empathy (Webb et al., 2017).

"When I see synchrony and mimicry—whether it concerns yawning, laughing, dancing, or aping—I see social connection and bonding." —Primatologist Frans de Waal, "The Empathy Instinct," 2009

Social networks serve as contagious pathways for moods, such as happiness and loneliness, drug use, and even the behavior patterns that lead to obesity and sleep loss (Christakis & Fowler, 2009). On websites, positive ratings generate more positive ratings—a phenomenon called *positive herding* (Muchnik et al., 2013). In a massive experiment on the 2010 U.S. congressional election day, Facebook showed 61 million people a message that encouraged voting, with a link to a local voting place and a clickable "I voted" button. For some recipients, the messages also contained pictures of Facebook friends who had already voted. Those who received "tell your friends you voted" messages were slightly more likely to vote, and that difference generated an estimated 282,000 additional votes.

Suggestibility and mimicry can also lead to tragedy. Following highly publicized mass shootings, people are more likely to purchase guns and threaten violence (Cooper, 1999; Porfiri et al., 2019). Spikes in suicide rates sometimes also follow a highly publicized suicide (Phillips, 1985; Phillips et al., 1989).

What causes behavior clusters? Do people act similarly because they influence one another? Or because they are simultaneously exposed to the same events and conditions? Seeking answers to such questions, social psychologists have conducted experiments on conformity.

NON SEQUITUR
by WILEY
BANKING on the YOUTH MARKET...
TATTOO & PIERCING
BE LIKE ALL YOUR FRIENDS AND EXPRESS YOUR INDIVIDUALITY
OPEN
WWW.NON-SEQUITUR.NET
Reprinted by permission of Anderws McMeel. © 1997 Wiley.

Conformity and Social Norms

Suggestibility and mimicry are subtle types of **conformity**. To study conformity, Solomon Asch (1955) devised a simple test. Imagine yourself as a participant in a supposed study of visual perception. You arrive in time to take a seat at a table with five other people. The experimenter asks the group members to state, one by one, which of three comparison lines is identical to a standard line. You see clearly that the answer is Line 2, and you wait your turn to say so. Your boredom begins to show when the next set of lines proves equally easy.

conformity adjusting our behavior or thinking to coincide with a group standard.

normative social influence influence resulting from a person's desire to gain approval or avoid disapproval.

Now comes the third trial, and the correct answer seems just as clear-cut (**FIGURE 42.1**). But the first person gives what strikes you as a wrong answer: "Line 3." When the second person and then the third and fourth give the same wrong answer, you sit up straight and squint. When the fifth person agrees with the first four, you feel your heart begin to pound. The experimenter then looks to you for your answer. Torn between the unanimity voiced by the five others and the evidence of your own eyes, you feel tense and suddenly unsure. You hesitate before answering, wondering whether you should suffer the discomfort of being the oddball. What answer do you give?

In Asch's experiments, college students, answering questions alone, erred less than 1 percent of the time. But what happened when several others—accomplices of the experimenter—answered incorrectly? Although most people told the truth even when others did not, Asch was disturbed by his result: More than one-third of the time, these "intelligent and well-meaning" college students were "willing to call white black" by going along with the group (Asch, 1955).

Later investigations have not always found as much conformity as Asch found, but they have revealed that we are more likely to conform when we

- are made to feel incompetent or insecure.
- are in a group with at least three other people.
- are in a group in which everyone else agrees. (If just one other person disagrees, the odds of our disagreeing greatly increase.)
- admire the group's status and attractiveness.
- have not made a prior commitment to any response.
- know that others in the group will observe our behavior.
- are from a culture that strongly encourages respect for social standards.

Why do we so often do as others do and think as they think? Why, when asked controversial questions, are students' answers more similar when they raise their hands and more diverse when they use anonymous electronic clickers (Stowell et al., 2010)? Why do we clap when others clap, eat as others eat, believe what others believe, say what others say, even see what others see?

Frequently, we conform to avoid rejection or to gain social approval. In such cases, we are responding to **normative social influence**. We need to belong. People are most conforming to social norms in collectivist and tight cultures, which prize group harmony (Stamkou et al., 2019). People also are responsive to "dynamic norms"—to how norms are *changing,* such as toward eating less meat, consuming fewer sugary drinks, or supporting gay rights (Sparkman & Walton, 2017, 2019).

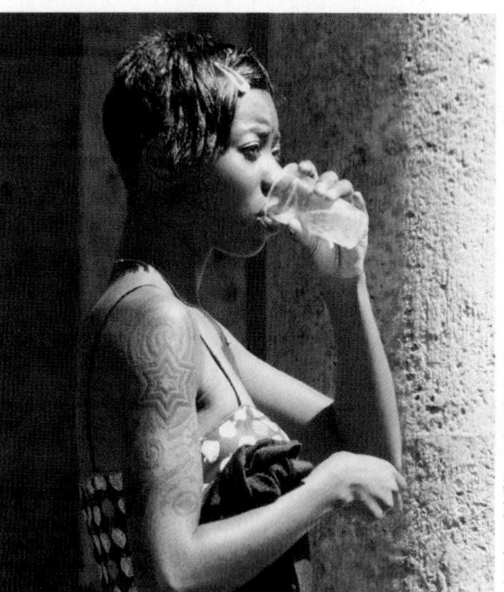

Gerda & Helmut Schill/Anzenberger/Redux Pictures

Tattoos: Yesterday's nonconformity, today's conformity? Steven Pinker (2019) recalls the unnoticed irony of the college administrator who bragged: "Our students are nonconformists. They all have tattoos and piercings."

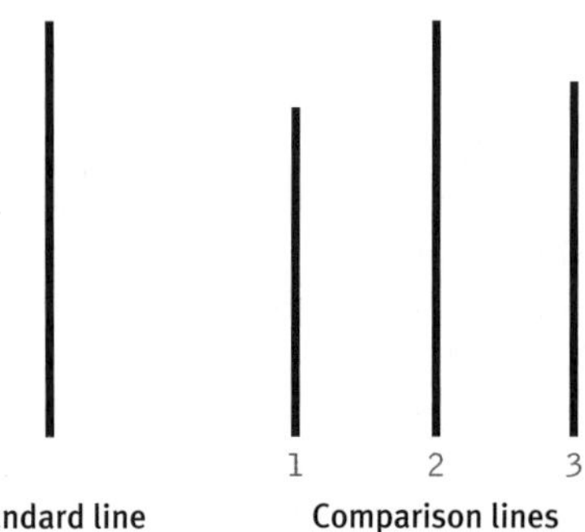
1
2
3
Standard line
Comparison lines

5
6
7

William Vendivert/Scientific American

FIGURE 42.1
Asch's conformity experiments Which of the three comparison lines is equal to the standard line? What do you suppose most people would say after hearing five others say, "Line 3"? In this photo from one of Asch's experiments, the student in the center shows the severe discomfort that comes from disagreeing with the responses of other group members (in this case, accomplices of the experimenter).

"I love the little ways you're identical to everyone else."

Mike Twohy/Cartoon Stock

At other times, we conform because we want to be accurate. Groups provide information, and only an uncommonly stubborn person will never listen to others. When we accept others' opinions about reality, as when reading online movie and product reviews, we are responding to **informational social influence**. Sometimes it pays to assume others are right and to follow their lead. One Welsh driver set a record for the longest distance driven on the wrong side of a British divided highway—30 miles, with only one minor sideswipe, before the motorway ran out and police were able to puncture her tires. The driver, who was intoxicated, later explained that she thought the hundreds of other drivers coming at her were all on the wrong side of the road (Woolcock, 2004).

Is conformity bad or good? Conformity can be bad—leading people to agree with falsehoods or go along with bullying. Or it can be good—leading people to give more generously after observing others' generosity (Nook et al., 2016). The answer also depends partly on our culturally influenced values. People in many Asian, African, and Latin American countries place a high value on *collectivism* (emphasizing group standards). Western Europeans and people in most English-speaking countries tend to prize *individualism* (emphasizing an independent self). Experiments across more than two dozen countries have found lower conformity rates in individualist and loose cultures (Bond & Smith, 1996; Gelfand et al., 2011).

"I don't know where we're going, but I'm following the crowd."—Derrick Evans (January 6, 2021), live-streaming himself among the mob invading the U.S. Capitol

Like humans, migrating and herding animals conform for both informational and normative reasons (Claidière & Whiten, 2012). Following others is informative; compared with a solo goose, a flock of geese migrates more accurately. (There is wisdom in the crowd.) And staying with the herd also sustains group membership.

ASK YOURSELF

How have you found yourself conforming, or perhaps "conforming to nonconformity"? In what ways have you seen others identifying themselves with those of the same culture or subculture?

RETRIEVAL PRACTICE

RP-1 Which of the following strengthens conformity to a group?

a. Finding the group attractive
b. Feeling secure
c. Coming from an individualist culture
d. Having made a prior commitment

RP-2 Despite her mother's pleas to use a more ergonomic backpack, Antonia insists on carrying all of her books to school in an oversized purse, the way her fashionable friends do. Antonia is affected by what type of social influence?

ANSWERS IN APPENDIX E

Obedience: Following Orders

LOQ 42-2 What did Milgram's obedience experiments teach us about the power of social influence?

Social psychologist Stanley Milgram (1963, 1974), a student of Solomon Asch, knew that people often give in to social pressures. But what about outright commands? Would they respond as did those who carried out Holocaust atrocities? (Some of Milgram's family members had survived Nazi concentration camps.) To find out, the 26-year-old Yale professor undertook what have become social psychology's most famous and controversial experiments (Benjamin & Simpson, 2009).

Imagine yourself as one of the nearly 1000 people, mostly White men aged 20 to 50, who took part in Milgram's 23 experiments. You respond to an ad for participants in a Yale University psychology study of the effect of punishment on learning. Professor Milgram's assistant asks you and another person to draw slips from a hat to see who will be the "teacher" and who will be the "learner." You draw a "teacher" slip (unknown to you, both slips say "teacher"). The supposed learner, a mild and submissive-seeming man, is led to an adjoining room and strapped into a chair. From the chair, wires run through the wall to a shock machine. You sit down in front of the machine and are given your task: Teach and then test the learner on a list of word pairs. If the learner gives a wrong answer, you are to flip a switch to deliver a brief electric shock. For the first wrong answer, you will flip the switch labeled "15 Volts—Slight Shock." With each

Stanley Milgram (1933–1984) This social psychologist's obedience experiments "belong to the self-understanding of literate people in our age" (Sabini, 1986).

Macmillan Learning

informational social influence influence resulting from a person's willingness to accept others' opinions about reality.

succeeding error, you will move to the next higher voltage. With each flip of a switch, lights flash and electronic switches buzz.

The experiment begins, and you deliver the shocks after the first and second wrong answers. If you continue, you hear the learner grunt when you flick the third, fourth, and fifth switches. After you activate the eighth switch ("120 Volts—Moderate Shock"), the learner cries out that the shocks are painful. After the tenth switch ("150 Volts—Strong Shock"), he begins shouting: "Get me out of here! I won't be in the experiment anymore! I refuse to go on!" You draw back, but the stern experimenter prods you: "Please continue—the experiment requires that you continue." You resist, but the experimenter insists, with statements such as, "It is absolutely essential that you continue," or "You have no other choice, you *must* go on."

If you obey, you hear the learner shriek in apparent agony as you continue to raise the shock level after each new error. After the 330-volt level, the learner refuses to answer and falls silent. Still, the experimenter pushes you toward the final, 450-volt switch. "Ask the question," he says, "and if no correct answer is given, administer the next shock level."

Would you follow the experimenter's commands to shock someone? At what level would you refuse to obey? Previously, Milgram had asked nonparticipants what they would do. Most were sure they would stop soon after the learner first indicated pain, certainly before he shrieked in agony. Forty psychiatrists agreed with that prediction. Were the predictions accurate? Not even close. When Milgram actually conducted the experiment, he was astonished. More than 60 percent complied fully—right up to the last switch. When he ran a new study, with 40 new "teachers" and a learner who complained of a "slight heart condition," the results were similar. A full 65 percent of the new teachers obeyed the experimenter, right up to 450 volts (**FIGURE 42.2**). In 10 later studies, women obeyed at rates similar to men's (Blass, 1999).

Were Milgram's results a product of the 1960s U.S. mindset? *No.* In a decades-later replication, 70 percent of the California participants obeyed up to the 150-volt point (only a modest reduction from Milgram's 83 percent at that level) (Burger, 2009). A Polish research team found 90 percent obedience to the same level (Doliński et al., 2017). And when a French reality TV show replicated Milgram's study, 81 percent of participants, egged on by a cheering audience, obeyed and tortured a screaming "victim" (Beauvois et al., 2012).

Did Milgram's teachers figure out the hoax—that no real shock was being delivered and the learner was in fact an accomplice pretending to feel pain? Did they realize the experiment was really testing their willingness to comply with commands to inflict punishment? Some did, and then became willing to play along, report Milgram's critics

FIGURE 42.2
Milgram's follow-up obedience experiment

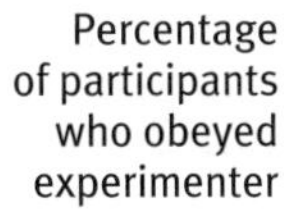
Percentage
of participants
who obeyed
experimenter

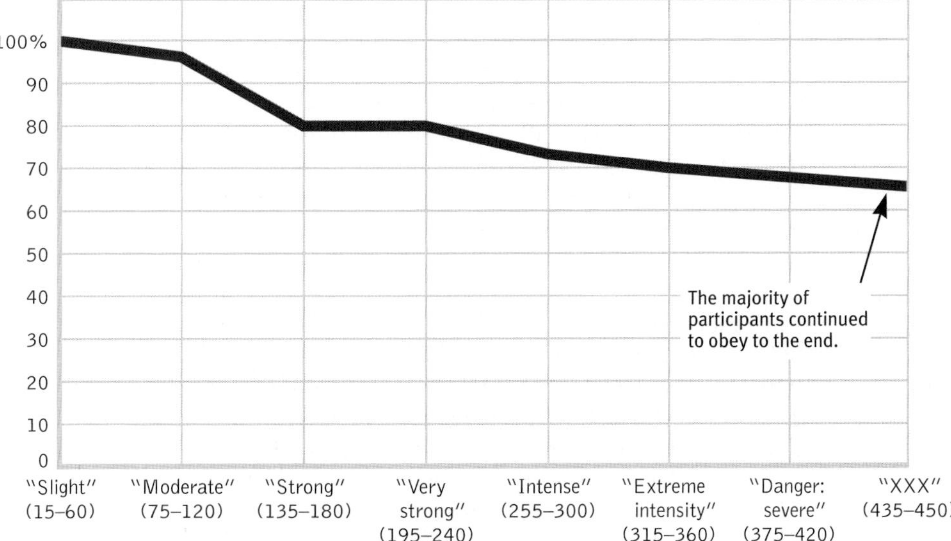
100%
90
80
70
60
50
40
30
20
10
0
The majority of participants continued to obey to the end.
"Slight" (15–60)
"Moderate" (75–120)
"Strong" (135–180)
"Very strong" (195–240)
"Intense" (255–300)
"Extreme intensity" (315–360)
"Danger: severe" (375–420)
"XXX" (435–450)
Shock levels in volts

Stanley and Alexandra Milgram

Stanley Milgram, from the film "Obedience." Rights held by Alexandra Milgram

(Griggs et al., 2020), though Milgram reported that the teachers were often genuinely distressed: Many sweated, trembled, laughed nervously, and bit their lips.

Milgram's use of deception and stress triggered a debate over his research ethics. In his own defense, Milgram pointed out that, after the participants learned of the deception and actual research purposes, virtually none regretted taking part (though perhaps by then the participants had reduced their *cognitive dissonance*—the discomfort they felt when their actions conflicted with their attitudes). When a psychiatrist later interviewed 40 of the teachers who had agonized most, none appeared to be suffering emotional aftereffects. All in all, said Milgram, the experiments provoked less enduring stress than university students experience when facing and failing big exams (Blass, 1996). Other scholars, however, after delving into Milgram's archives, report that his debriefing was less extensive and his participants' distress greater than he had suggested (Nicholson, 2011; Perry, 2013). Critics have also speculated that participants may have been identifying with the researcher and his scientific goals rather than merely being blindly obedient (Haslam et al., 2014, 2016).

In later experiments, Milgram discovered some conditions that influence people's behavior. When he varied the situation, full obedience ranged from 0 to 93 percent. Obedience was highest when

- ***the person giving the orders was close at hand and was perceived as a legitimate authority figure.*** This was the case in 2005 when Temple University's basketball coach sent a 250-pound bench player, Nehemiah Ingram, into a game with instructions to commit "hard fouls." Following orders, Ingram fouled out in 4 minutes after breaking an opposing player's right arm.
- ***a powerful or prestigious institution supported the authority figure.*** Compliance was somewhat lower when Milgram dissociated his experiments from Yale University. People have wondered: Why, during the 1994 Rwandan genocide, did so many Hutu citizens slaughter their Tutsi neighbors? It was partly because they were part of "a culture in which orders from above, even if evil," were understood as having the force of law (Kamatali, 2014).
- ***the victim was depersonalized or at a distance, even in another room.*** Similarly, many soldiers in combat either have not fired their rifles at an enemy they could see, or have not aimed them properly. Such refusals to kill are rarer among soldiers operating long-distance artillery or aircraft weapons (Padgett, 1989). Those who kill from a distance—by operating remotely piloted drones—also suffer stress, though much less posttraumatic stress than do veterans of on-the-ground conflict in Afghanistan and Iraq (G. Miller, 2012).
- ***there were no role models for defiance.*** "Teachers" did not see any other participant disobey the experimenter.

"I was only following orders."—Adolf Eichmann, Director of Nazi deportation of Jews to concentration camps

The power of legitimate, close-at-hand authorities was apparent among those who followed orders to carry out the Nazis' Holocaust atrocities. Obedience alone does not explain the Holocaust—anti-Semitic ideology produced eager killers as well (Fenigstein, 2015; Mastroianni, 2015). But obedience was a factor. In the summer of 1942, nearly 500 middle-aged German reserve police officers were dispatched to German-occupied Jozefow, Poland. On July 13, the group's visibly upset commander informed his recruits, mostly family men, of their orders. They were to round up the village's Jews, who were said to be aiding the enemy. Able-bodied men would be sent to work camps, and the rest would be shot on the spot.

The commander gave the recruits a chance to refuse to participate in the executions. Only about a dozen immediately refused. Within 17 hours, the remaining 485 officers killed 1500 helpless citizens, including women, children, and the elderly, shooting them in the back of the head as they lay face down. Hearing the victims' pleas, and seeing the gruesome results, some 20 percent of the officers did dissent eventually, managing either to miss their victims or to slip away and hide until the slaughter was over (Browning, 1992). In real life, as in Milgram's experiments, those who resisted were the minority.

A different story played out in the French village of Le Chambon. There, villagers openly defied orders to cooperate with the "New Order": They sheltered French Jews destined for deportation to Germany, and they sometimes helped them escape across the Swiss border. The villagers' Protestant ancestors had themselves been persecuted, and their pastors taught them to "resist whenever our adversaries will demand of us obedience contrary to the orders of the Gospel" (Rochat, 1993). Ordered by police to give a list of sheltered Jews, the head pastor modeled defiance: "I don't know of Jews, I only know of human beings." At great personal risk, the people of Le Chambon made an initial commitment to resist. They suffered from poverty and were punished for their disobedience. Still, supported by their beliefs, their role models, their interactions with one another, and their own initial acts, they remained defiant to the war's end.

Lest we presume that obedience is always evil and resistance is always good, consider the heroic obedience of British soldiers who, in 1852, were traveling with civilians aboard the steamship *Birkenhead*. As they neared their South African port, the *Birkenhead* became impaled on a rock. The soldiers calmed passengers and helped them onto three available lifeboats—not nearly enough for everyone. "Steady, men!," ordered their officer as the lifeboats filled. Heroically, no one frantically rushed to claim a lifeboat seat. As the boat sank, all left onboard were plunged into the sea, most to be drowned or devoured by sharks. For almost a century, noted James Michener (1978), "the Birkenhead drill remained the measure by which heroic behavior at sea was measured."

Lessons From the Conformity and Obedience Studies

LOQ 42-3 What do the social influence studies teach us about ourselves? How much power do we have as individuals?

How do the laboratory experiments on social influence relate to everyday life? How does judging the length of a line or flicking a shock switch relate to everyday social behavior? Psychology's experiments aim not to re-create the actual, complex behaviors of everyday life but to capture and explore the underlying processes that shape those behaviors. Solomon Asch and Stanley Milgram devised experiments that forced a familiar choice: Do I adhere to my own standards, even when they conflict with the expectations of others?

In Milgram's experiments and their modern replications, participants were torn. Should they respond to the pleas of the victim or the orders of the experimenter? Their moral sense warned them not to harm another, yet it also prompted them to obey the experimenter and to be a good research participant. With kindness and obedience on a collision course, obedience usually won.

These experiments demonstrated that strong social influences induce many people to conform to falsehoods or capitulate to cruelty. Milgram saw this as the fundamental lesson of this work: "Ordinary people, simply doing their jobs, and without any particular hostility on their part, can become agents in a terrible destructive process" (1974, p. 6).

Focusing on the end point—450 volts, or someone's real-life violence—we can hardly comprehend the inhumanity. But Milgram did not entrap his teachers by asking them first to zap learners with enough electricity to make their hair stand on end. Using the *foot-in-the-door* technique, he instead began with a little tickle of electricity and escalated step by step. To those throwing the switches, the small action became justified, making the next act tolerable. So it happens when people succumb, gradually, to evil.

"All evil begins with 15 volts."—Philip Zimbardo, Stanford lecture, 2010

In any society, great evils often grow out of people's compliance with lesser evils. The Nazi leaders suspected that most German civil servants would resist shooting or gassing Jews directly, but they found them willing to handle the paperwork of the Holocaust (Silver & Geller, 1978). Milgram found a similar reaction in his experiments. When he asked 40 men to administer the learning test while someone else did the shocking, 93 percent complied. Cruelty does not require devilish villains. All it takes is ordinary people corrupted by an evil situation. Ordinary students may follow orders to haze initiates into their group. Ordinary employees may follow orders to produce and market harmful products. Among people abducted into a violent group, those forced to perpetrate violence are most likely then to identify with the group (Littman, 2018). Attitudes follow behavior.

"The Holocaust. . . did not start from gas chambers. This hatred gradually developed from words, stereotypes & prejudice through legal exclusion, dehumanisation & escalating violence."—Auschwitz Museum tweet, 2018

Sueddeutsche Zeitung Photo/Alamy Stock Photo

Minority influence To be August Landmesser, standing defiantly with arms folded as everyone else salutes their allegiance to the Nazi Party and Adolf Hitler, requires extraordinary courage. But sometimes such individuals have inspired others, demonstrating the power of minority influence.

In Jozefow and Le Chambon, as in Milgram's experiments, those who resisted usually did so early. After the first acts of compliance or resistance, attitudes began to follow and justify behavior.

What have social psychologists learned about the power of the individual? *Social control* (the power of the situation) and *personal control* (the power of the individual) interact. Much as water dissolves salt but not sand, so rotten situations turn some people into bad apples while others resist (Johnson, 2007).

When feeling pressured, some people react by doing the opposite of what is expected (Rosenberg & Siegel, 2018). The power of one or two individuals to sway majorities is *minority influence* (Moscovici, 1985). One research finding repeatedly stands out. When you are the minority, you are far more likely to sway the majority if you hold firmly to your position and don't waffle. This tactic won't make you popular, but it may make you influential, especially if your self-confidence stimulates others to consider why you think as you do. Even when a minority's influence is not yet visible, people may privately develop sympathy for the minority position and rethink their views (Wood et al., 1994).

The powers of social influence are enormous, but so are the powers of the committed individual. Were this not so, communism would have remained an obscure theory, Christianity would be a small Middle Eastern sect, and Rosa Parks' refusal to sit at the back of the bus would not have ignited the U.S. civil rights movement. Social forces matter. But individuals matter, too.

RETRIEVAL PRACTICE

RP-3 Psychology's most famous obedience experiments, in which most participants obeyed an authority figure's demands to inflict presumed painful, dangerous shocks on an innocent participant, were conducted by social psychologist ________________.

RP-4 What situations have researchers found to be most likely to encourage obedience in participants?

ANSWERS IN APPENDIX E

The power of one In August, 2018, 15-year-old Greta Thunberg sat alone outside the Swedish Parliament—the first school strike protesting climate change. Thirteen months after her act ignited a movement, some 4 million people worldwide joined her for the September, 2019, climate strike, and *Time* magazine honored her as their 2019 Person of the Year.

SKOLSTREJK
FÖR
KLIMATET

Michael Campanella/Getty Images

WE DIDN'T START THE FIRE
YOLO
LOVE YOUR MOTHER SHE DIES WE DIE
THE SEAS ARE RISING AND SO ARE WE

Michael Nigro/Pacific Press Agency/Alamy Stock Photo

PERSON of the YEAR
TIME
GRETA THUNBERG
THE POWER OF YOUTH

Macmillan Learning

Group Behavior

LOQ 42-4 How does the presence of others influence our actions, via social facilitation, social loafing, and deindividuation?

Imagine standing in a room holding a fishing pole. Your task is to wind the reel as fast as you can. On some occasions you wind in the presence of another participant, who is also winding as fast as possible. Will the other's presence affect your own performance?

In one of social psychology's first experiments, Norman Triplett (1898) reported that adolescents would wind a fishing reel faster in the presence of someone doing the same thing. Although a modern reanalysis revealed that the difference was modest (Stroebe, 2012), Triplett inspired later social psychologists to study how others' presence affects our behavior. Group influences operate both in simple groups—one person in the company of another—and in more complex groups.

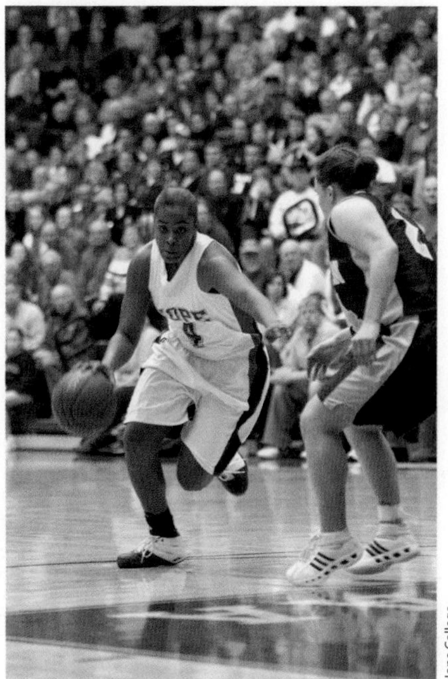

Hope College

Social facilitation Skilled athletes often find they are "on" before an audience. What they do well, they do even better when people are watching.

Social Facilitation

Triplett's claim—of strengthened performance in others' presence—is called **social facilitation**. But further studies revealed that the truth is more complicated. The presence of others strengthens our most *likely* response—the correct one on an easy task, an incorrect one on a difficult task (Guerin, 1986; Zajonc, 1965). Why? Because when others observe us, we become aroused, and this arousal amplifies our reactions. Perhaps you, like most people, tend to eat more when eating with others (Ruddock et al., 2019)? Or consider the expert pool players who made 71 percent of their shots when alone, and 80 percent when four people came to watch them (Michaels et al., 1982). Poor shooters, who made 36 percent of their shots when alone, made only 25 percent when watched.

The energizing effect of an enthusiastic audience helps explain the home-team advantage. Studies of more than a quarter-million college and professional athletic events in various countries have shown a home team advantage of 54 percent in Major League Baseball games, 60 percent in National Basketball Association games, and 63 percent in English Premier League football (soccer) games (Allen & Jones, 2014; Jamieson, 2010; Moskowitz & Wertheim, 2011). But in pandemic-era empty stadiums, the home advantage dissipated or disappeared in European professional football matches (Hamilton, 2021; Leitner & Richlan, 2021; Tilp & Thaller, 2020).

The point to remember: What you do well, you are likely to do even better in front of an audience, especially a friendly audience. What you usually find difficult may seem all but impossible when you are being watched.

Social facilitation also helps explain a funny effect of crowding. Comedians know that a "good house" is a full one. What they may not know is that crowding triggers arousal. Comedy routines that are mildly amusing in an uncrowded room seem funnier in a densely packed room (Aiello et al., 1983; Freedman & Perlick, 1979). When seated close to one another, people like a friendly person even more and an unfriendly person even less (Schiffenbauer & Schiavo, 1976; Storms & Thomas, 1977). So, to energize your next event, choose a room or set up seating that will just barely accommodate everyone.

Social Loafing

Social facilitation experiments test the effect of others' presence on the performance of an individual task, such as shooting pool. But what happens when people perform as a group—say, in a team tug-of-war? Would you exert more, less, or the same effort as in a one-on-one match?

To find out, a University of Massachusetts research team asked blindfolded students "to pull as hard as [they] can" on a rope. When they fooled the students into believing three others were also pulling behind them, students exerted only 82 percent as much effort as when they knew they were pulling alone (Ingham et al., 1974). And consider what happened when blindfolded people seated in a group clapped or shouted as loudly as they could while hearing (through headphones) other people clapping or shouting loudly (Latané, 1981). When they thought they were part of a group effort, the participants produced about one-third less noise than when clapping or shouting "alone."

social facilitation in the presence of others, improved performance on simple or well-learned tasks, and worsened performance on difficult tasks.

This diminished effort is called **social loafing** (Jackson & Williams, 1988; Latané, 1981). Experiments in the United States, India, Thailand, Japan, China, and Taiwan have found social loafing on various tasks, though it was especially common among men in individualist cultures (Karau & Williams, 1993). What causes social loafing? When people act as part of a group, they may

- ***feel less accountable*** and therefore worry less about what others think.
- ***view individual contributions as dispensable*** (Harkins & Szymanski, 1989; Kerr & Bruun, 1983).
- ***overestimate their own contributions,*** downplaying others' efforts (Schroeder et al., 2016).
- ***free ride on others' efforts.*** Unless highly motivated and strongly identified with the group, people may slack off (as you may have observed on group assignments)—especially when they share equally in the benefits, regardless of how much they contribute.

23
Jessica Kourkounis/Reuters/Newscom

Deindividuation In the excitement that followed the Philadelphia Eagles winning their first National Football League Super Bowl in 2018, some fans, disinhibited by social arousal and the anonymity provided by their "underdog" masks, became destructive.

ASK YOURSELF

What steps could you take to reduce social loafing in your next group project assignment?

Deindividuation

We've seen that the presence of others can arouse people (social facilitation), or it can diminish their feelings of responsibility (social loafing). But sometimes the presence of others does both. The uninhibited behavior that results can range from a food fight to vandalism or rioting. This process of losing self-awareness and self-restraint, called **deindividuation**, often occurs when group participation makes people both *aroused* and *anonymous*. Compared with identifiable women in a control group, New York University women dressed in depersonalizing Ku Klux Klan–style hoods delivered twice as much presumed electric shock to a victim (Zimbardo, 1970).

Deindividuation thrives in many settings. Internet anonymity enables people to feed and freely express their anger, sometimes with bullying and hate speech (Chetty & Alathur, 2018; Kowalski et al., 2018). Online trolls report enjoying their unleashed abuse of others (Buckels et al., 2014; Sest & March, 2017). They might never say "You're disgusting!" to someone's face, but they can hide behind their anonymity online. One study showed that tribal warriors wearing face paint or masks were more likely than those with exposed faces to kill, torture, or mutilate captured enemies (Watson, 1973). When we shed self-awareness and self-restraint—whether in a mob, at a concert, at a ball game, or at worship—we become more responsive to the group experience, bad or good. For a comparison of social facilitation, social loafing, and deindividuation, see **TABLE 42.1**.

* * *

We have examined the conditions under which the *presence* of others can motivate people to exert themselves or tempt them to free ride on the efforts of others, make easy tasks easier and difficult tasks harder, and enhance humor or fuel mob violence. Research also shows that *interacting* with others can similarly have both bad and good effects.

"**Groups tend to be more immoral than individuals.**" —Martin Luther King, Jr., "Letter from Birmingham Jail," 1963

TABLE 42.1 Behavior in the Presence of Others: Three Phenomena

Phenomenon	Social context	Psychological effect of others' presence	Behavioral effect
Social facilitation	Individual being observed	Increased arousal	Amplified dominant behavior, such as doing better what one does well, or doing worse what is difficult
Social loafing	Group projects	Diminished feelings of responsibility when not individually accountable	Decreased effort
Deindividuation	Group setting that fosters arousal and anonymity	Reduced self-awareness	Lowered self-restraint

social loafing the tendency for people in a group to exert less effort when pooling their efforts toward attaining a common goal than when individually accountable.

deindividuation the loss of self-awareness and self-restraint occurring in group situations that foster arousal and anonymity.

group polarization the enhancement of a group's prevailing inclinations through discussion within the group.

Group Polarization

LOQ 42-5 How can group interaction enable group polarization?

We live in an increasingly polarized world. The Middle East is torn by warring factions. The European Union is struggling with nationalist divisions. In 1990, a 1-minute speech in the U.S. Congress would enable you to guess the speaker's party just 55 percent of the time; by 2009, partisanship was evident 83 percent of the time (Gentzkow et al., 2016). In 2016, for the first time in survey history, most U.S. Republicans and Democrats reported having "*very* unfavorable" views of the other party (Doherty & Kiley, 2016). People in both parties believe that "my side" is objective, and the other side is biased (Schwalbe et al., 2020). U.S. polarization reached an extreme in early 2021, when pro-Trump insurrectionists invaded the U.S. Capitol and anti-Trump citizens were outraged.

A powerful principle helps us understand this increasing polarization: The beliefs and attitudes we bring to a group grow stronger as we discuss them with like-minded others. This process, called **group polarization**, can have beneficial results, as when low-prejudice students become even more accepting while discussing racial issues. As George Bishop and I [DM] discovered, it can also be socially toxic, as when high-prejudice students who discuss racial issues together become *more* prejudiced (Myers & Bishop, 1970) (**FIGURE 42.3**). Our repeated finding: Like minds polarize.

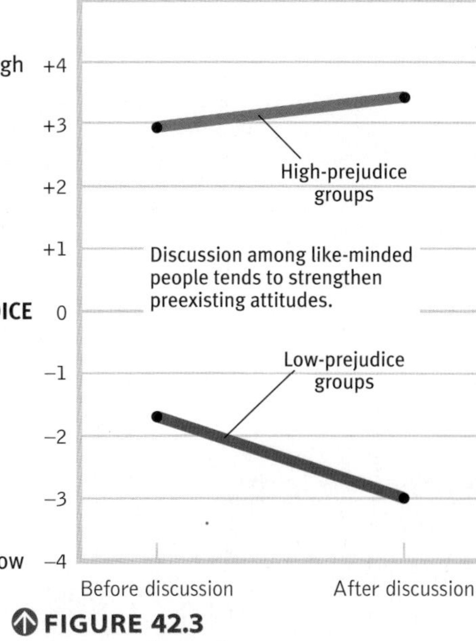
High
Low
PREJUDICE
+4
+3
+2
+1
0
−1
−2
−3
−4
High-prejudice groups
Discussion among like-minded people tends to strengthen preexisting attitudes.
Low-prejudice groups
Before discussion
After discussion

FIGURE 42.3
Group polarization

Analyses of terrorist organizations reveal that the terrorist mentality emerges slowly among those who share a grievance (McCauley, 2002; McCauley & Segal, 1987; Merari, 2002). As susceptible individuals interact in isolation (sometimes with other "brothers" and "sisters" in camps or prisons), their views grow more extreme. Increasingly, they categorize the world as "us" against "them" (Chulov, 2014; Moghaddam, 2005). Knowing that group polarization occurs when like-minded people segregate, a 2006 U.S. National Intelligence estimate speculated that "the operational threat from self-radicalized cells will grow."

NO EXIT
© Andy Singer
TECHNOLOGY'S A MIXED BAG
SOCIAL MEDIA HELPS ME CONNECT WITH OTHER GAY AND BISEXUAL KIDS AND FEEL LESS ISOLATED IN MY SMALL TOWN.
SOCIAL MEDIA HELPS ME CONNECT WITH NAZIS AND WHITE SUPREMACISTS AND FEEL LESS ISOLATED IN MY SMALL TOWN.
SINGER

Technology is a Mixed Bag by Andy Singer/Cagle Cartoons, Inc.

The internet offers us a connected global world, yet also provides an easily accessible medium for group polarization. When I [DM] got my start in social psychology with experiments on group polarization, I never imagined the potential power of polarization in *virtual* groups. Progressives friend progressives and share links to sites that affirm their shared views. Conservatives connect with conservatives and likewise share conservative perspectives. With news feeds and retweets, we fuel one another with information—and misinformation—and click on content we agree with (Hills, 2019). Social media echo chambers may amplify extremist messages, which tend to be more visible and more likely to be shared (Bail, 2021). The result is an outrage machine: Our biases may lead us to welcome and share misinformation that supports our beliefs, which strengthens our biases, and leads to even more polarization. In 2018, a U.S. man sent over a dozen pipe bombs to prominent Democrats and their perceived supporters after venting his partisan resentments on the internet, which "echoed them back. It validated and cultivated them. It took something dark and colored it darker still" (Bruni, 2018).

Mindful of the viral false-news phenomenon, tech companies are working on ways to promote media information literacy. For more on the internet's role in group polarization—toward ends that are good as well as bad—see Thinking Critically About: The Internet as Social Amplifier.

"Dear Satan, thank you for having my internet news feeds tailored especially for ME!" —Comedian Steve Martin, 2016

Shay Horse/NurPhoto/Getty Images

Toxic group polarization As illustrated in this 2017 Charlottesville, Virginia, white nationalist rally, the interaction of like minds—both online and face-to-face—can strengthen preexisting attitudes. The 2019 U.S. Department of Homeland Security's *Strategic Framework for Countering Terrorism and Targeted Violence* declared, "Similar to how ISIS inspired and connected with potential terrorists, white supremacist violent extremists connect with like-minded individuals online."

Thinking Critically About:
The Internet as Social Amplifier

LOQ **42-6** What role does the internet play in group polarization?

The internet connects like-minded people.
These connections can bring emotional healing, such as for cancer survivors and bereaved parents.
Grieving for a lost child
Online sharing can also strengthen social movements.
ANTISOCIAL
White supremacy
Vaccine skeptics
Climate change skeptics
#neveragain
#timesup
#blacklivesmatter
PROSOCIAL
Electronic communication and social networking can encourage people to isolate themselves from those with different opinions.
On social media, we often share political content with like-minded others.[1]
Supporting Candidate A
Supporting Candidate B
Like-minded separation + conversation
group polarization

1. Bakshy et al., 2015; Barberá et al., 2015.

Groupthink

LOQ 42-7 How can group interaction enable groupthink?

Does group influence ever distort important national decisions? Consider the Bay of Pigs fiasco. In 1961, U.S. President John F. Kennedy and his advisers decided to invade Cuba with 1400 CIA-trained Cuban exiles. When the invaders were easily captured and quickly linked to the U.S. government, Kennedy wondered aloud, "How could I have been so stupid?"

Social psychologist Irving Janis (1982) studied the decision-making process leading to the ill-fated invasion. He discovered that the soaring morale of the recently elected president and his advisers fostered undue confidence. To preserve the good feeling, group members suppressed or self-censored their dissenting views, especially after President Kennedy voiced his enthusiasm for the scheme. Since no one spoke strongly against the idea, everyone assumed the support was unanimous. To describe this harmonious but unrealistic group thinking, Janis coined the term **groupthink**.

Later studies showed that groupthink—fed by overconfidence, conformity, self-justification, and group polarization—contributed to other fiascos. Among them were the failure to anticipate the 1941 Japanese attack on Pearl Harbor; the escalation of the Vietnam war; the U.S. Watergate cover-up; the Chernobyl nuclear reactor accident (Reason, 1987); the U.S. space shuttle *Challenger* explosion (Esser & Lindoerfer, 1989); and the Iraq war, launched on the false belief that Iraq had weapons of mass destruction (U.S. Senate Intelligence Committee, 2004).

"One of the dangers in the White House, based on my reading of history, is that you get wrapped up in groupthink and everybody agrees with everything, and there's no discussion and there are no dissenting views." —Barack Obama, December 1, 2008, press conference

Despite the dangers of groupthink, two heads are often better than one. Great minds often don't think alike. Knowing this, Janis also studied instances in which U.S. presidents and their advisers collectively made good decisions, such as when the Truman administration formulated the Marshall Plan, which offered assistance to Europe after World War II, and when the Kennedy administration successfully prevented the Soviets from installing missiles in Cuba. His conclusion? Groupthink is prevented when a leader—whether in government or in business—welcomes various opinions, invites experts' critiques of developing plans, and assigns people to identify possible problems. Just as the suppression of dissent bends a group toward bad decisions, open debate often shapes good ones. This is especially the case with small but diverse groups, whose varied backgrounds and perspectives often enable creative or superior outcomes (Shi et al., 2019; J. Wang, et al., 2019; L. Wu et al., 2019). None of us is as smart as all of us.

"If evil is contagious, so is goodness." —Pope Francis tweet, 2017

ASK YOURSELF

Have you witnessed or experienced group polarization online?

RETRIEVAL PRACTICE

RP-5 What is *social facilitation*, and why does it improve performance with a well-learned task?

RP-6 People tend to exert less effort when working with a group than they would alone, which is called ____________ ____________.

RP-7 You are organizing a meeting of fiercely competitive political candidates and their supporters. To add to the fun, friends have suggested handing out masks of the candidates' faces for supporters to wear. What phenomenon might these masks engage?

RP-8 When like-minded groups discuss a topic, and the result is the strengthening of the prevailing opinion, this is called ____________ ____________.

RP-9 When a group's desire for harmony overrides its realistic analysis of other options, ____________ has occurred.

ANSWERS IN APPENDIX E

groupthink the mode of thinking that occurs when the desire for harmony in a decision-making group overrides a realistic appraisal of alternatives. 

MODULE 42 REVIEW Social Influence

LEARNING OBJECTIVES

Test Yourself Answer these repeated Learning Objective Questions on your own (before "showing" the answers here, or checking the answers in Appendix D) to improve your retention of the concepts (McDaniel et al., 2009, 2015).

LOQ 42-1 How is social contagion a form of conformity, and how do conformity experiments reveal the power of social influence?

LOQ 42-2 What did Milgram's obedience experiments teach us about the power of social influence?

LOQ 42-3 What do the social influence studies teach us about ourselves? How much power do we have as individuals?

LOQ 42-4 How does the presence of others influence our actions, via social facilitation, social loafing, and deindividuation?

LOQ 42-5 How can group interaction enable group polarization?

LOQ 42-6 What role does the internet play in group polarization?

LOQ 42-7 How can group interaction enable groupthink?

TERMS AND CONCEPTS TO REMEMBER

Test Yourself Write down the definition in your own words, then check your answer.

norms, p. 475
conformity, p. 477
normative social influence, p. 477
informational social influence, p. 478
social facilitation, p. 483
social loafing, p. 484
deindividuation, p. 484
group polarization, p. 485
groupthink, p. 487

MODULE TEST

Test Yourself Answer the following questions on your own first, then "show" the answers here, or check your answers in Appendix E.

1. Researchers have found that a person is most likely to conform to a group if
a. the group members have diverse opinions.
b. the person feels competent and secure.
c. the person admires the group's status.
d. no one else will observe the person's behavior.

2. In Milgram's experiments, the rate of obedience was highest when
a. the "learner" was at a distance from the "teacher."
b. the "learner" was close at hand.
c. other "teachers" refused to go along with the experimenter.
d. the "teacher" disliked the "learner."

3. Dr. Huang, a popular music professor, delivers fascinating lectures on music history but gets nervous and makes mistakes when describing exam statistics in front of the class. Why does his performance vary by task?

4. In a group situation that fosters arousal and anonymity, a person sometimes loses self-consciousness and self-control. This phenomenon is called ________________.

5. Sharing our opinions with like-minded others tends to strengthen our views, a phenomenon referred to as ________________ ________________.

MODULE 43 Antisocial Relations

Social psychology studies how we think about and influence one another, and also how we *relate* to one another. What causes people sometimes to hate and harm, and other times to love and help? And when conflicts arise, how can we move toward a just peace? In this section we ponder insights into *antisocial* relations gleaned by researchers who have studied prejudice, aggression, and conflict.

Prejudice

prejudice an unjustifiable and usually negative attitude toward a group and its members. Prejudice generally involves stereotyped beliefs, negative feelings, and a predisposition to discriminatory action.

LOQ 43-1 What is *prejudice?* How do explicit and implicit prejudice differ?

Prejudice means "prejudgment." It is an unjustifiable and usually negative *attitude* toward a group and its members, who often are people of a particular racial or ethnic group, gender, mental health or physical ability group, or sexual orientation. Attitudes are feelings, influenced by beliefs, that predispose us to act in certain ways. The ingredients in prejudice's three-part mixture are

- *negative emotions,* such as fear or disgust. Strong negative emotions are not problematic alone, but when they are projected toward another group without justification, they can be harmful. Feeling scared when approached by someone with mental illness can lead us to avoid or reject them (Hinshaw, 2009). Feeling disgust in response to others' differing sexual orientation can lead to disapproval of such differences (Inbar et al., 2009).
- **stereotypes**, or generalized beliefs about a group of people such as "corrupt media" or "vulture capitalists." Our stereotypes sometimes reflect reality (Jussim & Honeycutt, 2021). Senator Ted Cruz of Texas once observed, "It's a stereotype that Texans like barbecue. It also happens that pretty much all Texans like barbecue" (Flegenheimer, 2018). Other stereotypes—like those based on astrological signs—fail to predict personality or performance (Lu et al., 2020). Stereotypes often overgeneralize or exaggerate group traits and behaviors, and can even push people into undesirable roles that fit the stereotype (Eagly & Koenig, 2021). In the United States, for example, strongly partisan Republicans and Democrats exhibit a "perception gap"—they overestimate the extremism of the other side (Yudkin et al., 2019). Moreover, Democrats greatly overestimate the percent of Republicans who earn more than $250,000 a year and Republicans greatly overestimate the percent of Democrats who are LGBTQ (Ahler & Sood, 2018).
- a predisposition to **discriminate**—to *act* in harmful and unjustifiable ways toward members of the group. Sometimes prejudice is blatant. People with anti-Black attitudes, for example, are less likely to judge as guilty a White police officer who killed a Black man (Cooley et al., 2019). Other times, it is more subtle, taking the form of *microaggressions,* such as being ignored at the deli counter (Williams, 2021). In experiments, people seeking Airbnb reservations have received worse treatment when calling themselves Jamal rather than John, or Lakisha rather than Emily (Edelman et al., 2017).

People also experience prejudice because of their weight, age, or physical appearance (Lippens et al., 2022; Stier & Hinshaw, 2017; Zhu et al., 2022). To automatically perceive an older person as incapable or a less attractive person as incompetent is to be prejudiced. To reject a qualified job candidate who is older than most other applicants or is a woman instead of a man is to discriminate.

Body weight bias: **In data collected from 4 million U.S. adults, explicit biases against those of a particular sex, disability, age, or race were greatly exceeded by biases in response to body weight (Charlesworth & Banaji, 2019).**

Explicit and Implicit Prejudice

Again and again, we have seen that our brain processes thoughts, memories, and attitudes on two different tracks. Sometimes that processing is *explicit*—on the radar screen of our awareness. More often, it is *implicit*—an unthinking knee-jerk response operating below the radar, leaving us unaware of how our attitudes influence our behavior. In 2015, the U.S. Supreme Court, in upholding the Fair Housing Act, recognized **implicit bias** research, noting that "unconscious prejudices" can cause discrimination even when people do not consciously intend to discriminate.

Psychologists study implicit prejudice by

- ***testing for automatic group associations.*** Tests in which people quickly pair a person's image with a trait demonstrate that even people who deny any racial prejudice may exhibit negative associations (Greenwald & Banaji, 2017). Millions of people have taken the Implicit Association Test (as you can, too, at Implicit.Harvard.edu). Critics question the test's reliability and caution against using it to assess or label individuals (Kvam et al., 2022; Oswald et al., 2015). But defenders counter that implicit biases predict behaviors ranging from simple acts of friendliness to work quality (Greenwald et al., 2022). Implicit biases have also mirrored cultural trends toward greater acceptance of various groups. In the United States between 2007 and 2020, for example, people's implicit biases regarding sexual orientation and race decreased (Charlesworth & Banaji, 2022).
- ***considering automatic patronization.*** In one experiment, White university women assessed flawed student essays they believed had been written by either a White or a Black student. The women gave low evaluations, often with harsh comments,

stereotype a generalized (sometimes accurate but often overgeneralized) belief about a group of people.

discrimination unjustifiable negative behavior toward a group or its members.

implicit bias automatic associations that can influence individual judgments of or behavior toward people of a particular race, gender, or other group.

Beata Zawrzel/NurPhoto/Getty Images

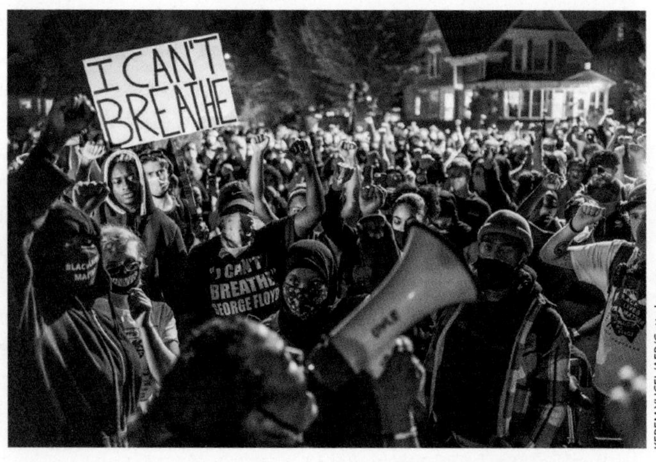
I CAN'T
BREATHE
KEREM YUCEL/AFP/Getty Images

Implicit bias, explicit prejudice? In May, 2020, a White police officer killed George Floyd by kneeling on his neck for more than 9 minutes while Floyd cried "I can't breathe!" and compliant subordinate officers stood by without intervening. Had Floyd been White, would he have been perceived and treated the same way?

to the essays supposedly written by a White student. Their assessment was more positive when the same essay was attributed to a Black student (Harber, 1998). In follow-up studies, male and female research participants similarly patronized female authors. When evaluating an author's essay, participants offered uplifting but inaccurate feedback to women, but not to men (Jampol & Zayas, 2021). In real-world evaluations, such low expectations and the resulting "white lies" of inflated praise and insufficient criticism could hinder minority student and female achievement. To reduce implicit bias, teachers may read essays without knowing the authors' race and gender.

- ***monitoring reflexive bodily responses.*** Even people who consciously express little prejudice may give off telltale signals as their body responds selectively to an image of a person from another ethnic group. Neuroscientists can detect signals of implicit prejudice in the viewer's facial-muscle responses and in the activation of the emotion-processing amygdala (Cunningham et al., 2004; Eberhardt, 2005; Stanley et al., 2008).

"But who can detect their errors? Clear me from hidden faults." —Psalm 19:12

Targets of Prejudice

LOQ 43-2 What groups tend to experience prejudice?

RACIAL AND ETHNIC PREJUDICE Expressed racial attitudes in the United States have undergone a sea change. Support for interracial marriage between Black and White people, for example, increased from a mere 4 percent approval in 1958 to 94 percent in 2021 (Gallup, 2021). Three in four Americans (including nearly 9 in 10 college graduates) now agree that their nation's having "many different races and ethnicities" is good for the country (Horowitz, 2019). The diversity benefit appeared in one analysis of 9 million scientific papers and 6 million scientists: Ethnically diverse scientific teams produced the most influential research (AlShebli et al., 2018).

"Data show [long-term] plunges in extreme poverty, illiteracy, war, violent crime, racism, sexism, homophobia, domestic violence, disease, lethal accidents and just about every other scourge." —Psychologist Steven Pinker, "Scared by the News? Take the Long View," 2018

Yet interracial prejudice persists:

- ***Colorism.*** Among Black and Hispanic people, and also among people in India and some East Asian cultures, those with darker skin tones experience greater prejudice and discrimination (Bettache, 2020; Gonzales-Barrera, 2019; Landor & Smith, 2019; Yasir & Gettleman, 2020).
- ***Criminal stereotypes.*** Black men are judged more harshly than White men when they commit "stereotypically Black" crimes (drive-by shooting, gang violence, street gambling). But this bias disappears when Black men commit "stereotypically White" crimes (embezzlement, computer hacking, and insider trading) (Petsko & Bodenhausen, 2019).
- ***Medical care.*** Health professionals allocate more resources to treat White patients than to treat equally unhealthy Black patients (Obermeyer et al., 2019). In one study of medical care in Louisiana, inequalities in medical treatment helped explain why Black Americans were more likely than White Americans to die from Covid (Hu et al., 2022).

Why does such prejudice persist? One reason is that few people muster the courage to challenge prejudicial or hate speech. Although many *say* they would feel upset with someone making racist (or homophobic) comments, they often respond indifferently when hearing prejudice-laden language (Kawakami et al., 2009). *The bottom line:* If you disapprove of prejudice, ask yourself, "What message am I sending when I remain silent while others make racist, homophobic, or sexist remarks?"

As noted, prejudice is not just subtle, but often automatic and unintended (implicit). An Implicit Association Test found 9 in 10 White respondents taking longer to identify pleasant words (such as *peace* and *paradise*) as "good" when presented with Black-sounding names (such as *Latisha* and *Darnell*) than when shown White-sounding names (such as *Katie* and *Ian*). Moreover, people who more quickly associate good things with White names or faces also are the quickest to perceive anger and apparent threat in Black faces (Hugenberg & Bodenhausen, 2003). Those demonstrating explicit *or* implicit prejudice were less likely to vote for then-presidential candidate Barack Obama. Multiple studies showed, however, that Obama's election reduced implicit prejudice (Bernstein et al., 2010; Payne et al., 2010; Stephens-Davidowitz, 2014).

Implicit bias can literally get "under the skin." Although the number of Black medical students has increased, only 5 percent of U.S. physicians are Black (AAMC, 2019; Murphy, 2022). Because Black medical providers may challenge people's stereotypes of doctors, researchers examined whether White patients would show less responsiveness to Black medical providers' treatment. In one experiment, White patients were exposed to a treatment that caused a mild allergic reaction (Howe et al., 2022). By random assignment, patients received "an antihistamine cream that will reduce allergic reaction and itching" from a Black, Asian, or White medical provider. In actuality, the cream was a placebo containing no medicine. Even after controlling for explicit attitudes toward Black medical providers, White patients who were assigned a Black medical provider showed the strongest initial allergic reaction and the weakest response to the placebo medical treatment.

Implicit bias can have deadly consequences. In 1999, Amadou Diallo, who was Black, was accosted as he approached his New York doorway by police officers looking for a rapist. When he pulled out his wallet, the officers, perceiving a gun, riddled his body with 19 bullets from 41 shots. In one analysis of 59 unarmed suspect shootings in Philadelphia over seven years, 49 involved the misidentification of an object (such as a phone) or movement (such as pants tugging). Black suspects were more than twice as likely to be misperceived as threatening, even by Black officers (Blow, 2015). Similarly, Black men are about 2.5 times more likely than White men to be killed by a police officer in the United States, even when unarmed (Edwards et al., 2019; Peeples, 2020). Researchers have analyzed implicit bias scores from more than 2 million Americans, while accounting for several other factors. Their finding: A region's implicit bias toward Black Americans predicted its number of Black Americans stopped and killed by police (Hehman et al., 2018; Stelter et al., 2022). And an analysis of more than 2 million U.S. 911 calls revealed that White officers sent to Black neighborhoods fired their guns five times as often as Black officers sent for similar calls in the same neighborhoods (Peeples, 2020).

Recognizing the reality of implicit bias, many police departments, colleges, and companies have given their staff implicit bias training. (Microsoft makes its online implicit bias training available to anyone at tinyurl.com/BiasTrain.) Although such single-session diversity or bias training sessions may modestly change attitudes, real behavior is harder to modify (Greenwald et al., 2022). "The enthusiasm for, and monetary investment in, diversity training," say social psychologists Patricia Devine and Tory Ash (2022), "has outpaced the available evidence that such programs are effective."

To better understand implicit prejudice, researchers have also simulated situations (Correll et al., 2007, 2015; Plant & Peruche, 2005; Sadler et al., 2012). They asked viewers to press buttons quickly to "shoot" or not shoot men who suddenly appeared on screen. Some of the on-screen men held a gun. Others held a harmless hand tool. People (both Black and White, including police officers) more often shot Black men holding harmless objects than they shot White men holding harmless objects. Priming people with a

© Inti St Clair/Blend Images/Corbis
(a)

JLP/Jose L. Pelaez/Corbis
(b)

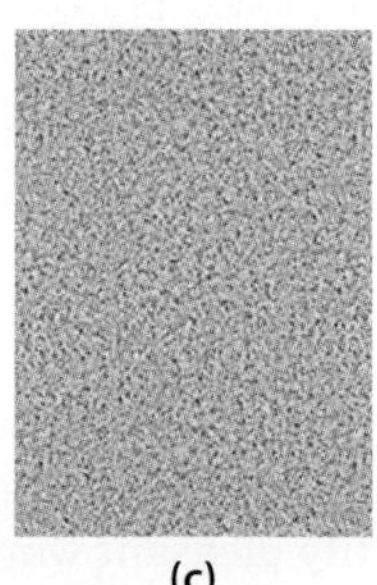
(c)

FIGURE 43.1
Race primes perceptions In experiments by Keith Payne (2006), people viewed (a) a White or Black face, immediately followed by (b) a flashed gun or hand tool, which was then followed by (c) a masking screen. Participants were more likely to misperceive a tool as a gun when it was preceded by a Black rather than a White face.

flashed Black face rather than a White face also made them more likely to misperceive a flashed tool as a gun (**FIGURE 43.1**). Fatigue, which diminishes one's conscious control and increases automatic reactions, amplifies racial bias in shooting decisions (Ma et al., 2013).

GENDER PREJUDICE In the early eighteenth century, Dr. James Barry became Britain's first female doctor. Because women were not allowed to attend university, Barry applied to the University of Edinburgh as a man, and went on to a storied career as a military surgeon. Barry's assigned sex was only revealed upon his death. Since then, and especially since 1950, expressed gender stereotypes and prejudice have decreased (Eagly et al., 2020). The one-third of Americans who in 1937 told Gallup pollsters that they would vote for a qualified woman whom their party nominated for president soared to 95 percent in 2012 (Jones, 2012; Newport, 1999). And 94 percent of people surveyed across 34 countries now agree "it is important for women to have the same rights as men" (Horowitz & Fetterolf, 2020).

Nevertheless, both implicit and explicit gender prejudice and discrimination persist. Consider:

- ***Work and pay.*** In Western countries, we pay more to those (usually men) who care for our streets than to those (usually women) who care for our children. Despite expressed support for women having the "same rights," 40 percent of the global survey respondents agreed that men have more right to a job when work is scarce. (Agreement varied greatly by country, ranging from 7 percent in Sweden to about 80 percent in India and Tunisia.)
- ***Leadership.*** From 2007 through 2016, male directors of 1000 popular films (the top 100 for each year) outnumbered female directors by 24 to 1 (Smith et al., 2017). Implicit gender bias also contributes to females' not being selected for prestigious scientific research positions (Régner et al., 2019).
- ***Perceived intelligence and intellectual interests.*** Gender bias even applies to beliefs about intelligence: Despite equality between males and females in intelligence test scores, people have tended to perceive their fathers as more intelligent than their mothers and their sons as brighter than their daughters (Furnham, 2016). Children's books often plant the seeds of such gender stereotypes, with girls portrayed as emotional and good readers and boys depicted as interested in tools and excelling in math (Lewis et al., 2022).
- ***Masculine norms.*** Organizations often value and reward masculine ideas, values, and interaction styles (Cheryan & Markus, 2020). For example, people are encouraged to work independently, nominate themselves for awards and promotions, and use an assertive interaction style to influence others. These "masculine defaults" can reduce women's sense of belonging and increase their feelings of being an imposter (Vial et al., 2022).

"Until I was a man, I had no idea how good men had it at work. . . . The first time I spoke up in a meeting in my newly low, quiet voice and noticed that sudden, focused attention, I was so uncomfortable that I found myself unable to finish my sentence." —Thomas Page McBee, 2016, after transitioning from female to male

Unwanted female infants are no longer left on a hillside to die of exposure, as was the practice in ancient Greece. Yet the average male-to-female newborn ratio (105-to-100) doesn't explain the world's millions of "missing women." In many cultures, parents value sons more than daughters. In India, there have been 3.5 times more Google searches asking how to conceive a boy than how to conceive a girl (Stephens-Davidowitz, 2014). With scientific testing that enables sex-selective abortions, some countries are experiencing a shortfall in female births (**FIGURE 43.2**). India's newborn sex ratio was recently 111 boys for every 100 girls—though after a "Save the Girl Child" campaign has dropped to a still-high 108 (Tong, 2022). China's has been 111 to 100, despite China's declaring sex-selective abortions a criminal offense (CIA, 2014). In China and India, which together have 50 million more males than females under age 20, many men will be without mates (Denyer & Gowen, 2018; Gupta, 2017). When men outnumber women, there is often increased crime, violence, and trafficking of women (Brooks, 2012).

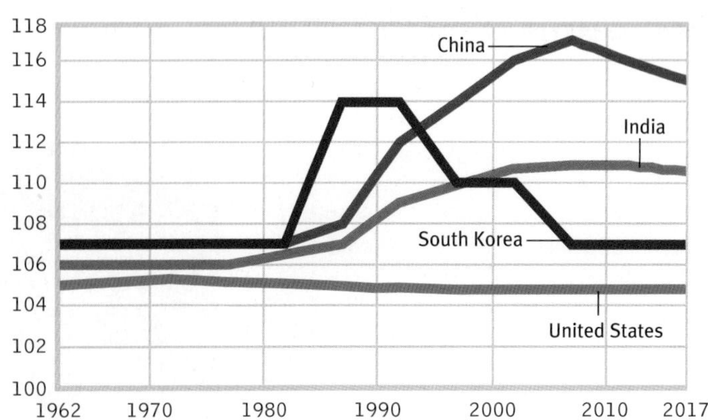

Number of newborn boys for every 100 newborn girls
118
116
114
112
110
108
106
104
102
100
1962
1970
1980
1990
2000
2010
2017
Year
China
India
South Korea
United States

FIGURE 43.2
Boy bias Biologically, the expected sex ratio would be 105 newborn boys for every 100 newborn girls. In reality, most countries show a significant boy bias. (Data from Our World in Data and World Bank/UN.)

LGBTQ PREJUDICE In most of the world, gay, lesbian, and transgender people cannot openly and comfortably disclose who they are and whom they love. Although 32 countries allowed same-sex marriage by 2022, dozens more had laws criminalizing same-sex relationships. Cultural variation is enormous—ranging from 94 percent in Sweden who believe "homosexuality should be accepted" to 7 percent in Nigeria who agree with that statement (Pew, 2020). Worldwide, anti-gay attitudes have been most common among men, older adults, and those who are unhappy, unemployed, and less educated (Haney, 2016; Jäckle & Wenzelburger, 2015).

Explicit anti-LGBTQ prejudice persists, even in countries with legal protections in place. When U.S. and UK experimenters sent thousands of responses to employment ads, those whose resumes included "Treasurer, Progressive and Socialist Alliance" received more replies than did those whose resumes specified "Treasurer, Gay and Lesbian Alliance" (Agerström et al., 2012; Bertrand & Mullainathan, 2004; Drydakis, 2009, 2015).

Do attitudes and practices that label, disparage, and discriminate against gay, lesbian, and transgender people increase their risk of psychological disorder and ill health? *Yes.* In U.S. states without protections against LGBTQ hate crime and discrimination, gay and lesbian people experience substantially higher rates of depression and related disorders, even after controlling for income and education differences. In communities where anti-gay prejudice is high, so are gay and lesbian suicide and cardiovascular deaths. In 16 states that banned same-sex marriage between 2001 and 2005, gay and lesbian people (but not straight people) experienced a 37 percent increase in depressive disorder rates, a 42 percent increase in alcohol use disorder, and a 248 percent increase in generalized anxiety disorder. Meanwhile, gay and lesbian people in other states did not experience increased psychiatric disorders (Hatzenbuehler, 2014). So, do laws that promote acceptance of gay, lesbian, and transgender people *reduce* bias? Again, *Yes.* As happened after the passage of desegregation and civil rights laws, attitudes have followed the newly legislated behavior. In various U.S. states, people became more gay-supportive when and where same-sex marriages became legal (Ofuso et al., 2019).

Roots of Prejudice

LOQ 43-3 What are some social, emotional, and cognitive roots of prejudice, and what are some ways to reduce prejudice?

Prejudice springs from a culture's divisions, the heart's passions, and the mind's natural workings.

THERE IS NO JUSTICE IN THE WORLD.
THERE IS SOME JUSTICE IN THE WORLD.
THE WORLD IS JUST.
MANKOFF
Robert Mankoff/Cartoon Stock

SOCIAL INEQUALITIES AND DIVISIONS When some people have money, power, and prestige and others do not, the "haves" usually develop attitudes that justify things as they are. The **just-world phenomenon** reflects an idea we commonly teach our children—that good is rewarded and evil is punished. From this, it is but a short and sometimes automatic leap to assume that those who succeed must be good and those who suffer must be bad. Such reasoning enables wealthy people to see both their own riches and the misfortunes of those living in poverty as justly deserved. When slavery existed in the United States, slaveholders perceived enslaved people as innately lazy, ignorant, and irresponsible—as having the very traits that supposedly justified enslaving them. Stereotypes rationalize inequalities.

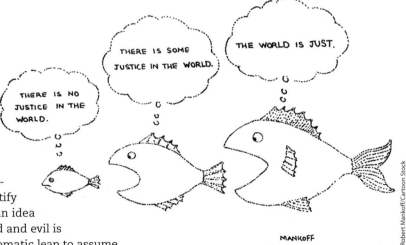

just-world phenomenon the tendency for people to believe that the world is just and people therefore get what they deserve and deserve what they get. 

Mike Hewitt/Getty Images

The ingroup Scotland's famed "Tartan Army" soccer fans, shown here during a match against archrival England, share a social identity that defines "us" (the Scottish ingroup) and "them" (the English outgroup).

People who experience discrimination may react in ways that feed prejudice through the classic *blame-the-victim* dynamic (Allport, 1954). Do the circumstances of poverty breed a higher crime rate? If so, that higher crime rate can be used to justify discrimination against those who live in poverty.

Dividing the world into "us" and "them" can result in conflict, racism, and war, but it also provides the benefits of communal solidarity. Thus, we cheer for our groups, kill for them, die for them. Indeed, we define who we are—our *social identity*—partly in terms of our groups (Thomas et al., 2020; Whitehouse, 2018). When Margarita identifies herself as a woman, a Brit, a Liverpool native, and a Brexit supporter, she knows who she is, and so do we.

Mentally drawing a circle defines "us," the **ingroup**. But the social definition of who we are also states who we are not. People outside that circle are "them," the **outgroup**. An **ingroup bias** soon follows. In experiments, children and adults have favored their own group when dividing rewards—even a group that is created by a mere coin toss (Tajfel, 1982; Wynn et al., 2018). Across 17 countries, ingroup bias appears more as ingroup favoritism than as harm to the outgroup (Romano et al., 2017). Discrimination is triggered less by outgroup hostility than by ingroup networking and mutual support—such as hiring a friend's child at the expense of other candidates (Greenwald & Pettigrew, 2014).

We have inherited our Stone Age ancestors' need to belong, to live and love in groups. There was safety in solidarity: Whether hunting, defending, or attacking, 10 hands were better than 2. Evolution prepared us, when encountering strangers, to make instant judgments: friend or foe? This urge to distinguish enemies from friends, and to dehumanize or "otherize" those not like us, predisposes prejudice against strangers (Kteily & Landry, 2022; Whitley, 1999). To Greeks of the classical era, all non-Greeks were "barbarians." In our own era, most children believe their school is better than all other schools in town. Many high school students form cliques—athletes, choir members, theater actors—and disparage those outside their own group. Even chimpanzees have been seen to wipe clean the spot where they were touched by a chimpanzee from another group (Goodall, 1986). They also display ingroup empathy by yawning more after seeing ingroup (rather than outgroup) members yawn (Campbell & de Waal, 2011). Although an ideal world might prioritize justice and love for all, in our real world, ingroup love often outranks universal justice.

ASK YOURSELF

What are some examples of ingroup bias in your own life, and in your community? How can you help break down barriers that you or others may face?

ingroup "us"—people with whom we share a common identity.

outgroup "them"—those perceived as different or apart from our ingroup.

ingroup bias the tendency to favor our own group.

NEGATIVE EMOTIONS Negative emotions nourish prejudice. When facing death, fearing threats, or experiencing frustration, people cling more tightly to their ingroup. When frustrated by extreme inequality, people worldwide wish for a strong leader to restore order (Sprong et al., 2019). Fearing terrorism increases patriotism, along with loathing and aggression toward those perceived as threats (Pyszczynski et al., 2002, 2008).

Scapegoat theory proposes that when things go wrong, finding someone to blame can provide a target for our negative emotions. From 2015 to 2020, as white nationalist political talk surged, FBI-reported U.S. hate crimes increased 38 percent (FBI, 2016, 2021). Social psychologists therefore wondered: Do political leaders' words merely voice common prejudices and grievances? Or do they also amplify them?

They do both. Leaders cater to their audiences. And when prominent leaders voice prejudices, it becomes more acceptable for their followers to do the same. Thus counties that hosted Trump rallies in 2016, where then-candidate Donald Trump had targeted Muslims and immigrants, reportedly experienced a doubled rate of hate crimes thereafter (Feinberg et al., 2019).

Researchers also have found that "frequent and repetitive exposure to hate speech leads to desensitization" to such speech and to "increasing outgroup prejudice" (Soral et al., 2018). Political leaders influence norms, and norms matter: "People express the prejudices that are socially acceptable and they hide the ones that are not" (Crandall & White, 2016).

Following the 2016 anti-immigrant Brexit referendum in England and Wales, hate crimes soared from 52,000 in 2015/2016 to 103,000 in 2018/2019 (Home Office, 2019). There, and in the United States, anti-Semitic crimes have also increased (ADL, 2022; Goodwin & Greene, 2022). During the Covid-19 pandemic, some government officials in White-majority countries referred to the virus as "Chinese" or "China virus." Associating the virus with a country fueled prejudice and discrimination, with 1 in 3 Asian Americans experiencing racial or ethnic slurs since the outbreak, and 1 in 4 fearing physical attack (Ruiz et al., 2020). U.S. psychologists have documented increased anti-Asian prejudice and called for greater advocacy to educate people about Covid-19 racial bias and build empathy toward Asian Americans (Cheng et al., 2021).

Evidence for the scapegoat theory comes in two forms: (1) *Social trends*: Economically frustrated people often express heightened prejudice, and during economic downturns, racial prejudice intensifies (Bianchi et al., 2018); and (2) *Experiments*: Temporarily frustrating people intensifies their prejudice. Researchers have found that students who experience failure or are made to feel insecure often restore their self-esteem by disparaging a rival school or another person (Cialdini & Richardson, 1980; Crocker et al., 1987). Denigrating others may boost our own sense of status, which explains why a rival's misfortune sometimes provides a twinge of pleasure. (The German language has a word—*schadenfreude*—for this secret joy that we sometimes take in another's failure.) By contrast, those made to feel loved and supported become more open to and accepting of others who differ (Mikulincer & Shaver, 2001).

STOP ASIAN HATE!!
WE BELONG
FOREVER
Ron Adar/Alamy Stock Photo

Fighting Covid-fueled prejudice U.S. demonstrators protest the rise of anti-Asian prejudice, which increased 339 percent between 2020 and 2021 (Yam, 2022).

SCHADENFREUDE
NEXT 20 MILES
SIPRESS
David Sipress/Cartoon Stock

"The misfortunes of others are the taste of honey." —Japanese saying

COGNITIVE SHORTCUTS Stereotyped beliefs are a by-product of how we cognitively simplify the world. To help understand the world around us, we frequently form categories. Chemists categorize molecules as organic and inorganic. Therapists categorize psychological disorders. We all categorize people by gender, ethnicity, race, age, and many other characteristics—including their warmth and their competence (Fiske, 2018). But when we categorize people into groups, we often stereotype. We recognize how greatly *we* differ from other individuals in *our* groups. But we overestimate the extent to which members of other groups are alike (Bothwell et al., 1989). We perceive *outgroup homogeneity*—uniformity of attitudes, personality, and appearance. Our greater recognition for individual own-race faces—called the **other-race effect** (or *cross-race effect* or *own-race bias*)—emerges during infancy, between 3 and 9 months of age, also a period when babies learn to distinguish the sounds of their language (Anzures et al., 2013; Telzer et al., 2013). Infant brains become attuned to small differences in familiar sounds and faces. (We also have an *own-age bias*—better recognition memory for faces of our own age group [Cronin et al., 2021; Rhodes & Anastasi, 2012]).

Sometimes, however, people don't fit easily into our racial categories. When that happens, we often assign them to their outgroup identity. Researchers believe this happens because, after learning the features of a familiar racial group, the observer's *selective attention* is drawn to the distinctive features of the less-familiar outgroup. One study illustrated this learned-association effect by showing research participants blended Chinese-White faces (Halberstadt et al., 2011). Compared with participants of Chinese

scapegoat theory the theory that prejudice offers an outlet for anger by providing someone to blame. 

other-race effect the tendency to recall faces of one's own race more accurately than faces of other races. Also called the *cross-race effect* and the *own-race bias.*

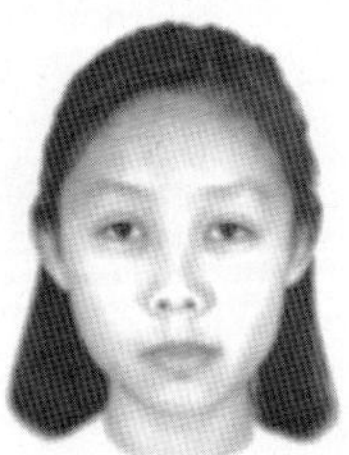
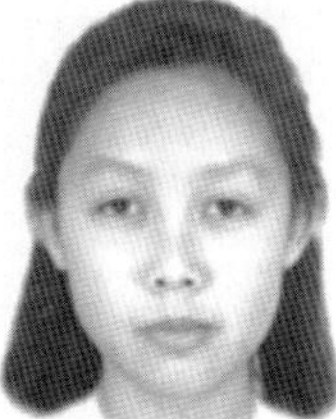

100% Chinese | 80% Chinese 20% White | 60% Chinese 40% White | 40% Chinese 60% White | 20% Chinese 80% White | 100% White

Dr. Jamin Halberstadt

FIGURE 43.3
Categorizing mixed-race people When research participants quickly classified 104 photos by race, those of European descent more often than those of Chinese descent classified the ambiguous middle two as Chinese (Halberstadt et al., 2011). The actual digital morphing mix is shown beneath each photo.

descent, European-descent participants more readily classified ambiguous faces as Chinese (**FIGURE 43.3**). With effort and experience, people get better at recognizing individual faces from another group (Hugenberg et al., 2010; Young et al., 2012).

REMEMBERING VIVID CASES We also simplify our world by employing *heuristics—mental* shortcuts that enable snap judgments. The *availability heuristic* is the tendency to estimate the frequency of an event by how readily it comes to mind. Vivid cases come to mind easily, so it's no surprise that they feed our stereotypes. In a classic experiment, researchers showed two groups of students lists containing information about 50 men (Rothbart et al., 1978). The first group's list included 10 men arrested for *nonviolent* crimes, such as forgery. The second group's list included 10 men arrested for *violent* crimes, such as assault. Later, both groups were asked how many men on their list had committed *any* sort of crime. The second group overestimated the number. Violent crimes form vivid memories (**FIGURE 43.4**).

YOU'RE BOB? SORRY, YOU RESEARCHERS ALL LOOK ALIKE TO ME.

© Dave Coverly/speedbump.com

VICTIM BLAMING As we noted earlier, people often justify their prejudices by blaming victims. If the world is just, they assume, people must get what they deserve, and believing this makes us feel better (Napier et al., 2020). As one German civilian is said to have remarked when visiting the Bergen-Belsen concentration camp shortly after World War II, "What terrible criminals these prisoners must have been to receive such treatment."

Hindsight bias amplifies victim blaming (Carli & Leonard, 1989). Have you ever heard people say that rape victims, abused spouses, or people with AIDS got what they deserved? In some countries, such as Pakistan, rape victims have been sentenced to severe punishment for violating adultery prohibitions (Mydans, 2002). In one experiment, two groups received a detailed account of a date (Janoff-Bulman et al., 1985). The first group's account ended with the woman being raped. Members of that group perceived the woman's behavior as at least partly to blame, and in hindsight, they thought, "She should have known better." The second group, given the same account with the rape ending deleted, did not perceive the woman's behavior as inviting rape. In the first group, hindsight bias promoted a blame-the-victim mentality. Blaming the victim reassures people that it couldn't happen to them.

People also tend to justify their culture's social systems (Jost, 2020). We're inclined to see the way things are as the way they ought to be and deserve to be: If people are rich, they must be smart (Hussak & Cimpian, 2015). This natural resistance to change makes it difficult to legislate major social changes, such as health care improvements or climate change policies. Once policies are in place, "system justification" tends to preserve them.

Muslims

Terrorism

FIGURE 43.4
Vivid cases feed stereotypes Memorable incidents of global terrorism have fed a stereotype of Muslims as terrorism-prone. Actually, reported a U.S. National Research Council panel on terrorism (which offered this inexact illustration), most terrorists are *not* Muslim.

* * *

If your own gut-check reveals you sometimes have feelings you would rather not have about other people, remember this: It is what we *do* with our feelings that matters. By monitoring our feelings and actions, by replacing old habits with new ones, and by seeking out new friendships, we can work to free ourselves from prejudice.

RETRIEVAL PRACTICE

RP-1 When prejudice causes us to blame an innocent person for a problem, we are using that person as a ________________.

ANSWERS IN APPENDIX E

Aggression

LOQ 43-4 How does psychology's definition of *aggression* differ from everyday usage? What biological factors make us more prone to hurt one another?

aggression any physical or verbal behavior intended to harm someone physically or emotionally.

In psychology, **aggression** is any physical or verbal behavior intended to harm someone, whether done out of hostility or as a calculated means to an end. The assertive, persistent salesperson is not aggressive. Nor is the dentist who makes you wince with pain. But the gossip who passes along a vicious rumor about you, the bully who torments you in person or online, and the attacker who robs you are aggressive. Remember, aggression is a behavior; you must *do* something to act aggressively. Feeling anger or thinking aggressive thoughts don't qualify as aggression.

Aggression emerges from the interaction of biology and experience. For a gun to fire, the trigger must be pulled; with some people, as with hair-trigger guns, it doesn't take much to trip an explosion. What do you think: Do guns in the home save or take more lives? "Personal safety/protection" is the number one reason people in the United States have given for gun ownership (Swift, 2013). However, firearm ownership can backfire: Guns in the home are much more often used to kill family members or oneself than in self-defense (Kivisto et al., 2019; Stroebe et al., 2017). In 2020, 45,222 Americans died from firearms; nearly 6 in 10 were suicides (CDC, 2022). Over the last half-century more than 1.5 million Americans have suffered nonwar firearm deaths—more than all war deaths in U.S. history (Jacobson, 2015). Compared with people of the same sex, race, age, and neighborhood, those who keep a gun in their home have been twice as likely to be murdered and three times as likely to die by suicide (Anglemyer et al., 2014; Stroebe, 2013). U.S. states with high gun ownership rates also tend to have high gun homicide rates (correlation $r = .82$) (**FIGURE 43.5**). It takes Japan nearly a decade to accumulate as many violent gun deaths as occur in an average U.S. day. More guns → more deaths.

In the discussions that follow, we will look first at some biological factors that influence our thresholds for aggressive behavior, then at the psychological factors that pull the trigger.

The Biology of Aggression

Aggression varies too widely from culture to culture, era to era, and person to person to be considered an unlearned instinct. But biology does *influence* aggression. We can look for biological influences at three levels—genetic, neural, and biochemical.

GENETIC INFLUENCES Genes influence aggression. Animals have been bred for aggressiveness—sometimes for sport, sometimes for research. The effect of genes also appears in human twin studies (Miles & Carey, 1997; Rowe et al., 1999). If one identical twin admits to "having a violent temper," the other twin will often independently admit the same. Fraternal twins are much less likely to respond similarly.

Gilbert Laurie/Getty Images

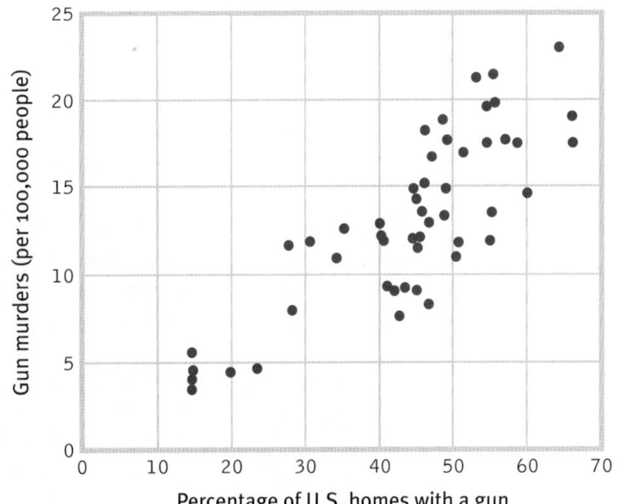

Gun murders (per 100,000 people)
25
20
15
10
5
0
0
10
20
30
40
50
60
70
Percentage of U.S. homes with a gun

FIGURE 43.5
Gun ownership and murder rates across the 50 U.S. states Information from CDC (2022) and Learish & Fieldstadt (2022).

Donald Reilly/Cartoon Stock

"It's a guy thing."

Researchers continue to search for genetic markers in those who commit violent acts. One is already well known and is carried by half the human race: the Y chromosome. Men are four times more likely than women to commit violent crime (FBI, 2022). Another such marker is the *monoamine oxidase A (MAOA) gene,* sometimes called the "warrior gene," which is involved in breaking down neurotransmitters such as dopamine and serotonin. People who have low MAOA gene expression tend to behave aggressively when provoked. In one experiment, low (compared with high) MAOA gene carriers gave more unpleasant hot sauce to someone who provoked them (McDermott et al., 2009; Tiihonen et al., 2015).

NEURAL INFLUENCES There is no one spot in the brain that controls aggression. Aggression is a complex behavior, and it occurs in particular contexts. But animal and human brains have neural systems that, given provocation, will either inhibit or facilitate aggression (Falkner et al., 2016; Fields, 2019). Consider:

- Researchers implanted a radio-controlled electrode in the brain of the domineering leader of a caged monkey colony. The electrode was in an area that, when stimulated, inhibited the leader's aggression. When researchers placed the control button for the electrode in the colony's cage, one small monkey learned to push it every time the boss became threatening.
- A neurosurgeon, seeking to diagnose a disorder, implanted an electrode in the amygdala of a mild-mannered woman. Because the brain has no sensory receptors, she was unable to feel the stimulation. But at the flick of a switch she snarled, "Take my blood pressure. Take it now," then stood up and began to strike the doctor (Moyer, 1983).
- If the frontal lobes are damaged, inactive, disconnected, or not yet fully mature, aggression may be more likely (Amen et al., 1996; Davidson et al., 2000; Raine, 2013). One study of 203 convicted murderers revealed reduced tissue in the frontal lobes (Sajous-Turner et al., 2020).

BIOCHEMICAL INFLUENCES Our genes engineer our individual nervous systems, which operate electrochemically. The hormone testosterone, for example, circulates in the bloodstream and influences the neural systems that influence aggression. A raging bull becomes a gentle giant when castration reduces its testosterone level. Conversely, when injected with testosterone, gentle, castrated mice become aggressive.

Humans are less sensitive to hormonal changes. But as men's testosterone levels diminish with age, hormonally charged, aggressive 17-year-olds mature into quieter and gentler 50-year-olds. Drugs that sharply reduce testosterone levels subdue men's aggressive tendencies.

"We could avoid two-thirds of all crime simply by putting all able-bodied young men in cryogenic sleep from the age of 12 through 28." —David T. Lykken, *The Antisocial Personalities*, 1995

Another drug that sometimes circulates in the bloodstream—alcohol—unleashes aggressive responses to frustration. Across police data, prison surveys, and experiments, aggression-prone people are more likely to drink, and to become violent when intoxicated (White et al., 1993). Alcohol is a disinhibitor—it slows the brain activity that controls judgment and inhibitions. Under its influence, people may interpret ambiguous acts (such as being bumped in a crowd) as provocations and react aggressively

Chris Courteau/AGE Fotostock

A lean, mean fighting machine—the testosterone-laden female hyena The hyena's unusual embryology pumps testosterone into female fetuses. The result is revved-up young female hyenas who seem born to fight.

(Bègue et al., 2010; Giancola & Corman, 2007). Alcohol consumption has been a factor in 1 in 3 U.S. homicides (Alpert et al., 2022). In countries that have restricted alcohol sales—by reducing alcohol's availability or increasing its price—homicides have dropped (Trangenstein et al., 2021).

Just *thinking* you've imbibed alcohol can increase aggression (Bègue et al., 2009). But so, too, does unknowingly ingesting alcohol slipped into a drink. Thus, alcohol affects aggression both biologically and psychologically (Bushman, 1993; Ito et al., 1996).

Teresa Burns Parkhurst/Cartoon Stock

"I just stubbed my toe and need you to come in here so I can scream at you."

Psychological and Social-Cultural Factors in Aggression

LOQ 43-5 What psychological and social-cultural factors may trigger aggressive behavior?

Biological factors influence how easily aggression is triggered. But what psychological and social-cultural factors pull the trigger?

AVERSIVE EVENTS: HURT PEOPLE HURT PEOPLE Suffering sometimes builds character. In both laboratory experiments and everyday life, however, those made miserable have often made others miserable (Berkowitz, 1983, 1989; O'Connor et al., 2021). Aversive stimuli—hot temperatures, physical pain, personal insults, foul odors, cigarette smoke, crowding, and a host of others—can evoke hostility. Even hunger can feed anger—making people "hangry" (Bushman et al., 2014). A prime example of this phenomenon is the **frustration-aggression principle**: Frustration creates anger, which can spark aggression.

The frustration-aggression link was illustrated in an analysis of 27,667 hit-by-pitch Major League Baseball incidents between 1960 and 2004 (Timmerman, 2007). Pitchers were most likely to hit batters when the previous batter had hit a home run, the current batter had hit a home run the last time at bat, or a pitch had hit the pitcher's teammate in the previous half-inning. A separate study found a similar link between rising temperatures and the number of hit batters (Reifman et al., 1991; see **FIGURE 43.6**). Overheated temperatures → overheated tempers.

Worldwide, violent crime and spousal abuse rates have been higher during hotter years, seasons, months, and days (Anderson et al., 1997; Heilmann & Kahn, 2019). Studies from archaeology, economics, geography, political science, and psychology converge in finding that throughout human history, higher temperatures have predicted increased individual violence, wars, and revolutions (Hsiang et al., 2013). One projection from available data estimates that global warming of 4 degrees Fahrenheit (about 2 degrees Celsius) could induce tens of thousands of additional assaults and murders (Miles-Novelo & Anderson, 2022). And that's before the added violence inducements from climate change–related drought, poverty, food insecurity, and migration.

frustration-aggression principle the principle that frustration—the blocking of an attempt to achieve some goal—creates anger, which can generate aggression.

Brita Meng Outzen/AP Photo

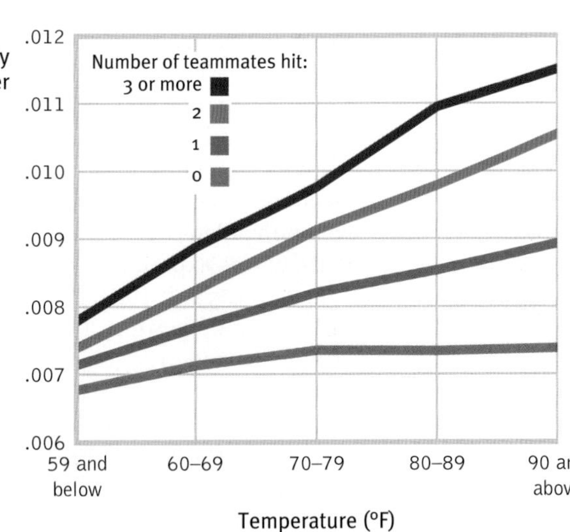

Probability of hit batter
.012
.011
.010
.009
.008
.007
.006
Number of teammates hit:
3 or more
2
1
0
59 and below
60–69
70–79
80–89
90 and above
Temperature (°F)

FIGURE 43.6
Temperature, tempers, and retaliation Researchers looked for occurrences of batters hit by pitches during 4,566,468 pitcher-batter matchups across 57,293 Major League Baseball games between 1952 and 2009 (Larrick et al., 2011). The probability of a hit batter increased if one or more of the pitcher's teammates had been hit, and also with higher temperatures.

REINFORCEMENT AND MODELING Aggression may naturally follow aversive events, but learning can alter natural reactions. We learn when our behavior is reinforced, and we learn by watching others.

In situations where experience has taught us that aggression pays, we are likely to act aggressively again. Children whose aggression has successfully intimidated other children may become bullies. Animals that have successfully fought to get food or mates become increasingly ferocious. To foster a kinder, gentler world we had best model and reward sensitivity and cooperation from an early age, perhaps by training parents to discipline without modeling violence. Parent-training programs often advise parents to avoid screaming and hitting; instead, they can reward desirable behaviors and frame statements positively (Kazdin, 2018). Rather than say, "If you don't clean your room, you'll be in big trouble," Say "When you clean your room, you can go play."

Different cultures model, reinforce, and evoke different tendencies toward violence. Between 1882 and 1926, lynch mobs in the U.S. state of Georgia murdered 514 people. The best predictors of this collective violence were cultural norms that encouraged and supported lynching (Ritchey & Rubak, 2018). But other factors also matter: Crime rates have been higher and average happiness lower in times and places marked by a great disparity between rich and poor (Messias et al., 2011; Oishi et al., 2011; Wilkinson & Pickett, 2009). And fathers matter (Triandis, 1994). Even after controlling for parental education, race, income, and teen motherhood, U.S. male youths from father-absent homes have been incarcerated at twice the rate of their peers (Harper & McLanahan, 2004).

Violence can vary by culture within a country. The U.S. South, for example, has long had a "culture of honor." Richard Nisbett and Dov Cohen (1996) analyzed violence among White Americans in southern towns settled by Scots-Irish herders whose tradition encouraged violent response to insult, the use of arms to protect one's flock, and slavery. Compared with their White counterparts in New England towns settled by the more traditionally peaceful Puritan, Quaker, and Dutch farmer-artisans, the cultural descendants of those herders had triple the homicide rates and were more supportive of physically punishing children, of wars, and of uncontrolled gun ownership. Today's culture of honor traditions remain influential, encouraging people to use weapons to defend their honor and to not "back down" (Gul et al., 2021; Lantz & Wenger, 2021).

MEDIA MODELS FOR VIOLENCE Television, films, video games, and the internet offer supersized portions of violence. An adolescent boy faced with a real-life challenge may "act like a man"—at least like an action-film man—by intimidating or eliminating the threat. Media violence teaches us **social scripts**—culturally provided mental files for how to act in certain situations. As more than 100 studies confirm, we sometimes imitate what we've viewed. Watching media depictions of risk-glorifying behaviors (dangerous driving, extreme sports, unprotected sex) increases real-life risk-taking (Fischer et al., 2011). Watching violent behaviors (murder, robbery) can increase real-life aggressiveness (Anderson et al., 2017).

Music lyrics also teach us social scripts. In one study, German university men who listened to woman-hating lyrics poured the hottest chili sauce for a woman to consume. They also recalled more negative feelings and beliefs about women. Listening to man-hating lyrics similarly affected women (Fischer & Greitemeyer, 2006).

How does repeatedly watching pornographic films affect viewers? Just as repeated viewing of on-screen violence helps immunize us to aggression, repeated viewing of pornography—even nonviolent pornography—has made sexual aggression seem less serious (Harris, 1994). In one experiment, undergraduates viewed six brief films weekly for 6 weeks (Zillmann & Bryant, 1984). Some viewed sexually explicit films; others viewed films with no sexual content. Three weeks later, both groups, after reading a report about a man convicted of raping a female hitchhiker, suggested an appropriate prison term. Compared with sentences recommended by the control group, the sex film viewers recommended terms that were half as long. In other studies that explored pornography's effects on aggression toward relationship partners, pornography consumption predicted both self-reported aggression and participants' willingness to administer laboratory noise blasts to their partner (Lambert et al., 2011; Peter & Valkenburg, 2016).

social script a culturally modeled guide for how to act in various situations.

Pornography acts mostly by adding fuel to a fire: It heightens the risk of sexual aggression primarily among aggression-prone men (Malamuth, 2018).

Researchers debate pornography's influence on healthy relationships and sexuality (Grubbs & Kraus, 2021; Zimbardo & Coulombe, 2021). Some experiments suggest that pornography with violent sexual content can increase men's readiness to behave aggressively toward women. As a long-ago statement by 21 social scientists noted, "Pornography that portrays sexual aggression as pleasurable for the victim increases the acceptance of the use of coercion in sexual relations" (Surgeon General, 1986). Analyzing 166 studies involving 125,000 participants, some of today's researchers reached a similar conclusion: "Exposure to sexualized media, especially in combination with violence, has negative effects on women, particularly on what people think about them and how aggressively they treat them" (Burnay et al., 2022).

Cathal McNaughton/REUTERS/Alamy Stock Photo

Coincidence or cause? In 2011, a Norwegian terrorist killed eight people by bombing government buildings, and then shot and killed 69 people, mostly teens, at a youth camp. Describing his murderous actions, the shooter stirred debate when he commented that "I see MW2 *[Modern Warfare 2]* more as a part of my training-simulation than anything else." Did his violent game playing—and that of the 2022 mass murderer of Uvalde, Texas' elementary school children and teachers—contribute to the violence, or was it a merely coincidental association? Psychologists explore such questions with experimental research.

DO VIOLENT VIDEO GAMES TEACH SOCIAL SCRIPTS FOR VIOLENCE? Experiments worldwide indicate that playing positive games produces positive effects (Greitemeyer & Mügge, 2014; Prot et al., 2014). For example, playing the classic video game *Lemmings,* where a goal was to help others, increased real-life helping. So, might a similar effect occur after playing games that enact violence? Violent video games became an issue for public debate after teenagers in more than a dozen places seemed to mimic the carnage in the first-person shooter games they had so often played (Anderson, 2004, 2013).

Such incidents of violent mimicry make us wonder: What *are* the effects of actively role-playing aggression? Does it cause people to become less sensitive to violence and more open to violent acts? Amid conflicting findings, nearly 400 studies of 130,000 people offer some answers (Calvert et al., 2017; Kim et al., 2021). Violent video game playing tends to make us less sensitive to cruelty (Arriaga et al., 2015). Video games can prime aggressive thoughts, decrease empathy, and induce us to respond aggressively when provoked. University men who spend the most hours playing violent video games have also tended to be the most physically aggressive (Anderson & Dill, 2000). For example, they more often acknowledged having hit or attacked someone else. More than two dozen longitudinal studies have found that violent video game playing predicts more bullying and physical violence (Prescott et al., 2018; Teng et al., 2022).

In experiments, people who were randomly assigned to play a game involving bloody murders with groaning victims (rather than to play nonviolent games) became more hostile. On a follow-up task, they were more likely to blast intense noise at a fellow student. Studies of young adolescents revealed that those who played a lot of violent video games became more aggressive and saw the world as more hostile (Bushman, 2016; Exelmans et al., 2015; Gentile, 2009). Compared with nongaming kids, they got into more arguments and fights and earned poorer grades. In another experiment, children who played a video game with gun violence (rather than sword violence or no violence) later became more likely to touch, pick up, and pull the trigger on a real (but disabled) gun (Chang & Bushman, 2019).

Ah, but is this merely because naturally hostile kids are drawn to such games (Greitemeyer et al., 2019)? Apparently not. Comparisons of both gamers and nongamers who scored low on hostility measures revealed a difference in the number of fights they reported. Almost 4 in 10 violent-game players had been in fights, compared with only 4 in 100 of the nongaming kids (Anderson, 2004). Some researchers believe that, due partly to the more active participation and rewarded violence of game play, violent video games have even greater effects on aggressive behavior and cognition than do violent TV shows and movies (Anderson & Warburton, 2012).

Other researchers are unimpressed by such findings (Ferguson et al., 2020; Markey & Ferguson, 2018). They note that although video game sales have increased, youth violence has declined. They argue that the best studies find minimal effects and that other factors—depression, family violence, peer influence, and a gun-toting culture—better predict aggression. Although some commentators have tried to blame modern mass shootings on violent video games, most researchers agree that they are, at worst, only one modest contributor to social violence (APA, 2019; Mathur & VanderWeele, 2019).

"Research demonstrates a consistent relation between violent video game use and increases in aggressive behavior, aggressive cognitions and aggressive affect, and decreases in prosocial behavior, empathy and sensitivity to aggression." —American Psychological Association Task Force on Violent Media, 2015

"Study finds exposure to violent children causes increased aggression in video game characters." —*The* [satirical] *Onion*, March 6, 2017

FIGURE 43.7
Biopsychosocial understanding of aggression Because many factors contribute to aggressive behavior, there are many ways to change such behavior, including learning anger management and communication skills, and avoiding violent media and video games.

Biological influences:
- heredity
- biochemical factors, such as testosterone and alcohol
- neural factors, such as a severe head injury

Psychological influences:
- dominating behavior (which boosts testosterone levels in the blood)
- believing that alcohol has been ingested (whether it has or not)
- frustration
- aggressive role models
- rewards for aggressive behavior
- low self-control

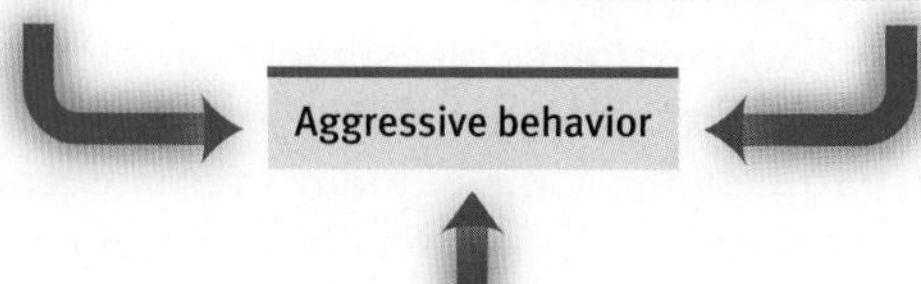
Aggressive behavior

Social-cultural influences:
- *deindividuation*, or a loss of self-awareness and self-restraint
- challenging environmental factors, such as crowding, heat, and direct provocations
- parental models of aggression
- minimal father involvement
- rejection from a group
- exposure to violent media

* * *

To sum up, research reveals biological, psychological, and social-cultural influences on aggressive behavior. Complex behaviors, including violence, have many causes, making any single explanation an oversimplification. Asking what causes violence is therefore like asking what causes cancer. Those who study the effects of asbestos exposure on cancer rates may remind us that asbestos is indeed a cancer cause, but it is only one among many. Like so much else, aggression is a biopsychosocial phenomenon (**FIGURE 43.7**).

A happy concluding note: Historical trends suggest that the world is becoming less violent over time (Pinker, 2011, 2018). That people vary across time and place reminds us that environments differ. Yesterday's plundering Vikings have become today's peace-promoting Scandinavians. Like all behavior, aggression arises from the interaction of persons and situations.

ASK YOURSELF

In what ways have you been affected by social scripts for aggression? Have your viewing and gaming habits influenced these social scripts?

RETRIEVAL PRACTICE

RP-2 What biological, psychological, and social-cultural influences interact to produce aggressive behaviors?

ANSWERS IN APPENDIX E

MODULE 43 REVIEW Antisocial Relations

LEARNING OBJECTIVES

Test Yourself Answer these repeated Learning Objective Questions on your own (before "showing" the answers here, or checking the answers in Appendix D) to improve your retention of the concepts (McDaniel et al., 2009, 2015).

LOQ 43-1 What is *prejudice*? How do explicit and implicit prejudice differ?

LOQ 43-2 What groups tend to experience prejudice?

LOQ 43-3 What are some social, emotional, and cognitive roots of prejudice, and what are some ways to reduce prejudice?

LOQ 43-4 How does psychology's definition of *aggression* differ from everyday usage? What biological factors make us more prone to hurt one another?

LOQ 43-5 What psychological and social-cultural factors may trigger aggressive behavior?

TERMS AND CONCEPTS TO REMEMBER

Test Yourself Write down the definition in your own words, then check your answer.

prejudice, p. 488
stereotype, p. 489
discrimination, p. 489
implicit bias, p. 489
just-world phenomenon, p. 493
ingroup, p. 494
outgroup, p. 494
ingroup bias, p. 494
scapegoat theory, p. 495
other-race effect, p. 495
aggression, p. 497
frustration-aggression principle, p. 499
social script, p. 500

MODULE TEST

Test Yourself Answer the following questions on your own first, then "show" the answers here, or check your answers in Appendix E.

1. Prejudice toward a group involves negative feelings, a tendency to discriminate, and overly generalized beliefs referred to as ____________.

2. If several well-publicized murders are committed by members of a particular group, we may tend to react with fear and suspicion toward all members of that group. In other words, we
a. blame the victim.
b. overgeneralize from vivid, memorable cases.
c. view the world as just.
d. rationalize inequality.

3. The other-race effect occurs when we assume that other groups are ____________ (more/less) homogeneous than our own group.

4. Evidence of a biochemical influence on aggression is the finding that
a. aggressive behavior varies widely from culture to culture.
b. animals can be bred for aggressiveness.
c. stimulation of an area of the brain produces aggressive behavior.
d. a higher-than-average level of the hormone testosterone is associated with violent behavior in males.

5. When those who feel frustrated become angry and aggressive, this is referred to as the ____________-____________ ____________.

6. Studies show that delinquent young people tend to have parents who used physical force to enforce discipline. This suggests that aggression can be
a. learned through direct rewards.
b. triggered by exposure to violent media.
c. learned through observation of aggressive models.
d. caused by hormone changes at puberty.

7. A conference of social scientists studying the effects of pornography unanimously agreed that violent pornography
a. has little effect on most viewers.
b. is the primary cause of reported and unreported rapes.
c. leads viewers to be more accepting of coercion in sexual relations.
d. has no effect, other than short-term arousal and entertainment.

8. The aspect of heterosexual pornography that most directly influences men's aggression toward women seems to be the
a. time spent viewing
b. eroticism portrayed.
c. depictions of sexual violence.
d. attractiveness of the actors.

MODULE
44

Prosocial Relations

As social animals—as people who need people—we often approach others not with closed fists, but with open arms. Social psychologists focus not only on the dark side of social relationships, but also on this bright side, by studying *prosocial behavior*—behavior that intends to help or benefit someone. Our positive behaviors toward others are evident from explorations of attraction, altruism and compassion, and peacemaking.

"We humans are social beings. We come into the world as the result of others' actions. We survive here in dependence on others. Whether we like it or not, there is hardly a moment of our lives when we do not benefit from others' activities. For this reason, it is hardly surprising that most of our happiness arises in the context of our relationships with others."—Dalai Lama XIV, *Ethics for the New Millennium*, 2019

Attraction

Pause a moment and think about your relationships. What led to you becoming close friends with someone, or stirred your romantic feelings for someone else? What psychological chemistry binds us together in friendship or love? Social psychology suggests some answers.

Brendan Beirne/REX/Shutterstock

Familiarity breeds acceptance When this rare white penguin was born in the Sydney, Australia, zoo, his tuxedoed peers ostracized him. Zookeepers thought they would need to dye him black to gain acceptance. But after three weeks of contact, the other penguins came to accept him.

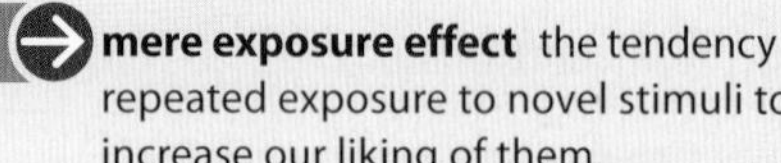

mere exposure effect the tendency for repeated exposure to novel stimuli to increase our liking of them.

The Psychology of Attraction

LOQ 44-1 Why do we befriend or fall in love with some people but not others?

We spend a lot of time thinking about how we can win others' affection and what makes our own affections flourish or fade. Does familiarity breed contempt, or does it amplify affection? Do birds of a feather flock together, or do opposites attract? Is it what's inside that counts, or does physical attractiveness matter, too? To explore these questions, let's consider three ingredients of our liking for one another: proximity, attractiveness, and similarity.

PROXIMITY Before friendships become close, they must begin. *Proximity*—geographic nearness—is one of friendship's most powerful predictors (Eagle et al., 2009; Nahemow & Lawton, 1975). Proximity can provide opportunities for aggression. But much more often it breeds liking (and sometimes romance) among those who live in the same neighborhood, sit nearby in class, work in the same office, share the same parking lot, or eat in the same dining hall. Look around. Mating starts with meeting.

The power of proximity was illustrated at a "Seeds of Peace" Israeli summer camp (White et al., 2021). The camp sought to reduce intergroup conflict among outgroup pairs (Jewish and Palestinian teens) with one of three strategies: Share a sleeping bunk, eat at the same table, or attend the same 110-minute dialogue group. Proximity mattered most. Outgroup pairs who shared a sleeping bunk, versus those who did not, were 11 times more likely to become friends. Keep your enemies close and they might become your friends.

Proximity breeds liking partly because of the **mere exposure effect**. Repeated exposure to novel visual stimuli increases our liking for them. By age 3 months, infants prefer photos of the race they most often see—usually their own race (Kelly et al., 2007). Familiarity with a face also makes it look happier (Carr et al., 2017). For our ancestors, this mere exposure effect likely had survival value. What was familiar was generally safe and approachable. What was unfamiliar was more often dangerous and threatening. Evolution may therefore have hard-wired into us the tendency to bond with those who look familiar and to be wary of those who look unfamiliar (Sofer et al., 2015; Zajonc, 1998).

Mere exposure leads to familiarity and thus increases our liking not only for faces, but also for musical selections, geometric figures, Chinese characters (for Chinese language learners), and for the letters of our own name (Moreland & Zajonc, 1982; Nuttin, 1987; Reis et al., 2011; Zajonc, 2001). Mere exposure even increases *unconscious* liking of nonsense syllables—strings of letters presented so quickly our minds don't consciously process them (Van Dessel et al., 2019). So, up to a point (after which the effect wears off), familiarity feeds fondness (Bornstein, 1989, 1999; Montoya et al., 2017). This would come as no surprise to the young Taiwanese man who wrote more than 700 letters to his girlfriend, urging her to marry him. She did marry—the mail carrier (Steinberg, 1993). No face is more familiar than your own. And that helps explain an interesting finding by Lisa DeBruine (2002, 2004): We like other people when their faces incorporate some morphed features of our own. When McMaster University students played an electronic game with a supposed other player, they were more trusting and cooperative when the other person's image had some of their own facial features morphed into it. In me I trust.

(a)

(b)

Anthony Behar/Sipa USA/Alamy Stock Photo

Which is the real Simu Liu? The mere exposure effect applies even to ourselves. Because the human face is not perfectly symmetrical, the face we see in the mirror is not the same face our friends see. Most of us prefer the familiar mirror image, while our friends like the reverse (Mita et al., 1977). The person actor Simu Liu sees in the mirror each morning is (b) and that's the photo he would probably prefer over the version that other people see in (a).

MODERN MATCHMAKING Those who have not found a romantic partner in their immediate proximity may cast a wider net. Millions search for love online. Despite some risks—which, for about half of young U.S. women using online dating sites and apps, include receiving unwanted sexual messages (Anderson et al., 2020; Brown, 2020)—an estimated 77 million people worldwide use online matchmaking services (Statista, 2022).

Online matchmaking expands the pool of potential mates, especially for same-sex couples (Finkel et al., 2012a,b; Rosenfeld et al., 2019). Among couples surveyed in 2017 that had met during the internet age, 39 percent of straight couples and 65 percent of same-sex couples met online (Rosenfeld et al., 2019; see **FIGURE 44.1**). Compared to couples meeting offline, those who meet online more often differ in race or ethnicity (Brown, 2019).

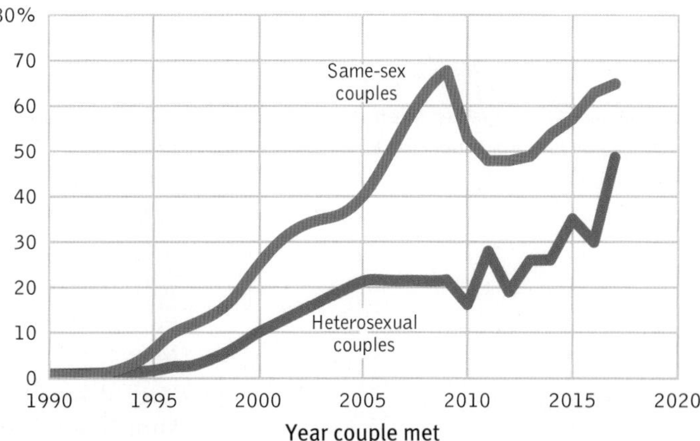
Percentage of couples who met online
80%
70
60
50
40
30
20
10
0
Same-sex couples
Heterosexual couples
1990
1995
2000
2005
2010
2015
2020
Year couple met

FIGURE 44.1
The changing way we meet our partners
The internet's increasing role is clear in U.S. surveys of straight and same-sex couples. (Data from Rosenfeld, 2011; Rosenfeld et al., 2018, 2019)

How effective is the matchmaking? Compared with friendships and romances that began in person, internet-formed relationships are, on average, slightly more likely to last and be satisfying (Bargh & McKenna, 2004; Bargh et al., 2002; Cacioppo et al., 2013). In one study, people disclosed more, with less posturing, to those whom they met online (McKenna et al., 2002). When talking via text or chat with someone for 20 minutes, they felt more liking for that person than they did for someone they had met and talked with face-to-face. This was true even when (unknown to them) it was the same person!

Speed dating pushes the search for romance into high gear. At these events, which were pioneered by a matchmaking Jewish rabbi, people meet a succession of prospective partners, either in person or via webcam (Bower, 2009). After a brief 3- to 8-minute conversation, people move on to the next prospect. Those who want to meet again can arrange for future contact. For many participants, a few minutes is enough time to form a feeling about a conversational partner and to register whether the partner likes them (Finkel & Eastwick, 2008).

For researchers, speed dating offers a unique opportunity for studying influences on our first impressions of potential romantic partners. Some findings:

- ***People who fear rejection often elicit rejection.*** After a 3-minute speed date, those who most feared rejection were least often selected for a follow-up date (McClure & Lydon, 2014).
- ***Given more options, people make more superficial choices.*** When people meet lots of potential partners, they focus on more easily assessed characteristics, such as height and weight (Lenton & Francesconi, 2010).
- ***Similarity is in the eye of the beholder.*** After interacting with dating candidates for 4 minutes each, people's perceived—but not actual—similarity with each person predicted their romantic interest (Tidwell et al., 2013).

e flake

Emily Flake/Cartoon Stock

"...and if anyone here suspects that the algorithm that put these two together might be flawed, speak now..."

PHYSICAL ATTRACTIVENESS Once proximity affords us contact, what most affects our first impressions? The person's sincerity? Intelligence? Personality? Hundreds of experiments reveal that it is something more superficial: physical appearance. This finding is unnerving for those of us taught that "beauty is only skin deep" and "appearances can be deceiving."

In one early study, researchers randomly matched new students for heterosexual blind dates in a Welcome Week dance (Walster et al., 1966). Before the dance, the researchers gave each student a battery of personality and aptitude tests, and they rated each student's physical attractiveness. The couples danced and talked for more than 2 hours and then took a brief intermission to rate their dates. What predicted whether they liked each other? Only one thing: appearance. Both the men and the women liked good-looking dates best. Women are more likely than men to say that another's looks don't affect them (Lippa, 2007). But studies show that a man's looks do affect women's behavior (Eastwick et al., 2014a,b). In speed-dating experiments, attractiveness influences first impressions and liking for men and women (Belot & Francesconi, 2006; Finkel & Eastwick, 2008).

Physical attractiveness also predicts how often people date and how popular they feel. And it affects initial impressions of people's personalities. We perceive attractive people as healthier, happier, more sensitive, more successful, and more socially skilled

(Eagly et al., 1991; Fink & Penton-Voak, 2002). We dehumanize unattractive people, especially women (Alaei et al., 2022). This dehumanization can have deadly results: When asked whether they would be willing to kill one person to save five people, participants were more willing to sacrifice the life of an unattractive person.

"Personal beauty is a greater recommendation than any letter of introduction."
—Aristotle, *Apothegems*, 330 B.C.E.

For those who find the importance of looks unfair, sexist, or unenlightened, three other findings offer some reassurance.

- People's attractiveness is unrelated to their self-esteem and happiness (Diener et al., 1995; Major et al., 1984). And unless we have just compared ourselves with extremely attractive people, few of us (thanks, perhaps, to the mere exposure effect) view ourselves as highly unattractive (Greitemeyer, 2020; Thornton & Moore, 1993).
- Very attractive people are sometimes suspicious that praise for their work may simply be a reaction to their looks. Less attractive people have been more likely to accept praise as sincere (Berscheid, 1981).
- For couples who were friends before lovers—who became romantically involved long after first meeting—looks matter less (Hunt et al., 2015). With slow-cooked love, shared values and interests matter more.

Peter Steiner/Cartoon Stock

"Cosmetic dentistry changed my life."

Beauty is also in the eye of the culture. People across the globe have modified their bodies in different ways, driven by cultural ideas of attractiveness. They have pierced and tattooed their bodies, lengthened their necks, bound their feet, artificially lightened or darkened their skin or hair, and bulked up their muscles. They have applied chemicals to rid themselves of unwanted hair or to regrow wanted hair, and used undergarments to change the proportions of waists, hips, and breasts. Cultural ideals also change over time and with context. For women in North America, for example, the ultrathin ideal of the Roaring Twenties gave way to the soft, voluptuous Marilyn Monroe ideal of the 1950s and then to today's more athletic ideal look.

Some aspects of sexual attractiveness, however, do cross place and time (Cunningham et al., 2005; Langlois et al., 2000). By providing reproductive clues, bodies influence sexual attraction. As some evolutionary psychologists explain, straight men in cultures worldwide judge romantic partners as more attractive if they have a youthful, fertile appearance (Walter et al., 2020). Straight women feel attracted to men who are healthy- and fertile-looking, but are most attracted to men who seem mature, dominant, and affluent (Feingold, 1990; Gallup & Frederick, 2010; Gangestad et al., 2010). One review reported that straight men may place higher value on physical attractiveness than straight women (Feingold, 1990). Gay and bisexual women have reported a preference for larger body figures (Cohen & Tannenbaum, 2001).

People's attractiveness influences our first impressions: We tend to think that what is beautiful is also good. But we also perceive what is good as beautiful (He et al., 2022). Our feelings color our attractiveness judgments. Imagine two people: One is honest, humorous, and polite. The other is rude, unfair, and abusive. Which one is more attractive? Most people perceive the person with the appealing traits as more physically attractive (Lewandowski et al., 2007). Or imagine being paired with a stranger of the gender

What is "attractive"? The answer varies by culture and over time. Yet some adult physical features, such as a healthy appearance and a relatively symmetrical face, seem attractive everywhere. Some people use a photo filter that makes their face symmetrical (as has been applied to the face on the right, above) for social media presentation (Garelick, 2022).

Morsa Images/DigitalVision/Getty Images

you find attractive—someone who listens intently to your self-disclosures. Might you feel a twinge of sexual attraction toward that empathic person? Student volunteers did, in several experiments (Birnbaum & Reis, 2012). People find smiling potential partners more attractive (Mehrabian & Blum, 2018). Those we like we find attractive.

Shakespeare said it in *A Midsummer Night's Dream:* "Love looks not with the eyes, but with the mind." As we see our loved ones repeatedly, their physical imperfections grow less noticeable and their attractiveness grows more apparent (Beaman & Klentz, 1983; Gross & Crofton, 1977). Come to love someone and watch beauty grow. Love sees loveliness.

SIMILARITY So, proximity has brought you into contact with someone, and your appearance has made an acceptable first impression. What influences whether you will become friends? As you get to know each other, will the chemistry be better if you are opposites or if you are alike?

It makes a good story—extremely different types liking or loving each other: unlikely friends Frog and Toad in Arnold Lobel's books, unlikely couple Hermione and Ron in the Harry Potter series.

But in many real-life situations, opposites retract (Montoya & Horton, 2013; Oosterhoff et al., 2022; Rosenbaum, 1986). Tall people often find true love with other tall people; short people show a soft spot for other short people (Yengo et al., 2018). Compared with randomly paired people, friends and couples are far more likely to share—and to like those with whom they share—attitudes, beliefs, interests, and even personality traits (and, for that matter, age, religion, race, education, intelligence, smoking behavior, and economic status). Most people's immediate neighbors tend to be from the same political party (Brown & Enos, 2021). As C. S. Lewis (1960) observed, "What draws people to be friends is that they see the same truth."

While there is some evidence that among married, same-sex couples, similarity in personality may not predict long-term happiness (Shiota & Levinson, 2007), for most relationships, the more alike people are, the more their liking endures (Byrne, 1971; Hartl et al., 2015). One journalist was right to suppose that love lasts "when the lovers love many things together, and not merely each other" (Lippmann, 1929).

Proximity, attractiveness, and similarity are not the only determinants of attraction. We also like those who like us. When we believe someone likes us, we feel good and respond to them warmly, which leads them to like us even more (Curtis & Miller, 1986). To be liked is powerfully rewarding. Moreover, there is a *liking gap*: After two strangers interact, both tend to report liking the other person more than they presume the other liked them. This is good news to remember: Most people immediately like us more than we realize (Boothby et al., 2018; Wolf et al., 2021).

Indeed, all the findings we have considered so far can be explained by a simple *reward theory of attraction:* We will like those whose behavior is rewarding to us, including those who are both able and willing to help us achieve our goals (Montoya & Horton, 2014). When people live or work in close proximity to us, it requires less time and effort to develop the friendship and enjoy its benefits. When people are attractive, they are aesthetically pleasing, and associating with them can be socially rewarding. When people share our views, they reward us by validating our own beliefs.

YOU'RE WHITE WITH BLACK STRIPES, I'M BLACK WITH WHITE STRIPES. MAYBE WE'RE JUST TOO DIFFERENT FOR THIS TO WORK.

Similarity attracts; perceived dissimilarity does not.

ASK YOURSELF

To what extent have your closest relationships been affected by proximity, physical attractiveness, and similarity?

RETRIEVAL PRACTICE

RP-1 People tend to marry someone who lives or works nearby. This is an example of the ________ ________ ________ in action.

RP-2 How does being physically attractive influence others' perceptions?

ANSWERS IN APPENDIX E

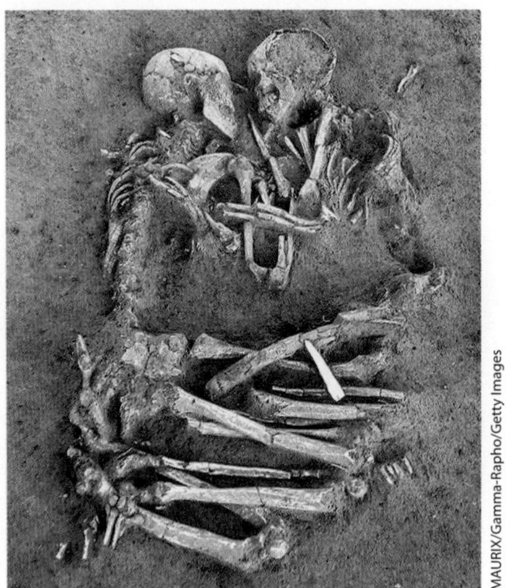

MAURIX/Gamma-Rapho/Getty Images

Love is an ancient thing This 5000- to 6000-year-old "Romeo and Juliet" young couple was unearthed locked in embrace, near Rome.

Romantic Love

LOQ 44-2 How does romantic love typically change as time passes?

Sometimes people move from initial impressions to friendship to the more intense, complex, and mysterious state of new romantic love. If love endures, temporary *passionate love* will mellow into a lingering *companionate love* (Hatfield, 1988; Fehr et al., 2014).

PASSIONATE LOVE **Passionate love** mixes something new with something positive (Aron et al., 2000; Coulter & Malouff, 2013). We intensely desire to be with our partner, and seeing our partner stimulates blood flow to brain regions linked to craving and obsession (Acevedo et al., 2012; Hatfield et al., 2015).

The *two-factor theory of emotion* can help us understand the intense positive absorption of passionate love (Hatfield, 1988). It assumes that

- emotions have two ingredients—*physical arousal* plus *cognitive appraisal*.
- arousal from any source can enhance one emotion or another, depending on how we interpret and label the arousal.

In one classic experiment, researchers studied straight men crossing two bridges above British Columbia's rocky Capilano River (Dutton & Aron, 1974, 1989). One, a swaying footbridge, was 230 feet (70 meters) above the rocks; the other was low and solid. As the men came off each bridge, an attractive young woman (working for the researchers) intercepted them and asked them to fill out a short questionnaire. She then offered her phone number in case they wanted to hear more about her project. Far more of the men who had just crossed the high bridge—which left their hearts pounding—accepted the number and later called the woman.

To be revved up and to associate some of that arousal with a desirable person is to feel the pull of passion. So, if you're looking for romance, perhaps take your date to a climbing gym. Adrenaline makes the heart grow fonder. Sexual desire + a growing attachment = passionate love (Berscheid, 2010).

Tom Toro/Cartoon Stock

"I think I know where the passion in our marriage has gone."

COMPANIONATE LOVE Although the desire and attachment of romantic love often endure, the intense absorption in the other, the thrill of the romance, the giddy "floating on a cloud" feelings typically fade. Does this mean the French are correct in saying that "love makes the time pass and time makes love pass"? Or can friendship and commitment keep a relationship going after the passion cools?

As love matures, it typically becomes a steadier **companionate love**—a deep, affectionate attachment (Hatfield, 1988). For people worldwide, as relationships mature they evolve: Passion subsides and commitment grows (Sorokowski et al., 2021). Like a passing storm, the flood of passion-facilitating hormones (testosterone, dopamine, adrenaline) subsides. But another hormone, *oxytocin*, remains, supporting feelings of trust, calmness, and bonding with the mate. This shift from passion to attachment has adaptive value (Reis & Aron, 2008). Passionate love often produces children; companionate love aids children's survival as the parents lose their obsession with each other.

In the most satisfying marriages, attraction and sexual desire endure, minus the obsession of early romance (Acevedo & Aron, 2009). Recognizing the short duration of obsessive passionate love, some societies deem such feelings an irrational reason for marrying. Better, they say, to seek (or have someone seek for you) a partner with a compatible background and interests. Cultures where people rate love as less important for marriage do have lower divorce rates (Levine et al., 1995).

passionate love an aroused state of intense positive absorption in another, usually present at the beginning of a romantic relationship.

companionate love the deep affectionate attachment we feel for someone with whom our life is intertwined.

equity a condition in which people receive from a relationship in proportion to what they give to it.

One key to a gratifying and enduring relationship is **equity**. When equity exists—when both partners receive in proportion to what they give—the chances for sustained and satisfying companionate love are good (Gray-Little & Burks, 1983; Van Yperen & Buunk, 1990). In one national survey, "sharing household chores" ranked third, after "having shared interests" and a "satisfying sexual relationship," on a list of seven things people associated with successful marriages (Geiger, 2016). As the saying goes, "I like hugs. I like kisses. But what I really love is help with the dishes."

Equity's importance extends beyond marriage. Mutually sharing one's self and possessions, making decisions together, giving and getting emotional support, promoting and caring about each other's welfare—all of these acts are at the core of every type of loving relationship (Sternberg & Grajek, 1984). It's true for lovers, for parent and child, and for close friends.

Sharing includes **self-disclosure**, revealing intimate details about ourselves—our likes and dislikes, our dreams and worries, our proud and shameful moments. "When I am with my friend," noted the Roman statesman Seneca, "methinks I am alone, and as much at liberty to speak anything as to think it." Self-disclosure breeds liking, and liking breeds self-disclosure (Collins & Miller, 1994). As one person reveals a little, the other reciprocates, the first then reveals more, and on and on, as lovers (and friends) move to deeper levels of intimacy (Baumeister & Bratslavsky, 1999).

One experiment marched some student pairs through 45 minutes of increasingly self-disclosing conversation—from "What is the greatest accomplishment of your life?" to "When did you last cry in front of another person? By yourself?" Other pairs spent the time with small-talk questions, such as "What was your high school like?" (Aron et al., 1997). By the experiment's end, those experiencing the escalating intimacy felt much closer to their conversation partner than did the small-talkers. Likewise, after dating couples spent 45 minutes answering such questions, they felt increased love (Welker et al., 2014).

In addition to equity and self-disclosure, a third key to enduring love is *positive support*. For happy couples in enduring relationships, positive interactions (compliments, touches, laughing) outnumber negative interactions (sarcasm, disapproval, insults) by at least 5 to 1 (Gottman & Gottman, 2022). In the mathematics of love, self-disclosing intimacy + mutually supportive equity = enduring companionate love.

Relationship conflicts are inevitable, but hurtful communications are not. Do we more often express sarcasm or support, scorn or sympathy, sneers or smiles? In romance, a rejection hurts more and for longer than an acceptance pleases (Dobson et al., 2020). For unhappy couples, disagreements, criticisms, and put-downs are routine. It takes multiple compliments to equal the attention-getting and emotion-affecting power of one criticism.

Couples benefit from making space for positive communication. In one experiment, some couples were randomly assigned to once a week spend 15 minutes with their partner writing down "three *good* things that happened to you as a couple during the week" and noting "why did this good thing happen?" After six weekly repetitions, these couples reported increased satisfaction and intimacy (Boiman-Meshita & Littman-Ovadia, 2021).

RETRIEVAL PRACTICE

RP-3 How does the two-factor theory of emotion help explain *passionate love*?

RP-4 Two vital components for maintaining *companionate love* are ____________ and ____________-____________.

ANSWERS IN APPENDIX E

Altruism

LOQ 44-3 What is *altruism*? When are people most—and least—likely to help?

"We are made for goodness," observed South African Archbishop Desmond Tutu (1931–2021). "Why else do we get so outraged by wrong?"

So it seemed during the first two weeks of March, 2021. Outraged by Russia's violence against Ukraine, people from 165 countries booked more than 430,000 nights at Ukrainian Airbnbs, most belonging to people they did not know (Friedman, 2022). The purchasers had no intention of using the reservation; they simply wanted to donate money to people who were hurting. In the invasion's first two weeks, nearly $400 million in additional donations were made by people from around the world to support Ukrainians (Roohi, 2022).

Among those fleeing Ukraine were cousins Lesia Orshoko and Alona Chugai. On their arrival in Israel, they were welcomed by Sharon Bass, a Jew who owed her existence to the long-ago altruism of the cousins' "righteous Gentile" Ukrainian

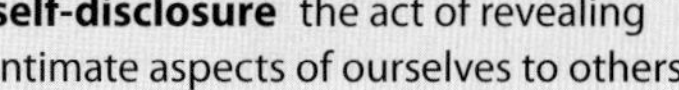

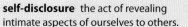

self-disclosure the act of revealing intimate aspects of ourselves to others.

Sharon Bass

Altruism across generations Israeli Sharon Bass (middle) is pictured here with Ukrainian refugees Lesia Orshoki (left) and Alona Chugai (right).

grandmother, Maria Blyshchik. For 2 years Blyshchik hid Bass's grandmother, Fania Rosenfeld, then a teen, sparing her from the Holocaust that killed her parents and five siblings.

After later relocating to Israel, Fania Rosenfeld Bass would tell the story "over and over to her children and grandchildren, letting them know about the good people who held on to their humanity and quietly rebelled against the horrors of the war" (Greenbaum, 2022). Eight decades later, as war ravaged Ukraine, Sharon Bass reciprocated that heroic goodness by enabling the cousins' escape to Israel and welcoming them into her home. For as long as they wish, she said, her house is their house.

Such acts of **altruism** show that humans are capable of great evil, but also, as we shall see, of great goodness.

Altruism became a major concern of social psychologists after a widely publicized incident. On March 13, 1964, a stalker repeatedly stabbed Kitty Genovese, then raped her as she lay dying outside her Queens, New York, apartment at 3:30 A.M. "Oh, my God, he stabbed me!" Genovese screamed into the early morning stillness. "Please help me!" Windows opened and lights went on as some neighbors heard her screams. Her attacker fled and then returned to stab and rape her again. No one called the police or came to her aid until it was too late.

Bystander Intervention

Newspaper accounts of the murder, which misreported the number of witnesses and their responses to Genovese's cries, triggered public outrage over the bystanders' apparent "apathy" and "indifference." However, social psychologists John Darley and Bibb Latané (1968) attributed bystanders' inaction not to character flaws or moral choices, but to an important situational factor—the presence of others. Given certain circumstances, they suspected, most of us would behave similarly. To paraphrase the French writer Voltaire, we all are guilty of the good we did not do.

After staging emergencies under various conditions, Darley and Latané assembled their findings into a decision scheme: We will help only if the situation enables us first to *notice* the incident, then to *interpret* it as an emergency, and finally to *assume responsibility* for helping (FIGURE 44.2). At each step, the presence of others can turn us away from the path that leads to helping.

One of Darley and Latané's experiments staged a fake emergency as students in separate laboratory rooms took turns talking over an intercom. Only the person whose microphone was switched on could be heard. When his turn came, one student (actually an accomplice) pretended to have an epileptic seizure, and he called for help (Darley & Latané, 1968).

How did the others react? As FIGURE 44.3 shows, those who believed only they could hear the victim—and therefore thought they alone were responsible for helping him—usually went to his aid. Students who thought others could also hear the victim's cries were more likely to do nothing. When more people shared responsibility for helping—when there was a **diffusion of responsibility**—any single listener was less likely to help. Indeed, inattention and diffused responsibility contribute to "global bystander nonintervention" as millions of far-away people die of hunger, disease, and genocide (Pittinsky & Diamante, 2015).

Hundreds of additional experiments have confirmed this **bystander effect**. For example, researchers and their assistants took 1497 elevator rides in three cities and

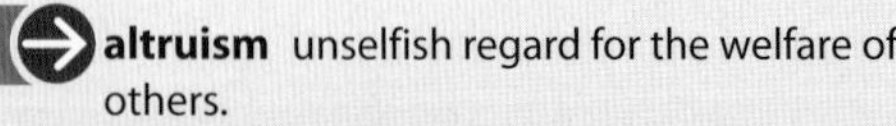

altruism unselfish regard for the welfare of others.

diffusion of responsibility when a person takes less responsibility for something, or is less likely to act in a situation, due to the presence of others.

bystander effect the tendency for any given bystander to be less likely to give aid if other bystanders are present.

Viviane Moos/Getty Images

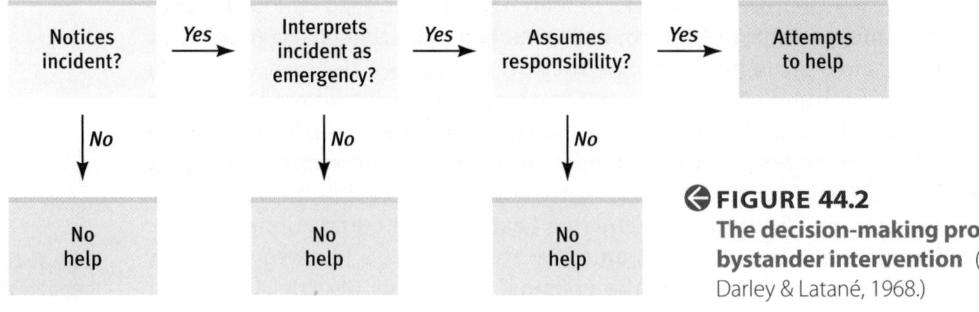
Notices incident?
Yes
Interprets incident as emergency?
Yes
Assumes responsibility?
Yes
Attempts to help
No
No
No
No help
No help
No help

FIGURE 44.2
The decision-making process for bystander intervention (Data from Darley & Latané, 1968.)

"accidentally" dropped coins or pencils in front of 4813 fellow passengers (Latané & Dabbs, 1975). When alone with the person in need, 40 percent helped; in the presence of 5 other bystanders, only 20 percent helped.

When reflecting on the bystander research—or on the conformity and obedience experiments in Module 42—it's tempting to think that, unlike many of the participants, we would have responded with moral courage. We may tell ourselves that, unlike so many others who lived before us, we would have taken steps to protect Jews from the Nazi genocide or intervened as George Floyd was slowly killed by a police officer. But research suggests we do not always act according to the better angels of our nature. In experiments, people greatly overestimate the odds of their protesting a sexist remark or a racial slur (Swim & Hyers, 1999).

Although the presence of other bystanders reduces the chance that an individual will offer help, often, people *do* help. In CCTV surveillance of arguments and fights caught on the streets of Amsterdam, Lancaster, and Cape Town, 9 times out of 10 at least one bystander and usually more did something to help (Philpot et al., 2019). Another research team planted 17,303 "lost" wallets in 40 countries, walking into public places such as hotels, post offices, and banks and explaining to a clerk: "I found this on the street around the corner. Someone must have lost it. I'm in a hurry and have to go. Can you please take care of it?" Forty percent of those given cashless wallets alerted the owner. Surprisingly to economists surveyed, those receiving wallets with cash were even *more* likely (51 percent) to help (Cohn et al., 2019).

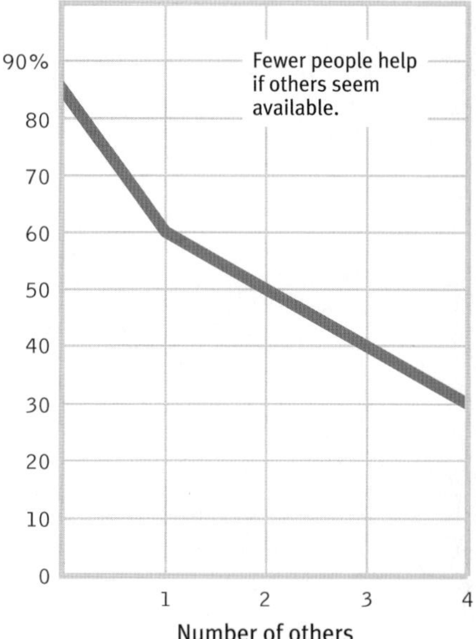
Percentage attempting to help
90%
80
70
60
50
40
30
20
10
0
Fewer people help if others seem available.
1
2
3
4
Number of others presumed available to help

FIGURE 44.3
Responses to a simulated emergency When people thought they alone heard the calls for help from a person they believed to be having an epileptic seizure, they usually helped. But when they thought four others were also hearing the calls, fewer than one-third responded. (Data from Darley & Latané, 1968.)

Observations of behavior in thousands of these situations—relaying an emergency phone call, aiding a stranded motorist, donating blood, picking up dropped books, contributing money, giving time—show that the odds of our helping someone depend on the characteristics of that person, the situation, and our own internal state. The odds of helping are highest when

- the person appears to need and deserve help.
- the person is in some way similar to us.
- the person is a woman.
- we have just observed someone else being helpful.
- we are not in a hurry.
- we are in a small town or rural area.
- we are feeling guilty.
- we are focused on others and not preoccupied.
- we are in a good mood.

The "good mood" result—that happy people are helpful people—is one of psychology's most consistent findings. As poet Robert Browning (1868) observed, "Oh, make us happy and you make us good!" It doesn't matter how we are cheered. Whether by being made to feel successful and intelligent, by thinking happy thoughts, by finding money, or even by receiving a posthypnotic suggestion, we become more generous and more eager to help (Aknin et al., 2019). Moreover, the world's happiest countries are also countries where people more often volunteer, give money, and even offer organ donations (Rhoads et al., 2021). And if our feeling of elevation follows witnessing or learning of someone else's self-giving deed, our helping will become even more pronounced (Schnall et al., 2010).

So, happiness begets helpfulness. But it's also true that helpfulness breeds happiness (Hui et al., 2020). Helping those in need activates brain areas associated with reward (Harbaugh et al., 2007; Kawamichi et al., 2015). That helps explain a curious finding: People who give money away are happier than those who spend it almost entirely on themselves. In one controlled experiment, researchers gave people money and instructed one group to spend it on themselves, and another group to spend it on others (Aknin et al., 2020). Which group was happiest afterward? It was, indeed, those assigned to the spend-it-on-others condition. Worldwide, people in both rich and developing countries were happier with their lives if they had donated to a charity in the last month (Dunn et al., 2008). You can likely recall a mood boost merely from giving directions to a stranger. *The lesson:* Doing good feels good.

Happy to give a dog a bone In an experiment, pet owners who spent money on their pets felt happier than did pet owners who spent money on themselves (White et al., 2022).

Zinkevych/iStock/Getty Images

ASK YOURSELF

Imagine being a newcomer needing directions at a busy bus station. What could you do to increase the odds that someone will assist you, and what sort of person would be most likely to help?

RETRIEVAL PRACTICE

RP-5 What social psychology principle did the Kitty Genovese incident illustrate?

ANSWERS IN APPENDIX E

Norms for Helping

LOQ 44-4 How do social exchange theory and social norms explain helping behavior?

Why do we help? One widely held view is that self-interest underlies all human interactions, that our constant goal is to maximize rewards and minimize costs. Accountants call it *cost-benefit analysis*. Philosophers call it *utilitarianism*. Social psychologists call it **social exchange theory**. For example, if you are considering donating blood, you may weigh the costs of doing so (time, discomfort, anxiety) against the benefits (reduced guilt, social approval, good feelings). If the rewards exceed the costs, you will donate blood.

Others believe we help because we have been socialized to do so, through norms that prescribe how we *ought* to behave (Everett et al., 2015). Two such norms are the *reciprocity norm* and the *social-responsibility norm*.

The **reciprocity norm** is the expectation that we should help, not harm, those who have helped us. Those for whom we do favors will often return favors. (Be kind to others and you may elicit future kindness from them.) With similar others, the reciprocity norm motivates us to give (in favors, gifts, or social invitations) about as much as we receive. Sometimes this means "paying it forward": In one experiment people who were treated generously became more likely to be generous to a stranger (Tsvetkova & Macy, 2014). Returning favors feels good, so we tend to find the reciprocity norm a pleasant way to help others (Hein et al., 2016).

The reciprocity norm kicked in after Dave Tally found $3300 in a backpack that an Arizona State University student had misplaced on his way to buy a used car (Lacey, 2010). Tally was homeless at the time, but instead of using the cash for much-needed bike repairs, food, and shelter, he turned the backpack in to the social service agency where he volunteered. To reciprocate Tally's help, the backpack's owner thanked him with a cash reward. Hearing about Tally's selfless deed, dozens of others also sent him money and job offers.

Invoking the social-responsibility norm

Healthier Scotland
Scottish Government
By wearing a face covering, you're **protecting** those around you

The Scottish Government

The **social-responsibility norm** is the expectation that we should help those who need our help—such as young children and newcomers—even if the costs outweigh the benefits. Europeans are most responsive to help sought by the most vulnerable asylum seekers—those, for example, who have been tortured or have no surviving family (Bansak et al., 2016). During the Covid-19 pandemic, many people—despite the risk of infection—cared for the sick, shopped for older neighbors, and donated money to help those in need (Fridman et al., 2022). Many people also responded affirmatively to persuasion that defined mask-wearing as an act of kindness and concern for others (Van Bavel et al., 2020).

We're especially likely to respond to requests for help when asked face-to-face, rather than by phone or email (Roghanizad & Bohns, 2022). People often hesitate to ask others to, for example, take their photo at a picturesque place. But experiments show that they underestimate others' willingness to help and underestimate how positively helpers will feel (Zhao et al., 2022). So, when you could use a favor, just ask. More often than you suppose, people—even strangers—will gladly help and feel good about doing so.

Many world religions encourage their followers to practice the social-responsibility norm, and sometimes this leads to prosocial behavior (Henrich, 2020). Between 2006 and 2008, Gallup polls sampled more than 300,000 people across 140 countries, comparing the "highly religious" (who said religion was important to them and who had attended

social exchange theory the theory that our social behavior is an exchange process, the aim of which is to maximize benefits and minimize costs.

reciprocity norm an expectation that people will help, not hurt, those who have helped them.

social-responsibility norm an expectation that people will help those needing their help.

a religious service in the prior week) to those less religious. The highly religious, despite being poorer, were about 50 percent more likely to report having "donated money to a charity in the last month" and to have volunteered time to an organization (Pelham & Crabtree, 2008). New surveys of 8000 Australians and 32,000 New Zealanders replicated this association of religious engagement with volunteerism (Petrovic et al., 2021; Van Tongeren et al., 2021). In more than two dozen "God-priming" studies, merely reminding people of God led them to cheat less and help more (Henrich, 2020).

Denis Poroy/AP Photo

Heroic helping In 2019, when a gunman entered a California synagogue, 60-year-old Lori Gilbert-Kaye was murdered when she selflessly used her body to shield her rabbi. Social psychologists study what prompts people to help.

From Conflict to Peace

Positive social norms encourage generosity and enable group living. But conflicts often divide us. One response to recent conflict- and scarcity-driven migrations has been anti-immigrant nationalism and nativism (favoring native-born citizens over newcomers). Psychologists have wondered: What in the human mind causes destructive conflict? How might a spirit of cooperation replace the perceived threats of social diversity?

Elements of Conflict

LOQ 44-5 How do social traps and mirror-image perceptions fuel social conflict?

To a social psychologist, a **conflict** is a perceived incompatibility of actions, goals, or ideas. The elements of conflict are much the same, whether partners sparring, political groups feuding, or nations at war. In each situation, conflict may seed positive change, or it may be a destructive process that can produce unwanted results. Among the destructive processes are *social traps* and *distorted perceptions*.

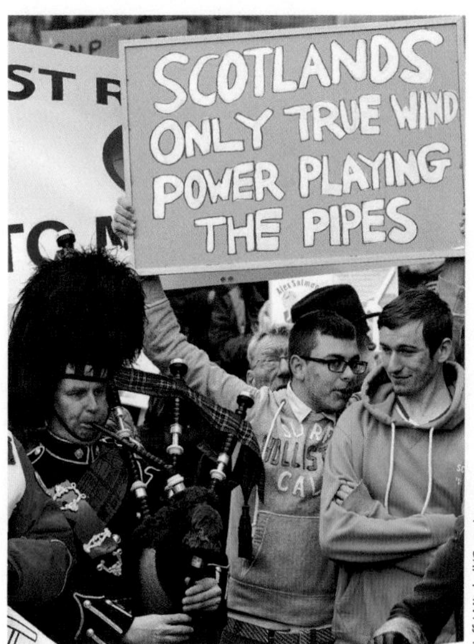
SCOTLANDS
ONLY TRUE WIND
POWER PLAYING
THE PIPES

Jeff J Mitchell/Getty Images

Not in my ocean! Many people support alternative energy sources, including wind turbines. But proposals to construct wind farms in real-world places elicit less support. Wind turbines in the Highlands and off the coast of Scotland have produced heated debate over the benefits of clean energy versus the costs of altering treasured scenic views.

SOCIAL TRAPS In some situations, pursuing our personal interests also supports our collective well-being: A person may choose to get vaccinated for self-protection from a contagious disease, but their decision means that they are also less likely to pass that disease on to others, and the whole community benefits from it. In other situations, we *harm* our collective well-being by pursuing our personal interests. Such situations are **social traps**.

Researchers have created mini social traps in laboratory games that require two participants to choose between pursuing their immediate self-interest, at others' expense, versus cooperating for mutual benefits. Many real-life situations similarly pit our individual interests against our communal well-being. Individual fish trawlers reasoned that the fish they took would not threaten the species and that if they didn't take them, others would anyway. The result: depleted fish stocks. Anticipating Covid-19-related shutdowns, people bought and hoarded toilet paper, leaving shelves empty for others. Individual car owners and homeowners reason, "Electric cars are more expensive. Besides, the fuel that I burn in my one car doesn't noticeably add to the greenhouse gases." When enough people reason similarly, the collective result threatens disaster—climate change, rising seas, and more extreme weather.

Social traps challenge us to reconcile our right to pursue our personal well-being with our responsibility for the well-being of all. Psychologists have therefore explored ways to convince people to cooperate for their mutual betterment—through agreed-upon *regulations,* through better *communication,* and through promoting *awareness* of our responsibilities toward community, nation, and the whole of humanity (Dawes, 1980; Kraft-Todd et al., 2015; Linder, 1982; Sato, 1987). Given effective regulations, communication, and awareness, people more often cooperate, whether playing a laboratory game or the real game of life.

ENEMY PERCEPTIONS Psychologists have noted that those in conflict have a curious tendency to form diabolical images of one another. These distorted images are, ironically, so similar that we call them **mirror-image perceptions**: As we see "them"—as untrustworthy, with evil intentions—so "they" see us. Each demonizes the other: "My political party, unlike the other party, has the nation's best interests at heart" (Waytz et al., 2014).

Mirror-image perceptions can often feed a vicious cycle of hostility. If Juan believes Maria is annoyed with him, he may snub her, causing her to act in ways that justify his

conflict a perceived incompatibility of actions, goals, or ideas.

social trap a situation in which two parties, by each pursuing their self-interest rather than the good of the group, become caught in mutually destructive behavior.

mirror-image perceptions mutual views often held by conflicting parties, as when each side sees itself as ethical and peaceful and views the other side as evil and aggressive.

perception. As with individuals, so with countries. Perceptions can become **self-fulfilling prophecies**—beliefs that confirm themselves by influencing the other country to react in ways that seem to justify those beliefs. In the real world, we make what we believe.

Individuals and nations alike tend to see their own actions as responses to provocation, not as the causes of what happens next. Perceiving themselves as returning tit for tat, they often hit back harder, as University College London volunteers did in one experiment (Shergill et al., 2003). Their task: After feeling pressure on their own finger, they used a mechanical device to press on another volunteer's finger. Although told to reciprocate with the same amount of pressure, they typically responded with about 40 percent more force than they had just experienced. Despite seeking only to respond in kind, their touches soon escalated to hard presses, much as when each child involved in a fight asserts "I just touched them, but they hit me!" Mirror-image perceptions feed similar cycles of hostility on the world stage. To most people, torture seems more justified when done by "us" rather than "them" (Tarrant et al., 2012).

The point is not that truth must lie midway between two such views (one may be more accurate). The point is that enemy perceptions often form mirror images.

RETRIEVAL PRACTICE

RP-6 How does group identity enable sports fans to feel a sense of satisfaction when their archrival team loses? Do such feelings, in other settings, make conflict resolution more challenging?

ANSWERS IN APPENDIX E

Promoting Peace

LOQ 44-6 What can we do to promote peace?

How can we make peace? Can contact, cooperation, communication, and conciliation transform the antagonisms fed by prejudice and conflicts into attitudes that promote peace? Research indicates that, in some cases, they can.

CONTACT Does it help to put two conflicting parties into close contact? It depends. Negative contact increases disliking (Kotzur & Wagner, 2021). But positive contact—especially noncompetitive contact between parties of equal status, such as fellow store clerks—typically helps. Initially prejudiced co-workers of different races have, in such circumstances, usually come to accept one another. This finding is confirmed by studies of face-to-face contact between majority people and outgroups, such as ethnic minorities, older people, LGBTQ people, and people with disabilities. Among the quarter-million people studied across 38 nations, contact has correlated with (and in experiments has led to) more positive and empathic attitudes and reduced dehumanization (Bruneau et al., 2021; Pettigrew & Tropp, 2011; Tropp & Barlow, 2018). Some examples:

- Countries and U.S. states that have the most immigrants tend to be the most supportive of immigrants; outgroup prejudice is strongest in places with few immigrants (Myers, 2018; Shrira, 2020; Wagner et al., 2020).
- Straight, cisgender people's attitudes toward gay and transgender people are influenced not only by *what* they know but also by *whom* they know (Brown, 2017; DellaPosta, 2018). In surveys, the reason people most often give for becoming more supportive of same-sex marriage is "having friends, family, or acquaintances who are gay or lesbian" (Pew, 2013). And in the United States, where 87 percent of people now say they know someone who is gay, attitudes toward same-sex marriage have become more accepting (McCarthy, 2019; Pew, 2016). Friendly contact—say, between Black and White students assigned to share a college dorm room—improves explicit and implicit attitudes toward others of the different race, and even toward other racial groups (Bruneau et al., 2021; Onyeador et al., 2020).
- More than 100 studies reveal that even "extended contact"—knowing that ingroup friends have outgroup friends—improves attitudes toward the outgroup (Zhou et al., 2019). Straight people often are more accepting of gay people if their straight friends have gay friends.

self-fulfilling prophecy a belief that leads to its own fulfillment.

superordinate goals shared goals that override differences among people and require their cooperation.

However, contact is not always enough. Despite laws that forbid school segregation, ethnic groups often resegregate themselves in lunchrooms, in classrooms, and elsewhere on school grounds (Alexander & Tredoux, 2010; Clack et al., 2005; Schofield, 1986). People in each group often think that they would welcome more contact with the other group, but they assume the other group does not reciprocate the wish (Richeson & Shelton, 2007). "I don't reach out to them because I don't want to be rebuffed; they don't reach out to me, because they're just not interested." When such mirror-image misperceptions are corrected, friendships may form and prejudices melt.

Rosalind Beckton

Strangers coming together When a family got stuck in a Florida rip current, no less than 80 of their fellow beachgoers formed a human chain, rescuing them. One of the witnesses, Rosalind Beckton, wrote: "All races & ages join[ed] together to save lives" (AP, 2017).

COOPERATION To see if enemies could overcome their differences, researcher Muzafer Sherif (1966) set a conflict in motion. He randomly separated 22 Oklahoma City boys into two separate camp areas. Then he had the two groups compete for prizes in a series of activities. Before long, each group became intensely proud of itself and hostile to the other group's "sneaky," "smart-alecky stinkers." Food wars broke out. Cabins were ransacked. Fistfights had to be broken up by camp counselors. Brought together, the two groups avoided each other, except to taunt and threaten. Little did they know that within a few days, they would be friends.

Sherif accomplished this by giving them **superordinate goals**—shared goals that could be achieved only through cooperation. When he arranged for the camp water supply to "fail," all 22 boys had to work together to restore the water. To rent a movie in those pre-streaming days, they all had to pool their resources. To move a stalled truck, everyone needed to combine their strength, pulling and pushing together. Having used isolation and competition to make strangers into enemies, Sherif used shared predicaments and goals to turn enemies into friends. What reduced conflict was not mere contact, but *cooperative* contact. When diverse people team up as equals and collaborate toward a shared goal, animosities abate and friendships form.

"Prejudice is learned behavior that can be unlearned." —Desmond & Leah Tutu Legacy Foundation, 2019

Critics suggest that Sherif's research team encouraged the conflict, hoping the study would illustrate their expectations about socially toxic competition and socially beneficial cooperation (Perry, 2018). Yet, shared predicaments or a common enemy do have powerfully unifying effects. Those facing rejection or discrimination have developed strong ingroup identification (Bauer et al., 2014; Ramos et al., 2012). Youth exposed to war also typically bond with one another (Bauer et al., 2014). Israeli children growing up in conflict areas often develop conflict-supportive perceptions, beliefs, and emotions regarding their shared adversary (Nasie et al., 2016). Such interpretations build ingroup solidarity but also insensitivity to the pain experienced by those in the outgroup (Levy et al., 2016). In the aftermath of a divisive U.S. primary election, party members will usually reunify when facing their shared threat—the opposing party candidate. At such times, cooperation can lead people to define a new, inclusive group that dissolves their former subgroups (Dovidio & Gaertner, 1999). If serving as a peacemaker, you might seat members of two groups not on opposite sides, but alternately around a table. Give them a new, shared name. Have them work together. Enable them to see each other as part of one larger group. Then watch "us" and "them" become "we."

"Me against my brother, my brothers and me against my cousins, then my cousins and me against strangers." —Bedouin proverb

Superordinate goals override differences Teaming up as equals and cooperating to achieve a shared goal is an optimal way to break down social barriers. When Iraqi Christians were assigned to play with Muslims on the same soccer team (as opposed to playing on all-Christian teams), they were later more likely to train with Muslims and register to play on a Christian-Muslim mixed soccer team (Mousa, 2020).

STANFORD
Rabie Zakaria

If cooperative contact between rival group members encourages positive attitudes, might this principle bring diverse students together? Could cooperative learning in classrooms create interracial friendships, while also enhancing student achievement? Experiments with adolescents from many countries confirm that the answer to both questions is *Yes* (Tropp et al., 2022). In the classroom as in the sports arena, members of multiethnic groups who work together on projects typically come to feel friendly toward one another. Knowing this, thousands of teachers have made multiethnic cooperative learning part of their classroom experience.

The power of cooperative activity to make friends of former enemies has led psychologists to urge increased international exchange and cooperation. Some experiments have

"Most of us have overlapping identities which unite us with very different groups. We *can* love what we are, without hating what—and who—we are *not*. We can thrive in our own tradition, even as we learn from others." —UN Secretary-General Kofi Annan, Nobel Peace Prize lecture, 2001

found that just imagining the shared threat of global climate change reduces international hostilities (Pyszczynski et al., 2012). From adjacent Brazilian tribes to European countries, formerly conflicting groups have managed to build interconnections, interdependence, and a shared social identity as they seek common goals (Fry, 2012). As we engage in mutually beneficial trade, as we work to protect our common destiny on this fragile planet, and as we become more aware that our hopes and fears are shared, we can transform misperceptions that feed conflict into feelings of solidarity based on common interests.

Byron Buck

Finding common ground In local communities across the United States, mediators are helping "red" (conservative) and "blue" (liberal) citizens discover their common ground and form friendships (see BraverAngels.org). My Country Talks is an international platform with similar goals. They set up "one-on-one discussions between people with completely different views" to encourage civil political dialogue (MyCountryTalks.org, 2021).

COMMUNICATION When real-life conflicts become intense, a third-party mediator—a marriage counselor, labor mediator, diplomat, community volunteer—may facilitate much-needed communication (Rubin et al., 1994). Mediators help each party voice its viewpoint and understand the other's needs and goals. If successful, mediators can replace a competitive *win-lose* orientation with a cooperative *win-win* orientation that leads to a mutually beneficial resolution. A classic example: Two friends, after quarreling over an orange, agreed to split it. One squeezed his half for juice. The other used the peel from her half to flavor a cake. If only the two had communicated their motives to one another, they could have hit on the win-win solution of one having all the juice, the other all the peel.

CONCILIATION Understanding and cooperative resolution are most needed, yet least likely, in times of anger or crisis (Bodenhausen et al., 1994; Tetlock, 1988). When conflicts intensify, images become more stereotyped, judgments more rigid, and communication more difficult. Each party is likely to threaten, coerce, or retaliate. In the weeks before the 1990 Gulf War, U.S. President George H. W. Bush threatened, in the full glare of publicity, to "kick Saddam's ass." Iraqi president Saddam Hussein communicated in kind, threatening to make Americans "swim in their own blood."

Under such conditions, is there an alternative to war or surrender? Social psychologist Charles Osgood (1962, 1980) advocated a strategy of *Graduated and Reciprocated Initiatives in Tension-Reduction*, nicknamed **GRIT**. In applying GRIT, one side first announces its recognition of mutual interests and its intent to reduce tensions. It then initiates one or more small, conciliatory acts. Without weakening one's retaliatory capability, this modest beginning opens the door for reciprocity by the other party. Should the enemy respond with hostility, one reciprocates in kind. But so, too, with any conciliatory response.

Warren Miller/Cartoon Stock

"To begin with, I would like to express my sincere thanks and deep appreciation for the opportunity to meet with you. While there are still profound differences between us, I think the very fact of my presence here today is a major breakthrough."

In laboratory experiments, small conciliatory gestures—a smile, a touch, a word of apology—have allowed both parties to begin edging down the tension ladder to a safer rung where communication and mutual understanding can begin (Lindskold, 1978; Lindskold & Han, 1988). In a real-world international conflict, U.S. President John F. Kennedy's gesture of stopping atmospheric nuclear tests began a series of reciprocated conciliatory acts that culminated in the 1963 atmospheric test-ban treaty between the United States and the Soviet Union.

As working toward shared goals reminds us, we are more alike than different. Civilization advances not by conflict and cultural isolation, but by tapping the knowledge, the skills, and the arts that are each culture's legacy to the whole human race. Open societies are enriched by cultural sharing (Sowell, 1991). We have China to thank for paper and printing and for the magnetic compass that opened the great explorations. We have Egypt to thank for trigonometry. We have the Islamic world and India's Hindus to thank for our Arabic numerals. While celebrating and claiming these diverse cultural legacies, we can also welcome the continuing enrichment of today's cultural diversity. We can view ourselves as instruments in a human orchestra. And we can therefore each affirm our own culture's heritage while building bridges of communication, understanding, and cooperation across our cultural traditions.

GRIT Graduated and Reciprocated Initiatives in Tension-Reduction—a strategy designed to decrease international tensions.

ASK YOURSELF

Do you regret arguing with a friend or not getting along with a family member? How might you use these peace-promoting principles to resolve such conflicts, now or in the future?

"Peace is not just the absence of conflict; peace is the creation of an environment where all can flourish, regardless of race, color, creed, religion, gender, class, caste, or any other social markers of difference." — Former President of South Africa and anti-apartheid activist Nelson Mandela (2004).

RETRIEVAL PRACTICE

RP-7 What are some ways to reconcile conflicts and promote peace?

ANSWERS IN APPENDIX E

MODULE

44 REVIEW Prosocial Relations

LEARNING OBJECTIVES

Test Yourself Answer these repeated Learning Objective Questions on your own (before "showing" the answers here, or checking the answers in Appendix D) to improve your retention of the concepts (McDaniel et al., 2009, 2015).

LOQ 44-1 Why do we befriend or fall in love with some people but not others?

LOQ 44-2 How does romantic love typically change as time passes?

LOQ 44-3 What is *altruism*? When are people most — and least — likely to help?

LOQ 44-4 How do social exchange theory and social norms explain helping behavior?

LOQ 44-5 How do social traps and mirror-image perceptions fuel social conflict?

LOQ 44-6 What can we do to promote peace?

TERMS AND CONCEPTS TO REMEMBER

Test Yourself Write down the definition in your own words, then check your answer.

mere exposure effect, p. 504
passionate love, p. 508
companionate love, p. 508
equity, p. 508
self-disclosure, p. 509
altruism, p. 510
diffusion of responsibility, p. 510
bystander effect, p. 510
social exchange theory, p. 512
reciprocity norm, p. 512
social-responsibility norm, p. 512
conflict, p. 513
social trap, p. 513
mirror-image perceptions, p. 513
self-fulfilling prophecy, p. 514
superordinate goals, p. 515
GRIT, p. 516

MODULE TEST

Test Yourself Answer the following questions on your own first, then "show" the answers here, or check your answers in Appendix E.

1. The more familiar a stimulus becomes, the more we tend to like it. This exemplifies the ________________ ________________ effect.
2. A happy couple celebrating their fiftieth wedding anniversary is likely to experience deep ________________ love, even though their ________________ love has probably decreased over the years.
3. After vigorous exercise, you meet an attractive person, and you are suddenly seized by romantic feelings for that person. This response supports the two-factor theory of emotion, which assumes that emotions, such as passionate love, consist of physical arousal plus
   a. a reward.
   b. proximity.
   c. companionate love.
   d. our interpretation of that arousal.
4. The bystander effect states that a particular bystander is less likely to give aid if
   a. the victim is similar to the bystander in appearance.
   b. no one else is present.
   c. other people are present.
   d. the incident occurs in a deserted or rural area.
5. Our enemies often have many of the same negative impressions of us as we have of them. This exemplifies the concept of ________________-________________ perceptions.
6. One way of resolving conflicts and fostering cooperation is by giving rival groups shared goals that help them override their differences. These are called ________________ goals.

CHAPTER
14
eyecrave productions/E+/Getty Images

Personality (Modules 45–47)

Lady Gaga dazzles millions with her unique musical arrangements, tantalizing outfits, and memorable performances. Her most predictable trait is her unpredictability. At an MTV Video Music Awards show, she stirred up debate by wearing a meat dress. A decade later, she performed the National Anthem at the most mainstream of events, the inauguration of U.S. President Joseph Biden.

Yet even unpredictable Lady Gaga exhibits distinctive and enduring ways of thinking, feeling, and behaving. Her fans and critics alike can depend on her openness to new experiences and the energy she gets from the spotlight. And they can also rely on her painstaking dedication to her performances. She describes her high school self as "very dedicated, very studious, and very disciplined." Now, in adulthood, she shows similar self-discipline: "I'm very detailed — every minute of the show has got to be perfect." Modules 45, 46, and 47 focus on our *personality* — our unique and persistent patterns of thinking, feeling, and behaving.

Much of this book deals with personality. Other modules consider biological influences on personality; personality development across the life span; how personality relates to learning, motivation, emotion, and health; social influences on personality; and disorders of personality. These modules focus on personality itself — what it is and how researchers study it.

We begin with two important theories of personality that have become part of Western culture: *psychodynamic theories* and *humanistic theories* (Modules 45 and 46). These sweeping perspectives on human nature laid the foundation for later personality theories and for what Module 47 presents: newer scientific explorations of personality.

MODULE

45 Introduction to Personality and Psychodynamic Theories

Today's personality researchers study the basic dimensions of personality, and the interaction of persons and environments. They also study self-esteem, self-serving bias, and cultural influences on our concept of self—that sense of "Who I am." And they study the unconscious mind—with findings that probably would have surprised even Freud.

What Is Personality?

LEARNING OBJECTIVE QUESTION LOQ **45-1** What is *personality*, and what theories inform our understanding of personality?

Psychologists have varied ways to view and study **personality**—our characteristic pattern of thinking, feeling, and acting. Sigmund Freud's *psychoanalytic theory* proposed that childhood sexuality and unconscious motivations influence personality. The *humanistic theories* focused on our inner capacities for growth and self-fulfillment. Later theorists built upon these two broad perspectives. *Trait theories* examine characteristic patterns of behavior *(traits)*. *Social-cognitive theories* explore the interaction between people's traits (including their thinking) and their social context. Let's begin with Freud's work, and its modern-day descendant, *psychodynamic theories*.

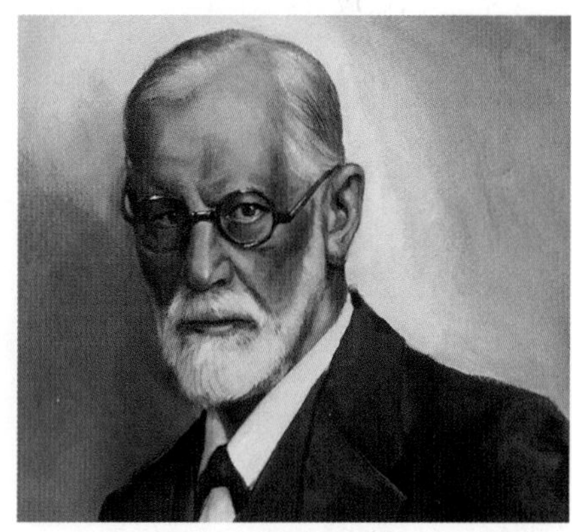
Macmillan Learning

Sigmund Freud (1856–1939) "I was the only worker in a new field."

Psychodynamic Theories

Psychodynamic theories of personality view human behavior as a dynamic interaction between the conscious mind and unconscious mind, including associated motives and conflicts. These theories descended from Freud's **psychoanalysis**—his theory of personality and the associated treatment techniques. Freud was the first to focus clinical attention on our unconscious mind.

Freud's Psychoanalytic Perspective: Exploring the Unconscious

LOQ **45-2** How did Freud's treatment of psychological disorders lead to his view of the unconscious mind?

On the first day of class, when I [ND] ask students to name one psychologist, they always mention Freud. Although today's psychologists question many of his ideas, Freud remains psychology's best-known person (Diener et al., 2014). In the popular mind, he is to psychology what Louis Armstrong is to jazz music. Freud's influence lingers not only in psychiatry and clinical psychology, but also in literary and film interpretation. Almost 9 in 10 U.S. college courses that reference psychoanalysis have been outside of psychology departments (Cohen, 2007). Freud's early twentieth-century concepts penetrate our twenty-first-century language. Without realizing their source, we may speak of *ego, repression, projection, complex* (as in "inferiority complex"), *sibling rivalry, Freudian slips,* and *fixation*. So, who was Freud, and what did he teach?

Like all of us, Sigmund Freud was a product of his times. The late 1800s, the tail end of the Victorian era, was a time of tremendous discovery and scientific advancement,

personality an individual's characteristic pattern of thinking, feeling, and acting.

psychodynamic theories theories that view personality with a focus on the unconscious mind and the importance of childhood experiences.

psychoanalysis Freud's theory of personality that attributes thoughts and actions to unconscious motives and conflicts; the techniques used in treating psychological disorders by seeking to expose and interpret unconscious tensions.

unconscious according to Freud, a reservoir of mostly unacceptable thoughts, wishes, feelings, and memories. According to contemporary psychologists, information processing of which we are unaware.

free association in psychoanalysis, a method of exploring the unconscious in which the person relaxes and says whatever comes to mind, no matter how trivial or embarrassing.

id a reservoir of unconscious psychic energy that, according to Freud, strives to satisfy basic sexual and aggressive drives. The id operates on the *pleasure principle,* demanding immediate gratification.

"The female . . . acknowledges the fact of her castration, and with it, too, the superiority of the male and her own inferiority; but she rebels against this unwelcome state of affairs." —Sigmund Freud, *Female Sexuality,* 1931

but also of sexual suppression and men's dominance. Gender roles were clearly defined, with men's superiority assumed. Only men's sexuality was generally acknowledged (discreetly), whereas women's sexuality was dismissed or ignored. These assumptions influenced Freud's thinking about personality. He believed that psychological troubles resulted from men's and women's unresolved conflicts with their expected roles.

Long before entering the University of Vienna in 1873, young Freud showed signs of independence and brilliance. He so loved reading plays, poetry, and philosophy that he once ran up a bookstore debt beyond his means. As a teen he often took his evening meal in his tiny bedroom in order to focus on his studies. After medical school he set up a private practice specializing in nervous disorders. Before long, however, he faced patients whose disorders made no neurological sense. A patient might have lost all feeling in a hand—yet there is no sensory nerve that, if damaged, would numb the entire hand and nothing else. Freud's search for a cause for such disorders set his mind running in a direction destined to change human self-understanding.

Do some neurological disorders have psychological causes? Observing patients led Freud to his "discovery" of the **unconscious**. He speculated that lost feeling in one's hand might be caused by a fear of touching one's genitals; that unexplained blindness or deafness might be caused by not wanting to see or hear something that aroused intense anxiety. After some early unsuccessful trials with hypnosis, Freud turned to **free association**, in which he told the patient to relax and say whatever came to mind, no matter how embarrassing or trivial. He assumed that a line of mental dominoes had fallen from his patients' distant past to their troubled present. Free association, he believed, would allow him to retrace that line, following a chain of thought leading into the patient's unconscious. There, painful unconscious memories, often from childhood, could be retrieved, reviewed, and released.

Basic to Freud's theory was this belief that the mind is mostly hidden (**FIGURE 45.1**). Our *conscious* awareness is like the part of an iceberg that floats above the surface. Beneath this awareness is the larger *unconscious* mind, with its thoughts, wishes, feelings, and memories. We store some of these thoughts temporarily in a *preconscious* area, from which we can retrieve them into conscious awareness. Of greater interest to Freud was the mass of unacceptable passions and thoughts that he believed we *repress,* or forcibly block from our consciousness because they would be too unsettling to acknowledge. Freud believed that without our awareness, these troublesome feelings and ideas powerfully influence us, sometimes gaining expression in disguised forms—the work we choose, the beliefs we hold, our daily habits, our upsetting symptoms.

FIGURE 45.1
Freud's idea of the mind's structure
Psychologists have used an iceberg image to illustrate Freud's idea that the mind is mostly hidden beneath the conscious surface.

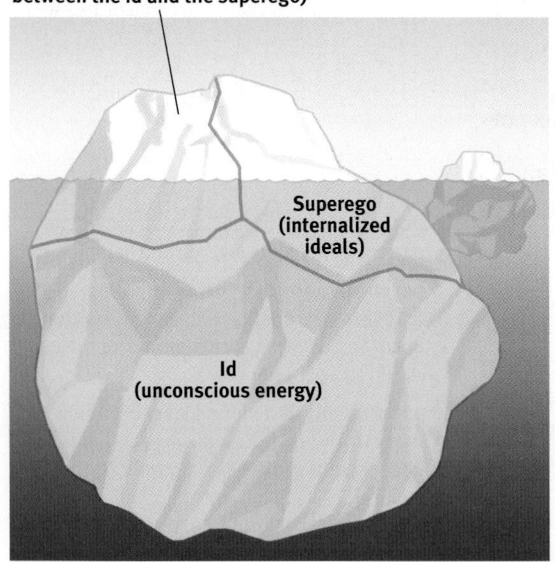
Ego
(mostly conscious; makes peace between the id and the superego)
Superego
(internalized ideals)
Id
(unconscious energy)
Conscious mind
Preconscious
(outside awareness but accessible)
Unconscious mind

PERSONALITY STRUCTURE

LOQ 45-3 What was Freud's view of personality?

Freud believed that human personality, including its emotions and strivings, arises from a conflict between impulse and restraint—between our aggressive, pleasure-seeking biological urges and our internalized social controls over these urges. Freud believed personality springs from our efforts to resolve this basic conflict—to express these impulses in ways that bring satisfaction without also bringing guilt or punishment. To understand the mind's dynamics during this conflict, Freud proposed three interacting systems: the *id, ego,* and *superego* (Figure 45.1).

The **id** stores unconscious energy, including our *libido*—a sexual energy force that fuels our pleasure-seeking. Freud argued that the id tries to satisfy our basic drives to survive, reproduce, and act aggressively. The id operates on the *pleasure principle:* It seeks immediate gratification. To understand the id's power, think of a newborn infant crying out for satisfaction, caring nothing for the outside world's conditions and demands. Or think of people who focus on the present more than the future—those who misuse tobacco, alcohol, or other drugs, and would sooner party now than sacrifice today's temporary pleasure for future success and happiness (Fernie et al., 2013; Friedel et al., 2014; Keough et al., 1999).

As the **ego** develops, a young child responds to the real world. The ego, operating on the *reality principle,* seeks to gratify the id's impulses in realistic ways to bring long-term pleasure. (Imagine what would happen if, lacking an ego, we acted on our unrestrained sexual or aggressive impulses.) The ego contains our partly conscious perceptions, thoughts, judgments, and memories.

Around age 4 or 5, Freud theorized, a child's ego recognizes the demands of the newly emerging **superego**, the partly conscious voice of our moral compass (conscience) that forces the ego to consider not only the real but also the *ideal*. The superego focuses on how we *ought* to behave. It strives for perfection, judging actions and producing positive feelings of pride or negative feelings of guilt. Someone with an exceptionally strong superego may be virtuous yet guilt-ridden; another with a weak superego may be outrageously self-indulgent and remorseless.

Because the superego's demands often oppose the id's, the ego struggles to reconcile the two. The ego is the personality "executive," mediating among the impulsive demands of the id, the restraining demands of the superego, and the real-life demands of the external world. If virtuous Conner feels sexually attracted to Tatiana, he might make an ego-driven decision to satisfy both his id and superego by joining an organization where Tatiana volunteers regularly.

ego the partly conscious, "executive" part of personality that, according to Freud, mediates among the demands of the id, the superego, and reality. The ego operates on the *reality principle,* satisfying the id's desires in ways that will realistically bring pleasure rather than pain.

superego the partly conscious part of personality that, according to Freud, represents internalized ideals and provides standards for judgment (the conscience) and for future aspirations.

psychosexual stages the childhood stages of development (oral, anal, phallic, latency, genital) during which, according to Freud, the id's pleasure-seeking energies focus on distinct *erogenous zones.*

Oedipus [ED-uh-puss] complex according to Freud, a boy's sexual desires toward his mother and feelings of jealousy and hatred for the rival father.

identification the process by which, according to Freud, children incorporate their parents' values into their developing superegos.

PERSONALITY DEVELOPMENT

LOQ 45-4 What developmental stages did Freud propose?

Analysis of his patients' histories convinced Freud that personality forms during life's first few years. He concluded that children pass through a series of **psychosexual stages**, during which the id's pleasure-seeking energies focus on distinct pleasure-sensitive areas of the body called *erogenous zones* (**TABLE 45.1**). Each stage offers its own challenges, which Freud saw as conflicting tendencies.

Freud believed that during the *phallic stage,* for example, boys develop both unconscious sexual desires for their mother and jealousy and hatred for their father, whom they consider a rival. Such was Freud's (1897) own experience: "I have found, in my own case too, [the phenomenon of] being in love with my mother and jealous of my father, and I now consider it a universal event in early childhood." He believed these feelings cause boys to feel guilty and to fear punishment, perhaps by castration, from their father. He called this collection of feelings the **Oedipus complex** after the Greek legend of Oedipus, whose failure to understand his unconscious desires led him to unknowingly kill his father and marry his mother. In Freud's era, some psychoanalysts believed that girls experience a parallel *Electra complex* (named after a mythological daughter who helped kill her mother to avenge her father's murder).

Children eventually cope with the threatening feelings, said Freud, by repressing them and by identifying with (trying to become like) the rival parent. It's as though something inside the child decides, "If you can't beat 'em [the same-sex parent], join 'em." Through this **identification** process, children's superegos gain strength as they incorporate many of their parents' values. Freud believed that identification with the same-sex parent provided what psychologists now understand more broadly as our *gender identity*—our sense of being male, female, neither, or some combination

S. Harris
Sidney Harris/Cartoon Stock

"I heard that as soon as we become aware of our sexual impulses, whatever they are, we'll have to hide them."

TABLE 45.1 Freud's Psychosexual Stages

Stage	Focus
Oral (0–18 months)	Pleasure centers on the mouth—sucking, biting, chewing
Anal (18–36 months)	Pleasure focuses on bowel and bladder elimination; coping with demands for control
Phallic (3–6 years)	Pleasure zone is the genitals; coping with incestuous sexual feelings
Latency (6 years to puberty)	A phase of dormant sexual feelings
Genital (puberty on)	Maturation of sexual interests

fixation in psychoanalytic theory, a lingering focus of pleasure-seeking energies at an earlier psychosexual stage, in which conflicts were unresolved.

defense mechanisms in psychoanalytic theory, the ego's protective methods of reducing anxiety by unconsciously distorting reality.

repression in psychoanalytic theory, the basic defense mechanism that banishes from consciousness anxiety-arousing thoughts, feelings, and memories.

of male and female. Freud presumed that our early childhood relations—especially with our parents and other caregivers—influence our developing identity, personality, and frailties.

In Freud's view, conflicts unresolved during earlier psychosexual stages could surface as maladaptive behavior in the adult years. At any point in the oral, anal, or phallic stages, strong conflict could lock, or **fixate**, the person's pleasure-seeking energies in that stage. A person who had been either orally overindulged or deprived (perhaps by abrupt, early weaning) might fixate at the oral stage. This orally fixated adult could exhibit either passive dependence (like that of a nursing infant) or an exaggerated denial of this dependence (by acting tough or uttering biting sarcasm). Or the person might continue to seek oral gratification by smoking or excessive eating. In such ways, Freud suggested, the twig of personality is bent at an early age.

DEFENSE MECHANISMS

LOQ 45-5 How did Freud think people defended themselves against anxiety?

Anxiety, said Freud, is the price we pay for civilization. As members of social groups, we must control our sexual and aggressive impulses, not act them out. But sometimes the ego fears losing control of this inner id-superego war. The presumed result is a dark cloud of unfocused anxiety that leaves us feeling unsettled but unsure why.

Freud proposed that the ego protects itself with **defense mechanisms**—tactics that reduce or redirect anxiety by distorting reality (**TABLE 45.2**). For Freud, *all defense mechanisms functioned indirectly and unconsciously.* Just as the body unconsciously defends itself against disease, the ego also unconsciously defends itself against anxiety. For example, **repression** banishes anxiety-arousing wishes and feelings from consciousness. According to Freud, *repression underlies all the other defense mechanisms*. However, because repression is often incomplete, repressed urges may appear as symbols in dreams or as slips of the tongue in conversation.

Freud believed he could glimpse the unconscious seeping through when a financially stressed patient, not wanting any large pills, said, "Please do not give me any bills, because I cannot swallow them." (Today we call these "Freudian slips.") Freud also viewed jokes as expressions of repressed sexual and aggressive tendencies, and dreams as the "royal road to the unconscious." The remembered content of dreams

TABLE 45.2 Six Defense Mechanisms

Freud believed that *repression*, the basic mechanism that banishes anxiety-arousing impulses, enables other defense mechanisms, six of which are listed here.

Defense Mechanism	Unconscious Process Employed to Avoid Anxiety-Arousing Thoughts or Feelings	Example
Regression	Retreating to an earlier psychosexual stage, where some psychic energy remains fixated	A child reverts to the oral comfort of thumb sucking in the car on the way to their first day of school.
Reaction formation	Switching unacceptable impulses into their opposites	Repressing angry feelings, a person displays exaggerated friendliness.
Projection	Disguising one's own threatening impulses by attributing them to others	"The thief thinks everyone else is a thief" (an El Salvadoran saying).
Rationalization	Offering self-justifying explanations in place of the real, more threatening unconscious reasons for one's actions	A habitual drinker says they drink with their friends "just to be sociable."
Displacement	Shifting sexual or aggressive impulses toward a more acceptable or less threatening object or person	After being put in a time out, a child kicks the family dog.
Denial	Refusing to believe or even perceive painful realities	A partner denies evidence of their loved one's affair.

Nacivet/Getty Images

Regression

venues." One analysis of 40,000 typing errors suggested that such mistakes are probably random typos (Stephens-Davidowitz, 2017).

History also has failed to support Freud's idea that suppressed sexuality causes psychological disorders. From Freud's time to ours, sexual inhibition has diminished; psychological disorders have not. Psychologists further criticize Freud's theory for its scientific shortcomings. It's important to remember that good scientific theories explain observations and offer testable hypotheses. Freud's theory rests on few objective observations, and parts of it offer few testable hypotheses. For Freud, his own recollections and interpretations of patients' free associations, dreams, and slips—sometimes selected to support his theory—were evidence enough.

What is the most serious problem with Freud's theory? It offers after-the-fact explanations of any characteristic (of one person's smoking, another's fear of horses, another's sexual orientation), yet fails to *predict* such behaviors and traits. If you feel angry at your mother's death, you illustrate Freud's theory because "your unresolved childhood dependency needs are threatened." If you do not feel angry, you again illustrate his theory because "you are repressing your anger." That "is like betting on a horse after the race has been run" (Hall & Lindzey, 1978, p. 68). A good theory makes testable predictions.

So, should psychology post an "Allow Natural Death" order on this old theory? Freud's supporters object. To criticize Freudian theory for not making testable predictions is, they say, like criticizing baseball for not being an aerobic exercise—something it was never intended to be. Freud never claimed that psychoanalysis was predictive science. He merely claimed that, looking back, psychoanalysts could find meaning in our state of mind (Rieff, 1979).

Freud's supporters also note that some of his ideas *are* enduring. It was Freud who drew our attention to the unconscious and the irrational, at a time when such ideas were not popular. Many researchers have since studied our irrationality (Ariely, 2010; Thaler, 2015). Psychologist Daniel Kahneman (in 2002) and behavioral economist Richard Thaler (in 2017) each won Nobel Prizes for their studies of our faulty decision making. Freud also drew our attention to the importance of human sexuality, and to the tension between our biological impulses and our social well-being. It was Freud who challenged our self-righteousness, exposed our self-protective defenses, and reminded us of our potential for evil.

MODERN RESEARCH CHALLENGES THE IDEA OF REPRESSION Psychoanalytic theory hinges on the assumption that our mind often *represses* offending wishes, banishing them into the unconscious until they resurface, like a long-lost cat that finds its way home. Recover and resolve childhood's conflicted wishes, and emotional healing should follow. Repression became a widely accepted concept, used to explain hypnotic phenomena and psychological disorders. Some psychodynamic followers extended repression to explain apparently lost and recovered memories of childhood traumas (Boag, 2006; Cheit, 1998; Erdelyi, 2006). These psychodynamic beliefs have made their way into popular culture. In one survey, 88 percent of university students believed that painful experiences commonly get pushed out of awareness and into the unconscious (Garry et al., 1994).

Today's researchers agree that we sometimes preserve our self-esteem by neglecting threatening information (Green et al., 2008). Yet they also find that repression is rare, even in response to terrible trauma. Even those who have witnessed a parent's murder or survived Nazi death camps have retained their unrepressed memories of the horror (Helmreich, 1992, 1994; Malmquist, 1986; Pennebaker, 1990).

Some researchers do believe that extreme, prolonged stress, such as the stress some severely abused children experience, might disrupt memory by damaging the hippocampus (Schacter, 1996). But the far more common reality is that high stress and associated stress hormones *enhance* memory. Indeed, rape, torture, and other traumatic events haunt survivors, who experience unwanted flashbacks. They are seared onto the soul. "You see the babies," said Holocaust survivor Sally H. (1979). "You see the screaming mothers. You see hanging people. You sit and you see that face there. It's something you don't forget."

"During the Holocaust, many children . . . were forced to endure the unendurable. For those who continue to suffer [the] pain is still present, many years later, as real as it was on the day it occurred." —Eric Zillmer, Molly Harrower, Barry Ritzler, and Robert Archer, *The Quest for the Nazi Personality*, 1995

THE MODERN UNCONSCIOUS MIND

LOQ 45-8 How has modern research developed our understanding of the unconscious?

Freud was right about a big idea that underlies today's psychodynamic thinking: We have limited access to all that goes on in our mind (Erdelyi, 1985, 1988; Norman, 2010). Our two-track mind has a vast unseen realm. Some researchers even argue that "most of a person's everyday life is determined by unconscious thought processes" (Bargh & Chartrand, 1999). (Perhaps, for example, you can recall being sad or angry without consciously knowing why.)

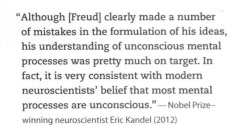

"Although [Freud] clearly made a number of mistakes in the formulation of his ideas, his understanding of unconscious mental processes was pretty much on target. In fact, it is very consistent with modern neuroscientists' belief that most mental processes are unconscious." —Nobel Prize–winning neuroscientist Eric Kandel (2012)

Many research psychologists now think of the unconscious not as seething passions and repressive censoring but as information processing that occurs without our awareness. To these researchers, the unconscious also involves

- the *schemas* that automatically control our perceptions and interpretations.
- the *priming* by stimuli to which we have not consciously attended.
- the right-hemisphere activity that enables the *split-brain* patient's left hand to carry out an instruction the patient cannot verbalize.
- the *implicit memories* of learned skills that operate without conscious recall, even in those with amnesia.
- the *emotions* that activate instantly, before conscious analysis.
- the *stereotypes* and *implicit prejudice* that automatically and unconsciously influence how we process information about others.

More than we realize, we fly on autopilot. Our lives are guided by off-screen, out-of-sight, unconscious information processing. The unconscious mind is vast. However, our current understanding of unconscious information processing is more like the pre-Freudian view of an underground, unattended stream of thought from which spontaneous behavior and creative ideas surface (Bargh & Morsella, 2008).

Research also supports two of Freud's defense mechanisms. One study demonstrated *reaction formation* (trading unacceptable impulses for their opposite) in men who reported strong anti-gay attitudes. Compared with those who did not report such attitudes, these anti-gay men experienced greater physiological arousal (assessed with a device that measured blood flow to the penis) when watching videos of gay men having sex, even though they said the films did not make them sexually aroused (Adams et al., 1996). Likewise, some evidence suggests that people who have an unconscious same-sex sexual orientation—but who consciously identify as straight—report more negative attitudes toward gay men and lesbians (Weinstein et al., 2012).

Freud's *projection* (attributing our own threatening impulses to others) has also been confirmed. People do tend to see their traits, attitudes, and goals in others (Baumeister et al., 1998; Maner et al., 2005). Shown an ambiguous face, aggressive people often see anger (Brennan & Baskin-Sommers, 2020). Today's researchers call this the *false consensus effect*—the tendency to overestimate the extent to which others share our beliefs and behaviors. People who binge-drink or break speed limits tend to think many others do the same. Shortly before the 2020 U.S. presidential election, 83 percent of Democrats and 84 percent of Republicans predicted that voters would elect *their* party's presidential candidate (ISR, 2020). As we are, so we see others.

CAJ
Carolita Johnson/Cartoon Stock

"It says, Someday you will die."

Finally, research has supported Freud's idea that we unconsciously defend ourselves against anxiety. Researchers have proposed that one source of anxiety is "the terror resulting from our awareness of vulnerability and death" (Greenberg et al., 1997). Hundreds of experiments testing **terror-management theory** show that thinking about one's mortality—for example, by writing a short essay on dying and its associated emotions—provokes various terror-management defenses (Burke et al., 2010). For example, death anxiety increases aggression toward rivals and heightens esteem for oneself (Cohen & Solomon, 2011; Koole et al., 2006).

terror-management theory a theory of death-related anxiety; explores people's emotional and behavioral responses to reminders of their impending death.

Faced with a threatening world, people act not only to enhance their self-esteem but also to adhere more strongly to worldviews that answer questions about life's meaning. The prospect of death promotes religious sentiments, and deep religious convictions enable people to be less defensive—less likely to rise in defense of their worldview—when reminded of death (Jonas & Fischer, 2006; Norenzayan & Hansen, 2006). Moreover, when contemplating death, people prioritize their close relationships (Cox & Arndt, 2012; Mikulincer et al., 2003). The actual death of loved ones can provoke protective responses as well. For years, I [ND] have studied the way people respond to thoughts about death—but it took the shock of my own mother's unexpected death to motivate me to start running again, and to live a healthier lifestyle (Hayasaki, 2014; Kashdan et al., 2014). Facing death can inspire us to affirm life.

ASK YOURSELF

What understandings and impressions of Freud did you bring to this course? Are you surprised to find that some of his ideas have value, or that others have been called into question?

RETRIEVAL PRACTICE

RP-4 What big ideas have survived from Freud's psychoanalytic theory? In what ways has Freud's theory been criticized?

RP-5 Which elements of traditional psychoanalysis have modern-day *psychodynamic* theorists and therapists retained, and which elements have they mostly left behind?

ANSWERS IN APPENDIX E

Assessing Unconscious Processes

LOQ 45-9 What are *projective tests*, how are they used, and what are some criticisms of them?

Personality tests reflect the basic ideas of particular personality theories. So, what might be the assessment tool of choice for someone working in the Freudian tradition? It would need to provide some sort of road into the unconscious—to unearth the residue of early childhood experiences, move beneath surface thoughts, and reveal hidden conflicts and impulses. Objective assessment tools, such as agree-disagree or true-false questionnaires, would be inadequate because they would merely tap the conscious surface.

Henry Murray (1933) demonstrated a possible basis for such a test at a party hosted by his 11-year-old daughter. Murray engaged the children in a frightening game called "Murder." When shown some photographs after the game, the children perceived the photos as more malicious than they had before the game. These children, it seemed to Murray, had *projected* their inner feelings into the pictures.

A few years later, Murray introduced the **Thematic Apperception Test (TAT)**—a **projective test** in which people view ambiguous pictures and then make up stories about them. Shown a daydreaming boy, those who imagine he is fantasizing about an achievement are presumed to be projecting their own goals. "As a rule," said Murray, "the subject leaves the test happily unaware that he has presented the psychologist with what amounts to an X-ray of his inner self" (quoted by Talbot, 1999).

Numerous studies suggest that Murray was right: The TAT provides a valid and reliable map of people's implicit motives (Jenkins, 2017). For example, such storytelling has been used to assess *achievement* and *affiliation motivation* (Drescher & Schultheiss, 2016; Schultheiss et al., 2014).

Swiss psychiatrist Hermann Rorschach [ROAR-shock; 1884–1922] created the most widely used projective test. He based his famous **Rorschach inkblot test** (FIGURE 45.2) on a childhood game. Unlike the TAT's natural life images, Rorschach and his friends would drip ink on a paper, fold it, and then say what they saw in the resulting inkblot (Sdorow, 2005). Do you see predatory animals or weapons? A Rorschach interpreter might speculate that you have aggressive tendencies. But is this a reasonable assumption, considering that inkblots don't have any real-life meaning? The answer varies.

Some clinicians cherish the Rorschach test, convinced that it projects a client's inner motives to the outside world. Others view the test as a source of suggestive leads, an icebreaker, or a revealing interview technique.

FIGURE 45.2
The Rorschach test In this projective test, people tell what they see in a series of symmetrical inkblots.

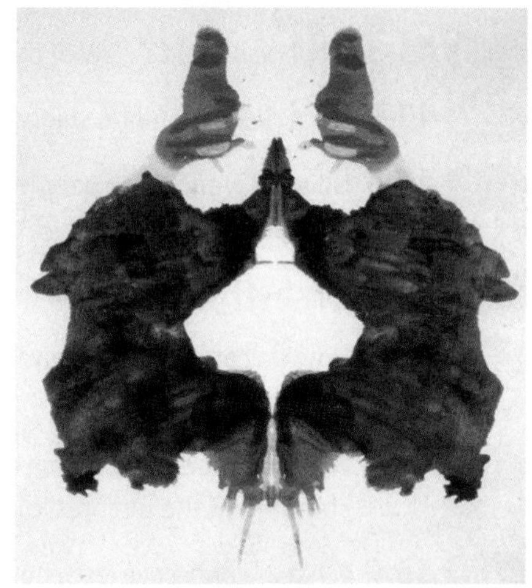

Spencer Grant/Science Source

Thematic Apperception Test (TAT) a projective test in which people express their inner feelings and interests through the stories they make up about ambiguous scenes.

projective test a personality test, such as the TAT or Rorschach, that provides ambiguous images designed to trigger projection of people's inner dynamics.

Rorschach inkblot test a projective test designed by Hermann Rorschach; seeks to identify people's inner feelings by analyzing how they interpret 10 inkblots.

"The Rorschach [inkblot test] has the dubious distinction of being, simultaneously, the most cherished and the most reviled of all psychological assessment tools."
—John Hunsley and J. Michael Bailey (1999)

But critics insist the Rorschach is no emotional MRI. They argue that only a few of the many Rorschach-derived scores, such as those for cognitive impairment and thought disorder, have demonstrated reliability and validity (Mihura et al., 2013, 2015; Wood et al., 2015). And inkblot assessments have inaccurately diagnosed many healthy adults as pathological (Wood, 2003; Wood et al., 2006).

RETRIEVAL PRACTICE

RP-6 ________ tests ask test-takers to respond to an ambiguous image by describing it or telling a story about it.

ANSWERS IN APPENDIX E

MODULE 45 REVIEW Introduction to Personality and Psychodynamic Theories

LEARNING OBJECTIVES

Test Yourself Answer these repeated Learning Objective Questions on your own (before "showing" the answers here, or checking the answers in Appendix D) to improve your retention of the concepts (McDaniel et al., 2009, 2015).

LOQ 45-1 What is *personality*, and what theories inform our understanding of personality?

LOQ 45-2 How did Freud's treatment of psychological disorders lead to his view of the unconscious mind?

LOQ 45-3 What was Freud's view of personality?

LOQ 45-4 What developmental stages did Freud propose?

LOQ 45-5 How did Freud think people defended themselves against anxiety?

LOQ 45-6 Which of Freud's ideas did his followers accept or reject?

LOQ 45-7 How do contemporary psychologists view Freud's psychoanalysis?

LOQ 45-8 How has modern research developed our understanding of the unconscious?

LOQ 45-9 What are *projective tests*, how are they used, and what are some criticisms of them?

TERMS AND CONCEPTS TO REMEMBER

Test Yourself Write down the definition in your own words, then check your answer.

personality, p. 519
psychodynamic theories, p. 519
psychoanalysis, p. 519
unconscious, p. 520
free association, p. 520
id, p. 520
ego, p. 521
superego, p. 521
psychosexual stages, p. 521
Oedipus [ED-uh-puss] complex, p. 521
identification, p. 521
fixation, p. 522
defense mechanisms, p. 522
repression, p. 522
collective unconscious, p. 523
terror-management theory, p. 526
Thematic Apperception Test (TAT), p. 527
projective test, p. 527
Rorschach inkblot test, p. 527

MODULE TEST

Test Yourself Answer the following questions on your own first, then "show" the answers here, or check your answers in Appendix E.

1. According to Freud's view of personality structure, the "executive" system, the ________, seeks to gratify the impulses of the ________ in more acceptable ways.
   a. id; ego
   b. ego; superego
   c. ego; id
   d. id; superego
2. Freud proposed that the development of the "voice of our moral compass" is related to the ________, which internalizes ideals and provides standards for judgments.
3. According to the psychoanalytic view of development, we all pass through a series of psychosexual stages, including the oral, anal, and phallic stages. Conflicts unresolved at any of these stages may lead to
   a. dormant sexual feelings.
   b. fixation at that stage.
   c. preconscious blocking of impulses.
   d. a distorted gender identity.
4. Freud believed that defense mechanisms are unconscious attempts to distort or disguise reality, all in an effort to reduce our ________.
5. Freud believed that we may block painful or unacceptable thoughts, wishes, feelings, or memories from consciousness through an unconscious process called ________.

6. In general, neo-Freudians such as Adler and Horney accepted many of Freud's views but placed more emphasis than he did on
   a. development throughout the life span.
   b. the collective unconscious.
   c. the role of the id.
   d. social interactions.
7. Modern-day psychodynamic theorists and therapists agree with Freud about
   a. the existence of unconscious mental processes.
   b. the Oedipus complex.
   c. the predictive value of Freudian theory.
   d. the superego's role as the executive part of personality.
8. Which of the following is NOT part of the contemporary view of the unconscious?
   a. Repressed memories of anxiety-provoking events
   b. Schemas that influence our perceptions and interpretations
   c. Stereotypes that affect our information processing
   d. Instantly activated emotions and implicit memories of learned skills

MODULE 46 Humanistic Theories and Trait Theories

By the 1960s, some personality psychologists had become discontented with the sometimes bleak focus on drives and conflicts in psychodynamic theory, and the mechanistic psychology of B. F. Skinner's *behaviorism*. Two pioneering theorists—Abraham Maslow and Carl Rogers—offered a *third-force perspective* that emphasized our potential for healthy personal growth.

Macmillan Learning

Abraham Maslow (1908–1970) "Any theory of motivation that is worthy of attention must deal with the highest capacities of the healthy and strong person as well as with the defensive maneuvers of crippled spirits" (*Motivation and Personality,* 1970, p. 33).

Humanistic Theories

LOQ 46-1 How did humanistic psychologists view personality, and what was their goal in studying personality?

In contrast to Sigmund Freud's emphasis on disorders born out of dark conflicts, the **humanistic theorists** emphasized the ways people strive for self-determination and self-realization. In contrast to behaviorism's scientific objectivity, they studied people through self-reported experiences and feelings.

Abraham Maslow's Self-Actualizing Person

Maslow proposed that we are motivated by a **hierarchy of needs**. If our physiological needs are met, we become concerned with personal safety. If we achieve a sense of security, we then seek to love and to be loved. With our love needs satisfied, we seek self-esteem. Having achieved self-esteem, we ultimately seek **self-actualization** (the process of fulfilling our potential) and **self-transcendence** (meaning, purpose, and identity beyond the self).

Maslow (1970) developed his ideas by studying healthy, creative people rather than clinical cases of troubled people. His description of self-actualization grew out of his study of people, such as Abraham Lincoln, who seemed notable for their meaningful and productive lives. Maslow reported that such people shared certain characteristics: They were self-aware and self-accepting, open and spontaneous, loving and caring, and not paralyzed by others' opinions (Kaufman, 2018). Secure in their sense of who they were, their interests were task-centered rather than self-centered. Curious about the world, they embraced uncertainties and stretched themselves to seek out new experiences (Compton, 2018; Kashdan, 2009). Once they focused their energies on a particular task, they often regarded it as their life mission, or "calling" (Hall & Chandler, 2005). Most enjoyed a few deep relationships rather than many superficial ones. Many had

humanistic theories theories that view personality with a focus on the potential for healthy personal growth.

hierarchy of needs Maslow's five levels of human needs, beginning with physiological needs. Often visualized as a pyramid, with basic needs providing the foundation supporting higher-level needs.

self-actualization according to Maslow, one of the ultimate psychological needs that arises after basic physical and psychological needs are met and self-esteem is achieved; the motivation to fulfill one's potential.

self-transcendence according to Maslow, the striving for identity, meaning, and purpose beyond the self.

FIGURE 46.1
Characteristics of Self-Actualization Scale (CSAS) This shortened version of the CSAS represents the 10 self-actualization characteristics studied by Scott Barry Kaufman (2018).

Characteristics of Self-Actualization Scale (CSAS)

Here are a number of characteristics that may or may not describe you. Please select the answer that best indicates the extent to which you agree or disagree with each statement. Be as honest as possible, but rely on your initial feeling and do not think too much.

1	2	3	4	5
Strongly disagree	**Disagree**	**Neutral**	**Agree**	**Strongly agree**

1. ___I often feel gratitude for the good in my life no matter how many times I encounter it.
2. ___I accept all sides of myself, including my shortcomings.
3. ___I take responsibility for my actions.
4. ___I am often undisturbed and unruffled by things that seem to bother most people.
5. ___I have a purpose in life that will help the good of humankind.
6. ___I often have a clear perception of reality.
7. ___I have a genuine desire to help the human race.
8. ___I often have experiences in which I feel one with all people and things on this planet.
9. ___I have a strong sense of right and wrong in my daily life.
10. ___I bring a generally creative attitude to all of my work.

Scoring Guide:
Add up your scores and divide by 10 for your total score. The items above represent the 10 characteristics of self-actualization studied by Scott Barry Kaufman (2018):
(1) Continued freshness of appreciation, (2) Acceptance, (3) Authenticity, (4) Equanimity (mental calmness), (5) Purpose, (6) Truth seeking, (7) Humanitarianism (concern with human welfare), (8) Peak experiences, (9) Good moral intuition, and (10) Creative spirit.

Kaufman found that those with higher scores experienced "greater life satisfaction, self-acceptance, positive relations, personal growth, purpose in life, and self-transcendent experiences" as well as "creativity across multiple domains of achievement."

Information from Kaufman (2018)

been moved by spiritual or personal *peak experiences* that surpassed ordinary consciousness. These, said Maslow (1970), are mature adult qualities found in those who have learned enough about life to be compassionate, to have outgrown their mixed feelings toward their parents, to have found their calling, to have "acquired enough courage to be unpopular, to be unashamed about being openly virtuous." (Test your own level of self-actualization in **FIGURE 46.1**.)

Macmillan Learning

Carl Rogers (1902–1987) "The curious paradox is that when I accept myself just as I am, then I can change" (*On Becoming a Person,* 1961).

Carl Rogers' Person-Centered Perspective

Fellow humanistic psychologist Carl Rogers agreed with much of Maslow's thinking. Rogers' *person-centered perspective* held that people are basically good and are endowed with self-actualizing tendencies. Unless thwarted by an environment that inhibits growth, each of us is like an acorn, primed for growth and fulfillment. Rogers (1980) believed that a growth-promoting social climate provides

- ***acceptance.*** When people are *accepting,* they offer **unconditional positive regard**, an attitude of grace that values us even knowing our failings. It is a profound relief to drop our pretenses, confess our worst feelings, and discover that we are still accepted. In a good marriage, a close family, or an intimate friendship, we are free to be spontaneous without fearing the loss of others' esteem.
- ***genuineness.*** When people are *genuine,* they are open with their own feelings, drop their facades, and are transparent and self-disclosing.
- ***empathy.*** When people are *empathic,* they share and mirror others' feelings and reflect their meanings. "Rarely do we listen with real understanding, true empathy," said Rogers. "Yet listening, of this very special kind, is one of the most potent forces for change that I know."

unconditional positive regard a caring, accepting, nonjudgmental attitude, which Carl Rogers believed would help people develop self-awareness and self-acceptance.

Acceptance, genuineness, and empathy are, Rogers believed, the water, Sun, and nutrients that enable people to grow from acorns into vigorous oak trees. For "as persons are accepted and prized, they tend to develop a more caring attitude toward themselves" (Rogers, 1980, p. 116). When heard and accepted, people can listen to and accept their thoughts and feelings.

The educator Alice Stewart Trillin discovered acceptance and genuineness at a camp for children with severe disorders. L., a "magical child," had genetic diseases that meant she had to be tube-fed and could walk only with difficulty. Trillin wondered "what this child's parents could have done . . . to make her the most optimistic, most enthusiastic, most hopeful human being I had ever encountered" (quoted in Trillin, 2006). One day Trillin spotted a note that L. received from her mom: "If God had given us all of the children in the world to choose from, L., we would only have chosen you." Inspired, Trillin approached a co-worker. "Quick. Read this," she whispered. "It's the secret of life."

Maslow and Rogers would have smiled knowingly. For them, a central feature of personality is one's **self-concept**—all the thoughts and feelings we have in response to the question, "Who am I?" If our self-concept is positive, we tend to act and perceive the world positively. If it is negative—if we fall far short of our *ideal self*—said Rogers, we feel dissatisfied and unhappy. A worthwhile goal for therapists, parents, teachers, and friends is therefore, he said, to help others know, accept, and be true to themselves.

Leo Cullum/Cartoon Stock

"Yes, Doreen. I think I am capable of unconditional love."

ASK YOURSELF

Think back to a conversation you had when you knew someone was just waiting for their turn to speak instead of listening to you. Now consider the last time someone heard you with empathy. How did those two experiences differ?

stefanamer/iStock/Getty Images

The picture of empathy Being open and sharing confidences is easier when the listener shows real understanding. Within such relationships we can relax and fully express our true selves.

Assessing the Self

LOQ 46-2 How did humanistic psychologists assess a person's sense of self?

Humanistic psychologists sometimes assessed personality by asking people to fill out questionnaires that would evaluate their self-concept. One questionnaire, inspired by Carl Rogers, asked people to describe themselves both as they would *ideally* like to be and as they *actually* are. When the ideal and the actual self are nearly alike, said Rogers, the self-concept is positive. Assessing his clients' personal growth during therapy, he looked for successively closer ratings of actual and ideal selves.

Some humanistic psychologists believed that any standardized assessment of personality, even a questionnaire, is depersonalizing. Rather than forcing the person to respond to narrow categories, these humanistic psychologists presumed that interviews and intimate conversation would provide a better understanding of each person's unique experiences. Some researchers today believe our identity may be revealed using the *life story approach*—collecting a rich narrative detailing a person's unique life history (Adler et al., 2016; McAdams & Guo, 2015). A lifetime of stories can show more of a person's complete identity than can the responses to a few questions (Waters et al., 2019).

Evaluating Humanistic Theories

LOQ 46-3 How have humanistic theories influenced psychology? What criticisms have they faced?

One thing said of Freud can also be said of the humanistic psychologists: Their impact has been pervasive. Maslow's and Rogers' ideas have influenced counseling, education, child raising, and management. And they laid the groundwork for today's scientific *positive psychology* subfield.

These theorists have also influenced—sometimes in unintended ways—much of today's popular psychology. Is a positive self-concept the key to happiness and success? Do acceptance and empathy nurture positive feelings about ourselves? Are people basically good and capable of self-improvement? Many people answer *Yes, Yes,* and *Yes.* In 2006, U.S. high school students reported notably higher self-esteem and greater

self-concept all our thoughts and feelings about ourselves, in answer to the question, "Who am I?" 

expectations of future career success than did students living in 1975, before humanistic psychology's feel-good philosophy infused U.S. culture (Twenge & Campbell, 2008). Given a choice, North American college students have said they'd rather get a self-esteem boost, such as a compliment or good grade on a paper, than enjoy a favorite food or sexual activity (Bushman et al., 2011). Humanistic psychology's message has been heard.

But the prominence of the humanistic perspective set off a backlash of criticism. First, said the critics, its concepts are vague and subjective. Consider Maslow's description of self-actualizing people as open, spontaneous, loving, self-accepting, and productive. Is this a scientific description? Or is it merely a description of the theorist's own values and ideals? Maslow, noted M. Brewster Smith (1978), offered impressions of his own personal heroes, such as Abraham Lincoln and Albert Einstein. Imagine another theorist who began with a different set of heroes—perhaps French military conqueror Napoleon and former U.S. President Donald Trump. This theorist might describe self-actualizing people as "undeterred by others' opinions," "motivated to achieve," and "comfortable with power."

Critics also objected to the idea that, as Rogers (1985) put it, "The only question which matters is, 'Am I living in a way which is deeply satisfying to me, and which truly expresses me?'" (quoted in Wallach & Wallach, 1985). This emphasis on *individualism*—trusting and acting on one's feelings, being true to oneself, fulfilling oneself—could lead to self-indulgence, selfishness, and an erosion of moral restraint (Campbell & Specht, 1985; Wallach & Wallach, 1983). Imagine working on a group project with people who refuse to complete any task that is not deeply satisfying or does not truly express their identity.

Igor Bobic/Huffington Post

Are we humans born to be bad or good? The lessons of psychological science mirror our cultural experience, where forces of good and bad sometimes collide, as Capitol Police Officer Eugene Goodman's bravery and quick-thinking protected lawmakers and staff from an invading mob that breached the U.S. Capitol in 2021.

Humanistic psychologists have replied that a secure, nondefensive self-acceptance is actually the first step toward loving others. Indeed, people who feel intrinsically liked and accepted—for who they are, not just for their achievements—exhibit less defensive attitudes (Schimel et al., 2001). Those feeling liked and accepted by a romantic partner report being happier in their relationships and acting more kindly toward their partner (Gordon & Chen, 2010).

A final criticism leveled against humanistic psychology is that it is naive—that it fails to appreciate the reality of our human capacity for evil (May, 1982). Psychological science reminds us of this unfortunate capacity. Some situations can prompt us to believe lies or act cruelly (see the Social Psychology modules). *Deindividuation, groupthink,* and *group polarization* may accentuate our worst tendencies. And mere dislike can become prejudiced hatred. But as the humanistic psychologists remind us, there is another mountain of research that testifies to our potential for goodness—for growth and gratitude, for humility and hope, for empathy and compassion.

Faced with a climate crisis, economic woes, and systemic racism, we may become apathetic from either of two rationalizations. One is a starry-eyed optimism that denies the threat ("People are basically good; everything will work out"). The other is a dark despair ("It's hopeless; why try?"). Action requires enough realism to fuel concern and enough optimism to provide hope. (Pessimism often fulfills its own predictions, by restraining our efforts at change.) Humanistic psychology, say the critics, encourages the needed hope but not the equally necessary realism about threats.

RETRIEVAL PRACTICE

RP-1 How did the *humanistic theories* provide a fresh perspective?

RP-2 What does it mean to be *empathic*? How about *self-actualized*? Which humanistic psychologists used these terms?

ANSWERS IN APPENDIX E

Trait Theories

LOQ 46-4 How do psychologists use traits to describe personality?

Rather than focusing on unconscious forces and thwarted growth opportunities, some researchers attempt to define personality in terms of stable and enduring behavior patterns, such as Lady Gaga's self-discipline and openness to new experiences. This perspective can be traced in part to a remarkable meeting in 1919, when Gordon Allport, a curious 22-year-old psychology student, interviewed Sigmund Freud in Vienna. Allport soon discovered just how preoccupied the founder of psychoanalysis was with finding hidden motives, even in Allport's own behavior during the interview. That experience ultimately led Allport to do what Freud did not do: to describe personality in terms of fundamental **traits**, or people's characteristic behaviors and conscious motives (such as the curiosity that actually motivated Allport to see Freud). Meeting Freud, said Allport, "taught me that [psychoanalysis], for all its merits, may plunge too deep, and that psychologists would do well to give full recognition to manifest motives before probing the unconscious." Allport came to define personality in terms of identifiable behavior patterns. He was concerned less with *explaining* individual traits than with *describing* them.

James Stevenson/Cartoon Stock

"Hello. This is Dial-a-Grump. What the hell do you want?"

Like Allport, Isabel Briggs Myers (1987) and her mother, Katharine Briggs, wanted to describe important personality differences. They attempted to sort people according to Carl Jung's *personality types*, based on their responses to 126 questions. The *Myers-Briggs Type Indicator (MBTI)*, available in 20+ languages, has been taken by millions of people, mostly for counseling, leadership training, and work-team development (CPP, 2017). It offers choices, such as "Do you usually value sentiment more than logic, or value logic more than sentiment?" Then it counts the test-taker's preferences, labels them as indicating, say, a "feeling type" or "thinking type," and feeds them back to the person in complimentary terms. Feeling types, for example, are told they are "sympathetic, appreciative, and tactful"; thinking types are told they are "good at analyzing." (Every type has its strengths, so everyone is affirmed.)

Most people agree with their announced MBTI profile, which mirrors their declared preferences. They may also accept their label as a basis for being matched with work or dating partners, and with tasks that supposedly suit their temperaments. But a National Research Council report noted that despite the test's popularity in business and career counseling, its use has outrun research on its validity as a job performance predictor: "The popularity of this instrument in the absence of proven scientific worth is troublesome" (Druckman & Bjork, 1991, p. 101; see also Pittenger, 1993). Although research on the MBTI has been accumulating since those cautionary words were expressed, the test remains mostly a counseling and coaching tool, not a research instrument. Fortunately, newer research offers reliable and valid tools to explore traits.

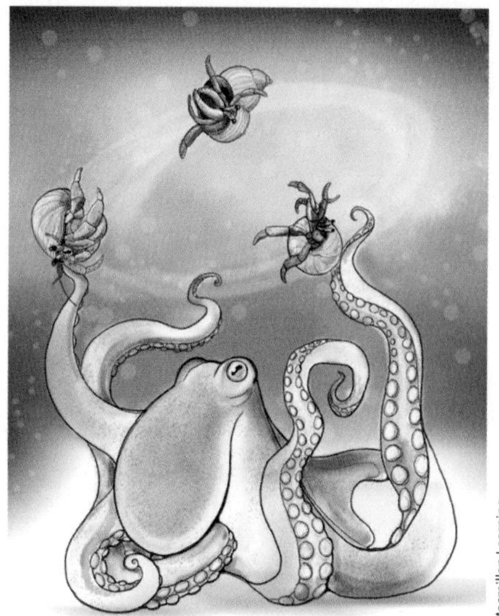
Macmillan Learning

Octopus personality The real-life Otto the octopus seems to love getting attention from visitors. But when his German aquarium closes during the winter, Otto acts like a bored prankster. He has juggled hermit crabs, squirted water at staff members, and broken his light by spraying it with water.

Exploring Traits

We are each a unique complex of multiple traits. So how can we describe our personalities in a way that captures our individuality? We might describe an apple by placing it along several trait dimensions—relatively large or small, red or green, sweet or tart. By placing people on several trait dimensions simultaneously, psychologists can describe countless individual personality variations.

What trait dimensions describe personality? If you were looking at profiles on a dating app, what personality traits would give you the most useful information about each person? Allport and his associate H. S. Odbert (1936) counted all the words in an unabridged dictionary that could be used to describe people. There were almost 18,000! How, then, could psychologists condense the list to a manageable number of basic traits?

FACTOR ANALYSIS One technique is *factor analysis*, a statistical procedure that identifies clusters (factors) of test items that tap basic components of a trait (McCabe & Fleeson, 2016). Imagine that people who describe themselves as outgoing also tend to say that they like excitement and practical jokes and dislike quiet reading. Such a statistically correlated cluster of behaviors reflects a basic factor, or trait—in this case, *extraversion*.

British psychologists Hans Eysenck and Sybil Eysenck [EYE-zink] believed that we can reduce many of our individual variations to two dimensions: *extraversion–introversion* and *emotional stability–instability* (**FIGURE 46.2**).[1] People in 35 countries worldwide took

trait a characteristic pattern of behavior or a disposition to feel and act in certain ways, as assessed by self-report inventories and peer reports. 

[1] Some of the late Hans Eysenck's views have been deemed racist and some of his other research has been judged untrustworthy, but his personality concepts remain accepted (O'Grady, 2020).

HBO/Photofest

UNSTABLE

Moody
Anxious
Rigid
Sober
Pessimistic
Reserved
Unsociable
Quiet

Touchy
Restless
Aggressive
Excitable
Changeable
Impulsive
Optimistic
Active

INTROVERTED — EXTRAVERTED

Passive
Careful
Thoughtful
Peaceful
Controlled
Reliable
Even-tempered
Calm

Sociable
Outgoing
Talkative
Responsive
Easygoing
Lively
Carefree
Dominant

STABLE

Abaca Press/Sipa/AP Photo

FIGURE 46.2
Two personality dimensions Mapmakers can tell us a lot by using two axes (north–south and east–west). Two primary personality factors (extraversion–introversion and stability–instability) are similarly useful as axes for describing personality variation. Varying combinations define other, more specific traits (Eysenck & Eysenck, 1963). Although many actors are extraverted, some, such as Issa Rae, are introverts—particularly capable of solitary study to become each character they portray. Professional comedians, such as Jimmy Fallon, are often natural extraverts (Irwing et al., 2020).

the *Eysenck Personality Questionnaire*. When their answers were analyzed, the extraversion and emotionality (later called *neuroticism*) factors inevitably emerged as basic personality dimensions (Eysenck, 1990, 1992). The Eysencks believed, and research confirms, that these factors are genetically influenced.

BIOLOGY AND PERSONALITY Brain-activity scans of extraverts add to the growing list of traits and mental states now being explored. Such studies indicate that extraverts seek stimulation because their normal brain arousal is relatively low. For example, PET scans have shown that a frontal lobe area involved in behavior inhibition is less active in extraverts than in introverts (Johnson et al., 1999).

Our biology influences our personality. As we know from twin and adoption studies, compared with fraternal twins, identical twin personalities are much more similar (Loehlin & Martin, 2018; Mõttus et al., 2019). What's true of so much of human nature is also true of personality and life outcomes, which are influenced by many genes having small effects (Smith-Wooley et al., 2019; van den Berg et al., 2016). Our genes also influence the *temperament* and behavioral style that shape our personality. Jerome Kagan (2010), for example, has attributed differences in children's shyness and inhibition to their autonomic nervous system reactivity. Those with a reactive autonomic nervous system respond to stress with greater anxiety and inhibition. The fearless, curious child may become the extreme skier or mountain biker with a GoPro. (See Thinking Critically About: The Stigma of Introversion.)

Personality differences among dogs (in energy, affection, reactivity, and curious intelligence) are as evident, and as consistently judged, as personality differences among humans (Gosling et al., 2003; Jones & Gosling, 2005). Monkeys, bonobos, chimpanzees, orangutans, dolphins, orcas, sea lions, and even birds and fish also have distinct and stable personalities (Altschul et al., 2018; Morton et al., 2021; Úbeda et al., 2018; Weiss et al., 2017). Even conscientiousness varies among individual animals, from chimps to bees (Delgado & Sulloway, 2017). Through selective breeding, researchers can produce bold or shy birds. Both personality types have their place in natural history: In lean years, bold birds are more likely to find food; in abundant years, shy birds feed with less risk.

"I come from many tribes—immigrant, introvert, working class, Korean. . . . Talking is painful because we expose our ideas for evaluation; however, . . . talking is powerful because our ideas . . . have value and require expression." —Writer and lecturer Min Jin Lee (2019)

RETRIEVAL PRACTICE

RP-3 Which two primary dimensions did Hans Eysenck and Sybil Eysenck propose for describing personality variation?

ANSWERS IN APPENDIX E

Thinking Critically About:
The Stigma of Introversion

LOQ 46-5 What are some common misunderstandings about introversion?

Western cultures are hard on introverts:

Extraverts are often celebrated in comics and film. Black Panther unites five tribes of people with his engaging strength of character. Take-charge Elastigirl saves the day in *The Incredibles*.

87% of Westerners want to be more extraverted.[1]

Being introverted seems to imply that we don't have the "right stuff."[2]

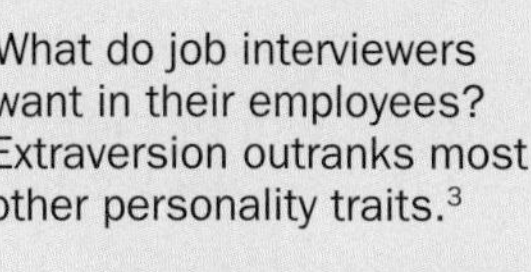

What do job interviewers want in their employees? Extraversion outranks most other personality traits.[3]

Attractive, successful people are presumed to be extraverts.[4]

What is introversion?

Introverts tend to gain energy from time alone, and may find social interactions exhausting. Extraverts, by contrast, tend to draw energy from time spent with others.

Introverts are not "shy." (Shy people remain quiet because they fear others will evaluate them negatively.)

Introverted people seek low levels of stimulation from their environment because they have more sensitive nervous systems. For example, when given lemon juice, introverted people salivated more than extraverted people.[5]

Introversion has many benefits:

- Introverted leaders outperform extraverted leaders in some contexts, such as when their employees voice new ideas and challenge existing norms.[6]
- Introverts handle conflict well. In response, they seek solitude rather than revenge.[7]
- Many introverts have flourished, including Sir Isaac Newton, Mother Teresa, and Oprah Winfrey. "A true extravert," Winfrey explains, "gets energy,...feeds off people,...and I get sucked dry."[8]

1. Hudson & Roberts, 2014. 2. Cain, 2012. 3. Kluemper et al., 2015; Salgado & Moscoso, 2002. 4. McCord & Joseph, 2020. 5. Corcoran, 1964. 6. A. Grant et al., 2011. 7. Ren et al., 2016. 8. OWN, 2018.

Assessing Traits

LOQ 46-6 What are *personality inventories*, and what are their strengths and weaknesses as trait-assessment tools?

If stable and enduring traits guide our actions, can we devise valid and reliable tests of them? Several trait-assessment techniques exist—some more valid than others. Some provide quick assessments of a single trait, such as extraversion, anxiety, or self-esteem. **Personality inventories**—longer **self-report** questionnaires covering a wide range of feelings and behaviors—assess several traits at once.

The classic personality inventory is the **Minnesota Multiphasic Personality Inventory (MMPI)**. Although the MMPI was originally developed to identify emotional disorders (still considered its most appropriate use), it also assesses people's personality traits. One of its creators, Starke Hathaway (1960), compared his effort with that of Alfred Binet. Binet, the founder of modern intelligence testing, developed the first intelligence test by selecting items that identified children who would likely struggle to progress in French schools. Like Binet's items, the MMPI items were **empirically derived**: From a large pool of items, Hathaway and his colleagues selected those on which particular diagnostic groups differed. "My hands and feet are usually warm enough" may seem superficial, but it just so happened that anxious people were more likely to answer *False*. The researchers grouped the questions into 10 clinical scales, including scales that assess depressive tendencies, masculinity–femininity, and introversion–extraversion. Today's MMPI-2 has additional scales that assess work attitudes, family problems, and anger.

Whereas most projective tests (such as the Rorschach) are scored subjectively, personality inventories are scored objectively. Objectivity does not, however, guarantee validity. For example, individuals taking the MMPI for employment purposes can give socially desirable answers to create a good impression. But in so doing they may also

personality inventory a questionnaire (often with *true-false* or *agree-disagree* items) on which people respond to items designed to gauge a wide range of feelings and behaviors; used to assess selected personality traits.

self-report a method of recording participants' descriptions of their personality traits, often using surveys, questionnaires, or tests.

Minnesota Multiphasic Personality Inventory (MMPI) the most widely researched and clinically used of all personality tests. Originally developed to identify emotional disorders (still considered its most appropriate use), this test is now used for many other screening purposes.

empirically derived test a test (such as the MMPI) created by selecting from a pool of items those that discriminate between groups.

score high on a *lie scale* that assesses faking (as when people respond *False* to a universally true statement such as "I get angry sometimes"). In other cases, the MMPI can be used to identify people pretending to have a disorder in order to avoid their responsibilities (Chmielewski et al., 2017). The MMPI's objectivity has contributed to its popularity and its translation into more than 100 languages.

People have had fun spoofing the MMPI with their own mock items: "Weeping brings tears to my eyes," "Frantic screams make me nervous," and "I stay in the bathtub until I look like a raisin" (Frankel et al., 1983).

The Big Five Factors

LOQ 46-7 Which traits seem to provide the most useful information about personality variation?

Today's trait researchers believe that simple trait factors, such as the Eysencks' introversion–extraversion and stability–instability dimensions, are important, but they do not tell the whole story. A slightly expanded set of factors—dubbed the **Big Five factors** (also called the *five-factor model*)—does a better job (Costa & McCrae, 2011; Soto & John, 2017). If a test specifies where you are on the five dimensions (*openness, conscientiousness, extraversion, agreeableness,* and *neuroticism;* see **TABLE 46.1**), it has said much of what there is to say about your personality. The Big Five factors can also be used to understand both psychological flourishing and dysfunction (Bleidorn et al., 2020; Oltmanns et al., 2018; Wimmelmann et al., 2020).

Around the world—across 56 nations and 29 languages in one study (Schmitt et al., 2007)—people describe others in terms roughly consistent with this list. The Big Five—today's "common currency for personality psychology" (Funder, 2001)—has been the most active personality research topic since the early 1990s and is currently our best approximation of the basic trait dimensions.

Big Five research has explored various questions:

- ***How stable are these traits?*** Research teams have analyzed the traits of Americans, Australians, Icelanders, and Germans in adolescence and again 20 to 30 years later (Damian et al., 2019; Hoff et al., 2020; Wagner et al., 2019). The participants' personalities remained generally stable, but most people exhibited a *maturity principle:* From adolescence onward, they became more conscientious and agreeable, and less neurotic (emotionally unstable) (Allemand et al., 2019; Atherton et al., 2021). People in Japan, who more often adapt their personality to their social environment, show somewhat more Big Five trait variation (Haas & vanDellen, 2020).
- ***Do self-ratings on these traits match others' ratings?*** The ratings of family and friends of our Big Five trait levels do resemble the ratings we give ourselves (Finnigan & Vazire, 2018; Luan et al., 2019).
- ***Do these traits reflect differing brain structure?*** The size and thickness of brain tissue correlates with several Big Five traits (DeYoung & Allen, 2019; Li et al., 2017; Riccelli et al., 2017). For example, those who score high on conscientiousness tend

TABLE 46.1 The "Big Five" Personality Factors

Researchers use a self-report inventory to assess and score the Big Five personality factors.
(*Memory tip:* Picturing an **OCEAN** will help you recall these.)

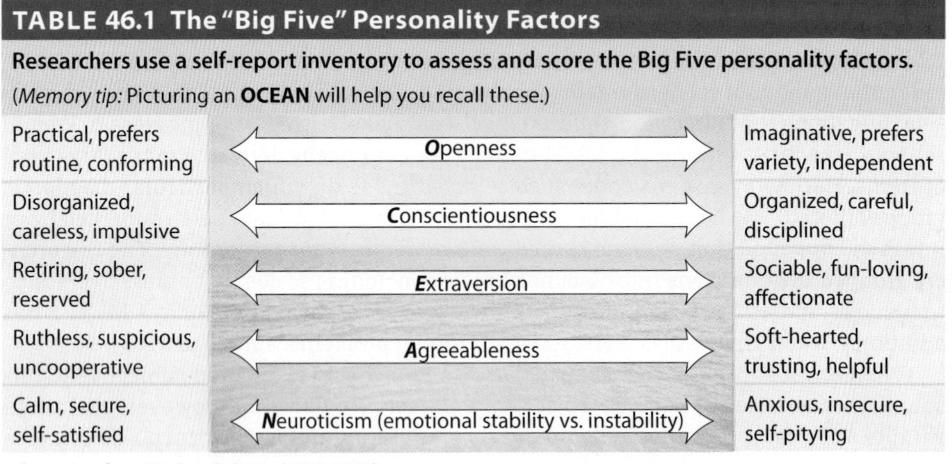

Practical, prefers routine, conforming	**O**penness	Imaginative, prefers variety, independent
Disorganized, careless, impulsive	**C**onscientiousness	Organized, careful, disciplined
Retiring, sober, reserved	**E**xtraversion	Sociable, fun-loving, affectionate
Ruthless, suspicious, uncooperative	**A**greeableness	Soft-hearted, trusting, helpful
Calm, secure, self-satisfied	**N**euroticism (emotional stability vs. instability)	Anxious, insecure, self-pitying

Aaron Foster/The Image Bank/Getty Images

Information from McCrae & Costa (1986, 2008).

Big Five factors researchers identified five factors—*openness, conscientiousness, extraversion, agreeableness,* and *neuroticism*—that describe personality. (Also called the *five-factor model.*)

to have a larger frontal lobe area that aids in planning and controlling behavior. Brain connections also influence the Big Five traits (Toschi et al., 2018). People high in neuroticism have brains that are wired to experience stress intensely (Shackman et al., 2016; Xu & Potenza, 2012).

- ***Do these traits reflect birth order?*** After controlling for other variables such as family size, are first-born children, for example, more conscientious and agreeable? Contrary to popular opinion, several massive studies failed to find any association between birth order and personality (Damian & Roberts, 2015; Harris, 2009; Rohrer et al., 2015).
- ***How well do these traits apply to various cultures?*** The Big Five dimensions describe personality in various cultures reasonably well (H. Kim et al., 2018; Minkov et al., 2019; Schmitt et al., 2007). From herders in Kenya and Tanzania to gardeners in Mali, these traits help us understand basic features of personality (Thalmayer et al., 2020). After studying people from 50 cultures, Robert McCrae and 79 co-researchers concluded that Big Five traits "are common to all human groups" (2005).
- ***Do the Big Five traits predict our everyday behaviors?*** Yes, Big Five traits reliably predict important life outcomes (Soto, 2021). Conscientiousness predicts better school performance and workplace success (Mammadov, 2022; Nickel et al., 2019). (Maybe nice people finish first?) Agreeable people are caring and law-abiding, and were more likely to follow mobility restrictions to minimize Covid-19 spread (Chan et al., 2021; Zajenkowski et al., 2020). Extraverts post more on social media, more often become leaders, and spend less time at home (true even during the Covid pandemic) (Bowden-Green, 2020; Götz et al., 2021; Matz & Harari, 2021; Scott & Medeiros, 2020). People high in neuroticism were more stressed during the pandemic (Kroenke et al., 2020).

By exploring such questions, Big Five research has sustained trait psychology and has renewed appreciation for the importance of personality. (To describe your personality, try the brief self-assessment in **FIGURE 46.3**.) Traits matter.

How do you shop and vote? Let me count the likes Researchers can use Facebook likes to predict individuals' Big Five traits, opinions, and political attitudes (Youyou et al., 2015). Companies sell "big data" for advertisers (who then personalize the ads you see) and to political campaigns, which can then target certain users with persuasive messages (Matz et al., 2017).

FIGURE 46.3
The Big Five self-assessment

How Do You Describe Yourself?

Describe yourself as you generally are now, not as you wish to be in the future. Describe yourself as you honestly see yourself, in relation to other people you know of the same sex and roughly the same age. Use the scale below to enter a number for each statement. Then, use the scoring guide at the bottom to see where you fall on the spectrum for each of the Big Five traits.

1	2	3	4	5
Very Inaccurate	**Moderately Inaccurate**	**Neither Accurate Nor Inaccurate**	**Moderately Accurate**	**Very Accurate**

1. ___Am the life of the party
2. ___Sympathize with others' feelings
3. ___Get stressed out easily
4. ___Am always prepared
5. ___Am full of ideas
6. ___Start conversations
7. ___Take time out for others
8. ___Follow a schedule
9. ___Worry about things
10. ___Have a vivid imagination

SCORING GUIDE SORTED BY BIG FIVE PERSONALITY TRAITS

Openness: statements 5, 10
Conscientiousness: statements 4, 8
Extraversion: statements 1, 6
Agreeableness: statements 2, 7
Neuroticism: statements 3, 9

How to score:
Separate your responses by each Big Five personality trait, as noted at left, and divide by two to obtain your score for each trait. So, for example, for the "Agreeableness" trait let's say you scored 3 for statement 2 ("Sympathize with others' feelings") and 4 for statement 7 ("Take time out for others"). That means on a scale from 1 to 5, your overall score for the "Agreeableness" trait is 3 + 4 = 7 ÷ 2 = 3.5.

Scale data from: International Personality Item Pool: A Scientific Collaboratory for the Development of Advanced Measures of Personality Traits and Other Individual Differences (ipip.ori.org)

ASK YOURSELF

Before trying the self-assessment in Figure 46.3, where would you have placed yourself on the Big Five personality dimensions? Where might your family and friends place you? Did the actual results surprise you, and do you think these results would surprise them?

RETRIEVAL PRACTICE

RP-4 What are the *Big Five* personality factors, and why are they scientifically useful?

ANSWERS IN APPENDIX E

Evaluating Trait Theories

LOQ 46-8 Does research support the consistency of personality traits over time and across situations?

Are our personality traits stable and enduring? Or does our behavior depend on where and with whom we find ourselves? Cheerful, friendly children do tend to become cheerful, friendly adults. At a college reunion, I [DM] was amazed to find that my jovial former classmates were still jovial, the shy ones still shy, the happy-seeming people still smiling and laughing 50 *years later*. But it's also true that a fun-loving jokester can suddenly turn serious and respectful at a job interview. New situations and major life events can shift the personality traits we express. Transitioning from high school to university or the workforce, we often become more agreeable, conscientious, and open-minded, and less neurotic (Bleidorn et al., 2018). Losing our job may make us less agreeable and open-minded (Boyce et al., 2015). But when we retire—losing our job *by choice*—we often become more agreeable and open-minded (Schwaba & Bleidorn, 2019).

"There is as much difference between us and ourselves, as between us and others." —Michel de Montaigne, *Essays*, 1588

THE PERSON-SITUATION CONTROVERSY Our behavior is influenced by the interaction of our inner disposition with our environment. Still, the question lingers: Which is more important? When we explore this *person-situation controversy*, we look for genuine personality traits that persist over time and across situations. Are some people dependably conscientious and others unreliable, some cheerful and others dour, some outgoing and others quiet? If we are to consider friendliness a trait, friendly people must act friendly at different times and places. Do they?

Longitudinal research follows lives through time. Some scholars (especially those who study infants) are impressed with personality change; others are struck by personality stability during adulthood. As **FIGURE 46.4** illustrates, data from 152 longitudinal studies reveal that personality trait scores are positively correlated with scores obtained an average of 7 years later, and that as people grow older, their personality stabilizes. Interests may change—the avid tropical-fish collector may become an avid gardener. Careers may change—the determined salesperson may become a determined social worker. Relationships may change—the hostile son may become a hostile husband. But most people come to recognize and accept who they are. As researchers Robert McCrae and Paul Costa (1994) observed, our recognizing the inevitability of our personality is "the culminating wisdom of a lifetime."

FIGURE 46.4
Personality stability With age, personality traits become more stable, as reflected in the stronger correlation of trait scores with follow-up scores 7 years later. (Data from Roberts & DelVecchio, 2000.)

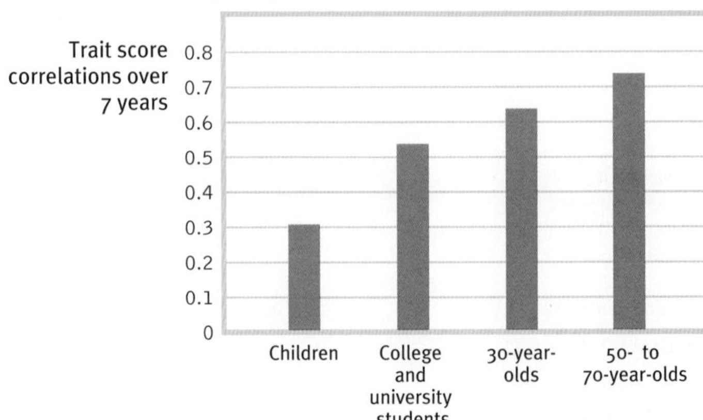
Trait score correlations over 7 years
0.8
0.7
0.6
0.5
0.4
0.3
0.2
0.1
0
Children
College and university students
30-year-olds
50- to 70-year-olds

So most people—including most psychologists—would probably presume the stability of personality traits. Moreover, our traits are socially significant. They influence our health, our thinking, and our job choices and performance (Hogan, 1998; Jackson et al., 2012; Mueller et al., 2018). Studies that follow thousands of lives through time show that personality traits rival socioeconomic status and cognitive ability as predictors of mortality, divorce, and occupational attainment (Graham et al., 2017; Roberts et al., 2007).

Although our personality *traits* may be both stable and potent, the consistency of our specific *behaviors* from one situation to the next is another matter. What relationship would you expect to find between being conscientious in one situation (say, showing up for class on time) and being conscientious in another (say, avoiding unhealthy foods)? If you've noticed how outgoing you are in some situations and how reserved you are in others, perhaps you said, "Very little." That's what researchers have found—only a small correlation (Mischel, 1968; Sherman et al., 2015). This inconsistency in behaviors also makes personality test scores weak predictors of behaviors. People's scores on an extraversion test, for example, do not neatly predict how sociable they will be on any given occasion.

If we remember such results, we will be more cautious about labeling and pigeonholing individuals (Mischel, 1968). Years in advance, science can tell us the phase of the Moon for any date. A day in advance, meteorologists can predict the weather. But we are much further from being able to predict how *you* will feel and act tomorrow.

However, people's *average* outgoingness, happiness, or carelessness over many situations is predictable (Epstein, 1983a,b). This tendency toward trait-consistent actions occurs worldwide, from the United States to Venezuela to Japan (Locke et al., 2017). By tracking their daily phone activity, researchers confirmed that extraverts really do talk and text more (Harari et al., 2020). I [DM] kept vowing to cut back on my jabbering and joking during my noontime pickup basketball games. Alas, moments later, the irrepressible chatterbox would inevitably reoccupy my body. Likewise, when buying groceries, I [ND] always end up chatting with the cashier! As our best friends can verify, we do have persistent (genetically influenced) personality traits. And our personality traits get expressed in our

- ***music preferences.*** Your playlist reveals something of your personality. Folk, classical, and ambient music lovers tend to be open to experience and verbally intelligent. Agreeable people tend to like jazz and avoid punk rock music. Blues, classic country, and soul music lovers tend to be emotionally stable. Extraverts like country music, R&B, and funk—and enjoy listening to their friends' playlists (Anderson et al., 2021). People also gravitate toward musicians who share their personality traits (Greenberg et al., 2021). Extraverts prefer extraverted Lil Wayne and Jay Z; agreeable people prefer the agreeable Norah Jones and Carrie Underwood.
- ***written communications.*** If you have ever felt you could detect someone's personality from their writing voice, you are right!! What a cool finding!!! 😊 People's writings—even their brief tweets and Facebook posts—often express their extraversion, self-esteem, and agreeableness (Bowden-Green et al., 2020; Park et al., 2015; Pennebaker, 2011). "Off to meet a friend. Woohoo!!!" posted one Facebook user who had scored high on extraversion (Kern et al., 2014). Extraverts also use more adjectives.
- ***online and personal spaces.*** Are online profiles, websites, and avatars a canvas for self-expression? Or are they an opportunity for people to present themselves in false or misleading ways? It's more the former (Akhtar et al., 2018; Hinds & Joinson, 2019). People who seemed most likable on Facebook or Twitter also seemed most likable in person (Qiu et al., 2012; Weisbuch et al., 2009). Photos show people's clothes, expressions, and postures, and can therefore give clues to personality and how people act in person (Gunyadin et al., 2017; Naumann et al., 2009). Our living and working spaces also help us express our identity, offering clues to our extraversion, agreeableness, conscientiousness, and openness (Back et al., 2010; Fong & Mar, 2015; Gosling, 2008).

Mike Twohy/Cartoon Stock

"You tend to overuse the exclamation point."

In unfamiliar, formal situations (perhaps as a guest in the home of a person from another culture) our traits remain hidden as we carefully attend to social cues. In familiar, informal situations (just hanging out with friends), we feel less constrained, allowing our traits to emerge (Buss, 1989). In these informal situations, our expressive styles—our animation, manner of speaking, and gestures—are impressively consistent. Viewing "thin slices" of someone's behavior, such as seeing a photo for a mere fraction of a second, or seeing several 2-second clips of a teacher in action, can tell us a lot about the person's basic personality traits (Ambady, 2010; Tackett et al., 2016).

Some people are naturally expressive (and therefore talented at pantomime and charades); others are less expressive (and therefore better poker players). To evaluate people's voluntary control over their expressiveness, Bella DePaulo and her colleagues (1992) asked people to *act* as expressive or inhibited as possible while stating opinions.

Room with a cue Even at "zero acquaintance," people can catch a glimpse of others' personality from looking at their online and personal spaces. So, what's your read on the occupants of these two rooms?

James Woodson/Getty Images

Their remarkable findings: Inexpressive people, even when feigning expressiveness, were less expressive than expressive people acting naturally. Similarly, expressive people, even when trying to seem inhibited, were less inhibited than inexpressive people acting naturally. It's hard to be someone you're not, or not to be who you are.

To sum up, we can say that at any moment the immediate situation powerfully influences a person's behavior. Social psychologists have learned that this is especially so when a "strong situation" makes clear demands (Cooper & Withey, 2009). We can better predict drivers' behavior at traffic lights from knowing the color of the lights than from knowing the drivers' personalities. Thus, professors may perceive certain students as subdued (based on their classroom behavior), but friends may perceive them as pretty wild (based on their party behavior). Averaging our behavior across many occasions does, however, reveal distinct personality traits. Traits exist. We differ. And our differences matter.

ASK YOURSELF

How do you think your own personality traits shine through in your music preferences, communication style, and online and personal spaces?

RETRIEVAL PRACTICE

RP-5 How well do personality test scores predict our behavior? Explain.

ANSWERS IN APPENDIX E

MODULE 46 REVIEW Humanistic Theories and Trait Theories

LEARNING OBJECTIVES

Test Yourself Answer these repeated Learning Objective Questions on your own (before "showing" the answers here, or checking the answers in Appendix D) to improve your retention of the concepts (McDaniel et al., 2009, 2015).

LOQ 46-1 How did humanistic psychologists view personality, and what was their goal in studying personality?

LOQ 46-2 How did humanistic psychologists assess a person's sense of self?

LOQ 46-3 How have humanistic theories influenced psychology? What criticisms have they faced?

LOQ 46-4 How do psychologists use traits to describe personality?

LOQ 46-5 What are some common misunderstandings about introversion?

LOQ 46-6 What are *personality inventories*, and what are their strengths and weaknesses as trait-assessment tools?

LOQ 46-7 Which traits seem to provide the most useful information about personality variation?

LOQ 46-8 Does research support the consistency of personality traits over time and across situations?

TERMS AND CONCEPTS TO REMEMBER

Test Yourself Write down the definition in your own words, then check your answer.

MODULE TEST

Test Yourself Answer the following questions on your own first, then "show" the answers here, or check your answers in Appendix E.

1. Maslow's hierarchy of needs proposes that we must satisfy basic physiological and safety needs before we seek ultimate psychological needs, such as self-actualization. Maslow based his ideas on
   a. Freudian theory.
   b. his experiences with patients.
   c. a series of laboratory experiments.
   d. his study of healthy, creative people.
2. How might Rogers explain how environment influences the development of a criminal?
3. The total acceptance Rogers advocated as part of a growth-promoting environment is called ________________ ________________ ________________.
4. ________________ theories of personality focus on describing characteristic behavior patterns, such as agreeableness or extraversion.
5. The most widely used personality inventory is the
   a. Extraversion–Introversion Scale.
   b. Person-Situation Inventory.
   c. MMPI.
   d. Big Five.
6. Which of the following is NOT one of the Big Five personality factors?
   a. Conscientiousness
   b. Anxiety
   c. Extraversion
   d. Agreeableness
7. Our scores on personality tests best predict
   a. our behavior on a specific occasion.
   b. our average behavior across many situations.
   c. behavior involving a single trait, such as conscientiousness.
   d. behavior that depends on the situation or context.

MODULE 47 Social-Cognitive Theories and the Self

Roughly speaking, the outside influences on behavior are the focus of *social psychology* (see the Social Psychology modules), and the inner influences are the focus of *personality psychology.* But behavior always depends on the interaction of persons with situations.

Social-Cognitive Theories

LOQ 47-1 How do social-cognitive theorists view personality development, and how do they explore behavior?

The **social-cognitive perspective** on personality, proposed by Albert Bandura (1986, 2006, 2008), emphasizes the interaction of our traits with our social situations.

Social-cognitive theorists believe we learn many of our behaviors either through conditioning or by observing and imitating others. (That's the "social" part.) They also emphasize the importance of mental processes: What we *think* about a situation affects our resulting behavior. (That's the "cognitive" part.) Instead of focusing solely on how our environment *controls* us (behaviorism), social-cognitive theorists focus on how we and our environment *interact:* How do we interpret and respond to external events? How do our schemas, our memories, and our expectations influence our behavior patterns?

social-cognitive perspective a view of behavior as influenced by the interaction between people's traits (including their thinking) and their social context.

reciprocal determinism the interacting influences of behavior, internal cognition, and environment.

Reciprocal Influences

Bandura (1986, 2006) views the person-environment interaction as **reciprocal determinism**. "Behavior, internal personal factors, and environmental influences,"

FIGURE 47.1
Reciprocal determinism

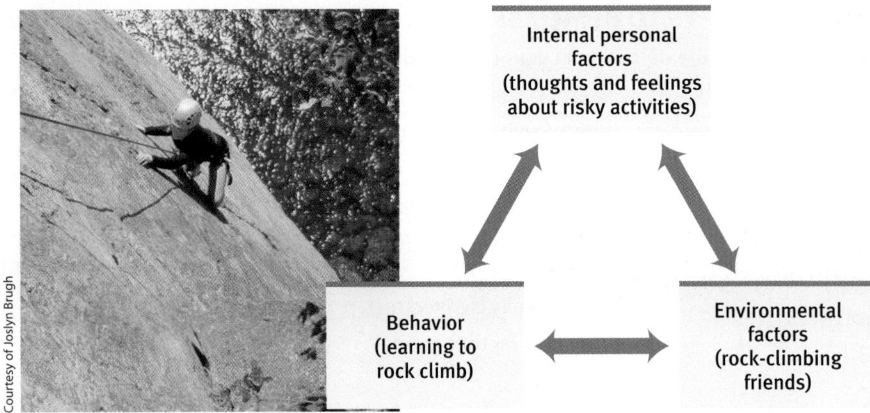
Internal personal factors (thoughts and feelings about risky activities)
Behavior (learning to rock climb)
Environmental factors (rock-climbing friends)
Courtesy of Joslyn Brugh

he said, "all operate as interlocking determinants of each other" (**FIGURE 47.1**). We can see this interaction as people's relationships affect their self-esteem, and as their self-esteem also affects their relationships (de Moor et al., 2021; Harris & Orth, 2020). For example, Rosa's past romantic experiences (her behaviors) influence her romantic attitudes (internal factor), which affect how she now responds to Ryan (environmental factor).

Consider three specific ways in which individuals and environments interact:

1. *Different people choose different environments.* The reading we do, the social media we use, the careers we pursue, the music we listen to, the friends we associate with—all are part of the environment we have chosen, based partly on our disposition (Denissen et al., 2018; Funder, 2009). And the environments we choose then shape us. People with inflated self-esteem may post frequent selfies, which may lead to public attention and praise, and to even greater self-love (Halpern et al., 2016).
2. *Our personalities shape how we interpret and react to events.* If we perceive the world as threatening, we will watch for threats and be prepared to defend ourselves. Anxious people often attend to and react strongly to relationship threats, such as when they feel ignored or excluded (Campbell & Marshall, 2011).
3. *Our personalities help create situations to which we react.* How we view and treat people influences how they then treat us. If we expect that others will not like us, our efforts to win their approval (such as bragging) might actually cause them to reject us (Scopelliti et al., 2015).

FIGURE 47.2
The biopsychosocial approach to the study of personality As with other psychological phenomena, personality is fruitfully studied at multiple levels.

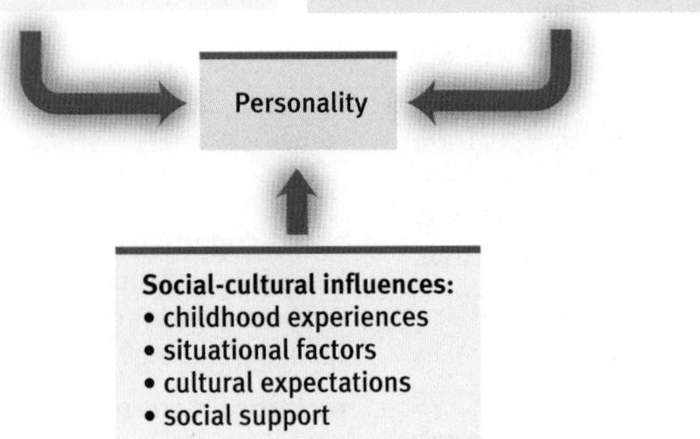
Biological influences:
• genetically determined temperament
• autonomic nervous system reactivity
• brain activity
Psychological influences:
• learned responses
• unconscious thought processes
• expectations and interpretations
Personality
Social-cultural influences:
• childhood experiences
• situational factors
• cultural expectations
• social support

In addition to the interaction of internal personal factors, the environment, and our behaviors, we also experience *gene–environment interaction.* Our genetically influenced traits evoke certain responses from others, which may nudge us in one direction or another. In one well-replicated finding, those with the interacting factors of (1) having a specific gene associated with aggression and (2) being raised in a difficult environment were most likely to demonstrate adult antisocial behavior (Byrd & Manuck, 2014; Caspi et al., 2002).

In such ways, we are both the products and the architects of our environments: *Behavior emerges from the interplay of external and internal influences.* Boiling water turns an egg hard and a potato soft. A threatening environment turns one person into a hero, another into a scoundrel. Extraverts experience focused concentration—what psychologists call *flow*—in social situations; introverts more often experience flow when alone (Liu & Csikszentmihalyi, 2020). *At every moment,* our behavior is influenced by our biology, our social and cultural experiences, and our cognition and dispositions (**FIGURE 47.2**).

ASK YOURSELF

How have your experiences shaped your personality? How has your personality helped shape your environment?

RETRIEVAL PRACTICE

RP-1 Albert Bandura proposed the ________________-________________ perspective on personality, which emphasizes the interaction of people with their environment. To describe the interacting influences of behavior, thoughts, and environment, he used the term ________________ ________________.

ANSWERS IN APPENDIX E

Assessing Behavior in Situations

To predict behavior, social-cognitive psychologists often observe behavior in realistic situations. One ambitious example was the U.S. Army's World War II strategy for assessing candidates for spy missions. Rather than using paper-and-pencil tests, Army psychologists subjected the candidates to simulated undercover conditions. They tested their ability to handle stress, solve problems, maintain leadership, and withstand intense interrogation without blowing their cover. Although time-consuming and expensive, this assessment of behavior in a realistic situation helped predict later success on actual spy missions (OSS Assessment Staff, 1948).

Military and educational organizations and many Fortune 500 companies have adopted similar strategies, known as the *assessment center* approach (Bray & Byham, 1991, 1997; Eurich et al., 2009). The U.S. telecommunications giant AT&T has observed prospective managers doing simulated managerial work. Some European universities give student applicants material to study, and then test their learning—thus mimicking the educational program (Niessen & Meijer, 2017). Many colleges assess nursing students' potential by observing their clinical work. And they assess potential faculty members' teaching abilities by observing them teach.

Shutterstock

Teaching success Many education programs require students to complete a supervised instructional experience. The student teaching program presumes a valid point: People's behavior in job-relevant situations helps predict their job performance.

The assessment center approach exploits the principle that the best means of predicting behavior is neither a personality test nor an interviewer's intuition. Rather, *the best predictor of future behavior is the person's past behavior patterns in similar situations* (Lyons et al., 2011; Mischel, 1981; Schmidt & Hunter, 1998). As long as the situation and the person remain much the same, the best predictor of future job performance is past job performance; the best predictor of future grades is past grades; the best predictor of future aggressiveness is past aggressiveness. People who have used marital infidelity websites at home will also be more likely to behave immorally at work (Griffin et al., 2019). If you can't check the person's past behavior, the next best thing is to create an assessment situation that simulates the task so you can see how the person handles it (Lievens et al., 2009; Meriac et al., 2008).

"What's past is prologue." —William Shakespeare, *The Tempest*, 1611

Evaluating Social-Cognitive Theories

LOQ 47-2 What criticisms have social-cognitive theories faced?

Social-cognitive theories of personality sensitize researchers to how situations affect, and are affected by, individuals. More than other personality theories (see **TABLE 47.1**), they build from psychological research on learning and cognition.

Critics charge that social-cognitive theories focus so much on the situation that they fail to appreciate the person's inner traits. Where is the person in this view of personality, ask the dissenters, and where are human emotions? True, the situation does guide our behavior. But in many instances our unconscious motives, our emotions, and our pervasive traits shine through. Personality traits predict behavior at work, in love, and at play. Our biologically influenced traits really do matter. Consider Percy Ray Pridgen and Charles Gill. Each faced the same situation: They had jointly won a $90 million lottery jackpot (Harriston, 1993). When Pridgen learned of the winning numbers, he began trembling uncontrollably, huddled with a friend behind a bathroom door while confirming the win, and then sobbed. When Gill heard the news, he told his wife and then went to sleep.

TABLE 47.1 Comparing the Major Personality Theories

Personality Theory	Key Proponents	Assumptions	View of Personality	Personality Assessment Methods
Psychoanalytic	Freud	Emotional disorders spring from unconscious dynamics, such as unresolved sexual and other childhood conflicts, and fixation at various developmental stages. Defense mechanisms fend off anxiety.	Personality consists of pleasure-seeking impulses (the id), a reality-oriented executive (the ego), and an internalized set of ideals (the superego).	Free association, projective tests, dream analysis
Psychodynamic	Adler, Horney, Jung	The unconscious and conscious minds interact. Childhood experiences and defense mechanisms are important.	The dynamic interplay of conscious and unconscious motives and conflicts shapes our personality.	Projective tests, therapy sessions
Humanistic	Maslow, Rogers	Rather than focusing on disorders born of dark conflicts, it's better to emphasize how healthy people may strive for self-realization.	If our basic human needs are met, we will strive toward self-actualization. In a climate of unconditional positive regard, we can develop self-awareness and a more realistic and positive self-concept.	Questionnaires, therapy sessions, life story approach
Trait	Allport; Costa; H. Eysenck; S. Eysenck; McCrae	We have certain stable and enduring characteristics, influenced by genetic predispositions.	Scientific study of traits has isolated important dimensions of personality, such as the Big Five traits (openness, conscientiousness, extraversion, agreeableness, and neuroticism).	Personality inventories
Social-cognitive	Bandura	Our traits interact with the social context to produce our behaviors.	Conditioning and observational learning interact with cognition to create behavior patterns. Our behavior in one situation is best predicted by considering our past behavior in similar situations.	Observing behavior in realistic situations

RETRIEVAL PRACTICE

RP-2 What is the best way to predict a person's future behavior?

ANSWERS IN APPENDIX E

Exploring the Self

LOQ 47-3 Why has psychology generated so much research on the self?

Our personality feeds our sense of self. Asked to consider "Who I am," people draw on their distinctive and enduring ways of thinking, feeling, and acting. Psychology's concern with our sense of self dates back at least to William James, who devoted more than 100 pages of his 1890 *Principles of Psychology* to the topic. By 1943, Gordon Allport lamented that the self had become "lost to view." Although humanistic psychology's later emphasis on the self did not instigate much scientific research, it did help renew the concept of self and keep it alive. Now, more than a century after James, the self is one of Western psychology's most vigorously researched topics. Every year, new studies galore appear on self-esteem, self-disclosure, self-awareness, self-schemas, self-monitoring, and more. Even neuroscientists have searched for the self, by identifying a central frontal lobe region that activates when people respond to self-reflective questions about their traits and dispositions (Damasio, 2010; Mitchell, 2009; Pauly et al., 2013). The **self**, as organizer of our thoughts, feelings, and actions, occupies the center of personality.

self in contemporary psychology, assumed to be the center of personality, the organizer of our thoughts, feelings, and actions.

Consider the concept of *possible selves* (Markus & Nurius, 1986; Rathbone et al., 2016). Your possible selves include your visions of the self you dream of becoming (the rich self, the successful self, the loved and admired self), and also the self you fear becoming (the unemployed self, the academically failed self, the lonely and unpopular self). Possible selves motivate us to lay out specific goals that direct our energy effectively and efficiently (Landau et al., 2014). Eighth- and ninth-grade students whose families struggle financially are more likely to earn high grades if they have a clear vision of themselves succeeding in school (Duckworth et al., 2013). Dreams do often give birth to achievements.

Our self-focused perspective may motivate us, but it can also lead us to presume too readily that others are noticing and evaluating us, a phenomenon called the **spotlight effect**. In one experiment, university students who were asked to put on an embarrassing T-shirt before meeting other students guessed that nearly half their peers would notice the shirt. But only 23 percent did (Gilovich, 1996). To turn down the spotlight's brightness, we can use two strategies. The first is simply to know and remember the spotlight effect. Public speakers perform better if they understand that their natural nervousness is hardly noticeable (Savitsky & Gilovich, 2003). The second is to take the audience's perspective. When we imagine audience members empathizing with our situation, we usually expect to be judged less harshly (Epley et al., 2002). The point to remember: *We stand out less than we imagine,* even with dorky clothes and bad hair, and even after a blunder like setting off a library alarm (Gilovich & Savitsky, 1999; Savitsky et al., 2001).

ASK YOURSELF

What possible selves do you dream of—or fear—becoming? To what extent do these imagined selves motivate you now?

The Benefits of Self-Esteem

LOQ 47-4 How important is self-esteem to our well-being?

Self-esteem—our feelings of high or low self-worth—matters. So does **self-efficacy**, our sense of competence on a task (Bandura, 1977, 2018). (A student might feel high self-efficacy in a math course yet low overall self-esteem.) People who feel good about themselves (who strongly agree with self-affirming questionnaire statements, such as "I am fun to be with") have fewer sleepless nights. They tend to be outgoing, responsible, and open to new experiences (Fetvadjiev & He, 2019). Online and in person, they communicate positively, causing others to like and include them more (Cameron & Granger, 2019; Mahadevan et al., 2019). They feel less shy, anxious, and lonely, and are just plain happier (Greenberg, 2008; Orth & Robins, 2014; Swann et al., 2007). Our self-esteem grows from venturesome experiences and achievement, and therefore changes as we age (Hutteman et al., 2015). Self-esteem often increases dramatically from adolescence to middle adulthood, continuing to climb until peaking between ages 50 and 60 (Bleidorn et al., 2016; Orth et al., 2018; von Soest et al., 2018).

Dear diary,
Sorry to bother you again.
LOW SELF-ESTEEM

Mike Twohy/Cartoon Stock

But most psychologists doubt that high self-esteem is "the armor that protects kids" from life's problems (Baumeister & Vohs, 2018; McKay, 2000; Seligman, 2002). Children's academic self-efficacy—their confidence that they can do well in a subject—predicts school achievement. But general self-image does not (Marsh & Craven, 2006; Swann et al., 2007; Trautwein et al., 2006). Maybe self-esteem is a side effect of meeting challenges and surmounting difficulties, or a gauge that reports the state of our relationships with others (Bleidorn et al., 2021; Reitz et al., 2016). If so, isn't pushing the gauge artificially higher with empty compliments much like forcing a car's low fuel gauge to display "full"?

"When kids increase in self-control, their grades go up later. But when kids increase their self-esteem, there is no effect on their grades." —Angela Duckworth, *In Character* interview, 2009

If feeling good *follows* doing well, then giving praise in the absence of good performance may actually harm people. After receiving weekly self-esteem-boosting messages, struggling students earned *lower-than-expected* grades (Forsyth et al., 2007). Other research showed that giving people random rewards hurt their productivity. Martin Seligman (2012) reported that "when good things occurred that weren't earned, like nickels coming out of slot machines, it did not increase people's well-being. It produced helplessness. People gave up and became passive."

spotlight effect overestimating others' noticing and evaluating our appearance, performance, and blunders (as if we presume a spotlight shines on us).

self-esteem our feelings of high or low self-worth.

self-efficacy our sense of competence and effectiveness.

"The enthusiastic claims of the self-esteem movement mostly range from fantasy to hogwash. The effects of self-esteem are small, limited, and not all good." —Roy Baumeister (1996)

There are, however, important effects when self-esteem is threatened. When researchers temporarily deflated people's self-image (by telling them they did poorly on an aptitude test or by disparaging their personality), those participants became more likely to disparage others or to express heightened racial prejudice (vanDellen et al., 2011; van Dijk et al., 2011; Ybarra, 1999). Self-image threat even increases *unconscious* racial bias (Allen & Sherman, 2011). Those who are negative about themselves have also tended to be oversensitive and judgmental (Baumgardner et al., 1989; Pelham, 1993). Such findings are consistent with humanistic psychology's ideas about the benefits of a healthy self-image. Accept yourself and you'll find it easier to accept others. Disparage yourself and you will be prone to the floccinaucinihilipilification[1] of others. People who are down on themselves tend to be down on others.

The Costs of Self-Esteem

LOQ 47-5 How do excessive optimism, blindness to one's own incompetence, and self-serving bias reveal the costs of self-esteem, and how do defensive and secure self-esteem differ?

EXCESSIVE OPTIMISM Positive thinking in the face of adversity can pay dividends, but so, too, can a dash of realism (Schneider, 2001). Realistic anxiety over possible future failures can fuel energetic efforts to avoid the dreaded fate (Goodhart, 1986; Norem, 2001; Showers, 1992). Concerned about failing an upcoming exam, students may study thoroughly and outperform their equally able but more confident peers. Asian American students have expressed somewhat greater pessimism than their European American counterparts, which may help explain their often impressive academic achievements (Chang, 2001). Success requires enough optimism to provide hope and enough pessimism to prevent complacency. We want our airline pilots to be mindful of worst-possible outcomes.

Excessive optimism can blind us to real risks (Tenney et al., 2015). More than 1000 studies have shown how our natural positive thinking bias can promote "unrealistic optimism" (Shepperd et al., 2015; Weinstein, 1980). When 56 percent of twelfth graders believed they would earn a graduate degree—though only 9 percent were likely to do so—that was unrealistic optimism (Reynolds et al., 2006). When most people of opposing political views optimistically believed that *their* views would become more widely held, many were in error (Rogers et al., 2017). When students believed they were more likely than their classmates to get a high-paying job and own a nice home, and less likely to have a heart attack or get cancer, that, too, was unrealistic optimism (Waters et al., 2011). If overconfident of our ability to control an impulse such as the urge to smoke, we are more likely to expose ourselves to temptations—and to fail (Nordgren et al., 2009). Blind optimism can be self-defeating, as we can see in those who optimistically deny the addictive toxicity of smoking, venture into ill-fated relationships, and invest money in risky schemes.

Our natural positive thinking bias does seem to vanish, however, when we are awaiting feedback, such as exam results (Carroll et al., 2006). Across many studies in both the real world (awaiting bar exam scores) and laboratory (awaiting intelligence test results), people "brace for the worst" (Sweeny & Falkenstein, 2017). (Perhaps you, too, can recall shifting toward pessimism as a moment of truth approaches?) Positive illusions also vanish after a traumatic personal experience—as they did for victims of a catastrophic California earthquake, who had to give up their illusions of being less vulnerable than others to earthquakes (Helweg-Larsen, 1999).

BLINDNESS TO ONE'S OWN INCOMPETENCE Ironically, people often are most overconfident when most incompetent. They are often "unskilled and unaware of it," observed Justin Kruger and David Dunning (1999), after finding that most students scoring at the low end of grammar and logic tests *believed* they had scored in the top half. This "ignorance of one's own incompetence," now famously called the *Dunning-Kruger effect,*

[1] We couldn't resist throwing that in. But don't worry, you won't be tested on *floccinaucinihilipilification,* which is the act of estimating something as worthless (and was the longest nontechnical word in the first edition of the *Oxford English Dictionary*).

can produce overconfidence among political leaders. It also has a parallel among those of us with hearing loss, as I [DM] can confirm. Because we are unaware of what we don't hear, we may overestimate our hearing. If I fail to hear my friend calling my name, the friend notices my inattention. But for me it's a nonevent. I hear what I hear—which, to me, seems pretty normal. As comedian Trevor Noah (2020) quipped, "This is the problem when the dumbest person in the room thinks they're the smartest."

Because it takes competence to recognize competence, "Our ignorance is invisible to us," summarizes Dunning (2019). "The first rule of the Dunning-Kruger club," he says, "is you don't know you're a member of the Dunning-Kruger club." Thus, to judge our competence and predict our future performance, it pays to invite others' assessments (Dunning, 2006; Grossmann & Kross, 2014).

"What I'd dearly love would be to be able to see [myself] having a Dunning-Kruger moment. But according to my own theory, I'll never have it." —Psychologist David Dunning, NPR, 2016

Based on studies in which both individuals and their acquaintances predict their future, we can hazard some advice: Ask your peers for their candid prediction. If you're in love and want to predict whether it will last, don't listen to your heart—ask your roommate.

SELF-SERVING BIAS Imagine dashing to class, hoping not to miss the first few minutes. But you arrive 5 minutes late, huffing and puffing. As you sink into your seat, what sorts of thoughts go through your mind? Do you go through a negative door, thinking "I'm such a loser"? Or do you go through a positive door, telling yourself, "At least I made it to class"?

Personality psychologists have found that most people choose the second door because it leads to positive self-thoughts. We have a good reputation with ourselves. We show a **self-serving bias**—a readiness to perceive ourselves favorably (Myers, 2010). Consider:

People accept more responsibility for good deeds than for bad, and for successes than for failures. Athletes often privately credit their victories to their own prowess, and their losses to bad breaks, lousy officiating, or the other team's exceptional performance (Allen et al., 2020). Most students who receive poor exam grades criticize the exam or the instructor, not themselves. Drivers filling out insurance claims have explained their accidents in such words as "A pedestrian hit me and went under my car." The question "What have I done to deserve this?" is one we usually ask of our troubles, not our successes. Although a self-serving bias can lead us to avoid uncomfortable truths, it can also motivate us to approach difficult tasks with confidence instead of despair (Tomaka et al., 1992; von Hippel & Trivers, 2011). Indeed, across many studies, self-enhancement predicts emotional well-being (Dufner et al., 2019).

Sophia Warren/Cartoon Stock

"That's strange. I remember it differently, in a way that aligns with my world view and casts me in a positive light."

Most people see themselves as better than average. Compared with most other people, how intelligent are you? How friendly? On each question, where would you rank yourself, from the 1st to the 99th percentile? Most people put themselves well above the 50th percentile. This better-than-average effect appears for nearly any subjectively assessed and socially desirable trait or behavior. Most people rate themselves as having above average intelligence, kindness, humor, and ethics (Zell et al., 2020). Nine in ten drivers rate themselves as more skilled than the average driver (Koppel et al., 2021). Most people in the United Kingdom, the United States, and Germany believed that, compared with other same-aged citizens, they had a better-than-average chance of not catching Covid-19 (Kuper-Smith et al., 2020). The average person thinks they're better than average. Self-serving bias is weaker in Asia, where social practices emphasize modesty (Church et al., 2014; Falk et al., 2009). Yet in every one of 53 countries surveyed, people expressed self-esteem above the midpoint of the most widely used scale (Schmitt & Allik, 2005).

PEANUTS

WHY ARE YOU ALWAYS SO ANXIOUS TO CRITICIZE ME?
© 1989 United Feature Syndicate, Inc.

I JUST THINK I HAVE A KNACK FOR SEEING OTHER PEOPLE'S FAULTS..
4-25

WHAT ABOUT YOUR OWN FAULTS?
I HAVE A KNACK FOR OVERLOOKING THEM..
SCHULZ

Andrews McMeel Syndication

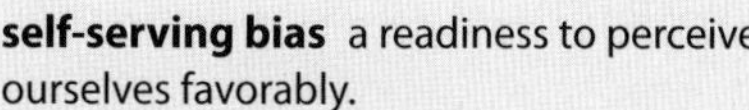

self-serving bias a readiness to perceive ourselves favorably.

"Fun fact: The average man [thinks] he would be better than 63 percent of other men if he had to survive a zombie apocalypse." —Mathematician Spencer Greenberg and economist Seth Stephens-Davidowitz, 2019

Self-serving bias often underlies conflicts, such as blaming a partner for relationship problems or a colleague for work problems. All of us also tend to see our own *groups*—our school, organization, region, or country—as superior. Although there are 50 U.S. states, Americans on average estimate that their home state made 18 percent of the contributions to U.S. history (Putnam et al., 2018). Likewise, people from 35 countries rate their own country as making outsized contributions to world history (Zaromb et al., 2018). Such *group-serving bias*—my group is better—fueled the trans-Atlantic slave trade, Nazi horrors, and Rwandan genocide. No wonder literature and religion so often warn against the perils of self-love and pride. Ingroup love often feeds outgroup hate (Golec de Zavala & Lantos, 2020).

Finding their self-esteem threatened, some people with inflated egos may react violently. Researchers Brad Bushman and Roy Baumeister (1998; Bushman et al., 2009) had undergraduate volunteers write a brief essay, in response to which another supposed student gave them either praise ("Great essay!") or stinging criticism ("One of the worst essays I have read!"). The essay writers were then allowed to lash out at their evaluators by blasting them with unpleasant noise. Can you anticipate the result? After criticism, those with inflated self-esteem were "exceptionally aggressive." They delivered three times the auditory torture than did those with average self-esteem. Over 80 studies have replicated the dangerous effect of **narcissism** (excessive self-love and self-focus) on aggression (Rasmussen, 2016). Researchers have concluded that "conceited, self-important individuals turn nasty toward those who puncture their bubbles of self-love" (Baumeister, 2001).

After tracking self-importance across several decades, psychologist Jean Twenge (2006; Twenge & Foster, 2010) reported that what she called *Generation Me*—born in the 1980s and early 1990s—expressed more narcissism (by agreeing more often with statements such as, "If I ruled the world, it would be a better place," or "I think I am a special person"). Why does a rise in narcissism matter? Narcissists tend to be materialistic, desire fame, have inflated expectations, hook up more often without commitment, and gamble and cheat more—all of which have been increasing as narcissism has increased. Humility, by contrast, is the attitude that, no matter your accomplishments, you are not entitled to special treatment (Banker & Leary, 2020).

Narcissistic people (who are more often men) tend to be unforgiving, take a game-playing, sexually forceful approach to romantic relationships, and are more likely to become divorced (Johnson, 2020; Lamarche & Seery, 2019; Wetzel et al., 2020). They're often charismatic and ambitious, making them popular until others tire of their cold-hearted arrogance (Leckelt et al., 2020; Poorthuis et al., 2019). From moment to moment, they crave status and adulation and often become defensive or enraged when criticized (Grapsas et al., 2020; Sedikides, 2021). Many had parents who told them they were superior to others (Brummelman et al., 2015). Reality TV stars are often especially narcissistic (Rubinstein, 2016; Young & Pinsky, 2006).

"The [self-]portraits that we actually believe, when we are given freedom to voice them, are dramatically more positive than reality can sustain." —Shelley Taylor, *Positive Illusions*, 1989

Despite the demonstrated perils of pride, many people object that the idea of self-serving bias overlooks those who feel worthless and unlovable. If self-serving bias prevails, why do so many people disparage themselves? For five reasons:

1. Sometimes self-directed put-downs are *subtly strategic*—they elicit reassuring strokes. Saying "No one likes me" may at least elicit "But not everyone has met you!"
2. Other times, such as before a game or an exam, self-disparaging comments *prepare us for possible failure.* The coach who extols the superior strength of the upcoming opponent makes a loss understandable, a victory noteworthy.
3. A self-disparaging "How could I have been so stupid!" also helps us *learn from our mistakes.*
4. Sometimes false humility is actually a *humblebrag:* "I barely studied, so I'm amazed I got an A" (Sezer et al., 2018).
5. Self-disparagement frequently *pertains to one's old self.* Asked to remember their really bad behaviors, people recall things from long ago; good behaviors more easily

narcissism excessive self-love and self-absorption.

come to mind from their recent past (Escobedo & Adolphs, 2010). Even when they have not changed, people are much more critical of their distant past selves than of their current selves (Wilson & Ross, 2001). Chumps yesterday, champs today: "At 18, I was a jerk; today I'm more sensitive."

Even so, all of us some of the time (and some of us much of the time) do feel inferior. This is especially true when we compare ourselves with those who are a step or two higher on the ladder of status, looks, income, or ability. The more frequently we feel comparatively inferior, the more unhappy or even depressed we become. But for most people, thinking has a naturally positive bias.

"If you compare yourself with others, you may become vain and bitter; for always there will be greater and lesser persons than yourself." —Max Ehrmann, "Desiderata," 1927

Some researchers identify two types of self-esteem—defensive and secure (Kernis, 2003; Lambird & Mann, 2006; Ryan & Deci, 2004). *Defensive self-esteem* is fragile. It focuses on sustaining itself, which makes failure and criticism feel threatening. Defensive people may respond to such perceived threats with anger or aggression (Crocker & Park, 2004; Donnellan et al., 2005).

Secure self-esteem is less fragile, because it is less contingent on external evaluations. To feel accepted for who we are, and not for our looks, wealth, or acclaim, relieves pressures to succeed and enables us to focus beyond ourselves. Those who accept their own flaws also more compassionately accept others' flaws (Zhang et al., 2020).

By losing ourselves in relationships and purposes larger than ourselves, we may achieve a more secure self-esteem, satisfying relationships, and greater quality of life (Crocker & Park, 2004). Authentic pride, rooted in actual achievement, supports self-confidence and leadership (Tracy et al., 2009; Weidman et al., 2016; Williams & DeSteno, 2009).

"True humility is not thinking less of yourself; it is thinking of yourself less." —C. S. Lewis, *Mere Christianity*, 1952

RETRIEVAL PRACTICE

RP-3 What are the positive and negative effects of high self-esteem?

RP-4 The tendency to accept responsibility for success and blame circumstances or bad luck for failure is called ______-______ ______.

RP-5 ______ (Secure/Defensive) self-esteem is linked to angry and aggressive behavior. ______ (Secure/Defensive) self-esteem is a healthier self-image that allows us to focus beyond ourselves and enjoy a higher quality of life.

ANSWERS IN APPENDIX E

MODULE 47 REVIEW Social-Cognitive Theories and the Self

LEARNING OBJECTIVES

Test Yourself Answer these repeated Learning Objective Questions on your own (before "showing" the answers here, or checking the answers in Appendix D) to improve your retention of the concepts (McDaniel et al., 2009, 2015).

LOQ 47-1 How do social-cognitive theorists view personality development, and how do they explore behavior?

LOQ 47-2 What criticisms have social-cognitive theories faced?

LOQ 47-3 Why has psychology generated so much research on the self?

LOQ 47-4 How important is self-esteem to our well-being?

LOQ 47-5 How do excessive optimism, blindness to one's own incompetence, and self-serving bias reveal the costs of self-esteem, and how do defensive and secure self-esteem differ?

TERMS AND CONCEPTS TO REMEMBER

Test Yourself Write down the definition in your own words, then check your answer.

social-cognitive perspective, p. 541
reciprocal determinism, p. 541
self, p. 544
spotlight effect, p. 545
self-esteem, p. 545
self-efficacy, p. 545
self-serving bias, p. 547
narcissism, p. 548

MODULE TEST

Test Yourself Answer the following questions on your own first, then "show" the answers here, or check your answers in Appendix E.

1. The social-cognitive perspective proposes our personality is shaped by a process called *reciprocal determinism*, as personal factors, environmental factors, and behaviors interact. An example of an environmental factor is

a. the presence of books in a home.
b. a preference for outdoor play.
c. the ability to read at a fourth-grade level.
d. the fear of violent action on television.

2. Critics say that ______________-______________ personality theories are very sensitive to an individual's interactions with particular situations, but that they give too little attention to the person's enduring traits.

3. The tendency to overestimate others' attention to and evaluation of our appearance, performance, and blunders is called the ______________ ______________.

4. Researchers have found that low self-esteem tends to be linked with life problems. How should this link be interpreted?

a. Life problems cause low self-esteem.
b. The answer isn't clear because the link is correlational and does not indicate cause and effect.
c. Low self-esteem leads to life problems.
d. Because of the self-serving bias, we must assume that external factors cause low self-esteem.

5. A fortune cookie advises, "Love yourself and happiness will follow." Is this good advice?

CHAPTER
15

Clique Images/Shutterstock

Psychological Disorders (Modules 48–53)

You lose entire blocks of your day to obsessive thoughts or actions. I spend so much time finishing songs in my car before I can get out or redoing my entire shower routine because I lost count of how many times I scrubbed my left arm.

Kelly, diagnosed with obsessive-compulsive disorder (from Schuster, 2015)

Whenever I get depressed it's because I've lost a sense of self. I can't find reasons to like myself. I think I'm ugly. I think no one likes me.

Greta, diagnosed with depression (from Thorne, 1993, p. 21)

Voices, like the roar of a crowd, came. I felt like Jesus; I was being crucified.

Stuart, diagnosed with schizophrenia (from Emmons et al., 1997)

Now and then, we all feel, think, or act in ways that resemble a psychological disorder. We feel anxious, depressed, withdrawn, or suspicious. So it's no wonder we are drawn to try to understand disordered psychological states—we sometimes see ourselves in the mental illnesses we study.

Worldwide, nearly a billion people live with mental or behavioral disorders (GBD, 2022). Many of us will know—or love someone who knows—the bewilderment and pain of unexplained physical symptoms, irrational fears, or a feeling that life is not worth living. In a survey of first-year university students in eight countries, 1 in 3 reported a mental health problem during the prior year (Auerbach et al., 2018).

Each year, mental or behavioral disorders contribute to an estimated 8 million deaths (Walker et al., 2015). Although their rates and symptoms vary by culture, no known society is free of two serious disorders — major *depressive disorder* and *schizophrenia* (Baumeister & Härter, 2007; Jablensky, 1999; Susser & Martínez-Alés, 2018). These modules examine mental disorders; the Therapy modules consider scientifically-studied treatments for them.

MODULE

48 Introduction to Psychological Disorders

Most people would agree that someone who is depressed and stays mostly in bed for 3 months has a psychological disorder. But what about a grieving father who, 3 months after his child has died, can't resume his usual social activities? Where should we draw the line between understandable grief and clinical depression? Between a fear and a phobia? Between typical distractedness and attention-deficit/hyperactivity disorder?

And how do race and socioeconomic status influence mental illness diagnoses and treatment? For example, why are incarcerated people in the United States more likely to receive a mental health diagnosis if they are White, whereas those who are Black are more likely to be labeled merely as criminals (Bronson & Berzofsky, 2017; Prins et al., 2012)? Why are White defendants more often offered substance use disorder treatment as an alternative to prosecution, while Black defendants in similar circumstances more often receive a felony conviction (Schlesinger, 2013)? And why do people in poverty have an increased risk for depression and anxiety—and often struggle for equitable access to high-quality mental health care (Hodgkinson et al., 2017; Ridley et al., 2020)? Scientists and clinicians are asking these and other questions:

- How should we *define* psychological disorders?
- How should we *understand* what causes disorders? How do underlying biological factors contribute? How do troubling environments influence our well-being? And how do these effects of nature and nurture interact?
- How should we *classify* psychological disorders? And can we do so in a way that allows us to help people without stigmatizing or labeling them?
- Are those with psychological disorders at risk of harming themselves or others?
- What do we know about rates of psychological disorders? How many people have them? Who is vulnerable, and when are they most likely to develop a new disorder?

"Who in the rainbow can draw the line where the violet tint ends and the orange tint begins? Distinctly we see the difference of the colors, but where exactly does the one first blendingly enter into the other? So with sanity and insanity." — Herman Melville, *Billy Budd, Sailor*, 1924

Defining Psychological Disorders

LEARNING OBJECTIVE QUESTION LOQ **48-1** How should we draw the line between typical behavior and a disorder?

A **psychological disorder** is a syndrome (a collection of symptoms) marked by a "clinically significant disturbance in an individual's cognition, emotion regulation, or behavior" (American Psychiatric Association, 2013). Thoughts, emotions, or behaviors are described as *dysfunctional* or *maladaptive* when they interfere with day-to-day quality

psychological disorder a disturbance in people's thoughts, emotions, or behaviors that causes distress or suffering and impairs their daily lives.

of life. Believing your home must be thoroughly cleaned every weekend is not a disorder; but if compulsive daily cleaning rituals interfere with work and leisure, they may indicate a disorder. Occasional sadness is to be expected; sadness that persists for weeks and becomes disabling likewise signals a psychological disorder. Feeling energized is common; feeling so hyped or excited that you sleep too little, drive dangerously, or spend money recklessly—perhaps worrying your loved ones—can be a sign of a disorder.

Distress often accompanies such dysfunction. Kelly, Greta, and Stuart were all distressed by their thoughts, emotions, or behaviors.

Over time, definitions of what constitutes a "significant disturbance" have varied. In 1973, the American Psychiatric Association voted that "homosexuality" should no longer be classified as a psychological disorder. The organization made this change because more and more of its members viewed same-sex attraction as a natural biological predisposition that did not cause people distress or impair their daily lives. Such is the power of shifting societal beliefs. Despite cultural progress toward reducing stigma and prejudice toward various groups, U.S. children and adolescents who identify as transgender or gender nonconforming have been seven times more likely than their peers to be diagnosed with a psychological disorder (Becerra-Culqui et al., 2018). This is due largely to the continued stigma and stress they often experience (Hatzenbuehler et al., 2009; Meyer, 2003). In the twenty-first century, controversies swirl over other new or altered diagnoses in the most recent edition of psychiatry's manual for describing disorders (Conway et al., 2019; Widiger et al., 2019).

RETRIEVAL PRACTICE

RP-1 Anika, a lawyer, is distressed by feeling the need to wash her hands 100 times a day. She has little time to meet with clients, and her colleagues are wondering about her competence. Her behavior would probably be labeled disordered, because it is ____________________—that is, it interferes with her quality of life.

ANSWERS IN APPENDIX E

Understanding Psychological Disorders

LOQ 48-2 How do the medical model and the biopsychosocial approach influence our understanding of psychological disorders?

The way we view a problem influences how we try to solve it. In earlier times, people often viewed strange behaviors as evidence of strange forces at work—the movements of the stars, godlike powers, or evil spirits. Had you lived during the Middle Ages, you might have said, "The devil made me do it." Believing that, you might have approved of a harsh cure that would drive out the evil demon. Thus, people experiencing "madness" (as mental illness was then known) have been caged or given "therapies" such as genital mutilation, beatings, removal of teeth or lengths of intestines, or transfusions of animal blood (Farina, 1982).

Reformers, such as Philippe Pinel (1745–1826) in France, opposed such brutal treatments. Madness is not demonic possession, Pinel insisted, but a sickness of the mind caused by severe stress and inhumane conditions. He argued that curing the illness requires *moral treatment,* including boosting patients' spirits by unchaining them and talking with them. He and others worked to replace brutality with gentleness, isolation with activity, and filth with clean air and sunshine.

In some places, cruel treatments for mental illness—including chaining people to beds or confining them in spaces with wild animals—linger even today. The World Health Organization has launched a reform that aims to transform hospitals "into patient-friendly and humane places with minimum restraints" (WHO, 2014).

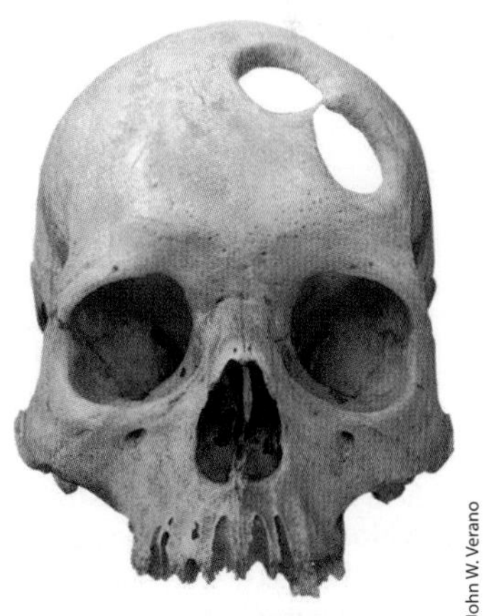

John W. Verano

Yesterday's "therapy"? Through the ages, people with psychological disorders have endured brutal treatments, including the trephination evident in this Stone Age patient's skull. Drilling skull holes like these may have been an attempt to release evil spirits and cure those with psychological disorders. Do you think a patient would have survived this kind of "cure"?

The Medical Model

A medical breakthrough around the year 1900 prompted further reforms. Researchers discovered that syphilis, a sexually transmitted infection, invades the brain and distorts the mind. This discovery triggered an eager search for physical causes and effective

medical model the concept that diseases, in this case psychological disorders, have physical causes that can be *diagnosed, treated,* and, in most cases, *cured,* often through treatment in a *hospital.*

epigenetics "above" or "in addition to" *(epi)* genetics; the study of the molecular mechanisms by which environments can influence genetic expression (without a DNA change).

treatments of other mental disorders. Hospitals replaced asylums, and the **medical model** of mental disorders was born. A mental *illness* (also called a psycho*pathology*) needs to be *diagnosed* based on its *symptoms.* It needs to be *treated* through *therapy,* which may include time in a psychiatric *hospital.* Recent discoveries have energized the medical model, demonstrating that many genes together influence the brain and that biochemical abnormalities contribute to all major disorders (Smoller, 2019). A growing number of clinical psychologists work in medical hospitals, where they collaborate with physicians.

The Biopsychosocial Approach

To call psychological disorders "sicknesses" tilts research toward the influence of biology. But as in so many other areas, biological, psychological, and social-cultural influences together weave the fabric of our human experience. As individuals, we differ in how much stress we experience and how we cope with stressors. Cultures also differ in their sources of stress and in their ways of coping. We are physically embodied and socially embedded.

Two disorders—major depressive disorder and schizophrenia—occur worldwide. Other disorders tend to be associated with specific cultures. In Latin America, some experience *susto*—severe anxiety or panic in response to emotional trauma or fear of black magic. In Japanese culture, people may experience *taijin kyofusho*—*social* anxiety about physical appearance, a readiness to blush, and a fear of eye contact. The eating disorders *anorexia nervosa* and *bulimia nervosa* occur mostly in food-abundant Western cultures. These varied disorders may share an underlying dynamic (such as anxiety) while differing in the symptoms (an eating problem or a specific fear) manifested in a particular culture.

The biopsychosocial approach emphasizes that mind and body are inseparable (**FIGURE 48.1**). Negative emotions can trigger physical problems and vice versa. The biopsychosocial approach gave rise to the *vulnerability-stress model,*[1] which assumes that individual dispositions combine with environmental stressors to influence psychological disorder (Monroe & Simons, 1991; Zuckerman, 1999). Research on **epigenetics** supports the vulnerability-stress model by showing how environment interacts with our DNA. A gene may be *expressed* in one environment, but not in another. For some, that will be the difference between developing a disorder or not.

Disorders often accompany one another (Jacobson & Newman, 2017; Plana-Ripoll et al., 2019). People diagnosed with one disorder, such as major depressive disorder, are at higher risk for being diagnosed with another, such as an anxiety disorder. Such *comorbidity* results from several factors, such as having overlapping genes that predispose different disorders (Brainstorm Consortium, 2018; Tylee et al., 2022). In one

FIGURE 48.1
The biopsychosocial approach to psychological disorders Today's psychology studies how biological, psychological, and social-cultural factors interact to produce specific psychological disorders.

Biological influences:
• evolution
• individual genes
• brain structure and chemistry
Psychological influences:
• stress
• trauma
• learned helplessness
• mood-related perceptions and memories
Psychological disorder
Social-cultural influences:
• roles
• expectations
• definitions of *disorder*

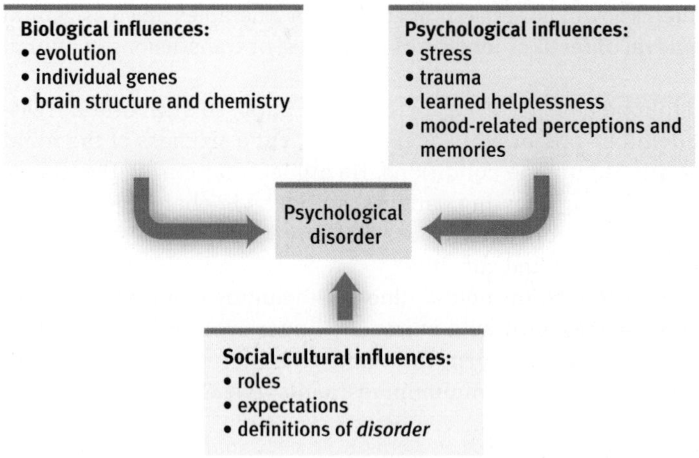

[1]Also called the *diathesis-stress model.* ("Diathesis"—meaning "predisposed vulnerability"—derives from a Greek word for "predisposition.")

U.S. national sample, 51 percent of people with one disorder were also diagnosed with at least one other disorder (Barr et al., 2022). Comorbidity is common.

RETRIEVAL PRACTICE

RP-2 Are psychological disorders universal or culture-specific? Explain with examples.

RP-3 What is the biopsychosocial approach, and why is it important in our understanding of psychological disorders?

ANSWERS IN APPENDIX E

Classifying Disorders — and Labeling People

LOQ 48-3 How and why do clinicians classify psychological disorders, and why do some psychologists criticize diagnostic labels?

In biology, classification creates order. To classify an animal as a "mammal" says a great deal—that it is likely warm-blooded, has hair or fur, and produces milk to nourish its young. In psychiatry and psychology, too, classification aims to order and describe symptoms. To classify a person's disorder as "schizophrenia" suggests that the person talks incoherently, has irrational beliefs, shows either little emotion or inappropriate emotion, or is completely withdrawn. "Schizophrenia" is a quick way to describe a complex disorder.

Moreover, diagnostic classification gives more than a thumbnail sketch of a disorder. In psychiatry and psychology, classification also aims to *predict* a disorder's future course, *suggest* appropriate treatment, and *guide* research into its causes. To study a disorder, we must first name and describe it.

In many countries, the most common tool for describing disorders is the American Psychiatric Association's *Diagnostic and Statistical Manual of Mental Disorders,* released in 2022 as an updated Text Revision of the fifth edition (**DSM-5-TR**).[2] Physicians and mental health workers use the detailed DSM-5-TR to guide diagnoses and treatment. The DSM-5-TR represents a *categorical* approach (symptoms are present or absent). For example, someone who meets all of the criteria in **TABLE 48.1** may be diagnosed with *insomnia disorder.* Other disorders, such as *posttraumatic stress disorder* and major depressive disorder require people to meet only a certain number of criteria to be diagnosed. The DSM-5-TR includes diagnostic codes from the World Health Organization's *International Classification of Diseases* (ICD), which makes it easy to track worldwide trends in psychological disorders.

In real-world tests *(field trials)* assessing the DSM-5 categories' reliability, some diagnoses fared well and others fared poorly (Freedman et al., 2013). Clinician agreement on adult posttraumatic stress disorder and childhood *autism spectrum disorder,* for example, was near 70 percent. (If one psychiatrist or psychologist diagnosed someone with one

TABLE 48.1 Insomnia Disorder

- Feeling unsatisfied with amount or quality of sleep (trouble falling asleep, staying asleep, or returning to sleep)
- Sleep disruption causes distress or diminished everyday functioning
- Happens three or more nights each week
- Occurs during at least three consecutive months
- Happens even with sufficient sleep opportunities
- Independent from other sleep disorders (such as narcolepsy)
- Independent from substance use or abuse
- Independent from other mental disorders or medical conditions

Information from: American Psychiatric Association (2022).

[2]Many examples in the psychological disorders modules were drawn from case studies in a previous DSM edition.

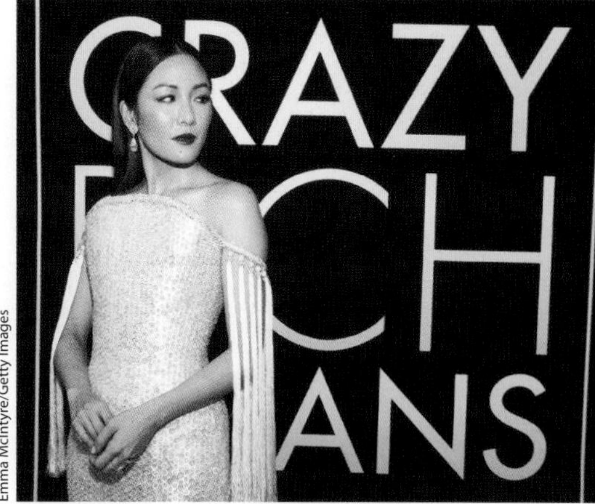
CRAZY
ANS

Emma McIntyre/Getty Images

Making a scene Actor Constance Wu has achieved acclaim for her roles in the television sitcom *Fresh Off the Boat* and the movies *Crazy Rich Asians* and *Hustlers.* She has also experienced mental health problems, which led her to attempt suicide. "Asian Americans don't talk about mental health enough," she said. "While we're quick to celebrate representation wins, there's a lot of avoidance around the more uncomfortable issues within our community" (Kim, 2022). In her memoir *Making a Scene,* she portrays how sexism and racism in Hollywood harm Asian American women's mental health (Wu, 2019).

Sidney Harris/Cartoon Stock

"I'm always like this, and my family was wondering if you could prescribe a mild depressant."

DSM-5-TR the American Psychiatric Association's *Diagnostic and Statistical Manual of Mental Disorders, Fifth Edition, Text Revision*; a widely used categorical system for classifying psychological disorders.

of these disorders, there was a 70 percent chance that another mental health worker would independently give the same diagnosis.) But for *antisocial personality disorder* and *generalized anxiety disorder,* agreement was closer to 20 percent.

Critics have long faulted the DSM for casting too wide a net and bringing "almost any kind of behavior within the compass of psychiatry" (Eysenck et al., 1983). Some worried that the DSM-5's (2013) even wider net would extend the pathologizing of everyday behavior. For example, the DSM-5 classified severe grief following the death of a loved one as a possible *depressive disorder.* Critics wondered whether such grief—which one grieving person described as "not a problem to be solved, but a process to be lived through"—might instead be considered a common human reaction to tragic life events (Perry, 2022). The DSM-5-TR (2022) responded to this concern with the newly classified *prolonged grief disorder,* diagnosed only when bereavement-related grief lasts more than a year (or 6 months for children and adolescents) and disrupts daily life. Yet grief varies in duration—for some 3 months, for some a year, and for some, a lifetime. "There is no uniform expiration date on normal grief," argue Joanne Cacciatore and Allen Francis (2022). "Pathologizing grief is an insult to the dignity of loving relationships."

A newer *dimensional* approach to classification (in which symptoms are present along a continuum) that builds on the DSM is the U.S. National Institute of Mental Health's Research Domain Criteria (RDoC) project (Cuthbert, 2022; NIMH, 2022). This dimensional approach argues that mental health problems are a common part of day-to-day life and that people who have one symptom of a disorder are just as worthy of receiving treatment as those who have all of a disorder's symptoms. The RDoC framework fosters "new research approaches that will lead to better diagnosis, prevention, intervention, and cures" (NIMH, 2022). Clinical psychologists, for example, may explore how neural, genetic, and childhood trauma factors influence the development of mental disorders (Damme et al., 2022; Li et al., 2022; Tiecher et al., 2022). Other dimensional approaches, such as the Hierarchical Taxonomy of Psychopathology (HiTOP), recognize different numbers of symptoms and the connections between disorders (Kotov et al., 2017).

"Portray [people with mental illness] sympathetically, and portray them in all the richness and depth of their experience as people, and not as diagnoses."—American legal scholar and professor Elyn Saks, diagnosed with schizophrenia (TED talk, A Tale of Mental Illness, 2012)

Other critics of classification register a more basic complaint—that diagnostic labels, whether categorical or dimensional, can be subjective or even value judgments masquerading as science. Once we label a person, we view that person differently. Labels can change reality by putting us on alert for evidence that confirms our view. If we hear that a new co-worker is mean-spirited, we may treat them suspiciously. They may, in turn, react to us as a mean-spirited person would. Ditto if we're led to believe that someone is smart. Teachers who were told certain students were "gifted" then acted in ways that elicited the behaviors they expected (Snyder, 1984). Labels can be self-fulfilling, and if negative, they convey a stigma.

The struggle is real Actor Dwayne "The Rock" Johnson has been vocal about his struggle with depression. "Struggle and pain is real," he said. "I was devastated and depressed" (Parker, 2018). He also "found that, with depression, one of the most important things you could realize is that you're not alone" (Mosbergen, 2015).

OTICE
NETFLIX
Kevin Mazur/Getty Images

In one study, therapists watched recorded interviews. If told the interviewees were job applicants, the therapists perceived the interviewees as typical people (Langer & Abelson, 1974; Langer & Imber, 1980). Other therapists who were told they were watching cancer or psychiatric patients perceived the same interviewees as "different from most people." Therapists who thought they were watching an interview of a psychiatric patient perceived him as "frightened of his own aggressive impulses," a "passive, dependent type," and so forth. People, especially in high-income countries, tend to stigmatize those with psychological disorders (Wüsten & Lincoln, 2022). Increasing mental health education, and promoting contact between those who have psychological disorders and those who do not, can reduce this stigma (Corrigan et al., 2012, 2014).

Labels also have power outside the laboratory. Getting a job or finding a place to rent can be a challenge for people recently released from a psychiatric hospital. Label someone as "mentally ill" and people may fear them as potentially violent. That reaction is fading as people increase their understanding of psychological disorders. Public figures have helped foster this understanding by speaking openly about their own struggles with disorders such as anxiety, depression, and substance abuse—and about how beneficial it was to seek help, receive a diagnosis, and get better through treatment.

So, labels matter. Despite their risks, diagnostic labels have benefits. They help mental health professionals communicate about their cases and study the causes and treatments of disorders. Clients are often relieved to learn that their challenges have a name, and that they are not alone in experiencing their symptoms.

ASK YOURSELF

Have you or someone you know been diagnosed with a psychological disorder? How do you think a diagnostic label has helped or hurt?

RETRIEVAL PRACTICE

RP-4 What is the value, and what are the dangers, of labeling people with disorders?

ANSWERS IN APPENDIX E

Risk of Harm to Self and Others

People with psychological disorders are more likely to harm themselves than are people without such disorders. Are they also more likely to harm others?

Understanding Suicide

LOQ 48-4 What factors increase the risk of suicide, and what do we know about nonsuicidal self-injury?

Each year some 160,000 Americans are among the drug, alcohol, or suicide "deaths of despair" (Case & Deaton, 2020). Have you ever, in a moment of despair, considered suicide? If so, you have much company. Among the many who entertain the thought, each year some 703,000 despairing people worldwide will complete the act, electing a permanent solution to what might have been a temporary problem (WHO, 2022a). Someone will likely die by suicide in the 40 or so seconds it takes you to read this paragraph.

For those who have been anxious, the risk of suicide is tripled, and for those who have been depressed, the risk is quintupled (Bostwick & Pankratz, 2000; Kanwar et al., 2013). Yet people seldom elect suicide while in the depths of depression, when energy and initiative are lacking. The risk increases when they begin to rebound and become capable of following through (Chu et al., 2016).

Comparing the suicide rates of different groups, researchers have found

- *national differences:* Guyana has more than double the suicide rate of the United States, which has double that of Spain (WHO, 2022b). Within Europe, Lithuanians have been five times more likely to die by suicide than Greeks.
- *racial differences:* Within the United States, White and Native American people die by suicide roughly twice as often as Black, Hispanic, and Asian people (Curtin & Hedegaard, 2019). The rate among Indigenous Canadians is triple that of other Canadians (Kumar & Tjepkema, 2019).
- *gender differences:* Women are much more likely than men to consider or attempt suicide. But worldwide, men are twice as likely to actually die by suicide (ONS, 2019; Ritchie et al., 2019; WHO, 2022b). The methods men use, such as firing a bullet into the head, are more lethal. In the United States, for example, only 13 percent of all suicide attempts end in death—but for those using firearms, that number mushrooms to 90 percent (Juskalian, 2019).
- *trait differences:* Suicidal thoughts increase when perfectionists feel driven to reach a goal or standard—to become thin or straight or rich—and find it unattainable (Chatard & Selimbegović, 2011; Smith et al., 2018).
- *age differences:* In late adulthood, rates increase worldwide, with the highest rate among those over age 70 (Ritchie et al., 2019).
- *other group differences:* Suicide rates have been much higher among the high-income, the nonreligious, and the unmarried (Chen et al., 2020; Norko et al., 2017; VanderWeele et al., 2016, 2017). Gay, transgender, and gender-nonconforming youth who face an unsupportive environment, including family or peer rejection, are also at increased risk of attempting suicide (Goldfried, 2001; Haas et al., 2011; Hatzenbuehler, 2011; Testa et al., 2017). One in two transgender adults has contemplated suicide, and one in four has attempted suicide (Adams & Vincent, 2019; Yockey et al., 2022).

"But life, being weary of these worldly bars,
Never lacks power to dismiss itself."
—William Shakespeare, *Julius Caesar*, 1599

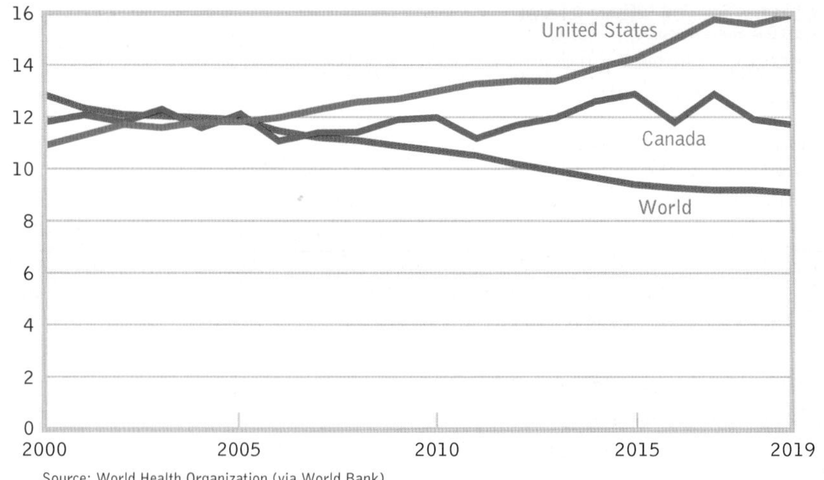

16
14
12
10
8
6
4
2
0
United States
Canada
World
2000
2005
2010
2015
2019
Source: World Health Organization (via World Bank)

FIGURE 48.2
Suicide death rates, 2000 to 2019 The annual number of suicide deaths per 100,000 people has trended downward worldwide, but upward in the United States (Ritchie et al., 2022).

- ***seasonal differences:*** Suicide rates are highest in April and May, and not (as commonly believed) over the winter holidays (Nock, 2016).
- ***year-by-year differences:*** In most countries, suicide deaths have been decreasing. But in the United States and Canada, suicide deaths have trended upward (**FIGURE 48.2**). For example, between 2009 and 2019, U.S. high school students' suicide rate increased by 62 percent (CDC, 2019; SAMHSA, 2019). (See the What Drives Us modules for a discussion of social media and teen mental health.)

Social suggestion may trigger suicidal thinking and behavior. One analysis of 17 million Twitter users' data showed that sharing suicidal thoughts had a ripple effect, spreading suicidal thinking through one's social network (Cero & Witte, 2020). Following highly publicized suicides and TV programs featuring suicide, rates of suicide sometimes increase (Niederkrotenthaler et al., 2019). Sometimes, suicide reverberates throughout a family tree. One 36-year Danish study tracked suicides among 4.4 million people between 1980 and 2016 (Ranning et al., 2022). People were 3.2 times more likely to die by suicide if exposed to a parent's suicide.

Suicide is rarely an act of hostility or revenge. People—especially older adults—may choose death as an alternative to current or future suffering, a way to switch off unendurable pain or relieve a perceived burden on family members. Suicidal urges typically arise when people feel like they don't belong or are a burden to others, when they feel demoralized, or when they are unable to experience joy (Chu et al., 2018; Costanza et al., 2022). Three examples of difficult life circumstances increasing suicide risk:

- The Covid-19 pandemic brought widespread unemployment and social isolation, and a tripling of suicidal thinking (CDC, 2020).
- Following the January 6, 2021, attack on the U.S. Capitol, four of its police officers died by suicide.
- In Britain, 35 percent of women attempting suicide had experienced intimate partner violence in the past year (McManus et al., 2022).

Suicide prevention Rapper Lil Nas X was the Trevor Project's 2021 Suicide Prevention Advocate of the Year. The Trevor Project, which works to prevent suicide and crisis among LGBTQ young people, cited Lil Nas X's mental health advocacy and openness about his sexual orientation and suicidal ideation.

MARIO ANZUONI/REUTERS/Alamy Stock Photo

In hindsight, families and friends may recall signs they believe should have forewarned them—verbal hints, giving possessions away, a sudden mood change, or withdrawal and preoccupation with death (Bagge et al., 2017). To judge from surveys of 84,850 people across 17 nations, about 9 percent of people at some point in their lives contemplate suicide. About 3 in 10 of those who think about it will actually attempt suicide; of those, fewer than 1 in 20 will die by suicide (Han et al., 2016; Nock et al., 2008; WHO, 2020).

Suicide is difficult to predict. Over the past 50 years, researchers have conducted hundreds of studies examining suicide risk factors, which have yielded little conclusive evidence on whether a person will die by suicide (Knipe et al., 2022). Today's researchers continue to try to solve the suicide puzzle with newer methods and technologies. Using an app that harvests phone data, investigative teams have gained clues to suicide risk by studying teen volunteers' tone of voice, language, photos, music choice, sleep disturbances, and angry words in text messages (Glenn et al., 2020; Servick, 2019). Other researchers are seeking to identify *epigenetic* marks that predict suicide death (Punzi et al., 2022). And still other research teams are developing suicide-predicting AI (artificial intelligence) algorithms using psychological assessments, health records, or social media posts (Ribeiro et al., 2019; Simon et al., 2018; Walsh et al., 2017).

About 46,000 Americans a year die by suicide, half using guns (CDC, 2022). (Poison and drug overdoses account for about 80 percent of suicide *attempts,* but only 14 percent of suicide fatalities.) U.S. states with high gun ownership are states with high suicide rates, even after controlling for poverty and urbanization (Siegel & Rothman, 2016). After Missouri repealed its tough handgun law, its suicide rate went up 15 percent; when Connecticut enacted such a law, its suicide rate dropped 16 percent (Crifasi et al., 2015). Thus, although U.S. gun owners often keep a gun to feel safer, having a gun in the home makes one less safe, because it substantially *increases* the odds of a family member dying by suicide or homicide (Miller et al., 2022; VPC, 2015; Vyse, 2016).

How can we be helpful to someone who is talking about suicide—who says, for example, "I wish I could just end it all" or "I hate my life; I can't go on"? If people write such things online, you can anonymously contact various social media safety teams (including on Facebook, Twitter, Instagram, YouTube, and Snapchat). If a classmate, friend, or family member talks about suicide, you can

1. ***listen,*** empathize, and offer hope;
2. ***connect*** the person with their campus counseling center; with (in the United States) the 988 Suicide & Crisis Lifeline (by dialing 988) or Crisis Text Line (by texting HOME to 741741); or with support services in other countries (such as CrisisServicesCanada.ca); and
3. ***protect*** someone who appears at immediate risk by seeking help from your campus health or counseling service, a doctor, the nearest hospital emergency room, or 911. Better to disclose a secret than to attend a funeral. Remain connected—online or in person—until the person gets the help they need.

"People desire death when two fundamental needs are frustrated to the point of extinction: The need to belong with or connect to others, and the need to feel effective with or to influence others." —Thomas Joiner (2006, p. 47)

By synthesizing the available evidence, experts have outlined a variety of strategies for community-based suicide prevention (**TABLE 48.2**). Developing and implementing policies and programs based on these strategies—involving the cooperation of educators, health care providers, government officials, and community activists—aims to enhance individual and community resilience, reducing suicide risk for all.

TABLE 48.2 Community-Based Suicide Prevention Strategies

Strategy	Example
Build economic security	Make sure people have enough money to meet their basic needs (food, shelter), such as by offering job skills training or public housing.
Ensure access to mental health care providers	Lobby health insurance companies to cover mental health conditions. Create programs in communities to ensure enough money to hire mental health care providers.
Create safe environments	Reduce access to firearms among people at risk of suicide. Create community policies to reduce excessive alcohol use.
Promote social connections	Promote programs that bring people together and foster a connection to the local community.
Teach coping and problem-solving skills	Offer free programs teaching parenting skills and relationship strategies.
Identify and support people at risk	Train people to identify warning signs of suicide risk in others and get them the help they need.
Prevent future risk	Encourage those at risk to regularly check in with mental health care providers.

Information from: Stone et al., 2017

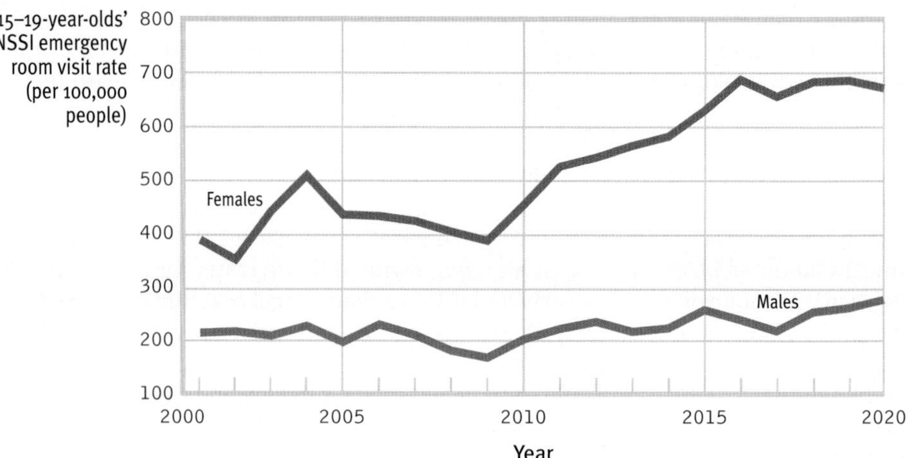
15–19-year-olds' NSSI emergency room visit rate (per 100,000 people)
800
700
600
500
400
300
200
100
Females
Males
2000
2005
2010
2015
2020
Year

FIGURE 48.3
Rates of U.S. nonsuicidal self-injury emergency room visits Self-injury rates peak higher for 15- to 19-year-old females than for same-age males (Mercado et al., 2017). Other countries, including Canada and England, have simultaneously experienced the same gender difference and upward trend (Ritchie et al., 2022).

Nonsuicidal Self-Injury

Self-harm takes many forms. Some people—mostly adolescents and females—engage in *nonsuicidal self-injury (NSSI)* (Mercado et al., 2017) (**FIGURE 48.3**). They may, for example, cut or burn their skin, hit themselves, or insert objects under their nails or skin.

Those who engage in NSSI often have experienced harassment, stress, or bullying (either as the target of bullies, or as bullies themselves) (Miller et al., 2019; Nesi et al., 2021). They are generally less able to tolerate and regulate emotional distress (Hamza et al., 2015). They are often both self-critical and impulsive (Beachaine et al., 2019; Cassels et al., 2020).

NSSI is often self-reinforcing (Cummings et al., 2021). People who engage in NSSI may

- find relief from intense negative thoughts through the distraction of pain.
- attract attention and possibly get help.
- relieve guilt by punishing themselves.
- get others to change their negative behavior (bullying, criticism).
- fit in with a peer group.

Does NSSI lead to suicide? Usually not. Those who engage in NSSI are typically suicide gesturers, not suicide attempters (Liu et al., 2022; Nock & Kessler, 2006). Nevertheless, NSSI is a risk factor for suicidal thoughts and future suicide attempts, especially when co-existing with a bipolar disorder (Geulayov et al., 2019). If people do not find help, their nonsuicidal behavior may escalate to suicidal thoughts and, finally, to suicide attempts. Thankfully, various forms of psychotherapy can benefit people who engage in NSSI (Prada et al., 2018; Turner et al., 2014).

Does Disorder Equal Danger?

LOQ 48-5 Do psychological disorders predict violent behavior?

September 16, 2013, started like any other Monday at the Navy Yard in Washington, DC, with people arriving early to begin work. Then government contractor Aaron Alexis entered the building and began shooting. An hour later, 13 people were dead—including Alexis, who had a history of mental illness and had earlier written that an "ultra low frequency attack is what I've been subject to for the last three months. And to be perfectly honest, that is what has driven me to this."

This mass shooting, like many others since, reinforced public perceptions that people with psychological disorders pose a threat (Barry et al., 2013; Jorm et al., 2012). "People with mental illness are getting guns and committing these mass shootings," said U.S. Speaker of the House Paul Ryan (2015). In one survey, 84 percent of Americans agreed that "increased government spending on mental health screening and treatment" would be a "somewhat" or "very" effective "approach to preventing mass shootings at schools" (Newport, 2012). "Anybody who shoots somebody else has a mental health challenge,"

ROBB
ELEMENTARY
SCHOOL

Eric Gay/AP Photo

Marco Bello/REUTERS/Alamy Stock Photo

Mental health and mass shootings Following mass shootings such as the 2022 Uvalde, Texas, slaughter of 19 schoolchildren and 2 adults, people wondered: Could mental health workers identify people who are violence-prone and remove their right to gun ownership? Not likely. Most homicide "is committed by healthy people in the grip of everyday emotions using guns" (Friedman, 2017).

said Texas Governor Greg Abbott in the aftermath of the 2022 Uvalde, Texas, school massacre (Hixenbaugh & Siemaszko, 2022).

Can clinicians indeed foretell who is likely to do harm? *No.* Most violent criminals and mass murderers are not mentally ill, and most mentally ill people are not violent (Brucato et al., 2021; Whiting et al., 2021). Moreover, clinical prediction of violence is unreliable. The few people with disorders who commit violent acts tend to be either those, like the Navy Yard shooter, who experience threatening delusions and hallucinated voices that command them to act, or those who abuse substances (Douglas et al., 2009; Elbogen et al., 2016; Fazel et al., 2009, 2010).

People with disorders are more likely to be *victims* than perpetrators of violence (Buchanan et al., 2019). According to the U.S. Surgeon General's Office (1999, p. 7), "there is very little risk of violence or harm to a stranger from casual contact with an individual who has a mental disorder." Better predictors of violence are alcohol or drug use, previous violence, gun availability, and—as in the case of the repeatedly head-injured and ultimately homicidal National Football League player Aaron Hernandez—brain damage (Belson, 2017). Mass-killing shooters have one more thing in common: They are mostly young males.

ASK YOURSELF

Why do you think people often believe those with psychological disorders are dangerous?

RETRIEVAL PRACTICE

RP-5 The presence of a gun in a home makes it less likely that a family member will die. True or false?

RP-6 Those with psychological disorders are more likely to be victims of violence rather than perpetrators of violence. True or false?

ANSWERS IN APPENDIX E

Rates of Psychological Disorders

LOQ 48-6 How many people have, or have had, a psychological disorder? What are some of the risk factors?

Who is most vulnerable to psychological disorders? At what times of life? To answer such questions, many countries have conducted lengthy structured interviews with their citizens. After asking hundreds of questions that probed for symptoms (for example, "Has there ever been a period of two weeks or more when you felt like you wanted to die?"), researchers have estimated the current, prior-year, and lifetime prevalence of various disorders. (See **TABLE 48.3**.)

Do rates of psychological disorder vary by place? The Global Burden of Disease Study estimated the prevalence of mental disorders in 204 countries and territories (GBD, 2022;

TABLE 48.3 Percentage in the U.S. Reporting Selected Psychological Disorders "in the Past Year"

Psychological Disorder	Percentage
Phobia of specific object or situation	9.1
Major depressive disorder	7.8
Social anxiety disorder	7.1
Attention-deficit/hyperactivity disorder (ADHD)	4.4
Posttraumatic stress disorder (PTSD)	3.6
Bipolar disorders	2.8
Generalized anxiety disorder	2.7
Obsessive-compulsive disorder (OCD)	1.2
Schizophrenia	< 0.5

Data from: National Institute of Mental Health (2018).

FIGURE 48.4). Cultures vary. For example, the highest rates of eating disorders are in high-income Monaco and Australia, and the lowest rates in low-income Somalia.

Moreover, immigrants to the United States from Mexico, Africa, and Asia averaged better mental health than their U.S.-born counterparts with the same ethnic heritage (Breslau et al., 2007; Maldonado-Molina et al., 2011). For example, compared with Mexican Americans born in the United States, Mexican Americans who have recently immigrated are less at risk for mental disorders—a phenomenon known as the *immigrant paradox* (Salas-Wright et al., 2018).

What increases vulnerability to mental disorders? As TABLE 48.4 indicates, there are various risk and protective factors for mental disorders. One predictor—poverty—crosses ethnic and gender lines. The incidence of serious psychological disorders is 2.5 times higher among those below the poverty line (CDC, 2014). This poverty-disorder correlation raises further questions: Does poverty cause disorders? Or do disorders cause poverty? The answer varies with the disorder. Schizophrenia understandably leads to poverty. Yet poverty can cause distress that increases the risk of certain disorders. A recession-related financial, job, or housing loss may produce lingering depression and anxiety (Forbes & Krueger, 2019).

TABLE 48.4 Risk and Protective Factors for Mental Disorders

Level	Risk factors	Protective factors
Individual attributes	Low self-esteem	Self-esteem, confidence
	Cognitive/emotional immaturity	Ability to solve problems and manage stress or adversity
	Difficulties in communicating	Communication skills
	Medical illness, substance use	Physical health, fitness
Social circumstances	Loneliness, bereavement	Social support of family and friends
	Neglect, family conflict	Good parenting/positive family interaction
	Exposure to violence/abuse	Physical security and safety
	Low income and poverty	Economic security
	Difficulties or failure at school	Scholastic achievement
	Work stress, unemployment	Satisfaction and success at work
Environmental factors	Poor access to basic services	Equality of access to basic services
	Injustice and discrimination	Social justice, tolerance, integration
	Social and gender inequalities	Social and gender equality
	Exposure to war or disaster	Physical security and safety

Information from WHO, 2012.

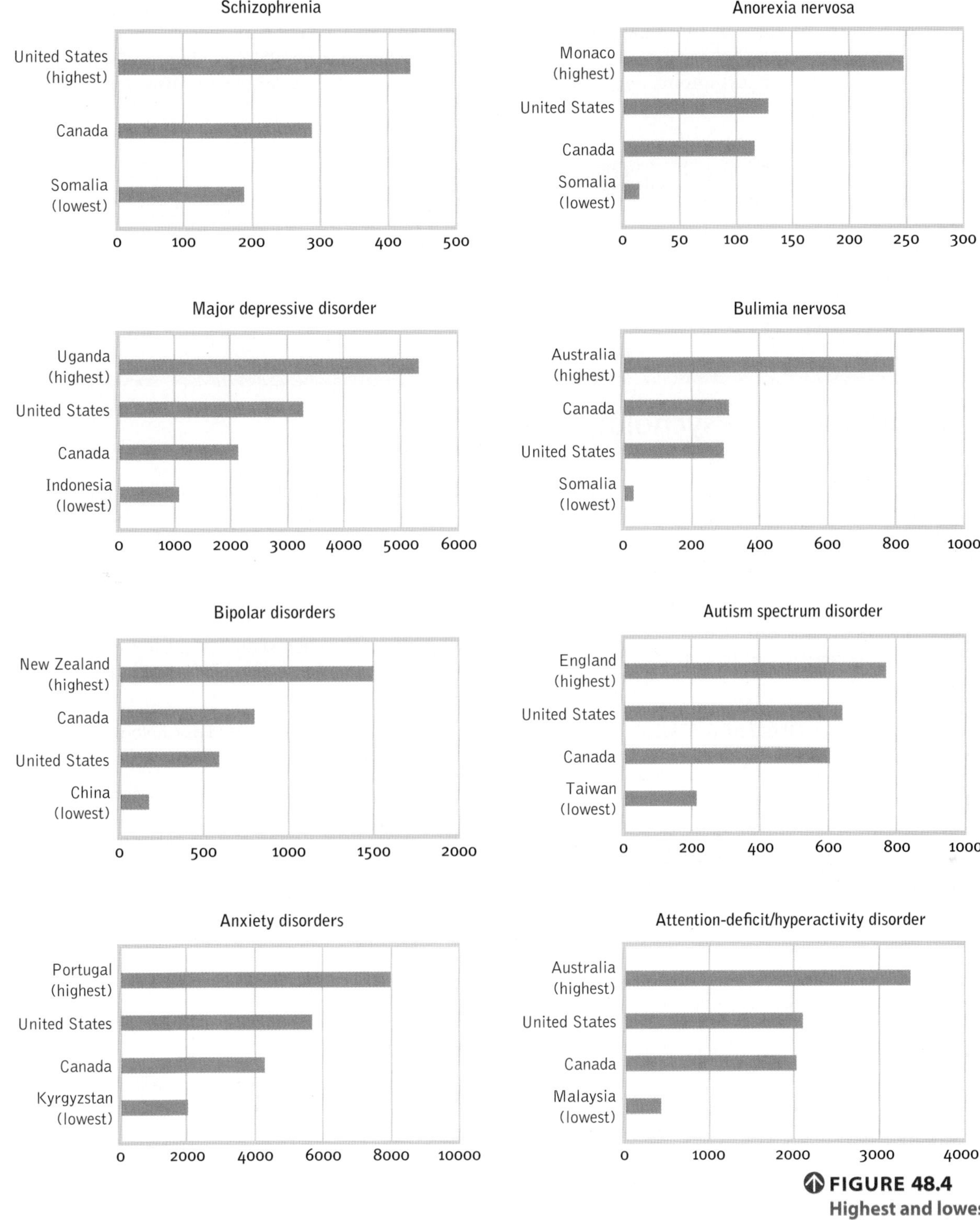
Schizophrenia
United States (highest)
Canada
Somalia (lowest)
0 100 200 300 400 500
Anorexia nervosa
Monaco (highest)
United States
Canada
Somalia (lowest)
0 50 100 150 200 250 300
Major depressive disorder
Uganda (highest)
United States
Canada
Indonesia (lowest)
0 1000 2000 3000 4000 5000 6000
Bulimia nervosa
Australia (highest)
Canada
United States
Somalia (lowest)
0 200 400 600 800 1000
Bipolar disorders
New Zealand (highest)
Canada
United States
China (lowest)
0 500 1000 1500 2000
Autism spectrum disorder
England (highest)
United States
Canada
Taiwan (lowest)
0 200 400 600 800 1000
Anxiety disorders
Portugal (highest)
United States
Canada
Kyrgyzstan (lowest)
0 2000 4000 6000 8000 10000
Attention-deficit/hyperactivity disorder
Australia (highest)
United States
Canada
Malaysia (lowest)
0 1000 2000 3000 4000

FIGURE 48.4
Highest and lowest rates of selected disorders worldwide These data, from an investigation of 204 countries and territories, show the number of cases per 100,000 people (controlling for age). The United States and Canada are shown for comparison. (Data from GBD, 2022.)

As economic development enabled a dramatic poverty-rate reduction for the North Carolina Eastern Band of Cherokee Indians, researchers saw the opportunity for a natural experiment that could investigate the poverty-pathology link. They tracked the community's rates of children's behavior problems over time. When the study began, children of poverty exhibited more deviant and aggressive behaviors. After 4 years, children whose families had moved above the poverty line exhibited a 40 percent decrease in behavior problems. But children whose families remained in poverty or were never in poverty exhibited no change (Costello et al., 2003).

At what times of life do disorders strike? About half of people with a disorder experience their first symptoms by the mid-teens, and three-quarters do so by the mid-twenties

(Kessler et al., 2007; Robins & Regier, 1991). Among the earliest to appear are the symptoms of antisocial personality disorder (median age 8) and of phobias (median age 10). Alcohol use disorder, obsessive-compulsive disorder, bipolar disorders, and schizophrenia symptoms appear at a median age near 20. Major depressive disorder often hits somewhat later, at a median age of 25.

RETRIEVAL PRACTICE

RP-7 What is the relationship between poverty and psychological disorders?

ANSWERS IN APPENDIX E

MODULE 48 REVIEW Introduction to Psychological Disorders

LEARNING OBJECTIVES

Test Yourself Answer these repeated Learning Objective Questions on your own (before "showing" the answers here, or checking the answers in Appendix D) to improve your retention of the concepts (McDaniel et al., 2009, 2015).

LOQ 48-1 How should we draw the line between typical behavior and a disorder?

LOQ 48-2 How do the medical model and the biopsychosocial approach influence our understanding of psychological disorders?

LOQ 48-3 How and why do clinicians classify psychological disorders, and why do some psychologists criticize diagnostic labels?

LOQ 48-4 What factors increase the risk of suicide, and what do we know about nonsuicidal self-injury?

LOQ 48-5 Do psychological disorders predict violent behavior?

LOQ 48-6 How many people have, or have had, a psychological disorder? What are some of the risk factors?

TERMS AND CONCEPTS TO REMEMBER

Test Yourself Write down the definition in your own words, then check your answer.

psychological disorder, p. 552
medical model, p. 554
epigenetics, p. 554
DSM-5-TR, p. 555

MODULE TEST

Test Yourself Answer the following questions on your own first, then "show" the answers here, or check your answers in Appendix E.

1. Two major disorders that are found worldwide are schizophrenia and ________________ ________________.
2. Robert is embarrassed that it takes him several minutes to parallel park his car. He usually gets out of the car once or twice to inspect his distance, both from the curb and from the nearby cars. Should he worry about having a psychological disorder?
3. A therapist says that psychological disorders are illnesses, and people with these disorders should be treated as patients in a hospital. This therapist's belief reflects the ________________ model.
4. What is an example of a culturally related psychological disorder?
5. Many psychologists reject the disorder-as-illness view and instead contend that other factors may also be involved—for example, the person's level of stress and ways of coping. This view represents the ________________ approach.
   a. medical
   b. epigenetics
   c. biopsychosocial
   d. diagnostic
6. Why is the DSM, and the DSM-5 in particular, considered controversial?
7. ________________ (Women/Men) are more likely than ________________ (women/men) to die by suicide.
8. The symptoms of ________________ appear around age 10; ________________ tend[s] to appear later, around age 25.
   a. schizophrenia; bipolar disorders
   b. bipolar disorders; schizophrenia
   c. major depressive disorder; phobias
   d. phobias; major depressive disorder

MODULE

49 Anxiety Disorders, Obsessive-Compulsive and Related Disorders, Trauma- and Stressor-Related Disorders, and Somatic Symptom and Related Disorders

Anxiety is part of life. Speaking in front of a class, peering down from a ladder, or waiting to learn the results of a final exam can make any of us feel anxious.

Anxiety can both help us and hurt us. Anxiety, it has been said, keeps us alive while also diminishing our living. A little anxiety prompts action and keeps us safe, but persistent anxiety can overwhelm and paralyze us. It may cause us to avoid talking or making eye contact—"shyness," we call it. Fortunately for most people, this uneasiness is neither intense nor persistent.

Some people, however, are especially prone to fearing the unknown and noticing and remembering perceived threats—as if living while horror-movie background music plays (Gorka et al., 2017; Mitte, 2008). When the brain's danger-detection system becomes hyperactive—with fearsome pop-up thoughts—we are at greater risk for an *anxiety disorder* and three other disorders involving anxiety: *obsessive-compulsive disorder (OCD)*, *posttraumatic stress disorder (PTSD)*, and the *somatic symptom disorders*.

Anxiety Disorders

LOQ 49-1 How do generalized anxiety disorder, panic disorder, and specific phobias differ?

The **anxiety disorders** are marked by distressing, persistent anxiety or by dysfunctional anxiety-reducing behaviors. For example, people with **social anxiety disorder** become extremely anxious in social settings where others might judge them, such as parties, class presentations, or even eating in public. People with social anxiety may experience palpitations, tremors, blushing, and sweating when giving a presentation, taking an exam, or meeting an authority figure, fearing embarrassment or rejection. By avoiding eye contact or staying home, they can temporarily avoid anxious feelings. But in the long run, such strategies are maladaptive: Avoiding others prevents them from learning to cope and leaves them feeling lonely (Günther et al., 2021; Oren-Yagoda et al., 2022; Rapee et al., 2022).

Let's take a closer look at three other anxiety disorders:

- *generalized anxiety disorder,* in which a person, for no apparent reason, worries about many different things they cannot control and is continually tense and uneasy;
- *panic disorder,* in which a person experiences one or more *panic attacks*—sudden episodes of intense dread and "fight or flight" arousal—and fears a future panic attack; and
- *specific phobias,* in which a person is intensely and excessively afraid of a specific object, activity, or place.

Generalized Anxiety Disorder

For two years, Tom, a 27-year-old electrician, was bothered by dizziness, sweating palms, and heart palpitations. He felt on edge and sometimes found himself shaking. Tom mostly hid his symptoms from his family and co-workers. But he allowed himself few other social contacts, and occasionally he felt so anxious he would leave work. Neither his family doctor nor a neurologist could find any physical problem.

Tom's experiences suggest **generalized anxiety disorder**, which is marked by excessive and uncontrollable worry that persists for 6 months or more. People with this condition (two-thirds are women) worry continually, and they are often jittery, agitated, and sleep-deprived (McLean & Anderson, 2009). Their *autonomic nervous system* arousal may

anxiety disorders a group of disorders characterized by excessive fear and anxiety and related maladaptive behaviors.

social anxiety disorder intense fear and avoidance of social situations.

generalized anxiety disorder an anxiety disorder in which a person is continually tense, apprehensive, and in a state of autonomic nervous system arousal.

panic disorder an anxiety disorder marked by unpredictable, minutes-long episodes of intense dread in which a person may experience terror and accompanying chest pain, choking, or other frightening sensations; often followed by worry over a possible next attack.

specific phobia an anxiety disorder marked by a persistent, irrational fear and avoidance of a specific object, activity, or situation.

leak out through furrowed brows, twitching eyelids, trembling, perspiration, or fidgeting. Concentration suffers, as everyday worries demand continual attention. Emotions can feel overwhelming, confusing, and hard to manage (Mennin et al., 2005).

Those affected usually cannot identify, relieve, or avoid their anxiety. To use Sigmund Freud's term, the anxiety is *free-floating* (not linked to a specific stressor or threat). Generalized anxiety disorder often co-occurs with a depressed mood. But even without depression, generalized anxiety disorder tends to be disabling. Moreover, it may lead to physical problems, such as high blood pressure. As time passes, however, emotions tend to mellow, and by age 50, generalized anxiety disorder becomes relatively rare (Rubio & López-Ibor, 2007).

© Walt Disney Pictures/Entertainment Pictures/Alamy Stock Photo

Understanding panic At age 7, actor Emma Stone started having panic attacks. While playing at a friend's house, she became convinced that the house was on fire. "There was nothing in me that didn't think we were going to die," she said (Gonzalez, 2018). Therapy and meditation have helped Stone cope with her anxiety. Today, she says, publicly discussing her anxiety helps her "own it and realize that this is something that is part of me but it's not who I am."

Panic Disorder

Some people experience intense anxiety that escalates into a terrifying panic attack—a several-minutes-long episode of intense fear that something horrible is about to happen. The body's fight-or-flight system goes into overdrive: Irregular heartbeat, chest pains, shortness of breath, choking, trembling, or dizziness may accompany the panic. One woman recalled suddenly feeling

> hot and as though I couldn't breathe. My heart was racing and I started to sweat and tremble and I was sure I was going to faint. Then my fingers started to feel numb and tingly and things seemed unreal. It was so bad I wondered if I was dying and asked my husband to take me to the emergency room. By the time we got there (about 10 minutes) the worst of the attack was over and I just felt washed out (Greist et al., 1986).

For the 3 percent of people with **panic disorder**, panic attacks recur. These anxiety tornados strike suddenly, wreak havoc, and disappear, but are not forgotten. Ironically, worries about anxiety—perhaps fearing another panic attack, or fearing anxiety-related symptoms in public—can amplify anxiety symptoms (Olatunji & Wolitzky-Taylor, 2009). After several panic attacks, people may avoid situations where panic might strike (**FIGURE 49.1**). People with panic disorder are two to three times more likely than the general population to think about or attempt suicide (Zhang et al., 2022).

If their fear is intense enough, people with panic disorder may also develop *agoraphobia*—fear or avoidance of public situations from which escape might be difficult. People with agoraphobia may avoid being outside the home, in a crowd, or at a coffee shop or grocery store. Smokers have at least a doubled risk of panic disorder and greater symptoms when they do have an attack (Knuts et al., 2010; Zvolensky & Bernstein, 2005). Because nicotine is a stimulant, lighting up doesn't lighten us up.

Charles Darwin began experiencing panic disorder at age 28, after spending 5 years sailing the world. He moved to the country, avoided social gatherings, and traveled only in his wife's company. But the relative seclusion did free him to elaborate his evolutionary theory. "Even ill health," he reflected, "has saved me from the distraction of society and its amusements" (quoted in Ma, 1997).

Specific Phobias

We all live with some fears. But people with **specific phobias** are consumed by a persistent, excessive fear and avoidance of some object, activity, or place—for example, animals, insects, heights, blood, or enclosed spaces (**FIGURE 49.2**). Many people avoid the

FIGURE 49.1
A person who experiences four or more of the symptoms noted here may be having a *panic attack* (APA, 2022). They may be diagnosed with a *panic disorder* if a disruptive fear of future panic attacks persists for a month or more (and if the symptoms are not better explained by substance use, a medical condition, or another mental disorder).

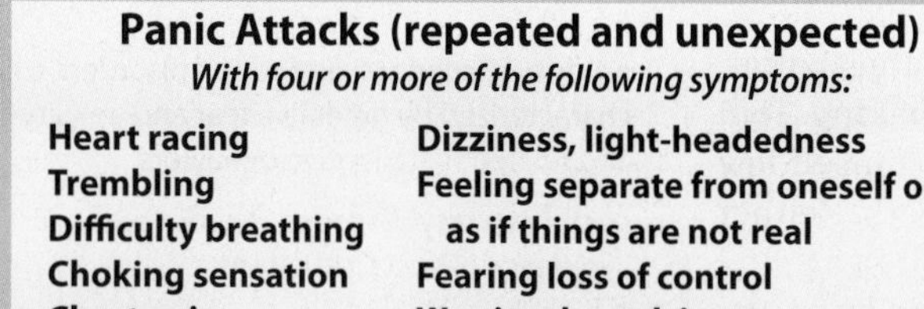
Panic Attacks (repeated and unexpected)
With four or more of the following symptoms:
Heart racing
Trembling
Difficulty breathing
Choking sensation
Chest pain
Sweating
Hot flashes/chills
Dizziness, light-headedness
Feeling separate from oneself or as if things are not real
Fearing loss of control
Worries about dying
Intestinal distress or nausea
Feelings of numbness or tingling
+

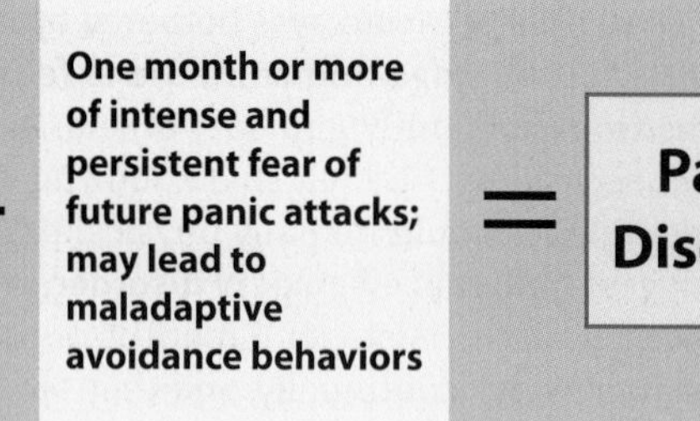
One month or more of intense and persistent fear of future panic attacks; may lead to maladaptive avoidance behaviors
=

Panic Disorder

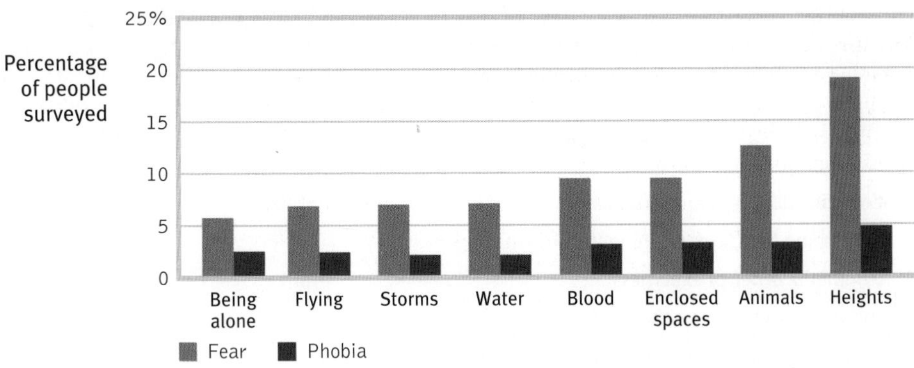
25%
20
15
10
5
0
Percentage of people surveyed
Being alone
Flying
Storms
Water
Blood
Enclosed spaces
Animals
Heights
Fear
Phobia

FIGURE 49.2
Some common specific fears Researchers surveyed Dutch people to identify the most common events or objects they feared. An intense fear becomes a specific phobia if it provokes a compelling, irrational desire to avoid the dreaded object or situation. (Data from Depla et al., 2008.)

triggers (such as high places) that arouse their fear, and they manage to live with their phobia. Others are incapacitated. Marilyn, an otherwise healthy and happy 28-year-old, feared thunderstorms so much that she felt anxious as soon as a weather forecaster mentioned possible storms later in the week. If her husband was away when a storm was forecast, she often stayed with a close relative. During a storm, she hid from windows and buried her head to avoid seeing the lightning.

RETRIEVAL PRACTICE

RP-1 Unfocused tension, apprehension, and arousal are symptoms of ______ ______ disorder.

RP-2 Those who experience unpredictable periods of terror and intense dread, accompanied by frightening physical sensations, may be diagnosed with ______ disorder.

RP-3 If a person is focusing anxiety on specific feared objects, activities, or situations, that person may have a ______ ______.

ANSWERS IN APPENDIX E

Obsessive-Compulsive and Related Disorders

LOQ 49-2 What is *OCD*?

Obsessive-compulsive and related disorders are characterized by the presence of obsessions and compulsions. *Obsessive thoughts* are unwanted, intrusive, and persistent. *Compulsive behaviors* are responses to those thoughts. As with the anxiety disorders, we can see aspects of **obsessive-compulsive disorder (OCD)** in our everyday behavior.

We are all at times obsessed with thoughts, and we may behave compulsively. Have you ever felt a bit anxious about how your living space will appear to others and found yourself checking and cleaning one last time before your guests arrived? Or, perhaps worried about an upcoming exam, you caught yourself lining up your study materials "just so" before studying? Our everyday lives are full of little rehearsals and fussy behaviors. They cross the fine line between "typical" and "disordered" only when they *persistently interfere* with everyday living and cause distress. Checking that you locked the door is typical; checking 10 times is not. (**TABLE 49.1** offers more examples.) At some time during their lives, often during their late teens or early adulthood, about 2 percent of people cross that line from typical preoccupations and fussiness to debilitating disorder (Kessler et al., 2012). Although people know their anxiety-fueled obsessive thoughts are irrational, the thoughts can become so haunting, and the compulsive rituals so intensely time-consuming, that effective functioning—including healthy sleep and school success—becomes nearly impossible (Pérez-Vigil et al., 2018; Segal & Carmona, 2022).

OCD is more common among teens and young adults than among older people (Samuels & Nestadt, 1997). A 40-year follow-up study of 144 Swedes diagnosed with the disorder found that, for most, the obsessions and compulsions had gradually lessened, though only 1 in 5 had completely recovered (Skoog & Skoog, 1999).

Kelly Sullivan/Getty Images

Writing with OCD Author John Green's personal experience with obsessive-compulsive disorder informed his novel, *Turtles All the Way Down* (Flood, 2017). Green explained: "It's like there is an invasive weed that just spreads out of control. It starts out with one little thought and then slowly that becomes the only thought that you're able to have, the thought that you're . . . trying desperately to distract yourself from" (Gross, 2018).

obsessive-compulsive disorder (OCD) a disorder characterized by unwanted and repetitive thoughts (obsessions), actions (compulsions), or both.

posttraumatic stress disorder (PTSD) a disorder characterized by haunting memories, nightmares, hypervigilance, avoidance of trauma-related stimuli, social withdrawal, jumpy anxiety, numbness of feeling, and/or insomnia that lingers for 4 weeks or more after a traumatic experience.

trauma- and stressor-related disorders a group of disorders in which exposure to a traumatic or stressful event is followed by psychological distress.

TABLE 49.1 Common Obsessions and Compulsions Among Children and Adolescents With Obsessive-Compulsive Disorder

Thought or Behavior	Percentage Reporting Symptom
Obsessions (repetitive *thoughts*)	
Concern with dirt, germs, or toxins	40
Something terrible happening (fire, death, illness)	24
Symmetry, order, or exactness	17
Compulsions (repetitive *behaviors*)	
Excessive hand washing, bathing, toothbrushing, or grooming	85
Repeating rituals (in/out of a door, up/down from a chair)	51
Checking doors, locks, appliances, car brakes, homework	46

Data from: Rapoport, 1989.

Lila Ash/Cartoon Stock

"Wait—did you wash your hands?"

Some people experience other OCD-related disorders, such as *hoarding disorder* (cluttering their space with acquired possessions they can't part with), *body dysmorphic disorder* (preoccupation with perceived body defects; repeatedly checking their appearance in the mirror), *trichotillomania* (hair-pulling disorder), or *excoriation* (skin-picking) *disorder*. Many people have some clutter in their living space or feel sensitive about their appearance. But for these common behaviors and feelings to be considered an OCD-related disorder, they must occur frequently and disrupt people's lives—their social life, work, or daily functioning.

Trauma- and Stressor-Related Disorders

LOQ 49-3 What is *PTSD*?

While serving overseas, one soldier, Jesse, saw the killing "of children and women. It was just horrible for anyone to experience." Back home, he experienced "real bad flashbacks" (Welch, 2005). Jesse is not alone. In one study of 104,000 veterans returning from Iraq and Afghanistan, 25 percent were diagnosed with a psychological disorder (Seal et al., 2007). The most frequent diagnosis was **posttraumatic stress disorder (PTSD)**, one of the **trauma- and stressor-related disorders**. Survivors of terror, torture, sexual assault, earthquakes, and refugee displacement have also exhibited PTSD (Charlson et al., 2016; Nichter et al., 2022). The hallmark symptoms are recurring vivid, distressing memories and nightmares. PTSD also often entails laser-focused attention on possible threats, social withdrawal, and jumpy anxiety (Clauss et al., 2022; Fried et al., 2018). To cope with PTSD symptoms, people sometimes engage in harmful alcohol use (Luciano et al., 2022).

Many of us will experience a traumatic event at some point in our lives. Yet most people, after traumatic experiences, display *resiliency* by returning to their baseline of healthy functioning (Galatzer-Levy et al., 2018). During the early months of the Covid pandemic, people's self-reported anxiety and depression rose sharply, and then—displaying human resilience—subsided (Banks et al., 2021; Fancourt et al., 2021).

PTSD in Parkland In the 2018 Parkland, Florida, school shooting, Samantha Fuentes (at right) witnessed friends dying, and shrapnel struck her face and legs. She later reported PTSD symptoms, including a fear of returning to the school, and jumping at the sound of a slammed door. Two other student survivors died by suicide in 2019, including one diagnosed with PTSD (Mazzei, 2019).

MARCH
FOR OUR
LIVES

Chip Somodevilla/Getty Images

Although philosopher Friedrich Nietzsche's (1889/1990) idea that "what does not kill me makes me stronger" is not true for all, about half of trauma survivors report *posttraumatic growth*—marked by a greater appreciation for life and its close relationships, more compassion, or increased spirituality and life purpose (X. Wu et al., 2019). The trauma remains a negative, but it can change one's perspective for the better. Sometimes, tears enable triumphs.

Why do some 5 to 10 percent of people develop PTSD after a traumatic event while others do not (Bonanno et al., 2011)? Multiple factors, including personality and social support, matter. One important influence is the amount of emotional distress: The higher the distress (such as the level of physical torture suffered by prisoners of war), the greater the risk for posttraumatic symptoms (King et al., 2015; Ozer et al., 2003). In a study of child survivors of the 2020 Beirut port explosion—which killed 200 people and injured 7,000—children who were near the blast (compared to children who were in the region, but far from the site of the catastrophe) had quadruple the risk of a subsequent PTSD diagnosis (Maalouf et al., 2022).

What else influences PTSD development? Individual differences in memory processing matter. In memory testing of people affected by a Paris terror attack, those who experienced PTSD exhibited more difficulty inhibiting unwanted memories than did those not experiencing PTSD (Mary et al., 2020).

Fadel Itani/NurPhoto/Alamy Stock Photo

Closeness to terror In the 2020 Beirut port explosion (pictured here), the 2001 terrorist attack in New York, and the 2011 massacre at a Norwegian summer camp, the closer survivors were to the heart of the terror, the more likely PTSD became (Bonanno et al., 2006; Glad et al., 2020).

Exposure to violence also increases the risk of experiencing PTSD. African American and Puerto Rican people who experienced repeated violent crime, such as being threatened with a weapon or assaulted, also faced a higher-than-average risk of experiencing PTSD (Pahl et al., 2020). Other studies show that 1 in 4 U.S. college women experience sexual assault, and those who were assaulted had a higher-than-average risk of PTSD (AAU, 2020; Dworkin et al., 2017).

Some people may have a more sensitive emotion-processing limbic system that floods their bodies with stress hormones (Duncan et al., 2017; Kosslyn, 2005). Genes and gender also matter. Twins, compared with nontwin siblings, more commonly share PTSD risk factors (Gilbertson et al., 2006). And after a traumatic event, women experience PTSD more often than do men (Olff et al., 2007; Ozer & Weiss, 2004).

Some psychologists believe that PTSD has been overdiagnosed (Dobbs, 2009; McNally, 2003). Too often, say critics, PTSD gets stretched to include typical stress-related bad memories and dreams. And some well-intentioned procedures—such as "debriefing" people by asking them to revisit the experience and vent their emotions immediately after the traumatic event—may worsen stress reactions (Bonanno et al., 2010; Wakefield & Spitzer, 2002).

RETRIEVAL PRACTICE

RP-4 Those who experience unwanted repetitive thoughts or actions may have ____________-____________ disorder.

RP-5 Those with symptoms of recurring memories and nightmares, social withdrawal, jumpy anxiety, numbness of feeling, and/or insomnia for weeks after a traumatic event may be diagnosed with ____________ ____________ disorder.

ANSWERS IN APPENDIX E

Somatic Symptom and Related Disorders

LOQ 49-4 What is a *somatic symptom disorder*?

Among the common problems bringing people into doctors' offices are "medically unexplained illnesses" (Johnson, 2008). Earl becomes dizzy and nauseated shortly before he expects his wife home. Neither his primary care physician nor a neurologist can identify a physical cause. They suspect his symptoms have an unconscious psychological origin, possibly triggered by his feelings about his wife. Earl has a **somatic symptom disorder** (formerly known as *somatoform disorder*).

We have all experienced inexplicable physical symptoms under stress. Being told the problem is "all in your head" gives no comfort. Although the symptoms may be psychological in origin, they are genuinely felt. One person may have a variety of complaints—vomiting, dizziness, blurred vision, difficulty swallowing. Another may experience severe and prolonged pain. Such symptoms become a disorder when they are associated with significant distress and impaired functioning.

Cultural context greatly affects people's physical complaints and how they explain them (Kirmayer & Sartorius, 2007). In China, anxiety disorders are the most common psychological disorder (Huang et al., 2019). Yet psychological explanations of anxiety and depression are socially less acceptable there than in many Western countries, so people less often

somatic symptom disorder a psychological disorder in which the symptoms take a somatic (bodily) form without apparent physical cause.

express the emotional aspects of distress. The Chinese appear more sensitive to—and more willing to report—the physical symptoms of their distress (Ryder et al., 2008).

Somatic symptom and related disorders send people not to a psychologist or psychiatrist but to a physician. This is especially true of those who experience **illness anxiety disorder** (previously called *hypochondriasis*). People with this relatively common disorder interpret normal sensations (a stomach cramp today, a headache tomorrow) as symptoms of a dreaded disease. No amount of reassurance by any physician convinces the patient that the trivial symptoms do not reflect a serious illness. So, the patient moves on to another physician—seeking and receiving more medical attention, but failing to confront the disorder's psychological roots. Other patients with illness anxiety disorder cope with their fears by avoiding medical care.

ASK YOURSELF

Can you recall (as most people can) times when you have fretted needlessly over a normal bodily sensation?

RETRIEVAL PRACTICE

RP-6 What does *somatic* mean, and how does it apply to a *somatic symptom disorder*?

ANSWERS IN APPENDIX E

Understanding Anxiety Disorders, Obsessive-Compulsive and Related Disorders, Trauma- and Stressor-Related Disorders, and Somatic Symptom and Related Disorders

LOQ 49-5 How do learning, cognition, and biology contribute to the feelings and thoughts that mark anxiety disorders, OCD, PTSD, and somatic symptom disorders?

Anxiety is a feeling. It is also a cognition—a doubt-laden self-evaluation. How do these anxious feelings and thoughts arise? Most psychologists attribute them to learning, cognition, and biology.

Learning

Through *classical conditioning* (see Learning modules), our fear responses can become linked with formerly neutral objects and events. To understand the link between learning and anxiety, researchers have given lab rats unpredictable electric shocks (Schwartz, 1984). The rats were like assault survivors who report feeling anxious when returning to the scene of the crime: They learned to become uneasy in their lab environment.

Likewise, anxious or traumatized people learn to associate their anxiety with certain cues (Christian & Levinson, 2022). In one survey, 58 percent of those with social anxiety disorder experienced their disorder after a traumatic event (Öst & Hugdahl, 1981). Anxiety or an anxiety-related disorder is more likely to develop when bad events happen unpredictably and uncontrollably (Field, 2006; Mineka & Oehlberg, 2008). Black people residing in the United States and Canada who experience frequent racial discrimination—a type of bad event that is both unpredictable and out of their control—are at greater risk of anxiety (Paradies et al., 2015; Kogan et al., 2022). Even a single painful and frightening event may trigger a full-blown phobia, thanks to classical conditioning's *stimulus generalization* and operant conditioning's *reinforcement*.

Stimulus generalization occurs when a person experiences a fear-provoking event and later develops a fear of similar events. My [DM's] car was once struck by a driver who missed a stop sign. For months afterward, I felt a twinge of unease when any car approached from a side street. Combat veterans exposed to frequent explosions may experience panic attacks and flashbacks at the sound of fireworks.

Reinforcement helps maintain learned fears and anxieties. Anything that enables us to avoid or escape a feared situation can reinforce maladaptive behaviors. Fearing a panic

illness anxiety disorder a disorder in which a person interprets normal physical sensations as symptoms of a disease. (Formerly called *hypochondriasis*.)

attack, we may decide not to leave the house. Reinforced by feeling calmer, we are likely to repeat that behavior (Antony et al., 1992). So, too, with compulsive behaviors. If washing our hands relieves our feelings of anxiety, we may rewash our hands when those feelings return.

Cognition

Conditioning influences our feelings of anxiety, but so do our thoughts, memories, interpretations, and expectations. By observing others, we can learn to fear what they fear. Nearly all monkeys raised in the wild fear snakes, but lab-raised monkeys do not. Surely, most wild monkeys do not actually suffer snake bites. Do they learn their fear through observation?

To find out, Susan Mineka (1985, 2002) experimented with six monkeys raised in the wild (all strongly fearful of snakes) and their lab-raised offspring (virtually none of which feared snakes). After repeatedly observing the wild-raised monkeys refuse to reach for food in the presence of a snake, the lab-raised monkeys developed a similar strong fear of snakes that persisted when retested 3 months later. We humans similarly learn fears by observing others (Helsen et al., 2011; Olsson et al., 2007).

Although it pays to be alert to dangers, anxiety is often a response to the "fake news" we produce ourselves. One study that followed people with anxiety disorders found that more than 9 in 10 of their worries proved groundless (LaFreniere & Newman, 2020). Such people tend to be *hypervigilant*. They more often *interpret* stimuli as threatening (Everaert et al., 2018). A pounding heart signals a heart attack; a lone spider indicates an infestation; an everyday disagreement with a friend spells a doomed relationship. And they more often *remember* threatening events (Van Bockstaele et al., 2014). Anxiety is especially common when people cannot switch off such intrusive thoughts and feel helpless (Franklin & Foa, 2011).

ASK YOURSELF

What is a fear that you have learned? How were conditioning or cognition involved?

Biology

Conditioning and cognition can't explain all aspects of anxiety disorders, OCD, or trauma-related disorders like PTSD. Our biology also plays a role. Physically stronger people, for example, tend to be less anxious (Kerry & Murray, 2021). And men, who are often physically stronger than women, also tend to live with less self-protective anxiety (Benenson et al., 2021; Courtright et al., 2013).

GENES Among monkeys, fearfulness runs in families. A monkey reacts more strongly to stress if its close biological relatives are anxiously reactive (Suomi, 1986). So, too, with people. Although twins, in general, are not at higher risk for disorders, if one identical twin has an anxiety disorder, the other is also at risk (Polderman et al., 2015). Even when raised separately, identical twins may develop similar specific phobias (Carey, 1990; Eckert et al., 1981). One pair of separated identical twins independently became so afraid of water that each would wade into the ocean backward and only up to her knees. Another pair of twins with OCD rarely left their house, took hours-long showers, used five bottles of disinfecting rubbing alcohol daily, and, tragically, died together in an apparent suicide pact (Schmidt, 2018).

Given the genetic contribution to anxiety disorders, researchers are sleuthing the culprit genes. Researchers have identified gene variations associated with typical anxiety disorder symptoms (Purves et al., 2020). Other teams have found genes associated specifically with OCD or PTSD (Girgenti et al., 2021; Lin et al., 2022). But remember that behavior is typically influenced by *many genes each having small effects*. Thus, large-scale research further explores how the whole of our genome predicts anxiety (Smoller, 2020).

Some genes may influence anxiety disorders by regulating brain levels of neurotransmitters. These neurotransmitters include

- *serotonin,* which influences sleep, mood, and attending to threats;
- *glutamate,* which heightens activity in the brain's alarm centers; and
- GABA, which inhibits neural activity to produce a calming effect (Pergamin-Hight et al., 2012; Ross et al., 2021; Welch et al., 2007).

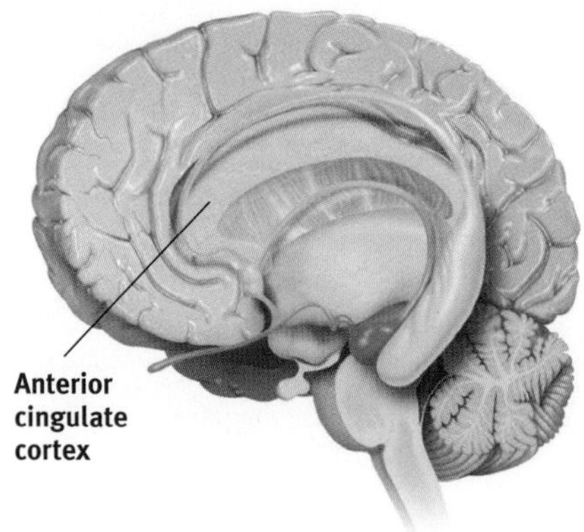
Anterior cingulate cortex

FIGURE 49.3
An obsessive-compulsive brain When people engaged in a challenging cognitive task, those with OCD showed the most activity in the anterior cingulate cortex in the brain's frontal lobe (Maltby et al., 2005).

So genes matter. Some people have genes that make them like orchids—fragile, yet capable of beauty under favorable circumstances. Others are like dandelions—hardy, and able to thrive in varied circumstances (Ellis & Boyce, 2008; Pluess & Belsky, 2013).

But experience affects gene expression. A history of wartime trauma or child abuse can leave long-term *epigenetic marks*. These molecular tags attach to our chromosomes and turn certain genes on or off. Thus, traumatic experiences can increase the likelihood that a genetic vulnerability to a disorder such as PTSD will be expressed (Wang et al., 2022; Zannas et al., 2015).

THE BRAIN Our experiences change our brain, paving new pathways. Traumatic fear-learning experiences can leave tracks in the brain, altering fear circuits within the amygdala (Couette et al., 2022; Kredlow et al., 2022). These fear pathways create easy inroads for more fear experiences (Armony et al., 1998).

Social anxiety disorder, generalized anxiety disorder, panic attacks, specific phobias, OCD, and PTSD express themselves biologically as overarousal of brain areas involved in impulse control and habitual behaviors. These disorders reflect the brain's danger-detection system gone hyperactive—producing anxiety when little danger exists. In OCD, for example, when the brain detects that something is amiss, it seems to generate a mental hiccup of repeating thoughts (obsessions) or actions (compulsions) (Gehring et al., 2000). Brain scans of people with OCD reveal elevated activity in specific brain areas during behaviors such as compulsive hand washing, checking, organizing, or hoarding (Insel, 2010; Mataix-Cols et al., 2004, 2005). The *anterior cingulate cortex*, a brain region that monitors our actions and checks for errors, is often especially hyperactive (Chavanne & Robinson, 2021) (**FIGURE 49.3**).

Some antidepressant drugs dampen this fear circuit activity and its associated obsessive-compulsive behavior. Fears can also be blunted by giving people drugs as they recall and then rerecord ("reconsolidate") a traumatic experience (Kindt et al., 2009; Norberg et al., 2008). Although they don't forget the experience, the associated emotion is largely erased.

NATURAL SELECTION We seem biologically prepared to fear threats faced by our ancestors. Our specific phobias focus on particular fears such as spiders, snakes, and other animals; enclosed spaces and heights; storms and darkness. Those fearless about these occasional threats were less likely to survive and leave descendants. Nine-month-old infants attend more to sounds signaling ancient threats (hisses, thunder) than they do to sounds representing modern threats (a bomb exploding, breaking glass) (Erlich et al., 2013). It is easy to condition and hard to extinguish fears of such "evolutionarily relevant" stimuli (Coelho & Purkis, 2009; Davey, 1995; Öhman, 2009). Some of our modern fears (such as of flying) can also have an evolutionary explanation (a biological predisposition to fear confinement and heights).

Just as our specific phobias sometimes focus on dangers faced by our ancestors, so our compulsive acts typically exaggerate behaviors that contributed to our species' survival. Grooming had survival value. Gone wild, it becomes compulsive hair pulling. Washing up becomes relentless hand washing. And securing territorial boundaries becomes checking and rechecking already locked doors (Rapoport, 1989).

Fearless The biological perspective helps us understand why most people fear heights more than Alex Honnold does. In 2017, he became the first person to free solo (climb without safety ropes) Yosemite National Park's massive El Capitan granite wall. (*Free Solo*, a documentary about this feat, won a 2019 Oscar.) When psychologist Jane Joseph showed Honnold fear-inducing images in the lab, an fMRI scan found his fear-processing amygdala minimally responsive (Donovan, 2019). (The red and yellow indicate increased amygdala activation in the control subject—also a rock climber—while Honnold's brain shows less activation in that region.)

Peter Bohler/Redux Pictures

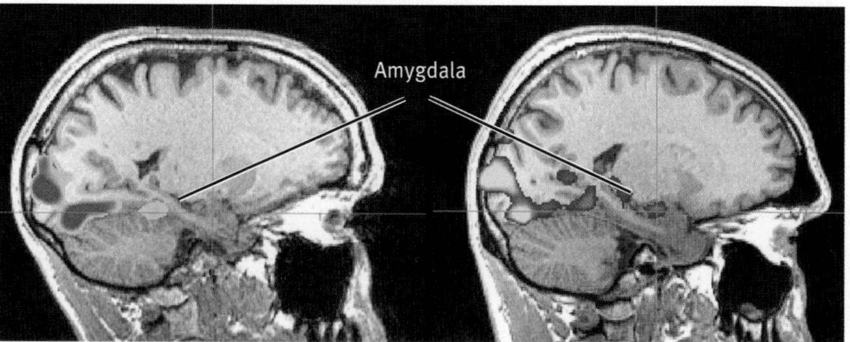
Amygdala
Alex Honnold
Control subject
Jane E. Joseph

RETRIEVAL PRACTICE

RP-7 In addition to conditioning and cognition, what *biological* factors contribute to anxiety disorders, OCD, PTSD, and somatic symptom disorders?

ANSWERS IN APPENDIX E

MODULE 49 REVIEW Anxiety Disorders, Obsessive-Compulsive and Related Disorders, Trauma- and Stressor-Related Disorders, and Somatic Symptom and Related Disorders

LEARNING OBJECTIVES

Test Yourself Answer these repeated Learning Objective Questions on your own (before "showing" the answers here, or checking the answers in Appendix D) to improve your retention of the concepts (McDaniel et al., 2009, 2015).

LOQ **49-1** How do generalized anxiety disorder, panic disorder, and specific phobias differ?

LOQ **49-2** What is *OCD*?

LOQ **49-3** What is *PTSD*?

LOQ **49-4** What is a *somatic symptom disorder*?

LOQ **49-5** How do learning, cognition, and biology contribute to the feelings and thoughts that mark anxiety disorders, OCD, PTSD, and somatic symptom disorders?

TERMS AND CONCEPTS TO REMEMBER

Test Yourself Write down the definition in your own words, then check your answer.

anxiety disorders, p. 565
social anxiety disorder, p. 565
generalized anxiety disorder, p. 565
panic disorder, p. 566
specific phobia, p. 566
obsessive-compulsive disorder (OCD), p. 567
posttraumatic stress disorder (PTSD), p. 568
trauma- and stressor-related disorders, p. 568
somatic symptom disorder, p. 569
illness anxiety disorder, p. 570

MODULE TEST

Test Yourself Answer the following questions on your own first, then "show" the answers here, or check your answers in Appendix E.

1. An episode of intense dread that can be accompanied by chest pains, choking, or other frightening sensations is called
   a. an obsession.
   b. a compulsion.
   c. a panic attack.
   d. a specific phobia.
2. Anxiety that takes the form of an irrational and maladaptive fear of a specific object, activity, or situation is called a ________ ________.
3. Marino became consumed with the need to clean the entire house and refused to participate in any other activities. His family consulted a therapist, who diagnosed him as having ________-________ disorder.
4. When a person with an anxiety disorder eases anxiety by avoiding or escaping a situation that inspires fear, this is called
   a. free-floating anxiety.
   b. reinforcement.
   c. an epigenetic mark.
   d. hypervigilance.
5. The learning perspective proposes that specific phobias are
   a. the result of individual genetic makeup.
   b. a way of repressing unacceptable impulses.
   c. conditioned fears.
   d. a symptom of having been abused as a child.

MODULE 50 Depressive Disorders and Bipolar Disorders

LOQ **50-1** How do depressive disorders and bipolar disorders differ?

What separates depression from sadness? We feel sad when bad things happen—a poor exam grade, a breakup, a job loss. But when feelings of despair or emptiness last for weeks (or even months), psychologists consider this more than just ordinary sadness—it may be depression.

"The first thing that goes is happiness. You cannot gain pleasure from anything."
—Andrew Solomon, *The Noonday Demon: An Atlas of Depression*, 2001

"My life had come to a sudden stop. I was able to breathe, to eat, to drink, to sleep. I could not, indeed, help doing so; but there was no real life in me." —Leo Tolstoy, *My Confession*, 1887

Have you ever been diagnosed with depression? If so, you are not alone. In one national survey, 27 percent of U.S. college students answered *Yes* (ACHA, 2022). If depressed, you might feel deeply discouraged about the future, dissatisfied with your life, or socially isolated. You may lack the energy to get things done, to see people, or even to force yourself out of bed. You may be unable to concentrate or eat. You may struggle to fall or stay asleep (Pan et al., 2022). Occasionally, you may think about death and even wonder if you would be better off gone (Li et al., 2022). Perhaps academic success came easily to you before, but now you find that disappointing grades jeopardize your perfectionist goals (Levine et al., 2020). Maybe loneliness or a romantic breakup has plunged you into despair. And perhaps low self-esteem increases your brooding, worsening your self-torment (Orth et al., 2016). Comparing yourself to seemingly happy, successful others on social media, you may think it's just you feeling this way (Jordan et al., 2011). Most of us will have some direct or indirect experience with depression: Misery has more company than we think.

As anxiety can be a response to the threat of future loss, depression is often a response to past and current stress, such as family traumas or repeatedly experienced racism (Chen et al., 2022; Hankerson et al., 2022; Macjejewski et al., 2021). To feel bad in reaction to profoundly sad events, such as the loss of a friend or family member, is to be in touch with reality. In such times, depression is like a car's low-fuel light—a signal to stop and take appropriate measures. As one book title reminds us, there are "good reasons for bad feelings."

"If someone offers you a pill that would make you happy 100 percent of the time, you should run fast in the other direction. . . . What good is a compass if it's always stuck on north?" —Daniel Gilbert (Lambert, 2007)

People with *major depressive disorder,* however, experience hopelessness and lethargy that doesn't always match the situation, and that lasts several weeks or months (Rottenberg & Hindash, 2015). *Persistent depressive disorder* (also called *dysthymia*) is similar, but with milder depressive symptoms that last 2 years or more. Those with *bipolar disorders* (formerly called *manic-depressive disorder*) alternate between depression and overexcited hyperactivity.

"Depression is a silent, slow motion tsunami of dark breaking over me." —Effy Redman, "Waiting for Depression to Lift," 2017

Biologically speaking, life's purpose is not constant happiness but survival and reproduction. Coughing, vomiting, and pain protect the body from dangerous toxins and stimuli. Similarly, depression compels us to slow us down and conserve energy (Beck & Bredemeier, 2016; Gershon et al., 2016). When we grind temporarily to a halt and reassess our life, as depressed people do, we can consider how to redirect our energy in ways that may reduce our depression (Watkins, 2008). There can be sense to some suffering.

Even temporary sadness helps people process and recall faces more accurately (Hills et al., 2017). Sadness can also help us be more cooperative, compassionate, and attuned to others (Gruber et al., 2011; Ong et al., 2017). It can enhance our critical thinking (and lessen our chances of being fooled) by increasing our attention to details (Forgas, 2009, 2013, 2017). Bad moods sometimes serve good purposes. But sometimes depression becomes seriously maladaptive. How do we recognize the fine line between a blue mood and a depressive disorder?

NEUROTOPLEX
1 MY INSECURITIES
2 MY INNER GUILT
3 MY SELF-LOATHING
4 MY PARENTS

Jack Ziegler/Cartoon Stock

Depression involves multiple symptoms.

ASK YOURSELF

Has student life ever made you feel down or depressed? What advice would you have for new students (perhaps advice you wish someone had given to you)?

major depressive disorder a disorder in which a person experiences five or more symptoms lasting 2 or more weeks. In the absence of drug use or a medical condition, at least one symptom must be either (1) depressed mood or (2) loss of interest or pleasure.

depressive disorders a group of disorders characterized by an enduring sad, empty, or irritable mood, along with physical and cognitive changes that affect a person's ability to function.

Depressive Disorders

Joy, contentment, sadness, and despair are different points on a continuum—points at which any of us may be found at any given moment. The difference between a blue mood after bad news and **major depressive disorder**—the most common of the **depressive disorders**—is like the difference between breathlessness after climbing a few flights of stairs and chronic breathing problems (**TABLE 50.1**).

Depression varies. You can be depressed in different ways and for different amounts of time. You can be depressed for 2 weeks or more, in the case of major depressive disorder, or for a much longer time (but with milder symptoms) in the case of persistent depressive disorder. You might feel unusually depressed a week before your menses

TABLE 50.1 Diagnosing Major Depressive Disorder

The DSM-5-TR classifies major depressive disorder as the presence of at least five of the following symptoms over 2 weeks (must include depressed mood or reduced interest) (American Psychiatric Association, 2022).
• Depressed mood most of the time
• Dramatically reduced interest or enjoyment in most activities most of the time
• Significant challenges regulating appetite and weight
• Significant challenges regulating sleep
• Physical agitation or lethargy
• Feeling listless or with much less energy
• Feeling worthless, or feeling unwarranted guilt
• Problems in thinking, concentrating, or making decisions
• Thinking repetitively of death and suicide

bipolar disorders disorders in which a person experiences the overexcited state of mania (or milder hypomania), and usually experiences periods of depression. (Formerly called *manic-depressive disorder.*)

mania an unusually excited and overly ambitious mood state in which people show dangerously poor judgment, less need for sleep, and increased energy (part of bipolar disorders).

(premenstrual dysphoric disorder), experience parts of depression and anxiety at the same time *(mixed anxiety-depressive disorder)*, or feel depressed alongside severe irritability that starts at a young age *(disruptive mood dysregulation disorder)* (American Psychiatric Association, 2022).

Depression—the number-one reason people seek mental health services—is "a global health crisis," according to a World Psychiatric Association commission (Herrman et al., 2022). In surveys conducted in 15 countries, 5 percent of people reported experiencing a major depressive episode during the prior year (Vigo et al., 2022). U.S. rates were even higher, with 17 percent of adolescents and 8 percent of adults experiencing such an episode (SAMHSA, 2021). Worldwide, depression levels rose dramatically during the Covid-19 pandemic (Zhang & Chen, 2021). Younger adults, women, medical workers, people of color, and those who were unemployed were hardest hit (Fitzpatrick et al., 2020; Gruber et al., 2021; Rossi et al., 2020; Twenge & Joiner, 2020). Michelle Obama (2020) spoke for many: "There have been periods throughout this quarantine where I just have felt too low. . . . I am dealing with some form of low-grade depression."

NEWS 4 U
DEPRESSION CURED!
TURNS OUT WE JUST NEEDED TO "CHEER UP"

If only it were so easy.

Bipolar Disorders

People with **bipolar disorders** have periods of extremely excited mood and increased energy that can last several days or more. Like depressive disorders, bipolar disorders take different forms depending on how severe the symptoms are and how long they last (see FIGURE 50.1). People with *bipolar I disorder*, the most severe form, experience a euphoric, talkative, highly energetic and overly ambitious state called **mania** that lasts a week or longer. Psychiatrist Kay Redfield Jamison described her mania: "When you're high it's tremendous. The ideas and feelings are fast and frequent like shooting stars, and you follow them until you find better and brighter ones" (Jamison, 1996).

But before long, many people with bipolar I disorder can plunge into depression. Sometimes they go back and forth, experiencing *rapid cycling* between the highs and lows. Those with *bipolar II disorder* move between depression and a milder *hypomania*.

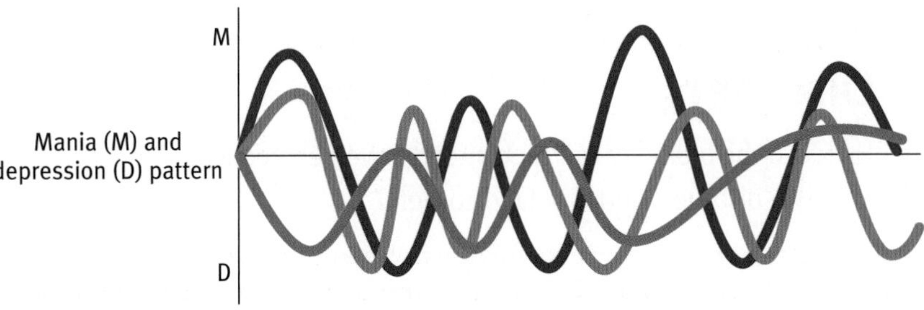
M
Mania (M) and depression (D) pattern
D
Time
Bipolar type I
Bipolar type II
Major Depressive Disorder

FIGURE 50.1 Mood fluctuation in bipolar disorders, compared with major depressive disorder For those with major depressive disorder, moods move up and down but barely make it above the midline. For those with bipolar I, there is deeper depression than for major depressive disorder, along with dramatic swings into mania. Those with bipolar II experience similar depression but less severe mania (called hypomania).

Pills make you weak
Can't you just calm down?
Stop feeling so sorry for yourself
I don't get why you can't just act normal
Don't you have pills for this?
I keep trying to help you but you don't want it
Life as a Two-Headed Beast
BIPOLAR
What do you have to be depressed about?
What's wrong with you?
You're deluded

Life as a Two-Headed Beast: Bipolar, Abigail Southworth

Bipolar disorders Artist Abigail Southworth illustrated her experience of a bipolar disorder.

If depression is living in slow motion, mania is fast forward. Thinking fast feels good, but it also increases risk-taking (Chandler & Pronin, 2012; Pronin, 2013). During the manic phase, people with a bipolar disorder typically have less need for sleep. They show fewer sexual inhibitions. They set overly ambitious goals—like becoming famous or winning the Nobel Prize—and rarely follow through with them (Johnson, 2005). They may be excited and highly positive, no matter what the circumstances (Gruber, 2011). They have trouble regulating their emotions, which can lead to inappropriately persistent positive emotions (Gruber et al., 2019; Miola et al., 2022). Their speech is rapid, flighty, and hard to interrupt. They may ignore advice. Yet they might need assistance to prevent them from engaging in harmful behaviors, such as out-of-control spending, too-fast driving, or unsafe sex.

Dave Bedrosian/ZUMA Press/Newscom

Axelle/Bauer-Griffin/Getty Images

Creativity and bipolar disorders There have been many creative artists, composers, writers, and musical performers with a bipolar disorder. Some, like Russell Brand, have also developed a substance use disorder. Others struggle secretly, as did Mariah Carey for 17 years.

Mania's energy and flood of ideas can fuel creativity. Genes associated with high creativity increase the likelihood of a bipolar disorder, and risk factors for developing a bipolar disorder predict greater creativity (Taylor, 2017). George Frideric Handel (1685–1759), who may have experienced a bipolar disorder, composed his nearly 3-hour-long *Messiah* (1742) during 3 weeks of intense, creative energy (Keynes, 1980). Robert Schumann composed 51 musical works during 2 years of mania (1840 and 1849) but none during 1844, when he experienced severe depression (Slater & Meyer, 1959). Composers, artists, poets, novelists, and entertainers seem especially prone to bipolar disorders (Jamison, 1993, 1996; Kaufman & Baer, 2002; Ludwig, 1995). Indeed, one analysis of over a million people showed that the only psychiatric condition linked to working in a creative profession was a bipolar disorder (Kyaga et al., 2013).

People in the United States are more likely than people in other countries to have been diagnosed with a bipolar disorder, especially among adolescents (GBD, 2022; Merikangas et al., 2011). From 2000 to 2010, U.S. children and adolescents were an astonishing 72 times more likely than English adolescents to receive a bipolar disorder diagnosis (James et al., 2014). The DSM-5-TR (2022) classifications became stricter, resulting in a reduced number of child and adolescent bipolar diagnoses.

Understanding Depressive Disorders and Bipolar Disorders

LOQ 50-2 How can the biological and social-cognitive perspectives help us understand depressive disorders and bipolar disorders?

Today's psychologists continue to investigate why people have depressive disorders and bipolar disorders, and to design more effective treatments and prevention strategies. Here, we focus on major depressive disorder. One research group summarized the facts that any theory of depression must explain (Lewinsohn et al., 1985, 1998, 2003):

- ***Behaviors and thoughts change with depression.*** People in a depressed mood become inactive and feel alone, empty, and without a meaningful future. They have more negative thoughts about themselves *(I am a failure),* the world *(everything is worthless),* and the future *(the future is hopeless).* Depression may be triggered by a sad or stressful event (LeMoult, 2020). Yet even when nothing bad happens, people with major depressive disorder often feel a heavy sadness. They also recall and expect negative happenings (my team will lose, my grades will fall, my love will fail) (Zetsche et al., 2019).
- ***Depression is widespread, with women everywhere at greater risk.*** Worldwide, 280 million people have depressive disorders and 40 million people have a bipolar disorder (WHO, 2022). There is, however, a considerable depression *gender gap.* Globally, women's risk for major depressive disorder is roughly double men's (GBD, 2022). The gap is especially pronounced among adolescent girls (Kuehner, 2017; see also **FIGURE 50.2**). In general, women are more vulnerable to disorders involving internal states, such as depression, anxiety, and inhibited sexual desire. Women also experience more situations that increase their risk for depression, such as receiving less pay for equal work, experiencing sexual harassment and assault, juggling multiple roles, and more often caring for children and older family members (Freeman & Freeman, 2013). Men's disorders tend to be more external—alcohol use disorder, and disorders related to antisocial conduct and lack of impulse control. Women often get sadder than men do; men often get madder than women do.
- ***Depression sometimes returns.*** For many people, depression comes and, after sustained struggle, it often goes. But for about half of these people, the depression returns (Curry et al., 2011; Klein & Kotov, 2016). For about 20 percent, the condition will be chronic (Klein, 2010).
- ***Stress and negative events often precede depression.*** About 1 person in 4 diagnosed with depression has experienced significant loss or trauma, such as a loved one's death, a ruptured marriage, a physical assault, or a lost job (LeMoult, 2020). Moving to a new culture also increases risk for depression, especially among younger people who have not yet formed their identities (Zhang et al., 2013). And childhood maltreatment and emotional abuse doubles a person's risk of later adult depression (Nelson et al., 2017).
- ***Compared with generations past, depression strikes earlier and more often, with the highest rates among older teens and young adults*** (Cross-National Collaborative Group, 1992; Kessler et al., 2010; Olfson et al., 2015). From 2010 to 2020, depression rates doubled among U.S. 12- to 17-year-olds (SAMHSA, 2021).
- ***Most people with depression can recover on their own and thrive.*** Therapy often speeds recovery. But even without professional help, many people recover amazingly well, do not experience future depression, and achieve "optimal well-being" (Rottenberg & Kashdan, 2022). An enduring recovery is more likely if: The first episode strikes later in life, there were no previous episodes, the person experiences minimal physical or psychological stress, and there is ample social support (Fuller-Thomson et al., 2016).

FIGURE 50.2
Worldwide gender gap in depression
Teen depression—especially among girls—has risen sharply since 2010 (see the What Drives Us modules). Researchers Rachel Salk, Janet Hyde, and Lyn Abramson (2017) found that, compared with males, females have twice the risk of depression, and a tripled rate during early adolescence. For many girls, the early teen years are tough.

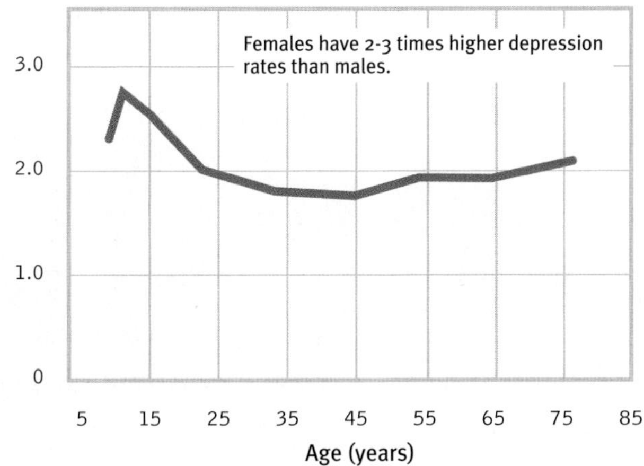
Female-to-male depression ratio
3.0
2.0
1.0
0
Females have 2-3 times higher depression rates than males.
5
15
25
35
45
55
65
75
85
Age (years)

The Biological Perspective

Depression is a whole-body disorder. It involves genetic predispositions and biochemical imbalances, as well as negative thoughts and a gloomy mood.

GENETIC INFLUENCES Major depressive disorder and bipolar disorders run in families. As one researcher noted, emotions are "postcards from our genes" (Plotkin, 1994). The risk of being diagnosed with one of these disorders increases if your parent or sibling has the disorder

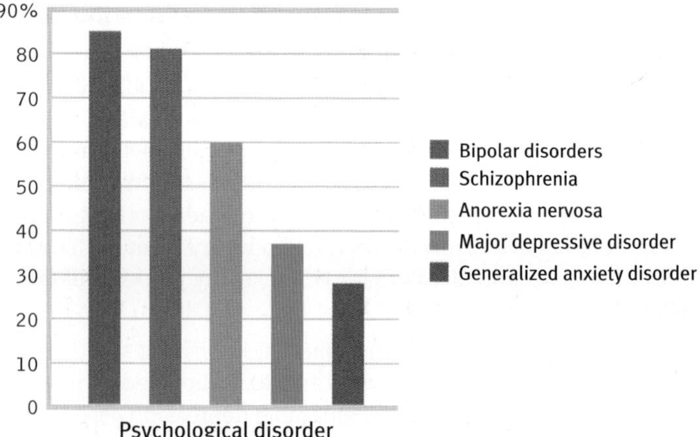
90%
80
70
60
50
40
30
20
10
0
Heritability estimates (percentage of variation due to genetic influence)
Psychological disorder
Bipolar disorders
Schizophrenia
Anorexia nervosa
Major depressive disorder
Generalized anxiety disorder

FIGURE 50.3
The heritability of various psychological disorders Using aggregated data from studies of identical and fraternal twins, researchers estimated the heritability of bipolar disorders, schizophrenia, anorexia nervosa, major depressive disorder, and generalized anxiety disorder (Bienvenu et al., 2011). (Heritability was calculated by a formula that compares the extent of similarity among identical versus fraternal twins.)

(Sullivan et al., 2000; Weissman et al., 2016). If one identical twin is diagnosed with major depressive disorder, the chances are about 1 in 2 that at some time the other twin will be, too. If one identical twin has a bipolar disorder, the chances of a similar diagnosis for the co-twin are even higher—7 in 10—even for twins raised apart (DiLalla et al., 1996).

Summarizing the major twin studies, two research teams independently estimated the *heritability*—the extent to which individual differences are attributable to genes—of major depressive disorder at nearly 40 percent (Kendler et al., 2018; Polderman et al., 2015; see also **FIGURE 50.3**). But nurture matters, too. A Swedish national study examined children who had a biological parent with depression. In families where at least one child was raised by the parent with depression and another child was adopted into a different family, those raised in the adoptive homes "had a significantly reduced risk for major depression" (Kendler et al., 2020).

To tease out the genes that put people at risk for depression, researchers may use *linkage analysis*. First, geneticists find families in which the disorder appears across several generations. Next, the researchers look for differences in DNA from affected and unaffected family members. Linkage analysis points them to a chromosome neighborhood; "A house-to-house search is then needed to find the culprit gene" (Plomin & McGuffin, 2003). But depression is a complex condition. *Many genes* work together, each producing small effects that interact with other factors to increase depression risk. Today's researchers are analyzing the entire human genome to identify genetic variations in depressive and bipolar disorders that may open the door to more personalized and effective drug therapy (Howard et al., 2019; Palmer et al., 2022; Peterson, 2021).

BRAIN STRUCTURE AND ACTIVITY Nearly 150 studies have identified unique brain circuitry linked with depression (Zhukovsky et al., 2021). Neuroscientists have also discovered altered brain structures in people with a bipolar disorder, including thin frontal lobes and enlarged fluid-filled ventricles (Angelescu et al., 2021; Zhu et al., 2022).

Scanning devices offer a window into the brain's activity during depressed and manic states. One study gave 13 elite Canadian swimmers the wrenching experience of watching a video of the swim in which they failed to make the Olympic team or failed at the Olympic games (Davis et al., 2008). Functional MRI scans showed the disappointed swimmers experiencing brain activity patterns similar to those of people with depressed moods.

Many studies have found diminished brain activity during slowed-down depressive states, and more activity during periods of mania (**FIGURE 50.4**). Depression can cause the brain's reward centers to become less active, whereas bipolar mania can increase activity in these centers (Dutra et al., 2015; Nusslock et al., 2012).

At least two neurotransmitter systems are at work during the periods of altered brain activity that accompany major depressive disorder and bipolar disorders.

FIGURE 50.4
The ups and downs of a bipolar disorder These top-facing PET scans show that brain energy consumption rises and falls with the patient's emotional changes. Red areas are where the brain rapidly consumes *glucose*, an important energy source.

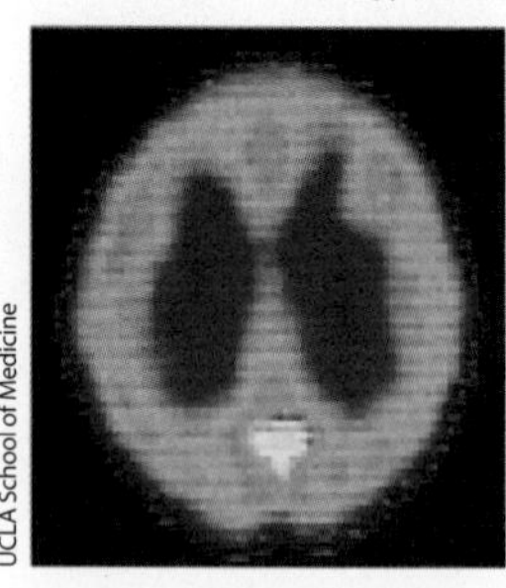
Depressed state (May 17)

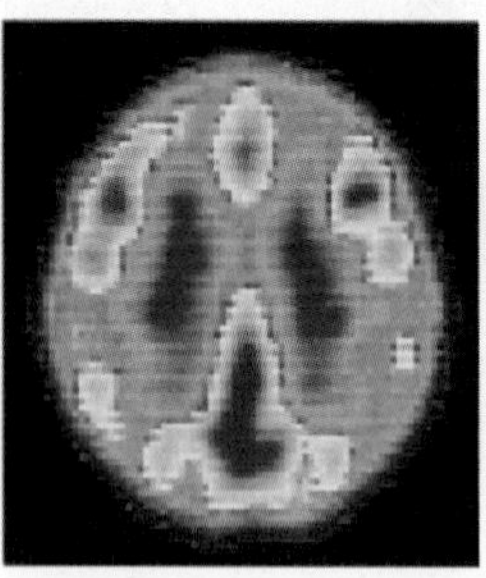
Manic state (May 18)

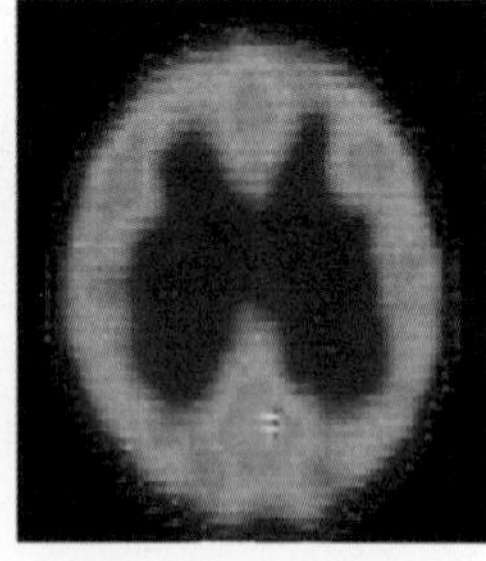
Depressed state (May 27)

Norepinephrine, which increases arousal and boosts mood, is scarce during depression and overabundant during mania. Drugs that decrease mania reduce norepinephrine. *Serotonin* is also often scarce or inactive during depression, increasing when depression fades (Carver et al., 2008; Svensson et al., 2021). The story of neurotransmitters is still being written, as other researchers have begun to question the reliability of associations between neurotransmitter levels and depression (Moncrieff et al., 2022).

Drugs that relieve depression tend to increase norepinephrine or serotonin supplies by blocking either their reuptake (as Prozac, Zoloft, and Paxil do with serotonin) or their chemical breakdown. Repetitive physical exercise, such as jogging, reduces depression in part because it increases serotonin, which affects mood and arousal (Wipfli et al., 2011; Morres et al., 2019). To run away from a bad mood, some people use their own two feet.

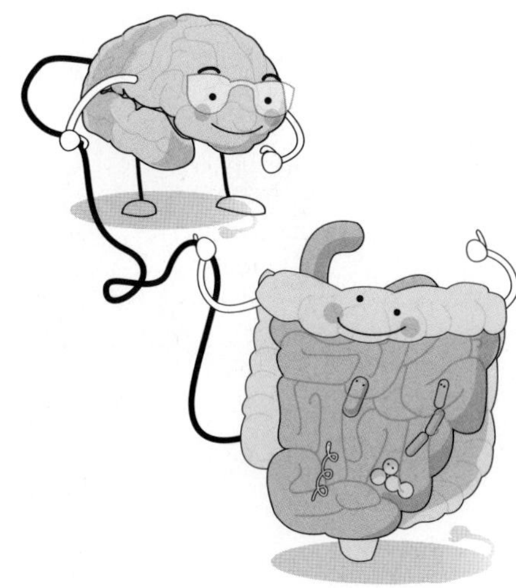

Minding the gut Does food modify mood? Digestive system bacteria produce serotonin and other neurotransmitters that influence emotions. Although some researchers think the happy gut/happy brain relationship is overhyped, healthy, diverse gut microbes predict less risk of anxiety, depression, and bipolar disorders (Nikolova et al., 2021). There is, it seems, a biochemistry behind "gut feelings."

NUTRITIONAL EFFECTS Certain foods, such as refined sugar and red meat, have been linked to *inflammation* (a persistent immune response that can affect many body systems). Inflammation and depression often go hand in hand (Mousten et al., 2022; Osimo et al., 2019). Conversely, what's good for the body is also good for the brain and mind. People who eat a healthy "Mediterranean diet" (heavy on vegetables, fish, whole grains, and olive oil) reduce inflammation levels, thereby diminishing their risk of depression (Kaplan et al., 2015; Psaltopoulou et al., 2013; Rechenberg, 2016). Excessive alcohol use also correlates with depression, partly because depression can increase alcohol use but mostly because alcohol misuse *leads* to depression (Fergusson et al., 2009).

The Social-Cognitive Perspective

Biological influences contribute to depression, but in the nature–nurture dance, our life experiences also play a part. Diet, drugs, stress, and other environmental influences lay down epigenetic marks, those molecular genetic tags that can turn certain genes on or off. Animal studies suggest long-lasting epigenetic influences on depression (Nestler, 2011).

Thinking matters, too. The *social-cognitive perspective* explores how people's assumptions and expectations influence what they perceive. Many depressed people have intensely negative views of themselves, their situation, and their future (Nieto et al., 2020). Norman, a Canadian university professor, recalled his depression this way:

> I [despaired] of ever being human again. I honestly felt subhuman, lower than the lowest vermin. Furthermore, I was self-deprecatory and could not understand why anyone would want to associate with me, let alone love me. . . . I was positive that I was a fraud and a phony and that I didn't deserve my Ph.D. . . . I didn't deserve the research grants I had been awarded; I couldn't understand how I had written books and journal articles. . . . I must have conned a lot of people. (Endler, 1982, pp. 45–49)

Expecting the worst, depressed people magnify bad experiences and minimize good ones (Wenze et al., 2012). Their *self-defeating beliefs* and their *negative explanatory style* feed their depression.

NEGATIVE THOUGHTS AND NEGATIVE MOODS Do you agree or disagree with this statement: "I feel frequently overwhelmed by all I have to do"? In a national survey, 55 percent of women and 28 percent of men entering U.S. colleges and universities agreed (Stolzenberg et al., 2020). Relationship stresses also affect teen girls more than boys (Hamilton et al., 2015). Why are women nearly twice as vulnerable as men to depression, and twice as likely to take antidepressant drugs (Pratt et al., 2017)?

This higher risk may relate to women's tendency to *ruminate*—to overthink, fret, or brood (Nolen-Hoeksema, 2003; Spinoven et al., 2018). Staying focused on a problem—thanks to the continuous activation of an attention-sustaining frontal lobe area—can be adaptive (Altamirano et al., 2010; Andrews & Thomson, 2009a,b). But relentless, self-focused **rumination** can distract us, intensify negative emotion, and increase depression symptoms (Johnson et al., 2016; Stefanovic et al., 2022; Yang et al., 2017). We can even ruminate about our excessive rumination—by thinking too much about how we're thinking about something too much.

Comparisons can also feed rumination. Lonely Lori scrolls through her social media feed and sees Maria having a blast at a party, Angelique enjoying a family vacation, and

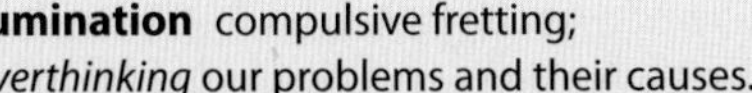

rumination compulsive fretting; *overthinking* our problems and their causes.

I NEVER KNOW WHAT TO SAY TO PEOPLE.
NO ONE WANTS TO BE AROUND ME.
WILL I EVER GET A JOB?!
DO I SMELL BAD? I'M SO UGLY.

Rumination runs wild We all think about our flaws. But dwelling constantly on negative thoughts—particularly negative thoughts about ourselves—makes it difficult to feel confident and self-assured. People sometimes seek therapy to reduce their rumination.

Amira looking super in a swimsuit. In response, Lori broods: "My life is terrible" and "Why can't I look like her?" (See the What Drives Us modules for the debate over whether social media-enabled comparisons have fueled the rise in teen girls' depression.)

But why do life's unavoidable failures lead only some people to become depressed? The answer lies partly in their *explanatory style*—who or what they blame for their failures. Think of how you might feel if you failed a test. If you externalize the blame ("What an unfair test!"), you are more likely to feel angry. If you blame yourself, you probably will feel stupid and depressed ("I can't do anything right!").

Depression-prone people respond to bad events in an especially self-focused, self-blaming way (LeMoult & Gotlib, 2019). As **FIGURE 50.5** illustrates, they explain bad events in terms that are *stable, global,* and *internal.*

Self-defeating beliefs may arise from *learned helplessness,* the hopelessness and passive resignation that humans and other animals learn when they experience uncontrollable painful events (Maier & Seligman, 2016). Pessimistic, overgeneralized, self-blaming attributions may create a depressing sense of hopelessness (Abramson et al., 1989; Groß et al., 2017). As researcher Martin Seligman has noted, "A recipe for severe depression is preexisting pessimism encountering failure" (1991, p. 78).

What, then, might we expect of new college students who exhibit a pessimistic explanatory style? Lauren Alloy and her colleagues (1999) monitored several hundred students every 6 weeks for 2.5 years. Among those identified as having a pessimistic thinking style, 17 percent had a first episode of major depression, as did only 1 percent of those who began college with an optimistic thinking style. This massive difference was no fluke: A large follow-up study showed that extreme feelings of hopelessness increased the odds of major depression tenfold (Liu et al., 2021).

Why is depression so common among young Westerners? Seligman (1991, 1995) has pointed to the rise of individualism and the decline of commitment to religion and family. In non-Western cultures, where close-knit relationships and cooperation are the norm, major depressive disorder is less common and less tied to self-blame for failure (De Vaus et al., 2018; Ferrari et al., 2013). In Japan, for example, depressed people instead tend to report feeling shame over letting others down (Draguns, 1990).

Critics note a chicken-and-egg problem nesting in the social-cognitive explanation of depression. Which comes first? The pessimistic explanatory style, or the depressed mood? The negative explanations *coincide* with a depressed mood, and they are *indicators* of depression. But do they *cause* depression? Experiments reveal that a depressed mood triggers pessimism. Temporarily putting people in a bad or sad mood makes their memories, judgments, and expectations more pessimistic.

FIGURE 50.5
Explanatory style and depression

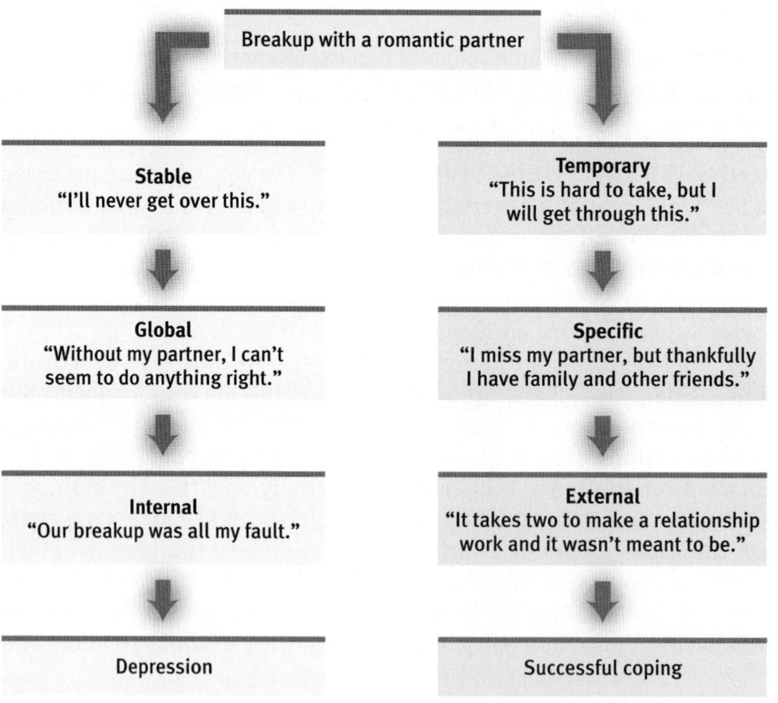
Breakup with a romantic partner
Stable
"I'll never get over this."
Temporary
"This is hard to take, but I will get through this."
Global
"Without my partner, I can't seem to do anything right."
Specific
"I miss my partner, but thankfully I have family and other friends."
Internal
"Our breakup was all my fault."
External
"It takes two to make a relationship work and it wasn't meant to be."
Depression
Successful coping

Memory researchers call this tendency to recall experiences that fit our current good or bad mood *state-dependent memory*.

DEPRESSION'S VICIOUS CYCLE Depression is both a cause and an effect of stressful experiences that disrupt our sense of who we are and why we matter. Such disruptions can lead to brooding, which amplifies negative feelings. Being withdrawn, self-focused, and complaining can, in turn, elicit rejection (Furr & Funder, 1998; Gotlib & Hammen, 1992). Indeed, people in the throes of depression are at high risk for divorce, job loss, and other stressful life events. Weary of the person's fatigue, hopeless attitude, and negativity, a spouse may threaten to leave, or a boss may begin to question the person's competence. (This provides another example of gene–environment interaction: People genetically predisposed to depression more often experience depressing events.) Rejection and depression feed each other. Misery may love another's company, but company does not love another's misery.

We can now assemble the pieces of the depression puzzle (**FIGURE 50.6**): (1) Stressful experiences interpreted through (2) a ruminating, pessimistic explanatory style create (3) a hopeless, depressed state that (4) hampers the way the person thinks and acts. This, in turn, fuels (1) further stressful experiences such as rejection. Depressed people "are prone to behaviors that reinforce their depressive symptoms" (Hart et al., 2021). Depression is a snake that bites its own tail.

It is a cycle we can all recognize. Bad moods feed on themselves: When we feel down, we think negatively and remember bad experiences. Britain's Prime Minister Winston Churchill called depression a "black dog" that periodically hounded him. U.S. President Abraham Lincoln was so withdrawn and brooding as a young man that his friends feared he might take his own life (Kline, 1974). Poet Emily Dickinson was so afraid of bursting into tears in public that she spent much of her adult life in seclusion (Patterson, 1951). As their lives remind us, "depression" can be an anagram for "I pressed on." Many people struggle through depression and regain their capacity to love, to work, and to succeed.

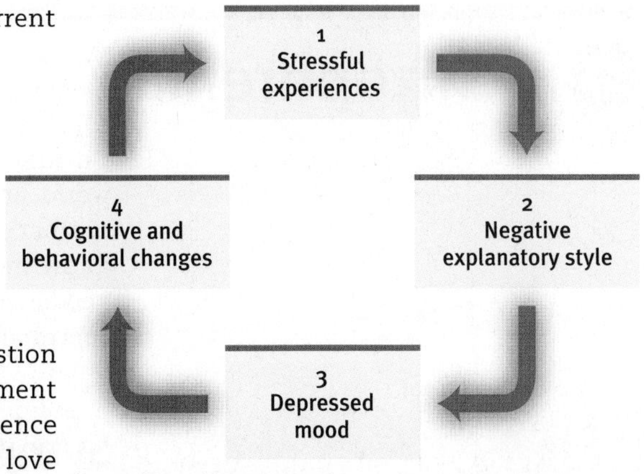

1 Stressful experiences → 2 Negative explanatory style → 3 Depressed mood → 4 Cognitive and behavioral changes → 1

FIGURE 50.6
The vicious cycle of depressed thinking Therapists recognize this cycle, and they work to help depressed people break out of it by changing their negative thinking, turning their attention outward, and engaging them in more pleasant and competent behavior.

RETRIEVAL PRACTICE

RP-1 What does it mean to say that "depression is a whole-body disorder"?

ANSWERS IN APPENDIX E

MODULE 50 REVIEW Depressive Disorders and Bipolar Disorders

LEARNING OBJECTIVES

Test Yourself Answer these repeated Learning Objective Questions on your own (before "showing" the answers here, or checking the answers in Appendix D) to improve your retention of the concepts (McDaniel et al., 2009, 2015).

LOQ 50-1 How do depressive disorders and bipolar disorders differ?

LOQ 50-2 How can the biological and social-cognitive perspectives help us understand depressive disorders and bipolar disorders?

TERMS AND CONCEPTS TO REMEMBER

Test Yourself Write down the definition in your own words, then check your answer.

major depressive disorder, p. 574
depressive disorders, p. 574
bipolar disorders, p. 575
mania, p. 575
rumination, p. 579

MODULE TEST

Test Yourself Answer the following questions on your own first, then "show" the answers here, or check your answers in Appendix E.

1. The gender gap in depression refers to the finding that ________ (men's/women's) risk of depression is roughly double that of ________ (men's/women's).
2. U.S. rates of bipolar disorders ________ between 1990 and 2019.
   a. increased.
   b. decreased.
   c. were consistent.
3. Treatment for depression often includes drugs that increase supplies of the neurotransmitters ________ and ________.
4. Psychologists who emphasize how negative perceptions, beliefs, and thoughts enable depression are working within the ________-________ perspective.

MODULE 51 Schizophrenia

During their most severe periods, people with **schizophrenia** live in a private inner world, preoccupied with the strange ideas and images that haunt them. The word itself means "split" *(schizo)* "mind" *(phrenia)*. It refers *not* to a multiple identity split but rather to the mind's split from reality. People with schizophrenia have disturbed perceptions and beliefs, disorganized speech, and diminished, inappropriate emotions and actions. Schizophrenia is the chief example of a **psychotic disorder**.

Symptoms of Schizophrenia

LOQ **51-1** What patterns of perceiving, thinking, and feeling characterize schizophrenia?

Schizophrenia comes in varied forms. People with schizophrenia display symptoms that are *positive* (*inappropriate* behaviors are *present*) or *negative* (*appropriate* behaviors are *absent*). Those with positive symptoms may experience disturbed perceptions, talk in disorganized and deluded ways, or exhibit inappropriate laughter, tears, or rage. Those with negative symptoms may exhibit an absence of emotion in their voices, expressionless faces, or mute and rigid bodies.

Disturbed Perceptions and Beliefs

People with schizophrenia sometimes *hallucinate*—they see, hear, feel, taste, or smell things that exist only in their minds. Most often, the hallucinations are voices, which sometimes make insulting remarks or give orders. The voices may tell the person that they are bad or that they must hurt themselves. Imagine your own reaction if a dream broke into your waking consciousness, making it hard to separate your experience from your imagination. When the unreal seems real, the resulting perceptions are at best bizarre, at worst terrifying.

Hallucinations are false *perceptions*. People with schizophrenia also have disorganized, fragmented thinking, often distorted by false *beliefs* called **delusions**. If they have *paranoid* delusions, they may interpret events in ways that make them feel threatened or pursued (Trotta et al., 2021).

One cause of disorganized thinking may be a breakdown in *selective attention*. Normally, we have a remarkable capacity to give our undivided attention to one set of sensory stimuli while filtering out others. People with schizophrenia are easily distracted by tiny unrelated stimuli, such as the grooves on a brick or tones in a voice. As Elyn Saks (2007) described it, "every sight, every sound, every smell coming at you carries equal weight; every thought, feeling, memory, and idea presents itself to you with an equally strong and demanding intensity." This selective-attention difficulty is but one of dozens of cognitive differences associated with schizophrenia (Reichenberg & Harvey, 2007).

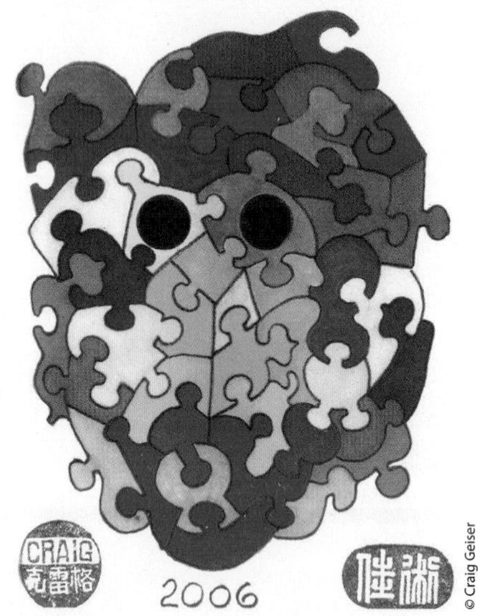
CRAIG
2006

© Craig Geiser

Art by someone with schizophrenia After his schizophrenia diagnosis, Michigan artist Craig Geiser said he "started drawing as a way to relax and escape the real world" (Geiser, 2021). Medication and therapy have helped quiet Geiser's hallucinations and delusions, enabling him to lead a meaningful life (Geiser, 2019).

Disorganized Speech

Maxine, a young woman with schizophrenia, believed she was Mary Poppins. Communicating with Maxine was difficult because her thoughts spilled out in no logical order. Her biographer, Susan Sheehan (1982, p. 25), observed her saying aloud to no one in particular, "This morning, when I was at Hillside [Hospital], I was making a movie. I was surrounded by movie stars. . . . Is this room painted blue to get me upset? My grandmother died four weeks after my eighteenth birthday."

Jumbled ideas may make no sense even within sentences, forming what is known as *word salad*. One young man begged for "a little more allegro in the treatment," and suggested that "liberationary movement with a view to the widening of the horizon" will "ergo extort some wit in lectures."

schizophrenia a disorder characterized by delusions, hallucinations, disorganized speech, and/or diminished, inappropriate emotional expression.

psychotic disorders a group of disorders marked by irrational ideas, distorted perceptions, and a loss of contact with reality.

delusion a false belief, often of persecution or grandeur, that may accompany psychotic disorders.

Diminished or Inappropriate Emotions

The expressed emotions of schizophrenia are often utterly inappropriate, split off from reality (Kring & Caponigro, 2010). Maxine laughed after recalling her grandmother's death. On other occasions, she cried when others laughed, or became angry for no apparent reason. Others with schizophrenia lapse into an emotionless *flat affect* state of no apparent feeling.

Most also have an *impaired theory of mind*—they have difficulty reading other peoples' facial expressions and states of mind (Bora & Pantelis, 2016). Unable to understand others' mental states, those with schizophrenia struggle to feel sympathy and compassion (Bonfils et al., 2016). These emotional deficiencies occur early in the illness and have a genetic basis (Bora & Pantelis, 2013). *Motor behavior* may also be inappropriate and disruptive. Those with schizophrenia may experience *catatonia,* characterized by motor behaviors ranging from a physical stupor (remaining motionless for hours), to senseless, compulsive actions (such as continually rocking or rubbing an arm), to severe and dangerous agitation.

As you can imagine, such disturbed perceptions and beliefs, disorganized speech, and out of place emotions profoundly disrupt social and work relationships. During their most severe periods, people with schizophrenia live in a private inner world, preoccupied with illogical ideas and unreal images. As with other disorders, many have sleep problems, which can increase night eating and obesity (Baglioni et al., 2016; Palmese et al., 2011). Given a supportive environment and medication, over 40 percent of people with schizophrenia will have periods of a year or more of normal life experience (Jobe & Harrow, 2010). But only 1 in 7 will have a full and enduring recovery (Jääskeläinen et al., 2013).

Onset and Development of Schizophrenia

LOQ 51-2 How do *chronic schizophrenia* and *acute schizophrenia* differ?

An estimated 20 million people worldwide—about 1 in 270—have schizophrenia (WHO, 2019). This disorder knows no national boundaries and it typically strikes as young people are maturing into adulthood (**TABLE 51.1**). Men tend to be diagnosed more often than women, and to be struck earlier and with more severity (Aleman et al., 2003; Eranti et al., 2013; Picchioni & Murray, 2007).

When schizophrenia is a slow-developing process, called **chronic schizophrenia**, recovery is doubtful (Harrison et al., 2001; Jääskeläinen et al., 2013). This was the case with Maxine, whose schizophrenia took a slow course, emerging after a long history of social difficulties and poor school performance (MacCabe et al., 2008). Although people with both chronic and *acute schizophrenia* can exhibit positive or negative symptoms, social withdrawal—a negative symptom—is often found among those with chronic

TABLE 51.1 Onset of Psychological Disorders

A digest of nearly 200 studies of more than 700,000 people reveals the *median* age (midpoint of the recorded ages) at which various disorders are first diagnosed (Solmi et al., 2022). In each case the most frequent *(modal)* age of onset is somewhat younger than the median age shown below.

Disorder	Median Age of Onset
Neurodevelopmental disorders	12
Anxiety disorders	17
Eating disorders	18
Obsessive-compulsive disorder	19
Substance use disorders	25
Schizophrenia	25
Personality disorders	25
Depressive disorders	30

chronic schizophrenia (also called *process schizophrenia*) a form of schizophrenia in which symptoms usually appear by late adolescence or early adulthood. As people age, psychotic episodes last longer and recovery periods shorten. 

acute schizophrenia (also called *reactive schizophrenia*) a form of schizophrenia that can begin at any age, frequently occurs in response to a traumatic event, and from which recovery is much more likely.

schizophrenia (Kirkpatrick et al., 2006). Men more often exhibit negative symptoms and chronic schizophrenia (Räsänen et al., 2000).

When previously well-adjusted people develop schizophrenia rapidly following particular life stresses, this is called **acute schizophrenia**, and recovery is much more likely. They more often have positive symptoms that respond to drug therapy (Fenton & McGlashan, 1991, 1994; Fowles, 1992).

Understanding Schizophrenia

Schizophrenia is one of the most heavily researched psychological disorders. Studies now link it with abnormal brain tissue and genetic predispositions. Schizophrenia is a disease of the brain manifested in symptoms of the mind.

Brain Abnormalities

LOQ 51-3 What brain abnormalities are associated with schizophrenia?

Might chemical imbalances in the brain underlie schizophrenia? Scientists have long known that strange behavior can have strange chemical causes. The saying "as mad as a hatter" is often thought to refer to the psychological deterioration of British hatmakers whose brains, it was later discovered, were slowly poisoned by the mercury-laden felt material (Smith, 1983). Could schizophrenia symptoms have a similar biochemical key? Scientists are searching for blood proteins that might predict schizophrenia onset (Chan et al., 2015). And they are tracking the mechanisms by which chemicals produce hallucinations and other symptoms.

DOPAMINE OVERACTIVITY One possible answer emerged when researchers examined schizophrenia patients' brains after death. They found an excess number of *dopamine* receptors, including a sixfold excess for the dopamine receptor D4 (Seeman et al., 1993; Wong et al., 1986). Such a hyper-responsive dopamine system may intensify brain signals in schizophrenia, creating positive symptoms such as hallucinations and paranoia (Maia & Frank, 2017). Drugs that block dopamine receptors often lessen these symptoms. Drugs that increase dopamine levels, such as nicotine, amphetamines, and cocaine, sometimes intensify them (Basu & Basu, 2015; Farnia et al., 2014).

Storing and studying brains Psychiatrist E. Fuller Torrey has collected the brains of hundreds of people with disorders such as schizophrenia and bipolar disorders who died as young adults.

ABNORMAL BRAIN ACTIVITY AND ANATOMY Abnormal brain activity and brain structures accompany schizophrenia. Some people diagnosed with schizophrenia have abnormally low brain activity in the frontal lobes, areas that help us reason, plan, and solve problems (Morey et al., 2005; Pettegrew et al., 1993; Resnick, 1992). Brain scans also show a noticeable decline in the brain waves that reflect synchronized neural firing in the frontal lobes (Spencer et al., 2004; Symond et al., 2005).

One study took PET scans of brain activity while people with schizophrenia were hallucinating (Silbersweig et al., 1995). When participants heard a voice or saw something, their brain became vigorously active in several core regions. One was the thalamus, the structure that filters incoming sensory signals and transmits them to the brain's cortex. Another PET scan study of people with paranoia found increased activity in the amygdala, a fear-processing center (Epstein et al., 1998).

In schizophrenia, fluid-filled brain cavities called *ventricles* become enlarged; cerebral tissue also shrinks (Goldman et al., 2009; van Haren et al., 2016). People often inherit these brain differences. If one affected identical twin shows brain abnormalities, the odds are at least 1 in 2 that the other twin's brain will have them (van Haren et al., 2012). Some studies have even found these abnormalities in people who *later* developed the disorder (Karlsgodt et al., 2010). The greater the brain shrinkage, the more severe the thought disorder (Collinson et al., 2003; Nelson et al., 1998; Shenton, 1992).

Smaller-than-normal areas may include the cortex, the hippocampus, and the corpus callosum connecting the brain's two hemispheres (Arnone et al., 2008; Bois et al., 2016). Often, the thalamus is also smaller than normal, which may explain why people with schizophrenia have difficulty filtering sensory input and focusing attention (Andreasen et al., 1994; Ellison-Wright et al., 2008). Schizophrenia also tends to involve a loss of neural connections across the brain network (Bohlken et al., 2016; Kambeitz et al., 2016). *The bottom line:* Schizophrenia involves not one isolated brain abnormality but problems with several brain regions and their interconnections (Andreasen, 1997, 2001; Arnedo et al., 2015).

Prenatal Environment and Risk

LOQ 51-4 What prenatal events are associated with increased risk of developing schizophrenia?

What causes these brain abnormalities in people with schizophrenia? Some scientists point to prenatal development or delivery (Fatemi & Folsom, 2009; Walker et al., 2010). Risk factors include low birth weight, maternal diabetes, older paternal age, and oxygen deprivation during delivery (King et al., 2010). Famine may also increase risks. People conceived during the peak of World War II's Dutch famine and during the famine of 1959 to 1961 in eastern China later developed schizophrenia at twice the normal rate (St. Clair et al., 2005; Susser et al., 1996). And extreme maternal stress may be a culprit: A large Israeli study showed that maternal exposure to terror attacks during pregnancy doubled children's risk of schizophrenia (Weinstein et al., 2018).

Let's consider another possible culprit. Might a midpregnancy viral infection impair fetal brain development (Brown & Patterson, 2011)? Can you imagine some ways to test this fetal-virus idea? Scientists have asked the following:

- ***Are people at increased risk of schizophrenia if their country experienced a flu epidemic during the middle of their fetal development?*** The repeated answer has been *Yes* (Mednick et al., 1994; Murray et al., 1992; Wright et al., 1995).
- ***Are people born in densely populated areas, where viral diseases spread more readily, at greater risk for schizophrenia?*** The answer, confirmed in a study of 1.75 million Danes, has again been *Yes* (Jablensky, 1999; Mortensen, 1999).
- ***Are those born during the winter and spring months—those who were in utero during the fall-winter flu season—also at increased risk?*** The answer is again *Yes* (Fox, 2010; Schwartz, 2011; Torrey & Miller, 2002; Torrey et al., 1997).
- ***In the Southern Hemisphere, where the seasons are the reverse of the Northern Hemisphere, are the months of above-average pre-schizophrenia births similarly reversed?*** Again, the answer has been *Yes*. In Australia, people born between August and October are at greater risk. But people born in the Northern Hemisphere who later moved to Australia still have a greater risk if they were born between January and March (McGrath et al., 1995; McGrath & Welham, 1999).
- ***Are those who report being sick with influenza during pregnancy more likely to bear children who develop schizophrenia?*** In one study of nearly 8000 women, the answer was *Yes*. The schizophrenia risk increased from the customary 1 percent to about 2 percent—but only when infections occurred during the second trimester (Brown et al., 2000). Maternal influenza infection during pregnancy affects brain development in monkeys as well (Short et al., 2010).
- ***Do blood samples collected from pregnant participants whose offspring develop schizophrenia show higher-than-normal levels of antibodies that suggest a viral infection?*** In several studies—including one that collected blood samples from some 20,000 pregnant participants—the answer has again been *Yes* (Brown et al., 2004; Buka et al., 2001; Canetta et al., 2014).

These converging lines of evidence suggest that fetal-virus infections contribute to the development of schizophrenia. They also strengthen the World Health Organization's (2017) recommendation that those who are pregnant be given high priority for the seasonal flu vaccine.

Genetic Factors

LOQ 51-5 How do genes influence schizophrenia? What factors may be early warning signs of schizophrenia in children?

Fetal-virus infections may increase the odds that a child will develop schizophrenia. But many women get the flu during their second trimester of pregnancy, and only 2 percent

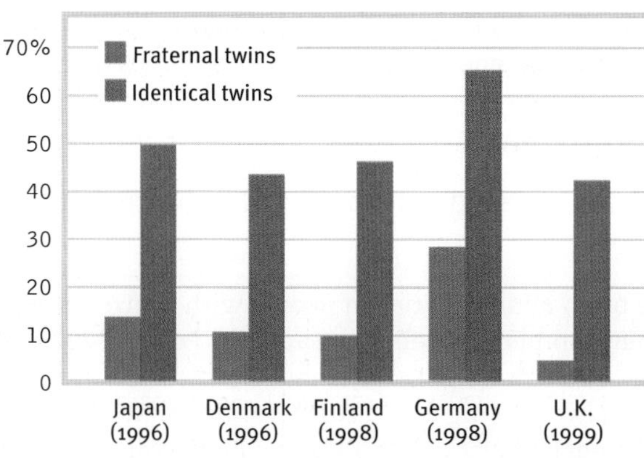
Schizophrenia risk for twins of those diagnosed with schizophrenia
70%
60
50
40
30
20
10
0
Fraternal twins
Identical twins
Japan (1996)
Denmark (1996)
Finland (1998)
Germany (1998)
U.K. (1999)

FIGURE 51.1
Risk of developing schizophrenia The lifetime risk of developing schizophrenia varies with a person's genetic relatedness to someone who has this disorder. Worldwide, barely more than 1 in 10 fraternal twins, but some 5 in 10 identical twins, share a schizophrenia diagnosis. (Data from Gottesman, 2001; Hilker et al., 2018.)

of them bear children who develop schizophrenia. Why are only some children at risk? Might some people be more genetically vulnerable to schizophrenia? *Yes.* The roughly 1-in-270 lifetime odds of any person being diagnosed with schizophrenia become about 1 in 10 among those who have a sibling or parent with the disorder. If the affected sibling is an identical twin, the odds increase to nearly 1 in 2 (**FIGURE 51.1**). Those odds remain the same even when the twins are raised apart (Plomin et al., 1997). (Only about a dozen such cases are on record.)

Remember, though, that identical twins share more than their genes. They also share a prenatal environment. About two-thirds share a placenta and the blood it supplies; the other third have separate placentas. Shared placentas matter. If the co-twin of an identical twin with schizophrenia shared the placenta, the chances of developing the disorder are 6 in 10. If the identical twins had separate placentas, the co-twin's chances of developing schizophrenia drop to 1 in 10 (Davis et al., 1995; Davis & Phelps, 1995; Phelps et al., 1997). Twins who share a placenta are more likely to share the same prenatal viruses. So perhaps shared germs as well as shared genes produce identical twin schizophrenia similarities (**FIGURE 51.2**).

Adoption studies help untangle genetic and environmental influences. Children adopted by someone who develops schizophrenia do not "catch" the disorder. Rather, adopted children have an elevated risk if a *biological* parent has schizophrenia (Gottesman, 1991). Genes indeed matter.

Although genes matter, the genetic formula is not straightforward as with inheritance of eye color. Schizophrenia is influenced by (no surprise by now) many genes, each with small effects (Binder, 2019; Weinberger, 2019). The search is on for specific genes that, in some combination, predispose schizophrenia-inducing brain abnormalities. In the largest genetic studies of schizophrenia, scientists analyze worldwide data from the genomes of tens of thousands of people with and without schizophrenia (Lam et al., 2019; Pardiñas et al., 2018). One analysis found 176 genome locations linked with this disorder, some affecting dopamine and other neurotransmitters. Another study of more than 100,000 people—nearly half with schizophrenia and the rest without—identified 413 schizophrenia-associated genes (Huckins et al., 2019).

FIGURE 51.2
Schizophrenia in only one identical twin When identical twins differ, only the brain of the twin with schizophrenia typically has enlarged, fluid-filled cranial cavities (b) (Suddath et al., 1990). The difference between the twins implies some nongenetic factor, such as a virus, is also at work.

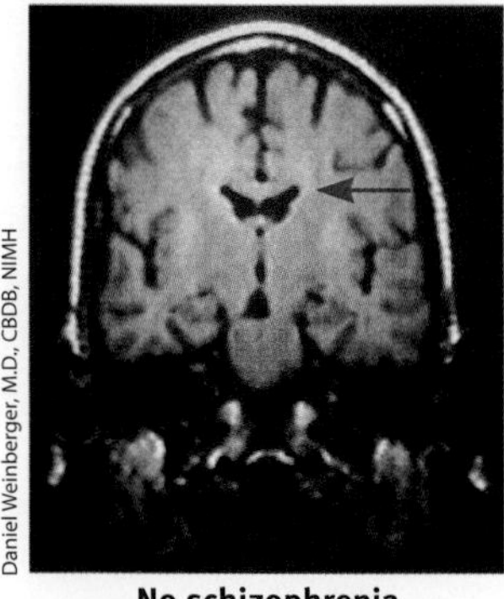
Daniel Weinberger, M.D., CBDB, NIMH
No schizophrenia
(a)

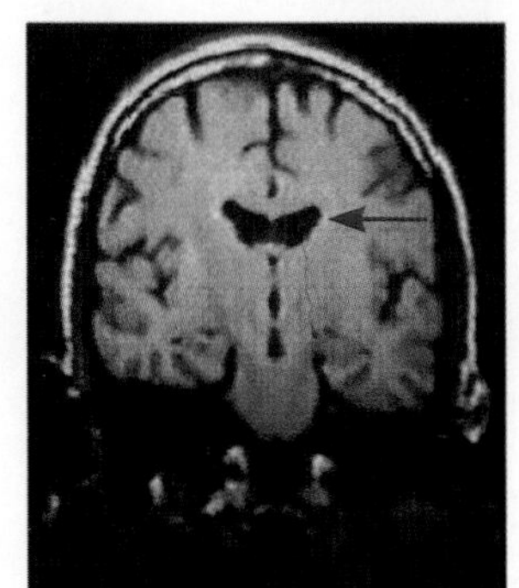
Schizophrenia
(b)

Moreover, as we see in so many different contexts, nature and nurture interact. *Epigenetic* factors influence whether genes will be expressed. Like hot water activating a tea bag, environmental factors such as viral infections, nutritional deprivation, and maternal or severe life stress can "turn on" the genes that put some of us at higher risk for schizophrenia. Identical twins' differing histories in the womb and beyond explain why they may show differing gene expressions (Dempster et al., 2013; Walker et al., 2010). Our heredity and our life experiences work together. Neither hand claps alone.

Thanks to our expanding understanding of genetic and brain influences on disorders such as schizophrenia, the general public increasingly recognizes the potency of biological factors in psychiatric disorders

(Pescosolido et al., 2010). So, will future scientists develop genetic tests that reveal who is at risk—for schizophrenia, or for other psychological disorders? If so, will people undergo testing for themselves, their embryos, or their children to determine risk? And how will they use that information? In this twenty-first-century world, such questions await answers.

Environmental Triggers for Schizophrenia

If prenatal viruses and genetic predispositions do not, by themselves, cause schizophrenia, neither do family or social factors alone. It remains true, as Susan Nicol and Irving Gottesman (1983) noted over three decades ago, that "no environmental causes have been discovered that will invariably, or even with moderate probability, produce schizophrenia in persons who are not related to" a person with schizophrenia.

Hoping to identify environmental triggers of schizophrenia, researchers have compared the experiences of high-risk children (for example, those with relatives with schizophrenia) and low-risk children. In one 2.5-year study that followed 163 teens and early-twenties adults who had two relatives with schizophrenia, the 20 percent of participants who developed schizophrenia showed social withdrawal or other abnormal behavior before the onset of the disorder (Johnstone et al., 2005). Researchers identified other possible early warning signs, including a mother whose schizophrenia was severe and long-lasting; birth complications (often involving oxygen deprivation and low birth weight); frequent childhood hospitalizations for viral and other infections; separation from parents; short attention span and poor muscle coordination; disruptive or withdrawn behavior; emotional unpredictability; poor peer relations and solo play; and childhood physical, sexual, or emotional abuse (Abel et al., 2010; Debost et al., 2019; Freedman et al., 1998; Schiffman et al., 2001; Susser, 1999; Welham et al., 2009).

* * *

Few of us can relate to the strange thoughts, perceptions, and behaviors of schizophrenia. Sometimes our thoughts jump around, but we rarely talk nonsensically. Occasionally we feel unjustly suspicious of someone, but we do not fear that the world is plotting against us. Often our perceptions err, but rarely do we see or hear things that are not there. We feel regret after laughing at someone's misfortune, but we rarely giggle in response to our own bad news. At times we just want to be alone, but we do not retreat into fantasy worlds. However, millions of people worldwide do talk strangely, experience delusions, hear nonexistent voices, see things that are not there, laugh or cry at inappropriate times, or withdraw into private imaginary worlds. The quest to solve the cruel puzzle of schizophrenia therefore continues, more vigorously than ever.

ASK YOURSELF

Can you recall a time when you heard something or someone casually (and inaccurately) described as "schizophrenic"? Now that you know more about this disorder, how might you correct such descriptions?

RETRIEVAL PRACTICE

RP-1 A person with schizophrenia who has ____________ (positive/negative) symptoms may have an expressionless face and toneless voice. Those with ____________ (positive/negative) symptoms are likely to experience delusions.

RP-2 What factors contribute to the onset and development of schizophrenia?

ANSWERS IN APPENDIX E

MODULE

51 REVIEW Schizophrenia

LEARNING OBJECTIVES

Test Yourself Answer these repeated Learning Objective Questions on your own (before "showing" the answers here, or checking the answers in Appendix D) to improve your retention of the concepts (McDaniel et al., 2009, 2015).

LOQ **51-1** What patterns of perceiving, thinking, and feeling characterize schizophrenia?

LOQ **51-2** How do *chronic schizophrenia* and *acute schizophrenia* differ?

LOQ **51-3** What brain abnormalities are associated with schizophrenia?

LOQ **51-4** What prenatal events are associated with increased risk of developing schizophrenia?

LOQ **51-5** How do genes influence schizophrenia? What factors may be early warning signs of schizophrenia in children?

TERMS AND CONCEPTS TO REMEMBER

Test Yourself Write down the definition in your own words, then check your answer.

schizophrenia, p. 582
psychotic disorders, p. 582
delusion, p. 582
chronic schizophrenia, p. 583
acute schizophrenia, p. 584

MODULE TEST

Test Yourself Answer the following questions on your own first, then "show" the answers here, or check your answers in Appendix E.

1. Valencia exclaims, "The weather has been so schizophrenic lately; it's hot one day and freezing the next!" In addition to being insensitive, this comparison is inaccurate. Why?

2. A person with positive symptoms of schizophrenia is most likely to experience

a. catatonia.
b. delusions.
c. withdrawal.
d. flat emotion.

3. People with schizophrenia may hear voices urging self-destruction, an example of a(n) ______________.

4. Chances for recovery from schizophrenia are best when

a. onset is sudden, in response to stress.
b. deterioration occurs gradually, during childhood.
c. no environmental causes can be identified.
d. there is a detectable brain abnormality.

MODULE

52 Dissociative, Personality, and Eating Disorders

Next we will consider the dissociative, personality, and eating disorders.

Dissociative Disorders

LOQ **52-1** What are *dissociative disorders*, and why are they controversial?

Among the most bewildering disorders are the rare **dissociative disorders**, in which a person's conscious awareness *dissociates* (separates) from painful memories, thoughts, and feelings. The result may be a *dissociative fugue state*, a sudden loss of memory or change in identity, often in response to an overwhelmingly stressful situation (Harrison et al., 2017). Such was the case for one Vietnam War veteran who was haunted by his comrades' deaths, and who had left his World Trade Center office shortly before the 9/11 terrorist attack. Later, he disappeared. Six months later, when he was discovered in a Chicago homeless shelter, he reported no memory of his identity or family (Stone, 2006).

dissociative disorders a controversial, rare group of disorders characterized by a disruption of or discontinuity in the normal integration of consciousness, memory, identity, emotion, perception, body representation, motor control, and behavior.

dissociative identity disorder (DID) a rare dissociative disorder in which a person exhibits two or more distinct and alternating identities. (Formerly called *multiple personality disorder.*)

Dissociative Identity Disorder

Dissociation itself is not so rare. Any one of us may have a fleeting sense of being unreal, of being separated from our body, of watching ourselves as if in a movie. A massive dissociation of self from ordinary consciousness occurs in **dissociative identity disorder (DID)**, in which two or more distinct identities—each with its own voice and mannerisms—seem to control a person's behavior. Thus, the person may be prim and proper one moment, loud and flirtatious the next. Typically, the original identity denies any awareness of the other(s).

Collection Christophel/Alamy Stock Photo

Multiple identities in the movies Chris Sizemore's story, told in the 1957 book and movie *The Three Faces of Eve*, gave early visibility to what is now called dissociative identity disorder. This controversial disorder continues to influence modern media, as in the 2019 movie *Glass*, where James McAvoy's character (pictured here) displays 24 different identities.

UNDERSTANDING DISSOCIATIVE IDENTITY DISORDER Skeptics question DID. Are clinicians who discover multiple identities merely triggering role-playing by fantasy-prone people in a particular social context (Giesbrecht et al., 2008, 2010; Lynn et al., 2014; Merskey, 1992)? After all, clients do not enter therapy saying "Allow me to introduce myselves." Instead, charge the critics, some therapists go fishing for multiple identities: "Have you ever felt like another part of you does things you can't control?" "Does this part of you have a name? Can I talk to the angry part of you?" Once clients permit a therapist to talk, by name, "to the part of you that says those angry things," they begin acting out the fantasy. Like actors who lose themselves in their roles, vulnerable patients may "become" the parts they are acting out. The result may be the experience of another self. Or perhaps dissociative identities are simply a more extreme version of the varied "selves" we sometimes present—a goofy self around our friends, a subdued self around our employer.

Skeptics also find it suspicious that the disorder has such a short and localized history. Between 1930 and 1960, the number of North American DID diagnoses averaged 2 per decade. By the 1980s, when the *Diagnostic and Statistical Manual of Mental Disorders* (DSM) contained the first formal code for this disorder, the number had exploded to more than 20,000 (McHugh, 1995). The average number of displayed identities also mushroomed—from 3 to 12 per patient (Goff & Simms, 1993). And although diagnoses have been increasing in countries where DID has been publicized, the disorder is much less prevalent outside North America (Lilienfeld, 2017). As skeptics note, once a disorder is made "official," reported cases of it tend to soar.

"Though this be madness, yet there is method in 't." —William Shakespeare, *Hamlet*, 1600

Despite some hoaxes, other researchers and clinicians believe DID is a real disorder. They cite findings of distinct body and brain states associated with differing identities (Putnam, 1991). Abnormal brain anatomy and activity can also accompany DID. Brain scans show shrinkage in areas that aid memory and detection of threat (Vermetten et al., 2006). Heightened activity appears in brain areas associated with the control and inhibition of traumatic memories (Elzinga et al., 2007).

Both the psychodynamic and learning perspectives have interpreted DID symptoms as ways of coping with anxiety. Some psychodynamic theorists see them as defenses against the anxiety caused by the eruption of unacceptable impulses. In this view, a second identity enables the discharge of forbidden impulses. Learning theorists see dissociative disorders as behaviors reinforced by anxiety reduction.

Some clinicians include dissociative disorders under the umbrella of posttraumatic stress disorder as a natural, protective response to traumatic experiences during childhood (Brand et al., 2016; Spiegel, 2008). Many people being treated for DID recall being physically, sexually, or emotionally abused as children (Gleaves, 1996; Lilienfeld et al., 1999). Critics wonder, however, whether such recollections are false memories (Kihlstrom, 2005; McNally, 2007). So the scientific debate continues.

Widespread dissociation Shirley Mason was a psychiatric patient diagnosed with dissociative identity disorder. Her life formed the basis of the bestselling book, *Sybil* (Schreiber, 1973), and of two movies. The book and movies' popularity contributed to increased DID diagnoses. Audio recordings later revealed that Mason's psychiatrist manipulated her and that she did not actually have the disorder (Nathan, 2011).

MBR/KRT/Newscom

ASK YOURSELF

Do you ever flip between displays of different aspects of your identity depending on the situation? How is your experience similar to and different from the described symptoms of dissociative identity disorder?

RETRIEVAL PRACTICE

RP-1 The psychodynamic and learning perspectives agree that dissociative identity disorder symptoms are ways of dealing with anxiety. How do their explanations differ?

ANSWERS IN APPENDIX E

Personality Disorders

LOQ 52-2 What are the three clusters of personality disorders? What behaviors and brain activity characterize antisocial personality disorder?

The inflexible and enduring behavior patterns of **personality disorders** interfere with social functioning. These 10 disorders in the DSM-5-TR tend to form three clusters (**TABLE 52.1**):

- In Cluster A, people appear ***eccentric or odd,*** as in the suspiciousness of *paranoid personality disorder*; the social detachment of *schizoid personality disorder*; or the magical thinking of *schizotypal personality disorder.*
- In Cluster B, people appear ***dramatic, emotional, or erratic,*** as in the unstable, attention-getting *borderline personality disorder;* the self-focused and self-inflating *narcissistic personality disorder;* the excessively emotional *histrionic personality disorder;* and—what we next discuss as an in-depth example—the callous, and often dangerous, *antisocial personality disorder.*
- In Cluster C, people appear ***anxious or fearful,*** as in the fearful sensitivity to rejection that predisposes the withdrawn *avoidant personality disorder;* the clinging behavior of *dependent personality disorder;* and the preoccupation with orderliness, perfectionism, and control that characterizes *obsessive-compulsive personality disorder.*

BANK

Leo Cullum/Cartoon Stock

"Thursday is out. I have jury duty."
Many criminals, like this one, display a sense of conscience and responsibility in other areas of their life, and thus do not exhibit antisocial personality disorder.

Antisocial Personality Disorder

People with **antisocial personality disorder**, usually male, can display symptoms by age 8. Their lack of conscience becomes plain before age 15, as they begin to lie, steal, fight, or display unrestrained sexual behavior (Cale & Lilienfeld, 2002). Not all children with these traits become antisocial adults, and for many males, antisocial behavior often subsides after adolescence (Moffitt, 2018). (Note that *antisocial* means socially harmful and remorseless, not merely unsociable.) Those who do develop the disorder—about half—will generally act in violent or otherwise criminal ways, be unable to keep a job, and behave irresponsibly toward family members (Farrington, 1991).

But criminality is not an essential component of antisocial behavior (Skeem & Cooke, 2010). And many criminals do not exhibit antisocial personality disorder; rather, they show responsible concern for their friends and family members. In contrast with most criminals, people with antisocial personality disorder (sometimes called

TABLE 52.1 Personality Disorders

The DSM-5-TR identifies 10 personality disorders (APA, 2022).

Cluster A

- **Paranoid personality disorder:** suspiciousness; distrust of others
- **Schizoid personality disorder:** social detachment; limited emotional expression
- **Schizotypal personality disorder:** intense social discomfort; distorted cognitions or perceptions; behavioral eccentricity

Cluster B

- **Borderline personality disorder:** impulsivity; unstable relationships and self-image
- **Narcissistic personality disorder:** grandiosity; admiration-seeking behavior; deficient empathy
- **Histrionic personality disorder:** extreme emotional expression; a need for attention
- **Antisocial personality disorder:** indifference to (and willingness to violate) others' rights; impulsiveness; criminal behavior

Cluster C

- **Avoidant personality disorder:** social inhibition; feeling inadequate; sensitivity to criticism
- **Dependent personality disorder:** submissive behavior; emotional neediness
- **Obsessive-compulsive personality disorder:** a fixation on orderliness; the need for perfection and control

personality disorders a group of disorders characterized by enduring inner experiences or behavior patterns that differ from the person's cultural norms and expectations, are pervasive and inflexible, begin in adolescence or early adulthood, are stable over time, and cause distress or impairment.

antisocial personality disorder a personality disorder in which a person (usually a man) exhibits a lack of conscience for wrongdoing, even toward friends and family members; may be aggressive and ruthless or a clever con artist.

John Mantha/Reuters/Newscom

No remorse Bruce McArthur, a 66-year-old landscaper shown here in a courtroom sketch, was convicted in 2019 of killing eight people over 8 years. He often targeted men who were gay, immigrants, or experiencing homelessness, storing their remains in boxes at his job sites. McArthur exhibited the extreme lack of remorse that marks antisocial personality disorder.

sociopaths or *psychopaths*) are more socially deficient. They often exhibit less *emotional intelligence*—the ability to understand, manage, and perceive emotions (Ermer et al., 2012; Gillespie et al., 2019).

Antisocial personalities behave impulsively, and then feel and fear little (Fowles & Dindo, 2009). Their impulsivity can have horrific consequences, including homicide (Camp et al., 2013; Fox & DeLisi, 2019). Consider the case of Tommy Lynn Sells. He said he killed his first victim when he was 15. He felt little regret then or later. During his years of crime, he brutally murdered at least 17 adults and children. "I am hatred," Sells told one interviewer while on death row (ABC, 2014). "When you look at me, you look at hate."

UNDERSTANDING ANTISOCIAL PERSONALITY DISORDER Antisocial personality disorder is woven of both biological and psychological strands. Twin and adoption studies reveal that biological relatives of people with antisocial and unemotional tendencies are at increased risk for antisocial behavior (Frisell et al., 2012; Kendler et al., 2015). People with antisocial personalities sometimes spread their genes to future generations by marrying others who have antisocial personalities (B. Weiss et al., 2017). No single gene codes for a complex behavior such as crime. But genes that predispose lower mental ability and self-control predict a higher crime risk (Wertz et al., 2018). As with other disorders, geneticists have also identified specific genes that are more common in those with antisocial personality disorder (Gunter et al., 2010; Tielbeek et al., 2017). The genes that put people at risk for antisocial behavior also put people at risk for substance use disorders (Dick, 2007).

The genetic vulnerability of people with antisocial tendencies appears as low arousal in response to threats. Awaiting aversive events, such as electric shocks or loud noises, they show little autonomic nervous system arousal (Hare, 1975; Ling et al., 2019). Long-term studies show that their stress hormone levels were lower than average as teenagers, before they had ever committed a crime (**FIGURE 52.1**). And those who were slow to develop conditioned fears at age 3 were also more likely to commit a crime later in life (Gao et al., 2010). Likewise, preschool boys who later become aggressive or antisocial adolescents tend to be impulsive, uninhibited, unconcerned with social rewards, and low in anxiety (Caspi et al., 1996; Tremblay et al., 1994).

Traits such as fearlessness and dominance can be adaptive. If channeled in more productive directions, fearlessness may lead to athletic stardom, adventurism, or courageous heroism (Costello et al., 2018; Patton et al., 2018). Indeed, 42 U.S. presidents exhibited higher than usual fearlessness and dominance (Lilienfeld et al., 2012, 2016). Patient S. M., a 49-year-old woman with amygdala damage, showed fearlessness and impulsivity but also heroism: She gave a man in need her only coat and scarf, and donated her hair to the Locks of Love charity after befriending a child with cancer (Lilienfeld et al., 2017). Lacking a sense of social responsibility, however, the same disposition may produce a cool con artist or killer (Lykken, 1995).

Brain structure matters, too: People with antisocial criminal tendencies have a smaller-than-usual amygdala, which controls emotions, and a smaller and thinner brain cortex (Carlisi et al., 2020; Pardini et al., 2014). The frontal lobes are also less active,

FIGURE 52.1

Cold-blooded arousability and risk of crime Researchers measured levels of the stress hormone adrenaline in two groups of 13-year-old Swedish boys, and followed up on them as young adults. Those who would later be convicted of a crime as 18- to 26-year-olds showed relatively low arousal when they were younger, in both stressful and nonstressful situations. (Data from Magnusson, 1990.)

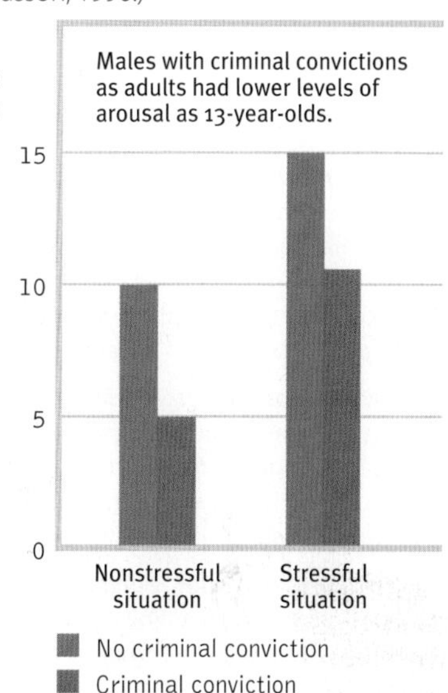
Adrenaline excretion (ng/min)
Males with criminal convictions as adults had lower levels of arousal as 13-year-olds.
15
10
5
0
Nonstressful situation
Stressful situation
No criminal conviction
Criminal conviction

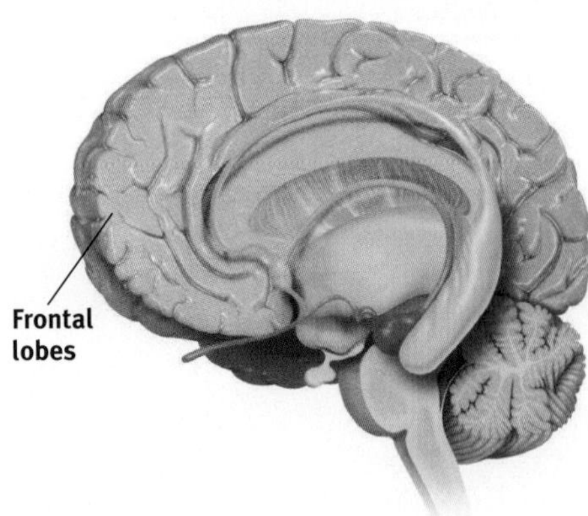
Frontal lobes

FIGURE 52.2
Murderous minds Researchers have found reduced activation in a murderer's frontal lobes. This brain area (shown in a left-facing brain) helps curb impulsive, aggressive behavior (Raine, 1999).

as shown by PET scans of 41 murderers' brains compared with those from people of similar age and sex (Raine, 1999, 2005; **FIGURE 52.2**). The frontal lobes help control impulses. The reduced activation was especially apparent in those who murdered impulsively. In a follow-up study, Adrian Raine and his team (2000) found that violent repeat offenders had 11 percent less frontal lobe tissue than is typical. This helps explain why people with antisocial personality disorder exhibit marked deficits in frontal lobe cognitive functions, such as planning, organization, and inhibition (Morgan & Lilienfeld, 2000). Compared with people who feel and display empathy, their brains also respond less to facial displays of others' distress, which may contribute to their lower emotional intelligence (Deeley et al., 2006).

Genetic influences often combine with negative environmental factors—such as childhood abuse, family instability, or poverty—to wire the brain (Dodge, 2009). This gene–environment combination also occurs in chimpanzees, which, like humans, vary in antisocial (mean/bold/disinhibited) tendencies (Latzman et al., 2017). In another Raine-led study (1996), researchers checked criminal records on nearly 400 Danish men at ages 20 to 22. All these men either had biological risk factors at birth (such as premature birth) or came from family backgrounds marked by poverty and family instability. The researchers then compared each of these two groups with a third *biosocial* group (people whose lives were marked by *both* those biological and social risk factors). The biosocial group had double the risk of committing a crime. Similar findings emerged from a famous study that followed 1037 children for a quarter-century: Two combined factors—childhood maltreatment and a gene that altered neurotransmitter balance—predicted antisocial problems (Caspi et al., 2002). Neither "bad" genes alone nor a "bad" environment alone predisposed later antisocial behavior. Rather, genes predisposed some children to be more sensitive to maltreatment. Within "genetically vulnerable segments of the population," environmental influences matter—for better or for worse (Belsky & Pluess, 2009; Moffitt, 2005).

With antisocial behavior—as with so much else—nature and nurture interact. Once again, the biopsychosocial perspective helps us understand the whole story. To further investigate the neural basis of antisocial personality disorder, neuroscientists are exploring the antisocial brain (Brazil & Buades-Rotger, 2020). Shown emotionally evocative photographs, such as a man holding a knife to a woman's throat, criminals with antisocial personality disorder display blunted heart rate and perspiration responses, and less activity in brain areas that typically respond to emotional stimuli (Harenski et al., 2010; Kiehl & Buckholtz, 2010). They also have a larger and hyperreactive dopamine reward system, which predisposes their impulsive drive to do something rewarding despite the consequences (Buckholtz et al., 2010; Glenn et al., 2010). Such data provide another reminder: Everything psychological is also biological.

RETRIEVAL PRACTICE

RP-2 How do biological and psychological factors contribute to antisocial personality disorder?

ANSWERS IN APPENDIX E

Eating Disorders

LOQ 52-3 What are the three main eating disorders, and how do biological, psychological, and social-cultural influences make some people more vulnerable to them?

Our bodies are naturally disposed to maintain a steady weight, including storing energy for times when food becomes unavailable. But sometimes psychological influences overwhelm biological wisdom. This becomes painfully clear in three eating disorders.

- In **anorexia nervosa**, people—most often adolescent girls, but some women, men, and boys as well—starve themselves. Anorexia often begins as an attempt to lose weight, but the dieting becomes a habit (Steinglass et al., 2018). Regardless of their actual weight, a person with anorexia feels fat, fears being fat, and focuses obsessively on losing weight, sometimes exercising excessively.

anorexia nervosa an eating disorder in which a person (most often an adolescent female) maintains a starvation diet despite being significantly underweight, and has an inaccurate self-perception; sometimes accompanied by excessive exercise.

bulimia nervosa an eating disorder in which a person's binge eating (usually of high-calorie foods) is followed by weight-loss-promoting behavior, such as vomiting, laxative use, fasting, or excessive exercise.

binge-eating disorder significant binge-eating episodes, followed by distress, disgust, or guilt, but without the compensatory behavior that marks bulimia nervosa.

- In **bulimia nervosa**, a cycle of repeated episodes of binge eating alternates with behaviors to compensate, such as vomiting, laxative use, fasting, or excessive exercise (Wonderlich et al., 2007). Unlike anorexia, bulimia is marked by weight fluctuations within or above typical ranges, making the disorder easier to hide.
- Those with **binge-eating disorder**—the world's most common eating disorder—are preoccupied with food and engage in significant bouts of bingeing, followed by remorse. But they do not purge, fast, or exercise excessively (Santomauro et al., 2021).

At some point during their lifetime, about 2.6 million Americans (0.8 percent) have met the DSM-5-TR-defined criteria for anorexia, 2.6 million for bulimia, and 2.7 million for binge-eating disorder (Udo & Grilo, 2019). All three disorders can be deadly. They harm the body and mind, resulting in shorter life expectancy and greater risk of suicide and nonsuicidal self-injury (Cucchi et al., 2016; Fichter & Quadflieg, 2016; Mandelli et al., 2019).

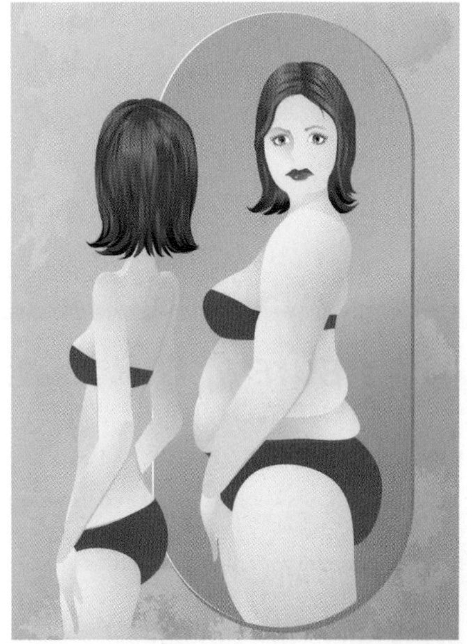
artbyjulie/Getty Images

A distorted body image underlies anorexia.

Understanding Eating Disorders

Eating disorders are *not* (as some have speculated) a telltale sign of childhood sexual abuse (Smolak & Murnen, 2002; Stice, 2002). The family environment may influence eating disorders in other ways, however. For example, the families of those with anorexia tend to be competitive, high-achieving, and protective (Ahrén et al., 2013; Berg et al., 2014; Yates, 1989, 1990).

Eating disorders share some commonalities with anxiety disorders (Schaumberg et al., 2021). Those with eating disorders often have low body satisfaction, set perfectionist standards, and ruminate about falling short of expectations and how others perceive them (Farstad et al., 2016; Smith et al., 2018; S. Wang et al., 2019). Some of these factors also predict teen boys' pursuit of unrealistic muscularity (Karazsia et al., 2017; Ricciardelli & McCabe, 2004).

Heredity also matters. Identical twins share these disorders more often than do fraternal twins—with 50 to 60 percent *heritability* for anorexia (Yilmaz et al., 2015). Scientists are searching for culprit genes. The largest study identified gene differences by comparing the genomes of nearly 17,000 people with anorexia with 56,000 others who did not have the disorder (Watson et al., 2019).

But eating disorders also have cultural and gender components. Ideal shapes vary across culture and time. Hungry people find larger bodies more attractive (Saxton et al., 2020). In countries with high poverty rates, plump may mean prosperity and thin may signal poverty or illness (Knickmeyer, 2001; Swami et al., 2010). Not so in high-income Western cultures. In one analysis of 222 studies, the rise in eating disorders in the last half of the twentieth century coincided with a dramatic decline in Western women's body image (Feingold & Mazzella, 1998). Women have come to overestimate the female thinness that straight men prefer, while men overestimate the male muscularity that straight women prefer (Lei & Perrett, 2021).

BOVINE BARBIE
Leigh Rubes/Creators Syndicate, Inc.

"Up until that point, Bernice had never once had a problem with low self-esteem."

Today's weight-obsessed culture—which sends the message that "fat is bad" in countless ways—motivates millions of women to diet constantly, and invites eating binges by pressuring women to live in a constant state of semistarvation. One former model recalled walking into a meeting with her agent, starving and with her organs failing due to anorexia (Carroll, 2013). Her agent's greeting: "Whatever you are doing, keep doing it." Women who view real and doctored images of unnaturally thin models and celebrities often feel ashamed, depressed, and dissatisfied with their own bodies—the very attitudes that predispose eating disorders (Bould et al., 2018; Tiggemann & Miller, 2010). Even ultrathin models do not reflect the impossible standard of the original Barbie doll, who had, when adjusted to a height of 5 feet 7 inches, a 32-inch bust, 16-inch waist, and 29-inch hips (in centimeters, 82–41–73) (Norton et al., 1996).

"Why do women have such low self-esteem? There are many complex psychological and societal reasons, by which I mean Barbie." —Humorist Dave Barry, 1999

Most people diagnosed with an eating disorder do improve. In one 22-year study, 2 in 3 women with anorexia nervosa or bulimia nervosa had recovered (Eddy et al., 2017). Prevention is also possible. Interactive programs that teach teen girls to accept their bodies have reduced the risk of eating disorders (Beintner et al., 2012; Melioli et al., 2016; Vocks et al., 2010). By combating cultural learning, those at risk may instead live long and healthy lives.

RETRIEVAL PRACTICE

RP-3 People with ________________ (anorexia nervosa/bulimia nervosa) continue to want to lose weight even when they are underweight. Those with ________________ (anorexia nervosa/bulimia nervosa) tend to have a weight that fluctuates within or above typical ranges.

ANSWERS IN APPENDIX E

MODULE 52 REVIEW Dissociative, Personality, and Eating Disorders

LEARNING OBJECTIVES

Test Yourself Answer these repeated Learning Objective Questions on your own (before "showing" the answers here, or checking the answers in Appendix D) to improve your retention of the concepts (McDaniel et al., 2009, 2015).

LOQ **52-1** What are *dissociative disorders*, and why are they controversial?

LOQ **52-2** What are the three clusters of personality disorders? What behaviors and brain activity characterize antisocial personality disorder?

LOQ **52-3** What are the three main eating disorders, and how do biological, psychological, and social-cultural influences make some people more vulnerable to them?

TERMS AND CONCEPTS TO REMEMBER

Test Yourself Write down the definition in your own words, then check your answer.

dissociative disorders, p. 588
dissociative identity disorder (DID), p. 588
personality disorders, p. 590
antisocial personality disorder, p. 590
anorexia nervosa, p. 592
bulimia nervosa, p. 592
binge-eating disorder, p. 592

MODULE TEST

Test Yourself Answer the following questions on your own first, then "show" the answers here, or check your answers in Appendix E.

1. Dissociative identity disorder is controversial because
   a. dissociation is quite rare.
   b. it was reported frequently in the 1920s but is rarely reported today.
   c. it is almost never reported outside North America.
   d. its symptoms are nearly identical to those of obsessive-compulsive disorder.
2. A personality disorder, such as antisocial personality, is characterized by
   a. depression.
   b. hallucinations.
   c. enduring inner experiences and behavior patterns that cause distress or impairment.
   d. an elevated level of autonomic nervous system arousal.
3. PET scans of murderers' brains have revealed
   a. higher-than-normal activation in the frontal lobes.
   b. lower-than-normal activation in the frontal lobes.
   c. more frontal lobe tissue than normal.
   d. no differences in brain structures or activity.
4. Which of the following statements is true of bulimia nervosa?
   a. People with bulimia continue to want to lose weight even when they are underweight.
   b. Bulimia is marked by weight fluctuations within or above typical ranges.
   c. Those with bulimia do not follow food binges with compensating behaviors.
   d. If one twin is diagnosed with bulimia, the chances of the other twin sharing the disorder are greater if they are fraternal rather than identical twins.

MODULE 53 Neurodevelopmental Disorders

Our thoughts and behaviors change as we grow older. For people with **neurodevelopmental disorders**, these typical changes are disrupted in childhood because of unusual features of the central nervous system. These disorders include *intellectual developmental disorders, autism spectrum disorder,* and *attention-deficit/hyperactivity disorder.*

Intellectual Developmental Disorder

LOQ **53-1** What is *intellectual developmental disorder*?

Intellectual developmental disorder is apparent before age 18, often with a known physical cause. *Down syndrome,* for example, is a disorder of varying intellectual and physical severity caused by an extra copy of chromosome 21 in the person's genetic makeup.

To be diagnosed with intellectual developmental disorder, a young person must meet two criteria. The first is low intellectual functioning as reflected in a low intelligence test score. Guidelines specify test score performance that is in the lowest 3 percent of the general population, or about 70 or below (Schalock et al., 2010). The second criterion is that the person must have difficulty adapting to the normal demands of independent living, as expressed in three areas, or skills: *conceptual* (language, reading, and concepts of money, time, and number); *social* (interpersonal skills, being socially responsible, following basic rules and laws, avoiding being victimized); and *practical* (health and personal care, occupational skill, and travel). Intellectual developmental disorder results from a combination of genetic and environmental factors (Reichenberg et al., 2016).

neurodevelopmental disorders central nervous system developmental differences (usually in the brain) that start in childhood and alter thinking and behavior (as in intellectual limitations or a psychological disorder).

intellectual developmental disorder a condition of limited mental ability, indicated by an intelligence test score of 70 or below and difficulty adapting to the demands of life. (May also be referred to as *intellectual disability.*)

autism spectrum disorder (ASD) a disorder that appears in childhood and is marked by limitations in communication and social interaction, and by rigidly fixated interests and repetitive behaviors.

RETRIEVAL PRACTICE

RP-1 What criteria must be met for someone to be diagnosed with intellectual developmental disorder?

ANSWERS IN APPENDIX E

Autism Spectrum Disorder

LOQ **53-2** What is *autism spectrum disorder?*

Autism spectrum disorder (ASD) is a cognitive and social-emotional disorder that is marked by social deficiencies and repetitive behaviors. Once believed to affect 1 in 2500 children (and referred to simply as *autism*), ASD is now diagnosed in 1 in 38 children in South Korea, 1 in 54 in the United States, 1 in 62 in Canada, and 1 in 166 in Germany (CDC, 2020; Chiarotti & Venerosi, 2020). The increase in ASD diagnoses has been offset by a decrease in the number of children with a "cognitive disability" or "learning disability," which suggests a relabeling of children's disorders (Gernsbacher et al., 2005; Grinker, 2007; Shattuck, 2006).

martinedoucet/E+/Getty Images

Comforting connections In this shelter for battered and abandoned animals, children with a neurodevelopmental disorder learn to connect with the animals as a way of building their own strengths.

The underlying source of ASD's symptoms seems to be poor communication among brain regions that typically work together to let us take another's viewpoint. From age 2 months on, children typically spend more and more time looking into others' eyes; those who later develop ASD do so less and less (Baron-Cohen, 2017; Wang et al., 2020). Researchers are debating whether autistic people have an *impaired theory of mind* (Gernsbacher & Yergeau, 2019; Matthews & Goldberg, 2018; Velikonja et al., 2019). Reading faces *(Is that face conveying a smile or a sneer?)* or even recognizing faces is often difficult for those with ASD (Griffin et al., 2021). Autistic people have difficulty inferring how others think differently than they do (Deschrijver & Palmer, 2020). For example, they may not appreciate that playmates and parents might view things differently, or understand that their teachers know more than they do (Boucher et al., 2012; Frith & Frith, 2001; Knutsen et al., 2015).

A national survey of parents and school staff reported that 46 percent of adolescents with ASD had endured the taunts and torments of bullying—four times the 11 percent rate for other children (Sterzing et al., 2012). Children with ASD do make friends, but their peers often find such relationships emotionally unsatisfying (Mendelson et al., 2016). This helps explain why people with ASD have a quadrupled risk of experiencing depression in their lifetime (Hudson et al., 2019).

"I'm autistic, which means everyone around me has a disorder that makes them . . . creepily stare into my eyeballs." —Facebook.com/autisticnotweird, 2020

ASD has differing levels of severity. Some (those diagnosed with what used to be called *Asperger syndrome*) function at a high level, with average intelligence, often accompanied by exceptional skill or talent in a specific area. But those with more severe ASD may lack the motivation and ability to interact and communicate socially, and they tend to become distracted by irrelevant stimuli (Clements et al., 2018; Remington et al., 2009). Those at the spectrum's most severe end struggle to use language.

"Autism makes my life difficult, but it also makes my life beautiful. When everything is more intense, then the everyday, the mundane, the typical, the normal—those things become outstanding." —Erin McKinney, "The Best Way I Can Describe What It's Like to Have Autism," 2015

ASD gets diagnosed in about four boys for every girl, perhaps partly because girls may be more skilled in hiding ASD-related traits (CDC, 2020; Dean et al., 2017; Loomes et al., 2017). Psychologist Simon Baron-Cohen (2010), who has been knighted for his autism research, believes the imbalance is because boys—whether or not they have ASD—are "systemizers." They tend to understand things according to rules or laws, as in mathematical and mechanical systems. Girls, he contends, are more often predisposed to be "empathizers." They tend to excel at reading facial expressions, predicting what others will feel, and knowing what to do in social situations. Whether male or female, those with ASD are systemizers who have more difficulty reading facial expressions, intuitively knowing what others feel, and understanding how to have smooth social interactions (Greenberg et al., 2018; Velikonja et al., 2019). People working in STEM (science, technology, engineering, or mathematics) careers are also somewhat more likely than others to exhibit some ASD-like traits (Ruzich et al., 2015).

Justin Sellers/The Clarion Ledger/USA TODAY NETWORK/Imagn Content Services

"Autism" case number 1 In 1943, Donald Gray Triplett, an "odd" child with unusual gifts and social limitations, was the first person to receive the diagnosis of "autism." (After a 2013 change in the diagnosis manual, his condition is now called *autism spectrum disorder.*) At age 82, Triplett—a retired bank teller who often played golf—was living independently in his family home and Mississippi town (Atlas, 2016). He is shown here (left) walking with his brother.

Biological factors contribute to ASD (Ecker et al., 2021; J. Zhou et al., 2019). Prenatal environment matters, especially when altered by maternal infection, psychiatric drug use, or stress hormones (NIH, 2013; Wang, 2014). Genes also matter. One five-nation study of 2 million people found the hereditability of ASD was near 80 percent (Bai et al., 2019). If one identical twin is diagnosed with ASD, the chances are near 9 in 10 that the co-twin will be as well, though such twins often differ in symptom severity (Castelbaum et al., 2020). No one "autism gene" accounts for the disorder. Rather, many genes—with more than 400 identified so far—contribute (Krishnan et al., 2016; Yuen et al., 2016). Random genetic mutations in sperm cells may also play a role. As men age, these mutations become more frequent, which helps explain why a man over age 40 has a much higher risk of fathering a child with ASD than does a man under age 30 (Wu et al., 2017).

Researchers are also sleuthing ASD's telltale signs in the brain's structure. Several studies have revealed "underconnectivity"—fewer-than-normal fiber tracts connecting the front of the brain to the back (Picci et al., 2016). With underconnectivity, there is less of the whole-brain synchrony that, for example, integrates visual and emotional information. In children as young as 3 months, EEG-recorded brain activity can foretell ASD (Bosl et al., 2018).

Biology's role in ASD also appears in the brain's functioning. People without ASD often yawn after seeing others yawn. And as they view and imitate another's smiling or frowning, they feel something of what the other is feeling. Not so among those with ASD, who are less imitative and show less activity in brain areas involved in mirroring others' actions (Edwards, 2014; Yang & Hoffmann, 2015). When people with ASD watch another person's hand movements, for example, their brain displays less mirroring activity than is typical (Oberman & Ramachandran, 2007; Théoret et al., 2005). Scientists are exploring whether treatment with oxytocin, the hormone that promotes social bonding, might improve social understanding in those with ASD (Gordon et al., 2013; Lange & McDougle, 2013).

There is overwhelming evidence that childhood vaccinations, which—despite a fraudulent 1998 study claiming otherwise—have *no connection* to ASD. In fact, in one recent study following nearly 700,000 Danish children, those receiving the measles/mumps/rubella vaccine were slightly *less* likely to later be among the 6517 children diagnosed with ASD (Hviid et al., 2019). *The bottom line:* When deciding whether to vaccinate their children, parents should trust the scientific evidence. Childhood vaccinations do not increase the risk for ASD.

Attention-Deficit/Hyperactivity Disorder

For children who experience the challenging symptoms of **attention-deficit/hyperactivity disorder (ADHD)**, diagnosis and treatment can help (Kupfer, 2012; Maciejewski et al., 2016). The DSM has broadened the diagnostic criteria for this disorder, prompting critics to wonder whether the criteria are now too broad (Frances, 2013). Shall we say such a child is hyperactive—or energetic? Impulsive—or spontaneous? Excessively talkative—or excited? One 10-year study in Sweden found children's attentional behaviors unchanging, while national ADHD diagnoses increased fivefold (Rydell et al., 2018). (See Thinking Critically About: ADHD—Natural High Energy or Disordered Behavior?)

attention-deficit/hyperactivity disorder (ADHD) a psychological disorder marked by extreme inattention and/or hyperactivity and impulsivity.

* * *

The bewilderment, fear, and sorrow caused by psychological disorders are real. But, as the Therapy modules show, hope, too, is real.

Thinking Critically About:

ADHD—Natural High Energy or Disordered Behavior?

LOQ 53-3 Why is there controversy over attention-deficit/hyperactivity disorder?

Diagnosis in the U.S.

9.4%[1] 2- to 17-year-olds

2.5%[2] adults

Less often in many other countries, such as Norway and Sweden[3]

Twice as often in BOYS as in girls

Symptoms

- inattention and distractibility[4]
- hyperactivity[5]
- impulsivity

SKEPTICS note:

Energetic child + **boring school** = **ADHD overdiagnosis**

- Children are not meant to sit for hours in chairs inside.
- The youngest children in a class tend to be more fidgety—and more often diagnosed.[6]
- Older students may seek out stimulant ADHD prescription drugs–"good-grade pills."[7]
- We don't know the long-term effects of drug treatment.
- There is no clear explanation for increases in ADHD diagnoses and drugs.[8]

SUPPORTERS note:

- More diagnoses reflect increased awareness.
- "ADHD is a real neurobiological disorder whose existence should no longer be debated."[9]
- ADHD is associated with abnormal brain structure, abnormal brain activity patterns, and future risky or antisocial behavior.[10]

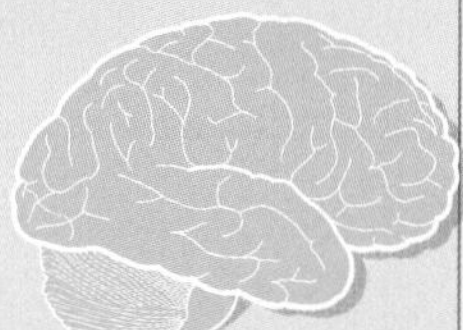

Causes?

- May co-exist with a learning disorder or with defiant and temper-prone behavior.
- May be genetic.[11]

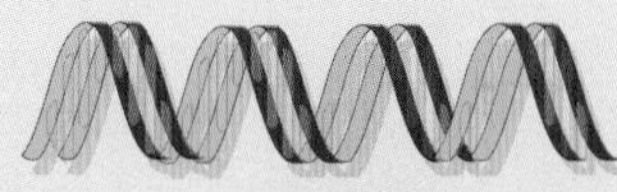

Treatment

- Stimulant drugs (Ritalin and Adderall) calm hyperactivity, and increase ability to sit and focus.[12] So do behavior therapy and aerobic exercise.[13]
- Psychological therapies help with the distress of ADHD.[14]

The bottom line:

Extreme inattention, hyperactivity, and impulsivity can derail social, academic, and work achievements. These symptoms can be treated with medication and other therapies. But the debate continues over whether normal high energy is too often diagnosed as a psychiatric disorder, and whether there is a cost to the long-term use of stimulant drugs in treating ADHD.

1. CDC, 2019. 2. Simon et al., 2009. 3. MacDonald et al., 2019; Smith, 2017. 4. Martel et al., 2016. 5. Kofler et al., 2016. 6. M. Chen et al., 2016. 7. Schwarz, 2012. 8. Ellison, 2015. Hales et al., 2018; Sayal et al., 2017. 9. World Federation for Mental Health, 2005. 10. Ball et al, 2019; Hoogman et al., 2019. 11. Nikolas & Burt, 2010; Poelmans et al., 2011; Volkow et al., 2009; Williams et al., 2010. 12. Barbaresi et al., 2007. 13. Cerrillo-Urbina et al., 2015; Pelham et al., 2016. 14. Fabiano et al., 2008.

MODULE 53 REVIEW Neurodevelopmental Disorders

LEARNING OBJECTIVES

Test Yourself Answer these repeated Learning Objective Questions on your own (before "showing" the answers here, or checking the answers in Appendix D) to improve your retention of the concepts (McDaniel et al., 2009, 2015).

LOQ 53-1 What is *intellectual developmental disorder*?

LOQ 53-2 What is *autism spectrum disorder*?

LOQ 53-3 Why is there controversy over attention-deficit/hyperactivity disorder?

TERMS AND CONCEPTS TO REMEMBER

Test Yourself Write down the definition in your own words, then check your answer.

neurodevelopmental disorders, p. 595

intellectual developmental disorder, p. 595

autism spectrum disorder (ASD), p. 595

attention-deficit/hyperactivity disorder (ADHD), p. 596

MODULE TEST

Test Yourself Answer the following questions on your own first, then "show" the answers here, or check your answers in Appendix E.

1. Which of the following statements is true of intellectual developmental disorder?
   a. People with this condition can generally adapt to the normal demands of independent living.
   b. This condition typically presents with no known physical cause.
   c. People with this condition have an intelligence test score of about 70 or below.
   d. People with this condition are systemizers who tend to have difficulty reading facial expressions.
2. What differences in brain structure and function are characteristic of ASD?
3. Some critics believe that the DSM-5-TR may pathologize everyday life and typical behaviors. How does the ADHD controversy relate to this concern?

CHAPTER
16

xavierarnau/E+/Getty Images

Therapy (Modules 54–56)

Psychologist Kay Redfield Jamison, a renowned expert on the emotional extremes of bipolar disorders, knows her subject firsthand. As she recalled in *An Unquiet Mind:*

> For as long as I can remember, I was frighteningly, although often wonderfully, beholden to moods. Intensely emotional as a child, mercurial as a young girl, first severely depressed as an adolescent, and then unrelentingly caught up in the cycles of manic-depressive illness [now known as *bipolar I disorder*] by the time I began my professional life, I became, both by necessity and intellectual inclination, a student of moods. (1995, pp. 4–5)

Jamison's life was blessed with times of intense sensitivity and passionate energy. But like her father's, it was also sometimes plagued by reckless spending, racing conversation, and sleeplessness, alternating with swings into "the blackest caves of the mind."

Then, "in the midst of utter confusion," she made a life-changing decision. Risking professional embarrassment, she made an appointment with a therapist, a psychiatrist she would visit weekly for years to come.

> He kept me alive a thousand times over. He saw me through madness, despair, wonderful and terrible love affairs, disillusionments and triumphs, recurrences of illness, an almost fatal suicide attempt, the death of a man I greatly loved, and the enormous pleasures and aggravations of my professional life. . . . He was very tough, as well as very kind, and even though he understood more than anyone how much I felt I was losing — in energy, vivacity, and originality — by taking medication, he never [lost] sight of the overall perspective of how costly, damaging, and life threatening my illness was. . . . Although I went to him to be treated for an illness, he taught me . . . the total beholdenness of brain to mind and mind to brain. (pp. 87–88)

These modules explore healing options available to therapists and those who seek their help. We begin by exploring and evaluating *psychotherapies* (Modules 54 and 55), and then focus on *biomedical therapies* and preventing disorders (Module 56).

MODULE 54 Introduction to Therapy and the Psychological Therapies

John Shearer/Getty Images

Kevin Winter/Getty Images for Variety

Value of therapy Actor Kerry Washington and singer Katy Perry have spoken publicly about the benefits of psychotherapy. "I've been going to therapy for about five years," Perry said, "and I think it has really helped my mental health incredibly" (Chen, 2017).

The long history of treating psychological disorders has included a bewildering mix of harsh and gentle methods. Would-be healers have cut holes in people's heads and restrained, bled, or "beat the devil" out of them. But they also have given warm baths and massages and placed people in sunny, serene environments. They have given them helpful drugs. And they have talked with them about childhood experiences, current feelings, and negative thoughts and behaviors.

Reformers Philippe Pinel (1745–1826) and Dorothea Dix (1802–1887) pushed for gentler, more humane treatments and for constructing psychiatric hospitals. Since the 1950s, the introduction of effective drug therapies and community-based treatment programs has emptied most of those hospitals. Unfortunately, this *deinstitutionalization* has left many people with mental illness untreated, which has contributed to their increased homelessness and incarceration.

Treating Psychological Disorders

LEARNING OBJECTIVE QUESTION LOQ 54-1 How do *psychotherapy* and the *biomedical therapies* differ?

Modern Western therapies take two main forms.

- In **psychotherapy**, a trained therapist uses psychological techniques to help someone overcome difficulties and achieve personal growth. The therapist may explore a client's early relationships, encourage the client to adopt new ways of thinking, or coach the client in replacing old behaviors with new ones.
- **Biomedical therapy** offers medication or other biological treatments for psychological disorders. For example, a person with severe depression may receive antidepressants, electroconvulsive therapy (ECT), or brain stimulation.

Today, 1 in 5 Americans annually receives some form of mental health therapy (Olfson et al., 2019). The care provider's training and expertise, and the disorder itself, influence the choice of treatment. Psychotherapy and medication are often combined to treat psychological disorders. Kay Redfield Jamison received psychotherapy and took medications to control her dramatic mood swings.

Let's look first at some influential psychotherapy options. Each is built on one or more of psychology's major theories: psychodynamic, humanistic, behavioral, and cognitive. Most of these techniques can be used one-on-one or in groups. Therapy often occurs in person, but people may also receive treatment by phone or online via *teletherapy*.

The history of treatment Visitors to eighteenth-century psychiatric hospitals paid to gawk at patients, as though they were viewing zoo animals. William Hogarth's (1697–1764) painting captured one of these visits to London's St. Mary of Bethlehem hospital (commonly called Bedlam).

The Granger Collection

Some therapists combine techniques. Indeed, many psychotherapists describe their approach as **eclectic** or integrative, using a blend of therapies.

Macmillan Learning

Dorothea Dix "I . . . call your attention to the state of the Insane Persons confined within this Commonwealth, in cages" (*Memorial to the Legislature of Massachusetts*, 1843).

Psychoanalysis and Psychodynamic Therapies

LOQ 54-2 What are the goals and techniques of psychoanalysis, and how have they been adapted in psychodynamic therapy?

The first major psychological therapy was Sigmund Freud's **psychoanalysis**. Although few clinicians today practice therapy as Freud did, his work deserves discussion. It helped form the foundation for treating psychological disorders, and it continues to influence contemporary therapists working from the modern *psychodynamic* perspective.

The Goals of Psychoanalysis

Freud believed that in therapy, people could achieve healthier, less anxious living by releasing the energy they had previously devoted to *id-ego-superego* conflicts (Personality modules). Freud believed that there are things we *repress*—things we do not want to know because they may cause distress, so we deny or avoid them. Psychoanalysis was Freud's method of helping people bring these repressed feelings into conscious awareness. By helping them reclaim their unconscious thoughts and feelings, and by giving them *insight* into the origins of their distress, the therapist *(analyst)* could help them reduce growth-impeding inner conflicts.

The Techniques of Psychoanalysis

Psychoanalytic theory emphasizes the power of early life experiences to mold the adult. It aims to unearth the past in the hope of loosening its hold on the present. After discarding hypnosis as an unreliable excavator, Freud turned to *free association*.

Imagine yourself as a patient using free association. You begin by relaxing, perhaps by lying on a couch. The psychoanalyst, who sits out of your line of vision, asks you to say aloud whatever comes to mind. At one moment, you're relating a childhood memory. At another, you're describing a disturbing dream and then what you ate for breakfast. Your thoughts may jump from one thing to the next. It sounds easy, but soon you notice how often you edit your thoughts as you speak. You pause for a second before uttering an embarrassing thought. You omit what seems trivial, irrelevant, or shameful. Sometimes your mind goes blank or you clutch up, unable to remember important details. You may joke or change the subject to something less threatening.

Freud thought that these mental blocks were signs of **resistance**. They hint that anxiety lurks and you are defending against uncomfortable material. An analyst would note your resistance and then provide insight into its meaning. If offered at the right moment, this **interpretation**—of, say, your reluctance to call or message your mother—may illuminate the underlying wishes, feelings, and conflicts you are avoiding. The analyst may also offer an explanation of how this resistance fits with other pieces of your psychological puzzle, including those based on analysis of your dream content.

Over many such sessions, your relationship patterns surface in your interaction with your analyst. You may find yourself experiencing strong positive or negative feelings for this confidant. The analyst may suggest you are **transferring** feelings, such as dependency or mingled love and anger, that you experienced in earlier relationships with family members or other important people. By exposing such feelings, you may gain insight into your current relationships.

Today's therapists rarely offer Freud's traditional psychoanalysis. Much of its underlying theory is not supported by scientific research. Analysts' interpretations cannot be proven or disproven. Psychoanalysis takes considerable time and money, often years of several sessions per week. Some of these problems have been addressed in the modern *psychodynamic perspective* that has evolved from psychoanalysis.

psychotherapy treatment involving psychological techniques; consists of interactions between a trained therapist and someone seeking to address psychological difficulties or achieve personal growth.

biomedical therapy prescribed medications or procedures that act directly on the person's physiology.

eclectic approach an approach to psychotherapy that uses techniques from various forms of therapy.

psychoanalysis Sigmund Freud's therapeutic technique. Freud believed the patient's free associations, resistances, and dreams—and the analyst's interpretations of them—released previously repressed feelings, allowing the patient to gain self-insight.

resistance in psychoanalysis, the blocking from consciousness of unpleasant or anxiety-laden material.

interpretation in psychoanalysis, the analyst's noting of dream meanings, resistances, and other significant behaviors and events in order to promote insight and growth.

transference in psychoanalysis, the patient's transfer to the analyst of emotions linked with other relationships (such as love or hatred for a parent).

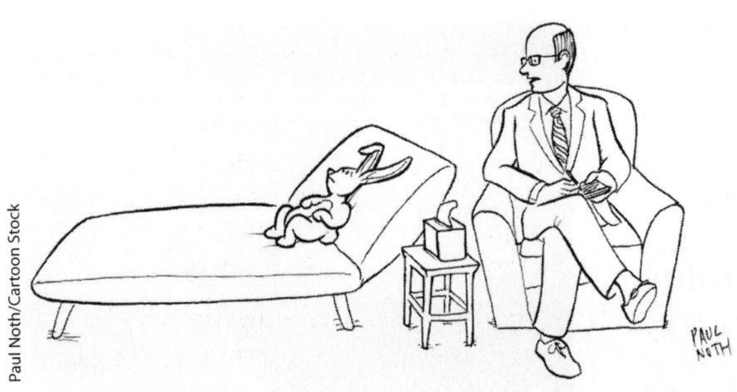
PAUL NOTH

Paul Noth/Cartoon Stock

"I'm more interested in hearing about the eggs you're hiding from yourself."

RETRIEVAL PRACTICE

RP-1 In psychoanalysis, when patients experience strong feelings for their analyst, this is called __________. Patients are said to demonstrate anxiety when they put up mental blocks around sensitive memories, indicating __________. The analyst will attempt to provide insight into the underlying anxiety by offering a(n) __________ of the mental blocks.

ANSWERS IN APPENDIX E

Psychodynamic Therapy

Although influenced by Freud's ideas, **psychodynamic therapists** don't talk much about symbolic id-ego-superego conflicts. Instead, they try to help people understand their current thoughts and feelings by focusing on important relationships and events, including early childhood experiences and the therapist-client relationship. "We can have loving feelings and hateful feelings toward the same person," observed psychodynamic therapist Jonathan Shedler (2009), and "we can desire something and also fear it." Client-therapist sessions occur weekly (rather than several times per week) and often for only a few weeks or months (rather than years). Clients meet with their therapist in person, over the phone, or online. And in contrast to Freud's prescribing cocaine to his depressed patients(!), today's psychodynamic therapists might prescribe antidepressant drugs that have been researched, tested, and deemed safe for use (Driessen et al., 2020).

In their sessions, clients explore and gain perspective on defended-against thoughts and feelings. Therapist David Shapiro (1999, p. 8) illustrated this with the case of a young man who had told women he loved them but knew that he didn't. The client's explanation: They expected it, so he said it. But later, with his wife, who wished he would say that he loved her, he found himself unable—"I don't know why, but I can't."

> ***Therapist:*** Do you mean, then, that if you could, you would like to?
>
> ***Patient:*** Well, I don't know. . . . Maybe I can't say it because I'm not sure it's true. Maybe I don't love her.

Further interactions revealed that the client could not express real love because it would feel "mushy" and "soft" and therefore unmanly. He was "in conflict with himself, and . . . cut off from the nature of that conflict." Shapiro noted that with such patients, who are estranged from themselves, therapists using psychodynamic techniques "are in a position to introduce them to themselves. We can restore their awareness of their own wishes and feelings, and their awareness, as well, of their reactions against those wishes and feelings."

Humanistic Therapies

LOQ 54-3 What are the basic themes of humanistic therapy? What are the goals and techniques of Rogers' person-centered approach?

The *humanistic* perspective emphasizes people's innate goodness and potential for self-fulfillment. To this end, humanistic therapists help clients discover new insights. Indeed, because they share this goal, the psychodynamic and humanistic therapies are often referred to as **insight therapies**. But humanistic therapies differ from psychodynamic therapies in many ways, including their focus on three main ideas:

1. *Growth*. Humanistic therapists focus not on illness, but on helping people grow in self-awareness and self-acceptance. Thus, they call those in therapy "persons" or "clients" rather than "patients" (a change many other therapists have adopted).
2. *The present*. Humanistic psychologists believe the present and the future are more important than the past. Rather than uncovering hidden internal conflicts from the past, they encourage clients to take immediate responsibility for their current feelings and actions.

psychodynamic therapy therapy deriving from the psychoanalytic tradition; views individuals as responding to unconscious forces and childhood experiences, and seeks to enhance self-insight.

insight therapies therapies that aim to improve psychological functioning by increasing a person's awareness of underlying motives and defenses.

3. *The conscious mind.* Humanistic therapies focus on clients' conscious thoughts, which they believe are more important than unconscious thoughts.

These themes are present in the widely used **person-centered therapy**, a humanistic technique that Carl Rogers (1902–1987) developed. In this *nondirective* therapy, the client leads the discussion. The therapist listens, without judging or interpreting, and refrains from directing the client toward certain insights. Believing that most people possess the resources for growth, Rogers (1961, 1980) encouraged therapists to foster that growth through acceptance, genuineness, and empathy. By being *accepting*, therapists may help clients feel freer and more open to change. By being *genuine*, therapists hope to encourage clients to express their true feelings. By being *empathic*, therapists try to sense and reflect their clients' feelings, helping them experience a deeper self-understanding and self-acceptance (Hill & Nakayama, 2000). As Rogers (1980) explained nearly a half century ago,[1]

> Hearing has consequences. When I truly hear a person and the meanings that are important to him at that moment, hearing not simply his words, but him, and when I let him know that I have heard his own private personal meanings, many things happen. There is first of all a grateful look. He feels released. He wants to tell me more about his world. He surges forth in a new sense of freedom. He becomes more open to the process of change.
>
> I have often noticed that the more deeply I hear the meanings of the person, the more there is that happens. Almost always, when a person realizes he has been deeply heard, his eyes moisten. I think in some real sense he is weeping for joy. It is as though he were saying, "Thank God, somebody heard me. Someone knows what it's like to be me." (p. 10)

person-centered therapy a humanistic therapy, developed by Carl Rogers, in which the client directs the discussion and the therapist uses techniques such as *active listening* within an accepting, genuine, empathic environment to facilitate clients' growth. (Also called *client-centered therapy*.)

active listening empathic listening in which the listener echoes, restates, and seeks clarification. A feature of Rogers' person-centered therapy.

To Rogers, "hearing" was **active listening**. The therapist echoes, restates, and seeks clarification of what the person expresses (verbally or nonverbally). The therapist also acknowledges those expressed feelings. Active listening is now an accepted part of counseling practices in many schools, colleges, and clinics. Counselors listen attentively. They interrupt only to restate and confirm feelings, to accept what is being expressed, or to seek clarification. In the following brief excerpt, note how Rogers tried to provide a psychological mirror that would help the client see himself more clearly (Meador & Rogers, 1984, p. 167):

Rogers: Feeling that now, hm? That you're just no good to yourself, no good to anybody. Never will be any good to anybody. Just that you're completely worthless, huh?—Those really are lousy feelings. Just feel that you're no good at all, hm?

Client: Yeah. *(Muttering in low, discouraged voice)* That's what this guy I went to town with just the other day told me.

Rogers: This guy that you went to town with really told you that you were no good? Is that what you're saying? Did I get that right?

Client: M-hm.

Rogers: I guess the meaning of that if I get it right is that here's somebody that meant something to you and what does he think of you? Why, he's told you that he thinks

Michael Rougier/The LIFE Picture Collection/Getty Images

Active listening Carl Rogers (right) empathized with a client during this group therapy session.

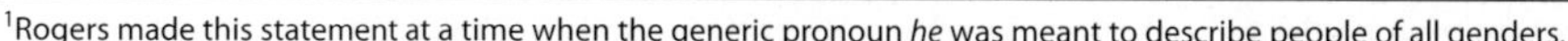

[1]Rogers made this statement at a time when the generic pronoun *he* was meant to describe people of all genders.

unconditional positive regard a caring, accepting, and nonjudgmental attitude, which Carl Rogers believed would help clients develop self-awareness and self-acceptance.

behavior therapy therapy that uses learning principles to reduce unwanted behaviors and increase desirable behaviors.

you're no good at all. And that just really knocks the props out from under you. *(Client weeps quietly.)* It just brings the tears. *(Silence of 20 seconds)*

Client: (Rather defiantly) I don't care though.

Rogers: You tell yourself you don't care at all, but somehow I guess some part of you cares because some part of you weeps over it.

Can a therapist be a perfect mirror, without selecting and interpreting what is reflected? Rogers conceded that one cannot be *totally* nondirective. Nevertheless, he said, the therapist's most important contribution is to accept and understand the client. Given a nonjudgmental, grace-filled environment that provides **unconditional positive regard**, people may accept even their worst traits and still feel valued and whole.

How can we improve communication in our own relationships by listening more actively? Three Rogers-inspired hints may help:

1. ***Paraphrase.*** Check your understanding by summarizing the person's words out loud, in your own words. "You felt disappointed when your friend canceled your plans. Is that right?"
2. ***Invite clarification.*** "What might be an example of that?" may encourage the person to say more.
3. ***Reflect feelings.*** "It sounds frustrating" might mirror what you're sensing from the person's body language and intensity.

ASK YOURSELF

Think of your closest friends. Do they tend to express more empathy than those you feel less close to? How might *you* more deeply and actively listen to your friends?

Behavior Therapies

LOQ 54-4 How does the basic assumption of behavior therapy differ from the assumptions of psychodynamic and humanistic therapies? What classical conditioning techniques are used in exposure therapies and aversive conditioning?

The insight therapies assume that self-awareness and psychological well-being go hand in hand. For example, psychodynamic therapists expect people's problems to diminish as they gain insight into their unresolved and unconscious tensions. And humanistic therapists expect problems to diminish as people get in touch with their feelings. **Behavior therapists**, however, doubt the healing power of self-awareness. Rather than delving deeply below the surface looking for inner causes, behavior therapists assume that problem behaviors *are* the problems. (You can become aware of why you are highly anxious during exams and still be anxious.) If specific phobias, sexual dysfunctions, or other maladaptive symptoms are learned behaviors, why not apply the learning principles of classical and operant conditioning to replace them with new, constructive behaviors?

Classical Conditioning Techniques

One cluster of behavior therapies derives from principles developed in Ivan Pavlov's early twentieth-century conditioning experiments. As Pavlov and others showed, we learn various behaviors and emotions through *classical conditioning* (Learning modules). If a dog attacks us, we may thereafter have a conditioned fear response when other dogs approach. If our fear generalizes and all dogs become conditioned stimuli, we may even develop a specific phobia for dogs.

What's the nature of the trouble, and when did it begin?
Let's drive it around and see what happens.
FREUDIAN
BEHAVIOR THERAPIST
S. Harris
Sidney Harris/Cartoon Stock

Could maladaptive symptoms be examples of conditioned responses? If so, might reconditioning be a solution? Learning theorist O. H. Mowrer (1907–1982) thought so. He developed a successful conditioning therapy for chronic bed-wetting, using a liquid-sensitive pad connected to an alarm. If the sleeping child wets the bed pad, moisture triggers the alarm, waking the child. After several trials, the child associates bladder relaxation with waking. In three out of four cases, the treatment has been effective and the success has boosted the child's self-esteem (Christophersen & Edwards, 1992; Houts et al., 1994).

Can we unlearn fear responses, such as to public speaking or flying, through new conditioning? Many people have. An example: The fear of riding in an elevator is often a learned aversion to being in a confined space. **Counterconditioning**, such as with *exposure therapy*, pairs the trigger stimulus (in this case, the enclosed space of the elevator) with a new relaxation response that is incompatible with fear. Therapists use such techniques as slow and deep breathing or imagining peaceful images.

RETRIEVAL PRACTICE

RP-2 What might a psychodynamic therapist say about Mowrer's therapy for bed-wetting? How might a behavior therapist defend it?

ANSWERS IN APPENDIX E

EXPOSURE THERAPIES Picture this scene: Behavioral psychologist Mary Cover Jones is working with 3-year-old Peter, who is petrified of rabbits and other furry objects. To rid Peter of his fear, Jones plans to associate the fear-evoking rabbit with the pleasurable, relaxed response associated with eating a favorite snack. As Peter begins his mid-afternoon snack, she introduces a caged rabbit on the other side of the huge room. Peter, eagerly munching away on his crackers and drinking his milk, hardly notices. On succeeding days, she gradually moves the rabbit closer and closer. Within 2 months, Peter is holding the rabbit in his lap, even stroking it while he eats. Moreover, his fear of other furry objects subsides as well, having been *countered*, or replaced, by a relaxed state that cannot coexist with fear (Fisher, 1984; Jones, 1924).

Unfortunately for many who might have been helped by Jones' counterconditioning procedures, her story of Peter and the rabbit didn't become well-known when it was reported in 1924. It was more than 30 years before psychiatrist Joseph Wolpe (1958; Wolpe & Plaud, 1997) refined Jones' counterconditioning technique into the **exposure therapies** used today. These therapies, in a variety of ways, try to change people's reactions by repeatedly exposing them to stimuli that trigger unwanted reactions. We all experience this process in everyday life. A person moving to a new apartment may be annoyed by nearby loud traffic noise, but only for a while. With repeated exposure, the person adapts. So, too, with people who have fear reactions to specific events, such as people with PTSD (Thompson-Hollands et al., 2018). Exposed repeatedly to the situation that once petrified them, with support from talk therapy, they can learn to react less anxiously (Holder et al., 2020). Exposure therapy is neither pleasant nor easy, so it helps to have supportive family and friends (Meis et al., 2019).

One exposure therapy used to treat specific phobias is **systematic desensitization**. You cannot simultaneously be anxious and relaxed. Therefore, if you can repeatedly relax when facing anxiety-provoking stimuli, you can gradually eliminate your anxiety. The trick is to proceed gradually. If you fear public speaking, a behavior therapist might first help you construct an *anxiety hierarchy*—a kind of ladder of speaking situations that trigger increasing anxiety levels. Yours might range from mildly anxiety-provoking situations (perhaps speaking up in a small group of friends) to panic-provoking situations (having to address a large audience).

Next, the therapist would train you in *progressive relaxation*. You would learn to release tension in one muscle group after another, until you achieve a comfortable, complete state of relaxation. Then the therapist might ask you to imagine, with your eyes closed, a mildly anxiety-arousing situation: You are having coffee with a group of friends and are trying to decide whether to speak up. If imagining the scene causes you to feel any anxiety, you are told to signal by raising your finger. Seeing the signal, the therapist will instruct you to switch off the mental image and go back to deep relaxation. This imagined scene is repeatedly paired with relaxation until you feel no trace of anxiety.

The therapist will then move to the next item in your anxiety hierarchy, again using relaxation techniques to desensitize you to each imagined situation. After several sessions, you move to actual situations and practice what you had only imagined before, beginning with relatively easy tasks (like speaking up among friends) and gradually

counterconditioning behavior therapy procedures that use classical conditioning to evoke new responses to stimuli that are triggering unwanted behaviors; includes *exposure therapies* and *aversive conditioning*.

exposure therapies behavioral techniques that treat anxieties by exposing people (in imaginary or actual situations) to the things they fear and avoid.

systematic desensitization a type of exposure therapy that associates a pleasant relaxed state with gradually increasing anxiety-triggering stimuli. Commonly used to treat specific phobias.

FIGURE 54.1
Scary spider Guided by a therapist, virtual reality technology exposes people to vivid simulations of feared stimuli and helps them gradually overcome their fear.

moving to more anxiety-filled ones (like giving a public speech). Conquering your anxiety in an actual situation, not just in your imagination, will increase your self-confidence (Foa & Kozak, 1986; Williams, 1987). Eventually, you may even become a confident public speaker. Often people fear not just a situation, such as public speaking, but also being incapacitated by their own fear response. As their fear subsides, so also does their fear of the fear.

"According to most studies, people's number one fear is public speaking. Number two is death. Does that sound right? This means to the average person, if you go to a funeral, you are better off in the casket than doing the eulogy." —Comedian Jerry Seinfeld

If anxiety-arousing situations (such as those that evoke fears of flying, heights, particular animals, and public speaking) are too expensive, difficult, or risky to re-create, the therapist may recommend **virtual reality exposure therapy**. Imagine donning a head-mounted display unit that projects a lifelike three-dimensional virtual world tailored to your particular fear (**FIGURE 54.1**). If you fear flying, for example, you could peer out of a simulated plane, feel the engine's vibrations, and hear it roar as the plane taxis down the runway and takes off. If you fear social interactions, you could experience simulated stressful situations, such as entering a roomful of people. In controlled studies, people treated with virtual reality exposure therapy have experienced relief from real-life fear and social anxiety (Meyerbröker & Morina, 2021).

AVERSIVE CONDITIONING Exposure therapy helps you learn what you *should* do; it enables a more relaxed, positive response to an upsetting *harmless* stimulus. **Aversive conditioning** helps you learn what you *should not* do; it creates a negative (aversive) response to a *harmful* stimulus (such as alcohol). The aversive conditioning procedure is simple: It associates the unwanted behavior with unpleasant feelings. To treat compulsive nail biting, the therapist may suggest painting the fingernails with a nasty-tasting nail polish (Brush, 2014). To treat alcohol use disorder, the therapist may offer the client appealing alcoholic drinks laced with a drug that produces severe nausea. If that therapy links alcohol with violent nausea, the person's reaction to alcohol may change from positive to negative (**FIGURE 54.2**).

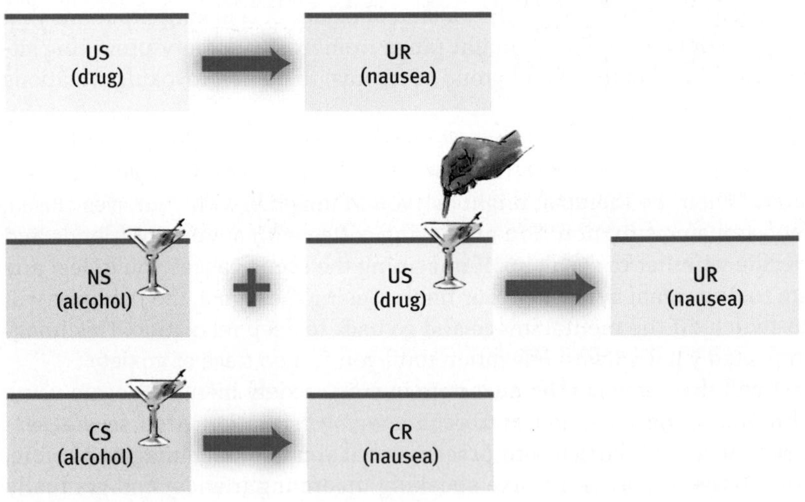
US
(drug)
UR
(nausea)
NS
(alcohol)
US
(drug)
UR
(nausea)
CS
(alcohol)
CR
(nausea)

FIGURE 54.2
Aversion therapy for alcohol use disorder After repeatedly imbibing an alcoholic drink mixed with a drug that produces severe nausea, some people with a history of alcohol use disorder develop at least a temporary conditioned aversion to alcohol. (Remember: US is unconditioned stimulus, UR is unconditioned response, NS is neutral stimulus, CS is conditioned stimulus, and CR is conditioned response.)

Taste aversion learning has been a successful alternative to killing predators in some animal protection programs (Dingfelder, 2010; Garcia & Gustavson, 1997). After being sickened by eating a tainted sheep, wolves may later avoid sheep. Does aversive conditioning also transform humans' reactions to alcohol? In the short run it may. In one classic study, 685 participants with alcohol use disorder completed an aversion therapy program (Wiens & Menustik, 1983). Over the next year, they returned for several booster treatments that paired alcohol with sickness. At the end of that year, 63 percent were not drinking alcohol. But the effects diminished when the boosters stopped: After three years, only 33 percent were alcohol free.

In therapy, as in research, cognition influences conditioning. People know that outside the therapist's office they can drink without fear of nausea. This ability to discriminate between the therapy situation and all others can limit aversive conditioning's effectiveness. Thus, therapists often combine aversive conditioning with other treatments.

virtual reality exposure therapy a counterconditioning technique that treats anxiety through creative electronic simulations in which people can safely face specific fears, such as flying, spiders, or public speaking.

aversive conditioning associates an unpleasant state (such as nausea) with an unwanted behavior (such as drinking alcohol).

token economy an operant conditioning procedure in which people earn a token for exhibiting a desired behavior and can later exchange tokens for privileges or treats.

Operant Conditioning Techniques

LOQ 54-5 What is the main premise of behavior therapy based on operant conditioning principles, and what are the views of its proponents and critics?

If you have learned to swim, you learned to hold your breath with your head under water, to pull your body through the water, to bring your face above water to breathe, and perhaps even to dive safely. Operant conditioning shaped your swimming. You were reinforced for safe, effective behaviors. And you were naturally punished, as when you swallowed water, for improper swimming behaviors.

Consequences strongly influence our voluntary behaviors. Knowing this basic principle of operant conditioning, behavior therapists can apply *behavior modification*. They reinforce desirable behaviors, and they fail to reinforce—or sometimes punish—undesirable behaviors.

Using operant conditioning to solve specific behavior problems has raised hopes for some seemingly hopeless cases. Children with intellectual developmental disorder have been taught to care for themselves. Socially withdrawn children with autism spectrum disorder (ASD) have learned to interact. People with schizophrenia have been helped to behave more rationally. In such cases, therapists use positive reinforcers to *shape* behavior. In a step-by-step manner, they reward closer and closer approximations of the desired behavior.

Rewards used to modify behavior vary. For some people, the reinforcing power of attention or praise is sufficient. Others require concrete rewards, such as food. In institutional settings, therapists may create a **token economy**. When people display a desired behavior, such as getting out of bed, washing, dressing, eating, talking coherently, cleaning up their rooms, or playing cooperatively, they receive a token or plastic coin. Later, they can exchange a number of these tokens for rewards, such as candy, TV time, day trips, or better living quarters. Token economies have proven successful in a number of settings, including group homes, classrooms, and correctional institutions, and among people with various disabilities (Matson & Boisjoli, 2009). They have been widely used for children with ADHD, ASD, and other behavioral difficulties (Coehlo et al., 2015; Gilley & Ringdahl, 2014; Kazdin, 1982).

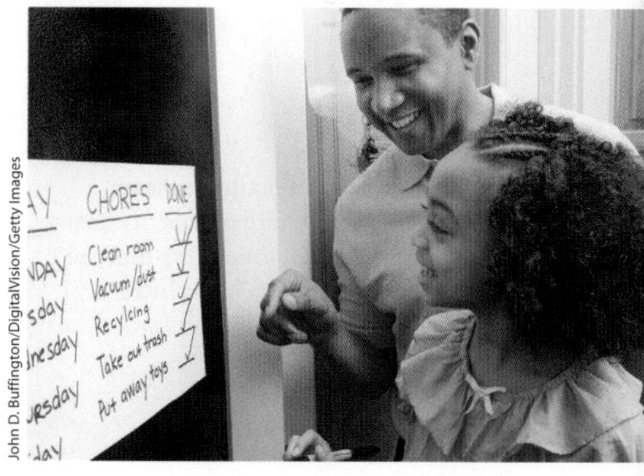
CHORES
DONE
Clean room
Vacuum/dust
Recycling
Take out trash
Put away toys
John D. Buffington/DigitalVision/Getty Images

Behavior modification critics express two concerns:

- ***How durable are the behaviors?*** Will people become so dependent on extrinsic rewards that the desired behaviors will stop when reinforcers stop? Behavior modification advocates believe the behaviors will endure if therapists wean people from the tokens by shifting them toward other, real-life rewards, such as social approval. Further, they point out, the desired behaviors themselves can be rewarding. As people become more socially competent, the intrinsic satisfaction of social interaction may sustain the behaviors.
- ***Is it right for one human to control another's behavior?*** Those who set up token economies deprive people of something they desire and decide which behaviors to reinforce. To critics, this whole process feels authoritarian. Advocates reply that control already exists: People's destructive behavior patterns are being maintained

cognitive therapy therapy that teaches people new, more adaptive ways of thinking; based on the assumption that thoughts intervene between events and our emotional reactions.

and perpetuated by natural reinforcers and punishers in their environments. Isn't using positive rewards to reinforce adaptive behavior more humane than institutionalizing or punishing people? Advocates also argue that the right to effective treatment and an improved life justifies temporary deprivation.

ASK YOURSELF

What is your judgment of behavior modification techniques, such as those used in token economies? Do you agree or disagree with this approach?

RETRIEVAL PRACTICE

RP-3 What are the *insight therapies*, and how do they differ from behavior therapies?

RP-4 Some maladaptive behaviors are learned. What hope does this fact provide?

RP-5 Exposure therapies and aversive conditioning are applications of ________________ conditioning. Token economies are an application of ________________ conditioning.

ANSWERS IN APPENDIX E

Cognitive Therapies

LOQ 54-6 What are the goals and techniques of the cognitive therapies and of cognitive-behavioral therapy?

People with specific fears and problem behaviors may respond to behavior therapy. But how might behavior therapists modify the wide assortment of behaviors that accompany depressive disorders? Or treat people with generalized anxiety disorder, where unfocused anxiety doesn't lend itself to a neat list of anxiety-triggering situations? The *cognitive revolution* that has profoundly changed other areas of psychology since the 1960s has also influenced therapy.

"You have power over your mind." —Marcus Aurelius (121–180 C.E.), *Meditations*

The **cognitive therapies** assume that our *thinking* colors our *feelings* (**FIGURE 54.3**). Between an event and our response lies the mind. Anxiety, for example, can arise from an "attention bias to threat" (MacLeod & Clarke, 2015). Self-blaming and overgeneralized explanations of bad events feed depression. If depressed, we may interpret a suggestion as criticism, disagreement as dislike, praise as flattery, friendliness as pity. Dwelling on such thoughts (ruminating) sustains or worsens negative thinking.

If feeling depressed is sometimes nature's way of getting us to slow down and solve a problem, cognitive therapies may speed up that problem solving (Hollon, 2020). Cognitive therapies help people change their mind with new, more constructive ways of perceiving and interpreting events (Burns, 1981; Persons, 2016; Schmidt et al., 2019).

"Life does not consist mainly, or even largely, of facts and happenings. It consists mainly of the storm of thoughts that are forever blowing through one's head." —Writer Mark Twain, *Autobiography, Volume 1*, 1924

Beck's Cognitive Therapy

In the late 1960s, a woman left a party early. Things had not gone well. She felt disconnected from the other partygoers and assumed no one liked her. A few days later, she visited cognitive therapist Aaron Beck. Rather than go down the traditional path to her childhood, Beck questioned her current thinking. After she then listed a dozen people who *did* like her, Beck realized that challenging people's automatic negative thoughts could be therapeutic. After trying this approach with other clients, he developed cognitive

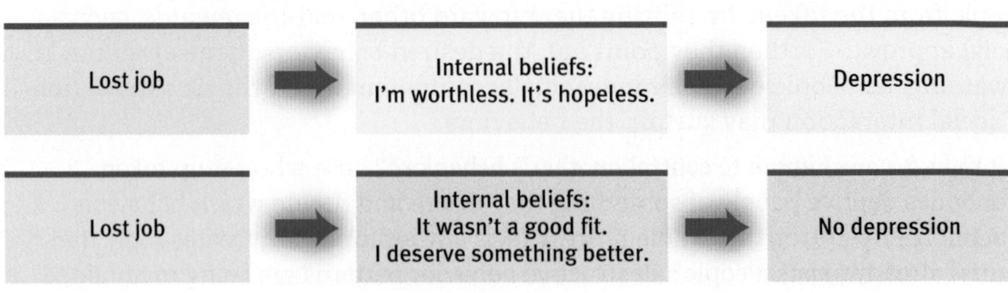
Lost job
Internal beliefs:
I'm worthless. It's hopeless.
Depression
Lost job
Internal beliefs:
It wasn't a good fit.
I deserve something better.
No depression

FIGURE 54.3
A cognitive perspective on psychological disorders The person's emotional reactions are produced not directly by the event, but by the person's thoughts in response to the event.

therapy, which assumes that changing people's thinking can change their functioning (Spiegel, 2015).

People with depression, Beck found, often reported dreams with negative themes of loss, rejection, and abandonment. These themes extended into their waking thoughts, and even into therapy, as clients recalled and rehearsed their failings and worst impulses (Kelly, 2000). Beck and his colleagues (1979) used cognitive therapy to reverse clients' negativity about themselves, their situations, and their futures. With this technique, gentle questioning seeks to reveal irrational thinking, and then to persuade people to remove the dark glasses through which they view life (Beck et al., 1979):

Client: I agree with the descriptions of me but I guess I don't agree that the way I think makes me depressed.

Beck: How do you understand it?

Client: I get depressed when things go wrong. Like when I fail a test.

Beck: How can failing a test make you depressed?

Client: Well, if I fail I'll never get into law school.

Beck: So failing the test means a lot to you. But if failing a test could drive people into clinical depression, wouldn't you expect everyone who failed the test to have a depression? . . . Did everyone who failed get depressed enough to require treatment?

Client: No, but it depends on how important the test was to the person.

Beck: Right, and who decides the importance?

Client: I do.

Beck: And so, what we have to examine is your way of viewing the test (or the way that you think about the test) and how it affects your chances of getting into law school. Do you agree?

Client: Right.

Beck: Do you agree that the way you interpret the results of the test will affect you? You might feel depressed, you might have trouble sleeping, not feel like eating, and you might even wonder if you should drop out of the course.

Client: I have been thinking that I wasn't going to make it.

Beck: Now what did failing mean?

Client: *(tearful)* That I couldn't get into law school.

Beck: And what does that mean to you?

Client: That I'm just not smart enough.

Beck: Anything else?

Client: That I can never be happy.

Beck: And how do these thoughts make you feel?

Client: Very unhappy.

Beck: So it is the meaning of failing a test that makes you very unhappy. In fact, believing that you can never be happy is a powerful factor in producing unhappiness. So, you get yourself into a trap—by definition, failure to get into law school equals "I can never be happy." (pp. 145–146)

We often think in words. Therefore, getting people to change what they say to themselves is an effective way to change their thinking. Perhaps you can identify with the anxious students who, before an exam, make matters worse with self-defeating thoughts: "This exam's going to be impossible. All these other students are so confident. I didn't study hard enough. I'll probably forget everything." Psychologists call this sort of relentless, overgeneralized, self-blaming behavior *catastrophizing*.

To change such negative *self-talk*, cognitive therapists have offered *stress inoculation training*: teaching people to restructure their thinking in stressful situations (Meichenbaum, 1977, 1985). Sometimes it may be enough simply to say more positive things to yourself: "Relax. The exam may be hard, but it will

Macmillan Learning

Aaron Beck (1921–2021) "Cognitive therapy seeks to alleviate psychological stresses by correcting faulty conceptions and beliefs. By correcting erroneous beliefs we can lower excessive reactions" (Beck, 1978).

LIFE IS RARELY ALL ONE WAY, CHARLIE BROWN
YOU WIN A FEW, AND YOU LOSE A FEW!
REALLY?
GEE, THAT'D BE NEAT!!
SCHULZ
9/17/01
www.snoopy.com
© 1973 United Feature Syndicate, Inc.

Drawing by Charles Schultz; ©1956. Reprinted by permission of Andrews McMeel Syndication

TABLE 54.1 Selected Cognitive Therapy Techniques

Aim of Technique	Technique	Therapists' Directives
Reveal beliefs	Question your interpretations	Explore your beliefs, revealing faulty assumptions such as "I must be liked by everyone."
	Rank thoughts and emotions	Gain perspective by ranking your thoughts and emotions from mildly to extremely upsetting.
Test beliefs	Examine consequences	Explore difficult situations, assessing possible consequences and challenging faulty reasoning.
	Decatastrophize thinking	Work through the actual worst-case consequences of the situation you face (it is often not as bad as imagined). Then determine how to cope with the real situation you face.
Change beliefs	Take appropriate responsibility	Challenge total self-blame and negative thinking, noting aspects for which you may be truly responsible, as well as aspects that aren't your responsibility.
	Resist extremes	Develop new ways of thinking and feeling to replace maladaptive habits. For example, change from thinking "I am a total failure" to "I got a failing grade on that paper, and I can make these changes to succeed next time."

be hard for everyone else, too. I studied harder than most people. Besides, I don't need a perfect score to get a good grade." After learning to "talk back" to negative thoughts, depression-prone children, teens, and college students have shown a greatly reduced rate of future depression (Reivich et al., 2013; Seligman et al., 2009). Ditto for anxiety (Krueze et al., 2018). To a large extent, it is the thought that counts. For a sampling of commonly used cognitive therapy techniques, see **TABLE 54.1**.

It's not just depressed people who can benefit from positive self-talk. We all talk to ourselves (thinking "I wish I hadn't said that," for example, can protect us from repeating the blunder). The findings of nearly three dozen sport psychology studies show that self-talk interventions can even enhance the learning of athletic skills (Hatzigeorgiadis et al., 2011). Novice basketball players may be trained to think "focus" and "follow through," swimmers to think "high elbow," and tennis players to think "look at the ball." People anxious about public speaking have grown in confidence if asked to recall a speaking success and then asked this: "Explain WHY you were able to achieve such a successful performance" (Zunick et al., 2015).

ASK YOURSELF

Have you ever struggled to reach a goal at school or work because of your own self-defeating thoughts? How could you challenge those thoughts?

artursfoto/iStock/Getty Images

CBT for eating disorders aided by journaling Cognitive-behavioral therapists guide people with eating disorders toward new ways of explaining their good and bad food-related experiences (Linardon et al., 2017). By recording positive events and how she has enabled them, this woman may become more aware of her self-control and more optimistic.

Cognitive-Behavioral Therapy

"The trouble with most therapy," said therapist Albert Ellis (1913–2007), "is that it helps you to feel better. But you don't get better. You have to back it up with action, action, action." **Cognitive-behavioral therapy (CBT)** takes a combined approach to treating depression, anxiety, and many other disorders. This widely practiced *integrative* therapy aims to alter not only the way people *think* but also the way they *act*. Like other cognitive therapies, CBT seeks to make people aware of their irrational negative thinking and to replace it with new ways of thinking. And like other behavior therapies, it trains people to *practice* the more positive approach in everyday settings.

Anxiety, depressive, and bipolar disorders share a common problem: unhealthy emotion regulation (Aldao & Nolen-Hoeksema, 2010; Gruber et al., 2011; Szkodny et al., 2014). An effective CBT program for these emotional disorders trains people both to replace their catastrophizing *thinking* with more realistic appraisals, and, as homework, to practice *behaviors* that are incompatible with their problem (Kazantzis et al., 2010; Moses & Barlow, 2006). A person might record daily situations associated with negative and positive emotions, and engage more in activities that increase well-being. Those who fear social situations might learn to restrain the negative thoughts surrounding their social anxiety and practice approaching people.

CBT is an effective treatment for people with obsessive-compulsive and related disorders (Öst et al., 2015; Tolin et al., 2019). In one classic study, people learned to prevent their compulsive behaviors by relabeling their obsessive thoughts (Schwartz et al., 1996). Feeling the urge to wash their hands again, they would tell themselves, "I'm having a compulsive urge." They would explain to themselves that the hand-washing urge was a result of their brain's abnormal activity, which they had previously viewed in PET scans. Then, instead of giving in, they would spend 15 minutes in an enjoyable, alternative behavior—practicing an instrument, taking a walk, gardening. This helped "unstick" the brain by shifting attention and engaging other brain areas. For two or three months, the weekly therapy sessions continued, with relabeling and refocusing practice at home. By the study's end, most participants' symptoms had diminished and their PET scans revealed normalized brain activity. Many other studies confirm CBT's effectiveness for treating other disorders, such as PTSD and alcohol or other substance use disorders (Lewis et al., 2020; Magill et al., 2020).

cognitive-behavioral therapy (CBT) a popular integrative therapy that combines cognitive therapy (changing self-defeating thinking) with behavior therapy (changing behavior).

group therapy therapy conducted with groups rather than individuals, providing benefits from group interaction.

CBT variations have added new angles to treat clients' thinking and behavior. For example, *dialectical behavior therapy (DBT)* helps change harmful and even suicidal behavior patterns (Linehan, 2020; McCauley et al., 2018). *Dialectical* means "opposing," and this therapy attempts to make peace between two opposing forces—acceptance and change. Therapists create an accepting and encouraging environment, helping clients feel they have an ally who will offer them constructive feedback and guidance. In individual sessions, clients learn new ways of thinking that help them tolerate distress and regulate their emotions. They may also receive training in social skills and in *mindfulness meditation*, which helps alleviate depression and anxiety (Haller et al., 2021; Wielgosz et al., 2019). Group training sessions offer additional opportunities to practice new skills in a social context, with further practice as homework.

Acceptance and commitment therapy (ACT) helps clients learn to *accept* their feelings and *commit* to actions that are more consistent with their life values (Hayes et al., 2009). ACT effectively treats depression and anxiety, and even chronic pain (Bai et al., 2020; van Agteren et al., 2021).

RETRIEVAL PRACTICE

RP-6 How do the humanistic and cognitive therapies differ?

RP-7 A critical attribute of the ________ ________ developed by Aaron Beck focuses on the belief that changing people's thinking can change their functioning.

RP-8 What is *cognitive-behavioral therapy,* and what sorts of problems does this therapy best address?

ANSWERS IN APPENDIX E

Group Therapy, Couples Therapy, and Family Therapy

LOQ 54-7 What are the aims and benefits of group therapy, couples therapy, and family therapy?

Group Therapy

Except for traditional psychoanalysis, most therapies may also occur in small groups. **Group therapy** does not provide the same degree of therapist involvement with each client. However, it offers other benefits:

- ***It saves therapists' time and clients' money,*** and often is no less effective than individual therapy (Burlingame et al., 2016).
- ***It offers a social laboratory for exploring social behaviors and developing social skills.*** Therapists frequently suggest group therapy for people experiencing frequent conflicts or whose behavior distresses others. The therapist guides people's interactions as they discuss issues and try out new behaviors.
- ***It enables people to see that others share their problems.*** It can be a relief to discover that others have experienced similar stressors, troublesome feelings, and behaviors (Rahman et al., 2019).

Andrew Toos/Cartoon Stock

"We are communicating better, but we are still not out of woods."

family therapy therapy that treats people in the context of their family system. Views an individual's unwanted behaviors as influenced by, or directed at, other family members.

- *It helps clients understand their feelings around others.* Sometimes our most difficult feelings happen in our close relationships. Couples therapy helps people understand and work through unhealthy emotions and communication patterns with their partners.
- *It provides feedback as clients try out new ways of behaving.* Hearing that you look or sound poised, even though you feel anxious and self-conscious, can be very reassuring.

Family Therapy

One special type of group interaction, **family therapy**, assumes that no person is an island (Baucom & Crenshaw, 2019). We live and grow in relation to others, especially our family. We struggle to differentiate ourselves from our families, but we also need to connect with them emotionally. These two opposing tendencies can create stress for both the individual and the family.

Family therapists view families as systems, in which each person's actions trigger reactions from others. A child's rebellion, for example, affects and is affected by other family tensions. Therapists are often successful in helping family members identify their roles within the family's social system, improve communication, and discover new ways of preventing or resolving conflicts (Hazelrigg et al., 1987; Shadish et al., 1993). Family-focused treatments focus on understanding and building healthier and more supportive family interactions, especially for younger family members who have mood difficulties (Miklowitz & Chung, 2016).

Self-Help Groups

More than 100 million in the United States have belonged to religious, special-interest, or support groups that meet regularly—with 9 in 10 reporting that group members "support each other emotionally" (Gallup, 1994). Self-help groups often provide support to people who struggle to find it elsewhere (Dingle et al., 2021). One analysis of more than 14,000 self-help groups reported that most focus on stigmatized, hard-to-discuss problems (Davison et al., 2000).

Many self-help groups use a 12-step program modeled on that of Alcoholics Anonymous (AA), the grandparent of support groups. Such a program asks members to admit their powerlessness, to seek help from a higher power and from one another, and (the twelfth step) to take the message to others in need of it (Galanter, 2016). Studies of 12-step programs such as AA have found that they help reduce alcohol use disorder at rates comparable to other treatment interventions (Ferri et al., 2006; Moos & Moos, 2005). An 8-year, $27 million investigation found that AA participants reduced their drinking sharply, as did those assigned to CBT or an alternative therapy (Project Match, 1997). The more meetings AA members attend, the greater their alcohol abstinence (Moos & Moos, 2006). Those whose personal stories include a "redemptive narrative"—who see something good as having come from their struggles—more often sustain sobriety (Dunlop & Tracy, 2013).

With close to 2 million members in 180 countries, AA is said to be "the largest organization on Earth that nobody wanted to join" (Finlay, 2000).

Hispanolistic/E+/Getty Images

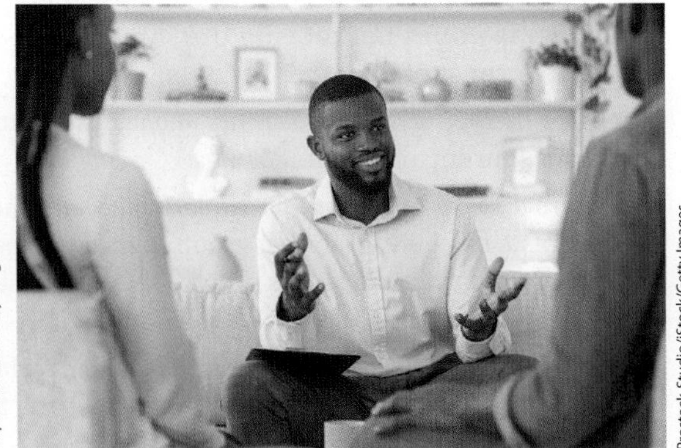

Prostock-Studio/iStock/Getty Images

Group and couples therapy People in group therapy may find comfort in knowing others share their challenges. *Couples therapy* focuses on how romantic partners' ways of relating to each other create problems, and how they might change their interactions. Couples therapy often increases emotional intimacy, healthy communication, and relationship satisfaction (Roddy et al., 2020).

TABLE 54.2 Comparing Modern Psychotherapies

Therapy	Targeted Problem	Therapy Aim	Therapy Technique
Psychodynamic	Unconscious conflicts from childhood experiences	Reduce anxiety through self-insight.	Interpret clients' memories, dreams, and feelings.
Person-centered	Barriers to self-understanding and self-acceptance	Enable growth via unconditional positive regard, acceptance, genuineness, and empathy.	Listen actively and reflect clients' feelings.
Behavior	Dysfunctional behaviors	Learn adaptive behaviors; extinguish problem behaviors.	Use classical conditioning (via exposure or aversion therapy) or operant conditioning (as in token economies).
Cognitive	Negative, self-defeating thinking	Promote healthier thinking and self-talk.	Train people to dispute their negative thoughts and attributions.
Cognitive-behavioral	Self-harmful thoughts and behaviors	Promote healthier thinking and adaptive behaviors.	Train people to counter self-harmful thoughts and to act out their new ways of thinking.
Group, couples, and family	Stressful relationships	Heal relationships.	Develop an understanding of family and other social systems, explore roles, and improve communication.

In an individualist age, with more and more people living alone or feeling isolated, the popularity of support groups—for the addicted, the bereaved, the divorced, or simply those seeking fellowship and growth—may reflect a longing for community and connectedness.

* * *

For a synopsis of these modern psychotherapies, see **TABLE 54.2**.

MODULE 54 REVIEW Introduction to Therapy and the Psychological Therapies

LEARNING OBJECTIVES

Test Yourself Answer these repeated Learning Objective Questions on your own (before "showing" the answers here, or checking the answers in Appendix D) to improve your retention of the concepts (McDaniel et al., 2009, 2015).

LOQ 54-1 How do *psychotherapy* and the *biomedical therapies* differ?

LOQ 54-2 What are the goals and techniques of psychoanalysis, and how have they been adapted in psychodynamic therapy?

LOQ 54-3 What are the basic themes of humanistic therapy? What are the goals and techniques of Rogers' person-centered approach?

LOQ 54-4 How does the basic assumption of behavior therapy differ from the assumptions of psychodynamic and humanistic therapies? What classical conditioning techniques are used in exposure therapies and aversive conditioning?

LOQ 54-5 What is the main premise of behavior therapy based on operant conditioning principles, and what are the views of its proponents and critics?

LOQ 54-6 What are the goals and techniques of the cognitive therapies and of cognitive-behavioral therapy?

LOQ 54-7 What are the aims and benefits of group therapy, couples therapy, and family therapy?

TERMS AND CONCEPTS TO REMEMBER

Test Yourself Write down the definition in your own words, then check your answer.

psychotherapy, p. 601
biomedical therapy, p. 601
eclectic approach, p. 601
psychoanalysis, p. 601
resistance, p. 601
interpretation, p. 601
transference, p. 601
psychodynamic therapy, p. 602
insight therapies, p. 602
person-centered therapy, p. 603
active listening, p. 603
unconditional positive regard, p. 604
behavior therapy, p. 604
counterconditioning, p. 605
exposure therapies, p. 605
systematic desensitization, p. 605
virtual reality exposure therapy, p. 607
aversive conditioning, p. 607
token economy, p. 607
cognitive therapy, p. 608
cognitive-behavioral therapy (CBT), p. 611
group therapy, p. 611
family therapy, p. 612

MODULE TEST

Test Yourself Answer the following questions on your own first, then "show" the answers here, or check your answers in Appendix E.

1. A therapist who helps clients search for the unconscious roots of their problem and offers interpretations of their behaviors, feelings, and dreams is drawing from

a. psychoanalysis.
b. humanistic therapies.
c. person-centered therapy.
d. behavior therapy.

2. ________________ therapies are designed to help individuals discover the unconscious thoughts and feelings that guide their motivation and behavior.

3. Compared with psychoanalysts, humanistic therapists are more likely to emphasize
   a. hidden or repressed feelings.
   b. childhood experiences.
   c. psychological disorders.
   d. self-fulfillment and growth.

4. A therapist who restates and clarifies the client's statements is practicing the technique of ________________ ________________.

5. The goal of behavior therapy is to
   a. identify and treat the underlying causes of the problem.
   b. improve learning and insight.
   c. eliminate the unwanted behavior.
   d. improve communication and social sensitivity.

6. Behavior therapies often use ________________ techniques, such as systematic desensitization and aversive conditioning, to encourage clients to produce new responses to old stimuli.

7. The technique of ________________ ________________ teaches people to relax in the presence of progressively more anxiety-provoking stimuli.

8. After a near-fatal car accident, Rico developed such an intense fear of driving on the highway that he takes lengthy alternative routes to work each day. Which psychological therapy might best help Rico overcome his specific phobia, and why?

9. At a treatment center, people who display a desired behavior receive coins that they can later exchange for other rewards. This is an example of a(n) ________________ ________________.

10. Cognitive therapy has been especially effective in treating
    a. nail biting.
    b. specific phobias.
    c. alcohol use disorder.
    d. depressive disorders.

11. ________________-________________ therapy helps people to change their self-defeating ways of thinking and to act out those changes in their daily behavior.

12. In family therapy, the therapist assumes that
    a. only one family member needs to change.
    b. each person's actions trigger reactions from other family members.
    c. dysfunctional family behaviors are based largely on genetic factors.
    d. therapy is most effective when clients are treated apart from the family unit.

MODULE 55

Evaluating Psychotherapies

© Jon Carter/Cartertoons
SO HOW LONG HAVE YOU WANTED TO BE A THERAPIST?
THAT'S WHAT I WOULD LIKE TO ASK YOU.
ED WAS IN THERAPY FOR BELIEVING HE WAS A THERAPIST.
Jon Carter/Cartoon Stock

Many people presume **psychotherapy's** effectiveness. "Seek counseling" or "Ask your partner to find a therapist," advice columnists often urge. Before 1950, psychiatrists were the primary providers of mental health care. Today's providers include clinical and counseling psychologists; clinical social workers; pastoral, marital, abuse, and school counselors; and psychiatric nurses. With such an enormous outlay of time as well as money and effort, it is important to ask: Are the millions of people worldwide justified in placing their hopes in psychotherapy?

psychotherapy treatment involving psychological techniques; consists of interactions between a trained therapist and someone seeking to overcome psychological difficulties or achieve personal growth.

Is Psychotherapy Effective?

LOQ 55-1 Does psychotherapy work? How can we know?

The question, though simply put, is not simply answered. If an infection quickly clears, we may assume an antibiotic has been effective. But how can we assess psychotherapy's effectiveness? By how we feel about our progress? By how our therapist feels about it? By how our friends and family feel about it? By how our behavior has changed?

Client Perceptions

If client testimonials were the only measuring stick, we could strongly affirm psychotherapy's effectiveness. Consider one early survey of 2900 *Consumer Reports* readers who related their experiences with mental health professionals (*Consumer Reports*, 1995; Kotkin et al., 1996; Seligman, 1995). How many were at least "fairly well satisfied"? Almost 90 percent. Among those who recalled feeling *fair* or *very poor* when beginning therapy, 9 in 10 now were feeling *very good*, *good*, or at least *so-so*. Worldwide, most people report benefiting from psychotherapy (Stein et al., 2020). We have clients' word for it—and who should know better?

We should not dismiss these testimonials. But consider some reasons for skepticism:

People often enter therapy in crisis. When, with the normal ebb and flow of events, the crisis passes, people may attribute their improvement to the therapy. Depressed people often get better no matter what they do.

Clients believe that treatment will be effective. The *placebo effect* is the healing power of positive expectations.

Clients generally speak kindly of their therapists. Even if the problems remain, clients "work hard to find something positive to say. The therapist had been very understanding, the client had gained a new perspective, [they] learned to communicate better, [their] mind was eased, anything at all so as not to have to say treatment was a failure" (Zilbergeld, 1983, p. 117).

Clients want to believe the therapy was worth the effort. If you invested time and money in something, wouldn't you be motivated to find something positive about it? Psychologists call this *effort justification*.

Consider the testimonials gathered in a massive experiment with over 500 Massachusetts boys, aged 5 to 13 years, many of whom seemed bound for delinquency. By the toss of a coin, half the boys were assigned to a 5-year treatment program. The treated boys were visited by counselors twice a month. They participated in community programs, and they received academic tutoring, medical attention, and family assistance as needed. Some 30 years later, Joan McCord (1978, 1979) located 485 participants, sent them questionnaires, and checked public records from courts, psychiatric hospitals, and other sources. Was the treatment successful?

Client testimonials were glowing. Some men noted that, had it not been for their counselors, "I would probably be in jail," "My life would have gone the other way," or "I think I would have ended up in a life of crime." Court records offered apparent support: Even among the "difficult" boys in the treatment group, 66 percent had no official juvenile crime record.

But recall psychology's most powerful tool for sorting reality from wishful thinking: the *control group*. For every boy in the treatment group, there was a similar boy in a control group receiving no counseling. Of these untreated men, *70 percent* had no juvenile record. On several other measures, such as a record of having committed a second crime, alcohol use disorder, death rate, and job satisfaction, the untreated men exhibited slightly *fewer* problems. Unfortunately, the glowing testimonials of those treated were misleading.

Clinician Perceptions

If clinician perceptions were proof of therapy's effectiveness, we would have even more reason to celebrate. Case studies of successful treatment abound. The problem is that clients enter psychotherapy focused on their unhappiness and leave it focused on their well-being. Therapists treasure compliments from those clients saying good-bye or later expressing their gratitude. But they hear little from clients who experience only temporary relief and seek out new therapists for their recurring problems. Thus, therapists are most aware of the failures of *other* therapists. With the same recurring anxieties, depression, or marital difficulty, the same person may be a "success" story in several therapists' files. Moreover, therapists, like the rest of us, are vulnerable to cognitive errors. **Confirmation bias** can lead them to unconsciously seek evidence that confirms their beliefs and to ignore contradictory evidence, and *illusory correlations* can lead them to perceive associations that don't really exist (Lilienfeld et al., 2015).

Outcome Research

How, then, can we objectively measure the effectiveness of psychotherapy? What *outcomes* can we expect—what types of people and problems are helped, and by what type of psychotherapy?

In search of answers, psychologists have turned to the well-traveled path of controlled research. In the 1800s, skeptical physicians began to realize that many patients

confirmation bias a tendency to search for information that supports our preconceptions and to ignore or distort contradictory evidence.

Feng Li/Getty Images

Trauma and resilience Those who suffer through trauma, such as these women in China mourning the devastating loss of lives and homes in the 2010 Yushu earthquake, may benefit from counseling. But many people recover on their own or with the help of supportive relationships with family and friends. "Life itself still remains a very effective therapist," noted psychodynamic therapist Karen Horney (*Our Inner Conflicts*, 1945).

were dying despite receiving then-mainstream treatments (such as bloodletting), and many others were getting better on their own. Sorting fact from superstition required observing patients and recording outcomes with and without a particular treatment. Typhoid fever patients, for example, often improved after bloodletting, convincing most physicians that the treatment worked. But when a control group was given mere bed rest, 5 weeks later 70 percent had improved, showing that the bloodletting was worthless (as reported in Thomas, 1992).

A similar result—and spirited debate—followed the summary of 24 studies of psychotherapy outcomes (Eysenck, 1952). Two-thirds of people who received psychotherapy for disorders not involving hallucinations or delusions improved markedly. To this day, no one disputes that optimistic estimate. But there was a catch. Similar improvement occurred among people who were *untreated*, such as those who sought treatment but were placed on waiting lists. With or without psychotherapy, roughly two-thirds improved noticeably. Time was a great healer.

Later research revealed shortcomings in the 24-study summary's analyses and methods. The sample was small—only 24 outcome studies in 1952, compared with thousands available today. The best of these are *randomized clinical trials*, in which researchers randomly assign people on a waiting list to therapy or to no therapy. Later, they evaluate everyone and compare outcomes, using tests and assessments done by others who don't know whether therapy was given.

A glimpse of psychotherapy's overall effectiveness can then be provided by means of a **meta-analysis**, a statistical procedure that combines the conclusions of a large number of different studies. Simply said, a meta-analysis summarizes lots of studies' results. Therapists welcomed the first meta-analysis of some 475 psychotherapy outcome studies. It showed that the average therapy client ends up better off than 80 percent of the untreated individuals on waiting lists (**FIGURE 55.1**). Psychologist Mary Lee Smith and her colleagues summed it up: "Psychotherapy benefits people of all ages as reliably as schooling educates them, medicine cures them, or business turns a profit" (Smith et al., 1980, p. 183).

Dozens of subsequent summaries have now examined psychotherapy's effectiveness. Their verdict replicated earlier results: *Those not undergoing therapy often improve, but those undergoing therapy are more likely to improve—and to improve more quickly and with less risk of relapse* (Eckshtain et al., 2020; Weisz et al., 2017). (One qualification: Compared with studies that find no therapy benefit, those that do find a positive therapy effect are more likely to get published [Driessen et al., 2015].) After therapy, many people exhibit improved insight and emotional awareness, with a more patient, outgoing personality (Høglend & Hagtvet, 2019; Roberts et al., 2017). Some people with depression or anxiety also experience sudden symptom reductions between their treatment sessions (Aderka et al., 2012). Those *sudden gains* bode well for long-term improvement (Shalom & Aderka, 2020).

Psychotherapy also can be cost-effective. Studies show that when people seek psychological treatment, their search for other medical treatment drops substantially—by

FIGURE 55.1
Treatment worked, as shown by the outcomes of treated versus untreated clients

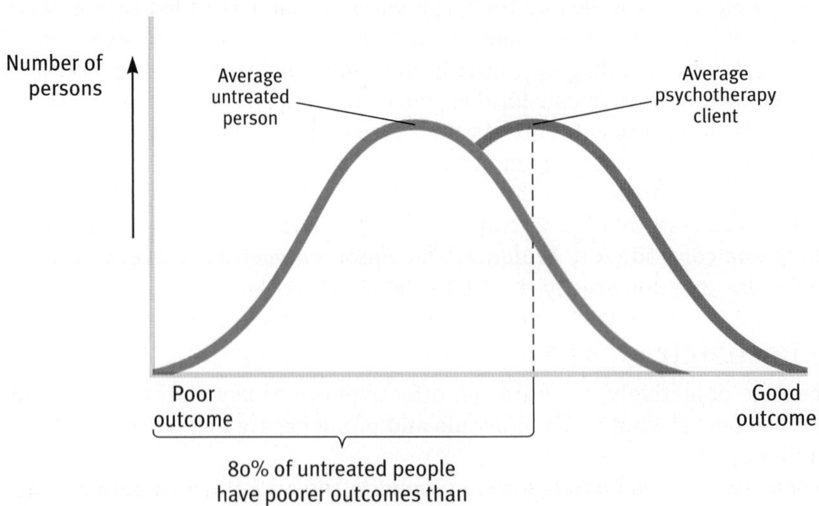
Number of persons
Average untreated person
Average psychotherapy client
Poor outcome
Good outcome
80% of untreated people have poorer outcomes than the average treated person.

meta-analysis a statistical procedure for analyzing the results of multiple studies to reach an overall conclusion.

16 percent in one digest of 91 studies (Chiles et al., 1999). Substance abuse and other psychological disorders exert a staggering cost on society, including crime, accidents, and lost work. By one estimate, the opioid epidemic cost the United States more than $1 trillion between 2001 and 2017 (Altarum, 2018). Given such costs, psychotherapy is a good investment, much like investing time and money in healthy foods and exercise (de Oliveira et al., 2020; Johnson et al., 2019). Both reduce long-term costs. Boosting employees' psychological well-being can lower medical costs, improve work efficiency, and diminish absenteeism. It's no wonder that U.S. health insurers and the National Health Service in Britain have increasingly funded therapy (Hockenberry et al., 2019; NHS, 2020).

But note that the claim—that psychotherapy, *on average*, is somewhat effective—refers to no one therapy in particular. It is like reassuring lung-cancer patients that "on average," medical treatment of health problems is effective. But what distressed people—and those paying for their therapy—want to know is whether a *particular* treatment is effective for their specific problems.

RETRIEVAL PRACTICE

RP-1 How might the *placebo effect* bias clients' and clinicians' appraisals of the effectiveness of psychotherapies?

ANSWERS IN APPENDIX E

Which Psychotherapies Work Best?

LOQ 55-2 Are some psychotherapies more effective than others for specific disorders?

The early statistical summaries and surveys did not find that any one type of psychotherapy is generally superior (Smith & Glass, 1977; Smith et al., 1980). Later studies have similarly found that clients can benefit from psychotherapy regardless of their clinicians' experience, training, supervision, and licensing (Cuijpers, 2017; Kivlighan et al., 2015; Wampold et al., 2017). Were clients treated by a psychiatrist, psychologist, social worker, marriage counselor, or other mental health professional? Were they seen in a group or individual context? Did the therapist have extensive or relatively limited training and experience? It didn't matter.

So, was *Alice in Wonderland*'s dodo bird right: "Everyone has won and all must have prizes"? Not quite. One general finding emerges from the studies: The more specific the problem, the greater the hope that psychotherapy might solve it (Singer, 1981; Westen & Morrison, 2001). Those who experience panic or specific phobias, who are unassertive, or who are frustrated by sexual performance problems can hope for improvement. Those with less-focused problems, such as depression and anxiety, usually benefit in the short term but often relapse later. There often is also an overlapping of disorders (*comorbidity*), which can make successful treatment more challenging.

Nevertheless, some forms of therapy do get prizes for effectively treating *particular* problems:

"Different sores have different salves."
—English proverb

Cognitive and cognitive-behavioral therapies: primarily anxiety, panic disorder, posttraumatic stress disorder, insomnia, and depression (Qaseem et al., 2016; Scaini et al., 2016; Tolin, 2010).

Behavioral conditioning therapies: behavior problems such as bed-wetting, specific phobias, compulsions, marital difficulties, and sexual dysfunctions (Baker et al., 2008; Hunsley & DiGiulio, 2002; Shadish & Baldwin, 2005).

Psychodynamic therapy: depression and anxiety (Driessen et al., 2010; Leichsenring & Rabung, 2008; Shedler, 2010). Some analyses suggest that psychodynamic therapy and cognitive-behavioral therapy are equally effective in reducing depression (Driessen et al., 2017; Steinert et al., 2017).

Nondirective (person-centered) counseling: mild to moderate depression (Cuijpers et al., 2012).

The tendency of many disordered states of mind to return to healthy states, combined with the placebo effect (the healing power of mere belief in a treatment), creates fertile soil for pseudotherapies. No prizes—and no scientific support—go to these alternative therapies (Arkowitz & Lilienfeld, 2006; Lilienfeld et al., 2015). We would all be wise to avoid therapies that propose to manipulate invisible "energy fields," therapies that reenact the supposed trauma of a client's birth, and therapies that use "facilitated communication," in which "responders" guide noncommunicative people's arms or hands to point to letters to compose messages.

Like some medical treatments, some psychological treatments are not only ineffective but also harmful. The American Psychiatric Association, the Canadian Psychological Association, and the British Psychological Society have warned against conversion therapies that purport to change people's gender identity or sexual orientation. APA president Barry Anton has described such therapies as an attempt to "repair . . . something that is not a mental illness and therefore does not require therapy" (2015). Indeed, conversion therapy entails "a significant risk of harm" (APA, 2018; Turban et al., 2020). Such evidence has led to conversion therapy bans in many cities, states, and countries, especially for minors. Other initiatives have been found ineffective or harmful (Walton & Wilson, 2018). These failed programs include the Scared Straight program designed to curb teenage delinquency and the police-promoted D.A.R.E. anti-drug effort. Numerous weight-reduction programs, and several pedophile rehabilitation efforts have also proven unsuccessful.

The evaluation question—which therapies get prizes and which do not?—lies at the heart of what some call psychology's civil war. To what extent should science guide both clinical practice and insurers' willingness to pay for psychotherapy? On one side are research psychologists using scientific methods to extend the list of well-defined and validated therapies for various disorders. They decry clinicians who seem to "give more weight to their personal experience than to science" (Baker et al., 2008). On the other side are some therapists who view their practice as more art than science, arguing that people are too complex and psychotherapy is too intuitive to describe in a manual or test in an experiment.

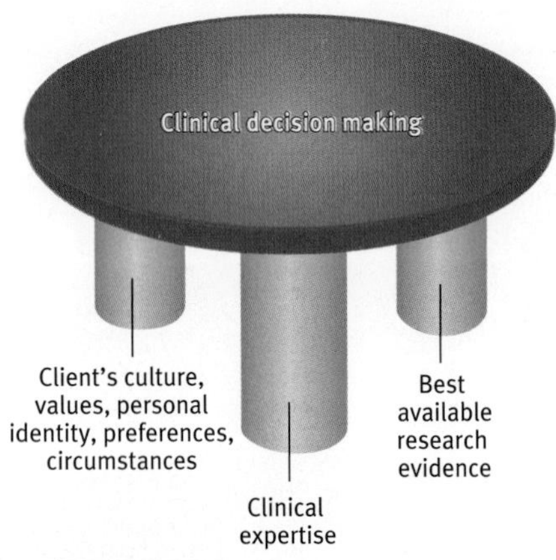
Clinical decision making
Client's culture, values, personal identity, preferences, circumstances
Clinical expertise
Best available research evidence

FIGURE 55.2
Evidence-based practice Ideal clinical decision making can be visualized as a three-legged stool, upheld by research evidence, clinical expertise, and knowledge of the client.

Between these two factions stand the science-oriented clinicians calling for **evidence-based practice**, which has been endorsed by the American Psychological Association and others (APA, 2006; Holmes et al., 2018; Sakaluk et al., 2019; **FIGURE 55.2**). After rigorous evaluation, clinicians apply therapies suited to their own skills and their clients' unique situations. Some are using technology, too. By analyzing many pieces of clients' information, computer programs can help clinicians offer personalized therapeutic solutions (Ewbank et al., 2019; Webb et al., 2020). Increasingly, insurer and government support for mental health services require evidence-based practice.

RETRIEVAL PRACTICE

RP-2 Therapy is most likely to be helpful for those with problems that ________ (are/are not) well-defined.

RP-3 What is *evidence-based practice*?

ANSWERS IN APPENDIX E

How Do Psychotherapies Help People?

LOQ 55-3 What three elements are shared by all effective forms of psychotherapy?

Why have studies found little correlation between therapists' training and experience and clients' outcomes? One answer seems to be that all effective psychotherapies share three basic benefits (Cuijpers et al., 2019; Frank, 1982; Wampold, 2007):

- ***Hope for discouraged people*** People seeking therapy typically feel anxious, depressed, self-disapproving, and incapable of turning things around. What any psychotherapy offers is the expectation that, with commitment from the therapy seeker, things can and will get better. This belief, apart from any therapeutic technique, may improve morale, create feelings of self-efficacy, and diminish symptoms (Corrigan, 2014; Meyerhoff & Rohan, 2016).

evidence-based practice clinical decision making that integrates the best available research with clinical expertise and client characteristics and preferences.

- *A new perspective* Every therapy offers people a plausible explanation of their symptoms. Armed with a believable fresh perspective, they may approach life with a new attitude, open to making changes in their behaviors and their views of themselves.
- *An empathic, trusting, caring relationship* No matter what technique they use, effective therapists are empathic. They seek to understand the client's experience. They communicate care and concern, and they earn trust through respectful listening and guidance (Ovenstad et al., 2020). These qualities were clear in recorded therapy sessions from 36 recognized master therapists (Goldfried et al., 1998). Some took a cognitive-behavioral approach. Others used psychodynamic principles. Although the master therapists used different approaches, they showed some striking *similarities*. They helped clients evaluate themselves, link one aspect of their life with another, and gain insight into their interactions with others. The emotional bond between therapist and client—the **therapeutic alliance**—helps explain why empathic, caring therapists are especially effective (Flückiger et al., 2020). Whether experienced in Canada or Cambodia, a strong therapeutic alliance fosters psychological health (Falkenström et al., 2019; Gold, 2019). It may even save lives. In one analysis of a dozen studies, a strong therapeutic alliance predicted less frequent suicidal thoughts, self-harming behaviors, and suicide attempts (Dunster-Page et al., 2017).

Mort Gerberg/Cartoon Stock

"The thing is, you have to really want to change."

These three common elements—hope, a fresh perspective, and an empathic, caring relationship—help us understand why *paraprofessionals* (briefly trained caregivers, who sometimes have firsthand experience with a specific mental health challenge) can assist many troubled people so effectively (Bryan & Arkowitz, 2015; Christensen & Jacobson, 1994). They are also part of what the growing numbers of in-person and online *self-help and support groups* offer their members. And they are part of what traditional healers have offered (Jackson, 1992). Healers everywhere—special people to whom others disclose their suffering, whether psychiatrists or shamans—have listened to understand and to empathize, reassure, advise, console, interpret, or explain (Torrey, 1986). Such qualities may explain why people who feel supported by close relationships—who enjoy the fellowship and friendship of caring people—have been less likely to seek therapy (Frank, 1982; O'Connor & Brown, 1984).

FRIENDSHIP BENCH

Rainer Kwiotek/Friendship Bench

Friendship bench Some Zimbabwe health clinics have added outdoor "friendship benches," where paraprofessional community health workers offer therapy (Chibanda et al., 2016). Psychiatrist Dixon Chibanda created this free therapy for rural communities after a client, lacking bus fare to get to Chibanda's office, died by suicide. "We have to take [psychiatry] to the community," Chibanda said (Rosenberg, 2019).

* * *

To recap, people who seek help usually improve. So do many of those who do not, which is a tribute to our human resourcefulness and our capacity to care for one another. Nevertheless, though the therapist's orientation and experience appear not to matter much, people who receive some psychotherapy usually improve more than those who do not. People with clear-cut, specific problems tend to improve the most.

ASK YOURSELF

Based on what you've read, would you seek therapy if you were struggling with a mental health challenge? Why or why not? If you've experienced therapy, does what you've learned here influence your feelings about the experience?

RETRIEVAL PRACTICE

RP-4 Those who undergo psychotherapy are ____________ (more/less) likely to show improvement than those who do not undergo psychotherapy.

ANSWERS IN APPENDIX E

Human Diversity and Psychotherapy

LOQ 55-4 What personal factors influence the therapist-client relationship?

All psychotherapies offer hope, and nearly all psychotherapists attempt to enhance their clients' sensitivity, openness, personal responsibility, and sense of purpose

therapeutic alliance a bond of trust and mutual understanding between a therapist and client, who work together constructively to overcome the client's problem. 

AAMIR QURESHI/AFP/Getty Images

Meeting the needs of the community In 2021, the Pakistani government opened this Transgender Protection Center to provide legal aid, health services, and psychological counseling for the transgender community.

(Jensen & Bergin, 1988). But in matters of culture, values, and personal identity, psychotherapists differ from one another and may differ from their clients (Delaney et al., 2007; Kelly, 1990).

These differences can create a mismatch—for example, when a therapist from one culture interacts with a client from another. Therapists tend to prefer clients who are culturally similar to themselves (Desai et al., 2021). In North America, Europe, and Australia, most psychotherapists reflect their culture's *individualism*, which often gives priority to personal desires and identity. Clients with a *collectivist* perspective, as with many from Asian cultures, may be more mindful of social and family responsibilities, harmony, and group goals. These clients may have trouble relating to therapists who ask them to think only of their own well-being (Markus & Kitayama, 1991). In one experiment, Asian American clients matched with counselors who shared their cultural values (rather than mismatched with those who did not) perceived more counselor empathy and felt a stronger alliance with the counselor (Kim et al., 2005).

Client-psychotherapist mismatches may also stem from other personal differences. Highly religious people may prefer and benefit from religiously similar therapists who share their values and beliefs (Masters, 2010; Pearce et al., 2015). Likewise, therapists' attitudes toward LGBTQ people can affect the client-therapist relationship. Transgender people, for example, may understandably seek out therapists who affirm them (Bettergarcia & Israel, 2018).

Cultural differences help explain some groups' reluctance to use mental health services (Eken et al., 2021). People living in "cultures of honor" (Social Psychology modules) prize being strong and tough. They may feel that seeking mental health care is an admission of weakness rather than an opportunity for growth (Brown et al., 2014). Refugees, despite having frequently endured trauma and discrimination, tend to avoid seeking mental health services due to distrust, poverty, and language barriers (Byrow et al., 2020). And some cultural groups tend to be both reluctant to seek therapy and quick to leave it (Chen et al., 2009; Sue et al., 2009). Hesitancy to seek psychotherapy is often higher among African Americans than for other groups, due to social pressure against seeking help, mistrust of therapists, and microaggressions experienced during therapy (Taylor & Kuo, 2018).

The bottom line: By building their *cultural competence*—understanding and respecting different cultural groups' values, beliefs, and traditions—therapists can better serve their clients (Soto et al., 2018).

Seeking Psychotherapy

LOQ 55-5 When should people seek therapy, and what should they look for when selecting a therapist?

Life for everyone is marked by a mix of serenity and stress, blessing and bereavement, good moods and bad. So, when should we seek a mental health professional's help? The American Psychological Association offers these trouble signals:

- Feelings of hopelessness
- Deep and lasting depression
- Self-destructive behavior, such as substance abuse and self-injury
- Disruptive fears
- Sudden mood shifts
- Thoughts of suicide
- Compulsive rituals, such as lock checking
- Sexual difficulties
- Hearing voices or seeing things that others don't experience
- Struggling to understand others' thoughts and emotions

In looking for a psychotherapist, you may want to have a preliminary session with two or three. Meeting with more than one therapist gives you multiple opportunities to find someone with whom you feel comfortable. College or university health centers are

TABLE 55.1 Therapists and Their Training

Type	Description
Clinical psychologists	Most are psychologists with a Ph.D. (includes research training) or Psy.D. (focuses on therapy) supplemented by a supervised internship and, often, postdoctoral training. About half work in agencies and institutions, half in private practice.
Psychiatrists	Psychiatrists are physicians who specialize in the treatment of psychological disorders. Not all psychiatrists have had extensive training in psychotherapy, but as M.D.s or D.O.s they can prescribe medications. Thus, they tend to see those with the most serious problems. Many have their own private practice.
Clinical or psychiatric social workers	A master of social work (M.S.W.) plus postgraduate supervision prepares some social workers to offer psychotherapy, mostly to people with everyday personal and family problems. About half of U.S. social workers have earned the National Association of Social Workers' designation of clinical social worker.
Counselors	Family and couples counselors specialize in problems arising from family relations. Clergy provide counseling to countless people. Counselors may work with people with substance use disorders and with spouse and child abusers and victims of abuse. Mental health and other counselors may be required to have a master's degree.

generally good starting points; you may be able to access qualified therapists and some free services by browsing their web page or visiting in person. You may also get a referral from your primary care provider or visit a walk-in clinic. If you have insurance coverage, your provider may supply a list of participating therapists. Many people also use the internet to search for therapists, and many receive help online or via one of the more than 10,000 mental health apps (Kocsis, 2018; Levin et al., 2018; Nielssen et al., 2019). Therapist-guided treatment online or via apps can help reduce depression, social anxiety disorder, and panic disorder (Niles et al., 2021). Being able to meet remotely with a therapist has helped people who may struggle to attend in-person sessions (Guo et al., 2020; Markowitz et al., 2021). Such online therapy also offered a useful alternative solution when it was unsafe to attend in-person therapy sessions during the Covid-19 pandemic.

During your in-person or remote session, you can describe your problem and learn each therapist's treatment approach. You can ask questions about the therapist's values, credentials (**TABLE 55.1**), and fees. And you can assess your own feelings about each therapist. The emotional bond between therapist and client is perhaps the most important factor in effective therapy.

The American Psychological Association recognizes the importance of a strong therapeutic alliance, and it welcomes diverse therapists who can relate well to diverse clients. It accredits programs that provide training in cultural sensitivity (for example, to differing values, communication styles, and languages) and that recruit underrepresented cultural groups.

Macmillan Learning

Therapy for all Therapy was once available only for the wealthy and well-connected. Teletherapy, low-cost and no-cost community programs, and mental health apps have put help just a few clicks away.

"Being physically present with a client does not appear essential to generating therapeutic outcomes."—Psychologist Ashley Batastini and colleagues (2020)

Ethical Principles in Psychotherapy

LOQ 55-6 What ethical principles guide psychotherapy and psychological research on mental illness?

Psychotherapists use different approaches to help reduce their clients' suffering. Likewise, researchers apply many methods to understand how to lessen people's disordered thoughts, feelings, and behaviors. But before psychotherapists or researchers begin their treatment or investigation, they must follow their country's ethical principles and code of conduct (APA, 2017).

According to the American Psychological Association, your therapist should follow these principles:

- Seek to benefit you and do you no harm.
- Establish a feeling of trust and a defined role as your therapist, as well as be of service to the therapeutic community.
- Be honest, truthful, and accurate.
- Be fair and promote justice for you and others, helping everyone to have access to the benefits of therapy.
- Respect the dignity and worth of you and others, recognizing the right to privacy, confidentiality, and self-determination.

Psychological researchers use the same ethical guidelines when studying how to lessen mental illness. They aim to benefit others, to be honest and truthful, and to never expose people to experiences that pose greater than a *minimal risk*—to more than what people may encounter in their daily lives.

RETRIEVAL PRACTICE

RP-5 There are many acceptable mental health treatment and study approaches, but all therapists and psychological researchers must follow ______________ principles.

ANSWERS IN APPENDIX E

MODULE

55 REVIEW Evaluating Psychotherapies

LEARNING OBJECTIVES

Test Yourself Answer these repeated Learning Objective Questions on your own (before "showing" the answers here, or checking the answers in Appendix D) to improve your retention of the concepts (McDaniel et al., 2009, 2015).

LOQ 55-1 Does psychotherapy work? How can we know?

LOQ 55-2 Are some psychotherapies more effective than others for specific disorders?

LOQ 55-3 What three elements are shared by all effective forms of psychotherapy?

LOQ 55-4 What personal factors influence the therapist-client relationship?

LOQ 55-5 When should people seek therapy, and what should they look for when selecting a therapist?

LOQ 55-6 What ethical principles guide psychotherapy and psychological research on mental illness?

TERMS AND CONCEPTS TO REMEMBER

Test Yourself Write down the definition in your own words, then check your answer.

psychotherapy, p. 614
confirmation bias, p. 615
meta-analysis, p. 616
evidence-based practice, p. 618
therapeutic alliance, p. 619

MODULE TEST

Test Yourself Answer the following questions on your own first, then "show" the answers here, or check your answers in Appendix E.

1. The most enthusiastic or optimistic view of the effectiveness of psychotherapy comes from
a. outcome research.
b. randomized clinical trials.
c. reports of clinicians and clients.
d. a government study of treatment for depression.

2. Studies show that ______________ therapy is the most effective treatment for most psychological disorders.
a. behavior
b. humanistic
c. psychodynamic
d. no one type of

3. What are the three components of evidence-based practice?

4. Psychotherapies help people by providing ______________, a new perspective, and an empathic, trusting, caring relationship.

MODULE

56 The Biomedical Therapies and Preventing Psychological Disorders

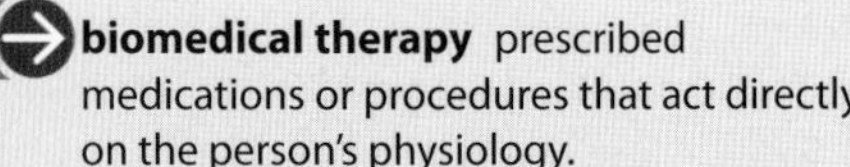

biomedical therapy prescribed medications or procedures that act directly on the person's physiology.

Psychotherapy is one way to treat psychological disorders. The other is **biomedical therapy**. Biomedical treatments can change the brain's chemistry with drugs; affect its circuitry with electrical stimulation, magnetic impulses, or psychosurgery; or influence its responses with lifestyle changes.

Are you surprised to find *lifestyle changes* in this list? We find it convenient to talk of separate psychological and biological influences, but everything psychological is also biological. Thus, our lifestyle—exercise, sleep, nutrition, relationships, recreation, relaxation, religious or spiritual engagement, and our service to others—affects our mental health (Bennie et al., 2020; Walsh, 2011). (See Thinking Critically About: Therapeutic Lifestyle Change.)

Every thought and feeling depends on the functioning brain. Every creative idea, every moment of joy or anger, every experience of depression emerges from the electrochemical activity of the living brain. Anxiety disorders, obsessive-compulsive disorder, posttraumatic stress disorder, depressive disorders, bipolar disorders, and schizophrenia are all biological events. Some psychologists even see psychotherapy as a biological treatment: Changing the way we think and act is brain-changing (Kandel, 2013). When psychotherapy relieves behaviors associated with obsessive-compulsive disorder, depression, or schizophrenia, PET scans reveal a less agitated brain (Habel et al., 2010; Kennedy et al., 2007; Porto et al., 2009). As we have seen over and over, *a human being is an integrated biopsychosocial system.*

RETRIEVAL PRACTICE

RP-1 What are some examples of lifestyle changes people can make to enhance their mental health?

ANSWERS IN APPENDIX E

Drug Therapies

LOQ 56-2 What are the drug therapies? How do double-blind studies help researchers evaluate a drug's effectiveness?

By far the most widely used biomedical treatments today are the drug therapies. Most drugs for anxiety and depression are prescribed by primary care providers, followed by psychiatrists and, in some U.S. states, psychologists.

Peter C. Vey/Cartoon Stock

"If this doesn't help you don't worry, it's a placebo."

Since the 1950s, **psychopharmacology** discoveries have revolutionized the treatment of people with severe disorders, liberating hundreds of thousands from hospital confinement. Thanks to drug therapies and community mental health programs, today's resident population of psychiatric hospitals has dropped to a small fraction of what it once was. For some who are unable to care for themselves, however, release from hospitals has meant experiencing homelessness, not liberation.

Almost any new treatment, including a drug therapy, is greeted by an initial wave of enthusiasm as many people apparently improve. But that enthusiasm often diminishes on closer examination. To evaluate any new drug's effectiveness, researchers also need to know the following:

- How many people recover *without* treatment, and how quickly?
- How does the drug therapy's effectiveness compare to that of nondrug treatments, like psychotherapy?

Is recovery due to the drug or to the placebo effect? When clients or mental health workers expect positive results, they may see what they expect, not what really happens. Even mere exposure to advertising about a drug's supposed effectiveness can increase its effect (Kamenica et al., 2013).

To control for these influences, drug researchers often give about half of study participants the drug, and the other half a similar-appearing placebo. Because neither the staff nor the participants know who gets which, this is called a *double-blind procedure.* The good news: Worldwide, double-blind studies show that several types of drugs effectively treat psychological disorders in children, adolescents, and adults (Correll et al., 2022; Leichsenring et al., 2022).

Antipsychotic Drugs

An accidental discovery launched a treatment revolution for people with hallucinations or delusions—what psychologists call *psychoses.* The discovery: Certain drugs, originally

psychopharmacology the study of the effects of drugs on the mind and behavior.

Thinking Critically About:

Therapeutic Lifestyle Change

LOQ 56-1 Why is therapeutic lifestyle change considered an effective biomedical therapy, and how does it work?

LIFESTYLE (exercise, nutrition, relationships, recreation, service to others, relaxation, and religious or spiritual engagement) → **influences our BRAIN AND BODY** → **affects our MENTAL HEALTH**[1]

Our shared history has prepared us to be physically active and socially engaged.

Our ancestors hunted, gathered, and built in groups.

Modern researchers have found that outdoor activity in a natural environment reduces stress and promotes health.[2]

APPLICATION TO THERAPY

Training seminars promote therapeutic lifestyle change.[3] Small groups of people with depression undergo a 12-week training program with the following goals:

Aerobic exercise, 30 minutes a day, at least three times weekly (increases fitness and vitality, stimulates endorphins)

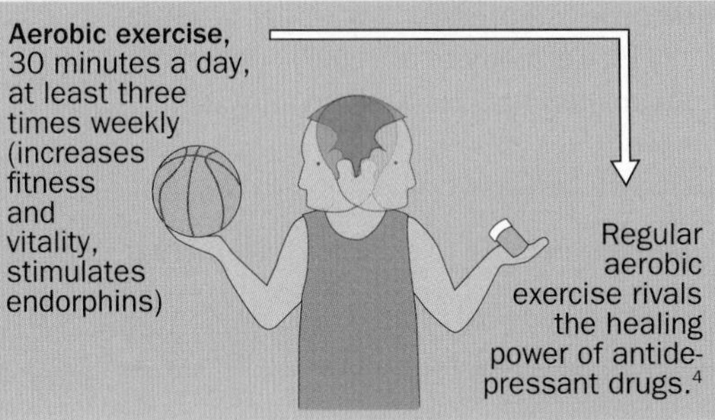

Regular aerobic exercise rivals the healing power of antidepressant drugs.[4]

Adequate sleep, with a goal of 7 to 8 hours per night.

A complete night's sleep boosts immunity and increases energy, alertness, and mood.[5]

Light exposure, 15 to 30 minutes each morning with a light box (amplifies arousal, influences hormones)

Social connection, with less alone time and at least two meaningful social engagements weekly (helps satisfy the human need to belong)

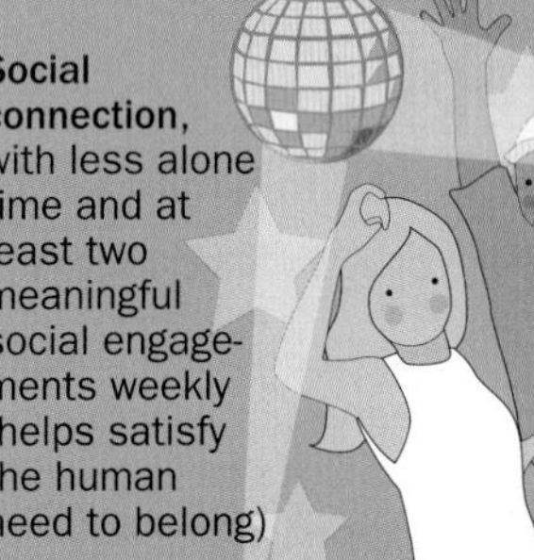

Reducing rumination, by identifying and redirecting negative thoughts (enhances positive thinking)

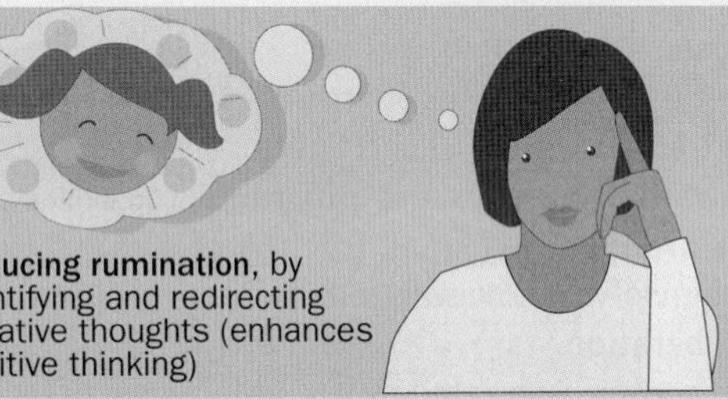

Nutritional supplements, including a daily supplement with omega-3 fatty acids (reduces aggressive behavior)[6]

Initial small study (74 participants)[7]

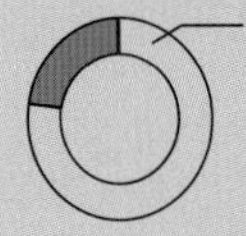

77% of those who completed the program experienced relief from depressive symptoms.

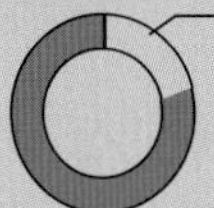

Only 19% of those assigned to a treatment-as-usual control group showed similar results.

Future research will try to identify which parts of the treatment produce the therapeutic effect.

The biomedical therapies assume that mind and body are a unit:

Affect one and you will affect the other.

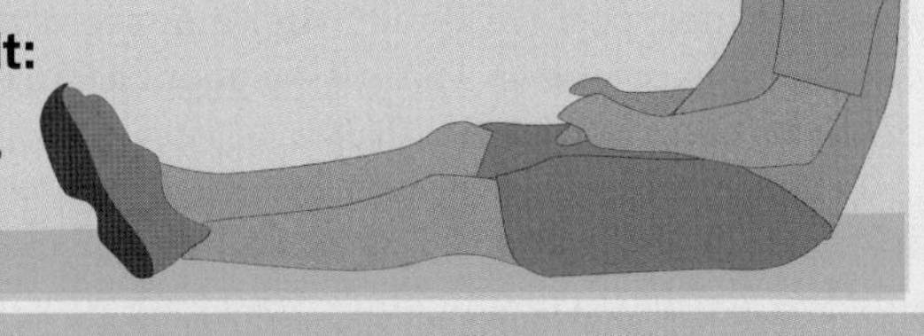

1. Sánchez-Villegas et al., 2015; Marques et al., 2022; Walsh, 2011. 2. Huynh et al., 2022; MacKerron & Mourato, 2013; NEEF, 2020; Phillips, 2011. 3. Ilardi, 2009. 4. Babyak et al., 2000; Salmon, 2001; Schuch et al., 2016. 5. Irwin et al., 2022; Scott et al., 2021. 6. Bègue et al., 2018; Raine et al., 2018. 7. Ilardi, 2009, 2016.

developed to reduce presurgical agitation, calmed these patients' split from reality. First-generation **antipsychotic drugs**, such as chlorpromazine (sold as Thorazine), helped people with schizophrenia who were experiencing auditory hallucinations and paranoia (Leucht et al., 2018). (Antipsychotic drugs are less effective in changing negative symptoms, such as apathy and withdrawal.)

The molecules of most conventional antipsychotic drugs are similar enough to molecules of the neurotransmitter dopamine to occupy its receptor sites and block its activity. This finding reinforces the idea that an overactive dopamine system contributes to schizophrenia. Second-generation antipsychotics also act on serotonin systems.

Antipsychotics have powerful side effects. Some produce sluggishness, tremors, and twitches similar to those of Parkinson's disease (Kaplan & Sadock, 1989). Long-term use of antipsychotics can produce *tardive dyskinesia*, with involuntary motor movements of the facial muscles (such as grimacing), tongue, and limbs. Second-generation antipsychotics, such as clozapine (Clozaril), quetiapine (Seroquel), and olanzapine (Zyprexa), are less likely than first-generation antipsychotics to cause these effects. These drugs may, however, increase the risk of obesity and diabetes (Buchanan et al., 2010; Tiihonen et al., 2009). To identify doses that reduce symptoms with fewer side effects, researchers have combed through data for more than 20 antipsychotic medications (Leucht et al., 2020).

Antipsychotics, combined with life-skills programs and support from family and close others, have given new hope to many people with schizophrenia (Goff et al., 2017; Guo et al., 2010). Computer programs are beginning to help clinicians identify which people with schizophrenia will benefit from specific antipsychotic medications (Lee et al., 2018; Yu et al., 2018). Hundreds of thousands have returned to work and to near-typical lives due to symptom relief from these medications (Leucht et al., 2003; Saks, 2007).

USC Gould School of Law

Effective treatment Elyn Saks, a University of Southern California law professor, has written about what it's like to live with schizophrenia. Thanks to her treatment, which combines an antipsychotic drug and psychotherapy, she says, "Now I'm mostly well. I'm mostly thinking clearly. I do have episodes, but it's not like I'm struggling all of the time to stay on the right side of the line" (Saks, 2007).

Perhaps you can guess an occasional side effect of L-dopa, a drug that raises dopamine levels for Parkinson's patients: hallucinations.

Antianxiety Drugs

Antianxiety drugs, such as Xanax, Klonopin, and Ativan, depress central nervous system activity. Some antianxiety drugs have been successfully combined with psychological therapy to enhance exposure therapy's extinction of learned fears and to help relieve the symptoms of anxiety-related disorders, including posttraumatic stress disorder and obsessive-compulsive disorder (Davis, 2005; Kushner et al., 2007). Antianxiety drugs depress central nervous system activity, so they should not be used in combination with alcohol.

Some critics fear that antianxiety drugs may reduce symptoms without resolving underlying problems, especially when used as an ongoing treatment. "Popping a Xanax" at the first sign of tension can create a learned response: The immediate relief reinforces a person's tendencies to take drugs when anxious and avoid learning how to cope with distressing situations. Antianxiety drugs can also be addictive. Regular users who stop taking these drugs may experience increased anxiety, insomnia, and other withdrawal symptoms.

Antidepressant Drugs

The **antidepressant drugs** were named for their ability to lift people up from a state of depression, and this was their main use until recently. These drugs are now also increasingly used to treat anxiety disorders, obsessive-compulsive and related disorders, and posttraumatic stress disorder (Beaulieu et al., 2019; Merz et al., 2019; Slee et al., 2019). Many antidepressant drugs work by increasing the availability of neurotransmitters, such as norepinephrine or serotonin, which elevate arousal and mood and are scarce when a person experiences feelings of depression or anxiety.

The most prescribed drugs in this group, including Prozac and its cousins Zoloft and Paxil, work by prolonging the time serotonin molecules remain in the brain's synapses. They do this by blocking the normal reuptake process. Given their use in treating disorders other than depressive ones—from anxiety to strokes—these particular drugs are most often called *SSRIs (selective serotonin reuptake inhibitors)* rather than antidepressants (Kramer, 2011).

But be advised: Patients with depression who begin taking antidepressants do not wake up the next morning singing, "It's a beautiful day!" Antidepressants begin to

antipsychotic drugs drugs used to treat schizophrenia and other psychotic disorders.

antianxiety drugs drugs used to control anxiety and agitation.

antidepressant drugs drugs used to treat depressive disorders, anxiety disorders, obsessive-compulsive and related disorders, and posttraumatic stress disorder. (Several widely used antidepressant drugs are *selective serotonin reuptake inhibitors—SSRIs.*)

influence neurotransmission within hours, but their full psychological effect may take 4 weeks. One possible reason for the delay is that increased serotonin promotes neural changes, including new synapses and *neurogenesis*—the birth of new brain cells—perhaps reversing stress-induced neuron loss (Launay et al., 2011; Nord et al., 2021).

Cognitive therapy, by helping people reverse their habitual negative thinking style, helps prevent depression, boosts drug-aided relief from depression, and reduces posttreatment relapses (Amick et al., 2015; Cuijpers et al., 2021). Some clinicians, for example, attack youth depression and anxiety from both below and above (Strawn et al., 2022): They use antidepressant drugs to work, bottom-up, on the emotion-related limbic system. And they use cognitive-behavioral therapy to work, top-down, to change frontal lobe activity and thinking.

Researchers agree that many people with depression often improve after a month on antidepressant drugs. But after allowing for natural recovery and the placebo effect, how big is the effect? The effect is consistent but, critics argue, not very big (Cipriani et al., 2018; Kirsch, 2010). In double-blind clinical trials, placebos produced improvement comparable to about 75 percent of the active drug's effect. For those with severe depression, there is less of a placebo effect and the added drug benefit is somewhat greater (Fournier et al., 2010; Kirsch et al., 2008; Olfson & Marcus, 2009). Antidepressants can have negative side effects, such as increased appetite, nausea, fatigue, reduced sex drive, and withdrawal symptoms when discontinued (Horowitz & Wilcock, 2022). So some clinicians advise beginning with psychotherapy before introducing antidepressants (Strayhorn, 2019; Svaldi et al., 2019). "If [drugs] are to be used at all," notes Irving Kirsch (2016), "it should be as a last resort."

Paul Noth/Cartoon Stock

"Of course you feel great. These things are loaded with antidepressants."

Antidepressant drugs are not the only way to boost our mental health. Aerobic exercise can also reduce anxiety and depression. Combining exercise with psychotherapy produces a particularly powerful antidepressant effect (Lee et al., 2021). For adults worldwide, three or more weekly exercise hours predicts a lower risk of future depression and a greater sense of life purpose (Choi et al., 2019; Schuch et al., 2018; Yemiscigil & Vlaev, 2021). *The point to remember*: If you're concerned about your mental health, consult a mental health professional to determine the best treatment for you.

Psychedelic Drugs

For those who have a depressive or anxiety disorder, suicidal thoughts, posttraumatic stress disorder (PTSD), or a substance use disorder, researchers are assessing possible benefits of small doses of **psychedelic drugs** (Reiff et al., 2021). Proponents claim that, when psychedelics are administered under guided conditions and in combination with psychotherapy, *microdosing* works quickly and with few side effects.

After preparatory talk therapy sessions, the typical client might swallow a pill that administers a small drug dose in a safe, comfortable setting. Over the next several hours, the lying-down client, perhaps wearing eyeshades and listening to calm music, may experience striking visions, emotions, and memories. Talk therapy then helps the client process the experience, which they may repeat in additional sessions.

"One good way to understand a complex system is to disturb it and then see what happens." —Michael Pollan, *How to Change Your Mind: What the New Science of Psychedelics Teaches Us About Consciousness, Dying, Addiction, Depression, and Transcendence*, 2018

The drugs in this group include ketamine (an anesthetic that is also sometimes used as a risky party drug), psilocybin (the active ingredient in "magic mushrooms"), and MDMA (also known as Ecstasy).

Ketamine. Dozens of experiments show that ketamine can provide relief from depression and suicidal thinking within hours (Alnefeesi et al., 2022; Riggs & Gould, 2021). Those dependent on alcohol use have also become more abstinent after ketamine treatment (Dakwar et al., 2019; Grabski et al., 2022). But ketamine is not a magic bullet. Relief often dissipates, which raises questions about the risks of repeated use (Schatzberg, 2019; Zimmermann et al., 2020). Given that ketamine acts as an opioid, one skeptic wonders if ketamine clinics are "nothing more than modern opium dens" (George, 2018). But others note that ketamine stimulates new synapses, which for some aids lasting change (Beyeler, 2019).

psychedelic drugs hallucinogenic drugs used to treat depressive disorders, anxiety disorders, posttraumatic stress disorder, and substance use disorders. These drugs cause temporary visual, psychological, and auditory changes, and an altered state of consciousness (often called a psychedelic experience or "trip").

Psilocybin. Experiments have found psilocybin-assisted therapy benefits at least equal to those of antidepressant drugs, and with fewer side effects (Carhart-Harris et al., 2021; Davis et al., 2021; Gukasyan et al., 2022). Microdosing psilocybin has also produced relief from excessive drinking. In one experiment, nearly half of those receiving psilocybin were abstinent 8 months later, as were only a quarter of those who received a placebo (Bogenschutz et al., 2022). One apparent reason for the lessened depression and alcohol use: The drug-assisted treatment stimulates brain cell growth and increases neural network connections (Daws et al., 2022). But the mind matters, too. Psilocybin's benefits are enhanced when patients have positive expectations (Gill et al., 2022; Kaertner et al., 2021).

MDMA. When paired with psychotherapy, MDMA has offered relief to people who for years had struggled with severe PTSD. In one experiment, 90 people across clinical sites in Canada, the United States, and Israel received either MDMA in three 8-hour sessions, or a placebo (Mitchell et al., 2021). By the end of the 18-week study, 67 percent of those who microdosed MDMA, and 32 percent of those who received the placebo, no longer had clinical PTSD.

Stay tuned. More clinical trials (experiments) are underway, and as many as 50 companies are working to make psychedelics into a billion-dollar business (Smith, 2022). Soon we will know whether psychedelic-assisted therapy is a revolutionary therapeutic aid—for many, the trip of a lifetime—or another therapeutic fad that flourishes and fades.

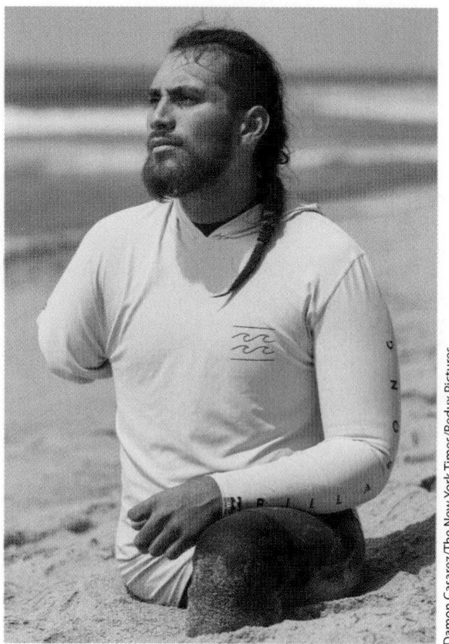

Damon Casarez/The New York Times/Redux Pictures

Psychedelics offer a new perspective Jose Martinez is a former Army gunner whose legs and right arm were blown off by a roadside bomb in Afghanistan. To cope with chronic pain and suicidal thoughts, Martinez has turned to the psychedelic drug psilocybin. "Psychedelics helped me realize that my problems are small compared to the world's bigger problems," he says (Jacobs, 2021).

Mood-Stabilizing Medications

In addition to antipsychotic, antianxiety, and antidepressant drugs, psychiatrists have *mood-stabilizing drugs* in their arsenal. One of them, Depakote, was originally used to treat epilepsy. It also controlled the manic episodes associated with bipolar disorders. Another, the simple salt *lithium*, effectively levels the emotional highs and lows of bipolar disorders.

In the 1940s, Australian physician John Cade discovered that lithium calmed guinea pigs. Wondering if it might do the same for humans, he first tried it himself (to confirm its safety) and then on 10 people with mania—all of whom improved dramatically (W. Brown, 2019). About 7 in 10 people with bipolar disorders benefit from a long-term daily dose of this cheap salt, which helps prevent or ease manic episodes and, to a lesser extent, lifts depression (Solomon et al., 1995). Kay Redfield Jamison (1995) described the effect:

> Lithium prevents my seductive but disastrous highs, diminishes my depressions, clears out the wool and webbing from my disordered thinking, slows me down, gentles me out, keeps me from ruining my career and relationships, keeps me out of a hospital, alive, and makes psychotherapy possible. (pp. 88–89)

Among people with bipolar disorders, taking lithium also correlates with a greatly lowered risk of suicide (Oquendo et al., 2011). Naturally occurring lithium in drinking water has also correlated with lower suicide rates (across 808 Japanese cities and towns) and lower crime rates (across 27 Texas counties) (Kugimiya et al., 2021; Schrauzer & Shrestha, 1990, 2010). Lithium works.

RETRIEVAL PRACTICE

RP-2 How do researchers determine if particular drug therapies are effective?

RP-3 The drugs given most often to treat depression are called ______________. Schizophrenia is often treated with ______________ drugs.

ANSWERS IN APPENDIX E

Brain Stimulation

LOQ 56-3 How are brain stimulation and psychosurgery used in treating specific disorders?

Electroconvulsive Therapy

Another biomedical treatment, **electroconvulsive therapy (ECT)**, manipulates the brain with mild electric shocks. When ECT was introduced in 1938, the wide-awake person was strapped to a table and jolted with electricity to the brain. This early ECT, which produced convulsions and brief unconsciousness, gained a barbaric image. Today's ECT is much kinder and gentler, and no longer "convulsive." The person receives a general

electroconvulsive therapy (ECT) a biomedical therapy for severe and treatment-resistant depression in which a brief electric current is sent through the brain of an anesthetized person.

anesthetic and a muscle relaxant (to prevent bodily convulsions). A psychiatrist then delivers a brief electrical pulse, sometimes only to the brain's right side, which triggers a 30- to 60-second brain seizure (McCall et al., 2017). Within 30 minutes, the person awakens and remembers nothing of the treatment or of the preceding hours. The mysteriously effective treatment is roughly similar to rebooting a computer.

Many studies confirm that ECT effectively treats severe depression in "treatment-resistant" people who have not responded to drug therapy (Fink, 2009; Giacobbe et al., 2018; Ross et al., 2018). After three such sessions each week for 2–4 weeks, 70 percent or more of those receiving today's ECT improve markedly, with less memory loss than with earlier versions of ECT and without discernible brain damage or increased dementia risk (Osler et al., 2018). ECT also reduces suicidal thoughts, making it "often life-saving" (Maixner et al., 2021; Rhee et al., 2021). A *Journal of the American Medical Association* editorial concluded that "the results of ECT in treating severe depression are among the most positive treatment effects in all of medicine" (Glass, 2001).

How does ECT alleviate severe depression—and, in some newer studies, mania (Elias et al., 2021)? After more than 80 years, no one knows for sure. One recipient likened ECT to the smallpox vaccine, which was saving lives before we knew how it worked. Perhaps the brief electric current calms neural centers where overactivity produces depression. Some research indicates that ECT stimulates neurogenesis (new neurons) and new synaptic connections (An & Wang, 2022).

The medical use of electricity is an ancient practice. Physicians treated the Roman Emperor Claudius (10 B.C.E.–54 C.E.) for headaches by pressing electric eels to his temples. Today, about 17 people per 100,000—people whose depression has not responded to other treatments—have received ECT (Lesage et al., 2016).

No matter how impressive the results, the idea of electrically shocking a person's brain still strikes many as barbaric, especially given our ignorance about why ECT works. Moreover, the mood boost may not last long. Many ECT-treated people eventually relapse back into depression, although relapses are somewhat fewer for those who also receive antidepressant drugs or do aerobic exercise (Rosenquist et al., 2016; Salehi et al., 2016). *The bottom line*: In the minds of many psychiatrists and clients, ECT is a lesser evil than severe depression's anguish and risk of suicide. After ECT, psychiatrist Rebecca Barchas (2021) reported "regaining my joie de vivre, my high level of motivation, and my ability to make decisions."

Alternative Neurostimulation Therapies

Three other neural stimulation techniques—transcranial direct current stimulation, transcranial magnetic stimulation, and deep brain stimulation—also aim to treat the depressed brain (**FIGURE 56.1**).

TRANSCRANIAL DIRECT CURRENT STIMULATION In contrast to ECT, which produces a brain seizure with about 800 milliamps of electricity, *transcranial direct current stimulation (tDCS)* administers a weak 1- to 2-milliamp current to the scalp. Skeptics argue that such a current is too weak to penetrate the brain (Underwood, 2016). But research suggests that tDCS is a modestly effective treatment for depression and obsessive-compulsive disorder (Gao et al., 2022; Razza et al., 2020).

FIGURE 56.1
A stimulating experience Today's neurostimulation therapies apply strong or mild electricity, or magnetic energy, either to the skull's surface or directly to brain neurons.

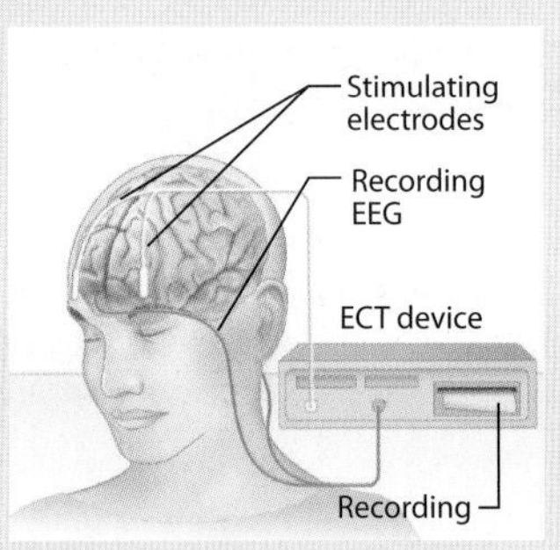
Stimulating electrodes
Recording EEG
ECT device
Recording

Electroconvulsive therapy (ECT) Psychiatrist administers a strong current, which triggers a brain seizure in the anesthetized patient.

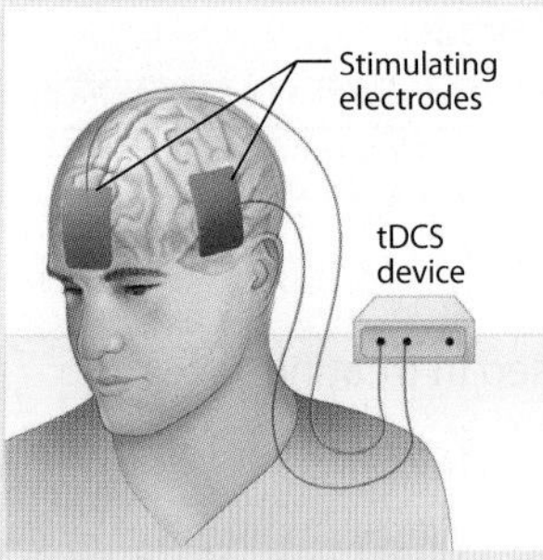
Stimulating electrodes
tDCS device

Transcranial direct current stimulation (tDCS) Psychiatrist applies a weak current to the scalp.

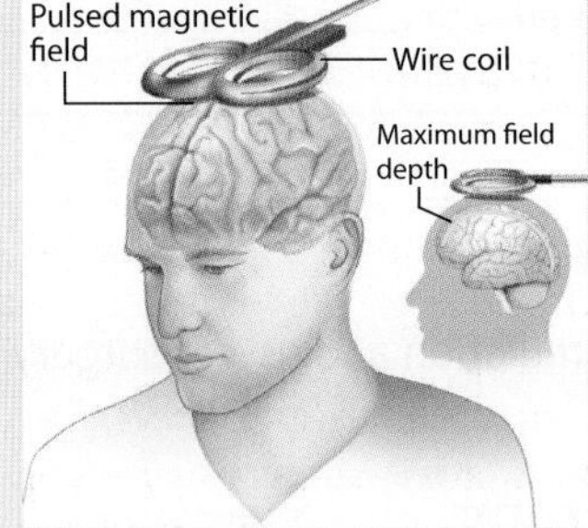
Pulsed magnetic field
Wire coil
Maximum field depth

Transcranial magnetic stimulation (TMS) Psychiatrist sends a painless magnetic field through the skull to the surface of the cortex to alter brain activity.

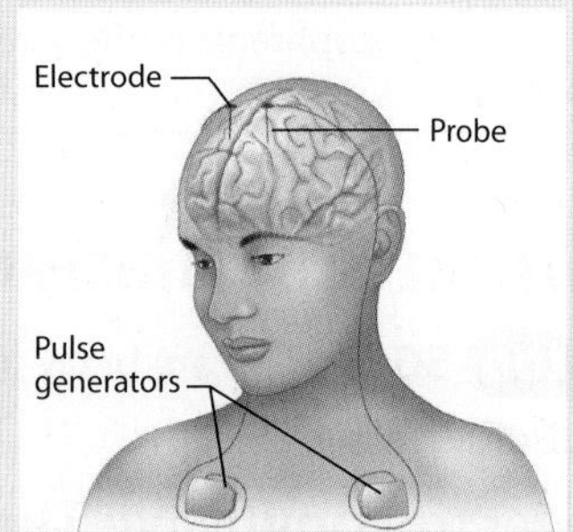
Electrode
Probe
Pulse generators

Deep brain stimulation (DBS) Psychiatrist stimulates electrodes implanted in "sadness centers" to calm those areas.

Jared Siskin/Patrick McMullan/Getty Images

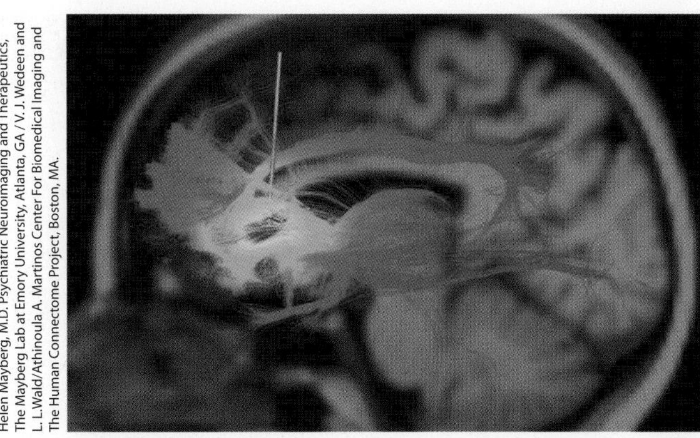

Helen Mayberg, M.D. Psychiatric Neuroimaging and Therapeutics, The Mayberg Lab at Emory University, Atlanta, GA / V. J. Wedeen and L. L. Wald/Athinoula A. Martinos Center For Biomedical Imaging and The Human Connectome Project, Boston, MA.

A depression switch? By comparing the brains of clients with and without depression, researcher Helen Mayberg identified a brain area (highlighted in red) that appears active in people who are depressed or sad, and whose activity may be calmed by deep brain stimulation.

TRANSCRANIAL MAGNETIC STIMULATION Depressed moods also sometimes improve when a painless procedure called **transcranial magnetic stimulation (TMS)** is performed on wide-awake patients in sessions over several weeks. Repeated pulses surging through a magnetic coil held close to the skull can stimulate or suppress activity in areas of the cortex. Like tDCS (and unlike ECT), the TMS procedure produces no memory loss or other serious side effects, aside from possible headaches.

Results are mixed. Some studies have found that, for 30 to 40 percent of people with depression, TMS works, although it is less effective than ECT (Carmi et al., 2019; Mutz et al., 2019). But researchers are exploring higher-dose and precisely targeted stimulation techniques that hold promise of greater relief (Cole et al., 2022; Ferrarelli & Phillips, 2021).

TMS also reduces some schizophrenia symptoms, such as social apathy and memory loss (Osoegawa et al., 2018; Xiu et al., 2020). How it works is unclear. Repeated stimulation may cause nerve cells to form new functioning circuits through *long-term potentiation*. Another possible explanation is a placebo effect: People benefit when, after being given a credible explanation, they *believe* TMS will work (Geers et al., 2019; Yesavage et al., 2018).

DEEP BRAIN STIMULATION Other clients have benefited from an experimental treatment pinpointing a neural hub that bridges the thinking frontal lobes to the limbic system (Becker et al., 2016; Brunoni et al., 2017; Ryder & Holtzheimer, 2016). This area, which is overactive in the brain of a depressed or temporarily sad person, typically calms when treated by ECT or antidepressants. If not calmed, then to activate neurons that inhibit this negative activity, neuroscientist Helen Mayberg applied *deep brain stimulation (DBS)* technology, sometimes used to treat Parkinson's tremors. Since 2003, she and her colleagues have used DBS to treat more than 200 depressed patients via implanted electrodes in a brain area that functions as the neural "sadness center" (Lozano & Mayberg, 2015; Scangos et al., 2021). For some clients, DBS produces large and enduring reductions in depression (Crowell et al., 2019; Scangos et al., 2021). "The bottom line," notes Mayberg, "is that if you get better, you stay better" (Carey, 2019).

New York Times Co./Getty Images

Failed lobotomy This 1940 photo shows Rosemary Kennedy (center) at age 22 with brother (and future U.S. president) John and their sister Jean. When doctors suggested that a lobotomy would control Rosemary's reportedly violent mood swings, her father approved the procedure. The lobotomy, performed after this photo was taken, left her confined to a hospital with an infantile mentality for the next 63 years, until her death in 2005.

Psychosurgery

Because its effects are irreversible, **psychosurgery** is the most drastic and least-used biomedical intervention for changing behavior. In the 1930s, Portuguese physician Egas Moniz developed what would become the best-known psychosurgical operation: the **lobotomy**. Moniz found that cutting the nerves connecting the frontal lobes with the inner brain's emotion-controlling centers calmed uncontrollably emotional and violent patients. In what would later become, in others' hands, a crude but relatively simple procedure, a neurosurgeon would shock the patient into a coma, hammer an icepick-like instrument through the top of each eye socket into the brain, and then wiggle it to sever connections running up to the frontal lobes. Between 1936 and 1954, tens of thousands of people with mental illness were "lobotomized," including 35,000 in the United States alone (Valenstein, 1986).

Although the intention was simply to disconnect emotion from thought, the effect was often more drastic. A lobotomy usually decreased misery or tension, but also produced a permanently lethargic, immature, uncreative person. During the 1950s, when calming drugs became available, psychosurgery became scorned.

transcranial magnetic stimulation (TMS)  the application of repeated pulses of magnetic energy to the brain; used to stimulate or suppress brain activity.

psychosurgery surgery that removes or destroys brain tissue to change behavior.

lobotomy a psychosurgical procedure once used to calm uncontrollably emotional or violent patients. The procedure cut the nerves that connect the frontal lobes to the emotion-controlling centers of the inner brain.

TABLE 56.1 Comparing Biomedical Therapies

Therapy	Targeted Problem	Therapy Aim	Therapy Technique
Therapeutic lifestyle change	Anxiety and depressive disorders	Restore healthy biological state.	Alter lifestyle through adequate exercise, sleep, nutrition, and other changes.
Drug therapies	Neurotransmitter malfunction	Control symptoms of psychological disorders.	Alter brain chemistry through drugs.
Brain stimulation	Depressive disorders and mania (ECT is used for severe, treatment-resistant depressive disorders, mania, and catatonia)	Alleviate depression and mania, especially when it is unresponsive to drugs or other forms of therapy.	Stimulate brain through electroconvulsive shock, mild electrical stimulation, magnetic pulses, or deep brain stimulation.
Psychosurgery	Brain malfunction	Relieve severe disorders.	Remove or destroy brain tissue.

Today, lobotomies are history. More precise, microscale psychosurgery is sometimes used in extreme cases. For example, if a person experiences uncontrollable seizures, surgeons can deactivate the specific nerve clusters that cause or transmit the convulsions. MRI-guided precision surgery is also occasionally done to cut the circuits involved in severe major depressive disorder and obsessive-compulsive disorder (Carey, 2009, 2011; M. Kim et al., 2018; Sachdev & Sachdev, 1997). Because these procedures are irreversible, neurosurgeons perform them only as a last resort.

* * *

TABLE 56.1 summarizes some aspects of the biomedical therapies we've discussed.

ASK YOURSELF

What were your impressions of biomedical therapies before reading this section? Are any of your views different now? Why or why not?

RETRIEVAL PRACTICE

RP-4 Severe depression that has not responded to other therapy may be treated with ________ ________, which can cause some memory loss of the preceding hours. More moderate neural stimulation techniques designed to help alleviate depression include transcranial ________ ________ stimulation, transcranial ________ stimulation, and ________ ________ stimulation.

ANSWERS IN APPENDIX E

Preventing Psychological Disorders and Building Resilience

LOQ 56-4 What may help prevent psychological disorders, and why is it important to develop resilience?

THIS ANTI-DEPRESSANT WORKS BEST IF YOU TAKE IT WITH WATER LAPPING NEAR YOUR HAMMOCK ON A CARIBBEAN BEACH.
SPEEDBUMP.COM
DIST. BY CREATORS
Dave Coverly/Speed Bump

Psychotherapies and biomedical therapies locate the cause of psychological disorders within the person. We infer that people who act cruelly must be cruel and that people who act "crazy" must be "sick." We attach labels to such people, thereby distinguishing them from "normal" folks. It follows, then, that we try to treat people with mental disorders by giving them insight into their problems, by changing their thinking, by helping them gain control with drugs.

There is an alternative viewpoint: We could interpret many psychological disorders as understandable responses to a disturbing and stressful world. According to this view, it is not just the person who needs treatment. Rather, as the soaring mental health problems during the Covid-19 pandemic illustrated, it's also the person's social context. It is better to prevent problems by reforming an unhealthy situation and developing people's coping competencies than to wait for and treat the problems that develop.

Life's stresses and challenges endure, and thus so do psychological disorders. Medical interventions such as antibiotics and vaccinations have greatly lengthened our life expectancy. Yet our growing understanding of suicide risks has not diminished suicide.

Our understanding the neuroscience of addiction has been followed by *increased* overdose deaths. And more widely available psychotherapy has not reduced U.S. rates of depression and anxiety (Insel, 2022). So, what might we do to alleviate the root causes of such problems?

resilience the personal strength that helps people cope with stress and recover from adversity and even trauma.

Preventive Mental Health

A story about the rescue of a drowning person from a rushing river illustrates this viewpoint: Having successfully administered first aid to the victim, the rescuer spots another struggling person and pulls that person out, too. After a half-dozen repetitions, the rescuer suddenly turns and starts running away while the river sweeps yet another floundering person into view. "Aren't you going to rescue that person?" asks a bystander. "No way," the rescuer replies. "I'm going upstream to find out what's pushing all these people in."

"It is better to prevent than to cure."
—Peruvian folk wisdom

Preventive mental health is upstream work. It seeks to prevent psychological casualties by identifying and alleviating the conditions that cause them. As clinical psychologist George Albee (1986, 2006) pointed out, there is abundant evidence that poverty, safety concerns, lack of meaningful work, constant criticism, unemployment, and discrimination undermine people's sense of competence, personal control, and self-esteem. Such stresses increase their risk of depression, substance use disorder, and suicide. To prevent psychological casualties we should, Albee contended, support programs that work to improve these distressing situations.

Preventing psychological problems means empowering those who have learned an attitude of helplessness, and changing environments that breed loneliness, suicidal thinking, and excessive alcohol and drug use. It means teaching children how to manage their emotions, get along with others, and keep up with academic demands (Godwin, 2020). It means harnessing positive psychology interventions to enhance human flourishing. One intervention taught adolescents that personality isn't fixed—people can change—and reduced their chances of future depression by 40 percent (Miu & Yeager, 2015). This result is no fluke: Preventive therapies have consistently reduced the risk for depression (Breedvelt et al., 2018).

In short, "everything aimed at improving the human condition, at making life more fulfilling and meaningful, may be considered part of primary prevention of mental or emotional disturbance" (Kessler & Albee, 1975, p. 557). Prevention can sometimes provide a double payoff. People with a strong sense of life's meaning are more engaging socially (Stillman et al., 2011). By strengthening people's sense of meaning in life, we may also lessen their loneliness as they become more engaging companions.

Among the upstream prevention workers are *community psychologists*. Mindful of how people interact with their environment, they focus on creating environments that support psychological health. Through their research and social action, community psychologists aim to empower people and to enhance their competence, health, and well-being.

"Mental disorders arise from physical ones, and likewise physical disorders arise from mental ones."—*The Mahabharata*, 200 B.C.E.

Building Resilience

Preventive mental health includes efforts to build individuals' **resilience**.

Faced with extreme suffering or trauma, some people experience lasting harm, some experience stable resilience, and some experience growth (Myers, 2019). In the aftermath

© Stephen Voss 2020/Redux Pictures

(a)

Chip Somodevilla/Getty Images

(b)

Disability and resilience (a) "I get to appreciate the gift of sight—any sight at all," said U.S. Congressman and Retired Navy SEAL Dan Crenshaw, who lost his eye to an improvised explosive device in the war in Afghanistan. (b) "Sometimes it takes dealing with a disability—the trauma, the relearning, the months of rehabilitation therapy—to uncover our true abilities and how we can put them to work for us in ways we may have never imagined," said U.S. Senator and Retired Lieutenant Colonel Tammy Duckworth, who lost both legs as an Army helicopter pilot in the Iraq War.

posttraumatic growth positive psychological changes following a struggle with extremely challenging circumstances and life crises.

of the September 11, 2001, terror attacks, many New Yorkers exhibited resilience. This resilience was especially true for those who enjoyed supportive close relationships and who had not recently experienced other stressful events (Bonanno et al., 2007). More than 9 in 10 New Yorkers, although stunned and grief-stricken by 9/11, did *not* have a dysfunctional stress reaction. Among those who did, the stress symptoms were mostly gone by the following January (Person et al., 2006). The initial isolation during the Covid-19 pandemic increased the rate of depressive disorders. But many people quickly adapted and their mental health returned to prepandemic levels (Robinson et al., 2022).

Struggling with challenging crises can lead to **posttraumatic growth.** Many people who have lost a loved one to suicide have reported a greater appreciation for life, more meaningful relationships, and a richer spiritual life (Levi-Belz et al., 2021). Out of even our worst experiences, some good can come, especially when we can imagine new possibilities (Mangelsdorf et al., 2019; Roepke, 2015). As with positive experiences, suffering can beget sensitivity and strength.

Thema Bryant
AJ SHORTER
PHOTOGRAPHY
AJ Shorter Photography

Power and healing to the people APA President Thema Bryant aims to reduce negative outcomes among members of marginalized communities. "APA and the science of psychology," she says, "are ideally situated to address the triple threat of trauma, loss and inequities that currently plagues our society" (APA, 2021).

RETRIEVAL PRACTICE

RP-5 What is the difference between preventive mental health and the psychological or biomedical therapies?

ANSWERS IN APPENDIX E

If you just finished reading this book, your introduction to psychological science is completed. Our tour of psychological science has taught us much—and you, too?—about our moods and memories, about the reach of our unconscious, about how we flourish and struggle, about how we perceive our physical and social worlds, and about how our biology and culture shape us. As your guides on this tour, we hope that you have shared our fascination, grown in your understanding and compassion, and sharpened your critical thinking. And we hope you enjoyed the ride.

With every good wish in your life journey ahead,

David G. Myers
DavidMyers.org; @DavidGMyers

C. Nathan DeWall
@cndewall

June Gruber
@junegruber

Let the globe, if nothing else, say this is true:
That even as we grieved, we grew
That even as we hurt, we hoped
That even as we tired, we tried
—Poet Amanda Gorman, "The Hill We Climb" (U.S. Presidential inaugural poem, 2021)

MODULE 56 REVIEW The Biomedical Therapies and Preventing Psychological Disorders

LEARNING OBJECTIVES

Test Yourself Answer these repeated Learning Objective Questions on your own (before "showing" the answers here, or checking the answers in Appendix D) to improve your retention of the concepts (McDaniel et al., 2009, 2015).

LOQ 56-1 Why is therapeutic lifestyle change considered an effective biomedical therapy, and how does it work?

LOQ 56-2 What are the drug therapies? How do double-blind studies help researchers evaluate a drug's effectiveness?

LOQ 56-3 How are brain stimulation and psychosurgery used in treating specific disorders?

LOQ 56-4 What may help prevent psychological disorders, and why is it important to develop resilience?

TERMS AND CONCEPTS TO REMEMBER

Test Yourself Write down the definition in your own words, then check your answer.

biomedical therapy, p. 622
psychopharmacology, p. 623
antipsychotic drugs, p. 625
antianxiety drugs, p. 625
antidepressant drugs, p. 625
psychedelic drugs, p. 626
electroconvulsive therapy (ECT), p. 627
transcranial magnetic stimulation (TMS), p. 629
psychosurgery, p. 629
lobotomy, p. 629
resilience, p. 631
posttraumatic growth, p. 632

MODULE TEST

Test Yourself Answer the following questions on your own first, then "show" the answers here, or check your answers in Appendix E.

1. Some antipsychotic drugs, used to calm people with schizophrenia, can have unpleasant side effects, most notably
   a. hyperactivity.
   b. momentary memory loss.
   c. sluggishness, tremors, and twitches.
   d. paranoia.

2. Drugs such as Xanax and Ativan, which depress central nervous system activity, can become addictive when used as ongoing treatment. These drugs are referred to as ____________ drugs.

3. A simple salt that often brings relief to people with bipolar disorders is ____________.

4. When drug therapies have not been effective, electroconvulsive therapy (ECT) may be used as a treatment for people with
   a. severe obsessive-compulsive disorder.
   b. severe depression.
   c. schizophrenia.
   d. anxiety disorders.

5. An approach that seeks to identify and alleviate conditions that put people at higher risk for developing psychological disorders is called
   a. deep brain stimulation.
   b. the mood-stabilizing perspective.
   c. spontaneous recovery.
   d. preventive mental health.

The Story of Psychology: A Timeline

Charles L. Brewer, *Furman University* and **Salena Brody,** *University of Texas, Dallas*

B.C.E.

387— Plato, who believed in innate ideas, suggests that the brain is the seat of mental processes.

335— Aristotle, who denied the existence of innate ideas, suggests that the heart is the seat of mental processes.

C.E.

1604— Johannes Kepler describes the inverted image on the retina.

Lens
Pupil
Retina
Fovea (point of central focus)
Iris
Cornea
Optic nerve to brain's visual cortex
Blind spot

Inverted image on the retina

Pascal Goetgheluck/ Science Source

1605— Francis Bacon publishes *The Proficiency and Advancement of Learning.*

1637— René Descartes, the French philosopher and mathematician who proposed mind–body interaction and the doctrine of innate ideas, publishes *A Discourse on Method.*

1690— John Locke, the British philosopher who rejected Descartes' notion of innate ideas and insisted that the mind at birth is a "blank slate" *(tabula rasa),* publishes *An Essay Concerning Human Understanding,* which stresses empiricism over speculation.

1774— Franz Mesmer, an Austrian physician, performs his first supposed cure using "animal magnetism" (later called mesmerism and hypnosis). In **1777,** he was expelled from the practice of medicine in Vienna.

1793— Philippe Pinel releases the first psychiatric patients from their chains at the Bicêtre Asylum in France and advocates for more humane treatment of psychiatric patients.

1802— Thomas Young publishes *A Theory of Color Vision* in England. (His theory was later called the trichromatic theory.)

1808— Franz Joseph Gall, a German physician, describes phrenology, the false belief that the shape of a person's skull reveals mental faculties and character traits.

1813— The first private psychiatric hospital in the United States opens in Philadelphia.

1834— Ernst Heinrich Weber publishes *The Sense of Touch,* in which he discusses the "just noticeable difference (jnd)" and what we now call Weber's law.

All Portraits: Macmillan Learning

1840— Dorothea Dix begins advocating for humane treatment of people in mental health institutions, persuading politicians to construct psychiatric hospitals.

Dorothea Dix (1802–1887)

1844— In Philadelphia, 13 superintendents form *the Association of Medical Superintendents of American Institutions for the Insane* (now known as the American Psychiatric Association).

1848— Phineas Gage suffers massive brain damage when a large iron rod accidentally pierces his brain, leaving his intellect and memory intact but altering his personality.

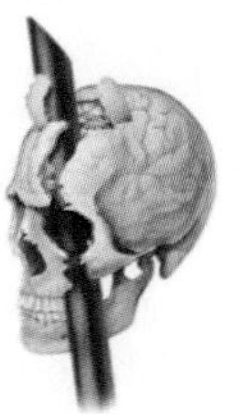

Warren Anatomical Museum in the Francis A. Countway Library of Medicine. Gift of Jack and Beverly Wilgus.

Phineas Gage

1850— Hermann von Helmholtz measures the speed of the nerve impulse.

1859— Charles Darwin publishes *On the Origin of Species by Means of Natural Selection,* synthesizing much previous work on the theory of evolution, including that of Herbert Spencer, who coined the phrase "survival of the fittest."

1861— Paul Broca, a French physician, discovers an area in the left frontal lobe of the brain (now called Broca's area) that is critical for the production of spoken language.

1869— Francis Galton, Charles Darwin's cousin, publishes *Hereditary Genius,* in which he claims that intelligence is inherited. In **1876,** he coins the expression "nature and nurture" to correspond with "heredity and environment." Later, Galton proposes harmful ideas about how to improve the genetic quality of human populations (called *eugenics*) that would inform prejudiced and discriminatory policies.

1874— Carl Wernicke, a German neurologist and psychiatrist, shows that damage to a specific area in the left temporal lobe (now called Wernicke's area) disrupts ability to comprehend or produce spoken or written language.

1878— G. Stanley Hall receives from Harvard University's Department of Philosophy the first U.S. Ph.D. degree based on psychological research.

1879— Wilhelm Wundt establishes at the University of Leipzig, Germany, the first psychology laboratory, which becomes a mecca for psychology students from all over the world.

Wilhelm Wundt (1832–1920)

1883— G. Stanley Hall, student of Wilhelm Wundt, establishes the first formal U.S. psychology laboratory at Johns Hopkins University.

1885— Hermann Ebbinghaus publishes *On Memory,* summarizing his extensive research on learning and memory, including the "forgetting curve."

1886— Joseph Jastrow receives from Johns Hopkins University the first Ph.D. degree awarded by a U.S. Department of Psychology.

1889— Henri-Étienne Beaunis and Alfred Binet establish France's first psychology laboratory at the Sorbonne.

Alfred Binet (1857–1911)

— The first International Congress of Psychology meets in Paris.

1890— William James, Harvard University philosopher and psychologist, publishes *The Principles of Psychology,* describing psychology as "the science of mental life."

William James (1842–1910)

1891— James Mark Baldwin establishes the first psychology laboratory in the British Commonwealth at the University of Toronto.

1892— G. Stanley Hall spearheads the founding of the American Psychological Association (APA) and becomes its first president.

1893— Mary Whiton Calkins and Christine Ladd-Franklin are the first women elected to membership in the APA.

Mary Whiton Calkins (1863–1930) **Christine Ladd-Franklin (1847–1930)**

1894— Margaret Floy Washburn is the first woman to receive a Ph.D. degree in psychology (Cornell University).

— Harvard University denies Mary Whiton Calkins admission to doctoral candidacy because of her gender. She goes on to publish more than 100 scientific articles related to memory and the self.

1896— John Dewey publishes "The Reflex Arc Concept in Psychology," helping to formalize the school of psychology called functionalism.

1898— In *Animal Intelligence,* Edward L. Thorndike describes his learning experiments with cats in "puzzle boxes." In **1905**, he proposes the "law of effect."

— Doctoral student Alice Lee uses published data from the *Journal of Anatomy* to debunk the popular phrenology and eugenics arguments that skull size predicts intelligence.

1900— Sigmund Freud publishes *The Interpretation of Dreams,* his major theoretical work on psychoanalysis.

1901— Ten founders establish the British Psychological Society.

1904— Ivan Pavlov is awarded the Nobel Prize for Physiology or Medicine for his studies on the physiology of digestion.

1905— Mary Whiton Calkins becomes the first woman president of the APA.

— Ivan Pavlov begins publishing studies of conditioning in animals.

Ivan Pavlov (1849–1936)

— Alfred Binet and Théodore Simon produce the first intelligence test for assessing the abilities and academic progress of Parisian schoolchildren.

1909— Sigmund Freud makes his only trip to America to deliver a series of lectures at Clark University.

Sigmund Freud (1856–1939)

1913— John B. Watson outlines the tenets of behaviorism in a *Psychological Review* article, "Psychology as the Behaviorist Views It."

John Watson (1878–1958)

1914— Lilian Gilbreth publishes *Principles of Management,* a foundational text for the field of industrial-organizational psychology.

— During World War I, Robert Yerkes and his staff develop a group intelligence test for evaluating U.S. military personnel, which increases the U.S. public's acceptance of psychological testing.

1920— 
Leta Stetter Hollingworth publishes *The Psychology of Subnormal Children,* an early classic. In **1921,** she is cited in *American Men of Science* for her research on the psychology of women.

Leta Stetter Hollingworth (1886–1939)

— 
Francis Cecil Sumner becomes the first Black person in the U.S. to receive a Ph.D. degree in psychology (Clark University). He later co-founds the psychology department at Howard University.

Francis Cecil Sumner (1895–1954)

— John B. Watson and Rosalie Rayner report conditioning a fear reaction in a child called "Little Albert."

1921— Hermann Rorschach, a Swiss psychiatrist, introduces the Rorschach inkblot test.

1923— Developmental psychologist Jean Piaget publishes *The Language and Thought of the Child.*

1924— Mary Cover Jones reports reconditioning a fear reaction in a child (Peter), a forerunner of systematic desensitization developed by Joseph Wolpe.

1927— In *Introduction to the Technique of Child Analysis,* Anna Freud discusses psychoanalysis in the treatment of children.

1929— Wolfgang Köhler publishes *Gestalt Psychology,* which criticizes behaviorism and outlines essential elements of the gestalt theory.

1931— 
Margaret Floy Washburn becomes the first female psychologist (and the second female scientist in any discipline) elected to the U.S. National Academy of Sciences.

Margaret Floy Washburn (1871–1939)

1932— In *The Wisdom of the Body,* Walter B. Cannon coins the term "homeostasis," discusses the fight-or-flight response, and identifies hormonal changes associated with stress.

1933— 
Inez Beverly Prosser becomes the first Black woman to receive a Ph.D. degree in psychology from a U.S. institution (University of Cincinnati).

Inez Beverly Prosser (1895–1934)

1934— 
Ruth Winifred Howard becomes the second Black woman in the U.S. to receive a Ph.D. degree in psychology (University of Minnesota) and spends her career doing clinical work with children and young people.

Ruth Winifred Howard (1900–1997)

1935— Christiana Morgan and Henry Murray introduce the Thematic Apperception Test to elicit fantasies from people undergoing psychoanalysis.

1936— Egas Moniz, a Portuguese physician, publishes work on the first frontal lobotomies performed on humans.

1938— B. F. Skinner publishes *The Behavior of Organisms,* which describes operant conditioning of animals.

— In *Primary Mental Abilities,* Louis L. Thurstone proposes seven such abilities.

— Ugo Cerletti and Lucio Bini introduce electroshock treatment with a human patient.

1939— David Wechsler publishes the Wechsler–Bellevue intelligence test, forerunner of the Wechsler Intelligence Scale for Children (WISC) and the Wechsler Adult Intelligence Scale (WAIS).

— 
Mamie Phipps Clark receives a master's degree from Howard University. She later earns her doctorate and, with Kenneth B. Clark, provides joint research cited in the U.S. Supreme Court's 1954 decision to end racial segregation in public schools.

Mamie Phipps Clark (1917–1983)

— Edward Alexander Bott helps found the Canadian Psychological Association. He becomes its first president in 1940.

— World War II provides many opportunities for psychologists to enhance the popularity and influence of psychology, especially in applied areas.

1941— Raymond Cattell and John Horn distinguish fluid and crystallized intelligence. Decades later, John Carroll synthesizes these ideas as a bridge between a general intelligence factor (*g*) and specific abilities, to create the Cattell-Horn-Carroll (CHC) theory of intelligence.

1943— Psychologist Starke Hathaway and physician J. Charnley McKinley publish the Minnesota Multiphasic Personality Inventory (MMPI).

1945— 
Karen Horney, who criticized Freud's theory of female sexual development, publishes *Our Inner Conflicts.*

Karen Horney (1885–1952)

1946— U.S. Congress creates the National Institute of Mental Health, making mental health a national priority.

— Benjamin Spock's first edition of *The Commonsense Book of Baby and Child Care* appears; the book will influence child raising in North America for several decades.

1948— Alfred Kinsey and his colleagues publish *Sexual Behavior in the Human Male,* and they publish *Sexual Behavior in the Human Female* in **1953.**

— B. F. Skinner's novel, *Walden Two,* describes a utopian community based on positive reinforcement, which becomes a clarion call for applying psychological principles in everyday living, especially communal living.

B. F. Skinner (1904–1990)

— Ernest R. Hilgard publishes *Theories of Learning,* which was required reading for several generations of psychology students in North America.

1949— Raymond B. Cattell publishes the Sixteen Personality Factor Questionnaire (16PF).

— The scientist-practitioner model of training is approved at the Boulder Conference on Graduate Education in Clinical Psychology.

— In *The Organization of Behavior: A Neuropsychological Theory,* Canadian psychologist Donald O. Hebb outlines a new and influential conceptualization of how the nervous system functions.

1950— Solomon Asch publishes studies of effects of conformity on judgments of line length.

— In *Childhood and Society,* Erik Erikson outlines his stages of psychosocial development.

1951— Carl Rogers publishes *Client-Centered Therapy.*

1952— The American Psychiatric Association publishes the *Diagnostic and Statistical Manual of Mental Disorders,* an influential book that will be updated periodically.

1953— Eugene Aserinski and Nathaniel Kleitman describe rapid eye movements (REM) that occur during sleep.

— Janet Taylor's Manifest Anxiety Scale appears in the *Journal of Abnormal Psychology.*

1954— In *Motivation and Personality,* Abraham Maslow proposes a hierarchy of motives ranging from physiological needs to self-actualization. (Maslow later updates the hierarchy to include self-transcendence needs.)

— James Olds and Peter Milner, McGill University neuropsychologists, describe the rewarding effects of electrical stimulation of the hypothalamus in rats.

— Gordon Allport publishes *The Nature of Prejudice.*

1956— In his *Psychological Review* article titled "The Magical Number Seven, Plus or Minus Two: Some Limits on Our Capacity for Processing Information," George Miller coins the term "chunk" for memory researchers.

1957— Robert Sears, Eleanor Maccoby, and Harry Levin publish *Patterns of Child Rearing.*

— Charles Ferster and B. F. Skinner publish *Schedules of Reinforcement.*

1958— Harry Harlow publishes "The Nature of Love," outlining his work on attachment in monkeys.

1959— Noam Chomsky's critical review of B. F. Skinner's *Verbal Behavior* appears in the journal *Language.*

— Keturah Whitehurst becomes the first Black person in the U.S. to be licensed as a psychologist. She later co-founds a human development and learning laboratory that provides educational opportunities to children in need.

Keturah Whitehurst (1912–2000)

— Eleanor Gibson and Richard Walk report their research on infants' depth perception in "The Visual Cliff."

— Lloyd Peterson and Margaret Peterson, in the *Journal of Experimental Psychology* article, "Short-Term Retention of Individual Verbal Items," highlight the importance of rehearsal in memory.

— John Thibaut and Harold Kelley publish *The Social Psychology of Groups.*

1960— George Sperling publishes "The Information Available in Brief Visual Presentations."

1961— Georg von Békésy receives a Nobel Prize for research on the physiology of hearing.

— David McClelland publishes *The Achieving Society.*

1962— Jerome Kagan and Howard Moss publish *Birth to Maturity.*

— Martha E. Bernal becomes the first Latina to earn a U.S. doctoral degree (Ph.D. in clinical psychology, Indiana University).

Martha E. Bernal (1931–2001)

— Stanley Schachter and Jerome Singer publish findings that support the two-factor theory of emotion.

— Albert Ellis' *Reason and Emotion in Psychotherapy* is published; it is a milestone in the development of rational-emotive therapy (RET).

1963— Stanley Milgram's "Behavioral Study of Obedience" appears in the *Journal of Abnormal and Social Psychology.*

1964— Marigold Linton becomes the first Native American to receive a doctoral degree in psychology (University of California, Los Angeles). She is a founding member of both the Society for Advancement of Chicanos and Native Americans in Science, and the National Indian Education Association.

Marigold Linton (born 1936)

1965— Canadian researcher Ronald Melzack and British researcher Patrick Wall propose the gate-control theory of pain.

— The Archives of the History of American Psychology is founded at the University of Akron.

1966— Nancy Bayley becomes the first woman to receive the APA's Distinguished Scientific Contribution Award.

— Jerome Bruner and colleagues at Harvard University's Center for Cognitive Studies publish *Studies in Cognitive Growth*.

— William Masters and Virginia Johnson publish results of their research in *Human Sexual Responses*.

— Allen Gardner and Beatrix Gardner begin training a chimpanzee named Washoe in American Sign Language at the University of Nevada, Reno. (Washoe dies in 2007.)

— John Garcia and Robert Koelling publish a study on taste aversion in rats.

John Garcia (1917–1983)

— David M. Green and John A. Swets publish *Signal Detection Theory and Psychophysics*.

— Julian Rotter publishes research on locus of control.

1967— Publication of Ulric Neisser's *Cognitive Psychology*, which helps to steer psychology away from behaviorism and toward cognitive processes.

— Martin Seligman and Steven Maier publish the results of their research on "learned helplessness" in dogs.

1968— Richard Atkinson and Richard Shiffrin's influential three-stage memory model appears in *The Psychology of Learning and Motivation*.

— Neal E. Miller's article in *Science*, describing instrumental conditioning of autonomic responses, stimulates research on biofeedback.

1969— Albert Bandura publishes *Principles of Behavior Modification*.

— The Association for Women in Psychology is founded. E. Kitch Childs is instrumental in this effort, pioneering therapy techniques grounded in "intersectionality" (considering how race, class, and other aspects of identity may combine to create discrimination or disadvantage).

— George Miller, in his APA presidential address, "Psychology as a Means of Promoting Human Welfare," emphasizes the importance of "giving psychology away."

1970— Psychologist Reiko Homma True lobbies successfully to open the Asian American Community Mental Health program—the first to focus on a minority population.

Reiko Homma True (born 1933)

1971— Kenneth B. Clark becomes the first Black president of the APA. He spends his career studying racial bias in schools. His research helps desegregate U.S. schools and leads the federal government to prioritize spending to improve Black children's educational experiences.

Kenneth B. Clark (1914–2005)

— Albert Bandura publishes *Social Learning Theory*.

— B. F. Skinner publishes *Beyond Freedom and Dignity*.

1972— Elliot Aronson publishes *The Social Animal*.

— Fergus Craik and Robert Lockhart's "Levels of Processing: A Framework for Memory Research" appears in the *Journal of Verbal Learning and Verbal Behavior*.

— Robert Rescorla and Allan Wagner publish their associative model of Pavlovian conditioning.

— Under the leadership of Derald Wing Sue and Stanley Sue, the Asian American Psychological Association is founded.

Derald Wing Sue (born 1942)

Stanley Sue (born 1944)

1973— APA votes to remove "homosexuality" as a psychological disorder from the *Diagnostic and Statistical Manual of Mental Disorders*.

— Ethologists Karl von Frisch, Konrad Lorenz, and Nikolaas Tinbergen receive the Nobel Prize for their research on animal behavior.

1974— APA's Division 2 first publishes its journal, *Teaching of Psychology*, with Robert S. Daniel as editor.

— Eleanor Maccoby and Carol Jacklin publish *The Psychology of Sex Differences*.

1975— Biologist Edward O. Wilson's *Sociobiology* is published; it will be a controversial precursor to evolutionary psychology.

1976— Sandra Wood Scarr and Richard A. Weinberg publish "IQ Test Performance of Black Children Adopted by White Families" in *American Psychologist*.

— Psychologist Robert V. Guthrie publishes *Even the Rat Was White*, the first history of Black psychologists in the U.S.

Robert V. Guthrie (1930–2005)

— Saundra Murray Nettles chairs the Task Force on Black Women's Priorities, which leads to the creation of APA's Division 35, Section 1: The Psychology of Black Women.

— Psychologist Carolyn Payton becomes Director of the U.S. Peace Corps, the first woman and the first Black person to serve in that role.

1978— Psychologist Herbert A. Simon, Carnegie-Mellon University, wins a Nobel Prize for pioneering research on computer simulations of human thinking and problem solving.

1979 — James J. Gibson publishes *The Ecological Approach to Visual Perception*.

— Elizabeth Loftus publishes *Eyewitness Testimony*, showing that eyewitness memory is often inaccurate.

1981 — David Hubel and Torsten Wiesel receive a Nobel Prize for research on single-cell recordings that identified feature detector cells in the visual cortex.

— Roger Sperry receives a Nobel Prize for research on split-brain patients.

— U.S. sociologist Harriette Pipe McAdoo publishes *Black Families*, an anthology of work done with John Lewis McAdoo on middle class Black families. Previous studies had focused on dysfunctional families, such as those in contact with prison and drug treatment programs.

— Paleontologist Stephen Jay Gould publishes *The Mismeasure of Man*, highlighting the debate concerning biological determination of intelligence.

1983 — In his *Frames of Mind*, Howard Gardner outlines his theory of multiple intelligences.

1984 — 44 Society for the Psychology of Sexual Orientation and Gender Diversity

The APA creates Division 44 (Society for the Psychology of Sexual Orientation and Gender Diversity).

1987 — Elizabeth Scarborough and Laurel Furumoto publish *Untold Lives: The First Generation of American Women Psychologists*.

— Fluoxetine (Prozac) is introduced as a treatment for depression.

— Wilbert J. McKeachie, University of Michigan, receives the first APA Award for Distinguished Career Contributions to Education and Training in Psychology.

1988 — The American Psychological Society is founded. The organization changes its name to the Association for Psychological Science in **2006**.

1990 — Psychiatrist Aaron Beck receives the Distinguished Scientific Award for the Applications of Psychology for advancing understanding and treatment of psychopathology, including pivotal contributions to the development of cognitive therapy.

— B. F. Skinner receives APA's first Citation for Outstanding Lifetime Contributions to Psychology and presents his last public address, "Can Psychology Be a Science of Mind?" (He died a few days later at age 86.)

1991 — Martin Seligman publishes *Learned Optimism*, which foreshadows the "positive psychology" movement.

1992 — Teachers of Psychology in Secondary Schools (TOPSS) is established as part of the APA.

— About 3000 U.S. secondary school students take the first Advanced Placement (AP) Examination in Psychology.

1993 — Psychologist Judith Rodin is elected president of the University of Pennsylvania, becoming the first female president of an Ivy League school.

1996 — Dorothy Cantor becomes the first president of the APA with a Psy.D. degree.

1998 — *The Handbook of Asian American Psychology* is published.

2002 — New Mexico becomes the first U.S. state to allow qualified clinical psychologists to prescribe certain drugs. Many U.S. states now allow nurse practitioners and other providers to prescribe psychiatric medication.

— Psychologist Daniel Kahneman, Princeton University, receives a Nobel Prize for research on decision making later summarized in his **2011** book, *Thinking Fast and Slow*.

2009 — Psychologist Judy Chu becomes the first Chinese American woman elected to the U.S. Congress.

2011 — Proposed by participants at the 2008 national conference at the University of Puget Sound, the document "Principles for Quality Undergraduate Education in Psychology," is approved as official APA policy.

— Melba J. T. Vasquez becomes the first Latina president of the APA.

Melba J. T. Vasquez (born 1951)

2013 — U.S. President Barack Obama announces $100 million in funding for an interdisciplinary project to advance understanding of the human brain.

2015 — The *Independent Review Relating to APA Ethics Guidelines, National Security Interrogations, and Torture* is presented to the APA.

2018 — Kristina Olson becomes the first psychologist to receive the National Science Foundation's Waterman Award. She also receives a 2018 MacArthur Fellowship for her work studying the social and cognitive development of transgender and gender-nonconforming youth.

2020 — MacArthur Fellowship awardee and implicit bias researcher Jennifer L. Eberhardt receives multiple awards for authoring *Biased: Uncovering the Hidden Prejudice That Shapes What We See, Think, and Do*.

— Cognitive neuroscientist Damien Fair wins a MacArthur award for his work studying neurodiverse children.

2021 — The APA issues an official "Apology to People of Color for APA's Role in Promoting, Perpetuating, and Failing to Challenge Racism, Racial Discrimination, and Human Hierarchy in the U.S."

Career Fields in Psychology

Jennifer Zwolinski, *University of San Diego*

What can you do with a degree in psychology? Lots!

As a psychology major, you will graduate with a scientific mindset and an awareness of basic principles of human behavior (biological mechanisms, nature–nurture interactions, life-span development, cognition, psychological disorders, social interaction). This background will prepare you for success in many areas, including business, the helping professions, health services, marketing, law, sales, and teaching. You may even go on to graduate school for specialized training to become a psychology professional. This appendix provides an overview of some of psychology's key career fields, most of which require a graduate degree in psychology.[1] For an expanded discussion, see ***Pursuing a Psychology Career*** in Achieve, where you can learn more about the many interesting options available to those with bachelor's, master's, and doctoral degrees in psychology. You can also read about the professional skills and abilities a psychology major (or even psychology coursework, if you are a non-major) can provide, how to articulate those skills and abilities to potential employers, and other steps you can take to help you secure a job after graduation.

If you are like most psychology students, you may be unaware of the wide variety of specialties and work settings available in psychology (Terre & Stoddart, 2000). To date, the American Psychological Association (APA) has 54 divisions that represent the popular subfields and interest groups of APA members (**TABLE B.1**). APA Division 2 (Society for the Teaching of Psychology) offers an excellent career exploration resource for those interested in learning about the hundreds of career options available for students with an undergraduate degree in psychology.

TABLE B.1 APA Divisions by Number and Name

No.	Division	No.	Division
1.	Society for General Psychology	31.	State, Provincial and Territorial Psychological Association Affairs
2.	Society for the Teaching of Psychology	32.	Society for Humanistic Psychology
3.	Society for Experimental Psychology and Cognitive Science	33.	Intellectual and Developmental Disabilities/Autism Spectrum Disorder
4.	*There is no active Division 4.*	34.	Society for Environmental, Population and Conservation Psychology
5.	Quantitative and Qualitative Methods	35.	Society for the Psychology of Women
6.	Society for Behavioral Neuroscience and Comparative Psychology	36.	Society for the Psychology of Religion and Spirituality
7.	Developmental Psychology	37.	Society for Child and Family Policy and Practice
8.	Society for Personality and Social Psychology	38.	Society for Health Psychology
9.	Society for the Psychological Study of Social Issues (SPSSI)	39.	Society for Psychoanalysis and Psychoanalytic Psychology
10.	Society for the Psychology of Aesthetics, Creativity and the Arts	40.	Society for Clinical Neuropsychology
11.	*There is no active Division 11.*	41.	American Psychology-Law Society
12.	Society of Clinical Psychology	42.	Psychologists in Independent Practice
13.	Society of Consulting Psychology	43.	Society for Couple and Family Psychology
14.	Society for Industrial and Organizational Psychology	44.	Society for the Psychology of Sexual Orientation and Gender Diversity
15.	Educational Psychology	45.	Society for the Psychological Study of Culture, Ethnicity and Race
16.	School Psychology	46.	Society for Media Psychology and Technology
17.	Society of Counseling Psychology	47.	Society for Sport, Exercise and Performance Psychology
18.	Psychologists in Public Service	48.	Society for the Study of Peace, Conflict and Violence: Peace Psychology Division
19.	Society for Military Psychology	49.	Society of Group Psychology and Group Psychotherapy
20.	Adult Development and Aging	50.	Society of Addiction Psychology
21.	Applied Experimental and Engineering Psychology	51.	Society for the Psychological Study of Men and Masculinities
22.	Rehabilitation Psychology	52.	International Psychology
23.	Consumer Psychology	53.	Society of Clinical Child and Adolescent Psychology
24.	Society for Theoretical and Philosophical Psychology	54.	Society of Pediatric Psychology
25.	Behavior Analysis	55.	Society for Prescribing Psychology
26.	Society for the History of Psychology	56.	Trauma Psychology
27.	Society for Community Research and Action: Division of Community Psychology		
28.	Psychopharmacology and Substance Abuse		
29.	Society for the Advancement of Psychotherapy		
30.	Society of Psychological Hypnosis		

Information from: American Psychological Association (2020).

The following paragraphs (arranged alphabetically) describe some of psychology's main career fields.

BIOLOGICAL PSYCHOLOGISTS Biological psychologists seek to understand and explain how biological and psychological processes influence behavior. Biological psychologists typically use advanced technologies in research settings with human participants or animals to investigate the influence of biological factors on sensation, learning, memory, motivation, and emotion. Although many biological psychologists work in academic research or teaching environments, the interdisciplinary nature of their training prepares them to work in various other settings, including private consulting, public or government health, and the pharmaceutical, biotechnology, or medical industries. Subfields of biological psychology include neuropsychology, behavioral neuroscience, and cognitive neuroscience.

CLINICAL PSYCHOLOGISTS Clinical psychologists promote psychological health in individuals, groups, and organizations. Some clinical psychologists specialize in specific psychological disorders. Others treat a range of disorders, from adjustment difficulties to severe psychopathology. Clinical psychologists often provide therapy but may also engage in research, teaching, assessment, and consultation. Clinical psychologists work in a variety of settings, including private practice, mental health service organizations, schools, universities, industry, legal systems, medical systems, counseling centers, government agencies, correctional facilities, nonprofit organizations, and military services.

To become a clinical psychologist, you will need to earn a doctorate from a clinical psychology program. The APA sets the standards for clinical psychology graduate programs, offering *accreditation* (official recognition) to those who meet their standards. To serve clients representing a variety of races, ethnicities, genders, ages, socioeconomic backgrounds, sexual orientations, and physical abilities, the APA also encourages professional psychologists to seek ongoing diversity training throughout their careers. In all U.S. states, clinical psychologists working in independent practice must obtain a license to offer services such as therapy and testing.

COGNITIVE PSYCHOLOGISTS Cognitive psychologists study thought processes and focus on such topics as perception, language, attention, problem solving, memory, judgment and decision making, and intelligence. Research interests include designing computer-based models of thought processes and identifying biological correlates of cognition. As a cognitive psychologist, you might work as a professor, industrial consultant, or human factors specialist in an educational or business setting.

COMMUNITY PSYCHOLOGISTS Community psychologists move beyond focusing on specific individuals or families and deal with broad problems of mental health in community settings. These psychologists believe that human behavior is powerfully influenced by the interaction between people and their physical, social, political, and economic environments. Community psychologists value the uniqueness of individuals, communities, and social groups, and they actively integrate their clients' diverse backgrounds into their work. With this understanding and appreciation, they seek to promote psychological health by enhancing environmental settings—focusing on preventive measures and crisis intervention, with special attention to the problems of underserved and underrepresented groups. Many community psychologists collaborate with professionals in other areas, such as public health, with a shared emphasis on prevention. As a community psychologist, your work settings could include federal, state, and local departments of mental health, corrections, and welfare. You might conduct research or help evaluate research in health service settings, serve as an independent consultant for a private or

Cognitive consulting Cognitive psychologists may advise businesses on how to operate more effectively by understanding the human factors involved.

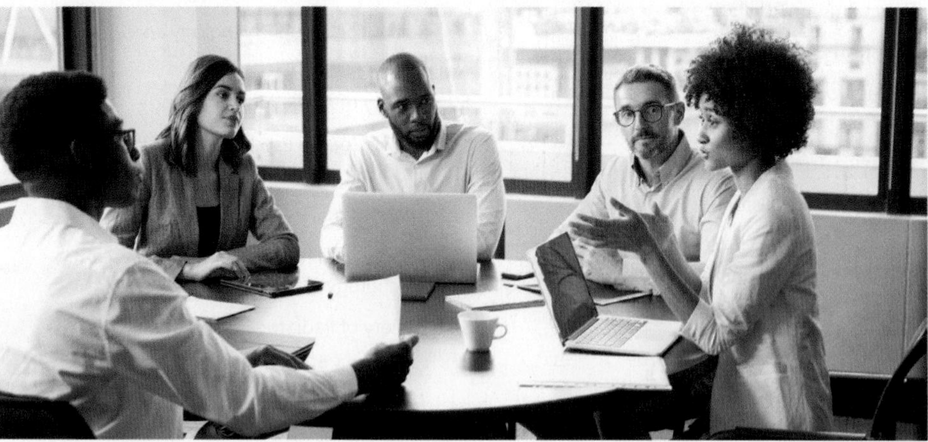

iStock/Getty Images

government agency, or teach and consult as a college or university faculty member.

AP Photo

Community care Community psychologists have helped people in Haiti to work through the ongoing emotional challenges that come with enduring repeated natural disasters.

COUNSELING PSYCHOLOGISTS Counseling psychologists help people adjust to life transitions or make lifestyle changes. Although similar to clinical psychologists, counseling psychologists typically help people with adjustment problems rather than severe psychopathology. Like clinical psychologists, counseling psychologists conduct therapy and provide assessments to individuals and groups. As a counseling psychologist, you would likely emphasize your clients' strengths, helping them to use their own skills, interests, and abilities to cope during transitions. You might find yourself working in an academic setting as a faculty member or administrator or in a university counseling center, community mental health center, business, or private practice. As with clinical psychology, if you plan to work in independent practice you will need to obtain a state license to provide counseling services to the public. And, as is the case for clinical psychology, the APA promotes diversity and cultural awareness and competencies across all phases of career development—from graduate training to continuing education after licensure.

DEVELOPMENTAL PSYCHOLOGISTS Developmental psychologists conduct research on age-related behavioral changes and apply their scientific knowledge to educational, child-care, policy, and related settings. As a developmental psychologist, you would investigate change across a broad range of topics, including the biological, psychological, cognitive, and social aspects of development. Developmental psychology informs a number of applied fields, including educational psychology, school psychology, child psychopathology, and gerontology. This field also informs public policy in areas such as education and child-care reform, maternal and child health, and attachment and adoption. You would probably specialize in a specific stage of the life span, such as infancy, childhood, adolescence, or middle or late adulthood. Your work setting could be an educational institution, day-care center, youth group program, or senior center.

EDUCATIONAL PSYCHOLOGISTS Educational psychologists are interested in the psychological processes involved in learning. They study the relationship between learning and physical and social environments, and they develop strategies for enhancing the learning process. As an educational psychologist working in a university psychology department or school of education, you might conduct basic research on topics related to learning, or develop innovative methods of teaching to enhance the learning process. You might design effective tests, including measures of aptitude and achievement. You might be employed by a school or government agency or charged with designing and implementing effective employee-training programs in a business setting.

ENVIRONMENTAL PSYCHOLOGISTS Environmental psychologists study the interaction of individuals with their natural and built (urban) environments. They are interested in how we influence and are affected by these environments. As an environmental psychologist, you might study wildlife conservation, the impact of urbanization on health, or cognitive factors involved in sustainable lifestyle choices. Environmental psychologists tend to address these kinds of issues by working with other professionals as part of an interdisciplinary team. As an environmental psychologist, you might work in a consulting firm, an academic setting, the nonprofit sector, or the government.

EXPERIMENTAL PSYCHOLOGISTS Experimental psychologists are a diverse group of scientists who investigate a variety of basic behavioral processes in humans and

Rick Wood/Milwaukee Journal-Sentinel/AP Photo

Forensics in court Forensic psychologists may be called on to assist police officers who are investigating a crime scene, but most forensic work occurs in the lab and for the judicial system.

other animals. Prominent areas of experimental research include comparative methods of science, motivation, learning, thought, attention, memory, perception, and language. Most experimental psychologists identify with a particular subfield, such as cognitive psychology, depending on their interests and training. Experimental research methods are not limited to the field of experimental psychology; many other subfields rely on experimental methodology to conduct studies. As an experimental psychologist, you would most likely work in an academic setting, teaching courses and supervising students' research in addition to conducting your own research. Or you might be employed by a research institution, zoo, business, or government agency.

FORENSIC PSYCHOLOGISTS Forensic psychologists apply psychological principles to legal issues. They conduct research on the interface of law and psychology, help to create public policies related to mental health, help law enforcement agencies in criminal investigations, or consult on jury selection and deliberation processes. They also provide assessment to assist the legal community. Although most forensic psychologists are clinical psychologists, many have expertise in other areas of psychology, such as social or cognitive psychology. Some also hold law degrees. As a forensic psychologist, you might work in a university psychology department, law school, research organization, community mental health agency, law-enforcement agency, court, or correctional setting.

HEALTH PSYCHOLOGISTS Health psychologists are researchers and practitioners concerned with psychology's contribution to promoting health and preventing disease. As applied psychologists or clinicians, they may help individuals lead healthier lives by designing, conducting, and evaluating programs to stop smoking, lose weight, improve sleep, manage pain, prevent the spread of sexually transmitted infections, or treat psychosocial problems associated with chronic and terminal illnesses. As researchers and clinicians, they identify conditions and practices associated with health and illness to help create effective interventions. In public service, health psychologists study and work to improve government policies and health care systems. As a health psychologist, you could be employed in a hospital, medical school, rehabilitation center, public health agency, college or university, or, if you are also a clinical psychologist, in private practice.

INDUSTRIAL-ORGANIZATIONAL (I/O) PSYCHOLOGISTS Industrial-organizational psychologists study the relationship between people and their working environments. They may develop new ways to increase productivity, improve personnel selection, or promote job satisfaction in an organizational setting. Their interests include organizational structure and change, consumer behavior, and personnel selection and training. As an I/O psychologist, you might conduct workplace training or provide organizational analysis and development. You may find yourself working in business, industry, the government, or a college or university. Or you may be self-employed as a consultant or work for a management consulting firm. (For more on I/O psychology, see Appendix C, Psychology at Work.)

NEUROPSYCHOLOGISTS Neuropsychologists investigate the relationship between neurological processes (structure and function of the brain and nervous system) and behavior. As a neuropsychologist you might assess, diagnose, or treat central nervous system disorders, such as Alzheimer's disease or stroke. You might also evaluate individuals for evidence of head injuries; specific learning disorders; and neurodevelopmental disorders, such as autism spectrum disorder and attention-deficit/hyperactivity disorder (ADHD). If you are a *clinical neuropsychologist*, you might work in a hospital's neurology, neurosurgery, or psychiatric unit. Neuropsychologists also work in academic settings, where they conduct research and teach.

PERSONALITY PSYCHOLOGISTS Personality psychologists study how individuals differ in their feelings, thoughts, motivations, and behaviors. Because their interests are complementary, personality psychologists and social psychologists often collaborate to understand how both individual and social factors impact phenomena such as romantic attraction, persuasion, prosocial behavior, and conformity. As a personality psychologist, you would probably be a researcher or college or university faculty member. Your research might take place in a laboratory, clinic, or field setting, and your work might focus on factors that impact personality development or how personality is related to other areas, such as law, business, or education. You might also work in the private sector, as a consultant to businesses, or in a public nonprofit organization.

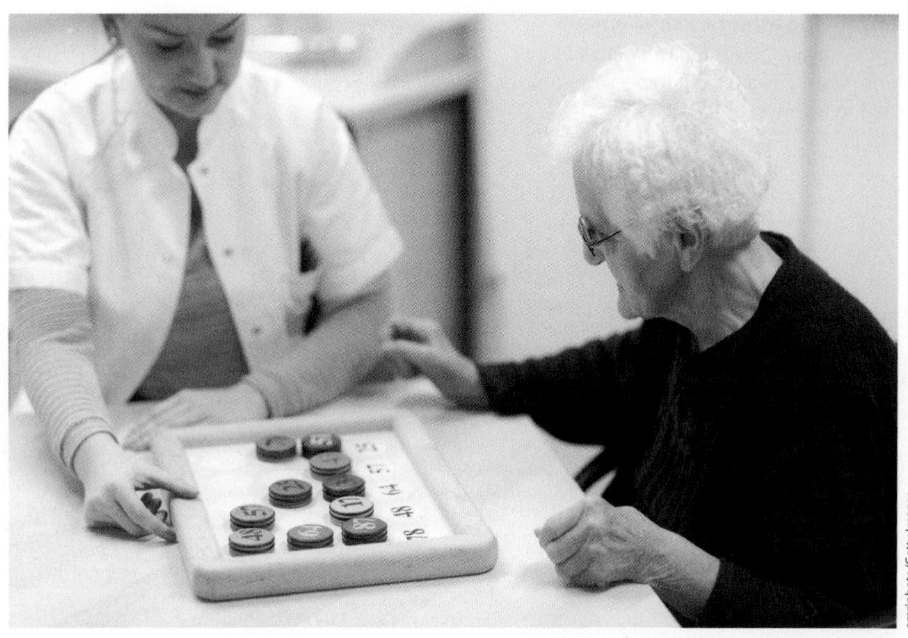

amriphoto/Getty Images

Evaluating cognitive functioning The APA projects that by 2030, those age 65 and older will be the U.S. age group requiring the most psychological care (APA, 2018). Psychologists can use neuropsychological assessments to evaluate cognitive capacities, helping to diagnose, treat, and manage psychological disorders such as Alzheimer's disease.

PSYCHOMETRIC AND QUANTITATIVE PSYCHOLOGISTS Psychometric and quantitative psychologists study the methods and techniques used to acquire psychological knowledge. A psychometric psychologist may update existing neurocognitive or personality tests, or devise new tests for use in clinical settings, in schools and other institutional settings, and in business and industry. These psychologists also administer, score, and interpret such tests. Quantitative psychologists collaborate with researchers to design, analyze, and interpret the results of research programs. As a psychometric or quantitative psychologist, you would need to be well trained in research methods, statistics, and computational software. You would most likely be employed by a university or college, a testing company, a private research firm, or a government agency.

REHABILITATION PSYCHOLOGISTS Rehabilitation psychologists are researchers and practitioners who work with people who have lost optimal functioning after an accident, illness, or other event. As a rehabilitation psychologist, you would probably work in a medical rehabilitation facility or hospital. You might also work in a medical school, university, or government vocational rehabilitation agency, or in private practice serving people with physical disabilities.

SCHOOL PSYCHOLOGISTS School psychologists are involved in the assessment of and intervention for children in educational settings. They diagnose and treat cognitive, social, and emotional problems that may negatively influence children's learning or overall functioning at school. As a school psychologist, you would collaborate with teachers, parents, and administrators, making recommendations to improve student learning. You might work at a school or child guidance center, for a government agency, or at a behavioral research laboratory.

© Spencer Grant/PhotoEdit

Assessing and supporting children School psychologists may find themselves working with children individually or in groups. They receive interdisciplinary training in mental health assessment and behavior analysis, research methods and design, and special needs education. They work primarily in schools, but also in a range of other settings.

SOCIAL PSYCHOLOGISTS Social psychologists are interested in our interactions with others. Social psychologists study how our beliefs, feelings, and behaviors are affected by and influence other people. They study topics such as attitudes, aggression, prejudice, interpersonal attraction, group behavior, and leadership. In an initiative to use social psychological and personality research to address social problems, APA's Division 8 (Society for Personality and Social Psychology) has established a frequently updated repository of research, videos, and other resources to increase public awareness of racism, bias, and diversity in general. As a social psychologist, you would probably be a college or university faculty member. You might also work in organizational consultation, market research, or other applied psychology fields, including social neuroscience. Some social psychologists work for hospitals, government agencies, social networking sites, or businesses performing applied research.

SPORT PSYCHOLOGISTS Sport psychologists study the psychological factors that influence, and are influenced by, participation in sports and other physical activities.

Nigel French/EMPICS/Getty Images

Improving athletic achievement Sussex cricket player Stuart Meaker gathers input from sport psychologist Rebecca Symes during warmup.

Their professional activities include coach education and athlete preparation, as well as research and teaching. Sport psychologists who also have a clinical or counseling degree can apply those skills to working with individuals with psychological problems, such as anxiety or substance use disorder, that might interfere with optimal performance. As a sport psychologist, if you were not working in an academic or research setting, you would most likely work as part of a team or an organization, or in a private capacity.

* * *

The next time someone asks you what you will do with your psychology degree, tell them you have lots of options. You might use your acquired skills and understanding to get a job and succeed in any number of fields, or you might pursue graduate school and then career opportunities in associated professions. In any case, what you have learned about behavior and mental processes will surely enrich your life (Hammer, 2003).

APPENDIX
C

Psychology at Work

For many people, to live is to work. Work supports us, enabling food, water, and shelter. Work connects us, meeting our social needs. Work helps define us. Meeting people and wondering about their identity, we may ask, "So, what do you do?"

We vary in our job satisfaction: On the day we leave the workforce, some of us will sadly bid our former employer farewell, while others will gladly bid them good riddance. We vary in the predictability of our career path: We will change jobs, some of us often, for a variety of reasons—cutbacks, a desire for better work-life balance, or to pursue a passion project. And we vary in how we view our work as a way to earn a paycheck or to pursue a meaningful calling, an opportunity to do the bare minimum or to maximize our potential. Let's take a look at how psychologists can help explain these differences.

Work and Life Satisfaction

People across various occupations vary in their attitudes toward their work. Some view their work as a *job*, a possibly unfulfilling but necessary way to make money. Others view their work as a *career*, an opportunity to advance from one position to a better position. The rest—those who view their work as a *calling*, a fulfilling and socially useful activity—report the highest satisfaction with their work and with their lives (Dik & Duffy, 2012; Wrzesniewski & Dutton, 2001).

The jobs people do: Columnist Gene Weingarten (2002) noted that sometimes a humorist knows "when to just get out of the way." Here are some sample self-reported job titles from the U.S. Department of Labor: animal impersonator, human projectile, banana ripening-room supervisor, impregnator, impregnator helper, dope sprayer, finger waver, rug scratcher, egg smeller, bottom buffer, cookie breaker, brain picker, hand pouncer, bosom presser, and mother repairer.

Flow at Work

LEARNING OBJECTIVE QUESTION LOQ **C-1** What is *flow?*

The work satisfaction findings would not have surprised Mihaly Csikszentmihalyi [chick-SENT-me-hi] (1934–2021). He observed that our quality of life increases when we are purposefully engaged. Between the anxiety of being overwhelmed and stressed, and the apathy of being underwhelmed and bored, lies the experience of **flow** (Csikszentmihalyi, 1990, 1999). "Flow," Csikszentmihalyi noted, "occurs in that delicate zone between anxiety and boredom" (Goleman, 1986). We might experience it when we clean a kitchen, organize a spreadsheet, or read a psychology text. (Are you experiencing flow right now?) Perhaps you can recall being in a zoned-out flow state while scrolling social media.

"Some people have *jobs*. Some people have *careers*. . . . When you've got a career, there ain't enough time in the day. . . . When you've got a job, there's too much time."
—Comedian Chris Rock

Csikszentmihalyi formulated the flow concept after studying artists who spent hour after hour painting or sculpting with focused concentration. Immersed in a project, they worked as if nothing else mattered, and then, when finished, they promptly moved on. The artists seemed driven less by external rewards—money, praise, promotion—than by the intrinsic rewards of creating their art. Nearly 200 other studies confirm that *intrinsic motivation* enhances performance (Cerasoli et al., 2014).

Csikszentmihalyi studied dancers, chess players, surgeons, writers, parents, mountain climbers, sailors, and farmers. His research included Australian, North American, Korean, Japanese, and Italian participants, who ranged in age from the teen years to the golden years. A clear principle emerged: It's exhilarating to flow with an activity that fully engages our skills (Fong et al., 2015). Flow experiences boost our sense of self-esteem, competence, and well-being. One research team studying 10,000 Swedes found that frequent flow experiences reduced their risk of depression and burnout (Mosing et al., 2018). A focused mind is a happy mind.

flow a completely involved, focused state, with diminished awareness of self and time; results from fully engaging our skills.

Jacob Ammentorp Lund/iStock/Getty Images

Attention theft It takes energy to resist checking our phones, and time to refocus mental concentration after each disruption. Such frequent interruptions disrupt flow. A solution: Disable notifications, and check the phone only during scheduled breaks.

Idleness may sound like bliss. You may dream of a future filled with streaming movies, sleeping in, and no responsibilities. In reality, purposeful work enriches our lives. People who leave the workforce tend to become unhappy, but rejoining the workforce rapidly improves their mood (Y. Zhou et al., 2019). Busy people are often happy people (Hsee et al., 2010; Robinson & Martin, 2008).

Finding Your Own Flow, and Matching Interests to Work

Want to identify your own path to flow? You can start by pinpointing your strengths and the types of work that may prove satisfying and successful. Marcus Buckingham and Donald Clifton (2001) suggested asking yourself four questions:

1. What activities give me pleasure? Bringing order out of chaos? Playing host? Helping others? Challenging sloppy thinking?
2. What activities leave me wondering, "When can I do this again?" rather than, "When will this be over?"
3. What sorts of challenges do I relish? And which do I dread?
4. What sorts of tasks do I learn easily? And which do I struggle with?

Have you ever noticed that when you are immersed in an activity, time flies? And that when you are watching the clock, it seems to move more slowly? French researchers have confirmed that the more we attend to an event's duration, the longer it seems to last (Couli et al., 2004).

You may find your skills engaged and time flying when teaching or selling or writing or cleaning or consoling or creating or repairing. If an activity feels good, if it comes easily, if you look forward to it, then look deeper. You'll see your strengths at work (Buckingham, 2007). For a free (requires registration) assessment of your own strengths, take the "Brief Strengths Test" at tinyurl.com/AssessStrengths.

The U.S. Department of Labor also offers a career interest questionnaire through its Occupational Information Network (O*NET). At MyNextMove.org/explore/ip you will need about 10 minutes to respond to 60 items, indicating how much you would like or dislike activities ranging from building kitchen cabinets to playing a musical instrument. You will then receive feedback on how strongly your responses reflect six interest types (Holland, 1996):

- *Realistic* (hands-on doers)
- *Investigative* (thinkers)
- *Artistic* (creators)
- *Social* (helpers, teachers)
- *Enterprising* (persuaders, deciders)
- *Conventional* (organizers)

"Find a job you love, and you'll never work another day of your life." —Popular saying expressed in a Facebook hiring video, 2016

Finally, depending on how much training or schooling you are willing to complete, you will be shown occupations that fit your interest pattern (selected from a national database of 900+ occupations).

Michael Maslin/The Cartoon Bank

"Let's face it: you and this organization have never been a good fit."

Do what you love and you will love what you do. Career counseling science aims, first, to assess people's differing values, personalities, and, especially, *interests,* which are remarkably stable and predictive of future life choices and outcomes (Hanna & Rounds, 2020). (Your job may change, but your interests today will likely still be your interests in 10 years.) Second, it aims to alert people to well-matched vocations—vocations with a good *person-environment fit.* It pays to have a job that fits your personality. People high in openness earn more if they hold jobs that demand openness; people who are highly extraverted earn more if they work in jobs that require extraversion (Denissen et al., 2018).

One study assessed 400,000 high school students' interests and then followed the students over time. The take-home finding: "Interests uniquely predict academic and career success over and above cognitive ability and personality" (Rounds & Su, 2014). Sixty other studies confirm the point both for students in school and workers on the job: Interests predict both performance and persistence (Nye et al., 2012). Lack of job fit can fuel frustration, resulting in unproductive and even hostile work behavior (Harold et al., 2016). *Industrial-organizational psychologists* put career counseling science into action. First, they use surveys to assess people's interests, values, personalities, and workplace culture preferences. Next, they use the data to suggest occupations and connect respondents with job listings.

ASK YOURSELF

What have you discovered about your own strengths and about the kind of career you might see yourself pursuing?

RETRIEVAL PRACTICE

RP-1 What is the value of finding flow in our work?

ANSWERS IN APPENDIX E

Industrial-Organizational Psychology

LOQ C-2 What are industrial-organizational psychology's three key areas of study?

In developed nations, work has expanded, from farming to manufacturing to *knowledge work*. More and more work is outsourced to temporary employees and consultants, or to workers telecommuting from off-site workplaces (Gallup, 2020). (The three-author team for this book and its teaching package is aided immeasurably by a team of people across North America, from Alberta to Florida.)

The Covid pandemic dramatically increased remote work and virtual teamwork. This raised new issues for I/O psychologists to study (Kniffin et al., 2021):

- How will remote work affect workers' attitudes toward their employer and co-workers?
- How does remote versus in-person work affect workers' well-being?
- How can leaders best communicate with and mentor remote workers?
- How can remote work inclusively support and connect workers of all ages, abilities, cultural backgrounds, and ethnicities?

As work has changed, have our attitudes toward our work also changed? Has our satisfaction with work increased or decreased? Has the *psychological contract—the* sense of mutual obligation between workers and employers—become more or less trusting and secure? How can psychologists help organizations make work more satisfying and productive? These are among the questions that fascinate **industrial-organizational (I/O) psychologists** as they apply psychology's principles to the workplace (TABLE C.1).

- The I/O psychology subfield of **personnel psychology** applies psychology's methods and principles to selecting, placing, training, and evaluating workers. Personnel psychologists match people with jobs by identifying and placing well-suited candidates.
- The **organizational psychology** subfield considers how work environments and management styles influence worker motivation, satisfaction, and productivity. It focuses on modifying jobs and supervision in ways that boost morale and productivity.
- **Human factors psychology,** a distinct field allied with I/O psychology, explores how machines and environments can be optimally designed to fit human abilities. Human factors psychologists study people's natural perceptions and inclinations, using this research to create user-friendly machines and work settings.

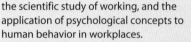

industrial-organizational (I/O) psychology the scientific study of working, and the application of psychological concepts to human behavior in workplaces. 

personnel psychology an I/O psychology subfield that helps with job seeking, and with employee recruitment, selection, placement, training, appraisal, and development.

organizational psychology an I/O psychology subfield that examines organizational influences on worker satisfaction and productivity and facilitates organizational change.

human factors psychology a field of psychology allied with I/O psychology that explores how people and machines interact and how machines and physical environments can be made safe and easy to use.

Collaboration across the miles The editorial and production team that guides the development of this book and its resources works from far-flung places across North America.

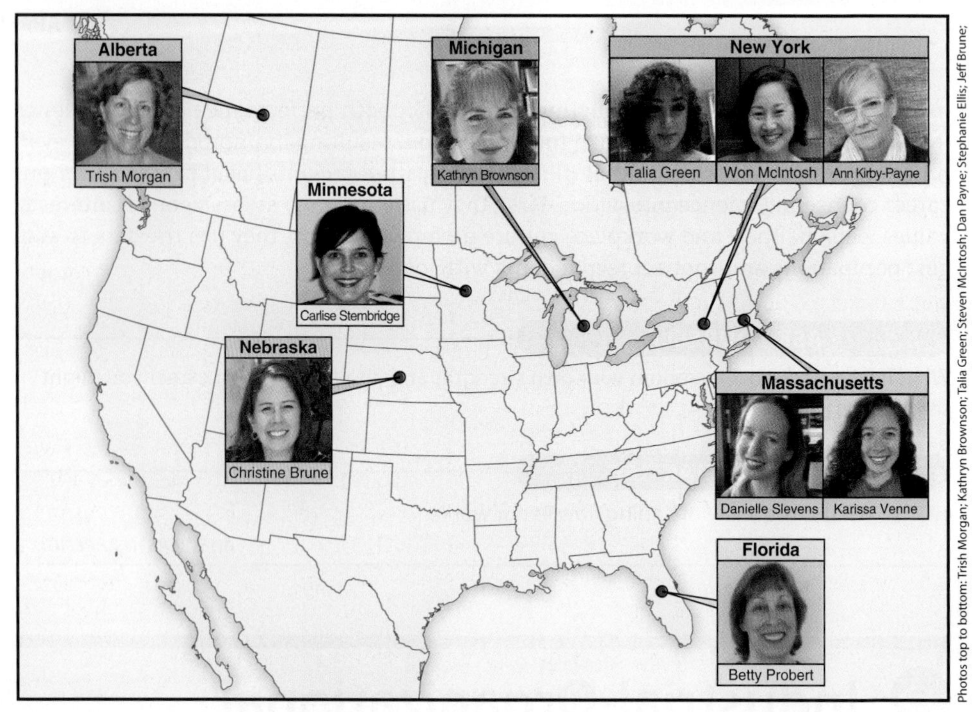
Alberta
Trish Morgan
Michigan
Kathryn Brownson
New York
Talia Green
Won McIntosh
Ann Kirby-Payne
Minnesota
Carlise Stembridge
Nebraska
Christine Brune
Massachusetts
Danielle Slevens
Karissa Venne
Florida
Betty Probert

Photos top to bottom: Trish Morgan; Kathryn Brownson; Talia Green; Steven McIntosh; Dan Payne; Stephanie Ellis; Jeff Brune; Danielle Slevens; ©2022 Macmillan, Photo by Karissa Venne; Don Probert

TABLE C.1 I/O Psychology and Human Factors Psychology at Work

As scientists, consultants, and management professionals, industrial-organizational (I/O) psychologists may be found helping organizations to resolve work-family conflicts, build employee retention, improve organizational spirit, or promote teamwork. Human factors psychologists also contribute to human safety and improved designs.

Personnel Psychology: Maximizing Human Potential	Organizational Psychology: Building Better Organizations
Developing training programs to increase job seekers' success **Selecting and placing employees** • Developing and testing assessment tools for selecting, placing, and promoting workers • Analyzing job content • Optimizing worker placement **Training and developing employees** • Identifying needs • Designing training programs, including for ethical and diverse workplaces • Evaluating training programs **Appraising performance** • Developing guidelines • Measuring individual performance • Measuring organizational performance	**Developing organizations** • Analyzing organizational structures • Maximizing worker satisfaction and productivity • Facilitating organizational change **Enhancing quality of work life** • Expanding individual productivity • Identifying elements of satisfaction • Redesigning jobs • Balancing work and nonwork life in an era of social media, smartphones, and rapid technological change **Human Factors Psychology: Optimizing Machines and Environments** • Designing optimal work environments • Optimizing person-machine interactions • Developing systems technologies

Information from the Society of Industrial and Organizational Psychology. For more information about I/O psychology, more than 500 North American I/O graduate programs, and related job opportunities, visit SIOP.org.

Personnel Psychology

LOQ C-3 How do personnel psychologists facilitate job seeking, employee selection, work placement, and performance appraisal?

Psychologists assist organizations at various stages of selecting and assessing employees. They may help identify needed job skills, develop effective selection methods, recruit and evaluate diverse applicants, introduce and train new employees, appraise performance, and facilitate team building among people with differing cultural backgrounds. They also seek to enhance the well-being and productivity of *neurodiverse* workers—those on the autism spectrum, or those challenged by ADHD, a learning disorder, or brain injury (Weinberg & Doyle, 2017).

Psychologists also assist job seekers. Across four dozen studies, training programs (which teach job-search skills, improve self-presentation, boost self-confidence, promote goal setting, and enlist support) have nearly tripled job seekers' success (Liu et al., 2014).

Using Strengths for Successful Selection

As a new AT&T human resources executive, psychologist Mary Tenopyr (1997) was assigned to solve a problem: Customer-service representatives were failing at a high rate. After concluding that many of the hires were ill-matched to the demands of their new job, Tenopyr developed a new selection instrument:

1. She asked new applicants to respond to various test questions (without as yet making any use of their responses).
2. She followed up later to assess which of the applicants excelled on the job.
3. She identified the earlier test questions that best predicted success.

The happy result of her data-driven work was a new test that enabled AT&T to identify likely-to-succeed representatives. Personnel selection techniques such as this one aim to recruit people with strengths that will enable them and their organization to flourish. Marry the strengths of people with the tasks of organizations and the results are often prosperity, profit, and pleased employees.

Do Interviews Predict Performance?

Employee selection usually includes an interview, and many interviewers feel confident of their ability to predict long-term job performance from a get-acquainted *(unstructured)* interview. What's therefore shocking is how error-prone interviewers' predictions may be when predicting job or graduate school success. General mental ability has been a better predictor, especially for complex jobs—for which it indicates people's ability to learn new skills (Schmidt & Hunter, 2004; Warne, 2020). Informal interviews are less informative than aptitude tests, work samples, job knowledge tests, and past job performance. After studying thousands of informal interviews and later job success, Google found "zero relationship. It's a complete random mess" (Bock, 2013).

Unstructured Interviews and the Interviewer Illusion

Traditional, unstructured interviews can provide a sense of someone's personality—their expressiveness, warmth, and verbal ability, for example. But these informal interviews also give interviewees considerable power to control the impression they are making in the interview situation (Barrick et al., 2009). Why, then, do many interviewers have such faith in their ability to discern interviewees' fitness for a job? "I have excellent interviewing skills," I/O psychology consultants often hear, "so I don't need reference checking as much as someone who doesn't have my ability to read people." Overrating one's ability to predict people's futures is called the *interviewer illusion* (Dana et al., 2013; Nisbett, 1987). Five factors explain interviewers' overconfidence:

- ***Interviewers presume that people are what they seem to be in the interview situation.*** An unstructured interview may create a false impression of a person's behavior toward others in different situations. Some interviewees may feign desired attitudes; others may be nervous. As social psychologists explain, when meeting others, we commit the *fundamental attribution error:* We discount the enormous influence of varying situations and mistakenly presume that what we see is what we will get. But research on everything from chattiness to conscientiousness reveals that how we behave reflects not only our enduring traits, but also the details of the particular situation (such as wanting to impress in a job interview).

- ***Interviewers' preconceptions and moods color how they perceive interviewees' responses*** (Cable & Gilovich, 1998; Macan & Dipboye, 1994). If interviewers instantly like a person who perhaps is similar to themselves (opening the door to unintended racial or gender bias), they may interpret the person's assertiveness as indicating "confidence" rather than "arrogance." If told certain applicants have been prescreened, interviewers are disposed to judge them more favorably. Such interviewers are showing *confirmation bias:* They search for information that supports their preconceptions about a job candidate and ignore or distort contradictory evidence (Skov & Sherman, 1986).
- ***Interviewers judge people relative to those interviewed just before and after them*** (Simonsohn & Gino, 2013). If you are being interviewed for a job or graduate program, hope for a day when the other interviewees have been weak.
- ***Interviewers more often follow the successful careers of those they have hired than the successful careers of those they have rejected.*** This missing feedback prevents interviewers from getting a reality check on their hiring ability.
- ***Interviews disclose the interviewee's good intentions, which are less revealing than habitual behaviors*** (Ouellette & Wood, 1998). Intentions matter. People can change. But the best predictor of our future habits will be our past habits. Educational attainments predict job performance partly because people who have the ability and motivation to show up for school each day and stay on task also tend to show up for work and stay on task (Ng & Feldman, 2009). Wherever we go, we take ourselves along.

Hoping to improve prediction and selection, personnel psychologists have put people in simulated work situations, sought information on past performance, aggregated evaluations from multiple interviews, administered tests, and developed job-specific interviews.

Structured Interviews

Unlike casual conversation aimed at getting a feel for someone, **structured interviews** offer a disciplined method of collecting information. A personnel psychologist may analyze a job, script questions, and train interviewers. The interviewers then ask all applicants the same questions, in the same order, and rate each applicant on established scales.

In an unstructured interview, someone might ask, "How organized are you?" "How well do you get along with people?" or "How do you handle stress?" Street-smart applicants know how to score high: "Although I sometimes drive myself too hard, I handle stress by prioritizing and delegating, and leaving time for sleep and exercise."

By contrast, structured interviews pinpoint strengths (attitudes, behaviors, knowledge, and skills) that distinguish high performers in a particular line of work. The process includes outlining job-specific situations and asking candidates to explain how they would handle them, and how they handled similar situations in their prior employment. "Tell me about a time when you were caught between conflicting demands, without time to accomplish both. How did you handle that?" In its interviews, Google has asked, "Give me an example of a time when you solved an analytically difficult problem" (Bock, 2013).

To reduce memory distortions and bias, the interviewer takes notes, makes ratings as the interview proceeds, and avoids irrelevant and follow-up questions. The structured interview therefore feels less friendly, but that can be explained to the applicant: "This conversation won't typify how we relate to each other in this organization."

A review of 150 findings revealed that structured interviews had double the predictive accuracy of unstructured interviews (Schmidt & Hunter, 1998; Wiesner & Cronshaw, 1988). Structured interviews also reduce bias, such as against overweight applicants (Kutcher & Bragger, 2004).

If, instead, we let our intuitions bias the hiring process, noted Malcolm Gladwell (2000, p. 86), then "all we will have done is replace the old-boy network, where you hired your nephew, with the new-boy network, where you hire whoever impressed you most when you shook his hand. Social progress, unless we're careful, can merely be the means by which we replace the obviously arbitrary with the not so obviously arbitrary."

structured interview an interview process that asks the same job-relevant questions of all applicants, each of whom is rated on established scales.

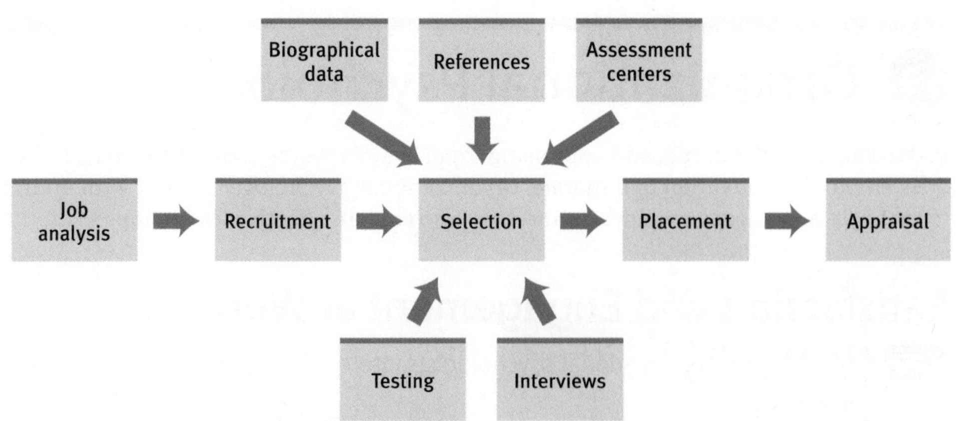
Biographical data
References
Assessment centers
Job analysis
Recruitment
Selection
Placement
Appraisal
Testing
Interviews

FIGURE C.1
Personnel psychologists at work Personnel psychologists consult in human resources activities, from job definition to recruitment to employee appraisal. The *assessment center* approach (see the Personality modules), which includes simulated job tasks, may be used to evaluate potential and existing employees.

To recap, personnel psychologists help train job seekers, and they assist organizations in analyzing jobs, recruiting well-suited applicants, and selecting and placing employees. They also appraise employees' performance (**FIGURE C.1**)—our next topic.

Appraising Performance

Performance appraisal serves organizational purposes: It helps decide who to keep on staff, how to appropriately reward and pay people, and how to better harness employee strengths, sometimes with job shifts or promotions. Performance appraisal also serves individual purposes: Feedback affirms workers' strengths and helps motivate needed improvements.

Performance appraisal methods include

- ***checklists*** on which supervisors simply check specific behaviors that describe the worker ("always attends to customers' needs"; "takes long breaks").
- ***graphic rating scales*** on which a supervisor checks, perhaps on a five-point scale, how often a worker is dependable, productive, and so forth.
- ***behavior rating scales*** on which a supervisor checks scaled behaviors that describe a worker's performance. If rating the extent to which a worker "follows procedures," the supervisor might mark the employee somewhere between "often takes shortcuts" and "always follows established procedures" (Levy, 2003).

In some organizations, performance feedback comes not only from supervisors, but also from all organizational levels. If you join an organization that practices *360-degree feedback* (**FIGURE C.2**), you will rate yourself, your manager, and your other colleagues, and you will be rated by your manager, other colleagues, and customers (Green, 2002). The net result is often more open communication and more complete appraisal.

Performance appraisal, like other social judgments, is vulnerable to bias (Murphy & Cleveland, 1995). *Halo errors* occur when one's overall evaluation of an employee, or of a personal trait such as their friendliness, biases ratings of their specific work-related behaviors, such as their reliability. *Leniency* and *severity errors* reflect evaluators' tendencies to be either too easy or too harsh on everyone. *Recency errors* occur when raters focus only on easily remembered recent behavior. By using multiple raters and developing objective, job-relevant performance measures, personnel psychologists seek to support their organizations while also helping employees perceive the appraisal process as fair.

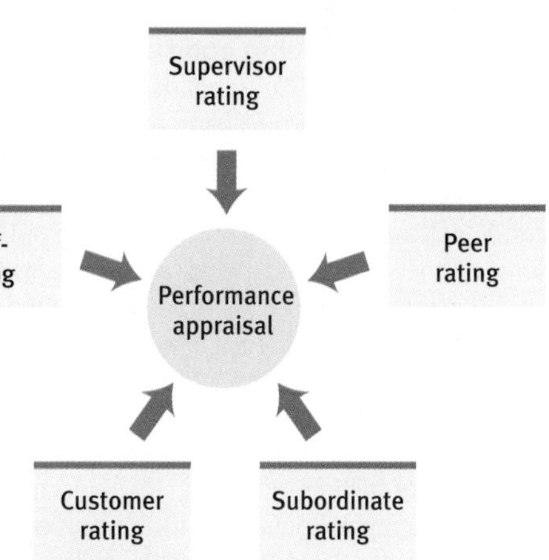
Supervisor rating
Self-rating
Performance appraisal
Peer rating
Customer rating
Subordinate rating

FIGURE C.2
360-degree feedback With multisource 360-degree feedback, our knowledge, skills, and behaviors are rated by ourselves and surrounding others. Professors, for example, may be rated by their department chairs, their students, and their colleagues. After receiving all these ratings, professors discuss the 360-degree feedback with their department chair.

RETRIEVAL PRACTICE

RP-2 A human resources director explains to you that "I don't bother with tests or references. It's all about the interview." Based on I/O psychology research, what concerns does this raise?

ANSWERS IN APPENDIX E

 Organizational Psychology

Recruiting, hiring, training, and appraising capable and diverse workers matters, but so does employee motivation and morale. Organizational psychologists assist with efforts to motivate and engage employees, and they also explore effective leadership.

Satisfaction and Engagement at Work

LOQ **C-4** Why are organizational psychologists interested in employee satisfaction and engagement?

I/O psychologists have found that satisfaction with work, and a desirable work-life balance, feed overall satisfaction with life (Bowling et al., 2010). Lower job stress (sometimes enabled by telecommuting) supports better health (Allen et al., 2015).

Satisfied employees also contribute to successful organizations. Positive moods at work enhance creativity, persistence, and helpfulness (Ford et al., 2011; Jeffrey et al., 2014; Shockley et al., 2012). Are engaged, happy workers also less often absent? Less likely to quit? Less prone to theft? More punctual? More productive? Statistical digests of prior research have found a modest positive correlation between individual job satisfaction and performance (Judge et al., 2001; Ng et al., 2009). In one analysis, employee job satisfaction at 31 firms predicted those firms' profitability over the ensuing 4 years (Kessler et al., 2020).

Some organizations seem to have a knack for cultivating more engaged and productive employees. In the United States, *Fortune*'s "100 Best Companies to Work For" have also produced markedly higher-than-average returns for their investors (Yoshimoto & Frauenheim, 2018). And consider a huge study of more than 198,000 employees in nearly 8000 business units of 36 large companies (including some 1100 bank branches, 1200 stores, and 4200 teams or departments). James Harter, Frank Schmidt, and Theodore Hayes (2002) explored correlations between various measures of organizational success and *employee engagement*—the extent of workers' involvement, enthusiasm, and

Courtesy of New Lanark Trust

Doing well while doing good—"the great experiment" At the end of the 1700s, the New Lanark, Scotland, cotton mill had more than 1000 workers. Many were children drawn from Glasgow's poorhouses. They worked 13-hour days and lived in grim conditions.

On a visit to Glasgow, Welsh-born Robert Owen—an idealistic young cotton-mill manager—met and married the mill owner's daughter. Owen and some partners purchased the mill and on the first day of the 1800s began what he called "the most important experiment for the happiness of the human race that had yet been instituted at any time in any part of the world" (Owen, 1814). The exploitation of child and adult labor was, he observed, producing unhappy and inefficient workers. Owen showed *transformational leadership* (discussed later in this appendix) when he undertook numerous innovations: a nursery for preschool children, education for older children (with encouragement rather than corporal punishment), Sundays off, health care, paid sick days, unemployment pay for days when the mill could not operate, and a company store selling goods at reduced prices. He also innovated a goals- and worker-assessment program that included detailed records of daily productivity and costs but with "no beating, no abusive language."

The ensuing commercial success fueled a humanitarian reform movement. By 1816, with decades of profitability still ahead, Owen believed he had demonstrated "that society may be formed so as to exist without crime, without poverty, with health greatly improved, with little if any misery, and with intelligence and happiness increased a hundredfold." Although his utopian vision has not been fulfilled, Owen's great experiment laid the groundwork for employment practices that have today become accepted in much of the world.

TABLE C.2 Three Types of Employees

- ***Engaged:*** Working with commitment and energy, and feeling connected to their company or organization.
- ***Not engaged:*** Putting in the time but investing little passion or energy in their work.
- ***Actively disengaged:*** Unhappy workers undermining what their colleagues accomplish.

Information from Gallup via Crabtree, 2005.

leadership an individual's ability to motivate and influence others to contribute to their group's success.

identification with their organizations (**TABLE C.2**). They found that engaged workers (compared with not-engaged workers who are just putting in their time) knew what was expected of them, had what they needed to do their work, felt fulfilled in their work, had regular opportunities to do what they do best, perceived that they were part of something significant, and had opportunities to learn and develop. They also found that business units with engaged employees had more loyal customers, lower turnover rates, higher productivity, and greater profits.

What percentage of employees are engaged? One massive study of 6.4 million people in 159 countries showed that only about 15 percent of workers reported being engaged (Gallup, 2017, 2020). Engagement is highest among people who have knowledge-based jobs, flexible hours, and freedom to work remotely. More organizations now offer such benefits in the hope of increasing employee engagement (Eisenberger et al., 2019).

An engaged employee Mohamed Mamow, left, was joined by his employer in saying the Pledge of Allegiance as he became a U.S. citizen. Mamow and his wife met in a Somali refugee camp. Since then, he has supported his family by working as a machine operator at a Michigan packaging company. Mindful of his responsibility—"I don't like to lose my job. I have a responsibility for my children and my family"—he would arrive for work a half hour early and tend to every detail on his shift. "He is an extremely hard-working employee," noted his employer, and "a reminder to all of us that we are really blessed" (Roelofs, 2010).

But what causal arrows explain this correlation between business success and employee morale and engagement? Does success boost morale, or does high morale boost success? A longitudinal study of 142,000 workers found that, over time, employee attitudes predicted *future* business success (more than the other way around) (Harter et al., 2010). Many other studies confirm that happy workers tend to be good workers (Kleine et al., 2019; Walsh et al., 2018). A longitudinal study of 102 companies showed that employee engagement predicted future company success (Schneider et al., 2018). It pays to have engaged employees.

Effective Leadership

LOQ C-5 How can leaders be most effective?

Engaged employees don't just happen. Most have effective **leaders**—people who motivate and enable their group's success, and who engage their employees' interests and loyalty (Royal, 2019). Great managers support employees' well-being, articulate goals clearly, and lead in ways that suit the situation and consider the cultural context.

tdub_video/Getty Images

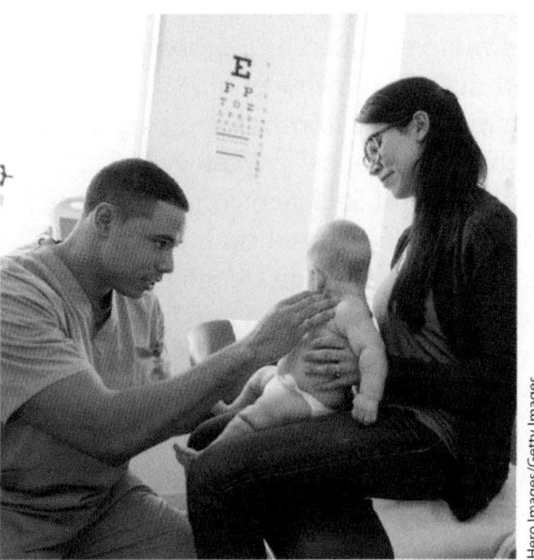

Hero Images/Getty Images

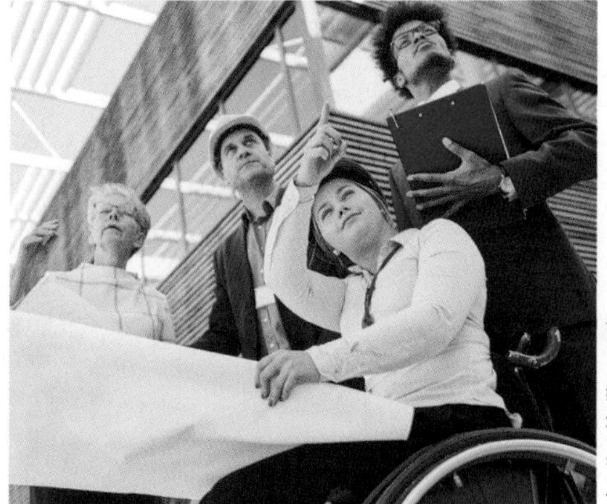

Robert Kneschke/Shutterstock

Task significance People find their work meaningful and engaging when it has *task significance*—when they view their work as benefiting others (Allan, 2017).

"Good leaders don't ask more than their constituents can give, but they often ask—and get—more than their constituents intended to give or thought it was possible to give." —John W. Gardner, *Excellence*, 1984

Setting Specific, Challenging Goals

Measurable objectives, such as "finish gathering the history paper information by Friday," focus our attention and stimulate us to persist and to be creative. Goals motivate achievement, especially when combined with progress reports (Harkin et al., 2016). Action plans increase the odds of on-time completion when they (1) break large goals into smaller steps (subgoals), (2) specify *implementation intentions* (when, where, and how to achieve those steps), and (3) engage accountability (progress checks) (Fishbach et al., 2006; Gollwitzer & Sheeran, 2006). We best sustain our mood and motivation through a task's ups and downs when we focus on immediate goals (such as daily study) rather than distant goals (such as a course grade). Better to have our nose to the grindstone than our eye on the ultimate prize (Houser-Marko & Sheldon, 2008).

HE'D BE BETTER IF HE WERE MORE DECISIVE.
HE'S GOOD ON IDEAS, BUT NOT SO GOOD ON FOLLOW-THROUGH.
AUTOCRATIC.
HIS PROBLEM IS HE DOESN'T KNOW HOW TO SET CLEAR GOALS.
I'D LIKE HIM BETTER IF HE WERE MORE COMPASSIONATE.
HE DOESN'T TAKE CRITICISM WELL AT ALL.
NOT CONSISTENT.
OPEN TO SUGGESTIONS.
Anthony
Anthony Taber/Cartoon Stock

Thus, before beginning each new edition of this book, our author-editor team *manages by objectives*—we agree on target dates for completion of each module draft. Each week, we monitor our progress and make necessary adjustments. If we focus on achieving each of these short-term goals, then the prize—an on-time book—takes care of itself. So, to motivate high productivity, effective leaders work with people to define explicit goals, subgoals, and implementation plans, and then provide feedback on progress. Such goals are SMART—*s*pecific, *m*easurable, *a*ctionable, *r*ealistic, and *t*ime-bound (SIOP, 2018).

Choosing an Appropriate Leadership Style

Effective leaders of laboratory groups, work teams, and large corporations often exude *charisma* (Goethals & Allison, 2014; Tskhay et al., 2018). Charismatic people inspire others' loyalty and focus their enthusiasm (Grabo & van Vugt, 2016).

Charisma can bolster leadership, especially when combined with practical managerial skills (Vergauwe et al., 2018). What other qualities help? Leadership styles vary, depending on both the qualities of the leader and the demands of the situation (Badura et al., 2019). In some situations (think of a commander leading troops into battle), a *directive* style may be needed (Fiedler, 1981). In other situations—developing a comedy show, for example—a leader might get better results using a *democratic* style that welcomes team member creativity.

Luiz Rampelotto/NurPhoto/Getty Images

Social leadership Former Liberian president Ellen Johnson Sirleaf was Africa's first female elected head of state. After earlier being arrested for her opposition to government corruption, her charismatic leadership and achievements led to her receiving the 2011 Nobel Peace Prize for her "non-violent struggle for the safety of women and for women's rights to full participation in peace-building work."

Leaders differ in the personal qualities they bring to the job. Some excel at **task leadership.** To keep the group centered on its mission, task leaders typically use a directive style, which can work well if the leader gives good directions (Fiedler, 1987).

Other managers excel at **social leadership.** They explain decisions, help group members solve conflicts, and build teams that work well together (Bisbey et al., 2019; Pfaff et al., 2013). Social leaders, many of whom are women, often have a democratic style. They share authority and welcome team members' opinions. Social leadership and team-building increases morale and productivity (Shuffler et al., 2011, 2013). We usually feel more satisfied and motivated, and perform better, when we can participate in decision making (Cawley et al., 1998; Pereira & Osburn, 2007). Moreover, when members are sensitive to one another and participate equally, groups solve problems with greater "collective intelligence" (Woolley et al., 2010).

In one study of 50 Dutch companies, the firms with the highest morale had chief executives who most inspired their colleagues "to transcend their own self-interests for the sake of the collective" (de Hoogh et al., 2004). *Transformational leadership* of this kind motivates others to identify with and fully commit themselves to the group's mission. Transformational leaders, many of whom are natural extraverts, articulate high standards, inspire people to share their vision, and offer personal attention (Bono & Judge, 2004). The frequent result is more engaged, trusting, and effective workers (Turner et al., 2002). Women more than men tend to exhibit transformational leadership qualities (G. Wang et al., 2018).

Studies in India, Taiwan, and Iran suggest that effective managers—whether in coal mines, banks, or government offices—often exhibit a high degree of *both* task and social

task leadership goal-oriented leadership that sets standards, organizes work, and focuses attention on goals.

social leadership group-oriented leadership that builds teamwork, mediates conflict, and offers support.

leadership (Smith & Tayeb, 1989). As achievement-minded people, effective managers care about how well work is done, yet they are sensitive to their subordinates' needs. Workers in family-friendly organizations that offer flexible hours report feeling greater job satisfaction and loyalty to their employers (Butts et al., 2013; Roehling et al., 2001). Social virtues work.

POSITIVE REINFORCEMENT Effective leadership often builds on a basic principle of *operant conditioning:* To teach a behavior, catch a person doing something right and reinforce it. It sounds simple, but many managers are like parents who, when a child brings home a near-perfect school report card, focus on the one low grade in a troublesome class and ignore the rest. "Sixty-five percent of Americans received NO praise or recognition in the workplace last year," reported the Gallup organization (2004).

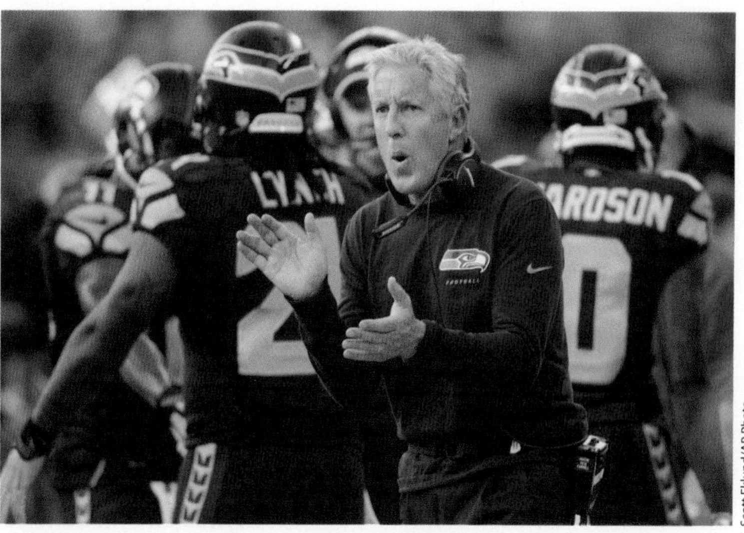
LYNCH
ARDSON

Scott Eklund/AP Photo

The power of positive coaching Football coach Pete Carroll, who led the University of Southern California to two national championships and the Seattle Seahawks to a Super Bowl championship, combined positive enthusiasm and fun workouts with "a commitment to a nurturing environment that allows people to be themselves while still being accountable to the team" (Trotter, 2014). "It shows you can win with positivity," noted former Seahawks defensive star Richard Sherman. "It's literally all positive reinforcement," said teammate Jimmy Graham (Belson, 2015).

FULFILLING THE NEED TO BELONG A work environment that satisfies employees' need to belong is energizing. Employees who enjoy high-quality colleague relationships engage in their work with more vigor (Carmeli et al., 2009). Gallup researchers have asked more than 15 million employees worldwide if they have a "best friend at work." The 30 percent who do "are *seven times* as likely to be engaged in their jobs" as those who don't, report Tom Rath and James Harter (2010). And, as we noted earlier, positive, engaged employees are a mark of thriving organizations.

PARTICIPATIVE MANAGEMENT Employee participation in decision making is common in Sweden, Japan, the United States, and elsewhere (Cawley et al., 1998; Sundstrom et al., 1990). Workers given a chance to voice their opinion and be part of the decision-making process have responded more positively to the final decision (van den Bos & Spruijt, 2002). They also feel more empowered, and are likely, therefore, to be more creative and committed (Hennessey & Amabile, 2010; Seibert et al., 2011).

The ultimate in employee participation is the employee-owned company. Approximately 6500 such companies exist in the United States—including Publix Supermarkets with its nearly 225,000 employees (Lapp, 2019; NCEO, 2022; Publix, 2022; Quinton, 2020). One such company in my [DM's] town is the Fleetwood Group, a thriving 165-employee manufacturer of educational furniture and wireless communication devices. Every employee owns part of the company, and as a group they own 100 percent. The more years employees work, the more they own, yet no one owns more than 5 percent. Like every corporate president, Fleetwood's president works for his stockholders—who also just happen to be his employees.

As a company that endorses faith-inspired "respect and care for each team member-owner," Fleetwood is free to place people above profits. Thus, when orders lagged during a recession, the employee-owners decided that job security meant more to them than profits. So the company paid otherwise idle workers to do community service, such as answering phones at nonprofit agencies and building Habitat for Humanity houses. Employee ownership attracts and retains talented people, which for Fleetwood has meant company success.

©Susan Camilleri Konar

Originally published in Harvard Business Review

"Department hug in five."

Cultural Influences on Leadership Styles

LOQ C-6 What cultural influences need to be considered when choosing an effective leadership style?

I/O psychology sprang from North American roots. So, how well do its leadership principles apply to cultures worldwide?

One worldwide investigation, Project GLOBE (Global Leadership and Organizational Behavior Effectiveness), has studied cultural variations in leadership expectations (House et al., 2001). Some cultures, for example, encourage collective sharing of resources and rewards; others are more individualist. Some cultures minimize and others accentuate traditional gender roles. Some cultures prioritize being friendly, caring, and kind, and others encourage a "me-first" attitude. The program's first research phase studied 17,300 leaders of 950 organizations in 61 countries (Brodbeck et al., 2008; Dorfman et al., 2012). One finding: Leaders who fulfill expectations, such as by being directive in some cultures or participative in others, tend to be successful. Cultures shape leadership and what makes for leadership success.

Nevertheless, some leader behaviors are universally effective. From its massive study of nearly 50,000 business units in 45 countries, Gallup observed that thriving companies tend to focus on identifying and enhancing employee *strengths* (rather than punishing their deficiencies). Doing so predicts increased employee engagement, customer satisfaction, and profitability (Rigoni & Asplund, 2016a,b). *Strengths-based* leadership pays dividends, supporting happier, more creative, more productive employees in workplaces with less absenteeism and turnover (Amabile & Kramer, 2011; De Neve et al., 2013).

Moreover, the same principles affect student satisfaction, retention, and future success (Larkin et al., 2013; Ray & Kafka, 2014). Students who feel supported by caring friends and mentors tend to persist and ultimately succeed during school and after graduation.

* * *

We have considered *personnel psychology* (the I/O psychology subfield that focuses on training job seekers, and assisting with employee selection, placement, appraisal, and development). And we have considered *organizational psychology* (the I/O psychology subfield that focuses on worker satisfaction and productivity, and on organizational change). Finally, we turn to *human factors psychology,* which explores the human-machine interface.

ASK YOURSELF

In what type of leadership role do you think you would most excel? If you already have leadership experience, how could you grow to become a more effective leader?

RETRIEVAL PRACTICE

RP-3 What characteristics are important for *transformational leaders?*

ANSWERS IN APPENDIX E

Human Factors Psychology

LOQ C-7 How do human factors psychologists work to create user-friendly machines and work settings?

Designs sometimes neglect the human factor. Cognitive scientist Donald Norman (2001) bemoaned the complexity of assembling his new HDTV, related components, and seven remotes into a usable home theater system: "I was VP of Advanced Technology at Apple. I can program dozens of computers in dozens of languages. I understand television, really, I do. . . . It doesn't matter: I am overwhelmed." Norman hosts a website (jnd.org) that illustrates good designs that fit people (**FIGURE C.3**).

Ride On Carry On

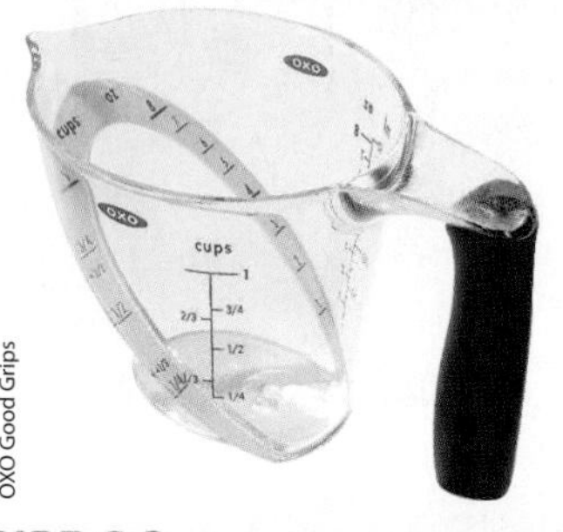
OXO
cups
OXO
cups
1
3/4
2/3
1/2
1/4

OXO Good Grips

FIGURE C.3
Designing products that fit people
Human factors expert Donald Norman offers these and other examples of effectively designed products. The Ride On Carry On foldable chair attachment, "designed by a flight attendant mom," enables a small suitcase to double as a stroller. The OXO measuring cup allows the user to see the quantity from above.

Human factors psychologists work with designers and engineers to tailor appliances, machines, and work settings to our natural perceptions and inclinations. Bank ATM machines are internally more complex than remote controls ever were, yet thanks to human factors engineering, ATMs are easier to operate. Digital recorders have solved the TV recording problem with a simple select-and-click menu system ("record that one"). Handheld and wearable technologies are increasingly making use of *haptic* (touch-based) feedback—opening a phone with a thumbprint, sharing your heartbeat via a smartwatch, or having GPS directional instructions ("turn left" arrow) "drawn" on your skin with other wrist-worn devices.

Human factors psychologists also help design efficient environments. An ideal kitchen layout, researchers have found, puts needed items close to their usage point and near eye level. It locates work areas to enable doing tasks in order, such as placing the refrigerator, stove, and sink in a triangle. It creates counters that enable hands to work at or slightly below elbow height (Boehm-Davis, 2005).

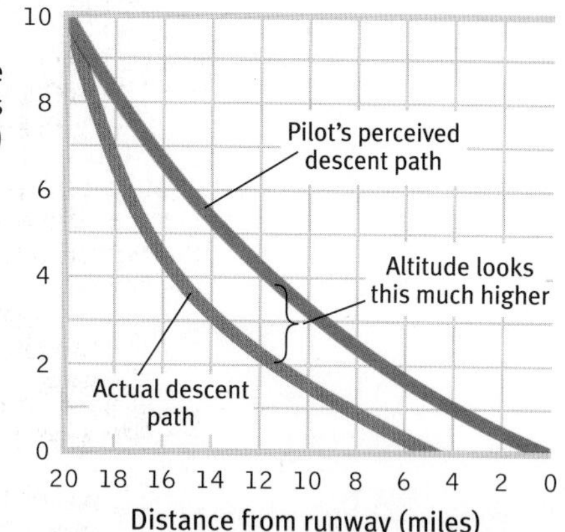
Altitude (thousands of feet)
10
8
6
4
2
0
Pilot's perceived descent path
Altitude looks this much higher
Actual descent path
20 18 16 14 12 10 8 6 4 2 0
Distance from runway (miles)

FIGURE C.4
The human factor in accidents Lacking distance cues when approaching a runway from over a dark surface, pilots simulating a night landing tended to fly too low. (Data from Kraft, 1978.)

Understanding human factors can help prevent accidents. By studying the human factor in driving accidents, psychologists seek to devise ways to reduce the distractions, fatigue, and inattention that contribute to 1.25 million annual worldwide traffic fatalities (WHO, 2016). At least two-thirds of commercial air accidents have been caused by human error (Shappell et al., 2007). After beginning commercial flights in the 1960s, the Boeing 727 was involved in several landing accidents caused by pilot error. Psychologist Conrad Kraft (1978) noted a common context for these accidents: All took place at night, and all involved landing short of the runway after crossing a dark stretch of water or unilluminated ground. Kraft reasoned that, on rising terrain, city lights beyond the runway would project a larger retinal image, making the ground seem farther away than it was. By re-creating these conditions in flight simulations, Kraft discovered that pilots were deceived into thinking they were flying higher than their actual altitudes (FIGURE C.4). Aided by Kraft's finding, airlines began requiring the co-pilot to monitor the altimeter—calling out altitudes during the descent—and the accidents diminished.

Human factors psychologists can also help us to function in other settings. Consider the available *assistive listening* technologies in various theaters, auditoriums, and places of worship. One technology, commonly available in the United States, requires a headset attached to a pocket-sized receiver. The well-meaning people who provide these systems correctly understand that the technology puts sound directly into the user's ears. Alas, few people with hearing loss elect the hassle and embarrassment of locating, requesting, wearing, and returning a conspicuous headset. Most such units therefore sit in closets. Britain, the Scandinavian countries, Australia, and now many parts of the United States have instead installed *loop systems* (see HearingLoop.org) that broadcast customized sound directly through a person's own hearing aid. When suitably equipped, a hearing aid can be transformed by a discreet touch of a switch into a customized in-the-ear speaker. When offered convenient, inconspicuous, personalized sound, many more people elect to use assistive listening.

Designs that enable safe, easy, and effective interactions between people and technology often seem obvious after the fact. Why, then, aren't they more common? Technology developers, like all of us, sometimes mistakenly assume that others share their expertise—that what's clear to them will similarly be clear to others (Camerer et al., 1989; Nickerson, 1999). When people rap their knuckles on a table to convey a familiar tune (try this with a friend), they often expect their listener to recognize it. But for the listener, this is a near-impossible task (Newton, 1991). When you know a thing, it's hard to mentally simulate what it's like not to know, and that is called the *curse of knowledge*.

The human factor in safe landings Advanced cockpit design and rehearsed emergency procedures aided pilot Chesley "Sully" Sullenberger, a U.S. Air Force Academy graduate who earned a master's degree in industrial psychology. In 2009, Sullenberger's instantaneous decisions safely guided his disabled airplane onto New York City's Hudson River, where all 155 of the passengers and crew were safely evacuated.

As psychologist Steven Pinker (2014) has noted, "The better you know something, the less you remember about how hard it was to learn."

The point to remember: Everyone benefits when designers and engineers tailor machines, technologies, and environments to fit human abilities and behaviors, when they user-test their work before production and distribution, and when they remain mindful of the curse of knowledge.

ASK YOURSELF

What situations have you experienced (using new technology, visiting buildings, using transportation) in which the design did not work well? What situations have you experienced in which planners did a particularly good job matching machines and physical environments to abilities and expectations?

RETRIEVAL PRACTICE

RP-4 What is the *curse of knowledge,* and what does it have to do with the work of human factors psychologists?

ANSWERS IN APPENDIX E

REVIEW Psychology at Work

LEARNING OBJECTIVES

Test Yourself Answer these repeated Learning Objective Questions on your own (before "showing" the answers here, or checking the answers in Appendix D) to improve your retention of the concepts (McDaniel et al., 2009, 2015).

LOQ C-1 What is *flow?*

LOQ C-2 What are industrial-organizational psychology's three key areas of study?

LOQ C-3 How do personnel psychologists facilitate job seeking, employee selection, work placement, and performance appraisal?

LOQ C-4 Why are organizational psychologists interested in employee satisfaction and engagement?

LOQ C-5 How can leaders be most effective?

LOQ C-6 What cultural influences need to be considered when choosing an effective leadership style?

LOQ C-7 How do human factors psychologists work to create user-friendly machines and work settings?

TERMS AND CONCEPTS TO REMEMBER

Test Yourself Write down the definition in your own words, then check your answer.

flow, p. C-1
industrial-organizational (I/O) psychology, p. C-3
personnel psychology, p. C-3
organizational psychology, p. C-3
human factors psychology, p. C-3
structured interview, p. C-6
leadership, p. C-9
task leadership, p. C-10
social leadership, p. C-10

APPENDIX TEST

Test Yourself Answer the following questions on your own first, then "show" the answers here, or check your answers in Appendix E.

1. People whose work fully engages their skills often experience __________, a focused state of consciousness, with diminished awareness of themselves and of time.

2. __________ psychologists assist with job seeking, and the recruitment, selection, placement, training, appraisal, and development of employees; __________ psychologists focus on how people and machines interact, and on optimizing devices and work environments.

3. A personnel psychologist scripted a set of questions to ask all applicants for a job opening. She then trained the firm's interviewers to ask only those questions, to take notes, and to rate applicants' responses. This technique is known as a(n)

   a. structured interview.

   b. unstructured interview.

   c. performance appraisal checklist.

   d. behavior rating scale.

4. In your job, you rate your own performance, your manager's, and your peers'. Your manager, your peers, and your customers in turn rate your performance. Your organization is using a form of performance appraisal called

   a. the assessment center approach.

   b. graphic feedback.

   c. structured interviews.

   d. 360-degree feedback.

5. What are SMART goals, and why are they effective?

6. Research indicates that women are often social leaders. They are also more likely than men to have a ______________ leadership style.

7. Effective managers often exhibit

   a. only task leadership.

   b. only social leadership.

   c. both task and social leadership, depending on the situation and the person.

   d. task leadership for building teams and social leadership for setting standards.

8. Human factors psychologists focus primarily on

   a. training and developing employees.

   b. appraising employee performance.

   c. maximizing worker satisfaction.

   d. improving the design of machines and environments.

Complete Module Reviews

CHAPTER 1

Thinking Critically With Psychological Science (Modules 1–3)

THE HISTORY AND SCOPE OF PSYCHOLOGY

1-1 How is psychology a science?

Psychology's findings, based on an empirical approach, are the result of careful observation and testing. Sifting reality from fantasy requires a scientific attitude.

1-2 What are the three key elements of the scientific attitude, and how do they support scientific inquiry?

The scientific attitude equips us to be curious, skeptical, and humble in scrutinizing competing ideas or our own observations. Curiosity triggers new ideas, skepticism encourages attention to the facts, and humility helps us both discard predictions that can't be verified by research and be open to surprises. Together, these three key elements make modern science possible.

1-3 How does critical thinking feed a scientific attitude, and smarter thinking for everyday life?

Critical thinking puts ideas to the test by examining assumptions, appraising the source, discerning hidden biases, evaluating evidence, and assessing conclusions.

1-4 What were some important milestones in psychology's early history?

Wilhelm Wundt established the first psychological laboratory in 1879 in Germany. Two early schools of thought in psychology were *structuralism* and *functionalism*. Mary Whiton Calkins and Margaret Floy Washburn were two of the first women in the field.

1-5 How did behaviorism, Freudian psychology, and humanistic psychology further the development of psychological science?

Early researchers defined *psychology* as "the science of mental life." In the 1920s, under the influence of John B. Watson and the behaviorists, the field's focus changed to the "scientific study of observable behavior." *Behaviorism* became one of psychology's two major forces well into the 1960s. However, the second major force of Freudian (psychoanalytic) psychology, along with the influence of *humanistic psychology*, revived interest in the study of mental processes.

1-6 How has contemporary psychology focused on cognition, on biology and experience, on culture and gender, and on human flourishing?

The *cognitive revolution* in the 1960s led psychology back to its early interest in the mind, and to its current definition as the science of behavior and mental processes. The field of *cognitive neuroscience* now examines the brain activity underlying mental activity. Our growing understanding of biology and experience has fed psychology's most enduring debate. The *nature–nurture issue* centers on the relative contributions of genes and experience, and their interaction in specific environments. Charles Darwin's view that *natural selection* shapes behaviors as well as bodies led to *evolutionary psychology*'s study of our similarities because of our common biology and evolutionary history, and *behavior genetics*' focus on the relative power and limits of genetic and environmental influences on behavior. Cross-cultural and gender studies have diversified psychology's assumptions while also reminding us of our similarities. Attitudes and behaviors may vary somewhat by gender or across *cultures*, but because of our shared human kinship, the underlying processes and principles are more similar than different. Psychology's traditional focus on understanding and treating troubles has expanded with *positive psychology*'s call for more research on human flourishing and its attempt to discover and promote traits that help people to thrive.

1-7 How do psychologists use the biopsychosocial approach, and how can it help us understand our diverse world?

The *biopsychosocial approach* integrates information from three differing but complementary *levels of analysis*: biological, psychological, and social-cultural. This approach offers a more complete understanding than could usually be reached by relying on only one of psychology's current theoretical perspectives (neuroscience, evolutionary, behavior genetics, psychodynamic, behavioral, cognitive, and social-cultural). The biopsychosocial approach can help us understand our diverse world: We share a biologically rooted nature, but many psychological and social-cultural influences fine-tune our assumptions, values, and behavior.

1-8 What are psychology's main subfields?

Within the science of psychology, researchers may conduct *basic research* to increase the field's knowledge base (often in biological, developmental, cognitive, personality, and social psychology) or *applied research* to solve practical problems (in industrial-organizational psychology and other areas). Those who engage in psychology as a helping profession may assist people as *counseling psychologists*, helping people with challenges and crises (including academic, vocational, and relationship issues) and to improve their personal and social functioning, or as *clinical psychologists*, assessing and treating people with mental, emotional, and behavior disorders. *Psychiatrists* also assess and treat people with disorders, but as medical doctors, they may prescribe drugs in addition to psychotherapy. *Community psychologists* work to create healthy social and physical environments (in schools and neighborhoods, for example).

1-9 How can psychological principles help you learn, remember, and thrive?

The *testing effect* shows that learning and memory are enhanced by actively retrieving, rather than simply rereading, previously studied material. The *SQ3R* study method—survey, question, read, retrieve, and review—applies principles derived from memory research and can help you learn and remember material. Four additional tips are (1) distribute your study time; (2) learn to think critically; (3) process class information actively; and (4) overlearn. Psychological research has shown that people who live happy, thriving lives manage their time to get a full night's sleep; make space for exercise; set long-term goals, with daily aims; have a growth mindset; and prioritize relationships.

2 RESEARCH STRATEGIES: HOW PSYCHOLOGISTS ASK AND ANSWER QUESTIONS

2-1 How does our everyday thinking sometimes lead us to a wrong conclusion?

Our everyday thinking can lead us astray because of three phenomena. *Hindsight bias* (the "I-knew-it-all-along phenomenon") is the tendency to believe, after learning an outcome, that we would have foreseen it. Overconfidence is often the result of our readiness to be more confident than correct. These tendencies, along with our eagerness to perceive patterns in random events, lead us to overestimate the weight of common-sense thinking. Scientific inquiry can help us overcome such biases and shortcomings.

2-2 Why are we so vulnerable to believing untruths?

In our modern "post-truth" culture, our emotions, beliefs, and group affiliations may color our judgments, prevent our acknowledgement of objective facts, and prompt us to accept only the information that confirms our views. Misinformation may spread as a result of repetition and memorable examples, contributing to the post-truth culture. Critical evaluation of information and a scientific mindset can help to combat our biases and distorted thinking.

2-3 How do theories advance psychological science?

Psychological *theories* apply an integrated set of principles to organize observations and to generate *hypotheses*. By testing their hypotheses, researchers can confirm, reject, or revise their theories. To enable other researchers to *replicate* the studies, researchers report them using precise *operational definitions* of their procedures and concepts. If others achieve similar results, confidence in the conclusion will be greater. More and more psychologists use *preregistration* to publicly communicate their planned study design, hypotheses, data collection, and analyses, which promotes openness and transparency. By combining the results of many studies, *meta-analysis* helps increase researchers' confidence in their results by avoiding the problem of small sample sizes.

2-4 How do psychologists use case studies, naturalistic observations, and surveys to observe and describe behavior, and why is random sampling important?

Descriptive methods, which include *case studies* (in-depth analyses of individuals or groups), *naturalistic observations* (recording many individuals' natural behavior), and *surveys* (asking people questions), show us what can happen, and they may offer ideas for further study. The best basis for generalizing about a *population* is a representative sample; in a *random sample*, every person in the entire population being studied has an equal chance of participating. Descriptive methods describe but do not *explain* behavior; they cannot show cause and effect because researchers cannot control variables.

2-5 What does it mean when we say two things are correlated, and what are positive and negative correlations?

Correlation is the degree to which two variables are related, and how well one predicts the other. In a positive correlation, two variables increase or decrease together; in a negative correlation, one variable increases as the other decreases. The strength and direction of their relationship is expressed as a *correlation coefficient*, which ranges from +1.00 (a perfect positive correlation) through 0 (no correlation) to –1.00 (a perfect negative correlation).

2-6 What are *illusory correlations*, and what is *regression toward the mean*?

Illusory correlations are random events that we notice and falsely assume are related.

2-7 Why do correlations enable prediction but not cause-effect explanation?

Correlations enable prediction because they show how two factors are related—either positively or negatively. A correlation can indicate the possibility of a cause-effect relationship, but it does not prove the direction of the influence, or whether an underlying third factor may explain the correlation.

2-8 What are the characteristics of experimentation that make it possible to isolate cause and effect?

To discover cause-effect relationships, psychologists conduct *experiments*, manipulating one or more variables of interest and controlling other variables. Using *random assignment*, they can minimize confounding variables, such as preexisting differences between the *experimental group* (exposed to the treatment) and the *control group* (not given the treatment). The *independent variable* is the factor the experimenter manipulates to study its effect; the *dependent variable* is the factor the experimenter measures to discover any changes occurring in response to the manipulation of the independent variable. Studies may use a *double-blind procedure* to avoid the *placebo effect* and researcher bias.

2-9 How would you know which research design to use?

Psychological scientists design studies and choose research methods that will best provide meaningful results. Researchers generate testable questions, and then carefully consider the best design to use in studying those questions (experimental, correlational, case study, naturalistic observation, twin study, longitudinal, or cross-sectional). Next, psychologists measure the variables they are studying, and finally they interpret their results, keeping possible confounding variables in mind. (The online *How Would You Know?* research activities allow you to play the role of the researcher, making choices about the best ways to test interesting questions.)

2-10 How can simplified laboratory experiments help us understand general principles of behavior?

Researchers intentionally create a controlled, artificial environment in the laboratory to test general theoretical principles. It is the general principles—not the specific findings—that help explain everyday behaviors.

2-11 Why do psychologists study animals, and what ethical research guidelines safeguard human and animal welfare? How do psychologists' values influence what they study and how they apply their results?

Some psychologists are primarily interested in animal behavior; others want to better understand the physiological and psychological processes shared by humans and other species. Government agencies have established standards for animal care and housing. Professional associations and funding agencies also have guidelines for protecting animals' well-being. The ethics codes of the American Psychological Association (APA) and the British Psychological

Society (BPS) outline standards for safeguarding human participants' well-being, including obtaining their *informed consent* and *debriefing* them later. Universities and research organizations have Institutional Review Boards to screen research proposals and ensure participants' well-being. Scientific scrutiny and replication help to guard against the fabrication of data, which has the potential to cause great harm. Psychologists' values influence their choice of research topics, their theories and observations, and their labels for behavior. Applications of psychology's principles have been used mainly in the service of humanity

3 STATISTICAL REASONING IN EVERYDAY LIFE

3-1 Why does statistical literacy matter?

Statistical literacy involves not only the ability to understand numbers and basic math, but also the ability to think about what numbers mean in context. Improving your statistical literacy will give you a more accurate understanding of the world and the people around you, and a clearer sense of the risks that affect your life.

3-2 How do we describe data using three measures of central tendency?

Researchers use descriptive statistics to measure and describe characteristics of groups under study. A measure of central tendency is a single score that represents a whole set of scores. Three such measures that we use to describe data are the *mode* (the most frequently occurring score), the *mean* (the arithmetic average), and the *median* (the middle score in a group of data).

3-3 What is the relative usefulness of the two measures of variation?

Measures of central tendency neatly summarize data; measures of variation tell us how diverse data are. Two measures of variation are the *range* (which describes the gap between the highest and lowest scores) and the *standard deviation* (which states how much scores vary around the mean, or average, score). Scores often form a *normal* (or bell-shaped) *curve*.

3-4 How do we know whether an observed difference can be generalized to other populations?

Researchers use inferential statistics (which include ways of determining the reliability and significance of an observed difference between the results for different groups) to determine if results can be generalized to a larger population. Reliable differences are based on samples that are representative of the larger population being studied; that demonstrate low variability, on average; that consist of many cases; and that comprise multiple studies (using *meta-analysis*). The effect size—the size of the difference between groups—helps determine *statistical significance*: When the sample averages are reliable and the difference between them is large, we can reject the null hypothesis of no existing differences. Many psychological tests provide *p-values*, which indicate the probability of the null hypothesis being true given the sample data.

CHAPTER 2

The Biology of Mind (Modules 4–7)

4 NEURAL AND HORMONAL SYSTEMS

4-1 Why are psychologists concerned with human biology?

Psychologists working from a *biological* perspective study the links between biological processes and psychological processes. We are biopsychosocial systems, in which biological, psychological, and social-cultural factors interact to influence behavior.

4-2 How do biology and experience together enable neuroplasticity?

Neuroplasticity enables our brain to build new neural pathways as we adjust to new experiences; so, our brain is sculpted by both genes and life. While neuroplasticity is lifelong, it is greatest early in life. With practice, our brain develops unique patterns that reflect our life experiences.

4-3 What are *neurons*, and how do they transmit information?

Neurons are the elementary components of the nervous system, the body's speedy electrochemical information system. A neuron (a *cell body* and its branching fibers) receives signals through its often bushy, branching *dendrites* and sends signals through its *axons*. Some axons are encased in a *myelin sheath*, which enables faster transmission. *Glial cells* support, nourish, and protect neurons and also play a role in learning, thinking, and memory. If the combined signals received by a neuron exceed a minimum *threshold*, the neuron fires, transmitting an electrical impulse (the *action potential*) down its axon by means of a chemistry-to-electricity process. Neurons need a short rest called the *refractory period*, after which they can fire again. The neuron's reaction is an *all-or-none response*.

4-4 How do nerve cells communicate with other nerve cells?

When action potentials reach the end of an axon (the button-like axon terminals), they stimulate the release of *neurotransmitters*. These chemical messengers carry a message from the sending neuron across a *synapse* to receptor sites on a receiving neuron. The sending neuron, in a process called *reuptake*, then normally reabsorbs the excess neurotransmitter molecules in the synaptic gap. If incoming signals are strong enough, the receiving neuron generates its own action potential and relays the message to other cells.

4-5 How do neurotransmitters influence behavior, and how do drugs and other chemicals affect neurotransmission?

Neurotransmitters travel designated pathways in the brain and may influence specific behaviors and emotions. Acetylcholine (ACh) enables muscle action, learning, and memory. *Endorphins* are natural opioids released in response to pain and exercise. Drugs and other chemicals affect brain chemistry at synapses. *Agonists* increase a neurotransmitter's action, and may do so in various ways. *Antagonists* decrease a neurotransmitter's action by blocking production or release.

4-6 What are the functions of the nervous system's main divisions, and what are the three main types of neurons?

The *central nervous system (CNS)*—the brain and the spinal cord—is the *nervous system's* decision maker. The *peripheral nervous system (PNS)*, which connects the CNS to the rest of the body by means of *nerves*, gathers information and transmits CNS decisions to the rest of the body. The two main PNS divisions are the *somatic nervous system* (which enables voluntary control of the skeletal muscles) and the *autonomic nervous system* (which controls involuntary muscles and glands by means of its *sympathetic* and *parasympathetic* divisions). The three types of neurons cluster into working networks: (1) *Sensory (afferent) neurons* carry incoming information from the body's tissues and sensory receptors to the brain and spinal cord. (2) *Motor (efferent) neurons* carry outgoing information from the brain and spinal cord to the muscles and glands. (3) *Interneurons* communicate within the brain and spinal cord and process information between the sensory inputs and motor outputs.

4-7 How does the endocrine system transmit information and interact with the nervous system?

The *endocrine system's* glands and fat tissue secrete *hormones* into the bloodstream; these hormones travel through the body and affect other tissues, including the brain. The endocrine system's master gland, the *pituitary*, influences hormone release by other glands, including the *adrenal glands*. In an intricate feedback system, the brain's hypothalamus influences the pituitary gland, which influences other glands, which release hormones, which in turn influence the brain.

TOOLS OF DISCOVERY: HAVING OUR HEAD EXAMINED

5-1 How do neuroscientists study the brain's connections to behavior and mind?

Clinical observations and lesioning reveal the general effects of brain damage. Electrical, chemical, or magnetic stimulation can also reveal aspects of information processing in the brain. MRI scans show anatomy. EEG, MEG, PET, and fMRI (functional MRI) recordings reveal brain function.

BRAIN REGIONS AND STRUCTURES

6-1 What are the *hindbrain, midbrain,* and *forebrain?*

Vertebrate brains have three main divisions. The *hindbrain* contains brainstem structures that direct essential survival functions, such as breathing, sleeping, arousal, coordination, and balance. The *midbrain* connects the hindbrain with the forebrain; it controls some movement and transmits information that enables seeing and hearing. The *forebrain* manages complex cognitive activities, sensory and associative functions, and voluntary motor activities.

6-2 What structures make up the brainstem, and what are the functions of the brainstem, thalamus, reticular formation, and cerebellum?

The *brainstem* is responsible for automatic survival functions. It includes the *medulla* (which controls heartbeat and breathing), the pons (which helps coordinate movements and control sleep), and the *reticular formation* (which filters incoming stimuli, relays information to other brain areas, and affects arousal). The *thalamus*, sitting above the brainstem, acts as the brain's sensory control center. The *cerebellum*, attached to the rear of the brainstem, coordinates voluntary movement and balance and enables nonverbal learning and memory.

6-3 What are the limbic system's structures and functions?

The *limbic system* is linked to emotions, memory, and drives. Its neural centers include the *amygdala* (involved in behavioral and emotional responses, such as aggression and fear); the *hypothalamus* (directs various bodily maintenance functions, helps govern the endocrine system, and is linked to emotion and reward); and the *hippocampus* (helps process explicit, conscious memories). The hypothalamus controls the pituitary (the "master gland") by stimulating it to trigger the release of hormones.

6-4 What four lobes make up the cerebral cortex, and what are the functions of the motor cortex, somatosensory cortex, and association areas?

The *cerebral cortex* has two hemispheres, and each hemisphere has four lobes: *frontal, parietal, occipital,* and *temporal*. Each lobe performs many functions and interacts with other areas of the cortex. The *motor cortex*, at the rear of the frontal lobes, controls voluntary movements. The *somatosensory cortex*, at the front of the parietal lobes, registers and processes body touch and movement sensations. Body parts requiring precise control (in the motor cortex) or those that are especially sensitive (in the somatosensory cortex) occupy the greatest amount of space. Most of the brain's cortex—the major portion of each of the four lobes—is devoted to uncommitted *association areas*, which integrate information involved in higher mental functions such as learning, remembering, thinking, and speaking. Our mental experiences arise from coordinated brain activity.

6-5 Is it true that 90 percent of our brain isn't really used?

The unresponsiveness of our association areas to electrical probing led to the false claim that we use only 10 percent of our brain. But these vast areas of the brain are responsible for interpreting, integrating, and acting on sensory information and linking it with stored memories. Evidence from brain damage shows that the neurons in association areas are busy with higher mental functions; a bullet would not land in an "unused" area.

DAMAGE RESPONSES AND BRAIN HEMISPHERES

7-1 To what extent can a damaged brain reorganize itself, and what is *neurogenesis*?

While brain and spinal cord neurons usually do not regenerate, some neural tissue can reorganize in response to damage. The damaged brain may demonstrate neuroplasticity, especially in young children, as new pathways are built and functions migrate to other brain regions. Reassignment of functions to different areas of the brain may also occur in blindness and deafness, or as a result of damage and disease. Some research suggests that the brain may sometimes mend itself by forming new neurons, a process known as *neurogenesis*.

7-2 What do split brains reveal about the functions of our two brain hemispheres?

Split-brain research (experiments on people with a severed *corpus callosum*) has confirmed that in most people, the left hemisphere is the more verbal. The right hemisphere excels in visual perception and making inferences, and helps us modulate our speech and orchestrate our self-awareness. Studies of the intact brain in healthy people confirm that each hemisphere makes unique contributions to the integrated functioning of the whole brain.

CHAPTER 3

Consciousness and the Two-Track Mind (Modules 8–10)

BASIC CONSCIOUSNESS CONCEPTS

8-1 What is the place of *consciousness* in psychology's history?

After initially claiming consciousness as their area of study in the nineteenth century, psychologists abandoned it in the first half of the twentieth century, turning instead to the study of observable behavior because they believed consciousness was too difficult to study scientifically. Since the 1960s, our awareness of ourselves and our environment—our *consciousness*—has reclaimed its place as an important area of research, such as in the interdisciplinary field of *cognitive neuroscience*.

8-2 How does *selective attention* direct our perceptions?

We *selectively attend* to, and process, a very limited portion of incoming information, blocking out much and often shifting the spotlight of our attention from one thing to another. Focused intently on one task, we often display *inattentional blindness* to other events, including *change blindness* to changes around us.

8-3 What is the *dual processing* being revealed by today's cognitive neuroscience?

Scientists studying the brain mechanisms underlying consciousness and cognition have discovered that the mind processes information on two separate tracks, one operating at a conscious level *(sequential processing)* and the other at an unconscious level *(parallel processing)*. Parallel processing takes care of the routine business, while sequential processing is best for solving new problems that require our attention. Together, this *dual processing*—conscious and unconscious—affects our perception, memory, attitudes, and other cognitions.

9 SLEEP AND DREAMS

9-1 What is *sleep?*

Sleep is the periodic, natural loss of normal consciousness—as distinct from unconsciousness resulting from a coma, general anesthesia, or hibernation.

9-2 How do our biological rhythms influence our daily functioning?

Our bodies have an internal biological clock, roughly synchronized with the 24-hour cycle of night and day. This *circadian rhythm* appears in our daily patterns of body temperature, arousal, sleeping, and waking. Age and experience can alter these patterns, resetting our biological clock.

9-3 What is the biological rhythm of our sleeping and dreaming stages?

Younger adults cycle through four distinct sleep stages about every 90 minutes. (The sleep cycle repeats more frequently for older adults.) Leaving the *alpha waves* of the awake, relaxed stage, we descend into the irregular brain waves of N1 sleep, often with *hallucinations*. N2 sleep (in which we spend about half our sleep time) follows, lasting about 20 minutes, with its characteristic sleep spindles. We then enter N3 sleep, lasting about 30 minutes, with large, slow *delta waves*. About an hour after falling asleep, we ascend from our initial sleep dive and begin periods of *REM* (rapid eye movement or R) *sleep*. REM sleep, which includes most dreaming, is described as a paradoxical sleep stage because of internal arousal but external calm (near paralysis). During a normal night's sleep, N3 sleep shortens and REM and N2 sleep lengthen.

9-4 How do biology and environment interact in our sleep patterns?

Our biology—our circadian rhythm as well as our age and our body's production of melatonin (influenced by the brain's *suprachiasmatic nucleus*)—interacts with social, cultural, and economic influences and individual emotions and behaviors to determine our sleeping and waking patterns. Being bathed in (or deprived of) light disrupts our 24-hour biological clock. Those who are chronically deprived of natural sunlight, such as night-shift workers, may experience desynchronization. Artificial light, including from light-emitting electronic devices, delays sleep and affects sleep quality.

9-5 What are sleep's functions?

Sleep may have played a protective role in human evolution by keeping people safe during potentially dangerous periods. Sleep also helps restore the immune system and repair damaged neurons. Sleep consolidates our memories by replaying recent learning and strengthening neural connections. Sleep promotes creative problem solving the next day. During slow-wave sleep, the pituitary gland secretes a growth hormone necessary for muscle development. As a result of these benefits, a regular full night's sleep can greatly enhance athletic performance.

9-6 How does sleep loss affect us, and what are the major sleep disorders?

Sleep deprivation causes fatigue and irritability, and it impairs concentration and memory consolidation. It can also lead to depression, obesity, joint inflammation, a suppressed immune system, and slowed performance (with greater vulnerability to accidents). Sleep disorders include *insomnia* (recurring problems in falling or staying asleep); *narcolepsy* (sudden uncontrollable sleepiness, sometimes lapsing directly into REM sleep); *sleep apnea* (the repeated stopping of breathing while asleep; associated with obesity, especially in men); *REM sleep behavior disorder* (acting out dreams by moving or speaking while asleep); *night terrors* (high arousal and the appearance of being terrified; N3 disorder found mainly in children); sleepwalking; and sleeptalking.

9-7 What do we dream, and what functions have theorists proposed for dreams?

We usually *dream* of ordinary events and everyday experiences, most involving some anxiety or misfortune. Fewer than 10 percent of dreams among men (and fewer still among women) have any sexual content. Most dreams occur during REM sleep. There are five major views of the function of dreams. (1) Freud's wish fulfillment: Dreams provide a psychic "safety valve," with *manifest content* (story line) acting as a censored version of *latent content* (underlying meaning that gratifies our unconscious wishes). (2) Information processing: Dreams help us sort out the day's events and consolidate them in memory. (3) Neurocognitive function: REM sleep preserves memory and processes emotional information. (4) Activation synthesis: The brain attempts to make sense of neural static by weaving it into a story line. (5) Cognitive development: Dreams reflect the dreamers' level of development—their knowledge and understanding. Most sleep theorists agree that REM sleep and its associated dreams serve an important function, as shown by the *REM rebound* that occurs following REM deprivation in humans and other species.

10 DRUGS AND CONSCIOUSNESS

10-1 What are *substance use disorders?*

Those with a *substance use disorder* experience continued substance craving and use despite significant life disruption and/or physical risk. *Psychoactive drugs* alter perceptions and moods. A substance/medication-induced disorder occurs when drug use causes changes that resemble a psychological disorder.

10-2 What roles do tolerance and addiction play in substance use disorders, and how has the concept of *addiction* changed?

Psychoactive drugs may produce *tolerance*—requiring larger doses to achieve the desired effect, a result of neuroadaptation—and *withdrawal*—the discomfort and distress that follow discontinuing an addictive drug or behavior. Addiction prompts users to crave the drug and to continue use despite known adverse consequences. Therapy or group support may help; it helps to believe that addictions are controllable and that people can change. Although psychologists try to avoid overuse of the term *addiction* to label driven, excessive behaviors, there are some behavior addictions (such as gambling disorder and internet gaming disorder) in which behaviors become compulsive and dysfunctional.

10-3 What are *depressants*, and what are their effects?

Depressants, such as alcohol, *barbiturates*, and the *opioids*, reduce neural activity and slow body functions. Alcohol disinhibits, increasing the likelihood that we will act on our impulses, whether harmful or helpful. It also impairs judgment by slowing neural processing, disrupts memory processes by suppressing REM sleep, and reduces self-awareness and self-control. User expectations strongly influence alcohol's behavioral effects. Alcohol can shrink the brain in those with *alcohol use disorder* (marked by tolerance, withdrawal if use is suspended, and a drive to continue problematic use).

10-4 What are *stimulants*, and what are their effects?

Stimulants—including caffeine, nicotine, cocaine, the amphetamines, methamphetamine, and Ecstasy—excite neural activity and speed up body functions, triggering energy and mood changes. Stimulants can be highly addictive. *Nicotine's* effects make tobacco product use a difficult habit to kick, yet repeated attempts to quit seem to pay off. *Cocaine* gives users a fast high, followed shortly by a crash. Its risks include cardiac arrest, respiratory failure, convulsions, and emotional disturbances. *Amphetamines* stimulate neural activity, leading to heightened energy and mood. *Methamphetamine* use may permanently reduce dopamine production. *Ecstasy (MDMA)* is a combined stimulant and mild hallucinogen that produces euphoria and feelings of intimacy. Its users risk immune system suppression, permanent damage to mood, memory impairment, and (if taken during physical activity) dehydration and escalating body temperatures.

10-5 What are *hallucinogens*, and what are their effects?

Hallucinogens, such as *LSD* and marijuana, distort perceptions and evoke hallucinations. The user's mood and expectations influence the effects of LSD, but common experiences are hallucinations and emotions varying from euphoria to panic. Marijuana's main ingredient, *THC*, may trigger feelings of disinhibition, euphoria, relaxation, relief from pain, and intense sensitivity to sensory stimuli, but may increase the risk of psychological disorders and lead to impaired attention, learning, and memory.

10-6 Why do some people become regular users of consciousness-altering drugs?

Some people may be biologically vulnerable to particular drugs. Psychological factors (such as stress, depression, and anxiety) and social factors (such as peer pressure and cultural influences) combine to lead many people to experiment with—and sometimes become addicted to—drugs. Cultural and ethnic groups have differing rates of drug use. Each type of influence—biological, psychological, and social-cultural—offers a possible path for drug misuse prevention and treatment programs.

CHAPTER 4

Nature, Nurture, and Human Diversity (Modules 11–13)

BEHAVIOR GENETICS: PREDICTING INDIVIDUAL DIFFERENCES

11-1 What are *chromosomes, DNA, genes*, and the human *genome*? How do behavior geneticists explain our individual differences?

Genes are the biochemical units of *heredity* that make up *chromosomes*, the threadlike coils of *DNA*. When genes are expressed, they provide the code for creating the proteins that form our body's building blocks. The human *genome* is the shared genetic profile that distinguishes humans from other species, consisting at an individual level of all the genetic material in an organism's chromosomes. *Behavior geneticists* study the relative power and limits of genetic and *environmental* influences on behavior. Most of our differing traits are polygenic, and are influenced by the interaction of our individual environments with these genetic predispositions.

11-2 How do twin and adoption studies help us understand the effects and interactions of nature and nurture?

Studies of *identical (monozygotic) twins* versus *fraternal (dizygotic) twins*, separated twins, and biological versus adoptive relatives allow researchers to consider the effects of shared environment and shared genes, which sheds light on how nature and nurture influence our traits. Shared family environments have surprisingly little effect on personality, though parenting does influence other factors.

11-3 What have psychologists learned about temperament?

The stability of *temperament*, a person's characteristic emotional reactivity and intensity, from the first weeks of life suggests a genetic predisposition. The genetic effect appears in physiological differences such as heart rate and nervous system reactivity.

11-4 What is *heritability*, and how does it relate to individuals and groups?

Heritability is the proportion of variation among individuals in a group that can be attributed to genes. Heritable individual differences (in traits such as height or intelligence) need not imply heritable group differences. Genes mostly explain why some people are taller than others, but not why people are taller today than they were a century ago.

11-5 How is molecular genetics research changing our understanding of the effects of nature and nurture?

Our genetic predispositions and our specific environments *interact*. Environments can trigger genetic expression, and genetically influenced traits can influence the experiences we seek and the responses we evoke from others. *Molecular geneticists* study the molecular structure and function of genes, including those that affect behavior. One goal of *molecular behavior genetics* is to identify specific genes—or, more often, teams of genes—that together orchestrate complex traits (such as body weight, sexual orientation, and impulsivity) or put people at risk for disorders. The field of *epigenetics* studies the molecular mechanisms by which environments can trigger or block genetic expression.

12 EVOLUTIONARY PSYCHOLOGY: EXPLAINING HUMAN NATURE AND NURTURE

12-1 How do evolutionary psychologists use natural selection to explain behavior tendencies?

Evolutionary psychologists attempt to understand how *natural selection* has shaped traits and behavior tendencies found in all people. Genetic variations that increase the odds of reproducing and surviving in a particular environment are most likely to be passed on to future generations. Some variations arise from *mutations*, others from new gene combinations at conception. Humans share a genetic legacy and are predisposed to behaviors that promoted our ancestors' survival and reproduction. Charles Darwin's theory of evolution is one of biology's fundamental organizing principles. He anticipated today's application of evolutionary principles in psychology.

12-2 How might an evolutionary psychologist explain male-female differences in sexuality and mating preferences?

Females tend to be more selective than males when choosing sexual partners. Evolutionary psychologists reason that male's attraction to multiple fertile-appearing partners increases their chances of spreading their genes widely. Because females incubate and nurse babies, they increase their own and their children's chances of survival by searching for mates with the potential for long-term investment in their joint offspring.

12-3 What are the key criticisms of evolutionary explanations of human sexuality, and how do evolutionary psychologists respond?

Critics argue that evolutionary psychologists start with an effect and work backward to an explanation, minimize contemporary social and cultural influences (including learned *social scripts*), and relieve people from taking responsibility for their sexual behavior, including sexual aggression. Evolutionary psychologists respond that they recognize the importance of social and cultural influences, but note the value of testable predictions based on evolutionary principles: Understanding our predispositions can help us overcome them.

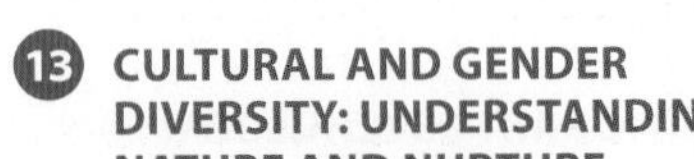
13

CULTURAL AND GENDER DIVERSITY: UNDERSTANDING NATURE AND NURTURE

13-1 How do early experiences modify the brain?

The brain's nerve cells are sculpted by heredity and experience. As a child's brain develops, neural connections grow more numerous and complex. Experiences then prompt a pruning process, in which unused connections weaken and heavily used ones strengthen. Early childhood is an important period for shaping the brain, but thanks to neuroplasticity, the brain modifies itself throughout our lives in response to our learning.

13-2 In what ways do parents and peers shape children's development?

Family environment and parental expectations can affect children's motivation and future success. Personality, however, is mostly not attributable to the effects of nurture. As children attempt to fit in with peers, they tend to adopt their peers' culture.

13-3 How does culture affect our behavior?

A *culture* is an enduring set of behaviors, ideas, attitudes, values, and traditions shared by a group and transmitted from one generation to the next. Culture enables innovation and division of labor. Cultural *norms*, which differ across time and place, are understood rules that inform members of a culture about accepted and expected behaviors. Cultures differ in how strictly people follow norms: People more often obey norms in *tight cultures*, but those in *loose cultures* expect greater variability.

13-4 How do individualist and collectivist cultures shape values and goals?

Our personality is culturally influenced. Although individuals vary, different cultures tend to emphasize either individualism or collectivism. Cultures based on self-reliant *individualism* tend to value personal independence and individual achievement. They define identity in terms of self-esteem, personal goals and attributes, and personal rights and liberties. Cultures based on socially connected *collectivism* tend to value group goals, social identity, and commitments. They define identity in terms of interdependence, tradition, and harmony.

13-5 How does the meaning of *gender* differ from the meaning of *sex?*

Gender refers to the behavioral characteristics that people associate with boy, girl, man, and woman. *Sex* refers to the biologically influenced characteristics by which people define *male*, *female*, and *intersex*. Our understanding of gender arises from the interplay between our biology and our experiences.

13-6 What are some of the ways males and females tend to be alike and to differ?

Whether male, female, or intersex, most of us receive 23 chromosomes from our mother and 23 from our father, of which 45 are unisex. Humans are in most ways alike, thanks to similar genetic makeup—they see, learn, and remember similarly, with comparable creativity, intelligence, and emotions. Male-female differences include age of onset of puberty, life expectancy, emotional expressiveness, and vulnerability to certain disorders. Men display more *aggression* than women do, and they are more likely to be physically (rather than *relationally*) aggressive. In most societies, men have more social power. Males tend to be more independent, while females tend to be more interdependent. Women often focus more on social connectedness than do men, and they "tend and befriend."

13-7 What factors contribute to gender bias in the workplace?

Workplace gender bias is revealed in differences in perception, compensation, and family-care responsibility. Social norms, interaction styles, and everyday behaviors also contribute. Men's leadership style tends to be directive, whereas women's tends to be more democratic. In their everyday behaviors and interactions, men tend to act more assertive and opinionated; women tend to act more supportive and apologetic.

13-8 How do sex hormones influence prenatal and adolescent sexual development?

Both sex chromosomes and sex hormones influence development. About seven weeks after conception, a gene on the Y *chromosome* from the father—who can contribute either this or an X *chromosome* (the mother always contributes the latter)—triggers the production of *testosterone*. This promotes male sex organ development. *Estrogens* contribute to female sex characteristics and are secreted in greater amounts by females than by males. During the fourth and fifth prenatal months, sex hormones bathe the fetal brain, with different patterns developing due to the male's greater testosterone and the female's estrogens. Prenatal exposure of females to unusually high levels of male hormones can later dispose them to more male-typical interests.

Males prenatally exposed to low male hormone levels tend to grow up with more female-typical interests. Another flood of hormones occurs in *puberty*, triggering a growth spurt, the development of *primary* and *secondary sex characteristics*, and the landmark events of *menarche* and *spermarche*. Sexual development variations may occur through unusual combinations of male and female chromosomes, hormones, and anatomy.

13-9 What are some cultural influences on gender roles?

Gender roles—a set of expected behaviors, attitudes, and traits for men and women—vary across place and time. Gender roles in many parts of the world have changed dramatically in the last century. Expectations about gender roles also influence cultural attitudes about *sexual aggression*.

13-10 What are the effects of sexual aggression? How have cultural views changed, and how can we reduce sexual aggression?

Sexual aggression, which includes sexual harassment and sexual assault, can increase anxiety, depression, and the risk of posttraumatic stress disorder; disrupt sleep; harm physical health; and make it difficult to trust new relationship partners. Cultural views of sexual aggression differ across time and place, with some cultures continuing to blame survivors, but changes in global norms over the last half-century have made such blaming less acceptable. Therapy for sexual aggressors has not proven effective, but we may reduce sexual aggression by encouraging people to report and share their experiences, empowering survivors, and educating communities about preventive bystander intervention strategies.

13-11 How do we form our gender identity?

Social learning theory proposes that we learn our *gender identity*—our personal sense of being male, female, neither, or some combination of male and female—in the same way that we learn other things: through reinforcement, punishment, and observation. But *gender typing* varies from child to child, indicating that imitation and reward, alone, do not explain gender identity. Some children organize themselves into "boy worlds" and "girl worlds"; others prefer *androgyny*. For people who identify as cisgender, gender identity corresponds with birth-assigned sex. For those who identify as *transgender*, gender identity differs from what is typical for that person's birth-assigned sex. Gender identity is distinct from sexual orientation; transgender people may be sexually attracted to people of any gender or to no one at all.

13-12 How do nature, nurture, and our own choices influence gender roles and sexuality?

Individual development results from the interaction of biological, psychological, and social-cultural influences. Biological influences include our shared human genome; individual variations; prenatal environment; and sex-related genes, hormones, and physiology. Psychological influences include gene–environment interactions; the effect of early experiences on neural networks; responses evoked by our own characteristics, such as gender and temperament; and personal beliefs, feelings, and expectations. Social-cultural influences include parental and peer influences; cultural traditions and values; and cultural gender norms. And our individual choices affect the way all of these influences interact.

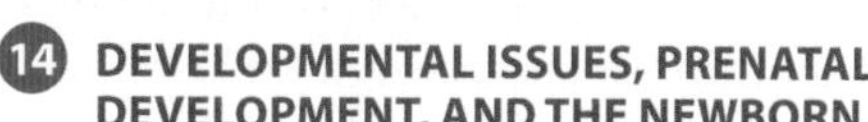
CHAPTER 5

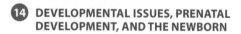

Developing Through the Life Span (Modules 14–17)

14 DEVELOPMENTAL ISSUES, PRENATAL DEVELOPMENT, AND THE NEWBORN

14-1 What three issues have engaged developmental psychologists?

Developmental psychologists study physical, cognitive, and social changes across the life span. They often use *cross-sectional* (comparing people of different ages at one point in time) and *longitudinal studies* (retesting the same people over a period of years) to explore three issues: nature and nurture (the interaction between our genetic inheritance and our experiences); continuity and stages (which aspects of development are gradual and continuous and which change relatively abruptly); and stability and change (whether our traits endure or change as we age).

14-2 What is the course of prenatal development, and how do teratogens affect that development?

The life cycle begins at conception, when one sperm cell unites with an egg to form a *zygote*. The zygote's inner cells become the *embryo*, and the outer cells become the placenta. In the next 6 weeks, body organs begin to form and function, and by 9 weeks, the *fetus* is recognizably human. *Teratogens* are potentially harmful agents that can pass through the placenta and harm the developing embryo or fetus, as happens with *fetal alcohol syndrome*.

14-3 What are some newborn abilities, and how do researchers explore infants' mental abilities?

Babies are born with sensory equipment and reflexes that facilitate their survival and their social interactions with adults. For example, they quickly learn to discriminate their mother's smell, and they prefer the sound of human voices. Researchers use techniques that test *habituation* to explore infants' abilities.

15 INFANCY AND CHILDHOOD

15-1 During infancy and childhood, how do the brain and motor skills develop?

The brain's nerve cells are sculpted by heredity and experience. As a child's brain develops, neural connections grow more numerous and complex. Experiences then trigger a pruning process, in which unused connections weaken and heavily used ones strengthen. In childhood, complex motor skills—sitting, standing, walking—develop in a predictable sequence, though the timing of that sequence is a function of individual *maturation* and culture. We have few or no conscious memories of events occurring before about age 4. This infantile amnesia occurs in part because major brain areas have not yet matured.

15-2 How did Piaget broaden our understanding of the way a child's mind develops, and how have today's researchers built on his work?

As he studied children's *cognitive* development, Jean Piaget proposed that they actively construct and modify their understanding of the world through the processes of *assimilation* and *accommodation*. They form *schemas* that help them organize their experiences. Progressing from the simplicity of the *sensorimotor stage* of the first 2 years, in which they develop *object permanence*, children move to more complex ways of thinking. In the *preoperational stage* (about age 2 to about 6 or 7), children are *egocentric* and unable to perform simple logical operations. By about age 7, they enter the *concrete operational stage* and are able to comprehend the principle of *conservation*. By age 12, children enter the *formal operational stage* and can reason systematically. Research supports the sequence Piaget proposed, but it also shows that young children are more capable, and their development more continuous, than he believed.

15-3 How did Vygotsky view children's cognitive development?

Lev Vygotsky's studies of child development focused on the ways a child's mind grows by interacting with the social environment. In his view, parents, teachers, and other children provide temporary *scaffolds* enabling children to step to higher levels of thinking.

15-4 What does it mean to develop a *theory of mind*, and how is this impaired in those with autism spectrum disorder?

Our *theory of mind*—our ideas about our own and others' mental states—develops during early childhood. Children with *autism spectrum disorder (ASD)* have an impaired theory of mind: They have difficulty understanding others' state of mind, as well as reflecting on their own.

15-5 How do caregiver-infant attachment bonds form?

At about 8 months, soon after object permanence develops, children separated from their caregivers display *stranger anxiety*. Infants form *attachments* with caregivers who gratify biological needs but, more importantly, who are comfortable, familiar, and responsive. Many birds and other animals have a more rigid attachment process, called *imprinting*, that occurs during a *critical period*.

15-6 How have psychologists studied attachment differences, and what have they learned?

Attachment has been studied in strange situation experiments, which show that some children are securely attached and others are insecurely (anxiously or avoidantly) attached. Infants' differing attachment styles reflect both their individual temperament and the responsiveness of their parents and child-care providers. Adult relationships seem to reflect the attachment styles of early childhood, lending support to Erik Erikson's idea that *basic trust* is formed in infancy by our experiences with responsive caregivers.

15-7 How does experiencing adversity affect children's social development?

Most children growing up under adversity are resilient, and they may be hardier when facing future stresses. But extreme trauma in childhood may alter the brain, affecting our stress responses or leaving epigenetic marks. Children who experience neglect, bullying, poverty, wartime atrocities, or severe or prolonged abuse are at increased risk for health problems, psychological disorders, substance abuse, and criminality.

15-8 How do children's self-concepts develop?

Self-concept, an understanding and evaluation of who we are, emerges gradually. By 15 to 18 months, children recognize themselves in a mirror. By school age, they can describe many of their own traits and by age 8 or 10 their self-image is stable.

15-9 What are the four main parenting styles?

The main parenting styles are authoritarian (coercive), permissive (unrestraining), neglectful (uninvolved), and authoritative (confrontive).

15-10 What outcomes are associated with each parenting style?

Authoritative parenting is associated with greater self-esteem, self-reliance, self-regulation, and social competence; authoritarian parenting with lower self-esteem, less social skill, and a brain that overreacts to mistakes; permissive parenting with greater aggression and immaturity; and neglectful parenting with poor academic and social outcomes. However, correlation does not equal causation (it's possible that children with positive characteristics are more likely to bring out positive parenting methods).

16 ADOLESCENCE AND EMERGING ADULTHOOD

16-1 How is *adolescence* defined, and how do physical changes affect developing teens?

Adolescence is the transition period from childhood to adulthood, extending from *puberty* to social independence. Early maturation can be a challenge for developing adolescents. The brain's frontal lobes mature and myelin growth increases during adolescence and the early twenties, enabling improved judgment, impulse control, and long-term planning.

16-2 How did Piaget, Kohlberg, and later researchers describe adolescent cognitive and moral development?

Piaget theorized that adolescents develop a capacity for formal operations and that this development is the foundation for moral judgment. Lawrence Kohlberg proposed a stage theory of moral reasoning, from a preconventional morality of self-interest, to a conventional morality concerned with upholding laws and social rules, to (in some people) a postconventional morality of basic rights and self-defined ethical principles. Other researchers believe that morality lies in moral intuition and moral action as well as thinking. Kohlberg's critics note that the postconventional level is culturally limited (representing morality only from the perspective of an individualist society), and male-focused (since women more often emphasize care for those in need over what is "fair"). Life success can grow from the ability to delay gratification.

16-3 What are the social tasks and challenges of adolescence?

Erik Erikson proposed eight stages of psychosocial development across the life span. He believed we need to achieve trust, autonomy, initiative, competency, *identity* (in adolescence), *intimacy* (in young adulthood), generativity, and integrity. Each life stage has its own psychosocial task. Solidifying one's sense of self in adolescence means trying out a number of different roles. *Social identity* is the part of the self-concept that comes from a person's group memberships.

16-4 How do parents and peers influence adolescents?

During adolescence, parental influence diminishes and peer influence increases. Adolescents adopt their peers' ways of dressing, acting, and communicating. Positive parent-teen relationships correlate with positive peer relationships, however. Personalities and temperaments are shaped by both nature and nurture, including parental and peer influences.

16-5 What is *emerging adulthood?*

Due to earlier sexual maturity and later independence, the transition from adolescence to adulthood is taking longer than it once did. *Emerging adulthood* is the period from age 18 to the mid-twenties, when many young people are not yet fully independent. This stage is found mostly in today's Western cultures.

 ADULTHOOD

17-1 What physical changes occur during middle and late adulthood?

Muscular strength, reaction time, sensory abilities, and cardiac output begin to almost imperceptibly decline in the mid-twenties; this downward trajectory accelerates through middle and late adulthood, varying considerably with personal health and exercise habits. Women's period of fertility ends with *menopause* around age 50; men experience a more gradual decline. In late adulthood, the immune system weakens, increasing susceptibility to life-threatening illnesses. But exercising can slow aging, enhancing physical health as well as boosting memory, improving judgment, and reducing the risk of severe cognitive decline.

17-2 How does memory change with age?

Recall begins to decline, especially for meaningless information, but recognition memory remains strong. Developmental researchers study age-related changes such as in memory with cross-sectional studies and longitudinal studies. "Terminal decline" describes the cognitive decline in the final few years of life.

17-3 How do neurocognitive disorders and Alzheimer's disease affect cognitive ability?

Neurocognitive disorders (NCDs) are acquired (not lifelong) disorders marked by cognitive deficits, which are often related to Alzheimer's disease, brain injury or disease, or substance abuse. This damage to brain cells results in the erosion of mental abilities that is not typical of normal aging. *Alzheimer's disease* causes the deterioration of memory, then reasoning. After 5 to 20 years, the person becomes emotionally flat, disoriented, disinhibited, incontinent, and finally mentally vacant.

17-4 What themes and influences mark our social journey from early adulthood to death?

Adults do not progress through an orderly sequence of age-related social stages. Chance events can determine life choices. The *social clock* is a culture's preferred timing for events such as marriage, parenthood, and retirement. Many people in Western cultures today feel freer about setting their own timing. Adulthood's dominant themes are love and work (Erikson's intimacy and generativity).

17-5 How does our well-being change across the life span?

Surveys show that until the very end, life satisfaction is unrelated to age. Positive emotions increase after midlife and negative ones decrease; with age come fewer extremes of emotion and mood. While older adults do have smaller social networks, with fewer friendships and greater loneliness, they also experience fewer relationship problems.

17-6 What range of reactions does a loved one's death trigger?

People do not grieve in predictable stages, as was once supposed, and bereavement therapy is not significantly more effective than grieving without such aid. Life can be affirmed even at death, especially for those who experience what Erikson called a sense of integrity—a feeling that one's life has been meaningful.

CHAPTER 6

Sensation and Perception (Modules 18–20)

 BASIC CONCEPTS OF SENSATION AND PERCEPTION

18-1 What are *sensation* and *perception?* What do we mean by *bottom-up processing* and *top-down processing?*

Sensation is the process by which our *sensory receptors* and nervous system receive and represent stimulus energies from our environment. *Perception* is the process of organizing and interpreting this information, enabling recognition of meaningful objects and events. Sensation and perception are one continuous process. *Bottom-up processing* is sensory analysis that begins at the entry level, with information flowing from the sensory receptors to the brain. *Top-down processing* is information processing guided by high-level mental processes, as when we construct perceptions by filtering information through our experience and expectations.

18-2 What three steps are basic to all of our sensory systems?

Our senses (1) receive sensory stimulation, often using specialized receptor cells; (2) transform that stimulation into neural impulses; and (3) deliver the neural information to the brain. *Transduction* is the process of converting energy into a form that our brain can use. Researchers in *psychophysics* study the relationships between stimuli's physical characteristics and our psychological experience of them.

18-3 How do *absolute thresholds* and *difference thresholds* differ?

Our *absolute threshold* for any stimulus is the minimum stimulation necessary for us to detect it 50 percent of the time. *Signal detection theory* predicts how and when we will detect a faint stimulus amid background noise. Individual absolute thresholds vary, depending on the strength of the signal and also on our experience, expectations, motivation, and alertness. Our *difference threshold* (also called the *just noticeable difference*, or *jnd*) is the minimum difference we can discern between two stimuli 50 percent of the time. *Weber's law* states that two stimuli must differ by a constant minimum percentage (not a constant amount) to be perceived as different.

18-4 How are we affected by subliminal stimulation?

We do sense some stimuli *subliminally*—less than 50 percent of the time—and can be affected by these sensations. But although we can be *primed*, subliminal sensations have no powerful, enduring influence.

18-5 What is the function of sensory adaptation?

Sensory adaptation (our diminished sensitivity to constant or routine odors, sounds, and touches) focuses our attention on informative changes in our environment.

18-6 How do our expectations, contexts, motivation, and emotions influence our perceptions?

Perceptual set is a mental predisposition that functions as a lens through which we perceive the world. Our learned concepts (schemas) prime us to organize and interpret ambiguous stimuli in certain ways. Our expectations, contexts, motivation, and emotions can color our interpretation of events and behaviors.

19 VISION: SENSORY AND PERCEPTUAL PROCESSING

19-1 What are the characteristics of the energy that we see as visible light? What structures in the eye help focus that energy?

What we see as light is only a thin slice of the broad spectrum of electromagnetic energy. The portion visible to humans extends from the shorter blue-violet wavelengths to the longer red light wavelengths. After entering the eye through the cornea, passing through the pupil and iris, and being focused by a lens, light energy particles strike the eye's inner surface, the *retina*. The *hue* we perceive in a light depends on its *wavelength*, and its brightness depends on its *intensity*.

19-2 How do the rods and cones process information, and what is the path information travels from the eye to the brain?

Light entering the eye triggers chemical changes that convert light energy into neural impulses. Photoreceptors called *cones* and *rods* at the back of the retina each provide a special sensitivity—cones to detail and color, rods to faint light and peripheral motion. After processing by bipolar and ganglion cells, neural impulses travel from the retina through the *optic nerve* to the thalamus, and on to the visual cortex. A lack of receptor cells at the point where the optic nerve leaves the eye creates a *blind spot* in the field of vision.

19-3 How do we perceive color in the world around us?

According to the *Young-Helmholtz trichromatic (three-color) theory*, the retina contains three types of color receptors. Contemporary research has found three types of cones, each most sensitive to the wavelengths of one of the three primary colors of light (red, green, or blue). According to Hering's *opponent-process theory*, there are three additional sets of opposing retinal processes (red-green, blue-yellow, black-white). Research has confirmed that, en route to the brain, neurons in the retina and the thalamus code the color-related information from the cones into pairs of opponent colors. These two theories, and the research supporting them, show that color processing occurs in two stages.

19-4 Where are feature detectors located, and what do they do?

Feature detectors, specialized nerve cells in the visual cortex, respond to specific features of the visual stimulus, such as shape, angle, or movement. Feature detectors pass information on to other cortical areas, where supercell clusters respond to more complex patterns.

19-5 How does the brain use parallel processing to construct visual perceptions?

Through *parallel processing*, the brain handles many aspects of vision (color, movement, form, and depth) simultaneously. Other neural teams integrate the results, comparing them with stored information and enabling perceptions.

19-6 How did the Gestalt psychologists understand perceptual organization, and how do figure-ground and grouping principles contribute to our perceptions?

Gestalt psychologists searched for rules by which the brain organizes fragments of sensory data into *gestalts*, or meaningful forms. In pointing out that the whole may exceed the sum of its parts, they noted that we filter sensory information and construct our perceptions. To recognize an object, we must first perceive it (see it as a *figure*) as distinct from its surroundings (the *ground*). We bring order and form to stimuli by organizing them into meaningful *groups*, following such rules as proximity, continuity, and closure.

19-7 How do binocular and monocular cues enable three-dimensional vision, and how does motion perception occur?

For those of us with vision, *depth perception* is the ability to see objects in three dimensions and to judge distance. The *visual cliff* and other research demonstrate that many species perceive the world in three dimensions at, or very soon after, birth. *Binocular cues*, such as *retinal disparity*, are depth cues that rely on information from both eyes. *Monocular cues* (such as relative height, relative size, relative motion, linear perspective, and interposition) let us judge depth using information transmitted by only one eye. The brain computes motion imperfectly, based partly on its assumption that shrinking objects are retreating and enlarging objects are approaching. A quick succession of images on the retina can create an illusion of movement, as in stroboscopic movement or the *phi phenomenon*.

19-8 How do perceptual constancies help us construct meaningful perceptions?

Perceptual constancies, such as in color, brightness (or lightness), shape, or size, enable us to perceive objects as stable despite the changing image they cast on our retinas. Our brain constructs our experience of an object's color or brightness through comparisons with other surrounding objects. Knowing an object's size gives us clues to its distance; knowing its distance gives clues about its size, but we sometimes misread monocular distance cues and reach the wrong conclusions, as in the Moon illusion.

19-9 What does research on restored vision, sensory restriction, and perceptual adaptation reveal about the effects of experience on perception?

Experience guides our perceptual interpretations. People blind from birth who gain sight after surgery lack the experience to visually recognize shapes and forms. Sensory restriction research indicates that there is a critical period for some aspects of sensory and perceptual development. Without early stimulation, the brain's neural organization does not develop normally. People given glasses that shift the world slightly to the left or right, or even upside down, experience *perceptual adaptation*. They are initially disoriented, but they manage to adapt to their new context.

20 HEARING, SKIN, CHEMICAL, AND BODY SENSES

20-1 What are the characteristics of the air pressure waves that we hear as sound?

Sound waves are bands of compressed and expanded air. Our ears detect these changes in air pressure and transform them into neural impulses, which the brain decodes as sound. Sound waves vary in amplitude, which we perceive as differing loudness (with sound intensity measured in decibels), and in *frequency* (measured in hertz), which we experience as differing *pitch*.

20-2 How does the ear transform sound energy into neural messages?

The *middle ear* is the chamber between the eardrum and cochlea; the *inner ear* consists of the cochlea, semicircular canals, and vestibular sacs. Sound waves traveling through the auditory canal cause tiny vibrations in the eardrum. The bones of the middle ear amplify the vibrations and relay them to the fluid-filled cochlea. Rippling of the basilar membrane, caused by pressure changes in the cochlear fluid, causes movement of the tiny hair cells, triggering neural messages to be sent (via the thalamus) to the auditory cortex in the brain. *Sensorineural hearing loss* (or nerve deafness) results from damage to the cochlea's hair cells or their associated nerves. *Conduction hearing loss* results from damage to the mechanical system that transmits sound waves to the cochlea. *Cochlear implants* can restore hearing for some people.

20-3 How do we detect loudness, discriminate pitch, and locate sounds?

Loudness is not related to the intensity of a hair cell's response, but rather to the number of activated hair cells. *Place theory* (place coding) explains how we hear high-pitched sounds, and *frequency theory* (temporal coding) extended by the volley principle explains how we hear low-pitched sounds. A combination of the two theories explains how we hear pitches in the middle range. Sound waves strike one ear sooner and more intensely than the other. To locate sounds, the brain analyzes the minute differences in the sounds received by the two ears and computes the sound's source.

20-4 What are the four basic touch sensations, and how do we sense touch?

Our sense of touch is four basic sensations—pressure, warmth, cold, and pain—that combine to produce other sensations, such as "itchy" or "wet."

20-5 What biological, psychological, and social-cultural influences affect our experience of pain? How do placebos, distraction, and hypnosis help control pain?

The biopsychosocial perspective views our perception of pain as the sum of biological, psychological, and social-cultural influences. Pain reflects bottom-up sensations and top-down processes. One theory of pain is that a *"gate"* in the spinal cord either opens to permit pain signals traveling up small nerve fibers to reach the brain, or closes to prevent their passage. Pain treatments often combine physical and psychological elements. Combining a placebo with distraction, and amplifying the effect with *hypnosis* (which increases our response to suggestions), can help relieve pain. *Posthypnotic suggestion* is used by some clinicians to control undesired symptoms and behavior.

20-6 In what ways are our senses of taste and smell similar, and how do they differ?

Taste and smell are both chemical senses. Taste (*gustation*) is a composite of five basic sensations—sweet, sour, salty, bitter, and umami—and of the aromas that interact with information from the taste receptor cells of the taste buds. There are no basic sensations for smell *(olfaction)*. From the top of each nasal cavity, some 20 million olfactory receptor cells for smell send messages to the brain's olfactory bulb and then onward to the temporal lobe's primary smell cortex and to the parts of the limbic system involved in memory and emotion.

20-7 How do we sense our body's position and movement?

Position and motion sensors in muscles, tendons, and joints called proprioceptors enable *kinesthesia*, our sense of the position and movement of our body parts. We monitor our head's (and thus our body's) position and movement, and maintain our balance, with our *vestibular sense*, which relies on the semicircular canals and vestibular sacs to sense the tilt or rotation of our head.

20-8 How does *sensory interaction* influence our perceptions, and what is *embodied cognition?*

Our senses influence one another. This *sensory interaction* occurs, for example, when the smell of a favorite food amplifies its taste. *Embodied cognition* is the influence of bodily sensations, gestures, and other states on cognitive preferences and judgments.

20-9 What are the claims of ESP, and what have most research psychologists concluded after putting these claims to the test?

Parapsychology is the study of paranormal phenomena, including *extrasensory perception (ESP)* and psychokinesis. The three most testable forms of ESP are telepathy (mind-to-mind communication), clairvoyance (perceiving remote events), and precognition (perceiving future events). To refute those who say there is no ESP, one need only produce a single person who can demonstrate a single, reproducible ESP event. Although study continues, researchers have been unable to replicate ESP phenomena under controlled conditions.

CHAPTER 7

Learning (Modules 21–23)

BASIC LEARNING CONCEPTS AND CLASSICAL CONDITIONING

21-1 How do we define *learning*, and what are some basic forms of learning?

Learning is the process of acquiring through experience new and relatively enduring information or behaviors. In *associative learning*, we learn that certain events occur together. In classical conditioning, we learn to associate two *stimuli* and thus to anticipate events. Automatically responding to stimuli we do not control is called *respondent behavior*. In operant conditioning, we learn to associate a response and its consequence. These associations produce *operant behaviors*. Through *cognitive learning*, we acquire mental information that guides our behavior. For example, in observational learning, we learn new behaviors by observing events and watching others.

21-2 What is behaviorism's view of learning?

Ivan Pavlov's work on classical conditioning laid the foundation for *behaviorism*, the view that psychology should be an objective science that studies behavior without reference to mental processes. The behaviorists believed that the basic laws of learning are the same for all species, including humans.

21-3 Who was Pavlov, and what are the basic components of classical conditioning?

Ivan Pavlov, a Russian physiologist, created novel experiments on learning. His early twentieth-century research over the last three decades of his life demonstrated that classical conditioning is a basic form of learning. *Classical conditioning* is a type of learning in which an organism comes to associate stimuli and anticipate events. A *UR* (unconditioned response) is an event that occurs naturally (such as salivation), in response to some stimulus. A *US* (unconditioned stimulus) is something that naturally and automatically (without learning) triggers the unlearned response (as food in the mouth triggers salivation).

A CS (conditioned stimulus) is originally an NS (neutral stimulus, such as a tone) that, after association with a US (such as food) comes to trigger a CR. A CR (conditioned response) is the learned response (salivating) to the originally neutral (but now conditioned) stimulus.

21-4 In classical conditioning, what are the processes of *acquisition, extinction, spontaneous recovery, generalization*, and *discrimination?*

In classical conditioning, the first stage is *acquisition*, associating an NS with the US so that the NS begins triggering the CR. Acquisition occurs most readily when the NS is presented just before (ideally, about a half-second before) a US, preparing the organism for the upcoming event. This finding supports the view that classical conditioning is biologically adaptive. *Extinction* is diminished responding, which occurs if the CS appears repeatedly by itself without the US. *Spontaneous recovery* is the reappearance of a weakened conditioned response, following a rest period. *Generalization* is the tendency to respond to stimuli that are similar to a CS. *Discrimination* is the learned ability to distinguish between a CS and other irrelevant stimuli.

21-5 Why does Pavlov's work remain so important?

Pavlov taught us that significant psychological phenomena can be studied objectively and that classical conditioning is a basic form of learning that applies to all species.

21-6 What have been some applications of Pavlov's work to human health and well-being? How did Watson apply Pavlov's principles to learned fears?

Classical conditioning techniques are used to improve human health and well-being in many areas, including behavioral therapy for some types of psychological disorders. The body's immune system may also respond to classical conditioning. Pavlov's work also provided a basis for Watson's idea that human emotions and behaviors, though biologically influenced, are mainly a bundle of conditioned responses. Watson applied classical conditioning principles in his studies of "Little Albert" to demonstrate how specific fears might be conditioned.

22 OPERANT CONDITIONING

22-1 What is *operant conditioning?*

Operant conditioning is a type of learning in which behavior becomes more likely to recur if followed by a reinforcer or less likely to recur if followed by a punisher.

22-2 Who was Skinner, and how is operant behavior reinforced and shaped?

B. F. Skinner was a college English major and aspiring writer who later entered graduate school for psychology. He became modern behaviorism's most influential and controversial figure. Expanding on Edward Thorndike's *law of effect*, Skinner and others found that the behavior of rats or pigeons placed in an *operant chamber* (Skinner box) can be *shaped* by using reinforcers to guide successive approximations of the desired behavior.

22-3 How do positive and negative reinforcement differ, and what are the basic types of reinforcers?

Reinforcement is any event that strengthens the behavior it follows. *Positive reinforcement* adds a desirable stimulus to increase the frequency of a behavior. *Negative reinforcement* reduces or removes an aversive stimulus to increase the frequency of a behavior. *Primary reinforcers* (such as receiving food when hungry or having nausea end during an illness) are innately satisfying—no learning is required. *Conditioned* (or secondary) *reinforcers* (such as money) are satisfying because we have learned to associate them with more basic rewards (such as the desirable things we buy). Immediate reinforcers (such as a food reward given right after a desired behavior) offer immediate payback; delayed reinforcers (such as a paycheck) require the ability to delay gratification.

22-4 How do different reinforcement schedules affect behavior?

A *reinforcement schedule* defines how often a response will be reinforced. In *continuous reinforcement* (reinforcing desired responses every time they occur), learning is rapid, but so is extinction if rewards cease. In *partial (intermittent) reinforcement* (reinforcing responses only sometimes), initial learning is slower, but the behavior is much more resistant to extinction. *Fixed-ratio schedules* reinforce behaviors after a set number of responses; *variable-ratio schedules*, after an unpredictable number. *Fixed-interval schedules* reinforce behaviors after set time periods; *variable-interval schedules*, after unpredictable time periods.

22-5 How does punishment differ from negative reinforcement, and how does punishment affect behavior?

Punishment aims to decrease the frequency of a behavior (such as a child's disobedience). Positive punishment administers, or adds, an undesirable consequence (such as a speeding ticket) or withdraws something desirable (such as taking away a favorite toy). Negative punishment aims to increase the frequency of a behavior (such as putting on your seat belt) by withdrawing, or subtracting, something undesirable (the annoying beeping).

This desired consequence (silencing the annoying beeping) increases the likelihood that the behavior (putting on your seat belt) will be repeated. Physical punishment can have undesirable side effects, such as suppressing rather than changing unwanted behaviors, failing to provide a direction for appropriate behavior, encouraging discrimination (so that the undesirable behavior appears when the punisher is not present), creating fear, and teaching aggression.

22-6 Why did Skinner's ideas provoke controversy, and how might his operant conditioning principles be applied?

Critics of Skinner's principles believed the approach dehumanized people by neglecting their personal freedom and seeking to control their actions. Skinner replied that people's actions are already controlled by external consequences and that reinforcement is more humane than punishment as a means for controlling behavior. Teachers can use shaping techniques to guide students' behaviors and use interactive media such as online adaptive quizzing to provide immediate feedback. (The LearningCurve adaptive quizzing system available with this text provides such feedback and allows students to direct the pace of their own learning.) Coaches can build players' skills and self-confidence by rewarding small improvements. Computer programmers and game developers can use reinforcement principles to train artificial intelligence (AI) machines that simulate human learning. Managers can boost productivity and morale by rewarding well-defined and achievable behaviors. Parents can reward desired behaviors but not undesirable ones. We can shape our own behaviors by stating realistic goals, planning how to work toward those goals, monitoring the frequency of desired behaviors, reinforcing desired behaviors, and gradually reducing rewards as behaviors become habitual.

22-7 How does operant conditioning differ from classical conditioning?

In operant conditioning, an organism learns associations between its own behavior and resulting events; this form of conditioning involves operant behavior (behavior that operates on the environment, producing rewarding or punishing consequences). In classical conditioning, the organism forms associations between stimuli—events it does not control; this form of conditioning involves respondent behavior (automatic responses to some stimulus).

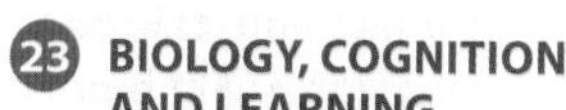

23 BIOLOGY, COGNITION, AND LEARNING

23-1 How do biological constraints affect classical and operant conditioning?

An animal's capacity for conditioning is limited by biological constraints, so some associations are easier to learn. Each species has a biological predisposition to learn associations that aid its survival—a phenomenon called *preparedness*. Those who readily learned taste aversions were unlikely to eat the same toxic food again and were more likely to survive and leave descendants. Nature constrains each species' capacity for both classical conditioning and operant conditioning. Our preparedness to associate a CS with a US that follows predictably and immediately is often (but not always) adaptive. During operant training, animals may display *instinctive drift* by reverting to biologically predisposed patterns.

23-2 How do cognitive processes affect classical and operant conditioning?

In classical conditioning, animals may learn when to expect a US and may be aware of the link between stimuli and responses. In operant conditioning, *cognitive mapping* and *latent learning* research demonstrate the importance of cognitive processes in learning.

23-3 What is *observational learning?*

Observational learning (also called *social learning*) involves learning by watching and imitating, rather than through direct experience.

23-4 How may observational learning be enabled by neural mirroring?

Our brain's frontal lobes have a demonstrated ability to mirror the activity of another's brain, which may enable imitation and observational learning. Some scientists argue that *mirror neurons* are responsible for this ability, while others attribute it to distributed brain networks.

23-5 What is the impact of prosocial modeling and of antisocial modeling?

Children tend to imitate what a model does and says, whether the behavior being *modeled* is *prosocial* (positive, constructive, and helpful) or antisocial. If a model's actions and words are inconsistent, children may imitate the hypocrisy they observe.

23-6 What is the violence-viewing effect?

Media violence can contribute to aggression. This violence-viewing effect may be prompted by imitation and desensitization. Correlation does not equal causation, but study participants have reacted more cruelly to provocations when they have viewed violence (instead of entertaining nonviolence).

CHAPTER 8

Memory (Modules 24–26)

24 STUDYING AND ENCODING MEMORIES

24-1 What is *memory*, and how is it measured?

Memory is learning that has persisted over time, through the encoding, storage, and retrieval of information. Evidence of memory may be seen in an ability to *recall* information, *recognize* it, or *relearn* it more easily on a later attempt. Psychologists can measure these different forms of memory separately.

24-2 How do memory models help us study memory, and how has later research updated the three-stage information-processing model?

Psychologists use memory models to think about and explain how our brain forms and retrieves memories. Information-processing models involve three processes: *encoding*, *storage*, and *retrieval*. Our agile brain processes many things simultaneously by means of *parallel processing*. The connectionism information-processing model focuses on this multitrack processing, viewing memories as products of interconnected neural networks. The three processing stages in the Atkinson-Shiffrin model are *sensory memory*, *short-term memory*, and *long-term memory*. This model has since been updated to include newer concepts, such as working memory (the active "scratch pad" processing that occurs at the stage when our short-term memories combine with our long-term memories) and *automatic processing* (which occurs behind the scenes to allow information to slip into long-term memory without the need to consciously attend to it).

24-3 How do explicit and implicit memories differ?

The human brain processes information on dual tracks, consciously and unconsciously. Many *explicit* (declarative) *memories*—our conscious memories of facts and experiences—form through *effortful processing*, which requires conscious effort and attention. *Implicit* (nondeclarative) *memories*—of learned skills and classically conditioned associations—happen without our awareness, through *automatic processing*.

24-4 What information do we process automatically?

In addition to skills and classically conditioned associations, we automatically process incidental information about space, time, and frequency and familiar or well-learned information, such as sounds, smells, and word meanings.

24-5 How does sensory memory work?

Sensory memory feeds some information into working memory for active processing there. An *iconic memory* is a very brief (a few tenths of a second) sensory memory of visual stimuli; an *echoic memory* is a three- or four-second sensory memory of auditory stimuli.

24-6 What is our short-term memory capacity?

Short-term memory capacity is about seven bits of information, plus or minus two, but this information disappears from memory quickly without rehearsal. Our working memory capacity for active processing varies, depending on age and other factors, but everyone does better and more efficient work by avoiding task-switching.

24-7 What are some effortful processing strategies that can help us remember new information?

Effective effortful processing strategies include *chunking*, *mnemonics*, and hierarchies. Each boosts our ability to form new memories.

24-8 How do distributed practice, deep processing, and making new material personally meaningful aid memory?

Distributed practice sessions (the *spacing effect*) produce better long-term recall. The *testing effect* is the finding that consciously retrieving, rather than simply rereading, information enhances memory. Depth of processing also affects long-term retention. In *shallow processing*, we encode words based on their structure or sound. Retention is best when we use *deep processing*, encoding words based on their meaning. We also more easily remember material when we learn and rephrase it into personally meaningful terms—the self-reference effect.

 STORING AND RETRIEVING MEMORIES

25-1 What is the capacity of long-term memory? Are our long-term memories processed and stored in specific locations?

Our long-term memory capacity is essentially unlimited. Memories are not stored intact in the brain in single spots. Many parts of the brain interact as we encode, store, and retrieve memories.

25-2 What roles do the frontal lobes and hippocampus play in memory processing?

The frontal lobes and *hippocampus* are parts of the brain network dedicated to explicit memory formation. Many brain regions send information to the frontal lobes for processing. The hippocampus, with the help of nearby brain networks, registers and temporarily holds elements of explicit memories (which are either *semantic* or *episodic*) before moving them to other brain regions for long-term storage. The neural storage of long-term memories, which is supported by sleep, is called *memory consolidation*.

25-3 What roles do the cerebellum and basal ganglia play in memory processing?

The cerebellum and basal ganglia are parts of the brain network dedicated to implicit memory formation. The cerebellum is important for storing classically conditioned memories. The basal ganglia are involved in motor movement and help form procedural memories for skills. Many reactions and skills learned during our first 4 years continue into our adult lives, although we cannot consciously remember learning these associations and skills (infantile amnesia).

25-4 How do emotions affect our memory processing?

Emotional arousal causes an outpouring of stress hormones, which leads the amygdala to boost activity in the brain's memory-forming areas. Significantly stressful events can trigger very clear *flashbulb memories*. Through rehearsal, memory of personally important experiences largely endures.

25-5 How do changes at the synapse level affect our memory processing?

Long-term potentiation (LTP) is the neural basis for learning and memory. In LTP, neurons become more efficient at releasing and sensing the presence of neurotransmitters, and more connections develop between neurons.

25-6 How do external cues, internal emotions, and order of appearance influence memory retrieval?

External cues activate associations that help us retrieve memories; this process may occur without our awareness, as it does in *priming*. The *encoding specificity principle* is the idea that cues and contexts specific to a particular memory will be most effective in helping us recall it. Returning to the same physical context or emotional state *(mood congruency)* in which we formed a memory can help us retrieve it. The *serial position effect* is our tendency to recall best the last items (which may still be in working memory) and the first items (which we've spent more time rehearsing) in a list.

 FORGETTING, MEMORY CONSTRUCTION, AND IMPROVING MEMORY

26-1 Why do we forget?

Some people experience *anterograde amnesia*, an inability to form new memories, or *retrograde amnesia*, an inability to retrieve old memories. Normal forgetting can happen because we have never encoded information (encoding failure); because the physical memory trace has decayed (storage decay); or because we cannot retrieve what we have encoded and stored (retrieval failure). Retrieval problems may result from *proactive* (forward-acting) *interference*, when prior learning interferes with recall of new information, or from *retroactive* (backward-acting) *interference*, when new learning disrupts recall of old information. Motivated forgetting occurs, but researchers have found little evidence of *repression*.

26-2 How do misinformation, imagination, and source amnesia influence our memory construction? How do we decide whether a memory is real or false?

Memories can be continually revised when retrieved, a process memory researchers call *reconsolidation. The misinformation effect* (exposure to misleading information) and imagination inflation may corrupt our stored memories of what actually happened. When we reassemble a memory during retrieval, we may attribute it to the wrong source *(source amnesia)*. Source amnesia may help explain *déjà vu*. Since memory involves reconstruction as well as reproduction, and the misinformation effect and source amnesia occur outside our awareness, it is difficult to separate false memories from real ones.

26-3 Why have reports of repressed and recovered memories been so hotly debated?

The debate focuses on whether memories of early childhood abuse are repressed and can be recovered during therapy. Unless the victim was a child too young to remember, such traumas are usually remembered vividly, not repressed. Psychologists agree that childhood sexual abuse happens; injustice happens; forgetting happens; recovered memories are common; memories of events that happened before age 4 are unreliable; memories "recovered" under hypnosis are especially unreliable; and memories, whether real or false, can be emotionally upsetting.

26-4 How reliable are young children's eyewitness descriptions?

Children's eyewitness descriptions are subject to the same memory influences that distort adult reports, and suggestive interviewing techniques can lead to false memories. But if questioned by a carefully trained interviewer who asks nonleading questions—and especially if they have not spoken to involved adults prior to the interview—children can accurately recall events and people involved in them.

26-5 How can you use memory research findings to do better in this and other courses?

Memory research findings suggest the following strategies for improving memory: Rehearse repeatedly, make the material meaningful, activate retrieval cues, use mnemonic devices, minimize proactive and retroactive interference, sleep more, and test yourself to be sure you can retrieve, as well as recognize, material.

CHAPTER 9

Thinking and Language (Modules 27–28)

 THINKING

27-1 What are *cognition* and *metacognition*, and what are the functions of concepts?

Cognition refers to all the mental activities associated with thinking, knowing, remembering, and communicating. *Metacognition* is cognition about our cognition or keeping track of and evaluating our mental processes. We use *concepts*, mental groupings of similar objects, events, ideas, or people, to simplify and order the world around us. We form most concepts around *prototypes* or best examples of a category.

27-2 What cognitive strategies assist our problem solving, and what obstacles hinder it?

An *algorithm* is a methodical, logical rule, or procedure (such as a step-by-step description for evacuating a building during a fire) that guarantees a solution to a problem. A *heuristic* is a simpler strategy—a mental shortcut (such as running for an exit if you smell smoke)—that is usually speedier than an algorithm but is also more error prone. *Insight* is not a strategy-based solution but rather a sudden flash of inspiration that solves a problem. Obstacles to problem solving include *confirmation bias*, which predisposes us to verify rather than challenge our preconceptions, and *fixation*, which may prevent us from taking the fresh perspective that would lead to a solution.

27-3 What is *intuition*, and how can the representativeness and availability heuristics influence our decisions and judgments?

Intuition is the effortless, immediate, automatic feelings, or thoughts, we often use instead of systematic reasoning. Heuristics enable snap judgments. Using the *representativeness heuristic*, we judge the likelihood of events based on how well they seem to represent particular prototypes. Using the *availability heuristic*, we judge the likelihood of things based on how readily they come to mind.

27-4 What factors exaggerate our fear of unlikely events?

We tend to be afraid of what our ancestral history has prepared us to fear, what we cannot control, what is immediate, and what is most readily available in memory. We fear too little the ongoing threats that claim lives one by one, such as traffic accidents and diseases.

27-5 How are our decisions and judgments affected by overconfidence, belief perseverance, and framing?

Overconfidence can lead us to overestimate the accuracy of our beliefs. When a belief we have formed and explained has been discredited, *belief perseverance* may cause us to cling to that belief. A remedy for belief perseverance is to consider how we might have explained an opposite result. *Framing* is the way an issue is posed. Subtle differences in presentation can dramatically alter our responses and *nudge* us toward particular decisions.

27-6 How do smart thinkers use intuition?

Smart thinkers welcome their intuitions (which are usually adaptive) but also know when to override them. When making complex decisions we may benefit from gathering as much information as possible and then taking time to let our two-track mind process it.

27-7 What is *creativity*, and what fosters it?

Creativity, the ability to produce novel and valuable ideas, is supported by a certain level of aptitude but is more than what intelligence tests reveal. Aptitude tests require *convergent thinking*, but creativity requires *divergent thinking*. Robert Sternberg has proposed that creativity involves expertise; imaginative thinking skills; a venturesome personality; intrinsic motivation; and a creative environment that sparks, supports, and refines creative ideas.

27-8 What do we know about thinking in other species?

Researchers make inferences about other species' consciousness and intelligence based on behavior and neural activity. Evidence from studies of various species shows that many other animals use concepts, numbers, and tools and that they transmit learning from one generation to the next (cultural transmission). And, like humans, some other species show insight, self-awareness, altruism, cooperation, and grief.

28 LANGUAGE AND THOUGHT

28-1 What are the structural components of a language?

Phonemes are a *language's* basic units of sound. *Morphemes* are the elementary units of meaning. *Grammar—the* system of rules that enables us to communicate—includes semantics (rules for deriving meaning from sounds) and *syntax* (rules for ordering words into sentences).

28-2 How do we acquire language, and what did Chomsky mean by *universal grammar?*

As our biology and experience interact, we readily learn the specific grammar and vocabulary of the language we experience as children. Linguist Noam Chomsky has proposed that humans are born with a built-in predisposition to learn grammar rules, which he called universal grammar. Human languages do share some commonalities, but other researchers note that children learn grammar as they discern language patterns.

28-3 What are the milestones in language development, and when is the critical period for acquiring language?

Language development's timing varies, but all children follow the same sequence. Receptive language (the ability to understand what is said to or about you) develops before productive language (the ability to produce words). At about 4 months of age, infants *babble*, making sounds found in languages from all over the world, which by about 10 months includes only the sounds found in their household language. Around 12 months of age, children begin to speak in single words. This *one-word stage* evolves into *two-word* and other short, *telegraphic* utterances before their second birthday, after which they begin speaking in full sentences. Childhood is a critical period for learning language. Children who get a late start on language learning follow the usual developmental sequence, though at a faster pace. But children not exposed to either a spoken or a signed language until age 7 will never be able to fully comprehend or use any language. The importance of early language experiences is often evident in deaf children born to hearing-nonsigning parents.

28-4 What brain areas are involved in language processing and speech?

Aphasia is an impairment of language, usually caused by left-hemisphere damage. Two important language- and speech-processing areas are *Broca's area*, a region of the left frontal lobe that controls language expression, and *Wernicke's area*, a region in the left temporal lobe that controls language reception. Language processing is spread across other brain areas as well, with different neural networks handling specific linguistic subtasks.

28-5 What is the relationship between thinking and language, and what is the value of thinking in images?

Although Benjamin Lee Whorf's *linguistic determinism* hypothesis suggested that language determines thought, it is more accurate to say that language influences thought *(linguistic relativism)*. Different languages embody different ways of thinking, and bilingualism can enhance thinking. We often think in images when we use implicit (nondeclarative, procedural) memory. Thinking in images can increase our skills when we mentally practice an activity. Process simulation (focusing on the steps needed to reach a goal) is effective, but outcome simulation (fantasizing about having achieved the goal) does little.

28-6 What do we know about other species' capacity for language?

Chimpanzees and bonobos have learned to communicate with humans by signing or by pushing buttons. Some have developed vocabularies of nearly 400 words, communicated by stringing these words together, and have demonstrated some understanding of syntax. While only humans communicate in complex sentences, other animals' impressive abilities to think and communicate challenge humans to consider what this means about the moral rights of other species.

CHAPTER 10

Intelligence (Modules 29–31)

 WHAT IS INTELLIGENCE?

29-1 How do psychologists define *intelligence?*

Intelligence is the ability to learn from experience, solve problems, and use knowledge to adapt to new situations.

29-2 What are the arguments for *g?*

Charles Spearman proposed that we have one *general intelligence (g)* underlying all other specific mental abilities. Through his work with factor analysis, a statistical procedure that identifies clusters of related variables, he noted that those who score high in one area typically score higher than average in other areas.

29-3 How have the concepts of *fluid intelligence* and *crystallized intelligence*, and the *CHC theory*, affected our understanding of intelligence?

Raymond Cattell and John Horn formulated a theory of general ability based on two factors: *fluid intelligence (Gf)* and *crystallized intelligence (Gc)*. The *Cattell-Horn-Carroll (CHC) theory* affirms a general intellectual ability factor, but also identifies more specific abilities (such as reading and writing ability, memory capacity, and processing speed).

29-4 How do Gardner's and Sternberg's theories of multiple intelligences differ, and what criticisms have they faced?

Howard Gardner proposed eight relatively independent intelligences (linguistic, logical-mathematical, musical, spatial, bodily kinesthetic, intrapersonal, interpersonal, and naturalist), as well as a possible ninth (existential intelligence). The different intelligences of people with *savant syndrome* and certain kinds of brain damage seem to support this view. Robert Sternberg's triarchic theory proposes three intelligence areas that contribute to life success: analytical (academic problem solving), creative (innovative smarts), and practical (required for everyday tasks). Critics note that research has confirmed a general intelligence factor, which widely predicts performance. Highly successful people also tend to be conscientious and doggedly energetic; their achievements arise from both ability *and* deliberate practice.

29-5 What are the four components of emotional intelligence?

Emotional intelligence, which is an aspect of social intelligence, includes the abilities to perceive, understand, manage, and use emotions. Emotionally intelligent people tend to be happy, healthy, and more successful personally and professionally.

30 INTELLIGENCE ASSESSMENT AND DYNAMICS

30-1 What is an *intelligence test*, and how do *achievement tests* and *aptitude tests* differ?

An *intelligence test* assesses a person's mental aptitudes and compares them with those of others, using numerical scores. *Aptitude tests* measure the ability to learn, while *achievement tests* measure what has already been learned.

30-2 When and why were intelligence tests created, and how do today's tests differ from early intelligence tests?

Francis Galton, who was fascinated with measuring what he believed to be hereditary genius (so that those with exceptional abilities might be encouraged to reproduce), attempted but failed to construct a simple intelligence test in the late 1800s. Alfred Binet, who tended toward an environmental explanation of intelligence differences, started the modern intelligence-testing movement in France in the early 1900s, when he developed questions to help predict children's future progress in the Paris school system. Binet hoped his test, which measured children's *mental age*, would improve children's education; but he feared it might also be used to label children. During the early twentieth century, Lewis Terman of Stanford University revised Binet's work for use in the United States. Terman thought his *Stanford-Binet* could help guide people toward appropriate opportunities, but his belief that intelligence was fixed at birth and differed among ethnic groups realized Binet's fear that intelligence tests would be used to limit children's opportunities. William Stern contributed the concept of the *IQ (intelligence quotient)*. The most widely used intelligence tests today are the *Wechsler Adult Intelligence Scale*

(WAIS) and Wechsler's tests for children. These tests differ from their predecessors by offering an overall intelligence score as well as scores for verbal comprehension, perceptual reasoning, working memory, and processing speed.

30-3 What is a *normal curve*, and what does it mean to say that a test has been *standardized* and is *reliable* and *valid?*

The distribution of test scores often forms a *normal* (bell-shaped) *curve* around the central average score, with fewer and fewer scores at the extremes. *Standardization* establishes a basis for meaningful score comparisons by giving a test to a representative sample of future test-takers. *Reliability* is the extent to which a test yields consistent results (on two halves of the test, on alternative forms of the test, or on retesting). *Validity* is the extent to which a test measures or predicts what it is supposed to. A test has *predictive validity* if it predicts a behavior it was designed to predict. (Aptitude tests have predictive validity if they can predict future achievements; their predictive power is best for the early school years.)

30-4 What are the traits of those at the low and high intelligence extremes?

People who score at the two extremes of the normal curve differ noticeably in intelligence test performance. An intelligence test score of or below 70 is one diagnostic factor in the diagnosis of intellectual developmental disorder; limited conceptual, social, and practical skills are other factors. People at the high intelligence extreme—such as those with IQ scores of over 135 whom Terman studied—tend to be healthy and well adjusted, as well as unusually successful academically. "Gifted" and "remedial" programs may create self-fulfilling prophecies, but can be effective when students are appropriately placed.

30-5 What are *cross-sectional studies* and *longitudinal studies*, and why is it important to know which method was used?

Cross-sectional studies, which study people of different ages at the same point in time, compare people of different eras and life circumstances. This can provide an excellent snapshot of a particular moment, but *longitudinal studies—which* follow and retest the same people over time—are superior for tracing the evolution of traits over a longer period. When studying intelligence, psychologists using the cross-sectional method concluded that mental ability declines with age, but those using the longitudinal method learned that it remains stable (or even increases).

30-6 How stable are intelligence test scores over the life span?

The stability of intelligence test scores increases with age. At age 4, scores begin to predict adolescent and adult scores. By age 11, scores are very stable and predictive.

30-7 How does aging affect crystallized intelligence *(Gc)* and fluid intelligence *(Gf)?*

The answers to age-and-intelligence questions depend on what we assess and how we assess it. Fluid intelligence *(Gf)* declines in older adults, who lose recall memory and processing speed; but accumulated knowledge, reflected in crystallized intelligence *(Gc)*, tends to increase with age.

31 GENETIC AND ENVIRONMENTAL INFLUENCES ON INTELLIGENCE

31-1 What is *heritability*, and what do twin and adoption studies tell us about the nature and nurture of intelligence?

Heritability is the proportion of variation among individuals in a group that can be attributed to genes. Studies of twins, family members, and adoptive parents and siblings indicate a significant hereditary contribution to intelligence scores. Intelligence is polygenic.

31-2 How can environmental influences affect cognitive development?

Studies of children raised in impoverished environments with minimal social interaction indicate that life experiences significantly influence cognitive development. No evidence supports the idea that typical, healthy children can be molded into geniuses by growing up in an exceptionally enriched environment. Environments that foster a *growth mindset* do not alter intelligence, but can positively impact achievement.

31-3 How and why do the genders differ in mental ability scores?

Girls and boys have the same average intelligence test scores, but they tend to differ in some specific abilities. Girls, on average, are better spellers, more verbally fluent, better at reading and at locating objects, better at detecting emotions, and more sensitive to touch, taste, and color. Boys outperform girls at spatial ability and complex mathematics, though boys and girls hardly differ in math computation and overall math performance. Boys also outnumber girls at both the low and high extremes of mental abilities. Evolutionary and cultural explanations have been proposed for these gender differences.

31-4 How and why do racial and ethnic groups differ in mental ability scores?

Racial and ethnic groups differ in their average intelligence test scores. Evidence suggests that environmental differences are responsible for these group differences.

31-5 Are intelligence tests biased or unfair? What is *stereotype threat*, and how does it affect test-takers' performance?

The scientific meaning of bias hinges on a test's ability to predict future behavior for all test-takers, not just for some. In this sense, most experts consider the major U.S. aptitude tests unbiased. However, if we consider bias to mean that a test may be influenced by the test-taker's education and cultural experiences, then intelligence tests, by that definition, may be considered unfair. *Stereotype threat*, a self-confirming concern that we will be evaluated based on a negative stereotype, affects performance on all kinds of tests. Some research findings suggest effective strategies for reducing stereotype threat.

CHAPTER 11

What Drives Us: Hunger, Sex, Belongingness, and Achievement (Modules 32–35)

32 BASIC MOTIVATIONAL CONCEPTS

32-1 How do psychologists define *motivation?* What are four key motivation theories?

Motivation is a need or desire that energizes and directs behavior. The *instinct/* evolutionary perspective explores genetic influences on complex behaviors. *Drive-reduction theory* explores how *physiological needs* create aroused, motivated states (drives) that direct us to satisfy those needs. Environmental *incentives* can intensify drives. Drive-reduction's goal is *homeostasis*, maintaining a steady internal state. Arousal theory proposes that some behaviors (such as those driven by curiosity) do not reduce physiological needs but rather are prompted by a search for an optimal level of arousal. The *Yerkes-Dodson law* describes the relationship between arousal and performance. Abraham Maslow's *hierarchy of needs* proposes a pyramid of human needs, from basic needs up to higher-level needs.

33 HUNGER

33-1 What physiological factors produce hunger?

Hunger pangs correspond to stomach contractions, but hunger also has other causes. Neural areas in the brain, some within the hippocampus and hypothalamus, monitor blood chemistry (including level of *glucose*) and incoming information about the body's state. Appetite hormones include ghrelin (secreted by an empty stomach), orexin (secreted by the hypothalamus), leptin (secreted by fat cells), and PYY (secreted by the digestive tract). *Basal metabolic rate* is the body's resting rate of energy expenditure. The body may have a *set point* (a biologically fixed tendency to maintain a given weight) or a looser settling point (also influenced by the environment).

33-2 What cultural and situational factors influence hunger?

Hunger reflects our memory of when we last ate and our expectation of when we should eat again. Humans as a species prefer certain tastes (such as sweet and salty), but our individual preferences are also influenced by conditioning, culture, and situation. Some taste preferences have survival value. Situational influences include the presence of others, serving size, the variety of foods offered, and the way food is presented.

33-3 How does obesity affect physical and psychological health? What factors are involved in weight management?

Obesity, defined by a body mass index (BMI) of 30 or above, is associated with increased depression (especially among women) and bullying, and with many physical health risks. Genes and environment interact to produce obesity. Storing fat was adaptive to our ancestors, and fat requires less food intake to maintain than it did to gain. Set point and metabolism matter. Twin and adoption studies indicate that body weight is also genetically influenced. Environmental influences include sleep loss, social influence, and food and activity levels. Those seeking healthier eating habits are advised to adopt a healthy attitude; exercise and get enough sleep; minimize exposure to unhealthy food cues; limit variety and eat healthy foods; reduce and relabel portions; time your intake to avoid nighttime eating and eat heavier meals earlier in the day; monitor your moods; eat unhurriedly; plan ahead before eating with others; allow for an occasional treat; chart and share your progress; and connect to a support group.

34 SEXUAL MOTIVATION

34-1 How do hormones influence human sexual motivation?

Our *sexuality* consists of feelings and behaviors that reflect both physiological and psychological influences. For all but those of us who are *asexual*, dating and mating often become a high priority from puberty on. The primary female sex hormones (the estrogens, such as estradiol) and male sex hormone (testosterone) influence human sexual behavior less directly than they influence sexual behavior in other species. More than other female mammals, however, women's sexuality is responsive to their testosterone level. Testosterone level also varies in men, partly in response to stimulation.

34-2 What is the human *sexual response cycle*, and how do sexual dysfunctions and paraphilias differ?

William Masters and Virginia Johnson described four stages in the human *sexual response cycle:* excitement, plateau, orgasm, and resolution. During resolution there is a *refractory period* (briefer for women) in which renewed arousal and orgasm are impossible. *Sexual dysfunctions* are problems that consistently impair sexual arousal or functioning. They include *erectile disorder* and *female orgasmic disorder*, and can often be successfully treated by behaviorally oriented therapy or drug therapy. *Paraphilias* are considered disordered if a person experiences distress from an unusual sexual interest or if it entails harm or risk of harm.

34-3 How can sexually transmitted infections be prevented?

Safe-sex practices help prevent sexually transmitted infections (STIs). Condoms are especially effective in preventing transmission of HIV, the virus that causes *AIDS*. Knowing one's STI status, and telling one's sexual partner, is an important first step in STI prevention.

34-4 How do external and imagined stimuli contribute to sexual arousal?

External stimuli can trigger sexual arousal. Sexually explicit material may diminish relationship satisfaction, and extensive online pornography exposure may warp expectations and desensitize young adults to normal sexuality. Viewing sexually coercive material can lead to increased acceptance of violence toward women. Imagined stimuli (dreams and fantasies) also influence sexual arousal.

34-5 What factors influence teenagers' sexual behaviors and use of contraceptives?

Teen sexuality varies from culture to culture and era to era. Factors contributing to these variations include communication about sex and contraception, impulsivity, alcohol use, and mass media. High intelligence, religious engagement, father presence, comprehensive sex education, and service-learning participation predict teen sexual restraint.

34-6 What do we know about sexual orientation?

Sexual orientation is the direction of our sexual attraction, as reflected in our longings and fantasies. We may have sexual attraction that is female-male (heterosexual orientation), to our own sex (same-sex orientation), to males and females (bisexual orientation), or to no one at all (asexual orientation). Attitudes toward same-sex attractions vary across cultures and over time. Regardless of whether a culture condemns or accepts same-sex unions, heterosexuality is most common, but same-sex attraction and other variations exist. The number of people who self-report as gay or bisexual has increased with increased social acceptance. Scientists have been unable to find specific environmental influences that contribute to sexual orientation. Evidence for biological influences includes same-sex attraction in other species, gay-straight trait and brain differences, genetic influences, and prenatal influences.

34-7 What role do social factors play in our sexuality?

Scientific research on sexual motivation does not attempt to define the personal meaning of sex in our lives, which is influenced by many social factors. Sex is a socially significant act. Sexual desire motivates people to form intimate, committed relationships, which in turn enable satisfying sex; sexual desire and love feed each other. Sex at its human best is life uniting and love renewing.

 AFFILIATION AND ACHIEVEMENT

35-1 What evidence points to our human affiliation need—our need to belong?

Our *affiliation need*—to feel connected and identified with others—had survival value for our ancestors, which may explain why humans in every society live in groups. According *to self-determination theory*, we strive to satisfy our needs for competence, autonomy, and relatedness. Social bonds help us to be healthier and happier, and feeling loved activates brain regions associated with reward and safety systems. *Ostracism* is the deliberate social exclusion of individuals or groups. Social isolation can put us at risk mentally and physically.

35-2 How does social networking influence us?

We connect with others through social networking, strengthening our relationships, meeting new friends or romantic partners, and finding support at difficult times. But increased online time displaces other activities, and social media leads people to compare their lives with others. Researchers are investigating possible connections between increasing screen time and a rise in teen mental health problems. When networking, people tend toward increased self-disclosure. People with high *narcissism* are especially active on social networking sites. Working out strategies for self-control and disciplined usage can help people maintain a healthy balance between their real-world and online time.

35-3 What is *achievement motivation*, and what are some ways to encourage achievement?

Achievement motivation is a desire for significant accomplishment, for mastery of skills or ideas, for control, and for attaining a high standard. High achievement motivation leads to greater success, especially when combined with determined, persistent *grit*. Research shows that excessive rewards (driving *extrinsic motivation*) can undermine *intrinsic motivation*. To achieve our own goals, we can make a resolution; announce the goal; develop an implementation plan; create short-term rewards; monitor and record progress; create a supportive environment; and transform the behavior into a habit.

CHAPTER 12

Emotions, Stress, and Health (Modules 36–40)

 INTRODUCTION TO EMOTION

36-1 How do arousal, expressive behavior, and cognition interact in emotion?

Emotions are responses of the whole organism, involving bodily arousal, expressive behaviors, and conscious experience resulting from one's interpretations. Theories of emotion generally address two major questions: (1) Does physiological arousal come before or after emotional feelings? And (2) How do feeling and cognition interact? The *James-Lange theory* maintains that emotion occurs when we become aware of our body's response to emotion-inducing stimuli (we observe our heart pounding and feel fear). The *Cannon-Bard theory* proposes that our physiological response to an emotion-inducing stimulus occurs at the same time as our subjective experience of the emotion (one does not cause the other).

36-2 To experience emotions, must we consciously interpret and label them?

The Schachter-Singer *two-factor theory* holds that our emotions have two ingredients: physical arousal and a cognitive label. The cognitive labels we put on our states of arousal are an essential ingredient of emotion. But Zajonc and LeDoux have contended that some simple emotional responses occur instantly, not only outside our conscious awareness, but before any cognitive processing occurs. This interplay between emotion and cognition illustrates our two-track mind. Lazarus agreed that some emotional responses do not require conscious thinking, but he asserted that appraisals can occur outside of conscious awareness and give rise to emotions.

36-3 What is the link between emotional arousal and the autonomic nervous system?

The arousal component of emotion is regulated by the autonomic nervous system's sympathetic (arousing) and parasympathetic (calming) divisions. In a crisis, the fight-or-flight response automatically mobilizes your body for action.

36-4 How do emotions activate different physiological and brain-pattern responses?

The large-scale body changes that accompany fear, anger, and sexual arousal are very similar (increased perspiration, breathing, and heart rate), though they feel different. Emotions may be similarly arousing, but some subtle physiological responses (such as facial muscle movements) distinguish them. More meaningful differences have been found in activity in some brain pathways and cortical areas.

36-5 How effective are polygraphs in using body states to detect lies?

Polygraphs (machines used in attempts to detect lies) measure several emotion-linked physiological changes, but are not accurate enough to justify widespread use in business and law enforcement. Using the Concealed Information Test may produce better indications of lying.

 EXPRESSING EMOTION

37-1 How do we communicate emotions nonverbally?

Much of our communication is through body movements, facial expressions, and vocal tones. Even seconds-long filmed slices of behavior can reveal feelings.

37-2 How do men and women differ in nonverbal communication?

Women tend to read emotional cues more easily and to be more empathic. They also show greater emotional responsiveness and expressiveness, especially for positive emotions.

37-3 How are gestures and facial expressions understood within and across cultures?

The meaning of gestures and some facial expressions varies by culture, but happy facial expressions are similarly understood all over the world. Context and culture can influence the interpretation of facial expressions; cultural display rules also influence when we express emotions, which emotions we express, and the amount of emotion expressed.

37-4 How do our external facial expressions influence our internal feelings?

Research on the *facial feedback effect* shows that our facial expressions can trigger emotional feelings and signal our body to respond accordingly. We also mimic others' expressions, which helps us empathize. A similar *behavior feedback effect* is the tendency of behavior to influence our own and others' thoughts, feelings, and actions.

38 EXPERIENCING EMOTION

38-1 What are some of the basic emotions?

Most emotion scientists agree that anger, fear, disgust, sadness, and happiness are basic human emotions. Carroll Izard's 10 basic emotions are joy, interest-excitement, surprise, sadness, anger, disgust, contempt, fear, shame, and guilt. Other researchers have identified as many as 28 emotions. Emotions are categorized along two dimensions: valence (positive versus negative) and arousal (low versus high).

38-2 What are the causes and consequences of anger?

Facing a threat or a challenge may trigger anger, and chronic hostility is linked to heart disease. Our culture can influence how we express anger. Emotional venting may be temporarily calming, but it does not reduce anger; expressing anger can make us angrier. Experts suggest reducing the level of physiological arousal of anger by waiting, finding a healthy distraction or support, and trying to move away from the situation mentally. Controlled assertions of feelings may resolve conflicts, and expressing grievances in ways that promote reconciliation can benefit a relationship.

38-3 What is happiness? Why does happiness matter?

Happiness means we have more positive feelings than negative feelings. Happy people tend to be healthy, energized, and have higher levels of *subjective well-being* (satisfaction with life). They also are more willing to help others (the *feel-good, do-good phenomenon*).

38-4 How do time, wealth, adaptation, and comparison affect our happiness levels?

With time, our positive and negative emotions tend to balance out—even over the course of the day. Even significantly bad events are usually not permanently depressing. Having enough money to assure comfort, security, and a sense of control predicts happiness; having more than enough does not increase it. Economic growth in many countries has produced rising inequality, which predicts unhappiness; in countries and states with greater inequality, people with lower incomes experience more ill health, social problems, and mental disorders. Happiness is relative to our own experiences (the *adaptation-level phenomenon*) and to others' success (the *relative deprivation principle*).

38-5 What predicts happiness, and how can we be happier?

Some people, because of their genetic predispositions and personal histories, are happier than others. Cultures, which vary in the traits they value and the behaviors they expect and reward, also influence personal levels of happiness. Tips for increasing happiness levels: Take charge of your schedule, label your feelings, seek meaningful work and leisure, buy shared experiences rather than things, exercise, sleep enough, foster friendships, find meaning beyond the self, challenge negative thinking, take time to express and record your gratitude, nurture your spirituality, and take an "awe walk."

39 STRESS AND ILLNESS

39-1 How does our appraisal of an event affect our stress reaction, and what are the three main types of stressors?

Stress is the process by which we perceive and respond to stressors that we appraise as challenging or threatening. If we appraise an event as challenging, we will be aroused and focused in preparation for success; if we appraise it as a threat, we will experience a stress reaction, and our health may suffer. The three main types of stressors are catastrophes; significant life changes; and daily hassles, which include social stress. Daily hassles and social stress may include inequality and prejudice, chronic workplace stress (which may lead to worker "burnout"), and the conflicts we face between our different *approach and avoidance motives*.

39-2 How do we respond and adapt to stress?

Walter Cannon viewed the stress response as a fight-or-flight system. Hans Selye proposed a general three-phase (alarm, resistance, exhaustion) *general adaptation syndrome* (GAS). People may react to stress by withdrawing. Others, especially women, may have a *tend-and-befriend* response.

39-3 How does stress make us more vulnerable to disease?

Psychoneuroimmunology is the study of how psychological, neural, and endocrine processes together affect our immune system and resulting health. Along with other factors such as age, nutrition, and genetics, stress can prompt the immune system either to overreact (causing an allergic reaction or autoimmune disease) or underreact (allowing an infection to flare or cancer cells to multiply). Stress diverts energy from the immune system, inhibiting the activities of its B and T lymphocytes, macrophages, and NK cells. Stress does not cause illness, but by altering our immune functioning it may make us more vulnerable to diseases and influence their progression.

39-4 Why are some of us more prone than others to coronary heart disease?

Coronary heart disease has been linked with the reactive, anger-prone *Type A* personality. Compared with relaxed, easygoing *Type B* personalities, Type A people's more active sympathetic nervous system may divert blood flow from the liver to the muscles, leaving excess cholesterol and fat circulating in the bloodstream for eventual deposit around the heart. Chronic stress also contributes to persistent inflammation, which is associated with heart and other health problems, including depression.

39-5 So, does stress *cause* illness?

Stress may not directly cause illness, but it does make us more vulnerable, by influencing our physiology and our behaviors.

40 HEALTH AND COPING

40-1 In what two ways do people try to alleviate stress?

We use *problem-focused coping* to change the stressor or the way we interact with it. We use *emotion-focused coping* to avoid or ignore stressors and attend to emotional needs related to stress reactions.

40-2 How does a perceived lack of control affect health?

A perceived lack of *personal control* provokes a rise in stress hormones and blood pressure and a lowered immune response, which puts people's health at risk. Being unable to avoid repeated aversive events can lead to *learned helplessness.* Poverty entails less control, which helps explain the link between economic status and longevity. People who perceive an *internal locus of control* achieve more, enjoy better health, and are happier than those who perceive an *external locus of control.* Belief in free will is linked to more helpful behavior, better learning, and superior persistence, performance, and satisfaction at work.

40-3 Why is self-control important, and can our self-control be depleted?

Self-control requires attention and energy, but predicts good health, higher income, and better school performance; it does better than an intelligence test score in predicting future academic and life success. Self-control tends to weaken after use, recover after rest, and grow stronger when exercised. Researchers disagree about whether self-control can be depleted, but strengthening self-control can lead to a healthier, happier, and more successful life.

40-4 How does an optimistic outlook affect health and longevity?

Studies of people with an optimistic outlook show that they are more likely than pessimists to have optimal health, to be successful, and to have a longer life expectancy.

40-5 How does controlling our feelings affect our well-being and health?

Emotion regulation refers to how we manage our emotions, including which emotions we allow ourselves to feel, when we feel them, and how we express those emotions. Strategies for emotion regulation include: changing the situation (situation selection); changing how you think about a situation (cognitive reappraisal); and hiding or dampening your emotional expression (suppression).

40-6 How does social support promote good health?

Social support promotes health by calming us, improving our sleep, and reducing blood pressure, and it fosters stronger immune functioning. We can significantly reduce our stress and increase our health by building and maintaining relationships, and by confiding rather than suppressing painful feelings.

40-7 How effective is aerobic exercise as a way to manage stress and improve well-being?

Aerobic exercise helps fight heart disease, predicts longevity, and, in later life, is associated with better cognitive functioning. It boosts mood by promoting muscle relaxation and sounder sleep, triggering the production of neurotransmitters, fostering neurogenesis, and enhancing self-image. It increases arousal and can reduce or prevent depression and anxiety.

40-8 In what ways might relaxation and meditation influence stress and health?

Relaxation and meditation have been shown to lower stress, improve immune functioning, and lessen anxiety and depression. *Mindfulness meditation* is a reflective practice of attending to current experiences in a nonjudgmental and accepting manner. Massage also promotes relaxation and reduces depression.

40-9 What is the *faith factor,* and what are some possible explanations for the link between faith and health?

The faith factor is the finding that religiously active people tend to live longer than those who are not religiously active do. Possible explanations may include intervening variables such as the healthy behaviors, social support, or positive emotions often found among people who regularly attend religious services.

CHAPTER 13

Social Psychology (Modules 41–44)

41 SOCIAL THINKING

41-1 What do social psychologists study? How do we tend to explain others' behavior and our own?

Social psychologists use scientific methods to study how people think about, influence, and relate to one another. They study the social influences that explain why the same person will act differently in different situations. When explaining others' behavior, we may—especially if we come from an individualist Western culture—commit the *fundamental attribution error,* by underestimating the influence of the situation and overestimating the effects of stable, enduring traits. When explaining our own behavior, we more readily attribute it to the influence of the situation.

41-2 How do attitudes and actions interact?

Our *attitudes* and our actions influence one another. When other influences are minimal, attitudes that are stable, specific, and easily recalled can affect our actions. Actions can modify attitudes, as in the *foot-in-the-door phenomenon* and *role* playing. When our attitudes don't fit with our actions, *cognitive dissonance theory* suggests that we will reduce tension by changing our attitudes to match our actions.

41-3 How do *peripheral route persuasion* and *central route persuasion* differ?

Peripheral route persuasion uses attention-getting cues (such as celebrity endorsement) to trigger fast but relatively thoughtless judgments. *Central route persuasion* offers evidence and arguments to trigger thoughtful responses.

41-4 How can we share our views more effectively?

To persuade people with views that differ from your own, avoid yelling at, humiliating, or boring them with complicated or forgettable information. Instead, identify shared goals and relate your aim to their motives. It also helps to make your message vivid, to repeat it, and to engage others in restating it.

42 SOCIAL INFLUENCE

42-1 How is social contagion a form of conformity, and how do conformity experiments reveal the power of social influence?

Social contagion (the chameleon effect)—our tendency to unconsciously imitate others' behavior, expressions, postures, voice tones, and moods—is a form of *conformity.* Social networks serve as contagious pathways for moods, both good and bad. Solomon Asch and others found that we are most likely to adjust our behavior or thinking to coincide with a group standard when we feel incompetent or insecure, our group has at least three people, everyone else agrees, we admire the group's status and attractiveness, we have not already committed to another response, we know we are being observed, and our culture encourages respect for social standards. We may conform to gain approval (*normative social influence*) or because we are willing to accept others' opinions as new information (*informational social influence*).

42-2 What did Milgram's obedience experiments teach us about the power of social influence?

Stanley Milgram's experiments—in which people obeyed orders even when they thought they were harming another person—demonstrated that strong social influences can make ordinary people conform to falsehoods or capitulate to cruelty. Obedience was highest when the person giving orders was nearby and was perceived as a legitimate authority figure, the research was supported by a prestigious institution, the victim was depersonalized or at a distance, and there were no role models for defiance.

42-3 What do the social influence studies teach us about ourselves? How much power do we have as individuals?

These experiments have demonstrated that strong social influences can influence behavior. The power of the individual (personal control) and the power of the situation (social control) interact. Minority influence can also be powerful: A small minority that consistently expresses its views may sway the majority, as may even a single committed individual.

42-4 How does the presence of others influence our actions, via social facilitation, social loafing, and deindividuation?

In *social facilitation*, the mere presence of others arouses us, improving our performance on easy or well-learned tasks but decreasing it on difficult ones. In *social loafing*, group work makes us feel less responsible, and we may free ride on others' efforts. When the presence of others both arouses us and makes us feel anonymous, we may experience *deindividuation*—loss of self-awareness and self-restraint.

42-5 How can group interaction enable group polarization?

In *group polarization*, group discussions with like-minded others strengthen members' prevailing beliefs and attitudes.

42-6 What role does the internet play in group polarization?

Internet communication magnifies the effect of connecting like-minded people, for better and for worse. People find support, which strengthens their ideas, but also often isolation from those with different opinions. Separation plus conversation may thus lead to group polarization.

42-7 How can group interaction enable groupthink?

Groupthink is driven by a desire for harmony within a decision-making group, overriding realistic appraisal of alternatives. Group leaders can harness the benefits of group interaction by assigning people to identify possible problems, and by welcoming various opinions and expert critique. Small but diverse groups, with varied backgrounds and perspectives, can enable superior outcomes.

43 ANTISOCIAL RELATIONS

43-1 What is *prejudice?* How do explicit and implicit prejudice differ?

Prejudice is an unjustifiable, usually negative attitude toward a group and its members. Prejudice's three components are beliefs (often *stereotypes*), emotions, and predispositions to action (*discrimination*). Prejudice may be explicit (overt), or it may be implicit—an unthinking knee-jerk response operating below conscious awareness. Implicit prejudice can cause discrimination even when people do not consciously intend to discriminate.

43-2 What groups tend to experience prejudice?

Prejudice involves explicit and implicit negative attitudes toward people of a particular racial or ethnic group, gender, or sexual orientation. In the United States, frequently targeted groups include Black Americans, women, and LGBTQ people.

43-3 What are some social, emotional, and cognitive roots of prejudice, and what are some ways to reduce prejudice?

The social roots of prejudice include social inequalities and divisions. Higher-status groups often justify their privileged position with the *just-world phenomenon*. We tend to favor our own group (*ingroup bias*) as we divide ourselves into "us" (the *ingroup*) and "them" (the *outgroup*). Prejudice can also be a tool for protecting our emotional well-being, as when we focus our anger by blaming events on a *scapegoat*. The cognitive roots of prejudice grow from our natural ways of processing information: forming categories, remembering vivid cases, and believing that the world is just (and that our own and our group's ways of doing things are the right ways). Monitoring our feelings and actions, as well as developing new friendships, can help us free ourselves from prejudice.

43-4 How does psychology's definition of *aggression* differ from everyday usage? What biological factors make us more prone to hurt one another?

In psychology's more specific meaning, *aggression* is any physical or verbal behavior intended to harm someone physically or emotionally. Biology influences our threshold for aggressive behaviors at three levels: genetic (inherited traits), neural (activity in key brain areas), and biochemical (such as alcohol or excess testosterone in the bloodstream). Aggression is a complex behavior resulting from the interaction of biology and experience.

43-5 What psychological and social-cultural factors may trigger aggressive behavior?

Frustration (the *frustration-aggression principle*), previous reinforcement for aggressive behavior, and observing aggressive role models all contribute to aggression. Media violence provides *social scripts* that children learn to follow. Viewing sexual violence contributes to greater aggression toward women. Playing violent video games can increase aggressive thoughts, emotions, and behaviors.

44 PROSOCIAL RELATIONS

44-1 Why do we befriend or fall in love with some people but not others?

Proximity (geographical nearness) increases liking, in part because of the *mere exposure effect*—exposure to novel stimuli increases liking of those stimuli. Physical attractiveness increases social opportunities and improves the way we are perceived. Similarity of attitudes and interests greatly increases liking, especially as relationships develop. We also like those who like us.

44-2 How does romantic love typically change as time passes?

Intimate love relationships start with *passionate love*—an intensely aroused state. Over time, the strong affection of *companionate love* may develop, especially if enhanced by an *equitable* relationship, intimate *self-disclosure*, and positive support.

44-3 What is *altruism?* When are people most—and least—likely to help?

Altruism is unselfish regard for the well-being of others. We are most likely to help when we notice an incident, interpret it as an emergency, and assume responsibility for helping. Other factors, including our mood and our similarity to the victim, also affect our willingness to help. We are least likely to help if other bystanders are present (the *bystander effect*).

44-4 How do social exchange theory and social norms explain helping behavior?

Social exchange theory is the view that we help others because it is in our own self-interest; in this view, the goal of social behavior is maximizing personal benefits and minimizing costs. Others believe that helping results from socialization, in which we are taught guidelines for expected behaviors in social situations, such as the *reciprocity norm* and the *social-responsibility norm*.

44-5 How do social traps and mirror-image perceptions fuel social conflict?

Social traps are situations in which people in *conflict* pursue their own individual self-interest, harming the collective well-being. Individuals and cultures in conflict also tend to form *mirror-image perceptions:* Each party views itself as an ethical, peaceful victim, and the opponent as untrustworthy and evil-intentioned. Perceptions can become *self-fulfilling prophecies*.

44-6 What can we do to promote peace?

Peace can result when individuals or groups work together to achieve *superordinate* (shared) *goals*. Research indicates that contact, cooperation, communication, and conciliation—such as the Graduated and Reciprocated Initiatives in Tension-Reduction (*GRIT*) strategy—help promote peace.

CHAPTER 14

Personality (Modules 45–47)

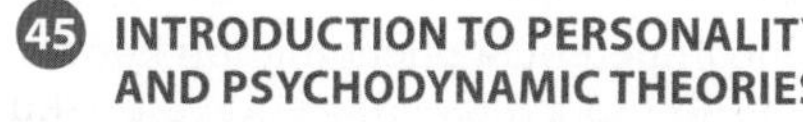

INTRODUCTION TO PERSONALITY AND PSYCHODYNAMIC THEORIES

45-1 What is *personality,* and what theories inform our understanding of personality?

Personality is an individual's characteristic pattern of thinking, feeling, and acting. Psychoanalytic (and later psychodynamic) theory and humanistic theory have become part of Western culture. They also laid the foundation for later theories, such as trait and social-cognitive theories of personality.

45-2 How did Freud's treatment of psychological disorders lead to his view of the unconscious mind?

Psychodynamic theories of personality view behavior as a dynamic interaction between the conscious and unconscious mind. These theories trace their origin to Sigmund Freud's theory of *psychoanalysis*. In treating patients whose disorders had no clear physical explanation, Freud concluded that these problems reflected unacceptable thoughts and feelings, hidden away in the *unconscious* mind. To explore this hidden part of a patient's mind, Freud used *free association* and dream analysis.

45-3 What was Freud's view of personality?

Freud believed that personality results from conflict arising from the interaction among the mind's three systems: the *id* (pleasure-seeking impulses), *ego* (reality-oriented executive), and *superego* (internalized set of ideals, or conscience).

45-4 What developmental stages did Freud propose?

He believed children pass through five *psychosexual stages* (oral, anal, phallic, latency, and genital). He proposed that boys develop the *Oedipus complex* during the phallic stage, but then gradually incorporate their father's values into their superegos in a process called *identification*. According to this view, unresolved conflicts at any stage can leave a person's pleasure-seeking impulses *fixated* (stalled) at that stage.

45-5 How did Freud think people defended themselves against anxiety?

For Freud, anxiety was the product of tensions between the demands of the id and superego. The ego copes by using unconscious *defense mechanisms,* such as *repression,* which he viewed as the basic mechanism underlying and enabling all the others.

45-6 Which of Freud's ideas did his followers accept or reject?

Freud's early followers, the neo-Freudians, accepted many of his ideas. They differed in placing more emphasis on the conscious mind and in stressing social motives more than sex or aggression. Most contemporary psychodynamic theorists and therapists reject Freud's emphasis on sexual motivation. They stress, with support from modern research findings, that much of our mental life is unconscious, and they believe that our childhood experiences influence our adult personality and attachment patterns. Many also believe that our species' shared evolutionary history shaped some universal predispositions.

45-7 How do contemporary psychologists view Freud's psychoanalysis?

Freud is credited with drawing attention to the unconscious and the irrational, the importance of human sexuality and the conflict between biological impulses and social restraints, and for formulating some science-backed defense mechanisms. But his concept of repression, and his view of the unconscious as a collection of repressed and unacceptable thoughts, wishes, feelings, and memories, cannot survive scientific scrutiny. Freud offered after-the-fact explanations, which are hard to test scientifically. Research does not support many of Freud's specific ideas, such as the view that development (which we now know is lifelong) is fixed in childhood.

45-8 How has modern research developed our understanding of the unconscious?

Research confirms that we do not have full access to all that goes on in our mind, though today's science views the unconscious as a separate and parallel track of information processing that occurs outside our awareness. This processing includes schemas that control our perceptions, priming, implicit memories of learned skills, instantly activated emotions, and the implicit prejudice and stereotypes that filter our information processing of others' traits and characteristics. Research also supports reaction formation and projection (the false consensus effect), and the idea that we unconsciously defend ourselves from anxiety (as seen in experiments testing *terror-management theory*).

45-9 What are *projective tests,* how are they used, and what are some criticisms of them?

Projective tests show people stimuli that are open to many possible interpretations, treating their answers as revelations of inner dynamics. The *Thematic Apperception Test (TAT)* and the *Rorschach inkblot test* are two such tests. The TAT provides a valid and reliable map of people's implicit motives that is consistent over time. The Rorschach has low reliability and validity, but some clinicians value it as a source of suggestive leads, an icebreaker, or a revealing interview technique.

46 HUMANISTIC THEORIES AND TRAIT THEORIES

46-1 How did humanistic psychologists view personality, and what was their goal in studying personality?

The *humanistic* psychologists' view of personality focused on the potential for healthy personal growth and people's striving for self-determination and self-realization. Abraham Maslow proposed that human motivations form a *hierarchy of needs;* if basic needs are fulfilled, people will strive toward *self-actualization* and *self-transcendence.* Carl Rogers believed that the ingredients of a growth-promoting environment are acceptance (including *unconditional positive regard*), genuineness, and empathy. *Self-concept* was a central feature of personality for both Maslow and Rogers.

46-2 How did humanistic psychologists assess a person's sense of self?

Some rejected any standardized assessments and relied on interviews and conversations. Others, like Rogers, sometimes used questionnaires in which people described their ideal and actual selves; these were later used to judge progress during therapy. Some now use the life story approach, enabling a rich narrative detailing each person's unique life history.

46-3 How have humanistic theories influenced psychology? What criticisms have they faced?

Humanistic psychology has had pervasive cultural impact; it also laid the groundwork for today's scientific subfield of positive psychology. Critics have said that humanistic psychology's concepts are vague and subjective, its values self-centered, and its assumptions naively optimistic.

46-4 How do psychologists use traits to describe personality?

Trait theorists see personality as a stable and enduring pattern of behavior. They have been more interested in trying to describe our differences than in explaining them. Using factor analysis, they identify clusters of behavior tendencies that occur together. Genetic predispositions influence many traits.

46-5 What are some common misunderstandings about introversion?

Western cultures prize extraversion, but introverts have different, equally important skills. Introversion does not equal shyness, and introverted leaders outperform extraverts in some contexts. Introverts handle conflict well, seeking solitude rather than revenge.

46-6 What are *personality inventories*, and what are their strengths and weaknesses as trait-assessment tools?

Personality inventories (such as the *MMPI*) are questionnaires on which people respond (*self-report*) to items designed to gauge a wide range of feelings and behaviors. Test items are *empirically derived,* and the tests are objectively scored. Objectivity does not guarantee validity; people can fake their answers to create a good impression (but may then score high on a lie scale that assesses faking).

46-7 Which traits seem to provide the most useful information about personality variation?

The *Big Five* personality factors—openness, conscientiousness, extraversion, agreeableness, and neuroticism (OCEAN)—currently offer our best approximation of the basic trait dimensions. These factors are generally stable and describe people in various cultures reasonably well. Many genes, each having small effects, combine to influence our traits.

46-8 Does research support the consistency of personality traits over time and across situations?

A person's average traits persist over time and are predictable over many different situations. But traits cannot predict behavior in any one situation.

47 SOCIAL-COGNITIVE THEORIES AND THE SELF

47-1 How do social-cognitive theorists view personality development, and how do they explore behavior?

Albert Bandura's *social-cognitive perspective* emphasizes the interaction of our traits with our situations. Social-cognitive researchers apply principles of learning, cognition, and social behavior to personality. *Reciprocal determinism* describes the interaction and mutual influence of behavior, internal cognition, and environment. Assessment situations involving simulated conditions exploit the principle that the best predictor of future behavior is a person's actions in similar situations.

47-2 What criticisms have social-cognitive theories faced?

Social-cognitive theories build on well-established concepts of learning and cognition, sensitizing researchers to the ways situations affect, and are affected by, individuals. They have been faulted for underemphasizing the importance of unconscious motives, emotions, and biologically influenced traits.

47-3 Why has psychology generated so much research on the self?

The *self* is vigorously researched as the center of personality, organizing our thoughts, feelings, and actions. Considering possible selves helps motivate us toward positive development, but focusing too intensely on ourselves can lead to the *spotlight effect.*

47-4 How important is self-esteem to our well-being?

High *self-esteem* and *self-efficacy* correlate with benefits such as higher school achievement and with being able to meet challenges. But the direction of the correlation is unclear. Rather than unrealistically promoting self-worth, it's better to reward achievements, thus promoting feelings of competence.

47-5 How do excessive optimism, blindness to one's own incompetence, and self-serving bias reveal the costs of self-esteem, and how do defensive and secure self-esteem differ?

Excessive optimism can lead to complacency and prevent us from seeing real risks, while blindness to one's own incompetence may lead us to make the same mistakes repeatedly. People are often most overconfident when they are most incompetent, a phenomenon known as the Dunning-Kruger effect. Asking others for a candid assessment can help us to counter the self-serving bias that would otherwise lead us to overestimate our own skills. *Self-serving bias* is our tendency to perceive ourselves favorably, as when viewing ourselves as better than average or when accepting credit for our successes but not blame for our failures. Excessive self-love leads to *narcissism*. Defensive self-esteem is fragile, focuses on sustaining itself, and views failure or criticism as a threat. Secure self-esteem enables us to feel accepted for who we are.

CHAPTER 15

Psychological Disorders (Modules 48–53)

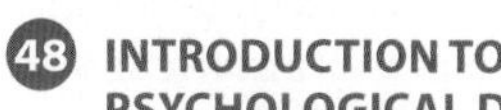

48 INTRODUCTION TO PSYCHOLOGICAL DISORDERS

48-1 How should we draw the line between typical behavior and a disorder?

According to psychologists and psychiatrists, *psychological disorders* are marked by a clinically significant disturbance in an individual's cognition, emotion regulation, or behavior. Such dysfunctional or maladaptive thoughts, emotions, or behaviors—which are often accompanied by distress—interfere with daily life, and thus are disordered.

48-2 How do the medical model and the biopsychosocial approach influence our understanding of psychological disorders?

The *medical model* assumes that psychological disorders have physical causes that can be diagnosed, treated, and often cured through therapy, sometimes in a hospital. The biopsychosocial perspective assumes that disordered behavior comes from the interaction of biological characteristics, psychological dynamics, and social-cultural circumstances. This approach has given rise to the vulnerability-stress model, in which individual characteristics and environmental stressors combine to increase or decrease the likelihood of developing a psychological disorder, a model supported by *epigenetics* research.

48-3 How and why do clinicians classify psychological disorders, and why do some psychologists criticize diagnostic labels?

The American Psychiatric Association's DSM-5-TR (*Diagnostic and Statistical Manual of Mental Disorders*, Fifth Edition, Text Revision) contains diagnostic labels and descriptions that provide a common language and shared concepts for communication and research. Critics of the DSM say it casts too wide a net, pathologizing typical behaviors. A complementary approach to classification is the U.S. National Institute of Mental Health's Research Domain Criteria (RDoC) project, a framework that organizes disorders according to behaviors and brain activity along several dimensions. The Hierarchical Taxonomy of Psychopathology (HiTOP) is another approach that emphasizes the different numbers of people's symptoms and the connections between disorders. Any classification attempt produces diagnostic labels that may create preconceptions, which bias perceptions of the labeled person's past and present behavior.

48-4 What factors increase the risk of suicide, and what do we know about nonsuicidal self-injury?

Suicide rates differ by nation, race, gender, age group, income, religious involvement, marital status, and other factors. In most countries, suicide rates have been decreasing, but in the United States and Canada they have been increasing. Those lacking social support, such as many gay, transgender, and gender nonconforming youth, are at increased risk, as are people who have been anxious or depressed. Isolation and unemployment can also heighten risk. Forewarnings of suicide may include verbal hints, giving away possessions, social withdrawal, and preoccupation with death. People who talk about suicide should be taken seriously: Listen and empathize, connect them to help, and protect those who appear at immediate risk. Nonsuicidal self-injury (NSSI) does not usually lead to suicide but may escalate to suicidal thoughts and acts if untreated. People who engage in NSSI do not tolerate stress well and tend to be self-critical and impulsive.

48-5 Do psychological disorders predict violent behavior?

Mental disorders seldom lead to violence, and clinicians cannot predict who is likely to harm others. Most people with disorders are nonviolent and are more likely to be victims than attackers. Better predictors of violence are alcohol or drug use, previous violence, gun availability, and brain damage.

48-6 How many people have, or have had, a psychological disorder? What are some of the risk factors?

Psychological disorder rates vary, depending on the time and place of the survey. Poverty is a risk factor. But some disorders, such as schizophrenia, can also drive people into poverty. Immigrants to the United States may average better mental health than their U.S.-born counterparts with the same ethnic heritage (a phenomenon known as the immigrant paradox).

49 ANXIETY DISORDERS, OBSESSIVE-COMPULSIVE AND RELATED DISORDERS, TRAUMA- AND STRESSOR-RELATED DISORDERS, AND SOMATIC SYMPTOM AND RELATED DISORDERS

49-1 How do generalized anxiety disorder, panic disorder, and specific phobias differ?

Anxiety disorders are psychological disorders characterized by distressing, persistent anxiety or maladaptive behaviors that reduce anxiety. People with *generalized anxiety disorder* feel persistently and uncontrollably tense and apprehensive, for no apparent reason. In the more extreme *panic disorder*, anxiety escalates into episodes of intense dread. Those with a *specific phobia* show an intense and irrational fear of a particular object, activity, or situation.

49-2 What is *OCD?*

Persistent and repetitive thoughts (obsessions), actions (compulsions), or both characterize *obsessive-compulsive disorder (OCD)*.

49-3 What is *PTSD?*

Symptoms of *posttraumatic stress disorder (PTSD)* include 4 or more weeks of haunting memories, nightmares, hypervigilance, avoidance of trauma-related stimuli, social withdrawal, jumpy anxiety, numbness of feeling, and/or sleep problems following a traumatic event.

49-4 What is a *somatic symptom disorder?*

People who experience bodily symptoms without any apparent physical cause may be experiencing *somatic symptom disorder*. Those with *illness anxiety disorder* (previously known as hypochondriasis) interpret normal physical sensations as symptoms of a disease.

49-5 How do learning, cognition, and biology contribute to the feelings and thoughts that mark anxiety disorders, OCD, PTSD, and somatic symptom disorders?

The learning perspective views these disorders as products of fear conditioning, stimulus generalization, fearful-behavior reinforcement, and observational learning of others' fears and cognitions. The cognitive perspective focuses on the effects of our thoughts, memories, interpretations, and expectations in what we learn to fear. The biological perspective considers genetic predispositions, brain overarousal, and the role that fears of life-threatening dangers played in natural selection and evolution.

 DEPRESSIVE DISORDERS AND BIPOLAR DISORDERS

50-1 How do depressive disorders and bipolar disorders differ?

Depressive disorders are characterized by an enduring sad, empty, or irritable mood, along with physical and cognitive changes that affect a person's ability to function. A person with *major depressive disorder* experiences at least five symptoms of depression (including either depressed mood or loss of interest or pleasure) for 2 or more weeks. A person with a *bipolar disorder* experiences not only depression but also *mania*—episodes of hyperactive and wildly optimistic, impulsive behavior.

50-2 How can the biological and social-cognitive perspectives help us understand depressive disorders and bipolar disorders?

The biological perspective on depressive disorders and bipolar disorders focuses on genetic predispositions, unusual brain structure and activity (including activity within neurotransmitter systems), and nutritional effects. The social-cognitive perspective views depression as an ongoing cycle of stressful experiences—interpreted through negative beliefs, attributions, and memories, often with relentless *rumination*—leading to negative moods, thoughts, and actions, thereby fueling new stressful experiences.

 SCHIZOPHRENIA

51-1 What patterns of perceiving, thinking, and feeling characterize schizophrenia?

Schizophrenia is a *psychotic disorder* characterized by *delusions,* hallucinations, disorganized speech, and/or diminished, inappropriate emotional expression. Hallucinations are sensory experiences without sensory stimulation; delusions are false beliefs. Schizophrenia symptoms may be positive (the presence of inappropriate behaviors) or negative (the absence of appropriate behaviors).

51-2 How do *chronic schizophrenia* and *acute schizophrenia* differ?

Schizophrenia typically strikes during late adolescence or early adulthood, affects slightly more men than women, and occurs in all cultures. In *chronic* (or process) *schizophrenia,* development of symptoms is gradual and recovery is doubtful. In *acute* (or reactive) *schizophrenia,* onset is sudden, in reaction to stress, and prospects for recovery are brighter.

51-3 What brain abnormalities are associated with schizophrenia?

People with schizophrenia have an excess number of dopamine receptors, which may intensify brain signals, creating positive symptoms such as hallucinations and paranoia. Brain scans have revealed abnormal activity in the frontal lobes, thalamus, and amygdala, as well as a loss of neural connections across the brain network. Brain abnormalities associated with schizophrenia include enlarged, fluid-filled areas and corresponding shrinkage and thinning of cerebral tissue. Smaller-than-normal areas may include the cortex, the hippocampus, the corpus callosum, and the thalamus.

51-4 What prenatal events are associated with increased risk of developing schizophrenia?

Possible contributing factors include maternal diabetes; older paternal age; viral infections, famine conditions, or extreme maternal stress during pregnancy; and low weight or oxygen deprivation at birth.

51-5 How do genes influence schizophrenia? What factors may be early warning signs of schizophrenia in children?

Twin and adoption studies indicate that the predisposition to schizophrenia is inherited. Multiple genes probably interact to produce schizophrenia. No environmental causes invariably produce schizophrenia, but environmental events (such as prenatal viruses or maternal stress) may "turn on" genes in those who are predisposed to this disorder. Possible early warning signs of schizophrenia include social withdrawal; a mother with severe and long-lasting schizophrenia; birth complications; short attention span; poor muscle coordination; emotional unpredictability; poor peer relations and solo play; separation from parents; and childhood abuse.

 DISSOCIATIVE, PERSONALITY, AND EATING DISORDERS

52-1 What are *dissociative disorders*, and why are they controversial?

Dissociative disorders are controversial, rare disorders characterized by a disruption of or discontinuity in the normal integration of consciousness, memory, identity, emotion, perception, body representation, motor control, and behavior. Skeptics note that diagnoses of *dissociative identity disorder (DID)* increased dramatically in the late twentieth century, is rarely found outside North America, and may reflect role playing by people vulnerable to therapists' suggestions. Others view DID as a manifestation of feelings of anxiety, or as a response learned when behaviors are reinforced by anxiety reduction.

52-2 What are the three clusters of personality disorders? What behaviors and brain activity characterize antisocial personality disorder?

Personality disorders are characterized by enduring inner experiences or behavior patterns that differ from someone's cultural norms and expectations, are pervasive and inflexible, begin in adolescence or early adulthood, are stable over time, and cause distress or impairment. The 10 DSM-5-TR disorders tend to form three clusters, characterized by eccentric or odd behaviors (Cluster A); dramatic, emotional, or erratic behaviors (Cluster B); and anxious or fearful behaviors (Cluster C). *Antisocial personality disorder* (one of those in Cluster B) is characterized by a lack of conscience and, sometimes, by aggressive and fearless behavior. The amygdala is smaller, the brain cortex is smaller and thinner, and the frontal lobes are less active in people with this disorder, leading to impaired frontal lobe cognitive functions and decreased responsiveness to others' distress. Genetic predispositions may interact with the environment to produce these characteristics.

52-3 What are the three main eating disorders, and how do biological, psychological, and social-cultural influences make some people more vulnerable to them?

In those with eating disorders, psychological factors overwhelm the body's tendency to maintain a healthy weight. Regardless of their actual weight, people with *anorexia nervosa* (usually adolescent girls) maintain a starvation diet, sometimes exercise excessively, and have an inaccurate self-perception. Those with *bulimia nervosa* binge and then compensate by purging, fasting, or excessively exercising. Bulimia is marked by weight fluctuations within or above typical ranges. Those with *binge-eating disorder* are preoccupied with food and engage in significant bouts of bingeing, but they do not follow binges with purging, fasting, or exercising. Cultural pressures, low self-esteem, and negative emotions interact with stressful life experiences and genetics to produce eating disorders.

 NEURODEVELOPMENTAL DISORDERS

53-1 What is *intellectual developmental disorder?*

Intellectual developmental disorder is marked by limited mental ability, which is indicated by an intelligence score of 70 or below and difficulty adapting to the demands of life in three skill areas: conceptual, social, and practical.

53-2 What is *autism spectrum disorder?*

Autism spectrum disorder (ASD) is a cognitive and social-emotional disorder that appears in childhood and is marked by limitations in communication and social interaction, as well as rigidly fixated interests and repetitive behaviors.

53-3 Why is there controversy over attention-deficit/hyperactivity disorder?

A child (or, less commonly, an adult) who displays extreme inattention and/or hyperactivity and impulsivity may be diagnosed with *attention-deficit/hyperactivity disorder (ADHD)*. Controversies center on whether the growing number of ADHD cases reflects overdiagnosis or increased awareness of the disorder, and on the long-term effects of stimulant-drug treatment.

CHAPTER 16

Therapy (Modules 54–56)

 INTRODUCTION TO THERAPY AND THE PSYCHOLOGICAL THERAPIES

54-1 How do *psychotherapy* and the *biomedical therapies* differ?

Psychotherapy is treatment involving psychological techniques that consists of interactions between a trained therapist and someone seeking to overcome psychological difficulties or achieve personal growth. The major psychotherapies derive from psychology's psychodynamic, humanistic, behavioral, and cognitive perspectives, with many psychotherapists taking an *eclectic approach* that blends therapies. *Biomedical therapy* treats psychological disorders with medications or procedures that act directly on a person's physiology.

54-2 What are the goals and techniques of psychoanalysis, and how have they been adapted in psychodynamic therapy?

Through *psychoanalysis,* Sigmund Freud tried to give people self-insight and relief from their disorders by bringing anxiety-laden feelings and thoughts into conscious awareness. Psychoanalytic techniques included using free association and *interpretation* of instances of *resistance* and *transference. Psychodynamic therapy* has been influenced by traditional psychoanalysis but differs from it in many ways, including little attention to the concepts of id, ego, and superego. This contemporary therapy is briefer, less expensive, and more focused on helping the client find relief from current symptoms. Psychodynamic therapists help clients understand how past relationships create themes that may be acted out in present relationships.

54-3 What are the basic themes of humanistic therapy? What are the goals and techniques of Rogers' person-centered approach?

Both psychodynamic and humanistic therapies are *insight therapies*—they attempt to improve functioning by increasing people's awareness of motives and defenses. Humanistic therapy's goals include helping people grow in self-awareness and self-acceptance; promoting personal growth rather than curing illness; helping people take responsibility for their own growth; focusing on conscious thoughts rather than unconscious motivations; and seeing the present and future as more important than the past. Carl Rogers' *person-centered therapy* proposed that therapists' most important contribution is to function as a psychological mirror through *active listening* and to provide a growth-fostering environment of *unconditional positive regard.*

54-4 How does the basic assumption of behavior therapy differ from the assumptions of psychodynamic and humanistic therapies? What classical conditioning techniques are used in exposure therapies and aversive conditioning?

Behavior therapies are not insight therapies, and instead assume that problem behaviors *are* the problem. Their goal is to apply learning principles to modify these problem behaviors. Classical conditioning techniques, including *exposure therapies* (such as *systematic desensitization* or *virtual reality exposure therapy*) and *aversive conditioning,* attempt to change behaviors through *counterconditioning*—*evoking* new responses to old stimuli that trigger unwanted behaviors.

54-5 What is the main premise of behavior therapy based on operant conditioning principles, and what are the views of its proponents and critics?

Operant conditioning operates under the premise that voluntary behaviors are strongly influenced by their consequences. Therapy based on operant conditioning principles therefore uses behavior modification techniques to change unwanted behaviors by positively reinforcing desired behaviors and ignoring or punishing undesirable behaviors. Critics maintain that (1) techniques such as those used in *token economies* may produce behavior changes that disappear when rewards end, and (2) deciding which behaviors should change is authoritarian and unethical. Proponents argue that treatment with positive rewards is more humane than punishing people or institutionalizing them for undesired behaviors.

54-6 What are the goals and techniques of the cognitive therapies and of cognitive-behavioral therapy?

The *cognitive therapies,* such as Aaron Beck's cognitive therapy for depression, assume that our thinking colors our feelings, and that the therapist's role is to change clients' self-defeating thinking by training them to perceive and interpret events in more constructive ways. The widely researched and practiced *cognitive-behavioral therapy (CBT)* combines cognitive therapy and behavior therapy by helping clients regularly try out their new ways of thinking and behaving in their everyday life. Dialectical behavior therapy (DBT) combines cognitive tactics for tolerating distress and regulating emotions with social skills training and mindfulness meditation. Acceptance and commitment therapy (ACT) helps clients learn to accept their feelings and act in ways that reflect their life values.

54-7 What are the aims and benefits of group therapy, couples therapy, and family therapy?

Group therapy sessions can help more people with less cost than individual therapy. Clients may benefit in person or online from exploring feelings and developing social skills in a group situation, from learning that others have similar problems, and from getting feedback on new ways of behaving. *Couples therapy* focuses on how romantic partners can improve their interactions, which can increase emotional intimacy, healthy communication, and relationship satisfaction. *Family therapy* aims to help family members discover the roles they play within the family's interactive social system, improve communication, and learn new ways to prevent or resolve conflicts.

55 EVALUATING PSYCHOTHERAPIES

55-1 Does psychotherapy work? How can we know?

Clients' and therapists' positive testimonials cannot prove that psychotherapy is effective, and the placebo effect and *confirmation bias* make it difficult to judge whether improvement occurred because of the treatment. Using *meta-analyses* to statistically combine the results of hundreds of randomized psychotherapy outcome studies, researchers have found that those not undergoing treatment often improve, but those undergoing psychotherapy are more likely to improve—and to improve more quickly and with less risk of relapse.

55-2 Are some psychotherapies more effective than others for specific disorders?

No one type of psychotherapy is generally superior to all others. Therapy is most effective for those with clear-cut, specific problems. Some therapies—such as behavior conditioning for treating specific phobias and compulsions—are more effective for particular disorders. Cognitive and cognitive-behavioral therapies have been effective in coping with anxiety, panic disorder, posttraumatic stress disorder, insomnia, and depression; behavioral conditioning therapies with specific behavior problems; psychodynamic therapy for depression and anxiety; and nondirective (client-centered) counseling for mild to moderate depression. Abnormal states tend to return to normal on their own, and the placebo effect can create the impression that a treatment has been effective. *Evidence-based practice* integrates the best available research with clinicians' expertise and clients' culture, values, personality, identity, and circumstances.

55-3 What three elements are shared by all effective forms of psychotherapy?

All psychotherapies offer new hope for demoralized people; a fresh perspective; and (if the therapist is effective) an empathic, trusting, and caring relationship. The emotional bond of trust and understanding between therapist and client—the *therapeutic alliance*—is an important element in effective therapy.

55-4 What personal factors influence the therapist-client relationship?

Therapists differ in the values that influence their goals in therapy and their views of progress. They may also differ from their clients. These differences may create problems if therapists and clients differ in their cultural, religious, or personal values and perspectives.

55-5 When should people seek therapy, and what should they look for when selecting a therapist?

Campus health centers are generally good starting points for counseling options, and they may offer some free services. A person seeking therapy may want to ask about the therapist's treatment approach, values, credentials, and fees. An important consideration is whether the therapy seeker feels comfortable and able to establish a bond with the therapist. Recognizing the importance of a strong therapeutic alliance, the American Psychological Association accredits programs that provide training in cultural sensitivity and that recruit underrepresented cultural groups.

55-6 What ethical principles guide psychotherapy and psychological research on mental illness?

Psychotherapists and psychological researchers on mental health must follow their country's ethical principles and code of conduct, aiming to benefit others, to be honest and truthful, and to never expose people to greater risks than would be encountered in everyday life.

56 THE BIOMEDICAL THERAPIES AND PREVENTING PSYCHOLOGICAL DISORDERS

56-1 Why is therapeutic lifestyle change considered an effective biomedical therapy, and how does it work?

Therapeutic lifestyle change is considered a biomedical therapy because it influences the way the brain responds. Mind and body are a unit; affect one and you will affect the other. Our exercise, nutrition, relationships, recreation, service to others, relaxation, and religious or spiritual engagement affect our mental health. People who undergo a program of aerobic exercise, adequate sleep, light exposure, social engagement, rumination reduction, and better nutrition have gained relief from depressive symptoms.

56-2 What are the drug therapies? How do double-blind studies help researchers evaluate a drug's effectiveness?

Psychopharmacology has helped make drug therapy the most widely used biomedical therapy. *Antipsychotic drugs* are used in treating schizophrenia; some block dopamine activity. Side effects may include tardive dyskinesia (involuntary movements of facial muscles, tongue, and limbs) or increased risk of obesity and diabetes. *Antianxiety drugs*, which depress central nervous system activity, are used to treat anxiety disorders, obsessive-compulsive disorder, and posttraumatic stress disorder, and can be addictive. *Antidepressant drugs*, which often increase the availability of serotonin and norepinephrine, are used to treat depression, anxiety disorders, obsessive-compulsive and related disorders, and posttraumatic stress disorder. Given their use in treating disorders other than depressive ones (from anxiety to strokes), these drugs are more often called SSRIs (selective serotonin reuptake inhibitors) rather than antidepressants. Quicker-acting antidepressants may include ketamine and microdoses of psychedelic drugs such as psilocybin. Lithium and Depakote are mood stabilizers prescribed for those with a bipolar disorder. Studies may use a double-blind procedure to avoid the placebo effect and researcher bias.

56-3 How are brain stimulation and psychosurgery used in treating specific disorders?

Electroconvulsive therapy (ECT), in which a brief electric current is sent through the brain of an anesthetized patient, is an effective treatment for severe depression in people who have not responded to other therapy. Newer alternative treatments for depression include transcranial direct current stimulation (tDCS), *transcranial magnetic stimulation (TMS)*, and deep-brain stimulation (DBS; may calm an overactive brain region linked with negative emotions in some patients). *Psychosurgery* removes or destroys brain tissue in hopes of modifying behavior. Radical psychosurgical procedures such as *lobotomy* are no longer performed. Today's microscale psychosurgery and MRI-guided precision brain surgery are rare, last-resort treatments because the effects are irreversible.

56-4 What may help prevent psychological disorders, and why is it important to develop resilience?

Preventive mental health programs are based on the idea that many psychological disorders could be prevented by identifying and alleviating the conditions that cause them, such as poverty, lack of meaningful work, constant criticism, unemployment, and discrimination. Community psychologists work to prevent psychological disorders by turning destructive environments into ones that support psychological health. This includes efforts to build people's *resilience*, helping them cope and recover from stress. Struggling with challenges can lead to *posttraumatic growth*.

NOTE: There are no learning objective questions in Appendix A, The Story of Psychology: A Timeline; and Appendix B, Career Fields in Psychology.

APPENDIX C

Psychology at Work

WORK AND LIFE SATISFACTION

C-1 What is *flow?*

Flow is a completely involved, focused state of consciousness with diminished awareness of self and time. It results from fully engaging one's skills. Interests predict both performance and persistence, so people should aim to find vocations with a strong person-environment fit.

INDUSTRIAL-ORGANIZATIONAL PSYCHOLOGY

C-2 What are industrial-organizational psychology's three key areas of study?

Three key areas of study related to *industrial-organizational (I/O) psychology* are *personnel, organizational,* and *human factors psychology.* Each uses psychological principles to study and benefit the wide range of today's workers, workplaces, and work activities.

PERSONNEL PSYCHOLOGY

C-3 How do personnel psychologists facilitate job seeking, employee selection, work placement, and performance appraisal?

Personnel psychologists work to provide training programs for job seekers, devise selection methods for new employees, recruit and evaluate diverse applicants, design and evaluate training programs, identify people's interests and strengths, analyze job content, appraise individual and organizational performance, and facilitate team building. Unstructured, subjective interviews foster the interviewer illusion; *structured interviews* pinpoint job-relevant strengths and are better predictors of performance. Checklists, graphic rating scales, and behavior rating scales are useful performance appraisal methods.

ORGANIZATIONAL PSYCHOLOGY

C-4 Why are organizational psychologists interested in employee satisfaction and engagement?

Organizational psychologists examine influences on worker satisfaction and productivity and facilitate organizational change. Employee satisfaction and engagement tend to correlate with organizational success; in fact, employee attitudes predict future business success.

C-5 How can leaders be most effective?

Effective leaders set specific, challenging goals and choose an appropriate *leadership style.* Leadership style may be goal-oriented *(task leadership)*, group-oriented *(social leadership)*, or some combination of the two. Effective management often involves positive reinforcement, fulfilling the need to belong, and participative management.

C-6 What cultural influences need to be considered when choosing an effective leadership style?

Project GLOBE studies cultural variations in leadership expectations. Leaders who fulfill expectations (being directive in some cultures or participative in others) tend to be successful. But thriving companies worldwide tend to focus on identifying and enhancing employee strengths; strengths-based leadership pays dividends everywhere.

HUMAN FACTORS PSYCHOLOGY

C-7 How do human factors psychologists work to create user-friendly machines and work settings?

Human factors psychologists contribute to human safety and improved design by encouraging developers and designers to consider human abilities and behaviors, to user-test their work before production and distribution, and to remain mindful of the curse of knowledge.

Answers to the *Retrieval Practice* and *Module Test* Questions

Thinking Critically With Psychological Science (Modules 1–3)

1 THE HISTORY AND SCOPE OF PSYCHOLOGY

RETRIEVAL PRACTICE ANSWERS

RP-1 Examining our own assumptions, appraising the source, discerning hidden biases, and assessing conclusions are essential parts of critical thinking. **RP-2** Scientific psychology began in Germany in 1879, when Wilhelm Wundt opened the first psychology laboratory. **RP-3** People's self-reports varied, depending on the experience and the person's intelligence and verbal ability. **RP-4** structuralism; functionalism. **RP-5** behaviorism; Freudian. **RP-6** It recaptured the field's early interest in mental processes and made them legitimate topics for scientific study. **RP-7** Natural selection is the process by which nature selects from chance variations the traits that best enable an organism to survive and reproduce in a particular environment. **RP-8** Psychological events often stem from the interaction of nature and nurture, rather than from either of them acting alone. **RP-9** By incorporating three different levels of analysis, the biopsychosocial approach can provide a more complete view than any one perspective could offer. **RP-10** social-cultural; behavioral. **RP-11** i. b, ii. c, iii. a. **RP-12** testing effect. **RP-13** Survey, Question, Read, Retrieve, Review.

MODULE TEST ANSWERS

1. Critical thinking is smart thinking. When evaluating media claims (even about topics you might not know much about), look for empirical evidence. Ask the following questions in your analysis: Are the claims based on scientific findings? Have several studies replicated the findings and confirmed them? Are any experts cited? If so, are they affiliated with a credible institution? Have they conducted or written about scientific research? What agenda might they have? What alternative explanations are possible? **2.** Wilhelm Wundt. **3.** a. **4.** a. **5.** b. **6.** The environment (nurture) has an influence on us, but that influence is constrained by our biology (nature). Nature and nurture interact. People predisposed to be very tall (nature), for example, are unlikely to become Olympic gymnasts, no matter how hard they work (nurture). **7.** b. **8.** positive psychology. **9.** d. **10.** psychiatrist. **11.** c.

2 RESEARCH STRATEGIES: HOW PSYCHOLOGISTS ASK AND ANSWER QUESTIONS

RETRIEVAL PRACTICE ANSWERS

RP-1 We often suffer from hindsight bias—after we've learned a situation's outcome, that outcome seems familiar and therefore obvious. **RP-2** A good theory *organizes* observed facts and implies hypotheses that offer testable *predictions* and, sometimes, practical applications. It also often stimulates further research. **RP-3** When other investigators are able to replicate an experiment with the same (or stronger) results, scientists can confirm the result and become more confident of its reliability. **RP-4** Case studies involve only one individual or group, so we can't know for sure whether the principles observed would apply to a larger population. **RP-5** Naturalistic observation does not explain behavior, and it does not control for all the factors that may influence behavior. Nevertheless, the descriptions it provides can be revealing, expanding our understanding and paving the way for future studies. **RP-6** An unrepresentative sample is a group that does not represent the population being studied. *Random sampling* helps researchers form a representative sample, because each member of the population has an equal chance of being included. **RP-7** 1. Negative correlation, 2. Positive correlation, 3. Positive correlation, 4. Negative correlation. **RP-8** The team's poor performance was not their typical behavior. The return to their more typical play—their winning streak—may just have been a case of regression toward the mean. **RP-9** In this case, as in many others, a third factor can explain the correlation: Golden anniversaries and baldness both accompany aging. **RP-10** Research designed to prevent the placebo effect randomly assigns participants to an *experimental group* (which receives the real treatment) or to a *control group* (which receives a placebo). A double-blind procedure prevents people's beliefs and hopes from affecting the results, because neither the participants nor those collecting the data know who receives the placebo. A comparison of the results will demonstrate whether the real treatment produces better results than *belief* in that treatment. **RP-11** confounding variables. **RP-12** i. c, ii. a, iii. b. **RP-13** We learn more about the drug's effectiveness when we can compare the results of those who took the drug (the experimental group) with the results of those who did not (the control group). If we gave the drug to all 1000 participants, we would have no way of knowing whether the drug is serving as a placebo or is actually medically effective. **RP-14** Animal protection legislation, laboratory regulation and inspection, and local and university ethics committees (which screen research proposals) attempt to safeguard animal welfare. International psychological organizations urge researchers involving human participants to obtain *informed consent*, protect them from greater-than-usual harm and discomfort, treat their personal information confidentially, and *debrief* them fully at the end of the experiment. Institutional Review Boards serve to enforce these standards.

MODULE TEST ANSWERS

1. Hindsight bias. **2.** d. **3.** hypothesis. **4.** c. **5.** random. **6.** negative. **7.** scatterplot. **8.** a. **9.** positive. **10.** Regression toward the mean is a statistical phenomenon describing the tendency of extreme scores or outcomes to return to average after an unusual event. Without knowing this, we may inaccurately decide the return to average was a result of our own behavior. **11.** a. **12.** (a) *Alcohol use is associated with violence. (One interpretation: Drinking triggers or unleashes aggressive behavior.)* Perhaps anger triggers drinking, or perhaps the same genes or child-raising practices are predisposing both drinking and aggression. (Here researchers have learned that drinking does indeed trigger aggressive behavior.) (b) *Educated people live longer, on average, than less-educated people. (One interpretation: Education lengthens life and* *enhances health.)* Perhaps richer people can afford more education and better health care. (Research supports this conclusion.) (c) *Teens engaged in team sports are less likely to use drugs, smoke, have sex, carry weapons, and eat junk food than are teens who do not engage in team sports. (One interpretation: Team sports encourage healthy living.)* Perhaps some third factor explains this correlation—teens who use drugs, smoke, have sex, carry weapons, and eat junk food may be "loners" who do not enjoy playing on any team. (d) *Adolescents who frequently see smoking in movies are more likely to smoke. (One interpretation: Movie stars' behavior influences impressionable teens.)* Perhaps adolescents who smoke and attend movies frequently have less parental supervision and more access to spending money than other adolescents. **13.** experiments. **14.** placebo. **15.** c. **16.** independent variable. **17.** b. **18.** d.

3 STATISTICAL REASONING IN EVERYDAY LIFE

RETRIEVAL PRACTICE ANSWERS

RP-1 Note how the y-axis of each graph is labeled. The range for the y-axis label in graph (a) is only from 95 to 100. The range for graph (b) is from 0 to 100. All the trucks rank as 95 percent and up, so almost all are still functioning after 10 years, which graph (b) makes clear. **RP-2** mean; mode; median. **RP-3** range; standard deviation. **RP-4** Averages based on fewer courses are more variable, which guarantees a greater number of extremely low and high marks at the end of the first term. **RP-5** Descriptive; inferential.

MODULE TEST ANSWERS

1. b. **2.** d. **3.** normal curve. **4.** a.

CHAPTER 2

The Biology of Mind (Modules 4–7)

4 NEURAL AND HORMONAL SYSTEMS

RETRIEVAL PRACTICE ANSWERS

RP-1 They share a focus on the links between the brain and behavior. Phrenology faded because it had no scientific basis—skull bumps don't reveal mental traits and abilities. **RP-2** Thanks to its *neuroplasticity*, our brain changes in response to the experiences we have. Learning and practicing a new skill, like playing an instrument, can promote the development of new neural pathways and cause lasting changes in brain organization. **RP-3** dendrites, cell body, axon. **RP-4** Stronger stimuli (the slap) cause more neurons to fire and to fire more frequently than happens with weaker stimuli (the tap). **RP-5** Neurons send neurotransmitters (chemical messengers) across this tiny space between one neuron's terminal branch and the next neuron's dendrite or cell body. **RP-6** Reuptake occurs when excess neurotransmitters are reabsorbed by the sending neuron. Neurotransmitters can also drift away or be broken down by enzymes. **RP-7** neurotransmitters. **RP-8** Morphine is an agonist; curare is an antagonist. **RP-9** i. c, ii. a, iii. b. **RP-10** The sympathetic division of the autonomic nervous system would have directed arousal (accelerated heartbeat, inhibited digestion, and so forth), and the parasympathetic division would have directed calming. **RP-11** Responding to signals from the hypothalamus, the pituitary releases hormones that trigger other endocrine glands to secrete hormones, which in turn influence brain and behavior. **RP-12** Both of these communication systems produce chemical molecules that act on the body's receptors to influence our behavior and emotions. The endocrine system, which secretes hormones into the bloodstream, delivers its messages much more slowly than the speedy nervous system, and the effects of the endocrine system's messages tend to linger much longer than those of the nervous system.

MODULE TEST ANSWERS

1. The human brain is uniquely designed to be flexible; it can reorganize after damage and build new pathways based on experience. This neuroplasticity enables us to adapt to our changing world. **2.** axon. **3.** c. **4.** a. **5.** neurotransmitters. **6.** b. **7.** c. **8.** autonomic. **9.** central. **10.** a. **11.** adrenal glands.

5 TOOLS OF DISCOVERY: HAVING OUR HEAD EXAMINED

RETRIEVAL PRACTICE ANSWERS

RP-1 i. b, ii. a, iii. c.

MODULE TEST ANSWERS

1. lesioning. **2.** a. **3.** a. **4.** c.

6 BRAIN REGIONS AND STRUCTURES

RETRIEVAL PRACTICE ANSWERS

RP-1 brainstem. **RP-2** (a) cerebellum, (b) thalamus, (c) reticular formation, (d) medulla. **RP-3** The sympathetic nervous system. **RP-4** (a) The *amygdala* is involved in aggression and fear responses. (b) The *hypothalamus* is involved in bodily maintenance, pleasurable rewards, and control of the hormonal systems. (c) The *hippocampus* processes memories of facts and events. **RP-5** The cerebral cortex. **RP-6** (a) The right limbs' opposed activities interfere with each other because both are controlled by the same (left) side of your brain. (b) Opposite sides of your brain control your left and right limbs, so the reversed motion causes less interference. **RP-7** somatosensory; motor. **RP-8** Association areas are involved in higher mental functions—interpreting, integrating, and acting on information processed in other areas.

MODULE TEST ANSWERS

1. b. **2.** d. **3.** c. **4.** cerebellum. **5.** b. **6.** amygdala. **7.** b. **8.** hypothalamus. **9.** d. **10.** The visual cortex is a neural network of sensory neurons connected via interneurons to other neural networks, including auditory networks. If you can see and hear, this allows you to integrate visual and auditory information to respond when a friend you recognize greets you at a party. **11.** c. **12.** frontal. **13.** association areas.

7 DAMAGE RESPONSES AND BRAIN HEMISPHERES

RETRIEVAL PRACTICE ANSWERS

RP-1 (a) yes, (b) no, (c) green.

MODULE TEST ANSWERS

1. c. **2.** ON; HER. **3.** a. **4.** b.

CHAPTER 3

Consciousness and the Two-Track Mind (Modules 8–10)

8 BASIC CONSCIOUSNESS CONCEPTS

RETRIEVAL PRACTICE ANSWERS

RP-1 cognitive neuroscience. **RP-2** Our *selective attention* allows us to focus on only a limited portion of our surroundings. *Inattentional blindness* explains why we don't perceive some things when we are distracted. *Change blindness*, for example, happens when we fail to notice a relatively unimportant change in our environment. These principles help magicians fool us, as they direct our attention elsewhere to perform their tricks. **RP-3** Our mind simultaneously processes information on a conscious track and an unconscious track (dual processing) as we organize and interpret information.

MODULE TEST ANSWERS

1. inattentional blindness. **2.** unconscious; conscious. **3.** selective.

9 SLEEP AND DREAMS

RETRIEVAL PRACTICE ANSWERS

RP-1 With each refugee cycling through the sleep stages independently, at any given time at least one of them will likely be in an easily awakened stage. **RP-2** REM, N1, N2, N3; we typically move through N1, then N2, then N3, then back up through N2 before we experience REM sleep. **RP-3** i. b, ii. c, iii. a. **RP-4** suprachiasmatic; circadian. **RP-5** (1) Sleep has survival value. (2) Sleep helps us restore the immune system, heal from infection, and repair brain tissue. (3) During sleep we consolidate memories. (4) Sleep fuels creativity. (5) Sleep plays a role in the growth process. **RP-6** quick reaction times; gain weight. **RP-7** (1) Freud's wish fulfillment (dreams are a psychic safety valve), (2) information processing (dreams sort the day's events and consolidate memories), (3) neurocognitive function (REM sleep expands neural pathways, preserving memory and processing emotional information), (4) activation synthesis (REM sleep triggers random neural activity that the mind weaves into stories), and (5) cognitive development (dreams reflect the dreamer's developmental stage).

MODULE TEST ANSWERS

1. circadian rhythm. **2.** b. **3.** N3. **4.** It increases in duration. **5.** c. **6.** With narcolepsy, the person periodically falls directly into REM sleep, with no warning; with sleep apnea, the person repeatedly awakens during the night. **7.** d. **8.** The activation-synthesis theory suggests that dreams are the brain's attempt to synthesize random neural activity. **9.** The information-processing explanation of dreaming proposes that brain activity during REM sleep enables us to sift through the daily events and activities we have been thinking about *(what one has dwelt on by day)*. **10.** REM rebound.

10 DRUGS AND CONSCIOUSNESS

RETRIEVAL PRACTICE ANSWERS

RP-1 With repeated exposure to a psychoactive drug, the user's brain chemistry adapts and the drug's effect lessens. Thus, it takes bigger doses to get the desired effect. **RP-2** Unless it becomes compulsive or dysfunctional, simply having a strong interest in shopping is not the same as having a physical addiction to a drug. It typically does not involve obsessive craving in spite of known negative consequences. **RP-3** depressants. **RP-4** Nicotine-withdrawal symptoms include strong cravings, insomnia, anxiety, irritability, and distractibility. However, if your friend sticks with it, the craving and withdrawal symptoms will gradually dissipate over about 6 months. **RP-5** Psychoactive drugs create pleasure by altering brain chemistry. With repeated use of the drug, the user develops tolerance and needs more of the drug to achieve the desired effect. Discontinuing use of the substance then produces painful or psychologically unpleasant withdrawal symptoms. **RP-6** Nicotine is powerfully addictive, and those who start paving the neural pathways when young may find it very hard to stop using it. As a result, tobacco product companies may have lifelong customers. Moreover, evidence suggests that if these companies haven't hooked customers by early adulthood, they most likely won't. **RP-7** Possible explanations include (a) biological factors (a person could have a biological predisposition to both early use and later abuse, or alcohol use could modify a person's neural pathways); (b) psychological factors (early use could establish taste preferences for alcohol); and (c) social-cultural factors (early use could influence enduring habits, attitudes, activities, or peer relationships that could foster alcohol use disorder).

MODULE TEST ANSWERS

1. tolerance. **2.** a. **3.** Alcohol is a disinhibitor—it makes us more likely to do what we would have done when sober, whether that is being helpful or being aggressive. **4.** d. **5.** hallucinogenic. **6.** a. **7.** b.

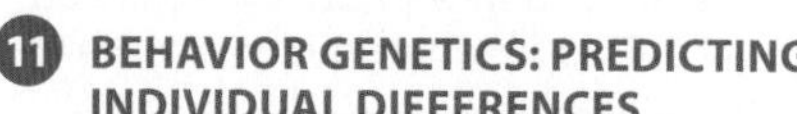

CHAPTER 4

Nature, Nurture, and Human Diversity (Modules 11–13)

11 BEHAVIOR GENETICS: PREDICTING INDIVIDUAL DIFFERENCES

RETRIEVAL PRACTICE ANSWERS

RP-1 gene, chromosome, nucleus. **RP-2** Researchers use twin and adoption studies to understand how much variation among individuals is due to genetic makeup and how much is due to environmental factors. Some studies compare the traits and behaviors of identical twins (same genes) and fraternal twins (different genes, as in any two siblings). They also compare adopted children with their adoptive and biological parents. Some studies compare the traits and behaviors of twins raised together or separately. **RP-3** genes. **RP-4** i. c, ii. b, iii. a.

MODULE TEST ANSWERS

1. chromosomes. **2.** gene. **3.** b. **4.** c. **5.** Identical. **6.** b. **7.** temperament. **8.** Heritability. **9.** environments.

12 EVOLUTIONARY PSYCHOLOGY: EXPLAINING HUMAN NATURE AND NURTURE

RETRIEVAL PRACTICE ANSWERS

RP-1 Over many generations, Belyaev and Trut selected and bred foxes that exhibited a trait they desired: tameness. This process is similar to naturally occurring selection, but it differs in that natural selection is much slower, and normally favors traits (including those arising from mutations) that contribute to reproduction and survival. **RP-2** Evolutionary psychologists theorize that females have inherited their ancestors' tendencies to be more cautious sexually because of the challenges associated with incubating and nurturing offspring. Males have inherited a tendency to be more casual about sex, because their act of fathering requires a smaller investment. **RP-3** (1) It starts with an effect and works backward to propose an explanation. (2) This explanation may overlook the effects of cultural expectations and socialization. (3) Men could use such explanations to rationalize irresponsible behavior toward women.

MODULE TEST ANSWERS

1. differences; commonalities. **2.** c. **3.** *Natural selection* favors traits and behaviors that enable survival and reproduction. Evolutionary psychologists argue that women are choosier about their mates because of the investment required to conceive, birth, nurse, and protect children. Straight women tend to prefer men who seem capable of supporting and protecting their joint offspring. Men, who have less at stake, tend to be more casual about sex, and straight men tend to prefer women whose traits convey health and fertility.

13 CULTURAL AND GENDER DIVERSITY: UNDERSTANDING NATURE AND NURTURE

RETRIEVAL PRACTICE ANSWERS

RP-1 Adolescents tend to *select* similar others and to sort themselves into like-minded groups. For an athletic teen, this could lead to finding other athletic teens and joining school teams together. **RP-2** Individualists give priority to personal goals over group goals and tend to define their identity in terms of their own personal attributes. Collectivists give priority to group goals over individual goals and tend to define their identity in terms of group identifications. **RP-3** Women; men. **RP-4** seven; puberty. **RP-5** *Gender roles* are social rules or norms for expected behavior for women and men. The norms associated with various roles, including gender roles, vary widely in different cultural contexts, which is proof that we are able to learn and adapt to the social demands of different environments. **RP-6** The biopsychosocial approach considers all the factors that influence our individual development: biological factors (including evolution and our genes, hormones, and brain), psychological factors (including our experiences, beliefs, feelings, and expectations), and social-cultural factors (including parental and peer influences, cultural individualism or collectivism, and gender norms).

MODULE TEST ANSWERS

1. b. **2.** sex; gender. **3.** c. **4.** Y. **5.** d. **6.** 10; 12. **7.** intersex. **8.** b. **9.** gender identity.

CHAPTER 5

Developing Through the Life Span (Modules 14–17)

DEVELOPMENTAL ISSUES, PRENATAL DEVELOPMENT, AND THE NEWBORN

RETRIEVAL PRACTICE ANSWERS

RP-1 continuity; stages. **RP-2** (1) Stage theory is supported by the work of Piaget (cognitive development), Kohlberg (moral development), and Erikson (psychosocial development). (2) Some traits, such as temperament, exhibit remarkable stability across many years. **RP-3** zygote; fetus; embryo. **RP-4** habituation.

MODULE TEST ANSWERS

1. Cross-sectional studies compare people of different ages at one point in time. Longitudinal studies restudy and retest the same people over a long period of time. **2.** continuity/stages. **3.** b. **4.** c. **5.** teratogens. **6.** a.

INFANCY AND CHILDHOOD

RETRIEVAL PRACTICE ANSWERS

RP-1 maturation. **RP-2** Object permanence for the sensorimotor stage, pretend play for the preoperational stage, conservation for the concrete operational stage, and abstract logic for the formal operational stage. **RP-3** i. d, ii. b, iii. c, iv. c, v. a, vi. b. **RP-4** Theory of mind focuses on our ability to understand our own and others' mental state. It enables us to infer other people's feelings, perceptions, and thoughts, and the behaviors these might predict. Those with autism spectrum disorder struggle with this ability. **RP-5** Attachment is the normal process by which we form emotional ties with important others. Imprinting occurs only in certain animals that have a critical period very early in their development during which they must form their attachments, and they do so in an inflexible manner. **RP-6** The authoritarian style would be described as too hard, the permissive style too soft, the neglectful style too uncaring, and the authoritative style just right. Parents using the authoritative style tend to have children with high self-esteem, self-reliance, self-regulation, and social competence.

MODULE TEST ANSWERS

1. frontal. **2.** b. **3.** We consciously recall little from before age 4, in part because major brain areas have not yet matured. **4.** Infants in Piaget's *sensorimotor stage* tend to be focused only on their own perceptions of the world and may, for example, be unaware that objects continue to exist when unseen. A child in the *preoperational stage* is still egocentric and incapable of appreciating simple logic, such as the reversibility of operations. A preteen in the *concrete operational stage* is beginning to think logically about concrete events but not about abstract concepts. **5.** a. **6.** stranger anxiety. **7.** Before these studies, many psychologists believed that infants simply became attached to those who nourished them.

ADOLESCENCE AND EMERGING ADULTHOOD

RETRIEVAL PRACTICE ANSWERS

RP-1 preconventional; postconventional; conventional. **RP-2** Kohlberg's work reflected an individualist worldview, so his theory is less culturally universal than he supposed. **RP-3** i. g, ii. h, iii. c, iv. f, v. e, vi. d, vii. a, viii. b.

MODULE TEST ANSWERS

1. b. **2.** formal operational. **3.** b. **4.** emerging adulthood.

ADULTHOOD

RETRIEVAL PRACTICE ANSWERS

RP-1 love; work. **RP-2** Challenges: decline of muscular strength, reaction times, stamina, sensory keenness, cardiac output, and immune system functioning. Risk of cognitive decline increases. Rewards: positive feelings tend to grow; negative emotions subside; and anger, stress, worry, and social-relationship problems decrease.

MODULE TEST ANSWERS

1. a. **2.** generativity. **3.** c.

CHAPTER 6

Sensation and Perception (Modules 18–20)

BASIC CONCEPTS OF SENSATION AND PERCEPTION

RETRIEVAL PRACTICE ANSWERS

RP-1 *Sensation* is the bottom-up process by which your sensory receptors and your nervous system receive and represent stimuli. *Perception* is the top-down process by which your brain creates meaning by organizing and interpreting what your senses detect. **RP-2** *Absolute threshold* is the minimum stimulation needed to detect a particular sound (such as an approaching bike on the sidewalk behind you) 50 percent of the time. *Subliminal stimulation* happens when, without your awareness, your sensory system processes a sound that is below your absolute threshold. A *difference threshold* is the minimum difference needed to distinguish between two stimuli (such as between the sound of a bike and the sound of a runner coming up behind you) 50 percent of the time. **RP-3** The shoes provide constant stimulation. Thanks to *sensory adaptation*, we tend to focus primarily on changing stimuli. **RP-4** *Perceptual set* involves top-down processing, because it draws on your experiences, assumptions, and expectations when interpreting stimuli.

MODULE TEST ANSWERS

1. b. **2.** perception. **3.** d. **4.** just noticeable difference. **5.** b. **6.** d. **7.** a.

VISION: SENSORY AND PERCEPTUAL PROCESSING

RETRIEVAL PRACTICE ANSWERS

RP-1 For those with vision, the blind spot is on the nose side of each retina, which means that objects to the right may fall onto the right eye's blind spot. Objects to the left may fall on the left eye's blind spot. The blind spot does not normally impair vision, because the eyes are moving and because one eye catches what the other misses. Moreover, even with only one eye open, the brain provides a perception without a hole in it. **RP-2** rods; cones; color. **RP-3** pupils. **RP-4** The *Young-Helmholtz trichromatic theory* shows that the retina contains color receptors for red, green, and blue. The *opponent-process theory* shows that we have opponent-process cells in the retina and thalamus for red-green, blue-yellow, and white-black. These theories are complementary and outline the two stages of color vision. First, the retina's receptors for red, green, and blue respond to different color stimuli. Second, the receptors' signals are then processed by the opponent-process cells on their way to the visual cortex in the brain. **RP-5** Light waves reflect off the person and travel into the eyes. Receptor cells in the retina convert the light waves' energy into neural impulses sent to the brain. The brain's detector cells and work teams process the subdimensions of this visual input—including color, movement, form, and depth—separately but simultaneously. The brain interprets this information, based on previously stored information and our expectations, and forms a conscious perception of that friend. **RP-6** figure;

ground. **RP-7** Gestalt psychologists used this saying to describe our perceptual tendency to organize clusters of sensations into meaningful forms or coherent groups. **RP-8** People typically are able to perceive depth thanks to both binocular cues (such as retinal disparity) and monocular cues (which include relative height, relative size, relative motion, linear perspective, and interposition).

MODULE TEST ANSWERS

1. wavelength. **2.** a. **3.** c. **4.** c. **5.** d. **6.** The brain constructs this perception of color in two stages. In the first stage, the lemon reflects light energy into the eyes, where it is transformed into neural messages. Three sets of cones, each sensitive to a different light frequency (red, blue, and green) process color. In this case, the light energy stimulates both red-sensitive and green-sensitive cones. In the second stage, opponent-process cells sensitive to paired opposites of color (red/green, blue/yellow, and black/white) evaluate the incoming neural messages as they pass through the optic nerve to the thalamus and visual cortex. When the yellow-sensitive opponent-process cells are stimulated, the viewer identifies the lemon as yellow. **7.** feature detectors. **8.** parallel processing. **9.** a. **10.** d. **11.** b. **12.** c. **13.** monocular. **14.** b. **15.** b. **16.** perceptual adaptation.

20 HEARING, SKIN, CHEMICAL, AND BODY SENSES

RETRIEVAL PRACTICE ANSWERS

RP-1 loudness. **RP-2** lower; lower. **RP-3** place theory; frequency theory. **RP-4** c. **RP-5** We have four basic touch senses and five basic taste sensations. But we have no specific smell receptors. Instead, different combinations of odor receptors send messages to the brain, enabling us to recognize some 1 trillion different smells. **RP-6** Kinesthetic receptors, called proprioceptors, are located in our joints, tendons, and muscles. Vestibular sense receptors are located in our inner ear. **RP-7** The ESP event would need to be replicated in other scientific studies.

MODULE TEST ANSWERS

1. cochlea. **2.** The outer ear collects sound waves, which are translated into mechanical waves by the *middle ear* and turned into fluid waves in the *inner ear*. The *auditory nerve* then translates the energy into electrical waves and sends them to the brain, which perceives and interprets the sound. **3.** Place; frequency; volley. **4.** nociceptors. **5.** c. **6.** Our experience of pain is influenced by biological factors (such as genetic differences in endorphin production), psychological factors (such as our attention), and social-cultural factors (such as the presence of others). **7.** We have specialized receptors for detecting sweet, salty, sour, bitter, and umami tastes. Being able to detect pleasurable tastes enabled our ancestors to seek out energy- or protein-rich foods. Detecting aversive tastes deterred them from eating toxic substances, increasing their chances of survival. **8.** Kinesthesia; vestibular sense. **9.** Your vestibular sense regulates balance and body positioning through kinesthetic receptors triggered by fluid in your inner ear. Wobbly legs and a spinning world are signs that these receptors are still responding to the ride's turbulence. As your vestibular sense adjusts to solid ground, your balance will be restored. **10.** d. **11.** d.

CHAPTER 7

Learning (Modules 21–23)

BASIC LEARNING CONCEPTS AND CLASSICAL CONDITIONING

RETRIEVAL PRACTICE ANSWERS

RP-1 Habits form when we repeat behaviors in a given context and, as a result, learn associations—often without our awareness. For example, we may have eaten a sweet pastry with a cup of coffee often enough to associate the flavor of the coffee with the treat, so that the cup of coffee alone just doesn't seem right anymore! **RP-2** NS = tone before conditioning; US = air puff; UR = blink to air puff; CS = tone after conditioning; CR = blink to tone. **RP-3** The pie (including its taste and aroma) is the US. The photo of the apple pie is the CS. Salivation to the photo is the CR. **RP-4** acquisition; extinction. **RP-5** generalization. **RP-6** If viewing a favorite fictional character (a US) elicits a positive response (a UR), then pairing the US with a new NS (a particular brand of car) could turn that brand of car into a conditioned stimulus (CS) that also prompts a positive, conditioned response (CR). **RP-7** The US was the loud noise; the UR was the fear response to the noise; the NS was the rat before it was paired with the noise; the CS was the rat after pairing; the CR was fear of the rat.

MODULE TEST ANSWERS

1. information; behaviors. **2.** c. **3.** conditioned. **4.** discrimination. **5.** b. **6.** A sexual image is a US that triggers a UR of interest or arousal. Before the ad pairs a product with a sexual image, the product is an NS. Over time the product can become a CS that triggers the CR of interest or arousal.

22 OPERANT CONDITIONING

RETRIEVAL PRACTICE ANSWERS

RP-1 do not; resulting. **RP-2** The baby negatively reinforces her parents' behavior when she stops crying once they grant her wish. Her parents positively reinforce her cries by letting her sleep with them. **RP-3** Spammers are reinforced on a variable-ratio schedule (receiving a response after sending a varying number of emails). Cookie checkers are reinforced on a fixed-interval schedule. Sandwich shop rewards programs use a fixed-ratio schedule. **RP-4** 1. PR (positive reinforcement); 2. NP (negative punishment); 3. PP (positive punishment); 4. NR (negative reinforcement). **RP-5** If Joslyn is seeking attention, the teacher's scolding may be reinforcing rather than punishing. To change Joslyn's behavior, her teacher could offer reinforcement (such as praise) each time she behaves well. The teacher might encourage Joslyn toward increasingly appropriate behavior through shaping, or by rephrasing rules as rewards instead of punishments. ("You can use the blocks if you play nicely with the other children" [reward] rather than "You may not use the blocks if you misbehave!" [punishment].) **RP-6** respondent; operant.

MODULE TEST ANSWERS

1. Skinner. **2.** shaping. **3.** c. **4.** They fuss or cry until they are fed. When providing food removes something aversive (baby's cry), the baby negatively reinforces the caregiver's desired behavior (feeding). **5.** partial (intermittent). **6.** a. **7.** variable-interval. **8.** c.

23 BIOLOGY, COGNITION, AND LEARNING

RETRIEVAL PRACTICE ANSWERS

RP-1 Garcia and Koelling demonstrated that rats may learn an aversion to tastes, on which their survival depends, but not to sights or sounds. **RP-2** The success of operant conditioning is affected not just by environmental cues, but also by biological and cognitive factors. **RP-3** Hannah may be more likely to speed. Observational learning studies suggest that children tend to do as others do and say what they say. **RP-4** i. c (You've probably learned your way by latent learning), ii. d (Observational learning may have contributed to your brother's imitating the actions seen in the movie), iii. a (Through classical conditioning you have associated the smell with the anticipated tasty result), iv. e (You are biologically predisposed to develop a conditioned taste aversion to foods associated with illness), v. b (Through operant conditioning your dog may have come to associate approaching excitedly with attention, petting, and a treat).

MODULE TEST ANSWERS

1. taste-aversion. **2.** This finding supports Darwin's principle that natural selection favors traits that aid survival. **3.** cognitive map. **4.** latent learning. **5.** observational learning. **6.** vicarious; vicarious. **7.** a. **8.** mirror. **9.** c.

CHAPTER 8

Memory (Modules 24–26)

STUDYING AND ENCODING MEMORIES

RETRIEVAL PRACTICE ANSWERS

RP-1 recognition; recall. **RP-2** It would be better to test your memory with *recall* (such as with short-answer or fill-in-the-blank self-test questions) rather than *recognition* (such as with multiple-choice questions). Recalling information is harder than recognizing it. So if you can recall it, that means your retention of the material is better than if you could only recognize it. Your chances of test success are, therefore, greater. **RP-3** The Atkinson-Shiffrin model viewed short-term memory as a temporary holding space for briefly storing recent thoughts and experiences. The newer idea of *working memory* expands our understanding of Atkinson-Shiffrin's short-term memory stage, emphasizing the conscious, active processing that takes place as the brain makes sense of new experiences and links them with our long-term memories. **RP-4** Working memory's two basic functions are active integration of new information with existing long-term memories and focusing of our spotlight of attention. **RP-5** *Automatic* processing occurs unconsciously (automatically) for such things as the sequence and frequency of a day's events, and reading and comprehending words in our own language(s). *Effortful* processing requires attentive awareness and happens, for example, when we work hard to learn new material in class, or new lines for a play. **RP-6** sensory memory. **RP-7** Although cramming and rereading may lead to short-term gains in knowledge, distributed practice, and repeated self-testing will result in the greatest long-term retention. **RP-8** Making material personally meaningful involves processing at a deep level, because you are processing *semantically*—based on the meaning of the words. Deep processing leads to greater retention.

MODULE TEST ANSWERS

1. recall. **2.** encoding; storage; retrieval. **3.** a. **4.** iconic; echoic. **5.** seven. **6.** mnemonics.

STORING AND RETRIEVING MEMORIES

RETRIEVAL PRACTICE ANSWERS

RP-1 The cerebellum and basal ganglia are important for *implicit* memory processing, and the frontal lobes and hippocampus are key to *explicit* memory formation. **RP-2** Our *explicit* conscious memories of facts and episodes differ from our *implicit* memories of skills (such as tying shoelaces) and classically conditioned responses. The parts of the brain involved in explicit memory processing (the frontal lobes and hippocampus) may have sustained damage in the accident, while the parts involved in implicit memory processing (the cerebellum and basal ganglia) appear to have escaped harm. **RP-3** the amygdala. **RP-4** long-term potentiation. **RP-5** *Priming* is the activation (often without our awareness) of associations. Seeing a gun, for example, might temporarily predispose someone to interpret an ambiguous face as threatening or to recall a boss as nasty. **RP-6** serial position.

MODULE TEST ANSWERS

1. a. **2.** implicit. **3.** c. **4.** retrieval cues. **5.** Memories are stored within a web of many associations, one of which is mood. When you recall happy moments from your past, you activate these positive links. You may then experience mood-congruent memory and recall other happy moments, which could improve your mood and brighten your interpretation of current events. **6.** a.

FORGETTING, MEMORY CONSTRUCTION, AND IMPROVING MEMORY

RETRIEVAL PRACTICE ANSWERS

RP-1 First, through *encoding failure:* Unattended information never entered our memory system. Second, through *storage decay:* Information fades from our memory. Third, through *retrieval failure:* We cannot access stored information accurately, sometimes due to interference or motivated forgetting. **RP-2** repress. **RP-3** Real experiences would be confused with those we dreamed. When seeing people we know, we might, therefore, be unsure whether we were reacting to something they previously did or to something we dreamed they did. **RP-4** It will be important to remember the key points agreed upon by most researchers and professional associations: Sexual abuse, injustice, forgetting, and memory construction all happen; recovered memories are common; memories from before age 4 are unreliable; memories claimed to be recovered through hypnosis are especially unreliable; and memories, whether real or false, can be emotionally upsetting. **RP-5** Spend more time rehearsing or actively thinking about the material to boost long-term recall. Consider a study group so you can verbalize your learning. Schedule spaced (not crammed) study times. Make the material personally meaningful, with well-organized and vivid associations. Refresh your memory by returning to contexts and moods to activate retrieval cues. Use mnemonic devices. Minimize proactive and retroactive interference. Plan ahead to ensure a complete night's sleep. Test yourself repeatedly—retrieval practice is a proven retention strategy.

MODULE TEST ANSWERS

1. d. **2.** d. **3.** retroactive. **4.** repression. **5.** b. **6.** Eliza's immature hippocampus and minimal verbal skills made it impossible for her to encode an explicit memory of the wedding reception at the age of two. It's more likely that Eliza learned information (from hearing the story repeatedly) that she eventually constructed into a memory that feels very real. **7.** source amnesia. **8.** déjà vu. **9.** b. **10.** b.

CHAPTER 9

Thinking and Language (Modules 27–28)

THINKING

RETRIEVAL PRACTICE ANSWERS

RP-1 If a tragic event, such as a plane crash, makes the news, it is noteworthy and unusual, unlike much more common bad events, such as traffic accidents. Knowing this, we can worry less about unlikely events and think more about improving the safety of our everyday activities. (For example, we can wear a seat belt when in a vehicle and use the crosswalk when walking.) **RP-2** i. b, ii. c, iii. e, iv. d, v. a, vi. f, vii. h, viii. j, ix. i, x. g, xi. k.

MODULE TEST ANSWERS

1. concept. **2.** algorithm. **3.** Omar will need to guard against *confirmation bias* (searching for support for his own views and ignoring contradictory evidence) as he seeks out opposing viewpoints. Even if Omar encounters new information that disproves his beliefs, *belief perseverance* may lead him to cling to these views anyway. It will take more compelling evidence to change his political beliefs than it took to create them. **4.** c. **5.** availability. **6.** framing. **7.** b. **8.** neural networks.

28 LANGUAGE AND THOUGHT

RETRIEVAL PRACTICE ANSWERS

RP-1 Two morphemes—*cat* and *s*, and four phonemes—*c, a, t,* and *s*. **RP-2** Chomsky maintained that humans are biologically predisposed to learn the grammar rules of language. **RP-3** Infants typically start developing *receptive language* skills (ability to understand what is said to and about them) around 4 months of age. Then, starting with babbling at 4 months and beyond, infants typically start building *productive language* skills (ability to produce sounds and eventually words). **RP-4** Our brain's *critical period* for language learning is in childhood, when we can absorb language structure almost effortlessly. As we move past that stage in our brain's development, our ability to learn a new language diminishes dramatically. **RP-5** Broca's area; Wernicke's area. **RP-6** linguistic determinism. **RP-7** Mental practice uses visual imagery to mentally rehearse future behaviors, activating some of the same brain areas used during the actual behaviors. Visualizing the details of the process is more effective than visualizing only your end goal. **RP-8** These are definitely communications. But if language consists of words and the grammatical rules we use to combine them to communicate meaning, few scientists would label a dog's barking and yipping as language.

MODULE TEST ANSWERS

1. c. **2.** phonemes; morphemes; grammar. **3.** telegraphic speech. **4.** universal grammar. **5.** a.

CHAPTER 10

Intelligence (Modules 29–31)

 WHAT IS INTELLIGENCE?

RETRIEVAL PRACTICE ANSWERS

RP-1 People with savant syndrome have limited mental ability overall but possess one or more exceptional skills. According to Howard Gardner, this suggests that our abilities come in separate packages rather than being fully expressed by one general intelligence that encompasses all of our talents. **RP-2** The CHC theory proposes that there is a general ability based on *two* factors—fluid intelligence and crystallized intelligence—but also that there are more specific abilities, such as reading and writing ability, memory capacity, and processing speed.

MODULE TEST ANSWERS

1. general intelligence. **2.** c. **3.** analytical; creative; practical. **4.** d.

 INTELLIGENCE ASSESSMENT AND DYNAMICS

RETRIEVAL PRACTICE ANSWERS

RP-1 Binet hoped that determining the child's mental age (the age that typically corresponds to a certain level of performance) would help identify appropriate school placements. **RP-2** 125($5/4 \times 100 = 125$) **RP-3** aptitude; achievement. **RP-4** A psychological test must be *standardized* (pretested on a representative sample of people), *reliable* (yielding consistent results), and *valid* (measuring and predicting what it is supposed to). **RP-5** disagreement; down; zero; agreement; up. **RP-6** Researcher A should develop a *longitudinal study* to examine how intelligence changes in the same people over the life span. Researcher B should develop a *cross-sectional study* to examine the intelligence of people now at various life stages.

MODULE TEST ANSWERS

1. d. ($9/6 \times 100 = 150$). **2.** c. **3.** reliability. **4.** c. **5.** Writers' work relies more on *Gc* (crystallized intelligence)—accumulated knowledge that increases with age. For top performance, scientists doing research may need more *Gf* (the speedy and abstract reasoning of fluid intelligence), which tends to decrease with age.

 GENETIC AND ENVIRONMENTAL INFLUENCES ON INTELLIGENCE

RETRIEVAL PRACTICE ANSWERS

RP-1 a. (Heritability—variation within a group explained by genetic influences—will increase as environmental variation decreases.) **RP-2** Perfectly equal opportunity would create 100 percent heritability, because genes alone would account for any human differences. **RP-3** A test may be *culturally* biased (unfair) if higher scores are achieved by those with certain cultural experiences. That same test is not scientifically biased as long as it has *predictive validity*—if it predicts what it is supposed to predict. For example, the SAT may favor those with experience in the U.S. school system, but it does still accurately predict U.S. college success. **RP-4** stereotype threat.

MODULE TEST ANSWERS

1. c. **2.** a. **3.** c. **4.** Stereotype threat.

CHAPTER 11

What Drives Us: Hunger, Sex, Belongingness, and Achievement (Modules 32–35)

 BASIC MOTIVATIONAL CONCEPTS

RETRIEVAL PRACTICE ANSWERS

RP-1 (a) Well-practiced runners tend to excel when aroused by competition. (b) High anxiety about a difficult exam may disrupt test-takers' performance. **RP-2** According to Maslow, our drive to meet the physiological needs of hunger and thirst takes priority over our safety needs, prompting us to take risks at times.

MODULE TEST ANSWERS

1. b. **2.** a. **3.** incentive. **4.** Arousal. **5.** b. **6.** a.

 HUNGER

RETRIEVAL PRACTICE ANSWERS

RP-1 low; high. **RP-2** You have learned to respond to the sight and aroma that signal the food about to enter your mouth. Both *physiological* cues (low blood sugar) and *psychological* cues (anticipation of the tasty meal) heighten your experienced hunger. **RP-3** Genetically influenced set/settling points, metabolism, and other factors (such as adequate sleep) influence the way our body burns calories.

MODULE TEST ANSWERS

1. Maslow's hierarchy of needs supports this statement because it addresses the primacy of some motives over others. Once our basic physiological needs are met, safety concerns are addressed next, followed by belongingness and love needs (such as the desire to kiss). **2.** set. **3.** c. **4.** low. **5.** basal metabolic. **6.** d. **7.** Sanjay's plan is problematic. After he gains weight, the extra fat will require less energy to maintain than it did to gain in the first place. Sanjay may have a hard time getting rid of it later, when his metabolism slows down in an effort to retain his body weight.

34 SEXUAL MOTIVATION

RETRIEVAL PRACTICE ANSWERS

RP-1 estrogens; testosterone. **RP-2** sexual dysfunction; paraphilia. **RP-3** Influences include biological factors such as sexual maturity and sex hormones, psychological factors such as environmental stimuli and fantasies, and social-cultural factors such as the values and expectations absorbed from family and the surrounding culture. **RP-4** a, c, d. **RP-5** b, c, e.

MODULE TEST ANSWERS

1. b. **2.** b. **3.** Sexual dysfunctions are problems that consistently impair arousal or sexual function. Paraphilias are conditions, which may be classified as psychological disorders, in which sexual arousal is associated with nonhuman objects, the suffering of self or others, and/or nonconsenting persons. **4.** does; doesn't. **5.** c. **6.** Researchers have found no evidence that any environmental factor (parental relationships, childhood experiences, peer relationships, or dating experiences) influences the development of our sexual orientation.

 AFFILIATION AND ACHIEVEMENT

RETRIEVAL PRACTICE ANSWERS

RP-1 They engaged in more self-defeating behaviors and displayed more disparaging and aggressive behavior. These students' basic *need to belong* seems to have been disrupted. **RP-2** strengthen; increase. **RP-3** self-discipline *(grit)*.

MODULE TEST ANSWERS

1. c. **2.** Monitor our time spent online, as well as our feelings about that time. Change our online status to unavailable when we don't want to be contacted. Check our devices less often. Get outside and away from technology regularly. **3.** should; should.

CHAPTER 12

Emotions, Stress, and Health (Modules 36–40)

 INTRODUCTION TO EMOTION

RETRIEVAL PRACTICE ANSWERS

RP-1 simultaneously; sequentially (first the physiological response, and then the experienced emotion). **RP-2** cognitive. **RP-3** Zajonc and LeDoux suggested that we experience some emotions without any conscious, cognitive appraisal. Lazarus, Schachter, and Singer emphasized the importance of appraisal and cognitive labeling in our experience of emotion. **RP-4** The *sympathetic division* of the ANS arouses us for more intense experiences of emotion, pumping out the stress hormones epinephrine and norepinephrine to prepare our body for fight or flight. The *parasympathetic division* of the ANS takes over when a crisis passes, restoring our body to a calm physiological and emotional state.

MODULE TEST ANSWERS

1. James-Lange. **2.** b. **3.** c. **4.** A polygraph measures emotion-linked physiological changes, such as in perspiration, heart rate, and breathing. But the measure cannot distinguish between emotions with similar physiology (such as anxiety and guilt).

 EXPRESSING EMOTION

RETRIEVAL PRACTICE ANSWERS

RP-1 Women. **RP-2** Some facial expressions, such as those of happiness and sadness, tend to be universally recognizable and thus likely rooted in biology. Context and culture, however, can influence the way facial expressions are interpreted. Like most psychological events, facial expressions are best understood not only as biological and cognitive phenomena, but also as social-cultural phenomena. **RP-3** (a) Most students report feeling more happy than sad when their cheeks are raised upward. (b) Most students report feeling more sad than happy when their cheeks are pulled downward.

MODULE TEST ANSWERS

1. facial feedback. **2.** Aiden's droopy posture could negatively affect his mood thanks to the behavior feedback effect, which tends to make us feel the way we act.

 EXPERIENCING EMOTION

RETRIEVAL PRACTICE ANSWERS

RP-1 b. **RP-2** a. Age does NOT effectively predict happiness levels. Better predictors are personality traits, sleep and exercise, and religious faith.

MODULE TEST ANSWERS

1. d. **2.** Positive. **3.** b. **4.** relative deprivation.

 STRESS AND ILLNESS

RETRIEVAL PRACTICE ANSWERS

RP-1 sympathetic; increase; muscles; fight-or-flight. **RP-2** psychoneuroimmunology. **RP-3** Stress tends to reduce our immune system's ability to function properly, so that higher stress generally leads to greater risk of physical illness. **RP-4** Feeling angry and negative much of the time.

MODULE TEST ANSWERS

1. b. **2.** d. **3.** resistance; exhaustion. **4.** tend; befriend. **5.** immune system. **6.** Type A people frequently experience negative emotions (anger, impatience), during which the sympathetic nervous system diverts blood away from the liver. This leaves fat and cholesterol circulating in the bloodstream for deposit near the heart and other organs, increasing the risk of heart disease and other health problems. Thus, Type A people actually harm themselves by directing anger at others.

 HEALTH AND COPING

RETRIEVAL PRACTICE ANSWERS

RP-1 problem; emotion. **RP-2** b. **RP-3** Aerobic exercise, relaxation, meditation, and active spiritual engagement.

MODULE TEST ANSWERS

1. emotion. **2.** b. **3.** internal. **4.** By allowing ourselves to feel our natural negative and positive emotions, we are better able to navigate the realities of our lives—including good times and bad times. Suppressing or ignoring our feelings has negative consequences, leaving us less able to manage stress or build authentic relationships. **5.** d. **6.** aerobic. **7.** c.

CHAPTER 13

Social Psychology (Modules 41–44)

 SOCIAL THINKING

RETRIEVAL PRACTICE ANSWERS

RP-1 By attributing the other person's behavior to the person ("What a terrible driver") and his own to the situation ("These roads are awful"), Marco has exhibited the *fundamental attribution error.* **RP-2** Our attitudes often influence our actions as we behave in ways consistent with our beliefs. However, our actions also influence our attitudes; we come to believe in what we have done. **RP-3** cognitive dissonance. **RP-4** Avoid yelling at, humiliating, or boring your audience. It's more effective to identify shared values, appeal to others' admirable motives, make your message vivid and repeat it, and get your audience to actively engage with your message.

MODULE TEST ANSWERS

1. fundamental attribution. **2.** foot-in-the-door. **3.** *Cognitive dissonance theory* best supports this suggestion. If Jamala acts confident, her behavior will contradict her negative self-thoughts, creating cognitive dissonance. To relieve the tension, Jamala may realign her attitudes with her actions by viewing herself as more outgoing and confident. **4.** peripheral.

 SOCIAL INFLUENCE

RETRIEVAL PRACTICE ANSWERS

RP-1 a. **RP-2** normative social influence. **RP-3** Stanley Milgram. **RP-4** The Milgram studies showed that people were most likely to follow orders when the experimenter was nearby and was perceived to be a legitimate authority figure, the authority figure was supported by a powerful or prestigious institution, the victim was depersonalized or at a distance, and there were no models for defiance. **RP-5** This improved performance in the presence of others is most likely to occur with a well-learned task, because the added arousal caused by an audience tends to strengthen the most likely response. This also predicts poorer performance on a difficult task in others' presence. **RP-6** social loafing. **RP-7** The anonymity provided by the masks, combined with the arousal of the contentious setting, might create deindividuation (lessened self-awareness and self-restraint). **RP-8** group polarization. **RP-9** groupthink.

MODULE TEST ANSWERS

1. c. **2.** a. **3.** The presence of a large audience generates arousal and strengthens Dr. Huang's most likely response: enhanced performance on a task he has mastered (teaching music history) and impaired performance on a task he finds difficult (statistics). **4.** deindividuation. **5.** group polarization.

 ANTISOCIAL RELATIONS

RETRIEVAL PRACTICE ANSWERS

RP-1 scapegoat. **RP-2** Our biology (our genes, neural systems, and biochemistry—including testosterone and alcohol levels) influences our aggressive tendencies. Psychological factors (such as frustration, previous rewards for aggressive acts, and observation of others' aggression) can trigger any aggressive tendencies we may have. Social influences, such as exposure to violent media, and cultural influences, such as whether we've grown up in a "culture of honor" or a father-absent home, can also affect our aggressive responses.

MODULE TEST ANSWERS

1. stereotypes. **2.** b. **3.** more. **4.** d. **5.** frustration-aggression principle. **6.** c. **7.** c. **8.** c.

 PROSOCIAL RELATIONS

RETRIEVAL PRACTICE ANSWERS

RP-1 mere exposure effect. **RP-2** Being physically attractive tends to elicit positive first impressions. People tend to assume that attractive people are healthier, happier, more sensitive, more successful, and more socially skilled than others are. **RP-3** Emotions consist of (1) physical arousal and (2) our interpretation of that arousal. Researchers have found that any source of arousal may be interpreted as passion in the presence of a desirable person. **RP-4** equity; self-disclosure. **RP-5** In the presence of others, an individual is less likely to notice a situation, correctly interpret it as an emergency, and take responsibility for offering help. The inaction of neighbors who heard Kitty Genovese's cries for help demonstrated this *bystander effect,* as each witness assumed many others were also aware of the event. **RP-6** Sports fans may feel they are a part of an *ingroup* (fans of their preferred team) that sets itself apart from an *outgroup* (fans of the archrival team). Ingroup bias tends to develop, leading to prejudice and the view that the outgroup "deserves" misfortune. So, the archrival team's loss may seem justified. In conflicts, this kind of thinking is problematic, especially when each side in the conflict develops *mirror-image perceptions* of the other (distorted, negative images that are ironically similar). **RP-7** Peacemakers should encourage equal-status contact, cooperation to achieve *superordinate goals* (shared goals that override differences), understanding through communication, and reciprocated conciliatory gestures (each side gives a little).

MODULE TEST ANSWERS

1. mere exposure. **2.** companionate; passionate. **3.** d. **4.** c. **5.** mirror-image. **6.** superordinate.

CHAPTER 14

Personality (Modules 45–47)

 INTRODUCTION TO PERSONALITY AND PSYCHODYNAMIC THEORIES

RETRIEVAL PRACTICE ANSWERS

RP-1 ego; id; superego. **RP-2** fixation. **RP-3** unconsciously; anxiety. **RP-4** Freud is credited with first drawing attention to the importance of childhood experiences, to the existence of the unconscious mind, and to our self-protective defense mechanisms. Freud's theory has been criticized as not scientifically testable and offering after-the-fact explanations, focusing too much on sexual conflicts in childhood, and being based on the idea of repression, which has not been supported by modern research. **RP-5** Today's psychodynamic theorists and therapists still use Freud's interviewing techniques, and they still tend to focus on childhood experiences and attachments, unresolved conflicts, and unconscious influences. However, they are not likely to dwell on fixation at any psychosexual stage, or the idea that sexual issues are the basis of our personality. **RP-6** Projective.

MODULE TEST ANSWERS

1. c. **2.** superego. **3.** b. **4.** anxiety. **5.** repression. **6.** d. **7.** a. **8.** a.

 HUMANISTIC THEORIES AND TRAIT THEORIES

RETRIEVAL PRACTICE ANSWERS

RP-1 The humanistic theories sought to turn psychology's attention away from drives and conflicts and toward our growth potential. This movement's focus on the way people strive for self-determination and self-realization was in contrast to Freudian theory and strict behaviorism. **RP-2** To be *empathic* is to share and mirror another person's feelings. Carl Rogers believed that people nurture growth in others by being empathic. Abraham Maslow proposed that *self-actualization* is the motivation to fulfill one's potential, and one of the ultimate psychological needs (another is self-transcendence). **RP-3** extraversion–introversion and emotional stability–instability. **RP-4** The Big Five personality factors are openness, conscientiousness, extraversion, agreeableness, and neuroticism (emotional stability vs. instability): OCEAN. These factors may be objectively measured, they are relatively stable over the life span, and they apply fairly well to all cultures in which they have been studied. **RP-5** Our scores on personality tests predict our *average* behavior across many situations much better than they predict our specific behavior in any given situation.

MODULE TEST ANSWERS

1. d. **2.** Rogers might assert that the criminal was raised in an environment lacking acceptance (unconditional positive regard), genuineness, and empathy, which inhibited psychological growth and led to a negative self-concept. **3.** unconditional positive regard. **4.** Trait. **5.** c. **6.** b. **7.** b.

 SOCIAL-COGNITIVE THEORIES AND THE SELF

RETRIEVAL PRACTICE ANSWERS

RP-1 social-cognitive; reciprocal determinism. **RP-2** To predict someone's future behavior, examine the person's past behavior patterns in similar situations. **RP-3** People who feel confident in their abilities tend to be outgoing, responsible, and open to new experiences, and are often happier, less anxious, and less lonely. Inflated self-esteem can lead to the Dunning-Kruger effect, self-serving bias, greater aggression, and narcissism. **RP-4** self-serving bias. **RP-5** Defensive; Secure.

MODULE TEST ANSWERS

1. a. **2.** social-cognitive. **3.** spotlight effect. **4.** b. **5.** Yes, if that self-love is of the *secure* type. Secure self-esteem promotes a focus beyond the self and a higher quality of life. Excessive self-love may promote artificially high or defensive self-esteem, which is fragile; perceived threats may be met with anger or aggression.

CHAPTER 15

Psychological Disorders (Modules 48–53)

48 INTRODUCTION TO PSYCHOLOGICAL DISORDERS

RETRIEVAL PRACTICE ANSWERS

RP-1 dysfunctional or maladaptive. **RP-2** Some psychological disorders are culture-specific. For example, anorexia nervosa occurs mostly in Western cultures, and *taijin kyofusho* appears largely in Japan. Other disorders, such as major depressive disorder and schizophrenia, are universal—they occur in all cultures. **RP-3** Biological, psychological, and social-cultural influences combine to produce psychological disorders. This approach helps us understand that our well-being is affected by our genes, brain functioning, inner thoughts and feelings, and the influences of our social and cultural environment. **RP-4** Therapists and others apply disorder labels to communicate with one another using a common language, and to share concepts during research. Clients may benefit from knowing that they are not the only ones with these symptoms. The dangers of labeling people are that (1) overly broad classifications may pathologize typical behavior, and (2) the labels can trigger assumptions that will change people's behavior toward those who are labeled. **RP-5** false. **RP-6** true. **RP-7** Poverty-related stresses can help trigger disorders, but disabling disorders can also contribute to poverty. Thus, poverty and disorder are often a chicken-and-egg situation; it's hard to know which came first.

MODULE TEST ANSWERS

1. major depressive disorder. **2.** No. Robert's behavior is unusual, causes distress, and may make him a few minutes late on occasion, but it does not appear to significantly disrupt his ability to function. Like most of us, Robert demonstrates some unusual behaviors. Since they are not disabling or dysfunctional, they do not suggest a psychological disorder. **3.** medical. **4.** There are various culture-linked disorders, including *susto* (in Latin America), *taijin kyofusho* (in Japan), and eating disorders (in food-abundant Western cultures). **5.** c. **6.** Critics have expressed concerns about the negative effects of labeling by the DSM and other classification systems. Labels have the potential to be both subjective and stigmatizing. Further, critics suggest that the DSM-5 cast too wide a net on disorders, pathologizing typical behavior. **7.** Men; women. **8.** d.

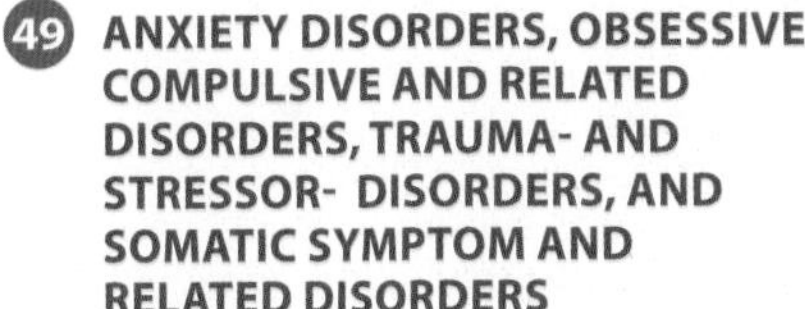

49 ANXIETY DISORDERS, OBSESSIVE-COMPULSIVE AND RELATED DISORDERS, TRAUMA- AND STRESSOR- DISORDERS, AND SOMATIC SYMPTOM AND RELATED DISORDERS

RETRIEVAL PRACTICE ANSWERS

RP-1 generalized anxiety. **RP-2** panic. **RP-3** specific phobia. **RP-4** obsessive-compulsive. **RP-5** posttraumatic stress. **RP-6** Somatic means "relating to the body"; somatic symptom disorders produce distressing bodily symptoms that have no apparent physical cause. **RP-7** Biological factors include inherited temperament and other gene variations; experience-altered brain pathways; and outdated, inherited responses that had survival value for our distant ancestors.

MODULE TEST ANSWERS

1. c. **2.** specific phobia. **3.** obsessive-compulsive. **4.** b. **5.** c.

DEPRESSIVE DISORDERS AND BIPOLAR DISORDERS

RETRIEVAL PRACTICE ANSWERS

RP-1 Many factors contribute to depression, including the biological influences of genetics and brain function. Social-cognitive factors also matter, including the interaction of explanatory style, mood, our responses to stressful experiences, changes in our patterns of thinking and behaving, and cultural influences. Depression involves the whole body and may disrupt sleep, energy levels, and concentration.

MODULE TEST ANSWERS

1. women's; men's. **2.** a. **3.** norepinephrine; serotonin. **4.** social-cognitive.

SCHIZOPHRENIA

RETRIEVAL PRACTICE ANSWERS

RP-1 negative; positive. **RP-2** Biological factors include abnormalities in brain structure and function and a genetic predisposition to the disorder. Environmental factors such as nutritional deprivation, exposure to virus, and maternal stress contribute to activating the genes that increase risk. Exposure to many environmental triggers can increase the odds of developing schizophrenia.

MODULE TEST ANSWERS

1. Schizophrenia involves the altered perceptions, emotions, and behaviors of a mind split from reality. It does not involve the rapid changes in mood or identity suggested by this comparison. **2.** b. **3.** hallucination. **4.** a.

DISSOCIATIVE, PERSONALITY, AND EATING DISORDERS

RETRIEVAL PRACTICE ANSWERS

RP-1 The psychodynamic explanation of DID symptoms is that they are defenses against anxiety generated by unacceptable urges. The learning perspective attempts to explain these symptoms as behaviors that have been reinforced by relieving anxiety. **RP-2** Twin and adoption studies show that biological relatives of people with antisocial personality disorder are at increased risk for antisocial behavior. Researchers have also observed differences in the brain activity and structure of antisocial criminals. Negative environmental factors, such as poverty or childhood abuse, may channel genetic traits such as fearlessness in more dangerous directions—toward aggression and away from social responsibility. **RP-3** anorexia nervosa; bulimia nervosa.

MODULE TEST ANSWERS

1. c. **2.** c. **3.** b. **4.** b.

NEURODEVELOPMENTAL DISORDERS

RETRIEVAL PRACTICE ANSWERS

RP-1 To be diagnosed with an intellectual developmental disorder, a person's intelligence test score must be in the lowest 3 percent of the general population, or about 70 or below. In addition, the person must have difficulty adapting to the normal demands of independent living: conceptual (language, reading, and concepts of money, time, and number); social (interpersonal skills, being socially responsible, following basic rules and laws, not being victimized); and practical (health and personal care, occupational skill, and travel).

MODULE TEST ANSWERS

1. c. **2.** Several studies have revealed "underconnectivity" in the brains of people with ASD, which makes it more difficult for different parts of the brain to work together and integrate information. Those with ASD are also less imitative and show less activity in brain areas involved in mirroring others' actions. **3.** The DSM has broadened the diagnostic criteria for ADHD, leading to an increase in diagnoses without concurrent changes in children's attentional behavior. Critics suggest that these criteria are now too broad and may pathologize behaviors, labeling everyday childish rambunctiousness as a disorder.

CHAPTER 16

Therapy (Modules 54–56)

INTRODUCTION TO THERAPY AND THE PSYCHOLOGICAL THERAPIES

RETRIEVAL PRACTICE ANSWERS

RP-1 transference; resistance; interpretation. **RP-2** A psychodynamic therapist might be more interested in helping the child develop insight about the underlying problems that have caused the bed-wetting response. A behavior therapist would be more likely to agree with Mowrer that the bed-wetting is the problem, and that counterconditioning the unwanted behavior would indeed bring emotional relief. **RP-3** The *insight therapies*—psychodynamic and humanistic therapies—seek to relieve problems by providing an understanding of their origins. *Behavior therapies* assume the problem behavior is the problem and treat it directly, paying less attention to its origins. **RP-4** If a behavior can be learned, it can be *un*learned and replaced by other, more adaptive responses. **RP-5** classical; operant. **RP-6** By reflecting people's feelings in a nondirective setting, the *humanistic therapies* attempt to foster personal growth by helping people become more self-aware and self-accepting. By making people aware of self-defeating patterns of thinking, *cognitive therapies* guide them toward more adaptive ways of thinking about themselves and their world. **RP-7** cognitive therapy. **RP-8** *Cognitive-behavioral therapy* helps people change self-defeating thinking and behavior. It has been shown to be effective for those with anxiety disorders, obsessive-compulsive and related disorders, depressive disorders, bipolar disorders, ADHD, eating disorders, and alcohol or other substance use disorders.

MODULE TEST ANSWERS

1. a. **2.** Insight. **3.** d. **4.** active listening. **5.** c. **6.** counterconditioning. **7.** systematic desensitization. **8.** Behavior therapies are often the best choice for treating specific phobias. Viewing Rico's fear of the highway as a learned response, a behavior therapist might help Rico learn to replace his anxious response to highway driving with a relaxation response. **9.** token economy. **10.** d. **11.** Cognitive-behavioral. **12.** b.

 EVALUATING PSYCHOTHERAPIES

RETRIEVAL PRACTICE ANSWERS

RP-1 The *placebo effect* is the healing power of belief in a treatment. Patients and therapists who expect a treatment to be effective may believe it was effective. **RP-2** are. **RP-3** When using an evidence-based approach, therapists make decisions about treatment based on research evidence, clinical expertise, and knowledge of the client. **RP-4** more. **RP-5** ethical.

MODULE TEST ANSWERS

1. c. **2.** d. **3.** research evidence, clinical expertise, and knowledge of the patient. **4.** hope.

 THE BIOMEDICAL THERAPIES AND PREVENTING PSYCHOLOGICAL DISORDERS

RETRIEVAL PRACTICE ANSWERS

RP-1 Exercise regularly, get enough sleep, get more exposure to light (get outside or use a light box), nurture important relationships, redirect negative thinking, and eat a diet rich in omega-3 fatty acids. **RP-2** Researchers assign people to treatment and no-treatment conditions to see if those who receive the drug therapy improve more than those who don't. Double-blind controlled studies are most effective. If neither the therapist nor the client knows which participants have received the drug treatment, then any difference between the treated and untreated groups will reflect the drug treatment's actual effect. **RP-3** antidepressants; antipsychotic. **RP-4** electroconvulsive therapy; direct current; magnetic; deep brain. **RP-5** Psychological or biomedical therapies attempt to relieve people's suffering from psychological disorders. Preventive mental health attempts to prevent suffering by identifying and eliminating the conditions that cause disorders, as well as by building resilience.

MODULE TEST ANSWERS

1. c. **2.** antianxiety. **3.** lithium. **4.** b. **5.** d.

APPENDIX C

Psychology at Work

WORK AND LIFE SATISFACTION

RETRIEVAL PRACTICE ANSWERS

RP-1 We become more likely to view our work as socially useful, and we experience higher self-esteem, feelings of competence, and overall well-being. **RP-2** (1) Interviewers may presume people are what they seem to be in interviews. (2) Interviewers' preconceptions and moods color how they perceive interviewees' responses. (3) Interviewers judge people relative to other recent interviewees. (4) Interviewers tend to track the successful careers of those they hire, not the successful careers of those they reject. (5) Interviews tend to disclose prospective workers' good intentions, not their habitual behaviors. **RP-3** *Transformational leaders* are able to inspire others to share a vision and commit themselves to a group's mission. They tend to be naturally extraverted and set high standards. **RP-4** To develop safer machines and work environments, human factors psychologists stay mindful of the curse of knowledge—the tendency for experts to mistakenly assume that others share their knowledge.

MODULE TEST ANSWERS

1. flow. **2.** Personnel; human factors. **3.** a. **4.** d. **5.** Focusing on SMART goals—goals that are *specific, measurable, actionable, realistic,* and *time-bound* (such as maintaining a regular study schedule)—will be more helpful than focusing on more distant general goals (such as earning a good grade in this class). **6.** transformational. **7.** c. **8.** d.

Glossary

absolute threshold the minimum stimulus energy needed to detect a particular stimulus 50 percent of the time.

accommodation (1) adapting our current schemas (understandings) to incorporate new information. (2) the process by which the eye's lens changes shape to focus near or far objects on the retina.

achievement motivation the desire for significant accomplishment, for mastery of skills or ideas, for control, and for attaining a high standard.

achievement test a test designed to assess what a person has learned.

acquisition in classical conditioning, the initial stage—when one links a neutral stimulus and an unconditioned stimulus so that the neutral stimulus begins triggering the conditioned response. (In operant conditioning, the strengthening of a reinforced response.)

action potential a neural impulse; a brief electrical charge that travels down an axon.

active listening empathic listening in which the listener echoes, restates, and seeks clarification. A feature of Rogers' person-centered therapy.

acute schizophrenia (also called *reactive schizophrenia*) a form of schizophrenia that can begin at any age, frequently occurs in response to a traumatic event, and from which recovery is much more likely.

adaptation-level phenomenon our tendency to form judgments (of sounds, of lights, of income) relative to a neutral level defined by our prior experience.

addiction an everyday term for compulsive substance use (and sometimes for dysfunctional behavior patterns, such as out-of-control gambling) that continues despite harmful consequences. (See also *substance use disorder*.)

adolescence the transition period from childhood to young adulthood, extending from puberty to independence.

adrenal [ah-DREEN-el] glands a pair of endocrine glands that sits just above the kidneys and secretes hormones (epinephrine and norepinephrine) that help arouse the body in times of stress.

aerobic exercise sustained exercise that increases heart and lung fitness; also helps alleviate depression and anxiety.

affiliation need the need to build and maintain relationships and to feel connected to a group.

aggression any physical or verbal behavior intended to harm someone physically or emotionally.

agonist a molecule that increases a neurotransmitter's action.

AIDS (acquired immune deficiency syndrome) a life-threatening condition caused by the *human immunodeficiency virus (HIV)*, a sexually transmitted infection. AIDS depletes the immune system, leaving the person vulnerable to infections.

alcohol use disorder (commonly known as *alcoholism*) alcohol use marked by a combination of symptoms that may include tolerance, withdrawal, and a drive to continue problematic use.

algorithm a methodical, logical rule, or procedure that guarantees solving a particular problem. Contrasts with the usually speedier—but also more error-prone—use of *heuristics*.

all-or-none response a neuron's reaction of either firing (with a full-strength response) or not firing.

alpha waves the relatively slow brain waves of a relaxed, awake state.

altruism unselfish regard for the welfare of others.

Alzheimer's disease a neurocognitive disorder marked by neural plaques, often with onset after age 80, and entailing a progressive decline in memory and other cognitive abilities.

amphetamines drugs (such as *methamphetamine*) that stimulate neural activity, causing accelerated body functions and associated energy and mood changes.

amygdala [uh-MIG-duh-la] two almond-shaped neural clusters in the limbic system; linked to emotion.

androgyny blending traditionally masculine and traditionally feminine psychological characteristics.

anorexia nervosa an eating disorder in which a person (most often an adolescent female) maintains a starvation diet despite being significantly underweight, and has an inaccurate self-perception; sometimes accompanied by excessive exercise.

antagonist a molecule that inhibits or blocks a neurotransmitter's action.

anterograde amnesia an inability to form new memories.

antianxiety drugs drugs used to control anxiety and agitation.

antidepressant drugs drugs used to treat depressive disorders, anxiety disorders, obsessive-compulsive and related disorders, and post-traumatic stress disorder. (Several widely used antidepressant drugs are *selective serotonin reuptake inhibitors—SSRIs*.)

antipsychotic drugs drugs used to treat schizophrenia and other psychotic disorders.

antisocial behavior negative, destructive, harmful behavior. The opposite of prosocial behavior.

antisocial personality disorder a personality disorder in which a person (usually a man) exhibits a lack of conscience for wrongdoing, even toward friends and family members; may be aggressive and ruthless or a clever con artist.

anxiety disorders a group of disorders characterized by excessive fear and anxiety and related maladaptive behaviors.

aphasia impairment of language, usually caused by left hemisphere damage either to Broca's area (impairing speaking) or to Wernicke's area (impairing understanding).

applied research a scientific study that aims to solve practical problems.

approach and avoidance motives the drive to move toward (approach) or away from (avoid) a stimulus.

aptitude test a test designed to predict a person's future performance; *aptitude* is the capacity to learn.

asexual having no sexual attraction toward others.

assimilation interpreting our new experiences in terms of our existing schemas.

association areas areas of the cerebral cortex that are not involved in primary motor or sensory functions; rather, they are involved in higher mental functions such as learning, remembering, thinking, and speaking.

associative learning learning that certain events occur together. The events may be two stimuli (as in classical conditioning) or a response and its consequence (as in operant conditioning).

attachment an emotional tie with others; shown in young children by their seeking closeness to caregivers and showing distress on separation.

attention-deficit/hyperactivity disorder (ADHD) a psychological disorder marked by extreme inattention and/or hyperactivity and impulsivity.

attitude feelings, often influenced by our beliefs, that predispose us to respond in a particular way to objects, people, and events.

attribution theory the theory that we explain someone's behavior by crediting either the situation or the person's disposition.

audition the sense or act of hearing.

autism spectrum disorder (ASD) a disorder that appears in childhood and is marked by limitations in communication and social interaction, and by rigidly fixated interests and repetitive behaviors.

automatic processing unconscious encoding of incidental information, such as space, time, and frequency, and of familiar or well-learned information, such as sounds, smells, and word meanings.

autonomic [aw-tuh-NAHM-ik] nervous system (ANS) the part of the peripheral nervous system that controls the glands and the muscles of the internal organs (such as the heart). Its *sympathetic* division arouses; its *parasympathetic* division calms.

availability heuristic judging the likelihood of events based on their availability in memory; if instances come readily to mind (perhaps because of their vividness), we presume such events are common.

aversive conditioning associates an unpleasant state (such as nausea) with an unwanted behavior (such as drinking alcohol).

axon the segmented neuron extension that passes messages through its branches to other neurons, muscles, or glands.

babbling stage the stage in speech development, beginning around 4 months, during which an infant spontaneously utters various sounds that are not all related to the household language.

barbiturates drugs that depress central nervous system activity, reducing anxiety but impairing memory and judgment.

basal metabolic rate the body's resting rate of energy output.

basic research pure science that aims to increase the scientific knowledge base.

basic trust according to Erik Erikson, a sense that the world is predictable and trustworthy; said to be formed during infancy by appropriate experiences with responsive caregivers.

behavior feedback effect the tendency of behavior to influence our own and others' thoughts, feelings, and actions.

behavior genetics the study of the relative power and limits of genetic and environmental influences on behavior.

behaviorism the view that psychology (1) should be an objective science that (2) studies behavior without reference to mental processes. Most research psychologists today agree with (1) but not with (2).

behavior therapy therapy that uses learning principles to reduce unwanted behaviors and increase desirable behaviors.

belief perseverance the persistence of one's initial conceptions after the basis on which they were formed has been discredited.

Big Five factors researchers identified five factors—*openness, conscientiousness, extraversion, agreeableness,* and *neuroticism*—that describe personality. (Also called the *five-factor model.*)

binge-eating disorder significant binge-eating episodes, followed by distress, disgust, or guilt, but without the compensatory behavior that marks bulimia nervosa.

binocular cue a depth cue, such as retinal disparity, that depends on the use of two eyes.

biological psychology the scientific study of the links between biological (genetic, neural, hormonal) and psychological processes. Some biological psychologists call themselves *neuroscientists, neuropsychologists, behavior geneticists, physiological psychologists,* or *biopsychologists.*

biomedical therapy prescribed medications or procedures that act directly on the person's physiology.

biopsychosocial approach an integrated approach that incorporates biological, psychological, and social-cultural levels of analysis.

bipolar disorders disorders in which a person experiences the overexcited state of mania (or milder hypomania), and usually experiences periods of depression. (Formerly called *manic-depressive disorder.*)

blindsight a condition in which a person can respond to a visual stimulus without consciously experiencing it.

blind spot the point at which the optic nerve leaves the eye, creating a "blind" spot because no receptor cells are located there.

bottom-up processing information processing that begins with the sensory receptors and works up to the brain's integration of sensory information.

brainstem the central core of the brain, beginning where the spinal cord swells as it enters the skull; the brainstem is responsible for automatic survival functions.

Broca's area a frontal lobe brain area, usually in the left hemisphere, that helps control language expression by directing the muscle movements involved in speech.

bulimia nervosa an eating disorder in which a person's binge eating (usually of high-calorie foods) is followed by weight-loss-promoting behavior, such as vomiting, laxative use, fasting, or excessive exercise.

bystander effect the tendency for any given bystander to be less likely to give aid if other bystanders are present.

Cannon-Bard theory the theory that an emotion-arousing stimulus simultaneously triggers (1) physiological responses and (2) the subjective experience of emotion.

case study a descriptive technique in which one individual or group is studied in depth in the hope of revealing universal principles.

Cattell-Horn-Carroll (CHC) theory the theory that our intelligence is based on general intelligence (*g*) as well as specific abilities, bridged by fluid intelligence (*Gf*) and crystallized intelligence (*Gc*).

cell body the part of a neuron that contains the nucleus; the cell's life-support center.

central nervous system (CNS) the brain and spinal cord.

central route persuasion occurs when interested people's thinking is influenced by considering evidence and arguments.

cerebellum [sehr-uh-BELL-um] the hindbrain's "little brain" at the rear of the brainstem; functions include processing sensory input, coordinating movement output and balance, and enabling nonverbal learning and memory.

cerebral [seh-REE-bruhl] cortex the intricate fabric of interconnected neural cells covering the forebrain's cerebral hemispheres; the body's ultimate control and information-processing center.

change blindness failing to notice changes in the environment; a form of *inattentional blindness.*

chromosomes threadlike structures made of DNA molecules that contain the genes.

chronic schizophrenia (also called *process schizophrenia*) a form of schizophrenia in which symptoms usually appear by late adolescence or early adulthood. As people age, psychotic episodes last longer and recovery periods shorten.

chunking organizing items into familiar, manageable units; often occurs automatically.

circadian [ser-KAY-dee-an] rhythm our biological clock; regular bodily rhythms (for example, of temperature and wakefulness) that occur on a 24-hour cycle.

classical conditioning a type of learning in which we link two or more stimuli; as a result, to illustrate with Pavlov's classic experiment, the first stimulus (a tone) comes to elicit behavior (drooling) in anticipation of the second stimulus (food).

clinical psychology a branch of psychology that studies, assesses, and treats people with psychological disorders.

cocaine a powerful and addictive stimulant derived from the coca plant; produces temporarily increased alertness and euphoria.

cochlea [KOHK-lee-uh] a coiled, bony, fluid-filled tube in the inner ear; sound waves traveling through the cochlear fluid trigger nerve impulses.

cochlear implant a device for converting sounds into electrical signals and stimulating the auditory nerve through electrodes threaded into the cochlea.

cognition all the mental activities associated with thinking, knowing, remembering, and communicating.

cognitive-behavioral therapy (CBT) a popular integrative therapy that combines cognitive therapy (changing self-defeating thinking) with behavior therapy (changing behavior).

cognitive dissonance theory the theory that we act to reduce the discomfort (dissonance) we feel when two of our thoughts (cognitions) are inconsistent. For example, when we become aware that our attitudes and our actions clash, we can reduce the resulting dissonance by changing our attitudes.

cognitive learning the acquisition of mental information, whether by observing events, by watching others, or through language.

cognitive map a mental representation of the layout of one's environment. For example, after exploring a maze, rats act as if they have learned a cognitive map of it.

cognitive neuroscience the interdisciplinary study of the brain activity linked with cognition (perception, thinking, memory, and language).

cognitive psychology the study of the mental processes involved in perceiving, learning, remembering, thinking, communicating, and solving problems.

cognitive therapy therapy that teaches people new, more adaptive ways of thinking; based on the assumption that thoughts intervene between events and our emotional reactions.

cohort a group of people sharing a common characteristic, such as being from a given time period.

collective unconscious Carl Jung's concept of a shared, inherited reservoir of memory traces from our species' history.

collectivism a cultural pattern that prioritizes the goals of important groups (often one's extended family or work group).

community psychology a branch of psychology that studies how people interact with their social environments and how social institutions (such as schools and neighborhoods) affect individuals and groups.

companionate love the deep affectionate attachment we feel for someone with whom our life is intertwined.

concept a mental grouping of similar objects, events, ideas, or people.

concrete operational stage in Piaget's theory, the stage of cognitive development (from about 7 to 11 years of age) at which children gain the mental operations that enable them to think logically about concrete events.

conditioned reinforcer a stimulus that gains its reinforcing power through its association with a primary reinforcer. (Also known as a *secondary reinforcer.*)

conditioned response (CR) in classical conditioning, a learned response to a previously neutral (but now conditioned) stimulus (CS).

conditioned stimulus (CS) in classical conditioning, an originally neutral stimulus that, after association with an unconditioned stimulus (US), comes to trigger a conditioned response (CR).

conduction hearing loss a less common form of hearing loss, caused by damage to the mechanical system that conducts sound waves to the cochlea.

cones retinal receptors that are concentrated near the center of the retina and that function in daylight or in well-lit conditions. Cones detect fine detail and give rise to color sensations.

confirmation bias a tendency to search for information that supports our preconceptions and to ignore or distort contradictory evidence.

conflict a perceived incompatibility of actions, goals, or ideas.

conformity adjusting our behavior or thinking to coincide with a group standard.

confounding variable in an experiment, a variable other than the variable being studied that might influence a study's results.

consciousness our subjective awareness of ourselves and our environment.

conservation the principle (which Piaget believed to be a part of concrete operational reasoning) that properties such as mass, volume, and number remain the same despite changes in the forms of objects.

continuous reinforcement schedule reinforcing the desired response every time it occurs.

control group in an experiment, the group *not* exposed to the treatment; contrasts with the experimental group and serves as a comparison for evaluating the effect of the treatment.

convergent thinking narrowing the available problem solutions to determine the single best solution.

coping alleviating stress using emotional, cognitive, or behavioral methods.

coronary heart disease the clogging of the vessels that nourish the heart muscle; a leading cause of death in many developed countries.

corpus callosum [KOR-pus kah-LOW-sum] the large band of neural fibers connecting the two brain hemispheres and carrying messages between them.

correlation a measure of the extent to which two factors vary together, and thus of how well either factor *(variable)* predicts the other.

correlation coefficient a statistical index of the direction and strength of the relationship between two things (from –1.00 to +1.00).

counseling psychology a branch of psychology that assists people with problems in living (often related to school, work, or relationships) and in achieving greater well-being.

counterconditioning behavior therapy procedures that use classical conditioning to evoke new responses to stimuli that are triggering unwanted behaviors; include *exposure therapies* and *aversive conditioning.*

creativity the ability to produce new and valuable ideas.

critical period an optimal period early in the life of an organism when exposure to certain stimuli or experiences produces typical development.

critical thinking thinking that does not automatically accept arguments and conclusions. Rather, it examines assumptions, appraises the source, discerns hidden biases, evaluates evidence, and assesses conclusions.

cross-sectional study research that compares people of different ages at the same point in time.

crystallized intelligence (Gc) our accumulated knowledge and verbal skills; tends to increase with age.

culture the enduring behaviors, ideas, attitudes, values, and traditions shared by a group of people and transmitted from one generation to the next.

debriefing the post experimental explanation of a study, including its purpose and any deceptions, to its participants.

deep processing encoding semantically, based on the meaning of the words; tends to yield the best retention.

defense mechanisms in psychoanalytic theory, the ego's protective methods of reducing anxiety by unconsciously distorting reality.

deindividuation the loss of self-awareness and self-restraint occurring in group situations that foster arousal and anonymity.

déjà vu that eerie sense that "I've experienced this before." Cues from the current situation may unconsciously trigger retrieval of an earlier experience.

delta waves the large, slow brain waves associated with deep sleep.

delusion a false belief, often of persecution or grandeur, that may accompany psychotic disorders.

dendrites a neuron's often bushy, branching extensions that receive and integrate messages from axons, conducting impulses toward the cell body.

dependent variable in an experiment, the variable that is measured; the variable that may change when the independent variable is manipulated.

depressants drugs (such as alcohol, barbiturates, and opioids) that reduce neural activity and slow body functions.

depressive disorders a group of disorders characterized by an enduring sad, empty, or irritable mood, along with physical and cognitive changes that affect a person's ability to function.

depth perception the ability to see objects in three dimensions, although the images that strike the retina are two-dimensional; allows us to judge distance.

descriptive statistics using statistical methods to provide a simple summary of data.

developmental psychology a branch of psychology that studies physical, cognitive, and social development throughout the life span.

difference threshold the minimum difference between two stimuli required for detection 50 percent of the time. We experience the difference threshold as a *just noticeable difference* (or *jnd*).

diffusion of responsibility when a person takes less responsibility for something, or is less likely to act in a situation, due to the presence of others.

discrimination (1) in classical conditioning, the learned ability to distinguish between a conditioned stimulus and similar stimuli that do not signal an unconditioned stimulus. (In operant conditioning, the ability to distinguish responses that are reinforced from similar responses that are not reinforced.) (2) unjustifiable negative behavior toward a group or its members.

dissociation a split in consciousness, which allows some thoughts and behaviors to occur simultaneously with others.

dissociative disorders a controversial, rare group of disorders characterized by a disruption of or discontinuity in the normal integration of consciousness, memory, identity, emotion, perception, body representation, motor control, and behavior.

dissociative identity disorder (DID) a rare dissociative disorder in which a person exhibits two or more distinct and alternating identities. (Formerly called *multiple personality disorder.)*

divergent thinking expanding the number of possible problem solutions; creative thinking that diverges in different directions.

DNA (deoxyribonucleic acid) a complex molecule containing the genetic information that makes up the chromosomes.

double-blind procedure an experimental procedure in which both the research participants and the research staff are uninformed (blind) about whether the research participants have received the treatment or a placebo. Commonly used in drug-evaluation studies.

dream a sequence of images, emotions, and thoughts passing through a sleeping person's mind.

drive-reduction theory the idea that a physiological need creates an aroused state (a drive) that motivates an organism to satisfy the need.

DSM-5-TR the American Psychiatric Association's *Diagnostic and Statistical Manual of Mental Disorders, Fifth Edition, Text Revision;* a widely used categorical system for classifying psychological disorders.

dual processing the principle that information is often simultaneously processed on separate conscious and unconscious tracks.

echoic memory a momentary sensory memory of auditory stimuli; if attention is elsewhere, sounds and words can still be recalled within 3 or 4 seconds.

eclectic approach an approach to psychotherapy that uses techniques from various forms of therapy.

Ecstasy (MDMA) a synthetic stimulant and mild hallucinogen. Produces euphoria and social intimacy, but with short-term health risks and longer-term harm to serotonin-producing neurons and to mood and cognition.

EEG (electroencephalogram) an amplified recording of the waves of electrical activity sweeping across the brain's surface. These waves are measured by electrodes placed on the scalp.

effortful processing encoding that requires attention and conscious effort.

ego the partly conscious, "executive" part of personality that, according to Freud, mediates among the demands of the id, the superego, and reality. The ego operates on the *reality principle,* satisfying the id's desires in ways that will realistically bring pleasure rather than pain.

egocentrism in Piaget's theory, the preoperational child's difficulty taking another's point of view.

electroconvulsive therapy (ECT) a biomedical therapy for severe and treatment-resistant depression in which a brief electric current is sent through the brain of an anesthetized person.

embodied cognition the influence of bodily sensations, gestures, and other states on cognitive preferences and judgments.

embryo the developing human organism from about 2 weeks after fertilization through the second month.

emerging adulthood a period from about age 18 to the mid-twenties, when many in Western cultures are no longer adolescents but have not yet achieved full independence as adults.

emotion a response of the whole organism, involving (1) physiological arousal, (2) expressive behaviors, and, most importantly, (3) conscious experience resulting from one's interpretations.

emotional intelligence the ability to perceive, understand, manage, and use emotions.

emotion-focused coping attempting to alleviate stress by avoiding or ignoring a stressor and attending to emotional needs related to our stress reaction.

emotion regulation how we manage our emotions, including which emotions we allow ourselves to feel, when we feel them, and how we express those emotions.

empirical approach an evidence-based method that draws on observation and experimentation.

empirically derived test a test (such as the MMPI) created by selecting from a pool of items those that discriminate between groups.

encoding the process of getting information into the memory system—for example, by extracting meaning.

encoding specificity principle the idea that cues and contexts specific to a particular memory will be most effective in helping us recall it.

endocrine [EN-duh-krin] system the body's "slow" chemical communication system; glands and fat tissue that secrete hormones into the bloodstream.

endorphins [en-DOR-fins] "morphine within"—natural, opiate-like neurotransmitters linked to pain control and to pleasure.

environment every nongenetic influence, from prenatal nutrition to the people and things around us.

epigenetics "above" or "in addition to" *(epi)* genetics; the study of the molecular mechanisms by which environments can influence genetic expression (without a DNA change).

episodic memory explicit memory of personally experienced events; one of our two conscious memory systems (the other is *semantic memory*).

equity a condition in which people receive from a relationship in proportion to what they give to it.

erectile disorder inability to develop or maintain an erection due to insufficient blood flow to the penis.

estrogens sex hormones, such as estradiol, that contribute to female sex characteristics and are secreted in greater amounts by females than by males.

evidence-based practice clinical decision making that integrates the best available research with clinical expertise and client characteristics and preferences.

evolutionary psychology the study of the evolution of behavior and the mind, using principles of natural selection.

experiment a research method in which an investigator manipulates one or more variables (independent variables) to observe the effect on some behavior or mental process (the dependent variable). By *random assignment* of participants, the experimenter aims to control other relevant variables that may change the research outcome.

experimental group in an experiment, the group exposed to the treatment, that is, to one version of the independent variable.

explicit memory retention of facts and experiences that we can consciously know and "declare." (Also called *declarative memory*.)

exposure therapies behavioral techniques that treat anxieties by exposing people (in imaginary or actual situations) to the things they fear and avoid.

external locus of control the perception that outside forces beyond our personal control determine our fate.

extinction in classical conditioning, the diminishing of a conditioned response—when an unconditioned stimulus does not follow a conditioned stimulus. (In operant conditioning, when a response is no longer reinforced.)

extrasensory perception (ESP) the controversial claim that perception can occur apart from sensory input; includes telepathy, clairvoyance, and precognition.

extrinsic motivation the desire to perform a behavior to receive promised rewards or avoid threatened punishment.

facial feedback effect the tendency of facial muscle activation, alone, to trigger corresponding feelings such as fear, anger, or happiness.

family therapy therapy that treats people in the context of their family system. Views an individual's unwanted behaviors as influenced by, or directed at, other family members.

feature detectors nerve cells in the brain's visual cortex that respond to specific features of the stimulus, such as shape, angle, or movement.

feel-good, do-good phenomenon our tendency to be helpful when in a good mood.

female orgasmic disorder distress due to weak orgasmic feelings or infrequently or never experiencing orgasm.

fetal alcohol syndrome (FAS) physical and cognitive function deficits in children caused by their mother's heavy drinking during pregnancy. In severe cases, symptoms include a small, out-of-proportion head and distinct facial features.

fetus the developing human organism from 9 weeks after conception to birth.

fight-or-flight response an emergency response, including activation of the sympathetic nervous system, that mobilizes energy and activity for attacking or escaping a threat.

figure-ground the organization of the visual field into objects (the *figures*) that stand out from their surroundings (the *ground*).

fixation (1) in cognition, the inability to see a problem from a new perspective; an obstacle to problem solving. (2) in psychoanalytic theory, a lingering focus of pleasure-seeking energies at an earlier psychosexual stage, in which conflicts were unresolved.

fixed-interval schedule in operant conditioning, a reinforcement schedule that reinforces a response only after a specified time has elapsed.

fixed-ratio schedule in operant conditioning, a reinforcement schedule that reinforces a response only after a specified number of responses.

flashbulb memory a clear memory of an emotionally significant moment or event.

flow a completely involved, focused state, with diminished awareness of self and time; results from fully engaging our skills.

fluid intelligence *(Gf)* our ability to reason speedily and abstractly; tends to decrease with age, especially during late adulthood.

fMRI (functional MRI) a technique for revealing blood flow and, therefore, brain activity by comparing successive MRI scans. fMRI scans show brain function as well as structure.

foot-in-the-door phenomenon the tendency for people who have first agreed to a small request to comply later with a larger request.

forebrain consists of the cerebral cortex, thalamus, and hypothalamus; manages complex cognitive activities, sensory and associative functions, and voluntary motor activities.

formal operational stage in Piaget's theory, the stage of cognitive development (usually beginning about age 12) at which people begin to think logically about abstract concepts.

fovea the central focal point in the retina, around which the eye's cones cluster.

framing the way an issue is posed; how an issue is framed can significantly affect decisions and judgments.

fraternal (dizygotic) twins individuals who developed from separate fertilized eggs. They are genetically no closer than ordinary siblings, but shared a prenatal environment.

free association in psychoanalysis, a method of exploring the unconscious in which the person relaxes and says whatever comes to mind, no matter how trivial or embarrassing.

frequency the number of complete wavelengths that pass a point in a given time (for example, per second).

frequency theory in hearing, the theory that the rate of nerve impulses traveling up the auditory nerve matches the frequency of a tone, thus enabling us to sense its pitch. (Also called *temporal coding*.)

frontal lobes the portion of the cerebral cortex lying just behind the forehead; involved in speaking and muscle movements and in making plans and judgments.

frustration-aggression principle the principle that frustration—the blocking of an attempt to achieve some goal—creates anger, which can generate aggression.

functionalism an early school of thought promoted by James and influenced by Darwin; explored how mental and behavioral processes function—how they enable the organism to adapt, survive, and flourish.

fundamental attribution error the tendency, when analyzing others' behavior, to underestimate the impact of the situation and to overestimate the impact of personal disposition.

gate-control theory the theory that the spinal cord contains a neurological "gate" that blocks pain signals or allows them to pass on to the brain. The "gate" is opened by the activity of pain signals traveling up small nerve fibers and is closed by activity in larger fibers or by information coming from the brain.

gender in psychology, the behavioral characteristics that people associate with *boy, girl, man,* and *woman.* (See also *gender identity.*)

gender identity our personal sense of being male, female, neither, or some combination of male and female.

gender role a set of expected behaviors, attitudes, and traits for men and for women.

gender typing the acquisition of a traditional masculine or feminine role.

general adaptation syndrome (GAS) Selye's concept of the body's adaptive response to stress in three phases—alarm, resistance, exhaustion.

general intelligence (*g*) according to Spearman and others, underlies all mental abilities and is, therefore, measured by every task on an intelligence test.

generalization (also called *stimulus generalization*) in classical conditioning, the tendency, once a response has been conditioned, for stimuli similar to the conditioned stimulus to elicit similar responses. (In operant conditioning, when responses learned in one situation occur in other, similar situations.)

generalized anxiety disorder an anxiety disorder in which a person is continually tense, apprehensive, and in a state of autonomic nervous system arousal.

genes the biochemical units of heredity that make up the chromosomes; small segments of DNA capable of synthesizing proteins.

genome the complete instructions for making an organism, consisting of all the genetic material in that organism's chromosomes.

gestalt an organized whole. Gestalt psychologists emphasized our tendency to integrate pieces of information into meaningful wholes.

glial cells (glia) cells in the nervous system that support, nourish, and protect neurons; they also play a role in learning, thinking, and memory.

glucose the form of sugar that circulates in the blood and provides the major source of energy for body tissues. When its level is low, we feel hunger.

grammar in a language, a system of rules that enables us to communicate with and understand others. *Semantics* is the language's set of rules for deriving meaning from sounds, and *syntax* is its set of rules for combining words into grammatically sensible sentences.

GRIT (1) in psychology, passion and perseverance in the pursuit of long-term goals. (2) Graduated and Reciprocated Initiatives in Tension-Reduction—a strategy designed to decrease international tensions.

grouping the perceptual tendency to organize stimuli into coherent groups.

group polarization the enhancement of a group's prevailing inclinations through discussion within the group.

group therapy therapy conducted with groups rather than individuals, providing benefits from group interaction.

groupthink the mode of thinking that occurs when the desire for harmony in a decision-making group overrides a realistic appraisal of alternatives.

growth mindset a focus on learning and growing rather than viewing abilities as fixed.

gustation our sense of taste.

habituation decreasing responsiveness with repeated stimulation. As infants gain familiarity with repeated exposure to a stimulus, their interest wanes and they look away sooner.

hallucinations sensory experiences without sensory stimulation, such as seeing something in the absence of an external visual stimulus.

hallucinogens psychedelic ("mind-manifesting") drugs, such as LSD, that distort perceptions and evoke sensory images in the absence of sensory input.

happiness an enduring prevalence of positive emotions.

health psychology a subfield of psychology that contributes to behavioral medicine.

heredity the genetic transfer of characteristics from parents to offspring.

heritability the proportion of variation among individuals in a group that we can attribute to genes. The heritability of a trait may vary, depending on the range of populations and environments studied.

heuristic a simple thinking strategy—a mental shortcut—that often allows us to make judgments and solve problems efficiently; usually speedier but also more error-prone than an *algorithm.*

hierarchy of needs Maslow's five levels of human needs, beginning with physiological needs. Often visualized as a pyramid, with basic needs providing the foundation supporting higher-level needs.

higher-order conditioning a procedure in which the conditioned stimulus in one conditioning experience is paired with a new neutral stimulus, creating a second (often weaker) conditioned stimulus. For example, an animal that has learned that a tone predicts food might then learn that a light predicts the tone and begin responding to the light alone. (Also called *second-order conditioning.*)

hindbrain consists of the medulla, pons, and cerebellum; directs essential survival functions, such as breathing, sleeping, and wakefulness, as well as coordination and balance.

hindsight bias the tendency to believe, after learning an outcome, that one would have foreseen it. (Also known as the *I-knew-it-all-along phenomenon.*)

hippocampus a neural center located in the limbic system that helps process explicit (conscious) memories—of facts and events—for storage.

homeostasis a tendency to maintain a balanced or constant internal state; the regulation of any aspect of body chemistry, such as blood glucose, around a particular level.

hormones chemical messengers that are manufactured by the endocrine glands, travel through the bloodstream, and affect other tissues.

hue the dimension of color that is determined by the wavelength of light; what we know as the color names *blue, green,* and so forth.

human factors psychology a field of psychology allied with I/O psychology that explores how people and machines interact and how machines and physical environments can be made safe and easy to use.

humanistic psychology a historically significant perspective that emphasized human growth potential.

humanistic theories theories that view personality with a focus on the potential for healthy personal growth.

hypnosis a social interaction in which one person (the hypnotist) suggests to another (the subject) that certain perceptions, feelings, thoughts, or behaviors will spontaneously occur.

hypothalamus [hi-po-THAL-uh-muss] a limbic system neural structure lying below (*hypo*) the thalamus; it directs several maintenance activities (eating, drinking, body temperature), helps govern the endocrine system via the pituitary gland, and is linked to emotion and reward.

hypothesis a testable prediction, often implied by a theory.

iconic memory a momentary sensory memory of visual stimuli; a photographic or picture-image memory lasting no more than a few tenths of a second.

id a reservoir of unconscious psychic energy that, according to Freud, strives to satisfy basic sexual and aggressive drives. The id operates on the *pleasure principle,* demanding immediate gratification.

identical (monozygotic) twins individuals who developed from a single fertilized egg that split in two, creating two genetically identical organisms.

identification the process by which, according to Freud, children incorporate their parents' values into their developing superegos.

identity our sense of self; according to Erikson, the adolescent's task is to solidify a sense of self by testing and integrating various roles.

illness anxiety disorder a disorder in which a person interprets normal physical sensations as symptoms of a disease. (Formerly called *hypochondriasis.*)

illusory correlation perceiving a relationship where none exists, or perceiving a stronger-than-actual relationship.

implicit bias automatic associations that can influence individual judgments of or behavior toward people of a particular race, gender, or other group.

implicit memory retention of learned skills or classically conditioned associations independent of conscious recollection. (Also called *nondeclarative memory.*)

imprinting the process by which certain animals form strong attachments during early life.

inattentional blindness failing to see visible objects when our attention is directed elsewhere.

incentive a positive or negative environmental stimulus that motivates (or *pulls*) behavior.

independent variable in an experiment, the variable that is manipulated; the variable whose effect is being studied.

individualism a cultural pattern that emphasizes people's own goals over group goals and defines identity mainly in terms of unique personal attributes.

industrial-organizational (I/O) psychology the scientific study of working, and the application of psychological concepts to human behavior in workplaces.

inferential statistics using statistical methods to interpret data meaningfully.

informational social influence influence resulting from a person's willingness to accept others' opinions about reality.

informed consent giving potential participants enough information about a study to enable them to choose whether they wish to participate.

ingroup "us"—people with whom we share a common identity.

ingroup bias the tendency to favor our own group.

inner ear the innermost part of the ear, containing the cochlea, semicircular canals, and vestibular sacs.

insight a sudden realization of a problem's solution; contrasts with strategy-based solutions.

insight therapies therapies that aim to improve psychological functioning by increasing a person's awareness of underlying motives and defenses.

insomnia recurring problems in falling or staying asleep.

instinct a complex behavior that is rigidly patterned throughout a species and is unlearned.

instinctive drift the tendency of learned behavior to gradually revert to biologically predisposed patterns.

intellectual developmental disorder a condition of limited mental ability, indicated by an intelligence test score of 70 or below and difficulty adapting to the demands of life. (May also be referred to as *intellectual disability*.)

intelligence the ability to learn from experience, solve problems, and use knowledge to adapt to new situations.

intelligence quotient (IQ) defined originally as the ratio of mental age *(ma)* to chronological age *(ca)* multiplied by 100 (thus, $IQ = ma/ca \times 100$). On contemporary intelligence tests, the average performance for a given age is assigned a score of 100.

intelligence test a method for assessing an individual's mental aptitudes and comparing them with those of others, using numerical scores.

intensity the amount of energy in a light wave or sound wave, which influences what those with typical vision or hearing perceive as brightness or loudness. Intensity is determined by the wave's amplitude (height).

interaction the interplay that occurs when the effect of one factor (such as environment) depends on another factor (such as heredity).

internal locus of control the perception that we control our own fate.

interneurons neurons within the brain and spinal cord; they communicate internally and process information between the sensory inputs and motor outputs.

interpretation in psychoanalysis, the analyst's noting of dream meanings, resistances, and other significant behaviors and events in order to promote insight and growth.

intersex possessing male and female biological sexual characteristics at birth.

intimacy in Erikson's theory, the ability to form close, loving relationships; a primary developmental task in young adulthood.

intrinsic motivation a desire to perform a behavior effectively for its own sake.

intuition an effortless, immediate, automatic feeling or thought, as contrasted with explicit, conscious reasoning.

James-Lange theory the theory that our experience of emotion occurs when we become aware of our physiological responses to an emotion-arousing stimulus.

just-world phenomenon the tendency for people to believe that the world is just and people therefore get what they deserve and deserve what they get.

kinesthesia [kin-ehs-THEE-zhuh] our movement sense—our system for sensing the position and movement of individual body parts.

language our spoken, written, or signed words and the ways we combine them to communicate meaning.

latent content according to Freud, the underlying meaning of a dream (as distinct from its *manifest content*).

latent learning learning that occurs but is not apparent until there is an incentive to demonstrate it.

law of effect Thorndike's principle that behaviors followed by favorable consequences become more likely, and that behaviors followed by unfavorable consequences become less likely.

leadership an individual's ability to motivate and influence others to contribute to their group's success.

learned helplessness the hopelessness and passive resignation humans and other animals learn when unable to avoid repeated aversive events.

learning the process of acquiring through experience new and relatively enduring information or behaviors.

lesion [LEE-zhuhn] tissue destruction. Brain lesions occur naturally (disease or trauma), in surgery, or experimentally (using electrodes to destroy brain cells).

levels of analysis the differing complementary views, from biological to psychological to social-cultural, for analyzing any given phenomenon.

limbic system neural system located mostly in the forebrain—below the cerebral hemispheres—that includes the *amygdala, hypothalamus*, and *hippocampus;* associated with emotions and drives.

linguistic determinism Whorf's hypothesis that language determines the way we think.

linguistic relativism the idea that language influences the way we think.

lobotomy a psychosurgical procedure once used to calm uncontrollably emotional or violent patients. The procedure cut the nerves that connect the frontal lobes to the emotion-controlling centers of the inner brain.

longitudinal study research that follows and retests the same people over time.

long-term memory the relatively permanent and limitless archive of the memory system. Includes knowledge, skills, and experiences.

long-term potentiation (LTP) an increase in a nerve cell's firing potential after brief, rapid stimulation; a neural basis for learning and memory.

loose culture places with flexible and informal norms.

LSD (lysergic acid diethylamide) a powerful hallucinogenic drug; also known as *acid*.

magnetoencephalography (MEG) a brain-imaging technique that measures magnetic fields from the brain's natural electrical activity.

major depressive disorder a disorder in which a person experiences five or more symptoms lasting 2 or more weeks. In the absence of drug use or a medical condition, at least one symptom must be either (1) depressed mood or (2) loss of interest or pleasure.

mania an unusually excited and overly ambitious mood state in which people show dangerously poor judgment, less need for sleep, and increased energy (part of bipolar disorders).

manifest content according to Freud, the symbolic, remembered story line of a dream (as distinct from its *latent*, or hidden, content).

maturation biological growth processes that enable orderly changes in behavior, relatively uninfluenced by experience.

mean the arithmetic average of a distribution, obtained by adding the scores and then dividing by the number of scores.

median the middle score in a distribution; half the scores are above it and half are below it.

medical model the concept that diseases, in this case psychological disorders, have physical causes that can be *diagnosed, treated,* and, in most cases, *cured,* often through treatment in a *hospital.*

medulla [muh-DUL-uh] the hindbrain structure that is the brainstem's base; controls heartbeat and breathing.

memory the persistence of learning over time through the encoding, storage, and retrieval of information.

memory consolidation the neural storage of a long-term memory.

menarche [meh-NAR-key] the first menstrual period.

menopause the time of natural cessation of menstruation; also refers to the biological changes a woman experiences as her ability to reproduce declines.

mental age a measure of intelligence test performance devised by Binet; the level of performance typically associated with children of a certain chronological age. Thus, a child who does as well as an average 8-year-old is said to have a mental age of 8.

mental set a tendency to approach a problem in one particular way, often a way that has been successful in the past.

mere exposure effect the tendency for repeated exposure to novel stimuli to increase our liking of them.

meta-analysis a statistical procedure for analyzing the results of multiple studies to reach an overall conclusion.

metacognition cognition about our cognition; keeping track of and evaluating our mental processes.

methamphetamine a powerfully addictive drug that stimulates the central nervous system, with accelerated body functions and associated energy and mood changes; over time, reduces baseline dopamine levels.

midbrain found atop the brainstem; connects the *hindbrain* with the *forebrain,* controls some motor movement, and transmits auditory and visual information.

middle ear the chamber between the eardrum and cochlea containing three tiny bones—hammer (malleus), anvil (incus), and stirrup (stapes)—that concentrate the vibrations of the eardrum on the cochlea's oval window.

mindfulness meditation a reflective practice in which people attend to current experiences in a nonjudgmental and accepting manner.

Minnesota Multiphasic Personality Inventory (MMPI) the most widely researched and clinically used of all personality tests. Originally developed to identify emotional disorders (still considered its most appropriate use), this test is now used for many other screening purposes.

mirror-image perceptions mutual views often held by conflicting parties, as when each side sees itself as ethical and peaceful and views the other side as evil and aggressive.

mirror neurons frontal lobe neurons that some scientists believe fire when we perform certain actions or observe another doing so. The brain's mirroring of another's action may enable imitation and empathy.

misinformation effect occurs when a memory has been corrupted by misleading information.

mnemonics [nih-MON-iks] memory aids, especially those techniques that use vivid imagery and organizational devices.

mode the most frequently occurring score(s) in a distribution.

modeling the process of observing and imitating a specific behavior.

molecular behavior genetics the study of how the structure and function of genes interact with our environment to influence behavior.

molecular genetics the subfield of biology that studies the molecular structure and function of genes.

monocular cue a depth cue, such as interposition or linear perspective, available to either eye alone.

mood-congruent memory the tendency to recall experiences that are consistent with one's current good or bad mood.

morpheme in a language, the smallest unit that carries meaning; may be a word or a part of a word (such as a prefix).

motivation a need or desire that energizes and directs (or *pushes*) behavior.

motor cortex a cerebral cortex area at the rear of the frontal lobes that controls voluntary movements.

motor (efferent) neurons neurons that carry outgoing information from the brain and spinal cord to the muscles and glands.

MRI (magnetic resonance imaging) a technique that uses magnetic fields and radio waves to produce computer-generated images of soft tissue. MRI scans show brain anatomy.

mutation a random error in gene replication that leads to a change.

myelin [MY-uh-lin] sheath a fatty tissue layer segmentally encasing the axons of some neurons; enables vastly greater transmission speed as neural impulses hop from one node to the next.

narcissism excessive self-love and self-absorption.

narcolepsy a sleep disorder characterized by uncontrollable sleep attacks. The sufferer may lapse directly into REM sleep, often at inopportune times.

naturalistic observation a descriptive technique of observing and recording behavior in naturally occurring situations without changing or controlling the situation.

natural selection the principle that inherited traits that better enable an organism to survive and reproduce in a particular environment will (in competition with other trait variations) most likely be passed on to succeeding generations.

nature–nurture issue the longstanding controversy over the relative contributions that genes and experience make to the development of psychological traits and behaviors. Today's science sees traits and behaviors arising from the interaction of nature and nurture.

near-death experience an altered state of consciousness reported after a close brush with death (such as cardiac arrest); often similar to drug-induced hallucinations.

negative punishment an event that decreases behavior by removing a rewarding stimulus.

negative reinforcement increasing behaviors by stopping or reducing an aversive stimulus. A negative reinforcer is any stimulus that, when *removed* after a response, strengthens the response. (*Note:* Negative reinforcement is not punishment.)

nerves bundled axons that form neural cables connecting the central nervous system with muscles, glands, and sensory organs.

nervous system the body's speedy, electrochemical communication network, consisting of all the nerve cells of the peripheral and central nervous systems.

neurocognitive disorders (NCDs) acquired (not lifelong) disorders marked by cognitive deficits; often related to Alzheimer's disease, brain injury or disease, or substance abuse. Also called *dementia* in older adults.

neurodevelopmental disorder central nervous system developmental differences (usually in the brain) that start in childhood and alter thinking and behavior (as in intellectual limitations or a psychological disorder).

neurogenesis the formation of new neurons.

neuron a nerve cell; the basic building block of the nervous system.

neuroplasticity the brain's ability to change, especially during childhood, by reorganizing after damage or by building new pathways based on experience.

neurotransmitters chemical messengers that cross the synaptic gap between neurons. When released by the sending neuron, neurotransmitters travel across the synapse and bind to receptor sites on the receiving neuron, thereby influencing whether that neuron will generate a neural impulse.

neutral stimulus (NS) in classical conditioning, a stimulus that elicits no response before conditioning.

nicotine a stimulating and highly addictive psychoactive drug in tobacco products.

night terrors a sleep disorder characterized by high arousal and an appearance of being terrified; unlike nightmares, night terrors occur during N3 sleep, within 2 or 3 hours of falling asleep, and are seldom remembered.

normal curve a symmetrical, bell-shaped curve that describes the distribution of many types of data; most scores fall near the mean (about 68 percent fall within one standard deviation of it) and fewer and fewer near the extremes. (Also called a *normal distribution.*)

normative social influence influence resulting from a person's desire to gain approval or avoid disapproval.

norms understood rules for accepted and expected behavior. Norms prescribe "proper" behavior.

nudge framing choices in a way that encourages people to make beneficial decisions.

obesity defined as a body mass index (BMI) measurement of 30 or higher, which is calculated from our weight-to-height ratio. (Individuals who are *overweight* have a BMI of 25 or higher.)

object permanence the awareness that things continue to exist even when not perceived.

observational learning learning by observing others. (Also called *social learning.*)

obsessive-compulsive disorder (OCD) a disorder characterized by unwanted and repetitive thoughts (obsessions), actions (compulsions), or both.

occipital [ahk-SIP-uh-tuhl] lobes the portion of the cerebral cortex lying at the back of the head; includes areas that receive information from the visual fields.

Oedipus [ED-uh-puss] complex according to Freud, a boy's sexual desires toward his mother and feelings of jealousy and hatred for the rival father.

olfaction our sense of smell.

one-word stage the stage in speech development, from about age 1 to 2, during which a child speaks mostly in single words.

operant behavior behavior that operates on the environment, producing a consequence.

operant chamber in operant conditioning research, a chamber (also known as a *Skinner box*) containing a bar or key that an animal can manipulate to obtain a food or water reinforcer; attached devices record the animal's rate of bar pressing or key pecking.

operant conditioning a type of learning in which a behavior becomes more likely to recur if followed by a reinforcer or less likely to recur if followed by a punisher.

operational definition a carefully worded statement of the exact procedures (operations) used in a research study. For example, *human intelligence* may be operationally defined as what an intelligence test measures. (Also known as *operationalization.*)

opioids opium and its derivatives, such as morphine and heroin; depress neural activity, temporarily lessening pain and anxiety.

opponent-process theory the theory that opposing retinal processes (red-green, blue-yellow, white-black) enable color vision. For example, some cells are stimulated by green and inhibited by red; others are stimulated by red and inhibited by green.

optic nerve the nerve that carries neural impulses from the eye to the brain.

organizational psychology an I/O psychology subfield that examines organizational influences on worker satisfaction and productivity and facilitates organizational change.

ostracism deliberate social exclusion of individuals or groups.

other-race effect the tendency to recall faces of one's own race more accurately than faces of other races. Also called the *cross-race effect* and the *own-race bias.*

outgroup "them"—those perceived as different or apart from our ingroup.

overconfidence the tendency to be more confident than correct—to overestimate the accuracy of our beliefs and judgments.

panic disorder an anxiety disorder marked by unpredictable, minutes-long episodes of intense dread in which a person may experience terror and accompanying chest pain, choking, or other frightening sensations; often followed by worry over a possible next attack.

parallel processing processing multiple aspects of a stimulus or problem simultaneously.

paraphilias sexual arousal from fantasies, behaviors, or urges involving nonhuman objects, the suffering of self or others, and/or nonconsenting persons.

parapsychology the study of paranormal phenomena, including ESP and psychokinesis (also called *telekinesis*).

parasympathetic nervous system the division of the autonomic nervous system that calms the body, conserving its energy.

parietal [puh-RYE-uh-tuhl] lobes the portion of the cerebral cortex lying at the top of the head and toward the rear; receives sensory input for touch and body position.

partial (intermittent) reinforcement schedule reinforcing a response only part of the time; results in slower acquisition of a response but much greater resistance to extinction than does continuous reinforcement.

passionate love an aroused state of intense positive absorption in another, usually present at the beginning of a romantic relationship.

peer reviewers scientific experts who evaluate a research article's theory, originality, and accuracy.

perception the process by which our brain organizes and interprets sensory information, enabling us to recognize objects and events as meaningful.

perceptual adaptation the ability to adjust to changed sensory input, including an artificially displaced or even inverted visual field.

perceptual constancy perceiving objects as unchanging (having consistent color, brightness, shape, and size) even as illumination and retinal images change.

perceptual set a mental predisposition to perceive one thing and not another.

peripheral nervous system (PNS) the sensory and motor neurons that connect the central nervous system (CNS) to the rest of the body.

peripheral route persuasion occurs when people are influenced by attention-getting cues, such as a speaker's attractiveness.

personal control our sense of being in charge of our environment rather than feeling helpless.

personality an individual's characteristic pattern of thinking, feeling, and acting.

personality disorders a group of disorders characterized by enduring inner experiences or behavior patterns that differ from the person's cultural norms and expectations, are pervasive and inflexible, begin in adolescence or early adulthood, are stable over time, and cause distress or impairment.

personality inventory a questionnaire (often with *true-false* or *agree-disagree* items) on which people respond to items designed to gauge a wide range of feelings and behaviors; used to assess selected personality traits.

person-centered therapy a humanistic therapy, developed by Carl Rogers, in which the client directs the discussion and the therapist uses techniques such as *active listening* within an accepting, genuine, empathic environment to facilitate clients' growth. (Also called *client-centered therapy*.)

personnel psychology an I/O psychology subfield that helps with job seeking, and with employee recruitment, selection, placement, training, appraisal, and development.

PET (positron emission tomography) a technique for detecting brain activity that displays where a radioactive form of glucose goes while the brain performs a given task.

phi phenomenon an illusion of movement created when two or more adjacent lights blink on and off in quick succession.

phoneme in a language, the smallest distinctive sound unit.

physiological need a basic bodily requirement.

pitch a tone's experienced highness or lowness; depends on frequency.

pituitary gland the endocrine system's most influential gland. Under the influence of the hypothalamus, the pituitary regulates growth and controls other endocrine glands.

placebo [pluh-SEE-bo; Latin for "I shall please"] effect experimental results caused by expectations alone; any effect on behavior caused by the administration of an inert substance or condition, which the recipient assumes is an active agent.

place theory in hearing, the theory that links the pitch we hear with the place where the cochlea's membrane is stimulated. (Also called *place coding.*)

polygraph a machine used in attempts to detect lies; measures emotion-linked changes in perspiration, heart rate, and breathing.

population all those in a group being studied, from which random samples may be drawn. (*Note:* Except for national studies, this does *not* refer to a country's whole population.)

positive psychology the scientific study of human flourishing, with the goals of discovering and promoting strengths and virtues that help individuals and communities to thrive.

positive punishment an event that decreases a behavior by administering a negative stimulus.

positive reinforcement increasing behaviors by presenting a pleasurable stimulus. A positive reinforcer is any stimulus that, when *presented* after a response, strengthens the response.

posthypnotic suggestion a suggestion, made during a hypnosis session, to be carried out after the subject is no longer hypnotized; used by some clinicians to help control undesired symptoms and behaviors.

posttraumatic growth positive psychological changes following a struggle with extremely challenging circumstances and life crises.

posttraumatic stress disorder (PTSD) a disorder characterized by haunting memories, nightmares, hypervigilance, avoidance of trauma-related stimuli, social withdrawal, jumpy anxiety, numbness of feeling, and/or insomnia that lingers for 4 weeks or more after a traumatic experience.

predictive validity the success with which a test predicts the behavior it is designed to predict; it is assessed by computing the correlation between test scores and the criterion behavior. (Also called *criterion-related validity.*)

prejudice an unjustifiable and usually negative attitude toward a group and its members. Prejudice generally involves stereotyped beliefs, negative feelings, and a predisposition to discriminatory action.

preoperational stage in Piaget's theory, the stage (from about 2 to 6 or 7 years of age) at which a child learns to use language but does not yet comprehend the mental operations of concrete logic.

preparedness a biological predisposition to learn associations, such as between taste and nausea, that have survival value.

preregistration publicly communicating planned study design, hypotheses, data collection, and analyses.

primary reinforcer an innately reinforcing stimulus, such as one that satisfies a biological need.

primary sex characteristics the body structures (ovaries, testes, and external genitalia) that make sexual reproduction possible.

priming the activation, often unconsciously, of certain associations, thus predisposing one's perception, memory, or response.

proactive interference the forward-acting disruptive effect of older learning on the recall of *new* information.

problem-focused coping attempting to alleviate stress directly—by changing the stressor or the way we interact with that stressor.

projective test a personality test, such as the TAT or Rorschach, that provides ambiguous images designed to trigger projection of people's inner dynamics.

prosocial behavior positive, constructive, helpful behavior. The opposite of antisocial behavior.

prototype a mental image or best example of a category. Matching new items to a prototype provides a quick and easy method for sorting items into categories (as when comparing feathered creatures to a prototypical bird, such as a crow).

psychedelic drugs hallucinogenic drugs used to treat depressive disorders, anxiety disorders, posttraumatic stress disorder, and substance use disorders. These drugs cause temporary visual, psychological, and auditory changes, and an altered state of consciousness (often called a psychedelic experience or "trip").

psychiatry a branch of medicine dealing with psychological disorders; practiced by physicians who provide medical (for example, drug) treatments as well as psychological therapy.

psychoactive drug a chemical substance that alters the brain, causing changes in perceptions and moods.

psychoanalysis (1) Freud's theory of personality that attributes thoughts and actions to unconscious motives and conflicts. (2) Freud's therapeutic technique. Freud believed the patient's free associations, resistances, and dreams—and the analyst's interpretations of them—released previously repressed feelings, allowing the patient to gain self-insight.

psychodynamic theories theories that view personality with a focus on the unconscious mind and the importance of childhood experiences.

psychodynamic therapy therapy deriving from the psychoanalytic tradition; views individuals as responding to unconscious forces and childhood experiences, and seeks to enhance self-insight.

psychological disorder a disturbance in people's thoughts, emotions, or behaviors that causes distress or suffering and impairs their daily lives.

psychology the science of behavior and mental processes.

psychoneuroimmunology the study of how psychological, neural, and endocrine processes together affect our immune system and resulting health.

psychopharmacology the study of the effects of drugs on the mind and behavior.

psychophysics the study of relationships between the physical characteristics of stimuli, such as their intensity, and our psychological experience of them.

psychosexual stages the childhood stages of development (oral, anal, phallic, latency, genital) during which, according to Freud, the id's pleasure-seeking energies focus on distinct *erogenous zones*.

psychosurgery surgery that removes or destroys brain tissue to change behavior.

psychotherapy treatment involving psychological techniques; consists of interactions between a trained therapist and someone seeking to address psychological difficulties or achieve personal growth.

psychotic disorders a group of disorders marked by irrational ideas, distorted perceptions, and a loss of contact with reality.

puberty the period of sexual maturation, during which a person usually becomes capable of reproducing.

random assignment assigning participants to experimental and control groups by chance, thus minimizing preexisting differences between the different groups.

random sample a sample that fairly represents a population because each member has an equal chance of inclusion.

range the difference between the highest and lowest scores in a distribution.

recall a measure of memory in which the person must retrieve information learned earlier, as on a fill-in-the-blank test.

reciprocal determinism the interacting influences of behavior, internal cognition, and environment.

reciprocity norm an expectation that people will help, not hurt, those who have helped them.

recognition a measure of memory in which the person identifies items previously learned, as on a multiple-choice test.

reconsolidation a process in which previously stored memories, when retrieved, are potentially altered before being stored again.

reflex a simple, automatic response to a sensory stimulus, such as the knee-jerk reflex.

refractory period (1) in neural processing, a brief resting pause that occurs after a neuron has fired; subsequent action potentials cannot occur until the axon returns to its resting state. (2) in human sexuality, a resting period that occurs after orgasm, during which a person cannot achieve another orgasm.

regression toward the mean the tendency for extreme or unusual scores or events to fall back (regress) toward the average.

reinforcement in operant conditioning, any event that *strengthens* the behavior it follows.

reinforcement schedule a pattern that defines how often a desired response will be reinforced.

relational aggression an act of aggression (physical or verbal) intended to harm a person's relationship or social standing.

relative deprivation the perception that we are worse off relative to those with whom we compare ourselves.

relearning a measure of memory that assesses the amount of time saved when learning material again.

reliability the extent to which a test yields consistent results, as assessed by the consistency of scores on two halves of the test, on alternative forms of the test, or on retesting.

REM rebound the tendency for REM sleep to increase following REM sleep deprivation.

REM sleep rapid eye movement sleep; a recurring sleep stage during which vivid dreams commonly occur. Also known as *paradoxical sleep*, because the muscles are relaxed (except for minor twitches) but other body and brain systems are active. (Sometimes called *R sleep*.)

REM sleep behavior disorder a sleep disorder characterized by acting out dreams while sleeping, through physical movements (such as kicking or striking out) and vocal behaviors (such as talking or yelling).

replication repeating the essence of a research study, usually with different participants in different situations, to see whether the basic finding can be reproduced.

representativeness heuristic judging the likelihood of events in terms of how well they seem to represent, or match, particular prototypes; may lead us to ignore other relevant information.

repression in psychoanalytic theory, the basic defense mechanism that banishes from consciousness anxiety-arousing thoughts, feelings, and memories.

resilience the personal strength that helps people cope with stress and recover from adversity and even trauma.

resistance in psychoanalysis, the blocking from consciousness of unpleasant or anxiety-laden material.

respondent behavior behavior that occurs as an automatic response to some stimulus.

reticular formation a nerve network that travels through the brainstem into the thalamus; filters information and plays an important role in controlling arousal.

retina the light-sensitive back inner surface of the eye, containing the receptor rods and cones plus layers of neurons that begin the processing of visual information.

retinal disparity a binocular cue for perceiving depth. By comparing retinal images from the two eyes, the brain computes distance—the greater the disparity (difference) between the two images, the closer the object.

retrieval the process of getting information out of memory storage.

retroactive interference the backward-acting disruptive effect of newer learning on the recall of *old* information.

retrograde amnesia an inability to remember information from one's past.

reuptake a neurotransmitter's reabsorption by the sending neuron.

rods retinal receptors that detect black, white, and gray, and are sensitive to movement. Rods are necessary for peripheral and twilight vision, when cones don't respond.

role a set of expectations *(norms)* about a social position, defining how those in the position ought to behave.

Rorschach inkblot test a projective test designed by Hermann Rorschach; seeks to identify people's inner feelings by analyzing how they interpret 10 inkblots.

rumination compulsive fretting; *overthinking* our problems and their causes.

savant syndrome a condition in which a person otherwise limited in mental ability has an exceptional specific skill, such as in computation or drawing.

scaffold in Vygotsky's theory, a framework that offers children temporary support as they develop higher levels of thinking.

scapegoat theory the theory that prejudice offers an outlet for anger by providing someone to blame.

scatterplot a graphed cluster of dots, each of which represents the values of two variables. The slope of the points suggests the direction of the relationship between the two variables. The amount of scatter suggests the strength of the correlation (little scatter indicates high correlation).

schema a concept or framework that organizes and interprets information.

schizophrenia a disorder characterized by delusions, hallucinations, disorganized speech, and/or diminished, inappropriate emotional expression.

secondary sex characteristics nonreproductive sexual traits, such as female breasts and hips, male voice quality, and body hair.

selective attention focusing conscious awareness on a particular stimulus.

self in contemporary psychology, assumed to be the center of personality, the organizer of our thoughts, feelings, and actions.

self-actualization according to Maslow, one of the ultimate psychological needs that arises after basic physical and psychological needs are met and self-esteem is achieved; the motivation to fulfill one's potential.

self-concept all our thoughts and feelings about ourselves, in answer to the question, "Who am I?"

self-control the ability to control impulses and delay short-term gratification for greater long-term rewards.

self-determination theory the theory that we feel motivated to satisfy our needs for competence, autonomy, and relatedness.

self-disclosure the act of revealing intimate aspects of ourselves to others.

self-efficacy our sense of competence and effectiveness.

self-esteem our feelings of high or low self-worth.

self-fulfilling prophecy a belief that leads to its own fulfillment.

self-report a method of recording participants' descriptions of their personality traits, often using surveys, questionnaires, or tests.

self-serving bias a readiness to perceive ourselves favorably.

self-transcendence according to Maslow, the striving for identity, meaning, and purpose beyond the self.

semantic memory explicit memory of facts and general knowledge; one of our two conscious memory systems (the other is *episodic memory*).

sensation the process by which our sensory receptors and nervous system receive and represent stimulus energies from our environment.

sensorimotor stage in Piaget's theory, the stage (from birth to nearly 2 years of age) at which infants know the world mostly in terms of their sensory impressions and motor activities.

sensorineural hearing loss the most common form of hearing loss, caused by damage to the cochlea's receptor cells or to the auditory nerve; also called *nerve deafness*.

sensory adaptation diminished sensitivity as a consequence of constant stimulation.

sensory (afferent) neurons neurons that carry incoming information from the body's tissues and sensory receptors to the brain and spinal cord.

sensory interaction the principle that one sense can influence another, as when the smell of food influences its taste.

sensory memory the immediate, very brief recording of sensory information in the memory system.

sensory receptors sensory nerve endings that respond to stimuli.

sequential processing processing one aspect of a stimulus or problem at a time; generally used to process new information or to solve difficult problems.

serial position effect our tendency to recall best the last *(recency effect)* and first *(primacy effect)* items in a list.

set point the point at which the "weight thermostat" may be set. When the body falls below this weight, increased hunger and a lowered metabolic rate may combine to restore lost weight.

sex in psychology, the biologically influenced characteristics by which people define *male*, *female*, and *intersex*.

sexual aggression any physical or verbal behavior of a sexual nature that is unwanted or intended to harm someone physically or emotionally. Can be expressed as either *sexual harassment* or *sexual assault*.

sexual dysfunction a problem that consistently impairs sexual arousal or functioning at any point in the sexual response cycle.

sexuality our thoughts, feelings, and actions related to our physical attraction to another.

sexual orientation the direction of our sexual attractions, as reflected in our longings and fantasies.

sexual response cycle the four stages of sexual responding described by Masters and Johnson—excitement, plateau, orgasm, and resolution.

shallow processing encoding on a basic level, based on the structure or appearance of words.

shaping an operant conditioning procedure in which reinforcers guide behavior toward closer and closer approximations of the desired behavior.

short-term memory briefly activated memory of a few items (such as digits of a phone number while calling) that is later stored or forgotten.

signal detection theory a theory predicting how and when we detect the presence of a faint stimulus *(signal)* amid background stimulation *(noise)*. Assumes there is no single absolute threshold and that detection depends partly on a person's experience, expectations, motivation, and alertness.

sleep a periodic, natural loss of consciousness—as distinct from unconsciousness resulting from a coma, general anesthesia, or hibernation. (Information from Dement, 1999.)

sleep apnea a sleep disorder characterized by temporary cessations of breathing during sleep and repeated momentary awakenings.

social anxiety disorder intense fear and avoidance of social situations.

social clock the culturally preferred timing of social events such as marriage, parenthood, and retirement.

social-cognitive perspective a view of behavior as influenced by the interaction between people's traits (including their thinking) and their social context.

social exchange theory the theory that our social behavior is an exchange process, the aim of which is to maximize benefits and minimize costs.

social facilitation in the presence of others, improved performance on simple or well-learned tasks, and worsened performance on difficult tasks.

social identity the "we" aspect of our self-concept; the part of our answer to "Who am I?" that comes from our group memberships.

social leadership group-oriented leadership that builds teamwork, mediates conflict, and offers support.

social learning theory the theory that we learn social behavior by observing and imitating and by being rewarded or punished.

social loafing the tendency for people in a group to exert less effort when pooling their efforts toward attaining a common goal than when individually accountable.

social psychology the scientific study of how we think about, influence, and relate to one another.

social script a culturally modeled guide for how to act in various situations.

social-responsibility norm an expectation that people will help those needing their help.

social trap a situation in which two parties, by each pursuing their self-interest rather than the good of the group, become caught in mutually destructive behavior.

somatic nervous system the division of the peripheral nervous system that controls the body's skeletal muscles. Also called the *skeletal nervous system*.

somatic symptom disorder a psychological disorder in which the symptoms take a somatic (bodily) form without apparent physical cause.

somatosensory cortex a cerebral cortex area at the front of the parietal lobes that registers and processes body touch and movement sensations.

source amnesia faulty memory for how, when, or where information was learned or imagined. (Also called *source misattribution*.) Source amnesia, along with the misinformation effect, is at the heart of many false memories.

spacing effect the tendency for distributed study or practice to yield better long-term retention than is achieved through massed study or practice.

specific phobia an anxiety disorder marked by a persistent, irrational fear and avoidance of a specific object, activity, or situation.

spermarche [sper-MAR-key] the first ejaculation.

split brain a condition resulting from surgery that separates the brain's two hemispheres by cutting the fibers (mainly those of the corpus callosum) connecting them.

spontaneous recovery the reappearance, after a pause, of a weakened conditioned response.

spotlight effect overestimating others' noticing and evaluating our appearance, performance, and blunders (as if we presume a spotlight shines on us).

SQ3R a study method incorporating five steps: Survey, Question, Read, Retrieve, Review.

standard deviation a computed measure of how much scores vary around the mean score.

standardization defining uniform testing procedures and meaningful scores by comparison with the performance of a pretested group.

Stanford-Binet the widely used U.S. revision (by Terman at Stanford University) of Binet's original intelligence test.

statistical significance a statistical statement of how likely it is that an obtained result (such as a difference between samples) occurred by chance, assuming there is no difference between the populations being studied.

statistics using mathematical methods to understand numerical information *(data)*.

stereotype a generalized (sometimes accurate but often overgeneralized) belief about a group of people.

stereotype threat a self-confirming concern that one will be evaluated based on a negative stereotype.

stimulants drugs (such as caffeine, nicotine, and the more powerful cocaine, amphetamines, methamphetamine, and Ecstasy) that excite neural activity and speed up body functions.

stimulus any event or situation that evokes a response.

storage the process of retaining encoded information over time.

stranger anxiety the fear of strangers that infants commonly display, beginning by about 8 months of age.

stress the process by which we perceive and respond to certain events, called *stressors,* that we appraise as threatening or challenging.

structuralism an early school of thought promoted by Wundt and Titchener; used introspection to reveal the structure of the human mind.

structured interviews an interview process that asks the same job-relevant questions of all applicants, each of whom is rated on established scales.

subjective well-being self-perceived satisfaction with life. Used along with measures of objective well-being (for example, physical and economic indicators) to judge our quality of life.

subliminal stimulation presenting something below one's absolute threshold for conscious awareness.

substance use disorder a disorder characterized by continued substance use despite significant life disruption.

superego the partly conscious part of personality that, according to Freud, represents internalized ideals and provides standards for judgment (the conscience) and for future aspirations.

superordinate goals shared goals that override differences among people and require their cooperation.

suprachiasmatic nucleus (SCN) a pair of cell clusters in the hypothalamus that controls circadian rhythm. In response to light, the SCN causes the pineal gland to adjust melatonin production, thus modifying our feelings of sleepiness.

survey a descriptive technique for obtaining the self-reported attitudes or behaviors of a particular group, usually by questioning a representative, *random sample* of the group.

sympathetic nervous system the division of the autonomic nervous system that arouses the body, mobilizing its energy.

synapse [SIN-aps] the junction between the axon tip of the sending neuron and the dendrite or cell body of the receiving neuron. The tiny gap at this junction is called the *synaptic gap* (or *synaptic cleft*).

syntax the correct way to string words together to form sentences for a given language.

systematic desensitization a type of exposure therapy that associates a pleasant relaxed state with gradually increasing anxiety-triggering stimuli. Commonly used to treat specific phobias.

task leadership goal-oriented leadership that sets standards, organizes work, and focuses attention on goals.

telegraphic speech the early speech stage in which a child speaks like a telegram—"go car"—using mostly nouns and verbs.

temperament a person's characteristic emotional reactivity and intensity.

temporal lobes the portion of the cerebral cortex lying roughly above the ears; includes the auditory areas, each receiving information primarily from the opposite ear.

tend-and-befriend response under stress, people (especially women) often provide support to others *(tend)* and bond with and seek support from others *(befriend)*.

teratogens agents, such as chemicals and viruses, that can reach the embryo or fetus during prenatal development and cause harm.

terror-management theory a theory of death-related anxiety; explores people's emotional and behavioral responses to reminders of their impending death.

testing effect enhanced memory after retrieving, rather than simply rereading, information. Also referred to as a *retrieval practice effect* or *test-enhanced learning.*

testosterone the most important male sex hormone. Males and females have it, but the additional testosterone in males stimulates the growth of the male sex organs during the fetal period, and the development of the male sex characteristics during puberty.

thalamus [THAL-uh-muss] the forebrain's sensory control center, located on top of the brainstem; it directs messages to the sensory receiving areas in the cortex and transmits replies to the cerebellum and medulla.

THC (delta-9-tetrahydrocannabinol) the major mind-altering ingredient in marijuana.

Thematic Apperception Test (TAT) a projective test in which people express their inner feelings and interests through the stories they make up about ambiguous scenes.

theory an explanation using an integrated set of principles that organizes observations and predicts behaviors or events.

theory of mind people's ideas about their own and others' mental states—about their feelings, perceptions, and thoughts, and the behaviors these might predict.

therapeutic alliance a bond of trust and mutual understanding between a therapist and client, who work together constructively to overcome the client's problem.

threshold the level of stimulation required to trigger a neural impulse.

tight culture places with clearly defined and reliably imposed norms.

token economy an operant conditioning procedure in which people earn a token for exhibiting a desired behavior and can later exchange tokens for privileges or treats.

tolerance the diminishing effect with regular use of the same dose of a drug, requiring the user to take larger and larger doses before experiencing the drug's effect.

top-down processing information processing guided by higher-level mental processes, as when we construct perceptions drawing on our experience and expectations.

trait a characteristic pattern of behavior or a disposition to feel and act in certain ways, as assessed by self-report inventories and peer reports.

transcranial magnetic stimulation (TMS) the application of repeated pulses of magnetic energy to the brain; used to stimulate or suppress brain activity.

transduction conversion of one form of energy into another. In sensation, the transforming of physical energy, such as sights, sounds, and smells, into neural impulses our brain can interpret.

transference in psychoanalysis, the patient's transfer to the analyst of emotions linked with other relationships (such as love or hatred for a parent).

transgender an umbrella term describing people whose gender identity differs from that associated with their sex assigned at birth.

trauma- and stressor-related disorders a group of disorders in which exposure to a traumatic or stressful event is followed by psychological distress.

two-factor theory the Schachter-Singer theory that to experience emotion one must (1) be physically aroused and (2) cognitively label the arousal.

two-word stage the stage in speech development, beginning about age 2, during which a child speaks mostly in two-word sentences.

Type A Friedman and Rosenman's term for competitive, hard-driving, impatient, verbally aggressive, and anger-prone people.

Type B Friedman and Rosenman's term for easygoing, relaxed people.

unconditional positive regard a caring, accepting, and nonjudgmental attitude, which Carl Rogers believed would help clients develop self-awareness and self-acceptance.

unconditioned response (UR) in classical conditioning, an unlearned, naturally occurring response (such as salivation) to an unconditioned stimulus (US) (such as food in the mouth).

unconditioned stimulus (US) in classical conditioning, a stimulus that unconditionally—naturally and automatically—triggers an unconditioned response (UR).

unconscious according to Freud, a reservoir of mostly unacceptable thoughts, wishes, feelings, and memories. According to contemporary psychologists, information processing of which we are unaware.

validity the extent to which a test measures or predicts what it is supposed to. (See also *predictive validity*.)

variable anything that can vary and is practical and ethical to measure.

variable-interval schedule in operant conditioning, a reinforcement schedule that reinforces a response at unpredictable time intervals.

variable-ratio schedule in operant conditioning, a reinforcement schedule that reinforces a response after an unpredictable number of responses.

vestibular sense our balance sense—our sense of body movement and position that enables our sense of balance.

virtual reality exposure therapy a counterconditioning technique that treats anxiety through creative electronic simulations in which people can safely face specific fears, such as flying, spiders, or public speaking.

visual cliff a laboratory device for testing depth perception in infants and young animals.

wavelength the distance from the peak of one light or sound wave to the peak of the next. Electromagnetic wavelengths vary from the short blips of gamma rays to the long pulses of radio transmission.

Weber's law the principle that, to be perceived as different, two stimuli must differ by a constant minimum percentage (rather than a constant amount).

Wechsler Adult Intelligence Scale (WAIS) the WAIS and its companion versions for children are the most widely used intelligence tests; they contain verbal and performance (nonverbal) subtests.

Wernicke's area a brain area, usually in the left temporal lobe, involved in language comprehension and expression.

withdrawal the discomfort and distress that follow discontinuing an addictive drug or behavior.

working memory a newer understanding of short-term memory; conscious, active processing of both (1) incoming sensory information and (2) information retrieved from long-term memory.

X chromosome the sex chromosome found in females and males. Females typically have two X chromosomes; males typically have one. An X chromosome from each parent produces a female child.

Y chromosome the sex chromosome typically found only in males. When paired with an X chromosome from the mother, it produces a male child.

Yerkes-Dodson law the principle that performance increases with arousal only up to a point, beyond which performance decreases.

Young-Helmholtz trichromatic (three-color) theory the theory that the retina contains three different types of color receptors—one most sensitive to red, one to green, one to blue—which, when stimulated in combination, can produce the perception of any color.

zygote the fertilized egg; it enters a 2-week period of rapid cell division and develops into an embryo.

References

Note: As your authors, we aim to report psychology's current state, including each sub-discipline's latest research insights. We've incorporated over 1200 citations dated 2019–2022, highlighted here in blue.

AAA. (2015). *Teen driver safety: Environmental factors and driver behaviors in teen driver crashes* [PDF file]. AAA Foundation for Traffic Safety. https://aaafoundation.org/wp-content/uploads/2015/03/TeenCrashCausation_2015_FACTSHEET.pdf

AAMC (Association of American Medical Colleges). (2014). *Medical students, selected years, 1965–2013* [PDF file]. https://www.aamc.org/system/files/reports/1/2015table1.pdf

AAMC. (2018). *Total enrollment by U.S. medical school and sex, 2014–2015 through 2018–2019.* https://www.aamc.org/data-reports/students-residents/report/facts

AAMC. (2019). *Diversity in medicine: Facts and figures 2019.* Figure 18: Percentage of all active physicians by race/ethnicity, 2018. https://www.aamc.org/data-reports/workforce/interactive-data/figure-18-percentage-all-active-physicians-race/ethnicity-2018

AAMC. (2021, December). 2021 Fall applicant, matriculant, and enrollment data tables. https://www.aamc.org/media/57761/download?attachment

Aarts, H., & Custers, R. (2012) Unconscious goal pursuit: Nonconscious goal regulation and motivation. In R. M. Ryan (Ed.), *The Oxford handbook of human motivation* (pp. 232–247). Oxford University Press.

AAU (Association of American Universities). (2020). *Report on the AAU Campus Climate Survey on sexual assault and misconduct* [PDF file]. https://tinyurl.com/2um55y42

Abbey, A. (1987). Misperceptions of friendly behavior as sexual interest: A survey of naturally occurring incidents. *Psychology of Women Quarterly, 11,* 173–194.

ABC. (2014). *Tommy Lynn Sells—the mind of a psychopath* [YouTube video]. Nightline. https://www.youtube.com/watch?v=6V7EL-Yg8Gg&feature=youtu.be

Abel, K. M., Drake, R., & Goldstein, J. M. (2010). Sex differences in schizophrenia. *International Review of Psychiatry, 22,* 417–428.

Ablaza, C., Kabátek, J., & Perales, F. (2022) Are sibship characteristics predictive of same sex marriage? An examination of fraternal birth order and female fecundity effects in population-level administrative data from the Netherlands. *Journal of Sex Research, 59,* 671–683.

Abrams, D. B., & Wilson, G. T. (1983). Alcohol, sexual arousal, and self-control. *Journal of Personality and Social Psychology, 45,* 188–198.

Abrams, L. (2008). Tip-of-the-tongue states yield language insights. *American Scientist, 96,* 234–239.

Abrams, M. (2002, June). Sight unseen—Restoring a blind man's vision is now a real possibility through stem-cell surgery. But even perfect eyes cannot see unless the brain has been taught to use them. *Discover, 23,* 54–60.

Abramson, L. Y., Metalsky, G. I., & Alloy, L. B. (1989). Hopelessness depression: A theory-based subtype. *Psychological Review, 96,* 358–372.

Abramson, L. Y., Seligman, M. E. P., & Teasdale, J. D. (1978). Learned helplessness in humans: Critique and reformulation. *Journal of Abnormal Psychology, 87,* 49–74.

Abuhamdeh, S., Csikszentmihalyi, M., & Jalal, B. (2015). Enjoying the possibility of defeat: Outcome uncertainty, suspense, and intrinsic motivation. *Motivation and Emotion, 39,* 1–10.

Academy of Science of South Africa. (2015). *Diversity in human sexuality: Implications for policy in Africa.* https://research.assaf.org.za/handle/20.500.11911/38

Acevedo, B. P., & Aron, A. (2009). Does a long-term relationship kill romantic love? *Review of General Psychology, 13,* 59–65.

Acevedo, B. P., Aron, A., Fisher, H. E., & Brown, L. L. (2012). Neural correlates of long-term intense romantic love. *Social Cognitive and Affective Neuroscience, 7,* 145–159.

ACHA (American College Health Association). (2022). *Publications and reports: ACHA-NCHA III.* Spring 2022. https://www.acha.org/NCHA/ACHA-NCHA_Data/Publications_and_Reports/NCHA/Data/Reports_ACHA-NCHAIII.aspx

Achterberg, M., van Duijvenvoorde, A. C. K., van IJzendoorn, M. H., Bakermans-Kranenburg, M. J., & Crone, E. A. (2020). Longitudinal changes in DLPFC activation during childhood are related to decreased aggression following social rejection. *PNAS, 117*(15), 8602–8610.

Ackerman, D. (2004). *An alchemy of mind: The marvel and mystery of the brain.* Scribner.

Ackerman, P. L. (2014). Adolescent and adult intellectual development. *Current Directions in Psychological Science, 23,* 246–251.

ACMD (Advisory Council on the Misuse of Drugs). (2009). *MDMA ('Ecstasy'): A review of its harms and classification under the Misuse of Drugs Act 1971* [PDF file]. https://assets.publishing.service.gov.uk/government/uploads/system/uploads/attachment_data/file/119088/mdma-report.pdf

Adachi, T., Fujino, H., Nakae, A., Mashimo, T., & Sasaki, J. (2014). A meta-analysis of hypnosis for chronic pain problems: A comparison between hypnosis, standard care, and other psychological interventions. *International Journal of Clinical and Experimental Hypnosis, 62,* 1–28.

Adams, H. E., Wright, L. W., Jr., & Lohr, B. A. (1996). Is homophobia associated with homosexual arousal? *Journal of Abnormal Psychology, 105,* 440–446.

Adams, N. J., & Vincent, B. (2019). Suicidal thoughts and behaviors among transgender adults in relation to education, ethnicity, and income: A systematic review. *Transgender Health, 4*(1), 226–246.

Adams, Z. W., Sieverdes, J. C., Brunner-Jackson, B., Mueller, M., Chandler, J., Diaz, V., Patel, S., Sox, L. R., Wilder, S., & Treiber, F. A. (2018). Meditation smartphone application effects on prehypertensive adults' blood pressure: Dose-response feasibility trial. *Health Psychology, 37,* 850–860.

Addis, D. R., Leclerc, C. M., Muscatell, K. A., & Kensinger, E. A. (2010). There are age-related changes in neural connectivity during the encoding of positive, but not negative, information. *Cortex, 46,* 425–433.

Adelmann, P. K., Antonucci, T. C., Crohan, S. F., & Coleman, L. M. (1989). Empty nest, cohort, and employment in the well-being of midlife women. *Sex Roles, 20,* 173–189.

Ader, R., & Cohen, N. (1985). CNS-immune system interactions: Conditioning phenomena. *Behavioral and Brain Sciences, 8,* 379–394.

Aderka, I. M., Nickerson, A., Bøe, H. J., & Hofmann, S. G. (2012). Sudden gains during psychological treatments of anxiety and depression: A meta-analysis. *Journal of Consulting and Clinical Psychology, 80,* 93–101.

Adetunji, J. (2014, February 17). *Genes predispose obesity but it's fullness that makes you fat.* The Conversation. https://theconversation.com/genes-predispose-obesity-but-its-fullness-that-makes-you-fat-23335

ADL (Anti-Defamation League). (2022). *Audit of antisemitic incidents 2021.* https://www.adl.org/resources/report/audit-antisemitic-incidents-2021

Adler, J. (2012). Erasing painful memories. *Scientific American, 306,* 56–61.

Adler, J. M., Lodi-Smith, J., Philippe, F. L., & Houle, I. (2016). The incremental validity of narrative identity in predicting well-being: A review of the field and recommendations for the future. *Personality and Social Psychology Review, 20,* 142–175.

Admon, R., Vaisvaser, S., Erlich, N., Lin, T., Shapira-Lichter, I., Fruchter, E., Gazit, T., & Hendler, T. (2018). The role of the amygdala in enhanced remembrance of negative episodes and acquired negativity of related neutral cues. *Biological Psychology, 139,* 17–24.

Adolph, K. E., & Hoch, J. E. (2019). Motor development: Embodied, embedded, enculturated, and enabling. *Annual Review of Psychology, 70,* 141–164.

Adolph, K. E., Kretch, K. S., & LoBue, V. (2014). Fear of heights in infants? *Current Directions in Psychological Science, 23,* 60–66.

Affleck, G., Tennen, H., Urrows, S., & Higgins, P. (1994). Person and contextual features of daily stress reactivity: Individual differences in relations of undesirable daily events with mood disturbance and chronic pain intensity. *Journal of Personality and Social Psychology, 66,* 329–340.

Afzali, M. H., Sunderland, M., Stewart, S., Masse, B., Seguin, J., Newton, N., Teesson, M., & Conrod, P. (2019). Machine-learning prediction of adolescent alcohol use: A cross-study, cross-cultural validation. *Addiction, 114,* 662–671.

Agerström, J., Björklund, F., Carlsson, R., & Rooth, D.-O. (2012). Warm and competent Hassan = cold and incompetent Eric: A harsh equation of real-life hiring discrimination. *Basic and Applied Social Psychology, 34*, 359–366.

Agrawal, M., Peterson, J. C., & Griffiths, T. L. (2020). Scaling up psychology via Scientific Regret Minimization. *PNAS, 117*(16), 8825–8835.

Agrawal, Y., Platz, E. A., & Niparko, J. K. (2008). Prevalence of hearing loss and differences by demographic characteristics among US adults: Data from the National Health and Nutrition Examination Survey, 1999–2004. *Archives of Internal Medicine, 168*, 1522–1530.

Agrigoroaei, S., & Lachman, M. E. (2011). Cognitive functioning in midlife and old age: Combined effects of psychosocial and behavioral factors. *The Journals of Gerontology. Series B: Psychological Sciences and Social Sciences, 66*(suppl 1), 1130–1140.

Agudelo, L. Z., Femenía, T., Orhan, F., Porsmyr-Palmertz, M., Goiny, M., Martinez-Redondo, V., Correia, J. C., Izadi, M., Bhat, M., Schuppe-Koistinen, I., Pettersson, A. T., Ferreira, D. M. S., Krook, A., Barres, R., Zierath, J. R., Erhardt, S., & Ruas, J. L. (2014). Skeletal muscle PGC-1α1 modulates kynurenine metabolism and mediates resilience to stress-induced depression. *Cell, 159*, 33–45.

Ahler, D. J., & Sood, G. (2018). The parties in our heads: Misperceptions about party composition and their consequences. *Journal of Politics, 80*, 964–981.

Ahrén, J. C., Chiesa, F., Koupil, I., Magnusson, C., Dalman, C., & Goodman, A. (2013). We are family—parents, siblings, and eating disorders in a prospective total-population study of 250,000 Swedish males and females. *International Journal of Eating Disorders, 46*, 693–700.

Aichele, S., Rabbitt, P., & Ghisletta, P. (2016). Think fast, feel fine, live long: A 29-year study of cognition, health, and survival in middle-aged and older adults. *Psychological Science, 27*, 518–529.

Aiello, J. R., Thompson, D. D., & Brodzinsky, D. M. (1983). How funny is crowding anyway? Effects of room size, group size, and the introduction of humor. *Basic and Applied Social Psychology, 4*, 193–207.

Aikins, J. W., Simon, V. A., & Prinstein, M. J. (2010). Romantic partner selection and socialization of young adolescents' substance use and behavior problems. *Journal of Adolescence, 33*(6), 813–826.

Ainsworth, M. D. S. (1973). The development of infant-mother attachment. In B. Caldwell & H. Ricciuti (Eds.), *Review of child development research* (Vol. 3). University of Chicago Press.

Ainsworth, M. D. S. (1979). Infant-mother attachment. *American Psychologist, 34*, 932–937.

Ainsworth, M. D. S. (1989). Attachments beyond infancy. *American Psychologist, 44*, 709–716.

Ajiboye, A. B., Willett, F. R., Young, D. R., Memberg, W. D., Murphy, B. A., Miller, J. P., Walter, B. L., Sweet, J. A., Hoyen, H. A., Keith, M. W., Peckham, P. H., Simeral, J. D., Donoghue, J. P., Hochberg, L. R., & Kirsch, R. F. (2017). Restoration of reaching and grasping in a person with tetraplegia through brain-controlled muscle stimulation: A proof-of-concept demonstration. *The Lancet, 389*, 1821–1830.

Ajilore, O., & Thames, A. D. (2020). The fire this time: The stress of racism, inflammation and COVID-19. *Brain, Behavior, and Immunity, 88*, 66.

Akanbi, M. O., Carroll, A. J., Achenbach, C., O'Dwyer, L. C., Jordan, N., Hitsman, B., Bilaver, L. A., McHugh, M. C., & Murphy, R. (2019). The efficacy of smoking cessation interventions in low- and middle-income countries: A systematic review and meta-analysis. *Addiction, 114*, 620–635.

Akee, R. K. Q., Copeland, W. E., Keeler, G., Angold, A., & Costello, E. J. (2010). Parents' incomes and children's outcomes: A quasi-experiment using transfer payments from casino profits. *American Economic Journal: Applied Economics, 2*(1), 86–115.

Åkerlund, D., Golsteyn, B. H., Grönqvist, H., & Lindahl, L. (2016). Time discounting and criminal behavior. *PNAS, 113*, 6160–6165.

Akers, K. G., Martinez-Canabal, A., Restivo, L., Yiu, A. P., De Cristofara, A., Hsiang, H.-L., Wheeler, A. L., Guskjolen, A., Niibori, Y., Shoji, H., Richards, B. A., Miyakawa, T., Josselyn, S. A., & Frankland, P. W. (2014). Hippocampal neurogenesis regulates forgetting during adulthood and infancy. *Science, 344*, 598–602.

Akhtar, R., Winsborough, D., Ort, U., Johnson, A., & Chamorro-Premuzic, T. (2018). Detecting the dark side of personality using social media status updates. *Personality and Individual Differences, 132*, 90–97.

Akiyama, M., Okada, Y., Kanai, M., Takahashi, A., Momozawa, Y., Ikeda, M., Iwata, N., Ikegawa, S., Hirata, M., Matsuda, K., & Iwasaki, M. (2017). Genome-wide association study identifies 112 new loci for body mass index in the Japanese population. *Nature Genetics, 49*, 1458–1467.

Aknin, L. B., Broesch, T., Kiley Hamlin, J., & Van de Vondervoort, J. W. (2015). Prosocial behavior leads to happiness in a small-scale rural society. *Journal of Experimental Psychology: General, 144*, 788–795.

Aknin, L.B., De Neve, J.-E., Dunn, E., Fancourt, D., Goldberg, E., Helliwell, J., Jones, S. P., Karam, E., Layard, R., Lyubomirsky, S., Rzepa, A., Saxena, S., Thornton, E., VanderWeele, T., Whillans, A., Zaki, J., Caman, O. K., & Amour, Y. B. (2022). Mental health during the first year of the COVID-19 pandemic: A review and recommendations for moving forward. *Perspectives on Psychological Science, 17*, 915–936.

Aknin, L. B., Dunn, E. W., Proulx, J., Lok, I., & Norton, M. I. (2020). Does spending money on others promote happiness?: A registered replication report. *Journal of Personality and Social Psychology, 119*(2), e15–e26.

Aknin, L. B., & Human, L. J. (2015). Give a piece of you: Gifts that reflect givers promote closeness. *Journal of Experimental Social Psychology, 60*, 8–16.

Aknin, L. B., Whillans, A. V., Norton, M. I., & Dunn, E. W. (2019). Happiness and prosocial behavior: An evaluation of the evidence (Chapter 4). In J. Helliwell, R. Layard, & J. Sachs (Eds.), *World happiness report 2019*. Sustainable Development Solutions Network.

Akpinar, E., & Berger, J. (2015). Drivers of cultural success: The case of sensory metaphors. *Journal of Personality and Social Psychology, 109*, 20–34.

Alaei, R., Deska, J. C., Hugenberg, K., & Rule, N. O. (2022). People attribute humanness to men and women differently based on their facial appearance. *Journal of Personality and Social Psychology, 123*(2), 400–422.

Al Aïn, S., Poupon, D., Hétu, S., Mercier, N., Steffener, J., & Frasnelli, J. (2019). Smell training improves olfactory function and alters brain structure. *NeuroImage, 189*, 45–54.

al-Asaadi, M. (2016). "We sleep afraid, we wake up afraid": A child's life in Yemen. *The New York Times*. https://www.nytimes.com/2016/10/12/world/middleeast/yemen-children-in-a-war-zone.html

Al Ibraheem, B., Kira, I. A., Aljakoub, J., & Al Ibraheem, A. (2017). The health effect of the Syrian conflict on IDPs and refugees. *Peace and Conflict: Journal of Peace Psychology, 23*, 140–152.

Alang, S., VanHook, C., Judson, J., Ikiroma, A., & Adkins-Jackson, P. B. (2022). Police brutality, heightened vigilance, and the mental health of Black adults. *Psychology of Violence, 12*(4), 211–220.

Alanko, K., Santtila, P., Harlaar, N., Witting, K., Varjonen, M., Jern, P., Johansson, A., von der Pahlen, B., & Sandnabba, N. K. (2010). Common genetic effects of gender atypical behavior in childhood and sexual orientation in adulthood: A study of Finnish twins. *Archives of Sexual Behavior, 39*, 81–92.

Albee, G. W. (1986). Toward a just society: Lessons from observations on the primary prevention of psychopathology. *American Psychologist, 41*, 891–898.

Albee, G. W. (2006). Historical overview of primary prevention of psychopathology: Address to the 3rd world conference on the promotion of mental health and prevention of mental and behavioral disorders. September 15–17, 2004, Auckland, New Zealand. *Journal of Primary Prevention, 27*, 449–456.

Alcock, J. E. (2011, March/April). Back from the future: Parapsychology and the Bem affair. *Skeptical Inquirer*, pp. 31–39.

Aldao, A., & Nolen-Hoeksema, S. (2010). Emotion-regulation strategies across psychopathology: A meta-analytic review. *Clinical Psychology Review, 30*, 217–237.

Aldao, A., Nolen-Hoeksema, S., & Schweizer, S. (2010). Emotion-regulation strategies across psychopathology: A meta-analytic review. *Clinical Psychology Review, 30*(2), 217–237.

Aleman, A., Kahn, R. S., & Selten, J.-P. (2003). Sex differences in the risk of schizophrenia: Evidence from meta-analysis. *Archives of General Psychiatry, 60*, 565–571.

Alexander, L., & Tredoux, C. (2010). The spaces between us: A spatial analysis of informal segregation. *Journal of Social Issues, 66*, 367–386.

Alfonsi, V., Palmizio, R., Rubino, A., Scarpelli, S., Gorgoni, M., D'Atri, A., Pazzaglia, M., Ferrara, M., Giuliano, S., & De Gennaro, L. (2020). The association between school start time and sleep duration, sustained attention, and academic performance. *Nature and Science of Sleep, 12*, 1161–1172.

Alimujiang, A., Wiensch, A., Boss, J., Fleischer, N. L., Mondul, A. M., McLean, K., Mukherjee, B., & Pearce, C. L. (2019). Association between life purpose and mortality among U.S. adults older than 50 years. *JAMA Network Open, 2*(5). https://jamanetwork

.com/journals/jamanetworkopen/fullarticle/2734064

Al-Kontar, H. (2020). *This pandemic has made refugees of us all.* CBC. https://www.cbc.ca/news/canada/british-columbia/hassan-al-kontar-covid-oped-1.5529447

Allan, B. A. (2017). Task significance and meaningful work: A longitudinal study. *Journal of Vocational Behavior, 102*, 174–182.

Allard, F., & Burnett, N. (1985). Skill in sport. *Canadian Journal of Psychology, 39*, 294–312.

Allcott, H., Braghieri, L., Eichmeyer, S., & Gentzkow, M. (2020). The welfare effects of social media. *American Economic Review, 110*(3), 629–676.

Allemand, M., Job, V., & Mroczek, D. K. (2019). Self-control development in adolescence predicts love and work in adulthood. *Journal of Personality and Social Psychology, 117*, 621–634.

Allen, J., Weinrich, M., Hoppitt, W., & Rendell, L. (2013). Network-based diffusion analysis reveals cultural transmission of lobtail feeding in humpback whales. *Science, 340*, 485–488.

Allen, J. P., Uchino, B. N., & Hafen, C. A. (2015). Running with the pack: Teen peer-relationship qualities as predictors of adult physical health. *Psychological Science, 26*, 1574–1583.

Allen, K. (2003). Are pets a healthy pleasure? The influence of pets on blood pressure. *Current Directions in Psychological Science, 12*, 236–239.

Allen, M. S., & Jones, M. V. (2014). The "home advantage" in athletic competitions. *Current Directions in Psychological Science, 23*, 48–53.

Allen, M. S., Robson, D. A., Martin, L. J., & Laborde, S. (2020). Systematic review and meta-analysis of self-serving attribution biases in the competitive context of organized sport. *Personality and Social Psychology Bulletin, 46*, 1027–1043.

Allen, M. W., Gupta, R., & Monnier, A. (2008). The interactive effect of cultural symbols and human values on taste evaluation. *Journal of Consumer Research, 35*, 294–308.

Allen, T., & Sherman, J. (2011). Ego threat and intergroup bias: A test of motivated-activation versus self-regulatory accounts. *Psychological Science, 22*, 331–333.

Allesøe, K., Hundrup, V. A., Thomsen, J. F., & Osler, M. (2010). Psychosocial work environment and risk of ischaemic heart disease in women: The Danish Nurse Cohort Study. *Occupational and Environmental Medicine, 67*, 318–322.

Alloy, L. B., Abramson, L. Y., Whitehouse, W. G., Hogan, M. E., Tashman, N. A., Steinberg, D. L., Rose, D. T., & Donovan, P. (1999). Depressogenic cognitive styles: Predictive validity, information processing and personality characteristics, and developmental origins. *Behaviour Research and Therapy, 37*, 503–531.

Allport, G. W. (1954). *The nature of prejudice.* Addison-Wesley.

Allport, G. W., & Odbert, H. S. (1936). Trait-names: A psycho-lexical study. *Psychological Monographs, 47*(1), i–171.

Almas, A. N., Degnan, K. A., Nelson, C. A., Zeanah, C. H., & Fox, N. A. (2017). IQ at age 12 following a history of institutional care: Findings from the Bucharest Early Intervention Project. *Developmental Psychology, 52*, 1858–1866.

Almås, I., Cappelen, A. W., Sørensen, E. Ø., & Tungodden, B. (2010). Fairness and the development of inequality acceptance. *Science, 328*, 1176–1178.

Almazan, A. N., & Keuroghlian, A. S. (2021). Association between gender-affirming surgeries and mental health outcomes. *JAMA Surgery, 156*, 611–618.

Almeida, J., He, D., Chen, Q., Mahon, B. Z., Zhang, F., Gonçalves, Ó. F., Fang, F., & Bi, Y. (2015). Decoding visual location from neural patterns in the auditory cortex of the congenitally deaf. *Psychological Science, 26*, 1771–1782.

Almond, D., & Du, X. (2020). Later bedtimes predict President Trump's performance. *Economics Letters, 197*. https://www.sciencedirect.com/science/article/pii/S0165176520303554

Alnefeesi, Y., Chen-Li, D., Krane, E., Jawad, M. H., Rodrigues, N. B., Ceban, F., Di Vincenzo, J. D., Meshkat, S., Ho, R. C. M., Gill, H., Teopiz, K. M., Cao, B., Lee, Y., McIntyre, R. S., & Rosenblat, J. D. (2022). Real-world effectiveness of ketamine in treatment-resistant depression: A systematic review & meta-analysis. *Journal of Psychiatric Research, 151*, 693–709.

Alpert, H. R., Slater, M. E., Yoon, Y.-H., Chen, C. M., Winstanley, N., & Esser, M. B. (2022). Alcohol consumption and 15 causes of fatal injuries: A systematic review and meta-analysis. *American Journal of Preventive Medicine, 63*(2), 286–300.

al-Sharif, M. (2019, April 10). We finally won the right to drive in Saudi Arabia. But the kingdom's war on women is only getting worse. *Time Magazine.* https://time.com/5567330/saudi-arabia-women-rights-drive/

AlShebli, B. K., Rahwan, T., & Woon, W. L. (2018). The preeminence of ethnic diversity in scientific collaboration. *Nature Communications, 9*. https://www.nature.com/articles/s41467-018-07634-8

Altamirano, L. J., Miyake, A., & Whitmer, A. J. (2010). When mental inflexibility facilitates executive control: Beneficial side effects of ruminative tendencies on goal maintenance. *Psychological Science, 21*, 1377–1382.

Altarum. (2018). *Economic toll of opioid crisis in U.S. exceeded $1 trillion since 2001.* https://altarum.org/news/economic-toll-opioid-crisis-us-exceeded-1-trillion-2001

Altschul, D. M., Hopkins, W. D., Herrelko, E. S., Inoue-Murayama, M., Matsuzawa, T., King, J. E., Ross, S. R., & Weiss, A. (2018). Personality links with lifespan in chimpanzees. *eLife, 7*. https://bit.ly/3BQoxQc

Alvarez, L., & Schwartz, J. (2014, May 30). On death row with low I.Q., and new hope for a reprieve. *The New York Times.* https://www.nytimes.com/2010/09/22/us/22execute.html

Alves, H., Högden, F., Gast, A., Aust, F., & Unkelbach, C. (2020). Attitudes from mere co-occurrences are guided by differentiation. *Journal of Personality and Social Psychology, 119*(3), 560–581.

Alving, C. R. (2011, March 2). *Carl Alving: Idea for vaccine patch came to me in dream* [Podcast]. American Association for the Advancement of Science.

Alwin, D. F. (1990). Historical changes in parental orientations to children. In N. Mandell (Ed.), *Sociological studies of child development* (Vol. 3). JAI Press.

Amabile, T. M., & Hennessey, B. A. (1992). The motivation for creativity in children. In A. K. Boggiano & T. S. Pittman (Eds.), *Achievement and motivation: A social-developmental perspective.* Cambridge University Press.

Amabile, T. M., & Kramer, S. J. (2011). *The progress principle: Using small wins to ignite joy, engagement, and creativity at work.* Harvard Business Review Press.

Amalric, M., & Dehaene, S. (2019). A distinct cortical network for mathematical knowledge in the human brain. *NeuroImage, 189*, 19–31.

Ambady, N. (2010). The perils of pondering: Intuition and thin slice judgments. *Psychological Inquiry, 21*, 271–278.

Amedi, A., Merabet, L. B., Bermpohl, F., & Pascual-Leone, A. (2005). The occipital cortex in the blind: Lessons about plasticity and vision. *Current Directions in Psychological Science, 14*, 306–311.

Amen, D. G., Stubblefield, M., Carmichael, B., & Thisted, R. (1996). BrainSPECT findings and aggressiveness. *Annals of Clinical Psychiatry, 8*, 129–137.

American Academy of Pediatrics. (2009). Media violence. *Pediatrics, 124*(5), 1495–1503.

American Academy of Pediatrics. (2013). *Promoting the well-being of children whose parents are gay or lesbian.* https://pediatrics.aappublications.org/content/131/4/827

American Psychiatric Association. (2013). *Diagnostic and statistical manual of mental disorders* (5th ed.). American Psychiatric Publishing.

American Psychiatric Association. (2022). *Diagnostic and statistical manual of mental disorders, 5th edition, text revision, DSM-5-TR.*

American Sociological Association. (2013, February 28). Brief of *Amicus Curiae* American Sociological Association in support of respondent Kristin M. Perry and respondent Edith Schlain Windsor. Supreme Court of the United States, Nos. 12–144, 12–307.

Amick, H. R., Gartlehner, G., Gaynes, B. N., Forneris, C., Asher, G. N., Morgan, L. C., Coker-Schwimmer, E., Boland, E., Lux, L. J., Gaylord, S., Bann, C., Pieri, C. B., & Lohr, K. N. (2015). Comparative benefits and harms of second generation antidepressants and cognitive behavioral therapies in initial treatment of major depressive disorder: Systematic review and meta-analysis. *BMJ: British Medical Journal, 351*. https://www.bmj.com/content/351/bmj.h6019

Ammori, B. (2013, January 4). Viewpoint: Benefits of bariatric surgery. *GP.* https://www.gponline.com/viewpoint-benefits-bariatric-surgery/obesity/bariatric-surgery/article/1164873

An, X., & Wang, Y. (2022). Electroconvulsive shock increases neurotrophy and neurogenesis: Time course and treatment session effects. *Psychiatry Research, 309*. https://doi.org/10.1016/j.psychres.2022.114390

Ananth, M., Hetelekides, E. M., Hamilton, J., & Thanos, P. K. (2019). Dopamine D4 receptor gene expression plays important role in extinction and reinstatement of cocaine-seeking behavior in mice. *Behavioural Brain Research, 365*, 1–6.

Andersen, M. M., Schjoedt, U., Price, H., Rosas, F. E., Scrivner, C., & Clasen, M. (2020). Playing with fear: A field study in recreational horror. *Psychological Science, 31*, 1497–1510.

Andersen, R. (2019, April). The intention machine. *Scientific American*, pp. 25–31.

Andersen, R. A., Hwang, E. J., & Mulliken, G. H. (2010). Cognitive neural prosthetics. *Annual Review of Psychology, 61*, 169–190.

Andersen, S. M. (1998, September). *Service learning: A national strategy for youth development*. Institute for Communitarian Policy Studies, George Washington University.

Anderson, C. A. (2004). An update on the effects of playing violent video games. *Journal of Adolescence, 27*, 113–122.

Anderson, C. A. (2013, June). Guns, games, and mass shootings in the U.S. *Bulletin of the International Society for Research on Aggression*, pp. 14–19.

Anderson, C. A., Brion, S., Moore, D. A., & Kennedy, J. A. (2012). A status enhancement account of overconfidence. *Journal of Personality and Social Psychology, 103*, 718–735.

Anderson, C. A., Bushman, B. J., & Groom, R. W. (1997). Hot years and serious and deadly assault: Empirical tests of the heat hypothesis. *Journal of Personality and Social Psychology, 73*, 1213–1223.

Anderson, C. A., & Delisi, M. (2011). Implications of global climate change for violence in developed and developing countries. In J. Forgas, A. Kruglanski, & K. Williams (Eds.), *The psychology of social conflict and aggression* (pp. 249–265). Psychology Press.

Anderson, C. A., & Dill, K. E. (2000). Video games and aggressive thoughts, feelings, and behavior in the laboratory and in life. *Journal of Personality and Social Psychology, 78*, 772–790.

Anderson, C. A., & Warburton, W. A. (2012). The impact of violent video games: An overview. In W. Warburton & D. Braunstein (Eds.), *Growing up fast and furious: Reviewing the impacts of violent and sexualized media on children* (pp. 56–84). Federation Press.

Anderson, C. A., Suzuki, K., Swing, E. L., Groves, C. L., Gentile, D. A., Prot, S., Lam, C. P., Sakamoto, A., Horiuchi, Y., Krahé, B., Jelic, M., Liuqing, W., Toma, R., Warburton, W. A., Zhang, X. M., Tajima, S., Qing, F., & Petrescu, P. (2017). Media violence and other aggression risk factors in seven nations. *Personality and Social Psychology Bulletin, 43*, 986–998.

Anderson, E., Siegel, E., White, D., & Barrett, L. F. (2012). Out of sight but not out of mind: Unseen affective faces influence evaluations and social impressions. *Emotion, 12*, 1210–1221.

Anderson, F. T., & McDaniel, M. A. (2019). Hey buddy, why don't we take it outside: An experience sampling study of prospective memory. *Memory & Cognition, 47*, 47–62.

Anderson, I., Gil, S., Gibson, C., Wolf, S., Shapiro, W., Semerci, O., & Greenberg, D. M. (2021). "Just the way you are": Linking music listening on Spotify and personality. *Social Psychological and Personality Science, 12*(4), 561–572.

Anderson, M., Vogels, E. A., & Turner, E. (2020, February 6). *The virtues and downsides of online dating*. Pew Research Center. https://www.pewresearch.org/internet/2020/02/06/the-virtues-and-downsides-of-online-dating/

Anderson, R. C., Pichert, J. W., Goetz, E. T., Schallert, D. L., Stevens, K. V., & Trollip, S. R. (1976). Instantiation of general terms. *Journal of Verbal Learning and Verbal Behavior, 15*, 667–679.

Anderson, S. E., Dallal, G. E., & Must, A. (2003). Relative weight and race influence average age at menarche: Results from two nationally representative surveys of U.S. girls studied 25 years apart. *Pediatrics, 111*, 844–850.

Andreasen, N. C. (1997). Linking mind and brain in the study of mental illnesses: A project for a scientific psychopathology. *Science, 275*, 1586–1593.

Andreasen, N. C. (2001). *Brave new brain: Conquering mental illness in the era of the genome*. Oxford University Press.

Andreasen, N. C., Arndt, S., Swayze, V., II, Cizadlo, T., & Flaum, M. (1994). Thalamic abnormalities in schizophrenia visualized through magnetic resonance image averaging. *Science, 266*, 294–298.

Andrews, P. W., & Thomson, J. A., Jr. (2009a). The bright side of being blue: Depression as an adaptation for analyzing complex problems. *Psychological Review, 116*, 620–654.

Andrews, P. W., & Thomson, J. A., Jr. (2009b). Depression's evolutionary roots. *Scientific American Mind, 20*, 56–61.

Andrillon, T., Nir, Y., Cirelli, C., Tononi, G., & Fried, I. (2015). Single-neuron activity and eye movements during human REM sleep and awake vision. *Nature Communications, 6*. https://www.nature.com/articles/ncomms8884

Angelakis, I., Gillespie, E. L., & Panagioti, M. (2019). Childhood maltreatment and adult suicidality: A comprehensive systematic review with meta-analysis. *Psychological Medicine, 49*, 1057–1078.

Angelescu, I., Brugger, S. P., Borgan, F., Kaar, S. J., & Howes, O. D. (2021). The magnitude and variability of brain structural alterations in bipolar disorder: A double meta-analysis of 5534 patients and 6651 healthy controls. *Journal of Affective Disorders, 291*, 171–176.

Anglada-Tort, M., Baker, T., & Müllensiefen, D. (2019). False memories in music listening: Exploring the misinformation effect and individual difference factors in auditory memory. *Memory, 27*, 612–627.

Anglemyer, A., Horvath, T., & Rutherford, G. (2014). The accessibility of firearms and risk for suicide and homicide victimization among household members. *Annals of Internal Medicine, 160*, 101–112.

Anglim, J., Horwood, S., Smillie, L. D., Marrero, R. J., & Wood, J. K. (2020). Predicting psychological and subjective well-being from personality: A meta-analysis. *Psychological Bulletin, 146*, 279–323.

Anglin, S. M. (2019). Do beliefs yield to evidence? Examining belief perseverance vs. change in response to congruent empirical findings. *Journal of Experimental Social Psychology, 82*, 176–199.

Annese, J., Schenker-Ahmed, N. M., Bartsch, H., Maechler, P., Sheh, C., Thomas, N., Kayano, J., Ghatan, A., Bresler, N., Frosch, M. P., Klaming, R., & Corkin, S. (2014). Postmortem examination of patient H. M.'s brain based on histological sectioning and digital 3D reconstruction. *Nature Communications, 5*, 3122.

Ansari, A., Purtell, K., & Gershoff, E. (2015). Classroom age composition and the school readiness of 3- and 4-year-olds in the Head Start program. *Psychological Science, 27*, 53–63.

Ansere, V. A., & Freeman, W. M. (2020). Exercising your mind. *Science, 369*, 144–145.

Anton, B. S. (2015, June). Quoted in, APA applauds President Obama's call to end use of therapies intended to change sexual orientation. *Monitor, 46*, 10.

Antoniou, M. (2019). The advantages of bilingualism debate. *Annual Reviews, 5*, 395–415.

Antony, M. M., Brown, T. A., & Barlow, D. H. (1992). Current perspectives on panic and panic disorder. *Current Directions in Psychological Science, 1*, 79–82.

Antrobus, J. (1991). Dreaming: Cognitive processes during cortical activation and high afferent thresholds. *Psychological Review, 98*, 96–121.

Anumanchipalli, G. K., Chartier, J., & Chang, E. F. (2019). Speech synthesis from neural decoding of spoken sentences. *Nature, 568*, 493–498.

Anzures, G., Quinn, P. C., Pascalis, O., Slater, A. M., Tanaka, J. W., & Lee, K. (2013). Developmental origins of the other-race effect. *Current Directions in Psychological Science, 22*, 173–178.

Aonuma, H., Totani, Y., Kaneda, M., Nakamura, R., Watanabe, T., Hatakeyama, D., Dyakonova, V. E., Lukowiak, K., & Ito, E. (2018). Effects of 5-HT and insulin on learning and memory formation in food-deprived snails. *Neurobiology of Learning and Memory, 148*, 20–29.

AP (Associated Press). (2009, May 9). *AP-mtvU AP 2009 Economy, College Stress and Mental Health Poll*. https://dokument.pub/2009-mtvuap-poll-half-of-us-flipbook-pdf.html

AP. (2017). *Strangers on beach form 80-link human chain, rescue family from rip current*. CBC. https://www.cbc.ca/news/world/human-chain-saves-family-in-water-1.4199181

APA (American Psychological Association). (2006). Evidence-based practice in psychology (from APA Presidential Task Force on Evidence-Based Practice). *American Psychologist, 61*, 271–285.

APA. (2010, accessed July 31). *Answers to your questions about transgender individuals and gender identity* [PDF file]. https://www.apa.org/topics/lgbt/transgender.pdf

APA. (2012). *Guidelines for ethical conduct in the care and use of nonhuman animals in research*.

APA. (2014). *Strengthening the common core of the introductory psychology course* [PDF file]. APA Board of Educational Affairs Working Group. https://www.apa.org/ed/governance/bea/intro-psych-report.pdf

APA. (2017). *Ethical principles of psychologists and code of conduct* [PDF file]. https://www.apa.org/ethics/code/ethics-code-2017.pdf

APA. (2018). *APA fact sheet series on psychologist supply and demand projections 2015–2030: Demand across age groups* [PDF file]. https://www.apa.org/workforce/publications/supply-demand/demand-age-groups.pdf

APA. (2018). *Position statement on conversion therapy and LGBTQ patients* [PDF file]. https://www.psychiatry.org/getattachment/3d23f2f4-1497-4537-b4de-fe32fe8761bf/Position-Conversion-Therapy.pdf

APA. (2019, February). *Resolution on physical discipline of children by parents* [PDF file]. https://www.apa.org/about/policy/physical-discipline.pdf

APA. (2019, October). *APA task force report on violent video games* [PDF file]. https://www.apa.org/science/leadership/bsa/report-violent-video-games.pdf

APA. (2021, November 4). *APA elects Pepperdine professor Bryant 2023 president*. https://www.apa.org/news/press/releases/2021/11/bryant-2023-president

APA. (2021). *CWS data tool: Degrees in psychology*. https://www.apa.org/workforce/data-tools/degrees-psychology

APA Task Force on Violent Media. (2015). *Technical report on the review of the violent video game literature* [PDF file]. https://www.apa.org/pi/families/review-video-games.pdf

Apostolou, M. (2022). The direct reproductive cost of same-sex attraction: Evidence from two nationally representative U.S. samples. *Archives of Sexual Behavior, 51*, 1857–1864.

Apostolou, M., & Khalil, M. (2019). Aggressive and humiliating sexual play: Occurrence rates and discordance between the sexes. *Archives of Sexual Behavior, 48*, 2187–2200.

Apostolova, L. G., Dutton, R. A., Dinov, I. D., Hayashi, K. M., Toga, A. W., Cummings, J. L., & Thompson, P. M. (2006). Conversion of mild cognitive impairment to Alzheimer disease predicted by hippocampal atrophy maps. *Archives of Neurology, 63*, 693–699.

Archer, J. (2000). Sex differences in aggression between heterosexual partners: A meta-analytic review. *Psychological Bulletin, 126*, 651–680.

Archer, J. (2004). Sex differences in aggression in real-world settings: A meta-analytic review. *Review of General Psychology, 8*, 291–322.

Archer, J. (2007). A cross-cultural perspective on physical aggression between partners. *Issues in Forensic Psychology, 6*, 125–131.

Archer, J. (2009). Does sexual selection explain human sex differences in aggression? *Behavioral and Brain Sciences, 32*, 249–311.

Arendt, H. (1963). *Eichmann in Jerusalem: A report on the banality of evil*. Viking.

Ariel, R., & Karpicke, J. D. (2018). Improving self-regulated learning with a retrieval practice intervention. *Journal of Experimental Psychology: Applied, 24*, 43–56.

Ariely, D. (2010). *Predictably irrational, revised and expanded edition: The hidden forces that shape our decisions*. Harper Perennial.

Ariely, D., & Loewenstein, G. (2006). The heat of the moment: The effect of sexual arousal on sexual decision making. *Journal of Behavioral Decision Making, 19*, 87–98.

Aries, E. (1987). Gender and communication. In P. Shaver & C. Henrick (Eds.), *Review of Personality and Social Psychology, 7*, 149–176.

Arkowitz, H., & Lilienfeld, S. O. (2006, April/May). Psychotherapy on trial. *Scientific American: Mind*, pp. 42–49.

Armony, J. L., Quirk, G. J., & LeDoux, J. E. (1998). Differential effects of amygdala lesions on early and late plastic components of auditory cortex spike trains during fear conditioning. *Journal of Neuroscience, 18*, 2592–2601.

Armstrong, E. A., England, P., & Fogarty, A. C. K. (2012). Accounting for women's orgasm and sexual enjoyment in college hookups and relationships. *American Sociological Review, 77*, 435–462.

Arnedo, J., Mamah, D., Baranger, D. A., Harms, M. P., Barch, D. M., Svrakic, D. M., de Erausquin, G. A., Cloninger, C. R., & Zwir, I. (2015). Decomposition of brain diffusion imaging data uncovers latent schizophrenias with distinct patterns of white matter anisotropy. *NeuroImage, 120*, 43–54.

Arnett, J. J. (1999). Adolescent storm and stress, reconsidered. *American Psychologist, 54*, 317–326.

Arnett, J. J. (2006). Emerging adulthood: Understanding the new way of coming of age. In J. J. Arnett & J. L. Tanner (Eds.), *Emerging adults in America: Coming of age in the 21st century* (pp. 3–19). American Psychological Association.

Arnett, J. J. (2007). Socialization in emerging adulthood: From the family to the wider world, from socialization to self-socialization. In J. E. Grusec & P. D. Hastings (Eds.), *Handbook of socialization: Theory and research* (pp. 208–230). Guilford Press.

Arnett, J. J. (2015). The cultural psychology of emerging adulthood. In L. A. Jensen (Ed.), *The Oxford handbook of human development and culture: An interdisciplinary perspective* (pp. 487–501). Oxford University Press.

Arnold, K. M., Umanath, S., Thio, K., Reilly, W. B., McDaniel, M. A., & Marsh, E. J. (2017). Understanding the cognitive processes involved in writing to learn. *Journal of Experimental Psychology: Applied, 23*, 115–127.

Arnone, D., McIntosh, A. M., Tan, G. M. Y., & Ebmeier, K. P. (2008). Meta-analysis of magnetic resonance imaging studies of the corpus callosum in schizophrenia. *Schizophrenia Research, 101*, 124–132.

Aron, A., Aron, E. N., & Smollan, D. (1992). Inclusion of Other in the Self Scale and the structure of interpersonal closeness. *Journal of Personality and Social Psychology, 63*(4), 596–512.

Aron, A., Aron, E. N., Tudor, M., & Nelson, G. (1991). Close relationships as including other in the self. *Journal of Personality and Social Psychology, 60*(2), 241–253.

Aron, A., Melinat, E., Aron, E. N., Vallone, R. D., & Bator, R. J. (1997). The experimental generation of interpersonal closeness: A procedure and some preliminary findings. *Personality and Social Psychology Bulletin, 23*, 363–377.

Aron, A., Norman, C. C., Aron, E. N., McKenna, C., & Heyman, R. E. (2000). Couples' shared participation in novel and arousing activities and experienced relationship quality. *Journal of Personality and Social Psychology, 78*, 273–284.

Aronson, E. (2001, April 13). *Newsworthy violence* [Email to Society for Personality and Social Psychology discussion list, drawing from *Nobody left to hate: Teaching compassion after Columbine*. (2000)]. Freeman.

Arriaga, P., Adrião, J., Madeira, F., Cavaleiro, I., Maia e Silva, A., Barahona, I., & Esteves, F. (2015). A "dry eye" for victims of violence: Effects of playing a violent video game on pupillary dilation to victims and on aggressive behavior. *Psychology of Violence, 5*, 199–208.

Arsenio, W. F. (2018). The wealth of nations: International judgments regarding actual and ideal resource distributions. *Current Directions in Psychological Science, 27*, 357–362.

Arslan, R. C., Schilling, K. M., Gerlach, T. M., & Penke, L. (2021). Using 26,000 diary entries to show ovulatory changes in sexual desire and behavior. *Journal of Personality and Social Psychology, 121*, 410–431.

Aryawibawa, I. N., & Ambridge, B. (2018). Is syntax semantically constrained? Evidence from a grammaticality judgment study of Indonesian. *Cognitive Science, 42*(8), 3135–3148.

Arzi, A., Shedlesky, L., Ben-Shaul, M., Nasser, K., Oksenberg, A., Hairston, I. S., & Sobel, N. (2012). Humans can learn new information during sleep. *Nature Neuroscience, 15*, 1460–1465.

Ascády, L., & Harris, K. D. (2017). Synaptic scaling in sleep. *Science, 355*, 457.

Asch, S. E. (1955). Opinions and social pressure. *Scientific American, 193*, 31–35.

Aserinsky, E. (1988, January 17). Personal communication.

Ashbrook, L. H., Krystal, A. D., Fu, Y. H., & Ptáček, L. J. (2020). Genetics of the human circadian clock and sleep homeostat. *Neuropsychopharmacology, 45*(1), 45–54.

Ashton, K., Bellis, M., Davies, A., Hardcastle, K., & Hughes, K. (2016). *Adverse childhood experiences and their association with chronic disease and health service use in the Welsh adult population*. Welsh Adverse Childhood Experiences (ACE) Study, NHS Wales Public Trust.

Askay, S. W., & Patterson, D. R. (2007). Hypnotic analgesia. *Expert Review of Neurotherapeutics, 7*, 1675–1683.

Asperholm, M., Högman, N., Rafi, J., & Herlitz, A. (2019). What did you do yesterday? A meta-analysis of sex differences in episodic memory. *Psychological Bulletin, 145*, 785–821.

Aspinwall, L. G., Brown, T. R., & Tabery, J. (2012). The double-edged sword: Does biomechanism increase or decrease judges' sentencing of psychopaths? *Science, 337*, 846–849.

Aspinwall, L. G., & Tedeschi, R. G. (2010). The value of positive psychology for health psychology: Progress and pitfalls in examining the relation of positive phenomena to health. *Annals of Behavioral Medicine, 39*, 4–15.

Assanand, S., Pinel, J. P. J., & Lehman, D. R. (1998). Personal theories of hunger and eating. *Journal of Applied Social Psychology, 28*, 998–1015.

Associated Press. (1999, April 26). Airline passengers mistakenly told plane would crash. *Grand Rapids Press*, p. A3.

Atherton, O. E., Grijalva, E., Roberts, B. W., & Robins, R. W. (2021). Stability and change in personality traits and major life goals from college to midlife. *Personality and Social Psychology Bulletin, 47*(5), 841–858.

Atkinson, R. C., & Shiffrin, R. M. (1968). Human memory: A control system and its control processes. In K. Spence (Ed.), *The psychology of learning and motivation* (Vol. 2, pp. 89–195). Academic Press.

Atkinson, R. C., & Shiffrin, R. M. (2016). Human memory: A proposed system and its control processes. In R. J. Sternberg, S. T. Fiske, & D. J. Foss (Eds.), *Scientists making a difference: One hundred eminent behavioral and brain scientists talk about their most important contributions*. Cambridge University Press.

Atlas, D. (2016, January 29). *Autism's first-ever patient, now 82, 'has continued to grow his whole life.'* People. https://people.com/celebrity/donald-triplett-autisms-first-ever-patient-now-82-has-continued-to-grow/

Attard-Johnson, J., Bindemann, M., & Ciardha, C. Ó. (2016). Pupillary response as an age-specific measure of sexual interest. *Archives of Sexual Behavior, 45*, 855–870.

Attard-Johnson, J., Bindemann, M., & Ciardha, C. Ó. (2017). Heterosexual, homosexual, and bisexual men's pupillary responses to persons at different stages of sexual development. *Journal of Sex Research, 54*, 1085–1096.

Aubrey, A. (2019, August 29). *Surgeon General sounds alarm on risk of marijuana addiction and harm*. National Public Radio. https://www.npr.org/sections/health-shots/2019/08/29/755423290/

Auerbach, R. P., Mortier, P., Bruffaerts, R., Alonso, J., Benjet, C., Cuijpers, P., Demyttenaere, K., Ebert, D. D., Green, J. G., Hasking, P., Murray, E., Nock, M. K., Pinder-Amaker, S., Sampson, N. A., Stein, D. J., Vilagut, G., Zaslavsky, A. M., Kessler, R. C., & WHO WMH-ICS Collaborators. (2018). WHO world mental health surveys international college student project: Prevalence and distribution of mental disorders. *Journal of Abnormal Psychology, 127*, 623–638.

Aumann, L., Titzmann, P. F., & Lee, R. M. (2022). Striking a new path to study the adaptation processes of immigrant adolescents: Changes in language use and family interactions. *Developmental Psychology, 58*, 1163–1175.

Austen, I. (2022). With discovery of unmarked graves, Canada's Indigenous seek reckoning. *The New York Times*. https://www.nytimes.com/2021/06/26/world/canada/indigenous-residential-schools-grave.html

Austen, J. M., & Sanderson, D. J. (2019). Delay of reinforcement versus rate of reinforcement in Pavlovian conditioning. *Journal of Experimental Psychology: Animal Learning and Cognition, 45*, 203–221.

Austin, E. J., Deary, I. J., Whiteman, M. C., Fowkes, F. G. R., Pedersen, N. L., Rabbitt, P., Bent, N., & McInnes, L. (2002). Relationships between ability and personality: Does intelligence contribute positively to personal and social adjustment? *Personality and Individual Differences, 32*, 1391–1411.

Averill, J. R. (1983). Studies on anger and aggression: Implications for theories of emotion. *American Psychologist, 38*, 1145–1160.

Averill, J. R. (1993). William James's other theory of emotion. In M. E. Donnelly (Ed.), *Reinterpreting the legacy of William James*. American Psychological Association.

Aviv, R. (2017, June 19). Remembering the murder you didn't commit. *The New Yorker*. https://www.newyorker.com/magazine/2017/06/19/remembering-the-murder-you-didnt-commit

Awad, E., Dsouza, S., Shariff, A., Rahwan, I., & Bonnefon, J.-F. (2020). Universals and variations in moral decisions made in 42 countries by 70,000 participants. *PNAS, 117*(5), 2332–2337.

Ayan, S. (2009). Laughing matters. *Scientific American Mind, 20*, 24–31.

Ayling, K., Jia, R., Coupland, C., Chalder, T., Massey, A., Broadbent, E., & Vedhara, K. (2022). Psychological predictors of self-reported COVID-19 outcomes: Results from a prospective cohort study. *Annals of Behavioral Medicine, 56*(5), 484–497.

Azar, B. (1998, June). Why can't this man feel whether or not he's standing up? *APA Monitor*. www.apa.org/monitor/jun98/touch.html

Baars, B. J. (2002). The conscious access hypothesis: Origins and recent evidence. *Trends in Cognitive Sciences, 6*, 47–52.

Babyak, M., Blumenthal, J. A., Herman, S., Khatri, P., Doraiswamy, M., Moore, K., Craighead, W. E., Baldewicz, T. T., & Krishnan, K. R. (2000). Exercise treatment for major depression: Maintenance of therapeutic benefit at ten months. *Psychosomatic Medicine, 62*, 633–638.

Bachman, J., O'Malley, P. M., Schulenberg, J. E., Johnston, L. D., Freedman-Doan, P., & Messersmith, E. E. (2007). *The education-drug use connection: How successes and failures in school relate to adolescent smoking, drinking, drug use, and delinquency*. Erlbaum.

Back, M. D., Stopfer, J. M., Vazire, S., Gaddis, S., Schmukle, S. C., Egloff, B., & Gosling, S. D. (2010). Facebook profiles reflect actual personality, not self-idealization. *Psychological Science, 21*, 372–374.

Backman, L., & Dixon, R. A. (1992). Psychological compensation: A theoretical framework. *Psychological Bulletin, 112*, 259–283.

Backman, L., & MacDonald, S. W. S. (2006). Death and cognition: Synthesis and outlook. *European Psychologist, 11*, 224–235.

Baddeley, A. D. (1982). *Your memory: A user's guide*. Macmillan.

Baddeley, A. D. (2002, June). Is working memory still working? *European Psychologist, 7*, 85–97.

Baddeley, A. D., Thomson, N., & Buchanan, M. (1975). Word length and the structure of short-term memory. *Journal of Verbal Learning and Verbal Behavior, 14*, 575–589.

Baddeley, J. L., & Singer, J. A. (2009). A social interactional model of bereavement narrative disclosure. *Review of General Psychology, 13*, 202–218.

Badura, K. L., Grijalva, E., Galvin, B. M., Owens, B. P., & Joseph, D. L. (2019). Motivation to lead: A meta-analysis and distal-proximal model of motivation and leadership. *Journal of Applied Psychology, 105*, 331–354.

Bagemihl, B. (1999). *Biological exuberance: Animal homosexuality and natural diversity*. St. Martins.

Bagge, C. L., Littlefield, A. K., & Glenn, C. R. (2017). Trajectories of affective response as warning signs for suicide attempts: An examination of the 48 hours prior to a recent suicide attempt. *Clinical Psychological Science, 5*, 259–271.

Baglioni, C., Nanovska, S., Regen, W., Spiegelhalder, K., Feige, B., Nissen, C., Reynolds, C. F., & Riemann, D. (2016). Sleep and mental disorders: A meta-analysis of polysomnographic research. *Psychological Bulletin, 142*, 969–990.

Bago, B., Rand, D. G., & Pennycook, G. (2020). Fake news, fast and slow: Deliberation reduces belief in false (but not true) news headlines. *Journal of Experimental Psychology, General, 149*(8), 1608–1613.

Bahrick, H. P. (1984). Semantic memory content in permastore: 50 years of memory for Spanish learned in school. *Journal of Experimental Psychology: General, 111*, 1–29.

Bahrick, H. P., Bahrick, P. O., & Wittlinger, R. P. (1975). Fifty years of memory for names and faces: A cross-sectional approach. *Journal of Experimental Psychology: General, 104*, 54–75.

Bai, D., Yip, B. H. K., & Windham, G. C. (2019). Association of genetic and environmental factors with autism in a 5-country cohort. *JAMA Psychiatry, 76*, 1035–1043.

Bai, Y., Ocampo, J., Jin, G., Chen, S., Benet-Martinez, V., Monroy, M., Anderson, C., & Keltner, D. (2021). Awe, daily stress, and elevated life satisfaction. *Journal of Personality and Social Psychology, 120*(4), 837.

Bai, Z., Luo, S., Zhang, L., Wu, S., & Chi, I. (2020). Acceptance and Commitment Therapy (ACT) to reduce depression: A systematic review and meta-analysis. *Journal of Affective Disorders, 260*, 728–737.

Bail, C. (2021). *Breaking the social media prism: How to make our platforms less polarizing*. Princeton University Press.

Bailey, J. M., Gaulin, S., Agyei, Y., & Gladue, B. A. (1994). Effects of gender and sexual orientation on evolutionary relevant aspects of human mating psychology. *Journal of Personality and Social Psychology, 66*, 1081–1093.

Bailey, J. M., Vasey, P. L., Diamond, L. M., Breedlove, S. M., Vilain, E., & Epprecht, M. (2016). Sexual orientation, controversy, and science. *Psychological Science in the Public Interest, 17*, 45–101.

Bailey, P. E., & Leon, T. (2019). A systematic review and meta-analysis of age-related differences in trust. *Psychology and Aging, 34*, 674–685.

Bailey, R. E., & Gillaspy, J. A., Jr. (2005). Operant psychology goes to the fair: Marian and Keller Breland in the popular press, 1947–1966. *The Behavior Analyst, 28*, 143–159.

Baillargeon, R., Scott, R. M., & Bian, L. (2016). Psychological reasoning in infancy. *Annual Review of Psychology, 67*, 159–186.

Baird, H. M., Webb, T. L., Sirois, F. M., & Gibson-Miller, J. (2021). Understanding the effects of time perspective: A meta-analysis testing a self-regulatory framework. *Psychological Bulletin, 147*, 233–267.

Bakadorova, O., & Raufelder, D. (2018). The essential role of the teacher-student relationship in students' need satisfaction during adolescence. *Journal of Applied Developmental Psychology, 58*, 57–65.

Baker, D. H., & Cass, J. R. (2013). A dissociation of performance and awareness during binocular rivalry. *Psychological Science, 24*, 2563–2568.

Baker, J. T., Dillon, D. G., Patrick, L. M., Roffman, J. L., Brady, R. O., Pizzagalli, D. A., Öngür, D., & Holmes, A. J. (2019). Functional connectomics of affective and psychotic pathology. *PNAS, 116*, 9050–9059.

Baker, K. E., Wilson, L. M., Sharma, R., Dukhanin, V., McArthur, K., & Robinson, K. A.

(2021). Hormone therapy, mental health, and quality of life among transgender people: A systematic review. *Journal of the Endocrine Society,* 5(4). https://academic.oup.com/jes/article/5/4/bvab011/6126016?login=false

Baker, M., Strickland, A., & Fox, N. D. (2019). Choosing a meal to increase your appeal: How relationship status, sexual orientation, dining partner sex, and attractiveness impact nutritional choices in social dining scenarios. *Appetite, 133,* 262–269.

Baker, T. B., McFall, R. M., & Shoham, V. (2008). Current status and future prospects of clinical psychology: Toward a scientifically principled approach to mental and behavioral health care. *Psychological Science in the Public Interest, 9,* 67–103.

Bakermans-Kranenburg, M. J., van IJzendoorn, M. H., & Juffer, F. (2003). Less is more: Meta-analyses of sensitivity and attachment interventions in early childhood. *Psychological Bulletin, 129,* 195–215.

Bakshy, E., Messing, S., & Adamic, L. A. (2015). Exposure to ideologically diverse news and opinion on Facebook. *Science, 348,* 1130–1132.

Balcetis, E., & Dunning, D. (2010). Wishful seeing: More desired objects are seen as closer. *Psychological Science, 21,* 147–152.

Ball, G., Adamson, C., Beare, R., & Seal, M. L. (2017). Modelling neuroanatomical variation due to age and sex during childhood and adolescence. *Scientific Reports.* https://www.nature.com/articles/s41598-017-18253-6

Ball, G., Malpas, C. B., Genc, S., Efron, D., Sciberras, E., Anderson, V., Nicholson, J. M., & Silk, T. J. (2019). Multimodal structural neuroimaging markers of brain development and ADHD symptoms. *American Journal of Psychiatry, 176,* 57–66.

Balter, M. (2010). Animal communication helps reveal roots of language. *Science, 328,* 969–970.

Balter, M. (2014). Science misused to justify Ugandan antigay law. *Science, 343,* 956.

Balter, M. (2015). Can epigenetics explain homosexuality puzzle? *Science, 350,* 148.

Bancroft, J., Loftus, J., & Long, J. S. (2003). Distress about sex: A national survey of women in heterosexual relationships. *Archives of Sexual Behavior, 32,* 193–208.

Bandura, A. (1977). Self-efficacy: Toward a unifying theory of behavior. *Psychological Review, 84,* 191–215.

Bandura, A. (1982). The psychology of chance encounters and life paths. *American Psychologist, 37,* 747–755.

Bandura, A. (1986). *Social foundations of thought and action: A social-cognitive theory.* Prentice-Hall.

Bandura, A. (2005). The evolution of social cognitive theory. In K. G. Smith & M. A. Hitt (Eds.), *Great minds in management: The process of theory development* (pp. 9–35). Oxford University Press.

Bandura, A. (2006). Toward a psychology of human agency. *Perspectives on Psychological Science, 1,* 164–180.

Bandura, A. (2008). An agentic perspective on positive psychology. In S. J. Lopez (Ed.), *The science of human flourishing.* Praeger.

Bandura, A. (2017). The Bobo Doll legacy. *Psychology Review, 22*(3), 2–6.

Bandura, A. (2018). Toward a psychology of human agency: Pathways and reflections. *Perspectives on Psychological Science, 13,* 130–136.

Bandura, A., Ross, D., & Ross, S. A. (1961). Transmission of aggression through imitation of aggressive models. *Journal of Abnormal and Social Psychology, 63,* 575–582.

Bang, J. W., Shibata, K., Frank, S. M., Walsh, E. G., Greenlee, M. W., Watanabe, T., & Sasaki, Y. (2018). Consolidation and reconsolidation share behavioural and neurochemical mechanisms. *Nature Human Behaviour, 2,* 507–513.

Banker, C. C., & Leary, M. R. (2020). Hypo-egoic nonentitlement as a feature of humility. *Personality and Social Psychology Bulletin, 46,* 738–753.

Banks, J., Fancourt, D., & Xu, X. (2021, March 20). *Mental health and the COVID-19 pandemic.* Figure 5.6. World Happiness Report. https://worldhappiness.report/ed/2021/mental-health-and-the-covid-19-pandemic/

Bansak, K., Hainmueller, J., & Hangartner, D. (2016). How economic, humanitarian, and religious concerns shape European attitudes toward asylum seekers. *Science, 354,* 217–222.

Banville, J. (2012, April). APA weighs in on the constitutionality of life without parole for juvenile offenders. *Monitor on Psychology,* p. 12.

Barash, D. P. (2012). *Homo mysterious: Evolutionary puzzles of human nature.* Oxford University Press.

Barbaresi, W. J., Katusic, S. K., Colligan, R. C., Weaver, A. L., & Jacobsen, S. J. (2007). Modifiers of long-term school outcomes for children with attention deficit/hyperactivity disorder: Does treatment with stimulant medication make a difference? Results from a population-based study. *Journal of Developmental and Behavioral Pediatrics, 28,* 274–287.

Barberá, P., Jost, J. T., Nagler, J., Tucker, J. A., & Bonneau, R. (2015). Tweeting from left to right: Is online political communication more than an echo chamber? *Psychological Science, 26,* 1531–1542.

Barchas, R. E. (2021). My benefits from electroconvulsive therapy—what a psychiatrist learned by being a patient. *Psychiatric Services, 72*(3), 347–348.

Bargh, J. A., & Chartrand, T. L. (1999). The unbearable automaticity of being. *American Psychologist, 54,* 462–479.

Bargh, J. A., & McKenna, K. Y. A. (2004). The internet and social life. *Annual Review of Psychology, 55,* 573–590.

Bargh, J. A., McKenna, K. Y. A., & Fitzsimons, G. M. (2002). Can you see the real me? Activation and expression of the "true self" on the internet. *Journal of Social Issues, 58,* 33–48.

Bargh, J. A., & Morsella, E. (2008). The unconscious mind. *Perspectives on Psychological Science, 3,* 73–79.

Barinaga, M. B. (1992). The brain remaps its own contours. *Science, 258,* 216–218.

Barinaga, M. B. (1997). How exercise works its magic. *Science, 276,* 1325.

Barinaga, M. B. (1999). Salmon follow watery odors home. *Science, 286,* 705–706.

Barker, A. J., Veviurko, G., Bennett, N. C., Hart, D. W., Mograby, L., & Lewin, G. R. (2021). Cultural transmission of vocal dialect in the naked mole-rat. *Science, 371*(6528), 503–507.

Barkley-Levenson, E., & Galván, A. (2014). Neural representation of expected value in the adolescent brain. *PNAS, 111,* 1646–1651.

Barlow, F. K. (2019). Nature vs. nurture is nonsense: On the necessity of an integrated genetic, social, developmental, and personality psychology. *Australian Journal of Psychology, 71,* 68–79.

Barlow, M., Woodman, T., & Hardy, L. (2013). Great expectations: Different high-risk activities satisfy different motives. *Journal of Personality and Social Psychology, 105,* 458–475.

Barlow, M. A., Wrosch, C., Gouin, J. P., & Kunzmann, U. (2019). Is anger, but not sadness, associated with chronic inflammation and illness in older adulthood? *Psychology and Aging, 34,* 330–340.

Barnier, A. J., & McConkey, K. M. (2004). Defining and identifying the highly hypnotizable person. In M. Heap, R. J. Brown, & D. A. Oakley (Eds.), *The highly hypnotizable person: Theoretical, experimental and clinical issues* (pp. 30–60). Brunner-Routledge.

Baron, C. E., Smith, T. W., Uchino, B. N., Baucom, B. R., & Birmingham, W. C. (2016). Getting along and getting ahead: Affiliation and dominance predict ambulatory blood pressure. *Health Psychology, 35,* 253–261.

Baron, K. G., Abbott, S., Jao, N., Manalo, N., & Mullen, R. (2017). Orthosomnia: Are some patients taking the quantified self too far? *Journal of Clinical Sleep Medicine, 13*(2), 351–354.

Baron-Cohen, S. (2010). Autism and the empathizing-systemizing (E-S) theory. In P. D. Zelazo, M. Chandler, & E. Crone (Eds.), *Developmental social cognitive neuroscience* (pp. 125–138). Psychology Press.

Baron-Cohen, S. (2017). The eyes as window to the mind. *American Journal of Psychiatry, 174,* 1–2.

Baron-Cohen, S., Leslie, A. M., & Frith, U. (1985). Does the autistic child have a "theory of mind"? *Cognition, 21,* 37–46.

Barr, P. B., Bigdeli, T. B., & Meyers, J. L. (2022). Prevalence, comorbidity, and sociodemographic correlates of psychiatric disorders reported in the All of Us research program. *JAMA Psychiatry, 79*(6), 622–628.

Barr, S. M., Budge, S. L., & Adelson, J. L. (2016). Transgender community belongingness as a mediator between strength of transgender identity and well-being. *Journal of Counseling Psychology, 63,* 87.

Barrett, D. (2011, November/December). Answers in your dreams. *Scientific American Mind,* pp. 26–33.

Barrett, H. C., Bolyanatz, A., Crittenden, A. N., Fessler, D. M., Fitzpatrick, S., Gurven, M., Henrich, J., Kanovsky, M., Kushnick, G., Pisor, A., Scelza, B. A., Stich, S., von Rueden, C., Zhao, W., & Laurence, S. (2016). Small-scale societies exhibit fundamental variation in the role of intentions in moral judgment. *PNAS, 113,* 4688–4693.

Barretto, R. P., Gillis-Smith, S., Chandrashekar, J., Yarmolinsky, D. A., Schnitzer, M. J., Ryba, N. J., & Zuker, C. S. (2015). The neural representation of taste quality at the periphery. *Nature, 517,* 373–376.

Barrick, M. R., Shaffer, J. A., & DeGrassi, S. W. (2009). What you see may not be what you get: Relationships among self-presentation tactics and ratings of interview and job performance. *Journal of Applied Psychology, 94*, 1304–1411.

Barrouillet, P., Portrat, S., & Camos, V. (2011). On the law relating processing to storage in working memory. *Psychological Review, 118*, 175–192.

Barry, C. L., McGinty, E. E., Vernick, J. S., & Webster, D. W. (2013). After Newtown—Public opinion on gun policy and mental illness. *New England Journal of Medicine, 368*, 1077–1081.

Barry, D. (1985). *Dave Barry's stay fit and healthy until you're dead.* Rodale.

Barry, D. (1995, September 17). Teen smokers, too, get cool, toxic, waste-blackened lungs. *Asbury Park Press*, p. D3.

Bartels, M. (2015). Genetics of wellbeing and its components with life, happiness, and quality of life: A review of meta-analysis of heritability studies. *Behavior Genetics, 45*, 137–156.

Bartoshuk, L. (2010, June 18). Quoted by K. Travis, Interview: Linda Bartoshuk. *Science*. https://blogs.sciencemag.org/sciencecareers/2010/06/linda-bartoshuk.html

Bartoshuk, L. M. (2000). Comparing sensory experiences across individuals: Recent psychophysical advances illuminate genetic variation in taste perception. *Chemical Senses, 25*, 447–460.

Bartoshuk, L. M., Sims, C. A., Colquhoun, T. A., & Snyder, D. J. (2019). What Aristotle didn't know about flavor. *American Psychologist, 74*, 1003–1011.

Basak, C., Qin, S., & O'Connell, M. A. (2020). Differential effects of cognitive training modules in healthy aging and mild cognitive impairment: A comprehensive meta-analysis of randomized controlled trials. *Psychology and Aging*, 35(2), 220–249.

Bashore, T. R., Ridderinkhof, K. R., & van der Molen, M. W. (1997). The decline of cognitive processing speed in old age. *Current Directions in Psychological Science, 6*, 163–169.

Bassett, D. S., Zurn, P., & Gold, J. I. (2018). On the nature and use of models in network neuroscience. *Nature Reviews Neuroscience, 19*, 566–578.

Basu, S., & Basu, D. (2015). The relationship between psychoactive drugs, the brain and psychosis [PDF file]. *International Archives of Addiction Research and Medicine, 1*. https://clinmedjournals.org/articles/iaarm/iaarm-1-003.pdf

Batastini, A. B., Paprzycki, P., Jones, A. C. T., & MacLean, N. (2021). Are videoconferenced mental and behavioral health services just as good as in-person? A meta-analysis of a fast-growing practice. *Clinical Psychology Review, 83*. doi: 10.1016/j.cpr.2020.101944

Bat-Chava, Y. (1993). Antecedents of self-esteem in deaf people: A meta-analytic review. *Rehabilitation Psychology, 38*, 221–234.

Bat-Chava, Y. (1994). Group identification and self-esteem of deaf adults. *Personality and Social Psychology Bulletin, 20*, 494–502.

Bates, T. C. (2015). The glass is half full and half empty: A population-representative twin study testing if optimism and pessimism are distinct systems. *Journal of Positive Psychology, 10*, 533–542.

Batruch, A., Autin, F., Bataillard, F., & Butera, F. (2019). School selection and the social class divide: How tracking contributes to the reproduction of inequalities. *Personality and Social Psychology Bulletin, 45*, 477–490.

Batsell, W. R., Perry, J. L., Hanley, E., & Hostetter, A. B. (2017). Ecological validity of the testing effect: The use of daily quizzes in introductory psychology. *Teaching of Psychology, 44*, 18–23.

Battal, C., Occelli, V., Bertonati, G., Falagiarda, F., & Collignon, O. (2020). General enhancement of spatial hearing in congenitally blind people. *Psychological Science, 31*, 1129–1139.

Batterink, L. J. (2017). Rapid statistical learning supporting word extraction from continuous speech. *Psychological Science, 28*, 921–928.

Batz-Barbarich, C., Tay, L., Kuykendall, L., & Cheung, H. K. (2018). A meta-analysis of gender differences in subjective well-being: Estimating effect sizes and associations with gender inequality. *Psychological Science, 29*, 1491–1503.

Baucom, B. R. W., & Crenshaw, A. O. (2019). Evaluating the efficacy of couple and family therapy. In B. H. Fiese, M. Celano, K. Deater-Deckard, E. N. Jouriles, & M. A. Whisman (Eds.), *APA handbook of contemporary family psychology: Family therapy and training* (pp. 69–86). American Psychological Association.

Bauer, C. M., Hirsch, G. V., Zajac, L., Koo, B.-B., Collignon, O., & Merabet, L. B. (2017). Multimodal MR-imaging reveals large-scale structural and functional connectivity changes in profound early blindness. *PLOS ONE, 12*. https://journals.plos.org/plosone/article?id=10.1371/journal.pone.0173064

Bauer, M., Cassar, A., Chytilová, J., & Henrich, J. (2014). War's enduring effects on the development of egalitarian motivations and in-group biases. *Psychological Science, 25*, 47–57.

Bauer, P. J., & Larkina, M. (2014). The onset of childhood amnesia in childhood: A prospective investigation of the course and determinants of forgetting of early-life events. *Memory, 22*, 907–924.

Bault, N., di Pellegrino, G., Puppi, M., Opolczynski, G., Monti, A., Braghittoni, D., Thibaut, F., Rustichini, A., & Coricelli, G. (2019). Dissociation between private and social counterfactual value signals following ventromedial prefrontal cortex damage. *Journal of Cognitive Neuroscience, 31*, 639–656.

Baumann, J., & DeSteno, D. (2010). Emotion guided threat detection: Expecting guns where there are none. *Journal of Personality and Social Psychology, 99*, 595–610.

Baumeister, H., & Härter, M. (2007). Prevalence of mental disorders based on general population surveys. *Social Psychiatry and Psychiatric Epidemiology, 42*, 537–546.

Baumeister, R. F. (1996). Should schools try to boost self-esteem? Beware the dark side. *American Educator, 20*, 43.

Baumeister, R. F. (2000). Gender differences in erotic plasticity: The female sex drive as socially flexible and responsive. *Psychological Bulletin, 126*, 347–374.

Baumeister, R. F. (2001). Violent pride: Do people turn violent because of self-hate, or self-love? *Scientific American, 17*, 96–101.

Baumeister, R. F. (2010). *Is there anything good about men? How cultures flourish by exploiting men.* Oxford.

Baumeister, R. F. (2015). Toward a general theory of motivation: Problems, challenges, opportunities, and the big picture. *Motivation and Emotion, 40*, 1–10.

Baumeister, R. F., & Bratslavsky, E. (1999). Passion, intimacy, and time: Passionate love as a function of change in intimacy. *Personality and Social Psychology Review, 3*, 49–67.

Baumeister, R. F., Bratslavsky, E., Muraven, M., & Tice, D. M. (1998). Ego depletion: Is the active self a limited resource? *Journal of Personality and Social Psychology, 74*, 1252–1265.

Baumeister, R. F., Catanese, K. R., & Vohs, K. D. (2001). Is there a gender difference in strength of sex drive? Theoretical views, conceptual distinctions, and a review of relevant evidence. *Personality and Social Psychology Review, 5*, 242–273.

Baumeister, R. F., Dale, K., & Sommer, K. L. (1998). Freudian defense mechanisms and empirical findings in modern personality and social psychology: Reaction formation, projection, displacement, undoing, isolation, sublimation, and denial. *Journal of Personality, 66*, 1081–1125.

Baumeister, R. F., Hofmann, W., Summerville, A., Reiss, P. T., & Vohs, K. D. (2020). Everyday thoughts in time: Experience Sampling studies of mental time travel. *Personality and Social Psychology Bulletin, 46*(12), 1631–1648.

Baumeister, R. F., & Leary, M. R. (1995). The need to belong: Desire for interpersonal attachments as a fundamental human motivation. *Psychological Bulletin, 117*, 497–529.

Baumeister, R. F., & Tice, D. M. (1986). How adolescence became the struggle for self: A historical transformation of psychological development. In J. Suls & A. G. Greenwald (Eds.), *Psychological perspectives on the self* (Vol. 3, pp. 183–201). Erlbaum.

Baumeister, R. F., Tice, D. M., & Vohs, K. D. (2018). The strength model of self-regulation: Conclusions from the second decade of willpower research. *Perspectives on Psychological Science, 13*, 141–145.

Baumeister, R. F., & Vohs, K. D. (2016). Strength model of self-regulation as limited resource: Assessment, controversies, update. *Advances in Experimental Social Psychology, 54*, 67–127.

Baumeister, R. F., & Vohs, K. D. (2018). Revisiting our reappraisal of the (surprisingly few) benefits of high self-esteem. *Perspectives on Psychological Science, 13*, 137–140.

Baumgardner, A. H., Kaufman, C. M., & Levy, P. E. (1989). Regulating affect interpersonally: When low esteem leads to greater enhancement. *Journal of Personality and Social Psychology, 56*, 907–921.

Baumrind, D. (1966). Effects of authoritative parental control on child behavior. *Child Development, 37*(4), 887–907.

Baumrind, D. (1989). Rearing competent children. In W. Damon (Ed.), *Child development today and tomorrow* (pp. 349–378). Jossey-Bass.

Baumrind, D. (1991). The influence of parenting style on adolescent competence and substance abuse. *Journal of Early Adolescence, 11*, 56–95.

Baumrind, D. (1996). The discipline controversy revisited. *Family Relations, 45*, 405–414.

Baumrind, D. (2013). Is a pejorative view of power assertion in the socialization process justified? *Review of General Psychology, 17*, 420–427.

Baur, E., Forsman, M., Santtila, P., Johansson, A., Sandnabba, K., & Långström, N. (2016). Paraphilic sexual interests and sexually coercive behavior: A population-based twin study. *Archives of Sexual Behavior, 45*, 1163–1172.

Bavelier, D., Newport, E. L., & Supalla, T. (2003). Children need natural languages, signed or spoken. *Cerebrum, 5*, 19–32.

Bavelier, D., Tomann, A., Hutton, C., Mitchell, T., Corina, D., Liu, G., & Neville, H. (2000). Visual attention to the periphery is enhanced in congenitally deaf individuals. *Journal of Neuroscience, 20*, 1–6.

Baye, A., & Monseur, C. (2016). Gender differences in variability and extreme scores in an international context. *Large-Scale Assessments in Education, 4*, 1.

Bazzi, S., Fiszbein, M., & Gebresilasse, M. (2020). *Rugged individualism and collective (in) action during the COVID-19 pandemic* [PDF file]. NBER Working Paper Series. https://www.nber.org/system/files/working_papers/w27776/w27776.pdf

BBC (British Broadcasting Corporation). (2017). *'I only have half a brain.'* https://www.bbc.com/news/av/magazine-39117532

Beam, C. R., Emery, R. E., Reynolds, C. A., Gatz, M., Turkheimer, R., & Pedersen, N. L. (2016). Widowhood and the stability of late life depressive symptomatology in the Swedish Adoption Twin Study of Aging. *Behavior Genetics, 46*, 100–113.

Beaman, A. L., & Klentz, B. (1983). The supposed physical attractiveness bias against supporters of the women's movement: A meta-analysis. *Personality and Social Psychology Bulletin, 9*, 544–550.

Beames, J. R., Schofield, T. P., & Denson, T. F. (2017). A meta-analysis of improving self-control with practice. In D. T. D. de Ridder, M. A. Adriaanse, & K. Fujita (Eds.), *Handbook of self-control in health and well-being*. Routledge.

Beauchaine, T. P., Hinshaw, S. P., & Bridge, J. A. (2019). Nonsuicidal self-injury and suicidal behaviors in girls: The case for targeted prevention in preadolescence. *Clinical Psychological Science, 7*, 643–667.

Beauchamp, G. K. (1987). The human preference for excess salt. *American Scientist, 75*, 27–33.

Beaulieu, A. M., Tabasky, E., & Osser, D. N. (2019). The psychopharmacology algorithm project at the Harvard South Shore Program: An algorithm for adults with obsessive-compulsive disorder. *Psychiatry Research, 281*. doi: 10.1016/j.psychres.2019.112583

Beauvois, J.-L., Courbet, D., & Oberlé, D. (2012). The prescriptive power of the television host: A transposition of Milgram's obedience paradigm to the context of TV game show. *European Review of Applied Psychology/Revue Européenne de Psychologie Appliquée, 62*, 111–119.

Becerra-Culqui, T. A., Liu, Y., Nash, R., Cromwell, L., Flanders, W. D., Getahun, D., Giammattei, S. V., Hunkeler, E. M., Lash, T. L., Millman, A., Quinn, V. P., Robinson, B., Roblin, D., Sandberg, D. E., Silverberg, M. J., Tangpricha, V., & Goodman, M. (2018). Mental health of transgender and gender nonconforming youth compared with their peers. *Pediatrics, 141*. https://tinyurl.com/398v67pf

Bechara, A., Berridge, K. C., Bickel, W. K., Morón, J. A., Williams, S. B., & Stein, J. S. (2019). A neurobehavioral approach to addiction: Implications for the opioid epidemic and the psychology of addiction. *Psychological Science in the Public Interest, 20*, 96–127.

Beck, A. T. (1978). *Cognitive therapy and the emotional disorders*. Penguin Publishing Group.

Beck, A. T., & Bredemeier, K. (2016). A unified model of depression: Integrating clinical, cognitive, biological, and evolutionary perspectives. *Clinical Psychological Science, 4*, 596–619.

Beck, A. T., Rush, A. J., Shaw, B. F., & Emery, G. (1979). *Cognitive therapy of depression*. Guilford Press.

Beck, D. M. (2010). The appeal of the brain in the popular press. *Perspectives on Psychological Science, 5*, 762–766.

Becker, D. V., Kenrick, D. T., Neuberg, S. L., Blackwell, K. C., & Smith, D. M. (2007). The confounded nature of angry men and happy women. *Journal of Personality and Social Psychology, 92*, 179–190.

Becker, J. E., Maley, C., Shultz, E., & Taylor, W. D. (2016). Update on transcranial magnetic stimulation for depression and other neuropsychiatric illnesses. *Psychiatric Annals, 46*, 637–641.

Becklen, R., & Cervone, D. (1983). Selective looking and the noticing of unexpected events. *Memory and Cognition, 11*, 601–608.

Bediou, B., Adams, D. M., Mayer, R. E., Tipton, E., Green, C. S., & Bavelier, D. (2018). Meta-analysis of action video game impact on perceptual, attentional, and cognitive skills. *Psychological Bulletin, 144*, 77–110.

Beeman, M. J., & Chiarello, C. (1998). Complementary right- and left-hemisphere language comprehension. *Current Directions in Psychological Science, 7*, 2–8.

Bègue, L., Bushman, B. J., Giancola, P. R., Subra, B., & Rosset, E. (2010). "There is no such thing as an accident," especially when people are drunk. *Personality and Social Psychology Bulletin, 36*, 1301–1304.

Bègue, L., Subra, B., Arvers, P., Muller, D., Bricout, V., & Zorman, M. (2009). A message in a bottle: Extrapharmacological effects of alcohol on aggression. *Journal of Experimental Social Psychology, 45*, 137–142.

Bègue, L., Zaalberg, A., Shankland, R., Duke, A., Jacquet, J., Kaliman, P., Pennel, L., Chanove, M., Arvers, P., & Bushman, B. J. (2018). Omega-3 supplements reduce self-reported physical aggression in healthy adults. *Psychiatry Research, 261*, 307–311.

Beil, L. (2018, July 21). The clean cycle. *Science News*, pp. 22–26.

Beilin, H. (1992). Piaget's enduring contribution to developmental psychology. *Developmental Psychology, 28*, 191–204.

Beilock, S. (2010). *Choke: What the secrets of the brain reveal about getting it right when you have to*. Free Press.

Beintner, I., Jacobi, C., & Taylor, C. B. (2012). Effects of an Internet-based prevention programme for eating disorders in the USA and Germany: A meta-analytic review. *European Eating Disorders Review, 20*, 1–8.

Bekkali, S., Youssef, G. J., Donaldson, P. H., Albein-Urios, N., Hyde, C., & Enticott, P. G. (2021). Is the putative mirror neuron system associated with empathy? A systematic review and meta-analysis. *Neuropsychology Review, 31*, 14–57.

Bell, A. P., Weinberg, M. S., & Hammersmith, S. K. (1981). *Sexual preference: Its development in men and women*. Indiana University Press.

Bellet, B. W., Jones, P. J., Meyersburg, C. A., Brenneman, M. M., Morehead, K. E., & McNally, R. J. (2020). Trigger warnings and resilience in college students: A preregistered replication and extension. *Journal of Experimental Psychology: Applied, 26*(4), 717–723.

Bellos, A. (2014). *'Seven' triumphs in poll to discover world's favourite number*. The Guardian. https://www.theguardian.com/science/alexs-adventures-in-numberland/2014/apr/08/seven-worlds-favourite-number-online-survey

Belluck, P. (2012, July 16). Footprints to cognitive decline and Alzheimer's are seen in gait. *The New York Times*. https://www.nytimes.com/2012/07/17/health/research/signs-of-cognitive-decline-and-alzheimers-are-seen-in-gait.html

Belluck, P. (2013, February 5). People with mental illness more likely to be smokers, study finds. *The New York Times*. https://www.nytimes.com/2013/02/06/health/more-smoking-found-by-mentally-ill-people.html

Belluck, P. (2021). Tapping into the brain to help a paralyzed man speak. *The New York Times*. https://www.nytimes.com/2021/07/14/health/speech-brain-implant-computer.html

Belot, M., & Francesconi, M. (2006, November). *Can anyone be "the one"? Evidence on mate selection from speed dating*. Centre for Economic Policy Research.

Belsky, J., & Pluess, M. (2009). Beyond diathesis stress: Differential susceptibility to environmental influences. *Psychological Bulletin, 135*, 885–908.

Belson, K. (2015, September 6). No foul mouths on this field: Football with a New Age twist. *The New York Times*. https://www.nytimes.com/2015/09/07/sports/football/no-foul-mouths-on-pete-carrolls-field-football-with-a-new-age-twist.html

Belson, K. (2017, September 21). Aaron Hernandez had severe C.T.E. when he died at age 27. *The New York Times*. https://www.nytimes.com/2017/09/21/sports/aaron-hernandez-cte-brain.html

Bem, D., Tressoldi, P., Rabeyron, T., & Duggan, M. (2015). Feeling the future: A meta-analysis of 90 experiments on the anomalous anticipation of random future events. *F1000Research, 4*, 1188.

Bem, D. J. (1984). Quoted in *The Skeptical Inquirer, 8*, 194.

Bem, D. J. (2011). Feeling the future: Experimental evidence for anomalous retroactive influences on cognition and affect. *Journal of Personality and Social Psychology, 100*, 407–425.

Bem, S. L. (1987). Masculinity and femininity exist only in the mind of the perceiver. In J. M. Reinisch, L. A. Rosenblum, & S. A. Sanders (Eds.), *Masculinity/femininity: Basic perspectives* (pp. 304–311). Oxford University Press.

Bem, S. L. (1993). *The lenses of gender: Transforming the debate on sexual inequality.* Yale University Press.

Benartzi, S., Beshears, J., Milkman, K. L., Sunstein, C. R., Thaler, R. H., Shankar, M., Tucker-Ray, W., Congdon, W. J., & Galing, S. (2017). Should governments invest more in nudging? *Psychological Science, 28,* 1041–1055.

Bencharit, L. Z., Ho, Y. W., Fung, H. H., Yeung, D., Stephens, N., Romero-Canyas, R., & Tsai, J. L. (2019). Should job applicants be excited or calm? The role of culture and ideal affect in employment settings. *Emotion, 19,* 377–401.

Bendixen, M., Asao, K., Wyckoff, J. P., Buss, D. M., & Kennair, L. E. O. (2017). Sexual regret in US and Norway: Effects of culture and individual differences in religiosity and mating strategy. *Personality and Individual Differences, 116,* 246–251.

Benedict, C., Brooks, S. J., O'Daly, O. G., Almén, M. S., Morell, A., Åberg, K., Gingnell, M., Schultes, B., Hallschmid, M., Broman, J. E., Larsson, E. M., & Schiöth, H. B. (2012). Acute sleep deprivation enhances the brain's response to hedonic food stimuli: An fMRI study. *Journal of Clinical Endocrinology and Metabolism, 97,* 2011–2759.

Benenson, J. F., Gauthier, E., & Markovits, H. (2021). Girls exhibit greater empathy than boys following a minor accident. *Scientific Reports, 11,* 7965.

Benenson, J. F., Markovits, H., Fitzgerald, C., Geoffroy, D., Flemming, J., Kahlenberg, S. M., & Wrangham, R. W. (2009). Males' greater tolerance of same-sex peers. *Psychological Science, 20,* 184–190.

Benenson, J. F., Webb, C. E., & Wrangham, R. W. (2021). Self-protection as an adaptive female strategy. *Behavioral and Brain Sciences, 45.* doi: 10.1017/S0140525X2100247

Benjamin, L. T., Jr., & Simpson, J. A. (2009). The power of the situation: The impact of Milgram's obedience studies on personality and social psychology. *American Psychologist, 64,* 12–19.

Benjamins, M. R., Ellison, C. G., & Rogers, R. G. (2010). Religious involvement and mortality risk among pre-retirement aged U.S. adults. In C. E. Ellison & R. A. Hummer (Eds.), *Religion, families, and health: Population-based research in the United States.* Rutgers University Press.

Ben Malek, B. H., Philippi, H., Botzung, A., Cretin, B., Berna, F., Manning, L., & Blanc, F. (2019). Memories defining the self in Alzheimer's disease. *Memory, 27,* 698–704.

Bennett, W. I. (1995). Beyond overeating. *New England Journal of Medicine, 332,* 673–674.

Bennie, J. A., De Cocker, K., Biddle, S. J. H., & Teychenne, M. J. (2020). Joint and dose-dependent associations between aerobic and muscle-strengthening activity with depression: A cross-sectional study of 1.48 million adults between 2011 and 2017. *Depression & Anxiety, 37*(2), 166–178.

Ben-Shakhar, G., & Elaad, E. (2003). The validity of psychophysiological detection of information with the guilty knowledge test: A meta-analytic review. *Journal of Applied Psychology, 88,* 131–151.

Berenbaum, S. A., & Beltz, A. M. (2021). Evidence and implications from a natural experiment of prenatal androgen effects on gendered behavior. *Current Directions in Psychological Science, 30,* 202–210.

Berg, J. M., Wall, M., Larson, N., Eisenberg, M. E., Loth, K. A., & Neumark-Sztainer, D. (2014). The unique and additive associations of family functioning and parenting practices with disordered eating behaviors in diverse adolescents. *Journal of Behavioral Medicine, 37,* 205–217.

Bergen, B. K. (2014). *Universal grammar.* Response to 2014 Edge question: What scientific idea is ready for retirement? Edge. https://www.edge.org/response-detail/25539

Berk, L. E. (1994). Why children talk to themselves. *Scientific American, 271,* 78–83.

Berk, L. S., Felten, D. L., Tan, S. A., Bittman, B. B., & Westengard, J. (2001). Modulation of neuroimmune parameters during the eustress of humor-associated mirthful laughter. *Alternative Therapies, 7,* 62–76.

Berken, J. A., Gracco, V. L., Chen, J., Soles, J., Watkins, K. E., Baum, S., Callahan, M., & Klein, D. (2015). Neural activation in speech production and reading aloud in native and non-native languages. *NeuroImage, 112,* 208–217.

Berkovich-Ohana, A., Glickson, J., & Goldstein, A. (2014). Studying the default mode and its mindfulness-induced changes using EEF functional connectivity. *Social Cognitive and Affective Neuroscience, 9,* 1616–1624.

Berkowitz, L. (1983). Aversively stimulated aggression: Some parallels and differences in research with animals and humans. *American Psychologist, 38,* 1135–1144.

Berkowitz, L. (1989). Frustration-aggression hypothesis: Examination and reformulation. *Psychological Bulletin, 106,* 59–73.

Berman, M. G., Jonides, J., & Kaplan, S. (2008). The cognitive benefits of interacting with nature. *Psychological Science, 19,* 1207–1212.

Bernal-Gamboa, R., Rosas, J. M., & Nieto, J. (2018). Extinction makes acquisition context-specific in conditioned taste aversion regardless of the context where acquisition and testing take place. *Journal of Experimental Psychology: Animal Learning and Cognition, 44,* 385–395.

Berndt, T. J. (1992). Friendship and friends' influence in adolescence. *Current Directions in Psychological Science, 1,* 156–159.

Bernieri, F., Davis, J., Rosenthal, R., & Knee, C. (1994). Interactional synchrony and rapport: Measuring synchrony in displays devoid of sound and facial affect. *Personality and Social Psychology Bulletin, 20,* 303–311.

Bernstein, B. O., Lubinski, D., & Benbow, C. P. (2019). Psychological constellations assessed at age 13 predict distinct forms of eminence 35 years later. *Psychological Science, 30,* 444–454.

Bernstein, D. M., & Loftus, E. F. (2009). The consequences of false memories for food preferences and choices. *Perspectives on Psychological Science, 4,* 135–139.

Bernstein, M. J., Young, S. G., & Claypool, H. M. (2010). Is Obama's win a gain for Blacks? Changes in implicit racial prejudice following the 2008 election. *Social Psychology, 41,* 147–151.

Berridge, K. C., Robinson, T. E., & Aldridge, J. W. (2009). Dissecting components of reward: "liking", "wanting", and learning. *Current Opinion in Pharmacology, 9,* 65–73.

Berry, C. M., & Sackett, P. R. (2009). Individual differences in course choice result in underestimation of the validity of college admissions systems. *Psychological Science, 20,* 822–830.

Berry, C. M., & Zhao, P. (2015). Addressing criticisms of existing predictive bias research: Cognitive ability test scores still overpredict African Americans' job performance. *Journal of Applied Psychology, 100,* 162–179.

Berry, K. M., Erickson, D. J., Berger, A. T., Wahlstrom, K., Iber, C., Full, K. M., Redline, S., & Widome, R. (2021). Association of delaying school start time with sleep-wake behaviors among adolescents. *Journal of Adolescent Health, 69*(5), 831–837.

Berscheid, E. (1981). An overview of the psychological effects of physical attractiveness and some comments upon the psychological effects of knowledge of the effects of physical attractiveness. In G. W. Lucker, K. Ribbens, & J. A. McNamara (Eds.), *Psychological aspects of facial form* (Craniofacial Growth Series). Center for Human Growth and Development, University of Michigan.

Berscheid, E. (1985). Interpersonal attraction. In G. Lindzey & E. Aronson (Eds.), *The handbook of social psychology.* Random House.

Berscheid, E. (2010). Love in the fourth dimension. *Annual Review of Psychology, 61,* 1–25.

Berti, A., Cottini, G., Gandola, M., Pia, L., Smania, N., Stracciari, A., Castiglioni, I., Vallar, G., & Paulesu, E. (2005). Shared cortical anatomy for motor awareness and motor control. *Science, 309,* 488–491.

Bértolo, H. (2005). Visual imagery without visual perception? *Psicológica, 26,* 173–188.

Bertrand, M., & Mullainathan, S. (2004). Are Emily and Greg more employable than Lakisha and Jamal? A field experiment on labor market discrimination. *American Economic Review, 94,* 991–1013.

Bessone, P., Rao, G., Schilbach, F., Schofield, H., & Toma, M. (2021). The economic consequences of increasing sleep among the urban poor. *Quarterly Journal of Economics, 136*(3), 1887–1941.

Bettache, K. (2020). A call to action: The need for a cultural psychological approach to discrimination on the basis of skin color in Asia. *Perspectives on Psychological Science, 15,* 1131–1139.

Bettergarcia, J. N., & Israel, T. (2018). Therapist reactions to transgender identity exploration: Effects on the therapeutic relationship in an analogue study. *Psychology of Sexual Orientation and Gender Diversity, 5,* 423–431.

Beyeler, A. (2019). Do antidepressants restore lost synapses? *Science, 364,* 129–130.

Bhatt, R. S., Wasserman, E. A., Reynolds, W. F., Jr., & Knauss, K. S. (1988). Conceptual behavior in pigeons: Categorization of both familiar and novel examples from four classes of natural and artificial stimuli. *Journal of Experimental Psychology: Animal Behavior Processes, 14,* 219–234.

Bialystok, E. (2017). The bilingual adaptation: How minds accommodate experience. *Psychological Bulletin, 143,* 233–262.

Bianchi, E. C., Hall, E. V., & Lee, S. (2018). Reexamining the link between economic downturns and racial antipathy: Evidence that prejudice against blacks rises during recessions. *Psychological Science, 29*, 1584–1597.

Bianco, V., Berchicci, M., Gigante, E., Perri, R. L., Quinzi, F., Mussini, E., & Di Russo, F. (2022). Brain plasticity induced by musical expertise on proactive and reactive cognitive functions. *Neuroscience, 483*, 1–12.

Bianconi, E., Piovesan, A., Facchin, F., Beraudi, A., Casadei, R., Frabetti, F., Vitale, L., Pelleri, M. C., Tassani, S., Piva, F., Perez-Amodio, S., Strippoli, P., & Canaider, S. (2013). An estimation of the number of cells in the human body. *Annals of Human Biology, 40*, 463–471.

Biddlestone, M., Green, R., & Douglas, K. M. (2020). Cultural orientation, power, belief in conspiracy theories, and intentions to reduce the spread of COVID-19. *British Journal of Social Psychology, 59*(3), 663–673.

Biden, J. (2021, January 27). *Memorandum on restoring trust in government through scientific integrity and evidence-based policymaking.* Executive order on the President's Council of Advisors on Science and Technology. The White House. https://bit.ly/3AG0GB2

Bienvenu, O. J., Davydow, D. S., & Kendler, K. S. (2011). Psychiatric "diseases" versus behavioral disorders and degree of genetic influence. *Psychological Medicine, 41*, 33–40.

Bilefsky, D. (2009, March 11). Europeans debate castration of sex offenders. *The New York Times.* https://www.nytimes.com/2009/03/11/world/europe/11castrate.html

Billock, V. A., & Tsou, B. H. (2012). Elementary visual hallucinations and their relationships to neural pattern-forming mechanisms. *Psychological Bulletin, 138*, 744–774.

Binder, E. B. (2019). Polygenic risk scores in schizophrenia: Ready for the real world? *American Journal of Psychiatry, 176*, 783–784.

Binet, A. (1909). *Les idées modernes sur les enfants* [Modern ideas about children]. Flammarion. Quoted in Clarke, A., & Clarke, A. (2006), Born to be bright. *The Psychologist, 19*, 409.

Binning, K. R., Kaufmann, N., McGreevy, E. M., Fotuhi, O., Chen, S., Marshman, E., Kalender, Z. Y., Limeri, L. B., Betancur, L., & Singh, C. (2020). Changing social contexts to foster equity in college science courses: An ecological-belonging intervention. *Psychological Science, 31*, 1059–1070.

Bird, C. D., & Emery, N. J. (2009). Rooks use stones to raise the water level to reach a floating worm. *Current Biology, 19*, 1410–1414.

Birnbaum, G. E. (2018). The fragile spell of desire: A functional perspective on changes in sexual desire across relationship development. *Personality and Social Psychology Review, 22*, 101–127.

Birnbaum, G. E., & Reis, H. T. (2012). When does responsiveness pique sexual interest? Attachment and sexual desire in initial acquaintanceships. *Personality and Social Psychology Bulletin, 38*, 946–958.

Biro, D., Humle, T., Koops, K., Sousa, C., Hayashi, M., & Matsuzawa, T. (2010). Chimpanzee mothers at Bossou, Guinea carry the mummified remains of their dead infants. *Current Biology, 20*, R351–R352.

Biro, F. M., Galvez, M. P., Greenspan, L. C., Succop, P. A., Vangeepuram, N., Pinney, S. M., Teitelbaum, S., Windham, G. C., Kushi, L. H., & Wolff, M. S. (2010). Pubertal assessment method and baseline characteristics in a mixed longitudinal study of girls. *Pediatrics, 126*, e583–e590.

Biro, F. M., Greenspan, L. C., & Galvez, M. P. (2012). Puberty in girls of the 21st century. *Journal of Pediatric and Adolescent Gynecology, 25*, 289–294.

Bisbey, T. M., Reyes, D. L., Traylor, A. M., & Salas, E. (2019). Teams of psychologists helping teams: The evolution of the science of team training. *American Psychologist, 74*, 278–289.

Bishop, D. I., Weisgram, E. S., Holleque, K. M., Lund, K. E., & Wheeler, J. R. (2005). Identity development and alcohol consumption: Current and retrospective self-reports by college students. *Journal of Adolescence, 28*, 523–533.

Bishop, G. D. (1991). Understanding the understanding of illness: Lay disease representations. In J. A. Skelton & R. T. Croyle (Eds.), *Mental representation in health and illness* (pp. 32–59). Springer-Verlag.

Bisra, K., Liu, Q., Nesbit, J. C., Salimi, F., & Winne, P. H. (2018). Inducing self-explanation: A meta-analysis. *Educational Psychology Review, 30*, 703–725.

Bjork, E. L., & Bjork, R. (2011). Making things hard on yourself, but in a good way: Creating desirable difficulties to enhance learning. In M. A. Gernsbacher, M. A. Pew, L. M. Hough, & J. R. Pomerantz (Eds.), *Psychology and the real world* (pp. 55–64). Worth.

Bjork, R. (2011, January 20). Quoted by P. Belluck in, To really learn, quit studying and take a test. *The New York Times.* https://www.nytimes.com/2011/01/21/science/21memory.html

Bjork, R. A., & Bjork, E. L. (2019). Forgetting as the friend of learning: Implications for teaching and self-regulated learning. *Advances in Physiology Education, 43*, 164–167.

Bjorklund, D. F., & Green, B. L. (1992). The adaptive nature of cognitive immaturity. *American Psychologist, 47*, 46–54.

Black, M. C., Basile, K. C., Breiding, M. J., Smith, S. G., Walters, M. L., Merrick, M. T., Chen, J., & Stevens, M. R. (2011). *The National Intimate Partner and Sexual Violence Survey (NISVS): 2010 summary report.* National Center for Injury Prevention and Control, Centers for Disease Control and Prevention.

Blake, A., Nazarian, M., & Castel, A. (2015). The Apple of the mind's eye: Everyday attention, metamemory, and reconstructive memory for the Apple logo. *Quarterly Journal of Experimental Psychology, 68*, 858–865.

Blake, K. R., & Gangestad, S. (2020). On attenuated interactions, measurement error, and statistical power: Guidelines for social and personality psychologists. *Personality & Social Psychology Bulletin, 46*(12), 1702–1711.

Blake, K. R., O'Dean, S. M., Lian, J., & Denson, T. F. (2021). Misogynistic tweets correlate with violence against women. *Psychological Science, 32*, 315–325.

Blakemore, S. (2018). Avoiding social risk in adolescence. *Current Directions in Psychological Science, 27*, 116–122.

Blakemore, S. J. (2008). Development of the social brain during adolescence. *Quarterly Journal of Experimental Psychology, 61*, 40–49.

Blakemore, S.-J., Wolpert, D. M., & Frith, C. D. (1998). Central cancellation of self-produced tickle sensation. *Nature Neuroscience, 1*, 635–640.

Blakeslee, S. (2006, January 10). Cells that read minds. *The New York Times.* https://www.nytimes.com/2006/01/10/science/cells-that-read-minds.html

Blanchard, R. (2004). Quantitative and theoretical analyses of the relation between older brothers and homosexuality in men. *Journal of Theoretical Biology, 230*, 173–187.

Blanchard, R. (2008). Review and theory of handedness, birth order, and homosexuality in men. *Laterality, 13*, 51–70.

Blanchard, R. (2018). Fraternal birth order, family size, and male homosexuality: Meta-analysis of studies spanning 25 years. *Archives of Sexual Behavior, 47*, 1–15.

Blanchard, R. (2019). Recent findings on fraternal birth order and homosexuality in males. *Archives of Sexual Behavior, 48*, 1899–1900.

Blanchard, R., Beier, K. M., Gómez Jiménez, F. R., Grundmann, D., Krupp, J., Semenyna, S. W., & Vasey, P. L. (2021). Meta-analyses of fraternal and sororal birth order effects in homosexual pedophiles, hebephiles, and teleiophiles. *Archives of Sexual Behavior, 50*, 779–796.

Blanchard, R., & Skorska, M. N. (2022). New data on birth order in homosexual men and women and a reply to Vilsmeier et al. (2021a, 2021b). *Archives of Sexual Behavior, 51*(7), 3319–3349.

Blanchard-Fields, F. (2007). Everyday problem solving and emotion: An adult developmental perspective. *Current Directions in Psychological Science, 16*, 26–31.

Blascovich, J., & Mendes, W. B. (2010). Social psychophysiology and embodiment. In S. T. Fiske, D. T. Gilbert, & G. Lindzey (Eds.), *The handbook of social psychology* (5th ed., pp. 194–227). Wiley.

Blasi, D. E., Wichmann, S., Hammarström, H., Stadler, P. F., & Christiansen, M. H. (2016). Sound-meaning association biases evidenced across thousands of languages. *PNAS, 113*, 10818–10823.

Blass, T. (1996). Stanley Milgram: A life of inventiveness and controversy. In G. A. Kimble, C. A. Boneau, & M. Wertheimer (Eds.), *Portraits of pioneers in psychology* (Vol. II). American Psychological Association and Lawrence Erlbaum.

Blass, T. (1999). The Milgram paradigm after 35 years: Some things we now know about obedience to authority. *Journal of Applied Social Psychology, 29*, 955–978.

Blazer, D. G., & Tucci, D. L. (2019). Hearing loss and psychiatric disorders: A review. *Psychological Medicine, 49*, 891–897.

Blechert, J., Testa, G., Georgii, C., Klimesch, W., & Wilhelm, F. H. (2016). The Pavlovian craver: Neural and experiential correlates of single trial naturalistic food conditioning in humans. *Physiology & Behavior, 158*, 18–25.

Bleidorn, W., Arslan, R. C., Denissen, J. J. A., Rentfrow, P. J., Gebauer, J. E., Potter, J., & Gosling, S. D. (2016). Age and gender differences in self-esteem—a cross-cultural window. *Journal of Personality and Social Psychology, 111*, 396–410.

Bleidorn, W., Hopwood, C. J., Ackerman, R. A., Witt, E. A., Kandler, C., Riemann,

R., Samuel, D. B., & Donnellan, M. B. (2020). The healthy personality from a basic trait perspective. *Journal of Personality and Social Psychology, 118*(6), 1207–1225.

Bleidorn, W., Hopwood, C. J., & Lucas, R. E. (2018). Life events and personality trait change. *Journal of Personality, 86*, 83–96.

Bleidorn, W., Schwaba, T., Denissen, J. J. A., & Hopwood, C. J. (2021). Charting self-esteem during marital dissolution. *Journal of Personality, 89*(1), 9–22.

Blix, I., & Brennen, T. (2011). Mental time travel after trauma: The specificity and temporal distribution of autobiographical memories and future-directed thoughts. *Memory, 19*, 956–967.

Bloom, B. C. (Ed.). (1985). *Developing talent in young people*. Ballantine.

Bloom, F. E. (1993, January/February). What's new in neurotransmitters. *BrainWork*, pp. 7–9.

Bloom, P. (2000). *How children learn the meanings of words*. MIT Press.

Blow, C. M. (2015, March 26). Officers' race matters less than you think. *The New York Times*. https://www.nytimes.com/2015/03/26/opinion/charles-blow-officer-race-matters-less-than-you-think.html

BLS (U.S. Bureau of Labor Statistics). (2011, June 22). *American time use survey summary*. https://www.scribd.com/document/154489647/American-Time-Use-Survey-Summary

Blum, D. (2011). *Love at Goon Park: Harry Harlow and the science of affection* (2nd ed.). Perseus.

Blum, K., Cull, J. G., Braverman, E. R., & Comings, D. E. (1996). Reward deficiency syndrome. *American Scientist, 84*, 132–145.

Blum, K., Thanos, P. K., & Gold, M. S. (2014). Dopamine and glucose, obesity, and reward deficiency syndrome. *Frontiers in Psychology, 5*, 919.

Blumenstein, B., & Orbach, I. (2012). *Mental practice in sport: Twenty case studies*. Novinka/Nova Science Publishers.

Boag, S. (2006). Freudian repression, the common view, and pathological science. *Review of General Psychology, 10*, 74–86.

Bock, L. (2013, June 19). Interview by Adam Bryant, "In head-hunting, big data may not be such a big deal." *The New York Times*. https://www.nytimes.com/2013/06/20/business/in-head-hunting-big-data-may-not-be-such-a-big-deal.html

Bocklandt, S., Horvath, S., Vilain, E., & Hamer, D. H. (2006). Extreme skewing of X chromosome inactivation in mothers of homosexual men. *Human Genetics, 118*, 691–694.

Bockting, W. O. (2014). Transgender identity development. In D. L. Tolman & L. M. Diamond (Eds.), *APA handbook of sexuality and psychology: Vol. 1. Person-based approaches* (pp. 739–758). American Psychological Association.

Bodenhausen, G. V., Sheppard, L. A., & Kramer, G. P. (1994). Negative affect and social judgment: The differential impact of anger and sadness. *European Journal of Social Psychology, 24*, 45–62.

Boecker, H., Sprenger, T., Spilker, M. E., Henriksen, G., Koppenhoefer, M., Wagner, K. J., Valet, M., Berthele, A., & Tolle, T. R. (2008). The runner's high: Opioidergic mechanisms in the human brain. *Cerebral Cortex, 18*, 2523–2531.

Boehm, J. K., & Kubzansky, L. D. (2012). The heart's content: The association between positive psychological well-being and cardiovascular health. *Psychological Bulletin, 138*, 655–691.

Boehm, J. K., Trudel-Fitzgerald, C., Kivimaki, M., & Kubzansky, L. D. (2015). The prospective association between positive psychological well-being and diabetes. *Health Psychology, 34*, 1013–1021.

Boehm-Davis, D. A. (2005). Improving product safety and effectiveness in the home. In R. S. Nickerson (Ed.), *Reviews of human factors and ergonomics* (Vol. 1, pp. 219–253). Human Factors and Ergonomics Society.

Boesch-Achermann, H., & Boesch, C. (1993). Tool use in wild chimpanzees: New light from dark forests. *Current Directions in Psychological Science, 2*, 18–21.

Bogaert, A. F. (2003). Number of older brothers and sexual orientation: New texts and the attraction/behavior distinction in two national probability samples. *Journal of Personality and Social Psychology, 84*, 644–652.

Bogaert, A. F. (2004). Asexuality: Prevalence and associated factors in a national probability sample. *Journal of Sex Research, 41*, 279–287.

Bogaert, A. F. (2006). Biological versus nonbiological older brothers and men's sexual orientation. *PNAS, 103*, 10771–10774.

Bogaert, A. F. (2015). Asexuality: What it is and why it matters. *Journal of Sex Research, 52*, 362–379.

Bogaert, A. F., Friesen, C., & Klentrou, P. (2002). Age of puberty and sexual orientation in a national probability sample. *Archives of Sexual Behavior, 31*, 73–81.

Bogaert, A. F., Skorska, M. N., Wang, C., Gabrie, J., MacNeil, A. J., Hoffarth, M. R., VanderLaan, D. P., Zucker, K. J., & Blanchard, R. (2018). Male homosexuality and maternal immune responsivity to the Y-linked protein NLGN4Y. *PNAS, 115*, 302–306.

Bogen, J. E. & Vogel, P. J. (1962). Cerebral commissurotomy in man: Preliminary case report. *Bulletin Los Angeles Neurological Society, 27*, 169–172.

Bogenschutz, M. P., Ross, S., Bhatt, S., Baron, T., Forcehimes, A. A., Laska, E., Mennenga, S. E., O'Donnell, K., Owens, L. T., Podrebarac, S., Rotrosen, J., Tonigan, J. S., & Worth, L. (2022). Percentage of heavy drinking days following psilocybin-assisted psychotherapy vs placebo in the treatment of adult patients with alcohol use disorder: A randomized clinical trial. *JAMA Psychiatry, 79*(10), 953–962.

Boggiano, A. K., Harackiewicz, J. M., Bessette, M. M., & Main, D. S. (1985). Increasing children's interest through performance-contingent reward. *Social Cognition, 3*, 400–411.

Boggiano, M. M., Chandler, P. C., Viana, J. B., Oswald, K. D., Maldonado, C. R., & Wauford, P. K. (2005). Combined dieting and stress evoke exaggerated responses to opioids in binge-eating rats. *Behavioral Neuroscience, 119*, 1207–1214.

Bohlken, M. M., Brouwer, R. M., Mandl, R. C. W., Van, d. H., Hedman, A. M., De Hert, M., Cahn, W., Kahn, R. S., & Pol, H. E. H. (2016). Structural brain connectivity as a genetic marker for schizophrenia. *JAMA Psychiatry, 73*, 11–19.

Bohman, M., & Sigvardsson, S. (1990). Outcome in adoption: Lessons from longitudinal studies. In D. Brodzinsky & M. Schechter (Eds.), *The psychology of adoption* (pp. 93–106). Oxford University Press.

Boiman-Meshita, M., & Littman-Ovadia, H. (2021). The marital version of three good things: A mixed-method study. *Journal of Positive Psychology, 16*, 367–378.

Bois, C., Levita, L., Ripp, I., Owens, D. C. G., Johnstone, E. C., Whalley, H. C., & Lawrie, S. M. (2016). Longitudinal changes in hippocampal volume in the Edinburgh High Risk Study of Schizophrenia. *Schizophrenia Research, 173*, 146–151.

Bolger, N., DeLongis, A., Kessler, R. C., & Schilling, E. A. (1989). Effects of daily stress on negative mood. *Journal of Personality and Social Psychology, 57*, 808–818.

Bolmont, M., Cacioppo, J. T., & Cacioppo, S. (2014). Love is in the gaze: An eye-tracking study of love and sexual desire. *Psychological Science, 25*, 1748–1756.

Boly, M., Garrido, M. I., Gosseries, O., Bruno, M.-A., Boveroux, P., Schnakers, C., Massimini, M., Litvak, V., Laureys, S., & Friston, K. (2011). Preserved feed-forward but impaired top-down processes in the vegetative state. *Science, 332*, 858–862.

Bonanno, G. A. (2004). Loss, trauma, and human resilience: Have we underestimated the human capacity to thrive after extremely aversive events? *American Psychologist, 59*, 20–28.

Bonanno, G. A. (2009). *The other side of sadness: What the new science of bereavement tells us about life after loss*. Basic Books.

Bonanno, G. A. (2021, September 4). What 9/11 taught us about trauma and resilience. *The Wall Street Journal*. https://www.wsj.com/articles/what-9-11-taught-us-about-trauma-and-resilience-11630728061

Bonanno, G. A., Brewin, C. R., Kaniasty, K., & La Greca, A. M. (2010). Weighing the costs of disaster: Consequences, risks, and resilience in individuals, families, and communities. *Psychological Science in the Public Interest, 11*, 1–49.

Bonanno, G. A., Galea, S., Bucciarelli, A., & Vlahov, D. (2006). Psychological resilience after disaster. *Psychological Science, 17*, 181–186.

Bonanno, G. A., Galea, S., Bucciarelli, A., & Vlahov, D. (2007). What predicts psychological resilience after disaster? The role of demographics, resources, and life stress. *Journal of Consulting and Clinical Psychology, 75*, 671–682.

Bonanno, G. A., & Kaltman, S. (1999). Toward an integrative perspective on bereavement. *Psychological Bulletin, 125*, 760–777.

Bonanno, G. A., Westphal, M., & Mancini, A. D. (2011). Resilience to loss and potential trauma. *Annual Review of Clinical Psychology, 11*, 511–535.

Bond, C. F., Jr., & DePaulo, B. M. (2006). Accuracy of deception judgments. *Personality and Social Psychology Review, 10*, 214–234.

Bond, M. H., Lun, V. M.-C., Chan, J., Chan, W. W.-Y., & Wong, D. (2012). Enacting modesty in Chinese culture: The joint contribution of personal characteristics and contextual features. *Asian Journal of Social Psychology, 15,* 14–25.

Bond, R., & Smith, P. B. (1996). Culture and conformity: A meta-analysis of studies using Asch's (1952, 1956) line judgment task. *Psychological Bulletin, 119,* 111–137.

Bonezzi, A., Brendl, C. M., & DeAngelis, M. (2011). Stuck in the middle: The psychophysics of goal pursuit. *Psychological Science, 22,* 607–612.

Bonfils, K. A., Lysaker, P. H., Minor, K. S., & Salyers, M. P. (2016). Affective empathy in schizophrenia: A meta-analysis. *Schizophrenia Research, 175,* 109–117.

Bono, J. E., & Judge, T. A. (2004). Personality and transformational and transactional leadership: A meta-analysis. *Journal of Applied Psychology, 89,* 901–910.

Bookheimer, S. H., Strojwas, M. H., Cohen, M. S., Saunders, A. M., Pericak-Vance, M. A., Mazziotta, J. C., & Small, G. W. (2000). Patterns of brain activation in people at risk for Alzheimer's disease. *New England Journal of Medicine, 343,* 450–456.

Bookwala, J., & Gaugler, T. (2020). Relationship quality and 5-year mortality risk. *Health Psychology, 39,* 633–641.

Booth, F. W., & Neufer, P. D. (2005). Exercise controls gene expression. *American Scientist, 93,* 28–35.

Boothby, E. J., & Bohns, V. K. (2021). Why a simple act of kindness is not as simple as it seems: Underestimating the positive impact of our compliments on others. *Personality and Social Psychology Bulletin, 47,* 826–840.

Boothby, E. J., Cooney, G., Sandstrom, G. M., & Clark, M. S. (2018). The liking gap in conversations: Do people like us more than we think? *Psychological Science, 29,* 1742–1756.

Bopp, K. L., & Verhaeghen, P. (2020). Aging and n-back performance: A meta-analysis. *Journals of Gerontology: Series B, 75*(2), 229–240.

Bor, D. (2010). The mechanics of mind reading. *Scientific American, 21,* 52–57.

Bora, E., & Pantelis, C. (2013). Theory of mind impairments in first-episode psychosis, individuals at ultra-high risk for psychosis and in first-degree relatives of schizophrenia: Systematic review and meta-analysis. *Schizophrenia Research, 144,* 31–36.

Bora, E., & Pantelis, C. (2016). Social cognitive in schizophrenia in comparison to bipolar disorder: A meta-analysis. *Schizophrenia Research, 175,* 72–78.

Bordalo, P., Coffman, K., Gennaioli, N., Schwerter, F., & Shleifer, A. (2021). Memory and representativeness. *Psychological Review,* 128(1), 71–85.

Borgogna, N. C., McDermott, R. C., Aita, S. L., & Kridel, M. M. (2019). Anxiety and depression across gender and sexual minorities: Implications for transgender, gender nonconforming, pansexual, demisexual, asexual, queer, and questioning individuals. *Psychology of Sexual Orientation and Gender Diversity, 6,* 54–63.

Boring, E. G. (1930). A new ambiguous figure. *American Journal of Psychology, 42,* 444–445.

Boring, E. G. (1959). *Lewis Madison Terman, 1877–1956.* National Academy of Sciences.

Borman, G. D., Rozek, C. S., Pyne, J., & Hanselman, P. (2019). Reappraising academic and social adversity improves middle school students' academic achievement, behavior, and well-being. *PNAS, 116,* 16286–16291.

Bornstein, M. H., Cote, L. R., Maital, S., Painter, K., Park, S.-Y., Pascual, L., Pêcheux, M. G., Ruel, J., Venuti, P., & Vyt, A. (2004). Cross-linguistic analysis of vocabulary in young children: Spanish, Dutch, French, Hebrew, Italian, Korean, and American English. *Child Development, 75,* 1115–1139.

Bornstein, M. H., Tal, J., Rahn, C., Galperin, C. Z., Pêcheux, M.-G., Lamour, M., Toda, S., Azuma, H., Ogino, M., & Tamis-LeMonda, C. S. (1992). Functional analysis of the contents of maternal speech to infants of 5 and 13 months in four cultures: Argentina, France, Japan, and the United States. *Developmental Psychology, 28,* 593–603.

Bornstein, M. H., Tamis-LeMonda, C. S., Tal, J., Ludemann, P., Toda, S., Rahn, C. W., Pêcheux, M. G., Azuma, H., & Vardi, D. (1992). Maternal responsiveness to infants in three societies: The United States, France, and Japan. *Child Development, 63,* 808–821.

Bornstein, R. F. (1989). Exposure and affect: Overview and meta-analysis of research, 1968–1987. *Psychological Bulletin, 106,* 265–289.

Bornstein, R. F. (1999). Source amnesia, misattribution, and the power of unconscious perceptions and memories. *Psychoanalytic Psychology, 16,* 155–178.

Bornstein, R. F., Galley, D. J., Leone, D. R., & Kale, A. R. (1991). The temporal stability of ratings of parents: Test-retest reliability and influence of parental contact. *Journal of Social Behavior and Personality, 6,* 641–649.

Boroditsky, L. (2009, June 12). *How does our language shape the way we think?* Edge. https://www.edge.org/conversation/lera_boroditsky-how-does-our-language-shape-the-way-we-think

Boroditsky, L. (2011, February). How language shapes thought. *Scientific American,* pp. 63–65.

Boroditsky, L. (2017). *How language shapes the way we think* [TED talk/video]. https://www.ted.com/talks/lera_boroditsky_how_language_shapes_the_way_we_think/transcript?language=en

Bos, H. M. W., Knox, J. R., van Rijn-van Gelderen, L., & Gartrell, N. K. (2016). Same-sex and different-sex parent households and child health outcomes: Findings from the national survey of children's health. *Journal of Developmental and Behavioral Pediatrics, 37,* 179–187.

Bosl, W. J., Tager-Flusberg, H., & Nelson, C. A. (2018). EEG analytics for early detection of autism spectrum disorder: A data-driven approach. *Scientific Reports, 8.* https://www.nature.com/articles/s41598-018-24318-x

Bosma, H., Marmot, M. G., Hemingway, H., Nicolson, A. C., Brunner, E., & Stansfeld, S. A. (1997). Low job control and risk of coronary heart disease in Whitehall II (prospective cohort) study. *British Medical Journal, 314,* 558–565.

Bosma, H., Peter, R., Siegrist, J., & Marmot, M. (1998). Two alternative job stress models and the risk of coronary heart disease. *American Journal of Public Health, 88,* 68–74.

Bostean, G., & Gillespie, B. J. (2018). Acculturation, acculturative stressors, and family relationships among Latina/o immigrants. *Cultural Diversity and Ethnic Minority Psychology, 24,* 126–138.

Bostwick, J. M., & Pankratz, V. S. (2000). Affective disorders and suicide risk: A re-examination. *American Journal of Psychiatry, 157,* 1925–1932.

Bothwell, R. K., Brigham, J. C., & Malpass, R. S. (1989). Cross-racial identification. *Personality and Social Psychology Bulletin, 15,* 19–25.

Botvinick, M., Ritter, S., Wang, J. X., Kurth-Nelson, Z., Blundell, C., & Hassabis, D. (2019). Reinforcement learning, fast and slow. *Trends in Cognitive Sciences, 23,* 408–422.

Bouchard, T. J., Jr. (2009). Genetic influences on human intelligence (Spearman's *g*): How much? *Annals of Human Biology, 36,* 527–544.

Boucher, J., Mayes, A., & Bigham, S. (2012). Memory in autistic spectrum disorder. *Psychological Bulletin, 138,* 458–496.

Boudesseul, J., Gildersleeve, K. A., Haselton, M. G., & Bègue, L. (2019). Do women expose themselves to more health-related risks in certain phases of the menstrual cycle? A meta-analytic review. *Neuroscience and Biobehavioral Reviews, 107,* 505–524.

Bould, H., Carnegie, R., Allward, H., Bacon, E., Lambe, Sapseid, M., Button, K. S., Lewis, G., Skinner, A., Broome, M. R., Park, R., Harmer, C. J., Penton-Boak, I. S., & Munafó, M. R. (2018). Effects of exposure to bodies of different sizes on perception of and satisfaction with own body size: Two randomized studies. *Royal Society Open Science, 5.* https://royalsocietypublishing.org/doi/10.1098/rsos.171387

Bourgault, S., Peterman, A., & O'Donnell, M. (2021). *Violence against women and children during COVID-19—One year on and 100 papers in: A fourth research roundup.* Center for Global Development. https://www.cgdev.org/publication/violence-against-women-and-children-during-covid-19-one-year-and-100-papers-fourth

Bourke, A., Boduszek, D., Kelleher, C., McBride, O., & Morgan, K. (2014). Sex education, first sex and sexual health outcomes in adulthood: Findings from a nationally representative sexual health survey. *Sex Education,* 14(3), 299–309.

Bowden, E. M., & Beeman, M. J. (1998). Getting the right idea: Semantic activation in the right hemisphere may help solve insight problems. *Psychological Science, 9,* 435–440.

Bowden-Green, T., Hinds, J., & Joinson, A. (2020). How is extraversion related to social media use? A literature review. *Personality and Individual Differences, 164.* https://doi.org/10.1016/j.paid.2020.110040

Bowdring, M. A., & Sayette, M. A. (2018). Perception of physical attractiveness when consuming and not consuming alcohol: A meta-analysis. *Addiction, 113,* 1585–1597.

Bower, B. (2009, February 14). The dating go round. *Science News,* pp. 22–25.

Bower, G. (1973, October). How to ... uh ... remember! *Psychology Today,* pp. 63–70.

Bower, G. H. (1981). Mood and memory. *American Psychologist,* 36(2), 129–148.

Bower, G. H. (1986). Prime time in cognitive psychology. In P. Eelen (Ed.), *Cognitive research and behavior therapy: Beyond the conditioning paradigm* (pp. 22–47). North-Holland Publishing Company.

Bower, G. H., Clark, M. C., Lesgold, A. M., & Winzenz, D. (1969). Hierarchical retrieval schemes in recall of categorized word lists. *Journal of Verbal Learning and Verbal Behavior, 8*, 323–343.

Bower, G. H., & Morrow, D. G. (1990). Mental models in narrative comprehension. *Science, 247*, 44–48.

Bowers, J. S. (2009). On the biological plausibility of grandmother cells: Implications for neural network theories in psychology and neuroscience. *Psychological Review, 116*, 220–251.

Bowers, J. S., Mattys, S. L., & Gage, S. H. (2009). Preserved implicit knowledge of a forgotten childhood language. *Psychological Science, 20*, 1064–1069.

Bowker, E., & Dorstyn, D. (2016). Hypnotherapy for disability-related pain: A meta-analysis. *Journal of Health Psychology, 21*, 526–539.

Bowling, N. A., Eschleman, K. J., & Wang, Q. (2010). A meta-analytic examination of the relationship between job satisfaction and subjective well-being. *Journal of Occupational and Organizational Psychology, 83*, 915–934.

Boxer, P., Huesmann, L. R., Bushman, B. J., O'Brien, M., & Moceri, D. (2009). The role of violent media preference in cumulative developmental risk for violence and general aggression. *Journal of Youth and Adolescence, 38*, 417–428.

Boyatzis, C. J. (2012). Spiritual development during childhood and adolescence. In L. J. Miller (Ed.), *The Oxford handbook of psychology and spirituality* (pp. 151–164). Oxford University Press.

Boyatzis, C. J., Matillo, G. M., & Nesbitt, K. M. (1995). Effects of the "Mighty Morphin Power Rangers" on children's aggression with peers. *Child Study Journal, 25*, 45–55.

Boyce, C. J., & Wood, A. M. (2011). Personality prior to disability determines adaptation: Agreeable individuals recover lost life satisfaction faster and more completely. *Psychological Science, 22*, 1397–1402.

Boyce, C. J., Wood, A. M., Daly, M., & Sedikides, C. (2015). Personality change following unemployment. *Journal of Applied Psychology, 100*, 991–1011.

Boyce, R., Glasgow, S. D., Williams, S., & Adamantidis, A. (2016). Causal evidence for the role of REM sleep theta rhythm in contextual memory consolidation. *Science, 352*, 812–816.

Boyden, E. S. (2014). Let there be light. *Scientific American, 25*, 62–69.

Boyle, A. (2021, April 6). *Horses can recognize themselves in a mirror—new study.* The Conversation. https://theconversation.com/horses-can-recognise-themselves-in-a-mirror-new-study-158447

Boynton, R. M. (1979). *Human color vision.* Holt, Rinehart & Winston.

Braat, M., Engelen, J., van Gemert, T., & Verhaegh, S. (2020). The rise and fall of behaviorism: The narrative and the numbers. *History of Psychology, 23*(3), 252–280.

Braden, J. P. (1994). *Deafness, deprivation, and IQ.* Plenum.

Bradley, D. R., Dumais, S. T., & Petry, H. M. (1976). Reply to Cavonius. *Nature, 261*, 78.

Bradley, R. B., Binder, E. B., Epstein, M. P., Tan, Y.-L., Nair, H. P., Liu, W., Gillespie, C. F., Berg, T., Evces, M., Newport, D. J., Stowe, Z. N., Heim, C. M., Nemeroff, C. B., Schwartz, A., Cubells, J. F., & Ressler, K. (2008). Influence of child abuse on adult depression: Moderation by the corticotropin-releasing hormone receptor gene. *Archives of General Psychiatry, 65*, 190–200.

Bradshaw, C., Sawyer, A., & O'Brennan, L. (2009). A social disorganization perspective on bullying-related attitudes and behaviors: The influence of school context. *American Journal of Community Psychology, 43*, 204–220.

Brady, W. J., Wills, J. A., Jost, J. T., Tucker, J. A., & Van Bavel, J. J. (2017). Emotion shapes the diffusion of moralized content in social networks. *PNAS, 114*, 7313–7318.

Braiker, B. (2005, October 18). A quiet revolt against the rules on SIDS. *The New York Times*. https://www.nytimes.com/2005/10/18/health/a-quiet-revolt-against-the-rules-on-sids.html

Brainerd, C. J. (1996). Piaget: A centennial celebration. *Psychological Science, 7*, 191–195.

Brainstorm Consortium. (2018). Analysis of shared heritability in common disorders of the brain. *Science, 360*, 1313.

Brakefield, T. A., Mednick, S. C., Wilson, H. W., De Neve, J., Christakis, N. A., & Fowler, J. H. (2014). Same-sex sexual attraction does not spread in adolescent social networks. *Archives of Sexual Behavior, 43*, 335–344.

Brand, B. L., Sar, V., Stavropoulos, P., Krüger, C., Korzekwa, M., Martínez-Taboas, A., & Middleton, W. (2016). Separating fact from fiction: An empirical examination of six myths about dissociative identity disorder. *Harvard Review of Psychiatry, 24*, 257–270.

Brandon, S., Boakes, J., Glaser, & Green, R. (1998). Recovered memories of childhood sexual abuse: Implications for clinical practice. *British Journal of Psychiatry, 172*, 294–307.

Brang, D., Edwards, L., Ramachandran, V. S., & Coulson, S. (2008). Is the sky 2? Contextual priming in grapheme-color synaesthesia. *Psychological Science, 19*, 421–428.

Brannan, D., Biswas-Diener, R., Mohr, C., Mortazavi, S., & Stein, N. (2013). Friends and family: A cross-cultural investigation of social support and subjective well-being among college students. *Journal of Positive Psychology, 8*, 65–75.

Bransford, J. D., & Johnson, M. K. (1972). Contextual prerequisites for understanding: Some investigations of comprehension and recall. *Journal of Verbal Learning and Verbal Behavior, 11*, 717–726.

Brasel, S. A., & Gips, J. (2011). Media multitasking behavior: Concurrent television and computer usage. *Cyberpsychology, Behavior, and Social Networking, 14*, 527–534.

Brashier, N. M., & Schacter, D. L. (2020). Aging in an era of fake news. *Current Directions in Psychological Science, 29*, 316–323.

Braun, S. (2001, Spring). Seeking insight by prescription. *Cerebrum*, pp. 10–21.

Braunstein, G. D., Sundwall, D. A., Katz, M., Shifren, J. L., Buster, J. E., Simon, J. A., Bachman, G., Aguirre, O. A., Lucas, J. D., Rodenberg, C., Buch, A., & Watts, N. B. (2005). Safety and efficacy of a testosterone patch for the treatment of hypoactive sexual desire disorder in surgically menopausal women: A randomized, placebo-controlled trial. *Archives of Internal Medicine, 165*, 1582–1589.

Bray, D. W., & Byham, W. C. (1991, Winter). Assessment centers and their derivatives. *Journal of Continuing Higher Education*, pp. 8–11.

Bray, D. W., & Byham, W. C., interviewed by Mayes, B. T. (1997). Insights into the history and future of assessment centers: An interview with Dr. Douglas W. Bray and Dr. William Byham. *Journal of Social Behavior and Personality, 12*, 3–12.

Brayne, C., Spiegelhalter, D. J., Dufouil, C., Chi, L. Y., Dening, T. R., Paykel, E. S., O'Connor, D. W., Ahmed, A., McGee, M. A., & Huppert, F. A. (1999). Estimating the true extent of cognitive decline in the old old. *Journal of the American Geriatrics Society, 47*, 1283–1288.

Brazil, I. A., & Buades-Rotger, M. (2020). Staring at the (sur)face of the antisocial brain. *Lancet Psychiatry, 7*, 218–219.

Breda, T., & Napp, C. (2019). Girls' comparative advantage in reading can largely explain the gender gap in math-related fields. *PNAS, 116*, 15435–15440.

Breedlove, S. M. (1997). Sex on the brain. *Nature, 389*, 801.

Breedlove, S. M. (2017). Prenatal influences on human sexual orientation: Expectations versus data. *Archives of Sexual Behavior, 46*, 1583–1592.

Breedvelt, J. J. F., Kandola, A., Kousoulis, A. A., Brouwer, M. E., Karyotaki, E., Bockting, C. L. H., & Cuijpers, P. M. W. (2018). What are the effects of preventative interventions on major depressive disorder (MDD) in young adults? A systematic review and meta-analysis of randomized controlled trials. *Journal of Affective Disorders, 239*, 18–29.

Brenan, M. (2019, July 26). *40% of Americans believe in creationism.* Gallup. https://news.gallup.com/poll/261680/americans-believe-creationism.aspx

Brenan, M. (2020, January 29). *Women still handle main household tasks in U.S.* Gallup. https://news.gallup.com/poll/283979/women-handle-main-household-tasks.aspx

Brennan, G. M., & Baskin-Sommers, A. (2020). Aggressive realism: More efficient processing of anger in physically aggressive individuals. *Psychological Science, 31*, 568–581.

Brennan, Z. (2010, April 8). *The Goering who saved Jews: While Hermann masterminded the Final Solution his brother Albert rescued Gestapo victims.* Daily Mail. https://www.dailymail.co.uk/news/article-1264738/The-Goering-saved-Jews-A-new-book-reveals-Hermann-masterminded-Final-Solution-brother-Albert-rescued-Gestapo-victims.html

Brescoll, V. L., & Uhlmann, E. L. (2008). Can an angry woman get ahead? Status conferral, gender, and expression of emotion in the workplace. *Psychological Science, 19*(3), 268–275.

Bresin, K., Mekawi, Y., & Verona, E. (2018). The effect of laboratory manipulations of negative affect on alcohol craving and use: A meta-analysis. *Psychology of Addictive Behaviors, 32*, 617–627.

Breslau, J., Aguilar-Gaxiola, S., Borges, G., Kendler, K. S., Su, M., & Kessler, R. C. (2007). Risk for psychiatric disorder among immigrants and their US-born descendants. *Journal of Nervous and Mental Disease, 195*, 189–195.

Brethel-Haurwitz, K. M., & Marsh, A. A. (2014, March). Geographical differences in subjective well-being predict extraordinary altruism. *Psychological Science, 25*, 762–771.

Brewer, M. B., & Chen, Y.-R. (2007). Where (who) are collectives in collectivism? Toward conceptual clarification of individualism and collectivism. *Psychological Review, 114*, 133–151.

Brewer, W. F. (1977). Memory for the pragmatic implications of sentences. *Memory & Cognition, 5*, 673–678.

Brewin, C. R., & Andrews, B. (2017). Creating memories for false autobiographical events in childhood: A systematic review. *Applied Cognitive Psychology, 31*, 2–23.

Brewin, C. R., Kleiner, J. S., Vasterling, J. J., & Field, A. P. (2007). Memory for emotionally neutral information in posttraumatic stress disorder: A meta-analytic investigation. *Journal of Abnormal Psychology, 116*, 448–463.

Bridgman, T., Cummings, S., & Ballard, J. (2019). Who built Maslow's pyramid? A history of the creation of management studies' most famous symbol and its implications for management education. *Academy of Management Learning & Education, 18*, 81–98.

Briscoe, D. (1997, February 16). Women lawmakers still not in charge. *Grand Rapids Press*, p. A23.

Brislin, R. W. (1988). Increasing awareness of class, ethnicity, culture, and race by expanding on students' own experiences. In I. Cohen (Ed.), *The G. Stanley Hall Lecture Series*. American Psychological Association.

Britton, W. B. (2019). Can mindfulness be too much of a good thing? The value of a middle way. *Current Opinion in Psychology, 28*, 159–165.

Broadbent, E., Kakokehr, A., Booth, R. J., Thomas, J., Windsor, J. A., Buchanan, C. M., Wheeler, B. R., Sammour, T., & Hill, A. G. (2012). A brief relaxation intervention reduces stress and improves surgical wound healing response: A randomized trial. *Brain, Behavior, and Immunity, 26*, 212–217.

Broda, M., Yun, J., Schneider, B., Yeager, D. S., Walton, G. M., & Diemer, M. (2018). Reducing inequality in academic success for incoming college students: A randomized trial of growth mindset and belonging interventions. *Journal of Research on Educational Effectiveness, 11*, 317–338.

Brodbeck, F. C., Chhokar, J. S., & House, R. J. (2008). Culture and leadership in 25 societies: Integration, conclusions, and future directions. In J. S. Chhokar, F. C. Brodbeck, & R. J. House (Eds.), *Culture and leadership across the world: The GLOBE book of in-depth studies of 25 societies* (pp. 1023–1099). Erlbaum.

Brody, G. H., Yu, T., Chen, E., Ehrlich, K. B., & Miller, G. E. (2018). Racial discrimination, body mass index, and insulin resistance: A longitudinal analysis. *Health Psychology, 37*, 1107–1114.

Brody, J. E. (2018, August 13). Quoted in An underappreciated key to college success: Sleep. *The New York Times*. https://www.nytimes.com/2018/08/13/well/an-underappreciated-key-to-college-success-sleep.html

Brody, J. E. (2019, April 29). Virtual reality as therapy for pain. *The New York Times*. https://www.nytimes.com/2019/04/29/well/live/virtual-reality-as-therapy-for-pain.html

Brody, S., & Tillmann, H. C. (2006). The post-orgasmic prolactin increase following intercourse is greater than following masturbation and suggests greater satiety. *Biological Psychology, 71*, 312–315.

Broks, P. (2007, April). The mystery of consciousness. *Prospect*. https://www.prospectmagazine.co.uk/magazine/themysteryofconsciousness

Bronson, J., & Berzofsky, M. (2017). *Indicators of mental health problems reported by prisoners and jail inmates, 2011–12* [PDF file]. U. S. Department of Justice. https://bjs.ojp.gov/content/pub/pdf/imhprpji1112.pdf

Brooks, R. (2012). "Asia's missing women" as a problem in applied evolutionary psychology? *Evolutionary Psychology, 12*, 910–925.

Brooks, R., Singleton, J. L., & Meltzoff, A. N. (2020). Enhanced gaze-following behavior in Deaf infants of Deaf parents. *Developmental Science, 23*(2). doi: 10.1111/desc.12900

Brooks, S. (2015). Does personal social media usage affect efficiency and well-being? *Computers in Human Behavior, 46*, 26–37.

Brookwood, M. (2021). *The orphans of Davenport*. Liveright.

Brose, A., de Roover, K., Ceulemans, E., & Kuppens, P. (2015). Older adults' affective experiences across 100 days are less variable and less complex than younger adults'. *Psychology and Aging, 30*, 194–208.

Brown, A. (2017, November 8). *Republicans, Democrats have starkly different views on transgender issues*. Pew Research Center. https://www.pewresearch.org/fact-tank/2017/11/08/transgender-issues-divide-republicans-and-democrats/

Brown, A. (2019, June 24). *Couples who meet online are more diverse than those who meet in other ways, largely because they're younger*. Pew Research Center. https://pewrsr.ch/34xMQBE

Brown, A. (2020). *Nearly half of U.S. adults say dating has gotten harder for most people in the last 10 years* [PDF file]. Pew Research Center. https://www.pewsocialtrends.org/wp-content/uploads/sites/3/2020/08/PSDT_08.20.20.dating-relationships.final_.pdf

Brown, A. (2022, June 7). *About 5% of young adults in the U.S. say their gender is different from their sex assigned at birth*. Pew Research Center. https://pewrsr.ch/3RMNZfB

Brown, A. S., Begg, M. D., Gravenstein, S., Schaefer, C. A., Wyatt, R. J., Bresnahan, M., Babulas, V. P., & Susser, E. S. (2004). Serologic evidence of prenatal influenza in the etiology of schizophrenia. *Archives of General Psychiatry, 61*, 774–780.

Brown, A. S., & Patterson, P. H. (2011). Maternal infection and schizophrenia: Implications for prevention. *Schizophrenia Bulletin, 37*, 284–290.

Brown, A. S., Schaefer, C. A., Wyatt, R. J., Goetz, R., Begg, M. D., Gorman, J. M., & Susser, E. S. (2000). Maternal exposure to respiratory infections and adult schizophrenia spectrum disorders: A prospective birth cohort study. *Schizophrenia Bulletin, 26*, 287–295.

Brown, E. L., & Deffenbacher, K. (1979). *Perception and the senses*. Oxford University Press.

Brown, J. A. (1958). Some tests of the decay theory of immediate memory. *Quarterly Journal of Experimental Psychology, 10*, 12–21.

Brown, J. R., & Enos, R. D. (2021). The measurement of partisan sorting for 180 million voters. *Nature Human Behaviour, 5*, 998–1008.

Brown, K. W., Goodman, R. J., & Inzlicht, M. (2013). Dispositional mindfulness and the attenuation of neural responses to emotional stimuli. *Social Cognitive and Affective Neuroscience, 8*, 93–99.

Brown, M. I., Wai, J., & Chabris, C. F. (2021). Can you ever be too smart for your own good? Comparing linear and nonlinear effects of cognitive ability on life outcomes. *Perspectives on Psychological Science, 16*(6), 1337–1359.

Brown, R. (1986). Linguistic relativity. In S. H. Hulse & B. F. Green, Jr. (Eds.), *One hundred years of psychological research in America*. Johns Hopkins University Press.

Brown, R., & Kulik, J. (1977). Flashbulb memories. *Cognition, 5*(1), 73–99.

Brown, R. L., LeRoy, A. S., Chen, M. A., Suchting, R., Jaremka, L. M., Liu, J., Heijnen, C., & Fagundes, C. P. (2022). Grief symptoms promote inflammation during acute stress among bereaved spouses. *Psychological Science, 33*(6), 859–873.

Brown, R. P., Imura, M., & Mayeux, L. (2014). Honor and the stigma of mental healthcare. *Personality and Social Psychology Bulletin, 40*, 1119–1131.

Brown, S., Cockett, P., & Yuan, Y. (2019). The neuroscience of Romeo and Juliet: An fMRI study of acting. *Royal Society Open Science, 6*. https://www.researchgate.net/publication/331715646_The_neuroscience_of_Romeo_and_Juliet_An_fMRI_study_of_acting

Brown, S. L., Brown, R. M., House, J. S., & Smith, D. M. (2008). Coping with spousal loss: Potential buffering effects of self-reported helping behavior. *Personality and Social Psychology Bulletin, 34*, 849–861.

Brown, S. L., Stykes, J. B., & Manning, W. D. (2016). Trends in children's family instability, 1995–2010. *Journal of Marriage and Family, 78*, 1173–1183.

Brown, W. A. (2019). *Lithium: A doctor, a drug, and a breakthrough*. Liveright.

Browning, C. (1992). *Ordinary men: Reserve police battalion 101 and the final solution in Poland*. HarperCollins.

Browning, R. (1868). *The ring and the book. IV—Tertium quid*. Thomas Y. Crowell.

Brucato, G., Appelbaum, P., Hesson, H., Shea, E., Dishy, G., Lee, K., Pia, T., Syed, F., Villalobos, A., Wall, M. M., Lieberman, J. A., & Girgis, R. (2021). Psychotic symptoms in mass shootings v. mass murders not involving firearms: Findings from the Columbia mass murder database. *Psychological Medicine*. doi:10.1017/S0033291721000076

Bruce, S. M., & Vargas, C. (2012). Assessment and instruction of object permanence in children with blindness and multiple disabilities. *Journal of Visual Impairment & Blindness, 106*(11), 717–727.

Bruck, M., & Ceci, S. J. (1999). The suggestibility of children's memory. *Annual Review of Psychology, 50*, 419–439.

Bruck, M., & Ceci, S. J. (2004). Forensic developmental psychology: Unveiling four common misconceptions. *Current Directions in Psychological Science, 15*, 229–232.

Brummelman, E., Thomaes, S., Nelemans, S. A., Orobio de Castro, B., Overbeek, G., & Bushman, B. J. (2015). Origins of narcissism in children. *PNAS, 112*, 3659–3662.

Brune, A. (2021). Pandemic nursing stories. Antonia Brune, RN. *Nebraska Nurse, 54*(1), 7.

Bruneau, E., Hameiri, B., Moore-Berg, S. L., & Kteily, N. (2021). Intergroup contact reduces dehumanization and meta-dehumanization: Cross-sectional, longitudinal, and quasi-experimental evidence from 16 samples in five countries. *Personality and Social Psychology Bulletin, 47*(6), 906–920.

Brunet, A., Saumier, D., Liu, A., Streiner, D. L., Tremblay, J., & Pitman, R. K. (2018). Reduction of PTSD symptoms with pre-reactivation propranolol therapy: A randomized controlled trial. *American Journal of Psychiatry, 175*, 427–433.

Bruni, F. (2018, October 30). The internet will be the death of us. *The New York Times*. https://www.nytimes.com/2018/10/30/opinion/internet-violence-hate-prejudice.html

Brunoni, A. R., Chaimani, A., Moffa, A. H., Razza, L. B., Gattaz, W. F., Daskalakis, Z. J., & Carvalho, A. F. (2017). Repetitive transcranial magnetic stimulation for the acute treatment of major depressive episodes: A systematic review with network meta-analysis. *JAMA Psychiatry, 74*, 143–152.

Brush, F. R. (Ed.). (2014). *Aversive conditioning and learning*. Academic Press.

Bryan, A. D., Gillman, A. S., & Hansen, N. S. (2016). Changing the context is important and necessary, but not sufficient, for reducing adolescent risky sexual behavior: A reply to Steinberg (2015). *Perspectives on Psychological Science, 11*, 535–538.

Bryan, A. E. B., & Arkowitz, H. (2015). Meta-analysis of the effects of peer-administered psychosocial interventions on symptoms of depression. *American Journal of Community Psychology, 55*, 455–471.

Bryant, G. A., Fessler, D. M. T., Fusaroli, R., Clint, E., Amir, D., Chávez, B., Denton, K. K., Diaz, C., Duran, L. T., Fanćovićová, J., Fux, M., Ginting, E. F., Hasan, Y., Hu, A., Kamble, S. V., Kameda, T., Kuroda, K., Li, N. P., Luberti, F. R., ... Zhou, Y. (2018). The perception of spontaneous and volitional laughter across 21 societies. *Psychological Science, 29*, 1515–1525.

Bryson, B. (2019). *The body: A guide for occupants* (p. 179). Knopf Doubleday.

Bub, K. L., Robinson, L. E., & Curtis, D. S. (2016). Longitudinal associations between self-regulation and health across childhood and adolescence. *Health Psychology, 35*, 1235–1245.

Buchanan, A., Sint, K., Swanson, J., & Rosenheck, R. (2019). Correlates of future violence in people being treated for schizophrenia. *American Journal of Psychiatry, 176*, 694–701.

Buchanan, R. W., Kreyenbuhl, J., Kelly, D. L., Noel, J. M., Boggs, D. L., Fischer, B. A., Himelhoch, S., Fang, B., Peterson, E., Aquino, P. R., Keller, W., & Schizophrenia Patient Outcomes Research Team (PORT). (2010). The 2009 schizophrenia PORT psychopharmacological treatment recommendations and summary statements. *Schizophrenia Bulletin, 36*, 71–93.

Buchanan, T. W. (2007). Retrieval of emotional memories. *Psychological Bulletin, 133*, 761–779.

Buck, L. B., & Axel, R. (1991). A novel multigene family may encode odorant receptors: A molecular basis for odor recognition. *Cell, 65*, 175–187.

Buckell, J., & Sindelar, J. L. (2019). The impact of flavors, health risks, secondhand smoke and prices on young adults' cigarette and e-cigarette choices: A discrete choice experiment. *Addiction, 114*, 1427–1435.

Buckels, E. E., Trapnell, P. D., & Paulhus, D. L. (2014). Trolls just want to have fun. *Personality and Individual Differences, 67*, 97–102.

Buckholtz, J. W., Treadway, M. T., Cowan, R. L., Woodward, N. D., Benning, S. D., Li, R., Ansari, M. S., Baldwin, R. M., Schwartzman, A. N., Shelby, E. S., Smith, C. E., Cole, D., Kessler, R. M., & Zald, D. H. (2010). Mesolimbic dopamine reward system hypersensitivity in individuals with psychopathic traits. *Nature Neuroscience, 13*, 419–421.

Buckingham, M. (2007). *Go put your strengths to work: 6 powerful steps to achieve outstanding performance*. Free Press.

Buckingham, M., & Clifton, D. O. (2001). *Now, discover your strengths*. Free Press.

Buckner, J. D., Walukevich Dienst, K., & Zvolensky, M. J. (2019). Distress tolerance and cannabis craving: The impact of laboratory-induced distress. *Experimental and Clinical Psychopharmacology, 27*, 38–44.

Buecker, S., Simacek, T., Ingwersen, B., Terwiel, S., & Simonsmeier, B. A. (2020). Physical activity and subjective well-being in healthy individuals: A meta-analytic review. *Health Psychology Review*. https://www.researchgate.net/publication/340741946_Physical_Activity_and_Subjective_Well-Being_in_Healthy_Individuals_A_Meta-Analytic_Review

Buehler, R., Griffin, D., & Ross, M. (1994). Exploring the "planning fallacy": Why people underestimate their task completion times. *Journal of Personality and Social Psychology, 67*, 366–381.

Buehler, R., Griffin, D., & Ross, M. (2002). Inside the planning fallacy: The causes and consequences of optimistic time predictions. In T. Gilovich, D. Griffin, & D. Kahneman (Eds.), *Heuristics and biases: The psychology of intuitive judgment* (pp. 250–270). Cambridge University Press.

Buffardi, L. E., & Campbell, W. K. (2008). Narcissism and social networking web sites. *Personality and Social Psychology Bulletin, 34*, 1303–1314.

Buffett, W. (2006). Quoted by B. Obama in, *The audacity of hope: Thoughts on reclaiming the American dream*. Penguin.

Buhle, J. T., Stevens, B. L., Friedman, J. J., & Wager, T. D. (2012). Distraction and placebo: Two separate routes to pain control. *Psychological Science, 23*, 246–253.

Buka, S. L., Tsuang, M. T., Torrey, E. F., Klebanoff, M. A., Wagner, R. L., & Yolken, R. H. (2001). Maternal infections and subsequent psychosis among offspring. *Archives of General Psychiatry, 58*, 1032–1037.

Bunde, J., & Suls, J. (2006). A quantitative analysis of the relationship between the Cook-Medley Hostility Scale and traditional coronary artery disease risk factors. *Health Psychology, 25*, 493–500.

Buquet, R. (1988). Le reve et les deficients visuels [Dreams and the visually impaired]. *Psychanalyse-a-l'Universite, 13*, 319–327.

Burelli, J. (2008). *Thirty-three years of women in S&E faculty positions* (Publication No. NSF 08-308). National Science Foundation. wayback.archive-it.org/5902/20160210152800/http://www.nsf.gov/statistics/infbrief/nsf08308/

Burger, J. M. (2009). Replicating Milgram: Would people still obey today? *American Psychologist, 64*, 1–11.

Burger, J. M., Bender, T. J., Day, L., DeBolt, J. A., Guthridge, L., How, H. W., Meyer, M., Russell, K. A., & Taylor, S. (2015). The power of one: The relative influence of helpful and selfish models. *Social Influence, 10*, 77–84.

Bürgin, D., Varghese, N., Eckert, A., Clemens, V., Unternährer, E., Boonmann, C., O'Donovan, A., & Schmid, M. (2022). Higher hair cortisol concentrations associated with shorter leukocyte telomere length in high-risk young adults. *Scientific Reports, 12*. https://www.nature.com/articles/s41598-022-14905-4

Burgoyne, A. P., Hambrick, D. Z., & Macnamara, B. N. (2020). How firm are the foundations of mind-set theory? The claims appear stronger than the evidence. *Psychological Science, 31*(3), 258–267.

Buri, J. R., Louiselle, P. A., Misukanis, T. M., & Mueller, R. A. (1988). Effects of parental authoritarianism and authoritativeness on self-esteem. *Personality and Social Psychology Bulletin, 14*, 271–282.

Burish, T. G., & Carey, M. P. (1986). Conditioned aversive responses in cancer chemotherapy patients: Theoretical and developmental analysis. *Journal of Counseling and Clinical Psychology, 54*, 593–600.

Burk, W. J., Denissen, J., Van Doorn, M. D., Branje, S. J. T., & Laursen, B. (2009). The vicissitudes of conflict measurement: Stability and reliability in the frequency of disagreements. *European Psychologist, 14*, 153–159.

Burke, B. L., Martens, A., & Faucher, E. H. (2010). Two decades of terror management theory: A meta-analysis of mortality salience research. *Personality and Social Psychology Review, 14*, 155–195.

Burke, D. M., & Shafto, M. A. (2004). Aging and language production. *Current Directions in Psychological Science, 13*, 21–24.

Burlingame, G. M., Seebeck, J. D., Janis, R. A., Whitcomb, K. E., Barkowski, S., Rosendahl, J., & Strauss, B. (2016). Outcome differences between individual and group formats when identical and nonidentical treatments, patients, and doses are compared: A 25-year meta-analytic perspective. *Psychotherapy, 53*, 446–461.

Burnay, J., Kepes, S., & Bushman, B. J. (2022). Effects of violent and nonviolent sexualized media on aggression-related thoughts, feelings, attitudes, and behaviors: A meta-analytic review. *Aggressive Behavior, 48*(1), 111–136.

Burns, D. D. (1981). *Feeling good*. Signet Book.

Burns, S. M., Barnes, L. N., McCulloh, I. A., Dagher, M. M., Falk, E. B., Storey, J. D., & Lieberman, M. D. (2019). Making social neuroscience less WEIRD: Using fNIRS to measure neural signatures of persuasive influence in a Middle East participant sample. *Journal of Personality and Social Psychology, 116*, e1–e11.

Burris, J. L., Oleas, D., Reider, L., Buss, K. A., Pérez-Edgar, K., & LoBue, V. (2019). Biased attention to threat: Answering old questions with young infants. *Current Directions in Psychological Science, 28*(6), 534–539.

Burrow, A. L., Hill, P. L., & Sumner, R. (2016). Leveling mountains: Purpose attenuates links between perceptions of effort and steepness. *Personality and Social Psychology Bulletin, 42*, 94–103.

Burton, C. M., & King, L. A. (2008). Effects of (very) brief writing on health: The two-minute miracle. *British Journal of Health Psychology, 13*, 9–14.

Busby, D. M., Carroll, J. S., & Willoughby, B. J. (2010). Compatibility or restraint? The effects of sexual timing on marriage relationships. *Journal of Family Psychology, 24*, 766–774.

Bushdid, C., Magnasco, M. O., Vosshall, L. B., & Keller, A. (2014). Humans can discriminate more than 1 trillion olfactory stimuli. *Science, 343*, 1370–1372.

Bushman, B. J. (1993). Human aggression while under the influence of alcohol and other drugs: An integrative research review. *Current Directions in Psychological Science, 2*, 148–152.

Bushman, B. J. (2002). Does venting anger feed or extinguish the flame? Catharsis, rumination, distraction, anger, and aggressive responding. *Personality and Social Psychology Bulletin, 28*, 724–731.

Bushman, B. J. (2016). Violent media and hostile appraisals: A meta-analytic review. *Aggressive Behavior, 42*, 605–613.

Bushman, B. J. (2018). Teaching students about violent media effects. *Teaching of Psychological Science, 45*, 200–206.

Bushman, B. J., & Anderson, C. A. (2009). Comfortably numb: Desensitizing effects of violent media on helping others. *Psychological Science, 20*, 273–277.

Bushman, B. J., & Baumeister, R. F. (1998). Threatened egotism, narcissism, self-esteem, and direct and displaced aggression: Does self-love or self-hate lead to violence? *Journal of Personality and Social Psychology, 75*, 219–229.

Bushman, B. J., Baumeister, R. F., Thomaes, S., Ryu, E., Begeer, S., & West, S. G. (2009). Looking again, and harder, for a link between low self-esteem and aggression. *Journal of Personality, 77*, 427–446.

Bushman, B. J., DeWall, C. N., Pond, R. S., Jr., & Hanus, M. D. (2014). Low glucose relates to greater aggression in married couples. *PNAS, 111*, 6254–6257.

Bushman, B. J., & Huesmann, L. R. (2010). Aggression. In S. T. Fiske, D. T. Gilbert, & G. Lindzey (Eds.), *Handbook of social psychology* (5th ed., pp. 833–863). John Wiley & Sons.

Bushman, B. J., Moeller, S. J., & Crocker, J. (2011). Sweets, sex, or self-esteem? Comparing the value of self-esteem boosts with other pleasant rewards. *Journal of Personality, 79*, 993–1012.

Bushman, B. J., Ridge, R. D., Das, E., Key, C. W., & Busath, G. L. (2007). When God sanctions killing: Effects of scriptural violence on aggression. *Psychological Science, 18*, 204–207.

Buss, A. H. (1989). Personality as traits. *American Psychologist, 44*, 1378–1388.

Buss, D. M. (1991). Evolutionary personality psychology. *Annual Review of Psychology, 42*, 459–491.

Buss, D. M. (2008). *Female sexual psychology*. Edge. https://www.edge.org/response-detail/10356

Buss, D. M. (2021). *When men behave badly: The hidden roots of sexual deception, harassment, and assault*. Little, Brown Spark.

Buss, D. M., & Schmitt, D. P. (2019). Mate preferences and their behavioral manifestations. *Annual Review of Psychology, 70*, 77–110.

Buss, D. M., & von Hippel, W. (2018). Psychological barriers to evolutionary psychology: Ideological bias and coalitional adaptations. *Archives of Scientific Psychology*, 6, 148–158.

Buster, J. E., Kingsberg, S. A., Aguirre, O., Brown, C., Breaux, J. G., Buch, A., Rodenberg, C. A., Wekselman, K., & Casson, P. (2005). Testosterone patch for low sexual desire in surgically menopausal women: A randomized trial. *Obstetrics and Gynecology*, 105, 944–952.

Bustos, V. P., Bustos, S. S., Mascaro, A., Del Corral, G., Forte, A. J., Ciudad, P., Kim, E. A., Langstein, H. N., & Manrique, O. J. (2021). Regret after gender-affirmation surgery: A systematic review and meta-analysis of prevalence. *Plastic and Reconstructive Surgery. Global Open*, 9(3). https://journals.lww.com/prsgo/Fulltext/2022/04000/Regret_after_Gender_affirmation_Surgery_A.63.aspx

Butler, J. D. (2017). The complex intersection of education and therapy in the drama therapy classroom. *The Arts in Psychotherapy, 53*, 28–35.

Butler, R. A. (1954, February). Curiosity in monkeys. *Scientific American*, pp. 70–75.

Butterfield, R. D., Silk, J. S., Lee, K. H., Siegle, G. S., Dahl, R. E., Forbes, E. E., Ryan, N. D., Hooley, J. M., & Ladouceur, C. D. (2021). Parents still matter! Parental warmth predicts adolescent brain function and anxiety and depressive symptoms 2 years later. *Development and Psychopathology, 33*(1), 226–239.

Butterworth, G. (1992). Origins of self-perception in infancy. *Psychological Inquiry*, 3, 103–111.

Buttrick, N., Choi, H., Wilson, T. D., Oishi, S., Boker, S. M., Gilbert, D. T., Alper, S., Aveyard, M., Cheong, W., Čolić, M. V., Dalgar, I., Doğulu, C., Karabati, S., Kim, E., Knežević, G., Komiya, A., Laclé, C. O., Ambrosio Lage, C., Lazarević, L. B., … Wilks, D. C. (2019). Cross-cultural consistency and relativity in the enjoyment of thinking versus doing. *Journal of Personality and Social Psychology*, 117(5), e71–e83.

Buttrick, N., & Oishi, S. (2021). The cultural dynamics of declining residential mobility. *American Psychologist, 76*, 904–916.

Butts, M. M., Casper, W. J., & Yang, T. S. (2013). How important are work-family support policies? A meta-analytic investigation of their effects on employee outcomes. *Journal of Applied Psychology, 98*, 1–25.

Byers-Heinlein, K., Burns, T. C., & Werker, J. F. (2010). The roots of bilingualism in newborns. *Psychological Science, 21*, 343–348.

Byrc, K., Durand, E. Y., Macpherson, J. M., Reich, D., & Mountain, J. L. (2015). The genetic ancestry of African Americans, Latinos, and European Americans across the United States. *American Journal of Human Genetics, 96*, 37–53.

Byrd, A. L., & Manuck, S. B. (2014). MAOA, childhood maltreatment, and antisocial behavior: Meta-analysis of a gene-environment interaction. *Biological Psychiatry, 75*, 9–17.

Byrd, A. L., Manuck, S. B., Hawes, S. W., Vebares, T. J., Nimgaonkar, V., Chowdari, K. V., Hipwell, A. E., Keenan, K., & Stepp, S. D. (2019). The interaction between monoamine oxidase A (MAOA) and childhood maltreatment as a predictor of personality pathology in females: Emotional reactivity as a potential mediating mechanism. *Development and Psychopathology, 31*, 361–377.

Byrne, D. (1971). *The attraction paradigm*. Academic Press.

Byrne, D. (1982). Predicting human sexual behavior. In A. G. Kraut (Ed.), *The G. Stanley Hall lecture series* (Vol. 2, pp. 211–254). American Psychological Association.

Byrne, R. W. (1991, May/June). Brute intellect. *The Sciences*, pp. 42–47.

Byrne, R. W., Bates, L. A., & Moss, C. J. (2009). Elephant cognition in primate perspective. *Comparative Cognition & Behavior Reviews, 4*, 1–15.

Byron, K., & Khazanchi, S. (2011). A meta-analytic investigation of the relationship of state and trait anxiety to performance on figural and verbal creative tasks. *Personality and Social Psychology Bulletin, 37*, 269–283.

Byrow, Y., Pajak, R., Specker, P., & Nickerson, A. (2020). Perceptions of mental health and perceived barriers to mental health help-seeking amongst refugees: A systematic review. *Clinical Psychology Review, 75*. https://www.sciencedirect.com/science/article/abs/pii/S0272735819303241

Cable, D. M., & Gilovich, T. (1998). Looked over or overlooked? Prescreening decisions and post-interview evaluations. *Journal of Personality and Social Psychology, 83*, 501–508.

Cacciatore, J., & Francis, A. (2022). DSM-5-TR turns normal grief into a mental disorder. *The Lancet, 9*, e32.

Cacioppo, J. T., Cacioppo, S., Capitanio, J. P., & Cole, S. W. (2015). The neuroendocrinology of social isolation. *Annual Review of Psychology, 66*, 733–767.

Cacioppo, J. T., Cacioppo, S., Gonzaga, G. C., Ogburn, E. L., & VanderWeele, T. J. (2013). Marital satisfaction and break-ups differ across on-line and off-line meeting venues. *PNAS, 110*, 10135–10140.

Cacioppo, S., Bianchi-Demicheli, F., Frum, C., Pfaus, J. G., & Lewis, J. W. (2012). The common neural bases between sexual desire and love: A multilevel kernel density fMRI analysis. *Journal of Sexual Medicine, 12*, 1048–1054.

Cacioppo, S., Capitanio, J. P., & Cacioppo, J. T. (2014). Toward a neurology of loneliness. *Psychological Bulletin, 140*, 1464–1504.

Cadar, D., Robitaille, A., Pattie, A., Deary, I. J., & Muniz-Terrera, G. (2020). The long arm of childhood intelligence on terminal decline: Evidence from the Lothian Birth Cohort 1921. *Psychology and Aging*, 35(6), 806–817.

Caemmerer, J. M., Keith, T. Z., & Reynolds, M. R. (2020). Beyond individual intelligence tests: Application of Cattell-Horn-Carroll theory.

Intelligence, 79. https://doi.org/10.1016/j.intell.2020.101433

Cain, S. (2012). *Quiet: The power of introverts in a world that can't stop talking*. Crown.

Caldwell, J. A. (2012). Crew schedules, sleep deprivation, and aviation performance. *Current Directions in Psychological Science, 21*, 85–89.

Cale, E. M., & Lilienfeld, S. O. (2002). Sex differences in psychopathy and antisocial personality disorder: A review and integration. *Clinical Psychology Review, 22*, 1179–1207.

Callaghan, T., Rochat, P., Lillard, A., Claux, M. L., Odden, H., Itakura, S., Tapanya, S., & Singh, S. (2005). Synchrony in the onset of mental-state reasoning. *Psychological Science, 16*, 378–384.

Callan, M. J., Shead, N. W., & Olson, J. M. (2011). Personal relative deprivation, delay discounting, and gambling. *Journal of Personality and Social Psychology, 101*, 955–973.

Calvan, B., & Melley, B. (2022, October 10). 'Nothing's left': Hurricane Ian leaves emotional toll behind. *Los Angeles Times*. https://www.latimes.com/world-nation/story/2022-10-10/hurricane-ian-leaves-emotional-toll-behind

Calvert, S. L., Appelbaum, M., Dodge, K. A., Graham, S., Nagayama Hall, G. C., Hamby, S., Fasig-Caldwell, L. G., Citkowicz, M., Galloway, D. P., & Hedges, L. V. (2017). The American Psychological Association Task Force assessment of violent video games: Science in the service of public interest. *American Psychologist, 72*, 126–143.

Calvo-Merino, B., Glaser, D. E., Grèzes, J., Passingham, R. E., & Haggard, P. (2004). Action observation and acquired motor skills: An fMRI study with expert dancers. *Cerebral Cortex, 15*, 1243–1249.

Calzo, J. P., Mays, V. M., Björkenstam, C., Björkenstam, E., Kosidou, K., & Cochran, S. D. (2019). Parental sexual orientation and children's psychological well-being: 2013–2015 National Health Interview Survey. *Child Development, 90*, 1097–1108.

Camerer, C. F., Loewenstein, G., & Weber, M. (1989). The curse of knowledge in economic settings: An experimental analysis. *Journal of Political Economy, 97*, 1232–1254.

Cameron, J. J., & Granger, S. (2019). Does self-esteem have an interpersonal imprint beyond self-reports? A meta-analysis of self-esteem and objective interpersonal indicators. *Personality and Social Psychology Review, 23*, 73–102.

Cameron, L. D., & Overall, N. C. (2018). Suppression and expression as distinct emotion-regulation processes in daily interactions: Longitudinal and meta-analyses. *Emotion, 18*, 465–480.

Camp, J. P., Skeem, J. L., Barchard, K., Lilienfeld, S. O., & Poythress, N. G. (2013). Psychopathic predators? Getting specific about the relation between psychopathy and violence. *Journal of Consulting and Clinical Psychology, 81*, 467–480.

Campbell, D. T., & Specht, J. C. (1985). Altruism: Biology, culture, and religion. *Journal of Social and Clinical Psychology, 3*, 33–42.

Campbell, L., & Marshall, T. (2011). Anxious attachment and relationship processes: An interactionist perspective. *Journal of Personality, 79*, 1219–1249.

Campbell, M. W., & de Waal, F. B. M. (2011). Ingroup-outgroup bias in contagious yawning by chimpanzees supports link to empathy. *PLOS ONE, 6*. https://tinyurl.com/jnz3jmr2

Campbell, S. (1986). *The Loch Ness Monster: The evidence*. Aquarian Press.

Camperio-Ciani, A., Corna, F., & Capiluppi, C. (2004). Evidence for maternally inherited factors favouring male homosexuality and promoting female fecundity. *Proceedings of the Royal Society of London B, 271*, 2217–2221.

Camperio-Ciani, A., Lemmola, F., & Blecher, S. R. (2009). Genetic factors increase fecundity in female maternal relatives of bisexual men as in homosexuals. *Journal of Sexual Medicine, 6*, 449–455.

Camperio-Ciani, A., & Pellizzari, E. (2012). Fecundity of paternal and maternal non-parental female relatives of homosexual and heterosexual men. *PLOS ONE, 7*. https://www.ncbi.nlm.nih.gov/pmc/articles/PMC3515521/

Campitelli, G., & Gobet, F. (2011). Deliberate practice: Necessary but not sufficient. *Current Directions in Psychological Science, 20*, 280–285.

Campos, B., Schoebi, D., Gonzaga, G. C., Gable, S. L., & Keltner, D. (2015). Attuned to the positive? Awareness and responsiveness to others' positive emotion experience and display. *Motivation and Emotion, 39*, 780–794.

Campos, J. J., Bertenthal, B. I., & Kermoian, R. (1992). Early experience and emotional development: The emergence of wariness of heights. *Psychological Science, 3*, 61–64.

Canadian Press. (2018, March 14). *Calgary researchers develop tool to literally shine light on concussions*. https://www.cbc.ca/news/canada/calgary/calgary-university-concussions-brain-imaging-research-dunn-1.4575645

Canavello, A., & Crocker, J. (2017). Compassionate goals and affect in social situations. *Motivation and Emotion, 41*, 158–179.

Canetta, S., Sourander, A., Surcel, H., Hinkka-Yli-Salomäki, S., Leiviskä, J., Kellendonk, C., McKeague, I. W., & Brown, A. S. (2014). Elevated maternal C-reactive protein and increased risk of schizophrenia in a national birth cohort. *American Journal of Psychiatry, 171*, 960–968.

Canivet, C., Bolduc, R., & Godbout, N. (2022). Exploring variations in individuals' relationships to sexual fantasies: A latent class analysis. *Archives of Sexual Behavior, 51*, 589–600.

Canning, E. A., Murphy, M. C., & Emerson, K. T. U., Chatman, J. A., Dweck, C. S., & Kray, L. J. (2020). Cultures of genius at work: Organizational mindsets predict cultural norms, trust, and commitment. *Personality and Social Psychology Bulletin, 46*(4), 626–642.

Cannon, W. B. (1929). *Bodily changes in pain, hunger, fear, and rage*. Branford.

Cannon, W. B., & Washburn, A. L. (1912). An explanation of hunger. *American Journal of Physiology, 29*, 441–454.

Cantor, N., & Kihlstrom, J. F. (1987). *Personality and social intelligence*. Prentice-Hall.

Caplan, N., Choy, M. H., & Whitmore, J. K. (1992, February). Indochinese refugee families and academic achievement. *Scientific American*, pp. 36–42.

Caprariello, P. A., & Reis, H. T. (2013). To do, to have, or to share? Valuing experiences over material possessions depends on the involvement of others. *Journal of Personality and Social Psychology, 104*, 199–215.

Capraro, V., Jagfeld, G., Klein, R., Mul, M., & van de Pol, I. (2019). Increasing altruistic and cooperative behaviour with simple moral nudges. *Scientific Reports, 9*, 1–11.

Cardeña, E. (2018). The experimental evidence for parapsychological phenomena: A review. *American Psychologist, 73*, 663–677.

Carey, B. (2009, November 27). Surgery for mental ills offers both hope and risk. *The New York Times*. https://www.nytimes.com/2009/11/27/health/research/27brain.html

Carey, B. (2010). Seeking emotional clues without facial cues. *The New York Times*. https://www.nytimes.com/2010/04/06/health/06mind.html

Carey, B. (2011, February 14). Wariness on surgery of the mind. *The New York Times*. https://www.nytimes.com/2011/02/15/health/15brain.html

Carey, B. (2019). Brain stimulation shows promise in treating severe depression. *The New York Times*. https://www.nytimes.com/2019/10/04/health/deep-brain-stimulation-depression.html

Carey, G. (1990). Genes, fears, phobias, and phobic disorders. *Journal of Counseling and Development, 68*, 628–632.

Carey, I. M., Shah, S. M., DeWilde, S., Harris, T., Victor, C. R., & Cook, D. G. (2014). Increased risk of acute cardiovascular events after partner bereavement: A matched cohort study. *JAMA Internal Medicine, 174*, 598–605.

Carhart-Harris, R., Giribaldi, B., Watts, R., Baker-Jones, M., Murphy-Beiner, A., Murphy, R., Martell, J., Blemings, A., Erritzoe, D., & Nutt, D. J. (2021). Trial of psilocybin versus escitalopram for depression. *New England Journal of Medicine, 384*, 1402–1411.

Carhart-Harris, R. L., Muthukumaraswamy, S., Roseman, L., Kaelen, M., Droog, W., Murphy, K., Tagliazucchi, E., Schenberg, E. E., Nest, T., Orban, C., Leech, R., Williams, L. T., Williams, T. M., Bolstridge, M., Sessa, B., McGonigle, J., Sereno, M. I., Nichols, D., Hellyer, P. J., ... Nutt, D. J. (2016). Neural correlates of the LSD experience revealed by multimodal neuroimaging. *PNAS, 113*, 4853–4858.

Carli, L. L., & Leonard, J. B. (1989). The effect of hindsight on victim derogation. *Journal of Social and Clinical Psychology, 8*, 331–343.

Carlisi, C. O., Moffitt, T. E., Knodt, A. R., Harrington, H., Ireland, D., Melzer, T. R., Poulton, R., Ramrakha, S., Caspi, A., Hariri, A. R., & Viding, E. (2020). Associations between life-course-persistent antisocial behaviour and brain structure in a population-representative longitudinal birth cohort. *Lancet Psychiatry, 7*, 245–253.

Carmeli, A., Ben-Hador, B., Waldman, D. A., & Rupp, D. E. (2009). How leaders cultivate social capital and nurture employee vigor: Implications for job performance. *Journal of Applied Psychology, 94*, 1553–1561.

Carmi, L., Tendler, A., Bystritsky, A., Hollander, E., Blumberger, D. M., Daskalakis, J., Ward, H., Lapidus, K., Goodman, W., Casuto, L., Feifel, D., Barnea-Ygael, N., Roth, Y., Zangen, A., & Zohar, J. (2019). Efficacy and safety of deep transcranial magnetic stimulation for obsessive-compulsive disorder: A prospective multicenter randomized double-blind place-controlled trial. *American Journal of Psychiatry, 176*, 931–938.

Carney, D. R., Cuddy, A. J. C., & Yap, A. J. (2015). Review and summary of research on the embodied effects of expansive (vs. contractive) nonverbal displays. *Psychological Science, 26*, 657–663.

Carpenter, S. (2001, February). Rediscovered data confirm link between early intellect and dementia. *APA Monitor, 32*(2), 46.

Carpusor, A., & Loges, W. E. (2006). Rental discrimination and ethnicity in names. *Journal of Applied Social Psychology, 36*, 934–952.

Carr, E. W., Brady, T. F., & Winkielman, P. (2017). Are you smiling, or have I seen you before? Familiarity makes faces look happier. *Psychological Science, 28*, 1087–1102.

Carragan, R. C., & Dweck, C. S. (2014). Rethinking natural altruism: Simple reciprocal interactions trigger children's benevolence. *PNAS, 111*, 17071–17074.

Carroll, D., Davey Smith, G., & Bennett, P. (1994, March). Health and socioeconomic status. *The Psychologist*, pp. 122–125.

Carroll, H. (2013, October). *Teen fashion model Georgina got so thin her organs were failing. But fashion designers still queued up to book her. Now she's telling her story to shame the whole industry.* The Daily Mail. https://www.dailymail.co.uk/femail/article-2442084/Anorexic-model-Georgina-Wilkin-organs-failing-designers-booked-her.html

Carroll, J. B. (1993). *Human cognitive abilities: A survey of factor-analytic studies.* Cambridge University Press.

Carroll, J. M., & Russell, J. A. (1996). Do facial expressions signal specific emotions? Judging emotion from the face in context. *Journal of Personality and Social Psychology, 70*, 205–218.

Carroll, P., Sweeny, K., & Shepperd, J. A. (2006). Forsaking optimism. *Review of General Psychology, 10*, 56–73.

Carstensen, L. L. (2011). *A long bright future: Happiness, health and financial security in an age of increased longevity.* PublicAffairs.

Carstensen, L. L., & Mikels, J. A. (2005). At the intersection of emotion and cognition: Aging and the positivity effect. *Current Directions in Psychological Science, 14*, 117–121.

Carstensen, L. L., Turan, B., Scheibe, S., Ram, N., Ersner-Hershfield, Samanez-Larkin, G. R., Brooks, K. P., & Nesselroade, J. R. (2011). Emotional experience improves with age: Evidence based on over 10 years of experience sampling. *Psychology and Aging, 26*(1), 21–33.

Carvalho, A. C., & Rodrigues, D. L. (2022). Sexuality, sexual behavior, and relationships of asexual individuals: Differences between aromantic and romantic orientation. *Archives of Sexual Behavior, 51*, 2159–2168.

Carver, C. S., Johnson, S. L., & Joormann, J. (2008). Serotonergic function, two-mode models of self-regulation, and vulnerability to depression: What depression has in common with impulsive aggression. *Psychological Bulletin, 134*, 912–943.

CASA (National Center on Addiction and Substance Use). (2003). *The formative years: Pathways to substance abuse among girls and young women ages 8–22.* Columbia University.

Casale, S., & Banchi, V. (2020). Narcissism and problematic social media use: A systematic literature review. *Addictive Behaviors Reports, 11*. https://www.sciencedirect.com/science/article/pii/S2352853219302391

Case, A., & Deaton, A. (2020). *Deaths of despair.* Princeton University Press.

Casetta, G., Nolfo, A. P., & Palagi, E. (2021). Yawn contagion promotes motor synchrony in wild lions, *Panthera leo. Animal Behaviour, 174*, 149–159.

Casey, B. J. (2015). Beyond simple models of self-control to circuit-based accounts of adolescent behavior. *Annual Review of Psychology, 66*(1), 295–319.

Caspi, A., Houts, R. M., Belsky, D. W., Harrington, H., Hogan, S., Ramrakha, S., Poulton, R., & Moffitt, T. E. (2016). Childhood forecasting of a small segment of the population with large economic burden. *Nature Human Behavior, 1*. https://www.ncbi.nlm.nih.gov/pmc/articles/PMC5505663/

Caspi, A., McClay, J., Moffitt, T., Mill, J., Martin, J., Craig, I. W., Taylor, A., & Poulton, R. (2002). Role of genotype in the cycle of violence in maltreated children. *Science, 297*, 851–854.

Caspi, A., Moffitt, T. E., Newman, D. L., & Silva, P. A. (1996). Behavioral observations at age 3 years predict adult psychiatric disorders: Longitudinal evidence from a birth cohort. *Archives of General Psychiatry, 53*, 1033–1039.

Cassels, M., Neufeld, S., van Harmelen, A.-L., Goodyer, I., & Wilkinson, P. (2020). Prospective pathways from impulsivity to non-suicidal self-injury among youth. *Archives of Suicide Research, 26*(2), 534–547.

Castelbaum, L., Sylvester, C. M., Zhang, Y., Yu, Q., & Constantino, J. N. (2020). On the nature of monozygotic twin concordance and discordance for autistic trait severity: A quantitative analysis. *Behavior Genetics, 50*, 263–272.

Catalan-Matamoros, D., Gomez-Conesa, A., Stubbs, B., & Vancampfort, D. (2016). Exercise improves depressive symptoms in older adults: An umbrella review of systematic reviews and meta-analyses. *Psychiatry Research, 244*, 202–209.

Catapano, R., Tormala, Z. L., & Rucker, D. D. (2019). Perspective taking and self-persuasion: Why "putting yourself in their shoes" reduces openness to attitude change. *Psychological Science, 30*, 424–435.

CATO Institute. (2017). *Criminal immigrants: Their numbers, demographics, and countries of origin.* https://www.cato.org/publications/immigration-reform-bulletin/criminal-immigrants-their-numbers-demographics-countries

Cattell, R. B. (1963). Theory of fluid and crystallized intelligence: A critical experiment. *Journal of Educational Psychology, 54*, 1–22.

Cavalli-Sforza, L., Menozzi, P., & Piazza, A. (1994). *The history and geography of human genes.* Princeton University Press.

Cavna, M. (2022). 'Lightyear' same-sex couple is part of an evolution at Pixar. *The Washington Post*. https://www.washingtonpost.com/comics/2022/06/17/lightyear-same-sex-couple-kiss/

Cawley, B. D., Keeping, L. M., & Levy, P. E. (1998). Participation in the performance appraisal process and employee reactions: A meta-analytic review of field investigations. *Journal of Applied Psychology, 83*, 615–633.

CBC (Canadian Broadcasting Corporation). (2019, August 15). *Men twice as likely to consume cannabis as women, StatsCan survey suggests.* https://www.cbc.ca/news/business/cannabis-statscan-data-1.5248307

CBS (CBS Broadcasting Inc.). (2021, July 19). *Biden nets positive marks for handling pandemic, but vaccine resistance, Delta concern remains—CBS News poll.* https://www.cbsnews.com/news/biden-pandemic-approval-covid-19-opinion-poll/

CCSA (Canadian Centre on Substance Use and Addiction). (2017, August). *Canadian drug use summary: Cannabis* [PDF file]. https://www.cpha.ca/sites/default/files/uploads/resources/cannabis/ccsa-canadian-drug-summary-cannabis-2017-en.pdf

CDC (Center for Disease Control and Prevention). (2013). *Tobacco-related mortality.* https://www.cdc.gov/tobacco/data_statistics/fact_sheets/health_effects/tobacco_related_mortality/index.htm

CDC. (2014, December). *Depression in the U.S. household population, 2009–2012.* NCHS Data Brief No. 172.

CDC. (2018). *Distracted driving* [PDF file]. https://www.cdc.gov/motorvehiclesafety/pdf/Distracted-Driving-Summary-Sheet-508.pdf

CDC. (2018). *What you need to know about marijuana use and pregnancy.* https://www.cdc.gov/marijuana/factsheets/pregnancy.htm

CDC. (2019). *Attention-deficit/hyperactivity disorder (ADHD).* https://www.cdc.gov/ncbddd/adhd/data.html

CDC. (2019). *Did not get 8 or more hours of sleep.* High School Youth Risk Behavior Survey, 2017. https://tinyurl.com/s2ck2zs

CDC. (2019). *Increase in measles cases—United States, January 1–April 26, 2019.* https://www.cdc.gov/mmwr/volumes/68/wr/mm6817e1.htm

CDC. (2019). STDs in adolescents and young adults [PDF file]. In *Sexually transmitted disease surveillance 2018.* https://www.cdc.gov/std/stats18/STDSurveillance2018-full-report.pdf

CDC. (2019). *Suicide and self-harm injury.* https://www.cdc.gov/nchs/fastats/suicide.htm

CDC. (2020, May 29). *Schools start too early.* https://www.cdc.gov/sleep/features/schools-start-too-early.html

CDC. (2020). *COVID-19 hospitalization and death by race/ethnicity.* https://www.cdc.gov/coronavirus/2019-ncov/covid-data/investigations-discovery/hospitalization-death-by-race-ethnicity.html

CDC. (2020). *Diagnoses of HIV infection in the United States and dependent areas, 2018. Risk by gender.* https://www.cdc.gov/hiv/library/reports/hiv-surveillance/vol-31/content/diagnoses.html#gender

CDC. (2020). *Fast facts: Smoking and tobacco use.* https://www.cdc.gov/tobacco/data_statistics/fact_sheets/fast_facts/index.htm

CDC. (2020). *Mental health, substance use, and suicidal ideation during the COVID-19 pandemic—United States, June 24–30, 2020.* https://www.cdc.gov/mmwr/volumes/69/wr/mm6932a1.htm

CDC. (2020). *Prevalence of autism spectrum disorder among children aged 8 years—Autism *and Developmental Disabilities Monitoring Network, 11 sites, United States, 2016*. https://www.cdc.gov/mmwr/volumes/69/ss/ss6904a1.htm?s_cid=ss6904a1_w

CDC. (2020). Trends in violence victimization and suicide risk by sexual identity among high school students. Your Risk Behavior Survey, United States, 2015–2019. *Morbidity and Mortality Weekly Report*, 69(supp 1), 19–27.

CDC. (2020). *Youth Risk Behavior Surveillance System* (YRBSS). www.cdc.gov/healthyyouth/data/yrbs/index.htm

CDC. (2021). *Weekly updates by select demographic and geographic characteristics. Provisional death counts for coronavirus disease 2019 (COVID-19)*. https://www.cdc.gov/nchs/nvss/vsrr/covid_weekly/index.htm

CDC. (2022, July 13). *All injuries*. https://www.cdc.gov/nchs/fastats/injury.htm

CDC. (2022, July 13). *Suicide and self-harm injury*. https://www.cdc.gov/nchs/fastats/suicide.htm

CEA (Council of Economic Advisers). (2014). *Nine facts about American families and work*. Office of the President of the United States: Council of Economic Advisers. https://obamawhitehouse.archives.gov/the-press-office/2014/06/20/white-house-report-nine-facts-about-american-families-and-work

Ceci, S. J. (1993). *Cognitive and social factors in children's testimony* [Master lecture]. Presented at the Annual Convention of the American Psychological Association.

Ceci, S. J., & Bruck, M. (1993). Child witnesses: Translating research into policy. *Social Policy Report (Society for Research in Child Development)*, 7, 1–30.

Ceci, S. J., & Bruck, M. (1995). *Jeopardy in the courtroom: A scientific analysis of children's testimony*. American Psychological Association.

Ceci, S. J., Huffman, M. L. C., Smith, E., & Loftus, E. F. (1994). Repeatedly thinking about a non-event: Source misattributions among preschoolers. *Consciousness and Cognition*, 3, 388–407.

Ceci, S. J., & Williams, W. M. (1997). Schooling, intelligence, and income. *American Psychologist*, 52, 1051–1058.

Ceci, S. J., & Williams, W. M. (2009). *The mathematics of sex: How biology and society conspire to limit talented women and girls*. Oxford University Press.

Ceci, S. J., & Williams, W. M. (2010). Sex differences in math-intensive fields. *Current Directions in Psychological Science*, 19, 275–279.

Ceci, S. J., & Williams, W. M. (2011). Understanding current causes of women's underrepresentation in science. *PNAS*, 108, 3157–3162.

Centerwall, B. S. (1989). Exposure to television as a risk factor for violence. *American Journal of Epidemiology*, 129, 643–652.

Cepeda, N. J., Pashler, H., Vul, E., Wixted, J. T., & Rohrer, D. (2006). Distributed practice in verbal recall tasks: A review and quantitative synthesis. *Psychological Bulletin*, 132, 354–380.

Cepeda, N. J., Vul, E., Rohrer, D., Wixed, J. T., & Pashler, H. (2008). Spacing effects in learning: A temporal ridgeline of optimal retention. *Psychological Science*, 19, 1095–1102.

Cerasoli, C. P., Nicklin, J. M., & Ford, M. T. (2014). Intrinsic motivation and extrinsic incentives jointly predict performance: A 40-year meta-analysis. *Psychological Bulletin*, 140, 980–1008.

Cero, I., & Witte, T. K. (2020). Assortativity of suicide-related posting on social media. *American Psychologist*, 75(3), 365–379.

Cerrillo-Urbina, A. J., García-Hermoso, A., Sánchez-López, M., Pardo-Guijarro, M. J., Santos Gómez, J. L., & Martínez-Vizcaíno, V. (2015). The effects of physical exercise in children with attention deficit hyperactivity disorder: A systematic review and meta-analysis of randomized control trials. *Child: Care, Health and Development*, 41, 779–788.

Cesario, J., Johnson, D. J., & Eisthen, H. L. (2020). Your brain is not an onion with a tiny reptile inside. *Current Directions in Psychological Science*, 29(3), 255–260.

CFI (Center for Inquiry International). (2003, July). *International developments*. Report.

Chabris, C. F., & Simons, D. (2010). *The invisible gorilla: And other ways our intuitions deceive us*. Crown.

Chae, D. H., Wang, Y., Martz, C. D., Slopen, N., Yip, T., Adler, N. E., Fuller-Rowell, T. E., Lin, J., Matthews, K. A., Brody, G. H., Spears, E. C., Puterman, E., & Epel, E. S. (2020). Racial discrimination and telomere shortening among African Americans: The Coronary Artery Risk Development in Young Adults (CARDIA) study. *Health Psychology*, 39(3), 209–219.

Chajut, E., Caspi, A., Chen, R., Hod, M., & Ariely, D. (2014). In pain thou shalt bring forth children: The peak-and-end rule in recall of labor pain. *Psychological Science*, 25, 2266–2271.

Chambel, M. J., Castanheira, F., Oliveira-Cruz, F., & Lopes, S. (2015). Work context support and Portuguese soldiers' well-being: The mediating role of autonomous motivation. *Military Psychology*, 27, 297–310.

Chamove, A. S. (1980). Nongenetic induction of acquired levels of aggression. *Journal of Abnormal Psychology*, 89, 469–488.

Champagne, F. A. (2010). Early adversity and developmental outcomes: Interaction between genetics, epigenetics, and social experiences across the life span. *Perspectives on Psychological Science*, 5, 564–574.

Champagne, F. A., Francis, D. D., Mar, A, & Meaney, M. J. (2003). Naturally-occurring variations in maternal care in the rat as a mediating influence for the effects of environment on the development of individual differences in stress reactivity. *Physiology & Behavior*, 79, 359–371.

Champagne, F. A., & Mashoodh, R. (2009). Genes in context: Gene-environment interplay and the origins of individual differences in behavior. *Current Directions in Psychological Science*, 18, 127–131.

Chan, H. F., Moon, J. W., Savage, D. A., Skali, A., Torgler, B., & Whyte, S. (2021). Can psychological traits explain mobility behavior during the COVID-19 pandemic? *Social Psychological and Personality Science*, 12(6), 1018–1029.

Chan, M. K., Krebs, M. O., Cox, D., Guest, P. C., Yolken, R. H., Rahmoune, H., Rothermundt, M., Steiner, J., Leweke, F. M., Van Beveren, N. J. M., Niebuhr, D., Weber, N. S., Cowan, D. N., Suarez-Pinilla, P., Crespo-Facorro, B., Mam-Lam-Fook, C., Bourgin, J., Wenstrup, R. J., Kaldate, R. R., ... Bahn, S. (2015, July 14). Development of a blood-based molecular biomarker test for identification of schizophrenia before disease onset. *Translational Psychiatry*, 5, e601.

Chancellor, J., Margolis, S., Jacobs Bao, K., & Lyubomirsky, S. (2018). Everyday prosociality in the workplace: The reinforcing benefits of giving, getting, and glimpsing. *Emotion*, 18, 507–517.

Chance News. (1997, November 25). More on the frequency of letters in texts. Dart. Chance@Dartmouth.edu

Chandler, J. J., & Pronin, E. (2012). Fast thought speed induces risk taking. *Psychological Science*, 23, 370–374.

Chandra, A., Mosher, W. D., & Copen, C. (2011, March 3). *Sexual behavior, sexual attraction, and sexual identity in the United States: Data from the 2006–2008 National Survey of Family Growth* [PDF file]. National Health Statistics Report No. 36. CDC. https://www.cdc.gov/nchs/data/nhsr/nhsr036.pdf

Chang, A.-M., Aeschbach, D., Duggy, J. F., & Czeisler, C. A. (2015). Evening use of light-emitting eReaders negatively affects sleep, circadian timing, and next-morning alertness. *PNAS*, 112, 1232–1237.

Chang, E. C. (2001). Cultural influences on optimism and pessimism: Differences in Western and Eastern construals of the self. In E. C. Chang (Ed.), *Optimism and pessimism* (pp. 257–280). APA Books.

Chang, J. H., & Bushman, B. J. (2019). Effect of exposure to fun violence in video games on children's dangerous behavior with real guns: A randomized clinical trial. *JAMA Network Open*, 2. https://jamanetwork.com/journals/jamanetworkopen/fullarticle/2734799

Chaplin, T. M. (2015). Gender and emotion expression: A developmental contextual perspective. *Emotion Review*, 7, 14–21.

Chaplin, T. M., & Aldao, A. (2013). Gender differences in emotion expression in children: A meta-analytic review. *Psychological Bulletin*, 139, 735–765.

Chaplin, W. F., Phillips, J. B., Brown, J. D., Clanton, N. R., & Stein, J. L. (2000). Handshaking, gender, personality, and first impressions. *Journal of Personality and Social Psychology*, 79, 110–117.

Charlesworth, T. E. S., & Banaji, M. R. (2019). Patterns of implicit and explicit attitudes: I. Long-term change and stability from 2007 to 2016. *Psychological Science*, 30, 174–192.

Charlesworth, T. E. S., & Banaji, M. R. (2022) Patterns of implicit and explicit attitudes: IV. Change and stability from 2007 to 2020. *Psychological Science*, 33(9), 1347–1371.

Charlson, F. J., Flaxman, A., Ferrari, A. J., Vos, T., Steel, Z., & Whiteford, H. A. (2016). Post-traumatic stress disorder and major depression in conflict-affected populations: An epidemiologic analysis. *Global Mental Health (Cambridge Core)*, 3, e4.

Charness, N., & Boot, W. R. (2009). Aging and information technology use. *Current Directions in Psychological Science*, 18, 253–258.

Charpak, G., & Broch, H. (2004). *Debunked! ESP, telekinesis, and other pseudoscience*. Johns Hopkins University Press.

Charpak, N., Montealegre-Pomar, S., & Bohorquez, A. (2021). Systematic review and meta-analysis suggest that the duration of kangaroo mother care has a direct impact on neonatal growth. *Acta PÆdiatrica, 110*(1), 45–59.

Charpak, N., Tessier, R., Ruiz, J. G., Hernandez, J. T., Uriza, F., Villegas, J., Nadeau, L., Mercier, C., Maheu, F., Marin, J., Cortes, D., Gallego, J. M., & Maldonado, D. (2017). Twenty-year follow-up of kangaroo mother care versus traditional care. *Pediatrics, 139*(1). doi: 10.1542/peds.2016-2063

Chartrand, T. L., & Bargh, J. A. (1999). The chameleon effect: The perception-behavior link and social interaction. *Journal of Personality and Social Psychology, 76*, 893–910.

Chartrand, T. L., & Lakin, J. (2013). The antecedents and consequences of human behavioral mimicry. *Annual Review of Psychology, 64*, 285–308.

Chartrand, T. L., & van Baaren, R. (2009). Human mimicry. In M. P. Zanna (Ed.), *Advances in experimental social psychology* (pp. 219–274). Elsevier Academic Press.

Chassin, M. R. L., & MacKinnon, D. P. (2015). Role transitions and young adult maturing out of heavy drinking: Evidence for larger effects of marriage among more severe premarriage problem drinkers. *Alcoholism: Clinical and Experimental Research, 39*, 1064–1074.

Chassy, P., & Gobet, F. (2011). A hypothesis about the biological basis of expert intuition. *Review of General Psychology, 15*, 198–212.

Chatard, A., & Selimbegović, L. (2011). When self-destructive thoughts flash through the mind: Failure to meet standards affects the accessibility of suicide-related thoughts. *Journal of Personality and Social Psychology, 100*, 587–605.

Chatterjee, R. (2015, October 3). Out of the darkness. *Science, 350*, 372–375.

Chavanne, A. V., & Robinson, O. J. (2021). The overlapping neurobiology of induced and pathological anxiety: A meta-analysis of functional neural activation. *American Journal of Psychiatry, 178*, 156–164.

Cheek, S. M., Goldston, D. B., Erkanli, A., Massing-Schaffer, M., & Liu, R. T. (2019). Social rejection and suicidal ideation and attempts among adolescents following hospitalization: A prospective study. *Journal of Abnormal Child Psychology, 48*(1), 123–133.

Cheesman, R., Hunjan, A., Coleman, J. R. I., Ahmadzadeh, Y., Plomin, R., McAdams, T. A., Eley, T. C., & Breen, G. (2020). Comparison of adopted and nonadopted individuals reveals gene–environment interplay for education in the UK biobank. *Psychological Science, 31*, 582–591.

Chein, J. M., & Schneider, W. (2012). The brain's learning and control architecture. *Current Directions in Psychological Science, 21*, 78–84.

Cheit, R. E. (1998). Consider this, skeptics of recovered memory. *Ethics & Behavior, 8*, 141–160.

Chekroud, S. R., Gueorguieva, R., Zheutlin, A. B., Paulus, M., Krumholz, H. M., Krystal, J. H., & Chekroud, A. M. (2018). Association between physical exercise and mental health in 1.2 million individuals in the USA between 2011 and 2015: A cross-sectional study. *Lancet Psychiatry, 5*, 739–746.

Chen, A. W., Kazanjian, A., & Wong, H. (2009). Why do Chinese Canadians not consult mental health services: Health status, language or culture? *Transcultural Psychiatry, 46*, 623–640.

Chen, E., Turiano, N. A., Mroczek, D. K., & Miller, G. E. (2016). Association of reports of childhood abuse and all-cause mortality rates in women. *JAMA Psychiatry, 73*, 920–927.

Chen, G., Wu, Z., Guo, Z., & Gearing, M. (2014). Tonic inhibition in dentate gyrus impairs long-term potentiation and memory in an Alzheimer's disease model. *Nature Communications, 5*, 4159.

Chen, H., Fan, Q., Nicholas, S., & Maitland, E. (2022). The long arm of childhood: The prolonged influence of adverse childhood experiences on depression during middle and old age in China. *Journal of Health Psychology, 27*, 2373–2389.

Chen, J. (2017, June 28). *Katy Perry defends her livestream therapy session: 'People think it's weird'*. Rolling Stone. https://www.rollingstone.com/music/music-news/katy-perry-defends-her-livestream-therapy-session-people-think-its-weird-194530/

Chen, J., & Zhou, X. (2021). Within-family patterns of intergenerational emotional closeness and psychological well-begin of older parents in China. *Aging & Mental Health, 25*(4), 711–719.

Chen, M.-H., Lan, W.-H., Bai, Y.-M., Huang, K.-L., Su, T.-P., Tsai, S.-J., Li, C. T., Lin, W. C., Chang, W. H., Pan, T. L., Chen, T. J., & Hsu, J.-W. (2016). Influence of relative age on diagnosis and treatment of attention-deficit hyperactivity disorder in Taiwanese children. *Journal of Pediatrics, 172*, 162–167.

Chen, S. X., & Bond, M. H. (2010). Two languages, two personalities? Examining language effects on the expression of personality in a bilingual context. *Personality and Social Psychology Bulletin, 36*, 1514–1528.

Chen, Y., Kawachi, I., Berkman, L. F., Trudel-Fitzgerald, C., & Kubzansky, L. D. (2018). A prospective study of marital quality and body weight in midlife. *Health Psychology, 37*, 247–256.

Chen, Y., Koh, H. K., Kawachi, I., Botticelli, M., & VanderWeele, T. J. (2020). Religious service attendance and deaths related to drugs, alcohol, and suicide among US health care professionals. *JAMA Psychiatry, 77*, 737–744.

Chen, Z., Poon, K.-T., DeWall, C. N., & Tonglin, J. (2021). Life lacks meaning without acceptance: Ostracism triggers suicidal thoughts. *Journal of Personality and Social Psychology, 119*(6), 1423–1443.

Cheng, H.-L., Kim, H. Y., Reynolds (Taewon Choi), J. D., Tsong, Y., & Joel Wong, Y. (2021). COVID-19 anti-Asian racism: A tripartite model of collective psychosocial resilience. *American Psychologist, 76*(4), 627–642.

Chernev, A., Böckenholt, U., & Goodman, J. (2015). Choice overload: A conceptual review and meta-analysis. *Journal of Consumer Psychology, 25*(2), 333–358.

Cherniss, C. (2010a). Emotional intelligence: New insights and further clarifications. *Industrial and Organizational Psychology, 3*, 183–191.

Cherniss, C. (2010b). Emotional intelligence: Toward clarification of a concept. *Industrial and Organizational Psychology, 3*, 110–126.

Chernyak, N., Kang, C., & Kushnir, T. (2019). The cultural roots of free will beliefs: How Singaporean and U.S. children judge and explain possibilities for action in interpersonal contexts. *Developmental Psychology, 55*, 866–876.

Cheryan, S., & Markus, H. R. (2020). Masculine defaults: Identifying and mitigating hidden cultural biases. *Psychological Review, 127*(6), 1022–1052.

Chesnutt, J. (2013). *Blind adventurer relies on his ears and a guide to ski*. Today. https://www.today.com/health/blind-adventurer-relies-his-ears-guide-ski-6C9567013

Chess, S., & Thomas, A. (1987). *Know your child: An authoritative guide for today's parents*. Basic Books.

Chester, D. S., & DeWall, C. N. (2016). The pleasure of revenge: Retaliatory aggression arises from a neural imbalance toward reward. *Social Cognitive and Affective Neuroscience, 11*, 1173–1182.

Chetty, N., & Alathur, S. (2018). Hate speech review in the context of online social networks. *Aggression and Violent Behavior, 40*, 108–118.

Cheung, F., & Lucas, R. E. (2015). When does money matter most? Examining the association between income and life satisfaction over the life course. *Psychology and Aging, 30*, 120–135.

Cheung, F., & Lucas, R. E. (2016). Income inequality is associated with stronger social comparison effects: The effect of relative income on life satisfaction. *Journal of Personality and Social Psychology, 110*, 332–341.

Chiang, J. J., Lam, P. H., Chen, E., & Miller, G. E. (2022). Psychological stress during childhood and adolescence and its association with inflammation across the lifespan: A critical review and meta-analysis. *Psychological Bulletin, 148*(1–2), 27–66.

Chiang, J. J., Turiano, N. A., Mroczek, D. K., & Miller, G. E. (2018). Affective reactivity to daily stress and 20-year mortality risk in adults with chronic illness: Findings from the National Study of Daily Experiences. *Health Psychology, 37*, 170–178.

Chiarotti, F., & Venerosi, A. (2020). Epidemiology of autism spectrum disorders: A review of worldwide prevalence estimates since 2014. *Brain Sciences, 10*(5), 274.

Chibanda, D., Weiss, H. A., Verhey, R., Simms, V., Munjoma, R., Rusakaniko, S., Chingono, A., Munetsi, E., Bere, T., Manda, E., Abas, M., & Araya, R. (2016). Effect of a primary care-based psychological intervention on symptoms of common mental disorders in Zimbabwe: A randomized clinical trial. *Journal of the American Medical Association, 316*, 2618–2626.

Chida, Y., & Hamer, M. (2008). Chronic psychosocial factors and acute physiological responses to laboratory-induced stress in healthy populations: A quantitative review of 30 years of investigations. *Psychological Bulletin, 134*, 829–885.

Chida, Y., & Steptoe, A. (2009). The association of anger and hostility with future coronary heart disease: A meta-analytic review of prospective evidence. *Journal of the American College of Cardiology, 17*, 936–946.

Chida, Y., Steptoe, A., & Powell, L. H. (2009). Religiosity/spirituality and mortality. *Psychotherapy and Psychosomatics, 78*, 81–90.

Chida, Y., & Vedhara, K. (2009). Adverse psychosocial factors predict poorer prognosis in HIV disease: A meta-analytic review of prospective investigations. *Brain, Behavior, and Immunity, 23*, 434–445.

Chiles, J. A., Lambert, M. J., & Hatch, A. L. (1999). The impact of psychological interventions on medical cost offset: A meta-analytic review. *Clinical Psychology: Science and Practice, 6*, 204–220.

Chivers, M. L. (2017). The specificity of women's sexual response and its relationship with sexual orientations: A review and ten hypotheses. *Archives of Sexual Behavior, 46*, 1161–1179.

Chivers, M. L., & Brotto, L. A. (2017). Controversies of women's sexual arousal and desire. *European Psychologist, 22*, 5–26.

Chivers, M. L., Seto, M. C., Lalumière, M. L., Laan, E., & Grimbos, T. (2010). Agreement of self-reported and genital measures of sexual arousal in men and women: A meta-analysis. *Archives of Sexual Behavior, 39*, 5–56.

Chmielewski, M., Zhu, J., Burchett, D., Bury, A. S., & Bagby, R. M. (2017). The comparative capacity of the Minnesota Multiphasic Personality Inventory–2 (MMPI–2) and MMPI–2 Restructured Form (MMPI-2-RF) validity scales to detect suspected malingering in a disability claimant sample. *Psychological Assessment, 29*, 199–208.

Cho, H. S., Cheah, C. S. L., Vu, K. T. T., Selçuk, B., Yavuz, H. M., Sen, H. H., & Park, S.-Y. (2021). Culturally shared and unique meanings and expressions of maternal control across four cultures. *Developmental Psychology, 57*(2), 284–301.

Choi, I., & Choi, Y. (2002). Culture and self-concept flexibility. *Personality and Social Psychology Bulletin, 28*(11), 1508–1517.

Choi, K. W., Zheutlin, A. B., Karlson, R. A., Wang, M. J., Dunn, E. C., Stein, M. B., Karlson, E. W., & Smoller, J. W. (2019). Physical activity offsets genetic risk for incident depression assessed via electronic health records in a biobank cohort study. *Depression and Anxiety, 37*(2), 106–114.

Choi, S. Y., Son, S. J., & Park, B. (2022). Shared genetic effects of emotion and subcortical volumes in healthy adults. *NeuroImage, 249*. https://www.sciencedirect.com/science/article/pii/S1053811922000246

Chomsky, N. (1972). *Language and mind.* Harcourt Brace.

Chopik, W. J., Edelstein, R. S., & Fraley, R. C. (2013). From the cradle to the grave: Age differences in attachment from early adulthood to old age. *Journal of Personality, 81*, 171–183.

Chopik, W., & O'Brien, E. (2017). Happy you, healthy me? Having a happy partner is independently associated with better health in oneself. *Health Psychology, 36*, 21–30.

Choudhary, E., Smith, M., & Bossarte, R. M. (2012). Depression, anxiety, and symptom profiles among female and male victims of sexual violence. *American Journal of Men's Health, 6*, 28–36.

Choudhury, S., Blakemore, S. J., & Charman, T. (2006). Social cognitive development during adolescence. *Social Cognitive and Affective Neuroscience, 1*(3), 165–174.

Christakis, D. A., Garrison, M. M., Herrenkohl, T., Haggerty, K., Rivara, K. P., Zhou, C., & Liekweg, K. (2013). Modifying media content for preschool children: A randomized control trial. *Pediatrics, 131*, 431–438.

Christakis, N. (2019, March 24). We are one: Obsession with human difference is out of step with scientific evidence on universals that connect us. *New York Daily News*. https://www.nydailynews.com/opinion/ny-oped-we-are-one-20190324-nmngbhbs3fcelfwawh3iibhpwu-story.html

Christakis, N. A., & Fowler, J. H. (2007). The spread of obesity in a large social network over 32 years. *New England Journal of Medicine, 357*, 370–379.

Christakis, N. A., & Fowler, J. H. (2008, May). The collective dynamics of smoking in a large social network. *New England Journal of Medicine, 358*, 2249–2258.

Christakis, N. A., & Fowler, J. H. (2009). *Connected: The surprising power of social networks and how they shape our lives.* Little, Brown.

Christensen, A., & Jacobson, N. S. (1994). Who (or what) can do psychotherapy: The status and challenge of nonprofessional therapies. *Psychological Science, 5*, 8–14.

Christian, C., & Levinson, C. A. (2022). An integrated review of fear and avoidance learning in anxiety disorders and application to eating disorders. *New Ideas in Psychology, 67*. https://doi.org/10.1016/j.newideapsych.2022.100964

Christiansen, P., Jennings, E., & Rose, A. K. (2016). Anticipated effects of alcohol stimulate craving and impair inhibitory control. *Psychology of Addictive Behaviors, 30*, 383–388.

Christophersen, E. R., & Edwards, K. J. (1992). Treatment of elimination disorders: State of the art 1991. *Applied & Preventive Psychology, 1*, 15–22.

Christov-Moore, L., Simpson, E. A., Coudé, G., Grigaityte, K., Iacoboni, M., & Ferrari, P. F. (2014). Empathy: Gender effects in brain and behavior. *Neuroscience and Biobehavioral Reviews, 46*(Pt 4), 604–627.

Chu, C., Podlogar, M. C., Hagan, C. R., Buchman-Schmitt, J. M., Silva, C., Chiurliza, B., Hames, J. L., Stanley, I. H., Lim, L. I., & Joiner, T. E. (2016). The interactive effects of the capability for suicide and major depressive episodes on suicidal behavior in a military sample. *Cognitive Therapy and Research, 40*, 22–30.

Chu, C., Walker, K. L., Stanley, I. H., Hirsch, J. K., Greenberg, J. H., Rudd, M. D., & Joiner, T. E. (2018). Perceived problem-solving deficits and suicidal ideation: Evidence for the explanatory roles of thwarted belongingness and perceived burdensomeness in five samples. *Journal of Personality and Social Psychology, 115*, 137–160.

Chu, P. S., Saucier, D. A., & Hafner, E. (2010). Meta-analysis of the relationships between social support and well-being in children and adolescents. *Journal of Social and Clinical Psychology, 29*, 624–645.

Chua, H. F., Boland, J. E., & Nisbett, R. E. (2005). Cultural variation in eye movements during scene perception. *PNAS, 102*, 12629–12633.

Chugani, H. T., & Phelps, M. E. (1986). Maturational changes in cerebral function in infants determined by 18FDG positron emission tomography. *Science, 231*, 840–843.

Chulov, M. (2014, December 11). *ISIS: The inside story.* The Guardian. https://www.theguardian.com/world/2014/dec/11/-sp-isis-the-inside-story

Church, A. T., Katigbak, M. S., Mazuera Arias, R., Rincon, B. C., Vargas-Flores, J., Ibáñez-Reyes, J., Wang, L., Alvarez, J. M., Wang, C., & Ortiz, F. A. (2014). A four-culture study of self-enhancement and adjustment using the social relations model: Do alternative conceptualizations and indices make a difference? *Journal of Personality and Social Psychology, 106*, 997–1014.

Churchland, P. S. (2013). *Touching a nerve: The self as brain.* Norton.

CIA. (2014, accessed April 23). Sex ratio. *The World Factbook.*

Cialdini, R. B. (1993). *Influence: Science and practice* (3rd ed.). HarperCollins.

Cialdini, R. B., & Richardson, K. D. (1980). Two indirect tactics of image management: Basking and blasting. *Journal of Personality and Social Psychology, 39*, 406–415.

Cialdini, R. B., Vincent, J. E., Lewis, S. K., Catalan, J., Wheeler, D., & Darby, B. L. (1975). Reciprocal concessions procedure for inducing compliance: The door-in-the-face technique. *Journal of Personality and Social Psychology, 31*(2), 206–215.

Cin, S. D., Gibson, B., Zanna, M. P., Shumate, R., & Fong, G. T. (2007). Smoking in movies, implicit associations of smoking with the self, and intentions to smoke. *Psychological Science, 18*, 559–563.

Cinelli, M., De Francisci Morales, G., Galeazzi, A., Quattrociocchi, W., & Starnini, M. (2021). The echo chamber effect on social media. *PNAS, 118*(9). https://www.pnas.org/doi/10.1073/pnas.2023301118

Cipriani, A., Furukawa, T. A., Salanti, G., Chaimani, A., Atkinson, L. Z., Ogawa, Y., Leucht, S., Ruhe, H. G., Turner, E. H., Higgins, J. P. T., Egger, M., Takeshima, N., Hayasaka, Y., Imai, H., Shinohara, K., Tajika, A., Ioannidis, J. P. A., & Geddes, J. R. (2018). Comparative efficacy and acceptability of 21 antidepressant drugs for the acute treatment of adults with major depressive disorder: A systematic review and network meta-analysis. *The Lancet, 391*, 1357–1366.

Citron, P. (Ed.) (1989). Letter written in November, 1856. *Correspondence générale* (Vol. 5, p. 390). Flammarion.

Claassen, J., Doyle, K., Matory, A., Couch, C., Burger, K. M., Velazquez, A., Okonkwo, J. U., King, J.-R., Park, S., Agarwal, S., Roh, D., Megjhani, M., Eliseyev, A., Connolly, E. S., & Rohaut, B. (2019). Detection of brain activation in unresponsive patients with acute brain injury. *New England Journal of Medicine, 380*, 2497–2505.

Clack, B., Dixon, J., & Tredoux, C. (2005). Eating together apart: Patterns of segregation in a multi-ethnic cafeteria. *Journal of Community and Applied Social Psychology, 15*, 1–16.

Claidière, N., & Whiten, A. (2012). Integrating the study of conformity and culture in humans and nonhuman animals. *Psychological Bulletin, 138*, 126–145.

Clancy, S. A. (2005). *Abducted: How people come to believe they were kidnapped by aliens.* Harvard University Press.

Clancy, S. A. (2010). *The trauma myth: The truth about the sexual abuse of children—and its aftermath.* Basic Books.

Clark, A., Seidler, A., & Miller, M. (2001). Inverse association between sense of humor and coronary heart disease. *International Journal of Cardiology, 80*, 87–88.

Clark, I. A., & Maguire, E. A. (2016). Remembering preservation in hippocampal amnesia. *Annual Review of Psychology, 67*, 51–82.

Clark, J. L., Algoe, S. B., & Green, M. C. (2018). Social network sites and well-being: The role of social connection. *Current Directions in Psychological Science, 27*, 32–37.

Clark, K. B., & Clark, M. P. (1947). Racial identification and preference in Negro children. In T. M. Newcomb & E. L. Hartley (Eds.), *Readings in social psychology*. Holt.

Clark, R. D., III, & Hatfield, E. (1989). Gender differences in receptivity to sexual offers. *Journal of Psychology & Human Sexuality, 2*, 39–55.

Clarke, E., Reichard, U. H., & Zuberbuehler, K. (2015). Context-specific close-range "hoo" calls in wild gibbons (Hylobates lar). *BMC Evolutionary Biology, 15*, 56.

Clausen, J., Fetz, E., Donoghue, J., Ushiba, J., Spöhase, J., Birbaummer, N., & Soekadar, S. R. (2017). Help, hope, and hype: Ethical dimensions of neuroprosthetics. *Science, 356*, 1338–1339.

Clauss, K., Gorday, J., & Bardeen, J. R. (2022). Eye tracking evidence of threat-related attentional bias in anxiety- and fear-related disorders: A systematic review and meta-analysis. *Clinical Psychology Review, 93*. https://www.sciencedirect.com/science/article/abs/pii/S0272735822000277

Cleare, S., Gumley, A., & O'Connor, R. C. (2019). Self-compassion, self-forgiveness, suicidal ideation, and self-harm: A systematic review. *Clinical Psychology & Psychotherapy, 26*(5), 511–530.

Cleary, A. M., & Claxton, A. B. (2018). Déjà vu: An illusion of prediction. *Psychological Science, 29*, 635–644.

Clements, C. C., Zoltowski, A. R., Yankowitz, L. D., Yerys, B. E., Schultz, R. T., & Herrington, J. D. (2018). Evaluation of the social motivation hypothesis of autism: A systematic review and meta-analysis. *JAMA Psychiatry, 75*, 797–808.

Clynes, T. (2016). How to raise a genius. *Nature, 537*, 152–155.

CMEC (Council of Ministers of Education, Canada). (2018). *Measuring up: Canadian results of the OECD PISA Study. The performance of Canada's youth in science, reading and mathematics* [PDF file]. https://www.cmec.ca/Publications/Lists/Publications/Attachments/396/PISA2018_PublicReport_EN.pdf

CNN (Cable News Network). (2009). *'Twilight' author: It started with a dream*. https://edition.cnn.com/2009/LIVING/worklife/11/18/o.twilight.newmoon.meyer/

Coan, J. A., Schaefer, H. S., & Davidson, R. J. (2006). Lending a hand: Social regulation of the neural response to threat. *Psychological Science, 17*, 1032–1039.

Coelho, C. M., & Purkis, H. (2009). The origins of specific phobias: Influential theories and current perspectives. *Review of General Psychology, 13*, 335–348.

Coelho, L. F., Barbosa, D. L. F., Rizzutti, S., Muszkat, M., Bueno, O. F. A., & Miranda, M. C. (2015). Use of cognitive behavioral therapy and token economy to alleviate dysfunctional behavior in children with attention-deficit hyperactivity disorder. *Frontiers in Psychiatry, 6*, 167.

Coffey, J. K. (2020). Cascades of infant happiness: Infant positive affect predicts childhood IQ and adult educational attainment. *Emotion, 20*, 1255–1265.

Cohen, A. B. (2009). Many forms of culture. *American Psychologist, 64*, 194–204.

Cohen, A. B., & Tannenbaum, I. J. (2001). Lesbian and bisexual women's judgments of the attractiveness of different body types. *Journal of Sex Research, 38*(3), 226–232.

Cohen, A. O., Breiner, K., Steinberg, L., Bonnie, R. J., Scott, E. S., Taylor-Thompson, K. A., Rudolph, M. D., Chein, J., Richeson, J. A., Heller, A. S., Silverman, M. R., Dellarco, D. V., Fair, D. A., Galván, A., & Casey, B. J. (2016). When is an adolescent an adult? Assessing cognitive control in emotional and nonemotional contexts. *Psychological Science, 27*, 549–562.

Cohen, F., & Solomon, S. (2011). The politics of mortal terror. *Current Directions in Psychological Science, 20*, 316–320.

Cohen, P. (2007, November 15). Freud is widely taught at universities, except in the psychology department. *The New York Times*. https://www.nytimes.com/2007/11/25/weekinreview/25cohen.html

Cohen, S. (2004). Social relationships and health. *American Psychologist, 59*, 676–684.

Cohen, S., Doyle, W. J., Skoner, D. P., Rabin, B. S., & Gwaltney, J. M., Jr. (1997). Social ties and susceptibility to the common cold. *Journal of the American Medical Association, 277*, 1940–1944.

Cohen, S., Janicki-Deverts, D., Turner, R. B., & Doyle, W. J. (2015). Does hugging provide stress-buffering social support? A study of susceptibility to upper respiratory infection and illness. *Psychological Science, 26*, 135–147.

Cohen, S., Kamarck, T., & Mermelstein, R. (1983). A global measure of perceived stress. *Journal of Health and Social Behavior, 24*, 385–396.

Cohen, S., Kaplan, J. R., Cunnick, J. E., Manuck, S. B., & Rabin, B. S. (1992). Chronic social stress, affiliation, and cellular immune response in nonhuman primates. *Psychological Science, 3*, 301–304.

Cohen, S., Tyrrell, D. A. J., & Smith, A. P. (1991). Psychological stress and susceptibility to the common cold. *New England Journal of Medicine, 325*, 606–612.

Cohn, A., Maréchal, M. A., Tannenbaum, D., & Zünd, C. L. (2019). Civic honesty around the globe. *Science, 365*, 70–73.

Cohn, D. (2013, February 13). *Love and marriage*. Pew Research Center. https://www.pewsocialtrends.org/2013/02/13/love-and-marriage/

Coker, A. L., Bush, H. M., Cook-Craig, P. G., DeGue, S. A., Clear, E. R., Brancato, C. J., Fisher, B. S., & Recktenwald, E. A. (2017). RCT testing bystander effectiveness to reduce violence. *American Journal of Preventative Medicine, 52*, 566–578.

Colapinto, J. (2000). *As nature made him: The boy who was raised as a girl*. HarperCollins.

Colarelli, S. M., Spranger, J. L., & Hechanova, M. R. (2006). Women, power, and sex composition in small groups: An evolutionary perspective. *Journal of Organizational Behavior, 27*, 163–184.

Colbert, S. (2014, November 18). *Tweet*. Twitter: @StephenAtHome

Cole, E. J., Phillips, A. L., Bentzley, B. S., Stimpson, K. H., Nejad, R., Barmak, F., Veerapal, C., Khan, N., Cherian, K., Felber, E., Brown, R., Choi, E., King, S., Pankow, H., Bishop, J. H., Azeez, A., Coetzee, J., Rapier, R., Odenwald, N., ... Williams, N. R. (2022). Stanford neuromodulation therapy (SNT): A double-blind randomized controlled trial. *American Journal of Psychiatry, 179*, 132–141.

Cole, J. D., Espinueva, D. F., Seib, D. R., Ash, A. M., Cooke, M. B., Cahill, S. P., O'Leary, T. P., Kwan, S. P., & Snyder, J. S. (2020). Adult-born hippocampal neurons undergo extended development and are morphologically distinct from neonatally-born neurons. *Journal of Neuroscience, 40*, 5740–5756.

Cole, K. C. (1998). *The universe and the teacup: The mathematics of truth and beauty*. Harcourt Brace.

Cole, M. W., Ito, T., & Braver, T. S. (2015). Lateral prefrontal cortex contributes to fluid intelligence through multinetwork connectivity. *Brain Connectivity, 5*, 497–504.

Coles, N. A., Larsen, J. T., & Lench, H. C. (2019). A meta-analysis of the facial feedback literature: Effects of facial feedback on emotional experience are small and variable. *Psychological Bulletin, 145*, 610–651.

Coley, R. L., Medeiros, B. L., & Schindler, H. (2008). Using sibling differences to estimate effects of parenting on adolescent sexual risk behaviors. *Journal of Adolescent Health, 43*, 133–140.

Collins, F. (2006). *The language of God*. Free Press.

Collins, N. L., & Miller, L. C. (1994). Self-disclosure and liking: A meta-analytic review. *Psychological Bulletin, 116*, 457–475.

Collins, W. A., Welsh, D. P., & Furman, W. (2009). Adolescent romantic relationships. *Annual Review of Psychology, 60*, 631–652.

Collinson, S. L., MacKay, C. E., James, A. C., Quested, D. J., Phillips, T., Roberts, N., & Crow, T. J. (2003). Brain volume, asymmetry and intellectual impairment in relation to sex in early-onset schizophrenia. *British Journal of Psychiatry, 183*, 114–120.

Colombo, J. (1982). The critical period concept: Research, methodology, and theoretical issues. *Psychological Bulletin, 91*, 260–275.

Comfort, A. (2002). *The joy of sex: Fully revised & completely updated for the 21st century*. Crown.

Compton, W. C. (2018). Self-actualization myths: What did Maslow really say? *Journal of Humanistic Psychology*. https://www.researchgate.net/publication/323921573_Self-Actualization_Myths_What_Did_Maslow_Really_Say

Confer, J. C., Easton, J. A., Fleischman, D. S., Goetz, C. D., Lewis, D. M. G., Perilloux, C., & Buss, D. M. (2010). Evolutionary psychology: Controversies, questions, prospects, and limitations. *American Psychologist, 65*, 110–126.

Conklin, Q. A., King, B. G., Zanesco, A. P., Lin, J., Hamidi, A. B., Pokorny, J. J., Álvarez-López, M. J., Cosin-Tomás, M., Huang, C., Kaliman, P., Epel, E. S., & Saron, C. D. (2018). Insight meditation and telomere biology: The effects of intensive retreat and the moderating role of personality. *Brain, Behavior, and Immunity, 70*, 233–245.

Conley, T. D. (2011). Perceived proposer personality characteristics and gender differences in acceptance of casual sex offers. *Journal of Personality and Social Psychology, 100*, 300–329.

Connor, C. E. (2010). A new viewpoint on faces. *Science, 330*, 764–765.

Connor-Smith, J. K., & Flachsbart, C. (2007). Relations between personality and coping: A meta-analysis. *Journal of Personality and Social Psychology, 93*, 1080–1107.

Consumer Reports. (1995, November). Does therapy help? pp. 734–739.

Converse, B. A., Juarez, L., & Hennecke, M. (2019). Self-control and the reasons behind our goals. *Journal of Personality and Social Psychology, 116*, 860–883.

Conway, C. C., Forbes, M. K., Forbush, K. T., Fried, E. I., Hallquist, M. N., Kotov, R., Mullins-Sweatt, S. N., Shackman, A. J., Skodol, A. E., South, S. C., Sunderland, M., Waszczuk, M. A., Zald, D. H., Afzali, M. H., Bornovalova, M. A., Carragher, N., Docherty, A. R., Jonas, K. G., Krueger, R. F., … Eaton, N. R. (2019). A hierarchical taxonomy of psychopathology can transform mental health research. *Perspectives on Psychological Science, 14*, 419–436.

Conway, M. A., Wang, Q., Hanyu, K., & Haque, S. (2005). A cross-cultural investigation of autobiographical memory: On the universality and cultural variation of the reminiscence bump. *Journal of Cross-Cultural Psychology, 36*, 739–749.

Cook, S., Kokmotou, K., Soto, V., Fallon, N., Tyson-Carr, J., Thomas, A., Giesbrecht, T., Field, M., & Stancak, A. (2017). Pleasant and unpleasant odour-face combinations influence face and odour perception: An event-related potential study. *Behavioural Brain Research, 333*, 304–313.

Cooke, L. J., Wardle, J., & Gibson, E. L. (2003). Relationship between parental report of food neophobia and everyday food consumption in 2–6-year-old children. *Appetite, 41*, 205–206.

Cooley, E., Lei, R., Brown-Iannuzzi, J., & Ellerkamp, T. (2019). Personal prejudice, other guilt: Explicit prejudice toward Black people predicts guilty verdicts for White officers who kill Black men. *Personality and Social Psychology Bulletin, 45*, 754–766.

Cooper, K. J. (1999, May 1). This time, copycat wave is broader. *The Washington Post.* https://www.washingtonpost.com/wp-srv/national/longterm/juvmurders/stories/copycat050199.htm

Cooper, W. H., & Withey, M. J. (2009). The strong situation hypothesis. *Personality and Social Psychology Review, 13*, 62–72.

Coopersmith, S. (1967). *The antecedents of self-esteem.* Freeman.

Copen, C. E., Chandra, A., & Febo-Vazquez, I. (2016, January 7). *Sexual behavior, sexual attraction, and sexual orientation among adults aged 18–44 in the United States: Data from the 2011–2013 National Survey of Family Growth* [PDF file]. National Health Statistics Reports No. 88. CDC. https://www.cdc.gov/nchs/data/nhsr/nhsr088.pdf

Corballis, M. C. (2002). *From hand to mouth: The origins of language.* Princeton University Press.

Corballis, M. C. (2003). From mouth to hand: Gesture, speech, and the evolution of right-handedness. *Behavioral and Brain Sciences, 26*, 199–260.

Corcoran, D. W. J. (1964). The relation between introversion and salivation. *American Journal of Psychology, 77*, 298–300.

Cordaro, D. T., Sun, R., Keltner, D., Kamble, S., Huddar, N., & McNeil, G. (2018). Universals and cultural variations in 22 emotional expressions across five cultures. *Emotion, 18*, 75–93.

Coren, S. (1996). *Sleep thieves: An eye-opening exploration into the science and mysteries of sleep.* Free Press.

Corey, D. P., Garcia-Añoveros, J., Holt, J. R., Kwan, K. Y., Lin, S. Y., Vollrath, M. A., & Zhang, D. S. (2004). TRPA1 is a candidate for the mechano-sensitive transduction channel of vertebrate hair cells. *Nature, 432*, 723–730.

Corina, D. P. (1998). The processing of sign language: Evidence from aphasia. In B. Stemmer & H. A. Whittaker (Eds.), *Handbook of neurolinguistics* (pp. 313–329). Academic Press.

Corina, D. P., Vaid, J., & Bellugi, U. (1992). The linguistic basis of left hemisphere specialization. *Science, 255*, 1258–1260.

Corkin, S. (2005, September). Quoted by R. Adelson in Lessons from H. M. *Monitor on Psychology*, p. 59.

Corkin, S. (2013). *Permanent present tense: The unforgettable life of the amnesic patient.* Basic Books.

Corneille, O., Huart, J., Becquart, E., & Brédart, S. (2004). When memory shifts toward more typical category exemplars: Accentuation effects in the recollection of ethnically ambiguous faces. *Journal of Personality and Social Psychology, 86*, 236–250.

Cornier, M.-A. (2011). Is your brain to blame for weight regain? *Physiology & Behavior, 104*, 608–612.

Cornil, Y., & Chandon, P. (2013). From fan to fat? Vicarious losing increases unhealthy eating, but self-affirmation is an effective remedy. *Psychological Science, 24*, 1936–1946.

Correll, C. U., Cortese, S., Croatto, G., Monaco, F., Krinitski, D., Arrondo, G., Ostinelli, E. G., Zangani, C., Fornaro, M., Estradé, A., Fusar-Poll, P., Carvalho, A. F., & Solmi, M. (2022). Efficacy and acceptability of pharmacological, psychosocial, and brain stimulation interventions in children and adolescents with mental disorders: An umbrella review. *World Psychiatry, 20*(2), 244–275.

Correll, J., Park, B., Judd, C. M., Wittenbrink, B., Sadler, M. S., & Keesee, T. (2007). Across the thin blue line: Police officers and racial bias in the decision to shoot. *Journal of Personality and Social Psychology, 92*, 1006–1023.

Correll, J., Wittenbrink, B., Crawford, M. T., & Sadler, M. S. (2015). Stereotypic vision: How stereotypes disambiguate visual stimuli. *Journal of Personality and Social Psychology, 108*, 219–233.

Corrigan, P. W. (2014). Can there be false hope in recovery? *British Journal of Psychiatry, 205*, 423–424.

Corrigan, P. W., Druss, B. G., & Perlick, D. A. (2014). The impact of mental illness stigma on seeking and participating in mental health care. *Psychological Science in the Public Interest, 15*(2), 37–70.

Corrigan, P. W., Morris, S. B., Michaels, P. J., Rafacz, J. D., & Rüsch, N. (2012). Challenging the public stigma of mental illness: A meta-analysis of outcome studies. *Psychiatric Services, 63*(10), 963–973.

Cortes, K., Leith, S., & Wilson, A. E. (2018). Relationship satisfaction and the subjective distance of past relational events. *Journal of Social and Personal Relationships, 35*, 1092–1117.

Costa, P. T., Jr., & McCrae, R. R. (2011). The five-factor model, five factor theory, and interpersonal psychology. In L. M. Horowitz & S. Strack (Eds.), *Handbook of interpersonal psychology: Theory, research, assessment, and therapeutic interventions* (pp. 91–104). John Wiley & Sons.

Costa, P. T., Jr., Terracciano, A., & McCrae, R. R. (2001). Gender differences in personality traits across cultures: Robust and surprising findings. *Journal of Personality and Social Psychology, 81*, 322–331.

Costanza, A., Vasileios, C., Ambrosetti, J., Shah, S., Amerio, A., Aguglia, A., Serafini, G., Piguet, V., Luthy, C., Cedraschi, C., Bondolfi, G., & Berardelli, I. (2022). Demoralization in suicide: A systematic review. *Journal of Psychosomatic Research, 157*. https://www.sciencedirect.com/science/article/pii/S0022399922000733

Costello, E. J., Compton, S. N., Keeler, G., & Angold, A. (2003). Relationships between poverty and psychopathology: A natural experiment. *Journal of the American Medical Association, 290*, 2023–2029.

Costello, T. H., Unterberger, A., Watts, A. L., & Lilienfeld, S. O. (2018). Psychopathy and pride: Testing Lykken's hypothesis regarding the implications of fearlessness for prosocial and antisocial behavior. *Frontiers in Psychology, 9*, 185.

Coudé, G., Toschi, G., Festante, F., Bimbi, M., Bonaiuto, J., & Ferrari, P. F. (2019). Grasping neurons in the ventral premotor cortex of macaques are modulated by social goals. *Journal of Cognitive Neuroscience, 31*, 299–313.

Couette, M., Mouchabac, S., Adrien, V., Cagnone, V., Bourla, A., & Ferreri, F. (2022). Functional neuro-anatomy of social cognition in posttraumatic stress disorders: A systematic review. *Psychiatry Research, 315*. doi: 10.1016/j.psychres.2022.114729

Couli, J. T., Vidal, F., Nazarian, B., & Macar, F. (2004). Functional anatomy of the attentional modulation of time estimation. *Science, 303*, 1506–1508.

Coulter, K. C., & Malouff, J. M. (2013). Effects of an intervention designed to enhance romantic relationship excitement: A randomized-control trial. *Couple and Family Psychology: Research and Practice, 2*, 34–44.

Courage, M. L., & Howe, M. L. (2002). From infant to child: The dynamics of cognitive change in the second year of life. *Psychological Bulletin, 128*, 250–277.

Courtright, S. H., McCormick, B. W., Postlethwaite, B. E., Reeves, C. J., & Mount, M. K. (2013). A meta-analysis of sex differences in physical ability: Revised estimates and strategies for reducing differences in selection contexts. *Applied Psychology, 98*(4), 623–641.

Cousins, J. N., Teo, T. B., Tan, Z. Y., Wong, K. F., & Chee, J. W. L. (2021). Sleep after learning aids the consolidation of factual knowledge, but not relearning. *Sleep, 44*(3). https://academic.oup.com/sleep/article/44/3/zsaa210/5920204

CovidCast. (2020). Delphi's COVID-19 Surveys. https://delphi.cmu.edu/covidcast/surveys/

Cowan, N. (1988). Evolving conceptions of memory storage, selective attention, and their mutual constraints within the human information-processing system. *Psychological Bulletin, 104,* 163–191.

Cowan, N. (2008). What are the differences between long-term, short-term, and working memory? *Progress in Brain Research, 169,* 323–338.

Cowan, N. (2010). The magical mystery four: How is working memory capacity limited, and why? *Current Directions in Psychological Science, 19,* 51–57.

Cowan, N. (2015). George Miller's magical number of immediate memory in retrospect: Observations on the faltering progression of science. *Psychological Review, 122,* 536–541.

Cowan, N. (2016). Working memory maturation: Can we get at the essence of cognitive growth? *Perspectives on Psychological Science, 11,* 239–264.

Cowart, B. J. (1981). Development of taste perception in humans: Sensitivity and preference throughout the life span. *Psychological Bulletin, 90,* 43–73.

Cowart, B. J. (2005). Taste, our body's gustatory gatekeeper. *Cerebrum, 7,* 7–22.

Cowell, J. M., & Decety, J. (2015). Precursors to morality in development as a complex interplay between neural, socioenvironmental, and behavioral facets. *PNAS, 112,* 12657–12662.

Cowen, A. S., & Keltner, D. (2020). What the face displays: Mapping 28 emotions conveyed by naturalistic expression. *American Psychologist, 75*(3), 349–364.

Cowen, A. S., Keltner, D., Schroff, F., Jou, B., Adam, H., & Prasad, G. (2021). Sixteen facial expressions occur in similar contexts worldwide. *Nature, 589,* 251–257.

Cox, C. R., & Arndt, J. (2012). How sweet it is to be loved by you: The role of perceived regard in the terror management of close relationships. *Journal of Personality and Social Psychology, 102,* 616–632.

Cox, D. A., & Bowman, K. (2020, April 2). *Fear, frustration, and faith: Americans respond to the coronavirus outbreak: Findings from the March 2020 American Perspectives Survey.* American Enterprise Institute. https://www.aei.org/research-products/report/fear-frustration-and-faith-americans-respond-to-the-coronavirus-outbreak

Cox, J. J., Reimann, F. Nicholas, A. K., Thornton, G., Roberts, E., Springell, K., & Woods, C. G. (2006). An SCN9A channelopathy causes congenital inability to experience pain. *Nature, 444,* 894–898.

Coye, C., Ouattara, K., Zuberbühler, K., & Lemasson, A. (2015). Suffixation influences receivers' behaviour in non-human primates. *Proceedings of the Royal Society B, 282,* 1807.

Coyne, S. M., Padilla-Walker, L., Holmgren, H. G., Davis, E. J., Collier, K. M., Memmott-Elison, M., & Hawkins, A. J. (2018). A meta-analysis of prosocial media on prosocial behavior, aggression, and empathic concern: A multidimensional approach. *Developmental Psychology, 54,* 331–347.

CPP. (2017). *Myers-Briggs Type Indicator® (MBTI®).* CPP, Inc. (cpp.com).

Crabbe, J. C. (2002). Genetic contributions to addiction. *Annual Review of Psychology, 53,* 435–462.

Crabtree, S. (2005, January 13). *Engagement keeps the doctor away.* Gallup. https://news.gallup.com/businessjournal/14500/engagement-keeps-doctor-away.aspx

Crabtree, S. (2011, December 12). *U.S. seniors maintain happiness highs with less social time.* Gallup. https://news.gallup.com/poll/151457/seniors-maintain-happiness-highs-less-social-time.aspx

Crabtree, S., & Lai, A. (2021, September 30). *The world prefers a calm life to an exciting life.* Gallup Blog. https://news.gallup.com/opinion/gallup/355133/world-prefers-calm-life-exciting-life.aspx

Craik, F. I. M., & Tulving, E. (1975). Depth of processing and the retention of words in episodic memory. *Journal of Experimental Psychology: General, 104,* 268–294.

Cramer, M., & Yuhas, A. (2021). Zaila Avant-garde makes spelling bee history, and other moments from the bee. *The New York Times.* https://www.nytimes.com/2021/07/09/us/zaila-avant-garde-spelling-bee-winner.html

Crandall, C., & White, M. (2016, November 17). *Trump and the social psychology of prejudice.* Undark. https://undark.org/2016/11/17/trump-social-psychology-prejudice-unleashed/

Credé, M., & Kuncel, N. R. (2008). Study habits, skills, and attitudes: The third pillar supporting collegiate academic performance. *Perspectives on Psychological Science, 3,* 425–453.

Creswell, J. D., Bursley, J. K., & Satpute, A. B. (2013). Neural reactivation links unconscious thought to decision making performance. *Social Cognitive and Affective Neuroscience, 8,* 863–869.

Creswell, J. D., Way, B. M., Eisenberger, N. I., & Lieberman, M. D. (2007). Neural correlates of dispositional mindfulness during affect labeling. *Psychosomatic Medicine, 69,* 560–565.

Creswell, K. G., Chung, T., Clark, D., & Martin, C. (2014). Solitary alcohol use in teens is associated with drinking in response to negative affect and predicts alcohol problems in young adulthood. *Clinical Psychological Science, 2,* 602–610.

Crews, F. T., He, J., & Hodge, C. (2007). Adolescent cortical development: A critical period of vulnerability for addiction. *Pharmacology, Biochemistry and Behavior, 86,* 189–199.

Crews, F. T., Mdzinarishvilli, A., Kim, D., He, J., & Nixon, K. (2006). Neurogenesis in adolescent brain is potently inhibited by ethanol. *Neuroscience, 137,* 437–445.

Crifasi, C. K., Meyers, J. S., Vernick, J. S., & Webster, D. W. (2015). Effects of changes in permit-to-purchase handgun laws in Connecticut and Missouri on suicide rates. *Preventive Medicine: An International Journal Devoted to Practice and Theory, 79,* 43–49.

Crivelli, C., Jarillo, S., Russell, J. A., & Fernández-Dols, J. M. (2016). Reading emotions from faces in two indigenous societies. *Journal of Experimental Psychology: General,* 145, 830–843.

Crivelli, C., Russell, J. A., Jarillo, S., & Fernández-Dols, J. M. (2016). The fear gasping face as a threat display in a Melanesian society. *PNAS, 113,* 12403–12407.

Crocker, J., & Park, L. E. (2004). The costly pursuit of self-esteem. *Psychological Bulletin, 130,* 392–414.

Crocker, J., Thompson, L. L., McGraw, K. M., & Ingerman, C. (1987). Downward comparison, prejudice, and evaluation of others: Effects of self-esteem and threat. *Journal of Personality and Social Psychology, 52,* 907–916.

Crockett, M. J. (2017). Moral outrage in the digital age. *Nature Human Behaviour, 1*(11), 769–771.

Crockford, C., Wittig, R. M., & Zuberbühler, K. (2017). Vocalizing in chimpanzees is influenced by social-cognitive processes. *Science Advances, 3.* https://www.science.org/doi/10.1126/sciadv.1701742

Croft, A., Schmader, T., Block, K., & Baron, A. S. (2014). The second shift reflected in the second generation: Do parents' gender roles at home predict children's aspirations? *Psychological Science, 25,* 1418–1428.

Croft, R. J., Klugman, A., Baldeweg, T., & Gruzelier, J. H. (2001). Electrophysiological evidence of serotonergic impairment in long-term MDMA ("Ecstasy") users. *American Journal of Psychiatry, 158,* 1687–1692.

Crombie, A. C. (1964, May). Early concepts of the senses and the mind. *Scientific American,* pp. 108–116.

Cronin, S. L., Craig, B. M., & Lipp, O. V. (2021). Stable middle-aged face recognition: No moderation of the own-age bias across contexts. *British Journal of Psychology, 112,* 645–661.

Crook, T. H., & West, R. L. (1990). Name recall performance across the adult lifespan. *British Journal of Psychology, 81,* 335–340.

Cross-National Collaborative Group. (1992). The changing rate of major depression. *Journal of the American Medical Association, 268,* 3098–3105.

Crowell, A. L., Riva-Posse, P., Holtzheimer, P. E., Garlow, S. J., Kelley, M. E., Gross, R. E., Denison, L., Quinn, S., & Mayberg, H. S. (2019). Long-term outcomes of subcallosal cingulate deep brain stimulation for treatment-resistant depression. *American Journal of Psychiatry, 176,* 949–956.

Crowell, J. A., & Waters, E. (1994). Bowlby's theory grown up: The role of attachment in adult love relationships. *Psychological Inquiry, 5,* 1–22.

Croy, I., Bojanowski, V., & Hummel, T. (2013). Men without a sense of smell exhibit a strongly reduced number of sexual relationships, women exhibit reduced partnership security: A reanalysis of previously published data. *Biological Psychology, 92,* 292–294.

Croy, I., Negoias, S., Novakova, L., Landis, B. N., & Hummel, T. (2012). Learning about the functions of the olfactory system from people without a sense of smell. *PLOS ONE, 7.* https://journals.plos.org/plosone/article?id=10.1371/journal.pone.0033365

Csikszentmihalyi, M. (1990). *Flow: The psychology of optimal experience.* Harper & Row.

Csikszentmihalyi, M. (1999). If we are so rich, why aren't we happy? *American Psychologist, 54,* 821–827.

Csikszentmihalyi, M., & Hunter, J. (2003). Happiness in everyday life: The uses of experience sampling. *Journal of Happiness Studies, 4,* 185–199.

Cuartas, J. (2021). Corporal punishment and early childhood development in 49 low- and middle-income countries. *Child Abuse & Neglect, 120*. https://www.sciencedirect.com/science/article/abs/pii/S0145213421002787

Cucchi, A., Ryan, D., Konstantakopoulos, G., Stroumpa, S., Kaçar, A. Ş., Renshaw, S., Landau, S., & Kravariti, E. (2016). Lifetime prevalence of non-suicidal self-injury in patients with eating disorders: A systematic review and meta-analysis. *Psychological Medicine, 46*, 1345–1358.

Cuijpers, P. (2017). Four decades of outcome research on psychotherapies for adult depression: An overview of a series of meta-analyses. *Canadian Psychology/Psychologie Canadienne, 58*, 7–19.

Cuijpers, P., Driessen, E., Hollon, S. D., van Oppen, P., Barth, J., & Andersson, G. (2012). The efficacy of non-directive supportive therapy for adult depression: A meta-analysis. *Clinical Psychology Review, 32*, 280–291.

Cuijpers, P., Pineda, B. S., Quero, S., Karyotaki, E., Struijs, S. Y., Figueroa, C. A., Llamas, J. A., Furukawa, T. A., & Muñoz, R. F. (2021). Psychological interventions to prevent the onset of depressive disorders: A meta-analysis of randomized controlled trials. *Clinical Psychology Review, 83*, 13.

Cuijpers, P., Reijnders, M., & Huibers, M. J. H. (2019). The role of common factors in psychotherapy outcomes. *Annual Review of Clinical Psychology, 15*, 207–231.

Cummings, J. R., & Tomiyama, A. J. (2019). Food loves company: Risky eating with friends increases interpersonal closeness. *Journal of Experimental Social Psychology, 81*, 61–69.

Cummings, L. R., Mattfeld, A. T., Pettit, J. W., & McMakin, D. L. (2021). Viewing nonsuicidal self-injury in adolescence through a developmental neuroscience lens: The impact of neural sensitivity to socioaffective pain and reward. *Clinical Psychological Science, 9*, 767–790.

Cunningham, G. B., Ferreira, M., & Fink, J. S. (2009). Reactions to prejudicial statements: The influence of statement content and characteristics of the commenter. *Group Dynamics: Theory, Research, and Practice, 13*, 59–73.

Cunningham, M. R., Roberts, A., Barbee, A. P., Druen, P. B., & Wu, C.-H. (2005). "Their ideas of beauty are, on the whole, the same as ours": Consistency and variability in the cross-cultural perception of female physical attractiveness. *Journal of Personality and Social Psychology, 68*, 261–279.

Cunningham, P. J., & Shahan, T. A. (2019). Rats engage in suboptimal choice when the delay to food is sufficiently long. *Journal of Experimental Psychology: Animal Learning and Cognition, 45*, 301–310.

Cunningham, W. A., Johnson, M. K., Raye, C. L., Gatenby, J. C., Gore, J. C., & Banaji, M. R. (2004). Separable neural components in the processing of Black and White faces. *Psychological Science, 15*, 806–813.

Cunningham, W. A., & Kirkland, T. (2014). The joyful, yet balanced, amygdala: Moderated responses to positive but not negative stimuli in trait happiness. *Social Cognitive and Affective Neuroscience, 9*, 760–766.

Curry, J., Silva, S., Rohde, P., Ginsburg, G., Kratochvil, C., Simons, A., Kirchner, J., May, D., Kennard, B., Mayes, T., Feeny, N., Albano, A. M., Lavanier, S., Reinecke, M., Jacobs, R., Becker-Weidman, E., Weller, E., Emslie, G., Walkup, J., ... March, J. (2011). Recovery and recurrence following treatment for adolescent major depression. *Archives of General Psychiatry, 68*, 263–269.

Curtin, S. C., & Hedegaard, H. (2019). *Suicide rates for females and males by race and ethnicity: United States, 1999 and 2017*. NCHS Health Statistics. https://www.cdc.gov/nchs/data/hestat/suicide/rates_1999_2017.htm

Curtis, R. C., & Miller, K. (1986). Believing another likes or dislikes you: Behaviors making the beliefs come true. *Journal of Personality and Social Psychology, 51*, 284–290.

Custers, R., & Aarts, H. (2010). The unconscious will: How the pursuit of goals operates outside of conscious awareness. *Science, 329*, 47–50.

Cuthbert, B. N. (2022). Research Domain Criteria (RDoC): Progress and potential. *Current Directions in Psychological Science, 31*(2), 107–114.

Cyders, M. A., & Smith, G. T. (2008). Emotion-based dispositions to rash action: Positive and negative urgency. *Psychological Bulletin, 134*, 807–828.

Czarna, A. Z., Leifeld, P., Śmieja, M., Dufner, M., & Salovey, P. (2016). Do narcissism and emotional intelligence win us friends? Modeling dynamics of peer popularity using inferential network analysis. *Personality and Social Psychology Bulletin, 42*, 1588–1599.

Czeisler, C. A., Allan, J. S., Strogatz, S. H., Ronda, J. M., Sanchez, R., & Rios, C. D. (1986). Bright light resets the human circadian pacemaker independent of the timing of the sleep-wake cycle. *Science, 233*, 667–671.

Czeisler, C. A., Duffy, J. F., Shanahan, T. L., Brown, E. N., Mitchell, J. F., Rimmer, D. W., Ronda, J. M., Silva, E. J., Allan, J. S., Emens, J. S., Dijk, D. J., & Kronauer, R. E. (1999). Stability, precision, and near-24-hour period of the human circadian pacemaker. *Science, 284*, 2177–2181.

Czeisler, C. A., Kronauer, R. E., Allan, J. S., & Duffy, J. F. (1989). Bright light induction of strong (Type O) resetting of the human circadian pacemaker. *Science, 244*, 1328–1333.

Dadds, M. R., & Tully, L. A. (2019). What is it to discipline a child: What should it be? A reanalysis of time-out from the perspective of child mental health, attachment, and trauma. *American Psychologist, 74*(7), 794–808.

Dahl, R. E. (2004). Adolescent brain development: A period of vulnerabilities and opportunities. *Annals of the New York Academy of Sciences, 1021*, 1–22.

Dahl, R. E., Allen, N. B., Wilbrecht, L., & Suleiman, A. B. (2018). Importance of investing in adolescence from a developmental science perspective. *Nature, 554*, 441–450.

Dakwar, E., Nunes, E. V., Hart, C. L., Foltin, R. W., Mathew, S. J., Carpenter, K. M., Choi, C. J. J., Basaraba, C. N., Pavlicova, M., & Levin, F. R. (2019). A single ketamine infusion combined with mindfulness-based behavioral modification to treat cocaine dependence: A randomized clinical trial. *American Journal of Psychiatry, 176*, 923–930.

Dalai Lama XIV, & Cutler, H. C. (2009). *The art of happiness in a troubled world*. Harmony.

Daley, J. (2011, July/August). What you don't know can kill you. *Discover*. https://www.discovermagazine.com/mind/what-you-dont-know-can-kill-you

Daly, M., Delaney, L., Egan, R. F., & Baumeister, R. F. (2015). Childhood self-control and unemployment throughout the life span: Evidence from two British cohort studies. *Psychological Science, 26*, 709–723.

Daly, M., Sutin, A. R., & Robinson, E. (2021). Depression reported by US adults in 2017–2018 and March and April 2020. *Journal of Affective Disorders, 278*, 131–135.

Damasio, A. R. (2003). *Looking for Spinoza: Joy, sorrow, and the feeling brain*. Harcourt.

Damasio, A. R. (2010). *Self comes to mind: Constructing the conscious brain*. Pantheon.

Damian, R. I., & Roberts, B. W. (2015). The associations of birth order with personality and intelligence in a representative sample of U.S. high school students. *Journal of Research in Personality, 58*, 96–105.

Damian, R. I., Spengler, M., Sutu, A., & Roberts, B. W. (2019). Sixteen going on sixty-six: A longitudinal study of personality stability and change across 50 years. *Journal of Personality and Social Psychology, 117*(3), 674–695.

Damme, K. S. F., Norton, E. S., Briggs-Gowan, M. J., Wakschlag, L. S., & Mittal, V. A. (2022). Developmental patterning of irritability enhances prediction of psychopathology in preadolescence: Improving RDoC with developmental science. *Journal of Psychopathology and Clinical Science, 131*(6), 556–566.

Damon, W., & Hart, D. (1982). The development of self-understanding from infancy through adolescence. *Child Development, 53*, 841–864.

Damon, W., & Hart, D. (1988). *Self-understanding in childhood and adolescence*. Cambridge University Press.

Damon, W., & Hart, D. (1992). Self-understanding and its role in social and moral development. In M. H. Bornstein & M. E. Lamb (Eds.), *Developmental psychology: An advanced textbook* (3rd ed.). Lawrence Erlbaum.

Dana, J., Dawes, R., & Peterson, N. (2013). Belief in the unstructured interview: The persistence of an illusion. *Judgment and Decision Making, 8*, 512–520.

Dandine-Roulland, C., Laurent, R., Dall'Ara, I., Toupance, B., & Chaix, R. (2019). Genomic evidence for MHC disassortative mating in humans. *Proceedings of the Royal Society B*, 286(1899). https://royalsocietypublishing.org/doi/10.1098/rspb.2018.2664

Danek, A. H., & Salvi, C. (2020). Moment of truth: Why aha! experiences are correct. *Journal of Creative Behavior, 54*(2), 484–486.

Dang, J., Barker, P., Baumert, A., Bentvelzen, M., Berkman, E., Buchholz, N., Buczny, J., Chen, Z., De Cristofaro, V., de Vries, L., Dewitte, S., Giacomantonio, M., Gong, R., Homan, M., Imhoff, R., Ismail, I., Jia, L., Kubiak, T., Lange, F., ... Zinkernagel, A. (2021). A multilab replication of the ego depletion effect. *Social Psychological and Personality Science, 12*(1), 14–24.

Daniel, T. A., & Katz, J. S. (2018). Primacy and recency effects for taste. *Journal of Experimental Psychology: Learning, Memory, and Cognition, 44*, 399–405.

Daniels, D. P., & Zlatev, J. J. (2019). Choice architects reveal a bias toward positivity and certainty. *Organizational Behavior and Human Decision Processes, 151*, 132–149.

Danner, D. D., Snowdon, D. A., & Friesen, W. V. (2001). Positive emotions in early life and longevity: Findings from the Nun Study. *Journal of Personality and Social Psychology, 80*, 804–813.

Danso, H., & Esses, V. (2001). Black experimenters and the intellectual test performance of White participants: The tables are turned. *Journal of Experimental Social Psychology, 37*, 158–165.

Dargue, N., Sweller, N., & Jones, M. P. (2019). When our hands help us understand: A meta-analysis into the effects of gesture on comprehension. *Psychological Bulletin, 145*, 765–784.

Darley, J. M., & Alter, A. (2013). Behavioral issues of punishment, retribution, and deterrence. In E. Shafir (Ed.), *The behavioral foundations of public policy* (pp. 181–194). Princeton University Press.

Darley, J. M., & Latané, B. (1968, December). When will people help in a crisis? *Psychology Today*, pp. 54–57, 70–71.

Darley, J. M., & Latané, B. (1968). Bystander intervention in emergencies: Diffusion of responsibility. *Journal of Personality and Social Psychology, 8*, 377–383.

Darwin, C. (1859). *On the origin of species by means of natural selection*. John Murray.

Darwin, C. (1872). *The expression of the emotions in man and animals*. John Murray.

Daum, I., & Schugens, M. M. (1996). On the cerebellum and classical conditioning. *Psychological Science, 5*, 58–61.

Davey, G. C. L. (1992). Classical conditioning and the acquisition of human fears and phobias: A review and synthesis of the literature. *Advances in Behavior Research and Therapy, 14*, 29–66.

Davey, G. C. L. (1995). Preparedness and phobias: Specific evolved associations or a generalized expectancy bias? *Behavioral and Brain Sciences, 18*, 289–297.

Davidoff, J. (2004). Coloured thinking. *The Psychologist, 17*, 570–572.

Davidson, R. J., Kabat-Zinn, J., Schumacher, J., Rosenkranz, M., Muller, D., Santorelli, S. F., Urbanowski, F., Harrington, A., Bonus, K., & Sheridan, J. F. (2003). Alterations in brain and immune function produced by mindfulness meditation. *Psychosomatic Medicine, 65*, 564–570.

Davidson, R. J., Putnam, K. M., & Larson, C. L. (2000). Dysfunction in the neural circuitry of emotion regulation—a possible prelude to violence. *Science, 289*, 591–594.

Davidson, T. L., & Riley, A. L. (2015). Taste, sickness, and learning. *American Scientist, 103*, 204–211.

Davies, P. (2007). *Cosmic jackpot: Why our universe is just right for life*. Houghton Mifflin.

Davis, A. K., Barrett, F. S., May, D. G., Cosimano, M. P., Sepeda, N. D., Johnson, M. W., Finan, P. H., & Griffiths, R. R. (2021). Effects of psilocybin-assisted therapy on major depressive disorder a randomized clinical trial. *JAMA Psychiatry, 78*, 481–489.

Davis, B. E., Moon, R. Y., Sachs, H. C., & Ottolini, M. C. (1998). Effects of sleep position on infant motor development. *Pediatrics, 102*, 1135–1140.

Davis, D. E., Choe, E., Meyers, J., Wade, N., Varias, K., Gifford, A., Quinn, A., Hook, J. N., Van Tongeren, D. R., Griffin, B. J., & Worthington, E. L. (2016). Thankful for the little things: A meta-analysis of gratitude interventions. *Journal of Counseling Psychology, 63*, 20–31.

Davis, E. P., Stout, S. A., Molet, J., Vegetabile, B., Glynn, L. M., Sandman, C. A., Heins, K., Stern, H., & Baram, T. Z. (2017). Exposure to unpredictable maternal sensory signals influences cognitive development across species. *PNAS, 114*, 10390–10395.

Davis, H., IV, Liotti, M., Ngan, E. T., Woodward, T. S., Van Sellenberg, J. X., van Anders, S. M., Smith, A., & Mayberg, H. S. (2008). fMRI BOLD signal changes in elite swimmers while viewing videos of personal failure. *Brain Imaging and Behavior, 2*, 84–93.

Davis, J. I., Senghas, A., Brandt, F., & Ochsner, K. N. (2010). The effects of BOTOX injections on emotional experience. *Emotion, 10*(3), 433–440.

Davis, J. O., & Phelps, J. A. (1995). Twins with schizophrenia: Genes or germs? *Schizophrenia Bulletin, 21*, 13–18.

Davis, J. O., Phelps, J. A., & Bracha, H. S. (1995). Prenatal development of monozygotic twins and concordance for schizophrenia. *Schizophrenia Bulletin, 21*, 357–366.

Davis, J. P., Lander, K., & Jansari, A. (2013). I never forget a face. *The Psychologist, 26*, 726–729.

Davis, K., Christodoulou, J., Seider, S., & Gardner, H. (2011). The theory of multiple intelligences. In R. J. Sternberg & S. B. Kaufman (Eds.), *Cambridge handbook of intelligence* (pp. 485–503). Cambridge University Press.

Davis, M. (2005). Searching for a drug to extinguish fear. *Cerebrum, 7*, 47–58.

Davison, K. P., Pennebaker, J. W., & Dickerson, S. S. (2000). Who talks? The social psychology of illness support groups. *American Psychologist, 55*, 205–217.

Davison, S. L., & Davis, S. R. (2011). Androgenic hormones and aging—The link with female function. *Hormones and Behavior, 59*, 745–753.

Dawes, R. M. (1980). Social dilemmas. *Annual Review of Psychology, 31*, 169–193.

Dawkins, L., Shahzad, F.-Z., Ahmed, S. S., & Edmonds, C. J. (2011). Expectation of having consumed caffeine can improve performance and moods. *Appetite, 57*, 597–600.

Dawkins, R. (1998). *Unweaving the rainbow*. Houghton Mifflin.

Dawkins, R. (2007, July 1). Inferior design. *The New York Times*. https://www.nytimes.com/2007/07/01/books/review/Dawkins-t.html

Daws, R. E., Timmermann, C., Giribaldi, B., Sexton, J. D., Wall, M. B., Erritzoe, D., Roseman, L., Nutt, D., & Carhart-Harris, R. (2022). Increased global integration in the brain after psilocybin therapy for depression. *Nature Medicine, 28*, 844–851.

Day, F. R., Thompson, D. J., Helgason, H., Chasman, D. I., Finucane, H., Sulem, P., Ruth, K. S., Whalen, S., Sarkar, A. K., Albrecht, E., Altmaier, E., Amini, M., Barbieri, C. M., Boutin, T., Campbell, A., Demerath, E., Giri, A., He, C., Hottenga, J. J., … Perry, J. R. B. (2017). Genomic analyses identify hundreds of variants associated with age at menarche and support a role for puberty timing in cancer risk. *Nature Genetics, 49*, 834–841.

Dean, G. (2012, November/December). Phrenology and the grand delusion of experience. *Skeptical Inquirer*, pp. 31–38.

Dean, M., & Ortoleva, P. (2019). The empirical relationship between nonstandard economic behaviors. *PNAS, 116*, 16262–16267.

Dean, M., Harwood, R., & Kasari, C. (2017). The art of camouflage: Gender differences in the social behaviors of girls and boys with autism spectrum disorder. *Autism, 21*, 678–689.

Deary, I. J., Batty, G. D., & Gale, C. R. (2008). Bright children become enlightened adults. *Psychological Science, 19*, 1–6.

Deary, I. J., Johnson, W., & Houlihan, L. M. (2009). Genetic foundations of human intelligence. *Human Genetics, 126*, 215–232.

Deary, I. J., Pattie, A., & Starr, J. M. (2013). The stability of intelligence from age 11 to age 90 years: The Lothian birth cohort of 1921. *Psychological Science, 24*, 2361–2368.

Deary, I. J., Strand, S., Smith, P., & Fernandes, C. (2007). Intelligence and educational achievement. *Intelligence, 35*, 13–21.

Deary, I. J., Thorpe, G., Wilson, V., Starr, J. M., & Whalley, L. J. (2003). Population sex differences in IQ at age 11: The Scottish mental survey 1932. *Intelligence, 31*, 533–541.

Deary, I. J., Whalley, L. J., & Starr, J. M. (2009). *A lifetime of intelligence: Follow-up studies of the Scottish Mental Surveys of 1932 and 1947*. American Psychological Association.

Deary, I. J., Whiteman, M. C., Starr, J. M., Whalley, L. J., & Fox, H. C. (2004). The impact of childhood intelligence on later life: Following up the Scottish mental surveys of 1932 and 1947. *Journal of Personality and Social Psychology, 86*, 130–147.

Deary, I. J., Yang, J., Davies, G., Harris, S. E., Tenesa, A., Liewald, D., Luciano, M., Lopez, L. M., Gow, A. J., Corley, J., Redmond, P., Fox, H. C., Rowe, S. J., Haggarty, P., McNeill, G., Goddard, M. E., Porteous, D. J., Whalley, L., J., Starr, J. M., & Visscher, P. M. (2012). Genetic contributions to stability and change in intelligence from childhood to old age. *Nature, 481*, 212–215.

deBettencourt, M. T., Keene, P. A., Awh, E., & Vogel, E. K. (2019). Real-time triggering reveals concurrent lapses of attention and working memory. *Nature Human Behaviour, 3*, 808–816.

de Boer, H., Donker, A. S., Kostons, D. D., & van der Werf, G. P. (2018). Long-term effects of metacognitive strategy instruction on student academic performance: A meta-analysis. *Educational Research Review, 24*, 98–115.

de Boysson-Bardies, B., Halle, P., Sagart, L., & Durand, C. (1989). A cross-linguistic investigation of vowel formants in babbling. *Journal of Child Language, 16*, 1–17.

de Courten-Myers, G. M. (2005, February 4). Personal communication.

Debost, J. C., Larsen, J. T., Munk-Olsen, T., Mortensen, P. B., Agerbo, E., & Petersen, L. V. (2019). Childhood infections and schizophrenia: The impact of parental SES and mental illness, and childhood adversities. *Brain, Behavior, and Immunity, 81*, 341–347.

Debowska, W. Wolak, T., Nowicka, A., Kozak, A., Szwed, M., & Kossut, M. (2016). Functional and structural neuroplasticity induced by short-term tactile training based on Braille reading. *Frontiers in Neuroscience, 10,* 460.

DeBruine, L. M. (2002). Facial resemblance enhances trust. *Proceedings of the Royal Society of London, 269,* 1307–1312.

DeBruine, L. M. (2004). Facial resemblance increases the attractiveness of same-sex faces more than other-sex faces. *Proceedings of the Royal Society of London B, 271,* 2085–2090.

DeCasper, A. J., & Spence, M. J. (1986). Prenatal maternal speech influences newborns' perception of speech sounds. *Infant Behavior and Development, 9,* 133–150.

DeCasper, A. J., Lecanuet, J.-P., Busnel, M.-C., Granier-Deferre, C., & Maugeais, R. (1994). Fetal reactions to recurrent maternal speech. *Infant Behavior and Development, 17,* 159–164.

de Chastelaine, M., Mattson, J. T., Wang, T. H., Donley, B. E., & Rugg, M. D. (2016). The neural correlates of recollection and retrieval monitoring: Relationships with age and recollection performance. *NeuroImage, 138,* 164–175.

Dechêne, A., Stahl, C., Hansen, J., & Wänke, M. (2010). The truth about the truth: A meta-analytic review of the truth effect. *Personality and Social Psychology Review, 14,* 238–257.

Dechesne, M., Pyszczynski, T., Arndt, J., Ransom, S., Sheldon, K. M., van Knippenberg, A., & Janssen, J. (2003). Literal and symbolic immortality: The effect of evidence of literal immortality on self-esteem striving in response to mortality salience. *Journal of Personality and Social Psychology, 84,* 722–737.

Deci, E. L., Koestner, R., & Ryan, R. M. (1999, November). A meta-analytic review of experiments examining the effects of extrinsic rewards on intrinsic motivation. *Psychological Bulletin, 125,* 627–668.

Deci, E. L., & Ryan, R. M. (2012). Motivation, personality, and development within embedded social contexts: An overview of self-determination theory. In R. M. Ryan (Ed.), *Oxford handbook of human motivation* (pp. 85–107). Oxford University Press.

Deckman, T., DeWall, C. N., Way, B., Gilman, R., & Richman, S. (2014). Can marijuana reduce social pain? *Social Psychological and Personality Science, 5,* 131–139.

De Dreu, C. K. W., Nijstad, B. A., Baas, M., Wolsink, I., & Roskes, M. (2012). Working memory benefits creative insight, musical improvisation, and original ideation through maintained task-focused attention. *Personality and Social Psychology Bulletin, 38,* 656–669.

Deeley, Q., Daly, E., Surguladze, S., Tunstall, N., Mezey, G., Beer, D., Ambikapathy, A., Robertson, D., Giampietro, V., Brammer, M. J., & Clark, A. (2006). Facial emotion processing in criminal psychopathy. *British Journal of Psychiatry, 189,* 533–539.

DeFranza, D., Mishra, H., & Mishra, A. (2020). How language shapes prejudice against women: An examination across 45 world languages. *Journal of Personality and Social Psychology, 119*(1), 7–22.

de Gee, J., Knapen, T., & Donner, T. H. (2014). Decision-related pupil dilation reflects upcoming choice and individual bias. *PNAS, 111,* E618–E625.

de Gelder, B. (2010). Uncanny sight in the blind. *Scientific American, 302,* 60–65.

de Graaf, N. M., Steensma, T. D., Carmichael, P., VanderLaan, D. P., Aitken, M., Cohen-Kettenis, P. T., de Vries, A. L. C., Kreukels, B. P. C., Wasserman, L., Wood, H., & Zucker, K. J. (2022). Suicidality in clinic-referred transgender adolescents. *European Child & Adolescent Psychiatry, 31*(1), 67–83.

Dehaene, S., & Changeux, J. P. (2011). Experimental and theoretical approaches to conscious processing. *Neuron, 70,* 200–227.

Dehne, K. L., & Riedner, G. (2005). *Sexually transmitted infections among adolescents: The need for adequate health services* [PDF file]. World Health Organization. https://apps.who.int/iris/bitstream/handle/10665/43221/9241562889.pdf?sequence=1&isAllowed=y

de Hoogh, A. H. B., den Hartog, D. N., Koopman, P. L., Thierry, H., van den Berg, P. T., van der Weide, J. G., & Wilderom, C. P. M. (2004). Charismatic leadership, environmental dynamism, and performance. *European Journal of Work and Organisational Psychology, 13,* 447–471.

De keersmaecker, J., Dunning, D., Pennycook, G., Rand, D. G., Sanchez, C., Unkelbach, C., & Roets, A. (2020). Investigating the robustness of the illusory truth effect across individual differences in cognitive ability, need for cognitive closure, and cognitive style. *Personality and Social Psychology Bulletin, 46*(2), 204–215.

Dekker, S., Lee, N. C., Howard-Jones, P., & Jolles, J. (2012). Neuromyths in education: Prevalence and predictors of misconceptions among teachers. *Frontiers in Psychology, 3,* 429.

DeLamater, J. D. (2012). Sexual expression in later life: A review and synthesis. *Journal of Sex Research, 49,* 125–141.

DeLamater, J. D., & Sill, M. (2005). Sexual desire in later life. *Journal of Sex Research, 42,* 138–149.

Delaney, H. D., Miller, W. R., & Bisonó, A. M. (2007). Religiosity and spirituality among psychologists: A survey of clinician members of the American Psychological Association. *Professional Psychology: Research and Practice, 38,* 538–546.

de Lange, M., Debets, L., Ruitenberg, K., & Holland, R. (2012). Making less of a mess: Scent exposure as a tool for behavioral change. *Social Influence, 7,* 90–97.

Delaunay-El Allam, M., Soussignan, R., Patris, B., Marlier, L., & Schaal, B. (2010). Long-lasting memory for an odor acquired at the mother's breast. *Developmental Science, 13,* 849–863.

Delgado, J. M. R. (1969). *Physical control of the mind: Toward a psychocivilized society.* Harper & Row.

Delgado, M. M., & Sulloway, F. J. (2017). Attributes of conscientiousness throughout the animal kingdom: An empirical and evolutionary overview. *Psychological Bulletin, 143,* 823–867.

DellaPosta, D. (2018). Gay acquaintanceship and attitudes toward homosexuality: A conservative test. *Socius: Sociological Research for a Dynamic World, 4,* 1–12.

DeLoache, J. S., & Brown, A. L. (1987, October–December). Differences in the memory-based searching of delayed and normally developing young children. *Intelligence, 11,* 277–289.

DeLoache, J. S., Chiong, C., Sherman, K., Islam, N., Vanderborght, M., Troseth, G. L., Strouse, G. A., & O'Doherty, K. (2010). Do babies learn from baby media? *Psychological Science, 21,* 1570–1574.

DelPriore, D. J., Schlomer, G. L., & Ellis, B. J. (2017). Impact of fathers on parental monitoring of daughters and their affiliation with sexually promiscuous peers: A genetically and environmentally controlled sibling study. *Developmental Psychology, 53,* 1330–1343.

DelPriore, D. J., Shakiba, N., Schlomer, G. L., Hill, S. E., & Ellis, B. J. (2019). The effects of fathers on daughters' expectations for men. *Developmental Psychology, 55,* 1523–1536.

Dement, W. C. (1978). *Some must watch while some must sleep.* Norton.

Dement, W. C., & Wolpert, E. A. (1958). The relation of eye movements, body mobility, and external stimuli to dream content. *Journal of Experimental Psychology, 55,* 543–553.

Demertzi, A., Tagliazucchi, E., Dehaene, S., Deco, G., Bartfield, P., Raimondo, F., Martial, C., Fernández-Espejo, D., Rohaut, B., Voss, H. U., Schiff, N. D., Owen, A. M., Laureys, S., Naccache, L., & Sitt, J. D. (2019). Human consciousness is supported by dynamic complex patterns of brain signal coordination. *Science Advances, 5*(2). https://www.science.org/doi/10.1126/sciadv.aat7603

De Meyer, G., Shapiro, F., Vanderstichele, H., Vanmechelen, E., Engelborghs, S., De Deyn, P. P., & Trojanowski, J. Q. (2010). Diagnosis-independent Alzheimer disease biomarker signature in cognitively normal elderly people. *Archives of Neurology, 67,* 949–956.

de Moor, E. L., Denissen, J. J. A., Emons, W. H. M., Bleidorn, W., Luhmann, M., Orth, U., & Chung, J. M. (2021). Self-esteem and satisfaction with social relationships across time. *Journal of Personality and Social Psychology, 120*(1), 173–191.

Dempster, E., Viana, J., Pidsley, R., & Mill, J. (2013). Epigenetic studies of schizophrenia: Progress, predicaments, and promises for the future. *Schizophrenia Bulletin, 39,* 11–16.

De Neve, J.-E., Diener, E., Tay, L., & Xuereb, C. (2013). The objective benefits of subjective well-being. In J. F. Helliwell, R. Layard, & J. Sachs (Eds.), *World happiness report 2013* (Vol. 2, pp. 54–79). UN Sustainable Network Development Solutions Network.

De Neve, K. M., & Cooper, H. (1998). The happy personality: A meta-analysis of 137 personality traits and subjective well-being. *Psychological Bulletin, 124,* 197–229.

Denissen, J. J. A., Bleidorn, W., Hennecke, M., Luhmann, M., Orth, U., Specht, J., & Zimmermann, J. (2018). Uncovering the power of personality to shape income. *Psychological Science, 29,* 3–13.

Deniz, F., Nunez-Elizalde, A. O., Huth, A. G., & Gallant, J. L. (2019). The representation of semantic information across human cerebral cortex during listening versus reading is invariant to stimulus modality. *Journal of Neuroscience, 39,* 7722–7736.

Dennett, D. C. (1996, September 9). Quoted by Ian Parker in Richard Dawkins' evolution. *The New Yorker*, pp. 41–45.

de Oliveira, C., Cho, E., Kavelaars, R., Jamieson, M., Bao, B., & Rehm, J. (2020). Economic analyses of mental health and substance use interventions in the workplace: A systematic literature review and narrative synthesis. *Lancet Psychiatry, 7*, 893–910.

Denyer, S., & Gowen, A. (2018, April 18). Too many men. *The Washington Post*. https://www.washingtonpost.com/

DePaulo, B. M., Blank, A. L., Swaim, G. W., & Hairfield, J. G. (1992). Expressiveness and expressive control. *Personality and Social Psychology Bulletin, 18*, 276–285.

De Pinto, J. (2019, April 19). *Support for marijuana legalization hits new high, CBS News poll finds*. CBS News. https://www.cbsnews.com/news/support-for-marijuana-legalization-hits-new-high-cbs-news-poll-finds/

Depla, M. F. I. A., ten Have, M. L., van Balkom, A. J. L. M., & de Graaf, R. (2008). Specific fears and phobias in the general population: Results from the Netherlands Mental Health Survey and Incidence Study (NEMESIS). *Social Psychiatry and Psychiatric Epidemiology, 43*, 200–208.

Depow, G. J., Francis, Z., & Inzlicht, M. (2021). The experience of empathy in everyday life. *Psychological Science, 32*, 1198–1213.

Derebery, M. J., Vermiglio, A., Berliner, K. I., Potthoff, M., & Holguin, K. (2012). Facing the music: Pre- and postconcert assessment of hearing in teenagers. *Otology & Neurotology, 33*, 1136–1141.

Deri, S., Davidai, S., & Gilovich, T. (2017). Home alone: Why people believe others' social lives are richer than their own. *Journal of Personality and Social Psychology, 113*, 858–877.

Desai, M. U., Paranamana, N., Restrepo-Toro, M., O'Connell, M., Davidson, L., & Stanhope, V. (2021). Implicit organizational bias: Mental health treatment culture and norms as barriers to engaging with diversity. *American Psychologist, 76*(1), 78–90.

Deschrijver, E., & Palmer, C. (2020). Reframing social cognition: Relational versus representational mentalizing. *Psychological Bulletin, 146*, 941–969.

Deslauriers, L., McCarthy, L. S., Miller, K., Callaghan, K., & Kestin, G. (2019). Measuring actual learning versus feeling of learning in response to being actively engaged in the classroom. *PNAS, 116*, 19251–19257.

Desmurget, M., Reilly, K. T., Richard, N., Szathmari, A., Mottolese, C., & Sirigu, A. (2009). Movement intention after parietal cortex stimulation in humans. *Science, 324*, 811–813.

DeSteno, D., Petty, R. E., Wegener, D. T., & Rucker, D. D. (2000). Beyond valence in the perception of likelihood: The role of emotion specificity. *Journal of Personality and Social Psychology, 78*, 397–416.

Dettman, S. J., Pinder, D., Briggs, R. J. S., Dowell, R. C., & Leigh, J. R. (2007). Communication development in children who receive the cochlear implant younger than 12 months: Risk versus benefits. *Ear and Hearing, 28*(suppl 2), 11S–18S.

Deutsch, J. A. (1972, July). Brain reward: ESP and ecstasy. *Psychology Today*, 46–48.

DeValois, R. L., & DeValois, K. K. (1975). Neural coding of color. In E. C. Carterette & M. P. Friedman (Eds.), *Handbook of perception: Vol. V. Seeing*. Academic Press.

De Vaus, J., Hornsey, M. J., Kuppens, P., & Bastian, B. (2018). Exploring the East-West divide in prevalence of affective disorder: A case for cultural differences in coping with negative emotion. *Personality and Social Psychology Review, 22*, 285–304.

Devine, P. G., & Ash, T. L. (2022). Diversity training goals, limitations, and promise: A review of the multidisciplinary literature. *Annual Review of Psychology, 73*, 403–429.

Dew, M. A., Hoch, C. C., Buysse, D. J., Monk, T. H., Begley, A. E., Houck, P. R., Hall, M., Kupfer, D. J., & Reynolds, C. F., III. (2003). Healthy older adults' sleep predicts all-cause mortality at 4 to 19 years of follow-up. *Psychosomatic Medicine, 65*, 63–73.

de Waal, F. (2016). *Are we smart enough to know how smart animals are?* Norton.

de Waal, F. (2019). *Mama's last hug: Animal emotions and what they tell us about ourselves*. Norton.

de Waal, F. (2022). *Different: Gender through the eyes of a primatologist*. Norton.

DeWall, C. N., Lambert, N. M., Slotter, E. B., Pond, R. S., Jr., Deckman, T., Finkel, E. J., Luchies, L. B., & Fincham, F. D. (2011). So far away from one's partner, yet so close to romantic alternatives: Avoidant attachment, interest in alternatives, and infidelity. *Journal of Personality and Social Psychology, 101*, 1302–1316.

DeWall, C. N., MacDonald, G., Webster, G. D., Masten, C. L., Baumeister, R. F., Powell, C., Combs, D., Schurtz, D. R., Stillman, T. F., Tice, D. M., & Eisenberger, N. I. (2010). Acetaminophen reduces social pain: Behavioral and neural evidence. *Psychological Science, 21*, 931–937.

DeWall, C. N., & Pond, R. S., Jr. (2011). Loneliness and smoking: The costs of the desire to reconnect. *Self and Identity, 10*, 375–385.

DeWall, C. N., Pond, R. S., Jr., Carter, E. C., McCullough, M. E., Lambert, N. M., Fincham, F. D., & Nezlek, J. B. (2014). Explaining the relationship between religiousness and substance use: Self-control matters. *Journal of Personality and Social Psychology, 107*, 339–351.

de Witte, M., Spruit, A., van Hooren, S., Moonen, X., & Stams, G. J. (2019). Effects of music interventions on stress-related outcomes: A systematic review and two meta-analyses. *Health Psychology Review, 15*, 1–31.

De Wolff, M. S., & van IJzendoorn, M. H. (1997). Sensitivity and attachment: A meta-analysis on parental antecedents of infant attachment. *Child Development, 68*, 571–591.

DeYoung, C. G., & Allen, T. A. (2019). Personality neuroscience: A developmental perspective. In D. P. McAdams, R. L. Shiner, & J. L. Tackett (Eds.), *Handbook of personality development*. Guilford Press.

Diaconis, P. (2002, August 11). Quoted by L. Belkin in, The odds of that. *The New York Times*. https://www.nytimes.com/2002/08/11/magazine/the-odds-of-that.html

Diaconis, P., & Mosteller, F. (1989). Methods for studying coincidences. *Journal of the American Statistical Association, 84*, 853–861.

Diamond, J. (1997). *Guns, germs, and steel: The fates of human societies*. W. W. Norton.

Diamond, L. M., Dickenson, J. A., & Blair, K. L. (2017). Stability of sexual attractions across different timescales: The roles of bisexuality and gender. *Archives of Sexual Behavior, 46*, 193–204.

Diamond, M. C., Krech, & Rosenzweig, M. R. (1964). The effects of an enriched environment on the histology of the rat cerebral cortex. *Journal of Comparative Neurology, 123*(1), 111–119.

Diamond, M. C., Law, F., Rhodes, H., Lindner, B., Rosenzweig, M. R., Krech, D., & Bennett, E. L. (1966). Increases in cortical depth and glia numbers in rats subjected to enriched environment. *Journal of Comparative Neurology, 128*(1), 117–125.

Diamond, M. C., Scheibel, A. B., Murphy, G. M., & Harvey, T. (1985). On the brain of a scientist: Albert Einstein. *Experimental Neurology, 88*(1), 198–204.

Di Carlo, D., Schulte-Cloos, J., & Saudelli, G. (2018, March 3). *Has immigration really led to an increase in crime in Italy?* London School of Economics and Political Science. https://blogs.lse.ac.uk/europpblog/2018/03/03/has-immigration-really-led-to-an-increase-in-crime-in-italy/

Dick, D. M. (2007). Identification of genes influencing a spectrum of externalizing psychopathology. *Current Directions in Psychological Science, 16*, 331–335.

Dickens, L. R. (2017). Using gratitude to promote positive change: A series of meta-analyses investigating the effectiveness of gratitude interventions. *Basic and Applied Social Psychology, 39*, 193–208.

Dickens, W. T., & Flynn, J. R. (2006). Black Americans reduce the racial IQ gap: Evidence from standardization samples. *Psychological Science, 17*, 913–920.

Dicker, D., Murray, C. J. L., & Gakidou, E. (2018). Global, regional, and national age-sex-specific mortality and life expectancy, 1950–2017: A systematic analysis for the Global Burden of Disease Study 2017. *The Lancet, 392*, 1684–1735.

Dickerson, S. S., Gable, S. L., Irwin, M. R., Aziz, N., & Kemeny, M. E. (2009). Social-evaluative threat and proinflammatory cytokine regulation: An experimental laboratory investigation. *Psychological Science, 20*, 1237–1243.

Dickerson, S. S., & Kemeny, M. E. (2004). Acute stressors and cortisol responses: A theoretical integration and synthesis of laboratory research. *Psychological Bulletin, 130*, 355–391.

Dickson, B. J. (2005, June 3). Quoted in E. Rosenthal, For fruit flies, gene shift tilts sex orientation. *The New York Times*. https://www.nytimes.com/2005/06/03/science/for-fruit-flies-gene-shift-tilts-sex-orientation.html

Dickson, N., van Roode, T., Cameron, C., & Paul, C. (2013). Stability and change in same-sex attraction, experience, and identity by sex and age in a New Zealand birth cohort. *Archives of Sexual Behavior, 42*, 753–763.

Diener, E., & Oishi, S. (2000). Money and happiness: Income and subjective well-being across nations. In E. Diener & E. M. Suh (Eds.), *Subjective well-being across cultures*. MIT Press.

Diener, E., Biswas-Diener, R., & Personal Happiness Committee. (2019). Well-being interventions to improve societies [PDF file]. In J. Sachs, R. Layard, & J. F. Helliwell (Eds.), *Global happiness policy report 2019*. Global Happiness Council. https://s3.amazonaws.com/ghwbpr-2019/UAE/GH19_Ch6.pdf

Diener, E., Nickerson, C., Lucas, R. E., & Sandvik, E. (2002). Dispositional affect and job outcomes. *Social Indicators Research, 59*, 229–259.

Diener, E., Oishi, S., & Lucas, R. E. (2003). Personality, culture, and subjective well-being: Emotional and cognitive evaluations of life. *Annual Review of Psychology, 54*, 403–425.

Diener, E., Oishi, S., & Lucas, R. E. (2015). National accounts of subjective well-being. *American Psychologist, 70*, 234–242.

Diener, E., Oishi, S., & Park, J. Y. (2014). An incomplete list of eminent psychologists of the modern era. *Archives of Scientific Psychology, 21*, 20–31.

Diener, E., Pressman, S. D., Hunter, J., & Delgadillo-Chase, D. (2017). If, why, and when subjective well-being influences health, and future needed research. *Applied Psychology: Health and Well-Being, 9*, 133–167.

Diener, E., Seligman, M. E., Choi, H., & Oishi, S. (2018). Happiest people revisited. *Perspectives on Psychological Science, 13*, 176–184.

Diener, E., & Tay, L. (2015). Subjective well-being and human welfare around the world as reflected in the Gallup world poll. *International Journal of Psychology, 50*, 135–149.

Diener, E., Tay, L., & Myers, D. G. (2011). The religion paradox: If religion makes people happy, why are so many dropping out? *Journal of Personality and Social Psychology, 101*, 1278–1290.

Diener, E., Wolsic, B., & Fujita, F. (1995). Physical attractiveness and subjective well-being. *Journal of Personality and Social Psychology, 69*, 120–129.

Dietze, P., & Knowles, E. D. (2016). Social class and the motivational relevance of other human beings: Evidence from visual attention. *Psychological Science, 27*(11), 1517–1527.

Dietze, P., & Knowles, E. D. (2021). Social class predicts emotion perception and perspective-taking performance in adults. *Personality and Social Psychology Bulletin, 47*(1), 42–56.

DiFranza, J. R. (2008). Hooked from the first cigarette. *Scientific American, 298*, 82–87.

Dijksterhuis, A., & Strick, M. (2016). A case for thinking without consciousness. *Perspectives on Psychological Science, 11*, 117–132.

Dik, B. J., & Duffy, R. D. (2012). *Make your job a calling: How the psychology of vocation can change your life at work*. Templeton Press.

DiLalla, D. L., Carey, G., Gottesman, I. I., & Bouchard, T. J., Jr. (1996). Heritability of MMPI personality indicators of psychopathology in twins reared apart. *Journal of Abnormal Psychology, 105*, 491–499.

Dimberg, U., Thunberg, M., & Elmehed, K. (2000). Unconscious facial reactions to emotional facial expressions. *Psychological Science, 11*, 86–89.

Dimitrov, S., Lange, T., Gouttefangeas, C., Jensen, A. T. R., Szczepanski, M., Lehnnolz, J., Soekadar, S., Rammensee, H. G., Born, J., & Besedovsky, L. (2019). Gα_s-coupled receptor signaling and sleep regulate integrin activation of human antigen-specific T cells. *Journal of Experimental Medicine, 216*, 517–526.

Dimsdale-Zucker, H. R., Flegal, K. E., Atkins, A. S., & Reuter-Lorenz, P. A. (2019). Serial position-dependent false memory effects. *Memory, 27*, 397–409.

Dindia, K., & Allen, M. (1992). Sex differences in self-disclosure: A meta-analysis. *Psychological Bulletin, 112*, 106–124.

Ding, F., O'Donnell, J., Xu, Q., Kang, N., Goldman, N., & Nedergaard, M. (2016). Changes in the composition of brain interstitial ions control the sleep-wake cycle. *Science, 352*, 550–555.

Ding, X., Liang, M., Wu, Y., Zhao, T., Qu, G., Zhang, J., Zhang, H., Han, T., Ma, S., & Sun, Y. (2021). The impact of prenatal stressful life events on adverse birth outcomes: A systematic review and meta-analysis. *Journal of Affective Disorders, 287*, 406–416.

Dinges, C. W., Varnon, C. A., Cota, L. D., Slykerman, S., & Abramson, C. I. (2017). Studies of learned helplessness in honey bees *(Apis mellifera ligustica)*. *Journal of Experimental Psychology: Animal Learning and Cognition, 43*, 147–158.

Dinges, N. G., & Hull, P. (1992). Personality, culture, and international studies. In D. Lieberman (Ed.), *Revealing the world: An interdisciplinary reader for international studies*. Kendall-Hunt.

Dingfelder, S. (2019). My life with face blindness. *The Washington Post*. https://www.washingtonpost.com/news/magazine/wp/2019/08/21/feature/my-life-with-face-blindness/

Dingfelder, S. F. (2010, November). A second chance for the Mexican wolf. *Monitor on Psychology*, pp. 20–21.

Dingle, G. A., Sharman, L. S., Haslam, C., Donald, M., Turner, C., Partanen, R., Lynch, J., Draper, G., & van Driel, M. L. (2021). The effects of social group interventions for depression: Systematic review. *Journal of Affective Disorders, 28*, 67–81.

Dion, K. K., & Dion, K. L. (1993). Individualistic and collectivistic perspectives on gender and the cultural context of love and intimacy. *Journal of Social Issues, 49*, 53–69.

Dirix, C. E. H., Nijhuis, J. G., Jongsma, H. W., & Hornstra, G. (2009). Aspects of fetal learning and memory. *Child Development, 80*, 1251–1258.

DiSantis, K. I., Birch, L. L., Davey, A., Serrano, E. L., Zhang, J., Bruton, Y., & Fisher, J. O. (2013). Plate size and children's appetite: Effects of larger dishware on self-served portions and intake. *Pediatrics, 131*, e1451–e1458.

Discover. (1996, May). A fistful of risks. pp. 82–83.

Ditre, J. W., Brandon, T. H., Zale, E. L., & Meagher, M. M. (2011). Pain, nicotine, and smoking: Research findings and mechanistic considerations. *Psychological Bulletin, 137*, 1065–1093.

Dixon, M. L., Thiruchselvam, R., Todd, R., & Christoff, K. (2017). Emotion and the prefrontal cortex: An integrative review. *Psychological Bulletin, 143*, 1033–1081.

Dobbs, D. (2009). The post-traumatic stress trap. *Scientific American, 300*, 64–69.

Dobson, K., Campbell, L., & Stanton, S. C. E. (2018). Are you coming on to me? Bias and accuracy in couples' perceptions of sexual advances. *Journal of Social and Personal Relationships, 35*, 460–484.

Dobson, K., Zhu, J., Balzarini, R. N., & Campbell, L. (2020). Responses to sexual advances and satisfaction in romantic relationships: Is yes good and no bad? *Social Psychological and Personality Science, 11*, 801–811.

Dodge, K. A. (2009). Mechanisms of gene-environment interaction effects in the development of conduct disorder. *Perspectives on Psychological Science, 4*, 408–414.

Dodge, K. A., Bai, Y., Ladd, H. F., & Muschkin, C. G. (2017). Impact of North Carolina's early childhood programs and policies on educational outcomes in elementary school. *Child Development, 88*, 996–1014.

Doherty, C., & Kiley, J. (2016, June 22). *Key facts about partisanship and political animosity in America*. Pew Research Center. https://www.pewresearch.org/fact-tank/2016/06/22/key-facts-partisanship/

Doherty, E. W., & Doherty, W. J. (1998). Smoke gets in your eyes: Cigarette smoking and divorce in a national sample of American adults. *Families, Systems, and Health, 16*, 393–400.

Dohrenwend, B. P., Pearlin, L., Clayton, P., Hamburg, B., Dohrenwend, B. S., Riley, M., & Rose, R. (1982). Report on stress and life events. In G. R. Elliott & C. Eisdorfer (Eds.), *Stress and human health: Analysis and implications of research* (A study by the Institute of Medicine/National Academy of Sciences). Springer.

Doidge, N. (2007). *The brain that changes itself*. Viking.

Dolezal, H. (1982). *Living in a world transformed*. Academic Press.

Dolinoy, D. C., Huang, D., & Jirtle, R. L. (2007). Maternal nutrient supplementation counteracts bisphenol A-induced DNA hypomethylation in early development. *PNAS, 104*, 13056–13061.

Doliński, D., Grzyb, T., Folwarczny, M., Grzybała, P., Krzyszycha, K., Martynowska, K., & Trojanowski, J. (2017). Would you deliver an electric shock in 2015? Obedience in the experimental paradigm developed by Stanley Milgram in the 50 years following the original studies. *Social Psychological and Personality Science, 8*, 927–933.

Dollfus, S., Lecardeur, L., Morello, R., & Etard, O. (2016). Placebo response in repetitive transcranial magnetic stimulation trials of auditory hallucinations in schizophrenia: A meta-analysis. *Schizophrenia Bulletin, 42*, 301–308.

Domhoff, G. W. (1996). *Finding meaning in dreams: A quantitative approach*. Plenum.

Domhoff, G. W. (2003). *The scientific study of dreams: Neural networks, cognitive development, and content analysis*. American Psychological Association.

Domhoff, G. W. (2007). Realistic simulations and bizarreness in dream content: Past findings and suggestions for future research. In D. Barrett & P. McNamara (Eds.), *The new science of dreaming: Content, recall, and personality characteristics*. Praeger.

Domhoff, G. W. (2010). *The case for a cognitive theory of dreams* [Unpublished manuscript]. University of California at Santa Cruz. https://bit.ly/3fyXNfB

Domhoff, G. W. (2011). The neural substrate for dreaming: Is it a subsystem of the default network? *Consciousness and Cognition, 20,* 1163–1174.

Domhoff, G. W. (2014, January 5). Personal communication.

Domingos, C., Pêgo, J. M., & Santos, N. C. (2021). Effects of physical activity on brain function and structure in older adults: A systematic review. *Behavioural Brain Research, 402.* https://www.sciencedirect.com/science/article/pii/S0166432820307609

Domingue, B. W., Belsky, D. W., Fletcher, J. M., Conley, D., Boardman, J. D., & Harris, K. M. (2018). The social genome of friends and schoolmates in the National Longitudinal Study of Adolescent to Adult Health. *PNAS, 115,* 702–707.

Dominus, S. (2015, July 9). The mixed-up brothers of Bogotá. *The New York Times Magazine.* https://www.nytimes.com/interactive/2015/07/09/magazine/twins-promo.html

Domjan, M. (1992). Adult learning and mate choice: Possibilities and experimental evidence. *American Zoologist, 32,* 48–61.

Domjan, M. (1994). Formulation of a behavior system for sexual conditioning. *Psychonomic Bulletin & Review, 1,* 421–428.

Domjan, M. (2005). Pavlovian conditioning: A functional perspective. *Annual Review of Psychology, 56,* 179–206.

Donahue, C. J., Glasser, M. F., Preuss, T. M., Rilling, J. K., & Van Essen, D. C. (2018). Quantitative assessment of prefrontal cortex in humans relative to nonhuman primates. *PNAS, 115,* E5183–E5192.

Donald, J. N., Sahdra, B. K., Van Zanden, B., Duineveld, J. J., Atkins, P. W., Marshall, S. L., & Ciarrochi, J. (2018). Does your mindfulness benefit others? A systematic review and meta-analysis of the link between mindfulness and prosocial behaviour. *British Journal of Psychology, 110,* 101–125.

Dong, M., van Prooijen, J.-W., Wu, S., & van Lange, P. A. M. (2022). Culture, status, and hypocrisy: High-status people who don't practice what they preach are viewed as worse in the United States than China. *Social Psychological and Personality Science, 13*(1), 60–69.

Dong, X., Talhelm, T., & Ren, X. (2019). Teens in Rice County are more interdependent and think more holistically than nearby Wheat County. *Social Psychological and Personality Science, 10,* 966–976.

Donnellan, M. B., Trzesniewski, K. H., Robins, R. W., Moffitt, T. E., & Caspi, A. (2005). Low self-esteem is related to aggression, antisocial behavior, and delinquency. *Psychological Science, 16,* 328–335.

Donnelly, G. E., Ksendzova, M., Howell, R. T., Vohs, K. D., & Baumeister, R. F. (2016). Buying to blunt negative feelings: Materialistic escape from the self. *Review of General Psychology, 20,* 272–316.

Donnelly, G. E., Zheng, T., Haisley, E., & Norton, M. I. (2018). The amount and source of millionaires' wealth (moderately) predict their happiness. *Personality and Social Psychology Bulletin, 44,* 684–699.

Donovan, B. (2019, March). *The science of risk: How a neuroscientist and professional climber learned from one another.* Medical University of South Carolina. https://web.musc.edu/about/news-center/2019/03/18/how-a-neuroscientist-and-professional-climber-learned-from-one-another

Dorfman, P., Javidan, M., Hanges, P., Dastmalchian, A., & House, R. (2012). GLOBE: A twenty-year journey into the intriguing world of culture and leadership. *Journal of World Business, 47,* 504–518.

Doss, B. D., Rhoades, G. K., Stanley, S. M., & Markman, H. J. (2009). The effect of the transition to parenthood on relationship quality: An 8-year prospective study. *Journal of Personality and Social Psychology, 96,* 601–619.

Dotan-Eliaz, O., Sommer, K. L., & Rubin, S. (2009). Multilingual groups: Effects of linguistic ostracism on felt rejection and anger, coworker attraction, perceived team potency, and creative performance. *Basic and Applied Social Psychology, 31,* 363–375.

Dotterer, H. L., Hyde, L. W., Swartz, J. R., Hariri, A. R., & Williamson, D. E. (2017). Amygdala reactivity predicts adolescent antisocial behavior but not callous-unemotional traits. *Developmental Cognitive Neuroscience, 24,* 84–92.

Doty, R. L. (2001). Olfaction. *Annual Review of Psychology, 52,* 423–452.

Dougherty, M. R., Slevc, L. R., & Grand, J. A. (2018). Making research evaluation more transparent: Aligning research philosophy, institutional values, and reporting. *Perspectives on Psychological Science, 14*(3), 361–375.

Douglas, K. S., Guy, L. S., & Hart, S. D. (2009). Psychosis as a risk factor for violence to others: A meta-analysis. *Psychological Bulletin, 135,* 679–706.

Dovidio, J. F., & Gaertner, S. L. (1999). Reducing prejudice: Combating intergroup biases. *Current Directions in Psychological Science, 8,* 101–105.

Downing, P. E., Jiang, Y., & Shuman, M. (2001). A cortical area selective for visual processing of the human body. *Science, 293,* 2470–2473.

Downs, E., & Smith, S. L. (2010). Keeping abreast of hypersexuality: A video game character content analysis. *Sex Roles, 62,* 721–733.

Doyle, R. (2005, March). Gay and lesbian census. *Scientific American,* p. 28.

Doyle, R. A., & Voyer, R. A. (2016). Stereotype manipulation effects on math and spatial test performance: A meta-analysis. *Learning and Individual Differences, 47,* 103–116.

Draganski, B., Gaser, C., Busch, V., Schuierer, G., Bogdahn, U., & May, A. (2004). Neuroplasticity: Changes in grey matter induced by training. *Nature, 427,* 311–312.

Draguns, J. G. (1990). Applications of cross-cultural psychology in the field of mental health. In R. W. Brislin (Ed.), *Applied cross-cultural psychology* (pp. 302–324). Sage.

Drake, R. A., & Myers, L. R. (2006). Visual attention, emotion, and action tendency: Feeling active or passive. *Cognition and Emotion, 20,* 608–622.

Drescher, A., & Schultheiss, O. C. (2016). Meta-analytic evidence for higher implicit affiliation and intimacy motivation scores in women, compared to men. *Journal of Research in Personality, 64,* 1–10.

Drewelies, J., Wagner, J., Tesch-Römer, C., Heckhausen, J., & Gerstorf, D. (2017). Perceived control across the second half of life: The role of physical health and social integration. *Psychology and Aging, 32,* 76–92.

Driessen, E., Cuijpers, P., de Maat, S. C. M., Abbas, A. A., de Jonghe, F., & Dekker, J. J. M. (2010). The efficacy of short-term psychodynamic psychotherapy for depression: A meta-analysis. *Clinical Psychology Review, 30,* 25–36.

Driessen, E., Dekker, J. J. M., Peen, J., Van, H. L., Maina, G., Rosso, G., Rigardetto, S., Cuniberti, F., Vitriol, V. G. Florenzano, R. U., Andreoli, A., Burnand, Y., López-Rodríguez, J., Villamil-Salcedo, V., Twisk, J. W. R., & Cuijpers, P. (2020). The efficacy of adding short-term psychodynamic psychotherapy to antidepressants in the treatment of depression: A systematic review and meta-analysis of individual participant data. *Clinical Psychology Review, 80.* doi: 10.1016/j.cpr.2020.101886

Driessen, E., Hollon, S. D., Bockting, C. L. H., Cuijpers, P., & Turner, E. H. (2015, September 30). Does publication bias inflate the apparent efficacy of psychological treatment for major depressive disorder? A systematic review and meta-analysis of U.S. National Institutes of Health-funded trials. *PLOS ONE, 10.* https://journals.plos.org/plosone/article?id=10.1371/journal.pone.0137864

Driessen, E., Van, H. L., Peen, J., Don, F. J., Twisk, J. W. R., Cuijpers, P., & Dekker, J. J. M. (2017). Cognitive-behavioral versus psychodynamic therapy for major depression: Secondary outcomes of a randomized clinical trial. *Journal of Consulting and Clinical Psychology, 85,* 653–663.

Druckman, D., & Bjork, R. A. (1991). *In the mind's eye: Enhancing human performance.* National Academy Press.

Druckman, J. N., & McGrath, M. C. (2019). The evidence for motivated reasoning in climate change preference formation. *Nature Climate Change, 9,* 111–119.

Drydakis, N. (2009). Sexual orientation discrimination in the labour market. *Labour Economics, 16,* 364–372.

Drydakis, N. (2015). Sexual orientation discrimination in the United Kingdom's labour market: A field experiment. *Human Relations, 68,* 1769–1796.

DSM-5-TR. (2022). *Diagnostic and statistical manual of mental disorders, fifth edition, text revision.* American Psychiatric Association.

Dubé, S., Lavoie, F., Blais, M., & Hébert, M. (2017). Consequences of casual sex relationships and experiences on adolescents' psychological well-being: A prospective study. *Journal of Sex Research, 54,* 1006–1017.

Duckworth, A. (2016). *Grit: The power of passion and perseverance.* Scribner.

Duckworth, A. L., & Seligman, M. E. P. (2005). Discipline outdoes talent: Self-discipline predicts academic performance in adolescents. *Psychological Science, 12,* 939–944.

Duckworth, A. L., & Seligman, M. E. P. (2017). The science and practice of self-control. *Perspectives on Psychological Science, 12,* 715–718.

Duckworth, A. L., Gendler, T. S., & Gross, J. J. (2016). Situational strategies for self-control. *Perspectives on Psychological Science, 11,* 35–55.

Duckworth, A. L., Milkman, K. L., & Laibson, D. (2018). Beyond willpower: Strategies for reducing failures of self-control. *Psychological Science in the Public Interest, 19,* 102–129.

Duckworth, A. L., Quinn, P. D., Lynam, D. R., Loeber, R., & Stouthamer-Loeber, M. (2011). Role of test motivation in intelligence testing. *PNAS, 108,* 7716–7720.

Duckworth, A. L., Tsukayama, E., & Kirby, T. A. (2013). Is it really self-control? Examining the predictive power of the delay of gratification task. *Personality and Social Psychology Bulletin, 39,* 843–855.

Duclos, S. E., Laird, J. D., Sexter, M., Stern, L., & Van Lighten, O. (1989). Emotion-specific effects of facial expressions and postures on emotional experience. *Journal of Personality and Social Psychology, 57,* 100–108.

Duffy, M. E., Twenge, J. M., & Joiner, T. E. (2019). Trends in mood and anxiety symptoms and suicide-related outcomes among U.S. undergraduates, 2007–2018: Evidence from two national surveys. *Journal of Adolescent Health, 65,* 590–598.

Dufner, M., Gebauer, J. E., Sedikides, C., & Denissen, J. J. (2019). Self-enhancement and psychological adjustment: A meta-analytic review. *Personality and Social Psychology Review, 23,* 48–72.

Dugatkin, L. A., & Trut, L. (2017). How to take a fox and build a dog. *American Scientist, 105,* 240–247.

Duggan, J. P., & Booth, D. A. (1986). Obesity, overeating, and rapid gastric emptying in rats with ventromedial hypothalamic lesions. *Science, 231,* 609–611.

DuMont, K. A., Widom, C. S., & Czaja, S. J. (2007). Predictors of resilience in abused and neglected children grown-up: The role of individual and neighborhood characteristics. *Child Abuse & Neglect, 31,* 255–274.

Dunbar, R. (2021). *Friends: Understanding the power of our most important relationships.* Little, Brown.

Dunbar, R. I. M. (1993). Coevolution of neocortical size, group size and language in humans. *Behavioral and Brain Sciences, 16*(4), 681–694.

Dunbar, R. I. M., Baron, R., Frangou, A., Pearce, E., van Leeuwin, E. J. C., Stow, J., Partridge, G., MacDonald, I., Barra, V., & van Vugt, M. (2011). Social laughter is correlated with an elevated pain threshold. *Proceedings of the Royal Society B, 279,* 1161–1167.

Duncan, L., Yilmaz, Z., Gaspar, H., Walters, R., Goldstein, J., Anttila, V., Bulik-Sullivan, B., Ripke, S., Eating Disorders Working Group of the Psychiatric Genomics Consortium, Thornton, L., Hinney, A., Daly, M., Sullivan, P. F., Zeggini, E., Breen, G., & Bulik, C. M. (2017). Significant locus and metabolic genetic correlations revealed in genome-wide association study of anorexia nervosa. *American Journal of Psychiatry, 174,* 850–858.

Dunlop, W. L., & Tracy, J. L. (2013). Sobering stories: Narratives of self-redemption predict behavioral change and improved health among recovering alcoholics. *Journal of Personality and Social Psychology, 104,* 576–590.

Dunn, A. (2018, October 4). *Partisans are divided over the fairness of the U.S. economy—and why people are rich or poor.* Pew Research Center. https://pewrsr.ch/39o8yIL

Dunn, E. W., Aknin, L. B., & Norton, M. I. (2008). Spending money on others promotes happiness. *Science, 319,* 1687–1688.

Dunn, M., & Searle, R. (2010). Effect of manipulated prestige-car ownership on both sex attractiveness ratings. *British Journal of Psychology, 101,* 69–80.

Dunn, M. J., & Hill, A. (2014). Manipulated luxury-apartment ownership enhances opposite-sex attraction in females but not males. *Journal of Evolutionary Psychology, 12,* 1–17.

Dunning, D. (2006). Strangers to ourselves? *The Psychologist, 19,* 600–603.

Dunning, D. (2019, January 31). *An expert on human blind spots gives advice on how to think* [Interview with Brian Resnick]. Vox. https://lsa.umich.edu/psych/news-events/all-news/faculty-news/an-expert-on-human-blind-spots-gives-advice-on-how-to-think.html

Dunsmoor, J. E., Murty, V. P., Davachi, L., & Phelps, E. A. (2015). Emotional learning selectively and retroactively strengthens memories for related events. *Nature, 520,* 345–348.

Dunson, D. B., Colombo, B., & Baird, D. D. (2002). Changes with age in the level and duration of fertility in the menstrual cycle. *Human Reproduction, 17,* 1399–1403.

Dunster, G. P., de la Iglesia, L., Ben-Hamo, M., Nave, C., Fleischer, J. G., Panda, S., & Horacio, O. (2018). Sleepmore in Seattle: Later school start times are associated with more sleep and better performance in high school students. *Science Advances,* 4. https://www.science.org/doi/10.1126/sciadv.aau6200

Dunster-Page, C., Haddock, G., Wainwright, L., & Berry, K. (2017). The relationship between therapeutic alliance and patient's suicidal thoughts, self-harming behaviours and suicide attempts: A systematic review. *Journal of Affective Disorders, 223,* 165–174.

Durwood, L., McLaughlin, K. A., & Olson, K. R. (2017). Mental health and self-worth in socially transitioned transgender youth. *Journal of the American Academy of Child & Adolescent Psychiatry, 56*(2), 116–123.

Dutra, S. J., Cunningham, W. A., Kober, H., & Gruber, J. (2015). Elevated striatal reactivity across monetary and social rewards in bipolar I disorder. *Journal of Abnormal Psychology, 124*(4), 890.

Dutton, D. G., & Aron, A. P. (1974). Some evidence for heightened sexual attraction under conditions of high anxiety. *Journal of Personality and Social Psychology, 30,* 510–517.

Dutton, D. G., & Aron, A. P. (1989). Romantic attraction and generalized liking for others who are sources of conflict-based arousal. *Canadian Journal of Behavioural Sciences, 21,* 246–257.

Dutton, E., Bakhiet, S. F. A., Osman, H. A., Becker, D., Essa, Y. A. S., Blahmar, T. A. M., Lynn, R., & Hakami, S. M. (2018). A Flynn effect in Khartoum, the Sudanese capital, 2004–2016. *Intelligence, 68,* 82–86.

Dutton, J. (2018, April). 'She's afflicted by these memories… they flood her.' *The Psychologist, 31,* 28–30.

Dweck, C. (2018, August 20). Growth mindset interventions yield impressive results. *Character & Context.* http://www.spsp.org/news-center/blog/growth-mindset-interventions-results

Dweck, C. S., & Yeager, D. S. (2019). Mindsets: A view from two eras. *Perspectives on Psychological Science, 14,* 481–496.

Dworkin, E. R., Menon, S. V., Bystrynski, J., & Allen, N. E. (2017). Sexual assault victimization and psychopathology: A review and meta-analysis. *Clinical Psychology Review, 56,* 65–81.

Dygalo, N. N., & Shishkina, G. T. (2019). Optogenetic studies of the pathophysiological mechanisms and treatment of depression. *Neuroscience and Behavioral Physiology, 49,* 178–183.

Dyrdal, G. M., & Lucas, R. E. (2011). *Reaction and adaptation to the birth of a child: A couple level analysis* [Unpublished manuscript]. Michigan State University.

Eagle, N., Pentland, A., & Lazer, D. (2009). Inferring friendship network structure by using mobile phone data. *PNAS, 106*(36), 15274–15278.

Eagleman, D. (2011, September). Secret life of the mind. *Discover,* pp. 50–53.

Eagly, A. H., Ashmore, R. D., Makhijani, M. G., & Kennedy, L. C. (1991). What is beautiful is good, but …: A meta-analytic review of research on the physical attractiveness stereotype. *Psychological Bulletin, 110,* 109–128.

Eagly, A. H., & Carli, L. (2007). *Through the labyrinth: The truth about how women become leaders.* Harvard University Press.

Eagly, A. H., & Koenig, A. M. (2021). The vicious cycle linking stereotypes and social roles. *Current Directions in Psychological Science, 30*(4), 343–350.

Eagly, A. H., Nater, C., Miller, D. I., Kaufmann, M., & Sczesny, S. (2020). Gender stereotypes have changed: A cross-temporal meta-analysis of U.S. public opinion polls from 1946 to 2018. *American Psychologist, 75,* 301–315.

Eagly, A. H., & Revelle, W. (2022). Understanding the magnitude of psychological differences between women and men requires seeing the forest and the trees. *Perspectives on Psychological Science, 17*(5), 1139–1358.

Eagly, A. H., & Wood, W. (1999). The origins of sex differences in human behavior: Evolved dispositions versus social roles. *American Psychologist, 54,* 408–423.

Eagly, A. H., & Wood, W. (2013). The nature-nurture debates: 25 years of challenges in understanding the psychology of gender. *Perspectives on Psychological Science, 8,* 340–357.

Easterlin, R. A., & O'Connor, K. J. (2020, December). *The Easterlin paradox* [PDF file]. IZA Institute of Labor Economics. Discussion Paper No. 13923. https://ftp.iza.org/dp13923.pdf

Eastman, C. L., Boulos, Z., Terman, M., Campbell, S. S., Dijk, D.-J., & Lewy, A. J. (1995). Light treatment for sleep disorders: Consensus report. VI. Shift work. *Journal of Biological Rhythms, 10,* 157–164.

Eastwick, P. W., Luchies, L. B., Finkel, E. J., & Hunt, L. L. (2014a). The many voices of Darwin's descendants: Reply to Schmitt (2014). *Psychological Bulletin, 140,* 673–681.

Eastwick, P. W., Luchies, L. B., Finkel, E. J., & Hunt, L. L. (2014b). The predictive validity of ideal partner preferences: A review and meta-analysis. *Psychological Bulletin, 140*, 623–665.

Ebbinghaus, H. (1885). *Memory: A contribution to experimental psychology* (H. A. Ruger & C. E. Bussenius, Trans.). Dover.

Eberhardt, J. L. (2005). Imaging race. *American Psychologist, 60*, 181–190.

Ebersbach, M., Feierabend, M., & Nazari, K. B. B. (2020). Comparing the effects of generating questions, testing, and restudying on students' long-term recall in university learning. *Applied Cognitive Psychology, 34*(3), 724–736.

Ebert, T., Gebauer, J. E., Talman, J. R., & Rentfrow, P. J. (2020). Religious people only live longer in religious cultural contexts: A gravestone analysis. *Journal of Personality and Social Psychology, 119*, 1–6.

Eckensberger, L. H. (1994). Moral development and its measurement across cultures. In W. J. Lonner & R. Malpass (Eds.), *Psychology and culture*. Allyn & Bacon.

Ecker, D., Pretzsch, C. M., Bletsch, A., Mann, C., Schaefer, T., Ambrosino, S., Tillmann, J., Yousaf, A., Chiochetti, A., Lombardo, M. V., Warrier, V., Bast, N., Moessnang, C., Baumeister, S., Dell'Acqua, F., Floris, D. L., Zabihi, M., Marquand, A., Cliquet, F., … Murphy, D. G. M. (2022). Interindividual differences in cortical thickness and their genome underpinnings in autism spectrum disorder. *American Journal of Psychiatry, 179*(3), 242–254.

Eckert, E. D., Heston, L. L., & Bouchard, T. J., Jr. (1981). MZ twins reared apart: Preliminary findings of psychiatric disturbances and traits. In L. Gedda, P. Paris, & W. D. Nance (Eds.), *Twin research: Vol. 3. Pt. B. Intelligence, personality, and development*. Alan Liss.

Eckert-Lind, C., Busch, A. S. Petersen, J. H., Biro, F. M., Butler, G., Bräuner, E. V., & Juul, A. (2020). Worldwide secular trends in age at pubertal onset assessed by breast development among girls. *JAMA Pediatrics, 174*(4). https://jamanetwork.com/journals/jamapediatrics/article-abstract/2760573

Eckholm, E. (2010, September 21). Woman on death row runs out of appeals. *The New York Times*. https://www.nytimes.com/2010/09/22/us/22execute.html

Ecklund-Flores, L. (1992). *The infant as a model for the teaching of introductory psychology* [Paper]. Presented at the American Psychological Association annual convention.

Eckshtain, D., Kuppens, S., Ugueto, A., Ng, M. Y., Vaughn-Coaxum, R., Corteselli, K., & Weisz, J. R. (2020). Meta-analysis: 13-year follow-up of psychotherapy effects on youth depression. *Journal of the American Academy of Child and Adolescent Psychiatry, 59*(1), 45–63.

Eddy, K. T., Tabri, N., Thomas, J. J., Murray, H. B., Keshaviah, A., Hastings, E., Edkins, K., Krishna, M., Herzog, D. B., Keel, P. K., & Franko, D. L. (2017). Recovery from anorexia nervosa and bulimia nervosa at 22-year follow-up. *Journal of Clinical Psychiatry, 78*, 184–189.

Edelman, B., Luca, M., & Svirsky, D. (2017). Racial discrimination in the sharing economy: Evidence from a field experiment. *American Economic Journal: Applied Economics, 9*, 1–22.

Edelstein, R. S. (2022). Testosterone tradeoffs in close relationships. (Chapter Five.) *Advances in Experimental Social Psychology, 65*, 235–280.

Edsinger, E., & Dölen, G. (2018). A conserved role for serotonergic neurotransmission in mediating social behavior in octopus. *Current Biology, 28*, 3136–3142.

Edwards, A. C., & Kendler, K. S. (2012). A twin study of depression and nicotine dependence: Shared liability or causal relationship? *Journal of Affective Disorders, 142*, 90–97.

Edwards, F., Lee, H., & Esposito, M. (2019). Risk of being killed by police use of force in the United States by age, race–ethnicity, and sex. *PNAS, 116*, 16793–16798.

Edwards, L. A. (2014). A meta-analysis of imitation abilities in individuals with autism spectrum disorders. *Autism Research, 7*, 363–380.

Edwards, R. R., Campbell, C., Jamison, R. N., & Wiech, K. (2009). The neurobiological underpinnings of coping with pain. *Current Directions in Psychological Science, 18*, 237–241.

Effron, D. A., & Raj, M. (2020). Misinformation and morality: Encountering fake-news headlines makes them seem less unethical to publish and share. *Psychological Science, 31*, 75–87.

Egan, P. J., & Mullin, M. (2012). Turning personal experience into political attitudes: The effects of local weather on Americans' perceptions about global warming. *Journal of Politics, 74*, 796–809.

Ehrlinger, J., Burnette, J. L., Park, J., Harrold, M. L., & Orvidas, K. (2017). Incremental theories of weight and healthy eating behavior. *Journal of Applied Social Psychology, 47*, 320–330.

Eich, E. (1990). Learning during sleep. In R. B. Bootzin, J. F. Kihlstrom, & D. L. Schacter (Eds.), *Sleep and cognition*. American Psychological Association.

Eichstaedt, J. C., Schwartz, H. A., Kern, M. L., Park, G., Labarthe, D. R., Merchant, R. M., Jha, S., Agrawal, M., Dziurzynski, L. A., Sap, M., Weeg, C., Larson, E. E., Ungar, L. H., & Seligman, M. E. P. (2015). Psychological language on Twitter predicts county-level heart disease mortality. *Psychological Science, 26*, 159–169.

Ein-Dor, T., Mikulincer, M., Doron, G., & Shaver, P. R. (2010). The attachment paradox: How can so many of us (the insecure ones) have no adaptive advantages? *Perspectives on Psychological Science, 5*, 123–141.

Ein-Dor, T., & Perry, A. (2012). Scared saviors: Evidence that people high in attachment anxiety are more effective in alerting others to threat. *European Journal of Social Psychology, 42*, 667–671.

Ein-Dor, T., & Perry, A. (2013, April). Full house of fears: Evidence that people high in attachment anxiety are more accurate in detecting deceit. *Journal of Personality, 82*, 83–92.

Einstein, G. O., McDaniel, M. A., Richardson, S. L., Guynn, M. J., & Cunfer, A. R. (1995). Aging and prospective memory: Examining the influences of self-initiated retrieval processes. *Journal of Experimental Psychology: Learning, Memory, and Cognition, 21*, 996–1007.

Einstein, G. O., McDaniel, M. A., Smith, R. E., & Shaw, P. (1998). Habitual prospective memory and aging: Remembering intentions and forgetting actions. *Psychological Science, 9*, 284–288.

Eippert, F., Finsterbush, J., Bingel, U., & Bùchel, C. (2009). Direct evidence for spinal cord involvement in placebo analgesia. *Science, 326*, 404.

Eisenberger, N. I., Master, S. L., Inagaki, T. K., Taylor, S. E., Shirinyan, D., Lieberman, M. D., & Nalifoff, B. D. (2011). Attachment figures activate a safety signal-related neural region and reduce pain experience. *PNAS, 108*, 11721–11726.

Eisenberger, R., & Aselage, J. (2009). Incremental effects of reward on experienced performance pressure: Positive outcomes for intrinsic interest and creativity. *Journal of Organizational Behavior, 30*, 95–117.

Eisenberger, R., Rockstuhl, T., Shoss, M. K., Wen, X., & Dulebohn, J. (2019). Is the employee–organization relationship dying or thriving? A temporal meta-analysis. *Journal of Applied Psychology, 104*, 1036–1057.

Eken, H. N., Dee, E. C., Powers, III, A. R., & Jordan, A. (2021). Racial and ethnic differences in perception of provider cultural competence among patients with depression and anxiety symptoms: A retrospective, population-based, cross-sectional analysis. *Lancet Psychiatry, 8*(11), 957–968.

Ekman, P. (2016). What scientists who study emotion agree about. *Perspectives on Psychological Science, 11*, 31–34.

Ekman, P., Davidson, R. J., & Friesen, W. V. (1990). The Duchenne smile: Emotional expression and brain physiology: II. *Journal of Personality and Social Psychology, 58*(2), 342–353.

Ekman, P., & Friesen, W. V. (1975). *Unmasking the face*. Prentice-Hall.

Elbert, T., Pantev, C., Wienbruch, C., Rockstroh, B., & Taub, E. (1995). Increased cortical representation of the fingers of the left hand in string players. *Science, 270*, 305–307.

Elbeshbishi , S., & King, L. (2020). *Exclusive: Two-thirds of Americans say they won't get COVID-19 vaccines when it's first available, USA TODAY/Suffolk Poll shows*. USA Today. https://www.usatoday.com/story/news/politics/2020/09/04/covid-19-two-thirds-us-wont-take-vaccine-right-away-poll-shows/5696982002/

Elbogen, E. B., Dennis, P. A., & Johnson, S. C. (2016). Beyond mental illness: Targeting stronger and more direct pathways to violence. *Clinical Psychological Science, 4*, 747–759.

Elenbaas, L. (2019). Against unfairness: Young children's judgments about merit, equity, and equality. *Journal of Experimental Child Psychology, 186*, 73–82.

Elfenbein, H. A., & Ambady, N. (2002). On the universality and cultural specificity of emotion recognition: A meta-analysis. *Psychological Bulletin, 128*, 203–235.

Elias, A., Thomas, N., & Sackeim, H. (2021). Electroconvulsive therapy in mania: A review of 80 years of clinical experience. *American Journal of Psychiatry, 178*(3), 229–239.

Elias, S., Lozano, J., & Bentley, J. (2016). *How executive functioning, anxiety, and technology use impact university students'*

course performance [Paper]. Presented at the Western Psychological Association Convention.

Elkind, D. (1970). The origins of religion in the child. *Review of Religious Research, 12*, 35–42.

Elkins, G., Johnson, A., & Fisher, W. (2012). Cognitive hypnotherapy for pain management. *American Journal of Clinical Hypnosis, 54*, 294–310.

Ellenbogen, J. M., Hu, P. T., Payne, J. D., Titone, D., & Walker, M. P. (2007). Human relational memory requires time and sleep. *PNAS, 104*, 7723–7728.

Ellis, A., & Becker, I. M. (1982). *A guide to personal happiness*. Wilshire.

Ellis, B. J., Bates, J. E., Dodge, K. A., Fergusson, D. M., John, H. L., Pettit, G. S., & Woodward, L. (2003). Does father absence place daughters at special risk for early sexual activity and teenage pregnancy? *Child Development, 74*, 801–821.

Ellis, B. J., Bianchi, J., Griskevicius, V., & Frankenhuis, W. E. (2017). Beyond risk and protective factors: An adaptation-based approach to resilience. *Perspectives on Psychological Science, 12*, 561–587.

Ellis, B. J., & Boyce, W. T. (2008). Biological sensitivity to context. *Current Directions in Psychological Science, 17*, 183–187.

Ellis, B. J., Schlomer, G. L., Tilley, E. H., & Butler, E. A. (2012). Impact of fathers on risky sexual behavior in daughters: A genetically and environmentally controlled sibling study. *Development and Psychopathology, 24*, 317–332.

Ellis, L., & Ames, M. A. (1987). Neurohormonal functioning and sexual orientation: A theory of homosexuality-heterosexuality. *Psychological Bulletin, 101*, 233–258.

Ellison, K. (2015, November 9). A.D.H.D. rates rise around globe, but sympathy often lags. *The New York Times*. https://well.blogs.nytimes.com/2015/11/09/a-d-h-d-rates-rise-around-globe-but-sympathy-often-lags/

Ellison-Wright, I., Glahn, D. C., Laird, A. R., Thelen, S. M., & Bullmore, E. (2008). The anatomy of first-episode and chronic schizophrenia: An anatomical likelihood estimation meta-analysis. *American Journal of Psychiatry, 165*, 1015–1023.

Else-Quest, N. M., Hyde, J. S., & Linn, M. C. (2010). Cross-national patterns of gender differences in mathematics: A meta-analysis. *Psychological Bulletin, 136*, 103–127.

Elsey, J. W. B., Van Ast, V. A., & Kindt, M. (2018). Human memory reconsolidation: A guiding framework and critical review of the evidence. *Psychological Bulletin, 144*, 797–848.

Elson, M., Ferguson, C. J., Gregerson, M., Hogg, J. L., Ivory, J., Klisanin, D., Markey, P. M., Nichols, D., Siddiqui, S., & Wilson, J. (2019). Do policy statements on media effects faithfully represent the science? *Advances in Methods and Practices in Psychological Science*. https://journals.sagepub.com/doi/full/10.1177/2515245918811301?journalCode=ampa

Elzinga, B. M., Ardon, A. M., Heijnis, M. K., De Ruiter, M. B., Van Dyck, R., & Veltman, D. J. (2007). Neural correlates of enhanced working-memory performance in dissociative disorder: A functional MRI study. *Psychological Medicine, 37*, 235–245.

Emmons, S., Geisler, C., Kaplan, K. J., & Harrow, M. (1997). *Living with schizophrenia*. Taylor and Francis.

Empson, J. A. C., & Clarke, P. R. F. (1970). Rapid eye movements and remembering. *Nature, 227*, 287–288.

Enache, D., Pariante, C., & Mondelli, V. (2019). Markers of central inflammation in major depressive disorder: A systematic review and meta-analysis of studies examining cerebrospinal fluid, positron emission tomography and post-mortem brain tissue. *Brain, Behavior, and Immunity, 81*, 24–40.

Endendijk, J. J., Beltz, A. M., McHale, S. M., Bryk, K., & Berenbaum, S. A. (2016). Linking prenatal androgens to gender-related attitudes, identity, and activities: Evidence from girls with congenital adrenal hyperplasia. *Archives of Sexual Behavior, 45*, 1807–1815.

Endler, N. S. (1982). *Holiday of darkness: A psychologist's personal journey out of his depression*. Wiley.

Engel, G. L. (1981). The clinical application of the biopsychosocial model. *Journal of Medicine and Philosophy: A Forum for Bioethics and Philosophy of Medicine, 6*(2), 101–124.

Engeler, I., & Raghubir, P. (2018). Decomposing the cross-sex misprediction bias of dating behaviors: Do men overestimate or women underreport their sexual intentions? *Journal of Personality and Social Psychology, 114*, 95–109.

Engen, T. (1987). Remembering odors and their names. *American Scientist, 75*, 497–503.

Engle, R. W. (2002). Working memory capacity as executive attention. *Current Directions in Psychological Science, 11*, 19–23.

English, T., Davis, J., Wei, M., & Gross, J. J. (2017). Homesickness and adjustment across the first year of college: A longitudinal study. *Emotion, 17*, 1–5.

Ennis, D. (2015). *Discovering the guevedoces: The fascinating story of boys raised as girls*. Advocate. https://www.advocate.com/world/2015/9/29/discovering-guevedoces-fascinating-story-boys-raised-girls

Epel, E. S. (2009). Telomeres in a life-span perspective: A new "psychobiomarker"? *Current Directions in Psychological Science, 18*, 6–9.

Epel, E. S., Blackburn, E. H., Lin, J., Dhabhar, F. S., Adler, N. E., Morrow, J. D., & Cawthon, R. M. (2004). Accelerated telomere shortening in response to life stress. *PNAS, 101*(49), 17312–17315.

Epel, E. S., McEwen, B. S., & Ickovics, J. R. (1998). Embodying psychological thriving: Physical thriving in response to stress. *Journal of Social Issues, 54*(2), 301–322.

Epley, N., Keysar, B., Van Boven, L., & Gilovich, T. (2004). Perspective taking as egocentric anchoring and adjustment. *Journal of Personality and Social Psychology, 87*, 327–339.

Epley, N., Savitsky, K., & Gilovich, T. (2002). Empathy neglect: Reconciling the spotlight effect and the correspondence bias. *Journal of Personality and Social Psychology, 83*, 300–312.

Epley, N., & Schroeder, J. (2014). Mistakenly seeking solitude. *Journal of Experimental Psychology: General, 143*, 1980–1999.

Epstein, J., Stern, E., & Silbersweig, D. (1998). Mesolimbic activity associated with psychosis in schizophrenia: Symptom-specific PET studies. In J. F. McGinty (Ed.), *Advancing from the ventral striatum to the extended amygdala: Implications for neuropsychiatry and drug use: In honor of Lennart Heimer. Annals of the New York Academy of Sciences, 877*, 562–574.

Epstein, S. (1983a). Aggregation and beyond: Some basic issues on the prediction of behavior. *Journal of Personality, 51*, 360–392.

Epstein, S. (1983b). The stability of behavior across time and situations. In R. Zucker, J. Aronoff, & A. I. Rabin (Eds.), *Personality and the prediction of behavior*. Academic Press.

Eranti, S. V., MacCabe, J. H., Bundy, H., & Murray, R. M. (2013). Gender difference in age at onset of schizophrenia: A meta-analysis. *Psychological Medicine, 43*, 155–167.

Erdelyi, M. H. (1985). *Psychoanalysis: Freud's cognitive psychology*. Freeman.

Erdelyi, M. H. (1988). Repression, reconstruction, and defense: History and integration of the psychoanalytic and experimental frameworks. In J. Singer (Ed.), *Repression: Defense mechanism and cognitive style*. University of Chicago Press.

Erdelyi, M. H. (2006). The unified theory of repression. *Behavioral and Brain Sciences, 29*, 499–551.

Erel, O., & Burman, B. (1995). Interrelatedness of marital relations and parent–child relations: A meta-analytic review. *Psychological Bulletin, 118*, 108–132.

Erickson, M. F., & Aird, E. G. (2005). *The motherhood study: Fresh insights on mothers' attitudes and concerns*. The Motherhood Project, Institute for American Values. https://www.worldcat.org/title/70265670

Ericsson, K. A. (2001). Attaining excellence through deliberate practice: Insights from the study of expert performance. In M. Ferrari (Ed.), *The pursuit of excellence in education*. Erlbaum.

Ericsson, K. A. (2006). The influence of experience and deliberate practice on the development of superior expert performance. In K. A. Ericsson, N. Charness, P. J. Feltovich, & R. R. Hoffman (Eds.), *The Cambridge handbook of expertise and expert performance*. Cambridge University Press.

Ericsson, K. A. (2007). Deliberate practice and the modifiability of body and mind: Toward a science of the structure and acquisition of expert and elite performance. *International Journal of Sport Psychology, 38*, 4–34.

Ericsson, K. A., Cheng, X., Pan, Y., Ku, Y., Ge, Y., & Hu, Y. (2017). Memory skills mediating superior memory in a world-class memorist. *Memory, 25*, 1294–1302.

Ericsson, K. A., & Pool, R. (2016). *PEAK: Secrets from the new science of expertise*. Houghton Mifflin.

Ericsson, K. A., Roring, R. W., & Nandagopal, K. (2007). Giftedness and evidence for reproducibly superior performance: An account based on the expert performance framework. *High Ability Studies, 18*, 3–56.

Erikson, E. H. (1963). *Childhood and society*. Norton.

Erlandsson, A., Nilsson, A., Tinghög, G., & Västfjäll, D. (2018). Bullshit-sensitivity predicts prosocial behavior. *PLOS ONE, 13*. https://journals.plos.org/plosone/article?id=10.1371/journal.pone.0201474

Erlich, N., Lipp, O. V., & Slaughter, V. (2013). Of hissing snakes and angry voices: Human infants are differentially responsive to evolutionary fear-relevant sounds. *Developmental Science, 16*, 894–904.

Ermer, E., Cope, L. M., Nyalakanti, P. K., Calhoun, V. D., & Kiehl, K. A. (2012). Aberrant paralimbic gray matter in criminal psychopathy. *Journal of Abnormal Psychology, 121*, 649–658.

Ermer, E., Kahn, R. E., Salovey, P., & Kiehl, K. A. (2012). Emotional intelligence in incarcerated men with psychopathic traits. *Journal of Personality and Social Psychology, 103*, 194–204.

Ertmer, D. J., Young, N. M., & Nathani, S. (2007). Profiles of focal development in young cochlear implant recipients. *Journal of Speech, Language, and Hearing Research, 50*, 393–407.

Erzurumluoglu, A. M., Liu, M., Jackson, V. E., Barnes, D. R., Datta, G., Melbourne, C. A., Young, R., Batini, C., Surendran, P., Jiang, T., Adnan, S. D., Afaq, S., Agrawal, A., Altmaier, E., Antoniou, A. C., Asselbergs, F. W., Baumbach, C., Bierut, L., Bertelsen, S., … Howson, J. M. M. (2019). Meta-analysis of up to 622,409 individuals identifies 40 novel smoking behaviour associated genetic loci. *Molecular Psychiatry, 25*(10), 2392–2409.

Escasa, M. J., Casey, J. F., & Gray, P. B. (2011). Salivary testosterone levels in men at a U.S. sex club. *Archives of Sexual Behavior, 40*, 921–926.

Escobar-Chaves, S. L., Tortolero, S. R., Markham, C. M., Low, B. J., Eitel, P., & Thickstun, P. (2005). Impact of the media on adolescent sexual attitudes and behaviors. *Pediatrics, 116*, 303–326.

Escobedo, J. R., & Adolphs, R. (2010). Becoming a better person: Temporal remoteness biases autobiographical memories for moral events. *Emotion, 10*, 511–518.

Eskreis-Winkler, L., & Fishbach, A. (2019). Not learning from failure—the greatest failure of all. *Psychological Science, 30*, 1733–1744.

Esposito, G., Yoshida, S., Ohnishi, R., Tsuneoka, Y., Rostagno, M., Yokoto, S., Okabe, S., Kamiya, K., Hoshino, M., Shimizu, M., Venuti, P., Kikusui, T., Kato, T., & Kuroda, K. O. (2013). Infant calming responses during maternal carrying in humans and mice. *Current Biology, 23*, 739–745.

Esser, J. K., & Lindoerfer, J. S. (1989). Groupthink and the space shuttle *Challenger* accident: Toward a quantitative case analysis. *Journal of Behavioral Decision Making, 2*, 167–177.

Esses, V. M. (2021). Prejudice and discrimination toward immigrants. *Annual Review of Psychology, 72*, 503–531.

Esterson, A. (2001). The mythologizing of psychoanalytic history: Deception and self-deception in Freud's accounts of the seduction theory episode. *History of Psychiatry, 12*, 329–352.

Eurich, T. L., Krause, D. E., Cigularov, K., & Thornton, G. C., III. (2009). Assessment centers: Current practices in the United States. *Journal of Business Psychology, 24*, 387–407.

Euston, D. R., Tatsuno, M., & McNaughton, B. L. (2007). Fast-forward playback of recent memory sequences in prefrontal cortex during sleep. *Science, 318*, 1147–1150.

Evans, D. (2021, January 6). Quoted by TalkingPointsMemo in, *So who actually participated in the siege of the Capitol?* https://talkingpointsmemo.com/news/so-who-actually-participated-in-the-siege-of-the-capitol

Evans, G. W., Palsane, M. N., & Carrere, S. (1987). Type A behavior and occupational stress: A cross-cultural study of blue-collar workers. *Journal of Personality and Social Psychology, 52*, 1002–1007.

Evenson, K. R., Wen, F., & Herring, A. H. (2016). Associations of accelerometry-assessed and self-reported physical activity and sedentary behavior with all-cause and cardiovascular mortality among U.S. adults. *American Journal of Epidemiology, 184*, 621–632.

Everaert, J., Bronstein, M. V., Cannon, T. D., & Joormann, J. (2018). Looking through tinted glasses: Depression and social anxiety are related to both interpretation biases and inflexible negative interpretations. *Clinical Psychological Science, 6*, 517–528.

Everett, J. A. C., Caviola, L., Kahane, G., Savulescu, J., & Faber, N. S. (2015). Doing good by doing nothing? The role of social norms in explaining default effects in altruistic contexts. *European Journal of Social Psychology, 45*, 230–241.

Evers, A., Muñiz, J., Bartram, D., Boben, D., Egeland, J., Fernández-Hermida, J. R., Frans, Ö., Gintilienė, G., Hagemeister, C., Halama, P., Iliescu, D., Jaworowska, A., Jimenez, P., Manthouli, M., Matešić, K., Schittekatte, M., Sümer, H. C., & Urbánek, T. (2012). Testing practices in the 21st century: Developments and European psychologists' opinions. *European Psychologist, 17*, 300–319.

Everson, S. A., Goldberg, D. E., Kaplan, G. A., Cohen, R. D., Pukkala, E., Tuomilehto, J., & Salonen, J. T. (1996). Hopelessness and risk of mortality and incidence of myocardial infarction and cancer. *Psychosomatic Medicine, 58*, 113–121.

Ewbank, M. P., Cummins, R., Tablan, V., Bateup, S., Catarino, A., Martin, A. J., & Blackwell, A. D. (2019). Quantifying the association between psychotherapy content and clinical outcomes using deep learning. *JAMA Psychiatry, 77*, 35–43.

Exelmans, L., Custers, K., & Van den Bulck, J. (2015). Violent video games and delinquent behavior in adolescents: A risk factor perspective. *Aggressive Behavior, 41*, 267–279.

Exelmans, L., & Van den Bulck, J. (2018). Self-control depletion and sleep duration: The mediating role of television viewing. *Psychology & Health, 33*, 1251–1268.

Eysenck, H. J. (1952). The effects of psychotherapy: An evaluation. *Journal of Consulting Psychology, 16*, 319–324.

Eysenck, H. J. (1990, April 30). An improvement on personality inventory. *Current Contents: Social and Behavioral Sciences, 22*, 20.

Eysenck, H. J. (1992). Four ways five factors are *not* basic. *Personality and Individual Differences, 13*, 667–673.

Eysenck, H. J., & Grossarth-Maticek, R. (1991). Creative novation behavior therapy as a prophylactic treatment for cancer and coronary heart disease: Part II—Effects of treatment. *Behaviour Research and Therapy, 29*, 17–31.

Eysenck, H. J., Wakefield, J. A., Jr., & Friedman, A. F. (1983). Diagnosis and clinical assessment: The DSM-III. *Annual Review of Psychology, 34*, 167–193.

Eysenck, S. B. G., & Eysenck, H. J. (1963). The validity of questionnaire and rating assessments of extraversion and neuroticism, and their factorial stability. *British Journal of Psychology, 54*, 51–62.

Fabiano, G. A., Pelham, W. E., Jr., Coles, E. K., Gnagy, E. M., Chronis-Tuscano, A., & O'Connor, B. C. (2008). A meta-analysis of behavioral treatments for attention-deficit/hyperactivity disorder. *Clinical Psychology Review, 29*, 129–140.

Fabiansson, E. C., Denson, T. F., Moulds, M. L., Grisham, J. R., & Schira, M. M. (2012). Don't look back in anger: Neural correlates of reappraisal, analytical rumination, and angry rumination during a recall of an anger-inducing autobiographical memory. *NeuroImage, 59*, 2974–2981.

Facco, E. (2016). Hypnosis and anesthesia: Back to the future. *Minerva Anestesiologica, 82*, 1343–1356.

Fagan, J. F., & Holland, C. R. (2007). Racial equality in intelligence: Predictions from a theory of intelligence as processing. *Intelligence, 35*, 319–334.

Fagan, J. F., & Holland, C. R. (2009). Culture-fair prediction of academic achievement. *Intelligence, 37*, 62–67.

Fagundes, C. P., & Way, B. (2014). Early-life stress and adult inflammation. *Current Directions in Psychological Science, 23*, 277–283.

Fairbairn, C. E., Briley, D. A., Kang, D., Fraley, R. C., Hankin, B. L., & Ariss, T. (2018). A meta-analysis of longitudinal associations between substance use and interpersonal attachment security. *Psychological Bulletin, 144*, 532–555.

Fairbairn, C. E., & Sayette, M. A. (2014). A social-attributional analysis of alcohol response. *Psychological Bulletin, 140*, 1361–1382.

Fairfield, H. (2012, February 4). Girls lead in science exam, but NOT in the United States. *The New York Times*. https://archive.nytimes.com/www.nytimes.com/interactive/2013/02/04/science/girls-lead-in-science-exam-but-not-in-the-united-states.html

Falk, C. F., Heine, S. J., Yuki, M., & Takemura, K. (2009). Why do Westerners self-enhance more than East Asians? *European Journal of Personality, 23*, 183–203.

Falk, E. B., Hyde, L. W., Mitchell, C., Faul, J., Gonzalez, R., Heitzeg, M. M., Keating, D. P., Langa, K. M., Martz, M. E., Maslowsky, J., Morrison, F. J., Noll, D. C., Patrick, M. E., Pfeffer, F. T., Reuter-Lorenz, P. A., Thomason, M. E., Davis-Kean, P., Monk, C. D., & Schulenberg, J. (2013). What is a representative brain? Neuroscience meets population science. *PNAS, 110*, 17615–17622.

Falkenström, F., Kuria, M., Othieno, C., & Kumar, M. (2019). Working alliance predicts symptomatic improvement in public hospital–delivered psychotherapy in Nairobi, Kenya. *Journal of Consulting and Clinical Psychology, 87*, 46–55.

Falkner, A. L., Grosenick, L., Davidson, T. J., Deisseroth, K., & Lin, D. (2016). Hypothalamic control of male aggression-seeking behavior. *Nature Neuroscience, 19*, 596–604.

Fan, S. P., Liberman, Z., Keysar, B., & Kinzler, K. D. (2015). The exposure advantage: Early exposure to a multilingual environment promotes effective communication. *Psychological Science, 26*, 1090–1097.

Fan, W., & Williams, C. (2018). The mediating role of student motivation in the linking of perceived school climate and academic achievement in reading and mathematics. *Frontiers in Education, 3*, 50.

Fancourt, D., Steptoe, A., & Bu, F. (2021). Trajectories of anxiety and depressive symptoms during enforced isolation due to COVID-19 in England: A longitudinal observational study. *Lancet Psychiatry, 8*, 141–149.

Fang, Y., Forger, D. B., Frank, E., Srijan, S., & Goldstein, C. (2021). Day-to-day variability in sleep parameters and depression risk: A prospective cohort study of training physicians. *NPJ Digital Medicine, 4*. nature.com/articles/s41746-021-00400-z

Fang, Z., Spaeth, A. M., Ma, N., Zhu, S., Hu, S., Goel, N., Detre, J. A., Dinges, D. F., & Rao, H. (2015). Altered salience network connectivity predicts macronutrient intake after sleep deprivation. *Scientific Reports*, 5(8215). https://www.nature.com/articles/srep08215

Fanti, K. A., Vanman, E., Henrich, C. C., & Avraamides, M. N. (2009). Desensitization to media violence over a short period of time. *Aggressive Behavior, 35*, 179–187.

Farah, M. J. (2017). The neuroscience of socioeconomic status: Correlates, causes, and consequences. *Neuron, 96*, 56–71.

Farah, M. J., Rabinowitz, C., Quinn, G. E., & Liu, G. T. (2000). Early commitment of neural substrates for face recognition. *Cognitive Neuropsychology, 17*, 117–124.

Farb, N. A. S., Anderson, A. K., Mayberg, H., Bean, J., McKeon, D., & Segal, Z. V. (2010). Minding one's emotions: Mindfulness training alters the neural expression of sadness. *Emotion, 10*, 25–33.

Farina, A. (1982). The stigma of mental disorders. In A. G. Miller (Ed.), *In the eye of the beholder*. Praeger.

Farnia, V., Shakeri, J., Tatari, F., Juibari, T. A., Yazdchi, K., Bajoghli, H., Brand, S., Abdoli, N., & Aghaei, A. (2014). Randomized controlled trial of aripiprazole versus risperidone for the treatment of amphetamine-induced psychosis. *American Journal of Drug and Alcohol Abuse, 40*, 10–15.

Farr, R. H. (2017). Does parental sexual orientation matter? A longitudinal follow-up of adoptive families with school-age children. *Developmental Psychology, 53*, 252–264.

Farr, R. H., Bruun, S. T., Doss, K. M., & Patterson, C. J. (2018). Children's gender-typed behavior from early to middle childhood in adoptive families with lesbian, gay, and heterosexual parents. *Sex Roles, 78*, 528–541.

Farrington, D. P. (1991). Antisocial personality from childhood to adulthood. *The Psychologist: Bulletin of the British Psychological Society, 4*, 389–394.

Farstad, S. M., McGeown, L. M., & von Ranson, K. M. (2016). Eating disorders and personality, 2004–2016: A systematic review and meta-analysis. *Clinical Psychology Review, 46*, 91–105.

Fatemi, S. H., & Folsom, T. D. (2009). The neurodevelopmental hypothesis of schizophrenia, revisited. *Schizophrenia Bulletin, 35*, 528–548.

Fattore, L. (2016). Synthetic cannabinoids—further evidence supporting the relationship between cannabinoids and psychosis. *Biological Psychiatry, 79*, 539–548.

Fazel, S., Langstrom, N., Hjern, A., Grann, M., & Lichtenstein, P. (2009). Schizophrenia, substance abuse, and violent crime. *Journal of the American Medical Association, 301*, 2016–2023.

Fazel, S., Lichtenstein, P., Grann, M., Goodwin, G. M., & Långström, N. (2010). Bipolar disorder and violent crime: New evidence from population-based longitudinal studies and systematic review. *Archives of General Psychiatry, 67*, 931–938.

Fazio, L. K., Brashier, N. M., Payne, B. K., & Marsh, E. J. (2015). Knowledge does not protect against illusory truth. *Journal of Experimental Psychology: General, 144*, 993–1002.

Fazio, L. K., & Marsh, E. J. (2019). Retrieval-based learning in children. *Current Directions in Psychological Science, 28*, 111–116.

Fazio, L. K., & Sherry, C. L. (2020). The effect of repetition on truth judgments across development. *Psychological Science, 31*(9), 1150–1160.

FBI (Federal Bureau of Investigation). (2016). *2015 hate crime statistics*. Table 1: Incidents, offenses, victims, and known offenders. https://ucr.fbi.gov/hate-crime/2015/tables-and-data-declarations/1tabledatadecpdf

FBI. (2021, October 25). *FBI releases updated hate crime statistics*. https://www.fbi.gov/news/press-releases/press-releases/fbi-releases-updated-2020-hate-crime-statistics

FBI. (2022). *Trend of violent crime from 2011 to 2021*. Crime Data Explorer. https://crime-data-explorer.fr.cloud.gov/pages/explorer/crime/crime-trend

Fecher, N., & Johnson, E. K. (2019). By 4.5 months, linguistic experience already affects infants' talker processing abilities. *Child Development, 90*, 1535–1543.

Fedorenko, E., Scott, T. L., Brunner, P., Coon, W. G., Pritchett, B., Schalk, G., & Kanwisher, N. (2016). Neural correlate of the construction of sentence meaning. *PNAS, 113*, E6256–E6262.

Fedotova, N. O., & Rozin, P. (2018). Contamination, association, or social communication: An examination of alternative accounts for contagion effects. *Judgment & Decision Making, 13*, 150–162.

Feeney, D. M. (1987). Human rights and animal welfare. *American Psychologist, 42*, 593–599.

Fehr, B., Harasymchuk, C., & Sprecher, S. (2014). Compassionate love in romantic relationships: A review and some new findings. *Journal of Social and Personal Relationships, 31*(5), 575–600.

Feigenson, L., Carey, S., & Spelke, E. (2002). Infants' discrimination of number vs. continuous extent. *Cognitive Psychology, 44*, 33–66.

Feinberg, A., Branton, R., & Martinez-Ebers, V. (2019, March 22). Counties that hosted a 2016 Trump rally saw a 226 percent increase in hate crimes. *The Washington Post*. https://www.washingtonpost.com/

Feinberg, M., Willer, R., Antonenko, O., & John, O. P. (2012). Liberating reason from the passions: Overriding intuitionist moral judgments through emotion reappraisal. *Psychological Science, 23*, 788–795.

Feinberg, M., Willer, R., & Schultz, M. (2014). Gossip and ostracism promote cooperation in groups. *Psychological Science, 25*, 656–664.

Feinberg, T. E., & Mallatt, J. (2016). The nature of primary consciousness: A new synthesis. *Consciousness and Cognition, 43*, 113–127.

Feingold, A. (1990). Gender differences in effects of physical attractiveness on romantic attraction: A comparison across five research paradigms. *Journal of Personality and Social Psychology*, 59(5), 981.

Feingold, A., & Mazzella, R. (1998). Gender differences in body image are increasing. *Psychological Science, 9*, 190–195.

Feinstein, J. S., Buzza, C., Hurlemann, R., Follmer, R. L., Dahdaleh, N. S., Coryell, W. H., Welsh, M. J., Tranel, D., & Wemmie, J. A. (2013). Fear and panic in humans with bilateral amygdala damage. *Nature Neuroscience, 16*, 270–272.

Feinstein, J. S., Duff, M. C., & Tranel, D. (2010, April 27). Sustained experiences of emotion after loss of memory in patients with amnesia. *PNAS, 107*, 7674–7679.

Feldman, G., Farh, J. L., & Wong, K. F. E. (2018). Agency beliefs over time and across cultures: Free will beliefs predict higher job satisfaction. *Personality and Social Psychology Bulletin, 44*, 304–317.

Feldman Barrett, L. (2006). Are emotions natural kinds? *Perspectives on Psychological Science, 1*, 28–58.

Feldman Barrett, L. (2012). Emotions are real. *Emotion, 12*, 413–429.

Feldman Barrett, L. (2013). Quoted by Fischer, S. About face: Emotions and facial expressions may not be directly related. *Boston Magazine*. https://www.bostonmagazine.com/news/2013/06/25/emotions-facial-expressions-not-related/

Feldman Barrett, L. (2017). *How emotions are made: The secret life of the brain*. Houghton Mifflin Harcourt.

Feldman Barrett, L. (2020). *Seven and a half lessons about the human brain*. Houghton Mifflin Harcourt.

Feldman Barrett, L., Adolphs, R., Marsella, S., Martinez, A. M., & Pollak, S. D. (2019). Emotional expressions reconsidered: Challenges to inferring emotion from human facial movements. *Psychological Science in the Public Interest, 20*, 1–68.

Feldman Barrett, L., & Bliss-Moreau, E. (2009). She's emotional. He's having a bad day: Attributional explanations for emotion stereotypes. *Emotion, 9*, 649–658.

Feldman Barrett, L., Lane, R. D., Sechrest, L., & Schwartz, G. E. (2000). Sex differences in emotional awareness. *Personality and Social Psychology Bulletin, 26*, 1027–1035.

Feldman Barrett, L., & Russell, J. A. (1998). Independence and bipolarity in the structure of current affect. *Journal of Personality and Social Psychology, 74*(4), 967–984.

Fenigstein, A. (2015). Milgram's shock experiments and the Nazi perpetrators: A contrarian perspective on the role of obedience pressures during the Holocaust. *Theory and Psychology, 25*, 581–598.

Fenn, K. M., & Hambrick, D. Z. (2012). Individual differences in working memory capacity predict sleep-dependent memory consolidation. *Journal of Experimental Psychology: General, 141*, 404–410.

Fenton, W. S., & McGlashan, T. H. (1991). Natural history of schizophrenia subtypes: II. Positive and negative symptoms and long-term course. *Archives of General Psychiatry, 48*, 978–986.

Fenton, W. S., & McGlashan, T. H. (1994). Antecedents, symptom progression, and long-term outcome of the deficit syndrome in schizophrenia. *American Journal of Psychiatry, 151*, 351–356.

Ferguson, C. J. (2009, June 14). Not every child is secretly a genius. *The Chronicle Review*. https://www.chronicle.com/article/Not-Every-Child-Is-Secretly-a/48001

Ferguson, C. J. (2013). Spanking, corporal punishment and negative long-term outcomes: A meta-analytic review of longitudinal studies. *Clinical Psychology Review, 33*, 196–208.

Ferguson, C. J., Copenhaver, A., & Markey, P. (2020). Reexamining the findings of the American Psychological Association's 2015 task force on violent media: A meta-analysis. *Perspectives on Psychological Science, 15*(6), 1423–1443.

Ferguson, E. D. (2003). Social processes, personal goals, and their intertwining: Their importance in Adlerian theory and practice. *Journal of Individual Psychology, 59*, 136–144.

Ferguson, E. D. (2020). Adler's motivational theory: An historical perspective on belonging and the fundamental human striving. *Journal of Individual Psychology, 76*(1), 51–58.

Ferguson, M. J., & Zayas, V. (2009). Automatic evaluation. *Current Directions in Psychological Science, 18*, 362–366.

Fergusson, D. M., Boden, J. M., & Horwood, L. J. (2009). Tests of causal links between alcohol abuse or dependence and major depression. *Archives of General Psychiatry, 66*, 260–266.

Fernandes, M. A., Wammes, J. D., & Meade, M. E. (2018). The surprisingly powerful influence of drawing on memory. *Current Directions in Psychological Science, 27*, 302–308.

Fernández-Dols, J.-M., & Ruiz-Belda, M.-A. (1995). Are smiles a sign of happiness? Gold medal winners at the Olympic Games. *Journal of Personality and Social Psychology, 69*, 1113–1119.

Fernandez-Duque, E., Evans, J., Christian, C., & Hodges, S. D. (2015). Superfluous neuroscience information makes explanations of psychological phenomena more appealing *Journal of Cognitive Neuroscience, 27*, 926–944.

Fernie, G., Peeters, M., Gullo, M. J., Christianson, P., Cole, J. C., Sumnall, H., & Field, M. (2013). Multiple behavioral impulsivity tasks predict prospective alcohol involvement in adolescents. *Addiction, 108*, 1916–1923.

Fernyhough, C. (2008). Getting Vygotskian about theory of mind: Mediation, dialogue, and the development of social understanding. *Developmental Review, 28*, 225–262.

Ferrarelli, F., & Phillips, M. L. (2021). Examining and modulating neural circuits in psychiatric disorders with transcranial magnetic stimulation and electroencephalography: Present practices and future developments. *American Journal of Psychiatry, 178*, 400–413.

Ferrari, A. J., Charlson, F. J., Norman, R. E., Patten, S. B., Freedman, G., Murray, C. J. L., Vos, T., & Whiteford, H. A. (2013). Burden of depressive disorders by country, sex, age, and year: Findings from the Global Burden of Disease Study 2010. *PLOS Medicine, 10*. https://journals.plos.org/plosmedicine/article?id=10.1371/journal.pmed.1001547

Ferrer, R. A., & Cohen, G. L. (2018). Reconceptualizing self-affirmation with the trigger and channel framework: Lessons from the health domain. *Personality and Social Psychology Review, 23*(3), 285–304.

Ferreri, L., Mas-Herrero, E., Zatorre, R. J., Ripollés, P., Gomez-Andres, A., Alicart, H., Olivé, G., Marco-Pallarés, J., Antonijoan, R. M., Valle, M., Riba, J., & Rodriguez-Fornelis, A. (2019). Dopamine modulates the reward experiences elicited by music. *PNAS, 116*, 3793–3798.

Ferri, M., Amato, L., & Davoli, M. (2006). Alcoholics Anonymous and other 12-step programmes for alcohol dependence. *Cochrane Database of Systematic Reviews, 3*. https://www.cochranelibrary.com/cdsr/doi/10.1002/14651858.CD012880.pub2/full

Ferriman, K., Lubinski, D., & Benbow, C. P. (2009). Work preferences, life values, and personal views of top math/science graduate students and the profoundly gifted: Developmental changes and gender differences during emerging adulthood and parenthood. *Journal of Personality and Social Psychology, 97*, 517–522.

Ferris, C. F. (1996, March). The rage of innocents. *The Sciences*, pp. 22–26.

Festinger, L. (1957). *A theory of cognitive dissonance*. Stanford University Press.

Fetvadjiev, V. H., & He, J. (2019). The longitudinal links of personality traits, values, and well-being and self-esteem: A five-wave study of a nationally representative sample. *Journal of Personality and Social Psychology, 117*, 448–464.

Fichter, M. M., & Quadflieg, N. (2016). Mortality in eating disorders—results of a large prospective clinical longitudinal study. *International Journal of Eating Disorders, 49*, 391–401.

Fiedler, F. E. (1981). Leadership effectiveness. *American Behavioral Scientist, 24*, 619–632.

Fiedler, F. E. (1987, September). When to lead, when to stand back. *Psychology Today*, pp. 26–27.

Field, A. P. (2006). Is conditioning a useful framework for understanding the development and treatment of phobias? *Clinical Psychology Review, 26*, 857–875.

Field, T., Hernandez-Reif, M., Feijo, L., & Freedman, J. (2006). Prenatal, perinatal, and neonatal stimulation: A survey of neonatal nurseries. *Infant Behavior & Development, 29*, 24–31.

Fielder, R. L., Walsh, J. L., Carey, K. B., & Carey, M. P. (2013). Predictors of sexual hookups: A theory-based, prospective study of first-year college women. *Archives of Sexual Behavior, 42*, 1425–1441.

Fields, R. D. (2004, April). The other half of the brain. *Scientific American*, pp. 54–61.

Fields, R. D. (2005). Making memories stick. *Scientific American, 292*, 74–81.

Fields, R. D. (2013). Neuroscience: Map the other brain. *Nature, 501*, 25–27.

Fields, R. D. (2019, May). The roots of human aggression. *Scientific American*, pp. 65–71.

Fincham, F. D., & Bradbury, T. N. (1993). Marital satisfaction, depression, and attributions: A longitudinal analysis. *Journal of Personality and Social Psychology, 64*, 442–452.

Fingerman, K. L., & Charles, S. T. (2010). It takes two to tango: Why older people have the best relationships. *Current Directions in Psychological Science, 19*, 172–176.

Fink, A., Bay, J. U., Koschutnig, K., Prettenthaler, K., Rominger, C., Benedek, M., Papousek, I., Weiss, E. M., Seidel, A., & Memmert, D. (2019). Brain and soccer: Functional patterns of brain activity during the generation of creative moves in real soccer decision-making situations. *Human Brain Mapping, 40*, 755–764.

Fink, B., & Penton-Voak, I. (2002). Evolutionary psychology of facial attractiveness. *Current Directions in Psychological Science, 11*(5), 154–158.

Fink, H. A., MacDonald, R., Rutks, I. R., Nelson, D. B., & Wilt, T. J. (2002). Sildenafil for male erectile dysfunction. A systematic review and meta-analysis. *JAMA Internal Medicine, 162*(12), 1349–1360.

Fink, M. (2009). *Electroconvulsive therapy: A guide for professionals and their patients*. Oxford University Press.

Finkel, E. J. (2017). *The all-or-nothing marriage*. Dutton.

Finkel, E. J., & Eastwick, P. W. (2008). Speed-dating. *Current Directions in Psychological Science, 17*, 193–197.

Finkel, E. J., DeWall, C. N., Slotter, E. B., McNulty, J. K., Pond, R. S., Jr., & Atkins, D. C. (2012a). Using I3 theory to clarify when dispositional aggressiveness predicts intimate partner violence perpetration. *Journal of Personality and Social Psychology, 102*, 533–549.

Finkel, E. J., Eastwick, P. W., Karney, B. R., Reis, H. T., & Sprecher, S. (2012b, September/October). Dating in a digital world. *Scientific American Mind*, pp. 26–33.

Finkenauer, C., Buyukcan-Tetik, A., Baumeister, R. F., Schoemaker, K., Bartels, M., & Vohs, K. D. (2015). Out of control: Identifying the role of self-control strength in family violence. *Current Directions in Psychological Science, 24*, 261–266.

Finlay, S. W. (2000). Influence of Carl Jung and William James on the origin of alcoholics anonymous. *Review of General Psychology, 4*, 3–12.

Finnigan, K. M., & Vazire, S. (2018). The incremental validity of average state self-reports over global self-reports of personality. *Journal of Personality and Social Psychology, 115*, 321–337.

Fiore, M. C., Jaén, C. R., Baker, T. B., Bailey, W. C., Benowitz, N. L., Curry, S. J., Dorfman, S. F., Froelicher, E. S., Goldstein, M. G., Healton, C. G., Henderson, P. N., Heyman, R. B., Koh, H. K., Kottke, T. E., Lando, H. A., Mecklenburg, R. E., Mullen, P. D., Orleans, C. T., Robinson, L., … Wewers, M. E. (2008). *Treating tobacco use and dependence: 2008 update. Clinical practice guideline*. U.S. Department of Health and Human Services, Public Health Service.

Fiorella, L. (2020). The science of habit and its implications for student learning and well-being. *Educational Psychology Review, 32*, 603–625.

Firsov, M. L. (2019). Perspectives for the optogenetic prosthetization of the retina. *Neuroscience and Behavioral Physiology, 49*, 192–198.

Fischer, A., & LaFrance, M. (2015). What drives the smile and the tear: Why women are more emotionally expressive than men. *Emotion Review, 7*, 22–29.

Fischer, A. H., & Roseman, I. J. (2007). Beat them or ban them: The characteristics and social functions of anger and contempt. *Journal of Personality and Social Psychology, 93*(1), 103.

Fischer, P., & Greitemeyer, T. (2006). Music and aggression: The impact of sexual-aggressive song lyrics on aggression-related thoughts, emotions, and behavior toward the same and the opposite sex. *Personality and Social Psychology Bulletin, 32*, 1165–1176.

Fischer, P., Greitemeyer, T., Kastenmüller, A., Vogrincic, C., & Sauer, A. (2011). The effects of risk-glorifying media exposure on risk-positive cognitions, emotions, and behaviors: A meta-analytic review. *Psychological Bulletin, 137*, 367–390.

Fischer, R., & Boer, D. (2011). What is more important for national well-being: Money or autonomy? A meta-analysis of well-being, burnout, and anxiety across 63 societies. *Journal of Personality and Social Psychology, 101*, 164–184.

Fischer, R., & Karl, J. A. (2022). Predicting behavioral intentions to prevent or mitigate COVID-19: A cross-cultural meta-analysis of attitudes, norms, and perceived behavioral control effects. *Social Psychological and Personality Science, 13*(1), 264–276.

Fischhoff, B. (1982). Debiasing. In D. Kahneman, P. Slovic, & A. Tversky (Eds.), *Judgment under uncertainty: Heuristics and biases*. Cambridge University Press.

Fischhoff, B., Slovic, P., & Lichtenstein, S. (1977). Knowing with certainty: The appropriateness of extreme confidence. *Journal of Experimental Psychology: Human Perception and Performance, 3*, 552–564.

Fishbach, A., Dhar, R., & Zhang, Y. (2006). Subgoals as substitutes or complements: The role of goal accessibility. *Journal of Personality and Social Psychology, 91*, 232–242.

Fisher, H. E. (1993, March/April). After all, maybe it's biology. *Psychology Today*, pp. 40–45.

Fisher, H. T. (1984). Little Albert and Little Peter. *Bulletin of the British Psychological Society, 37*, 269.

Fiske, S. T. (2018). Stereotype content: Warmth and competence endure. *Current Directions in Psychological Science, 27*, 67–73.

Fitton, L., Yu, R., & Fazel, S. (2020). Childhood maltreatment and violent outcomes: A systematic review and meta-analysis of prospective studies. *Trauma, Violence, & Abuse, 21*(4), 754–768.

Fitz, N., Kushlev, K., Jagannathan, R., Lewis, T., Paliwal, D., & Ariely, D. (2019). Batching smartphone notifications can improve well-being. *Computers in Human Behavior, 101*, 84–94.

Fitzgerald, R. J., & Price, H. L. (2015). Eyewitness identification across the life span: A meta-analysis of age differences. *Psychological Bulletin, 141*, 1228–1265.

Fitzpatrick, K. M., Harris, C., & Drawve, G. (2020). Living in the midst of fear: Depressive symptomatology among US adults during the COVID-19 pandemic. *Depression & Anxiety, 37*(10), 957–964.

Fivush, R., Brotman, M. A., Buckner, J. P., & Goodman, S. H. (2000). Gender differences in parent–child emotion narratives. *Sex Roles, 43*, 233–253.

Flack, W. F. (2006). Peripheral feedback effects of facial expressions, bodily postures, and vocal expressions on emotional feelings. *Cognition and Emotion, 20*, 177–195.

Flagg, A. (2018, March 30). The myth of the criminal immigrant. *The New York Times*. https://www.nytimes.com/interactive/2018/03/30/upshot/crime-immigration-myth.html

Flagg, A. (2019, May 13). Is there a connection between undocumented immigrants and crime? *The New York Times*. https://www.nytimes.com/2019/05/13/upshot/illegal-immigration-crime-rates-research.html

Flaherty, D. K. (2011). The vaccine-autism connection: A public health crisis caused by unethical medical practices and fraudulent science. *Annals of Pharmacotherapy, 45*, 1302–1304.

Flegal, K. M., Carroll, M. D., Kit, B. K., & Ogden, C. L. (2012). Prevalence of obesity and trends in the distribution of body mass index among US adults, 1999–2010. *Journal of the American Medical Association, 307*, 491–497.

Flegal, K. M., Carroll, M. D., Ogden, C. L., & Curtin, L. R. (2010). Prevalence and trends in obesity among US adults, 1999–2008. *Journal of the American Medical Association, 303*, 235–241.

Flegal, K. M., Kruszon-Moran, D., Carroll, M. D., Fryar, C. D., & Ogden, C. L. (2016). Trends in obesity among adults in the United States, 2005 to 2014. *Journal of the American Medical Association, 315*, 2284–2291.

Flegenheimer, M. (2018). Beto O'Rourke dreams of one Texas. Ted Cruz sees another clearly. *The New York Times*. https://www.nytimes.com/2018/08/31/us/politics/beto-orourke-dreams-of-one-texas-ted-cruz-sees-another-clearly.html

Fleming, I., Baum, A., & Weiss, L. (1987). Social density and perceived control as mediator of crowding stress in high-density residential neighborhoods. *Journal of Personality and Social Psychology, 52*, 899–906.

Fleming, J. H., & Scott, B. A. (1991). The costs of confession: The Persian Gulf War POW tapes in historical and theoretical perspective. *Contemporary Social Psychology, 15*, 127–138.

Flesher, S., Downey, J. E., Weiss, J. M., Hughes, C. L., Herrera, A. J., Tyler-Kabara, E. C., Boninger, M. L., Collinger, J. L., & Gaunt, R. A. (2021). A brain-computer interface that evokes tactile sensations improves robotic arm control. *Science, 372*(6544), 831–836.

Fletcher, G. J. O., Fitness, J., & Blampied, N. M. (1990). The link between attributions and happiness in close relationships: The roles of depression and explanatory style. *Journal of Social and Clinical Psychology, 9*, 243–255.

Flinker, A., Korzeniewska, A., Shestyuk, A. Y., Franaszczuk, P. J., Dronkers, N. F., Knight, R. T., & Crone, N. E. (2015). Redefining the role of Broca's area in speech. *PNAS, 112*, 2871–2875.

Flood, A. (2017, October 14). John Green: 'Having OCD is an ongoing part of my life.' *The Guardian*. https://www.theguardian.com/books/2017/oct/14/john-green-turtles-all-the-way-down-ocd-interview

Flora, S. R. (2004). *The power of reinforcement*. SUNY Press.

Flore, P. C., Mulder, J., & Wicherts, J. M. (2019). The influence of gender stereotype threat on mathematics test scores of Dutch high school students: A registered report. *Comprehensive Results in Social Psychology*. https://www.tandfonline.com/doi/full/10.1080/23743603.2018.1559647?scroll=top&needAccess=true

Flore, P. C., & Wicherts, J. M. (2015). Does stereotype threat influence performance of girls in stereotyped domains? A meta-analysis. *Journal of School Psychology, 53*, 25–44.

Floud, R., Fogel, R. W., Harris, B., & Hong, S. C. (2011). *The changing body: Health, nutrition, and human development in the western world since 1700*. Cambridge University Press.

Flouri, E., & Buchanan, A. (2004). Early father's and mother's involvement and child's later educational outcomes. *British Journal of Educational Psychology, 74*, 141–153.

Flückiger, C., Rubel, J., Del Re, A. C., Horvath, A. O., Wampold, B. E., Crits-Christoph, P., Atzil-Slonim, D., Compare, A., Falkenström, F., Ekeblad, A., Errázuriz, P., Fisher, H., Hoffart, A., Huppert, J. D., Kivity, Y., Kuman, M., Lutz, W., Muran, J. C., Strunk, D. R., … Barber, J. P. (2020). The reciprocal relationship between alliance and early treatment symptoms: A two-stage individual participant data meta-analysis. *Journal of Consulting and Clinical Psychology, 88*(9), 829–843.

Flynn, J. R. (1987). Massive IQ gains in 14 nations: What IQ tests really measure. *Psychological Bulletin, 101*, 171–191.

Flynn, J. R. (2009). Requiem for nutrition as the cause of IQ gains: Raven's gains in Britain 1938–2008. *Economics and Human Biology, 7*, 18–27.

Flynn, J. R. (2012). *Are we getting smarter? Rising IQ in the twenty-first century*. Cambridge University Press.

Flynn, J. R. (2018). Reflections about intelligence over 40 years. *Intelligence, 70*, 73–83.

Flynn, M. (2018, November 5). 'I wanted him to feel compassion': The Jewish nurse who treated the synagogue shooting suspect tells his story. *The Washington Post*. https://www.washingtonpost.com/

Foa, E. B., & Kozak, M. J. (1986). Emotional processing of fear: Exposure to corrective information. *Psychological Bulletin, 99*, 20–35.

Foell, J., Palumbo, I. M., Yancey, J. R., Vizueta, N., Demirakca, T., & Patrick, C. J. (2019). Biobehavioral threat sensitivity and amygdala volume: A twin neuroimaging study. *NeuroImage, 186*, 14–21.

Foer, J. (2011). *Moonwalking with Einstein: The art and science of remembering everything*. Penguin.

Foley, M. A. (2015). Setting the records straight: Impossible memories and the persistence of their phenomenological qualities. *Review of General Psychology, 19*, 230–248.

Foley, R. T., Whitwell, R. L., & Goodale, M. A. (2015). The two-visual-systems hypothesis and the perspectival features of visual experience. *Consciousness and Cognition, 35*, 225–233.

Fong, C. J., Zaleski, D. J., & Leach, J. K. (2015). The challenge–skill balance and antecedents of flow: A meta-analytic investigation. *Journal of Positive Psychology, 10*, 425–446.

Fong, K., & Mar, R. A. (2015). What does my avatar say about me? Inferring personality from avatars. *Personality and Social Psychology Bulletin, 41*, 237–249.

Forbes, L., Graham, J., Berglund, C., & Bell, R. (2018). Dietary change during pregnancy and women's reasons for change. *Nutrients, 10*. https://www.ncbi.nlm.nih.gov/pmc/articles/PMC6115730/

Forbes, M. K., & Krueger, R. F. (2019). The great recession and mental health in the United States. *Clinical Psychological Science, 7*, 900–913.

Ford, B. Q., & Troy, A. S. (2019). Reappraisal reconsidered: A closer look at the costs of an acclaimed emotion-regulation strategy. *Current Directions in Psychological Science, 28*, 195–203.

Ford, E. S. (2002). Does exercise reduce inflammation? Physical activity and B-reactive protein among U.S. adults. *Epidemiology, 13*, 561–569.

Ford, M. T., Cerasoli, C. P., Higgins, J. A., & Deccesare, A. L. (2011). Relationships between psychological, physical, and behavioural health and work performance: A review and meta-analysis. *Work & Stress, 25*, 185–204.

Foree, D. D., & LoLordo, V. M. (1973). Attention in the pigeon: Differential effects of food-getting versus shock-avoidance procedures. *Journal of Comparative and Physiological Psychology, 85*, 551–558.

Forest, A. L., Kille, D. R, Wood, J. V., & Stehouwer, L. R. (2015). Turbulent times, rocky relationships: Relational consequences of experiencing physical instability. *Psychological Science, 26*, 1261–1271.

Forgas, J. (2017, May 14). *Why bad moods are good for you: The surprising benefits of sadness*. The Conversation. https://theconversation.com/why-bad-moods-are-good-for-you-the-surprising-benefits-of-sadness-75402

Forgas, J. P. (2009, November/December). Think negative! *Australian Science*, pp. 14–17.

Forgas, J. P. (2013). Don't worry, be sad! On the cognitive, motivational, and interpersonal benefits of negative mood. *Current Directions in Psychological Science, 22*, 225–232.

Forgas, J. P., Bower, G. H., & Krantz, S. E. (1984). The influence of mood on perceptions of social interactions. *Journal of Experimental Social Psychology, 20*, 497–513.

Forman, D. R., Aksan, N., & Kochanska, G. (2004). Toddlers' responsive imitation predicts preschool-age conscience. *Psychological Science, 15*, 699–704.

Forrin, N. D., & MacLeod, C. M. (2018). This time it's personal: The memory benefit of hearing oneself. *Memory, 26*, 574–579.

Forster, S., & Spence, C. (2018). "What smell?" Temporarily loading visual attention induces a prolonged loss of olfactory awareness. *Psychological Science, 29*, 1642–1652.

Forsyth, D. R., Lawrence, N. K., Burnette, J. L., & Baumeister, R. F. (2007). Attempting to improve academic performance of struggling college students by bolstering their self-esteem: An intervention that backfired. *Journal of Social and Clinical Psychology, 26*, 447–459.

Foss, D. J., & Hakes, D. T. (1978). *Psycholinguistics: An introduction to the psychology of language*. Prentice-Hall.

Fothergill, E., Guo, J., Howard, L., Kerns, J. C., Knuth, J. D., Brychta, R., Chen, K. Y., Skarulis, M. C., Walter, M., Walter, P. J., & Hall, K. D. (2016). Persistent metabolic adaptation 6 years after "The Biggest Loser" competition. *Obesity, 24*, 1612–1619.

Foulk, T. A., Lanaj, K., & Krishnan, S. (2019). The virtuous cycle of daily motivation: Effects of daily strivings on work behaviors, need satisfaction, and next-day strivings. *Journal of Applied Psychology, 104*, 755–775.

Foulkes, D. (1999). *Children's dreaming and the development of consciousness*. Harvard University Press.

Fournier, J. C., DeRubeis, R. J., Hollon, S. D., Dimidjian, S., Amsterdam, J. D., Shelton, R. C., & Fawcett, J. (2010). Antidepressant drug effects and depression severity: A patient-level meta-analysis. *Journal of the American Medical Association, 303*, 47–53.

Fowles, D. C. (1992). Schizophrenia: Diathesis-stress revisited. *Annual Review of Psychology, 43*, 303–336.

Fowles, D. C., & Dindo, L. (2009). Temperament and psychopathy: A dual-pathway model. *Current Directions in Psychological Science, 18*, 179–183.

Fox, A. S., Harris, R. A., Del Rosso, L., Raveendran, M., Kamboj, S., Kinnally, E. L., Capitanio, J. P., & Rogers, J. (2021). Infant inhibited temperament in primates predicts adult behavior, is heritable, and is associated with anxiety-relevant genetic variation. *Molecular Psychiatry, 26*, 6609–6618.

Fox, A. S., Oler, J. A., Shackman, A. J., Shelton, S. E., Raveendran, M., McKay, D. R., Converse, A. K., Alexander, A., Davidson, R. J., Blangero, J., Rogers, J., & Kalin, N. H. (2015). Intergenerational neural mediators of early-life anxious temperament. *PNAS, 112*, 9118–9122.

Fox, B., & DeLisi, M. (2019). Psychopathic killers: A meta-analytic review of the psychopathy-homicide nexus. *Aggression and Violent Behavior, 44*, 67–79.

Fox, D. (2010, June). The insanity virus. *Discover*, pp. 58–64.

Fox, K. C. R., Nijeboer, S., Solomonova, E., Domhoff, G. W., & Christoff, K. (2013). Dreaming as mind wandering: Evidence from functional neuroimaging and first-person content reports. *Frontiers in Human Neuroscience, 7*, 412.

Fox, M. (2020, October 21). James Randi, magician who debunked paranormal claims, dies at 92. *The New York Times*. https://www.nytimes.com/2020/10/21/obituaries/james-randi-dead.html

Fox, M. L., Dwyer, D. J., & Ganster, D. C. (1993). Effects of stressful job demands and control on physiological and attitudinal outcomes in a hospital setting. *Academy of Management Journal, 36*, 289–318.

Fox, N. A., Bakermans-Kranenburg, M., Yoo, K. H., Bowman, L. C., Cannon, E. N., Vanderwert, R. E., Ferrari, P. F., & van IJzendoorn, M. H. (2016). Assessing human mirror activity with EEG mu rhythm: A meta-analysis. *Psychological Bulletin, 142*, 291–313.

Fragaszy, D. M. (2021). Comparative psychology's founding mother, Margaret Floy Washburn. *Journal of Comparative Psychology, 135*(1), 3–14.

Fragaszy, D. M., Eshchar, Y., Visalberghi, E., Resende, B., Laity, K., & Izar, P. (2017). Synchronized practice helps bearded capuchin monkeys learn to extend attention while learning a tradition. *PNAS, 114*, 7798–7805.

Fraley, R. C. (2019). Attachment in adulthood: Recent developments, emerging debates, and future directions. *Annual Review of Psychology, 70*, 401–422.

Fraley, R. C., Gillath, O., & Deboeck, P. R. (2021). Do life events lead to enduring changes in adult attachment styles? A naturalistic longitudinal investigation. *Journal of Personality and Social Psychology, 120*(6), 1567–1606.

Fraley, R. C., & Tancredy, C. M. (2012). Twin and sibling attachment in a nationally representative sample. *Personality and Social Psychology Bulletin, 38*, 308–316.

Frances, A. J. (2013). *Saving normal: An insider's revolt against out-of-control psychiatric diagnosis, DSM-5, Big Pharma, and the medicalization of ordinary life*. HarperCollins.

Francis, A. L. (2018). The embodied theory of stress: A constructionist perspective on the experience of stress. *Review of General Psychology, 22*, 398–405.

Frank, J. D. (1982). Therapeutic components shared by all psychotherapies. In J. H. Harvey & M. M. Parks (Eds.), *The master lecture series: Vol. 1. Psychotherapy research and behavior change*. American Psychological Association.

Frank, M., Braginsky, M., Marchman, V., & Yurovsky, D. (2019). Chapter 8, Consistency in early vocabulary comprehension. In *Variability and consistency in early language learning*. The Wordbank Project. https://langcog.github.io/wordbank-book/items-consistency.html

Frankel, A., Strange, D. R., & Schoonover, R. (1983). CRAP: Consumer rated assessment procedure. In G. H. Scherr & R. Liebmann-Smith (Eds.), *The best of The Journal of Irreproducible Results*. Workman.

Frankenbach, J., Weber, M., Loschelder, D. D., Kilger, H., & Friese, M. (2022). Sex drive: Theoretical conceptualization and meta-analytic review of gender differences. *Psychological Bulletin*. https://psyarxiv.com/9yk8e/

Frankenburg, W., Dodds, J., Archer, P., Shapiro, H., & Bresnick, B. (1992). The Denver II: A major revision and restandardization of the Denver Developmental Screening Test. *Pediatrics, 89*, 91–97.

Frankl, V. E. (1962). *Man's search for meaning: An introduction to logotherapy*. Beacon Press.

Franklin, A., & Merrifield, R. (2020, September 29). *Parrots removed from UK wildlife park after they started swearing at customers*. Mirror. https://www.mirror.co.uk/news/uk-news/parrots-removed-uk-wildlife-park-22758160

Franklin, M., & Foa, E. B. (2011). Treatment of obsessive-compulsive disorder. *Annual Review of Clinical Psychology, 7*, 229–243.

Franklin, R. G., Adams, R. B., Steiner, T. G., & Zebrowitz, L. A. (2019). Reading the lines in the face: The contribution of angularity and roundness to perceptions of facial anger and joy. *Emotion, 19*(2), 209–218.

Franz, E. A., Waldie, K. E., & Smith, M. J. (2000). The effect of callosotomy on novel versus familiar bimanual actions: A neural dissociation between controlled and automatic processes? *Psychological Science, 11*, 82–85.

Fraser, M. A., Shaw, M. E., & Cherubin, N. (2015). A systematic review and meta-analysis of longitudinal hippocampal atrophy in healthy human ageing. *NeuroImage, 112*, 364–374.

Frassanito, P., & Pettorini, B. (2008). Pink and blue: The color of gender. *Child's Nervous System, 24*, 881–882.

Frasure-Smith, N., & Lesperance, F. (2005). Depression and coronary heart disease: Complex synergism of mind, body, and environment. *Current Directions in Psychological Science, 14*, 39–43.

Frattaroli, J. (2006). Experimental disclosure and its moderators: A meta-analysis. *Psychological Bulletin, 132*, 823–865.

Frederick, S. (2005). Cognitive reflection and decision making. *Journal of Economic Perspectives, 4*, 25–42.

Fredrickson, B. L. (2013). Updated thinking on positivity ratios. *American Psychologist, 68*, 814–822.

Freedman, A. A., Papachristos, A. V., Smart, B. P., Keenan-Devlin, L. S., Khan, S. S., Borders, A., Kershaw, K. N., & Miller, G. E. (2022). Complaints about excessive use of police force in women's neighborhoods and subsequent perinatal and cardiovascular health. *Science Advances, 8*(3). https://www.science.org/doi/10.1126/sciadv.abl5417

Freedman, D. H. (2011, February). How to fix the obesity crisis. *Scientific American*, pp. 40–47.

Freedman, D. J., Riesenhuber, M., Poggio, T., & Miller, E. K. (2001). Categorical representation of visual stimuli in the primate prefrontal cortex. *Science, 291*, 312–316.

Freedman, J. L., & Fraser, S. C. (1966). Compliance without pressure: The foot-in-the-door technique. *Journal of Personality and Social Psychology, 4*, 195–202.

Freedman, J. L., & Perlick, D. (1979). Crowding, contagion, and laughter. *Journal of Experimental Social Psychology, 15*, 295–303.

Freedman, L. R., Rock, D., Roberts, S. A., Cornblatt, B. A., & Erlenmeyer-Kimling, L. (1998). The New York high-risk project: Attention, anhedonia and social outcome. *Schizophrenia Research, 30*, 1–9.

Freedman, R., Lewis, D. A., Michels, R., Pine, D. S., Schultz, S. K., Tamminga, C. A., Gabbard, G. O., Gau, S. S., Javitt, D. C., Oquendo, M. A., Shrout, P. E., Vieta, E., & Yager, J. (2013). The initial field trials of DSM-5: New blooms and old thorns. *American Journal of Psychiatry, 170*, 1–5.

Freeman, D., & Freeman, J. (2013). *The stressed sex: Uncovering the truth about men, women, and mental health*. Oxford University Press.

Freeman, E. C., & Twenge, J. M. (2010, January). *Using MySpace increases the endorsement of narcissistic personality traits* [Poster]. Presented at the annual conference of the Society for Personality and Social Psychology, Las Vegas, NV.

Freeman, S., Eddy, S. L., McDonough, M., Smith, M. K., Okoroafor, N., Jordt, H., & Wenderoth, M. P. (2014). Active learning increases student performance in science, engineering, and mathematics. *PNAS, 111*, 8410–8415.

Freeman, W. J. (1991, February). The physiology of perception. *Scientific American*, pp. 78–85.

Frenda, S. J., Patihis, L., Loftus, E. F., Lewis, H. C., & Fenn, K. M. (2014). Sleep deprivation and false memories. *Clinical Psychological Science, 25*, 1674–1681.

Freud, S. (1897, October 15). Letter of Freud to Fleiss. In J. M. Masson (Ed.). (1985). *The complete letters of Sigmund Freud to Wilhelm Fleiss, 1887–1904*. Harvard University Press.

Freud, S. (1935: reprinted 1960). *A general introduction to psychoanalysis*. Washington Square Press.

Frew, N. (2022, April 27). *Census data gives clearer picture of Alberta's transgender, non-binary community*. CBC News. https://www.cbc.ca/news/canada/edmonton/alberta-2021-census-gender-age-dwelling-1.6432469

Frey, M. C., & Detterman, D. K. (2004). Scholastic assessment or *g*? The relationship between the Scholastic Assessment Test and general cognitive ability. *Psychological Science, 15*, 373–378.

Freyd, J. J., DePrince, A. P., & Gleaves, D. H. (2007). The state of betrayal trauma theory: Reply to McNally—Conceptual issues and future directions. *Memory, 15*, 295–311.

Fridman, A., Gerson, R., & Gneezy, A. (2022). Increased generosity under COVID-19 threat. *Scientific Reports, 12*. https://tinyurl.com/4h27edck

Fried, E. I., Eidhof, M. B., Palic, S., Costantini, G., Huisman-van Dijk, H. M., Bockting, C. L. H., Engelhard, I., Armour, C., Nielsen, A. B., & Karstoft, K.-I. (2018). Replicability and generalizability of posttraumatic stress disorder (PTSD) networks: A cross-cultural multisite study of PTSD symptoms in four trauma patient samples. *Clinical Psychological Science, 6*, 335–351.

Friedel, J. E., DeHart, W. B., Madden, G. J., & Odum, A. L. (2014). Impulsivity and cigarette smoking: Discounting of monetary and consumable outcomes in current and non-smokers. *Psychopharmacology, 231*, 4517–4526.

Friedman, H. S., & Martin, L. R. (2012). *The longevity project*. Penguin (Plume).

Friedman, M., & Ulmer, D. (1984). *Treating Type A behavior—and your heart*. Knopf.

Friedman, R., & James, J. W. (2008). The myth of the stages of dying, death and grief. *Skeptic, 14*, 37–41.

Friedman, R. A. (2017, October 11). Psychiatrists can't stop mass killers. *The New York Times*. https://www.nytimes.com/2017/10/11/opinion/psychiatrists-mass-killers.html

Friedman, T. L. (2022, March 15). In the war over Ukraine, expect the unexpected. *The New York Times*. https://www.nytimes.com/2022/03/15/opinion/russia-ukraine-putin-war.html

Friesen, J. P., Campbell, T. H., & Kay, A. C. (2015). The psychological advantage of unfalsifiability: The appeal of untestable religious and political ideologies. *Journal of Personality and Social Psychology, 108*, 515–529.

Frimer, J. A., Brandt, M. J., Melton, Z., & Motyl, M. (2019). Extremists on the left and right use angry, negative language. *Personality and Social Psychology Bulletin, 45*, 1216–1231.

Frisell, T., Pawitan, Y., Långström, N., & Lichtenstein, P. (2012). Heritability, assortative mating and gender differences in violent crime: Results from a total population sample using twin, adoption, and sibling models. *Behavior Genetics, 42*, 3–18.

Frith, U., & Frith, C. (2001). The biological basis of social interaction. *Current Directions in Psychological Science, 10*, 151–155.

Frithsen, A., Stark, S. M., & Stark, C. E. (2019). Response bias, recollection, and familiarity in individuals with Highly Superior Autobiographical Memory (HSAM). *Memory, 27*, 739–749.

Fritz, C., Curtin, J., Poitevineau, J., & Tao, F.-C. (2017). Listener evaluations of new and old Italian violins. *PNAS, 114*, 5395–5400.

Fritz, H. L., Russek, L. N., & Dillon, M. M. (2017). Humor use moderates the relation of stressful life events with psychological distress. *Personality and Social Psychology Bulletin, 43*, 845–859.

Fritz, J., VoPham, T., Wright, K. P., Jr., & Vetter, C. (2020). A chronobiological evaluation of the acute effects of daylight saving time on traffic accident risk. *Current Biology, 30*(4), 729–735.

Fritz, N., & Paul, B. (2018). From orgasms to spanking: A content analysis of the agentic and objectifying sexual scripts in feminist, for women, and mainstream pornography. *Sex Roles, 77*, 639–652.

Fritz, N., Malic, V., Paul, B., & Zhou, Y. (2020). A descriptive analysis of the types, targets, and relative frequency of aggression in mainstream pornography. *Archives of Sexual Behavior, 49*(8), 3041–3053.

Fromkin, V., & Rodman, R. (1983). *An introduction to language* (3rd ed.). Holt, Rinehart & Winston.

Frühauf, S., Gerger, H., Schmidt, H. M., Munder, T., & Barth, J. (2013). Efficacy of psychological interventions for sexual dysfunction: A systematic review and meta-analysis. *Archives of Sexual Behavior, 42*, 915–933.

Fry, A. F., & Hale, S. (1996). Processing speed, working memory, and fluid intelligence: Evidence for a developmental cascade. *Psychological Science, 7*, 237–241.

Fry, D. P. (2012). Life without war. *Science, 336*, 879–884.

Fry, R. (2017, May 5). *It's becoming more common for young adults to live at home—and for longer stretches*. Pew Research Center. https://www.pewresearch.org/fact-tank/2017/05/05/its-becoming-more-common-for-young-adults-to-live-at-home-and-for-longer-stretches/

Fuligni, A. J. (2019). The need to contribute during adolescence. *Perspectives on Psychological Science, 14*, 331–343.

Fuligni, A. J., & Pedersen, S. (2002). Family obligation and the transition to young adulthood. *Developmental Psychology*, 38(5), 856.

Fuller-Rowell, T. E., Nichols, O. I., Burrow, A. L., Ong, A. D., Chae, D. H., & El-Sheikh, M. (2021). Day-to-day fluctuations in experiences of discrimination: Associations with sleep and the moderating role of internalized racism among African American college students. *Cultural Diversity and Ethnic Minority Psychology, 27*(1), 107–117.

Fuller-Thomson, E., Agbeyaka, S., LaFond, D. M., & Bern-Klug, M. (2016). Flourishing after depression: Factors associated with achieving complete mental health among those with a history of depression. *Psychiatry Research, 242*, 111–120.

Fulmer, C. A., Gelfand, M. J., Kruglanski, A. W., Kim-Prieto, C., Diener, E., Pierro, A., & Higgins, E. T. (2010). On "feeling right" in cultural contexts: How person–culture match affects self-esteem and subjective well-being. *Psychological Science, 21*, 1563–1569.

Funder, D. C. (2001). Personality. *Annual Review of Psychology, 52*, 197–221.

Funder, D. C. (2009). Persons, behaviors and situations: An agenda for personality psychology in the postwar era. *Journal of Research in Personality, 43*, 155–162.

Funk, C. (2019, February 6). *How highly religious Americans view evolution depends on how they're asked about it*. Pew Research Center. https://tinyurl.com/qszpfzc

Furnham, A. (1982). Explanations for unemployment in Britain. *European Journal of Social Psychology, 12*, 335–352.

Furnham, A. (2016). Whether you think you can, or you think you can't—You're right. In R. J. Sternberg, S. T. Fiske, & D. J. Foss (Eds.), *Scientists making a difference: One hundred eminent behavioral and brain scientists talk about their most important contributions*. Cambridge University Press.

Furnham, A. (2018). Myths and misconceptions in developmental and neuro-psychology. *Psychology, 9*, 249–259.

Furnham, A., & Baguma, P. (1994). Cross-cultural differences in the evaluation of male and female body shapes. *International Journal of Eating Disorders, 15*, 81–89.

Furr, R. M., & Funder, D. C. (1998). A multimodal analysis of personal negativity. *Journal of Personality and Social Psychology, 74*, 1580–1591.

Fuss, J., Steinle, J., Bindila, L., Auer, M. K., Kirchherr, H., Lutz, B., & Gass, P. (2015). A runner's high depends on cannabinoid receptors in mice. *PNAS, 112*, 13105–13108.

Futrell, R., Mahowald, K., & Gibson, E. (2015). Large-scale evidence of dependency length minimization in 37 languages. *PNAS, 112*, 10336–10341.

Futterman, M. (2021, April 8). Olympic bobsledder who killed himself likely had C.T.E. *The New York Times*. https://www.nytimes.com/2021/04/08/sports/olympics/bobsled-cte-concussions-sledhead.html

Gable, S. L., Hopper, E. A., & Schooler, J. W. (2019). When the muses strike: Creative ideas of physicists and writers routinely occur during mind wandering. *Psychological Science, 30*, 396–404.

Gächter, S., Starmer, C., & Tufano, F. (2015). Measuring the closeness of relationships: A comprehensive evaluation of the 'Inclusion of the Other in the Self' scale. *PLOS ONE*. https://journals.plos.org/plosone/article?id=10.1371/journal.pone.0129478#sec011

Gaddy, M. A., & Ingram, R. E. (2014). A meta-analytic review of mood-congruent implicit memory in depressed mood. *Clinical Psychology Review, 34*, 402–416.

Gaertner, L., Iuzzini, J., & O'Mara, E. M. (2008). When rejection by one fosters aggression against many: Multiple-victim aggression as a consequence of social rejection and perceived groupness. *Journal of Experimental Social Psychology, 44*, 958–970.

Gage, S. (2019). Cannabis and psychosis: Triangulating the evidence. *The Lancet, 6*, 364–365.

Gaissmaier, W., & Gigerenzer, G. (2012). 9/11, Act II: A fine-grained analysis of regional variations in traffic fatalities in the aftermath of the terrorist attacks. *Psychological Science, 23*, 1449–1454.

Galambos, N. L. (1992). Parent-adolescent relations. *Current Directions in Psychological Science, 1*, 146–149.

Galambos, N. L., Krahn, H. J., Johnson, M. D., & Lachman, M. E. (2020). The U shape of happiness across the life course: Expanding the discussion. *Perspectives on Psychological Science, 15*(4), 898–912.

Galanter, E. (1962). Contemporary psychophysics. In R. Brown, E. Galanter, E. H. Hess, & G. Mandler (Eds.), *New directions in psychology*. Holt Rinehart & Winston.

Galanter, M. (2016). *What is Alcoholics Anonymous?* Oxford University Press.

Galati, D., Scherer, K. R., & Ricci-Bitti, P. E. (1997). Voluntary facial expression of emotion: Comparing congenitally blind with normally sighted encoders. *Journal of Personality and Social Psychology, 73*, 1363–1379.

Galatzer-Levy, I., Huang, S. H., & Bonanno, G. A. (2018). Trajectories of resilience and dysfunction following potential trauma: A review and statistical evaluation. *Clinical Psychology Review, 63*, 41–55.

Gale, C. R., Batty, G. D., & Deary, I. J. (2008). Locus of control at age 10 years and health outcomes and behaviors at age 30 years: The 1970 British Cohort Study. *Psychosomatic Medicine, 70*, 397–403.

Gale, N., Swaine, T., Morgan, H., Parkinson, V., Bagnall-Oakeley, R., Clarke, J., Williams, C., Ross, M., Keogh, B., Wilson, S., Singh, R., Reeves, A., Saddington, P., Calderwood, C., Mathers, N., Ruddle, A., Andersen-Warren, M., Stewart, J., Davis, D., & Pollecoff, M. (2017). *Memorandum of understanding on conversion therapy in the UK, Version 2* [PDF file]. https://www.psychotherapy.org.uk/wp-content/uploads/2017/10/UKCP-Memorandum-of-Understanding-on-Conversion-Therapy-in-the-UK.pdf

Galinsky, A. M., & Sonenstein, F. L. (2013). Relationship commitment, perceived equity, and sexual enjoyment among young adults in the United States. *Archives of Sexual Behavior, 42*, 93–104.

Gallace, A. (2012). Living with touch. *The Psychologist, 25*, 896–899.

Gallace, A., & Spence, C. (2011). To what extent do Gestalt grouping principles influence tactile perception? *Psychological Bulletin, 137*, 538–561.

Gallo, W. T., Teng, H. M., Falba, T. A., Kasl, S. V., Krumholz, H. M., & Bradley, E. H. (2006). The impact of late career job loss on myocardial infarction and stroke: A 10-year follow up using the health and retirement survey. *Occupational and Environmental Medicine, 63*, 683–687.

Gallup. (2004, August 16). 65% of Americans receive NO praise or recognition in the workplace. E-mail from Tom Rath: bucketbook@gallup.com

Gallup. (2017). *State of the global workplace*. https://www.gallup.com/workplace/238079/state-global-workplace-2017.aspx

Gallup, G. G., Jr., & Frederick, D. A. (2010). The science of sex appeal: An evolutionary perspective. *Review of General Psychology, 14*, 240–250.

Gallup, G. G., Jr., & Suarez, S. D. (1986). Self-awareness and the emergence of mind in humans and other primates. In J. Suls & A. G. Greenwald (Eds.), *Psychological perspectives on the self* (Vol. 3.). Erlbaum.

Gallup, G. H., Jr. (1994, October). Millions finding care and support in small groups. *Emerging Trends*, pp. 2–5.

Gallup. (2019). *Illegal drugs*. Gallup News. https://news.gallup.com/poll/1657/illegal-drugs.aspx

Gallup. (2020, February 4). *Is working remotely effective? Gallup research says yes*. https://www.gallup.com/workplace/283985/working-remotely-effective-gallup-research-says-yes.aspx

Gallup. (2021, September). *U.S. approval of interracial marriage at new high of 94%*. https://news.gallup.com/poll/354638/approval-interracial-marriage-new-high.aspx

Gallup. (2021). *Crime*. https://news.gallup.com/poll/1603/crime.aspx

Gallup. (2022). *Global emotions report*. https://www.gallup.com/analytics/349280/gallup-global-emotions-report.aspx

Gampe, A., Wermelinger, S., & Daum, M. M. (2019). Bilingual children adapt to the needs of their communication partners, monolinguals do not. *Child Development, 90*, 98–107.

Gana, K., Broc, G., Saada, Y., Amieva, H., & Quintard, B. (2016). Subjective wellbeing and longevity: Findings from a 22-year cohort study. *Journal of Psychosomatic Research, 85*, 28–34.

Gandhi, A. V., Mosser, E. A., Oikonomou, G., & Prober, D. A. (2015). Melatonin is required for the circadian regulation of sleep. *Neuron, 85*, 1193–1199.

Gandhi, T. K., Ganesh, S., & Sinha, P. (2014). Improvement in spatial imagery following sight onset late in childhood. *Psychological Science, 25*, 693–701.

Gandhi, T. K., Singh, A. K., Swami, P., Ganesh, S., & Sinha, P. (2017). Emergence of categorical face perception after extended early-onset blindness. *PNAS, 114*, 6139–6143.

Gangestad, S. W., Thornhill, R., & Garver-Apgar, C. E. (2010). Men's facial masculinity predicts changes in their female partners' sexual interests across the ovulatory cycle, whereas men's intelligence does not. *Evolution and Human Behavior, 31*, 412–424.

Ganna, A., Verweij, K. J., Nivard, M. G., Maier, R., Wedow, R., Busch, A. S., Abdellaoui, A., Guo, S., Sathirapongsasuti, J. F., ..., & Zietsch, B. P. (2019). Large-scale GWAS reveals insights into the genetic architecture of same-sex sexual behavior. *Science, 365*(6456). https://tinyurl.com/465d62aj

Ganzach, Y., & Patel, P. (2018). Wages, mental abilities and assessments in large scale international surveys: Still not much more than *g*. *Intelligence, 69*, 1–7.

Gao, T., Du, J., Tian, S., & Liu, W. (2022). A meta-analysis of the effects of non-invasive brain stimulation on obsessive-compulsive disorder. *Psychiatry Research, 312*. doi: 10.1016/j.psychres.2022.114530

Gao, T., Han, X., Bang, D., & Han, S. (2022). Cultural differences in neurocognitive mechanisms underlying believing. *NeuroImage, 250*. https://www.sciencedirect.com/science/article/pii/S1053811922000830

Gao, Y., Raine, A., Venables, P. H., Dawson, M. E., & Mednick, S. A. (2010). Association of poor child fear conditioning and adult crime. *American Journal of Psychiatry, 167*, 56–60.

Garcia-Falgueras, A., & Swaab, D. F. (2010). Sexual hormones and the brain: An essential alliance for sexual identity and sexual orientation. *Endocrine Development, 17*, 22–35.

Garcia, J., & Gustavson, A. R. (1997, January). Carl R. Gustavson (1946–1996): Pioneering wildlife psychologist. *APS Observer*, pp. 34–35.

Garcia, J., & Koelling, R. A. (1966). Relation of cue to consequence in avoidance learning. *Psychonomic Science, 4*, 123–124.

Garcia, J. R., Reiber, C., Massey, S. G., & Merriwether, A. M. (2013, February). Sexual hook-up culture. *Monitor on Psychology*, pp. 60–66.

Garcia-Saenz, A., Sánchez de Miguel, A., Espinosa, A., Valentin, A., Aragonés, N., Llorca, J., Amiano, P., Sánchez, V. M., Guevara, M., Capelo, R., Tardón, A., Peiró-Perez, R., Jiménez-Moleón, Roca-Barceló, A., Pérez-Gómez, B., Dierssen-Sotos, T., Fernández-Villa, T., Moreno-Iribas, C., Moreno, V., ... & Kogevinas, M. (2018). Evaluating the association between artificial light-at-night exposure and breast and prostate cancer risk in Spain (MCC-Spain study). *Environmental Health Perspectives, 126*(4). https://ehp.niehs.nih.gov/doi/full/10.1289/EHP1837

Gardiner, G., Sauerberger, K., Lee, D., & Funder, D. (2022). What happy people do: The behavioral correlates of happiness in everyday situations [PDF file]. *Journal of Research in Personality, 99*. https://bit.ly/3SmnuP2

Gardner, H. (1983). *Frames of mind: The theory of multiple intelligences*. Basic Books.

Gardner, H. (1999). *Multiple views of multiple intelligence*. Basic Books.

Gardner, H. (2006). *The development and education of the mind: The selected works of Howard Gardner*. Routledge/Taylor & Francis.

Gardner, H. (2011). *The theory of multiple intelligences: As psychology, as education, as social science* [Address]. Upon the receipt of an honorary degree from José Cela University in Madrid and the Prince of Asturias Prize for Social Science.

Gardner, J., & Oswald, A. J. (2007). Money and mental well-being: A longitudinal study of medium-sized lottery wins. *Journal of Health Economics, 6*, 49–60.

Gardner, R. A., & Gardner, B. I. (1969). Teaching sign language to a chimpanzee. *Science, 165*, 664–672.

Garelick, R. (2022, October 23). When did we become so obsessed with being 'symmetrical'? *The New York Times*. https://www.nytimes.com/2022/08/23/style/is-your-face-symmetrical.html

Garfield, C. (1986). *Peak performers: The new heroes of American business*. Morrow.

Garland, P., Babbitt, D., Bondarenko, M., Sorichetta, A., Tatem, A. J., & Johnson, O. (2020). The COVID-19 pandemic as experienced by the individual [PDF file]. https://arxiv.org/pdf/2005.01167.pdf

Garon, N., Bryson, S. E., & Smith, I. M. (2008). Executive function in preschoolers: A review using an integrative framework. *Psychological Bulletin, 134*, 31–60.

Garrett-Bakelman, F. E., Darshi, M., Green, S. J., Gur, R. C., Lin, L., Macias, B. R., McKenna, M. J., Meydan, C., Mishra, T., Nasrini, J., Piening, B. D., Rizzardi, L. F., Sharma, K., Siamwala, J. H., Taylor, L., Vitaterna, M. H., Afkarian, M., Afshinnekoo, E., Ahadi, S., & Turek, F. W. (2019). The NASA Twins Study: A multidimensional analysis of a year-long human spaceflight. *Science, 364*(6436). https://www.science.org/doi/10.1126/science.aau8650

Garry, M., Loftus, E. F., & Brown, S. W. (1994). Memory: A river runs through it. *Consciousness and Cognition, 3*, 438–451.

Gartrell, N., & Bos, H. (2010). U.S. national longitudinal lesbian family study: Psychological adjustment of 17-year-old adolescents. *Pediatrics, 126*, 28–36.

Gasiorowska, A., Chaplin, L. N., Zaleskiewicz, T., Wygrab, S., & Vohs, K. D. (2016). Money cues increase agency and decrease prosociality among children: Early signs of market-mode behaviors. *Psychological Science, 27*, 331–344.

Gaskins, A. J., Rich-Edwards, J. W., Williams, P. L., Toth, T. L., Missmer, S. A., & Chavarro, J. E. (2018). Pre-pregnancy caffeine and caffeinated beverage intake and risk of spontaneous abortion. *European Journal of Nutrition, 57*, 107–117.

Gatchel, R. J., Peng, Y. B., Peters, M. L., Fuchs, P. N., & Turk, D. C. (2007). The biopsychosocial approach to chronic pain: Scientific advances and future directions. *Psychological Bulletin, 133*, 581–624.

Gavin, K. (2004, November 9). *U-M team reports evidence that smoking affects human brain's natural "feel good" chemical system* [Press release]. med.umich.edu/

Gavrilets, S., Friberg, U., & Rice, W. R. (2018). Understanding homosexuality: Moving on from patterns to mechanisms. *Archives of Sexual Behavior, 47*, 27–31.

Gawande, A. (1998, September 21). The pain perplex. *The New Yorker*, pp. 86–94.

Gawin, F. H. (1991). Cocaine addiction: Psychology and neurophysiology. *Science, 251*, 1580–1586.

Gaydos, R. (2019, February 21). *Two similar-looking baseball players take DNA tests to find out if they're related*. Fox Sports. https://www.foxnews.com/sports/two-similar-looking-baseball-players-take-dna-tests-to-prove-whether-they-are-related

Gazzaniga, M. (2006). *The ethical brain: The science of our moral dilemmas*. HarperPerennial.

Gazzaniga, M. S. (1967, August). The split brain in man. *Scientific American*, pp. 24–29.

Gazzaniga, M. S. (1983). Right hemisphere language following brain bisection: A 20-year perspective. *American Psychologist, 38*, 525–537.

Gazzola, V., Spezio, M. L., Etzel, J. A., Catelli, F., Adolphs, R., & Keysers, C. (2012). Primary somatosensory cortex discriminates affective significance in social touch. *PNAS, 109*, E1657–E1666.

GBD (Global Burden of Disease). (2017). Smoking prevalence and attributable disease burden in 195 countries and territories, 1990–2015: A systematic analysis from the Global Burden of Disease Study 2015. *The Lancet, 389*, 1885–1906.

GBD. (2022). Global, regional, and national burden of 12 mental disorders in 204 countries and territories, 1990–2019: A systematic analysis for the Global Burden of Disease Study 2019. *The Lancet, 9*(2), 137–150.

Geary, D. C. (2019). The spark of life and the unification of intelligence, health, and aging. *Current Directions in Psychological Science, 28*, 223–228.

Geary, D. C. (2021). Now you see them, and now you don't: An evolutionarily informed model of environmental influences on human sex differences. *Neuroscience & Biobehavioral Reviews, 125*, 26–32.

Gecewicz, C. (2018, October 1). *'New Age' beliefs common among both religious and nonreligious Americans*. Pew Research Center. https://www.pewresearch.org/fact-tank/2018/10/01/new-age-beliefs-common-among-both-religious-and-nonreligious-americans/

Geen, R. G., & Quanty, M. B. (1977). The catharsis of aggression: An evaluation of a hypothesis. In L. Berkowitz (Ed.), *Advances in experimental social psychology* (Vol. 10). Academic Press.

Geers, A. E., & Nicholas, J. G. (2013). Enduring advantages of early cochlear implantation for spoken language development. *Journal of Speech, Language, and Hearing Research, 56*, 643–653.

Geers, A. L., Briñol, P., & Petty, R. E. (2019). An analysis of the basic processes of formation and change of placebo expectations. *Review of General Psychology, 23*, 211–229.

Gehring, W. J., Wimke, J., & Nisenson, L. G. (2000). Action monitoring dysfunction in obsessive-compulsive disorder. *Psychological Science, 11*, 1–6.

Geier, A. B., Rozin, P., & Doros, G. (2006). Unit bias: A new heuristic that helps explain the effects of portion size on food intake. *Psychological Science, 17*, 521–525.

Geiger, A. W. (2016, November 30). *Sharing chores a key to good marriage, say majority of married adults*. Pew Research Center. https://www.pewresearch.org/fact-tank/2016/11/30/sharing-chores-a-key-to-good-marriage-say-majority-of-married-adults/

Geiser, C. (2019). *Dear God amen, I can. My art my life my schizophrenia*. Self-published.

Geiser, C. (2021, September 16–October 3). *Craig Geiser*. Art Prize. Grand Rapids, MI. https://beta.artprize.org/Craig-Geiser

Gelfand, M. (2018). *Rule makers, rule breakers: How tight and loose cultures wire our world*. Scribner.

Gelfand, M. J., Jackson, J. C., Pan, X., Nau, D., Pieper, D., Denison, E., Dagher, M., Van Lange, P. A. M., Chiu, C.-Y., & Wang, M. (2021). The relationship between cultural tightness-looseness and COVID-19 cases and deaths: A global analysis. *The Lancet, 22*, e135–144.

Gelfand, M. J., Raver, J. L., Nishii, L., Leslie, L. M., Lun, J., Lim, B. C., Duan, L., Almaliach, A., Ang, S., Amadottir, J., Aycan Z., Boehnke, K., Boski, P., Cabecinhas, R., Chan, D., Chhokar, J., D'Amato, A., Ferrer, M., Fischlmayr, I. C., ... Yamaguchi, S.

(2011). Differences between tight and loose cultures: A 33-nation study. *Science, 332*(6033), 1100–1104.

Gellis, L. A., Arigo, D., & Elliott, J. C. (2013). Cognitive refocusing treatment for insomnia: A randomized controlled trial in university students. *Behavior Therapy, 44*, 100–110.

Genesee, F., & Gándara, P. (1999). Bilingual education programs: A cross-national perspective. *Journal of Social Issues, 55*, 665–685.

Genschow, O., Westfal, M., Crusius, J., Bartosch, L., Feikes, K. I., Pallasch, N., & Wozniak, M. (2021). Does social psychology persist over half a century? A direct replication of Cialdini et al.'s (1975) classic door-in-the-face technique. *Journal of Personality and Social Psychology, 120*(2), e1–e7.

Gentile, D. A. (2009). Pathological video-game use among youth ages 8 to 18: A national study. *Psychological Science, 20*, 594–602.

Gentile, D. A., & Bushman, B. J. (2012). Reassessing media violence effects using a risk and resilience approach to understanding aggression. *Psychology of Popular Media Culture, 1*, 138–151.

Gentile, D. A., Coyne, S., & Walsh, D. A. (2011). Media violence, physical aggression and relational aggression in school age children: A short-term longitudinal study. *Aggressive Behavior, 37*, 193–206.

Gentner, D. (2016). Language as cognitive tool kit: How language supports relational thought. *American Psychologist, 71*, 650–657.

Gentzkow, M., Shapiro, J. M., & Taddy, M. (2016, July). *Measuring polarization in high-dimensional data: Method and application to congressional speech.* NBER Working Paper 22423. Stanford Institute for Economic Policy Research.

Geoffrey, M.-C., Arsenault, L., Girard, A., Ouellet-Morin, I., & Power, C. (2022). Association of childhood bullying victimisation with suicide deaths: Findings from a 50-year nationwide cohort study. *Psychological Medicine.* https://bit.ly/3eG3He8

Georgakis, M. K., Thomopoulos, T. P., Diamantaras, A.-A., Kalogirou, E. I., Skalkidou, A., Daskalopoulou, S. S., & Petridou, E. T. (2016). Association of age at menopause and duration of reproductive period with depression after menopause: A systematic review and meta-analysis. *JAMA Psychiatry, 73*(2), 139–149.

George, M. S. (2018). Is there really nothing new under the sun? Is low-dose ketamine a fast-acting antidepressant simply because it is an opioid? *American Journal of Psychiatry, 175*, 1157–1158.

Geraerts, E., Bernstein, D. M., Merckelbach, H., Linders, C., Raymaekers, L., & Loftus, E. F. (2008). Lasting false beliefs and their behavioral consequences. *Psychological Science, 19*, 749–753.

Geraerts, E., Schooler, J. W., Merckelbach, H., Jelicic, M., Hauer, B. J. A., & Ambadar, Z. (2007). The reality of recovered memories: Corroborating continuous and discontinuous memories of childhood sexual abuse. *Psychological Science, 18*, 564–568.

Gernsbacher, M. (2015). Video captions benefit everyone. *Policy Insights from the Brain and Behavioral Sciences, 2*, 195–202.

Gernsbacher, M. A., Dawson, M., & Goldsmith, H. H. (2005). Three reasons not to believe in an autism epidemic. *Current Directions in Psychological Science, 14*, 55–58.

Gernsbacher, M. A., & Yergeau, M. (2019). Empirical failures of the claim that autistic people lack a theory of mind. *Archives of Scientific Psychology, 7*, 102–118.

Gershoff, E. T., Goodman, G. S., Miller-Perrin, C., Holden, G. W., Jackson, Y., & Kazdin, A. E. (2019). There is still no evidence that physical punishment is effective or beneficial: Reply to Larzelere, Gunnoe, Ferguson, and Roberts (2019) and Rohner and Melendez-Rhodes (2019). *American Psychologist, 74*, 503–505.

Gershoff, E. T., & Grogan-Kaylor, A. (2016). Spanking and child outcomes: Old controversies and new meta-analyses. *Journal of Family Psychology, 30*, 453–469.

Gershoff, E. T., Grogan-Kaylor, A., Lansford, J. E., Chang, L., Zelli, A., Deater-Deckard, K., & Dodge, K. A. (2010). Parent discipline practices in an international sample: Associations with child behaviors and moderation by perceived normativeness. *Child Development, 81*, 487–502.

Gershoff, E. T., Sattler, K. M. P., & Ansari, A. (2018). Strengthening causal estimates for links between spanking and children's externalizing behavior problems. *Psychological Science, 29*, 110–120.

Gershon, A., Ram, N., Johnson, S. L., Harvey, A. G., & Zeitzer, J. M. (2016). Daily actigraphy profiles distinguish depressive and interepisode states in bipolar disorder. *Clinical Psychological Science, 4*, 641–650.

Gerst-Emerson, K., & Jayawardhana, J. (2015). Loneliness as a public health issue: The impact of loneliness on health care utilization among older adults. *American Journal of Public Health, 105*, 1013–1019.

Geulayov, G., Casey, D., Bale, L., Brand, F., Clements, C., & Farooq, B., Kapur, N., Ness, J., Waters, K., Tsiachristas, A., & Hawton, K. (2019). Suicide following presentation to hospital for non-fatal self-harm in the Multicentre Study of Self-Harm: A long-term follow-up study. *Lancet Psychiatry, 6*, 1021–1030.

Ghazi Sherbaf, F., Aarabi, M. H., Hosein Yazdi, M., & Haghshomar, M. (2019). White matter microstructure in fetal alcohol spectrum disorders: A systematic review of diffusion tensor imaging studies. *Human Brain Mapping, 40*, 1017–1036.

Ghorayshi, A. (2022, May 23). Puberty starts earlier than it used to. No one knows why. *The New York Times.* https://www.nytimes.com/2022/05/19/science/early-puberty-medical-reason.html

Ghorayshi, A. (2022). England overhauls medical care for transgender youth. *The New York Times.* https://www.nytimes.com/2022/07/28/health/transgender-youth-uk-tavistock.html

Giacobbe, P., Rakita, U., Penner-Goeke, K., Feffer, K., Flint, A. J., Kennedy, S. H., & Downar, J. (2018). Improvements in health-related quality of life with electroconvulsive therapy: A meta-analysis. *Journal of ECT, 34*, 87–94.

Giamalvo, E. (2021). Simone Biles said she got the 'twisties.' Gymnasts immediately understood. *The Washington Post.* https://www.washingtonpost.com/sports/olympics/2021/07/28/twisties-gymnastics-simone-biles-tokyo-olympics/

Giampietro, M., & Cavallera, G. M. (2007). Morning and evening types and creative thinking. *Personality and Individual Differences, 42*, 453–463.

Giancola, P. R., & Corman, M. D. (2007). Alcohol and aggression: A test of the attention-allocation model. *Psychological Science, 18*, 649–655.

Giancola, P. R., Josephs, R. A., Parrott, D. J., & Duke, A. A. (2010). Alcohol myopia revisited: Clarifying aggression and other acts of disinhibition through a distorted lens. *Perspectives on Psychological Science, 5*, 265–278.

Gibbons, F. X. (1986). Social comparison and depression: Company's effect on misery. *Journal of Personality and Social Psychology, 51*, 140–148.

Gibson, D. J., Glazier, J. J., & Olson, K. R. (2021, April 7). Evaluation of anxiety and depression in a community sample of transgender youth. *JAMA Network Open, 4*(4). https://jamanetwork.com/journals/jamanetworkopen/article-abstract/2778206

Gibson, E. J., & Walk, R. D. (1960, April). The "visual cliff." *Scientific American*, pp. 64–71.

Gibson, J. J. (1979). *The ecological approach to visual perception.* Houghton Mifflin.

Giedd, J. N. (2015, June). The amazing teen brain. *Scientific American*, pp. 33–37.

Giesbrecht, T., Lynn, S. J., Lilienfeld, S. O., & Merckelbach, H. (2008). Cognitive processes in dissociation: An analysis of core theoretical assumptions. *Psychological Bulletin, 134*, 617–647.

Giesbrecht, T., Lynn, S. J., Lilienfeld, S. O., & Merckelbach, H. (2010). Cognitive processes, trauma, and dissociation—Misconceptions and misrepresentations: Reply to Bremmer (2010). *Psychological Bulletin, 136*, 7–11.

Gigerenzer, G. (2004). Dread risk, September 11, and fatal traffic accidents. *Psychological Science, 15*, 286–287.

Gigerenzer, G. (2006). Out of the frying pan into the fire: Behavioral reactions to terrorist attacks. *Risk Analysis, 26*, 347–351.

Gigerenzer, G. (2010). *Rationality for mortals: How people cope with uncertainty.* Oxford University Press.

Gigerenzer, G. (2015). *Simply rational: Decision making in the real world.* Oxford University Press.

Gilbert, D. T. (2006). *Stumbling on happiness.* Knopf.

Gilbert, D. T., Pinel, E. C., Wilson, T. D., Blumberg, S. J., & Wheatley, T. P. (1998). Immune neglect: A source of durability bias in affective forecasting. *Journal of Personality and Social Psychology, 75*, 617–638.

Gilbertson, M. W., Paulus, L. A., Williston, S. K., Gurvits, T. V., Lasko, N. B., Pitman, R. K., & Orr, S. P. (2006). Neurocognitive function in monozygotic twins discordant for combat exposure: Relationship to posttraumatic stress disorder. *Journal of Abnormal Psychology, 115*, 484–495.

Gill, H., Puramat, P., Patel, P., Gill, B., Marks, C. A., Rodrigues, N. B., Castle, D., Cha, D. S., Mansur, R. B., Rosenblat, J. D., & McIntyre, R. S. (2022). The effects of psilocybin in adults with major depressive disorder and the general population: Findings from neuroimaging studies. *Psychiatry Research, 313*. doi: 10.1016/j.psychres.2022.114577

Gillen-O'Neel, C., Huynh, V. W., & Fuligni, A. J. (2013). To study or to sleep? The academic costs of extra studying at the expense of sleep. *Child Development, 84*, 133–142.

Gillespie, S. M., Rotshtein, P., Chapman, H., Brown, E., Beech, A. R., & Mitchell, I. J. (2019). Pupil reactivity to emotional faces among convicted violent offenders: The role of psychopathic traits. *Journal of Abnormal Psychology, 128*, 622–632.

Gilley, C., & Ringdahl, J. E. (2014). The effects of item preference and token reinforcement on sharing behavior exhibited by children with autism spectrum disorder. *Research in Autism Spectrum Disorders, 8*(11), 1425–1433.

Gilligan, C. (1982). *In a different voice: Psychological theory and women's development*. Harvard University Press

Gilligan, C. (2015). In a different voice: Women's conceptions of self and morality. In V. Burr (Ed.), *Gender and psychology* (Vol. II, pp. 33–74). Routledge/Taylor & Francis Group.

Gilovich, T. (1991). *How we know what isn't so: The fallibility of human reason in everyday life*. Free Press.

Gilovich, T. D. (1996). *The spotlight effect: Exaggerated impressions of the self as a social stimulus* [Unpublished manuscript]. Cornell University.

Gilovich, T. D., & Medvec, V. H. (1995). The experience of regret: What, when, and why. *Psychological Review, 102*, 379–395.

Gilovich, T. D., & Savitsky, K. (1999). The spotlight effect and the illusion of transparency: Egocentric assessments of how we are seen by others. *Current Directions in Psychological Science, 8*, 165–168.

Gingerich, O. (1994). Is there a role for natural theology today? Chapter 1. In M. Rae, H. Regan, & J. Stenhouse (Eds.), *Science and theology questions at the interface*. Bloomsbury Academic.

Gingerich, O. (2006). *God's universe*. Belknap Press.

Gino, G., Wilmuth, C. A., & Brooks, A. W. (2015). Compared to men, women view professional advancement as equally attainable, but less desirable. *PNAS, 112*, 12354–12359.

Ginsburg, H., Hu, Y., & Robinson, B. (2020). Little Albert's fear conditioning disappears when Watson's different presentations of the rate before and after conditioning are controlled. *North American Journal of Psychology, 22*, 661–678.

Girardeau, G., & Lopes-dos-Santos, V. (2021). Brain neural patterns and the memory function of sleep. *Science, 374*, 560–564.

Girgenti, M. J., Wang, J., Ji, D., Cruz, D. A., Traumatic Stress Brain Research Group, Stein, M. B., Gelernter, J., Young, K. A., Huber, B. R., Williamson, D. E., Friedman, M. J., Krystal, J. H., Zhao, H., & Duman, R. S. (2021). Transcriptomic organization of the human brain in posttraumatic stress disorder. *Nature Neuroscience, 24*, 24–33.

Girme, Y. U., Jones, R. E., Fleck, C., Simpson, J. A., & Overall, N. C. (2021). Infants' attachment insecurity predicts attachment-relevant emotion regulation strategies in adulthood. *Emotion, 21*(2), 260–272.

Giuliano, T. A., Barnes, L. C., Fiala, S. E., & Davis, D. M. (1998). *An empirical investigation of male answer syndrome* [Paper]. Presented at the Southwestern Psychological Association convention.

Giumetti, G. W., Kowalski, R. M., & Feinn, R. S. (2022). Predictors and outcomes of cyberbullying among college students: A two wave study. *Aggressive Behavior, 48*(1), 40–54.

Glad, K. A., Czajkowski, N. O., Dyb, G., & Hafstad, G. S. (2020). Cross-lagged association between symptoms of posttraumatic stress disorder and perceived centrality of a terrorist attack. *Clinical Psychological Science, 8*, 295–305.

Gladwell, M. (2000, May 9). The new-boy network: What do job interviews really tell us? *The New Yorker*, pp. 68–86.

Glanz, J., Carey, B., Holder, J., Watkins, D., Valentino-DeVries, J., Rojas, R., & Leatherby, L. (2020, April 2). Where America didn't stay home even as the virus spread. *The New York Times*. https://www.nytimes.com/interactive/2020/04/02/us/coronavirus-social-distancing.html

Glasman, L. R., & Albarracín, D. (2006). Forming attitudes that predict future behavior: A meta-analysis of the attitude-behavior relation. *Psychological Bulletin, 132*, 778–822.

Glass, R. M. (2001). Electroconvulsive therapy: Time to bring it out of the shadows. *Journal of the American Medical Association, 285*, 1346–1348.

Glasser, M. F., Coalson, T. S., Robinson, E. C., Hacker, C. D., Harwell, J., Yacoub, E., Ugurbil, K., Andersson, J., Beckmann, C. F., Jenkinson, M., Smith, S. M., & Van Essen, D. C. (2016). A multi-modal parcellation of human cerebral cortex. *Nature, 536*, 171–178.

Gleaves, D. H. (1996). The sociocognitive model of dissociative identity disorder: A reexamination of the evidence. *Psychological Bulletin, 120*, 42–59.

Glenn, A. L., & Raine, A. (2014). Neurocriminology: Implications for the punishment, prediction and prevention of criminal behavior. *Nature Reviews Neuroscience, 15*, 54–63.

Glenn, A. L., Raine, A., Yaralian, P. S., & Yang, Y. (2010). Increased volume of the striatum in psychopathic individuals. *Biological Psychiatry, 67*, 52–58.

Glenn, J. J., Nobles, A. L., Barnes, L. E., & Teachman, B. A. (2020). Can text messages identify suicide risk in real time? A within-subjects pilot examination of temporally sensitive markers of suicide risk. *Clinical Psychological Science, 8*, 704–722.

Gliklich, E., Guo, R., & Bergmark, R. W. (2016). Texting while driving: A study of 1211 U.S. adults with the Distracted Driving Survey. *Preventive Medicine Reports, 4*, 486–489.

Global Burden of Disease. (2021). Hearing loss prevalence and years lived with disability, 1990–2019: Findings from the Global Burden of Disease Study 2019. *The Lancet, 397*(10278), 996–1009.

GLSEN (Gay, Lesbian & Straight Education Network). (2012). *The 2011 national school climate survey*. https://www.glsen.org/news/2011-national-school-climate-survey

Gobbi, G., Atkin, T., Zytynski, T., Wang, S., Askari, S., Boruff, J., Ware, M., Marmorstein, N., Cipriani, A., Dendukuri, N., & Mayo, N. (2019). Association of cannabis use in adolescence and risk of depression, anxiety, and suicidality in young adulthood: A systematic review and meta-analysis. *JAMA Psychiatry, 76*, 426–434.

Godart, F. C., Maddux, W. W., Shipilov, A. V., & Galinsky, A. D. (2015). Fashion with a foreign flair: Professional experiences abroad facilitate the creative innovations of organizations. *Academy of Management Journal, 58*, 195–220.

Goddard, M. J. (2018). Extending B.F. Skinner's selection by consequences to personality change, implicit theories of intelligence, skill learning, and language. *Review of General Psychology, 22*, 421–426.

Godden, D. R., & Baddeley, A. D. (1975). Context-dependent memory in two natural environments: On land and underwater. *British Journal of Psychology, 66*, 325–331.

Godlee, F. (2011). Wakefield's article linking MMR vaccine and autism was fraudulent. *British Medical Journal, 342*, c7452.

Godwin, J. W. (2020). The Fast Track intervention's impact on behaviors of despair in adolescence and young adulthood. *PNAS, 117*(50), 31748–31753.

Goethals, G. R., & Allison, S. T. (2014). Kings and charisma, Lincoln and leadership: An evolutionary perspective. In G. R. Goethals, S. T. Allison, R. M. Kramer, & D. M. Messick (Eds.), *Conceptions of leadership: Enduring ideas and emerging insights* (pp. 111–124). Palgrave Macmillan.

Goetz, S. M. M., Tang, L., Thomason, M. E., Diamond, M. P., Hariri, A. R., & Carré, J. (2014). Testosterone rapidly increases neural reactivity to threat in healthy men: A novel two-step pharmacological challenge paradigm. *Biological Psychiatry, 76*, 324–331.

Goff, D. C., Falkai, P., Fleischhacker, W. W., Girgis, R. R., Kahn, R. M., Uchida, H., Zhao, J., & Lieberman, J. A. (2017). The long-term effects of antipsychotic medication on clinical course in schizophrenia. *American Journal of Psychiatry, 174*, 840–849.

Goff, D. C., & Simms, C. A. (1993). Has multiple personality disorder remained consistent over time? *Journal of Nervous and Mental Disease, 181*, 595–600.

Gold, M. (2019, January 21). New York passes a ban on 'conversion therapy' after years-long efforts. *The New York Times*. https://www.nytimes.com/2019/01/21/nyregion/conversion-therapy-ban.html

Gold, M., & Yanof, D. S. (1985). Mothers, daughters, and girlfriends. *Journal of Personality and Social Psychology, 49*, 654–659.

Goldberg, J. (2007). The quivering bundles that let us hear [PDF file]. In *Seeing, hearing, and smelling the world* (p. 32). Report from the Howard Hughes Medical Institute. http://www.alchemical.org/optics/Senses-HowardHughesMedCenter.pdf

Goldberg, S. B., Riordan, K. M., Sun, S., & Davidson, R. J. (2021). The empirical status of mindfulness-based interventions: A systematic review of 44 meta-analyses of randomized controlled trials. *Perspectives on Psychological Science*. https://tinyurl.com/4h8pvr2u

Goldberg, S. B., Tucker, R. P., Greene, P. A., Davidson, R. J., Kearney, D. J., & Simpson, T. L. (2019). Mindfulness-based cognitive therapy for the treatment of current depressive symptoms: A meta-analysis. *Cognitive Behaviour Therapy, 48*, 445–462.

Goldberg, S. B., Tucker, R. P., Greene, P. A., Davidson, R. J., Wampold, B. E., Kearney, D. J., & Simpson, T. L. (2018). Mindfulness-based interventions for psychiatric disorders: A systematic review and meta-analysis. *Clinical Psychology Review, 59*, 52–60.

Golder, S. A., & Macy, M. W. (2011). Diurnal and seasonal mood vary with work, sleep, and day length across diverse cultures. *Science, 333*, 1878–1881.

Goldfarb, D., Goodman, G. S., Larson, R. P., Eisen, M. L., & Qin, J. (2019). Long-term memory in adults exposed to childhood violence: Remembering genital contact nearly 20 years later. *Clinical Psychological Science, 7*, 381–396.

Goldfried, M. R. (2001). Integrating gay, lesbian, and bisexual issues into mainstream psychology. *American Psychologist, 56*, 977–988.

Goldfried, M. R., Raue, P. J., & Castonguay, L. G. (1998). The therapeutic focus in significant sessions of master therapists: A comparison of cognitive–behavioral and psychodynamic–interpersonal interventions. *Journal of Consulting and Clinical Psychology, 66*, 803–810.

Goldinger, S. D., & Papesh, M. H. (2012). Pupil dilation reflects the creation and retrieval of memories. *Current Directions in Psychological Science, 21*, 90–95.

Goldman, A. L., Pezawas, L., Mattay, V. S., Fischl, B., Verchinski, B. A., Chen, Q., Weinberger, D. R., & Meyer-Lindenberg, A. (2009). Widespread reductions of cortical thickness in schizophrenia and spectrum disorders and evidence of heritability. *Archives of General Psychiatry, 66*, 467–477.

Goldstein, I., Lue, T. F., Padma-Nathan, H., Rosen, R. C., Steers, W. D., & Wicker, P. A. (1998). Oral sildenafil in the treatment of erectile dysfunction. *New England Journal of Medicine, 338*, 1397–1404.

Golec de Zavala, A., & Lantos, D. (2020). Collective narcissism and its social consequences: The bad and the ugly. *Current Directions in Psychological Science, 29*, 273–278.

Goleman, D. (1980, February). 1,528 little geniuses and how they grew. *Psychology Today*, pp. 28–53.

Goleman, D. (1986, March 4). Concentration is likened to euphoric states of mind. *The New York Times*. https://www.nytimes.com/1986/03/04/science/concentration-is-likened-to-euphoric-states-of-mind.html

Goleman, D. (2006). *Social intelligence*. Bantam Books.

Golkar, A., Selbing, I., Flygare, O., Öhman, A., & Olsson, A. (2013). Other people as means to a safe end: Vicarious extinction blocks the return of learned fear. *Psychological Science, 24*, 2182–2190.

Gollwitzer, P. M., & Oettingen, G. (2012). Goal pursuit. In P. M. Gollwitzer & G. Oettingen (Eds.), *The Oxford handbook of human motivation* (pp. 208–231). Oxford University Press.

Gollwitzer, P. M., & Sheeran, P. (2006). Implementation intentions and goal achievement: A meta-analysis of effects and processes. *Advances in Experimental Social Psychology, 38*, 69–119.

Gomes, C. M., Miranda, E. P., de Bessa Jr, J., Bellucci, C. H. S., Battistella, L. R., Abdo, C. H. N., Bruschini, H., Srougi, M., & Mulhall, J. P. (2017). Erectile function predicts sexual satisfaction in men with spinal cord injury. *Sexual Medicine, 5*, e148–e155.

Gómez-Robles, A., Hopkins, W. D., Schapiro, S. J., & Sherwood, C. C. (2015). Relaxed genetic control of cortical organization in human brains compared with chimpanzees. *PNAS, 112*, 14799–14804.

Gongola, J., Scurich, N., & Quas, J. A. (2017). Detecting deception in children: A meta-analysis. *Law and Human Behavior, 41*, 44–54.

Gonsalkorale, K., & Williams, K. D. (2006). The KKK would not let me play: Ostracism even by a despised outgroup hurts. *European Journal of Social Psychology, 36*, 1–11.

Gonsalves, B., Reber, P. J., Gitelman, D. R., Parrish, T. B., Mesulam, M.-M., & Paller, K. A. (2004). Neural evidence that vivid imagining can lead to false remembering. *Psychological Science, 15*, 655–659.

Gonzaga, G. C., Keltner, D., Londahl, E. A., & Smith, M. D. (2001). Love and the commitment problem in romantic relations and friendship. *Journal of Personality and Social Psychology, 81*(2), 247.

Gonzales, N. A., Johnson, M., Shirtcliff, E. A., Tein, J. Y., Eskenazi, B., & Deardorff, J. (2018). The role of bicultural adaptation, familism, and family conflict in Mexican American adolescents' cortisol reactivity. *Development and Psychopathology, 30*, 1571–1587.

Gonzalez, R. (2018, June 8). *How science helps the Warriors sleep their way to success*. Wired Magazine. https://www.wired.com/story/how-science-helps-the-warriors-sleep-their-way-to-success/

Gonzalez, S. (2018, October 2). *Emma Stone opens up about ongoing battle with anxiety*. CNN Entertainment. https://www.cnn.com/2018/10/02/entertainment/emma-stone-anxiety/index.html

Gonzalez-Barrera, A. (2019, July 2). *Hispanics with darker skin are more likely to experience discrimination than those with lighter skin*. Pew Research Center. https://pewrsr.ch/2wH7PoH

Goodale, M. A., & Milner, A. D. (2004). *Sight unseen: An exploration of conscious and unconscious vision*. Oxford University Press.

Goodall, J. (1986). *The chimpanzees of Gombe: Patterns of behavior*. Harvard University Press.

Goodall, J. (1998). Learning from the chimpanzees: A message humans can understand. *Science, 282*, 2184–2185.

Goode, E. (1999, April 13). If things taste bad, "phantoms" may be at work. *The New York Times*. https://www.nytimes.com/1999/04/13/science/if-things-taste-bad-phantoms-may-be-at-work.html

Goodhart, D. E. (1986). The effects of positive and negative thinking on performance in an achievement situation. *Journal of Personality and Social Psychology, 51*, 117–124.

Goodman, G. S. (2006). Children's eyewitness memory: A modern history and contemporary commentary. *Journal of Social Issues, 62*, 811–832.

Goodman, G. S., Ghetti, S., Quas, J. A., Edelstein, R. S., Alexander, K. W., Redlich, A. D., Cordon, I. M., & Jones, D. P. H. (2003). A prospective study of memory for child sexual abuse: New findings relevant to the repressed-memory controversy. *Psychological Science, 14*, 113–118.

Goodwin, A., & Greene, R. A. (2022, February 9). *UK anti-Semitism reaches record high in 2021, report says*. CNN. https://www.cnn.com/2022/02/09/europe/uk-anti-semitism-report-2021-intl/index.html

Gopnik, A. (2016). *The carpenter and the gardener*. Farrar, Straus and Giroux.

Gopnik, A., Griffiths, T. L., & Lucas, C. G. (2015). When younger learners can be better (or at least more open-minded) than older ones. *Current Directions in Psychological Science, 24*, 87–92.

Gopnik, A., & Meltzoff, A. N. (1986). Relations between semantic and cognitive development in the one-word stage: The specificity hypothesis. *Child Development, 57*, 1040–1053.

Goranson, A., Ritter, R. S., Waytz, A., Norton, M. I., & Gray, K. (2017). Dying is unexpectedly positive. *Psychological Science, 28*, 988–999.

Goranson, R. E. (1978). *The hindsight effect in problem solving*. Unpublished manuscript cited in G. Wood (1984), Research methodology: A decision-making perspective. In A. M. Rogers & C. J. Scheirer (Eds.), *The G. Stanley Hall lecture series* (Vol. 4, pp. 193–217). American Psychological Association.

Gorchoff, S. M., John, O. P., & Helson, R. (2008). Contextualizing change in marital satisfaction during middle age. *Psychological Science, 19*, 1194–1200.

Gordon, A. M., & Chen, S. (2010). When you accept me for me: The relational benefits of intrinsic affirmations from one's relationship partner. *Personality and Social Psychology Bulletin, 36*, 1439–1453.

Gordon, I., Vander Wyk, B. C., Bennett, R. H., Cordeaux, C., Lucas, M. V., Eilbott, J. A., Zagoory-Sharon, O., Leckman, J. F., Feldman, R., & Pelphrey, K. A. (2013). Oxytocin enhances brain function in children with autism. *PNAS, 110*, 20953–20958.

Gore, J., & Sadler-Smith, E. (2011). Unpacking intuition: A process and outcome framework. *Review of General Psychology, 15*, 304–316.

Gore-Felton, C., Koopman, C., Thoresen, C., Arnow, B., Bridges, E., & Spiegel, D. (2000). Psychologists' beliefs and clinical characteristics: Judging the veracity of childhood sexual abuse memories. *Professional Psychology: Research and Practice, 31*, 372–377.

Gorka, S. M., Lieberman, L., Shankman, S. A., & Phan, K. L. (2017). Startle potentiation to uncertain threat as a psychophysiological indicator of fear-based psychopathology: An examination across multiple internalizing disorders. *Journal of Abnormal Psychology, 126*, 8.

Gorlick, A. (2010, January 13). Stanford scientists link brain development to chances of recovering vision after blindness. *Stanford Report*. https://stanford.io/3ezVtEx

Gorman, J. (2019, December 3). Why are these foxes tame? Maybe they weren't so wild to begin with. *The New York Times*. https://www.nytimes.com/2019/12/03/science/foxes-tame-belyaev.html

Gormley, W., Kitchens, K., & Adelstein, S. (2013). *Do middle-class families benefit from high-quality pre-K?* CROCUS Policy Brief, July.

Center for Research on Children in the U.S., Georgetown University.

Gorno-Tempini, M. L., & Price, C. J. (2001). Identification of famous faces and buildings: A functional neuroimaging study of semantically unique items. *Brain, 124*, 2087–2097.

Gorrese, A., & Ruggieri, R. (2012). Peer attachment: A meta-analytic review of gender and age differences and associations with parent attachment. *Journal of Youth and Adolescence, 41*, 650–672.

Gosling, S. D. (2008). *Snoop: What your stuff says about you.* Basic Books.

Gosling, S. D., Kwan, V. S. Y., & John, O. P. (2003). A dog's got personality: A cross-species comparative approach to personality judgments in dogs and humans. *Journal of Personality and Social Psychology, 85*, 1161–1169.

Gotink, R. A., Meijboom, R., Vernooij, M. W., Smits, M., & Hunink, M. G. M. (2016). 8-week mindfulness based stress reduction induces brain changes similar to traditional long-term meditation practice—A systematic review. *Brain and Cognition, 108*, 32–41.

Gotlib, I. H., & Hammen, C. L. (1992). *Psychological aspects of depression: Toward a cognitive-interpersonal integration.* Wiley.

Gottesman, I. I. (1991). *Schizophrenia genesis: The origins of madness.* Freeman.

Gottesman, I. I. (2001). Psychopathology through a life span—Genetic prism. *American Psychologist, 56*, 867–881.

Gottfredson, L. S. (2002a). Where and why *g* matters: Not a mystery. *Human Performance, 15*, 25–46.

Gottfredson, L. S. (2002b). *g*: Highly general and highly practical. In R. J. Sternberg & E. L. Grigorenko (Eds.), *The general factor of intelligence: How general is it?* (pp. 331–380). Erlbaum.

Gottfredson, L. S. (2003a). Dissecting practical intelligence theory: Its claims and evidence. *Intelligence, 31*, 343–397.

Gottfredson, L. S. (2003b). On Sternberg's "Reply to Gottfredson." *Intelligence, 31*, 415–424.

Gottfried, A. W., Gottfried, A. E., & Guerin, D. W. (2006). The Fullerton Longitudinal Study: A long-term investigation of intellectual and motivational giftedness. *Journal for the Education of the Gifted, 29*, 430–450.

Gottman, J. M., & Gottman, J. S. (2018). *The science of couples and family therapy: Behind the scenes at the "love lab."* W. W. Norton.

Gottman, J., & Gottman, J. S. (2022). *The love prescription: Seven days to more intimacy, connection, and joy.* Penguin.

Götz, F. M., Gvirtz, A., Galinsky, A. D., & Jachimowicz, J. M. (2021). How personality and policy predict pandemic behavior: Understanding sheltering-in-place in 55 countries at the onset of COVID-19. *American Psychologist, 76*(1), 39–49.

Gould, E. (2007). How widespread is adult neurogenesis in mammals? *Nature Neuroscience, 8*, 481–488.

Gould, E., Simhon, A., & Weinberg, B. A. (2019, January). *Does parental quality matter? Evidence on the transmission of human capital using variation in parental influence from death, divorce, and family size.* NBER Working Paper No. 25495. https://www.nber.org/papers/w25495

Gould, K. L., Gilbertson, K. E., Hrvol, A. J., Nelson, J. C., Seyfer, A. L., Brantner, R. M., & Kamil, A. C. (2013). Differences in relative hippocampus volume and number of hippocampus neurons among five corvid species. *Brain, Behavior and Evolution, 81*, 56–70.

Gould, S. J. (1981). *The mismeasure of man.* Norton.

Goyal, M., Singh, S., Sibinga, E. S., Gould, N. F., Rowland-Seymour, A., Sharma, R., Berger, Z., Sleicher, D., Maron, D. D., Shihab, H. M., Ranasinghe, P. D., Linn, S., Saha, S., Bass, E. B., & Haythornthwaite, J. A. (2014). Meditation programs for psychological stress and well-being: A systematic review and meta-analysis. *JAMA Internal Medicine, 174*, 357–368.

Graafland, J., & Lous, B. (2019). Income inequality, life satisfaction inequality and trust: A Cross Country Panel Analysis. *Journal of Happiness Studies, 20*, 1717–1737.

Grabo, A., & van Vugt, M. (2016). Charismatic leadership and the evolution of cooperation. *Evolution and Human Behavior, 37*, 399–406.

Grabski, M., McAndrew, A., Lawn, W., Marsh, B., Raymen, L., Stevens, T., Hardy, L., Warren, F., Bloomfield, M., Borissova, A., Maschauer, E., Broomby, R., Price, R., Coathup, R., Gilhooly, D., Palmer, E., Gordon-Williams, R., Hill, R., Harris, J., ... Morgan, C. J. A. (2022). Adjunctive ketamine with relapse prevention–based psychological therapy in the treatment of alcohol use disorder. *American Journal of Psychiatry, 179*, 152–162.

Gradisar, M., Kahn, M., Micic, G., Short, M., Reynolds, C., Orchard, F., Bauducco, S., Bartel, K., & Richardson, C. (2022). Sleep's role in the development and resolution of adolescent depression. *Nature Reviews Psychology, 1*, 512–523.

Graham, A. M., Fisher, P. A., & Pfeifer, J. H. (2013). What sleeping babies hear: A functional MRI study of interparental conflict and infants' emotion processing. *Psychological Science, 24*, 782–789.

Graham, E. K., Rutsohn, J. P., Turiano, N. A., Bendayan, R., Batterham, P. J., Gerstorf, D., Katz, M. J., Reynolds, C. A., Sharp, E. S., Yoneda, T. B., Bastarache, E. D., Elleman, L. G., Zelinski, E. M., Johansson, B., Kuh, D., Barnes, L. L., Bennett, D. A., Deeg, D. J. H., Lipton, R. B., ... Mroczek, D. K. (2017). Personality predicts mortality risk: An integrative data analysis of 15 international longitudinal studies. *Journal of Research in Personality, 70*, 174–186.

Graham, M., Winter, A. K., Ferrari, M., Grenfell, B., Moss, W. J., Azman, A. S., Metcalf, J. E., & Lessler, J. (2019). Measles and the canonical path to elimination. *Science, 364*, 584–587.

Gramlich, J. (2018, October 24). *8 facts about Americans and Facebook.* The Universal News Network.

Gramlich, J. (2020). *What the data says (and doesn't say) about crime in the United States.* Pew Research Center. https://www.pewresearch.org/fact-tank/2020/11/20/facts-about-crime-in-the-u-s/

Grand, J. A. (2016). Brain drain? An examination of stereotype threat effects during training on knowledge acquisition and organizational effectiveness. *Journal of Applied Psychology, 102*, 115–150.

Grandner, M. A., & Fernandez, F.-X. (2021). The translational neuroscience of sleep: A contextual framework. *Science, 374*, 568–573.

Granqvist, P., Mikulincer, M., & Shaver, P. R. (2010). Religion as attachment: Normative processes and individual differences. *Personality and Social Psychology Review, 14*, 49–59.

Granqvist, P., Vestbrant, K., Döllinger, L., Liuzza, M. T., Olsson, M. J., Blomkvist, A., & Lundström, J. N. (2019). The scent of security: Odor of romantic partner alters subjective discomfort and autonomic stress responses in an adult attachment-dependent manner. *Physiology & Behavior, 198*, 144–150.

Grant, A. M., Gino, F., & Hofmann, D. A. (2011). Reversing the extraverted leadership advantage: The role of employee proactivity. *Academy of Management Journal, 54*, 528–550.

Grant, N., Wardle, J., & Steptoe, A. (2009). The relationship between life satisfaction and health behavior: A cross-cultural analysis of young adults. *International Journal of Behavioral Medicine, 16*, 259–268.

Grapsas, S., Brummelman, E., Back, M. D., & Denissen, J. J. A. (2020). The "why" and "how" of narcissism: A process model of narcissistic status pursuit. *Perspectives on Psychological Science, 15*, 150–172.

Graybiel, A. M., & Smith, K. S. (2014, June). Good habits, bad habits. *Scientific American*, pp. 39–43.

Gray-Little, B., & Burks, N. (1983). Power and satisfaction in marriage: A review and critique. *Psychological Bulletin, 93*, 513–538.

Greaves, L. M., Sibley, C. G., Fraser, G., & Barlow, F. K. (2019). Comparing pansexual- and bisexual-identified participants on demographics, psychological well-being, and political ideology in a New Zealand National Sample. *Journal of Sex Research, 56*(9), 1083–1090.

Green, B. (2002). Listening to leaders: Feedback on 360-degree feedback one year later. *Organizational Development Journal, 20*, 8–16.

Green, J. D., Sedikides, C., & Gregg, A. P. (2008). Forgotten but not gone: The recall and recognition of self-threatening memories. *Journal of Experimental Social Psychology, 44*, 547–561.

Green, J. T., & Woodruff-Pak, D. S. (2000). Eyeblink classical conditioning: Hippocampal formation is for neutral stimulus associations as cerebellum is for association-response. *Psychological Bulletin, 126*, 138–158.

Greenbaum, D. (2022, March 14). A Jewish girl was saved by a Ukrainian family during World War II. Now her grandchildren are returning the favor. *The Washington Post.* https://www.washingtonpost.com/lifestyle/2022/03/12/sharon-bass-israel-refugee-ukraine/

Greenberg, D. M., Matz, S. C., Schwartz, H. A., & Fricke, K. R. (2021). The self-congruity effect of music. *Journal of Personality and Social Psychology, 121*(1), 137–150.

Greenberg, D. M., Warrier, V., Allison, C., & Baron-Cohen, S. (2018). Testing the Empathizing–Systemizing theory of sex differences and the Extreme Male Brain theory of autism in half a million people. *PNAS, 114*(48), 12152–12157.

Greenberg, J. (2008). Understanding the vital human quest for self-esteem. *Perspectives on Psychological Science, 3*, 48–55.

Greenberg, J., Solomon, S., & Pyszczynski, T. (1997). Terror management theory of self-esteem and cultural worldviews: Empirical assessments and conceptual refinements. *Advances in Social Psychology, 29*, 61–142.

Greenberg, S., & Stephens-Davidowitz, S. (2019, April 6). You are not as good at kissing as you think. But you are better at dancing. *The New York Times.* https://www.nytimes.com/2019/04/06/opinion/sunday/overconfidence-men-women.html

Greene, J. (2010). *Remarks to an Edge conference: The new science of morality.* Edge. https://www.edge.org/event/the-new-science-of-morality

Greene, J., Sommerville, R. B., Nystrom, L. E., Darley, J. M., & Cohen, J. D. (2001). An fMRI investigation of emotional engagement in moral judgment. *Science, 293*, 2105.

Greene, M. F. (2020, July/August). 30 years ago, Romania deprived thousands of babies of human contact. *The Atlantic.* https://www.theatlantic.com/magazine/archive/2020/07/can-an-unloved-child-learn-to-love/612253/

Greenwald, A. G. (1992). *Subliminal semantic activation and subliminal snake oil* [Paper]. Presented to the American Psychological Association Convention, Washington, DC.

Greenwald, A. G., & Banaji, M. R. (2017). The implicit revolution: Reconceiving the relation between conscious and unconscious. *American Psychologist, 72*, 861–871.

Greenwald, A. G., Dasgupta, N., Dovidio, J. F., Kang, J., Moss-Racusin, C., & Teachman, B. A. (2022). Implicit-bias remedies: Treating discriminatory bias as a public-health problem. *Psychological Science in the Public Interest, 23*(1), 7–40.

Greenwald, A. G., & Lai, C. K. (2020). Implicit social cognition. *Annual Review of Psychology, 71*, 419–445.

Greenwald, A. G., & Pettigrew, T. F. (2014). With malice toward none and charity for some: Ingroup favoritism enables discrimination. *American Psychologist, 69*, 645–655.

Greenwald, A. G., Spangenberg, E. R., Pratkanis, A. R., & Eskenazi, J. (1991). Double-blind tests of subliminal self-help audiotapes. *Psychological Science, 2*, 119–122.

Greenwood, M. (2021). An open invitation to address anti-Indigenous systemic racism. *The Lancet, 379*(10293), 2458–2459.

Greer, S. G., Goldstein, A. N., & Walker, M. P. (2013). The impact of sleep deprivation on food desire in the human brain. *Nature Communications, 4*, 3259.

Gregory, A. M., Rijksdijk, F. V., Lau, J. Y., Dahl, R. E., & Eley, T. C. (2009). The direction of longitudinal associations between sleep problems and depression symptoms: A study of twins aged 8 and 10 years. *Sleep, 32*, 189–199.

Gregory, R. L. (1978). *Eye and brain: The psychology of seeing* (3rd ed.). McGraw-Hill.

Gregory, R. L., & Gombrich, E. H. (Eds.). (1973). *Illusion in nature and art.* Charles Scribner's Sons.

Greist, J. H., Jefferson, J. W., & Marks, I. M. (1986). *Anxiety and its treatment: Help is available.* American Psychiatric Press.

Greitemeyer, T. (2020). Unattractive people are unaware of their (un)attractiveness. *Scandinavian Journal of Psychology, 61*(4), 471–483.

Greitemeyer, T., & Mügge, D. O. (2014). Video games do affect social outcomes: A meta-analytic review of the effects of violent and prosocial video game play. *Personality and Social Psychology Bulletin, 40*, 578–589.

Greitemeyer, T., Weiß, N., & Heuberger, T. (2019). Are everyday sadists specifically attracted to violent video games and do they emotionally benefit from playing those games? *Aggressive Behavior, 45*, 206–213.

Grèzes, J., & Decety, J. (2001). Functional anatomy of execution, mental simulation, observation, and verb generation of actions: A meta-analysis. *Human Brain Mapping, 12*, 1–19.

Griesbauer, E.-M., Manley, E., Wiener, J. M., & Spiers, H. J. (2022). London taxi drivers: A review of neurocognitive studies and an exploration of how they build their cognitive map of London. *Hippocampus, 32*(1), 3–20.

Griesler, P. C., Hu, M. C., Wall, M. M., & Kandel, D. B. (2019). Nonmedical prescription opioid use by parents and adolescents in the US. *Pediatrics, 143*(3). https://tinyurl.com/5xe8je73

Griffin, E. A., Jr., Melas, P. A., Zhou, R., Li, Y., Mercado, P., & Kemp, K. A. (2017). Prior alcohol use enhances vulnerability to compulsive cocaine self-administration by promoting degradation of HDAC4 and HDAC5. *Science Advances, 3*(11). https://www.science.org/doi/10.1126/sciadv.1701682

Griffin, J. M., Kruger, S., & Maturana, G. (2019). Personal infidelity and professional conduct in 4 settings. *PNAS, 116*, 16268–16273.

Griffin, J. W., Bauer, R., & Scherf, K. S. (2021). A quantitative meta-analysis of face recognition deficits in autism: 40 years of research. *Psychological Bulletin, 147*, 268–292.

Griffiths, M. (2001). Sex on the internet: Observations and implications for internet sex addiction. *Journal of Sex Research, 38*, 333–342.

Griggs, R. A., Blyler, J., & Jackson, S. L. (2020). Using research ethics as a springboard for teaching Milgram's obedience study as a contentious classic. *Scholarship of Teaching and Learning in Psychology, 6*, 350–356.

Grilo, C. M., & Pogue-Geile, M. F. (1991). The nature of environmental influences on weight and obesity: A behavior genetic analysis. *Psychological Bulletin, 110*, 520–537.

Grinberg, N., Joseph, K., Friedland, L., Swire-Thompson, B., & Lazer, D. (2019). Fake news on Twitter during the 2016 U.S. presidential election. *Science, 363*, 374–378.

Grinker, R. R. (2007). *Unstrange minds: Remapping the world of autism.* Basic Books.

Grobstein, C. (1979, June). External human fertilization. *Scientific American*, pp. 57–67.

Grønnerød, C., Grønnerød, J. S., & Grøndahl, P. (2015). Psychological treatment of sexual offenders against children: A meta-analytic review of treatment outcome studies. *Trauma, Violence, & Abuse, 16*, 280–290.

Gross, A. E., & Crofton, C. (1977). What is good is beautiful. *Sociometry, 40*, 85–90.

Gross, J. J. (1998). The emerging field of emotion regulation: An integrative review. *Review of General Psychology, 2*, 271–299.

Gross, J. J. (1998). Antecedent- and response-focused emotion regulation: Divergent consequences for experience, expression, and physiology. *Journal of Personality and Social Psychology, 74*(1), 224.

Gross, J. J. (2013). Emotion regulation: Taking stock and moving forward. *Emotion, 13*, 359–365.

Gross, J. J. (2015). The extended process model of emotion regulation: Elaborations, applications, and future directions. *Psychological Inquiry, 26*(1), 130–137.

Gross, J. J., Richards, J. M., & John, O. P. (2006). Emotion regulation in everyday life. In D. K. Snyder, J. A. Simpson, & J. N. Hughes (Eds.), *Emotion regulation in couples and families: Pathways to dysfunction and health* (pp. 13–35). American Psychological Association.

Gross, J. J., Sheppes, G., & Urry, H. L. (2011). Emotion generation and emotion regulation: A distinction we should make (carefully). *Cognition and Emotion, 25*, 765–781.

Gross, T. (2018, September 14). *For novelist John Green, OCD is like an 'invasive weed' inside his mind.* NPR Fresh Air. https://www.npr.org/2018/09/14/647848731/for-novelist-john-green-ocd-is-like-an-invasive-weed-inside-his-mind

Grossberg, S. (1995). The attentive brain. *American Scientist, 83*, 438–449.

Grossman, S., Gueta, C., Pesin, S., Malach, R., & Landau, A. N. (2019). Where does time go when you blink? *Psychological Science, 30*, 907–916.

Grossmann, I., & Kross, E. (2014). Exploring Solomon's paradox: Self-distancing eliminates the self-other asymmetry in wise reasoning about close relationships in younger and older adults. *Psychological Science, 25*, 1571–1580.

Grossmann, I., Na, J., Varnum, M. E. W., Park, D. C., Kitayama, S., & Nisbett, R. E. (2010). Reasoning about social conflicts improves into old age. *PNAS, 107*, 7246–7250.

Grossmann, I., & Varnum, M. E. W. (2015). Social structure, infectious diseases, disasters, secularism, and cultural change in America. *Psychological Science, 26*, 311–324.

Groß, J., Blank, H., & Bayen, U. J. (2017). Hindsight bias in depression. *Clinical Psychological Science, 5*, 771–788.

Grotzinger, A. D., Mallard, T. T., Akingbuwa, W. A., Ip, H. F., Adams, M. J., Lewis, C. M., McIntosh, A. M., Grove, J., Dalsgaard, S., Lesch, K.-P., Strom, N., Meier, S. M., Mattheisen, M., Børglum, A. D., Mors, O., Breen, G., iPSYCH, Tourette Syndrome and Obsessive Compulsive Disorder Working Group of the Psychiatric Genetics Consortium, Bipolar Disorder Working Group of the Psychiatric Genetics Consortium, ... Nivard, M. G. (2022). Genetic architecture of 11 major psychiatric disorders at biobehavioral, functional genomic and molecular genetic levels of analysis. *Nature Genetics, 54*, 548–559.

Grover, S., & Helliwell, J. F. (2014, December). *How's life at home? New evidence on marriage and the set point for happiness.* NBER Working Paper No. 20794. https://www.nber.org/papers/w20794

Grubbs, J. B., & Kraus, S. W. (2021). Pornography use and psychological science: A call for consideration. *Current Directions in Psychological Science, 30*, 68–75.

Gruber, J. (2011). Can feeling too good be bad? Positive emotion persistence (PEP) in bipolar disorder. *Current Directions in Psychological Science, 20*(4), 217–221.

Gruber, J., Prinstein, M. J., Clark, L. A., Rottenberg, J., Abramowitz, J. S., Albano, A. M., Aldao, A., Borelli, J., Chung, T., Davila, J., Forbes, E. E., Gee, D. G., Hall, G. C. N., Hallion, L. S., Hinshaw, S. P., Hofmann, S. G., Hollon, S. D., Joormann, J., Kazdin, A. E., ...Klein, D. N. (2021). Mental health and clinical psychological science in the time of COVID-19: Challenges, opportunities, and a call to action. *American Psychologist*. 76(3: 409–426. doi: 10.1037/amp0000707

Gruber, J., Eidelman, P., Johnson, S. L., Smith, B., & Harvey, A. G. (2011). Hooked on a feeling: Rumination about positive and negative emotion in inter-episode bipolar disorder. *Journal of Abnormal Psychology, 120*(4), 956.

Gruber, J., Mendle, J., Lindquist, K. A., Schmader, T., Clark, L. A., Bliss-Moreau, E., Akinola, M., Atlas, L., Barch, D. M., Feldman Barrett, L., Borelli, J. L., Brannon, T. N., Bunge, S. A., Campos, B., Cantlon, J., Carter, R., Carter-Sowell, A. R., Chen, S., Craske, M. G., ... Williams, L. A. (2021). The future of women in psychological science. *Perspectives on Psychological Science, 16*(3), 483–516.

Gruber, J., Oveis, C., Keltner, D., & Johnson, S. L. (2011). A discrete emotions approach to positive emotion disturbance in depression. *Cognition and Emotion, 25(1)*, 40–52.

Gruber, J., Prinstein, M. J., Clark, L. A., Rottenberg, J., Abramowitz, J. S., Albano, A. M., Aldao, A., Borelli, J. L., Chung, T., Davila, J., Forbes, E. E., Gee, D. G., Hall, G. C. N., Hallion, L. S., Hinshaw, S. P., Hofmann, S. G., Hollon, S. D., Joormann, J., Kazdin, A. E., ... Weinstock, L. M. (2021). Mental health and clinical psychological science in the time of COVID-19: Challenges, opportunities, and a call to action. *American Psychologist, 76*, 409–426.

Gruber, J., Villanueva, C., Burr, E., Purcell, J. R., & Karoly, H. (2019). Understanding and taking stock of positive emotion disturbance. *Social and Personality Psychology Compass, 14*(1). https://doi.org/10.1111/spc3.12515

Gu, X., Lohrenz, T., Salas, R., Baldwin, P. R., Soltani, A., Kirk, U., Cinciripini, P. M., & Montague, P. R. (2015). Belief about nicotine selectively modulates value and reward prediction error signals in smokers. *PNAS, 112*, 2539–2544.

Guéguen, N. (2011). Effects of solicitor sex and attractiveness on receptivity to sexual offers: A field study. *Archives of Sexual Behavior, 40*, 915–919.

Guerin, B. (1986). Mere presence effects in humans: A review. *Journal of Personality and Social Psychology, 22*, 38–77.

Guertin, C., Pelletier, L. G., Émond, C., & Lalande, G. (2017). Change in physical and psychological health over time in patients with cardiovascular disease: On the benefits of being self-determined, physically active, and eating well. *Motivation and Emotion, 41*(3), 294–307.

Guinness World Records. (2019). *Guinness world records 2019*. Guinness World Records Limited.

Guiso, L., Monte, F., Sapienza, P., & Zingales, L. (2008). Culture, gender, and math. *Science, 320*, 1164–1165.

Gukasyan, N., Davis, A. K., Barrett, F. S., Cosimano, M. P., Sepeda, N. D., Johnson, M. W., & Griffiths, R. R. (2022). Efficacy and safety of psilocybin-assisted treatment for major depressive disorder: Prospective 12-month follow-up. *Journal of Psychopharmacology, 36*, 151–158.

Gul, P., Cross, S. E., & Uskul, A. K. (2021). Implications of culture of honor theory and research for practitioners and prevention researchers. *American Psychologist, 76*(3), 502–515.

Gülgöz, S., Glazier, J. J., Enright, E. A., Alonso, D. J, Durwood, L. J., Fast, A. A., Lowe, R., Ji, C., Heer, J., Martin, C. L., & Olson, K. R. (2019). Similarity in transgender and cisgender children's gender development. *PNAS, 116*, 24480–24485.

Gunaydin, G., Selcuk, E., & Zayas, V. (2017). Impressions based on a portrait predict, 1-month later, impressions following a live interaction. *Social Psychological and Personality Science, 8*, 36–44.

Gunderson, E. A., Gripshover, S. J., Romero, C., Dweck, C. S., Goldin-Meadow, S., & Levine, S. C. (2013). Parent praise to 1- to 3-year-olds predicts children's motivational frameworks 5 years later. *Child Development, 84*, 1526–1541.

Gunn, R. L., Norris, A. L., Sokolovsky, A., Micalizzi, L., Merrill, J. E., & Barnett, N. P. (2018). Marijuana use is associated with alcohol use and consequences across the first 2 years of college. *Psychology of Addictive Behaviors, 32*, 885–894.

Gunnerud, H. L., ten Braak, D., Reikerås, E. K. L., Donolato, E., & Melby-Lervåg, M. (2020). *Psychological Bulletin, 146*(12), 1059–1083.

Gunnery, S. D., & Ruben, M. A. (2016). Perceptions of Duchenne and non-Duchenne smiles: A meta-analysis. *Cognition and Emotion, 30*, 501–515.

Gunter, T. D., Vaughn, M. G., & Philibert, R. A. (2010). Behavioral genetics in antisocial spectrum disorders and psychopathy: A review of the recent literature. *Behavioral Sciences and the Law, 28*, 148–173.

Günther, V., Kropidlowski, A., Schmidt, F. M., Koelkebeck, K., Kersting, A., & Suslow, T. (2021). Attentional processes during emotional face perception in social anxiety disorder: A systematic review and meta-analysis of eye-tracking findings. *Progress in Neuro-Psychopharmacology & Biological Psychiatry, 111*. doi: 10.1016/j.pnpbp.2021.110353

Guo, S., Deng, W., Wang, H., Liu, J., Liu, X., Yang, X., He, C., Zhang, Q., Liu, B., Dong, X., Yang, Z., Li, Z., & Li, X. (2020). The efficacy of internet-based cognitive behavioural therapy for social anxiety disorder: A systematic review and meta-analysis. *Clinical Psychology & Psychotherapy, 28*(3), 656–668.

Guo, X., Zhai, J., Liu, Z., Fang, M., Wang, B., Wang, C., Hu, B., Sun, X., Lv, L., Lu, Z., Ma, C., He, X., Gui, T., Xie, S., Wu, R., Xue, Z., Chen, J., Twamley, E. W., Jin, H., & Zhao, J. (2010). Effect of antipsychotic medication alone vs combined with psychosocial intervention on outcomes of early-stage schizophrenia. *Archives of General Psychiatry, 67*, 895–904.

Gupta, M. D. (2017, September). Return of the missing daughters. *Scientific American*, pp. 78–85.

Gurung, R. A. R., Hackathorn, J., Enns, C., Frantz, S., Cacioppo, J. T., Loop, T., & Freeman, J. E. (2016). Strengthening introductory psychology: A new model for teaching the introductory course. *American Psychologist, 71*(2), 112–124.

Gustavson, C. R., Garcia, J., Hankins, W. G., & Rusiniak, K. W. (1974). Coyote predation control by aversive conditioning. *Science, 184*, 581–583.

Gustavson, C. R., Kelly, D. J., & Sweeney, M. (1976). Prey lithium aversions I: Coyotes and wolves. *Behavioral Biology, 17*, 61–72.

Gutchess, A. (2014). Plasticity in the aging brain: New directions in cognitive neuroscience. *Science, 346*, 579–582.

Guthier, C., Dormann, C., & Voelkle, M. C. (2020). Reciprocal effects between job stressors and burnout: A continuous time meta-analysis of longitudinal studies. *Psychological Bulletin, 146*(12), 1146–1173.

Guttmacher Institute. (1994). *Sex and America's teenagers* [PDF file]. https://www.guttmacher.org/sites/default/files/pdfs/pubs/archive/SaAT.pdf

H., Sally. (1979, August). Videotape recording number T-3. Fortunoff Video Archive of Holocaust Testimonies. Yale University Library.

Haaker, J., Yi, J., Petrovic, P., & Olsson, A. (2017). Endogenous opioids regulate social threat learning in humans. *Nature Communications, 8*. https://www.nature.com/articles/ncomms15495

Haas, A. P., Eliason, M., Mays, V. M., Mathy, R. M., Cochran, S. D., D'Augelli, A. R., Silverman, M. M., Fisher, P. W., Hughes, T., Rosario, M., Russell, S. T., Malley, E., Reed, J., Litts, D. A., Haller, E., Sell, R. L., Remafedi, G., Bradford, J., Beautrais, A. L., ... Clayton, P. J. (2011). Suicide and suicide risk in lesbian, gay, bisexual, and transgender populations: Review and recommendations. *Journal of Homosexuality, 58*, 10–51.

Haas, B. W., & vanDellen, M. R. (2020). Culture is associated with the experience of long-term self-concept changes. *Social Psychological and Personality Science, 11*(8), 1047–1056.

Habel, U., Koch, K., Kellerman, T., Reske, M., Frommann, N., Wölwer, W., Zilles, K., Shah, N. J., & Schneider, F. (2010). Training of affect recognition in schizophrenia: Neurobiological correlates. *Social Neuroscience, 5*, 92–104.

Haber, R. N. (1970). How we remember what we see. *Scientific American*, pp. 104–112.

Habib, A. M., Okorkov, A. L., Hill, M. N., Bras, J. T., Lee, M-C., Li, S., Gossage, S. J., van Drimmelen, M., Morena, M., Houlden, H., Ramirez, J. D., Bennett, D. L. H., Srivastava, D., & Cox, J. J. (2019). Microdeletion in a *FAAH* pseudogene identified in a patient with high anandamide concentrations and pain insensitivity. *British Journal of Anaesthesia, 123*, e249–e253.

Hadjistavropoulos, T., Craig, K. D., Duck, S. Cano, A., Goubert, L., Jackson, P. L., Mogil, J. S., Rainville, P., Sullivan, M. J. L., Williams, A. C. C., Vervoort, T., & Fitzgerald, T. D.

(2011). A biopsychosocial formulation of pain communication. *Psychological Bulletin, 137*, 910–939.

Hafenbrack, A. C., Kinias, Z., & Barsade, S. G. (2014). Debiasing the mind through meditation: Mindfulness and the sunk-cost bias. *Psychological Science, 25*, 369–376.

Hagger, M. S., & Chatzisarantis, N. L. (2016). The trans-contextual model of autonomous motivation in education: Conceptual and empirical issues and meta-analysis. *Review of Educational Research, 86*, 360–407.

Hagger, M. S., Chatzisarantis, N. L. D., Alberts, H., Anggono, C. O., Birt, A., Brand, R., Brandt, M. J., Brewer, G., Bruyneel, S., Calvillo, D., Campbell, W., Cannon, P., Carlucci, M., Carruth, N., Cheung, T., Crowell, A., Ridder, D., Dewitte, S., & Elson, M. (2016). A multi-lab pre-registered replication of the ego-depletion effect. *Perspectives on Psychological Science, 11*, 546–573.

Hahn, A., Kranz, G., Sladky, R., Kaufmann, U., Ganger, S., Hummer, A., Seiger, R., Spies, M., Vanicek, T., Winkler, D., Kasper, S., Windischberger, C., Swabb, D. F., & Lanzenberger, R. (2016). Testosterone affects language areas of the adult human brain. *Human Brain Mapping, 37*, 1738–1748.

Haidt, J. (2000). The positive emotion of elevation. *Prevention and Treatment, 3*(1), Article 3c.

Haidt, J. (2001). The emotional dog and its rational tail: A social intuitionist approach to moral judgment. *Psychological Review, 108*(4), 814–834.

Haidt, J. (2021a, September 14). Tweet at @JonHaidt.

Haidt, J. (2021b, November 21). *The dangerous experiment on teen girls*. The Atlantic. https://www.theatlantic.com/ideas/archive/2021/11/facebooks-dangerous-experiment-teen-girls/620767/

Haidt, J. (2022, May 4). *Teen mental health is plummeting and social media is a major contributing cause* [PDF File]. Testimony before the U.S. Senate Judiciary Committee, Subcommittee on Technology, Privacy, and the Law. https://www.judiciary.senate.gov/imo/media/doc/Haidt%20Testimony.pdf

Haidt, J., & Twenge, J. (2021). *Social media use and mental health: A collaborative review*. https://bit.ly/2OoPUsJ

Hainey, M. (2016). *Lin-Manuel Miranda thinks the key to parenting is a little less parenting*. GQ Magazine. https://www.gq.com/story/unexpected-lin-manuel-miranda

Hajek, P., Phillips-Waller, A., Przulj, D., Pesola, F., Smith, K. M., Bisal, N., Li, J., Parrott, S., Sasieni, P., Dawkins, L., Ross, L., Goniewicz, M., Wu, Q., & McRobbie, H. J. (2019). A randomized trial of e-cigarettes versus nicotine-replacement therapy. *New England Journal of Medicine, 380*, 620–637.

Hajhosseini, B., Stewart, B., Tan, J. C., Busque, S., & Melcher, M. L. (2013). Evaluating deceased donor registries: Identifying predictive factors of donor designation. *American Surgeon, 79*, 235–241.

Halberstadt, J. B., Niedenthal, P. M., & Kushner, J. (1995). Resolution of lexical ambiguity by emotional state. *Psychological Science, 6*, 278–281.

Halberstadt, J., Sherman, S. J., & Sherman, J. W. (2011). Why Barack Obama is Black. *Psychological Science, 22*, 29–33.

Haldeman, D. C. (1994). The practice and ethics of sexual orientation conversion therapy. *Journal of Consulting and Clinical Psychology, 62*, 221–227.

Haldeman, D. C. (2002). Gay rights, patient rights: The implications of sexual orientation conversion therapy. *Professional Psychology: Research and Practice, 33*, 260–264.

Hales, C. M., Kit, B. K., Gu, Q., & Ogden, C. L. (2018). Trends in prescription medication use among children and adolescents—United States, 1999–2014. *Journal of the American Medical Association, 319*(19), 2009–2020.

Hall, C. S., Dornhoff, W., Blick, K. A., & Weesner, K. E. (1982). The dreams of college men and women in 1950 and 1980: A comparison of dream contents and sex differences. *Sleep, 5*, 188–194.

Hall, C. S., & Lindzey, G. (1978). *Theories of personality* (2nd ed.). Wiley.

Hall, D. T., & Chandler, D. E. (2005). Psychological success: When the career is a calling. *Journal of Organizational Behavior, 26*, 155–176.

Hall, G. (1997). Context aversion, Pavlovian conditioning, and the psychological side effects of chemotherapy. *European Psychologist, 2*, 118–124.

Hall, G. S. (1904). *Adolescence: Its psychology and its relations to physiology, anthropology, sex, crime, religion and education* (Vol. 1). Appleton-Century-Crofts.

Hall, J. A., Gunnery, S. D., & Horgan, T. G. (2016). Gender differences in interpersonal accuracy. In J. A. Hall, M. S. Mast, & T. V. West (Eds.), *The social psychology of perceiving others accurately* (pp. 309–327), Cambridge University Press.

Hall, K. M., Knudson, S. T., Wright, J., Charlifue, S. W., Graves, D. E., & Warner, P. (1999). Follow-up study of individuals with high tetraplegia (C1-C4) 14 to 24 years postinjury. *Archives of Physical Medicine and Rehabilitation, 80*, 1507–1513.

Hall, M. H., Brindle, R. C., & Buysse, D. J. (2018). Sleep and cardiovascular disease: Emerging opportunities for psychology. *American Psychologist, 73*, 994–1006.

Hall, P. A. (2016). Executive-control processes in high-calorie food consumption. *Current Directions in Psychological Science, 25*, 91–98.

Hall, S. S. (2004, May). The good egg. *Discover*, pp. 30–39.

Hall, S. S., Knox, D., & Shapiro, K. (2017). "I have," "I would," "I won't": Hooking up among sexually diverse groups of college students. *Psychology of Sexual Orientation and Gender Diversity, 4*, 233–240.

Hallal, P. C., Andersen, L. B., Bull, F. C., Guthold, R., Haskell, W., & Ekelund, U. (2012). Global physical activity levels: Surveillance progress, pitfalls, and prospects. *The Lancet, 380*, 247–257.

Haller, H., Breilmann, P., Schröter, M., Dobos, G., & Cramer, H. (2021). A systematic review and meta-analysis of acceptance- and mindfulness-based interventions for DSM-5 anxiety disorders. *Scientific Reports, 11*. https://www.nature.com/articles/s41598-021-99882-w

Haller, R., Rummel, C., Henneberg, S., Pollmer, U., & Köster, E. P. (1999). The influence of early experience with vanillin on food preference later in life. *Chemical Senses, 24*, 465–467.

Halmburger, A., Baumert, A., & Schmitt, M. (2015). Anger as driving factor of moral courage in comparison with guilt and global mood: A multimethod approach. *European Journal of Social Psychology, 45*, 39–51.

Halpern, D., Valenzuela, S., & Katz, J. E. (2016). "Selfie-ists" or "Narci-selfiers"?: A cross-lagged panel analysis of selfie taking and narcissism. *Personality and Individual Differences, 97*, 98–101.

Halpern, D. F., Benbow, C. P., Geary, D. C., Gur, R. C., Hyde, J. S., & Gernsbacher, M. A. (2007). The science of sex differences in science and mathematics. *Psychological Science in the Public Interest, 8*, 1–51.

Hamamura, T. (2012). Are cultures becoming individualistic? A cross-temporal comparison of individualism–collectivism in the United States and Japan. *Personality and Social Psychology Review, 16*(1), 3–24.

Hambrick, D. Z. (2014, December 2). Brain training doesn't make you smarter. *Scientific American*. https://www.scientificamerican.com/article/brain-training-doesn-t-make-you-smarter/

Hambrick, D. Z., Altmann, E. M., Oswald, F. L., Meinz, E. J., Gobet, F., & Campitelli, G. (2014a). Accounting for expert performance: The devil is in the details. *Intelligence, 45*, 112–114.

Hambrick, D. Z., & Meinz, E. J. (2011). Limits on the predictive power of domain-specific experience and knowledge in skilled performance. *Current Directions in Psychological Science, 20*, 275–279.

Hambrick, D. Z., Oswald, F. L., Altmann, E. M., Meinz, E. J., Gobet, F., & Campitelli, G. (2014b). Deliberate practice: Is that all it takes to become an expert? *Intelligence, 45*, 34–45.

Hamer, M., Kivimaki, M., Stamatakis, E., & Batty, G. D. (2019). Psychological distress and infectious disease mortality in the general population. *Brain, Behavior, and Immunity, 76*, 280–283.

Hamid, A. A., Pettibone, J. R., Mabrouk, O. S., Hetrick, V. L., Schmidt, R., Vander Weele, C. M., Kennedy, R. T., Aragona, B. J., & Berke, J. D. (2016). Mesolimbic dopamine signals the value of work. *Nature Neuroscience, 19*, 117–126.

Hamilton, J. L., Stange, J. P., Abramson, L. Y., & Alloy, L. B. (2015). Stress and the development of cognitive vulnerabilities to depression explain sex differences in depressive symptoms during adolescence. *Clinical Psychological Science, 3*, 702–714.

Hamilton, T. (2021, February 12). *Premier League's home edge has gone in pandemic era: The impact of fan-less games in England and Europe*. ESPN. https://tinyurl.com/pwa7rw7d

Hamlat, E. J., Laraia, B., Bleil, M., Deardorff, J., Tomiyama, A. J., Mujahid, M., Shields, G. S., Brownell, K., Slavich, G. M., & Epel, E. S. (2022). Effects of early life adversity on pubertal timing and tempo in Black and White girls: The National Growth and Health study. *Psychosomatic Medicine, 84*, 297–305.

Hamlin, J. K., Wynn, K., & Bloom, P. (2007). Social evaluation by preverbal infants. *Nature, 450*(7169), 557–559.

Hamlin, J. K., Wynn, K., Bloom, P., & Mahajan, N. (2011). How infants and toddlers reach to antisocial others. *PNAS, 108*, 19931–19936.

Hammack, P. L., (2005). The life course development of human sexual orientation: An integrative paradigm. *Human Development, 48*, 267–290.

Hammer, E. (2003). How lucky you are to be a psychology major. *Eye on Psi Chi*, 4–5.

Hammersmith, S. K. (1982, August). *Sexual preference: An empirical study from the Alfred C. Kinsey Institute for Sex Research* [Paper]. Presented at the 90th Annual Convention of the American Psychological Association, Washington, DC.

Hammond, D. C. (2008). Hypnosis as sole anesthesia for major surgeries: Historical and contemporary perspectives. *American Journal of Clinical Hypnosis, 51*, 101–121.

Hampton, R. S., Kwon, J. Y., & Varnum, M. E. W. (2021). Variations in the regulation of affective neural responses across three cultures. *Emotion, 21*(2), 283–296.

Hamza, C. A., Willoughby, T., & Heffer, T. (2015). Impulsivity and nonsuicidal self-injury: A review and meta-analysis. *Clinical Psychology Review, 38*, 13–24.

Han, B., Kott, P. S., Hughes, A., McKeon, R., Blanco, C., & Compton, W. M. (2016). Estimating the rates of deaths by suicide among adults who attempt suicide in the United States. *Journal of Psychiatric Research, 77*, 125–133.

Han, L. K. M., Aghajani, M., Clark, S. L., Chan, R. F., Hattab, M. W., Shabalin, A. A., Zhao, M., Kumar, G., Xie, L. Y., Jansen, R., Milaneschi, Y., Den, B., Aberg, K. A., van den Oord, D. J. C. G., & Penninx, B. W. J. H. (2018). Epigenetic aging in major depressive disorder. *American Journal of Psychiatry, 175*, 774–782.

Hanc, J. (2021, April 28). Doctors harness the power of human connections. *The New York Times*. https://www.nytimes.com/2021/04/28/health/social-medicine-programs.html

Haney, J. L. (2016). Predictors of homonegativity in the United States and the Netherlands using the fifth wave of the World Values Survey. *Journal of Homosexuality, 63*, 1355–1377.

Hänggi, J., Koeneke, S., Bezzola, L., & Jäncke, L. (2010). Structural neuroplasticity in the sensorimotor network of professional female ballet dancers. *Human Brain Mapping*, 31, 1196–1206.

Hankerson, S. H., Moise, N., Wilson, D., Waller, B. Y., Arnold, K. T., Duarte, C., Lugo-Candelas, C., Weissman, M. M., Wainberg, M., Yehuda, R., & Shim, R. (2022). The intergenerational impact of structural racism and cumulative trauma on depression. *American Journal of Psychiatry*, 179, 434–439.

Hanna, A., & Rounds, J. (2020). How accurate are interest inventories? A quantitative review of career choice hit rates. *Psychological Bulletin*, 146(9), 765–796.

Hanniball, K. B., Aknin, L. B., Douglas, K. S., & Viljoen, J. L. (2019). Does helping promote well-being in at-risk youth and ex-offender samples? *Journal of Experimental Social Psychology*, 82, 307–317.

Hansen, A., Turpyn, C. C., Mauro, K., Thompson, J. C., & Chaplin, T. M. (2019). Adolescent brain response to reward is associated with a bias toward immediate reward. *Developmental Neuropsychology, 44*(5), 417–428.

Harari, G. M., Müller, S. R., Stachl, C., Wang, R., Wang, W., Bühner, M., Rentfrow, P. J., Campbell, A. T., & Gosling, S. D. (2020). Sensing sociability: Individual differences in young adults' conversation, calling, texting, and app use behaviors in daily life. *Journal of Personality and Social Psychology, 119*(1), 204–228.

Harbaugh, W. T., Mayr, U., & Burghart, D. R. (2007). Neural responses to taxation and voluntary giving reveal motives for charitable donations. *Science, 316*, 1622–1625.

Harber, K. D. (1998). Feedback to minorities: Evidence of a positive bias. *Journal of Personality and Social Psychology, 74*, 622–628.

Harden, K. P. (2012). True love waits? A sibling-comparison study of age at first sexual intercourse and romantic relationships in young adulthood. *Psychological Science, 23*, 1324–1336.

Harden, K. P. (2021). *The genetic lottery: Why DNA matters for social equality*. Princeton University Press.

Harden, K. P., & Mendle, J. (2011). Why don't smart teens have sex? A behavioral genetic approach. *Child Development, 82*, 1327–1344.

Hards, E., Ellis, J., Fisk, J., & Reynolds, S. (2019). Memories of the self in adolescence: Examining 6558 self-image norms. *Memory, 27*, 1–7.

Hardt, O., Einarsson, E. O., & Nader, K. (2010). A bridge over troubled water: Reconsolidation as a link between cognitive and neuro-scientific memory research traditions. *Annual Review of Psychology, 61*, 141–167.

Hare, R. D. (1975). Psychophysiological studies of psychopathy. Chapter 3. In D. C. Fowles (Ed.), *Clinical applications of psychophysiology*. Columbia University Press.

Harenski, C. L., Harenski, K. A., Shane, M. W., & Kiehl, K. A. (2010). Aberrant neural processing of moral violations in criminal psychopaths. *Journal of Abnormal Psychology, 119*, 863–874.

Harker, L., & Keltner, D. (2001). Expressions of positive emotion in women's college yearbook pictures and their relationship to personality and life outcomes across adulthood. *Journal of Personality and Social Psychology*, 80(1), 112.

Harkin, B., Webb, T. L., Chang, B. P. I., Prestwich, A., Conner, M., Kellar, I., Benn, Y., & Sheeran, P. (2016). Does monitoring goal progress promote goal attainment? A meta-analysis of the experimental evidence. *Psychological Bulletin*, 142, 198–229.

Harkins, S. G., & Szymanski, K. (1989). Social loafing and group evaluation. *Journal of Personality and Social Psychology*, 56, 934–941.

Harlow, H. F., Harlow, M. K., & Suomi, S. J. (1971). From thought to therapy: Lessons from a primate laboratory. *American Scientist*, 59, 538–549.

Harmon-Jones, E., Abramson, L. Y., Sigelman, J., Bohlig, A., Hogan, M. E., & Harmon-Jones, C. (2002). Proneness to hypomania/mania symptoms or depression symptoms and asymmetrical frontal cortical responses to an anger-evoking event. *Journal of Personality and Social Psychology*, 82, 610–618.

Harnett, N. G., Shumen, J. R., Wagle, P. A., Wood, K. H., Wheelock, M. D., Baños, J. H., & Knight, D. C. (2016). Neural mechanisms of human temporal fear conditioning. *Neurobiology of Learning and Memory, 136*, 97–104.

Harold, C. M., Oh, I.-S., Holtz, B. C., Han, S., & Giacalone, R. A. (2016). Fit and frustration as drivers of targeted counterproductive work behaviors: A multifoci perspective. *Journal of Applied Psychology*, 101, 1513–1535.

Harper, C., & McLanahan, S. (2004). Father absence and youth incarceration. *Journal of Research on Adolescence, 14*, 369–397.

Harrington, M. O., Ashton, J. E., Sankarasubramanian, S., Anderson, M. C., & Cairney, S. A. (2021). Losing control: Sleep deprivation impairs the suppression of unwanted thoughts. *Clinical Psychological Science*, 9, 97–113.

Harris, B. (1979). Whatever happened to Little Albert? *American Psychologist, 34*, 151–160.

Harris, E. A., & Van Bavel, J. J. (2021). Preregistered replication of "Feeling superior is a bipartisan issue: Extremity (not direction) of political views predicts perceived belief superiority." *Psychological Science*, 32(3), 451–458.

Harris, J. R. (1998). *The nurture assumption*. Free Press.

Harris, J. R. (2000). Beyond the nurture assumption: Testing hypotheses about the child's environment. In J. G. Borkowski & S. L. Ramey (Eds.), *Parenting and the child's world: Influences on academic, intellectual, and social-emotional development*. APA Books.

Harris, J. R. (2007, August 8). Do pals matter more than parents? [PDF]. *The Times*. https://www.nyman.org/Judith%20Rich%20Harris.pdf

Harris, J. R. (2009). *The nurture assumption: Why children turn out the way they do. Revised and updated*. Free Press.

Harris, M. A., & Orth, U. (2020). The link between self-esteem and social relationships: A meta-analysis of longitudinal studies. *Journal of Personality and Social Psychology*, 119(6), 1459–1477.

Harris, R. J. (1994). The impact of sexually explicit media. In J. Brant & D. Zillmann (Eds.), *Media effects: Advances in theory and research* (pp. 247–272). Erlbaum.

Harrison, G., Hopper, K. I. M., Craig, T., Laska, E., Siegel, C., Wanderling, J., Dube, K. C., Ganev, K, Giel, R., Der Heiden, W. A., Holmberg, S. K., Janca, A., Lee, P. W., León, C. A., Malhotra, S., Marsella, A. J., Nakane, Y., Sartorius, N., Shen, Y., … Wiersma, D. (2001). Recovery from psychotic illness: A 15-and 25-year international follow-up study. *British Journal of Psychiatry*, 178, 506–517.

Harrison, L. A., Hurlemann, R., & Adolphs, R. (2015). An enhanced default approach bias following amygdala lesions in humans. *Psychological Science, 26*, 1543–1555.

Harrison, N. A., Johnston, K., Corno, F., Casey, S. J., Friedner, K., Humphreys, K., Jaldow, E. J., Pitkanen, M., & Kopelman, M. D. (2017). Psychogenic amnesia: Syndromes, outcome, and patterns of retrograde amnesia. *Brain: A Journal of Neurology*, 140, 2498–2510.

Harriston, K. A. (1993, December 24). 1 shakes, 1 snoozes: Both win $45 million. *The*

Washington Post release in Tacoma News Tribune, pp. A1, A2.

Hart, W., Breeden, C. J., Richardson, K., & Kinrade, C. (2021). Depression and the adoption of faux depression symptoms: Novel evidence for a self-verification perspective. *Clinical Psychological Science, 9*, 598–614.

Harter, J. K., Schmidt, F. L., & Hayes, T. L. (2002). Business-unit-level relationship between employee satisfaction, employee engagement, and business outcomes: A meta-analysis. *Journal of Applied Psychology, 87*, 268–279.

Harter, J. K., Schmidt, F. L., Asplund, J. W., Killham, E. A., & Agrawal, S. (2010). Causal impact of employee work perceptions on the bottom line of organizations. *Perspectives on Psychological Science, 5*, 378–389.

Hartl, A. C., Laursen, B., & Cillessen, A. H. (2015). A survival analysis of adolescent friendships: The downside of dissimilarity. *Psychological Science, 26*, 1304–1315.

Hartshorne, J. K., Tenenbaum, J. B., & Pinker, S. (2018). A critical period for second language acquisition: Evidence from 2/3 million English speakers. *Cognition, 177*, 263–277.

Hartwig, M., & Bond, C. F., Jr. (2011). Why do lie-catchers fail? A lens model meta-analysis of human lie judgments. *Psychological Bulletin, 137*, 643–659.

Harvard Business School. (2019). Admissions—Class of 2020 profile. (hbs.edu).

Harvey, P. D. (2019). Smoking cannabis and acquired impairments in cognition: Starting early seems like a really bad idea. *American Journal of Psychiatry, 176*, 90–91.

Harvey, S. B., Øverland, S., Hatch, S. L., Wessely, S., Mykletun, A., & Hotopf, M. (2018). Exercise and the prevention of depression: Results of the HUNT Cohort Study. *American Journal of Psychiatry, 175*, 28–36.

Harward, S. C., Hedrick, N. G., Hall, C. E., Parra-Bueno, P., Milner, T. A., Pan, E., Laviv, T., Hempstead, B. L., Yasuda, R., & McNamara, J. O. (2016). Autocrine BDNF–TrkB signalling within a single dendritic spine. *Nature, 538*, 99–103.

Hasell, J. (2018). *Is income inequality rising around the world?* Our World in Data. https://ourworldindata.org/income-inequality-since-1990

Haslam, C., Cruwys, T., Chang, M. X. L., Bentley, S. V., Haslam, S. A., Dingle, G. A., & Jetten, J. (2019). GROUPS 4 HEALTH reduces loneliness and social anxiety in adults with psychological distress: Findings from a randomized controlled trial. *Journal of Consulting and Clinical Psychology, 87*, 787–801.

Haslam, S. A., & Reicher, S. (2007). Beyond the banality of evil: Three dynamics of an interactionist social psychology of tyranny. *Personality and Social Psychology Bulletin, 33*, 615–622.

Haslam, S. A., & Reicher, S. D. (2012). Contesting the "nature" of conformity: What Milgram and Zimbardo's studies really show. *PLOS Biology, 10*. https://www.ncbi.nlm.nih.gov/pmc/articles/PMC3502509/

Haslam, S. A., Reicher, S. D., & Birney, M. E. (2014). Nothing by mere authority: Evidence that in an experimental analogue of the Milgram paradigm participants are motivated not by orders but by appeals to science. *Journal of Social Issues, 70*, 473–488.

Haslam, S. A., Reicher, S. D., & Birney, M. E. (2016). Questioning authority: New perspectives on Milgram's "obedience" research and its implications for intergroup relations. *Current Opinion in Psychology, 11*, 6–9.

Hassan, B., & Rahman, Q. (2007). Selective sexual orientation-related differences in object location memory. *Behavioral Neuroscience, 121*, 625–633.

Hassin, R. R. (2013). Yes it can: On the functional abilities of the human unconscious. *Perspectives on Psychological Science, 8*, 195–207.

Hatano, K., Sugimura, K., Crocetti, E., & Meeus, W. (2020). Diverse-and-dynamic pathways in educational and interpersonal identity formation during adolescence: Longitudinal links with psychosocial functioning. *Child Development, 91*(4), 1203–1218.

Hatfield, E. (1988). Passionate and companionate love. In R. J. Sternberg & M. L. Barnes (Eds.), *The psychology of love* (pp. 191–217). Yale University Press.

Hatfield, E., Mo, Y., & Rapson, R. L. (2015). Love, sex, and marriage across cultures. In L. A. Jensen (Ed.), *The Oxford handbook of human development and culture: An interdisciplinary perspective* (pp. 570–585). Oxford University Press.

Hathaway, S. R. (1960). *An MMPI handbook* (Vol. 1, Foreword). University of Minnesota Press (rev. ed.), 1972.

Hatzenbuehler, M. L. (2011). The social environment and suicide attempts in lesbian, gay, and bisexual youth. *Pediatrics, 127*, 896–903.

Hatzenbuehler, M. L. (2014). Structural stigma and the health of lesbian, gay, and bisexual populations. *Current Directions in Psychological Science, 23*, 127–132.

Hatzenbuehler, M. L., Nolen-Hoeksema, S., & Dovidio, J. (2009). How does stigma "get under the skin?" The mediating role of emotion regulation. *Psychological Science, 20*, 1282–1289.

Hatzigeorgiadis, A., Zourbanos, N., Galanis, E., & Theodorakis, Y. (2011). Self-talk and sports performance: A meta-analysis. *Perspectives on Psychological Science, 6*, 348–356.

Hauser, M. D., Chomsky, N., & Fitch, W. T. (2002). The faculty of language: What is it, who has it, and how did it evolve? *Science, 298*, 1569–1579.

Hawkley, L. C., Hughes, M. E., Waite, L. J., Masi, C. M., Thisted, R. A., & Cacioppo, J. T. (2008). From social structure factors to perceptions of relationship quality and loneliness: The Chicago Health, Aging, and Social Relations Study. *Journal of Gerontology: Series B, 63*, S375–S384.

Haworth, C. M. A., Wright, M. J., Luciano, M., Martin, N. G., de Geus, E. J., van Beijsterveldt, C. E., Bartels, M., Posthuma, D., Boomsma, D. I., Davis, O. S., Kovas, Y., Corley, R. P., Defries, J. C., Hewitt, J. K., Olson, R. K., Rhea, S. A., Wadsworth, S. J., Iacono, W. G., McGue, M., … Plomin, R. (2010). The heritability of general cognitive ability increases linearly from childhood to young adulthood. *Molecular Psychiatry, 15*, 1112–1120.

Haworth, C. M. A., Wright, M. J., Martin, N. W., Martin, N. G., Boomsma, D. I., Bartels, M., Posthuma, D., Davis, O. S., Brant, A. M., Corley, R. P., Hewitt, J. K., Iacono, W. G., McGue, M., Thompson, L. A., Hart, S. A., Petrill, S. A., Lubinski, D., & Plomin, R. (2009). A twin study of the genetics of high cognitive ability selected from 11,000 twin pairs in sex studies from four countries. *Behavior Genetics, 39*, 359–370.

Haxby, J. V. (2001, July 7). Quoted by B. Bower in, Faces of perception. *Science News*, pp. 10–12. See also J. V. Haxby, M. I. Gobbini, M. L. Furey, A. Ishai, J. L. Schouten, & P. Pietrini (2001), Distributed and overlapping representations of faces and objects in ventral temporal cortex. *Science, 293*, 2425–2430.

Hayasaki, E. (2014, July). Want to know when you'll die? 'Big data' could tell you. *Newsweek*. https://www.newsweek.com/2014/08/01/want-know-when-youll-die-big-data-could-tell-you-260883.html

Hayashi, Y., Kashiwagi, M., Yasuda, K., Ando, R., Kanuka, M., Sakai, K., & Itohara, S. (2015). Cells of a common developmental origin regulate REM/non-REM sleep and wakefulness in mice. *Science, 350*, 957–961.

Hayes, S. C., Strosahl, K. D., & Wilson, K. G. (2009). *Acceptance and commitment therapy.* American Psychological Association.

Haynes, A., Kersbergen, I., Sutin, A., Daly, M., & Robinson, E. (2019). Does perceived overweight increase risk of depressive symptoms and suicidality beyond objective weight status? A systematic review and meta-analysis. *Clinical Psychology Review, 73*. doi: 10.1016/j.cpr.2019.101753

Hays, C., & Carver, L. J. (2014). Follow the liar: The effects of adult lies on children's honesty. *Developmental Science, 17*, 977–983.

Hazan, C., & Shaver, P. R. (1994). Attachment as an organizational framework for research on close relationships. *Psychological Inquiry, 5*, 1–22.

Hazelrigg, M. D., Cooper, H. M., & Borduin, C. M. (1987). Evaluating the effectiveness of family therapies: An integrative review and analysis. *Psychological Bulletin, 101*, 428–442.

HBVA (Honour Based Violence Awareness Network). (2018). *Honour killings by region, South and Central Asia.* http://hbv-awareness.com/regions/

He, A. X., Huang, S., Waxman, S., & Arunachalam, S. (2020). Two-year-olds consolidate verb meanings during a nap. *Cognition, 198*. https://www.ncbi.nlm.nih.gov/pmc/articles/PMC9034726/

He, D., Workman, C. I., He, X., & Chatterjee, A. (2022). What is good is beautiful (and what isn't, isn't): How moral character affects perceived facial attractiveness [PDF file]. *Psychology of Aesthetics, Creativity, and the Arts*. https://neuroaesthetics.med.upenn.edu/assets/user-content/documents/publications/he-et-al.,-2022-what-is-good-is-beautiful-(and-what-isn't,-isn't).pdf

He, Z., & Jin, Y. (2016). Intrinsic control of axon regeneration. *Neuron, 90*, 437–451.

Headey, B., Muffels, R., & Wagner, G. G. (2010). Long-running German panel survey shows that personal and economic choices, not just genes, matter for happiness. *PNAS, 107*, 17922–17926.

Healy, A. F., Jones, M., Lalchandani, L. A., & Tack, L. A. (2017). Timing of quizzes during learning: Effects on motivation and retention. *Journal of Experimental Psychology: Applied, 23*, 128–137.

Heathcote, R. J., Darden, S. K., Troscianko, J., Lawson, M. R., Brown, A. M., Laker, P. R., Naisbett-Jones, L. C., MacGregor, H. E. A., Ramnarine, I., & Croft, D. P. (2018). Dynamic eye colour as an honest signal of aggression. *Current Biology, 28,* R652–R653.

Hebb, D. O. (1949). *The organization of behavior: A neuropsychological theory.* Psychology Press.

Heberle, A. E., & Carter, A. S. (2015). Cognitive aspects of young children's experience of economic disadvantage. *Psychological Bulletin, 141,* 723–746.

Heckert, J. (2012, November 15). The hazards of growing up painlessly. *The New York Times.* https://www.nytimes.com/2012/11/18/magazine/ashlyn-blocker-feels-no-pain.html

Heckman, J. J., & Karapakula, G. (2019). *Intergenerational and intragenerational externalities of the Perry Preschool Project* (No. w25889). National Bureau of Economic Research.

Hehman, E., Flake, J. K., & Calanchini, J. (2018). Disproportionate use of lethal force in policing is associated with regional racial biases of residents. *Social Psychological Personality Science, 9*(4), 393–401.

Heider, F. (1958). *The psychology of interpersonal relations.* Wiley.

Heilmann, K., & Kahn, M. E. (2019, June) *The urban crime and heat gradient in high and low poverty areas.* NBER Working Paper No. 25961. https://www.nber.org/papers/w25961

Heiman, J. R. (1975, April). The physiology of erotica: Women's sexual arousal. *Psychology Today,* pp. 90–94.

Hein, G., Morishima, Y., Leiberg, S., Sul, S., & Fehr, E. (2016). The brain's functional network architecture reveals human motives. *Science, 351,* 1074–1078.

Heine, S. J., Proulx, T., & Vohs, K. D. (2006). Meaning maintenance model: On the coherence of human motivations. *Personality and Social Psychology Review, 10,* 88–110.

Hejmadi, A., Davidson, R. J., & Rozin, P. (2000). Exploring Hindu Indian emotion expressions: Evidence for accurate recognition by Americans and Indians. *Psychological Science, 11,* 183–187.

Heller, S. B. (2014). Summer jobs reduce violence among disadvantaged youth. *Science, 346,* 1219–1222.

Heller, W. (1990, May/June). Of one mind: Second thoughts about the brain's dual nature. *The Sciences,* pp. 38–44.

Helliwell, J., Layard, R., & Sachs, J. (Eds.) (2013). *World happiness report.* The Earth Institute, Columbia University.

Helliwell, J. F., & Wang, S. (2015). How was the weekend? How the social context underlies weekend effects in happiness and other emotions for US workers. *PLOS ONE, 10.* https://journals.plos.org/plosone/article?id=10.1371/journal.pone.0145123

Helmreich, W. B. (1992). *Against all odds: Holocaust survivors and the successful lives they made in America.* Simon & Schuster.

Helmreich, W. B. (1994). Personal correspondence. Department of Sociology, City University of New York.

Helms, J. E., Jernigan, M., & Mascher, J. (2005). The meaning of race in psychology and how to change it: A methodological perspective. *American Psychologist, 60,* 27–36.

Helsen, K., Goubert, L., Peters, M. L., & Vlaeyen, J. W. S. (2011). Observational learning and pain-related fear: An experimental study with colored cold pressor tasks. *Journal of Pain, 12,* 1230–1239.

Helweg-Larsen, M. (1999). (The lack of) optimistic biases in response to the 1994 Northridge earthquake: The role of personal experience. *Basic and Applied Social Psychology, 21,* 119–129.

Hembree, R. (1988). Correlates, causes, effects, and treatment of test anxiety. *Review of Educational Research, 58,* 47–77.

Henderlong, J., & Lepper, M. R. (2002). The effects of praise on children's intrinsic motivation: A review and synthesis. *Psychological Bulletin, 128,* 774–795.

Henderson, J. M. (2007). Regarding scenes. *Current Directions in Psychological Science, 16,* 219–222.

Henig, R. M. (2010, August 18). What is it about 20-somethings? *The New York Times Magazine.* https://www.nytimes.com/2010/08/22/magazine/22Adulthood-t.html

Henley, N. M. (1989). Molehill or mountain? What we know and don't know about sex bias in language. In M. Crawford & M. Gentry (Eds.), *Gender and thought: Psychological perspectives* (pp. 59–78). Springer-Verlag.

Hennenlotter, A., Dresel, C., Castrop, F., Ceballos Baumann, A., Wohschlager, A., & Haslinger, B. (2008). The link between facial feedback and neural activity within central circuitries of emotion: New insights from botulinum toxin-induced denervation of frown muscles. *Cerebral Cortex, 19,* 537–542.

Hennessey, B. A., & Amabile, T. M. (2010). Creativity. *Annual Review of Psychology, 61,* 569–598.

Henrich, J. (2020). *The WEIRDest people in the world: How the West became psychologically peculiar and particularly prosperous.* Farrar, Straus and Giroux.

Henry, J. D., MacLeod, M. S., Phillips, L. H., & Crawford, J. R. (2004). A meta-analytic review of prospective memory and aging. *Psychology and Aging, 19,* 27–39.

Hensley, C., Browne, J. A., & Trentham, C. E. (2018). Exploring the social and emotional context of childhood animal cruelty and its potential link to adult human violence. *Psychology, Crime & Law, 24,* 489–499.

Hepper, P. (2005). Unravelling our beginnings. *The Psychologist, 18,* 474–477.

Herbenick, D., Reece, M., Schick, V., & Sanders, S. A. (2014). Erect penile length and circumference dimensions of 1,661 sexually active men in the United States. *Journal of Sexual Medicine, 11,* 93–101.

Herculano-Houzel, S. (2020). Birds do have a brain cortex—and think. *Science, 369,* 1567–1568.

Herman, C. P., & Polivy, J. (1980). Restrained eating. In A. J. Stunkard (Ed.), *Obesity.* Saunders.

Herman, C. P., Polivy, J., Pliner, P., & Vartanian, L. R. (2015). Mechanisms underlying the portion-size effect. *Physiology & Behavior, 144,* 129–136.

Herman, J. L., Flores, A. R., & O'Neill, K. K. (2022). *How many adults and youth identify as transgender in the United States?* UCLA Williams Institute. https://williamsinstitute.law.ucla.edu/publications/trans-adults-united-states/

Herman-Giddens, M. E. (2013). The enigmatic pursuit of puberty in girls. *Pediatrics, 132,* 1125–1126.

Herman-Giddens, M. E., Steffes, J., Harris, D., Slora, E., Hussey, M., Dowshen, S. A., Wasserman, R., Serwint, J. F., Smitherman, L., & Reiter, E. O. (2012). Secondary sexual characteristics in boys: Data from the pediatric research in office settings network. *Pediatrics, 130,* 1058–1068.

Hernandez, A. E., & Li, P. (2007). Age of acquisition: Its neural and computational mechanisms. *Psychological Bulletin, 133,* 638–650.

Hernandez, R., Kershaw, K. N., Siddique, J., Boehm, J. K., Kubzansky, L. D., Diez-Roux, A., Ning, H., & Lloyd-Jones, D. M. (2015). Optimism and cardiovascular health: Multi-Ethnic Study of Atherosclerosis (MESA). *Health Behavior and Policy Review, 2,* 62–73.

Herrero, N., Gadea, M., Rodríguez-Alarcón, G., Espert, R., & Salvador, A. (2010). What happens when we get angry? Hormonal, cardiovascular and asymmetrical brain responses. *Hormones and Behavior, 57,* 276–283.

Herrman, H., Patel, V., Kieling, C., Berk, M., Buchweitz, C., Cuijpers, P., Furukawa, T. A., Kessler, R. C., Kohrt, B. A., Maj, M., McGorry, P., Reynolds, C. F., III, Weissman, M. M., Chibanda, D., Dowrick, C., Howard, L. M., Hoven, C. W., Knapp, M., Mayberg, H. S., … Wolpert, M. (2022). Time for united action on depression: A Lancet-World Psychiatric Association commission. *The Lancet,* 399(10328), 957–1022.

Herrmann, E., Call, J., Hernández-Lloreda, M. V., Hare, B., & Tomasello, M. (2007). Humans have evolved specialized skills of social cognition: The cultural intelligence hypothesis. *Science, 317,* 1360–1365.

Herrnstein, R. J., & Loveland, D. H. (1964). Complex visual concept in the pigeon. *Science, 146,* 549–551.

Hershenson, M. (1989). *The moon illusion.* Erlbaum.

Hertenstein, M. J., Hansel, C., Butts, S., & Hile, S. (2009). Smile intensity in photographs predicts divorce later in life. *Motivation and Emotion, 33,* 99–105.

Hertenstein, M. J., Keltner, D., App, B., Bulleit, B., & Jaskolka, A. (2006). Touch communicates distinct emotions. *Emotion, 6,* 528–533.

Herz, R. (2007). *The scent of desire: Discovering our enigmatic sense of smell.* Morrow/HarperCollins.

Herz, R. (2012, January 28). You eat that? *The Wall Street Journal.* https://www.wsj.com/articles/SB10001424052970204661604577186843056231170

Herz, R. S. (2001, October). Ah, sweet skunk! Why we like or dislike what we smell. *Cerebrum,* pp. 31–47.

Herz, R. S., Beland, S. L., & Hellerstein, M. (2004). Changing odor hedonic perception through emotional associations in humans. *International Journal of Comparative Psychology, 17,* 315–339.

Hess, E. H. (1956, July). Space perception in the chick. *Scientific American,* pp. 71–80.

Hess, M. J., & Hough, S. (2012). Impact of spinal cord injury on sexuality: Broad-based clinical practice intervention and practical application. *Journal of Spinal Cord Medicine, 35*, 211–218.

Hess, U., & Fischer, A. H. (Eds.). (2016). *Emotional mimicry in social context*. Cambridge University Press.

Hess, U., & Thibault, P. (2009). Darwin and emotion expression. *American Psychologist, 64*, 120–128.

Heu, L. C., van Zomeren, M., & Hansen, N. (2019). Lonely alone or lonely together? A cultural-psychological examination of individualism–collectivism and loneliness in five European countries. *Personality and Social Psychology Bulletin, 45*, 780–793.

Hewett, R., & Conway, N. (2015). The undermining effect revisited: The salience of everyday verbal rewards and self-determined motivation. *Journal of Organizational Behavior, 37*, 436–455.

Hewlett, B. S. (1991). Demography and childcare in preindustrial societies. *Journal of Anthropological Research, 47*, 1–37.

HHS (Department of Health and Human Services). (2020). *Smoking cessation. A report of the Surgeon General*. Office on Smoking and Health. https://www.cdc.gov/tobacco/data_statistics/sgr/2020-smoking-cessation/index.html

HHS. (2020). *Young adult coverage*. https://bit.ly/2G6HRzH

Hickok, G., Bellugi, U., & Klima, E. S. (2001, June). Sign language in the brain. *Scientific American*, pp. 58–65.

Hilgard, E. R. (1986). *Divided consciousness: Multiple controls in human thought and action*. Wiley.

Hilgard, E. R. (1992). Dissociation and theories of hypnosis. In E. Fromm & M. R. Nash (Eds.), *Contemporary hypnosis research*. Guilford.

Hilker, R., Helenius, D., Fagerlund, B., Skytthe, A., Christensen, K., Werge, T. M., Nordentoft, N., & Glenthøj, B. (2018). Heritability of schizophrenia and schizophrenia spectrum based on the nationwide Danish twin register. *Biological Psychiatry, 83*, 492–498.

Hill, C. E., & Nakayama, E. Y. (2000). Client-centered therapy: Where has it been and where is it going? A comment on Hathaway. *Journal of Clinical Psychology, 56*, 961–875.

Hill, D. B. (2019). Andocentrism and the great man narrative in psychology textbooks. *Journal of Research in Gender Studies, 9*, 9–37.

Hills, P. J., Marquardt, Z., Young, I., & Goodenough, I. (2017). Explaining sad people's memory advantage for faces. *Frontiers in Psychology, 8*, 207.

Hills, T. T. (2019). The dark side of information proliferation. *Perspectives on Psychological Science, 14*, 323–330.

Hindley, G., Beck, K., Borgan, F., Ginestet, C. E., McCutcheon, R., Kleinloog, D., Ganesh, S., Radhakrishnan, R., D'Souza, D. C., & Howes, O. D. (2020). Psychiatric symptoms caused by cannabis constituents: A systematic review and meta-analysis. *Lancet Psychiatry, 7*, 344–353.

Hinds, J., & Joinson, A. (2019). Human and computer personality prediction from digital footprints. *Current Directions in Psychological Science, 28*, 204–211.

Hines, M. (2004). *Brain gender*. Oxford University Press.

Hingson, R. W., Heeren, T., & Winter, M. R. (2006). Age at drinking onset and alcohol dependence. *Archives of Pediatrics & Adolescent Medicine, 160*, 739–746.

Hinnant, J. B., McConnell, L. M., Yanes, J. A., McCormick, M. J., Murphy, J. E., Erath, S. A., & Robinson, J. L. (2019). Rewarding safe choices in peer contexts: Adolescent brain activity during decision making. *Biological Psychology, 142*, 45–53.

Hinshaw, S. P. (2009). *The mark of shame: Stigma of mental illness and an agenda for change*. Oxford University Press.

Hintzman, D. L. (1978). *The psychology of learning and memory*. Freeman.

Hirsh-Pasek, K., Adamson, L. B., Bakeman, R., Owen, M. T., Golinkoff, R. M., Pace, A., Yust, P. K., & Suma, K. (2015). The contribution of early communication quality to low-income children's language success. *Psychological Science, 26*, 1071–1083.

Hirst, W., & Echterhoff, G. (2012). Remembering in conversations: The social sharing and reshaping of memories. *Annual Review of Psychology, 63*, 55–79.

Hirst, W., & Phelps, E. A. (2016). Flashbulb memories. *Current Directions in Psychological Science, 25*, 36–41.

Hirst, W., Phelps, E. A., Meksin, R., Vaidya, C. J., Johnson, M. K., Mitchell, K. J., Buckner, R. L., Budson, A. E., Gabrieli, J. D., Lustig, C., Mather, M., Ochsner, K. N., Schacter, D., Simons, J. S., Lyle, K. B., Cuc, A. F., & Olsson, A. (2015). A ten-year follow-up of a study of memory for the attack of September 11, 2001: Flashbulb memories and memories for flashbulb events. *Journal of Experimental Psychology: General, 144*, 604.

Hixenbaugh, M., & Siemaszko, C. (2022). *Abbott calls Texas school shooting a mental health issue but cut state spending for it*. NBC News. https://www.nbcnews.com/news/us-news/abbott-calls-texas-school-shooting-mental-health-issue-cut-state-spend-rcna30557

Hjelmborg, J. V. B., Fagnani, C., Silventoinen, K., McGue, M., Korkeila, M., Christensen, K., Rissanen, A., & Kaprio, J. (2008). Genetic influences on growth traits of BMI: A longitudinal study of adult twins. *Obesity, 16*, 847–852.

Hjelmgaard, K. (2019, March 27). Head transplant doctors Xiaoping Ren and Sergio Canavero claim spinal cord progress. *USA Today*. https://conspiracy411.info/head-transplant-doctors-xiaoping-ren-and-sergio-canavero-claim-spinal-cord-progress/

HMHL (Harvard Mental Health Letter). (2002, January). *Disaster and trauma*. pp. 1–5.

Ho, T., Chong, J. K., & Xia, X. (2017). Yellow taxis have fewer accidents than blue taxis because yellow is more visible than blue. *PNAS, 114*, 3074–3078.

Hobaiter, C., Poisot, T., Zuberbühler, K., Hoppitt, W., & Gruber, T. (2014). Social network analysis shows direct evidence for social transmission of tool use in wild chimpanzees. *PLOS Biology, 12*. https://journals.plos.org/plosbiology/article?id=10.1371/journal.pbio.1001960

Hobbs, W. R., Burke, M., Christakis, N. A., & Fowler, J. H. (2016). Online social integration is associated with reduced mortality risk. *PNAS, 113*, 12980–12984.

Hobson, J. A. (2003). *Dreaming: An introduction to the science of sleep*. Oxford.

Hochberg, L. R., Serruya, M. D., Friehs, G. M., Mukand, J. A., Saleh, M., Caplan, A. H., Branner, A., Chen, D., Penn, R. D., & Donoghue, J. P. (2006). Neuronal ensemble control of prosthetic devices by a human with tetraplegia. *Nature, 442*, 164–171.

Hockenberry, J. M., Joski, P., Yarbrough, C., & Druss, B. G. (2019). Trends in treatment and spending for patients receiving outpatient treatment of depression in the United States, 1998–2015. *JAMA Psychiatry, 76*, 810–817.

Hodgkinson, S., Godoy, L., Beers, L. S., & Lewin, A. (2017). Improving mental health access for low-income children and families in the primary care setting. *Pediatrics, 139*(1). https://www.ncbi.nlm.nih.gov/pmc/articles/PMC5192088/

Hoebel, B. G., & Teitelbaum, P. (1966). Weight regulation in normal and hypothalamic hyperphagic rats. *Journal of Comparative and Physiological Psychology, 61*(2), 189–193.

Hoeft, F., Watson, C. L., Kesler, S. R., Bettinger, K. E., & Reiss, A. L. (2008). Gender differences in the mesocorticolimbic system during computer game-play. *Journal of Psychiatric Research, 42*, 253–258.

Hofer, M. K., Whillans, A. V., & Chen, F. S. (2018). Olfactory cues from romantic partners and strangers influence women's responses to stress. *Journal of Personality and Social Psychology, 114*, 1–9.

Hoff, K. A., Briley, D. A., Wee, C. J. M., & Rounds, J. (2018). Normative changes in interests from adolescence to adulthood: A meta-analysis of longitudinal studies. *Psychological Bulletin, 144*, 426–451.

Hoff, K. A., Song, Q. C., Einarsdóttir, S., Briley, D. A., & Rounds, J. (2020). Developmental structure of personality and interests: A four-wave, 8-year longitudinal study. *Journal of Personality and Social Psychology, 118*(5), 1044–1064.

Hoffman, B. M., Babyak, M. A., Craighead, W. E., Sherwood, A., Doraiswamy, P. M., Coons, M. J., & Blumenthal, J. A. (2011). Exercise and pharmacotherapy in patients with major depression: One-year follow-up of the SMILE study. *Psychosomatic Medicine, 73*, 127–133.

Hoffman, D. D. (1998). *Visual intelligence: How we create what we see*. Norton.

Hoffman, H. (2012). Considering the role of conditioning in sexual orientation. *Archives of Sexual Behavior, 41*, 63–71.

Hoffman, H. G. (2004, August). Virtual-reality therapy. *Scientific American*, pp. 58–65.

Hoffman, J. (2019, August 26). Johnson & Johnson ordered to pay $572 million in landmark opioid trial. *The New York Times*. https://www.nytimes.com/2019/08/26/health/oklahoma-opioids-johnson-and-johnson.html

Hoffman, Y. S. G., Shrira, A., Cohen-Fridel, S., Grossman, E. S., & Bodner, E. (2016). The effect of exposure to missile attacks on posttraumatic stress disorder symptoms as a function of perceived media control and locus of control. *Psychiatry Research, 244*, 51–56.

Hoffmann, H. (2017). Situating human sexual conditioning. *Archives of Sexual Behavior, 46*, 2213–2229.

Hogan, R. (1998). Reinventing personality. *Journal of Social and Clinical Psychology, 17*, 1–10.

Høglend, P., & Hagtvet, K. (2019). Change mechanisms in psychotherapy: Both improved insight and improved affective awareness are necessary. *Journal of Consulting and Clinical Psychology, 87*, 332–344.

Hohmann, G. W. (1966). Some effects of spinal cord lesions on experienced emotional feelings. *Psychophysiology, 3*, 143–156.

Hokanson, J. E., & Edelman, R. (1966). Effects of three social responses on vascular processes. *Journal of Personality and Social Psychology, 3*, 442–447.

Holahan, C. K., & Sears, R. R. (1995). *The gifted group in later maturity.* Stanford University Press.

Holden, C. (2008). Poles apart. *Science, 321*, 193–195.

Holden, G. W., & Miller, P. C. (1999). Enduring and different: A meta-analysis of the similarity in parents' child rearing. *Psychological Bulletin, 125*, 223–254.

Holder, N., Shiner, B., Li, Y., Madden, E., Neylan, T. C., Seal, K. H., Lujan, C., Patterson, O. V., DuVall, S. L., & Maguen, S. (2020). Determining the median effective dose of prolonged exposure therapy for veterans with posttraumatic stress disorder. *Behaviour Research and Therapy*, 135. doi: 10.1016/j.brat.2020.103756

Holland, D., Chang, L., Ernst, T. M., Curran, M., Buchthal, S. D., Alicata, D., Skranes, J., Johansen, H., Hernandez, A., Yamakawa, R., Kuperman, J. M., & Dale, A. M. (2014). Structural growth trajectories and rates of change in the first 3 months of infant brain development. *JAMA Neurology, 71*, 1266–1274.

Holland, J. L. (1996). Exploring careers with a typology: What we have learned and some new directions. *American Psychologist, 51*, 397–406.

Holland, K. J., Gustafson, A. M., Cortina, L. M., & Cipriano, A. E. (2020). Supporting survivors: The roles of rape myths and feminism in university resident assistants' response to sexual assault disclosure scenarios. *Sex Roles, 82*, 206–218.

Holle, H., Warne, K., Seth, A. K., Critchley, H. D., & Ward, J. (2012). Neural basis of contagious itch and why some people are more prone to it. *PNAS, 109*, 19816–19821.

Holliday, R. E., & Albon, A. J. (2004). Minimizing misinformation effects in young children with cognitive interview mnemonics. *Applied Cognitive Psychology, 18*, 263–281.

Hollis, K. L. (1997). Contemporary research on Pavlovian conditioning: A "new" functional analysis. *American Psychologist, 52*, 956–965.

Hollon, S. D. (2020). Is cognitive therapy enduring or antidepressant medications iatrogenic? Depression as an evolved adaptation. *American Psychologist, 75*, 1207–1218.

Holmes, E. A., Ghaderi, A., Harmer, C. J., Ramchandani, P. G., Cuijpers, P., Morrison, A. P., Roiser, J. P., Bockting, C. L., O'Connor, R. C., Shafran, R., Moulds, M. L., & Craske, M. G. (2018). The *Lancet Psychiatry* Commission on psychological treatments research in tomorrow's science. *Lancet Psychiatry, 5*, 237–286.

Holt, L. (2002, August). Reported in "From mouth to mind," in *Scientific American*, p. 26, and in personal correspondence, July 18, 2002.

Holt-Lunstad, J. (2021). The major health implications of social connection. *Current Directions in Psychological Science, 30*(3), 251–259.

Holt-Lunstad, J., Robles, T. F., & Sbarra, D. A. (2017). Advancing social connection as a public health priority in the United States. *American Psychologist, 72*, 517–530.

Holt-Lunstad, J., Smith, T. B., Baker, M., Harris, T., & Stephenson, D. (2015). Loneliness and social isolation as risk factors for mortality: A meta-analytic review. *Perspectives on Psychological Science, 10*, 227–237.

Holt-Lunstad, J., Smith, T. B., & Layton, J. B. (2010). Social relationships and mortality risk: A meta-analytic review. *PLoS Medicine, 7*. https://journals.plos.org/plosmedicine/article?id=10.1371/journal.pmed.1000316

Holwerda, T. J., Deeg, D. J., Beekman, A. T., van Tilburg, T. G., Stek, M. L., Jonker, C., & Schoevers, R. A. (2014). Feelings of loneliness, but not social isolation, predict dementia onset: Results from the Amsterdam Study of the Elderly (AMSTEL). *Journal of Neurology, Neurosurgery, and Psychiatry, 85*, 135–142.

Home Office. (2019). *Hate crime, England and Wales, 2018 to 2019*. https://www.gov.uk/government/statistics/hate-crime-england-and-wales-2018-to-2019

Homer, B. D., Solomon, T. M., Moeller, R. W., Mascia, A., DeRaleau, L., & Halkitis, P. N. (2008). Methamphetamine abuse and impairment of social functioning: A review of the underlying neurophysiological causes and behavioral implications. *Psychological Bulletin, 134*, 301–310.

Hoogman, M., Muetzel, R., Guimaraes, J. P., Shumskaya, E., Mennes, M., Zwiers, M. P., Jahanshad, N., Sudre, G., Wolfers, T., Earl, E. A., Soliva Vila, J. C., Vives-Gilabert, Y., Khadka, S., Novotny, S. E., Hartman, C., Heslenfeld, D. J., Schweren, L. J. S., Ambrosino, S., Oranje, B., ... Franke, B. (2019). Brain imaging of the cortex in ADHD: A coordinated analysis of large-scale clinical and population-based samples. *American Journal of Psychiatry, 176*, 531–542.

Hoojimans, C. R., Hlavica, M., Schuler, F. A. F., Good, N., Good, A., Baumgartner, L., Galeno, G., Schneider, M. P., Jung, T., de Vries, R., & Ineichen, B. V. (2019). Remyelination promoting therapies in multiple sclerosis animal models: A systematic review and meta-analysis. *Scientific Reports, 9*. https://www.nature.com/articles/s41598-018-35734-4

Hooker, S. A., & Masters, K. S. (2018). Daily meaning salience and physical activity in previously inactive exercise initiates. *Health Psychology, 37*, 344–354.

Hooper, J., & Teresi, D. (1986). *The three-pound universe.* Macmillan.

Hopkins, E. D., & Cantalupo, C. (2008). Theoretical speculations on the evolutionary origins of hemispheric specialization. *Current Directions in Psychological Science, 17*, 233–237.

Hopper, L. M., Lambeth, S. P., Schapiro, S. J., & Whiten, A. (2008). Observational learning in chimpanzees and children studied through "ghost" conditions. *Proceedings of the Royal Society, 275*, 835–840.

Hörder, H., Johansson, L., Guo, X., Grimby, G., Kern, S., Östling, S., & Skoog, I. (2018). Midlife cardiovascular fitness and dementia: A 44-year longitudinal population study in women. *Neurology, 90*, e1298–e1305.

Horne, K. S., Filmer, H., Nott, Z. E., Hawi, Z., Pugsley, K., Mattingley, J. B., & Dux, P. E. (2021). Evidence against benefits from cognitive training and transcranial direct current stimulation in healthy older adults. *Nature Human Behaviour, 5*, 146–158.

Horne, Z., Powell, D., Hummel, J. E., & Holyoak, K. J. (2015). Countering antivaccination attitudes. *PNAS, 112*, 10321–10324.

Horowitz, J. M. (2019, April 9). *How Americans see the state of race relations.* Pew Research Center. https://www.pewsocialtrends.org/2019/04/09/how-americans-see-the-state-of-race-relations/

Horowitz, J. M., & Fetterolf, J. (2020, April 30). *Worldwide optimism about future of gender equality, even as many see advantages for men.* Pew Research Center. https://www.pewresearch.org/global/2020/04/30/worldwide-optimism-about-future-of-gender-equality-even-as-many-see-advantages-for-men/

Horowitz, M., & Wilcock, M. (2022). Newer generation antidepressants and withdrawal effects: Reconsidering the role of anti-depressants and helping patients to stop. *Drug and Therapeutics Bulletin, 60*, 7–12.

Horowitz, S. S. (2012, November 9). The science and art of listening. *The New York Times*. https://www.nytimes.com/2012/11/11/opinion/sunday/why-listening-is-so-much-more-than-hearing.html

Horsthemke, B. (2018). A critical view on transgenerational epigenetic inheritance in humans. *Nature Communications, 9*. https://www.nature.com/articles/s41467-018-05445-5

Horwood, L. J., & Fergusson, D. M. (1998). Breastfeeding and later cognitive and academic outcomes. *Pediatrics, 101*(1), e9.

Hostetter, A. B. (2011). When do gestures communicate? A meta-analysis. *Psychological Bulletin, 137*, 297–315.

Hou, W.-H., Chiang, P.-T., Hsu, T.-Y., Chiu, S.-Y., & Yen, Y.-C. (2010). Treatment effects of massage therapy in depressed people: A meta-analysis. *Journal of Clinical Psychiatry, 71*, 894–901.

House, R., Jarvis, N., & Burdsey, D. (2022). Representation matters: Progressing research in plurisexuality and bisexuality in sport. *Journal of Homosexuality, 69*(8), 1301–1321.

House, R., Javidan, M., & Dorfman, P. (2001). Project GLOBE: An introduction. *Applied Psychology: An International Review, 50*, 489–505.

Houser-Marko, L., & Sheldon, K. M. (2008). Eyes on the prize or nose to the grindstone? The effects of level of goal evaluation on mood and motivation. *Personality and Social Psychology Bulletin, 34*, 1556–1569.

Houts, A. C., Berman, J. S., & Abramson, H. (1994). Effectiveness of psychological and pharmacological treatments for nocturnal enuresis. *Journal of Consulting and Clinical Psychology, 62*, 737–745.

Hovland, C. I., & Sears, R. R. (1938). Experiments on motor conflict. I. Types of conflict and their modes of resolution. *Journal of Experimental Psychology, 23*, 477–493.

Howansky, K., Wilton, L. S., Young, D. M., Abrams, S., & Clapham, R. (2021). (Trans) gender stereotypes and the self: Content and consequences of gender identity stereotypes. *Self and Identity, 20*(4), 478–495.

Howard, D. M., Adams, M. J., Clarke, T.-K., Hafferty, J. D., Gibson, J., Shirali, M., Coleman, J. R. I., Hagenaars, S. P., Ward, J., Wigmore, E. M., Alloza, C., Shen, X., Barbu, M. C., Xu, E. Y., Whalley, H. C., Marioni, R. E., Porteous, D. J., Davies, G., Deary, I. J., … McIntosh, A. M. (2019). Genome-wide meta-analysis of depression identifies 102 independent variants and highlights the importance of the prefrontal brain regions. *Nature Neuroscience, 22*, 343–352.

Howard, J. L., Gagné, M., & Bureau, J. S. (2017). Testing a continuum structure of self-determined motivation: A meta-analysis. *Psychological Bulletin, 143*, 1346–1377.

Howe, L. C., Hardebeck, E. J., & Eberhardt, J. L. (2022). White patients' physical responses to healthcare treatments are influenced by provider race and gender. *PNAS, 119*(27). https://www.pnas.org/doi/10.1073/pnas.2007717119

Hsee, C. K., Yang, A. X., & Wang, L. (2010). Idleness aversion and the need for justifiable busyness. *Psychological Science, 21*, 926–930.

Hsiang, S. M., Burke, M., & Miguel, E. (2013). Quantifying the influence of climate on human conflict. *Science, 341*, 1212.

Hsiao, J. H., An, J., Zheng, Y., & Chan, A. B. (2021). Do portrait artists have enhanced face processing abilities? Evidence from hidden Markov modeling of eye movements. *Cognition, 211*. https://www.sciencedirect.com/science/article/pii/S0010027721000354

Hsin, A., & Xie, Y. (2014). Explaining Asian Americans' academic advantage over Whites. *PNAS, 111*, 8416–8421.

Hsu, N., Badura, K. L., Newman, D. A., & Speach, M. E. P. (2021). Gender, "masculinity," and "femininity": A meta-analytic review of gender differences in agency and communion. *Psychological Bulletin, 147*, 987–1011.

Hu, G., Hamovit, N., Croft, K., & Niemeier, D. (2022). Assessing inequities underlying racial disparities of COVID-19 mortality in Louisiana parishes. *PNAS, 119*(27). https://www.pnas.org/doi/10.1073/pnas.2123533119

Huang, J., Chaloupka, F. J., & Fong, G. T. (2013). Cigarette graphic warning labels and smoking prevalence in Canada: A critical examination and reformulation of the FDA regulatory impact analysis. *Tobacco Control, 23*, i7–i12.

Huang, L., Zhen, O., Wang, B., & Zhang, Z. (2022). Individualism and the fight against COVID-19. *Humanities and Social Sciences Communications, 9*. https://www.nature.com/articles/s41599-022-01124-5

Huang, Y., Wang, Y., Wang, H., Liu, Z., Yu, X., Yan, J., Yu, Y., Kou, C., Xu, X., Lu, J., Wang, Z., He, S., Xu, Y., He, Y., Li, T., Guo, W., Tian, H., Xu, G., Xu, X., … Wu, Y. (2019). Prevalence of mental disorders in China: A cross-sectional epidemiological study. *Lancet Psychiatry, 6*, 211–224.

Huart, J., Corneille, O., & Becquart, E. (2005). Face-based categorization, context-based categorization, and distortions in the recollection of gender ambiguous faces. *Journal of Experimental Social Psychology, 41*, 598–608.

Hubbard, E. M., Arman, A. C., Ramachandran, V. S., & Boynton, G. M. (2005). Individual differences among grapheme-color synesthetes: Brain-behavior correlations. *Neuron, 45*, 975–985.

Hubel, D. H. (1979, September). The brain. *Scientific American*, pp. 45–53.

Hubel, D. H., & Wiesel, T. N. (1963). Receptive fields of cells in striate cortex of very young, visually inexperienced kittens. *Journal of Neurophysiology, 26*, 994–1002.

Hubel, D. H., & Wiesel, T. N. (1979, September). Brain mechanisms of vision. *Scientific American*, pp. 150–162.

Huber, E., Webster, J. M., Brewer, A. A., MacLeod, D. I. A., Wandell, B. A., Boynton, G. M., Wade, A. R., & Fine, I. (2015). A lack of experience-dependent plasticity after more than a decade of recovered sight. *Psychological Science, 26*, 393–401.

Hucker, S. J., & Bain, J. (1990). Androgenic hormones and sexual assault. In W. L. Marshall, D. R. Laws, & H. E. Barbaree (Eds.), *Handbook of sexual assault: Issues, theories, and treatment of the offender* (pp. 209–229). Plenum Press.

Huckins, L. M. (2017). Linking cannabis use to depression and suicidal thoughts and behaviours. *Lancet Psychiatry, 4*, 654–656.

Huckins, L. M., Dobbyn, A., Ruderfer, D. M., Hoffman, Wang, W., Pardi⊠as, A. F., Rajagopal, V. M., Als, T. D., Nguyen, H. T., Girdhar, K., Boocock, J., Roussos, P., Fromer, M., Kramer, R., Domenici, E., Gamazon, E. R., Purcell, S., CommonMind Consortium, Schizophrenia Working Group of the Psychiatric Genomis Consortium, iPSYCH-GEMS Schizophrenia Working Group, … Stahl, E. A. (2019). Gene expression imputation across multiple brain regions provides insights into schizophrenia risk. *Nature Genetics, 51*, 659–674.

Hudson, C. C., Hall, L., & Harkness, K. L. (2019). Prevalence of depressive disorders in individuals with autism spectrum disorder: A meta-analysis. *Journal of Abnormal Child Psychology, 47*, 165–175.

Hudson, N. W., & Roberts, B. W. (2014). Goals to change personality traits: Concurrent links between personality traits, daily behavior, and goals to change oneself. *Journal of Research in Personality, 53*, 68–83.

Hufer, A., Kornadt, A. E., Kandler, C., & Riemann, R. (2020). Genetic and environmental variation in political orientation in adolescence and early adulthood: A Nuclear Twin Family analysis. *Journal of Personality and Social Psychology, 118*(4), 762–776.

Hugenberg, K., & Bodenhausen, G. V. (2003). Facing prejudice: Implicit prejudice and the perception of facial threat. *Psychological Science, 14*, 640–643.

Hugenberg, K., Young, S. G., Bernstein, M. J., & Sacco, D. F. (2010). The categorization–individuation model: An integrative account of the other-race recognition deficit. *Psychological Review, 117*, 1168–1187.

Hughes, J. R. (2010). Craving among long-abstinent smokers: An Internet survey. *Nicotine & Tobacco Research, 12*, 459–462.

Hughes, M. L., Geraci, L., & De Forrest, R. L. (2013). Aging 5 years in 5 minutes: The effect of taking a memory test on older adults' subjective age. *Psychological Science, 24*, 2481–2488.

Hughes, S. M., Aung, T., Harrison, M. A., LaFayette, J. N., & Gallup, G. G., Jr. (2021). Experimental evidence for sex differences in sexual variety preferences: Support for the Coolidge Effect in humans. *Archives of Sexual Behavior, 50*, 495–509.

Hui, B. P. H., Ng, J. C. K., Berzaghi, E., Cunningham-Amos, L., & Kogan, A. (2020). Rewards of kindness? A meta-analysis of the link between prosociality and well-being. *Psychological Bulletin, 146*, 1084–1116.

Hull, H. R., Morrow, M. L., Dinger, M. K., Han, J. L., & Fields, D. A. (2007, November 20). Characterization of body weight and composition changes during the sophomore year of college. *BMC Women's Health, 7*, 21.

Hull, J. M. (1990). *Touching the rock: An experience of blindness*. Vintage Books.

Hull, S. J., Hennessy, M., Bleakley, A., Fishbein, M., & Jordan, A. (2011). Identifying the causal pathways from religiosity to delayed adolescent sexual behavior. *Journal of Sex Research, 48*, 543–553.

Hülsheger, U. R., Anderson, N., & Salgado, J. F. (2009). Team-level predictors of innovation at work: A comprehensive meta-analysis spanning three decades of research. *Journal of Applied Psychology, 94*, 1128–1145.

Hummer, R. A., Rogers, R. G., Nam, C. B., & Ellison, C. G. (1999). Religious involvement and U.S. adult mortality. *Demography, 36*, 273–285.

Humphrey, S. E., Nahrgang, J. D., & Morgeson, F. P. (2007). Integrating motivational, social, and contextual work design features: A meta-analytic summary and theoretical extension of the work design literature. *Journal of Applied Psychology, 92*, 1332–1356.

Humphreys, L. G., & Davey, T. C. (1988). Continuity in intellectual growth from 12 months to 9 years. *Intelligence, 12*, 183–197.

Hunsberger, J. G., Newton, S. S., Bennett, A. H., Duman, C. H., Russell, D. S., Salton, S. R., & Duman, R. S. (2007). Antidepressant actions of the exercise-regulated gene VGF. *Nature Medicine, 13*, 1476–1482.

Hunsley, J., & Bailey, J. M. (1999). The clinical utility of the Rorschach: Unfulfilled promises and an uncertain future. *Psychological Assessment, 11*, 266–277.

Hunsley, J., & Di Giulio, G. (2002). Dodo bird, phoenix, or urban legend? The question of psychotherapy equivalence. *Scientific Review of Mental Health Practice, 1*, 11–22.

Hunt, J. M. (1982). Toward equalizing the developmental opportunities of infants and preschool children. *Journal of Social Issues, 38*, 163–191.

Hunt, L. L., Eastwick, P. W., & Finkel, E. J. (2015). Leveling the playing field: Longer acquaintance predicts reduced assortative mating on attractiveness. *Psychological Science, 26*, 1046–1053.

Hunt, M. (1990). *The compassionate beast: What science is discovering about the humane side of humankind*. William Morrow.

Hunt, M. (1993). *The story of psychology*. Doubleday.

Hurst, Y., & Fukuda, H. (2018). Effects of changes in eating speed on obesity in patients with diabetes: A secondary analysis of longitudinal health check-up data. *BMJ Open, 8*(1). doi: 10.1136/bmjopen-2017-019589

Hussain, Z. (2020). An expert advantage in detecting unfamiliar visual signals in noise. *PNAS, 117*(41), 25935–25941.

Hussak, L. J., & Cimpian, A. (2015). An early-emerging explanatory heuristic promotes support for the status quo. *Journal of Personality and Social Psychology, 109*, 739–752.

Hussong, A. M., Ennett, S. T., McNeish, D. M., Cole, V. T., Gottfredson, N. C., Rothenberg, W. A., & Faris, R. W. (2020). Social network isolation mediates associations between risky symptoms and substance use in the high school transition. *Development and Psychopathology, 32*(2), 615–630.

Hutchinson, R. (2006). *Calum's road*. Birlinn Limited.

Hutchison, K. A., Smith, J. L., & Ferris, A. (2013). Goals can be threatened to extinction using the Stroop task to clarify working memory depletion under stereotype threat. *Social and Personality Psychological Science, 4*, 74–81.

Hutteman, R., Nestler, S., Wagner, J., Egloff, B., & Back, M. D. (2015). Wherever I may roam: Processes of self-esteem development from adolescence to emerging adulthood in the context of international student exchange. *Journal of Personality and Social Psychology, 108*, 767–783.

Huynh, L. T. M., Gasparatos, A., Lam, R. D., Grant, E. I., & Fukushi, K. (2022). Linking the nonmaterial dimensions of human-nature relations and human well-being through cultural ecosystem services. *Science Advances, 8*(31). https://www.science.org/doi/10.1126/sciadv.abn8042

Hviid, A., Hansen, J. V., Frisch, M., & Melbye, M. (2019). Measles, mumps, rubella vaccination and autism: A nationwide cohort study. *Annals of Internal Medicine, 170*, 513–520.

Hyde, J. S. (2014). Gender similarities and differences. *Annual Review of Psychology, 65*, 373–398.

Hyde, J. S., Bigler, R. S., Joel, D., Tate, C. C., & van Anders, S. M. (2019). The future of sex and gender in psychology: Five challenges to the gender binary. *American Psychologist, 74*, 171–193.

Hyde, J. S., & Mertz, J. E. (2009). Gender, culture, and mathematics performance. *PNAS, 106*, 8801–8807.

Hymowitz, K., Carroll, J. S., Wilcox, W. B., & Kaye, K. (2013). *Knot yet: The benefits and costs of delayed marriage in America* [PDF file]. National Marriage Project, University of Virginia. http://nationalmarriageproject.org/wordpress/wp-content/uploads/2013/04/KnotYet-FinalForWeb-041413.pdf

Iacoboni, M. (2008). *Mirroring people: The new science of how we connect with others*. Farrar, Straus and Giroux.

Iacoboni, M. (2009). Imitation, empathy, and mirror neurons. *Annual Review of Psychology, 60*, 653–670.

Ibbotson, P., & Tomasello, M. (2016, November). Language in a new key. *Scientific American*, pp. 71–75.

Idson, L. C., & Mischel, W. (2001). The personality of familiar and significant people: The lay perceiver as a social-cognitive theorist. *Journal of Personality and Social Psychology, 80*, 585–596.

Ihsen, E., Troester, H., & Brambring, M. (2010). The role of sound in encouraging infants with congenital blindness to reach for objects. *Journal of Visual Impairment & Blindness, 104*(8), 478–488.

Ikegaya, Y., & Matsumoto, N. (2019). Spikes in the sleeping brain. *Science, 366*, 306–307.

Ikizer, E. G., & Blanton, H. (2016). Media coverage of "wise" interventions can reduce concern for the disadvantaged. *Journal of Experimental Psychology: Applied, 22*, 135–147.

Ilardi, S. (2016). *Therapeutic lifestyle change (TLC)*. University of Kansas. tlc.ku.edu

Ilardi, S. S. (2009). *The depression cure: The six-step program to beat depression without drugs*. De Capo Lifelong Books.

Iliescu, A. F., Hall, J., Wilkinson, L. S., Dwyer, D. M., & Honey, R. C. (2018). The nature of phenotypic variation in Pavlovian conditioning. *Journal of Experimental Psychology: Animal Learning and Cognition, 44*, 358–369.

Ilieva, I. P., Hook, C. J., & Farah, M. J. (2015). Prescription stimulants' effects on healthy inhibitory control, working memory, and episodic memory: A meta-analysis. *Journal of Cognitive Neuroscience, 27*, 1069–1089.

Illes, J., & McDonald, P. J. (2017). Head transplants: Ghoulish takes on new definition. *AJOB Neuroscience, 8*, 211–212.

Im, S., Varma, K., & Varma, S. (2017). Extending the seductive allure of neuroscience explanations effect to popular articles about educational topics. *British Journal of Educational Psychology, 87*, 518–534.

Imada, T. (2012). Cultural narratives of individualism and collectivism: A content analysis of textbook stories in the United States and Japan. *Journal of Cross-Cultural Psychology, 43*(4), 576–591.

Imperato-McGinley, J., Guerrero, L., Gautier, T., & Peterson, R. E. (1974). Steroid 5alpha-reductase deficiency in man: An inherited form of male pseudohermaphroditism. *Science, 186*(4170), 1213–1215.

Inagaki, B., & Ross, L. P. (2021). A body-to-mind perspective on social connection: Physical warmth potentiates brain activity to close others and subsequent feelings of social connection. *Emotion, 21*(4), 812–822.

Inagaki, T. K., Hazlett, L. I., & Andreescu, C. (2019). Naltrexone alters responses to social and physical warmth: Implications for social bonding. *Social Cognitive and Affective Neuroscience, 14*, 471–479.

Inbar, Y., Cone, J., & Gilovich, T. (2010). People's intuitions about intuitive insight and intuitive choice. *Journal of Personality and Social Psychology, 99*, 232–247.

Inbar, Y., & Pizarro, D. A. (2022). Chapter 3. How disgust affects social judgments. *Advances in Experimental Social Psychology, 65*, 109–166.

Inbar, Y., Pizarro, D., & Bloom, P. (2012). Disgusting smells cause decreased liking of gay men. *Emotion, 12*(1), 23–27.

Inbar, Y., Pizarro, D. A., Knobe, J., & Bloom, P. (2009). Disgust sensitivity predicts intuitive disapproval of gays. *Emotion, 9*(3), 435.

İnel Manav, A., & Simsek, N. (2019). The effect of reminiscence therapy with Internet-based videos on cognitive status and apathy of older people with mild dementia. *Journal of Geriatric Psychiatry and Neurology, 32*, 104–113.

Infurna, F. J., & Luthar, S. S. (2016). Resilience to major life stressors is not as common as thought. *Perspectives on Psychological Science, 11*, 175–194.

Infurna, F. J., & Luthar, S. S. (2016). The multidimensional nature of resilience to spousal loss. *Journal of Personality and Social Psychology, 112*, 926–947.

Ingham, A. G., Levinger, G., Graves, J., & Peckham, V. (1974). The Ringelmann effect: Studies of group size and group performance. *Journal of Experimental Social Psychology, 10*, 371–384.

Inglehart, R. (1990). *Culture shift in advanced industrial society*. Princeton University Press.

Inglehart, R., Foa, R., Peterson, C., & Welzel, C. (2008). Development, freedom, and rising happiness: A global perspective (1981–2007). *Perspectives on Psychological Science, 3*, 264–285.

Inman, M. L., & Baron, R. S. (1996). Influence of prototypes on perceptions of prejudice. *Journal of Personality and Social Psychology, 70*, 727–739.

Innocence Project. (2021). *DNA exonerations in the United States*. https://innocenceproject.org/dna-exonerations-in-the-united-states/

Insel, T. (2022). *Healing: Our path from mental illness to mental health*. Penguin Press.

Insel, T. R. (2010). Faulty circuits. *Scientific American, 302*, 44–51.

Inzlicht, M., & Kang, S. K. (2010). Stereotype threat spillover: How coping with threats to social identity affects aggression, eating, decision making, and attention. *Journal of Personality and Social Psychology, 99*, 467–481.

IPPA (International Positive Psychology Association). (2022). Communication from International Positive Psychology Association.

Ipsos. (2019). *It's a fact ... scientists are the most trusted people in the world*. https://www.ipsos.com/en/its-fact-scientists-are-most-trusted-people-world

IPU (Inter-Parliamentary Union). (2022, accessed July 5). *Gender equality*. https://www.ipu.org/our-impact/gender-equality

Ireland, M. E., & Pennebaker, J. W. (2010). Language style matching in writing: Synchrony in essays, correspondence, and poetry. *Journal of Personality and Social Psychology, 99*, 549–571.

Ironson, G., Solomon, G. F., Balbin, E. G., O'Cleirigh, C., George, A., Kumar, M., Larson, D., & Woods, T. E. (2002). The Ironson-Woods Spiritual/Religiousness Index is associated with long survival, health behaviors, less distress, and low cortisol in people with HIV/AIDS. *Annals of Behavioral Medicine, 24*, 34–48.

Irwin, M. R., Carrillo, C., Sadeghi, N., Bjurstrom, M. F., Breen, E. C., & Olmstead, R. (2022). Prevention of incident and recurrent major depression in older adults with insomnia: A randomized clinical trial. *JAMA Psychiatry, 79*, 33–41.

Irwin, M. R., Cole, J. C., & Nicassio, P. M. (2006). Comparative meta-analysis of behavioral interventions for insomnia and their efficacy in middle-aged adults and in older adults 55+ years of age. *Health Psychology, 25*, 3–14.

Irwing, P., Cook, C., Pollet, T. V., & Hughes, D. J. (2020). Comedians' trait level and stage personalities: Evidence for goal-directed personality adaptation. *Personality and Social Psychology Bulletin, 46*(4), 590–602.

Isaacowitz, D. M. (2012). Mood regulation in real time: Age differences in the role of looking. *Current Directions in Psychological Science, 21*, 237–242.

Isen, A. M., & Levin, P. F. (1972). Effect of feeling good on helping: Cookies and kindness. *Journal of Personality and Social Psychology, 21*, 384.

Isen, A. M., & Levin, P. F. (1978). Affect, accessibility of material in memory, and behavior: A cognitive loop? *Journal of Personality and Social Psychology, 36*(1), 1–12.

Ishiyama, S., & Brecht, M. (2017). Neural correlates of ticklishness in the rat somatosensory cortex. *Science, 354*, 757–760.

Islam, S. S., & Johnson, C. (2003). Correlates of smoking behavior among Muslim Arab-American adolescents. *Ethnicity & Health, 8*, 319–337.

Iso-Markku, P., Waller, K., Vuoksimaa, E., Heikkilä, K., Rinne, J., Kaprio, J., & Kujala, U. M. (2016). Midlife physical activity and cognition later in life: A prospective twin study. *Journal of Alzheimer's Disease, 54*, 1303–1317.

ISR (Institute for Social Research). (2020, July). *Expected election winner by party affiliation*. University of Michigan.

Ito, T. A., Miller, N., & Pollock, V. E. (1996). Alcohol and aggression: A meta-analysis on the moderating effects of inhibitory cues, triggering events, and self-focused attention. *Psychological Bulletin, 120*, 60–82.

ITU (International Telecommunication Union). (2021). *Facts and figures 2021*. https://www.itu.int/itu-d/reports/statistics/facts-figures-2021/

Itzchakov, G., Reis, H. T., & Weinstein, N. (2022). How to foster perceived partner responsiveness: High-quality listening is key. *Social and Personality Psychology Compass*, 16(1). https://compass.onlinelibrary.wiley.com/doi/epdf/10.1111/spc3.12648

Ives-Deliperi, V. L., Solms, M., & Meintjes, E. M. (2011). The neural substrates of mindfulness: An fMRI investigation. *Social Neuroscience, 6*, 231–242.

Iyengar, S., & Westwood, S. J. (2015). Fear and loathing across party lines: New evidence on group polarization. *American Journal of Political Science, 59*, 690–707.

Iyengar, S. S., & Lepper, M. R. (2000). When choice is demotivating: Can one desire too much of a good thing? *Journal of Personality and Social Psychology, 79*, 995–1006.

Izard, C. E. (1977). *Human emotions*. Plenum Press.

Izard, C. E. (1994). Innate and universal facial expressions: Evidence from developmental and cross-cultural research. *Psychological Bulletin, 114*, 288–299.

Izawa, S., Matsudaira, K., Miki, K., Arisaka, M., & Tsuchiya, M. (2017). Psychosocial correlates of cortisol levels in fingernails among middle-aged workers. *The International Journal on the Biology of Stress, 20*, 386–389.

Jääskeläinen, E., Juola, P., Hirvonen, N., McGrath, J. J., Saha, S., Isohanni, M., Veijola, J., & Miettunen, J. (2013). A systematic review and meta-analysis of recovery in schizophrenia. *Schizophrenia Bulletin, 39*, 1296–1306.

Jablensky, A. (1999). Schizophrenia: Epidemiology. *Current Opinion in Psychiatry, 12*, 19–28.

Jachimowicz, J., Wihler, A., Bailey, E., & Galinsky, A. (2018). Why grit requires perseverance and passion to positively predict performance. *PNAS, 115*, 9980–9985.

Jäckle, S., & Wenzelburger, G. (2015). Religion, religiosity, and the attitudes toward homosexuality—A multilevel analysis of 79 countries. *Journal of Homosexuality, 62*, 207–241.

Jackson, J. J., Thoemmes, F., Jonkmann, K., Lüdtke, O., & Trautwien, U. (2012). Military training and personality trait development: Does the military make the man, or does the man make the military? *Psychological Science, 23*, 270–277.

Jackson, J. M., & Williams, K. D. (1988). *Social loafing: A review and theoretical analysis* [Unpublished manuscript]. Fordham University.

Jackson, M., & Holzman, B. (2020). A century of educational inequality in the United States. *PNAS, 117*(32), 19108–19115.

Jackson, S. W. (1992). The listening healer in the history of psychological healing. *American Journal Psychiatry, 149*, 1623–1632.

Jacobs, A. (2021). Veterans have become unlikely lobbyists in push to legalize psychedelic drugs. *The New York Times*. https://www.nytimes.com/2021/11/11/health/veterans-psychedelics-ptsd-depression.html

Jacobs, B. L. (1994). Serotonin, motor activity, and depression-related disorders. *American Scientist, 82*, 456–463.

Jacobs, J. (2019, May 7). James Holzhauer was told to smile to get on 'Jeopardy!' He's smiling now. *The New York Times*. https://www.nytimes.com/2019/05/07/arts/television/james-holzhauer-jeopardy.html

Jacobs, J. M., Maaravi, Y., & Stessman, J. (2021). Optimism and longevity beyond age 85. *Journals of Gerontology: Series A, 76*(10), 1806–1813.

Jacobson, L. (2015, August 27). *Nicholas Kristof stated on August 27, 2015 in his column in The New York Times: "More Americans have died from guns in the United States since 1968 than on battlefields of all the wars in American history."* Politifact. https://bit.ly/2JlMDYg

Jacobson, N. C., & Newman, M. G. (2017). Anxiety and depression as bidirectional risk factors for one another: A meta-analysis of longitudinal studies. *Psychological Bulletin, 143*, 1155–1200.

Jacoby, L. L., & Rhodes, M. G. (2006). False remembering in the aged. *Current Directions in Psychological Science, 15*, 49–53.

Jacques, C., & Rossion, B. (2006). The speed of individual face categorization. *Psychological Science, 17*, 485–492.

Jacques-Tiura, A. J., Abbey, A., Parkhill, M. R., & Zawacki, T. (2007). Why do some men misperceive women's sexual intentions more frequently than others do? An application of the confluence model. *Personality and Social Psychology Bulletin, 33*, 1467–1480.

Jaderberg, M., Czarnecki, W. M., Dunning, I., Marris, L., Lever, G., Castañeda, A. G., Beattie, C., Rabinowitz, N. C., Morcos, A. S., Ruderman, A., Sonnerat, N., Green, T., Deason, L., Leibo, J. Z., Silver, D., Hassabis, D., Kavukcuoglu, K., & Graepel, T. (2019). Human-level performance in 3D multiplayer games with population-based reinforcement learning. *Science, 364*, 859–865.

Jaffe, E. (2004, October). Peace in the Middle East may be impossible: Lee D. Ross on naive realism and conflict resolution. *APS Observer*, pp. 9–11.

Jakubiak, B. K., & Feeney, B. C. (2017). Affectionate touch to promote relational, psychological, and physical well-being in adulthood: A theoretical model and review of the research. *Personality and Social Psychology Review, 21*, 228–252.

Jakubiak, B. K., & Feeney, B. C. (2019). Hand-in-hand combat: Affectionate touch promotes relational well-being and buffers stress during conflict. *Personality and Social Psychology Bulletin, 45*, 431–446.

Jakubowski, K. P., Cundiff, J. M., & Matthews, K. A. (2018). Cumulative childhood adversity and adult cardiometabolic disease: A meta-analysis. *Health Psychology, 37*, 701–715.

James, A., Hoang, U., Seagroatt, V., Clacey, J., Goldacre, M., & Leibenluft, E. (2014). A comparison of American and English hospital discharge rates for pediatric bipolar disorder, 2000 to 2010. *Journal of the American Academy of Child and Adolescent Psychiatry, 53*(6), 614–624.

James, K. (1986). Priming and social categorizational factors: Impact on awareness of emergency situations. *Personality and Social Psychology Bulletin, 12*, 462–467.

James, S. E., Herman, J. L., Rankin, S., Keisling, M., Mottet, L., & Anafi, M. (2016). *The report of the 2015 U.S. Transgender Survey*. National Center for Transgender Equality. https://www.ustranssurvey.org/reports

James, W. (1890). *The principles of psychology* (Vol. 2). Holt.

James, W. (1902). *The varieties of religious experience: A study in human nature*. Longmans, Green & Co.

Jameson, D. (1985). Opponent-colors theory in light of physiological findings. In D. Ottoson & S. Zeki (Eds.), *Central and peripheral mechanisms of color vision* (pp. 83–102). Macmillan.

Jamieson, J. P. (2010). The home field advantage in athletics: A meta-analysis. *Journal of Applied Social Psychology, 40*, 1819–1848.

Jamieson, J. P., Nock, M. K., & Mendes, W. B. (2012). Mind over matter: Reappraising arousal improves cardiovascular and cognitive responses to stress. *Journal of Experimental Psychology: General, 141*(3), 417–422.

Jamison, K. R. (1993). *Touched with fire: Manic-depressive illness and the artistic temperament*. Free Press.

Jamison, K. R. (1995). *An unquiet mind*. Knopf.

Jamison, K. R. (1996). *An unquiet mind: A memoir of moods and madness*. Vintage.

Jamison, P. (2020). Anti-vaccination leaders seize on coronavirus to push resistance to inoculation. *The Washington Post*. https://www.washingtonpost.com/dc-md-va/2020/05/05/anti-vaxxers-wakefield-coronavirus-vaccine/

Jampol, L., & Zayas, V. (2021). Gendered white lies: Women are given inflated performance feedback compared with men. *Personality and Social Psychology Bulletin, 47*(1), 57–69.

Janis, I. L. (1982). *Groupthink: Psychological studies of policy decisions and fiascoes*. Houghton Mifflin.

Janis, I. L. (1986). Problems of international crisis management in the nuclear age. *Journal of Social Issues, 42*, 201–220.

Janoff-Bulman, R., Timko, C., & Carli, L. L. (1985). Cognitive biases in blaming the victim. *Journal of Experimental Social Psychology, 21*, 161–177.

Jansen, P. R., Watanabe, K., Stringer, S., Skene, N., Bryois, J., Hammerschlag, A. R., de Leeuw, C. A., Benjamins, J. S., Muñoz-Manchado, A. B., Nagel, M., Savage, J. E., Tiemeier, H., White, T., 23andMe Research Team, Tung, J. Y., Hinds, D. A., Vacic, V., Wang, X., Sullivan, P. F., & Posthuma, D. (2019). Genome-wide analysis of insomnia in 1,331,010 individuals identifies new risk loci and functional pathways. *Nature Genetics, 51*, 394–403.

Janssen, S. M. J., Rubin, D. C., & Conway, M. A. (2012). The reminiscence bump in the temporal distribution of the best football players of all time: Pelé, Cruijff or Maradona? *Quarterly Journal of Experimental Psychology, 65*, 165–178.

Jansson-Fröjmark, M., Evander, J., & Alfonsson, S. (2019). Are sleep hygiene practices related to the incidence, persistence and remission of insomnia? Findings from a prospective community study. *Journal of Behavioral Medicine, 42*, 128–138.

Jaroslawska, A. J., & Rhodes, S. (2019). Adult age differences in the effects of processing on storage in working memory: A meta-analysis. *Psychology and Aging, 34*, 512–530.

Jayakar, R., King, T. Z., Morris, R., & Na, S. (2015). Hippocampal volume and auditory attention on a verbal memory task with adult survivors of pediatric brain tumor. *Neuropsychology, 29*, 303–319.

Jebb, A. T., Morrison, M., Tay, L., & Diener, E. (2020). Subjective well-being around the world: Trends and predictors across the life span. *Psychological Science, 31*, 293–305.

Jebb, A. T., Tay, L., Diener, E., & Oishi, S. (2018). Happiness, income satiation and turning points around the world. *Nature: Human Behaviour, 2*, 33–38.

Jeffrey, K., Mahoney, S., Michaelson, J., & Abdallah, S. (2014). *Well-being at work: A review of the literature*. New Economics Foundation. https://neweconomics.org/2014/03/wellbeing-at-work

Jelbert, S. A., Hosking, R. J., Taylor, A. H., & Gray, R. D. (2018). Mental template matching is a potential cultural transmission mechanism for New Caledonian crow tool manufacturing traditions. *Scientific Reports, 8*. https://www.nature.com/articles/s41598-018-27405-1/

Jena, A. B., Jain, A., & Hicks, T. R. (2018). Do 'Fast and Furious' movies cause a rise in speeding? *The New York Times*. https://www.nytimes.com/2018/01/30/upshot/do-fast-and-furious-movies-cause-a-rise-in-speeding.html

Jenkins, J. G., & Dallenbach, K. M. (1924). Obliviscence during sleep and waking. *American Journal of Psychology, 35*, 605–612.

Jenkins, J. M., & Astington, J. W. (1996). Cognitive factors and family structure associated with theory of mind development in young children. *Developmental Psychology, 32*, 70–78.

Jenkins, R., Dowsett, A. J., Burton, A. M. (2018) How many faces do people know? *Proceedings of the Royal Society, 285*(1888). https://royalsocietypublishing.org/doi/10.1098/rspb.2018.1319

Jenkins, S. R. (2017). Not your same old story: New rules for Thematic Apperceptive Techniques (TATs). *Journal of Personality Assessment, 99*, 238–253.

Jennings, W., & Wlezien, C. (2018). Election polling errors across time and space. *Nature Human Behaviour, 2*, 276–283.

Jensen, A. R. (1980). *Bias in mental testing*. Free Press.

Jensen, J. P., & Bergin, A. E. (1988). Mental health values of professional therapists: A national interdisciplinary survey. *Professional Psychology: Research and Practice, 19*, 290–297.

Jensen, M., George, M. J., Russell, M. A., Lippold, M. A., & Odgers, C. L. (2021). Daily parent-adolescent digital exchanges. *Research on Child and Adolescent Psychopathology, 49*, 1125–1138.

Jensen, M. P. (2008). The neurophysiology of pain perception and hypnotic analgesia: Implications for clinical practice. *American Journal of Clinical Hypnosis, 51*, 123–147.

Jeon, H., & Lee, S.-H. (2018). From neurons to social beings: Short review of the mirror neuron system research and its socio-psychological and psychiatric implications. *Clinical Psychopharmacology and Neuroscience, 16*(1), 18–31.

Jepson, C., Krantz, D. H., & Nisbett, R. E. (1983). Inductive reasoning: Competence or skill. *The Behavioral and Brain Sciences, 3*, 494–501.

Jerrim, J., Parker, P., & Shure, N. (2019, April). *Bullshitters. Who are they and what do we know about their lives?* Discussion Paper Series. Institute of Labor Economics, Bonn, Germany.

Jessberger, S., Aimone, J. B., & Gage, F. H. (2008). Neurogenesis. In J. H. Byrne (Ed.), *Learning and memory: A comprehensive reference: Vol. 4. Molecular mechanisms of memory* (pp. 839–858). Elsevier.

Jesse, D. (2019, February 8). Second wave of more than 160 Nassar survivors fight for acknowledgement. *Detroit Free Press*. https://www.freep.com/story/news/education/2019/02/08/second-wave-nassar-survivors-fight-acknowledgement/2794436002/

Jiang, H., White, M. P., Greicius, M. D., Waelde, L. C., & Spiegel, D. (2016). Brain activity and functional connectivity associated with hypnosis. *Cerebral Cortex, 27*, 4083–4093.

Jiang, M., Wong, S., Chung, H., Hsiao, J., Sui, J., & Humphreys, G. (2019). Cultural orientation of self bias in perceptual matching. *Frontiers in Psychology, 10*, 1469.

Jiang, S., Simpkins, S. D., & Eccles, J. S. (2020). Individuals' math and science motivation and their subsequent STEM choices and achievement in high school and college: A longitudinal study of gender and college generation status differences. *Developmental Psychology, 56*(11), 2137–2151.

Jiang, Y., Costello, P., Fang, F., Huang, M., & He, S. (2006). A gender- and sexual orientation-dependent spatial attentional effect of invisible things. *PNAS, 103*, 17048–17052.

Jin, M., Onie, S., Curby, K. M., & Most, S. B. (2018). Aversive images cause less perceptual interference among violent video game players: Evidence from emotion-induced blindness. *Visual Cognition, 26*, 753–763.

Job, V., Dweck, C. S., & Walton, G. M. (2010). Ego depletion—Is it all in your head?: Implicit theories about willpower affect self-regulation. *Psychological Science, 21*, 1686–1693.

Jobe, T. H., & Harrow, M. (2010). Schizophrenia course, long-term outcome, recovery, and prognosis. *Current Directions in Psychological Science, 19*, 220–225.

Jobson, L., & Cheraghi, S. (2016). Influence of memory theme and posttraumatic stress disorder on memory specificity in British and Iranian trauma survivors. *Memory, 24*, 1015–1022.

Joel, D., Berman, Z., Tavor, I., Wexler, N., Gaber, O., Stein, Y., Shefi, N., Pool, J., Urchs, S., Margulies, D. S., Liem, F., Hänggi, J., Jäncke, L., & Assaf, Y. (2015, December). Sex beyond the genitalia: The human brain mosaic. *PNAS, 112*, 15468–15473.

Joel, S., Eastwick, P. W., & Finkel, E. J. (2017). Is romantic desire predictable? Machine learning applied to initial romantic attraction. *Psychological Science, 28*, 1478–1489.

John, S., & Jaeggi, A. V. (2021). Oxytocin levels tend to be lower in autistic children: A meta-analysis of 31 studies. *Autism, 25*(8), 2152–2161.

Johnson, A. W., & Earle, T. K. (2000). *The evolution of human societies: From foraging group to agrarian state*. Stanford University Press.

Johnson, D. F. (1997). Margaret Floy Washburn. *Psychology of Women Newsletter*, pp. 17, 22.

Johnson, D. L., Wiebe, J. S., Gold, S. M., Andreasen, N. C., Hichwa, R. D., Watkins, G. L., & Ponto, L. L. B. (1999). Cerebral blood flow and personality: A positron emission tomography study. *American Journal of Psychiatry, 156*, 252–257.

Johnson, D., Thorpe, R., McGrath, J., Jackson, W., & Jackson, C. (2018). Black–White differences in housing type and sleep duration as well as sleep difficulties in the United States. *International Journal of Environmental Research and Public Health, 15*, 564.

Johnson, D. P., Rhee, S. H., Friedman, N. P., Corley, R. P., Munn-Chernoff, M., Hewitt, J. K., & Whisman, M. A. (2016). A twin study examining rumination as a transdiagnostic correlate of psychopathology. *Clinical Psychological Science, 4*, 971–987.

Johnson, E. J., & Goldstein, D. (2003). Do defaults save lives? *Science, 302*, 1338–1339.

Johnson, J. A. (2007, June 26). *Not so situational*. Commentary on the SPSP listserv. https://www.psychologicalscience.org/observer/not-so-situational

Johnson, J. E., Stout, R. L., Miller, T. R., Zlotnick, C., Cerbo, L. A., Andrade, J. T., Nargiso, J., Bonner, J., & Wiltsey-Stirman, S. (2019). Randomized cost-effectiveness trial of group interpersonal psychotherapy (IPT) for prisoners with major depression. *Journal of Consulting and Clinical Psychology, 87*, 392–406.

Johnson, J. S., & Newport, E. L. (1991). Critical period effects on universal properties of language: The status of subjacency in the acquisition of a second language. *Cognition, 39*, 215–258.

Johnson, L. K. (2020). Narcissistic people, not narcissistic nations: Using multilevel modelling to explore narcissism across countries. *Personality and Individual Differences, 163*. https://doi.org/10.1016/j.paid.2020.110079

Johnson, M. D., & Chen, J. (2015). Blame it on the alcohol: The influence of alcohol consumption during adolescence, the transition to adulthood, and young adulthood on one-time sexual hookups. *Journal of Sex Research, 52*, 570–579.

Johnson, M. H. (1992). Imprinting and the development of face recognition: From chick to man. *Current Directions in Psychological Science, 1*, 52–55.

Johnson, M. P. (2008). *A typology of domestic violence: Intimate terrorism, violent resistance, and situational couple violence*. Northeastern University Press.

Johnson, R. (2017, August 12). The mystery of S. The man with an impossible memory. *The New Yorker*. https://www.newyorker.com/books/page-turner/the-mystery-of-s-the-man-with-an-impossible-memory

Johnson, S. C., Schmitz, T. W., Moritz, C. H., Meyerand, M. E., Rowley, H. A., Alexander, A. L., Hansen, K. W., Gleason, C. E., Carlsson, C. M., Ries, M. L., Asthana, S., Chen, K., Reiman, E. M., & Alexander, G. E. (2006). Activation of brain regions vulnerable to Alzheimer's disease: The effect of mild cognitive impairment. *Neurobiology of Aging, 27*, 1604–1612.

Johnson, S. L. (2005). Mania and dysregulation in goal pursuit: A review. *Clinical Psychology Review, 25*(2), 241–262.

Johnson, W., Carothers, A., & Deary, I. J. (2008). Sex differences in variability in general intelligence: A new look at the old question. *Perspectives on Psychological Science, 3*, 518–531.

Johnson, W., Gow, A. J., Corley, J., Starr, J. M., & Deary, I. J. (2010). Location in cognitive and residential space at age 70 reflects a lifelong trait over parental and environmental circumstances: The Lothian Birth Cohort 1936. *Intelligence, 38*, 403–411.

Johnson, W., Turkheimer, E., Gottesman, I. I., & Bouchard, Jr., T. J. (2009). Beyond heritability: Twin studies in behavioral research. *Current Directions in Psychological Science, 18*, 217–220.

Johnston, L. D., Miech, R. A., O'Malley P. M., Bachman, J. G., Schulenberg, J. E., & Patrick, M. E. (2020). *Monitoring the Future national survey results on drug use 1975–2019: Overview, key findings on adolescent drug use*. Institute for Social Science Research, University of Michigan. https://www.drugabuse.gov/drug-topics/trends-statistics/monitoring-future

Johnstone, E. C., Ebmeier, K. P., Miller, P., Owens, D. G. C., & Lawrie, S. M. (2005). Predicting schizophrenia: Findings from the Edinburgh High-Risk Study. *British Journal of Psychiatry, 186*, 18–25.

Joiner, T. E., Jr. (2006). *Why people die by suicide*. Harvard University Press.

Jokela, M., Elovainio, M., Archana, S.-M., & Kivimäki, M. (2009). IQ, socioeconomic status, and early death: The U.S. National Longitudinal Survey of Youth. *Psychosomatic Medicine, 71*, 322–328.

Jolley, D., & Douglas, K. M. (2017). Prevention is better than cure: Addressing anti-vaccine conspiracy theories. *Journal of Applied Social Psychology, 47*, 459–469.

Jonas, E., & Fischer, P. (2006). Terror management and religion: Evidence that intrinsic religiousness mitigates worldview defense following mortality salience. *Journal of Personality and Social Psychology, 91*, 553–567.

Jones, A. C., & Gosling, S. D. (2005). Temperament and personality in dogs (*Canis familiaris*): A review and evaluation of past research. *Applied Animal Behaviour Science, 95*, 1–53.

Jones, B., Reedy, E. J., & Weinberg, B. A. (2014, January). *Age and scientific genius*. NBER Working Paper Series. nber.org/papers/w19866

Jones, E. (1957). *Sigmund Freud: Life and work* (Vol. 3, Pt. 1., Ch. 4). Basic Books.

Jones, J. M. (2012, June 21). *Atheists, Muslims see most bias as presidential candidates*. Gallup. https://news.gallup.com/poll/155285/atheists-muslims-bias-presidential-candidates.aspx

Jones, J. M. (2021, February 24). *LGBT identification rises to 5.6% in latest U.S. estimate*. Gallup. https://news.gallup.com/poll/329708/lgbt-identification-rises-latest-estimate.aspx

Jones, M. (2018, February 7). What teenagers are learning from online porn. *The New York Times Magazine*. https://www.nytimes.com/2018/02/07/magazine/teenagers-learning-online-porn-literacy-sex-education.html

Jones, M. C. (1924). A laboratory study of fear: The case of Peter. *Journal of Genetic Psychology, 31*, 308–315.

Jones, S. (2017). Can newborn infants imitate? *WIREs Cognitive Science, 8*(1–2), 1–13.

Jones, S. E., Lane, J. M., Wood, A. R., van Hees, V. T., Tyrell, J., Beaumont, R. N., Jeffries, A. R., Dashti, H. S., Hillsdon, M., Ruth, K. S., Tuke, M. A., Yaghootkar, H., Sharp, S. A., Jie, Y., Thompson, W. D., Harrison, J. W., Dawes, A., Dyrne, E. M., Tiemeier, H., ... Weedon, M. N. (2019). Genome-wide association analyses of chronotype in 697,828 individuals provides insights into circadian rhythms. *Nature Communications, 10*, 343.

Jones, S. R., & Abes, E. S. (2013). *Identity development of college students: Advancing frameworks for multiple dimensions of identity*. John Wiley & Sons.

Jones, S. S. (2007). Imitation in infancy: The development of mimicry. *Psychological Science, 18*, 593–599.

Jones, W. H., Carpenter, B. N., & Quintana, D. (1985). Personality and interpersonal predictors of loneliness in two cultures. *Journal of Personality and Social Psychology, 48*, 1503–1511.

Joo, M., Terzino, K. A., Cross, S. E., Yamaguchi, N., & Ohbuchi, K. I. (2019). How does culture shape conceptions of forgiveness? Evidence from Japan and the United States. *Journal of Cross-Cultural Psychology, 50*, 676–702.

Jordan, A. H., Monin, B., Dweck, C. S., Lovett, B. J., John, O. P., & Gross, J. J. (2011). Misery has more company than people think: Underestimating the prevalence of others' negative emotions. *Personality and Social Psychology Bulletin, 37*, 120–135.

Jorm, A. F., Reavley, N. J., & Ross, A. M. (2012). Belief in the dangerousness of people with mental disorders: A review. *Australian and New Zealand Journal of Psychiatry, 46*, 1029–1045.

Joseph, J. (2001). Separated twins and the genetics of personality differences: A critique. *American Journal of Psychology, 114*, 1–30.

Joshanloo, M., & Jovanović, V. (2021). Similarities and differences in predictors of life satisfaction across age groups: A 150-country study. *Journal of Health Psychology, 26*(3), 401–411.

Jost, J. T. (2020). *A theory of system justification*. Harvard University Press.

Jovanovic, T., Blanding, N. Q., Norrholm, S. D., Duncan, E., Bradley, B., & Ressler, K. J. (2009). Childhood abuse is associated with increased startle reactivity in adulthood. *Depression and Anxiety, 26*, 1018–1026.

Juarez, B., Liu, Y., Zhang, L., & Han, M. H. (2019). Optogenetic investigation of neural mechanisms for alcohol use disorders. *Alcohol, 74*, 29–38.

Judge, T. A., Thoresen, C. J., Bono, J. E., & Patton, G. K. (2001). The job satisfaction/job performance relationship: A qualitative and quantitative review. *Psychological Bulletin, 127*, 376–407.

Julian, K. (2018, December). Why are young people having so little sex? *The Atlantic*. https://www.realclearpolitics.com/2018/11/13/why_are_young_people_having_so_little_sex_458984.html

Jung, H., Herrenkohl, T. I., Skinner, M. L., Lee, J. O., Klika, J. B., & Rousson, A. N. (2019). Gender differences in intimate partner violence: A predictive analysis of IPV by child abuse and domestic violence exposure during early childhood. *Violence Against Women, 25*, 903–924.

Jung, H., Seo, E., Han, E., Henderson, M. D., & Patall, E. A. (2020). Prosocial modeling: A meta-analytic review and synthesis. *Psychological Bulletin, 146*(8), 635–663.

Jung, R. E., & Haier, R. J. (2013). Creativity and intelligence: Brain networks that link and differentiate the expression of genius. In O. Vartanian, A. S. Bristol, & J. C. Kaufman (Eds.), *Neuroscience of creativity*. MIT Press.

Jung, S. J., Woo, H., Cho, S., Park, K., Jeong, S., Lee, Y. J., Kang, D., & Shin, A. (2017). Association between body size, weight change and depression: Systematic review and meta-analysis. *British Journal of Psychiatry, 211*, 14–21.

Jung-Beeman, M., Bowden, E. M., Haberman, J., Frymiare, J. L., Arambel-Liu, S., Greenblatt, R., Reber, P. J., & Kounios, J. (2004). Neural activity when people solve verbal problems with insight. *PLOS Biology, 2*, e111.

Juskalian, R. (2019, September/October). The science of fun violence. *Discover*, pp. 31–37.

Jussim, L., & Honeycutt, N. (2021, September 8). *The accuracy of stereotypes: Data and implications*. Report No. 3. Center for the Study of Partisanship and Ideology.

Just, M. A., Keller, T. A., & Cynkar, J. (2008). A decrease in brain activation associated with driving when listening to someone speak. *Brain Research, 1205*, 70–80.

Kabat-Zinn, J. (2001). Mindfulness-based interventions in context: Past, present, and future. *Clinical Psychology: Science and Practice, 10*, 144–156.

Kadohisa, M. (2013). Effects of odor on emotion, with implications. *Frontiers in Systems Neuroscience, 7*, 6.

Kaertner, L. S., Steinborn, M. B., Kettner, H., Spriggs, M. J., Roseman, L., Buchborn, T., Balaet, M., Timmermann, C., Erritzoe, D., & Carhart-Harris, R. L. (2021). Positive expectations predict improved mental-health outcomes linked to psychedelic microdosing. *Scientific Reports, 11*(1), 1941.

Kagan, J. (1976). Emergent themes in human development. *American Scientist, 64*, 186–196.

Kagan, J. (1995). On attachment. *Harvard Review of Psychiatry, 3*, 104–106.

Kagan, J. (2010). *The temperamental thread: How genes, culture, time, and luck make us who we are.* Dana Press.

Kagan, J., & Snidman, N. (2004). *The long shadow of temperament.* Belknap Press.

Kahldun, I. (1377). *The muqaddimah* [PDF file]. (F. Rosenthal, Trans). https://delong.typepad.com/files/muquaddimah.pdf

Kahneman, D. (1985, June). Quoted by K. McKean in Decisions, decisions [PDF file]. *Discover.* http://d1m3qhodv9fjlf.cloudfront.net/wp-content/uploads/2013/01/Decisions_Decisions.pdf

Kahneman, D. (1999). Objective happiness. In D. Kahneman, E. Diener, & N. Schwartz (Eds.), *Well-being. Foundations of hedonic psychology.* Russell Sage Foundation.

Kahneman, D. (2005, January 13). What were they thinking? Q&A with Daniel Kahneman. *Gallup Management Journal.* https://news.gallup.com/businessjournal/14503/what-were-they-thinking.aspx

Kahneman, D. (2011). *Thinking, fast and slow.* Farrar, Straus and Giroux.

Kahneman, D. (2015, July 18). Quoted by D. Shariatmadari in, Daniel Kahneman, 'What would I eliminate if I had a magic wand? Overconfidence.' *The Guardian.* https://www.theguardian.com/books/2015/jul/18/daniel-kahneman-books-interview

Kahneman, D., Fredrickson, B. L., Schreiber, C. A., & Redelmeier, D. A. (1993). When more pain is preferred to less: Adding a better end. *Psychological Science, 4*, 401–405.

Kahneman, D., Krueger, A. B., Schkade, D. A., Schwarz, N., & Stone, A. A. (2004). A survey method for characterizing daily life experience: The day reconstruction method. *Science, 306*, 1776–1780.

Kail, R. (1991). Developmental change in speed of processing during childhood and adolescence. *Psychological Bulletin, 109*, 490–501.

Kaiser, J. (2020, November 6). Growth spurt for height genetics. *Science, 370*, 645.

Kaiser Family Foundation. (2010, January). *Generation M2: Media in the lives of 8- to 18-year-olds* [PDF file]. By V. J. Rideout, U. G. Foeher, & D. F. Roberts. https://files.eric.ed.gov/fulltext/ED527859.pdf

Kakinami, L., Barnett, T. A., Séguin, L., & Paradis, G. (2015). Parenting style and obesity risk in children. *Preventive Medicine, 75*, 18–22.

Kalkusch, I., Jaggy, A.-K., Bossi, C. B., Weiss, B., Sticca, F., & Perren, S. (2020). Promoting social pretend play in preschool age: Is providing roleplay material enough? *Early Education and Development, 32*(8), 1136–1152. https://www.tandfonline.com/doi/full/10.1080/10409289.2020.1830248

Kállay, É. (2015). Physical and psychological benefits of written emotional expression: Review of meta-analyses and recommendations. *European Psychologist, 20*, 242–251.

Kamatali, J.-M. (2014, April 4). Following orders in Rwanda. *The New York Times.* https://www.nytimes.com/2014/04/05/opinion/following-orders-in-rwanda.html

Kambeitz, J., Kambelitz-Ilankovic, L., Cabral, C., Dwyer, D. B., Calhoun, V. C., van den Heuvel, M. P., Falkai, P., Koutsouleris, N., & Malchow, B. (2016). Aberrant functional whole-brain network architecture in patients with schizophrenia: A meta-analysis. *Schizophrenia Bulletin, 42*(suppl 1), S13–S21.

Kamel, N. S., & Gammack, J. K. (2006). Insomnia in the elderly: Cause, approach, and treatment. *American Journal of Medicine, 119*, 463–469.

Kamenica, E., Naclerio, R., & Malani, A. (2013). Advertisements impact the physiological efficacy of a branded drug. *PNAS, 110*, 12931–12935.

Kamil, A. C., & Cheng, K. (2001). Way-finding and landmarks: The multiple-bearings hypothesis. *Journal of Experimental Biology, 204*, 103–113.

Kaminski, J., Cali, J., & Fischer, J. (2004). Word learning in a domestic dog: Evidence for "fast mapping." *Science, 304*, 1682–1683.

Kämpf, M. S., Liebermann, H., Kerschreiter, R., Krause, S., Nestler, S., & Schmukle, S. C. (2018). Disentangling the sources of mimicry: Social relations analyses of the link between mimicry and liking. *Psychological Science, 29*, 131–138.

Kandel, E. (2008, October/November). Quoted in S. Avan, Speaking of memory. *Scientific American Mind*, pp. 16–17.

Kandel, E. (2013, September 6). The new science of mind. *The New York Times.* https://www.nytimes.com/2013/09/08/opinion/sunday/the-new-science-of-mind.html

Kandel, E. R. (2012, March 5). A quest to understand how memory works [Interview with Claudia Dreifus]. *The New York Times.* https://www.nytimes.com/2012/03/06/science/a-quest-to-understand-how-memory-works.html

Kandel, E. R., & Schwartz, J. H. (1982). Molecular biology of learning: Modulation of transmitter release. *Science, 218*, 433–443.

Kandler, C., Bleidorn, W., Riemann, R., Angleitner, A., & Spinath, F. M. (2012). Life events as environmental states and genetic traits and the role of personality: A longitudinal twin study. *Behavior Genetics, 42*, 57–72.

Kandler, C., Riemann, R., & Angleitner, A. (2013). Patterns and sources of continuity and change of energetic and temporal aspects of temperament in adulthood: A longitudinal twin study of self- and peer reports. *Developmental Psychology, 49*, 1739–1753.

Kane, J. M., & Mertz, J. E. (2012). Debunking myths about gender and mathematics performance. *Notices of the American Mathematical Society, 59*, 10–21.

Kane, M. J., Brown, L. H., McVay, J. C., Silvia, P. J., Myin-Germeys, I., & Kwapil, T. R. (2007). For whom the mind wanders, and when: An experience-sampling study of working memory and executive control in daily life. *Psychological Science, 18*, 614–621.

Kanwar, A., Malik, S., Prokop, L. J., Sim, L. A., Feldstein, D., Wang, Z., & Murad, M. H. (2013). The association between anxiety disorders and suicidal behaviors: A systematic review and meta-analysis. *Depression and Anxiety, 30*, 917

Kapadia, R. (2021, February 17). *Women are still scarce at top of corporate ranks even after diversity talk. Here's why.* Barron's. https://www.barrons.com/articles/women-are-still-scarce-at-top-of-corporate-ranks-even-after-diversity-talk-heres-why-51613527237

Kaplan, B. J., Rucklidge, J. J., Romijn, A., & McLeod, K. (2015). The emerging field of nutritional mental health: Inflammation, the microbiome, oxidative stress, and mitochondrial function. *Clinical Psychological Science, 3*, 964–980.

Kaplan, H. I., & Sadock, B. J. (Eds.). (1989). *Comprehensive textbook of psychiatry.* Williams and Wilkins.

Kaplan, K. A. (2020). Sleep and sleep treatments in bipolar disorder. *Current Opinion in Psychology, 34*, 117–122.

Kaprio, J., Koskenvuo, M., & Rita, H. (1987). Mortality after bereavement: A prospective study of 95,647 widowed persons. *American Journal of Public Health, 77*, 283–287.

Karacan, I., Goodenough, D. R., Shapiro, A., & Starker, S. (1966). Erection cycle during sleep in relation to dream anxiety. *Archives of General Psychiatry, 15*, 183–189.

Karasik, L. B., Adolph, K. E., Tamis-LeMonda, C. S., & Bornstein, M. H. (2010). WEIRD walking: Cross-cultural research on motor development. *Behavioral and Brain Sciences, 33*, 95–96.

Karau, S. J., & Williams, K. D. (1993). Social loafing: A meta-analytic review and theoretical integration. *Journal of Personality and Social Psychology, 65*, 681–706.

Karazsia, B. T., Murnen, S. K., & Tylka, T. L. (2017). Is body dissatisfaction changing across time? A cross-temporal meta-analysis. *Psychological Bulletin, 143*, 293–320.

Kardas, M., Kumar, A., & Epley, N. (2022). Overly shallow?: Miscalibrated expectations create a barrier to deeper conversation. *Journal of Personality and Social Psychology, 122*(3), 367–398.

Kardas, M., & O'Brien, E. (2018). Easier seen than done: Merely watching others perform can foster an illusion of skill acquisition. *Psychological Science, 29*, 521–536.

Kark, J. D., Shemi, G., Friedlander, Y., Martin, O., Manor, O., & Blondheim, S. H. (1996). Does religious observance promote health? Mortality in secular vs. religious kibbutzim in Israel. *American Journal of Public Health, 86*, 341–346.

Karlsgodt, K. H., Sun, D., & Cannon, T. D. (2010). Structural and functional brain abnormalities in schizophrenia. *Current Directions in Psychological Science, 19*, 226–231.

Karni, A., Meyer, G., Rey-Hipolito, C., Jezzard, P., Adams, M. M., Turner, R., & Ungerleider, L. G. (1998). The acquisition of skilled motor performance: Fast and slow experience-driven changes in primary motor cortex. *PNAS, 95*, 861–868.

Karni, A., & Sagi, D. (1994). Dependence on REM sleep for overnight improvement of perceptual skills. *Science, 265*, 679–682.

Karns, C. M., Dow, M. W., & Neville, H. J. (2012). Altered cross-modal processing in the primary auditory cortex of congenitally deaf adults: A visual-somatosensory fMRI study with a double-flash illusion. *Journal of Neuroscience, 32*, 9626–9638.

Karpicke, J. D. (2012). Retrieval-based learning: Active retrieval promotes meaningful learning. *Current Directions in Psychological Science, 21*, 157–163.

Karremans, J. C., Frankenhis, W. E., & Arons, S. (2010). Blind men prefer a low waist-to-hip ratio. *Evolution and Human Behavior, 31*, 182–186.

Karsay, K., Knoll, J., & Matthes, J. (2018). Sexualizing media use and self-objectification: A meta-analysis. *Psychology of Women Quarterly, 42*, 9–28.

Kasen, S., Chen, H., Sneed, J., Crawford, T., & Cohen, P. (2006). Social role and birth cohort influences on gender-linked personality traits in women: A 20-year longitudinal analysis. *Journal of Personality and Social Psychology, 91*, 944–958.

Kashdan, T., DeWall, C. N., Schurtz, D., Deckman, T., Lykins, E. L. B., Evans, D., McKenzie, J., Segerstrom, S. C., Gailliot, M. T., & Brown, K. (2014). More than words: Contemplating death enhances positive emotional word use. *Personality and Individual Differences, 71*, 171–175.

Kashdan, T. B. (2009). *Curious? Discover the missing ingredient to a fulfilling life.* William Morrow.

Kashima, Y., Bain, P. G., & Perfors, A. (2019). The psychology of cultural dynamics: What is it, what do we know, and what is yet to be known? *Annual Review of Psychology, 70*, 499–529.

Kashubeck-West, S., & Meyer, J. (2008). The well-being of women who are late deafened. *Journal of Counseling Psychology, 55*, 463–472.

Kasser, T. (2018). Materialism and living well. In E. Diener, S. Oishi, & L. Tay (Eds.), *Handbook of well-being.* DEF Publishers.

Kassing, F., Godwin, J., Lochman, J. E., Coie, J. D., & Conduct Problems Prevention Research Group. (2019). Using early childhood behavior problems to predict adult convictions. *Journal of Abnormal Child Psychology, 47*, 765–778.

Katz, J. Goodnough, A., & Sanger-Katz, M. (2020). In shadow of pandemic, U.S. drug overdose deaths resurge to record. *The New York Times.* https://www.nytimes.com/interactive/2020/07/15/upshot/drug-overdose-deaths.html

Katz-Wise, S. L., Priess, H. A., & Hyde, J. S. (2010). Gender-role attitudes and behavior across the transition to parenthood. *Developmental Psychology, 46*, 18–28.

Kaufman, J. C., & Baer, J. (2002). I bask in dreams of suicide: Mental illness, poetry, and women. *Review of General Psychology, 6*, 271–286.

Kaufman, L., & Kaufman, J. H. (2000). Explaining the moon illusion. *PNAS, 97*, 500–505.

Kaufman, S. B. (2018). Self-actualizing people in the 21st century: Integration with contemporary theory and research on personality and well-being [PDF file]. *Journal of Humanistic Psychology, 63*(5). https://scottbarrykaufman.com/wp-content/uploads/2018/11/Kaufman-self-actualization-2018.pdf

Kaufman, S. B. (2020). *Transcend: The new science of self-actualization.* TarcherPerigee.

Kaufmann, R. K., Mann, M. L., Gopal, S., Liederman, J. A., Howe, P. D., Pretis, F., Tang, X., & Gilmore, M. (2017). Spatial heterogeneity of climate change as an experiential basis for skepticism. *PNAS, 114*, 67–71.

Kaunitz, L. N., Rowe, E. G., & Tsuchiya, N. (2016). Large capacity of conscious access for incidental memories in natural scenes. *Psychological Science, 27*, 1266–1277.

Kawakami, K., Dunn, E., Karmali, F., & Dovidio, J. F. (2009). Mispredicting affective and behavioral responses to racism. *Science, 323*, 276–278.

Kawamichi, H., Yoshihara, K., Sugawara, S. K., Matsunaga, M., Makita, K., Hamano, Y. H., Tanabe, H. C., & Sadato, N. (2015). Helping behavior induced by empathic concern attenuates anterior cingulate activation in response to others' distress. *Social Neuroscience, 11*, 109–122.

Kaye, L. K., Malone, S. A., & Wall, H. J. (2017). Emojis: Insights, affordances, and possibilities for psychological science. *Trends in Cognitive Sciences, 21*(2), 66–68.

Kayser, C. (2007, April/May). Listening with your eyes. *Scientific American Mind*, pp. 24–29.

Kazantzis, N., Whittington, C., & Dattilio, F. M. (2010). Meta-analysis of homework effects in cognitive and behavioral therapy: A replication and extension. *Clinical Psychology: Science and Practice, 17*, 144–156.

Kazdin, A. E. (1982). The token economy: A decade later. *Journal of Applied Behavior Analysis, 15*(3), 431–445.

Kazdin, A. E. (2018). Developing treatments for antisocial behavior among children: Controlled trials and uncontrolled tribulations. *Perspectives on Psychological Science, 13*(5), 634–650.

Kearns, M. C., Ressler, K. J., Zatzick, D., & Rothbaum, B. O. (2012). Early interventions for PTSD: A review. *Depression and Anxiety, 29*, 833–842.

Keefe, P. R. (2016, August 15). *The detectives who never forget a face.* NPR. https://www.npr.org/2016/08/17/490314062/new-yorker-the-detectives-who-never-forget-a-face

Keesey, R. E., & Corbett, S. W. (1984). Metabolic defense of the body weight set-point. In A. J. Stunkard & E. Stellar (Eds.), *Eating and its disorders* (pp. 87–96). Raven Press.

Keiser, H. N., Sackett, P. R., Kuncel, N. R., & Brothen, T. (2016). Why women perform better in college than admission scores would predict: Exploring the roles of conscientiousness and course-taking patterns. *Journal of Applied Psychology, 101*, 569–581.

Keith, S. W., Redden, D. T., Katzmarzyk, P. T., Boggiano, M. M., Hanlon, E. C., Benca, R. M., Ruden, D., Pietrobelli, A., Barger, J. L., Fontaine, K. R., Wang, C., Aronne, L. J. Wright, S. M., Baskin, M., Dhurandhar, N. V., Lijoi, M. C., Grilo, C. M., DeLuca, M., Westfall, A. O., & Allison, D. B. (2006). Putative contributors to the secular increase in obesity: Exploring the roads less traveled. *International Journal of Obesity, 30*, 1585–1594.

Kell, H. J., Lubinski, D., & Benbow, C. P. (2013). Who rises to the top? Early indicators. *Psychological Science, 24*, 648–659.

Keller, C., Hartmann, C., & Siegrist, M. (2016). The association between dispositional self-control and longitudinal changes in eating behaviors, diet quality, and BMI. *Psychology & Health, 31*, 1311–1327.

Keller, P. S., Haak, E. A., DeWall, C. N., & Renzetti, C. (2019). Poor sleep is associated with greater marital aggression: The role of self-control. *Behavioral Sleep Medicine, 17*, 174–180.

Kellerman, J., Lewis, J., & Laird, J. D. (1989). Looking and loving: The effects of mutual gaze on feelings of romantic love. *Journal of Research in Personality, 23*, 145–161.

Kelling, S. T., & Halpern, B. P. (1983). Taste flashes: Reaction times, intensity, and quality. *Science, 219*, 412–414.

Kelly, A. E. (2000). Helping construct desirable identities: A self-presentational view of psychotherapy. *Psychological Bulletin, 126*, 475–494.

Kelly, D. J., Quinn, P. C., Slater, A. M., Lee, K., Ge, L., & Pascalis, O. (2007). The other-race effect develops during infancy: Evidence of perceptual narrowing. *Psychological Science, 18*, 1084–1089.

Kelly, S. D., Özyürek, A., & Maris, E. (2010). Two sides of the same coin: Speech and gesture mutually interact to enhance comprehension. *Psychological Science, 21*, 260–267.

Kelly, T. A. (1990). The role of values in psychotherapy: A critical review of process and outcome effects. *Clinical Psychology Review, 10*, 171–186.

Kelly, Y., Zilanawala, A., Booker, C., & Sacker, A. (2019). Social media use and adolescent mental health: Findings from the UK Millennium Cohort Study. *EClinicalMedicine (The Lancet), 6*, 59–68.

Kempe, R. S., & Kempe, C. C. (1978). *Child abuse.* Harvard University Press.

Kempermann, G., Gage, F. H., Aigner, L., Song, H., Curtis, M. A., Thuret, S., Kuhn, H. G., Jessberger, S., Frankland, P. W., Cameron, H. A., Gould, E., Hen, R., Abrous, D. N., Toni, N., Schinder, A. F., Zhao, X., Lucassen, P. J., & Frisén, J. (2018). Human adult neurogenesis: Evidence and remaining questions. *Cell Stem Cell, 23*, 25–30.

Kendall-Tackett, K. A., Williams, L. M., & Finkelhor, D. (1993). Impact of sexual abuse on children: A review and synthesis of recent empirical studies. *Psychological Bulletin, 113*, 164–180.

Kendler, K. S. (1996). Parenting: A genetic-epidemiologic perspective. *American Journal of Psychiatry, 153*, 11–20.

Kendler, K. S., Maes, H. H., Lönn, S. L., Morris, N. A., Lichtenstein, P., Sundquist, J., & Sundquist, K. (2015). A Swedish national twin study of criminal behavior and its violent, white-collar and property subtypes. *Psychological Medicine, 45*, 2253–2262.

Kendler, K. S., Neale, M. C., Kessler, R. C., Heath, A. C., & Eaves, L. J. (1994). Parent treatment and the equal environment assumption in twin studies of psychiatric illness. *Psychological Medicine, 24*, 579–590.

Kendler, K. S., Ohlsson, H., Lichtenstein, P., Sundquist, J., & Sundquist, K. (2018). The genetic epidemiology of treated major depression in Sweden. *American Journal of Psychiatry, 175*, 1137–1144.

Kendler, K. S., Ohlsson, H., Sundquist, J., & Sundquist, K. (2016). Alcohol use disorder and mortality across the lifespan: A longitudinal cohort and co-relative analysis. *JAMA Psychiatry, 73*, 575–581.

Kendler, K. S., Ohlsson, H., Sundquist, J., & Sundquist, K. (2020). The rearing environment and risk for major depression: A Swedish national high-risk home-reared and adopted-away co-sibling control study. *American Journal of Psychiatry, 46*(7), 1359–1366.

Kendler, K. S., Sundquist, K., Ohlsson, H., Palmer, K., Maes, H., Winkleby, M. A., & Sundquist, J. (2012). Genetic and familiar environmental influences on the risk for drug abuse: A Swedish adoption study. *Archives of General Psychiatry, 69*, 690–697.

Kendler, K. S., Turkheimer, E., Ohlsson, H., Sundquist, J., & Sundquist, K. (2015). Family environment and the malleability of cognitive ability: A Swedish national home-reared and adopted-away cosibling control study. *PNAS, 112*, 4612–4617.

Kendrick, K. M., & Feng, J. (2011). Neural encoding principles in face perception revealed using non-primate models. In G. Rhodes, A. Calder, M. Johnson, & J. V. Haxby (Eds.), *The Oxford handbook of face perception*. Oxford University Press.

Kennedy, S., & Over, R. (1990). Psychophysiological assessment of male sexual arousal following spinal cord injury. *Archives of Sexual Behavior, 19*, 15–27.

Kennedy, S. H., Konarski, J. Z., Segal, Z. V., Lau, M. A., Bieling, P. J., McIntyre, R. S., & Mayberg, H. S. (2007). Differences in brain glucose metabolism between responders to CBT and venlafaxine in a 16-week randomized controlled trial. *American Journal of Psychiatry, 164*(5), 778–788.

Kennis, M., Gerritsen, L., van Dalen, M., Williams, A., Cuijpers, P., & Bockting, C. (2020). Prospective biomarkers of major depressive disorder: A systematic review and meta-analysis. *Molecular Psychiatry, 25*, 321–338.

Kenrick, D. T., Nieuweboer, S., & Bunnk, A. P. (2009). Universal mechanisms and cultural diversity: Replacing the blank slate with a coloring book. In M. Schaller, S. Heine, A. Norenzayan, T. Yamagishi, & T. Kameda (Eds.), *Evolution, culture, and the human mind* (pp. 257–271). Erlbaum.

Kensinger, E. A. (2007). Negative emotion enhances memory accuracy: Behavioral and neuroimaging evidence. *Current Directions in Psychological Science, 16*, 213–218.

Kent de Grey, R. G., Uchino, B. N., Trettevik, R., Cronan, S., & Hogan, J. N. (2018). Social support and sleep: A meta-analysis. *Health Psychology, 37*, 787–798.

Keough, K. A., Zimbardo, P. G., & Boyd, J. N. (1999). Who's smoking, drinking, and using drugs? Time perspective as a predictor of substance use. *Basic and Applied Social Psychology, 2*, 149–164.

Keramati, M., Durand, A., Girardeau, P., Gutkin, B., & Ahmed, S. H. (2017). Cocaine addiction as a homeostatic reinforcement learning disorder. *Psychological Review, 124*, 130–153.

Keresztes, A., Bender, A. R., Bodammer, N. C., Lindenberger, U., Shing, Y. L., & Werkle-Bergner, M. (2017). Hippocampal maturity promotes memory distinctiveness in childhood and adolescence. *PNAS, 114*, 9212–9217.

Kern, M. L., Eichstaedt, J. C., Schwartz, H. A., Dziurzynski, L., Ungar, L. H., Stillwell, D. J., Kosinski, M., Ramones, S. M., & Seligman, M. E. P. (2014). The online social self: An open vocabulary approach to personality. *Assessment, 21*, 158–169.

Kernis, M. H. (2003). Toward a conceptualization of optimal self-esteem. *Psychological Inquiry, 14*, 1–26.

Kerns, J. C., Guo, J., Fothergill, E., Howard, L., Knuth, N. D., Brychta, R., Chen, K. Y., Skaruli, M. C., Walter, P. J., & Hall, K. D. (2017). Increased physical activity associated with less weight regain six years after "The Biggest Loser" competition. *Obesity, 25*, 1838–1843.

Kerr, N. L., & Bruun, S. E. (1983). Dispensability of member effort and group motivation losses: Free-rider effects. *Journal of Personality and Social Psychology, 44*, 78–94.

Kerry, N., & Murray, D. R. (2021). Physical strength partly explains sex differences in trait anxiety in young Americans. *Psychological Science, 32*, 809–815.

Kessler, M., & Albee, G. (1975). Primary prevention. *Annual Review of Psychology, 26*, 557–591.

Kessler, R. C., Amminger, G. P., Aguilar-Gaxiola, S., Alonso, J., Lee, S., & Üstün, T. B. (2007). Age of onset of mental disorders: A review of recent literature. *Current Opinion in Psychiatry, 20*, 359–364.

Kessler, R. C., Brinbaum, H. G., Shahly, V., Bromet, E., Hwang, I., McLaughlin, K. A., Sampson, N., Andrade, L. H., De Girolamo, G., Demyttenaere, K., Haro, J. M., Karam, A. N., Kostyuchenko, S., Kovess, V., Lara, C., Levinson, D., Matschinger, H., Nakane, Y., Oakley, B., … Stein, D. J. (2010). Age differences in the prevalence and co-morbidity of DSM-IV major depressive episodes: Results from the WHO World Mental Health Survey Initiative. *Depression and Anxiety, 27*, 351–364.

Kessler, R. C., Petukhova, M., Sampson, N. A., Zaslavsky, A. M., & Wittchen, H.-A. (2012). Twelve-month and lifetime morbid risk of anxiety and mood disorders in the United States. *International Journal of Methods in Psychiatric Research, 21*, 169–184.

Kessler, S. R., Lucianetti, L., Pindek, S., Zhu, Z., & Spector, P. E. (2020). Job satisfaction and firm performance: Can employees' job satisfaction change the trajectory of a firm's performance? *Journal of Applied Social Psychology, 10*, 563–572.

Keyes, K. M., Cerdá, M., Brady, J. E., Havens, J. R., & Galea, S. (2014). Understanding the rural–urban differences in nonmedical prescription opioid use and abuse in the United States. *American Journal of Public Health, 104*, e52–e59.

Keyes, K. M., Maslowsky, J., Hamilton, A., & Schulenberg, J. (2015). The great sleep recession: Changes in sleep duration among U.S. adolescents, 1991–2012. *Pediatrics, 135*, 460–468.

Keynes, M. (1980, December 20/27). Handel's illnesses. *The Lancet*, pp. 1354–1355.

Keys, A., Brozek, J., Henschel, A., Mickelsen, O., & Taylor, H. L. (1950). *The biology of human starvation*. University of Minnesota Press.

KFF (Kaiser Family Foundation). (2021, August 4). KFF COVID-19 Vaccine Monitor: July 2021. https://www.kff.org/coronavirus-covid-19/poll-finding/kff-covid-19-vaccine-monitor-july-2021/

Khanna, S., & Greyson, B. (2014). Daily spiritual experiences before and after near-death experiences. *Psychology of Religion and Spirituality, 6*, 302–309.

Khanna, S., & Greyson, B. (2015). Near-death experiences and posttraumatic growth. *Journal of Nervous and Mental Disease, 203*, 749–755.

Khera, M., Bhattacharya, R. K., Blick, G., Kushner, H., Nguyen, D., & Miner, M. M. (2011). Improved sexual function with testosterone replacement therapy in hypogonadal men: Real-world data from the Testim Registry in the United States (TriUS). *Journal of Sexual Medicine, 8*, 3204–3213.

Khodagholy, D., Gelinas, J. N., & Buzsáki, G. (2017). Learning-enhanced coupling between ripple oscillations in association cortices and hippocampus. *Science, 358*, 369–372.

Kiatpongsan, S., & Norton, M. (2014). How much (more) should CEOs make? A universal desire for more equal pay. *Perspectives on Psychological Science, 9*, 587–593.

Kiecolt-Glaser, J. K. (2009). Psychoneuroimmunology: Psychology's gateway to the biomedical future. *Perspectives on Psychological Science, 4*, 367–369.

Kiecolt-Glaser, J. K., Loving, T. J., Stowell, J. R., Malarkey, W. B., Lemeshow, S., Dickinson, S. L., & Glaser, R. (2005). Hostile marital interactions, proinflammatory cytokine production, and wound healing. *Archives of General Psychiatry, 62*, 1377–1384.

Kiecolt-Glaser, J. K., Page, G. G., Marucha, P. T., MacCallum, R. C., & Glaser, R. (1998). Psychological influences on surgical recovery: Perspectives from psychoneuroimmunology. *American Psychologist, 53*, 1209–1218.

Kiehl, K. A., & Buckholtz, J. W. (2010). Inside the mind of a psychopath. *Scientific American Mind, 21*, 22–29.

Kiesow, H., Dunbar, R. I. M., Kable, J. W., Kalenscher, T., Vogeley, K., Schilbach, L., Marquand, A. F., Wiecki, T. V., & Bzdok, D. (2020). 10,000 social brains: Sex differentiation in human brain anatomy. *Science Advances, 6*(12). https://www.science.org/doi/10.1126/sciadv.aaz1170

Kihlstrom, J. (2019). The motivational unconscious. *Social and Personality Psychology Compass, 13*(5), 1–18.

Kihlstrom, J. F. (2005). Dissociative disorders. *Annual Review of Clinical Psychology, 1*, 227–253.

Kilgore, A. (2017, November 9). Aaron Hernandez suffered from most severe CTE ever found in a person his age. *The Washington Post*. https://tinyurl.com/ycj8mx64

Kille, D. R., Forest, A. L., & Wood, J. V. (2013). Tall, dark, and stable: Embodiment motivates mate selection preferences. *Psychological Science, 24*, 112–114.

Killingsworth, M. A. (2021). Experienced well-being rises with income, even above $75,000 per year. *PNAS, 118*(4). https://www.pnas.org/doi/10.1073/pnas.2016976118

Kilpatrick, L. A., Suyenobu, B. Y., Smith, S. R., Bueller, J. A., Goodman, T., Creswell, J. D., Tillisch, K., Mayer, E. A., & Naliboff, B. D. (2011). Impact of mindfulness-based stress reduction training on intrinsic brain activity. *Neuroimage, 56*, 290–298.

Kilpeläinen, T. O., Qi, L. Brage, S., Sharp, S. J., Sonestedt, E., Demerath, E., Ahmad, T., Mora, S., Kaakinen, M., Sandholt, C. H., Holzapfel, C., Autenrieth, C. S., Hyppönen, E., Cauchi, S., He, M., Kutalik, Z., Kumari, M., Stan⊠áková, A., Meidtner, K., ... Loos, R. J. F. (2012). Physical activity attenuates the influence of FTO variants on obesity risk: A meta-analysis of 218,166 adults and 19,268 children. *PLOS Medicine, 8*(11). https://www.ncbi.nlm.nih.gov/pmc/articles/PMC3206047/

Kim, B. S. K., Ng, G. F., & Ahn, A. J. (2005). Effects of client expectation for counseling success, client-counselor worldview match, and client adherence to Asian and European American cultural values on counseling process with Asian Americans. *Journal of Counseling Psychology, 52*, 67–76.

Kim, E.-L., Anderson, C. A., & Gentile, D. A. (2021). 7 ± 2 deadly sins of video game violence research. In V. Strasburger (Ed.), *Masters of media, Volume 1: Controversies and solutions*. Rowman and Littlefield.

Kim, E. S., Hagan, K. A., Grodstein, F., DeMeo, D. L., De Vivo, I., & Kubzansky, L. D. (2017). Optimism and cause-specific mortality: A prospective cohort study. *American Journal of Epidemiology, 185*, 21–29.

Kim, E. S., Ryff, C., Hassett, A., Brummett, C., Yeh, C., & Strecher, V. (2020). Sense of purpose in life and likelihood of future illicit drug use or prescription medication misuse. *Psychosomatic Medicine, 82*(7), 715–721.

Kim, H., & Markus, H. R. (1999). Deviance or uniqueness, harmony or conformity? A cultural analysis. *Journal of Personality and Social Psychology, 77*, 785–800.

Kim, H., Schimmack, U., Oishi, S., & Tsutsui, Y. (2018). Extraversion and life satisfaction: A cross-cultural examination of student and nationally representative samples. *Journal of Personality, 86*, 604–618.

Kim, J. (2022). *Constance Wu's reveal speaks to the profound pressure Asian American women face*. NPR. https://www.npr.org/2022/07/18/1112055817/constance-wu-asian-american-women

Kim, J., Suh, W., Kim, S., & Gopalan, H. (2012). Coping strategies to manage acculturative stress: Meaningful activity participation, social support, and positive emotion among Korean immigrant adolescents in the USA. *International Journal of Qualitative Studies on Health and Well-Being, 7*, 1–10.

Kim, J., Wang, C., Nunez, N., Kim, S., Smith, T., & Sahgal, N. (2015). Paranormal beliefs: Using survey trends from the USA to suggest a new area of research in Asia. *Asian Journal for Public Opinion Research, 2*, 279–306.

Kim, M., Kim, C.-H., Jung, H. H., Kim, S. J., & Chang, J. W. (2018). Treatment of major depressive disorder via magnetic resonance-guided focused ultrasound surgery. *Biological Psychiatry, 83*, e17–e18.

Kim, M. Y., Ford, B. Q., Mauss, I., & Tamir, M. (2015). Knowing when to seek anger: Psychological health and context-sensitive emotional preferences. *Cognition and Emotion, 29*(6), 1126–1136.

Kim, S. H., Hwang, J. H., Park, H. S., & Kim, S. E. (2008). Resting brain metabolic correlates of neuroticism and extraversion in young men. *NeuroReport, 19*, 883–886.

Kim, S. H., Vincent, L. C., & Goncalo, J. A. (2013). Outside advantage: Can social rejection fuel creative thought? *Journal of Experimental Psychology: General, 142*, 605–611.

Kimble, G. A. (1956). *Principles of general psychology*. Ronald Press.

Kimble, G. A. (1981). *Biological and cognitive constraints on learning*. In L. T. Benjamin, Jr. (Ed.), *The G. Stanley Hall lecture series*, Vol. 1 (pp. 11–60). American Psychological Association.

Kimble, M., Flack, W., Koide, J., Bennion, K., Brenneman, M., & Meyersburg, C. (2021). Student reactions to traumatic material in literature: Implications for trigger warnings. *PLOS ONE, 16*(3). https://journals.plos.org/plosone/article?id=10.1371/journal.pone.0247579

Kindt, M., Soeter, M., & Vervliet, B. (2009). Beyond extinction: Erasing human fear responses and preventing the return of fear. *Nature Neuroscience, 12*, 256–258.

King, D. W., King, L. A., Park, C. L., Lee, L. O., Pless Kaiser, A., Spiro, A., III, Moore, J. L., Kaloupek, D. G., & Keane, T. M. (2015). Positive adjustment among American repatriated prisoners of the Vietnam War: Modeling the long-term effects of captivity. *Clinical Psychological Science, 3*, 861–876.

King, L. A., Heintzelman, S. J., & Ward, S. J. (2016). Beyond the search for meaning: A contemporary science of the experience of meaning in life. *Current Directions in Psychological Science, 25*, 211–216.

King, S., St.-Hilaire, A., & Heidkamp, D. (2010). Prenatal factors in schizophrenia. *Current Directions in Psychological Science, 19*, 209–213.

Kingston, D. A., & Bradford, J. M. (2013). Hypersexuality and recidivism among sexual offenders. *Sexual Addiction & Compulsivity, 20*, 91–105.

Kinney, J. (2010). *EXCERPT: 'The Diary of a Wimpy Kid,' by Jeff Kinney*. ABC News. https://abcnews.go.com/GMA/excerpt-diary-wimpy-kid-jeff-kinney/story?id=12368623

Kinnier, R. T., & Metha, A. T. (1989). Regrets and priorities at three stages of life. *Counseling and Values, 33*, 182–193.

Kinsella, E. L., Hughes, S., Lemon, S., Stonebridge, N., & Sumner, R. C. (2022). "We shouldn't waste a good crisis": The lived experience of working on the frontline through the first surge (and beyond) of COVID-19 in the UK and Ireland. *Psychology & Health, 37*(2), 151–177.

Kipnis, J. (2018, August). The seventh sense. *Scientific American*, pp. 28–35.

Kirby, D. (2002). Effective approaches to reducing adolescent unprotected sex, pregnancy, and childbearing. *Journal of Sex Research, 39*, 51–57.

Kirk, M., Rasmussen, K. W., Overgaard, S. B., & Berntsen, D. (2019). Five weeks of immersive reminiscence therapy improves autobiographical memory in Alzheimer's disease. *Memory, 27*, 441–454.

Kirkpatrick, B., Fenton, W. S., Carpenter, W. T., Jr., & Marder, S. R. (2006). The NIMH-MATRICS consensus statement on negative symptoms. *Schizophrenia Bulletin, 32*, 214–219.

Kirkpatrick, L. (1999). Attachment and religious representations and behavior. In J. Cassidy & P. R. Shaver (Eds.), *Handbook of attachment*. Guilford.

Kirmayer, L. J., & Sartorius, N. (2007). Cultural models and somatic syndromes. *Psychosomatic Medicine, 69*, 832–840.

Kirsch, I. (2010). *The emperor's new drugs: Exploding the antidepressant myth*. Basic Books.

Kirsch, I. (2016). *The emperor's new drugs: Medication and placebo in the treatment of depression*. In Behind and beyond the brain. Symposium conducted by the Bial Foundation, March 30–April 2.

Kirsch, I., Deacon, B. J., Huedo-Medina, T. B., Scoboria, A., Moore, T. J., & Johnson, B. T. (2008). Initial severity and antidepressant benefits: A meta-analysis of data submitted to the Food and Drug Administration. *Public Library of Science Medicine, 5*, e45.

Kisley, M. A., Wood, S., & Burrows, C. L. (2007). Looking at the sunny side of life: Age-related change in an event-related potential measure of the negativity bias. *Psychological Science, 18*, 838–843.

Kisor, H. (1990). *What's that pig outdoors? A memoir of deafness*. Hill and Wang.

Kitahara, C. M., Flint, A. J., de Gonzalez, A. B., Bernstein, L., Brotzman, M., MacInnis, R. J., Moore, S. C., Robien, K., Rosenberg, P. S., Singh, P. H., Weiderpass, E., Adami, H. O., Anton-Culver, H., Ballard-Barbash, R., Buring, J. E., Freedman, D. M., Fraser, G. E., Beane Freeman, L. E., Gapstur, S. M., ... Hartge, P. (2014, July 8). Association between class III obesity (BMI of 40–59 kg/m^2) and mortality: A pooled analysis of 20 prospective studies. *PLoS Medicine, 11*(7). https://journals.plos.org/plosmedicine/article?id=10.1371/journal.pmed.1001673

Kitaoka, A. (2016, September 11). Facebook post. https://bit.ly/38TZ7Cy

Kitayama, S., Berg, M. K., & Chopik, W. J. (2020). Culture and well-being in late adulthood: Theory and evidence. *American Psychologist, 75*(4), 567–576.

Kitayama, S., Conway, L. G., III, Pietromonaci, P. R., Park, H., & Plaut, V. C. (2010). Ethos of independence across regions in the United States: The production-adoption model of cultural change. *American Psychologist, 65*, 559–574.

Kitayama, S., Ishii, K., Imada, T., Takemura, K., & Ramaswamy, J. (2006). Voluntary settlement and the spirit of independence: Evidence from Japan's "northern frontier." *Journal of Personality and Social Psychology, 91*, 369–384.

Kitayama, S., Park, H., Sevincer, A. T., Karasawa, M., & Uskul, A. K. (2009). A cultural task analysis of implicit independence: Comparing North America, Western Europe, and East Asia. *Journal of Personality and Social Psychology, 97*, 236–255.

Kitayama, S., Park, J., Boylan, J. M., Miyamoto, Y., Levine, C. S., Markus, H. R., Karasawa, M., Coe, C. L., Kawakami, N., Love, G. D., & Ryff, C. D. (2015). Expression of anger and ill health in two cultures: An examination of inflammation and cardiovascular risk. *Psychological Science, 26*, 211–220.

Kivimaki, M., Leino-Arjas, P., Luukkonen, R., Rihimaki, H., & Kirjonen, J. (2002). Work stress and risk of cardiovascular mortality: Prospective cohort study of industrial employees. *British Medical Journal, 325*, 857.

Kivipelto, M., & Håkansson, K. (2017, April). A rare success against Alzheimer's. *Scientific American*, pp. 33–37.

Kivisto, A. J., Magee, L. A., Phalen, P. L., & Ray, B. R. (2019). Firearm ownership and domestic versus nondomestic homicide in the U.S. *American Journal of Preventive Medicine, 57*, 311–320.

Kivlighan, D. M., Goldberg, S. B., Abbas, M., Pace, B. T., Yulish, N. E., Thomas, J. G., Cullen, M. M., Flückiger, C., & Wampold, B. E. (2015). The enduring effects of psychodynamic treatments vis-à-vis alternative treatments: A multilevel longitudinal meta-analysis. *Clinical Psychology Review, 40*, 1–14.

Klahr, A. M., & Burt, S. A. (2014). Elucidating the etiology of individual differences in parenting: A meta-analysis of behavioral genetic research. *Psychological Bulletin, 140*, 544–586.

Klaiber, P., Wen, J. H., DeLongis, A., & Sin, N. L. (2021). The ups and downs of daily life during COVID-19: Age differences in affect, stress, and positive events. *Journals of Gerontology: Series B, 76*, e30–e37.

Klapilová, K., Demidova, L. Y., Elliott, H., Flinton, C. A., Weiss, P., & Fedoroff, J. P. (2019). Psychological treatment of problematic sexual interests: Cross-country comparison. *International Review of Psychiatry, 31*(2), 169–180.

Klayman, J., & Ha, Y.-W. (1987). Confirmation, disconfirmation, and information in hypothesis testing. *Psychological Review, 94*, 211–228.

Klein, D. N. (2010). Chronic depression: Diagnosis and classification. *Current Directions in Psychological Science, 19*, 96–100.

Klein, D. N., & Kotov, R. (2016). Course of depression in a 10-year prospective study: Evidence for qualitatively distinct subgroups. *Journal of Abnormal Psychology, 125*, 337–348.

Kleine, A.-K., Rudolph, C. W., & Zacher, H. (2019). Thriving at work: A meta-analysis. *Journal of Organizational Behavior, 40*(9–10), 973–999.

Kleinke, C. L. (1986). Gaze and eye contact: A research review. *Psychological Bulletin, 1000*, 78–100.

Kleinmuntz, B., & Szucko, J. J. (1984). A field study of the fallibility of polygraph lie detection. *Nature, 308*, 449–450.

Kleitman, N. (1960, November). Patterns of dreaming. *Scientific American*, pp. 82–88.

Klemm, W. R. (1990). Historical and introductory perspectives on brainstem-mediated behaviors. In W. R. Klemm & R. P. Vertes (Eds.), *Brainstem mechanisms of behavior* (pp. 3–32). Wiley.

Klimstra, T. A., Hale, W. W., III, Raaijmakers, Q. A. W., Branje, S. J. T., & Meeus, W. H. J. (2009). Maturation of personality in adolescence. *Journal of Personality and Social Psychology, 96*, 898–912.

Klimstra, T. A., Kuppens, P., Luyckx, K., Branje, S., Hale, W. W., Oosterwegel, A., Koot, H. M., & Meeus, W. H. J. (2015). Daily dynamics of adolescent mood and identity. *Journal of Research on Adolescence, 26*, 459–473.

Kline, D., & Schieber, F. (1985). Vision and aging. In J. E. Birren & K. W. Schaie (Eds.), *Handbook of the psychology of aging* (2nd ed., pp. 296–331). Van Nostrand Reinhold.

Kline, N. S. (1974). *From sad to glad*. Ballantine Books.

Klinke, R., Kral, A., Heid, S., Tillein, J., & Hartmann, R. (1999). Recruitment of the auditory cortex in congenitally deaf cats by long-term cochlear electrostimulation. *Science, 285*, 1729–1733.

Kluemper, D. H., McLarty, B. D., Bishop, T. R., & Sen, A. (2015). Interviewee selection test and evaluator assessments of general mental ability, emotional intelligence and extraversion: Relationships with structured behavioral and situational interview performance. *Journal of Business and Psychology, 30*, 543–563.

Knapp, S., & VandeCreek, L. (2000). Recovered memories of childhood abuse: Is there an underlying professional consensus? *Professional Psychology: Research and Practice, 31*, 365–371.

Knickmeyer, E. (2001, August 7). In Africa, big is definitely better. *Seattle Times*, p. A7.

Kniffin, K. M., Narayanan, J., Anseel, F., Antonakis, J., Ashford, S. P., Bakker, A. B., Bamberger, P., Bpuji, H., Bhave, D. P., Choi, V. K., Creary, S. J., Demerouti, E., Flynn, F. J., Gelfand, M. J., Greer, L. L., Johns G., Kesebir, S., Klein, P. G., Lee, S. Y., ... van Vugt, M. (2021). COVID-19 and the workplace: Implications, issues, and insights for future research and action. *American Psychologist, 76*(1), 63–77.

Knight, W. (2004, August 2). *Animated face helps deaf with phone chat*. New Scientist. https://www.newscientist.com/article/dn6228-animated-face-helps-deaf-with-phone-chat/

Knipe, D., Padmanathan, P., Newton-Howes, G., Chang, L. F., & Kapur, N. (2022). Suicide and self-harm. *The Lancet*, 399(10338), 1903–1916.

Knoblich, G., & Oellinger, M. (2006, October/November). The Eureka moment. *Scientific American Mind*, pp. 38–43.

Knolle, F., Goncalves, R. P., & Morton, J. A. (2017, November 8). Sheep recognize familiar and unfamiliar human faces from two-dimensional images. *Royal Society Open Science*, 4. https://royalsocietypublishing.org/doi/10.1098/rsos.171228

Knuts, I. J. E., Cosci, F., Esquivel, G., Goossens, L., van Duinen, M., Bareman, M., Overbeek, T., Griez, E. J., & Schruers, K. R. J. (2010). Cigarette smoking and 35% CO_2 induced panic in panic disorder patients. *Journal of Affective Disorders*, 124, 215–218.

Knutsen, J., Mandell, D. S., & Frye, D. (2015). Children with autism are impaired in the understanding of teaching. *Developmental Science, 20*. doi: 10.1111/desc.12368

Knutsson, A., & Bøggild, H. (2010). Gastrointestinal disorders among shift workers. *Scandinavian Journal of Work, Environment & Health*, 36(2), 85–95.

Ko, A., Pick, C. M., Kwon, J. Y., Barlev, M., Krems, J. A., Varnum, M. E. W., Neel, R., Peysha, M., Boonyasiriwat, W., Brandstätter, E., Crispim, A. C., Cruz, J. E., David, D., David, O. A., de Felipe Pereira, R., Fetvadjiev, V. H., Fischer, R., Galdi, S., Galindo, O., ... Kenrick, D. T. (2020). Family matters: Rethinking the psychology of human social motivation. *Perspectives on Psychological Science*, 15(1), 173–201.

Kocevar, G., Suprano, I., Stamile, C., Hannoun, S., Fourneret, P., Revol, O., Nusbaum, F., & Sappey-Marinier, D. (2019). Brain structural connectivity correlates with fluid intelligence in children: A DTI graph analysis. *Intelligence, 72*, 67–75.

Koch, C. (2015, January/February). The face as entryway to the self. *Scientific American Mind*, pp. 26–29.

Koch, C. (2016, November/December). Sleeping while awake. *Scientific American Mind*, pp. 20–23.

Koch, C. (2021, June). The brain electric. *Scientific American*, pp. 71–75.

Kocsis, J. H. (2018). Internet-based psychotherapy: How far can we go? *American Journal of Psychiatry, 175*, 202–203.

Koenig, H. G., & Larson, D. B. (1998). Use of hospital services, religious attendance, and religious affiliation. *Southern Medical Journal, 91*, 925–932.

Koenig, L. B., & Vaillant, G. E. (2009). A prospective study of church attendance and health over the life-span. *Health Psychology, 28*, 117–124.

Koerner, B. (2003, March 28). *What does a "thumbs up" mean in Iraq?* Slate. https://slate.com/news-and-politics/2003/03/what-does-a-thumbs-up-mean-in-iraq.html

Kofler, M. J., Raiker, J. S., Sarver, D. E., Wells, E. L., & Soto, E. F. (2016). Is hyperactivity ubiquitous in ADHD or dependent on environmental demands? Evidence from meta-analysis. *Clinical Psychology Review, 46*, 12–24.

Kogan, C. S., Noorishad, P.-G., Ndengeyingoma, A., Guerrier, M., & Cénat, J. M. (2022). Prevalence and correlates of anxiety symptoms among Black people in Canada: A significant role for everyday racial discrimination and racial microaggressions. *Journal of Affective Disorders, 308*, 545–553.

Koh, A. W. L., Lee, S. C., & Lim, S. W. H. (2018). The learning benefits of teaching: A retrieval practice hypothesis. *Applied Cognitive Psychology, 32*, 401–410.

Kohlberg, L. (1981). *The philosophy of moral development: Essays on moral development* (Vol. I). Harper & Row.

Kohlberg, L. (1984). *The psychology of moral development: Essays on moral development* (Vol. II). Harper & Row.

Kohler, I. (1962, May). Experiments with goggles. *Scientific American*, pp. 62–72.

Köhler, W. (1925; reprinted 1957). *The mentality of apes*. Pelican.

Kolb, B., & Whishaw, I. Q. (1998). Brain plasticity and behavior. *Annual Review of Psychology, 49*, 43–64.

Kolb, B., & Whishaw, I. Q. (2006). *An introduction to brain and behavior* (2nd ed.). Worth.

Kolla, B., Coombes, B. J., Morgenthaler, T. I., & Mansukhani, M. P. (2020). 0173 spring forward, fall back: Increased patient safety-related adverse events following the spring time change. *Sleep, 43*, A69.

Komisaruk, B. R., & Whipple, B. (2011). Non-genital orgasms. *Sexual and Relationship Therapy, 26*, 356–372.

Kondoh, K., Lu, Z., Olson, D. P., Lowell, B. B., & Buck, L. B. (2016). A specific area of olfactory cortex involved in stress hormone responses to predator odours. *Nature, 532*, 103–106.

Kong, A., Thorleifsson, G., Frigge, M. L., Vilhjalmsson, B. J., Young, A. I., Thorgeirsson, T. E., Benonisdottir, S., Oddsson, A., Halldorsson, B. V., Masson, G., Gudbjartsson, D. F., Helgason, A., Bjornsdottir, G., Thorsteinsdottir, U., & Stefansson, K. (2018). The nature of nurture: Effects of parental genotypes. *Science, 359*, 424–428.

Konkle, T., Brady, T. F., Alvarez, G. A., & Oliva, A. (2010). Conceptual distinctiveness supports detailed visual long-term memory for real-world objects. *Journal of Experimental Psychology: General, 139*, 558–578.

Kontula, O., & Haavio-Mannila, E. (2009). The impact of aging on human sexual activity and sexual desire. *Journal of Sex Research, 46*, 46–56.

Koole, S. L., Greenberg, J., & Pyszczynski, T. (2006). Introducing science to the psychology of the soul. *Current Directions in Psychological Science, 15*, 212–216.

Kopp, S. J., Sockol, L. E., & Multhaup, K. S. (2020). Age-related differences in flashbulb memories: A meta-analysis. *Psychology and Aging, 35*, 459–472.

Koppel, L., Andersson, D., Tinghög, G. Västfjäll, D., & Feldman, G. (2021). We are all less risky and more skillful than our fellow drivers: Replication and extension of Svenson (1981). https://psyarxiv.com/2ewb9/

Kornell, N., & Bjork, R. A. (2008). Learning concepts and categories: Is spacing the "enemy of induction?" *Psychological Science, 19*, 585–592.

Kosslyn, S. M. (2005). Reflective thinking and mental imagery: A perspective on the development of posttraumatic stress disorder. *Development and Psychopathology, 17*, 851–863.

Kosslyn, S. M., & Koenig, O. (1992). *Wet mind: The new cognitive neuroscience.* Free Press.

Kotchick, B. A., Shaffer, A., & Forehand, R. (2001). Adolescent sexual risk behavior: A multi-system perspective. *Clinical Psychology Review, 21*, 493–519.

Kotkin, M., Daviet, C., & Gurin, J. (1996). The *Consumer Reports* mental health survey. *American Psychologist, 51*, 1080–1082.

Kotov, R., Krueger, R. F., Watson, D., Achenbach, T. M., Althoff, R. R., Bagby, R. M., Brown, T. A., Carpenter, W. T., Caspi, A., Clark, L. A., Eaton, N. R., Forbes, M. K., Forbush, K. T., Goldberg, D., Hasin, D., Hyman, S. E., Ivanova, M. Y., Lynam, D. R., Markon, K., … Zimmerman, M. (2017). The Hierarchical Taxonomy of Psychopathology (HiTOP): A dimensional alternative to traditional nosologies. *Journal of Abnormal Psychology, 126*(4), 454.

Kotzur, P. F., & Wagner, U. (2021). The dynamic relationship between contact opportunities, positive and negative intergroup contact, and prejudice: A longitudinal investigation. *Journal of Personality and Social Psychology, 120*(2), 418–442.

Kounios, J., & Beeman, M. (2014). The cognitive neuroscience of insight. *Annual Review of Psychology, 65*, 71–93.

Kovács, Á. M., Téglás, E., & Endress, A. D. (2010). The social sense: Susceptibility to others' beliefs in human infants and adults. *Science, 330*, 1830–1834.

Kovelman, I., Shalinsky, M. H., Berens, M. S., & Petitto, L. (2014). Words in the bilingual brain: An fNIRS brain imaging investigation of lexical processing in sign-speech bimodal bilinguals. *Frontiers in Human Neuroscience, 8*. https://www.frontiersin.org/articles/10.3389/fnhum.2014.00606/full

Kowalski, R. M., Limber, S. P., & McCord, A. (2018). A developmental approach to cyberbullying: Prevalence and protective factors. *Aggression and Violent Behavior, 45*, 20–32.

Koyanagi, A., Oh, H., Carvalho, A. F., Smith, L., Haro, J. M., Vancampfort, D., Stubbs, B., & Devylder, J. E. (2019). Bullying victimization and suicide attempt among adolescents aged 12–15 years from 48 countries. *Journal of the American Academy of Child & Adolescent Psychiatry, 58*, 907–918.

Kraft, C. (1978). A psychophysical approach to air safety: Simulator studies of visual illusions in night approaches. In H. L. Pick, H. W. Leibowitz, J. E. Singer, A. Steinschneider, & H. W. Stevenson (Eds.), *Psychology: From research to practice.* Plenum Press.

Kraft, T., & Pressman, S. (2012). Grin and bear it: The influence of the manipulated facial expression on the stress response. *Psychological Science, 23*, 1372–1378.

Kraft-Todd, G., Yoeli, E., Bhanot, S., & Rand, D. (2015). Promoting cooperation in the field. *Current Opinion in Behavioral Sciences, 3*, 96–101.

Krahé, B., & Berger, A. (2017). Longitudinal pathways of sexual victimization, sexual self-esteem, and depression in women and men. *Psychological Trauma: Theory, Research, Practice, and Policy, 9*, 147–155.

Krahé, B., Lutz, J., & Sylla, I. (2018). Lean back and relax: Reclined seating position buffers the effect of frustration on anger and aggression. *European Journal of Social Psychology, 48*, 718–723.

Krakow, B., Germain, A., Warner, T. D., Schrader, R., Koss, M. P., Hollifeld, M., Tandberg, D., Melendrez, D., & Johnston, L. (2001). The relationship of sleep quality and posttraumatic stress to potential sleep disorders in sexual assault survivors with nightmares, insomnia, and PTSD. *Journal of Traumatic Stress, 14*, 647–665.

Krakow, B., Schrader, R., Tandberg, D., Hollifeld, M., Koss, M. P., Yau, C. L., & Cheng, D. T. (2002). Nightmare frequency in sexual assault survivors with PTSD. *Journal of Anxiety Disorders, 16*, 175–190.

Kramer, A. (2010). Personal communication.

Kramer, A. F., & Erickson, K. I. (2007). Capitalizing on cortical plasticity: Influence of physical activity on cognition and brain function. *Trends in Cognitive Sciences, 11*, 342–348.

Kramer, P. D. (2011, July 9). In defense of antidepressants. *The New York Times.* https://www.nytimes.com/2011/07/10/opinion/sunday/10antidepressants.html

Kranz, F., & Ishai, A. (2006). Face perception is modulated by sexual preference. *Current Biology, 16*, 63–68.

Kraus, M. W., Piff, P. K., Mendoza-Denton, R., Rheinschmidt, M. L., & Keltner, D. (2012). Social class, solipsism, and contextualism: How the rich are different from the poor. *Psychological Review, 119*(3), 546–572.

Kredlow, M. A., Fenster, R. J., Laurent, E. S., Ressler, K. J., & Phelps, E. A. (2022). Prefrontal cortex, amygdala, and threat processing: Implications for PTSD. *Neuropsychopharmacology, 47*, 247–259.

Krems, J. A., Ko, A., Moon, J. W., & Varnum, M. E. W. (2021). Lay beliefs about gender and sexual behavior: First evidence for a pervasive, robust (but seemingly unfounded) stereotype. *Psychological Science, 32*(6), 871–889.

Kret, M. E., & De Dreu, C. K. W. (2019). The power of pupil size in establishing trust and reciprocity. *Journal of Experimental Psychology: General, 148*(8), 1299–1311.

Kretch, K. S., Franchak, J. M., & Adolph, K. E. (2014). Crawling and walking infants see the world differently. *Child Development, 85*, 1503–1518.

Kring, A. M., & Caponigro, J. M. (2010). Emotion in schizophrenia: Where feeling meets thinking. *Current Directions in Psychological Science, 19*, 255–259.

Kring, A. M., & Gordon, A. H. (1998). Sex differences in emotion: Expression, experience, and physiology. *Journal of Personality and Social Psychology, 74*, 686–703.

Kringelbach, M. L., & Berridge, K. C. (2012, August). The joyful mind. *Scientific American*, pp. 40–45.

Krishnan, A., Zhang, R., Yao, V., Theesfeld, C. L., Wong, A. K., Tadych, A., Volfovsky, N., Packer, A., Lash, A., & Troyanskaya, O. G. (2016). Genome-wide prediction and functional characterization of the genetic basis of autism spectrum disorder. *Nature Neuroscience, 19*, 1454–1462.

Kristal, A. S., Whillans, A. V., Bazerman, M. H., Gino, F., Shu, L. L., Mazar, N., & Ariely, D. (2020). Signing at the beginning versus at the end does not decrease dishonesty. *PNAS, 117*(13), 7103–7107.

Kristof, N. (2017, February 11). Husbands are deadlier than terrorists. *The New York Times* https://www.nytimes.com/2017/02/11/opinion/sunday/husbands-are-deadlier-than-terrorists.html

Kristof, N. (2019, March 16). This 8-year-old chess champion will make you smile. *The New York Times.* https://www.nytimes.com/2019/03/16/opinion/sunday/chess-champion-8-year-old-homeless-refugee-.html

Krittanawong, C., Maitra, N. S., Virk, H. U. H., Fogg, S., Wang, Z., Kaplin, S., Gritsch, D., Storch, E. A., Tobler, P. N., Charney, D. S., & Levine, G. N. (2022). Association of optimism with cardiovascular events and all-cause mortality: Systematic review and meta-analysis. *American Journal of Medicine, 135*(7), 856–863.

Krizan, Z., & Hisler, G. (2019). Sleepy anger: Restricted sleep amplifies angry feelings. *Journal of Experimental Psychology: General, 148*, 1239–1250.

Kroenke, L., Geukes, K., Utesch, T., Kuper, N., & Back, M. D. (2020). Neuroticism and emotional risk during the COVID-19 pandemic. *Journal of Research in Personality, 89*. https://www.sciencedirect.com/science/article/pii/S0092656620301276

Krosnick, J. A., & Alwin, D. F. (1989). Aging and susceptibility to attitude change. *Journal of Personality and Social Psychology, 57*, 416–425.

Krosnick, J. A., Betz, A. L., Jussim, L. J., & Lynn, A. R. (1992). Subliminal conditioning of attitudes. *Personality and Social Psychology Bulletin, 18*, 152–162.

Kross, E., & Ayduk, O. (2011). Making meaning out of negative experiences by self-distancing. *Current Directions in Psychological Science, 20*, 187–191.

Kross, E., Berman, M., Mischel, W., Smith, E. E., & Wager, T. (2011). Social rejection shares somatosensory representations with physical pain. *PNAS, 108*, 6270–6275.

Kross, E., Bruehlman-Senecal, E., Park, J., Burson, A., Dougherty, A., Shablack, H., Bremner, R., Moser, J., & Ayduk, O. (2014). Self-talk as a regulatory mechanism: How you do it matters. *Journal of Personality and Social Psychology, 106*, 304–324.

Krueze, L. J., Pijnenborg, G. H. M., de Jonge, Y. B., & Nauta, M. H. (2018). Cognitive-behavior therapy for children and adolescents with anxiety disorders: A meta-analysis of secondary outcomes. *Journal of Anxiety Disorders, 60*, 43–57.

Kruger, J., & Dunning, D. (1999). Unskilled and unaware of it: How difficulties in recognizing one's own incompetence lead to inflated self-assessments. *Journal of Personality and Social Psychology, 77*, 1121–1134.

Kruger, J., Epley, N., Parker, J., & Ng, Z.-W. (2005). Egocentrism over e-mail: Can we communicate as well as we think? *Journal of Personality and Social Psychology, 89*, 925–936.

Krüger, T. H. C., Schulze, J., Bechinie, A., Neumann, I., Jung, S., Sperling, C., Engel, J., Müller, A., Kneer, J., Kahl, K. G., Karst, M., Herrmann, J., Fournier-Kaiser, L., Peters, L., Jürgensen, F., Nagel, M., Prager, W., Dulz, B., Wohlmuth, P., ... Wollmer, M. A. (2022). Neuronal effects of glabellar botulinum toxin injections using a valenced inhibition task in borderline personality disorder. *Scientific Reports, 12*. https://www.nature.com/articles/s41598-022-17509-0

Krumhansl, C. L. (2010). Plink: "Thin slices" of music. *Music Perception, 27*, 337–354.

Krynen, R. C., & McBeath, M. K. (2019). Baseball's sight-audition farness effect (SAFE) when umpiring baserunners: Judging precedence of competing visual versus auditory events. *Journal of Experimental Psychology: Human Perception and Performance, 45*, 67–81.

Kteily, N. S., & Landry, A. P. (2022). Dehumanization: Trends, insights, and challenges. *Trends in Cognitive Sciences, 26*(3), 222–240.

Kubzansky, L. D., Koenen, K. C., Jones, C., & Eaton, W. W. (2009). A prospective study of posttraumatic stress disorder symptoms and coronary heart disease in women. *Health Psychology, 28*, 125–130.

Kuehn, B. (2019). Vaping and pregnancy. *Journal of the American Medical Association, 321*, 1344.

Kuehner, C. (2017). Why is depression more common among women than among men? *Lancet Psychiatry, 4*, 146–158.

Kugimiya, T., Ishii, N., Kohno, K., Kanehisa, M., Hatano, K., Hirakawa, H., & Terao, T. (2021). Lithium in drinking water and suicide prevention: The largest nationwide epidemiological study from Japan. *Bipolar Disorders, 23*, 33–40.

Kuhl, P. K. (2015, November). Baby talk. *Scientific American*, pp. 65–69.

Kuhl, P. K., & Meltzoff, A. N. (1982). The bimodal perception of speech in infancy. *Science, 218*, 1138–1141.

Kuhl, P. K., Ramírez, R. R., Bosseler, A., Lin, J. L., & Imada, T. (2014). Infants' brain responses to speech suggest analysis by synthesis. *PNAS, 111*, 11238–11245.

Kumar, A., & Epley, N. (2018). Undervaluing gratitude: Expressers misunderstand the consequences of showing appreciation. *Psychological Science, 29*, 1423–1435.

Kumar, A., & Epley, N. (2022). A little good goes an unexpectedly long way: Underestimating the positive impact of kindness on recipients. *Journal of Experimental Psychology: General*, 152(1), 236–252.

Kumar, A., & Gilovich, T. (2013). *Talking about what you did and what you have: The differential story utility of experiential and material purchases* [Paper]. Presented at the Association for Consumer Research Annual Conference, Chicago, IL.

Kumar, A., & Gilovich, T. (2015). Some "thing" to talk about? Differential story utility from experiential and material purchases. *Personality and Social Psychology Bulletin, 41*, 1320–1331.

Kumar, M. B., & Tjepkema, M. (2019). *Suicide among First Nations people, Métis and Inuit (2011–2016): Findings from the 2011 Canadian census health and environment cohort* (CanCHEC). Statistics Canada. https://www150.statcan.gc.ca/n1/pub/99-011-x/99-011-x2019001-eng.htm

Kuncel, N. R., & Hezlett, S. A. (2007). Standardized tests predict graduate students' success. *Science, 315*, 1080–1081.

Kuncel, N. R., & Hezlett, S. A. (2010). Fact and fiction in cognitive ability testing for admissions and hiring decisions. *Current Directions in Psychological Science, 19*, 339–345.

Kunst-Wilson, W., & Zajonc, R. (1980). Affective discrimination of stimuli that cannot be recognized. *Science, 207*, 557–558.

Kuper-Smith, B., Doppelhofer, L., Oganian, Y., Rosenblau, G., & Korn, C. (2020). Optimistic beliefs about the personal impact of COVID-19. https://www.researchgate.net/publication/340047943_Optimistic_beliefs_about_the_personal_impact_of_COVID-19

Kupfer, D. J. (2012, June 1). *Dr. Kupfer defends* DSM-5. Medscape. https://medscape.com/viewarticle/764735

Kurtycz, L. M. (2015). Choice and control for animals in captivity. *The Psychologist, 28*, 892–893.

Kushlev, K., & Dunn, E. W. (2015). Checking email less frequently reduces stress. *Computers in Human Behavior, 43*, 220–228.

Kushlev, K., Heintzelman, S. J., Lutes, L. D., Wirtz, D., Kanippayoor, J. M., Leitner, D., & Diener, E. (2020). Does happiness improve health? Evidence from a randomized controlled trial. *Psychological Science, 31*, 807–821.

Kushlev, K., Radosic, N., & Diener, E. (2022). Subjective well-being and prosociality around the globe: Happy people give more of their time and money to others. *Social Psychological and Personality Science, 13*(4). https://doi.org/10.1177/19485506211043379

Kushner, M. G., Kim, S. W., Conahue, C., Thuras, P., Adson, D., Kotlyar, M., McCabe, J., Peterson, J., & Foa, E. B. (2007). D-cycloserine augmented exposure therapy for obsessive-compulsive disorder. *Biological Psychiatry, 62*, 835–838.

Kutas, M. (1990). Event-related brain potential (ERP) studies of cognition during sleep: Is it more than a dream? In R. R. Bootzin, J. F. Kihlstrom, & D. Schacter (Eds.), *Sleep and cognition*. American Psychological Association.

Kutcher, E. J., & Bragger, J. D. (2004). Selection interviews of overweight job applicants: Can structure reduce the bias? *Journal of Applied Social Psychology, 34*, 1993–2022.

Kuttler, A. F., La Greca, A. M., & Prinstein, M. J. (1999). Friendship qualities and social–emotional functioning of adolescents with close, cross-sex friendships. *Journal of Research on Adolescence, 9*, 339–366.

Kuzawa, C. W., Chugani, H. T., Grossman, L. I., Lipovich, L., Muzik, O., Hof, P. R., Wildman, D. E., Sherwood, C. C., Leonard, W. R., & Lange, N. (2014). Metabolic costs and evolutionary implications of human brain development. *PNAS, 111*, 13010–13015.

Kvam, P. D., Smith, C., Irving, L. H., & Sokratous, K. (2022, April). Improving the reliability and validity of the IAT with a dynamic model driven by associations. https://www.researchgate.net/publication/359724201_Improving_the_reliability_and_validity_of_the_IAT_with_a_dynamic_model_driven_by_associations

Kwauk, C., Petrova, D., & Robinson, J. P. (2016). *Sesame Street: Combining education and entertainment to bring early childhood education to children around the world.* Center for Universal Education at Brookings. https://bit.ly/38Pje3x

Kwong, A. S. F., Manley, D., Timpson, N. J., Pearson, R. M., Heron, J., Sallis, H., Stergiakouli, E., Davis, O. S. P., & Leckie, G. (2019). Identifying critical points of trajectories of depressive symptoms from childhood to young adulthood. *Journal of Youth and Adolescence*, 48(4), 815–827.

Kyaga, S., Landén, M., Boman, M., Hultman, C. M., Långström, N., & Lichtenstein, P. (2013). Mental illness, suicide, and creativity: 40-year prospective total population study. *Journal of Psychiatric Research, 47*, 83–90.

Labella, M. H., Johnson, W. F., Martin, J., Ruiz, S. K., Shankman, J. L., Englund, M. M., Collins, W. A., Roisman, G. I., & Simpson, J. A. (2018). Multiple dimensions of childhood abuse and neglect prospectively predict poorer adult romantic functioning. *Personality and Social Psychology Bulletin, 44*, 238–251.

Lacey, M. (2010, December 11). He found bag of cash, but did the unexpected. *The New York Times*. https://www.nytimes.com/2010/12/12/us/12backpack.html

Lachman, M. E. (2004). Development in midlife. *Annual Review of Psychology, 55*, 305–331.

Ladd, G. T. (1887). *Elements of physiological psychology.* Scribner's.

Laeng, B., & Sulutvedt, U. (2014). The eye pupil adjusts to imaginary light. *Psychological Science, 25*, 188–197.

LaFreniere, L. S., & Newman, M. G. (2020). Exposing worry's deceit: Percentage of untrue worries in generalized anxiety disorder treatment. *Behavior Therapy, 51*(3), 413–423.

Lai, C. K., & Wilson, M. E. (2021). Measuring implicit intergroup biases. *Social and*

Personality Psychology Compass, 15(1). https://doi.org/10.1111/apc3.12573

Laird, J. D. (1974). Self-attribution of emotion: The effects of expressive behavior on the quality of emotional experience. *Journal of Personality and Social Psychology, 29*, 475–486.

Laird, J. D. (1984). The real role of facial response in the experience of emotion: A reply to Tourangeau and Ellsworth, and others. *Journal of Personality and Social Psychology, 47*, 909–917.

Laird, J. D., & Lacasse, K. (2014). Bodily influences on emotional feelings: Accumulating evidence and extensions of William James's theory of emotion. *Emotion Review, 6*, 27–34.

Lakin, J. L., Chartrand, T. L., & Arkin, R. M. (2008). I am too just like you: Nonconscious mimicry as an automatic behavioral response to social exclusion. *Psychological Science, 19*, 816–822.

Lally, P., Van Jaarsveld, C. H. M., Potts, H. W. W., & Wardle, J. (2010). How are habits formed: Modelling habit formation in the real world. *European Journal of Social Psychology, 40*, 998–1009.

La Londe, K. B., Mahoney, A., Edwards, T. L., Cox, C., Weetjens, B., Durgin, A., & Poling, A. (2015). Training pouched rats to find people. *Journal of Applied Behavior Analysis, 48*, 1–10.

Lam, C. B., & McBride-Chang, C. A. (2007). Resilience in young adulthood: The moderating influences of gender-related personality traits and coping flexibility. *Sex Roles, 56*, 159–172.

Lam, M., Chen, C. Y., Li, Z., Martin, A. R., Bryois, J., Ma, X., Gaspar, H., Ikeda, M., Benyamin, B., Brown, B. C., Liu, R., Zhou, W., Guan, L., Kamatani, Y., Kim, S.-W., Kubo, M., Kusumawardhani, A. A., Liu, C.-M., Ma, H., ... Huang, H. (2019). Comparative genetic architectures of schizophrenia in East Asian and European populations. *Nature Genetics, 51*, 1670–1678.

Lamarche, V. M., & Seery, M. D. (2019). Come on, give it to me baby: Self-esteem, narcissism, and endorsing sexual coercion following social rejection. *Personality and Individual Differences, 149*, 315–325.

Lambert, C. (2007, January–February). *The science of happiness.* Harvard Magazine. https://www.harvardmagazine.com/2007/01/the-science-of-happiness.html

Lambert, J.-C., Ibrahim-Verbaas, C. A., Harold, D., Naj, A. C., Sims, R., Bellenguiez, C., DeStafano, A. L., Bis, J. C., Beecham, G. W., Grenier-Boley, B., Russo, G., Thornton-Wells, T. A., Jones, N., Smith, A. V., Chouraki, V., Thomas, C., Ikram, M. A., Zelenika, D., Vardarajan, B. N., ... Amouyel, P. (2013). Meta-analysis of 74,046 individuals identifies 11 new susceptibility loci for Alzheimer's disease. *Nature Genetics, 45*, 1452–1458.

Lambert, N. M., DeWall, C. N., Bushman, B. J., Tillman, T. F., Fincham, F. D., Pond, R. S., Jr., & Gwinn, A. M. (2011). *Lashing out in lust: Effect of pornography on nonsexual, physical aggression against relationship partners* [Paper]. Presented at the Society for Personality and Social Psychology convention.

Lambert, W. E. (1992). Challenging established views on social issues: The power and limitations of research. *American Psychologist, 47*, 533–542.

Lambert, W. E., Genesee, F., Holobow, N., & Chartrand, L. (1993). Bilingual education for majority English-speaking children. *European Journal of Psychology of Education, 8*, 3–22.

Lambird, K. H., & Mann, T. (2006). When do ego threats lead to self-regulation failure? Negative consequences of defensive high self-esteem. *Personality and Social Psychology Bulletin, 32*, 1177–1187.

Lammers, J., & Baldwin, M. (2018). Past-focused temporal communication overcomes conservatives' resistance to liberal political ideas. *Journal of Personality and Social Psychology, 114*, 599–619.

Lampert, M. (2017). *Majority of humanity say we are not alone in the universe.* Glocalities. http://www.glocalities.com/reports/majority-of-humanity-say-we-are-not-alone-in-the-universe

Landau, E., Verjee, Z., & Mortensen, A. (2014, February 24). *Uganda president: Homosexuals are "disgusting."* CNN. https://www.cnn.com/2014/02/24/world/africa/uganda-homosexuality-interview/index.html

Landor, A. M., & Smith, S. M. (2019). Skin-tone trauma: Historical and contemporary influences on the health and interpersonal outcomes of African Americans. *Perspectives on Psychological Science, 14*, 797–815.

Landry, M. J. (2002). MDMA: A review of epidemiologic data. *Journal of Psychoactive Drugs, 34*, 163–169.

Landy, J. F., Jia, M., Ding, I. L., Viganola, D., Tierney, W., Dreber, A., Johannesson, M., Pfeiffer, T., Ebersole, C. R., Gronau, Q. F., Ly, A., van den Bergh, D., Marsman, M., Derks, K., Wagenmakers, E.-J., Proctor, A., Bartels, D. M., Bauman, C. W., Brady, W. J., ... Uhlmann, E. L. (2020). Crowdsourcing hypothesis tests: Making transparent how design choices shape research results. *Psychological Bulletin, 146*(5), 451–479.

Lange, N., & McDougle, C. J. (2013). Help for the child with autism. *Scientific American, 25*, 72–77.

Lange, S., Probst, C., Gmel, G., Rehm, J., Burd, L., & Popova, S. (2017). Global prevalence of fetal alcohol spectrum disorder among children and youth: A systematic review and meta-analysis. *JAMA Pediatrics, 171*, 948–956.

Langer, E. J. (1983). *The psychology of control.* Sage.

Langer, E. J., & Abelson, R. P. (1974). A patient by any other name ...: Clinician group differences in labeling bias. *Journal of Consulting and Clinical Psychology, 42*, 4–9.

Langer, E. J., & Imber, L. (1980). The role of mindlessness in the perception of deviance. *Journal of Personality and Social Psychology, 39*, 360.

Langer, E. J., & Rodin, J. (1976). The effects of choice and enhanced personal responsibility for the aged: A field experiment in an institutional setting. *Journal of Personality and Social Psychology, 34*(2), 191–198.

Langlois, J. H., Kalakanis, L., Rubenstein, A. J., Larson, A., Hallam, M., & Smoot, M. (2000). Maxims or myths of beauty? A meta-analytic and theoretical review. *Psychological Bulletin, 126*, 390–423.

Långström, N. H., Rahman, Q., Carlström, E., & Lichtenstein, P. (2010). Genetic and environmental effects on same-sex sexual behavior: A population study of twins in Sweden. *Archives of Sexual Behavior, 39*, 75–80.

Lantz, B., & Wenger, M. R. (2021). Guns, groups, and the Southern culture of honor: Considering the role of co-offenders in Southern firearm violence. *Psychology of Violence, 11*(4), 405–416.

Lapp, D. (2019, December 17). *Gellert Dornay on the benefits of employee-ownership: 5 questions with family studies.* Institute for Family Studies. https://ifstudies.org/blog/gellert-dornay-on-the-benefits-of-employee-ownership-5-questions-with-family-studies

Larkin, J. E., Brasel, A. M., & Pines, H. A. (2013). Cross-disciplinary applications of I/O psychology concepts: Predicting student retention and employee turnover. *Review of General Psychology, 17*, 82–92.

Larkin, K., Resko, J. A., Stormshak, F., Stellflug, J. N., & Roselli, C. E. (2002, November). *Neuroanatomical correlates of sex and sexual partner preference in sheep* [Paper]. Presented at the annual meeting of the Society for Neuroscience, Orlando, FL.

Larrick, R. P., Timmerman, T. A., & Carton, A. M., & Abrevaya, J. (2011). Temper, temperature, and temptation: Heat-related retaliation in baseball. *Psychological Science, 22*, 423–428.

Larsen, R. J., & Diener, E. (1987). Affect intensity as an individual difference characteristic: A review. *Journal of Research in Personality, 21*, 1–39.

Larson, R. W., & Verma, S. (1999). How children and adolescents spend time across the world: Work, play, and developmental opportunities. *Psychological Bulletin, 125*, 701–736.

Larzelere, R. E. (2000). Child outcomes of non-abusive and customary physical punishment by parents: An updated literature review. *Clinical Child and Family Psychology Review, 3*, 199–221.

Larzelere, R. E., Gunnoe, M. L., Ferguson, C. J., & Roberts, M. W. (2019). The insufficiency of the evidence used to categorically oppose spanking and its implications for families and psychological science: Comment on Gershoff et al. (2018). *American Psychologist, 74*, 497–499.

Lashley, K. S. (1950). In search of the engram. In J. F. Danielli & R. Brown (Eds.), *Symposia of the Society for Experimental Biology: Vol. 4. Physiological mechanisms in animal behaviour* (pp. 454–482). Cambridge University Press.

Lassek, W. D., & Gaulin, S. J. C. (2018). Do the low WHRs and BMIs judged most attractive indicate higher fertility? *Evolutionary Psychology, 16*(4). https://www.researchgate.net/publication/328168587_Do_the_Low_WHRs_and_BMIs_Judged_Most_Attractive_Indicate_Better_Health

Lassek, W. D., & Gaulin, S. J. C. (2019). Evidence supporting nubility and reproductive value as the key to human female physical attractiveness. *Evolution and Human Behavior, 40*, 408–419.

Lassiter, G. D., & Irvine, A. A. (1986). Videotaped confessions: The impact of camera point of view on judgments of coercion.

Journal of Personality and Social Psychology, 16, 268–276.

Latané, B. (1981). The psychology of social impact. *American Psychologist, 36*, 343–356.

Latané, B., & Dabbs, J. M., Jr. (1975). Sex, group size and helping in three cities. *Sociometry, 38*, 180–194.

Latzman, R. D., Patrick, C. J., Freeman, H. D., Schapiro, S. J., & Hopkins, W. D. (2017). Etiology of triarchic psychopathy dimensions in chimpanzees *(Pan troglodytes)*. *Clinical Psychological Science, 5*, 341–354.

Laudenslager, M. L., & Reite, M. L. (1984). Losses and separations: Immunological consequences and health implications. *Review of Personality and Social Psychology, 5*, 285–312.

Lauer, J. E., Yhang, E., & Lourenco, S. F. (2019). The development of gender differences in spatial reasoning: A meta-analytic review. *Psychological Bulletin, 145*, 537–565.

Laukka, P., & Elfenbein, H. A. (2021). Cross-cultural emotion recognition and in-group advantage in vocal expression: A meta-analysis. *Emotion Review, 13*(1), 3–11.

Launay, J. M., Mouillet-Richard, S., Baudry, A., Pietri, M., & Kellermann, O. (2011). Raphe-mediated signals control the hippocampal response to SRI antidepressants via miR-16. *Translational Psychiatry, 1*, e56.

Lavi, I., Katz, L. F., Ozer, E. J., & Gross, J. J. (2019). Emotion reactivity and regulation in maltreated children: A meta-analysis. *Child Development, 90*, 1503–1524.

Lawrence, J. A., Kawachi, I., White, K., Bassett, M. T., Priest, N., Masunga, J. G., Cory, H. J., Mita, C., & Williams, D. R. (2022). A systematic review and meta-analysis of the Everyday Discrimination Scale and biomarker outcomes. *Psychoneuroendocrinology, 142*. https://www.sciencedirect.com/science/article/pii/S0306453022001135

Laws, K. R., & Kokkalis, J. (2007). Ecstasy (MDMA) and memory function: A meta-analytic update. *Human Psychopharmacology: Clinical and Experimental, 22*, 381–388.

Lazaruk, W. (2007). Linguistic, academic, and cognitive benefits of French immersion. *Canadian Modern Language Review, 63*, 605–628.

Lazarus, R. S. (1990). Theory-based stress measurement. *Psychological Inquiry, 1*, 3–13.

Lazarus, R. S. (1991). Progress on a cognitive-motivational-relational theory of emotion. *American Psychologist, 46*, 352–367.

Lazarus, R. S. (1998). *Fifty years of the research and theory of R. S. Lazarus: An analysis of historical and perennial issues*. Erlbaum.

Lea, S. E. G. (2000). Towards an ethical use of animals. *The Psychologist, 13*, 556–557.

Leaper, C., & Ayres, M. M. (2007). A meta-analytic review of gender variations in adults' language use: Talkativeness, affiliative speech, and assertive speech. *Personality and Social Psychology Review, 11*, 328–363.

Learish, J., & Fieldstadt, E. (2022, April). *Gun map: Ownership by state*. CBS News. https://www.cbsnews.com/pictures/gun-ownership-rates-by-state/

Lebedev, A. V., Lövdén, M., Rosenthal, G., Feilding, A., Nutt, D. J., & Carhart-Harris, R. L. (2015). Finding the self by losing the self: Neural correlates of ego-dissolution under psilocybin. *Human Brain Mapping, 36*, 3137–3153.

Leckelt, M., Geukes, K., Küfner, A. C., Niemeyer, L. M., Hutteman, R., Osterholz, S., Egloff, B., Nestler, S., & Back, M. D. (2020). A longitudinal field investigation of narcissism and popularity over time: How agentic and antagonistic aspects of narcissism shape the development of peer relationships. *Personality and Social Psychology Bulletin, 46*(4), 463–659.

Leding, J. K. (2019). Adaptive memory: Animacy, threat, and attention in free recall. *Memory & Cognition, 47*, 383–394.

LeDoux, J. (2015). *Anxious: Using the brain to understand and treat fear and anxiety*. Viking.

LeDoux, J. E. (1996). *The emotional brain: The mysterious underpinnings of emotional life*. Simon & Schuster.

LeDoux, J. E. (2002). *The synaptic self*. Macmillan.

LeDoux, J. E. (2009, July/August). Quoted by K. McGowan in, Out of the past. *Discover*, pp. 28–37.

LeDoux, J. E., & Armony, J. (1999). Can neurobiology tell us anything about human feelings? In D. Kahneman, E. Diener, & N. Schwartz (Eds.), *Well-being: The foundations of hedonic psychology* (pp. 489–499). Sage.

LeDoux, J. E., & Brown, R. (2017). A higher-order theory of emotional consciousness. *PNAS, 114*, E2016–E2025.

Lee, B. S., McIntyre, R. S., Gentle, J. E., Park, N. S., Chiriboga, D. A., Lee, Y., Singh, S., & McPherson, M. A. (2018). A computational algorithm for personalized medicine in schizophrenia. *Schizophrenia Research, 192*, 131–136.

Lee, C. A., Derefinko, K. J., Milich, R., Lynam, D. R., & DeWall, C. N. (2017). Longitudinal and reciprocal relations between delay discounting and crime. *Personality and Individual Differences, 111*, 193–198.

Lee, D. S., Kim, E., & Schwarz, N. (2015). Something smells fishy: Olfactory suspicion cues improve performance on the Moses illusion and Wason rule discovery task. *Journal of Experimental Social Psychology, 59*, 47–50.

Lee, G. Y., & Kisilevsky, B. S. (2014). Fetuses respond to father's voice but prefer mother's voice after birth. *Developmental Psychobiology, 56*, 1–11.

Lee, I.-M., Shiroma, E. J., Kamada, M., Bassett, D. R., Matthews, C. E., & Buring, J. E. (2019). Association of step volume and intensity with all-cause mortality in older women. *JAMA Internal Medicine, 179*(8), 1105–1112.

Lee, J., Gierc, M., Vila-Rodriguez, F., Puterman, E., & Faulkner, G. (2021). Efficacy of exercise combined with standard treatment for depression compared to standard treatment alone: A systematic review and meta-analysis of randomized controlled trials. *Journal of Affective Disorders, 295*, 1494–1511.

Lee, J. C., Hall, D. L., & Wood, W. (2018). Experiential or material purchases? Social class determines purchase happiness. *Psychological Science, 29*, 1031–1039.

Lee, J. J., Wedow, R., Okbay, A., Kong, E., Maghzian, O., Zacher, M., Nguyen-Viet, T. A., Bowers, P., Sidorenko, J., Linnér, R. K., Fontana, M. A., Kundu, T., Lee, C., Li, H., Li, R., Royer, R., Timshel, P. N., Walters, R. I., Willoughby, E. A., ... Fontana, M. A. (2018). Gene discovery and polygenic prediction from a genome-wide association study of educational attainment in 1.1 million individuals. *Nature Genetics, 50*, 1112–1121.

Lee, L., Frederick, S., & Ariely, D. (2006). Try it, you'll like it: The influence of expectation, consumption, and revelation on preferences for beer. *Psychological Science, 17*, 1054–1058.

Lee, L. O., James, P., Zevon, E. S., Kim, E. S., Trudel-Fitzgerald, C., Spiro, A., Grodstein, F., & Kubzansky, L. D. (2019). Optimism is associated with exceptional longevity in 2 epidemiologic cohorts of men and women. *PNAS, 116*, 18357–18362.

Lee, M. J. (2019). Breaking my own silence. *The New York Times*. https://www.nytimes.com/2019/05/20/opinion/confidence-public-speaking.html

Lee, M. R., Boness, C. L., McDowell, Y. E., Vergés, A., Steinley, D. L., & Sher, K. J. (2018). Desistance and severity of alcohol use disorder: A lifespan-developmental investigation. *Clinical Psychological Science, 6*, 90–105.

Lee, S. J., Zhang, J., Neale, M. C., Styner, M., Zhu, H., & Gilmore, J. H. (2019). Quantitative tract-based white matter heritability in 1-and 2-year-old twins. *Human Brain Mapping, 40*, 1164–1173.

Lee, S. W. S., & Schwartz, N. (2020). Grounded procedures: A proximate mechanism for the psychology of cleansing and other physical actions. *Behavioral and Brain Sciences, 44*, 1–78.

Lees, B., Mewton, L., Jacobus, J., Valadez, E. A., Stapinski, L. A., Teesson, M., Tapert, S. F., & Squeglia, L. M. (2020). Association of prenatal alcohol exposure with psychological, behavioral, and neurodevelopmental outcomes in children from the adolescent brain cognitive development study. *American Journal of Psychiatry, 177*, 1060–1072.

Lefcourt, H. M. (1982). *Locus of control: Current trends in theory and research*. Erlbaum.

Leger, K. A., Gloger, E. M., Maras, J., & Marshburn, C. K. (2022). Discrimination and health: The mediating role of daily stress processes. *Health Psychology, 41*(5), 332–342.

Lehman, D. R., Wortman, C. B., & Williams, A. F. (1987). Long-term effects of losing a spouse or child in a motor vehicle crash. *Journal of Personality and Social Psychology, 52*, 218–231.

Lei, X., & Perrett, D. (2021). Misperceptions of opposite-sex preferences for thinness and muscularity. *British Journal of Psychology, 112*, 247–264.

Leichsenring, F., & Rabung, S. (2008). Effectiveness of long-term psychodynamic psychotherapy: A meta-analysis. *Journal of the American Medical Association, 300*, 1551–1565.

Leichsenring, F., Steinert, C., Rabung, S., & Ioannidis, J. P. A. (2022). The efficacy of psychotherapies and pharmacotherapies for mental disorders in adults: An umbrella review and meta-analytic evaluation of recent meta-analyses. *World Psychiatry, 21*(1), 133–145.

Leitenberg, H., & Henning, K. (1995). Sexual fantasy. *Psychological Bulletin, 117*, 469–496.

Leitner, M. C., & Richlan, F. (2021). No fans–no pressure: Referees in professional football during the COVID-19 pandemic. *Frontiers in Sports and Active Living, 3*. https://

www.frontiersin.org/articles/10.3389/fspor.2021.720488/full

Leland, J. (2022). How loneliness is damaging our health. *The New York Times*. https://www.nytimes.com/2022/04/20/nyregion/loneliness-epidemic.html

Lemonick, M. D. (2002, June 3). Lean and hungrier. *Time*, p. 54.

LeMoult, J. (2020). From stress to depression: Bringing together cognitive and biological science. *Current Directions in Psychological Science, 29*, 592–598.

LeMoult, J., & Gotlib, I. H. (2019). Depression: A cognitive perspective. *Clinical Psychology Review, 69*, 51–66.

L'Engle, M. (1973). *A wind in the door*. Farrar, Straus and Giroux.

Lenneberg, E. H. (1967). *Biological foundations of language*. Wiley.

Lennox, B. R., Bert, S., Park, G., Jones, P. B., & Morris, P. G. (1999). Spatial and temporal mapping of neural activity associated with auditory hallucinations. *The Lancet, 353*, 644.

Lenton, A. P., & Francesconi, M. (2010). How humans cognitively manage an abundance of mate options. *Psychological Science, 21*, 528–533.

Leong, R. L. F., Cheng, G. H.-L., Chee, M. W. L., & Lo, J. C. (2020). The effects of sleep on prospective memory: A systematic review and meta-analysis. *Sleep Medicine Reviews, 47*, 18–27.

Leonhardt, D. (2021, February 19). [Twitter thread] https://twitter.com/DLeonhardt/status/1362767520764203011

Lepp, A., Barkley, J. E., & Karpinski, A. C. (2014). The relationship between cell phone use, academic performance, anxiety, and satisfaction with life in college students. *Computers in Human Behavior, 31*, 343–350.

Lesage, A., Lemasson, M., Medina, K., Tsopmo, J., Sebti, N., Potvin, S., & Patry, S. (2016). The prevalence of electroconvulsive therapy use since 1973: A meta-analysis. *Journal of ECT, 32*, 236–242.

Leschak, C. J., & Eisenberger, N. L. (2019). Two distinct immune pathways linking social relationships with health: Inflammatory and antiviral processes. *Psychosomatic Medicine, 81*, 711–719.

Leucht, S., Barnes, T. R. E., Kissling, W., Engel, R. R., Correll, C., & Kane, J. M. (2003). Relapse prevention in schizophrenia with new-generation antipsychotics: A systematic review and exploratory meta-analysis of randomized, controlled trials. *American Journal of Psychiatry, 160*, 1209–1222.

Leucht, S., Chaimani, A., Leucht, C., Huhn, M., Mavridis, D., Helfer, B., Samara, M., Cipriani, A., Geddes, J. R., Salanti, G., & Davis, J. M. (2018). 60 years of placebo-controlled antipsychotic drug trials in acute schizophrenia: Meta-regression of predictors of placebo response. *Schizophrenia Research, 201*, 315–323.

Leucht, S., Crippa, A., Siafis, S., Patel, M. X., Orsini, N., & Davis, J. M. (2020). Dose-response meta-analysis of antipsychotic drugs for acute schizophrenia. *American Journal of Psychiatry, 177*(4), 342–353.

LeVay, S. (1991). A difference in hypothalamic structure between heterosexual and homosexual men. *Science, 253*, 1034–1037.

LeVay, S. (2011). *Gay, straight, and the reason why: The science of sexual orientation*. Oxford University Press.

Levenson, R. M., Krupinski, E. A., Navarro, V. M., & Wasserman, E. A. (2015, November 18). Pigeons *(Columba livia)* as trainable observers of pathology and radiology breast cancer images. *PLOS ONE, 10*. https://journals.plos.org/plosone/article?id=10.1371/journal.pone.0141357

Levi-Belz, Y., Krysinska, K., & Andriessen, K. (2021). "Turning personal tragedy into triumph": A systematic review and meta-analysis of studies on posttraumatic growth among suicide-loss survivors. *Psychological Trauma: Theory, Research, Practice, and Policy, 13*(3), 322–332.

Levin, M. E., Stocke, K., Pierce, B., & Levin, C. (2018). Do college students use online self-help? A survey of intentions and use of mental health resources. *Journal of College Student Psychotherapy, 32*, 181–198.

Levine, J. A., Lanningham-Foster, L. M., McCrady, S. K., Krizan, A. C., Olson, L. R., Kane, P. H., Jensen, M. D., & Clark, M. M. (2005). Interindividual variation in posture allocation: Possible role in human obesity. *Science, 307*, 584–586.

Levine, R. (2016). *Stranger in the mirror: The scientific search for self*. Princeton University Press.

Levine, R., Sato, S., Hashimoto, T., & Verma, J. (1995). Love and marriage in eleven cultures. *Journal of Cross-Cultural Psychology, 26*, 554–571.

Levine, R. V., & Norenzayan, A. (1999). The pace of life in 31 countries. *Journal of Cross-Cultural Psychology, 30*, 178–205.

Levine, S. L., Milyavskaya, M., & Zuroff, D. C. (2020). Perfectionism in the transition to university: Comparing diathesis-stress and downward spiral models of depressive symptoms. *Clinical Psychological Science, 8*, 52–64.

Levy, B., & Langer, E. (1992). *Avoidance of the memory loss stereotype: Enhanced memory among the elderly deaf* [Paper]. Presented at American Psychological Association convention, Washington, DC.

Levy, D. J., Heissel, J. A., Richeson, J. A., & Adam, E. K. (2016). Psychological and biological responses to race-based social stress as pathways to disparities in educational outcomes. *American Psychologist, 71*, 455–473.

Levy, N., Harmon-Jones, C., & Harmon-Jones, E. (2018). Dissonance and discomfort: Does a simple cognitive inconsistency evoke a negative affective state? *Motivation Science, 4*, 95–108.

Levy, P. E. (2003). *Industrial/organizational psychology: Understanding the workplace*. Houghton Mifflin.

Lewald, J. (2007). More accurate sound localisation induced by short-term light deprivation. *Neuropsychologia, 45*, 1215–1222.

Lewandowski, G. W., Jr., Aron, A., & Gee, J. (2007). Personality goes a long way: The malleability of opposite-sex physical attractiveness. *Personality Relationships, 14*, 571–585.

Lewin, K. (1935). *A dynamic theory of personality*. McGraw-Hill.

Lewinsohn, P. M., Hoberman, H., Teri, L., & Hautziner, M. (1985). An integrative theory of depression. In S. Reiss & R. Bootzin (Eds.), *Theoretical issues in behavior therapy* (pp. 331–359). Academic Press.

Lewinsohn, P. M., Petit, J., Joiner, T. E., Jr., & Seeley, J. R. (2003). The symptomatic expression of major depressive disorder in adolescents and young adults. *Journal of Abnormal Psychology, 112*, 244–252.

Lewinsohn, P. M., Rohde, P., & Seeley, J. R. (1998). Major depressive disorder in older adolescents: Prevalence, risk factors, and clinical implications. *Clinical Psychology Review, 18*, 765–794.

Lewis, C., Roberts, N. P., Andrew, M., Starling, E., & Bisson, J. I. (2020). Psychological therapies for post-traumatic stress disorder in adults: Systematic review and meta-analysis. *European Journal of Psychotraumatology, 11*(1). doi: 10.1080/20008198.2020.1729633

Lewis, C. S. (1960). *Mere Christianity*. Macmillan.

Lewis, C. S. (1960). *The four loves*. Geoffrey Bles.

Lewis, C. S. (1967). *Christian reflections*. Eerdmans.

Lewis, D. M. G., Al-Shawaf, L., Conroy-Beam, D., Asao, K., & Buss, D. M. (2017). Evolutionary psychology: A how-to guide. *American Psychologist, 72*, 353–373.

Lewis, D. M. G., Russell, E. M., Al-Shawaf, L., & Buss, D. M. (2015). Lumbar curvature: A previously undiscovered standard of attractiveness. *Evolution and Human Behavior, 36*, 345–350.

Lewis, D. O., Pincus, J. H., Bard, B., Richardson, E., Prichep, L. S., Feldman, M., & Yeager, C. (1988). Neuropsychiatric, psychoeducational, and family characteristics of 14 juveniles condemned to death in the United States. *American Journal of Psychiatry, 145*, 584–589.

Lewis, L. D. (2021). The interconnected causes and consequences of sleep in the brain. *Science, 374*, 564–568.

Lewis, M. (2016). *The undoing project: A friendship that changed our minds*. W.W. Norton & Co.

Lewis, M., Borkenhagen, M. C., Converse, E., Lupyan, G., & Seidenberg, M. S. (2022). What might books be teaching young children about gender? *Psychological Science, 33*(1), 33–47.

Lewis, M., & Lupyan, G. (2020). Gender stereotypes are reflected in the distributional structure of 25 languages. *Nature Human Behaviour, 4*, 1021–1028.

Lewis, M. B. (2018). The interactions between botulinum-toxin-based facial treatments and embodied emotions. *Scientific Reports, 8*, 14720.

Lewis, N. A., Jr., & Earl, A. (2018). Seeing more and eating less: Effects of portion size granularity on the perception and regulation of food consumption. *Journal of Personality and Social Psychology, 114*, 786–803.

Lewontin, R. (1982). *Human diversity*. Scientific American Library.

Li, J., Laursen, T. M., Precht, D. H., Olsen, J., & Mortensen, P. B. (2005). Hospitalization for mental illness among parents after the death of a child. *New England Journal of Medicine, 352*, 1190–1196.

Li, J., Zhao, Y., Lin, L., Chen, J., & Wang, S. (2018). The freedom to persist: Belief in free will predicts perseverance for long-term goals among Chinese adolescents. *Personality and Individual Differences, 121*, 7–10.

Li, J. J., Zhang, Q., Wang, Z., & Lu, Q. (2022). Research Domain Criteria (RDoC) mechanisms of transdiagnostic polygenic risk for trajectories of depression: From early adolescence to adulthood. *Journal of Psychopathology and Clinical Science, 131*(6), 567–574.

Li, L., & Tomasello, M. (2021). On the moral functions of language. *Social Cognition, 39*(1), 99–116.

Li, L., Wang, Y. Y., Wang, S. B., Zhang, L., Li, L., Xu, D. D., Ng, C. H., Ungvari, G. S., Cui, X., Liu, Z.-M., De Li, S., Jia, F.-J., & Xiang, Y.-T. (2018). Prevalence of sleep disturbances in Chinese university students: A comprehensive meta-analysis. *Journal of Sleep Research, 27*(3). doi: 10.1111/jsr.12648

Li, N., & DiCarlo, J. J. (2008). Unsupervised natural experience rapidly alters invariant object representation in visual cortex. *Science, 321*, 1502–1506.

Li, N. P., & Kanazawa, S. (2016). Country roads, take me home ... to my friends: How intelligence, population density, and friendship affect modern happiness. *British Journal of Psychology, 107*, 675–697.

Li, S., Stampfer, M. J., Williams, D. R., & VanderWeele, T. J. (2016). Association of religious service attendance with mortality among women. *JAMA Internal Medicine, 176*, 777–785.

Li, S.-B., Damonte, V. M., Chen, C., Wang, G., Kebschull, J. M., Yamaguchi, H., Bian, W.-J., Purmann, C., Pattni, R., Urban, A. E., Mourrain, P., Kauer, J. A., Scherrer, G., & de Lecea, L. (2022). Hyperexcitable arousal circuits drive sleep instability during aging. *Science, 375*, 838.

Li, T., Yan, X., Li, Y., Wang, J., Li, Q., Li, H., & Li, J. (2017). Neuronal correlates of individual differences in the Big Five personality traits: Evidences from cortical morphology and functional homogeneity. *Frontiers in Neuroscience, 11*, 414.

Li, X., Han, M., Cohen, G. L., & Markus, H. R. (2021). Passion matters but not equally everywhere: Predicting achievement from interest, enjoyment, and efficacy in 59 societies. *Psychological and Cognitive Sciences, 118*(11). https://www.pnas.org/doi/10.1073/pnas.2016964118

Li, X., Mu, F., Liu, D., Zhu, J., Yue, S., Liu, M., Liu, Y., & Wang J. (2022). Predictors of suicidal ideation, suicide attempt and suicide death among people with major depressive disorder: A systematic review and meta-analysis of cohort studies. *Journal of Affective Disorders, 302*, 332–351.

Li, Z. H., Jiang, D., Pepler, D., & Craig, W. (2010). Adolescent romantic relationships in China and Canada: A cross-national comparison. *International Journal of Behavioral Development, 34*, 113–120.

Liberman, M. C. (2015, August). Hidden hearing loss. *Scientific American*, pp. 49–53.

Libertus, M. E., & Brannon, E. M. (2009). Behavioral and neural basis of number sense in infancy. *Current Directions in Psychological Science, 18*, 346–351.

Licata, A., Taylor, S., Berman, M., & Cranston, J. (1993). Effects of cocaine on human aggression. *Pharmacology Biochemistry and Behavior, 45*, 549–552.

Lichtenstein, E., Zhu, S.-H., & Tedeschi, G. J. (2010). Smoking cessation quitlines: An underrecognized intervention success story. *American Psychologist, 65*, 252–261.

Liddle, J. R., Shackelford, T. K., & Weekes-Shackelford, V. W. (2012). Why can't we all just get along? Evolutionary perspectives on violence, homicide, and war. *Review of General Psychology, 16*, 24–36.

Lieberman, M. D., & Eisenberger, N. I. (2015). The dorsal anterior cingulate is selective for pain: Results from large-scale fMRI reverse inference. *PNAS, 12*, 15250–15255.

Lieberman, M. D., Eisenberger, N. I., Crockett, M. J., Tom, S. M., Pfeifer, J. H., & Way, B. M. (2007). Putting feelings into words: Affect labeling disrupts amygdala activity in response to affective stimuli. *Psychological Science, 18*, 421–428.

Lieberman, M. D., Straccia, M. A., Meyer, M. L., Du, M., & Tan, K. M. (2019). Social, self, (situational), and affective processes in medial prefrontal cortex (MPFC): Causal, multivariate, and reverse inference evidence. *Neuroscience & Biobehavioral Reviews, 99*, 311–328.

Lievens, F., Dilchert, S., & Ones, D. S. (2009). The importance of exercise and dimension factors in assessment centers: Simultaneous examinations of construct-related and criterion-related validity. *Human Performance, 22*, 375–390.

Lifton, R. J. (1961). *Thought reform and the psychology of totalism: A study of "brainwashing" in China.* Norton.

Lilienfeld, S. O. (2009, Winter). Tips for spotting psychological pseudoscience: A student-friendly guide. *Eye on Psi Chi*, pp. 23–26.

Lilienfeld, S. O. (2017). Clinical psychological science: Then and now. *Clinical Psychological Science, 5*, 3–13.

Lilienfeld, S. O., Lynn, S. J., Kirsch, I., Chaves, J. F., Sarbin, T. R., Ganaway, G. K., & Powell, R. A. (1999). Dissociative identity disorder and the sociocognitive model: Recalling the lessons of the past. *Psychological Bulletin, 125*, 507–523.

Lilienfeld, S. O., Marshall, J., Todd, J. T., & Shane, H. C. (2015). The persistence of fad interventions in the face of negative scientific evidence: Facilitated communication for autism as a case example. *Evidence-Based Communication Assessment and Intervention, 8*, 62–101.

Lilienfeld, S. O., Sauvigné, K. C., Reber, J., Watts, A. L., Hamann, S., Smith, S. F., Patrick, C. J., Bowes, S. M., & Tranel, D. (2017). Potential effects of severe bilateral amygdala damage on psychopathic features: A case report. *Personality Disorders: Theory, Research, and Treatment, 9*, 112–121.

Lilienfeld, S. O., Smith, S. F., & Watts, A. L. (2016). Fearless dominance and its implications for psychopathy: Are the right stuff and the wrong stuff flip sides of the same coin? In V. Zeigler-Hill & D. K. Marcus (Eds.), *The dark side of personality: Science and practice in social, personality, and clinical psychology* (pp. 65–86). American Psychological Association.

Lilienfeld, S. O., Waldman, I. D., Landfield, K., Watts, A. L., Rubenzer, S., & Fashingbauer, T. R. (2012). Fearless dominance and the U.S. presidency: Implications of psychopathic personality traits for successful and unsuccessful political leadership. *Journal of Personality and Social Psychology, 103*, 489–505.

Lillard, D. (2015). [Tweet.] https://twitter.com/dame_lillard/status/555485512492785665?lang=en

Lim, D., & DeSteno, D. (2016). Suffering and compassion: The links among adverse life experiences, empathy, compassion, and prosocial behavior. *Emotion, 16*(2), 175–182.

Lim, J., & Dinges, D. F. (2010). A meta-analysis of the impact of short-term sleep deprivation on cognitive variables. *Psychological Bulletin, 136*, 375–389.

Lin, F. R., Ferrucci, L., Metter, E. J., An, Y., Zonderman, A. B., & Resnick, S. M. (2011a). Hearing loss and cognition in the Baltimore longitudinal study of aging. *Neuropsychology, 25*, 763–770.

Lin, F. R., Metter, E. J., O'Brien, R. J., Resnick, S. M., Zonderman, A. B., & Ferrucci, L. (2011b). Hearing loss and incident dementia. *Archives of Neurology, 68*, 214–220.

Lin, G. N., Song, W., Wang, W., Wang, P., Yu, H., Cai, W., Jiang, X., Huang, W., Qian, W., Chen, Y., Chen, M., Yu, S., Xu, T., Jiao, Y., Liu, Q., Zhang, C., Yi, Z., Fan, Q., Chen, J., & Wang, Z. (2022). De novo mutations identified by whole-genome sequencing implicate chromatin modifications in obsessive-compulsive disorder. *Science Advances, 8*(2). doi: 10.1126/sciadv.abi6180

Lin, P. (2016). Risky behaviors: Integrating adolescent egocentrism with the theory of planned behavior. *Review of General Psychology, 20*, 392–398.

Lin, X., Chen, W., Wei, F., Ying, M., Wei, W., & Xie, X. (2015). Night-shift work increases morbidity of breast cancer and all-cause mortality: A meta-analysis of 16 prospective cohort studies. *Sleep Medicine, 16*, 1381–1387.

Lin, Y., & Oyserman, D. (2021). Upright and honorable: People use space to understand honor, affecting choice and perception. *Personality and Social Psychology Bulletin, 47*(1), 3–19.

Lin, Z., & Murray, S. O. (2015). More power to the unconscious: Conscious, but not unconscious, exogenous attention requires location variation. *Psychological Science, 26*, 221–230.

Linardon, J., Wade, T. D., de la Piedad Garcia, X., & Brennan, L. (2017). The efficacy of cognitive-behavioral therapy for eating disorders: A systematic review and meta-analysis. *Journal of Consulting and Clinical Psychology, 85*, 1080–1094.

Lindau, S. T., Schumm, L. P., Laumann, E. O., Levinson, W., O'Muircheartaigh, C. A., & Waite, L. J. (2007). A study of sexuality and health among older adults in the United States. *New England Journal of Medicine, 357*, 762–774.

Lindberg, S. M., Hyde, J. S., Linn, M. C., & Petersen, J. L. (2010). New trends in gender and mathematics performance: A meta-analysis. *Psychological Bulletin, 136*, 1125–1135.

Lindenberger, U., & Lövdén, M. (2019). Brain plasticity in human lifespan development: The exploration-selection-refinement model. *Annual Review of Developmental Psychology, 1*, 197–222.

Linder, D. (1982). Social trap analogs: The tragedy of the commons in the laboratory. In V. J. Derlega & J. Grzelak (Eds.), *Cooperative and helping behavior: Theories and research.* Academic Press.

Lindley, L., Anzani, A., & Galupo, M. P. (2022). Gender dysphoria and sexual well-being among trans masculine and nonbinary individuals. *Archives of Sexual Behavior, 51,* 2049–2063.

Lindner, I., Echterhoff, G., Davidson, P. S. R., & Brand, M. (2010). Observation inflation: Your actions become mine. *Psychological Science, 21,* 1291–1299.

Lindqvist, E., Östling, R., & Cesarini, D. (2020). Long-run effects of lottery wealth on psychological well-being. *Review of Economic Studies, 87,* 2703–2726.

Lindskold, S. (1978). Trust development, the GRIT proposal, and the effects of conciliatory acts on conflict and cooperation. *Psychological Bulletin, 85,* 772–793.

Lindskold, S., & Han, G. (1988). GRIT as a foundation for integrative bargaining. *Personality and Social Psychology Bulletin, 14,* 335–345.

Lindson-Hawley, N., Banting, M., West, R., Michie, S., Shinkins, B., & Aveyard, P. (2016). Gradual versus abrupt smoking cessation: A randomized, controlled noninferiority trial. *Annals of Internal Medicine, 164,* 585–592.

Lindström, B., Bellander, M., Schultner, D. T., Chang, A., Tobler, P. N., & Amodio, D. M. (2021, February 26). A computational reward learning account of social media engagement. *Nature Communications, 12,* 1311. https://www.nature.com/articles/s41467-020-19607-x

Lindström, B., Golkar, A., Jangard, S., Tobler, P. N., & Olsson, A. (2019). Social threat learning transfers to decision making in humans. *PNAS, 116,* 4732–4737.

Linehan, M. M. (2016). Behavior therapy: Where we were, where we are and where we need to be going. *Cognitive and Behavioral Practice, 23*(4), 451–453.

Linehan, M. M. (2020). *Building a life worth living: A memoir.* Random House.

Ling, S., Umbach, R., & Raine, A. (2019). Biological explanations of criminal behavior. *Psychology, Crime & Law, 25,* 626–640.

Lionetti, F., Palladino, B. E., Moses Passini, C., Casonato, M., Hamzallari, O., Ranta, M., Dellagiulia, A., & Keijsers, L. (2019). The development of parental monitoring during adolescence: A meta-analysis. *European Journal of Developmental Psychology, 16,* 552–580.

Lippa, R. A. (2007). The relation between sex drive and sexual attraction to men and women: A cross-national study of heterosexual, bisexual, and homosexual men and women. *Archives of Sexual Behavior, 36,* 209–222.

Lippa, R. A. (2009). Sex differences in sex drive, sociosexuality, and height across 53 nations: Testing evolutionary and social structural theories. *Archives of Sexual Behavior, 38,* 631–651.

Lippens, L., Vermeiren, S., & Baert, S. (2022). *The state of hiring discrimination: A meta-analysis of (almost) all recent correspondence experiments.* IZA discussion paper No. 14966. https://papers.ssrn.com/sol3/papers.cfm?abstract_id=4114491

Lippmann, W. (1929). *A preface to morals* (p. 309). Macmillan.

Lipsitt, L. P. (2003). Crib death: A biobehavioral phenomenon? *Current Directions in Psychological Science, 12,* 164–170.

Liptak, A. (2022). 27 years in solitary confinement, then another plea for help in Texas. *The New York Times.* https://www.nytimes.com/2022/02/14/us/supreme-court-solitary-confinement.html?smid=fb-nytimes&smtyp=cur

Lisak, D., Gardinier, L., Nicksa, S. C., & Cote, A. M. (2010). False allegations of sexual assault: An analysis of ten years of reported cases. *Violence Against Women, 16,* 1318–1334.

Littlewood, D. L., Kyle, S. D., Carter, L. A., Peters, S., Pratt, D., & Gooding, P. (2019). Short sleep duration and poor sleep quality predict next-day suicidal ideation: An ecological momentary assessment study. *Psychological Medicine, 49,* 403–411.

Littman, R. (2018). Perpetrating violence increases identification with violent groups: Survey evidence from former combatants. *Personality and Social Psychology Bulletin, 44,* 1077–1089.

Liu, J., Zhao, S., Chen, X., Falk, E., & Albarracín, D. (2017). The influence of peer behavior as a function of social and cultural closeness: A meta-analysis of normative influence on adolescent smoking initiation and continuation. *Psychological Bulletin, 143,* 1082–1115.

Liu, J. J. W., Ein, N., Gervasio, J., & Vickers, K. (2019). The efficacy of stress reappraisal interventions on stress responsivity: A meta-analysis and systematic review of existing evidence. *PLOS ONE, 14*(2). https://tinyurl.com/4d53y8tb

Liu, Q., Martin, N. C., Findling, R. L., Youngstrom, E. A., Garber, J., Curry, J. F., Hyde, J. S., Essex, M. J., Compas, B. E., Goodyer, I. M., Rohde, P., Stark, D., Slattery, M. J., Forehand, R., & Cole, D. A. (2021). Hopelessness and depressive symptoms in children and adolescents: An integrative data analysis. *Journal of Abnormal Psychology, 130*(6), 594–607.

Liu, R. T., Walsh, R. F. L., Sheehan, A. E., Cheek, S. M., & Sanzari, C. M. (2022). Prevalence and correlates of suicide and nonsuicidal self-injury in children. A systematic review and meta-analysis. *JAMA Psychiatry, 79*(7), 718–726.

Liu, S., Huang, J. L., & Wang, M. (2014). Effectiveness of job search interventions: A meta-analytic review. *Psychological Bulletin, 140,* 1009–1041.

Liu, T., & Csikszentmihalyi, M. (2020). Flow among introverts and extraverts in solitary and social activities. *Personality and Individual Differences, 167.* https://doi.org/10.1016/j.paid.2020.110197

Liu, Y., Balaraman, Y., Wang, G., Nephew, K. P., & Zhou, F. C. (2009). Alcohol exposure alters DNA methylation profiles in mouse embryos at early neurulation. *Epigenetics, 4,* 500–511.

Livi, A., Lanzilotto, M., Maranesi, M., Fogassi, L., Rizzolatti, G., & Bonini, L. (2019). Agent-based representations of objects and actions in the monkey pre-supplementary motor area. *PNAS, 116,* 2691–2700.

Livingston, G. (2019, February 20). *The way U.S. teens spend their time is changing, but differences between boys and girls persist.* Pew Research Center. https://pewrsr.ch/2ILALhO

Livingston, G., & Parker, K. (2011). *A tale of two fathers: More are active, but more are absent.* Pew Research Center. https://www.pewsocialtrends.org/2011/06/15/a-tale-of-two-fathers/

Livingston, G., & Thomas, D. (2019, August 2). *Why is the teen birth rate falling?* Pew Research Center. https://www.pewresearch.org/fact-tank/2019/08/02/why-is-the-teen-birth-rate-falling/

LMIC (Labour Market Information Council). (2020). *Post-secondary graduate earnings.* https://lmic-cimt.ca/projects/studentoutcomes/

Lo, J. C., Chong, P. L., Ganesan, S., Leong, R. L., & Chee, M. W. (2016). Sleep deprivation increases formation of false memory. *Journal of Sleep Research, 25,* 673–682.

Locke, K. D., Church, A. T., Mastor, K. A., Curtis, G. J., Sadler, P., McDonald, K., Vargas-Flores, J. J., Ibáñez-Reyes, J., Morio, H., Reyes, J. A. S., Cabrera, H. F., Mazuera Arias, R., Rincon, B. C., Albornoz Arias, N. C., Muñoz, A., & Ortiz, F. A. (2017). Cross-situational self-consistency in nine cultures: The importance of separating influences of social norms and distinctive dispositions. *Personality and Social Psychology Bulletin, 43,* 1033–1049.

Lodder, P., Ong, H. H., Grasman, R. P., & Wicherts, J. M. (2019). A comprehensive meta-analysis of money priming. *Journal of Experimental Psychology: General, 148,* 688–712.

Loehlin, J. C. (2016). What can an adoption study tell us about the effect of prenatal environment on a trait? *Behavior Genetics, 46,* 329–333.

Loehlin, J. C., Horn, J. M., & Ernst, J. L. (2007). Genetic and environmental influences on adult life outcomes: Evidence from the Texas adoption project. *Behavior Genetics, 37,* 463–476.

Loehlin, J. C., & Martin, N. G. (2018). Personality types: A twin study. *Personality and Individual Differences, 122,* 99–103.

Loehlin, J. C., & Nichols, R. C. (1976). *Heredity, environment, and personality.* University of Texas Press.

Loewenstein, G., Krishnamurti, T., Kopsic, J., & McDonald, D. (2015). Does increased sexual frequency enhance happiness? *Journal of Economic Behavior & Organization, 116,* 206–218.

Loftus, E. F. (2001, November). Imagining the past. *The Psychologist, 14,* 584–587.

Loftus, E. F. (2012, July). *Manufacturing memories* [Invited address]. International Congress of Psychology, Cape Town.

Loftus, E. F., & Ketcham, K. (1994). *The myth of repressed memory: False memories and allegations of sexual abuse.* St. Martin's Press.

Loftus, E. F., Levidow, B., & Duensing, S. (1992). Who remembers best? Individual differences in memory for events that occurred in a science museum. *Applied Cognitive Psychology, 6,* 93–107.

Loftus, E. F., & Loftus, G. R. (1980). On the permanence of stored information in the human brain. *American Psychologist, 35,* 409–420.

Loftus, E. F., & Palmer, J. C. (October, 1974). Reconstruction of automobile destruction: An example of the interaction between language and memory. *Journal of Verbal Learning & Verbal Behavior, 13,* 585–589.

Logan, G. D. (2018). Automatic control: How experts act without thinking. *Psychological Review, 125,* 453–485.

Logan, J. A., Justice, L. M., Yumus, M., & Chaparro-Moreno, L. J. (2019). When children are not read to at home: The million word gap. *Journal of Developmental & Behavioral Pediatrics*, 40, 383–386.

Logan, T. K., Walker, R., Cole, J., & Leukefeld, C. (2002). Victimization and substance abuse among women: Contributing factors, interventions, and implications. *Review of General Psychology*, 6, 325–397.

Logel, C., Kathmandu, A., & Cohen, G. L. (2019). Affirmation prevents long-term weight gain. *Journal of Experimental Social Psychology, 81*, 70–75.

Logue, A. W. (1998a). Laboratory research on self-control: Applications to administration. *Review of General Psychology*, 2, 221–238.

Logue, A. W. (1998b). Self-control. In W. T. O'Donohue (Ed.), *Learning and behavior therapy* (pp. 252–273). Allyn & Bacon.

London, P. (1970). The rescuers: Motivational hypotheses about Christians who saved Jews from the Nazis. In J. Macaulay & L. Berkowitz (Eds.), *Altruism and helping behavior.* Academic Press.

Loomba, S., de Figueiredo, A., Piatek, S. J., de Graaf, K., & Larson, H. J. (2021). Measuring the impact of COVID-19 vaccine misinformation on vaccination intent in the UK and USA. *Nature Human Behaviour*, 5, 337–348.

Loomes, R., Hull, L., & Mandy, W. P. L. (2017). What is the male-to-female ratio in autism spectrum disorder? A systematic review and meta-analysis. *Journal of the American Academy of Child & Adolescent Psychiatry*, 56, 466–474.

Lopez, D. J. (2002, January/February). Snaring the fowler: Mark Twain debunks phrenology. *Skeptical Inquirer*. https://skepticalinquirer.org/2002/01/snaring-the-fowler-mark-twain-debunks-phrenology/

Lopez-Quintero, C., de los Cobos, P., Hasin, D. S., Okuda, M., Wang, S., Grant, B. F., & Blanco, C. (2011). Probability and predictors of transition from first use to dependence on nicotine, alcohol, cannabis, and cocaine: Results of the national epidemiologic survey on alcohol and related conditions (NESARC). *Drug and Alcohol Dependence*, 115, 120–130.

Loprinzi, P. D., Loenneke, J. P., & Blackburn, E. H. (2015). Movement-based behaviors and leukocyte telomere length among US adults. *Medical Science and Sports Exercise*, 47, 2347–2352.

Lord, C. G., Lepper, M. R., & Preston, E. (1984). Considering the opposite: A corrective strategy for social judgment. *Journal of Personality and Social Psychology*, 47, 1231–1247.

Lord, C. G., Ross, L., & Lepper, M. (1979). Biased assimilation and attitude polarization: The effects of prior theories on subsequently considered evidence. *Journal of Personality and Social Psychology*, 37, 2098–2109.

Lorenz, K. (1937). The companion in the bird's world. *Auk*, 54, 245–273.

Loughrey, D. G., Kelly, M. E, Kelley, G. A., Brennan, S., & Lawlor, B. A. (2018). Association of age-related hearing loss with cognitive function, cognitive impairment, and dementia: A systematic review and meta-analysis. *JAMA Otolaryngology Head Neck Surgery*, 144, 115–126.

Louie, K., & Wilson, M. A. (2001). Temporally-structured replay of awake hippocampal ensemble activity during rapid eye movement sleep. *Neuron*, 29, 145–156.

Lourenco, O., & Machado, A. (1996). In defense of Piaget's theory: A reply to 10 common criticisms. *Psychological Review*, 103, 143–164.

Lövdén, M., Fratiglioni, L., Glymour, M. M., Lindenberger, U., Tucker-Drob, E. M. (2020). Education and cognitive functioning across the life span. *Psychological Science in the Public Interest*, 21(1), 6–41.

Lowe, H., Haddock, G., Mulligan, L. D., Gregg, L., Carter, L.-A., Fuzellier-Hart, A., & Kyle, S. D. (2019). Does exercise improve sleep for adults with insomnia? A systematic review with quality appraisal. *Clinical Psychology Review*, 68, 1–12.

Lowicki, P., & Zajenkowski, M. (2020). Empathy and exposure to credible religious acts during childhood independently predict religiosity. *International Journal for the Psychology of Religion*, 30(2), 128–141.

Lozano, A. M., & Mayberg, H. S. (2015, February). Treating depression at the source. *Scientific American*, pp. 68–73.

Lu, J. G., Liu, X. L., Liao, H., & Wang, L. (2020). Disentangling stereotypes from social reality: Astrological stereotypes and discrimination in China. *Journal of Personality and Social Psychology*, 119, 1359–1379.

Lu, J. G., Martin, A., Usova, A., & Galinsky, A. D. (2018). Creativity and humor across cultures: Where Aha meets Haha. In S. R. Luria, J. Baer, & J. C. Kaufman (Eds.), *Creativity and humor* (pp. 183–203). Academic Press.

Lu, Z.-L., Williamson, S. J., & Kaufman, L. (1992). Behavioral lifetime of human auditory sensory memory predicted by physiological measures. *Science*, 258, 1668–1670.

Luan, Z., Poorthuis, A. M., Hutteman, R., Denissen, J. J., Asendorpf, J. B., & van Aken, M. A. (2019). Unique predictive power of other-rated personality: An 18-year longitudinal study. *Journal of Personality*, 87, 532–545.

Lubinski, D. (2016). From Terman to today: A century of findings on intellectual precocity. *Review of Educational Research*, 86, 900–944.

Lubinski, D., Benbow, C. P., & Kell, H. J. (2014). Life paths and accomplishments of mathematically precocious males and females four decades later. *Psychological Science*, 25, 2217–2232.

Luby, J. L., Belden, A., Harms, M. P., Tillman, R., & Barch, D. M. (2016). Preschool is a sensitive period for the influence of maternal support on the trajectory of hippocampal development. *PNAS*, 113, 5742–5747.

Lucas, B. J., & Nordgren, L. F. (2020). The creative cliff illusion. *PNAS*, 117(33), 19830–19836.

Lucas, R. E., Clark, A. E., Georgellis, Y., & Diener, E. (2004). Unemployment alters the set point for life satisfaction. *Psychological Science*, 15, 8–13.

Luciano, M., Gow, A. J., Harris, S. E., Hayward, C., Allerhand, M., Starr, J. M., Visscher, P. M., & Deary, I. J. (2009). Cognitive ability at age 11 and 70 years, information processing speed, and APOE variation: The Lothian birth cohort 1936 study. *Psychology and Aging*, 24, 129–138.

Luciano, M. T., Acuff, S. F., Olin, C. C., Lewin, R. K., Strickland, J. C., McDevitt-Murphy, M. E., & Murphy, J. G. (2022). Posttraumatic stress disorder, drinking to cope, and harmful alcohol use: A multivariate meta-analysis of the self-medication hypothesis. *Journal of Psychopathology and Clinical Science*, 131(5), 447–456.

Ludwig, A. M. (1995). *The price of greatness: Resolving the creativity and madness controversy.* Guilford Press.

Ludwig, D. S., & Friedman, M. I. (2014). Increasing adiposity: Consequence or cause of overeating? *Journal of the American Medical Association*, 311, 2167–2168.

Luhmann, M., & Hawkley, L. C. (2016). Age differences in loneliness from late adolescence to oldest old age. *Developmental Psychology*, 52, 943–959.

Luhmann, M., Hofmann, W., Eid, M., & Lucas, R. E. (2012). Subjective well-being and adaptation to life events: A meta-analysis. *Journal of Personality and Social Psychology*, 102, 592–615.

Luna, V. M., Anacker, C., Burghardt, N. S., Khandaker, H., Andreu, V., Millette, A., Leary, P., Ravenelle, R., Jimenez, J. C. Mastrodonato, A., Denny, C. A., Fenton, A. A., Scharfman, H. E., & Hen, R. (2019). Adult-born hippocampal neurons bidirectionally modulate entorhinal inputs into the dentate gyrus. *Science*, 364, 578–583.

Lundy, A. C. (1985). The reliability of the Thematic Apperception Test. *Journal of Personality Assessment*, 49, 141–145.

Luningham, J. M., Merrilees, C. E., Taylor, L. K., Goeke-Morey, M., Shirlow, P., Wentz, B., & Cummings, E. M. (2021). Relations among father's presence, family conflict, and adolescent adjustment in Northern Ireland. *Child Development*, 92(3), 904–918.

Luria, A. M. (1968). *The mind of a mnemonist.* L. Solotaroff (Trans.). Basic Books.

Lustig, C., & Buckner, R. L. (2004). Preserved neural correlates of priming in old age and dementia. *Neuron*, 42, 865–875.

Lutgendorf, S. K., Russell, D., Ullrich, P., Harris, T. B., & Wallace, R. (2004). Religious participation, interleukin-6, and mortality in older adults. *Health Psychology*, 23, 465–475.

Lutz, P. E., Gross, J. A., Dhir, S. K., Maussion, G., Yang, J., Bramoullé, A., Meaney, M. J., & Turecki, G. (2017). Epigenetic regulation of the kappa opioid receptor by child abuse. *Biological Psychiatry*, 84, 751–761.

Luyckx, K., Tildesley, E. A., Soenens, B., Andrews, J. A., Hampson, S. E., Peterson, M., & Duriez, B. (2011). Parenting and trajectories of children's maladaptive behaviors: A 12-year prospective community study. *Journal of Clinical Child and Adolescent Psychology*, 40, 468–478.

Lyall, S. (2005, November 29). What's the buzz? Rowdy teenagers don't want to hear it. *The New York Times*. https://www.nytimes.com/2005/11/29/world/europe/whats-the-buzz-rowdy-teenagers-dont-want-to-hear-it.html

Lykes, V. A., & Kemmelmeier, M. (2014). What predicts loneliness? Cultural difference between individualistic and collectivistic societies in Europe. *Journal of Cross-Cultural Psychology*, 45, 468–490.

Lykken, D. T. (1991). *Science, lies, and controversy: An epitaph for the polygraph* [Invited address]. Upon receipt of the Senior Career Award for

Distinguished Contribution to Psychology in the Public Interest, American Psychological Association convention.

Lykken, D. T. (1995). *The antisocial personalities.* Erlbaum.

Lykken, D. T. (2006). The mechanism of emergenesis. *Genes, Brain & Behavior, 5*, 306–310.

Lynch, G. (2002). Memory enhancement: The search for mechanism-based drugs. *Nature Neuroscience, 5*(suppl), 1035–1038.

Lynch, G., Palmer, L. C., & Gall, C. M. (2011). The likelihood of cognitive enhancement. *Pharmacology, Biochemistry and Behavior, 99*, 116–129.

Lynch, G., & Staubli, U. (1991). Possible contributions of long-term potentiation to the encoding and organization of memory. *Brain Research Reviews, 16*, 204–206.

Lynch, R., Aspelund, T., Kormáksson, M., Flores-Torres, M. H., Hauksdóttir, A., Arnberg, F. K., Lajous, M., Kirschbaum, C., & Valdimarsdóttir, U. (2022). Lifetime exposure to violence and other life stressors and hair cortisol concentration in women. *Stress, 25*(1). https://www.tandfonline.com/doi/full/10.1080/10253890.2021.2011204

Lynn, M. (1988). The effects of alcohol consumption on restaurant tipping. *Personality and Social Psychology Bulletin, 14*, 87–91.

Lynn, R. (2009). What has caused the Flynn effect? Secular increases in the development quotients of infants. *Intelligence, 37*, 16–24.

Lynn, R., & Harvey, J. (2008). The decline of the world's intelligence. *Intelligence, 36*, 112–120.

Lynn, S. J., Laurence, J., & Kirsch, I. (2015). Hypnosis, suggestion, and suggestibility: An integrative model. *American Journal of Clinical Hypnosis, 57*, 314–329.

Lynn, S. J., Lilienfeld, S. O., Merckelbach, H., Giesbrecht, T., McNally, R. J., Loftus, E. F., Bruck, M., Garry, M., & Malaktaris, A. (2014). The trauma model of dissociation: Inconvenient truths and stubborn fictions. Comment on Dalenberg et al. (2012). *Psychological Bulletin, 140*, 896–910.

Lynn, S. J., Rhue, J. W., & Weekes, J. R. (1990). Hypnotic involuntariness: A social cognitive analysis. *Psychological Review, 97*, 169–184.

Lyons, A. (2015). Resilience in lesbians and gay men: A review and key findings from a nationwide Australian survey. *International Review of Psychiatry, 27*, 435–443.

Lyons, B. D., Hoffman, B. J., Michel, J. W., & Williams, K. J. (2011). On the predictive efficiency of past performance and physical ability: The case of the National Football League. *Human Performance, 24*, 158–172.

Lyons, D. E., Young, A. G., & Keil, F. C. (2007). The hidden structure of overimitation. *PNAS, 104*, 19751–19756.

Lyons, L. (2004, February 3). *Growing up lonely: Examining teen alienation.* Gallup. https://news.gallup.com/poll/10465/growing-lonely-examining-teen-alienation.aspx

Lyons, M. J., Panizzon, M. S., Liu, W., McKenzie, R., Bluestone, N. J., Grant, M. D., Franz, C. E., Vuoksimaa, E. P., Toomey, R., Jacobson, K. C., Reynolds, C. A., Kremen, W. S., & Xian, H. (2017). A longitudinal twin study of general cognitive ability over four decades. *Developmental Psychology, 53*, 1170–1177.

Lyubomirsky, S. (2001). Why are some people happier than others? The role of cognitive and motivational processes in well-being. *American Psychologist, 56*, 239–249.

Lyubomirsky, S. (2013). *The myths of happiness: What should make you happy, but doesn't, what shouldn't make you happy, but does.* Penguin Press.

Lyubomirsky, S., Sousa, L., & Dickerhoof, R. (2006). The costs and benefits of writing, talking, and thinking about life's triumphs and defeats. *Journal of Personality and Social Psychology, 90*, 690–708.

Ma, A., Landau, M. J., Narayanan, J., & Kay, A. C. (2017). Thought-control difficulty motivates structure seeking. *Journal of Experimental Psychology: General, 146*, 1067–1072.

Ma, D. S., Correll, J., Wittenbrink, B., Bar-Anan, Y., Sriram, N., & Nosek, B. A. (2013). When fatigue turns deadly: The association between fatigue and racial bias in the decision to shoot. *Basic and Applied Social Psychology, 35*, 515–524.

Ma, L. (1997, September). On the origin of Darwin's ills. *Discover*, p. 27.

Ma, X., Tamir, M., & Miyamoto, Y. (2018). A socio-cultural instrumental approach to emotion regulation: Culture and the regulation of positive emotions. *Emotion, 18*(1), 138–152.

Maalouf, F. T., Haidar, R., Mansour, F., Elbejjani, M., Khoury, J. E., Khoury, B., & Ghandour, L. A. (2022). Anxiety, depression and PTSD in children and adolescents following the Beirut port explosion. *Journal of Affective Disorders, 302*, 58–65.

Maas, J. B., & Robbins, R. S. (2010). *Sleep for success: Everything you must know about sleep but are too tired to ask.* Author House.

Macan, T. H., & Dipboye, R. L. (1994). The effects of the application on processing of information from the employment interview. *Journal of Applied Social Psychology, 24*, 1291–1314.

MacCabe, J. H., Lambe, M. P., Cnattingius, S., Torrång, A., Björk, C., Sham, P. C., David, A. S., Murray, R. M., & Hultman, C. M. (2008). Scholastic achievement at age 16 and risk of schizophrenia and other psychoses: A national cohort study. *Psychological Medicine, 38*, 1133–1140.

MacCann, C., Jiang, Y., Brown, L. E. R., Double, K. S., Bucich, M., & Minbashian, A. (2020). Emotional intelligence predicts academic performance: A meta-analysis. *Psychological Bulletin, 146*, 150–186.

Macchia, L., Plagnol, A. C., & Powdthavee, N. (2020). Buying happiness in an unequal world: Rank of income more strongly predicts well-being in more unequal countries. *Personality and Social Psychology Bulletin, 46*, 769–780.

Maccoby, E. (1980). *Social development: Psychological growth and the parent-child relationship.* Harcourt Brace Jovanovich.

Maccoby, E. E. (1990). Gender and relationships: A developmental account. *American Psychologist, 45*, 513–520.

Maccoby, E. E. (1998). *The paradox of gender.* Harvard University Press.

Maccoby, E. E. (2002). Gender and group process: A developmental perspective. *Current Directions in Psychological Science, 11*, 54–58.

Maccoby, E. E., & Martin, J. A. (1983). Socialization in the context of the family: Parent-child interaction. In P. H. Mussen & E. M. Hetherington (Eds.), *Handbook of child psychology: Vol. 4. Socialization, personality, and social development* (pp. 1–101). Wiley.

MacCormack, J. K., & Lindquist, K. A. (2016). Bodily contribution to emotion: Schachter's legacy for a psychological constructionist view on emotion. *Emotion Review, 9*, 36–45.

MacDonald, B., Pennington, B. F., Willcutt, E. G., Dmitrieva, J., Samuelsson, S., Byrne, B., & Olson, R. K. (2019). Cross-country differences in parental reporting of symptoms of ADHD. *Journal of Cross-Cultural Psychology, 50*, 806–824.

MacDonald, G., & Leary, M. R. (2005). Why does social exclusion hurt? The relationship between social and physical pain. *Psychological Bulletin, 131*, 202–223.

Macdonald, K., Germine, L., Anderson, A., Christodoulou, J., & McGrath, L. M. (2017). Dispelling the myth: Training in education or neuroscience decreases but does not eliminate beliefs in neuromyths. *Frontiers in Psychology, 8*, 16.

MacDonald, T. K., & Hynie, M. (2008). Ambivalence and unprotected sex: Failure to predict sexual activity and decreased condom use. *Journal of Applied Social Psychology, 38*, 1092–1107.

MacDonald, T. K., Zanna, M. P., & Fong, G. T. (1995). Decision making in altered states: Effects of alcohol on attitudes toward drinking and driving. *Journal of Personality and Social Psychology, 68*, 973–985.

MacFarlane, A. (1978, February). What a baby knows. *Human Nature*, pp. 74–81.

Macfarlane, J. W. (1964). Perspectives on personality consistency and change from the guidance study. *Vita Humana, 7*, 115–126.

Maciejewski, D., van Sprang, E., Spinhoven, P., & Penninx, B. (2021). Longitudinal associations between negative life events and depressive symptoms—A 9-year longitudinal study on between-person and within-person effects and the role of family history. *Journal of Personality and Social Psychology, 121*, 707–721.

Maciejewski, P. K., Maercker, A., Boelen, P. A., & Prigerson, H. G. (2016). "Prolonged grief disorder" and "persistent complex bereavement disorder", but not "complicated grief," are one and the same diagnostic entity: An analysis of data from the Yale Bereavement Study. *World Psychiatry, 15*, 266–275.

MacInnis, C. C., & Hodson, G. (2015). Do American states with more religious or conservative populations search more for sexual content on Google? *Archives of Sexual Behavior, 44*, 137–147.

Mack, A., & Rock, I. (2000). *Inattentional blindness.* MIT Press.

Mackenzie, J. L., Aggen, S. H., Kirkpatrick, R. M., Kendler, K. S., & Amstadter, A. B. (2015). A longitudinal twin study of insomnia symptoms in adults. *Sleep, 38*, 1423–1430.

MacKenzie, M. J., Nicklas, E., Waldfogel, J., & Brooks-Gunn, J. (2013). Spanking and child development across the first decade of life. *Pediatrics, 132*, e1118–e1125.

MacKerron, G., & Mourato, S. (2013). Happiness is greater in natural environments. *Global Environmental Change, 23*, 992–1000.

Mackey, S., Allgaier, N., Chaarani, B., Spechler, P., Orr, C., Bunn, J., Allen, N. B., Alia-Klein, N., Batalla, A., Blaine, S., Brooks, S., Caparelli, E., Chye, Y. Y., Cousijn, J., Dagher, A., Desrivieres, S., Feldstein-Ewing, S., Foxe, J. J., Goldstein, R. Z., ... ENIGMA Addiction Working Group. (2019). Mega-analysis of gray matter volume in substance dependence: General and substance-specific regional effects. *American Journal of Psychiatry, 176*, 119–128.

MacLeod, C. M., & Bodner, G. E. (2017). The production effect in memory. *Current Directions in Psychological Science, 26*, 390–395.

MacLeod, C., & Clarke, P. J. F. (2015). The attentional bias modification approach to anxiety intervention. *Clinical Psychological Science, 3*, 58–78.

Macmillan, M., & Lena, M. L. (2010). Rehabilitating Phineas Gage. *Neuropsychological Rehabilitation, 17*, 1–18.

Macnamara, B. N., Hambrick, D. Z., & Oswald, F. L. (2014). Deliberate practice and performance in music, games, sports, education, and professions: A meta-analysis. *Psychological Science, 25*, 1608–1618.

Macnamara, B. N., Moreau, D., & Hambrick, D. Z. (2016). The relationship between deliberate practice and performance in sports: A meta-analysis. *Perspectives on Psychological Science, 11*, 333–350.

MacNeilage, P. F., Rogers, L. J., & Vallortigara, G. (2009, July). Origins of the left and right brain. *Scientific American*, pp. 60–67.

MacPherson, S. E., Turner, M. S., Bozzali, M., Cipolotti, L., & Shallice, T. (2016). The Doors and People Test: The effect of frontal lobe lesions on recall and recognition memory performance. *Neuropsychology, 30*, 332–337.

Maddieson, I. (1984). *Patterns of sounds*. Cambridge University Press.

Madigan, S., Cyr, C., Eirich, R., Fearon, R. P., Ly, A., Rash, C., Poole, J. C., & Alink, L. R. (2019). Testing the cycle of maltreatment hypothesis: Meta-analytic evidence of the intergenerational transmission of child maltreatment. *Development and Psychopathology, 31*, 23–51.

Madison, A., Andridge, R., Shrout, M. R., Renna, M. E., Bennett, J. M., Jaremka, L. M., Fagundes, C. P., Belury, M. A., Malarkey, W. B., & Kiecolt-Glaser, J. K. (2022). Frequent interpersonal stress and inflammatory reactivity predict depressive-symptom increases: Two tests of the social-signal-transduction theory of depression. *Psychological Science, 33*(1), 152–164.

Madison, G., Mosling, M. A., Verweij, K. J. H., Pedersen, N. L., & Ullen, F. (2016). Common genetic influences on intelligence and auditory simple reaction time in a large Swedish sample. *Intelligence, 59*, 157–162.

Maes, H. H., Neale, M. C., & Eaves, L. J. (1997). Genetic and environmental factors in relative body weight and human adiposity. *Behavior Genetics, 27*, 325–351.

Maes, H. H., Neale, M. C., Ohlsson, H., Zahery, M., Lichtenstein, P., Sundquist, K., Sundquist, J., & Kendler, K. S. (2016). A bivariate genetic analysis of drug abuse ascertained through medical and criminal registries in Swedish twins, siblings and half-siblings. *Behavior Genetics, 46*, 735–741.

Maestripieri, D. (2003). Similarities in affiliation and aggression between cross-fostered rhesus macaque females and their biological mothers. *Developmental Psychobiology, 43*, 321–327.

Maestripieri, D. (2005). Early experience affects the intergenerational transmission of infant abuse in rhesus monkeys. *PNAS, 102*, 9726–9729.

Magill, M., Tonigan, J. S., Kiluk, B., Ray, L., Walthers, J., & Carroll, K. (2020). The search for mechanisms of cognitive behavioral therapy for alcohol or other drug use disorders: A systematic review. *Behaviour Research and Therapy, 131*. doi: 10.1016/j.brat.2020.103648

Magnuson, K. A., Ruhm, C., & Waldfogel, J. (2007). Does prekindergarten improve school preparation and performance? *Economics of Education Review, 26*, 33–51.

Magnusson, D. (1990). Personality research—challenges for the future. *European Journal of Personality, 4*, 1–17.

Maguire, E. A., Gadian, D. G., Johnsrude, I. S., Good, C. D., Ashburner, J., Frackowiak, R. S. J., & Frith, C. D. (2000). Navigation-related structural change in the hippocampi of taxi drivers. *PNAS, 97*, 4398–4403.

Maguire, E. A., Spiers, H. J., Good, C. D., Hartley, T., Frackowiak, R. S. J., & Burgess, N. (2003). Navigation expertise and the human hippocampus: A structural brain imaging analysis. *Hippocampus, 13*, 250–259.

Maguire, E. A., Valentine, E. R., Wilding, J. M., & Kapur, N. (2003). Routes to remembering: The brains behind superior memory. *Nature Neuroscience, 6*, 90–95.

Mah, C. D., Mah, K. E., Kezirian, E. J., & Dement, W. C. (2011). The effects of sleep extension on the athletic performance of collegiate basketball players. *Sleep, 34*, 943–950.

Mahadevan, N., Gregg, A. P., & Sedikides, C. (2019). Is self-regard a sociometer or a hierometer? Self-esteem tracks status and inclusion, narcissism tracks status. *Journal of Personality and Social Psychology, 116*, 444.

Maharani, A., Dawes, P., Nazroo, J., Tampubolon, G., & Pendleton, N. (2018), Longitudinal relationship between hearing aid use and cognitive function in older Americans. *Journal of the American Geriatrics Society, 66*, 1130–1136.

Maher, S., Ekstrom, T., & Chen, Y. (2014). Greater perceptual sensitivity to happy facial expression. *Perception, 43*, 1353–1364.

Mahoney, J. L., Weissberg, R. P., Greenberg, M. T., Dusenbury, L., Jagers, R. J., Niemi, K., Schlinger, M., Schlund, J., Shriver, T. P., VanAusdal, K., & Yoder, N. (2021). Systemic social and emotional learning: Promoting educational success for all preschool to high school students. *American Psychologist, 76*(7), 1128–1142.

Mai, Q. D., Hill, T. D., Vila-Henninger, L., & Grandner, M. A. (2019). Employment insecurity and sleep disturbance: Evidence from 31 European countries. *Journal of Sleep Research, 28*(9). https://bit.ly/3TxdHpK

Maia, T. V., & Frank, M. J. (2017). An integrative perspective on the role of dopamine in schizophrenia. *Biological Psychiatry, 81*, 52–66.

Maier, A., Gieling, C., Heinen-Ludwig, L., Stefan, V., Schultz, J., Güntürkün, O., Becker, B., Hurlemann, R., & Scheele, D. (2020). Association of childhood maltreatment with interpersonal distance and social touch preferences in adulthood. *American Journal of Psychiatry, 177*, 37–46.

Maier, M., & Abdel Rahman, R. (2018). Native language promotes access to visual consciousness. *Psychological Science, 29*, 1757–1772.

Maier, S. F., & Seligman, M. E. P. (2016). Learned helplessness at fifty: Insights from neuroscience. *Psychological Review, 123*, 349–367.

Maier, S. F., Watkins, L. R., & Fleshner, M. (1994). Psychoneuroimmunology: The interface between behavior, brain, and immunity. *American Psychologist, 49*, 1004–1017.

Maisto, D., Barca, L., Van den Bergh, O., & Pezzulo, G. (2021). Perception and misperception of bodily symptoms from an active inference perspective: Modelling the case of panic disorder. *Psychological Review, 128*(4), 690–710.

Maiti, S., Kumar, K. H. B. G., Castellini, C. A., O'Reilly, R., & Singh, S. M. (2011). Ontonogenetic de novo copy number variations (CNVs) as a source of genetic individuality: Studies on two families with MZD twins for schizophrenia. *PLOS ONE, 6*. https://www.ncbi.nlm.nih.gov/pmc/articles/PMC3047561/

Maixner, D. F., Weiner, R., Reti, I. M., Hermida, A. P., Husain, M. M., Larsen, D., & McDonald, W. M. (2021). Electroconvulsive therapy is an essential procedure. *American Journal of Psychiatry, 178*, 381–382.

Major, B., Carrington, P. I., & Carnevale, P. J. D. (1984). Physical attractiveness and self-esteem: Attribution for praise from an other-sex evaluator. *Personality and Social Psychology Bulletin, 10*, 43–50.

Major, B., Schmidlin, A. M., & Williams, L. (1990). Gender patterns in social touch: The impact of setting and age. *Journal of Personality and Social Psychology, 58*, 634–643.

Makel, M. C., Kell, H. J., Lubinski, D., Putallaz, M., & Benbow, C. P. (2016). When lightning strikes twice: Profoundly gifted, profoundly accomplished. *Psychological Science, 27*, 1004–1018.

Malamuth, N. (2018). "Adding fuel to the fire"? Does exposure to non-consenting adult or to child pornography increase risk of sexual aggression? *Aggression and Violent Behavior, 41*, 74–89.

Malani, P., Singer, D., Clark, S., Kirch, M., & Solway, E. (2018, May). *Let's talk about sex*. National poll on healthy aging. University of Michigan. https://www.healthyagingpoll.org/report/lets-talk-about-sex

Maldonado-Molina, M. M., Reingle, J. M., Jennings, W. G., & Prado, G. (2011). Drinking and driving among immigrant and US-born Hispanic young adults: Results from a longitudinal and nationally representative study. *Addictive Behaviors, 36*, 381–388.

Malkiel, B. G. (2016). *A random walk down Wall Street: The time-tested strategy for successful investing* (11th ed.). Norton.

Malle, B. F. (2006). The actor–observer asymmetry in attribution: A (surprising) meta-analysis. *Psychological Bulletin, 132*, 895–919.

Malle, B. F., Knobe, J. M., & Nelson, S. E. (2007). Actor–observe asymmetries in explanations of behavior: New answers to an old question. *Journal of Personality and Social Psychology, 93*, 491–514.

Malmquist, C. P. (1986). Children who witness parental murder: Post-traumatic aspects. *Journal of the American Academy of Child Psychiatry, 25*, 320–325.

Malouff, J. M., & Schutte, N. S. (2017). Can psychological interventions increase optimism? A meta-analysis. *The Journal of Positive Psychology, 12*, 594–604.

Maltby, N., Tolin, D. F., Worhunsky, P., O'Keefe, T. M., & Kiehl, K. A. (2005). Dysfunctional action monitoring hyperactivates frontal-striatal circuits in obsessive-compulsive disorder: An event-related fMRI study. *NeuroImage, 24*, 495–503.

Mammadov, S. (2022). Big Five personality traits and academic performance: A meta-analysis. *Journal of Personality, 90*(2), 222–255.

Mampe, B., Friederici, A. D., Christophe, A., & Wermke, K. (2009). Newborns' cry melody is shaped by their native language. *Current Biology, 19*, 1–4.

Mandela, N. (2004). *Message from Mr N R Mandela for the Global Convention on Peace and Nonviolence in New Delhi on 31 January 2004*. http://db.nelsonmandela.org/speeches/pub_view.asp?pg=item&ItemID=NMS914&txtstr

Mandelli, L., Arminio, A., Atti, A. R., & De Ronchi, D. (2019). Suicide attempts in eating disorder subtypes: A meta-analysis of the literature employing DSM-IV, DSM-5, or ICD-10 diagnostic criteria. *Psychological Medicine, 49*, 1237–1249.

Mandsager, K., Harb, S., Cremer, P., Phelan, D., Nissen, S. E., & Jaber, W. (2018). Association of cardiorespiratory fitness with long-term mortality among adults undergoing exercise treadmill testing. *JAMA Network Open, 1*(6). https://jamanetwork.com/journals/jamanetworkopen/fullarticle/2707428

Maner, J. K., Kenrick, D. T., Neuberg, S. L., Becker, D. V., Robertson, T., Hofer, B., Neuberg, S. L., Delton, A. W., Butner, J., & Schaller, M. (2005). Functional projection: How fundamental social motives can bias interpersonal perception. *Journal of Personality and Social Psychology, 88*, 63–78.

Mangelsdorf, J., Eid, M., & Luhmann, M. (2019). Does growth require suffering? A systematic review and meta-analysis on genuine posttraumatic and postecstatic growth. *Psychological Bulletin, 145*, 302–338.

Mani, A., Mullainathan, S., Shafir, E., & Zhao, J. (2013). Poverty impedes cognitive function. *Science, 341*, 976–980.

Mann, T., Tomiyama, A. J., & Ward, A. (2015). Promoting public health in the context of the "obesity epidemic": False starts and promising new directions. *Perspectives on Psychological Science, 10*, 706–710.

Manson, J. E. (2002). Walking compared with vigorous exercise for the prevention of cardiovascular events in women. *New England Journal of Medicine, 347*, 716–725.

Manuck, S. B., & McCaffery, J. M. (2014). Gene-environment interaction. *Annual Review of Psychology, 65*, 41–70.

Mapes, L. (2021). *Orca: Shared waters, shared home*. Braided River.

Maquet, P. (2001). The role of sleep in learning and memory. *Science, 294*, 1048–1052.

Maquet, P., Peters, J.-M., Aerts, J., Delfiore, G., Degueldre, C., Luxen, A., & Franck, G. (1996). Functional neuroanatomy of human rapid-eye-movement sleep and dreaming. *Nature, 383*, 163–166.

Mar, R. A., & Oatley, K. (2008). The function of fiction is the abstraction and simulation of social experience. *Perspectives on Psychological Science, 3*, 173–192.

Mar, R. A., Oatley, K., & Peterson, J. B. (2009). Exploring the link between reading fiction and empathy: Ruling out individual differences and examining outcomes. *Communications: The European Journal of Communication, 34*, 407–428.

Marangolo, P., Fiori, V., Sabatini, U., De Pasquale, G., Razzano, C., Caltagirone, C., & Gili, T. (2016). Bilateral transcranial direct current stimulation language treatment enhances functional connectivity in the left hemisphere: Preliminary data from aphasia. *Journal of Cognitive Neuroscience, 28*, 724–738.

Marceau, K., McMaster, M. T. B., Smith, T. F., Daams, J. G., van Beijsterveldt, C. E. M., Boomsma, D. I., & Knopik, V. S. (2016). The prenatal environment in twin studies: A review on chorionicity. *Behavior Genetics, 46*, 286–303.

Maria, J. L., Mariano, S., & Diego, A. G. (2020). Effects of lockdown on human sleep and chronotype during the COVID-19 pandemic. *Current Biology, 30*(16). https://www.sciencedirect.com/science/article/pii/S0960982220310071

Marin, M.-F., Bilodeau-Houle, A., Morand-Beaulieu, S., Brouillard, A., Herringa, R. J., & Milad, M. R. (2020). Vicarious conditioned fear acquisition and extinction in child-parent dyads. *Scientific Reports, 10*. https://www.nature.com/articles/s41598-020-74170-1

Marinak, B. A., & Gambrell, L. B. (2008). Intrinsic motivation and rewards: What sustains young children's engagement with text? *Literacy Research and Instruction, 47*, 9–26.

Marken, S. (2022, April 27). *A third of U.S. college students consider withdrawing*. Gallup. https://bit.ly/3QDg9Jr

Markey, P. M., & Ferguson, C. J. (2017). *Moral combat: Why the war on violent video games is wrong*. BenBella Books.

Markfelder, T., & Pauli, P. (2020). Fear of pain and pain intensity: Meta-analysis and systemic review. *Psychological Bulletin, 146*, 411–450.

Markowitz, J. C., Milrod, B., Heckman, T. G., Bergman, M., Amsalem, D., Zalman, H., Ballas, T., & Neria, Y. (2021). Psychotherapy at a distance. *American Journal of Psychiatry, 178*(3), 240–246.

Marks, A. K., Patton, F., & Coll, C. G. (2011). Being bicultural: A mixed-methods study of adolescents' implicitly and explicitly measured multiethnic identities. *Developmental Psychology, 47*, 270–288.

Marks, E. H., Franklin, A. R., & Zoellner, L. A. (2018). Can't get it out of my mind: A systematic review of predictors of intrusive memories of distressing events. *Psychological Bulletin, 144*, 584–640.

Markus, G. B. (1986). Stability and change in political attitudes: Observe, recall, and "explain." *Political Behavior, 8*, 21–44.

Markus, H. R., & Kitayama, S. (1991). Culture and the self: Implications for cognition, emotion, and motivation. *Psychological Review, 98*, 224–253.

Markus, H. R., & Nurius, P. (1986). Possible selves. *American Psychologist, 41*, 954–969.

Markus, H. R., Uchida, Y., Omoregie, H., Townsend, S. S. M., & Kitayama, S. (2006). Going for the gold: Models of agency in Japanese and American contexts. *Psychological Science, 17*, 103–112.

Marmot, M. G., Bosma, H., Hemingway, H., Brunner, E., & Stansfeld, S. (1997). Contribution to job control and other risk factors to social variations in coronary heart disease incidents. *The Lancet, 350*, 235–239.

Marques, A., Ihle, A., Souza, A., Peralta, M., & de Matos, M. G. (2022). Religious-based interventions for depression: A systematic review and meta-analysis of experimental studies. *Journal of Affective Disorders, 309*, 289–296.

Marsh, A. A., Rhoads, S. A., & Ryan, R. M. (2019). A multi-semester classroom demonstration yields evidence in support of the facial feedback effect. *Emotion, 19*(8), 1500–1504.

Marsh, H. W., & Craven, R. G. (2006). Reciprocal effects of self-concept and performance from a multidimensional perspective: Beyond seductive pleasure and unidimensional perspectives. *Perspectives on Psychological Science, 1*, 133–163.

Marsh, H. W., Parker, P. D., Guo, J., Pekrun, R., & Basarkod, G. (2020). Psychological comparison processes and self-concept in relation to five distinct frame-of-reference effects: Pan-human cross-cultural generalizability over 68 countries. *European Journal of Personality, 34*, 180–202.

Marsh, H. W., Xu, K. M., Parker, P. D., Hau, K., Pekrun, R., Elliot, A., Guo, J., Dicke, T., & Basarkod, G. (2021). Moderation of the big-fish-little-pond effect: Juxtaposition of evolutionary (Darwinian-economic) and achievement motivation theory predictions based on a Delphi approach. *Educational Psychology Review, 33*, 1353–1378.

Marshall, M. J. (2002). *Why spanking doesn't work*. Bonneville Books.

Marshall, P. J., & Meltzoff, A. N. (2014). Neural mirroring mechanisms and imitation in human infants. *Philosophical Transactions of the Royal Society: Series B, 369*(1644). https://royalsocietypublishing.org/doi/10.1098/rstb.2013.0620

Martel, M. M., Levinson, C. A., Langer, J. K., & Nigg, J. T. (2016). A network analysis of developmental change in ADHD symptom structure from preschool to adulthood. *Clinical Psychological Science, 4*, 988–1001.

Martela, F., & Steger, M. F. (2016). The three meanings of meaning in life: Distinguishing coherence, purpose, and significance. *Journal of Positive Psychology, 11*, 531–545.

Martial, C., Cassol, H., Charland-Verville, V., Pallavicini, C., Sanz, C., Zamberlan, F., Martínez Vivot, R., Erowid, F., Erowid, E., Laureys, S., Greyson, B., & Tagliazucchi, E. (2019). Neurochemical models of near-death experiences: A large-scale study based on the semantic similarity of written reports. *Consciousness and Cognition: An International Journal, 69*, 52–69.

Martial, C., Cassol, H., Laureys, S., & Gosseries, O. (2020). Near-death experience as a probe to explore (disconnected) consciousness. *Trends in Cognitive Sciences, 24*(3), 173–183.

Martin, C. K., Anton, S. D., Walden, H., Arnett, C., Greenway, F. L., & Williamson, D. A. (2007). Slower eating rate reduces the food intake of men, but not women: Implications for behavioural weight control. *Behaviour Research and Therapy, 45*, 2349–2359.

Martin, C. L., Ruble, D. N., & Szkrybalo, J. (2002). Cognitive theories of early gender development. *Psychological Bulletin, 128*, 903–933.

Martín, R., Bajo-Grañeras, R., Moratalla, R., Perea, G., & Araque, A. (2015). Circuit-specific signaling in astrocyte-neuron networks in basal ganglia pathways. *Science, 349*, 730–734.

Martín-María, N., Miret, M., Caballero, F. F., Rico-Uribe, L., Steptoe, A., Chatterji, S., & Ayuso-Mateos, J. (2017). The impact of subjective well-being on mortality: A meta-analysis of longitudinal studies in the general population. *Psychosomatic Medicine, 79*, 565–575.

Martínez-Rivera, F. J., Martínez, N. A., Martínez, M., Ayala-Pagán, R. N., Silva, W. I., & Barreto-Estrada, J. L. (2019). Neuroplasticity transcript profile of the ventral striatum in the extinction of opioid-induced conditioned place preference. *Neurobiology of Learning and Memory, 163*. doi:10.1016/j.nlm.2019.107031

Martini, M., Bufalari, I., Stazi, M. A., & Aglioti, S. M. (2015). Is that me or my twin? Lack of self-face recognition advantage in identical twins. *PLOS ONE, 10*. https://journals.plos.org/plosone/article?id=10.1371/journal.pone.0120900

Martins, N., & Weaver, A. (2019). The role of media exposure on relational aggression: A meta-analysis. *Aggression and Violent Behavior, 47*, 90–99.

Martins, Y., Preti, G., Crabtree, C. R., & Wysocki, C. J. (2005). Preference for human body odors is influenced by gender and sexual orientation. *Psychological Science, 16*, 694–701.

Marty-Dugas, J., Ralph, B. C. W., Oakman, J. M., & Smilek, D. (2018). The relation between smartphone use and everyday inattention. *Psychology of Consciousness: Theory, Research, and Practice, 5*, 46–62.

Mary, A., Dayan, J., Leone, G., Postel, C., Fraisse, F., Malle, C., Vallée, T., Klein-Peschanski, C., Viader, F., de la Sayette, V., Peschanski, D., Eustache, F., & Gagnepain, P. (2020). Resilience after trauma: The role of memory suppression. *Science, 367*, 1–13.

Marzoli, D., Custodero, M., Pagliara, A., & Tommasi, L. (2013). Sun-induced frowning fosters aggressive feelings. *Cognition and Emotion, 27*, 1513–1521.

Mascetti, G. G. (2019, June). One eye open. *Scientific American*, pp. 41–45.

Mashour, G. A. (2018). The controversial correlates of consciousness. *Science, 360*, 493–494.

Maslow, A. H. (1970). *Motivation and personality* (2nd ed.). Harper & Row.

Maslow, A. H. (1971). *The farther reaches of human nature*. Viking Press.

Mason, A. E., Sbarra, D. A., & Mehl, M. R. (2010). Thin-slicing divorce: Thirty seconds of information predict changes in psychological adjustment over 90 days. *Psychological Science, 21*, 1420–1422.

Mason, C., & Kandel, E. R. (1991). Central visual pathways. In E. R. Kandel, J. H. Schwartz, & T. M. Jessell (Eds.), *Principles of neural science* (3rd ed.). Elsevier.

Mason, R. A., & Just, M. A. (2004). How the brain processes causal inferences in text. *Psychological Science, 15*, 1–7.

Mason, R. A., & Just, M. A. (2016). Neural representations of physics concepts. *Psychological Science, 27*, 904–913.

Massimini, M., Ferrarelli, F., Huber, R., Esser, S. K., Singh, H., & Tononi, G. (2005). Breakdown of cortical effective connectivity during sleep. *Science, 309*, 2228–2232.

Masten, A. S. (2001). Ordinary magic: Resilience processes in development. *American Psychologist, 56*, 227–238.

Masters, K. S. (2010). The role of religion in therapy: Time for psychologists to have a little faith? *Cognitive and Behavioral Practice, 17*, 393–400.

Masters, K. S., & Hooker, S. A. (2013). Religiousness/spirituality, cardiovascular disease, and cancer: Cultural integration for health research and intervention. *Journal of Consulting and Clinical Psychology, 81*, 206–216.

Masters, W. H., & Johnson, V. E. (1966). *Human sexual response*. Little, Brown.

Mastroianni, G. R. (2015). Obedience in perspective: Psychology and the Holocaust. *Theory and Psychology, 25*, 657–669.

Mastroianni, G. R., & Reed, G. (2006). Apples, barrels, and Abu Ghraib. *Sociological Focus, 39*, 239–250.

Masuda, T., Ellsworth, P. C., Mesquita, B., Leu, J., Tanida, S., & Van de Veerdonk, E. (2008). Placing the face in context: Cultural differences in the perception of facial emotion. *Journal of Personality and Social Psychology, 94*, 365–381.

Mata, R., Josef, A. K., & Hertwig, R. (2016). Propensity for risk taking across the life span and around the globe. *Psychological Science, 27*, 231–243.

Mataix-Cols, D., Rosario-Campos, M. C., & Leckman, J. F. (2005). A multidimensional model of obsessive-compulsive disorder. *American Journal of Psychiatry, 162*, 228–238.

Mataix-Cols, D., Wooderson, S., Lawrence, N., Brammer, M. J., Speckens, A., & Phillips, M. L. (2004). Distinct neural correlates of washing, checking, and hoarding symptom dimensions in obsessive-compulsive disorder. *Archives of General Psychiatry, 61*, 564–576.

Mather, M. (2016). The affective neuroscience of aging. *Annual Review of Psychology, 67*, 213–238.

Mather, M., Cacioppo, J. T., & Kanwisher, N. (2013). How fMRI can inform cognitive theories. *Perspectives on Psychological Science, 8*, 108–113.

Mather, M., Canli, T., English, T., Whitfield, S., Wais, P., Ochsner, K., Gabrieli, J. D., & Carstensen, L. L. (2004). Amygdala responses to emotionally valenced stimuli in older and younger adults. *Psychological Science, 15*, 259–263.

Mather, M., & Sutherland, M. (2012, February). *The selective effects of emotional arousal on memory*. APA Science Brief. https://www.apa.org/science/about/psa/2012/02/emotional-arousal

Mathur, M. B., & VanderWeele, T. J. (2019). Finding common ground in meta-analysis "wars" on violent video games. *Perspectives on Psychological Science, 14*, 705–708.

Matson, J. L., & Boisjoli, J. A. (2009). The token economy for children with intellectual disability and/or autism: A review. *Research on Developmental Disabilities, 30*, 240–248.

Matsumoto, D. (1994). *People: Psychology from a cultural perspective*. Brooks/Cole.

Matsumoto, D., Frank, M. G., & Hwang, H. C. (2015). The role of intergroup emotions on political violence. *Current Directions in Psychological Science, 24*, 369–373.

Matsumoto, D., Willingham, B., & Olide, A. (2009). Sequential dynamics of culturally moderated facial expressions of emotion. *Psychological Science, 20*, 1269–1275.

Mattanah, J. F., Lopez, F. G, & Govern, J. M. (2011). The contributions of parental attachment bonds to college student development and adjustment: A meta-analytic review. *Journal of Counseling Psychology, 58*, 565–596.

Matthews, N. L., & Goldberg, W. A. (2018). Theory of mind in children with and without autism spectrum disorder: Associations with the sibling constellation. *Autism, 22*, 311–321.

Matthews, R. N., Domjan, M., Ramsey, M., & Crews, D. (2007). Learning effects on sperm competition and reproductive fitness. *Psychological Science, 18*, 758–762.

Matz, S. C., & Harari, G. M. (2021). Personality–place transactions: Mapping the relationships between big five personality traits, states, and daily places. *Journal of Personality and Social Psychology, 120*, 1367–1385.

Matz, S. C., Kosinski, M., Nave, G., & Stillwell, D. J. (2017). Psychological targeting as an effective approach to digital mass persuasion. *PNAS, 114*, 12714–12719.

Maurer, D., & Maurer, C. (1988). *The world of the newborn*. Basic Books

Mauss, I. B., & Tamir, M. (2014). Emotion goals: How their content, structure, and operation shape emotion regulation. In J. J. Gross (Ed.), *Handbook of emotion regulation* (pp. 361–375). Guilford Press.

Maxwell, J. A., & McNulty, J. K. (2019). No longer in a dry spell: The developing understanding of how sex influences romantic relationships. *Current Directions in Psychological Science, 28*, 102–107.

May, C., & Hasher, L. (1998). Synchrony effects in inhibitory control over thought and action. *Journal of Experimental Psychology: Human Perception and Performance, 24*, 363–380.

May, J. (2019). Précis of Regard for reason in the moral mind. *Behavioral and Brain Sciences, 42*, e146.

May, P. A., Chambers, C. D., Kalberg, W. O., Zellner, J., Feldman, H., Buckley, D., Kopald, D., Hasken, J. M., Xu, R., Honerkamp-Smith, G., Taras, H., Manning, M. A., Robinson, L. K., Adam, M. P., Abdul-Rahman, M. D., Vaux, K., Jewett, T., Elliott, A. J., Kable, J. A., … Hoyme, E. (2018). Prevalence of fetal alcohol spectrum disorders in 4 US communities. *Journal of the American Medical Association, 319*, 474–482.

May, R. (1982). The problem of evil: An open letter to Carl Rogers. *Journal of Humanistic Psychology, 22*, 10–21.

Mayer, J. D., Caruso, D. R., & Salovey, P. (2016). The ability model of emotional intelligence: Principles and updates. *Emotion Review, 8*, 290–300.

Mayer, J. D., Salovey, P., & Caruso, D. R. (2002). *The Mayer-Salovey-Caruso Emotional Intelligence Test (MSCEIT)*. Multi-Health Systems, Inc.

Mayer, J. D., Salovey, P., & Caruso, D. R. (2012). The validity of the MSCEIT: Additional analyses and evidence. *Emotion Review, 4*, 403–408.

Mayr, U., & Freund, A. M. (2020). Do we become more prosocial as we age, and if so, why? *Current Directions in Psychological Science, 29*, 248–254.

Mazei, J., Hüffmeier, J., Freund, P. A., Stuhlmacher, A. F., Bilke, L., & Hertel, G. (2015). A meta-analysis on gender differences in negotiation outcomes and their moderators. *Psychological Bulletin, 141*, 85–104.

Mazza, S., Gerbier, E., Gustin, M. P., Kasikci, Z., Koenig, O., Toppino, T. C., & Magnin, M. (2016). Relearn faster and retain longer: Along with practice, sleep makes perfect. *Psychological Science, 27*, 1321–1330.

Mazzei, P. (2019, March 24). After 2 apparent student suicides, Parkland grieves again. *The New York Times*. https://www.nytimes.com/2019/03/24/us/parkland-suicide-marjory-stoneman-douglas.html

Mazzoni, G., Scoboria, A., & Harvey, L. (2010). Nonbelieved memories. *Psychological Science, 21*, 1334–1340.

Mazzoni, G., & Vannucci, M. (2007). Hindsight bias, the misinformation effect, and false autobiographical memories. *Social Cognition, 25*, 203–220.

McAdams, D. P., & Guo, J. (2015). Narrating the generative life. *Psychological Science, 26*, 475–483.

McBurney, D. H. (1996). *How to think like a psychologist: Critical thinking in psychology.* Prentice-Hall.

McBurney, D. H., & Collings, V. B. (1984). *Introduction to sensation and perception* (2nd ed.). Prentice-Hall.

McBurney, D. H., & Gent, J. F. (1979). On the nature of taste qualities. *Psychological Bulletin, 86*, 151–167.

McCabe, K. O., & Fleeson, W. (2016). Are traits useful? Explaining trait manifestations as tools in the pursuit of goals. *Journal of Personality and Social Psychology, 110*, 287–301.

McCabe, S. E., Veliz, P., & Schulenberg, J. E. (2018). How collegiate fraternity and sorority involvement relates to substance use during young adulthood and substance use disorders in early midlife: A national longitudinal study. *Journal of Adolescent Health, 62*(3S), S35–S43.

McCall, W. V., Lisanby, S. H., Rosenquist, P. B., Dooley, M., Husain, M. M., Knapp, R. G., Petrides, G., Rudorfer, M. V., Young, R. C., McClintock, S. M., Mueller, M., Prudic, J., Greenberg, R. M., Weiner, R. D., Bailine, S. H., Riley, M. A., McCloud, L., Kellner, C. H., & CORE/PRIDE Work Group. (2017). Effects of a right unilateral ultrabrief pulse electroconvulsive therapy course on health related quality of life in elderly depressed patients. *Journal of Affective Disorders, 209*, 39–45.

McCann, I. L., & Holmes, D. S. (1984). Influence of aerobic exercise on depression. *Journal of Personality and Social Psychology, 46*, 1142–1147.

McCann, U. D., Eligulashvili, V., & Ricaurte, G. A. (2001). (+–)3,4–Methylenedioxymethamphetamine ('Ecstasy')-induced serotonin neurotoxicity: Clinical studies. *Neuropsychobiology, 42*, 11–16.

McCarthy, J. (2017, June 28). *Americans more positive about effects of immigration.* Gallup. https://news.gallup.com/poll/213146/americans-positive-effects-immigration.aspx

McCarthy, J. (2018, October 22). *Two in three Americans now support legalizing marijuana.* Gallup News. https://news.gallup.com/poll/243908/two-three-americans-support-legalizing-marijuana.aspx

McCarthy, J. (2019, May 22). *U.S. support for same-sex marriage stable, at 63%.* Gallup. https://news.gallup.com/poll/257705/support-gay-marriage-stable.aspx

McCarthy, J. (2021, May 26). *Mixed views among Americans on transgender issues.* Gallup. https://news.gallup.com/poll/350174/mixed-views-among-americans-transgender-issues.aspx

McCarthy, P. (1986, July). Scent: The tie that binds? *Psychology Today*, pp. 6, 10.

McCauley, C. R. (2002). Psychological issues in understanding terrorism and the response to terrorism. In C. E. Stout (Ed.), *The psychology of terrorism* (Vol. 3, pp. 3–29). Praeger/Greenwood.

McCauley, C. R., & Segal, M. E. (1987). Social psychology of terrorist groups. In C. Hendrick (Ed.), *Group processes and intergroup relations: Review of personality and social psychology* (Vol. 9, pp. 231–256). Sage.

McCauley, E., Berk, M. S., Asarnow, J. R., Adrian, M., Cohen, J., Korslund, K., Avina, C., Hughes, J., Harned, M, Gallop, R., & Linehan, M. M. (2018). Efficacy of dialectical behavior therapy for adolescents at high risk for suicide: A randomized clinical trial. *JAMA Psychiatry, 75*, 777–785.

McClendon, B. T., & Prentice-Dunn, S. (2001). Reducing skin cancer risk: An intervention based on protection motivation theory. *Journal of Health Psychology, 6*, 321–328.

McClintock, M. K., & Herdt, G. (1996, December). Rethinking puberty: The development of sexual attraction. *Current Directions in Psychological Science, 5*, 178–183.

McClung, M., & Collins, D. (2007). "Because I know it will!": Placebo effects of an ergogenic aid on athletic performance. *Journal of Sport & Exercise Psychology, 29*, 382–394.

McClure, E. B. (2000). A meta-analytic review of sex differences in facial expression processing and their development in infants, children, and adolescents. *Psychological Bulletin, 126*, 424–453.

McClure, M. J., & Lydon, J. E. (2014). Anxiety doesn't become you: How attachment compromises relational opportunities. *Journal of Personality and Social Psychology, 106*, 89–111.

McConnell, A. R., Brown, C. M., Shoda, T. M., Stayton, L. E., & Martin, C. E. (2011). Friends with benefits: On the positive consequences of pet ownership. *Journal of Personality and Social Psychology, 101*, 1239–1252.

McCord, J. (1978). A thirty-year follow-up on treatment effects. *American Psychologist, 33*, 284–289.

McCord, J. (1979). Following up on Cambridge-Somerville. *American Psychologist, 34*, 727.

McCord, M. A., & Joseph, D. L. (2020). A framework of negative responses to introversion at work. *Personality and Individual Differences, 161*. https://doi.org/10.1016/j.paid.2020.109944

McCrae, R. R., & Costa, P. T., Jr. (1986). Clinical assessment can benefit from recent advances in personality psychology. *American Psychologist, 41*, 1001–1003.

McCrae, R. R., & Costa, P. T., Jr. (1990). *Personality in adulthood.* Guilford.

McCrae, R. R., & Costa, P. T., Jr. (1994). The stability of personality: Observations and evaluations. *Current Directions in Psychological Science, 3*, 173–175.

McCrae, R. R., & Costa, P. T., Jr. (2008). The Five-Factor Theory of personality. In O. P. John, R. W., Robins, & L. A. Pervin (Eds.), *Handbook of personality: Theory and research (3rd ed.).* Guilford.

McCrae, R. R., Terracciano, A., & 78 members of the Personality Profiles and Cultures Project. (2005). Universal features of personality traits from the observer's perspective: Data from 50 cultures. *Journal of Personality and Social Psychology, 88*, 547–561.

McCrink, K., & Wynn, K. (2004). Large-number addition and subtraction by 9-month-old infants. *Psychological Science, 15*, 776–781.

McCrory, E. J., De Brito, S. A., Sebastian, C. L., Mechelli, A., Bird, G., Kelly, P. A., & Viding, E. (2011). Heightened neural reactivity to threat in child victims of family violence. *Current Biology, 21*, R947–948.

McCullough, M. E., Hoyt, W. T., Larson, D. B., Koenig, H. G., & Thoresen, C. (2000). Religious involvement and mortality: A meta-analytic review. *Health Psychology, 19*, 211–222.

McCullough, M. E., & Laurenceau, J.-P. (2005). Religiousness and the trajectory of self-rated health across adulthood. *Personality and Social Psychology Bulletin, 31*, 560–573.

McCullough, M. E., & Willoughby, B. L. B. (2009). Religion, self-regulation, and self-control: Associations, explanations, and implications. *Psychological Bulletin, 135*, 69–93.

McDaniel, M. A., Bugg, J. M., Liu, Y., & Brick, J. (2015). When does the test-study-test sequence optimize learning and retention? *Journal of Experimental Psychology: Applied, 21*, 370–382.

McDaniel, M. A., Howard, D. C., & Einstein, G. O. (2009). The read-recite-review study strategy: Effective and portable. *Psychological Science, 20*, 516–522.

McDermott, K. B. (2021). Practicing retrieval facilitates learning. *Annual Review of Psychology, 72*, 609–633.

McDermott, R., Tingley, D., Cowden, J., Frazzetto, G., & Johnson, D. D. P. (2009). Monoamine oxidase A gene (MAOA) predicts behavioral aggression following provocation. *PNAS, 106*, 2118–2123.

McDonald, P. (2012). Workplace sexual harassment 30 years on: A review of the literature. *International Journal of Management Reviews, 14*, 1–17.

McDuff, D., Kodra, E., el Kallouby, R., & LaFrance, M. (2017). A large-scale analysis of sex differences in facial expressions. *PLOS ONE, 12*. doi: 10.1371/journal.pone.0173942

McElwain, N. L., Ravindran, N., Emery, H. T., & Swartz, R. (2019). Theory of mind as a mechanism linking mother–toddler relationship quality and child–friend interaction during the preschool years. *Social Development, 28*, 998–1015.

McEvoy, S. P., Stevenson, M. R., McCartt, A. T., Woodward, M., Haworth, C., Palamara, P., & Ceracelli, R. (2005). Role of mobile phones in motor vehicle crashes resulting in hospital attendance: A case-crossover study. *British Medical Journal, 331*, 428.

McEvoy, S. P., Stevenson, M. R., & Woodward, M. (2007). The contribution of passengers versus mobile phone use to motor vehicle crashes resulting in hospital attendance by the driver. *Accident Analysis and Prevention, 39*, 1170–1176.

McFarland, C., & Ross, M. (1987). The relation between current impressions and memories of self and dating partners. *Psychological Bulletin, 13*, 228–238.

McGaugh, J. L. (1994). Quoted by B. Bower in, Stress hormones hike emotional memories. *Science News, 146*, 262.

McGaugh, J. L. (2003). *Memory and emotion: The making of lasting memories.* Columbia University Press.

McGaugh, J. L. (2015). Consolidating memories. *Annual Review of Psychology, 66*, 1–24.

McGaugh, J. L., & LePort, A. (2014, February). Remembrance of all things past. *Scientific American*, pp. 41–45.

McGeehan, P. (2018, February 6). Failure to screen for sleep apnea led to two recent train crashes. *The New York Times*. https://www.nytimes.com/2018/02/06/nyregion/train-crash-sleep-apnea.html

McGhee, P. E. (1976, June). Children's appreciation of humor: A test of the cognitive congruency principle. *Child Development, 47*, 420–426.

McGonigal, K. (2019). *The joy of movement: How exercise helps us find happiness, hope, connection, and courage.* Penguin.

McGrath, J. J., & Welham, J. L. (1999). Season of birth and schizophrenia: A systematic review and meta-analysis of data from the Southern hemisphere. *Schizophrenia Research, 35*, 237–242.

McGrath, J. J., Welham, J., & Pemberton, M. (1995). Month of birth, hemisphere of birth and schizophrenia. *British Journal of Psychiatry, 167*, 783–785.

McGrath, R. E. (2015). Character strengths in 75 nations: An update. *Journal of Positive Psychology, 10*, 41–52.

McGue, M. (2010). The end of behavioral genetics? *Behavioral Genetics, 40*, 284–296.

McGue, M., & Bouchard, T. J., Jr. (1998). Genetic and environmental influences on human behavioral differences. *Annual Review of Neuroscience, 21*, 1–24.

McGue, M., Bouchard, T. J., Jr., Iacono, W. G., & Lykken, D. T. (1993). Behavioral genetics of cognitive ability: A life-span perspective. In R. Plomin & G. E. McClearn (Eds.), *Nature, nurture and psychology.* American Psychological Association.

McGurk, H., & MacDonald, J. (1976). Hearing lips and seeing voices. *Nature, 264*, 746–748.

McHugh, P. R. (1995). Witches, multiple personalities, and other psychiatric artifacts. *Nature Medicine, 1*, 110–114.

McIntyre, K. M., Puterman, E., Scodes, J. M., Choo, T.-H., Choi, C. J., Pavlicova, M., & Sloan, R. P. (2020). The effects of aerobic training on subclinical negative affect: A randomized controlled trial. *Health Psychology, 39*(4), 255–264.

McIntyre, L. (2021). Talking to science deniers and sceptics is not hopeless. *Nature, 596*, 165.

McKay, J. (2000). Building self-esteem in children. In M. McKay & P. Fanning (Eds.), *Self-esteem.* New Harbinger/St. Martins.

McKenna, K. E. (2022). What is the trigger for sexual climax? *Archives of Sexual Behavior, 51*(1), 383–390.

McKenna, K. Y. A., Green, A. S., & Gleason, M. E. J. (2002). What's the big attraction? Relationship formation on the internet. *Journal of Social Issues, 58*, 9–31.

McKinney, B. C. (2017). Epigenetic programming: A putative neurobiological mechanism linking childhood maltreatment and risk for adult psychopathology. *American Journal of Psychiatry, 174*, 1134–1136.

McKinnon, M. C., Palombo, D. J., Nazarov, A., Kumar, N., Khuu, W., & Levine, B. (2015). Threat of death and autobiographical memory a study of passengers from Flight AT236. *Clinical Psychological Science, 3*, 487–502.

McKone, E., Kanwisher, N., & Duchaine, B. C. (2007). Can generic expertise explain special processing for faces? *Trends in Cognitive Sciences, 11*, 8–15.

McLaughlin, K. A., & King, K. (2015). Developmental trajectories of anxiety and depression in early adolescence. *Journal of Abnormal Child Psychology, 43*(2), 311–323.

McLaughlin, K. A., Weissman, D., & Bitrán, D. (2019). Childhood adversity and neural development: A systematic review. *Annual Review of Developmental Psychology, 1*, 277–312.

McLean, C. P., & Anderson, E. R. (2009). Brave men and timid women? A review of the gender differences in fear and anxiety. *Clinical Psychology Review, 29*, 496–505.

McManus, S., Walby, S., Barbosa, E. C., Appleby, L., Brugha, T., Bebbington, P. E., Cook, E. A., & Knipe, D. (2022). Intimate partner violence, suicidality, and self-harm: A probability sample survey of the general population in England. *Lancet Psychiatry, 9*(7), 574–583.

McMurray, B. (2007). Defusing the childhood vocabulary explosion. *Science, 317*, 631.

McNally, R. J. (2003). *Remembering trauma.* Harvard University Press.

McNally, R. J. (2007). Betrayal trauma theory: A critical appraisal. *Memory, 15*, 280–294.

McNally, R. J. (2012). Are we winning the war against posttraumatic stress disorder? *Science, 336*, 872–874.

McNally, R. J., & Geraerts, E. (2009). A new solution to the recovered memory debate. *Perspectives on Psychological Science, 4*, 126–134.

McNulty, J. K., Olson, M. A., Jones, R. E., & Acosta, L. M. (2017). Automatic associations between one's partner and one's affect as the proximal mechanism of change in relationship satisfaction: Evidence from evaluative conditioning. *Psychological Science, 28*, 1031–1040.

Meador, B. D., & Rogers, C. R. (1984). Person-centered therapy. In R. J. Corsini (Ed.), *Current psychotherapies* (3rd ed.). Peacock.

Mednick, S. A., Huttunen, M. O., & Machon, R. A. (1994). Prenatal influenza infections and adult schizophrenia. *Schizophrenia Bulletin, 20*, 263–267.

Meeussen, L., Van Laar, C., & Verbruggen, M. (2019). Looking for a family man? Norms for men are toppling in heterosexual relationships. *Sex Roles, 80*, 429–442.

Mehlig, K., Nehmtallah, T., Rosvall, M., Hunsberger, M., Rosengren, A., & Lissner, L. (2020). Negative life events predict weight gain in a 13-year follow-up on an adult Swedish population. *Journal of Psychosomatic Research, 132*. https://www.sciencedirect.com/science/article/abs/pii/S0022399919311730

Mehrabian, A., & Blum, J. S. (2018). Physical appearance, attractiveness, and the mediating role of emotions. In N. Pallone (Ed.), *Love, romance, and sexual interaction: Research perspectives from* "Current Psychology" (pp. 1–30). Routledge.

Meichenbaum, D. (1977). *Cognitive-behavior modification: An integrative approach.* Plenum Press.

Meichenbaum, D. (1985). *Stress inoculation training.* Pergamon.

Meier, M., Haub, K., Schramm, M.-L., Hamma, M., Bentele, U. U., Dimitroff, S. J., Gärtner, R., Denk, B. F., Benz, A. B. E., Unternaehrer, E., & Pruessner, J. C. (2022). Validation of an online version of the trier social stress test in adult men and women. *Psychoneuroendocrinology, 142*. https://www.sciencedirect.com/science/article/pii/S0306453022001597

Meis, L. A., Noorbaloochi, S., Hagel Campbell, E. M., Erbes, C. R., Polusny, M. A., Velasquez, T. L., Bangerter, A., Cutting, A., Eftekhari, A., Rosen, C. S., Tuerk, P. W., Burmeister, L. B., & Spoont, M. R. (2019). Sticking it out in trauma-focused treatment for PTSD: It takes a village. *Journal of Consulting and Clinical Psychology, 87*, 246–256.

Melioli, T., Bauer, S., Franko, D. L., Moessner, M., Ozer, F., Chabrol, H., & Rodgers, R. F. (2016). Reducing eating disorder symptoms and risk factors using the internet: A meta-analytic review. *International Journal of Eating Disorders, 49*, 19–31.

Mellers, B., Stone, E., Atanasov, P., Rohrbaugh, N., Metz, S. E., Ungar, L., Bishop, M. M., Horowitz, M., Merkle, E., & Tetlock, P. (2015). The psychology of intelligence analysis: Drivers of prediction accuracy in world politics. *Journal of Experimental Psychology: Applied, 21*, 1–14.

Meltzer, A. L., Makhanova, A., Hicks, L. L., French, J. E., McNulty, J. K., & Bradbury, T. N. (2017). Quantifying the sexual afterglow: The lingering benefits of sex and their implications for pair-bonded relationships. *Psychological Science, 28*, 587–598.

Meltzoff, A. N. (1988). Infant imitation after a 1-week delay: Long-term memory for novel acts and multiple stimuli. *Developmental Psychology, 24*, 470–476.

Meltzoff, A. N., & Moore, M. K. (1989). Imitation in newborn infants: Exploring the range of gestures imitated and the underlying mechanisms. *Developmental Psychology, 25*, 954–962.

Meltzoff, A. N., Kuhl, P. K., Movellan, J., & Sejnowski, T. J. (2009). Foundations for a new science of learning. *Science, 325*, 284–288.

Meltzoff, A. N., & Moore, M. K. (1997). Explaining facial imitation: A theoretical model. *Early Development and Parenting, 6*, 179–192.

Melzack, R. (1992, April). Phantom limbs. *Scientific American*, pp. 120–126.

Melzack, R. (1998, February). Quoted in "Phantom limbs." *Discover*, p. 20.

Melzack, R. (2005). Evolution of the neuromatrix theory of pain. *Pain Practice, 5*, 85–94.

Melzack, R., & Katz, J. (2013). Pain. *Wiley Interdisciplinary Reviews: Cognitive Science, 4*, 1–15.

Melzack, R., & Wall, P. D. (1965). Pain mechanisms: A new theory. *Science, 150*, 971–979.

Melzack, R., & Wall, P. D. (1983). *The challenge of pain.* Basic Books.

Mende-Siedlecki, P., Said, C. P., & Todorov, A. (2013). The social evaluation of faces: A meta-analysis of functional neuroimaging studies. *SCAN, 8*, 285–299.

Mendelson, J. L., Gates, J. A., & Lerner, M. D. (2016). Friendship in school-age boys with autism spectrum disorders: A meta-analytic summary and developmental, process-based model. *Psychological Bulletin, 142*, 601–622.

Mendes, E. (2010, June 2). *U.S. exercise levels up, but demographic differences remain.* Gallup. https://news.gallup.com/poll/139340/exercise-levels-demographic-differences-remain.aspx

Mendolia, M., & Kleck, R. E. (1993). Effects of talking about a stressful event on arousal: Does what we talk about make a difference? *Journal of Personality and Social Psychology, 64*, 283–292.

Meng, S.-Q., Cheng, J.-L., Li, Y.-Y., Yang, X.-Q., Zheng, J.-W., Chang, X.-W., Shi, Y., Chen, Y., Lu, L., Sun, Y., Bao, Y.-P., & Shi, J. (2022). Global prevalence of digital addiction in general population: A systematic review and meta-analysis. *Clinical Psychology Review*, 92. doi: 10.1016/j.cpr.2022.102128

Mennella, J. A., Coren, P., Jagnow, M. S., & Beauchamp, G. K. (2001). Prenatal and postnatal flavor learning by human infants. *Pediatrics, 107*, E88.

Mennig, M., Tennie, S., & Barke, A. (2022). Self-perceived problematic use of online pornography is linked to clinically relevant levels of psychological distress and psychopathological symptoms. *Archives of Sexual Behavior, 51*, 1313–1321.

Mennin, D. S., Heimberg, R. G., Turk, C. L., & Fresco, D. M. (2005). Preliminary evidence for an emotion dysregulation model of generalized anxiety disorder. *Behaviour Research and Therapy*, 43(10), 1281–1310.

Merari, A. (2002). *Explaining suicidal terrorism: Theories versus empirical evidence* [Invited address]. American Psychological Association.

Mercado, M. C., Holland, K., Leemis, R. W., Stone, D. M., & Wang, J. (2017). Trends in emergency department visits for nonfatal self-inflicted injuries among youth aged 10 to 24 years in the United States, 2001–2015. *Journal of the American Medical Association, 318*, 1931–1933.

Mercer, T. (2015). Wakeful rest alleviates interference-based forgetting. *Memory, 23*, 127–137.

Meriac, J. P., Hoffman, B. J., Woehr, D. J., & Fleisher, M. S. (2008). Further evidence for the validity of assessment center dimensions: A meta-analysis of the incremental criterion-related validity of dimension ratings. *Journal of Applied Psychology, 93*, 1042–1052.

Merikangas, K. R., Jin, R., He, J. P., Kessler, R. C., Lee, S., Sampson, N. A., Viana, M. C., Andrade, L. H., Hu, C., Karam, E. G., Ladea, M., Medina-Mora, M. E., Ono, Y., Posada-Villa, J., Sagar, R., Wells, J. E., & Zarkov, Z. (2011). Prevalence and correlates of bipolar spectrum disorder in the World Mental Health Survey initiative. *Archives of General Psychiatry, 68*, 241–251.

Merskey, H. (1992). The manufacture of personalities: The production of multiple personality disorder. *British Journal of Psychiatry, 160*, 327–340.

Merz, J., Schwarzer, G., & Gerger, H. (2019). Comparative efficacy and acceptability of pharmacological, psychotherapeutic, and combination treatments in adults with posttraumatic stress disorder: A network meta-analysis. *JAMA Psychiatry, 76*, 904–913.

Mesman, J., van Ijzendoorn, M., Behrens, K., Carbonell, O. A., Cárcamo, R., Cohen-Paraira, I., Kondo-Ikemura, K., Mels, C., Mooya, H., Murtisari, S., Nóblega, M., Ortiz, J. A., Sagi-Schwartz, A., Sichimba, F., Soares, I., Steele, H., Steele, M., Pape, M., van Ginkel, J., ... Zreik, G. (2015). Is the ideal mother a sensitive mother? Beliefs about early childhood parenting in mothers across the globe. *International Journal of Behavioral Development, 40*, 385–397.

Mesoudi, A. (2009). How cultural evolutionary theory can inform social psychology and vice versa. *Psychological Review, 116*, 929–952.

Mesquita, B. (2022). *Between us: How cultures create emotions.* Norton & Company.

Messias, E., Eaton, W. W., & Grooms, A. N. (2011). Economic grand rounds: Income inequality and depression prevalence across the United States: An ecological study. *Psychiatric Services, 62*, 710–712.

Meston, C. M., & Buss, D. M. (2007). Why humans have sex. *Archives of Sexual Behavior, 36*, 477–507.

Metcalfe, J. (1986). Premonitions of insight predict impending error. *Journal of Experimental Psychology: Learning, Memory, and Cognition, 12*, 623–634.

Metzler, D. (2011, Spring). Vocabulary growth in adult cross-fostered chimpanzees. *Friends of Washoe, 32*(3), 11–13.

Meyer, A., Carlton, C., Chong, L. J., & Wissemann, K. (2019). The presence of a controlling parent is related to an increase in the error-related negativity in 5–7 year-old children. *Journal of Abnormal Child Psychology, 47*, 935–945.

Meyer, I. H. (2003). Prejudice, social stress, and mental health in lesbian, gay, and bisexual populations: Conceptual issues and research evidence. *Psychological Bulletin, 129*, 674–697.

Meyer-Bahlburg, H. F. L. (1995). Psychoneuroendocrinology and sexual pleasure: The aspect of sexual orientation. In P. R. Abramson & S. D. Pinkerton (Eds.), *Sexual nature/sexual culture* (pp. 135–153). University of Chicago Press.

Meyerbröker, K., & Morina, N. (2021). The use of virtual reality in assessment and treatment of anxiety and related disorders. *Clinical Psychology & Psychotherapy, 28*(3), 466–476.

Meyerhoff, J., & Rohan, K. J. (2016). Treatment expectations for cognitive-behavioral therapy and light therapy for seasonal affective disorder: Change across treatment and relation to outcome. *Journal of Consulting and Clinical Psychology, 84*, 898–906.

Mez, J., Daneshvar, D. H., Kiernan, P. T., Abdolmohammadi, B., Alvarez, V. E., Huber, B. R., Alosco, M. L., Solomon, T. M., Nowinski, C. J., McHale, L., Cormier, K. A., Kubilius, C. A., Martin, B. M., Murphy, L., Baugh, C. M., Montenigro, P. H., Chaisson, C. E., Tripodis, Y., Kowall, N. W., ... McKee, A. C. (2017). Clinicopathological evaluation of chronic traumatic encephalopathy in players of American football. *Journal of the American Medical Association, 318*, 360–370.

Miao, C., Humphrey, R. H., & Qian, S. (2016). Leader emotional intelligence and subordinate job satisfaction: A meta-analysis of main, mediator, and moderator effects. *Personality and Individual Differences, 102*, 13–24.

Michael, R. B., Garry, M., & Kirsch, I. (2012). Suggestion, cognition, and behavior. *Current Directions in Psychological Science, 21*, 151–156.

Michaels, E. K., Board, C., Mujahid, M. S., Riddell, C. A., Chae, D. H., Johnson, R. C., & Allen, A. M. (2022). Area-level racial prejudice and health: A systematic review. *Health Psychology, 41*, 211–224.

Michaels, J. W., Bloomel, J. M., Brocato, R. M., Linkous, R. A., & Rowe, J. S. (1982). Social facilitation and inhibition in a natural setting. *Replications in Social Psychology, 2*, 21–24.

Michalka, S. W., Kong, L., Rosen, M. L., Shinn-Cunningham, B., & Somers, D. C. (2015). Short-term memory for space and time flexibly recruit complementary sensory-biased frontal lobe attention networks. *Neuron, 87*, 882–892.

Michel, M., Beck, D., Block, N., Blumenfeld, H., Brown, R., Carmel, D., Dehaene, S., Fleming, S. M., Frith, C., Haggard, P., He, B. J., Heyes, C., Goodale, M. A., Irvine, L., Kawato, M., Kentridge, R., King, J. R., Knight, R. T., Kouider, S., ... Yoshida, M. (2019). Opportunities and challenges for a maturing science of consciousness. *Nature Human Behaviour, 3*, 104–107.

Michener, J. A. (1978, February 3). *External forces and inner voices.* Speech at the Chapel of the Four Chaplains, Philadelphia, PA.

Middlebrooks, J. C., & Green, D. M. (1991). Sound localization by human listeners. *Annual Review of Psychology, 42*, 135–159.

Miech, R., Patrick, M. E., O'Malley, P. M., & Johnston, L. D. (2017). E-cigarette use as a predictor of cigarette smoking: Results from a 1-year follow-up of a national sample of 12th grade students. *Tobacco Control, 26*, e2.

Miech, R. A., Schulenberg, J. E., Johnston, L. D., Bachman, J. G., O'Malley, P. M., & Patrick, M. E. (2019, December 19). *National adolescent drug trends in 2019: Findings released. Monitoring the Future.* Institute for Social Research. https://www.ncbi.nlm.nih.gov/pmc/articles/PMC6411424/

Miers, R. (2009, Spring). Calum's road. *Scottish Life*, pp. 36–39, 75.

Mihailova, S., & Jobson, L. (2020). Cross-cultural exploration of the characteristics, content and themes of intrusive autobiographical memories recalled during depression. *Memory, 38*(5), 701–711.

Mihura, J. L., Meyer, G. J., Bombel, G., & Dumitrascu, N. (2015). Standards, accuracy, and questions of bias in Rorschach meta-analyses: Reply to Wood, Garb, Nezworski, Lilienfeld, and Duke (2015). *Psychological Bulletin, 141*, 250–260.

Mihura, J. L., Meyer, G. J., Dumitrascu, N., & Bombel, G. (2013). The validity of individual Rorschach variables: Systematic reviews and meta-analyses of the comprehensive system. *Psychological Bulletin, 139*, 548–605.

Mikalson, P., Pardo, S., & Green, J. (2012). *First, do no harm: Reducing disparities for lesbian, gay, bisexual, transgender, queer and questioning populations in California*. National Council on Crime & Delinquency. https://www.nccdglobal.org/newsroom/news-of-interest/first-do-no-harm-reducing-disparities-lesbian-gay-bisexual-transgender

Mikhail, J. (2007). Universal moral grammar: Theory, evidence and the future. *Trends in Cognitive Sciences, 11*, 143–152.

Mikkelsen, T. S., & The Chimpanzee Sequencing and Analysis Consortium. (2005). Initial sequence of the chimpanzee genome and comparison with the human genome. *Nature, 437*, 69–87.

Miklowitz, D. J., & Chung, B. (2016). Family-focused therapy for bipolar disorder: Reflections on 30 years of research. *Family Process*, 55(3), 483–499.

Mikulincer, M., Florian, V., & Hirschberger, G. (2003). The existential function of close relationships: Introducing death into the science of love. *Personality and Social Psychology Review, 7*, 20–40.

Mikulincer, M., & Shaver, P. R. (2001). Attachment theory and intergroup bias: Evidence that priming the secure base schema attenuates negative reactions to out-groups. *Journal of Personality and Social Psychology, 81*, 97–115.

Mikulincer, M., & Shaver, P. R. (2020). Broaden-and-build effects of contextually boosting the sense of attachment security in adulthood. *Current Directions in Psychological Science, 29*, 22–26.

Milek, A., Butler, E. A., Tackman, A. M., Kaplan, D. M., Raison, C. L., Sbarra, D. A., Vazire, S., & Mehl, M. R. (2018). "Eavesdropping on happiness" revisited: A pooled, multisample replication of the association between life satisfaction and observed daily conversation quantity and quality. *Psychological Science, 29*, 1451–1462.

Miles, D. R., & Carey, G. (1997). Genetic and environmental architecture of human aggression. *Journal of Personality and Social Psychology, 72*, 207–217.

Miles-Novelo, A., & Anderson, C. A. (2022). *Climate change and human behavior: Impacts of a rapidly changing climate on human aggression and violence*. Cambridge University Press.

Milgram, S. (1963). Behavioral study of obedience. *Journal of Abnormal & Social Psychology, 67*, 371–378.

Milgram, S. (1974). *Obedience to authority*. Harper & Row.

Miller, A. B., Eisenlohr-Moul, T., Glenn, C. R., Turner, B. J., Chapman, A. L., Nock, M. K., & Prinstein, M. J. (2019). Does higher-than-usual stress predict nonsuicidal self-injury? Evidence from two prospective studies in adolescent and emerging adult females. *Journal of Child Psychology and Psychiatry, 60*, 1076–1084.

Miller, A. L., Fassett, I. T., & Palmer, D. L. (2021). Achievement goal orientation: A predictor of student engagement in higher education. *Motivation and Emotion, 45*, 327–344.

Miller, B. G., Kors, S., & Macfie, J. (2017). No differences? Meta-analytic comparisons of psychological adjustment in children of gay fathers and heterosexual parents. *Psychology of Sexual Orientation and Gender Diversity, 4*, 14–22.

Miller, G. (2004). Axel, Buck share award for deciphering how the nose knows. *Science, 306*, 207.

Miller, G. (2012). Drone wars: Are remotely piloted aircraft changing the nature of war? *Science, 336*, 842–843.

Miller, G. (2012). How are memories retrieved? *Science, 338*, 30–31.

Miller, G. A. (1956). The magical number seven, plus or minus two: Some limits on our capacity for processing information. *Psychological Review, 63*, 81–97.

Miller, G. E., & Blackwell, E. (2006). Turning up the heat: Inflammation as a mechanism linking chronic stress, depression, and heart disease. *Current Directions in Psychological Science*, 15, 269–272.

Miller, J. F., Neufang, M., Solway, A., Brandt, A., Trippel, M., Mader, I., Hefft, S., Merkow, M., Polyn, S. M., Jacobs, J., Kahana, M. J., & Schulze-Bonhage, A. (2013). Neural activity in human hippocampal formation reveals the spatial context of retrieved memories. *Science, 342*, 1111–1114.

Miller, L. K. (1999). The savant syndrome: Intellectual impairment and exceptional skill. *Psychological Bulletin, 125*, 31–46.

Miller, M., Zhang, Y., Prince, L., Swanson, S. A., Wintemute, G. J., Holsinger, E. E., & Studdert, D. M. (2022). Suicide deaths among women in California living with handgun owners vs those living with other adults in handgun-free homes, 2004–2016. *JAMA Psychiatry, 79*(6), 582–588.

Miller, M. A., Kruisbrink, M., Wallace, J., Ji, C., & Cappuccio, F. P. (2018). Sleep duration and incidence of obesity in infants, children, and adolescents: A systematic review and meta-analysis of prospective studies. *Sleep*, 41(4). doi: 10.1093/sleep/zsy018

Miller, N. E. (1985, February). Rx: Biofeedback. *Psychology Today*, pp. 54–59.

Miller, P. (2012, January). A thing or two about twins. *National Geographic*, pp. 38–65.

Miller, S. L., & Maner, J. K. (2010). Scent of a woman: Men's testosterone responses to olfactory ovulation cues. *Psychological Science, 21*, 276–283.

Miller, S. L., & Maner, J. K. (2011). Ovulation as a male mating prime: Subtle signs of women's fertility influence men's mating cognition and behavior. *Journal of Personality and Social Psychology*, 100, 295–308.

Milling, L. S., Gover, M. C., & Moriarty, C. L. (2018). The effectiveness of hypnosis as an intervention for obesity: A meta-analytic review. *Psychology of Consciousness: Theory, Research, and Practice*, 5, 29–45.

Milling, L. S., Kirsch, I., Meunier, S. A., & Levine, M. R. (2002). Hypnotic analgesia and stress inoculation training: Individual and combined effects in analog treatment of experimental pain. *Cognitive Therapy and Research*, 26, 355–371.

Milner, A. D., & Goodale, M. A. (2008). Two visual systems reviewed. *Neuropsychologia, 46*, 774–785.

Milner, B. (2017, November 20). *Pioneering brain scientist still working at 99*. AARP. https://www.psychologicalscience.org/news/pioneering-brain-scientist-still-working-at-99.html

Mineka, S. (1985). The frightful complexity of the origins of fears. In F. R. Brush & J. B. Overmier (Eds.), *Affect, conditioning and cognition: Essays on the determinants of behavior*. Erlbaum.

Mineka, S. (2002). Animal models of clinical psychology. In N. Smelser & P. Baltes (Eds.), *International encyclopedia of the social and behavioral sciences*. Elsevier Science.

Mineka, S., & Oehlberg, K. (2008). The relevance of recent developments in classical conditioning to understanding the etiology and maintenance of anxiety disorders. *Acta Psychologica, 127*, 567–580.

Minkov, M., van de Vijver, Fons J. R., & Schachner, M. (2019). A test of a new short Big-Five tool in large probabilistic samples from 19 countries. *Personality and Individual Differences*, 151. https://doi.org/10.1016/j.paid.2019.109519

Miola, A., Cattarinussi, G., Antiga, G., Caiolo, S., Solmi, M., & Sambataro, F. (2022). Difficulties in emotion regulation in bipolar disorder: A systematic review and meta-analysis. *Journal of Affective Disorders, 302*, 352–360.

Mischel, W. (1968). *Personality and assessment*. Wiley.

Mischel, W. (1981). Current issues and challenges in personality. In L. T. Benjamin, Jr. (Ed.), *The G. Stanley Hall lecture series* (Vol. 1). American Psychological Association.

Mischel, W. (2014). *The marshmallow test: Mastering self-control*. Little, Brown.

Mischkowski, D., Kross, E., & Bushman, B. (2012). Flies on the wall are less aggressive: Self-distancing "in the heat of the moment" reduces aggressive thoughts, angry feelings and aggressive behavior. *Journal of Experimental Social Psychology, 48*, 1187–1191.

Miserandino, M. (1991). Memory and the seven dwarfs. *Teaching of Psychology, 18*, 169–171.

Mishkin, M. (1982). A memory system in the monkey. *Philosophical Transactions of the Royal Society of London: Biological Sciences, 298*, 83–95.

Mishkin, M., Suzuki, W. A., Gadian, D. G., & Vargha-Khadem, F. (1997). Hierarchical organization of cognitive memory. *Philosophical Transactions of the Royal Society of London: Biological Sciences*, 352, 1461–1467.

Mita, T. H., Dermer, M., & Knight, J. (1977). Reversed facial images and the mere-exposure hypothesis. *Journal of Personality and Social Psychology*, 35, 597–601.

Mitani, J. C., Watts, D. P., & Amsler, S. J. (2010). Lethal intergroup aggression leads to territorial expansion in wild chimpanzees. *Current Biology, 20*, R507–R509.

Mitchell, G. (2012). Revisiting truth or triviality: The external validity of research in the psychological laboratory. *Perspectives on Psychological Science, 7*, 109–117.

Mitchell, J. M., Bogenschutz, M., Lilienstein, A., Harrison, C., Kleiman, S., Parker-Guilbert, K., Ot'Alora, M., Garas, W., Paleos, C., Gorman, I., Nicholas, C., Mithoefer, M., Carlin, S., Poulter, B., Mithoefer, A., Quevedo, S., Wells, G., Klaire, S. S., van der Kolk, B., ... Doblin, R. (2021). MDMA-assisted therapy for severe PTSD: A randomized, double-blind, placebo-controlled phase 3 study. *Nature Medicine, 27*, 1025–1033.

Mitchell, J. P. (2009). Social psychology as a natural kind. *Cell*, 13, 246–251.

Mitricheva, E., Kimura, R., Logothetis, N. K., & Noori, H. R. (2019). Neural substrates of sexual arousal are not sex dependent. *PNAS, 116*, 15671–15676.

Mitte, K. (2008). Memory bias for threatening information in anxiety and anxiety disorders: A meta-analytic review. *Psychological Bulletin, 134*, 886–911.

Miu, A. S., & Yeager, D. S. (2015). Preventing symptoms of depression by teaching adolescents that people can change: Effects of a brief incremental theory of personality intervention at 9-month follow-up. *Clinical Psychological Science, 3*, 726–743.

Miyamoto, Y., & Kitayama, S. (2018). Cultural differences in correspondence bias are systematic and multifaceted. *Advances in Methods and Practices in Psychological Science, 1*, 497–498.

Miyatsu, T., Nguyen, K., & McDaniel, M. A. (2018). Five popular study strategies: Their pitfalls and optimal implementations. *Perspectives on Psychological Science, 13*, 390–407.

Mobbs, D., Yu, R., Meyer, M., Passamonti, L., Seymour, B., Calder, A. J., Schweizer, S., Frith, C. D., & Dalgeish, T. (2009). A key role for similarity in vicarious reward. *Science, 324*, 900.

Moffitt, T. E. (2005). The new look of behavioral genetics in developmental psychopathology: Gene-environment interplay in antisocial behaviors. *Psychological Bulletin, 131*, 533–554.

Moffitt, T. E. (2018). Male antisocial behavior in adolescence and beyond. *Nature Human Behavior, 2*, 177–186.

Moffitt, T. E., Arsenault, L., Belsky, D., Dickson, N., Hancox, R. J., Harrington, H., Houts, R., Poulton, R., Roberts, B. W., Ross, S., Sears, M. R., Thompson, W. M., & Caspi, A. (2011). A gradient of childhood self-control predicts health, wealth, and public safety. *PNAS, 108*, 2693–2698.

Moffitt, T. E., Caspi, A., Harrington, H., & Milne, B. J. (2002). Males on the life-course-persistent and adolescence-limited antisocial pathways: Follow-up at age 26 years. *Development and Psychopathology, 14*, 179–207.

Moffitt, T. E., Poulton, R., & Caspi, A. (2013). Lifelong impact of early self-control. *American Scientist, 101*, 352–359.

Moghaddam, F. M. (2005). The staircase to terrorism: A psychological exploration. *American Psychologist, 60*, 161–169.

Moghaddam, F. M. (2019). The psychological citizen, democracy, and peace. *Peace and Conflict: Journal of Peace Psychology, 25*, 273–275.

Mogilner, C., & Norton, M. I. (2016). Time, money, and happiness. *Current Opinion in Psychology, 10*, 12–16.

Moholdt, T., Lavie, C., & Nauman, J. (2018). Sustained physical activity, not weight loss, associated with improved survival in coronary heart disease. *Journal of the American College of Cardiology. 71*, 1094–1101.

Möller-Levet, C. S., Archer, S. N., Bucca, G., Laing, E. E., Slak, A., Kabiljo, R., Lo, J. C. Y., Santhi, N., von Schantz, M., Smith, C. P., & Dijk, D.-J. (2013). Effects of insufficient sleep on circadian rhythmicity and expression amplitude of the human blood transcriptome. *PNAS, 110*, E1132–E1141.

Mommersteeg, P. M. C., Schoemaker, R. G., Naudé, P. J., Eisel, U. L., Garrelds, I. M., Schalkwijk, C. G., Westerhuis, B. W. J. J. M., Kop, W. J., & Denollet, J. (2016). Depression and markers of inflammation as predictors of all-cause mortality in heart failure. *Brain, Behavior, and Immunity, 57*, 144–150.

Monaro, M., Maldera, S., Scarpazza, C., Sartori, G., & Navarin, N. (2022). Detecting deception through facial expressions in a dataset of videotaped interviews: A comparison between human judges and machine learning models. *Computers in Human Behavior, 127*(3). https://www.sciencedirect.com/science/article/abs/pii/S0747563221003861

Moncrieff, J., Cooper, R. E., Stockmann, T., Amendola, S., Hengartner, M. P., & Horowitz, M. A. (2022). The serotonin theory of depression: A systematic umbrella review of the evidence. *Molecular Psychiatry.* https://www.nature.com/articles/s41380-022-01661-0

Mondloch, C. J., Lewis, T. L., Budreau, D. R., Maurer, D., Dannemiller, J. L., Stephens, B. R., & Kleiner-Gathercoal, K. A. (1999). Face perception during early infancy. *Psychological Science, 10*, 419–422.

Money, J. (1987). Sin, sickness, or status? Homosexual gender identity and psychoneuroendocrinology. *American Psychologist, 42*, 384–399.

Money, J., Berlin, F. S., Falck, A., & Stein, M. (1983). *Antiandrogenic and counseling treatment of sex offenders.* Johns Hopkins University School of Medicine, Department of Psychiatry and Behavioral Sciences.

Monroe, S. M., & Simons, A. D. (1991). Diathesis-stress theories in the context of life stress research: Implications for the depressive disorders. *Psychological Bulletin, 110*, 406–425.

Montagne, A., Barnes, S. R., Sweeney, M. D., Halliday, M. R., Sagare, A. P., Zhao, Z., Toga, A. W., Jacobs, R. E., Liu, C. Y., Amezcua, L., Harrington, M. G., Chui, H. C., Law, M., & Zlokovic, B. V. (2015). Blood-brain barrier breakdown in the aging human hippocampus. *Neuron, 85*, 296–302.

Montgomery, G. H., DuHamel, K. N., & Redd, W. H. (2000). A meta-analysis of hypnotically induced analgesia: How effective is hypnosis? *International Journal of Clinical and Experimental Hypnosis, 48*, 138–153.

Montoya, R. M., & Horton, R. S. (2013). A meta-analytic investigation of the processes underlying the similarity-attraction effect. *Journal of Social and Personal Relationships, 30*, 64–94.

Montoya, R. M., & Horton, R. S. (2014). A two-dimensional model for the study of interpersonal attraction. *Personality and Social Psychology Review, 18*, 59–86.

Montoya, R. M., Horton, R. S., Vevea, J. L., Citkowicz, M., & Lauber, E. A. (2017). A re-examination of the mere exposure effect: The influence of repeated exposure on recognition, familiarity, and liking. *Psychological Bulletin, 143*, 459–498.

Mook, D. G. (1983). In defense of external invalidity. *American Psychologist, 38*, 379–387.

Moon, C., Lagercrantz, H., & Kuhl, P. K. (2013). Language experienced in utero affects vowel perception after birth: A two-country study. *Acta Paediatrica, 102*, 156–160.

Moorcroft, W. H. (2003). *Understanding sleep and dreaming.* Kluwer Academic/Plenum Press.

Moore, D. W. (2004, December 17). *Sweet dreams go with a good night's sleep.* Gallup News Service. https://news.gallup.com/poll/14380/sweet-dreams-good-nights-sleep.aspx

Moore, S. C., Lee, I., Weiderpass, E., Campbell, P. T., Sampson, J. N., Kitahara, C. M., Keadle, S. K., Arem, H., Berrington de Gonzalez, A., Hartge, P., Adami, H. O., Blair, C. K., Borch, K. B., Boyd, E., Check, D. P., Fournier, A., Freedman, N. D., Gunter, M., Johannson, M., ... Patel, A. V. (2016). Association of leisure-time physical activity with risk of 26 types of cancer in 1.44 million adults. *JAMA Internal Medicine, 176*, 816–825.

Moos, R. H., & Moos, B. S. (2005). Sixteen-year changes and stable remission among treated and untreated individuals with alcohol use disorders. *Drug and Alcohol Dependence, 80*, 337–347.

Moos, R. H., & Moos, B. S. (2006). Participation in treatment and Alcoholics Anonymous: A 16-year follow-up of initially untreated individuals. *Journal of Clinical Psychology, 62*, 735–750.

More, H. L., Hutchinson, J. R., Collins, D. F., Weber, D. J., Aung, S. K. H., & Donelan, J. M. (2010). Scaling of sensorimotor control in terrestrial mammals. *Proceedings of the Royal Society: Series B, 277*, 3563–3568.

Moreira, M. T., Smith, L. A., & Foxcroft, D. (2009). Social norms interventions to reduce alcohol misuse in university or college students [PDF]. *Cochrane Database of Systematic Reviews, 11*(3). https://tinyurl.com/mpdrcb4s

Moreland, R. L., & Zajonc, R. B. (1982). Exposure effects in person perception: Familiarity, similarity, and attraction. *Journal of Experimental Social Psychology, 18*, 395–415.

Morewedge, C. K., & Norton, M. I. (2009). When dreaming is believing: The (motivated) interpretation of dreams. *Journal of Personality and Social Psychology, 96*, 249–264.

Morey, R. A., Inan, S., Mitchell, T. V., Perkins, D. O., Lieberman, J. A., & Belger, A. (2005). Imaging frontostriatal function in ultra-high-risk, early, and chronic schizophrenia during executive processing. *Archives of General Psychiatry, 62*, 254–262.

Morgan, A. B., & Lilienfeld, S. O. (2000). A meta-analytic review of the relation between antisocial behavior and neuropsychological measures of executive function. *Clinical Psychology Review, 20*, 113–136.

Morgan, C., Webb, R. T., Carr, M. J., Kontopantelis, E., Green, J., Chew-Graham, C. A., Kapur, N., & Ashcroft, D. M. (2017). Incidence, clinical management, and mortality risk following self-harm among children and adolescents: Cohort study in primary care. *British Medical Journal, 359*, j4351

Morgenthaler, T. I., Hashmi, S., Croft, J. B., Dort, L., Heald, J. L., & Mullington, J. (2016). High school start times and the impact on high school students: What we know and what we hope to learn. *Journal of Clinical Sleep Medicine, 12*, 1681–1689.

Mori, K., & Mori, H. (2009). Another test of the passive facial feedback hypothesis: When your face smiles, you feel happy. *Perceptual and Motor Skills, 109*, 1–3.

Morres, I. D., Hatzigeorgiadis, A., Stathi, A., Comoutos, N., Arpin-Cribbie, C., Krommidas, C., & Theodorakis, Y. (2019). Aerobic exercise for adult patients with major depressive disorder in mental health services: A systematic review and meta-analysis. *Depression & Anxiety, 36*(1), 39–53.

Morris, G., Baker-Ward, L., & Bauer, P. J. (2010). What remains of that day: The survival of children's autobiographical memories across time. *Applied Cognitive Psychology, 24,* 527–544.

Morris, J. N., Heady, J. A, Raffle, P. A., Roberts, C. G., & Parks, J. W. (1953). Coronary heart-disease and physical activity of work. *The Lancet, 262*(6795), 1053–1057.

Morris, M. C., Wang, Y., Barnes, L. L., Bennett, D. A., Dawson-Hughes, B., & Booth, S. L. (2018). Nutrients and bioactives in green leafy vegetables and cognitive decline: Prospective study. *Neurology, 90*(3), e214–e222.

Mortensen, P. B. (1999). Effects of family history and place and season of birth on the risk of schizophrenia. *New England Journal of Medicine, 340,* 603–608.

Morton, F. B., Robinson, L. M., Brando, S., & Weiss, A. (2021). Personality structure in bottlenose dolphins *(Tursiops truncates). Journal of Comparative Psychology, 135,* 219–231.

Mosbergen, D. (2015, November 18). *Dwayne 'The Rock' Johnson opens up about his battle with depression.* HuffPost. https://www.huffpost.com/entry/dwayne-johnson-the-rock-depression_n_564c2533e4b06037734bb59d

Moscovici, S. (1985). Social influence and conformity. In G. Lindzey & E. Aronson (Eds.), *The handbook of social psychology* (3rd ed., pp. 347–412). Erlbaum.

Moser, M.-B. (2014). *May-Britt Moser. Nobel Prize in Physiology or Medicine 2014.* Nobel Prize. https://www.nobelprize.org/womenwhochangedscience/stories/may-britt-moser?keyword=brain

Moses, D. A., Metzger, S. L., Liu, J. R., Anumanchipalli, G. K., Makin, J. G., Sun, P. F., Chartier, J., Dougherty, M. E., Liu, P. M., Abrams, G. M., Tu-Chan, A., Ganguly, K., & Chang, E. F. (2021). Neuroprosthesis for decoding speech in a paralyzed person with anarthria. *New England Journal of Medicine, 385,* 217–227.

Moses, E. B., & Barlow, D. H. (2006). A new unified treatment approach for emotional disorders based on emotion science. *Current Directions in Psychological Science, 15,* 146–150.

Mosher, C. E., & Danoff-Burg, S. (2008). Agentic and communal personality traits: Relations to disordered eating behavior, body shape concern, and depressive symptoms. *Eating Behaviors, 9,* 497–500.

Mosher, W. D., Chandra, A., & Jones, J. (2005, September 15). Sexual behavior and selected health measures: Men and women 15–44 years of age, United States, 2002. *Advance Data, 362,* 1–55.

Mosing, M. A., Butkovic, A., & Ullen, F. (2018). Can flow experiences be protective of work-related depressive symptoms and burnout? A genetically informative approach. *Journal of Affective Disorders, 226,* 6–11.

Mosing, M. A., Zietsch, B. P., Shekar, S. N., Wright, M. J., & Martin, N. G. (2009). Genetic and environmental influences on optimism and its relationship to mental and self-rated health: A study of aging twins. *Behavior Genetics, 39,* 597–604.

Moskowitz, T. J., & Wertheim, L. J. (2011). *Scorecasting: The hidden influences behind how sports are played and games are won.* Crown Archetype.

Mosnier, I., Bebear, J.-P., Marx, M., Fraysse, B., Truy, E., Lina-Granade, G., Mondain, M., Sterkers-Artières, F., Bordure, P., Robier, A., Godey, B., Meyer, B., Frachet, B., Poncet-Wallet, C., Bouccara, D., & Sterkers, O. (2015). Improvement of cognitive function after cochlear implantation in elderly patients. *JAMA Otolaryngology—Head & Neck Surgery, 141,* 442–450.

Moss, A. C., & Albery, I. P. (2009). A dual-process model of the alcohol-behavior link for social drinking. *Psychological Bulletin, 135,* 516–530.

Moss, A. J., Allen, K. F., Giovino, G. A., & Mills, S. L. (1992, December 2). *Recent trends in adolescent smoking, smoking-update correlates, and expectations about the future.* CDC. Advance Data No. 221.

Moss, S. A., Serbetci, D., O'Brien, K., & Alexi, N. (2022). The validated features of psychological interventions for weight loss: An integration. *Behavioral Medicine, 48*(3), 147–161.

Mõttus, R., Briley, D. A., Zheng, A., Mann, F. D., Engelhardt, L. E., Tackett, J. L., Harden, K. P., & Tucker-Drob, E. M. (2019). Kids becoming less alike: A behavioral genetic analysis of developmental increases in personality variance from childhood to adolescence. *Journal of Personality and Social Psychology, 117,* 635–658.

Moulin, S., Waldfogel, J., & Washbrook, E. (2014). Baby bonds: Parenting, attachment, and a secure base for children. *Sutton Trust,* 1–42.

Mousa, S. (2020). Building social cohesion between Christians and Muslims through soccer in post-ISIS Iraq. *Science, 369,* 866–870.

Mousten, I. V., Sørensen, N. V., Christensen, R. H. B., & Benros, M. E. (2022). Cerebrospinal fluid biomarkers in patients with unipolar depression compared with healthy control individuals. A systematic review and meta-analysis. *JAMA Psychiatry, 79*(6), 571–581.

Moxley, J. H., Ericsson, K. A., Charness, N., & Krampe, R. T. (2012). The role of intuition and deliberative thinking in experts' superior tactical decision-making. *Cognition, 124,* 72–78.

Moyer, K. E. (1983). The physiology of motivation: Aggression as a model. In C. J. Scheier & A. M. Rogers (Eds.), *G. Stanley Hall lecture series* (Vol. 3). American Psychological Association.

Muchnik, L., Aral, S., Taylor, S. J. (2013). Social influence bias: A randomized experiment. *Science, 341,* 647–651.

Mueller, P. A., & Oppenheimer, D. M. (2014). The pen is mightier than the keyboard: Advantages of longhand over laptop note-taking. *Psychological Science, 25,* 1159–1168.

Mueller, S., Wagner, J., Smith, J., Voelkle, M. C., & Gerstorf, D. (2018). The interplay of personality and functional health in old and very old age: Dynamic within-person interrelations across up to 13 years. *Journal of Personality and Social Psychology, 115,* 1127.

Muenks, K., Yang, J. S., & Wigfield, A. (2018). Associations between grit, motivation, and achievement in high school students. *Motivation Science, 4,* 158–176.

Muhlnickel, W. (1998). Reorganization of auditory cortex in tinnitus. *PNAS, 95,* 10340–10343.

Muise, A., Schimmack, U., & Impett, E. A. (2016). Sexual frequency predicts greater well-being, but more is not always better. *Social Psychological and Personality Science, 7,* 295–302.

Mulcahy, N. J., & Call, J. (2006). Apes save tools for future use. *Science, 312,* 1038–1040.

Muldoon, S., Taylor, S. C., & Norma, C. (2016). The survivor master narrative in sexual assault. *Violence Against Women, 22,* 565–587.

Mull, A. (2019, May 31). *What 10,000 steps will really get you.* The Atlantic. https://www.theatlantic.com/health/archive/2019/05/10000-steps-rule/590785/

Mullin, C. R., & Linz, D. (1995). Desensitization and resensitization to violence against women: Effects of exposure to sexually violent films on judgments of domestic violence victims. *Journal of Personality and Social Psychology, 69,* 449–459.

Murayama, K., Pekrun, R., Lichtenfeld, S., & vom Hofe, R. (2013). Predicting long-term growth in students' mathematics achievement: The unique contributions of motivation and cognitive strategies. *Child Development, 84,* 1475–1490.

Mure, L. S., Le, H. D., Benegiamo, G., Chang, M. W., Rios, L., Jillani, N., Ngotho, M., Kariuki, T., Dkhissi-Benyahya, O., Cooper, H. M., & Panda, S. (2018). Diurnal transcriptome atlas of a primate across major neural and peripheral tissues. *Science, 359*(6381). doi: 10.1126/science.aao0318

Murphy, B. (2022, January 27). *2021 medical school class sees enrollment diversity grow.* AMA. https://www.ama-assn.org/education/medical-school-diversity/2021-medical-school-class-sees-enrollment-diversity-grow

Murphy, D. H., & Castel, A. D. (2021). Responsible remembering and forgetting as contributors to memory for important information. *Memory & Cognition, 49,* 895–911.

Murphy, G., Loftus, E. F., Grady, R. F., Levine, L. J., & Greene, C. M. (2019). False memories for fake news during Ireland's abortion referendum. *Psychological Science, 30,* 1449–1459.

Murphy, G., Loftus, E., Grady, R. H., Levine, L. J., & Greene, C. M. (2020). Fool me twice: How effective is debriefing in false memory studies? *Memory, 28*(7), 938–949.

Murphy, K. R., & Cleveland, J. N. (1995). *Understanding performance appraisal: Social, organizational, and goal-based perspectives.* Sage.

Murphy, S., & Dalton, P. (2016). Out of touch? Visual load induces inattentional numbness. *Journal of Experimental Psychology: Human Perception and Performance, 42,* 761–765.

Murphy, S., & Dalton, P. (2018). Inattentional numbness and the influence of task difficulty. *Cognition, 178,* 1–6.

Murphy, S. T., Monahan, J. L., & Zajonc, R. B. (1995). Additivity of nonconscious affect: Combined effects of priming and exposure. *Journal of Personality and Social Psychology, 69,* 589–602.

Murray, G., Allen, N. B., & Trinder, J. (2002). Mood and the circadian system: Investigation of a circadian component in positive affect. *Chronobiology International, 19*(6), 1151–1169.

Murray, H. (1938). *Explorations in personality.* Oxford University Press.

Murray, H. A. (1933). The effect of fear upon estimates of the maliciousness of other personalities. *Journal of Social Psychology, 4,* 310–329.

Murray, H. A., & Wheeler, D. R. (1937). A note on the possible clairvoyance of dreams. *Journal of Psychology, 3,* 309–313.

Murray, R., Jones, P., O'Callaghan, E., Takei, N., & Sham, P. (1992). Genes, viruses, and neurodevelopmental schizophrenia. *Journal of Psychiatric Research, 26,* 225–235.

Murthy, V. (2017, September). Work and the loneliness epidemic. *Harvard Business Review.* https://hbr.org/cover-story/2017/09/work-and-the-loneliness-epidemic

Murthy, V. (2021, September 6). Quoted by J. Kenen in, *Why we can't turn the corner on COVID.* Politico. https://www.politico.com/news/magazine/2021/09/06/why-we-cant-turn-the-corner-on-covid-509349

Murty, V. P., Calabro, F., & Luna, B. (2016). The role of experience in adolescent cognitive development: Integration of executive, memory, and mesolimbic systems. *Neuroscience & Biobehavioral Reviews, 70,* 46–58.

Musick, M. A., Herzog, A. R., & House, J. S. (1999). Volunteering and mortality among older adults: Findings from a national sample. *Journals of Gerontology, 54B,* 173–180.

Mutz, J., Vipulananthan, V., Carter, B., Hurlemann, R., Fu, C. H. Y., & Young, A. H. (2019). Comparative efficacy and acceptability of non-surgical brain stimulation for the acute treatment of major depressive episodes in adults: Systematic review and network meta-analysis. *BMJ: British Medical Journal, 364,* 13.

Muusses, L. D., Kerkhof, P., & Finkenauer, C. (2015). Internet pornography and relationship quality: A longitudinal study of within and between partner effects of adjustment, sexual satisfaction and sexually explicit internet material among newlyweds. *Computers in Human Behavior, 45,* 77–84.

Muzzulini, B., Tinti, C., Conway, M. A., Testa, S., & Schmidt, S. (2020). Flashbulb memory: Referring back to Brown and Kulik's definition. *Memory, 28*(6), 766–782.

My Country Talks. (2021). Home page. https://www.mycountrytalks.org

Mydans, S. (2002, May 17). In Pakistan, rape victims are the 'criminals.' *The New York Times.* https://www.nytimes.com/2002/05/17/world/in-pakistan-rape-victims-are-the-criminals.html

Myers, D. G. (1993). *The pursuit of happiness.* Harper.

Myers, D. G. (2000). *The American paradox: Spiritual hunger in an age of plenty.* Yale University Press.

Myers, D. G. (2010). *Social psychology* (10th ed.). McGraw-Hill.

Myers, D. G. (2018, August 23). *Do more immigrants equal greater acceptance or greater fear of immigrants?* TalkPsych. Macmillan Learning. https://bit.ly/2UEvGNT

Myers, D. G. (2019, May). The likely aftermath of adversity: Harm, resilience, or growth? *APS Observer.* https://www.psychologicalscience.org/observer/teaching-current-directions-in-psychological-science-57#adversity

Myers, D. G., & Bishop, G. D. (1970). Discussion effects on racial attitudes. *Science, 169,* 778–779.

Myers, D. G., & Diener, E. (1995). Who is happy? *Psychological Science, 6,* 10–19.

Myers, D. G., & Diener, E. (1996, May). The pursuit of happiness [PDF file]. *Scientific American,* pp. 54–56. https://davidmyers.org/uploads/Pursuit.Happ.scientific-american.pdf

Myers, D. G., & Scanzoni, L. D. (2005). *What God has joined together: The Christian case for gay marriage.* HarperCollins Publishers.

Myers, I. B. (1987). *Introduction to type: A description of the theory and applications of the Myers-Briggs Type Indicator.* Consulting Psychologists Press.

Nagourney, A. (2002, September 25). For remarks on Iraq, Gore gets praise and scorn. *The New York Times.* https://www.nytimes.com/2002/09/25/us/threats-responses-former-vice-president-for-remarks-iraq-gore-gets-praise-scorn.html

Nagourney, A., Sanger, D. E., & Barr, J. (2018, January 13). Hawaii panics after alert about incoming missile is sent in error. *The New York Times.* https://www.nytimes.com/2018/01/13/us/hawaii-missile.html

Nahemow, L., & Lawton, M. P. (1975). Similarity and propinquity in friendship formation. *Journal of Personality and Social Psychology, 32*(2), 205–213.

Nakamura, Y., Gaetano, L., Matsushita, T., Anna, A., Sprenger, T., Radue, E. W., Wuerfel, J., Bauer, L., Amann, M., Shinoda, K., Isobe, N., Yamasaki, R., Saida, T., Kappos, L., & Isobe, N. (2018). A comparison of brain magnetic resonance imaging lesions in multiple sclerosis by race with reference to disability progression. *Journal of Neuroinflammation, 15,* 255.

Nancekivell, S. E., Shah, P., & Gelman, S. A. (2019). Maybe they're born with it, or maybe it's experience: Toward a deeper understanding of the learning style myth. *Journal of Educational Psychology, 112*(2), 221–235.

Napier, J. L., Bettinsoli, M. L., & Suppes, A. (2020). The palliative function of system-justifying ideologies. *Current Opinion in Behavioral Sciences, 34,* 129–134.

Napolitan, D. A., & Goethals, G. R. (1979). The attribution of friendliness. *Journal of Experimental Social Psychology, 15,* 105–113.

Nasie, M., Diamond, A. H., & Bar-Tal, D. (2016). Young children in intractable conflicts: The Israeli case. *Personality and Social Psychology Review, 20,* 365–392.

Nathan, D. (2011). *Sybil exposed: The extraordinary story behind the famous multiple personality case.* Free Press.

National Academies of Sciences, Engineering, and Medicine. (2017). *The health effects of cannabis and cannabinoids: The current state of evidence and recommendations for research.* National Academies Press.

National Academy of Sciences. (2019). *A roadmap to reducing child poverty.* The National Academies Press.

National Center for Health Statistics. (1990). *Health, United States, 1989.* U.S. Department of Health and Human Services.

National Council on Aging. (2000). The consequences of untreated hearing loss in older persons. *ORL-Head and Neck Nursing, 18*(1), 12–16.

National Highway Traffic Safety Administration. (2021). *Summary.* https://www-fars.nhtsa.dot.gov/Main/index.aspx

National Institute of Mental Health. (2018). *Statistics.* https://www.nimh.nih.gov/health/statistics/index.shtml

National Public Radio. (2020, September 12). *A COVID-19 vaccine may be only 50% effective. Is that good enough?* https://n.pr/30JgSE4

National Safety Council (NSC). (2021). *Deaths by transportation mode, United States 2007–2019.* https://injuryfacts.nsc.org/home-and-community/safety-topics/deaths-by-transportation-mode/

Natsuaki, M. N., Neiderhiser, J. M., Harold, G. T., Shaw, D. S., Reiss, D., & Leve, L. D. (2019). Siblings reared apart: A sibling comparison study on rearing environment differences. *Developmental Psychology, 55,* 1182–1190.

Nature. (2016). Character traits: Scientific virtue. *Nature, 532,* 139.

Naumann, L. P., Vazire, S., Rentfrow, P. J., & Gosling, S. D. (2009). Personality judgments based on physical appearance. *Personality and Social Psychology Bulletin, 35,* 1661–1671.

NCASA (National Center on Addiction and Substance Abuse). (2007). *Wasting the best and the brightest: Substance abuse at America's colleges and universities.* https://www.centeronaddiction.org/newsroom/op-eds/wasting-best-and-brightest-alcohol-and-drug-abuse-college-campuses

NCD Risk Factor Collaboration. (2016). Trends in adult body-mass index in 200 countries from 1975 to 2014: A pooled analysis of 1698 population-based measurement studies with 19.2 million participants. *The Lancet, 387,* 1377–1396.

NCEE (National Center on Education and the Economy). (2018, February 22). *Statistic of the month: How much time do students spend in school?* http://ncee.org/2018/02/statistic-of-the-month-how-much-time-do-students-spend-in-school/

NCEO (National Center for Employee Ownership). (2022). *What is employee ownership?* https://www.nceo.org/what-is-employee-ownership

NCHS (National Center for Health Statistics). (2020). *Anxiety and depression: Household pulse survey.* https://www.cdc.gov/nchs/covid19/pulse/mental-health.htm

Neatby, L. H., & Mercer, K. (2018). Sir John Franklin. *The Canadian encyclopedia.* https://www.thecanadianencyclopedia.ca/en/article/sir-john-franklin

Nedeltcheva, A. V., Kilkus, J. M., Imperial, J., Schoeller, D. A., & Penev, P. D. (2010). Insufficient sleep undermines dietary efforts to reduce adiposity. *Annals of Internal Medicine, 153,* 435–441.

NEEF (National Environmental Education Foundation). (2020). *Fact sheet: Children's health and nature fact sheet.* https://www.neefusa.org/resource/childrens-health-and-nature-fact-sheet

Neese, R. M. (1991, November/December). What good is feeling bad? The evolutionary benefits of psychic pain. *The Sciences,* pp. 30–37.

Neimeyer, R. A., & Currier, J. M. (2009). Grief therapy: Evidence of efficacy and emerging directions. *Current Directions in Psychological Science, 18,* 352–356.

Neisser, U. (1979). The control of information pickup in selective looking. In A. D. Pick (Ed.), *Perception and its development: A tribute to Eleanor J. Gibson* (pp. 209–219). Erlbaum.

Neisser, U., Boodoo, G., Bouchard, T. J., Jr., Boykin, A. W., Brody, N., Ceci, S. J., Halpern, D. F., Loehlin, J. C., Perloff, R., Sternberg, R. J., & Urbina, S. (1996). Intelligence: Knowns and unknowns. *American Psychologist, 51,* 77–101.

Neitz, J., Geist, T., & Jacobs, G. H. (1989). Color vision in the dog. *Visual Neuroscience, 3,* 119–125.

Nelles-McGee, T., Khoury, J., Kenny, M., Joshi, D., & Gonzalez, A. (2022). Biological embedding of child maltreatment: A systematic review of biomarkers and resilience in children and youth. *Psychological Trauma, 14*(S1), S50–S62.

Nelson, B. W., & Allen, N. B. (2018). Extending the passive-sensing toolbox: Using smart-home technology in psychological science. *Perspectives on Psychological Science, 13,* 718–733.

Nelson, C. A., III, Fox, N. A., & Zeanah, C. H., Jr. (2013, April). Anguish of the abandoned child. *Scientific American,* pp. 62–67.

Nelson, C. A., III, Furtado, E. Z., Fox, N. A., & Zeanah, C. H., Jr. (2009). The deprived human brain. *American Scientist, 97,* 222–229.

Nelson, J., Klumparendt, A., Doebler, P., & Ehring, T. (2017). Childhood maltreatment and characteristics of adult depression: Meta-analysis. *British Journal of Psychiatry, 210,* 96–104.

Nelson, L. D., Simmons, J., & Simonsohn, U. (2018). Psychology's renaissance. *Annual Review of Psychology, 69,* 511–534.

Nelson, L. J., & Chen, X. (2007). Emerging adulthood in China: The role of social and cultural factors. *Child Development Perspectives,* 1(2), 86–91.

Nelson, M. D., Saykin, A. J., Flashman, L. A., & Riordan, H. J. (1998). Hippocampal volume reduction in schizophrenia as assessed by magnetic resonance imaging. *Archives of General Psychiatry, 55,* 433–440.

Nelson, N. L., Hudspeth, K., & Russell, J. A. (2013). A story superiority effect for disgust, fear, embarrassment, and pride. *British Journal of Developmental Psychology, 31*(3), 334–348.

Nelson-Coffey, S. K., Killingsworth, M., Layous, K., Cole, S. W., & Lyubomirsky, S. (2019). Parenthood is associated with greater well-being for fathers than mothers. *Personality and Social Psychology Bulletin, 45,* 1378–1390.

Nes, R. B. (2010). Happiness in behaviour genetics: Findings and implications. *Journal of Happiness Studies, 11,* 369–381.

Nesi, J., Burke, T. A., Bettis, A. H., Kudinova, A. Y., Thompson, E. C., MacPherson, H. A., Fox, K. A., Lawrence, H. R., Thomas, S. A., Wolff, J. C., Altemus, M. K., Soriano, S., & Liu, R. T. (2021). Social media use and self-injurious thoughts and behaviors: A systematic review and meta-analysis. *Clinical Psychology Review, 87.* DOI: 10.1016/j.cpr.2021.102038

Ness, E. (2016, January/February). FDA OKs sex drug for women. *Discover,* p. 45.

Nestler, E. J. (2011). Hidden switches in the mind. *Scientific American, 305,* 76–83.

Nestoriuc, Y., Rief, W., & Martin, A. (2008). Meta-analysis of biofeedback for tension-type headache: Efficacy, specificity, and treatment moderators. *Journal of Consulting and Clinical Psychology, 76,* 379–396.

Nettle, D., Andrews, C., & Bateson, M. (2017). Food insecurity as a driver of obesity in humans: The insurance hypothesis. *Behavioral and Brain Sciences, 40.* https://www.ncbi.nlm.nih.gov/pmc/articles/PMC5266557/

Neumann, R., & Strack, F. (2000). "Mood contagion": The automatic transfer of mood between persons. *Journal of Personality and Social Psychology, 79,* 211–223.

Newbury, C. R., Crowley, R., Rastle, K., & Tamminen, J. (2021). Sleep deprivation and memory: Meta-analytic reviews of studies on sleep deprivation before and after learning. *Psychological Bulletin, 147,* 1215–1240.

Newell, B. R. (2015). "Wait! Just let me not think about that for a minute": What role do implicit processes play in higher-level cognition? *Current Directions in Psychological Science, 24,* 65–70.

Newell, F. N., & Mitchell, K. J. (2016). Multisensory integration and cross-modal learning in synaesthesia: A unifying model. *Neuropsychologia, 88,* 140–150.

Newman, L. S., & Ruble, D. N. (1988). Stability and change in self-understanding: The early elementary school years. *Early Child Development and Care, 40,* 77–99.

Newport, C., Wallis, G., Reshitnyk, Y., & Siebeck, U. E. (2016). Discrimination of human faces by archerfish *(Toxotes chatareus). Scientific Reports, 6,* 27523.

Newport, E. L. (1990). Maturational constraints on language learning. *Cognitive Science, 14,* 11–28.

Newport, F. (1999, accessed April 28, 2016). *Americans today much more accepting of a woman, Black, Catholic, or Jew as president.* Gallup. https://news.gallup.com/poll/3979/americans-today-much-more-accepting-woman-black-catholic.aspx

Newport, F. (2001, February). *Americans see women as emotional and affectionate, men as more aggressive.* Gallup. https://news.gallup.com/poll/1978/americans-see-women-emotional-affectionate-men-more-aggressive.aspx

Newport, F. (2012, December 19). *To stop shootings, Americans focus on police, mental health.* Gallup. https://news.gallup.com/poll/159422/stop-shootings-americans-focus-police-mental-health.aspx

Newport, F. (2013, July 31). *Most U. S. smokers want to quit, have tried multiple times.* Gallup. https://news.gallup.com/poll/163763/smokers-quit-tried-multiple-times.aspx

Newport, F. (2022, February 4). *Religion and wellbeing in the U.S.: Update.* Gallup. https://news.gallup.com/opinion/polling-matters/389510/religion-wellbeing-update.aspx

Newport, F., Argrawal, S., & Witters, D. (2010, December 23). *Very religious Americans lead healthier lives.* Gallup. https://news.gallup.com/poll/145379/religious-americans-lead-healthier-lives.aspx

Newton, E. L. (1991). The rocky road from actions to intentions. *Dissertation Abstracts International, 51,* 4105.

Newton, I. (1704). *Opticks: Or, a treatise of the reflexions, refractions, inflexions and colours of light.* Royal Society.

Newton, P. M., & Miah, M. (2017). Evidence-based higher education—is the learning styles 'myth' important? *Frontiers in Psychology, 8,* 444.

Ng, J. Y. Y., Ntoumanis, N., Thøgersen-Ntoumani, C., Deci, E. L., Ryan, R. M., Duda, J. L., & Williams, G. C. (2012). Self-determination theory applied to health contexts: A meta-analysis. *Perspectives on Psychological Science, 7,* 325–340.

Ng, S. H. (1990). Androcentric coding of man and his in memory by language users. *Journal of Experimental Social Psychology, 26,* 455–464.

Ng, T. W. H., & Feldman, D. C. (2009). How broadly does education contribute to job performance? *Personnel Psychology, 62,* 89–134.

Ng, T. W. H., Sorensen, K. L., & Eby, L. T. (2006). Locus of control at work: A meta-analysis. *Journal of Organizational Behavior, 27,* 1057–1087.

Ng, T. W. H., Sorensen, K. L., & Yim, F. H. K. (2009). Does the job satisfaction–job performance relationship vary across cultures? *Journal of Cross-Cultural Psychology, 40,* 761–796.

Nguyen, H.-H. D., & Ryan, A. M. (2008). Does stereotype threat affect test performance of minorities and women? A meta-analysis of experimental evidence. *Journal of Applied Psychology, 93,* 1314–1334.

Nguyen, T. T., Ryan, R. M., & Deci, E. L. (2018). Solitude as an approach to affective self-regulation. *Personality and Social Psychology Bulletin, 44,* 92–106.

Nguyen, T. V., Werner, K. M., & Soenens, B. (2019). Embracing me-time: Motivation for solitude during transition to college. *Motivation and Emotion, 43,* 571–591.

NHS (National Health Service England). (2020, accessed January 6). *Mental health.* https://www.england.nhs.uk/five-year-forward-view/next-steps-on-the-nhs-five-year-forward-view/mental-health/

NHTSA (National Highway Traffic Safety Administration). (2000). *Traffic safety facts 1999: Older population.* ntl.bts.gov

Nichols, E. S., Wild, C. J., Stojanoski, B., Battista, M. E., & Owen, A. M. (2020). Bilingualism affords no general cognitive advantages: A population study of executive function in 11,000 people. *Psychological Science, 31,* 548–567.

Nichols, H. (2018, October). Searching for the sandman. *Discover,* pp. 51–55.

Nicholson, I. (2011). "Torture at Yale": Experimental subjects, laboratory torment and the "rehabilitation" of Milgram's "Obedience to Authority." *Theory and Psychology, 21,* 737–761.

Nichter, B., Holliday, R., Monteith, L. L., Na, P. J., Hill, M. L., Kline, A. C., Norman, S. B., & Pietrzak, R. H. (2022). Military sexual trauma in the United States: Results from a population-based study. *Journal of Affective Disorders, 306,* 19–27.

Nickel, L. B., Roberts, B. W., & Chernyshenko, O. S. (2019). No evidence of a curvilinear relation between conscientiousness and relationship, work, and health outcomes. *Journal of Personality and Social Psychology, 116,* 296–312.

Nickell, J. (2005, July/August). The case of the psychic detectives. *Skeptical Inquirer.* https://skepticalinquirer.org/2005/07/the-case-of-the-psychic-detectives/

Nickerson, R. S. (1999). How we know—and sometimes misjudge—what others know: Imputing one's own knowledge to others. *Psychological Bulletin, 125,* 737–759.

Nickerson, R. S. (2002). The production and perception of randomness. *Psychological Review, 109*, 330–357.

Nickerson, R. S. (2005). Bertrand's chord, Buffon's needles, and the concept of randomness. *Thinking & Reasoning, 11*, 67–96.

Nicol, S. E., & Gottesman, I. I. (1983). Clues to the genetics and neurobiology of schizophrenia. *American Scientist, 71*, 398–404.

Nicolas, S., & Levine, Z. (2012). Beyond intelligence testing: Remembering Alfred Binet after a century. *European Psychologist, 17*, 320–325.

Nicolaus, L. K., Cassel, J. F., Carlson, R. B., & Gustavson, C. R. (1983). Taste-aversion conditioning of crows to control predation on eggs. *Science, 220*, 212–214.

NIDA (National Institute on Drug Abuse). (2002). Methamphetamine abuse and addiction. *Research Report Series*. NIH Publication Number 02–4210.

NIDA. (2005, May). Methamphetamine. *NIDA Info Facts*.

NIDA. (2017). *The science of drug use: Discussion points*. https://www.drugabuse.gov/related-topics/criminal-justice/science-drug-use-discussion-points

NIDA. (2018). *Overdose death rates*. https://drugabuse.gov/related-topics/trends-statistics/overdose-death-rates

Niedenthal, P. M., Rychlowska, M., Zhao, F., & Wood, A. (2019). Historical migration patterns shape contemporary cultures of emotion. *Perspectives on Psychological Science, 14*, 560–573.

Niederkrotenthaler, T., Stack, S., Till, B., Sinyor, M., Pirkis, J., Garcia, D., Rockett, I. R., & Tran, U. S. (2019). Association of increased youth suicides in the United States with the release of *13 Reasons Why*. *JAMA Psychiatry, 76*(9), 933–940.

NIEHS (National Institute of Environmental Health Sciences). (2019). Institutional review board. https://www.niehs.nih.gov/about/boards/committee/index.cfm

Nielsen, M., & Tomaselli, K. (2010). Overimitation in Kalahari Bushman children and the origins of human cultural cognition. *Psychological Science, 21*, 729–736.

Nielssen, O., Karin, E., Staples, L., Titov, N., Gandy, M., Fogliati, V. J., & Dear, B. F. (2019). Opioid use before and after completion of an online pain management program. *Journal of Consulting and Clinical Psychology, 87*, 904–917.

Niemiec, C. P., Ryan, R. M., & Deci, E. L. (2009). The path taken: Consequences of attaining intrinsic and extrinsic aspirations in post-college life. *Journal of Research in Personality, 43*, 291–306.

Niessen, A. S., & Meijer, R. R. (2017). On the use of broadened admission criteria in higher education. *Perspectives on Psychological Science, 12*, 436–448.

Nieto, I., Robles, E., & Vazquez, C. (2020). Self-reported cognitive biases in depression: A meta-analysis. *Clinical Psychology Review, 82*. doi: 10.1016/j.cpr.2020/101934

Nietzsche, F. (1889/1990). *Twilight of the idols and the Anti-Christ: Or how to philosophize with a hammer* (R. J. Hollindale, Trans.). Penguin Classics.

Nieuwenstein, M. R., Wierenga, T., Morey, R. D., Wicherts, J. M., Blom, T. N., Wagenmakers, E., & van Rijn, H. (2015). On making the right choice: A meta-analysis and large-scale replication attempt of the unconscious thought advantage. *Judgment and Decision Making, 10*, 1–17.

NIH. (2001, July 20). *Workshop summary: Scientific evidence on condom effectiveness for sexually transmitted disease (STD) prevention*. National Institute of Allergy and Infectious Diseases, National Institutes of Health.

NIH (National Institutes of Health). (2010). *Teacher's guide: Information about sleep*. https://nih.gov/

NIH. (2013, January 24). *Prenatal inflammation linked to autism risk*. https://www.nih.gov/news-events/news-releases/prenatal-inflammation-linked-autism-risk

NIH. (2021). *Epigenome*. National Human Genome Research Institute. https://www.genome.gov/genetics-glossary/Epigenome

NIH. (2022). National Institutes of Health All of Us Research Program [Home page]. https://allofus.nih.gov/

Nikitin, E. S., Roshchin, M. V., Ierusalimsky, V. N., Egorov, A. V., & Balaban, P. M. (2019). Optogenetic stimulation of the axons of visual cortex and hippocampus pyramidal neurons in living brain slices. *Neuroscience and Behavioral Physiology, 49*, 227–232.

Nikles, M., Stiefel, F., & Bourquin, C. (2017). What medical students dream of: A standardized and data-driven approach. *Dreaming, 27*, 177–192.

Nikolas, M. A., & Burt, A. (2010). Genetic and environmental influences on ADHD symptom dimensions of inattention and hyperactivity: A meta-analysis. *Journal of Abnormal Psychology, 119*, 1–17.

Nikolova, H., & Lamberton, C. (2016). Men and the middle: Gender differences in dyadic compromise effects. *Journal of Consumer Research, 43*, 355–371.

Nikolova, V. L., Hall, M. R. B., Hall, L. J., Cleare, A. J., Stone, J. M., & Young, A. H. (2021). Perturbations in gut microbiota composition in psychiatric disorders. A review and meta-analysis. *Jama Psychiatry, 78*(12), 1343–1354.

Niles, A. N., Axelsson, E., Andersson, E., Hedman-Lagerlöf, E., Carlbring, P., Andersson, G., Johansson, R., Widén, S., Driessen, J., Santoft, F., & Ljótsson, B. (2021). Internet-based cognitive behavior therapy for depression, social anxiety disorder, and panic disorder: Effectiveness and predictors of response in a teaching clinic. *Behaviour Research and Therapy, 136*. doi: 10.1016/j.brat.2020.103767

Niles, A. N., Craske, M. G., Lieberman, M. D., & Hur, C. (2015). Affect labeling enhances exposure effectiveness for public speaking anxiety. *Behavior Research and Therapy, 68*, 27–36.

NIMH. (2019). *Adolescent Brain Cognitive Development (ABCD) Study*. https://www.nimh.nih.gov/research/research-funded-by-nimh/research-initiatives/adolescent-brain-cognitive-development-abcd-study.shtml

NIMH (National Institute of Mental Health). (2022). *About RDoC*. https://www.nimh.nih.gov/research/research-funded-by-nimh/rdoc/about-rdoc

Ninio, J., & Stevens, K. A. (2000). Variations on the Hermann grid: An extinction illusion. *Perception, 29*, 1209–1217.

Niparko, J. K., Tobey, E. A., Thal, D. J., Eisenberg, L. S., Wang, N., Quittner, A. L., & Fink, N. E. (2010). Spoken language development in children following cochlear implantation. *Journal of the American Medical Association, 303*, 1498–1506.

Nir, S. M. (2020). The bird watcher, that incident and his feelings on the woman's fate. *The New York Times*. https://www.nytimes.com/2020/05/27/nyregion/amy-cooper-christian-central-park-video.html

Nir, Y., & Tononi, G. (2010). Dreaming and the brain: From phenomenology to neurophysiology. *Trends in Cognitive Sciences, 14*, 88–100.

Nisbett, R. E. (1987). Lay personality theory: Its nature, origin, and utility. In N. E. Grunberg, R. E. Nisbett, et al. (Eds.), *A distinctive approach to psychological research: The influence of Stanley Schachter*. Erlbaum.

Nisbett, R. E. (2003). *The geography of thought: How Asians and Westerners think differently … and why*. Free Press.

Nisbett, R. E. (2009). *Intelligence and how to get it: Why schools and culture count*. Norton.

Nisbett, R. E., Aronson, J., Blair, C., Dickens, W., Flynn, J., Halpern, D. F., & Turkheimer, E. (2012). Intelligence: New findings and theoretical developments. *American Psychologist, 67*, 130–159.

Nisbett, R. E., & Cohen, D. (1996). *Culture of honor: The psychology of violence in the South*. Westview Press.

Nisbett, R. E., & Ross, L. (1980). *Human inference: Strategies and shortcomings of social judgment*. Prentice-Hall.

Nivison, M. D., Vandell, D. L., Booth-LaForce, C., & Roisman, G. I. (2021). Convergent and discriminant validity of retrospective assessments of the quality of childhood parenting: Prospective evidence from infancy to age 26 years. *Psychological Science, 32*(5), 721–734.

Noah, T. (2020, April 27). Quote on "The Daily Show." T. Noah, J. Flanz, & J. Katz (executive producers).

Noah, T., Schul, Y., & Mayo, R. (2018). When both the original study and its failed replication are correct: Feeling observed eliminates the facial-feedback effect. *Journal of Personality and Social Psychology, 114*, 657–664.

Noble, W., & Spires-Jones, T. L. (2019). Sleep well to slow Alzheimer's progression? *Science, 363*, 813–814.

Nock, M. (2016, May 6). Five myths about suicide. *The Washington Post*. https://www.washingtonpost.com/opinions/five-myths-about-suicide/2016/05/06/5a537cbe-1236-11e6-81b4-581a5c4c42df_story.html

Nock, M. K., Borges, G., Bromet, E. J., Alonso, J., Angermeyer, M., Beautrais, A., Bruffaerts, R., Chiu, W. T., de Girolamo, G., Gluzman, S., de Graaf, R., Gureje, O., Haro, J. M., Huang, Y., Karam, E., Kessler, R. C., Lepine, J. P., Levinson, D., Medina-Mora, M. E., … Williams, D. (2008). Cross-national prevalence and risk factors for suicidal ideation, plans, and attempts. *British Journal of Psychiatry, 192*, 98–105.

Nock, M. K., & Kessler, R. C. (2006). Prevalence of and risk factors for suicide attempts versus suicide gestures: Analysis of the National Comorbidity Survey. *Journal of Abnormal Psychology, 115*, 616–623.

Noel, J. G., Forsyth, D. R., & Kelley, K. N. (1987). Improving the performance of failing students by overcoming their self-serving attributional biases. *Basic and Applied Social Psychology, 8*, 151–162.

Noice, H., & Noice, T. (2006). What studies of actors and acting can tell us about memory and cognitive functioning. *Current Directions in Psychological Science, 15*, 14–18.

Nolen-Hoeksema, S. (2003). *Women who think too much: How to break free of overthinking and reclaim your life.* Holt.

Nolen-Hoeksema, S., & Larson, J. (1999). *Coping with loss.* Erlbaum.

Nolen-Hoeksema, S., Stice, E., Wade, E., & Bohon, C. (2007). Reciprocal relations between rumination and bulimic, substance abuse, and depressive symptoms in female adolescents. *Journal of Abnormal Psychology, 116*(1), 198.

Nook, E. C., Ong, D. C., Morelli, S. A., Mitchell, J. P., & Zaki, J. (2016). Prosocial conformity: Prosocial norms generalize across behavior and empathy. *Personality and Social Psychology Bulletin, 42*, 1045–1062.

Norberg, M. M., Krystal, J. H., & Tolin, D. F. (2008). A meta-analysis of d-cycloserine and the facilitation of fear extinction and exposure therapy. *Biological Psychiatry, 63*, 1118–1126.

Nørby, S. (2015). Why forget? On the adaptive value of memory loss. *Perspectives on Psychological Science, 10*, 551–578.

NORC (National Opinion Research Center). (2016). *New insights into Americans' perceptions and misperceptions of obesity treatments, and the struggles many face* [PDF file]. National Opinion Research Center and the American Society for Metabolic and Bariatric Surgery. https://tinyurl.com/mrx2fx7u

NORC. (2019). *General social survey.* University of Chicago. https://gss.norc.org/

NORC. (2022). *General Social Survey data, 1972 through 2021.* Accessed via sda.berkeley.edu. https://bit.ly/3PfELXL

Nord, C. L., Barrett, L. F., Lindquist, K. A., Ma, Y., Marwood, L., Satpute, A. B., & Dalgleish, T. (2021). Neural effects of antidepressant medication and psychological treatments: A quantitative synthesis across three meta-analyses. *British Journal of Psychiatry, 219*, 546–550.

Nordgren, L. F., van Harreveld, F., & van der Pligt, J. (2009). The restraint bias: How the illusion of self-restraint promoted impulsive behavior. *Psychological Science, 20*, 1523–1528.

Norem, J. K. (2001). *The positive power of negative thinking: Using defensive pessimism to harness anxiety and perform at your peak.* Basic Books.

Norenzayan, A., & Hansen, I. G. (2006). Belief in supernatural agents in the face of death. *Personality and Social Psychology Bulletin, 32*, 174–187.

Norenzayan, A., Shariff, A. F., Gervais, W. M., Willard, A. K., McNamara, R. A., Slingerland, E., & Henrich, J. (2016). The cultural evolution of prosocial religions. *Behavioral and Brain Sciences, 39*, e1.

Norko, M. A., Freeman, D., Phillips, J., Hunter, W., Lewis, R., & Viswanathan, R. (2017). Can religion protect against suicide? *Journal of Nervous and Mental Disease, 205*, 9–14.

Norman, D. A. (2001). *The perils of home theater.* https://jnd.org/the_perils_of_home_theater/

Norman, E. (2010). "The unconscious" in current psychology. *European Psychologist, 15*, 193–201.

Norman, L. J., & Thaler, L. (2019). Retinotopic-like maps of spatial sound in primary 'visual' cortex of blind human echolocators. *Proceedings of the Royal Society B, 286*(1912). https://royalsocietypublishing.org/doi/10.1098/rspb.2019.1910

Norman, Y., Yeagle, E. M., Khuvis, S., Harel, M., Mehta, A. D., & Malach, R. (2019). Hippocampal sharp-wave ripples linked to visual episodic recollection in humans. *Science, 365*(6454). https://www.science.org/doi/10.1126/science.aax1030

Norris, A. L., Marcus, D. K., & Green, B. A. (2015). Homosexuality as a discrete class. *Psychological Science, 26*, 1843–1853.

Northey, J. M., Cherbuin, N., Pumpa, K. L., Smee, D. J., & Rattray, B. (2018). Exercise interventions for cognitive function in adults older than 50: A systematic review with meta-analysis. *British Journal of Sports Medicine, 52*, 154.

Norton, K. L., Olds, T. S., Olive, S., & Dank, S. (1996). Ken and Barbie at life size. *Sex Roles, 34*, 287–294.

Nosek, B. A., Ebersole, C. R., DeHaven, A. C., & Mellor, D. T. (2018). The preregistration revolution. *PNAS, 115*, 2600–2606.

Nosek, B. A., Hardwicke, T. E., Moshontz, H., Allard, A., Corker, K. S., Dreber, A., Fidler, F., Hilgard, J., Struhl, J. K., Nuijten, M., Rohrer, J., Romero, F., Scheel, A., Scherer, L., Schonbrodt, F., & Vazire, S. (2022). Replicability, robustness, and reproducibility in psychological science. *Annual Review of Psychology, 73*, 719–748.

Noveck, J. (2020, September 29). *In Hollywood, few believe harassers will be punished, survey shows.* Associated Press. https://www.cbc.ca/news/entertainment/anita-hill-survey-hollywood-1.5743114

Novén, M., Schremm, A., Nilsson, M., Horne, M., & Roll, M. (2019). Cortical thickness of Broca's area and right homologue is related to grammar learning aptitude and pitch discrimination proficiency. *Brain and Language, 188*, 42–47.

NPR (National Public Radio). (2009, July 11). *Afraid to fly? Try living on a plane.* https://www.npr.org/templates/story/story.php?storyId=106498235

NPR. (2018, October 1). *They always remember a face: What it takes to be a Scotland Yard 'super recognizer.'* NPR Here & Now. https://www.wbur.org/hereandnow/2018/10/01/skripal-poisoning-super-recognizer

NSC (National Safety Council). (2019). *Odds of dying.* https://injuryfacts.nsc.org/all-injuries/preventable-death-overview/odds-of-dying/data-details/

NSDUH (National Survey on Drug Use and Health). (2020, September 11). *2019 NSDUH detailed tables.* SAMHSA. https://www.samhsa.gov/data/report/2019-nsduh-detailed-tables

NSF (National Science Foundation). (2001, October 24). *Public bounces back after Sept. 11 attacks, national study shows.* https://www.nsf.gov/od/lpa/news/press/01/pr0185.htm

NSF. (2006). *The ABC's of back-to-school sleep schedules: The consequences of insufficient sleep.* National Sleep Foundation press release (sleepfoundation.org).

NSF. (2013). *2013 International Bedroom Poll: Summary of findings.* https://www.academia.edu/9103352/2013_International_Bedroom_Poll_on_Sleep

NSF. (2019). *Number of women with U.S. doctorates in science, engineering, or health employed in the United States more than doubles since 1997* [PDF file]. https://nsf.gov/statistics/2019/nsf19307/nsf19307.pdf

NSF (National Sleep Foundation). (2020). *Sleepwalking.* https://www.sleepfoundation.org/articles/sleepwalking

Nugent, N. R., Goldberg, A., & Uddin, M. (2016). Topical review: The emerging field of epigenetics: Informing models of pediatric trauma and physical health. *Journal of Pediatric Psychology, 41*, 55–64.

Nuñez, M., Beal, S. J., & Jacquez, F. (2022). Resilience factors in youth transitioning out of foster care: A systematic review. *Psychological Trauma, 14*(S1), S72–S81.

Nussinovitch, U., & Shoenfeld, Y. (2012). The role of gender and organ specific autoimmunity. *Autoimmunity Reviews, 11*, A377–A385.

Nusslock, R., Almeida, J. R. C., Forbes, E. E., Versace, A., Frank, E., LaBarbara, E. J., Klein, C. R., & Phillips, M. L. (2012). Waiting to win: Elevated striatal and orbitofrontal cortical activity during reward anticipation in euthymic bipolar disorder adults. *Bipolar Disorders, 14*(3), 249–260.

Nuttin, J. M., Jr. (1987). Affective consequences of mere ownership: The name letter effect in twelve European languages. *European Journal of Social Psychology, 17*, 381–402.

Nye, C. D., Su, R., Rounds, J., & Drasgow, F. (2012). Vocational interests and performance: A quantitative summary of over 60 years of research. *Perspectives on Psychological Science, 7*, 384–403.

Oakley, D. A., & Halligan, P. W. (2013). Hypnotic suggestion: Opportunities for cognitive neuroscience. *Nature Reviews Neuroscience, 14*, 565–576.

Obama, M. (2020, August 6). Quoted by D. B. Taylor in, Michelle Obama says she is dealing with 'low-grade depression.' *The New York Times.* https://www.nytimes.com/2020/08/06/us/michelle-obama-depression.html

Oberauer, K., Lewandowsky, S., Awh, E., Brown, G. D. A., Conway, A., Cowan, N., Donkin, C., Farrell, S., Hitch, G. J., Hurlstone, M. J., Ma, W. J., Morey, C. C., Nee, D. E., Schweppe, J., Vergauwe, E., & Ward, G. (2018). Benchmarks for models of short-term and working memory. *Psychological Bulletin, 144*, 885–958.

Oberman, L. M., & Ramachandran, V. S. (2007). The simulating social mind: The role of the mirror neuron system and simulation in the social and communicative deficits of autism spectrum disorders. *Psychological Bulletin, 133*, 310–327.

Obermeyer, Z., Powers, B., Vogeli, C., & Mullainathan, S. (2019). Dissecting racial bias in an algorithm used to manage the health of populations. *Science, 366*, 447–453.

O'Brien, E., & Ellsworth, P. C. (2012). Saving the last for best: A positivity bias for end experiences. *Psychological Science, 23*, 163–165.

O'Brien, E., & Smith, R. W. (2019). Unconventional consumption methods and enjoying things consumed: Recapturing the "first-time" experience. *Personality and Social Psychology Bulletin, 45*, 67–80.

O'Brien, F., Bible, J., Liu, D., & Simons-Morton, B. (2017). Do young drivers become safer after being involved in a collision? *Psychological Science, 28*, 407–413.

O'Brien, L., Albert, D., Chein, J., & Steinberg, L. (2011). Adolescents prefer more immediate rewards when in the presence of their peers. *Journal of Research on Adolescence, 21*, 747–753.

Obschonka, M., Zhou, M., Zhou, Y., Zhang, J., & Silbereisen, R. K. (2018). "Confucian" traits, entrepreneurial personality, and entrepreneurship in China: A regional analysis. *Small Business Economics*, 1–19.

O'Callaghan, C., Shine, J. M., Hodges, J. R., Andrews-Hanna, J. R., & Irish, M. (2019). Hippocampal atrophy and intrinsic brain network dysfunction relate to alterations in mind wandering in neurodegeneration. *PNAS, 116*, 3316–3321.

O'Callaghan, V. S., Hansell, N. K., Guo, W., Carpenter, J. S., Shou, H., Strike, L. T., Crouse, J. J., McAloney, K., McMahon, K. L., Byrne, E. M., Burns, J. M., Martin, N. G., Hickie, I. B., Merikangas, K. R., & Wright, M. J. (2021). Genetic and environmental influences on sleep-wake behaviors in adolescence. *Sleep Advances, 2*(1). https://academic.oup.com/sleepadvances/article/2/1/zpab018/6408541

Ochsner, K. N., Ray, R. R., Hughes, B., McRae, K., Cooper, J. C., Weber, J., Gabrieli, J. D., & Gross, J. J. (2009). Bottom-up and top-down processes in emotion generation: Common and distinct neural mechanisms. *Psychological Science, 20*, 1322–1331.

O'Connor, K. E., Sullivan, T. N., Ross, K. M., & Marshall, K. J. (2021). "Hurt people hurt people": Relations between adverse experiences and patterns of cyber and in-person aggression and victimization among urban adolescents. *Aggressive Behavior, 47*, 483–492.

O'Connor, P., & Brown, G. W. (1984). Supportive relationships: Fact or fancy? *Journal of Social and Personal Relationships, 1*, 159–175.

O'Connor, R. J., Fix, B. V., McNeill, A., Goniewicz, M. L., Bansal-Travers, M., Heckman, B. W., Cummings, M. K., Hitchman, S., Borland, R., Hammond, D., Levy, D. T., Gravely, S., & Fong, G. (2019). Characteristics of nicotine vaping products used by participants in the 2016 ITC Four Country Smoking and Vaping Survey. *Addiction, 114*(suppl 1), 15–23.

O'Donnell, L., Stueve, A., O'Donnell, C., Duran, R., San Doval, A., Wilson, R. F., Haber, E. P., & Pleck, J. H. (2002). Long-term reduction in sexual initiation and sexual activity among urban middle schoolers in the Reach for Health service learning program. *Journal of Adolescent Health, 31*, 93–100.

Odgers, C. L., Caspi, A., Nagin, D. S., Piquero, A. R., Slutske, W. S., Milne, B. J., Dickson, N., Poulton, R., & Moffitt, T. E. (2008). Is it important to prevent early exposure to drugs and alcohol among adolescents? *Psychological Science, 19*, 1037–1044.

Odgers, C. L., & Jensen, M. R. (2020). Annual research review: Adolescent mental health in the digital age: Facts, fears, and future directions. *Journal of Child Psychology and Psychiatry, 61*(3), 336–348.

OECD (Organisation for Economic Co-operation and Development). (2022). *Employment: Time spent in paid and unpaid work, by sex.* OECD. Stat. https://stats.oecd.org/index.aspx?queryid=54757

Offer, D., Ostrov, E., Howard, K. I., & Atkinson, R. (1988). *The teenage world: Adolescents' self-image in ten countries.* Plenum.

Ofosu, E. K., Chambers, M. K., Chen, J. M., & Hehman, E. (2019). Same-sex marriage legalization associated with reduced implicit and explicit antigay bias. *PNAS, 116*, 8846–8851.

Ogden, J. (2012, January 16). HM, the man with no memory. *Psychology Today.* https://www.psychologytoday.com/us/blog/trouble-in-mind/201201/hm-the-man-no-memory

Ogihara, Y., Fujita, H., Tominaga, H., Ishigaki, S., Kashimoto, T., Takahashi, A., Toyohara, K., & Uchida, Y. (2015). Are common names becoming less common? The rise in uniqueness and individualism in Japan. *Frontiers in Psychology, 6.* https://www.frontiersin.org/articles/10.3389/fpsyg.2015.01490/full

O'Grady, C. (2020). Famous psychologist faces posthumous reckoning. *Science, 369*, 233–234.

Ogunnaike, O., Dunham, Y., & Banaji, M. R. (2010). The language of implicit preferences. *Journal of Experimental Social Psychology, 46*, 999–1003.

O'Hara, R. E., Gibbons, F. X., Gerrard, M., Li, Z., & Sargent, J. D. (2012). Greater exposure to sexual content in popular movies predicts earlier sexual debut and increased sexual risk taking. *Psychological Science, 23*, 984–993.

Öhman, A. (2009). Of snakes and fears: An evolutionary perspective on the psychology of fear. *Scandinavian Journal of Psychology, 50*, 543–552.

Öhman, A., Lundqvist, D., & Esteves, F. (2001). The face in the crowd revisited: A threat advantage with schematic stimuli. *Journal of Personality and Social Psychology, 80*, 381–396.

Oishi, S., & Diener, E. (2014). Can and should happiness be a policy goal? *Policy Insights from Behavioral and Brain Sciences, 1*, 195–203.

Oishi, S., Diener, E. F., Lucas, R. E., & Suh, E. M. (1999). Cross-cultural variations in predictors of life satisfaction: Perspectives from needs and values. *Personality and Social Psychology Bulletin, 25*, 980–990.

Oishi, S., Kesebir, S., & Diener, E. (2011). Income inequality and happiness. *Psychological Science, 22*, 1095–1100.

Oishi, S., & Schimmack, U. (2010). Culture and well-being: A new inquiry into the psychological wealth of nations. *Perspectives in Psychological Science, 5*, 463–471.

Okimoto, T. G., & Brescoll, V. L. (2010). The price of power: Power seeking and backlash against female politicians. *Personality and Social Psychology Bulletin, 36*, 923–936.

Okuyama, T., Kitamura, T., Roy, D. S., Itohara, S., & Tonegawa, S. (2016). Ventral CA1 neurons store social memory. *Science, 353*, 1536–1541.

Olatunji, B. O., & Wolitzky-Taylor, K. B. (2009). Anxiety sensitivity and the anxiety disorders: A meta-analytic review and synthesis. *Psychological Bulletin, 135*, 974–999.

Olds, J. (1958). Self-stimulation of the brain. *Science, 127*, 315–324.

Olds, J. (1975). Mapping the mind onto the brain. In F. G. Worden, J. P. Swazey, & G. Adelman (Eds.), *The neurosciences: Paths of discovery* (pp. 375–400). MIT Press.

Olds, J., & Milner, P. (1954). Positive reinforcement produced by electrical stimulation of the septal area and other regions of rat brain. *Journal of Comparative and Physiological Psychology, 47*, 419–427.

O'Leary, K. D., O'Leary, S., & Becker, W. C. (1967). Modification of a deviant sibling interaction pattern in the home. *Behaviour Research and Therapy, 5*, 113–120.

O'Leary, T., Williams, A. H., Franci, A., & Marder, E. (2014). Cell types, network homeostasis, and pathological compensation from a biologically plausible ion channel expression model. *Neuron, 82*, 809–821.

Olenski, A. R., Zimerman, A., Coussens, S., & Jen, A. B. (2020). Behavioral heuristics in coronary-artery bypass graft surgery. *New England Journal of Medicine, 382*, 778–779.

Olff, M., Langeland, W., Draijer, N., & Gersons, B. P. R. (2007). Gender differences in posttraumatic stress disorder. *Psychological Bulletin, 135*, 183–204.

Olfson, M., Gerhard, T., Huang, C., Crystal, S., & Stroup, T. S. (2015). Premature mortality among adults with schizophrenia in the United States. *JAMA Psychiatry, 72*, 1172–1181.

Olfson, M., & Marcus, S. C. (2009). National patterns in antidepressant medication treatment. *Archives of General Psychiatry, 66*, 848–856.

Olfson, M., Wall, M. M., Liu, S.-M., & Blanco, C. (2018). Cannabis use and risk of prescription opioid use disorder in the United States. *American Journal of Psychiatry.* https://ajp.psychiatryonline.org/doi/full/10.1176/appi.ajp.2017.17040413

Olfson, M., Wall, M., Liu, S.-M., Morin, C. M. N., & Blanco, C. (2018). Insomnia and impaired quality of life in the United States. *Journal of Clinical Psychiatry, 79*(5). doi: 10.4088/JCP.17m12020

Olfson, M., Wang, S., Wall, M., Marcus, S. C., & Blanco, C. (2019). Trends in serious psychological distress and outpatient mental health care of U.S. adults. *JAMA Psychiatry, 76*, 152–161.

Oliner, S. P., & Oliner, P. M. (1988). *The altruistic personality: Rescuers of Jews in Nazi Europe.* Free Press.

Olivola, C. Y., & Todorov, A. (2010). Elected in 100 milliseconds: Appearance-based trait inferences and voting. *Journal of Nonverbal Behavior, 54*, 83–110.

Olshansky, S. J. (2011). Aging of U.S. presidents. *Journal of the American Medical Association, 306*, 2328–2329.

Olson, K. R., Durwood, L., DeMeules, M., & McLaughlin, K. A. (2016). Mental health of transgender children who are supported in their identities. *Pediatrics, 137*(3). https://doi.org/10.1542/peds.2015-3223

Olson, K. R., Durwood, L., Horton, R., Gallagher, N. M., & Devor, A. (2022). Gender identity 5 years after social transition. *Pediatrics, 150*(2). https://bit.ly/3Dks8bD

Olson, K. R., & Gülgöz, S. (2018). Early findings from the TransYouth Project: Gender development in transgender children. *Child Development Perspectives, 12*, 93–97.

Olson, K. R., Key, A. C., & Eaton, N. R. (2015). Gender cognition in transgender children. *Psychological Science, 26*, 467–474.

Olson, R. L., Hanowski, R. J., Hickman, J. S., & Bocanegra, J. (2009, September). *Driver distraction in commercial vehicle operations* [PDF file]. U.S. Department of Transportation, Federal Motor Carrier Safety Administration. https://www.fmcsa.dot.gov/sites/fmcsa.dot.gov/files/docs/DriverDistractionStudy.pdf

Olsson, A., Knapska, E., & Lindström, B. (2020). The neural and computational systems of social learning. *Nature Reviews Neuroscience, 21*, 197–212.

Olsson, A., Nearing, K. I., & Phelps, E. A. (2007). Learning fears by observing others: The neural systems of social fear transmission. *Social Cognitive and Affective Neuroscience, 2*, 3–11.

Olsson, M. I. T., Froehlich, L., Dorrough, A. R., & Martiny, S. E. (2021). The hers and his of prosociality across 10 countries. *British Journal of Social Psychology, 60*(1). https://www.researchgate.net/publication/350195015_The_hers_and_his_of_prosociality_across_10_countries

Oltmanns, J. R., Jackson, J. J., & Oltmanns, T. F. (2020). Personality change: Longitudinal self-other agreement and convergence with retrospective-reports. *Journal of Personality and Social Psychology, 118*, 1065–1079.

Oltmanns, J. R., Smith, G. T., Oltmanns, T. F., & Widiger, T. A. (2018). General factors of psychopathology, personality, and personality disorder: Across domain comparisons. *Clinical Psychological Science, 6*, 581–589.

O'Neill, M. J. (1993). *The relationship between privacy, control, and stress responses in office workers* [Paper]. Presented to the Human Factors and Ergonomics Society convention.

Oman, D., Kurata, J. H., Strawbridge, W. J., & Cohen, R. D. (2002). Religious attendance and cause of death over 31 years. *International Journal of Psychiatry in Medicine, 32*, 69–89.

Oman, D., & Syme, S. L. (2018). Weighing the evidence: What is revealed by 100+ meta-analyses and systematic reviews of religion/spirituality and health? In D. Oman (Ed.), *Why religion and spirituality matter for public health: Evidence, implications, and resources* (pp. 261–281). Springer.

Ong, D. C., Zaki, J., & Gruber, J. (2017). Increased cooperative behavior across remitted bipolar I disorder and major depression: Insights utilizing a behavioral economic trust game. *Journal of Abnormal Psychology, 126*(1), 1.

ONS (Office of National Statistics). (2018). *Measuring national well-being: Quality of life in the UK, 2018*. https://www.ons.gov.uk/releases/measuringnationalwellbeinglifeintheukapril2018

ONS (Office for National Statistics). (2019, September 3). *Suicides in the UK: 2018 registrations*. https://bit.ly/34Y9a7c

Onyeador, I. N., Wittlin, N. M., Burke, S. E., Dovidio, J. F., Perry, S. P., Hardeman, R. R., Dyrbye, L. N., Herrin, J., Phelan, S. M., & van Ryn, M. (2020). The value of interracial contact for reducing anti-Black bias among non-Black physicians: A cognitive habits and growth evaluation (CHANGE) study report. *Psychological Science, 31*(1), 18–30.

Oosterhoff, B., Poppler, A., & Palmer, C. A. (2022). Early adolescents demonstrate peer-network homophily in political attitudes and values. *Psychological Science, 33*, 874–888.

Opp, M. R., & Krueger, J. M. (2015). Sleep and immunity: A growing field with clinical impact. *Brain, Behavior, and Immunity, 47*, 1–3.

Oquendo, M. A., Galfalvy, H. C., Currier, D., Grunebaum, M. F., Sher, L., Sullivan, G. M., Burke, A. K., Harkavy-Friedman, J., Sublette, M. E., Parsey, R. V., & Mann, J. J. (2011). Treatment of suicide attempters with bipolar disorder: A randomized clinical trial comparing lithium and valproate in the prevention of suicidal behavior. *American Journal of Psychiatry, 168*, 1050–1056.

Orben, A., Przybylski, A. K., Blakemore, S.-J., & Kievit, R. A. (2022). Windows of developmental sensitivity to social media. *Nature Communications, 13*, 1649.

O'Reilly, D. (2021, March 29). *Teens, parents, and religion*. Trust Magazine. https://www.pewtrusts.org/en/trust/archive/winter-2021/teens-parents-and-religion

Oren, D. A., & Terman, M. (1998). Tweaking the human circadian clock with light. *Science, 279*, 333–334.

Oren-Yagoda, R., Melamud-Ganani, I., & Aderka, I. M. (2022). All by myself: Loneliness in social anxiety disorder. *Journal of Psychopathology and Clinical Science, 131*(1), 4–13.

Orth, U., Dapp, L. C., Erol, R. Y., Krauss, S., & Luciano, E. C. (2021). Development of domain-specific self-evaluations: A meta-analysis of longitudinal studies. *Journal of Personality and Social Psychology, 120*, 145–172.

Orth, U., Erol, R. Y., & Luciano, E. C. (2018). Development of self-esteem from age 4 to 94 years: A meta-analysis of longitudinal studies. *Psychological Bulletin, 144*, 1045–1080.

Orth, U., & Robins, R. W. (2014). The development of self-esteem. *Current Directions in Psychological Science, 23*, 381–387.

Orth, U., Robins, R. W., Meier, L. L., & Conger, R. D. (2016). Refining the vulnerability model of low self-esteem and depression: Disentangling the effects of genuine self-esteem and narcissism. *Journal of Personality and Social Psychology, 110*, 133–149.

Osborne, L. (1999, October 27). A linguistic big bang. *The New York Times Magazine*. https://archive.nytimes.com/www.nytimes.com/library/magazine/home/19991024mag-sign-language.html

Osgood, C. E. (1962). *An alternative to war or surrender*. University of Illinois Press.

Osgood, C. E. (1980). *GRIT: A strategy for survival in mankind's nuclear age?* [Paper]. Presented at the Pugwash Conference on New Directions in Disarmament.

Osimo, E. F., Baxter, L. J., Lewis, G., Jones, P. B., & Khandaker, G. M. (2019). Prevalence of low-grade inflammation in depression: A systematic review and meta-analysis of CRP levels. *Psychological Medicine, 49*(12), 1958–1970.

Oskarsson, A. T., Van Boven, L., McClelland, G. H., & Hastie, R. (2009). What's next? Judging sequences of binary events. *Psychological Bulletin, 135*, 262–285.

Osler, M., Rozing, M. P., Christensen, G. T., Andersen, P. K., & Jørgensen, M. B. (2018). Electroconvulsive therapy and risk of dementia in patients with affective disorders: A cohort study. *Lancet Psychiatry, 5*, 348–356.

Osoegawa, C., Gomes, J. S., Grigolon, R. B., Brietzke, E., Gadelha, A., Lacerda, A. L., Dias, A. M., Cordeiro, Q., Laranjeira, R., de Jesus, D., Daskalakis, Z. J., Brunelin, J., Cordes, J., & Paulino Trevizol, A. (2018). Non-invasive brain stimulation for negative symptoms in schizophrenia: An updated systematic review and meta-analysis. *Schizophrenia Research, 197*, 34–44.

OSS Assessment Staff. (1948). *The assessment of men*. Rinehart.

Ossher, L., Flegal, K. E., & Lustig, C. (2012). Everyday memory errors in older adults. *Aging, Neuropsychology, and Cognition, 20*, 220–242.

Öst, L. G., Havnen, A., Hansen, B., & Kvale, G. (2015). Cognitive behavioral treatments of obsessive–compulsive disorder. A systematic review and meta-analysis of studies published 1993–2014. *Clinical Psychology Review, 40*, 156–169.

Öst, L. G., & Hugdahl, K. (1981). Acquisition of phobias and anxiety response patterns in clinical patients. *Behaviour Research and Therapy, 16*, 439–447.

Österman, K., Björkqvist, K., & Wahlbeck, K. (2014). Twenty-eight years after the complete ban on the physical punishment of children in Finland: Trends and psychosocial concomitants. *Aggressive Behavior, 40*, 568–581.

Ostfeld, A. M., Kasl, S. V., D'Atri, D. A., & Fitzgerald, E. F. (1987). *Stress, crowding, and blood pressure in prison*. Erlbaum.

O'Sullivan, M., Frank, M. G., Hurley, C. M., & Tiwana, J. (2009). Police lie detection accuracy: The effect of lie scenario. *Law and Human Behavior, 33*, 530–538.

Osvath, M., & Karvonen, E. (2012). Spontaneous innovation for future deception in a male chimpanzee. *PLOS ONE, 7*. https://journals.plos.org/plosone/article?id=10.1371/journal.pone.0036782

Oswald, F. L., Mitchell, G., Blanton, H., Jaccard, J., & Tetlock, P. E. (2015). Using the IAT to predict ethnic and racial discrimination: Small effect sizes of unknown societal significance. *Journal of Personality and Social Psychology, 108*, 562–571.

Otgaar, H., & Baker, A. (2018). When lying changes memory for the truth. *Memory, 1*, 2–14.

Otgaar, H., Howe, M. L., Dodier, O., Lilienfeld, S. O., Loftus, E. F., Lynn, S. J., Merckelbach, H., & Patihis, L. (2021). Belief in unconscious repressed memory persists. *Perspectives on Psychological Science, 16*(2), 454–460.

Ott, C. H., Lueger, R. J., Kelber, S. T., & Prigerson, H. G. (2007). Spousal bereavement in older adults: Common, resilient, and chronic grief with defining characteristics. *Journal of Nervous and Mental Disease, 195*, 332–341.

Otterman, S. (2020, December 14). 'I trust science,' says nurse who is first to get vaccine in U.S. *The New York Times*. https://www.nytimes.com/2020/12/14/nyregion/us-covid-vaccine-first-sandra-lindsay.html

Ou, Z., Pan, J., Tang, S., Duan, D., Yu, D., Nong, H., & Wang, Z. (2021). Global trends in the incidence, prevalence, and years lived with disability of Parkinson's disease in 204 countries/territories from 1990 to 2019. *Frontiers in Public Health, 9*. https://www.ncbi.nlm.nih.gov/pmc/articles/PMC8688697/

Ouellette, J. A., & Wood, W. (1998). Habit and intention in everyday life: The multiple processes by which past behavior predicts future behavior. *Psychological Bulletin, 124*, 54–74.

Ouimet, M. C., Brown, T. G., Corado, L., Paquette, M., & Robertson, R. D. (2020). The effects of alcohol dose, exposure to an in-vehicle alcohol feedback device, and subjective responses to alcohol on the decision to drink-drive in young drivers. *Accident Analysis and Prevention, 139*, 7.

Our World in Data. (2019). *Human height.* https://ourworldindata.org/human-height

Oveis, C., Gruber, J., Keltner, D., Stamper, J. L., & Boyce, W. T. (2009). Smile intensity and warm touch as thin slices of child and family affective style. *Emotion, 9*(4), 544.

Ovenstad, K. S., Ormhaug, S. M., Shirk, S. R., & Jensen, T. K. (2020). Therapists' behaviors and youths' therapeutic alliance during trauma-focused cognitive behavioral therapy. *Journal of Consulting and Clinical Psychology, 88*(4), 350–361.

Owczarski, W. (2018). Adaptive nightmares of Holocaust survivors: The Auschwitz camp in the former inmates' dreams. *Dreaming, 28*, 287–302.

Owen, A. (2017a). *Into the gray zone: A neuroscientist explores the border between life and death.* Scribner.

Owen, A. (2017b). Adrian Owen: At the flimsy border between life and death [Interview]. *The Psychologist.* https://www.bps.org.uk/psychologist/flimsy-border-between-life-and-death

Owen, A. M., Coleman, M. R., Boly, M., Davis, M. H., Laureys, S., & Pickard, J. D. (2006). Detecting awareness in the vegetative state. *Science, 313*, 1402.

Owen, R. (1814). First essay in *New view of society or the formation of character.* Quoted in *The story of New Lanark.* New Lanark Conservation Trust, 1993.

OWN. (2018, April 20). *Oprah and Amy Schumer on being secret introverts* [Video file]. http://www.oprah.com/own-supersoulsessions/oprah-and-amy-schumer-on-being-secret-introverts-video_2

Oxfam International. (2021, April 29). *COVID-19 cost women globally over $800 billion in lost income in one year.* https://www.oxfam.org/en/press-releases/covid-19-cost-women-globally-over-800-billion-lost-income-one-year

Özçaliskan, S., Lucero, C., & Goldin-Meadow, S. (2016). Is *seeing gesture* necessary to *gesture* like a native speaker? *Psychological Science, 27*, 737–747.

Ozer, E. J., Best, S. R., Lipsey, T. L., & Weiss, D. S. (2003). Predictors of posttraumatic stress disorder and symptoms in adults: A meta-analysis. *Psychological Bulletin, 1*, 52–73.

Ozer, E. J., & Weiss, D. S. (2004). Who develops posttraumatic stress disorder? *Current Directions in Psychological Science, 13*, 169–172.

Özgen, E. (2004). Language, learning, and color perception. *Current Directions in Psychological Science, 13*, 95–98.

Pace-Schott, E. P., & Spencer, R. M. C. (2011). Age-related changes in the cognitive function of sleep. *Progress in Brain Research, 191*, 75–89.

Pachankis, J. E., Mahon, C. P., Jackson, S. D., Fetzner, B. K., & Bränström, R. (2020). Sexual orientation concealment and mental health: A conceptual and meta-analytic review. *Psychological Bulletin, 146*(10), 831–871.

Padgett, V. R. (1989). *Predicting organizational violence: An application of 11 powerful principles of obedience* [Paper]. Presented to the American Psychological Association convention.

Pahl, K., Williams, S. Z., Lee, J. Y., Joseph, A., & Blau, C. (2020). Trajectories of violent victimization predicting PTSD and comorbidities among urban ethnic/racial minorities. *Journal of Consulting and Clinical Psychology, 88*(1), 39–47.

Pailian, H., Cary, S. E., & Pepperberg, I. M. (2020). Age and species comparisons of visual mental manipulation ability as evidence for its development and evolution. *Scientific Reports, 10*, 7689.

Painter, D. R., Dwyer, M. F., Kamke, M. R., & Mattingley, J. B. (2018). Stimulus-driven cortical hyperexcitability in individuals with Charles Bonnet hallucinations. *Current Biology, 28*, 3475–3480.

Palagi, E., Celeghin, A., Tamietto, M., Winkielman, P., & Norscia, I. (2020). The neuroethology of spontaneous mimicry and emotional contagion in human and non-human animals. *Neuroscience and Biobehavioral Reviews, 111*, 149–165.

Palladino, J. J., & Carducci, B. J. (1983). *"Things that go bump in the night": Students' knowledge of sleep and dreams* [Paper]. Presented at the meeting of the Southeastern Psychological Association.

Paller, K. A., & Oudiette, D. (2018, November). Sleep learning gets real. *Scientific American*, pp. 27–31.

Palmer-Bacon, J., Willis-Esqueda, C., & Spaulding, W. D. (2020). Stress, trauma, racial/ethnic group membership, and HPA function: Utility of hair cortisol. *American Journal of Orthopsychiatry, 90*(2), 193–200.

Palmer, B. (2013, May 9). *Investigative intuition: Do psychics ever solves crimes? Why do police consult them?* Slate. https://slate.com/news-and-politics/2013/05/psychic-sylvia-browne-said-amanda-berry-was-dead-why-do-police-consult-psychics.html

Palmer, C. A., & Alfano, C. A. (2017). Sleep and emotion regulation: An organizing, integrative review. *Sleep Medicine Reviews, 31*, 6–16.

Palmer, D. C. (1989). A behavioral interpretation of memory. In L. J. Hayes (Ed.), *Dialogues on verbal behavior: The first international institute on verbal relations* (pp. 261–279). Context Press.

Palmer, D. S., Howrigan, D. P., Chapman, S. B., Adolfsson, R., Bass, N., Blackwood, D., Boks, M. P. M., Chen, C.-Y., Churchhouse, C., Corvin, A. P., Craddock, N., Curtis, D., Di Florio, A., Dickerson, F., Freimer, N. B., Goes, F. S., Jia, X., Jones, I., Jones, L., … Neale, B. M. (2022). Exome sequencing in bipolar disorder identifies *AKAP11* as a risk gene shared with schizophrenia. *Nature Genetics, 54*, 541–547.

Palmese, L. B., DeGeorge, P. C., Ratliff, J. C., Srihari, V. H., Wexler, B. E., Krystal, A. D., & Tek, C. (2011). Insomnia is frequent in schizophrenia and associated with night eating and obesity. *Schizophrenia Research, 133*, 238–243.

Palombo, D. J., McKinnon, M. C., McIntosh, A. R., Anderson, A. K., Todd, R. M., & Levine, B. (2015). The neural correlates of memory for a life-threatening event: An fMRI study of passengers from Flight AT236. *Clinical Psychological Science, 4*, 312–319.

Pan, C., Ye, J., Wen, Y., Chu, X., Jia, Y., Cheng, B., Cheng, S., Liu, L., Yang, X., Liang, C., Wu, C., Wang, S., Wang, X., Ning, Y., Zhang, F., & Ma, X. (2022). The associations between sleep behaviors, lifestyle factors, genetic risk and mental disorders: A cohort study of 402 290 UK Biobank participants. *Psychiatry Research, 311*. https://doi.org/10.1016/j.psychres.2022.114488

Pandey, J., Sinha, Y., Prakash, A., & Tripathi, R. C. (1982). Right-left political ideologies and attribution of the causes of poverty. *European Journal of Social Psychology, 12*, 327–331.

Panichello, M. F., & Buschman, T. J. (2021). Shared mechanisms underlie the control of working memory and attention. *Nature, 592*, 601–605.

Panksepp, J. (2007). Neurologizing the psychology of affects: How appraisal-based constructivism and basic emotion theory can coexist. *Perspectives on Psychological Science, 2*, 281–295.

Pantazis, C. B., Gonzalez, L. A., Tunstall, B. J., Carmack, S. A., Koob, G. F., & Vendruscolo, L. F. (2021). Cues conditioned to withdrawal and negative reinforcement: Neglected but key motivational elements driving opioid addiction. *Science Advances, 7*(15). https://www.science.org/doi/10.1126/sciadv.abf0364

Pantev, C., Oostenveld, R., Engelien, A., Ross, B., Roberts, L. R., & Hoke, M. (1998). Increased auditory cortical representation in musicians. *Nature, 392*, 811–814.

Papadatou-Pastou, M., Gritzali, M., & Barrable, A. (2018, November). The learning styles educational neuromyth: Lack of agreement between teachers' judgments, self-assessment, and students' intelligence. In *Frontiers in Education* (Vol. 3, pp. 1–5).

Paradies, Y., Ben, J., Denson, N., Elias, A., Priest, N., Pieterse, A., Gupta, A., Kelaher, M., & Gee, G. (2015). Racism as a determinant of health: A systematic review and meta-analysis. *PLOS ONE, 10*(9). https://www.ncbi.nlm.nih.gov/pmc/articles/PMC4580597/

Pardiñas, A. F., Holmans, P., Pocklington, A. J., Escott-Price, V., Ripke, S., Carrera, N., Legge, S. E., Bishop, S., Cameron, D., Hamshere, M. L., Han, J., Hubbard, L., Lynham, A., Mantripragada, K., Rees, E., MacCabe, J. H., McCarroll, S. A., Baune, B. T., Breen, G., … Walters, J. T. R. (2018). Common schizophrenia alleles are enriched in mutation-intolerant genes and in regions under strong background selection. *Nature Genetics, 50*, 381–389.

Pardini, D. A., Raine, A., Erickson, K., & Loeber, R. (2014). Lower amygdala volume in men is associated with childhood aggression, early psychopathic traits, and future violence. *Biological Psychiatry, 75*, 73–80.

Park, C. L. (2007). Religiousness/spirituality and health: A meaning systems perspective. *Journal of Behavioral Medicine, 30*, 319–328.

Park, D. C., & McDonough, I. M. (2013). The dynamic aging mind: Revelations from functional neuroimaging research. *Perspectives on Psychological Science, 8*, 62–67.

Park, G., Schwartz, H. A., Eichstaedt, J. C., Kern, M. L., Kosinski, M., Stillwell, D. J., Ungar, L. H., & Seligman, M. E. P. (2015). Automatic personality assessment through social media language. *Journal of Personality and Social Psychology, 108*, 934–952.

Park, G., Yaden, D. R., Schwartz, H. A., Kern, M. L., Eichstaedt, J. C., Kosinski, M., Stillwell, D., Ungar, L. H., & Seligman, M. E. P. (2016). Women are warmer but no less assertive than men: Gender and language on Facebook. *PLOS ONE, 11*. https://journals.plos.org/plosone/article?id=10.1371/journal.pone.0155885

Park, K., Lee, S., Yang, J., Song, T., & Hong, G. R. S. (2019). A systematic review and meta-analysis on the effect of reminiscence therapy for people with dementia. *International Psychogeriatrics, 31*, 1581–1597.

Park, Y. C., & Pyszczynski, T. (2019). Reducing defensive responses to thoughts of death: Meditation, mindfulness, and Buddhism. *Journal of Personality and Social Psychology, 116*, 101–118.

Parker, E. S., Cahill, L., & McGaugh, J. L. (2006). A case of unusual autobiographical remembering. *Neurocase, 12*, 35–49.

Parker, K., & Wang, W. (2013). *Modern parenthood. Roles of moms and dads converge as they balance work and family* [PDF file]. Pew Research Center, Social & Demographic Trends. https://www.pewsocialtrends.org/wp-content/uploads/sites/3/2013/03/FINAL_modern_parenthood_03-2013.pdf

Parker, R. (2018, April 2). *Dwayne "The Rock" Johnson opens up about depression: "I was crying constantly."* Hollywood Reporter. https://bit.ly/3C3hdyB

Parkes, A., Wight, D., Hunt, K., Henderson, M., & Sargent, J. (2013). Are sexual media exposure, parental restrictions on media use and co-viewing TV and DVDs with parents and friends associated with teenagers' early sexual behavior? *Journal of Adolescence, 36*, 1121–1133.

Parrish, A. E., & Beran, M. J. (2021). Children and monkeys overestimate the size of high-contrast stimuli. *Attention, Perception, & Psychophysics, 83*, 2123–2135.

Partanen, E., Kujala, T., Näätänen, R., Liitola, A., Sambeth, A., & Huotilainen, M. (2013). Learning-induced neural plasticity of speech processing before birth. *PNAS, 110*, 15145–15150.

Parthasarathy, S., Vasquez, M. M., Halonen, M., Bootzin, R., Quan, S. F., Martinez, F. D., & Guerra, S. (2015). Persistent insomnia is associated with mortality risk. *American Journal of Medicine, 128*, 268–275.

Pascoe, E. A., Lattanner, M. R., & Richman, L. S. (2022). Meta-analysis of interpersonal discrimination and health-related behaviors. *Health Psychology* 41(5), 319–331.

Pascoe, E. A., & Richman, L. S. (2009). Perceived discrimination and health: A meta-analytic review. *Psychological Bulletin, 135*, 531–554.

Passell, P. (1993, March 9). Like a new drug, social programs are put to the test. *The New York Times*. https://www.nytimes.com/1993/03/09/science/like-a-new-drug-social-programs-are-put-to-the-test.html

Patihis, L. (2016). Individual differences and correlates of highly superior autobiographical memory. *Memory, 24*, 961–978.

Patihis, L., Ho, L. Y., Loftus, E. F., & Herrera, M. E. (2021). Memory experts' beliefs about repressed memory. *Memory*, 29(6), 823–828.

Patihis, L., Ho, L. Y., Tingen, I. W., Lilienfeld, S. O., & Loftus, E. F. (2014). Are the "memory wars" over? A scientist-practitioner gap in beliefs about repressed memory. *Psychological Science, 25*, 519–530.

Patterson, D. R., & Jensen, M. P. (2003). Hypnosis and clinical pain. *Psychological Bulletin, 129*, 495–521.

Patterson, F. (1978, October). Conversations with a gorilla. *National Geographic*, pp. 438–465.

Patterson, G. R., Chamberlain, P., & Reid, J. B. (1982). A comparative evaluation of parent training procedures. *Behavior Therapy, 13*, 638–650.

Patterson, G. R., Ray, R. S., & Shaw, D. A. (1968). Direct intervention in families of deviant children. *Oregon Research Institute Research Bulletin*, 8(No. 9). Oregon Research Institute and University of Oregon.

Patterson, R. (1951). *The riddle of Emily Dickinson*. Houghton Mifflin.

Patton, C. L., Smith, S. F., & Lilienfeld, S. O. (2018). Psychopathy and heroism in first responders: Traits cut from the same cloth? *Personality Disorders: Theory, Research, and Treatment, 9*, 354–368.

Pauker, K., Weisbuch, M., Ambady, N., Sommers, S. R., Adams, R. B., Jr., & Ivcevic, Z. (2009). Not so Black and White: Memory for ambiguous group members. *Journal of Personality and Social Psychology, 96*, 795–810.

Paulesu, E., Démonet, J.-F., Fazio, F., McCrory, E., Chanoine, V., Brunswick, N., Cappa, S. F., Cossu, G., Habib, M., Frith, C. D., & Frith, U. (2001). Dyslexia: Cultural diversity and biological unity. *Science, 291*, 2165–2167.

Pauletti, R. E., Menon, M., Cooper, P. J., Aults, C. D., & Perry, D. G. (2017). Psychological androgyny and children's mental health: A new look with new measures. *Sex Roles, 76*, 705–718.

Pauly, K., Finkelmeyer, A., Schneider, F., & Habel, U. (2013). The neural correlates of positive self-evaluation and self-related memory. *Social Cognitive and Affective Neuroscience, 8*, 878–886.

Paus, T., Zijdenbos, A., Worsley, K., Collins, D. L., Blumenthal, J., Giedd, J. N., Rapaport, J. L., & Evans, A. C. (1999). Structural maturation of neural pathways in children and adolescents: In vivo study. *Science, 283*, 1908–1911.

Pavlacic, J. M., Buchanan, E. M., Maxwell, N. P., Hopke, T. G., & Schulenberg, S. E. (2019). A meta-analysis of expressive writing on posttraumatic stress, posttraumatic growth, and quality of life. *Review of General Psychology, 23*, 230–250.

Pavlenko, A. (2014). *The bilingual mind and what it tells us about language and thought*. Cambridge University Press.

Pavlov, I. (1927). *Conditioned reflexes: An investigation of the physiological activity of the cerebral cortex*. Oxford University Press.

Payne, B. K. (2006). Weapon bias: Split-second decisions and unintended stereotyping. *Current Directions in Psychological Science, 15*, 287–291.

Payne, B. K., Krosnick, J. A., Pasek, J., Lelkes, Y., Akhtar, O., & Tompson, T. (2010). Implicit and explicit prejudice in the 2008 American presidential election. *Journal of Experimental Social Psychology, 46*, 367–374.

Payne, K. (2017). *The broken ladder: How inequality affects the way we think, live, and die*. Viking.

PBS (Public Broadcasting System). (2019). Alfred Kinsey's life, and sex research and social policies in America. *PBS American Experience*. https://www.pbs.org/wgbh/americanexperience/features/kinsey-timeline/

Pearce, M. J., Koenig, H. G., Robins, C. J., Nelson, B., Shaw, S. F., Cohen, H. J., & King, M. B. (2015). Religiously integrated cognitive behavioral therapy: A new method of treatment for major depression in patients with chronic medical illness. *Psychotherapy, 52*, 56–66.

Pedersen, A., Zachariae, R., & Bovbjerg, D. H. (2010). Influence of psychological stress on upper respiratory infection—A meta-analysis of prospective studies. *Psychosomatic Medicine, 72*, 823–832.

Peeples, L. (2020). Brutality and racial bias: What the data say. *Nature, 583*, 22–24.

Peigneux, P., Laureys, S., Fuchs, S., Collette, F., Perrin, F., Reggers, J., Phillips, C., Degueldre, C., Del Fiore, G., Aerts, J., Luxen, A., & Maquet, P. (2004). Are spatial memories strengthened in the human hippocampus during slow wave sleep? *Neuron, 44*, 535–545.

Pelham, B., & Crabtree, S. (2008, October 8). *Worldwide, highly religious more likely to help others*. Gallup. https://news.gallup.com/poll/111013/worldwide-highly-religious-more-likely-help-others.aspx

Pelham, B. W. (1993). On the highly positive thoughts of the highly depressed. In R. F. Baumeister (Ed.), *Self-esteem: The puzzle of low self-regard*. Plenum.

Pelham, W. E., Jr., Fabiano, G. A., Waxmonsky, J. G., Greiner, A. R., Gnagy, E. M., Pelham, W. E., III, Coxe, S., Verley, J., Bhatia, I., Hart, K., Karch, K., Konijnendijk, E., Tresco, K., Nahum-Shani, I., & Murphy, S. A. (2016). Treatment sequencing for childhood ADHD: A multiple-randomization study of adaptive medication and behavioral interventions. *Journal of Clinical Child and Adolescent Psychology, 45*, 396–415.

Pellicane, M. J., & Ciesla, J. A. (2022). Associations between minority stress, depression, and suicidal ideation and attempts in transgender and gender diverse (TGD) individuals: Systematic review and meta-analysis. *Clinical Psychology Review*, 91. https://doi.org/10.1016/j.cpr.2021.102113

Peng, K., & Nisbett, R. E. (1999). Culture, dialectics, and reasoning about contradiction. *American Psychologist*, 54(9), 741–754.

Peng, Y., & Tullis, J. G. (2020). Theories of intelligence influence self-regulated study choices and learning. *Journal of Experimental Psychology: Learning, Memory, and Cognition*, 46(3), 487–496.

Pennebaker, J. (1990). *Opening up: The healing power of confiding in others*. William Morrow.

Pennebaker, J. W. (1985). Traumatic experience and psychosomatic disease: Exploring the roles of behavioral inhibition, obsession, and confiding. *Canadian Psychology, 26*, 82–95.

Pennebaker, J. W. (2011). *The secret life of pronouns: What our words say about us*. Bloomsbury Press.

Pennebaker, J. W., Barger, S. D., & Tiebout, J. (1989). Disclosure of traumas and health among Holocaust survivors. *Psychosomatic Medicine, 51*, 577–589.

Pennebaker, J. W., Gosling, S. D., & Ferrell, J. D. (2013). Daily online testing in large classes: Boosting college performance while reducing achievement gaps. *PLOS ONE, 8*. https://www.ncbi.nlm.nih.gov/pmc/articles/PMC3835925/

Pennebaker, J. W., & O'Heeron, R. C. (1984). Confiding in others and illness rate among spouses of suicide and accidental death victims. *Journal of Abnormal Psychology, 93*, 473–476.

Pennycook, G., De Neys, W., Evans, J. S. B., Stanovich, K. E., & Thompson, V. A. (2018). The mythical dual-process typology. *Trends in Cognitive Sciences, 22*, 667–668.

Pennycook, G., & Rand, D. G. (2019). Fighting misinformation on social media using crowdsourced judgments of news source quality. *PNAS, 116*, 2521–2526.

Peplau, L. A., & Fingerhut, A. W. (2007). The close relationships of lesbians and gay men. *Annual Review of Psychology, 58*, 405–424.

Pepler, D., & Craig, W. (2012, November 15). *Health development depends on healthy relationships* [PDF file]. Prepared for the Division of Childhood and Adolescence, Centre for Health Promotion, Public Health Agency of Canada. https://www.iicrd.org/sites/default/files/resources/HealthyRelationshipsPaperFINAL_0_0.pdf

Pepperberg, I. M. (2009). *Alex & me: How a scientist and a parrot discovered a hidden world of animal intelligence—and formed a deep bond in the process*. Harper.

Pepperberg, I. M. (2012). Further evidence for addition and numerical competence by a grey parrot *(Psittacus erithacus)*. *Animal Cognition, 15*, 711–717.

Pepperberg, I. M. (2013). Abstract concepts: Data from a grey parrot. *Behavioural Processes, 93*, 82–90.

Perdue, K. L., Jensen, S. K., Kumar, S., Richards, J. E., Kakon, S. H., Haque, R., Petri, W. A., Jr., Lloyd-Fox, S., Elwell, C., & Nelson, C. A. (2019). Using functional near-infrared spectroscopy to assess social information processing in poor urban Bangladeshi infants and toddlers. *Developmental Science, 22*. doi: 10.1111/desc.12839

Pereira, G. M., & Osburn, H. G. (2007). Effects of participation in decision making on performance and employee attitudes: A quality circles meta-analysis. *Journal of Business Psychology, 22*, 145–153.

Pérez-Vigil, A., Fernández de, l. C., Brander, G., Isomura, K., Jangmo, A., Feldman, I., Hesselmark, E., Serlachius, E., Lázaro, L., Rück, C., Kuja-Halkola, R., D'Onofrio, B. M., Larsson, H., & Mataix-Cols, D. (2018). Association of obsessive-compulsive disorder with objective indicators of educational attainment: A nationwide register-based sibling control study. *JAMA Psychiatry, 75*, 47–55.

Pergamin-Hight, L., Bakermans-Kranenburg, M. J., van IJzendoorn, M. H., & Bar-Haim, Y. (2012). Variations in the promoter region of the serotonin transporter gene and biased attention for emotional information: A meta-analysis. *Biological Psychiatry, 71*, 373–379.

Perilloux, C., Easton, J. A., & Buss, D. M. (2012). The misperception of sexual interest. *Psychological Science, 23*, 146–151.

Perkins, A., & Fitzgerald, J. A. (1997). Sexual orientation in domestic rams: Some biological and social correlates. In L. Ellis & L. Ebertz (Eds.), *Sexual orientation: Toward biological understanding* (pp. 107–128). Praeger.

Perkins, A. M., Inchley-Mort, S. L., Pickering, A. D., Corr, P. J., & Burgess, A. P. (2012). A facial expression for anxiety. *Journal of Personality and Social Psychology, 102*, 910–924.

Perrachione, T. K., Del Tufo, S. N., & Gabrieli, J. D. E. (2011). Human voice recognition depends on language ability. *Science, 333*, 595.

Perrett, D. I., Harries, M., Mistlin, A. J., & Chitty, A. J. (1990). Three stages in the classification of body movements by visual neurons. In H. Barlow, C. Blakemore, & M. Weston-Smith (Eds.), *Images and understanding* (pp. 94–108). Cambridge University Press.

Perrett, D. I., Hietanen, J. K., Oram, M. W., & Benson, P. J. (1992). Organization and functions of cells responsive to faces in the temporal cortex. *Philosophical Transactions of the Royal Society of London: Series B, 335*, 23–30.

Perrett, D. I., May, K. A., & Yoshikawa, S. (1994). Facial shape and judgments of female attractiveness. *Nature, 368*, 239–242.

Perry, G. (2013). *Behind the shock machine: The untold story of the notorious Milgram psychology experiments*. New Press.

Perry, G. (2018). *The lost boys: Inside Muzafer Sherif's Robbers Cave experiment*. Scribe.

Perry, L. G. (2022, April 2). Prolonged grief: A mental disorder, or a natural process? *The New York Times*. https://www.nytimes.com/2022/04/02/opinion/letters/grief-mental-disorder.html

Perry, S. L. (2020). Pornography and relationship quality: Establishing the dominant pattern by examining pornography use and 31 measures of relationship quality in 30 national studies. *Archives of Sexual Behavior, 49*(4), 1199–1213.

Person, C., Tracy, M., & Galea, S. (2006). Risk factors for depression after a disaster. *Journal of Nervous and Mental Disease, 194*, 659–666.

Persons, J. B. (2016). Science in practice in cognitive behavior therapy. *Cognitive and Behavioral Practice, 23*(4), 454–458.

Pert, C. B. (1986). Quoted in J. Hooper & D. Teresi, *The three-pound universe*. Macmillan.

Pert, C. B., & Snyder, S. H. (1973). Opiate receptor: Demonstration in nervous tissue. *Science, 179*, 1011–1014.

Perugini, E. M., Kirsch, I., Allen, S. T., Coldwell, E., Meredith, J., Montgomery, G. H., & Sheehan, J. (1998). Surreptitious observation of responses to hypnotically suggested hallucinations: A test of the compliance hypothesis. *International Journal of Clinical and Experimental Hypnosis, 46*, 191–203.

Peschel, E. R., & Peschel, R. E. (1987). Medical insights into the castrati in opera. *American Scientist, 75*, 578–583.

Pescosolido, B. A., Martin, J. K., Long, J. S., Medina, T. R., Phelan, J. C., & Link, B. G. (2010). "A disease like any other?" A decade of change in public reactions to schizophrenia, depression, and alcohol dependence. *American Journal of Psychiatry, 167*, 1321–1330.

Pesko, M. F. (2014). Stress and smoking: Associations with terrorism and causal impact. *Contemporary Economic Policy, 32*, 351–371.

Peter, C. J., Fischer, L. K., Kundakovic, M., Garg, P., Jakovcevski, M, Dincer, A., Amaral, S. C., Ginns, E., Galdzicka, M., Bryce, C. P., Ratner, C., Waber, D. P., Mokler, D., Medford, G., Champagne, F. A., Rosene, D. L., McGaughy, J. A., Sharp, A. J., Galler, J. R., & Akbarian, S. (2016). DNA methylation signatures of early childhood malnutrition associated with impairments in attention and cognition. *Biological Psychiatry, 80*, 765–774.

Peter, J., & Valkenburg, P. M. (2016). Adolescents and pornography: A review of 20 years of research. *Journal of Sex Research, 53*, 509–531.

Peters, B. J., Reis, H. T., & Gable, S. L. (2018). Making the good even better: A review and theoretical model of interpersonal capitalization. *Social and Personality Psychology Compass, 12*(7). https://doi.org/10.1111/spc3.12407

Peters, J. R., Pullman, L. E., Kingston, D. A., & Lalumière, M. L. (2022). Orgasm frequency (total sexual outlet) in a national American sample. *Archives of Sexual Behavior, 51*, 1447–1460.

Petersen, J. L., & Hyde, J. S. (2010). A meta-analytic review of research on gender differences in sexuality, 1993–2007. *Psychological Bulletin, 136*, 21–38.

Petersen, J. L., & Hyde, J. S. (2011). Gender differences in sexual attitudes and behaviors: A review of meta-analytic results and large datasets. *Journal of Sex Research, 48*, 149–165.

Peterson, C., & Barrett, L. C. (1987). Explanatory style and academic performance among university freshmen. *Journal of Personality and Social Psychology, 53*, 603–607.

Peterson, C., Peterson, J., & Skevington, S. (1986). Heated argument and adolescent development. *Journal of Social and Personal Relationships, 3*, 229–240.

Peterson, C. C., & Siegal, M. (1999). Representing inner worlds: Theory of mind in autistic, deaf, and normal hearing children. *Psychological Science, 10*, 126–129.

Peterson, C. K., & Harmon-Jones, E. (2012). Anger and testosterone: Evidence that situationally-induced anger relates to situationally-induced testosterone. *Emotion, 12*, 899–902.

Peterson, G. B. (2004). A day of great illumination: B. F. Skinner's discovery of shaping. *Journal of the Experimental Analysis of Behavior, 82*, 317–328.

Peterson, L. R., & Peterson, M. J. (1959). Short-term retention of individual verbal items. *Journal of Experimental Psychology, 58*, 193–198.

Peterson, R. E. (2021). The genetics of major depression: Perspectives on the state of research and opportunities for precision medicine. *Psychiatric Annals, 51*, 165–169.

Petitto, L. A., & Marentette, P. F. (1991). Babbling in the manual mode: Evidence for the ontogeny of language. *Science, 251*, 1493–1496.

Petrov, N., & Robinson, O. (2020, April). Dreams and their relationship with waking emotion. *The Psychologist, 33*(4), 48–51.

Petrovic, K., Chapman, C. M., & Schofield, T. P. (2021). Religiosity and volunteering over time: Religious service attendance is associated with the likelihood of volunteering, and religious importance with time spent volunteering. *Psychology of Religion and Spirituality, 13*(2), 136–146.

Petsko, C. D., & Bodenhausen, G. V. (2019). Race–crime congruency effects revisited: Do we take defendants' sexual orientation into account? *Social Psychological and Personality Science, 10,* 73–81.

Pettegrew, J. W., Keshavan, M. S., & Minshew, N. J. (1993). 31P nuclear magnetic resonance spectroscopy: Neurodevelopment and schizophrenia. *Schizophrenia Bulletin, 19,* 35–53.

Pettersson, E., Lichtenstein, P., Larsson, H., Song, J., Attention Deficit/Hyperactivity Disorder Working Group of the iPSYCH-Broad-PGC Consortium, Autism Spectrum Disorder Working Group of the iPSYCH-Broad-PGC Consortium, Bipolar Disorder Working Group of the PGC, Eating Disorder Working Group of the PGC, Major Depressive Disorder Working Group of the PGC, Obsessive Compulsive Disorders and Tourette Syndrome Working Group of the PGC, Schizophrenia CLOZUK, Substance Use Disorder Working Group of the PGC, Agrawal, A., Børglum, A. D., Bulik, C. M., Daly, M. J., Davis, L. K., Demontis, D., Edenberg, H. J., ... Polderman, T. J. C. (2019). Genetic influences on eight psychiatric disorders based on family data of 4 408 646 full and half-siblings, and genetic data of 333 748 cases and controls. *Psychological Medicine, 49,* 1166–1173.

Pettigrew, T. F., & Tropp, L. R. (2011). *When groups meet: The dynamics of intergroup contact.* Psychology Press.

Pew. (2013, June 4). *The global divide on homosexuality.* Global Attitudes Project. https://www.pewresearch.org/global/2013/06/04/the-global-divide-on-homosexuality/

Pew. (2014, April 15). *Global morality.* Global Attitudes Project. https://www.pewresearch.org/global/interactives/global-morality/

Pew. (2015, November 4). *Raising kids and running a household: How working parents share the load.* https://www.pewsocialtrends.org/2015/11/04/raising-kids-and-running-a-household-how-working-parents-share-the-load/

Pew. (2016, September 28). *Where the public stands on religious liberty vs. nondiscrimination.* https://www.pewforum.org/2016/09/28/where-the-public-stands-on-religious-liberty-vs-nondiscrimination/

Pew. (2017). *Internet/broadband technology fact sheet.* Pew Research Center. pewinternet.org/fact-sheet/internet-broadband/

Pew. (2019, January 31). *Religion's relationship to happiness, civic engagement and health around the world.* https://www.pewforum.org/2019/01/31/religions-relationship-to-happiness-civic-engagement-and-health-around-the-world/

Pew. (2020). *Most Democrats who are looking for a relationship would not consider dating a Trump voter.* https://www.pewresearch.org/fact-tank/2020/04/24/most-democrats-who-are-looking-for-a-relationship-would-not-consider-dating-a-trump-voter/

Pew. (2020). *The global divide on homosexuality persists.* Pew Research Center. https://www.pewresearch.org/global/2020/06/25/global-divide-on-homosexuality-persists/

Pfaff, L. A., Boatwright, K. J., Potthoff, A. L., Finan, C., Ulrey, L. A., & Huber, D. M. (2013). Perceptions of women and men leaders following 360-degree feedback evaluations. *Performance Improvement Quarterly, 26,* 35–56.

Pfeifer, J. H., & Allen, N. B. (2021). Puberty initiates cascading relationships between neurodevelopmental, social, and internalizing processes across adolescence. *Biological Psychiatry, 89*(2), 99–108.

Phelps, E. A., & Hofmann, S. G. (2019). Memory editing from science fiction to clinical practice. *Nature, 572,* 43–50.

Phelps, J. A., Davis J. O., & Schartz, K. M. (1997). Nature, nurture, and twin research strategies. *Current Directions in Psychological Science, 6,* 117–120.

Philbeck, J. W., & Witt, J. K. (2015). Action-specific influences on perception and postperceptual processes: Present controversies and future directions. *Psychological Bulletin, 141,* 1120–1144.

Philip Morris. (2003). Philip Morris USA youth smoking prevention. Teenage attitudes and behavior study, 2002. In *Raising kids who don't smoke.* Series, Vol. 1(2).

Phillips, A. C., Batty, G. D., Gale, C. R., Deary, I. J., Osborn, D., MacIntyre, K., & Carroll, D. (2009). Generalized anxiety disorder, major depressive disorder, and their comorbidity as predictors of all-cause and cardiovascular mortality: The Vietnam Experience Study. *Psychosomatic Medicine, 71,* 395–403.

Phillips, A. L. (2011). A walk in the woods. *American Scientist, 69,* 301–302.

Phillips, D. P. (1985). Natural experiments on the effects of mass media violence on fatal aggression: Strengths and weaknesses of a new approach. In L. Berkowitz (Ed.), *Advances in experimental social psychology* (Vol. 19, pp. 207–250). Academic Press.

Phillips, D. P., Carstensen, L. L., & Paight, D. J. (1989). Effects of mass media news stories on suicide, with new evidence on the role of story content. In C. R. Pfeffer (Ed.), *Suicide among youth: Perspectives on risk and prevention* (pp. 101–116). American Psychiatric Press.

Phillips, J. L. (1969). *Origins of intellect: Piaget's theory.* Freeman.

Phillips, R., Kraeuter, A.-K., McDermott, B., Lupien, S., & Sarnyai, Z. (2021). Human nail cortisol as a retrospective biomarker of chronic stress: A systematic review. *Psychoneuroendocrinology, 123.* doi: 10.1016/j.psyneuen.2020.104903

Phillips, W. J., Fletcher, J. M., Marks, A. D. G., & Hine, D. W. (2016). Thinking styles and decision making: A meta-analysis. *Psychological Bulletin, 142,* 260–290.

Philpot, R., Liebst, L. S., Levine, M., Bernasco, W., & Lindegaard, M. R. (2019). Would I be helped? Cross-national CCTV footage shows that intervention is the norm in public conflicts. *American Psychologist, 75*(1), 66–75.

Piaget, J. (1930). *The child's conception of physical causality.* Routledge & Kegan Paul.

Piaget, J. (1932). *The moral judgment of the child.* Harcourt, Brace & World.

Picardi, A., Fagnani, C., Nisticò, L., & Stazi, M. A. (2011). A twin study of attachment style in young adults. *Journal of Personality, 79,* 965–992.

Picchioni, M. M., & Murray, R. M. (2007). Schizophrenia. *British Medical Journal, 335,* 91–95.

Picci, G., Gotts, S. J., & Scherf, K. S. (2016). A theoretical rut: Revisiting and critically evaluating the generalized under/over-connectivity hypothesis of autism. *Developmental Science, 19,* 524–549.

Picci, G., & Scherf, K. S. (2016). From caregivers to peers: Puberty shapes human face perception. *Psychological Science, 27,* 1461–1473.

Picheta, R., Borghese, L., & Armstrong, C. (2022, July 25). *Pope Francis visiting Canada to apologize for Indigenous abuse in Catholic residential schools.* CNN. https://www.cnn.com/2022/07/24/americas/pope-francis-canada-visit-intl/index.html

Piekarski, D. J., Routman, D. M., Schoomer, E. E., Driscoll, J. R., Park, J. H., Butler, M. P., & Zucker, I. (2009). Infrequent low dose testosterone treatment maintains male sexual behavior in Syrian hamsters. *Hormones and Behavior, 55,* 182–189.

Pierce, L. J., Klein, D., Chen, J., Delcenserie, A., & Genesee, F. (2014). Mapping the unconscious maintenance of a lost first language. *PNAS, 111,* 17314–17319.

Pierce, M., Hope, H., Ford, T., Hatch, S., Hotopf, M., John, A., Kontopantelis, E., Webb, R., Wessely, S., McManus, S., & Abel, K. M. (2020). Mental health before and during the COVID-19 pandemic: A longitudinal probability sample survey of the UK population. *Lancet Psychiatry, 7,* 883–892.

Pierson, E., Althoff, T., Thomas, D., Hillard, P., & Leskovec, J. (2021). Daily, weekly, seasonal and menstrual cycles in women's mood, behaviour and vital signs. *Nature Human Behaviour, 5,* 716–725.

Pietschnig, J., & Voracek, M. (2015). One century of global IQ gains: A formal meta-analysis of the Flynn effect (1909–2013). *Perspectives on Psychological Science, 10,* 282–306.

Piliavin, J. A. (2003). Doing well by doing good: Benefits for the benefactor. In C. L. M. Keyes & J. Haidt (Eds.), *Flourishing: Positive psychology and the life well-lived.* American Psychological Association.

Pillemer, D. B. (1998). *Momentous events, vivid memories.* Harvard University Press.

Pilley, J. W. (2013). *Chaser: Unlocking the genius of the dog who knows a thousand words.* Houghton Mifflin.

Pinker, S. (1995). The language instinct. *The General Psychologist, 31,* 63–65.

Pinker, S. (1998). Words and rules. *Lingua, 106,* 219–242.

Pinker, S. (2005, April 22). *The science of gender and science: A conversation with Elizabeth Spelke. Harvard University.* Edge. https://www.edge.org/event/the-science-of-gender-and-science-pinker-vs-spelke-a-debate

Pinker, S. (2008). *The sexual paradox: Men, women, and the real gender gap.* Scribner.

Pinker, S. (2010, June 10). Mind over mass media. *The New York Times.* https://www.nytimes.com/2010/06/11/opinion/11Pinker.html

Pinker, S. (2011, September 27). *A history of violence.* Edge. https://www.edge.org/3rd_culture/pinker07/pinker07_index.html

Pinker, S. (2014). *The sense of style: The thinking person 21st century.* Penguin Books.

Pinker, S. (2018). *Enlightenment now.* Viking.

Pinker, S. A. (2019, March 10). @sapinker [Tweet]. https://twitter.com/sapinker/status/1104610776420139008?lang=en

Pinquart, M. (2016). Associations of parenting styles and dimensions with academic achievement in children and adolescents: A meta-analysis. *Educational Psychology Review, 28,* 475–493.

Pinto, Y., de Haan, E. H. F., & Lamme, V. A. F. (2017). The split-brain phenomenon revisited: A single conscious agent with split perception. *Trends in Cognitive Sciences, 21*, 835–851.

Pipe, M.-E., Lamb, M. E., Orbach, Y., & Esplin, P. W. (2004). Recent research on children's testimony about experienced and witnessed events. *Developmental Review, 24*, 440–468.

Pipher, M. (2002). *The middle of everywhere: The world's refugees come to our town*. Harcourt Brace.

Pirrone, D., Zondervan-Zwijnenburg, M., Reitz, E., van den Eijnden, R. J. J. M., & ter Bogt, T. F. M. (2022). Pornography use profiles and the emergence of sexual behaviors in adolescence. *Archives of Sexual Behavior, 51*, 1141–1156.

Pitcher, D., Walsh, V., Yovel, G., & Duchaine, B. (2007). TMS evidence for the involvement of the right occipital face area in early face processing. *Current Biology, 17*, 1568–1573.

Pitman, R. K., Sanders, K. M., Zusman, R. M., Healy, A. R., Cheema, F., Lasko, N. B., Cahill, L., & Orr, S. P. (2002). Pilot study of secondary prevention of posttraumatic stress disorder with propranolol. *Biological Psychiatry, 51*, 189–192.

Pittenger, D. J. (1993). The utility of the Myers-Briggs Type Indicator. *Review of Educational Research, 63*, 467–488.

Pittinsky, T. L., & Diamante, N. (2015). Global bystander nonintervention. *Peace and Conflict: Journal of Peace Psychology, 21*, 226–247.

Place, S. S., Todd, P. M., Penke, L., & Asendorph, J. B. (2009). The ability to judge the romantic interest of others. *Psychological Science, 20*, 22–26.

PLAN USA. (2018). *The state of gender equality for U.S. adolescents* [PDF file]. https://www.planusa.org/docs/state-of-gender-equality-summary-2018.pdf

Plana-Ripoll, O., Pedersen, C. B., Holtz, Y., Benros, M. E., Dalsgaard, S., de Jonge, P., Fan, C. C., Degenhardt, L., Ganna, A., Greve, A. N., Gunn, J., Moesgaard Iburg, K., Vedel Kessing, L., Lee, B. K., Lim, C. C. W., Mors, O., Nordentoft, M., Prior, A., Roest, A. M., … McGrath, J. J. (2019). Exploring comorbidity within mental disorders among a Danish national population. *JAMA Psychiatry, 76*, 259–270.

Plant, E. A., & Peruche, B. M. (2005). The consequences of race for police officers' responses to criminal suspects. *Psychological Science, 16*, 180–183.

Plante, D. T. (2021). The evolving nexus of sleep and depression. *American Journal of Psychiatry, 178*, 896–902.

Plassmann, H., O'Doherty, J., Shiv, B., & Rangel, A. (2008). Marketing actions can modulate neural representations of experienced pleasantness. *PNAS, 105*, 1050–1054.

Pliner, P. (1982). The effects of mere exposure on liking for edible substances. *Appetite: Journal for Intake Research, 3*, 283–290.

Pliner, P., Pelchat, M., & Grabski, M. (1993). Reduction of neophobia in humans by exposure to novel foods. *Appetite, 20*, 111–123.

Plomin, R. (1999). Genetics and general cognitive ability. *Nature, 402*, C25–C29.

Plomin, R. (2011). Why are children in the same family so different? Nonshared environment three decades later. *International Journal of Epidemiology, 40*, 582–592.

Plomin, R. (2018, December 14). In the nature–nurture war, nature wins [Blog]. *Scientific American*. https://blogs.scientificamerican.com/observations/in-the-nature-nurture-war-nature-wins/

Plomin, R. (2018). *Blueprint: How DNA makes us who we are*. MIT Press.

Plomin, R., & Bergeman, C. S. (1991). The nature of nurture: Genetic influence on "environmental" measures. *Behavioral and Brain Sciences, 14*, 373–427.

Plomin, R., & DeFries, J. C. (1998). The genetics of cognitive abilities and disabilities. *Scientific American, 278*, 62–69.

Plomin, R., DeFries, J. C., Knopik, V. S., & Neiderhiser, J. M. (2016). Top 10 replicated findings from behavioral genetics. *Perspectives on Psychological Science, 11*, 3–23.

Plomin, R., DeFries, J. C., McClearn, G. E., & Rutter, M. (1997). *Behavioral genetics*. Freeman.

Plomin, R., McClearn, G. E., Pedersen, N. L., Nesselroade, J. R., & Bergeman, C. S. (1988). Genetic influence on childhood family environment perceived retrospectively from the last half of the life span. *Developmental Psychology, 24*, 37–45.

Plomin, R., & McGuffin, P. (2003). Psychopathology in the postgenomic era. *Annual Review of Psychology, 54*, 205–228.

Plomin, R., Reiss, D., Hetherington, E. M., & Howe, G. W. (1994, January). Nature and nurture: Genetic contributions to measures of the family environment. *Developmental Psychology, 30*, 32–43.

Plomin, R., & von Stumm, S. (2018). The new genetics of intelligence. *Nature Reviews Neuroscience, 19*, 148–159.

Plotkin, H. (1994). *Darwin machines and the nature of knowledge*. Harvard University Press.

Plotnik, J. M., Brubaker, D. L., Dale, R., Tiller, L. N., Mumby, H. S., & Clayton, N. S. (2019). Elephants have a nose for quantity. *PNAS, 116*, 12566–12571.

Plous, S., & Herzog, H. A. (2000). Poll shows researchers favor lab animal protection. *Science, 290*, 711.

Pluess, M., & Belsky, J. (2013). Vantage sensitivity: Individual differences in response to positive experiences. *Psychological Bulletin, 139*, 901–916.

Poelmans, G., Pauls, D. L., Buitelaar, J. K., & Franke, B. (2011). Integrated genomewide association study findings: Identification of a neurodevelopmental network for attention deficit hyperactivity disorder. *American Journal of Psychiatry, 168*, 365–377.

Poirazi, P., & Papoutsi, A. (2020). Illuminating dendritic function with computational models. *Nature Reviews Neuroscience, 21*, 303–321.

Polák, J., Rádlová, S., Janovcová, M., Flegr, J., Landová, E., & Frynta, D. (2020). Scary and nasty beasts: Self-reported fear and disgust of common phobic animals. *British Journal of Psychology, 111*(2), 297–321.

Polanin, J. R., Espelage, D. L., & Pigott, T. D. (2012). A meta-analysis of school-based bully prevention programs' effects on bystander intervention behavior. *School Psychology Review, 41*, 47–65.

Polderman, T. J. C., Benyamin, B., de Leeuw, C. A., Sullivan, P. F., van Bochoven, A., Visscher, P. M., & Posthuma, D. (2015). Meta-analysis of the heritability of human traits based on fifty years of twin studies. *Nature Genetics, 47*, 702–709.

Poldrack, R. A. (2018). *The new mind readers: What neuroimaging can and cannot reveal about our thoughts*. Princeton University Press.

Polivy, J., Herman, C. P., & Coelho, J. S. (2008). Caloric restriction in the presence of attractive food cues: External cues, eating, and weight. *Physiology and Behavior, 94*, 729–733.

Pollak, S., Cicchetti, D., & Klorman, R. (1998). Stress, memory, and emotion: Developmental considerations from the study of child maltreatment. *Developmental Psychopathology, 10*, 811–828.

Pollak, S. D., & Kistler, D. J. (2002). Early experience is associated with the development of categorical representations for facial expressions of emotion. *PNAS, 99*, 9072–9076.

Pollak, S. D., & Tolley-Schell, S. A. (2003). Selective attention to facial emotion in physically abused children. *Journal of Abnormal Psychology, 112*, 323–328.

Pollard, R. (1992). *100 years in psychology and deafness: A centennial retrospective* [Invited address]. American Psychological Association convention, Washington, DC.

Pollatsek, A., Romoser, M. R. E., & Fisher, D. L. (2012). Identifying and remediating failures of selective attention in older drivers. *Current Directions in Psychological Science, 21*, 3–7.

Pollick, A. S., & de Waal, F. B. M. (2007). Ape gestures and language evolution. *PNAS, 104*, 8184–8189.

Pomponio, R., Erus, G., Habes, M., Doshi, J., Srinivasan, D., Mamourian, E., Bashyam, V., Nasrallah, I. M., Satterthwaite, T. D., Fan, Y., Launer, L. J., Masters, C. L., Maruff, P., Zhuo, C., Völzke, H., Johnson, S. C., Fripp, J., Koutsouleris, N., Wolf, D. H., … Davatzikos, C. (2020). Harmonization of large MRI datasets for the analysis of brain imaging patterns throughout the lifespan. *NeuroImage, 208*. https://www.sciencedirect.com/science/article/pii/S1053811919310419

Ponnock, A., Muenks, K., Morell, M., Yang, J. S., Gladstone, J. R., & Wigfield, A. (2021). Grit and conscientiousness: Another jangle fallacy. *Journal of Research in Personality, 89*. https://doi.org/10.1016/j.jrp.2020.104021

Poorthuis, A. M., Slagt, M., van Aken, M. A., Denissen, J. J., & Thomaes, S. (2019). Narcissism and popularity among peers: A cross-transition longitudinal study. *Self and Identity*, 1–15.

Pope, D., & Simonsohn, U. (2011). Round numbers as goals: Evidence from baseball, SAT takers, and the lab. *Psychological Science, 22*, 71–79.

Pope Francis. (2015). *Encyclical letter* Laudato Si' *of the Holy Father Francis on care for our common home* (official English-language text of encyclical). https://bit.ly/2ycGx9Z

Popova, S., Lange, S., Shield, K., Burd, L., & Rehm, J. (2019). Prevalence of fetal alcohol spectrum disorder among special subpopulations: A systematic review and meta-analysis. *Addiction, 114*, 1150–1172.

Porfiri, M., Sattanapalle, R. R., Nakayama, S., Macinko, J., & Sipahi, R. (2019). Media coverage and firearm acquisition in the aftermath of a mass shooting. *Nature Human Behaviour, 3*, 913–921.

Poropat, A. E. (2014). Other-rated personality and academic performance: Evidence and implications. *Learning and Individual Differences, 34*, 24–32.

Porter, D., & Neuringer, A. (1984). Music discriminations by pigeons. *Journal of Experimental Psychology: Animal Behavior Processes, 10*, 138–148.

Porter, S., & Peace, K. A. (2007). The scars of memory: A prospective, longitudinal investigation of the consistency of traumatic and positive emotional memories in adulthood. *Psychological Science, 18*, 435–441.

Porter, S., Birt, A. R., Yuille, J. C., & Lehman, D. R. (2000, November). Negotiating false memories: Interviewer and rememberer characteristics relate to memory distortion. *Psychological Science, 11*, 507–510.

Porto, P. R., Oliveira, L., Mari, J., Volchan, E., Figueira, I., & Ventura, P. (2009). Does cognitive behavioral therapy change the brain? A systematic review of neuroimaging in anxiety disorders. *Journal of Neuropsychiatry and Clinical Neurosciences, 21*(2), 114–125.

Potter, G. D. M., Cade, J. E., & Hardie, L. J. (2017). Longer sleep is associated with lower BMI and favorable metabolic profiles in UK adults: Findings from the National Diet and Nutrition Survey. *PLOS ONE 12*(7). https://www.ncbi.nlm.nih.gov/pmc/articles/PMC5531652/

Poulton, R., Moffitt, T. E., & Silva, P. A. (2015). The Dunedin Multidisciplinary Health and Development Study: Overview of the first 40 years, with an eye to the future. *Social Psychiatry and Psychiatric Epidemiology, 50*, 679–693.

Poundstone, W. (2014). *How to predict the unpredictable. The art of outsmarting almost everyone.* OneWorld.

Poushter, J., & Kent, N. (2020, June 25). *The global divide on homosexuality persists* [PDF file]. Pew Research Center. https://www.pewresearch.org/global/wp-content/uploads/sites/2/2020/06/PG_2020.06.25_Global-Views-Homosexuality_FINAL.pdf

Powell, R. A., & Boer, D. P. (1994). Did Freud mislead patients to confabulate memories of abuse? *Psychological Reports, 74*, 1283–1298.

Powell, R. A., & Schmaltz, R. M. (2021). Did Little Albert actually acquire a conditioned fear of furry animals? What the film evidence tells us. *History of Psychology 24*(2), 164–181.

Prada, P., Perroud, N., Rüfenacht, E., & Nicastro, R. (2018). Strategies to deal with suicide and non-suicidal self-injury in borderline personality disorder, the case of DBT. *Frontiers in Psychology.* https://www.frontiersin.org/articles/10.3389/fpsyg.2018.02595/full

Prather, A. A., Janicki-Deverts, D., Hall, M. H., & Cohen, S. (2015). Behaviorally assessed sleep and susceptibility to the common cold. *Sleep, 38*, 1353–1359.

Prati, G., & Mancini, A. D. (2021). The psychological impact of COVID-19 pandemic lockdowns: A review and meta-analysis of longitudinal studies and natural experiments. *Psychological Medicine, 51*(2), 201–211.

Pratt, L. A., Brody, D. J., & Gu, Q. (2017, August). Antidepressant use among persons aged 12 and over: United States, 2011–2014. *NCHS Data Brief, 283*, 1–8.

Prause, N. (2011). The human female orgasm: Critical evaluations of proposed psychological sequelae. *Sexual and Relationship Therapy, 26*(4), 315–328.

Preckel, F., Lipnevich, A., Boehme, K., Branderner, L., Georgi, K., Könen, T., Mursin, K., & Roberts, R. (2013). Morningness–eveningness and educational outcomes: The lark has an advantage over the owl at high school. *British Journal of Educational Psychology, 83*, 114–134.

Preller, K. H., Razi, A., Zeidman, P., Stämpfli, P., Friston, K. J., & Vollenweider, F. X. (2019). Effective connectivity changes in LSD-induced altered states of consciousness in humans. *PNAS, 116*, 2743–2748.

Premack, D. G. (2007). Human and animal cognition: Continuity and discontinuity. *PNAS, 104*, 13861–13867.

Premack, D. G., & Woodruff, G. (1978). Does the chimpanzee have a theory of mind? *Behavioral and Brain Sciences, 1*, 515–526.

Prentice, D. A., & Miller, D. T. (1993). Pluralistic ignorance and alcohol use on campus: Some consequences of misperceiving the social norm. *Journal of Personality and Social Psychology, 64*, 243–256.

Prescott, A. T., Sargent, J. D., & Hull, J. G. (2018). Metaanalysis of the relationship between violent video game play and physical aggression over time. *PNAS, 115*, 9882–9888.

Primack, B. A., Shensa, A., Escobar-Viera, C. G., Barrett, E. L., Sidani, J. E., Colditz, J. B., & James, A. E. (2016). Use of multiple social media platforms and symptoms of depression and anxiety: A nationally-representative study among U.S. young adults. *Computers in Human Behavior, 69*, 1–9.

Prins, S. J., Osher, F. C., Steadman, H. J., Robbins, P. C., & Case, B. (2012). Exploring racial disparities in The Brief Jail Mental Health Screen. *Criminal Justice and Behavior, 39*(5), 635–645.

Pritchard, A., Richardson, M., Sheffield, D., & McEwan, K. (2019). The relationship between nature connectedness and eudaimonic well-being: A meta-analysis. *Journal of Happiness Studies, 21*, 1145–1167.

Prochaska, J. J. (2019). The public health consequences of e-cigarettes: A review by the National Academies of Sciences. A call for more research, a need for regulatory action. *Addiction, 114*, 587–589.

Prochazkova, E., Prochazkova, L., Giffin, M. R., Scholte, H. S., De Dreu, C. K., & Kret, M. E. (2018). Pupil mimicry promotes trust through the theory-of-mind network. *PNAS, 115*, E7265–E7274.

Profet, M. (1992). Pregnancy sickness as adaptation: A deterrent to maternal ingestion of teratogens. In J. H. Barkow, L. Cosmides, & J. Tooby (Eds). *The adapted mind: Evolutionary psychology and the generation of culture* (pp. 327–366). Oxford University Press.

Proffitt, D. R. (2006a). Distance perception. *Current Directions in Psychological Research, 15*, 131–135.

Proffitt, D. R. (2006b). Embodied perception and the economy of action. *Perspectives on Psychological Science, 1*, 110–122.

Project Match Research Group. (1997). Matching alcoholism treatments to client heterogeneity: Project MATCH posttreatment drinking outcomes. *Journal of Studies on Alcohol, 58*, 7–29.

Pronin, E. (2013). When the mind races: Effects of thought speed on feeling and action. *Current Directions in Psychological Science, 22*, 283–288.

Pronin, E., & Ross, L. (2006). Temporal differences in trait self-ascription: When the self is seen as another. *Journal of Personality and Social Psychology, 90*, 197–209.

Propper, R. E., Stickgold, R., Keeley, R., & Christman, S. D. (2007). Is television traumatic? Dreams, stress, and media exposure in the aftermath of September 11, 2001. *Psychological Science, 18*, 334–340.

Prot, S., Gentile, D., Anderson, C. A., Suzuli, K., Swing, E., Lim, K. M., Horiuchi, Y., Jelic, M., Krahé, B., Liuqing, W., Liau, A. K., Khoo, A., Petrescu, P. D., Sakamoto, A., Tajima, S., Toma, R. A., Warburton, W., Zhang, X., & Lam, B. C. P. (2014). Long-term relations among prosocial-media use, empathy, and prosocial behavior. *Psychological Science, 25*, 358–368.

Protzko, J., Aronson, J., & Blair, C. (2013). How to make a young child smarter: Evidence from the database of raising intelligence. *Perspectives on Psychological Science, 8*, 25–40.

Provine, R. R. (2001). *Laughter: A scientific investigation.* Penguin.

Provine, R. R. (2012). *Curious behavior: Yawning, laughing, hiccupping, and beyond.* Harvard University Press.

Pryor, L. (2019, March 15). Mental illness isn't all in your head. *The New York Times.* https://www.nytimes.com/2019/03/15/opinion/preventing-mental-illness.html

Przybylski, A. K., Weinstein, N., & Murayama, K. (2017). Internet gaming disorder: Investigating the clinical relevance of a new phenomenon. *American Journal of Psychiatry, 174*, 230–236.

Psaltopoulou, T., Sergentanis, T. N., Panagiotakos, D. B., Sergentanis, I. N., Kosti, R., & Scarmeas, N. (2013). Mediterranean diet, stroke, cognitive impairment, and depression: A meta-analysis. *Annals of Neurology, 74*, 580–591.

Psychologist. (2003). Who's the greatest? *The Psychologist, 16*, 170–175.

PTC (Parents Television Council). (2007, January 10). *Dying to entertain: Violence on prime time broadcast TV, 1998 to 2006* [PDF file]. https://www.parentstv.org/resources/PTC-DyingtoEnt-Jan07_200224_174746.pdf

Publix. (2022). *Facts and figures.* https://corporate.publix.com/about-publix/company-overview/facts-figures

Pugh, Z. H., Choo, S., Leshin, J. C., Lindquist, K. A., & Nam, C. S. (2022). Emotion depends on context, culture and their interaction: Evidence from effective connectivity. *Social Cognitive and Affective Neuroscience, 17*(2), 206–217.

Puhl, R. M., Latner, J. D., O'Brien, K., Luedicke, J., Forhan, M., & Danielsdottir, S. (2015). Cross-national perspectives about weight-based bullying in youth: Nature, extent and remedies. *Pediatric Obesity, 11*, 241–250.

Punamäki, R. L., & Joustie, M. (1998). The role of culture, violence, and personal factors affecting dream content. *Journal of Cross-Cultural Psychology, 29*, 320–342.

Punzi, G., Ursini, G., Chen, Q., Radulescu, E., Tao, E., Huuki, L. A., Di Carlo, P.,

Collado-Torres, L., Shin, J. H., Catanesi, R., Jaffe, A. E., Hyde, T. M., Kleinman, J. E., Mackay, T. F. C., & Weinberger, D. R. (2022). Genetics and brain transcriptomics of completed suicide. *American Journal of Psychiatry, 179*(3), 226–241.

Purves, K. L., Coleman, J. R. I., Meier, S. M., Rayner, C., Davis, K. A. S., Cheesman, R., Baekvad-Hansen, M., Børglum, A. D., Cho, S. W., Deckert, J. J., Gaspar, H. A., Bybjerg-Grauholm, J., Hettema, J. M., Hotopf, M., Hougaard, D., Hübel, C., Kan, C., McIntosh, A. M., Mors, O., ... Eley, T. C. (2020). A major role for common genetic variation in anxiety disorders. *Molecular Psychiatry, 25*, 3292–3303.

Puterman, E., Gemmill, A., Karasek, D., Weir, D., Adler, N. E., Prather, A. A., & Epel, E. S. (2016). Lifespan adversity and later adulthood telomere length in the nationally representative U.S. Health and Retirement Study. *PNAS, 113*, E6335–E6342.

Puterman, E., Weiss, J., Hives, B. A., Gemmill, A., Karasek, D., Berry Mendes, W., & Rehkopf, D. H. (2020). Predicting mortality from 57 economic, behavioral, social, and psychological factors. *PNAS, 117*(28), 16273–16282.

Putnam, A. L., Ross, M. Q., Soter, L. K., & Roediger, H. L. (2018). Collective narcissism: Americans exaggerate the role of their home state in appraising U.S. history. *Psychological Science, 29*, 1414–1422.

Putnam, F. W. (1991). Recent research on multiple personality disorder. *Psychiatric Clinics of North America, 14*, 489–502.

Puttonen, S., Kivimäki, M., Elovainio, M., Pulkki-Råback, L., Hintsanen, M., Vahtera, J., Telama, R., Juonala, M., Viikari, J. S., Raitakari, O. T., & Keltikangas-Järvinen, L. (2009). Shift work in young adults and carotid artery intima-media thickness: The Cardiovascular Risk in Young Finns study. *Atherosclerosis, 205*(2), 608–613.

Pyszczynski, T. A., Motyl, M., Vail, K. E., III, Hirschberger, G., Arndt, J., & Kesebir, P. (2012). Drawing attention to global climate change decreases support for war. *Peace and Conflict: Journal of Peace Psychology, 18*, 354–368.

Pyszczynski, T. A., Rothschild, Z., & Abdollahi, A. (2008). Terrorism, violence, and hope for peace: A terror management perspective. *Current Directions in Psychological Science, 17*, 318–322.

Pyszczynski, T. A., Solomon, S., & Greenberg, J. (2002). *In the wake of 9/11: The psychology of terror.* American Psychological Association.

Qaseem, A., Kansagara, D., Forciea, M. A., Cooke, M., & Denberg, T. D. (2016). Management of chronic insomnia disorder in adults: A clinical practice guideline from the American College of Physicians. *Annals of Internal Medicine, 165*, 125–133.

Qin, H.-F., & Piao, T.-J. (2011). Dispositional optimism and life satisfaction of Chinese and Japanese college students: Examining the mediating effects of affects and coping efficacy. *Chinese Journal of Clinical Psychology, 19*, 259–261.

Qiu, L., Lin, H., Ramsay, J., & Yang, F. (2012). You are what you tweet: Personality expression and perception on Twitter. *Journal of Research in Personality, 46*, 710–718.

Quaedflieg, C. W. E. M., & Schwabe, L. (2017). Memory dynamics under stress. *Memory, 26*, 364–376.

Quasha, S. (1980). *Albert Einstein: An intimate portrait.* Forest.

Quinn, P. C., Bhatt, R. S., Brush, D., Grimes, A., & Sharpnack, H. (2002). Development of form similarity as a Gestalt grouping principle in infancy. *Psychological Science, 13*, 320–328.

Quinn, P. C., Lee, K., & Pascalis, O. (2019). Face processing in infancy and beyond: The case of social categories. *Annual Review of Psychology, 70*, 165–189.

Quinton, S. (2020, February 3). *Seeking a more worker-friendly economy, some states push employee ownership.* Pew. https://bit.ly/3nXIOdz

Quiroga, R. Q., Fried, I., & Koch, C. (2013, February). Brain cells for grandmother. *Scientific American*, pp. 30–35.

Quispe-Torreblanca, E., Brown, G. D. A., Boyce, C. J., Wood, A. M., & De Neve, J. (2021). Inequality and social rank: Income increases buy more life satisfaction in more equal countries. *Personality and Social Psychology Bulletin, 47*, 519–539.

Quoidbach, J., Berry, E. V., Hansenne, M., & Mikolajczak, M. (2010). Positive emotion regulation and well-being: Comparing the impact of eight savoring and dampening strategies. *Personality and Individual Differences, 49*, 368–373.

Quoidbach, J., Gilbert, D. T., & Wilson, T. D. (2013). The end of history illusion. *Science, 339*, 96–98.

Quoidbach, J., Gruber, J., Mikolajczak, M., Kogan, A., Kotsou, I., & Norton, M. (2014). Emodiversity and the emotional ecosystem. *Journal of Experimental Psychology: General, 143*(6), 2057.

Quoidbach, J., Taquet, M., Desseilles, M., de Montjoye, Y., & Gross, J. J. (2019). Happiness and social behavior. *Psychological Science, 30*, 1111–1122.

Rabbitt, P. (2006). Tales of the unexpected: 25 years of cognitive gerontology. *The Psychologist, 19*, 674–676.

Rabin, R. C. (2022). U.S. life expectancy falls again in 'historic' setback. *The New York Times.* https://www.nytimes.com/2022/08/31/health/life-expectancy-covid-pandemic.html

Raby, K. L., Cicchetti, D., Carlson, E. A., Cutuli, J. J., Englund, M. M., & Egeland, B. (2012). Genetic and care-giving-based contributions to infant attachment: Unique associations with distress reactivity and attachment security. *Psychological Science, 23*, 1016–1023.

Raby, K. L., Roisman, G. I., Fraley, R. C., & Simpson, J. A. (2014). The enduring predictive significance of early maternal sensitivity: Social and academic competence through age 32 years. *Child Development, 86*, 695–708.

Radford, B. (2010, March 5). *Missing persons and abductions reveal psychics' failures.* DiscoveryNews. https://culteducation.com/group/1104-psychics/22804-missing-persons-and-abductions-reveal-psychics-failures.html

Rae, J. R., Gülgöz, S., Durwood, L., DeMeules, M., Lowe, R., Lindquist, G., & Olson, K. R. (2019). Predicting early-childhood gender transitions. *Psychological Science, 30*, 669–681.

Rahl, H. A., Lindsay, E. K., Pacilio, L. E., Brown, K. W., & Creswell, J. D. (2017). Brief mindfulness meditation training reduces mind wandering: The critical role of acceptance. *Emotion, 17*, 224–230.

Rahman, A., Khan, M. N., Hamdani, S. U., Chiumento, A., Akhtar, P., Nazir, H., Nisar, A., Masood, A., Din, I. U., Khan, N. A., Bryant, R. A., Dawson, K. S., Sijbrandij, M., Wang, D., & van Ommeren, M. (2019). Effectiveness of a brief group psychological intervention for women in a post-conflict setting in Pakistan: A single-blind, cluster, randomised controlled trial. *The Lancet, 393*(10182), 1733–1744.

Rahman, Q. (2015, July 24). "Gay genes": Science is on the right track, we're born this way. Let's deal with it. *The Guardian.* https://www.theguardian.com/science/blog/2015/jul/24/gay-genes-science-is-on-the-right-track-were-born-this-way-lets-deal-with-it

Rahman, Q., & Koerting, J. (2008). Sexual orientation-related differences in allocentric spatial memory tasks. *Hippocampus, 18*, 55–63.

Rahman, Q., & Wilson, G. D. (2003). Born gay? The psychobiology of human sexual orientation. *Personality and Individual Differences, 34*, 1337–1382.

Rahman, Q., Wilson, G. D., & Abrahams, S. (2004). Biosocial factors, sexual orientation and neurocognitive functioning. *Psychoneuroendocrinology, 29*, 867–881.

Rahnev, D., Desender, K., Lee, A. L. F., Adler, W. T., Aguilar-Lleyda, D., Akdo⊠an, B., Arbuzova, P., Atlas, L. Y., Balci, F., Bang, J. W., Bégue, I., Birney, D. P., Brady, T. F., Calder-Travis, J., Chetverikov, A., Clark, T. K., Davranche, K., Denison, R. N., Dildine, T. C., ... Zylberberg, A. (2020). The confidence database. *Nature Human Behaviour, 4*, 317–325.

Raichle, M. (2010, March). The brain's dark energy. *Scientific American*, pp. 44–49.

Raichlen, D. A., & Polk, J. D. (2013). Linking brains and brawn: Exercise and the evolution of human neurobiology. *Proceedings of the Royal Society Biology, 280*(1750). https://www.ncbi.nlm.nih.gov/pmc/articles/PMC3574441/

Raila, H., Scholl, B. J., & Gruber, J. (2015). Seeing the world through rose-colored glasses: People who are happy and satisfied with life preferentially attend to positive stimuli. *Emotion, 15*, 449–462.

Raine, A. (1999). Murderous minds: Can we see the mark of Cain? *Cerebrum: The Dana Forum on Brain Science, 1*, 15–29.

Raine, A. (2005). The interaction of biological and social measures in the explanation of antisocial and violent behavior. In D. M. Stoff & E. J. Susman (Eds.), *Developmental psychobiology of aggression* (pp. 13–42). Cambridge University Press.

Raine, A. (2013). *The anatomy of violence: The biological roots of crime.* Pantheon.

Raine, A., Ang, R. P., Choy, O., Hibbeln, J. R., Ho, R., Lim, C. G., Lim-Ashworth, N. S. J., Ling, S., Liu, J. C. J., Ooi, Y. P., Tan, Y. R., & Fung, D. S. S. (2018). Omega-3 (⊠-3) and social skills interventions for reactive aggression and childhood externalizing behavior problems: A randomized, stratified, double-blind, placebo-controlled, factorial trial. *Psychological Medicine, 261*, 307–311.

Raine, A., Brennan, P., Mednick, B., & Mednick, S. A. (1996). High rates of violence, crime, academic problems, and behavioral problems in males with both early neuromotor deficits and unstable family environments. *Archives of General Psychiatry, 53*, 544–549.

Raine, A., Lencz, T., Bihrle, S., LaCasse, L., & Colletti, P. (2000). Reduced prefrontal gray matter volume and reduced autonomic activity in antisocial personality disorder. *Archives of General Psychiatry, 57*, 119–127.

Raines, J., Holmes, L., Watts-Overall, T. M., Slettevold, E., Gruia, D. C., Orbell, S., & Rieger, G. (2021). Patterns of genital sexual arousal in transgender men. *Psychological Science, 32*(4), 485–495.

Rainville, P., Duncan, G. H., Price, D. D., Carrier, B., & Bushnell, M. C. (1997). Pain affect encoded in human anterior cingulate but not somatosensory cortex. *Science, 277*, 968–971.

Rajangam, S., Tseng, P. H., Yin, A., Lehew, G., Schwarz, D., Lebedev, M. A., & Nicolelis, M. A. (2016). Wireless cortical brain-machine interface for whole-body navigation in primates. *Scientific Reports, 6*. https://go.nature.com/3BvYtec

Raji, C. A., Merrill, D. A., Eyre, H., Mallam, S., Torosyan, N., Erickson, K.I., Lopez, O. L., Becker, J. T., Carmichael, O. T., Gach, H. M., Thompson, P. M., Longstreth, W. T., & Kuller, L. H. (2016). Longitudinal relationships between caloric expenditure and gray matter in the cardiovascular health study. *Journal of Alzheimer's Disease, 52*, 719–729.

Ramachandran, V. S., & Blakeslee, S. (1998). *Phantoms in the brain: Probing the mysteries of the human mind.* Morrow.

Ramírez-Esparza, N., Gosling, S. D., Benet-Martínez, V., Potter, J. P., & Pennebaker, J. W. (2006). Do bilinguals have two personalities? A special case of cultural frame switching. *Journal of Research in Personality, 40*, 99–120.

Ramos, M. R., Cassidy, C., Reicher, S., & Haslam, S. A. (2012). A longitudinal investigation of the rejection-identification hypothesis. *British Journal of Social Psychology, 51*, 642–660.

Ramot, M., Walsh, C., & Martin, A. (2019). Multifaceted integration: Memory for faces is subserved by widespread connections between visual, memory, auditory, and social networks. *Journal of Neuroscience, 39*, 4976–4985.

Rand, D. G., & Nowak, M. A. (2013). Human cooperation. *Trends in Cognitive Sciences, 17*(8), 413–425.

Rand, D. G., Tomlin, D., Bear, A., Ludvig, E. A., & Cohen, J. D. (2017). Cyclical population dynamics of automatic versus controlled processing: An evolutionary pendulum. *Psychological Review, 124*, 626–642.

Randall, D. K. (2012, September 22). Rethinking sleep. *The New York Times.* https://www.nytimes.com/2012/09/23/opinion/sunday/rethinking-sleep.html

Randi, J. (1999, February 4). 2000 club mailing list e-mail letter.

Randler, C. (2008). Morningness–eveningness and satisfaction with life. *Social Indicators Research, 86*, 297–302.

Randler, C. (2009). Proactive people are morning people. *Journal of Applied Social Psychology, 39*, 2787–2797.

Ranning, A., Madsen, T., Hawton, K., Nordentoft, M., & Erlangsen, A. (2022). Transgenerational concordance in parent-to-child transmission of suicidal behaviour: A retrospective, nationwide, register-based cohort study of 4419642 individuals in Denmark. *Lancet Psychiatry*, 9(5), 363–374.

Ranzini, M., & Girelli, L. (2019). Colours + numbers differs from colours of numbers: Cognitive and visual illusions in grapheme-colour synaesthesia. *Attention, Perception, & Psychophysics, 81*, 1500–1511.

Raoelison, M., Thompson, V. A., & De Neyes, W. (2020). The smart intuitor: Cognitive capacity predicts intuitive rather than deliberate thinking. *Cognition, 204*. https://doi.org/10.1016/j.cognition.2020.104381

Rapee, R. M., Magson, N. R, Forbes, M. K., Richardson, C. E., Johnco, C. J., Oar, E. L., & Fardouly, J. (2022). Risk for social anxiety in early adolescence: Longitudinal impact of pubertal development, appearance comparisons, and peer connections. *Behaviour Research and Therapy*, 154. doi: 10.1016/j.brat.2022.104126

Rapoport, J. L. (1989). The biology of obsessions and compulsions. *Scientific American, 260*, 83–89.

Räsänen, S., Pakaslahti, A., Syvalahti, E., Jones, P. B., & Isohanni, M. (2000). Sex differences in schizophrenia: A review. *Nordic Journal of Psychiatry, 54*, 37–45.

Rashbaum, W. K. (2019, April 23). For first time, pharmaceutical distributor faces federal criminal charges over opioid crisis. *The New York Times.* https://www.nytimes.com/2019/04/23/nyregion/opioid-crisis-drug-trafficking-rochester.html

Rasmussen, K. (2016). Entitled vengeance: A meta-analysis relating narcissism to provoked aggression. *Aggressive Behavior, 42*, 362–379.

Rath, T., & Harter, J. K. (2010, August 19). *Your friends and your social well-being: Close friendships are vital to health, happiness, and even workplace productivity.* Gallup Business Journal. https://news.gallup.com/businessjournal/127043/friends-social-wellbeing.aspx

Rathbone, C. J., Salgado, S., Akan, M., Havelka, J., & Berntsen, D. (2016). Imagining the future: A cross-cultural perspective on possible selves. *Consciousness and Cognition, 42*, 113–124.

Rathore, S., Habes, M., Iftikhar, M. A., Shacklett, A., & Davatzikos, C. (2017). A review on neuroimaging-based classification studies and associated feature extraction methods for Alzheimer's disease and its prodromal stages. *Neuroimage, 155*, 531–548.

Ravizza, S. M., Uitvlught, M. G., & Fenn, K. M. (2017). Logged in and zoned out. *Psychological Science, 28*, 171–180.

Ray, J. (2019). *Americans' stress, worry and anger intensified in 2018.* Gallup. https://news.gallup.com/poll/249098/americans-stress-worry-anger-intensified-2018.aspx

Ray, J., & Kafka, S. (2014, May 6). *Life in college matters for life after college.* Gallup. https://news.gallup.com/poll/168848/life-college-matters-life-college.aspx

Ray, O., & Ksir, C. (1990). *Drugs, society, and human behavior* (5th ed.). Times Mirror/Mosby.

Ray, R., Sanes, M., & Schmitt, J. (2013). No-vacation nation revisited. *Center for Economic and Policy Research*, 1–22.

Raynor, H. A., & Epstein, L. H. (2001). Dietary variety, energy regulation, and obesity. *Psychological Bulletin, 127*, 325–341.

Raz, A., Fan, J., & Posner, M. I. (2005). Hypnotic suggestion reduces conflict in the human brain. *PNAS, 102*, 9978–9983.

Razza, L. B., Palumbo, P., Moffa, A. H., Carvalho, A. F., Solmi, M., Loo, C. K., & Brunoni, A. R. (2020). A systematic review and meta-analysis on the effects of transcranial direct current stimulation in depressive episodes. *Depression & Anxiety, 37*(7), 594–608.

Reason, J. (1987). The Chernobyl errors. *Bulletin of the British Psychological Society, 40*, 201–206.

Reason, J., & Mycielska, K. (1982). *Absent-minded? The psychology of mental lapses and everyday errors.* Prentice-Hall.

Rebar, A. L., Stanton, R., Geard, D., Short, C., Duncan, M. J., & Vandelanotte, C. (2015). A meta-meta-analysis of the effect of physical activity on depression and anxiety in non-clinical adult populations. *Health Psychology Review, 9*, 366–378.

Reber, A. S., & Alcock, J. E. (2020). Searching for the impossible: Parapsychology's elusive quest. *American Psychologist, 75*, 391–399.

Rechenberg, K. (2016). Nutritional interventions in clinical depression. *Clinical Psychological Science, 4*, 144–162.

Rechsteiner, B., Compagnoni, M., Wullschleger, A., & Merki, K. M. (2021). Teachers' implicit theories of professional abilities in the domain of school improvement. *Frontiers in Education.* https://www.frontiersin.org/articles/10.3389/feduc.2021.635473/full

Redden, J. P., Mann, T., Vickers, Z., Mykerezi, E., Reicks, M., & Elsbernd, E. (2015). Serving first in isolation increases vegetable intake among elementary schoolchildren. *PLOS ONE, 10*. https://tinyurl.com/2p69m5me

Redmond, S., Jones, N. M., Holman, E. A., & Silver, R. C. (2019). Who watches an ISIS beheading—and why. *American Psychologist, 74*, 555–568.

Reed, D. (2012, January). Quoted by Miller, P. in, A thing or two about twins. *National Geographic.* https://www.nationalgeographic.com/magazine/2012/01/identical-twins-science-dna-portraits/

Rees, M. (1999). *Just six numbers: The deep forces that shape the universe.* Basic Books.

Refinetti, R., & Menaker, M. (1992). The circadian rhythm of body temperature. *Physiology & Behavior, 51*(3), 613–637.

Régner, I., Thinus-Blanc, C., Netter, A., Schmader, T., & Huguet, P. (2019). Committees with implicit biases promote fewer women when they do not believe gender bias exists. *Nature Human Behaviour, 3*, 1171–1179.

Reichenberg, A., Cederlöf, M., McMillan, A., Trzaskowski, M., Kapara, O., Fruchter, E., Ginat, K., Davidson, M., Weiser, M., Larsson, H., Plomin, R., & Lichtenstein, P. (2016). Discontinuity in the genetic and environmental causes of the intellectual disability spectrum. *PNAS, 113*, 1098–1103.

Reichenberg, A., & Harvey, P. D. (2007). Neuropsychological impairments in schizophrenia: Integration of performance-based and brain imaging findings. *Psychological Bulletin, 133*, 833–858.

Reichert, R. A., Robb, M. B., Fender, J. G., & Wartella, E. (2010). Word learning from baby videos. *Archives of Pediatrics & Adolescent Medicine, 164*, 432–437.

Reid, V. M., Dunn, K., Young, R. J., Amu, J., Donovan, T., & Reissland, N. (2017). The human fetus preferentially engages with face-like visual stimuli. *Current Biology, 27*, 1825–1828.

Reiff, C. M., Richman, E. E., Nemeroff, C. B., Carpenter, L. L., Widge, A. S., Rodriguez, C. I., Kalin, N. H., McDonald, W. M., & Work Group on Biomarkers and Novel Treatments. (2021). Psychedelics and psychedelic-assisted psychotherapy. *American Journal of Psychiatry, 177*, 391–410.

Reifman, A. S., Larrick, R. P., & Fein, S. (1991). Temper and temperature on the diamond: The heat-aggression relationship in Major League Baseball. *Personality and Social Psychology Bulletin, 17*, 580–585.

Reilly, D., Neumann, D. L., & Andrews, G. (2019). Gender differences in reading and writing achievement: Evidence from the National Assessment of Educational Progress (NAEP). *American Psychologist, 74*, 445–458.

Reimann, F., Cox, J. J., Belfer, I., Diatchenko, L., Zaykin, D. V., McHale, D. P., Drenth, J. P., Dai, F., Wheeler, J., Sanders, F., Wood, L., Wu, T. X., Karppinen, J., Nikolaisen, L., Männikkö, M., Max, M. B., Kiselycznyk, C., Poddar, M., Te Morsche, R. H., … Woods, C. G. (2010). Pain perception is altered by a nucleotide polymorphism in SCN9A. *PNAS, 107*, 5148–5153.

Reimão, R. N., & Lefévre, A. B. (1980). Prevalence of sleep-talking in childhood. *Brain and Development, 2*, 353–357.

Reis, H. T., & Aron, A. (2008). Love: What is it, why does it matter, and how does it operate? *Perspectives on Psychological Science, 3*, 80–86.

Reis, H. T., Maniaci, M. R., Caprariello, P. A., Eastwick, P. W., & Finkel, E. J. (2011). Familiarity does indeed promote attraction in live interaction. *Journal of Personality and Social Psychology, 101*(3), 557–570.

Reis, M., Ramiro, L., Camacho, I., Tomé, G., Brito, C., & Gaspar de Matos, G. (2017). Does having a pet make a difference? Highlights from the HBSC Portuguese study. *European Journal of Developmental Psychology, 15*, 548–564.

Reis, S. M. (2001). Toward a theory of creativity in diverse creative women. In M. Bloom & T. Gullotta (Eds.), *Promoting creativity across the life span* (pp. 231–275). CWLA Press.

Reisenzein, R. (1983). The Schachter theory of emotion: Two decades later. *Psychological Bulletin, 94*, 239–264.

Reitz, A. K., Motti-Stefanidi, F., & Asendorpf, J. B. (2016). Me, us, and them: Testing sociometer theory in a socially diverse real-life context. *Journal of Personality and Social Psychology, 110*, 908–920.

Reitzle, M. (2006). The connections between adulthood transitions and the self-perception of being adult in the changing contexts of East and West Germany. *European Psychologist, 11*, 25–38.

Reivich, K., Gillham, J. E., Chaplin, T. M., & Seligman, M. E. P. (2013). From helplessness to optimism: The role of resilience in treating and preventing depression in youth. In S. Goldstein & R. B. Brooks (Eds.), *Handbook of resilience in children* (2nd ed., pp. 201–214). Springer.

Rekker, R., Keijsers, L., Branje, S., & Meeus, W. (2015). Political attitudes in adolescence and emerging adulthood: Developmental changes in mean level, polarization, rank-order stability, and correlates. *Journal of Adolescence, 41*, 136–147.

Remick, A. K., Polivy, J., & Pliner, P. (2009). Internal and external moderators of the effect of variety on food intake. *Psychological Bulletin, 135*, 434–451.

Remington, A., Swettenham, J., Campbell, R., & Coleman, M. (2009). Selective attention and perceptual load in autism spectrum disorder. *Psychological Science, 20*, 1388–1393.

Remley, A. (1988, October). From obedience to independence. *Psychology Today*, pp. 56–59.

Ren, D., Wesselmann, E. D., & van Beest, I. (2021). Seeking solitude after being ostracized: A replication and beyond. *Personality and Social Psychology Bulletin, 47*, 426–440.

Ren, D., Wesselmann, E., & Williams, K. D. (2016). Evidence for another response to ostracism: Solitude seeking. *Social Psychological and Personality Science, 7*(3), 204–212.

Renner, M. J., & Renner, C. H. (1993). Expert and novice intuitive judgments about animal behavior. *Bulletin of the Psychonomic Society, 31*, 551–552.

Renner, M. J., & Rosenzweig, M. R. (1987). *Enriched and impoverished environments: Effects on brain and behavior.* Springer-Verlag.

Renninger, K. A., & Granott, N. (2005). The process of scaffolding in learning and development. *New Ideas in Psychology, 23*, 111–114.

Repacholi, B. M., Meltzoff, A. N., Toub, T. S., & Ruba, A. L. (2016). Infants' generalizations about other people's emotions: Foundations for trait-like attributions. *Developmental Psychology, 52*, 364.

Rescorla, R. A., & Wagner, A. R. (1972). A theory of Pavlovian conditioning: Variations in the effectiveness of reinforcement and nonreinforcement. In A. H. Black & W. F. Perokasy (Eds.), *Classical conditioning II: Current theory.* Appleton-Century-Crofts.

Resnick, M. D., Bearman, P. S., Blum, R. W., Bauman, K. E., Harris, K. M., Jones, J., Tabor, J., Beuhring, T., Sieving, R. E., Shew M., Ireland, M., Bearinger, L. H., & Udry, J. R. (1997). Protecting adolescents from harm. Findings from the National Longitudinal Study on Adolescent Health. *Journal of the American Medical Association, 278*, 823–832.

Resnick, S. M. (1992). Positron emission tomography in psychiatric illness. *Current Directions in Psychological Science, 1*, 92–98.

Retraction Watch. (2015, December 8). *Diederik Stapel now has 58 retractions.* https://www.retractionwatch.com/category/diederik-stapel

Retter, T. L., Jiang, F., Webster, M. A., & Rossion, B. (2020). All-or-none face categorization in the human brain. *NeuroImage, 213.* https://bit.ly/3eYuK58

Reyes-Jaquez, B., & Koenig, M. A. (2022). Early presence of a "power = males" association: Girls link power to their gender less often than boys but can be as motivated to gain it. *Journal of Experimental Child Psychology, 220.* https://doi.org/10.1016/j.jecp.2022.105419

Reynolds, G. (2009, November 18). Phys ed: Why exercise makes you less anxious. *The New York Times blog.* https://well.blogs.nytimes.com/2009/11/18/phys-ed-why-exercise-makes-you-less-anxious/

Reynolds, G. (2019, January 16). How exercise may help keep our memory sharp. *The New York Times.* https://www.nytimes.com/2019/01/16/well/move/exercise-brain-memory-irisin-alzheimer-dementia.html

Reynolds, J., Stewart, M., MacDonald, R., & Sischo, L. (2006). Have adolescents become too ambitious? High school seniors' educational and occupational plans, 1976 to 2000. *Social Problems, 53*, 186–206.

Rhee, T. G., Sint, K., Olfson, M., Gerhard, T., Busch, S. H., & Wilkinson, S. T. (2021). Association of ECT with risks of all-cause mortality and suicide in older Medicare patients. *American Journal of Psychiatry, 178*, 1089–1097.

Rhoads, S. A., Gunter, D., Ryan, R. M., & Marsh, A. A. (2021). Global variation in subjective well-being predicts seven forms of altruism. *Psychological Science, 32*, 1247–1261.

Rhodes, E. (2017, August). Back to academia … and elephants. *The Psychologist*, pp. 12–13.

Rhodes, M. G., & Anastasi, J. S. (2012). The own-age bias in face recognition: A meta-analytic and theoretical review. *Psychological Bulletin, 138*, 146–174.

Ribeiro, J. D., Huang, X., Fox, K. R., Walsh, C. G., & Linthicum, K. P. (2019). Predicting imminent suicidal thoughts and nonfatal attempts: The role of complexity. *Clinical Psychological Science, 7*, 941–957.

Riccelli, R., Toschi, N., Nigro, S., Terracciano, A., & Passamonti, L. (2017). Surface-based morphometry reveals the neuroanatomical basis of the five-factor model of personality. *Social Cognitive and Affective Neuroscience, 12*, 671–684.

Ricciardelli, L. A., & McCabe, M. P. (2004). A biopsychosocial model of disordered eating and the pursuit of muscularity in adolescent boys. *Psychological Bulletin, 130*, 179–205.

Rice, M. E., & Grusec, J. E. (1975). Saying and doing: Effects on observer performance. *Journal of Personality and Social Psychology, 32*, 584–593.

Rich, M., & Dooley, B. (2022, July 2). Japan's secret to taking the coronavirus: Peer pressure. *The New York Times.* https://www.nytimes.com/2022/07/02/world/asia/japan-covid.html

Richardson, G. B., La Guardia, A. C., & Klay, P. M. (2018). Determining the roles of father absence and age at menarche in female psychosocial acceleration. *Evolution and Human Behavior, 39*, 437–446.

Richardson, J. T. E., & Zucco, G. M. (1989). Cognition and olfaction: A review. *Psychological Bulletin, 105*, 352–360.

Richardson, M., Abraham, C., & Bond, R. (2012). Psychological correlates of university students' academic performance: A systematic review and meta-analysis. *Psychological Bulletin, 138*, 353–387.

Richeson, J. A., & Shelton, J. N. (2007). Negotiating interracial interactions. *Current Directions in Psychological Science, 16*, 316–320.

Richmond-Rakerd, L. S., Caspi, A., Ambler, A., d'Arbeloff, T., de Bruine, M., Elliott, M., Harrington, H., Hogan, S., Houts, R. M., Ireland, D., Keenan, R., Knodt, A. R., Melzer, T. R., Park, S., Poulton, R., Ramrakha, S., Hartmann Rasmussen, L. J., Sack, E., Schmidt, A. T., … Moffitt, T. E. (2021). Childhood self-control forecasts the pace of midlife aging and preparedness for old age. *PNAS, 118*(3). https://www.pnas.org/doi/10.1073/pnas.2010211118

Richtel, M., & Kaplan, S. (2018, August 27). Did Juul lure teenagers and get 'customers for life'? *The New York Times*. https://www.nytimes.com/2018/08/27/science/juul-vaping-teen-marketing.html

Richters, J., Yeung, A., Rissel, C., McGeechan, K., Caruana, T., & de Visser, R. (2022). Sexual difficulties, problems, and help-seeking in a national representative sample: The second Australian study of health and relationships. *Archives of Sexual Behavior, 51*, 1435–1446.

Rideout, V., Peebles, A., Mann, S., & Robb, M. B. (2022). *The Common Sense Census: Media use by tweens and teens, 2021*. Common Sense Media. https://www.commonsensemedia.org/research/the-common-sense-census-media-use-by-tweens-and-teens-2021

Ridley, M., Rao, G., Schilbach, F., & Patel, V. (2020). Poverty, depression, and anxiety: Causal evidence and mechanisms. *Science, 370*(6522), 1.

Rieff, P. (1979). *Freud: The mind of a moralist* (3rd ed.). University of Chicago Press.

Rieger, G., Savin-Williams, R., Chivers, M. L., & Bailey, J. M. (2016). Sexual arousal and masculinity-femininity of women. *Journal of Personality and Social Psychology, 111*, 265–283.

Riggs, L. M., & Gould, T. D. (2022). Ketamine and the future of rapid-acting antidepressants. *Annual Review of Clinical Psychology, 17*, 207–231.

Rigoni, J. B., & Asplund, J. (2016a, July 7). *Strengths-based development: The business results*. Gallup. https://www.gallup.com/workplace/236297/strengths-based-employee-development-business-results.aspx

Rigoni, J. B., & Asplund, J. (2016b, July 12). *Global study: ROI for strengths-based development*. Gallup. https://www.gallup.com/workplace/236288/global-study-roi-strengths-based-development.aspx

Rihm, J. S., Menz, M. M., Schultz, H., Bruder, L., Schilbach, L., Schmid, S. M., & Peters, J. (2019). Sleep deprivation selectively up-regulates an amygdala-hypothalamic circuit involved in food reward. *Journal of Neuroscience, 39*, 888–899.

Riley, L. D., & Bowen, C. (2005). The sandwich generation: Challenges and coping strategies of multigenerational families. *The Family Journal, 13*, 52–58.

Rincon, A. V., Deschner, T., Schülke, O., & Ostner, J. (2020). Oxytocin increases after affiliative interactions in male Barbary macaques. *Hormones and Behavior, 119*. https://doi.org/10.1016/j.yhbeh.2019.104661

Rindermann, H., & Becker, D. (2018). Flynn-effect and economic growth: Do national increases in intelligence lead to increases in GDP? *Intelligence, 69*, 87–93.

Rindermann, H., Becker, D., & Coyle, T. R. (2016). Survey of expert opinion on intelligence: The Flynn effect and the future of intelligence. *Personality and Individual Differences, 106*, 242–247.

Riordan, M. (2013, March 19). *Tobacco warning labels: Evidence of effectiveness*. The Campaign for Tobacco-Free Kids. http://tobaccofreekids.orgtobaccofreekids.org

Ritchey, A. J., & Ruback, R. B. (2018). Predicting lynching atrocity: The situational norms of lynchings in Georgia. *Personality and Social Psychology Bulletin, 44*, 619–637.

Ritchie, H. (2019, September 2). *Who smokes more, men or women?* Our World in Data. https://ourworldindata.org/who-smokes-more-men-or-women

Ritchie, H., & Roser, M. (2019). *Meat and dairy production*. Our World in Data. https://ourworldindata.org/meat-production#number-of-animals-slaughtered

Ritchie, H., Roser, M., & Ortiz-Ospina, E. (2019). *Suicide* (by age). Our World in Data. ourworldindata.org/suicide#suicide-by-age

Ritchie, H., Roser, M., & Ortiz-Ospina, E. (2019). *Suicide* (by gender). Our World in Data. ourworldindata.org/suicide#suicide-by-gender

Ritchie, H., Roser, M., & Ortiz-Espina, E. (2022). *Suicide*. Our World in Data. https://ourworldindata.org/suicide#summary

Ritchie, S. J., Cox, S. R., Shen, X., Lombardo, M. V., Reus, L. M., Alloza, C., Harris, M. A., Alderson, H. L., Hunter, S., Neilson, E., Liewald, D. C. M., Auyeung, B., Whalley, H. C., Lawrie, S. M., Gale, C. R., Bastin, M. E., McIntosh, A. M., & Deary, I. J. (2018). Sex differences in the adult human brain: Evidence from 5216 UK Biobank participants. *Cerebral Cortex, 28*, 2959–2975.

Ritchie, S. J., Dickie, D. A., Cox, S. R., Valdes Hernandez Mdel, C., Corley, J., Royle, N. A., Pattie, A., Aribisala, B. S., Redmond, P., Muñoz Maniega, S., Taylor, A. M., Sibbett, R., Gow, A. J., Starr, J. M., Bastin, M. E., Wardlaw, J. M., & Deary, I. J. (2015). Brain volumetric changes and cognitive ageing during the eighth decade of life. *Human Brain Mapping, 36*, 4910–4925.

Ritchie, S. J., & Tucker-Drob, E. M. (2018). How much does education improve intelligence? A meta-analysis. *Psychological Science, 29*, 1358–1369.

Ritchie, S. J., Wiseman, R., & French, C. C. (2012). Failing the future: Three unsuccessful attempts to replicate Bem's "retroactive facilitation of recall" effect. *PLOS ONE, 7*(3). https://journals.plos.org/plosone/article/file?id=10.1371/journal.pone.0033423&type=printable

Ritter, S. M., Damian, R. I., Simonton, D. K., van Baaren, R. B., Strick, M., Derks, J., & Dijksterhuis, A. (2012). Diversifying experiences enhance cognitive flexibility. *Journal of Experimental Social Psychology, 48*, 961–964.

Rivera, M., Locke, A. E., Corre, T., Czamara, D., Wolf, C., Ching-Lopez, A., Milaneschi, Y., Kloiber, S., Cohen-Woods, S., Rucker, J., Aitchison, K. J., Bergmann, S., Boomsma, D. I., Craddock, N., Gill, M., Holsboer, F., Hottenga, J. J., Korszun, A., Kutalik, Z., ... McGuffin, P. (2017). Interaction between the *FTO* gene, body mass index and depression: Metaanalysis of 13701 individuals. *British Journal of Psychiatry, 211*, 70–76.

Rizzo, S. (2021, May 12). Ron Johnson's unscientific use of vaccine and death data. *The Washington Post*. https://www.washingtonpost.com/politics/2021/05/12/ron-johnsons-unscientific-use-vaccine-death-data/

Rizzolatti, G., Fadiga, L., Fogassi, L., & Gallese, V. (2002). From mirror neurons to imitation: Facts and speculations. In A. N. Meltzoff & W. Prinz (Eds.), *The imitative mind: Development, evolution, and brain bases* (pp. 247–266). Cambridge University Press.

Rizzolatti, G., Fogassi, L., & Gallese, V. (2006, November). Mirrors in the mind. *Scientific American*, pp. 54–61.

Roberson, D., Davidoff, J., Davies, I. R. L., & Shapiro, L. R. (2004). The development of color categories in two languages: A longitudinal study. *Journal of Experimental Psychology: General, 133*, 554–571.

Roberson, D., Davies, I. R. L., Corbett, G. G., & Vandervyver, M. (2005). Free-sorting of colors across cultures: Are there universal grounds for grouping? *Journal of Cognition and Culture, 5*, 349–386.

Roberti, J. W., Storch, E. A., & Bravata, E. A. (2004). Sensation seeking, exposure to psychosocial stressors, and body modifications in a college population. *Personality and Individual Differences, 37*, 1167–1177.

Roberto, C. A. (2020). How psychological insights can inform food policies to address unhealthy eating habits. *American Psychologist, 75*, 265–273.

Roberts, B. W., & DelVecchio, W. F. (2000). The rank-order consistency of personality traits from childhood to old age: A quantitative review of longitudinal studies. *Psychological Bulletin, 126*, 3–25.

Roberts, B. W., Donnellan, M. B., & Hill, P. L. (2013). Personality trait development in adulthood. In H. Tennen, J. Suls, & I. B. Weiner (Eds.), *Handbook of psychology, Vol. 5: Personality and social psychology* (2nd ed.). Wiley.

Roberts, B. W., Kuncel, N. R., Shiner, R., Caspi, A., & Goldberg, L. R. (2007). The power of personality: The comparative validity of personality traits, socioeconomic status, and cognitive ability for predicting important life outcomes. *Perspectives on Psychological Science, 2*, 313–345.

Roberts, B. W., Luo, J., Briley, D. A., Chow, P. I., Su, R., & Hill, P. L. (2017). A systematic review of personality trait change through intervention. *Psychological Bulletin, 143*, 117–141.

Roberts, J. A., & David, M. E. (2016). My life has become a major distraction from my cell phone: Partner phubbing and relationship satisfaction among romantic partners. *Computers in Human Behavior, 54*, 134–141.

Roberts, P., & Stewart, B. A. (2018). Defining the 'generalist specialist' niche for Pleistocene Homo sapiens. *Nature Human Behaviour, 2*, 542–550.

Roberts, T.-A. (1991). Determinants of gender differences in responsiveness to others' evaluations. *Dissertation Abstracts International, 51*(8–B).

Robine, J.-M., & Allard, M. (1999). Jeanne Calment: Validation of the duration of her life. In B. Jeune & J. W. Vaupel (Eds.). *Validation of exceptional longevity*. Odense University Press. https://www.demogr.mpg.de/books/odense/6/09.htm

Robins, L., & Regier, D. (Eds.). (1991). *Psychiatric disorders in America*. Free Press.

Robins, L. N., Davis, D. H., & Goodwin, D. W. (1974). Drug use by U.S. Army enlisted men in Vietnam: A follow-up on their return home. *American Journal of Epidemiology, 99*, 235–249.

Robinson, E., Sutin, A. R., Daly, M., & Jones, A. (2022). A systematic review and meta-analysis of longitudinal cohort studies comparing mental health before versus during the COVID-19 pandemic in 2020. *Journal of Affective Disorders, 296*, 567–576.

Robinson, F. P. (1970). *Effective study.* Harper & Row.

Robinson, J. P., & Martin, S. (2008). What do happy people do? *Social Indicators Research, 89*, 565–571.

Robinson, T. E., & Berridge, K. C. (2003). Addiction. *Annual Review of Psychology, 54*, 25–53.

Robinson, T. N., Borzekowski, D. L. G., Matheson, D. M., & Kraemer, H. C. (2007). Effects of fast food branding on young children's taste preferences. *Archives of Pediatric and Adolescent Medicine, 161*, 792–797.

Robinson, V. M. (1983). Humor and health. In P. E. McGhee & J. H. Goldstein (Eds.), *Handbook of humor research: Vol. II: Applied studies.* Springer-Verlag.

Robson, D. A., Allen, M. S., & Howard, S. J. (2020). Self-regulation in childhood as a predictor of future outcomes: A meta-analytic review. *Psychological Bulletin, 146*, 324–354.

Rochat, F. (1993). *How did they resist authority? Protecting refugees in Le Chambon during World War II* [Paper]. Presented at the American Psychological Association convention.

Rock, I., & Palmer, S. (1990, December). The legacy of Gestalt psychology. *Scientific American*, pp. 84–90.

Roddy, M. K., Walsh, L. M., Rothman, K., Hatch, S. G., & Doss, B. D. (2020). Meta-analysis of couple therapy: Effects across outcomes, designs, timeframes, and other moderators. *Journal of Consulting and Clinical Psychology, 88*(7), 583–596.

Rodgers, A. (2021a). Quoted by R. Demovsky [Interview]. ESPN. https://es.pn/3oKiG8j

Rodgers, A. (2021b). *Aaron Rodgers tells Pat McAfee his side of vaccine situation* [YouTube video]. [Watch at the 18-minute mark.] https://www.youtube.com/watch?v=K3jM13A7OEw&t=1082s

Rodin, J. (1986). Aging and health: Effects of the sense of control. *Science, 233*, 1271–1276.

Rodriguez, D. N., & Strange, D. (2015). False memories for dissonance inducing events. *Memory, 23*, 203–212.

Roediger, H. L. (1980). Memory metaphors in cognitive psychology. *Memory & Cognition, 8*, 231–246.

Roediger, H. L., III. (2013). Applying cognitive psychology to education: Translational educational science. *Psychological Science in the Public Interest, 14*, 1–3.

Roediger, H. L., III., & DeSoto, K. A. (2016). Was Alexander Hamilton president? *Psychological Science, 27*, 644–650.

Roediger, H. L., III, & Finn, B. (2010, March/April). The pluses of getting it wrong. *Scientific American Mind*, pp. 39–41.

Roediger, H. L., III, & Karpicke, J. D. (2006). Test-enhanced learning: Taking memory tests improves long-term retention. *Psychological Science, 17*, 249–255.

Roediger, H. L., III, & McDaniel, M. A. (2007). Illusory recollection in older adults: Testing Mark Twain's conjecture. In M. Garry & H. Hayne (Eds.), *Do justice and let the sky fall: Elizabeth F. Loftus and her contributions to science, law, and academic freedom.* Erlbaum.

Roediger, H. L., III, & McDermott, K. B. (1995). Creating false memories: Remembering words not presented in lists. *Journal of Experimental Psychology: Learning, Memory, and Cognition, 21*, 803–814.

Roediger, H. L., III, Meade, M. L., & Bergman, E. T. (2001). Social contagion of memory. *Psychonomic Bulletin & Review, 8*, 365–371.

Roediger, H. L., III, Wheeler, M. A., & Rajaram, S. (1993). Remembering, knowing, and reconstructing the past. In D. L. Medin (Ed.), *The psychology of learning and motivation: Advances in research and theory* (Vol. 30). Academic Press.

Roehling, P. V., Roehling, M. V., & Moen, P. (2001). The relationship between work-life policies and practices and employee loyalty: A life course perspective. *Journal of Family and Economic Issues, 22*, 141–170.

Roelofs, T. (2010, September 22). Somali refugee takes oath of U.S. citizenship year after his brother. *The Grand Rapids Press.* https://www.mlive.com/news/grand-rapids/2010/09/somali_refugee_takes_oath_of_u.html

Roepke, A. M. (2015). Psychosocial interventions and posttraumatic growth: A meta-analysis. *Journal of Consulting and Clinical Psychology, 83*, 129.

Roese, N. J., & Summerville, A. (2005). What we regret most ... and why. *Personality and Social Psychology Bulletin, 31*, 1273–1285.

Roese, N. J., & Vohs, K. D. (2012). Hindsight bias. *Perspectives on Psychological Science, 7*, 411–426.

Roesser, R. (1998). *What you should know about hearing conservation.* betterhearing.org/

Rogers, C. R. (1961). *On becoming a person: A therapist's view of psychotherapy.* Houghton Mifflin.

Rogers, C. R. (1980). *A way of being.* Houghton Mifflin.

Rogers, C. R. (1985, February). Quoted by M. L. Wallach & L. Wallach, How psychology sanctions the cult of the self. *Washington Monthly*, pp. 46–56.

Rogers, T., & Milkman, K. L. (2016). Reminders through association. *Psychological Science, 27*, 973–986.

Rogers, T., Moore, D. A., & Norton, M. I. (2017). The belief in a favorable future. *Psychological Science, 28*, 1290–1301.

Roghanizad, M. M., & Bohns, V. K. (2022). Should I ask over Zoom, phone, email, or in-person? Communication channel and predicted versus actual compliance. *Social Psychological and Personality Science, 13*, 1163–1172.

Rohner, R. P., & Veneziano, R. A. (2001). The importance of father love: History and contemporary evidence. *Review of General Psychology, 5*, 382–405.

Rohrer, J. M., Egloff, B., Kosinski, M., Stillwell, D., & Schmukle, S. C. (2018). In your eyes only? Discrepancies and agreement between self- and other-reports of personality from age 14 to 29. *Journal of Personality and Social Psychology, 115*, 304–320.

Rohrer, J. M., Egloff, B., & Schmukle, S. C. (2015). Examining the effects of birth order on personality. *PNAS, 112*, 14224–14229.

Roiser, J. P., Cook, L. J., Cooper, J. D., Rubinsztein, D. C., & Sahakian, B. J. (2005). Association of a functional polymorphism in the serotonin transporter gene with abnormal emotional processing in Ecstasy users. *American Journal of Psychiatry, 162*, 609–612.

Rokach, A., Orzeck, T., Moya, M., & Exposito, F. (2002). Causes of loneliness in North America and Spain. *European Psychologist, 7*, 70–79.

Romano, A., Balliet, D., Yamagishi, T., & Liu, J. H. (2017). Parochial trust and cooperation across 17 societies. *PNAS, 114*, 12702–12707.

Romelsjö, A., Danielsson, A., Wennberg, P., & Hibell, B. (2014). Cannabis use and drug related problems among adolescents in 27 European countries: The utility of the prevention paradox. *Nordic Studies on Alcohol and Drugs, 31*, 359–369.

Romney, M. (2021, January 6). *Romney condemns insurrection at U.S. Capitol* [Press release]. https://www.romney.senate.gov/romney-condemns-insurrection-us-capitol

Ronay, R., & von Hippel, W. (2010). The presence of an attractive woman elevates testosterone and physical risk taking in young men. *Social Psychology and Personality Science, 1*, 57–64.

Roohi, E. (2022, March 11). *$397 million donated in support for Ukraine so far.* Alliance. https://www.alliancemagazine.org/blog/345-million-in-support-donated-for-ukraine-so-far/

Roos, L. L., Wall-Wieler, E., & Lee, J. B. (2019). Poverty and early childhood outcomes. *Pediatrics, 143*(6). https://bit.ly/3DLzyov

Roper, K. R. (2016, July 19). Public Facebook post. https://www.facebook.com/kate.riffleroper/posts/1746348308987959

Roper, S. D., & Chaudhari, N. (2017). Taste buds: Cells, signals, and synapses. *Nature Reviews Neuroscience, 18*, 485–497.

Roque, L., Verissimo, M., Oliveira, T. F., & Oliveira, R. F. (2012). Attachment security and HPA axis reactivity to positive and challenging emotional situations in child-mother dyads in naturalistic settings. *Developmental Psychobiology, 54*, 401–411.

Rosch, E. (1978). Principles of categorization. In E. Rosch & B. L. Lloyd (Eds.), *Cognition and categorization* (pp. 27–48). Erlbaum.

Rose, A. J., & Rudolph, K. D. (2006). A review of sex differences in peer relationship processes: Potential trade-offs for the emotional and behavioral development of girls and boys. *Psychological Bulletin, 132*, 98–131.

Roselli, C. E., Larkin, K., Schrunk, J. M., & Stormshak, F. (2004). Sexual partner preference, hypothalamic morphology and aromatase in rams. *Physiology and Behavior, 83*, 233–245.

Roselli, C. E., Resko, J. A., & Stormshak, F. (2002). Hormonal influences on sexual partner preference in rams. *Archives of Sexual Behavior, 31*, 43–49.

Rosenbaum, M. (1986). The repulsion hypothesis: On the nondevelopment of relationships. *Journal of Personality and Social Psychology, 51*, 1156–1166.

Rosenberg, B. D., & Siegel, J. T. (2018). A 50-year review of psychological reactance theory: Do not read this article. *Motivation Science, 4*, 281–300.

Rosenberg, E. L., Zanesco, A. P., King, B. G., Aichele, S. R., Jacobs, R. L., Bridwell, D. A., MacLean, K. A., Shaver, P. R., Ferrer, E., Sahdra, B. K., Lavy, S., Wallace, B. A., & Saron, C. D. (2015). Intensive meditation training influences emotional responses to suffering. *Emotion, 15*, 775–790.

Rosenberg, N. A., Pritchard, J. K., Weber, J. L., Cann, H. M., Kidd, K. K., Zhivotosky, L. A., & Feldman, M. W. (2002). Genetic structure of human populations. *Science, 298*, 2381–2385.

Rosenberg, T. (2010, November 1). The opt-out solution. *The New York Times.* https://archive.nytimes.com/opinionator.blogs.nytimes.com/2010/11/01/the-opt-out-solution/

Rosenberg, T. (2019, December 17). Five who spread hope in 2019. *The New York Times.* https://www.nytimes.com/2019/12/17/opinion/spread-hope-2019.html

Rosenblum, L. D. (2013, January). A confederacy of senses. *Scientific American,* pp. 73–78.

Rosenfeld, M. J. (2014). Couple longevity in the era of same-sex marriage in the United States. *Journal of Marriage and Family, 76,* 905–911.

Rosenfeld, M. J., Reuben, T. J., & Falcon, M. (2011). *How couples meet and stay together, Waves 1, 2, and 3: Public version 3.04.* Machine Readable Data File. Stanford University Libraries. https://data.stanford.edu/hcmst

Rosenfeld, M. J., & Roesler, K. (2019). Cohabitation experience and cohabitation's association with marital dissolution. *Journal of Marriage and Family, 81*(1), 42–58.

Rosenfeld, M. J., & Roesler, K. (2021). Premarital cohabitation and marital dissolution: A reply to Manning, Smock, and Kuperberg. *Journal of Marriage and Family, 83,* 260–267.

Rosenfeld, M. J., Thomas, R. J., & Hausen, S. (2018). *How couples meet and stay together 2017 fresh sample.* Stanford University Libraries. Social Science Data Collection. https://data.stanford.edu/hcmst2017

Rosenfeld, M. J., Thomas, R. J., & Hausen. S. (2019). Disintermediating your friends: How online dating in the United States displaces other ways of meeting. PNAS, 116, 17753–17758.

Rosenquist, P. B., McCall, W. V., & Youssef, N. (2016). Charting the course of electroconvulsive therapy: Where have we been and where are we headed? *Psychiatric Annals, 46,* 647–651.

Rosenzweig, M. R. (1984). Experience, memory, and the brain. *American Psychologist, 39,* 365–376.

Rosenzweig, M. R., Krech, D., Bennett, E. L., & Diamond, M. C. (1962). Effects of environmental complexity and training on brain chemistry and anatomy: A replication and extension. *Journal of Comparative and Physiological Psychology, 55,* 429–437.

Roser, M. (2019). *Life expectancy.* Our World in Data. https://ourworldindata.org/life-expectancy

Roser, M. (2021, February 22). *The economies that are home to the poorest billions of people need to grow if we want global poverty to decline.* Our World in Data. https://ourworldindata.org/poverty-growth-needed

Rosling, H., Rönnlund, A. R., & Rosling, O. (2018). *Factfulness: Ten reasons we're wrong about the world—and why things are better than you think.* Flatiron Books.

Ross, E. L., Zivin, K., & Maixner, D. F. (2018). Cost-effectiveness of electroconvulsive therapy vs pharmacotherapy/psychotherapy for treatment-resistant depression in the United States. *JAMA Psychiatry, 75,* 713–722.

Ross, I. M., Silveri, M. M., Olson, E. A., Jensen, J. E., & Ren, B. (2021). Regional specificity and clinical correlates of cortical GABA alterations in posttraumatic stress disorder. *Neuropsychopharmacology, 47,* 1055–1062.

Ross, L. (1977). The intuitive psychologist and his shortcomings: Distortions in the attribution process. In L. Berkowitz (Ed.), *Advances in experimental social psychology* (Vol. 10). Academic Press.

Ross, L. (2018). From the fundamental attribution error to the truly fundamental attribution error and beyond: My research journey. *Perspectives on Psychological Science, 13,* 750–769.

Ross, M., McFarland, C., & Fletcher, G. J. O. (1981). The effect of attitude on the recall of personal histories. *Journal of Personality and Social Psychology, 40,* 627–634.

Ross, M., Xun, W. Q. E., & Wilson, A. E. (2002). Language and the bicultural self. *Personality and Social Psychology Bulletin, 28,* 1040–1050.

Rossi, A. S., & Rossi, P. H. (1993). *Of human bonding: Parent-child relations across the life course.* Aldine de Gruyter.

Rossi, P. J. (1968). Adaptation and negative aftereffect to lateral optical displacement in newly hatched chicks. *Science, 160,* 430–432.

Rossi, R., Socci, V., Pacitti, F., Di Lorenzo, G., Di Marco, A., Siracusano, A., & Rossi, A. (2020, May 28). Mental health outcomes among frontline and second-line health care workers during the Coronavirus Disease 2019 (COVID-19) pandemic in Italy. *JAMA Network Open, 3*(5). https://jamanetwork.com/journals/jamanetworkopen/fullarticle/2766378

Rotge, J.-Y., Lemogne, C., Hinfray, S., Huguet, P., Grynszpan, O., Tartour, E., George, N., & Fossati, P. (2015). A meta-analysis of the anterior cingulate contribution to social pain. *Social Cognitive and Affective Neuroscience, 10,* 19–27.

Roth, B., Becker, N., Romeyke, S., Schäfer, S., Domnick, F., & Spinath, F. M. (2015). Intelligence and school grades: A meta-analysis. *Intelligence, 53,* 118–137.

Roth, G. A., Mensah, G. A., Johnson, C. O., Addolorato, G., Ammirati, E., Baddour, L. M., Barengo, N. C., Beaton, A. Z., Benjamin, E. J., Benziger, C. P., Bonny, A., Brauer, M., Brodmann, M., Cahill, T. J., Carapetis, J., Catapano, A. L., Chugh, S. S., Cooper, L. T., Coresh, J., ... Fuster, V. (2020). Global burden of cardiovascular diseases and risk factors, 1990–2019: Update from the GBD 2019 study. *Journal of the American College of Cardiology, 76,* 2982–3021.

Roth, T., Roehrs, T., Zwyghuizen-Doorenbos, A., Stpeanski, E., & Witting, R. (1988). Sleep and memory. In I. Hindmarch & H. Ott (Eds.), *Benzodiazepine receptor ligands, memory and information processing.* Springer-Verlag.

Rothbart, M., Fulero, S., Jensen, C., Howard, J., & Birrell, P. (1978). From individual to group impressions: Availability heuristics in stereotype formation. *Journal of Experimental Social Psychology, 14,* 237–255.

Rothbaum, F., & Tsang, B. Y.-P. (1998). Lovesongs in the United States and China: On the nature of romantic love. *Journal of Cross-Cultural Psychology, 29,* 306–319.

Rothblum, E. D. (2018). Slim chance for permanent weight loss. *Archives of Scientific Psychology, 6,* 63–69.

Rothwell, J. (2020, December 28). *Fear and social distancing: Global perceptions of risk vary.* Gallup Blog. https://bit.ly/3myktOy

Rottenberg, J., & Hindash, A. C. (2015). Emerging evidence for emotion context insensitivity in depression. *Current Opinion in Psychology, 4,* 1–5.

Rottenberg, J., & Kashdan, T. B. (2022). Well-being after psychopathology: A transformational research agenda. *Current Directions in Psychological Science, 31*(3), 280–287.

Rottensteiner, M., Leskinen, T., Niskanen, E., Aaltonen, S., Mutikainen, S., Wikgren, J., Heikkilä, K., Kovanen, V., Kainulainen, H., Kaprio, J., Tarkka, I. M., & Kujala, U. M. (2015). Physical activity, fitness, glucose homeostasis, and brain morphology in twins. *Medicine and Science in Sports and Exercise, 47,* 509–518.

Rounds, J., & Su, R. (2014). The nature and power of interests. *Current Directions in Psychological Science, 23,* 98–103.

Rovee-Collier, C. (1989). The joy of kicking: Memories, motives, and mobiles. In P. R. Solomon, G. R. Goethals, C. M. Kelley, & B. R. Stephens (Eds.), *Memory: Interdisciplinary approaches* (pp. 151–179). Springer-Verlag.

Rovee-Collier, C. (1993). The capacity for long-term memory in infancy. *Current Directions in Psychological Science, 2,* 130–135.

Rovee-Collier, C. (1999). The development of infant memory. *Current Directions in Psychological Science, 8,* 80–85.

Rowe, D. C. (1990). As the twig is bent? The myth of child-rearing influences on personality development. *Journal of Counseling and Development, 68,* 606–611.

Rowe, D. C., Almeida, D. M., & Jacobson, K. C. (1999). School context and genetic influences on aggression in adolescence. *Psychological Science, 10,* 277–280.

Rowe, D. C., Vazsonyi, A. T., & Flannery, D. J. (1994). No more than skin deep: Ethnic and racial similarity in developmental process. *Psychological Review, 101,* 396.

Rowe, D. C., Vazsonyi, A. T., & Flannery, D. J. (1995). Ethnic and racial similarity in developmental process: A study of academic achievement. *Psychological Science, 6,* 33–38.

Roy, J., & Forest, G. (2018). Greater circadian disadvantage during evening games for the National Basketball Association (NBA), National Hockey League (NHL) and National Football League (NFL) teams travelling westward. *Journal of Sleep Research, 27,* 86–89.

Royal, K. (2019, September 14). *Who's responsible for employee engagement.* Gallup. https://www.gallup.com/workplace/266822/engaged-employees-differently.aspx

Røysamb, E., & Nes, R. B. (2019). The role of genetics in subjective well-being. *Nature Human Behavior, 3*(1), 3.

Rozin, P., Dow, S., Mosovitch, M., & Rajaram, S. (1998). What causes humans to begin and end a meal? A role for memory for what has been eaten, as evidenced by a study of multiple meal eating in amnesic patients. *Psychological Science, 9,* 392–396.

Rozin, P., Haddad, B., Nemeroff, C., & Slovic, P. (2015). Psychological aspects of the rejection of recycled water: Contamination, purification and disgust. *Judgment and Decision Making, 10,* 50–63.

Rozin, P., Millman, L., & Nemeroff, C. (1986). Operation of the laws of sympathetic magic in disgust and other domains. *Journal of Personality and Social Psychology, 50,* 703–712.

Ruau, D., Liu, L. Y., Clark, J. D., Angst, M. S., & Butte, A. J. (2012). Sex differences in reported pain across 11,000 patients captured in electronic medical records. *Journal of Pain, 13*, 228–234.

Ruback, R. B., Carr, T. S., & Hopper, C. H. (1986). Perceived control in prison: Its relation to reported crowding, stress, and symptoms. *Journal of Applied Social Psychology, 16*, 375–386.

Rubenstein, J. S., Meyer, D. E., & Evans, J. E. (2001). Executive control of cognitive processes in task switching. *Journal of Experimental Psychology: Human Perception and Performance, 27*, 763–797.

Rubenstein, L. M., Freed, R. D., Shapero, B. G., Fauber, R. L., & Alloy, L. B. (2016, June). Cognitive attributions in depression: Bridging the gap between research and clinical practice. *Journal of Psychotherapy Integration, 26*, 103–115.

Ruberton, P. M., Gladstone, J., & Lyubomirsky, S. (2016). How your bank balance buys happiness. *Emotion, 16*, 575–580.

Rubin, D. C., Rahhal, T. A., & Poon, L. W. (1998). Things learned in early adulthood are remembered best. *Memory and Cognition, 26*, 3–19.

Rubin, J. Z., Pruitt, D. G., & Kim, S. H. (1994). *Social conflict: Escalation, stalemate, and settlement*. McGraw-Hill.

Rubin, L. B. (1985). *Just friends: The role of friendship in our lives*. Harper & Row.

Rubinstein, G. (2016). Modesty doesn't become me: Narcissism and the Big Five among male and female candidates for the *Big Brother* TV show. *Journal of Individual Differences, 37*, 223–230.

Rubio, G., & López-Ibor, J. J. (2007). Generalized anxiety disorder: A 40-year follow-up study. *Acta Psychiatrica Scandinavica, 115*, 372–379.

Rubio-Fernández, P., & Geurts, B. (2013). How to pass the false-belief task before your fourth birthday. *Psychological Science, 24*, 27–33.

Ruchlis, H. (1990). *Clear thinking: A practical introduction*. Prometheus Books.

Ruddock, H. K., Brunstrom, J. M., Vartanian, L. R., & Higgs, S. (2019). A systematic review and meta-analysis of the social facilitation of eating. *American Journal of Clinical Nutrition, 110*, 842–861.

Rudert, S. C., Keller, M. D., Hales, A. H., Walker, M., & Greifeneder, R. (2019). Who gets ostracized? A personality perspective on risk and protective factors of ostracism. *Journal of Personality and Social Psychology, 118*(6), 1247–1268.

Rueger, S. Y., Malecki, C. K., Pyun, Y., Aycock, C., & Coyle, S. (2016). A meta-analytic review of the association between perceived social support and depression in childhood and adolescence. *Psychological Bulletin, 142*, 1017–1067.

Ruffin, C. L. (1993). Stress and health—little hassles vs. major life events. *Australian Psychologist, 28*, 201–208.

Ruiz, N. G., Horowitz, J. M., & Tamir, C. (2020). *Many Black and Asian Americans say they have experienced discrimination amid the COVID-19 outbreak*. Pew Research Center. https://www.pewresearch.org/social-trends/2020/07/01/many-black-and-asian-americans-say-they-have-experienced-discrimination-amid-the-covid-19-outbreak/

Rule, B. G., & Ferguson, T. J. (1986). The effects of media violence on attitudes, emotions, and cognitions. *Journal of Social Issues, 42*, 29–50.

Rumbaugh, D. M. (1977). *Language learning by a chimpanzee: The Lana project*. Academic Press.

Ruotsalainen, H., Kyngäs, H., Tammelin, T., & Kääriäinen, M. (2015). Systematic review of physical activity and exercise interventions on body mass indices, subsequent physical activity and psychological symptoms in overweight and obese adolescents. *Journal of Advanced Nursing, 71*, 2461–2477.

Rusanen, M., Kivipelto, M., Quesenberry, C. P., Jr., Zhou, J., & Whitmer, R. A. (2011). Heavy smoking in midlife and long-term risk of Alzheimer disease and vascular dementia. *Archives of Internal Medicine, 171*, 333–339.

Rusch, H. L., Rosario, M., Levison, L. M., Olivera, A., Livingston, W. S., Wu, T., & Gill, J. M. (2019). The effect of mindfulness meditation on sleep quality: A systematic review and meta-analysis of randomized controlled trials. *Annals of the New York Academy of Sciences, 1445*, 5–16.

Rushton, J. P. (1975). Generosity in children: Immediate and long-term effects of modeling, preaching, and moral judgment. *Journal of Personality and Social Psychology, 31*, 459–466.

Russell, B. (1930/1985). *The conquest of happiness*. Unwin Paperbacks.

Ruthsatz, J., & Urbach, J. B. (2012). Child prodigy: A novel cognitive profile places elevated general intelligence, exceptional working memory and attention to detail at the root of prodigiousness. *Intelligence, 40*, 419–426.

Rutledge, R. B., Skandali, N., Dayan, P., & Dolan, R. J. (2014). A computational and neural model of momentary subjective well-being. *PNAS, 111*, 12252–12257.

Rutz, C., Klump, B. C., Komarczyk, L., Leighton, R., Kramer, R., Wischnewski, S., Sugasawa, S., Morrissey, M. B., James, R., St. Clair, J. J., Switzer, R. A., & Masuda, B. M. (2016). Discovery of species-wide tool use in the Hawaiian crow. *Nature, 537*, 403–407.

Ruzich, E., Allison, C., Chakrabarti, B., Smith, P., Musto, H., Ring, H., & Baron-Cohen, S. (2015). Sex and STEM occupation predict autism-spectrum quotient (AQ) scores in half a million people. *PLOS ONE* 10(10). https://www.ncbi.nlm.nih.gov/pmc/articles/PMC4619566/

Ryan, B. (2016, March 8). *Women's life ratings get better with full-time jobs*. Gallup. https://news.gallup.com/opinion/gallup/189854/women-life-ratings-better-full-time-jobs.aspx

Ryan, C. P., & Kuzawa, C. W. (2020). Germline epigenetic inheritance: Challenges and opportunities for linking human paternal experience with offspring biology and health. *Evolutionary Anthropology, 29*(4), 180–200.

Ryan, P. (2015, December 15). Quoted by Editorial Board of *The New York Times* in, Don't blame mental illness for gun violence. *The New York Times*. https://www.nytimes.com/2015/12/16/opinion/dont-blame-mental-illness-for-gun-violence.html

Ryan, R. M., & Deci, E. L. (2000). Self-determination theory and the facilitation of intrinsic motivation, social development, and well-being. *American Psychologist, 55*, 68–78.

Ryan, R. M., & Deci, E. L. (2004). Avoiding death or engaging life as accounts of meaning and culture: Comment on Pyszczynski et al. (2004). *Psychological Bulletin, 130*, 473–477.

Rychlowska, M., Miyamoto, Y., Matsumoto, D., Hess, U., Gilboa-Schechtman, E., Kamble, S., Muluk, H., Masuda, T., & Niedenthal, P. M. (2015). Heterogeneity of long-history migration explains cultural differences in reports of emotional expressivity and the functions of smiles. *PNAS, 112*(19). https://www.pnas.org/doi/10.1073/pnas.1413661112

Rydell, M., Lundström, S., Gillberg, C., Lichtenstein, P., & Larsson, H. (2018). Has the attention deficit hyperactivity disorder phenotype become more common in children between 2004 and 2014? Trends over 10 years from a Swedish general population sample. *Journal of Child Psychology and Psychiatry, 59*, 863–871.

Rydell, R. J., Rydell, M. T., & Boucher, K. L. (2010). The effect of negative performance stereotypes on learning. *Journal of Personality and Social Psychology, 99*, 883–896.

Ryder, A. G., Yang, J., Zhu, X., Yao, S., Yi, J., Heine, S. J., & Bagby, R. M. (2008). The cultural shaping of depression: Somatic symptoms in China, psychological symptoms in North America? *Journal of Abnormal Psychology, 117*, 300–313.

Ryder, J. G., & Holtzheimer, P. E. (2016). Deep brain stimulation for depression: An update. *Current Behavioral Neuroscience Reports, 3*, 102–108.

Saad, L. (2002, November 21). *Most smokers wish they could quit*. Gallup News Service. https://news.gallup.com/poll/7270/most-smokers-wish-they-could-quit.aspx

Saad, L. (2019, July 25). *Marijuana use similar to new lower rate of cigarette smoking*. Gallup. https://news.gallup.com/poll/261569/marijuana-similar-new-lower-rate-cigarette-smoking.aspx

Sabbagh, M. A., Xu, F., Carlson, S. M., Moses, L. J., & Lee, K. (2006). The development of executive functioning and theory of mind: A comparison of Chinese and U.S. preschoolers. *Psychological Science, 17*, 74–81.

Sabesan, R., Schmidt, B. P., Tuten, W. S., & Roorda, A. (2016). The elementary representation of spatial and color vision in the human retina. *Science Advances, 2*. https://www.science.org/doi/10.1126/sciadv.1600797

Sabia, S., Fayosse, A., Dumurgier, J, van Hees, V. T., Paquet, C., Sommerlad, A., Kivimäki, M., Dugravot, A., & Singh-Manoux, A. (2021). Association of sleep duration in middle and old age with incidence of dementia. *Nature Communications, 12*(2289). https://www.nature.com/articles/s41467-021-22354-2

Sabini, J. (1986). Stanley Milgram (1933–1984). *American Psychologist, 41*, 1378–1379.

Sachdev, P., & Sachdev, J. (1997). Sixty years of psychosurgery: Its present status and its future. *Australian and New Zealand Journal of Psychiatry, 31*, 457–464.

Sackett, P. R., Kuncel, N. R., Beatty, A. S., Rigdon, J. L., Shen, W., & Kiger, T. B. (2012). The role of socioeconomic status in SAT-grade relationships and in college admissions decisions. *Psychological Science, 23*, 1000–1007.

Sacks, O. (1985). *The man who mistook his wife for a hat*. Summit Books.

Sadato, N., Pascual-Leone, A., Grafman, J., Ibanez, V., Deiber, M.-P., Dold, G., & Hallett, M. (1996). Activation of the primary visual cortex by Braille reading in blind subjects. *Nature, 380*, 526–528.

Sadler, M. S., Correll, J., Park, B., & Judd, C. M. (2012). The world is not Black and White: Racial bias in the decision to shoot in a multiethnic context. *Journal of Social Issues, 68*, 286–313.

Saffran, J. A. (2009). What can statistical learning tell us about infant learning? In A. Woodward & A. Needham (Eds.), *Learning and the infant mind*. Oxford University Press.

Saffran, J. R., Aslin, R. N., & Newport, E. L. (1996). Statistical learning by 8-month-old infants. *Science, 274*, 1926–1928.

Sagan, C. (1977). *The dragons of Eden: Speculations on the evolution of human intelligence*. Ballantine.

Sagan, C. (1979). *Broca's brain: Reflections on the romance of science.* Random House.

Sagan, C. (1987, February 1). *The fine art of baloney detection* [PDF file]. https://www.inf.fu-berlin.de/lehre/pmo/eng/Sagan-Baloney.pdf

Sai, B., Liu, L., Li, L. H., Compton, B. J., & Heyman, G. D. (2020). Promoting honesty through overheard conversations. *Developmental Psychology, 56*(6), 1073–1079.

Saint Louis, C. (2017, February 2). Pregnant women turn to marijuana, perhaps harming infants. *The New York Times*. https://www.nytimes.com/2017/02/02/health/marijuana-and-pregnancy.html

Saito, A., Shinozuka, K., Ito, Y., & Hasegawa, T. (2019). Domestic cats (Felis catus) discriminate their names from other words. *Scientific Reports, 9*. https://www.nature.com/articles/s41598-019-40616-4

Sajous-Turner, A., Anderson, N. E., Widdows, M., Nyalakanti, P., Harenski, K., Harenski, C., Koenigs, M., Decety, J., & Kiehl, K. A. (2020). Aberrant brain gray matter in murderers. *Brain Imaging and Behavior, 14*(5), 2050–2061.

Sakaluk, J. K., Williams, A. J., Kilshaw, R. E., & Rhyner, K. T. (2019). Evaluating the evidential value of empirically supported psychological treatments (ESTs): A meta-scientific review. *Journal of Abnormal Psychology, 128*, 500–509.

Saks, E. (2007, August 27). *A memoir of schizophrenia*. Time. http://content.time.com/time/arts/article/0,8599,1656592,00.html

Sala, G., Tatlidil, K. S., & Gobet, F. (2021). Still no evidence that exergames improve cognitive ability: A commentary on Stanmore et al. (2017). *Neuroscience & Biobehavioral Reviews, 123*, 352–353.

Salas-Wright, C., Vaughn, M. G., Goings, T. C., Miller, D. P., & Schwartz, S. J. (2018). Immigrants and mental disorders in the United States: New evidence on the healthy migrant hypothesis. *Psychiatry Research, 267*, 438–445.

Salas-Wright, C. P., Vaughn, M. G., Hodge, D. R., & Perron, B. E. (2012). Religiosity profiles of American youth in relation to substance use, violence, and delinquency. *Journal of Youth and Adolescence, 41*, 1560–1575.

Salazar Kämpf, M., Liebermann, H., Kerschreiter, R., Krause, S., Nestler, S., & Schmukle, S. C. (2018). Disentangling the sources of mimicry: Social relations analyses of the link between mimicry and liking. *Psychological Science, 29*, 131–138.

Salehi, I., Hosseini, S. M., Haghighi, M., Jahangard, L., Bajoghli, H., Gerber, M., Pühse, U., Holsboer-Trachsler, E., & Brand, S. (2016). Electroconvulsive therapy (ECT) and aerobic exercise training (AET) increased plasma BDNF and ameliorated depressive symptoms in patients suffering from major depressive disorder. *Journal of Psychiatric Research, 76*, 1–8.

Salgado, J. F., & Moscoso, S. (2002). Comprehensive meta-analysis of the construct validity of the employment interview. *European Journal of Work and Organizational Psychology, 11*, 299–326.

Salk, R. H., Hyde, J. S., & Abramson, L. Y. (2017). Gender differences in depression in representative national samples: Meta-analyses of diagnoses and symptoms. *Psychological Bulletin, 143*, 783–822.

Salles, A., Bjaalie, J. G., Evers, K., Farisco, M., Fothergill, B. T., Guerrero, M., Maslen, H., Muller, J., Prescott, T., Stahl, B. C., Walter, H., Zilles, K., & Amunts, K. (2019). The Human Brain Project: Responsible brain research for the benefit of society. *Neuron, 101*, 380–384.

Salmon, P. (2001). Effects of physical exercise on anxiety, depression, and sensitivity to stress: A unifying theory. *Clinical Psychology Review, 21*, 33–61.

Salovey, P. (1990, January/February). Interview. *American Scientist*, pp. 25–29.

Salthouse, T. A. (2010). Selective review of cognitive aging. *Journal of the International Neuropsychological Society, 16*, 754–760.

Salthouse, T. A. (2014). Why are there different age relations in cross-sectional and longitudinal comparisons of cognitive functioning? *Current Directions in Psychological Science, 23*, 252–256.

Salthouse, T. A., & Mandell, A. R. (2013). Do age-related increases in tip-of-the tongue experiences signify episodic memory impairments? *Psychological Science, 24*, 2489–2497.

SAMHSA (Substance Abuse and Mental Health Services Administration). (2019). *Results from the 2018 National Survey on Drug Use and Health: Graphics from the key findings report*. Center for Behavioral Health Statistics and Quality, Substance Abuse and Mental Health Services Administration, U.S. Department of Health and Human Services.

SAMHSA. (2021). *Key substance use and mental health indicators in the United States: Results from the 2020 National Survey on Drug Use and Health* [PDF file]. HHS Publication No. PEP21-07-01-003, NSDUH Series H-56. Center for Behavioral Health Statistics and Quality. https://tinyurl.com/y2z8c9tz

Samson, D. R., Crittenden, A. N., Mabulla, I. A., Mabulla, A. Z. P., & Nunn, C. L. (2017). Chronotype variation drives night-time sentinel-like behaviour in hunter-gatherers [PDF file]. *Proceedings of the Royal Society B*, 284(1858). https://bit.ly/3DmoiOy

Samuels, J., & Nestadt, G. (1997). Epidemiology and genetics of obsessive-compulsive disorder. *International Review of Psychiatry, 9*, 61–71.

Samuelsson, J. G., Sundaram, P., Khan, S., Sereno, M. I., & Hämäläinen, M. S. (2020). Detectability of cerebellar activity with magnetoencephalography and electroencephalography. *Human Brain Mapping, 41*(9), 2357–2372.

Sánchez-Ávarez, N., Extremera, N., & Fernández-Berrocal, P. (2016). The relation between emotional intelligence and subjective well-being: A meta-analytic investigation. *Journal of Positive Psychology, 11*, 276–285.

Sanchez-Roige, S., Palmer, A. A., Fontanillas, P., Elson, S. L., 23andMe Research Team, the Substance Use Disorder Working Group of the Psychiatric Genomics Consortium, Adams, M. J., Howard, D. M., Edenberg, H. J., Davies, G., Crist, R. C., Deary, I. J., McIntosh, A. M., & Clarke, T. (2019). Genome-wide association study meta-analysis of the alcohol use disorders identification test (AUDIT) in two population-based cohorts. *American Journal of Psychiatry, 176*, 107–118.

Sánchez-Villegas, A., Henríquez-Sánchez, P., Ruiz-Canela, M., Lahortiga, F., Molero, P., Toledo, E., & Martínez-González, M. A. (2015). A longitudinal analysis of diet quality scores and the risk of incident depression in the SUN Project. *BMC Medicine, 13*, 1.

Sanders, A. R., Beecham, G. W., Guo, S., Dawood, K., Rieger, G., Badner, J. A., Gershon, E. S., Krishnappa, R. S., Kolundzija, A. B., Duan, J., MGS Collaboration, Gejman, P. V., Bailey, J. M., & Martin, E. R. (2017). Genome-wide association study of male sexual orientation. *Nature: Scientific Reports, 7*(1). https://www.nature.com/articles/s41598-017-15736-4

Sanders, A. R., Martin, E. R., Beecham, G. W., Guo, S., Dawood, K. Rieger, G., Badner, J. A., Gershon, E. S., Krishnappa, R. S., Kolundzija, A. B., Duan, J., Gejman, P. V., & Bailey, J. M. (2015). Genome-wide scan demonstrates significant linkage for male sexual orientation. *Psychological Medicine, 45*, 1379–1388.

Sandhu, A., Seth, M., & Gurm, H. S. (2014). Daylight savings time and myocardial infarction. *Open Heart, 1*(1). https://openheart.bmj.com/content/1/1/e000019

Sandler, W., Meir, I., Padden, C., & Aronoff, M. (2005). The emergence of grammar: Systematic structure in a new language. *PNAS, 102*, 2261–2265.

Sandstrom, G. M., & Dunn, E. W. (2014). Is efficiency overrated?: Minimal social interactions lead to belonging and positive affect. *Social Psychological and Personality Science, 5*(4), 437–442.

Sanson, M., Strange, D., & Garry, M. (2019). Trigger warnings are trivially helpful at reducing negative affect, intrusive thoughts, and avoidance. *Clinical Psychological Science, 7*, 778–793.

Santangelo, V., Pedale, T., Macrí, S., & Campolongo, P. (2020). Enhanced cortical specialization to distinguish older and newer memories in highly superior autobiographical memory. *Cortex, 128*, 476–483.

Santomauro, D. F., Melen, S., Mitchison, D., Vos, T., Whiteford, H., & Ferrari, A. J. (2021). The hidden burden of eating disorders: An extension of estimates from the global burden of disease study 2019. *Lancet Psychiatry, 8*, 320–328.

Santomauro, J., & French, C. C. (2009). Terror in the night. *The Psychologist, 22*, 672–675.

Santos, H. C., Varnum, M. E. W., & Grossmann, I. (2017). Global increases in individualism. *Psychological Science, 28*, 1228–1239.

Sanz, C., Blicher, A., Dalke, K., Gratton-Fabri, L., McClure-Richards, T., & Fouts, R. (1998, Winter–Spring). Enrichment object use: Five chimpanzees' use of temporary and semi-permanent enrichment objects. *Friends of Washoe, 19*(1,2), 9–14.

Sanz, C., Morgan, D., & Gulick, S. (2004). New insights into chimpanzees, tools, and termites from the Congo Basin. *American Naturalist, 164*, 567–581.

Sapadin, L. A. (1988). Friendship and gender: Perspectives of professional men and women. *Journal of Social and Personal Relationships, 5*, 387–403.

Sapolsky, R. (2003). Taming stress. *Scientific American, 289*, 86–95.

Sapolsky, R. (2005). The influence of social hierarchy on primate health. *Science, 308*, 648–652.

Sapolsky, R. (2010, November 14). This is your brain on metaphors. *The New York Times.* https://opinionator.blogs.nytimes.com/2010/11/14/this-is-your-brain-on-metaphors/

Sapolsky, R. (2017). *Behave: The biology of humans at our best and worst.* Penguin.

Saposnik, G., Redelmeier, D., Ruff, C. C., & Tobler, P. N. (2016). Cognitive biases associated with medical decisions: A systematic review. *BMC Medical Informatics and Decision Making, 16*, 138.

Sarrionandia, A., & Mikolajczak, M. (2020). A meta-analysis of the possible behavioural and biological variables linking trait emotional intelligence to health. *Health Psychology Review, 14*, 220–244.

Sarro, E. C., Wilson, D. A., & Sullivan, R. M. (2014). Maternal regulation of infant brain state. *Current Biology, 24*, 1664–1669.

Sarwer, D. B., & Heinberg, L. J. (2020). A review of the psychosocial aspects of clinically severe obesity and bariatric surgery. *American Psychologist, 75*, 252–264.

Sassenberg, K., & Ditrich, L. (2019). Research in social psychology changed between 2011 and 2016: Larger sample sizes, more self-report measures, and more online studies. *Advances in Methods and Practices in Psychological Science, 2*(2), 107–114.

Sasser, T. R., Bierman, K. L., Heinrichs, B., & Nix, R. L. (2017). Preschool intervention can promote sustained growth in the executive-function skills of children exhibiting early deficits. *Psychological Science, 28*, 1719–1730.

Sato, K. (1987). Distribution of the cost of maintaining common resources. *Journal of Experimental Social Psychology, 23*, 19–31.

Sauce, B., & Matzel, L. D. (2018). The paradox of intelligence: Heritability and malleability coexist in hidden gene-environment interplay. *Psychological Bulletin, 144*, 26–47.

Saulny, S. (2006, June 21). A legacy of the storm: Depression and suicide. *The New York Times.* https://www.nytimes.com/2006/06/21/us/a-legacy-of-the-storm-depression-and-suicide.html

Saunders, G. R. B., Elkins, I. J., Christensen, K., & McGue, M. (2018). The relationship between subjective well-being and mortality within discordant twin pairs from two independent samples. *Psychology and Aging, 33*, 439–447.

Saunders-Scott, D., Braley, M. B., & Stennes-Spidahl, N. (2018). Traditional and psychological factors associated with academic success: Investigating best predictors of college retention. *Motivation and Emotion, 42*, 459–465.

Saurat, M., Agbakou, M., Attigui, P., Golmard, J., & Arnulf, I. (2011). Walking dreams in congenital and acquired paraplegia. *Consciousness and Cognition, 20*, 1425–1432.

Savage, J. E., Jansen, P. R., Stringer, S., Watanabe, K., Bryois, J., de Leeuw, C. A., Nagel, M., Awasthi, S., Barr, P. B., Coleman, J., Grasby, K. L., Hammerschlag, A. R., Kaminski, J. A., Karlsson, R., Krapohl, E., Lam, M., Nygaard, M., Reynolds, C. A., Trampush, J. W., ... Grasby, K. L. (2018). Genome-wide association meta-analysis in 269,867 individuals identifies new genetic and functional links to intelligence. *Nature Genetics, 50*, 912–919.

Savage-Rumbaugh, E. S., Murphy, J., Sevcik, R. A., Brakke, K. E., Williams, S. L., & Rumbaugh, D. M., with commentary by Bates, E. (1993). Language comprehension in ape and child. *Monographs of the Society for Research in Child Development, 58*(233), 1–222.

Savage-Rumbaugh, E. S., Rumbaugh, D., & Fields, W. M. (2009). Empirical Kanzi: The ape language controversy revisited. *Skeptic, 15*, 25–33.

Savani, K., & Rattan, A. (2012). A choice mind-set increases the acceptance and maintenance of wealth inequality. *Psychological Science, 23*, 796–804.

Savelieva, K., Pulkki-Råback, L., Jokela, M., Kubzansky, L. D., Elovainio, M., Mikkilä, V., Tammelin, T., Juonala, M., Raitakari, O. T., & Keltikangas-Järvinen, L. (2016). Intergenerational transmission of socioeconomic position and ideal cardiovascular health: 32-year follow-up study. *Health Psychology, 36*, 270–279.

Savic, I., Berglund, H., & Lindstrom, P. (2005). Brain response to putative pheromones in homosexual men. *PNAS, 102*, 7356–7361.

Savin-Williams, R., Joyner, K., & Rieger, G. (2012). Prevalence and stability of self-reported sexual orientation identity during young adulthood. *Archives of Sexual Behavior, 41*, 103–110.

Savitsky, K., Epley, N., & Gilovich, T. D. (2001). Do others judge us as harshly as we think? Overestimating the impact of our failures, shortcomings, and mishaps. *Journal of Personality and Social Psychology, 81*, 44–56.

Savitsky, K., & Gilovich, T. D. (2003). The illusion of transparency and the alleviation of speech anxiety. *Journal of Experimental Social Psychology, 39*, 618–625.

Savoy, C., & Beitel, P. (1996). Mental imagery for basketball. *International Journal of Sport Psychology, 27*, 454–462.

Sawyer, A. C. P., Miller-Lewis, L. R., Searle, A. K., & Sawyer, M. G. (2015). Is greater improvement in early self-regulation associated with fewer behavioral problems later in childhood? *Developmental Psychology, 51*, 1740–1755.

Sawyer, S. M., Azzopardi, P. S., Wickremarathne, D., & Patton, G. C. (2018). The age of adolescence. *Lancet Child and Adolescent Health, 2*, 223–228.

Saxton, T. K., McCarty, K., Caizley, J., McCarrick, D., & Pollet, T. V. (2020). Hungry people prefer larger bodies and objects: The importance of testing boundary effects. *British Journal of Psychology, 111*, 492–507.

Sayal, K., Chudal, R., Hinkka-Yli-Salomäki, S., Joelsson, P., & Sourander, A. (2017). Relative age within the school year and diagnosis of attention-deficit hyperactivity disorder: A nationwide population-based study. *Lancet Psychiatry, 4*(11), 868–875.

Sayette, M. A., Loewenstein, G., Griffin, K. M., & Black, J. J. (2008). Exploring the cold-to-hot empathy gap in smokers. *Psychological Science, 19*, 926–932.

Sayette, M. A., Reichle, E. D., & Schooler, J. W. (2009). Lost in the sauce: The effects of alcohol on mind wandering. *Psychological Science, 20*, 747–752.

Sayette, M. A., Schooler, J. W., & Reichle, E. D. (2010). Out for a smoke: The impact of cigarette craving on zoning out during reading. *Psychological Science, 21*, 26–30.

Sayre, R. F. (1979). The parents' last lessons. In D. D. Van Tassel (Ed.), *Aging, death, and the completion of being.* University of Pennsylvania Press.

Sbarra, D. A., Briskin, J. L., & Slatcher, R. B. (2019). Smartphones and close relationships: The case for an evolutionary mismatch. *Perspectives on Psychological Science, 14*, 596–618.

Sbarra, D. A., Hasselmo, K., & Bourassa, K. J. (2015). Divorce and health: Beyond individual differences. *Current Directions in Psychological Science, 24*, 109–113.

Scaini, S., Belotti, R., Ogliari, A., & Battaglia, M. (2016). A comprehensive meta-analysis of cognitive-behavioral interventions for social anxiety disorder in children and adolescents. *Journal of Anxiety Disorders, 42*, 105–112.

Scangos, K. W., Khambhati, A. N., Daly, P. M., Makhoul, G. S., Sugrue, L. P., Zamanian, H., Liu, T. X., Rao, V. R., Sellers, K. K., Dawes, H. E., Starr, P. A., Krystal, A. D., & Chang, E. F. (2021). Closed-loop neuromodulation in an individual with treatment-resistant depression. *Nature Medicine, 10*, 1696–1700.

Scangos, K. W., Makhoul, G. S., Sugrue, L. P., Chang, E. F., & Krystal, A. D. (2021). State-dependent responses to intracranial brain stimulation in a patient with depression. *Nature Medicine, 27*, 229–231.

Scarborough, E., & Furumoto, L. (1987). *Untold lives: The first generation of American women psychologists.* Columbia University Press.

Scarf, D., Boy, K., Reinert, A. U., Devine, J., Güntürkün, O., & Colombo, M. (2016). Orthographic processing in pigeons (*Columba livia*). *PNAS, 113*, 11272–11276.

Scarr, S. (1984, May). What's a parent to do? A conversation with E. Hall. *Psychology Today*, pp. 58–63.

Scarr, S. (1990). Back cover comments on J. Dunn & R. Plomin (1990), *Separate lives: Why siblings are so different.* Basic Books.

Schab, F. R. (1991). Odor memory: Taking stock. *Psychological Bulletin, 109*, 242–251.

Schachter, S., & Singer, J. E. (1962). Cognitive, social and physiological determinants of emotional state. *Psychological Review, 69*, 379–399.

Schacter, D. L. (1992). Understanding implicit memory: A cognitive neuroscience approach. *American Psychologist, 47*, 559–569.

Schacter, D. L. (1996). *Searching for memory: The brain, the mind, and the past.* Basic Books.

Schaefer, J. D., Hamdi, N. R., Malone, S. M., & Iacono, W. G. (2021). Associations between adolescent cannabis use and young-adult functioning in three longitudinal twin studies. *PNAS, 118*(14). https://www.pnas.org/doi/10.1073/pnas.2013180118

Schaefer, J. D., Moffitt, T. E., Arseneault, L., Danese, A., Fisher, H. L., Houts, R., Sheridan, M. A., Wertz, J., & Caspi, A. (2018). Adolescent victimization and early-adult psychopathology: Approaching causal inference using a longitudinal twin study to rule out noncausal explanations. *Clinical Psychological Science, 6*, 352–371.

Schaefer, M., Cherkasskiy, L., Denke, C., Spies, C., Song, H., Malahy, S., Heinz, A., Ströhle, A., & Bargh, J. A. (2018). Incidental haptic sensations influence judgment of crimes. *Scientific Reports, 8*, 6039.

Schaie, K. W. (1994). The life course of adult intellectual abilities. *American Psychologist, 49*, 304–313.

Schaie, K. W., & Geiwitz, J. (1982). *Adult development and aging*. Little, Brown.

Schalbetter, S. M., Von Arx, A. S., Cruz-Ochoa, N., Dawson, K., Ivanov, A., Mueller, F. S., Lin, H.-Y., Amport, R., Mildenberger, W., Mattei, D., Beule, D., Földy, C., Greter, M., Notter, T., & Meyer, U. (2022). Adolescence is a sensitive period for prefrontal microglia to act on cognitive development. *Science Advances, 8*(9). https://www.science.org/doi/10.1126/sciadv.abi6672

Schalock, R. L., Borthwick-Duffy, S., Bradley, V. J., Buntinx, W. H. E., Coulter, D. L., Craig, E. M. (2010). *Intellectual disability: Definition, classification, and systems of supports* (11th ed.). American Association on Intellectual and Developmental Disabilities.

Schatzberg, A. F. (2019). A word to the wise about intranasal esketamine. *American Journal of Psychiatry, 176*, 422–424.

Schaumberg, K., Reilly, E. E., Gorrell, S., Levinson, C. A., Farrell, N. R., Brown, T. A., Smith, K. M., Schaefer, L. M., Essayli, J. H., Haynos, A. F., & Anderson, L. M. (2021). Conceptualizing eating disorder psychopathology using an anxiety disorders framework: Evidence and implications for exposure-based clinical research. *Clinical Psychology Review, 83*. https://doi.org/10.1016/j.cpr.2020.101952

Scheier, M. F., Swanson, J. D., Barlow, M. A., Greenhouse, J. B., Wrosch, C., & Tindle, H. A. (2021). Optimism versus pessimism as predictors of physical health: A comprehensive reanalysis of dispositional optimism research. *American Psychologist, 76*, 529–548.

Schein, E. H. (1956). The Chinese indoctrination program for prisoners of war: A study of attempted brainwashing. *Psychiatry, 19*, 149–172.

Schiffenbauer, A., & Schiavo, R. S. (1976). Physical distance and attraction: An intensification effect. *Journal of Experimental Social Psychology, 12*, 274–282.

Schiffer, L. P., & Roberts, T. A. (2018). The paradox of happiness: Why are we not doing what we know makes us happy? *Journal of Positive Psychology, 13*, 252–259.

Schiffman, J., Abrahamson, A., Cannon, T., LaBrie, J., Parnas, J., Schulsinger, F., & Mednick, S. (2001). Early rearing factors in schizophrenia. *International Journal of Mental Health, 30*, 3–16.

Schilt, T., de Win, M. M. L, Koeter, M., Jager, G., Korf, D. J., van den Brink, W., & Schmand, B. (2007). Cognition in novice Ecstasy users with minimal exposure to other drugs. *Archives of General Psychiatry, 64*, 728–736.

Schimel, J., Arndt, J., Pyszczynski, T., & Greenberg, J. (2001). Being accepted for who we are: Evidence that social validation of the intrinsic self reduces general defensiveness. *Journal of Personality and Social Psychology, 80*, 35–52.

Schink, T., Kreutz, G., Busch, V., Pigeot, I., & Ahrens, W. (2014). Incidence and relative risk of hearing disorders in professional musicians. *Occupational and Environmental Medicine, 71*, 472–476.

Schlegel, A. A., & Barry, H. (1991). *Adolescence: An anthropological inquiry*. Free Press.

Schlesinger, T. (2013). Racial disparities in pretrial diversion: An analysis of outcomes among men charged with felonies and processed in state courts. *Race and Justice, 3*(3), 210–238.

Schlomer, G. L., Del Giudice, M., & Ellis, B. J. (2011). Parent-offspring conflict theory: An evolutionary framework for understanding conflict within human families. *Psychological Review, 118*, 496–521.

Schloss, J. (2009). Does evolution explain human nature? Totally, for a Martian. In *Celebrating the bicentenary of the birth of Charles Darwin* [PDF file]. John Templeton Foundation. https://nanopdf.com/download/does-evolution-explain-human-nature_pdf

Schmid, S. M., Hallschmid, M., & Schultes, B. (2015). The metabolic burden of sleep loss. *Lancet Diabetes & Endocrinology, 3*, 52–62.

Schmidt, A., Dirk, J., & Schmiedek, F. (2019). The importance of peer relatedness at school for affective well-being in children: Between- and within-person associations. *Social Development, 28*, 873–892.

Schmidt, F. L., & Hunter, J. (2004). General mental ability in the world of work: Occupational attainment and job performance. *Journal of Personality and Social Psychology, 86*, 162–173.

Schmidt, F. L., & Hunter, J. E. (1998). The validity and utility of selection methods in personnel psychology: Practical and theoretical implications of 85 years of research findings. *Psychological Bulletin, 124*, 262–274.

Schmidt, I. D., Pfeifer, B. J., & Strunk, D. R. (2019). Putting the "cognitive" back in cognitive therapy: Sustained cognitive change as a mediator of in-session insights and depressive symptom improvement. *Journal of Consulting and Clinical Psychology, 87*, 446–456.

Schmidt, S. (2018, April 4). Twin sisters known for battle with debilitating OCD die in possible 'suicide pact' [Video]. *The Washington Post*. https://tinyurl.com/5xtvhazr

Schmitt, D. P. (2003). Universal sex differences in the desire for sexual variety; tests from 52 nations, 6 continents, and 13 islands. *Journal of Personality and Social Psychology, 85*, 85–104.

Schmitt, D. P. (2007). Sexual strategies across sexual orientations: How personality traits and culture relate to sociosexuality among gays, lesbians, bisexuals, and heterosexuals. *Journal of Psychology and Human Sexuality, 18*, 183–214.

Schmitt, D. P., & Allik, J. (2005). Simultaneous administration of the Rosenberg Self-esteem Scale in 53 nations: Exploring the universal and culture-specific features of global self-esteem. *Journal of Personality and Social Psychology, 89*, 623–642.

Schmitt, D. P., & Fuller, R. C. (2015). On the varieties of sexual experience: Cross-cultural links between religiosity and human mating strategies. *Psychology of Religion and Spirituality, 7*, 314–326.

Schmitt, D. P., Allik, J., McCrae, R. R., & Benet-Martínez, V. (2007). The geographic distribution of Big Five personality traits: Patterns and profiles of human self-description across 56 nations. *Journal of Cross-Cultural Psychology, 38*, 173–212.

Schmitt, D. P., & Pilcher, J. J. (2004). Evaluating evidence of psychological adaptation: How do we know one when we see one? *Psychological Science, 15*, 643–649.

Schmunk, R. (2020). *B.C. marks 3rd straight month with more than 170 overdose deaths*. CBC. https://www.cbc.ca/news/canada/british-columbia/bc-overdose-numbers-july-2020-1.5698795

Schnall, E., Wassertheil-Smoller, S., Swencionis, C., Zemon, V., Tinker, L., O'Sullivan, M. J., Van Horn, L., & Goodwin, M. (2010). The relationship between religion and cardiovascular outcomes and all-cause mortality in the women's health initiative observational study. *Psychology and Health, 25*, 249–263.

Schnall, S., Haidt, J., Clore, G. L., & Jordan, A. (2008). Disgust as embodied moral judgment. *Personality and Social Psychology Bulletin, 34*, 1096–1109.

Schneider, B., Yost, A. B., Kropp, A., Kind, C., & Lam, H. (2018). Workforce engagement: What it is, what drives it, and why it matters for organizational performance. *Journal of Organizational Behavior, 39*(4), 462–480.

Schneider, S. L. (2001). In search of realistic optimism: Meaning, knowledge, and warm fuzziness. *American Psychologist, 56*, 250–263.

Schneider, W. J., & McGrew, K. S. (2012). The Cattell-Horn-Carroll model of intelligence In D. P. Flanagan & P. L. Harrison (Eds.), *Contemporary intellectual assessment: Theories, tests, and issues* (3rd ed.). Guilford Press.

Schneier, B. (2007, May 17). *Virginia Tech lesson: Rare risks breed irrational responses*. Schneir on Security. https://www.schneier.com/essays/archives/2007/05/virginia_tech_lesson.html

Schnur, J. B., Kafer, I., Marcus, C., & Montgomery, G. H. (2008). Hypnosis to manage distress related to medical procedures: A meta-analysis. *Contemporary Hypnosis, 25*, 114–128.

Schoeneman, T. J. (1994). Individualism. In V. S. Ramachandran (Ed.), *Encyclopedia of human behavior* (Vol. 2, pp. 631–643). Academic Press.

Schofield, J. W. (1986). Black-White contact in desegregated schools. In M. Hewstone & R. Brown (Eds.), *Contact and conflict in intergroup encounters* (pp. 79–92). Basil Blackwell.

Scholaske, L., Buss, C., Wadhwa, P. D., & Entringer, S. (2018). Acculturation and interleukin (IL)-6 concentrations across pregnancy among Mexican-American women. *Brain, Behavior, and Immunity, 73*, 731–735.

Scholtz, S., Miras, A. D., Chhina, N., Prechtl, C. G., Sleeth, M. L., Daud, N. M., Ismail, N. A. Durighel, G., Ahmed, A. R., Olbers, T., Vincent, R. P., Alaghband-Zadeh, J., Ghatei, M. A., Waldman, A. D., Frost, G. S., Bell,

J. D., le Roux, C. W., & Goldstone, A. P. (2013). Obese patients after gastric bypass surgery have lower brain-hedonic responses to food than after gastric banding. *Gut, 63,* 891–902.

Schonfield, D., & Robertson, B. A. (1966). Memory storage and aging. *Canadian Journal of Psychology, 20,* 228–236.

Schooler, J. W., Gerhard, D., & Loftus, E. F. (1986). Qualities of the unreal. *Journal of Experimental Psychology: Learning, Memory, and Cognition, 12,* 171–181.

Schorr, E. A., Fox, N.A., van Wassenhove, V., & Knudsen, E. I. (2005). Auditory-visual fusion in speech perception in children with cochlear implants. *PNAS, 102,* 18748–18750.

Schrauzer, G. N., & Shrestha, K. P. (1990). Lithium in drinking water and the incidences of crimes, suicides, and arrests related to drug addictions. *Biological Trace Element Research, 25,* 105–113.

Schrauzer, G. N., & Shrestha, K. P. (2010). Lithium in drinking water. *British Journal of Psychiatry, 196,* 159.

Schreiber, F. R. (1973). *Sybil.* Regnery.

Schroeder, J., Caruso, E. M., & Epley, N. (2016). Many hands make overlooked work: Over-claiming of responsibility increases with group size. *Journal of Experimental Psychology: Applied, 22,* 238–246.

Schroeder, J., & Epley, N. (2015). The sound of intellect: Speech reveals a thoughtful mind, increasing a job candidate's appeal. *Psychological Science, 26,* 877–891.

Schroeder, J., & Epley, N. (2016). Mistaking minds and machines: How speech affects dehumanization and anthropomorphism. *Journal of Experimental Psychology: General, 145,* 1427–1437.

Schuch, F., Vancampfort, D., Firth, J., Rosenbaum, S., Ward, P., Silva, E. S., Hallgren, M., Ponce De Leon, A., Dunn, A. L., Deslandes, A. C., Fleck, M. P., Carvalho, A. F., & Stubbs, B. (2018). Physical activity and incident depression: A meta-analysis of prospective cohort studies. *American Journal of Psychiatry, 175,* 631–648.

Schuch, F. B., Vancampfort, D., Rosenbaum, S., Richards, J., Ward, P. B., & Stubbs, B. (2016). Exercise improves physical and psychological quality of life in people with depression: A meta-analysis including the evaluation of control group response. *Psychiatry Research, 241,* 47–54.

Schultheiss, O., Wiemers, U., & Wolf, O. (2014). Implicit need for achievement predicts attenuated cortisol responses to difficult tasks. *Journal of Research in Personality, 48,* 84–92.

Schultheiss, O. C., & Pang, J. S. (2007). Measuring implicit motives. In R. W. Robins, R. C. Fraley, & R. F. Krueger (Eds.), *Handbook of research methods in personality psychology* (pp. 322–345). Guilford Press.

Schultze, J., Neumann, I., Magid, M., Finzi, E., Sinke, C., Wollmer, M. A., & Krüger, T. H. C. (2021). Botulinum toxin for the management of depression: An updated review of the evidence and meta-analysis. *Journal of Psychiatric Research, 135,* 332–340.

Schuman, H., & Scott, J. (1989, June). Generations and collective memories. *American Sociological Review, 54,* 359–381.

Schumann, K., & Ross, M. (2010). Why women apologize more than men: Gender differences in thresholds for perceiving offensive behavior. *Psychological Science, 21,* 1649–1655.

Schuster, S. (2015). *17 quotes that prove OCD is so much more than being neat.* The Mighty. https://themighty.com/2015/10/what-ocd-feels-like/

Schuyler, A. C., Kintzle, S., Lucas, C. L., Moore, H., & Castro, C. A. (2017). Military sexual assault (MSA) among veterans in Southern California: Associations with physical health, psychological health, and risk behaviors. *Traumatology, 23,* 223–234.

Schwaba, T., & Bleidorn, W. (2019). Personality trait development across the transition to retirement. *Journal of Personality and Social Psychology, 116,* 651–665.

Schwalbe, M. C., Cohen, G. L., & Ross, L. D. (2020). The objectivity illusion and voter polarization in the 2016 presidential election. *PNAS, 117*(35). https://www.pnas.org/doi/10.1073/pnas.1912301117

Schwartz, B. (1984). *Psychology of learning and behavior* (2nd ed.). Norton.

Schwartz, B. (2000). Self-determination: The tyranny of freedom. *American Psychologist, 55,* 79–88.

Schwartz, B. (2004). *The paradox of choice: Why more is less.* Ecco/HarperCollins.

Schwartz, H. A., Eichstaedt, J. C., Kern, M. L., Dziurzynski, L., Ramones, S. M., Agrawal, M., Shah, A., Kosinski, M., Stillwell, D., Seligman, M. E. P., & Ungar, L. H. (2013). Personality, gender, and age in the language of social media: The open-vocabulary approach. *PLOS ONE, 8.* https://journals.plos.org/plosone/article?id=10.1371/journal.pone.0073791

Schwartz, J. M., Stoessel, P. W., Baxter, L. R., Jr., Martin, K. M., & Phelps, M. E. (1996). Systematic changes in cerebral glucose metabolic rate after successful behavior modification treatment of obsessive-compulsive disorder. *Archives of General Psychiatry, 53,* 109–113.

Schwartz, J. R., Thomas, E. B. K., Juckett, M. B., & Costanzo, E. S. (2022). Predictors of posttraumatic growth among hematopoietic cell transplant recipients. *Psychooncology, 31*(6), 1013–1021.

Schwartz, P. J. (2011). Season of birth in schizophrenia: A maternal-fetal chronobiological hypothesis. *Medical Hypotheses, 76,* 785–793.

Schwartz, S. H., & Rubel-Lifschitz, T. (2009). Cross-national variation in the size of sex differences in values: Effects of gender equality. *Journal of Personality and Social Psychology, 97,* 171–185.

Schwartz, S. J., Lilienfeld, S. O., Meca, A., & Sauvigné, K. C. (2016). The role of neuroscience within psychology: A call for inclusiveness over exclusiveness. *American Psychologist, 71,* 52–70.

Schwartzman-Morris, J., & Putterman, C. (2012). Gender differences in the pathogenesis and outcome of lupus and of lupus nephritis. *Clinical and Developmental Immunology, 2012.* https://www.ncbi.nlm.nih.gov/pmc/articles/PMC3368358/

Schwarz, A. (2012, June 9). Risky rise of the good-grade pill. *The New York Times.* https://www.nytimes.com/2012/06/10/education/seeking-academic-edge-teenagers-abuse-stimulants.html

Schwarz, N., Strack, F., Kommer, D., & Wagner, D. (1987). Soccer, rooms, and the quality of your life: Mood effects on judgments of satisfaction with life in general and with specific domains. *European Journal of Social Psychology, 17,* 69–79.

Schwemmer, M. A., Skomrock, N. D., Sederberg, P. B., Ting, J. E., Sharma, G., Bockbrader, M. A., & Friedenberg, D. A. (2018). Meeting brain–computer interface user performance expectations using a deep neural network decoding framework. *Nature Medicine, 24,* 1669–1676.

Scinicariello, F., Przybyla, J., Carroll, Y., Eichwald, J., Decker, J., & Breysse, P. N. (2019). Age and sex differences in hearing loss association with depressive symptoms: Analyses of NHANES 2011–2012. *Psychological Medicine, 49,* 962–968.

Sclafani, A. (1995). How food preferences are learned: Laboratory animal models. *PNAS, 54,* 419–427.

Scoboria, A., Wade, K. A., Lindsay, D. S., Azad, T., Strange, D., Ost, J., & Hyman, I. E. (2017). A mega-analysis of memory reports from eight peer-reviewed false memory implantation studies. *Memory, 25,* 146–163.

Scopelliti, I., Loewenstein, G., & Vosgerau, J. (2015). You call it "self-exuberance"; I call it "bragging": Miscalibrated predictions of emotional responses to self-promotion. *Psychological Science, 26,* 903–914.

Scott, A. J., Webb, T. L., Martyn-St James, M., Rowse, G., & Weich, S. (2021). Improving sleep quality leads to better mental health: A meta-analysis of randomised controlled trials. *Sleep Medicine Reviews, 60.* https://www.sciencedirect.com/science/article/pii/S1087079221001416

Scott, C., & Medeiros, M. (2020). Personality and political careers: What personality types are likely to run for office and get elected? *Personality and Individual Differences, 152.* https://doi.org/10.1016/j.paid.2019.109600

Scott, D. J., Stohler, C. S., Egnatuk, C. M., Wang, H., Koeppe, R. A., & Zubieta, J.-K. (2007). Individual differences in reward responding explain placebo-induced expectations and effects. *Neuron, 55,* 325–336.

Scott, K. M., Wells, J. E., Angermeyer, M., Brugha, T. S., Bromet, E., Demyttenaere, K., de Girolamo, G., Gureje, O., Haro, J. M., Jin, R., Karam, A. N., Kovess, V., Lara, C., Levinson, D., Ormel, J., Posada-Villa, J., Sampson, N., Takeshima, T., Zhang, M., & Kessler, R. C. (2010). Gender and the relationship between marital status and first onset of mood, anxiety and substance use disorders. *Psychological Medicine, 40,* 1495–1505.

Scullin, M. K. (2019). The eight hour sleep challenge during final exams week. *Teaching of Psychology, 46,* 55–63.

Scullin, M. K., & Bliwise, D. L. (2015). Sleep, cognition, and normal aging: Integrating a half century of multidisciplinary research. *Perspectives on Psychological Science, 10,* 97–137.

Scullin, M. K., Gao, C., & Fillmore, P. (2021). Bedtime music, involuntary musical imagery, and sleep. *Psychological Science, 32,* 985–997.

Scullin, M. K., & McDaniel, M. A. (2010). Remembering to execute a goal: Sleep on it! *Psychological Science, 21,* 1028–1035.

Scully, I. D., Napper, L. E., & Hupbach, A. (2017). Does reactivation trigger episodic memory change? A meta-analysis. *Neurobiology of Learning and Memory, 142*, 99–107.

Sdorow, L. M. (2005). The people behind psychology. In B. Perlman, L. McCann, & W. Buskist (Eds.), *Voices of experience: Memorable talks from the National Institute on the Teaching of Psychology*. American Psychological Society.

Seal, K. H., Bertenthal, D., Miner, C. R., Sen, S., & Marmar, C. (2007). Bringing the war back home: Mental health disorders among 103,788 U.S. veterans returning from Iraq and Afghanistan seen at Department of Veterans Affairs facilities. *Archives of Internal Medicine, 167*, 467–482.

Seamon, J., Punjabi, P., & Busch, E. (2010). Memorizing Milton's *Paradise Lost:* A study of a septuagenarian exceptional memoriser. *Memory, 18*, 498–503.

Seaton, E. K., & Zeiders, K. H. (2021). Daily racial discrimination experiences, ethnic–racial identity, and diurnal cortisol patterns among Black adults. *Cultural Diversity and Ethnic Minority Psychology, 27*(1), 145–155.

Sedikides, C. (2021). In search of Narcissus. *Trends in Cognitive Sciences, 25*(1), 67–80.

Sedley, W., Gander, P. E., Kumar, S., Oya, H., Kovach, C. K., Nourski, K. V., Kawasaki, H., Howard, M. A., & Griffiths, T. D. (2015). Intracranial mapping of a cortical tinnitus system using residual inhibition. *Current Biology, 25*, 1208–1214.

Sedlmeier, P., Eberth, J., Schwarz, M., Zimmermann, D., Haarig, F., Jaeger, S., & Kunze, S. (2012). The psychological effects of meditation: A meta-analysis. *Psychological Bulletin, 138*, 1139–1171.

Seehagen, S., Konrad, C., Herbert, J. S., & Schneider, S. (2015). Timely sleep facilitates declarative memory consolidation in infants. *PNAS, 112*, 1625–1629.

Seeman, P., Guan, H.-C., & Van Tol, H. H. M. (1993). Dopamine D4 receptors elevated in schizophrenia. *Nature, 365*, 441–445.

Seery, M. D. (2011). Resilience: A silver lining to experiencing adverse life events. *Current Directions in Psychological Science, 20*, 390–394.

Segal, N. L. (2005). *Indivisible by two: Lives of extraordinary twins*. Harvard University Press.

Segal, N. L. (2013). Personality similarity in unrelated look-alike pairs: Addressing a twin study challenge. *Personality and Individual Differences, 54*, 23–28.

Segal, N. L., McGuire, S. A., & Stohs, J. H. (2012). What virtual twins reveal about general intelligence and other behaviors. *Personality and Individual Differences, 53*, 405–410.

Segal, N. L., & Montoya, Y. S. (2018). *Accidental brothers: The story of twins exchanged at birth and the power of nature and nurture*. Macmillan.

Segal, S. C., & Carmona, N. E. (2022). A systematic review of sleep problems in children and adolescents with obsessive compulsive disorder. *Journal of Anxiety Disorders, 90*(6). https://doi.org/10.1016/j.janxdis.2022.102591

Segall, M. H., Dasen, P. R., Berry, J. W., & Poortinga, Y. H. (1990). *Human behavior in global perspective: An introduction to cross-cultural psychology*. Pergamon.

Segerstrom, S. C. (2007). Stress, energy, and immunity. *Current Directions in Psychological Science, 16*, 326–330.

Segerstrom, S. C., Taylor, S. E., Kemeny, M. E., & Fahey, J. L. (1998). Optimism is associated with mood, coping, and immune change in response to stress. *Journal of Personality and Social Psychology, 74*, 1646–1655.

Seibert, S. E., Wang, G., & Courtright, S. H. (2011). Antecedents and consequences of psychological and team empowerment in organizations: A meta-analytic review. *Journal of Applied Psychology, 96*, 981–1003.

Sejnowski, T. (2016, January 20). Quoted in *Memory capacity of brain is 10 times more than previously thought*. Salk News. https://www.salk.edu/news-release/memory-capacity-of-brain-is-10-times-more-than-previously-thought/

Self, C. E. (1994). *Moral culture and victimization in residence halls* [Unpublished master's thesis.]. Bowling Green University.

Seli, P., Risko, E. F., Smilek, D., & Schacter, D. L. (2016). Mind-wandering with and without intention. *Trends in Cognitive Sciences, 20*, 605–617.

Seligman, M. (2016). How positive psychology happened and where it is going. In R. J. Sternberg, S. T. Fiske, & D. J. Foss (Eds.), *Scientists making a difference: One hundred eminent behavioral and brain scientists talk about their most important contributions* (pp. 478–480). Cambridge University Press.

Seligman, M. E. P. (1975). *Helplessness: On depression, development and death*. Freeman.

Seligman, M. E. P. (1991). *Learned optimism: How to change your mind and your life*. Knopf.

Seligman, M. E. P. (1995). The effectiveness of psychotherapy: The *Consumer Reports* study. *American Psychologist, 50*, 965–974.

Seligman, M. E. P. (2002). *Authentic happiness: Using the new positive psychology to realize your potential for lasting fulfillment*. Free Press.

Seligman, M. E. P. (2012, May 8). Quoted in A. C. Brooks, America and the value of 'earned success.' *The Wall Street Journal*. https://www.wsj.com/articles/SB10001424052702304749904577385650652966894

Seligman, M. E. P., Ernst, R. M., Gillham, J., Reivich, K., & Linkins, M. (2009). Positive education: Positive psychology and classroom interventions. *Oxford Review of Education, 35*, 293–311.

Seligman, M. E. P., & Maier, S. F. (1967). Failure to escape traumatic shock. *Journal of Experimental Psychology, 74*, 1–9.

Seligman, M. E. P., Steen, T. A., Park, N., & Peterson, C. (2005). Positive psychology progress: Empirical validation of interventions. *American Psychologist, 60*, 410–421.

Seligman, M. E. P., & Yellen, A. (1987). What is a dream? *Behavior Research and Therapy, 25*, 1–24.

Selimbeyoglu, A., & Parvizi, J. (2010). Electrical stimulation of the human brain: Perceptual and behavioral phenomena reported in the old and new literature. *Frontiers in Human Neuroscience, 4*, 1–11.

Selvin, E., Burnett, A. L., & Platz, E. A. (2007). Prevalence and risk factors for erectile dysfunction in the U.S. *American Journal of Medicine, 120*(2), 151–157.

Selye, H. (1936). A syndrome produced by diverse nocuous agents. *Nature, 138*, 32.

Selye, H. (1976). *The stress of life*. McGraw-Hill.

Senft, N., Campos, B., Shiota, M. N., & Chentsova-Dutton, Y. E. (2021). Who emphasizes positivity? An exploration of emotion values in people of Latino, Asian, and European heritage living in the United States. *Emotion, 21*(4), 707.

Senghas, A., & Coppola, M. (2001). Children creating language: How Nicaraguan Sign Language acquired a spatial grammar. *Psychological Science, 12*, 323–328.

Sergeant, S., & Mongrain, M. (2014). An online optimism intervention reduces depression in pessimistic individuals. *Journal of Consulting and Clinical Psychology, 82*, 263–274.

Service, R. F. (1994). Will a new type of drug make memory-making easier? *Science, 266*, 218–219.

Servick, K. (2019). Warning signs. *Science, 365*, 742–744.

Sest, N., & March, E. (2017). Constructing the cyber-troll: Psychopathy, sadism, and empathy. *Personality and Individual Differences, 119*, 69–72.

Sethi, R. (2021). *Episode 7: "My parents keep expecting us to pay for them."* I Will Teach You to Be Rich. https://www.iwillteachyoutoberich.com/podcast/007-maria-barry/

Sezer, O., Gino, F., & Norton, M. I. (2018). Humblebragging: A distinct—and ineffective—self-presentation strategy. *Journal of Personality and Social Psychology, 114*, 52–74.

Sforzini, L., Pariante, C. M., Palacios, J. E., Tylee, A., Carvalho, L. A., Viganò, C. A., & Nikkheslat, N. (2019). Inflammation associated with coronary heart disease predicts onset of depression in a three-year prospective follow-up: A preliminary study. *Brain, Behavior, and Immunity, 81*, 659–664.

Shackman, A. J., Tromp, D. P., Stockbridge, M. D., Kaplan, C. M., Tillman, R. M., & Fox, A. S. (2016). Dispositional negativity: An integrative psychological and neurobiological perspective. *Psychological Bulletin, 142*, 1275–1314.

Shadish, W. R., & Baldwin, S. A. (2005). Effects of behavioral marital therapy: A meta-analysis of randomized controlled trials. *Journal of Consulting and Clinical Psychology, 73*, 6–14.

Shadish, W. R., Montgomery, L. M., Wilson, P., Wilson, M. R., Bright, I., & Okwumabua, T. (1993). Effects of family and marital psychotherapies: A meta-analysis. *Journal of Consulting and Clinical Psychology, 61*, 992–1002.

Shafir, E. (Ed.). (2013). *The behavioral foundations of public policy*. Princeton University Press.

Shafir, T., Taylor, S. F., Atkinson, A. P., Langenecker, S. A., & Zubieta, J. K. (2013). Emotion regulation through execution, observation, and imagery of emotional movements. *Brain and Cognition, 82*(2), 219–227.

Shaki, S. (2013). What's in a kiss? Spatial experience shapes directional bias during kissing. *Journal of Nonverbal Behavior, 37*, 43–50.

Shalev, I., Moffitt, T. E., Sugden, K., Williams, B., Houts, R. M., Danese, A., Mill, J., Arseneault, L., & Caspi, A. (2013). Exposure to violence during childhood is associated with telomere erosion from 5 to 10 years of age: A longitudinal study. *Molecular Psychiatry, 18*, 576–581.

Shalom, J. G., & Aderka, I. M. (2020). A meta-analysis of sudden gains in psychotherapy:

Outcome and moderators. *Clinical Psychology Review, 76*. doi: 10.1016/j.cpr.2020.101827

Shanahan, L., McHale, S. M., Osgood, D. W., & Crouter, A. C. (2007). Conflict frequency with mothers and fathers from middle childhood to late adolescence: Within- and between-families comparisons. *Developmental Psychology, 43*, 539–550.

Shandrashekar, A., Liu, J., Martinot, A. J., McMahan, K., Mercado, N. B., Peter, L., Tostanoski, L. H., Yu, J., Maliga, Z., Nekorchuk, M., Busman-Sahay, K., Terry, M., Wrijil, L. M., Ducat, S., Martinez, D. R., Atyeo, C., Fischinger, S., Burke, J. S., Slein, M. D., ... Barouch, D. H. (2020). SARS-CoV-2 infection protects against rechallenge in rhesus macaques. *Science, 369*(6505), 812–817.

Shannon, B. J., Raichle, M. E., Snyder, A. Z., Fair, D. A., Mills, K. L., Zhang, D., Bache, K., Calhoun, V. D., Nigg, J. T., Nagel, B. J., Stevens, A. A., & Kiehl, K. A. (2011). Premotor functional connectivity predicts impulsivity in juvenile offenders. *PNAS, 108*, 11241–11245.

Shapin, S. (2013, October 15). The man who forgot everything. *The New Yorker*. https://www.newyorker.com/books/page-turner/the-man-who-forgot-everything

Shapiro, D. (1999). *Psychotherapy of neurotic character*. Basic Books.

Shapiro, K. A., Moo, L. R., & Caramazza, A. (2006). Cortical signatures of noun and verb production. *PNAS, 103*, 1644–1649.

Shappell, S., Detweiler, C., Holcomb, K., Hackworth, C., Boquet, A., & Wiegmann, D. A. (2007). Human error and commercial aviation accidents: An analysis using the human factors analysis and classification system. *Human Factors, 49*, 227–242.

Shargorodsky, J., Curhan, S. G., Curhan, G. C., & Eavey, R. (2010). Changes of prevalence of hearing loss in US adolescents. *Journal of the American Medical Association, 304*, 772–778.

Shariff, A. F., Greene, J. D., Karremans, J. C., Luguri, J. B., Clark, C. J., Schooler, J. W., Baumeister, R. F., & Vohs, K. D. (2014). Free will and punishment: A mechanistic view of human nature reduces retribution. *Psychological Science, 25*, 1563–1570.

Sharma, A. R., McGue, M. K., & Benson, P. L. (1998). The psychological adjustment of United States adopted adolescents and their nonadopted siblings. *Child Development, 69*, 791–802.

Shattuck, P. T. (2006). The contribution of diagnostic substitution to the growing administrative prevalence of autism in US special education. *Pediatrics, 117*, 1028–1037.

Shave, R. E., Lieberman, D. E., Drane, A. L., Brown, M. G., Batterham, A. M., Worthington, S., Atencia, R., Feltrer, Y., Neary, J., Weiner, R. B., & Wasfy, M. M. (2019). Selection of endurance capabilities and the trade-off between pressure and volume in the evolution of the human heart. *PNAS, 116*, 19905–19910.

Shaw, J. (2018). How can researchers tell whether someone has a false memory? Coding strategies in autobiographical false memory research. A reply to Wade, Garry, and Pezdek. *Psychological Science, 29*, 477–480.

Shedler, J. (2009, March 23). *That was then, this is now: Psychoanalytic psychotherapy for the rest of us* [Unpublished manuscript]. Department of Psychiatry, University of Colorado Health Sciences Center, Aurora, CO.

Shedler, J. (2010). The efficacy of psychodynamic psychotherapy. *American Psychologist, 65*, 98–109.

Sheehan, S. (1982). *Is there no place on earth for me?* Houghton Mifflin.

Sheikh, S., & Janoff-Bulman, R. (2013). Paradoxical consequences of prohibitions. *Journal of Personality and Social Psychology, 105*, 301–315.

Sheldon, K. M., Corcoran, M., & Sheldon, M. (2021). Duchenne smiles as honest signals of chronic positive mood. *Perspectives on Psychological Science, 16*(3), 654–666.

Sheldon, K. M., Elliot, A. J., Kim, Y., & Kasser, T. (2001). What is satisfying about satisfying events? Testing 10 candidate psychological needs. *Journal of Personality and Social Psychology, 80*, 325–339.

Sheldon, K. M., & Lyubomirsky, S. (2012). The challenge of staying happier: Testing the hedonic adaptation prevention model. *Personality and Social Psychology Bulletin, 38*, 670–680.

Sheldon, K. M., & Lyubomirsky, S. (2021). Revisiting the Sustainable Happiness Model and pie chart: Can happiness be successfully pursued? *Journal of Positive Psychology, 16*(2), 145–154.

Shelton, L. T., Elliott, E. M., Matthews, R. A., Hill, B. H., & Gouvier, W. D. (2010). The relationships of working memory, secondary memory, and general fluid intelligence: Working memory is special. *Journal of Experimental Psychology, 36*, 813–820.

Shen, L., Fishbach, A., & Hsee, C. K. (2015, February). The motivating-uncertainty effect: Uncertainty increases resource investment in the process of reward pursuit. *Journal of Consumer Research, 41*, 1301–1315.

Shen, W., Yuan, Y., Liu, C., & Luo, J. (2017). The roles of the temporal lobe in creative insight: An integrated review. *Thinking & Reasoning, 23*, 321–375.

Shenton, M. E. (1992). Abnormalities of the left temporal lobe and thought disorder in schizophrenia: A quantitative magnetic resonance imaging study. *New England Journal of Medicine, 327*, 604–612.

Shepard, R. N. (1990). *Mind sights*. Freeman.

Shepperd, J. A., Waters, E., Weinstein, N. D., & Klein, W. M. P. (2015). A primer on unrealistic optimism. *Current Directions in Psychological Science, 24*, 232–237.

Shergill, S. S., Bays, P. M., Frith, C. D., & Wolpert, D. M. (2003). Two eyes for an eye: The neuroscience of force escalation. *Science, 301*, 187.

Sherif, M. (1966). *In common predicament: Social psychology of intergroup conflict and cooperation*. Houghton Mifflin.

Sherif, M., Radhakrishnan, R., D'Souza, D. C., & Ranganathan, M. (2016). Human laboratory studies on cannabinoids and psychosis. *Biological Psychiatry, 79*, 526–538.

Sherman, G. D., Lee, J. J., Cuddy, A. J. C., Renshon, J., Oveis, C., Gross, J. J., & Lerner, J. S. (2012). Leadership is associated with lower levels of stress. *PNAS, 109*, 17903–17907.

Sherman, L. E., Payton, A. A., Hernandez, L. M., Greenfield, P. M., & Dapretto, M. (2016). The power of the like in adolescence: Effects of peer influence on neural and behavioral responses to social media. *Psychological Science, 27*, 1027–1035.

Sherman, P. W., & Flaxman, S. M. (2001). Protecting ourselves from food. *American Scientist, 89*, 142–151.

Sherman, R. A., Rauthmann, J. F., Brown, N. A., Serfass, D. S., & Jones, A. B. (2015). The independent effects of personality and situations on real-time expressions of behavior and emotion. *Journal of Personality and Social Psychology, 109*, 872–888.

Sherry, D., & Vaccarino, A. L. (1989). Hippocampus and memory for food caches in black-capped chickadees. *Behavioral Neuroscience, 103*, 308–318.

Shettleworth, S. J. (1973). Food reinforcement and the organization of behavior in golden hamsters. In R. A. Hinde & J. Stevenson-Hinde (Eds.), *Constraints on learning: Limitations and predispositions*. Academic Press.

Shettleworth, S. J. (1993). Where is the comparison in comparative cognition? Alternative research programs. *Psychological Science, 4*, 179–184.

Shi, F., Teplitskiy, M., Duede, E., & Evans, J. A. (2019). The wisdom of polarized crowds. *Nature Human Behaviour, 3*, 329–336.

Shilsky, J. D., Hartman, T. J., Kris-Etherton, P. M., Rogers, C. J., Sharkey, N. A., & Nickols-Richardson, S. M. (2012). Partial sleep deprivation and energy balance in adults: An emerging issue for consideration by dietetics practitioners. *Journal of the Academy of Nutrition and Dietetics, 112*, 1785–1797.

Shimamura, A. P. (2010). Bridging psychological and biological science: The good, bad, and ugly. *Perspectives on Psychological Science, 5*, 772–775.

Shimizu, M., & Pelham, B. W. (2008). Postponing a date with the grim reaper. *Basic and Applied Social Psychology, 30*, 36–45.

Shin, J. E., Suh, E. M., Li, N. P., Eo, K., Chong, S. C., & Tsai, M. H. (2019). Darling, get closer to me: Spatial proximity amplifies interpersonal liking. *Personality and Social Psychology Bulletin, 45*, 300–309.

Shinkareva, S. V., Mason, R. A., Malave, V. L., Wang, W., Mitchell, T. M., & Just, M. A. (2008, January 2). Using fMRI brain activation to identify cognitive states associated with perceptions of tools and dwellings. *PLOS ONE, 3*. https://journals.plos.org/plosone/article?id=10.1371/journal.pone.0001394

Shiota, M. N., Campos, B., Oveis, C., Hertenstein, M. J., Simon-Thomas, E., & Keltner, D. (2017). Beyond happiness: Building a science of discrete positive emotions. *American Psychologist, 72*(7), 617.

Shiota, M. N., & Levenson, R. W. (2007). Birds of a feather don't always fly together: Similarity in Big Five personality predicts more negative marital satisfaction trajectories in long-term marriages. *Psychology and Aging, 22*(4), 666–675.

Shirazi, T. N., Self, H., Rosenfield, K. A., Dawood, K., Welling, L. L. M., Cárdenas, R., Bailey, J. M., Balasubramanian, R., Delaney, A., Breedlove, S. M., & Puts, D. A. (2022). Low perinatal androgens predict recalled childhood gender nonconformity in men. *Psychological Science, 33*(3), 343–353.

Shockley, K. M., Ispas, D., Rossi, M. E., & Levine, E. L. (2012). A meta-analytic investigation of the relationship between state affect, discrete emotions, and job performance. *Human Performance, 25*, 377–411.

Shor, E., Roelfs, D. J., Bugyi, P., & Schwartz, J. E. (2012). Meta-analysis of marital dissolution and mortality: Reevaluating the intersection of gender and age. *Social Science & Medicine, 75*, 46–59.

Shorey, S., Ng, E. D., & Wong, C. H. J. (2022). Global prevalence of depression and elevated depressive symptoms among adolescents: A systematic review and meta-analysis. *British Journal of Clinical Psychology, 61*(2), 287–305.

Shors, T. J. (2014). The adult brain makes new neurons, and effortful learning keeps them alive. *Current Directions in Psychological Science, 23*, 311–318.

Short, M., Gradisar, M., Wright, H., Dewald, J., Wolfson, A., & Carskadon, M. (2013). A cross-cultural comparison of sleep duration between U.S. and Australian adolescents: The effect of school start time, parent-set bedtimes, and extra-curricular load. *Health Education Behavior, 40*, 323–330.

Short, S. J., Lubach, G. R., Karasin, A. I., Olsen, C. W., Styner, M., Knickmeyer, R. C., Gilmore, J. H., & Coe, C. L. (2010). Maternal influenza infection during pregnancy impacts postnatal brain development in the rhesus monkey. *Biological Psychiatry, 67*, 965–973.

Showers, C. (1992). The motivational and emotional consequences of considering positive or negative possibilities for an upcoming event. *Journal of Personality and Social Psychology, 63*, 474–484.

Shrestha, A., Nohr, E. A., Bech, B. H., Ramlau-Hansen, C. H., & Olsen, J. (2011). Smoking and alcohol during pregnancy and age of menarche in daughters. *Human Reproduction, 26*, 259–265.

Shrira, I. (2020). Population diversity and ancestral diversity as distinct contributors to outgroup prejudice. *Personality and Social Psychology Bulletin, 46*(6), 885–895.

Shuffler, M. L., Burke, C. S., Kramer, W. S., & Salas, E. (2013). Leading teams: Past, present, and future perspectives. In M. G. Rumsey (Ed.), *The Oxford handbook of leadership*. Oxford University Press.

Shuffler, M. L., DiazGranados, D., & Salas, E. (2011). There's a science for that: Team development interventions in organizations. *Current Directions in Psychological Science, 20*, 365–372.

Shuwairi, S. M., & Johnson, S. P. (2013). Oculomotor exploration of impossible figures in early infancy. *Infancy, 18*, 221–232.

Shweder, R. A., Jensen, L. A., & Goldstein, W. M. (1995). Who sleeps by whom revisited: A method for extracting the moral goods implicit in practice. In J. J. Goodnow, P. J. Miller, & F. Kessel (Eds.), *New directions for child development, No. 67. Cultural practices as contexts for development* (pp. 21–39). Jossey Bass.

Siciliano, C. A. (2019, November 21). *Brain activity predicts which mice will become compulsive drinkers*. The Conversation. https://theconversation.com/brain-activity-predicts-which-mice-will-become-compulsive-drinkers-127313

Siclari, F., Baird, B., Perogamvros, L., Bernardi, G., LaRocque, J. J., Riedner, B., Boly, M., Postle, B. R., & Tononi, G. (2017). The neural correlates of dreaming. *Nature Neuroscience, 20*, 872–878.

Sidari, M. J., Lee, A. J., Murphy, S. C., Sherlock, J. M., Dixson, B. J. W., & Zietsch, B. P. (2021). Preferences for sexually dimorphic body characteristics revealed in a large sample of speed daters. *Social Psychological and Personality Science, 12*(2), 225–236.

Sieber, V., Flückiger, L., Mata, J., Bernecker, K., & Job, V. (2019). Autonomous goal striving promotes a nonlimited theory about willpower. *Personality and Social Psychology Bulletin, 45*, 1295–1307.

Siegel, E. H., Sands, M. K., Van den Noortgate, W., Condon, P., Chang, Y., Dy, J., Quigley, K. S., & Barrett, L. F. (2018). Emotion fingerprints or emotion populations? A meta-analytic investigation of autonomic features of emotion categories. *Psychological Bulletin, 144*, 343–393.

Siegel, J. M. (2009). Sleep viewed as a state of adaptive inactivity. *Nature Reviews Neuroscience, 10*, 747–753.

Siegel, J. M. (2012). Suppression of sleep for mating. *Science, 337*, 1610–1611.

Siegel, M., & Rothman, E. F. (2016). Firearm ownership and suicide rates among US men and women, 1981–2013. *American Journal of Public Health, 106*(7), 1316–1322.

Siegel, R. K. (1977, October). Hallucinations. *Scientific American*, pp. 132–140.

Siegel, R. K. (1980). The psychology of life after death. *American Psychologist, 35*, 911–931.

Siegel, R. K. (1982, October). Quoted by J. Hooper in, Mind tripping. *Omni*, pp. 72–82, 159–160.

Siegel, R. K. (1984, March 15). Personal communication.

Siegel, R. K. (1990). *Intoxication: Life in pursuit of artificial paradise*. Pocket Books.

Siegel, S. (2005). Drug tolerance, drug addiction, and drug anticipation. *Current Directions in Psychological Science, 14*, 296–300.

Silber, M. H., Ancoli-Israel, S., Bonnet, M. H., Chokroverty, S., Grigg-Damberger, M. M., Hirshkowitz, M., Kapen, S., Keenan, S. A., Kryger, M. H., Penzel, T., Pressman, M. R., & Iber, C. (2007). The visual scoring of sleep in adults. *Journal of Clinical Sleep Medicine, 3*, 121–131.

Silbersweig, D. A., Stern, E., Frith, C., Cahill, C., Holmes, A., Grootoonk, S., Seaward, J., McKenna, P., Chua, S. E., Schnorr, L., Jones, T., & Frackowiak, R. S. J. (1995). A functional neuroanatomy of hallucinations in schizophrenia. *Nature, 378*, 176–179.

Silston, B., Bassett, D. S., & Mobbs, D. (2018). How dynamic brain networks tune social behavior in real time. *Current Directions in Psychological Science, 27*, 413–421.

Silva, C. E., & Kirsch, I. (1992). Interpretive sets, expectancy, fantasy proneness, and dissociation as predictors of hypnotic response. *Journal of Personality and Social Psychology, 63*, 847–856.

Silver, M., & Geller, D. (1978). On the irrelevance of evil: The organization and individual action. *Journal of Social Issues, 34*, 125–136.

Silver, N. (2012). *The signal and the noise: Why so many predictions fail—but some don't*. Penguin.

Silver, R. C., Holman, E. A., McIntosh, D. N., Poulin, M., & Gil-Rivas, V. (2002). Nationwide longitudinal study of psychological responses to September 11. *Journal of the American Medical Association, 288*, 1235–1244.

Silverman, K., Evans, S. M., Strain, E. C., & Griffiths, R. R. (1992). Withdrawal syndrome after the double-blind cessation of caffeine consumption. *New England Journal of Medicine, 327*, 1109–1114.

Silverstein, B. H., Snodgrass, M., Shevrin, H., & Kushwaha, R. (2015). P3b, consciousness, and complex unconscious processing. *Cortex, 73*, 216–227.

Simek, T. C., & O'Brien, R. M. (1981). *Total golf: A behavioral approach to lowering your score and getting more out of your game*. B-MOD Associates.

Simek, T. C., & O'Brien, R. M. (1988). A chaining-mastery, discrimination training program to teach Little Leaguers to hit a baseball. *Human Performance, 1*, 73–84.

Simon, G. E., Johnson, E., Lawrence, J. M., Rossom, R. C., Ahmedani, B., Lynch, F. L., Beck, A., Waitzfelder, B., Ziebell, R., Penfold, R. B., & Shortreed, S. M. (2018). Predicting suicide attempts and suicide deaths following outpatient visits using electronic health records. *American Journal of Psychiatry, 175*, 951–960.

Simon, V., Czobor, P., Bálint, S., Mésáros, A., & Bitter, I. (2009). Prevalence and correlates of adult attention-deficit hyperactivity disorder: Meta-analysis. *British Journal of Psychiatry, 194*, 204–211.

Simon-Kutscher, K., Wanke, N., Hiller, C., & Schwabe, L. (2019). Fear without context: Acute stress modulates the balance of cue-dependent and contextual fear learning. *Psychological Science, 30*(8), 1123–1135.

Simons, D. J., & Chabris, C. F. (1999). Gorillas in our midst: Sustained inattentional blindness for dynamic events. *Perception, 28*, 1059–1074.

Simons, D. J., & Chabris, C. F. (2011). What people believe about how memory works: A representative survey of the U.S. population. PLOS ONE, 6. https://journals.plos.org/plosone/article/file?id=10.1371/journal.pone.0022757&type=printable

Simons, D. J., Boot, W. R., Charness, N., Gathercole, S. E., Chabris, C. F., Hambrick, D. Z., & Stine-Morrow, E. A. L. (2016). Do "brain-training" programs work? *Psychological Science in the Public Interest, 17*, 103–186.

Simons, D. J., & Levin, D. T. (1998). Failure to detect changes to people during a real-world interaction. *Psychonomic Bulletin & Review, 5*, 644–649.

Simonsohn, U., & Gino, F. (2013). Daily horizons: Evidence of narrow bracketing in judgment from 10 years of M.B.A. admissions interviews. *Psychological Science, 24*, 219–224.

Simonton, D. K. (1988). Age and outstanding achievement: What do we know after a century of research? *Psychological Bulletin, 104*, 251–267.

Simonton, D. K. (1990). Creativity in the later years: Optimistic prospects for achievement. *The Gerontologist, 30*, 626–631.

Simonton, D. K. (1992). The social context of career success and course for 2,026 scientists and inventors. *Personality and Social Psychology Bulletin, 18*, 452–463.

Simonton, D. K. (2000). Methodological and theoretical orientation and the long-term disciplinary impact of 54 eminent psychologists. *Review of General Psychology, 4*, 13–24.

Simonton, D. K. (2012a). Teaching creativity: Current findings, trends, and controversies in the psychology of creativity. *Teaching of Psychology, 39*, 217–222.

Simonton, D. K. (2012b, November–December). The science of genius. *Scientific American Mind*, pp. 35–41.

Sims, C. R. (2018). Efficient coding explains the universal law of generalization in human perception. *Science, 360*, 652–656.

Sin, N. L., & Lyubomirsky, S. (2009). Enhancing well-being and alleviating depressive symptoms with positive psychology interventions: A practice-friendly meta-analysis. *Journal of Clinical Psychology: In Session, 65*, 467–487.

Sinclair, R. C., Hoffman, C., Mark, M. M., Martin, L. L., & Pickering, T. L. (1994). Construct accessibility and the misattribution of arousal: Schachter and Singer revisited. *Psychological Science, 5*, 15–18.

Singer, J. L. (1981). Clinical intervention: New developments in methods and evaluation. In L. T. Benjamin, Jr. (Ed.), *The G. Stanley Hall lecture series* (Vol. 1). American Psychological Association.

Singer, T., Seymour, B., O'Doherty, J., Kaube, H., Dolan, R. J., & Frith, C. (2004). Empathy for pain involves the affective but not sensory components of pain. *Science, 303*, 1157–1162.

Singh, D. (1993). Adaptive significance of female physical attractiveness: Role of waist-to-hip ratio. *Journal of Personality and Social Psychology, 65*, 293–307.

Singh, D., & Randall, P. K. (2007). Beauty is in the eye of the plastic surgeon: Waist-hip ratio (WHR) and women's attractiveness. *Personality and Individual Differences, 43*, 329–340.

Singh, L., Quinn, P. C., Qian, M., & Lee, K. (2020). Bilingualism is associated with less racial bias in preschool children. *Developmental Psychology, 56*(5), 888–896.

Singh, S. (1997). *Fermat's enigma: The epic quest to solve the world's greatest mathematical problem*. Bantam Books.

Sinha, I. P., Lee, A. R., Bennett, D., McGeehan, L., Abrams, E. M., Mayell, S. J., Harwood, R., Hawcutt, D. B., Gilchrist, F. J., Auth, M. K. H., Simba, J. M., & Taylor-Robinson, D. C. (2020). Child poverty, food insecurity, and respiratory health during the COVID-19 pandemic. *The Lancet: Respiratory Medicine, 8*(8), 762–763.

Sinha, N., Berg, C. N., Yassa, M. A., & Gluck, M. A. (2021). Increased dynamic flexibility in the medial temporal lobe network following an exercise intervention mediates generalization of prior learning. *Neurobiology of Learning and Memory, 177*. doi: 10.1016/j.nlm.2020.107340

Sio, U. N., Monahan, P., & Ormerod, T. (2013). Sleep on it, but only if it is difficult: Effects of sleep on problem solving. *Memory and Cognition, 41*, 159–166.

SIOP (Society for Industrial and Organizational Psychology). (2018, August 28). *Materials for incorporating I-O into an introductory psychology textbook*. https://www.siop.org/Events-Education/Educators/Incorporating-I-O

Sipski, M. L., Alexander, C. J., & Rosen, R. C. (1999). Sexual response in women with spinal cord injuries: Implications for our understanding of the able bodied. *Journal of Sexual & Marital Therapy, 25*, 11–22.

Sireteanu, R. (1999). Switching on the infant brain. *Science, 286*, 59, 61.

Sivertsen, B., Pallesen, S., Friborg, O., Nilsen, K. B., Bakke, Ø. K., Goll, J. B., & Hopstock, L. A. (2020). Sleep patterns and insomnia in a large population-based study of middle-aged and older adults: The Tromsø study 2015–2016. *Journal of Sleep Research*. doi: 10.1111/jsr.13095

Skeem, J. L., & Cooke, D. J. (2010). Is criminal behavior a central component of psychopathy? Conceptual directions for resolving the debate. *Psychological Assessment, 22*, 433–445.

Skinner, B. F. (1938/1966). *The behavior of organisms: An experimental analysis*. Appleton-Century-Crofs. (Original work published 1938.)

Skinner, B. F. (1953). *Science and human behavior*. Macmillan.

Skinner, B. F. (1956). A case history in scientific method. *American Psychologist, 11*, 221–233.

Skinner, B. F. (1960). Pigeons in a pelican. *American Psychologist, 15*, 28–37.

Skinner, B. F. (1961, November). Teaching machines. *Scientific American*, pp. 91–102.

Skinner, B. F. (1983, September). Origins of a behaviorist. *Psychology Today*, pp. 22–33.

Skinner, B. F. (1989). Teaching machines. *Science, 243*, 1535.

Skoog, G., & Skoog, I. (1999). A 40-year follow-up of patients with obsessive-compulsive disorder. *Archives of General Psychiatry, 56*, 121–127.

Skoog, T., & Kapetanovic, S. (2022). The role of pubertal timing in the development of peer victimization and offending from early- to mid-adolescence. *Journal of Early Adolescence, 42*, 5–32.

Skov, R. B., & Sherman, S. J. (1986). Information-gathering processes: Diagnosticity, hypothesis-confirmatory strategies, and perceived hypothesis confirmation. *Journal of Experimental Social Psychology, 22*, 93–121.

Slagt, M., Dubas, J. S., Deković, M., & van Aken, M. A. (2016). Differences in sensitivity to parenting depending on child temperament: A meta-analysis. *Psychological Bulletin, 142*, 1068–1110.

Slater, E., & Meyer, A. (1959). *Confinia psychiatra*. S. Karger AG.

Slaughter, V., Imuta, K., Peterson, C. C., & Henry, J. D. (2015). Meta-analysis of theory of mind and peer popularity in the preschool and early school years. *Child Development, 86*, 1159–1174.

Slee, A., Nazareth, I., Bondaronek, P., Liu, Y., Cheng, Z., & Freemantle, N. (2019). Pharmacological treatments for generalised anxiety disorder: A systematic review and network meta-analysis. *The Lancet, 393*, 768–777.

Slemp, G. R., Kern, M. L., Patrick, K. J., & Ryan, R. M. (2018). Leader autonomy support in the workplace: A meta-analytic review. *Motivation and Emotion, 42*, 706–724.

Sloan, R. P. (2005). *Field analysis of the literature on religion, spirituality, and health* [PDF file]. Columbia University. https://metanexus.net/archive/templetonadvancedresearchprogram/pdf/TARP-Sloan.pdf

Sloan, R. P., & Bagiella, E. (2002). Claims about religious involvement and health outcomes. *Annals of Behavioral Medicine, 24*, 14–21.

Sloan, R. P., Bagiella, E., & Powell, T. (1999). Religion, spirituality, and medicine. *The Lancet, 353*, 664–667.

Sloan, R. P., Bagiella, E., VandeCreek, L., & Poulos, P. (2000). Should physicians prescribe religious activities? *New England Journal of Medicine, 342*, 1913–1917.

Slopen, N., Glynn, R. J., Buring, J., & Albert, M. A. (2010, November 23). Abstract A18520: Job strain, job insecurity, and incident cardiovascular disease in the Women's Health Study. *Circulation, 122*(suppl 21). https://www.ahajournals.org/doi/10.1161/circ.122.suppl_21.A18520

Slovic, P., Västfjälla, D., Erlandsson, A., & Gregory, R. (2017). Iconic photographs and the ebb and flow of empathic response to humanitarian disasters. *PNAS, 114*, 640–644.

Slutske, W. S., Moffitt, T. E., Poulton, R., & Caspi A. (2012). Under-controlled temperament at age 3 predicts disordered gambling at age 32: A longitudinal study of a complete birth cohort. *Psychological Science, 23*, 510–516.

Smaldino, P. E., & McElreath, R. (2016). The natural selection of bad science. *Royal Society Open Science, 3*. https://bit.ly/3d60t38

Small, M. F. (1997). Making connections. *American Scientist, 85*, 502–504.

Smedley, A., & Smedley, B. D. (2005). Race as biology is fiction, racism as a social problem is real: Anthropological and historical perspectives on the social construction of race. *American Psychologist, 60*, 16–26.

Smeeth, D., Beck, S., Karam, E. G., & Pluess, M. (2021). The role of epigenetics in psychological resilience. *Lancet Psychiatry, 8*(7), 621–629.

Smith, A. (1983). Personal correspondence.

Smith, B. C. (2011, January 16). *The senses and the multi-sensory*. Edge. https://www.edge.org/response-detail/11677

Smith, C. (2006, January 7). Nearly 100, LSD's father ponders his "problem child." *The New York Times*. https://www.nytimes.com/2006/01/07/pageoneplus/world/the-saturday-profile-nearly-100-lsds-father-ponders-his.html

Smith, D. G. (2022, July 15). Taking the magic out of magic mushrooms. *The New York Times*. https://www.nytimes.com/2022/07/15/opinion/hallucinations-psychedelics-depression.html

Smith, G. E. (2016). Healthy cognitive aging and dementia prevention. *American Psychologist, 71*, 268–275.

Smith, J. C., Nielson, K. A., Woodard, J. L., Seidenberg, M., Durgerian, S., Hazlett, K. E., Figueroa, C. M., Kandah, C. C., Kay, C. D., Matthews, M. A., & Rao, S. M. (2014, April 23). Physical activity reduces hippocampal atrophy in elders at genetic risk for Alzheimer's disease. *Frontiers in Aging Neuroscience, 6*, 61.

Smith, K. (2018). Sex and drugs and self-control: How the teen brain navigates risk. *Nature, 554*, 426–428.

Smith, K. V., Wild, J., & Ehlers, A. (2020). The masking of mourning: Social disconnection after bereavement and its role in psychological distress. *Clinical Psychological Science, 8*, 464–476.

Smith, M. (2017). Hyperactive around the world? The history of ADHD in global perspective. *Social History of Medicine, 30*, 767–787.

Smith, M. B. (1978). Psychology and values. *Journal of Social Issues, 34*, 181–199.

Smith, M. L., & Glass, G. V. (1977). Meta-analysis of psychotherapy outcome studies. *American Psychologist, 32*, 752–760.

Smith, M. L., Asada, N., & Malenka, R. C. (2021). Anterior cingulate inputs to nucleus accumbens control the social transfer of pain and analgesia. *Science, 371*(6525), 153–159.

Smith, M. L., Glass, G. V., & Miller, R. L. (1980). *The benefits of psychotherapy*. Johns Hopkins Press.

Smith, M. M., Sherry, S. B., Chen, S., Saklofske, D. H., Mushquash, C., Flett, G. L., & Hewitt, P. L. (2018). The perniciousness of perfectionism: A meta-analytic review of the perfectionism–suicide relationship. *Journal of Personality, 86*, 522–542.

Smith, P. B., & Tayeb, M. (1989). Organizational structure and processes. In M. Bond (Ed.), *The cross-cultural challenge to social psychology*. Sage.

Smith, S. L., Pieper, K., & Choueiti, M. (2017, February). *Inclusion in the director's chair? Gender, race, & age of film directors across 1,000 films from 2007–2016*. Media, Diversity, & Social Change Initiative, University of Southern California Annenberg School for Communications and Journalism.

Smith, T. W., & Baucom, B. R. W. (2017). Intimate relationships, individual adjustment, and coronary heart disease: Implications of overlapping associations in psychosocial risk. *American Psychologist, 72*, 578–589.

Smith-Woolley, E., Selzam, S., & Plomin, R. (2019). Polygenic score for educational attainment captures DNA variants shared between personality traits and educational achievement. *Journal of Personality and Social Psychology, 117*, 1145–1163.

Smits, I. A. M., Dolan, C. V., Vorst, H. C. M., Wicherts, J. M., & Timmerman, M. E. (2011). Cohort differences in big five personality traits over a period of 25 years. *Journal of Personality and Social Psychology, 100*, 1124–1138.

Smolak, L., & Murnen, S. K. (2002). A meta-analytic examination of the relationship between child sexual abuse and eating disorders. *International Journal of Eating Disorders, 31*, 136–150.

Smoller, J. W. (2019). Psychiatric genetics begins to find its footing. *American Journal of Psychiatry, 176*, 609–614.

Smoller, J. W. (2020). Anxiety genetics goes genomic. *American Journal of Psychiatry, 177*, 190–194.

Snedeker, J., Geren, J., & Shafto, C. L. (2007). Starting over: International adoption as a natural experiment in language development. *Psychological Science, 18*, 79–86.

Snell, J., & Grainger, J. (2019). Readers are parallel processors. *Trends in Cognitive Sciences, 23*, 537–546.

Snipes, D. J., Calton, J. M., Green, B. A., Perrin, P. B., & Benotsch, E. G. (2017). Rape and posttraumatic stress disorder (PTSD): Examining the mediating role of explicit sex-power beliefs for men versus women. *Journal of Interpersonal Violence, 32*, 2453–2470.

Snodgrass, S. E., Higgins, J. G., & Todisco, L. (1986). *The effects of walking behavior on mood* [Paper]. Presented at the American Psychological Association convention.

Snyder, F., & Scott, J. (1972). The psychophysiology of sleep. In N. S. Greenfield & R. A. Sterbach (Eds.), *Handbook of psychophysiology*. Holt, Rinehart & Winston.

Snyder, S. H. (1984). Neurosciences: An integrative discipline. *Science, 225*, 1255–1257.

Soderstrom, N. C., Kerr, T. K., & Bjork, R. A. (2016). The critical importance of retrieval—and spacing—for learning. *Psychological Science, 27*, 223–230.

Sofer, C., Dotsch, R., Wigboldus, D. H. J., & Todorov, A. (2015). What is typical is good: The influence of face typicality on perceived trustworthiness. *Psychological Science, 26*, 39–47.

Solano, I., Eaton, N. R., & O'Leary, K. D. (2018). Pornography consumption, modality and function in a large internet sample. *Journal of Sex Research, 57*(1), 92–103.

Sole-Smith, V. (2020, July). Treating patients without the scale. *Scientific American*, pp. 23–31.

Solmi, M., Radua, J., Olivola, M., Croce, E., Soardo, L., Salazar de Pablo, G., Shin, J. I., Kirkbride, J. B., Jones, P., Kim, J. H., Kim, J. Y., Carvalho, A. F., Seeman, M. V., Correll, C., & Fusar-Poli, P. (2022). Age at onset of mental disorders worldwide: Large-scale meta-analysis of 192 epidemiological studies. *Molecular Psychiatry, 27*, 281–295.

Solomon, D. A., Keitner, G. I., Miller, I. W., Shea, M. T., & Keller, M. B. (1995). Course of illness and maintenance treatments for patients with bipolar disorder. *Journal of Clinical Psychiatry, 56*, 5–13.

Soloski, A. (2019, May 26). Asia Kate Dillon: 'This is who I am.' *The New York Times*. https://www.nytimes.com/2019/05/26/arts/television/asia-kate-dillon-billions.html

Somerville, L. H., Fani, N., & McClure-Tone, E. B. (2011). Behavioral and neural representation of emotional facial expressions across the lifespan. *Developmental Neuropsychology, 36*(4), 408–428.

Somerville, L. H., Jones, R. M., Ruberry, E. J., Dyke, J. P., Glover, G., & Casey, B. J. (2013). The medial prefrontal cortex and the emergence of self-conscious emotion in adolescence. *Psychological Science, 24*, 1554–1562.

Sommet, N., Morselli, D., & Spini, D. (2018). Income inequality affects the psychological health of only the people facing scarcity. *Psychological Science, 29*, 1911–1921.

Song, S. (2006, March 27). Mind over medicine. *Time*, p. 47.

Song, Z., Li, W.-D., Jin, X., & Fan, Q. (2022). Genetics, leadership position, and well-being: An investigation with a large-scale GWAS. PNAS, 199(12). https://www.pnas.org/doi/10.1073/pnas.2114271119

Soral, W., Bilewicz, M., & Winiewski, M. (2018). Exposure to hate speech increases prejudice through desensitization. *Aggressive Behavior, 44*, 136–146.

Sorokowski, P., Sorokowska, A., Karwowski, M., Groyecka, A., Aavik, T., Akello, G., Alm, C., Amjad, N., Anjum, A., Asao, K., Atama, C. S., Atamtürk Duyar, D., Ayebare, R., Batres, C., Bendixen, M., Bensafia, A., Bizumic, B., Boussena, M., Buss, D. M., ... Sternberg, R. J. (2021). Universality of the Triangular Theory of Love: Adaptation and psychometric properties of the Triangular Love Scale in 25 countries. *Journal of Sex Research, 58*(1), 106–115.

Soto, A., Smith, T. B., Griner, D., Rodríguez, M. D., & Bernal, G. (2018). Cultural adaptations and therapist multicultural competence: Two meta-analytic reviews. *Journal of Clinical Psychology, 74*(11), 1907–1923.

Soto, C. J. (2021). Do links between personality and life outcomes generalize? Testing the robustness of trait–outcome associations across gender, age, ethnicity, and analytic approaches. *Social Psychological and Personality Science, 12*(1), 118–130.

Soto, C. J., & John, O. P. (2017). The next big five inventory (BFI-2): Developing and assessing a hierarchical model with 15 facets to enhance bandwidth, fidelity, and predictive power. *Journal of Personality and Social Psychology, 113*, 117–143.

Soussignan, R. (2001). Duchenne smile, emotional experience, and autonomic reactivity: A test of the facial feedback hypothesis. *Emotion, 2*, 52–74.

South, S. C., Krueger, R. F., Johnson, W., & Iacono, W. G. (2008). Adolescent personality moderates genetic and environmental influences on relationships with parents. *Journal of Personality and Social Psychology, 94*, 899–912.

Sowell, T. (1991, May/June). Cultural diversity: A world view. *American Enterprise*, pp. 44–55.

Spanos, N. P., & Coe, W. C. (1992). A social-psychological approach to hypnosis. In E. Fromm & M. R. Nash (Eds.), *Contemporary hypnosis research*. Guilford.

Sparkman, G., & Walton, G. M. (2017). Dynamic norms promote sustainable behavior, even if it is counternormative. *Psychological Science, 28*, 1663–1674.

Sparkman, G., & Walton, G. M. (2019). Witnessing change: Dynamic norms help resolve diverse barriers to personal change. *Journal of Experimental Social Psychology, 82*, 238–252.

Sparrow, E. P., Swirsky, L. T., Kudus, F., & Spaniol, J. (2021). Aging and altruism: A meta-analysis. *Psychology and Aging, 36*(1), 49–56.

Spearman, C. (1904). "General intelligence," objectively determined and measured. *American Journal of Psychology, 15*, 201–292.

Spector, T. (2012). *Identically different: Why you can change your genes*. Weidenfeld & Nicolson.

Speer, N. K., Reynolds, J. R., Swallow, K. M., & Zacks, J. M. (2009). Reading stories activates neural representations of visual and motor experiences. *Psychological Science, 20*, 989–999.

Spelke, E. S., Bernier, E. P., & Skerry, A. E. (2013). Core social cognition. In M. R. Banaji & S. A. Gelman (Eds.), *Navigating the social world: What infants, children, and other species can teach us*. Oxford University Press.

Spencer, K. M., Nestor, P. G., Perlmutter, R., Niznikiewicz, M. A., Klump, M. C., Frumin, M., Shenton, M. E., & McCarley, R. W. (2004). Neural synchrony indexes disordered perception and cognition in schizophrenia. *PNAS, 101*, 17288–17293.

Spencer, S. J., Logel, C., & Davies, P. G. (2016). Stereotype threat. *Annual Review of Psychology, 67*, 415–437.

Spencer, S. J., Steele, C. M., & Quinn, D. M. (1999). Stereotype threat and women's math performance. *Journal of Experimental Social Psychology, 35*(1), 4–28.

Sperry, R. W. (1964). *Problems outstanding in the evolution of brain function*. The James Arthur Lecture, delivered at the American Museum of Natural History, New York, NY. Cited by R. Ornstein (1977), *The psychology of consciousness* (2nd ed.). Harcourt Brace Jovanovich.

Sperry, R. W. (1985). Changed concepts of brain and consciousness: Some value implications. *Zygon, 20*, 41–57.

Spiegel, A. (2015, January 8). *Dark thoughts*. From "Invisibilia." National Public Radio. https://www.npr.org/2015/01/09/375928124/dark-thoughts

Spiegel, D. (2007). The mind prepared: Hypnosis in surgery. *Journal of the National Cancer Institute, 99*, 1280–1281.

Spiegel, D. (2008, January 31). *Coming apart: Trauma and the fragmentation of the self*. Dana Foundation. https://www.dana.org/article/coming-apart-trauma-and-the-fragmentation-of-the-self/

Spielberger, C., & London, P. (1982). Rage boomerangs. *American Health, 1*, 52–56.

Spielmann, J., Feng, S., Briley, D. A., & Stern, C. (2022). Mental health contributors among transgender people in a non-WEIRD society: Evidence from China. *Social Psychological and Personality Science, 13*(3), 747–757.

Spinhoven, P., van Hemert, A. M., & Penninx, B. W. (2018). Repetitive negative thinking as a predictor of depression and anxiety: A longitudinal cohort study. *Journal of Affective Disorders, 241*, 216–225.

Spitzer, M. (2020). Masked education? The benefits and burdens of wearing face masks in schools during the current Corona pandemic. *Trends in Neuroscience and Education, 20*. https://www.ncbi.nlm.nih.gov/pmc/articles/PMC7417296/

Sprecher, S., O'Sullivan, L. F., Drouin, M., Verette-Lindenbaum, J., & Willetts, M. C. (2022). Perhaps it was too soon: College students' reflections on the timing of their sexual debut. *Journal of Sex Research, 59*, 39–52.

Sprecher, S., Treger, S., & Sakaluk, J. K. (2013). Premarital sexual standards and sociosexuality: Gender, ethnicity, and cohort differences. *Archives of Sexual Behavior, 42*, 1395–1405.

Spring, B., Pingitore, R., Bourgeois, M., Kessler, K. H., & Bruckner, E. (1992). *The effects and non-effects of skipping breakfast: Results of three studies* [Paper]. Presented at the American Psychological Association convention.

Sproesser, G., Schupp, H. T., & Renner, B. (2014). The bright side of stress-induced eating: Eating more when stressed but less when pleased. *Psychological Science, 25*, 58–65.

Sprong, S., Jetten, J., Wang, Z., Peters, K., Verkuyten, M., Bastian, B., Ariyanto, A., Autin, F., Ayub, N., Badea, C., Besta, T., Butera, F., Costa-Lopes, R., Cui, L., Fantini, C., Finchilescu, G., Gaertner, L., Gollwitzer, M., Gómez, Á., … Wohl, J. A. (2019). "Our country needs a strong leader right now": Economic inequality enhances the wish for a strong leader. *Psychological Science, 30*(11), 1625–1637.

Squire, L. R., & Zola-Morgan, S. (1991, September 20). The medial temporal lobe memory system. *Science, 253*, 1380–1386.

Srivastava, A., Locke, E. A., & Bartol, K. M. (2001). Money and subject wellbeing: It's not the money, it's the motives. *Journal of Personality and Social Psychology, 80*, 959–971.

Srivastava, S., McGonigal, K. M., Richards, J. M., Butler, E. A., & Gross, J. J. (2006). Optimism in close relationships: How seeing things in a positive light makes them so. *Journal of Personality and Social Psychology, 91*, 143–153.

Stafford, T., & Dewar, M. (2014). Tracing the trajectory of skill learning with a very large sample of online game players. *Psychological Science, 25*, 511–518.

Stager, C. L., & Werker, J. F. (1997). Infants listen for more phonetic detail in speech perception than in word-learning tasks. *Nature, 388*, 381–382.

Stahl, A. E., & Feigenson, L. (2015). Observing the unexpected enhances infants' learning and exploration. *Science, 348*, 91–94.

Stamkou, E., van Kleef, G. A., Homan, A. C., Gelfand, M. J., van de Vijver, F. J., van Egmond, M. C., Boer, D., Phiri, N., Ayub, N., Kinias, Z., Cantarero, K., Efrat Treister, D., Figueiredo, A., Hashimoto, H., Hofmann, E. B., Lima, R. P., & Lee, I. C. (2019). Cultural collectivism and tightness moderate responses to norm violators: Effects on power perception, moral emotions, and leader support. *Personality and Social Psychology Bulletin, 45*, 947–964.

Stanley, D., Phelps, E., & Banaji, M. (2008). The neural basis of implicit attitudes. *Current Directions in Psychological Science, 17*, 164–170.

Stanley, S., & Rhoades, G. (2016a, July 19). *Testing a relationship is probably the worst reason to cohabit*. Institute for Family Studies. https://ifstudies.org/blog/testing-a-relationship-is-probably-the-worst-reason-to-cohabit

Stanley, S., & Rhoades, G. (2016b, July/August). The perils of sowing your wild oats. *Psychology Today*, pp. 40–42.

Stanovich, K. E., West, R. F., & Toplak, M. E. (2016). *The rationality quotient: Toward a test of rational thinking*. MIT Press.

Starcke, K., & Brand, M. (2016). Effects of stress on decisions under uncertainty: A meta-analysis. *Psychological Bulletin, 142*, 909–933.

Starzynski, L. L., Ullman, S. E., & Vasquez, A. L. (2017). Sexual assault survivors' experiences with mental health professionals: A qualitative study. *Women & Therapy, 40*, 228–246.

Statista. (2022, June). *Matchmaking - worldwide*. www.statista.com/outlook/dmo/eservices/dating-services/matchmaking/worldwide#revenue

Statista. (2022). *Total number of SMS and MMS messages sent in the United States from 2005 to 2020*. https://www.statista.com/statistics/185879/number-of-text-messages-in-the-united-states-since-2005/

Statistics Canada. (2016). *Chart 10: Prevalence of fair/poor mental health and mood disorders, female population aged 12 to 19, Canada, 2003 to 2014*. https://www150.statcan.gc.ca/n1/pub/89-503-x/2015001/article/14324/c-g/c-g10-eng.htm

Statistics Canada. (2019). *Bilingualism among Canadian children and youth* [PDF file]. https://www150.statcan.gc.ca/n1/en/pub/11-627-m/11-627-m2019090-eng.pdf?st=giS_k41l

Statistics Canada. (2019). *Mental health characteristics: Ability to handle stress and sources of stress*. https://www150.statcan.gc.ca/t1/tbl1/en/tv.action?pid=1310080201

Staub, E. (1989). *The roots of evil: The psychological and cultural sources of genocide*. Cambridge University Press.

Stavrinos, D., Pope, C. N., Shen, J., & Schwebel, D. C. (2017). Distracted walking, bicycling, and driving: Systematic review and meta-analysis of mobile technology and youth crash risk. *Child Development, 89*(1), 118–128.

Stavrova, O., & Ehlebracht, D. (2019). The cynical genius illusion: Exploring and debunking lay beliefs about cynicism and competence. *Personality and Social Psychology Bulletin, 45*(2), 254–269.

St. Clair, D., Xu, M., Wang, P., Yu, Y., Fang, Y., Zhang, F., Zheng, X., Gu, N., Feng, G., Sham, P., & He, L. (2005). Rates of adult schizophrenia following prenatal exposure to the Chinese famine of 1959–1961. *Journal of the American Medical Association, 294*, 557–562.

Steel, P., Schmidt, J., & Schultz, J. (2008). Refining the relationship between personality and subject well-being. *Psychological Bulletin, 134*, 138–161.

Steele, C. M. (1990, May). A conversation with Claude Steele. *APS Observer*, pp. 11–17.

Steele, C. M. (1995, August 31). Black students live down to expectations. *The New York Times*. https://www.nytimes.com/1995/08/31/opinion/black-students-live-down-to-expectations.html

Steele, C. M. (2010). *Whistling Vivaldi: And other clues to how stereotypes affect us*. Norton.

Steele, C. M., & Josephs, R. A. (1990). Alcohol myopia: Its prized and dangerous effects. *American Psychologist, 45*, 921–933.

Steele, C. M., Spencer, S. J., & Aronson, J. (2002). Contending with group image: The psychology of stereotype and social identity threat. *Advances in Experimental Social Psychology, 34*, 379–440.

Stefanovic, M., Rosenkranz, T., Ehring, T., Watkins, E. R., & Takano, K. (2022). Is a high association between repetitive negative thinking and negative affect predictive of depressive symptoms? A clustering approach for experience-sampling data. *Clinical Psychological Science, 10*(1), 74–89.

Stein, D. J., Harris, M. G., Vigo, D. V., Chiu, W. T., Sampson, N., Alonso, J., Altwaijri, Y., Caldas-de-Almeida, J. M., Cía, A., Ciutan, M., Degenhardt, L., Gureje, O., Karam, A., Karam, E. G., Lee, S., Medina-Mora, M. E., Mneimneh, Z., Navarro-Mateu, F., Posada-Villa, J., … Kessler, R. C. (2020). Perceived helpfulness of treatment for posttraumatic stress disorders: Findings from the World Mental Health Surveys. *Depression & Anxiety, 37*(10), 972–994.

Stein, R. (2018, December 18). *Surgeon General warns youth vaping is now an 'epidemic.'* National Public Radio. https://www.npr.org/sections/health-shots/2018/12/18/677755266/surgeon-general-warns-youth-vaping-is-now-an-epidemic

Steinberg, L. (1987, September). Bound to bicker. *Psychology Today*, pp. 36–39.

Steinberg, L. (2012, Spring). Should the science of adolescent brain development inform public policy? *Issues in Science and Technology, 28*, pp. 67–78.

Steinberg, L. (2013). The influence of neuroscience on U.S. Supreme Court decisions involving adolescents' criminal culpability. *Nature Reviews Neuroscience, 14*, 513–518.

Steinberg, L. (2015). How to improve the health of American adolescents. *Perspectives on Psychological Science, 10*, 711–715.

Steinberg, L., & Icenogle, G. (2019). Using developmental science to distinguish adolescents and adults under the law. *Annual Review of Developmental Psychology, 1*, 21–40.

Steinberg, L., Icenogle, G., Shulman, E. P., Breiner, K., Chein, J., Bacchini, D., Chang, L., Chaudhary, N., Giunta, L. D., Dodge, K. A., Fanti, K. A., Lansford, J. E., Malone, P. S., Oburu, P., Pastorelli, C., Skinner, A. T., Sorbring, E., Tapanya, S., Tirado, L. M. U., ... Takash, H. M. S. (2018). Around the world, adolescence is a time of heightened sensation seeking and immature self-regulation. *Developmental Science, 21*. https://doi.org/10.1111/desc.12532.

Steinberg, L., Lamborn, S. D., Darling, N., Mounts, N. S., & Dornbusch, S. M. (1994). Over-time changes in adjustment and competence among adolescents from authoritative, authoritarian, indulgent, and neglectful families. *Child Development, 65*, 754–770.

Steinberg, L., & Morris, A. S. (2001). Adolescent development. *Annual Review of Psychology, 52*, 83–110.

Steinberg, L., & Scott, E. S. (2003). Less guilty by reason of adolescence: Developmental immaturity, diminished responsibility, and the juvenile death penalty. *American Psychologist, 58*, 1009–1018.

Steinberg, L., Cauffman, E., Woolard, J., Graham, S., & Banich, M. (2009). Are adolescents less mature than adults? Minors' access to abortion, the juvenile death penalty, and the alleged APA "flip-flop." *American Psychologist, 64*, 583–594.

Steinberg, N. (1993, February). Astonishing love stories (from an earlier United Press International report). *Games*, p. 47.

Steiner, J. L., Murphy, E. A., McClellan, J. L., Carmichael, M. D., & Davis, J. M. (2011). Exercise training increases mitochondrial biogenesis in the brain. *Journal of Applied Physiology, 111*, 1066–1071.

Steinert, C., Munder, T., Rabung, S., Hoyer, J., & Leichsenring, F. (2017). Psychodynamic therapy: As efficacious as other empirically supported treatments? A meta-analysis testing equivalence of outcomes. *American Journal of Psychiatry, 174*, 943–953.

Steinglass, J. E, Glasofer, D. R., Walsh, E., Guzman, G., Peterson, C. B., Walsh, B. T., Attia, E., & Wonderlich, S. A. (2018). Targeting habits in anorexia nervosa: A proof-of-concept randomized trial. *Psychological Medicine, 48*, 2584–2591.

Stelter, M., Essien, I., Sander, C., & Degner, J. (2022). Racial bias in police traffic stops: White residents' county-level prejudice and stereotypes are related to disproportionate stopping of Black drivers. *Psychological Science, 33*(4), 483–496.

Stephan, Y., Sutin, A. R., Kornadt, A., Caudroit, J., & Terracciano, A. (2018). Higher IQ in adolescence is related to a younger subjective age in later life: Findings from the Wisconsin Longitudinal Study. *Intelligence, 69*, 195–199.

Stephens-Davidowitz, S. (2013, December 7). How many American men are gay? *The New York Times*. https://www.nytimes.com/2013/12/08/opinion/sunday/how-many-american-men-are-gay.html

Stephens-Davidowitz, S. (2014). The effects of racial animus on a black candidate: Evidence using Google search data. *Journal of Public Economics, 118*, 26–40.

Stephens-Davidowitz, S. (2017). *Everybody lies: Big data, new data, and what the internet can tell us about who we really are.* HarperCollins.

Steptoe, A., & Wardle, J. (2011). Positive affect measured using ecological momentary assessment and survival in older men and woman. *PNAS, 108*, 18244–18248.

Steptoe, A., & Wardle, J. (2017). Life skills, wealth, health, and wellbeing later in life. *PNAS, 114*, 4354–4359.

Sterling, R. (2003). *The traveling curmudgeon: Irreverent notes, quotes, and anecdotes on dismal destinations, excess baggage, the full upright position, and other reasons not to go there* (p. 102). Sasquatch Book.

Stern, M., & Karraker, K. H. (1989). Sex stereotyping of infants: A review of gender labeling studies. *Sex Roles, 20*, 501–522.

Sternberg, E. M. (2009). *Healing spaces: The science of place and well-being.* Harvard University Press.

Sternberg, R. (2017). ACCEL: A new model for identifying the gifted. *Roeper Review, 39*, 152–169.

Sternberg, R. J. (1985). *Beyond IQ: A triarchic theory of human intelligence.* Cambridge University Press.

Sternberg, R. J. (1988). Applying cognitive theory to the testing and teaching of intelligence. *Applied Cognitive Psychology, 2*, 231–255.

Sternberg, R. J. (2003). Our research program validating the triarchic theory of successful intelligence: Reply to Gottfredson. *Intelligence, 31*, 399–413.

Sternberg, R. J. (2015). Successful intelligence: A model for testing intelligence beyond IQ tests. *European Journal of Education and Psychology, 8*, 76–84.

Sternberg, R. J., & Grajek, S. (1984). The nature of love. *Journal of Personality and Social Psychology, 47*, 312–329.

Sternberg, R. J., & Kaufman, J. C. (1998). Human abilities. *Annual Review of Psychology, 49*, 479–502.

Sternberg, R. J., & Lubart, T. I. (1991). An investment theory of creativity and its development. *Human Development, 34*, 1–31.

Sternberg, R. J., & Lubart, T. I. (1992). Buy low and sell high: An investment approach to creativity. *Psychological Science, 1*, 1–5.

Sterzing, P. R., Shattuck, P. T., Narendorf, S. C., Wagner, M., & Cooper, B. P. (2012). Bullying involvement and autism spectrum disorders: Prevalence and correlates of bullying involvement among adolescents with an autism spectrum disorder. *Archives of Pediatric and Adolescent Medicine, 166*, 1058–1064.

Stetter, F., & Kupper, S. (2002). Autogenic training: A meta-analysis of clinical outcome studies. *Applied Psychophysiology and Biofeedback, 27*, 45–98.

Stevenson, R. J. (2014). Flavor binding: Its nature and cause. *Psychological Bulletin, 140*, 487–510.

Stevenson, R. J., & Francis, H. M. (2017). The hippocampus and the regulation of human food intake. *Psychological Bulletin, 143*, 1011–1032.

Steyvers, M., Hawkins, G. E., Karayanidis, F., & Brown, S. D. (2019). A large-scale analysis of task switching practice effects across the lifespan. *PNAS, 116*, 17735–17740.

Stice, E. (2002). Risk and maintenance factors for eating pathology: A meta-analytic review. *Psychological Bulletin, 128*, 825–848.

Stickgold, R. (2000, March 7). Quoted by S. Blakeslee in, For better learning, researchers endorse, "sleep on it" adage. *The New York Times*. https://www.nytimes.com/2000/03/07/science/for-better-learning-researchers-endorse-sleep-on-it-adage.html

Stier, A., & Hinshaw, S. P. (2007). Explicit and implicit stigma against individuals with mental illness. *Australian Psychologist, 42*(2), 106–117.

Stillman, T. F., Baumeister, R. F., Vohs, K. D., Lambert, N. M., Fincham, F. D., & Brewer, L. E. (2010). Personal philosophy and personnel achievement: Belief in free will predicts better job performance. *Social Psychological and Personality Science, 1*, 43–50.

Stillman, T. F., Lambet, N. M., Fincham, F. D., & Baumeister, R. F. (2011). Meaning as magnetic force: Evidence that meaning in life promotes interpersonal appeal. *Social Psychological and Personality Science, 2*, 13–20.

Stinson, D. A., Logel, C., Zanna, M. P., Holmes, J. G., Camerson, J. J., Wood, J. V., & Spencer, S. J. (2008). The cost of lower self-esteem: Testing a self- and social-bonds model of health. *Journal of Personality and Social Psychology, 94*, 412–428.

Stipek, D. (1992). The child at school. In M. H. Bornstein & M. E. Lamb (Eds.), *Developmental psychology: An advanced textbook.* Erlbaum.

Stith, S. M., Rosen, K. H., Middleton, K. A., Busch, A. L., Lunderberg, K., & Carlton, R. P. (2000). The intergenerational transmission of spouse abuse: A meta-analysis. *Journal of Marriage and the Family, 62*, 640–654.

Stjepanovic, D., & LaBar, K. S. (2018). Fear learning. In J. T. Wixted (Ed.), *Stevens' handbook of experimental psychology (4th ed., Vol. 1).* Wiley.

Stockton, M. C., & Murnen, S. K. (1992, June). *Gender and sexual arousal in response to sexual stimuli: A meta-analytic review* [Paper]. Presented at the Fourth Annual Convention of the American Psychological Society, San Diego, CA.

Stokoe, W. C. (1960). Sign language structure: An outline of the visual communication systems of the American Deaf. *Studies in linguistics: Occasional papers* (No. 8). Dept. of Anthropology and Linguistics, University of Buffalo.

Stolzenberg, E. B., Aragon, M. C., Romo, E., Couch, V., McLennan, D., Eagan, M. K., & Kang, N. (2020). *The American freshman: National norms fall 2019* [PDF file.] CIRP. https://www.heri.ucla.edu/monographs/TheAmericanFreshman2019.pdf

Stolzenberg, E. B., Eagan, M. K., Romo, E., Tamargo, E. J., Aragon, M.C., Luedke, M.,

& Kang, N. (2019). *The American freshman: National norms fall 2018*. Higher Education Research Institute, UCLA.

Stone, A. A., & Neale, J. M. (1984). Effects of severe daily events on mood. *Journal of Personality and Social Psychology, 46*, 137–144.

Stone, A. A., Schwartz, J. E., Broderick, J. E., & Deaton, A. (2010). A snapshot of the age distribution of psychological well-being in the United States. *PNAS, 107*, 9985–9990.

Stone, A. A., Schwartz, J. E., Broderick, J. E., & Shiffman, S. S. (2005). Variability of momentary pain predicts recall of weekly pain: A consequences of the peak (or salience) memory heuristic. *Personality and Social Psychology Bulletin, 31*, 1340–1346.

Stone, D. M., Holland, K. M., Bartholow, B., Crosby, A. E., Davis, S., & Wilkins, N. (2017). *Preventing suicide: A technical package of policies, programs, and practices*. National Center for Injury Prevention and Control, Centers for Disease Control and Prevention.

Stone, G. (2006, February 17). *Homeless man discovered to be lawyer with amnesia*. ABC News. https://abcnews.go.com/US/story?id=1629645&page=1

Stone, M., & Vogelstein, R. (2019, March 7). *Celebrating #MeToo's global impact*. Foreign Policy. https://foreignpolicy.com/2019/03/07/metooglobalimpactinternationalwomens-day/

St-Onge, M. P., McReynolds, A., Trivedi, Z. B., Roberts, A. L., Sy, M., & Hirsch, J. (2012). Sleep restriction leads to increased activation of brain regions sensitive to food stimuli. *American Journal of Clinical Nutrition, 95*, 818–824.

Stop Street Harassment. (2018). *The facts behind the #MeToo movement: A national study on sexual harassment and assault* [PDF file]. http://www.stopstreetharassment.org/wp-content/uploads/2018/01/Executive-Summary-2018-National-Study-on-Sexual-Harassment-and-Assault.pdf

Storbeck, J., Robinson, M. D., & McCourt, M. E. (2006). Semantic processing precedes affect retrieval: The neurological case for cognitive primary in visual processing. *Review of General Psychology, 10*, 41–55.

Storm, B. C., & Jobe, T. A. (2012). Retrieval-induced forgetting predicts failure to recall negative autobiographical memories. *Psychological Science, 23*, 1356–1363.

Storm, L., Tressoldi, P. E., & Di Risio, L. (2010a). A meta-analysis with nothing to hide: Reply to Hyman (2010). *Psychological Bulletin, 136*, 491–494.

Storm, L., Tressoldi, P. E., & Di Risio, L. (2010b). Meta-analysis of free-response studies, 1992–2008: Assessing the noise reduction model in parapsychology. *Psychological Bulletin, 136*, 471–485.

Storms, M. D. (1973). Videotape and the attribution process: Reversing actors' and observers' points of view. *Journal of Personality and Social Psychology, 27*, 165–175.

Storms, M. D. (1981). A theory of erotic orientation development. *Psychological Review, 88*, 340–353.

Storms, M. D., & Thomas, G. C. (1977). Reactions to physical closeness. *Journal of Personality and Social Psychology, 35*, 412–418.

Stothart, C., Mitchum, A., & Yehnert, C. (2015). The attentional cost of receiving a cell phone notification. *Journal of Experimental Psychology: Human Perception and Performance, 41*, 893–897.

Stout, D. M., Glenn, D. E., Acheson, D. T., Spadoni, A. D., Risbrough, V. B., & Simmons, A. N. (2018). Neural measures associated with configural threat acquisition. *Neurobiology of Learning and Memory, 150*, 99–106.

Stowell, J. R., Oldham, T., & Bennett, D. (2010). Using student response systems ("clickers") to combat conformity and shyness. *Teaching of Psychology, 37*, 135–140.

Strack, F. (2016). Reflection on the Smiling Registered Replication Report. *Perspectives on Psychological Science, 11*, 929–930.

Stramaccia, D. F., Meyer, A.-K., Rischer, K. M., Fawcett, J. M., & Benoit, R. G. (2021). Memory suppression and its deficiency in psychological disorders: A focused meta-analysis. *Journal of Experimental Psychology: General, 150*(5), 828–850.

Strange, D., Hayne, H., & Garry, M. (2008). A photo, a suggestion, a false memory. *Applied Cognitive Psychology, 22*, 587–603.

Stratton, G. M. (1896). Some preliminary experiments on vision without inversion of the retinal image. *Psychological Review, 3*, 611–617.

Strauss, M. (2018, August 16). *Americans are divided over the use of animals in scientific research*. Pew Research Center. https://www.pewresearch.org/fact-tank/2018/08/16/americans-are-divided-over-the-use-of-animals-in-scientific-research/

Strawbridge, W. J. (1999). *Mortality and religious involvement: A review and critique of the results, the methods, and the measures* [Paper]. Presented at a Harvard University conference on religion and health, sponsored by the National Institute for Health Research and the John Templeton Foundation.

Strawbridge, W. J., Cohen, R. D., & Shema, S. J. (1997). Frequent attendance at religious services and mortality over 28 years. *American Journal of Public Health, 87*, 957–961.

Strawn, J. R., Mills, J. A., Suresh, V., Peris, T. S., Walkup, J. T., & Croarkin, P. E. (2022). Combining selective serotonin reuptake inhibitors and cognitive behavioral therapy in youth with depression and anxiety. *Journal of Affective Disorders, 298, Part A*, 292–300.

Strayhorn, J., Jr. (2019). Editorial: Cognitive-behavior therapy versus serotonin reuptake inhibitors for pediatric obsessive-compulsive disorder. *Journal of the American Academy of Child & Adolescent Psychiatry, 59*, 219–221.

Strick, M., Dijksterhuis, A., Bos, M. W., Sjoerdsma, A., & van Baaren, R. B. (2011). A meta-analysis on unconscious thought effects. *Social Cognition, 29*, 738–762.

Strick, M., Dijksterhuis, A., & van Baaren, R. B. (2010). Unconscious thought effects take place off-line, not on-line. *Psychological Science, 21*, 484–488.

Strickland, B. (1992, February 20). *Gender differences in health and illness* [Lecture]. Sigma Xi national lecture delivered at Hope College, Michigan.

Striem-Amit, E., Vannuscorps, G., & Caramazza, A. (2018). Plasticity based on compensatory effector use in the association but not primary sensorimotor cortex of people born without hands. *PNAS, 115*, 7801–7806.

Strittmatter, A., Sunde, U., & Zegners, D. (2020). Life cycle patterns of cognitive performance over the long run. *PNAS, 117*, 27255–27261.

Stroebe, M., Finenauer, C., Wijngaards-de Meij, L., Schut, H., van den Bout, J., & Stroebe, W. (2013). Partner-oriented self-regulation among bereaved parents: The costs of holding in grief for the partner's sake. *Psychological Science, 24*, 395–402.

Stroebe, W. (2012). The truth about Triplett (1898), but nobody seems to care. *Perspectives on Psychological Science, 7*, 54–57.

Stroebe, W. (2013). Firearm possession and violent death: A critical review. *Aggression and Violent Behavior, 18*, 709–721.

Stroebe, W., Leander, N. P., & Kruglanski, A. W. (2017). Is it a dangerous world out there? The motivational bases of American gun ownership. *Personality and Social Psychology Bulletin, 43*, 1071–1085.

Stroebe, W., Schut, H., & Stroebe, M. S. (2005). Grief work, disclosure and counseling: Do they help the bereaved? *Clinical Psychology Review, 25*, 395–414.

Stroud, L. R., Panadonatos, G. D., Rodriguez, D., McCallum, M., Salisbury, A. L., Phipps, M. G., Lester, B., Huestis, M. A., Niaura, R., Padbury, J. F., & Marsit, C. J. (2014). Maternal smoking during pregnancy and infant stress response: Test of a prenatal programming hypothesis. *Psychoneuroendocrinology, 48*, 29–40.

Strully, K. W. (2009). Job loss and health in the U.S. labor market. *Demography, 46*, 221–246.

Stubbs, B., Vancampfort, D., Rosenbaum, S., Firth, J., Cosco, T., Veronese, N., Salum, G. A., & Schuch, F. B. (2017). An examination of the anxiolytic effects of exercise for people with anxiety and stress-related disorders: A meta-analysis. *Psychiatry Research, 249*, 102–108.

Studte, S., Bridger, E., & Mecklinger, A. (2017). Sleep spindles during a nap correlate with post sleep memory performance for highly rewarded word-pairs. *Brain and Language, 167*, 28–35.

Štulhofer, A., Šoh, D., Jelaska, N., Baćak, V., & Landripet, I. (2011). Religiosity and sexual risk behavior among Croatian college students, 1998–2008. *Journal of Sex Research, 48*, 360–371.

Sturm, V. E., Datta, S., Roy, A. R. K., Sible, I. J., Kosik, E. L., Veziris, C. R., Chow, T. E., Morris, N. A., Neuhaus, J., Kramer, J. H., Miller, B. L., Holley, S. R., & Keltner, D. (2020). Big smile, small self: Awe walks promote prosocial positive emotions in older adults [PDF file]. *Emotion*. Advance online publication. https://tinyurl.com/s4nbhn7b

Su, N., Buchin, Z. L., & Mulligan, N. W. (2021). Levels of retrieval and the testing effect. *Journal of Experimental Psychology: Learning, Memory, and Cognition, 47*(4), 652–670.

Subotnik, R. F., Olszewski-Kubilius, P., & Worrell, F. C. (2011). Rethinking giftedness and gifted education: A proposed direction forward based on psychological science. *Psychological Science in the Public Interest, 12*, 3–54.

Suchotzki, K., Verschuere, B., Van Bockstaele, B., Ben-Shakhar, G., & Crombez, G. (2017). Lying takes time: A meta-analysis on reaction time measures of deception. *Psychological Bulletin, 143*, 428–453.

Suddath, R. L., Christison, G. W., Torrey, E. F., Casanova, M. F., & Weinberger, D. R. (1990). Anatomical abnormalities in the brains of monozygotic twins discordant for schizophrenia. *New England Journal of Medicine, 322*, 789–794.

Suddendorf, T. (2018, September). Two key features created the human mind. *Scientific American*, pp. 43–47.

Sue, S., Zane, N., Hall, G. C. N., & Berger, L. K. (2009). The case for cultural competency in psychotherapeutic interventions. *Annual Review of Psychology, 60*, 525–548.

Suedfeld, P., & Mocellin, J. S. P. (1987). The "sensed presence" in unusual environments. *Environment and Behavior, 19*, 33–52.

Sugaya, L., Hasin, D. S., Olfson, M., Lin, K.-H., Grant, B. F., & Blanco, C. (2012). Child physical abuse and adult mental health: A national study. *Journal of Traumatic Stress, 25*, 384–392.

Sugimura, K. (2020). Adolescent identity development in Japan. *Child Development Perspectives, 14*(2), 71–77.

Sullivan, P. F., Neale, M. C., & Kendler, K. S. (2000). Genetic epidemiology of major depression: Review and meta-analysis. *American Journal of Psychiatry, 157*, 1552–1562.

Sulser, R. B., Patterson, B. D., Urban, D. J., Neander, A. I., & Luo, Z.-X. (2022). Evolution of inner ear neuroanatomy of bats and implications for echolocation. *Nature, 602*, 449–454.

Sumner, R., Burrow, A. L., & Hill, P. L. (2018). The development of purpose in life among adolescents who experience marginalization: Potential opportunities and obstacles. *American Psychologist, 73*, 740–752.

Sun, X., Zheng, B., Lv, J., Guo, Y., Bian, Z., Yang, L., Chen, Y., Fu, Z., Guo, H., Liang, P., Chen, Z., Chen, J., Li, L., Yu, C., & China Kadoorie Biobank (CKB) Collaborative Group. (2018). Sleep behavior and depression: Findings from the China Kadoorie Biobank of 0.5 million Chinese adults. *Journal of Affective Disorders, 229*, 120–124.

Sun, Y., Mensah, F. K., Azzopardi, P., Patton, G. C., & Wake, M. (2017). Childhood social disadvantage and pubertal timing: A national birth cohort from Australia. *Pediatrics, 139*(6), 1–10.

Sundstrom, E., De Meuse, K. P., & Futrell, D. (1990). Work teams: Applications and effectiveness. *American Psychologist, 45*, 120–133.

Sung, S., Simpson, J. A., Griskevicius, V., Sally, I., Kuo, C., Schlomer, G. L., & Belsky, J. (2016). Secure infant-mother attachment buffers the effect of early-life stress on age of menarche. *Psychological Science, 27*, 667–674.

Sunstein, C. R., Bobadilla-Suarez, S., Lazzaro, S. C., & Sharot, T. (2016). How people update beliefs about climate change: Good news and bad news [PDF file]. *Cornell Law Review, 102*(6). https://scholarship.law.cornell.edu/cgi/viewcontent.cgi?article=4736&context=clr

Sunstein, C. R., & Thaler, R. (2016, December 7). The two friends who changed how we think about how we think. *The New Yorker*. https://www.newyorker.com/books/page-turner/the-two-friends-who-changed-how-we-think-about-how-we-think

Suomi, S. J. (1986). Anxiety-like disorders in young nonhuman primates. In R. Gettleman (Ed.), *Anxiety disorders of childhood*. Guilford Press.

Suomi, S. J., Collins, M. L., Harlow, H. F., & Ruppenthal, G. C. (1976). Effects of maternal and peer separations on young monkeys. *Journal of Child Psychology and Psychiatry, 17*, 101–112.

Suppes, P. (1982). Quoted in R. H. Ennis, Children's ability to handle Piaget's propositional logic: A conceptual critique. In S. Modgil & C. Modgil (Eds.), *Jean Piaget: Consensus and controversy* (pp. 101–130). Praeger.

Surgeon General. (1986). *The Surgeon General's workshop on pornography and public health* [Report] June 22–24. Prepared by E. P. Mulvey & J. L. Haugaard and released by Office of the Surgeon General on August 4, 1986.

Surgeon General. (1999). *Mental health: A report of the Surgeon General*. Department of Health and Human Services. https://profiles.nlm.nih.gov/spotlight/nn/catalog/nlm:nlmuid-101584932X120-doc

Surgeon General. (2012). *Preventing tobacco use among youth and young adults: A report of the Surgeon General*. Department of Health and Human Services, Office of the Surgeon General.

Susser, E., & Martínez-Alés, G. (2018). Putting psychosis into sociocultural context: An international study in 17 locations. *JAMA Psychiatry, 75*, 9–10.

Susser, E. S. (1999). Life course cohort studies of schizophrenia. *Psychiatric Annals, 29*, 161–165.

Susser, E. S., Neugenbauer, R., Hoek, H. W., Brown, A. S., Lin, S., Labovitz, D., & Gorman, J. M. (1996). Schizophrenia after prenatal famine. *Archives of General Psychiatry, 53*, 25–31.

Svaldi, J., Schmitz, F., Baur, J., Hartmann, A. S., Legenbauer, T., Thaler, C., von Wietersheim, J., de Zwaan, M., & Tuschen-Caffier, B. (2019). Efficacy of psychotherapies and pharmacotherapies for bulimia nervosa. *Psychological Medicine, 49*, 898–910.

Svensson, J. E., Svanborg, C., Plavén-Sigray, P., Kaldo, V., Halldin, C., Schain, M., & Lundberg, J. (2021, May 10). Serotonin transporter availability increases in patients recovering from a depressive episode. *Translational Psychiatry, 11*(1), 264.

Swami, V. (2015). Cultural influences on body size ideals: Unpacking the impact of Westernization and modernization. *European Psychologist, 20*, 44–51.

Swami, V., Frederick, D. A., Aavik, T., Alcalay, L., Allik, J., Anderson, D., Andrianto, S., Arora, A., Brännström, A., Cunningham, J., Danel, D., Dorosqewicz, K., Forbes, G. B., Furnham, A., Greven, C. U., Halberstadt, J., Hao, S., Haubner, T., Hwang, C. S., ... Zivcic-Becirevic, I. (2010). The attractive female body weight and female body dissatisfaction in 26 countries across 10 world regions: Results of the International Body Project I. *Personality and Social Psychology Bulletin, 36*, 309–325.

Swann, W. B., Jr., Chang-Schneider, C., & McClarty, K. L. (2007). Do people's self-views matter: Self-concept and self-esteem in everyday life. *American Psychologist, 62*, 84–94.

Swartz, J. R., Hariri, A. R., & Williamson, D. E. (2016). An epigenetic mechanism links socioeconomic status to changes in depression-related brain function in high-risk adolescents. *Molecular Psychiatry, 22*, 209–214.

Sweeny, K., & Falkenstein, A. (2017). Even optimists get the blues: Interindividual consistency in the tendency to brace for the worst. *Journal of Personality, 85*, 807–816.

Swift, A. (2013, October 28). *Personal safety top reason Americans own guns today*. Gallup. https://news.gallup.com/poll/165605/personal-safety-top-reason-americans-own-guns-today.aspx

Swim, J. K., & Hyers, L. L. (1999). Excuse me—What did you just say?!: Women's public and private reactions to sexist remarks. *Journal of Experimental Social Psychology, 35*, 68–88.

Symbaluk, D. G., Heth, C. D., Cameron, J., & Pierce, W. D. (1997). Social modeling, monetary incentives, and pain endurance: The role of self-efficacy and pain perception. *Personality and Social Psychology Bulletin, 23*, 258–269.

Symond, M. B., Harris, A. W. F., Gordon, E., & Williams, L. M. (2005). "Gamma synchrony" in first-episode schizophrenia: A disorder of temporal connectivity? *American Journal of Psychiatry, 162*, 459–465.

Szasz, P. L., Szentagotai, A., & Hofmann, S. G. (2011). The effect of emotion regulation strategies on anger. *Behaviour Research and Therapy, 49*(2), 114–119.

Szkodny, L. E., Newman, M. G., & Goldfried, M. R. (2014). Clinical experiences in conducting empirically supported treatments for generalized anxiety disorder. *Behavior Therapy, 45*, 7–20.

Szutorisz, H., & Hurd, J. L. (2016). Epigenetic effects of cannabis exposure. *Biological Psychiatry, 79*, 586–594.

Tackett, J. L., Herzhoff, K., Kushner, S. C., & Rule, N. (2016). Thin slices of child personality: Perceptual, situational, and behavioral contributions. *Journal of Personality and Social Psychology, 110*, 150–166.

Taha, F. A. (1972). A comparative study of how sighted and blind perceive the manifest content of dreams. *National Review of Social Sciences, 9*, 28.

Taheri, S. (2004, December 20). Does the lack of sleep make you fat? *University of Bristol Research News*. https://www.bristol.ac.uk/news/2004/1113989409.html

Taheri, S., Lin, L., Austin, D., Young, T., & Mignot, E. (2004). Short sleep duration is associated with reduced leptin, elevated ghrelin, and increased body mass index. *PLOS Medicine, 1*. https://journals.plos.org/plosmedicine/article?id=10.1371/journal.pmed.0010062

Tajfel, H. (Ed.). (1982). *Social identity and intergroup relations*. Cambridge University Press.

Takahashi, Y., Zheng, A., Yamagata, S., & Ando, J. (2021). Genetic and environmental architecture of conscientiousness in adolescence. *Scientific Reports, 11*. https://www.nature.com/articles/s41598-021-82781-5

Takizawa, R., Maughan, B., & Arseneault, L. (2014). Adult health outcomes of childhood bullying victimization: Evidence from a five-decade longitudinal British birth cohort. *American Journal of Psychiatry, 171*, 777–784.

Talarico, J. M., & Moore, K. M. (2012). Memories of "The Rivalry": Differences in how fans of the winning and losing teams remember the same game. *Applied Cognitive Psychology, 26*, 746–756.

Talbot, L. S., McGlinchey, E. L., Kaplan, K. A., Dahl, R. E., & Harvey, A. G. (2010). Sleep deprivation in adolescents and adults: Changes in affect. *Emotion, 10*(6), 831.

Talbot, M. (1999, October). The Rorschach chronicles. *The New York Times*. https://www.nytimes.com/1999/10/17/magazine/the-rorschach-chronicles.html

Talhelm, T., Zhang, X., & Oishi, S. (2018). Moving chairs in Starbucks: Observational studies find rice-wheat cultural differences in daily life in China. *Science Advances, 4*. https://www.science.org/doi/10.1126/sciadv.aap8469

Talhelm, T., Zhang, X., Oishi, S., Shimin, C., Duan, D., Lan, X., & Kitayama, S. (2014). Large-scale psychological differences within China explained by rice versus wheat agriculture. *Science, 344*, 603–608.

Talvitie, E., Hintsanen, M., Pulkki-Råback, L., Lipsanen, J., Merjonen, P., Hakulinen, C., Elovainio, M., Rosenström, T., Lehtimäki, T., Raitakari, O., & & Keltikangas-Järvinen, L. (2019). Adverse childhood environment and self-reported sleep in adulthood: The Young Finns Study. *Health Psychology, 38*, 705–715.

Talwar, S. K., Xu, S., Hawley, E. S., Weiss, S. A., Moxon, K. A., & Chapin, J. K. (2002). Rat navigation guided by remote control. *Nature, 417*, 37–38.

Tam, T. (2018). *The Chief Public Health Officer's report on the state of public health in Canada 2018: Preventing problematic substance use in youth*. Public Health Agency of Canada. https://bit.ly/3qFTVg3

Tamir, M. (2009). What do people want to feel and why? Pleasure and utility in emotion regulation. *Current Directions in Psychological Science, 18*(2), 101–105.

Tamminen, J., & Mebude, M. (2019). Reinstatement of odour context cues veridical memories but not false memories. *Memory, 27*, 575–579.

Tamres, L. K., Janicki, D., & Helgeson, V. S. (2002). Sex differences in coping behavior: A meta-analytic review and an examination of relative coping. *Personality and Social Psychology Review, 6*, 2–30.

Tan, J. J. X., Kraus, M. W., Carpenter, N. C., & Adler, N. E. (2020). The association between objective and subjective socioeconomic status and subjective well-being: A meta-analytic review. *Psychological Bulletin, 146*(11), 970–1020.

Tan, L. L., & Kuner, R. (2021). Neocortical circuits in pain and pain relief. *Nature Reviews Neuroscience, 22*, 458–471.

Tang, A., Crawford, H., Morales, S., Degnan, K. A., Pine, D. S., & Fox, N. A. (2020). Infant behavioral inhibition predicts personality and social outcomes three decades later. *PNAS, 117*(18), 9800–9807.

Tang, S.-H., & Hall, V. C. (1995). The overjustification effect: A meta-analysis. *Applied Cognitive Psychology, 9*, 365–404.

Tang, X., Upadyaya, K., & Salmela-Aro, K. (2021). School burnout and psychosocial problems among adolescents: Grit as a resilience factor. *Journal of Adolescence, 86*, 77–89.

Tangney, J. P., Baumeister, R., & Boone, A. L. (2004). High self-control predicts good adjustment, less pathology, better grades, and interpersonal success. *Journal of Personality, 72*(2), 271–324.

Tannen, D. (1990). *You just don't understand: Women and men in conversation*. Morrow.

Tannen, D. (2001). *You just don't understand: Women and men in conversation*. Harper.

Tao, V. Y. K., Li, Y., Lam, K. H., Leung, C. W., Sun, C. I., & Wu, A. M. S. (2021). From teachers' implicit theories of intelligence to job stress: The mediating role of teachers' causal attribution of students' academic achievement. *Journal of Applied Social Psychology, 51*(5), 522–533.

Tardif, T., Fletcher, P., Liang, W., Zhang, Z., Kaciroti, N., & Marchman, V. A. (2008). Baby's first 10 words. *Developmental Psychology, 44*, 929–938.

Tarrant, M., Branscombe, N. R., Warner, R. H., & Weston, D. (2012). Social identity and perceptions of torture: It's moral when we do it. *Journal of Experimental Social Psychology, 48*, 513–518.

Tasbihsazan, R., Nettelbeck, T., & Kirby, N. (2003). Predictive validity of the Fagan test of infant intelligence. *British Journal of Developmental Psychology, 21*, 585–597.

Tasos, E. (2022). To what extent are prenatal androgens involved in the development of male homosexuality in humans? *Journal of Homosexuality, 69*(11), 1928–1963.

Tatlow, D. K. (2016). Doctor's plan for full-body transplants raises doubts even in daring China. *The New York Times*. https://www.nytimes.com/2016/06/12/world/asia/china-body-transplant.html

Taub, E. (2004). Harnessing brain plasticity through behavioral techniques to produce new treatments in neurorehabilitation. *American Psychologist, 59*, 692–698.

Taubes, G. (2001). The soft science of dietary fat. *Science, 291*, 2536–2545.

Taubes, G. (2002, July 7). What if it's all been a big fat lie? *The New York Times*. https://www.nytimes.com/2002/07/07/magazine/what-if-it-s-all-been-a-big-fat-lie.html

Tavernise, S. (2016, February 29). "Female Viagra" only modestly increases sexual satisfaction, study finds. *The New York Times*. https://www.nytimes.com/2016/03/01/health/female-viagra-addyi-flibanserin-sex-drive-women.html

Tavor, I., Botvinik-Nezer, R., Bernstein-Eliav, M., Tsarfaty, G., & Assaf, Y. (2020). Short-term plasticity following motor sequence learning revealed by diffusion magnetic resonance imaging. *Human Brain Mapping, 41*(2), 442–452.

Tavris, C. (1982, November). Anger defused. *Psychology Today*, pp. 25–35.

Tavris, C. (2022). Trans reality. *Skeptic, 27*(1), 19–22.

Tavris, C., & Aronson, E. (2007). *Mistakes were made (but not by me)*. Harcourt.

Tay, L., & Diener, E. (2011). Needs and subjective well-being around the world. *Journal of Personality and Social Psychology, 101*, 354–365.

Tay, R. Y. L., & Ng, B. C. (2019). Effects of affective priming through music on the use of emotion words. *PLOS ONE, 14*(4). https://journals.plos.org/plosone/article?id=10.1371/journal.pone.0214482

Taylor, C. (2017). Creativity and mood disorder: A systematic review and meta-analysis. *Perspectives on Psychological Science, 12*, 1040–1076.

Taylor, K., & Rohrer, D. (2010). The effects of interleaved practice. *Applied Cognitive Psychology, 24*, 837–848.

Taylor, P. (2014). *The next America: Boomers, millennials, and the looming generational showdown*. PublicAffairs.

Taylor, P. J., Russ-Eft, D. F., & Chan, D. W. L. (2005). A meta-analytic review of behavior modeling training. *Journal of Applied Psychology, 90*, 692–709.

Taylor, R. E., & Kuo, B. C. H. (2018). Black American psychological help-seeking intention: An integrated literature review with recommendations for clinical practice. *Journal of Psychotherapy Integration, 29*(4), 325–337.

Taylor, R. J., & Garry, M. (2019). People infuse their passwords with autobiographical information. *Memory, 27*, 581–591.

Taylor, S. E. (2002). *The tending instinct: How nurturing is essential to who we are and how we live*. Times Books.

Taylor, S. E. (2006). Tend and befriend: Biobehavioral bases of affiliation under stress. *Current Directions in Psychological Science, 15*, 273–277.

Taylor, S. E., Pham, L. B., Rivkin, I. D., & Armor, D. A. (1998). Harnessing the imagination: Mental simulation, self-regulation, and coping. *American Psychologist, 53*, 429–439.

Taylor-Covill, G. A., & Eves, F. F. (2016). Carrying a biological "backpack": Quasi-experimental effects of weight status and body fat change on perceived steepness. *Journal of Experimental Psychology: Human Perception and Performance, 42*, 331–338.

Teachman, B. A., McKay, D., Barch, D. M., Prinstein, M. J., Hollon, S. D., & Chambless, D. L. (2019). How psychosocial research can help the National Institute of Mental Health achieve its grand challenge to reduce the burden of mental illnesses and psychological disorders. *American Psychologist, 74*, 415–431.

Teasdale, T. W., & Owen, D. R. (2008). Secular declines in cognitive test scores: A reversal of the Flynn effect. *Intelligence, 36*, 121–126.

Teghtsoonian, R. (1971). On the exponents in Stevens' law and the constant in Ekman's law. *Psychological Review, 78*, 71–80.

Teicher, M. H., Gordon, J. B., & Nemeroff, C. B. (2022). Recognizing the importance of childhood maltreatment as a critical factor in psychiatric diagnoses, treatment, research, prevention, and education. *Molecular Psychiatry, 27*, 1331–1338.

te Lindert, B. H. W., Blanken, T., van der Meijden, W. P., Dekker, K., Wassing, R., van der Werf, Y. D., Ramautar, J. R., & Van Someren, E. J. W. (2020). Actigraphic multi-night home-recorded sleep estimates reveal three types of sleep misperception in insomnia disorder and good sleepers. *Journal of Sleep Research, 29*(1). doi: 10.1111/jsr.12937

Teller. (2009, April 20). Quoted by J. Lehrer in *Magic and the brain: Teller reveals the neuroscience of illusion*. Wired Magazine.

https://www.wired.com/2009/04/ff-neuroscienceofmagic/

Telzer, E. H., Flannery, J., Shapiro, M., Humphreys, K. L., Goff, B., Gabard-Durman, L., Gee, D. D., & Tottenham, N. (2013). Early experience shapes amygdala sensitivity to race: An international adoption design. *Journal of Neuroscience, 33,* 13484–13488.

Temming, M. (2021, August 28). The debate over gender-affirming health care. *Science News,* pp. 24–28.

ten Brinke, L., Vohs, K. D., & Carney. D. (2016). Can ordinary people detect deception after all? *Trends in Cognitive Sciences, 20,* 579–588.

Tenenbaum, H. R., & Leaper, C. (2002). Are parents' gender schemas related to their children's gender-related cognitions? A meta-analysis. *Developmental Psychology, 38,* 615–630.

Teng, Z., Chunyan, Y., Stomski, M., Nie, Q., & Guo, C. (2022). Violent video game exposure and bullying in early adolescence: A longitudinal study examining moderation of trait aggressiveness and moral identity. *Psychology of Violence, 12*(3), 149–159.

Teng, Z., Nie, Q., Guo, C., Zhang, Q., Liu, Y., & Bushman, B. J. (2019). A longitudinal study of link between exposure to violent video games and aggression in Chinese adolescents: The mediating role of moral disengagement. *Developmental Psychology,* 55, 184–195.

Tenney, E. R., Logg, J. M., & Moore, D. A. (2015). (Too) optimistic about optimism: The belief that optimism improves performance. *Journal of Personality and Social Psychology, 108,* 377–399.

Tenopyr, M. L. (1997). Improving the workplace: Industrial/organizational psychology as a career. In R. J. Sternberg (Ed.), *Career paths in psychology: Where your degree can take you.* American Psychological Association.

Terman, L. (1930). *Autobiography of Lewis Terman.* In C. A. Murchison & E. G. Boring (Eds.), *A history of psychology in autobiography.* Clark University Press.

Terrace, H. S. (1979, November). How Nim Chimpsky changed my mind. *Psychology Today,* pp. 65–76.

Terre, L., & Stoddart, R. (2000). Cutting edge specialties for graduate study in psychology. *Eye on Psi Chi,* 23–26.

Terry, P. C., Karageorghis, C. I., Curran, M. L., Martin, O. V., & Parsons-Smith, R. (2020). Effects of music in exercise and sport: A meta-analytic review. *Psychological Bulletin, 146,* 91–117.

Tesser, A., Forehand, R., Brody, G., & Long, N. (1989). Conflict: The role of calm and angry parent-child discussion in adolescent development. *Journal of Social and Clinical Psychology, 8,* 317–330.

Testa, R. J., Michaels, M. S., Bliss, W., Rogers, M. L., Balsam, K. F., & Joiner, T. (2017). Suicidal ideation in transgender people: Gender minority stress and interpersonal factors. *Journal of Abnormal Psychology, 126,* 125–136.

Teter, C. J., DiRaimo, C. G., West, B. T., Schepis, T. S., & McCabe, S. E. (2018). Nonmedical use of prescription stimulants among U.S. high school students to help study: Results from a national survey. *Journal of Pharmacy Practice, 33*(1), 38–47.

Tetlock, P. E. (1988). Monitoring the integrative complexity of American and Soviet policy rhetoric: What can be learned? *Journal of Social Issues, 44,* 101–131.

Tetlock, P. E. (1998). Close-call counterfactuals and belief-system defenses: I was not almost wrong but I was almost right. *Journal of Personality and Social Psychology, 75,* 639–652.

Tetlock, P. E. (2005). *Expert political judgement: How good is it? How can we know?* Princeton University Press.

Thaler, R. H. (2015, May 8). Unless you are Spock, irrelevant things matter in economic behavior. *The New York Times.* https://www.nytimes.com/2015/05/10/upshot/unless-you-are-spock-irrelevant-things-matter-in-economic-behavior.html

Thaler, R. H., & Sunstein, C. R. (2008). *Nudge: Improving decisions about health, wealth, and happiness.* Yale University Press.

Thalmann, M., Souza, A. S., & Oberauer, K. (2019). How does chunking help working memory? *Journal of Experimental Psychology: Learning, Memory, and Cognition, 45,* 37–55.

Thalmayer, A. G., Saucier, G., Ole-Kotikash, L., & Payne, D. (2020). Personality structure in East and West Africa: Lexical studies of personality in Maa and Supyire-Senufo. *Journal of Personality and Social Psychology, 19*(5), 1132–1152.

Tharmaratnam, T., Iskandar, M. A., Tabobondung, T. C., Tobbia, I., Gopee-Ramanan, P., & Tabobondung, T. A. (2018). Chronic traumatic encephalopathy in professional American football players: Where are we now? *Frontiers in Neurology, 9,* 445.

Thatcher, R. W., Walker, R. A., & Giudice, S. (1987). Human cerebral hemispheres develop at different rates and ages. *Science, 236,* 1110–1113.

Thayer, R. E. (1987). Energy, tiredness, and tension effects of a sugar snack versus moderate exercise. *Journal of Personality and Social Psychology, 52,* 119–125.

Thayer, R. E. (1993). Mood and behavior (smoking and sugar snacking) following moderate exercise: A partial test of self-regulation theory. *Personality and Individual Differences, 14,* 97–104.

Theobald, E. J., Hill, M. J., Tran, E., Agrawal, S., Arroyo, E. N., Behling, S., Chambwe, N., Laboy Cintrón, Cooper, J. D., Dunster, G., Grummer, J. A., Hennessey, K., Hsiao, J., Iranon, N., Jones II, L., Jordt, H., Keller, M., Lacey, M. E., Littlefield, C. E., … Freeman, S. (2020). Active learning narrows achievement gaps for underrepresented students in undergraduate science, technology, engineering, and math. *PNAS, 117*(12), 6476–6483.

Théoret, H., Halligan, H., Kobayashi, M., Fregni, F., Tager-Flusberg, H., & Pascual-Leone, A. (2005). Impaired motor facilitation during action observation in individuals with autism spectrum disorder. *Current Biology, 15,* R84–R85.

Thibodeau, R., Jorgensen, R. S., & Kim, S. (2006). Depression, anxiety, and resting frontal EEG asymmetry: A meta-analytic review. *Journal of Abnormal Psychology, 115,* 715–729.

Thiebaut de Schotten, M., Dell'Acqua, F., Ratiu, P., Leslie, A., Howells, H., Cabanis, E., Iba-Zizen, M. T., Plaisant, O., Simmons, A., Dronkers, N. F., Corkin, S., & Catani, M. (2015). From Phineas Gage and Monsieur Leborgne to HM: Revisiting disconnection syndromes. *Cerebral Cortex, 25,* 4812–4827.

Thiel, A., Hadedank, B., Herholz, K., Kessler, J., Winhuisen, L., Haupt, W. F., & Heiss, W. D. (2006). From the left to the right: How the brain compensates progressive loss of language function. *Brain and Language, 98,* 57–65.

Thomas, A., & Chess, S. (1986). The New York Longitudinal Study: From infancy to early adult life. In R. Plomin & J. Dunn (Eds.), *The study of temperament: Changes, continuities, and challenges.* Erlbaum.

Thomas, E. F., Zubielevitch, E., Sibley, C. G., & Osborne, D. (2020). Testing the social identity model of collective action longitudinally and across structurally disadvantaged and advantaged groups. *Personality and Social Psychology Bulletin, 46*(6), 823–838.

Thomas, L. (1974). *The lives of a cell.* Viking Press.

Thomas, L. (1992). *The fragile species.* Scribner's.

Thompson, G. (2010). The $1 million dollar challenge. *Skeptic Magazine, 15,* 8–9.

Thompson, J. K., Jarvie, G. J., Lahey, B. B., & Cureton, K. J. (1982). Exercise and obesity: Etiology, physiology, and intervention. *Psychological Bulletin, 91,* 55–79.

Thompson, L., Sarovic, D., Wilson, P., Sämfjord, A., & Gillberg, C. (2022). A PRISMA systematic review of adolescent gender dysphoria literature: 1) Epidemiology. *PLOS One Global Public Health.* https://journals.plos.org/globalpublichealth/article?id=10.1371/journal.pgph.0000245

Thompson, P. M., Giedd, J. N., Woods, R. P., MacDonald, D., Evans, A. C., & Toga, A. W. (2000). Growth patterns in the developing brain detected by using continuum mechanical tensor maps. *Nature, 404,* 190–193.

Thompson, P. M., Jahanshad, N., Ching, C. R. K., Salminen, L. E., Thomopoulos, S. I., Bright, J., Baune, B. T., Bertolín, S., Bralten, J., Bruin, W. B., Bülow, R., Chen, J., Chye, Y., Dannlowski, U., de Kovel, C. G. F., Donohoe, G., Eyler, L. T., Faraone, S. V., Favre, P., … Zelman, V. (2020). ENIGMA and global neuroscience: A decade of large-scale studies of the brain in health and disease across more than 40 countries. *Nature Translational Psychiatry, 10.* https://www.nature.com/articles/s41398-020-0705-1

Thompson, R., Emmorey, K., & Gollan, T. H. (2005). "Tip of the fingers" experiences by Deaf signers. *Psychological Science, 16,* 856–860.

Thomson, K. S., & Oppenheimer, D. M. (2016). Investigating an alternate form of the cognitive reflection test. *Judgment and Decision Making, 11,* 99–113.

Thompson-Hollands, J., Marx, B. P., Lee, D. J., Resick, P. A., & Sloan, D. M. (2018). Long-term treatment gains of a brief exposure-based treatment for PTSD. *Depression and Anxiety, 35,* 985–991.

Thompson-Schill, S. L., Ramscar, M., & Chrysikou, E. G. (2009). Cognition without control: When a little frontal lobe goes a long way. *Current Directions in Psychological Science, 18,* 259–263.

Thöni, C., & Volk, S. (2022). Converging evidence for greater male variability in time, risk, and social preferences. *PNAS, 118*(23).

https://www.pnas.org/doi/10.1073/pnas.2026112118#sec-1

Thorarinsdottir, E. H., Bjornsdottir, E., Benediktsdottir, B., Janson, C., Gislason, T., Aspelund, T., Kuna, S. T., Pack, A. I., & Arnardottir, E. S. (2019). Definition of excessive daytime sleepiness in the general population: Feeling sleepy relates better to sleep-related symptoms and quality of life than the Epworth Sleepiness Scale score. Results from an epidemiological study. *Journal of Sleep Research, 28*(6). doi: 10.1111/jsr.12852

Thorndike, E. L. (1898). Animal intelligence: An experimental study of the associative processes in animals. *Psychological Review Monograph Supplement, 2*, 4–160.

Thorne, J., with Larry Rothstein. (1993). *You are not alone: Words of experience and hope for the journey through depression.* HarperPerennial.

Thornton, B., & Moore, S. (1993). Physical attractiveness contrast effect: Implications for self-esteem and evaluations of the social self. *Personality and Social Psychology Bulletin, 19*, 474–480.

Thorpe, W. H. (1974). *Animal nature and human nature.* Methuen.

Tick, B., Bolton, P., Happé, F., Rutter, M., & Rijsdijk, F. (2016). Heritability of autism spectrum disorders: A meta-analysis of twin studies. *Journal of Child Psychology and Psychiatry, 57*, 585–595.

Tickle, J. J., Hull, J. G., Sargent, J. D., Dalton, M. A., & Heatherton, T. F. (2006). A structural equation model of social influences and exposure to media smoking on adolescent smoking. *Basic and Applied Social Psychology, 28*, 117–129.

Tidwell, N. D., Eastwick, P. W., & Finkel, E. J. (2013). Perceived, not actual, similarity predicts initial attraction in a live romantic context: Evidence from the speed-dating paradigm. *Personal Relationships, 20*(2), 199–215.

Tiedens, L. Z. (2001). Anger and advancement versus sadness and subjugation: The effect of negative emotion expressions on social status conferral. *Journal of Personality and Social Psychology, 80*, 86–94.

Tielbeek, J. J., Johansson, A., Polderman, T. J., Rautiainen, M. R., Jansen, P., Taylor, M., Tong, X., Lu, Q., Burt, A. S., Tiemeier, H., Viding, E., Plomin, R., Martin, N. G., Heath, A. C., Madden, P. A. F., Montgomery, G., Beaver, K. M., Waldman, I., Gelernter, J., … Broad Antisocial Behavior Consortium collaborators. (2017). Genome-wide association studies of a broad spectrum of antisocial behavior. *JAMA Psychiatry, 74*, 1242–1250.

Tigbe, W. W., Granat, M. H., Sattar, N., & Lean, M. E. J. (2017). Time spent in sedentary posture is associated with waist circumference and cardiovascular risk. *International Journal of Obesity, 41*, 689–696.

Tiggemann, M., & Miller, J. (2010). The internet and adolescent girls' weight satisfaction and drive for thinness. *Sex Roles, 63*, 79–90.

Tihonen, J., Lönnqvist, J., Wahlbeck, K., Klaukka, T., Niskanen, L., Tanskanen, A., & Haukka, J. (2009). 11-year follow-up of mortality in patients with schizophrenia: A population-based cohort study (FIN11 study). *The Lancet, 374*, 260–267.

Tiihonen, J., Rautiainen, M. R., Ollila, H. M., Repo-Tiihonen, E., Virkkunen, M., Palotie, A., Pietiläinen, O., Kristiansson, K., Joukamaa, M., Lauerma, H., Saarela, J., Tyni, S., Vartiainen, H., Paananen, J., Goldman, D., & Paunio, T. (2015). Genetic background of extreme violent behavior. *Molecular Psychiatry, 20*, 786–792.

Tilp, M., & Thaller, S. (2020). Covid-19 has turned home advantage into home disadvantage in the German Soccer Bundesliga. *Frontiers in Sports and Active Living.* https://www.ncbi.nlm.nih.gov/pmc/articles/PMC7739793/

Timerman, J. (1980). *Prisoner without a name, cell without a number.* University of Wisconsin Press.

Timmerman, T. A. (2007) "It was a thought pitch": Personal, situational, and target influences on hit-by-pitch events across time. *Journal of Applied Psychology, 92*, 876–884.

Timmermann, C., Spriggs, M. J., Kaelen, M., Leech, R., Nutt, D. J., Moran, R. J., Carhart-Harris, R. L., & Muthukumaraswamy, S. D. (2018). LSD modulates effective connectivity and neural adaptation mechanisms in an auditory oddball paradigm. *Neuropharmacology, 142*, 251–262.

Tinbergen, N. (1951). *The study of instinct.* Clarendon.

Tirrell, M. E. (1990). Personal communication.

Tobin, D. D., Menon, M., Menon, M., Spatta, B. C., Hodges, E. V. E., & Perry, D. G. (2010). The intrapsychics of gender: A model of self-socialization. *Psychological Review, 117*, 601–622.

Todd, R. M., MacDonald, M. J., Sedge, P., Robertson, A., Jetly, R., Taylor, M. J., & Pang, E. W. (2015). Soldiers with posttraumatic stress disorder see a world full of threat: Magnetoencephalography reveals enhanced tuning to combat-related cues. *Biological Psychiatry, 78*, 821–829.

Todes, D. P. (2014). *Ivan Pavlov: A Russian life in science.* Oxford University Press.

Todorva, R., & Zugaro, M. (2019). Isolated cortical computations during delta waves support memory consolidation. *Science, 366*, 377–381.

Toews, P. (2004, December 30). *Dirk Willems: A heart undivided.* Mennonite Brethren Historical Commission. https://mbhistory.org/profiles/dirk/

Tolin, D. F. (2010). Is cognitive-behavioral therapy more effective than other therapies? A meta-analytic review. *Clinical Psychology Review, 30*, 710–720.

Tolin, D. F., Wootton, B. M., Levy, H. C., Hallion, L. S., Worden, B. L., Diefenbach, G. J., Jaccard, J., & Stevens, M. C. (2019). Efficacy and mediators of a group cognitive–behavioral therapy for hoarding disorder: A randomized trial. *Journal of Consulting and Clinical Psychology, 87*, 590–602.

Tolman, E. C., & Honzik, C. H. (1930). Introduction and removal of reward, and maze performance in rats. *University of California Publications in Psychology, 4*, 257–275.

Tolstoy, L. (1904). *My confessions.* Dana Estes.

Tomaka, J., Blascovich, J., & Kelsey, R. M. (1992). Effects of self-deception, social desirability, and repressive coping on psychophysiological reactivity to stress. *Personality and Social Psychology Bulletin, 18*, 616–624.

Tomasello, M. (2019). The moral psychology of obligation [PDF file]. *Behavioral and Brain Sciences, 43.* https://www.eva.mpg.de/documents/Cambridge/Tomasello_Moral_BehBrainSci_2019_3232886.pdf

Tomita, K. K., Testa, R. J., & Balsam, K. F. (2019). Gender-affirming medical interventions and mental health in transgender adults. *Psychology of Sexual Orientation and Gender Diversity, 6*(2), 182–193.

Tompkins, D. A., Hobelmann, J. G., & Compton, P. (2017). Providing chronic pain management in the "Fifth Vital Sign" Era: Historical and treatment perspectives on a modern-day medical dilemma. *Drug and Alcohol Dependence, 173*, S11–S21.

Tong, Y. (2022, August 23). *India's sex ratio at birth begins to normalize.* Pew Research Center. https://www.pewresearch.org/religion/2022/08/23/indias-sex-ratio-at-birth-begins-to-normalize/

Toni, N., Buchs, P.-A., Nikonenko, I., Bron, C. R., & Muller, D. (1999). LTP promotes formation of multiple spine synapses between a single axon terminal and a dendrite. *Nature, 402*, 421–442.

Topolinski, S., & Reber, R. (2010). Gaining insight into the "aha" experience. *Current Directions in Psychological Science, 19*, 401–405.

Torres, J. G. (2019). A biopsychosocial perspective on bisexuality: A review for marriage and family therapists. *Journal of Bisexuality, 19*(1), 51–66.

Torrey, E. F. (1986). *Witchdoctors and psychiatrists.* Harper & Row.

Torrey, E. F., & Miller, J. (2002). *The invisible plague: The rise of mental illness from 1750 to the present.* Rutgers University Press.

Torrey, E. F., Miller, J., Rawlings, R., & Yolken, R. H. (1997). Seasonality of births in schizophrenia and bipolar disorder: A review of the literature. *Schizophrenia Research, 28*, 1–38.

Toschi, N., Riccelli, R., Indovina, I., Terracciano, A., & Passamonti, L. (2018). Functional connectome of the five-factor model of personality. *Personality Neuroscience, 1*, e2.

Totterdell, P., Kellett, S., Briner, R. B., & Teuchmann, K. (1998). Evidence of mood linkage in work groups. *Journal of Personality and Social Psychology, 74*, 1504–1515.

Towers, S., Gomez-Lievano, A., Khan, M., Mubayi, A., & Castillo-Chavez, C. (2015) Contagion in mass killings and school shootings. *PLOS ONE, 10.* https://journals.plos.org/plosone/article?id=10.1371/journal.pone.0117259

Townsend, S. S. M., Stephens, N. M., Smallets, S., & Hamedani, M. G. (2019). Empowerment through difference: An online difference-education intervention closes the social class achievement gap. *Personality and Social Psychology Bulletin, 45*(7), 1068–1083.

Tracy, J. L., Cheng, J. T., Robins, R. W., & Trzesniewski, K. H. (2009). Authentic and hubristic pride: The affective core of self-esteem and narcissism. *Self and Identity, 8*, 196–213.

Tracy, J. L., & Matsumoto, D. (2008). The spontaneous expression of pride and shame: Evidence for biologically innate nonverbal displays. *PNAS, 105*, 11655–11660.

Tracy, J. L., Shariff, A. F., Zhao, W., & Henrich, J. (2013). Cross-cultural evidence that the nonverbal expression of pride is an automatic status signal. *Journal of Experimental Psychology: General, 142,* 163–180.

Trahan, L. H., Stuebing, K. K., Fletcher, J. M., & Hiscock, M. (2014). The Flynn effect: A meta-analysis. *Psychological Bulletin, 140,* 1332–1360.

Tramontana, M. K. (2020, September 9). Why are men still explaining things to women? *The New York Times.* https://www.nytimes.com/2020/09/09/us/why-are-men-still-explaining-things-to-women-mansplaining-authority-gender.html

Trangenstein, P. J., Peddireddy, S. R., Cook, W. K., Rosshein, M. E., Monteiro, M. G., & Jernigan, D. H. (2021). Alcohol policy scores and alcohol-attributable homicide rates in 150 countries. *American Journal of Preventive Medicine, 61*(3), 311–319.

Trautwein, U., Lüdtke, O., Köller, O., & Baumert, J. (2006). Self-esteem, academic self-concept, and achievement: How the learning environment moderates the dynamics of self-concept. *Journal of Personality and Social Psychology, 90,* 334–349.

Traywick, J. (2020, October 30). Speaking from St. Vincent Healthcare hospital, Billings, Montana on MSNBC, *The Rachel Maddow Show.* V. Silverton-Peel (Producer).

Treanor, M., Brown, L. A., Rissman, J., & Craske, M. G. (2017). Can memories of traumatic experiences or addiction be erased or modified? A critical review of research on the disruption of memory reconsolidation and its applications. *Perspectives on Psychological Science, 12,* 290–305.

Treffert, D. A. (2010). *Islands of genius: The beautiful mind of the autistic, acquired, and sudden savant.* Jessica Kinsley Publishers.

Treffert, D. A., & Christensen, D. D. (2005, December). Inside the mind of a savant. *Scientific American,* pp. 108–113.

Tremblay, P., & Dick, A. S. (2016). Broca and Wernicke are dead, or moving past the classic model of language neurobiology. *Brain and Language, 162,* 60–71.

Tremblay, R. E., Pihl, R. O., Vitaro, F., & Dobkin, P. L. (1994). Predicting early onset of male antisocial behavior from preschool behavior. *Archives of General Psychiatry, 51,* 732–739.

Trevor Project. (2022). *The Trevor Project: 2022 National survey on LGBTQ youth mental health.* https://www.thetrevorproject.org/survey-2022/

Triandis, H. C. (1981). *Some dimensions of intercultural variation and their implications for interpersonal behavior* [Paper]. Presented at the American Psychological Association convention.

Triandis, H. C. (1994). *Culture and social behavior.* McGraw-Hill.

Trickett, E. (2009). Community psychology: Individuals and interventions in community context. *Annual Review of Psychology, 60,* 395–419.

Trillin, C. (2006, March 19). Alice off the page. *The New Yorker.* https://www.newyorker.com/magazine/2006/03/27/alice-off-the-page

Trimmer, C., Keller, A., Murphy, N. R., Snyder, L. L., Willer, J. R., Nagai, M. H., Katsanis, N., Vosshall, L. B., Matsunami, H., & Mainland, J. D. (2019). Genetic variation across the human olfactory receptor repertoire alters odor perception. *PNAS, 116,* 9475–9480.

Triplett, N. (1898). The dynamogenic factors in pacemaking and competition. *American Journal of Psychology, 9,* 507–533.

Troller-Renfree, S. V., Costanzo, M. A., & Duncan, G. J. (2022). The impact of a poverty reduction intervention on infant brain activity. *PNAS,* 119(5). https://www.pnas.org/doi/10.1073/pnas.2115649119

Tropp, L. R., & Barlow, F. K. (2018). Making advantaged racial groups care about inequality: Intergroup contact as a route to psychological investment. *Current Directions in Psychological Science, 27,* 194–199.

Tropp, L. R., White, F., Rucinski, C. L., & Tredoux, C. (2022). Intergroup contact and prejudice reduction: Prospects and challenges in changing youth attitudes. *Review of General Psychology, 26,* 342–360.

Trotta, A., Kang, J., Stahl, D., & Yiend, J. (2021). Interpretation bias in paranoia: A systematic review and meta-analysis. *Clinical Psychological Science, 9,* 3–23.

Trotter, J. (2014). *The power of positive coaching.* Sports Illustrated. https://www.si.com/nfl/2014/01/23/power-positive-coaching

Trubetskoy, V., Pardiñas, A. F., Qi, T., Panagiotaropoulou, G., Awasthi, S., Bigdeli, T. B., Bryois, J., Chen, C.-Y., Dennison, C. A., Hall, L. S., Lam, M., Watanabe, K., Frei, O., Ge, T., Harwood, J. C., Koopmans, F., Magnusson, S., Richards, A. L., Sidorenko, J., … O'Donovan, M. C. (2022). Mapping genomic loci implicates genes and synaptic biology in schizophrenia. *Nature, 604,* 502–508.

Trut, L. N. (1999). Early canid domestication: The farm-fox experiment. *American Scientist, 87,* 160–169.

Tsai, J. L. (2007). Ideal affect: Cultural causes and behavioral consequences. *Perspectives on Psychological Science, 2,* 242–259.

Tsai, J. L., Ang, J. Y. Z., Blevins, E., Goernandt, J., Fung, H. H., Jiang, D., Elliott, J., Kölzer, A., Uchida, Y., Lee, Y.-C., Lin, Y., Zhang, X., Govindama, Y., & Hoddouk, L. (2016). Leaders' smiles reflect cultural differences in ideal affect. *Emotion, 16*(2), 183–195.

Tsai, J. L., & Chentsova-Dutton, Y. (2003). Variation among European Americans in emotional facial expression. *Journal of Cross-Cultural Psychology, 34,* 650–657.

Tsai, J. L., Knutson, B., & Fung, H. H. (2006). Cultural variation in affect valuation. *Journal of Personality and Social Psychology, 90*(2), 288.

Tsai, J. L., Sims, T., Qu, Y., Thomas, E., Jiang, D., & Fung, H. H. (2018). Valuing excitement makes people look forward to old age less and dread it more. *Psychology and Aging, 33,* 975–992.

Tsang, Y. C. (1938). Hunger motivation in gastrectomized rats. *Journal of Comparative Psychology, 26,* 1–17.

Tsao, D. Y. (2019, February). Face values. *Scientific American,* pp. 23–29.

Tskhay, K. O., Zhu, R., Zou, C., & Rule, N. O. (2018). Charisma in everyday life: Conceptualization and validation of the General Charisma Inventory. *Journal of Personality and Social Psychology, 114,* 131–152.

Tsui, A. S. M., Byers-Heinlein, K., & Fennell, C. T. (2019). Associative word learning in infancy: A meta-analysis of the switch task. *Developmental Psychology, 55,* 934–950.

Tsvetkova, M., & Macy, M. W. (2014). The social contagion of generosity. *PLOS ONE, 9*(2). https://tinyurl.com/5n86x7ca

Tuber, D. S., Miller, D. D., Caris, K. A., Halter, R., Linden, F., & Hennessy, M. B. (1999). Dogs in animal shelters: Problems, suggestions, and needed expertise. *Psychological Science, 10,* 379–386.

Tucker-Drob, E. (2012). Preschools reduce early academic-achievement gaps: A longitudinal twin approach. *Psychological Science, 23,* 310–319.

Tucker-Drob, E., Brandmaier, A. M., & Lindenberger, U. (2019). Coupled cognitive changes in adulthood: A meta-analysis. *Psychological Bulletin, 145,* 273–301.

Tucker-Drob, E., & Briley, D. A. (2014). Continuity of genetic and environmental influences on cognition across the life span: A meta-analysis of longitudinal twin and adoption studies. *Psychological Bulletin, 140,* 949–979.

Tucker, R. P. (2019). Suicide in transgender veterans: Prevalence, prevention, and implications of current policy. *Perspectives on Psychological Science, 14,* 452–468.

Tuerk, P. W. (2005). Research in the high-stakes era: Achievement, resources, and No Child Left Behind. *Psychological Science, 16,* 419–425.

Tuk, M. A., Zhang, K., & Sweldens, S. (2015). The propagation of self-control: Self-control in one domain simultaneously improves self-control in other domains. *Journal of Experimental Psychology: General, 144,* 639–654.

Tullett, A. M., Kay, A. C., & Inzlicht, M. (2015). Randomness increases self-reported anxiety and neurophysiological correlates of performance monitoring. *Social Cognitive and Affective Neuroscience, 10,* 628–635.

Tully, T. (2003). Reply: The myth of a myth. *Current Biology, 13,* R426.

Turban, J. L., Beckwith, N., Reisner, S. L., & Keuroghlian, A. S. (2020). Association between recalled exposure to gender identity conversion efforts and psychological distress and suicide attempts among transgender adults. *JAMA Psychiatry, 77,* 68–76.

Turgeon, H., & Wright, J. (2022). Opinion: We're ignoring a major culprit behind the teen mental health crisis. *The Washington Post.* https://www.washingtonpost.com/opinions/2022/05/20/teen-mental-health-crisis-culprit-lack-of-sleep/

Turner, B. L., Caruso, E. M., Dilich, M. A., & Roese, N. J. (2019). Body camera footage leads to lower judgments of intent than dash camera footage. *PNAS, 116,* 1201–1206.

Turner, B., Austin, S. B., & Chapman, A. I. (2014). Treating nonsuicidal self-injury: A systematic review of psychological and pharmacological interventions. *Canadian Journal of Psychiatry, 59*(11), 576–585.

Turner, N., Barling, J., & Zacharatos, A. (2002). Positive psychology at work. In C. R. Snyder & S. J. Lopez (Eds.), *The handbook of positive psychology.* Oxford University Press.

Turnwald, B. P., Bertoldo, J. D., Perry, M. A., Policastro, P., Timmons, M., Bosso, C., Connors, P., Valgenti, R. T., Pine, L., Challamel, G., Gardner, C. D., & Crum, A. J. (2019). Increasing vegetable intake by emphasizing tasty and enjoyable attributes: A randomized controlled multisite intervention for taste-focused labeling. *Psychological Science, 30,* 1603–1615.

Turpin, A. (2005, April 3). The science of psi. *FT Weekend,* pp. W1, W2.

Tversky, A. (1985, June). Quoted in K. McKean, Decisions, decisions. *Discover Magazine,* pp. 22–31.

Tversky, A., & Kahneman, D. (1974). Judgment under uncertainty: Heuristics and biases. *Science, 185*, 1124–1131.

Tversky, A., & Kahneman, D. (1981). The framing of decisions and the psychology of choice. *Science, 211*(4481), 453–458.

Twenge, J. (2021). *Facebook's own internal documents offer a blueprint for making social media safer for teens*. The Conversation. https://theconversation.com/facebooks-own-internal-documents-offer-a-blueprint-for-making-social-media-safer-for-teens-169080

Twenge, J. (2022, April 11). *How much is social media to blame for teens' declining mental health?* Institute for Family Studies. https://ifstudies.org/blog/how-much-is-social-media-to-blame-for-teens-declining-mental-health

Twenge, J. M. (2006). *Generation me: Why today's young Americans are more confident, assertive, entitled—and more miserable than ever before*. Free Press.

Twenge, J. M. (2017). *iGen: Why today's super-connected kids are growing up less rebellious, more tolerant, less happy—and completely unprepared for adulthood—and what that means for the rest of us*. Atria Books.

Twenge, J. M. (2019). More time on technology, less happiness? Associations between digital media use and psychological well-being. *Current Directions in Psychological Science, 28*, 372–379.

Twenge, J. M., Baumeister, R. F., Tice, D. M., & Stucke, T. S. (2001). If you can't join them, beat them: Effects of social exclusion on aggressive behavior. *Journal of Personality and Social Psychology, 81*, 1058–1069.

Twenge, J. M., & Campbell, W. K. (2008). Increases in positive self-views among high school students: Birth-cohort changes in anticipated performance, self-satisfaction, self-liking, and self-competence. *Psychological Science, 19*, 1082–1086.

Twenge, J. M., & Campbell, W. K. (2019). Media use is linked to lower psychological well-being: Evidence from three datasets. *Psychiatric Quarterly, 90*, 311–331.

Twenge, J. M., Dawson, L., & Campbell, W. K. (2016). Still standing out: Children's names in the United States during the Great Recession and correlations with economic indicators. *Journal of Applied Social Psychology, 46*, 663–670.

Twenge, J. M., & Foster, J. D. (2010). Birth cohort increases in narcissistic personality traits among American college students, 1982–2009. *Social Psychological and Personality Science, 1*, 99–106.

Twenge, J. M., Gentile, B., DeWall, C. N., Ma, D., Lacefield, K., & Schurtz, D. R. (2010). Birth cohort increases in psychopathology among young Americans, 1938–2007: A cross-temporal meta-analysis of the MMPI. *Clinical Psychology Review, 30*, 145–154.

Twenge, J. M., Haidt, J., Blake, A. B., McAllister, C., Lemon, H., & Le Roy, A. (2022). Worldwide increases in adolescent loneliness. *Journal of Adolescence, 93*(1), 257–269.

Twenge, J. M., Haidt, J., Loazno, J., & Cummins, K. M. (2022). Specification curve analysis shows that social media use is linked to poor mental health, especially among girls. *Acta Psychologica, 224*. https://www.sciencedirect.com/science/article/pii/S0001691822000270

Twenge, J. M., & Joiner, T. E. (2020). Mental distress among U.S. adults during the COVID-19 pandemic. *Journal of Clinical Psychology, 76*(12), 2170–2182.

Twenge, J. M., & Joiner, T. E. (2020). U.S. Census Bureau-assessed prevalence of anxiety and depressive symptoms in 2019 and during the 2020 COVID-19 pandemic. *Depression & Anxiety, 37*(10), 954–956.

Twenge, J. M., & Park, H. (2019). The decline in adult activities among U.S. adolescents, 1976–2016. *Child Development, 90*, 638–654.

Twenge, J. M., Zhang, L., & Im, C. (2004). It's beyond my control: A cross-temporal meta-analysis of increasing externality in locus of control, 1960–2002. *Personality and Social Psychology Review, 8*, 308–319.

Twiss, C., Tabb, S., & Crosby, F. (1989). Affirmative action and aggregate data: The importance of patterns in the perception of discrimination. In F. Blanchard & F. Crosby (Eds.), *Affirmative action: Social psychological perspectives*. Springer-Verlag.

Tylee, D. S., Lee, Y. K., Wendt, F. R., Pathak, G. A., Levey, D. F., De Angelis, F., Gelernter, J., & Polimanti, R. (2022). An atlas of genetic correlations and genetically informed associations linking psychiatric and immune-related phenotypes. *JAMA Psychiatry, 79*(7), 667–676.

Tyson, A., Funk, C., Kennedy, B., & Johnson, C. (2021, September 15). *Majority in U.S. says public health benefits of COVID-19 restrictions worth the costs, even as large shares also see downsides*. Pew Research Center. https://pewrsr.ch/3TJQLDq

Úbeda, Y., Ortín, S., St. Leger, J., Llorente, M., & Almunia, J. (2018). Personality in captive killer whales (*Orcinus orca*): A rating approach based on the five-factor model. *Journal of Comparative Psychology, 133*, 252–261.

Uchida, Y., & Kitayama, S. (2009). Happiness and unhappiness in East and West: Themes and variations. *Emotion, 9*, 441–456.

Uchino, B. N., & Way, B. M. (2017). Integrative pathways linking close family ties to health: A neurochemical perspective. *American Psychologist, 72*, 590–600.

Udo, T., & Grilo, C. M. (2019). Psychiatric and medical correlates of DSM-5 eating disorders in a nationally representative sample of adults in the United States. *International Journal of Eating Disorders, 52*, 42–50.

Udry, J. R. (2000). Biological limits of gender construction. *American Sociological Review, 65*, 443–457.

Uga, V., Lemut, M. C., Zampi, C., Zilli, I., & Salzarulo, P. (2006). Music in dreams. *Consciousness and Cognition, 15*, 351–357.

Ullén, F., Hambrick, D. Z., & Mosing, M. A. (2016). Rethinking expertise: A multifactorial gene–environment interaction model of expert performance. *Psychological Bulletin, 142*, 427–446.

Uller, T., & Laland, K. N. (2019). *Evolutionary causation: Biological and philosophical reflections*. MIT Press.

Ullsperger, J. M., & Nikolas, M. A. (2017). A meta-analytic review of the association between pubertal timing and psychopathology in adolescence: Are there sex differences in risk? *Psychological Bulletin, 143*, 903–938.

Ulrich, R. E. (1991). Animal rights, animal wrongs and the question of balance. *Psychological Science, 2*, 197–201.

Underwood, E. (2016). Cadaver study challenges brain stimulation methods. *Science, 352*, 397.

UNDP (United Nations Development Programme). (2020). *Tackling social norms: A game changer for gender inequalities*. 2020 Human Development Perspectives.

UNFPA (United Nations Population Fund). (2016). *Changing attitudes towards gender equality: Update from the World Values Survey* [PDF file]. https://unstats.un.org/unsd/gender/Finland_Oct2016/Documents/UNFPA_abstract.pdf

Ungar, L. (2014). *Quiz: How long will you live?* Time Magazine. https://bit.ly/2tnbjdQ

Ungerleider, S. (2005). *Mental training for peak performance, revised & updated edition*. Rodale.

UNICEF (United Nations Children's Fund). (2020). *Violent discipline*. https://data.unicef.org/topic/child-protection/violence/violent-discipline/

United Nations. (2017). *World population prospects: The 2017 revision* [PDF file]. United Nations Division of Economic and Social Affairs. https://population.un.org/wpp/Publications/Files/WPP2017_DataBooklet.pdf

Univision. (2015). *Guevedoces* [YouTube video]. Primer Impacto. https://www.youtube.com/watch?v=oQ-k_hGotBY

UNODC (United Nations Office on Drugs and Crime). (2019). *Global study on homicide: Executive summary*.

Unsworth, N., & Engle, R. W. (2007). The nature of individual differences in working memory capacity: Active maintenance in primary memory and controlled search from secondary memory. *Psychological Review, 114*, 104–132.

Urcelay, G. P., & Jonkman, S. (2019). Delayed rewards facilitate habit formation. *Journal of Experimental Psychology: Animal Learning and Cognition, 45*(4), 413–421.

Urquhart, J. A., Sivakumaran, M. H., Macfarlane, J. A., & O'Connor, A. R. (2018). fMRI evidence supporting the role of memory conflict in the déjà vu experience. *Memory, 20*, 1–12.

Urry, H. L., & Gross, J. J. (2010). Emotion regulation in older age. *Current Directions in Psychological Science, 19*, 352–357.

Urry, H. L., Nitschke, J. B., Dolski, I., Jackson, D. C., Dalton, K. M., Mueller, C. J., Rosenkranz, M. A., Ryff, C. D., Singer, B. H., & Davidson, R. J. (2004). Making a life worth living: Neural correlates of well-being. *Psychological Science, 15*, 367–372.

USA FACTS. (2021). *Firearm deaths*. https://usafacts.org/data/topics/security-safety/crime-and-justice/firearms/firearm-deaths/

U.S. Census Bureau. (2021). *Median age at first marriage: 1890 to present* [PDF file]. https://www.census.gov/content/dam/Census/library/visualizations/time-series/demo/families-and-households/ms-2.pdf

U.S.E.E.O.C. (United States Equal Employment Opportunity Commission). (2018). *Sexual harassment*. https://www.eeoc.gov/laws/types/sexual_harassment.cfm

Uskul, A. K., & Over, H. (2017). Culture, social interdependence, and ostracism. *Current Directions in Psychological Science, 26*, 371–376.

U.S. Senate Select Committee on Intelligence. (2004, July 9). *Report of the Select Committee on*

Intelligence on the U.S. intelligence community's prewar intelligence assessments on Iraq. https://tinyurl.com/3fnykwxx

Uttal, W. R. (2001). *The new phrenology: The limits of localizing cognitive processes in the brain.* MIT Press.

Uysal, A., Aykutoglu, B., & Ascigil, E. (2020). Basic psychological need frustration and health: Prospective associations with sleep quality and cholesterol. *Motivation & Emotion, 44,* 209–225.

Vaci, N., Edelsbrunner, P., Stern, E., Neubauer, A., Bilalić, M., & Grabner, R. H. (2019). The joint influence of intelligence and practice on skill development throughout the life span. *PNAS, 116,* 18363–18369.

Vaillancourt, T., & Farrell, A. H. (2021). Mean kids become mean adults: Trajectories of indirect aggression from age 10 to 22. *Aggressive Behavior, 47*(4), 394–404.

Vaillant, G. (2013, May). *What makes us happy, revisited.* The Atlantic. http://theatlantic.com/magazine/archive/2013/05/thanks-mom/309287/

Vaillant, G. E. (1977). *Adaptation to life.* Little, Brown.

Vaillant, G. E. (2002). *Aging well: Surprising guideposts to a happier life from the landmark Harvard study of adult development.* Little, Brown.

Valenstein, E. S. (1986). *Great and desperate cures: The rise and decline of psychosurgery.* Basic Books.

Valentine, S. E., & Shipherd, J. C. (2018). A systematic review of social stress and mental health among transgender and gender non-conforming people in the United States. *Clinical Psychology Review, 66,* 24–38.

Valenza, E. Simion, F., Cassia, V. M., & Umiltà, C. (1996). Face preference at birth. *Journal of Experimental Psychology: Human Perception and Performance, 22,* 892–903.

Valkenburg, P. M., & Peter, J. (2009). Social consequences of the Internet for adolescents: A decade of research. *Current Directions in Psychological Science, 18,* 1–5.

Valluzzo, A. (2021, December 23). *Meet the blind explorer who takes Will Smith to the ends of the Earth in a new series.* Connecticut Magazine. https://www.ctinsider.com/connecticutmagazine/article/Meet-the-blind-explorer-who-takes-Will-Smith-to-17046489.php

van Agteren, J., Iasiello, M., Lo, L., Bartholomaeus, J., Kopsaftis, Z., Carey, M., & Kyrios, M. (2021). A systematic review and meta-analysis of psychological interventions to improve mental well-being. *Nature Human Behavior, 5,* 631–652.

Van Bavel, J. J., Baicker, K., Boggio, P., Capraro, V., Chichocka, A., Crockett, M., Cikara, M., Crum, A., Douglas, K., Druckman, J., Drury, J., Dube, O., Ellemers, N., Finkel, E. J., Fowler, J. H., Gelfand, M., Han, S., Haslam, S., Jetten, J., ... Willer, R. (2020). Using social and behavioural science to support COVID-19 pandemic response. *Nature Human Behaviour, 4,* 460–471.

van Beijsterveldt, C. E. M., Overbeek, L. I. H., Rozendaal, L., McMaster, M. T. B., Glasner, T. J., Bartels, M., Vink, M. J., Martin, N. G., Dolan, C. V., & Boomsma, D. I. (2016). Chorionicity and heritability estimates from twin studies: The prenatal environment of twins and their resemblance across a large number of traits. *Behavior Genetics, 46,* 304–314.

Van Bockstaele, B., Verschuere, B., Tibboel, H., De Houwer, J., Crombez, G., & Koster, E. H. W. (2014). A review of current evidence for the causal impact of attentional bias on fear and anxiety. *Psychological Bulletin, 140,* 682–721.

Van Boven, L., Ramos, J., Montal-Rosenberg, R., Kogut, T., Sherman, D. K., & Slovic, P. (2019). It depends: Partisan evaluation of conditional probability importance. *Cognition, 188,* 51–63.

Van Dam, N. T., van Vugt, M. K., Vago, D. R., Schmalzl, L., Saron, C. D., Olendzki, A., Meissner, T., Lazar, S. W., Kerr, C. E., Gorchov, J., Fox, K. C. R., Field, B. A., Britton, W. B., Brefczynski-Lewis, J. A., & Meyer, D. E. (2018). Mind the hype: A critical evaluation and prescriptive agenda for research on mindfulness and meditation. *Perspectives on Psychological Science, 13,* 36–61.

van de Bongardt, D., Reitz, E., Sandfort, T., & Deković, M. (2015). A meta-analysis of the relations between three types of peer norms and adolescent sexual behavior. *Personality and Social Psychology Review, 19,* 203–234.

van den Berg, S. M., de Moor, M. H., Verweij, K. J., Krueger, R. F., Luciano, M., Vasquez, A. A., Matteson, L. K., Derringer, J., Esko, T., Amin, N., Gordon, S. D., Hansell, N. K., Hart, A. B., Seppälä, I., Huffman, J. E., Konte, B., Lahti, J., Lee, M., Miller, M., ... Boomsma, D. I. (2016). Meta-analysis of genome-wide association studies for extraversion: Findings from the Genetics of Personality Consortium. *Behavior Genetics, 46,* 170–182.

van den Boom, D. C. (1994). The influence of temperament and mothering on attachment and exploration: An experimental manipulation of sensitive responsiveness among lower-class mothers with irritable infants. *Child Development, 65,* 1457–1477.

van den Bos, K., & Spruijt, N. (2002). Appropriateness of decisions as a moderator of the psychology of voice. *European Journal of Social Psychology, 32,* 57–72.

Van den Broeck, A., Ferris, D. L., Chang, C. H., & Rosen, C. C. (2016). A review of self-determination theory's basic psychological needs at work. *Journal of Management, 42,* 1195–1229.

Van den Bulck, J., Çetin, Y., Terzi, Ö., & Bushman, B. J. (2016). Violence, sex, and dreams: Violent and sexual media content infiltrate our dreams at night. *Dreaming, 26,* 271–279.

van der Helm, E., Yao, J., Dutt, S., Rao, V., Saletin, J. M., & Walker, M. P. (2011). REM sleep depotentiates amygdala activity to previous emotional experiences. *Current Biology, 21*(23), 2029–2032.

van der Linden, S. L., Leiserowitz, A. A., Feinberg, G. D., & Maibach, E. W. (2015). The scientific consensus on climate change as a gateway belief: Experimental evidence. *PLOS ONE, 10.* https://journals.plos.org/plosone/article?id=10.1371/journal.pone.0118489

Van Dessel, P., Mertens, G., Smith, C. T., & De Houwer, J. (2019). Mere exposure effects on implicit stimulus evaluation: The moderating role of evaluation task, number of stimulus presentations, and memory for presentation frequency. *Personality and Social Psychology Bulletin, 45,* 447–460.

van de Waal, E., Borgeaud, C., & Whiten, A. (2013). Potent social learning and conformity shape a wild primate's foraging decisions. *Science, 340,* 483–485.

van Dijk, W. W., Van Koningsbruggen, G. M., Ouwerkerk, J. W., & Wesseling, Y. M. (2011). Self-esteem, self-affirmation, and schadenfreude. *Emotion, 11,* 1445–1449.

Van Dyke, C., & Byck, R. (1982, March). Cocaine. *Scientific American,* pp. 128–141.

van Egmond, L., Ekman, M., & Benedict, C. (2019). Bed and rise times during the Age of Enlightenment: A case report. *Journal of Sleep Research, 28*(6). https://www.ncbi.nlm.nih.gov/pmc/articles/PMC6899797/

van Eijk, L., Zhu, D., Couvy-Duchesne, B., Strike, L. T., Lee, A. J., Hansell, N. K., Thompson, P. M., de Zubicaray, G. I., McMahon, K. L., Wright, M. J., & Zietsch, B. P. (2021). Are sex differences in human brain structure associated with sex differences in behavior? *Psychological Science, 32,* 1183–1197.

van Engen, M. L., & Willemsen, T. M. (2004). Sex and leadership styles: A meta-analysis of research published in the 1990s. *Psychological Reports, 94,* 3–18.

van Gelderen, M., Kautonen, T., Wincent, J., & Biniari, M. (2018). Implementation intentions in the entrepreneurial process: Concept, empirical findings, and research agenda. *Small Business Economics, 51,* 923–941.

van Haren, N. E., Rijsdijk, F., Schnack, H. G., Picchioni, M. M., Toulopoulou, T., Weisbrod, M., Sauer, H., van Erp, T. G., Cannon, T. D., Huttunen, M. O., Boomsma, D. I., Hulshoff Pol, H. E., Murray, R. M., & Kahn, R. S. (2012). The genetic and environmental determinants of the association between brain abnormalities and schizophrenia: The schizophrenia twins and relatives consortium. *Biological Psychiatry, 71,* 915–921.

van Haren, N. E., Schnack, H. G., Koevoets, M. G., Cahn, W., Pol, H. E. H., & Kahn, R. S. (2016). Trajectories of subcortical volume change in schizophrenia: A 5-year follow-up. *Schizophrenia Research, 173,* 140–145.

Van Horn, J., Irimia, A., Torgerson, C., Chambers, M., Kikinis, R., & Toga, A. (2012). Mapping connectivity damage in the case of Phineas Gage. *PLOS ONE, 7*(5). https://journals.plos.org/plosone/article?id=10.1371/journal.pone.0037454

van Ijzendoorn, M. H., Bakermans-Kranenburg, M. J., Duschinsky, R., Fox, N. A., Goldman, P. S., Gunnar, M. R., Johnson, D. E., Nelson, C. A., Reijman, S., Skinner, G. C. M., Zeanah, C. H., & Sonuga-Barke, E. J. S. (2020). Institutionalisation and deinstitutionalisation of children 1: A systematic and integrative review of evidence regarding effects on development [PDF file]. *Lancet Psychiatry.* https://bit.ly/39FEE6s

van IJzendoorn, M. H., & Juffer, F. (2006). The Emanual Miller Memorial Lecture 2006: Adoption as intervention. Meta-analytic evidence for massive catch-up and plasticity in physical, socio-emotional, and cognitive development. *Journal of Child Psychology and Psychiatry, 47,* 1228–1245.

van IJzendoorn, M. H., Juffer, F., & Poelhuis, C. W. K. (2005). Adoption and cognitive development: A meta-analytic comparison of adopted and nonadopted children's IQ and school performance. *Psychological Bulletin, 131*, 301–316.

van IJzendoorn, M. H., & Kroonenberg, P. M. (1988). Cross-cultural patterns of attachment: A meta-analysis of the strange situation. *Child Development, 59*, 147–156.

van IJzendoorn, M. H., Luijk, M. P. C. M., & Juffer, F. (2008). IQ of children growing up in children's homes: A meta-analysis on IQ delays in orphanages. *Merrill-Palmer Quarterly, 54*, 341–366.

Van Kleef, G. A., & Côté, S. (2007). Expressing anger in conflict: When it helps and when it hurts. *Journal of Applied Psychology, 92*(6), 1557.

Van Leeuwen, M. S. (1978). A cross-cultural examination of psychological differentiation in males and females. *International Journal of Psychology, 13*, 87–122.

Van Munster, C. E., Jonkman, L. E., Weinstein, H. C., Uitdehaag, B. M., & Geurts, J. J. (2015). Gray matter damage in multiple sclerosis: Impact on clinical symptoms. *Neuroscience, 303*, 446–461.

van Praag, H. (2009). Exercise and the brain: Something to chew on. *Trends in Neuroscience, 32*, 283–290.

Van Tongeren, D. R., DeWall, C. N., Chen, Z., Sibley, C. G., & Bulbulia, J. (2021). Religious residue: Cross-cultural evidence that religious psychology and behavior persist following deidentification. *Journal of Personality and Social Psychology, 120*(2), 484–503.

Van Tongeren, D. R., DeWall, C. N., Green, J. D., Cairo, A. H., Davis, D. E., & Hook, J. N. (2018). Self-regulation facilitates meaning in life. *Review of General Psychology, 22*, 95–106.

Van Yperen, N. W., & Buunk, B. P. (1990). A longitudinal study of equity and satisfaction in intimate relationships. *European Journal of Social Psychology, 20*, 287–309.

Van Zeijl, J., Mesman, J., Van IJzendoorn, M. H., Bakermans-Kranenburg, M. J., Juffer, F., Stolk, M. N., Koot, H. M., & Alink, L. R. A. (2006). Attachment-based intervention for enhancing sensitive discipline in mothers of 1- to 3-year-old children at risk for externalizing behavior problems: A randomized controlled trial. *Journal of Consulting and Clinical Psychology, 74*, 994–1005.

van Zuiden, M., Geuze, E., Willemen, H. L., Vermetten, E., Maas, M., Amarouchi, K., Kevelaars, A., & Heijnen, C. J. (2012). Glucocorticoid receptor pathway components predict posttraumatic stress disorder symptom development: A prospective study. *Biological Psychiatry, 71*, 309–316.

Vancampfort, D., Stubbs, B., Smith, L., Hallgren, M., Firth, J., Herring, M. P., Probst, M., & Koyanagi, A. (2018). Physical activity and sleep problems in 38 low-and middle-income countries. *Sleep Medicine, 48*, 140–147.

Vance, E. (2018, June). Can you super-charge your baby? *Scientific American*, pp. 35–39.

Vance, E. B., & Wagner, N. N. (1976). Written descriptions of orgasm: A study of sex differences. *Archives of Sexual Behavior, 5*, 87–98.

vanDellen, M. R., Campbell, W. K., Hoyle, R. H., & Bradfield, E. K. (2011). Compensating, resisting, and breaking: A meta-analytic examination of reactions to self-esteem threat. *Personality and Social Psychological Review, 15*, 51–74.

VanderLaan, D. P., Forrester, D. L., Petterson, L. J., & Vasey, P. L. (2012). Offspring production among the extended relatives of Samoan men and fa'afafine. *PLOS ONE, 7*(4). https://journals.plos.org/plosone/article?id=10.1371/journal.pone.0036088

VanderLaan, D. P., & Vasey, P. L. (2011). Male sexual orientation in Independent Samoa: Evidence for fraternal birth order and maternal fecundity effects. *Archives of Sexual Behavior, 40*, 495–503.

VanderWeele, T. (2021, October 26). *Baylor and Harvard researchers partner in long-term, global study of human flourishing* [Press release]. Templeton World Charity Foundation. https://bit.ly/3CccOg2

VanderWeele, T. J. (2017, May 30). What the *New York Times* gets wrong about marriage, health, and well-being. Institute for Family Studies. https://ifstudies.org/blog/what-the-new-york-times-gets-wrong-about-marriage-health-and-well-being

VanderWeele, T. J. (2018, September 18). *Religious upbringing and adolescence.* Institute for Family Studies. https://ifstudies.org/blog/religious-upbringing-and-adolescence

VanderWeele, T. J., Li, S., & Kawachi, I. (2017). Religious service attendance and suicide rates—reply. *JAMA Psychiatry, 74*, 197–198.

VanderWeele, T. J., Li, S., Tsai, A. C., & Kawachi, I. (2016). Association between religious service attendance and lower suicide rates among US women. *JAMA Psychiatry, 73*, 845–851.

Vanhalst, J., Soenens, B., Luyckx, K., Van Petegem, S., Weeks, M. S., & Asher, S. R. (2015). Why do the lonely stay lonely? Chronically lonely adolescents' attributions and emotions in situations of social inclusion and exclusion. *Journal of Personality and Social Psychology, 109*, 932–948.

Vasilev, M. R., Kirkby, J. A., & Angele, B. (2018). Auditory distraction during reading: A Bayesian meta-analysis of a continuing controversy. *Perspectives on Psychological Science, 13*, 567–597.

Vaz, A. P., Inati, S. K., Brunel, N., & Zaghloul, K. A. (2019). Coupled ripple oscillations between the medial temporal lobe and neocortex retrieve human memory. *Science, 363*, 975–978.

Vecera, S. P., Vogel, E. K., & Woodman, G. F. (2002). Lower region: A new cue for figure-ground assignment. *Journal of Experimental Psychology: General, 13*, 194–205.

Veenhoven, R. (2014, accessed March 17). *World database of happiness.* http://worlddatabaseofhappiness.eur.nl

Veenhoven, R. (2015). Informed pursuit of happiness: What we should know, do know and can get to know. *Journal of Happiness Studies, 16*, 1035–1071.

Vekassy, L. (1977). Dreams of the blind. *Magyar Pszichologiai Szemle, 34*, 478–491.

Velikonja, T., Fett, A.-K., & Velthorst, E. (2019). Patterns of nonsocial and social cognitive functioning in adults with autism spectrum disorder. A systematic review and meta-analysis. *JAMA Psychiatry, 76*(2), 135–151.

Verduyn, P., Gugushvili, N., & Kross, E. (2022). Do social networking sites influence well-being? The extended active-passive model. *Current Directions in Psychological Science, 31*(1), 62–68.

Vergauwe, J., Wille, B., Hofmans, J., Kaiser, R. B., & De Fruyt, F. (2018). The double-edged sword of leader charisma: Understanding the curvilinear relationship between charismatic personality and leader effectiveness. *Journal of Personality and Social Psychology, 114*, 110–130.

Vergunst, F., Tremblay, R. E., Nagin, D., Algan, Y., Beasley, E., Park, J., Galera, C., Vitaro, F., & Côté, S. M. (2019). Association between childhood behaviors and adult employment earnings in Canada. *JAMA Psychiatry, 76*, 1044–1051.

Verhaeghen, P., & Salthouse, T. A. (1997). Meta-analyses of age-cognition relations in adulthood: Estimates of linear and nonlinear age effects and structural models. *Psychological Bulletin, 122*, 231–249.

Verhulst, B., Neale, M. C., & Kendler, K. S. (2015). The heritability of alcohol use disorders: A meta-analysis of twin and adoption studies. *Psychological Medicine, 45*(5), 1061–1072.

Vermetten, E., Schmahl, C., Lindner, S., Loewenstein, R. J., & Bremner, J. D. (2006). Hippocampal and amygdalar volumes in dissociative identity disorder. *American Journal of Psychiatry, 163*, 630–636.

Verona, E., & Sullivan, E. A. (2008). Emotional catharsis and aggression revisited: Heart rate reduction following aggressive responding. *Emotion, 8*, 331–340.

Verschuere, B., & Meijer, E. H. (2014). What's on your mind? Recent advances in memory detection using the concealed information test. *European Psychologist, 19*, 162–171.

Vezzali, L., Stathi, S., Giovannini, D., Capozza, D., & Trifiletti, E. (2015). The greatest magic of Harry Potter: Reducing prejudice. *Journal of Applied Social Psychology, 45*, 105–121.

Vial, A. C., Muradoglu, M., Newman, G. E., & Cimpian, A. (2022). An emphasis on brilliance fosters masculinity-contest cultures. *Psychological Science, 33*(4), 395–612.

Vigil, J. M. (2009). A socio-relational framework of sex differences in the expression of emotion. *Behavioral and Brain Sciences, 32*, 375–428.

Vigliocco, G., & Hartsuiker, R. J. (2002). The interplay of meaning, sound, and syntax in sentence production. *Psychological Bulletin, 128*, 442–472.

Vigo, D., Haro, J. M., Hwang, I., Aguilar-Gaxiola, S., Alonso, J., Borges, G., Bruffaerts, R., Caldas-de-Almeida, J. M., de Girolamo, G., Florescu, S., Gureje, O., Karam, E., Karam, G., Kovess-Masfety, V., Lee, S., Navarro-Mateu, F., Ojagbemi, A., Posada-Villa, J., Sampson, N. A., … Kessler, R. C. (2022). Towards measuring effective treatment coverage: Critical bottlenecks in quality- and user-adjusted coverage for major depressive disorder. *Psychological Medicine, 52*(10), 1948–1958.

Vila, J. (2021). Social support and longevity: Meta-analysis-based evidence and psychobiological mechanisms. *Frontiers in*

Psychology, 13. https://www.frontiersin.org/articles/10.3389/fpsyg.2021.717164/full#h10

Villalba, D. K., Lindsay, E. K., Marsland, A. L., Greco, C. M., Young, S., Brown, K. W., Smyth, J. M., Walsh, C. P., Gray, K., Chin, B., & Creswell, J. D. (2019). Mindfulness training and systemic low-grade inflammation in stressed community adults: Evidence from two randomized controlled trials. *PLOS ONE, 14*. https://journals.plos.org/plosone/article?id=10.1371/journal.pone.0219120

Visich, P. S., & Fletcher, E. (2009). Myocardial infarction. In J. K. Ehrman, P. M. Gordon, P. S. Visich, & S. J. Keleyian (Eds.), *Clinical exercise physiology* (2nd ed.). Human Kinetics.

Vita, A. J., Terry, R. B., Hubert, H. B., & Fries, J. F. (1998). Aging, health risks, and cumulative disability. *New England Journal of Medicine, 338*, 1035–1041.

Vitello, P. (2012, August 1). George A. Miller. A pioneer in cognitive psychology, is dead at 92. *The New York Times*. https://www.nytimes.com/2012/08/02/us/george-a-miller-cognitive-psychology-pioneer-dies-at-92.html

Vitiello, M. V. (2009). Recent advances in understanding sleep and sleep disturbances in older adults: Growing older does not mean sleeping poorly. *Current Directions in Psychological Science, 18*, 316–320.

Vitória, P. D., Salgueiro, M. F., Silva, S. A., & De Vries, H. (2009). The impact of social influence on adolescent intention to smoke: Combining types and referents of influence. *British Journal of Health Psychology, 14*, 681–699.

Vlasenko, V. V., Rogers, E. G., & Waugh, C. E. (2021). Affect labelling increases the intensity of positive emotions. *Cognition and Emotion, 35*(7), 1350–1364.

Vlasic, B. (2015, February 4). Despite recalls, G.M. pays workers a big bonus. *The New York Times*. https://www.nytimes.com/2015/02/05/business/gm-reports-2-8-billion-profit-in-2014.html

Vocks, S., Tuschen-Caffier, B., Pietrowsky, R., Rustenbach, S. J., Kersting, A., & Herpertz, S. (2010). Meta-analysis of the effectiveness of psychological and pharmacological treatments for binge eating disorder. *International Journal of Eating Disorders, 43*, 205–217.

Vogel, G. (2010). Long-fought compromise reached on European animal rules. *Science, 329*, 1588–1589.

Vogel, N., Schilling, Wahl, H.-W., Beekman, A. T. F., & Penninx, B. W. J. H. (2013). Time-to-death-related change in positive and negative affect among older adults approaching the end of life. *Psychology and Aging, 28*, 128–141.

Vohs, K. D., Schmeichel, B. J., Lohmann, S., Gronau, Q. F., Finley, A. J., Ainsworth, S. E., Alquist, J. L., Baker, M. D., Brizi, A., Bunyi, A., Butschek, G. J., Campbell, C., Capaldi, J., Cau, C., Chambers, H., Chatzisarantis, N. L. D., Christensen, W. J., Clay, S. L., Curtis, J., ... Albarracin, D. (2021). A multisite reregistered paradigmatic test of the ego-depletion effect. *Psychological Science, 32*(10), 1566–1581.

Volkow, N. D., & Boyle, M. (2018). Neuroscience of addiction: Relevance to prevention and treatment. *American Journal of Psychiatry, 175*, 729–740.

Volkow, N. D., Wang, G. J., Kollins, S. H., Wigal, T. L., Newcorn, J. H., Telang, F., Fowler, J. S., Zhu, W., Logan, J., Ma, Y., Pradhan, K., Wong, C., & Swanson, J. M. (2009). Evaluating dopamine reward pathway in ADHD: Clinical implications. *Journal of the American Medical Association, 302*, 1084–1091.

Volkow, N. D., Wang, G.-J., Telang, F., Fowler, J. S., Alexoff, D., Logan, J., Jayne, M., Wong, C., & Tomasi, D. (2014). Decreased dopamine brain reactivity in marijuana abusers is associated with negative emotionality and addiction severity. *PNAS, 111*(30), E3149–E2156.

von Békésy, G. (1957, August). The ear. *Scientific American*, pp. 66–78. https://www.scientificamerican.com/article/the-ear/

von Dawans, B., Ditzen, B., Trueg, A., Fischbacher, U., & Heinrichs, M. (2019). Effects of acute stress on social behavior in women. *Psychoneuroendocrinology, 99*, 137–144.

von Hippel, W. (2007). Aging, executive functioning, and social control. *Current Directions in Psychological Science, 16*, 240–244.

von Hippel, W. (2015, July 17). *Do people become more prejudiced as they grow older?* BBC News Magazine. https://www.bbc.com/news/magazine-33523313

von Hippel, W., & Trivers, R. (2011). The evolution and psychology of self-deception. *Behavioral and Brain Sciences, 34*, 1–56.

von Senden, M. (1932). *The perception of space and shape in the congenitally blind before and after operation*. Free Press.

von Soest, T., Wagner, J., Hansen, T., & Gerstorf, D. (2018). Self-esteem across the second half of life: The role of socioeconomic status, physical health, social relationships, and personality factors. *Journal of Personality and Social Psychology, 114*, 945–958.

von Stumm, S., & d'Apice, K. (2022). From genome-wide to environment-wide: Capturing the environome. *Perspectives on Psychological Science, 17*(1), 30–40.

von Stumm, S., Hell, B., & Chamorro-Premuzic, T. (2011). The hungry mind: Intellectual curiosity is the third pillar of academic performance. *Perspectives on Psychological Science, 6*, 574–588.

Vonk, J., Jett, S. E., & Mosteller, K. W. (2012). Concept formation in American black bears, *Ursus americanus*. *Animal Behaviour, 84*, 953–964.

Vonk, R., & Visser, A. (2021). An exploration of spiritual superiority: The paradox of self-enhancement. *European Journal of Social Psychology, 51*(1), 152–165.

Vosberg, D. E., Syme, C., Parker, N., Richer, L., Pausova, Z., & Paus, T. (2021). Sex continuum in the brain and body during adolescence and psychological traits. *Nature Human Behaviour, 5*, 265–272.

Vosoughi, S., Roy, D., & Aral, S. (2018). The spread of true and false news online. *Science, 359*, 1146–1151.

Voss, U., Tuin, I., Schermelleh-Engel, K., & Hobson, A. (2011). Waking and dreaming: Related but structurally independent. Dream reports of congenitally paraplegic and deaf-mute persons. *Consciousness and Cognition, 20*, 673–687.

VPC (Violence Policy Center). (2015, June). *Firearm justifiable homicides and non-fatal self-defense gun use: An analysis of Federal Bureau of Investigation and National Crime Victimization Survey data* [PDF file]. https://biotech.law.lsu.edu/blog/justifiable15.pdf

Vrij, A., & Fisher, R. P. (2016). Which lie detection tools are ready for use in the criminal justice system? *Journal of Applied Research in Memory and Cognition, 5*, 302–307.

Vukovic, N., Hansen, B., Ellegaard Lund, T., Jespersen, S., & Shtyrov, Y. (2021). Rapid microstructural plasticity in the cortical semantic network following a short language learning session. *PLOS Biology, 19*(6). https://journals.plos.org/plosbiology/article?id=10.1371/journal.pbio.3001290

Vyas, S., Hathi, P., & Gupta, A. (2022). Social disadvantage, economic inequality, and life expectancy in nine Indian states. *PNAS, 119*(10). https://www.pnas.org/doi/10.1073/pnas.2109226119

Vyse, S. (2016, March/April). Guns: Feeling safe ≠ being safe. *Skeptical Inquirer*, pp. 27–30.

Waber, R. L., Shiv, B., Carmon, Z., & Ariely, D. (2008). Commercial features of placebo and therapeutic efficacy. *Journal of the American Medical Association, 299*, 1016–1017.

Wacker, J., Chavanon, M.-L., & Stemmler, G. (2006). Investigating the dopaminergic basis of extraversion in humans: A multilevel approach. *Journal of Personality and Social Psychology, 91*, 177–187.

Wade, K. A., Garry, M., & Pezdek, K. (2018). Deconstructing rich false memories of committing crime: Commentary on Shaw and Porter (2015). *Psychological Science, 29*, 471–476.

Wade, K. A., Garry, M., Read, J. D., & Lindsay, D. S. (2002). A picture is worth a thousand lies: Using false photographs to create false childhood memories. *Psychonomic Bulletin & Review, 9*, 597–603.

Wadley, J., & Lee, J. (2016, September 23). *Compared with Europe, American teens have high rates of illicit drug use*. Michigan News (University of Michigan). https://news.umich.edu/compared-with-europe-american-teens-have-high-rates-of-illicit-drug-use/

Wadman, M. (2018). Watching the teen brain grow. *Science, 359*, 13.

Wagemans, J., Elder, J. H., Kubovy, M., Palmer, S. E., Peterson, M. A., Singh, M., & von der Heydt, R. (2012a). A century of Gestalt psychology in visual perception: I. Perceptual grouping and figure–ground organization. *Psychological Bulletin, 138*, 1172–1217.

Wagemans, J., Feldman, J., Gepshtein, S., Kimchi, R., Pomerantz, J. R, van der Helm, P., & van Leeuwen, C. (2012b). A century of Gestalt psychology in visual perception: II. Conceptual and theoretical foundations. *Psychological Bulletin, 138*, 1218–1252.

Wagenmakers, E.-J. (2014, June 25). *Bem is back: A skeptic's review of a meta-analysis on psi*. Open Science Collaboration. http://osc.centerforopenscience.org/2014/06/25/a-skeptics-review/

Wagenmakers, E.-J., Wetzels, R., Borsboom, D., & van der Maas, H. (2011). Why psychologists must change the way they analyze their data: The case of psi. *Journal of Personality and Social Psychology, 100*, 1–12.

Wager, R. D., & Atlas, L. Y. (2013). How is pain influenced by cognition? Neuroimaging weighs in. *Perspectives on Psychological Science, 8*, 91–97.

Wagner, D., Becker, B., Koester, P., Gouzoulis-Mayfrank, E., & Daumann, J. (2012). A prospective study of learning, memory, and executive function in new MDMA users. *Addiction, 108*, 136–145.

Wagner, J., Lüdtke, O., & Robitzsch, A. (2019). Does personality become more stable with age? Disentangling state and trait effects for the big five across the life span using local structural equation modeling. *Journal of Personality and Social Psychology, 116*, 666–680.

Wagner, J., Ram, N., Smith, J., & Gerstorf, D. (2016). Personality trait development at the end of life: Antecedents and correlates of mean-level trajectories. *Journal of Personality and Social Psychology, 111*, 411–429.

Wagner, K., & Dobkins, K. R. (2011). Synaesthetic associations decrease during infancy. *Psychological Science, 22*, 1067–1072.

Wagner, U., Tachtsoglou, S., Kotzur, P. F., Friehs, M.-T., & Kemmesies, U. (2020). Proportion of foreigners negatively predicts the prevalence of xenophobic hate crimes within German districts. *Social Psychology Quarterly, 83*(2), 195–205.

Wagstaff, G. (1982). Attitudes to rape: The "just world" strikes again? *Bulletin of the British Psychological Society, 13*, 275–283.

Wai, J., Brown, M., & Chabris, C. (2018). Using standardized test scores to include general cognitive ability in education research and policy. *Journal of Intelligence, 6*, 37.

Wake, K., Green, J. A., & Zajac, R. (2020). Laypeople's beliefs about memory: Disentangling the effects of age and time. *Memory, 28*, 589–597.

Wakefield, J. C., & Spitzer, R. L. (2002). Lowered estimates—but of what? *Archives of General Psychiatry, 59*, 129–130.

Walasek, L., Juanchich, M., & Sirota, M. (2019). Adaptive cooperation in the face of social exclusion. *Journal of Experimental Social Psychology, 82*, 35–46.

Walasek, N., Frankenhuis, W. E., & Panchanathan, K. (2022). An evolutionary model of sensitive periods when the reliability of cues varies across ontogeny. *Behavioral Ecology, 33*(1), 101–114.

Walker, D. M., Cates, H. M., Loh, Y. H. E., Purushothaman, I., Ramakrishnan, A., Cahill, K. M., Lardner, C. K., Godino, A., Kronman, H. G., Rabkin, J., Lorsch, Z. S., Mews, P., Doyle, M. A., Feng, J., Labonté, B., Koo, J. W., Bagot, R. C., Logan, R. W., Seney, M. L., … Nestler, E. J. (2018). Cocaine self-administration alters transcriptome-wide responses in the brain's reward circuitry. *Biological Psychiatry, 84*, 867–880.

Walker, E., Shapiro, D., Esterberg, M., & Trotman, H. (2010). Neurodevelopment and schizophrenia: Broadening the focus. *Current Directions in Psychological Science, 19*, 204–208.

Walker, E. R., McGee, R. E., & Druss, B. G. (2015). Mortality in mental disorders and global disease burden implications. A systematic review and meta-analysis. *JAMA Psychiatry, 72*(4), 334–341.

Walker, M. (2007). *Why we sleep: Unlocking the power of sleep and dreams*. Scribner.

Walker, M. P. (2010). Sleep, memory and emotion. *Progress in Brain Research, 185*, 49–68.

Walker, M. P., & van der Helm, E. (2009). Overnight therapy? The role of sleep in emotional brain processing. *Psychological Bulletin, 135*, 731–748.

Wall, P. D. (2000). *Pain: The science of suffering*. Columbia University Press.

Wallace, D. S., Paulson, R. M., Lord, C. G., & Bond, C. F., Jr. (2005). Which behaviors do attitudes predict? Meta-analyzing the effects of social pressure and perceived difficulty. *Review of General Psychology, 9*, 214–227.

Wallace, L. E., Anthony, R., End, C. M., & Way, B. M. (2018). Does religion stave off the grave? Religious affiliation in one's obituary and longevity. *Social Psychological and Personality Science, 10*, 662–670.

Wallace, M. L., Kissel, N., Hall, M. H., Germain, A., Matthews, K. A., Troxel, W. M., Franzen, P. L., Buysse, D. J., Reynolds, C., III, Roecklein, K. A., Gunn, H. E., Hasler, B., Goldstein, T. R., McMakin, D. L., Szigethy, E., & Soehner, A. M. (2022). Age trends in actigraphy and self-report sleep across the life span: Findings from the Pittsburgh Lifespan Sleep Databank. *Psychosomatic Medicine, 84*(4), 410–420.

Wallach, M. A., & Wallach, L. (1983). *Psychology's sanction for selfishness: The error of egoism in theory and therapy*. Freeman.

Wallach, M. L., & Wallach, L. (1985, February). How psychology sanctions the cult of the self. *Washington Monthly*, pp. 46–56.

Walsh, C. G., Ribeiro, J. D., & Franklin, J. C. (2017). Predicting risk of suicide attempts over time through machine learning. *Clinical Psychological Science, 5*, 457–469.

Walsh, J. L., Fielder, R. L., Carey, K. B., & Carey, M. P. (2013). Female college students' media use and academic outcomes: Results from a longitudinal cohort study. *Emerging Adulthood, 1*, 219–232.

Walsh, L. C., Boehm, J. K., & Lyubomirsky, S. (2018). Does happiness promote career success? Revisiting the evidence. *Journal of Career Assessment, 26*, 199–219.

Walsh, R. (2011). Lifestyle and mental health. *American Psychologist, 66*, 579–592.

Walster (Hatfield), E., Aronson, V., Abrahams, D., & Rottman, L. (1966). Importance of physical attractiveness in dating behavior. *Journal of Personality and Social Psychology, 4*, 508–516.

Walter, K. V., Conroy-Beam, D., Buss, D. M., Asao, K., Sorokowska, A., Sorokowski, P., Sorokowski, P., Aavik, T., Akello, G., Alhabahba, M. M., Alm, C., Amjad, N., Anjum, A., Atama, C. S., Duyar, D. A., Ayebare, R., Batres, C., Bendixen, M., Bensafia, A., … Siddiqui, R. S. (2020). Sex differences in mate preferences across 45 countries: A large-scale replication. *Psychological Science, 31*, 408–423.

Walton, G. M. (2020). *Featured author—Gregory M. Walton*. Guilford Press. https://www.guilford.com/featured-author/december-2020-walton

Walton, G. M., & Spencer, S. J. (2009). Latent ability: Grades and test scores systematically underestimate the intellectual ability of negatively stereotyped students. *Psychological Science, 20*, 1132–1139.

Walton, G. M., & Wilson, T. D. (2018). Wise interventions: Psychological remedies for social and personal problems. *Psychological Review, 125*, 617–655.

Wampold, B. E. (2007). Psychotherapy: The humanistic (and effective) treatment. *American Psychologist, 62*, 857–873.

Wampold, B. E., Flückiger, C., Del Re, A. C., Yulish, N. E., Frost, N. D., Pace, B. T., Goldberg, S. B., Miller, S. D., Baardseth, T. P., Laska, K. M., & Hilsenroth, M. J. (2017). In pursuit of truth: A critical examination of meta-analyses of cognitive behavior therapy. *Psychotherapy Research, 27*, 14–32.

Wang, C. H. (2020). The cognitive gains of exercise. *Nature Human Behaviour, 4*, 565–566.

Wang, G., Holmes, R. M., Jr., Devine, R. A., & Bishoff, J. (2018). CEO gender differences in careers and the moderating role of country culture: A meta-analytic investigation. *Organizational Behavior and Human Decision Processes, 148*, 30–53.

Wang, J., Cheng, G. H., Chen, T., & Leung, K. (2019). Team creativity/innovation in culturally diverse teams: A meta-analysis. *Journal of Organizational Behavior, 40*, 693–708.

Wang, J., He, L., Liping, J., Tian, J., & Benson, V. (2015). The 'positive effect' is present in older Chinese adults: Evidence from an eye tracking study. *PLOS ONE, 10*. https://journals.plos.org/plosone/article?id=10.1371/journal.pone.0121372

Wang, J., Rao, Y., & Houser, D. E. (2017). An experimental analysis of acquired impulse control among adult humans intolerant to alcohol. *PNAS, 114*, 1299–1304.

Wang, J., Zhang, W. S., Jiang, C. Q., Zhu, F., Jin, Y. L., Cheng, K. K., Lam, T. H., & Xu, L. (2022). Associations of face-to-face and non-face-to-face social isolation with all-cause and cause-specific mortality: A 13-year follow-up of the Guangzhou Biobank Cohort study. *BMC Medicine, 20*. https://bmcmedicine.biomedcentral.com/articles/10.1186/s12916-022-02368-3

Wang, L., Zhou, C., Cheng, W., Rolls, E. T., Huang, P., Ma, N., Liu, Y., Zhang, Y., Guan, X., Guo, T., Wu, J., Gao, T., Xuan, M., Gu, Q., Xu, X., Zhang, B., Gong, W., Du, J., Zhang, W., … Zhang, M. (2022). Dopamine depletion and subcortical dysfunction disrupt cortical synchronization and metastability affecting cognitive function in Parkinson's disease. *Human Brain Mapping, 43*(5), 1598–1610.

Wang, Q. (2021). The cultural foundation of human memory. *Annual Review of Psychology, 72*, 151–179.

Wang, Q., Hoi, S. P., Wang, Y., Song, C., Li, T., Lam, C. M., Fang, F., & Yi, L. (2020). Out of mind, out of sight? Investigating abnormal face scanning in autism spectrum disorder using gaze-contingent paradigm. *Developmental Science, 23*(1). doi:10.1111/desc.12856

Wang, S. (2014, March 29). How to think about the risk of autism. *The New York Times*. https://www.nytimes.com/2014/03/30/opinion/sunday/how-to-think-about-the-risk-of-autism.html

Wang, S., Dai, J., Li, J., Wang, X., Chen, T., Yang, X., He, M., & Gong, Q. (2018). Neuroanatomical correlates of grit: Growth mindset mediates the association between gray matter structure and trait grit in late adolescence. *Human Brain Mapping, 39*, 1688–1699.

Wang, S. B., Haynos, A. F., Wall, M. M., Chen, C., Eisenberg, M. E., & Neumark-Sztainer, D. (2019). Fifteen-year prevalence, trajectories, and predictors of body dissatisfaction from adolescence to middle adulthood. *Clinical Psychological Science, 7*, 1403–1415.

Wang, S.-H., Baillargeon, R., & Brueckner, L. (2004). Young infants' reasoning about hidden objects: Evidence from violation-of-expectation tasks with test trials only. *Cognition, 93*, 167–198.

Wang, W., & Wilcox, W. B. (2019). *Less stable, less important: Cohabiting families' comparative disadvantage across the globe.* Institute for Family Studies. https://ifstudies.org/blog/less-stable-less-important-cohabiting-families-comparative-disadvantage-across-the-globe

Wang, X., Gallegos, D. A., Pogorelov, V. M., O'Hare, J. K., Calakos, N., Wetsel, W. C., & West, A. E. (2018). Parvalbumin interneurons of the mouse nucleus accumbens are required for amphetamine-induced locomotor sensitization and conditioned place preference. *Neuropsychopharmacology, 43*, 953–963.

Wang, X., & Qiao, Y. (2022). Parental phubbing, self-esteem, and suicidal ideation among Chinese adolescents: A longitudinal mediational analysis. *Journal of Youth and Adolescence, 51*(11), 2248–2260.

Wang, Y., & Olson, I. R. (2018). The original social network: White matter and social cognition. *Trends in Cognitive Sciences, 22*, 504–516.

Wang, Y., Jiao, Y., Nie, J., O'Neil, A., Huang, W., Zhang, L., Han, J., Liu, H., Zhu, Y., Yu, C., & Woodward, M. (2020). Sex differences in the association between marital status and the risk of cardiovascular, cancer, and all-cause mortality: A systematic review and meta-analysis of 7,881,040 individuals. *Global Health Research and Policy, 5*(4). https://www.ncbi.nlm.nih.gov/pmc/articles/PMC7047380/

Wang, Z., Hui, Q., Goldberg, J., Smith, N., Kaseer, B., Murrah, N., Levantsevych, O. M., Shallenberger, L., Diggers, E., Bremner, J. D., Vaccarino, V., & Sun, Y. V. (2022). Association between posttraumatic stress disorder and epigenetic age acceleration in a sample of twins. *Psychosomatic Medicine, 84*(2), 151–158.

Wang, Z., Lukowski, S. L., Hart, S. A., Lyons, I. M., Thompson, L. A., Kovas, Y., Mazzocco, M. M., Plomin, R., & Petrill, S. A. (2015). Is math anxiety always bad for math learning? The role of math motivation. *Psychological Science, 26*, 1863–1876.

Wann, J. P., Poulter, D. R., & Purcell, C. (2011). Reduced sensitivity to visual looming inflates the risk posed by speeding vehicles when children try to cross the road. *Psychological Science, 22*, 429–434.

Ward, A., & Mann, T. (2000). Don't mind if I do: Disinhibited eating under cognitive load. *Journal of Personality and Social Psychology, 78*, 753–763.

Ward, C. (1994). Culture and altered states of consciousness. In W. J. Lonner & R. Malpass (Eds.), *Psychology and culture.* Allyn & Bacon.

Ward, D. E., Park, L. E., Naragon-Gainey, K., Whillans, A. V., & Jung, H. Y. (2020). Can't buy me love (or friendship): Social consequences of financially contingent self-worth. *Personality and Social Psychology Bulletin, 46*, 1665–1681.

Ward, E. V., Berry, C. J., Shanks, D. R., Moller, P. L., & Czsiser, E. (2020). Aging predicts decline in explicit and implicit memory: A life-span study. *Psychological Science, 31*, 1071–1083.

Ward, K. D., Klesges, R. C., & Halpern, M. T. (1997). Predictors of smoking cessation and state-of-the-art smoking interventions. *Journal of Social Issues, 53*, 129–145.

Ward, L. M., Seabrook, R. C., Grower, P., Giaccardi, S., & Lippman, J. R. (2018). Sexual object or sexual subject? Media use, self-sexualization, and sexual agency among undergraduate women. *Psychology of Women Quarterly, 42*, 29–43.

Ward-Griffin, E., Klaiber, P., Collins, H. K., Owens, R. L., Coren, S., & Chen, F. S. (2018). Petting away pre-exam stress: The effect of therapy dog sessions on student well-being. *Stress and Health, 34*, 468–473.

Wardle, J., Cooke, L. J., Gibson, L., Sapochnik, M., Sheiham, A., & Lawson, M. (2003). Increasing children's acceptance of vegetables: A randomized trial of parent-led exposure. *Appetite, 40*, 155–162.

Wargo, E. (2007, December). Understanding the have-knots. *APS Observer*, pp. 18–21.

Warne, R. T. (2020). *In the know: Debunking 35 myths about human intelligence.* Cambridge University Press.

Warren, J. A. (2019). *Why were we caught napping at Pearl Harbor?* Daily Beast. https://www.thedailybeast.com/why-were-we-caught-napping-at-pearl-harbor

Warrier, V., Kwong, A. S. F., Luo, M., Dalvie, S., Croft, J., Sallis, H. M., Baldwin, J., Munafò, M. R., Nievergelt, C. M., Grant, A. J., Burgess, S., Moore, T. M., Barzilay, R., McIntosh, A., van IJzendoorn, M. H., & Cecil, C. A. M. (2021). Gene-environment correlations and causal effects of childhood maltreatment on physical and mental health: A genetically informed approach. *Lancet Psychiatry, 8*(5), 373–386.

Washburn, M. F. (1908). *The animal mind: A textbook of comparative psychology.* Macmillan.

Wason, P. C. (1960). On the failure to eliminate hypotheses in a conceptual task. *Quarterly Journal of Experimental Psychology, 12*, 129–140.

Wasserman, E. A. (1993). Comparative cognition: Toward a general understanding of cognition in behavior. *Psychological Science, 4*, 156–161.

Wasserman, E. A. (1995). The conceptual abilities of pigeons. *American Scientist, 83*, 246–255.

Wastell, C. A. (2002). Exposure to trauma: The long-term effects of suppressing emotional reactions. *Journal of Nervous and Mental Disorders, 190*, 839–845.

Waterman, A. S. (1988). Identity status theory and Erikson's theory: Commonalities and differences. *Developmental Review, 8*, 185–208.

Waters, E. A., Klein, W. M. P., Moser, R. P., Yu, M., Waldron, W. R., McNeel, T. S., & Freedman, A. N. (2011). Correlates of unrealistic risk beliefs in a nationally representative sample. *Journal of Behavioral Medicine, 34*, 225–235.

Waters, T. E., Köber, C., Raby, K. L., Habermas, T., & Fivush, R. (2019). Consistency and stability of narrative coherence: An examination of personal narrative as a domain of adult personality. *Journal of Personality, 87*, 151–162.

Watkins, E. R. (2008). Constructive and unconstructive repetitive thought. *Psychological Bulletin, 134*, 163–206.

Watson, D. (2000). *Mood and temperament.* Guilford Press.

Watson, H. J., Yilmaz, Z., Thornton, L. M., Hübel, C., Coleman, J. R., Gaspar, H. A., Bryois, J., Hinney, A., Leppä, V.M., Mattheisen, M., Medland, S. E., Ripke, S., Yao, S., Giusti-Rodríguez, P., Anorexia Nervosa Genetics Initiative, Hanscombe, K. B., Purves, K. L., Eating Disorders Working Group of the Psychiatric Genomics Consortium, Adan, R. A. H., ... Bulik, C. M. (2019). Genome-wide association study identifies eight risk loci and implicates metabo-psychiatric origins for anorexia nervosa. *Nature Genetics, 51*, 1207–1214.

Watson, J. B. (1913). Psychology as the behaviorist views it. *Psychological Review, 20*, 158–177.

Watson, J. B. (1924). The unverbalized in human behavior. *Psychological Review, 31*, 339–347.

Watson, J. B., & Rayner, R. (1920). Conditioned emotional reactions. *Journal of Experimental Psychology, 3*, 1–14.

Watson, R. I., Jr. (1973). Investigation into deindividuation using a cross-cultural survey technique. *Journal of Personality and Social Psychology, 25*, 342–345.

Watts, T. W., & Duncan, G. J. (2020). Controlling, confounding, and construct clarity: Responding to criticisms of "Revisiting the marshmallow test" by Doebel, Michaelson, and Munakata (2020) and Falk, Kosse, and Pinger (2020). *Psychological Science, 31*, 105–108.

Watts, T. W., Duncan, G. J., & Quan, H. (2018). Revisiting the marshmallow task: A conceptual replication investigating links between early delay of gratification and later outcomes. *Psychological Science, 29*, 1159–1177.

Way, B. M., Creswell, J. D., Eisenberger, N. I., & Lieberman, M. D. (2010). Dispositional mindfulness and depressive symptomatology: Correlations with limbic and self-referential neural activity during rest. *Emotion, 10*, 12–24.

Waytz, A., & Gray, K. (2018). Does online technology make us more or less sociable? A preliminary review and call for research. *Perspectives on Psychological Science, 13*, 473–491.

Waytz, A., Young, L. L., & Ginges, J. (2014). Motive attribution asymmetry for love vs. hate drives intractable conflict. *PNAS, 111*, 15687–15692.

Webb, C. A., Cohen, Z. D., Beard, C., Forgeard, M., Peckham, A. D., & Björgvinsson, T. (2020). Personalized prognostic prediction of treatment outcome for depressed patients in a naturalistic psychiatric hospital setting: A comparison of machine learning approaches. *Journal of Consulting and Clinical Psychology, 88*, 25–38.

Webb, C. E., Rossignac-Milon, M., & Higgins, E. T. (2017). Stepping forward together: Could walking facilitate interpersonal conflict resolution? *American Psychologist, 72*, 374–385.

Webb, J. R., Bumgarner, D. J., Conway-Williams, E., Dangel, T., & Hall, B. B. (2017). A consensus definition of self-forgiveness: Implications for assessment and treatment. *Spirituality in Clinical Practice, 4*(3), 216–227.

Webb, M. E., Cropper, S. J., & Little, D. R. (2019). "Aha!" is stronger when preceded by a "huh?": Presentation of a solution affects ratings of aha experience conditional on accuracy. *Thinking & Reasoning, 25*, 324–364.

Webb, W. B. (1992). *Sleep: The gentle tyrant*, Second edition. Anker Publishing Company.

Weber, B., Koschutnig, K., Schwerdtfeger, A., Rominger, C., Papousek, I., Weiss, E. M., Tilp, M., & Fink, A. (2019). Learning unicycling evokes manifold changes in gray and white matter networks related to motor and cognitive functions. *Scientific Reports, 9*, 4324.

Webster, G. D., DeWall, C. N., Pond, R. S., Jr., Deckman, T., Jonason, P. K., Le, B. M., Nichols, A. L., Schember, T. O., Crysel, L. C., Crosier, B. S., Smith, C. V., Paddock, E. L., Nezlek, J. B., Kirkpatrick, L. A., Bryan, A. D., & Bator, R. J. (2014). The Brief Aggression Questionnaire: Psychometric and behavioral evidence for an efficient measure of trait aggression. *Aggressive Behavior, 40*, 120–139.

Wechsler, D. (1972). "Hold" and "Don't Hold" tests. In S. M. Chown (Ed.), *Human aging*. Penguin.

Wegner, D. M. (2002). *The illusion of conscious will*. MIT Press.

Wegner, D. M., & Ward, A. F. (2013). How Google is changing your brain. *Scientific American, 309*, 58–61.

Wei, Q., Fentress, H. M., Hoversten, M. T., Zhang, L., Hebda-Bauer, E. K., Watson, S. J., Seasholtz, A. F., & Akil, H. (2012). Early-life forebrain glucocorticoid receptor overexpression increases anxiety behavior and cocaine sensitization. *Biological Psychiatry, 71*, 224–231.

Weichbold, V., Holzer, A., Newesely, G., & Stephan, K. (2012). Results from high-frequency hearing screening in 14- to 15-year old adolescents and their relation to self-reported exposure to loud music. *International Journal of Audiology, 51*, 650–654.

Weidman, A. C., & Kross, E. (2021). Examining emotional tool use in daily life. *Journal of Personality and Social Psychology, 120*, 1344–1366.

Weidman, A. C., Tracy, J. L., & Elliot, A. J. (2016). The benefits of following your pride: Authentic pride promotes achievement. *Journal of Personality, 84*, 607–622.

Weinberg, A., & Doyle, N. (2017). *Psychology at work: Improving wellbeing and productivity in the workplace*. British Psychological Society. https://www.bps.org.uk/news-and-policy/psychology-work-improving-wellbeing-and-productivity-workplace

Weinberger, D. R. (2019). Thinking about schizophrenia in an era of genomic medicine. *American Journal of Psychiatry, 176*, 12–20.

Weiner, J. (2017, October 6). The flagrant sexual hypocrisy of conservative men. *The New York Times*. https://www.nytimes.com/2017/10/06/opinion/sunday/conservative-men-abortion-hypocrisy.html

Weingarten, E., Chen, Q., McAdams, M., Yi, J., Hepler, J., & Albarracín, D. (2016). From primed concepts to action: A meta-analysis of the behavioral effects of incidentally presented words. *Psychological Bulletin, 142*, 472.

Weingarten, G. (2002, March 10). Below the beltway. *The Washington Post*, p. WO3.

Weinschenk, A., Rasmussen, S. H. R., Christensen, K., Dawes, C., & Kiemmensen, R. (2022). The five factor model of personality and heritability: Evidence from Denmark. *Personality and Individual Differences, 192*. https://www.sciencedirect.com/science/article/pii/S019188692200109X

Weinstein, N. D. (1980). Unrealistic optimism about future life events. *Journal of Personality and Social Psychology, 39*, 806–820.

Weinstein, N. D., Ryan, W. S., DeHaan, C. R., Przbylski, A. K., Legate, N., & Ryan, R. M. (2012). Parental autonomy support and discrepancies between implicit and explicit sexual identities: Dynamics of self-acceptance and defense. *Journal of Personality and Social Psychology, 102*, 815–832.

Weinstein, Y., Levav, I., Gelkopf, M., Roe, D., Yoffe, R., Pugachova, I., & Levine, S. Z. (2018). Association of maternal exposure to terror attacks during pregnancy and the risk of schizophrenia in the offspring: A population-based study. *Schizophrenia Research, 199*, 163–167.

Weir, K. (2013, May). Captive audience. *Monitor on Psychology*, pp. 44–49.

Weir, W. (2010, May 17). Middletown man, age 76, has memorized epic poem "Paradise Lost." *Hartford Courant*. https://www.courant.com/2010/05/17/middletown-man-age-76-has-memorized-epic-poem-paradise-lost/

Weisbuch, M., Ivcevic, Z., & Ambady, N. (2009). On being liked on the web and in the "real world": Consistency in first impressions across personal webpages and spontaneous behavior. *Journal of Experimental Social Psychology, 45*, 573–576.

Weiser, E. B. (2015). #Me: Narcissism and its facets as predictors of selfie-posting frequency. *Personality and Individual Differences, 86*, 477–481.

Weiskrantz, L. (2009). *Blindsight*. Oxford University Press.

Weiskrantz, L. (2010). Blindsight in hindsight. *The Psychologist, 23*, 356–358.

Weisman, K., Dweck, C. S., & Markman, E. M. (2017). Rethinking people's conceptions of mental life. *PNAS, 114*, 11374–11379.

Weiss, A., Wilson, M. L., Collins, D. A., Mhungu, D., Kamenya, S., Foerster, S., & Pusey, A. E. (2017). Personality in the chimpanzees of Gombe National Park. *Nature: Scientific Data, 4*. https://www.nature.com/articles/sdata2017146

Weiss, B., Lavner, J. A., & Miller, J. D. (2017). Self- and partner-reported psychopathic traits' relations with couples' communication, marital satisfaction trajectories, and divorce in a longitudinal sample. *Personality Disorders: Theory, Research, and Treatment, 9*, 239–249.

Weiss, D., & Kunzmann, U. (2020). Longitudinal changes in subjective social status are linked to changes in positive and negative affect in midlife, but not in later adulthood. *Psychology of Aging, 35*(7), 937–947.

Weissman, M. M., Wickramaratne, P., Gameroff, M. J., Warner, V., Pilowsky, D., Kohad, R. G., Verdeli, H., Skipper, J., & Talati, A. (2016). Offspring of depressed parents: 30 years later. *American Journal of Psychiatry, 173*, 1024–1032.

Weisz, J. R., Kuppens, S., Ng, M. Y., Eckshtain, D., Ugueto, A. M., Vaughn-Coaxum, R., Jensen-Doss, A., Hawley, K. M., Krumholz Marchette, L. S., Chu, B. C., Weersing, V. R., & Fordwood, S. R. (2017). What five decades of research tells us about the effects of youth psychological therapy: A multilevel meta-analysis and implications for science and practice. *American Psychologist, 72*, 79–117.

Welch, J. M., Lu, J., Rodriquiz, R. M., Trotta, N. C., Peca, J., Ding, J.-D., Feliciano, C., Chen, M., Adams, J. P., Luo, J., Dudek, S. M., Weinberg, R. J., Calakos, N., Wetsel, W. C., & Feng, G. (2007). Cortico-striatal synaptic defects and OCD-like behaviours in *Sapap3*-mutant mice. *Nature, 448*, 894–900.

Welch, W. W. (2005, February 28). *Trauma of Iraq war haunting thousands returning home*. USA Today. https://usatoday30.usatoday.com/news/world/iraq/2005-02-28-cover-iraq-injuries_x.htm

Welham, J., Isohanni, M., Jones, P., & McGrath, J. (2009). The antecedents of schizophrenia: A review of birth cohort studies. *Schizophrenia Bulletin, 35*, 603–623.

Welker, K. M., Baker, L., Padilla, A., Holmes, H., Aron, A., & Slatcher, R. B. (2014). Effects of self-disclosure and responsiveness between couples on passionate love within couples. *Personal Relationships, 21*, 692–708.

Weller, S. C., & Davis-Beaty, K. (2002). Condom effectiveness in reducing heterosexual HIV transmission. *Cochrane Database of Systematic Reviews*. https://tinyurl.com/ysdumc49

Wells, D. L. (2009). The effects of animals on human health and well-being. *Journal of Social Issues, 65*, 523–543.

Wells, G. L. (2020). Psychological science on eyewitness identification and its impact on police practices and policies. *American Psychologist, 75*(9), 1316–1329.

Wenze, S. J., Gunthert, K. C., & German, R. E. (2012). Biases in affective forecasting and recall in individuals with depression and anxiety symptoms. *Personality and Social Psychology Bulletin, 38*, 895–906.

Werchan, D. M., Kim, J.-S., & Gómez, R. L. (2021). A daytime nap combined with nighttime sleep promotes learning in toddlers. *Journal of Experimental Child Psychology, 202*. https://doi.org/10.1016/j.jecp.2020.105006

Werker, J. F., Yeung, H. H., & Yoshida, K. A. (2012). How do infants become experts at native-speech perception? *Current Directions in Psychological Science, 21*, 221–226.

Werner, L., Geisler, J., & Randler, C. (2015). Morningness as a personality predictor of punctuality. *Current Psychology, 34*, 130–139.

Wertz, J., Caspi, A., Belsky, D. W., Beckley, A. L., Arseneault, L., Barnes, J. C., Corcoran, D. L., Hogan, S., Houts, R. M., Morgan, N., Odgers, C. L., Prinz, J. A., Sugden, K., Williams, B. S., Poulton, R., & Moffitt, T. E. (2018). Genetics and crime: Integrating new genomic discoveries into psychological research about antisocial behavior. *Psychological Science, 29*, 791–803.

Westen, D. (1996). *Is Freud really dead? Teaching psychodynamic theory to introductory psychology* [Presentation]. Annual Institute on the Teaching of Psychology, St. Petersburg Beach, FL.

Westen, D. (1998). The scientific legacy of Sigmund Freud: Toward a psychodynamically informed psychological science. *Psychological Bulletin, 124*, 333–371.

Westen, D. (2007). *The political brain: The role of emotion in deciding the fate of the nation*. PublicAffairs.

Westen, D., & Morrison, K. (2001). A multidimensional meta-analysis of treatments for depression, panic, and generalized anxiety disorder: An empirical examination of the status of empirically supported therapies. *Journal of Consulting and Clinical Psychology, 69*, 875–899.

Westrick, P. A., Marini, J. P., Young, L., Ng, H., Shmueli, D., & Shaw, E. J. (2019). *Validity of the SAT® for predicting first-year grades and retention to the second year* [PDF file]. College Board. https://collegereadiness.collegeboard.org/pdf/national-sat-validity-study.pdf

Wetzel, E., Grijalva, E., Robins, R. W., & Roberts, B. W. (2020). You're still so vain: Changes in narcissism from young adulthood to middle age. *Journal of Personality and Social Psychology,* 119, 479–496.

Whalen, P. J., Shin, L. M., McInerney, S. C., Fisher, H., Wright, C. I., & Rauch, S. L. (2001). A functional MRI study of human amygdala responses to facial expressions of fear versus anger. *Emotion, 1*, 70–83.

Whaley, C. M., Koo, T., Arora, V. M., Ganguli, I., Gross, N., & Jena, A. B. (2021). Female physicians earn an estimated $2 million less than male physicians over a simulated 40-year career. *Health Affairs, 40*(12). 1856–1864.

Whelan, R., Conrod, P. J., Poline, J.-B., Lourdusamy, A., Banaschewski, T., Barker, G. J., Bellgrove, M. A., Büchel, C., Byrne, M., Cummins, T. D. R., Fauth-Bühler, Flor, H., Gallinat, J., Heinz, A., Ittermann, B., Mann, K., Martinot, J.-L., Lalor, E. C., Lathrop, M., ... IMAGEN Consortium. (2012). Adolescent impulsivity phenotypes characterized by distinct brain networks. *Nature Neuroscience,* 15, 920–925.

Whillans, A. (2019). Time poor and unhappy. *Harvard Business Review.*

Whillans, A. V., Christie, C. D., Cheung, S., Jordan, A. H., & Chen, F. S. (2017). From misperception to social connection: Correlates and consequences of overestimating others' social connectedness. *Personality and Social Psychology Bulletin, 43*, 1696–1711.

Whillans, A. V., Weidman, A. C., & Dunn, E. W. (2016). Valuing time over money is associated with greater happiness. *Social Psychological and Personality Science, 7*, 213–222.

Whitaker, K. J., Vértes, P. E., Romero-Garcia, R., Váša, F., Moutoussis, M., Prabhu, G., Weiskopf, N., Callaghan, M. F., Wagstyl, K., Rittman, T., Tait, R., Ooi, C., Suckling, J., Inkster, B., Fonagy, P., Dolan, R. J., Jones, P. B., Goodyer, I. M., NSPN Consortium, & Bullmore, E. T. (2016). Adolescence is associated with genomically patterned consolidation of the hubs of the human brain connectome. *PNAS, 113*, 9105–9110.

White, H. R., Brick, J., & Hansell, S. (1993). A longitudinal investigation of alcohol use and aggression in adolescence. *Journal of Studies on Alcohol*(supp 11), 62–77.

White, L., & Edwards, J. (1990). Emptying the nest and parental well-being: An analysis of national panel data. *American Sociological Review, 55*, 235–242.

White, M. W., Khan, N., Deren, J. S., Sim, J. J., & Majka, E. A. (2022). Give a dog a bone: Spending money on pets promotes happiness. *Journal of Positive Psychology, 17*(4), 589–595.

White, R. A. (1998). Intuition, heart knowledge, and parapsychology. *Journal of the American Society for Psychical Research, 92*, 158–171.

White, R. E., Kross, E., & Duckworth, A. L. (2015). Spontaneous self-distancing and adaptive self-reflection across adolescence. *Child Development, 86*, 1272–1281.

White, S., Schroeder, J., & Risen, J. L. (2021). When "enemies" become close: Relationship formation among Palestinians and Jewish Israelis at a youth camp. *Journal of Personality and Social Psychology, 121*(1), 76–94.

Whitehouse, H. (2018). Dying for the group: Towards a general theory of extreme self-sacrifice. *Behavioral and Brain Sciences, 7*, 1–64.

Whitehurst, L. N., Cellini, N., McDevitt, E. A., Duggan, K. A., & Mednick, S. C. (2016). Autonomic activity during sleep predicts memory consolidation in humans. *PNAS, 113*, 7272–7277.

Whiten, A. (2021a). The psychological reach of culture in animals' lives. *Current Directions in Psychological Science, 30*, 211–217.

Whiten, A. (2021b). The burgeoning reach of animal culture. *Science, 372*(6537). https://www.science.org/doi/10.1126/science.abe6514

Whiten, A., & Byrne, R. W. (1988). Tactical deception in primates. *Behavioral and Brain Sciences, 11*, 233–244, 267–273.

Whiten, A., Spiteri, A., Horner, V., Bonnie, K. E., Lambeth, S. P., Schapiro, S. J., & de Waal, F. B. M. (2007). Transmission of multiple traditions within and between chimpanzee groups. *Current Biology, 17*, 1038–1043.

Whiting, D., Lichtenstein, P., & Fazel, S. (2021). Violence and mental disorders: A structured review of associations by individual diagnoses, risk factors, and risk assessment. *Lancet Psychiatry, 8*, 150–161.

Whitley, B. E., Jr. (1999). Right-wing authoritarianism, social dominance orientation, and prejudice. *Journal of Personality and Social Psychology, 77*, 126–134.

Whitlock, J. R., Heynen, A. L., Shuler, M. G., & Bear, M. F. (2006). Learning induces long-term potentiation in the hippocampus. *Science, 313*, 1093–1097.

WHO (World Health Organization). (2000). *Effectiveness of male latex condoms in protecting against pregnancy and sexually transmitted infections.* Fact Sheet No. 243. Geneva. https://bit.ly/2vjBcN7

WHO. (2003). *The male latex condom: Specification and guidelines for condom procurement* [PDF file]. https://www.unfpa.org/sites/default/files/pub-pdf/male-latex-condom.pdf

WHO. (2012). *Risks to mental health.* https://www.who.int/publications/m/item/risks-to-mental-health

WHO. (2012, May). *Tobacco: Fact sheet N339.* https://www.ncbi.nlm.nih.gov/pmc/articles/PMC3850892/

WHO. (2014, accessed September 20). *Chain-free initiative.* https://www.mhinnovation.net/innovations/chain-free-initiative

WHO. (2014). *Global status report on alcohol and health 2014* [PDF file]. https://www.who.int/substance_abuse/publications/global_alcohol_report/msb_gsr_2014_1.pdf

WHO. (2016). *Global status on road safety 2015* [PDF file]. https://www.afro.who.int/publications/global-status-report-road-safety-2015

WHO. (2016). Growing recognition of transgender health. *Bulletin of the World Health Organization, 94*(11), 790–791.

WHO. (2017). *How to implement influenza vaccination of pregnant women.* https://www.who.int/publications/i/item/WHO-IVB-16.06

WHO. (2018). *Gaming disorder.* https://www.who.int/features/qa/gaming-disorder/en/

WHO. (2018). *Global status report on alcohol and health 2018.* V. Poznyak & D. Rekve (Eds.). https://www.who.int/substance_abuse/publications/global_alcohol_report/en/

WHO. (2019, accessed September 28). *Life expectancy.* Global Health Observatory (GHO) data. www.who.int

WHO. (2019, March 20). *Deafness and hearing loss.* https://www.who.int/news-room/fact-sheets/detail/deafness-and-hearing-loss

WHO. (2019). *Schizophrenia.* https://www.who.int/news-room/fact-sheets/detail/schizophrenia

WHO. (2020). *Suicide.* https://www.who.int/news-room/fact-sheets/detail/suicide

WHO. (2020). *Tobacco.* https://bit.ly/3qfJJs2

WHO. (2022a). *World mental health report: Transforming mental health for all.* https://www.who.int/publications/i/item/9789240049338

WHO. (2022b). *World health statistics 2022: Monitoring health for the SDGs, sustainable development goals.* https://www.who.int/publications/i/item/9789240051157

WHO. (2022). *World mental health report.* https://www.who.int/teams/mental-health-and-substance-use/world-mental-health-report

Whooley, M. A., de Jonge, P., Vittinghoff, E., Otte, C., Noos, R., Carney, R. M., Ali, S., Dowray, S., Na, B., Feldman, M. D., Schiller, N. B., & Browner, W. S. (2008). Depressive symptoms, health behaviors, and risk of cardiovascular events in patients with coronary heart disease. *Journal of the American Medical Association, 300*, 2379–2388.

Whorf, B. L. (1956). Science and linguistics. In J. B. Carroll (Ed.), *Language, thought, and reality: Selected writings of Benjamin Lee Whorf.* MIT Press.

Wicherts, J. M., Dolan, C. V., Carlson, J. S., & van der Maas, H. L. J. (2010). Raven's test performance of sub-Saharan Africans: Mean level, psychometric properties, and the Flynn effect. *Learning and Individual Differences, 20*, 135–151.

Wickelgren, I. (2009, September/October). I do not feel your pain. *Scientific American Mind,* pp. 51–57.

Wickelgren, W. A. (1977). *Learning and memory.* Prentice-Hall.

Widén, S. E., Båsjö, S., Möller, C., & Kähäri, K. (2017). Headphone listening habits and hearing thresholds in Swedish adolescents. *Noise & Health, 19*, 125–132.

Widiger, T. A., Sellbom, M., Chmielewski, M., Clark, L. A., DeYoung, C. G., Kotov, R., Krueger, R. F., Lynam, D. R., Miller, J. D., Mullins-Sweatt, S., Samuel., D. B., South, S. C., Tackett, J. L., Thomas, K. M., Watson, D., & Wright, A. G. C. (2019). Personality in a hierarchical model of psychopathology. *Clinical Psychological Science, 7*, 77–92.

Widman, L., Evans, R., Javidi, H., & Choukas-Bradley, S. (2019). Assessment of parent-based interventions for adolescent sexual health. A systematic review and meta-analysis. *JAMA Pediatrics, 173*(9), 866–877.

Widom, C. S. (1989). Does violence beget violence? A critical examination of the literature. *Psychological Bulletin, 106*, 3–28.

Wielgosz, J., Goldberg, S. B., Kral, T. R., Dunne, J. D., & Davidson, R. J. (2019). Mindfulness meditation and psychopathology. *Annual Review of Clinical Psychology, 15*, 285–316.

Wiens, A. N., & Menustik, C. E. (1983). Treatment outcome and patient characteristics in an aversion therapy program for alcoholism. *American Psychologist, 38*, 1089–1096.

Wierenga, L. M., Bos, M. G., van Rossenberg, F., & Crone, E. A. (2019). Sex effects on development of brain structure and executive functions: Greater variance than mean effects. *Journal of Cognitive Neuroscience, 31*, 730–753.

Wierenga, L. M., Doucet, G. E., Dima, D., Agartz, I., Aghajani, M., Akudjedu, T. N., Albajes-Eizagirre, A., Alnaes, D., Alpert, K. I., Andreassen, O. A., Anticevic, A., Asherson, P., Banaschewski, T., Bargallo, N., Baumeister, S., Baur-Streubel, R., Bertolino, A., Bonvino, A., Boomsma, D. I., ... Tammes, C. K. (2022). Greater male than female variability in regional brain structure across the lifespan. *Human Brain Mapping, 43*(1), 470–499.

Wierson, M., & Forehand, R. (1994). Parent behavioral training for child noncompliance: Rationale, concepts, and effectiveness. *Current Directions in Psychological Science, 3*, 146–149.

Wierzbicki, M. (1993). Psychological adjustment of adoptees: A meta-analysis. *Journal of Clinical Child Psychology, 22*, 447–454.

Wiese, C. W., Kuykendall, L., & Tay, L. (2018). Get active? A meta-analysis of leisure-time physical activity and subjective well-being. *Journal of Positive Psychology, 13*, 57–66.

Wiese, H., Tüttenberg, S. C., Ingram, B. T., Chan, C. Y., Gurbuz, Z., Burton, A. M., & Young, A. W. (2019). A robust neural index of high face familiarity. *Psychological Science, 30*, 261–272.

Wiesel, T. N. (1982). Postnatal development of the visual cortex and the influence of environment. *Nature, 299*, 583–591.

Wiesner, W. H., & Cronshaw, S. P. (1988). A meta-analytic investigation of the impact of interview format and degree of structure on the validity of the employment interview. *Journal of Occupational Psychology, 61*, 275–290.

Wigdor, A. K., & Garner, W. R. (1982). *Ability testing: Uses, consequences, and controversies.* National Academy Press.

Wilar, G., Shinoda, Y., Sasaoka, T., & Fukunaga, K. (2019). Crucial role of dopamine D2 receptor signaling in nicotine-induced conditioned place preference. *Molecular Neurobiology, 56*(12), 7911–7928.

Wilcox, W. B., & DeRose, L. (2017, March 27). *In Europe, cohabitation is stable ... right?* Brookings Institution. https://www.brookings.edu/blog/social-mobility-memos/2017/03/27/in-europe-cohabitation-is-stable-right/

Wilcox, W. B., Dew, J., & ElHage, A. (2019, February 7). *Cohabitation doesn't compare: Marriage, cohabitation, and relationship quality.* Institute for Family Studies. https://ifstudies.org/blog/cohabitation-doesnt-compare-marriage-cohabitation-and-relationship-quality

Wilcox, W. B., & Marquardt, E. (2011, December). *When baby makes three: How parenthood makes life meaningful and how marriage makes parenthood bearable.* National Marriage Project, University of Virginia.

Wilcox, W. B., & Wolfinger, N. H. (2017, February). *Men & marriage: Debunking the ball and chain myth* [PDF file]. Institute for Family Studies. https://ifstudies.org/wp-content/uploads/2017/02/IFSMenandMarriageResearchBrief2.pdf

Wilcox, W. B., Van Leeuwen, J., & Price, J. (2018, October 17). *The family geography of the American dream: New neighborhood data on single parenthood, prisons, and poverty.* Institute for Family Studies. https://ifstudies.org/blog/the-family-geography-of-the-american-dream-new-neighborhood-data-on-single-parenthood-prisons-and-poverty

Wildman, D. E., Uddin, M., Liu, G., Grossman, L. I., & Goodman, M. (2003). Implications of natural selection in shaping 99.4% nonsynonymous DNA identity between humans and chimpanzees: Enlarging genus Homo. *PNAS, 100*, 7181–7188.

Wiley, J., & Jarosz, A. F. (2012). Working memory capacity, attentional focus, and problem solving. *Current Directions in Psychological Science, 21*, 258–262.

Wilford, J. N. (1999, February 9). New findings help balance the cosmological books. *The New York Times.* https://www.nytimes.com/1999/02/09/science/new-findings-help-balance-the-cosmological-books.html

Wilkey, E. D., Cutting, L. E., & Price, G. R. (2018). Neuroanatomical correlates of performance in a state-wide test of math achievement. *Developmental Science, 21*(2). https://doi.org/10.1111/desc.12545

Wilkins, C. L., Wellman, J. D., Toosi, N. R., Miller, C. A., Lisnek, J. A., & Martin, L. A. (2022). Is LGBT progress seen as an attack on Christians?: Examining Christian/sexual orientation zero-sum beliefs. *Journal of Personality and Social Psychology, 122*(1), 73–101.

Wilkinson, G. (2021). 'Of the chaunge from one sex to another': Eye-witness accounts of Pliny the Elder (23–79) and Ambroise Paré (1510–1590) – psychiatry in literature. *British Journal of Psychiatry, 218*, 184.

Wilkinson, M. J., Manoogian, E. N., Zadourian, A., Lo, H., Fakhouri, S., Shoghi, A., Wang, X., Fleischer, J. G., Navlakha, S., Panda, S., & Taub, P. R. (2020). Ten-hour time-restricted eating reduces weight, blood pressure, and atherogenic lipids in patients with metabolic syndrome. *Cell Metabolism, 31*(1), 92–104.

Wilkinson, R., & Pickett, K. (2009). *The spirit level: Why greater equality makes societies stronger.* Bloomsbury Press.

Williams, J. E., & Best, D. L. (1990). *Measuring sex stereotypes: A multination study.* Sage.

Williams, K. D. (2007). Ostracism. *Annual Review of Psychology, 58*, 425–452.

Williams, K. D. (2009). Ostracism: A temporal need-threat model. *Advances in Experimental Social Psychology, 41*, 275–313.

Williams, L., Carrigan, A., Auffermann, W., Mills, M., Rich, A., Elmore, J., & Drew, T. (2021). The invisible breast cancer: Experience does not protect against inattentional blindness to clinically relevant findings in radiology. *Psychonomic Bulletin & Review, 28*, 503–511.

Williams, L. A., & DeSteno, D. (2009). Adaptive social emotion or seventh sin? *Psychological Science, 20*, 284–288.

Williams, M. T. (2021). Racial microaggressions: Critical questions, state of the science, and new directions. *Perspectives on Psychological Science, 16*(5), 880–885.

Williams, N. M., Zaharieva, I., Martin, A., Langley, K., Mantripragada, K., Fossdal, R., Steffanson, H., Steffanson, K., Magnusson, P., Gudmundsson, O. O., Gustafsson, O., Holmans, P., Owen, M. J., O'Donovan, M., & Thapar, A. (2010). Rare chromosomal deletions and duplications in attention-deficit hyperactivity disorder: A genome-wide analysis. *The Lancet, 376*, 1401–1408.

Williams, S. L. (1987). *Self-efficacy and mastery-oriented treatment for severe phobias* [Paper]. Presented to the American Psychological Association convention.

Williams, T. (2015, March 17). Missouri executes killer who had brain injury. *The New York Times.* https://www.nytimes.com/2015/03/18/us/missouri-executes-killer-who-had-brain-injury.html

Willingham, D. T. (2010, Summer). Have technology and multitasking rewired how students learn? *American Educator, 42*, 23–28.

Willingham, W. W., Lewis, C., Morgan, R., & Ramist, L. (1990). *Predicting college grades: An analysis of institutional trends over two decades.* Educational Testing Service.

Willis, B. L., Leonard, D., Barlow, C. E., Martin, S. B., DeFina, L. F., & Trivedi, M. H. (2018). Association of midlife cardiorespiratory fitness with incident depression and cardiovascular death after depression in later life. *JAMA Psychiatry, 75*, 911–917.

Willis, J., & Todorov, A. (2006). First impressions: Making up your mind after a 100-ms. exposure to a face. *Psychological Science, 17*, 592–598.

Willmuth, M. E. (1987). Sexuality after spinal cord injury: A critical review. *Clinical Psychology Review, 7*, 389–412.

Willoughby, B. J., Carroll, J. S., & Busby, D. M. (2014). Differing relationship outcomes when sex happens before, on, or after first dates. *Journal of Sex Research, 51*, 52–61.

Willoughby, E. A., Giannelis, A., Ludeke, S., Klemmensen, R., Nørgaard, A. S., Iacono, W. G., Lee, J. J., & McGue, M. (2021). Parent contributions to the development of political attitudes in adoptive and biological families. *Psychological Science, 32*, 2023–2034.

Willoughby, E. A., Love, A. C., McGue, M., Iacono, W. G., Quigley, J., & Lee, J. J. (2019). Free will, determinism, and intuitive judgments about the heritability of behavior. *Behavior Genetics, 49*, 136–153.

Willroth, E. C., Ong, A. D., Graham, E. K., & Mroczek, D. K. (2020). Being happy and becoming happier as independent predictors of physical health and mortality. *Psychosomatic Medicine, 82*, 650–657.

Wilson, A. E., & Ross, M. (2001). From chump to champ: People's appraisals of their earlier and present selves. *Journal of Personality and Social Psychology, 80*, 572–584.

Wilson, B., Smith, K., & Petkov, C. I. (2015). Mixed-complexity artificial grammar learning in humans and macaque monkeys: Evaluating learning strategies. *European Journal of Neuroscience, 41*, 568–578.

Wilson, B. S., Tucci, D. L., Merson, M. H., & O'Donoghue, G. M. (2017). Global hearing health care: New findings and perspectives. *The Lancet, 390*, 2503–2515.

Wilson, R. S. (1979). Analysis of longitudinal twin data: Basic model and applications to physical growth measures. *Acta Geneticae Medicae et Gemellologiae, 28*, 93–105.

Wilson, R. S., Arnold, S. E., Schneider, J. A., Tang, Y., & Bennett, D. A. (2007). The relationship between cerebral Alzheimer's disease pathology and odour identification in old age. *Journal of Neurology, Neurosurgery, and Psychiatry, 78*, 30–35.

Wilson, R. S., Beck, T. L., Bienias, J. L., & Bennett, D. A. (2007). Terminal cognitive decline: Accelerated loss of cognition in the last years of life. *Psychosomatic Medicine, 69*, 131–137.

Wilson, T. D. (2002). *Strangers to ourselves: Discovering the adaptive unconscious.* Harvard University Press.

Wilson, T. D., Reinhard, D. A., Westgate, E. C., Gilbert, D. T., Ellerbeck, N., Hahn, C., Brown, C. L., & Shaked, A. (2014). Just think: The challenges of the disengaged mind. *Science, 345*, 75–77.

Wimber, M., Alink, A., Charest, I., Kriegeskorte, N., & Anderson, M. C. (2015). Retrieval induces adaptive forgetting of competing memories via cortical pattern suppression. *Nature Neuroscience, 18*, 582–589.

Wimmelmann, C. L., Mortensen, E. L., Hegelund, E. R., Folker, A. P., Strizzi, J. M., Dammeyer, J., & Fiensborg-Madsen, T. (2020). Associations of personality traits with quality of life and satisfaction with life in a longitudinal study with up to 29 year follow-up. *Personality and Individual Differences, 156*. https://doi.org/10.1016/j.paid.2019.109725

Wimmer, R. D., Schmitt, L. I., Davidson, T. J., Nakajima, M., Deisseroth, K., & Halassa, M. M. (2015). Thalamic control of sensory selection in divided attention. *Nature, 526*, 705–709.

Windholz, G. (1989, April–June). The discovery of the principles of reinforcement, extinction, generalization, and differentiation of conditional reflexes in Pavlov's laboratories. *Pavlovian Journal of Biological Science, 26*, 64–74.

Windholz, G. (1997). Ivan P. Pavlov: An overview of his life and psychological work. *American Psychologist, 52*, 941–946.

Wingfield, A., McCoy, S. L., Peelle, J. E., Tun, P. A., & Cox, L. C. (2005). Effects of adult aging and hearing loss on comprehension of rapid speech varying in syntactic complexity. *Journal of the American Academy of Audiology, 17*, 487–497.

Winkler, A., Dòrsing, B., Rief, W., Shen, Y., & Glombiewski, J. A. (2013). Treatment of internet addiction: A meta-analysis. *Clinical Psychology Review, 33*, 317–329.

Winter, W. C., Hammond, W. R., Green, N. H., Zhang, Z., & Bilwise, D. L. (2009). Measuring circadian advantage in major league baseball: A 10-year retrospective study. *International Journal of Sports Physiology and Performance, 4*, 394–401.

Wipfli, B., Landers, D., Nagoshi, C., & Ringenbach, S. (2011). An examination of serotonin and psychological variables in the relationship between exercise and mental health. *Scandinavian Journal of Medicine & Science in Sports, 21*(3), 474–481.

Wirth, J. H., Sacco, D. F., Hugenberg, K., & Williams, K. D. (2010). Eye gaze as relational evaluation: Averted eye gaze leads to feelings of ostracism and relational devaluation. *Personality and Social Psychology Bulletin, 36*, 869–882.

Wiseman, R., & Greening, E. (2002). The Mind Machine: A mass participation experiment into the possible existence of extra-sensory perception. *British Journal of Psychology, 93*, 487–499.

Witelson, S. (2011). Sandra Witelson. http://www.science.ca/scientists/scientistprofile.php?pID=273

Witkower, Z., Hill, A. K., Koster, J., & Tracy, J. L. (2022). Is a downwards head tilt a cross-cultural signal of dominance? Evidence for a universal visual illusion. *Scientific Reports, 12*. https://www.nature.com/articles/s41598-021-04370-w

Witt, J. K., Linkenauger, S. A., & Proffitt, D. R. (2012). Get me out of this slump! Visual illusions improve sports performance. *Psychological Science, 23*, 397–399.

Witteman, H. O., Hendricks, M., Straus, S., & Tannenbaum, C. (2019). Are gender gaps due to evaluations of the applicant or the science? A natural experiment at a national funding agency. *The Lancet, 393*, 531–540.

Witters, D. (2014, October 20). *U.S. adults with children at home have greater joy, stress.* Gallup. https://news.gallup.com/poll/178631/adults-childrenhome-greaterjoy-stress.aspx

Witters, D., & Agrawal, S. (2022, March 18). *Poor sleep linked to $44 billion in lost productivity.* Gallup Poll. https://news.gallup.com/poll/390797/poor-sleep-linked-billion-lost-productivity.aspx

Witters, D., & Wood, J. (2015, January 14). *Heart attacks and depression closely linked.* Gallup. https://news.gallup.com/poll/180470/heart-attacks-depression-closely-linked.aspx

Wittgenstein, L. (1922). *Tractatus logico-philosophicus* (C. K. Ogden, Trans.). Harcourt, Brace.

Witvliet, C. V. O., & Vrana, S. R. (1995). Psychophysiological responses as indices of affective dimensions. *Psychophysiology, 32*, 436–443.

Wixted, J. T., & Ebbesen, E. B. (1991). On the form of forgetting. *Psychological Science, 2*, 409–415.

Wixted, J. T., Mickes, L., & Fisher, R. P. (2018). Rethinking the reliability of eyewitness memory. *Perspectives on Psychological Science, 13*, 324–335.

WKYT. (2017). *Kentucky fans set crowd roar world record.* https://www.wkyt.com/content/news/Kentucky-fans-set-crowd-roar-world-record-412059133.html

Wójcik, M. J., Nowicka, M. M., Bola, M., & Nowicka, A. (2019). Unconscious detection of one's own image. *Psychological Science, 30*, 471–480.

Wolf, W., Nafe, A., & Tomasello, M. (2021). The development of the liking gap: Children older than 5 years think that partners evaluate them less positively than they evaluate their partners. *Psychological Science, 32*, 789–798.

Wolfson, A. R., & Carskadon, M. A. (1998). Sleep schedules and daytime functioning in adolescents. *Child Development, 69*, 875–887.

Wolpe, J. (1958). *Psychotherapy by reciprocal inhibition.* Stanford University Press.

Wolpe, J., & Plaud, J. J. (1997). Pavlov's contributions to behavior therapy: The obvious and the not so obvious. *American Psychologist, 52*, 966–972.

Wolpe, P. (2018, June 12). *A human head transplant would be reckless and ghastly. It's time to talk about it.* Vox. https://www.vox.com/the-big-idea/2018/4/2/17173470/human-head-transplant-canavero-ethics-bioethics

Wonderlich, S. A., Joiner, T. E., Jr., Keel, P. K., Williamson, D. A., & Crosby, R. D. (2007). Eating disorder diagnoses: Empirical approaches to classification. *American Psychologist, 62*, 167–180.

Wondra, J. D., & Ellsworth, P. C. (2015). An appraisal theory of empathy and other vicarious emotional experiences. *Psychological Review, 122*, 411–428.

Wong, D. F., Wagner, H. N., Tune, L. E., Dannals, R. F., Pearlson, G. D., Links, J. M., Tamminga, C. A., Broussolle, E. P., Ravert, H. T., Wilson, A. A., Toung, J. K., Malat, J., Williams, J. A., O'Tuama, L. A., Snyder, S. H., Kuhar, M. J., & Gjedde, A. (1986). Positron emission tomography reveals elevated D2 dopamine receptors in drug-naive schizophrenics. *Science, 234*, 1588–1593.

Wong, M. M., & Csikszentmihalyi, M. (1991). Affiliation motivation and daily experience: Some issues on gender differences. *Journal of Personality and Social Psychology, 60*, 154–164.

Wong, M. M., Craun, E. A., Bravo, A. J., & Pearson, M. R. (2019). Insomnia symptoms, cannabis protective behavioral strategies, and hazardous cannabis use among U.S. college students. *Experimental and Clinical Psychopharmacology, 27*, 309–317.

Wong, T. K. Y., Konishi, C., & Kong, X. (2021). Parenting and prosocial behaviors: A meta-analysis. *Social Development, 30*(2), 343–373.

Wongupparaj, P., Kumari, V., & Morris, R. G. (2015). A cross-temporal meta-analysis of Raven's Progressive Matrices: Age groups and developing versus developed countries. *Intelligence, 49*, 1–9.

Wood, C. (2018, October 1). *Thought-reading AI helps a person with quadriplegia play Guitar Hero.* Popular Science. https://www.popsci.com/machine-learning-quadriplegia-brain-interface/

Wood, D., Bruner, J., & Ross, G. (1976). The role of tutoring in problem solving. *Journal of Child Psychology and Child Psychiatry, 17*, 89–100.

Wood, J. M. (2003, May 19). Quoted in R. Mestel, Rorschach tested: Blot out the famous method? Some experts say it has no place in psychiatry. *The Los Angeles Times.* http://articles.latimes.com/2003/may/19/health/he-rorschach19

Wood, J. M., Bootzin, R. R., Kihlstrom, J. F., & Schacter, D. L. (1992). Implicit and explicit memory for verbal information presented during sleep. *Psychological Science, 3*, 236–239.

Wood, J. M., Garb, H. N., Nezworski, M. T., Lilienfeld, S. O., & Duke, M. C. (2015). A second look at the validity of widely used Rorschach indices: Comment on Mihura, Meyer, Dumitrascu, and Bombel (2013). *Psychological Bulletin, 141*, 236–249.

Wood, J. M., Nezworski, M. T., Garb, H. N., & Lilienfeld, S. O. (2006). The controversy over the Exner Comprehensive System for the Rorschach: The critics speak. *Independent Practitioner, 26*.

Wood, W. (1987). Meta-analytic review of sex differences in group performance. *Psychological Bulletin, 102*, 53–71.

Wood, W. (2017). Habit in personality and social psychology. *Personality and Social Psychology Review, 21*, 389–403.

Wood, W., & Eagly, A. H. (2002). A cross-cultural analysis of the behavior of women and men: Implications for the origins of sex differences. *Psychological Bulletin, 128*, 699–727.

Wood, W., & Eagly, A. H. (2007). Social structural origins of sex differences in human mating. In S. W. Gagestad & J. A. Simpson (Eds.), *The evolution of mind: Fundamental questions and controversies* (pp. 383–390). Guilford Press.

Wood, W., Lundgren, S., Ouellette, J. A., Busceme, S., & Blackstone, T. (1994). Minority influence: A meta-analytic review of social influence processes. *Psychological Bulletin, 115*, 323–345.

Woods, S. A., Edmonds, G. W., Hampson, S. E., & Lievens, F. (2020). How our work influences who we are: Testing a theory of vocational and personality development over fifty years. *Journal of Research in Personality, 85*. https://www.sciencedirect.com/science/article/abs/pii/S0092656620300192

Woolcock, N. (2004, September 3). Driver thought everyone else was on wrong side. *The Times*, p. 22.

Woolford, S. J., Sidell, M., Li, X. Else, V., Young, D. R., Resnicow, K., & Koebnick, C. (2021). Changes in body mass index among children and adolescents during the COVID-19 pandemic. *Journal of the American Medical Association, 326*(14), 1434–1436.

Woollett, K., & Maguire, E. A. (2011). Acquiring "the knowledge" of London's layout drives structural brain changes. *Current Biology, 21*, 2109–2114.

Woolley, A. W., Chabris, C. F., Pentland, A., Hasmi, N., & Malone, T. W. (2010). Evidence for a collective intelligence factor in the performance of human groups. *Science, 330*, 686–688.

Woolley, K., & Fishbach, A. (2017). Immediate rewards predict adherence to long-term goals. *Personality and Social Psychology Bulletin, 43*, 151–162.

Woolley, K., & Fishbach, A. (2018). It's about time: Earlier rewards increase intrinsic motivation. *Journal of Personality and Social Psychology, 114*, 877–890.

Woolley, K., & Risen, J. L. (2018). Closing your eyes to follow your heart: Avoiding information to protect a strong intuitive preference. *Journal of Personality and Social Psychology, 114*, 230–245.

World Bank. (2019, accessed June 10). *Life expectancy at birth, total (years)*. https://data.worldbank.org/indicator/sp.dyn.le00.in

World Federation for Mental Health. (2005). *ADHD: The hope behind the hype* [PDF file]. http://webcontent.hkcss.org.hk/rh/rpp/ADHD_Hope_behind_Hype.pdf

Worthington, E. L., Jr., & Wade, N. G. (2019). *Handbook of forgiveness* (2nd ed.). Routledge/Taylor & Francis Group.

Worthman, C. M., & Trang, K. (2018). Dynamics of body time, social time and life history at adolescence. *Nature, 554*, 451–457.

Wortman, C. B., & Silver, R. C. (1989). The myths of coping with loss. *Journal of Consulting and Clinical Psychology, 57*, 349–357.

Wright, J. (2006, March 16). *Boomers in the bedroom: Sexual attitudes and behaviours in the boomer generation*. Ipsos. https://www.ipsos.com/en-ca/boomers-bedroom-sexual-attitudes-and-behaviours-boomer-generation

Wright, P. J., Bridges, A. J., Sun, C., Ezzell, M. B., Johnson, J. A. (2018). Personal pornography viewing and sexual satisfaction: A quadratic analysis. *Journal of Sex and Marital Therapy, 44*, 308–315.

Wright, P., Takei, N., Rifkin, L., & Murray, R. M. (1995). Maternal influenza, obstetric complications, and schizophrenia. *American Journal of Psychiatry, 152*, 1714–1720.

Wright, P. J., & Vangeel, L. (2019). Pornography, permissiveness, and sex differences: An evaluation of social learning and evolutionary explanations. *Personality and Individual Differences, 143*, 128–138.

Wrzesniewski, A., & Dutton, J. E. (2001). Crafting a job: Revisioning employees as active crafters of their work. *Academy of Management Review, 26*, 179–201.

Wrzesniewski, A., Schwartz, B., Cong, X., Kane, M., Omar, A., & Kolditz, T. (2014). Multiple types of motives don't multiply the motivation of West Point cadets. *PNAS, 111*, 10990–10995.

Wu, C. (2019). *Making a scene*. Scribner.

Wu, L., Wang, D., & Evans, J. A. (2019). Large teams develop and small teams disrupt science and technology. *Nature, 566*, 378–382.

Wu, S., Wu, F., Ding, Y., Hou, J., Bi, J., & Zhang, Z. (2017). Advanced parental age and autism risk in children: A systematic review and meta-analysis. *Acta Psychiatrica Scandinavica, 135*, 29–41.

Wu, W., & Small, S. A. (2006). Imaging the earliest stages of Alzheimer's disease. *Current Alzheimer Research, 3*, 529–539.

Wu, X., Kaminga, A. C., Dai, W., Deng, J., Wang, Z., Pan, X., & Liu, A. (2019). The prevalence of moderate-to-high posttraumatic growth: A systematic review and meta-analysis. *Journal of Affective Disorders, 243*, 408–415.

Wu, X., Zhang, Z., Zhao, F., Wang, W., Li, Y., Bi, L., Qian, Z. Z., Lu, S. S., Feng, F., Hu, C. Y., Gong, F. F., & Sun, Y. (2016). Prevalence of internet addiction and its association with social support and other related factors among adolescents in China. *Journal of Adolescence, 52*, 103–111.

Wüsten, C., & Lincoln, T. M. (2022). Cross-cultural comparisons of the effect of a schizophrenia label on stigmatizing family attitudes: A case vignette study. *Journal of Psychopathology and Clinical Science, 131*(1), 109–116.

Wyatt, J. K., & Bootzin, R. R. (1994). Cognitive processing and sleep: Implications for enhancing job performance. *Human Performance, 7*, 119–139.

Wynn, K. (1992). Addition and subtraction by human infants. *Nature, 358*, 749–759.

Wynn, K. (2000). Findings of addition and subtraction in infants are robust and consistent: Reply to Wakeley, Rivera, and Langer. *Child Development, 71*, 1535–1536.

Wynn, K. (2008). Some innate foundations of social and moral cognition. In K. Wynn (Ed.), *The innate mind. Volume 3: Foundations and the future* (pp. 330–347). Oxford University Press.

Wynn, K., Bloom, P., Jordan, A., Marshall, J., & Sheskin, M. (2018). Not noble savages after all: Limits to early altruism. *Current Directions in Psychological Science, 27*, 3–8.

Wynne, C. D. L. (2004). *Do animals think?* Princeton University Press.

Wynne, C. D. L. (2008). Aping language: A skeptical analysis of the evidence for nonhuman primate language. *Skeptic, 13*, 10–13.

Wysocki, C. J., & Gilbert, A. N. (1989). National Geographic Smell Survey: Effects of age are heterogeneous. *Annals of the New York Academy of Sciences, 561*, 12–28.

Xiong, Y., Qin, L., Wang, M., & Pomerantz, E. M. (2020). Parents' peer restriction in the United States and China: A longitudinal study of early adolescents. *Developmental Psychology, 56*(9), 1760–1774.

Xiu, M. H., Guan, H. Y., Zhao, J. M., Wang, K. Q., Pan, Y. F., Su, X. R., Wang, Y. H., Guo, J. M., Jiang, L., Liu, H. Y., Sun, S. G., Wu, H. R., Geng, H. S., Liu, X. W., Yu, H. J., Wei, B. C. Li, X. P., Trinh, T., Tan, S. P., & Zhang, X. Y. (2020). Cognitive enhancing effect of high-frequency neuronavigated rTMS in chronic schizophrenia patients with predominant negative symptoms: A double-blind controlled 32-week follow-up study. *Schizophrenia Bulletin, 46*(5), 1219–1230.

Xu, J., & Potenza, M. N. (2012). White matter integrity and five-factor personality measures in healthy adults. *NeuroImage, 59*, 800–807.

Xu, Y., & Corkin, S. (2001). H. M. revisits the Tower of Hanoi puzzle. *Neuropsychology, 15*, 69–79.

Xu, Y., Norton, S., & Rahman, Q. (2020). Sexual orientation and cognitive ability: A multivariate meta-analytic follow-up. *Archives of Sexual Behavior, 49*, 413–420.

Yam, K. (2022, January 31). *Anti-Asian hate crimes increased 339 percent nationwide last year, report says*. NBC News. https://www.nbcnews.com/news/asian-america/anti-asian-hate-crimes-increased-339-percent-nationwide-last-year-repo-rcna14282

Yamaguchi, M., Masuchi, A., Nakanishi, D., Suga, S., Konishi, N., Yu, Y. Y., & Ohtsubo, Y. (2015). Experiential purchases and prosocial spending promote happiness by enhancing social relationships. *Journal of Positive Psychology, 11*(5), 480–488.

Yanaoka, K., Michaelson, L. E., Guild, R. M., Dostart, G., Yonehiro, J., Saito, S., & Munakata, Y. (2022). Cultures crossing: The power of habit in delaying gratification. *Psychological Science, 33*(7), 1172–1181.

Yang, C., Luo, L., Vadillo, M. A., Yu, R., & Shanks, D. R. (2021). Testing (quizzing) boosts classroom learning: A systematic and meta-analytic review. *Psychological Bulletin, 147*(4), 399–435.

Yang, J., & Hofmann, J. (2015). Action observation and imitation in autism spectrum disorders: An ALE meta-analysis of fMRI studies. *Brain Imaging and Behavior, 10*, 960–969.

Yang, S. (2015). *Filial piety: Memoir of a good daughter.* Xlibris.

Yang, Y., Cao, S., Shields, G. S., Teng, Z., & Liu, Y. (2017). The relationships between rumination and core executive functions: A meta-analysis. *Depression and Anxiety, 34*, 37–50.

Yang, Y. C., Boen, C., Gerken, K., Li, T., Schorpp, K., & Harris, K. M. (2016). Social relationships and physiological determinants of longevity across the human life span. *PNAS, 113*, 578–583.

Yarnell, P. R., & Lynch, S. (1970, April 25). Retrograde memory immediately after concussion. *The Lancet, 1*, 863–865.

Yasir, S., & Gettleman, J. (2020, June 28). India debates skin-tone bias as beauty companies alter ads. *The New York Times.* https://www.nytimes.com/2020/06/28/world/asia/india-skin-color-unilever.html

Yates, A. (1989). Current perspectives on the eating disorders: I. History, psychological and biological aspects. *Journal of the American Academy of Child and Adolescent Psychiatry, 28*, 813–828.

Yates, A. (1990). Current perspectives on the eating disorders: II. Treatment, outcome, and research directions. *Journal of the American Academy of Child and Adolescent Psychiatry, 29*, 1–9.

Yau, J. O. Y., & McNally, G. P. (2018). Brain mechanisms controlling Pavlovian fear conditioning. *Journal of Experimental Psychology: Animal Learning and Cognition, 44*, 341–357.

Ybarra, O. (1999). Misanthropic person memory when the need to self-enhance is absent. *Personality and Social Psychology Bulletin, 25*, 261–269.

Yeager, D. S., Dahl, R. E., & Dweck, C. S. (2018). Why interventions to influence adolescent behavior often fail but could succeed. *Perspectives on Psychological Science, 13*, 101–122.

Yeager, D. S., Hanselman, P., Walton, G. M., Murray, J. S., Crosnoe, R., Muller, C., Tipton, E., Schneider, B., Hulleman, C. S., Hinojosa, C. P., Paunesku, D., Romero, C., Flint, K., Robert, A., Trott, J., Iachan, R., Buontempo, J., Yang, S. M., Carvalho, C. M., ... Dweck, C. S. (2019). A national experiment reveals where a growth mindset improves achievement. *Nature, 573*, 364–369.

Yemiscigil, A., & Vlaev, I. (2021). The bidirectional relationship between sense of purpose in life and physical activity: A longitudinal study. *Journal of Behavioral Medicine, 44*(5), 715–725.

Yengo, L., Robinson, M. R., Keller, M. C., Kemper, K. E., Yang, Y., Trzaskowski, M., Gratten, J., Turley, P., Cesarini, D., Banjamin, D. J., Wray, N. R., Goddard, M. E., Yang, J., & Visscher, P. M. (2018). Imprint of assortative mating on the human genome. *Nature Human Behaviour, 2*, 948–954.

Yeo, G. S. H., & O'Rahilly, S. (2021). Finding genes that control body weight. *Science, 373*, 30–31.

Yerkes, R. M., & Dodson, J. D. (1908). The relation of strength of stimulus to rapidity of habit-formation. *Journal of Comparative Neurology and Psychology, 18*, 459–482.

Yesavage, J. A., Fairchild, J. K., Mi, Z., Biswas, K., Davis-Karim, A., Phibbs, C. S., Forman, S. D., Thase, M., Williams, L. M., Etkin, A., O'Hara, R., Georgette, G., Beale, T., Huang, G. D., Noda, A., George, M. S., & VA Cooperative Studies Program Study Team. (2018). Effect of repetitive transcranial magnetic stimulation on treatment-resistant major depression in US veterans: A randomized clinical trial. *JAMA Psychiatry, 75*, 884–893.

Yilmaz, Z., Hardaway, J. A., & Bulik, C. M. (2015). Genetics and epigenetics of eating disorders. *Advances in Genomics and Genetics, 5*, 131–150.

Yip, T., Cheon, Y. M., Wang, Y., Cham, H., Tryon, W., & El-Sheikh, M. (2020). Racial disparities in sleep: Associations with discrimination among ethnic/racial minority adolescents. *Child Development, 91*(3), 914–931.

Yip, T., Wang, Y., Xie, M., Ip, P. S., Fowle, J., & Buckhalt, J. (2022). School start times, sleep, and youth outcomes: A meta-analysis. *Pediatrics, 149*(6). https://doi.org/10.1542/peds.2021-054068

Yockey, A., King, K., & Vidourek, R. (2022). Past-year suicidal ideation among transgender individuals in the United States. *Archives of Suicide Research, 26*(1), 70–80.

Yokum, D., Ravishankar, A., & Coppock, A. (2019). A randomized control trial evaluating the effects of police body-worn cameras. *PNAS, 116*. https://www.pnas.org/doi/10.1073/pnas.1814773116

Yong, H. H., Borland, R., Cummings, K. M., Gravely, S., Thrasher, J. F., McNeill, A., Hitchman, S., Greenhalgh, E., Thompson, M. E., & Fong, G. T. (2019). Reasons for regular vaping and for its discontinuation among smokers and recent ex-smokers: Findings from the 2016 ITC Four Country Smoking and Vaping Survey. *Addiction, 114*(suppl 1), 35–48.

Yopak, K. E., Lisney, T. J., Darlington, R. B., Collin, S. P., Montgomery, J. C., & Finlay, B. L. (2010). A conserved pattern of brain scaling from sharks to primates. *PNAS, 107*(29). https://tinyurl.com/yc7utn2u

Yoshimoto, C., & Frauenheim, E. (2018, February 27). *The best companies to work for are beating the marketplace.* Fortune. https://fortune.com/2018/02/27/the-best-companies-to-work-for-are-beating-the-market/

YouGov. (2021, April 9) *Half of vaccine rejectors believe it is safe to travel now, compared to 29% of vaccinated adults.* YouGovAmerica. https://today.yougov.com/topics/politics/articles-reports/2021/04/09/half-vaccine-rejectors-believe-safe-travel-now

Young, C., & Lim, C. (2014). Time as a network good: Evidence from unemployment and the standard workweek. *Sociological Science, 1*, 10–27.

Young, S. G., Hugenberg, K., Bernstein, M. J., & Sacco, D. F. (2012). Perception and motivation in face recognition: A critical review of theories of the cross-race effect. *Personality and Social Psychology Review, 16*, 116–142.

Young, S. M., & Pinsky, D. (2006). Narcissism and celebrity. *Journal of Personality, 40*, 463–471.

Youngentob, S. L., & Glendinning, J. I. (2009). Fetal ethanol exposure increases ethanol intake by making it smell and taste better. *PNAS, 106*, 5359.

Youngentob, S. L., Kent, P. F., Scheehe, P. R., Molina, J. C., Spear, N. E., & Youngentob, L. M. (2007). Experience-induced fetal plasticity: The effect of gestational ethanol exposure on the behavioral and neurophysiologic olfactory response to ethanol odor in early postnatal and adult rats. *Behavioral Neuroscience, 121*, 1293–1305.

Younger, J., Aron, A., Parke, S., Chatterjee, N., & Mackey, S. (2010) Viewing pictures of a romantic partner reduces experimental pain: Involvement of neural reward systems. *PLOS ONE, 5*. https://journals.plos.org/plosone/article?id=10.1371/journal.pone.0013309

Yount, K. M., James-Hawkins, L., Cheong, Y. F., & Naved, R. T. (2017). Men's perpetration of partner violence in Bangladesh: Community gender norms and violence in childhood. *Psychology of Men & Masculinity, 19*, 117–130.

Youyou, W., Kosinski, M., & Stillwell, D. (2015). Computer-based personality judgments are more accurate than those made by humans. *PNAS, 112*, 1036–1040.

Yu, H., McCoach, D. V., Gottfried, A. W., & Gottfried, A. E. (2018). Stability of intelligence from infancy through adolescence: An autoregressive latent variable model. *Intelligence, 69*, 8–15.

Yu, H., Yan, H., Wang, L., Li, J., Tan, L., Deng, W., Chen, Q., Yang, G., Zhang, F., Lu, T., Yang, J., Li, K., Lv, L., Tan, Q., Zhang, H., Xiao, X., Li, M., Ma, X., Yang, F., ... Chinese Antipsychotics Pharmacogenomics Consortium. (2018). Five novel loci associated with antipsychotic treatment response in patients with schizophrenia: A genome-wide association study. *Lancet Psychiatry, 5*, 327–338.

Yu, X., Zhao, G., Wang, D., Wang, S., Li, R., Li, A., Wang, H., Nollet, M., Chun, Y. Y., Zhao, T., Yustos, R., Li, H., Zhao, J., Li, J., Cai, M., Vyssotski, A., Li, Y., Dong, H., Franks, N. P., & Wisden, W. (2022). A specific circuit in the midbrain detects stress and induces restorative sleep. *Science, 377*(6601), 63–72.

Yudkin, D., Hawkins, S., Dixon, T. (2019, June). *The perception gap: How false impressions are pulling Americans apart* [PDF file]. More in Common. https://perceptiongap.us/media/zaslaroc/perception-gap-report-1-0-3.pdf

Yudkin, D. A., Van Bavel, J. J., & Rhodes, M. (2019). Young children police group members at personal cost. *Journal of Experimental Psychology: General, 149*, 182–191.

Yuen, R. K., Merico, D., Cao, H., Pellecchia, G., Alipanahi, B., Thiruvahindrapuram, B., Tong, X., Sun, Y., Cao, D., Zhang, T., Wu, X., Jin, X., Zhou, Z., Liu, X., Nalpathamkalam, T., Walker, S., Howe, J. L., Wang, Z., MacDonald, ... Schere, S. W. (2016). Genome-wide characteristics of de novo mutations in autism. *NPJ Genomic Medicine, 1*, 1–10.

Yuki, M., Maddux, W. W., & Masuda. T. (2007). Are the windows to the soul the same in the East and West? Cultural differences in using the eyes and mouth as cues to recognize emotions in Japan and the United States. *Journal of Experimental Social Psychology, 43*, 303–311.

Yuskaitis, C. J., Parviz, M., Loui, P., Wan, C. Y., & Pearl, P. L. (2015). Neural mechanisms underlying musical pitch perception and clinical applications including developmental dyslexia. *Current Neurology and Neuroscience Reports, 15*(8), 51.

Zadra, A., & Stickgold, R. (2021). *When brains dream: Exploring the science and mystery of sleep*. W. W. Norton.

Zagorsky, J. L. (2007). Do you have to be smart to be rich? The impact of IQ on wealth, income and financial distress. *Intelligence, 35*, 489–501.

Zahrt, O. H., & Crum, A. J. (2017). Perceived physical activity and mortality: Evidence from three nationally representative U.S. samples. *Health Psychology, 36*, 1017–1025.

Zajenkowski, M., Jonason, P. K., Leniarska, M., & Kozakiewicz, Z. (2020). Who complies with the restrictions to reduce the spread of COVID-19?: Personality and perceptions of the COVID-19 situation. *Personality and Individual Differences, 166*. https://www.ncbi.nlm.nih.gov/pmc/articles/PMC7296320/

Zajkowski, Z., Gullett, N., Walsh, A., Zonca, V., Pedersen, G. A., Souza, L., Kieling, C., Fisher, H. L., Kohrt, B. A., & Mondelli, V. (2022). Cortisol and development of depression in adolescence and young adulthood—a systematic review and meta-analysis. *Psychoneuroendocrinology, 136*. https://www.sciencedirect.com/science/article/pii/S0306453021004996

Zajonc, R. B. (1965). Social facilitation. *Science, 149*, 269–274.

Zajonc, R. B. (1980). Feeling and thinking: Preferences need no inferences. *American Psychologist, 35*, 151–175.

Zajonc, R. B. (1984). On the primacy of affect. *American Psychologist, 39*, 117–123.

Zajonc, R. B. (1998). Emotions. In D. Gilbert, S. T. Fiske, & G. Lindzey (Eds.), *Handbook of social psychology* (4th ed.). McGraw-Hill.

Zajonc, R. B. (2001). Mere exposure: A gateway to the subliminal. *Current Directions in Psychological Science, 10*, 224–228.

Zajonc, R. B., & Markus, G. B. (1975). Birth order and intellectual development. *Psychological Review, 82*, 74–88.

Zamore, Z., & Veasey, S. C. (2022). Neural consequences of chronic sleep disruption. *Trends in Neurosciences, 45*(9), 678–691.

Zanarini, M. C., Williams, A. A., Lewis, R. E., Reich, R. B., Vera, S. C., Marino, M. F., Levin, A., Yong, L., & Frankenburg, R. F. (1997). Reported pathological childhood experiences associated with the development of borderline personality disorder. *American Journal of Psychiatry, 154*, 1101–1106.

Zannas, A. S., Provençal, N., & Binder, E. B. (2015). Epigenetics of posttraumatic stress disorder: Current evidence, challenges, and future directions. *Biological Psychiatry, 78*, 327–335.

Zaromb, F. M., Liu, J. H., Páez, D., Hanke, K., Putnam, A. L., & Roediger, H. L. (2018). We made history: Citizens of 35 countries overestimate their nation's role in world history. *Journal of Applied Research in Memory and Cognition, 7*, 521–528.

Zaslavsky, O., Palgi, Y., Rillamas-Sun, E., LaCroix, A. Z., Schnall, E., Woods, N. F., Cochrane, B. B., Garcia, L., Hingle, M., Post, S., Seguin, R., Tindle, H., & Shrira, A. (2015). Dispositional optimism and terminal decline in global quality of life. *Developmental Psychology, 51*, 856–863.

Zauberman, G., & Lynch, J. G., Jr. (2005). Resource slack and propensity to discount delayed investments of time versus money. *Journal of Experimental Psychology: General, 134*, 23–37.

Zaval, L., Keenan, E. A., Johnson, E. J., & Weber, E. U. (2014). How warm days increase belief in global warming. *Nature Climate Change, 4*, 143–147.

Zeelenberg, R., Wagenmakers, E.-J., & Rotteveel, M. (2006). The impact of emotion on perception. *Psychological Science, 17*, 287–291.

Zeidner, M. (1990). Perceptions of ethnic group modal intelligence: Reflections of cultural stereotypes or intelligence test scores? *Journal of Cross-Cultural Psychology, 21*, 214–231.

Zeineh, M. M., Engel, S. A., Thompson, P. M., & Bookheimer, S. Y. (2003). Dynamics of the hippocampus during encoding and retrieval of face-name pairs. *Science, 299*, 577–580.

Zelenski, J. M., & Nisbet, E. K. (2014). Happiness and feeling connected: The distinct role of nature relatedness. *Environmental Behavior, 46*, 3–23.

Zell, E., Strickhouser, J. E., & Krizan, Z. (2018). Subjective social status and health: A meta-analysis of community and society ladders. *Health Psychology, 37*, 979–987.

Zell, E., Strickhouser, J. E., Sedikides, C., & Alicke, M. D. (2020). The better-than-average effect in comparative self-evaluation: A comprehensive review and meta-analysis. *Psychological Bulletin, 146*, 118–149.

Zeng, L.-N., Yang, Y., Feng, Y., Cui, X., Wang, R., Hall, B. J., Ungvari, G. S., Chen, L., & Xiang, Y.-T. (2019). The prevalence of depression in menopausal women in China: A meta-analysis of observational studies. *Journal of Affective Disorders, 256*, 337–343.

Zentner, M., & Eagly, A. H. (2015). A sociocultural framework for understanding partner preferences of women and men: Integration of concepts and evidence. *European Journal of Social Psychology, 26*, 328–373.

Zerr, C. L., Berg, J. J., Nelson, S. M., Fishell, A. K., Savalia, N. K., & McDermott, K. B. (2018). Learning efficiency: Identifying individual differences in learning rate and retention in healthy adults. *Psychological Science, 29*, 1436–1450.

Zerubavel, N., Hoffman, M. A., Reich, A., Ochsner, K. N., & Bearman, P. (2018). Neural precursors of future liking and affective reciprocity. *PNAS, 115*, 4375–4380.

Zetsche, U., Bürkner, P.-C., & Renneberg, B. (2019). Future expectations in clinical depression: Biased or realistic? *Journal of Abnormal Psychology, 128*, 678–688.

Zhang, D., & Tullis, J. G. (2021). Personal reminders: Self-generated reminders boost memory more than normatively related ones. *Memory & Cognition, 49*, 645–659.

Zhang, H., Gross, J., De Dreu, C., & Ma, Y. (2019). Oxytocin promotes coordinated out-group attack during intergroup conflict in humans. *eLife, 8*. https://bit.ly/3MVp7RK

Zhang, J. (2016, July 2). Personal correspondence from Dept. of Psychology and Behavioral Science, Zhejiang University, Hangzhou, China, based on 2015–2016 *Nationwide Psychology Specialty Ranking*.

Zhang, J., Fang, L., Yow-Wu, B. W., & Wieczorek, W. F. (2013). Depression, anxiety, and suicidal ideation among Chinese Americans: A study of immigration-related factors. *Journal of Nervous and Mental Disease, 201*, 17–22.

Zhang, J., Jin Y, Jia, P., Li, N., & Zheng, Z. J. (2021). Global gender disparities in premature death from cardiovascular disease, and their associations with country capacity for noncommunicable disease prevention and control. *International Journal of Environmental Research on Public Health, 18*(19). https://bit.ly/3d4ufFC

Zhang, J. W., Chen, S., & Tomova Shakur, T. K. (2020). From me to you: Self-compassion predicts acceptance of own and others' imperfections. *Personality and Social Psychology Bulletin, 46*, 228–242.

Zhang, M., Wu, S., Du, S., Qian, W., Chen, J., Qiao, L., Yang, Y., Tan, J., Yuan, Z., Peng, Q., Liu, Y., Navarro, N., Tang, K., Ruiz-Linares, A., Wang, J., Claes, P., Li, J., & Wang, S. (2022). Genetic variants underlying differences in facial morphology in East Asian and European populations. *Nature Genetics, 54*, 403–411.

Zhang, J. G. (2021). *We asked people who lost their taste to COVID: What do you eat in a day?* Eater. https://www.eater.com/2021/2/5/22267667/covid-19-loss-distorted-taste-smell-anosmia-parosmia-symptom-food-diaries

Zhang, S. X., & Chen, J. (2021). Scientific evidence on mental health in key regions under the COVID-19 pandemic—meta-analytical evidence from Africa, Asia, China, Eastern Europe, Latin America, South Asia, Southeast Asia, and Spain. *European Journal of Psychotraumatology, 12*(1). doi: 10.1080/20008198.2021.201192

Zhang, Y., Wang, J., Xiong, X., Jian, Q., Zhang, L., Xiang, M., Xhou, B., & Zou, Z. (2022). Suicidality in patients with primary diagnosis of panic disorder: A single-rate meta-analysis and systematic review. *Journal of Affective Disorders, 300*, 27–33.

Zhao, X., & Epley, N. (2022). Surprisingly happy to have helped: Underestimating prosociality creates a misplaced barrier to asking for help. *Psychological Science, 33*(10). https://doi.org/10.1177/09567976221097615

Zhong, C.-B., Dijksterhuis, A., & Galinsky, A. D. (2008). The merits of unconscious thought in creativity. *Psychological Science, 19*, 912–918.

Zhou, J., Park, C. Y., Theesfeld, C. L., Wong, A. K., Yuan, Y., Scheckel, C., Fak, J. J., Funk, J., Yao, K., Tajima, Y., Packer, A., Darnell, R. B., & Troyanskaya, O. G. (2019). Whole-genome deep-learning analysis identifies contribution of noncoding mutations to autism risk. *Nature Genetics, 51*, 973–980.

Zhou, J., Shi, Z., Zhou, L., Hu, Y., & Zhang, M. (2021). Occupational noise-induced hearing loss in China: A systematic review and meta-analysis. *BMJ Open. 10*(9). https://bmjopen.bmj.com/content/10/9/e039576

Zhou, N., Cao, H., Liu, F., Wu, L., Liang, Y., Xu, J., Meng, H., Zang, N., Hao, R., An, Y., Ma, S., Fang, X., & Zhang, J. (2020). A four-wave, cross-lagged model of problematic internet use and mental health among Chinese college students: Disaggregation of within-person and between-person effects. *Developmental Psychology, 56*(5), 1009–1021.

Zhou, S., DeFranco, J. P., Blaha, N. T., Dwivedy, P., Culver, A., Nallamala, H., Chelluri, S., & Dumas, T. C. (2019). Aversive conditioning in the tardigrade, *Dactylobiotus dispar*. *Journal of Experimental Psychology: Animal Learning and Cognition*, 45(4), 405–412.

Zhou, S., Page-Gould, E., Aron, A., Moyer, A., & Hewstone, M. (2019). The extended contact hypothesis: A meta-analysis on 20 years of research. *Personality and Social Psychology Review, 23*, 132–160.

Zhou, Y., Zou, M., Woods, S. A., & Wu, C.-H. (2019). The restorative effect of work after unemployment: An intraindividual analysis of subjective well-being recovery through reemployment. *Journal of Applied Psychology, 104*, 1195–1206.

Zhu, X., Smith, R. A., & Buteau, E. (2022). A meta-analysis of weight stigma and health behaviors. *Stigma and Health, 7*(1), 1–13.

Zhu, Z., Zhao, Y., Wen, K., Li, Q., Pan, N., Fu, S., Li, F., Radua, J., Vieta, E., Kemp, G. J., Biswa, B. B., & Gong, Q. (2022). Cortical thickness abnormalities in patients with bipolar disorder: A systematic review and meta-analysis. *Journal of Affective Disorders, 300*, 209–218.

Zhukovsky, P., Anderson, J. A. E., Coughlan, G., Mulsant, B. H., Cipriani, A., & Voineskos, A. N. (2021). Coordinate-based network mapping of brain structure in major depressive disorder in younger and older adults: A systematic review and meta-analysis. *American Journal of Psychiatry, 178*, 1119–1128.

Zietsch, B. P., Sidari, M. J., Abdellaoui, A., Maier, R., Långström, Guo, S., Beecham, G. W., Martin, E. R., Sanders, A. R., & Verweij, K. J. H. (2021). Genomic evidence consistent with antagonistic pleiotropy may help explain the evolutionary maintenance of same-sex sexual behaviour in humans. *Nature Human Behavior*, 5, 1251–1258.

Zilbergeld, B. (1983). *The shrinking of America: Myths of psychological change*. Little, Brown.

Zill, N. (2020, April 6). *Family still matters for key indicators of student performance*. Institute for Family Studies. https://ifstudies.org/blog/family-still-matters-for-key-indicators-of-student-performance

Zillmann, D., & Bryant, J. (1984). Effects of massive exposure to pornography. In N. Malamuth & E. Donnerstein (Eds.), *Pornography and sexual aggression* (pp. 115–138). Academic Press.

Zimbardo, P., & Coulombe, N. (2021, January 18). *Young men and society, Part 2: Social isolation, gaming, and porn*. Institute for Family Studies. https://ifstudies.org/blog/young-men-and-society-part-2-social-isolation-gaming-and-porn

Zimbardo, P., Wilson, G., & Coulombe, N. (2016). How porn is messing with your manhood. *Skeptic*. https://www.skeptic.com/reading_room/how-porn-is-messing-with-your-manhood

Zimbardo, P. G. (1970). The human choice: Individuation, reason, and order versus deindividuation, impulse, and chaos. In W. J. Arnold & D. Levine (Eds.), *Nebraska symposium on motivation, 1969*. University of Nebraska Press.

Zimbardo, P. G. (2007, September). Person x situation x system dynamics. *The Observer*. Association for Psychological Science. p. 43.

Zimmermann, K. S., Richardson, R., & Baker, K. D. (2020). Esketamine as a treatment for paediatric depression: Questions of safety and efficacy. *Lancet Psychiatry, 7*, 827–829.

Zimmermann, T. D., & Meier, B. (2006). The rise and decline of prospective memory performance across the lifespan. *Quarterly Journal of Experimental Psychology, 59*, 2040–2046.

Zinzow, H. M., Amstadter, A. B., McCauley, J. L., Ruggiero, K. J., Resnick, H. S., & Kilpatrick, D. G. (2011). Self-rated health in relation to rape and mental health disorders in a national sample of college women. *Journal of American College Health, 59*, 588–594.

Zisman, C., & Ganzach, Y. (2021). In a representative sample grit has a negligible effect on educational and economic success compared to intelligence. *Social Psychological and Personality Science, 12*(3), 296–303.

Zmigrod, L., Rentfrow, P. J., & Robbins, T. W. (2020). The partisan mind: Is extreme political partisanship related to cognitive inflexibility? *Journal of Experimental Psychology: General, 149*(3), 407–418.

Zogby, J. (2006, March). *Survey of teens and adults about the use of personal electronic devices and headphones*. Zogby International.

Zoma, M., & Gielen, U. P. (2015). How many psychologists are there in the world? *International Psychology Bulletin, 19*, 47–50.

Zoref, L., & Williams, P. (1980). A look at content bias in IQ tests. *Journal of Educational Measurement, 17*(4), 313–322.

Zou, L. Q., van Hartevelt, T. J., Kringelbach, M. L., Cheung, E. F., & Chan, R. C. (2016). The neural mechanism of hedonic processing and judgment of pleasant odors: An activation likelihood estimation meta-analysis. *Neuropsychology, 30*, 970–979.

Zubieta, J.-K., Bueller, J. A., Jackson, L. R., Scott, D. J., Xu, Y., Koeppe, R. A., Nichols, T. E., & Stohler, C. S. (2005). Placebo effects mediated by endogenous opioid activity on μ-opioid receptors. *Journal of Neuroscience, 25*, 7754–7762.

Zubieta, J.-K., Heitzeg, M. M., Smith, Y. R., Bueller, J. A., Xu, K., Xu, Y., Koeppe, R. A., Stohler, C. S., & Goldman, D. (2003). COMT val158met genotype affects μ-opioid neurotransmitter responses to a pain stressor. *Science, 299*, 1240–1243.

Zucco, G. M. (2003). Anomalies in cognition: Olfactory memory. *European Psychologist, 8*, 77–86.

Zucker, G. S., & Weiner, B. (1993). Conservatism and perceptions of poverty: An attributional analysis. *Journal of Applied Social Psychology, 23*, 925–943.

Zuckerman, M. (1979). *Sensation seeking: Beyond the optimal level of arousal*. Erlbaum.

Zuckerman, M. (1999). *Vulnerability to psychopathology: A biosocial model*. American Psychological Association.

Zuckerman, M. (2009). Sensation seeking. In M. R. Leary & R. H. Hoye (Eds.), *Handbook of individual differences in social behavior* (pp. 455–465). Guilford Press.

Zuckerman, M., Li, C., & Hall, J. A. (2016). When men and women differ in self-esteem and when they don't: A meta-analysis. *Journal of Research in Personality, 64*, 34–51.

Zunick, P. V., Fazio, R. H., & Vasey, M. W. (2015). Directed abstraction: Encouraging broad, personal generalizations following a success experience. *Journal of Personality and Social Psychology, 109*, 1–19.

Zvolensky, M. J., & Bernstein, A. (2005). Cigarette smoking and panic psychopathology. *Current Directions in Psychological Science, 14*, 301–305.

Zvolensky, M. J., Bakhshaie, J., Sheffer, C., Perez, A., & Goodwin, R. D. (2015). Major depressive disorder and smoking relapse among adults in the United States: A 10-year, prospective investigation. *Psychiatry Research, 226*, 73–77.

Name Index

Note: Page numbers followed by *f* indicate figures; those followed by t indicate tables. Page numbers preceded by A, B, or C refer to the appendices.

Subject Index

Note: Page numbers followed by *f* indicate figures; those followed by t indicate tables. Page numbers preceded by A, B, or C refer to the appendices.